P9-CKV-759

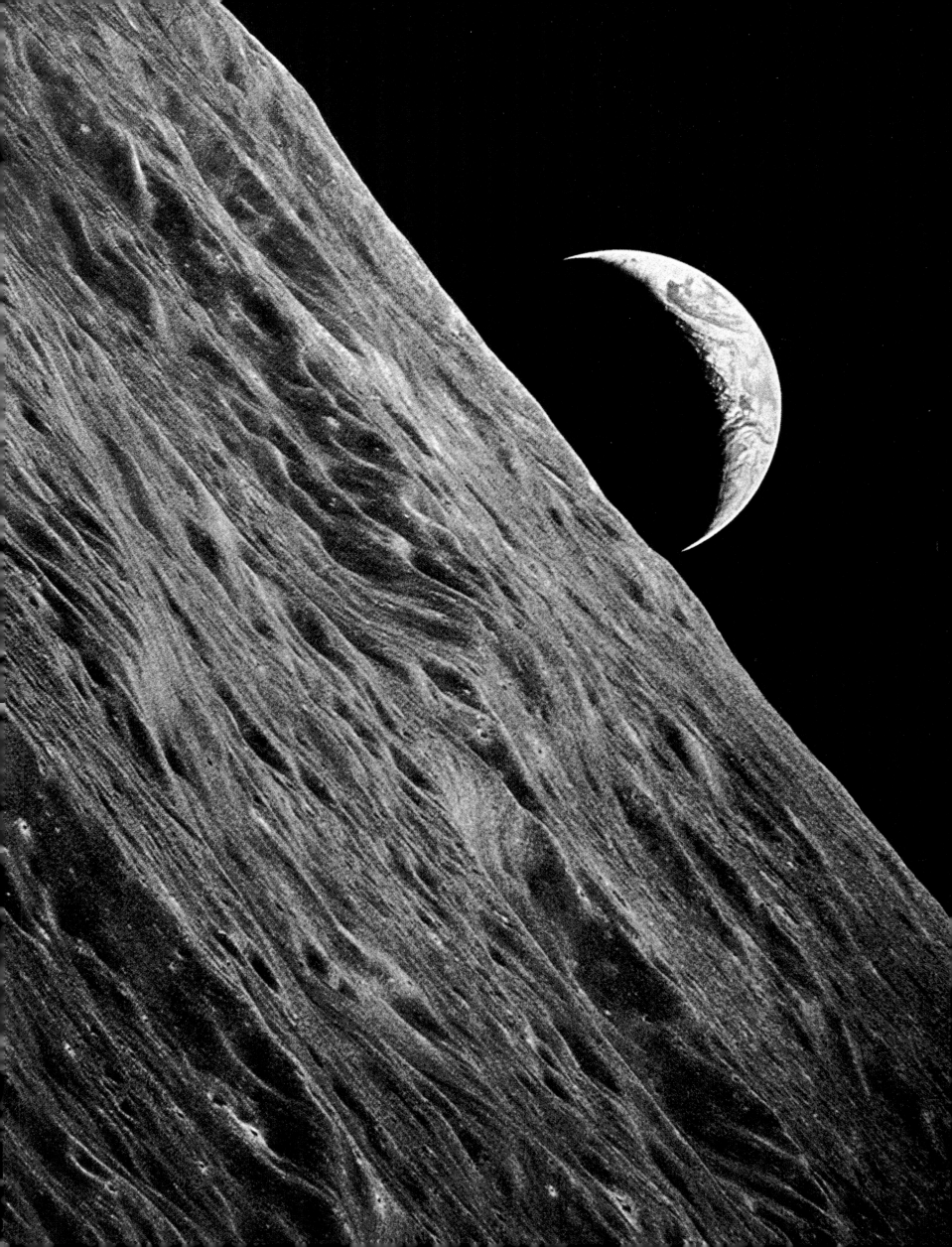

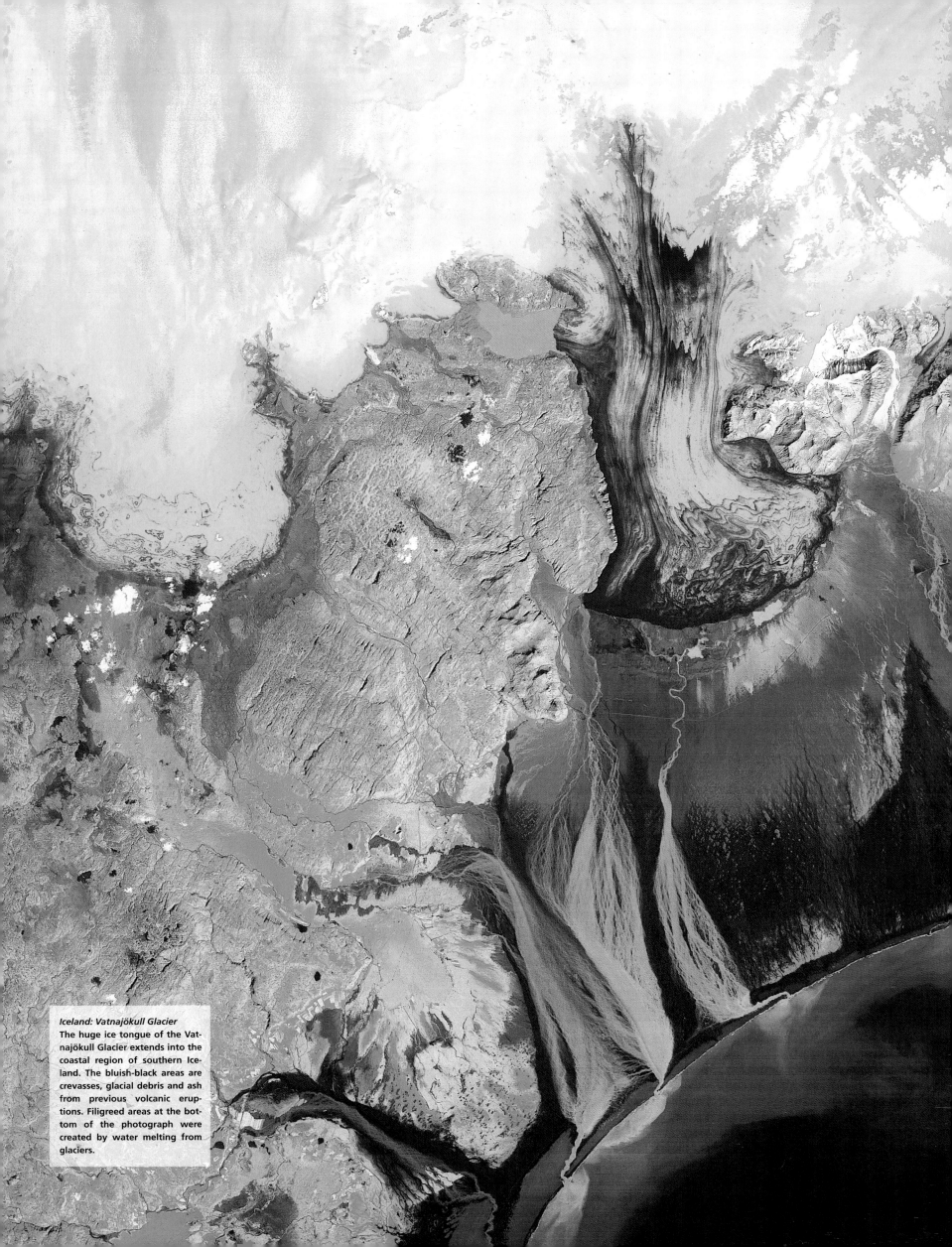

Iceland: Vatnajökull Glacier
The huge ice tongue of the Vatnajökull Glacier extends into the coastal region of southern Iceland. The bluish-black areas are crevasses, glacial debris and ash from previous volcanic eruptions. Filigreed areas at the bottom of the photograph were created by water melting from glaciers.

THE
MACMILLAN
WORLD ATLAS

Ref   The Macmillan
G   world atlas
1021
.M2382
1998

The Macmillan world atlas.
Ref G1021.M2382   70873

SOUTH PUGET SOUND COMM. COLLEG

LIBRARY-MEDIA CENTER
SOUTH PUGET SOUND COMM. COLLEGE
2011 MOTTMAN RD. S.W.
OLYMPIA, WA 98512-6292

MACMILLAN • USA

U.S.A.: New York City
The Greater New York area is one of the world's largest metropolitan areas. Between the Hudson River and the East River lies the borough of Manhattan with the green rectangle of famous Central Park. Brooklyn, the most populous borough, lies on the western tip of Long Island. Sandbars line the southern coast of Long Island.

60984 81800

"The world is a wonderful book, but it is only marginally useful to those who cannot read it."

- Carlo Goldoni

"We live in this world only as long as we love it."

- Rabindranath Tagore

The Earth is our home, both in the region where we happen to live and on the entire planet. We travel to Antarctica or Bali, have friends in Brisbane and Yokohama, place telephone calls to Johannesburg or perhaps even to Tierra del Fuego. Our stereo system was manufactured in Korea, our whiskies were distilled in Scotland or Kentucky. The planet is fast becoming a global village.

For millions of years humankind has been wandering across the face of the Earth, and today global travel has become a familiar feature of life. An increasingly large number of people are spending ever more time and money visiting foreign places. Three decades ago, only seventy million people were counted at international frontier crossings; that number has since increased sevenfold: the world has become mobile.

Modern communications technologies add another dimension to this mobility. An event happening right now in Beijing appears without delay on video screens around the world. No spectacular event can occur without immediately attracting the attention of the world community. Distances have become irrelevant as the continents seem to move closer together. And yet, far too much of the world still remains unknown and foreign to us. The vast expanses of Siberia and Australia, the island world of Oceania, the landscapes of central Africa, the far north and the extreme south of the two American continents: who can claim to have a clear, detailed mental image of these fascinating regions of our planet?

The *Macmillan World Atlas* is designed to meet the changing needs of a changing world. Although it follows in the tradition of Mercator and other cartographers, this new volume is a revolutionary innovation, a trailblazing geographic and cartographic databank. Its fundamental concept reflects two essential goals. First, it is a precise and detailed reference designed to meet the information needs of a contemporary people. It has been created with travelers, both business and leisure, in mind, and it also serves as an invaluable resource for families and students, politicians, scientists, and businesspeople. The maps in this volume have been drawn

to depict the actual state of today's world with unprecedented fidelity.

But beyond all that, The *Macmillan World Atlas* hopes to communicate a dream and a fascination: the fascination of our wonderful blue spaceship, a place where life is precious and worthwhile, a threatened oasis whose continued survival depends upon the cooperation and commitment of people around the world.

This book is the creation of the distinguished Bertelsmann Cartographic Institute, which has invested many years and many millions of dollars to create a revolutionary digital cartographic database for a major new atlas series. The 80 to 100 staff members and their expert advisers who have spent years designing (and who continually update) the cartographic database are passionately committed to the goals that define this atlas program. Worldwide cooperation is the guiding principle in all their work. To give just two examples: Chinese geographers and cartographers at the University of Nanking designed the cartography of China: and former employees of Sojus Karta in Moscow helped create the maps of the Commonwealth of Independent States that were born after the collapse of the Soviet Union. These collaborations are all the more remarkable in view of the fact that mapmakers have always been strongly influenced by the complex interplays of military and political forces.

The worldview embodied by *The Macmillan World Atlas* provides other examples of cartographic collaboration as well. New techniques and innovations in cartography have been harnessed in a variety of ways. The revolutionary technique of computer cartography – all map designs were digitally scanned, and all individual map elements are stored in a central databank – permits rapid reaction to changes of every sort. This is a milestone on the path to creating a truly up-to-date cartography commensurate with the actual state of the world.

In creating *The Macmillan World Atlas,* some antiquated cartographic conventions have been abandoned, new methods of representation have been developed, and different informational features have been emphasized. The most obvious example of

these improvements lies in the new, more realistic use of color. Subtle gradations of color represent fine distinctions in the world's ecological zones, which are depicted according to their particular climates and characteristic vegetation. Unlike the deserts and mountains in traditional atlases, where color is almost exclusively a function of elevation, the deserts in *The Macmillan World Atlas* are not green and mountains are not brown. Rather, coloration reflects more closely what you would see if you looked down at the Earth from an orbiting spaceship.

The inclusion of a detailed network of transportation arteries is another important feature, and one that will no doubt prove useful to leisure travelers and businesspeople alike. For the first time ever, *The Macmillan World Atlas* presents the world's entire continental network of roads and railways, complete with their exact routes, classifications and numbers. Emphasis has also been given to major cultural or natural sites that are likely to be of interest to tourists.

But perhaps the most important innovation of all has to do with the way we perceive the countries of the world in relation to one another. Previous atlases compel their readers to cope with maps whose scales vary from one page to the next. *The Macmillan World Atlas* puts an end to that by depicting our planet's land surfaces in a single, unified and detailed scale of 1:4.5 million. The scale is the same everywhere, from Nordkapp to Capetown, from Siberia to Australia and Oceania. In order to satisfy the desire for precise and detailed information, *The Macmillan World Atlas* also provides additional larger-scale maps depicting regions of particular interest to its primary audience: a detailed series of maps showing the United States and southern Canada in a scale of 1:2.25 million. As its users will quickly recognize, the policy of treating the continents and their countries with cartographic equality offers obvious practical advantages. Most of us grew up with atlases in which the map of England was nearly as big as the map of China and in which Europe was emphasized at the expense of marginally treated non-European continents. Cartographic misinformation has misled

generations of atlas users into forming mistaken notions about the relative sizes of the world's nations and cultural regions.

To deepen our understanding of our home planet and its topographic structures, *The Macmillan World Atlas* offers much more than mere cartography. Selected satellite photographs at the beginning of the volume provide fascinating insights into the world's characteristic natural and cultural landscapes. These images also show the actual models which the map colorations endeavor to represent faithfully.

The Macmillan World Atlas is conceived to serve as the ideal tool for discriminating people with global perspectives in their professional work and personal lifestyles. The atlas sets new standards in graphic design, information density and practical usability. The foundation for this new worldview is an enlightened perspective on humankind's responsibility to the universe. This responsibility involves both an ecologically sensitive attitude and a respect for the fundamental equality of human rights throughout the world. What may seem like a utopia today can and must become a reality – step by step. We hope that the *The Macmillan World Atlas* will help to carry this message.

Table of Contents

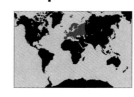

Key to Maps: Continents

North and Middle America · 1 : 4,500,000

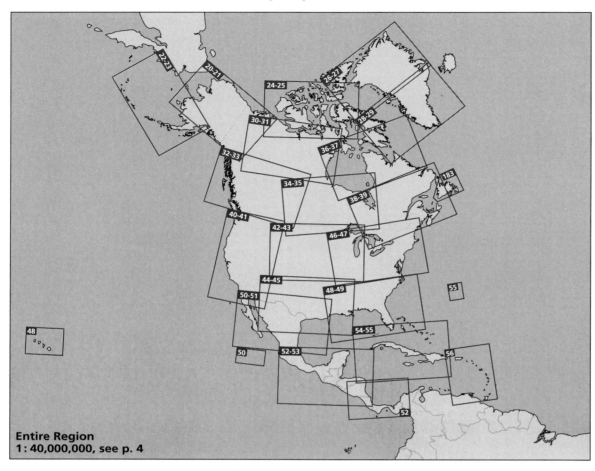

22-23
20-21
24-25
26-27
30-31
28-29
32-33
36-37
34-35
38-39
1 83
40-41
42-43
46-47
55
44-45
48-49
50-51
54-55
48
50
52-53
56
52

Entire Region
1 : 40,000,000, see p. 4

Europe · 1 : 4,500,000

86
86-87
90-91
94-95
92-93
98-99
100-101

Entire Region
1 : 40,000,000, see p. 8

South America · 1 : 4,500,000

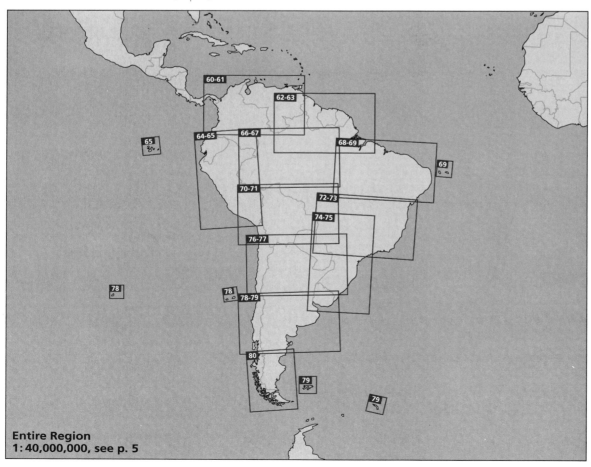

60-61
62-63
65
64-65
66-67
68-69
69
70-71
72-73
74-75
76-77
78
78
78-79
80
79
79

Entire Region
1 : 40,000,000, see p. 5

Asia · 1 : 4,500,000

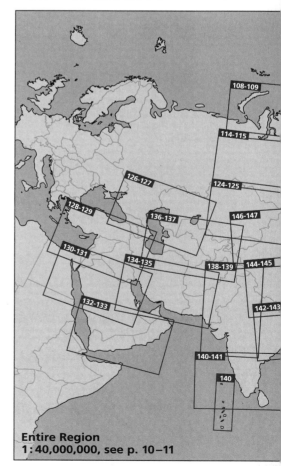

108-109
114-115
126-127
124-125
128-129
136-137
146-147
130-131
134-135
138-139
144-145
132-133
142-143
140-141
140

Entire Region
1 : 40,000,000, see p. 10–11

Australia and Oceania · 1 : 4,500,000

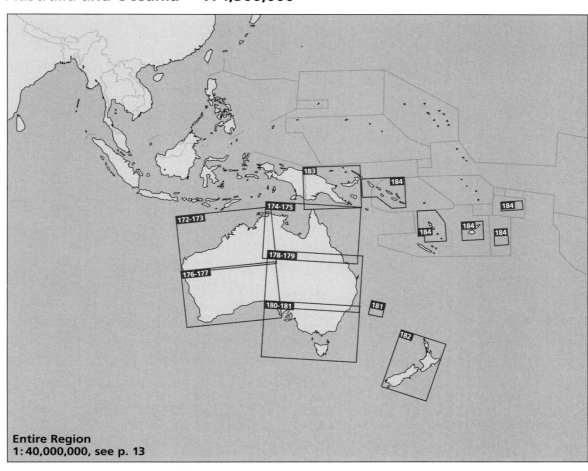

183
184
184
174-175
172-173
178-179
176-177
180-181
181
182

Entire Region
1 : 40,000,000, see p. 13

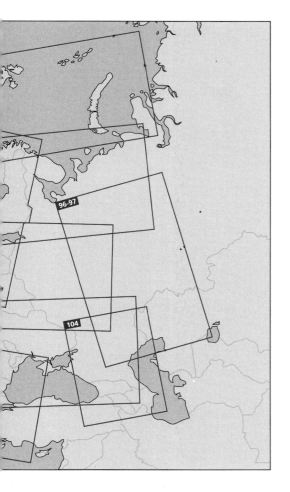

96-97
104

Africa · 1 : 4,500,000

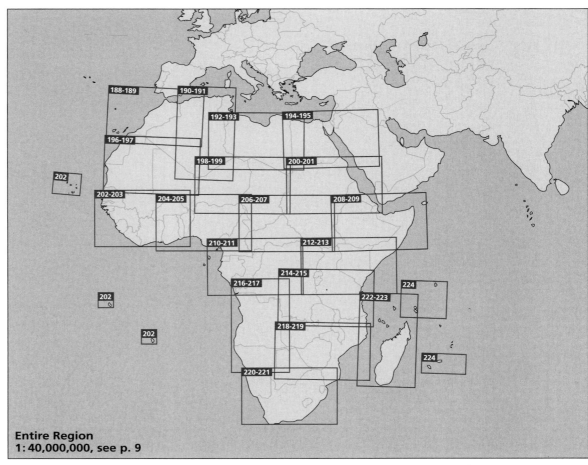

188-189
190-191
192-193
194-195
196-197
198-199
200-201
202
202-203
204-205
206-207
208-209
210-211
212-213
214-215
216-217
222-223
224
202
218-219
202
224
220-221

Entire Region
1 : 40,000,000, see p. 9

112-113
121
118-119
120-121
122-123
150-151
153
154-155
152
156-157
160-161
159
164-165
166-167
41 162-163
168
168

Key to Maps: United States of America and Southern Canada

United States of America and Southern Canada · 1:2,250,000

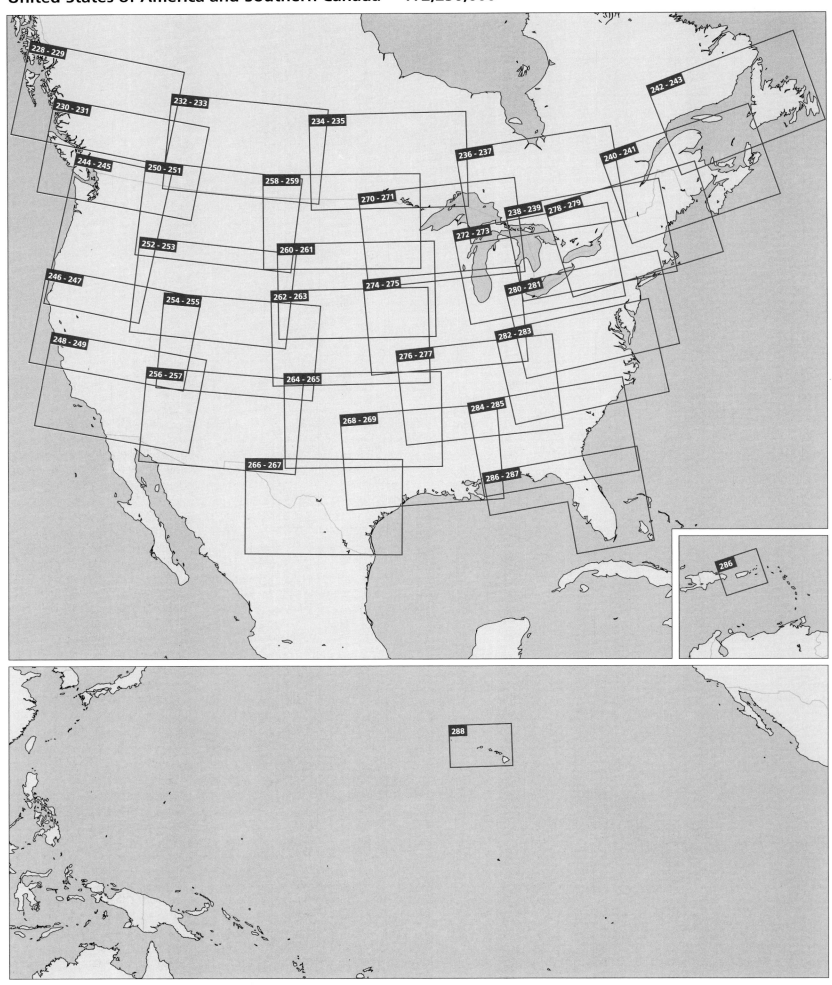

Map Samples

Satellite Imagery

Scale 1 : 40,000,000

Scale 1 : 4,500,000

Scale 1 : 2,250,000

Space travel has provided us with a new image of the Earth. Earth-observation satellites like those in the LANDSAT series orbit the Earth at an altitude of approximately 400 miles (700 kilometers). Sensors on board these satellites detect electromagnetic radiation reflected by the Earth, then transmit this information as photographic data to a global network of ground stations. But to arrive at brilliant satellite images like those selected for inclusion in this book, photographic data received from satellites must first be enhanced in a variety of ways.

Computers help make the gradations of color in the satellite images faithful renditions of their counterparts in nature. Various computer-assisted combinations of individually received spectral bands are used to achieve this accuracy. Filtering and contrast manipulation further enhance the images. Favorable photographic conditions are essential: optimum sunlight, ideal climatic conditions, and a minimum of cloud cover.

Of course, satellite photographs are no substitute for maps, but their multifaceted images do serve as a valuable complement to the cartographic information expressed in maps. Their brilliance is fascinating, and they provide views of the Earth from new and fantastic perspectives.

Space probes can photograph the whole Earth in its entirety as a heavenly body. Satellites in orbit closer to the Earth can photograph areas the size of continents or subcontinents. The view from an airplane reveals individual landscapes. A map's scale expresses the distance between the Earth and an imaginary observer. It determines the extent and contents of the map.

The scale of 1 : 40,000,000 is suitable for representing the Earth as a whole. The world map shows the Earth's major structures, its division into oceans and landmasses, the continents and their relative positions.

The various colors on the continents indicate major zones of vegetation. Bluish violet and yellowish red represent cold and dry deserts, green tones stand for various kinds of plant life. Since vegetation is largely a function of climate, a bluish green color indicates both coniferous forests and the colder climate of higher latitudes. Deep green, on the other hand, represents tropical rain forests in the hot, humid climate near the equator.

Shadings depict major topographic features of the Earth's crust: chains of folded mountains, highlands and basins, lowlands and low-mountain regions.

The majority of maps in this book are drawn in the scale of 1 : 4,500,000. All continents are thoroughly depicted in this scale, with the exception of Antarctica and some of the world's smaller islands. Maps on individual pages show parts of the continents. Settlements, transportation routes and political boundaries of various kinds are clearly visible against a color-coded background denoting the various topographies, climates and vegetation zones.

The spatial distribution and extent of settlements reflects population density. The few, widely spaced urban settlements in sparsely settled regions contrast with the urban sprawl of more densely populated regions. Maps also show the density of transportation networks, the presence or absence of roads and the accessibility of various places, as well as the distances between major intersections and the locations of railroads and airports. Political boundaries indicate international frontiers and national administrative subdivisions.

The representation of cultural sights is more than just an aid to tourists and leisure travelers. These sites are often focal points of ethnocultural traditions, important places of religious worship or national identity.

As a complement to the maps of the world and its continents, a special appendix provides maps depicting the United States and southern Canada in detailed scale of 1 : 2,250,000.

At this scale, maps show a particular wealth of detail. It is possible to distinguish individual forms within the network of rivers and lakes, as well as within the represented relief. These forms range from gently undulating moraine landscapes and lakelands to resurgence valleys in low mountain ranges or individual mountain ranges among high mountains, including their degree of glaciation. The representation of traffic networks shows similar detail. These maps clearly portray the adaptation of towns to the relief or the relationship between their location and other topographic features such as rivers emerging from mountains or mouths of rivers or ocean bays. They also indicate how far cities extend their developed land into the surrounding region. The larger scale permits a greater degree of precision, for example, in the positioning of the numerous topographic map symbols. Other advantages of this scale are the improved definition of locations and greater precision for measuring distances. Large-scale maps are useful for the planning of itineraries.

Explanation of Map Symbols Physical Aspects of the Earth

The Ocean

1. Coastline, shoreline
2. Island(s), archipelago
3. Tidal flat
4. Mangrove coast
5. Coral reef

Bathymetric Tints

6. 0   –   200 meters
7. 200   –   2,000 meters
8. 2000   –   4,000 meters
9. 4000   –   6,000 meters
10. 6000   –   8,000 meters
11. 8000   –   10,000 meters
12. Deeper than 10,000 meters
13. Water depth in meters

Coastlines are drawn with detail and precision in this atlas. As tides ebb and flow, certain sections of coast alternately belong to the mainland and the ocean. This is especially true of tidal flats and mangrove coasts, both of which are specially labeled on the maps.

Coral reefs in tropical oceans are remarkable features. Because of their low tolerance for changes in water temperature, salinity and deterioration in water quality, coral reefs are sensitive indicators of the quality of marine ecosystems.

Ocean depths are represented by bathymetric tints. The epicontinental shelf seas, which attain depths of 656 feet (200 m), are particularly important both politically and economically. During earlier geologic eras, some parts of these zones were dry land. Also known as continental shelves, these regions are rich in economically important resources. The ocean's deepest points are found near the edges of the continents. These deep sea trenches are depicted on individual map pages. Trenches are critical interfaces in the ongoing process of continental genesis and disappearance.

Hydrographic Features

1. Perennial stream or river
2. Tributary river with headwaters
3. Waterfall, rapids
4. Navigable canal
5. Non-navigable canal
6. Freshwater lake
7. Elevation of lake above sea level and depth of Lake
8. Reservoir with dam
9. Marsh, moor
10. Flood plain
11. Lake with variable shoreline

Mostly in Arid Regions

12. Seasonal lake
13. Salt lake
14. Salt swamp
15. River, drying up
16. Intermittent stream (wadi, arroyo)
17. Spring, well

The network of rivers and lakes provides a natural framework for the structures created by human beings in the process of developing and cultivating the land. Rivers and their mouths, bays and lake shores are preferred sites for human settlements. Rivers provide transportation routes, a source of hydroelectric power and water for irrigation. Above all, they supply us with our most basic need - potable water.

The maps depict the catchment areas of larger rivers with the treelike branching of their tributaries. Line thicknesses used in drawing the rivers correspond to their various sizes and to the hierarchy of main artery, major tributaries and headwaters. The paths of the blue lines represent the predominant characteristics of each natural watercourse with its meanders, branches, lakelike widenings and oxbows, as well as the comparatively rigid course of artificial waterways (canals). Agricultural and recreational uses are indicated by reservoirs and dams. The network of rivers and lakes reflects the world's gradient of water resources from abundance to aridity.

Glaciation

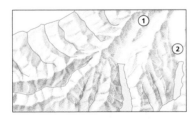

1. Glacier in high-mountain range
2. Glacial tongue

3. Continental ice sheet, icecap
4. Mean pack ice limit in summer
5. Mean pack ice limit in winter

The most recent ice age came to an end about 10,000 years ago. Its traces are still visible on roughly one-third of the Earth's landmasses, 11 percent of which are still covered by ice. The depiction of glaciers in the maps shows the worldwide distribution of these icy deserts. Continental ice sheets occupy by far the largest area, covering all of Antarctica and Greenland with sheets of ice as much as 10,000 feet (3,000 m) thick. Extensive surfaces of ocean, especially around the North Pole, are covered by sea or pack ice, and shelf ice is distributed along the edge of the Antarctic ice sheet. Alpine glaciers cover only a relatively insignificant 1 percent of the landmasses.

Glaciers are almost always in motion, usually at a very slow pace. Glacial tongues tend to move more rapidly. Sometimes reaching lengths of more than 125 miles (200 km), these tongues of ice stretch from continental glaciers to the ocean, where they calve icebergs. Glacial tongues are often the most impressive features of alpine glaciers; larger examples of these ice tongues are shown on the maps.

The Topography of the Earth's Surface

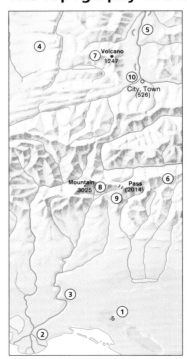

1. Depressed region (land below sea level with depth in meters below sea level)
2. River delta
3. Plain with depressed river valley
4. Hill country and highlands
5. Rift valley
6. Mountain range
7. Active volcano
8. Mountain (with elevation)
9. Pass (with elevation)
10. Approximate elevation of a city above sea level

Representing the third dimension – the topographic relief of the Earth's surface – is a special challenge for cartographers. The maps in this atlas derive their extraordinary plasticity from "relief shading." Gradations from pale to dark on the two-dimensional surface of the page help users visualize the Earth's actual three-dimensional topography. This impression is quantified with precise information about the elevations above sea level of mountains, passes and major cities.

The network of lakes and rivers is the counterpart to the relief depicted on the map. Waterways mark the locations of valleys that divide the topography. These two phenomena combine to provide an expressive picture of the major geographic regions and their underlying tectonic structures.

Particularly clear examples include the Great Rift Valley (which runs from the Near East to southern East Africa), the gigantic basins and high plateaus of central Asia (surrounded by the world's highest mountains), the generously watered lowlands of North and South America, and the mighty ranges of corrugated mountains that form the Andes.

The Biosphere: Continental Ecological Zones

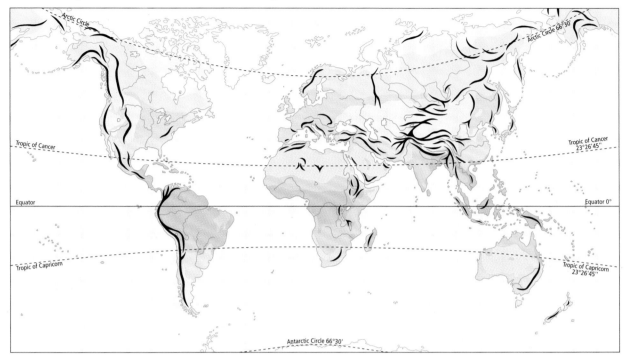

Tropics

I — Perennially humid climates
Tropical rain forest, moist savanna

II — Moist summer climates
Moist and dry savannas, deciduous forests

Subtropics

III — Subtropical-tropical semidesert and desert climates
Thorny scrub, desert

IV — Summer-humid to perennially moist climates
Monsoon forest, shrubs

V — Mediterranean climates with dry summers and moist winters
Shrubs, broadleaved evergreen forests

Temperature zones (middle latitudes)

VI — Winter-cold steppes, semidesert and desert climates
Grasslands (steppe, prairie), desert

VII — Maritime to continental moist climates
Broadleaved deciduous forests, mixed forests

Boreal zone

VIII — Taiga (needleleaved evergreen forests)

Polar and subpolar zone

IX —
a: continental ice, ice cap
b: tundra (lichens, mosses, dwarf shrubs)

High Mountains

Vertical arrangement of plant communities by altitude

Macroclimates are among the most significant of the many factors affecting the distribution of life on earth. Macroclimates influence soil formation and help shape surface topography, as well as affecting plant growth and animal communities, which in turn determine the suitability of a given geographic region for human habitation. All of these biotic and abiotic factors combine to create a complex web in which each factor influences the others in a variety of ways.

Based on climatic conditions and on the prevailing plant communities determined by those conditions, the earth's landmasses can be subdivided into various habitats and ecozones. The boundaries between these zones, however, are not sharply defined. Instead, each zone emanates from a central region with characteristics typical of that zone, makes a transition across a boundary belt, and then more or less gradually changes into the adjacent landscape zone.

Although the limits of continental ecozones generally correspond to latitude, these zones exhibit two important asymmetries: regions of winter rainfall (Mediterranean climate) occur only along the western edges of the continents; regions with moist summers (or perennially moist tropics) are located exclusively on the eastern edges (so-called "Shanghai climates").

Trees in Eurasia and America cannot grow beyond about 70 degrees of latitude; in South America tree-line occurs at 57 degrees, in New Zealand and Oceania at 48 degrees. The boreal or "northern" band of coniferous forests is entirely absent in the Southern Hemisphere because of the relatively limited extent of land area and the associated dominance of the ocean.

Arrangement of Ecological Zones by Altitude

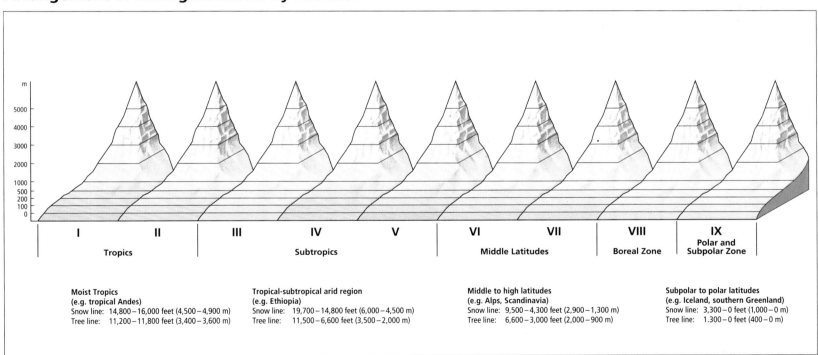

Moist Tropics
(e.g. tropical Andes)
Snow line: 14,800–16,000 feet (4,500–4,900 m)
Tree line: 11,200–11,800 feet (3,400–3,600 m)

Tropical-subtropical arid region
(e.g. Ethiopia)
Snow line: 19,700–14,800 feet (6,000–4,500 m)
Tree line: 11,500–6,600 feet (3,500–2,000 m)

Middle to high latitudes
(e.g. Alps, Scandinavia)
Snow line: 9,500–4,300 feet (2,900–1,300 m)
Tree line: 6,600–3,000 feet (2,000–900 m)

Subpolar to polar latitudes
(e.g. Iceland, southern Greenland)
Snow line: 3,300–0 feet (1,000–0 m)
Tree line: 1.300–0 feet (400–0 m)

An essential feature of geographic landscapes is their three-dimensional structure. The maps in this atlas provide clearly legible depictions of heights and depths on the face of the Earth. The arrangement of ecological zones is largely dependent upon latitude. This pattern, however, is overlaid by mountain ranges, which cut across latitudinally oriented climatic zones to create their own ecosystems where altitude creates characteristic ecological arrangements. A visible expression of the fact that biological conditions vary with altitude is the vertical arrangement of typical plant commu-

nities: generally forest (grassland) – meadows – cliffs (or talus) – ice (or glacier). This arrangement also creates characteristic ecological boundary lines: above, the tree line and the (climatic) snow line; and in arid regions, the lower tree line as well.

Elevations show typical climatic characteristics depending on a mountain range's location in the overall pattern of global climatic zones. Tropical mountains, for example, experience the same diurnal climatic variations typical of their neighboring lowlands.

The upper tree line in mountainous regions is caused by the lack of adequate warmth. The lower tree line found in arid regions is related to the lack of adequate moisture. This combination restricts the growth of forests in arid regions to more or less wide bands along the slopes of mountains.

Where a lower tree line is now found in humid high mountain regions, or where the band of forest is entirely absent in certain places, the causes of this deforestation are likely to be manmade.

Forests in mountainous regions provide abso-

lutely essential protection against avalanches and slope erosion.

The cultivation of crops in mountainous regions is likewise limited by prevailing climatic factors which, in turn, are primarily a function of elevation. In the Andes, for example, grains cannot be cultivated above 5,000 feet (1,500 m), although in the tropical Andes millet can be grown at elevations as high as 14,400 feet (4,400 m). With the exception of mining camps and settlements of shepherds at still higher elevations, these heights mark the upper limits of permanent human settlement.

Explanation of Map Symbols Manmade Features on Earth

The Map Margins

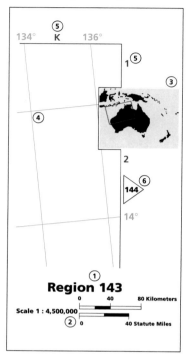

Region 143

Scale 1 : 4,500,000

① Page number and short title

② Numeric and graphic map scales
(scales in kilometers and miles)

③ Locator map showing the position and extent of
continental area covered by that particular map
page

④ Map grid (graticule) and its designation

	.0 degrees longitude (Meridian of Greenwich) = Gr.	
	Longitude 180 degrees to 1 degree west of Gr.	Longitude 1 degree to 180 degrees east of Gr.

Latitude 1 degree to 90 degrees north of the equator	Latitude 1 degree to 90 degrees north of the equator
Equator 0 degrees	**Equator 0 degrees**
Latitude 1 degree to 90 degrees south of the Equator	Latitude 1 degree to 90 degrees south of the Equator
Longitude 180 degrees to 1 degree west of Gr.	Longitude 1 degree to 180 degrees east of Gr.

0 degrees longitude of
Greenwich = Gr.

⑤ Grid search key as specified for each index entry:
Letters at top/bottom
Numbers at left/right
with graticule as searching grid

⑥ Page number of adjacent map page

Along with the short title and the page number, further aid in using the atlas is provided by the map overviews in the preface and by the locator maps at the beginning of each series of maps of individual continents. The number inside a small triangle on each map indicates the page where a map of the adjacent region can be found.

A locator map at the top right-hand corner of each double-page spread shows the area within the particular continent depicted by that particular map page. The scale notations in the lower margin are essential for determining geographic

distances. They express the relationship between a given distance on the map and a corresponding distance in the real world.

For centuries, the degree-calibrated latitude and longitude grid system has been used to define locations and plot courses on the face of the globe. The red letters along the top and bottom, together with the red numbers along the left and right margins, identify individual fields within the blue search grid.

Settlements and Transportation Routes

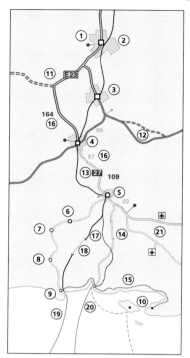

Town Symbols

① Urban area
(normally surrounding cities with populations over 100,000)

② Population over 5 million

③ 1,000,000 – 5,000,000

④ 500,000 – 1,000,000

⑤ 100,000 – 500,000

⑥ 50,000 – 100,000

⑦ 10,000 – 50,000

⑧ 5,000 – 10,000

⑨ Population less than 5,000

⑩ Settlement, hamlet, research station
(in remote areas often seasonally inhabited only)

Transportation Routes

⑪ Superhighway, four or more lanes, with number in blue

⑫ Highway under construction

⑬ Main road with number

⑭ Other road – road tunnel

⑮ Unpaved road, track

⑯ Distance in kilometers

⑰ Railway: main track – other track

⑱ Railway tunnel

⑲ Railway ferry

⑳ Car ferry – shipping line

㉑ International airport
Domestic airport

Town symbols correspond to the populations of their respective places. The density of these symbols on the map combines with their relative values to indicate a region's population density and settlement structure (urban area or smaller, equally distributed towns).

The representation of urban areas sheds light on the increasing concentration of humanity in major metropolitan areas. According to UNESCO, by the year 2000 approximately half of the world's population will live in cities occupying only about four percent of the Earth's total land area.

In the depiction of transportation routes, special emphasis has been given to the representation of continental road networks. This corresponds to the importance of such networks on the threshold of the 21st century. Transportation of economically important goods, tourism, and the migrations of people searching for work or fleeing disasters all take place primarily over roads. These routes have been classified and numbered according to their relative importance. Distance specifications help map users make accurate calculations of distances.

Political and Other Boundaries

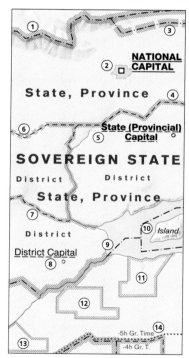

① International boundary

② Capital of a sovereign state

③ Disputed international boundary

④ 1st-order administrative boundary
(e.g. region, state, autonomous region, province)

⑤ Capital city (1st-order administrative seat)

⑥ Disputed 1st-order administrative boundary

⑦ 2nd-order administrative boundary
(e.g. region, area, province, country)

⑧ 2nd-order administrative seat

⑨ Boundary along watercourses or across bodies of water

⑩ Dependent region and specification of nation with jurisdiction

⑪ National park, national monument

⑫ Reservation

⑬ Restricted area

⑭ Boundary of a time zone with difference between local time and Greenwich Mean Time (GMT)

The documentation of territorial possessions was one of the reasons maps were invented. Maps play a central political role in border disputes and are an indispensable aid in interpreting or representing spatially related statistical data. The vast majority of statistical studies are based on national units or on regions within nations. Regardless of whether population distribution, buying power or cancer-incidence rates are measured, maps are the most convincing method of visually presenting and interpreting data.

International boundaries occupy first place in the hierarchy of political boundaries. They are therefore clearly marked in this atlas. First-order administrative boundaries, which define the limits of the major administrative units within a nation, come next in rank. Secondary boundaries are drawn when their political status merits it, providing their average surface area permits graphic representation on the scale involved. The maps also show capital cities or administrative seats of the depicted administrative entities.

Places and Points of Interest

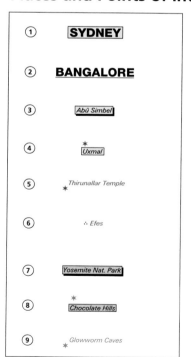

① Place of special interest

② Place of interest

③ UNESCO World Cultural Heritage Site

④ Cultural monument of special interest

⑤ Interesting cultural monument

⑥ Ancient monument or excavation

⑦ UNESCO World Natural Heritage Site

⑧ Natural monument of special interest

⑨ Interesting natural monument

The maps in this atlas provide the reader with a global view of the Blue Planet's most remarkable places and points of interest. These include exceptional monuments of natural or historico-cultural developments. Many of these places are important to national, ethnic or religious identity. This atlas places such sites in their geographical contexts. Graphic distinctions are made between natural and cultural monuments and according to their significance as magnets for tourism. UNESCO, a suborganization of the United Nations, has designated selected cultural sites and natural

monuments worldwide as part of the "heritage of mankind" and urged their special preservation. These sites are specially marked in the atlas. The volume thus provides not only an informative manual for globetrotters with widely ranging interests, but also serves as a helpful supplement for students of travel and nature guides or of relevant artistic and historico-cultural literature.

Lettering of Cities and Towns

① **TEHRĀN**
MONTEVIDEO

② **MIAMI**
LE HAVRE

③ MANHATTAN
VAIHINGEN

④ **Darwin**
Thimphu

⑤ Gallipolis
Grindelwald
Laugarvatn

⑥ **BOLZANO**
BOZEN

⑦ **HALAP**
(ALEPPO)

⑧ **FRANKFURT**
am Main

Type size indicates the relative importance and population of the town

① City with a population over one million
② Large city
③ Boroughs of large cities or of cities with populations over one million
④ Medium-sized city
⑤ Small town, rural community
⑥ Place names in region with two official languages
⑦ Place name, alternate or earlier form
⑧ Official supplement to a place name

This atlas includes carefully selected place names. Type size corresponds to the number of inhabitants; type face indicates the particular significance or function of the place. Place names in capital letters indicate large cities with more than 100,000 inhabitants.

Some names of important places, landscape features and bodies of water are written in the accepted American form, but as a general rule, place names are written in the official national spelling. In the case of countries having two official languages, both versions are given. This rule also applies to all other geographic names.

Letter-oriented transliteration or phonetic transcription is used to spell names from languages with non-Roman alphabets. Wherever possible, the atlas has followed accepted standards for such procedures.

Geographic names can offer valuable insights into historical developments and relationships.

Topographic Typography

① **CHILE**   *Réunion*   (France)

② *GOBI*   *Cappadocia*   *Kimberley*

③ **ANDES**   Nan Ling   *Tibesti*

④ Mt. McKinley   Simplonpass (2005)   Cabo de Hornos
6194

⑤ *JAVA*   *Galápagos Islands*   York Peninsula

⑥ *PACIFIC OCEAN*
Finskij zaliv   The Channel

⑦ *Niger*   *Panama Canal*   *Taj Hu*   *Niagara Falls*

⑧ *Yucatán Basin*   *Cayman Trench*

⑨ Nazca Ridge   Aves Ridge

⑩ *Aboriginal Land*   *Military Training Area*

⑪ 8848   *10540*   398

① Nation, administrative unit, designation of sovereignty
② Landscape, historical landscape
③ Mountains, mountain range, highland
④ Mountain with elevation above sea level, pass with elevation above sea level, cape
⑤ Island, archipelago, peninsula
⑥ Ocean, sea, gulf, bay, strait
⑦ River, canal, lake, waterfall
⑧ Undersea landscapes, trenches
⑨ Undersea mountains
⑩ Reservation, restricted areas
⑪ Elevation in meters above sea level
Depth in oceans and lakes, elevation of lake surface

Lettering and typeface help explain the various features on a map. They also serve to structure geographic data according to significance and rank. These distinctions are reflected by the use of either all capital letters or mixtures of capital and lower-case letters, and by various type faces and sizes. Color also supports these distinctions: for example, rivers are labeled in blue, political units in gray, and sites of natural interest in green. Colored backgrounds or colored underlining indicates sites of interest to tourists.

Geographic names are one of the ways human beings express their possession of the land. People have given names to the remotest islands, to minor coves in the inhospitable Antarctic and to barely defined coastal promontories. The maps in this atlas, as in any other atlas, can include only the most important of these geographic names. All of them are listed in alphabetical order in the index of geographic names, together with search-grid designations that make it easy to pinpoint them on individual maps.

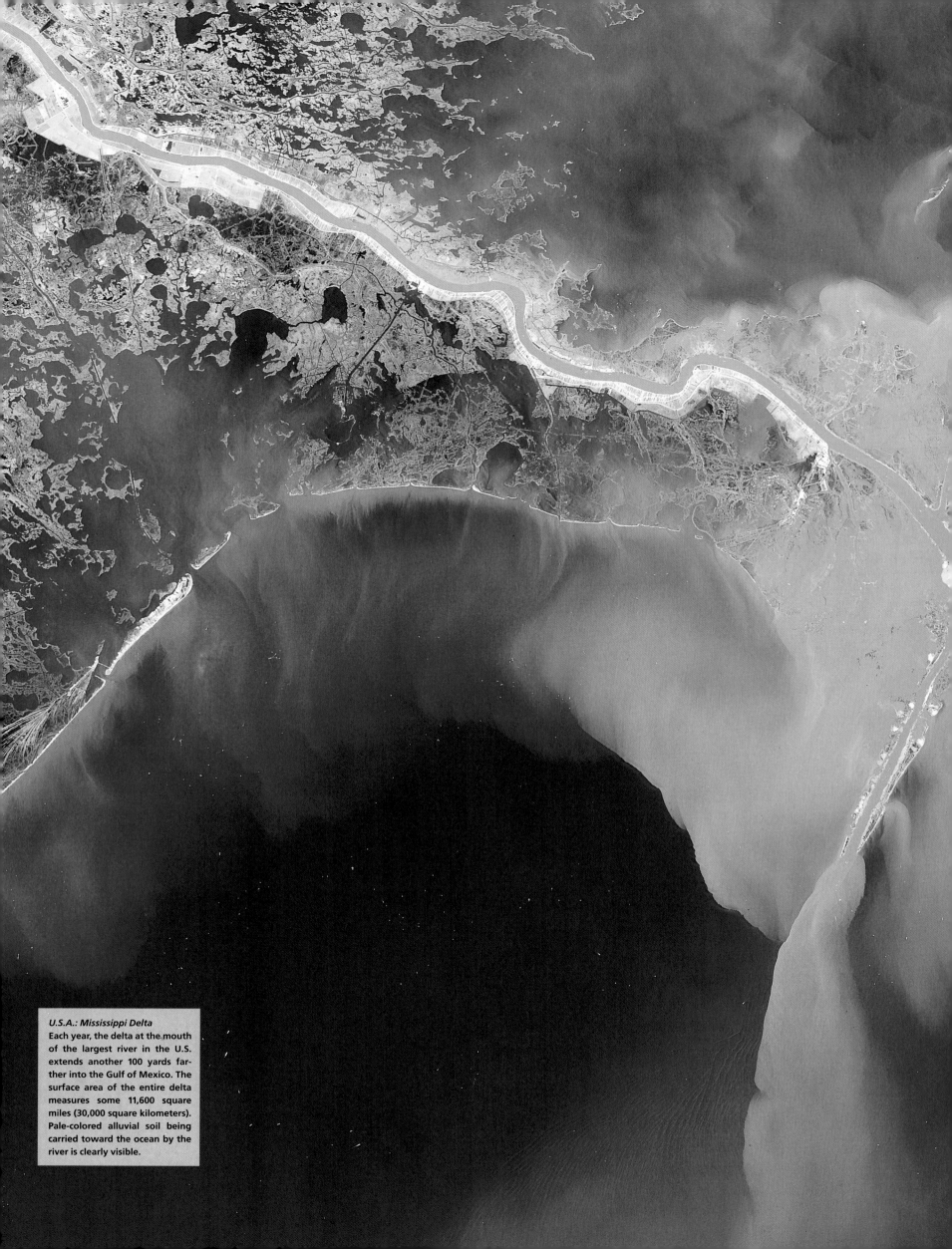

U.S.A.: Mississippi Delta
Each year, the delta at the mouth of the largest river in the U.S. extends another 100 yards farther into the Gulf of Mexico. The surface area of the entire delta measures some 11,600 square miles (30,000 square kilometers). Pale-colored alluvial soil being carried toward the ocean by the river is clearly visible.

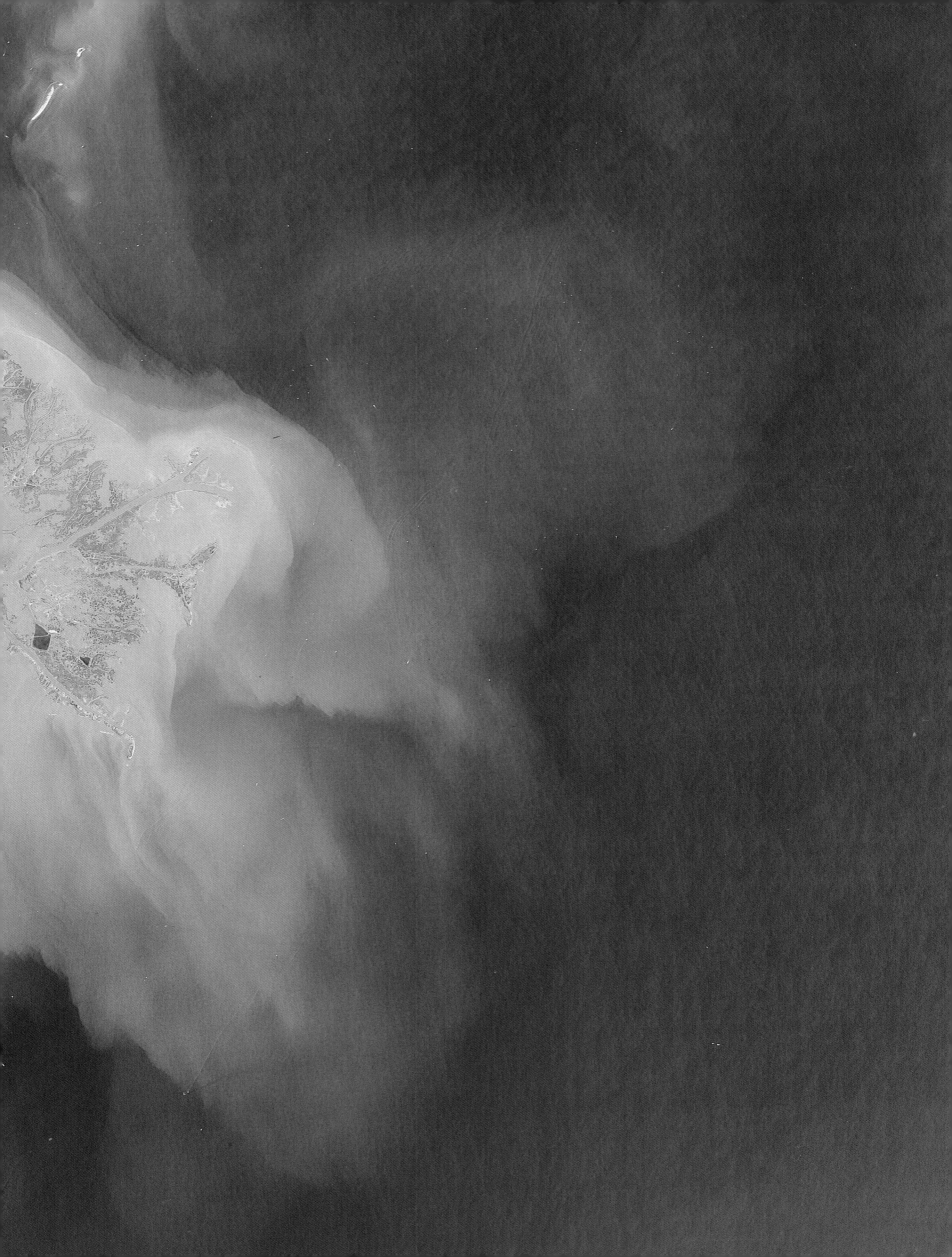

Brazil: Amazon River
To the east of the city of Manaus, the dark waters of the Rio Negro meet the coffee-colored waters of the Amazon. The gradual mixing of water from the two rivers is clearly visible at the photograph's upper right corner. The region's chief characteristic is the tropical rain forest, an endangered ecosystem.

Switzerland: Upper Rhône Valley
The valley of the Upper Rhône crosses the depicted region from the northeast to the southwest. Sickle-shaped Aletsch Glacier, the Alps' largest river of ice, can be seen at the center. Together with its branches, the glacier measures 15 miles (24 km) long with an area of 46 square miles (120 sq. km). Lake Brienz and Lake Thun at the upper left occupy valleys that have been deepened by glacial erosion.

Siberia: Taiga at the Ob River
The pale green region in the left-hand portion of the photograph shows the broad riparian meadows, traversed by the Ob River. The shallow gradient of the land in the west Siberian lowlands allows the river to form many side channels and twisting bends with oxbow lakes and ponds.

Sahara Desert/Algeria: Star Dunes
The photograph shows part of the Great Eastern Erg in eastern Algeria. The many-armed star dune formations are situated like pale yellow warts atop the flat, darker, faintly visible stripes of the longitudinal dunes. Star dunes attain heights of between 330 and 660 feet (100 and 200 meters).

The World

Among the planets of the solar system, the Earth is unique – not just because of its atmosphere, but above all because of its "face," whose features are the three oceans, occupying over two-thirds of the 196,911,000 square miles (510 million sq. km) of the surface of the Earth, and the seven continents. The Pacific Ocean alone is larger than all land areas together; the largest of these, in turn, is Eurasia, occupying a good third of the total. The highest elevations are reached in the Himalayas, where Mount Everest rises to 29,022 feet (8,846 m). Ten mountains over 26,000 feet can be found in this massive mountain range separating the Indian subcontinent from the rest of Asia. The longest mountain range is the Cordilleras, stretching the entire length of North and South America.

Not entirely up to date: This anonymous woodcut (1530) represents only the continents of the Old World and populates them with fantastic beasts taken from the prophesies of Daniel.

The deepest place on Earth is the Vitiaz Deep (–36,161 feet/ –11,022 m) in the Marianas Trench near the southeast Asian archipelagos. The deepest depression on Earth lies 1,312 feet (400 m) below sea level and is part of a rift valley system that includes the East African faults and the Red Sea. A trench is also the home of the deepest lake with the greatest water volume, Lake Baikal, with a depth of 5,315 feet (1,620 m). The face of the Earth is given further character by volcano chains, such as the Hawaiian Islands, as well as by the icy masses of Antarctica, Greenland and high mountain glaciers.

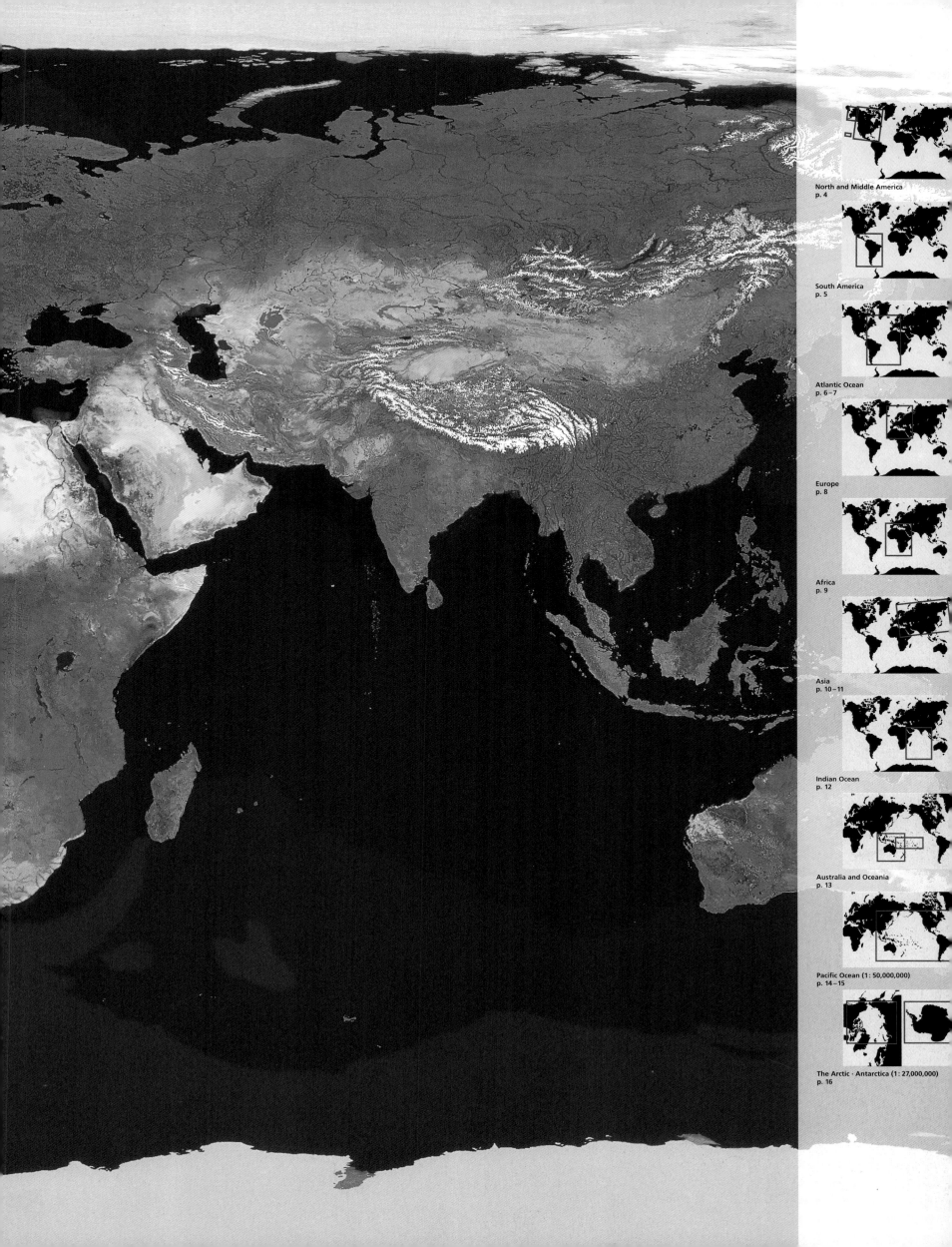

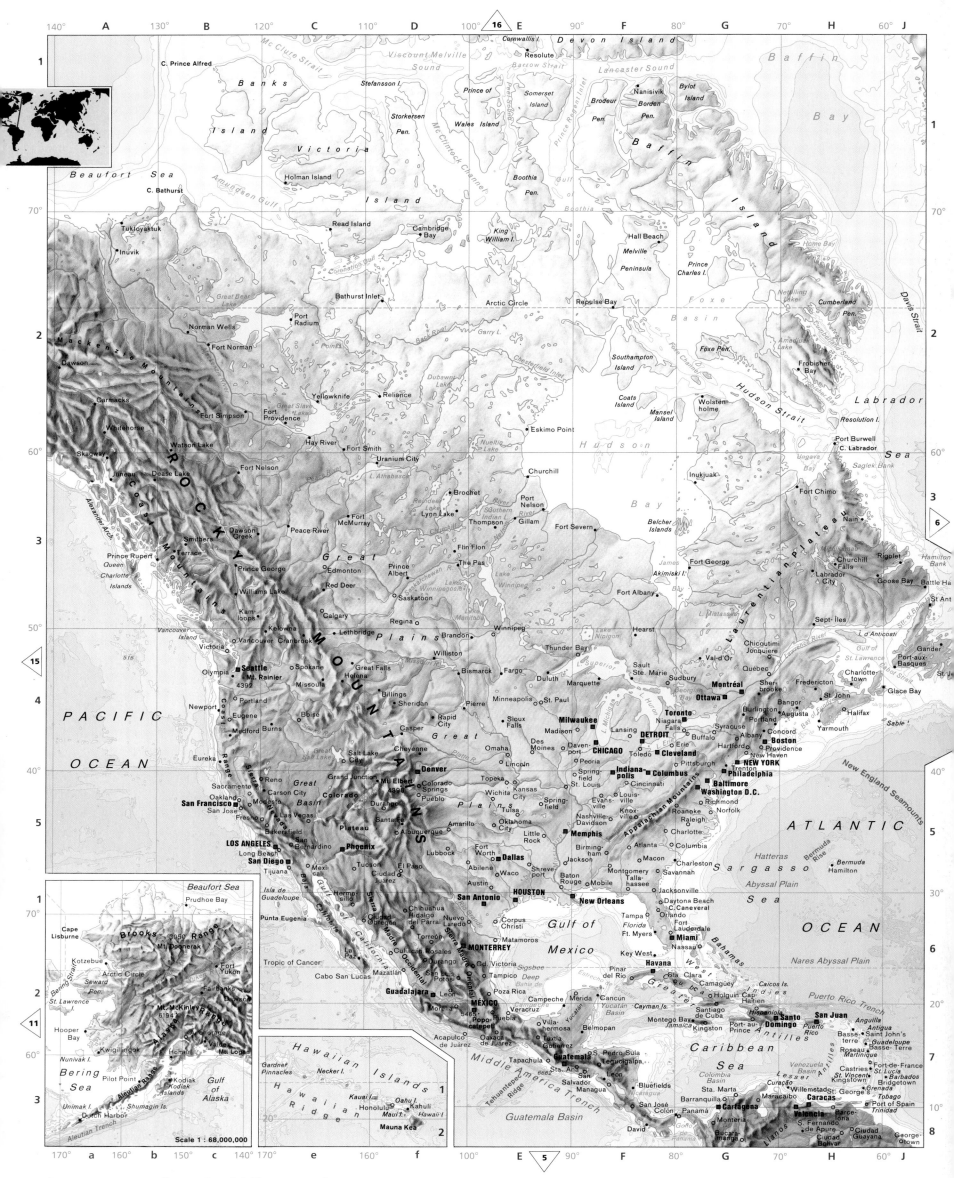

140° A **130°** B **120°** C **110°** D **100°** 16 E **90°** F **80°** G **70°** H **60°** J

1

Beaufort Sea

C. Prince Alfred

Banks

Island

Victoria

Island

McClure Strait

Viscount Melville
Sound

Stefansson I.

Prince of
Wales Island

Storkersen
Pen.

McClintock Channel

Somerset
Island

Boothia
Pen.

Prince Regent Inlet

Barrow Strait

Cornwallis I.
Resolute

Devon Island

Lancaster Sound

Brodeur
Pen.

Borden
Pen.

Nanisivik

Bylot
Island

Baffin

Bay

Baffin

Island

1

Holman Island

C. Bathurst

2

Tuktoyaktuk

Inuvik

Mackenzie Mountains

Dawson

Carmacks

Whitehorse

Skagway

Juneau

Norman Wells

Fort Norman

Great Bear
Lake

Port
Radium

Read Island

Cambridge
Bay

Bathurst Inlet

Coronation Gulf

Back River

Garry L.

King
William I.

Boothia

Gulf of

Repulse Bay

Arctic Circle

Hall Beach

Melville

Peninsula

Prince
Charles I.

Southampton
Island

Coats
Island

Mansel
Island

Wolsten-
holme

Foxe
Basin

Foxe Pen.

Netsilling
Lake

Frobisher
Bay

Cumberland
Pen.

Labrador

Davis Strait

2

70°

70°

Watson Lake

Dease Lake

Prince Rupert

Queen
Charlotte
Islands

Alexander Arch.

ROCKY

Smithers

Terrace

Prince George

Dawson
Creek

Fort Nelson

Fort Simpson

Fort
Providence

Yellowknife

Great Slave
Lake

Hay River

Reliance

Fort Smith

Uranium City

L. Athabasca

Dubawnt
Lake

Nueltin
Lake

Eskimo Point

Churchill

Hudson

Bay

James
Bay

Belcher
Islands

Akimiski I.

Fort George

Inukjuak

Ungava
Bay

Fort Chimo

Saglek Bank

Nain

Resolution I.

Port Burwell
C. Labrador

60°

Labrador

Sea

Laurentian Plateau

Churchill
Falls

Rigolet

Hamilton
Bank

Goose Bay

Battle Ha

60°

3

Peace River

Fort
McMurray

Great

Brochet

Lynn Lake

Reindeer
Lake

The Pas

Flin Flon

Southern
Indian Lake

Port
Nelson

Gillam

Thompson

Fort Severn

Fort Albany

Hearst

L. Mistassini

Chicoutimi
Jonquiere

Sept-Îles

Labrador
City

I. d'Anticosti

St Ant

St An

6

3

Prince George

Williams Lake

Kam-
loops

Kelowna

Cranbrook

Vancouver
Island

Victoria

Edmonton

Red Deer

Calgary

Lethbridge

Prince
Albert

Saskatoon

Regina

Brandon

Saskatchewan R.

Winnipegosis
Lake

Lake
Winnipeg

Plains

Williston

Winnipeg

Manitoba

Thunder Bay

L. Nipigon

L. Superior

Val-d'Or

Québec

Port-aux-
Basques

Charlotte-
town

Gander

Gulf of
St. Lawrence

St. Lawrence River

50°

50°

4

PACIFIC

OCEAN

Newport

Olympia

Seattle

Mt. Rainier
4392

Portland

Eugene

Medford

Burns

Bbise

Coast Range

Spokane

Great Falls

Missoula

Helena

Billings

Sheridan

Casper

Snake R.

MOUNTAINS

Salt
Lake
Great

Bismarck

Fargo

Duluth

Minneapolis

Pierre

Rapid
City

Great

St. Paul

Marquette

Sioux
Falls

Madison

Sault
Ste. Marie

Milwaukee

Lansing

Sudbury

L. Huron

Georgian
Bay

Toronto

L. Erie

L. Michigan

CHICAGO

DETROIT

Cleveland

Ottawa

Montréal

Niagara
Falls

Buffalo

Toledo

Erie

Pittsburgh

Sher-
brooke

Burlington

Syracuse

Hartford

Albany

Concord

St. John

Bangor

Augusta

Fredericton

Portland

New Haven

Boston

Halifax

Yarmouth

Glace Bay

Sable I.

40°

40°

5

Eureka

Sacramento

Oakland

San Francisco

San Jose

Fresno

Bakersfield

Reno

Carson City

Las Vegas

Sierra Nevada

Great

Basin

Salt Lake
City

Colorado

Denver

Grand Junction

Mt. Elbert
4395

Colorado
Springs

Durango

Plateau

Santafe

Albuquerque

Cheyenne

Platte R.

Lincoln

Omaha

Des
Moines

Daven-
port

Peoria

Spring-
field

St. Louis

Cincinnati

Topeka

Kansas
City

Wichita

Great

Plains

Tulsa

Oklahoma
City

Amarillo

Little
Rock

Spring-
field

Evans-
ville

Nashville
Davidson

Memphis

Indiana-
polis

Columbus

Louis-
ville

Knox-
ville

Appalachian Mountains

Roanoke

Richmond

Norfolk

Baltimore

Washington D.C.

Philadelphia

NEW YORK

Trenton

Raleigh

ATLANTIC

New England Seamounts

Bermuda
Rise

Bermuda

Hamilton

5

San Diego

LOS ANGELES

Long Beach

San
Bernardino

Phoenix

Tucson

Mexicali

Tijuana

El Paso

Ciudad
Juárez

Lubbock

Fort
Worth

Dallas

Abilene

Waco

Austin

San Antonio

Shreve-
port

Baton
Rouge

HOUSTON

New Orleans

Jackson

Birming-
ham

Atlanta

Montgomery

Talla-
hassee

Mobile

Macon

Charlotte

Columbia

Charleston

Savannah

Jacksonville

Daytona Beach

C. Canaveral

Orlando

Tampa

Florida

Ft. Myers

Ft.
Lauderdale

Miami

Nassau

Hatteras

Sargasso

Sea

Abyssal Plain

30°

6

San Diego

Isla de
Guadalupe

Punta Eugenia

Tropic of Cancer

Cabo San Lucas

La
Paz

Hermo-
sillo

Chihuahua

Hidalgo
del Parral

Ciudad
Obregon

Culiacán

Rosales

Durango

Mazatlán

Sierra Madre Occidental

Gulf of California

Sierra Madre Oriental

Nuevo
Laredo

Torreón

San Luis
Potosí

MONTERREY

Cd.
Victoria

Tampico

Poza Rica

Matamoros

Corpus
Christi

Gulf of

Mexico

Sigsbee
Deep

Bahía de
Campeche

Key West

Havana

Pinar
del Rio

Sta. Clara

Camagüey

Holguin

Santiago
de Cuba

Greater

Cuba

West Indies

Antilles

Caicos Is.

Haitien

Bahamas

Puerto Rico Trench

Nares Abyssal Plain

OCEAN

20°

Guadalajara

León

MÉXICO

Morelia

Popo-
catepetl

5465

Puebla

Toluca

Oaxaca
de Juárez

Acapulco
de Juárez

Veracruz

Mérida

Cancún

Yucatán

Campeche

Villa-
hermosa

Belmopan

Tuxtla
Gutiérrez

Tapachula

Middle America Trench

Tehuantepec

Yucatán
Basin

Montego Bay
Jamaica

Kingston

Cayman
Basin

Cayman Is.

Port-au-
Prince

Hispaniola

Santo
Domingo

Puerto
Rico

San Juan

Anguilla

Antigua

Saint John's

Basse-
terre

Guadeloupe
Basse-Terre

Lesser

Antilles

Martinique

Fort-de-France

Roseau

Castries

St. Lucia

St. Vincent

Kingstown

Barbados

Bridgetown

Grenada

George's

Tobago

Port of Spain

Trinidad

Caribbean

Sea

7

Guatemala Basin

Guatemala

Tegucigalpa

S. Pedro Sula

San
Salvador

Managua

Leon

S. Ana

Bluefields

Nicaragua

San
José

Colón

Panamá

David

Golfo

Monteria

Barranquilla

Sta. Marta

Cartagena

Maracaibo

Bucara-
manga

Cúcuta

Ciudad
Guayana

Ciudad
Bolívar

S. Fernando
de Apure

Barce-
lona

Valencia

CARACAS

Llanos

Colombia
Basin

Venezuela Basin

George-
Town

8

10°

8

Scale 1 : 68,000,000

Brooks Range

3050
Mt. Doonerak

Beaufort Sea

Prudhoe Bay

Cape
Lisburne

Kotzebue

Seward
Pen.

Arctic Circle

Fort
Yukon

Fairbanks

Dawson

Bering Strait

St. Lawrence
I.

Hooper
Bay

Nunivak I.

Pilot Point

St. Lawrence

Mt. McKinley
6194

Alaska Range

Kenai

Anchorage

Valdez

Mt. Logan
5959

Homer

Kodiak
Island

Kodiak

Bering

Sea

Kwigillingok

Unimak I.

Dutch Harbor

Shumagin Is.

Aleutian Trench

Aleutian Basin

Gulf of
Alaska

70°

60°

1

2

3

a 170° b 160° c 150° 140°

Hawaiian Islands

Hawaiian Ridge

Gardner
Pinnacles

Necker I.

Kauai I.

Oahu I.

Honolulu

Maui I.

Kahuli

Hawaii I.

Mauna Kea

1

2

e 170° f 160°

20°

4

North and Middle America

Scale at the equator 1:40,000,000

South America **5**

Scale at the equator 1:40,000,000

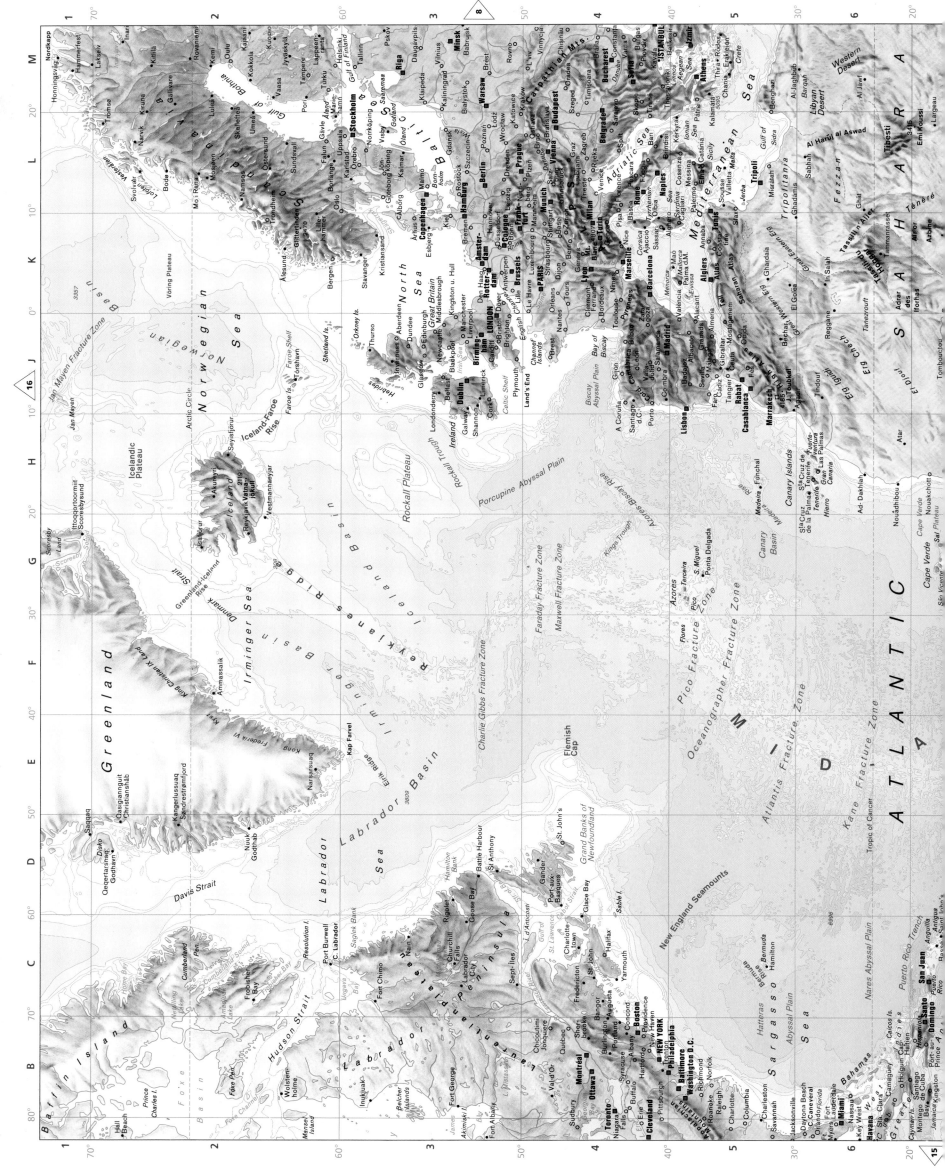

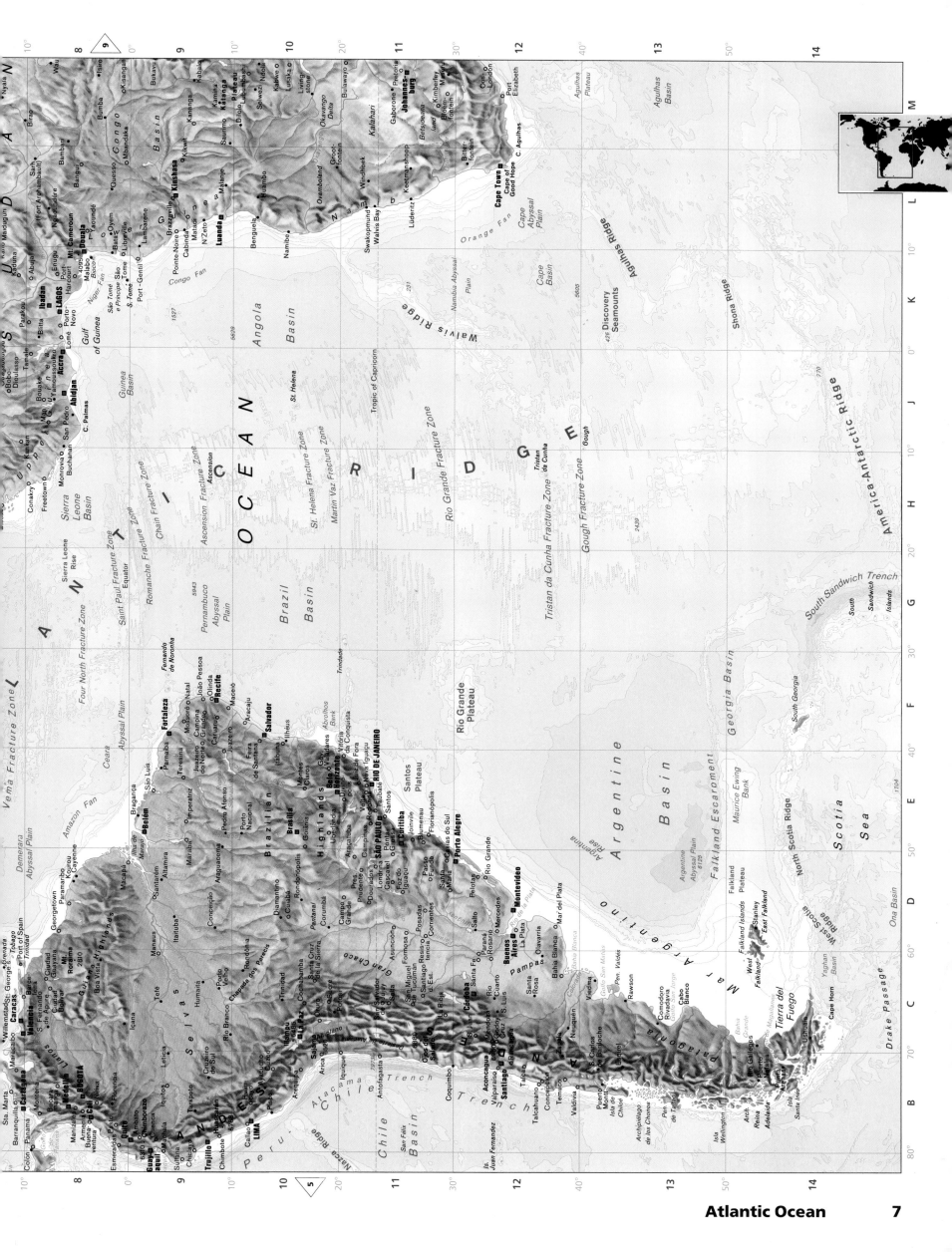

A 20°　　B 10°　　C 0°　　D 10°　　E 20°　　F 30°　　G 40°　　H 50°　　J 60°

Spitsbergen

Hopen

Greenland Sea

Shannon Ø

Barents Sea

Novaja Zemlja

Traill I.

Scoresby Land

Ittoqqortoormiit Scoresbysund

Jan Mayen Fracture Zone

3357

Jan Mayen

Icelandic Plateau

Vöring Plateau

Norwegian Basin

Murmanskoye Rise

70°

Nordkapp
Honningsvåg　Berlevåg
Hammerfest　Vadsø
Lakselv　Kirkenes

o. Vajgač

o. Kolguev

mys Kanin Nos

Tromsø

Murmansk　Mezen
Narvik　Kiruna
Kitilä
Bodø　Gällivare

Kola Peninsula

p-ov Kanin

Narjan-Mar

Ust'-Usa

Pečora

Isafjörur　Akureyri
Seyisfjörur

Iceland

2119 *Vatna-jökull*
Reykjavik

Vestmannaeyjar

Iceland-Faroe Rise

Faroe Is.　*Faroe Shelf*
Tórshavn

Shetland Is.

Mo i Rana

Mosjøen　Rovaniemi
Kuusamo
Namsos　Kemi　Belo-morsk
Umeå　Oulu

Trondheim

Ålesund　Östersund　Vaasa
Kajaani
Kokkola

Kuopio　Joensuu
Jyväskylä

White Sea

Arhangel'sk

Karelia

Onašskoe oz.

Ust'-Vaen'ga

Uchta

Syktyvkar

Kotlas

70°

Arctic Circle

North Sea

Rockall Plateau

Rockall Trough

Porcupine Abyssal Plain

Glittertinden 2470
Lille-hammer

Bergen　Oslo　Borlänge

Stavanger
Kristiansand

Orkney Is.

Hebrides
Thurso
Inverness　Aberdeen
Dundee
Glasgow　Edinburgh
Newcastle
Londonderry　Middlesbrough
Belfast　Blackpool
Manchester
Liverpool
Dublin　Kingston u. Hull

Falun　Gävle
Sundsvall

Petro-zavodsk

Ladožskoe oz.

Syktyvkar

Bereznik

Vjatka

Serov

60°

60°

Skellefteå
Luleå

Gulf of Bothnia

Pori
Tampere
Turku
Lappeen-ranta

Helsinki
Gulf of Finland
Tallinn
Novgorod

ST. PETERSBURG

Vologda

Rybinsk

Rybinskoe vdchr.

Tver'
Jaroslavl'

Niźnij Tagil

Perm

Ekaterinburg

Iževsk

Kazan'

Sarapul

Ufa

Magnito-gorsk

10

Great Britain

Karlstad
Örebro
Norrköping

STOCKHOLM

Visby

Åland
Marie-hamn

Vyborg

Gotland

Riga

Pskov
Velikie Luki

Smolensk

Vilnius

Sergijev-Posad

Kaluga

MOSCOW

Kolomna
Rjazan'

Ul'ja-simbirsk

Toljatti

Samara

Syzran

Orsk

Akt'ubinsk

Galway
Shannon
Limerick
Cork

Birming-ham
Cardiff
LONDON
Bristol
Plymouth

Ireland
Irish Sea

Den Haag　Hannover
Rotter-dam
Cologne　Leipzig
Brussels　Dresden

Dover
Brighton
English Channel

Land's End

Celtic Shelf

Channel Islands
Brest

Esbjerg

Kiel

Århus
Copenhagen　Malmö
Bornholm

Hamburg
Bremen

Berlin

Rostock
Szczecin

Gdańsk

Kaliningrad

Klaipeda

Daugávpils

Minsk

Homel'

Babrujsk

Brést

Orel

Kursk

Voronež

Tambov

Penza

Saratov

Èngel's

Ural'sk

50°

50°

Le Havre
PARIS
Orléans

Nantes
Tours

Düsseldorf
Bonn
Frank-furt
Nürn-berg
Mannheim

Luxembourg
Strasbourg
Stuttgart

Poznań
Łódź
Wrocław
Katowice

Warsaw

Białystok

Poznań

Prague
Plzeň
Brno
Ostrava

L'viv

Rovno

Žytomyr

Kiev

Kharkov

Dnipro-petrovs'k

Krivyj Rih

Luhans'k

Donec'k

Rostov n.D.

Zariżyn

Volgogradskoe vdchr.

Kamyšin

Atyrau

Astrahan'

Caspian Depression

Dijon
Clermont-Ferrand

Berno
Zürich
Munich
Salz-burg

Vienna
Bratislava

Budapest

Oradea

Szeged
Timisoara

Chişinău

Vinnycja

Odessa

Crimea

Sevastopol

Azovskoe more

Maryupol'

Krasnodar

Stavropol

Aktau

Ust'urt plato

ATLANTIC

Bordeaux
Toulouse
Nîmes

Lyon
Geneva
Mt. Blanc 4807
Turin

Milan
Venice

Ljubljana
Zagreb

Belgrade
Sarajevo

Bucharest

Danube

Braila

Constanta

Varna

Burgas

Sofia

Skopje

Tirane

Black Sea

Sinop
Samsun

Soči

Batumi

CAUCASUS

plato

Aral Sea

A Coruña
Santiago d.C.
Porto

Gijón
Cord. Cantábrica
Bilbao
Pyrenees

Vallad-olid
Zar-agoza

Marseille
Monaco
Nice

Corsica
Bastia

Ajaccio

Rome
Pisa
Florence

Olbia

Adriatic Sea

Pescara
Foggia
Bari
Brindisi

Split

Tirane

Plovdiv

ISTANBUL

Pontic Mts.

Trabzon

Tiflis

Yerevan

Baku

Ašhabad

Kopet-dag

40°

40°

Coimbra
Madrid
Lisbon

Badajoz
Sevilla

Cáceres
Albacete
Granada
Almería

València
Alacant

Barcelona

Menorca
Mallorca
Palma d.M.
Eivissa

Maò

Sardinia
Cagliari

Naples

Tyrrhenian Sea
Palermo
Messina

Cosenza

Etna
Catánia
Sicily

Ionian Sea

Kérkyra

Aegean Sea

Thessaloníki

Bursa
Balıkesir

Ankara

Sivas

Anatolia

Taurus Mts.

Konya
Adana

Diyarbakır

Euphrates

Mosul

Mesopotamia

Tabriz

Mašhad

Dašt-e Kavir

Faro
Cádiz
Málaga
Gibraltar
Ceuta
Tangier
Mostaganem

Algiers
Tell Atlas
Consta-ntine
Atlas

Tunis
Sousse
Sfax

Valletta
Malta

Jerba

Mediterranean Sea

Izmir
Antalya

Athens
Kalamáta
Thíra　Ródos
Chania

Crete
Erákleion

Patrai
5095

Larnaca
Cyprus
Nicosia
Pafos

Aleppo
Latakia
Syrian Desert

Al-Hims

Beirut

TEHERAN

Qom

Zagros Mts.

Isfahan

Daš-e Lut

50°

Rabat
Casablanca
Marrakech
J. Toubkal
Agadir

Fès
Middle Atlas
Oujda
High Atlas
Saharan Atlas
Béchar
Ghardaïa

Great Western Erg

El Goléa

Tripoli
Misrátah

Gulf of Sidra

Benghazi

Barqah

Damascus
Syrian Desert
Amman
Jerusalem
Tel Aviv-Yafo
Hefa
Elat
Port Said

Alexandria
Giza
CAIRO
Al-Fayyúm
Asyút

Tabúk

Sarm aš-Saih

an-Nafúd al-Kubrā

Hā'il

Kuwait

Medina

Rasi

Bağdad

Al Basra

Persian Gulf

Abādān

Kermán

Al-Manāma
Doha

Bandar-e Abbās
Strait of Hormuz
Dubai
Abu Dhabi
Muscat

Birğand

30°

30°

Canary Basin

Madeira
Funchal

Canary Islands

Ad-Dakhlah

Tropic of Cancer

Sta Cruz de la Palma
Sta Cruz de Tenerife
Tenerife
Hierro
Las Palmas
Gran Canaria
Fuerte-ventura

Ifni

Tindouf

Erg Iguidi

Reggane

In Salah

Great Eastern Erg

Ghadámis

Tripolitania

Sabhah

Al-Jaghbúb

Libyan Desert

Al Jawf

Western Desert

Al-Fayyúm
Asyút

Luxor
Aswan

Red Sea

Medina

Hā'il

Jiddah
Mecca

Abhā

Arabian Peninsula

ar-Rub' al-Hālī

Mirabit

Arabian Sea

Socotra

Nouâdhibou

Atar

El Djouf

Adrar des Iforhas

Tanezrouft

Erg Chech

Tassili du Hoggar

Tammanrasset

Aïr

Ténéré

Tibesti

3415
Emi Koussi

Fezzan

Ghät

Wādi Halfa

Nubian Desert

Bur Sudan

Wād Madai

Buhaira Nāsir

Asmara
Ras Dashen Terara 4620

Aden
Gulf of Aden

Al-Hudaida
Al-Mukalla

Sanaa
Jizan

20°

20°

Cape Verde

Sal Plateau

Nouakchott

Cape Verde Islands
Boa Vista
Santiago
Praia
Sal

Dakar
Banjul

SAHARA

SAHEL

Kaedi

Tombouctou

Gao

Mopti

Niamey

Bamako
Ouagadougou

Zinder

Kano
Maiduguri

Agadez

Azbine

Largeau

Abéché

Darfur

N'djaména

Tchad

Omdurman
Khartoum
Kassala

Kordofan
al Ubayyid

A 20°　　B 10°　　C 0°　　D 10°　　E 20°　　F 30°　　G 40°　　H 50°　　J 60°

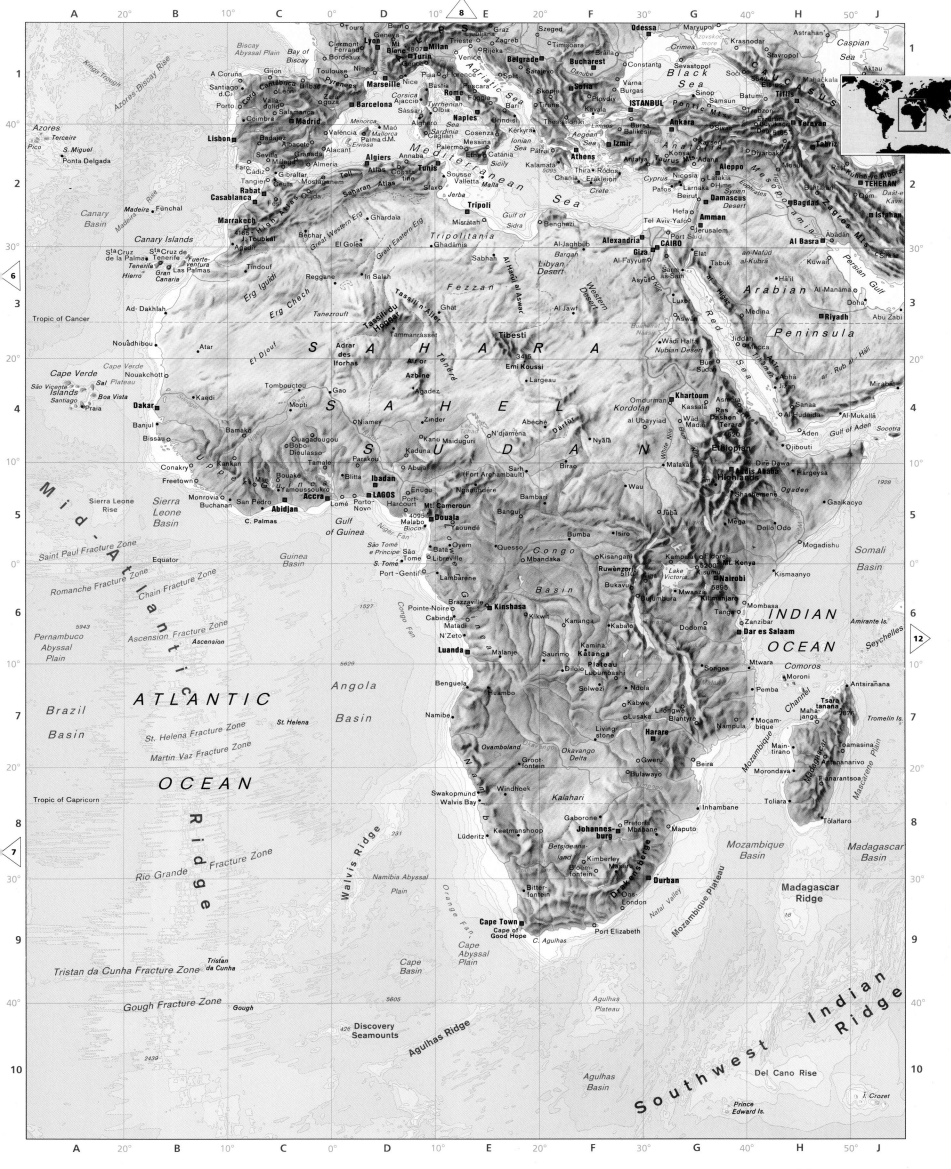

Scale at the equator 1:40,000,000

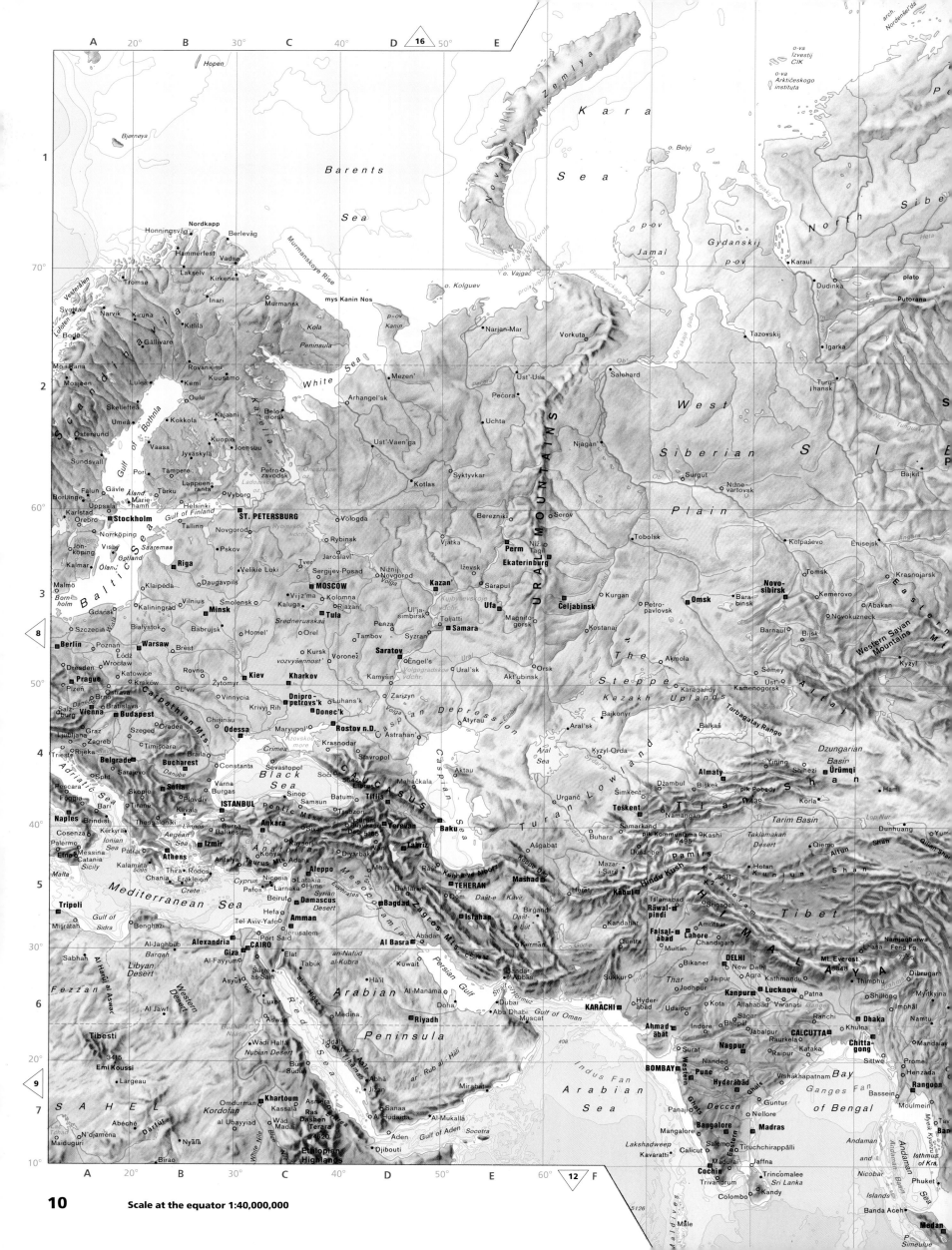

Scale at the equator 1:40,000,000

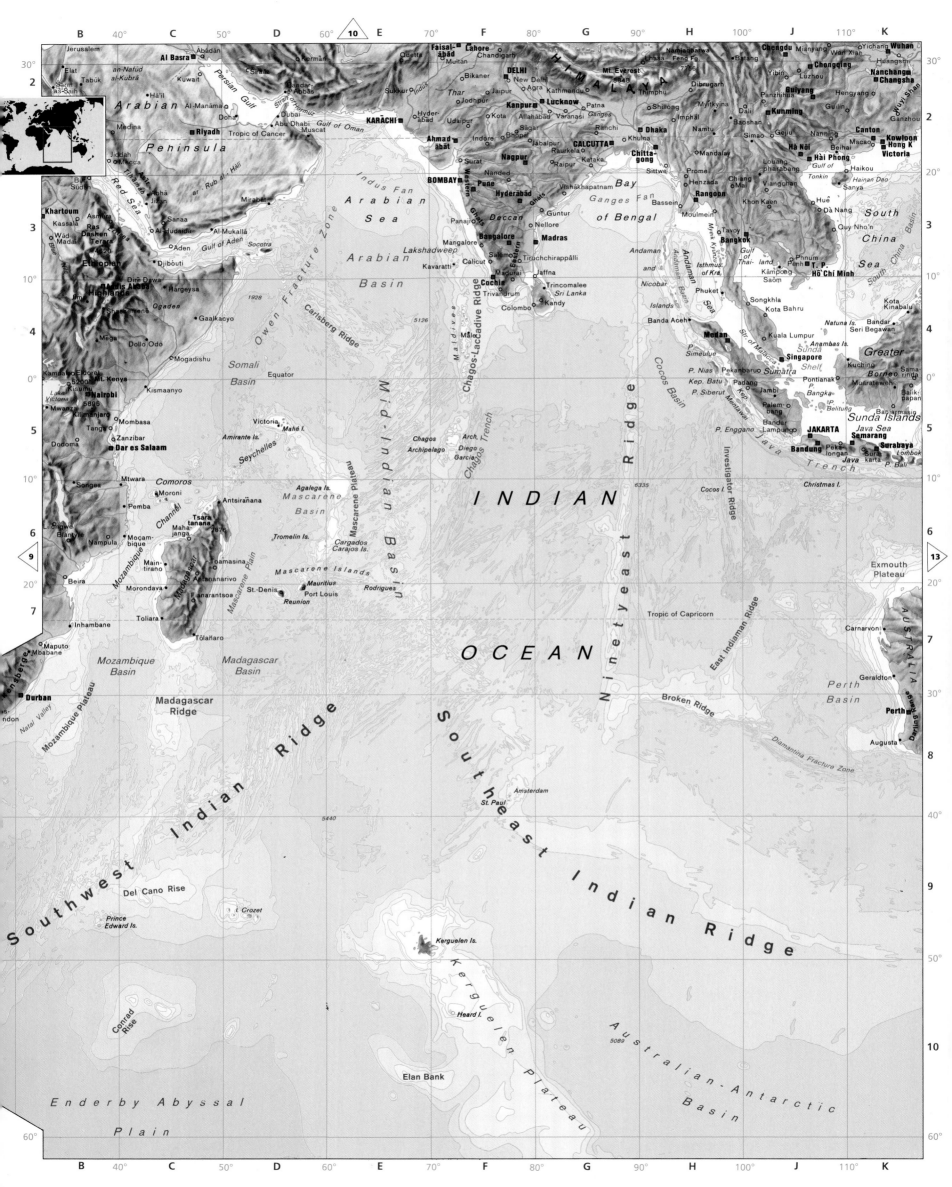

Jerusalem
Elat
Sarm
as-Saih
Tabūk

Al Basra
Ābādān
Sirāan
Kermān

Kuwait
an-Nafūd
al-Kubrā
Ha'il
al-Manāma
Persian Gulf
Bandar-
Abbās
Strait of
Hormuz
Dubai
Abu Dhabi
Doha
Gulf of Oman
Muscat

Faisal-
ābād
Lahore
Chandigarh
Multan
Quetta
Bikaner
Jaipur

Chengdu
Mianyang
Wan Xian
Yichang
Wuhan
Huangshi
Batang

Nangapārwa
Feng Fa
Lhāsa
HIMALAYA
Mt. Everest
8848
Dibrugarh
Thimphu

DELHI
New Delhi
Agra
Kathmandu
Shillong
Imphāl
Myitkyina
Namtu
Baoshan
Dali
Chongqing

Nanchang
Changsha

Kunming
Hengyang
Guilin
Canton

Medina
Jiddah
Mecca
Bi
Sudan

Riyadh

Arabian

Peninsula

Red Sea

Khartoum
Kassala
Wād
Madani
Blue
Nile
Asmara
Ras
Dashen Terara
4620

Sanaa
Al-Hudaida
Aden
Djibouti
Gulf of Aden
Socotra
Al-Mukallā
Mirbāt

Ahmad-
ābād
KARACHI
Hyder-
ābād

Sukkur
Indus
Jodhpur
Udaipur
Kota
Ajmer
Thar

Kanpur
LUCKNOW
Allahābād
Vārānasi
Patna
Ganges
Ranchi

Sāgar
Jabalpur
Raipur
Raurkela
Kataka

Mandalay
Namtu
Prome
Henzada
Rangoon
Chiang
Mai
Viangchan
Huế
Dà Nang
Hainan Dao
Sanya

Louang
phabang
Gulf of
Tonkin
Haikou

Ethiopian
Highlands
Addis Ababa
Jima
Dirē Dawa
Hargeysa
Ogaden

Indore
Bhopal
Nanded
Surat
BOMBAY

Nāgpur
PUNE
HYDERĀBĀD

CALCUTTA
Khulna
DHAKA
Chitta-
gong
Sittwe
Bassein
Moulmein

Arabian
Sea
Indus Fan
Arabian
Basin

Panajio
Mangalore
Bangalore
Salem
Calicut
Kavaratti
Lakshadweep

Deccan
Guntur
Nellore
Madras
Tiruchchirappālli
Madurai
Jaffna

Vishākhapatnam
Bay
of Bengal
Ganges Fan
Andaman
and
Nicobar
Islands

Andaman
Sea
Myeik Kyunzu
Isthmus
of Kra
Tavoy

Bangkok
Gulf
of
Thai-
land

South
China
Sea

Phnum
Penh
Kâmpong
Saôm
T. P.
Hồ Chí Minh

Quy Nho'n

Kota
Kinabalu

Arabian
Basin
5126
1928

Cochin
Trivandrum
Colombo
Sri Lanka
Trincomalee
Kandy
Māle

Maldives

Chagos-Laccadive Ridge
Western Ghats
Eastern Ghats

Songkhla
Banda Aceh
Kota Bahru

Phuket
Medan
P. Simeulue
P. Nias
Pekanbaru

Natuna Is.
Anambas Is.
Bandar
Seri Begawan
Kuching

Greater

Borneo
Sama-
rinda
Bali-
papan

Owen Fracture Zone
Carlsberg Ridge

Somali
Basin
Equator

Mogadishu
Kismaanyo

Nairobi
Mombasa
Mt. Kenya
5895
5200
Lake
Victoria
Kisumu
Kampala
Eldoret
Kilimanjaro
Tanga
Zanzibar
Dodoma
Mwanza
Dar es Salaam

Victoria
Mahé I.
Amirante Is.
Seychelles

Mid-Indian Basin

Chagos
Archipelago
Diego
Garcia
Arch.
Chagos Trench

INDIAN

Cocos Basin
Kep. Batu
P. Siberut
Padang
P. Enggano
Lampung
Sunda
Shelf
Singapore
Pontianak
Jambi
Palem-
bang
P. Bangka
P. Belitung

Banjarmasin
Java Sea
Sunda Islands

Ninetyeast Ridge
Investigator Ridge
Java

6335
Cocos I.
Christmas I.

Dire Dawa
Mega
Dollo Odo
Dollo
Gaalkacyo

Comoros
Moroni
Pemba
Mozambique
Channel
Tsara
tanana
2876
Maha-
janga

Mascarene
Basin
Mascarene Plateau
Tromelin Is.
Cargados
Carajos Is.
Agalega Is.

Songea
Mtwara

Lilongwe
Blantyre
Nampula

OCEAN

Jambi
Bandung
JAKARTA
Semarang
Sura
karta
Surabaya
Java
Pekalongan
P. Bali
Lombok

9
13

Beira
Inhambane
Maputo
Mbabane

Madagascar
Antananarivo
Morondava
Fianarantsoa
Toliara
Tôlañaro

Antsirañana
Toamasina
Main-
tirano

Mascarene Islands
St-Denis
Mauritius
Réunion
Port Louis
Rodrigues

Tropic of Capricorn

Exmouth
Plateau

Carnarvon

Mozambique
Basin

Madagascar
Basin

Madagascar
Ridge

Southwest Indian Ridge

Southeast Indian Ridge

Broken Ridge
East Indian Ridge

Perth
Basin

Geraldton
Perth

AUSTRALIA

Drakensberge
Durban
Natal Valley
Mozambique
Plateau

Amsterdam
St. Paul
5440

Diamantina Fracture Zone
Augusta

Del Cano Rise
I. Crozet

Prince
Edward Is.

Conrad
Rise

Kerguelen Is.

Kerguelen Plateau

Australian-Antarctic Basin

Heard I.
5089

Enderby Abyssal
Plain

Elan Bank

Scale at the equator 1:40,000,000

Australia and Oceania **13**

Scale at the equator 1:50,000,000

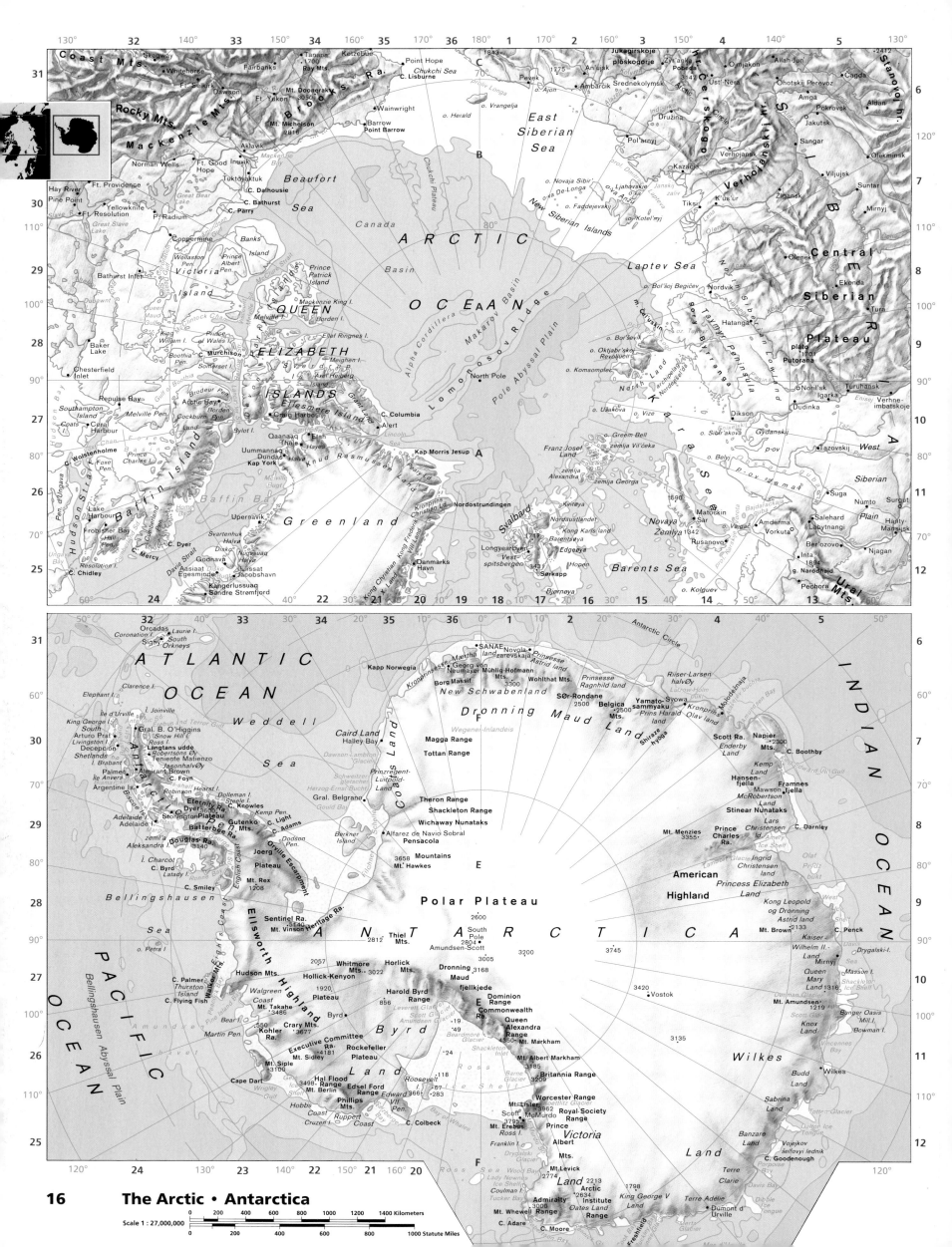

16 **The Arctic · Antarctica**

Scale 1 : 27,000,000

| 0 | 200 | 400 | 600 | 800 | 1000 | 1200 | 1400 Kilometers |
| 0 | 200 | 400 | 600 | 800 | 1000 Statute Miles |

70873

North and Middle America – one continent, two worlds

The North American continent, including Middle America and the West Indian archipelago, covers an area of 9,266,400 square miles (24 million sq. km). Thus the continent extends from the icy climate of the North Pole to the hot and humid tropics. One-quarter of the area consists of islands and peninsulas: in the north of the Canadian islands and Greenland, the largest island in the world; south of the Tropic of Cancer lie the Greater and Lesser Antilles. The entire area is made up of five elements: the Canadian Shield, the low range of the Appalachian Mountains, the central plains, the high ranges of the Rocky Mountains, and the West Indian islands. Due to the North-South orientation of the mountain ranges, the continent has no mountain barriers to prevent the exchange of polar and tropical air masses. The original population of North, Central and South America originates from Asia and has been displaced, with the exception of a few remaining enclaves, by European immigrants and their descendants. The resulting cultural areas come together at the southern border of the U.S.

"The Newe Islands That Lie Beyond Spain to the East By the Land of India." This depiction of America appeared in Sebastian Münster's "Cosmographia Universalis" (1550).

Alaska
p. 20–21

Aleutians
p. 22–23

Canada: Arctic Islands
p. 24–25

Greenland: Northern Region
p. 26–27

Greenland: Southern Region
p. 28–29

Canada: Barren Grounds
p. 30–31

Canada: British Columbia, Alberta, Saskatchewan p. 32–33

Canada: Manitoba, Ontario
p. 34–35

Canada: Labrador
p. 36–37

Canada: Atlantic Provinces
p. 38–39

U.S.A.: Pacific States
p. 40–41

U.S.A.: Central States, North
p. 42–43

U.S.A.: Central States, South
p. 44–45

U.S.A.: Great Lakes, Northeastern States p. 46–47

U.S.A.: Southeastern States (Inset: Hawaii) p. 48–49

Mexico: Northern Region
p. 50–51

Mexico: Southern Region Central America p. 52–53

Greater Antilles
p. 54–55

Lesser Antilles
p. 56

SOUTH PUGET SOUND LIBRARY

Top border (longitude and grid labels):
A 178° B 176° C 174° D 172° E 170° F 168° G 166° H 164° J 162° K 162° P

Latitude labels (left side): 2, 68°, 66°, 3, 64°, 4, 62°, 5, 60°, 6, 58°, 7

Bottom border:
F 168° G 166° H 164° J 162° K 23 160° L 158° M 156° N 154° O 152° P

20 — Scale 1 : 4,500,000 — 0 40 80 120 160 200 Kilometers — 0 40 80 120 160 Statute Miles

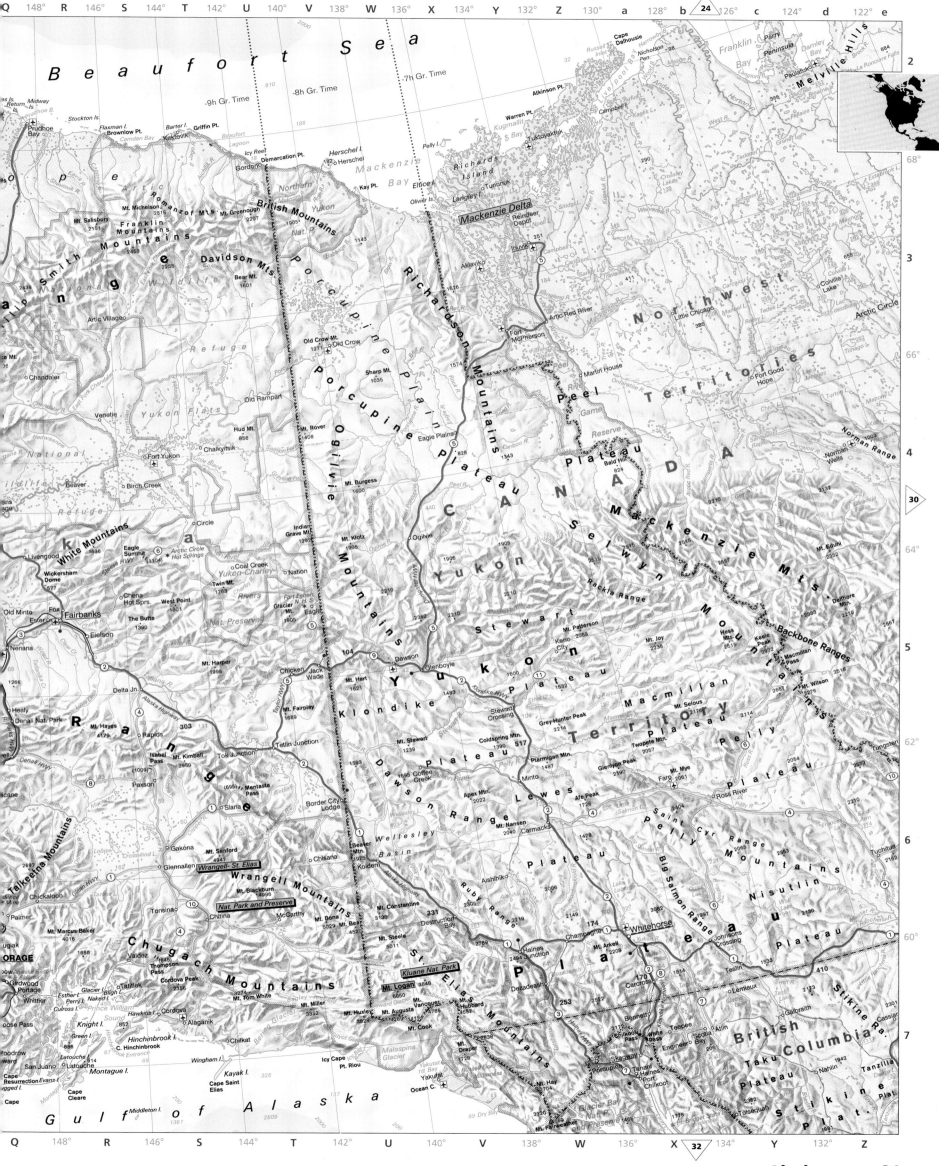

Alaska   21

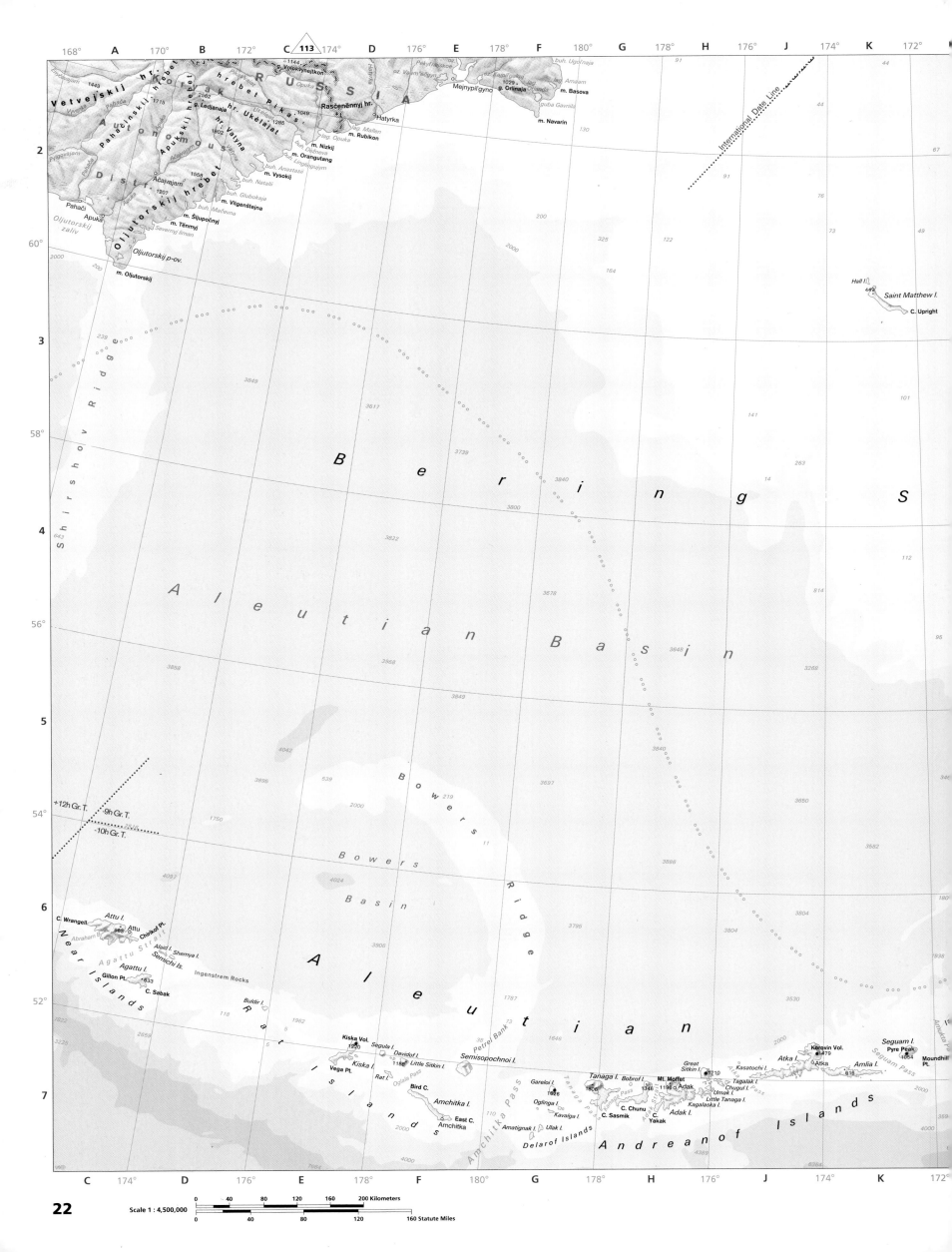

RUSSIA

Vetvejskij hr.
Koryak hr.
Pahačinskij hrebet
hrebet Pikas
Autonomous
Apukskij hrebet
District
Oljutorskij hrebet

1443
1715
2562
1049
1285
1802
1558
1207
1144

g. Volokvynejtkon
g. Ledjanaja
hr. Úkélajat
hr. Vatyna
Ačajvajam

Pahači
Apuka

Oljutorskij
zaliv

Oljutorskij p-ov.
m. Oljutorskij

Enylgyvajam
Pylgyvajam
pahača
Vyvenka

m. Nizkij
m. Rubikon
m. Orangutang
m. Vysokij
m. Mačevna
m. Vilgenštejna
m. Tènmyj
m. Šljupočnyj

buh. Dežneva
buh. Anastasii
buh. Natalii
buh. Glubokaja

Severnyj liman

Hatyrka
lag. Mallen
lag. Opuka
Lingljaguym

Mejnypil'gyno
m. Navarin

Pekvirejskoe
oz. Vaam'ečgyn
g. Orlinaja
m. Basova

Kajpil'gakuu
Ulak
Amaam
buh. Ugórnaja
lag. Gavriila

B   e   r   i   n   g   S

Bering Sea

A   l   e   u   t   i   a   n   B   a   s   i   n

Shirshov Ridge

Saint Matthew I.
Hall I.
C. Upright

Bowers Ridge
Bowers Basin

A   l   e   u   t   i   a   n

+12h Gr. T.   -9h Gr. T.
-10h Gr. T.

Near Islands
C. Wrangell
Attu I.
Attu
Chirikof Pt.
Abraham B.
Agattu Strait
Agattu I.
Gillon Pt.
C. Sabak
963
633

Alaid I.   Shemya I.
Semichi Is.
Ingenstrem Rocks

Buldir I.

Rat Islands

Kiska Vol.
Kiska I.
Vega Pt.
Segula I.
Davidof I.
Little Sitkin I.
Rat I.
Bird C.
Amchitka I.
East C.
Amchitka
1260
1188

Semisopochnoi I.
Oglala Pass
Petrel Bank

Amchitka Pass

Delarof Islands

Tanaga Pass

Garelof I.
1606
Oglinga
Amatignak I.
Ulak I.
1656
Tanaga I.
Bobrof I.
Mt. Moffet
1346
C. Chunu
Kavalga I.
C. Sasmik
Kagalaska I.
Adak I.
C. Yakak
Kanaga Pass
1196
Adak
Umak I.
Little Tanaga I.
Kagalaska I.
Chugul I.
1710
Great Sitkin
Kasatochi I.

Tagalak I.

Andreanof Islands

Korovin Vol.
1479
Atka I.
Atka
Amlia I.
616
Seguam I.
Pyre Peak
1054
Moundhill Pt.
Seguam Pass

International Date Line

Scale 1 : 4,500,000

0   40   80   120   160   200 Kilometers
0   40   80   120   160 Statute Miles

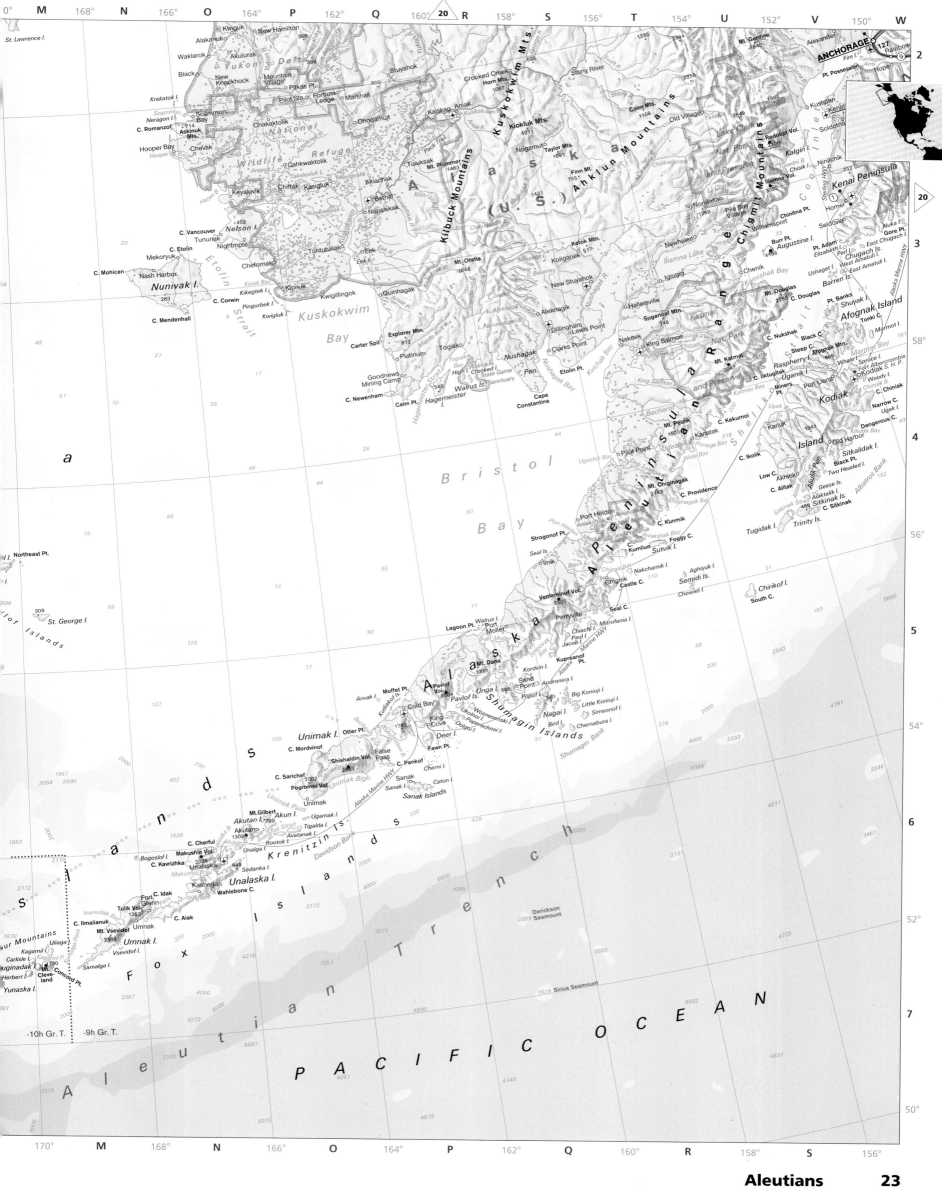

ARCTIC

Canada Basin

OCEAN

-8h Gr. Time   -7h Gr. Time

C. Isachsen

Prince

Gustav Adolf

C. Malloch

Borden Island   152

Sv Ellef Ring

Isachsen Pen.

Deer Bay

Noice Pen.

Isl

King Cha

Brock I.
C. Murray

Mackenzie King Island   457

Wilkins Strait

Sea

Maclean Strait

Kris

C. Leopold M'Clintock

Ballantyne Strait

Lougheed Island

Edmond Walker I.   218

Prince Patrick Island

C. Ludlow Rich

Hardinge Bay

Moore Bay

C. Hemphill

Emerald Isle   481

Hazen Strait

Findlay Group

Desbarats Strait

Blossom Pt.

Griffiths Pt.   97

Intrepid Inlet

Mould Bay

Hecla

Cameron I.

C. Manning

Dyer Bay   274

C. Mecham

Eglington I.

Crozier Channel

Fitzwilliam Strait

C. Scott

Sabine Pen.

C. George Richards

and

Vanier I.

Massey I.

Alexander

Canrober Hills   152

Griper

Donett Pt.

Weatherall Bay

Pell Inlet

Griper Bay

C. Russell   158

Kellett Strait

Purchase Bay

320

307

QUEEN ELIZABETH

Cape Prince Alfred   657

Cape Wrottesley   123   512

M'Clure Strait   427

Blue Hills   1067

Melville Island

Bailey Pt.

Hardy Bay

Liddon Gulf

Warrington Bay

Sabine Bay

Walker

Baldwin Ra.

Byam Martin Channel   298

Byam Martin I.   152   213

Austin Channel

S Graham

Bernard I.

Burnett Bay   27

200   296

457

62

C. James Ross

Dundas Peninsula   513   351

Mt. Hamelin   335

Bridport Inlet

Winter Harbour

Stefe Bay

Bernard R.

Storkerson Bay

Banks   105

Viscount   483   452   Melville   344   Sound

Meek Point

Island   33

Big R.

Peel Pt.

Melville Trough   482

C. Storkerson

Elvira I.

Stefansson Island

C. Joh

Cape Kellett   13

Sachs Harbour   200

Passage Pt.

Barnard Pt.

C. Elvira

Goldsmith Ch.

M'Clintock Cha

Thesiger Bay   2000

Kellett R.   Bernard R.

Stuart Colleton Inlet

232

Wynniatt Bay   224

Prince

Hadley Bay

Storkerson Peninsula

250

Omm

Cape Lambton   165   762

Cape Cardwell

Berkeley Pt.

Walker B.

Albert

Natkusiak Pen.

235

De Salis Bay

107

Cape Peter Richards

Fort Collinson

Peninsula   640

Shaler Mountains

C. Stang

Diamond Jennes Peninsula

Minto Inlet

Kuujjua R.

Victoria

Amundsen Gulf   215

Cape Pfarmigan

Holman Island

Albert Islands

Prince Albert Sound

Island

C. Michelsen

Russell Inlet

Cape Dalhousie

Baillie Is.   82   192

Cape Bathurst   26

Liverpool Bay

Harrowby B.

Nicholson Pen.   98

Northwest Passage

Wollaston

Mt. Bumpus   518

Cape Baring

Collins

Cape Parry

Booth Is.

Cape Parry

Franklin Bay

Parry Peninsula

Darnley B.   140   Cape Lyon

Peninsula

140

21

Paulatuko   366

Melville Hills

Brock R.

Deas Thompson Pt.

Clinton Point   124

C. Hope

Simpson Bay

C. Stang

Cambridge Bay   122

West R.   884

La Ronciare Falls

Clifton Pt.

Dolphin and Union Strait

Jenny Lind I.

Cape Young   609

Bluenose L.

Dease Strait

Camping I.

Lady Franklin Pt.

Richardson Is.

Turnagain Pt.   183   Mt. George

Kent Peninsula

Melbourne I.

Coronation Gulf

Queen Mau

N   o   r   t   h   w   e   s   t

Colville Lake   659

Horton L.   443

Locker Pt.

C. Kendall

Duke of York Arch.

Northwest Passage

Jameson Is.

Cockburn Is.

Campbell Bay

Whitebear Pt.   396

Arctic Circle

Horton R.   686

Coppermine

Richardson I.

Berens Is.

Lawford Is.

Melville Sound

Ritch I.   518

Dismal Les.

C   A   N

Barry Is.

Smith Arm

Ekka I.   852

C. McDonnel

Dease   Arm

Banks Pen.

James B.

Hood R.

Bathurst Inlet

Kokeragi Pt.

Etacho Pt.

Great Bear Lake

McTavish Arm   137

Echo Bay   Port Radium

Takijuak L.

MacAlpine

7h Gr. Time

Fort Franklin

Fox Pt.

Pt. Leith   Richardson I.

Sawmill Bay   529

Scale 1 : 4,500,000

0   40   80   120   160   200 Kilometers

0   40   80   120   160 Statute Miles

Islands

Axel
Heiberg
Island

Amund
Ringnes
Island

C. Sverre

Raanes
Peninsula

Ellesmere

Island

Mt. Leeds

Svendsen
Peninsula

Norwegian

Ammonite Mtn.
Bjorne
Peninsula

Northeast
Pt.

Graham
I.

Inglefield
Mts.

C. Mouat

C. Combermere

K. Robertson Siorapaluk
Murchison Sd.
Herbert Ø Qaanaaq
Thule

Steensby
Land

Hayes
Halvø
Arktik
Hovland

Nordgrønland

Haffner Bjerg

Natur

Kab Melville

Fisher
Øer

Cornwall
Island

Buckingham
I.

C. Torrens

North Lincoln
Land

C. Norton Shaw

Northumberland Ø
K. Powlett
K. Parry

Saunders Ø

Crimson Cliffs

Carey Øer

Wolstenholme Ø
K. Atholl
Dundas

Greenland
(Kalaallit Nunaat) (Denmark)

Ivnangneq Kap
York

Mt. Britannia

Grinnel
Peninsula

A
Bay

Simmon's
Peninsula

Phillips Pt.

Coburg
Island

Cambridge Pt.

Colin Archer
Pen.

Cape Vera

Eidsbotn West Fiord

Jones Sound

Lady Ann
Strait

Belcher
Pt.

C. Fitz Roy

Baffin

Bay

C. Becher

Queens
Channel

Baillie
Hamilton

Skruis
Pt.

Bear Bay

Sverdrup
Inlet

Philpots I.

Little
Cornwallis
I.

McDougall
Sound

Cornwallis
Island

Devon Island

Dundas Harbour

C. Sherard

C. Capel

Resolute

C. Hotham

Fellfoot
Pt.

C.
Ricketts

C. Bullen

Lancaster Sound

Lowther
I.

Griffith I.

Barrow Strait

Northwest Passage

Prince Leopold
I.

C. Clarence

C. Crauford

C. Charles Yorke

C. Hay

C. Liverpool

Bylot
Island

C. Graham Moore

C. Macculloch

Russell I.

C. Briggs

Somerset

Island

Hartz Mts.

Borden

Peninsula

Pond Inlet

Eclipse Sound

Nova Zembla

C. Jameson

Prescott
I.

Browne
Bay

Creswell
Bay

St. Joseph
Plateau

Uluksan
Pen.

Arctic Bay

Milne
Inlet

Mt. Emma

Prince

Brodeur

Peninsula

Magda
Plateau

Baffin

of

Mt. Walker

Brentford
Bay

C. Farrand

Steensby
Peninsula

Wales

Van Koenig
Pt.

Bernier Bay

Island

Easter C.

Charles
Dickens Is.

C.
Hobson

C.
Swinburne

Boothia

Peninsula

Gulf

C. Allington

C. St. Catherine

C. Margaret

C. North Hendon

Crown Prince
Frederik I.

C. Englefield

Pt.
Kendall C. Hallowell

Amherst

 Omande
Sevigny
Pt.

Jens Munk
I.

Koch I.

Bray
I.

Ikpik
Bay

Thom Bay

Astronomical
Society
Islands

of

Igloolik
Igloolik I.

Rowley
I.

Rowley I.

Baird
Pen.

Foley
I.

North
Tweedsmuir I.

South
Tweedsmuir I.

C. Felix

James Ross Str.

Harrison
Is.

C. Chapman

Boothia

C. Miles

Pinger Pt.

Hall Beach

North
Spicer I.

C. Burpee

Prince

Charles

Air
Force I.

Franklin Pt.

Tennent
Is.

Spence Bay

Matty I.

C. Richardson

Melville

South
Spicer I.

King

William

Island

C. Norton

St. Roch
Basin

Matheson
I.

Gjoa Haven

Royal
Geographical
Society Is.

Simpson

Peninsula

Pelly Bay

Peninsula

Parry

Committee

Amitikoe
Pen.

Kingora Pt.

Bay

Island

s

Gravell Pt.

Foxe

Arctic Circle

Basin

Adelaide

Peninsula

T e r r i t o r i e s

Wales

Bay

Peninsula

Cowie Pt.

Pt. Elizabeth

Grant Pt.

Ogle Pt.

Rasmussen

Basin

Rae
Isthmus

Repulse
Bay

Pt.
Clarke

C.
White

C. Penrhyn

C. Martineau
Sturges I.

Vansittart
I.

C. Dorchester

Repulse Bay

ARCTI

Lincoln Se

QUEEN

Meighen Island
C. Northwest
Sverdrup Channel
C. Thomas Hubbard
C. Woods
Alert Pt.
C. Egerton
C. Discovery
Ward Hunt I.
C. Aldrich
C. Colan
C. Joseph Henry

Axel Heiberg Island
Princess Margaret Range
Nansen Sound
British Empire Range
United States Range
Conger Range
Krieger Mountains
Grant Land
Mt. Oxford
Alert
C. Baird

ELLE
Sverdrup Islands
Eureka Sound
Fosheim Peninsula
Greely Fiord
Grinnell Land
Victoria and Albert Mts.
Judge Daly Promontory
Hall Basin
Polaris Forland
Nyeboe Land
Hendrik
Warming Land

Norwegian Bay
Graham I.
Raanes Peninsula
Svendsen Peninsula
Bjorne Peninsula
Sverdrup Pass
C. Collinson
C. Knorr
John Brown
Washington Land
Daugaard Jensen Land

TERRITOIRES
Buckingham
Northeast Pt.
C. Torrens
Ammonite Mtn.
Mt. Leeds
Alexandra Fiord
Johan Peninsula
Buchanan
Victoria Head
C. Albert
C. Hawk's
Kane Basin
K. Forbes
Humboldt Gletscher

Jones Sound
Skruis Pt.
Sverdrup Inlet
C. Sparbo
North Lincoln
Cadogan Gr.
Inglefield Mts.
C. Mouat
C. Combermere
K. Robertson
Siorapaluk
Herbert Ø
Etah
Brother John Gl.
C. Alexander
K. Isabella
Inglefield Land
Hayes
Knud Rasm

Devon Island
C. Vera
C. Bullen
Grise Fiord
South C.
C. Norton Shaw
Phillips Pt.
Coburg Island
Cambridge Pt.
C. Fitz Roy
Belcher Pt.
Northumberland Ø
K. Powlett
Prudhoe Land
Qaanaaq
Thule
Inglefield Bredning
K. Parry
Steensby Land
Camp Century
Naturreservat Lauge Koch Kyst

Lancaster Sound
C. Crauford
Dundas Harbour
Northwest Passage
C. Sherard
Philpots I.
Carey Øer
Saunders Ø
Wolstenholme Fj.
Uummannaq
Dundas
K. Athell
Halvø
Arktik / Hoyland
Haffner Bjerg

C. Charles Yorke
Hartz Mts.
C. Hay
C. Liverpool
Crimson Cliffs
Ivnangangal\\\ Kap York
Meteorit
Kap Melville
Melville Bugt
Kap Seddon
Steenstrup Gl.

Borden Peninsula
Bylot Island
Eclipse Sound
Pond Inlet
C. Graham Moore
Mt. Emma
Baffin Bay
Ryder Øer
Kullorsuaq
Holms Ø
Igdlulik
Vinter Øer
Vestg

CANADA
C. Macculloch
Nova Zembla
C. Jameson
Baffin
Bay
Qutdlikorssuit
Tugtorqutoq
Ikerasårssuk
Tasiussaq
Ivnarssuit
Upernavik
Aappilattoq

Baffin
Buchan Gulf
Baffin Island
Scott Inlet
Clyde Inlet
Basin
Upernavik Kujalleq
Søndre Upernavik
Kigatak
Qeqertaq
Ingineq

C. Thalbitzer
Koch I.
Bray I.
Rowley I.
Ikpik Bay
Erik Pt.
Clyde
Nunavik
Kap Cranstown
Karrats Fjord
Illorsuit
Ubekendt Ejland
Upernavik
Alfred Wegeners Halvø
Ukkusissat
Umanak
Appat
Niagornat
Saattut

Scale 1 : 4,500,000

0 40 80 120 160 200 Kilometers

0 40 80 120 160 Statute Miles

O C E A N

K. Christian IV
K. Morris Jesup
K Bridgman
K. John Flagler
Kap Eiler Rasmussen
Nordostrundingen

K. Payer
K. Hammock
Hazen
K. Benedict
Helland-Hansen Bugt
Prinsesse Margrethe
Station Nord
Flade Isblink

Roosevelt Fjelde
Herluf Trolles Land
Prinsesse Thyra
Prins Frederik Øer
Romer Sø
Antarctic Bugt

Kdrup Ø
Nansen
Land
1323
1920
1737
Peary
Land
Idefiville Land
Kap Rigsdagen
Prinsesse Dagmar
Eskimonæsset

Nares
Land
Freuchen
Land
1554
1646
Kronprins Christian Land

Mid Sophie Øe
Independence Fjord
670
Hagen Fjord
Mylius
Erichsen
Land
Holm Land
Kap H. N. Andersen

C. H. Ostenfeld
Gletscher
Heilprin
Land
1158
1097
1067
Hovgaards
Ø
Kap Anna Bistrup

1189
Amdrup
Højland
1433
Læegervallen
Kap Nansen
Norske
Øer

Niaghelfjordsfjorden
1097
Achton
Friis Ø
Belgica Bank

Lambert
Land
Franske Øer

Zachariaes Bræ
Schnauders
Øer
Pariserne
Amborten
Kap Merite Stigbeijlen
Kap Montpensier

Moltke
Nunatak
1768
Tuborg Fondet
Land
Jøkel-
bugten
Storøen
Île de France

Bjernesk
Kap Marie Valdemar
G r e e n l a n d

C. Silverberg Ø
Skærfjorden

Ymer
Nunatakker
1036
978
Germania
Land
Danmarkshavn
S e a

Dronning
Louise
Land
Edvard Ø
Godfried
Hansen Ø
Store
Koldewey
Dove
Bugt

Lindhard Ø
Bastrups Bræ
1036
Adolf S. Jensen
Land
Kap Alf Trolle

Carlsbergfondet
Land
2682
Bessel Fjord
Hochstetter
Balns Bierge
Mattenhorn
1824
Forland
Kap Bergen

Kong
Wilhelm
1850
C. H. Ostenfeld
Land
Kuhn Ø
Shannon
Kap Philip Broke

Ardencaple Fj.
Hochstetterbugten Øer
Pendulium Øer

Marianne
Nunatakker
1729
Payer
Land
1404
Wollaston
Forland
Daneborg
Sabine Ø

Holger Danskes
Tinde
2148
Glavering Ø
Gael Hamke
Bugt

Jakob Kjode
Bierg
1900
Ole
Roman
Land
Speth
Plateau
1569
Hold
with
Hope
Halvø

Strindberg
Land
2175
Hudson Land
2060
Kap Broer Ruys

Andrée
Land
2350
Gauss
Halvø
1679
Kap Franklin
Bontekoe Ø

Ymer Ø
Angelin
Bierg
1960
Joseph Fjord
Foster Bugt
Kap Mackenzie

Fraenkel
Land
Geographical
Society Ø
Kap Parry
Vega Sund

Petermann
Bjerg
2640
Suess Land
Sylva Man
Tinde
2216
Ella
Ø
Traill Ø
178

Goodenough
Land
Lyell Land
Nathorst
Land
King Oscar Fjord
Kong
Oscars
Fjord
Davy Sund
Kap Biot
Kap Wardlaw

2300
Stauning
Alper
Mesters Vig
762
Kap Hewitt

Sortehest
2450
Scoresby
Land
Kap Jones

Charcot
Land
3000
2450
8231
Kap Tobin

Hink Land
Sydkap
Bjørne
Ø
Jameson
Land
Ittaaimmit/
Kap Hope
Rathbon Ø
Ittoqqortoormiit/
Scoresbysund

Renland
1981
Kangikajip Appalia/
Kap Brewster

Charles Land
Milne Land
1650
Kap
Leslie
Uunartoq/
Kap Hope
Janus Ø
Kangikajip Appalia/
Kap Brewster

Denmark Ø
Hall Bredning
Kangertittivaq/
Scoresby Sund

Geaasland
643
Gaase
Pynt
Volquart Boon Kyst
Steward Ø
Manby Halvø

Knud Rasmussen Land
Kap Datton
Turner Ø
Neumann Fj.

Kap Barclay

Kong Frederik VIII Land
Kong Christian X Land

Nationalpark i
Nørdgrønland og
Østgrønland

T u n u /
Ø s t g r ø n l a n d

G r e e n l a n d
(K a l a a l l i t   N u n a a t)
(D e n m a r k)

nnaarsual/
dgrønland

2469
2164
2103
2225
2865
2530
2636
2935
3231

Q 48° R 46° S 44° T 42° U 40° V 38° W 36° 27 X 34° Y 32° Z 30° a 28° b 26° c 24° d 22° e

Greenland

(K a l a a l l i t   N u n a a t)

(D e n m a r k)

3147

2591

Kap Datton
616
Kap Barclay
Rungy Bugt
Kap Beaupré
Kap Tupinier
1120

Watkin Bjerge

Gunnbjørn Field

Blosseville Kyst

Kap Grivel
Kap Vedel
Kap Ravn
234
334

T u n u /

Kap Nansen

2652

2835

Søkongen Ø
238

Kong Christian IX Land

Kap Hammer
Kap J. C. Jacobsen

Ø s t g r ø n l a n d

Flad Ø   Kap Eduard Holm

547

Aggas Ø
Milait
Kap S. M. Jørgensen
245
365
625

Arctic Circle

173

Denmark Strait

ICELAND

3360
3243

Kap Gustav Holm
358

Greenland
Iceland Rise

Denmark Rise

Látrar
Isa fjör
Suðureyri

K i t a a /

2200

Schweizerland

2558

Kap Wandel
1006

Patreksfjörður

i k   I X

2284

Storø

g r ø n l a n d

Tinteqilaaq
Qianarteq
Ikkatteq

Kuummiit
Leifs Ø
Erik den
Rødes Ø

V

2774

745

Ammassalik
Isortoq
Kap Tiedo
Brahe

Kulusuk Kap Dan
Kulusuk

395

Kérssuaq
Danneborg Ø
Orla
Gråhs
Øer
Aflandshage
Qardlit Ikerat

Pikiutdleq / Køge Bugt

2458

Jens Munk Ø

Kap Løvenørn

1966

72

Upernagssivik
Umiivik
Bugt

Gyldenløves
Fjord
2743

Otte Klumpens Fj.

Tyrs Bjerge
1560
Kap Mestling Tvillingøen

Thors Land
fjord

Kap Harald Moltke

2042

A T L A N T I C

Skjoldungen
Skjoldungen

2917

62°

2760
Kong
Dans
Havn
Qutsigsormiut
Uivaq

Ebba Havn
Uumaanaq I.
Griffenfels Ø

2050

Nunarsuaq

Tingmiarmiut

1890

Uvdlorsivtit
Timmiarmiut
Jens Hedesens Fj.
Ikerniut

2190

arsssuaq

2804

Rud Ø

2195

Puisortoq
Gletscher

60°

2591

Napassorssuaq Fj.

3165

1643
2042

Kong Frederik VI Kyst

Kap Tordenskjøld

O C E A N

iut
nkshåb
orna
Arsuk
Ivittuut

Kangilinnguit/
Grønnedal

2225

Kap Herulf Trolle

Qassiarsuk   Narsarsuaq

Kap Fischer
Lindenfelduluk Fj.

Talloruit
Kobberminebug

Igaliku
1540

2499

Kap Dtscord
Iluileq

Kap Walløe
Banke

Qaqortoq
Julianehåb

Qaqlumiut 1977

Kap Walløe

Nunarsuit

Ammassivik
Sletten

2242

Tingmjarsuk Fjord

Kap Hvitfeldt

160

Saarloq

58°

Nanorta-Sermersoog
lik

Aappilattoq

1297

Angisoq
Loranstan.

Nanortalik
Narsaq Kujalleq
Frederiksdal

Prins Christian Sund

Banke

1372

Uummannarsuaq
Kap Farvel

Q 48° R 46° S 44° T 42° U 40° V -3h Gr. Time 38° W -1h Gr. Time 36° X 34° Y 32° Z

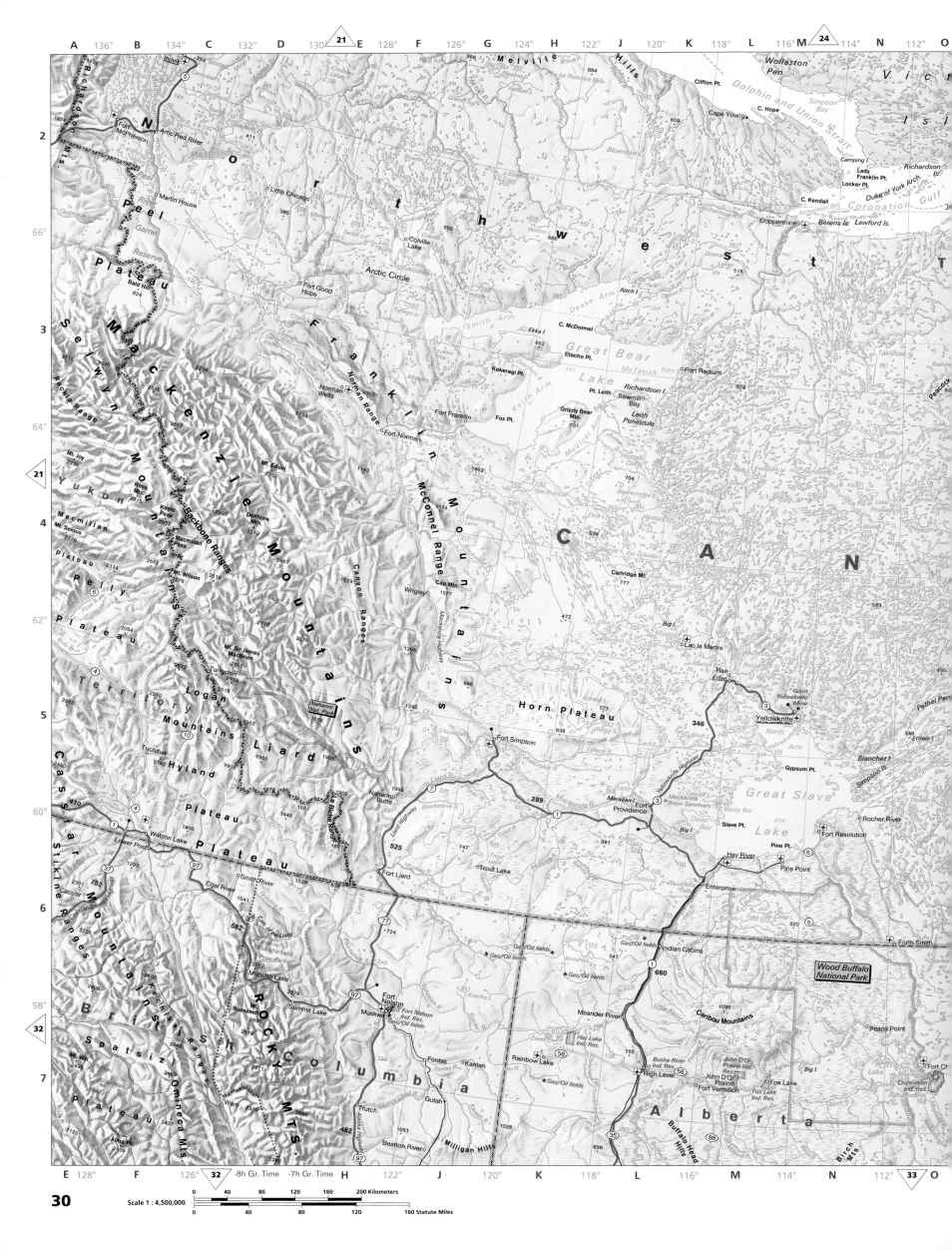

Melville Hills

Dolphin and Union Strait

Victo

Wollaston Pen.

Clifton Pt.

N o r t h w e s t

Richardson Mts.

Peel Plateau

Selwyn

Mackenzie Mountains

Franklin Mountains

McConnel Range

Yukon Plateau

Pelly Plateau

Territory

Logan Mountains

Hyland Plateau

Liard Plateau

Backbone Ranges

Canyon Ranges

Mackenzie Mountains

Nahanni Nat. Park

Cassiar Mountains

Stikine Ranges

British

Rocky Mts.

Omineca Mts.

Columbia

Spatsizi Plateau

C A N A

Great Bear Lake

Smith Arm

Dease Arm

McTavish Arm

Keith Arm

Horn Plateau

Great Slave Lake

Mackenzie Highway

Yellowknife Highway

Rae Edzo

Yellowknife

Fort Providence

Fort Simpson

Watson Lake

Lower Post

Fort Liard

Fort Nelson

Muncho Lake

Summit Lake

Ware

Wood Buffalo National Park

Alberta

Caribou Mountains

High Level

Meander River

Rainbow Lake

Indian Cabins

Hay River

Pine Point

Fort Resolution

Rocher River

Enterprise

Forth Smith

Fort Smith

Gas/Oil fields

Birch Mts.

Buffalo Head Hills

Milligan Hills

Arctic Circle

Fort Good Hope

Norman Wells

Fort Norman

Fort Franklin

Port Radium

Coppermine

Lac la Martre

Scale 1 : 4,500,000

0 40 80 120 160 200 Kilometers

0 40 80 120 160 Statute Miles

Canada: Barren Grounds

Canada: British Columbia, Alberta, Saskatchewan   33

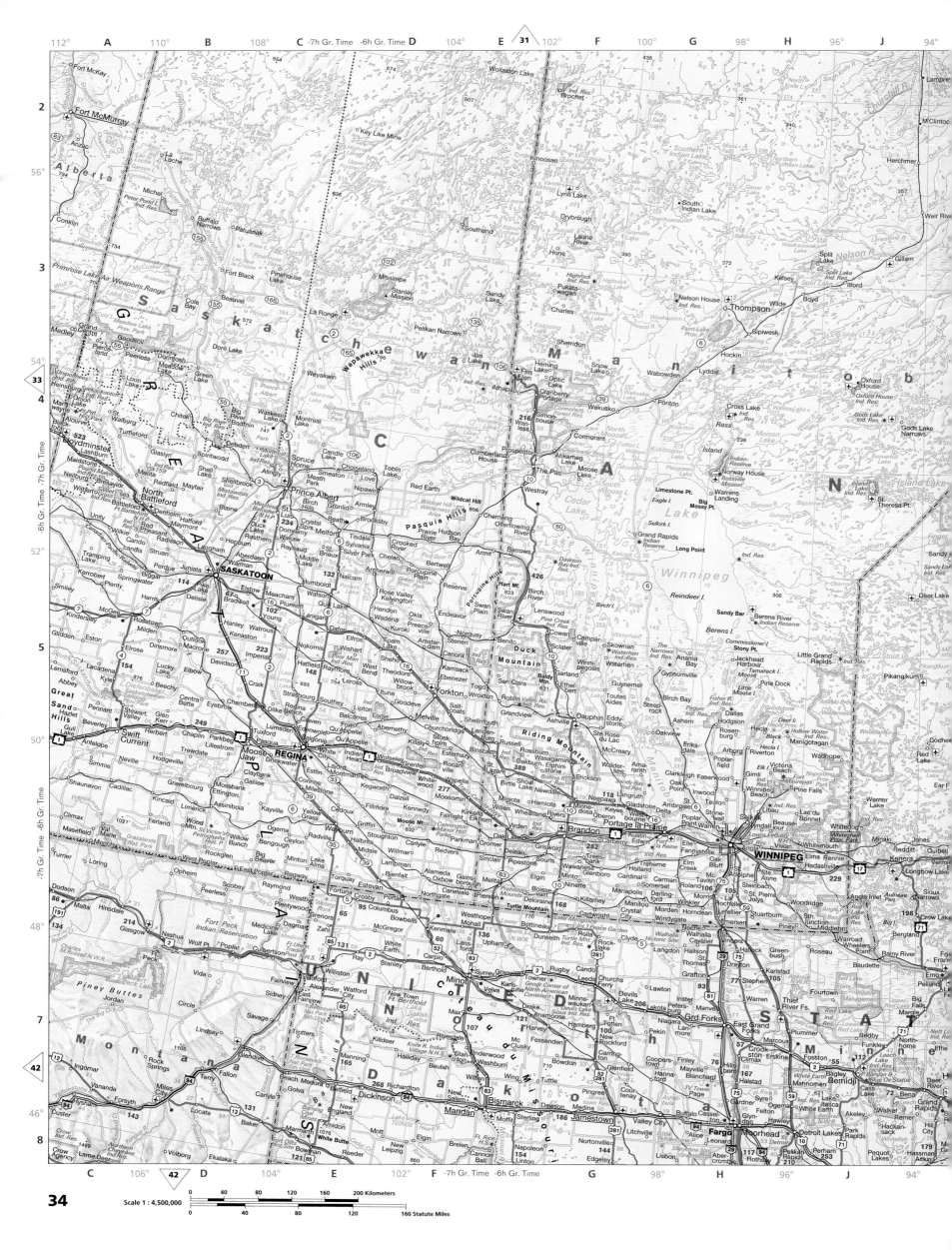

Canada: Manitoba, Ontario   **35**

Half Way Hills 183
Baker Lake
Baker Lake
122

C. Dominion
C. Ketorie
C. Dorchester
Nabukjuak B.
Finnie B.

N o r t h

Boywell
129
206
91
Winchester Inlet
Barrier R.

Welcome Sound
Savage Is.
354
116
C. Dobbs
White I.
Opposite I.
197
Vansittart

354

F o x e

Foxe Peninsula

154
130
Kaminuriak Lake
381
Hanbury
Cap Silumiut
Rockhouse I.
Chesterfield Inlet

Whale Pt.
C. Comfort
108
Ell Bay
S o u t h a m p t o n
Porsild Mts. 625
472
564
C. Welsford
298

C h a n n e l
352
106
15
Kinghait Range 293
137
Cape Dorset
Alareak

w e s t

Hanbury
63
159
Coral Harbour
Caribou
Bell Peninsula 226
King Charles C.
Okolli I.
Dorset I.
152
Mill I. 390
122
Chamberlain

C. Kendall
Bay of Gods Mercy
Manico Pt.
53
South Bay
East Bay
Ruin Pt.
Native Pt.
Bear Cove Pt. 108
Seahorse Pt. 312

T e r r i t

Pangertoot Pen.
Rankin Inlet
Marble I.
111
174
Leyson Pt.
Salisbury I. 305

Cape Jones
Port Rae
Corbett Inlet
114
18
96
C. Low
Evans Strait
Nottingham I. 244
H u d

Whale Cove
Term Pt.
154
Fisher Strait
Calanus Bay
C. Pembroke 152

Bibby I.
Angusko Pt.
16
Santianna Pt.
92
Coals Island
352

Austin I.
Maguse Pt.
Maguse River
Eskimo Point
124
C. Southampton
Shanun Bay

Digges Is.
C. Wolstenholme 385
Charles I. 162
Charles
C. de Nouvel

227
Mansel Island
231

Ivujivik
Déception Bay
447
Salluit
Déception

98
187
233
C. Acadia
Kovik Bay
661
479
Monts de Povungnituk
Crate Nouveau

119
162
60°
171
P é n i

187
Smith I.
C. Smith 308
Mosquito Bay
163
Pte. Demers
Pte. Cusson
Neakongul Bay

H u d s o n
257
144
162
Pte. Dufrost
Povungnituk
D' U n

Gilmour I.
Perley I.
40
Pte. aux Écucils

42
133
O t t a w a   I s l a n d s
Kogaluc B.
Kogaluc

49
155
Pte. Bonnissant
Elsje I.
Two Brothers
Cok I.

B a y
192
Farmer I.
Hopewell Islands
Inukjuak (Port Harrison) 164

C. Tatnam
Manitoba
18
Sleeper Is.
Kidney I. 91
King George Islands
Broughton I. 472

Kettle R.
Sachigo R.
197
133
Nkitskn R.
Black Duck R.
Fort Severn
Partridge I.
Niskibi R.
Beaver R.
Split I.
North Belcher Is.
Johnson I.
Bakers Dozen Is.
Davieau I.

162
97
Lillico Pt.
Belcher Kugong
Gushie Pt.
C. Bartlett 132
Gillies I.
Lac Minto

Limestone Rapids
Wood Creek
Islands
Tukarak I.
Belcher Islands
McLeary Pt.
Anderson I.
Belanger I.
Lac Guillaume-Delisle

O n t a r i o
Polar
Winisk
Wabuk Pt.
Peawanuck
18
Flaherty Island
Innetalling I.
Freakly Pt.
Snape I.
Sainsbury Pt.
Cairn
Castle I.
Merry I.

Big Trout Lake
Big Trout Lake Ind. Res.
Bear
Winisk R.
C. Lookout
C. Henrietta Maria
49
Hook Pt.
Provincial Park
James
Long I. 104
Long I.
C. Iones
Poste-de-la-Baleine
3724

Kasabonika
Lakitusaki R.
Indian Reserve
Bear I.
Bay
Pte. Kakachischuan
Julian I.

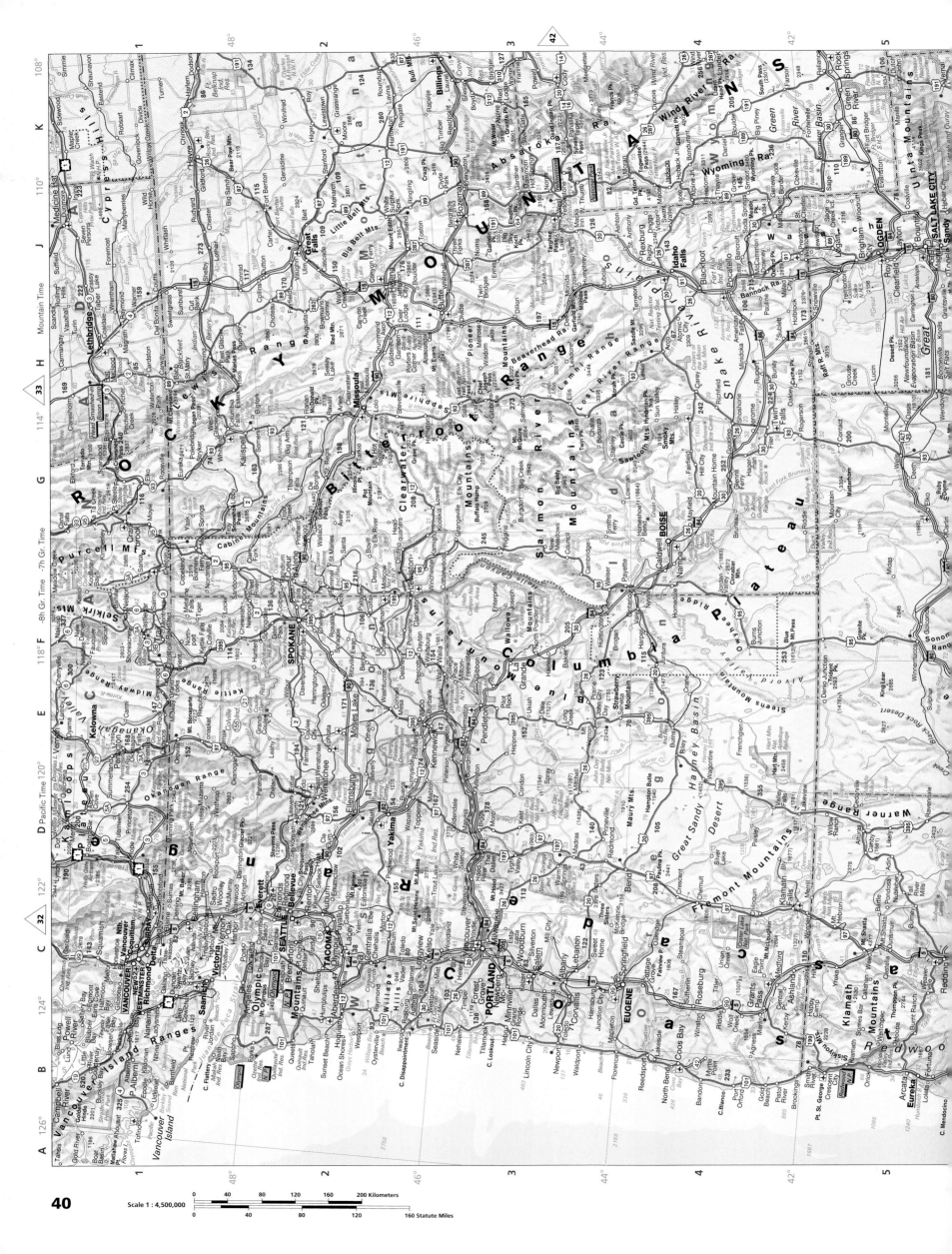

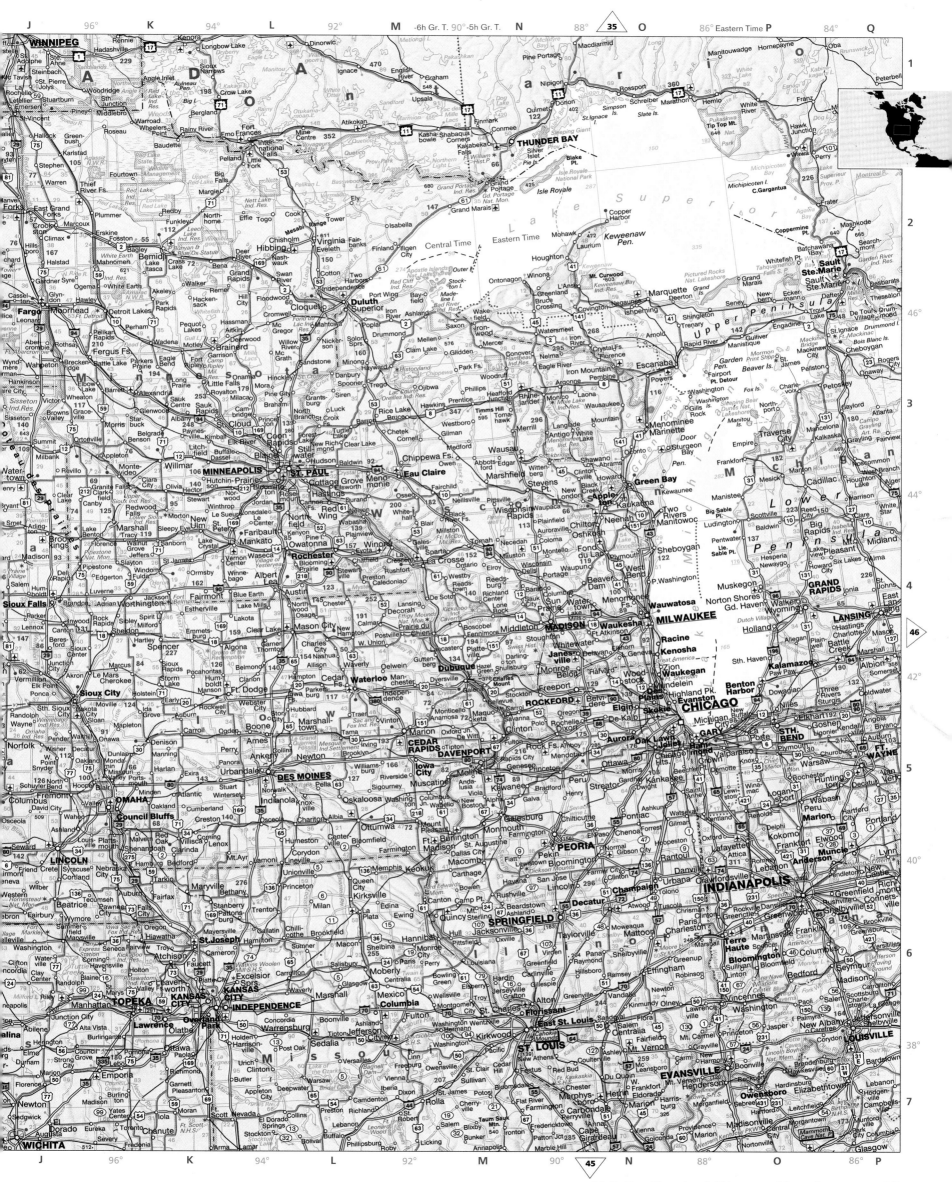

U.S.A.: Central States, North 43

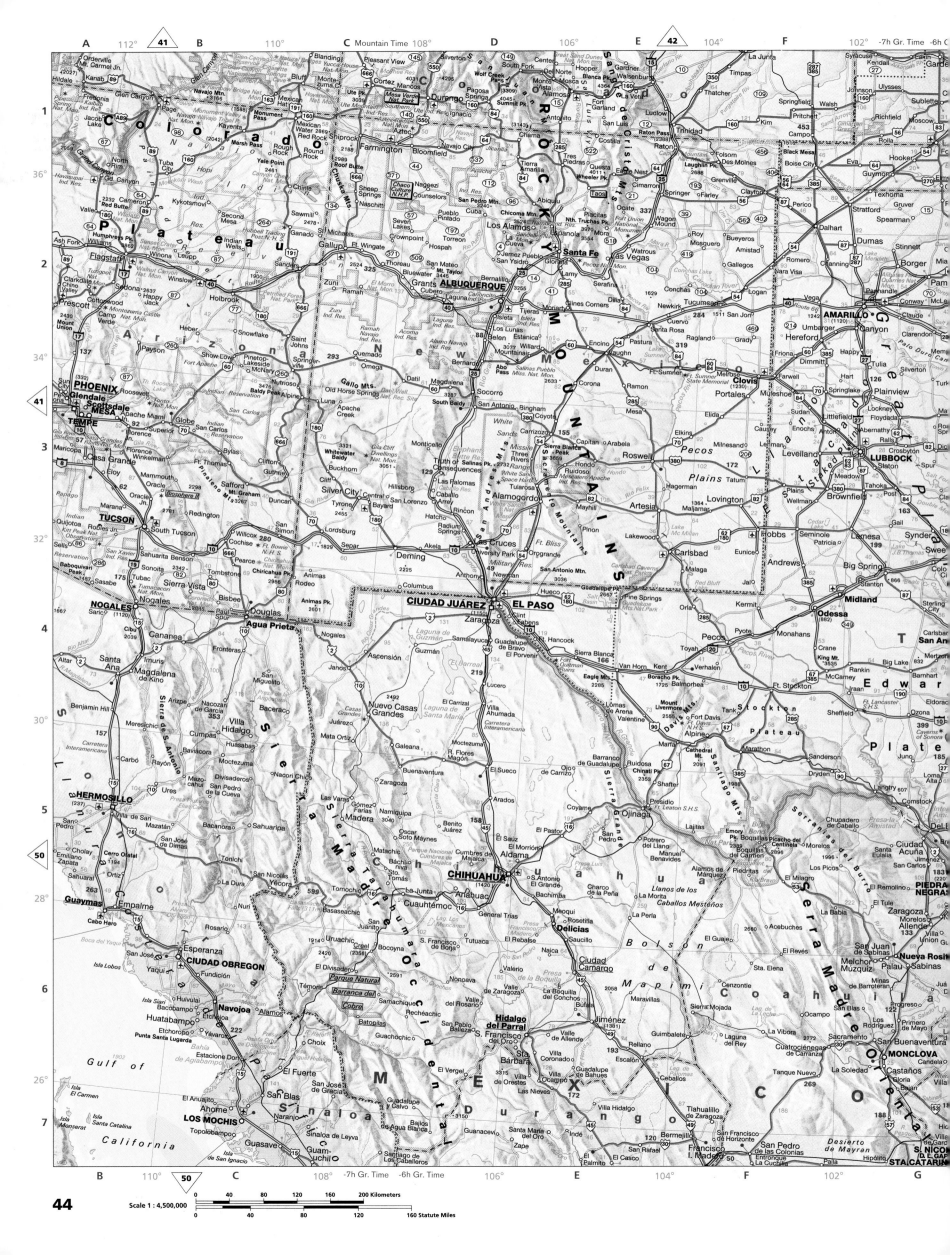

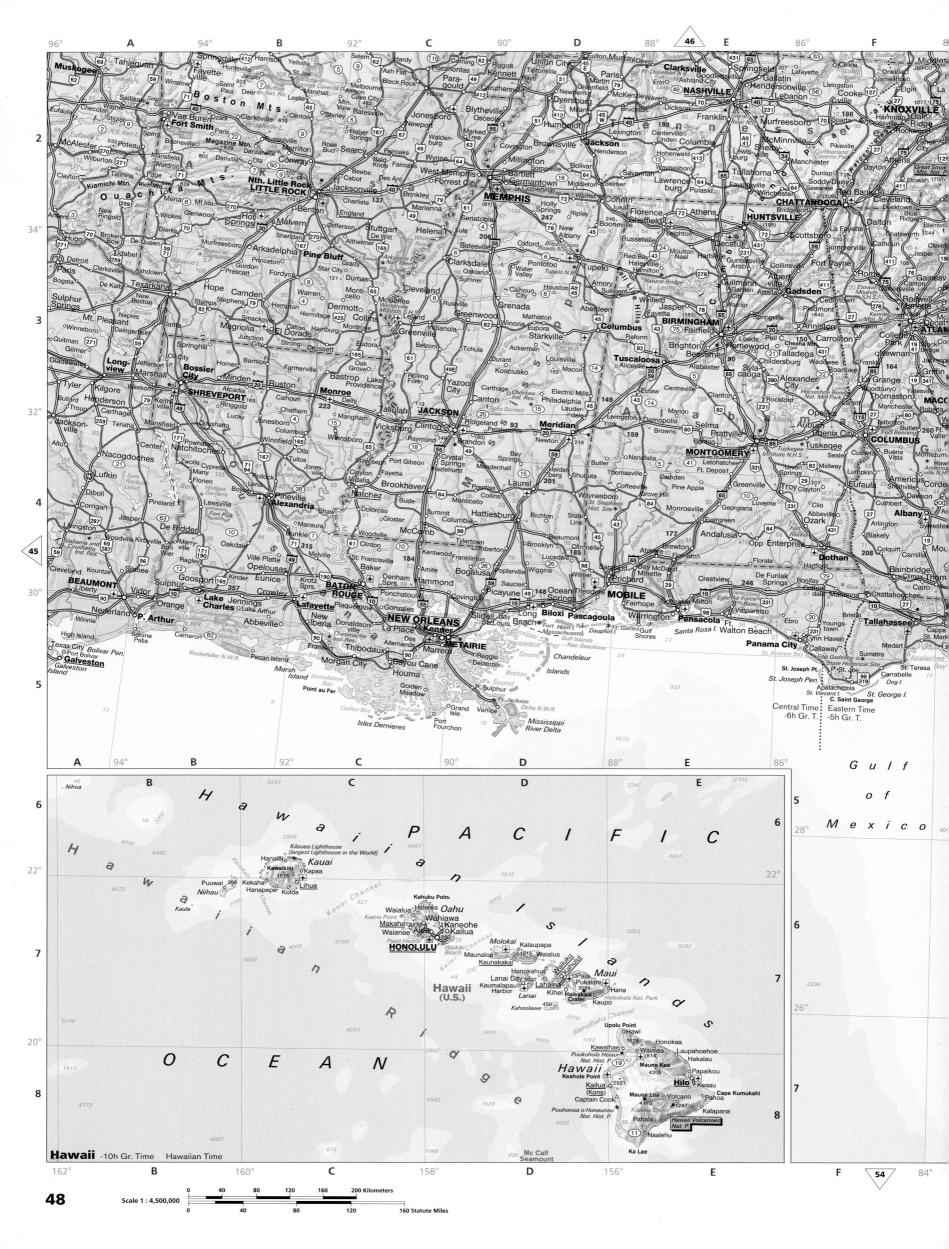

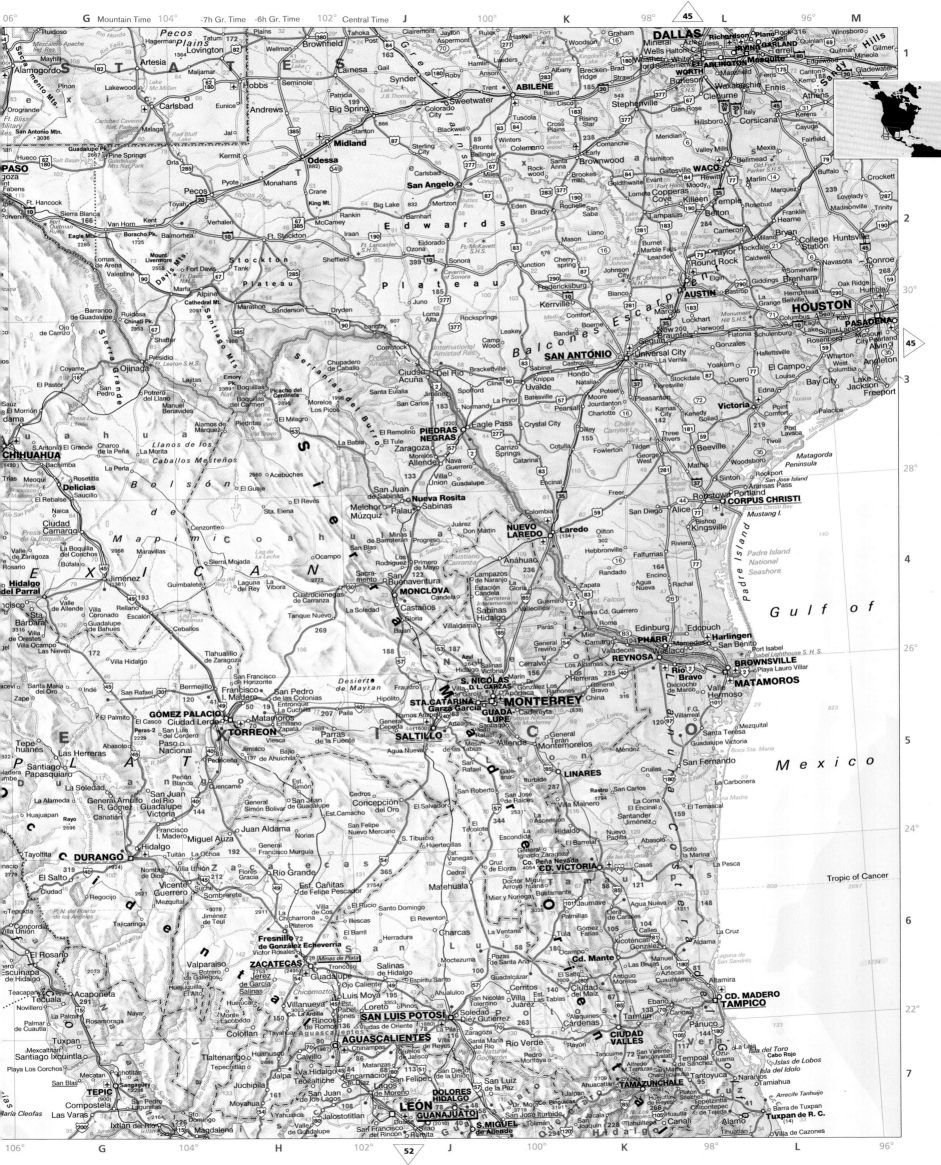

Mexico: Northern Region   51

Mexico: Southern Region • Central America   53

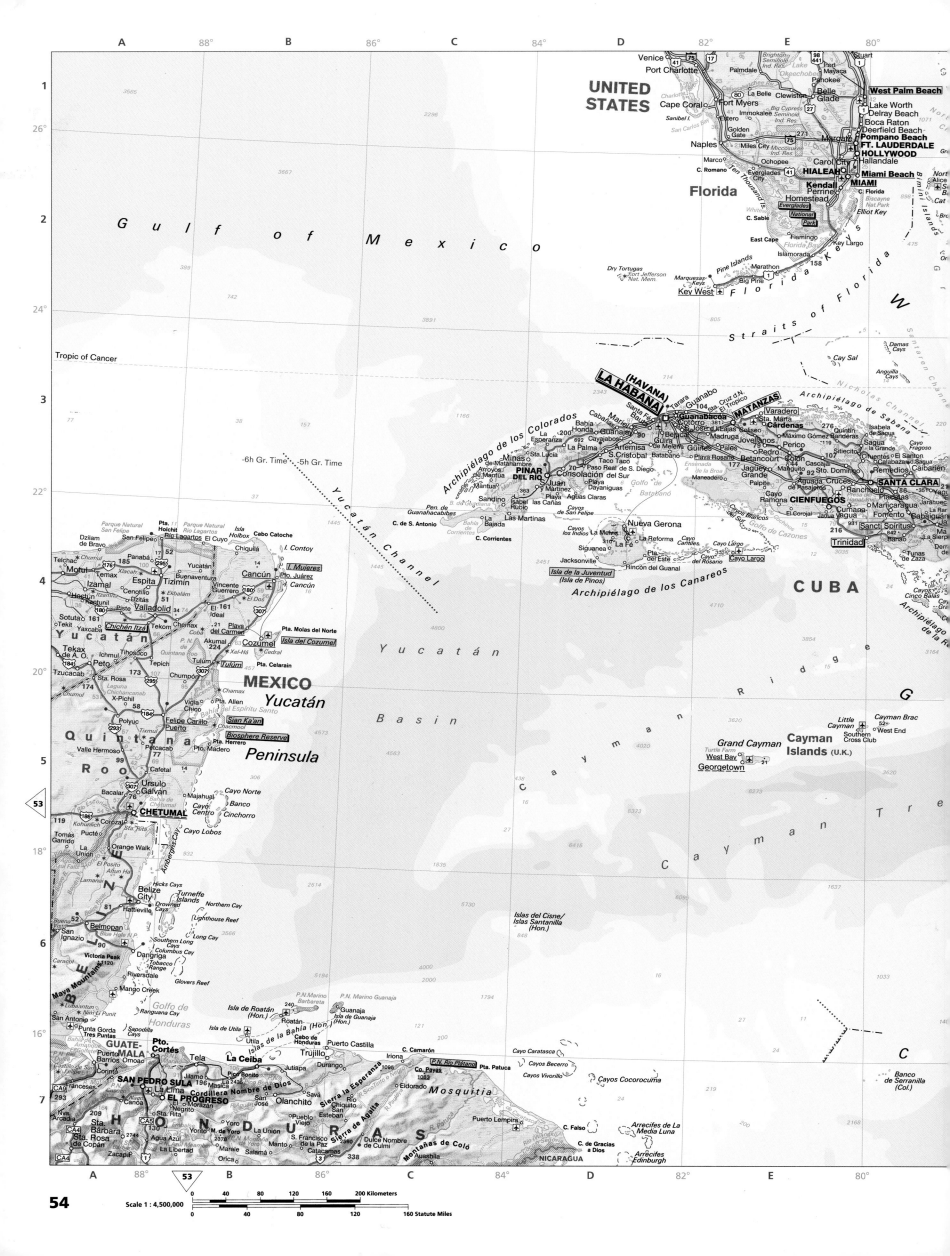

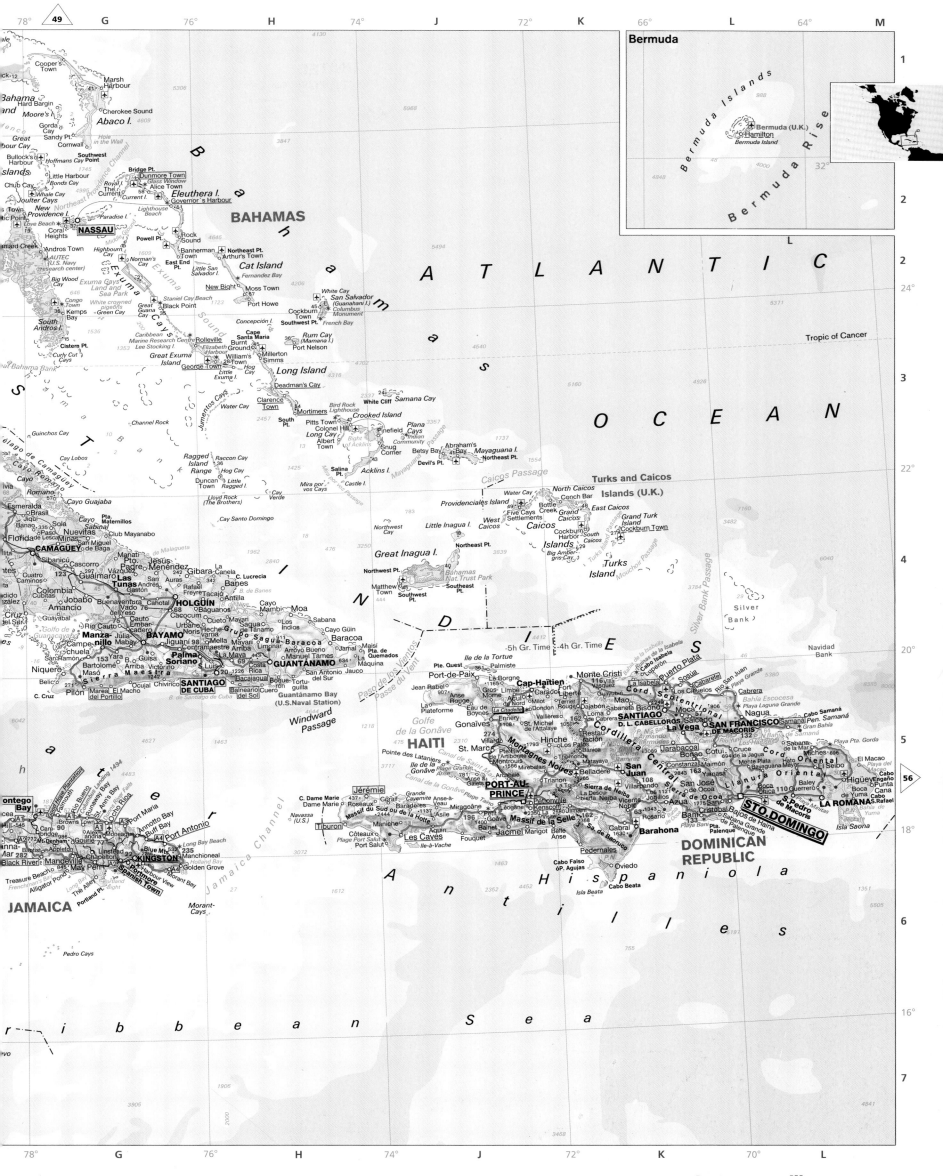

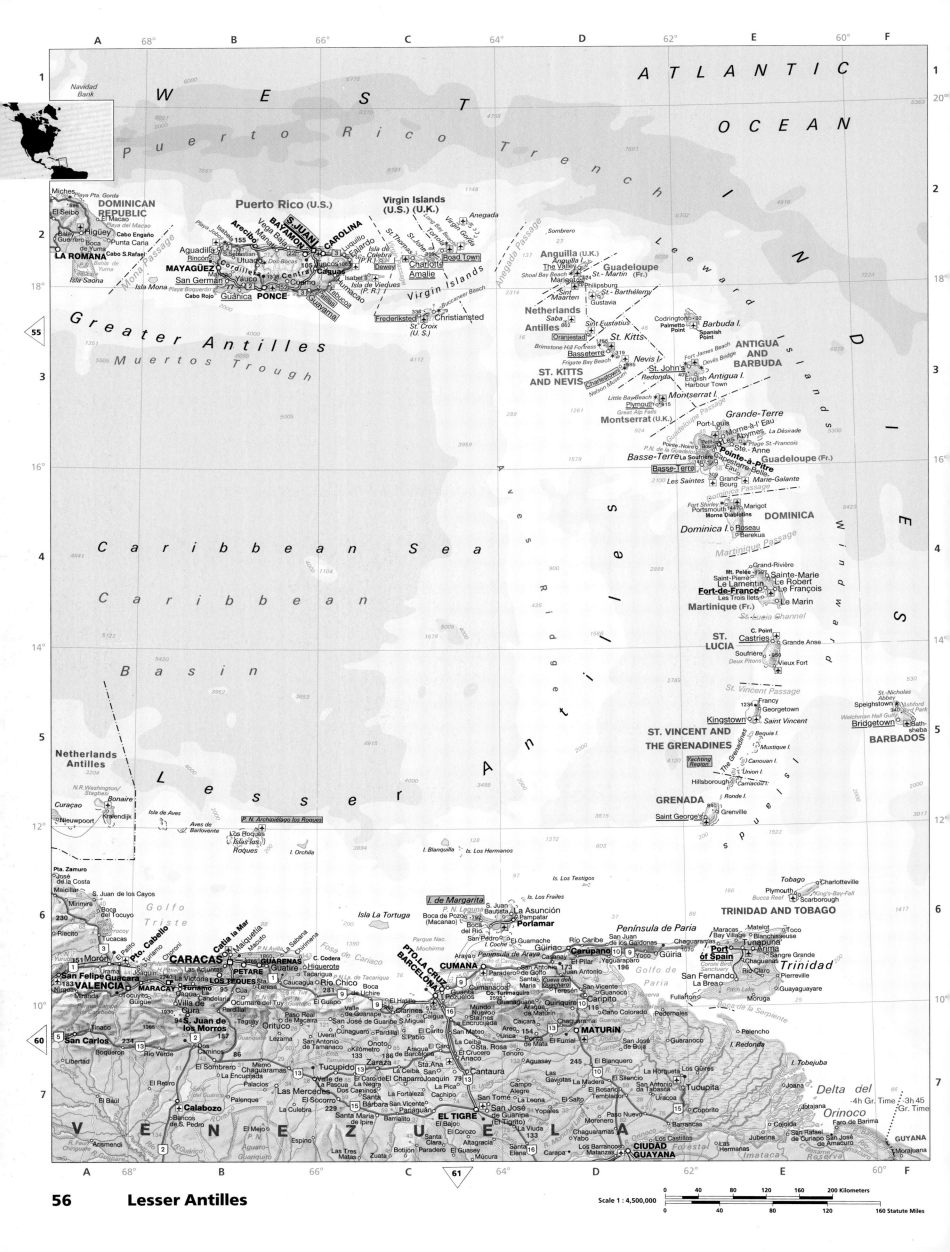

Scale 1 : 4,500,000

South America – continent of natural highlights

Since most of South America's 6,872,580 square miles (17.8 million sq. km) are located in the Southern Hemisphere, it is considered a southern continent, like Africa. The continent is even connected with the Antarctic via the Southern Antilles and submarine rises. With the exception of the polar ice region, all climatic and vegetation zones are represented on the continent; the tropical climate is predominant, however. The western part of the continent is characterized by the volcano-studded mountain range of the Cordilleras de Los Andes, which is close to 4,660 miles (7,500 km) long and reaches a height of almost 23,000 feet (7,000 m). Parallel to them runs a continuous deep-sea trench in the Pacific Ocean. Over half of the

An early documentation of inter-cultural encounter: Zacharias Wagner created this depiction of an Indian dance during his sojourn in Brazil (1634–37) and subsequently published it in his "Bestiary."

continent's land mass is taken up by the giant lowlands of the Orinoco, the Amazon and the Paraná. Adjacent to the southeastern coast is a broad continental shelf cresting in the Falkland Islands (called Islas Malvinas by Argentina). More animal and plant species are found in South America than anywhere else in the world: More than 250 of the 350 known flowering plant families originate there; it is home to one-third of all bird species, and the number of insect species is beyond estimation. The Amazon Basin not only is the largest river region on Earth but also contains the greatest area of tropical forest.

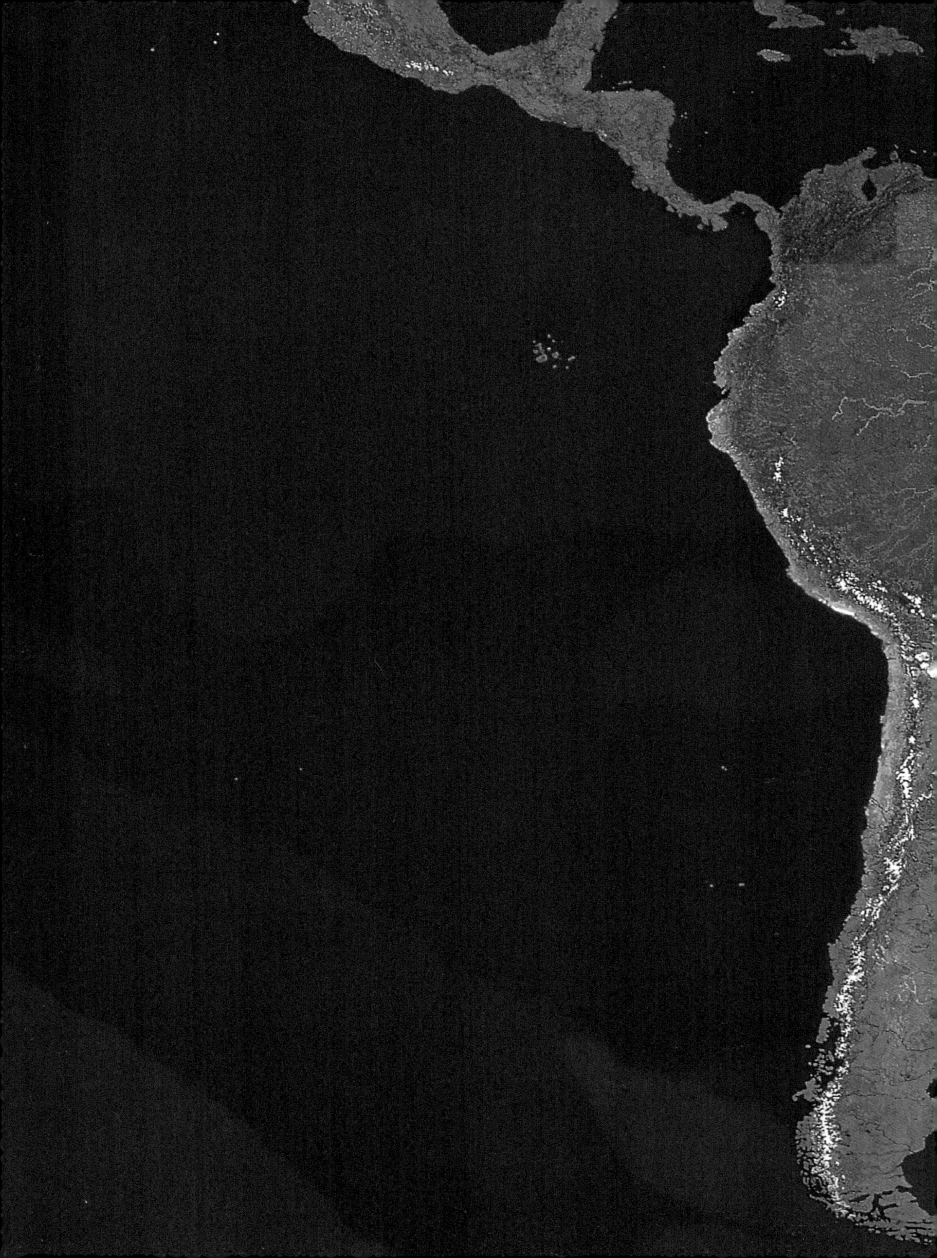

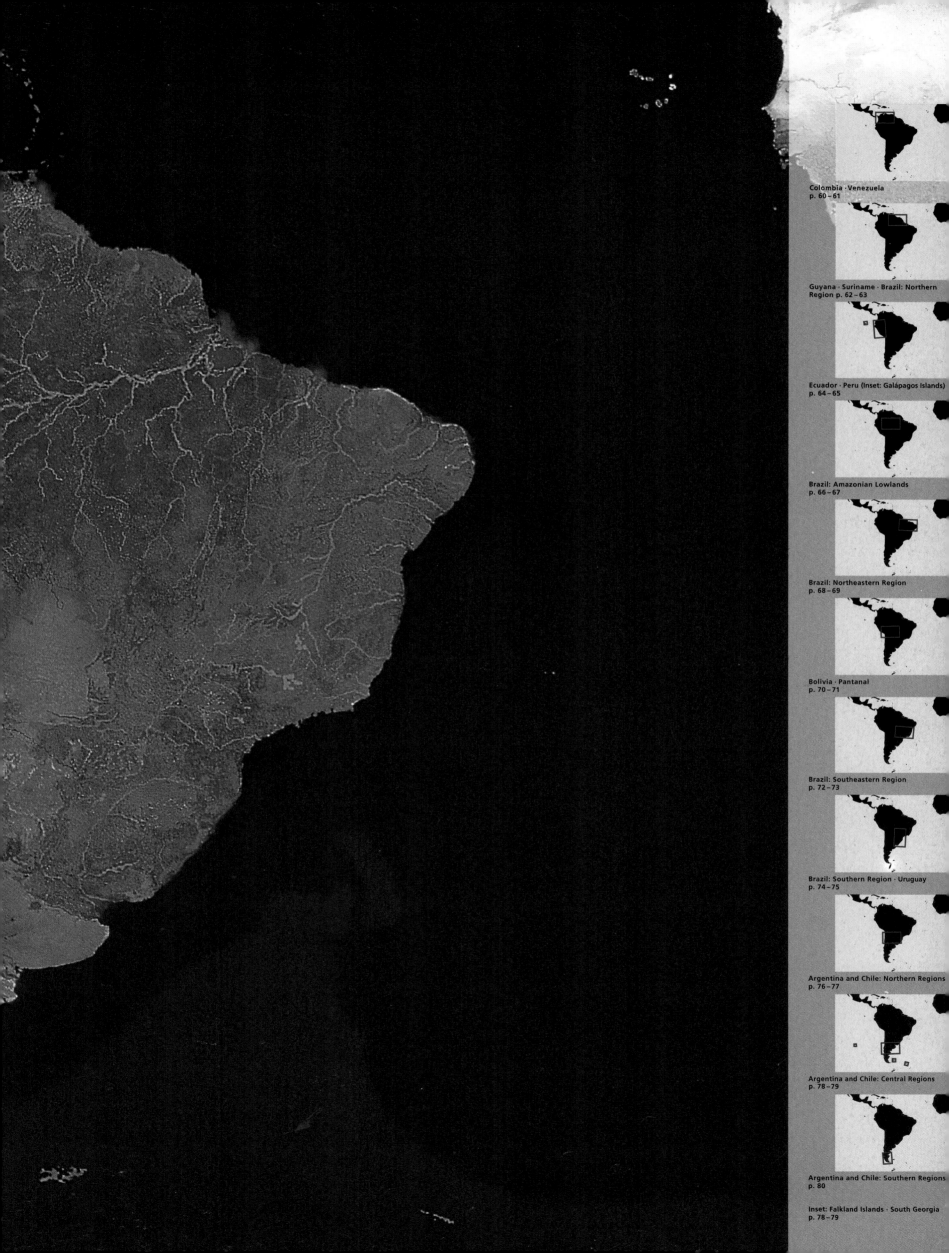

Colombia · Venezuela   **61**

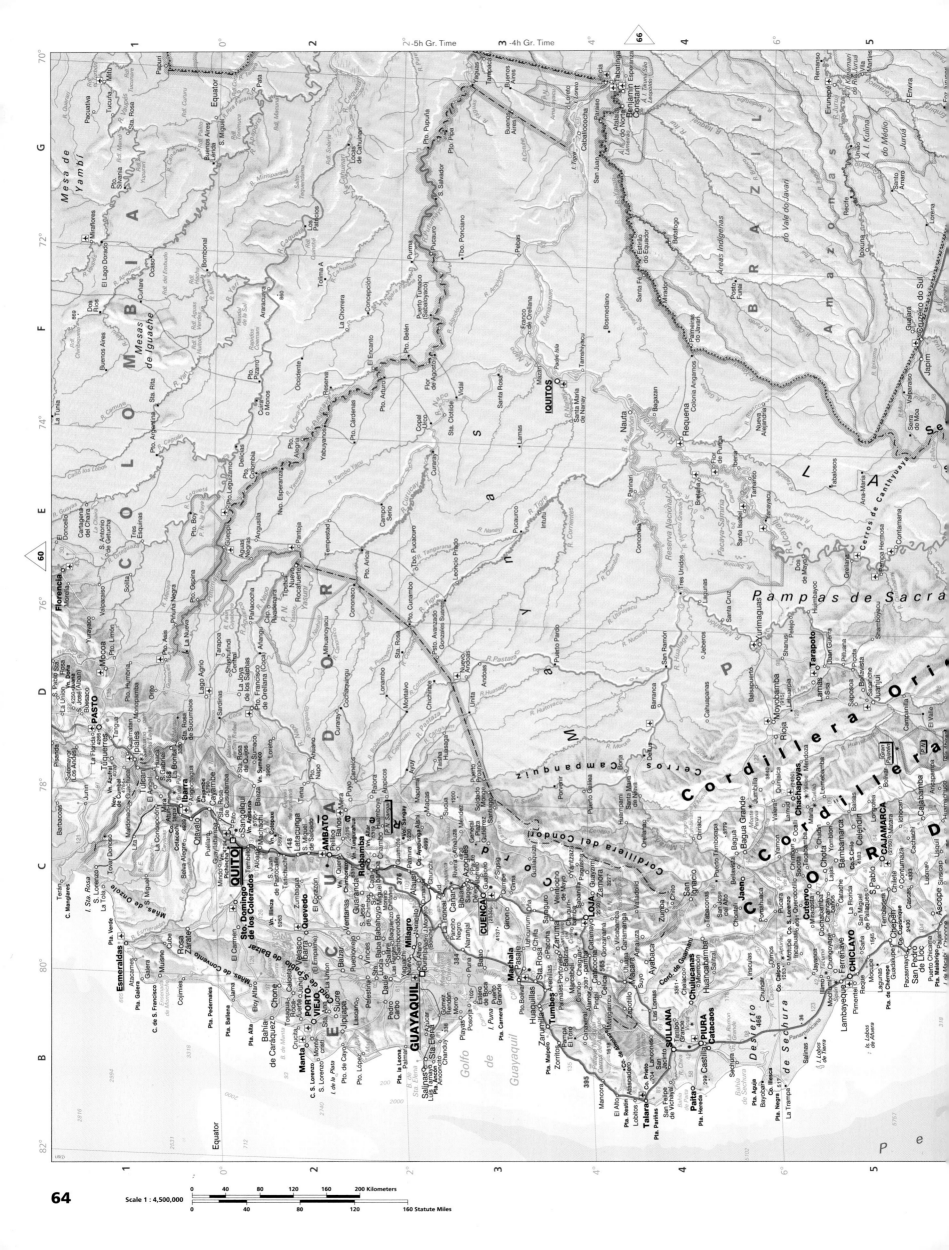

Galápagos Islands

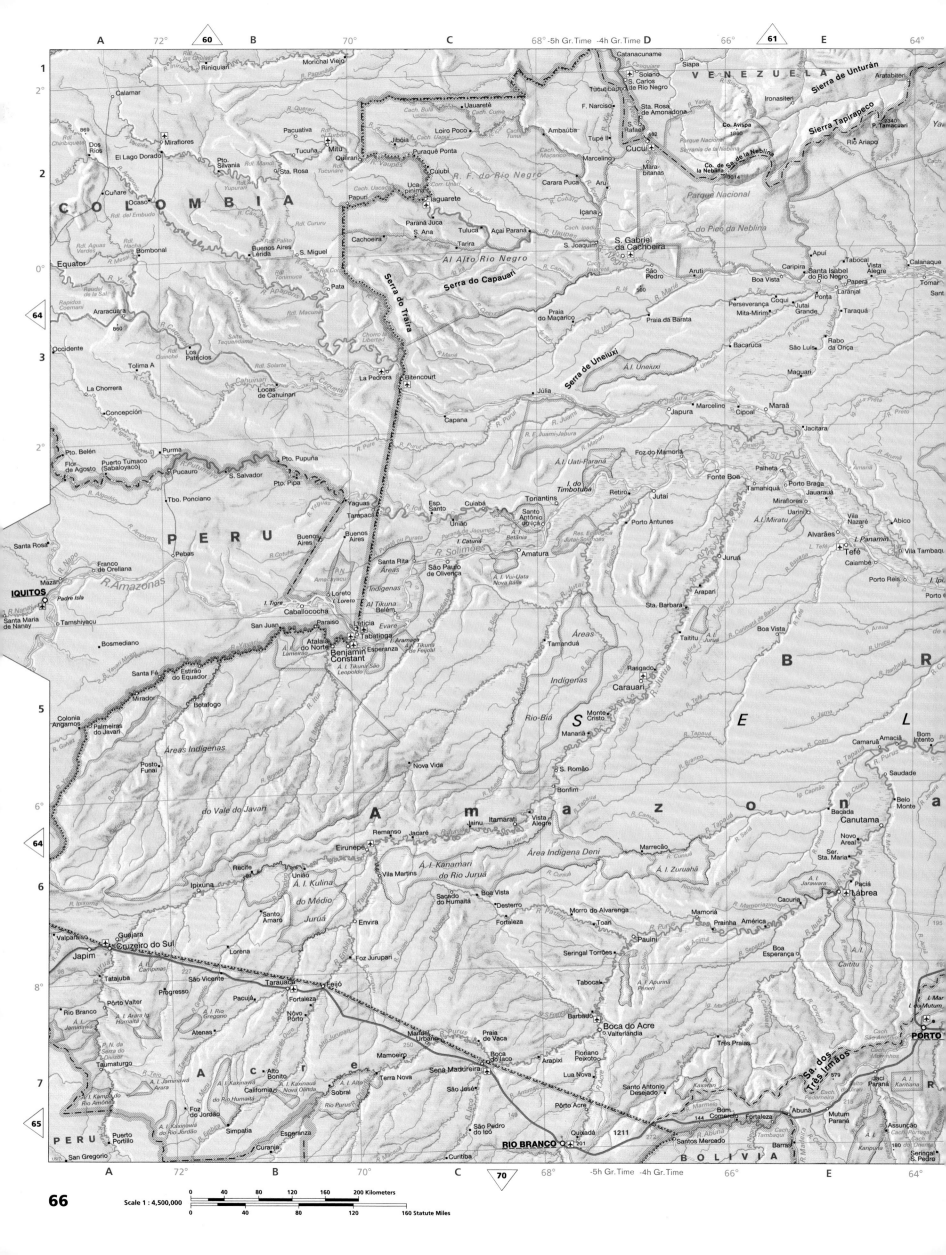

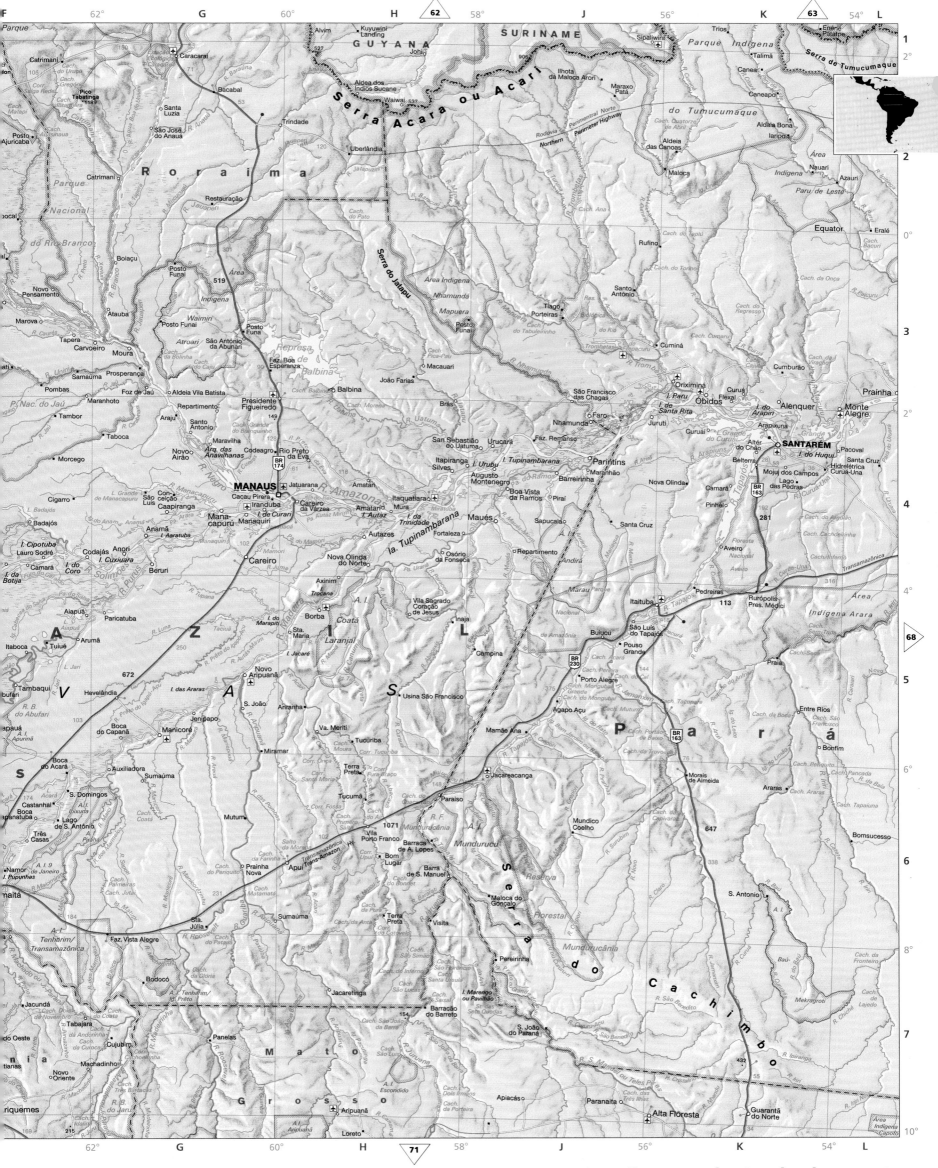

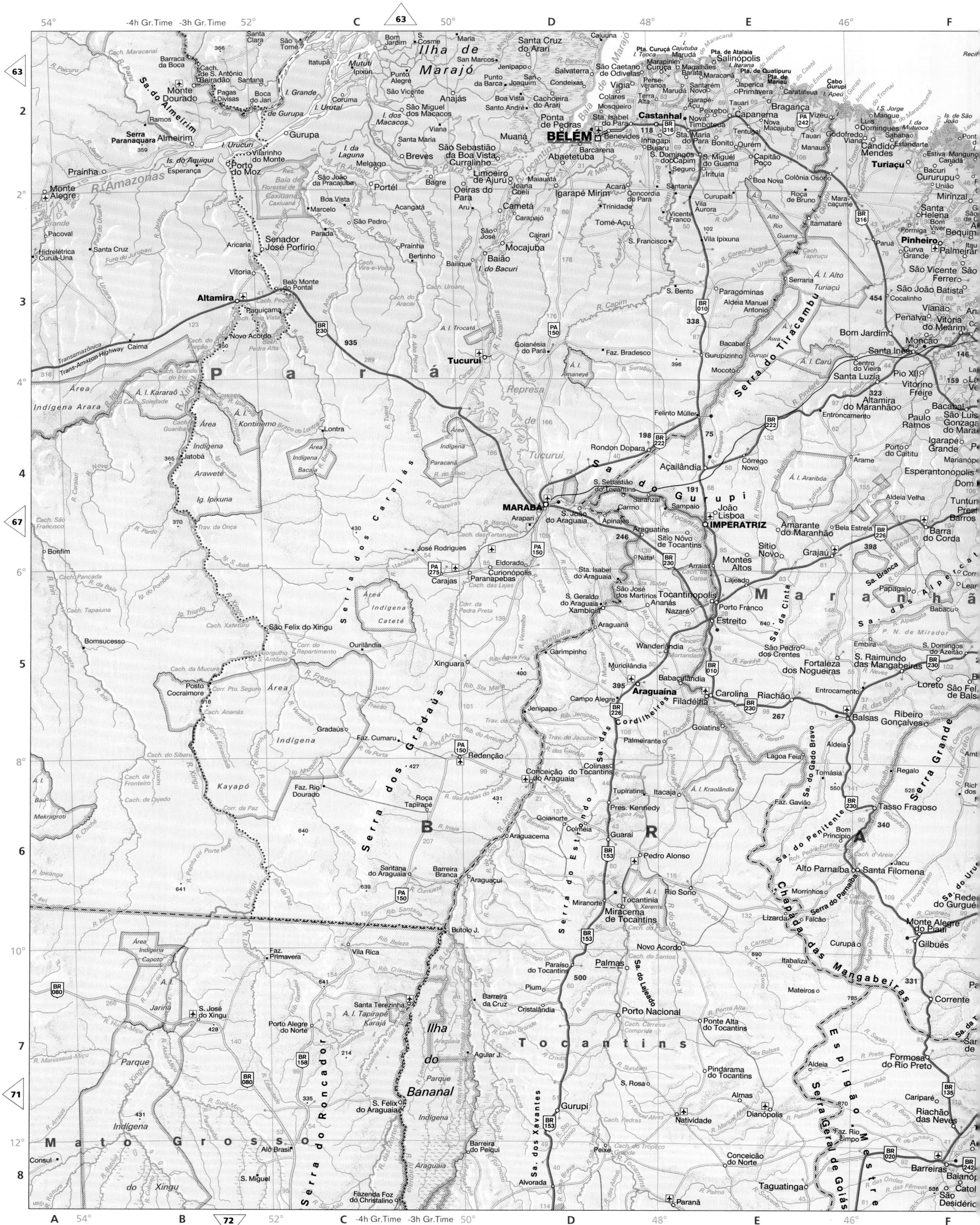

54° -4h Gr. Time -3h Gr. Time 52° 50° 48° 46°

Major labels and features:

Ilha de Marajó

BÉLEM

Castanhal

MARABÁ

IMPERATRIZ

Araguaína

Altamira

Tucuruí

Almeirim

Monte Alegre

Serra Paranaquara

Serra do Almeirim

Transamazônica / Trans-Amazon Highway

Represa de Tucuruí

P a r á

M a r a n h ã o

T o c a n t i n s

M a t o G r o s s o

Serra dos Carajás

Serra dos Gradaús

Serra do Roncador

Serra do Estrondo

Serra das Cordilheiras

Serra do Tiracambu

Chapada das Mangabeiras

Espigão Mestre

Serra Geral de Goiás

Palmas

Porto Nacional

Gurupi

Dianópolis

Natividade

Parque Nacional do Bananal

Ilha do Bananal

S. Félix do Araguaia

Kayapó

Parque do Xingu

Balsas

Carolina

Tasso Fragoso

Pinheiro

Turiaçu

Bragança

Capanema

Paragominas

Açailândia

Redenção

Carajás

São Félix do Xingu

Xinguara

Conceição do Araguaia

Scale 1 : 4,500,000

0 40 80 120 160 200 Kilometers

0 40 80 120 160 Statute Miles

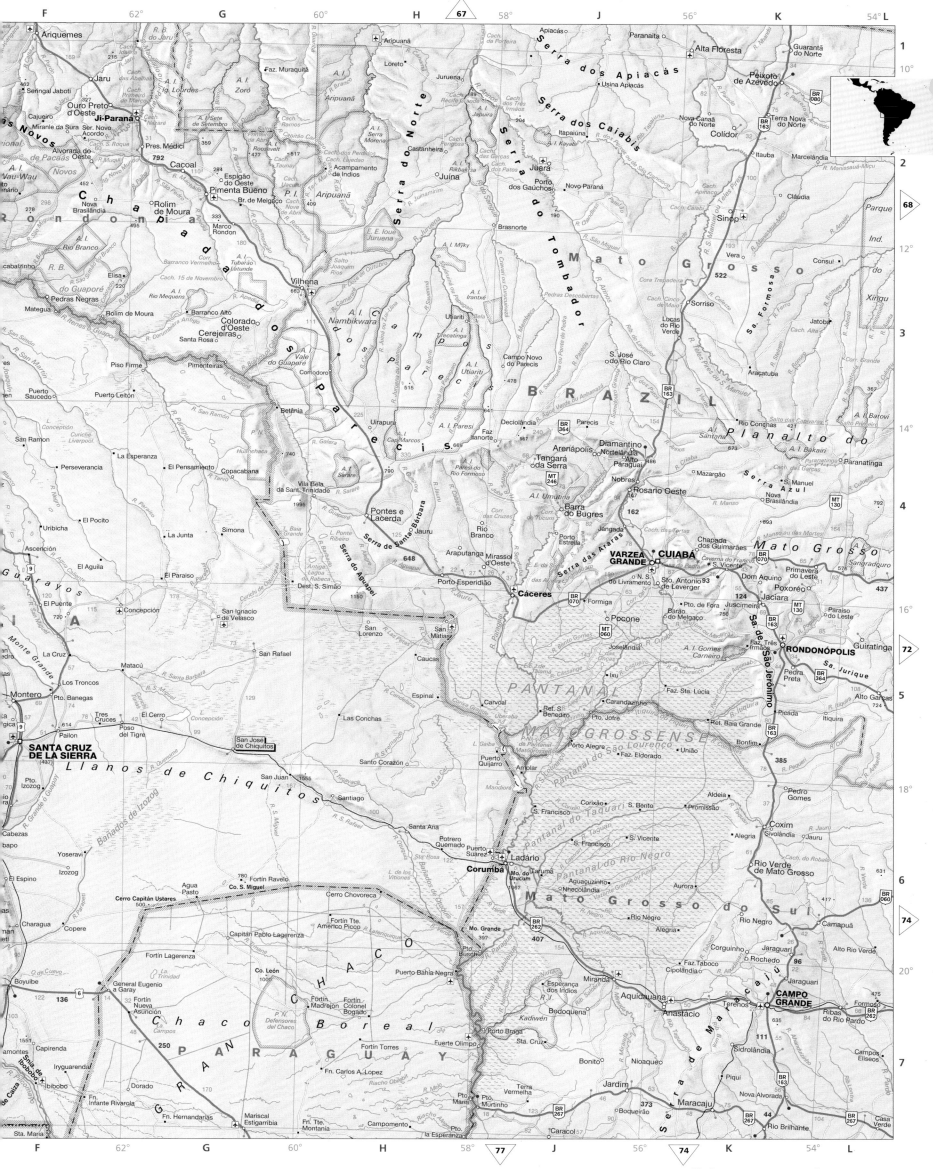

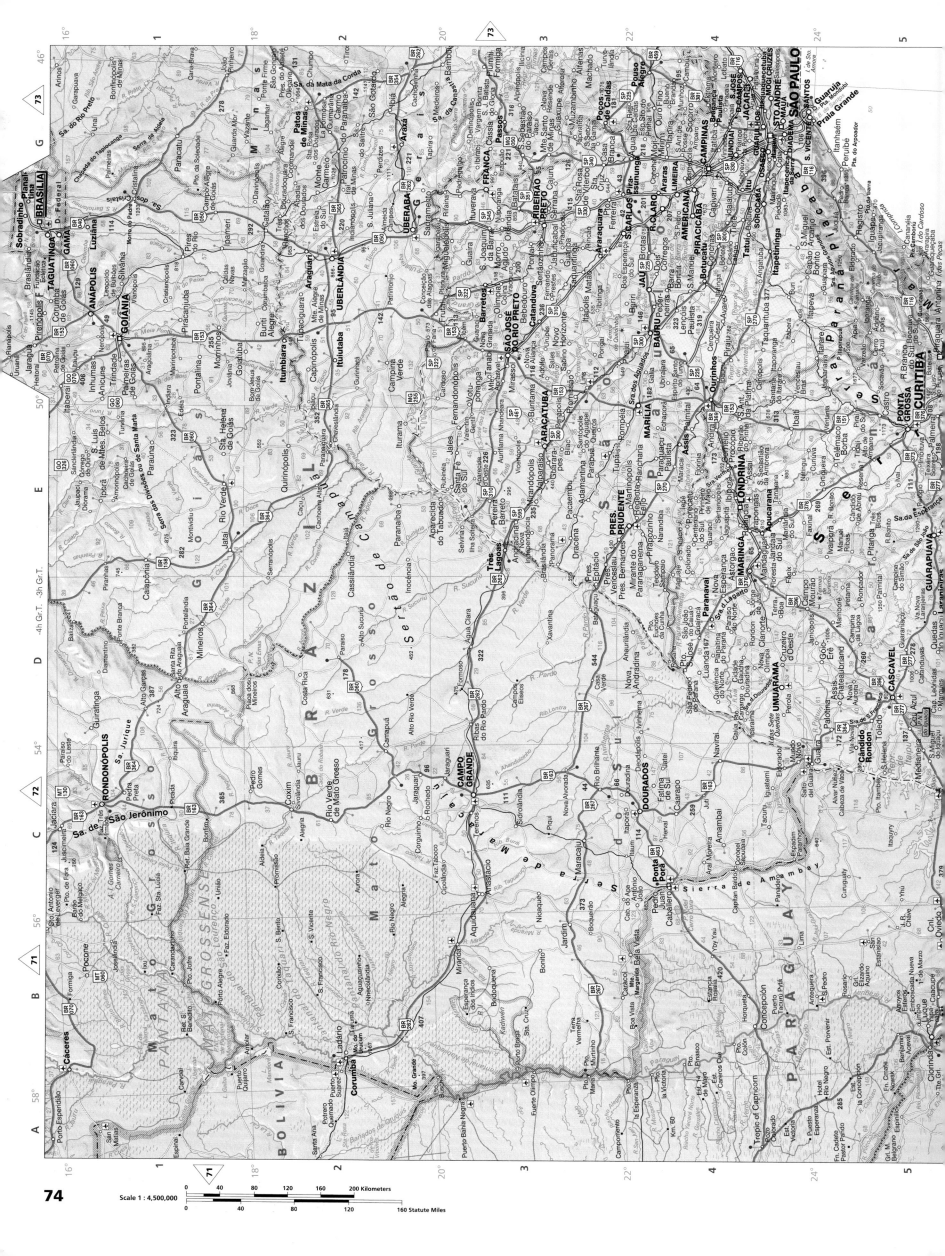

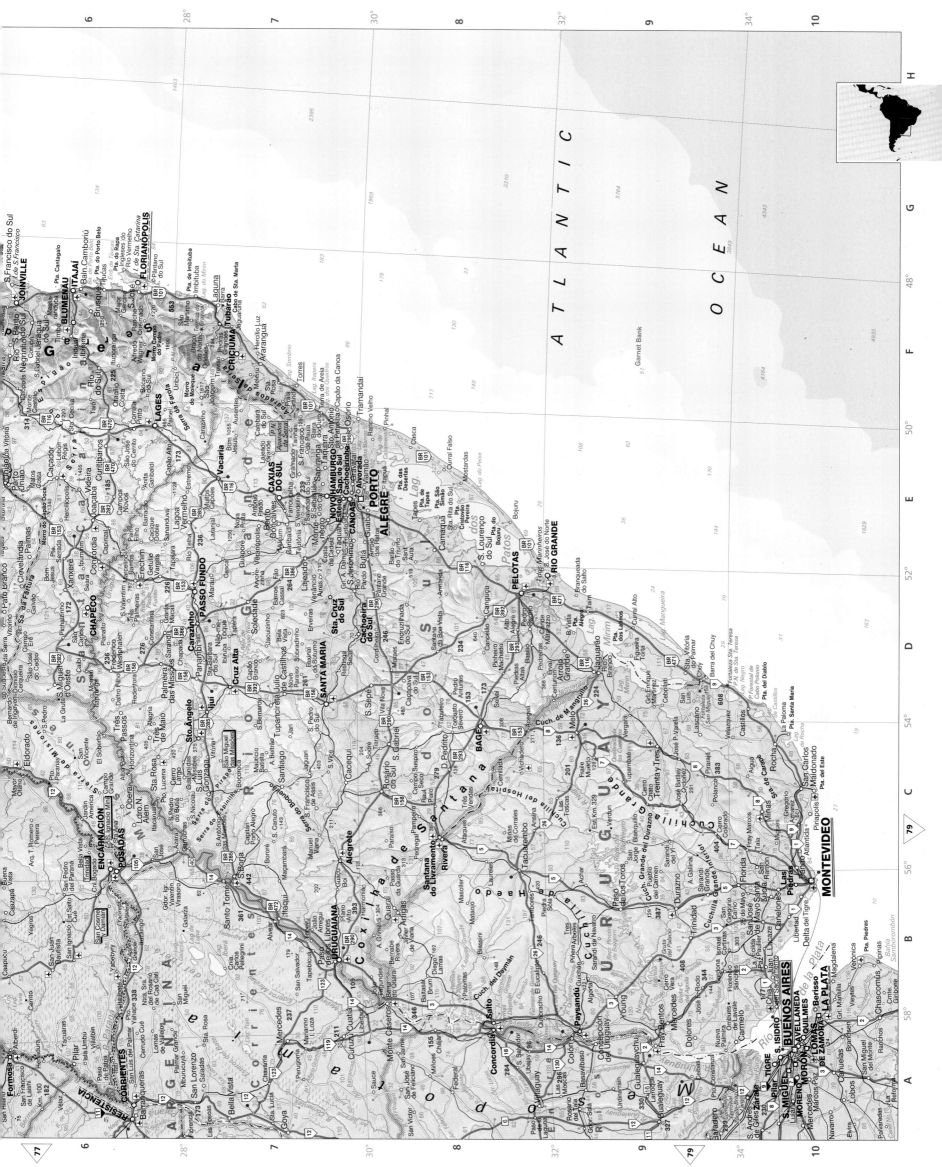

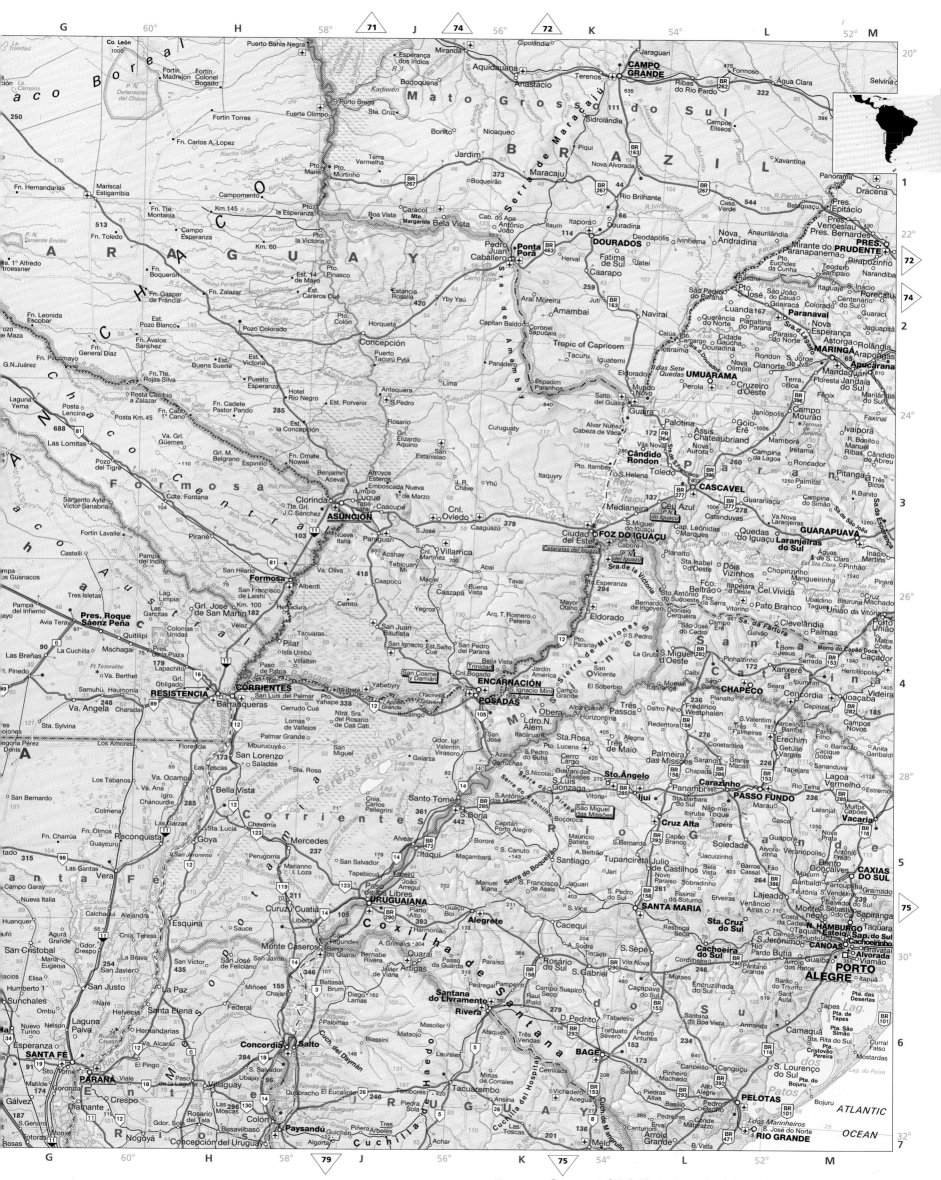

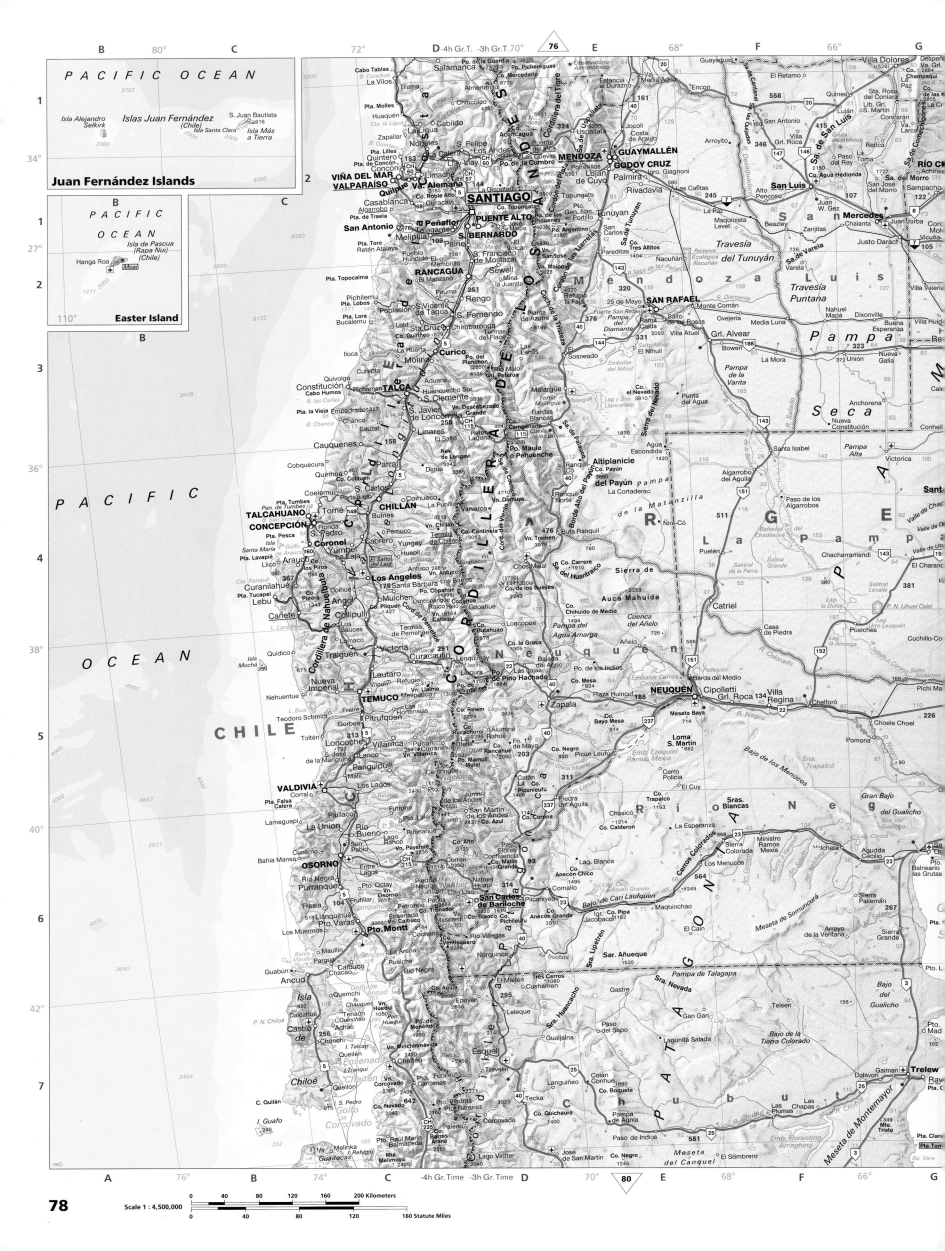

Argentina and Chile: Central Regions 79

Argentina and Chile: Southern Regions

Europe – a continent with border troubles

With an area of 4,054,050 sq. miles (10.5 million sq. km), Europe is the fourth largest continent. From the point of view of physical geography it merely represents a peninsula of Eurasia, jutting out to the west. Europe and Asia have the least well defined delimitation among all continents. The traditional borderline runs along the Ural Mountains the Ural River, the Caspian Sea, the northern edge of the Caucasus, the Black Sea, the Bosporus and the Aegean Sea. In Russia, which is part European and part Asian, this demarcation line is meaningless. A belt of high mountains in which the Alps are the highest range separates the South from the remainder of the continent. Adjacent to the North is the European

An aid to international trade: "New Map of Europe" including "the most noteworthy products and the foremost trading sites." J. Adams made this copperplate engraving in 1787.

medium-height mountainscape followed by a strip of lowlands that widens to the East. The British Isles are, geologically speaking, also part of the northern mountain areas. Its many islands and peninsulas interlace the continent with the Atlantic Ocean and the European Mediterranean Sea. Europe determined the destiny of the world some years into the twentieth century: The scientific research of the planet, the industrial revolution, great inventions and discoveries, but also colonization and thus the transmission of European influences to other parts of the world had their origins here.

Greenland

Sea

ARCTIC

Greenwich Time +1h Greenwich Time

+1h Greenwich Time +3h Gr. Time +4h Greenwich Time

Norskebanken

Sjubre- banken

Danckøya

Verlegen- huken

Phippsøya Sjuøyane
Nordkapp Martensøya
Parryøya Kapp
Platen

Fuglehuket

Spetsbergen

Nordaust-Svalbard nat-res

Grampianfjella
Prins Karls
Forlandet nasjonalpark

Oscar II land

Spitsbergen

Foynøya

Svalbard (Norway)

Kapp
Laura
Storøya

Nordaustlandet

Daudmannsodden

Gustav V land

Kvitøya (Nor.)

Natverøy

Wahlenbergfjorden

Gustav Adolf land

o. Viktorija (Rus.)

Nordaust-Svalbard nat-res
Svenskøya Kong Karls land Kongsøya Abeløya

Newtontoppen

Erik Eriksenstretet

Barentsøya

Olgastretet

Storfjorden

Haastbukta

Edgeøya

Stonepynten

Øyrlandsodden

Tjuvfjorden

Tusenøyane

Halvmåneøya

Storfjordrenna

Storfjordbanken

Hopen

Hopen Radio

Hopen- banken

Bjørnøya Bank

Bjørnøy Radio
Bjørnøya (Nor.) Tunheim

Perleporten

Norwegian

Barents

Sea

London

Fugløy Bank

Murmanskoje Rise

Knivskjelodden
Nordkapp
Magerøya
Havøysund Skarsvåg
Rolvsøya Nordkapp

Sørøya
Breivikbotn Honningsvåg
Hasvik Kjøllefjord Mehamn Gamvik

North Kap Bank

Arnøy
Skjervøy

Porsanger- halvøya

Nordkinn- halvøya

Berlevåg

Tromsø

Lyngseidet

Kjøllefjord

Ifjord
Langnes

Båtsfjord

Andenes

Alta
Hellerstranda

Lakselv Rastigaissa

Varanger- halvøya

Harstad

N O R W A Y

Finnmarks- vidda

Tanabru
Vadsø

Vardø

Narvik

Kautokeino

Karigasniemi

Utsjoki

Hurtigrute

Grense Jakobselv

S W E D E N

Kebnekaise

Karesuando Enontekiö

F I N L A N D

Nyrud

Sevettijärvi

Kikkenes

Neiden

Linahamari
Pečenga

Rybačij

mys Cypnavolok

Murmansk

R U S S I A

Nikel Zapoljarnyj

Pollarnyj

Uraguba

o. Kil'din

Scale 1 : 4,500,000

0 40 80 120 160 200 Kilometers

0 40 80 120 160 Statute Miles

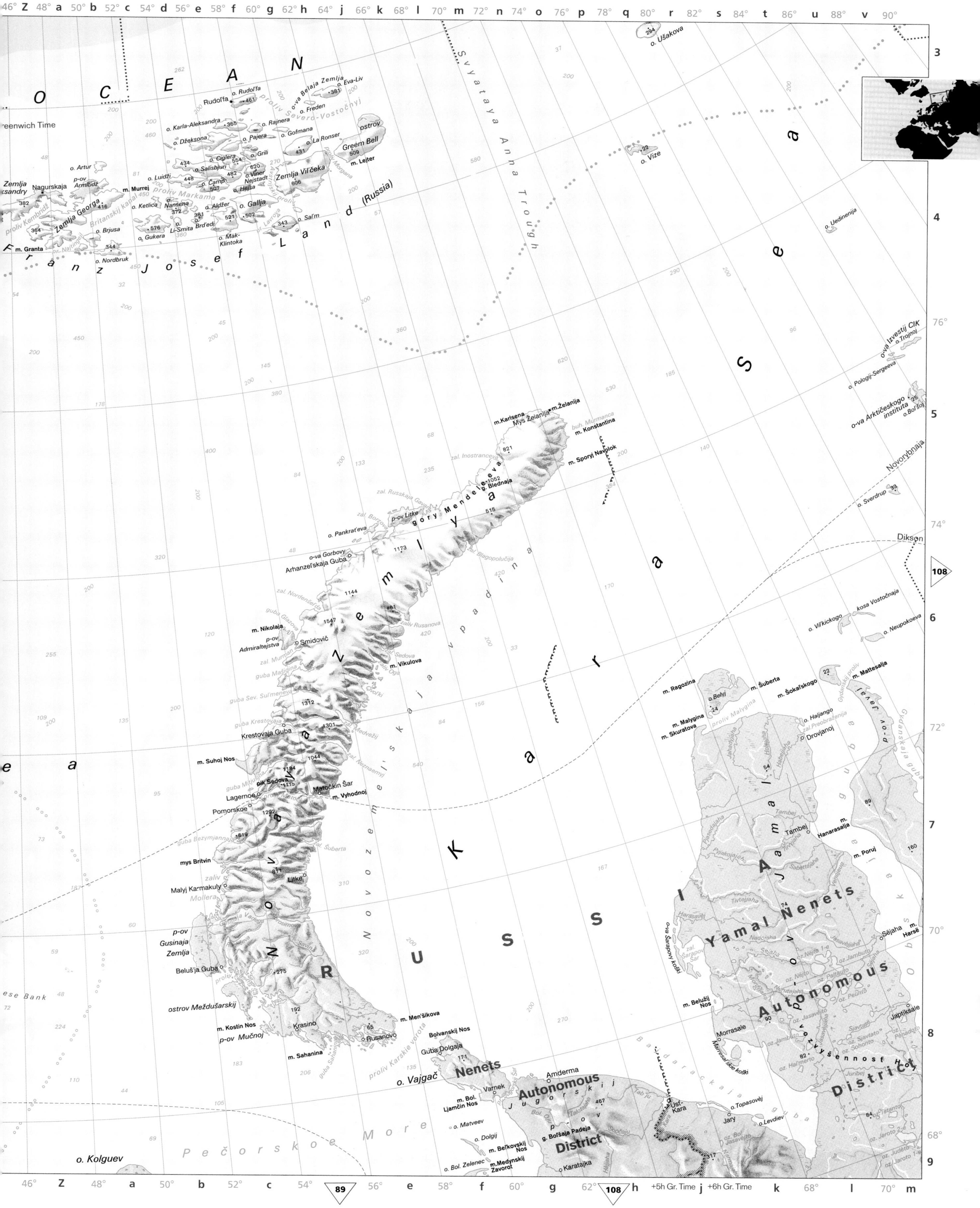

O C E A N

Greenwich Time

O

Svataya Anna Trough

o. Ušakova

o. Vize

Rudol'fa · o. Rudol'fa
·461
o-va Belaja Zemlja · o. Eva-Liv
·380
o. Freden
o. Karla-Aleksandra · 365 o. Rajnera
o. Džeksona o. Pajera o. Gofmana
434 o. Cigera 554 o. Grili La Ronser ostrov
o. Salisbjun 482 620 431 Green Bell
Zemlja p-ov 81 o. Luidži 448 · Čamp 502 Viner m. Lejter
ksandry Nagurskaja Armit'džâ m. Murrei 450 o. Hejsa Nejstadt 606
382 Zemlja Georga 416 o. Ketlica Nansena 372 o. Alžer Zemlja Vil'čeka
·416 o. Gukera 381 o. Gallja 509
proliv Kembridž 364 o. Brjusa 576 Li-Smita Brd'edi ·521 ·502
m. Granta 344 Mak- 343
o. Nordbruk Klintoka

Franz Josef Land (Russia)

o. Udinenija

o-va Izvestij CIK
o. Trojnoj
o-va Arktičeskogo o. Bol'šoj
instituta 25

Novorybnaja

o. Sverdrup 33

Dikson

108

o. Vil'kickogo kosa Vostočnaja

o. Neupokoeva

m. Karlsena m. Konstantina
Mys Želanija m. Želanija
821 buh. Murmanca
zal. Inostranceva m. Sporyj Navolok
·1052
g. Blednaja
515 gory Mendeleeva
p-ov Litke
o. Pankrat'eva zal. Russkaja Gavan'
o-va Gorbovy 1173 Blagopolučija
Arhanzel'skaja Guba
1144 Sedova
m. Nikolaja 1547 zaliv Rusanova
p-ov o. Smidovič
Admiraltejstva
m. Vikulova
1312
1301
Krestovaja Guba
m. Suhoj Nos 1044
1184
pik Sedova ·1115
Lagernoe Matočkin Šar
Pomorskoe 1292 m. Vyhodnoj
·1619
mys Britvin 611
Litke
Malyj Karmakuly
p-ov
Gusinaja
Zemlja
Beluš'ja Guba 275
ostrov Meždušarskij
192
m. Kostin Nos 65 Rusanovo
p-ov Mučnoj m. Men'šikova
m. Sahanina Bolvanskij Nos
Guba Dolgaja
o. Vajgač Nenets
Varnek Amderma
m. Bol. Autonomous
Ljamčin Nos 467
o. Matveev p-ov Ust-
o. Dolgij Jugorskij Kara Jary
o. Bel'kovskij Nos g. Bol'šaja Padeja Levdiev
o. Bol. Zelenec m. Medynskij District Topasovej
Zavorot Karatajka
o. Kolguev Pečorskoe More

Nenets
Autonomous
District

Yamal Nenets

Autonomous

District

m. Ragozina
o. Belyj
m. Šuberta
m. Malygina m. Šokal'skogo
m. Skuratova proliv Malygina
54
o. Hajango
zal. Preobraženija
Drovjanoj
m. Poruj
m. Tambej
m. Hanarasalja
160
Sèjaha m. Harše
Japtiksale
m. Belužij
Nos
Morrasale
Japtiksale

Gdanskaja guba

RUSSIA

Kara Sea

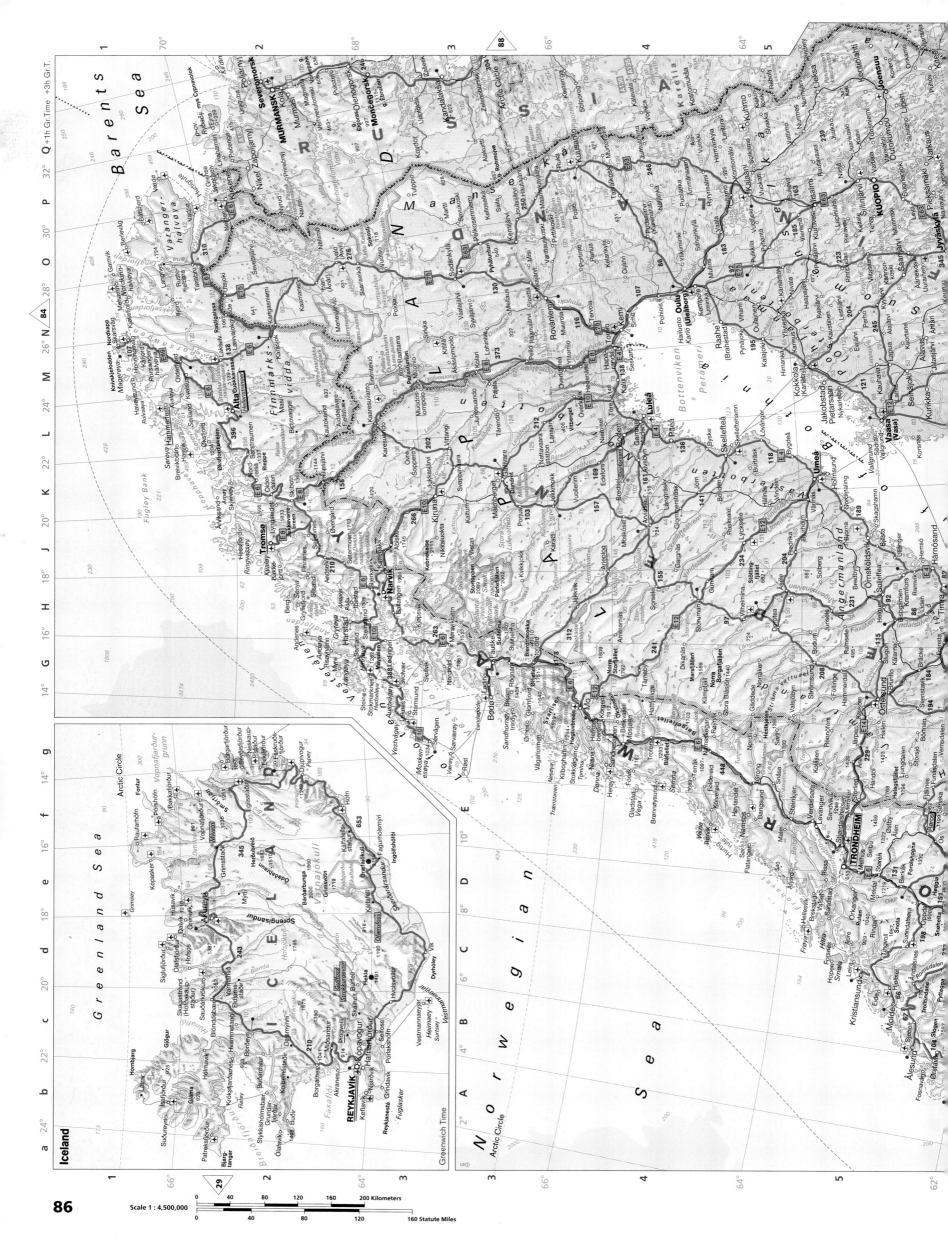

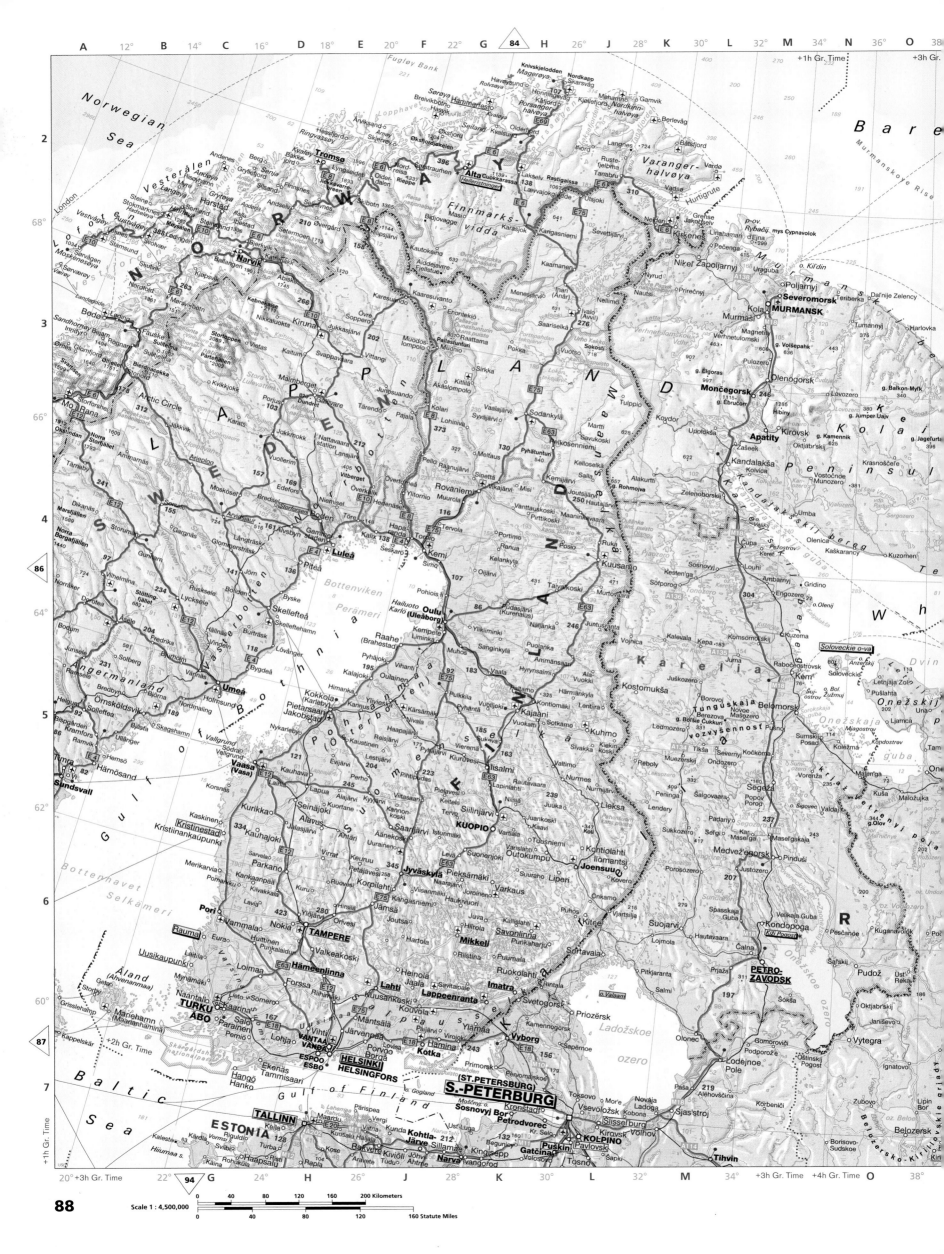

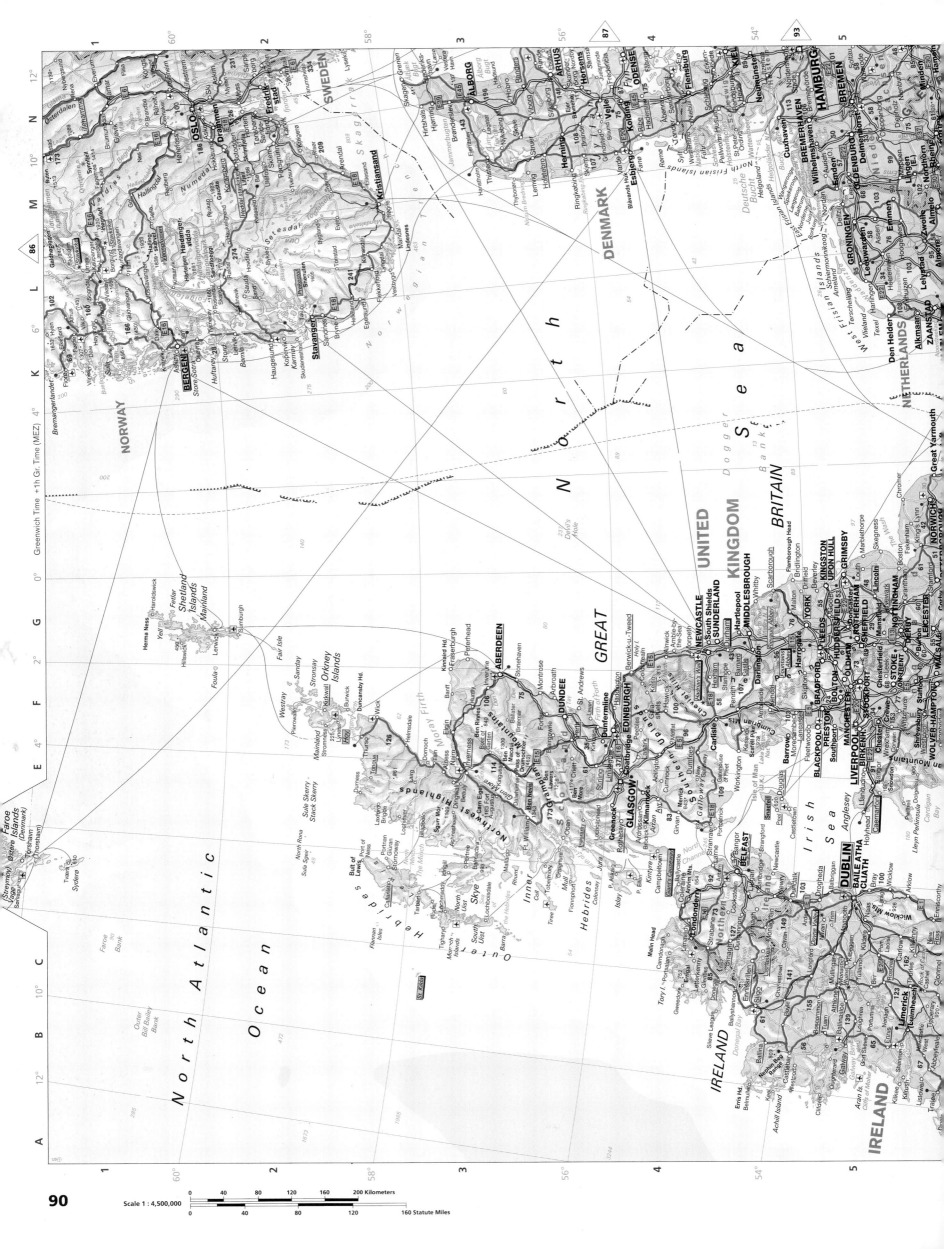

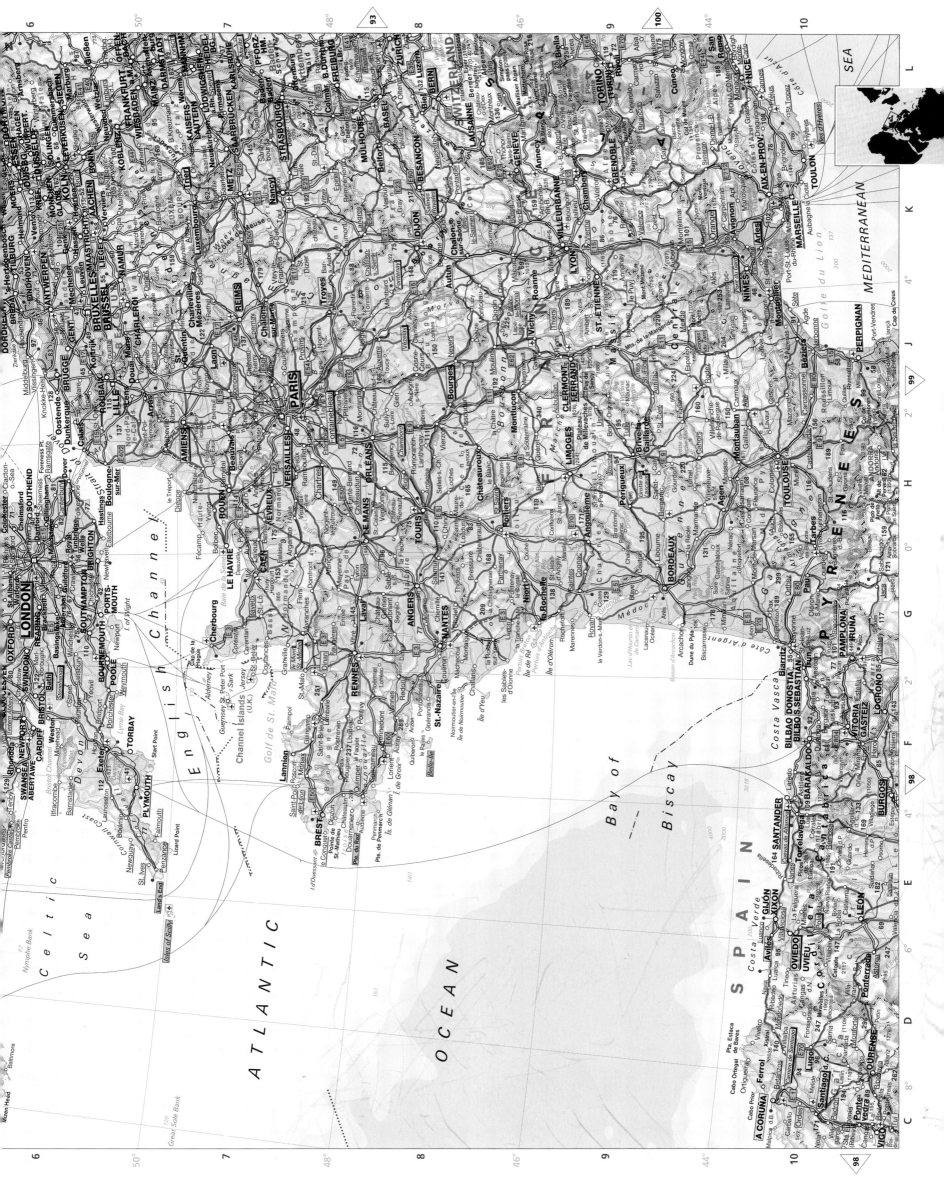

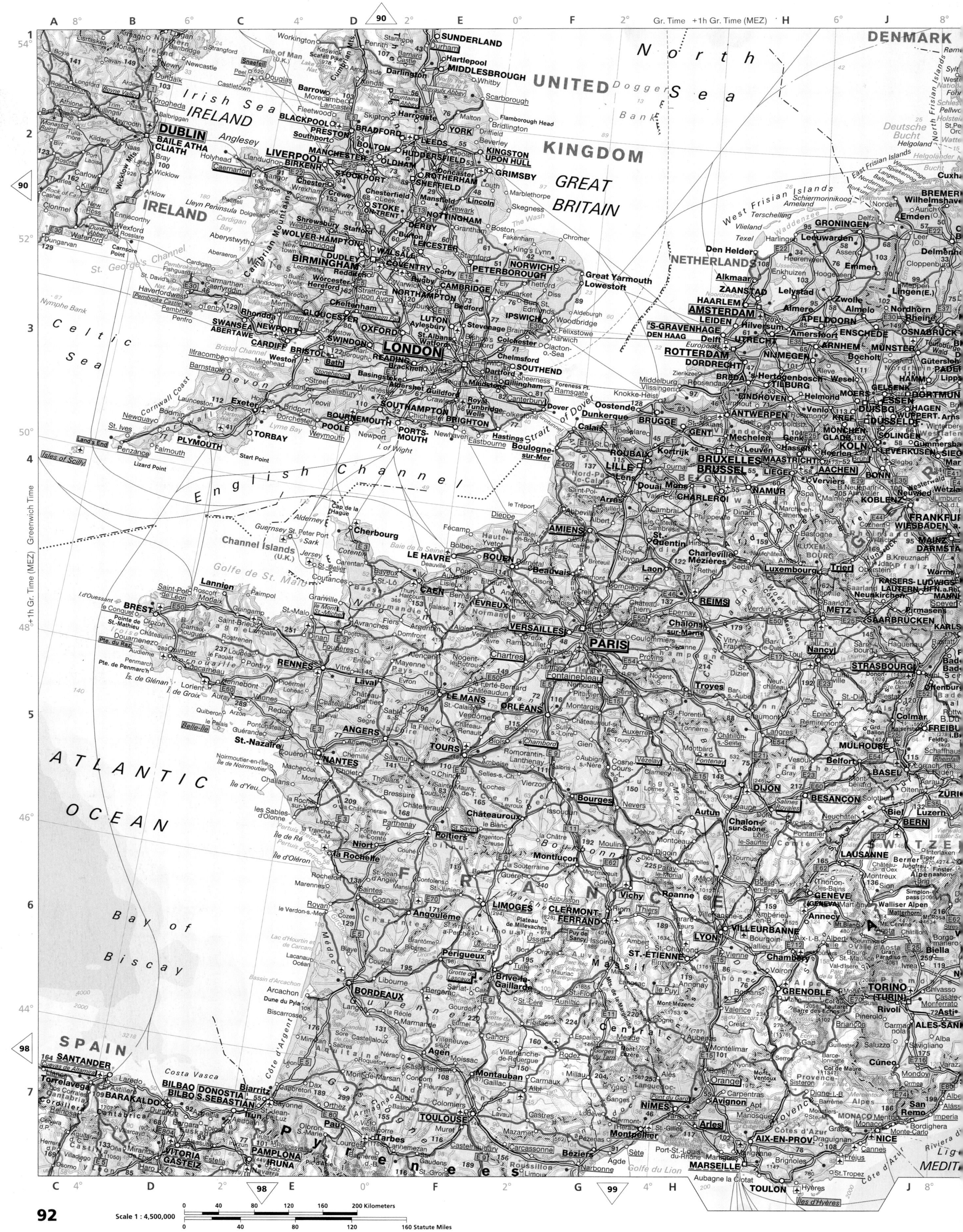
DENMARK
UNITED KINGDOM
GREAT BRITAIN
IRELAND
NETHERLANDS
BELGIUM
FRANCE
SPAIN
North Sea
Irish Sea
Celtic Sea
English Channel
ATLANTIC OCEAN
Bay of Biscay
Channel Islands (U.K.)
Golfe de St. Malo
Strait of Dover
St. George's Channel
Isle of Man (U.K.)
Pyrenees
Massif Central
Gr. Time
+1h Gr. Time (MEZ)
Greenwich Time
DUBLIN
BAILE ATHA CLIATH
LIVERPOOL
MANCHESTER
LEEDS
BIRMINGHAM
LONDON
CARDIFF
BRISTOL
PLYMOUTH
SOUTHAMPTON
AMSTERDAM
ROTTERDAM
ANTWERPEN
BRUXELLES
BRUSSEL
LILLE
PARIS
LE HAVRE
ROUEN
CAEN
RENNES
NANTES
TOURS
ORLÉANS
BORDEAUX
TOULOUSE
LYON
MARSEILLE
NICE
GENÈVE
TORINO
STRASBOURG
Luxembourg
BILBAO
DONOSTIA S.SEBASTIÁN
SANTANDER
PAMPLONA IRUÑA
VITORIA GASTEIZ

Scale 1 : 4,500,000

0 40 80 120 160 200 Kilometers

0 40 80 120 160 Statute Miles

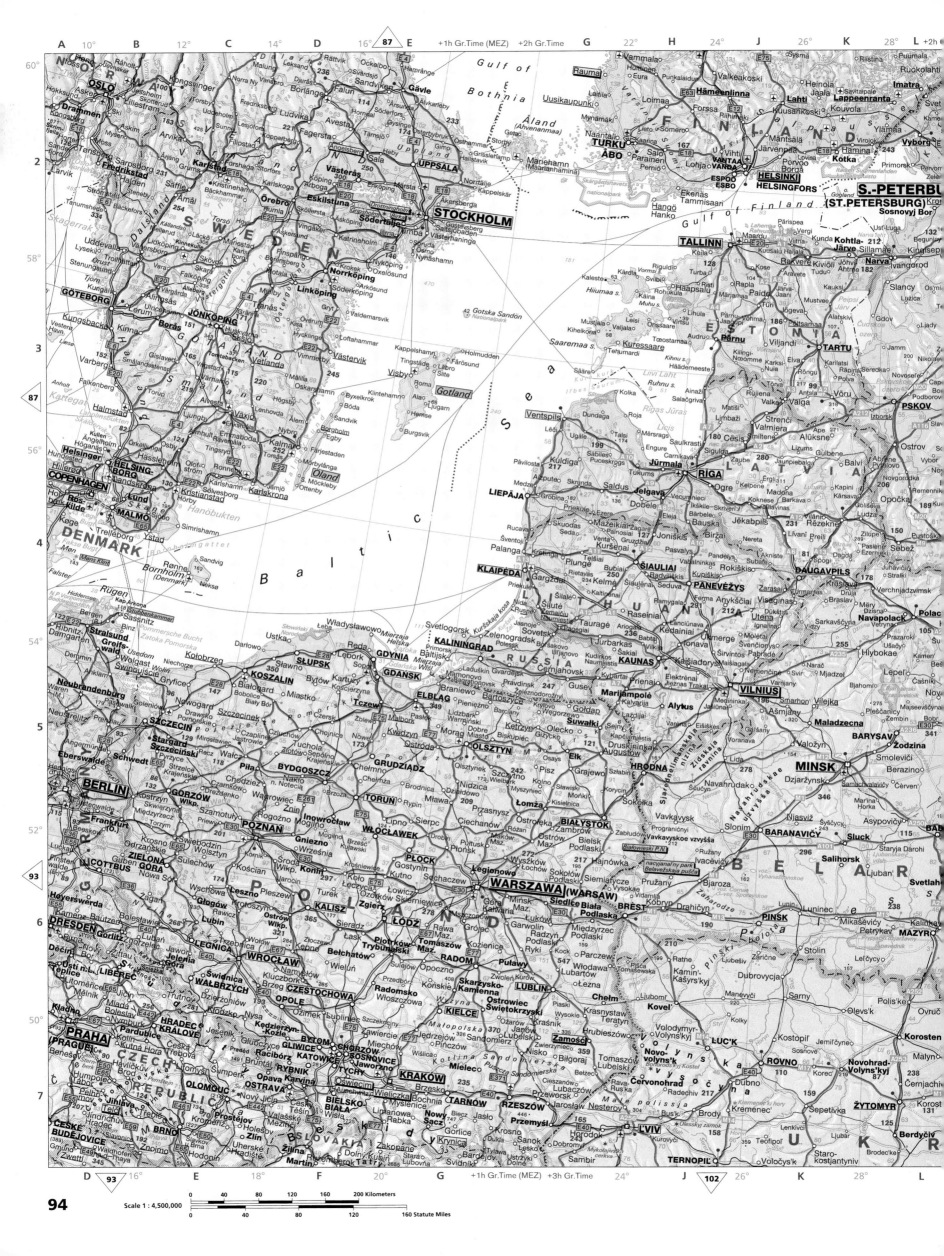

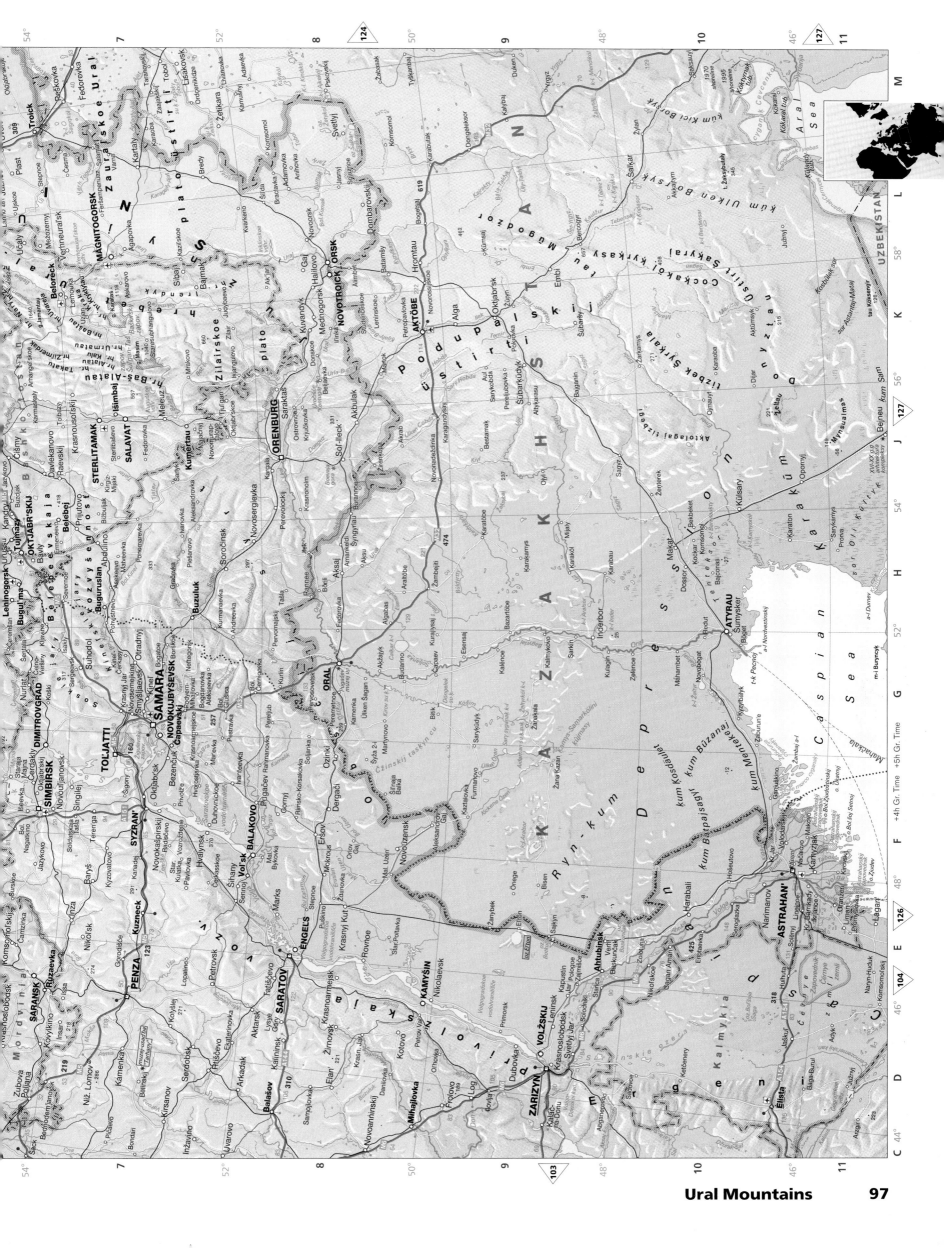

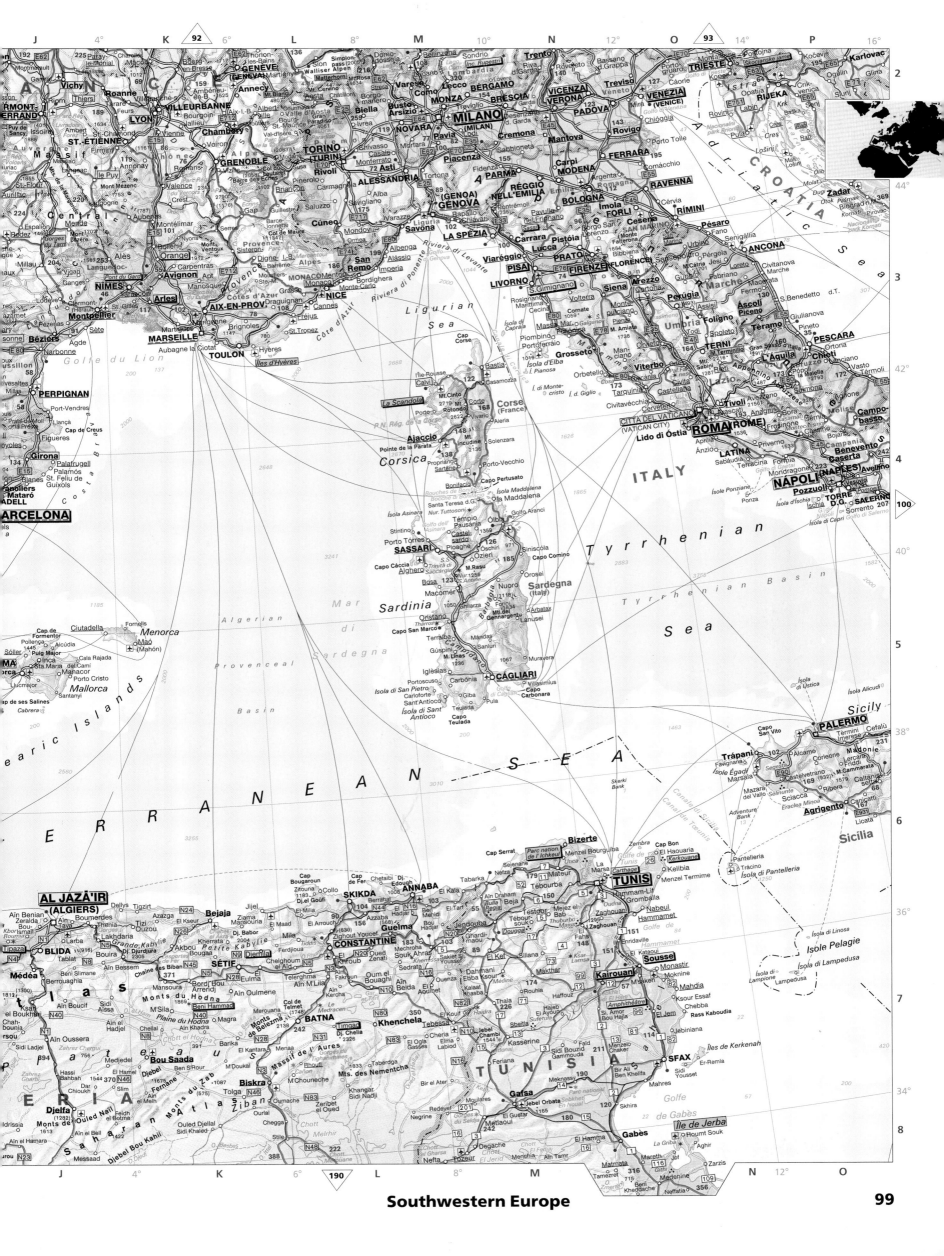

Scale 1 : 4,500,000

0   40   80   120   160   200 Kilometers

0   40   80   120   160 Statute Miles

36°

2

LIPECK
ELEC
Zmievka
Trosna
gorsk
E95
M2
Livny
ELEC
Zadonsk
395
Grjazi
Kotovsk
Znamenka
Inžavino
Serdobsk
Petrovsk
Sennoj
Sihany
Vol'sk
BALAKOVO
Pervo-
sovetsk
M32

Kolpny
Kšenskij
Dobrinka
Usman'
Mordovo
Žerdevka
Uvarovo
Arkadak
Aktarsk
Fatiščevo
Marks
Bol. Bykovka
Rimsko-Korsakovka
Soljanka
Gornyj
Peremetnoe

KURSK
160
274
Ščigry
Semiluki
VORONEŽ
Anna
Gribanovskij
SARATOV
ENGEL'S
Puškino
Stepnoe
Mokrous
Ersov
Dergači
Ozinki

218
233
Goršečnoe
Gremjače
ravnina
Rogačevka
Talovaja
Borisoglebsk
Balašov
Kalininsk
A144
310
105
Engel's
Krasnyj Kut
Krasn. Jar
Rovnoe
Star Poltavka
Novouzensk
Aleksandrov
Gaj
Kaztalovka
Furmanovo
Sarykūdyk
97

Obojan
Skorodnoe
Sinie Lipjagi
GEORGIU-DEZ
OSTROGOŽSK
Buturlinovka
Novohoperskij
Novonikolaevskij
Elan'-
Kolenovskij
Žirnovsk
221
Kotovo
Ol'hovka
Petrov Val
Nikolaevsk
KAMYŠIN
Jorskoe plo
Žanybek
Aleksandrov
Gaj

50°

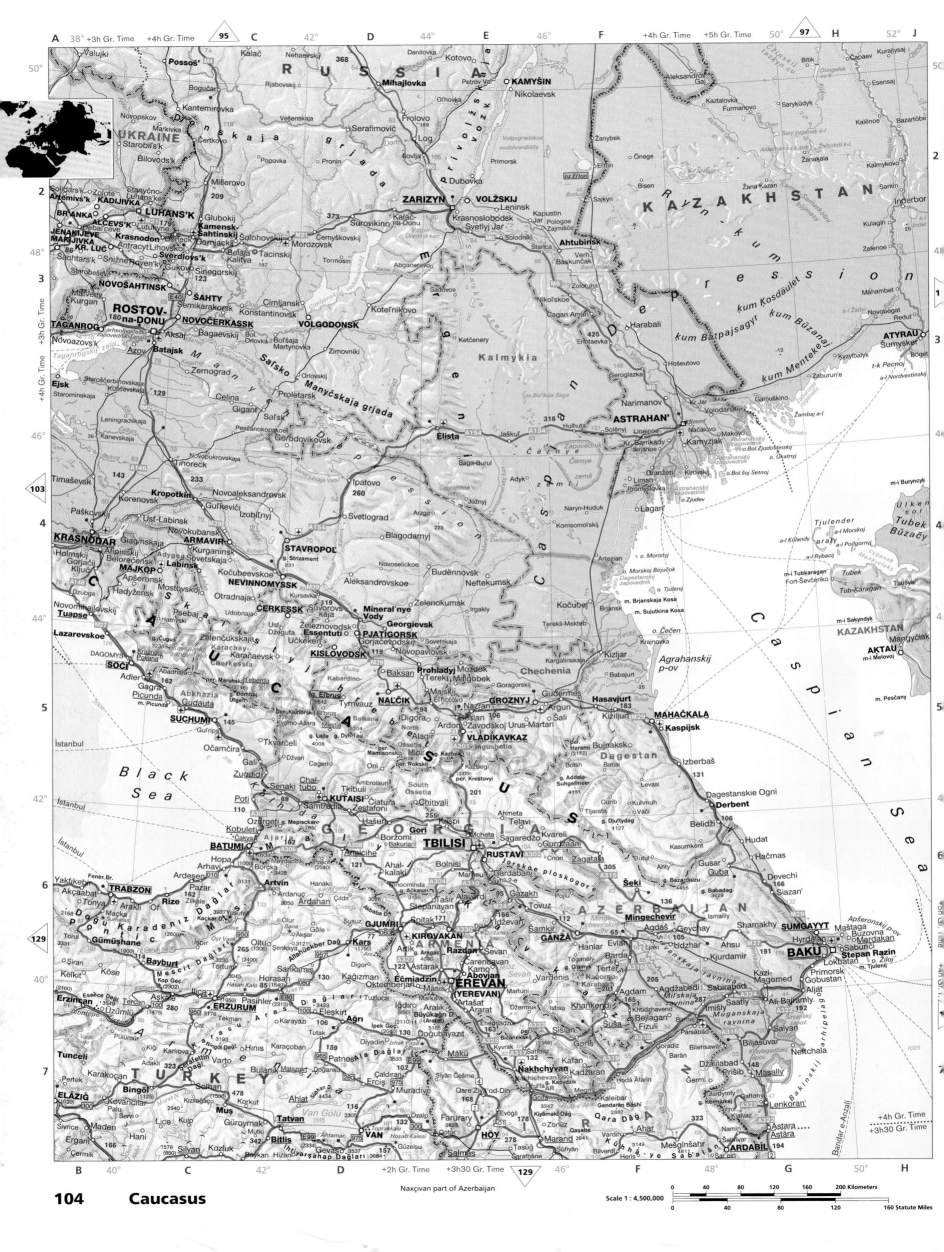

Naxçivan part of Azerbaijan

Scale 1 : 4,500,000

0   40   80   120   160   200 Kilometers

0   40   80   120   160 Statute Miles

Asia – continent of contrasts

This 17,142,840 square mile (4.4 million sq. km) continent, the largest in the world, incorporates all climatic and vegetation zones from the polar to the tropical region. The major landscapes of Europe continue in Asia to the East: in the North, the western Siberian lowlands, joined by the central Siberian ranges and the eastern Siberian mountains; farther South, the mountain chains converging on the node of Ararat, at the Hindu Kush and in Indochina, encircling several plateaus, including the Tibetan highlands, the highest such feature on Earth at 14,764 feet (4,500 m). South of the mountain chains lie the plateaus of Arabia and the Indian subcontinent. Toward the Pacific the continent is delimited by garlands of islands and by sea trenches.

Asia in a copperplate engraving: This detailed map with boundaries and relief features in color was drawn by imperial cartographer Johann Baptist Homann in Nuremberg (circa 1700).

Russia: West Siberian Plain, Northern Region p. 108–109

Russia: Central Siberian Plateau, Northern Region p. 110–111

Russia: Siberia, Northeastern Region p. 112–113

Russia: West Siberian Plain, Southern Region p. 114–115

Sayan Mountains · Lake Baikal p. 116–117

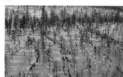

Transbaikal Region p. 118–119

Far East: Northern Region · Kamchatka p. 120–121

Far East: Southern Region · Sakhalin p. 122–123

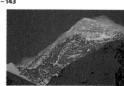

Kazakhstan: The Steppe p. 124–125

Caspian Depression · Aral Sea p. 126–127

Near East p. 128–129

Arabian Peninsula: Northern Region p. 130–131

Arabian Peninsula: Southern Region p. 132–133

Persian Gulf · Plateau of Iran p. 134–135

Central Asia p. 136–137

India: Northwestern Region · Indus Valley p. 138–139

India: Southern Region · Maldives · Sri Lanka p. 140–141

India: Northeastern Region · Bangladesh p. 142–143

Tibet p. 144–145

Sinkiang p. 146–147

Mongolia p. 148–149

Manchuria · Korea p. 150–151

Japan p. 152–153

China: Northern Region p. 154–155

China: Southern Region p. 156–157

Thailand · Cambodia p. 158–159

Philippines p. 160–161

Malaysia · Sumatra p. 162–163

Borneo · Sulawesi p. 164–165

Moluccas · West Irian p. 166–167

Java · Lesser Sunda Islands p. 168

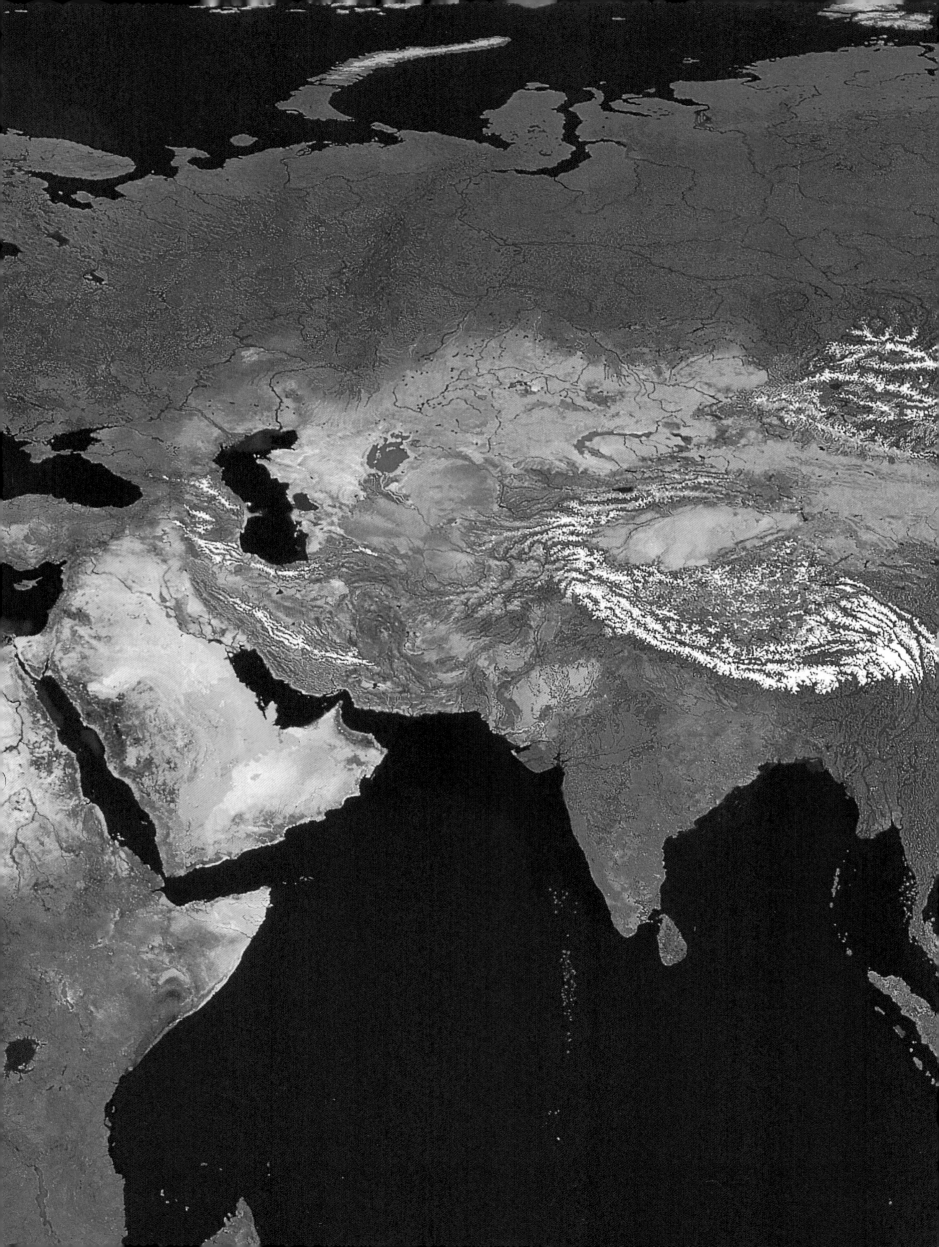

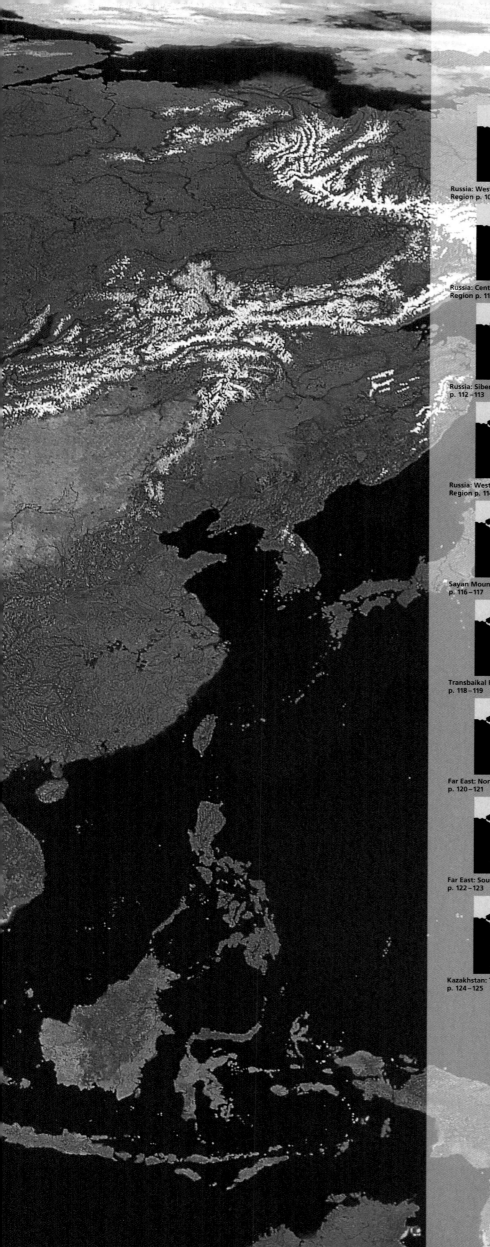

Z   94° a   b
m.
Arktičeskij
Y   c 100° d 102° e 104° f 106° g

E   54° F   56° G   58° H   60° J   62° K   64° L   66° M   68° N   70° O   72° P   74° Q   76° R

Inset map (top left): Severnaya Zemlya

m. Kujbyševa
Litvinova
m. Frunze
Iednik Akademii Nauk 781
o. Komsomolec
m. Rozy Ljuksemburg

Laptev Sea

S e v e r n a y a   Z e m l y a

o. Pioner 382
Krupskoj
Arhipelag Sedov
Iednik Vavilova
o. Oktjabr'skoj Revoljucii
m. Berga
m. Peščanyj
m. Ahmatova

Kara Sea
m. Mednyj
Universitetskij 725
Iednik 800
m. Sverdlova
o-va Krasnoflotskie
935
m. Cingera
mys Morozova

o. Dlinnyj
o. Voronina
m. Obryvistyj 258
o. Bol'ševik
m. Tajmyra
m. Vaigač

+8h Gr. Time

Main map:

B a r e n t s   S e a

Murmansk

72°

85

Arhangel'sk

70°

Pečorskoe More

+5h Gr. Time
+3h Gr. Time

68°

89

Narjan-Mar

Arctic Circle

Bol'šezemel'skaja tundra

Nenets Autonomous District

66°

Pečora

N o v a j a   Z e m l j a

m. Suhoj Nos
Krestovaja Guba
Pik Sedova
Lagernoe
Pomorskoe
mys Britvin
Malyj Karmakuly
Belušja Guba
p-ov Gusinaja Zemlja
m. Kostin Nos
p-ov Mučnoj
Krasino
m. Sahanina
o. Rusanovo
m. Men'šikova
proliv Karskie vorota
o. Vaigač

Matočkin Šar
m. Vyhodnoj
Litke

Bolvanskij Nos
Guba Dolgaja

p-ov Russkij Zavorot
o-va Guljaevskie Koški
o. Matveev
o. Dolgij
o. Bel'kovskij
Pesjakovo
Varandej
m. Bol. Ljamčin Nos
Varnek
Amderma

Jugorskij p-ov
Karataj ka

K a r a   S e a

m. Karlsena
Mys Želanija   m. Želanija
p-ov Litke
gory Mendeleva   g. Blednaja
m. Konstantina
m. Sporyj Navolok

m. Vikulova

Z e m l j a

N o v o z e m e l ' s k a j a   v p a d i n a

m. Ragozina   o. Belyj   o. Vil'kickogo   kosa Vostočna
m. Malygina   m. Šuberta
m. Skuratova   m. Šokal'skogo   o. Neupok
proliv Malygina

J a m a l

Drovjanoj
p-ov Javaj

Tambej
Hanarasalja
m. Poruj
m. Beluži Nos
Morrasale
Sejaha
m. Harse

Y a m a l   N e n e t s   A u t o n o m o u s   D i s t r i c t

Novyj Port
Labyntangi
Salehard   Aksarka   Salemal
Nyda
Kutop'jugan

G y d a n   p - o v

Juribejskaja grjada   Gydan
m. Čugor   Antipajuta
m. Trehbugornyj
Mys-Kamennyj   kosa Kamennaja
Japtiksale

T a z o v s k i j   p - o v

Nahodka

W e s t   S i b e r i a

VORKUTA
Komsomol'skij
Severnyj
Vorgašor
Eleckij
Sivomaskinskij
Abez'
Inta
Usinsk

Černy ševa grjada

Komi
hr. Obeiz
hr. Zap. Saledy

Tobseda
Timans kij bereg
g. Tonja Seda
Jušino
Čornaja
Horej-Ver
Mutnyj Materik
Novikbož
Ščeljabot
Ust'-Lyža
Synja
Kožva
Kadžerom
Konecbor

Scale 1 : 4,500,000

0   40   80   120   160   200 Kilometers
0   40   80   120   160 Statute Miles

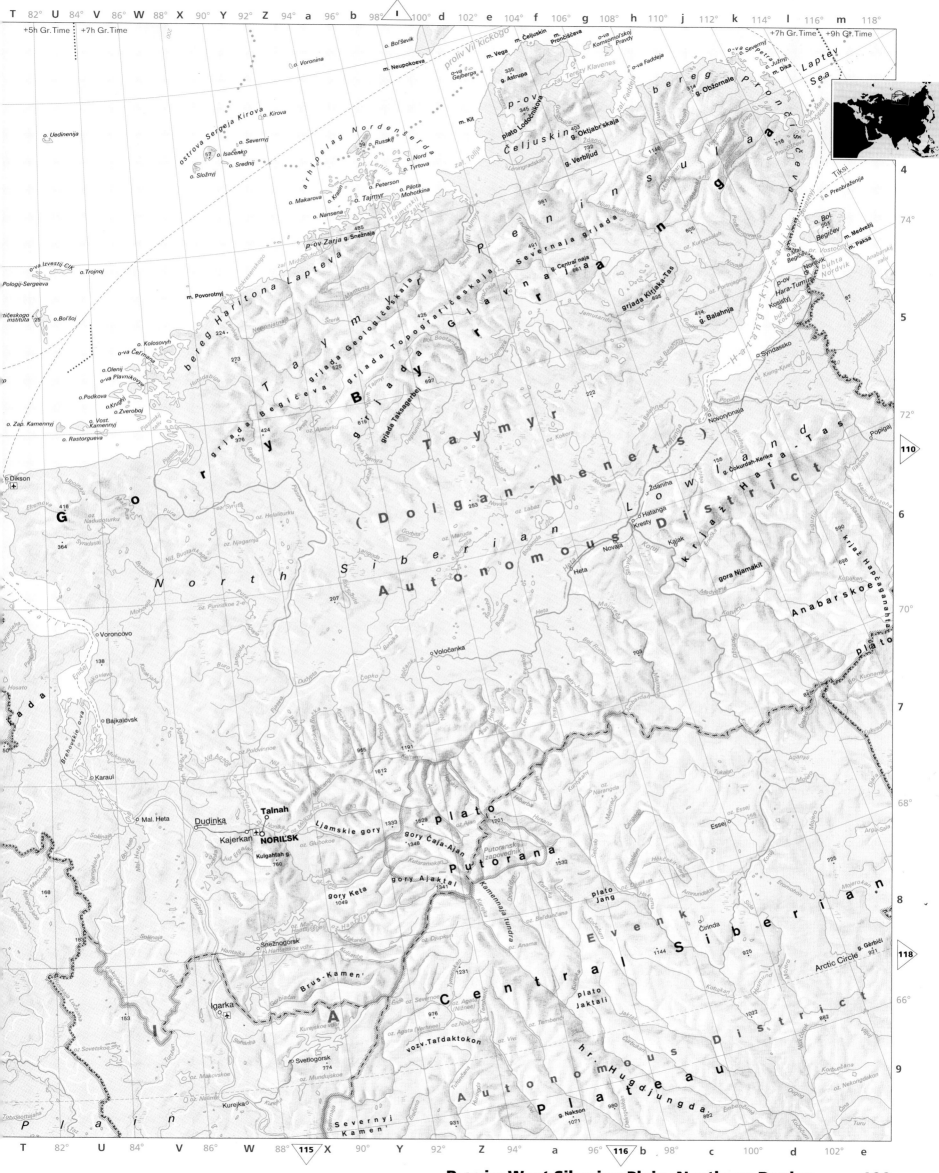

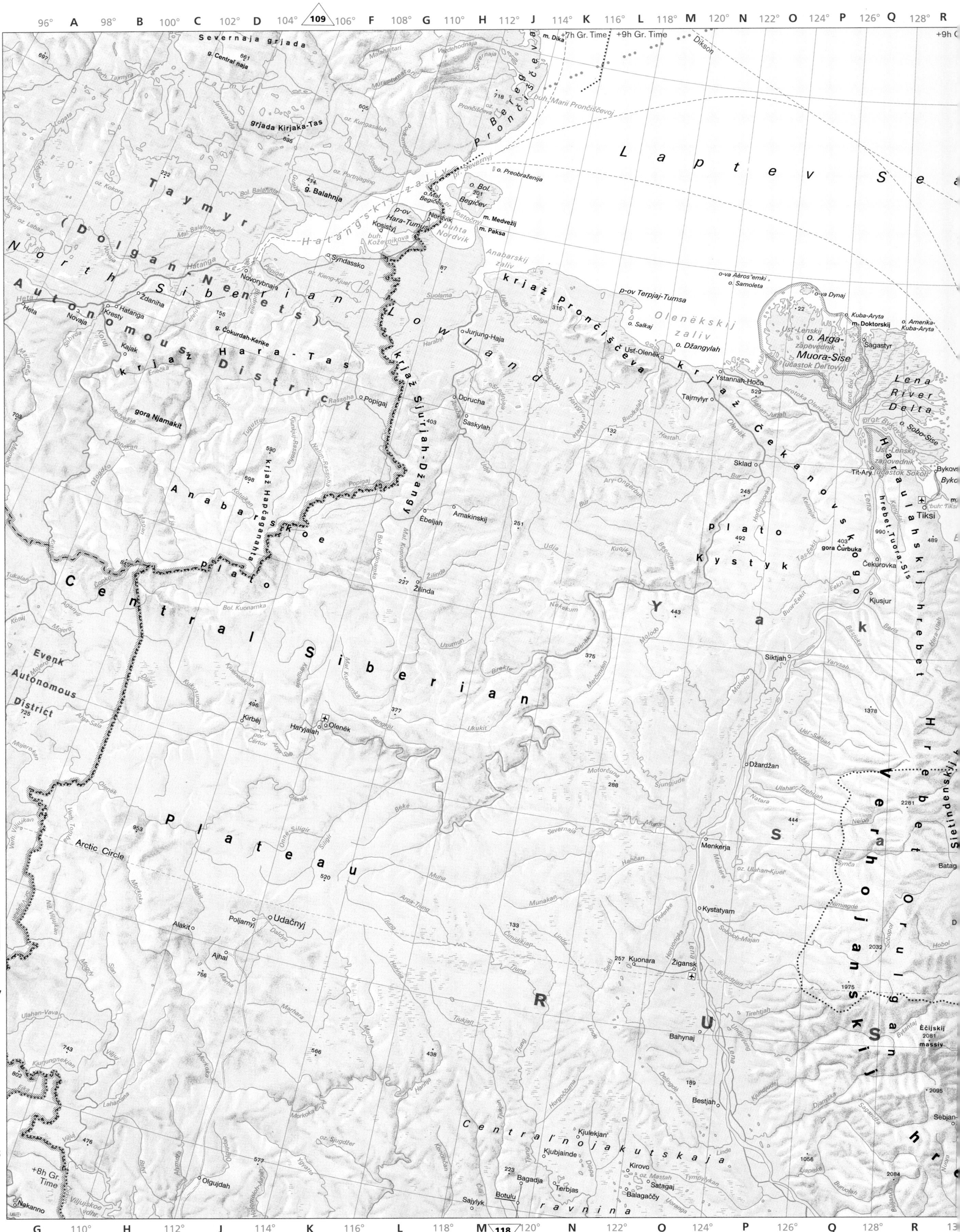

Severnaja grjada

g. Central'naja

grjada Kirjaka-Tas

g. Balahnja

Taymyr (Dolgan - Neenrets) North Siberian Autonomous District

L a p t e v   S e a

7h Gr. Time   +9h Gr. Time   +9h G

m. Dika   Dikson

o. Preobraženija

Bol. Begičev

Hara-Tumus   Nordvik   m. Medveži

Kosistyj   buhta Nordvik   m. Paksa

Hatanga   Novorybnaja   buh. Koževnikova

Ždaniha   Kresty

Hatanga   Syndassko   Kieng-Kjuel'

Novaja   Sirolama

p-ov Terpjaj-Tumsa

krjaž Prončiščeva

o-va Aёros"emki   o. Samoleta

o. Salkaj   o-va Dynaj

Ust-Olenёk   o. Džangylah   Kuba-Aryta

m. Doktorskij   Amerika-Kuba-Aryta

Ust-Lenskij zapovednik   Sagastyr

Kajak   Erečka   gora Njamakit

krjaž Hara-Tas   Hara-Tumus

Čokurdah-Kerike

o. Arga-Muora-Sise (učastok Del'tovyj)

Lena River Delta

krjaž Čekanovskogo

Rassoha   Popigaj   Jurjung-Haja   Harabyl

Ystannah-Hočo   protoka Olenёkskaja

Tajmylyr   gora Čurbuka

Harju-Jurjah   Bykovskij

Tit-Ary (učastok Sokol)   Bykov

Dorucha   Saskylah

krjaž Sjurjah-Džangy

plato Kystyk   Čekurovka   Tiksi   buh. Tiksi

Ёbeljah   Amakinskij

Žilinda   Žilinda

Anabarskoe plato   Kjusjur

Central   Siberian

Evenk Autonomous District

Siktjah

Kirbéj

Haryjalah   Olenёk   Sengkjuo

Džardžan   Hrebet Orulgan

Verhojanskij

Menkerja

Plateau

Arctic Circle

Udačnyj

Poljarnyj   Kystatyam

Alakit   Ajhal

Kuonara   Žigansk

Bahynaj

Bestjah

Kjulekjan   Central'nojakutskaja

Kjubjainde

Kirovo   Satagaj

Bagadja   Terbjas   Balagačči   ravnina

Botulu   Sajylyk

Nakanno   Olgujdah

+8h Gr. Time

Scale 1 : 4,500,000

0   40   80   120   160   200 Kilometers

0   40   80   120   160 Statute Miles

Russia: Central Siberian Plateau, Northern Region　**111**

Russia: Siberia, Northeastern Region 113

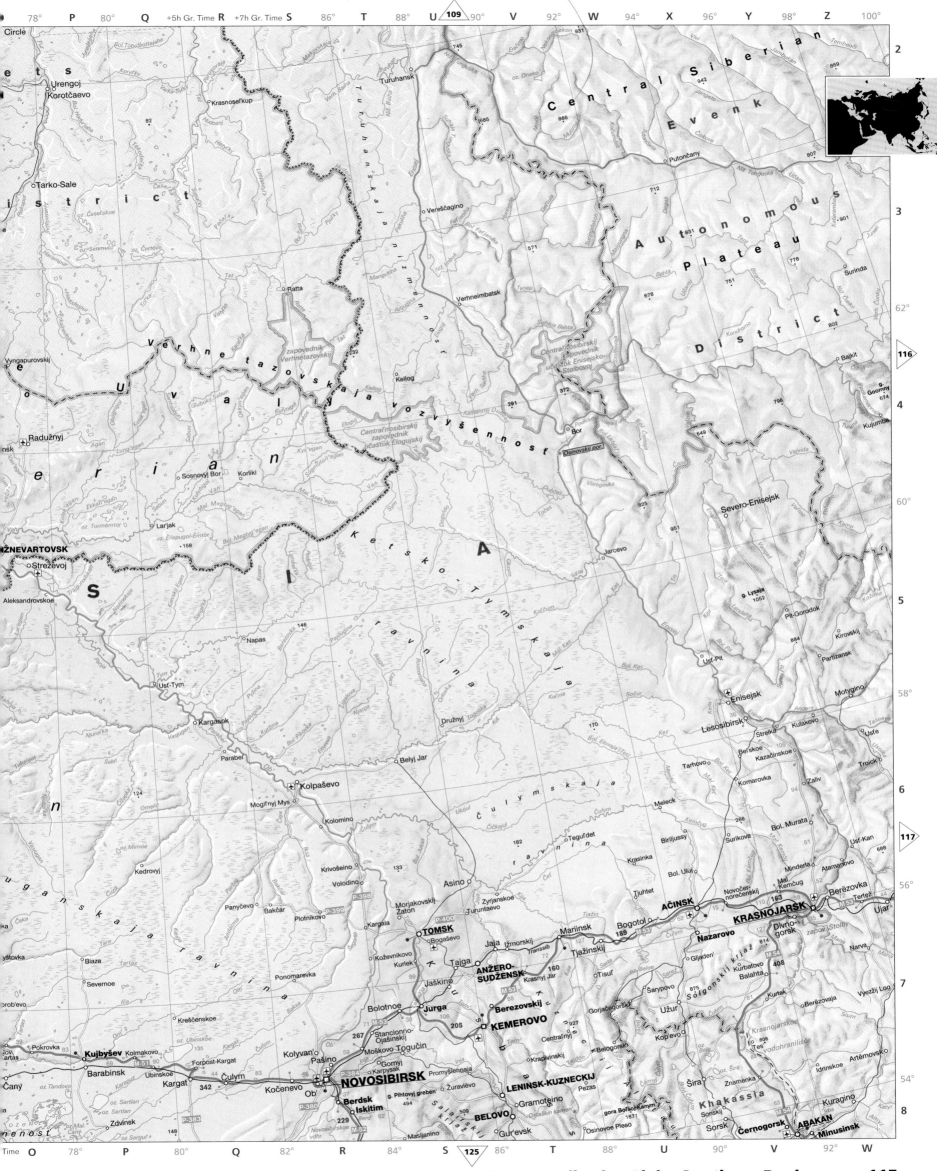

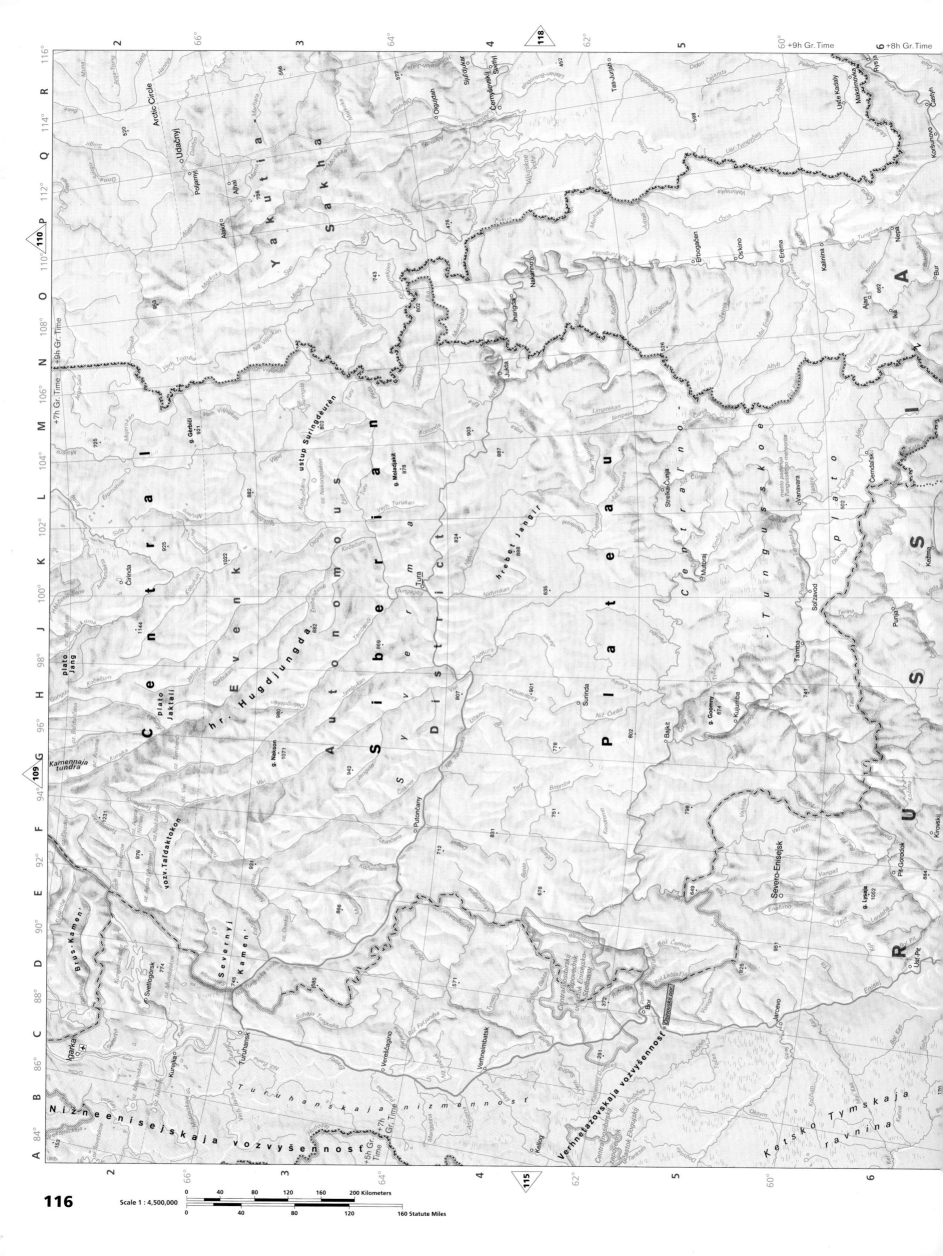

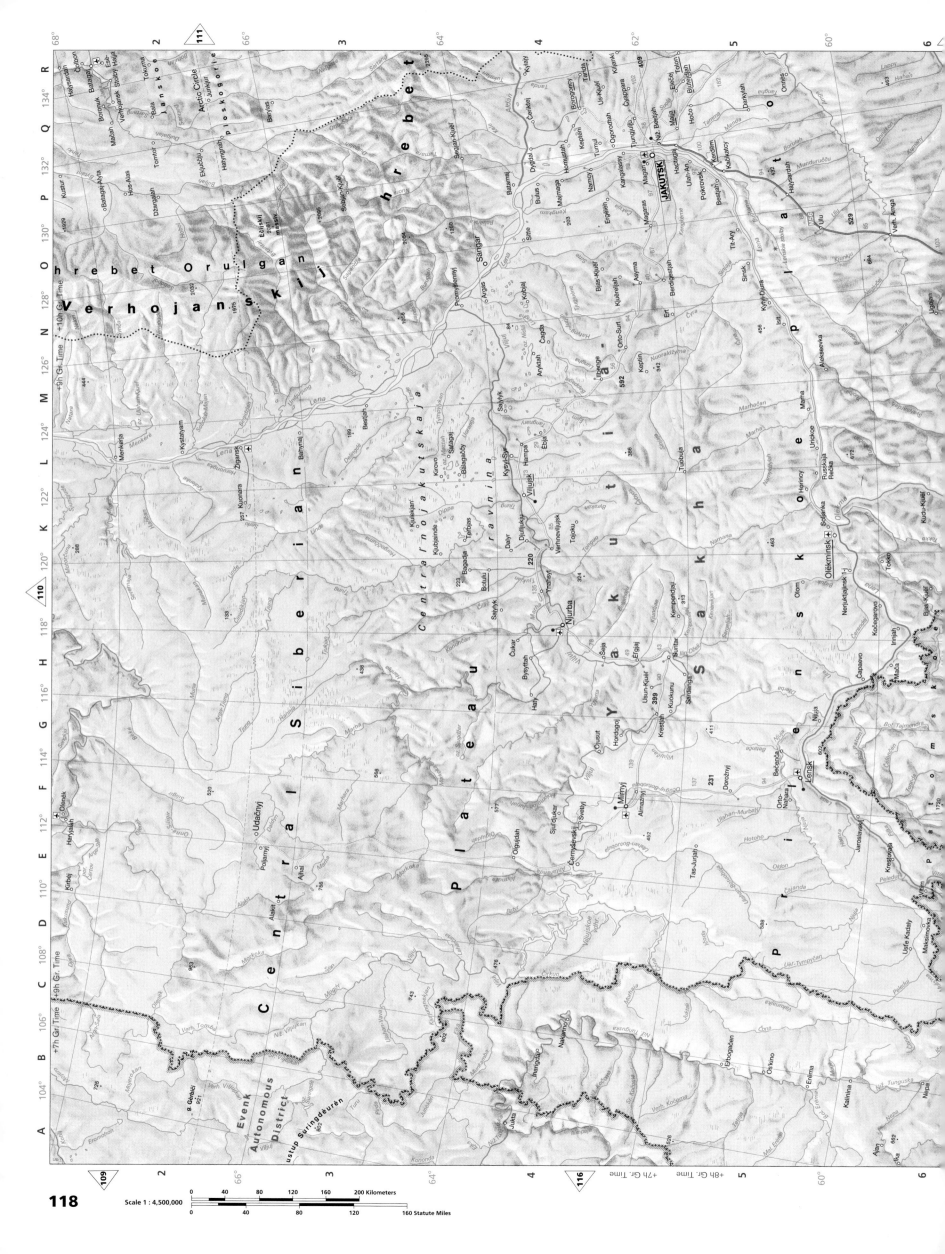

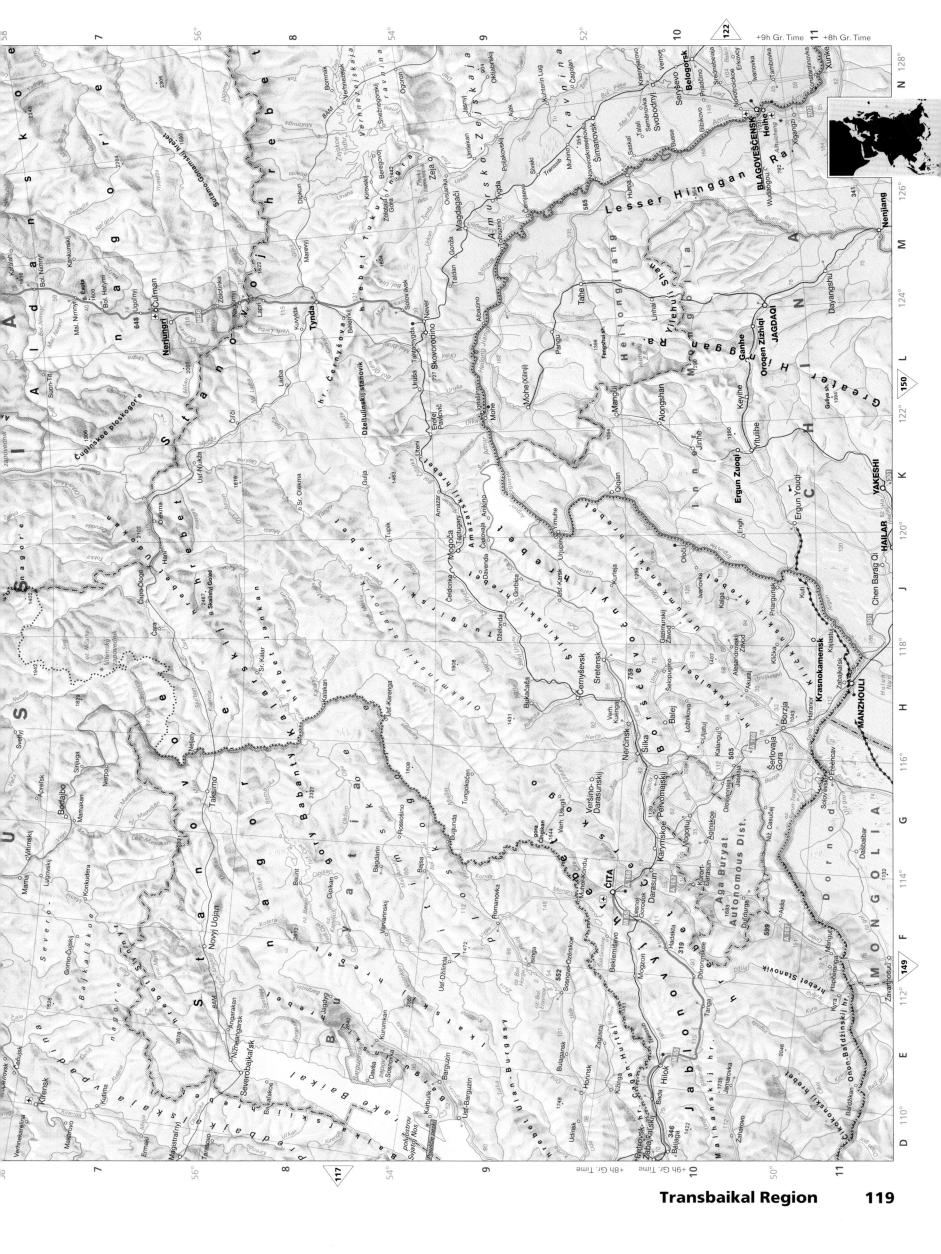

Scale 1 : 4,500,000

0 40 80 120 160 200 Kilometers

0 40 80 120 160 Statute Miles

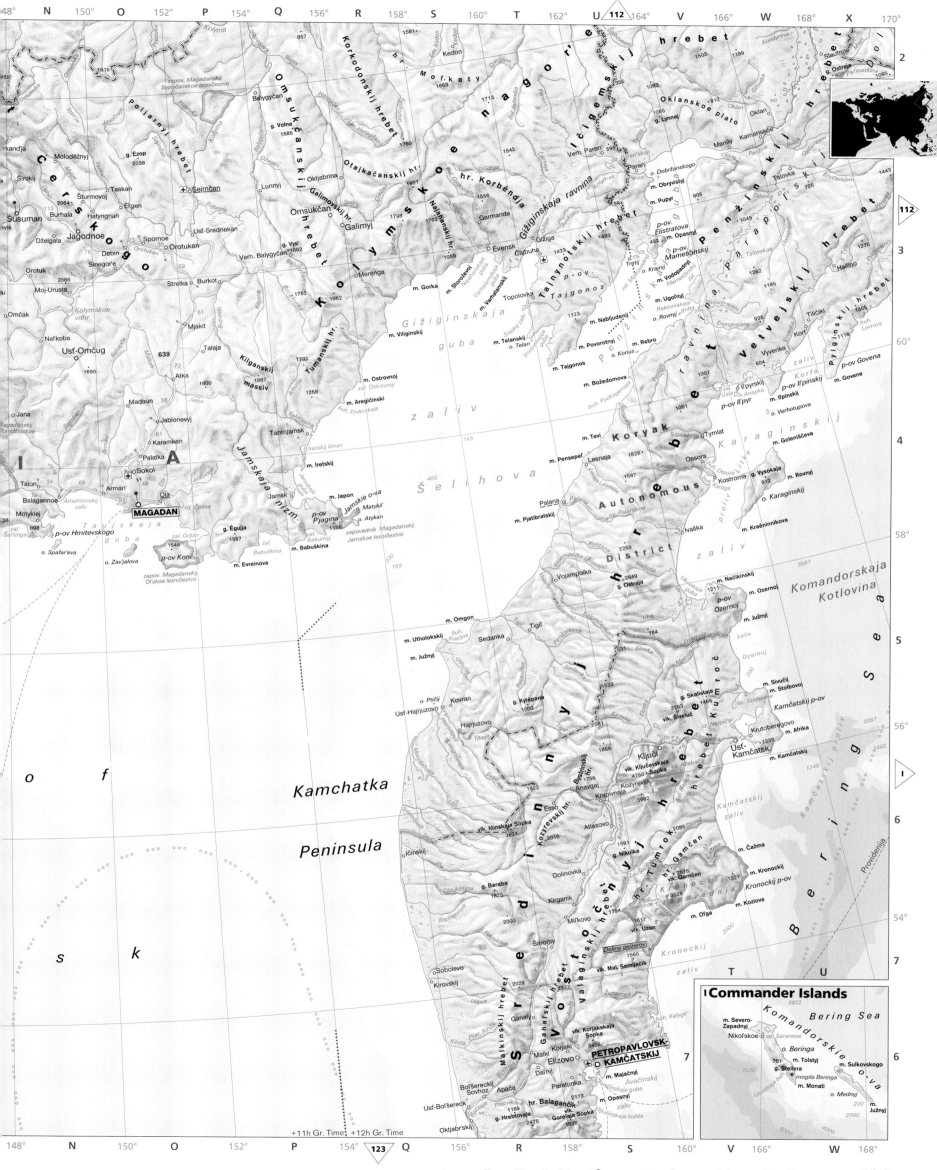

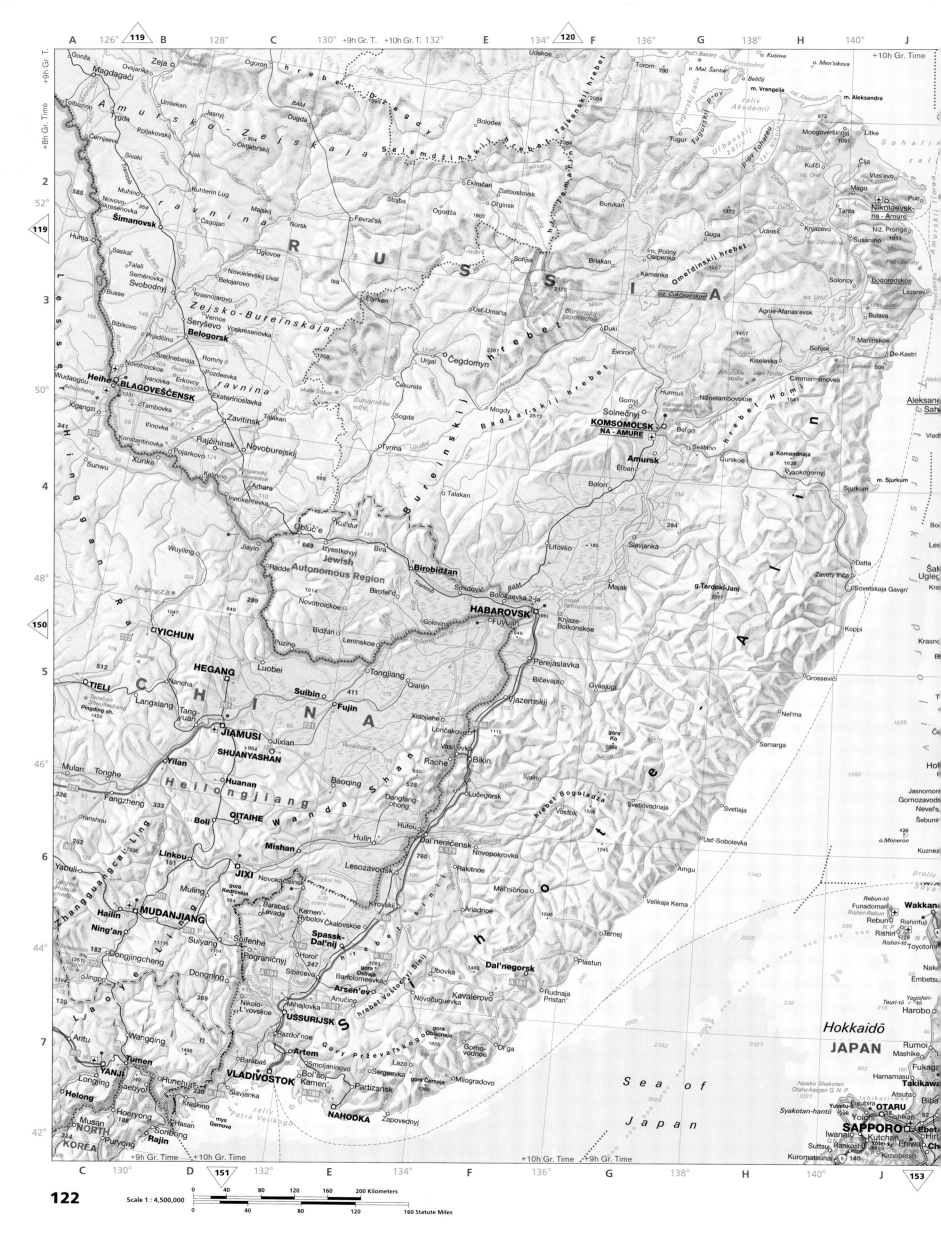

S e a   o f
O k h o t s k

Kamchatka
Peninsula

RUSSIA

Sakhalin

Terpenija

zaliv

PACIFIC

OCEAN

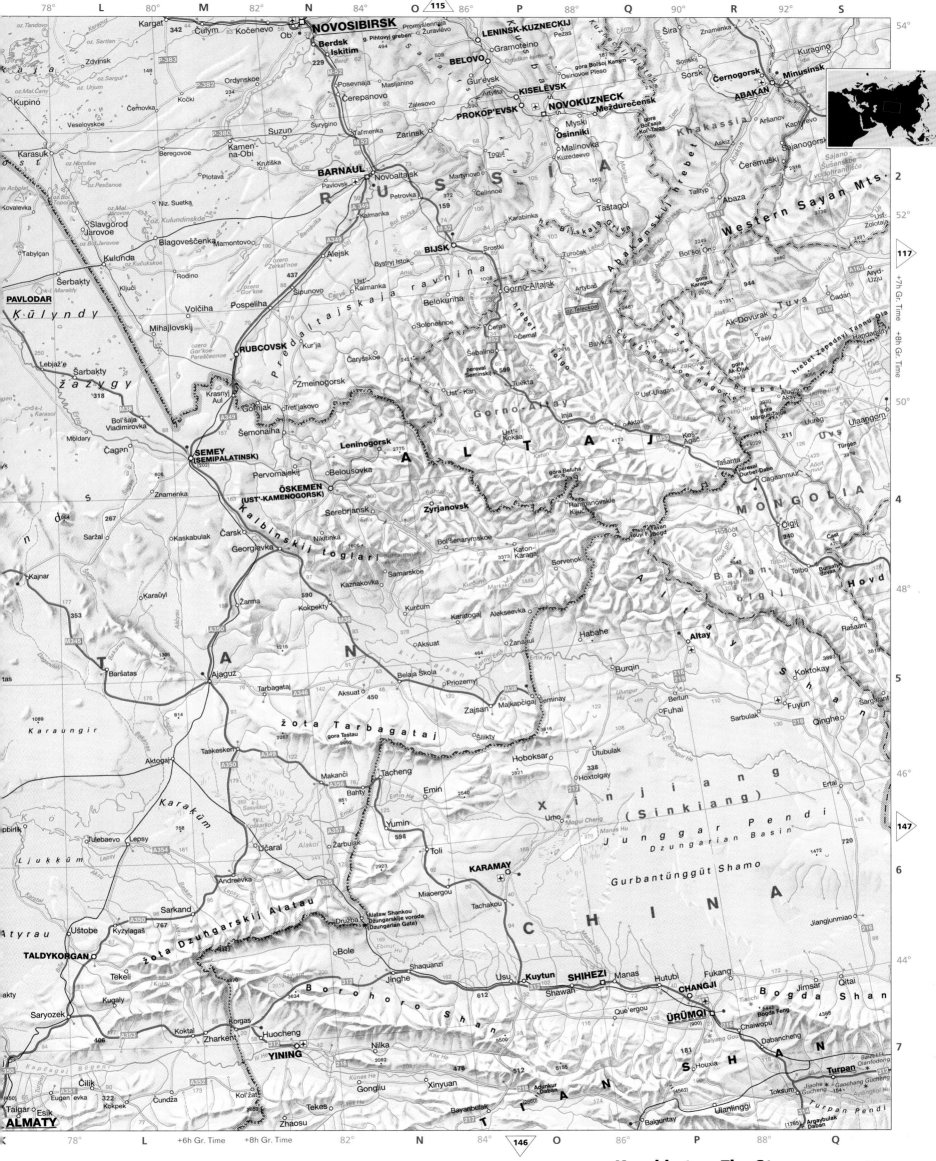

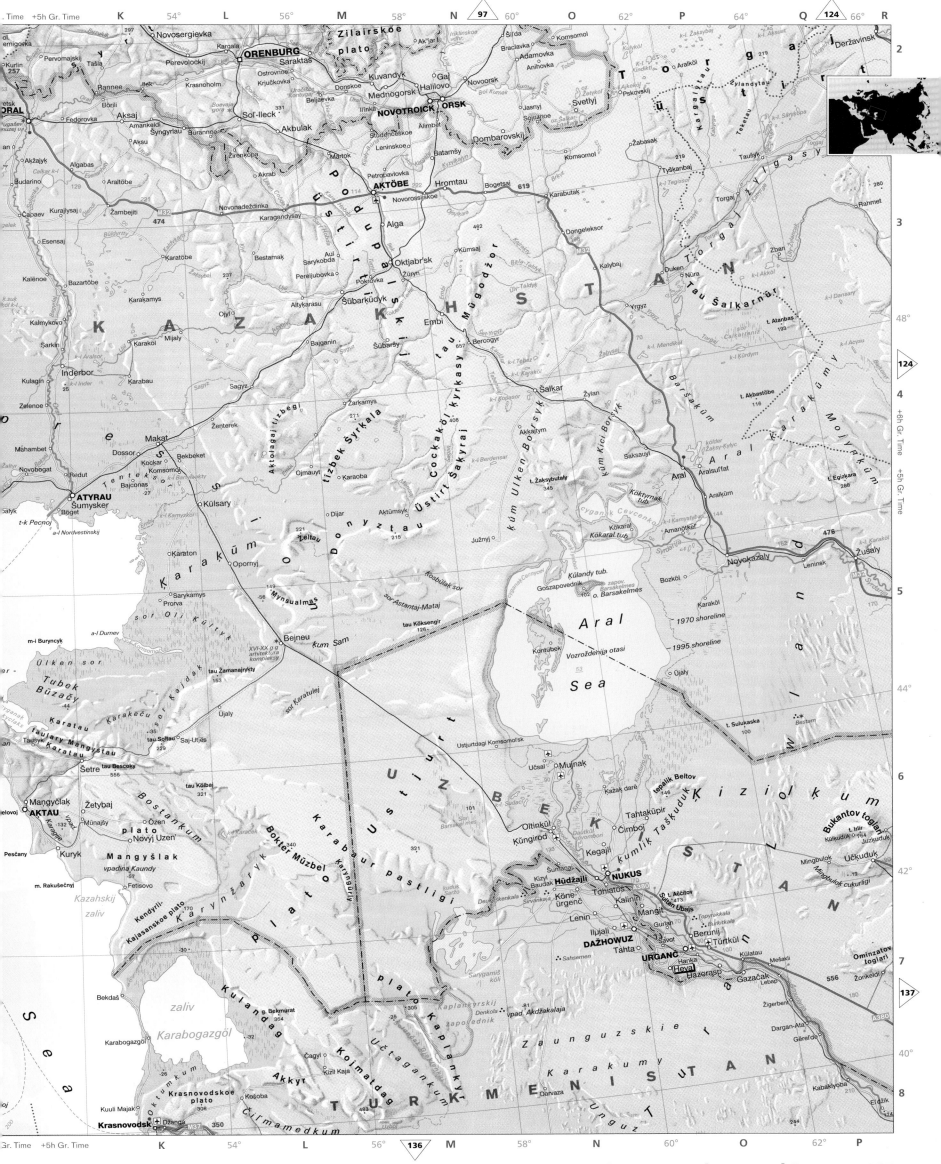

Novosergievka

ORENBURG

Zilairskoe
plato

Novotroick   **ORSK**

AKTÖBE

K A Z A K H S T A N

ATYRAU

AKTAU

Aral
Sea

1970 shoreline
1995 shoreline

U Z B E K I S T A N

NUKUS

DAŽHOWUZ

URGANČ

KarabogazGöl

Krasnovodsk

T U R K M E N I S T A N

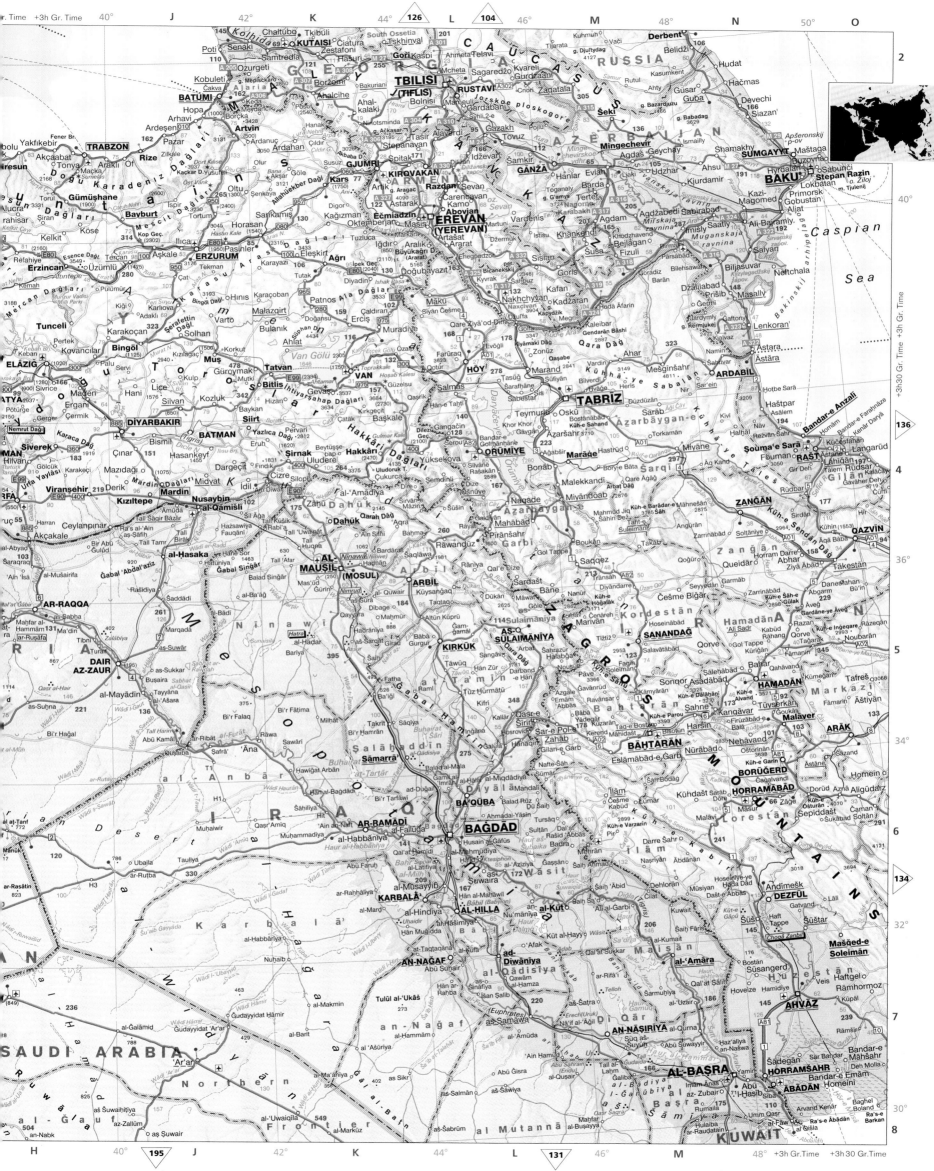

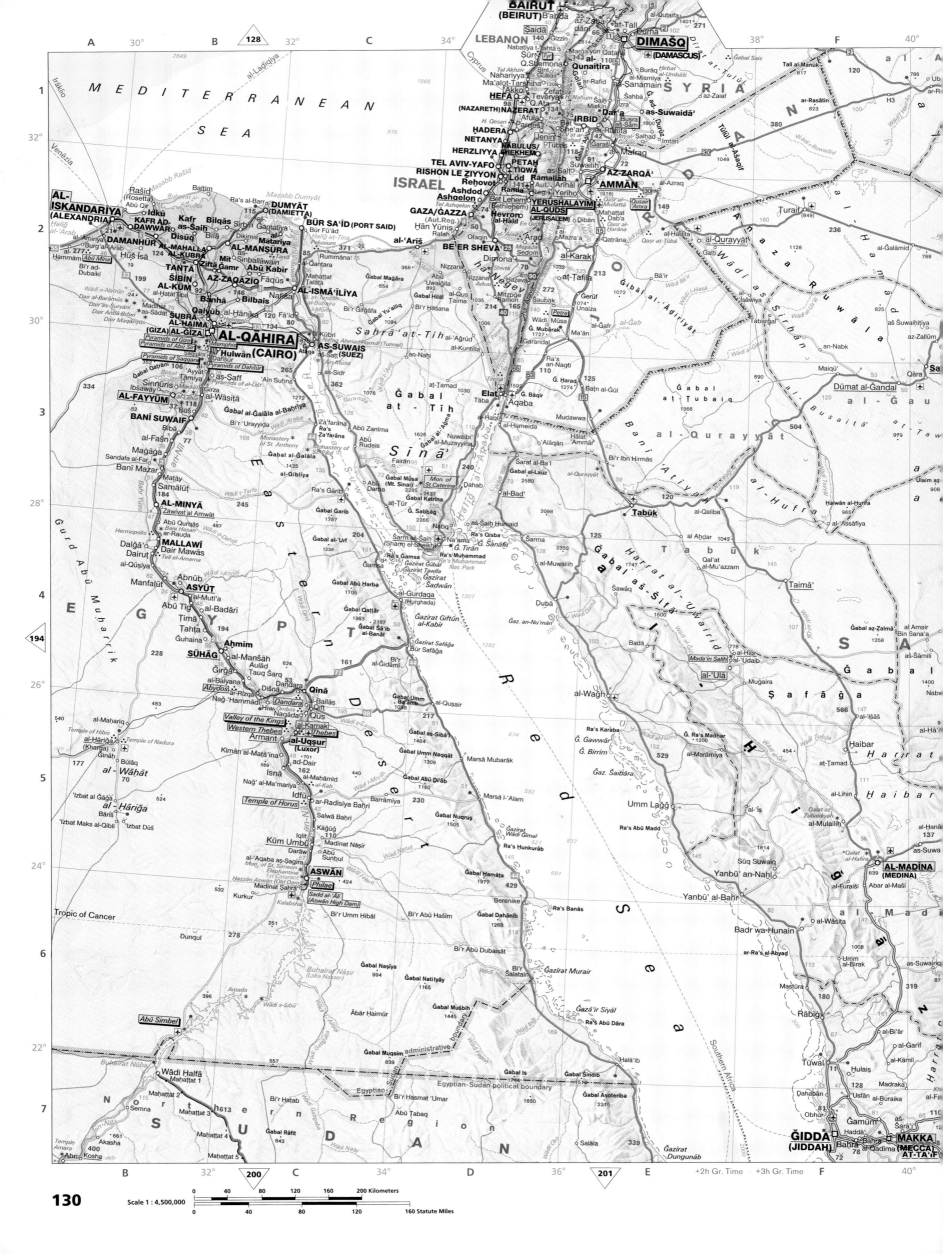

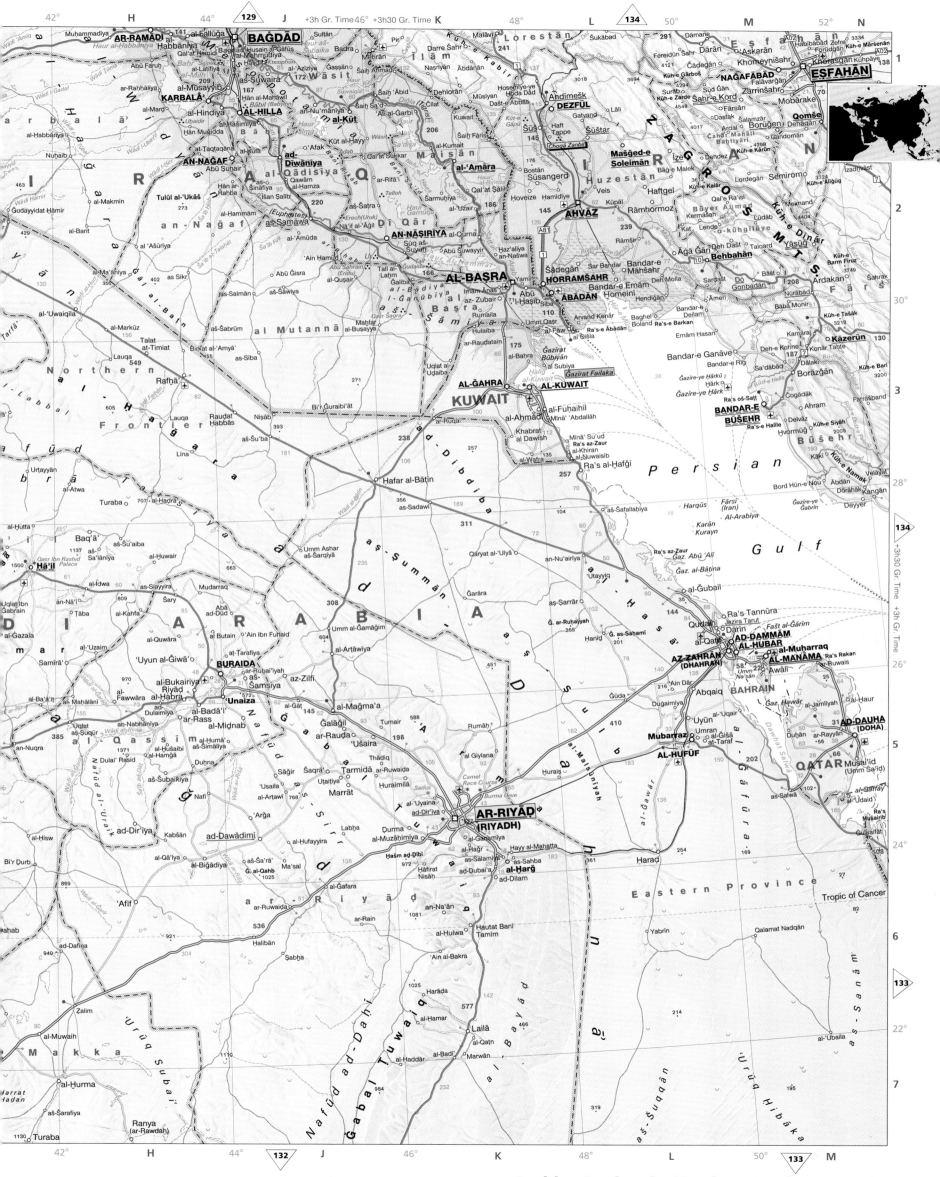

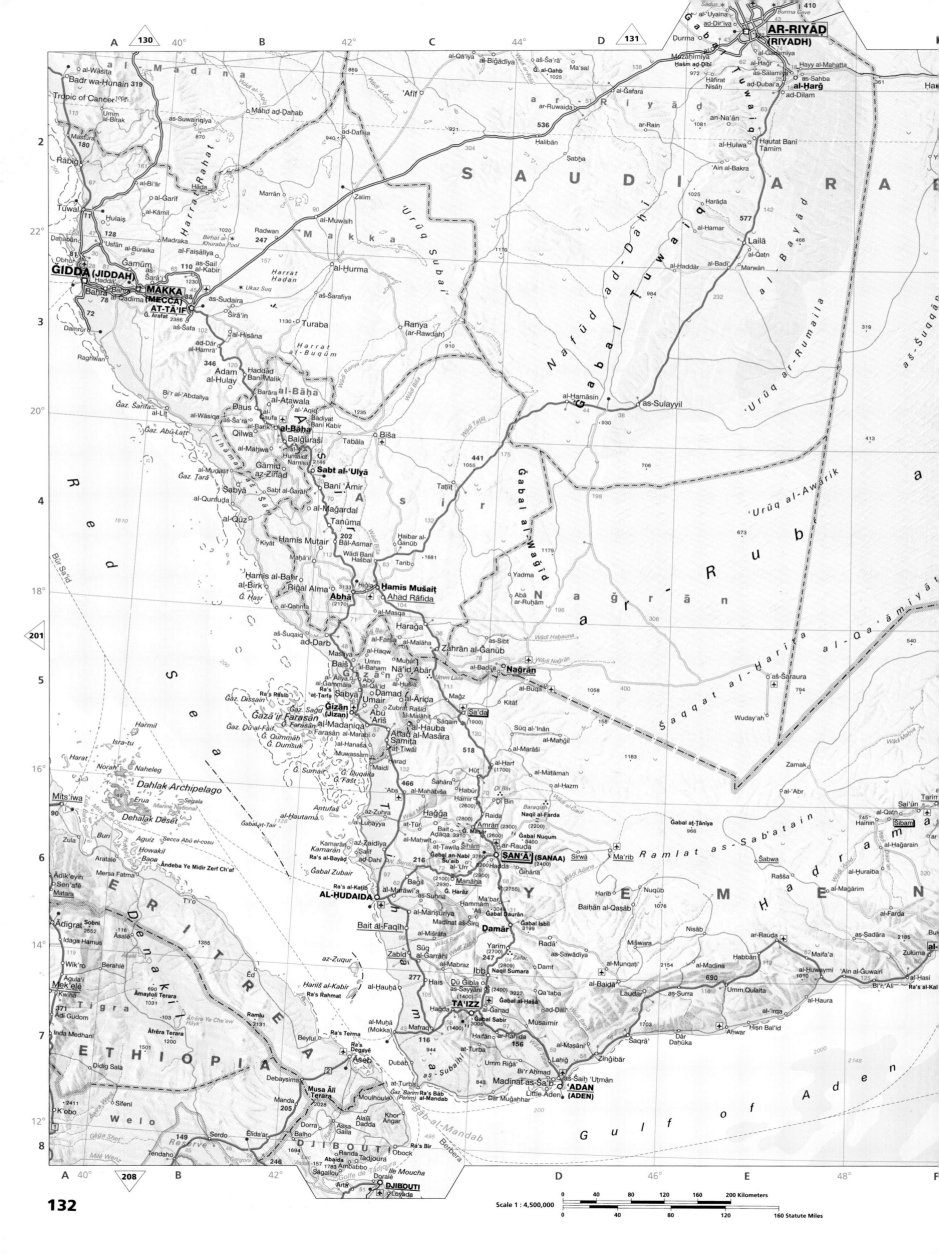

ABŪ ZABĪ *Sa'dīyat* 159 -176 88 Šinās
(ABU DHABI) al-Samha 107 al-Faq Sūḥār
Marawiḥ 27 Suwaihān 44 al-Liwā'
Ra's Mušairib Umm an-Naḥ 81 128 as-Sālābih Hili Maḥda 95
Sir Bani Yās 92 Ğubri al-Buraimi **AL-'AIN** Sahm
Guwaifat al-Yāsāt Gabal az-Zanna **AL-'AIN** ad-Daimānīyāt Matrah **Masqat** (Muscat)
Gananạ Ḃū Lifiyat Ru'ais al-Hābūra as-Sib **Ruwi** Tropic of Cancer

508 *B a y n ū n a* Giyatị 105 al-Fath al-Masā'iqa Sadam 238 al-Masṇa'a Barkā Yity
169 27 Habšān al-Masā'iqa Yanqul Wādi l-'Ulyā 34 53 38
Umm al-Aštān *az-Zafra* Dank 53 ar-Rustāq Samā'il Bidbid Qurayyāt
82 75 Ibri Gabal al-Aḥdạ Samā'il Dagmar
UNITED ARAB al-Hạtim 40 al-'Ain 2980 Nazwā Awābi
Qalamat Nadqān EMIRATES 'Arāḍa Qutūr Sāḥ Tarwānīya Hamim Kubārạ 272 al-Gāfat 153 Haġar aṣ-Šarqi Qalhāt
A as-Sanām al-Mahākik al-Jiwā' al-Huwair Oilfield 127 Bahla Izki Sa'id Bin Sarān Ibra al-Mudairib Sūr
al-Ubaila al-Mihrād Nuḥaida 1210 25 al-Kāmil al-Mintirib
'Urūq Hibāka'a al-Kidan ar-Rabbād Adam al-Mušallā Bilād Bani Bū Hasan
H 195 *E a s t e r n   P r o v i n c e* 120 Ramlat al-Ašḥara
Dikāka al-Hibāk Umm as-Samim 213 al-Wahība 161 Ra's al-Kabš

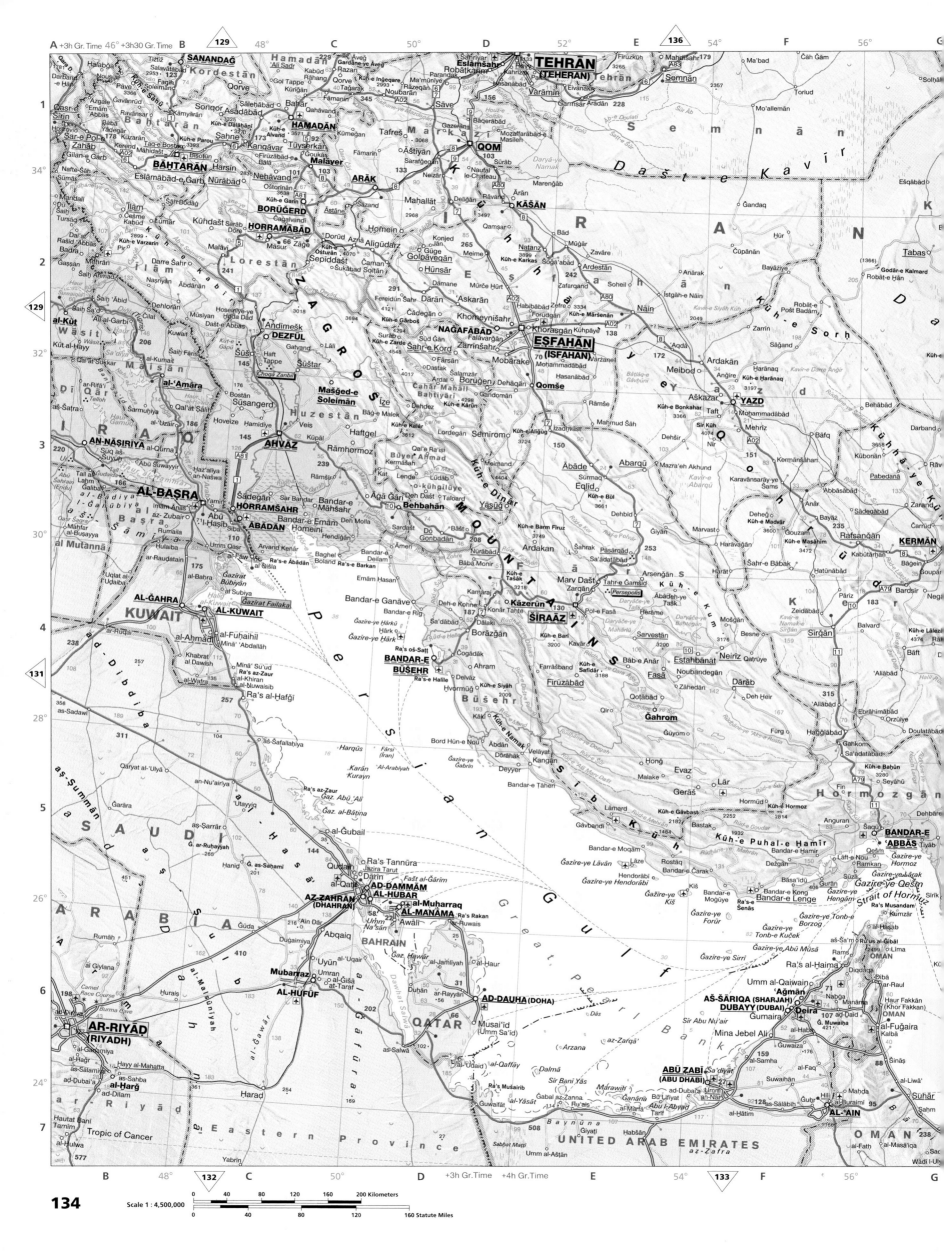

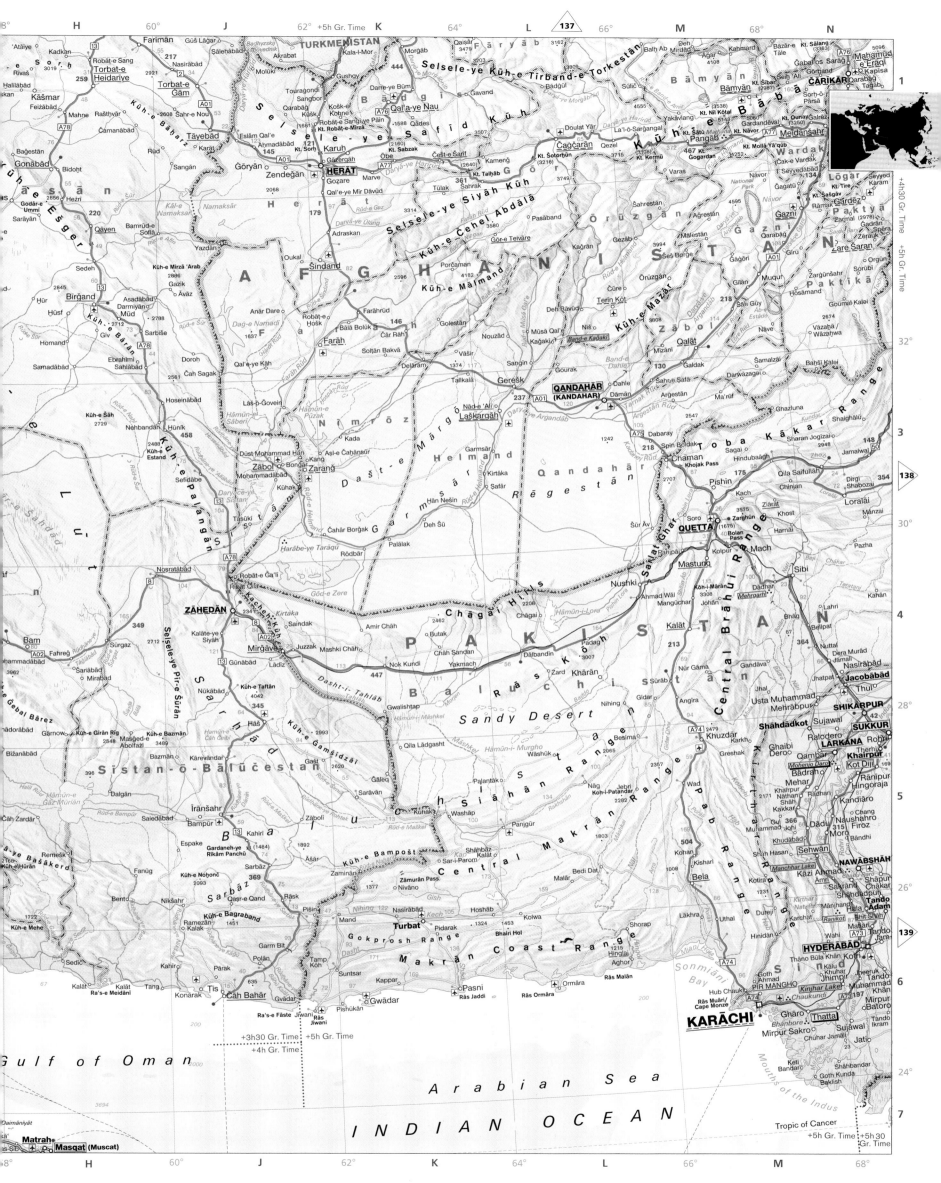

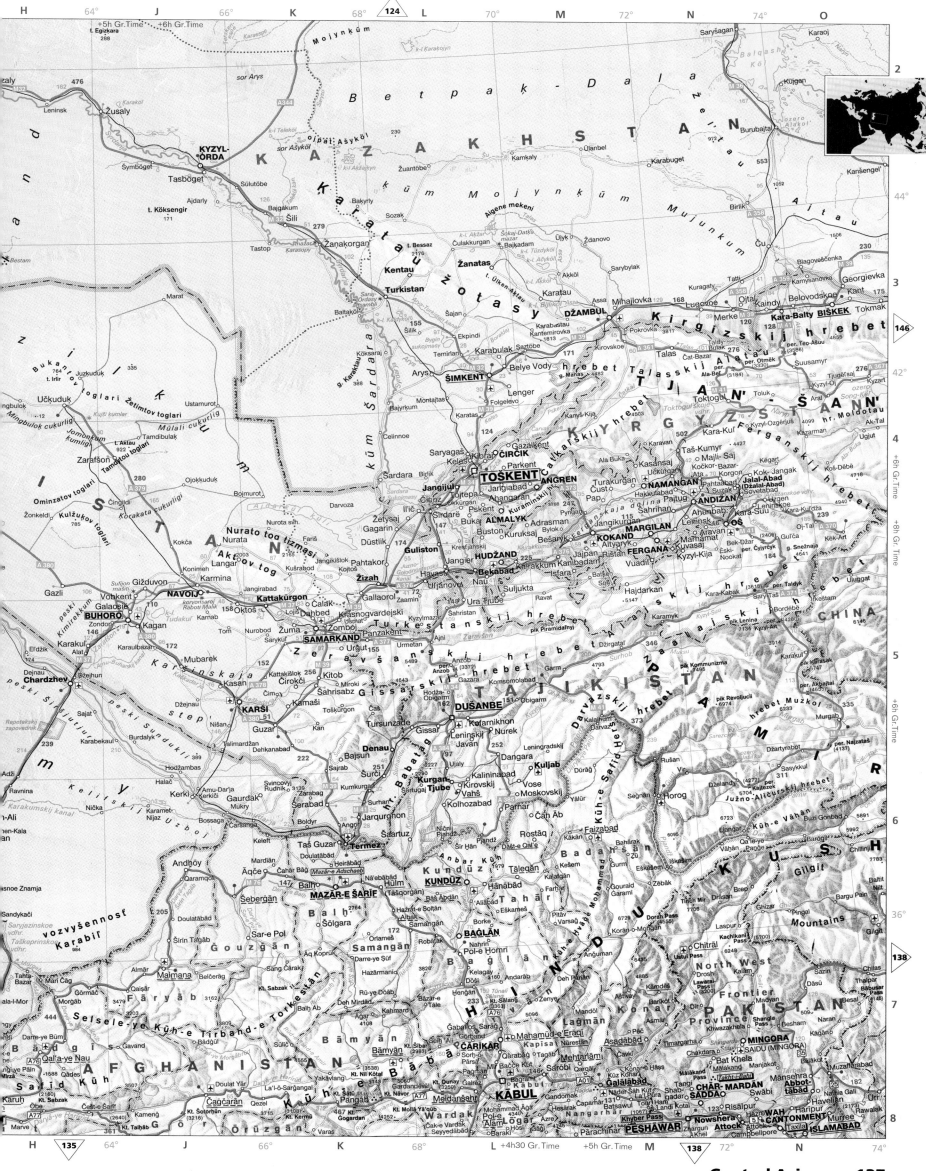

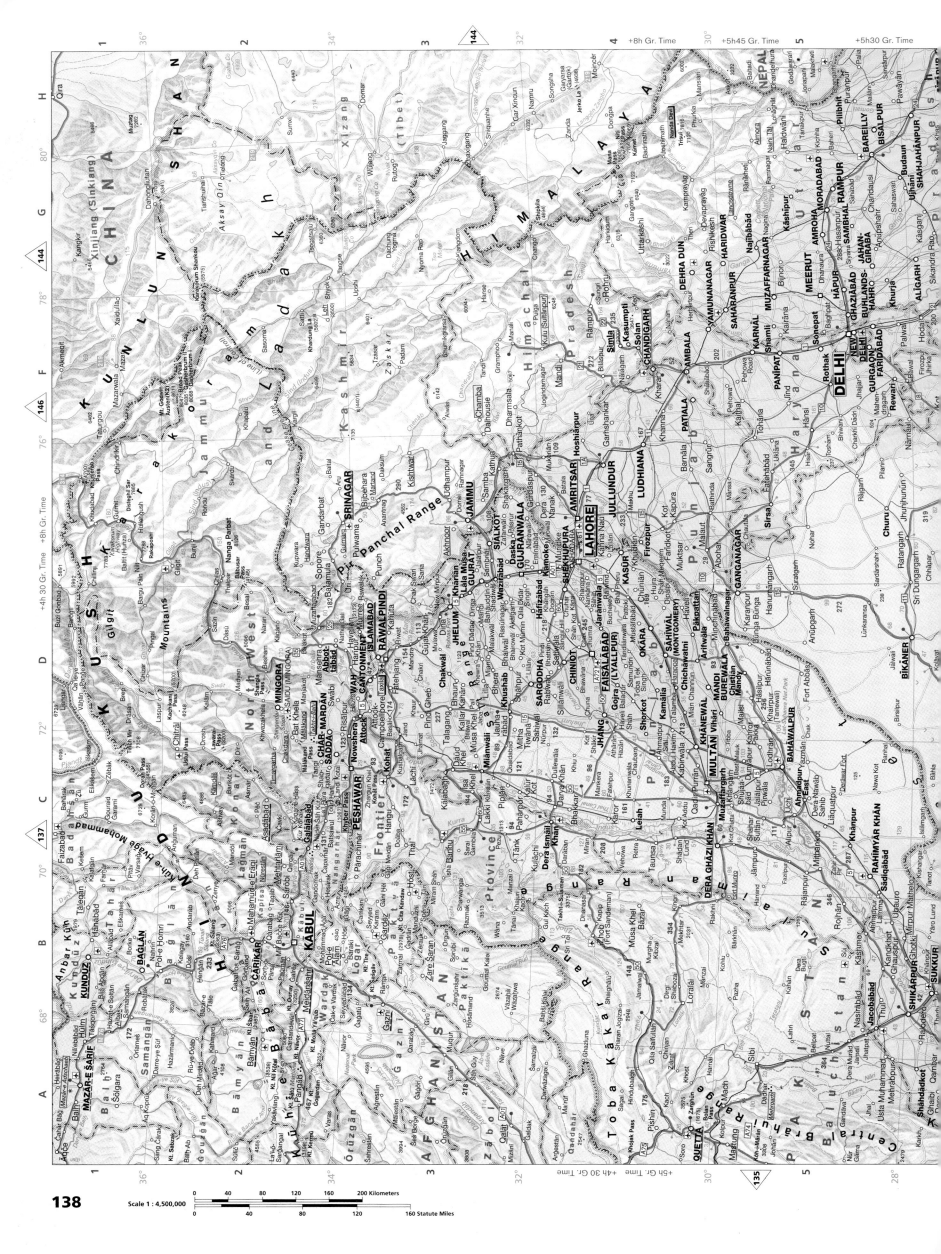

India: Northwestern Region • Indus Valley   139

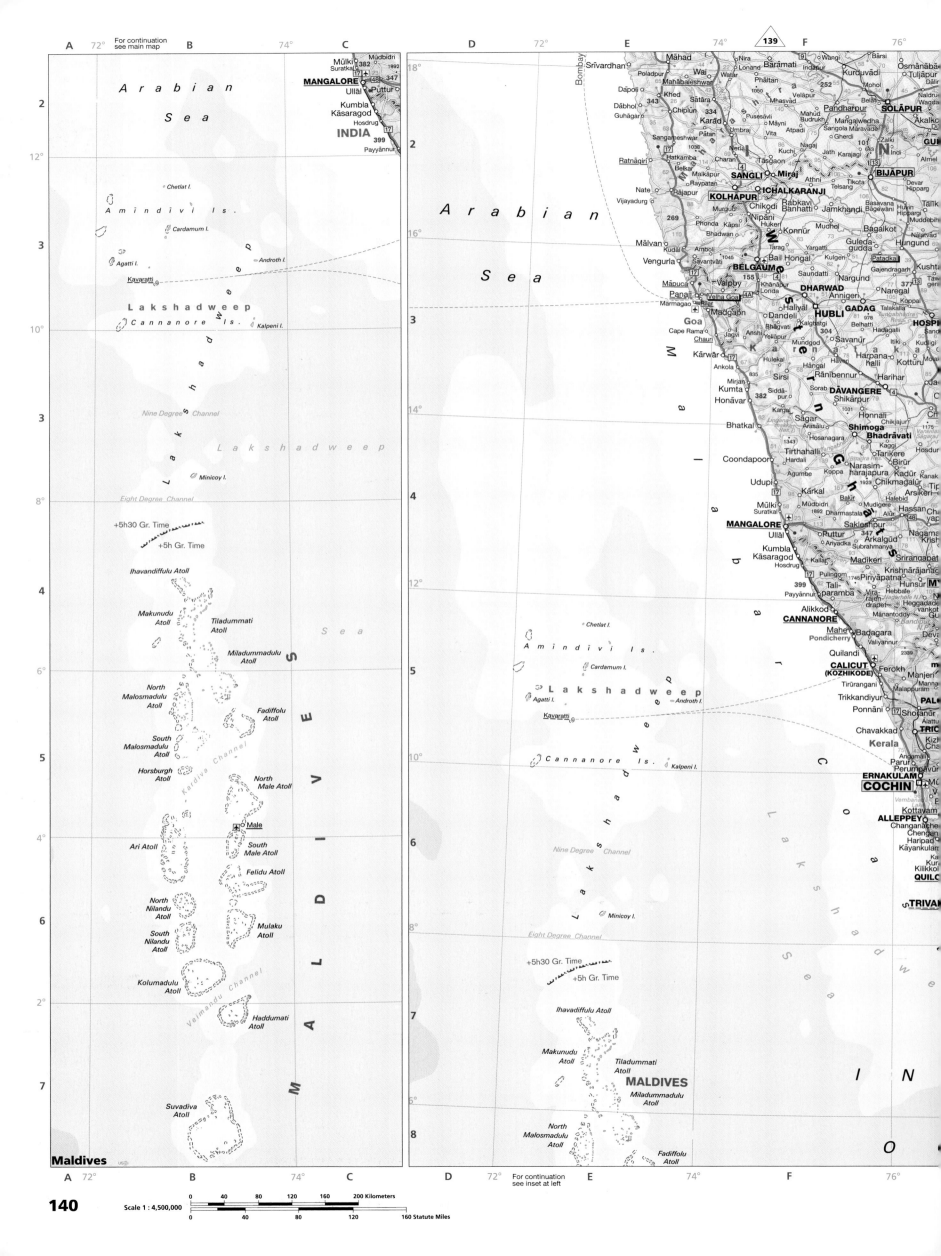

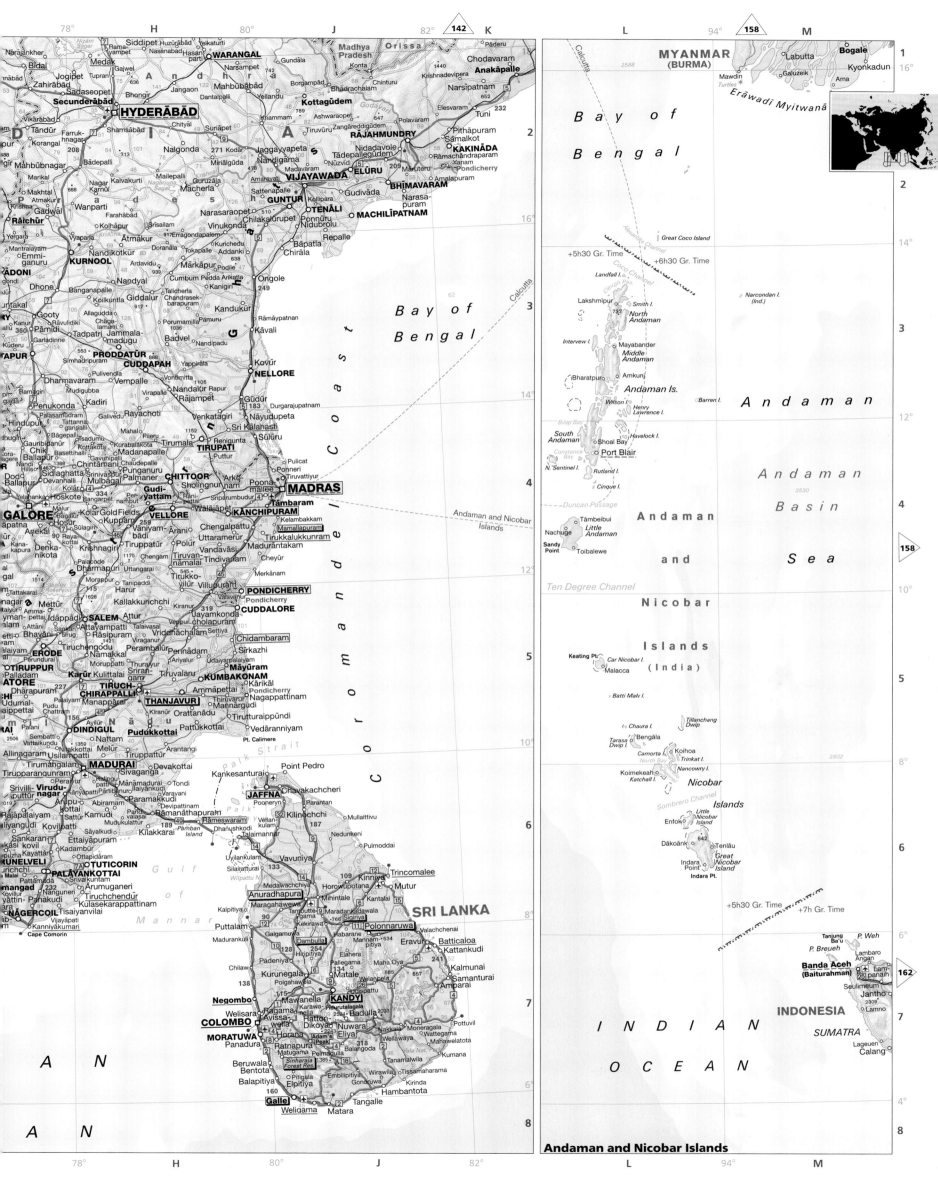

India: Northeastern Region • Bangladesh   **143**

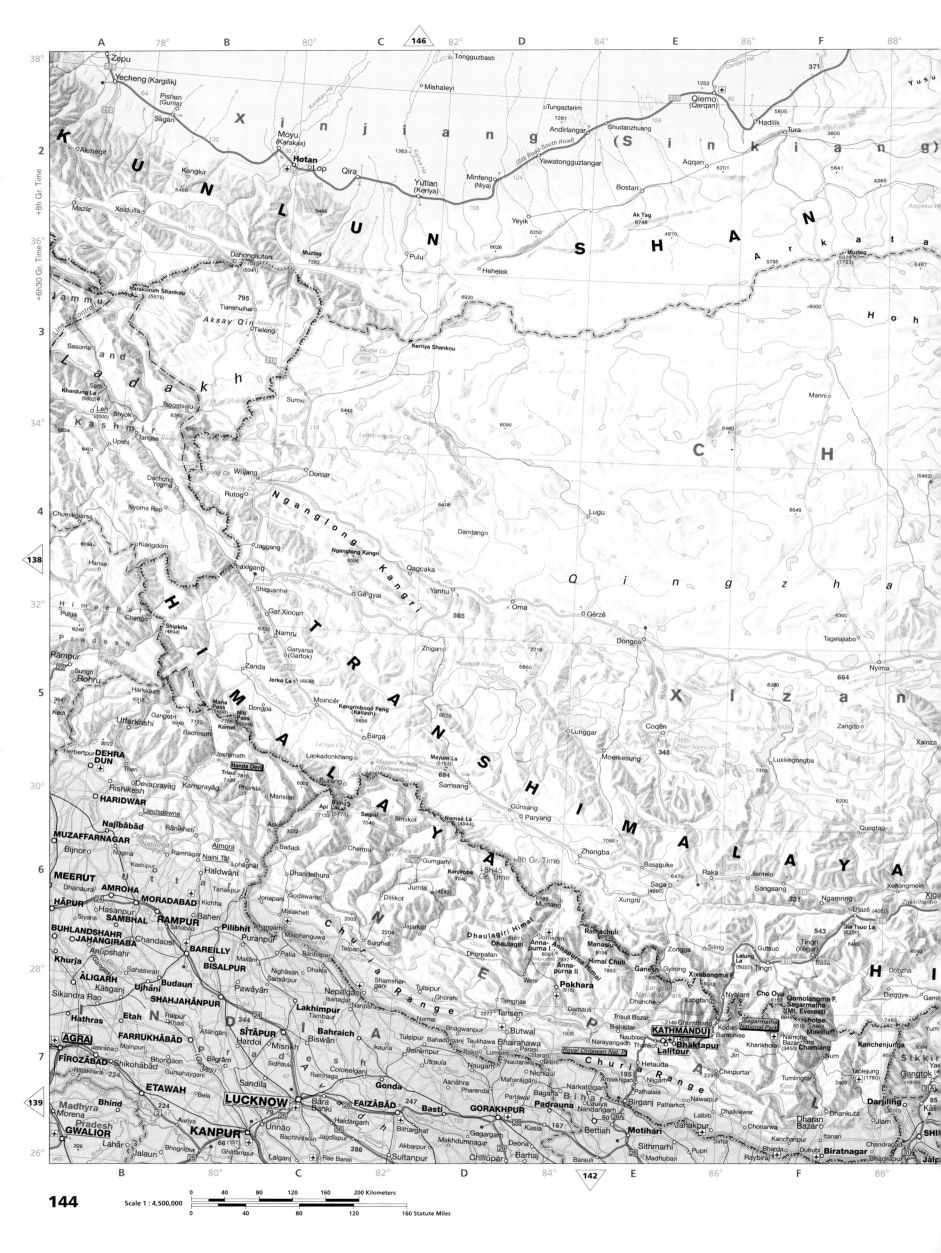

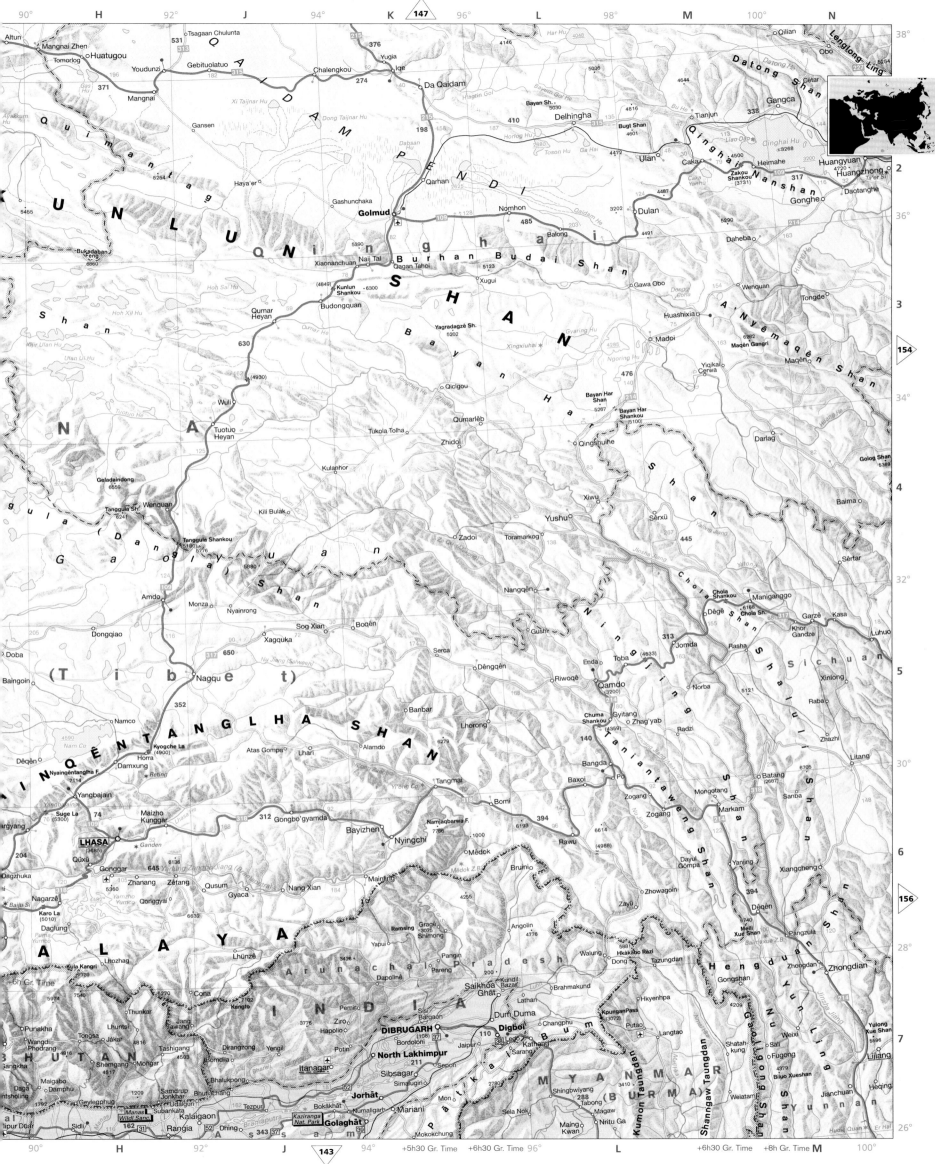

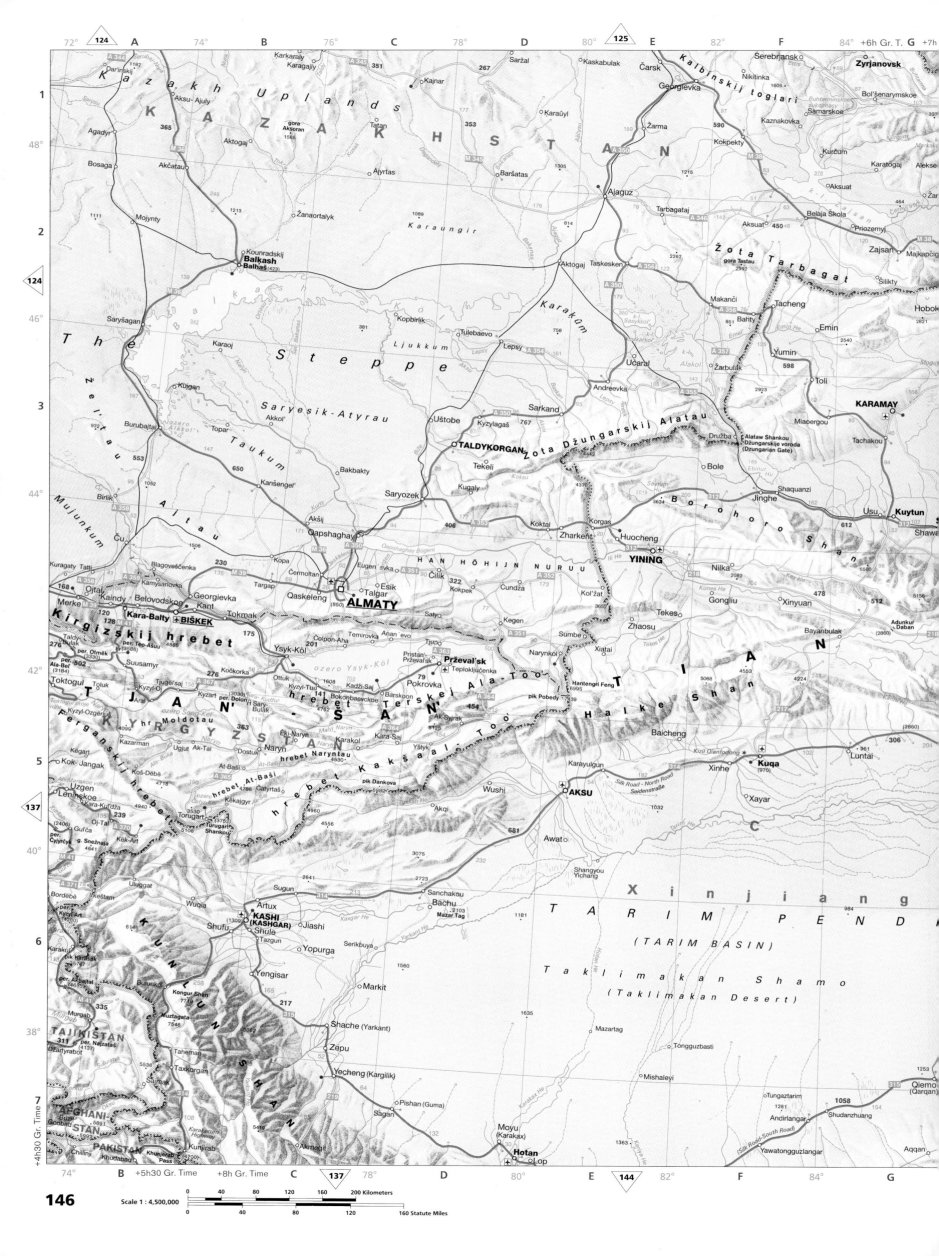

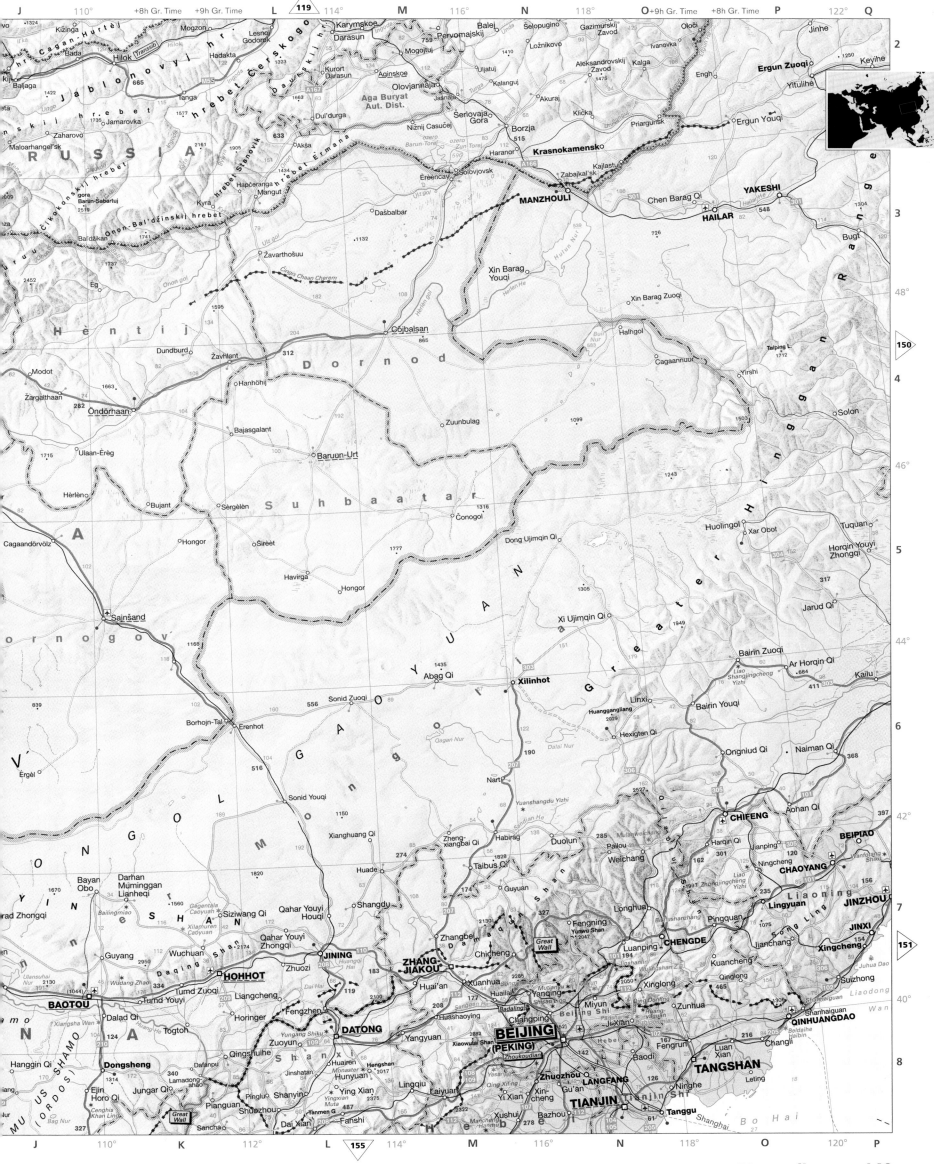

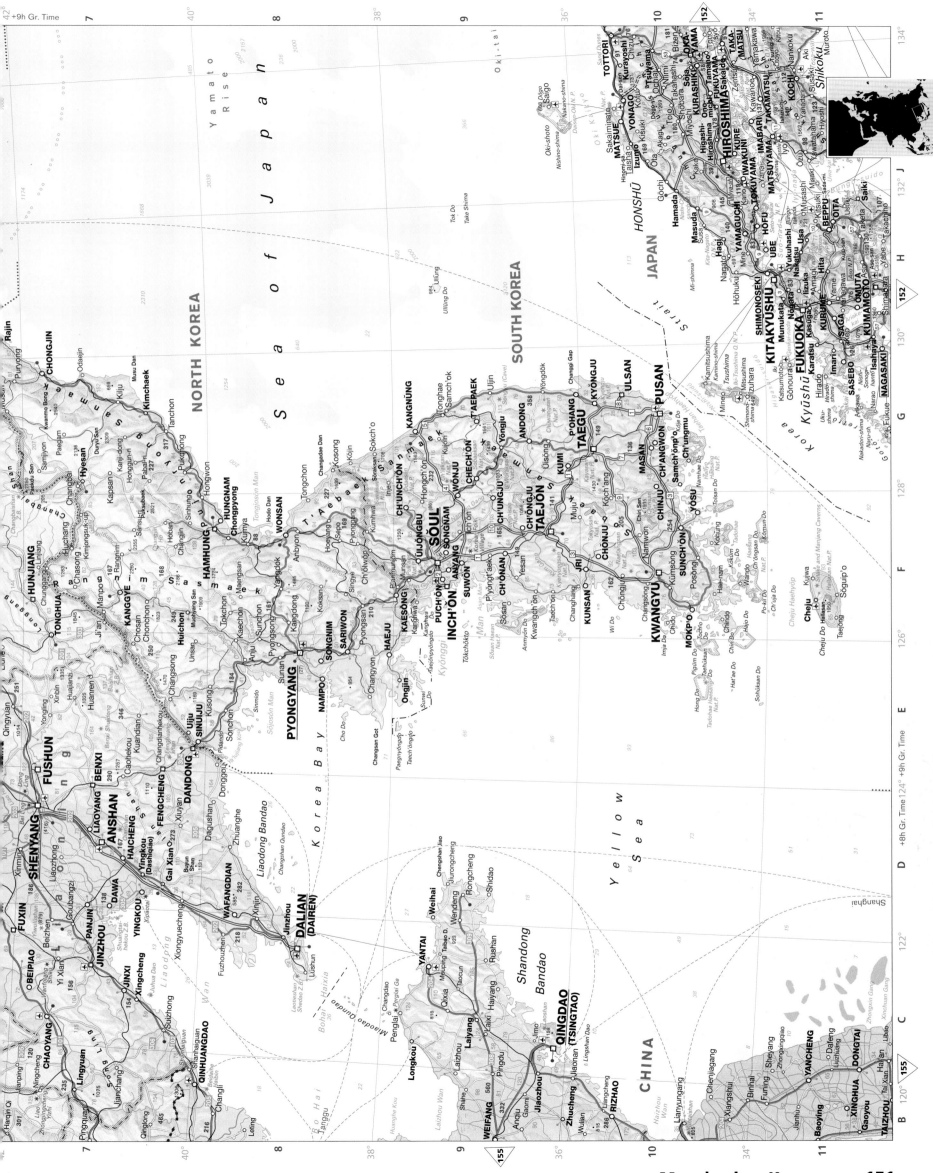

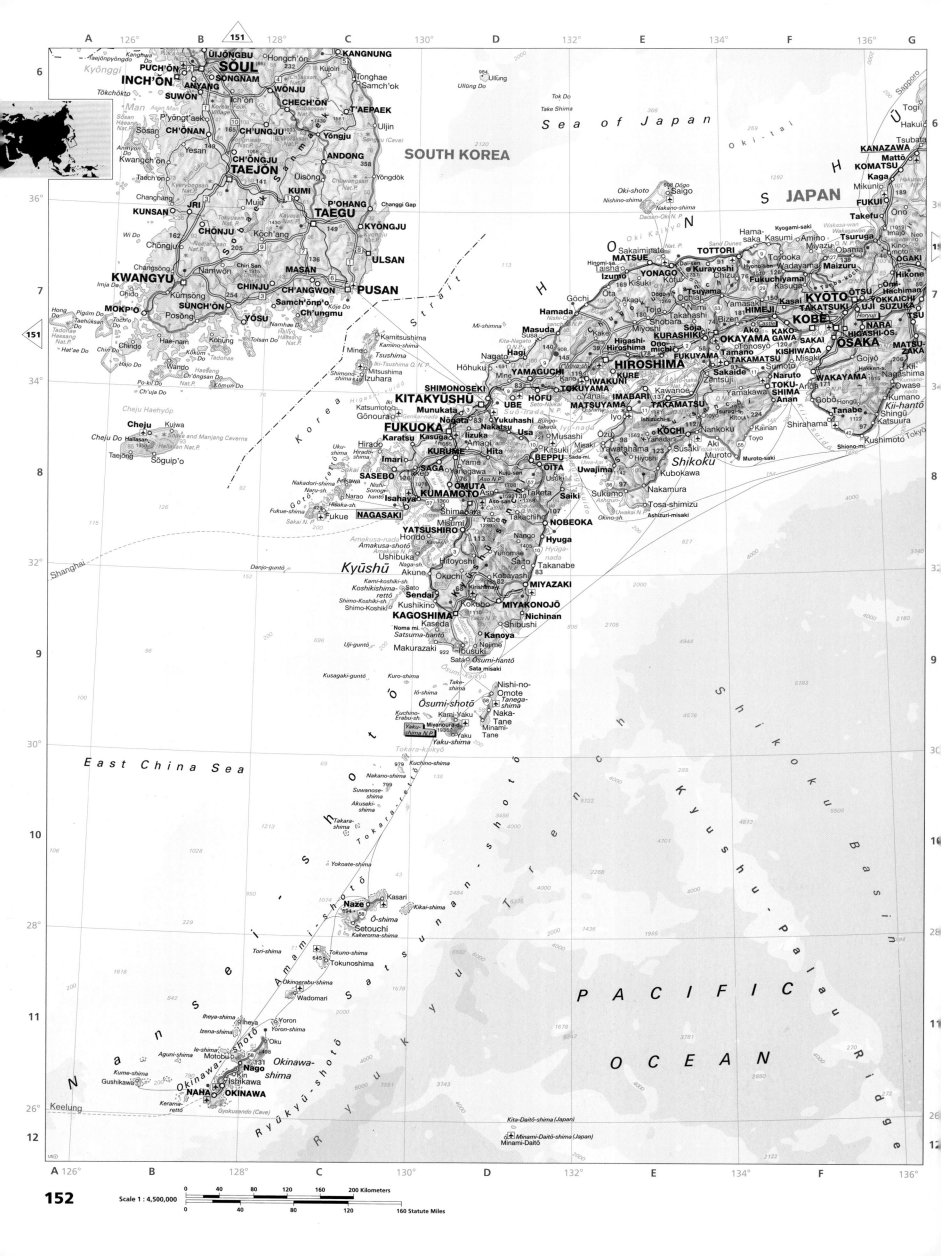

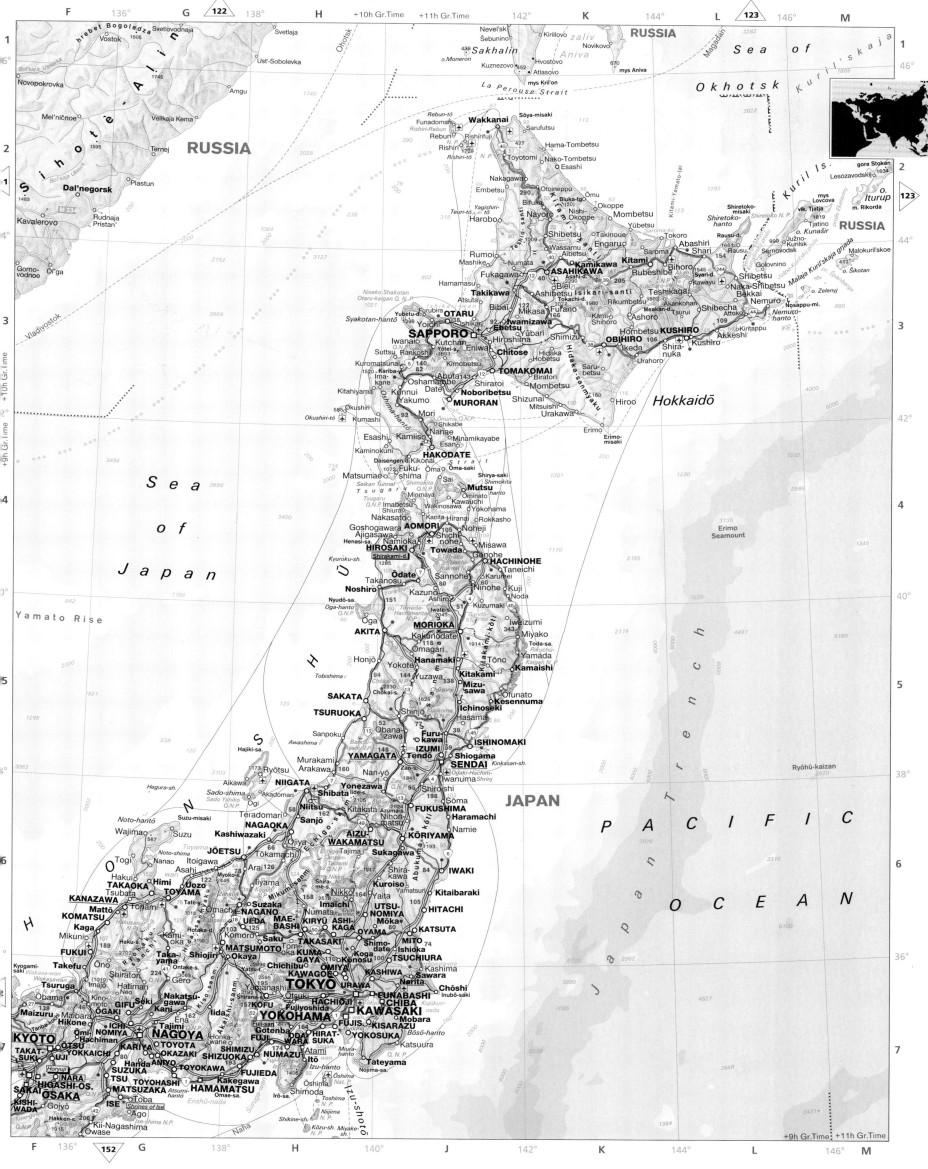

RUSSIA

Sea of
Okhotsk

RUSSIA

Sihote - Alin

RUSSIA

Sea
of
Japan

Yamato Rise

Hokkaidō

Wakkanai

OTARU
SAPPORO
Chitose
TOMAKOMAI
MURORAN
Noboribetsu

ASAHIKAWA
Takikawa
Iwamizawa
Ebetsu

Kitami
OBIHIRO KUSHIRO

HAKODATE

Mutsu

AOMORI
HIROSAKI
Towada
HACHINOHE
Ōdate
Noshiro

MORIOKA
AKITA
Hanamaki
Kitakami
Mizu-
sawa
Kamaishi

SAKATA
TSURUOKA

Ichinoseki
Kesennuma
Ofunato

Furu-
kawa
IZUMI
YAMAGATA Tendō
ISHINOMAKI
Shiogama
SENDAI

NIIGATA
Shibata
Yonezawa
Niitsu
NAGAOKA
Sanjō
KASHIWAZAKI
AIZU-
WAKAMATSU
JŌETSU

FUKUSHIMA
Haramachi
Namie

KORIYAMA
Sukagawa
Shira-
kawa
IWAKI

JAPAN

PACIFIC

OCEAN

KANAZAWA
TAKAOKA
Uozu
TOYAMA
KOMATSU
Kaga
FUKUI
Takefu
Tsuruga
Obama
Maizuru

NAGANO
UEDA
MAE-
BASHI
MATSUMOTO
KIRYŪ ASHI
KAGA
TAKASAKI
OYAMA

KATSUTA
HITACHI
Kitaibaraki

UTSU-
NOMIYA
Mōka

MITO
TSUCHIURA

KYŌTO
TAKAT-
SUKI
UJI
NARA
HIGASHI-OS.
OSAKA
SAKAI
KISHI-
WADA
ISE

GIFU
ŌGAKI
NAGOYA
TOYOTA
OKAZAKI
TOYOKAWA
TOYOHASHI
HAMAMATSU
SHIZUOKA
FUJIEDA
FUJI
NUMAZU

TOKYO
YOKOHAMA
KAWASAKI
CHIBA
FUNABASHI
URAWA
ŌMIYA
KAWAGOE
KONOSU
KASHIWA
Narita
Chōshi

China: Northern Region 155

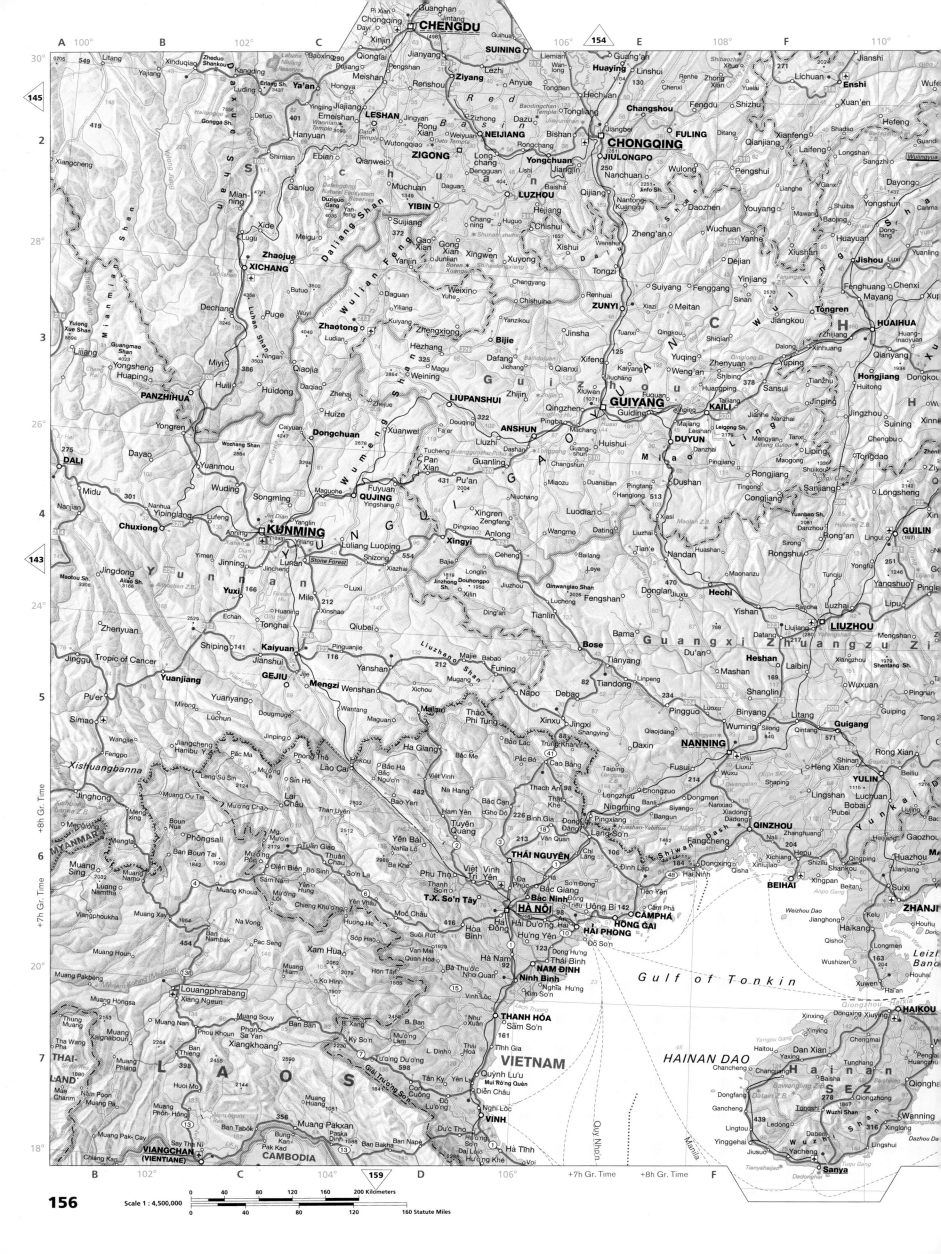

China: Southern Region   157

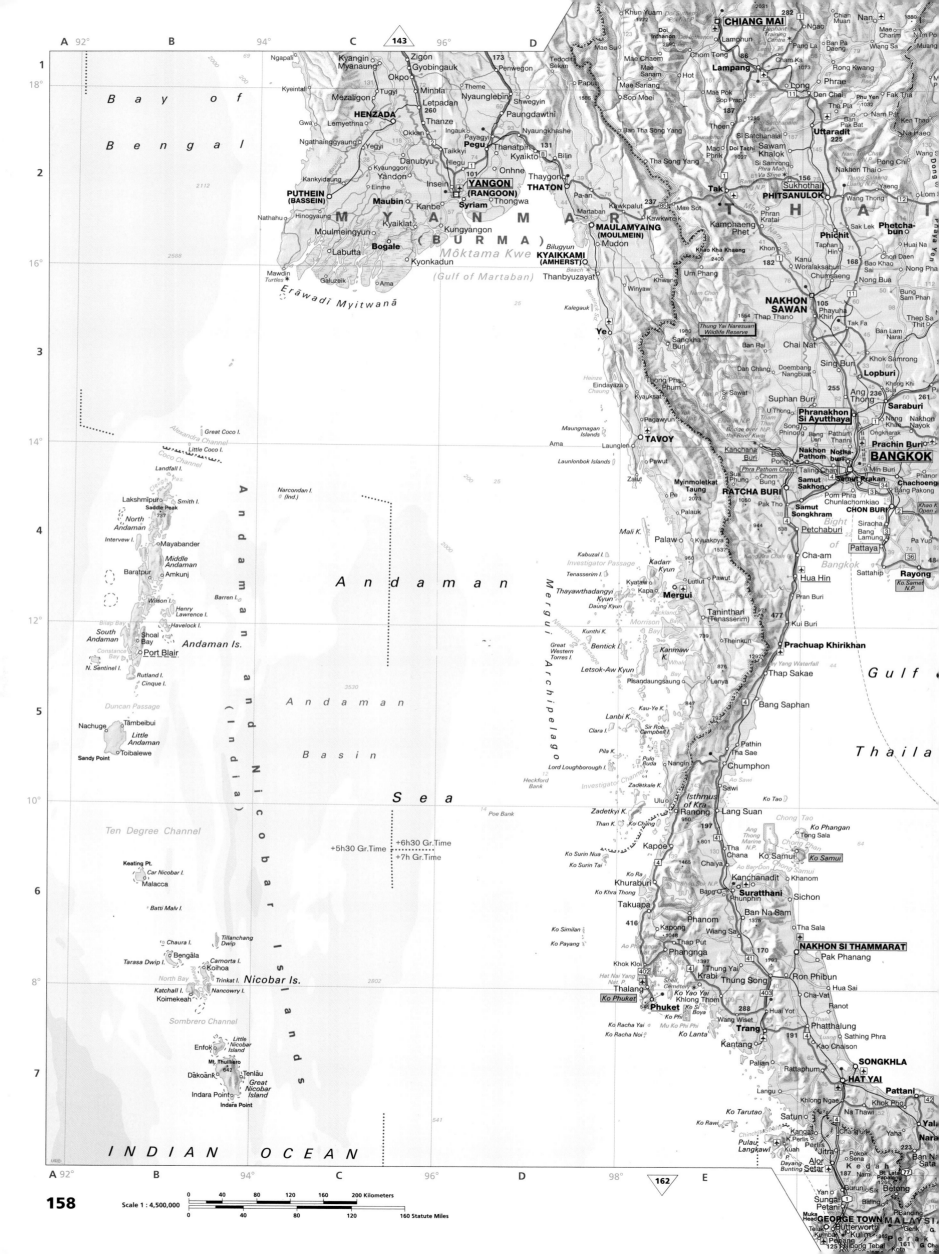

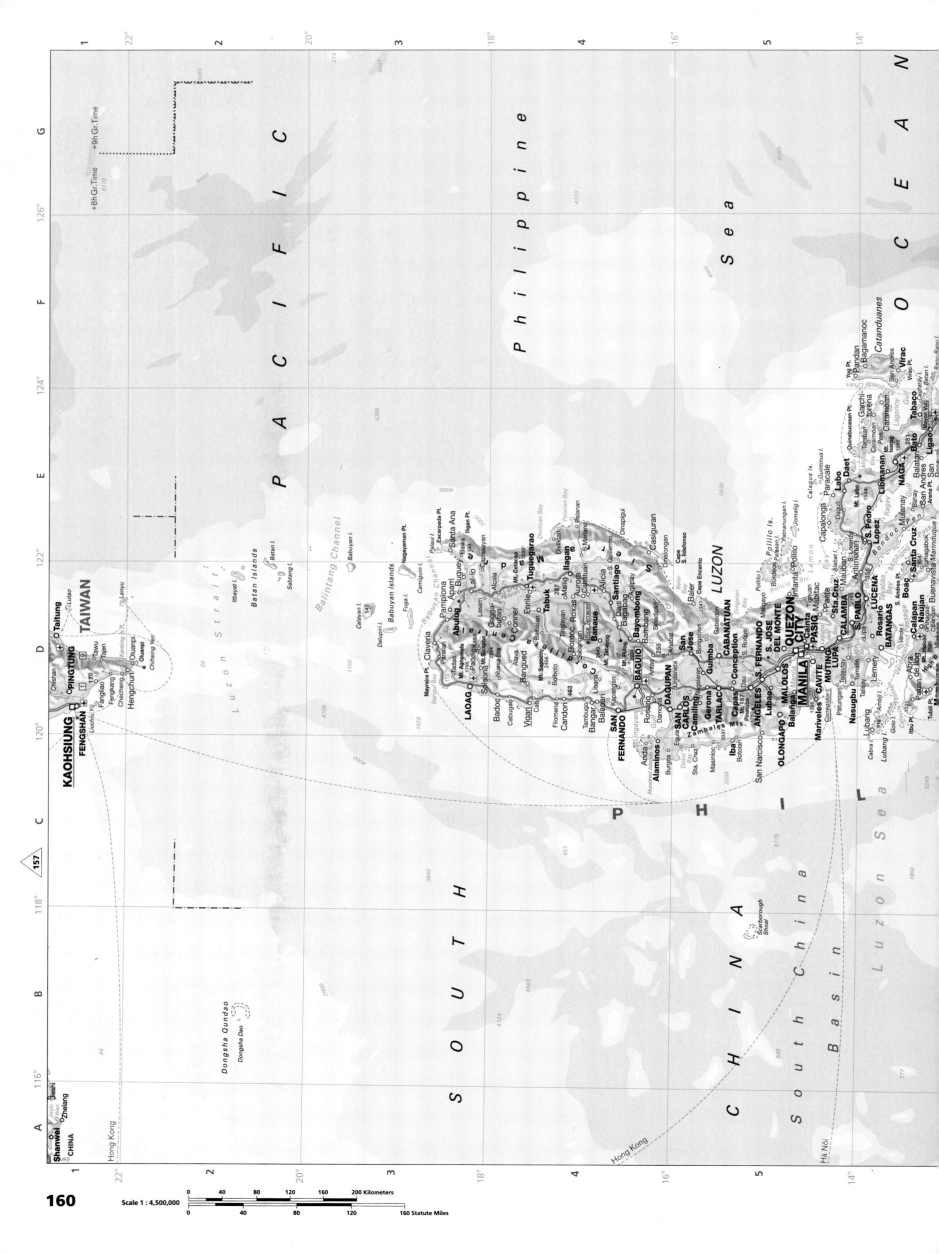

Scale 1 : 4,500,000

0 40 80 120 160 200 Kilometers

0 40 80 120 160 Statute Miles

CHINA
Shanwei
Zhelang
Jiesh
Jiesh Point

Hong Kong

KAOHSIUNG
FENGSHAN
OPINGTUNG
TAIWAN
Taitung

+8h Gr.Time   +9h Gr.Time
1 : 4,500,000

PACIFIC OCEAN

SOUTH CHINA SEA

South China Sea Basin

Luzon Sea

Luzon Strait

Balintang Channel

Babuyan Islands

Batan Islands

Dongsha Qundao
Dongsha Dao

Philippine Sea

LUZON

PHIL

MANILA
QUEZON CITY
LAOAG
VIGAN
BAGUIO
DAGUPAN
SAN FERNANDO
TARLAC
SAN CARLOS
CABANATUAN
ANGELES
OLONGAPO
BALANGA
MALOLOS
CALAMBA
BATANGAS
LUCENA
NAGA
DAET
LEGAZPI
Tuguegarao
Ilagan
Santiago
Bayombong
Bambang
Tabuk
Banaue
Aparri
Claveria
Santa Ana

Scarborough Shoal

Hong Kong

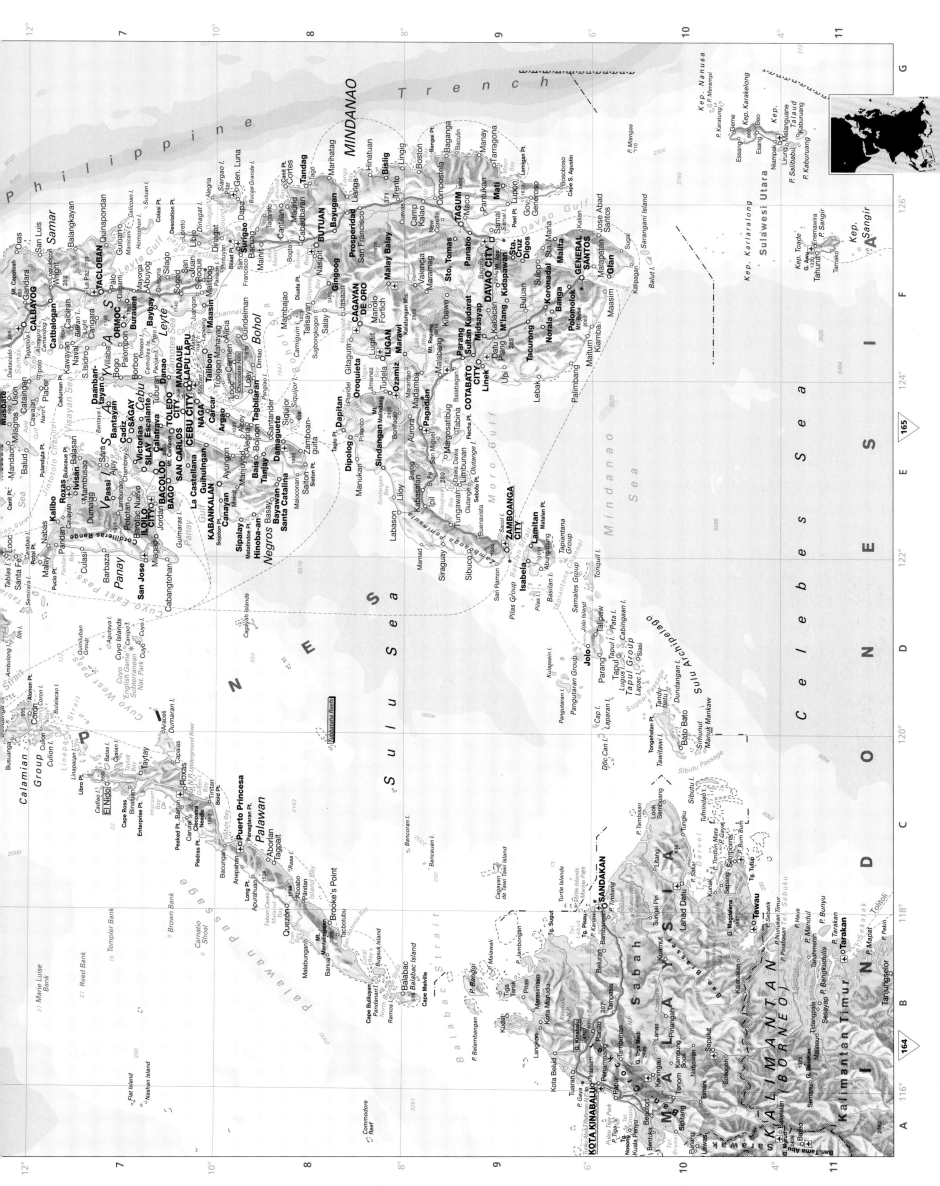

Philippines   **161**

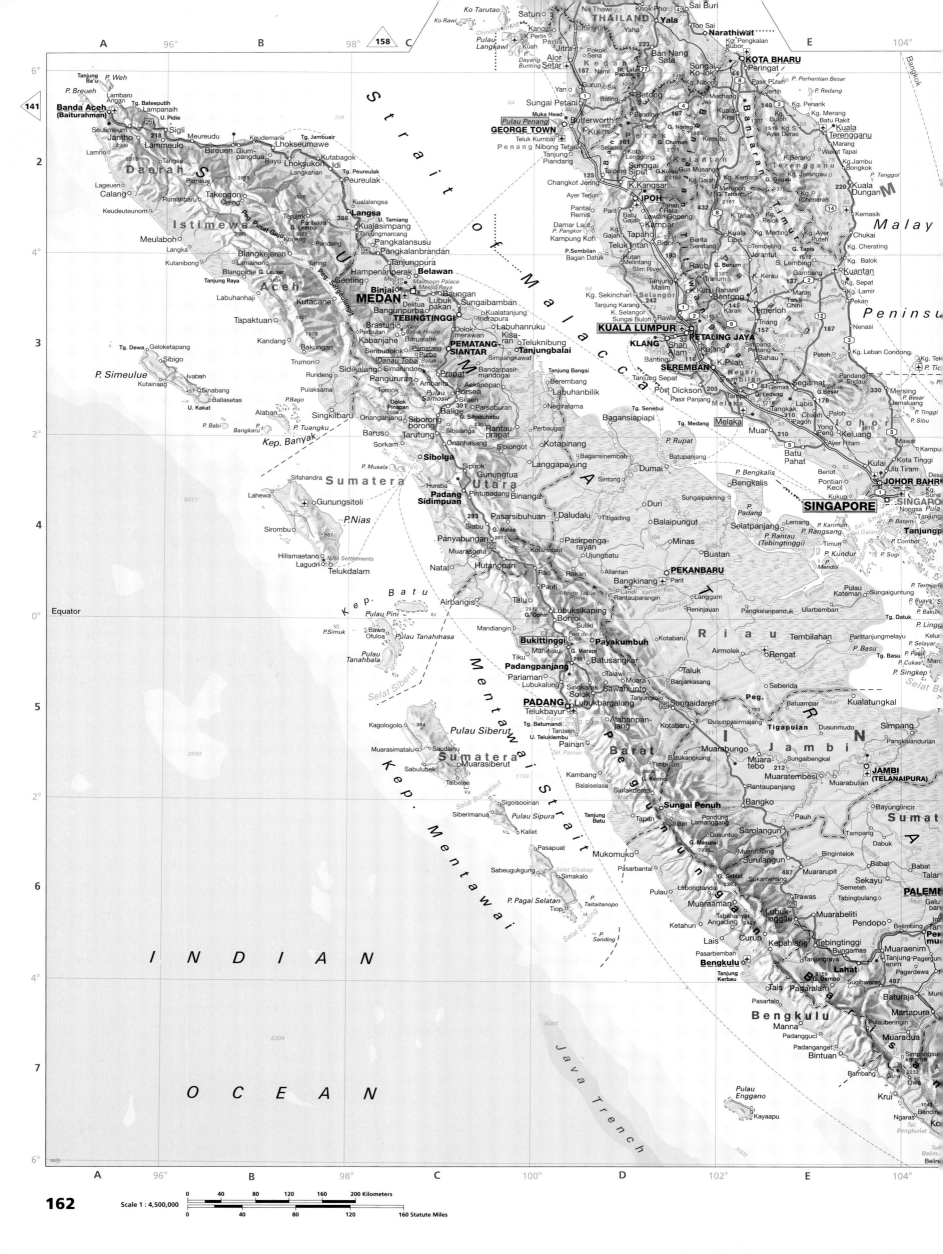

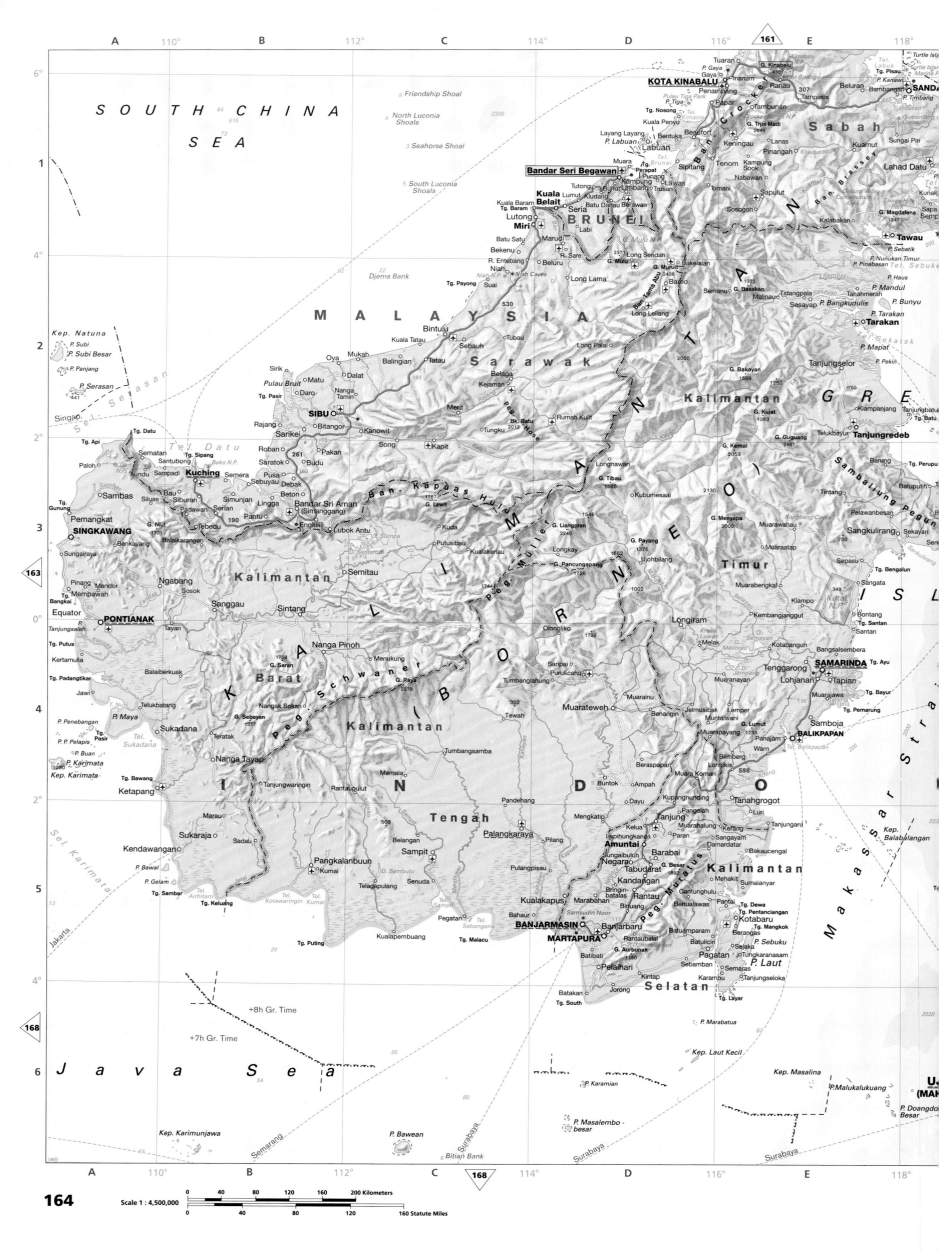

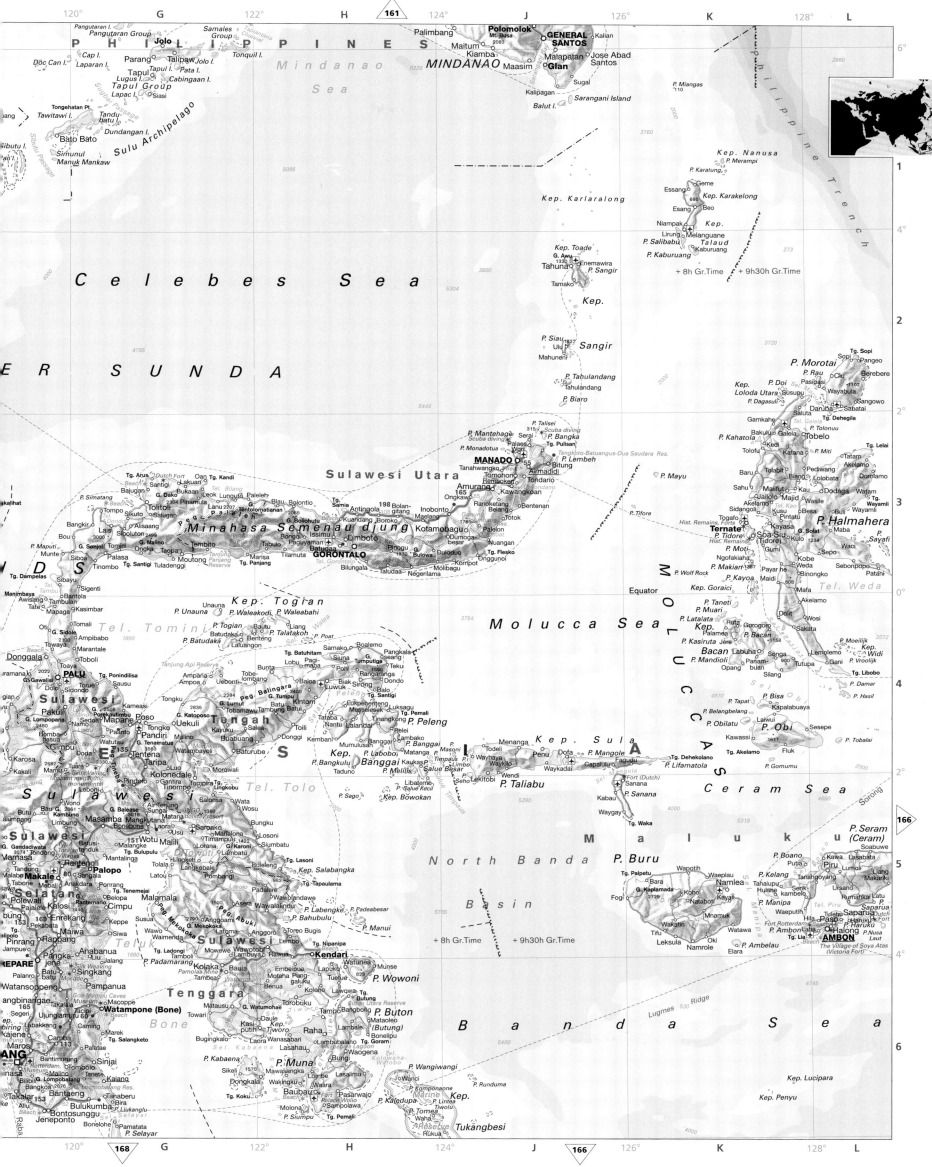

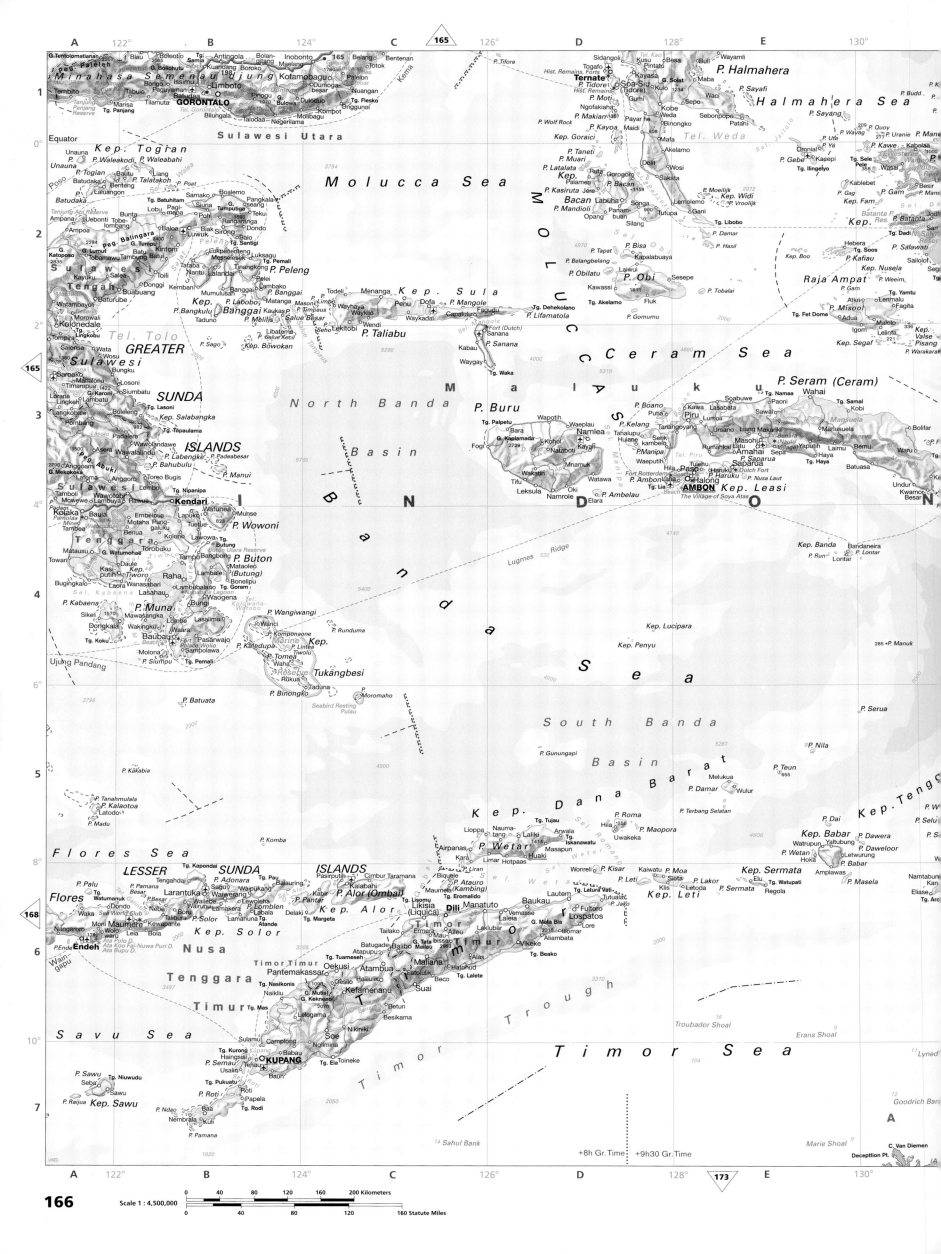

Scale 1 : 4,500,000

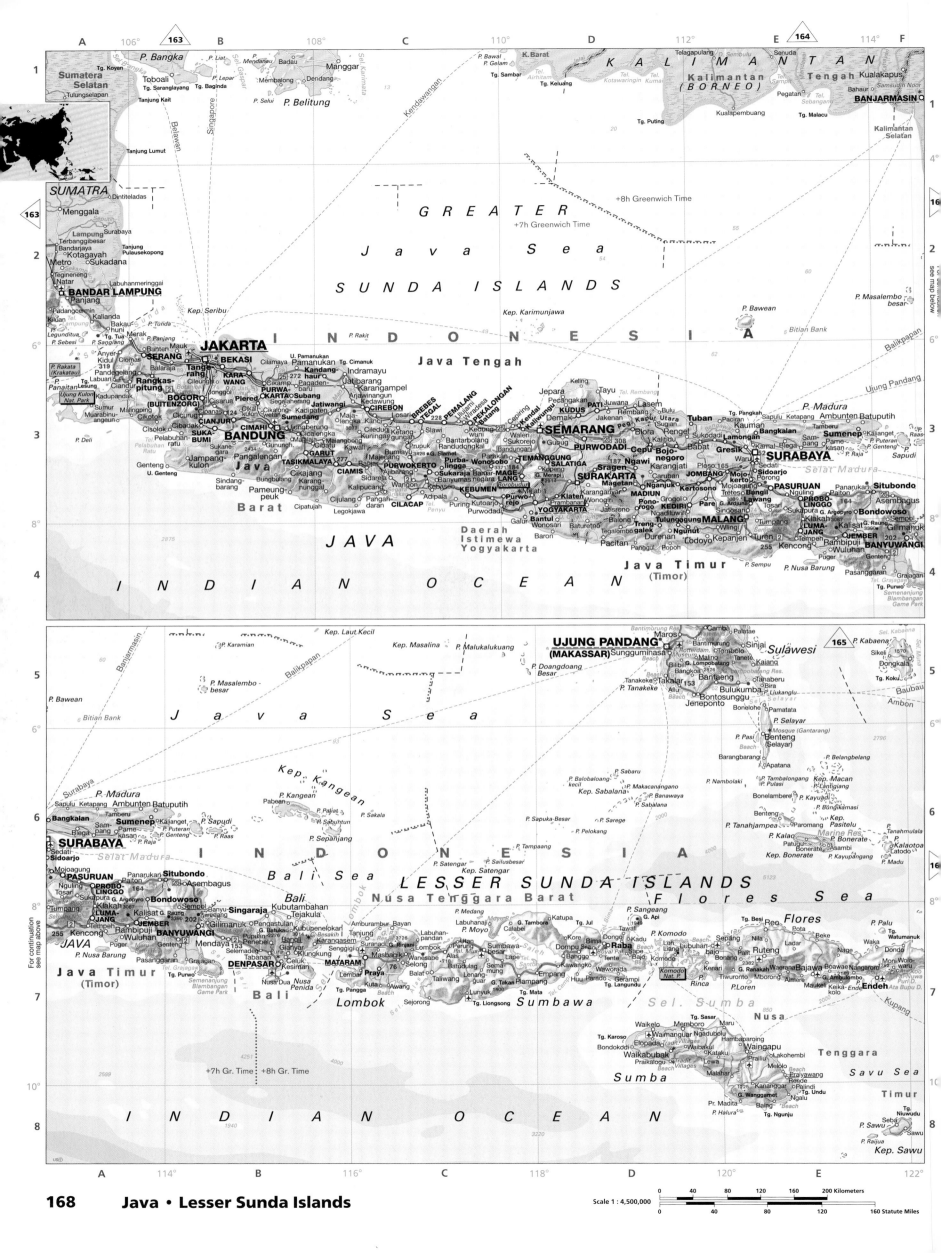

Australia and Oceania – a new world in the Pacific

The smallest continent (2,972,970 square miles/7.7 million sq. km) is also the one farthest from all the others. Australia's distance from Europe and the inaccessibility of its shores, due among other things to the coral reefs that extend north and east, were among the causes for its late exploration. Distinctive features are the western plateau with average heights of between 656 and 1,640 feet (200 – 500 m), the central lowlands with the internal drainage basin of Lake Eyre and the mountain areas in the East including the island of Tasmania. The archipelagos north and east of Australia, including the world's second largest island, New Guinea, and the two-island nation of New Zealand, are sometimes called Oceania, and comprise some 7,500 islands with an area of 501,930 square miles (1.3 million sq. km) dispersed over a sea area of 27,027,000 square miles (70 million sq. km). Melanesia and New Zealand constitute the outer arc of islands, Micronesia and Polynesia the inner. The islands sit partially on old mountains of volcanic origin beneath the sea and partially on elevated coral reefs. The 180th meridian, the dateline, runs through the middle of the region.

Australia as it was charted in 1644 by the Dutch Abel Tasman. It was not until 1770 that the eastern coast was explored by James Cook.

Australia: Northwestern Region
p. 172 – 173

Australia: Northeastern Region
p. 174 – 175

Australia: Southwestern Region
p. 176 – 177

Australia: Eastern Region
p. 178 – 179

Australia: Southeastern Region, Tasmania
p. 180 – 181

New Zealand
p. 182

Papua New Guinea
p. 183

Solomon Islands · Vanuatu · Fiji · Samoa · Tonga p. 184

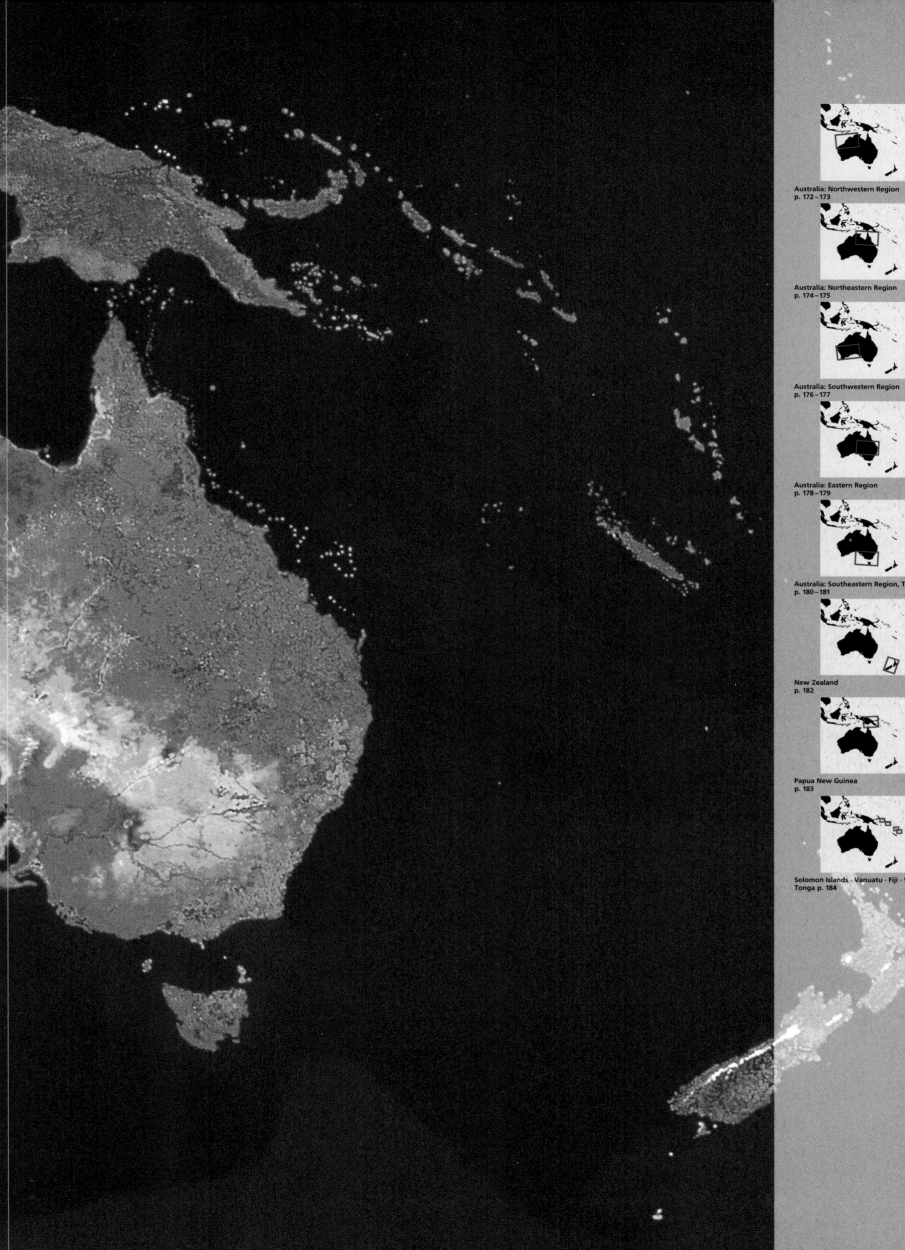

Australia: Northwestern Region
p. 172–173

Australia: Northeastern Region
p. 174–175

Australia: Southwestern Region
p. 176–177

Australia: Eastern Region
p. 178–179

Australia: Southeastern Region, Tasmania
p. 180–181

New Zealand
p. 182

Papua New Guinea
p. 183

Solomon Islands · Vanuatu · Fiji · Samoa · Tonga p. 184

1

Java Trench

6000

5820

3410

Hibern

INDIAN

12°

18

4000

200

Ashmore Reef

Sal

2

5815

North Australian

6733

9

Seringapatam Reef

Scott Reef

14°

Basin

6218

OCEAN

Lynher Reef

Adele I.

Mav

3

6036

5522

75

Buccaneer Arc
Mining
Yampi S

16°

Collier

C. Leveque

Lombadina
Pender Bay

Rowley Shoals

Mermaid Reef

Emeriau Pt.
Lacepede Is.
Beagle Bay

Beagle Bay
Abor. Land

Pt.
Torment

Clerke Reef

C. Baskerville
Carnot Bay

Beagle Bay

King Soun

4

Imperieuse Reef

Coulomb Pt.

C. Bertholet
Wildlife Sanct.

58

Dampier

Derb

Willare Brid
Roadhou

Land

Kilto

Manguel
Creek

Broome
Gantheaume Pt.
Roebuck
Bay

Roebuck
Roadhouse

Thangoo

Mowanjun

145

Cable Beach

C. Latouche Treville

18°

La Grange
Bay

La Grange

Dampier Downs

Babro
Tow

C. Bossut

Edgar
Ra.

64

Anna Plains

Nita Downs

W **e** **s**

5

Eighty Mile Beach

546

561

Wallal Downs

Mandora

Sandfire Flat
Roadhouse

Gr **e** **a** **t** **San**

Poissonnier
Point

C. Keraudren

Larrey Pt.

Pardoo
Roadhouse

Great Northern Hwy.

Spit Pt.

20°

C. Thouin

Port Hedland

Goldsworthy

131

Mount
Goldsworthy

Shay Gap

Legendre I.

Sloping
Pt.

C. Lambert
Pt. Samson
Wickham
Roebourne
(Hist. Town)

Strelley

138

Carlindi

170

Callawa

De Grey Riv.

Muccan

Yarrie

Warrawagine

A **u** **s** **t**

Montebello Is.

34

Dampier
Archipelago

Nickol
Bay

Karratha

Mundabul-
langana

Wallareenya

Lalla Rookh

Dampier

131

Eginbah

Bamboo
Creek

C. Dupuy

Barrow I.

C. Preston

Karratha
Roadhouse

Whim
Creek

Mallina

Gilliam

346

Marble Bar

Five Mile Hill
Mt. Edgar
371
Mount
Edgar

Barrow I.
Oil Field

South End
Pasco Island

Mardie I.

Maitland Riv.

Yandeearra

132

Yandeearra

440

Abydos

Isabelle

Woodi Woodi
Mining Centre

6

Barrow I.
Shoals

Mardie

223

Fortescue Riv.
Roadhouse

Millstream-
Chichester
Nat. P.

306

Mt. Richthofen
366

Mount
Florance

Mt.
Gratwick
393

Hillside

205

Nullagine Riv.

L. Waukarlycarly

Mary Anne Passage

Thevenard I.

Mary Anne
Group

718

Pannawonica

251

Mill-
stream

673

Tambrey
(Aband.)

Flora & Fauna
Reserve

Abor. Land

Gregory Ra.

Throssell Ra.

Telfer

Paterson Ra.

Beadon Pt.

Yarraloola

Mt. Enid
Mining Area

Mt.Elvire

Mt. Margaret
880

Bonney
Downs

Mt. Cooke

L. Dora

Onslow

1

Robe Riv.

Pk. Hester

Chichester Ra.

Nullagine

138

Eva Broadhurst L.

Peedamulla

Cane River

Red Hill

Hamersley
Ra.

Mount
Brockman
1132

1031

Wittenoom
Wittenoom
Gorge

826

421

Roy Hill
457

Mt. McKay

Mount Divide

Hanging Rock
536

Rudall River
National Park

Mt. Connaughton

L. Blanche

22°

Mt. Hollister

U.S.Navy's
SRC Base
Exmouth

315

C. Range
Nat. P.

Nanutarra
Roadhouse

Cane River

Mt.
Stuart

Duck Cr.

Mt. Brockman

Hamersley
1176

Mt.
Frederick

1235

Mt. George

Mt. Marsh

Roy Hill

146

Ethel Creek

Balfour Downs

Learmonth

Exmouth
Gulf

Tom-
Price

Mt. Bruce
(Iron Ore)

88

Cape Ra.

Giralia Ra.

Yanrey

Koordarrie

Wyloo

957

136

Mt. Wall

Tom Price
1083

Juna
Downs
1251

216

Walgun

McKay Ra.

No. 24 Well

7

Ningaloo

228

Bullara

Barradale
Roadhouse

N.W. Coastal Hwy.

Uaroo

418

Kooline

1075

Rocklea

Hamersley
Ranges
Nat. P.

Mt. Bennett
1064

1157

Mt. Meharry

95

Talawana

Robertson Ra.

Harbutt Ra.

Coral Bay

Winning

Towera

Mt. Palgrave
700

Ashburton
Downs

Paraburdoo

Parraburdu
Mining Area
(Iron Ore)

Mt. Robinson

Ophthalmia Ra.

Mt. Whaleback
Mining Area
(Iron Ore)
Spodelle Cr.

Newman

Jiggalong

Jiggalong
Abor. Land

Prairie
Downs

Savory Riv.

L. Disappointment

Runton Riv.

L. Winif

Scale 1 : 4,500,000

0   40   80   120   160   200 Kilometers

0   40   80   120   160 Statute Miles

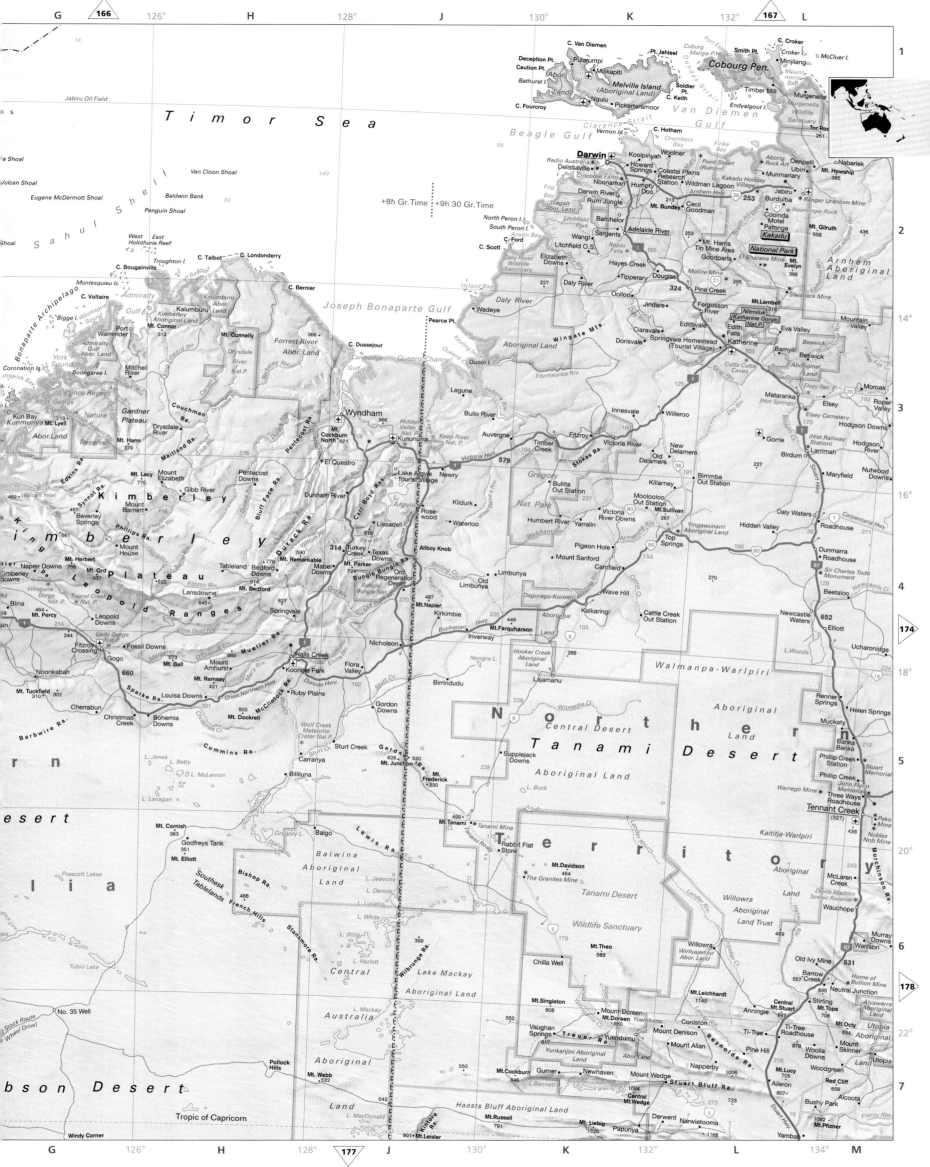

Australia: Northwestern Region   173

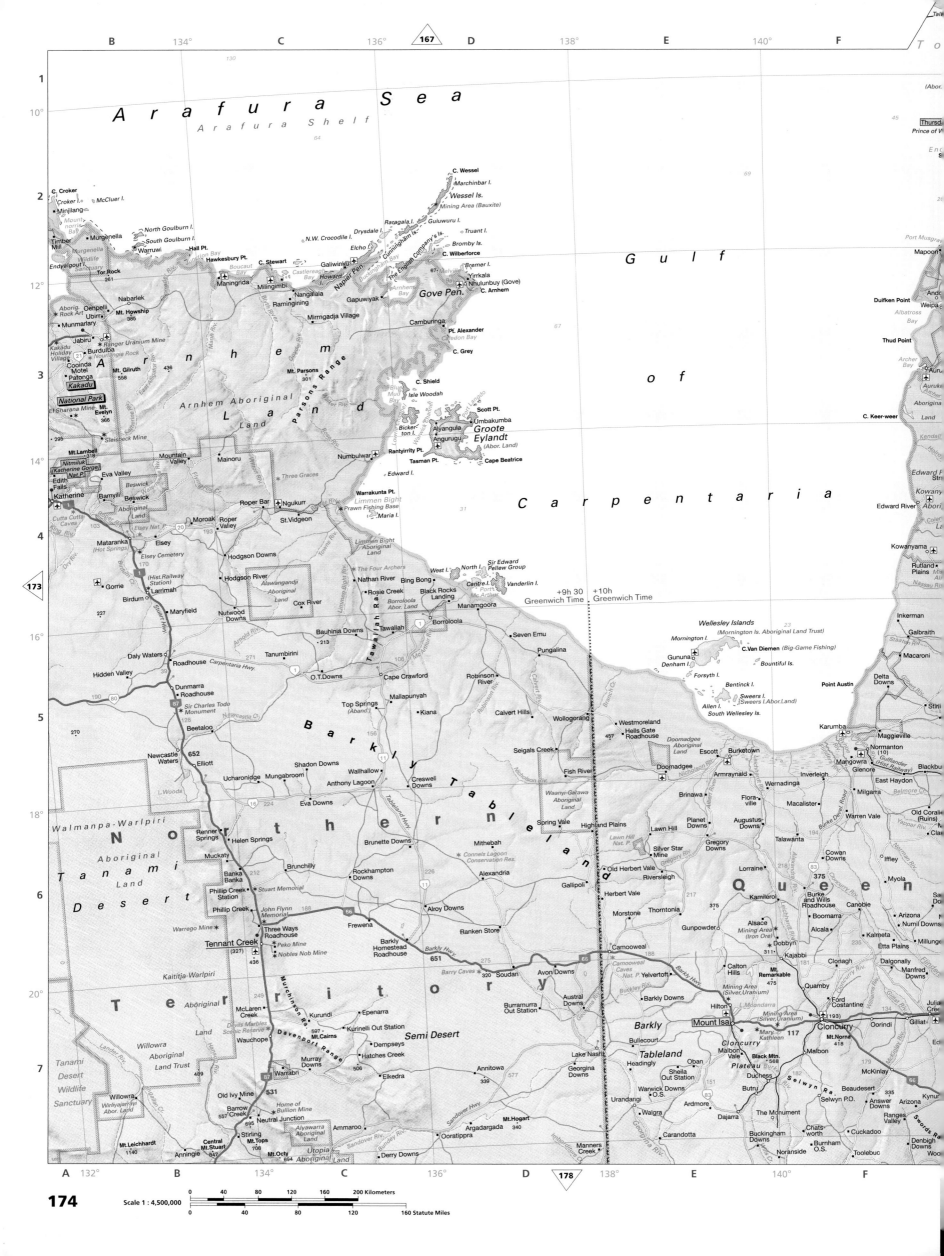

A r a f u r a   S e a

A r a f u r a   S h e l f

G u l f

o f

C a r p e n t a r i a

+9h 30 +10h
Greenwich Time | Greenwich Time

Arnhem Aboriginal Land

Kakadu National Park

N o r t h e r n   T a n a m i

Walmanpa-Warlpiri Aboriginal Land

D e s e r t

T e r r i t o r y

Tanami Desert Wildlife Sanctuary

B a r k l y   T a b l e l a n d

N o r t h e r n l a n d

Q u e e n

Barkly Tableland Plateau

Australia: Northeastern Region   175

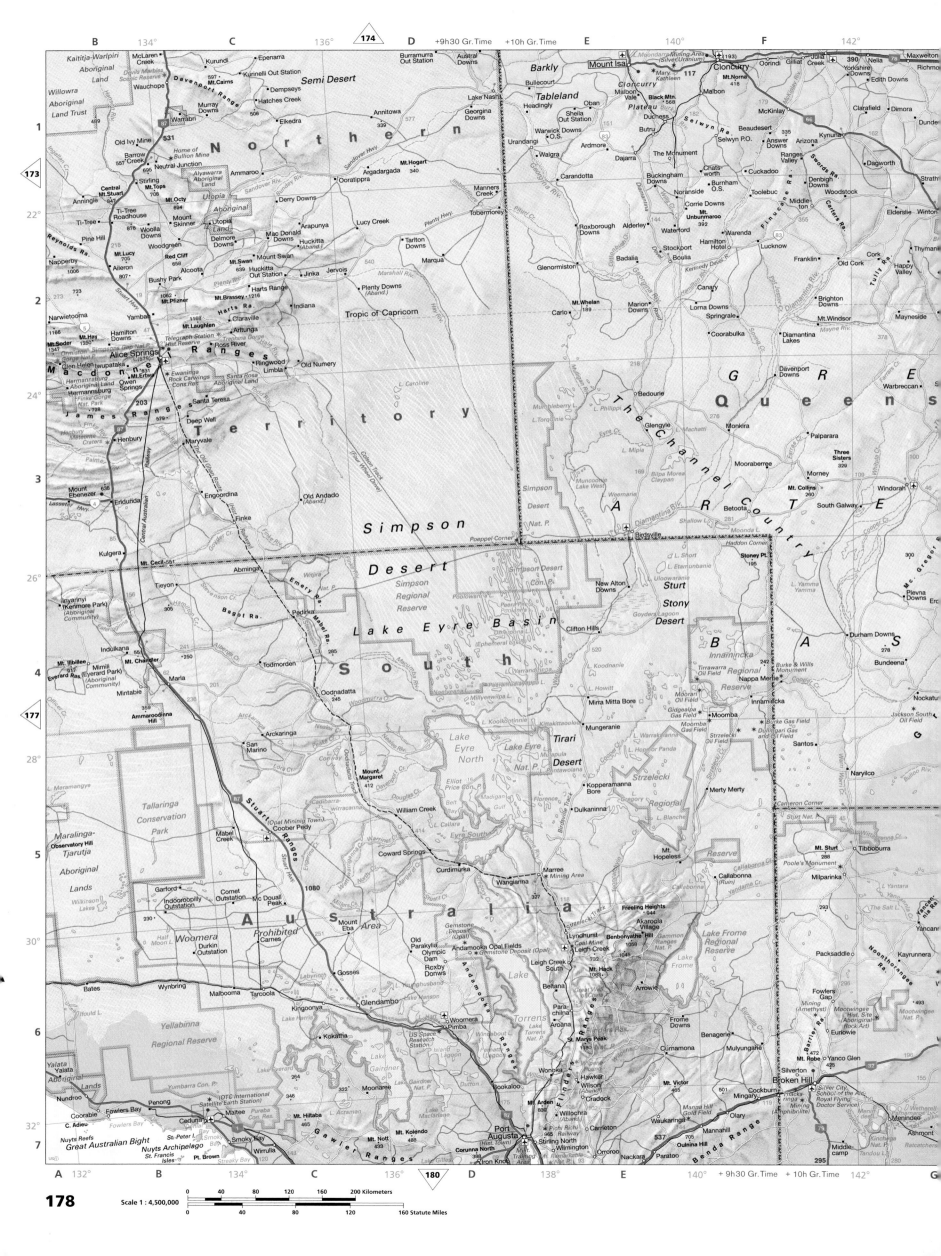

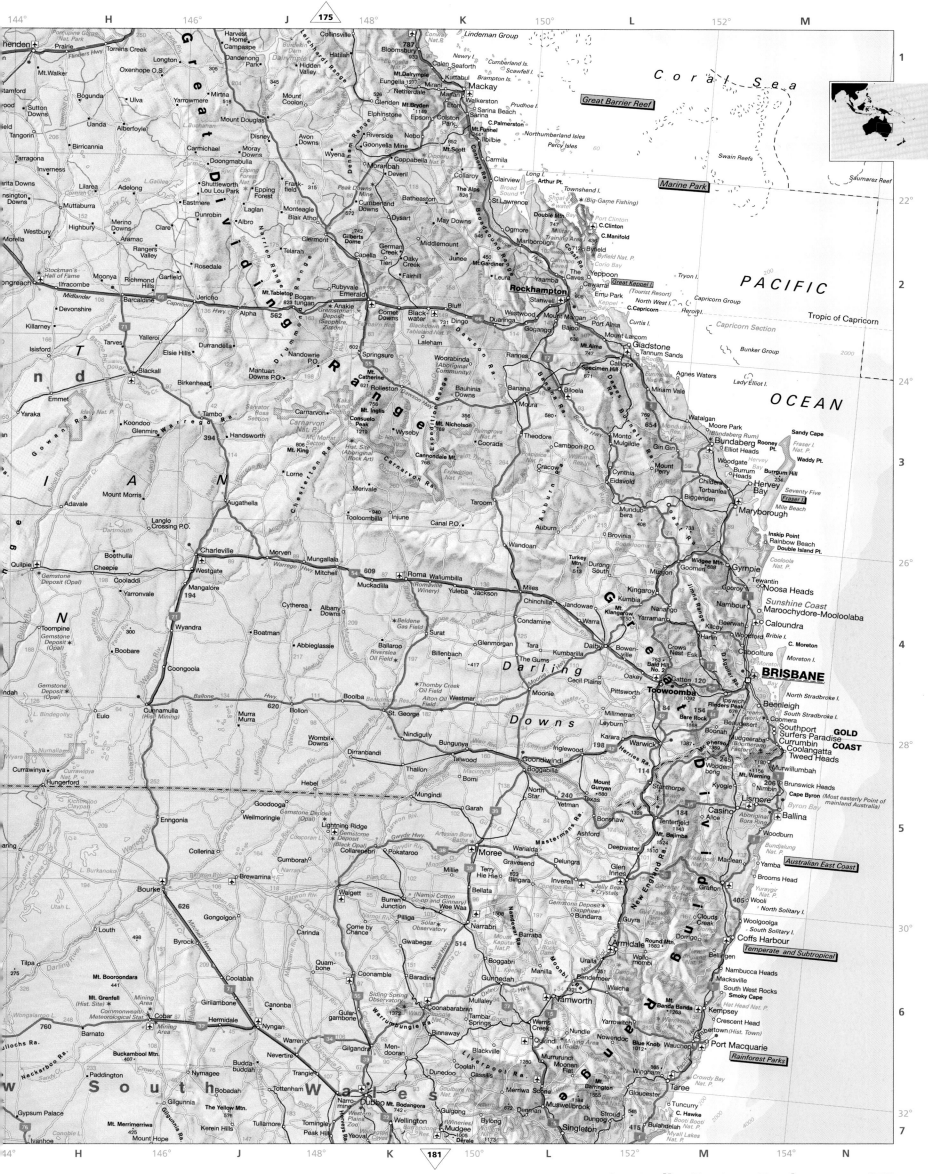

Australia: Eastern Region   179

Australia: Southeastern Region, Tasmania   **181**

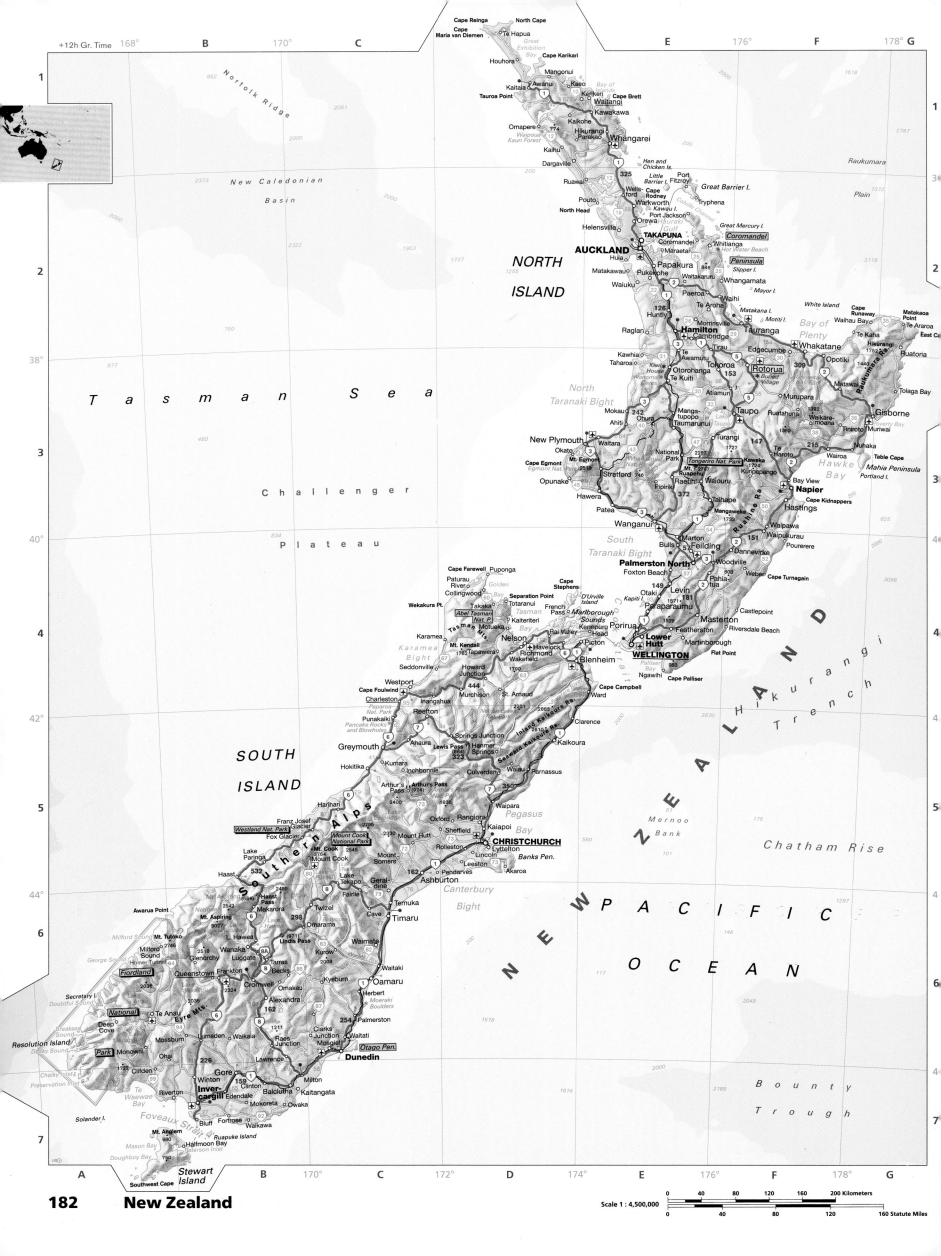

Cape Reinga North Cape
Cape Maria van Diemen Te Hapua
Great Exhibition Bay
Houhora Cape Karikari
Mangonui
Kaeo Bay of Islands
Awanui Kerikeri Cape Brett
Kaitala Waitangi
Tauroa Point Kawakawa

Omapere 774 Kaikohe
Waipoua Kauri Forest Hikurangi Parakao Whangarei Hen and Chicken Is. 1518
Kaihu 200 Port
Dargaville Little Fitzroy
325 Barrier I. Great Barrier I. 2787
Ruawai Wells-ford Cape Rodney Port Jackson Tryphena
Pouto Warkworth Kawau I. Coville Channel Great Mercury I.
North Head Orewa Coromandel Whitianga
Helensville Coromandel Hot Water Beach
TAKAPUNA Maraetai Peninsula Slipper I.
AUCKLAND Papakura Whangamata
Huia Matakawau Whakatane Mayor I.

NORTH Waiuku Pukekohe Paeroa Waihi
ISLAND Waiuku Te Aroha Matakana I. Motiti I. White Island Cape Runaway Matakaoa Point
126 Huntly Morrinsville Tauranga Waihau Bay Te Araroa
Raglan Hamilton Cambridge Tirau Edgecumbe Whakatane Te Kaha Hikurangi Ruatoria
Taharoa Te Awamutu Tokoroa Rotorua 309 Opotiki
Kawhia Otorohanga Te Kuiti Buried Murupara Matawai Tolaga Bay
North Taranaki Bight Village Gisborne
Mokau 242 Mangatupopo Atiamuri Waikaremoana Poverty Bay
Ohura Taumarunui Taupo Ruatahuna Tiniroto
Ahiti National Turangi Te Haroto Muriwai Table Cape
New Plymouth Waitara Park Kaweka Mahia Peninsula
Okato Stratford 147 Portland I.
Mt. Egmont 215 Wairoa
Cape Egmont Waikato Napier
Opunake Raetihi Taihape Hastings Cape Kidnappers
Hawera Patea Mangaweka Waipawa
Wanganui 372 Waipukurau
Bulls Marton 151 Dannevirke
South Taranaki Bight Feilding Woodville Weber Cape Turnagain
Palmerston North
Foxton Beach Pahiatua
149 Levin Masterton Castlepoint
Otaki Carterton
Paraparaumu Featherston Riversdale Beach
Cape Farewell Puponga Porirua Masterton
Collingwood Separation Point WELLINGTON Martinborough Flat Point
Takaka Totaranui Lower Hutt
Motueka French Pass Picton Cape Palliser
Nelson Blenheim Palliser Bay Ngawihi
SOUTH Karamea Havelock Richmond Cape Campbell
Seddonville Wakefield Ward
Westport Howard Junction
Cape Foulwind 444 Murchison St. Arnaud Clarence
Charleston Reefton Kaikoura
Punakaiki Springs Junction 350
Greymouth Ahaura Lewis Pass Hanmer Springs Waiau Parnassus
Hokitika Kumara Inchbonnie Culverden
Arthur's Pass Waipara
Harihari Oxford Rangiora Pegasus Bay
Franz Josef Glacier Sheffield Kaiapoi
Fox Glacier Mount Hutt CHRISTCHURCH Lyttelton
Lake Paringa Mt. Cook Rolleston Banks Pen.
Mount Cook Lincoln Akaroa
Haast 532 Mount Somers Leeston
Mt. Aspiring Lake Tekapo Geraldine Ashburton
Haast Pass Fairlie Temuka Canterbury Bight
298 Twizel Cave Timaru
Makarora Omarama Waimate
Milford Sound Lindis Pass Kurow
Mt. Tutoko L. Hawea Tarras Waitaki
Milford Wanaka Becks 85 Oamaru
Homer Tunnel Glenorchy Frankton 8A Kyeburn Herbert
Fiordland Luggate Cromwell Moeraki Boulders
Queenstown Omakau Palmerston
National 162 Alexandra 254 Waikouaiti
Te Anau Eyre Mts. Clarks Junction Mosgiel
Deep Cove Mossburn Lawrence DUNEDIN Otago Pen.
Park Monowai Lumsden Waikaia Milton
226 Ohai Gore Winton Clinton Balclutha
Invercargill 159 Kaitangata
Riverton Edendale Owaka
Mt. Anglem Bluff Fortrose Waikawa
Halfmoon Bay

Te Waewae Bay Foveaux Strait
Solander I. Ruapuke Island

Stewart Island
Southwest Cape

Tasman Sea
New Caledonian Basin
Challenger
Plateau

NEW ZEALAND
Hikurangi Trench

South Pacific Ocean

Mernoo Bank
Chatham Rise

Bounty Trough

Scale 1 : 4,500,000
0 40 80 120 160 200 Kilometers
0 40 80 120 160 Statute Miles

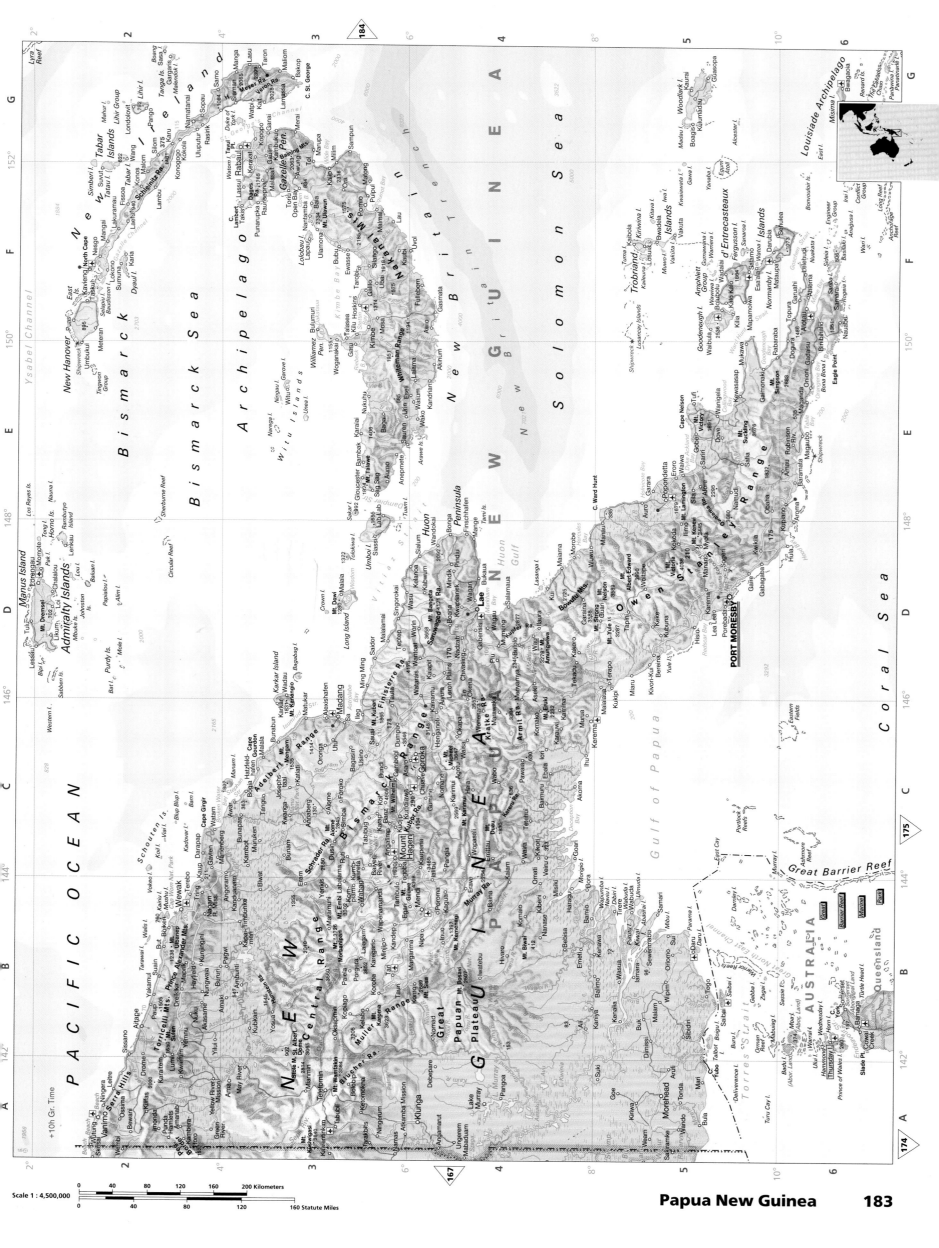

Scale 1 : 4,500,000

0   40   80   120   160   200 Kilometers

0   40   80   120   160 Statute Miles

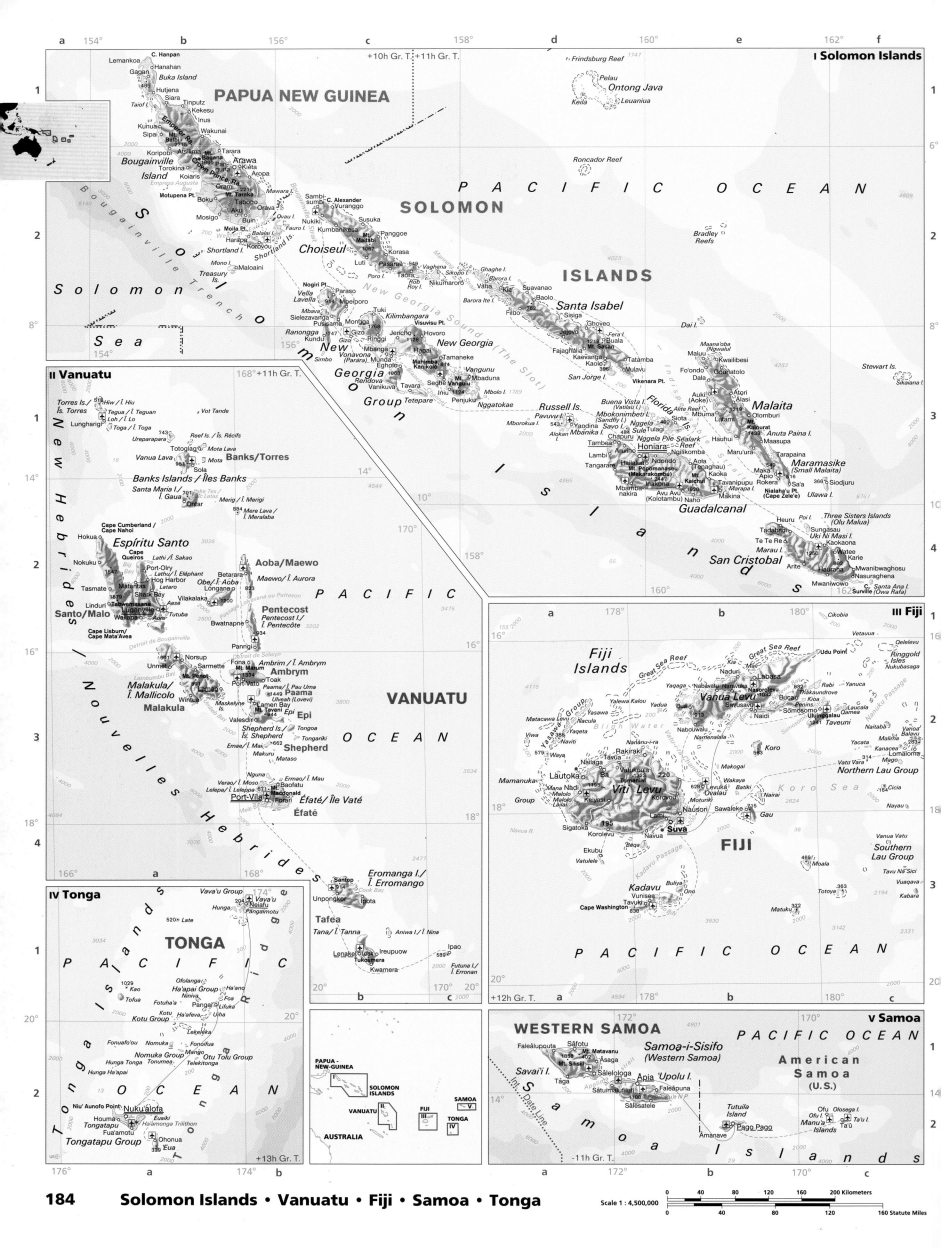

Africa – a continent of many faces

Africa, the second largest continent on Earth, takes up one-fifth of the total land mass on the planet. It is characterized by a coastline that contains few gulfs and peninsulas, the triangular southern cone with the northern trapeze on top and the division into Upper Africa in the southeast and Lower Africa in the northwest. The highlands with basins and rises as well as an extended rift valley system shape its surface. Africa contains all tropical landscape and climatic areas of the world, distributed primarily along the latitude lines on both sides of the Equator. One-third of Africa is occupied by the largest desert on Earth,

Johann Baptist Homann made this copperplate engraving of Africa around the year 1690, approximately 150 before Europeans first began to explore the continent's interior.

the Sahara. This environment, hostile to life, separates white Africa, mostly settled by Islamic Arab peoples, from black Africa, characterized by the Sudanese and Bantu peoples. Ethiopia has unique population and culture. Contrary to the imaginary picture of the "dark continent," Africa has a vibrant culture and history. This is where, over three million years ago, our early ancestors learned to walk upright, and nowadays its melange of peoples, races, languages and traditions is only beginning to be appreciated.

Morocco · Canary Islands
p. 188–189

Ghana · Togo · Benin · Nigeria · Camero
p. 204–205

Algeria · Tunisia
p. 190–191

Central African Republic · Sudan:
Southern Region p. 206–207

Libya
p. 192–193

Ethiopia · Somali Peninsula
p. 208–209

Egypt
p. 194–195

Lower Guinea
p. 210–211

Mauritania · Mali: Northern Region
p. 196–197

East Africa: Northern Region
p. 212–213

Niger · Chad
p. 198–199

East Africa: Southern Region
p. 214–215

Sudan: Northern Region · Eritrea
p. 200–201

Angola · Namibia: Northern Region
p. 216–217

Upper Guinea
p. 202–203

Zambia · Zimbabwe · Mozambique
p. 218–219

South Africa
220–221

Madagascar · Comoros
p. 222–223

Seychelles · Réunion · Mauritius
p. 224

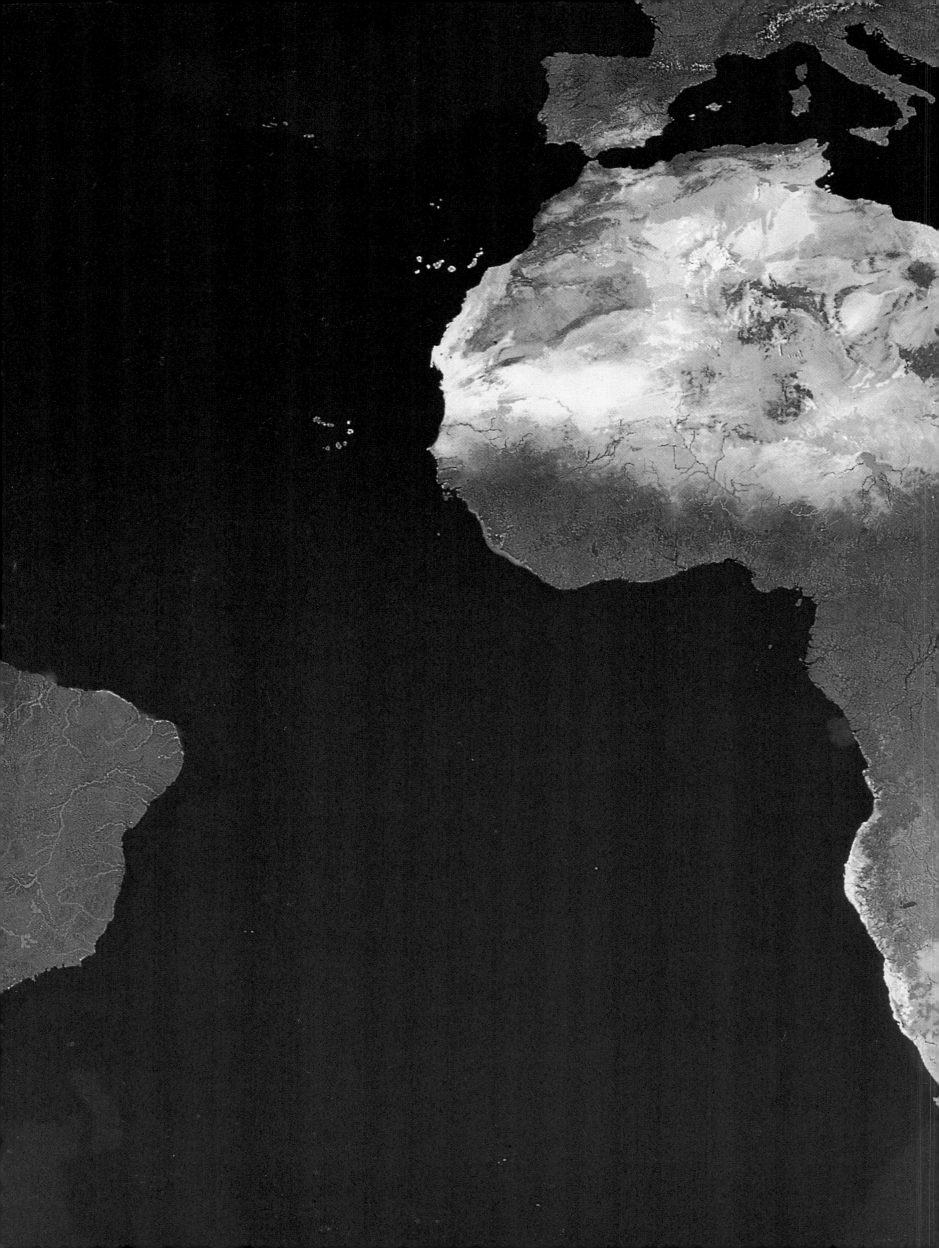

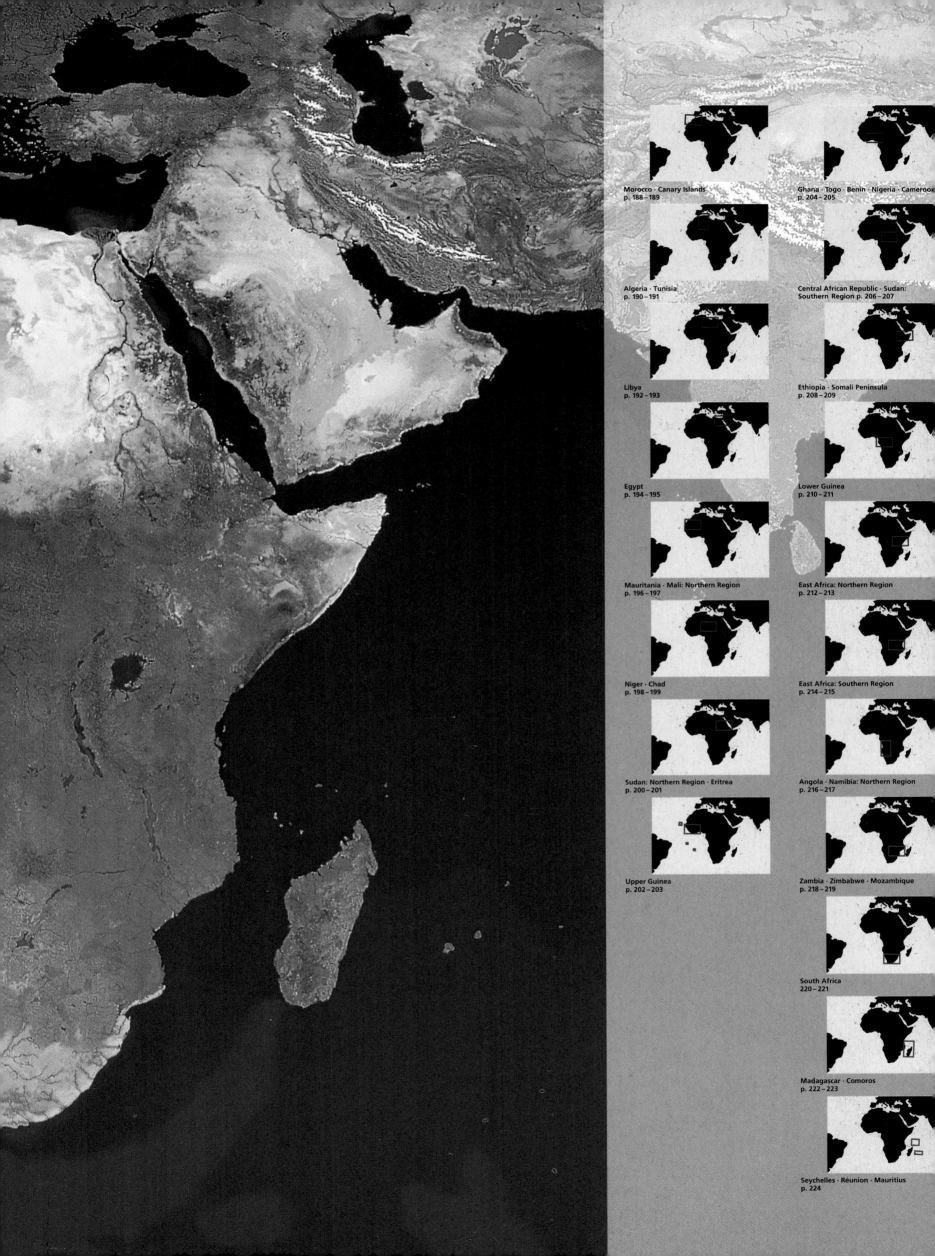

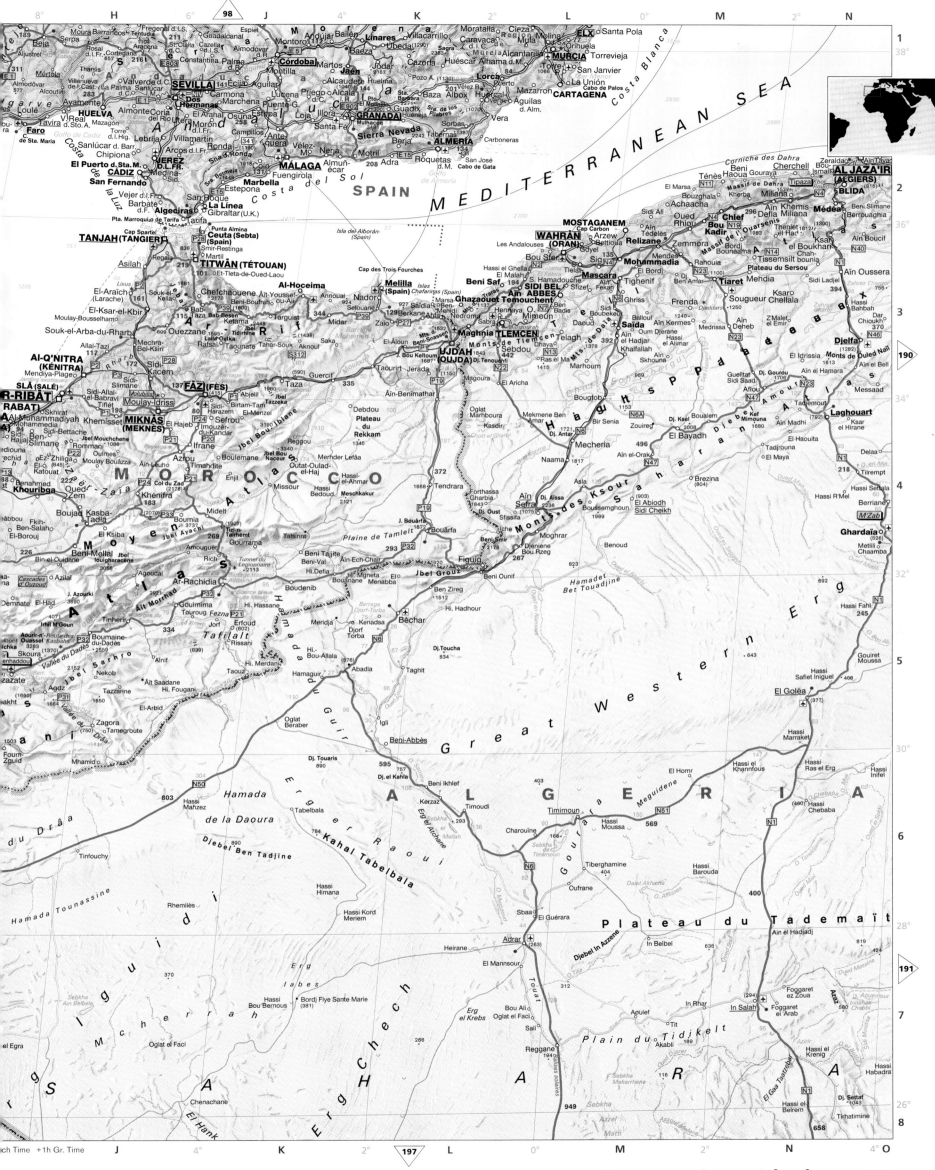

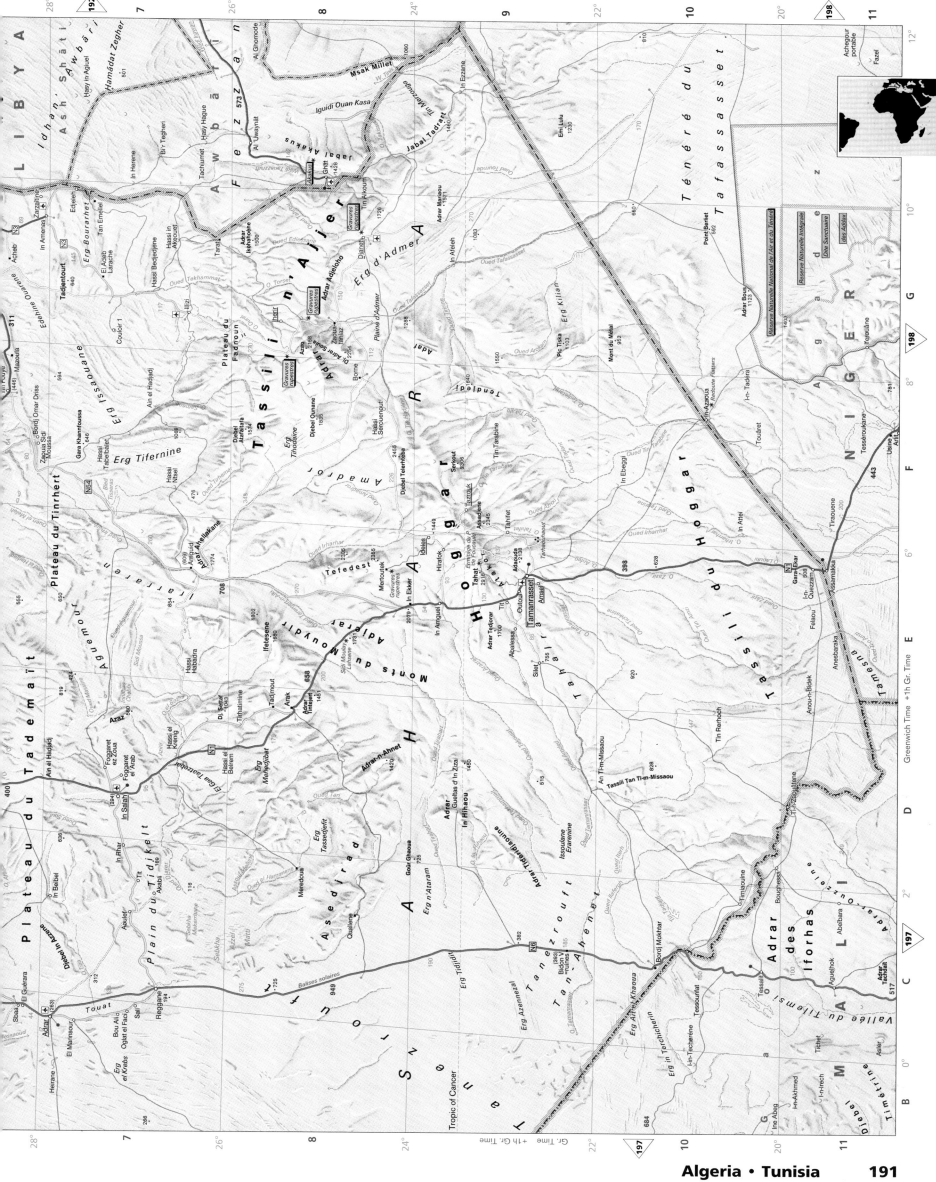

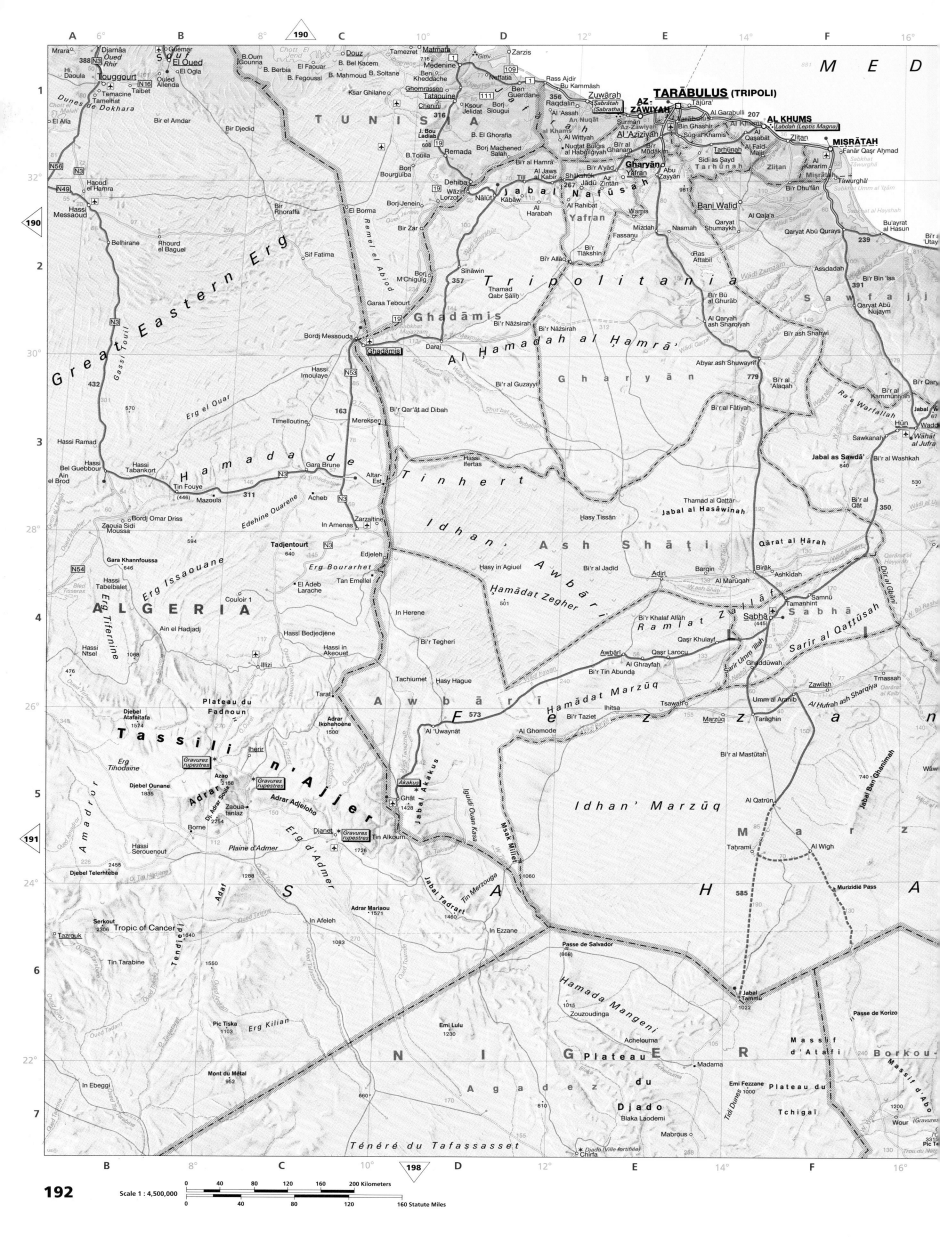

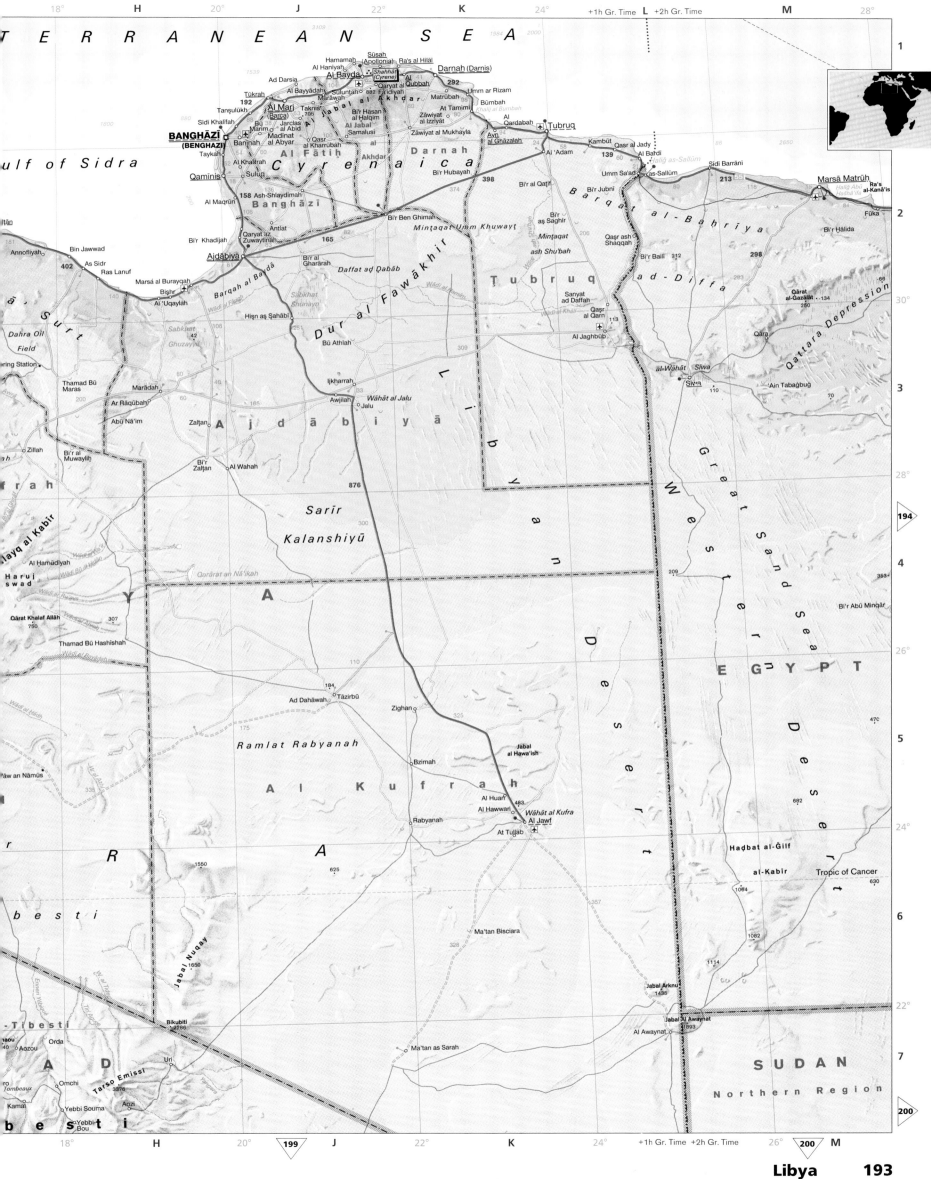

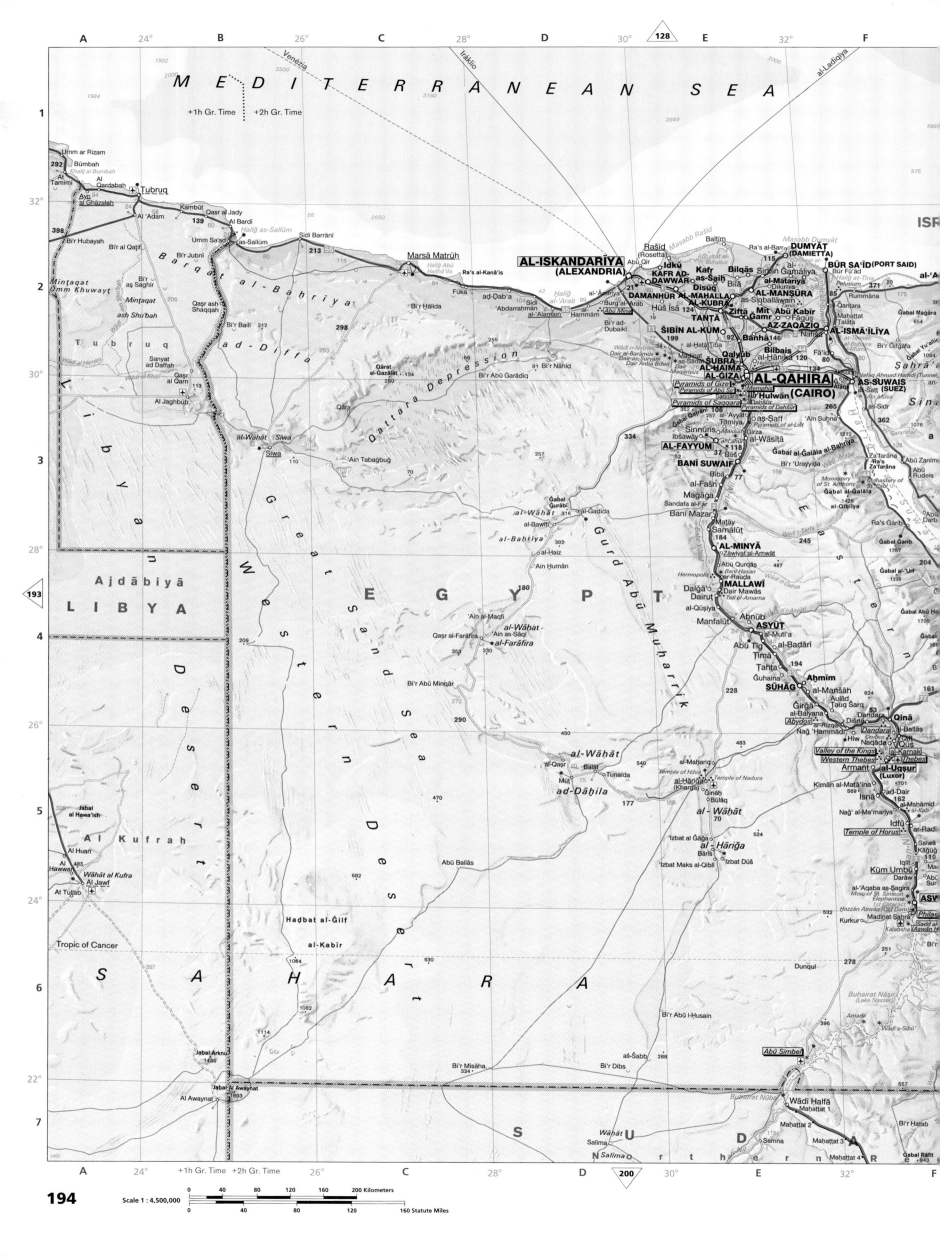

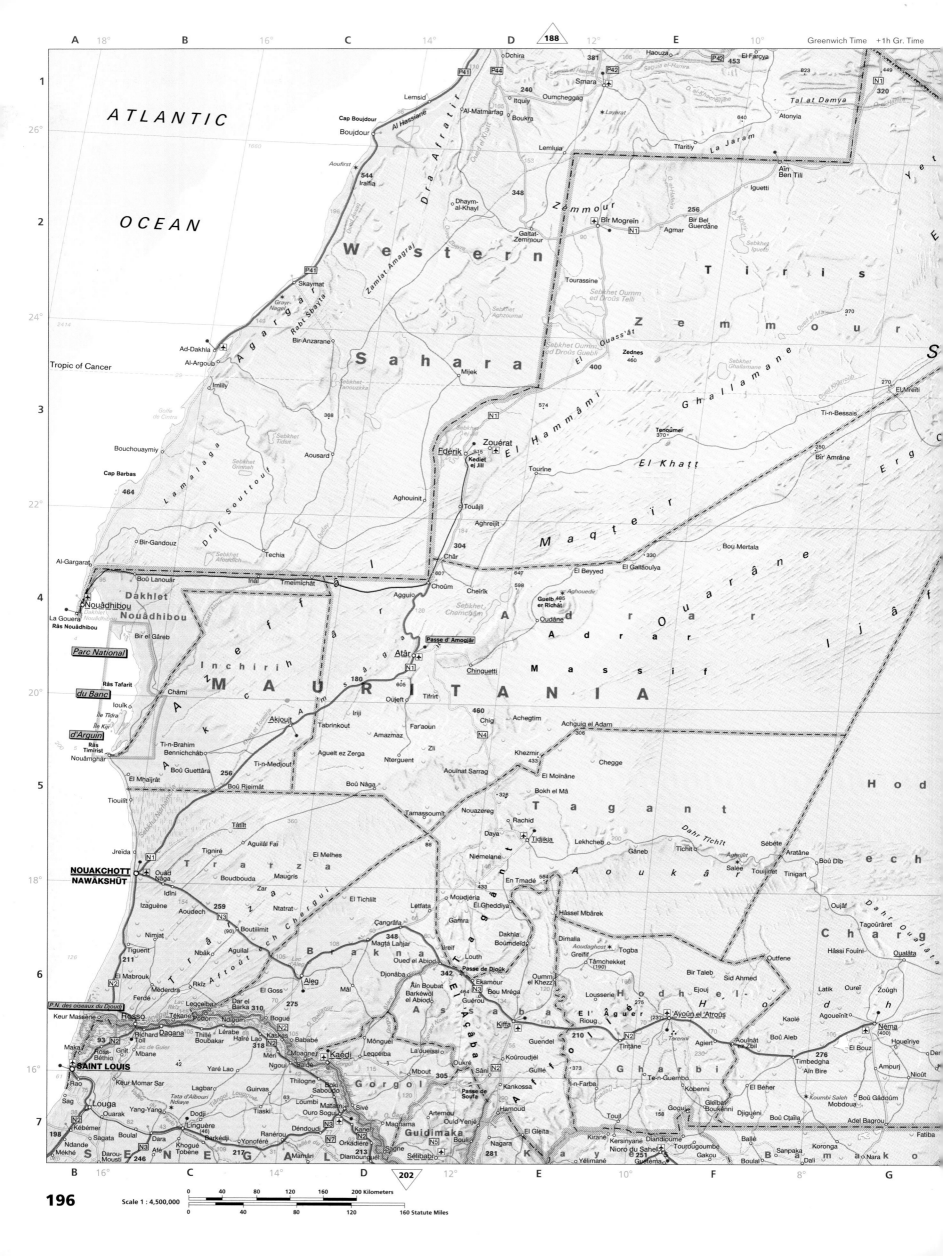

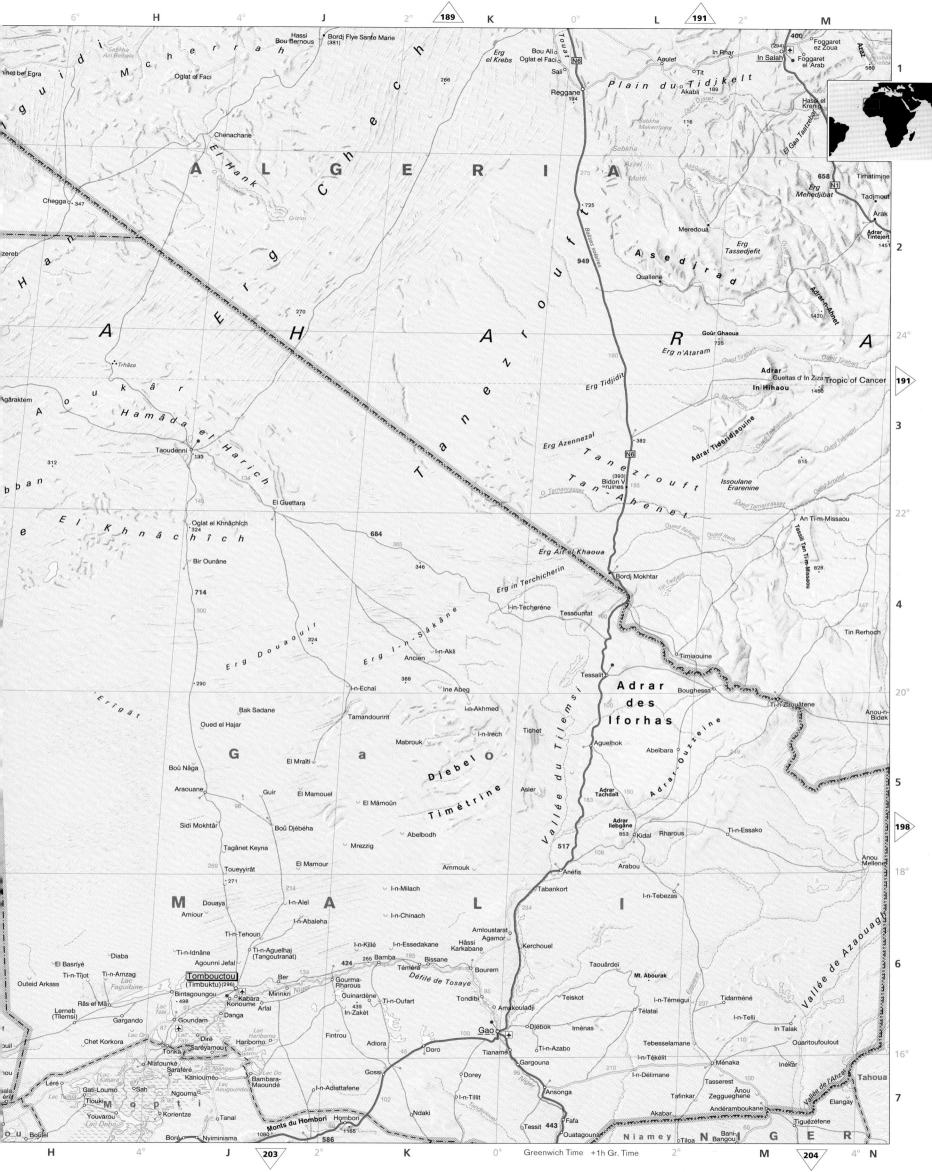

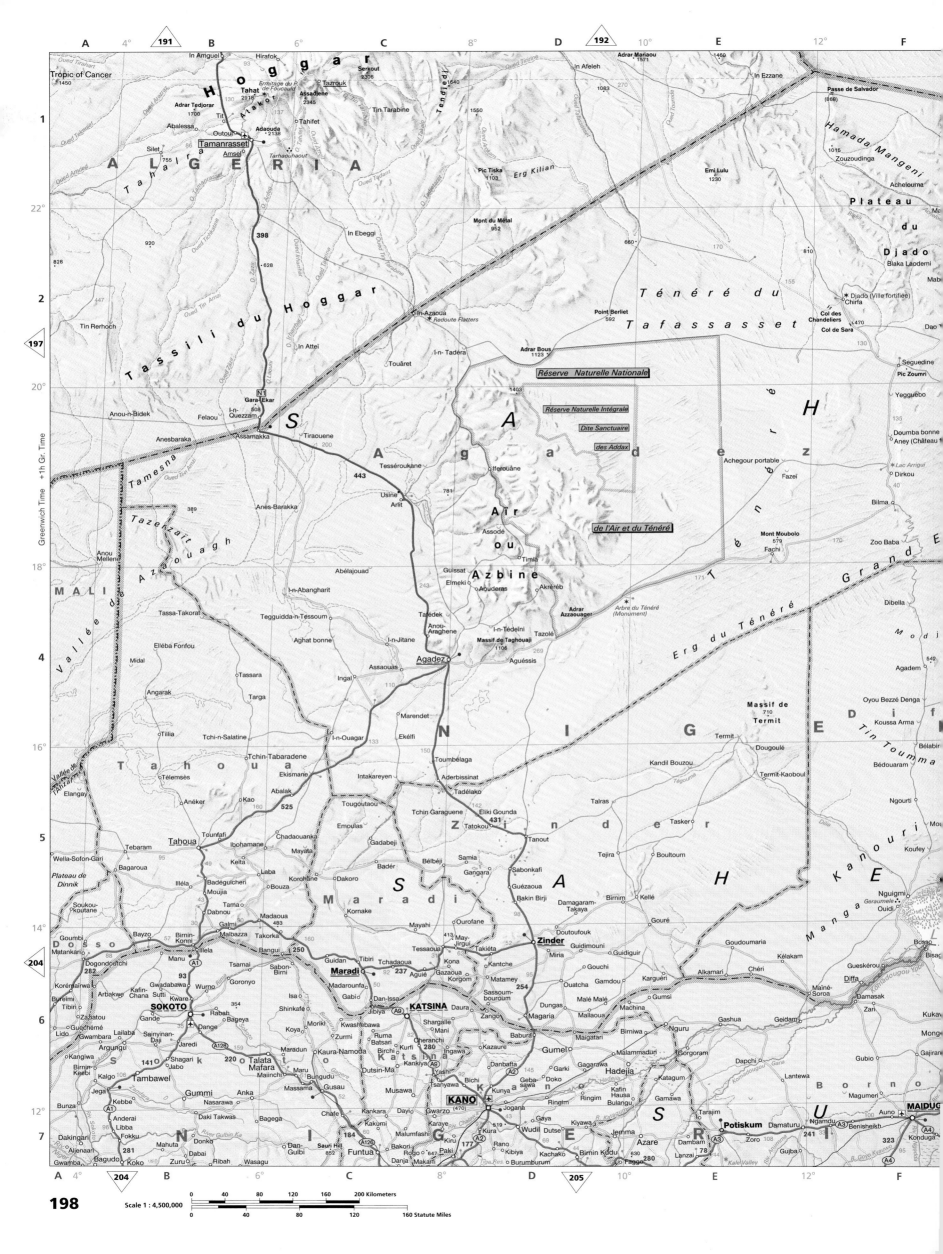

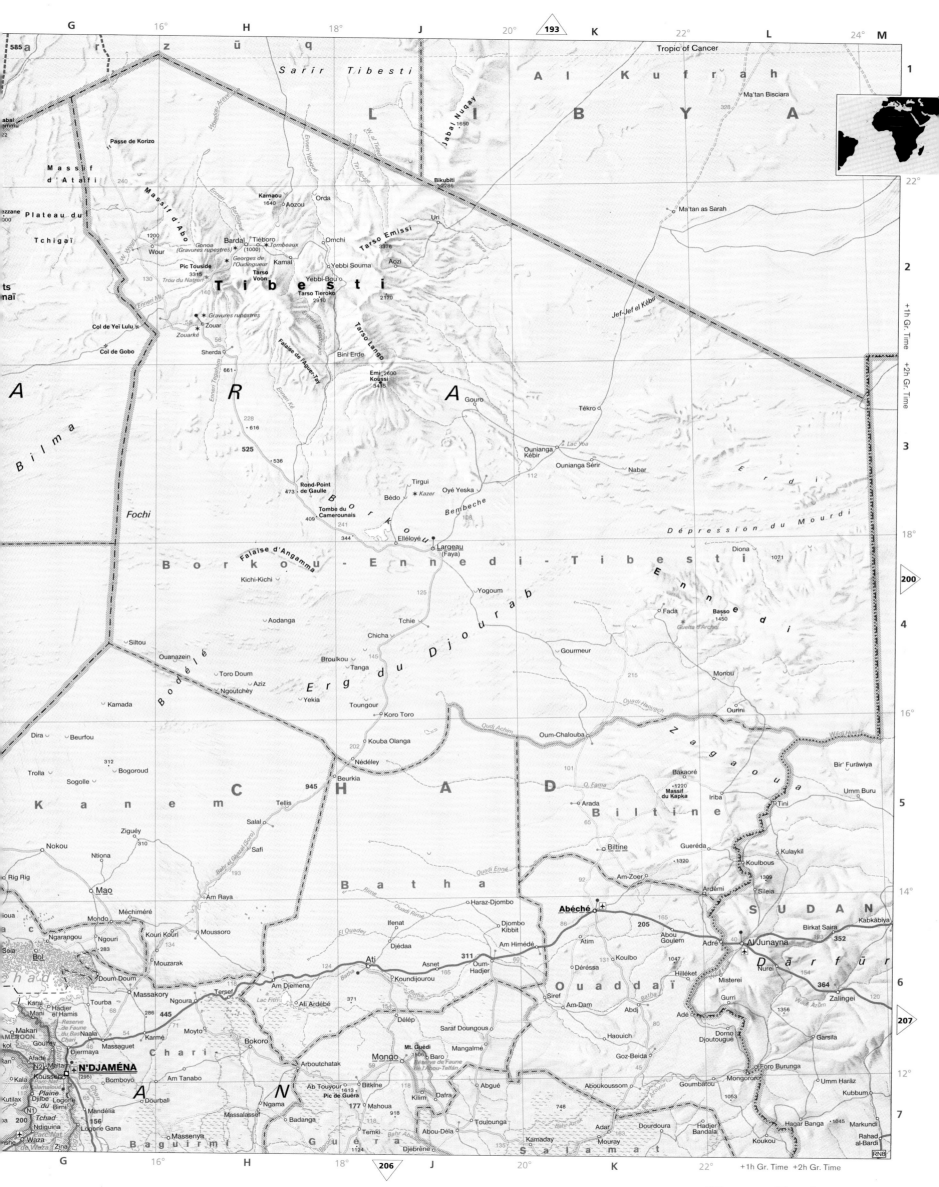

Tropic of Cancer

L I B Y A

Sarir Tibesti

Al Kufrah

Jabal Nugay

Ma'tan Bisciara

328

G a b a l
585 a

Massif
d'Atafi

Plateau du
Tchigaï

Passe de Korizo

Massif d'Abo

Karnaou
1640

Orda

Aozou

Bikubiti
2286

Ma'tan as Sarah

240

1200

Gonoa
(Gravures rupestres)
(1000)

Bardaï

Tiéboro

Tombeaux

Omchi

Uri

Pic Touside
3315

Georges de
l'Oudingueur

Kamal

Yebbi Souma

Aozi

130

Tärso
Voon

Yebbi-Bou

T i b e s t i

Tarso Emissi
3376

Jef-Jef el Kébir

Trou du Natron

140

Tarso Tieroko
2910

2170

Col de Yeï Lulu

Gravures rupestres

Zouar

58

Zouarké

56

A

Col de Gobo

Sherda

661

R

Falaise de l'Aguer-Tay

Bini Erde

Tarso Lango

Gouro

Tékro

Jef-Jef el Kébir

A

B i l m a

Fochi

525

228

616

536

Emi
Koussi
3415

2600

Bembeche
108

Ouníanga
Kébir

Lac Yoa

Ounianga Sérir

Nabar

E
r
d
i

112

Rond-Point
de Gaulle
473

Tirgui

Bédo

Kazer

Oyé Yeska

Dépression du Mourdi

B

Tombe du
Camerounais
409

241

o

r

k

344

Elléloyé

Largeau
(Faya)

Diona

1071

o

u

Falaise d'Angamma

B o r k o u - E n n e d i - T i b e s t i

200

Kichi-Kichi

125

Yogoum

E
n
n

Fada

Basso
1450

d i

Aodanga

Tchie

Guelta d'Archeï

Chicha

145

Gourmeur

Monou

E r g   d u   D j o u r a b

Broulkou

Tanga

215

Toro Doum

Aziz

Ngoutchèy

Yekia

Siltou

Ouanazein

B

o

d

é

l

é

Kamada

Toungour

Koro Toro

Ourini

Z

Dira

Beurfou

202

Kouba Olanga

Oued Achim

Oum-Chalouba

a

g

Bir' Furäwiya

312

Nédéley

101

O. Fama

Bakaoré

+1220
Massif
du Kapka

a

Umm Buru

Trolla

Bogoroud

945

Beurkia

Iriba

Tini

w

Sogolle

C

H

A

D

B i l t i n e

Tellis

Arada

a

Ziguéy

310

Salal

65

o

Nokou

Safi

K

a

n

e

m

Biltine

Guéréda

Koulbous

1309

Kulaykil

Rig Rig

193

1320

Am-Zoer

Ardémi

Sileia

Mao

Am Raya

B

a

t

h

a

Quadi Enne

92

Haraz-Djombo

Abéché

205

165

S U D A N

Birkat Saira

Kabkâbiya

Méchiméré

Mondo

Ifenat

Djombo
Kibbit

86

Atim

Abou
Goulem

Adré

40

Al Junayna

352

Ngarangou

Ngouri

134

Moussoro

Djédaa

Am Himédé

89

Koulbo

131

1047

D a r f u r

Bol

283

Mouzarak

Ati

Asnet

311

Oum-
Hadjer

Déréssa

Hilléket

Nurei

154

Doum Doum

124

Am Djemena

Baro

185

Koundijourou

Am-Dam

Abdj

Adé

1356

Gurri

364

Zalingei

120

Tourba

Tersef

Ali Ardébé

371

Siref

Saraf Doungous

Misteréi

Chari

445

Ngama

Moyto

Bokoro

154

Délép

Abou-
koussom

Haouich

Dorno
Djoutougué

Garsila

Karal
Mani

Hadjer
el Hamis

68

54

Karmé

Massaguet

Mongo

Mt. Guédi
1506

Mangalmé

Goz-Beida

45

Foro Burunga

Umm Haräz

Naala

Goulfey

Djermaya

Massakory

Arboutchatak

59

Reserve de Faune
du Bao-Bolo-Tellan

Goumbatou

1053

Mongororo

Kubbum

N'DJAMÉNA
(295)

Bomboyó

Am Tanabo

Bitkine

Abgué

748

Dourbali

Ab Touyour

Mahoua

Kilim

Dafra

Adar

Dourdoura

Hadjer
Bandala

Hagar Banga

1045

Markundi

156

Mandélia

Massalassét

Pic de Guéra

177

Ngama

918

Temkí

Touloungo

Kamaday

Mouray

Koukou

Rahad
al-Bardi

Ndiguina

Logone Gana

Massenya

Badanga

G u é r a

Bahr Abou

Abou-Déïa

1124

Djébrène

135

S a l a m a t

Waza

Zina

B a g u i r m i

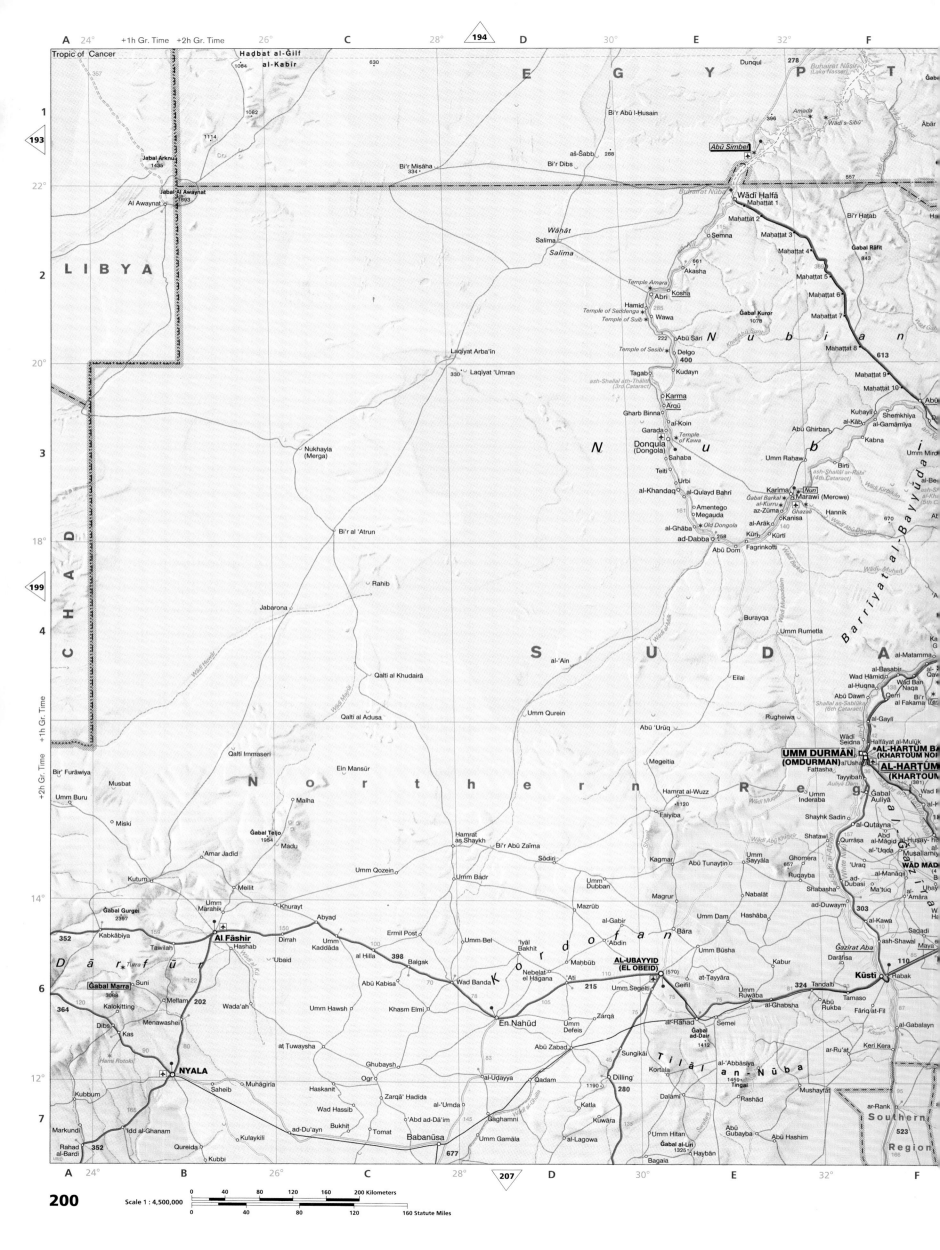

A 24° +1h Gr. Time +2h Gr. Time 26° C 28° ▽ 194 D 30° E 32° F

Tropic of Cancer

Ḥaḍbat al-Ǧilf al-Kabīr

E G Y P T

Dunqul
278
Buḥairat Nāṣir
(Lake Nasser)

1084
630
1082
1114
357

Bi'r Abū l-Ḥusain
Amada
396
Wādi s-Sibū'
Ābār

1

Jabal Arknu
1435

aš-Šabb
288
Abū Simbel

Bi'r Dibs

193

Bi'r Misāḥa
334

557

22°

Jabal Al Awaynat
1893

Al Awaynat

Wādī Halfā
Mahaṭṭat 1

Bi'r Ḥaṭab

Wāḥāt
Salīma

Mahaṭṭat 2
Semna

Mahaṭṭat 3

2 L I B Y A

Salīma

561
Akasha

Mahaṭṭat 4
Ǧabal Rāfit
843

Temple Amara
385

Mahaṭṭat 5

Abri
Kosha

Mahaṭṭat 6

Hamid
285
Temple of Seddenga
Temple of Sulb
Wawa

Ǧabal Kuror
1078

Mahaṭṭat 7

N u b i a n

Abū Sārī
222

Mahaṭṭat 8
613

Laqiyat Arba'īn

Temple of Sesibi
Delgo
400

20°

330
Laqiyat 'Umran

Tagab
Kudayn

ash-Shallāl ath-Thālit
(3rd Cataract)

Mahaṭṭat 9

Mahaṭṭat 10

Karma
Argū

Kuḥaylī
al-Kāb
Shemkhiya
al-Gamāmiya

Gharb Binna
al-Koin

Abū Ghirbān

Kabna
Umm Mird

N u b

3

Nukhayla
(Merga)

Garada
Temple of Kawa

Donqula
(Dongola)

Umm Rahaw

Birti
ash-Shallāl ar-Rābi'
(4th Cataract)

Sahaba

Teiti
Urbi

al-Bei

Karima
Nuri

al-Khandaq
al-Quļayd Bahrī

Ǧabal Barkal
al-Kurru
az-Zūma

Marawi (Merowe)
Hannik

Wādī Abū Dawm
(5th C

Bi'r al 'Atrun

Amentego
Megauda
161
Old Dongola
140

Ghazali
Kanisa

18°

al-Ghāba
ad-Dabba
258

Kūrī
Kūrtī

670
Ab

Abū Dom
Fagrinkotti

199

Rahib

Wādī Barkal
Wādī Muḥeit

Jabarona

4

Burayqa

Umm Rumetla

al-Matamma
Ka

Qalti al Khudairā

al-'Ain
Eilai

Wad Ḥāmid
al-Basabir
al-Qav

Abū Dawn
Shallāl as-Sablūka
(6th Cataract)

al-Huqna

Qerri
Bi'r
al Fakama

Wādī al-Milk

Wādī Howar

Qalti al Adusa

Umm Qurein

Rugheiwa

al-Gaylī

Abū 'Urūq

Wādī Seidna
Halfāyat al-Mulūk

Qalti Immaseri

Megeitia

AL-HARTŪM BA
(KHARTOUM NOR

Ein Mansūr

N o r t h e r n

al-'Usha
Fattasha

UMM DURMĀN
(OMDURMAN)

AL-HARTŪM
(KHARTOUM
381

Bi'r Furāwiya

Musbat

Malha

Hamrat al-Wuzz
1120

Tayyibah
Auliyā Daya

Umm Wad

Umm Buru

Miski

Faiyiba

Shaykh Sadin

al-Qutayna

al-Huṣay
Musallam

Ǧabal Teljo
1954

Madu

Hamrat
as Shaykh

Sōdiri

Inderaba

157
Shatawi

Abd
al-Māgid
Qurrāsa
'Uqda

WĀD MAD

5

'Amar Jadid

Bi'r Abū Zaīma

Kagmar

Abū Tunaytin

Umm
Sayyāla
657
Ghomera

Ruqayba

'Uraq
al-Managil
ad-Dubasi

Kutum

Mellit

Umm Qozein

Umm Bādr

Mazrūb

Umm
Dubban

Umm Dam

Magrur

Nabalāt

Shabasha

Ma'tūq

Uḥay
al-Amāra

Ǧabal Gurgei
2397

Umm
Marahik

Khurayt

al-Gabir

Hashāba

ad-Duwaym
303

al-Kawa

14°

352

Kabkābiya
159

Al Fāshir
150

Abyaḍ

Ermil Post

K o r d o f a n

Abdin

Umm Būsha

Ǧazīrat Aba
Darāfisa

ash-Shawal
Maya

110

Tawilah
Turra
122

Hashab
Dirrah

Umm
Kaddāda

al-Hilla
Umm Bel

'Iyāl
Bakhit

Mahbūb
Bāra

Kabur

D ā r f ū r

398
Balgak

Abū Kabisa
70

Wad Banda
78

Nebelat
el Hāgana
'Ati

AL-UBAYYID
(EL OBEID)
(570)

at-Tayyāra
Umm
Ruwāba
75

Abū
Rukba

324
Tandalti

Kūsti
Rabak

Ǧabal Marra
3088

Suni

Mellam
202

Wada'ah

Umm Hawsh

Khasm Elmi
105

215
Umm Segelti
Geifil

75
al-Ghabsha

Tamaso
Fāriq at-Fil
87

6

364
120

Kalokitting

Menawashei
90
80

aṭ Ṭuwaysha

En Nahūd

Umm
Defeis

Zārqā

75
ar-Rahad

Semei

al-Gabalayn

Dibs
Kas

Hami Rotoki

Ghubaysh

Ogr

Abū Zabad

Sungikai

Ǧabal
ad-Dair
1412

al-'Abbāsiya
1459
Tingal

Keri Kera

ar-Ru'at

12°

NYALA

Saheib
Muḥāgiria

Haskanit

Zarqā' Hadida

al-'Umda

Qadam

Kortala

Dilling

1190
280

Dalāmi

Rashād

T i l ā l   a n - Ñ u b a

Mushayfāt

ar-Rank

95

Kubbum

Markundi

'Idd al-Ghanam

Kulaykili

Wad Hassib

Bukhīt

'Abd ad-Dā'im
145

Gaghamni
135

al-Lagowa

Katla
Kūwāra

Umm Hitan

Abū
Gubayba

Ǧabal al-Liri
1325
Haybān

Bagaia

S o u t h e r n

7

352

Rahad
al-Bardi

Qureida
Kubbi

ad-Du'ayn
Tomat

Babanūsa
677

Umm Gamāla

523

R e g i o n

A 24° B 26° C 28° ▽ 207 D 30° E 32° F

200

Scale 1 : 4,500,000

0   40   80   120   160   200 Kilometers

0   40   80   120   160 Statute Miles

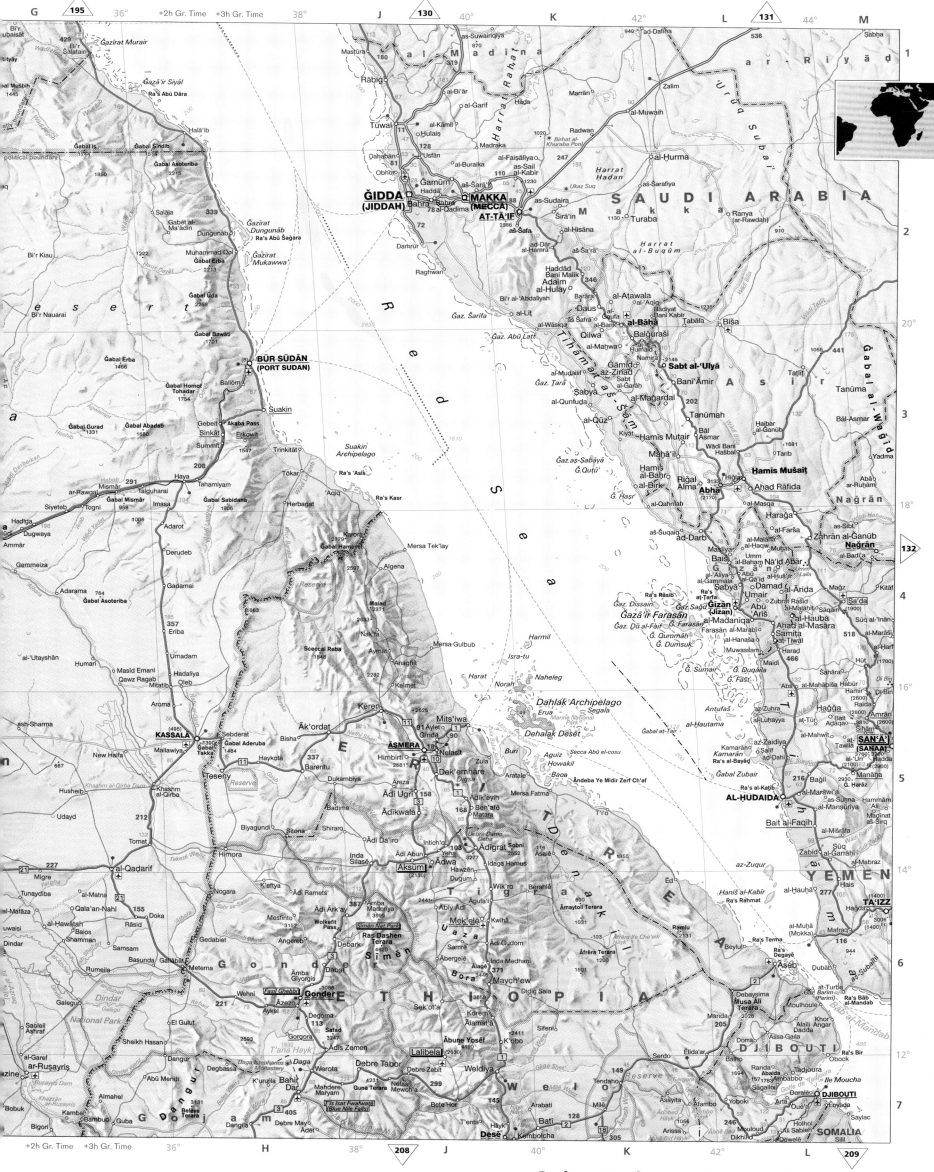

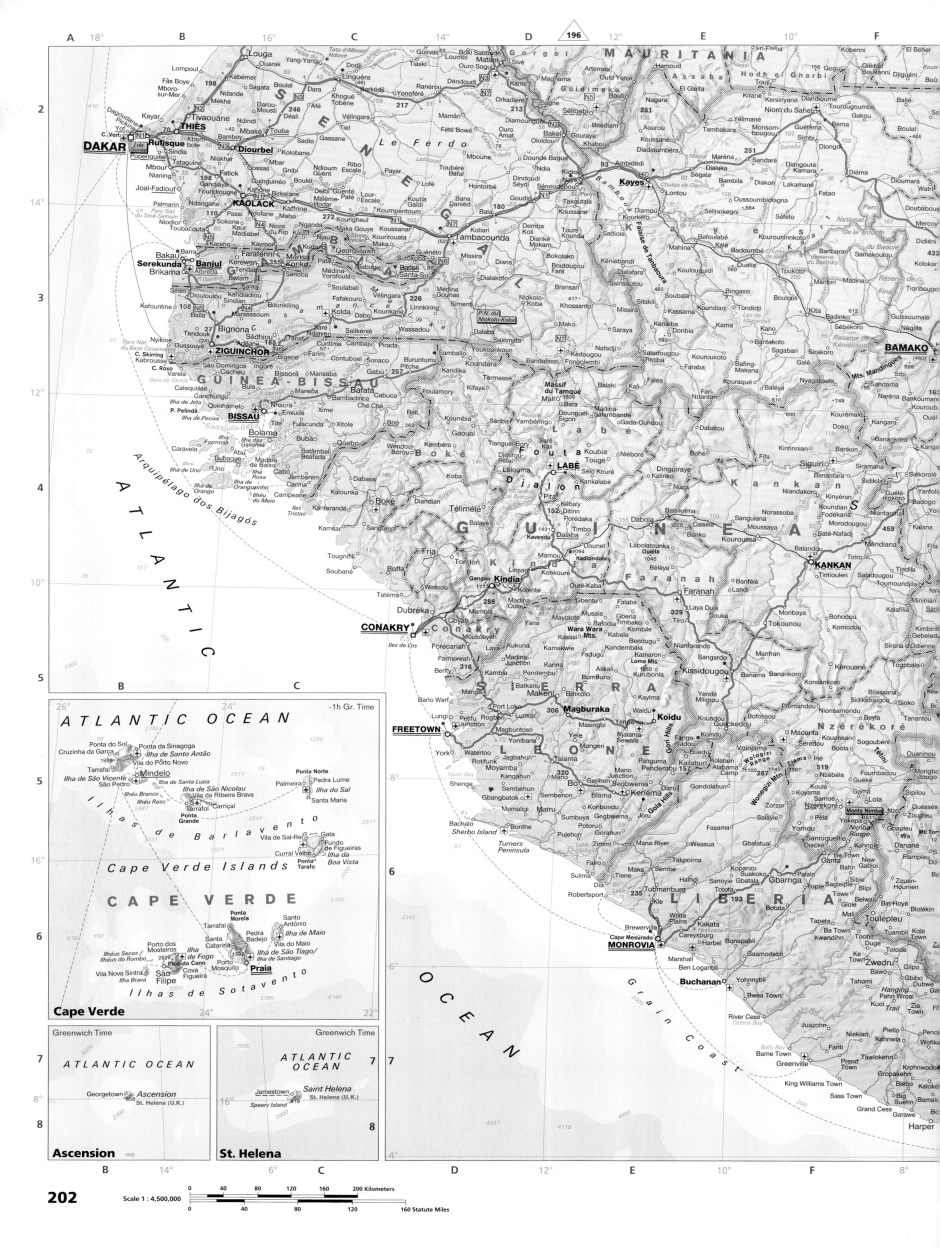

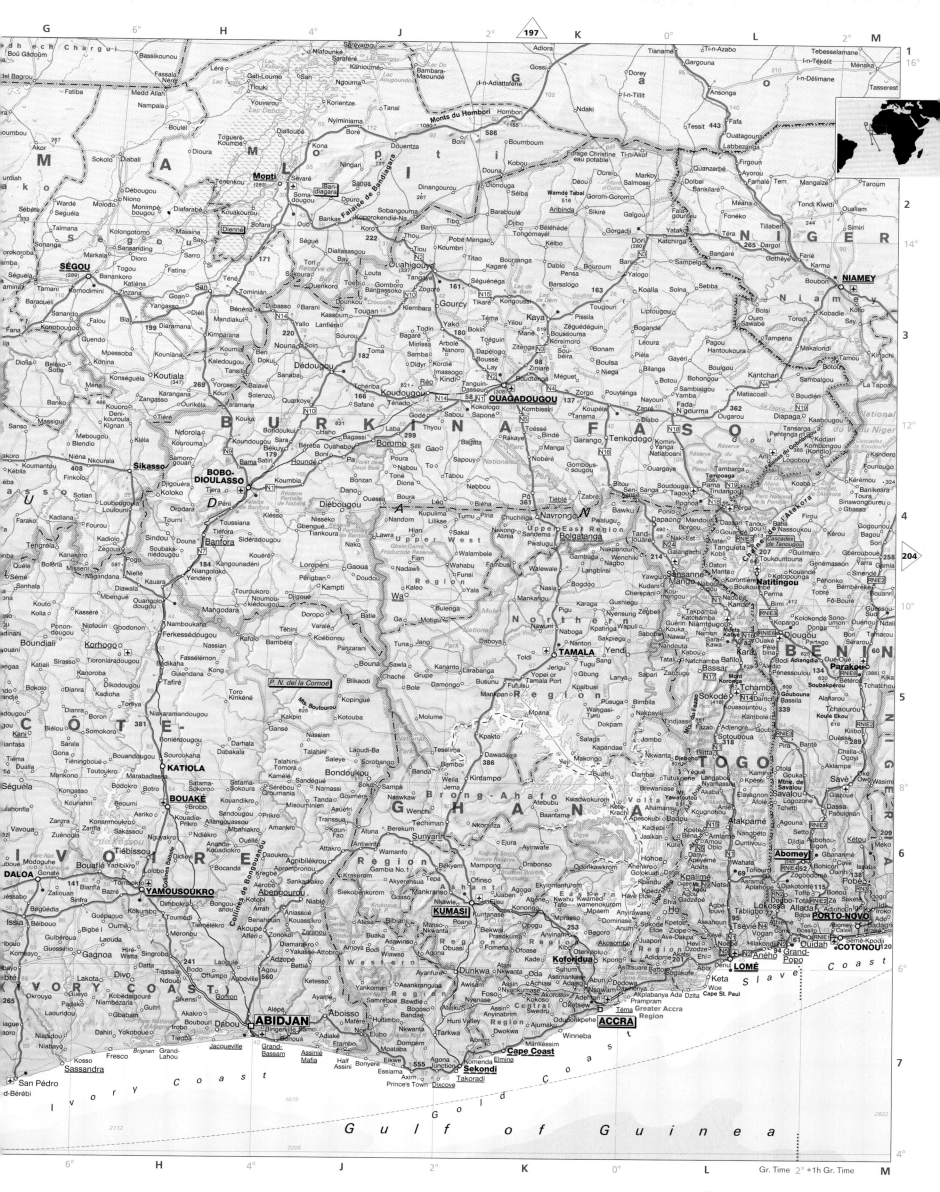

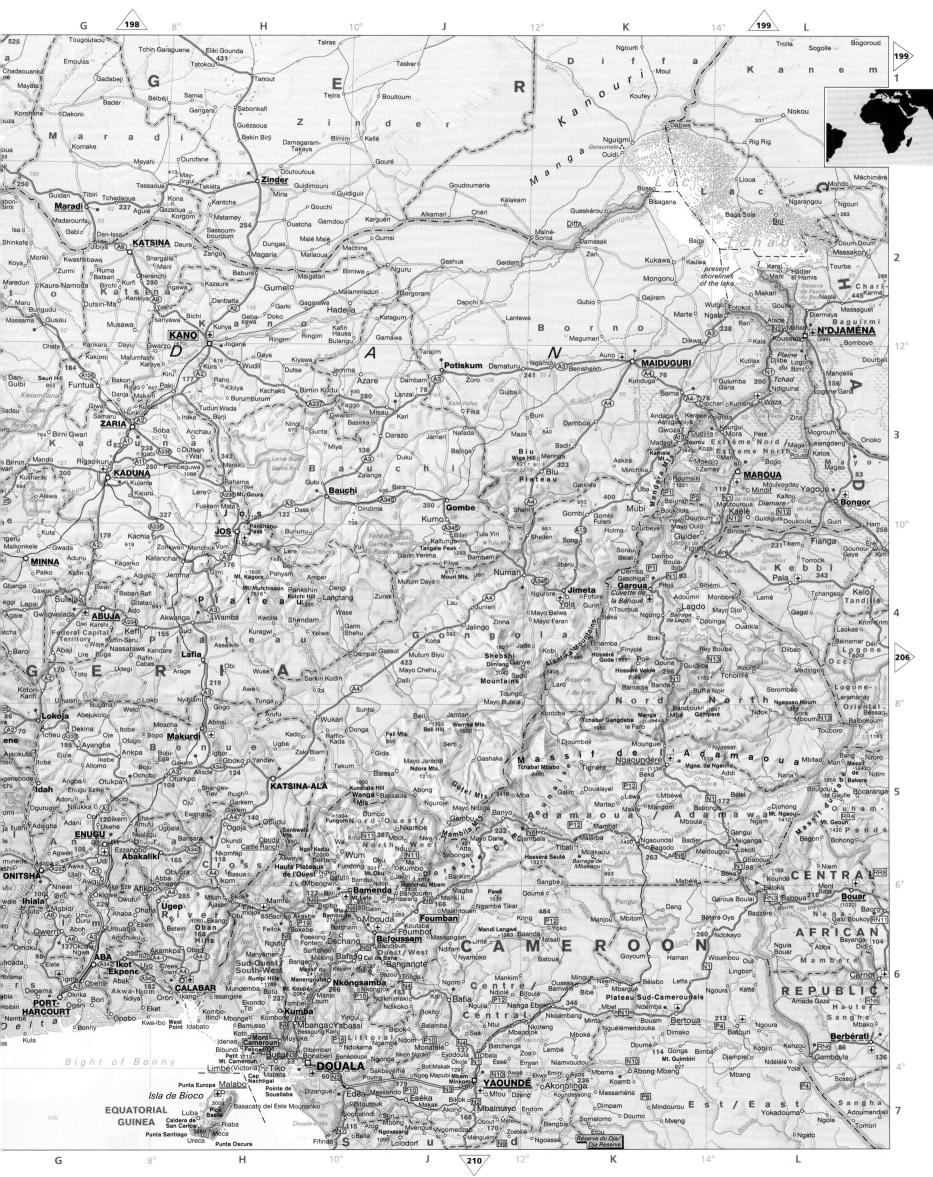

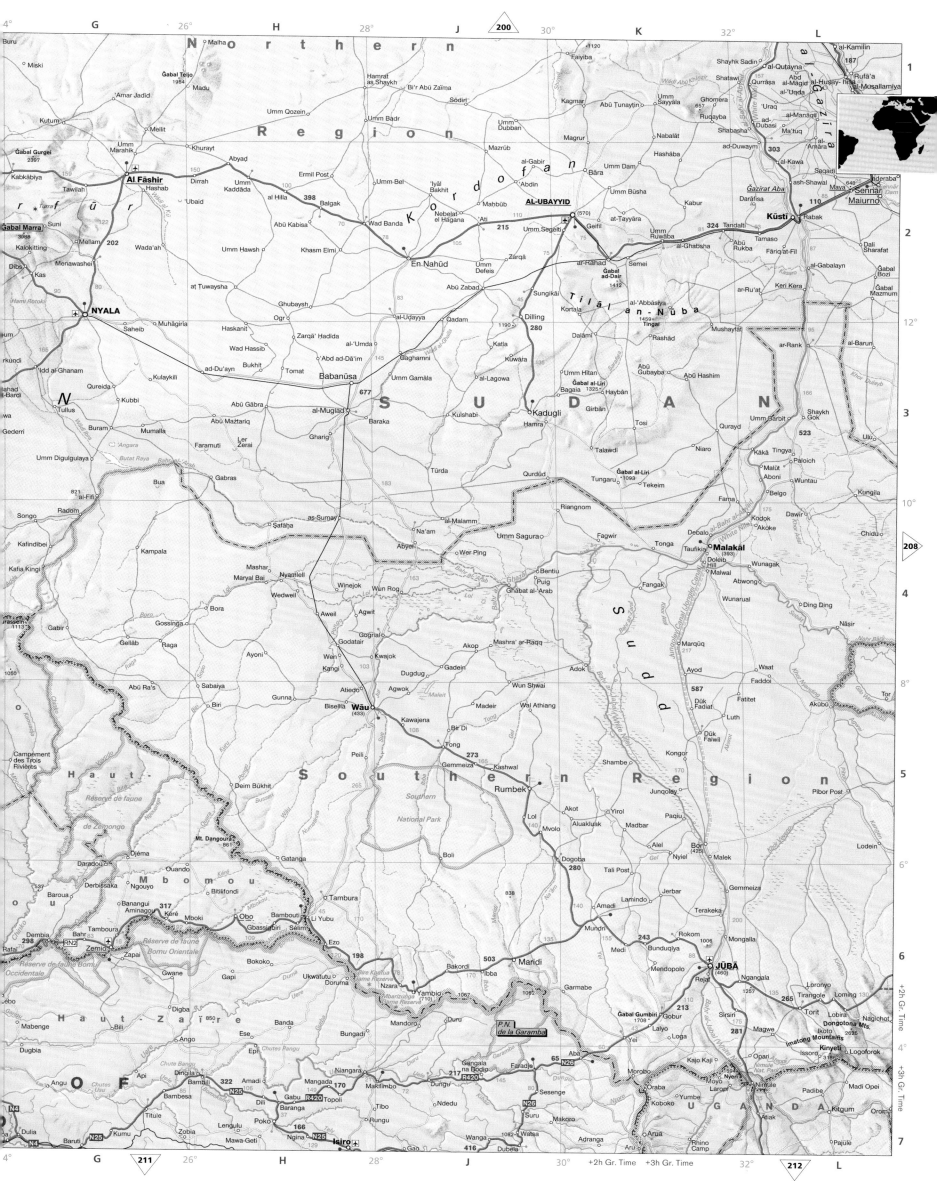

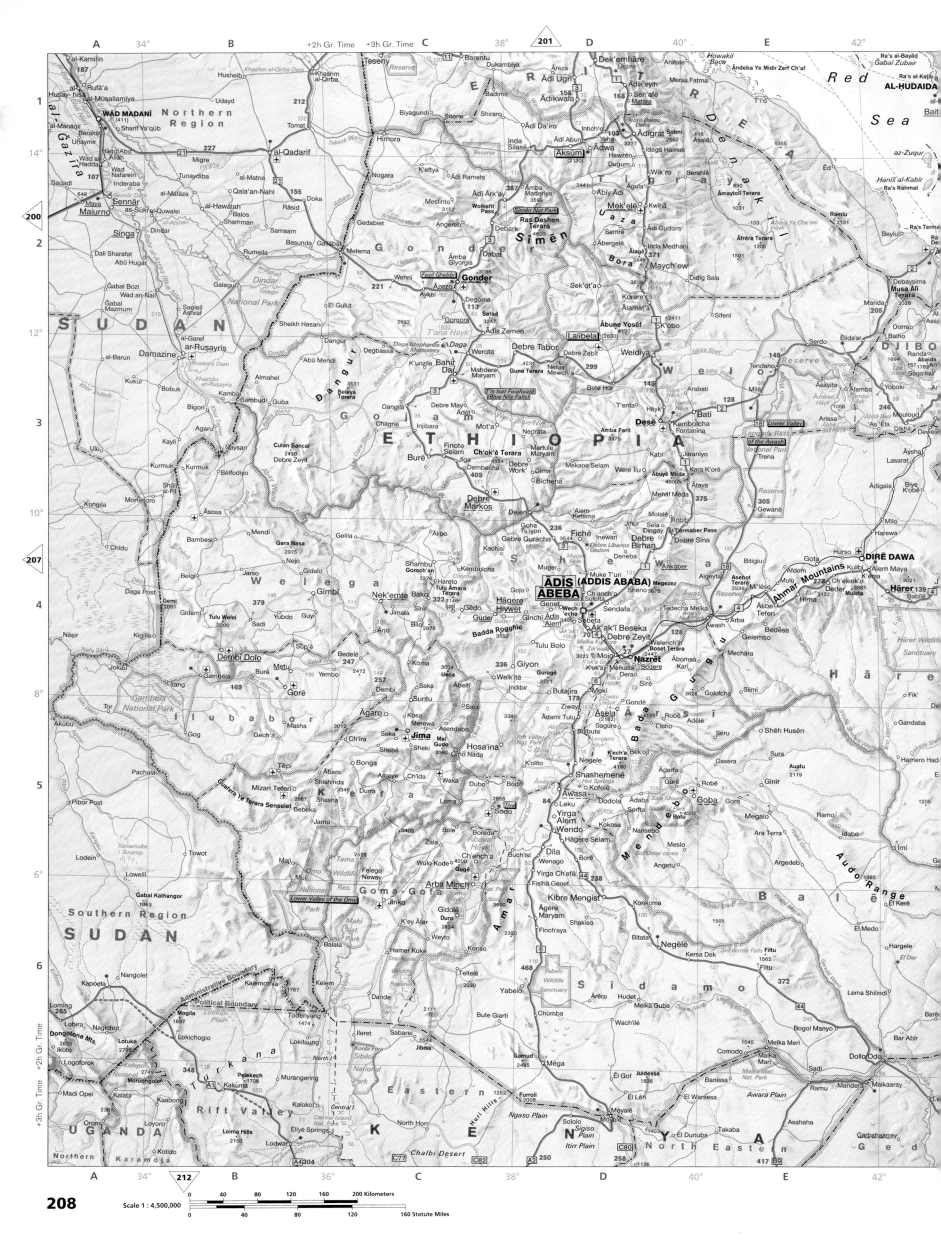

44° G 46° H 48° J 50° K 52° L

Y   E   M   E   N

Manāḥa
(2900)   (2755)
Ma'bar   Harib   Harib
Baihān al-Qasāb   al-Magārim   al-Magārim
Dammār   Gabal Isbil   Nisāb   1076   Tamnūn
Daurān   ·3199   al-Farda   1230
Yarim   Radā'   Miswara   Qusay'ir   Sarār
(2700)   Zafar   Damt   Buwais   Sarār
247   al-Sawādiya   al-Madina   2185   Gail Bāwazir   aṣ-Ṣuhair   as-Sihr   al-Hāmī   al-Gaida
Ibb   94   Habbān   82   Maifa'a   Zulūma   al-Mukallā
Dū Gibla   Qa'taba   690   al-Huwaymi   'Ain al-Guwairi   al-Hasi
as-Sayyāni   3227·   al-Baidā'   Laudar   1010   118   Bi'r 'Ali   Ra's al-Kalb
TA'IZZ   Gabal Sabir   63   aṣ-Ṣurra   Umm Qulaita   al-Haura
al-Ganad   ad-Dāli   1703   al-'Irqa   al-Haura
Musaimir   Saqrā'   Dār   Ahwar   200
Haifān   ar-Rāhida   156   al-Masāni   Dahūka
at-Turba   59   Lahig   2184
Umm Riga   843   58   Zingibār
Bi'r Ahmad   Madinat as-Sa'b   'ADAN
Dār   Little Aden   (ADEN)
Mughahhar

G   u   l   f   o   f   A   d   e   n

Socotra
(Yemen)   Qalansīya
Ra's Šu'b
Ra's Haisat   'Abd al-Kūrī   The Brothers
an-Naum   Samha   Darza

12°

Raas Caluula
(Ilaawe)
Caluula   Bereeda
Geesaley   Raas Caseyr
Bandar Murcaayo   (C. Gwardafuy)
Dhurbo   1510   Tooxin
Qandala   Ceel Gaal
Boosaaso   2135
(Bender Cassim)   togga Galal   914
Maydh   Karin   Bargaal
Laasqoray   585   645   Ceelayo   1810   Raas Binna
Maydh   940   2000   Buuraha Cal Madow   1450   Buuraha Cal Miskaat   570   3°
Xiis   2100   Hadaaftimo   Laaso Dawaco   Handa
Raas Khansiir   Shimbiris   2416   Ceerigaabo   Meeladeen   Hurdiyo   210   Raas Xaafuun
Karino   1531   Dayaxa   Ufeyn   370   Xaafuun   (Dante)
Laas   Subagle   Yufle   Buraan   Iskushuban
Musse   Ceel Afweyn   Samaysa Dheer
Berbera   1005   Sanaag   Bari   4020

b   a   n   877   158   148   1995   Buuraha Wagar   1998   Shiikh   Bannaanka   Xingalool   Rako Raxo   A   Bandarbeyla
a Galbeed   Dhubbato   Gubato   1510   Qardho   Adinsoone   togga Gono   Raas Macbar   10°
Dhubbato   Mandheera   Bannaanka Saraar   Garadag   Dhuudo   320
Hargeysa   Cadaadley   Burco   Xudun   Taleex   Xalin   830
Godhyogol   1370   Bandar Wanaag   268   Inaafmadow   120   togga Tog Dheer   Bannaanka   Dhoodi   Nugaal   Sinujiif   4°
Haro Shiikh   177   Kirit   Caynabo   1110   Laascaanood   132   Garoowe   Kalis
Salahleh/   Ceek   Wadamago   141   273   Rabaable   Garoowe   Raas Gabbac
Salahly   Inegub   Durukhsi   Daryaleh   1125   Eyl
Ãwarê   Deror   Shahda Bohotleh   260   Qooriga Neegro   Raas Ilig   8°
Degeh Bur   Misrak Gashemo   Domo   662   Laas Aano
Sasabeneh   Curale   Danot   Bur Tinle   Jirriiban
Bircot   188   1105   525   El Hamurre
O   g   a   d   e   ñ   Lebiolali   Bacaadweyn   Garacad
Warandab   Welwel   Geladi   Bardaale
696   Gedlegubê   Werdêr   Dudub   Beyra   I N D I A N
K'ebri Dehar   Ãgarsararēn   Gaalkacyo   Gal Adhale   Af Barwaarqo
Hadaluma   Yoube   Dagaari   Xingod   Dabaro   Raas Cabaad
K'orahê   85   Gellinsor   383   War Galoh   Iidaan
Shilabo   220   Cadaado   Colguula   4162
Gode   140   Godinlabe   Mirsale
K'elafo   Êl Ãbrêd   Mustahil   Dhuusa Mareeb   Wisil   O C E A N
Êl Bioba   Alaf Badane   Ferfêr   Sina Daqha   Hobyo
Êl K'oran   163   Galguduud   Bulacle   M   Ceel Huur   6°
Ted   Bagoosaar   Habar Cirir   Xarar
Beledweyne   406   Ceelbuur   Xarardheere
(Belet Weyne)   Hiiraan   Jacai   Gal Hareen
akool   Jiiqley   116   Maxaans   Derri   Nooleeye
Xuddur   Ceel Garas   O   Bud Bud   281
Totias   Buqda   Halgen   Muqaakoori
gari   Tayeeglow   Caqabe   Ceel Duubo
Golol   Buulobarde   El Dere
Bulo Balamal   566   Gal Tardo   'Aadan   Mareeq   Masagaweyn
Baydhabo   Magdad   El Cobias   Yabaal
256   Dalandole   S   Gialalassi   Massarole   332   Massaajid   Cali Guduud   4°
Bay   Baydhabo   Omar-Combon   Shabeellaha   Dhexe

44° G 46° H 48° J 50° K 52° L

Ethiopia · Somali Peninsula   209

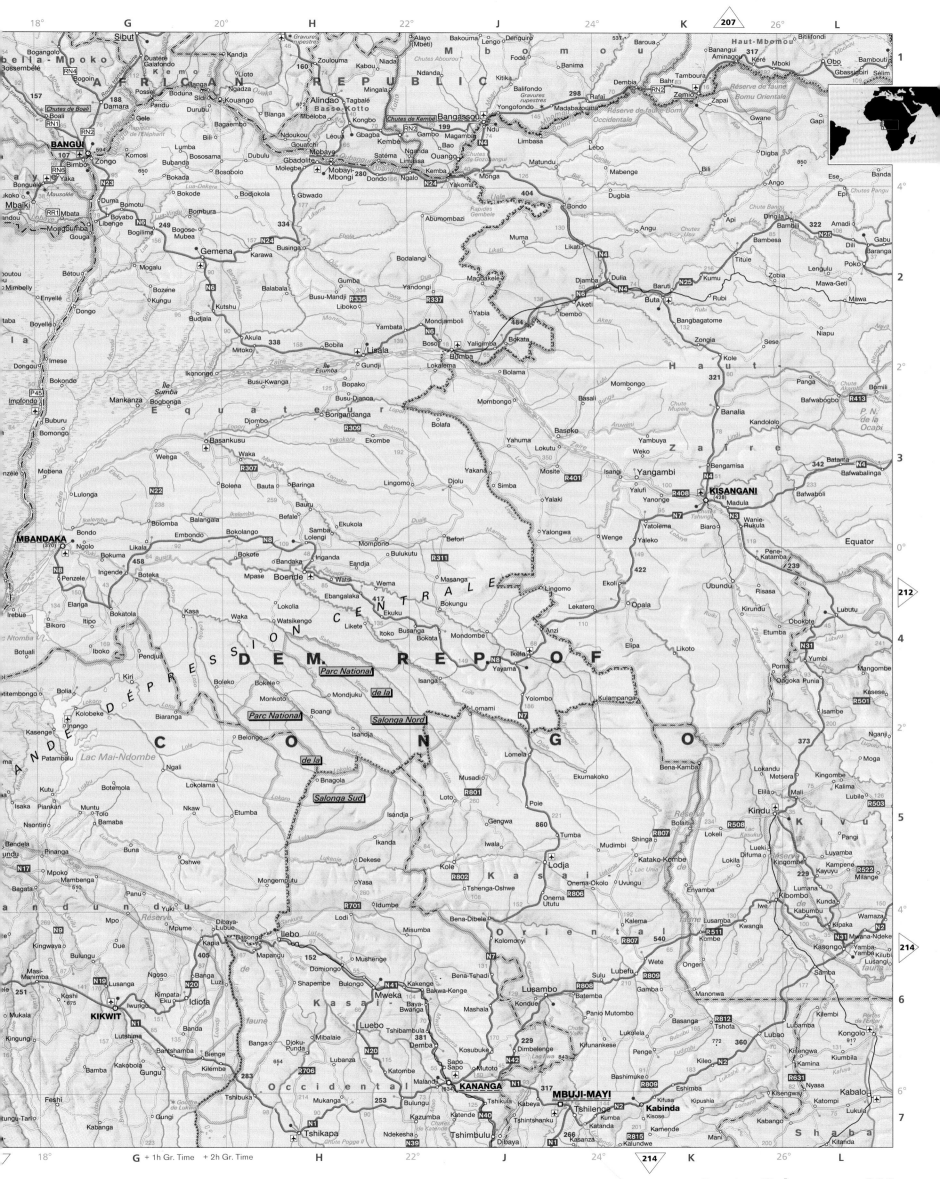

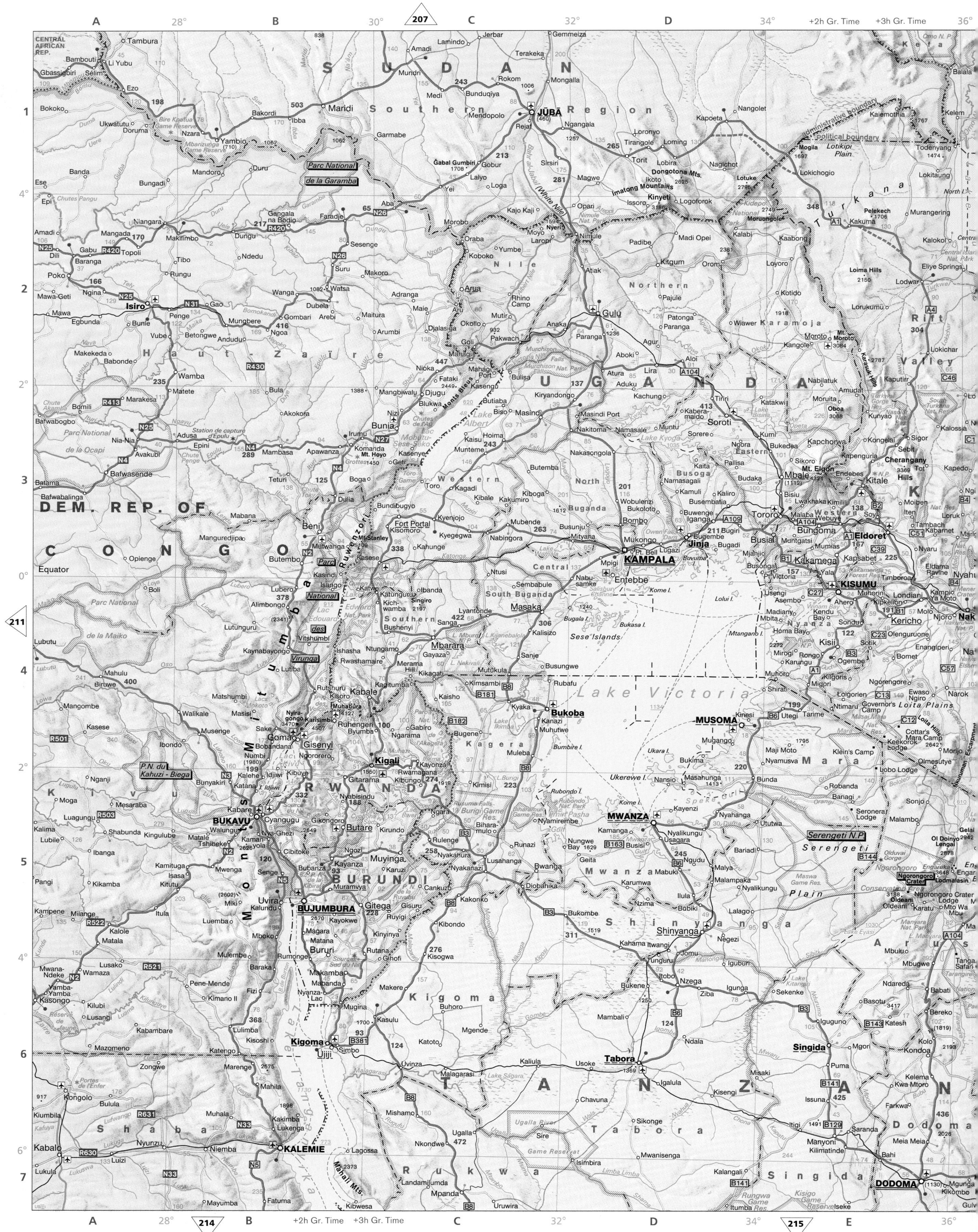

Scale 1 : 4,500,000

0 40 80 120 160 200 Kilometers

0 40 80 120 160 Statute Miles

East Africa: Northern Region   213

DEM. REP. OF CONGO

UGANDA

RWANDA

BURUNDI

ANGOLA

ZAMBIA

BUKAVU
BUJUMBURA
Kigali
Butare
Kigoma
KALEMIE
KANANGA
MBUJI-MAYI
Kabinda
Gandajika
Mwene-Ditu
Kamina
Kolwezi
LIKASI
LUBUMBASHI
CHILILABOMBWE
CHINGOLA
MUFULIRA
KITWE
Kalulushi
LUANSHYA
NDOLA
Mansa

Kasai Oriental
Shaba
Kivu
Copperbelt

P.N. de la Salonga Nord
P.N. Kahuzi-Biega
Parc National de l'Upemba
Parc National de Kundelungu

Scale 1 : 4,500,000

0 40 80 120 160 200 Kilometers

0 40 80 120 160 Statute Miles

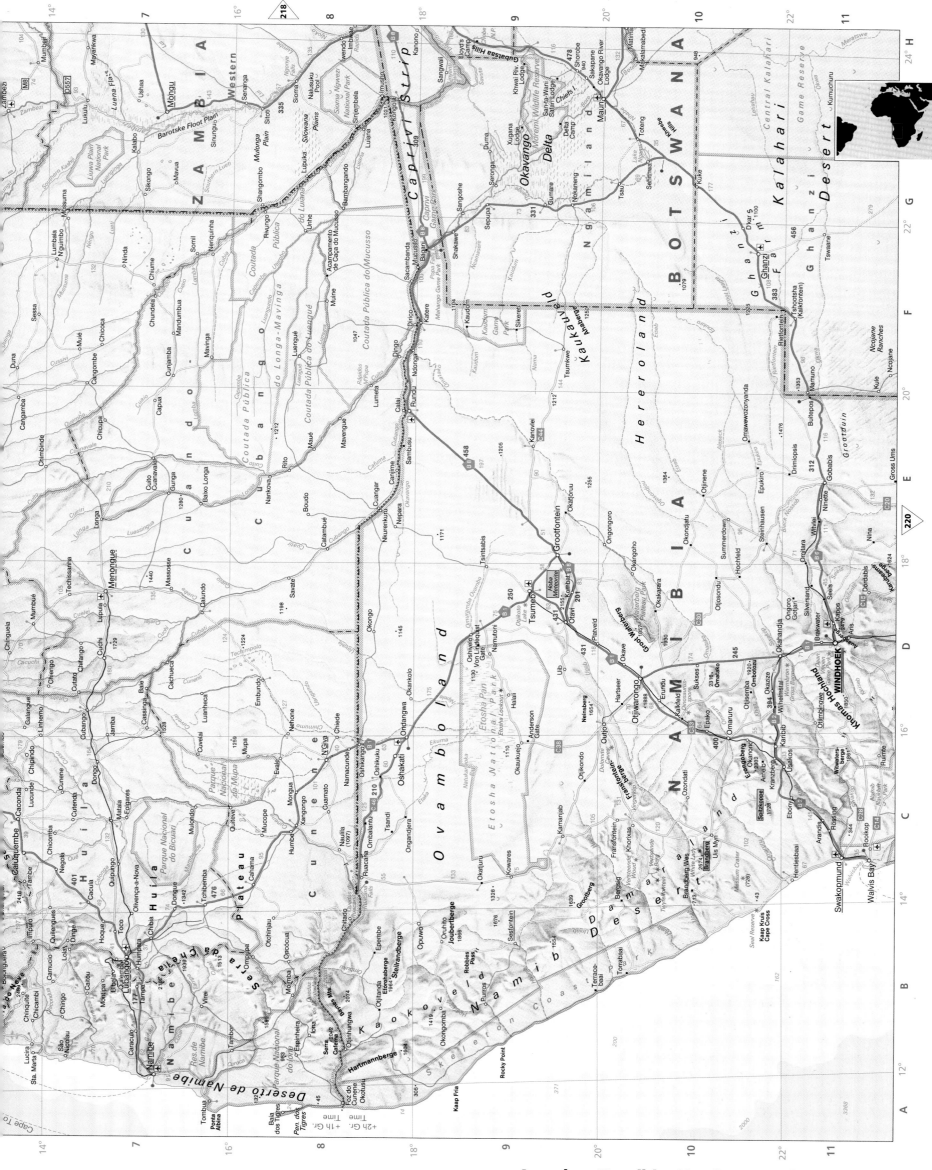

Angola • Namibia: Northern Region   217

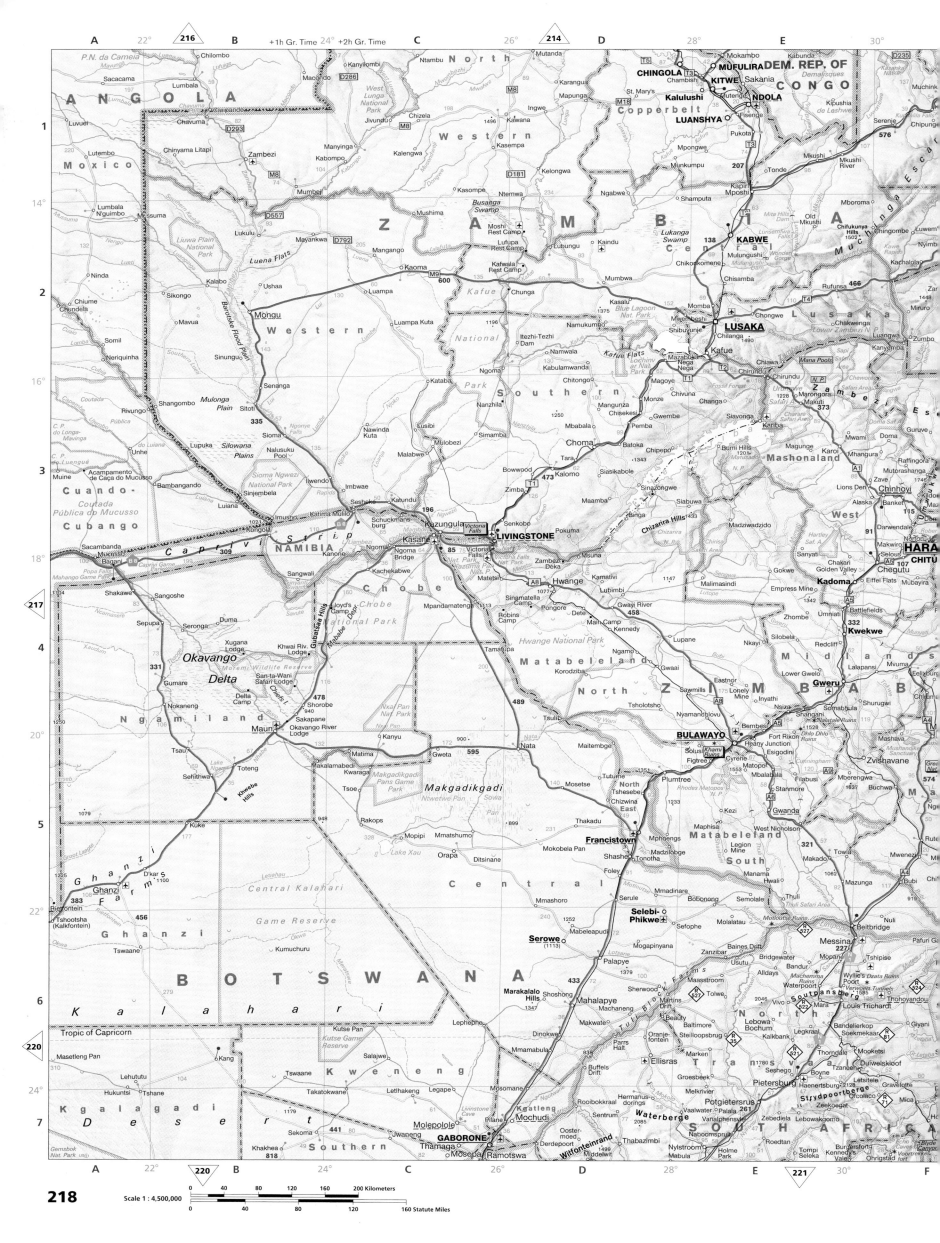

+1h Gr. Time   +2h Gr. Time

A   22°   B   24°   C   26°   D   28°   E   30°   F

A N G O L A

Moxico

Cuando-
Cubango

P.N. da Cameia

ANGOLA

Z A M B I A

Western

Western
National

North
Western

Central
Lusaka
LUSAKA
KABWE
Southern

Copperbelt
CHINGOLA   MUFULIRA   KITWE
Kalulushi
LUANSHYA   NDOLA
DEM. REP. OF
CONGO

NAMIBIA
Caprivi Strip

Kazungula   Kasane
Katima Mulilo
LIVINGSTONE
Victoria Falls

Chobe
Chobe National Park

BOTSWANA

Okavango
Delta
Ngamiland
Maun

Ghanzi

Kalahari   Desert

Kgalagadi
Desert

Central Kalahari
Game Reserve

Makgadikgadi
Makgadikgadi Pans Game Park

Francistown

Serowe
Selebi-
Phikwe

GABORONE
Molepolole
Mochudi
Ramotswa

Southern
Kweneng

Kgatleng

ZIMBABWE

Matabeleland
North

Hwange National Park

BULAWAYO

Matabeleland
South

GWERU
Kwekwe
Midlands

Mashonaland
HARARE
Chinhoyi
West

Kadoma
CHITUNGWIZA

Gwanda

Messina

SOUTH AFRICA

Soutpansberg
Pietersburg

Tropic of Capricorn

218

Scale 1 : 4,500,000

0   40   80   120   160   200 Kilometers
0   40   80   120   160 Statute Miles

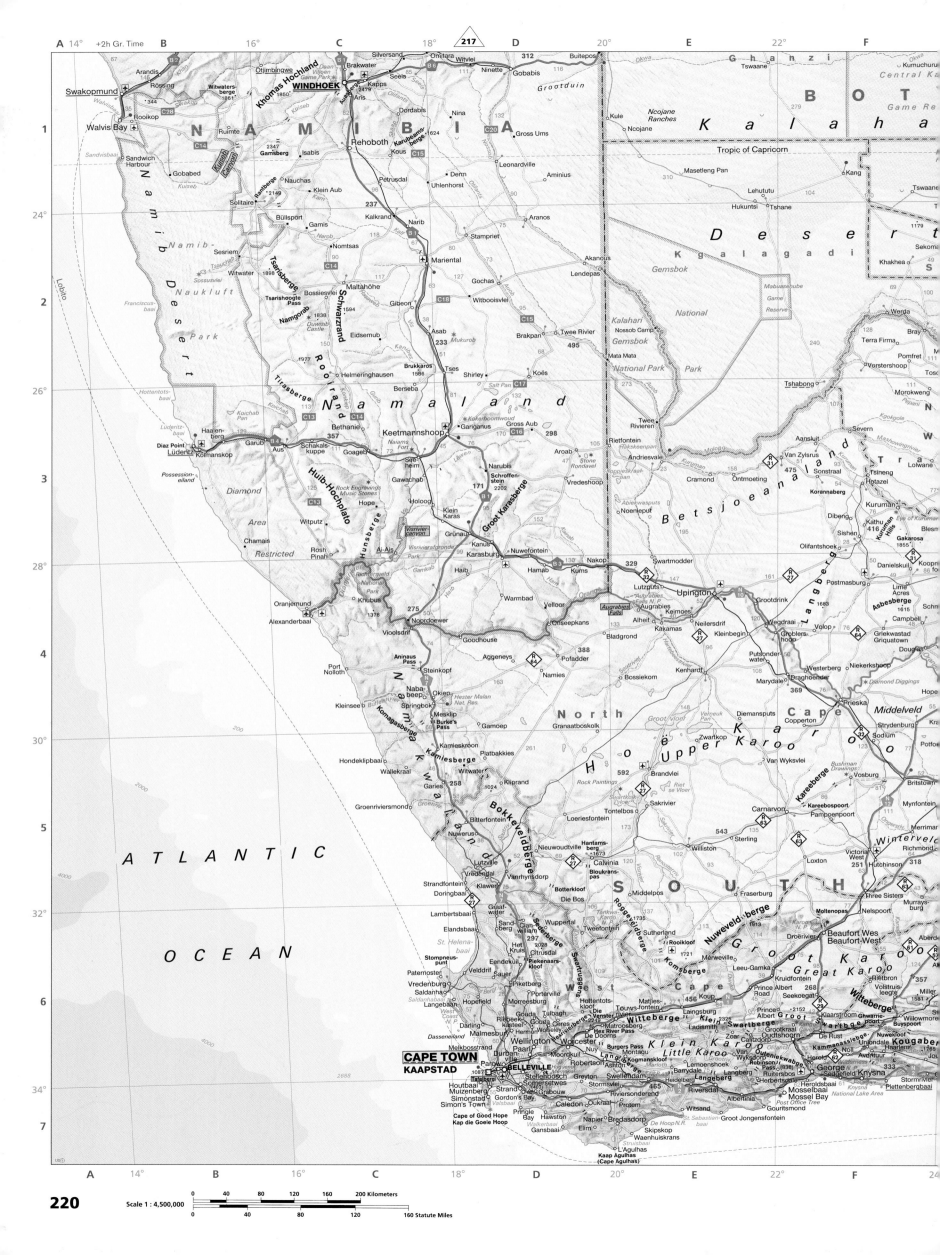

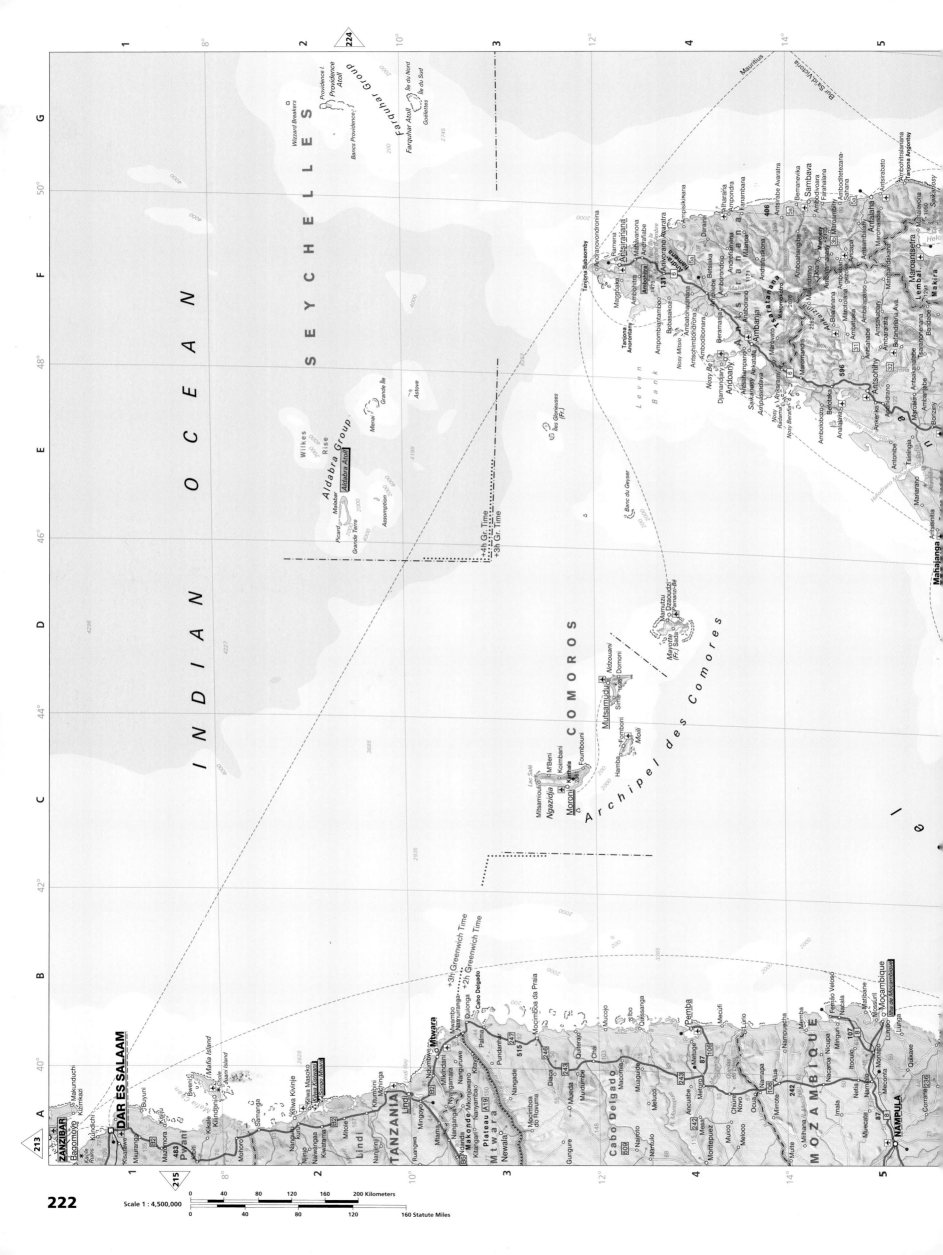

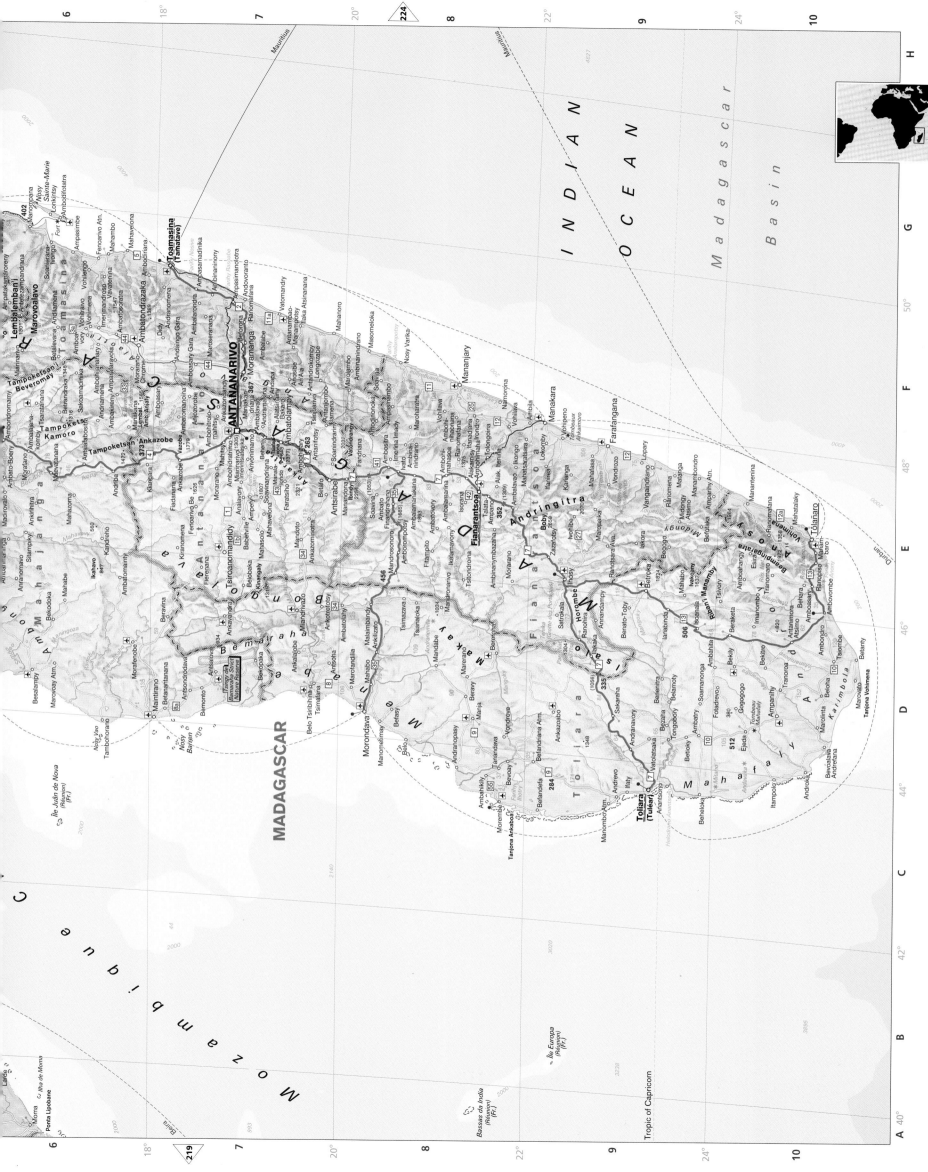

MADAGASCAR

INDIAN OCEAN

Madagascar Basin

Mozambique Channel

Tropic of Capricorn

ANTANANARIVO

Toamasina
(Tamatave)

Fianarantsoa

Toliara
(Tuléar)

Tôlañaro

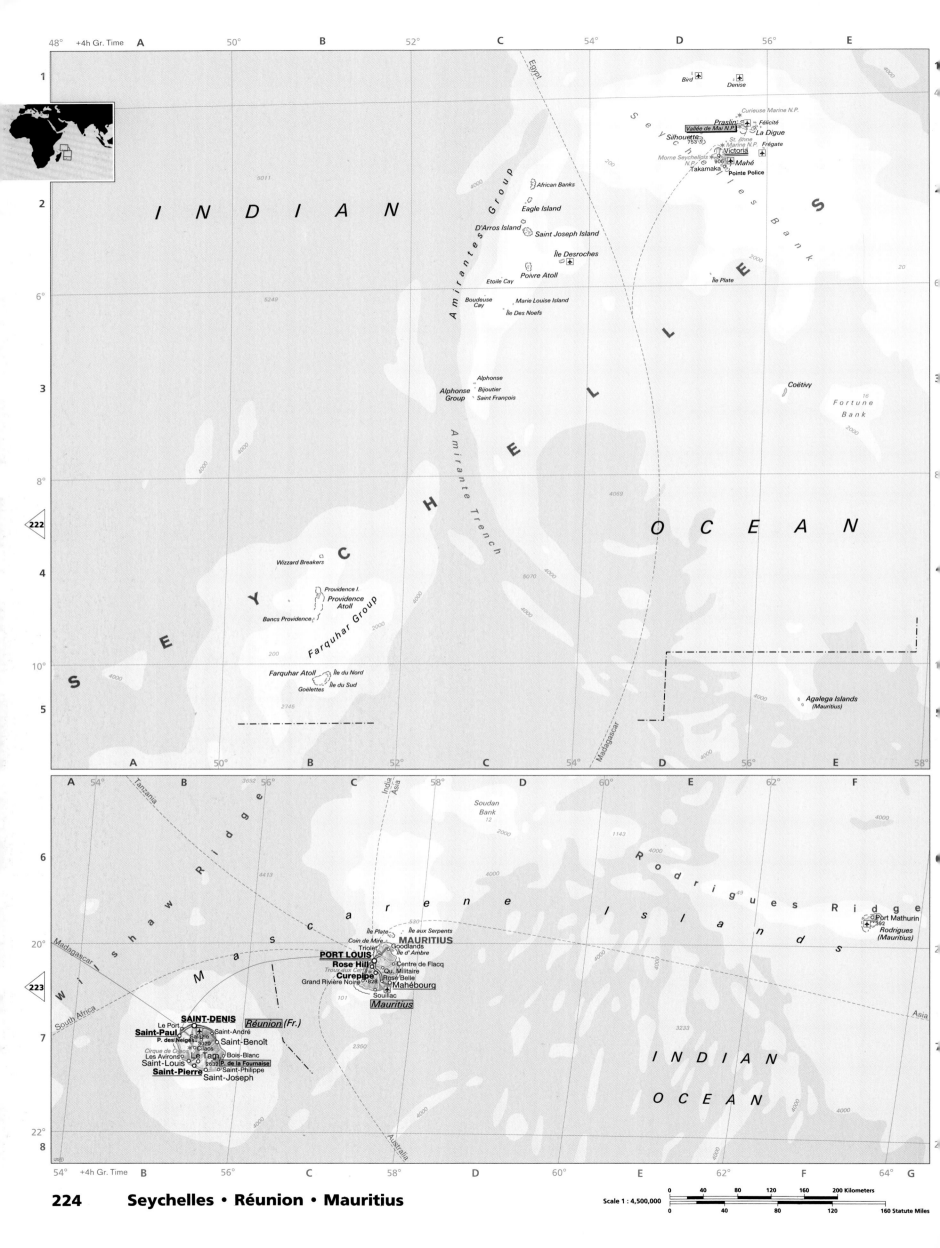

The U.S.A. and Southern Canada

The United States and the southern provinces of Canada occupy the entire center of North America. A clearly arranged topography characterizes this region between the Atlantic and Pacific Oceans. The mighty Rockies in the west and the narrow chain of the Appalachian Mountains in the east run more or less parallel to one another along their respective meridians of longitude. They enclose a huge plain whose expanse of arable land not only nourishes the native population, but also feeds millions of people in countries with less developed agriculture. Enormous coniferous and mixed forests and more than a million lakes are found in the north. The five Great Lakes lie between the two countries at their most productive point.

The Statue of Liberty, built "to glorify the Republic and Liberty," has become a symbol of freedom throughout the world. This lithograph was published in New York one year before "Lady Liberty" was unveiled on 28 October 1886.

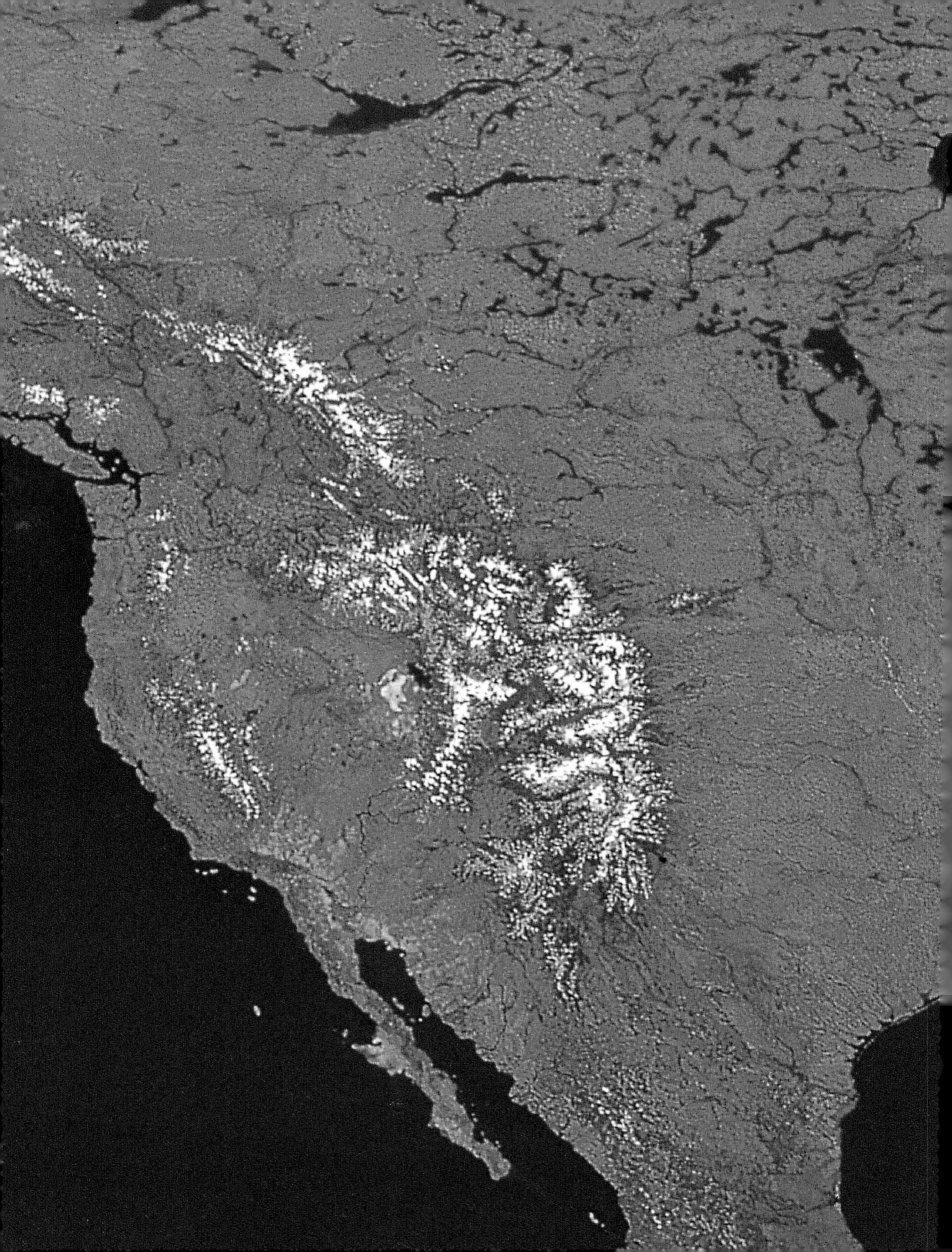

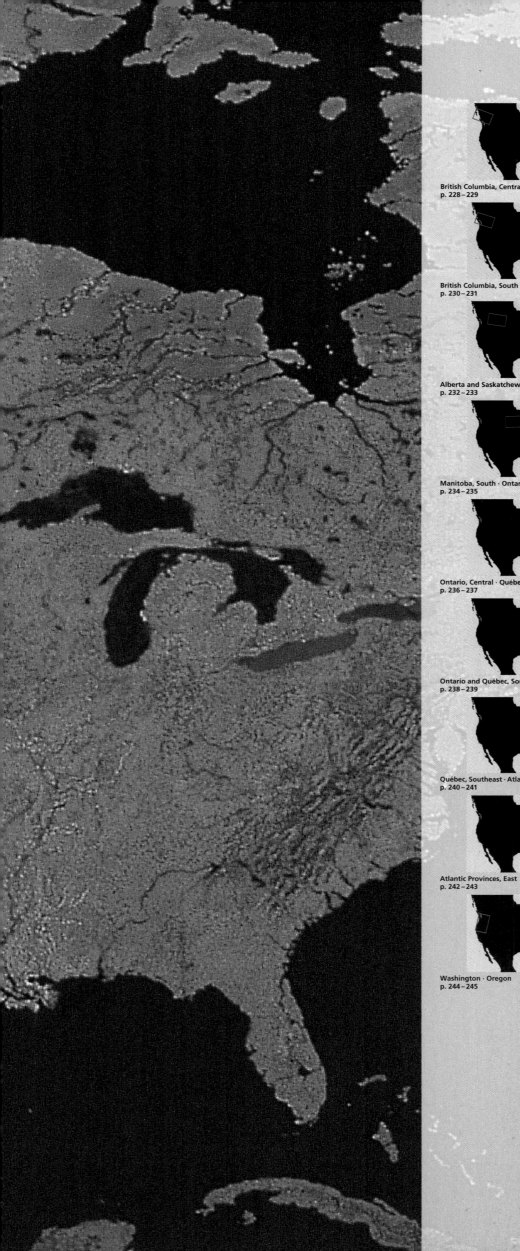

Cranberry
Junction
Baker I.
Craig
Hollis
Kasaan
Revillagigedo
Island
Old
Hogen
Bucareli B.
Prince of Wales
Island
Ward Cove
Anyox
Alice Arm
Mt. Weber
2007
37
Mt. Thomlinson
2438
2272
Takla Landing
C. Bartolome
Suemez I.
Waterfall
Hydaburg
Ketchikan
Mtn. Point
Gravina I.
Saxman
Kispiox
2286
New Aiyansh
Kitwancool
Hazelton
South
Hazelton
New Hazelton
Ksan Indian Village
Fort Babine
1946
Leo Creek
A L A S K A
(U.S.)
Metlakatla
Annette I.
Annette I.
Ind. Res.
Gitwinksihlkw
Nass Camp
Kitwanga
Kilseguecla
Seaton
Smithers
Landing
Old Fort
Sukkwan
I.
Misty Fjords
Nat. Mon.
812
Nisga'a
Mem.
2368
Kincolith
Greenville
Cedarvale
Woodcock
Moricetown
Granisle
Topley Landing
Dall I.
Long I.
South
Prince
of Wales
Wilderness
Duke I.
827
Peabody Mtns.
2007
Dorreen
2780
Evelyn
Driftwood
Creek
2388
Mt. Cronin
Telkwa
Tochopa L.
Trembleur L.
C. Muzon
Kaigani
C. Chacon
Wales I.
Port
Simpson
Pacific
16
Usk
Smithers
Telkwa Riv.
771
Cunningham L.
Dixon Entrance
336
Rosswood
2195
Terrace
Shames
Exstew
Thornhill
2743
Walcott
Perow
Topley
Pendelton
Bay
Donald
Landing
1613
C. Knox
Langara I.
Dundas I.
Metlakatla
Prince Rupert
Salvus
Du
Bose
Lakelse Lake
Barrett
Lake
Houston
Forestdale
16
Rose
Lake
Palling
Decker
Lake
Haida
Masset
Rose Pt.
McIntyre
Bay
Hooper Pt.
Port Edward
Skeena
242
Haysport
Kwinitsa
150
37
Francois L.
Burns Lake
Tintagel
58
Tian
Head
585
Graham I.
Naikoon
Prov. P.
Stephens I.
Hunts Inlet
Osland
Port Essington
Du Bose
Gitnadoix
River P. Rec.
Kitimat
Kitimaat
Village
Colleymount
Francois L.
Sheraton
End
Queen
Shannon
Bay
Port Clements
16
Juskatia
Tlell
Oona River
Kitkatla
McCauley I.
1202
Hawkesbury I.
Atna Peak
2755
Nadina
River
Tatalrose
Grassy Plains
Oosta L.
Charlotte
Kindakun Pt.
Lawnhill
Queen
Charlotte
Queen Charlotte
Is. Mus.
Skidegate Inlet
C. George
Porcher I.
Kemano
Wistaria
Marilla
Cheslatta L.
1250
Skidegate
Allford Bay
Sandspit
Banks I.
Hartley Bay
Gribbell I.
Michel Peak
2255
Nechako
Res.
Kenn
Islands
C. Henry
Moresby Camp
Cumshewa Head
Gil I.
Butedale
Eutsuk L.
Sewell
Inlet
1082
Louise I.
Campania
I.
1890
B
Tweedsmuir
2769
Tetachuck
Lake
Emteko R.
Englefield Bay
Tasu
Lyell I.
Estevan Group
Surf Inlet
Princess
Royal I.
Kalone Pk.
2557
Tsitsutl Pk.
2478
Far Mtn.
2393
Moresby I.
South Moresby
Gwaii Haanas
Nat. P. Reserve
719
Aristazabal I.
Klemtu
Roderick
I.
Swindle
I.
Pooley
I.
Kimsquit
Firvale
Atnarko
20
Anahi
Rose Harbour
Anthony I.
Kunghit I.
104
Price I.
790
Ocean Falls
Hagensborg
Stuie
Bella Coola
1125
Cape St. James
King Island
Mt. Saugstad
2929
Charlotte L.
Queen
Charlotte
Sound
Waglisla
Bella Bella
2318
Monarch Mtn.
3533
Namu
Hunter
Island
Hakai
Recreation
Area
Dawsons
Landing
Silverthrone Mtn.
2957
Mt. Waddington
4042
2000
4000
1045
Calvert
Island
Cape Calvert
Duncanby Landing
Goose Bay
Rivers Inlet
P A C I F I C   O C E A N
Cape Caution
Allison
Harbour
Bull
Harbour
Scott Is.
Nigei I.
Nahwitti
C. Scott
Cape Scott
Provincial Park
Port Hardy
Bear
Cove
Fort Rupert
Simoon Harbour
Kingcome Inlet
Thompson
Sound
Simoon
Sound
Glendale
Cove
Holberg
Coal Harbour
Pt. McNeill
Sointula
Alert Bay
Gilford I.
Minstrel
Island
Phillips
Arm
Winter Harbour
Rumble Beach
1272
Pt. Alice
Beaver Cove
Kokish
Cracroft I.
Pt. Neville
Hardwicke
Jackson
Bay
Thurlow
Quatsino Sd.
1372
V a n c o u v e r
Kelsey Bay
Blind
Channel
Sonora I.
Owen
Surge
Narrows
C. Cook
Brooks Peninsula
Provincial Recreation Area
Chamiss
Bay
Fair
Harbour
19
Schoen Lake
Provincial Park
Rock Bay
Granite
Bay
Quadra I.
Heriot Bay
Bloedel
Whalet
I s l a n d
Kynuquot
Zeballos
Tahsis
Victoria Pk.
2163
Black Creek
515
Campbell River
Esperanza Inl.
Ceepeecee
Hecate
Strathcona
Prov. Park
Gold River
28
19
Merville
Quathiaski
Cove
Mans

Scale 1 : 2,250,000

0   20   40   60   80   100 Kilometers
0   20   40   60   80 Statute Miles

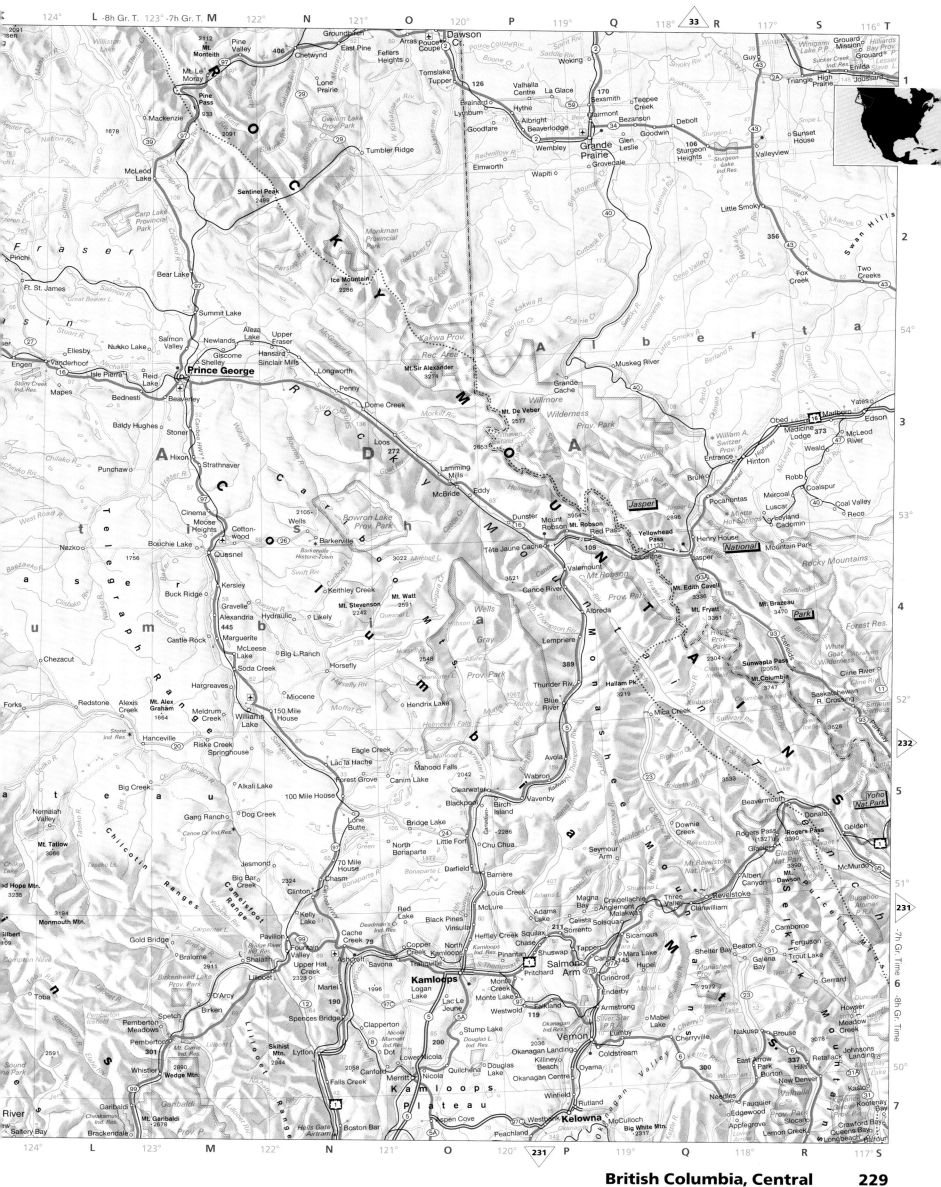

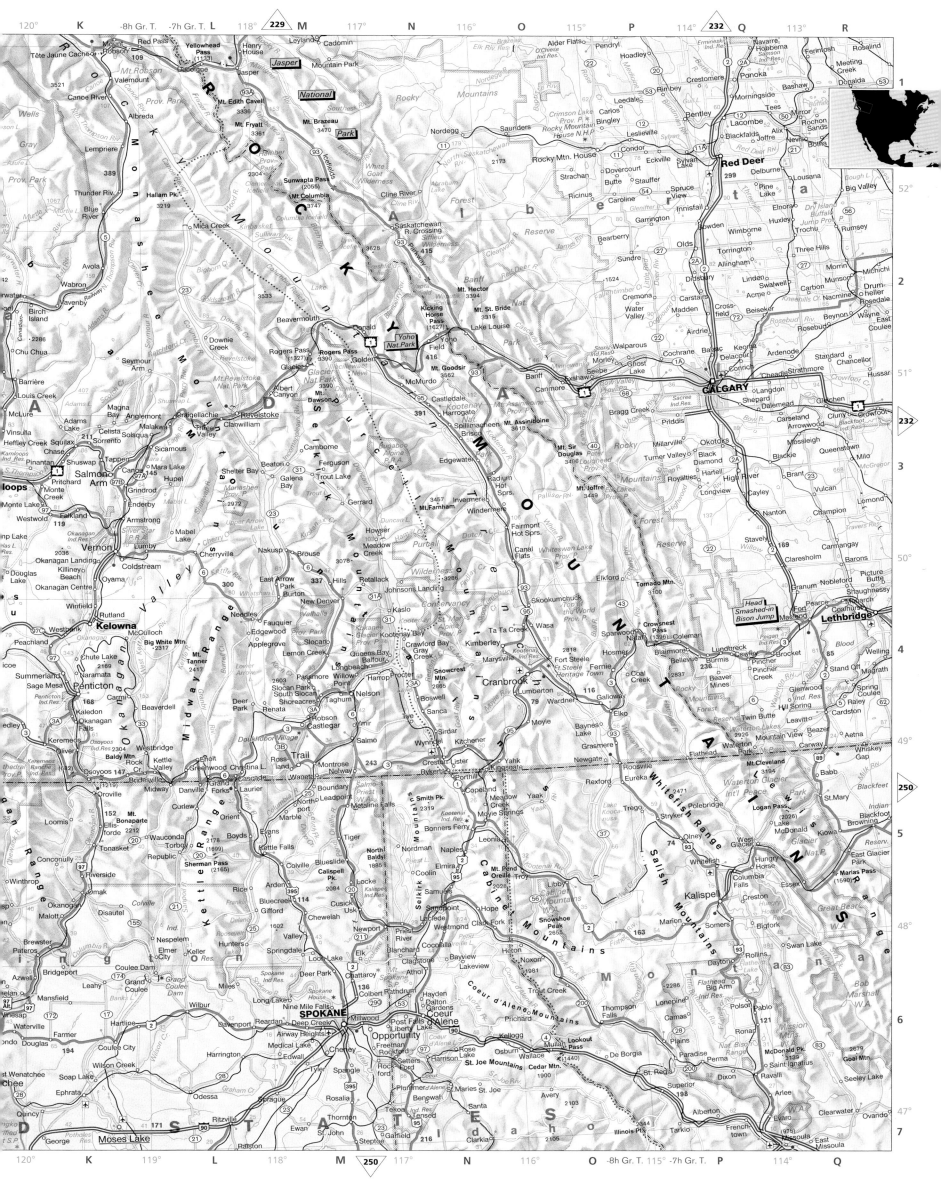

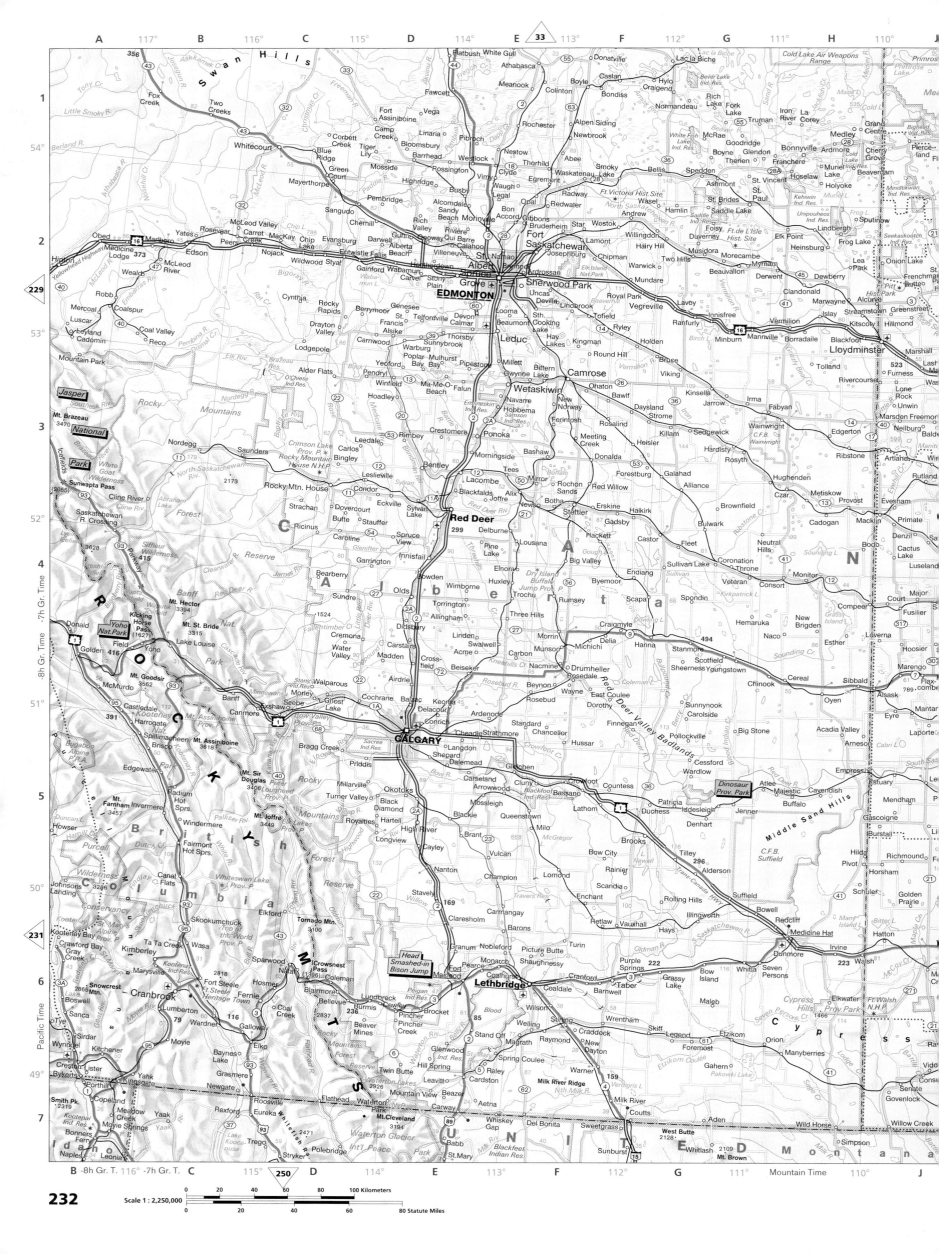

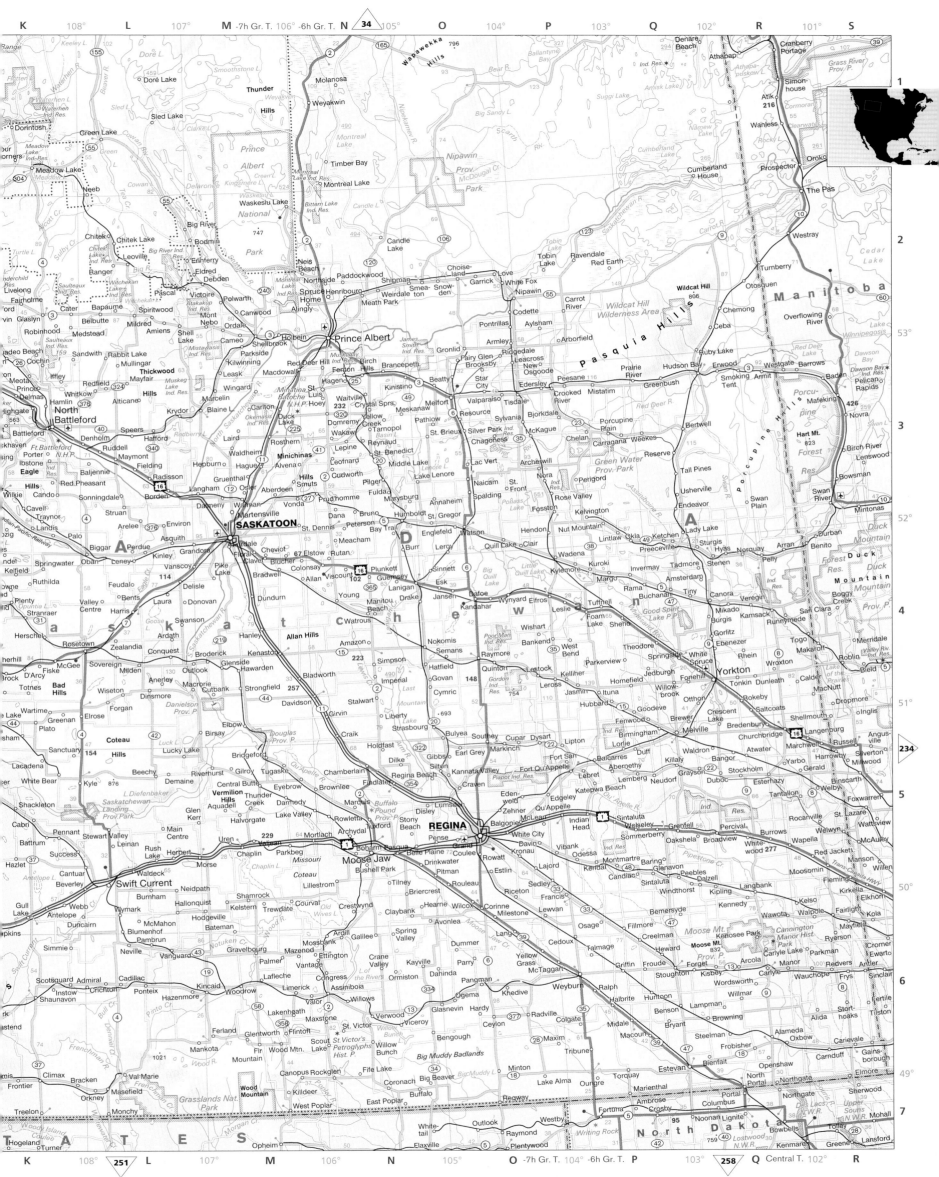

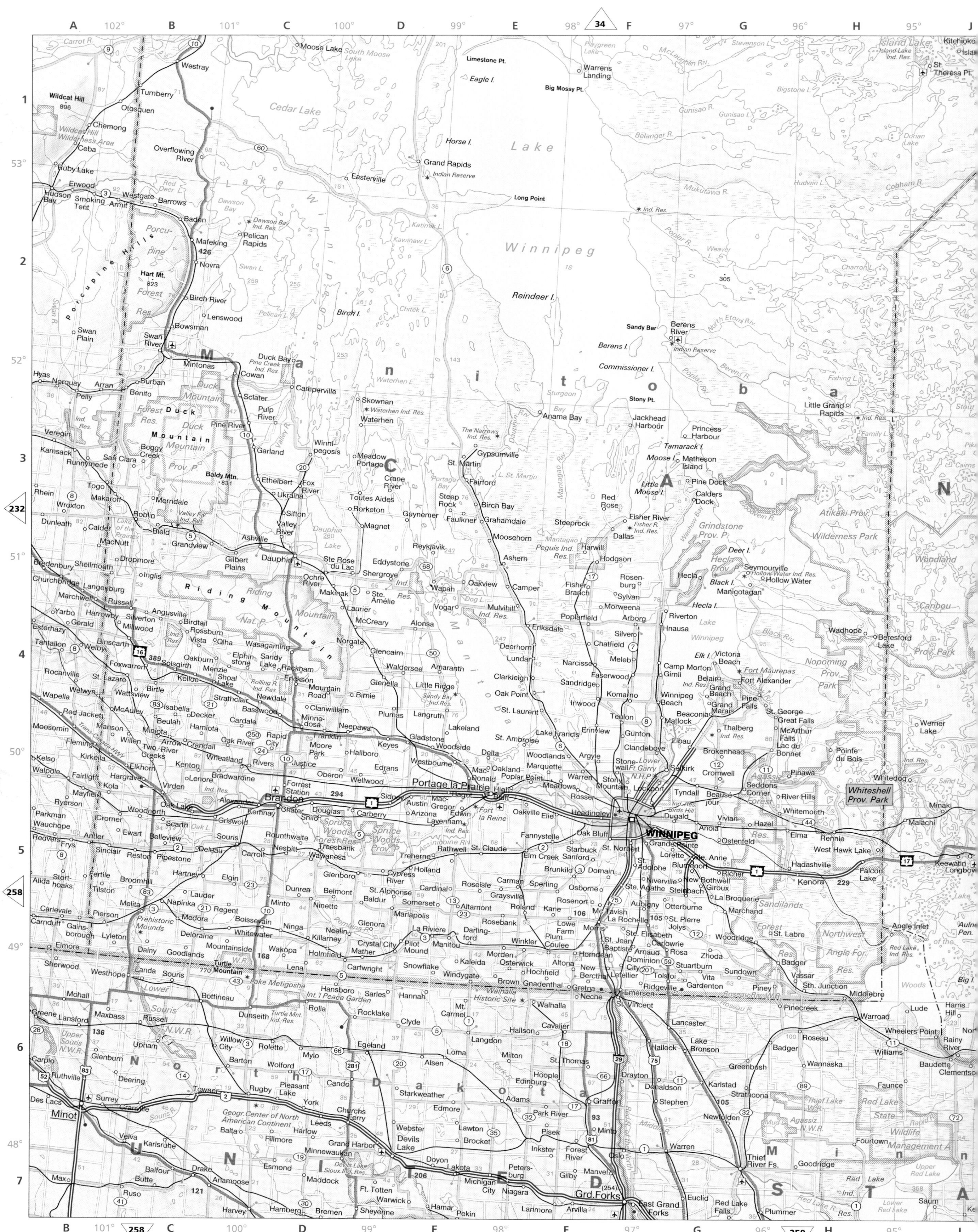

Carrot R.

Island Lake
Ind. Res.
Kitchioko
St. Theresa Pt.

Moose Lake
South Moose Lake

Limestone Pt.
Eagle I.
Playgreen Lake
Warrens Landing

Wildcat Hill
806
Westray
Turnberry
Otosquen
Big Mossy Pt.

Cedar Lake
Horse I.
Grand Rapids
Indian Reserve

Lake

Ruby Lake
Chemong
Ceba
Overflowing River
Easterville
Long Point

Winnipeg

Hudson Bay
Erwood
Smoking Tent
Armit
Westgate
Barrows
Baden

Dawson Bay
Dawson Bay Ind. Res.

Reindeer I.

Mafeking
426
Pelican Rapids
Novra

Sandy Bar
Berens River
Berens I.

Hart Mt.
823
Birch River

Commissioner I.

Swan Plain
Bowsman

Duck Bay
Pine Creek Ind. Res.
Cowan

Jackhead Harbour
Princess Harbour
Little Grand Rapids
Ind. Res.

Swan River
Mintonas

Camperville

Stony Pt.

Hyas
Norquay
Arran
Durban
Benito

Skownan
Waterhen Ind. Res.
Waterhen

Anama Bay

Tamarack I.

Pelly
Veregin
Kamsack
San Clara
Runnymede

Garland
Winnipegosis

The Narrows Ind. Res.

Gypsumville
St. Martin
Pine Dock
Calders Dock

Rhein
Wroxton
Togo
Makaroff
Merridale
Roblin

Ethelbert
Fox River
Ukraina
Sifton

Meadow Portage
Crane River
Toutes Aides
Rorketon
Magnet

St. Martin
Fairford

Birch Bay
Faulkner
Grahamdale
Moosehorn

Red Rose
Fisher River
Fisher R. Ind. Res.

Moose I.
Matheson Island

Dunleath
Calder
Bield
Grandview

Ashville
Valley River

Ste Rose du Lac
Shergrove
Reykjavik

Wapah
Oakview
Camper

Fisher Branch

Hecla

Bredenbury
Shellmouth
Inglis
Dropmore

Gilbert Plains
Dauphin
Ochre River
Makinak

Eddystone
Laurier
McCreary

Alonsa

Mulvihill
Ashern

Rosenburg
Black I.
Seymourville
Hollow Water Ind. Res.
Hollow Water
Manigotagan

Churchbridge
Langenburg
Marchwell
Russell

Angusville
Birdtail
Rossburn
Vista
Olha

Glencairn

Deerhorn
Lundar
Poplarfield
Morweena
Arborg
Riverton
Hnausa

Esterhazy
Yarbo
Gerald
Harrowby
Silverton
Millwood

Wasagaming
Elphinstone
Sandy Lake
Rackham
Erickson

Waldersee
Amaranth
Narcisse
Faserwood
Camp Morton
Gimli
Victoria Beach
Fort Maurepas

Binscarth
Welby
Foxwarren
Solsgirth
Menzie
Kelloe

Mountain Road
Glenella
Birnie
Plumas
Langruth
Clarkleigh
Oak Point
Sandridge
Komarno
Inwood
Winnipeg Beach
Belair
Grand Beach
Grand Marais

Rocanville
St. Lazare
Wattsview
Shoal Lake
Birtle
Strathclair
Basswood
Cardale
Minnedosa
Neepawa
Gladstone
Woodside
Lakeland
St. Laurent
Teulon
Stonewall
Clandeboye
Matlock
St. George
Great Falls
McArthur Falls
Lac du Bonnet

Wapella
Welwyn
Red Jacket
McAuley
Isabella
Decker
Hamiota
Rapid City
Franklin
Moore Park
Keyes
Woodstock
Delta
Oakland
Marquette
Warren
Meadows
Stone Mtn.
Lower Ft. Garry N.H.P.
Selkirk
Cromwell
Pinawa
Pointe du Bois

Moosomin
Fleming
Manson
Willen
Two Creeks
Arrow River
Crandall
Oak River
Wheatland
Rivers
Justice
Oberon
Edrans
Westbourne
Mac...
Donald
Poplar Pt.
Headingley
Tyndall
Beauséjour
River Hills
Whitedog

Kelso
Walpole
Fairlight
Elkhorn
Kirkella
Kenton
Lenore
Bradwardine
Virden
Sidney
Austin
MacGregor
Bagot
High Bluff
Oakville
Elie
Lockport
Birds Hill
Dugald
Vivian
Elma
Rennie
Malachi
Whiteshell Prov. Park

Parkman
Wauchope
Cromer
Woodnorth
Oak Lake
Alexander
Ghater
Kemnay
Douglas
Carberry
Arizona
Edwin
Fort la Reine
Portage la Prairie
Fort la Reine
Fannystelle
Oak Bluff
St. Norbert
WINNIPEG
Grande Pointe
Anola
Hazel
Ostenfeld

Ryerson
Mayfield
Antler
Belleview
Souris
Shilo
Lavenham
Rathwell
St. Claude
Treherne
Elm Creek
Sanford
Starbuck
St. Adolphe
Lorette
Ste. Anne
West Hawk Lake
Keewatin
Longbow

Redvers
Frys
Sinclair
Reston
Pipestone
Carroll
Wawanesa
Nesbitt
Rounthwaite
Treesbank
Holland
Glenboro
Cypress River
Roseisle
Brunkild
Domain
Niverville
Blumenfeld
New Bothwell
Richer
Kenora
Hadashville
Falcon Lake

Stortoaks
Alida
Fertile
Broomhill
Hartney
Elgin
Dunrea
Belmont
St. Alphonse
Baldur
Somerset
Altamont
Sperling
Osborne
Kane
Ste. Agathe
Steinbach
Giroux
La Broquerie
Marchand

Carievale
Pierson
Melita
Napinka
Regent
Minto
Ninette
Mariapolis
Roland
Rosebank
Lowe Farm
Morris
La Rochelle
Otterburne
St. Pierre
Jolys
St. Labre
Woodridge

Carnduff
Gainsborough
Lyleton
Medora
Boissevain
Ninga
Glenora
La Rivière
Darlingford
Winkler
Morden
Plum Coulee
Rosa
Zhoda
Badger

Elmore
Sherwood
Westhope
Dalny
Goodlands
Whitewater
Wakopa
Holmfield
Mather
Pilot Mound
Manitou
Osterwick
Altona
Horndean
St. Jean Baptiste
Carlowrie
Dominion City
Stuartburn
Sundown
Vassar

Mohall
Maxbass
Russell
Landa
Souris
Lena
Cartwright
Snowflake
Windygate
Kaleida
Hochfield
New Bergthal
Gretna
Letellier
Ridgeville
Gardenton
Piney
Sth. Junction
Middlebro

Turtle Mountain W.R.
770
Lake Metigoshe
Hansboro
International Peace Garden
Sarles
Walhalla Historic Site
Walhalla
Emerson
St. Vincent
Lancaster
Pinecreek
Warroad
Wheelers Point

Greene
Lansford
Bottineau
Dunseith
Turtle Mtn. Ind. Res.
Rolla
Rocklake
Hannah
Mt. Carmel
Hallson
Neche
Hallock
Lake Bronson
Roseau
Williams

Carpio
Ruthville
Glenburn
Upham
Willow City
Barton
Rolette
Clyde
Cavalier
Langdon
Milton
St. Thomas
Drayton
Karlstad
Greenbush
Wannaska
Badger

Des Lacs
Surrey
Deering
Wolford
Mylo
Cando
Loma
Hoople
Edinburg
Hallock
Karlstad
Strathcona
Faunce

Minot
Granville
Towner
Rugby
Pleasant Lake
York
Churchs Ferry
Leeds
Starkweather
Adams
Grafton
Stephen
Newfolden
Red Lake
W.R.

Velva
Karlsruhe
Geogr. Center of North American Continent
Balta
Harlow
Edmore
Webster
Lawton
Park River
Minto
Fourtown

Maxon
Balfour
Drake
Anamoose
Esmond
Minnewaukan
Devils Lake
Brocket
Pisek
Grafton
Oslo
Thief River Fs.
Goodridge
Red Lake

Ruso
Butte
Minnewaukan
Devils Lake
Sioux Ind. Res.
Ft. Totten
Warwick
Doyon
Michigan City
Niagara
Gilby
Manvel
Grand Forks
East Grand Forks
Red Lake Falls
Plummer

Scale 1 : 2,250,000

0 20 40 60 80 100 Kilometers
0 20 40 60 80 Statute Miles

Manitoba

North Dakota

Minnesota

UNITED STATES

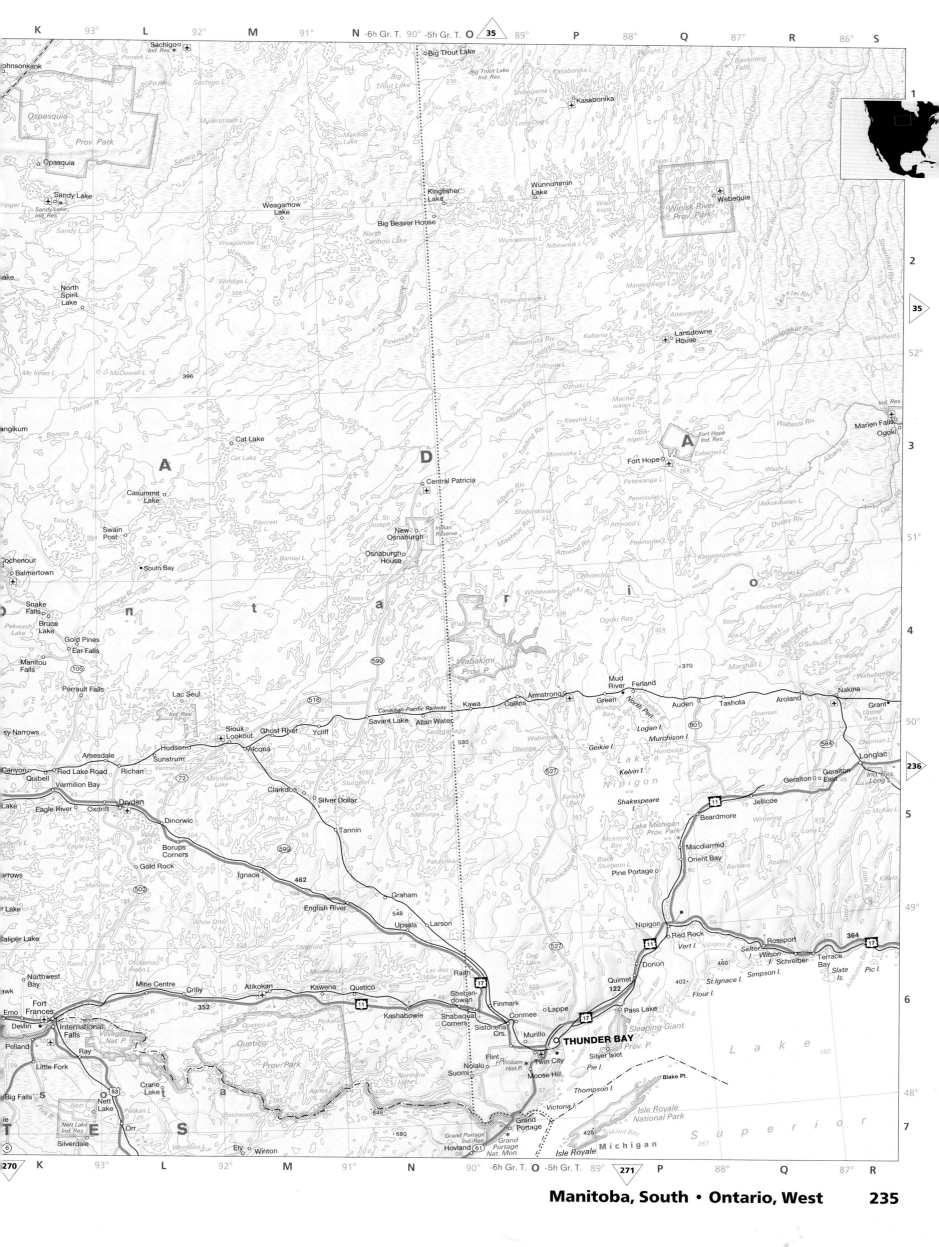

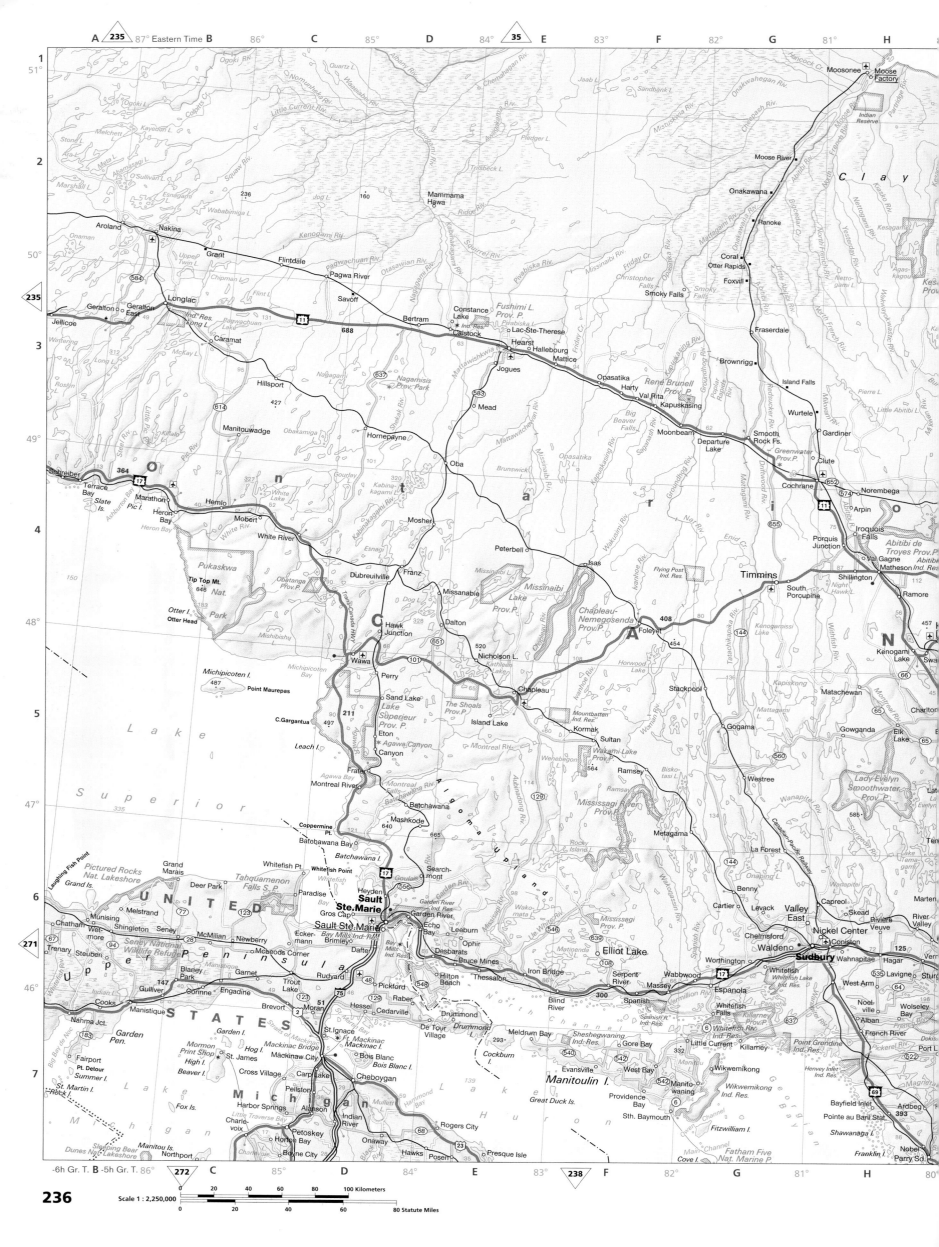

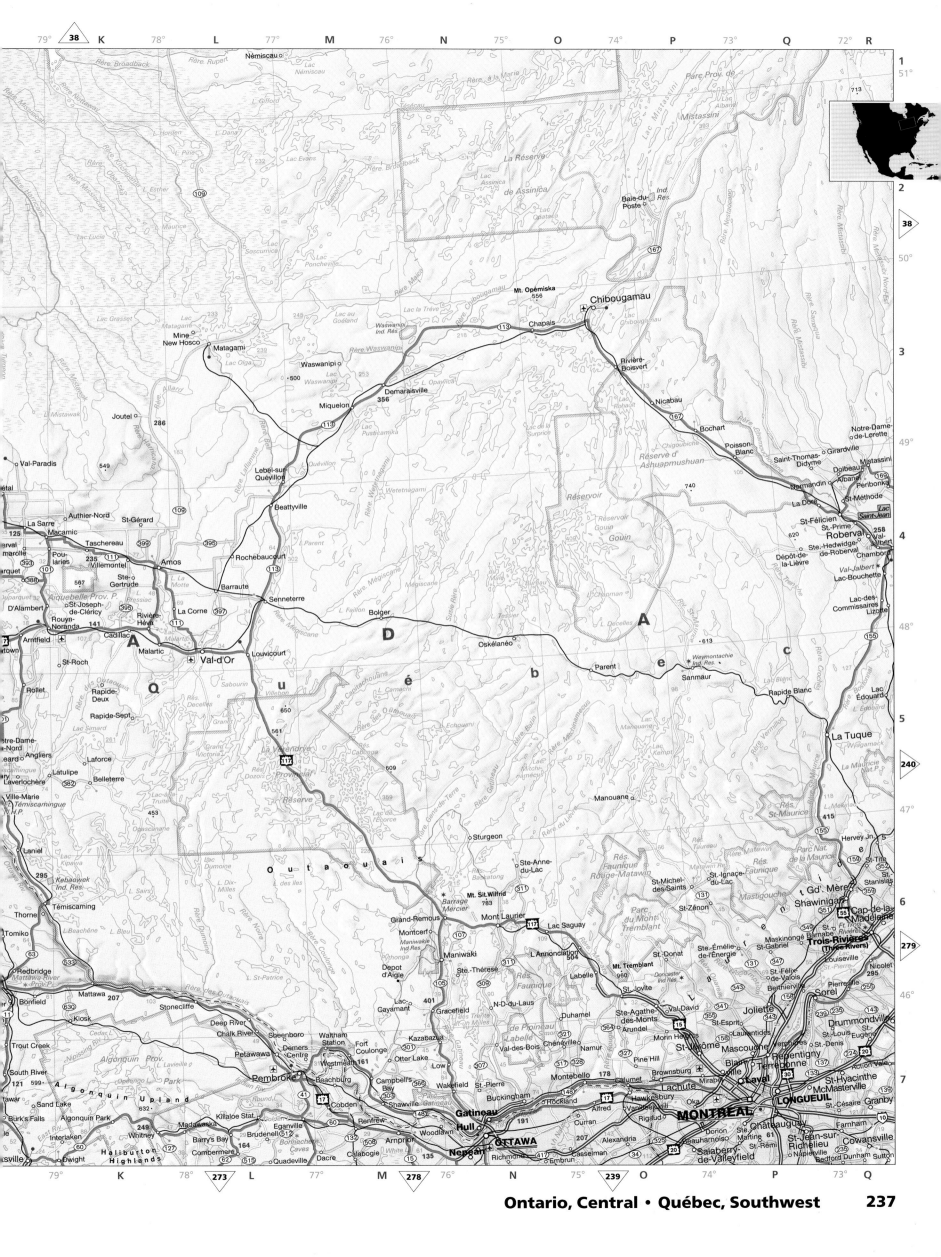

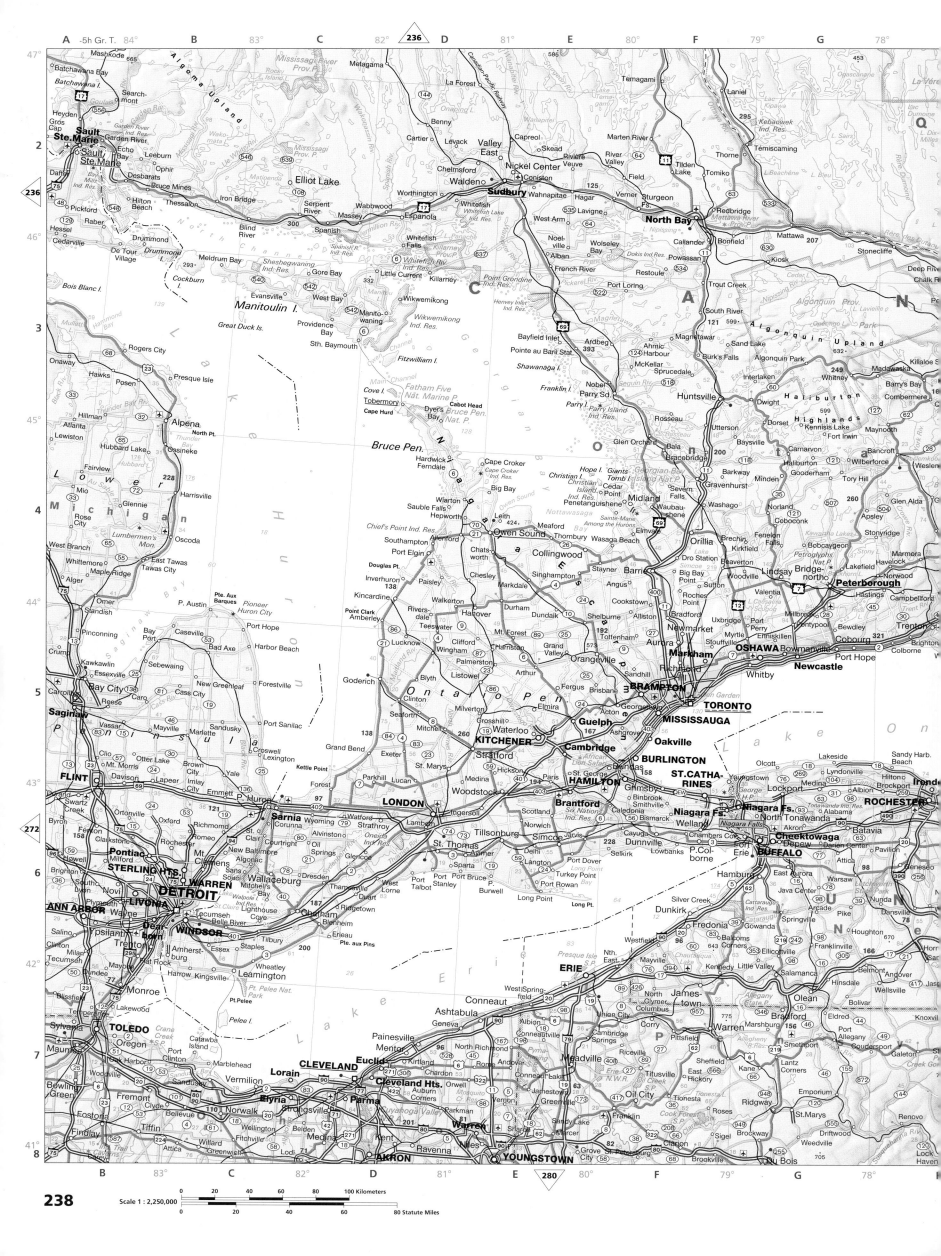

Scale 1 : 2,250,000

0   20   40   60   80   100 Kilometers

0   20   40   60   80 Statute Miles

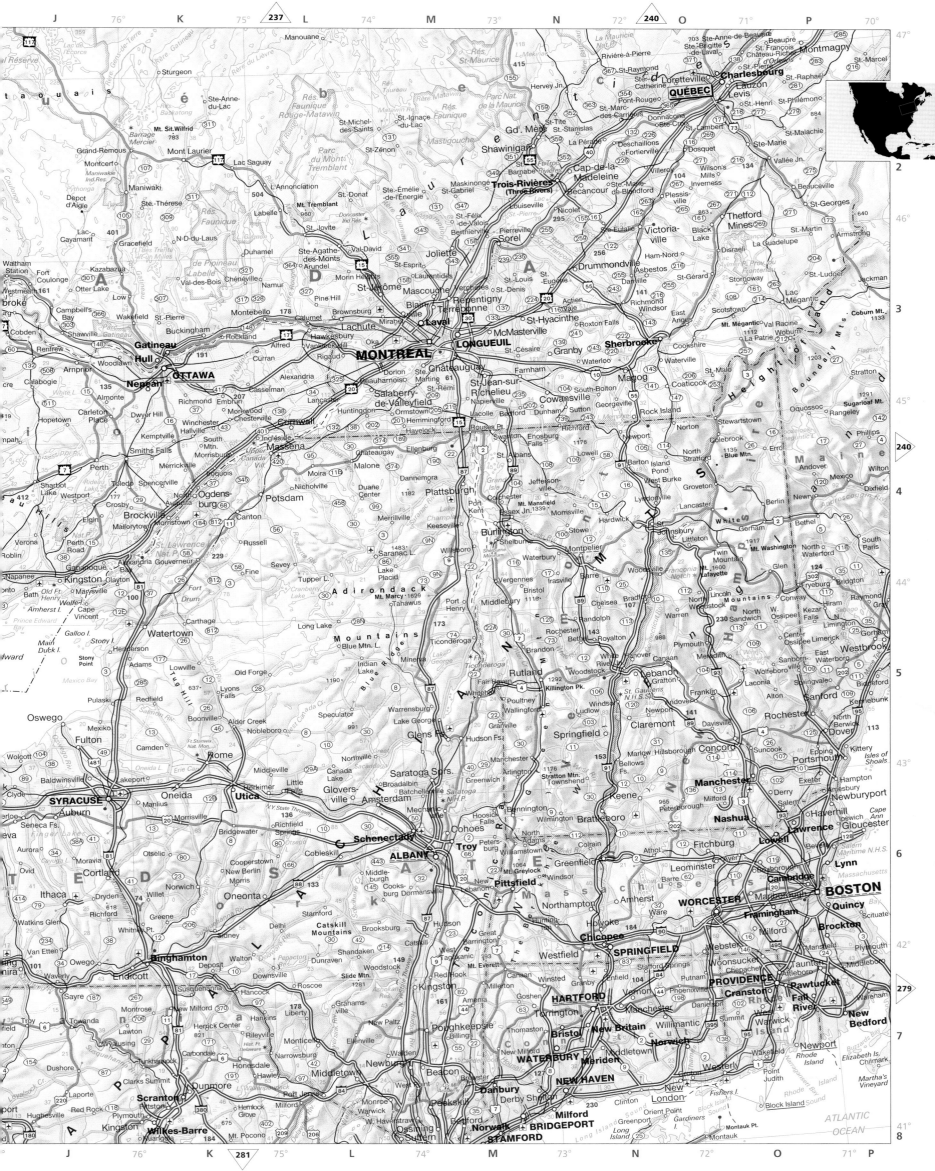

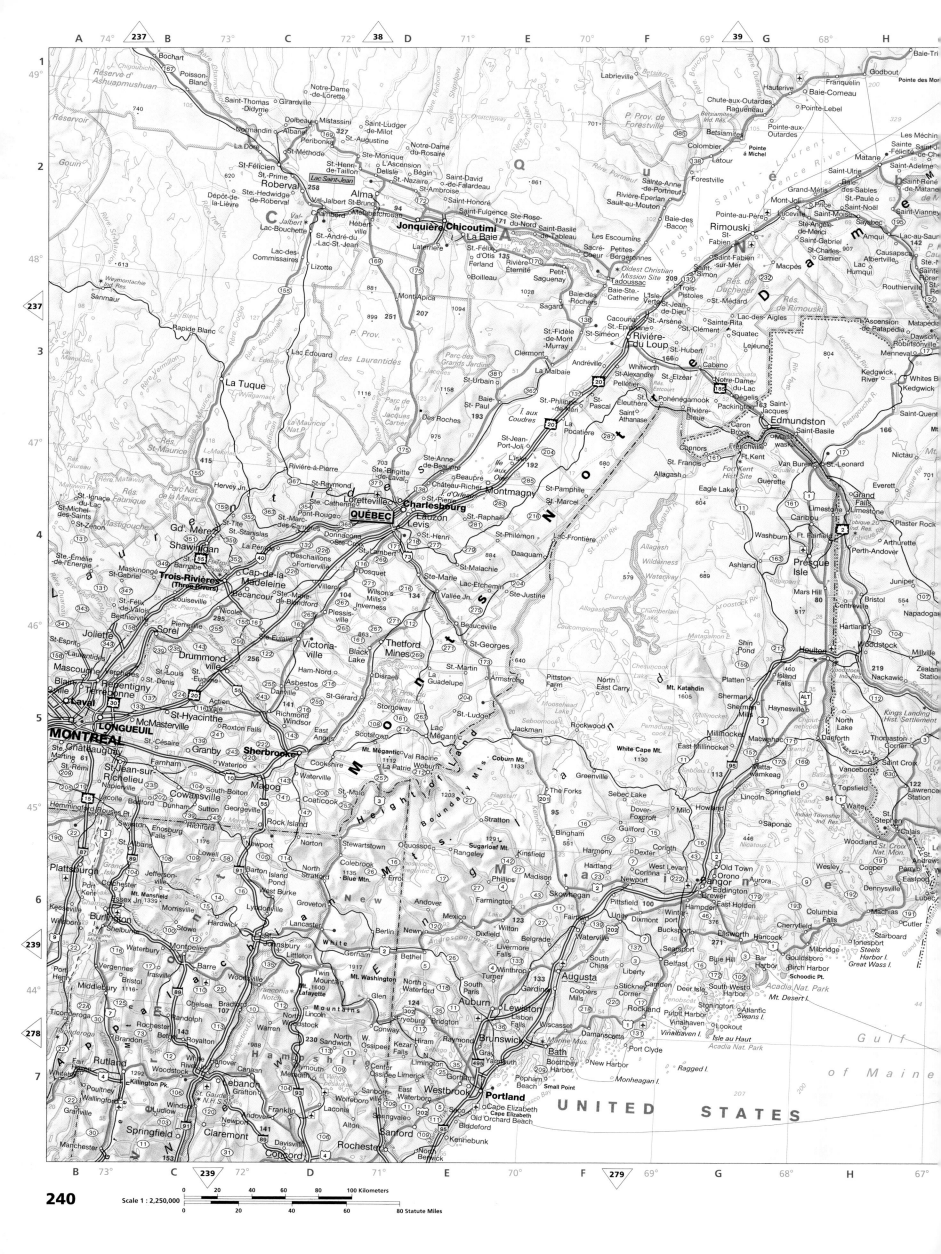

Scale 1 : 2,250,000

0 20 40 60 80 100 Kilometers

0 20 40 60 80 Statute Miles

Scale 1 : 2,250,000

0   20   40   60   80   100 Kilometers

0   20   40   60   80 Statute Miles

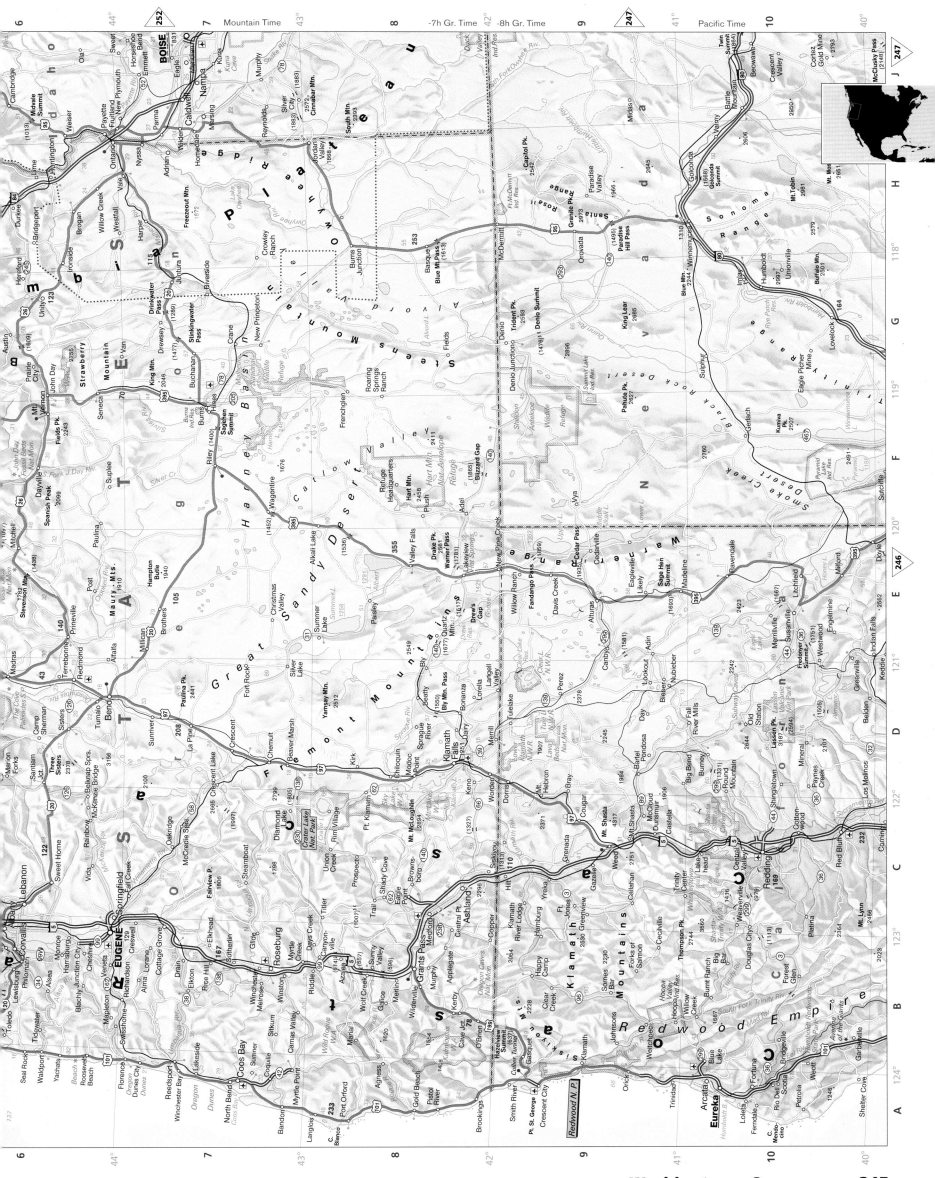

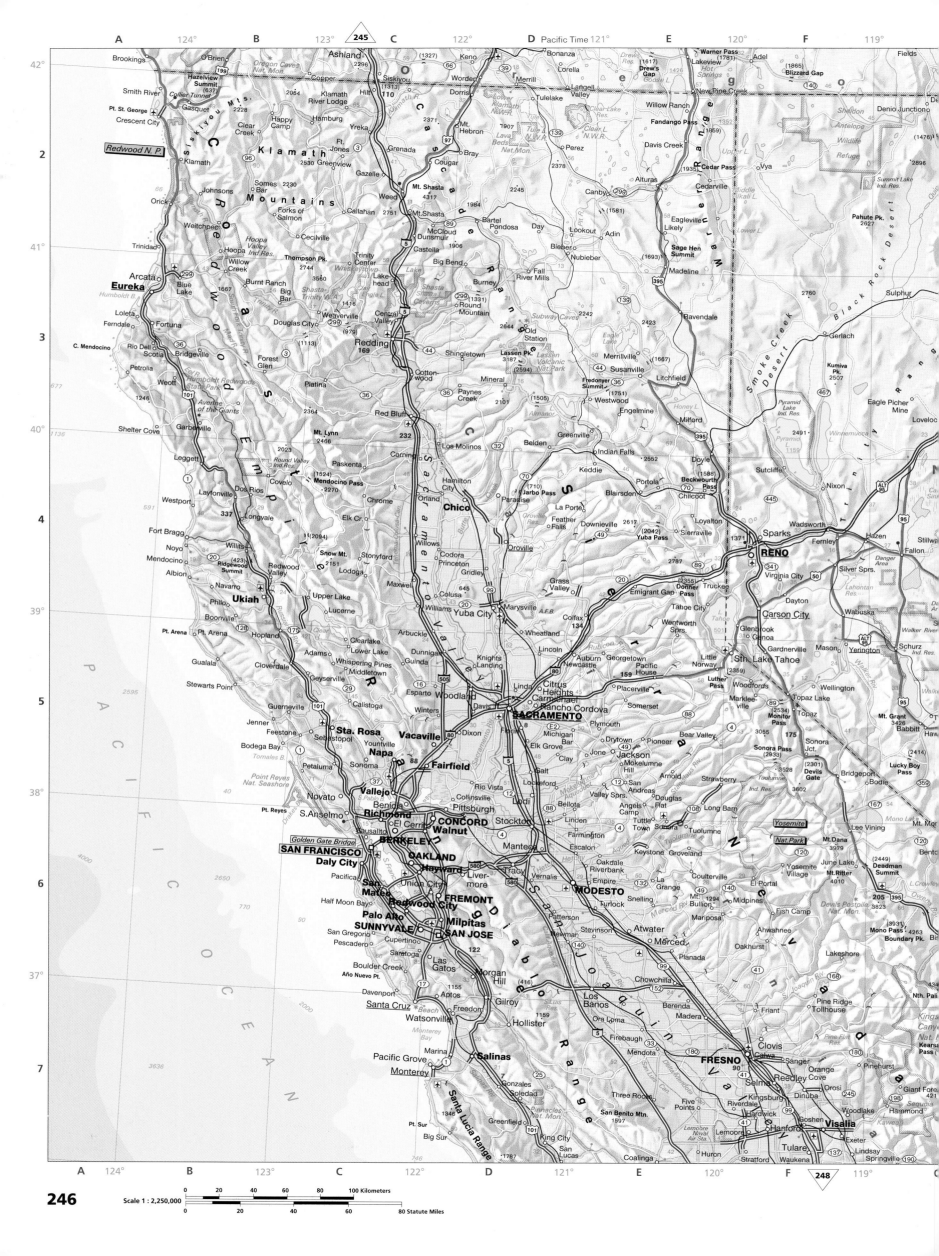

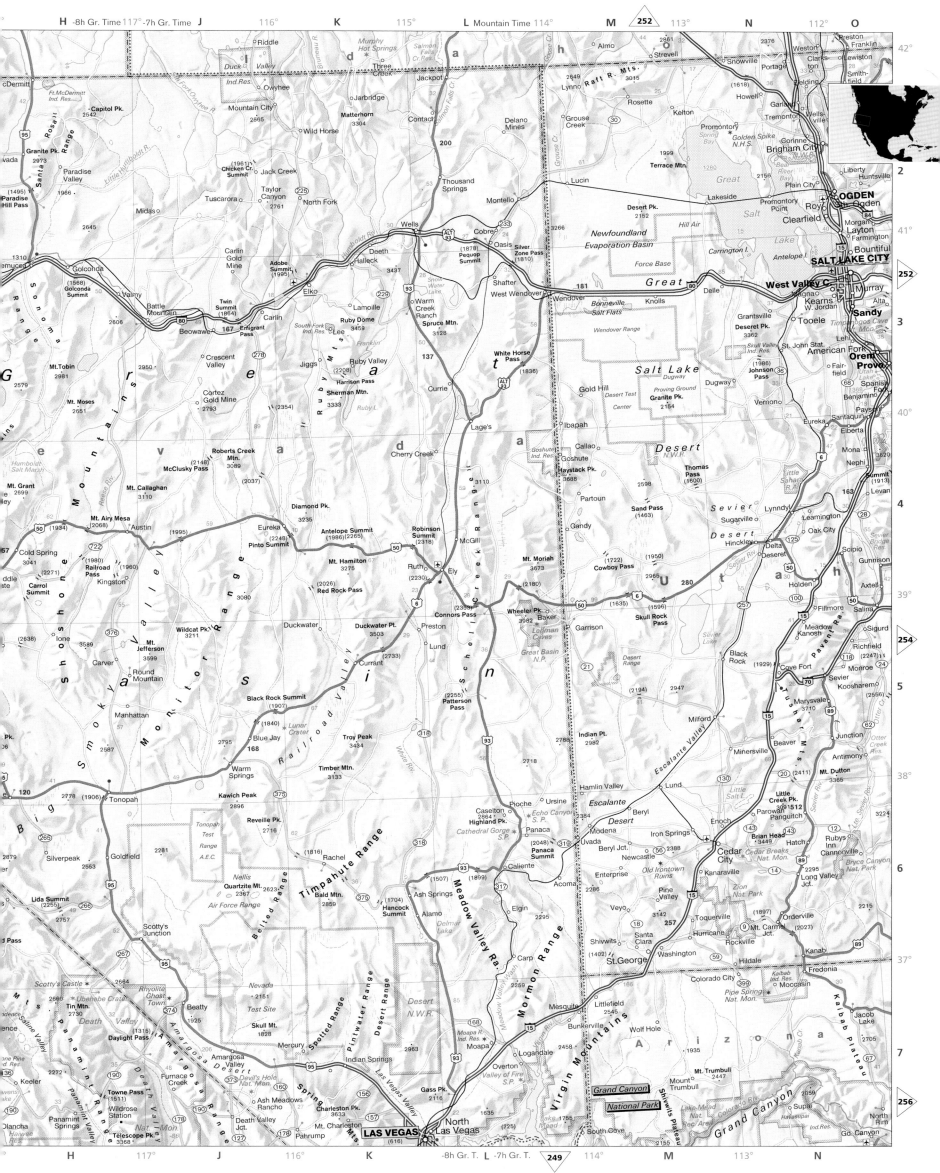

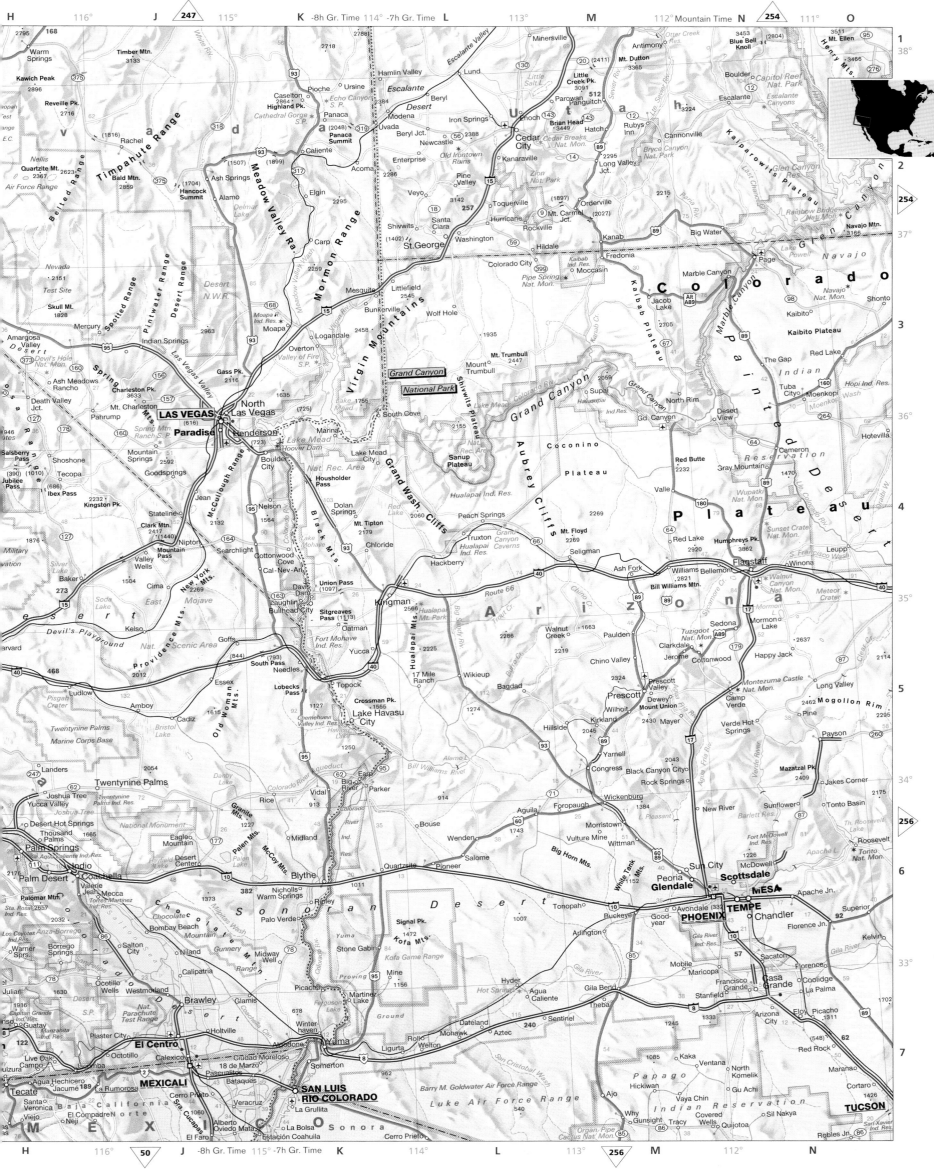

Scale 1 : 2,250,000

100 Kilometers

80 Statute Miles

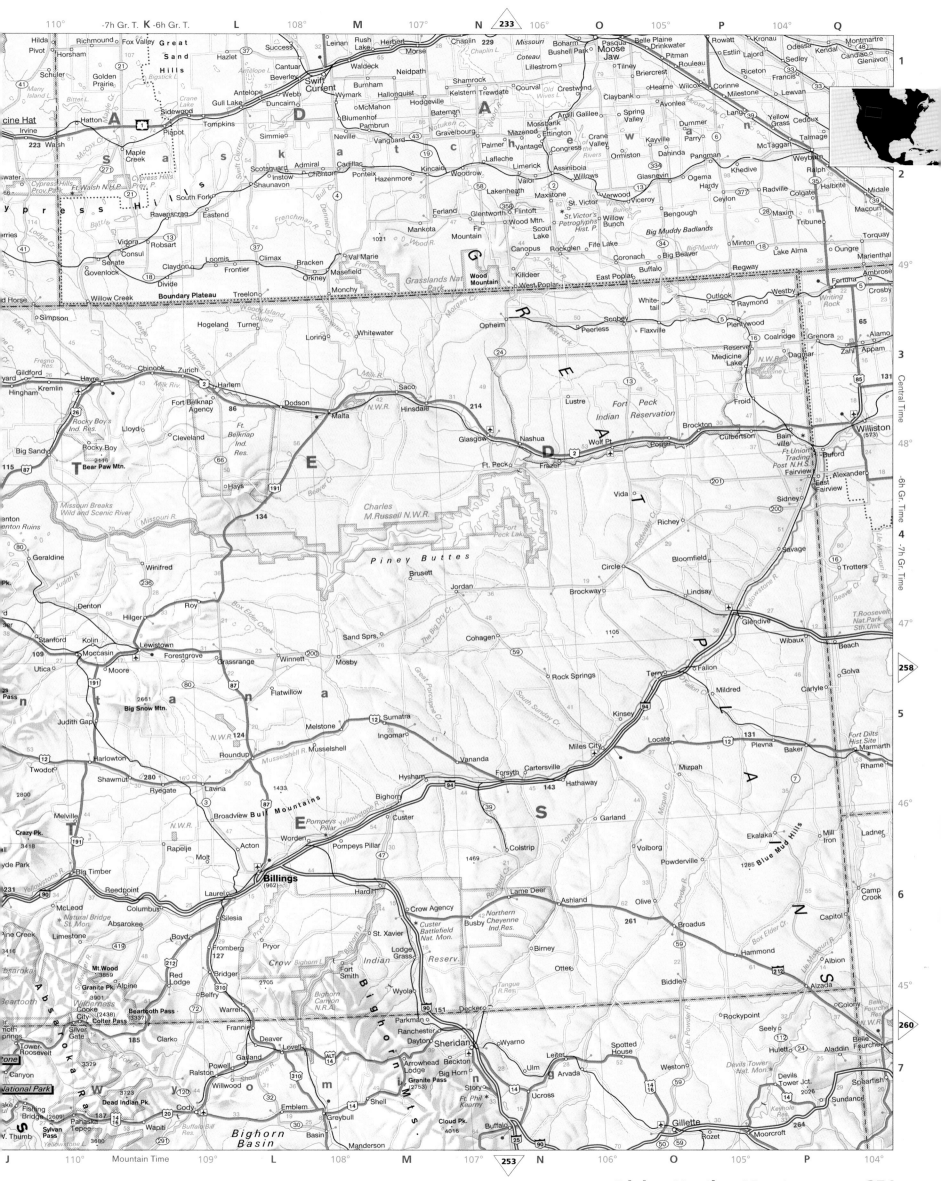

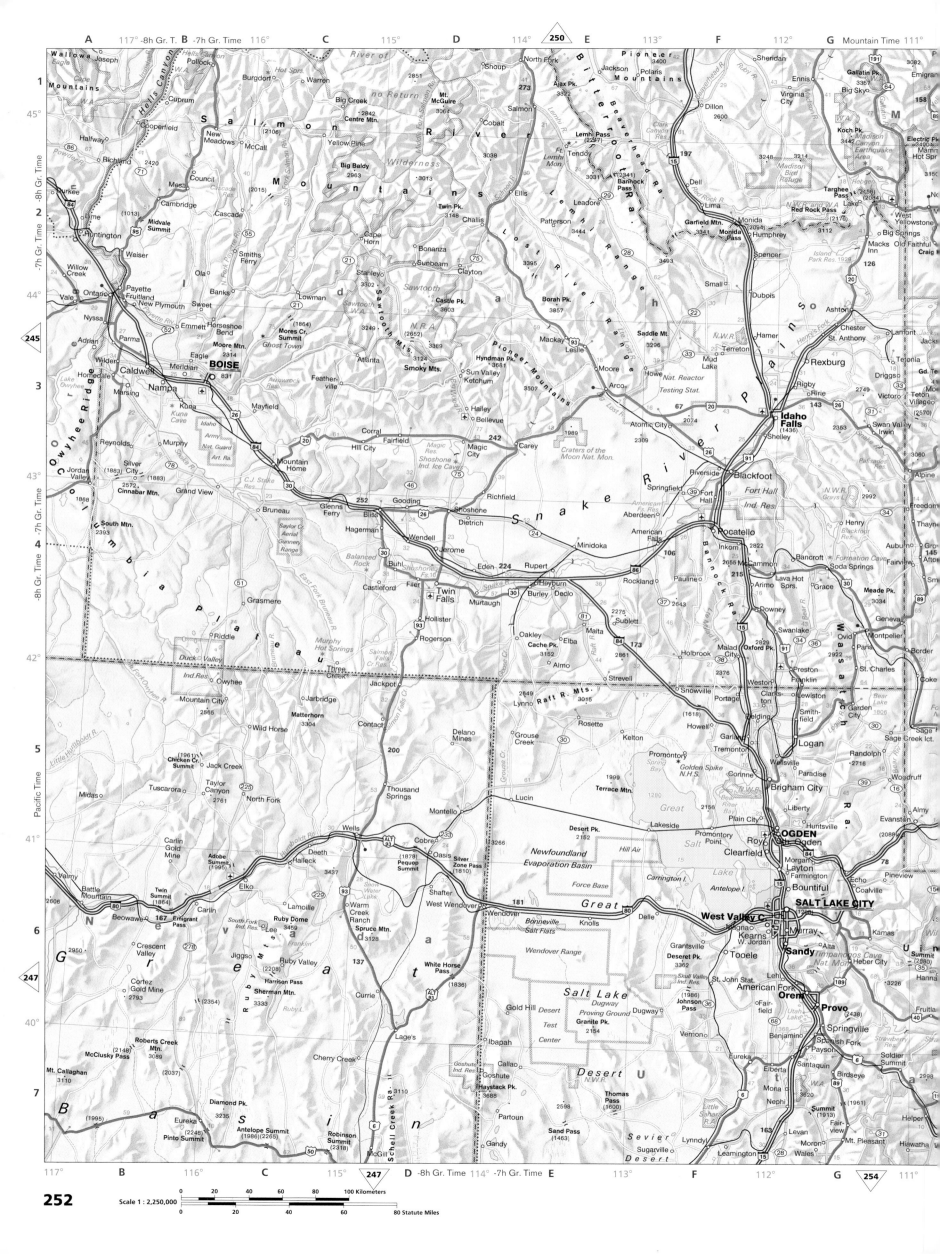

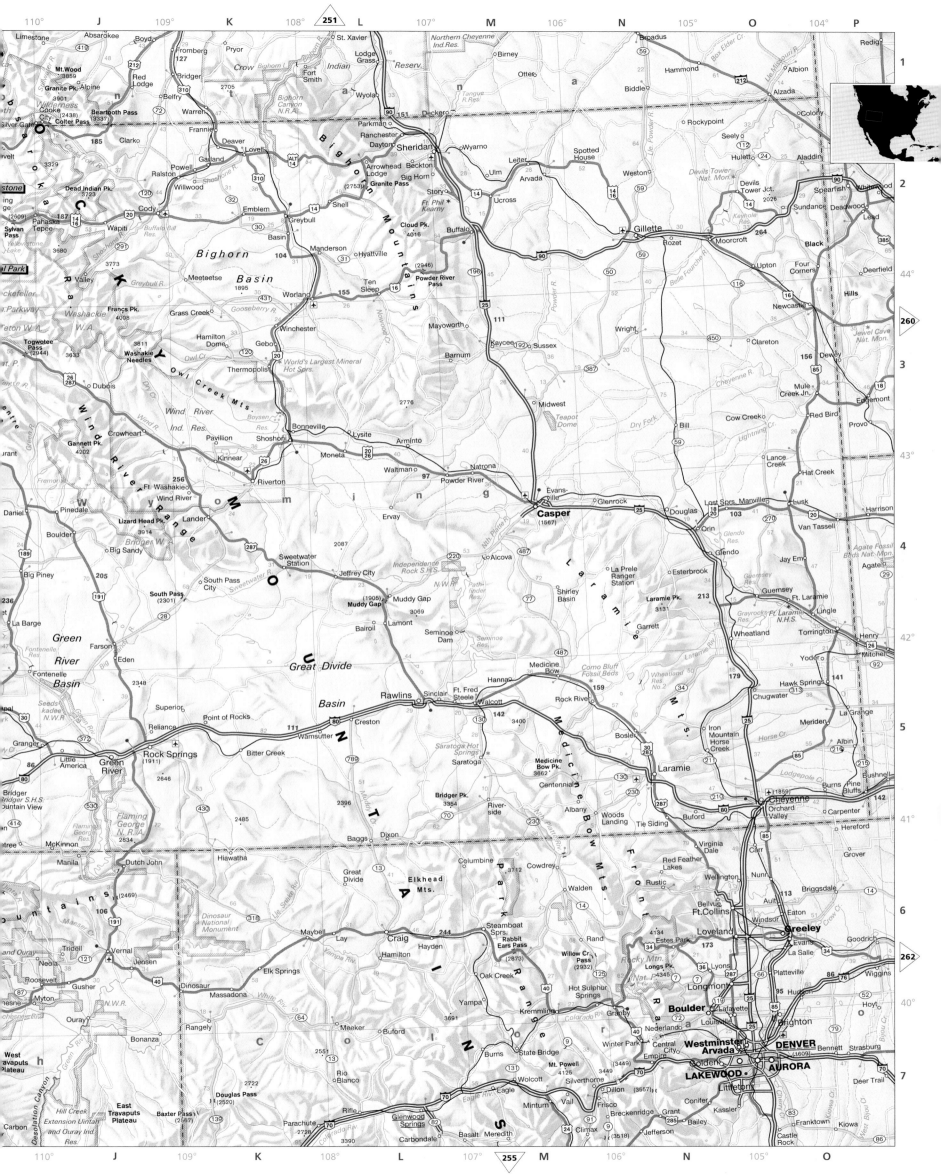

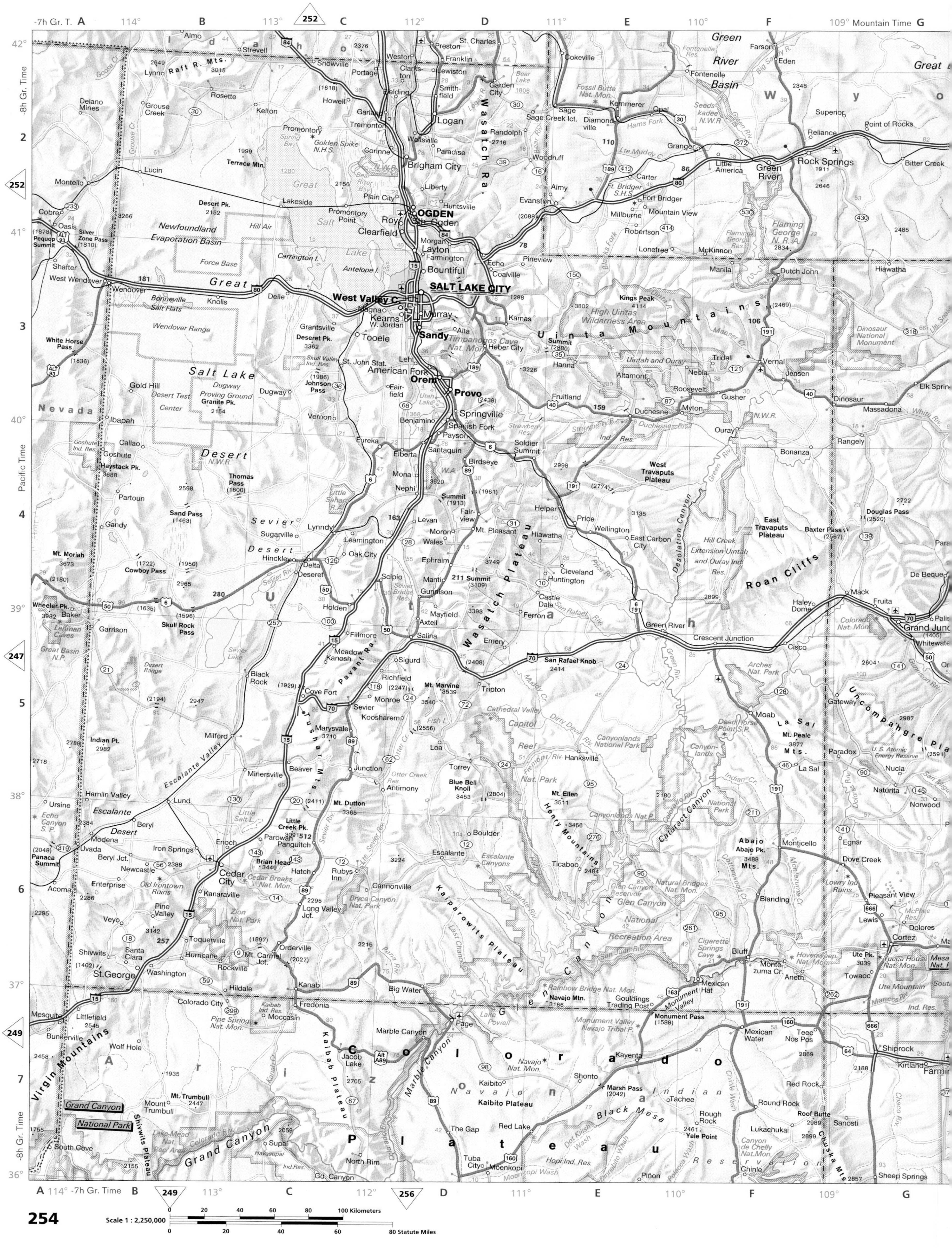

-8h Gr. Time

Pacific Time

-8h Gr. Time

42°
△252
41°
40°
△247
39°
△249
36°

Idaho

Wyoming

Great Basin

Green River

Farson · Eden
Fontenelle Res.
Fossil Butte Nat. Mon.
Kemmerer · Opal
Sage Creek Jct. · Diamondville
Hams Fork
Granger · Little America
Green River · Rock Springs 1911
Point of Rocks · Reliance · Bitter Creek
Superior
Fort Bridger S.H.S.
Evanston · Millburne · Mountain View · Robertson
Lonetree · McKinnon · Manila · Dutch John · Hiawatha
Flaming Gorge N.R.A. 2834

Cokeville · Sage
St. Charles · Preston · Franklin
Westor · Clarkston · Lewiston · Bear Lake · Garden City
Snowville · Portage · Smithfield
Almo · Strevell · Howell · Garland · Logan · Wellsville · Paradise
Lynne · Raft R. Mts. · Rosette · Tremonton · Corinne · Brigham City
Grouse Creek · Kelton · Promontory · Liberty · Huntsville · Woodruff
Delano Mines · Lucin · Golden Spike N.H.S. · Plain City · Randolph
Montello · Terrace Mtn. · Promontory Point
Lakeside · Huntsville
OGDEN
Roy · S. Ogden · Clearfield · Morgan · Echo · Coalville · Pineview
Layton · Farmington · Kaysville · Pineview
West Wendover · Wendover · Bonneville Salt Flats · Knolls · Delle
Bountiful · Coalville
SALT LAKE CITY
WEST VALLEY C. · Magna · Murray · Kamas
Kearns · W. Jordan · Sandy · Alta · Kings Peak 4114
Tooele · Deseret Pk. 3362 · Heber City · High Uintas Wilderness Area
Grantsville · Lehi · Timpanogos Cave Nat. Mon. · Uinta Mountains
St. John Stat. · American Fork · Hanna · Altamont · Tridell · Vernal
Johnson Pass · Fairfield · Orem · Provo · Summit · Neola · Jensen
Dugway · Vernon · Springville · Fruitland · Roosevelt · Gusher · Dinosaur
Gold Hill · Spanish Fork · Duchesne · Myton · Ouray · Massadona · Rangely
Ibapah · Benjamin · Payson · Soldier Summit · Duchesne River · Bonanza
Eureka · Santaquin · Helper
Callao · Goshute · Elberta · Mona · Nephi · Birdseye · Price · Wellington
Haystack Pk. 3688 · Thomas Pass · Levan · Fairview · Hiawatha · East Carbon City
Sugarville · Lynndyl · Moroni · Mt. Pleasant · Cleveland · Huntington
Partoun · Sand Pass · Leamington · Wales · Ephraim · Castle Dale · Ferron
Gandy · Oak City · Scipio · Manti · Gunnison · Green River
Mt. Moriah 3673 · Hinckley · Delta · Holden · Mayfield · Emery · Crescent Junction · Cisco
Cowboy Pass · Deseret · Axtell · Salina · Grand Junction
Wheeler Pk. 3982 · Baker · Garrison · Fillmore · Meadow · Sigurd · San Rafael Knob 2414 · Mack · Fruita
Great Basin N.P. · Kanosh · Richfield · Tripton · Green River · Colorado Nat. Mon.
Black Rock · Cove Fort · Monroe · Mt. Marvine 3539 · Gateway
Sevier · Koosharem · Cathedral Valley · Moab
Marysvale · Junction · Loa · Torrey · Hanksville · Mt. Peale 3877 · La Sal
Milford · Minersville · Beaver · Antimony · Blue Bell Knoll · Henry Mountains · Paradox
Indian Pt. 2982 · Hamlin Valley · Lund · Mt. Dutton 3365 · Mt. Ellen 3511 · Nucla · Naturita · Norwood
Escalante Desert · Beryl · Little Creek Pk. · Boulder · Escalante · Ticaboo · Abajo Pk. 3488 · Monticello · Egnar
Ursine · Modena · Enoch · Parowan · Brian Head 3449 · Panguitch · Cannonville · Blanding · Dove Creek
Panaca Summit · Beryl Jct. · Newcastle · Cedar City · Hatch · Ruby's Inn · Cannonville · Natural Bridges Nat. Mon. · Lewis · Dolores · Cortez
Acoma · Enterprise · Kanarraville · Cedar Breaks Nat. Mon. · Bryce Canyon Nat. Park · Glen Canyon · Pleasant View
Pine Valley · Long Valley Jct. · Escalante Canyons · Cigarette Springs Cave · Bluff · Ute Pk. 3039 · Hovenweep Nat. Mon.
Veyo · Toquerville · Orderville · Kaiparowits Plateau · Montezuma Cr. · Aneth · Towaoc
Shivwits · Santa Clara · Hurricane · Mt. Carmel Jct. · Rockville · Glen Canyon National Recreation Area · Monte · Yucca House Nat. Mon.
St. George · Washington · Zion Nat. Park · Kanab · Big Water · Navajo Mtn. 3166 · Mexican Hat · Ute Mountain Ind. Res.
Hildale · Fredonia · Page · Gouldings Trading Post · Monument Pass · Mexican Water · Teec Nos Pos · Shiprock
Mesquite · Littlefield · Colorado City · Pipe Spring Nat. Mon. · Moccasin · Marble Canyon · Navajo Nat'l Mon. · Monument Valley Navajo Tribal P. · Kayenta · Red Rock · Kirtland
Bunkerville · Wolf Hole · Jacob Lake · Lake Powell · Shonto · Round Rock · Roof Butte · Sanosti
Virgin Mountains · Mt. Trumbull 2447 · Marsh Pass · Lukachukai · Canyon de Chelly Nat. Mon.
Grand Canyon National Park · Supai · The Gap · Red Lake · Tuba City · Moenkopi · Yale Point · Rough Rock · Chinle · Sheep Springs
South Cove · North Rim · Kaibito Plateau · Black Mesa · Hopi Ind. Res. · Piñon
Grand Canyon · Gd. Canyon · Navajo Ind. Res. · Plateau

Nevada · Great Salt Lake Desert · Salt Lake · Sevier Desert · Great Salt Lake · Bonneville Salt Flats · Wasatch Range · Uinta Mountains · Wasatch Plateau · West Tavaputs Plateau · East Tavaputs Plateau · Roan Cliffs · Desolation Canyon · Uncompahgre Plateau · La Sal Mts. · Escalante Valley · Tushar Mts. · Pavant Ra. · Canyonlands National Park · Capitol Reef Nat. Park · Arches Nat. Park · Dead Horse Point S.P. · Colorado · Kaibab Plateau · Kaiparowits Plateau · Last Chance Ra. · Glen Canyon · Cataract Canyon · Dinosaur National Monument · Colorado National Monument

Scale 1 : 2,250,000

0 20 40 60 80 100 Kilometers

0 20 40 60 80 Statute Miles

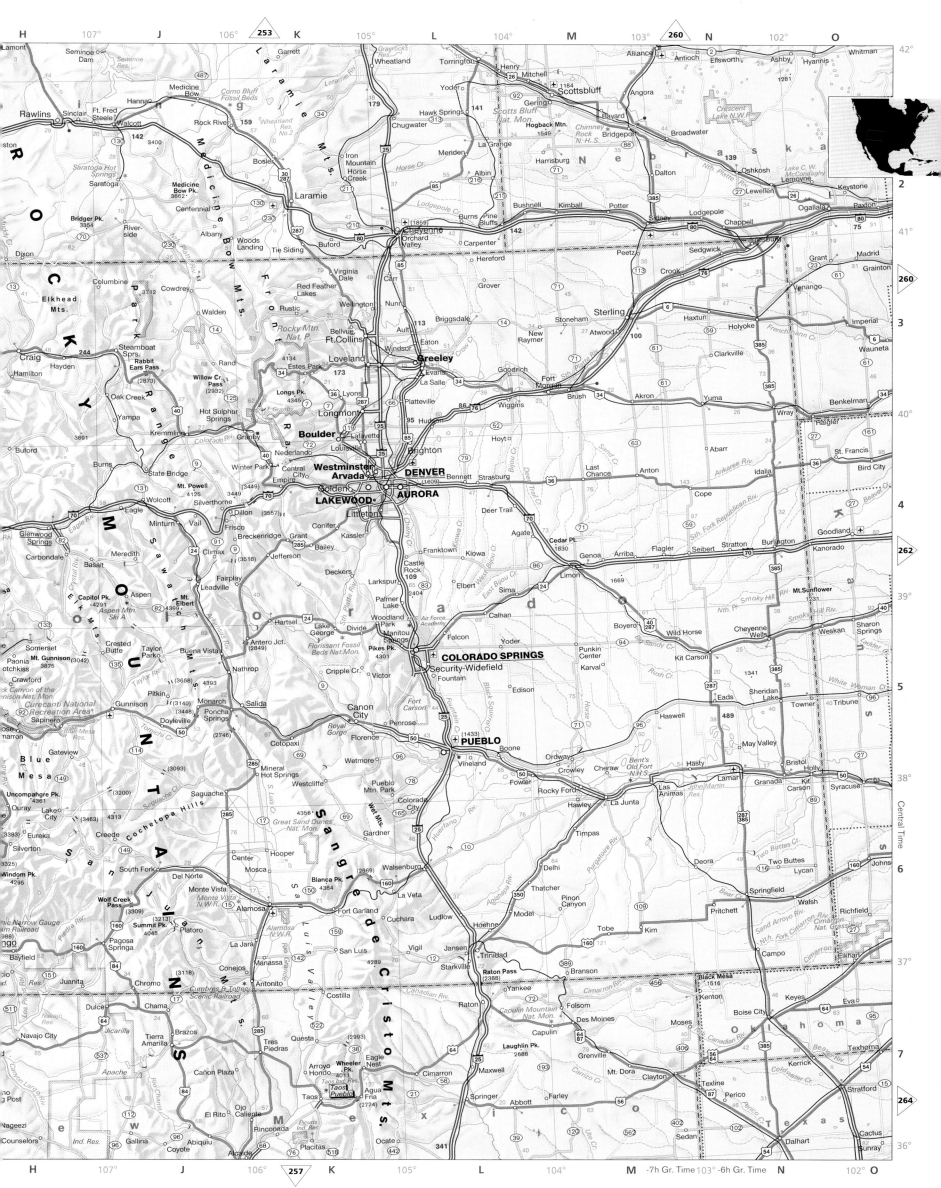

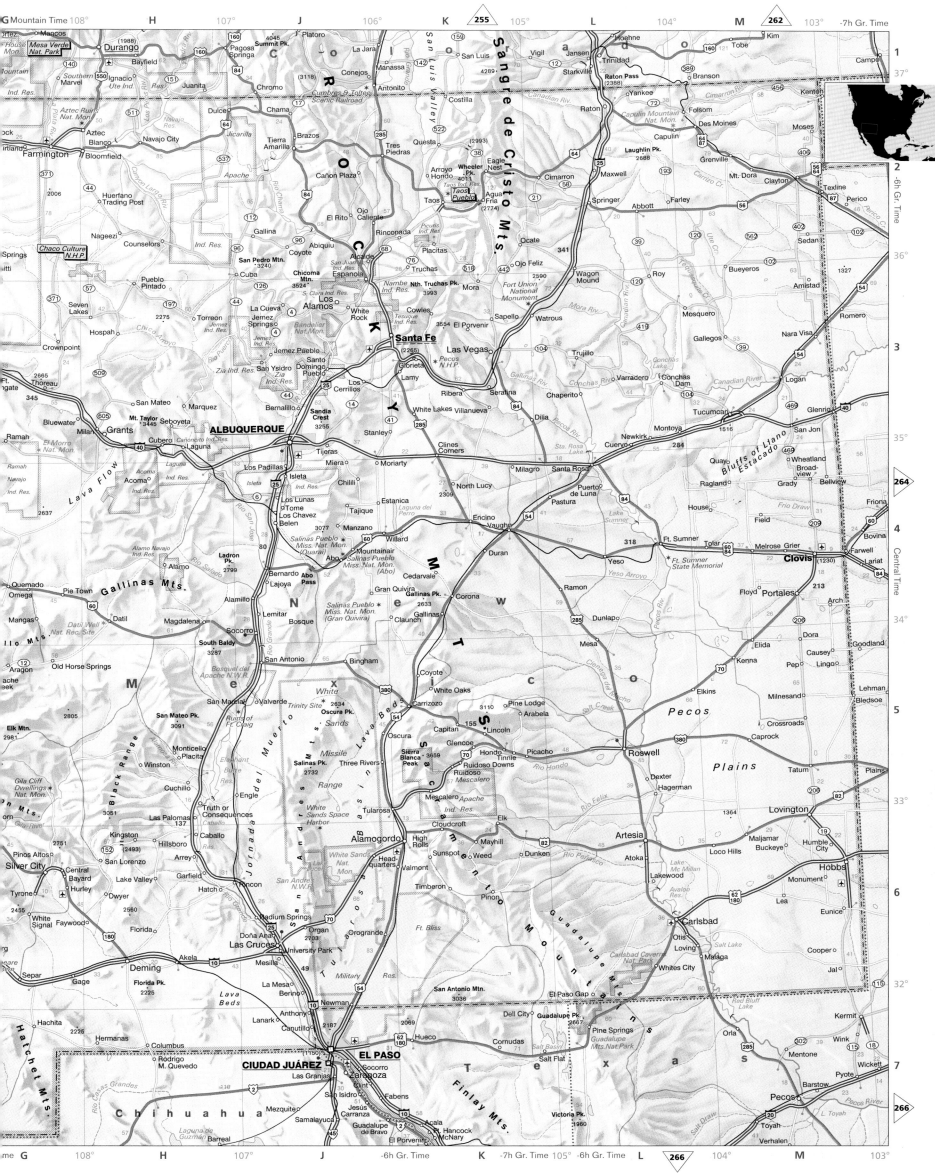

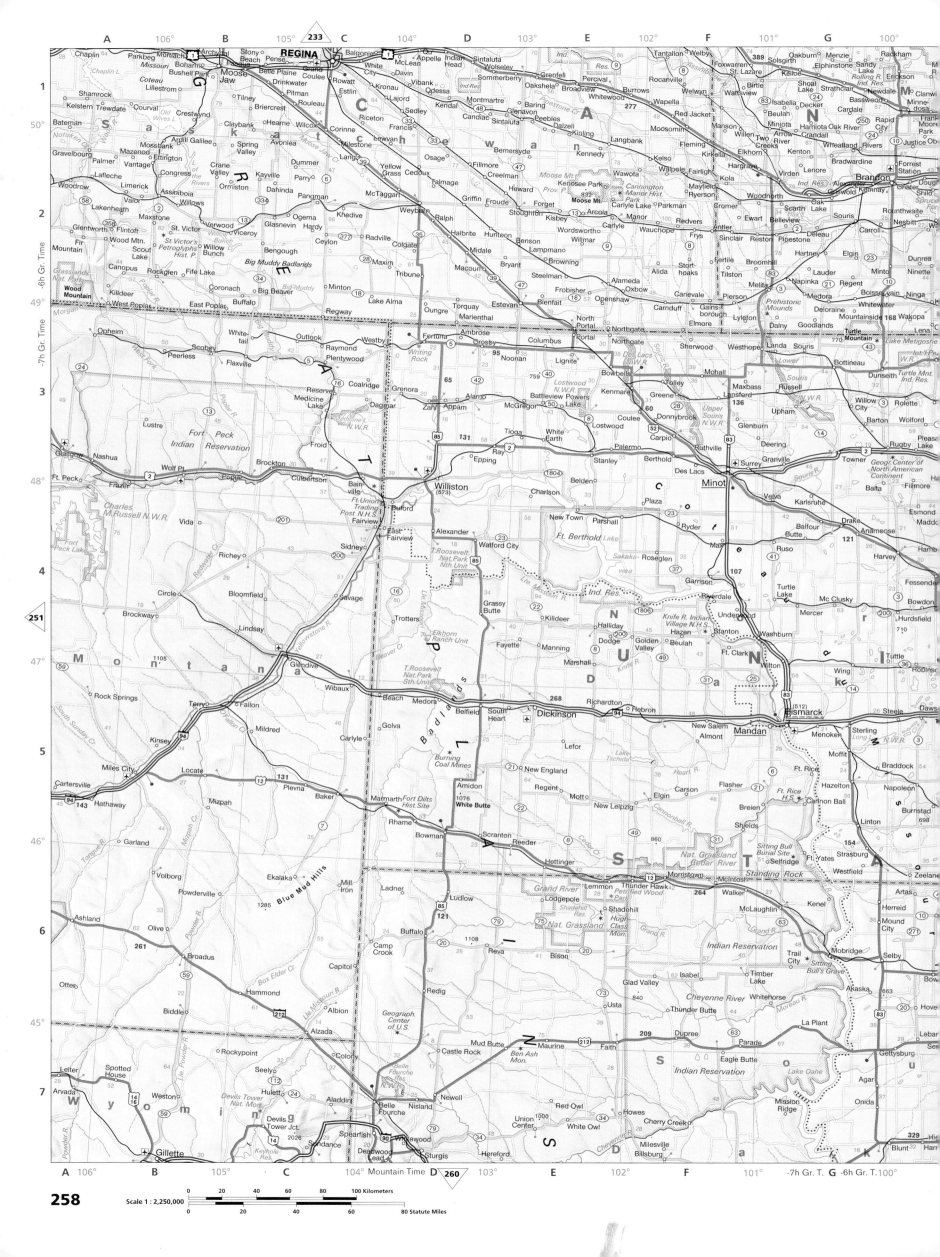

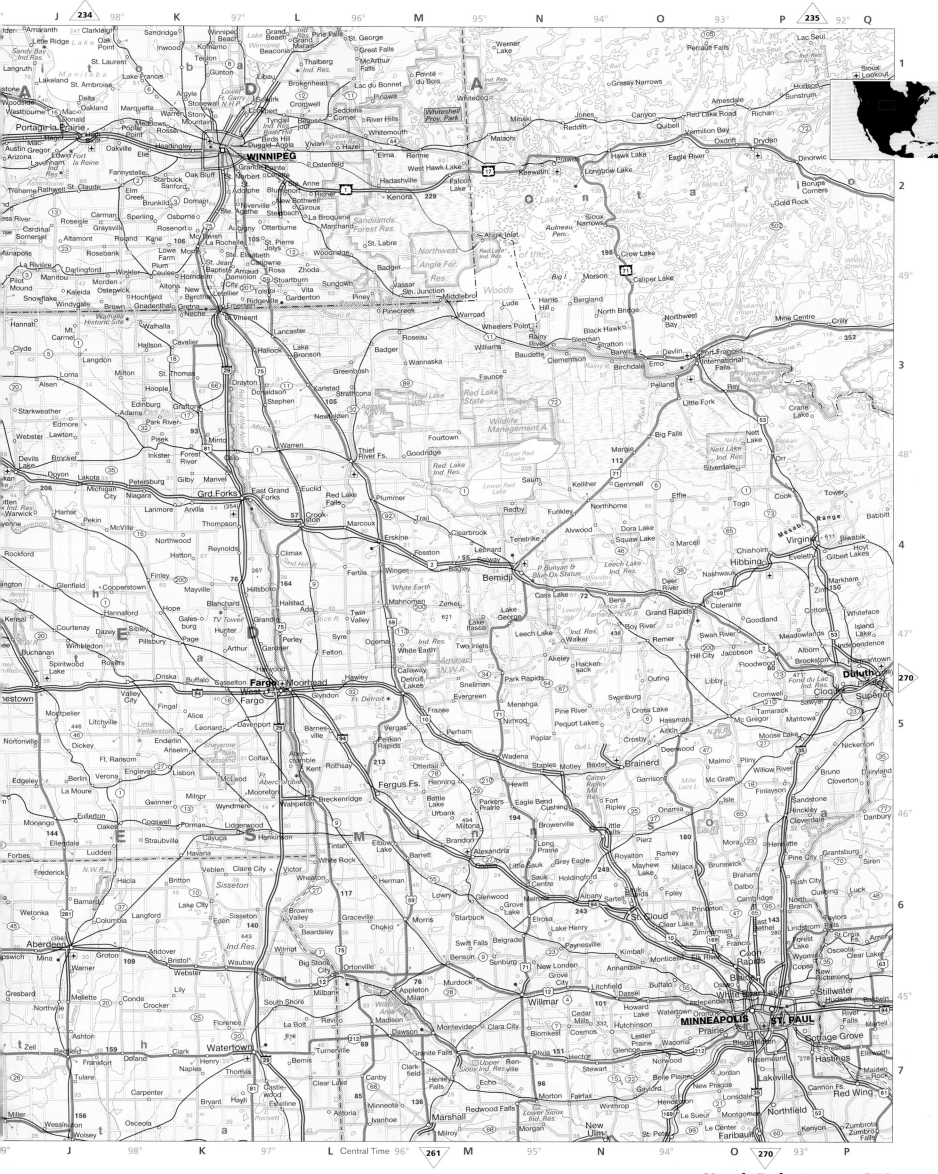

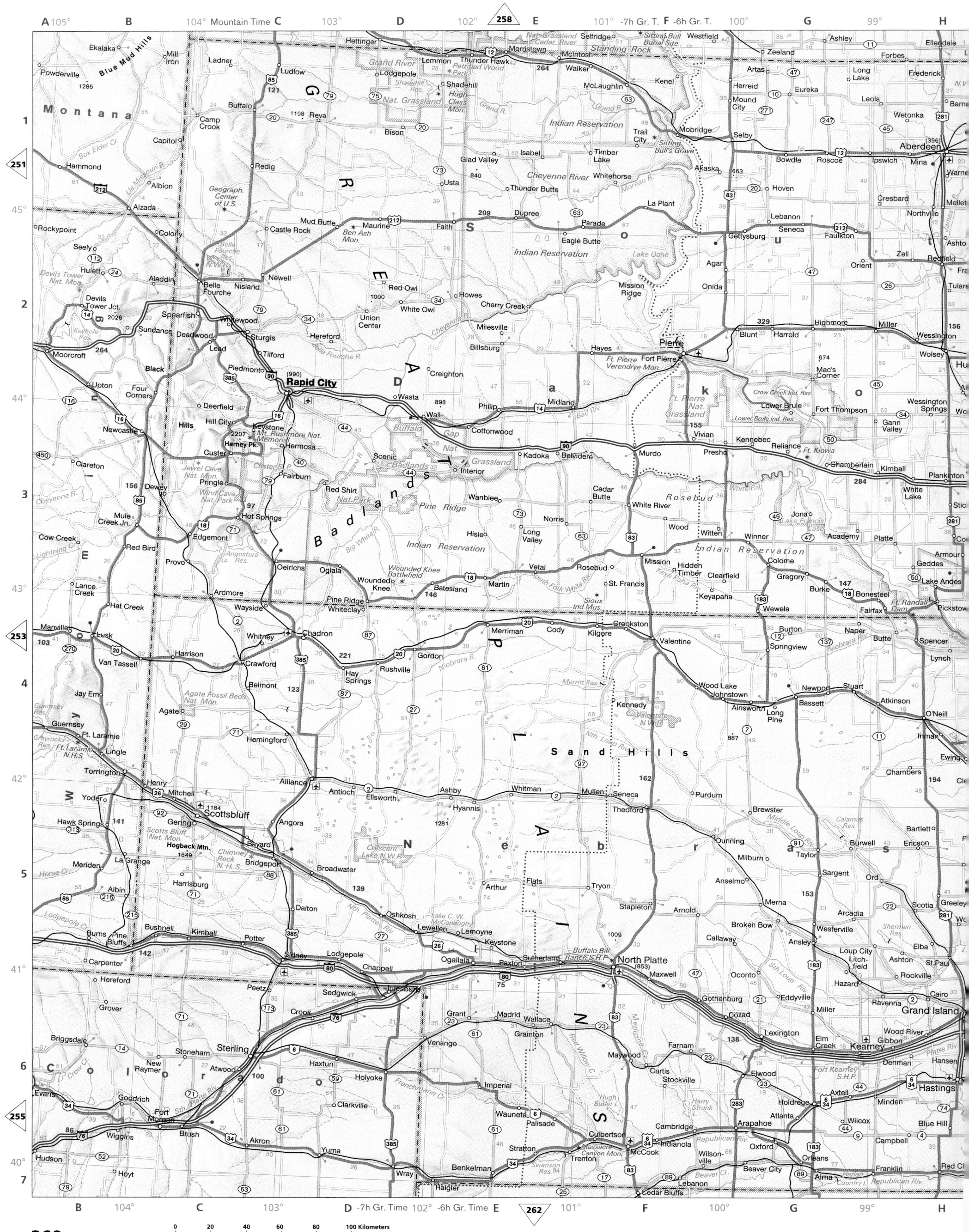

Scale 1 : 2,250,000

100 Kilometers
20 40 60 80

80 Statute Miles
20 40 60

-7h Gr. Time 102° -6h Gr. Time

Montana

Colorado

Rapid City

Badlands

Sand Hills

Black Hills

Aberdeen

Pierre

Fort Pierre

Scottsbluff

North Platte

Kearney

Grand Island

Hastings

Indian Reservation

Rosebud

Standing Rock

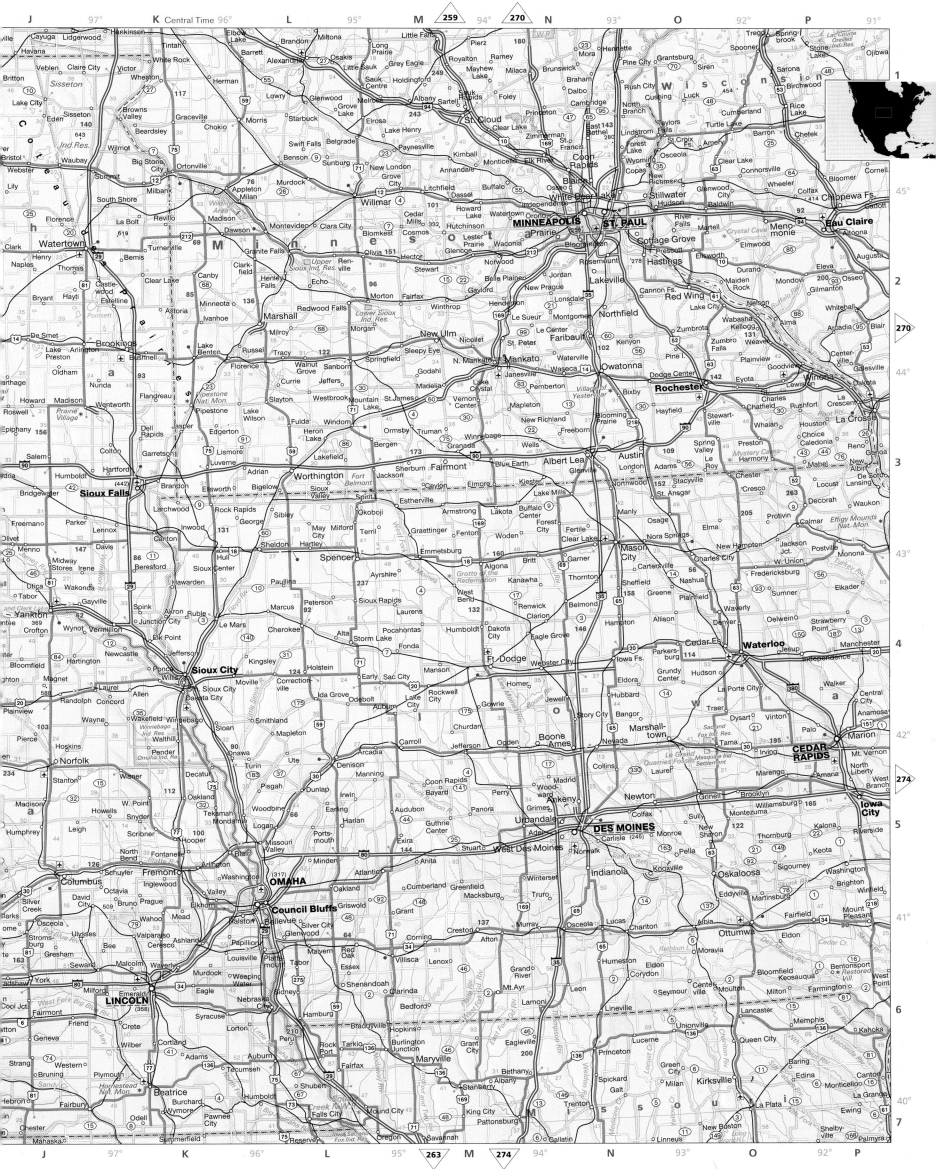

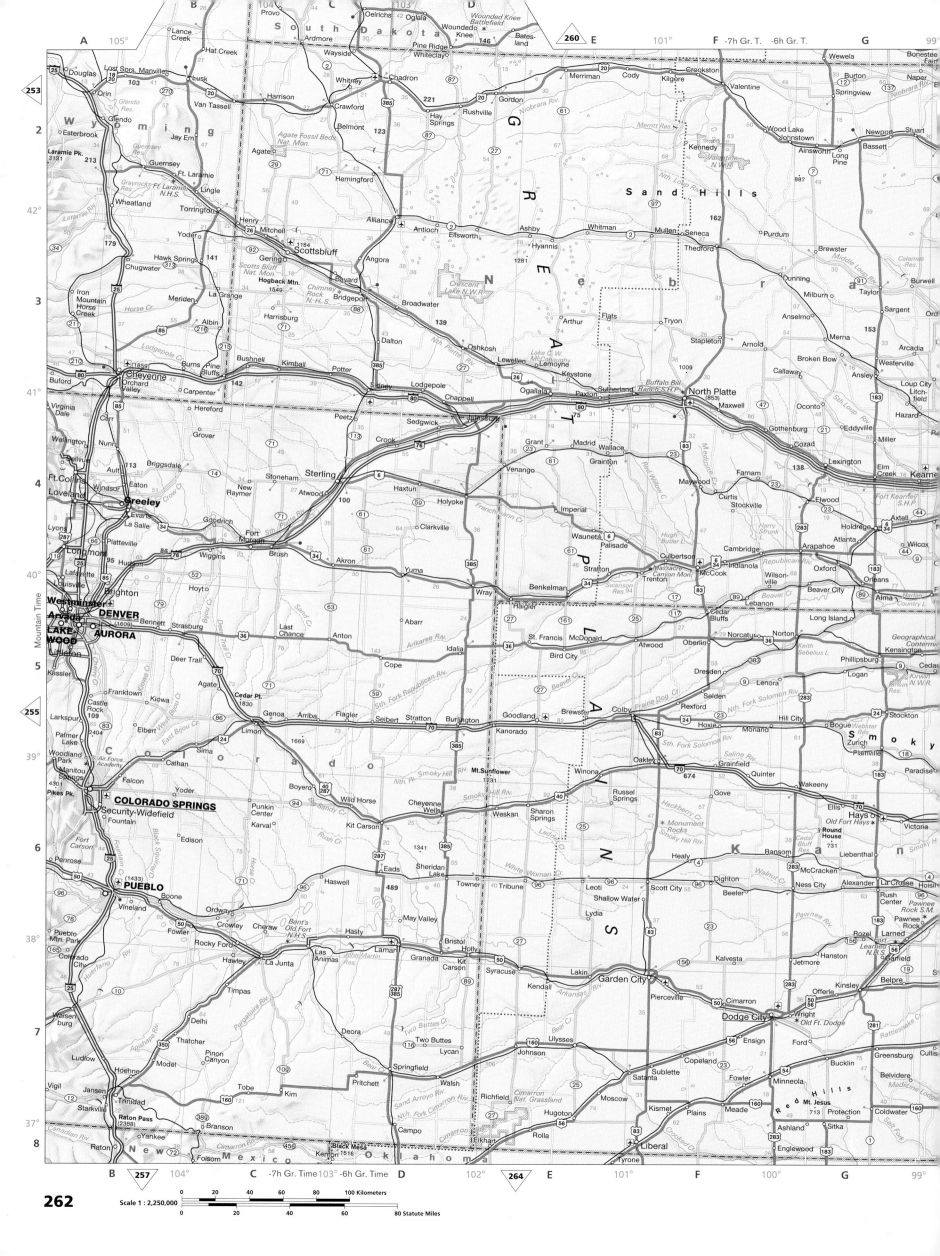

Scale 1 : 2,250,000

0   20   40   60   80   100 Kilometers

0   20   40   60   80 Statute Miles

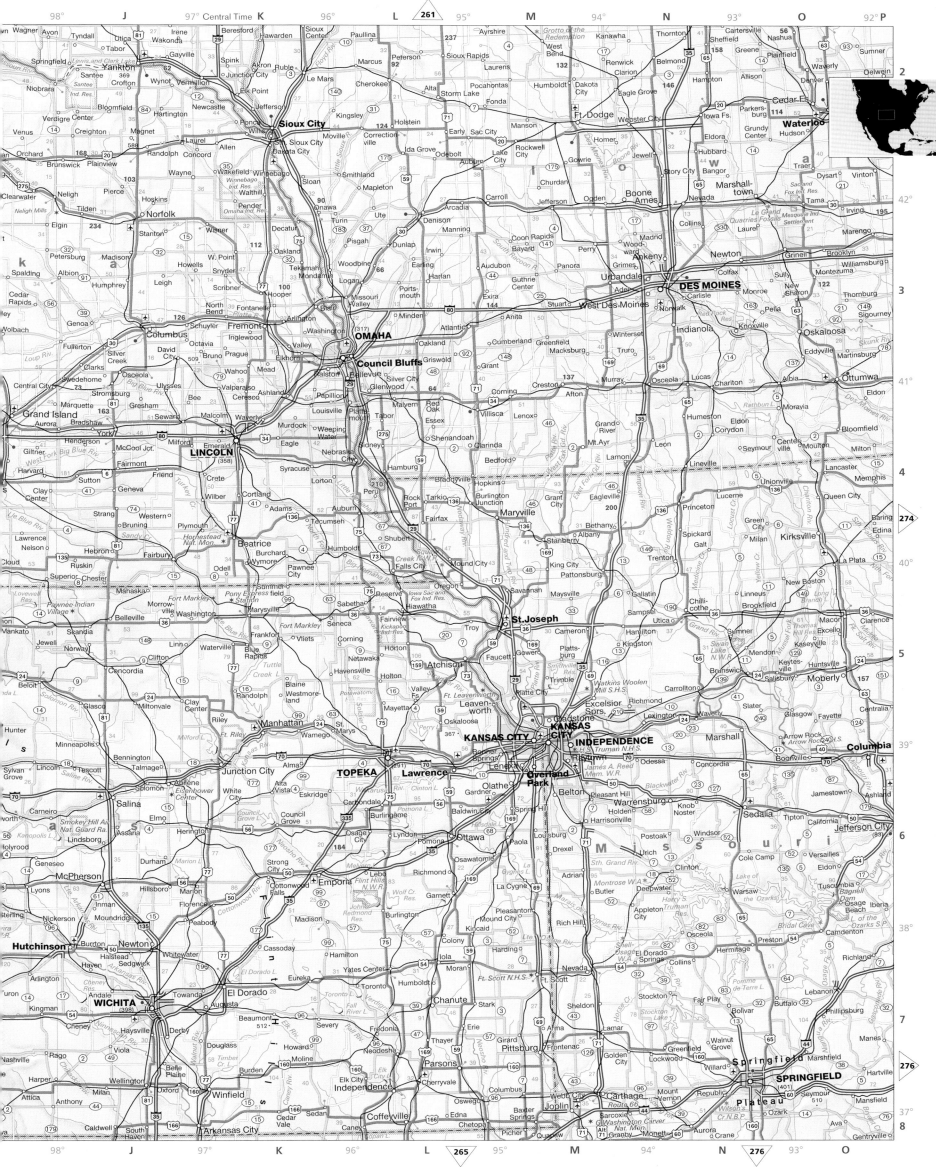

A 104° 103° Mountain Time B -7h Gr. Time 102° -6h Gr. Time C 101° D 100° E 99° F 98°

255

C o l o r a d o

Pinon Canyon • Deora • Two Buttes • Lycan • Ulysses • Ensign • Ford • Greensburg • Cullison • Pratt • Iuka • Kingman

Tobe • Kim • Springfield • Walsh • Johnson • Copeland • Bucklin • Belvidere • Sawyer • Nashville

1

Branson • Pritchett • Richfield • Moscow • Satanta • Fowler • Minneola • Red Hills • Mt. Jesus 713 • Protection • Coldwater • Medicine Lodge • Harper

K A N S A S

Folsom • Campo • Hugoton • Kismet • Plains • Meade • Ashland • Sitka • Englewood • Hardtner • Kiowa • Attica

Capulin Mountain Nat. Mon. • Kenton • Rolla • Elkhart • Liberal • Forgan • Rosston • Buffalo • Freedom • Avard • Alva • Cherokee • Hopeton

Capulin • Moses • Keyes • Hooker • Tyrone • Turpin • Beaver • Gate • Laverne • May • Fort Supply • Waynoka • Carmen • Jet • Goltry

2

Mt. Dora • Clayton • Texline • Guymon • Goodwell • Gray • Elmwood • Slapout • Woodward • Mooreland • Cleo Springs • Ringwood

O K L A H O M A

Sedan • Perico • Stratford • Texhoma • Gruver • Booker • Perryton • Follet • Fargo • Gage • Shattuck • Vici • Selling • Okeene • Canton L.

Bueyeros • Dalhart • Cactus • Morse • Spearman • Lipscomb • Higgins • Arnett • Camargo • Taloga • Canton

3

New Mexico • Amistad • Hartley • Dumas • Stinnett • Borger • Miami • Briscoe • Reydon • Cheyenne • Hammon • Arapaho • Weatherford • Calumet

Gallegos • Nara Visa • Romero • Channing • Fritch • Canadian • Allison • Rankin • Butler • Thomas • Geary

Logan • Tascosa • Pampa • Lefors • Mobeetie • Wheeler • Kelton • Sweetwater • Berlin • Foss • Clinton • Hinton • Binger

Tucumcari • Adriano • Vega • **AMARILLO** (1120) • White Deer • Panhandle • Groom • Alanreed • McLean • Sayre • Elk City 262 • Cordell

35° • San Jon • Glenrio • Wildorado • Bushland • Washburn • Conway • Lark • Shamrock • Texola • Erick • Alfalfa • Ft. Cobb

Quay • Wheatland • Umbarger • Claude • Goodnight • Lutie • Willow • Hobart • Gotebo • Carnegie

257 • Ragland • Bellview • Hereford • Canyon • Dawn • Ashtola • Clarendon • Hedley • Wellington • Vinson • Reed • Mangum • Blair • Roosevelt • Cyril

House • Field • Summerfield • Happy • Palo Duro Canyon S.P. • Hollis • Duke • Altus • Snyder • Cache • **Lawton**

4 • Melrose • Grier • Friona • Easter • Dimmitt • Tulia • Newlin • Estelline • Gould • Olustee • Tipton • 141

Clovis (1230) • Farwell • Bovina • Nazareth • Kress • Silverton • Turkey • Childress • Kirkland • Quanah • Chilicothe • Frederick • Grandfield • Temple

Floyd • Portales • Lariat • Muleshoe • Roy • Hart • Whitely • Quitaque • Flomot • Northfield • Goodlett • Davidson • Randlett

Elida • Dora • Goodland • Springlake • Olton • Aiken • Sth. Plains • Matador • Paducah • Dunlap • Swearingen • Vernon • Harrold • Electra • Burkburnett

34° • Kenna • Causey • Sudan • Amherst • Littlefield • Spade • Lockney • Whiteflat • Crowell • Thalia • **Wichita Falls**

Milnesand • Pep • Lingo • Enochs • Morton • Whitharral • Anton • Abernathy • Petersburg • Floydada • Roaring Springs • Dumont • Truscott • Iowa Park • Holliday

Crossroads • Bledsoe • Lehman • Whiteface • Levelland • New Deal • Idalou • Lorenzo • McAdoo • Dickens • Guthrie • Vera • Mabelle • Dundee • Henrietta

5 • Caprock • Smyer • **LUBBOCK** (988) • Ralls • Crosbyton • Benjamin • Seymour • Archer City • Windthorst

Wolfforth • Ropesville • Slaton • Spur • White River L. • Rochester • Knox City • Munday • Megargel • Olney • Jean

Tatum • Plains • Meadow • West Point • Southland • Kalgary • Jayton • Clairemont • Aspermont • Rule • Throckmorton • Elbert • Loving • Bryson

Brownfield • Tahoka • Post • Justiceburg • Swenson • Haskell • Newcastle • Graham

33° • Lovington • Seagraves • Wellman • New Moore • O'Donnell • Dermott • Rotan • Hamlin • Avoca • Lueders • Albany • Breckenridge • Caddo • Palo Pinto

Maljamar • Denver City • Loop • Welch • Gail • Key • Roby • Sylvester • Anson • Eliasville • Brad

Buckeye • Humble City • Lamesa • McCaulley • Moran • Ranger • Strawn • Santo • Gordon

6 • Hobbs • Seminole • Patricia • Ira • Dunn • Hermleigh • Inadale • Roscoe • **ABILENE** • Baird • Putnam • Cisco • Eastland • Morgan Mill

Lea • Monument • Ackerly • Vincent • Snyder • Hawley • Sweetwater • Merkel • View • Tuscola • Carbon • Stephenville

Eunice • Andrews • Tarzan • Fairview • Westbrook • Coahoma • Colorado City • Loraine • Gorman • De Leon • Dublin

32° • Cooper • North Cowden • Stanton • Lees • Big Spring (866) • Maryneal • Blackwell • Bradshaw • Lawn • Rowden • Rising Star • Proctor

Kermit • Gardendale • **Midland** • Garden City • Sterling City • Robert Lee • Bronte • Winters • Wingate • Comanche

7 • Notrees • Penwell • **Odessa** (882) • Midkiff • Water Valley • Tennyson • Ballinger • Rowena • Valera • Early • Brownwood • Lamkin • Zephyr • Priddy

Mentone • Wink • Monahans • Wickett

264

Scale 1 : 2,250,000

0 20 40 60 80 100 Kilometers
0 20 40 60 80 Statute Miles

A 103° B 266 102° C 101° D 100° E 267 99° F

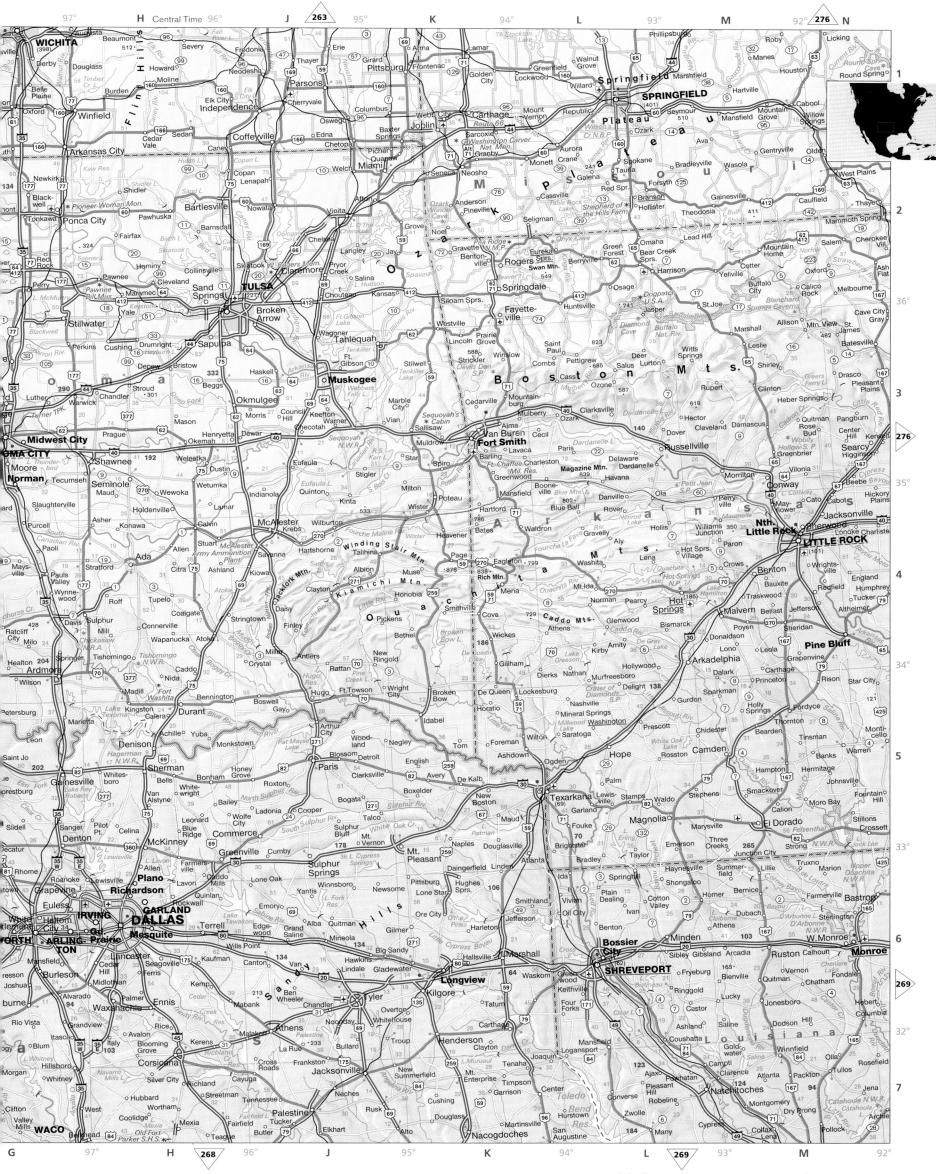

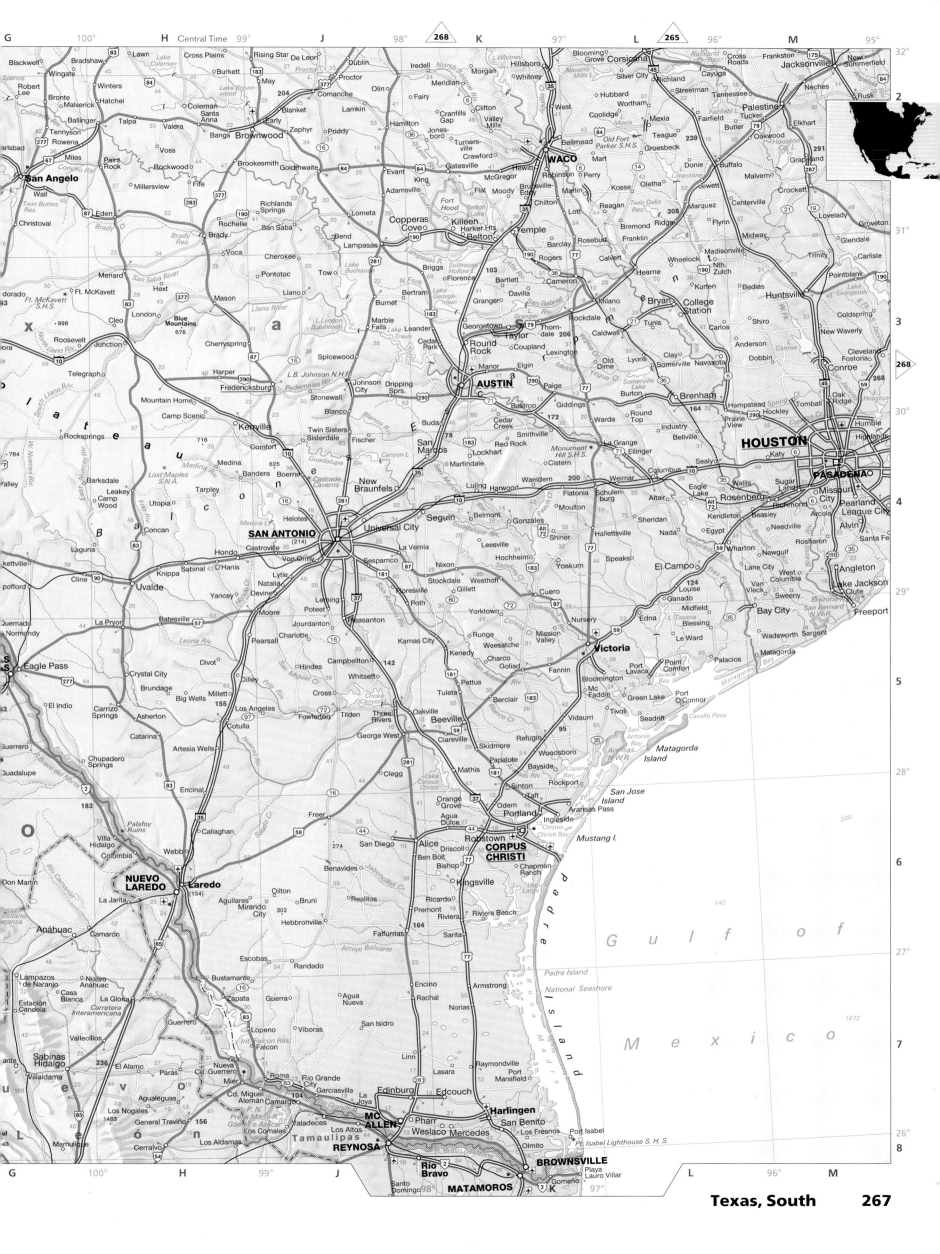

Scale 1 : 2,250,000

0 20 40 60 80 100 Kilometers

0 20 40 60 80 Statute Miles

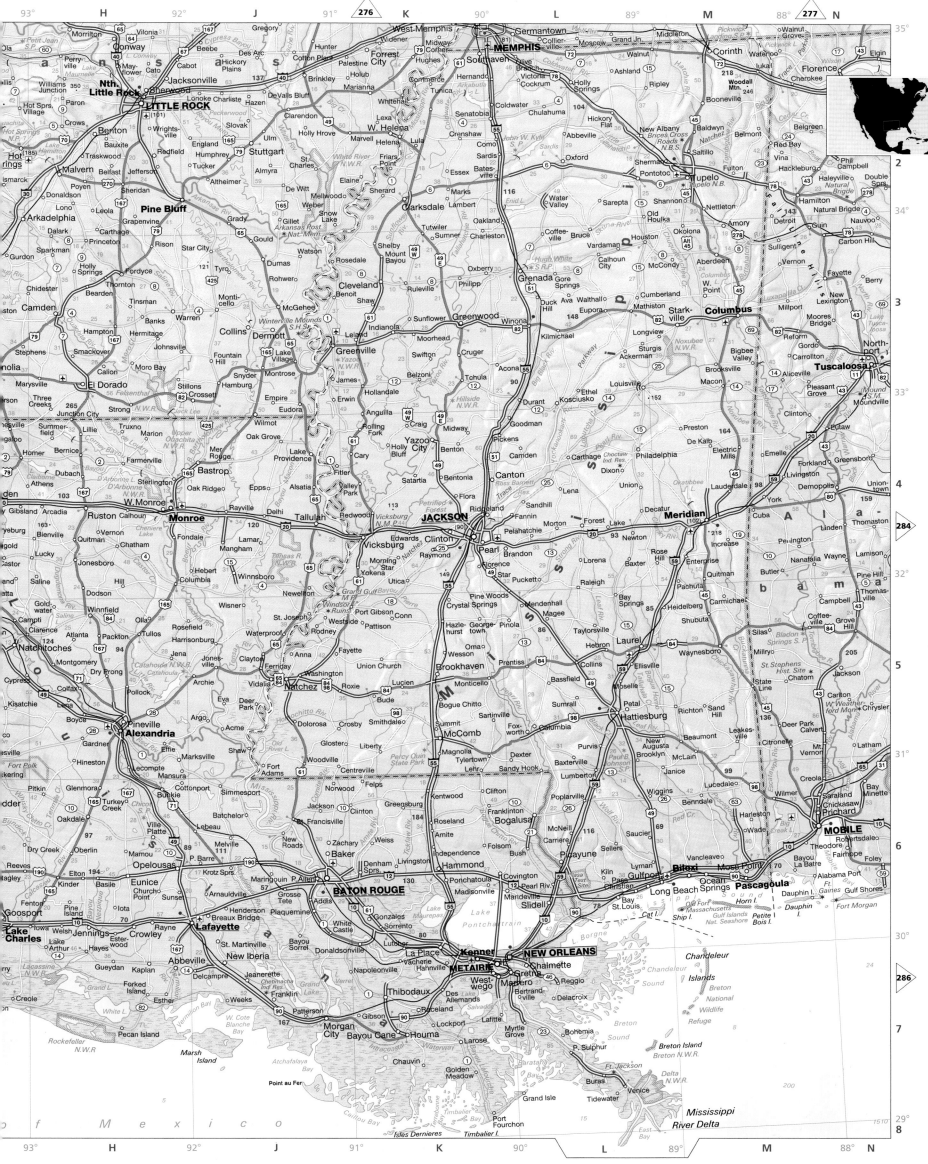

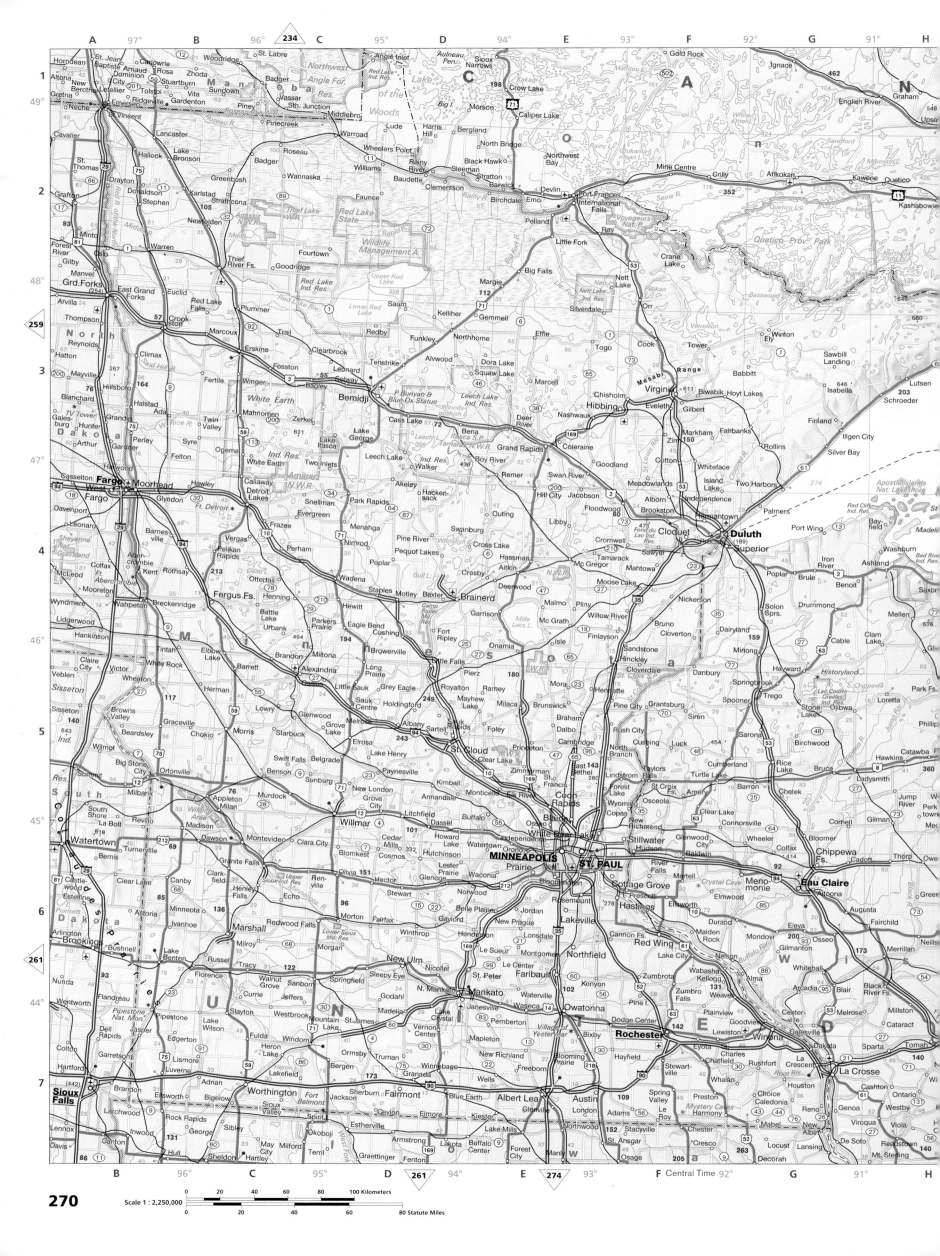

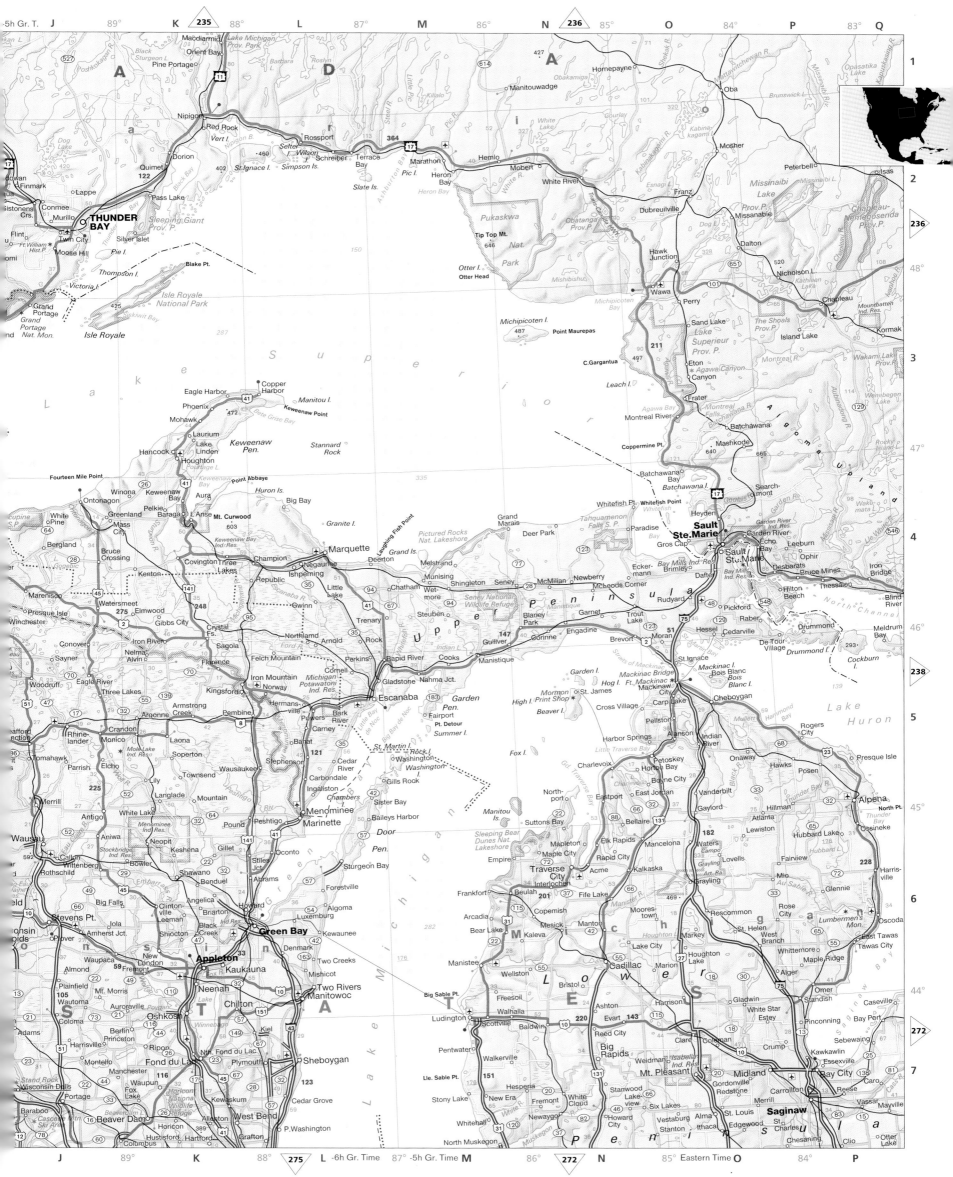

CHICAGO **MILWAUKEE** **DETROIT** **Green Bay** **Appleton** **GRAND RAPIDS** **LANSING** **FLINT** **ANN ARBOR** **Kalamazoo** **Saginaw** **Sault Ste.Marie** **FT. WAYNE** **SOUTH BEND** **GARY** **TOLEDO** **WARREN** **STERLING HTS.** **LIVONIA** **Pontiac** **WINDSOR** **Sarnia** **MANSFIELD**

Michigan Lower Peninsula Upper Peninsula Illinois Indiana Ohio Wisconsin

Lake Michigan Lake Huron Lake St. Clair Manitoulin I.

Escanaba Marinette Menominee Oshkosh Neenah Manitowoc Sheboygan Fond du Lac West Bend Waukesha Wauwatosa Racine Kenosha Waukegan Evanston Skokie Oak Lawn Aurora Joliet Elgin Hammond Traverse City Cadillac Ludington Muskegon Holland Battle Creek Jackson Mt. Pleasant Midland Bay City Alpena Petoskey Cheboygan Mackinaw City St. Ignace Gaylord Grayling Niles Elkhart Goshen Warsaw Kokomo Marion Huntington Lima Findlay Bowling Green Monroe Adrian

Scale 1 : 2,250,000

0 20 40 60 80 100 Kilometers
0 20 40 60 80 Statute Miles

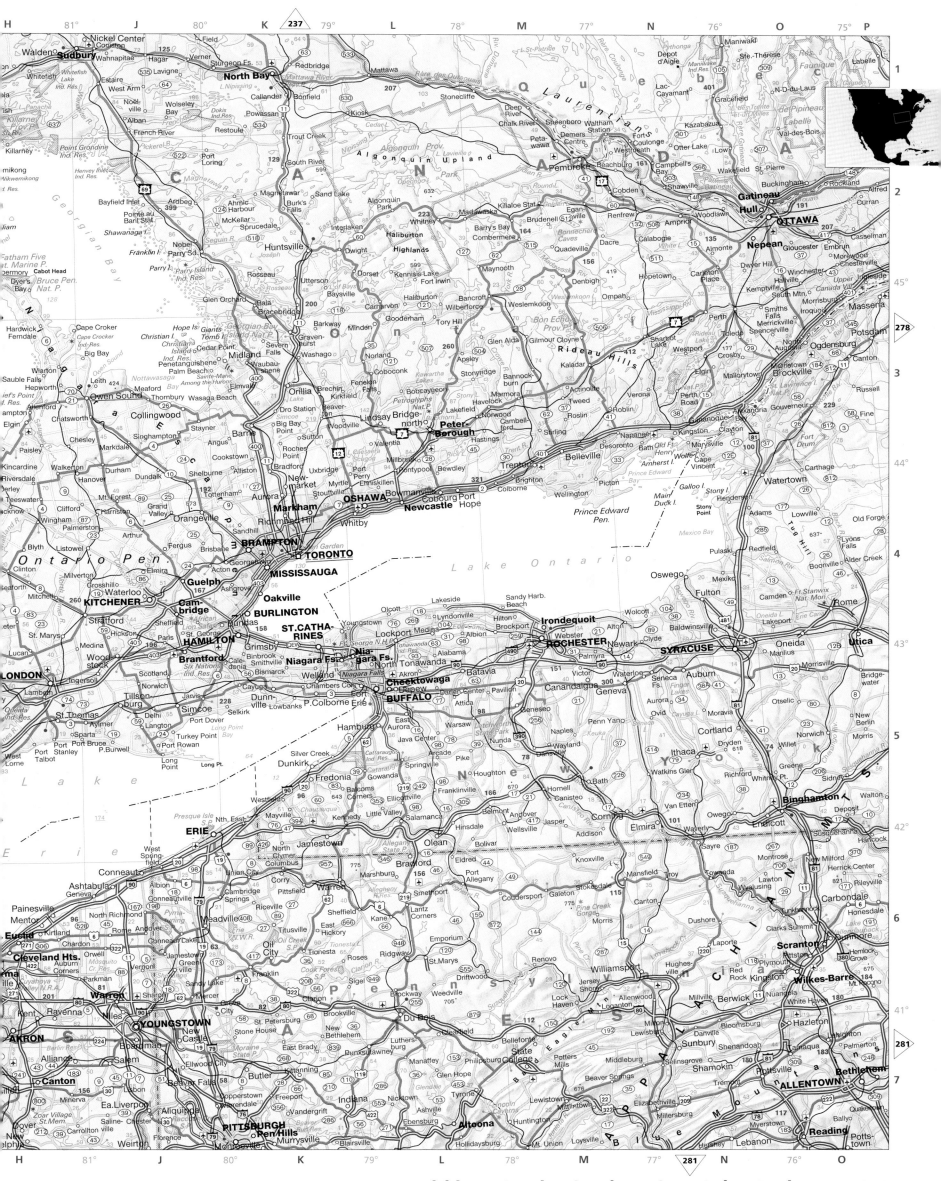

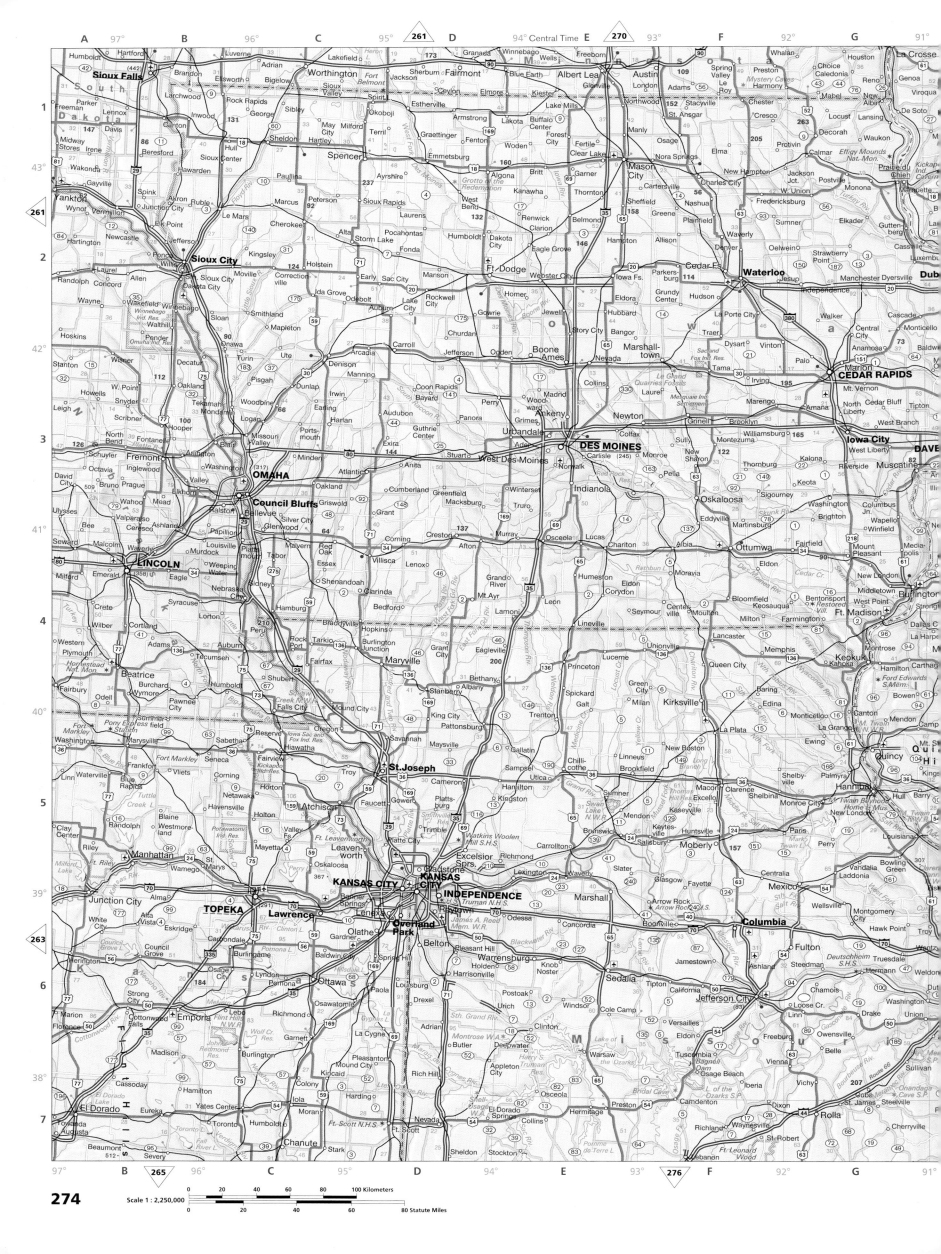

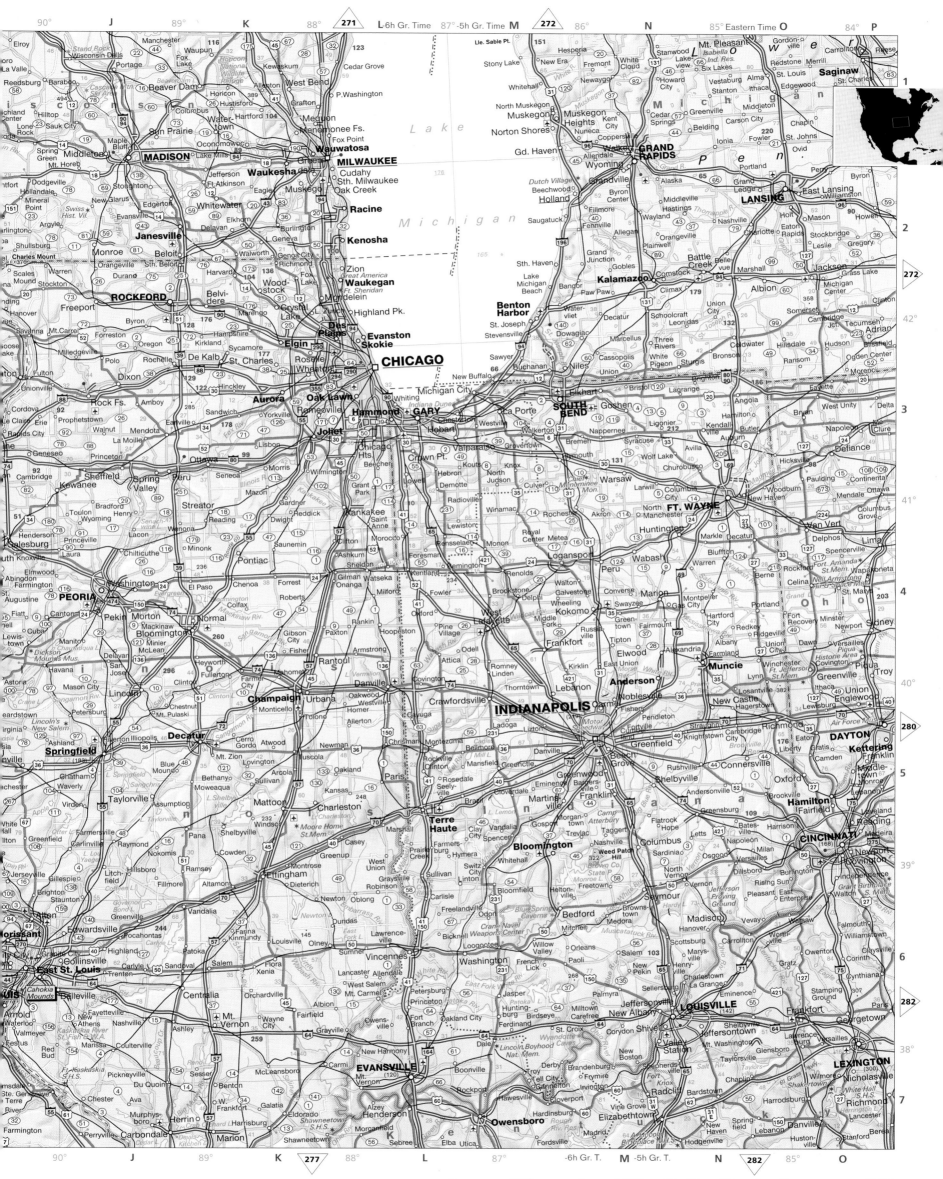

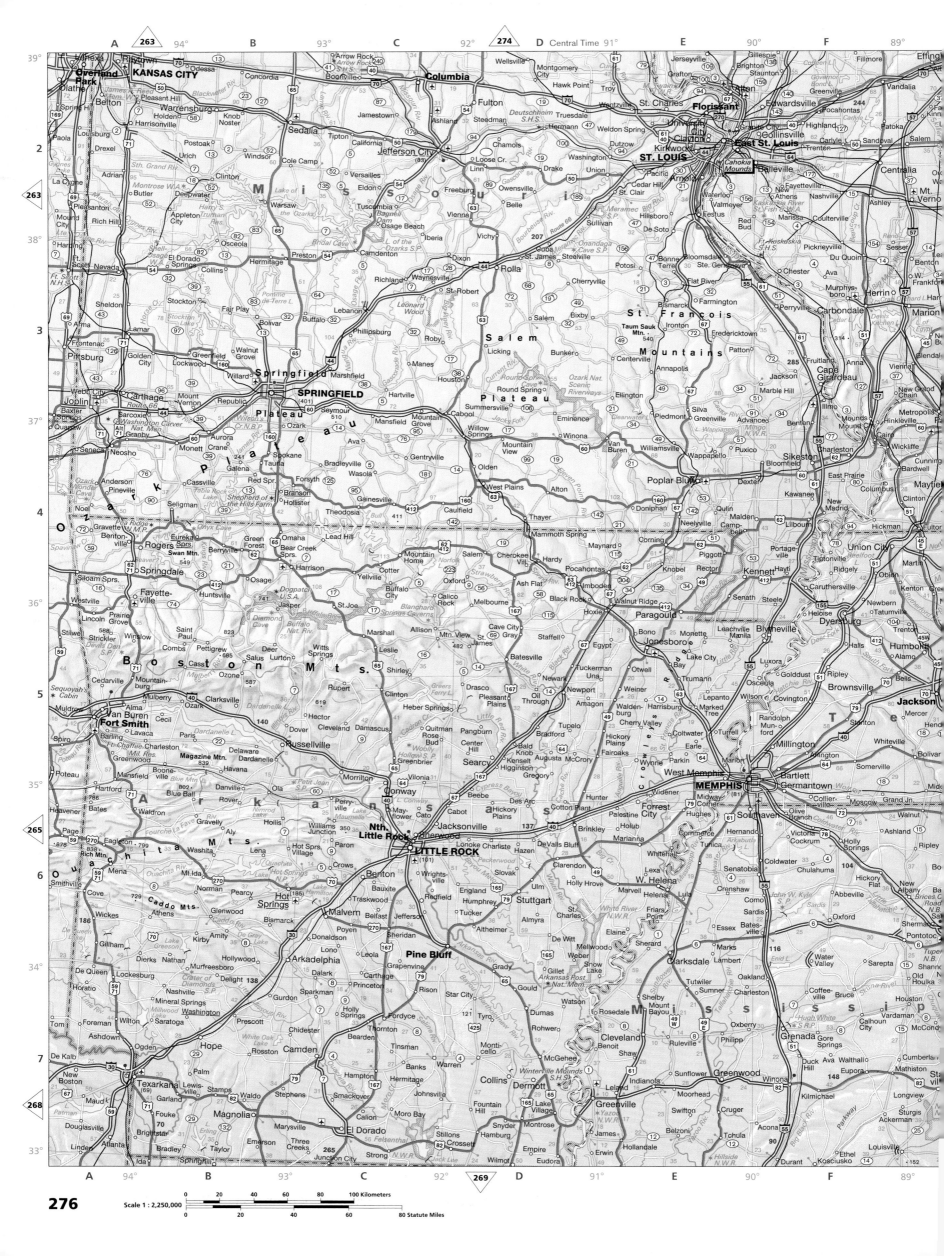

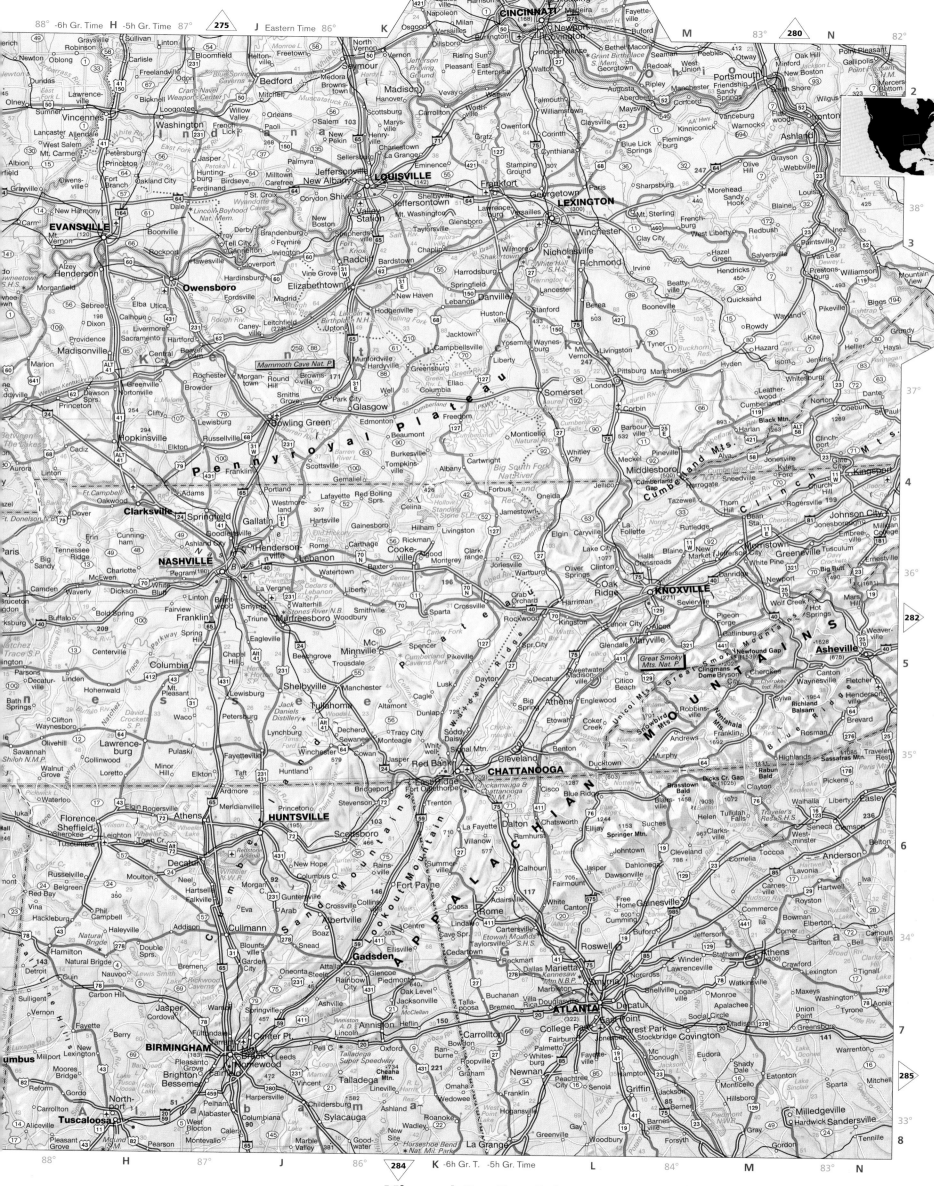

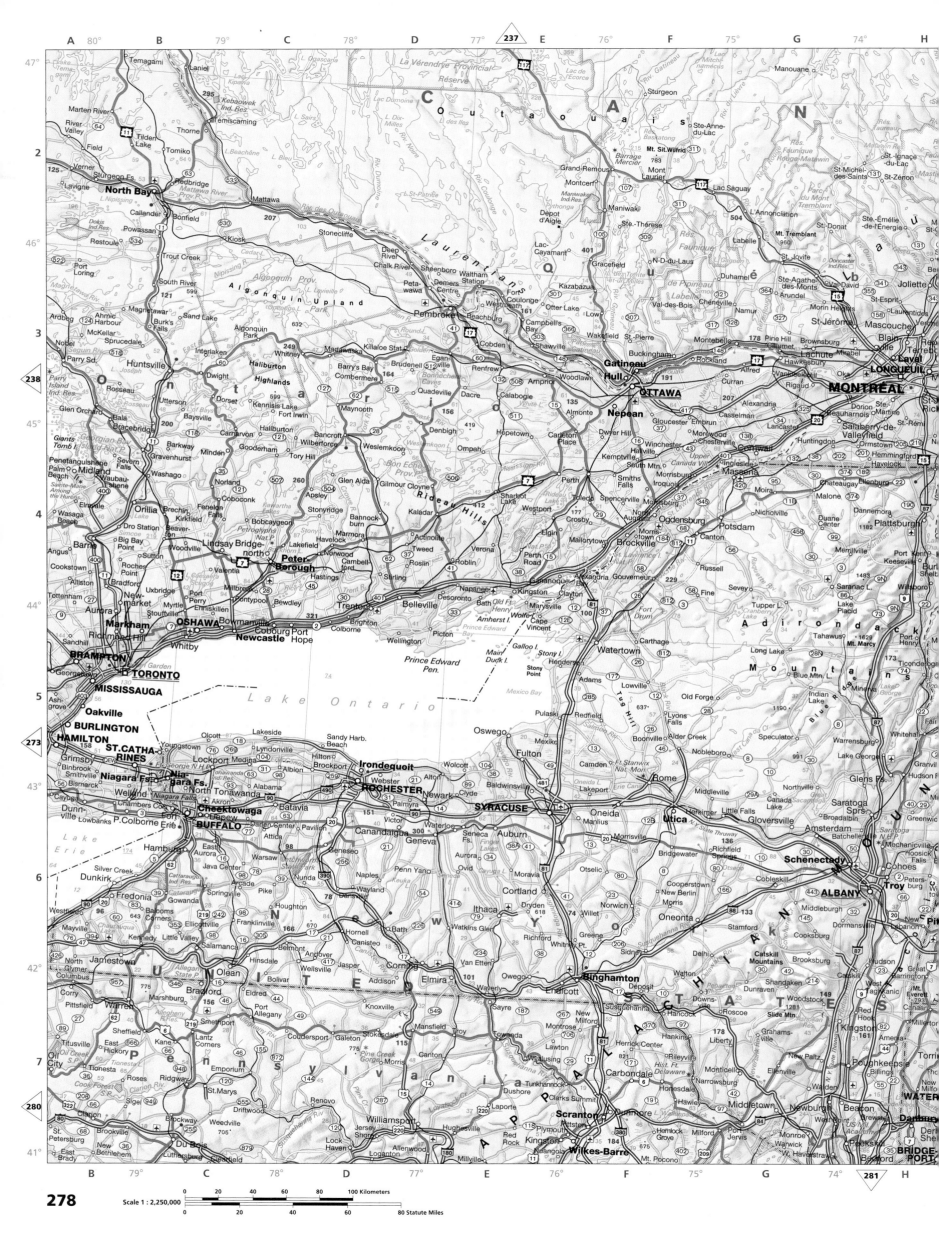

Scale 1 : 2,250,000

Scale 1 : 2,250,000

100 Kilometers

80 Statute Miles

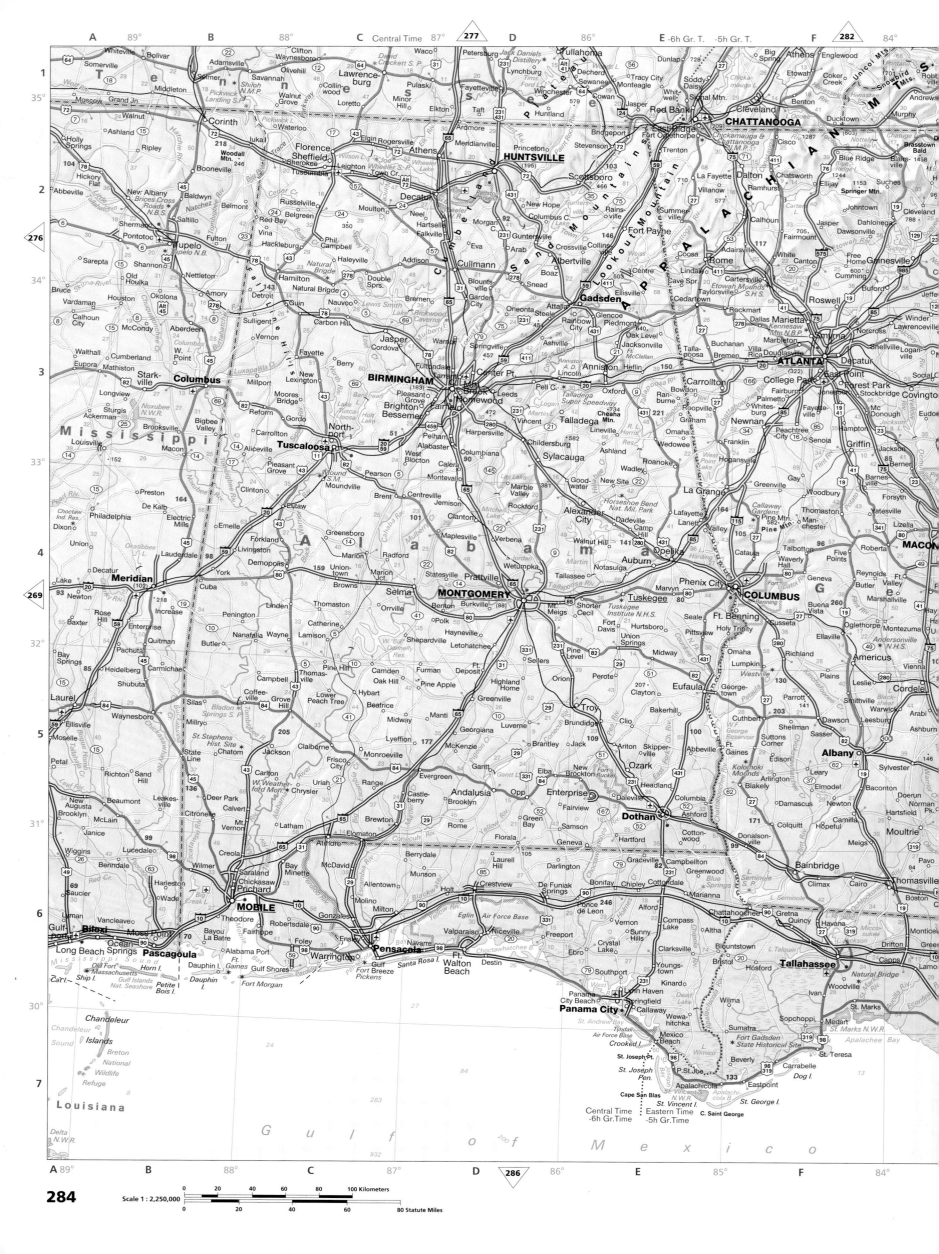

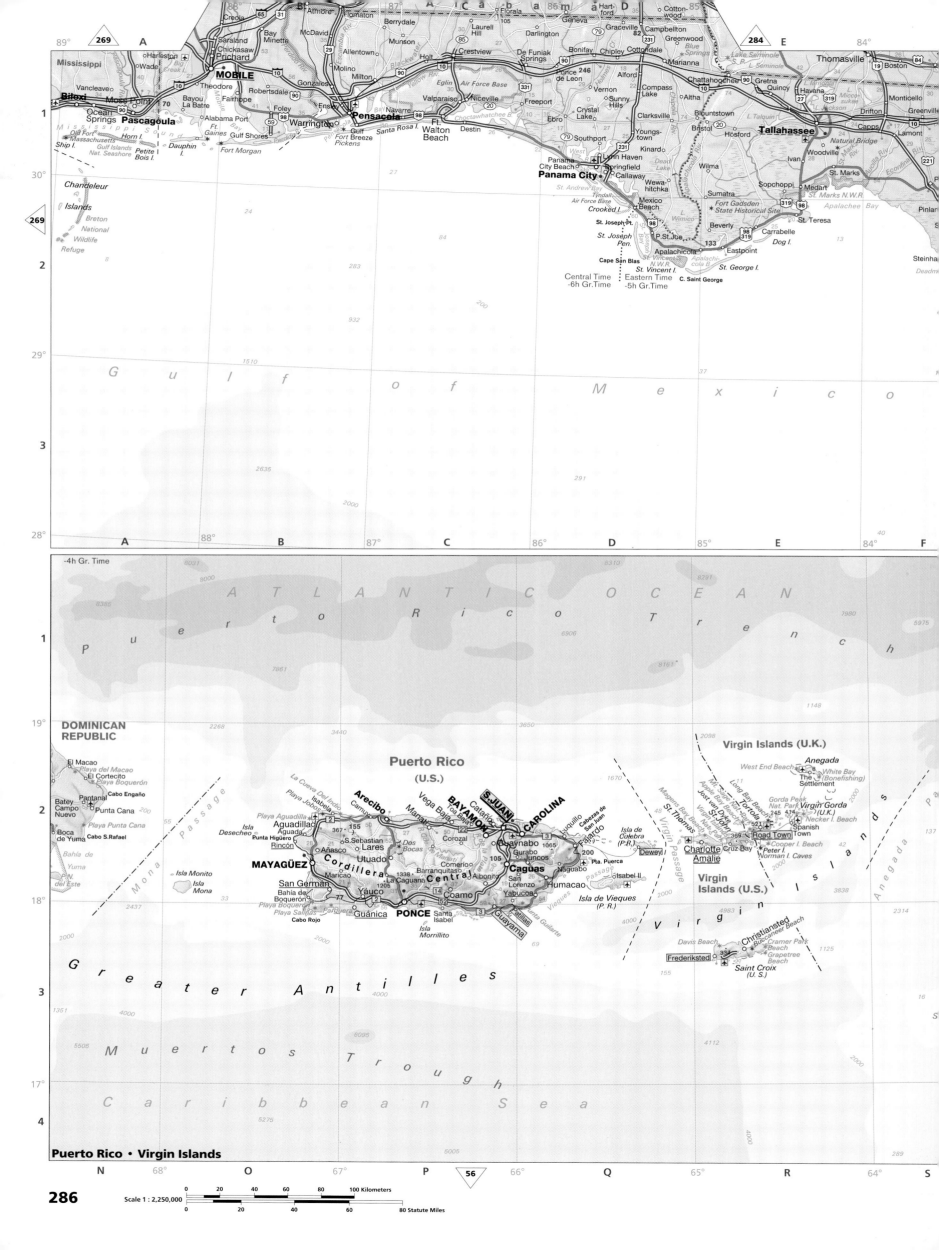

Puerto Rico • Virgin Islands

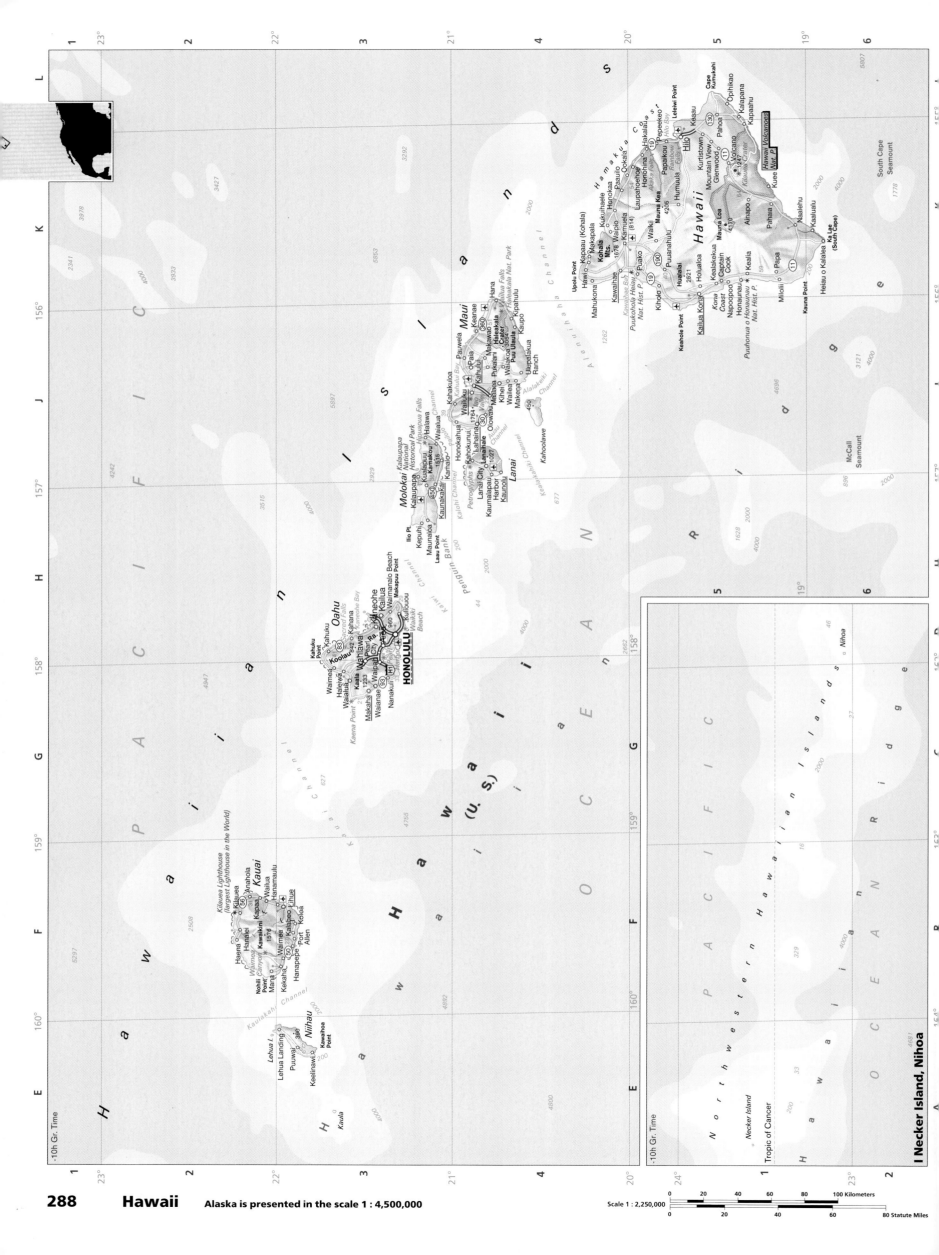

Alaska is presented in the scale 1 : 4,500,000

I Necker Island, Nihoa

Scale 1 : 2,250,000

Abbreviations

A

A.	Alm (Ger.) mountain meadow
Abb.	Abbaye (Fr.) abbey
Abor.	(Engl.) aboriginal
Aç.	Açude (Port.) small reservoir
Ad.	Adası (Turk.) island
A.F.B.	(Engl.) Air Force Base
Ag.	Agios (Gr.) saint
Á.I.	Área Indígena (Port.) Indian reservation
Ald.	Aldeia (Port.) village, hamlet
Arch.	(Engl.) archipelago
Arch.	Archipiélago (Span.) archipelago
Arh.	Arhipelag (Rus.) archipelago
Arq.	Arquipélago (Port.) archipelago
Arr.	Arroyo (Span.) brook
Art.Ra.	(Engl.) artillery range
Aut.	(Engl.) autonomous
Aut.Dist.	(Engl.) autonomous district
Aut.Reg.	(Engl.) autonomous region

B

B.	Baie (Fr.) bay
B.	Biológica, -o (Span.) biological
Ba.	Bahía (Span.) bay
Bal.	Balka (Rus.) gorge
Ban.	Banjaran (Mal.) mountains
Bel.	Belo, -yj, -aja, -oe (Rus.) white
Bk.	Bukit (Mal.) mountain, hill
Bol.	Boloto (Rus.) swamp
Bol.	Bolšoj, -aja, -oe (Rus.) big
Bot.	(Engl.) botanical
B.P.	(Engl.) battlefield park
Brj.	Baraj (Turk.) dam
Buch.	Buchta (Ukr.) bay
Buh.	Buhta (Rus.) bay

C

C.	Cap (Fr.) cape, point
C.	Cabo (Port., Span.) cape, point
Cab.	Cabeça (Port.) heights, summit
Cach.	Cachoeira (Port.) rapids
Cal.	Caleta (Span.) bay
Can.	Canalul (Rom.) canal
Can.	Canal (Span.) canal
Cast.	Castello (Ital.) castle, palace
Cd.	Ciudad (Span.) city
Cga.	Ciénaga (Span.) swamp, moor
Ch.	Chenal (Fr.) canal
Chr.	Chrebet (Ukr.) mountains
Co.	Cerro (Span.) mountain, hill
Col.	Colonia (Span.) colony
Conv.	Convento (Span.) monastery
Cord.	Cordillera (Span.) mountain chain
Corr.	Corredeira (Port.) rapids
Cpo.	Campo (Port.) field
Cr.	(Engl.) creek
Cs.	Cerros (Span.) mountain, hill

D

D.	Dake (Jap.) mountain
Dağl.	Dağlar (Turk.) mountains
Dist.	(Engl.) district
Df.	Dorf (Ger.) village
Dl.	Deal (Rom.) heights, hill

E

Ea.	Estancia (Span.) ranch
Ej.	Ejido (Span.) common
Emb.	Embalse (Span.) reservoir
Ens.	Enseada (Port.) small bay
Erm.	Ermita (Span.) hermitage
Ero.	Estero (Span.) estuary
Esp.	España (Span.) Spain
Est.	Estación (Span.) railroad terminal
Estr.	Estrecho (Span.) straight, sound
Ez.	Ezero (Bulg.) lake

F

Faz.	Fazenda (Port.) ranch
Fk.	(Engl.) fork
Fn.	Fortín (Span.) fort
Fr.	(Engl.) France
Fs.	(Engl.) falls, waterfall
Ft.	(Engl.) fort

G

Ğ.	Ğabal (Arab.) mountain
G.	Gawa (Jap.) lagoon
G.	Gîtul (Rom.) pass
G.	Golfo (Span.) bay, gulf
G.	Gora (Rus.) mountain
Gde.	Grande (Span.) big
Gds.	Grandes (Span.) big
Glac.	Glacier (Fr.) glacier
Gos.	Gosudarstvennyj, -aja (Rus.) national
Gr.	(Engl.) Greece
Gr.Br.	(Engl.) Great Britain
Grd.	Grand (Fr.) big
Grl.	General (Span.) general

H

H.	Hora (Ukr.) mountain
H.	Hütte (Ger.) mountain hut
Harb.	(Engl.) harbor
Hist.	(Engl.) historic
Hm.	Heim (Ger.) home
Hr.	Hrebet (Rus.) mountains
Hte.	Haute (Fr.) high
Hwy.	(Engl.) highway

I

I.	(Engl.) island
Î.	Île (Fr.) island
I.	Ilha (Port.) island
I.	Isla (Span.) island
Igl.	Iglesia (Span.) church
In.	Insulă (Rom.) island
Ind.	(Engl.) Indian
Ind.Res.	(Engl.) Indian reservation
Int.	(Engl.) international
Is.	(Engl.) islands
Is.	Islas (Span.) islands

J

Jaz.	Jazovir (Bulg.) reservoir
Jct.	(Engl.) junction
Jez.	Jezero (Slovenian) lake
Juž.	Južnyj, -aja (Rus.) southern

K

Kan.	Kanal (Ger.) canal
Kep.	Kepulauan (Indon.) archipelago
Kg.	Kampong (Indon.) village
K-l.	Köli (Kazakh.) lake
K-l.	Küli (Uzbek.) lake
Kör.	Körfez (Turk.) gulf, bay
Kp.	Kólpos (Gr.) gulf, bay
Kr.	Krasno, -yj, -aja, -oe (Rus.) red

L

L.	(Engl.) lake
L.	Lac (Fr.) lake
L.	Lacul (Rom.) lake
L.	Lago (Span.) lake
Lag.	Laguna (Rus.) lagoon
Lev.	Levyj, -aja (Rus.) left
Lim.	Liman (Rus.) lagoon
Lim.	Limni (Gr.) lake
Lte.	(Engl.) little

M

M.	Munte (Rom.) mountain
M.	Mys (Rus.) cape, point
Mal.	(Engl.) Malaysia
Mal.	Malo, -yj, -aja, -oe (Rus.) little
Man.	Manastir (Bulg.) monastery
Man.	Manastır (Turk.) monastery
Măn.	Mănăstire (Rom.) monastery
Mem.	(Engl.) memorial
Mgne.	Montagne (Fr.) mountain, mountains
Mi.	Misaki (Jap.) cape, point
Mil.Res.	(Engl.) military reservation
Milli P.	Milli Park (Turk.) national park
Min.	(Engl.) mineral
Mñas.	Montañas (Span.) mountains
Moh.	Mohyla (Ukr.) tomb
Mon.	Monasterio (Span.) monastery
M.P.	(Engl.) military park
Mt.	(Engl.) mount
Mte.	Monte (Span.) mountain
Mti.	Monti (Ital.) mountains
Mtn.	(Engl.) mountain
Mtns.	(Engl.) mountains
Mtn.S.P.	(Engl.) mountain state park
Mts.	(Engl.) mountains
Mts.	Montes (Span.) mountains
Munț.	Munții (Rom.) mountains
Mus.	(Engl.) museum

N

N.	Nehir/ Nehri (Turk.) river, stream
N.	Nudo (Span.) peak
Nac.	Nacional (Span.) national
Nac.	Nacional'nyj, -aja, -oe (Rus.) national
Nat.	(Engl.) national
Nat.Mon.	(Engl.) national monument
Nat.P.	(Engl.) national park
Nat.Seas.	(Engl.) national seashore
Naz.	Nazionale (Ital.) national
N.B.P.	(Engl.) national battlefield park
N.B.S.	(Engl.) national battlefield site
Ned.	Nederland (Neth.) Netherlands
Nev.	Nevado (Span.) snow-capped mountain
N.H.P.	(Engl.) national historic park
N.H.S.	(Engl.) national historic site
Niž.	Niže, -nij, -naja, -neje (Rus.) lower
Nizm.	Nizmennost' (Rus.) lowlands
N.M.P.	(Engl.) national military park
Nördl.	Nördlich (Ger.) northern
Nov.	Novo, -yj, -aja, -oe (Rus.) new
N.P.	(Engl.) national park
N.R.A.	(Engl.) national recreation area
Nsa.Sra.	Nossa Senhora (Port.) Our Lady
Nth.	(Engl.) north
Ntra.Sra.	Nuestra Señora (Span.) Our Lady
Nva.	Nueva (Span.) new
Nvo.	Nuevo (Span.) new
N.W.R.	(Engl.) national wildlife refuge

O

O.	Ostrov (Rus.) island
Obl.	Oblast (Rus.) district
Ö.	Östra (Swed.) eastern
Öv.	Övre (Swed.) upper
Of.	Oficina (Span.) office
Ostr.	Ostrov (Rom.) island
O-va.	Ostrova (Rus.) islands
Oz.	Ozero (Rus.) lake

P

P.	(Engl.) port
P.	Passe (Fr.) pass
P.	Pico (Span.) peak
P.	Pulau (Indon.) island
Peg.	Pegunungan (Indon.) mountains
Pen.	(Engl.) peninsula
Pen.	Peninsula (Span.) peninsula
Per.	Pereval (Rus.) pass
Picc.	Piccolo (Ital.) little
P-iv.	Pivostriv (Ukr.) peninsula
Pk.	(Engl.) peak
Pkwy.	(Engl.) parkway
Pl.	Planina (Bulg.) mountain, mountains
P.N.	Parque Nacional (Span.) national park
Po.	Paso (Span.) pass
Por.	Porog (Rus.) rapids
P-ov.	Poluostrov (Rus.) peninsula
Pr.	Proliv (Rus.) strait, sound
Pr.	Prohod (Bulg.) pass
Presq.	Presqu'île (Fr.) peninsula
Prov.	(Engl.) provincial
Prov.P.	(Engl.) provincial park
Pso.	Passo (Ital.) pass
Psto.	Puesto (Span.) outpost
Pt.	(Engl.) point
Pta.	Ponta (Port.) point
Pta.	Punta (Span.) point
Pte.	Pointe (Fr.) point
Pto.	Pôrto (Port.) port
Pto.	Puerto (Span.) port, pass
Pzo.	Pizzo (Ital.) point

Q

Q.N.P.	(Jap.) quasi national park

R

R.	Reka (Bulg.) river
R.	Reserva (Span.) reservation
R.	Rio (Port.) river
R.	Río (Span.) river
Ra.	(Engl.) range
Rch.	Riachão (Port.) small river
Rch.	Riacho (Span.) small river
Rdl.	Raudal (Span.) stream
Rep.	(Engl.) republic
Repr.	Represa (Port.) dam
Rère.	Rivière (Fr.) river
Res.	(Engl.) reservoir
Res.	Reserva (Port.) reservation
Resp.	Respublika (Rus.) republic
Rib.	Ribeira (Port.) shore
Rib.	Ribeiro (Port.) small river
Rif.	Rifugio (Ital.) mountain hut
Riv.	(Engl.) river

S

Rom.	(Engl.) Romania
Rom.	Romano, -na (Span.) Roman
Rus.	(Engl.) Russia
S.	San (Jap.) mountain, mountains
S.	San (Span.) saint
S.	São (Port.) saint
Sa.	Saki (Jap.) cape
Sa.	Serra (Port.) mountains
Sal.	Salar (Span.) salt desert, salt lagoon
Sanm.	Sanmyaku (Jap.) mountains
Sd.	(Engl.) sound
Sel.	Selat (Indon.) road
Sev.	Sever, -nyj, -naja, -noe (Rus.) north
Sf.	Sfîntu (Rom.) holy
Sh.	Shima (Jap.) island
S.H.P.	(Engl.) state historic park
S.H.S.	(Engl.) state historic site
S.M.	(Engl.) state monument
Sna.	Salina (Span.) salt flat
Snas.	Salinas (Span.) salt flats
Snía.	Serranía (Span.) ridge
S.P.	(Engl.) state park
Sr.	Sredne, -ij, -aja, -ee (Rus.) middle, central
Sra.	Sierra (Span.) mountains
St.	(Engl.) saint
St.	Saint (Fr., Span.) saint
Sta.	Santa (Span.) saint
Sta.	Staro, -ij, -aja, -oe (Rus.) old
Ste.	Sainte (Fr.) saint
Sth.	(Engl.) south
St.Mem.	(Engl.) state memorial
Sto.	Santo (Port.) saint
Str.	(Engl.) strait
Suh.	Suho, -aja (Rus.) dry
Sv.	Svet, -a, -o (Bulg.) saint
Sv.	Sveti (Croatian) saint

T

T.	Take (Jap.) peak, heights
Tel.	Teluk (Indon.) bay
Tg.	Tanjung (Indon.) cape
Tg.	Tôge (Jap.) pass
Tte.	Teniente (Span.) lieutenant

U

Ülk.	Ülken (Kazakh.) big
U.K.	(Engl.) United Kingdom
U.S.	(Engl.) United States

V

V.	Vallée (Fr.) valley
Va.	Villa (Span.) market town
Vda.	Vereda (Port.) path
Vdhr.	Vodohranilišče (Rus.) reservoir
Vdp.	Vodospad (Ukr.) waterfall
Vel.	Veliko, -ij, -aja, -oe (Rus.) big
Verh.	Verhnie, -yj, aja, -ee (Rus.) upper
Vf.	Virf (Rom.) peak, heights
Vill.	(Engl.) village
Vis.	Visočina (Bulg.) heights
Vjal.	Vjalikie (Belarus.) big
Vlk.	Vulkan (Ger.) volcano
Vn.	Volcán (Span.) volcano
Vod.	Vodopad (Rus.) waterfall
Vol.	Volcán (Span.) volcano
Vul.	Vulcano (Philip.) volcano

W

W.A.	(Engl.) wilderness area

Y

Y.	Yama (Jap.) mountain, mountains

Z

Zal.	Zaliv (Rus.) gulf, bay
Zap.	Zapadne, -ij, -aja, -noe (Rus.) west
Zapov.	Zapovednik (Rus.) protected area

Selected References

Index of Map Names

The index contains all names found on the maps in this atlas. The index's alphabetical listing corresponds to the sequence of letters in the Roman alphabet. Diacritical marks and special letters have been ignored in alphebetizing, e.g.:

A ....Á, À, Â, Ă, Å, Ą, Ā, Ã, Ä, Æ

The ligatures æ, œ are treated as ae and oe in the alphabetical listing.

Names that have been abbreviated on the maps are generally written in full in the index.

Generic concepts follow geographic names, e.g. Mexico, Gulf of; Ventoux, Mont. Exception: colors (e.g. Mount Blanc) and adjectives (e.g. Big, Little) come first. Official additions (e.g. Rothenburg ob der Tauber) are included in the alphabetizing.

To a certain degree, the index also includes official alternate forms, linguistic variants, renamings and other secondary denominations. In such cases, the index refers to names as they appear on the maps, e.g. Meran = Merano, Leningrad = Sankt-Peterburg.

Abbreviations in parentheses help distinguish between places bearing the same names. Abbreviations as used on international motor-vehicle license plates have been given priority; where this is insufficient, administrative information like federal lands, provinces, regions, etc. are indicated.

Icons, which immediately follow the names, are used to indicate fundamental geographic concepts.

New York	○••	**USA**	(NY)	280-281	N 3
① Search concept	② Icon	③ Nation	④ Administrative unit	⑤ Page	⑥ Search grid designation

② **Icons:**

■ ....Sovereign nation
□ ....Administrative unit
★ ....Capital city (national capital)
☆ ....State (provincial) capital
○ ....Place
⌢ ....Landscape
∩ ....Island
◡ ....Depression
▲▲ ....Mountains
▲ ....Mountain
▲ ....Active volcano
≈ ....Ocean, part of an ocean
○ ....Lake, salt lake
~ ....River, waterfall
⊂ ....glacier
< ....dam
≃ ....Undersea topography
⊥ ....National park
Ẋ ....Reservation
xx ....Military installation
II ....Transportation construction
✈ ....Airport
∴ ....Ruins, ruined city
••• ....World cultural or natural heritage site
•• ....Point of major interest
• ....Point of interest

③ **Souvereign States and Territories (Abbrevations in *italics:* Abbrevation not official)**

A	Austria
AFG	Afghanistan
AG	Antigua and Barbuda
AL	Albania
AND	Andorra
ANG	Angola
AR	Armenia
ARK	Antarctica
ARU	Aruba
AUS	Australia
AUT	Autonomous region
AZ	Azerbaijan
B	Belgium
BD	Bangladesh
BDS	Barbados
BF	Burkina Faso
BG	Bulgaria
BH	Belize
BHT	Bhutan
BIH	Bosnia and Herzegovina
BOL	Bolivia
BR	Brazil
BRN	Bahrain
BRU	Brunei
BS	Bahamas
BU	Burundi
BY	Belarus
C	Cuba
CAM	Cameroon
CDN	Canada
CH	Switzerland
CI	Côte d'Ivoire (Ivory Coast)
CL	Sri Lanka
CO	Colombia
COM	Comoros
CR	Costa Rica
CV	Cape Verde
CY	Cyprus
CZ	Czech Republic
D	Germany
DJI	Djibouti
DK	Denmark
DOM	Dominican Republic
DVR	North Korea
DY	Benin
DZ	Algeria
E	Spain
EAK	Kenya
EAT	Tanzania
EAU	Uganda
EC	Ecuador
ER	Eritrea
ES	El Salvador
EST	Estonia
ET	Egypt
ETH	Ethiopia
F	France
FIN	Finland
FJI	Fiji
FL	Liechtenstein
FR	Faroe Islands
FSM	Micronesia
G	Gabon
GB	United Kingdom
GBA	Alderney
GBG	Guernsey
GBJ	Jersey
GBM	Isle of Man
GBZ	Gibraltar
GCA	Guatemala
GE	Georgia
GH	Ghana
GNB	Guinea-Bissau
GQ	Equatorial Guinea
GR	Greece
GRØ	Greenland
GUY	Guyana
H	Hungary
HK	Hong Kong
HN	Honduras
HR	Croatia
I	Italy
IL	Israel
IND	India
IR	Iran
IRL	Ireland
IRQ	Iraq
IS	Iceland
J	Japan
JA	Jamaika
JOR	Jordan
K	Cambodia
KA	Kazakhstan
KAN	Saint Kitts and Nevis
KIB	Kiribati
KS	Kyrgyzstan
KSA	Saudi Arabia
KWT	Kuwait
L	Luxembourg
LAO	Laos
LAR	Libya
LB	Liberia
LS	Lesotho
LT	Lithuania
LV	Latvia
M	Malta
MA	Morocco
MAI	Marshall Islands
MAL	Malaysia
MAU	Mongolia
MC	Monaco
MD	Moldova
MEX	Mexico
MK	Macedonia
MOC	Mozambique
MS	Mauritius
MV	Maldives
MW	Malawi
MYA	Myanmar (Burma)
N	Norway
NA	Netherlands Antilles
NAM	Namibia
NAU	Nauru
NEP	Nepal
NIC	Nicaragua
NL	Netherlands
NZ	New Zealand
OM	Oman
P	Portugal
PA	Panama
PAL	Palau
PE	Peru
PK	Pakistan
PL	Poland
PNG	Papua New Guinea
PY	Paraguay
Q	Qatar
RA	Argentina
RB	Botswana
RC	Taiwan
RCA	Central African Republic
RCB	Congo
RCH	Chile
RG	Guinea
RH	Haiti
RI	Indonesia
RIM	Mauritania
RL	Lebanon
RM	Madagaskar
RMM	Mali
RN	Niger
RO	Romania
ROK	South Korea
ROU	Uruguay
RP	Philippines
RSM	San Marino
RT	Togo
RUS	Russia
RWA	Rwanda
S	Sweden
SCV	Vatican City
SD	Swaziland
SGP	Singapore
SK	Slovakia
SLO	Slovenia
SME	Suriname
SN	Senegal
SOL	Solomon Islands
SP	Somalia
STP	São Tomé and Príncipe
SUD	Sudan
SY	Seychelles
SYR	Syria
TCH	Chad
THA	Thailand
TJ	Tajikistan
TM	Turkmenistan
TN	Tunisia
TON	Tonga
TR	Turkey
TT	Trinidad and Tobago
TUV	Tuvalu
UA	Ukraine
UAE	United Arab Emirates
US	Uzbekistan
USA	United States
VAN	Vanuatu
VN	Vietnam
VRC	China
WAG	Gambia
WAL	Sierra Leone
WAN	Nigeria
WB	West Bank
WD	Dominica
WG	Grenada
WL	Saint Lucia
WS	Western Samoa
WSA	Western Sahara
WV	Saint Vincent and the Grenadines
Y	Yemen
YU	Yugoslavia
YV	Venezuela
Z	Zambia
ZA	South Africa
ZRE	Zaire
ZW	Zimbabwe

④ States of the U.S.A.

AK	Alaska	IL	Illinois	NC	North Carolina	SC	South Carolina
AL	Alabama	IN	Indiana	ND	North Dakota	SD	South Dakota
AR	Arkansas	KS	Kansas	NE	Nebraska	TN	Tennessee
AZ	Arizona	KY	Kentucky	NH	New Hampshire	TX	Texas
CA	California	LA	Louisiana	NJ	New Jersey	UT	Utah
CO	Colorado	MA	Massachusetts	NM	New Mexico	VA	Virginia
CT	Connecticut	MD	Maryland	NV	Nevada	VT	Vermont
DE	Delaware	ME	Maine	NY	New York	WA	Washington
FL	Florida	MI	Michigan	OH	Ohio	WI	Wisconsin
GA	Georgia	MN	Minnesota	OK	Oklahoma	WV	West Virginia
HI	Hawaii	MO	Missouri	OR	Oregon	WY	Wyoming
IA	Iowa	MS	Mississippi	PA	Pennsylvania		
ID	Idaho	MT	Montana	RI	Rhode Island		

A

Aachen ○··· **D** 92-93 J 3
Aačim, mys ▲ **RUS** 112-113 R 2
Aadan Yabaal ○ **SP** 212-213 L 2
'AA' Highway ǁ **USA** (KY) 276-277 M 2
Äänekoski ○ **FIN** 88-89 H 5
Aansluit ○ **ZA** 220-221 F 3
Aappilattoq ○ **GRØ** (VGR) 26-27 X 7
Aappilattoq ○ **GRØ** (VGR) 28-29 S 6
Aar, De ○ **ZA** 220-221 G 5
Aaratuba, Ilha ⌒ **BR** 66-67 G 4
Aarau ☆ **CH** 92-93 K 5
Aare ~ **CH** 92-93 J 5
Aasiaat = Egedesminde ○ **GRØ** 28-29 O 2
Aba ○ **VRC** 154-155 B 5
Aba ○ **WAN** 204-205 G 6
Aba ○ **ZRE** 212-213 C 2
Aba, Ğazīrat ⌒ **SUD** 200-201 F 6
Abā ad-Dūd ○ **KSA** 130-131 J 4
Abā ar-Ruḫām ○ **KSA** 132-133 D 4
Abacaxis, Rio ~ **BR** 66-67 H 5
Abaco Island ⌒ **BS** 54-55 G 1
Abadab, Ğabal ▲ **SUD** 200-201 G 3
Ābādān ○· **IR** 134-135 C 3
Ābādān, Ra's-e ▲ **IR** 134-135 C 4
Ābāde ○· **IR** 134-135 E 3
Ābādeh-ye Ṭašk ○ **IR** 134-135 E 4
Abadhara ○ **GE** 126-127 D 6
Abadia dos Dourados ○ **BR** 72-73 G 5
Abadla ○ **DZ** 188-189 K 5
Abaeté ○ **BR** 72-73 H 5
Abaeté, Rio ~ **BR** 72-73 H 5
Abaetetuba ○ **BR** 62-63 K 6
Abag Qi ○ **VRC** 148-149 M 5
Abaí ○ **PY** 76-77 K 4
Abaida ▲ **DJI** 208-209 F 3
Abaíra ○ **BR** 72-73 K 2
Abaj ○ **KA** 124-125 H 4
Abaji ○ **WAN** 204-205 G 4
Abajo Mountains ▲▲ **USA** (UT) 254-255 F 6
Abajo Peak ▲ **USA** (UT) 254-255 F 6
Abaj Takalik ∴· **GCA** 52-53 J 4
Abak ○ **WAN** 204-205 G 6
Abakaliki ○ **WAN** 204-205 H 5
Abakan ☆ **RUS** 116-117 E 9
Abakan ~ **RUS** 116-117 E 9
Abakan ~ **RUS** 124-125 Q 2
Abakanskij hrebet ▲▲ **RUS** 124-125 Q 2
Abala ○ **RCB** 210-211 E 4
Abala ○ **RN** 204-205 E 1
Abalak ○ **RN** 198-199 C 5
Abaleha, I-n- < **RMM** 196-197 J 6
Abalessa ○ **DZ** 190-191 E 9
Abali, Bahr ~ **TCH** 206-207 D 3
Abamasagi Lake ⬭ **CDN** (ONT) 234-235 Q 4
Aban ☆ **RUS** 116-117 H 7
Aban ~ **RUS** 116-117 H 7
Abancay ☆ **PE** 64-65 F 8
Abanga ~ **G** 210-211 C 4
Abangharit, I-n- < **RN** 198-199 C 4
Abapo ○ **BOL** 70-71 F 6
Abar al-Maši ○ **KSA** 130-131 F 5
Abaré ○ **BR** 68-69 J 6
Ābār Ḥaimūr < **ET** 194-195 F 6
Abarqū ○ **IR** 134-135 E 3
Abarqū, Kavīr-e ⬭ **IR** 134-135 E 3
Abarr ○ **USA** (CO) 254-255 N 4
Abashiri ○ **J** 152-153 L 2
Abasolo ○ **MEX** (DGO) 50-51 G 5
Abasolo ○ **MEX** (TAM) 50-51 K 5
Abasula < **EAK** 212-213 G 4
Abatskij ☆ **RUS** 114-115 L 6
Abaucán, Río ~ **RA** 76-77 D 5
Abaurai Island ⌒ **PNG** 183 B 5
Ābaya Häyk' ⬭ **ETH** 208-209 C 5
Abay Wenz = Blue Nile ~ **ETH** 208-209 C 3
Abaza ○ **RUS** 116-117 E 9
Abba ○ **RCA** 206-207 B 6
Abba-Omege ○ **WAN** 204-205 H 5
'Abbās, Bandar-e ☆· **IR** 134-135 G 5
'Abbāsābād ○ **IR** (KER) 134-135 F 3
'Abbāsābād ○ **IR** (MAZ) 136-137 B 6
'Abbāsābād ○ **IR** (SEM) 136-137 E 6
Abbaye, Point ▲ **USA** (MI) 270-271 K 4
Abbazia della Monte Oliveto Maggiore · **I** 100-101 C 3
Abbazia di Casamari · **I** 100-101 D 4
Abbazia di Montecassino · **I** 100-101 D 4
Abbeville ○ **F** 90-91 H 6
Abbeville ○ **USA** (AL) 284-285 E 5
Abbeville ○ **USA** (GA) 284-285 G 5
Abbeville ○ **USA** (LA) 268-269 H 7
Abbeville ○ **USA** (MS) 268-269 L 2
Abbeville ○ **USA** (SC) 284-285 H 2
Abbey ○ **CDN** (SAS) 232-233 K 5
Abbeyfeale = Mainistir na Féile ○ **IRL** 90-91 C 5
Abbieglassie ○ **AUS** 178-179 J 4
Abbot, Mount ▲ **AUS** 174-175 J 7
Abbotsford ○ **CDN** (BC) 230-231 G 4
Abbotsford ○ **USA** (WI) 270-271 H 6
Abbott ○ **USA** (NM) 256-257 L 2
Abbottābād ○ **PK** 138-139 D 2
'Abd ad-Dā'im ○ **SUD** 206-207 H 3
'Abdal'azīz, Ğabal ▲▲ **SYR** 128-129 J 4
'Abdalīyah, Bi'r al- ○ **KSA** 132-133 B 3
'Abd al-Kūrī ⌒ **Y** 132-133 H 7
'Abdallāh, Mīnā' ○ **KWT** 130-131 L 3
Abd al-Māgid ○ **SUD** 200-201 F 5
Ābdān ○ **IR** 134-135 D 4
Ābdānān ○ **IR** 134-135 B 1
'Abdīn ○ **SUD** 200-201 D 6
Abdj ○ **TCH** 198-199 K 6
Abdon, Pulau ⌒ **RI** 166-167 F 1
Abdoulaye, Réserve d' ⊥ **RT** 202-203 L 5
Abdul Hakīm ○ **PK** 138-139 D 4
Abdulino ☆ **RUS** 96-97 H 7
Ābdy Wenz ~ **ETH** 208-209 C 3
Āb-e Bāzoft ~ **IR** 134-135 C 2
Abéché ☆ **TCH** 198-199 K 6
Āb-e Estāde ⬭ **AFG** 134-135 M 2
Abeïbara ○ **RMM** 196-197 L 5
Abejukolo ○ **WAN** 204-205 G 5
Āb-e Kūhrang ~ **IR** 134-135 D 2
Abélajouad < **RN** 198-199 C 4
Abelbodh < **RMM** 196-197 K 5
Abelhas, Cachoeira das ~ **BR** 70-71 G 2
Abeløya ⌒ **N** 84-85 R 3
Abel Tasman National Park ⊥ **NZ** 182 D 4
Ābeltī ○ **ETH** 208-209 C 4
Abemama Atoll ⌒ **KIB** 13 J 3
Abemarre ○ **RI** 166-167 L 5
Abene ○ **GH** 202-203 K 6
Abengourou ☆· **CI** 202-203 J 6
Abenójar ○ **E** 98-99 E 5
Åbenrå ○· **DK** 86-87 D 9
Abeokuta ☆ **WAN** 204-205 E 5
Abepura ○ **RI** 166-167 L 3
Ābera ○ **ETH** 208-209 B 5
Aberaeron ○ **GB** 90-91 E 5
Abercrombie ○ **USA** (ND) 258-259 L 5
Abercrombie, Fort · **USA** (ND) 258-259 L 5
Abercrombie Caves · **AUS** 180-181 K 2
Abercrombie River ~ **AUS** 180-181 K 3
Aberdare National Park ⊥ **EAK** 212-213 F 4
Aberdeen ○ **CDN** (SAS) 232-233 M 3
Aberdeen ○· **GB** 90-91 F 3
Aberdeen ○ **USA** (ID) 252-253 F 4
Aberdeen ○ **USA** (MD) 280-281 K 4
Aberdeen ○ **USA** (MS) 268-269 M 3
Aberdeen ○ **USA** (NC) 282-283 H 5
Aberdeen ○ **USA** (OH) 280-281 C 5
Aberdeen ○ **USA** (SD) 260-261 H 1
Aberdeen ○ **USA** (WA) 244-245 B 4
Aberdeen ○ **ZA** 220-221 G 6
Aberdeen Lake ⬭ **CDN** 30-31 U 3
Aberdeen Proving Ground xx **USA** (MD) 280-281 K 4
Aberdeen Road ○ **ZA** 220-221 G 6
Abergavenny-y-Fenni ○ **GB** 90-91 F 6
Ābergelē ○ **ETH** 200-201 J 6
Abergowrie ○ **AUS** 174-175 H 6
Abernathy ○ **USA** (TX) 264-265 C 5
Abernethy ○ **CDN** (SAS) 232-233 P 5
Abertawe = Swansea ○ **GB** 90-91 F 6
Aberystwyth ○ **GB** 90-91 E 5
Āb-e Seimarre ~ **IR** 134-135 B 2
Āb-e Šūr ~ **IR** 134-135 C 3
Āb-e Šūr ~ **IR** 134-135 F 4
Abez' ○ **RUS** 108-109 J 8
Āb-e Zīmkān ~ **IR** 134-135 B 1
Abganerovo ○ **RUS** 96-97 D 9
Abgarm ○ **IR** 128-129 N 5
Abgué ○ **TCH** 206-207 D 3
Abhā ☆ **KSA** 132-133 C 4
Abhāna ○ **IND** 138-139 G 8
Abhar ○ **IR** 128-129 N 4
Abhar Rūd ~ **IR** 128-129 N 4
Ābhē Bad ⬭ **DJI** 208-209 E 3
Ābhē Bid Häyk' ⬭ **ETH** 208-209 E 3
Abico ○ **BR** 66-67 E 4
'Abīdīyah ○ **SUD** 200-201 F 3
Abidjan ☆·· **CI** 202-203 J 7
Abiekwasputs ⬭ **ZA** 220-221 E 3
Abi Hill ▲ **WAN** 204-205 F 4
Abilene ○ **USA** (KS) 262-263 J 6
Abilene ○ **USA** (TX) 264-265 E 6
Abingdon ○ **USA** (IL) 274-275 H 4
Abingdon ○ **USA** (VA) 280-281 E 7
Abingdon Downs ○ **AUS** 174-175 G 5
Abington ○ **GB** 90-91 F 4
Abinsi ○ **WAN** 204-205 H 5
Abiquiu ○ **USA** (NM) 256-257 J 2
Abirāmam ○ **IND** 140-141 H 6
Abisko ○ **S** 86-87 J 2
Abisko nationalpark ⊥·· **S** 86-87 J 2
Abitangka ○ **VRC** 144-145 G 5
Abitau River ~ **CDN** 30-31 P 5
Abitibi, Lake ⬭ **CDN** (ONT) 236-237 J 4
Abitibi de Troyes Provincial Park ⊥ **CDN** (ONT) 236-237 H 4
Abitibi Indian Reservation X **CDN** (ONT) 236-237 H 4
Abitibi River ~ **CDN** (ONT) 236-237 G 2
Ābīy Ādī ○ **ETH** 200-201 J 6
Abīyata Häyk' ⬭ **ETH** 208-209 D 5
Abjelil ○ **MA** 188-189 J 3
Abkhazia = Abchazskaja Avtonomnaja Respublika □ **GE** 126-127 D 6
Abminga ○ **AUS** 178-179 C 4
Abnūb ○ **ET** 194-195 E 4
Abo ○ **USA** (NM) 256-257 J 4
Abo, Massif d' ▲▲ **TCH** 198-199 G 2
Åbo = Turku ☆· **FIN** 88-89 G 6
Aboabo ○ **RP** 160-161 C 8
Aboh ○ **WAN** 204-205 G 6
Abohar ○ **IND** 138-139 E 4
Aboine, River ~ **WAN** 204-205 G 5
Aboisso ☆ **CI** 202-203 J 7
Aboki ○ **EAU** 212-213 D 2
Abomey ☆··· **DY** 202-203 L 6
Abomey-Calavi ○ **DY** 204-205 E 5
Ābomsa ○ **ETH** 208-209 E 4
Abong ○ **WAN** 204-205 J 5
Abong Mbang ○ **CAM** 210-211 D 2
Aboni ○ **SUD** 206-207 L 3
Abo Pass ▲ **USA** (NM) 256-257 J 4
Abor ○ **GH** 202-203 L 6
Aboriginal Bora Ring X **AUS** 178-179 M 5
Aboriginal Rock Art · **AUS** (NT) 172-173 L 2
Aboriginal Rock Art · **AUS** (QLD) 174-175 H 4
Aborlan ○ **RP** 160-161 C 8
Aboua ○ **G** 210-211 E 3
Abou-Deïa ○ **TCH** 206-207 D 3
Abou Goulem ○ **TCH** 198-199 K 6
Aboukoussom ○ **TCH** 206-207 E 3
Aboun ○ **G** 210-211 B 3
Abourak, Mont ▲ **RMM** 196-197 L 6
Abourou, Chutes ~ **RCA** 206-207 F 6
Abou-Telfân, Réserve de Faune de l' ⊥ **TCH** 198-199 J 6
Abovjan ○ **AR** 128-129 L 2
Abqaiq ○ **KSA** 130-131 L 5
'Abr, al- ○ **Y** 132-133 E 5
Abra, Lago del ⬭ **RA** 78-79 H 6
Abra de Ilog ○ **RP** 160-161 D 6
Abra de Lizoite ▲ **RA** 76-77 E 2
Abraham Bay ≈ 22-23 C 6
Abraham Bay ≈ 36-37 R 2
Abraham Lake ⬭ **CDN** (ALB) 232-233 B 3
Abraham's Bay ○ **BS** 54-55 J 3
Abra Huashuaccasa ▲ **PE** 64-65 F 9
Abraka ○ **WAN** 204-205 G 6
Abra la Cruz Chica ▲ **BOL** 76-77 E 1
Abrams ○ **USA** (WI) 270-271 K 6
Abrantes ○ **P** 98-99 C 5
Abra Pampa ○· **RA** 76-77 E 2
Abraq, Wādī al ~ **LAR** 192-193 H 4
Abra Tapuna ▲ **PE** 64-65 F 8
Abrem ○ **GH** 202-203 K 7
Abrene = Pytalovo ☆ **LV** 94-95 K 3
Abreojos, Punta ▲ **MEX** 50-51 C 4
Abreus ○ **BR** 68-69 H 7
Abri ○ **SUD** 200-201 E 2
Abril, 7 de ○ **RA** 76-77 E 4
Abrolhos, Arquipélago dos ⌒ **BR** 72-73 L 4
Abrolhos Bank ≃ 5 H 6
Abrosimova ~ **RUS** 108-109 F 5
Abrud ○ **RO** 102-103 C 4
Abruzzo □ **I** 100-101 D 3
Abruzzo, Parco Nazionale d' ⊥ **I** 100-101 D 4
'Abs ○ **Y** 132-133 C 5
Absaroka-Beartooth Wilderness ⊥ **USA** (MT) 250-251 J 6
Absaroka Range ▲▲ **USA** (WY) 252-253 H 1
Absarokee ○ **USA** (MT) 250-251 K 6
Absecon ○ **USA** (NJ) 280-281 M 4
Ab Touyour ○ **TCH** 206-207 D 3
Abu ○ **GNB** 202-203 C 4
Abū 'Alī, Ğazīrat ⌒ **KSA** 130-131 L 4
Abū 'Ammār ○ **SUD** 200-201 G 4
Abū 'Arīš ○ **KSA** 132-133 C 5
Abū Ballās < **ET** 194-195 C 5
Abū Dāra, Ra's ▲ **ET** 194-195 H 6
Abū Darba ○ **ET** 194-195 F 3
Abū Darīḥa ○ **SYR** 128-129 G 5
Abū Dā'ūd, Ra's ▲ **OM** 132-133 L 2
Abū Dawn ○ **SUD** 200-201 F 4
Abū Dawn, Wādī ~ **SUD** 200-201 F 3
Abū ḍ-Ḍuhūr ○ **SYR** 128-129 G 5
Abu Dhabi = Abū Ẓabī ★· **UAE** 134-135 F 6
Abū Ḏi'āb, Ğabal ▲ **ET** 194-195 G 5
Abū Dīs ○ **SUD** 200-201 F 3
Abū Dom ○ **SUD** 200-201 E 4
Abū Dubaisāt, Bi'r < **ET** 194-195 G 6
Abū Dulayq ○ **SUD** 200-201 F 5
Abufari ○ **BR** 66-67 F 5
Abufari, Reserva Biológica do ⊥ **BR** 66-67 F 5
Abū Faruḫ ○ **IRQ** 128-129 K 6
Abū Gābra ○ **SUD** 206-207 H 3
Abū Ġarādiq, Bi'r < **ET** 194-195 D 2
Abugi ○ **WAN** 204-205 G 4
Abū Ğisra ○ **IRQ** 130-131 J 2
Abū Gubaybah ○ **SUD** 206-207 K 3
Abū Ğulūd, Bi'r ○ **SYR** 128-129 H 4
Abū Ḥamad ○ **SUD** 200-201 F 3
Abū Ḥarāz ○ **SUD** 200-201 F 3
Abū Ḥarba, Ğabal ▲ **ET** 194-195 F 4
Abū Ḫašhā'ifa, Ḫalīğ ≈ 194-195 C 2
Abū Hashim ○ **SUD** 206-207 K 3
Abū Hašim, Bi'r < **ET** 194-195 G 6
Abū Hugar ○ **SUD** 200-201 F 6
Abuja ★ **WAN** 204-205 G 4
Abū Kabīr ○ **ET** 194-195 E 2
Abū Kabisa ○ **SUD** 200-201 C 6
Abū Kamāl ☆ **SYR** 128-129 J 5
Abū Khinzīr, Wādī ~ **SUD** 200-201 E 5
Abuki, Pegunungan ▲▲ **RI** 164-165 G 5
Abū Kulaywat ○ **SUD** 200-201 E 4
Abukuma-gawa ~ **J** 152-153 J 6
Abukuma-kōti ▲▲ **J** 152-153 J 6
Abu l-Abyaḍ ⌒ **UAE** 134-135 E 6
Abū Latt, Ğazīrat ⌒ **KSA** 132-133 B 4
Abū l-Ḫaṣīb ☆ **IRQ** 130-131 K 2
Abū l-Ḥusain, Bi'r < **ET** 194-195 D 6
Abulug ○ **RP** 160-161 D 3
Abulung ~ **RP** 160-161 D 3
Abū Madd, Ra's ▲ **KSA** 130-131 E 5
Abū Maṭariq ○ **SUD** 206-207 H 3
Abū Mendi ○ **ETH** 208-209 B 3
Abū Mīna ∴··· **ET** 194-195 D 2
Abū Minqār, Bi'r < **ET** 194-195 C 4
Abumombazi ○ **ZRE** 210-211 J 2
Abū Muḥarrik, Ġurd ∸ **ET** 194-195 D 3
Abū Mūsā, Ğazīre-ye ⌒ **IR** 134-135 F 6
Abunã ○ **BR** 66-67 E 7
Abuña, Río ~ **BOL** 66-67 D 7
Abunâ, Rio ~ **BR** 70-71 D 2
Abū Nā'im < **LAR** 192-193 H 3
Ābune Yosēf ▲ **ETH** 200-201 J 6
Abū Qīr ○ **ET** 194-195 E 2
Abū Qurqāṣ ○ **ET** 194-195 E 4
Abū Qurun ○ **SUD** 200-201 F 3
Abū Ra's ○ **SUD** 206-207 G 5
Abū Raṣāṣ, Ra's ▲ **OM** 132-133 L 3
Aburassein, Mont ▲ **RCA** 206-207 G 4
Abu Road ○ **IND** 138-139 D 7
Abū Rudeis ○ **ET** 194-195 F 3
Abū Rukbah ○ **SUD** 200-201 E 6
Abū Ṣaffār ○ **SUD** 200-201 F 4
Abū Šağara, Ra's ▲ **SUD** 200-201 H 2
Abū Šahrain ∴· **IRQ** 130-131 J 2
Abū Ṣāri ○ **SUD** 200-201 E 2
Abū Simbel ∴··· **ET** 194-195 E 6
Abū Sīr, Pyramids of ∴··· **ET** 194-195 E 3
Abū Ṣuḫair ☆ **IRQ** 128-129 L 7
Abū Sunbul ○ **ET** 194-195 F 5
Abū Sunṭ, Khor ~ **SUD** 200-201 E 2
Abuta ○ **J** 152-153 J 3
Abū Ṭabaq < **SUD** 200-201 G 2
Abū Tīg ○ **ET** 194-195 E 4
Abū Ṭunayṭin ○ **SUD** 200-201 E 5
Abū 'Urūq < **SUD** 200-201 E 5
Abū Ūwaiğila ○ **ET** 194-195 G 2
Abū 'Uwaiğila ○ **ET** 194-195 G 2
Ābuyē Meda ▲ **ETH** 208-209 D 3
Abuyog ○ **RP** 160-161 F 7
Abū Zabad ○ **SUD** 200-201 D 6
Abū Ẓabī ★· **UAE** 134-135 F 6
Abū Zaïma, Bi'r < **SUD** 200-201 D 5
Abū Zanīma ○ **ET** 194-195 F 3
Abu Zayyān ○ **LAR** 192-193 E 1
Abwong ○ **SUD** 206-207 L 4
Aby, Lagune ≈ 202-203 J 7
Abyaḍ ○ **SUD** 200-201 C 6
Abyaḍ, ar-Ra's al- ▲ **KSA** 130-131 F 6
Abyaḍ, Tall al- ☆ **SYR** 128-129 H 4
Abyar ash Shuwayrif ○ **LAR** 192-193 F 3
Abydos ○ **AUS** 172-173 D 6
Abydos ∴·· **ET** 194-195 E 4
Abyei ○ **SUD** 206-207 J 4
Ābyek ○ **IR** 136-137 B 6
Abyj ○ **RUS** 110-111 Z 5
Abymes, Les ○ **F** 56 E 3
Abyrabyt ~ **RUS** 110-111 U 5
Acacias ○ **CO** 60-61 E 6
Academy ○ **USA** (SD) 260-261 G 3
Academy Gletscher ⊂ **GRØ** 26-27 h 3
Acadia, Cape ▲ **CDN** 36-37 K 4
Acadia National Park ⊥ **USA** (ME) 278-279 N 4
Acadian Historic Village · **CDN** (NB) 240-241 L 3
Acadia Valley ○ **CDN** (ALB) 232-233 H 4
Acadie ∸ **CDN** (QUE) 240-241 J 2
Acadie Siding ○ **CDN** (NB) 240-241 K 4
Acahay ○ **PY** 76-77 J 3
Açailândia ○ **BR** 68-69 E 4
Açai Paraná ○ **BR** 66-67 C 2
Acajutla ○ **ES** 52-53 K 5
Ačajvajam ○ **RUS** 112-113 Q 6
Ačajvajam ~ **RUS** 112-113 Q 6
Acala ○ **MEX** 52-53 H 3
Acala ○ **USA** (TX) 266-267 B 2
Acámbaro ○ **MEX** 52-53 D 1
Acambuco, Arroyo ~ **RA** 76-77 E 2
Acampamento da Cameia ○ **ANG** 216-217 F 5
Acampamento de Indios ○ **BR** 70-71 H 2
Acampamento Grande ○ **BR** 62-63 H 5
Acancéh ○ **MEX** 52-53 K 1
Acandi ○ **CO** 60-61 C 3
Acangatá ○ **BR** 68-69 C 3
Acapetagua ○ **MEX** 52-53 H 4
Acaponeta ○ **MEX** 50-51 G 6
Acaponeta, Río ~ **MEX** 50-51 G 6
Acapu, Rio ~ **BR** 62-63 F 6
Acapulco de Juárez ○·· **MEX** 52-53 E 3
Acará ○ **BR** 62-63 K 6
Acará, Cachoeira ~ **BR** 66-67 J 5
Acará, Lago ⬭ **BR** 66-67 F 6
Acará, Rio ~ **BR** 62-63 K 6
Acará, Rio ~ **BR** 66-67 F 6
Acarai, Rio ~ **BR** 68-69 B 3
Acará-Mirim, Rio ~ **BR** 68-69 D 3
Acara ou Acarí, Serra ▲▲ **BR** 62-63 E 5
Acaraú ○ **BR** 68-69 H 3
Acaraú, Rio ~ **BR** 68-69 H 3
Acari ○ **PE** 64-65 E 9
Acari, Rio ~ **BR** 62-63 E 6
Acari, Rio ~ **BR** 66-67 H 6
Acari, Rio ~ **BR** 72-73 H 3
Acarigua ○ **YV** 60-61 G 3
Acasio ○ **BOL** 70-71 D 5
Acasta River ~ **CDN** 30-31 L 3
Acatayon ○ **GQ** 210-211 B 3
Acatic ○ **MEX** 52-53 C 1
Acatlán ○ **MEX** 52-53 F 2
Acatlán de Osorio ○ **MEX** 52-53 E 2
Acayucan ○ **MEX** 52-53 G 3
Aččen, ozero ⬭ **RUS** 112-113 X 4
Aččitov, togi ▲ **US** 136-137 G 3
Accomac ○ **USA** (VA) 280-281 L 6
Accra ★··· **GH** 202-203 K 7
Aččygyj-Taryn-Jurjah ~ **RUS** 110-111 Y 7
Acebuches ○ **MEX** 50-51 H 3
Aceguá ○ **BR** 76-77 K 6
Acequias ○ **YV** 60-61 F 3
Acequias, Las ○ **RA** 78-79 H 2
Achaacha ○ **DZ** 190-191 C 2
Achacachi ○ **BOL** 70-71 C 5
Achaguas ○ **YV** 60-61 G 4
Achalpur ○ **IND** 138-139 F 9
Achao ○ **RCH** 78-79 C 7
Achar ○ **ROU** 78-79 L 2
Acheb ○ **DZ** 190-191 G 6
Achegtim < **RIM** 196-197 E 5
Achelouma ~ **RN** 198-199 F 2
Achelouma < **RN** (AGA) 192-193 E 6
Acheng ○ **VRC** 150-151 F 5
Acheron River ~ **AUS** 180-181 H 4
Achguig el Adam < **RIM** 196-197 E 5
Achiasi ○ **GH** 202-203 K 7
Achibueno, Río ~ **RCH** 78-79 D 4
Achille ○ **USA** (OK) 264-265 H 5
Achill Island ⌒ **IRL** 90-91 B 5
Achim, Oudi ~ **TCH** 198-199 J 5
Achinsk = Ačinsk ☆ **RUS** 116-117 E 7
Achiras ○ **RA** 78-79 G 2
Achiri ○ **BOL** 70-71 C 5
Achnasheen ○ **GB** 90-91 E 3
Achoma ○ **PE** 70-71 B 4
Achton Friis Ø ⌒ **GRØ** 26-27 q 4
Acıgöl ⬭ **TR** 128-129 C 4
Acimã, Igarapé ~ **BR** 66-67 D 6
Āčin ○ **AFG** 138-139 C 2
Ačinsk ☆ **RUS** 116-117 E 7
Acıpayam ☆ **TR** 128-129 C 4
Acireale ○ **I** 100-101 E 6
Ačit ☆ **RUS** 96-97 K 5
Ačit nuur ⬭ **MAU** 116-117 E 11
Ačkasar, gora ▲ **AR** 128-129 L 2
Ackerly ○ **USA** (TX) 264-265 C 6
Ackerman ○ **USA** (MS) 268-269 L 3
Acklins, Bight of ≈ 54-55 H 3
Acklins Island ⌒ **BS** 54-55 J 3
Acme ○ **CDN** (ALB) 232-233 E 4
Acme ○ **USA** (LA) 268-269 J 5
Acme ○ **USA** (MI) 272-273 D 3
Acme ○ **USA** (WA) 244-245 C 2
Aco ○ **PE** 64-65 D 7
Acobamba ○ **PE** 64-65 E 8
Acoma ○ **USA** (NM) 256-257 H 4
Acoma ○ **USA** (NV) 248-249 K 2
Acoma Indian Reservation X **USA** (NM) 256-257 H 4
Acomayo ○ **PE** 70-71 B 3
Acona ○ **USA** (MS) 268-269 L 3
Aconcagua, Cerro ▲ **RA** 78-79 D 2
Aconcagua, Parque Nacional ⊥ **RA** 78-79 D 2
Aconquija, Sierra del ▲▲ **RA** 76-77 D 4
Acopiara ○ **BR** 68-69 J 5
Acos ○ **PE** 64-65 D 7
Acostambo ○ **PE** 64-65 E 8
Acraman, Lake ⬭ **AUS** 178-179 C 6
Acre □ **BR** 66-67 B 7
Acre, Rio ~ **BR** 66-67 D 7
Acre, Río ~ **BR** 70-71 B 2
Actinolite ○ **CDN** (ONT) 238-239 H 4
Action Vale ○ **CDN** (QUE) 238-239 N 3
Acton ○ **CDN** (ONT) 238-239 E 5
Acton ○ **USA** (MT) 250-251 L 6
Acton State Historic Site ∴ **USA** (TX) 264-265 G 6
Actopan ○ **MEX** 52-53 E 1
Acuã, Rio ~ **BR** 66-67 F 6
Açu da Torre ○ **BR** 72-73 L 2
Acufre, Paso de ▲ **RA** 76-77 B 6
Acula ○ **MEX** 52-53 G 2
Acul du Nord ○ **RH** 54-55 J 5
Acultzingo ○ **MEX** 52-53 F 2
Acurnam ○ **GQ** 210-211 C 3
Acyköl ⬭ **KA** 136-137 M 3
Acyojyl ~ **KA** 126-127 L 3
Acysu ~ **KA** 124-125 J 3
Acysu, köl ⬭ **KA** 124-125 D 5
Aczo ○ **PE** 64-65 D 6
Ada ○ **GH** 202-203 L 7
Ada ○ **USA** (MN) 270-271 B 3
Ada ○ **USA** (OH) 280-281 C 3
Ada ○ **USA** (OK) 264-265 H 4
Adab ∴· **IRQ** 128-129 L 7
Ādaba ○ **ETH** 208-209 D 5
Adad Cus, Uar < **SP** 212-213 J 2
Adadikam ○ **RI** 166-167 H 2
Adaevka ○ **RUS** 124-125 C 3
Adaf ▲▲ **DZ** 190-191 G 9
Adaigba ○ **WAN** 204-205 G 5
Adair, Bahía de ≈ 50-51 C 2
Adairsville ○ **USA** (GA) 284-285 F 2
Adaiso ○ **GH** 202-203 K 7
Adaja, Río ~ **E** 98-99 E 4
Adak ○ **USA** 22-23 H 7
Adak Island ⌒ **USA** 22-23 H 7
Adaklı ☆ **TR** 128-129 J 3
Adak Strait ≈ 22-23 H 7
Adalei ○ **SP** 212-213 K 2
Adam ○ **OM** 132-133 K 2
Adam, Mount ▲ **GB** 78-79 L 6
Adam, Point ▲ **USA** 22-23 U 3
Adam al-Hulay ○ **KSA** 132-133 B 3
Adamantina ○ **BR** 72-73 E 6
Adamaoua = Adamawa □ **CAM** 204-205 K 5
Adamaoua, Massif de l' ▲▲ **CAM** 204-205 K 5
Adamawa = Adamaoua □ **CAM** 204-205 K 5
Adamello ▲ **I** 100-101 C 1
Adaminaby ○ **AUS** 180-181 K 3
Ādamī Tulu ○ **ETH** 208-209 D 5
Adams ○ **USA** (CA) 246-247 C 5
Adams ○ **USA** (MN) 270-271 F 7
Adams ○ **USA** (ND) 258-259 J 3
Adams ○ **USA** (NE) 262-263 K 4
Adams ○ **USA** (NY) 278-279 E 5
Adams ○ **USA** (OR) 244-245 G 5
Adams ○ **USA** (TN) 276-277 H 4
Adams ○ **USA** (WI) 270-271 J 7
Adams, Cape ▲ **ARK** 16 F 30
Adams, Fort ○ **USA** (MS) 268-269 J 5
Adams, Mount ▲ **USA** (WA) 244-245 D 4
Adams Cove ○ **CDN** (NFL) 242-243 P 5
Adams Lake ○ **CDN** (BC) 230-231 K 3
Adams Lake ⬭ **CDN** (BC) 230-231 K 2
Adam's Peak ▲·· **CL** 140-141 J 7
Adams River ~ **CDN** (BC) 230-231 K 2
Adamsville ○ **USA** (TN) 276-277 G 5
Adamsville ○ **USA** (TX) 266-267 J 2
'Adan ○· **Y** 132-133 D 7
Adana ☆· **TR** 128-129 F 4
Aḏana, Wādī ~ **Y** 132-133 D 6
Adane ○ **G** 210-211 C 4
Adang, Teluk ≈ 164-165 E 4
Adani ○ **WAN** 204-205 G 5
Adaouda ▲ **DZ** 190-191 E 9
Adapazarı = Sakarya ○ **TR** 128-129 D 2
Adar ○ **TCH** 206-207 E 3
Adar, Khor ~ **SUD** 206-207 L 4
Adarama ○ **SUD** 200-201 G 4
Adarot ○ **SUD** 200-201 H 4
Adaut ○ **RI** 166-167 F 6
Adavale ○ **AUS** 178-179 H 3
Adda ~ **I** 100-101 B 1
Adda ~ **SUD** 206-207 G 4
aḍ-Ḍab'a ○ **ET** 194-195 D 2
ad-Dabbah ○ **SUD** 200-201 E 3
Ad Dahāwah < **LAR** 192-193 J 5
ad-Dāḫila, al-Wāḥāt ∸· **ET** 194-195 D 5
ad-Dakhla ○ **MA** 196-197 C 3
Addala-Suhgel'meer, gora ▲ **RUS** 126-127 G 6
ad-Dāmir ○ **SUD** 200-201 F 4
ad-Dammām ☆ **KSA** 134-135 D 5
Addanki ○ **IND** 140-141 H 3
ad-Dār al-Bayḍa ☆ **MA** 188-189 H 4
Ad Darsia ○ **LAR** 192-193 J 1
ad-Dauḥa ★ **Q** 134-135 D 6
ad-Dawwār, Kafr ○ **ET** 194-195 E 2
Addi ○ **CAM** 206-207 B 5
ad-Diffa ∸ **ET** 192-193 L 2
Addis ○ **USA** (LA) 268-269 J 6
Addis Ababa = Ādīs Ābeba ★·· **ETH** 208-209 D 4
Addison ○ **USA** (AL) 284-285 C 2
Addison ○ **USA** (NY) 278-279 D 6
Addo ○ **ZA** 220-221 G 6
Addoi, Uar < **SP** 212-213 H 2
Addo-Olifant National Park ⊥ **ZA** 220-221 G 6
ad-Du'ayn ○ **SUD** 206-207 H 3
ad-Dubaikī, Bi'r < **ET** 194-195 D 2
ad-Dubasi ○ **SUD** 200-201 F 5
ad-Duwaym ○ **SUD** 200-201 F 5
Adé ○ **TCH** 198-199 K 6
Adéane ○ **SN** 202-203 B 3
Adel ○ **USA** (GA) 284-285 G 5
Adel ○ **USA** (IA) 274-275 E 3
Adel ○ **USA** (OR) 244-245 F 8
Adelaide ☆· **AUS** 180-181 E 3
Adelaide ○ **ZA** 220-221 H 6
Adelaide Island ○ **ARK** 16 G 30
Adelaide Island ⌒ **ARK** 16 G 30
Adelaide Peninsula ⌣ **CDN** 24-25 X 6
Adelaide River ○· **AUS** 172-173 K 2
Adelanto ○ **USA** (CA) 248-249 G 5
Adel Bagrou ○ **RIM** 196-197 G 7
Adelbert Range ▲▲ **PNG** 183 C 3
Adēlē ○ **ETH** 208-209 D 5
Adele Island ⌒ **AUS** 172-173 F 3
Adelia María ○ **RA** 78-79 G 2
Adélie, Terre ∸ **ARK** 16 G 15
Adelong ○ **AUS** 178-179 H 2
Ademuz ○ **E** 98-99 G 4
Aden ○ **CDN** (ALB) 232-233 G 6
Aden = 'Adan ○· **Y** 132-133 D 7
Aden, Gulf of ≈ 208-209 G 3
Adendorp ○ **ZA** 220-221 G 6
Adentan ○ **GH** 202-203 K 7
Aderbissinat ○ **RN** 198-199 C 5
Aderpaëta ~ **RUS** 108-109 Q 7
Aderuba, Ğabal ▲ **ER** 200-201 H 5
Adéta ○ **RT** 202-203 L 6
'Adfā' ○ **KSA** 130-131 G 3
Adi, Pulau ⌒ **RI** 166-167 G 4
Ādī Abun ○ **ETH** 200-201 J 5
Adiaké ○ **CI** 202-203 J 7
Adiangdia ▲ **DY** 202-203 L 5
Ādī Ārk'ay ○ **ETH** 200-201 H 6
Adicora ○ **YV** 60-61 G 2
Ādī Da'iro ○ **ETH** 200-201 J 5
Adidome ○ **GH** 202-203 L 6
Adieu, Cape ▲ **AUS** 176-177 M 6
Adieu-Vat ○ **F** 62-63 H 3
Ādīgala ○ **ETH** 208-209 F 3
Àdige ~ **I** 100-101 D 2
Àdige = Etsch ~ **I** 100-101 C 1
Ādīgrat ○ **ETH** 200-201 J 5
Ādī Gudom ○ **ETH** 200-201 J 6
Ādīk'eyih ○ **ER** 200-201 J 5
Ādīkwala ○ **ER** 200-201 J 5
Adilābād ○ **IND** 138-139 G 10
Adin ○ **USA** (CA) 246-247 E 2
Adiora < **RMM** 196-197 K 6
Adipala ○ **RI** 168 C 3
Adīr ☆ **LAR** 192-193 E 4
Ādī Ramets' ○ **ETH** 200-201 H 6
'Āḏirīyāt, Ğibāl al- ▲▲ **JOR** 130-131 E 2

Aachen — 'Āḏirīyāt, Ğibā al- 293

Adirondack Mountains ▲▲ USA (NY)
278-279 G 4
'Ãdis Ãbeba o • ETH 208-209 D 4
Ãdis 'Alem o • ETH 208-209 D 4
Ãdis Zemen o ETH 200-201 H 6
Ãdi Ugri o ER 200-201 J 5
Adiyaman ☆ TR 128-129 H 4
Adjeloho, Adrar ▲▲ DZ 190-191 G 8
Adjengré o RT 202-203 L 5
Adjerar ▲▲ DZ 190-191 G 8
Adjiro o DY 202-203 L 5
Adjohoun o DY 204-205 L 5
Adjud o RO 102-103 E 4
Adjuntar, Presa de una MEX 50-51 K 6
Adjuntas, Las o YV (BOL) 60-61 J 4
Adjuntas, Las o YV (FED) 60-61 H 2
Adlavik Islands ∩ CDN 36-37 U 7
Adler o RUS 126-127 C 6
Admer, Erg d' ∴ DZ 190-191 G 8
Admer, Plaine d' ✓ DZ 190-191 G 8
Admiral o CDN (SAS) 232-233 L 6
Admiral Collinson, Cape ▲ CDN
24-25 V 5
Admiral's Beach o CDN (NFL)
242-243 P 5
Admiralteistva, poluostrov ∪ RUS
108-109 G 4
Admiralty Gulf ≈ 172-173 G 3
Admiralty Gulf Aboriginal Land ✗ AUS
172-173 G 3
Admiralty Inlet ≈ 24-25 c 4
Admiralty Inlet ≈ USA 244-245 B 2
Admiralty Island ∩ CDN 24-25 Y 7
Admiralty Island ∩ USA 32-33 C 3
Admiralty Island National Monument
Kootznoowoo Wilderness ⊥ • USA
32-33 C 3
Admiralty Islands ∩ PNG 183 D 2
Admiralty Range ▲▲ ARK 16 F 17
Admont o • A 92-93 N 5
Ado o WAN (OGU) 204-205 E 5
Ado o WAN (PLA) 204-205 E 5
Ado Awaiye o WAN 204-205 E 5
Adobes o USA (TX) 266-267 C 4
Ado-Ekiti o WAN 204-205 F 5
Adok o SUD 206-207 K 4
Adolfo o BR 72-73 F 6
Adolfo Gonzáles Chaves o RA 78-79 J 4
Adolfo López Mateos, Presa ✓ MEX
50-51 F 5
Adolf S. Jensen Land ⊥ GRØ 26-27 p 5
Adonara, Pulau ∩ RI 166-167 H 6
Ãdoni o IND 140-141 G 4
Adorf o D 92-93 M 3
Adoru o WAN 204-205 G 5
Ado-Tymovo o RUS 122-123 K 3
Adoumandjali o RCA 210-211 E 2
Adoumi o CAM 204-205 K 4
Adour ∼ F 90-91 G 10
Adra o E 98-99 F 6
Adranga o ZRE 212-213 C 2
Adrar ☆ • DZ (ADR) 188-189 L 7
Adrar ▲▲ DZ 190-191 F 8
Adrar Massif ▲▲ RIM 196-197 E 4
Adraskan o AFG 134-135 K 2
Adrasman o TJ 136-137 M 4
Adré o TCH 198-199 L 6
Adrian o USA (GA) 284-285 H 4
Adrian o USA (MI) 278-279 D 3
Adrian o USA (MN) 270-271 C 7
Adrian o USA (MO) 274-275 D 6
Adrian o USA (OR) 244-245 H 7
Adrian o USA (TX) 264-265 B 3
Adrianópolis o BR 74-75 F 5
Adriatic Sea ≈ 100-101 G 4
Adua o RI 166-167 E 2
Aduana o RCH 78-79 D 3
Aduana y Reten de Cuya o RCH
70-71 B 6
Aduku o KAU 212-213 D 2
Adunkur Daban ▲ VRC 146-147 G 4
Adunu o WAN 204-205 G 4
Adür o IND 140-141 G 6
Adura o WAN 204-205 G 4
Adusa o ZRE 212-213 B 3
Advance o USA (MO) 276-277 F 3
Advat ∴• IL 130-131 D 2
Adventure, Bahía ≈ 80 C 2
Adventure Beach o 100-101 C 6
Ãdwa o ETH 200-201 J 5
Adwana o IND 138-139 B 9
Ady o USA (TX) 264-265 B 3
Adyča ∼ RUS 110-111 V 6
Adygalah o RUS 120-121 M 2
Adygea = Adygée Respublikèm □ RUS
126-127 D 5
Adyk o RUS 126-127 F 5
Adzié o ROB 210-211 E 4
Adz'va ∼ RUS 108-109 J 8
Aegean Sea = Egéo Pélagos ≈ 8 F 5
Aegviidu o EST 94-95 J 2
Aekanopan o RI 162-163 C 3
'Ærø ∩ DK 86-87 E 9
Aérobo o 202-203 J 6
'Aèros'emki, ostrova ∪ RUS 110-111 N 3
Aesake, Lake o PNG 183 A 4
Aese ∩ VAN 184 II a 2
Aetna o CDN (ALB) 232-233 E 6
Aetós o GR 100-101 H 4
Afadé o CAM 198-199 G 6
'Afak ∩ IRQ 128-129 L 6
Afambo o ETH 208-209 E 3
Afanas'evo ☆ RUS 96-97 H 4
Afanas'evsk, Agnie- o RUS 122-123 H 3
'Afar, Tall ○ IRQ 128-129 K 4
Af Barwaaqo ☆ SP 206-207 J 5
Ãfdem o ETH 208-209 E 4
Afeleh, In ○ DZ 190-191 G 9
Afe Peak ▲ CDN 20-21 X 5
Afféri o CI 202-203 J 6
Afflisses, Oued ✓ DZ 190-191 C 6
Affollé ∴ RIM 196-197 E 6
Affon = Ouémé ∼ DY 202-203 L 5
Afghanistan = Afghänistän ■ AFG
134-135 J 2

Afgooye o SP 212-213 K 2
'Afif o KSA 130-131 H 6
Afikpo o WAN 204-205 G 6
Afin, Rüd-e- ∼ IR 134-135 H 2
Afipinskij o RUS 126-127 C 5
Ãfjord o N 86-87 E 5
Aflandshage ▲ GRØ 28-29 V 4
Aflou o DZ 190-191 D 3
Afmadow o SP 212-213 J 3
Afobaka o SME 62-63 G 3
Afogados da Ingazeira o BR 68-69 K 5
Afognak Island ∩ USA 22-23 U 3
Afolé o RT 202-203 L 6
Afonso Cláudio o BR 72-73 K 6
Afonso ∴ TR 128-129 E 5
Afouidich, Sebkhet o MA 196-197 C 4
Afrânio o BR 68-69 H 6
Ãfréra Terara ▲ ETH 200-201 K 6
Ãfréra Ye Ch'ew Häyk' o ETH
200-201 K 6
African Banks ∩ SY 224 C 2
African Lion Safari ⊥ CDN (ONT)
238-239 E 5
Afridi Lake o CDN 30-31 P 3
Afrika, mys ▲ RUS 120-121 U 5
'Afrin o SYR 128-129 G 4
Afşin o TR 128-129 G 3
Afton o USA (AL) 274-275 D 3
Afton o USA (OK) 264-265 K 2
Afton o USA (WY) 252-253 H 4
Afua o BR 62-63 J 6
Afua, fino- ▲ BR 62-63 K 6
Afuein o SP 212-213 K 3
'Afula ☆ IL 130-131 D 1
Afyon ☆• TR 128-129 D 3
Aga ∼ RUS 118-119 G 10
Ağā', Ğabal ▲▲ KSA 130-131 G 4
Agabama ✓ C 54-55 F 4
'Agâbsir o IR 128-129 L 4
Aga Buryat Autonomous District=Agin. Burj.
avt. okrug □ RUS 118-119 F 10
Agač, Koš ☆ RUS 124-125 Q 4
Agadem o RN 198-199 C 3
Agadez ☆ RN 198-199 C 3
Agadez ☆• RN (AGA) 198-199 C 4
Agãdir ▲ MAL 188-189 G 5
Agadyr' o KA 124-125 H 4
Ãğā Ğāri o IR 134-135 C 3
Agadro-gawa ∼ J 152-153 H 6
Agaie o WAN 204-205 G 4
Agapa o RUS 108-109 W 6
Agapo Açu o BR 66-67 J 5
Agapovka ☆ RUS 96-97 L 7
Ağar o AFG 136-137 K 7
Agar o USA (SD) 260-261 F 2
Ağāraktem o RIM 196-197 G 3
Agarfa o ETH 208-209 D 5
Agaro o ETH 208-209 C 5
Ãgarsararén ∩ ETH 208-209 G 5
Agartala ☆ IND 142-143 Q 4
Agaru o SUD 208-209 B 3
Agaskagou Lake o CDN (ONT)
236-237 H 4
Agassiz o CDN (BC) 230-231 H 4
Agassiz Forest Reserve ⊥ CDN (MAN)
234-235 G 5
Agassiz Fracture Zone ≈ 14-15 P 11
Agassiz National Wildlife Refuge ⊥ USA
(MN) 270-271 C 2
Agastya Malai ▲ IND 140-141 G 6
Agata (Nižnee), ozero o RUS
116-117 F 2
Agata (Verhnee), ozero o RUS
116-117 F 2
Agate o USA (CO) 254-255 M 4
Agate o USA (NE) 262-263 C 2
Agate Fossil Beds National Monument ∴•
USA (NE) 262-263 C 2
Agats o RI 166-167 K 4
Agattl Island ∩ IND 140-141 B 3
Agattu Island ∩ USA 22-23 C 6
Agattu Strait ≈ 22-23 C 6
Agawa Bay o CDN (ONT) 236-237 D 5
Agawa Canyon • CDN (ONT)
236-237 D 5
Agawa River ∼ CDN (ONT) 236-237 D 5
Agbabu o WAN 204-205 F 5
Agbado o DY 204-205 E 4
Agbara o WAN 204-205 E 5
Agbarha-Otor o WAN 204-205 F 6
Agbélouvé o RT 202-203 L 6
Agbohoutogon o DY 204-205 L 5
Agbor-Bojiboji o WAN 204-205 G 5
Agboville o CI 202-203 H 7
Agbozume o GH 202-203 L 6
Agdaš o AZ 128-129 N 2
Agde o F 90-91 J 10
Agdz o MA 188-189 H 5
Agdžabedi = Ağcabadi o AZ
128-129 M 2
Agege o WAN 204-205 E 5
Agen o F 90-91 H 9
Agenebode o WAN 204-205 G 5
Ãgere Maryam o ETH 208-209 D 6
Aggas ☆ GRØ 28-29 Y 3
Aggeneys o ZA 220-221 D 4
Aggi o RIM 196-197 D 4
Aghat bonne ∼ RIM 198-199 C 4
Aghir o TN 190-191 H 4
Aghiyuk Island ∩ USA 22-23 S 4
Aghor o PK 134-135 L 6
Aghoubir o RIM 196-197 E 4
Aghouint o MA 196-197 C 4
Aghreïjit ○ RIM 196-197 E 5
Aghrijit ∴• RIM 196-197 E 5
Aghzoumal, Sebkhet o MA 196-197 D 2
Agiabampo, Bahia de ≈ 50-51 E 4

Agia Galini o GR 100-101 K 7
Agia Napa o CY 128-129 E 5
Agiapuk River ∼ USA 20-21 G 4
Agia Triáda o GR 100-101 H 6
Agigea o RO 102-103 F 4
Ãgio Orous ☆ GR 100-101 K 4
Ágios Efstrátios ∩ GR 100-101 K 5
Ágios Kirikos o GR 100-101 L 6
Ágios Konstantinos o GR 100-101 J 5
Ágios Nikólaos o GR 100-101 J 4
Ãgiou Orous, Kólpos ≈ 100-101 J 4
Agita o RUS 118-119 H 9
Aglipay o RP 160-161 D 4
Aglou o RIM 196-197 D 4
Agnamala, Mount ▲ RP 160-161 D 3
Agnes o USA (TX) 264-265 G 6
Agnes Lake o USA (MN) 270-271 G 2
Agnesso o USA (OR) 244-245 A 8
Agnes Waters o AUS 178-179 L 3
Agnew o AUS 176-177 F 4
Agnibilékrou o CI 202-203 J 6
Agnie-Afanas'evsk o RUS 122-123 H 3
Agnita o RO 102-103 D 5
Agno ∼ RP 160-161 D 5
Agnone o I 100-101 F 4
Ago ☆ J 152-153 G 7
Ago-Are o WAN 204-205 E 4
Agogo o GH 202-203 K 6
Agona o GH 202-203 J 6
Agona Junction o GH 202-203 K 7
Agotu o PNG 183 C 4
Agou o CI 202-203 J 7
Agou, Mont ▲ RT 202-203 L 6
Agoudal o MA 188-189 J 4
Agoudim o RIM 196-197 G 3
Agouna o DY 202-203 L 5
Agounni Jefal o RIM 196-197 G 5
Agpamiut o GRØ 28-29 O 4
Agra o ••• IND 138-139 G 6
Agrado, El o CO 60-61 F 4
Agra-Emneke, gora ▲ RUS 110-111 X 5
Agrahanskij poluostrov ∪ RUS
126-127 G 6
Ãgreda o E 98-99 G 4
Ãgrestan o AFG 134-135 M 2
Ağrı ☆ TR 128-129 K 3
Agrigento o I 100-101 D 6
Agrinio o GR 100-101 H 5
Agrio, Rio ∼ RA 78-79 D 4
Agrirama • USA (GA) 284-285 G 5
Agrópoli o I 100-101 F 4
Agryz o RUS 96-97 H 5
Agua Amarga, Pampa del ⊥ RA
78-79 E 5
Agua Azúl o HN 52-53 L 4
Agua Azúl Cascades ∼• MEX 52-53 H 3
Agua Azúl Falls ∼ BH 52-53 K 3
Agua Blanca o YV 60-61 K 4
Água Boa o BR 72-73 J 4
Agua Boa o RA 76-77 C 6
Agua Boa do Univini, Rio ∼ BR
62-63 D 5
Água Braga o BR 72-73 F 2
Água Branca o BR 68-69 K 5
Água Branca, Igarapé ∼ BR 66-67 H 7
Agua Caliente o PE 64-65 E 6
Agua Caliente o USA (AZ) 256-257 B 6
Agua Caliente, Río o BOL 70-71 F 4
Agua Caliente Indian Reservation ✗ USA
(CA) 248-249 H 6
Aguacatán o GCA 52-53 J 4
Aguachica o CO 60-61 E 3
Água Clara o BR 72-73 D 6
Aguaçuzinho o BR 70-71 J 6
Agua Dulce o USA (AZ) 256-257 B 6
Água Dulce o USA (TX) 266-267 K 6
Agua Dulce o PA 52-53 P 7
Agua Escondida o RA 78-79 E 4
Água Fria o BR 68-69 J 7
Agua Fria o USA (NM) 256-257 M 6
Água Fria, Ribeiro ∼ BR 68-69 D 5
Agua Fria, Rio ∼ BR 72-73 D 4
Agua Fria River ∼ USA (AZ)
256-257 C 4
Agua Hedionda, Cerro ▲ RA 78-79 F 2
Aguaí o BR 72-73 G 7
Agua Linda o YV 60-61 G 2
Aguán, Rio ∼ HN 52-53 L 4
Aguanaval, Rio ∼ MEX 50-51 G 5
Agua Negra, Paso del ▲ RA 76-77 C 6
Agua Negra, Río ∼ RA 76-77 C 6
Aguanish o CDN (QUE) 242-243 F 2
Agua Nueva o MEX (COA) 50-51 J 5
Agua Nueva o MEX (TAM) 50-51 K 6
Agua Nueva o USA (TX) 266-267 J 7
Aguanus, Rivière ∼ CDN 38-39 N 3
Aguapaí, Rio ∼ BR 70-71 H 4
Agua Pasto o BOL 70-71 G 6
Aguapey, Rio ∼ RA 76-77 J 5
Aguapeí, Serra de ▲▲ BR 70-71 H 4
Água Preta, Igarapé ∼ BR 66-67 F 5
Água Prieta o MEX 50-51 E 2
Aguaray o RA 76-77 F 1
Aguaro-Guariquito, Parque Nacional ⊥ YV
60-61 H 3
Aguasay o YV 60-61 K 3
Aguas Belas o BR 68-69 K 6
Aguas Blancas o BOL 76-77 E 2
Aguas Blancas o RCH 76-77 C 3
Aguas Blancas, Cerro ▲ RA 76-77 C 4
Aguas Blancas, Quebrada de ∼ RCH
76-77 C 3

Aguas Blancas y Ãguas Negras, Reserva
Faunística ⊥ YV 60-61 F 3
Aguascalientes o RA 76-77 C 3
Aguascalientes ☆• MEX (AGS)
50-51 H 7
Aguas Calientes, Paso de ▲ RA
76-77 C 3
Aguas Calientes, Salar o RCH 76-77 C 3
Aguas Calientes, Sierra de ▲ RA
76-77 D 3
Aguas Claras o C 54-55 D 3
Aguas Claraso o C 54-55 G 4
Ãguas de São Clara o BR 74-75 E 5
Ãguas Formosas o BR 72-73 K 4
Aguas Negras o PE 64-65 E 2
Aguateca ∴ GCA 52-53 J 3
Agua Verde ou Anhanazá, Rio ∼ BR
70-71 J 4
Agua Viva o YV 60-61 F 3
Aguaytía o PE 64-65 E 6
Aguaytía, Río ∼ PE 64-65 E 5
Aguazul o CO 60-61 E 5
Agu Bay ≈ 24-25 c 5
Agudda Cecilio o RA 78-79 G 6
Agudos do Sul o BR 74-75 F 5
Agudos Grandes, Serra ▲▲ BR 74-75 F 5
Ãgueda o P 98-99 C 4
Aguelhok o RMM 196-197 L 5
Aguelt ez Zerga o RIM 196-197 C 5
Aguemour ⊥ DZ 190-191 E 7
Aguemour, Oued ∼ DZ 190-191 E 7
Aguéssis o RIM 198-199 D 4
Agues Verdes, Raudal ∼ CO 64-65 F 1
Aguga ∼ EAU 212-213 D 2
Ãguia Branca o BR 72-73 K 5
Aguiar Javaés o BR 68-69 D 7
Aguié o RN 198-199 C 6
Aguieira, Barragem da ✓ P 98-99 C 4
Aguila, El o BOL 70-71 F 4
Aguila, Gruta C. del ∼ ROU 78-79 L 2
Aguilaf Fai o RIM 196-197 C 5
Aguilal Faye o RIM 196-197 C 5
Aguilar, Cerro ▲ RA 76-77 E 2
Aguilar, El o RA 76-77 E 2
Aguilar, Salar de o RCH 76-77 C 3
Aguilar de Campoo o E 98-99 E 3
Aguilares o RA 76-77 E 2
Aguilares o USA (TX) 266-267 H 6
Águilas o E 98-99 G 6
Aguililla o MEX 52-53 C 2
Aguirre, Bahía ≈ 80 H 7
Aguirre, Centro o RA 78-79 D 7
Aguja, Cerro o RA 78-79 D 7
Aguja, Cerro ▲ RCH 80 F 7
Aguja, Punta ▲ PE 64-65 B 4
Agujar ∼ RUS 116-117 H 8
Agulhas, Cape = Agulhas, Kaap ▲ ZA
220-221 D 7
Agulhas, L' o ZA 220-221 D 7
Agulhas Basin ≈ 6-7 M 13
Agulhas Plateau ≈ 6-7 M 12
Agulhas Ridge ≈ 6-7 K 13
Agumbe o IND 140-141 F 4
Aguni-shima ∩ J 152-153 B 11
Agur o EAU 212-213 D 2
Agurã Grande o RA 76-77 G 6
Agusan ∼ RP 160-161 D 7
Agutaya Island ∩ RP 160-161 D 7
Agwampt ∼ SUD 200-201 G 3
Agwarra o WAN 204-205 G 4
Agweri o WAN 204-205 G 5
Agwok o SUD 206-207 J 5
Ahaba o WAN 204-205 G 6
Ahaberge ▲ NAM 216-217 F 9
Ahad al-Masára o KSA 132-133 C 5
Ahad Rãfida o KSA 132-133 C 4
Ahalcihe ☆ GE 126-127 E 7
Ahalkalaki o GE 126-127 E 7
Ahamansu o GH 202-203 L 6
Ahanduizinho, Rio ∼ BR 70-71 K 7
Ahangaran o US 136-137 L 4
Ahar o IR 128-129 M 3
Ahča-Kujma o TM 136-137 D 5
Ahdar, al-Ğabal al- ▲▲ OM 132-133 K 2
Ahellakane, Adrar ▲▲ DZ 190-191 E 7
Ahémé, Lac o DY 202-203 L 6
Ahenkro o GH 202-203 J 6
Ahero o EAK 212-213 E 4
Ahfir o MA 188-189 K 3
Ahillio o GR 100-101 J 5
Ahioma o PNG 183 F 6
Ahipara o NZ 182 H 2
Ahklun Mountains ▲▲ USA 20-21 M 6
Ahlat ☆ TR 128-129 K 3
Ahmad, Bi'r o Y 132-133 D 7
Ahmadābād o AFG 134-135 J 1
Ahmadābād o ••• IND 138-139 D 8
Ahmadal-Yasin o IRQ 128-129 L 5
Ahmadi, al- o KWT 130-131 K 3
Ahmadnagar ☆ IND 138-139 E 10
Ahmadpur o IND 138-139 G 9
Ahmadpur East o PK 138-139 C 4
Ahmadpur Lamma o PK 138-139 C 4
Ahmadpur Siãl o PK 138-139 D 4
Ahmad Wal o PK 134-135 L 4
Ahmar Mountains ▲ ETH 208-209 E 4
Ahmatova, zaliv ∼ RUS 108-109 e 2
Ahmeta o GE 126-127 F 7
Ahmic Harbour o CDN (ONT)
238-239 F 7
Ahmim ∼ ET 194-195 E 4
Ahnet ∴ DZ 190-191 D 8
Ahoada o WAN 204-205 G 6
Ahome o MEX 50-51 F 5
Ahoskie o USA (NC) 282-283 H 4
Ahousat o CDN (BC) 230-231 G 4
Ahram o IR 134-135 D 4
Ahraura o IND 142-143 C 3
Ahrweiler, Bad Neuenahr- o D 92-93 J 3

Ahsahka o USA (ID) 250-251 C 5
Ahsu = Ãgsu o AZ 128-129 N 2
Ahtamar o TR 128-129 K 3
Ahtaranda o RUS 118-119 F 3
Ãhtäri o FIN 88-89 H 5
Ahtarsk, Primorsko- o RUS 102-103 K 3
Ahtme, Jõhvi- o EST 94-95 K 2
Ahtuba ∼ RUS 96-97 E 10
Ahtubinsk o RUS 96-97 E 9
Ahty o RUS 126-127 G 7
Ahuacatlan o MEX 50-51 K 7
Ahuacatlán o MEX 52-53 F 1
Ahuachapán o ES 52-53 K 5
Ahualulco o MEX 50-51 J 6
Ahualulco de Mercata o MEX 52-53 C 1
Ahuano o EC 64-65 C 2
Ahunba o US 136-137 N 4
Ahurjan ∼ AR 128-129 K 2
Ahus, Pulau ∩ RI 164-165 J 2
Ahväz ☆ IR 134-135 C 3
Ahvenanmaa = Ãland □ FIN 88-89 F 6
Ahwa o IND 138-139 D 9
Ahwahnee o USA (CA) 248-249 E 2
Ahwar o Y 132-133 E 7
Ahwar, Wãdi ∼ Y 132-133 E 7
Ahzar, Vallée de l' ⊥ RMM 196-197 M 7
Ai-Ais o NAM 220-221 C 3
Aiak, Cape ▲ USA 22-23 N 6
Aiaktalik Island ∩ USA 22-23 U 4
Aialik Cape ▲ USA 20-21 Q 7
Aiani o GR 100-101 H 4
Aiapuá o BR 66-67 F 5
Aiapuá, Lago o BR 66-67 F 5
Aiari, Rio ∼ BR 66-67 C 2
Aibak ☆ AFG 136-137 K 6
Aibetsu o J 152-153 K 3
Aibonito o USA (PR) 286-287 P 2
Aichilik River ∼ USA 20-21 T 2
Aidarhan su ķoimaşy suķ ∼ KA 96-97 F 9
Aiddejavrre Fjelldstue o RN 198-199 C 3
Aiduma, Pulau ∩ RI 166-167 H 3
Aiduna o RI 166-167 H 4
Aiea o USA (HI) 288 H 4
Aiema River ∼ PNG 183 B 4
Aiere o WAN 204-205 G 5
Aigene mekeni ∴ KA 124-125 J 5
Aigle, l' o F 90-91 H 7
Aigles, Lac-des- o CDN (QUE)
240-241 G 3
Aigneau, Lac o CDN 36-37 O 6
Aigua o ROU 78-79 M 3
Aiguã'ul o ☆ ZA 220-221 D 7
Aigues ∼ F 90-91 K 9
Aiguilete, Cerro ▲ RCH 80 D 5
Aihuicheng • VRC 150-151 F 3
Aija o PE 64-65 C 6
Aikar, Tanjung ▲ RI 166-167 J 4
Aikawa ☆ J 152-153 H 5
Aiken o USA (SC) 284-285 J 3
Aiken o USA (TX) 264-265 C 4
Aikima o RI 166-167 L 4
Ailaoshan ▲ VRC 156-157 B 4
Aileron o AUS 178-179 B 2
Aileu o RI 166-167 G 6
Ailigandí o PA 52-53 E 7
Ailinglapalp ∼ MAI 13 J 1
Ail1k o CDN 36-37 U 7
Aim ∼ RUS 120-121 E 4
Aimere o RI 168 E 7
Aimogasta o RA 76-77 D 5
Aimorés o BR 72-73 K 5
Aimorés, Serra dos ▲▲ BR 72-73 K 4
Aimorés, Serra dos ▲▲ BR 72-73 K 5
'Ain ∼ F 90-91 K 8
'Ain, al- o UAE 132-133 H 4
'Ain, Ra's al- o SYR 128-129 J 4
'Ain al-Arnab o SYR 128-129 F 4
'Ain al-Bakra o KSA 130-131 K 6
Ãin as-Sãqi o ET 194-195 D 4
Ãin as-Sãqi o ET 194-195 D 4
Ainazi o LV 94-95 J 3
'Ain Beida o DZ 190-191 G 1
'Ain Benian o DZ 190-191 D 1
Ãin Ben Tili o RIM 196-197 F 2
'Ain Bessem o DZ 190-191 E 1
Ãin Bire o RIM 196-197 F 4
Ãin Boubat o RIM 196-197 F 4
'Ain Boucif o DZ 190-191 D 3
Ãin Bou Driss o RIM 196-197 E 5
Ãjax Peak ▲ USA 250-251 F 6
Ãjdãbíyã o LAR 192-193 J 2
Ãjdãbíyã o LAR 192-193 J 2
Ãjdar o UA 102-103 L 3
Ãjderkül, küli o US 136-137 K 4
Ãjderkülü, küli o US 136-137 K 4
Ãjer Terjun o MAL 162-163 J 4
Ãgyrial, tau ▲ KA 124-125 G 4
Ãjhal o RUS 110-111 H 7
Ãji, Isla ∩ CO 60-61 E 7
Ãjibarang o RI 162-163 F 7
Ãjigasawa o J 152-153 J 4
Ãjka o H 92-93 N 5
Ãjku o RUS 120-121 P 6
Ãjmer o IND 138-139 E 6
Ãjni o TJ 136-137 L 5
Ãjnianwãla o PK 138-139 E 3
Ãjnskoe, ozero o RUS 122-123 K 4
Ãjo o USA (AZ) 256-257 C 6
Ãjo Mountains ▲▲ USA (AZ) 256-257 C 6
Ãjon o RUS 112-113 O 2
Ãjon, ostrov ∩ RUS 112-113 P 2
Ãj-Plm ∼ RUS 114-115 L 3
Ãjrum o KA 124-125 K 4
Ãjry o KA 124-125 G 1

Ãjtau ▲▲ KA 124-125 J 6
Ãjtor, ozero o RUS 114-115 O 2
Ãjtos o BG 102-103 E 6
Ãjuly, Aksu- o KA 124-125 H 4
Ãjumaku o DA 202-203 K 7
Ãjumkan ∼ RUS 120-121 D 6
Ãjuy o RP 160-161 E 7
Ãjvasedapur ∼ RUS 114-115 O 2
Ãjvirtas o KA 124-125 K 4
Ãka ∼ GH 202-203 L 6
Ãkaba o RT 202-203 L 6
Ãkaba Pass ▲ SUD 200-201 K 3
Ãkabar o RMM 202-203 L 3
Ãkabli o DZ 190-191 C 7
Ãkačan o RUS 120-121 H 3
Ãkademii, zaliv ∼ RUS 120-121 G 6
Ãkademii Nauk, lednik ⊂ RUS
108-109 Z 1
Ãkademika Obručeva, hrebet ▲▲ RUS
116-117 Q 9
Ãkadomari o J 152-153 H 6
Ãka-Eze o WAN 204-205 G 6
Ãkagera ∼ RWA 212-213 C 5
Ãkagera, Parc national de l' ⊥ RWA
212-213 C 5
Ãkagi o J 152-153 E 7
Ãkaishi-sanmyaku ▲▲ J 152-153 H 7
Ãkaka o G 210-211 B 5
Ãkaka Falls ∼• USA (HI) 288 K 5
Ãk'ak'î Beseka o ETH 208-209 D 4
Ãkakro o CI 202-203 H 7
Ãkakus ••• LAR 190-191 H 7
Ãkakus, Jabal ▲ LAR 190-191 H 8
Ãkãlgarh o PK 138-139 D 3
Ãkalkot o IND 140-141 G 2
Ãkamba, Chute ∼ ZRE 210-211 L 3
Ãkam Ẽffak o G 210-211 C 3
Ãkamkpa o WAN 204-205 H 6
Ãkankohan o J 152-153 L 3
Ãkan National Park ⊥ J 152-153 L 3
Ãkanous o NAM 220-221 D 2
Ãkanyaru ∼ RWA 212-213 B 5
Ãkaroa o NZ 182 D 5
Ãkasame o PNG 183 B 2
Ãkasha o SUD 200-201 E 2
Ãkashi o J 152-153 F 7
Ãkaska o USA (SD) 260-261 F 1
Ãkãslompolo o FIN 88-89 H 3
Ãkassa o WAN 204-205 G 6
Ãkat Amnuai o THA 158-159 G 2
Ãkatsi o GH 202-203 L 6
Ãkbaba Dağı ▲ TR 128-129 J 3
Ãkbajtal, pereval ▲ TJ 136-137 N 5
Ãkbarpur o IND (BIH) 142-143 C 3
Ãkbarpur o IND (UTP) 142-143 C 2
Ãkbastöbe, tau ▲ KA 126-127 P 4
Ãkbou o DZ 190-191 E 2
Ãkbulak ∼ RUS 96-97 J 8
Ãkçaabat o TR 128-129 J 3
Ãkçadağ ☆ TR 128-129 H 3
Ãkçakale o TR 128-129 J 4
Ãkçakoca ☆ TR 128-129 D 2
Ãkçakoca Dağları ▲▲ TR 128-129 D 2
Ãkçali Dağları ▲▲ TR 128-129 E 4
Ãkçatau o KA 124-125 J 5
Ãkçay ∼ TR 128-129 C 4
Ãkchâr ∴ RIM 196-197 C 5
Ãk Dağlar ▲ TR 128-129 C 4
Ãk Dağlar ▲ TR 128-129 M 5
Ãkdağmadeni ☆ TR 128-129 F 3
Ãk-Dovurak o RUS 116-117 E 10
Ãkdym, tau ▲ KA 124-125 H 3
Ãkdžakala, vpadina ∪ TM 136-137 F 4
Ãkéboo ☆ RT 202-203 L 6
Ãkela o USA (NM) 256-257 H 6
Ãkelama ∼ RI 164-165 L 3
Ãkelamo o RI (MAL) 164-165 L 3
Ãkelamo o RI (MAL) 164-165 L 3
Ãkelamo o RI (MAL) 164-165 K 4
Ãkelamo, Tanjung ▲ RI 164-165 K 4
Ãkeley o USA (MN) 270-271 D 3
Ãkeonik o USA 20-21 K 1
Ãkeouet, Hassi in o DZ 190-191 D 7
Ãkera ∼ AZ 128-129 M 2
Ãkersberga ☆ S 86-87 J 7
Ãketi o ZRE 210-211 J 2
Ãketi o RO 210-211 K 2
Ãkhdar, Al Jabal al ▲ LAR 192-193 J 1
Ãkhicha, Dalet o DZ 190-191 C 6
Ãkhiok o USA 22-23 T 4
Ãkhisar ☆ TR 128-129 B 3
Ãkhmed, I-n- ∴ RMM 196-197 K 5
Ãkhnur o IND 138-139 E 3
Ãki o J 152-153 E 8
Ãkiachak o USA 20-21 L 6
Ãkiéni o G 210-211 D 4
Ãkimiski Island ∩ CDN 34-35 Q 4
Ãkıncı Burnu ▲ TR 128-129 F 4
Ãkinum o PNG 183 E 4
Ãkişma ∼ RUS 122-123 G 4
Ãkita ☆ J 152-153 J 5
Ãk'jar ☆ RUS 96-97 L 7
Ãkjoujt ☆ RIM 196-197 C 5
Ãkkajaure o S 86-87 H 3
Ãkkajtym o KA 126-127 N 4
Ãkkeshi o J 152-153 M 3
'Ãkko ☆• IL 130-131 D 1
Ãkkol o KA 124-125 J 6
Ãkköl o KA (DZA) 136-137 M 3
Ãkköl o KA (DZM) 136-137 M 3
Ãkköl o KA (KST) 126-127 P 3
Ãkkoshoulbak o RCA 206-207 L 4
Ãkkyr ▲▲ TM 136-137 D 4
Ãklampa o DY 204-205 L 5
Ãklavik o CDN 20-21 X 2
Ãkleimzon ∼ RUS 114-115 N 1
Ãklim, Adrar-n- ▲ MA 188-189 G 5
Ãkloa, Cascade d' ∼ RT 202-203 L 6
Ãkmeqit o VRC 146-147 C 7
Ãkmola o KA 124-125 H 3
Ãkmola, tau o USA 188-189 H 3
Ãkniste o LV 94-95 J 3
Ãknoul o MA 188-189 K 3
Ãko o J 152-153 F 7
Ãko'akas, Rochers = Ako'akas Rocks ∩
CAM 210-211 C 2

Ako'akas Rocks = Rochers Ako'akas • CAM 210-211 C 2
Akobo Wenz ~ ETH 208-209 B 5
Ākobo Wenz ~ ETH 208-209 B 5
Ak-Ojuk, gora ▲ RUS 124-125 Q 3
Akok o G 210-211 B 3
Akoke o SUD 206-207 L 4
Akokora o ZRE 212-213 B 3
Akola o IND 138-139 F 9
Akoma o PNG 183 C 4
Akom II o CAM 210-211 C 2
Akono o CAM 210-211 C 2
Akonolinga o CAM 210-211 D 2
Akop o SUD 206-207 J 4
Akor o RMM 202-203 G 2
Āk'ordat o ER 200-201 H 5
Akoroso o GH 202-203 K 7
Akosombo o • GH 202-203 L 6
Akot o IND 138-139 F 9
Akot o SUD 206-207 K 5
Akoupé o CI 202-203 J 6
Akpatok Island ∩ CDN 36-37 P 4
Akpınar ☆ TR 128-129 E 3
Akplabanya o GH 202-203 L 7
Akposso ⊥ RT 202-203 L 6
Akqi o VRC 146-147 D 5
Akrab o KA 126-127 L 2
Akrabat o TM 136-137 G 7
Akranes ☆ IS 86-87 b 2
Akráta o GR 100-101 J 5
Akra Ténaro ▲ GR 100-101 J 6
Akréréb o RN 198-199 D 4
Åkrestrømmen o N 86-87 E 6
Akrokorinthos •• GR 100-101 J 6
Akron o USA (CO) 254-255 M 3
Akron o USA (IA) 274-275 B 2
Akron o USA (IN) 274-275 M 3
Akron o USA (NY) 278-279 C 5
Akron o USA (OH) 280-281 E 2
Akša ☆ RUS 118-119 F 10
Aksaj ☆ KA 96-97 H 8
Ak-Saj ~ KS 146-147 C 5
Aksaj o RUS (ROS) 102-103 L 4
Aksaj ~ RUS 102-103 M 4
Aksaj ~ RUS 126-127 G 6
Aksaj Esaulovskij ~ RUS 102-103 N 4
Akşar o TR 128-129 K 2
Aksaray ☆ TR 128-129 F 3
Aksarka o RUS 108-109 N 8
Aksay o VRC 146-147 M 6
Aksay Qin ∩ IND 138-139 G 2
Aksayqin Co o VRC 144-145 B 3
Akşehir ☆ TR 128-129 D 3
Akşehir Gölü o TR 128-129 D 3
Akseki ☆ TR 128-129 D 4
'Aks-e Rostam, Rūdḫāne-ye ~ IR 134-135 F 4
Akši ~ KA 124-125 D 5
Akšij o KA 146-147 C 4
Aksoran, gora ▲ KA 124-125 J 4
Aksoran, tau ▲ KA 124-125 J 4
Aksu o KA 124-125 G 2
Aksu o KA (ZPK) 96-97 H 8
Aksu ☆ KA 124-125 K 2
Aksu ~ KA 124-125 L 6
Aksu ~ KA 124-125 L 5
Aksu ~ KS 146-147 B 4
Aksu o VRC 146-147 E 5
Aksu-Ajuly o KA 124-125 H 4
Aksu-Ajuly o KA 124-125 H 4
Aksuat o KA 124-125 N 4
Aksuat, köli o KA 124-125 D 3
Aksubaevo ☆ RUS 96-97 G 6
Aksu Çayı ~ TR 128-129 D 4
Aksum o ••• ETH 200-201 J 5
Ak-Syjrak o KS 146-147 D 5
Ak-Tal o KS 146-147 B 5
Aktanyš ☆ RUS 96-97 J 6
Aktarsk o RUS 96-97 D 8
Aktaš o RUS 124-125 P 3
Aktau o KA (KRG) 124-125 H 3
Aktau ☆ KA 126-127 J 6
Aktau ☆ KA (MNG) 126-127 J 6
Aktaz o KA 124-125 H 4
Aktaz o VRC 146-147 H 6
Aktöbe ☆ KA 126-127 M 2
Aktogaj o KA 124-125 J 4
Aktolagaj tizbegi ▲ KA 126-127 L 4
Aktov tog ▲ US 136-137 J 4
Aktümsyk o KA 126-127 M 4
Aku o PNG 184 I b 2
Akübü o SUD 206-207 L 5
Akugdleq, Ikertoog ≈ 28-29 O 3
Akula o ZRE 210-211 H 2
Akuliarusinguaq ∩ GRØ 26-27 Y 8
Akulurak o USA 20-21 H 5
Akumal o MEX 52-53 L 1
Akune o J 152-153 D 8
Akun Island ∩ USA 22-23 O 5
Akuraj o RUS 118-119 H 10
Akure ☆ WAN 204-205 F 5
Akureyri ☆ IS 86-87 d 2
Akuš, ozero o RUS 114-115 K 7
Akuseki-shima ∩ J 152-153 C 10
Akutan o USA 22-23 O 5
Akutan Island ∩ USA 22-23 N 5
Akutan Pass ≈ 22-23 N 5
Akutukpa o WAN 204-205 G 4
Akvinu River ~ CDN 32-33 N 4
Akwa-Ibom ■ WAN 204-205 G 6
Akwanga o WAN 204-205 H 4
Akwatuk Bay ≈ 38-39 E 2
Akwaya o CAM 204-205 H 5
Akwot ~ SUD 206-207 K 5
Akyab = Sittwe ☆ MYA 142-143 H 5
Akžajkyn, köl o KA 124-125 E 6
Akžajyk o KA 96-97 G 8
Akžar, k-l o KA 136-137 L 3
Akžar, ozero o KA 136-137 L 3
Alabama o USA (NY) 278-279 C 5
Alabama ■ USA (AL) 284-285 C 4
Alabama Camp o LB 202-203 F 5
Alabama & Coushatta Indian Reservation ⨯ USA (TX) 268-269 F 6
Alabama Port o USA (AL) 284-285 B 6
Alabama River ~ USA (AL) 284-285 C 5
Alabaster o USA (AL) 284-285 D 3
Alabat Island ∩ RP 160-161 D 5
al-'Abbāsīyah o SUD 200-201 E 6
Ala-Bel', pereval ▲ KS 136-137 N 3
Alabo ~ GH 202-203 L 6
Alabota, köli o KA (KKC) 124-125 G 2
Alabota, köli o KA (KST) 124-125 D 2
Ala Buka o KS 136-137 M 4
Ala-Buka ~ KS 146-147 B 5
Alaca ☆ TR 128-129 F 2
Alacahöyük •• TR 128-129 F 2
Alacalufe, Reserva Florestal ⊥ RCH 80 C 6
Alaçam ☆ TR 128-129 F 2
Alacant ☆ E 98-99 G 5
Alachua o USA (FL) 286-287 G 2
Alacranes, Presa < C 54-55 E 3
Aladağ ▲ TR 128-129 E 4
Ālādāğ, Kūh-e ▲ IR 136-137 E 6
Ala Dağlar ▲ TR 128-129 F 4
Ala Dağlar ▲ TR 128-129 K 3
al-'Adam o LAR 192-193 K 2
Aladdin o USA (WY) 252-253 O 2
Aladja o WAN 204-205 F 6
Aladža = Alağa o TM 136-137 C 5
Alaf Badane < ETH 208-209 G 6
Alafiarou o DY 204-205 E 4
Alaganik o USA 20-21 S 6
Alagapuram o IND 140-141 H 5
Alagé ▲ ETH 200-201 J 6
Alagir o RUS 126-127 F 6
al-'Ağma, Ğabal ▲ ET 194-195 G 3
Alag nuur o MAU 146-147 M 3
Alagoa Grande o BR 68-69 L 5
Alagoas ■ BR 68-69 K 6
Alagoinha o BR 68-69 K 6
Alagoinhas o BR 72-73 L 2
Alagón o E 98-99 G 4
Alagón, Río ~ E 98-99 D 4
al-'Ağrūd o ET 194-195 G 2
Alah ~ RP 160-161 F 9
Alahan Monastir •• TR 128-129 E 4
Alahanpanjang o RI 162-163 D 5
Alaid, vulkan ▲ RUS 122-123 Q 3
Alaid Island ∩ USA 22-23 C 6
al-Ain o ••• OM 132-133 K 2
al-'Ain < SUD 200-201 D 4
Alajärvi o FIN 88-89 G 5
Alajskij hrebet ▲ TJ 136-137 M 5
Alajuela ☆ CR 52-53 B 6
Alakamisy Ambohimaha o RM 222-223 E 8
Alakamisy Itenina o RM 222-223 E 8
Alakanuk o USA 20-21 H 5
Alakit o RUS 110-111 H 6
Alakit ~ RUS 110-111 H 6
Alakol', köli o KA 124-125 M 6
Alakol', ozero o KA 124-125 J 6
Alaktak o USA 20-21 N 1
Alakuko o WAN 204-205 F 5
Alakurtti o RUS 88-89 L 3
Alalakeiki Channel ≈ USA 288 J 4
al-'Alamain o • ET 194-195 D 2
Al 'Alaqah, Bi'r < LAR 192-193 F 3
Alalaú, Rio ~ BR 62-63 D 6
'Alali, al- o RL 128-129 F 6
al-'Ali Sadd < ET 194-195 F 6
Alamar o C 54-55 D 3
al-'Amarah o SUD 200-201 F 5
'Alā Marv Dašt, Rūd-e ~ IR 134-135 E 5
'Alamat'ā o ETH 200-201 J 6
Alameda o CDN (SAS) 232-233 Q 6
Alameda, La o MEX 50-51 G 5
Alamikamba o NIC 52-53 B 5
Alamillo o USA (NM) 256-257 J 4
Alaminos o RP 160-161 C 4
al-'Āmirīya o ET 194-195 D 2
Alamito Creek ~ USA (TX) 266-267 C 4
Alamo o MEX 52-53 F 1
Alamo o SP 208-209 F 6
Alamo o USA (ND) 258-259 D 3
Alamo o USA (NM) 256-257 H 4
Alamo o USA (NV) 248-249 J 2
Alamo o USA (TN) 276-277 F 5
Alamogordo o USA (NM) 256-257 K 6
Alamo Lake < USA (AZ) 256-257 B 4
Alamo Navajo Indian Reservation ⨯ USA (NM) 256-257 H 4
Alamor o EC 64-65 B 4
Alamos o MEX 50-51 E 4
Alamos, Los o USA (CA) 248-249 D 5
Alamos, Los o USA (NM) 256-257 J 3
Álamos, Río de los ~ MEX 50-51 J 3
Alamosa o USA (CO) 254-255 K 6
Alamosa National Wildlife Refuge ⊥ USA (CO) 254-255 K 6
Alamosa River ~ USA (NM) 256-257 H 5
Alamos de Márquez o MEX 50-51 H 3
Alampur o IND 140-141 H 3
Åland ∩ FIN 88-89 F 6
Aland o IND 140-141 G 2
Ålands Hav ≈ 86-87 J 6
Alang o IND 138-139 D 9
Alange o E 98-99 D 5
Alanreed o USA (TX) 264-265 D 3
Alanson o USA (MI) 272-273 E 2
Alantika Mountains ▲ WAN 204-205 K 4
Alanya o TR 128-129 E 4
Alaolo ~ SOL 184 I e 3
Alaotra ⊥ RM 222-223 F 6
Alaotra, Farihy o RM 222-223 F 6
Alapa o WAN 204-205 F 4
Alapaevsk o RUS 96-97 M 5
Alapaha o USA (GA) 284-285 G 5
Alapaha River ~ USA (FL) 286-287 F 1
Alapaha River ~ USA (GA) 284-285 G 6
al-'Aqaba, Ḫalīğ ≈ 194-195 G 3
al-'Aqaba as-Sağira o ET 194-195 F 5
'Alāqān o KSA 130-131 D 3
Alaquines o MEX 50-51 K 6
al-Arab, Bahr ~ SUD 206-207 G 3
al-'Arab, Bahr ~ SUD 206-207 J 4
al-'Arab, Ḫalīğ ≈ 194-195 D 2
al-Arāk o SUD 200-201 E 3
Alarcón, Embalse de < E 98-99 F 5
Alareak Island ∩ CDN 36-37 M 2
al-Argoub o MA 196-197 C 3
al-'Ariš ☆ ET 194-195 F 2
al-'Ariš, Wādī ~ ET 194-195 F 2
Alas o RI (NBA) 168 C 7
Alas o RI (TIT) 166-167 C 6
Alas ~ RI 162-163 B 3
Alaš ~ RUS 124-125 Q 3
Alas, Hos- o RUS 110-111 S 6
Alas, Selat ≈ 168 C 7
Alaşehir ☆ • TR 128-129 C 3
Alašeev buchta ≈ 16 G 5
Alashan Shamo ∩ VRC 148-149 E 7
Alasi o SOL 184 I e 3
al-'Āṣī, Nahr ~ SYR 128-129 G 5
Alaska o USA (MI) 272-273 D 5
Alaska ■ USA 20-21 K 4
Alaska o ZW 218-219 F 3
Alaska, Gulf of ≈ 14-15 O 2
Alaska Highway II CDN 32-33 K 3
Alaska Range ▲ USA 20-21 O 6
Al 'Assah o LAR 192-193 D 1
Alássio o • I 100-101 B 2
Alat o US 136-137 H 5
Alatau hrebet ▲ RUS 96-97 K 7
Alataw Shankou ▲ VRC 146-147 F 3
Al Atazar, Embalse de < E 98-99 F 4
Alati o CAM 210-211 D 2
Alatna River ~ USA 20-21 O 3
al-'Atrun, Bi'r < SUD 200-201 C 3
al-Atshan ~ SUD 200-201 G 6
Alatsinainy Bakaro o RM 222-223 E 7
Alatskivi o •• EST 94-95 K 2
Ālattur o IND 140-141 G 5
Alatyr' o RUS 96-97 E 6
Alausí o EC 64-65 C 3
Alava o RP 160-161 D 4
Alaverdi o AR 128-129 L 2
Ala-Vuokki o FIN 88-89 K 4
Alavus o FIN 88-89 G 5
Alawa o WAN 204-205 G 3
Alawa Game Reserve ⊥ WAN 204-205 G 3
Alawangandji Aboriginal Land ⨯ AUS 174-175 C 4
Al Awaynat o LAR 200-201 B 2
Al Awaynat, Jabal ▲ SUD 200-201 B 2
Alawoona o AUS 180-181 F 3
Alayo o RCA 206-207 F 6
al-'Ayun ☆ MA 188-189 E 7
al-'Ayyāt o ET 194-195 E 3
Alazani ~ AZ 128-129 M 2
Alazeja ~ RUS 110-111 b 5
Alazeja ~ RUS 112-113 H 1
Alazejskoe ploskogor'e ▲ RUS 110-111 a 6
Al 'Aziziyah ■ LAR 192-193 E 1
Al 'Aziziyah ☆ LAR 192-193 E 1
Alba o • I 100-101 B 2
Alba o USA (TX) 264-265 J 6
Albacete o E 98-99 G 5
Albacutya, Lake o AUS 180-181 F 3
al-Badārī o ET 194-195 E 4
Alba de Tormes o E 98-99 E 4
Ålbæk Bugt ≈ 86-87 E 8
al-Bahr al-Azraq ~ SUD 200-201 G 6
al-Bahriya, Barqat ⊥ ET 192-193 L 2
Alba Iulia ☆ • RO 102-103 C 4
Albāko o IND 142-143 B 6
al-Baliḫ, Nahr ~ SYR 128-129 H 4
al-Ballāṣ o ET 194-195 F 4
al-Balyana o ET 194-195 E 4
Alban o CDN (ONT) 238-239 E 2
Alban o CO 60-61 D 5
Alban = San José o CO 64-65 D 1
Albanel o CDN (QUE) 240-241 C 2
Albanel, Lac o CDN (QUE) 236-237 P 2
Albania = Shqipëri ■ AL 100-101 G 4
Albany o • AUS 176-177 D 7
Albany o USA (GA) 284-285 F 5
Albany o USA (IN) 274-275 N 4
Albany o USA (KY) 276-277 K 4
Albany o USA (MN) 270-271 D 5
Albany o USA (MO) 274-275 D 4
Albany o USA (OR) 244-245 B 6
Albany o USA (TX) 264-265 E 6
Albany o USA (WY) 252-253 M 5
Albany ☆ • USA (NY) 278-279 H 6
Albany Downs o AUS 178-179 K 4
Albany Highway II AUS 176-177 D 6
Albany Island ∩ CDN 34-35 Q 4
Albany River ~ CDN 34-35 O 5
Albany River ~ CDN (ONT) 234-235 O 3
Alba Posse o RA 76-77 K 4
al-Barāmūs, Dair ⊥ • ET 194-195 E 2
Al Bardī o LAR 192-193 L 2
Albarracín o • E 98-99 G 4
al-Barun o SUD 208-209 A 3
al-Basabir o SUD 200-201 F 4
al-Bāṭina, Ğazirat ∩ KSA 130-131 L 4
Albatros Bank ≃ 22-23 U 4
Albatross Bay ≈ 174-175 F 3
al-Bauga o SUD 200-201 F 3
al-Bawītī o ET 194-195 D 3
Al Bayādah, Wādī ~ LAR 192-193 H 4
Al Bayda ■ LAR 192-193 J 1
Al Bayda ☆ LAR 192-193 J 1
Al Baydā, Barqah ⊥ LAR 192-193 H 2
Albay Gulf ≈ 160-161 E 6
Al Bayyādah o LAR 192-193 J 1
Albazino o RUS 118-119 M 9
al-Begeir o SUD 200-201 F 3
Albemarle o USA (NC) 282-283 G 5
Albemarle Sound ≈ 48-49 K 1
Albemarle Sound ≈ USA 282-283 L 4
Albenga o • I 100-101 B 2
Alberche, La o • E 98-99 D 4
Alberdi o PY 76-77 H 4
Alberfoyle o AUS 178-179 I 1
Alberga Creek ~ AUS 178-179 C 4
Albergaria-a-Velha o P 98-99 C 4
Alberni o CDN (BC) 230-231 E 4
Alberni Inlet ≈ CDN 230-231 E 4
Alberobello o • I 100-101 F 4
Albert o F 90-91 J 6
Albert, Cape ▲ CDN 26-27 N 4
Albert, Lake o AUS 180-181 E 3
Albert, Lake o USA (OR) 244-245 E 8
Albert, Lake = Lac Mobutu-Sese-Seko o EAU 212-213 C 3
Albert, Port o • AUS 180-181 J 5
Alberta ■ CDN 32-33 L 4
Alberta o USA (VA) 280-281 J 7
Alberta Beach o CDN (ALB) 232-233 D 2
Albert Canyon o CDN (BC) 230-231 M 2
Albert Edward, Mount ▲ CDN (BC) 230-231 D 4
Albert Edward, Mount ▲ PNG 183 D 5
Albert Edward Bay ≈ 24-25 U 6
Alberti o RA 78-79 J 3
Albert I Land ⊥ N 84-85 G 3
Albertinia o ZA 220-221 E 7
Albert Law, Mont ▲ CDN 36-37 N 4
Albert Lea o USA (MN) 270-271 E 7
Albert Markham, Mount ▲ ARK 16 E 0
Albert Nile ~ EAU 212-213 C 2
Alberto de Agostini, Parque Nacional ⊥ RCH 80 E 7
Alberton o CDN (PEI) 240-241 L 4
Alberton o USA (MT) 250-251 E 4
Albert River ~ AUS 174-175 E 6
Albert Town o BS 54-55 H 3
Albert Town o JA 54-55 G 5
Albertville o CDN (QUE) 240-241 H 2
Albertville o • F 90-91 L 9
Albertville o USA (AL) 284-285 D 2
Albi ☆ • F 90-91 J 10
Albia o USA (IA) 274-275 F 3
Albin o USA (WY) 252-253 O 5
Albina ☆ SME 62-63 G 3
Albina, Ponta ▲ ANG 216-217 A 7
Albion o USA (CA) 246-247 B 4
Albion o USA (IL) 274-275 K 6
Albion o USA (MI) 272-273 E 5
Albion o USA (MT) 250-251 P 6
Albion o USA (NE) 262-263 J 3
Albion o USA (NY) 278-279 C 5
Albion o USA (OK) 264-265 J 4
Albion o USA (PA) 280-281 F 2
Alborán, Isla del ∩ E 98-99 F 7
Ålborg o •• DK 86-87 D 8
Ålborg Bugt ≈ 86-87 E 8
Alborn o USA (MN) 270-271 F 4
Alborz, Kūhhā-ye ▲ IR 136-137 B 6
Albox o E 98-99 F 6
Albreda o CDN (BC) 228-229 P 4
Albreda o • WAG 202-203 B 3
Albro o AUS 178-179 J 2
Albufeira o P 98-99 C 6
Albuquerque o • E 98-99 D 5
Albuquerque o • USA (NM) 256-257 J 3
Albuquerque, Cayos de ∩ CO 52-53 D 5
al-Burullus, Buhairat o ET 194-195 E 2
Albury-Wodonga o AUS 180-181 J 4
Alcácer do Sal o P 98-99 C 5
Alcáçovas o P 98-99 C 5
Alcala o AUS 174-175 F 6
Alcala o RP 160-161 D 4
Alcalá de Chivert = Alcalà de Xivert o E 98-99 H 4
Alcalá de Henares o • E 98-99 F 4
Alcalá del Júcar o E 98-99 G 5
Alcalà de Xivert o E 98-99 H 4
Alcalá la Real o E 98-99 F 6
Alcalde o USA (NM) 256-257 J 2
Alcalde, Punta ▲ RCH 76-77 B 5
Alcamo o I 100-101 D 6
Alcañices o E 98-99 D 4
Alcañiz o E 98-99 G 4
Alcântara o BR 68-69 F 3
Alcántara o E 98-99 D 5
Alcantara Lake o CDN 30-31 P 5
Alcantarilla o E 98-99 G 6
Alcaracejos o E 98-99 E 5
Alcaraz o E 98-99 F 5
Alcaraz, Sierra de ▲ E 98-99 F 5
Alcatrazes, Ilha do ∩ BR 72-73 H 8
Alcaudete o E 98-99 E 6
Alcázar •• E 98-99 E 6
Alcázar de San Juan o E 98-99 F 5
Alcedo, Volcán ▲ EC 64-65 B 10
Alcester Island ∩ PNG 183 G 5
Alčevs'k o UA 102-103 L 3
Alcira o RA 78-79 G 2
Alcoa o USA (TN) 282-283 D 5
Alcobaça o ••• P 98-99 C 5
Alcoi o E 98-99 G 5
Alcolea del Pinar o E 98-99 F 4
Alcomdale o CDN (ALB) 232-233 E 2
Alcona o CDN (ONT) 234-235 M 6
Alcoota o AUS 178-179 C 2
Alcorcón o E 98-99 F 4
Alcorta o RA 78-79 J 2
Alcott Creek ~ CDN (SAS) 232-233 K 2
Alcoutim o P 98-99 D 6
Alcova o USA (WY) 252-253 M 4
Alcovy River ~ USA (GA) 284-285 G 3
Alcoy o RP 160-161 E 8
Alcoy = Alcoi o E 98-99 G 5
Alcúdia o E 98-99 J 5
Alcúdia, l' o E 98-99 G 5
Alcurve o CDN (ALB) 232-233 H 2
Aldabra Atoll ⊥ ••• SY 222-223 E 2
Aldabra Group ⊥ SY 222-223 E 2
Aldaia Bona o BR 62-63 G 5
Aldama o MEX (CHA) 50-51 G 3
Aldama o MEX (TAM) 50-51 K 6
Aldamas, Los o MEX 50-51 K 4
Aldan ☆ • RUS (SAH) 118-119 M 6
Aldan ~ RUS 118-119 P 4
Aldan ~ RUS 118-119 L 7
Aldan ~ RUS 118-119 N 6
Aldan ~ RUS 120-121 F 2
Aldanskoe nagor'e ▲ RUS 118-119 K 6
Aldea, Isla ∩ RCH 80 C 4
Aldea dos Indios Sucane o GUY 62-63 E 5
Aldehuela Gallinal o ROU 78-79 M 2
Aldeia o BR (BAH) 68-69 E 7
Aldeia o BR (GSU) 70-71 K 6
Aldeia o BR (MAR) 68-69 E 5
Aldeia, Serra da ▲ BR 72-73 G 4
Aldeia Beltrão o BR 76-77 K 5
Aldeia Grimaldi o BR 76-77 J 6
Aldeia Manuel Antonio o BR 68-69 E 3
Aldeia Velha o BR 68-69 F 4
Aldeia Viçosa o ANG 216-217 C 4
Aldeia Vila Batista o BR 62-63 D 6
Alder o USA (MT) 250-251 G 6
Alder Creek o USA (NY) 278-279 F 5
Alder Flats o CDN (ALB) 232-233 D 3
Alderley o AUS 178-179 E 2
Alderley o ZA 220-221 J 6
Alderney ∩ GBA 90-91 F 7
Alder Peak ▲ USA (CA) 248-249 C 4
Alder Point ▲ USA (CA) 248-249 C 4
Alderson o CDN (ALB) 232-233 G 5
Aldoma o RUS 120-121 H 5
Aldoma ~ RUS 120-121 G 5
Aldrich, Cape ▲ CDN 26-27 Q 2
Aldžer, ostrov ∩ RUS 84-85 e 2
Alédjo o DY 202-203 L 5
Alédjo, Faille-d' ▲ • RT 202-203 L 5
Aledo o USA (IL) 274-275 H 3
Aleg ☆ RIM 196-197 D 6
Aleg, Lac d' o RIM 196-197 D 6
Alegre o BR (ESP) 72-73 K 6
Alegre o BR (MIN) 72-73 G 5
Alegre, Riacho ~ PY 76-77 H 1
Alegre, Rio ~ BR 70-71 H 4
Alegres Mountain ▲ USA (NM) 256-257 J 4
Alegrete o BR 76-77 K 5
Alegria o BR (GSU) 70-71 K 6
Alegria o BR (RSU) 76-77 K 4
Alegria o RP 160-161 E 8
Alegro, Ponta ▲ BR 74-75 D 9
Alëhovščina o RUS 94-95 N 1
Alei, I-n- < RMM 196-197 J 6
Aleiandia o CO 60-61 D 3
Alej ~ RUS 124-125 N 3
Alejandra o RA 76-77 H 5
Alejandria o BOL 70-71 E 3
Alejandro Selkirk, Isla ∩ RCH 78-79 B 1
Alejsk o RUS 124-125 N 2
Aleknagik o USA 22-23 R 3
Aleknagik, Lake o USA 22-23 R 3
Aleko-Kjuël' o RUS 110-111 d 5
Aleksandovskij, zaliv o RUS 122-123 J 3
Aleksandra, mys ▲ RUS 120-121 H 6
Aleksandra I, zemľa ⊥ ARK 16 G 29
Aleksandrija = Oleksandrivka o UA 102-103 H 3
Aleksandrov ☆ •• RUS 94-95 Q 3
Aleksandrov Gaj ☆ RUS 96-97 F 8
Aleksandrovka ☆ RUS 96-97 H 7
Aleksandrovsk ☆ RUS 114-115 D 5
Aleksandrovskij, Kus'e- o RUS 96-97 L 4
Aleksandrovskoe o RUS (STA) 126-127 E 5
Aleksandrovskoe o RUS (TOM) 114-115 O 4
Aleksandrovsk-Sahalinsij ☆ • RUS 122-123 K 3
Aleksandry, zaliv o RUS 120-121 H 6
Aleksandry, Zemlja ∩ RUS 84-85 Z 2
Alekseevka o RUS 102-103 L 2
Alekseevka o KA 124-125 O 4
Alekseevka ☆ KA 124-125 G 2
Alekseevka o RUS 118-119 M 5
Alekseevka ☆ RUS (SAM) 96-97 G 7
Alekseevskoe ☆ RUS 96-97 G 6
Aleksin ☆ • RUS 94-95 P 4
Aleksinac o YU 100-101 H 3
Alel o SUD 206-207 K 5
Ålem o S 86-87 H 8
Alemania o EC 64-65 B 10
Alèmbé o G 210-211 C 4
Alembé o RCB 210-211 E 4
'Alem Ketema o ETH 208-209 D 3
'Alem Maya o ETH 208-209 E 4
Além-Paraíba o BR 72-73 J 6
Ålen ☆ N 86-87 E 5
Alençon ☆ F 90-91 H 7
Alen Nkoma o G 210-211 C 3
Alenquer o BR 62-63 G 6
Alentejo ⊥ P 98-99 C 6
Alenuihaha Channel ≈ 48-49 D 7
Alenuihaha Channel ≈ USA 288 J 4
Alépé o CI 202-203 J 7
Aleppo = Halab ☆ ••• SYR 128-129 G 4
Alerces, Parque Nacional los ⊥ RA 78-79 D 7
Aleria o F 98-99 M 3
Alert o CDN 26-27 T 2
Alerta o PE 70-71 B 2
Alert Bay o CDN (BC) 230-231 C 3
Alert Point ▲ CDN 26-27 G 2
Alès o F 90-91 K 9
Alesandrovskij Zavod ☆ RUS 118-119 H 10
Alessándria ☆ I 100-101 B 2
Ålesund ☆ • N 86-87 C 5
Aleutian Basin ≃ 22-23 C 4
Aleutian Islands ∩ USA 22-23 H 6
Aleutian Range ▲ USA 22-23 R 4
Aleutian Trench ≃ 22-23 K 7
Aleutko o RUS 122-123 O 6
Alexander o CDN (MAN) 234-235 C 5
Alexander o USA (AK) 20-21 P 6
Alexander o USA (KS) 262-263 G 6
Alexander o USA (ND) 258-259 D 4
Alexander, Cape ▲ SOL 184 I c 2
Alexander, Kap ▲ GRØ 26-27 O 4
Alexander, Point ▲ AUS 174-175 D 3
Alexander Archipelago ∩ USA 32-33 B 3
Alexanderbaai = Alexander Bay o ZA 220-221 C 4
Alexander Bay = Alexanderbaai o ZA 220-221 C 4
Alexander City o USA (AL) 284-285 E 4
Alexander Graham Bell National Historic Park ⊥ • CDN (NS) 240-241 P 4
Alexander Inlet ≈ 28-29 G 2
Alexander Island ∩ CDN 24-25 U 3
Alexandra o AUS 180-181 H 4
Alexandra o NZ 182 B 6
Alexandra, Cape ▲ GB 78-79 O 7
Alexandra Bay ≈ 174-175 H 5
Alexandra Channel ≈ 140-141 L 2
Alexandra Falls ~ CDN 30-31 L 5
Alexandra Fiord o CDN 26-27 N 4
Alexandra River ~ AUS 174-175 F 6
Alexandria o AUS 174-175 D 6
Alexandria o BR 68-69 J 5
Alexandria o CDN (BC) 228-229 M 4
Alexandria o CDN (ONT) 238-239 L 3
Alexandria o GR 100-101 J 4
Alexandria o JA 54-55 G 5
Alexandria ☆ • RO 102-103 D 6
Alexandria o USA (IN) 274-275 N 4
Alexandria o USA (LA) 268-269 H 5
Alexandria o USA (MN) 270-271 C 5
Alexandria o USA (SD) 260-261 J 3
Alexandria o USA (VA) 280-281 J 5
Alexandria o ZA 220-221 H 6
Alexandria = al-Iskandarīya ☆ •• ET 194-195 D 2
Alexandria = Iskandariya, al- ☆ •• ET 194-195 D 2
Alexandria Bay o USA (NY) 278-279 F 4
Alexandrina, Lake o AUS 180-181 E 3
Alexandroúpoli ☆ GR 100-101 K 4
Alexeck ~ NAM 216-217 E 10
Alex Graham, Mount ▲ CDN (BC) 228-229 M 4
Alexis o USA (IL) 274-275 H 3
Alexis Bay ≈ 38-39 Q 2
Alexis Creek o CDN (BC) 228-229 L 4
Alexishafen o PNG 183 C 3
Alexis River ~ CDN 38-39 Q 2
Alex Morrison National Park ⊥ AUS 176-177 C 4
Aleza Lake o CDN (BC) 228-229 M 2
Al Faid-Majir o LAR 192-193 F 1
Alfalfa o USA (OK) 264-265 F 3
Alfalfa o USA (OR) 244-245 D 6
Alfarez de Navio Sobral o ARK 16 E 0
Alfa River ~ CDN 24-25 f 4
Alfarrás o E 98-99 H 4
Al Fāshir o • SUD 200-201 B 6
al-Fāshir o • SUD 200-201 B 6
al-Fašn o ET 194-195 E 3
Al Fāt, Wādī ~ LAR 192-193 F 3
Alfatar o BG 102-103 E 6
Al Fātih ■ LAR 192-193 J 1
Al Fātiyah, Bi'r < LAR 192-193 F 3
al-Fayyūm ☆ •• ET 194-195 E 3
Alfenas o BR 72-73 H 6
al-Fifi o SUD 206-207 G 3
Alford o USA (FL) 286-287 D 1
Ålfotbreen ⊂ N 86-87 B 6
Alfred o CDN (ONT) 238-239 L 3
Alfred o USA (TX) 266-267 K 6
Alfred, Cape ▲ CDN 24-25 V 6
Alfred and Marie Range ▲ AUS 176-177 H 2
Alfredo Chaves o BR 72-73 K 6
Alfredo M. Terrazas o MEX 50-51 K 7
Alfredo Wagner o BR 74-75 F 6
Alfred Wegeners Halvø ⌣ GRØ 26-27 Z 8
Alf Trolle, Kap ▲ GRØ 26-27 q 6
Al Fuqahā' o LAR 192-193 G 4
Alga ☆ KA 126-127 M 3
al-Gabalayn o SUD 200-201 F 6
Algabas o KA 96-97 H 8
al-Gabir o SUD 200-201 D 6
al-Ğadida o ET 194-195 D 3
al-Ğāhir, Ğabal ▲ Y 132-133 J 7
al-Ğalāla al-Bahriya, Ğabal ▲ ET 194-195 E 3
al-Ğalāla al-Qibliya, Ğabal ▲ ET 194-195 F 3
Algama ~ RUS 118-119 O 8
Algama ~ RUS 120-121 D 5
al-Ğamālīya o ET 194-195 E 2
al-Gamāmiyah o SUD 200-201 F 3
Algan ~ RUS 112-113 Q 4
Alganskij krjaž ▲ RUS 112-113 Q 4
Al Garabulli o LAR 192-193 E 1
al-Garef o SUD 200-201 G 6
al-Gargarat o MA 196-197 B 4
Algarrobal, Quebrada ~ RCH 76-77 B 5
Algarrobo o • RCH 78-79 D 2
Algarrobo del Aguila o RA 78-79 F 4
Algarve ⌣ P 98-99 C 6
al-Ğauf ■ KSA 132-133 F 2
al-Gayli o SUD 200-201 F 4
al-Ğazālāt, Qārat ▲ ET 194-195 C 2
al-Ğazira ⊥ SUD 200-201 F 5
Algeciras o E 98-99 E 6
Algena o ER 200-201 J 4
Alger o USA (MI) 272-273 E 3
Algeria = Al Jazā'ir ■ DZ 190-191 B 6
Algerian Provenceal Basin ≃ 98-99 K 4
Algeyta o ETH 208-209 E 4
al-Ghābah o SUD 200-201 E 3
al-Ghabshah o SUD 200-201 E 6
al-Ghalla, Wādī ~ SUD 206-207 J 3
Al Gharārah, Bi'r < LAR 192-193 J 2
al-Ghazāl, Bahr ~ SUD 206-207 J 4
Alghero o • I 100-101 B 4
Al Ghirāf, Wādī Bū ~ LAR 192-193 G 4
Al Ghomode < LAR 192-193 D 5
Al Ghrayfah o LAR 192-193 E 4
al-Ğidāmi, Bi'r < ET 194-195 F 4
Algiers = Al Jazā'ir ★ •• DZ 190-191 D 2
al-Ğilf al-Kabīr, Hadbat ▲ ET 192-193 L 6
al-Ğiza ☆ ET 194-195 E 2
al-Ğizi, Wādī ~ OM 132-133 K 1
Algoa Bay ≈ 220-221 G 6
Algodón, Río ~ PE 64-65 F 3
Algodones o USA (CA) 248-249 K 7
Algoma o USA (WI) 270-271 L 6
Algoma Upland ▲ CDN (ONT) 236-237 E 5
Algona o USA (IA) 274-275 D 1
Algonac o CDN (ONT) 238-239 C 6
Algonquin Park o CDN (ONT) 238-239 G 3
Algonquin Provincial Park ⊥ CDN (ONT) 238-239 G 3
Algonquin Upland ▲ CDN (ONT) 238-239 G 3
Algood o USA (TN) 276-277 K 4
Algorta o ROU 78-79 L 2
al-Ğurdaqa ☆ • ET 194-195 F 4
Al Guzayyil, Bi'r < LAR 192-193 D 3
al-Ḫābūr, Nahr ~ IRQ 128-129 K 4
Al Hādh, Wādī ~ LAR 192-193 G 5
al-Haiz o ET 194-195 D 3
Alhama de Murcia o E 98-99 G 6
Alhambra • E 98-99 F 6
Alhambra o USA (CA) 248-249 F 5
Al Hamim, Wādī ~ LAR 192-193 K 2
al-Hammām o ET 194-195 D 2
Al Ḥamrā', Al Hamadah ⊥ LAR 192-193 D 2
Al Hamrā', Bi'r < LAR 192-193 D 1
al-Hamsa, Bi'r < ET 192-193 L 2
Al Hamūdiyah < LAR 192-193 G 4
Alhančurtskij kanal < RUS 126-127 F 6
Alhandra o BR 68-69 L 5
al-Hānika o ET 194-195 E 2
Al Haniyah o LAR 192-193 J 1
Al Harabah o LAR 192-193 D 2
Al Hārah, Qārat ▲ LAR 192-193 F 4
al-Hāriğa ☆ • ET 194-195 E 5
al-Hāriğa, al-Wāhāt ⊥ • ET 194-195 E 5
al-Hartūm ★ •• SUD 200-201 F 5
al-Hartūm Baḥrī o SUD 200-201 F 5
Al Haruj al Aswad ▲ LAR 192-193 G 4
Al Hasāwinah, Jabal ▲ LAR 192-193 E 3
Al Hassiane ⊥ MA 188-189 D 7
al-Hatātiba o ET 194-195 E 2
al-Hawad, Wādī ~ SUD 200-201 F 4
Al Hawa'ish, Jabal ▲ LAR 192-193 K 5
al-Hawātah o SUD 200-201 G 6
Al Hawwari o LAR 192-193 K 5
Al Hayshah, Sabkhat o LAR 192-193 F 2
Al Hayyirah, Qarārat ~ LAR 192-193 F 4
Alheit o ZA 220-221 E 4
al-Hilla o SUD 200-201 C 6
Al Hoceima ☆ MA 188-189 K 3
Al Huan o LAR 192-193 K 5
Al Hufrah ash Sharqiyah ⊥ LAR 192-193 F 4
Al Hulayq al Kabir ▲ LAR 192-193 G 4
al-Huqnah o SUD 200-201 F 4
Ålhus o N 86-87 C 6
al-Husayhīsah o SUD 200-201 F 5
al-Huwair Oilfield o OM 132-133 J 2
Ali o PNG 183 B 4
'Ali, Bi'r o Y 132-133 F 6
'Aliābād o AFG 136-137 L 6
'Aliābād o IR 134-135 F 4
Aliābād o IR 136-137 D 6
Aliade o WAN 204-205 H 5
Aliaga o E 98-99 G 4
Aliağa ☆ TR 128-129 B 3
Aliákmon ~ GR 100-101 J 4
'Ali al-Ğarbi ☆ IRQ 128-129 M 6
Aliambata o RI 166-167 D 6
Aliança o BR 66-67 F 7
Aliantan o RI 162-163 D 4
Alianza, La o CO 60-61 C 6
Alibāg o IND 138-139 D 10
Ali-Bajramly = Ali Bayramlı o AZ 128-129 N 3
Alibates Flint Quarries National Monument ∴ USA (TX) 264-265 C 3
Alibo o ETH 208-209 C 4
Alibori ~ DY 204-205 E 3
Aliboy Knob ▲ AUS 172-173 J 4
Alicante = Alacant o E 98-99 G 5
Alice o AUS 178-179 M 5
Alice o USA (ND) 258-259 K 5
Alice o USA (TX) 266-267 J 6
Alice o ZA 220-221 H 6
Alice, Punta ▲ I 100-101 F 5
Alice Arm o CDN 32-33 F 4
Alice River ~ AUS 174-175 G 4
Alice River ~ AUS 178-179 H 2
Alice Springs ☆ AUS 176-177 B 2
Alice Town o BS 54-55 G 2
Alice Town o BS 54-55 F 2
Aliceville o USA (AL) 284-285 B 3
Alicia o RP 160-161 D 4
Alicudi, Ísola di ∩ I 100-101 E 5
Alida o CDN (SAS) 232-233 R 6
Aligarh o IND 138-139 G 6
Aligūdarz o IR 134-135 C 2
'Aliğūq, Kūh-e ▲ IR 134-135 D 3
Alikali o WAL 202-203 E 5
Alikazgan ~ RUS 126-127 G 6
Alikkod o IND 140-141 F 5
Alima ~ RCB 210-211 E 4
Alimbet o KA 126-127 N 2
Alimbongo o ZRE 212-213 B 4
Alim Island ∩ PNG 183 D 2
Alindao o RCA 206-207 E 6
Alingār, Darre-ye ~ AFG 136-137 M 7
Alingly o CDN (SAS) 232-233 N 2
Alingsås ☆ S 86-87 F 8
Alinshan ▲ VRC 144-145 C 4
Alipur o PK 138-139 C 5
Alipur Duār o IND 142-143 F 2
Aliquippa o USA (PA) 280-281 F 3
Aliquisanda o MOC 214-215 H 7
Alirājpur o IND 142-143 C 4
Alisaang o RI 164-165 G 3
Ali Sabīh o DJI 208-209 F 3
'Ali Sadr o IR 128-129 N 5
Aliseda o E 98-99 D 5
Alishan • RC 156-157 M 5
al-Iskandarīya = Alexandria ☆ •• ET 194-195 D 2
Aliskerovo o RUS 112-113 O 3
al-Ismā'iliya ☆ ET 194-195 F 2
Alitak, Cape ▲ USA 22-23 T 4
Alitak Bay ≈ 22-23 T 4
Alite Reef ∩ SOL 184 I e 3
Aliulik Peninsula ⌣ USA 22-23 U 4
Aliwal-Noord = Aliwal North o ZA 220-221 H 5
Aliwal North = Aliwal-Noord o ZA 220-221 H 5
Alix o CDN (ALB) 232-233 E 3
'Āliya, al- o KSA 132-133 C 5
Aliyābād o IND 140-141 H 4
'Aliyāb Gharb o SUD 200-201 F 4
'Aliyāb Sharq o SUD 200-201 F 4
Aliyak, Godār-e ▲ IR 136-137 E 6
al-Jabal, Bahr ~ SUD 206-207 K 6
al-Jabal, Bahr ~ SUD 206-207 K 4
Al Jabal al Akhdar ■ LAR 192-193 J 1
Al Jabal al Akhdar ▲ LAR 192-193 J 1
Al Jadid, Bi'r < LAR 192-193 E 4
Al Jaghbūb o LAR 192-193 L 3
Al Jalu, Wāhāt ⊥ LAR 192-193 J 3
Aljat o AZ 128-129 N 3
Aljaty o RUS 116-117 L 9
Al Jawf ☆ LAR 192-193 K 5
Al Jaws al Kabīr o LAR 192-193 D 2
Al Jazā'ir ★ •• DZ 190-191 D 2
Aljenaari o WAN 204-205 E 3
Aljezur o P 98-99 C 6
Al Jufra, Wāhāt ⊥ LAR 192-193 G 3

Ako'akas Rocks — Al Jufra, Wāhāt 295

Al Jufrah ◘ LAR 192-193 G 3
al-Junaynah o SUD 198-199 L 6
Aljustrel o P 98-99 C 6
al-Kab ∴• ET 194-195 F 5
al-Kāb o SUD 200-201 F 3
Al Kalb, Qarārat ⌣ LAR 192-193 G 4
Alkali Lake o CDN (BC) 230-231 H 2
Alkali Lake o USA (OR) 244-245 F 8
Alkamari o RN 198-199 E 6
Alkamergen, köli ⊖ KA 124-125 K 3
Alkamergen,köli ⊖ KA 124-125 K 3
Alkamergen, ozero = kölí Alkamergen ⊖ KA 124-125 K 3
al-Kāmilin o SUD 200-201 F 5
Al Kammūniyah, Bi'r < LAR 192-193 G 3
al-Kanā'is, Ra's ▲ ET 194-195 C 2
Al Kararim o LAR 192-193 F 1
al-Karnak o•• ET 194-195 F 5
al-Kawa o SUD 200-201 F 6
al-Khachbiyine, Oued ~ MA 188-189 F 7
Al Khadrah o LAR 192-193 J 2
Al Khāli, Wādi ~ LAR 192-193 K 2
al-Khāmis, ash-Shallāl = 5th Cataract ~ SUD 200-201 F 3
al-Khandaq o SUD 200-201 E 3
Al Khums ◘ LAR 192-193 E 1
Al Khums ☆ LAR (Akm) 192-193 F 1
Alkmaar o•• NL 92-93 H 2
al-Koin o SUD 200-201 E 3
al-Kū, Wādi ~ SUD 200-201 B 6
al-Kūbri o ET 194-195 F 2
Al Kufayfiyah o KSA 130-131 J 5
Al Kufra, Wāhāt ⊥ LAR 192-193 K 5
Al Kufrah ◘ LAR 192-193 J 5
al-Kuntilla o ET 194-195 G 3
al-Kurru • SUD 200-201 E 3
Allada o DY 204-205 E 5
Allagash o USA (ME) 278-279 M 1
Allagash Lake ⊖ USA (ME) 278-279 M 2
Allagash River ~ USA (ME) 278-279 M 2
Allagash Wilderness Waterway ⊥ USA (ME) 278-279 M 2
al-Lagowa o SUD 206-207 J 3
Allagudda o IND 140-141 H 3
Allahābād o• IND 142-143 B 3
Allāhganj o IND 138-139 G 6
Allah-Jun' o RUS 120-121 H 3
Allah-Jun' ~ RUS 120-121 F 3
Allahüekber Dağları ▲ TR 128-129 K 2
al-Lāhūn ∴• ET 194-195 E 3
Allaiha ~ RUS 110-111 Z 5
Allakaket o USA 20-21 O 3
Allal-bou-Fenzi o MA 188-189 G 5
Allal-Tazi o MA 188-189 H 3
Allamoore o USA (TX) 266-267 C 2
Allan o CDN (SAS) 232-233 M 4
Allangouassou o CI 202-203 H 6
Allan Hills ▲ CDN (SAS) 232-233 M 4
Allanmyo o MYA 142-143 J 6
Allanridge o ZA 220-221 H 3
Allan Water o CDN (ONT) 234-235 N 4
Allapalli o IND 142-143 B 6
Allard, Lac ⊖ CDN (QUE) 242-243 E 2
Allard, Rivière ~ CDN (QUE) 236-237 K 3
Allardville o CDN (NB) 240-241 K 3
Allariz o E 98-99 D 3
Allatoona Lake < USA (GA) 284-285 F 2
Alldays o ZA 218-219 E 6
Ålleberg ▲ S 86-87 F 7
Allegan o USA (MI) 272-273 D 5
Allegany State Park ⊥ USA (NY) 278-279 B 6
Allegheny Mountains ▲ USA (TN) 282-283 E 4
Allegheny River Reservoir < USA (PA) 280-281 H 2
Allemand, Lac ⊖ CDN 36-37 M 4
Allemands, Des o USA (LA) 268-269 K 7
Allemanskraaldam < ZA 220-221 H 4
Allen o RP 160-161 F 6
Allen o USA (NE) 262-263 K 2
Allen o USA (OK) 264-265 H 4
Allen o USA (TX) 264-265 H 5
Allendale o USA (IL) 274-275 L 6
Allendale o USA (MI) 272-273 D 5
Allendale o USA (SC) 284-285 J 3
Allende o MEX (COA) 50-51 J 3
Allende o MEX (NL) 50-51 J 5
Allenford o CDN (ONT) 238-239 D 4
Allen Island ⌒ AUS 174-175 E 5
Allensworth o USA (CA) 248-249 E 4
Allenton o USA (WI) 274-275 K 1
Allentown o USA (FL) 286-287 B 1
Allentown o• USA (PA) 280-281 L 3
Allenwood o USA (PA) 280-281 K 2
Allen Young Point ▲ CDN 24-25 V 4
Alleppey o IND 140-141 G 6
Allerton o USA (IL) 274-275 L 5
Allgäu ⊥ D 92-93 L 5
Alliance o CDN (ALB) 232-233 G 3
Alliance o USA (NE) 262-263 D 2
Alliance o USA (OH) 280-281 E 3
Allier ~ F 90-91 J 8
Alliford Bay o CDN (BC) 228-229 C 3
Alligator Lake ⊖ USA (NC) 282-283 L 5
Alligator Pond o JA 54-55 G 6
Alligator River ~ USA (NC) 282-283 L 5
Allinagaram o IND 140-141 G 5
Allingham o CDN (ALB) 232-233 E 4
Allington, Cape ▲ CDN 24-25 a 5
Allipen, Río ~ RCH 78-79 D 5
al-Liri, Ǧabal ▲ SUD 206-207 K 3
Allison o USA (AR) 276-277 C 5
Allison o USA (IA) 274-275 F 2
Allison o USA (TX) 264-265 D 3
Allison Harbour o CDN (BC) 230-231 B 2
Allison Pass ▲ CDN (BC) 230-231 J 4
al-Lišt, Pyramids of ∴• ET 194-195 E 3
Alliston o CDN (ONT) 238-239 F 4
Allomo o WAN 204-205 G 5
Allu o RI 164-165 F 6
Allumettes, Île des ⌒ CDN (QUE) 238-239 H 3
Āllūr o IND 140-141 J 3
Alluttoq ⌒ GRØ 28-29 P 2
Alluviaq, Fiord ≈ 36-37 R 5
Alluviaq, Rivière ~ CDN 36-37 R 5
Allyn o USA (WA) 244-245 C 3
Alma o CDN (NB) 240-241 L 5
Alma o CDN (QUE) 240-241 D 2
Al'ma ~ UA 102-103 H 5
Alma o USA (AR) 276-277 A 5
Alma o USA (GA) 284-285 H 5
Alma o USA (KS) 262-263 K 5
Alma o USA (MI) 272-273 E 4
Alma o USA (NE) 262-263 G 4
Alma o USA (OR) 244-245 B 7
Alma o USA (WI) 270-271 G 6
Alma, Mount ▲ AUS 178-179 L 2
Alma-Ata = Almaty ★ KA 146-147 C 4
Almaden o AUS 174-175 H 5
Almadén o E 98-99 E 5
al-Mafāza o SUD 200-201 G 6
Almagro o E 98-99 F 5
Almagro Island ⌒ RP 160-161 F 7
al-Mahalla al-Kubrā o ET 194-195 E 2
al-Mahāmid o ET 194-195 F 5
al-Mahariq o ET 194-195 E 5
Almahel o ETH 208-209 B 3
Al Majnīnīn, Wādī ~ LAR 192-193 E 1
al-Malamm o SUD 206-207 J 4
Almalyk o US 136-137 L 4
Almameda o USA (NM) 256-257 J 3
al-Manāqil o SUD 200-201 F 5
Almanor, Lake ⊖ USA (CA) 246-247 D 3
Almansa o E 98-99 G 5
Almansa, Puerto de ▲ E 98-99 G 5
al-Manšāh o ET 194-195 E 4
al-Manṣūra ☆ ET 194-195 E 2
al-Manzila, Buhairat ⊖ ET 194-195 E 2
Almanzor ▲ E 98-99 E 4
Alma Peak ▲ CDN 32-33 G 3
Al Maqrūn o LAR 192-193 J 2
Almār o AFG 136-137 J 7
Almara o AFG 138-139 B 3
Almarcha, La o E 98-99 F 5
Al Marj ☆•• LAR 192-193 J 1
Al Marūqah o LAR 192-193 F 4
Almas o BR 68-69 E 7
Almas, Rio das ~ BR 72-73 F 2
Almas, Rio das ~ BR 72-73 F 3
al-Massira, Barrage < MA 188-189 H 4
Al Mastūtah, Bi'r < LAR 192-193 F 5
al-Matamma o SUD 200-201 F 4
al-Matariya o ET 194-195 F 2
al-Matmarfag o MA 188-189 E 7
al-Matna o SUD 200-201 G 6
Almaty ★ KA 146-147 C 4
al-Mauṣil ☆ IRQ 128-129 K 4
Almazán o E 98-99 F 4
Almaznyj o RUS 118-119 G 4
Almeida o P 98-99 D 4
Almeida Campos o BR 72-73 G 5
Almeirim o BR 62-63 H 6
Almeirim o P 98-99 C 5
Almeirim, Serra do ▲ BR 62-63 H 6
Almel o IND 140-141 G 2
Almelo o NL 92-93 J 2
Almenara o BR 72-73 K 4
Almenar de Soria o E 98-99 F 4
Almendralejo o• E 98-99 D 5
Almendrillo o RCH 78-79 D 2
Al'menevo ☆ RUS 114-115 G 7
Almere o NL 92-93 H 2
Almería o E 98-99 F 6
Almería, Golfo de ≈ 98-99 F 6
Al'met'evsk ☆ RUS 96-97 H 6
Al'met'yevsk = Al'met'evsk ☆ RUS 96-97 H 6
Älmhult o S 86-87 G 8
al-Milk, Wādi ~ SUD 200-201 E 4
Almina, Punta ▲ E 98-99 E 7
al-Minyā ☆ ET 194-195 E 3
Almirantazgo, Seno ≈ 80 F 7
Almirant Brown o ARK 16 G 30
Almirante o PA 52-53 C 7
Almirante Montt, Golfo ≈ 80 D 5
Almirante Saldanha Seamount ≃ 72-73 M 7
Almirós o GR 100-101 J 5
Almo o USA (ID) 252-253 E 4
Almodôvar o P 98-99 C 6
Almodóvar del Río o E 98-99 E 6
Almond o USA (WI) 270-271 J 6
Almont o USA (ND) 258-259 F 5
Almonte o CDN (ONT) 238-239 J 3
Almonte o E 98-99 D 6
Almonte, Río ~ E 98-99 E 5
Almora o• IND 138-139 G 5
Almota o USA (WA) 244-245 H 4
al-Muglad o SUD 206-207 H 3
al-Mūh, Sabḥat ⊖ SYR 128-129 H 5
al-Muhammadiyah = Mohammedia o MA 188-189 H 4
al-Mukallā o•• Y 132-133 F 6
Almuñécar o E 98-99 F 6
Almunia de Doña Godina, La o E 98-99 G 4
Almus o TR 128-129 G 2
Al Muwaylih, Bi'r < LAR 192-193 H 3
Almy o USA (WY) 252-253 H 5
Almyra o USA (AR) 276-277 D 6
Alnaši ☆ RUS 96-97 H 5
Alness o GB 90-91 E 3
Alnif o MA 188-189 J 5
Alnwick o GB 90-91 G 4
Alóag o EC 64-65 C 2
Alô Brasil o BR 72-73 E 2
Aloi o EAU 212-213 D 2
Aloja o LV 94-95 J 3
Aloma, River ~ WAN 204-205 H 5
Alongshan o VRC 150-151 D 2
Alónissos ⌒ GR 100-101 J 5
Alonon Point ▲ RP 160-161 D 6
Alonsa o CDN (MAN) 234-235 E 4
Alor, Kepulauan ⌒ RI 166-167 C 6
Alor, Pulau ⌒ RI 166-167 C 6
Alor, Selat ≈ 166-167 B 6
Aloro, Río ~ BOL 76-77 D 1
Alor Setar ☆ MAL 162-163 D 2
Alot o IND 138-139 E 8
Alota o BOL 76-77 D 1
Alotau ☆ PNG 183 F 6
Alpachiri o RA 78-79 H 4
Alpamayo ▲ PE 64-65 D 6
Alpasinche o RA 76-77 D 5
Alpena o USA (MI) 272-273 F 2
Alpena o USA (SD) 260-261 H 2
Alpercata, Rio ~ BR 68-69 F 5
Alpercatas, Serra das ▲ BR 68-69 F 5
Alpha o AUS 178-179 J 2
Alpha o USA (IL) 274-275 H 3
Alpha Cordillera ≃ 16 A 30
Alpha Creek ~ AUS 178-179 J 2
Alphonse Group ⌒ SY 224 C 3
Alphonse Island ⌒ SY 224 C 3
Alpine o USA (AZ) 256-257 F 5
Alpine o USA (TX) 266-267 D 3
Alpine Junction o USA (WY) 252-253 H 3
Alpine Lakes Wilderness ⊥ USA (WA) 244-245 D 3
Alpine National Park ⊥ AUS 180-181 J 4
Alpinópolis o BR 72-73 G 6
Alpouro ~ DY 204-205 E 4
Alpowa o USA (WA) 244-245 H 4
Alps = Alpen ▲ 92-93 J 6
Alps, The ▲ AUS 178-179 K 2
Alpu ☆ TR 128-129 D 3
al-Qāhira ★ ••• ET 194-195 E 2
Al Qala'a o LAR 192-193 E 2
al-Qanṭara o ET 194-195 F 2
Al Qardabah o LAR 192-193 K 1
Al Qaṣabāt o LAR 192-193 F 1
al-Qāsh, Nahr ~ SUD 200-201 H 5
al-Qaṣr o ET 194-195 D 5
Al Qāt, Bi'r < LAR 192-193 F 3
Al Qatif, Bi'r < LAR 192-193 L 2
Al Qaṭrūn o LAR 192-193 F 5
Al Qaṭṭūsah, Sarir ⊥ LAR 192-193 F 4
al-Qawz o SUD 200-201 G 6
al-Qirbah Dam, Khashm < SUD 200-201 G 5
al-Q'nitra ☆ MA 188-189 H 3
Al Qubbah o• LAR 192-193 K 1
Alqueva, Barragem do < P 98-99 D 5
Alquízar o C 54-55 D 3
al-Qulayd Bahri o SUD 200-201 E 3
al-Qurayyāt ◘ KSA 130-131 E 3
al-Qusair o ET 194-195 G 4
al-Qūṣiya o ET 194-195 E 4
al-Qus Taima o ET 194-195 G 2
al-Qutaynah o SUD 200-201 F 5
al-Quwaisi o SUD 200-201 G 6
Al Rahibat o LAR 192-193 D 2
Alroy Downs o AUS 174-175 D 6
Alsace o AUS 174-175 E 6
Alsace ◘ F 90-91 L 8
Alsace ⊥ F 90-91 L 8
Alsask o CDN (SAS) 232-233 J 4
Alsasu o E 98-99 F 3
Alsatia o USA (LA) 268-269 J 4
Alsea o USA (OR) 244-245 B 6
Alsea River ~ USA (OR) 244-245 B 6
Alsek River ~ CDN 20-21 W 6
Alsen o USA (ND) 258-259 J 3
Alshi o EC 64-65 C 3
Alsike o CDN (ALB) 232-233 D 2
Alta o• N 86-87 L 2
Alta o USA (IA) 274-275 C 2
Alta o USA (UT) 254-255 D 3
Alta, Cachoeira ~ BR 70-71 K 3
Alta, Pampa ⊥ RA 78-79 G 4
Alta, Punta ▲ EC 64-65 B 2
Altaelva ~ N 86-87 L 2
Alta Floresta o BR 66-67 K 7
Alta Gracia o RA 76-77 E 6
Altagracia o YV (ANZ) 60-61 J 3
Altagracia o YV (ZUL) 60-61 F 2
Altair o USA (TX) 266-267 L 4
Altaj ▲ KA 124-125 N 3
Altaj ☆ MAU 148-149 C 4
Altaj = Bor-Üzüür o MAU 146-147 L 3
Altajn Caadah Gov' ⊥ MAU 146-147 M 3
Altajsk, Gorno ☆ RUS 124-125 O 3
Altajskij zapovednik ⊥ RUS 124-125 Q 3
Altamachi, Río ~ BOL 70-71 D 5
Altamaha River ~ USA (GA) 284-285 H 5
Altamaha Sound ≈ USA 284-285 J 5
Altamira o BR 68-69 B 3
Altamira o CO 60-61 D 6
Altamira o MEX 50-51 L 6
Altamira o RCH 76-77 C 3
Altamira o YV 60-61 F 3
Altamira, Cuevas de ••• E 98-99 E 3
Altamira do Maranhão o BR 68-69 F 4
Altamirano o MEX 52-53 H 3
Altamont o CDN (MAN) 234-235 E 5
Altamont o USA (IL) 274-275 K 6
Altamont o USA (OR) 244-245 D 8
Altamont o USA (TN) 276-277 K 5
Altamont o USA (UT) 254-255 E 3
Altamonte Springs o USA (FL) 286-287 H 3
Altamura o I 100-101 F 4
Altan Ovoo o MAU 148-149 E 4
Altan ovoo ▲ MAU 146-147 K 3
Altar o MEX 50-51 D 2
Altar, Desierto de ⊥ MEX 50-51 B 1
Altar, Río ~ MEX 50-51 D 2
Altar, Volcán ▲ EC 64-65 C 2
Altar de Sacrificios ∴• GCA 52-53 J 3
Altar-Est o DZ 190-191 G 6
Altata o MEX 50-51 F 5
Alta Vista o USA (KS) 262-263 K 6
Altavista o USA (VA) 280-281 G 6
Altay o VRC 146-147 J 2
Altay Mountains = Altaj ▲ KA 124-125 N 3
Altay Shan ▲ VRC 146-147 H 1
Altdorf ☆• CH 92-93 K 5
Altea o E 98-99 G 5
Altenburg o• D 92-93 M 3
Altér do Chão o BR 66-67 K 4
Alter do Chão o P 98-99 D 5
Alterosa o BR 72-73 G 6
Altevatnet ⊖ N 86-87 J 2
Altha o USA (FL) 286-287 D 1
Altheimer o USA (AR) 276-277 D 6
Alticane o CDN (SAS) 232-233 L 3
Al Tidedi, Wādi ~ LAR 192-193 H 6
Al Tikuna Evare, Áreas Indígena ⊼ BR 66-67 C 4
Altıntepe ∴• TR 128-129 H 3
Altiplanicie del Payún ▲ RA 78-79 E 4
Altmühl ~ D 92-93 L 4
Alto o USA (TX) 268-269 E 5
Alto, Cerro ▲ RA 78-79 D 6
Alto, El o PE 64-65 B 4
Alto, Raudal ~ YV 60-61 J 4
Alto Alegre o BR (PIA) 68-69 H 4
Alto Alegre o BR (RSU) 74-75 D 8
Alto Anapu, Rio ~ BR 68-69 C 3
Alto Araguaia o BR 72-73 D 4
Alto Bonito o BR 66-67 B 7
Alto Chandless, Río ~ PE 70-71 B 2
Alto Chicapa o ANG 216-217 E 5
Alto de Amparo o BR 74-75 E 5
Alto de Carrizal ▲ CO 60-61 C 4
Alto de la Sierra o RA 76-77 F 2
Alto del Carmen o RCH 76-77 B 5
Alto de los Colorados ▲ RA 76-77 C 4
Alto Garças o BR 72-73 D 4
Alto Hama o ANG 216-217 C 6
Alto Jurupari ~ BR 66-67 B 7
Alto Ligonha o MOC 218-219 K 2
Alto Longá o BR 68-69 G 4
Alto Madre de Dios, Río ~ PE 70-71 B 3
Alto Molócuè o MOC 218-219 J 2
Alton o USA (IA) 274-275 B 2
Alton o USA (IL) 274-275 H 6
Alton o USA (MO) 276-277 D 4
Alton o USA (NH) 278-279 K 5
Alton o USA (NY) 278-279 E 5
Altona o CDN (MAN) 234-235 F 5
Alto Nevado, Cerro ▲ RCH 80 D 2
Altoona o USA (PA) 280-281 H 3
Altoona o USA (WA) 244-245 B 4
Altoona o USA (WI) 270-271 G 6
Alto Pacaja, Rio ~ BR 68-69 C 3
Alto Paraguai o BR 70-71 J 4
Alto Paraíso de Goiás o BR 72-73 G 3
Alto Parnaíba o BR 68-69 F 6
Alto Pencoso o RA 78-79 F 2
Alto Purus, Río ~ PE 70-71 B 2
Alto Quiel o PA 52-53 C 7
Alto Quimarí ▲ CO 60-61 C 3
Alto Rabagão, Barragem do < P 98-99 D 4
Alto Rio Guama, Área Indígena ⊼ BR 68-69 E 3
Alto Rio Mayo o RA 80 E 2
Alto Rio Negro, Área Indígena ⊼ BR 66-67 C 3
Alto Rio Novo o BR 72-73 K 5
Alto Rio Purus, Área Indígena ⊼ BR 66-67 B 7
Alto Río Senguerr o RA 80 E 2
Alto Rio Verde o BR 72-73 D 5
Altos o BR 68-69 G 4
Altos de Talinay ▲ RCH 76-77 B 6
Alto Sucuriú o BR 72-73 D 5
Altotonga o MEX 52-53 F 2
Alto Turiaçu, Área Indígena ⊼ BR 68-69 E 3
Altsohl = Zvolen o SK 92-93 P 4
Altstadt = Staré Město o CZ 92-93 O 4
Altun o VRC 146-147 J 6
Altun Ha ∴• BH 52-53 K 3
Altun Küprü o IRQ 128-129 L 5
Altun Shan ▲ VRC 146-147 G 6
Alturas o USA (CA) 246-247 E 2
Altus o USA (OK) 264-265 E 4
Altus Reservoir < USA (OK) 264-265 E 4
Altvater = Praděd ▲ CZ 92-93 O 3
Altyaryk o US 136-137 M 4
Altyb ~ RUS 116-117 M 5
Altykarasu o KA 126-127 L 3
Alua o MOC 218-219 K 1
Aluakluak o SUD 206-207 K 5
al-Ubayyiḍ = El Obeid ☆• SUD 200-201 E 6
Alučin ~ RUS 112-113 N 3
Alucra ☆ TR 128-129 H 2
al-Udayya o SUD 200-201 D 6
Al Ugayb, Wādi < LAR 192-193 G 3
Aluize, Rio ~ MOC 218-219 G 6
Alūksne ☆•• LV 94-95 K 3
Alum Creek Lake ⊖ USA (OH) 280-281 D 3
al-'Umda o SUD 206-207 J 3
Aluminé o RA 78-79 D 5
Aluminé, Río ~ RA 78-79 D 5
A Lu'ö'i ☆ VN 158-159 J 2
Al 'Uqaylah o LAR 192-193 H 2
al-'Uqdah o SUD 200-201 F 5
al-Uqṣur o•• ET 194-195 F 5
Alūr o IND 140-141 F 4
Ālūr o IND 140-141 G 3
al-Urdunn, Nahr ~ JOR 130-131 D 2
al-'Urf, Ǧabal ▲ ET 194-195 F 4
Al 'Ushara o SUD 200-201 F 5
Alušta o•• UA 102-103 J 5
Al 'Utaylah, Bi'r < LAR 192-193 G 2
al-'Utayshān < SUD 200-201 G 4
Alut Oya o CL 140-141 J 6
Al 'Uwaynāt ⊥ LAR 190-191 H 8
al-'Uzaym, Nahr ~ IRQ 128-129 L 5
Alva o USA (KY) 276-277 M 4
Alva o USA (OK) 264-265 F 2
Alvand, Kūh-e ▲ IR 134-135 C 1
Alvarado o CO 60-61 D 5
Alvarado o MEX 52-53 G 2
Alvarado o USA (TX) 264-265 G 6
Alvarães o BR 66-67 E 4
Alvarenga o BR 72-73 K 5
Alvar Nuñez Cabeza de Vaca o PY 76-77 K 3
Álvaro Obregón, Presa ⊖ MEX 50-51 E 3
Álvaro Obregón, Presa ⊖ MEX 50-51 E 4
Alvdal ☆ N 86-87 E 5
Älvdalen o S 86-87 G 6
Alvear o RA 76-77 J 5
Alvena o CDN (SAS) 232-233 M 3
Alves o BR 72-73 L 2
Alvesta ☆ S 86-87 G 8
Alvim o GUY 62-63 E 4
Alvin o USA (TX) 268-269 E 7
Alvin o USA (WI) 270-271 K 4
Alvinston o CDN (ONT) 238-239 D 6
Alvito o P 98-99 D 5
Älvkarleby ☆ S 86-87 H 6
Alvorada o BR (RSU) 74-75 E 8
Alvorada o BR (TOC) 72-73 F 2
Alvorada do Norte o BR 72-73 G 3
Alvord o USA (TX) 264-265 G 5
Alvord Lake ⊖ USA (OR) 244-245 G 8
Alvord Valley ~ USA (OR) 244-245 G 8
Älvsbyn o• S 86-87 K 4
Alwood o USA (MN) 270-271 D 3
Al Wahah o LAR 192-193 J 3
al-Wāḥāt al-Baḥriya ⊥• ET 194-195 D 3
Al Wa'ir, Wādi ~ LAR 192-193 H 4
Alwar o• IND 138-139 F 6
Alwar Hills ▲ IND 138-139 F 6
Alwās o IND 138-139 E 5
Al Washkah, Bi'r < LAR 192-193 F 3
al-Wāsiṭā o ET 194-195 E 3
Alwero Wenz ~ ETH 208-209 B 4
Al Wigh o LAR 192-193 F 5
Al Wittyah o LAR 192-193 D 1
Alxa Gaoyuan ⊥ VRC 148-149 E 7
Alxa Youqi o VRC 154-155 B 2
Alxa Zuoqi o VRC 154-155 D 2
Aly o USA (AR) 276-277 B 6
Al Yaman ■ Y 132-133 E 6
Alyangula o AUS 174-175 D 3
Alyawarra Aboriginal Land ⊼ AUS 178-179 C 1
Alyeska Resort & Ski Area • USA 20-21 Q 6
Aly-Jurjah ~ RUS 112-113 H 4
Alymdža ~ RUS 118-119 E 4
Alyta, Batagaj- o RUS 110-111 S 6
Alytus ☆ LT 94-95 J 4
Alzada o USA (MT) 250-251 P 6
Alzamaj o RUS 116-117 J 8
Alzey o USA (KY) 276-277 H 3
Alzira o E 98-99 G 5
Ama o PNG 183 A 3
Amaam, laguna ⊖ RUS 112-113 U 5
Amacayacu, Parque Natural ⊥ CO 66-67 B 4
Amaciá o BR 66-67 E 5
Amacuzac, Río ~ MEX 52-53 E 2
Amada ∴• ET 194-195 F 6
Amada Gaza o RCA 206-207 B 6
Amadeus, Lake ⊖ AUS 176-177 L 2
Amadi o SUD 206-207 K 6
Amadi o ZRE 210-211 L 2
'Amādiya, al- ☆ IRQ 128-129 K 4
Amadjuak Bay ≈ 36-37 N 3
Amadjuak Lake ⊖ CDN 36-37 O 2
Amadjuak River ~ CDN 36-37 O 2
Amado o USA (AZ) 256-257 D 7
Amadora o P 98-99 C 5
Amadror ⊥ DZ 190-191 F 8
Amadror, Oued ~ DZ 190-191 F 8
Amaga o CO 60-61 D 4
Amagi o J 152-153 D 8
Amagon o USA (AR) 276-277 D 5
Amahai o RI 166-167 E 3
Amahtonskij, zaliv ⊖ RUS 120-121 N 4
Amair Bin Sana'a, al o KSA 130-131 G 4
Amajac, Río ~ MEX 52-53 E 1
Amaki o PNG 183 B 3
Amakinskij o RUS 110-111 K 4
Amakouladji o RMM 196-197 K 6
Amakusa-nada ≈ 152-153 C 8
Amakusa-shotō ⌒ J 152-153 D 8
Åmål ☆ S 86-87 F 7
Amala ~ EAK 212-213 E 4
Amalapuram o IND 140-141 K 2
Amalat ~ RUS 118-119 G 8
Amalfi o•• I 100-101 E 4
Amalia o ZA 220-221 G 3
Amaliáda o GR 100-101 H 6
Amalner o IND 138-139 E 9
Amaluza o EC (CAN) 64-65 C 3
Amaluza o EC (LOJ) 64-65 C 4
Amaluza, Embalse < EC 64-65 C 3
Amamá o RA 76-77 F 4
Amamapare o RI 166-167 J 4
Amamba o MOC 218-219 G 5
Amambai o BR 76-77 K 2
Amambai, Rio ~ BR 76-77 K 2
Amambay, Sierra de ▲ PY 76-77 K 2
Amami-shotō ⌒ J 152-153 C 11
Amana o USA (IA) 274-275 G 3
Amanã, Lago ⊖ BR 66-67 E 4
Amanã, Rio ~ BR 66-67 J 5
Amana, Río ~ YV 60-61 K 3
Amanab o PNG 183 A 2
Āmanave o USA 184 V b 2
Amancio o C 54-55 G 4
Amanda Park o USA (WA) 244-245 A 3
Amaneyé, Área Indígena ⊼ BR 68-69 D 3
Amangeldi ☆ KA 124-125 D 3
Amaniú o BR 68-69 H 7
Amankaragaj o KA 124-125 D 2
Amankeldi o KA 96-97 H 8
Amankro o CI 202-203 J 6
Amanōtkel' o KA 126-127 O 4
Amantani, Isla ⌒ PE 70-71 C 4
Amantea o I 100-101 F 5
Amantenango del Valle o MEX 52-53 H 3
Amantogaj ☆ KA 124-125 D 3
Amanzamnyama ~ ZW 218-219 D 4
Amanzimtoti o ZA 220-221 K 5
Amapá o BR 62-63 J 4
Amapá o BR 70-71 C 2
Amapá ◘ BR 62-63 H 5
Amapa Grande, Rio ~ BR 62-63 J 4
Amapari, Rio ~ BR 62-63 H 5
Amar ▲ ETH 208-209 C 6
Amar o RI 166-167 F 4
'Amāra, al- ☆• IRQ 128-129 M 7
Amara, Temple • SUD 200-201 E 2
Amarac National Wildlife Refuge ⊥ USA (MN) 270-271 C 3
Amaraji o BR 68-69 L 6
Amaramba, Lago ⊖ MOC 218-219 H 2
Amarante o BR 68-69 G 5
Amarante do Maranhão o BR 68-69 E 4
Amaranth o CDN (MAN) 234-235 E 4
Amarapura o MYA 142-143 K 4
Amarapuram o IND 140-141 G 3
Amarāvati o IND 140-141 J 2
Amaravati o• IND 140-141 J 2
Amardalaj o MAU 148-149 H 4
Amarga, Bañados de la ⊖ RA 78-79 G 3
Amarga, Laguna la ⊖ RA 78-79 F 5
Amargosa Desert ⊥ USA (NV) 248-249 H 3
Amargosa Range ▲ USA (CA) 248-249 H 3
Amargosa River ~ USA (CA) 248-249 H 4
Amargosa Valley o USA (NV) 248-249 H 3
Amarillo o USA (TX) 264-265 C 3
Amarinthos o GR 100-101 J 5
'Amar Jadid o SUD 200-201 B 5
Amarkantak o IND 142-143 B 4
Amarortalik ⌒ GRØ 26-27 Y 7
Amaru, Danau ⊖ RI 166-167 G 2
Amasu ~ KA 124-125 G 5
Amasya ☆•• TR 128-129 F 2
Amata ⊼ AUS 176-177 L 3
Amatari o BR 66-67 H 4
Amates, Los o GCA 52-53 K 4
Amatignak Island ⌒ USA 22-23 G 7
Amatique, Bahía de ≈ 52-53 K 4
Amatitlán o• GCA 52-53 J 4
Amatitlán de Cañas o MEX 52-53 B 1
Amatura o BR 66-67 C 4
Amau o PNG 183 E 6
Āmaytoli Terara ▲ ETH 200-201 K 6
Amazar o RUS 118-119 K 9
Amazar ~ RUS 118-119 K 9
Amazarskij hrebet ▲ RUS 118-119 K 9
Amazmaz < RIM 196-197 D 5
Amazon o CDN (SAS) 232-233 N 4
Amazonas ◘ BR 66-67 C 6
Amazon Canyon ≃ 62-63 K 5
Amazon Fan ≃ 62-63 K 4
Amazônia, Parque Nacional de ⊥ BR 66-67 J 5
Amazon Shelf ≃ 62-63 K 4
Ambabbo o DJI 208-209 F 3
Ambad o IND 138-139 E 10
Amba Farit ▲ ETH 208-209 D 3
Āmba Giyorgis o ETH 200-201 H 6
Ambahikily o RM 222-223 C 8
Ambahita o RM 222-223 D 10
Ambājogāi o IND 138-139 F 10
Ambakireny o RM 222-223 E 6
Ambala o IND 138-139 F 4
Ambalabe o RM 222-223 F 7
Ambalajanakomby o RM 222-223 E 6
Ambalakirajy o RM 222-223 F 5
Ambalamanakana o RM 222-223 E 8
Ambalamanasy o RM 222-223 F 5
Ambalamarina o RM 222-223 E 8
Ambalapaiso o RM 222-223 F 5
Ambalarondra o RM 222-223 F 7
Ambalavao o RM 222-223 E 8
Ambam o CAM 210-211 C 2
Āmba Maderiya o ETH 200-201 J 6
Ambang Reserve, Gunung ⊥• RI 164-165 J 3
Ambanja o RM 222-223 F 4
Ambanjabe o RM 222-223 E 5
Ambar o PE 64-65 D 7
Ambararata o RM 222-223 F 5
Ambarčik o RUS (KRN) 116-117 G 8
Ambarčik o RUS (SAH) 112-113 M 2
Ambardah ~ RUS 108-109 d 6
Ambargasta o RA 76-77 F 5
Ambargasta, Salinas de ⊖ RA 76-77 E 5
Ambargasta, Sierra ▲ RA 76-77 E 5
Ambarimaninga o RM 222-223 E 6
Ambarita • RI 162-163 C 3
Ambarnyj o RUS 88-89 M 4
Ambato ☆ EC 64-65 C 2
Ambato, Sierra de ▲ RA 76-77 D 5
Ambatoboeny o RM 222-223 E 6
Ambato Finandrahana o RM 222-223 E 8
Ambatoharanana o RM 222-223 F 4
Ambatolahy o RM 222-223 D 8
Ambatolampy o RM 222-223 E 7
Ambatomainty o RM 222-223 D 6
Ambatomanoina o RM 222-223 E 7
Ambatondrazaka o RM 222-223 F 6
Ambatosia o RM 222-223 F 5
Ambatosoratra o RM 222-223 F 6
Ambatovory o RM 222-223 E 8
Ambatry o RM 222-223 D 9
Ambaúba o BR 66-67 D 2
Ambazac o F 90-91 H 9
Ambe ~ ZRE 210-211 K 5
Ambelau, Pulau ⌒ RI 166-167 D 3
Amberg o D 92-93 L 4
Ambergris Cay ⌒ BH 52-53 L 3
Ambérieu-en-Bugey o F 90-91 K 9
Amberley o CDN (ONT) 238-239 D 4
Ambert o F 90-91 J 9
Ambidédi o RMM 202-203 E 2
Ambikāpur o IND 142-143 C 4
Ambila o RM 222-223 E 9
Ambil Island ⌒ RP 160-161 D 6
Ambilobe o RM 222-223 F 4
Ambinanindrano o RM 222-223 F 8
Ambinanindrano o RM 222-223 F 7
Ambinanymbazaha o RM 222-223 E 8
Ambition Mountain ▲ CDN 32-33 E 3
Ambitle Island ⌒ PNG 183 G 3
Amble-by-the-Sea o GB 90-91 G 4
Ambler o USA 20-21 M 3
Ambler River ~ USA 20-21 M 3
Ambleside o• GB 90-91 F 4
Ambo o PE 64-65 D 7
Amboahangibe o RM 222-223 F 4
Amboahangy o RM 222-223 E 10
Amboasary o RM 222-223 E 10
Amboasary Gara o RM 222-223 F 7
Amboavory o RM 222-223 F 6
Ambodiangezoka o RM 222-223 F 5
Ambodibonara o RM 222-223 F 4
Ambodifotatra o RM 222-223 F 6
Ambodiriana o RM 222-223 F 6
Ambodisatrana o RM 222-223 F 5
Ambodivoara o RM 222-223 G 5
Ambohibada o RM 222-223 F 4
Ambohibary o RM 222-223 E 7
Ambohidratrimo o RM 222-223 E 7
Ambohijanahary o RM 222-223 F 6
Ambohimahasoa o RM 222-223 E 8
Ambohimanga o RM 222-223 E 7
Ambohinihaonana o RM 222-223 E 8
Ambohipaky o RM 222-223 D 6
Ambohitra o RM (ASA) 222-223 F 4
Ambohitra ▲•• RM (ASA) 222-223 F 4
Ambohitralanana o RM 222-223 G 5
Ambohitrolomahitsy o RM 222-223 E 7
Amboi, Kepulauan ⌒ RI 166-167 J 2
Amboise o F 90-91 H 8
Amboiva o ANG 216-217 C 5
Amboli o IND 140-141 E 3
Ambolobozo o RM 222-223 E 5
Ambolomoty o RM 222-223 E 6
Ambolten ⌒ GRØ 26-27 q 4
Ambon ☆ RI 166-167 E 3
Ambon, Pulau ⌒ RI 166-167 D 3
Ambondro o RM 222-223 D 10
Ambondromamy o RM 222-223 E 6
Ambongo ⊥ RM 222-223 D 6
Amboni o EAT 212-213 G 6
Amboriala o RM 222-223 F 4
Amborompotsy o RM 222-223 E 8
Amborondolo o RM 222-223 F 6
Amboseli, Lake ⊖ EAK 212-213 F 5
Amboseli National Park ⊥ EAK 212-213 F 5
Ambositra o RM 222-223 E 8
Ambovombe o RM 222-223 E 10
Amboy o USA (CA) 248-249 J 5
Amboy o USA (IL) 274-275 J 3
Amboy o USA (WA) 244-245 C 5
Amboy Crater • USA (CA) 248-249 J 5
Ambre, Cap d' = Tanjona Babaomby ▲ RM 222-223 F 3
Ambre, Île d' ⌒ MS 224 C 7
Ambrim = Île Ambrym ⌒ VAN 184 II b 3
Ambriz o ANG 216-217 B 3
Ambriz, Coutada do ⊥ ANG 216-217 B 3
Ambrolauri o GE 126-127 E 6
Ambrose o USA (ND) 258-259 D 3
Ambrósio o BR 68-69 F 5
Ambrym ◘ VAN 184 II b 3
Ambrym, Île = Ambrim ⌒ VAN 184 II b 3
Ambuaki o RI 166-167 G 2
Ambulombo, Gunung ▲ RI 168 E 7
Ambulong Island ⌒ RP 160-161 D 6
Ambunten o RI 168 E 3
Ambunti o PNG 183 B 3
Ambur o IND 140-141 H 4
Amburambur o RI 168 C 7
Ambuve, Lake ⊖ PNG 183 A 4
Amchitka o USA 22-23 F 7
Amchitka Island ⌒ USA 22-23 F 7
Amchitka Pass ≈ 22-23 G 7
'Amd, Wādi ~ Y 132-133 F 6
Am Dafok o RCA 206-207 F 3
am-Dam o TCH 198-199 K 6
Amdāpur o IND 138-139 F 9
Amdassa o RI 166-167 F 6
Amded, Oued ~ DZ 190-191 D 9
Amderma o RUS 108-109 J 7
Am Djaména o RCA 206-207 E 4
Am Djemena o TCH 198-199 H 6
Amdo o VRC 144-145 H 4
Amdrup Højland ▲ GRØ 26-27 m 3
Amealco o MEX 52-53 D 1
Ameca o MEX 52-53 B 1
Ameca, Río ~ MEX 52-53 B 1
Amedići ~ RUS 118-119 L 7
Ameib o NAM 216-217 C 10
Ameland ⌒ NL 92-93 H 2
Amelia C.H. o USA (VA) 280-281 J 6
Amellougui o MA 188-189 H 5
Amenia o USA (NY) 280-281 N 2
Amentego o SUD 200-201 E 3
Ameralik ≈ 28-29 P 4
'Āmerī o IR 134-135 D 3
América o BR 66-67 E 6
America-Antarctic Ridge ≃ 6-7 H 14
América Dourada o BR 68-69 H 7
Americana o BR 72-73 G 7
American Falls o USA (ID) 252-253 F 4
American Falls Reservoir ⊖ USA (ID) 252-253 F 4
American Fork o USA (UT) 254-255 D 3
American Highland ▲ ARK 16 F 8
American Samoa ◘ USA 184 V c 1
Americus o USA (GA) 284-285 F 4
Amerika-Kuba-Aryta, ostrov ⌒ RUS 110-111 R 3
Amersfoort o• NL 92-93 H 2
Amersfoort o ZA 220-221 J 3
Amersham o GB 90-91 G 6
Amery o USA (WI) 270-271 F 5
Amery Ice Shelf ⊂ ARK 16 F 8
Ames o USA (IA) 274-275 E 2
Amesbury o USA (MA) 278-279 L 6
Amesdale o CDN (ONT) 234-235 L 4
Amethi o IND 142-143 B 2
Ameya o ETH 208-209 C 5
Amfilohia o GR 100-101 H 5
Amga ☆ RUS 120-121 D 3
Amga ~ RUS 118-119 L 6
Amga ~ RUS 120-121 D 3
Amginskij hrebet ▲ RUS 118-119 L 6
Amgotro o RI 166-167 L 3
Amgu o RUS 122-123 G 6
Amguèma ~ RUS 112-113 W 3
Amguèma, laguna ≈ 112-113 W 2
Amguemskaja vpadina ⊥ RUS 112-113 U 3
Amguid o DZ 190-191 E 7
Amgun' ~ RUS 122-123 F 3
Amgun ~ RUS 122-123 E 3
Amherst o CDN (NS) 240-241 L 5
Amherst o USA (MA) 278-279 J 6
Amherst o USA (TX) 264-265 B 4
Amherst o USA (VA) 280-281 G 6
Amherst = Kyaikkami o MYA 158-159 D 2
Amherstburg o CDN (ONT) 238-239 C 6
Amherst Island ⌒ CDN (NWT) 24-25 e 6
Amherst Island ⌒ CDN (ONT) 238-239 J 4
Amherst Junction o USA (WI) 270-271 J 6
Am Himédé o TCH 198-199 K 6
Ami ~ IND 142-143 C 2
Amiata, Monte ▲ I 100-101 C 3

296 Al Jufrah — Amiata, Monte

Amidon o USA (ND) 258-259 D 5
Amiens o CDN (SAS) 232-233 L 2
Amiens ☆ ··· F 90-91 J 7
Aminagou o RCA 206-207 G 6
Amindivi Islands ⌒ IND 140-141 E 5
Aminga o RA 76-77 D 5
Aminius ☆ NAM 220-221 D 1
Amino o J 152-153 F 7
Amiour < RMM 196-197 J 6
'Amiq, Qaṣr o IRQ 128-129 J 6
'Amiq, Wādi ~ IRQ 128-129 J 6
Amīrābād o IR 136-137 D 6
Amirantes Group ⌒ SY 224 C 3
Amirante Trench ≃ 224 C 3
Amir Chāh o PK 134-135 K 4
Amisk Lake o CDN 34-35 E 3
Amistad o USA (NM) 256-257 M 3
Amistad, Parque Internacional La ⊥ ··· CR 52-53 C 7
Amistad, Presa la < MEX 50-51 J 3
Amite o USA (LA) 268-269 K 6
Amite River ~ USA (LA) 268-269 K 6
Amitikoe Peninsula ⌄ CDN 24-25 f 6
Amity o USA (AR) 276-277 B 6
Amityville o USA (NY) 280-281 N 3
Amiuté, Ribeiro do ~ BR 68-69 D 5
Amizmiz o MA 188-189 G 5
Amka ~ RUS 120-121 J 4
Amkunj o IND 140-141 L 3
Amla o IND 138-139 G 9
Amlāgora o IND 142-143 E 4
Amlamé o RT 202-203 L 6
Amlapura = Karangasem o · RI 168 B 7
Amlekhganj o NEP 144-145 E 7
Amlia Island ⌒ USA 22-23 K 6
Amloustarat o RMM 196-197 L 6
'Ammān ★ · JOR 130-131 D 2
Ämmänsaari o FIN 88-89 K 4
Ammāpettai o IND 140-141 H 5
Ammapettai o IND 140-141 G 5
Ammarnäs o S 86-87 H 4
Ammaroo o AUS 178-179 C 1
Ammaroodinna Hill ▲ AUS 176-177 M 3
Ammassalik ☆ GRØ 28-29 W 4
Ammassivik = Sletten o GRØ 28-29 S 6
Ammer ~ D 92-93 L 4
Ammersee o D 92-93 L 5
Ammochostos o · TR 128-129 E 5
Ammon o USA (ID) 252-253 G 3
Ammouk < RMM 196-197 K 5
Amnat Charoen o THA 158-159 H 3
Amnja ~ RUS 114-115 J 3
Amnok Gang ~ DVR 150-151 E 7
Amnundakta ~ RUS 116-117 K 2
Amnura o BD 142-143 F 3
Amodinonoka o RM 222-223 E 8
Amogjâr, Passe d' ▲ RIM 196-197 D 4
Āmol o · IR 136-137 C 6
Amolar o BR 70-71 J 6
Amoltepec o MEX 52-53 F 3
Amon o MA 188-189 F 6
Amontada o BR 68-69 J 3
Amores, Arroyo ~ RA 76-77 H 5
Amores, Los o RA 76-77 H 5
Amorgós o GR 100-101 K 6
Amorgós ⌒ GR 100-101 K 6
Amorinópolis o BR 72-73 E 4
Amory o USA (MS) 268-269 M 3
Amos o CDN (QUE) 236-237 K 4
Amotape, Cerros de ▲ PE 64-65 B 4
Amotopo o SME 62-63 F 4
Amou ~ RT 202-203 L 6
Amouguèr o MA 188-189 J 4
Amou Oblo o RT 202-203 L 6
Amour, Djebel ▲ DZ 190-191 C 4
Amourj o RIM 196-197 G 6
Amoya o GH 202-203 J 6
Amozoc o MEX 52-53 E 2
Ampah o RI 164-165 D 4
Ampana o RI 164-165 G 4
Ampang o RI 168 C 7
Ampangalana, Lakandrano < RM 222-223 F 8
Ampanihy o RM 222-223 D 10
Amparafaravola o RM 222-223 F 6
Amparai o CL 140-141 J 7
Amparihy Atsinanana o RM 222-223 E 9
Amparo o BR 72-73 G 7
Amparo, El o YV 60-61 F 4
Ampasamadinika o RM 222-223 F 7
Ampasimanolotra o RM 222-223 F 7
Ampasimbe o RM 222-223 F 6
Ampasinambo o RM 222-223 E 8
Ampatakamaroreny o RM 222-223 F 6
Ampato, Cordillera de ▲ PE 64-65 F 9
Ampefy o RM 222-223 E 7
Amper o WAN 204-205 H 4
Ampère Seamount ≃ 188-189 E 3
Amphlett Group ⌒ PNG 183 F 5
Ampibako o RI 164-165 G 4
Ampisikinana o RM 222-223 F 4
Ampiyacu, Río ~ PE 64-65 F 3
Amplawas o RI 166-167 E 6
Ampoa o RI 164-165 G 4
Ampombiantambo o RM 222-223 F 4
Ampondra o RM 222-223 F 4
Amputa ~ RUS 114-115 O 3
Amqui o CDN (QUE) 240-241 H 2
'Amrān o · Y 132-133 C 6
Amrâne, Bîr' < RIM 196-197 F 3
Amrāvati o IND 138-139 F 9
Am Raya < TCH 198-199 H 5
Amreli o IND 138-139 C 9
Āmri o · PK 138-139 B 6
'Amrit o ·· SYR 128-129 F 5
Amritsar o · IND 138-139 E 4
Amroha o IND 138-139 G 5
Amsāga ⊥ RIM 196-197 C 4
Amsel o · DZ 190-191 E 9
Amsterdam o CDN (SAS) 232-233 Q 4
Amsterdam ★ ·· NL 92-93 H 2
Amsterdam o USA (NY) 278-279 G 6
Amsterdam o ZA 220-221 K 3
Amsterdam, Fort ∴ · NA 56 D 2
Amsterdam, Île ⌒ F 12 F 8
Amstetten o A 92-93 N 4
Am Tanabo o TCH 198-199 H 6
Am Timan ☆ TCH 206-207 E 3
Amu-Buharskij kanal < US 136-137 H 5
'Āmūdā o SYR 128-129 J 4
'Amūda, al- o IRQ 128-129 L 7
Amu-Dar'ja o TM 136-137 J 6
Amudar'ja ~ US 136-137 H 4
Amudarjo ~ US 136-137 F 3
Amudat o EAU 212-213 E 3
Amukta Island ⌒ USA 22-23 L 6
Amukta Pass ≈ 22-23 L 6
Amund Ringnes Island ⌒ CDN 24-25 X 1
Amundsen, Mount ▲ ARK 16 G 11
Amundsen Bay ≈ 16 G 5
Amundsen Glacier ⊂ ARK 16 E 0
Amundsen Gulf ≈ 24-25 J 5
Amundsen havet ≈ 16 G 26
Amundsen-Scott o ARK 16 E 0
Amungwiwa, Mount ▲ PNG 183 D 4
Amuntai o RI 164-165 D 5
Amur ~ RUS 118-119 K 9
Amur ~ RUS 122-123 E 4
Amur ~ RUS 122-123 J 2
'Amūr, Wādi ~ SUD 200-201 G 3
Amurang o RI 164-165 J 3
Amursk o RUS 122-123 G 3
Amurskie stolby · RUS 122-123 H 3
Amurskij liman ≈ 122-123 J 2
Amursko-Zejskaja ravnina ⌄ RUS 118-119 M 9
Amutu-Besar, Pulau ⌒ RI 166-167 G 3
Amyderya ~ TM 136-137 H 5
Amyl ~ RUS 116-117 F 9
Amzi, Oued Tin ~ DZ 198-199 B 2
Amzi, Oued Ti-n ~ RN 198-199 B 3
Am-Zoer o TCH 198-199 K 5
'Āna ☆ IRQ 128-129 J 5
Ana, Cachoeira ~ BR 62-63 F 5
Anabanua o RI 164-165 G 5
Anabar ~ RUS 110-111 J 4
Anabarskij zaliv ≈ 110-111 J 3
Anabarskoe plato ▲ RUS 110-111 F 4
Anabat o RP 160-161 D 4
Anaborano o RM 222-223 F 4
Anacadiña o YV 60-61 J 5
Anacapa Islands ⌒ USA (CA) 248-249 E 5
Anaco o YV 60-61 J 3
Anacoco o USA (LA) 268-269 G 5
Anacoco, Bayou ~ USA (LA) 268-269 G 6
Anaconda o USA (MT) 250-251 G 5
Anaconda-Pintler Wilderness ⊥ USA (MT) 250-251 F 5
Anacortes o USA (WA) 244-245 C 2
Anadarko o USA (OK) 264-265 F 3
Anadolu = Anatolia ⊥ 128-129 D 3
Anadyr' ☆ · RUS 112-113 T 4
Anadyr ~ RUS 112-113 S 4
Anadyr ~ RUS 112-113 Q 3
Anadyr' ~ RUS 112-113 P 4
Anadyrskaja nizmennost' ⌄ RUS 112-113 S 4
Anadyrskij liman ≈ 112-113 T 4
Anadyrskoe ploskogor'e ⊥ RUS 112-113 P 3
Anadyrskoye Ploskogor'ye = Anadyrskoe ploskogor'e ▲ RUS 112-113 P 3
Anáfi ⌒ GR 100-101 K 6
Anaghit o · ER 200-201 J 4
Anagni o · I 100-101 D 4
Anagusa Island ⌒ PNG 183 F 6
Anaharávi o GR 100-101 G 5
Anaheim o USA (CA) 248-249 G 6
Anahidrano o RM 222-223 E 5
Anahim Lake o CDN (BC) 228-229 J 4
Anahola o USA (HI) 288 F 2
Anáhuac o MEX (CHA) 50-51 F 3
Anáhuac o MEX (NL) 50-51 J 4
Anahuac o USA (TX) 268-269 F 7
Anahuac National Wildlife Refuge ⊥ USA (TX) 268-269 F 7
Anaimālai o IND 140-141 G 5
Anai Mudi ▲ IND 140-141 G 5
Anaj ~ RUS 116-117 N 9
Anajás o BR 62-63 K 6
Anajatuba o BR 68-69 F 3
Anajé o BR 72-73 K 3
Anaka o EAU 212-213 C 2
Anakalang o · RI 168 D 7
Anakāpalle o IND 142-143 C 7
Anakch o MA 188-189 E 7
Anakdara o RI 164-165 G 5
Anakie o AUS 178-179 J 2
Anaktuk o USA 20-21 L 1
Anaktuvuk Pass o USA 20-21 P 2
Anaktuvuk River ~ USA 20-21 P 2
Analalava o RM 222-223 E 5
Analamaitso ▲ RM 222-223 F 6
Analampotsy, Farihy o RM 222-223 F 8
Analasarotra o RM 222-223 E 5
Analavory o RM 222-223 E 7
Anamã o BR 66-67 G 4
Anamã, Igarapé do ~ BR 66-67 G 4
Anamã, Lago o BR 66-67 G 4
Anama, ozero o RUS 116-117 G 2
Anama Bay o CDN (MAN) 234-235 E 3
Ana Maria o PE 64-65 E 5
Ana Maria, Golfo de ≈ 54-55 F 4
Anambas, Kepulauan ⌒ RI 162-163 F 3
Anambra ◘ WAN 204-205 G 5
Anambra, River ~ WAN 204-205 G 5
Anamoose o USA (ND) 258-259 G 4
Anamosa o USA (IA) 274-275 G 2
Anamu, Rio ~ BR 62-63 F 5
Anamur ☆ TR 128-129 E 4
Anamur Burnu ▲ TR 128-129 E 4
Anan o J 152-153 F 8
Ananás o BR 68-69 D 5
Ananás, Cachoeira ~ BR 68-69 B 5
Ananda-Kouadiokro o CI 202-203 H 6
Anandpur o IND 142-143 E 5
Anan'evo o KS 146-147 C 4
Añangu o EC 64-65 D 2
Ananta, Lago o PE 70-71 B 4
Anantapur o IND 140-141 G 3
Anantnag o IND 138-139 E 3
Anantsono o RM 222-223 C 9
Anantsono, Helodrano ≈ 222-223 C 9
Anapka, zaliv o RUS 120-121 V 3
Anápolis o BR 72-73 F 4
Anapu, Rio ~ BR 68-69 C 3
Anār o IR 134-135 F 3
Anārak o IR 134-135 E 2
Anārbār, Rūd-e ~ IR 134-135 D 2
Anār Dare o AFG 134-135 J 2
Ānarjávri = Inarijärvi o ·· FIN 88-89 J 2
Ánarjohka ~ FIN 88-89 H 2
Anarnitsoq ⌒ GRØ 28-29 Q 6
Anastácio o BR 70-71 K 7
Anastácio, Rio ~ BR 72-73 E 7
Anastasii, buhta o RUS 112-113 R 6
Anatolia = Anadolu ⊥ TR 128-129 D 3
Anatolikí Macedonía Kai Thráki ◘ GR 100-101 K 4
Anatone o USA (WA) 244-245 H 4
Añatuya o RA 76-77 F 5
Anauá, Rio ~ BR 62-63 D 5
Anaunethat Lake o CDN 30-31 R 5
Anaurilândia o BR 72-73 D 7
Anavgaj o RUS 120-121 S 5
Anavilhanas, Arquipélago das ⌒ BR 66-67 G 4
'Anaza Ruwāla ▲ KSA 130-131 E 2
Anbā Bišwi, Dair ∴ ET 194-195 E 2
Anbār, al- ◘ IRQ 128-129 J 6
Anbar Kūh ▲ AFG 136-137 L 6
Anbyon o DVR 150-151 F 8
Anča ~ RUS 120-121 H 3
An Cabhán = Cavan ☆ IRL 90-91 D 5
An Caisleán Nua = Newcastle West o IRL 90-91 C 5
An Caol = Keel o IRL 90-91 B 5
Ancasti o del Alto, Sierra de ▲ RA 76-77 E 5
Ancenis o F 90-91 G 8
An Chathair = Caher o IRL 90-91 D 5
Anchau o WAN 204-205 H 3
Ancho o USA (NM) 256-257 K 5
Ancho, Canal ≈ 80 C 5
Anchorage o · USA 20-21 Q 6
Anchorena o RA 78-79 G 3
Ancien < RMM 196-197 K 4
Anciferova, ostrov ⌒ RUS 122-123 Q 3
Anclitas, Cayos ⌒ C 54-55 F 4
An Clochán = Clifden o · IRL 90-91 B 5
Anclote Keys ⌒ USA (FL) 286-287 G 3
An Cóbh = Cobh o IRL 90-91 C 6
An Coireán = Waterville o IRL 90-91 B 6
Ancon o PE 64-65 D 7
Ancon, Punta ▲ EC 64-65 B 3
Ancona ☆ · I 100-101 D 3
Anconcito o EC 64-65 B 3
Ancón de Sardinas, Bahía de ≈ 64-65 C 1
Ancuabe o MOC 214-215 K 7
Ancuaze o MOC 218-219 H 3
Ancud o RCH 78-79 C 6
Ancud, Golfo de ≈ 78-79 C 6
Anda o RP 160-161 C 4
Anda o VRC 150-151 E 4
Andacollo o RCH 76-77 B 6
Andaga o WAN 204-205 K 3
Andagua o PE 64-65 F 9
Andahuaylas o PE 64-65 F 8
Andaiá, Rio ~ BR 72-73 H 5
An Daingean = Dingle o IRL 90-91 B 5
Andaingo Gara o RM 222-223 F 7
Andakalaka o RM 222-223 E 5
Andale o USA (KS) 262-263 J 7
Andalgala o RA 76-77 D 4
Åndalsnes ☆ N 86-87 C 5
Andalucía ◘ E 98-99 D 6
Andalusia o USA (AL) 284-285 D 5
Andalusia o USA (IL) 274-275 H 3
Andām, Wādi ~ OM 132-133 L 3
Andaman and Nicobar Islands ◘ IND 140-141 L 4
Andaman Basin ≃ 158-159 C 5
Andaman Islands ⌒ IND 140-141 L 3
Andaman Sea ≈ 158-159 C 4
Andamarca o BOL 70-71 D 6
Andamooka Opal Fields o AUS 178-179 D 6
Andamooka Ranges ▲ AUS 178-179 D 6
Andapa o RM 222-223 E 7
Andarāb o AFG 136-137 L 7
Andaraí o BR 72-73 K 2
Andarma ~ RUS 114-115 Q 6
Andavaka · RM 222-223 D 10
Āndeba Ye Midir Zerf Ch'af ▲ ER 200-201 K 5
Andelys, les o F 90-91 H 7
Andenes o · N 86-87 H 2
Anderai o WAN 204-205 F 3
Andéramboukane o RMM 196-197 M 7
Ånderdalen nasjonalpark ⊥ N 86-87 H 2
Andermatt o CH 92-93 K 5
Andersen, Salto ~ RA 78-79 G 5
Anderson o USA (IN) 274-275 N 4
Anderson o USA (MO) 276-277 A 4
Anderson o USA (SC) 284-285 H 2
Anderson o USA (TX) 268-269 E 6
Anderson Channel ≈ 36-37 R 3
Anderson Creek ~ USA (TX) 264-265 K 5
Anderson Gate < NAM 216-217 C 9
Anderson Island ⌒ CDN 36-37 L 6
Anderson River ~ CDN 20-21 a 2
Anderson River ~ USA (IN) 274-275 M 6
Andersonville o USA (IN) 274-275 N 5
Andersonville National Historic Site · USA (GA) 284-285 F 4
Andes o CO 60-61 D 5
Andes = Andes, Cordillera de los ▲ 5 D 8
Andes, Los o RCH 78-79 D 2
Andes, Los = Sotomayor o CO 64-65 D 1
Andfjorden ≈ 86-87 H 2
Andhōy o AFG 136-137 J 6
Andhra Pradesh ◘ IND 140-141 H 2
Andijskoe Kojsu ~ RUS 126-127 G 6
Andikíthira ⌒ GR 100-101 J 7
Andilamena o RM 222-223 F 6
Andimešk o · IR 134-135 C 2
Anding o VRC 156-157 H 2
Andino, Parque Nacional ⊥ RCH 78-79 C 6
Andíparos ⌒ GR 100-101 K 6
Andira o BR 72-73 E 7
Andirá, Rio ~ BR 66-67 J 4
Andirá, Rio ~ BR 66-67 D 5
Andirá-Marau, Área Indígena ⚔ BR 66-67 J 4
Andırın ☆ TR 128-129 G 4
Andírio o GR 100-101 H 5
Andirlangar o VRC 144-145 D 2
Andižan ☆ US 136-137 N 4
Andižanskaja oblast' ◘ US 136-137 M 4
Andižanskoe vodohranilišče < KS 136-137 N 4
Andoain o E 98-99 F 3
Andoany o RM 222-223 F 4
Andoas o PE 64-65 D 3
Andohajango o RM 222-223 F 5
Andoi o RI 166-167 G 2
Andong o ROK 150-151 G 9
Andoom o AUS 174-175 F 3
Andorinha o BR 68-69 J 7
Andorinha, Cachoeira da ~ BR 66-67 G 7
Andørja ⌒ N 86-87 H 2
Andorra ■ AND 98-99 H 3
Andorra La Vella ★ · AND 98-99 H 3
Andorskaja grjada ▲ RUS 94-95 P 2
Andover o USA (ME) 278-279 L 4
Andover o USA (NH) 278-279 K 5
Andover o USA (NY) 278-279 D 6
Andover o USA (OH) 280-281 F 2
Andover o USA (SD) 260-261 J 1
Andovoranto o RM 222-223 F 7
Andøya ⌒ N 86-87 G 2
Andrada o ANG 216-217 F 3
Andradina o BR 72-73 E 6
Andrafainkona o RM 222-223 F 4
Andrafiabe o RM 222-223 F 4
Andrafiamena ▲ RM 222-223 F 4
Andramasina o RM 222-223 E 7
Andranavory o RM 222-223 D 9
Andranomena o RM 222-223 F 7
Andranomita · RM 222-223 D 8
Andranopasy o RM 222-223 C 8
Andranovondronina o RM 222-223 F 4
Andreafsky River ~ USA 20-21 J 5
Andreanof Islands ⌒ USA 22-23 H 7
Andrecyk Lake o CDN 30-31 R 5
Andrée Land ⊥ GRØ 26-27 m 7
Andrée land ~ N 84-85 J 3
Andreevka o KA 124-125 M 6
Andreevka o RUS 96-97 G 7
Andreevskoe, ozero o RUS 114-115 J 5
André Felix, Parc National ⊥ RCA 206-207 F 4
Andre Lake o CDN 36-37 R 7
Andrelândia o BR 72-73 H 6
Andrequicé o BR 72-73 H 5
Andréville o CDN (QUE) 240-241 F 3
Andrevo o RM 222-223 C 9
Andrew o CDN (ALB) 232-233 F 2
Andrew Gordon Bay ≈ 36-37 M 2
Andrew Lake o CDN 30-31 O 6
Andrew River ~ CDN 20-21 a 2
Andrews o USA (NC) 282-283 D 5
Andrews o USA (SC) 284-285 L 3
Andrews o USA (TX) 264-265 B 6
Ándria o I 100-101 F 4
Andriamena o RM 222-223 E 6
Andriamena, Lavarie d' · RM 222-223 E 6
Andriba o RM 222-223 E 6
Andrieskraal o ZA 220-221 G 6
Andriesvale o ZA 220-221 E 3
Andrijevica o · YU 100-101 G 3
Andringitra ▲ RM 222-223 E 8
Andrjuškino o RUS 112-113 H 2
Androfiamena o RM 222-223 F 4
Androhibe o RM 222-223 E 5
Androka o RM 222-223 D 10
Androna ⊥ RM 222-223 E 5
Andronica Island ⌒ USA 22-23 R 5
Andropov = Rybinsk ☆ RUS 94-95 Q 2
Andoranga ~ RM 222-223 F 5
Ándros ⌒ GR 100-101 K 6
Androscoggin River ~ USA (ME) 278-279 L 4
Andros Island ⌒ BS 54-55 F 2
Andros Town o · BS 54-55 G 2
Androth Island ⌒ IND 140-141 E 5
Androy ⊥ RM 222-223 D 10
Andru River ~ PNG 183 E 4
Andselv o N 86-87 J 2
Andudu o ZRE 212-213 B 2
Andújar o E 98-99 E 5
Andulo o ANG 216-217 D 5
Andyljvan ~ RUS 112-113 M 4
Anec, Lake o AUS 176-177 K 1
Anecón Chico, Cerro ▲ RA 78-79 E 6
Anecón Grande, Cerro ▲ RA 78-79 D 6
Anéfis o RMM 196-197 L 5
Anegada ⌒ GB 56 C 2
Anegada ⌒ GB (VI) 286-287 R 2
Anegada, Bahía ≈ 78-79 H 6
Anegada, Punta ▲ PA 52-53 D 8
Anegada Passage ≈ 56 D 2
Aného o · RT 202-203 L 6
Anekal o IND 140-141 G 4
Anéker o RN 198-199 B 5
Añelo o RA 78-79 E 5
Anemounon ∴ ·· TR 128-129 E 4
Anepahan o RP 160-161 C 8
Anepmete o PNG 183 E 3
Anerley o CDN (SAS) 232-233 L 4
Anesbaraka < DZ 198-199 B 3
Anes-Barakka < RN 198-199 C 3
Aneth o USA (UT) 254-255 F 6
Aneto, Pico de ▲ E 98-99 H 3
Anette Island ⌒ USA 32-33 E 4
Anette Island Indian Reservation ⚔ USA 32-33 E 4
Aney o RN 198-199 F 3
Anfeg, Oued ~ DZ 190-191 E 9
Anfu o VRC 156-157 J 3
Anga, Bol'šaja ~ RUS 116-117 N 8
Angading o RI 162-163 E 6
Angajurjualuk Lake o CDN 24-25 g 5
Angalimp o PNG 183 C 3
Angamāli o IND 140-141 G 5
Angamarut o PNG 183 A 4
Angamma, Falaise d' ▲ TCH 198-199 H 4
Angamos, Isla ⌒ RCH 80 C 4
Angamos, Punta ▲ RCH 76-77 B 2
Angangueo o MEX 52-53 D 2
Ang'ang Xi ∴ · VRC 150-151 D 4
Angara ~ RUS 116-117 F 6
Angara ~ RUS 116-117 K 6
Angara ~ RUS 116-117 L 9
'Angara o SUD 206-207 G 3
Angaradébou o DY 204-205 E 3
Angarakan o RUS 118-119 E 8
Angarka o RUS 112-113 N 3
Angarka ~ RUS 112-113 N 3
Angarsk o RUS 116-117 L 9
Angarskij krjaž ⊥ RUS 116-117 K 8
Angastaco o RA 76-77 D 3
Angaston o AUS 180-181 E 3
Angatuba o BR 72-73 F 7
Angavo ⊥ RM 222-223 E 7
Angba o WAN 204-205 G 5
Angel, El o EC 64-65 D 1
Angel, Salto ~ ·· YV 60-61 K 5
Ángel de la Guarda, Isla ⌒ MEX 50-51 C 3
Angeles o RP 160-161 D 5
Angeles, Los o RCH 78-79 C 4
Angeles, Los o USA (TX) 266-267 H 5
Angeles, Port o USA (WA) 244-245 B 2
Ängelholm o S 86-87 F 8
Angélica o RA 76-77 G 6
Angelica o USA (WI) 270-271 K 6
Angelim o BR 68-69 K 6
Angelina River ~ USA (TX) 268-269 E 5
Angelin Bjerg ▲ GRØ 26-27 n 7
Angellala Creek ~ AUS 178-179 J 4
Angelo River ~ AUS 176-177 D 1
Ängelsberg o ··· S 86-87 H 7
Angels Camp o USA (CA) 246-247 E 5
Angel's Cove o CDN (NFL) 242-243 O 5
Angelus Oaks o USA (CA) 248-249 H 5
Angemuk, Gunung ▲ RI 166-167 K 3
Angerburg = Węgorzewo o · PL 92-93 Q 1
Angereb o ETH 200-201 H 6
Angereb Wenz ~ ETH 200-201 H 6
Ångermanälven ~ S 86-87 H 5
Ångermanland ⊥ S 86-87 H 5
Angermünde o · D 92-93 N 2
Angers o F 90-91 G 8
Ängesån ~ S 86-87 L 3
Angetu o ETH 208-209 D 5
Anggoami o RI 164-165 G 5
Anggoro o RI 166-167 H 5
Angical o BR 68-69 F 7
Angicos o BR 68-69 K 4
Angier o USA (NC) 282-283 J 5
Angijak Island ⌒ CDN 36-37 T 2
Angikuni Lake o CDN 30-31 U 4
Angira o PK 134-135 M 4
Angìre o IR 134-135 F 2
Angisoq = Loransation o GRØ 28-29 S 7
Angkor Wat ··· K 158-159 H 4
Ángk Tasaôm o K 158-159 H 5
Angle Inlet o USA (MN) 270-271 C 1
Anglem, Mount ▲ NZ 182 A 7
Anglemont o CDN (BC) 230-231 K 3
Anglesea o AUS 180-181 H 5
Anglesey ⌒ GB 90-91 E 5
Angleton o USA (TX) 268-269 E 7
Angliers o CDN (QUE) 236-237 J 5
Angmagssalik Fjord ≈ 28-29 W 4
Ango o ZRE 206-207 G 6
Angochagua o EC 64-65 C 1
Angoche o MOC 218-219 K 3
Angohrān o IR 134-135 G 5
Angol o RCH 78-79 C 4
Angola ■ ANG 216-217 C 5
Angola o USA (IN) 274-275 N 3
Angola Abyssal Plain = Namibia Abyssal Plain ≃ 6-7 K 11
Angola Basin ≃ 6-7 K 10
Angola Swamp o USA (NC) 282-283 K 6
Angolin o IND 142-143 J 1
Angonia, Planalto de ▲ MOC 218-219 G 2
Angontsy, Tanjona ▲ RM 222-223 G 5
Angoon o USA 32-33 C 3
Angor o US 136-137 K 6
Angora o USA (NE) 262-263 C 3
Angoram o PNG 183 C 3
An Gort = Gort o IRL 90-91 C 5
Angostura, Presa de la < MEX (CHI) 52-53 H 3
Angostura, Presa de la < MEX (SON) 50-51 E 2
Angostura Reservoir < USA (SD) 260-261 C 3
Angoulême ☆ · F 90-91 H 9
Angpawing Bum ▲ MYA 142-143 J 3
Angra dos Reis o · BR 72-73 H 7
Angramios, Pulau ⌒ RI 166-167 H 3
Angren o US 136-137 M 4
Ang Thong Marine National Park ⊥ THA 158-159 E 6
Angu o ZRE 210-211 K 2
Anguilla ◘ GB 56 D 2
Anguilla o USA (MS) 268-269 K 3
Anguilla Cays ⌒ BS 54-55 F 3
Anguilla Island ⌒ GB 56 D 2
Anguille, Cape ▲ CDN (NFL) 242-243 J 5
Anguille Mountains ▲ CDN (NFL) 242-243 J 5
Angūman o AFG 136-137 M 7
Anguo o VRC 154-155 J 2
Angūrān o IR 128-129 M 4
Anguran o IR 134-135 F 5
Angurugu ⚔ AUS 174-175 D 3
Angus o CDN (ONT) 238-239 F 4
Angusilla o PE 64-65 E 2
Angusko Point ▲ CDN 30-31 X 5
Angusville o CDN (MAN) 234-235 B 4
Angwa ~ ZW 218-219 F 3
An Hāi ☆ VN 156-157 E 6
Anhanduí-Guaçu, Rio ~ BR 76-77 K 1
Anholt ⌒ DK 86-87 E 8
Anhua o VRC 156-157 G 2
Anhui ◘ VRC 154-155 K 5
Ani · TR 128-129 K 2
Aniak o USA 20-21 L 6
Aniakchak Crater · USA 22-23 R 4
Aniakchak National Monument and Preserve ⊥ USA 22-23 S 4
Aniak River ~ USA 20-21 L 6
Aniakshak Bay ≈ 22-23 S 4
Aniassue o CI 202-203 J 6
Aníbal Pinto, Lago o RCH 80 D 5
Anicuns o BR 72-73 F 4
Anié o RT (DPL) 202-203 L 6
Anié ~ RT 202-203 L 5
Anie, Pic d' ▲ F 90-91 G 10
Anihovka ☆ RUS 124-125 B 3
Anikino o RUS 118-119 K 9
Anil o BR 68-69 F 3
Anil, Igarapé do ~ BR 66-67 J 7
Animas o USA (NM) 256-257 G 7
Animas, Las o HN 52-53 L 4
Animas, Punta ▲ RCH 76-77 B 4
Animas, Quebrada de las ~ RCH 76-77 B 4
Animas Peak ▲ USA (NM) 256-257 G 7
Animas River ~ USA (CO) 254-255 H 6
Anina o RO 102-103 B 5
Aninaus Pass ▲ ZA 220-221 C 4
Anisij, mys ▲ RUS 110-111 W 1
Anita o USA (IA) 274-275 D 3
Anita Garibaldi o BR 74-75 E 6
Aniuk River ~ USA 20-21 M 2
Aniva o RUS 122-123 K 5
Aniva, mys ▲ RUS 122-123 K 5
Aniva, zaliv ≈ 122-123 K 5
Anivorano Avaratra o RM 222-223 F 4
Aniwa o USA (WI) 270-271 J 6
Aniwa Island = Île Nina ⌒ VAN 184 II b 4
Aniyo o J 152-153 G 7
Anjafy, Lembalemba Ambonin ▲ RM 222-223 E 6
Anjār o IND 138-139 C 8
Anji o VRC 154-155 L 6
Anjohibe · RM 222-223 E 5
Anjombony ~ RM 222-223 F 5
Anjou ⊥ F 90-91 G 8
Anjozorobe o RM 222-223 E 7
Anju o DVR 150-151 E 8
Anjuj ~ RUS 122-123 G 4
Anjuj, Bol'šoj ~ RUS 112-113 M 3
Anjuj, Malyj ~ RUS 112-113 O 3
Anjujsk o RUS 112-113 L 2
Anjujskij hrebet ▲ RUS 112-113 M 3
Anka o WAN 198-199 B 6
Ankaboa, Tanjona ▲ RM 222-223 C 8
Ankaimoro, Tombeaux · RM 222-223 E 9
Ankaizina ⊥ RM 222-223 F 5
Ankalalobe o RM 222-223 D 7
Ankang o VRC 154-155 F 5
Ankara ★ · TR 128-129 E 3
Ankaramy o RM 222-223 F 4
Ankaratra ▲ RM 222-223 E 7
Ankasa National Park ⊥ GH 202-203 J 7
Ankatafa o RM 222-223 F 4
Ankavanana ~ RM 222-223 F 5
Ankavandra o RM 222-223 D 7
Ankazoabo o RM 222-223 D 9
Ankazobe o RM 222-223 E 7
Ankazobe, Tampoketsan' ▲ RM 222-223 E 6
Ankazomborona o RM 222-223 E 6
Ankazomiriotra o RM 222-223 E 7
Ankazondandy o RM 222-223 E 7
Ankeny o USA (IA) 274-275 E 3
Ankerika o RM 222-223 E 5
An Khê o VN 158-159 K 4
Ankihalli o IND 140-141 F 4
Ankilizato o RM 222-223 D 8
Ankirihitra o RM 222-223 E 6
Anklam o D 92-93 M 2
Ankleshwar o IND 138-139 D 9
Ankli o IND 140-141 F 2
Ankober o · ETH 208-209 D 4
Ankobra ~ GH 202-203 J 7
Ankola o IND 140-141 F 3
Ankoro o ZRE 214-215 D 4
Ankotrofotsy o RM 222-223 D 7
Ankpa o WAN 204-205 G 5
An Láithreach = Laragh o · IRL 90-91 D 5
Anliu o VRC 156-157 J 5
Anllóns, Río ~ E 98-99 C 3
Anlong o VRC 156-157 D 4
An Longfort = Longford ☆ IRL 90-91 D 5
Ânlóng Vêng o K 158-159 H 3
Anlu o VRC 154-155 H 6
An Muileann-gCearr = Mullingar o IRL 90-91 D 5
Anmyŏn Do ⌒ ROK 150-151 F 9
Ann, Cape ▲ USA (MA) 278-279 L 6
Anna o RUS 102-103 M 2
Anna o USA (IL) 276-277 F 3
Anna o USA (MS) 268-269 J 5
Anna, Lake o USA (VA) 280-281 J 5
Annaba ☆ · DZ 190-191 F 2
Annaberg o PNG 183 C 3
Anna Bistrup, Kap ▲ GRØ 26-27 q 4
an-Nabk ☆ SYR 128-129 G 5
Annaheim o CDN (SAS) 232-233 O 3
an-Nahl o ET 194-195 F 3
An Nā'ikah, Qarārat o LAR 192-193 H 4
Anna Maria Island ⌒ USA (FL) 286-287 G 4
An Nāmūs, Wāw o LAR 192-193 G 5
Annandale o USA (MN) 270-271 D 5
Anna Plains o AUS 172-173 E 5
Annapolis o USA (MO) 276-277 E 3
Annapolis ☆ · USA (MD) 280-281 K 5
Annapolis Royal o CDN (NS) 240-241 K 6
Annapurna Himal ▲ NEP 144-145 D 6
Annapurna I ▲ NEP 144-145 D 6
Annapurna II ▲ NEP 144-145 E 6
Annapurna Sanctuary ⊥ · NEP 144-145 D 6
Ann Arbor o USA (MI) 272-273 F 5
Anna Regina o GUY 62-63 E 2
An Nás = Naas ☆ IRL 90-91 D 5
Annaville o CDN (QUE) 238-239 N 2
Anne, Mount ▲ AUS 180-181 J 7
Annean, Lake o AUS 176-177 E 3
Annecy o F 90-91 L 9
Annenkov Island ⌒ GB 78-79 O 7
Annigeri o IND 140-141 F 3
an-Nil ~ ET 194-195 E 3
Anning o VRC 156-157 C 4
Anningie o AUS 178-179 B 1
Anniston o USA (AL) 284-285 E 3
Anniston Army Depot ✕✕ USA (AL) 284-285 E 3
Annitowa o AUS 178-179 D 1
Annofiyah o LAR 192-193 G 2
Annonay o F 90-91 K 9
Annotto Bay o JA 54-55 G 5
Annoual o MA 188-189 K 3
an-Nugaym, Bi'r < SUD 200-201 G 3
An Nuqāt al Khams ◘ LAR 192-193 D 1
Anola o CDN (MAN) 234-235 G 5
An Ómaigh = Omagh ☆ · GB 90-91 D 4
Año Nuevo, Seno ≈ 80 F 7
Año Nuevo Point ▲ USA (CA) 248-249 B 2
Anony, Farihy o RM 222-223 E 10
Anori o BR 66-67 G 4
Anoritooq ≈ 28-29 T 6
Anorontany, Tanjona ▲ RM 222-223 F 4
Anosibe An'ala o RM 222-223 F 7
Anosy ▲ RM 222-223 E 10
Anpo Gang ~ VRC 156-157 F 6
Anqing o VRC 154-155 K 6
Anqiu o VRC 154-155 L 3
Anquincila o RA 76-77 E 5
Anranofasika o RM 222-223 E 6
Anranomavo o RM 222-223 D 6
Anriandampy o RM 222-223 D 9
Ansai o VRC 154-155 F 3
Ansas o RI 166-167 H 2
Ansbach o · D 92-93 L 4
Anse-à-Galets o RH 54-55 J 5
Anse-au-Loup Big Pond, L' o CDN (NFL) 242-243 M 1
Anse-à-Veau o RH 54-55 J 5
Änseba Shet' ~ ER 200-201 J 4
Anselm o USA (ND) 258-259 K 5
Anselmo o USA (NE) 262-263 G 3
Anse-Pleureuse o CDN (QUE) 242-243 C 3
Anserma o CO 60-61 D 5
Anse Rouge o RH 54-55 J 5
Anshan o VRC 150-151 D 7
Anshi o IND 140-141 F 3
Anshun o VRC 156-157 D 3
Ansilta, Cerro de ▲ RA 76-77 C 6
Ansilta, Cordillera de ▲ RA 76-77 C 6
Ansina o ROU 76-77 K 6
Ansley o USA (NE) 262-263 G 3
Anson o USA (TX) 264-265 E 6
Anson Bay ≈ 172-173 J 2
Ansonga o RMM 202-203 L 2
Answer Downs o AUS 178-179 F 4
Anta o PE 64-65 F 8
Anta, Cachoeira da ~ BR 66-67 H 6
Antabamba o PE 64-65 F 9
Antakya = Hatay ☆ TR 128-129 G 4
Antalaha o RM 222-223 G 5
Antalya ☆ TR 128-129 D 4
Antalya Körfezi ≈ 128-129 D 4
Antanambao Manampotsy o RM 222-223 F 7
Antananarivo ◘ RM 222-223 D 7
Antananarivo ★ · RM (ATN) 222-223 E 7
Antandrokomby o RM 222-223 F 7
Antanifotsy o RM 222-223 E 7
Antanimora Atsimo o RM 222-223 D 10
Antanjombolamena o RM 222-223 E 7
An tAonach = Nenagh o IRL 90-91 C 5
Antar, Djebel ▲ DZ 188-189 L 4
Antarctica ⊥ ARK 16 F 28
Antarctic Bugt ≈ 26-27 s 3
Antarctic Circle ARK 16 G 3
Antarctic Peninsula ⌄ ARK 16 G 30
Antarctic Sound ≈ 16 G 31
Antares, Gunung ▲ RI 166-167 L 4
Antas o BR 68-69 J 7
Antécume Pata o F 62-63 G 4
Antelope o CDN (SAS) 232-233 K 5
Antelope o USA (OR) 244-245 E 6
Antelope Island ⌒ USA (UT) 254-255 C 3
Antelope Lake o CDN (SAS) 232-233 K 5
Antelope Mine o ZW 218-219 E 5
Antelope Summit ▲ USA (NV) 246-247 K 4
Antelope Valley Indian Museum · USA (CA) 248-249 G 5
Antenor Navarro o BR 68-69 J 5
Antequera o E 98-99 E 6
Antequera o PY 76-77 J 3
Antero Junction o USA (CO) 254-255 K 5
Antetezampandrana o RM 222-223 F 6
An Thới, Quần Đảo ⌒ VN 158-159 H 6
Anthony o USA (KS) 262-263 H 7
Anthony o USA (TX) 256-257 A 2
Anthony Island ⌒ ··· CDN (BC) 228-229 C 4
Anthony Lagoon o AUS 174-175 C 5
Anthropological Museum ·· RI 166-167 L 3
Anti Atlas ▲ MA 188-189 G 6
Anticosti, Île d' ⌒ CDN (QUE) 242-243 E 3
Antiga Lagoa da Rabeca o BR 70-71 H 4
Antigo o BR 72-73 J 7
Antigo o USA (WI) 270-271 J 5
Antigonish o CDN (NS) 240-241 N 5
Antigua o · MEX 52-53 F 2
Antigua, Salina la o RA 76-77 E 5
Antigua and Barbuda ■ AG 56 E 3
Antigua Guatemala ☆ ··· GCA 52-53 J 4
Antigua Island ⌒ AG 56 E 3
Antiguo Cauce del Río Bermejo ~ RA 76-77 F 2
Antiguo Morelos o MEX 50-51 K 6
Antilla o C 54-55 H 4
Antimari, Rio ~ BR 66-67 C 7
An Ti-m-Missaou < DZ 196-197 M 4
Antimonan o RP 160-161 D 6
Antimony o USA (UT) 254-255 D 5

Amidon — Antimony 297

Atmakur ○ IND (ANP) 140-141 H 3
Atmis ~ RUS 94-95 S 5
Atmore ○ CDN 32-33 O 4
Atmore ○ USA (AL) 284-285 C 5
Atna Peak ▲ CDN (BC) 228-229 F 3
Atna Range ▲ CDN 32-33 G 4
Atnarko ○ CDN (BC) 228-229 J 4
Atnbrua ○ N 86-87 E 6
Atocha ○ BOL 70-71 D 7
Atog ○ CAM 210-211 C 2
Atoka ○ USA (NM) 256-257 L 6
Atoka ○ USA (OK) 264-265 H 4
Atoka Lake < USA (OK) 264-265 H 4
Atome ○ ANG 216-217 C 5
Atomic City ○ USA (ID) 252-253 F 3
Atongo-Bakari ○ RCA 206-207 E 6
Atonyia < MA 188-189 G 7
Atori ○ SOL 184 I e 3
Atotonilco ○ MEX 52-53 E 2
Atotonilco el Alto ○ MEX 52-53 C 1
Atotonilco El Grande ○ MEX 52-53 E 1
Atouat, Mount ▲ LAO 158-159 J 3
Atoyac, Río ~ MEX 52-53 E 2
Atoyac, Río ~ MEX 52-53 F 3
Atoyac de Alvarez ○ MEX 52-53 D 3
Atoyatempan ○ MEX 52-53 F 2
Atpadi ○ IND 140-141 F 2
Atqasuk ○ USA 20-21 M 1
Atrai ~ BD 142-143 F 3
Atrak, Rūd-e ~ IR 136-137 E 6
Ätran ~ S 86-87 F 8
Atrato, Río ~ CO 60-61 C 4
Atrek ~ TM 136-137 D 6
Atsion ○ USA (NJ) 280-281 M 4
Atsumi-hantō ⌣ J 152-153 G 7
Atsuta ○ J 152-153 J 3
Atsy ○ RI 166-167 K 4
Atta ○ CAM 204-205 J 5
Attakro ○ CI 202-203 J 6
Attalla ○ USA (AL) 284-285 D 2
aț-Ṭamad ○ ET 194-195 G 3
At Tamimi ○ LAR 192-193 K 1
aț-Ṭanf, Ǧabal ▲ SYR 128-129 H 6
Attāni ○ IND 140-141 G 5
Attapu ○ LAO 158-159 J 3
Attar, Oued el ~ DZ 190-191 E 4
Attawapiskat ○ CDN 34-35 P 4
Attawapiskat Lake ○ CDN (ONT) 234-235 Q 2
Attawapiskat River ~ CDN 34-35 O 4
Attawapiskat River ~ CDN (ONT) 234-235 R 2
Attayampatti ○ IND 140-141 H 5
at-Ṭayyārah ○ SUD 200-201 E 6
Atteï, in < DZ 198-199 C 2
Atterbury Reserve Training Center xx USA (IN) 274-275 M 5
Attica ○ USA (IN) 274-275 L 4
Attica ○ USA (KS) 262-263 H 7
Attica ○ USA (NY) 278-279 C 6
Attica ○ USA (OH) 280-281 D 2
at-Tih, Ǧabal ▲ ET 194-195 F 3
at-Tih, Ṣaḥrā' ⊥ ET 194-195 F 2
Attikamagen Lake ○ CDN 36-37 Q 7
at-Ṭina, Ḫalīǧ ≈ 194-195 F 2
Attingal ○ IND 140-141 G 6
Attipāra ○ IND 140-141 G 6
Attleboro ○ USA (RI) 278-279 K 7
Attobrou, Yakass- ○ CI 202-203 J 6
Attock ○• PK 138-139 D 3
Attock-Campbellpore ○ PK 138-139 D 3
Attoko ○ J 152-153 L 3
Attoyac River ~ USA (TX) 268-269 F 5
Attu ○ GRØ 28-29 O 3
Attu ○ USA 22-23 C 6
Attu Island ⌒ USA 22-23 C 6
At Tullab ○ LAR 192-193 K 5
at-Tūr ☆ ET 194-195 F 3
Attur ○ IND 140-141 H 5
aț-Ṭuwayshah ○ SUD 200-201 C 6
Attwood Lake ○ CDN (ONT) 234-235 P 3
Attwood River ~ CDN (ONT) 234-235 P 3
Attykeveem ~ RUS 112-113 N 2
Atucatiquini, Río ~ BR 66-67 C 6
Atuel, Río ~ RA 78-79 E 3
Atuka ○ RI 166-167 J 4
Atuna ○ GH 202-203 J 6
Atuntaqui ○ EC 64-65 C 1
Atura ○ EAU 212-213 D 2
Atures ○ YV 60-61 H 5
Atutia, Río ~ RA 76-77 B 6
Åtvidaberg ☆ S 86-87 H 7
Atwa, al- ○ KSA 130-131 H 3
Atwater ○ CDN (SAS) 232-233 Q 5
Atwater ○ USA (CA) 248-249 D 2
Atwood ○ USA (CO) 254-255 M 3
Atwood ○ USA (IL) 274-275 K 5
Atwood ○ USA (KS) 262-263 E 5
Atwood Cay = Samana Cays ⌒ BS 54-55 J 3
Atykan, ostrov ⌒ RUS 120-121 Q 4
Atžaksy ~ KA 126-127 M 3
Atzinging Lake ○ CDN 30-31 S 5
Aû, Chutes de l' ~• ZRE 212-213 C 3
Aua River ~ CDN 24-25 e 7
Auasberge ▲ NAM 216-217 D 11
Auasbila ○ HN 52-53 B 4
Auasinaua, Cachoeira ~ BR 66-67 F 2
Auatu ▲ ETH 208-209 E 5
Auau Channel ≈ USA 288 J 4
Aubagne ○ F 90-91 K 10
Aube ~ F 90-91 K 8
Aúbe ○ MOC 218-219 K 3
Aubenas ○ F 90-91 K 9
Aubigny ○ CDN (MAN) 234-235 F 5
Aubigny-sur-Nère ○ F 90-91 J 8
Aubinadong River ~ CDN (ONT) 236-237 E 5
Aubrey Cliffs ▲ USA (AZ) 256-257 B 3
Aubry Lake ○ CDN 30-31 G 2
Auburn ○ AUS (QLD) 178-179 L 3
Auburn ○ AUS (SA) 180-181 E 3
Auburn ○ USA (AL) 284-285 E 4
Auburn ○ USA (CA) 246-247 D 5
Auburn ○ USA (IA) 274-275 D 2
Auburn ○ USA (IN) 274-275 N 3
Auburn ○ USA (ME) 278-279 L 4
Auburn ○ USA (NE) 262-263 L 4
Auburn ○ USA (NY) 278-279 E 6
Auburn ○ USA (WA) 244-245 C 3
Auburn ○ USA (WY) 252-253 H 4
Auburn Corners ○ USA (OH) 280-281 E 2
Auburndale ○ USA (FL) 286-287 H 3
Auburn Range ▲ AUS 178-179 L 3
Auburn River ~ AUS 178-179 L 3
Aubusson ○ F 90-91 J 9
Auca Mahuida, Sierra de ▲ RA 78-79 E 4
Auçan, Cerro ▲ RCH 76-77 C 1
Aucara ○ PE 64-65 E 9
Aucayacu ○ PE 64-65 D 6
Auch ☆• F 90-91 H 10
Auchi ○ WAN 204-205 G 5
Aucilla River ~ USA (FL) 286-287 F 1
Auckland ○ NZ 182 E 2
Auckland Bay ≈ 158-159 E 4
Auckland Island ⌒ NZ 13 H 8
Aude ~ F 90-91 J 10
Auden ○ CDN (ONT) 234-235 Q 4
Audhild Bay ≈ 26-27 E 3
Audierne ○ F 90-91 E 7
Audo Range ▲ ETH 208-209 E 5
Audru ○• EST 94-95 J 2
Audubon ○ USA (IA) 274-275 D 3
Aue ○ D 92-93 M 3
Augathella ○ AUS 178-179 J 3
Augrabies ○ ZA 220-221 E 4
Augrabies Falls ~•• ZA 220-221 E 4
Augrabies Falls National Park ⊥ ZA 220-221 E 4
Augsburg ○•• D 92-93 L 4
Aug Thong ○ THA 158-159 F 3
Augusta ○• AUS 176-177 C 7
Augusta ○ I 100-101 E 6
Augusta ○ USA (AR) 276-277 D 5
Augusta ○ USA (GA) 284-285 J 3
Augusta ○ USA (IL) 274-275 H 4
Augusta ○ USA (KS) 262-263 K 7
Augusta ○ USA (MT) 250-251 G 4
Augusta ○ USA (OH) 280-281 B 5
Augusta ○ USA (WI) 270-271 G 6
Augusta ☆ USA (ME) 278-279 M 4
Augusta, Cabo ▲ CO 60-61 D 2
Augusta, Mount ▲ CDN 20-21 U 6
Augustina Libarona ○ RA 76-77 F 4
Augustin Codazzi ○ CO 60-61 E 2
Augustine Island ⌒ USA 22-23 U 3
Augusto Montenegro ○ BR 66-67 J 4
Augusto Severo ○ BR 68-69 K 4
Augustów ○ PL 92-93 R 2
Augustus, Mount ▲ AUS 176-177 D 2
Augustus Downs ○ AUS 174-175 E 6
Augustus Island ⌒ AUS 172-173 G 3
Augustus Island ⌒ CDN 36-37 Q 3
Auiita, Rio ~ BR 72-73 D 2
Auke Bay ○ USA 32-33 C 2
Auki = Aoke ☆ SOL 184 I e 3
Aukpar River ~ CDN 36-37 N 2
Aulād Ṭauq Šarq ○ ET 194-195 F 4
Aulander ○ USA (NC) 282-283 K 4
Auld, Lake ○ AUS 172-173 F 7
Auliräipāra ○ IND 142-143 G 4
Aulitivik Island ⌒ CDN 28-29 G 2
Auliyā Dam < SUD 200-201 F 5
Aulneau Peninsula ⌒ CDN (ONT) 234-235 J 5
Aul Sarykobda ○ KA 126-127 M 3
Ault ○ USA (CO) 254-255 L 3
Aumo ○ PNG 183 E 3
Auna ○ WAN 204-205 F 3
Aundah ○ IND 138-139 F 10
Auno ○ WAN 204-205 K 3
Auob ~ NAM 220-221 D 2
Aupwel ○ PNG 183 D 3
Aur, Pulau ⌒ MAL (KED) 162-163 F 3
Aura ○ USA (MI) 270-271 K 4
Aurahua ○ PE 64-65 E 8
Auram ~ NAM 220-221 C 3
Aurangabad ○ IND 142-143 D 3
Aurangābād ○• IND 138-139 E 10
Auras ○ C 54-55 G 4
Auray ○ F 90-91 F 8
Aurbunak, Gunung ▲ RI 164-165 D 5
Aure ☆ N 86-87 D 5
Aure River ~ PNG 183 C 4
Aures, Massif de l' ▲ DZ 190-191 F 3
Aure Scarp ▲ PNG 183 C 4
Auri, utes • RUS 122-123 J 2
Aurich (Ostfriesland) ○ D 92-93 J 2
Auriflama ○ BR 72-73 E 6
Aurillac ☆ F 90-91 J 9
Auriya ○ IND 138-139 G 6
Aurlandsvangen ○ N 86-87 C 6
Auro ○ PNG 183 E 5
Aurora ○ BR (CEA) 68-69 J 5
Aurora ○ BR (GSU) 70-71 K 6
Aurora ○ CDN (ONT) 238-239 F 5
Aurora ○ CDN (ONT) 238-239 F 4
Aurora ○ GUY 62-63 E 2
Aurora ○ RP (ISA) 160-161 D 4
Aurora ○ RP (ZAS) 160-161 E 9
Aurora ○ USA (AK) 20-21 H 4
Aurora ○ USA (CO) 254-255 L 4
Aurora ○ USA (IL) 274-275 K 3
Aurora ○ USA (KY) 276-277 G 4
Aurora ○ USA (ME) 278-279 N 4
Aurora ○ USA (MO) 276-277 B 4
Aurora ○ USA (NE) 262-263 H 4
Aurora ○ USA (NY) 278-279 E 6
Aurora, Île = Maewo ⌒ VAN 184 II b 2
Aurora, La ○ RA 76-77 E 4
Aurora do Tocantins ○ BR 72-73 G 2
Auroraville ○ USA (WI) 270-271 K 6
Aurukun X AUS 174-175 G 3
Aurukun Aboriginal Land X AUS 174-175 F 3
Aus ○ NAM 220-221 C 3
Ausa ○ IND 138-139 F 10
Au Sable River ~ USA (MI) 272-273 F 3
Auschwitz = Oświęcim ○••• PL 92-93 P 3
Ausentes ○ BR 74-75 E 7
Ausis < NAM 216-217 B 9
Aussig = Ústí nad Labem ○ CZ 92-93 N 3
Austerlitz = Slavkov u Brna ○ CZ 92-93 O 4
Austfonna ⊂ N 84-85 N 3
Austin ○ CDN (MAN) 234-235 E 5
Austin ○ USA (MN) 270-271 F 7
Austin ○ USA (NV) 246-247 H 4
Austin ○ USA (OR) 244-245 G 6
Austin ☆ USA (TX) 266-267 K 3
Austin, Lake ○ AUS 176-177 E 3
Austin, Point ▲ AUS 174-175 F 5
Austin Channel ≈ 24-25 U 3
Austin Island ⌒ CDN 30-31 X 5
Austral Downs ○ AUS 174-175 D 7
Austral Fracture Zone ≃ 14-15 Q 9
Australia ■ AUS 180-181 K 3
Australia ⊥ AUS 13 D 5
Australian-Antarctic Basin ≃ 12 G 10
Australian-Antarctic Discordance ≃ 13 C 7
Australian Capital Territory ■ AUS 180-181 K 3
Australind ○ AUS 176-177 C 6
Austria = Österreich ■ A 92-93 M 5
Austvågøy ⌒ N 86-87 G 2
Austwell ○ USA (TX) 266-267 L 5
Autás-Mirim, Rio ~ BR 66-67 G 5
Autaz, Ilha ⌒ BR 66-67 H 4
Autazes ○ BR 66-67 H 4
Autaz Mirim, Paraná ~ BR 66-67 H 4
Autec ∴• BS 54-55 G 2
Authier-Nord ○ CDN (QUE) 236-237 K 4
Autlán de Navarro ○ MEX 52-53 B 2
Autridge Bay ≈ 24-25 d 5
Autun ○• F 90-91 K 8
Auvergne ○ AUS 172-173 J 3
Auvergne ■ F 90-91 J 9
Aux Barques, Pointe ▲ USA (MI) 272-273 G 3
Auxerre ☆• F 90-91 J 8
Auxiliadora ○ BR 66-67 G 6
Auyan Tebuy ▲ YV 60-61 K 5
Auyuittuq National Park ⊥ CDN 28-29 G 3
Ava ○ MYA 142-143 J 5
Ava ○ USA (IL) 276-277 F 3
Ava ○ USA (MO) 276-277 C 4
Ava ○ USA (MS) 268-269 L 3
Avača ~ RUS 120-121 S 7
Avá-Canoeiro, Área Indígena X BR 72-73 F 2
Avačinskaja, guba ○ RUS 120-121 S 7
Avačinskij zaliv ≈ 120-121 S 7
Avadh ⊥ IND 142-143 B 2
Avadi ○ IND 140-141 J 4
Avakubi ○ ZRE 210-211 L 3
Avalik River ~ USA 20-21 L 1
Avaljak hrebet ▲ RUS 96-97 L 6
Avallon ○ F 90-91 J 8
Avalon ○ USA (CA) 248-249 F 6
Avalon ○ USA (TX) 264-265 H 6
Avalon Peninsula ⌣ CDN (NFL) 242-243 P 5
Avalon Reservoir ⌣ USA (NM) 256-257 L 6
Avalos, Arroyo ~ RA 76-77 H 5
Avanavero ○ SME 62-63 F 3
Avannaarsua = Nordgrønland ■ GRØ 26-27 V 4
Avard ○ USA (OK) 264-265 F 2
Avare ○ BR 72-73 F 7
Avarskoe Kojsu ~ RUS 126-127 G 6
Avatanak Island ⌒ USA 22-23 O 5
Avatanak Strait ≈ 22-23 O 5
Āvāz ○ IR 134-135 J 2
Ave, Rio ~ P 98-99 C 4
Ave-Dakpa ○ GH 202-203 L 6
Āveğ ○ IR 128-129 N 5
Āveğ, Gardāne-ye ▲ IR 128-129 N 5
Aveiro ○ BR 66-67 K 4
Aveiro ☆• P 98-99 C 4
Avekova ~ RUS 112-113 L 5
Avelino Lopes ○ BR 68-69 G 7
Avella ○ USA (PA) 280-281 F 3
Avellaneda ○ RA 78-79 K 3
Avellino ☆ I 100-101 E 4
Avenal ○ USA (CA) 248-249 D 3
Avenue of the Giants • USA (CA) 246-247 B 3
Avery ○ USA (ID) 250-251 D 4
Avery ○ USA (TX) 264-265 K 5
Aves, Isla de ⌒ YV 56 D 4
Aves, Islas de ⌒ YV 60-61 H 1
Aves de Barlovente ⌒ YV 60-61 H 2
Aves Ridge ≃ 56 D 5
Aveyron ~ F 90-91 J 9
Avezzano ○ I 100-101 D 3
Avia Teray ~ RA 76-77 G 4
Avignon ○•• F 90-91 K 10
Ávila de los Caballeros ○••• E 98-99 E 4
Avilés ○•• E 98-99 E 3
Avilla ○ USA (IN) 274-275 N 3
Avilla, Parque Nacional ⊥ YV 60-61 H 2
Avinurme ○ EST 94-95 K 2
Avirons, Les ○ F 224 B 7
Avis ○ P 98-99 D 5
Avispa, Cerro ▲ YV 66-67 E 2
Avissawella ○ CL 140-141 J 7
Avlandja, Bol'šaja ~ RUS 112-113 L 5
Avoca ○ AUS (TAS) 180-181 J 6
Avoca ○ AUS (VIC) 180-181 G 4
Avoca ○ USA (TX) 264-265 E 6
Avoca River ~ AUS 180-181 G 4
Avola ○ CDN (BC) 230-231 K 2
Avon ○ USA (MT) 250-251 G 5
Avon ○ USA (NC) 282-283 M 5
Avon ○ USA (SD) 260-261 H 3
Avon, Lake < AUS 180-181 L 3
Avondale ○ USA (AZ) 256-257 C 5
Avon Downs ○ AUS (NT) 174-175 D 7
Avon Downs ○ AUS (QLD) 178-179 J 1
Avonia ○ USA (PA) 280-281 F 1
Avon Park ○ USA (FL) 286-287 H 4
Avon Park Air Force Range xx USA (FL) 286-287 H 4
Avon River ~ AUS 176-177 D 6
Avontuur ○ ZA 220-221 F 6
Avranches ○ F 90-91 G 7
Avstrijskij proliv ≈ 84-85 f 2
Avu Avu = Kolotambu ○ SOL 184 I e 3
'Awābi ○ OM 132-133 K 2
Awaé ○ CAM 210-211 C 2
Awagakama River ~ CDN (ONT) 236-237 E 2
Awa Gurupi, Área Indígena X BR 68-69 E 3
Awai, Pulau ⌒ RI 166-167 J 2
Awaji-shima ⌒ J 152-153 F 7
Awakaba ○ RCA 206-207 E 4
'Awālī ○ BRN 134-135 D 5
Awang ○ RI 168 C 7
Awanui ○ NZ 182 D 1
Awar ○ PNG 183 C 3
Awara Plain ⊥ EAK 212-213 H 2
Awara soela ~ SME 62-63 G 4
Awaré ○ ETH 208-209 H 4
Awarua Point ▲ NZ 182 B 6
Āwasa ☆ ETH 208-209 D 5
Āwasa Hāyk' ○ ETH 208-209 D 5
Awashima ⌒ J 152-153 H 5
Āwash National Park ⊥ ETH 208-209 D 4
Āwash Reserve ⊥ ETH 208-209 D 4
Āwash Wenz ~ ETH 208-209 E 3
Awat ○ VRC 146-147 E 5
Āwat'a Shet' ~ ETH 208-209 D 6
Awatere River ~ NZ 182 D 4
Awbārī ○ LAR 190-191 H 7
Awbārī ☆ LAR 192-193 E 4
Awdheegle ○ SP 212-213 K 3
Awdiinle ○ SP 212-213 J 2
Awe ○ WAN 204-205 H 4
Aweil ○ SUD 206-207 H 4
Awendaw ○ USA (SC) 284-285 L 3
Awgu ○ WAN 204-205 G 5
Awio ○ PNG 183 F 4
Awio River ~ PNG 183 F 4
Āwira Wenz ~ ETH 200-201 K 6
Awisam ○ GH 202-203 K 7
Awisang ○ RI 164-165 F 4
Awjilah ○ LAR 192-193 J 3
Awka ○ WAN 204-205 G 5
Awrā, Wādī al ~ LAR 192-193 G 3
Awu, Gunung ▲ RI 164-165 J 2
Awun, River ~ WAN 204-205 F 4
Awuna River ~ USA 20-21 M 2
Awungi ○ PNG 183 F 3
Awyat, Tanjung ▲ RI 166-167 H 4
Awwal, Wādī ~ LAR 190-191 H 6
Axe Hill ▲ AUS 176-177 J 3
Axel Heiberg Island ⌒ CDN 26-27 C 3
Axim ○ GH 202-203 J 7
Axinim ○ BR 66-67 H 5
Axtell ○ USA (NE) 262-263 G 4
Axtell ○ USA (UT) 254-255 D 4
Axton ○ USA (VA) 280-281 G 7
Axui ○ BR 68-69 G 3
Ayabaca ○ PE 64-65 C 4
Ayachi, Ibel ▲ MA 188-189 J 4
Ayacucho ☆ PE 64-65 E 8
Ayacucho ○ RA 78-79 K 4
Ayakkum Hu ○ VRC 144-145 G 2
Ayamé ○ CI 202-203 J 7
Ayami, Tanjung ▲ RI 166-167 H 3
Ayamiken ○ GQ 210-211 C 2
Ayamonte ○• E 98-99 D 6
Ayancık ☆ TR 128-129 F 2
Ayanfuri ○ GH 202-203 K 7
Ayangba ○ WAN 204-205 G 5
Ayapata ○ PE 70-71 B 3
Ayapel ○ CO 60-61 D 3
Ayapel, Serranía de ▲ CO 60-61 D 4
Ayapunga, Cerro ▲ EC 64-65 C 3
Ayarde, Laguna ○ RA 76-77 G 3
Ayas ○ TR 128-129 E 2
Ayaviri ○ PE (LIM) 64-65 D 8
Ayaviri ○ PE (PUN) 70-71 B 4
Ayden ○ USA (NC) 282-283 K 5
Aydın ☆ TR 128-129 B 4
Aydın Dağları ▲ TR 128-129 B 4
Aydingkol Hu ○ VRC 146-147 J 4
Ayer ○ USA (MA) 278-279 K 6
Ayerbe ○ E 98-99 G 3
Ayer Deras, Kampung Sungai ○ MAL 162-163 E 2
Ayer Hitam ○• MAL 162-163 E 4
Ayer Puteh, Kampung ○ MAL 162-163 E 2
Ayers Rock ▲•• AUS 176-177 L 2
Ayilūr ○ IND 140-141 H 5
Ayina ~ G 210-211 D 2
Ayinwafe ○ GH 202-203 K 6
Ayiyak River ~ USA 20-21 O 2
Aykel ○ ETH 200-201 H 6
Aylesbury ○ GB 90-91 G 6
Āylet ○ ER 200-201 J 5
Ayllón ○ E 98-99 F 4
Aylmer ○ CDN (ONT) 238-239 E 6
Aylmer, Lac ○ CDN (QUE) 238-239 O 3
Aylmer Lake ○ CDN 30-31 P 3
Aylsham ○ CDN (SAS) 232-233 P 2
Aymat ○• ER 200-201 J 4
Ayn al Ghazalah ○ LAR 192-193 K 1
Aynor ○ USA (SC) 284-285 L 3
Ayo ○ PE 64-65 F 9
Ayod ○ SUD 206-207 K 4
Ayoni ○ SUD 206-207 H 4
Ayopaya, Río ~ BOL 70-71 D 5
Ayorou ○ RN 202-203 L 2
Ayos ○ CAM 210-211 D 2
'Ayoûn el 'Atroûs ☆ RIM 196-197 F 6
Ayr ○ AUS 174-175 J 6
Ayr ○• GB 90-91 E 4
Ayr Lake ○ CDN 26-27 Q 8
Ayrshire ○ USA (IA) 274-275 D 1
Aysha ○ ETH 208-209 F 3
Ayu, Kepulanan ⌒ RI 166-167 F 1
Ayu, Pulau ⌒ RI 166-167 F 1
Ayu, Tanjung ▲ RI 164-165 E 4
Ayungon ○ RP 160-161 E 8
Ayutla ○ MEX 52-53 B 1
Ayutla de los Libres ○ MEX 52-53 E 3
Ayuy ○ EC 64-65 D 3
Ayvacık ☆ TR 128-129 G 2
Ayvacık ☆ TR 128-129 B 3
Ayvalık ☆ TR 128-129 B 3
Ayyampettai ○ IND 140-141 H 5
Azabač'e, ozero ○ RUS 120-121 T 5
Azad Kashmir ⊥ IND 138-139 D 3
Āzād Šar ○ IR 136-137 D 6
Azahar, Costa del ▲ E 98-99 H 5
Azaila ○ E 98-99 G 4
Azalea ○ USA (OR) 244-245 B 8
Āzamgarh ○ IND 142-143 C 2
Azanaques, Cerro ▲ BOL 70-71 D 6
Azanaques, Cordillera de ▲ BOL 70-71 D 6
Azangaro ○ PE 70-71 B 4
Azao ▲ DZ 190-191 G 8
Azaouak, Vallée de l' ⊥ RMM 196-197 M 6
Azara ○ RA 76-77 K 5
Āzarbāyǧān-e Ġarbi ■ IR 128-129 L 3
Āzarbāyǧān-e Šarqi ■ IR 128-129 M 4
Azare ○ WAN 204-205 J 3
Āzaršahr ○ IR 128-129 L 4
Azas ~ RUS 116-117 H 9
Azas, ozero = Todža, ozero ○ RUS 116-117 H 9
Azauri ○ BR 62-63 G 5
Azaz ▲ DZ 190-191 D 7
A'zāz ☆ SYR 128-129 G 4
Azazga ○ DZ 190-191 E 2
Azbine, Aïr ou ⊥• RN 198-199 D 3
Až Bogd ▲ MAU 146-147 M 3
Azeffāl ⊥ RIM 196-197 C 5
Azemmour ○ MA 188-189 G 4
Azendjé ○ G 210-211 B 4
Azennezal, Erg ⊥ DZ 190-191 C 9
Azerbaijan = Azerbajdžan ■ AZ 128-129 M 2
Azero, Río ~ BOL 70-71 F 6
Azevedo Sodré ○ BR 76-77 K 6
Āzezo ○ ETH 200-201 H 6
Azgale ○ IR 134-135 A 1
Azilal ☆ MA 188-189 H 5
Azingo ○ G 210-211 B 4
Azingo, Lac ○ G 210-211 B 4
Azirir ○ DZ 190-191 D 7
Aziz < TCH 198-199 H 4
'Azīzīya, al- ○ IRQ 128-129 L 6
'Azīzīyah, Al ○ LAR 192-193 E 1
'Azīzīyah, Al ☆ LAR 192-193 E 1
Azlam, Wādī ~ KSA 130-131 E 4
Azle ○ USA (TX) 264-265 G 6
Azná ○ IR 134-135 C 2
Aznakaevo ☆ RUS 96-97 H 6
Azogues ☆ EC 64-65 C 3
Azoren ⌒ P 6-7 E 6
Azores = Açores, Archipélago dos ⌒ P 188-189 C 4
Azores-Biscaya Rise ≃ 6-7 G 4
Azores-Cape Saint Vincent Ridge ≃ 188-189 D 2
Azoum, Bahr ~ TCH 206-207 E 3
Azourki, Ibel ▲ MA 188-189 H 5
Azov ○• RUS 102-103 L 4
Azov, Sea of = Azovskoe more ≈ RUS 102-103 J 4
Azovskoe More ≈ 102-103 J 4
Azovy ○ RUS 114-115 H 2
Azpeitia ○ E 98-99 F 3
Azrak, Bahr ~ TCH 206-207 E 3
Azraq, al- ○ JOR 130-131 E 2
Azre ○ AFG 138-139 B 2
Azrou ○ MA 188-189 J 4
Azrou, Oued ~ DZ 190-191 F 9
Aztec ○ USA (AZ) 256-257 B 6
Aztec ○ USA (NM) 256-257 H 2
Aztecas, Los ○ MEX 50-51 K 6
Aztec Ruins National Monument ∴ USA (NM) 256-257 H 2
Azua ☆ DOM 54-55 K 5
Azuaga ○• E 98-99 E 5
Azúcar ○ EC 64-65 B 3
Azuer, Río ~ E 98-99 F 5
Azuero, Península de ⌣ PA 52-53 D 8
Azufral, Volcán ▲ CO 64-65 D 1
Azufre, Paso del ▲ RA 76-77 C 3
Azufre ó Copiapo, Cerro ▲ RCH 76-77 C 4
Azul ▲ MEX 50-51 J 4
Azul ○ RA 78-79 K 4
Azul, Arroyo del ~ RA 78-79 K 4
Azul, Cerro ▲ CR 52-53 B 7
Azul, Cerro ▲ EC 64-65 B 10
Azul, Cerro ▲ RA 78-79 D 6
Azul, Río ~ BR 64-65 F 5
Azul, Río ~ MEX 52-53 E 3
Azul, Río ~ MEX 52-53 K 3
Azul, Serra ▲ BR 70-71 K 4
Azul Meambar, Parque Nacional ⊥ HN 52-53 L 4
Azūm, Wādī ~ SUD 198-199 L 6
Azuma-san ▲ J 152-153 J 6
Azurduy ○ BOL 70-71 E 6
Azure Lake ○ CDN (BC) 228-229 O 4
Azwell ○ USA (WA) 244-245 F 3
Azzaba ○ DZ 190-191 F 2
az-Zāb al-Kabīr, Nahr ~ IRQ 128-129 K 5
az-Zāb aṣ-Ṣaġīr, Nahr ~ IRQ 128-129 L 5
az-Zāhirah ○ KSA 134-135 D 5
Azzaouager, Adrar ▲ RN 198-199 D 4
az-Zaqāzīq ☆ ET 194-195 E 2
az-Zaraf, Bahr ~ SUD 206-207 K 4
az-Zarqā' ⌒ UAE 134-135 E 6
az-Zāwiyah ■ LAR 192-193 E 1
az-Zāwiyah ☆ LAR 192-193 E 1
Azzel Matti, Sebkha ○ DZ 190-191 C 7
Az Zimām, Wādī ~ LAR 192-193 F 3
Az Zintān ○ LAR 192-193 E 2
az-Zūmah ○ SUD 200-201 E 3

B

Ba ○ FJI 184 III a 2
Baa ○• RI 166-167 B 7
Ba'āǧ, al- ○ IRQ 128-129 J 4
Ba'ā'iṭ, al- ○ KSA 130-131 G 4
Baantama ○ GH 202-203 K 6
Baardheere ○ SP 212-213 J 2
Bāb, al- ☆ SYR 128-129 G 4
Baba ○ EC 64-65 C 2
Baba ~ RCA 206-207 C 6
Bābā, Kūh-e ▲ AFG 134-135 M 1
Bababé ○ RIM 196-197 D 6
Baba Burnu ▲ TR 128-129 B 3
Babacu ○ BR 68-69 F 5
Babaçulândia ○ BR 68-69 E 5
Babadag ○• RO 102-103 F 5
Babadag, gora ▲ AZ 128-129 N 2
Babadayhan ○ TM 136-137 G 6
Babaera ○ ANG 216-217 C 6
Babaeski ☆ TR 128-129 B 2
Babaevo ○ RUS 94-95 O 2
Bābā Gurgur ○ IRQ 128-129 L 5
Babahoyo ☆ EC 64-65 C 2
Babai ~ NEP 144-145 C 6
Babajurt ○ RUS 126-127 G 6
Babalegi ○ ZA 220-221 J 2
Bāb al-Mandab ≈ 132-133 C 7
Bāb al-Mandab, Ra's ▲ Y 132-133 C 7
Bābā Monir ○ IR 134-135 D 3
Babana ○ RI 164-165 F 5
Babana ○ WAN 204-205 E 3
Baban Rafi ○ WAN 204-205 G 4
Babanty, gory ▲ RUS 118-119 F 8
Babanūsa ○ SUD 206-207 H 3
Babao ○ VRC 156-157 D 5
Babaomby, Tanjona ▲ RM 222-223 F 3
Babar, Kepulauan ⌒ RI 166-167 E 5
Babar, Pulau ⌒ RI 166-167 E 5
Babasa Island ⌒ PNG 183 G 3
Babat ○ RI (JTI) 168 E 3
Babat ○ RI (SUS) 162-163 F 6
Babat ○ RI (SUS) 162-163 E 6
Babatag, hrebet ▲ US 136-137 K 6
Babati ○ EAT 212-213 E 6
Babau ○ RI 166-167 B 7
Bābā Yādegār ○ IR 128-129 L 4
Babb ○ USA (MT) 250-251 F 3
Babbage River ~ CDN 20-21 V 2
Bab-Besen ▲ MA 188-189 J 3
Babbitt ○ USA (MN) 270-271 G 3
Babbitt ○ USA (NV) 246-247 G 5
Babcock ○ USA (FL) 286-287 H 5
B'abdā ☆ RL 128-129 F 6
Bab'e, ozero ○ RUS 88-89 P 3
Bāb-e Anār ○ IR 134-135 E 4
Babel, Mont de ▲ CDN 38-39 K 3
Băbeni ○ RO 102-103 D 5
Baberu ○ IND 142-143 B 3
Babetville ○ RM 222-223 E 7
Babi, Pulau ⌒ RI 162-163 B 3
Babia, La ○ MEX 50-51 H 3
Bābil ■ IRQ 128-129 L 6
Bābil (Babylon) ∴•• IRQ 128-129 L 6
Babilé ○ ETH 208-209 F 4
Babina ○ IND 138-139 G 7
Babinda ○ AUS 174-175 J 5
Babine Lake ○ CDN (BC) 228-229 J 2
Babine Mountains Provincial Recreation Area ⊥ CDN (BC) 228-229 G 2
Babine Range ▲ CDN 32-33 G 4
Babine River ~ CDN 32-33 G 4
Babo ○ RI 166-167 G 3
Bābol ○• IR 136-137 C 6
Bābolsar ○• IR 136-137 C 6
Babonde ○ ZRE 212-213 A 2
Babongo ○ CAM 206-207 B 5
Baboquivari Peak ▲ USA (AZ) 256-257 D 7
Babor, Djebel ▲ DZ 190-191 E 2
Baboua ○ RCA 206-207 B 6
Bābra ○ IND 138-139 C 9
Babrongan Tower ▲ AUS 172-173 F 5
Babrujsk ☆ BY 94-95 L 5
Babruysk = Babrujsk ☆ BY 94-95 L 5
Babtai ○ LT 94-95 H 4
Bab-Taza ○ MA 188-189 J 3
Babura ○ WAN 198-199 D 6
Bābusar Pass ▲ PK 138-139 E 2
Babuškin ○ RUS 116-117 N 10
Babuškina, mys ▲ RUS 120-121 Q 4
Babuškina, zaliv ○ RUS 120-121 P 4
Babuyan Channel ≈ 160-161 D 3
Babuyan Island ⌒ RP 160-161 D 3
Babuyan Islands ⌒ RP 160-161 D 3
Baca ⌒ ER 200-201 K 5
Bacaadweyn ○ SP 208-209 H 5
Bacabal ○ BR (AMA) 66-67 F 3
Bacabal ○ BR (MAR) 68-69 F 4
Bacabal ○ BR (MAR) 68-69 E 3
Bacabal ○ BR (ROR) 62-63 D 5
Bacabalzinho ○ BR 70-71 F 3
Bacada ○ BR 66-67 E 6
Bacaja, Área Indígena X BR 68-69 C 4
Bacaja, Rio ~ BR 68-69 C 3
Bacajagua ○ C 54-55 H 5
Bacalar ○ MEX 52-53 K 2
Bacan, Kepulauan ⌒ RI 164-165 K 4
Bacan, Pulau ⌒ RI 164-165 K 4
Bacanora ○ MEX 50-51 E 3
Bacarruca ○ BR 66-67 E 3
Bacateiro ○ BR 68-69 F 5
Bacău ☆• RO 102-103 E 4
Bắc Bình ○ VN 158-159 K 5
Baccaro ○ CDN (NS) 240-241 K 7
Bacchus Marsh ○ AUS 180-181 H 4
Bacerac ○ MEX 50-51 E 2
Bắc Giang ☆ VN 156-157 E 6
Bắc Hà ☆ VN 156-157 D 5
Bachalo ○ WAL 202-203 D 6
Bachaquero ○ YV 60-61 F 3
Bachčysaraj ☆• UA 102-103 H 5
Bache Peninsula ⌣ CDN 26-27 M 4
Bachhrāwān ○ IND 142-143 B 2
Bachimba ○ MEX 50-51 G 3
Bachiniva ○ MEX 50-51 F 3
Bachmač ○ UA 102-103 H 2
Bạch Thông ○ VN 156-157 D 5
Bachu ○ VRC 146-147 D 6
Bachuo Akakbe ○ CAM 204-205 H 6
Bačka Palanka ○ YU 100-101 G 2
Bačka Topola ○ YU 100-101 G 2
Back Bay ○ USA 280-281 L 7
Back Bay National Wildlife Refuge ⊥ USA (VA) 280-281 L 7
Backbone Mountain ▲ USA (MD) 280-281 G 4
Backbone Ranges ▲ CDN 30-31 E 4
Bäckefors ○ S 86-87 F 7
Bäckhammar ○ S 86-87 G 7
Back River ~ CDN 30-31 S 3
Backstairs Passage ≈ 180-181 D 3
Bắc Lạc ○ VN 156-157 D 5
Bắc Mê ☆ VN 156-157 D 5
Bắc Ngư'ờn ○ VN 156-157 D 5
Bắc Ninh ☆ VN 156-157 E 6
Baco, Mount ▲ RP 160-161 D 6
Bacobampo ○ MEX 50-51 E 4
Bacolod ☆ RP 160-161 E 7
Baconton ○ USA (GA) 284-285 F 5
Bắc Quang ○ VN 156-157 D 5
Bacqueville, Lac ○ CDN 36-37 M 5
Bactili ○ SP 212-213 H 3
Bacuag ○ RP 160-161 F 8
Bacungan ○ RP 160-161 C 8
Bacuri ○ BR 68-69 F 2
Bacuri, Cachoeira ~ BR 62-63 H 6
Bacuri, Ilha do ⌒ BR 68-69 D 3
Bacuri, Lago de ○ BR 68-69 G 3
Bād ○ IR 134-135 D 2
Bad', al- ○ KSA 130-131 D 3
Bada ▲ ETH 208-209 D 5
Badā ○ KSA 130-131 E 4
Bada ○ RUS 118-119 D 10
Bada Barabil ○ IND 142-143 D 4
Badagangshan Z.B. ⊥• VRC 156-157 F 2
Badagara ○ IND 140-141 F 5
Badago ○ RMM 202-203 F 4
Badagri ○ WAN 204-205 E 5
Badahšān ■ AFG 136-137 M 6
Badā'i', al- ○ KSA 130-131 H 4
Badain Jaran Shamo ⊥ VRC 148-149 E 7
Badajós ○ BR 66-67 F 4
Badajós, Lago ○ BR 66-67 F 4
Badajoz ○•• E 98-99 D 5
Badalia ○ AUS 178-179 E 2
Badaling • VRC 154-155 J 1
Badam ~ KA 136-137 L 3
Badanga ○ TCH 206-207 C 3
Badas, Kepulauau ⌒ RI 162-163 G 4
Badau ○ RI 162-163 G 6
Bada Valley ∴• RI 164-165 G 4
Bad Axe ○ USA (MI) 272-273 G 4
Badda Rogghie ▲ ETH 208-209 C 4
Baddeck ○ CDN (NS) 240-241 P 4
Baddo ~ PK 134-135 L 4
Bad Dürrheim ○ D 92-93 K 4
Badeggi ○ WAN 204-205 G 4
Badéguicheri ○ RN 198-199 B 5
Baden ○ A 92-93 O 5
Baden ○ CDN (MAN) 234-235 B 2
Baden ○ CH 92-93 K 5
Badena ~ SP 212-213 H 4
Baden-Baden ○• D 92-93 K 4
Baden-Württemberg ■ D 92-93 K 4
Bādepalli ○ IND 140-141 H 2
Badér ○ RN 198-199 C 5
Badgastein ○• A 92-93 M 5
Badger ○ CDN (MAN) 234-235 H 5
Badger ○ CDN (NFL) 242-243 M 4
Badger ○ USA (MN) 270-271 B 2
Badgingarra ○ AUS 176-177 C 5
Badgingarra National Park ⊥ AUS 176-177 C 5
Bādgīs ■ AFG 136-137 H 7
Badgūl ○ AFG 136-137 J 7
Bad Hersfeld ○ D 92-93 K 3
Bad Hills ▲ CDN (SAS) 232-233 K 4
Badhyzskij zapovednik ⊥ TM 136-137 G 7
Bādi, al- ○ IRQ 128-129 J 5
Badī', al- ○ KSA 130-131 K 6
Badī'a, al- ○ KSA 132-133 D 5
Badiara ~ SN 202-203 D 2
Badikaha ○ CI 202-203 H 5
Badime ○ ETH 200-201 H 5
Badin ○ PK 138-139 B 7
Badinko ○ RMM 202-203 F 3
Badinko, Reserve du ⊥ RMM 202-203 F 3
Badin Lake < USA (NC) 282-283 G 5
Badinn-Ko ~ RMM 202-203 F 3
Badir ○ WAN 204-205 K 3
Bad Ischl ○• A 92-93 M 5
Bādiyat Bani Kabir ○ KSA 132-133 B 3
Badjariha ~ RUS 110-111 Z 6
Badjer ○ CAM 204-205 K 5
Bad Kissingen ○ D 92-93 L 3
Bad Kreuznach ○ D 92-93 J 4
Badlands ⊥ USA (ND) 258-259 D 5
Badlands ⊥ USA (SD) 260-261 D 3
Badlands National Park ⊥ USA (SD) 260-261 D 3
Badnāwar ○ IND 138-139 E 8
Badnera ○ IND 138-139 F 9
Bad Neuenahr-Ahrweiler ○• D 92-93 J 3
Bado ○ RI 166-167 K 5
Badoc ○ RP 160-161 D 4
Ba Đồng ○ VN 158-159 J 6
Badong ○ VRC 154-155 G 6
Badou ○ RT 202-203 L 6
Badoumbé ○ RMM 202-203 E 3
Badplaas ○ ZA 220-221 K 2
Badra ☆ IRQ 128-129 L 6
Bādra ~ PK 134-135 M 4
Bad Radkersburg ○ A 92-93 N 5
Bādrah ○ PK 138-139 B 6
Badrānlū ○ IR 136-137 E 6
Bad Rapids ~ CDN 32-33 N 3
Bad Reichenhall ○ D 92-93 M 5
Badrinath ○ IND 138-139 G 4
Bad River ~ USA (SD) 260-261 E 2
Bad River Indian Reservation X USA (WI) 270-271 H 4
Badr wa-Hunain ○ KSA 130-131 F 6
Bad Segeberg ○• D 92-93 L 2
Bad Tölz ○ D 92-93 L 5
Badu ○ VRC 156-157 J 3
Badu Island ⌒ AUS 174-175 G 2
Badulla ○ CL 140-141 J 7
Badvel ○ IND 140-141 H 3
Badwater River ~ CDN 30-31 R 6
Badžal ~ RUS 122-123 F 3
Badžal'skij hrebet ▲ RUS 122-123 E 3
Badzéré ○ CAM 206-207 B 6
Baēdiam ○ RIM 202-203 E 2
Baer ○ VRC 144-145 B 4
Baerskin Lake ○ CDN 34-35 L 4
Baeza ○ E 98-99 F 6
Baeza ○ EC 64-65 D 2

300 Atmakur — Baeza

Baezaeko River ~ CDN (BC) 228-229 K 4
Bafang o CAM 204-205 J 6
Bafata ☆ GNB 202-203 C 3
Baffin Basin ≃ 26-27 R 7
Baffin Bay ≈ 26-27 P 7
Baffin Bay ≈ 44-45 J 6
Baffin Bay ≈ USA 266-267 K 6
Baffin-Greenland Rise ≃ 28-29 L 3
Baffin Island ⌒ CDN 24-25 e 5
Bafia o CAM 204-205 J 6
Bafilo o RT 202-203 L 5
Bafing ~ RMM 202-203 E 3
Bafing-Makana o RMM 202-203 E 3
Bafodia o WAL 202-203 E 5
Bafoulabé o RMM 202-203 E 3
Bafoussam ☆ CAM 204-205 J 6
Bāfq o IR 134-135 F 3
Bafra ☆ TR 128-129 F 2
Bafra Burnu ▲ TR 128-129 F 2
Bāft o IR 134-135 G 4
Bafu Bay ≈ 202-203 F 7
Bafut o• CAM 204-205 J 5
Bafwabalinga o ZRE 212-213 A 3
Bafwabogbo o ZRE 210-211 L 3
Bafwaboli o ZRE 210-211 L 3
Bafwasende o ZRE 212-213 A 3
Baga o WAN 198-199 F 6
Bagabag o RP 160-161 D 4
Bagabag Island ⌒ PNG 183 D 3
Baga-Burul o RUS 126-127 F 5
Bagaces o CR 52-53 B 6
Bagadja o RUS 118-119 J 3
Bagaembo o ZRE 206-207 E 6
Bagaevskij = stanica Bagaevskaja o RUS 102-103 M 4
Bagagem, Rio ~ BR 68-69 D 7
Bagai o PNG 183 E 3
Bagalkot o IND 140-141 F 2
Bagalūr o IND 140-141 G 4
Bagamanoc o RP 160-161 F 6
Bagan Datuk o MAL 162-163 D 2
Bagandou o RCA 210-211 F 2
Bagani o NAM 216-217 F 9
Bagansiapiapi o RI 162-163 D 3
Bagansinembah o RI 162-163 D 4
Baganuur = Nuurst o MAU 148-149 J 4
Bagaré o BF 202-203 J 3
Bagaroua o RN 198-199 B 5
Bagasin o PNG 183 C 3
Baga Sola o TCH 198-199 G 6
Bagassi o BF 202-203 J 4
Bagata o BF 202-203 K 4
Bagata o ZRE 210-211 F 5
Bagazan o PE 64-65 F 4
Bagbe ~ WAL 202-203 E 5
Baġdād ◘ IRQ 128-129 L 6
Baġdād ★•• IRQ 128-129 L 6
Bagdad o USA (AZ) 256-257 B 4
Bagdarin ☆ RUS 118-119 F 8
Bagé o BR 76-77 K 6
Bagega o WAN 204-205 F 3
Bāgein o IR 134-135 G 3
Bāġ-e Malek o IR 134-135 C 3
Bāgepalli o IND 140-141 G 4
Baġestān o IR 134-135 H 1
Bageya o WAN 198-199 B 6
Bāġġirān o IR 136-137 F 6
Baggs o USA (WY) 252-253 L 5
Baghdad = Baġdād ★•• IRQ 128-129 L 6
Baghel Boland o IR 134-135 C 3
Baghelkhand Plateau ▲ IND 142-143 B 4
Bagherhat o••• BD 142-143 F 4
Baghmara o IND 142-143 G 3
Baghpat o IND 138-139 F 5
Baġil o Y 132-133 C 6
Baginda, Tanjung ▲ RI 162-163 G 6
Baġlān ◘ AFG 136-137 L 7
Baġlān ☆ AFG 136-137 L 6
Bagley o USA (MN) 270-271 C 3
Bagley Icefield ⊂ USA 20-21 T 6
Bagnell Dam • USA (MO) 274-275 F 6
Bagnères-de-Bigorre o F 90-91 H 10
Bago o RP 160-161 E 7
Bago, Pulau ⌒ RI 162-163 B 3
Bagodar o IND 142-143 D 3
Bagodo o CAM 204-205 K 5
Bagodra o IND 138-139 D 8
Bagoé ~ RMM 202-203 G 3
Bagomoyo o• EAT 214-215 K 4
Bagoosaar o SP 208-209 G 6
Bagot o CDN (MAN) 234-235 E 5
Bagot Range ▲ AUS 178-179 C 4
Bagou o DY 204-205 E 3
Bagraband, Kūh-e ▲ IR 134-135 J 5
Bagrāmi o AFG 138-139 B 2
Bagrationovsk ☆•• RUS 94-95 G 4
Bagre o BR 62-63 J 6
Bag Tug ~ VRC 154-155 F 2
Bagua o PE 64-65 C 4
Bagua Grande o PE 64-65 C 4
Baguales, Cerro ▲ RA 80 F 4
Báguanos o C 54-55 G 4
Bagudo o WAN 204-205 F 3
Baguinéda o RMM 202-203 G 3
Baguio o RP (DAO) 160-161 F 9
Baguio o•• RP (BEN) 160-161 D 4
Bagyrlaj ~ KA 96-97 G 9
Bāha, al- ◘ KSA 132-133 B 3
Bāha, al- ☆ KSA 132-133 B 3
Bahādorābād o IR 134-135 G 4
Bahadurabad Ghat o BD 142-143 F 3
Bahādurganj o IND 142-143 E 2
Baham, Umm al- o KSA 132-133 C 5
Bahamas = Bahamas, The ■ BS 54-55 J 4
Bahamas National Trust Park ⊥ BS 54-55 J 4
Bahapča ~ RUS 120-121 O 3
Bahār o IR 134-135 C 1
Bahārāgora o IND 142-143 E 4
Bahārak o AFG 136-137 M 6
Baharampur o IND 142-143 F 3
Baharden o TM 136-137 E 5
Bahardok o TM 136-137 F 5
Bahariya Oasis = Bahriya, al-Wāhāt al- ⊥• ET 194-195 D 3
Bāharz, Kūh-e ▲ IR 136-137 F 7
Bahau o MAL 162-163 E 3
Bahaur o RI 164-165 D 5
Bahāwalnagar o PK 138-139 D 5
Bahāwalpur o• PK 138-139 C 5
Bahay o RP 160-161 E 6
Bahçe ☆ TR 128-129 G 4
Baheri o IND 138-139 G 5
Bahi o EAT 212-213 E 6
Bahia ◘ BR 68-69 H 7
Bahia ◘ BR 72-73 H 2
Bahía, Islas de la ⌒ HN 52-53 L 3
Bahia, Tanjung ▲ RI 166-167 H 4
Bahía Asunción o MEX 50-51 B 4
Bahía Blanca o RA 78-79 H 5
Bahía Bustamante o RA 80 G 2
Bahía Creek o RA 78-79 H 6
Bahía de Caráquez o EC 64-65 B 2
Bahía de Los Angeles o MEX 50-51 C 3
Bahía Honda o C 54-55 D 3
Bahía Kino o MEX 50-51 D 3
Bahía Laura o RA 80 G 4
Bahía Mansa o RCH 78-79 C 6
Bahías, Cabo dos ▲ RA 80 H 2
Bahía Solano o CO 60-61 C 4
Bahía Tortugas o MEX 50-51 B 4
Bahir, Che'w ⊂ ETH 208-209 C 6
Bahir Dar o ETH 208-209 C 3
Bāhla o IND 138-139 C 6
Bahla o••• OM 132-133 K 2
Baḥma o IRQ 128-129 L 4
Bahn o LB 202-203 F 6
Bahr o RCA 206-207 G 6
Bahra o KSA 132-133 A 3
Baḥra, al- o KWT 130-131 K 3
Bahra al-Qadima o KSA 132-133 A 3
Bahraich o IND 142-143 B 2
Bahrain = Baḥrain, al- ■ BRN 134-135 D 6
Bahr al-Milḥ < IRQ 128-129 K 6
Bahret Lut = Yam Hamelah ⊂ JOR 130-131 D 2
Baḥšī Kalai o AFG 138-139 B 4
Bahta ~ RUS 114-115 U 3
Bahta ~ RUS 116-117 F 4
Bāḫtarān ◘ IR 134-135 B 1
Bāḫtarān ☆• IR (BAH) 134-135 B 1
Baḫtegān, Daryāče-ye ⊂ IR 134-135 E 4
Bahtemir ~ RUS 126-127 G 5
Bahty o KA 124-125 N 5
Bahubulu, Pulau ⌒ RI 164-165 H 5
Bāhū Kalāt, Rūdḫāne-ye ~ IR 134-135 J 6
Bahusuai o RI 164-165 G 5
Bahynaj o RUS 110-111 O 6
Baia o PNG 183 F 3
Baía, Rio da ~ BR 68-69 B 5
Baía dos Tigres o ANG 216-217 A 8
Baía Farta o ANG 216-217 B 6
Baía Formosa o BR 68-69 L 5
Baía Grande, Lago ⊂ BR 70-71 G 4
Baia Mare ☆• RO 102-103 C 4
Baianópolis o BR 72-73 H 2
Baião o BR 68-69 D 3
Baia River ~ PNG 183 B 4
Baibokoum o TCH 206-207 B 5
Baicheng o VRC (JIL) 150-151 D 5
Baicheng o VRC (XUZ) 146-147 E 5
Băicoi o RO 102-103 D 5
Baiḍā', al- o Y 132-133 D 7
Baidā' Naṭil o KSA 130-131 G 4
Baidi Cheng • VRC 154-155 F 6
Baïdou ~ RCA 206-207 E 6
Baie, La o CDN (QUE) 240-241 E 2
Baie-Comeau o CDN 38-39 K 4
Baie-des-Bacon o CDN (QUE) 240-241 F 2
Baie-des-Rochers o CDN (QUE) 240-241 F 3
Baie-des-Sables o CDN (QUE) 240-241 H 2
Baie-du-Poste o CDN (QUE) 236-237 P 2
Baie-du-Renard o CDN (QUE) 242-243 G 3
Baie Johan Beetz o CDN (QUE) 242-243 F 2
Baie-Sainte-Catherine o CDN (QUE) 240-241 F 2
Baie-Sainte-Claire o CDN (QUE) 242-243 D 3
Baie-Trinité o CDN (QUE) 242-243 A 3
Ba'iğī o IRQ 128-129 K 5
Baiḥān al-Qasāb o Y 132-133 D 6
Baihe o VRC (JIL) 150-151 G 6
Baihe o VRC (SXI) 154-155 G 5
Baikal, Lake = Bajkal, ozero ⊂ RUS 116-117 N 9
Baikal-Amur-Magistrale = BAM II RUS 118-119 E 7
Baikoré, Bahr ~ TCH 206-207 E 3
Baikunthpur o IND 142-143 C 4
Baila o SN 202-203 B 3
Baila o VRC 144-145 F 6
Bailang o VRC 156-157 E 4
Baile Átha Cliath = Dublin ★•• IRL 90-91 D 5
Baile Átha Fhirdhia = Ardee o IRL 90-91 D 5
Baile Átha Luain = Athlone o IRL 90-91 D 5
Baile Átha Troim = Trim ☆• IRL 90-91 D 5
Baile Brigín = Balbriggan o IRL 90-91 D 5
Baile Chaisleáin Bhéarra = Castletown Bearhaven o IRL 90-91 C 6
Baile Chathail = Charlestown o IRL 90-91 C 5
Băile Herculane o RO 102-103 C 5
Baile Locha Riach = Loughrea o IRL 90-91 C 5
Baile Mhistéala = Mitchelstown o IRL 90-91 C 5
Bailén o E 98-99 F 5
Băileşti o RO 102-103 C 5
Bailey o USA (CO) 254-255 K 4
Bailey o USA (TX) 264-265 H 5
Bailey o ZA 220-221 H 5
Bailey Point ▲ CDN 24-25 O 3
Bailey Range ▲ AUS 176-177 G 4
Baileys Harbor o USA (WI) 270-271 L 5
Bail Hongal o IND 140-141 F 3
Baili, Bi'r < ET 192-193 L 2
Bailidujuan • VRC 156-157 E 3
Bailin o VRC 156-157 H 3
Bailingmiao • VRC 148-149 K 7
Bailique o BR (APA) 62-63 J 5
Bailique o BR (P) 68-69 D 3
Bailique, Ilha ⌒ BR 62-63 K 5
Baillargeon, Réserve ⊥ CDN (QUE) 240-241 L 2
Bailleul o F 90-91 J 6
Ba Illi o TCH 206-207 C 3
Ba Illi ~ TCH 206-207 C 3
Baillie Hamilton Island ⌒ CDN 24-25 Z 3
Baillie Islands ⌒ CDN 24-25 G 5
Baillie River ~ CDN 30-31 R 3
Bailong Jiang ~ VRC 154-155 D 5
Bailundo o ANG 216-217 C 6
Baima o VRC 154-155 B 5
Baimaxue Shan Z.B. ⊥• VRC 144-145 M 6
Baimka o RUS 112-113 N 3
Baimun o RI 166-167 H 5
Baimuru o PNG 183 C 4
Baina o PNG 183 B 4
Bainbridge o USA (GA) 284-285 F 6
Bainbridge Island o USA (WA) 244-245 C 3
Baines Drift o RB 218-219 E 6
Bainet o RH 54-55 J 5
Baing o RI 168 E 8
Baingoin o VRC 144-145 H 5
Baining Mountains ▲ PNG 183 G 3
Bainville o USA (MT) 250-251 P 3
Baiona o E 98-99 C 3
Baiquan o VRC 150-151 F 4
Bā'ir o JOR 130-131 E 2
Bā'ir, Wādi ~ JOR 130-131 E 2
Baird o USA (TX) 264-265 E 6
Baird, Cape ▲ CDN 26-27 S 3
Baird Inlet ≈ 20-21 H 6
Baird Mountains ▲ USA 20-21 K 3
Baird Peninsula ⌣ CDN 24-25 h 6
Bairds Table Mountain ▲ AUS 174-175 G 6
Baire o C 54-55 G 4
Bairiki ★ KIB 13 J 2
Bairin Youqi o VRC 148-149 O 6
Bairin Zuoqi o VRC 148-149 O 5
Bairnsdale o• AUS 180-181 J 4
Bairoil o USA (WY) 252-253 L 4
Bairūt ★ RL 128-129 F 6
Baiš o KSA 132-133 C 5
Bais o RP 160-161 E 8
Baiš, Wādi ~ KSA 132-133 C 5
Baise ~ F 90-91 H 10
Baisha o VRC (HAI) 156-157 F 7
Baisha o VRC (SIC) 156-157 E 2
Baishan o VRC 150-151 F 6
Bai Shan ▲ VRC 146-147 L 5
Baishanzu ▲ VRC 156-157 L 3
Baishilazi Z.B. ⊥• VRC 150-151 E 7
Baishiling • VRC 156-157 G 7
Baishui o VRC 154-155 F 4
Baishuijiang Z.B. ⊥• VRC 154-155 D 5
Baisogala o•• LT 94-95 H 4
Baissa o WAN 204-205 J 5
Bait Adāqa o Y 132-133 C 6
Baitadi o NEP 144-145 C 6
Bait al-Faqih o• Y 132-133 C 6
Bait Lahm = Bet Lehem ☆•• WB 130-131 D 2
Bait Range ▲ CDN 32-33 G 4
Baixa do Tubarã, Rio ~ BR 68-69 J 7
Baixa Grande o BR 68-69 H 7
Baixão o BR 72-73 K 2
Baixo Guandu o BR 72-73 K 5
Baixo Longa o ANG 216-217 E 7
Baiyang Gou • VRC 146-147 H 4
Baiyan Temple o VRC 154-155 G 3
Baiyer River o PNG 183 C 3
Baiyer River National Park ⊥ PNG 183 C 3
Baiyi o VRC 154-155 E 6
Baiyin o VRC 154-155 D 3
Baizeklik Qianfodong • VRC 146-147 J 4
Baja o H 92-93 P 5
Baja, Punta ▲ MEX (BCN) 50-51 B 3
Baja, Punta ▲ MEX (SON) 50-51 D 3
Baja California ⌣ MEX 50-51 B 2
Baja California Norte ◘ MEX 50-51 B 2
Baja California Sur ◘ MEX 50-51 C 4
Bajada, La o C 54-55 C 4
Bajada del Agrio o RA 78-79 D 5
Bajaga ~ RUS 120-121 E 2
Bajan o MAU 146-147 M 2
Baján o MEX 50-51 J 4
Bajanaul ☆•• KA 124-125 J 3
Bajanbulag o MAU 148-149 D 4
Bajančandman = Ih suuž o MAU 148-149 H 3
Bajandaj ☆ RUS 116-117 M 9
Bajandėlgėr =Širėėt o MAU 148-149 L 5
Bajangol=Baruunharaa o MAU 148-149 H 3
Bajan-Hongor ◘ MAU 148-149 D 4
Bajanhongor ☆ MAU 148-149 E 4
Bajanhošuu o MAU 146-147 K 1
Bajanlig = Hatansuudal o MAU 148-149 E 5
Bajanmönh = Ulaan-Ėrėg o MAU 148-149 J 4
Bajan-Ölgijo ◘ MAU 146-147 J 1
Bajan-Öndör = Bumbat o MAU 148-149 G 4
Bajan-Önzuul = Ihhairhan o MAU 148-149 H 4
Bajan-Ovoo o MAU 146-147 M 3
Bajan-Ovoo = Žavhlant o MAU 148-149 L 4
Bajantėėg o MAU 148-149 F 5
Bajan Uul = Bajan o MAU 146-147 M 2
Bajan-Uul = Žavarthošuu o MAU 148-149 L 3
Bajasgalant o MAU 148-149 L 4
Bajawa o RI 168 E 7
Bajdarackaja guba ≈ 108-109 L 7
Bajdarata ~ RUS 108-109 M 8
Bajdrag gol ~ MAU 148-149 D 4
Bajganin ☆ KA 126-127 M 3
Bajie o VRC 156-157 D 4
Bajimba, Mount ▲ AUS 178-179 M 5
Bajina Bašta o• YU 100-101 G 3
Bajío de Ahuichila o MEX 50-51 H 5
Bajíos de Agua Blanca o MEX 50-51 F 5
Bajkadam o KA 136-137 L 3
Bajkadam ☆ KA 136-137 L 3
Bajkal o RUS 116-117 M 10
Bajkal, zaliv ⊂ RUS 122-123 K 2
Bajkalovo o RUS 114-115 J 6
Bajkalovsk o RUS 108-109 U 6
Bajkal'sk o RUS 116-117 L 10
Bajkal'skij hrebet ▲ RUS 116-117 O 8
Bajkal'skij zapovednij ⊥ RUS 116-117 M 10
Bajkal'skoe o RUS 118-119 D 8
Bajki o RUS 96-97 K 6
Bajkit o RUS 116-117 H 5
Bajkonyr o KA 124-125 E 5
Bajkonyr ~ KA 124-125 D 5
Bajkovo o RUS 122-123 R 3
Bajmak ☆ RUS 96-97 L 7
Bajo o RI 168 D 7
Bajo, El o YV 60-61 J 3
Bajo Caracoles o RA 80 E 3
Bajoga o WAN 204-205 J 3
Bajo Hondo o RA 76-77 D 6
Bajo Nuevo ⌒ CO 54-55 F 7
Bajool o AUS 178-179 L 2
Bajo Pichanaqui o PE 64-65 E 7
Bajos de Haina o DOM 54-55 K 5
Bajram-Ali o TM 136-137 H 6
Bajsa o RUS 118-119 F 8
Bajsun o US 136-137 K 5
Bajugan o RI 164-165 G 3
Bajyrkům o KA 136-137 L 3
Baká o NIC 52-53 B 5
Bakaba o TCH 206-207 C 5
Bakairi, Área Indígena ⊻ BR 70-71 K 4
Bakal o RUS 96-97 L 6
Bakala o RCA (OMB) 206-207 C 6
Bakala o RCA (Oua) 206-207 E 5
Bakali ~ ZRE 210-211 F 6
Bakaly ☆ RUS 96-97 H 6
Bakanas ~ KA 124-125 L 5
Bakaoré o TCH 198-199 K 5
Bakau o• WAG 202-203 B 3
Bakaucengal o RI 164-165 E 5
Bakauhuni o RI 162-163 F 7
Bakayan, Gunung ▲ RI 164-165 E 2
Bakbakty o KA 124-125 K 6
Bakčar o RUS 114-115 R 6
Bakčar ~ RUS 114-115 R 6
Bakebe o CAM 204-205 H 6
Bakel o• SN 202-203 D 2
Bakelalan o MAL 164-165 D 2
Baker o USA (CA) 248-249 H 4
Baker o USA (LA) 268-269 J 6
Baker o USA (MT) 250-251 P 5
Baker o USA (NV) 246-247 L 4
Baker o USA (OR) 244-245 H 6
Baker o USA (WV) 280-281 H 4
Baker, Canal ≈ 80 C 3
Baker, Mount ▲ USA (WA) 244-245 D 2
Baker Creek ~ CDN (BC) 228-229 M 4
Bakerhill o USA (AL) 284-285 E 5
Baker Island ⌒ USA 13 K 2
Baker Island ⌒ USA 32-33 D 4
Baker Lake o AUS 176-177 J 3
Baker Lake o CDN (NWT) 30-31 V 3
Baker Lake ⊂ CDN (NWT) 30-31 W 3
Baker Lake ⊂ USA (WA) 244-245 D 2
Baker Range ▲ AUS 176-177 H 2
Bakers Dozen Islands ⌒ CDN 36-37 K 6
Baker Settlement o CDN (NS) 240-241 L 6
Bakersfield o USA (CA) 248-249 F 4
Bakersfield o USA (TX) 266-267 E 3
Bakerville o ZA 220-221 H 2
Ba Khe o VN 156-157 D 6
Bakhtiyārpur o IND 142-143 D 3
Bakı ★• AZ 128-129 N 2
Bakin Birji o RN 198-199 D 5
Bakinskij arhipelago ⌒ AZ 128-129 N 3
Bakırçay ~ TR 128-129 B 3
Bakkafjörður o IS 86-87 f 1
Bakkejord o N 86-87 J 2
Baknars Tāl ⊂ IND 142-143 C 2
Bako o CI 202-203 G 5
Bako o ETH 208-209 C 4
Bako National Park ⊥ MAL 162-163 J 4
Bakong, Pulau ⌒ RI 162-163 F 4
Bakongan o RI 162-163 B 3
Bakool ◘ SP 208-209 F 6
Bakop o PNG 183 G 3
Bakordi o SUD 206-207 J 6
Bakore, Massif de ▲ RCA 206-207 B 5
Bakori o WAN 204-205 G 3
Bakouma o RCA 206-207 F 6
Bakoumba o G 210-211 D 4
Bakoye ~ RMM 202-203 F 3
Baksa ~ RUS 114-115 R 7
Bak Sadane < RMM 196-197 J 5
Baksaj ~ KA 96-97 G 10
Baksan o RUS 126-127 E 6
Baksan ~ RUS 126-127 E 6
Baktalórántháza o H 92-93 R 5
Baku = Bakı ★• AZ 128-129 N 2
Bakulu o RI 164-165 K 3
Bakung, Pulau ⌒ RI 162-163 F 4
Bakuriani o GE 126-127 E 7
Bakwa-Kenge o ZRE 210-211 J 6
Baky ~ RUS 110-111 X 5
Bakyrly o KA 124-125 E 6
Bakyrly o KA 124-125 E 6
Bala o CDN (ONT) 238-239 F 3
Bala o RUS 110-111 T 6
Bala o SN 202-203 D 2
Balâ ☆ TR 128-129 E 3
Bala o WAN 204-205 F 4
Bala, Cerros de ▲ BOL 70-71 C 3
Balabac o RP 160-161 B 9
Balabac Island ⌒ RP 160-161 B 9
Balabac Strait ≈ 160-161 B 9
Balabagan o RP 160-161 F 9
Balabaiba o ANG 216-217 B 6
Ba'labakk ☆••• RL 128-129 G 5
Balabala o ZRE 210-211 H 2
Balabalangan, Kepulauan ⌒ RI 164-165 E 5
Bālā Bolūk o AFG 134-135 K 2
Balad al-Mala o IRQ 128-129 L 5
Balade o IR 136-137 B 6
Baladjie Lake ⊂ AUS 176-177 E 5
Balad Rūz o IRQ 128-129 L 6
Balad Sinğār o IRQ 128-129 J 4
Balagaččy o RUS 118-119 L 3
Balaganah o RUS 118-119 H 6
Balagančik, hrebet ▲ RUS 122-123 R 2
Balagannoe o RUS 120-121 N 4
Balagansk o RUS 116-117 L 9
Balagan-Taas • RUS 110-111 Z 6
Balaguer o E 98-99 H 4
Balahna o RUS 94-95 S 3
Balahnja, Bol'šaja ~ RUS 108-109 f 5
Balahnja, gora ▲ RUS 110-111 F 3
Balahta ☆ RUS 116-117 E 8
Ba Lai, Sông ~ VN 158-159 J 5
Balai Berkuak o RI 162-163 J 5
Balaikarangan o RI 162-163 J 4
Balaipungut o RI 162-163 D 4
Balaiselasa o RI 162-163 D 5
Balaka o MW 218-219 H 2
Balakbal ∴• MEX 52-53 K 3
Balakéte o RCA 206-207 D 5
Balaki o RG 202-203 D 4
Balaklava o AUS 180-181 E 3
Balaklija o UA 102-103 K 3
Bālākot o PK 138-139 D 2
Balakovo ☆ RUS 96-97 E 7
Balala o ETH 208-209 B 6
Balalai Island ⌒ SOL 184 I b 2
Balama o MOC 218-219 K 1
Balamba o CAM 204-205 J 6
Balambangan, Pulau ⌒ MAL 160-161 B 9
Balam Tākli o IND 138-139 E 10
Balancán de Domínguez o MEX 52-53 J 3
Balanced Rock ∴ USA (ID) 252-253 D 4
Balandou o RG 202-203 F 4
Balañga ☆ RP 160-161 D 5
Balanga o ZRE 214-215 E 5
Balangala o ZRE 210-211 G 3
Ba Làng An, Mũi ▲ VN 158-159 K 3
Balāngīr o IND 142-143 C 5
Balangkayan o RP 160-161 F 7
Balangoda o CL 140-141 J 7
Balao o EC 64-65 C 3
Balaoan o RP 160-161 D 4
Balapitiya o CL 140-141 J 7
Balaraja o RI 168 B 3
Balarāmpur o IND 142-143 E 4
Balasan o RP 160-161 E 7
Balašiha ☆ RUS 94-95 P 4
Bāl-Asmar o KSA 132-133 C 4
Balašov o RUS 102-103 N 2
Balassagyarmat o H 92-93 P 4
Balāt o ET 194-195 D 5
Balat (Labuhanbalat) o RI 168 C 7
Bala-Taldyk ~ KA 126-127 N 3
Balatan o RP 160-161 E 6
Balaton o H 92-93 O 5
Balatonfüred o H 92-93 O 5
Balauring o RI 166-167 B 6
Balavé o BF 202-203 H 3
Balaya o RG 202-203 D 4
Balazote o E 98-99 F 5
Balbalan o RP 160-161 D 4
Balbalasang o RP 160-161 D 4
Balbao o• PA 52-53 E 7
Balbi, Mount ▲ PNG 184 I b 1
Balbina o BR 62-63 E 6
Balbina, Cachoeira ~ BR 62-63 E 6
Balbina, Represa de < BR 62-63 E 6
Balboa o CO 60-61 D 5
Balbriggan = Baile Brigín o IRL 90-91 D 5
Balcad o SP 212-213 K 2
Balcarce o RA 78-79 K 4
Balcarres o CDN (SAS) 232-233 P 5
Bălceşti o RO 102-103 C 5
Balchaš, ozero = Balqash Köl ⊂ KA 124-125 H 6
Balčik o BG 102-103 F 6
Balclutha o NZ 182 B 7
Balcoms Corners o USA (NY) 278-279 E 6
Balcones Escarpment ▲ USA (TX) 266-267 H 4
Bald Eagle Mountain ▲ USA (PA) 280-281 J 3
Balde de la Mora o RA 76-77 E 6
Baldenburg = Biały Bór o• PL 92-93 O 2
Bald Head ▲ AUS 176-177 E 7
Bald Hill ▲ CDN 20-21 Z 4
Bald Hill No. 2 ▲ AUS 178-179 L 4
Bald Knob o USA (AR) 276-277 D 5
Bald Mountain ▲ USA (NV) 248-249 J 2
Baldock Lake ⊂ CDN 34-35 H 2
Baldur o CDN (MAN) 234-235 D 5
Baldwin o USA (FL) 286-287 H 1
Baldwin o USA (IA) 274-275 H 2
Baldwin o USA (MI) 272-273 D 4
Baldwin o USA (WI) 270-271 F 6
Baldwin, Parc Provincial ⊥ CDN (QUE) 240-241 K 2
Baldwin Bank ⌒ AUS 172-173 H 2
Baldwin City o USA (KS) 262-263 L 6
Baldwin Peninsula ⌣ USA 20-21 J 3
Baldwinsville o USA (NY) 278-279 E 5
Baldwinton o CDN (SAS) 232-233 J 3
Baldwyn o USA (MS) 268-269 M 2
Baldy Hughes o CDN (BC) 228-229 M 3
Baldy Mountain ▲ CDN (BC) 230-231 K 4
Baldy Mountain ▲ CDN (MAN) 234-235 C 3
Baldy Peak ▲ USA (AZ) 256-257 F 5
Bal'dżikan o RUS 118-119 E 11
Bale o ANG 216-217 D 7
Balē ◘ ETH 208-209 E 6
Balé ~ RG 202-203 E 4
Bale ~ RMM 202-203 F 4
Bâle = Basel ☆• CH 92-93 J 5
Baleares, Islas ◘ E 98-99 H 5
Balearic Islands = Balears, Illes ⌒ E 98-99 J 5
Balease ~ RI 164-165 G 5
Balease, Gunung ▲ RI 164-165 G 5
Baleh ~ MAL 162-163 K 4
Baleia, Ponta da ▲ BR 72-73 L 4
Baleine, Rivière à la ~ CDN 36-37 Q 5
Balej ☆ RUS 118-119 H 10
Balékoutou o TCH 206-207 D 4
Balelesberge ▲ ZA 220-221 K 3
Bale Mount National Park ⊥ ETH 208-209 D 5
Baleno o RP 160-161 E 6
Baler o RP 160-161 D 5
Baler Bay ≈ 160-161 D 5
Baleshwar o IND 142-143 E 5
Balestrand ☆• N 86-87 C 6
Baléya o RMM 202-203 F 3
Baleyara o RN 204-205 E 2
Baley Guerrero o DOM 54-55 L 5
Balezino ☆ RUS 96-97 H 5
Balfour o AUS 180-181 H 6
Balfour o CDN (BC) 230-231 N 4
Balfour o USA (ND) 258-259 G 4
Balfour o ZA (CAP) 220-221 H 6
Balfour o ZA (TRA) 220-221 J 3
Balfour Downs o AUS 172-173 E 7
Balgak o SUD 200-201 C 6
Balgazyn o RUS 116-117 G 10
Balgo ⊻ AUS 172-173 J 6
Balgonie o CDN (SAS) 232-233 O 5
Balguntay o VRC 146-147 H 4
Balğurašī o KSA 132-133 B 4
Balḫ o AFG 136-137 K 6
Balḫ ◘ AFG 136-137 K 6
Balḫ, Daryā-ye ~ AFG 136-137 K 6
Balḫ Ab o AFG 136-137 K 7
Balḫ Ab, Rūd-e ~ AFG 136-137 K 7
Balhaš = Balkash o KA 124-125 J 5
Balhaš, ozero = Balkash köl ⊂ KA 124-125 J 5
Balho o DJI 200-201 L 6
Bali o CAM 204-205 J 6
Bali o IND 142-143 F 4
Bali ◘ RI 168 B 6
Bali, Laut ≈ 168 B 6
Bali, Pulau ⌒ RI 168 B 7
Bali, Selat ≈ 168 B 7
Balibi o RCA 206-207 E 5
Balibo o RI 166-167 C 6
Baliem ~ RI 166-167 K 4
Baliem Valley ⌣ RI 166-167 K 3
Balifondo o RCA 206-207 F 6
Balige o RI 162-163 C 3
Balıkesir ☆ TR 128-129 B 3
Balikpapan o RI 164-165 E 4
Balikpapary, Teluk ≈ 164-165 E 4
Balimela Reservoir < IND 142-143 C 6
Balimo o PNG 183 B 5
Baling o MAL 162-163 D 2
Balingara, Pegunungan ▲ RI 164-165 G 4
Balingian o MAL 162-163 K 3
Balinn ~ RMM 202-203 E 3
Balintang Channel ≈ 160-161 D 3
Baliza o BR 72-73 D 4
Baljaga o RUS 116-117 O 10
Baljennie o CDN (SAS) 232-233 L 3
Balkan Mountains = Stara Planina ▲ BG 102-103 C 6
Balkaš o KA 124-125 J 5
Balkash köl ⊂ KA 124-125 H 6
Balkašty ☆ KA 124-125 E 2
Balkon-Myl'k, gora ▲ RUS 88-89 O 2
Ball, Mount ▲ AUS 172-173 H 5
Balladonia Motel o AUS 176-177 G 6
Ballangen o N 86-87 H 2
Ballantyne, Lac ⊂ CDN 36-37 P 5
Ballantyne Strait ≈ 24-25 O 2
Ballarat o AUS 180-181 G 4
Ballard, Lake ⊂ AUS 176-177 F 4
Ballaroo o AUS 178-179 K 4
Ballasetas o RI 162-163 B 3
Ballater o GB 90-91 F 3
Ballé o RMM 202-203 F 2
Ballena, Punta ▲ EC 64-65 B 2
Ballenas, Canal de ≈ 50-51 C 3
Ballenero, Canal ≈ 80 E 7
Ballia o IND 142-143 D 3
Ballidu o AUS 176-177 D 5
Ballina o AUS 178-179 M 5
Ballina = Béal an Átha o IRL 90-91 C 4
Ballinasloe = Béal Átha na Sluaighe o IRL 90-91 C 5
Ballinger o USA (TX) 266-267 H 2
Ball Lake ⊂ CDN (ONT) 234-235 K 4
Ballone Highway II AUS 178-179 J 4
Balloul o DZ 190-191 C 3
Ball's Pyramid ⌒ AUS 180-181 N 7
Bally o USA (PA) 280-281 L 3
Ballycastle o GB 90-91 D 4
Ballyshannon o IRL 90-91 C 4
Balmacara o GB 90-91 E 3
Balmaceda o RCH 80 E 2
Balmaceda, Cerro ▲ RCH 80 D 5
Balmaceda, Parque Nacional ⊥ RCH 80 D 5
Balmaceda, Sierra ▲ RCH 80 F 6
Balmertown o CDN (ONT) 234-235 K 3
Balmoral o AUS 180-181 F 4
Balmoral o ZA 220-221 J 2
Balmorhea o USA (TX) 266-267 D 2
Balnearia o RA 76-77 F 6
Balneário Camboriú o BR 74-75 F 6
Balneario del Sol o• C 54-55 H 5
Balneario las Grutas o RA 78-79 G 6
Balneario Massini o RA 78-79 H 6
Balo o RI 164-165 H 4
Baloa o RI 164-165 H 4
Balobaloang-Kecil, Pulau ⌒ RI 168 D 6
Balod o IND 142-143 B 5
Balohan, Teluk ≈ 162-163 A 2
Balok, Kampung o MAL 162-163 E 3
Balombo o ANG 216-217 C 6
Balombo ~ ANG 216-217 C 6
Balong o RI 168 D 3
Balong o VRC 144-145 L 2
Balonne River ~ AUS 178-179 K 5
Balotra o IND 138-139 D 7
Balqash Köl = Balkaš köli ⊂ KA 124-125 H 6
Balrāmpur o IND 142-143 C 2
Balranald o AUS 180-181 G 3
Balş o RO 102-103 D 5
Balsa Nova o BR 74-75 F 5
Balsapuerto o PE 64-65 D 4
Balsas o BR 68-69 E 5
Balsas o MEX 52-53 E 2
Balsas o PE 64-65 D 5
Balsas, Río ~ MEX 52-53 E 3
Balsas, Rio das ~ BR 68-69 F 5
Balsas, Rio das ~ BR 68-69 E 7
Balsinhas, Ribeiro ~ BR 68-69 F 5
Balta ☆ UA 102-103 F 4
Balta o USA (ND) 258-259 G 3
Balta Brăilei ⊥ RO 102-103 E 5
Baltaköl o KA 136-137 K 3
Baltakol' o KA 136-137 K 3
Baltal o IND 138-139 E 2
Baltasar Brum o ROU 76-77 J 6
Baltasi ☆ RUS 96-97 G 5
Baltazar o YV 60-61 H 6
Bălţi ☆ MD 102-103 E 4
Baltic Sea ≈ 86-87 H 9
Baltijsk o RUS 94-95 F 4
Baltîm o ET 194-195 E 2
Baltimore o USA (OH) 280-281 D 4
Baltimore o• USA (MD) 280-281 K 4
Baltimore o ZA 218-219 E 6
Baltimore = Dún na Séad o IRL 90-91 C 6
Baltit o PK 138-139 E 1
Baltiysk = Baltijsk o RUS 94-95 F 4
Baltra, Isla ⌒ EC 64-65 B 10
Baltrum ⌒ D 92-93 J 2
Ba Lụa, Quần Đảo ⌒ VN 158-159 H 5
Baluan Island ⌒ PNG 183 D 2
Baluarte, Arroyo ~ USA (TX) 266-267 J 6
Bālūčestān, Sīstān -ō- ◘ IR 134-135 H 5
Baluchistān ◘ PK 134-135 K 4
Baluchistan = Bālūčestan ⊥ IR 134-135 K 4
Balud o RP 160-161 E 6
Balui ~ MAL 164-165 D 2
Balūr o IND 140-141 F 4
Baluran Game Park ⊥ RI 168 B 6
Balut Island ⌒ RP 160-161 F 10
Balvard o IR 134-135 G 4
Balvi ☆•• LV 94-95 K 3
Balwāda o IND 138-139 E 8
Balwina Aboriginal Land ⊻ AUS 172-173 J 6
Balygyčan o RUS 112-113 H 5
Balygyčan ~ RUS 112-113 H 5
Balygyčan, Verhnij o RUS 112-113 H 5
Balyhta o RUS 116-117 M 8
Balykča o RUS 124-125 P 3
Balyktah ~ RUS 110-111 W 2
Balyktyg-Hem ~ RUS 116-117 H 10
Balzac o CDN (ALB) 232-233 D 4
Balzar o EC 64-65 C 2
Balzas o EC 64-65 C 3
Balž gol ~ MAU 148-149 K 3
Bam o IR 134-135 H 4
Bam o TCH 206-207 C 4
BAM = Baikal-Amur-Magistrale II RUS 118-119 E 7
Bam, Lac de o BF 202-203 K 3
Bama o• BF 202-203 H 4
Bama o VRC 156-157 E 4
Bama o WAN 204-205 K 3
Bamaba o ZRE 210-211 G 5
Bamaga ⊻ AUS 174-175 G 2
Bamaji Lake ⊂ CDN (ONT) 234-235 M 3
Bamake o LB 202-203 G 7
Bamako ◘ RMM 202-203 F 2
Bamako ★ RMM (BAM) 202-203 F 3
Bamba o EAK 212-213 G 5
Bamba ~ RCA 206-207 D 6
Bamba o RMM 196-197 K 6
Bamba o ZRE 210-211 G 6
Bambadinca o GNB 202-203 C 3
Bambak o PNG 183 E 3
Bambalang o CAM 204-205 J 6
Bambam o WAN 204-205 J 4
Bambama o RCB 210-211 D 5
Bambamarca o PE 64-65 C 5
Bambana, Río ~ NIC 52-53 B 5
Bambang o RI 162-163 F 7
Bambang o RP 160-161 D 4
Bambangan o MAL 160-161 B 10
Bambangando o ANG 218-219 B 3
Bambara o TCH 206-207 D 4
Bambara-Maoundé o RMM 202-203 J 2
Bambari ☆ RCA 206-207 E 6
Bambaroo o AUS 174-175 J 6
Bambéla o CI 202-203 J 5
Bamberg o• D 92-93 L 4
Bamberg o USA (SC) 284-285 J 3
Bambesa o ZRE 210-211 K 2
Bambesi o ETH 208-209 B 4
Bambey o• SN 202-203 B 2
Bambila o RMM 202-203 E 2
Bambili o ZRE 210-211 K 2
Bambio o RCA 210-211 F 2
Bamboesberg ▲ ZA 220-221 G 5
Bamboi o GH 202-203 J 5
Bamboo Creek o AUS 172-173 E 6
Bambouk ⊥ RMM 202-203 E 2
Bambouti o RCA 206-207 H 6
Bambouto, Monts ▲ CAM 204-205 J 6
Bambudi o ETH 208-209 B 3
Bambuí o BR 72-73 H 6
Bambui o CAM 204-205 J 5
Bambujka ~ RUS 118-119 G 8
Bamenda ☆ CAM 204-205 J 6
Bamendjing, Lac de ⊂ CAM 204-205 J 6
Bame Town o LB 202-203 F 7
Bamfield o CDN (BC) 230-231 D 5
Bami o TM 136-137 E 5
Bamingui o RCA 206-207 E 5
Bamingui ~ RCA 206-207 E 5
Bamingui-Bangoran ◘ RCA 206-207 D 4
Bamingui-Bangoran, Parc National du ⊥ RCA 206-207 D 4
Bamio o PNG 183 B 4

Baezaeko River — Bamio 301

Bam Island ⌒ PNG 183 C 2
Bamkeri o RI 166-167 F 2
Bampošt, Kūh-e ▲ IR 134-135 K 5
Bampūr o IR 134-135 J 5
Bampūr, Rūd-e ~ IR 134-135 H 5
Bamra Hills ▲ IND 142-143 D 5
Bamrūd-e Soflā o IR 134-135 J 2
Bamu River ~ PNG 183 B 4
Bamusso o CAM 204-205 H 6
Bāmyān ▫ AFG 134-135 M 1
Bāmyān ☆• AFG (BM) 134-135 M 1
Bāmyān ~ AFG 136-137 K 7
Bamyili ⚔ AUS 172-173 L 3
Ban o BF 202-203 J 2
Bana o CAM 204-205 J 6
Bana ∴• TR 128-129 K 2
Bana, Col de ▲ CAM 204-205 J 6
Banā, Wādī ~ Y 132-133 D 7
Banaadir ▫ SP 212-213 K 2
Banabuiú, Açude < BR 68-69 J 4
Banabuiú, Rio ~ BR 68-69 J 4
Bana Daniéd o SN 202-203 D 2
Banagi o EAT 212-213 E 5
Banaigarh o IND 142-143 D 5
Banalia o ZRE 210-211 K 3
Banama o RG 202-203 F 5
Banamba o RMM 202-203 G 3
Banana o AUS 178-179 L 3
Banana o ZRE 216-217 B 3
Bananal, Ilha do ⌒ BR 68-69 C 7
Bananal, Rio ~ BR 68-69 D 6
Banana Range ▲ AUS 178-179 L 3
Banana River ≈ USA 286-287 J 3
Banandjé o CI 202-203 G 5
Bananeiras o BR 68-69 L 5
Banantara o RG 202-203 F 4
Banangui o RCA 206-207 G 6
Banankoro o RG 202-203 F 5
Banankoro o RMM (SÉ) 202-203 G 3
Banankoro o RMM (SIK) 202-203 F 4
Banao o C (CG) 54-55 G 4
Banao o C (SS) 54-55 F 4
Banapur o IND 142-143 D 6
Banās ~ IND 138-139 E 7
Banas ~ IND 138-139 D 7
Banas ~ IND 142-143 B 3
Banās, Ra's ▲ ET 194-195 G 6
Banat o USA (MI) 270-271 L 5
Banaue ☆ RP 160-161 D 4
Banaz ☆ TR 128-129 C 3
Banaz Çayı ~ TR 128-129 C 3
Banba o RMM 202-203 G 4
Ban Bakha o LAO 156-157 D 7
Ban Ban o AUS 178-179 G 3
Ban Ban o LAO 156-157 C 7
Ban Ban o VN 156-157 D 7
Banbar o VRC 144-145 K 5
Banbaran o RMM 202-203 F 3
Banbirpur o IND 144-145 C 6
Ban Boun Tai o LAO 156-157 B 6
Banbridge o GB 90-91 D 4
Banbury o GB 90-91 G 5
Bancauan Island ⌒ RP 160-161 C 9
Banc d'Arguin, Parc National du ⊥••• RIM 196-197 B 4
Ban Chamrung o THA 158-159 G 4
Ban Chiang o••• THA 158-159 G 2
Banco, El o CO 60-61 E 3
Bancoran Island ⌒ RP 160-161 C 9
Bancos de San Pedro o YV 60-61 H 3
Bancroft o CDN (ONT) 238-239 H 3
Bancroft o USA (ID) 252-253 G 4
Bancs Providence ⌒ SY 224 B 4
Banda o CAM 204-205 K 4
Banda o GH 202-203 J 5
Banda o IND 138-139 G 7
Bānda o IND 142-143 B 3
Banda o ZRE (BAN) 210-211 G 6
Banda o ZRE (Hau) 206-207 H 6
Banda, Kepulauan (Nutmeg Kepulauan) ⌒•• RI 166-167 E 4
Banda, La o RA 76-77 E 4
Banda Aceh = Baiturahman ☆ RI 162-163 A 2
Banda Banda, Mount ▲ AUS 178-179 M 6
Bandabe o RM 222-223 F 5
Banda del Río Salí o RA 76-77 E 4
Bandae o GH 202-203 J 7
Banda Elat o RI 166-167 G 4
Bandafassi o SN 202-203 D 3
Bandai-Asahi National Park ⊥ J (NII) 152-153 H 6
Bandai-Asahi National Park ⊥ J (YAM) 152-153 H 5
Bandak o N 86-87 D 7
Bandaka o ZRE 210-211 H 4
Bandakami o ZRE 210-211 D 6
Ban Dakchoun o LAO 158-159 J 3
Bandama ~ CI 202-203 H 6
Bandama Blanc ~ CI 202-203 H 5
Bandama Rouge ~ CI 202-203 G 5
Bandaneira o•• RI 166-167 E 4
Bāndanwāra o IND 138-139 E 6
Bandar o MOC 218-219 H 3
Bandar o RI 168 C 3
Bandaragama o CL 140-141 H 7
Bandarban o BD 142-143 H 4
Bandarbeyla o SP 208-209 K 4
Bandar-e 'Abbās ☆• IR 134-135 G 5
Bandar-e Anzalī o• IR 128-129 N 4
Bandar-e Būšehr ☆• IR 134-135 D 4
Bandar-e Čarak o IR 134-135 F 5
Bandar-e Deilam o IR 134-135 D 3
Bandar-e Emām Ḫomeinī o IR 134-135 C 3
Bandar-e Ganāve o IR 134-135 D 4
Bandar-e Gaz o IR 136-137 C 6
Bandar-e Golmānḫāne o IR 128-129 L 4
Bandar-e Ḫamīr o IR 134-135 F 5
Bandar-e Kong o IR 134-135 F 5
Bandar-e Lenge o• IR 134-135 F 5
Bandar-e Māhšahr o IR 134-135 C 3
Bandar-e Moġūye o IR 134-135 F 5
Bandar-e Moqām o IR 134-135 E 5
Bandar-e Rīg o IR 134-135 D 4
Bandarlan Balagra o IND 138-139 D 3
Bandarjaya o RI 162-163 F 7
Bandar Lampung ☆ RI 162-163 F 7
Bandar Murcaayo o SP 208-209 K 3
Bandarpasirmandogai o RI 162-163 C 3
Bandar Seri Begawan ★•• BRU 164-165 D 1
Bandar Sri Aman (Simanggang) o MAL 162-163 J 4
Bandar Wanaag o SP 208-209 G 4
Banda Sea = Banda, Laut ≈ 166-167 C 3
Band-e Amīr, Rūd-e ~ AFG 136-137 K 7
Bandeira o BR 72-73 K 3
Bandeira, Pico da ▲ BR 72-73 K 6
Bandeirante, Rio ~ BR 72-73 E 7
Bandeirantes o BR (GOI) 72-73 E 2
Bandeirantes o BR (MAT) 70-71 J 2
Bandelierkop o ZA 218-219 E 6
Bandelier National Monument ∴ USA (NM) 256-257 J 3
Bandera o RA 76-77 F 5
Bandera o USA (TX) 266-267 H 4
Bandera Bajada o RA 76-77 F 4
Banderantes, Ilha dos ⌒ BR 72-73 D 7
Banderas, Bahía de ≈ 52-53 B 1
Banderilla o MEX 52-53 F 2
Bandhavagarh National Park ⊥ IND 142-143 B 4
Bāndhi o PK 138-139 B 6
Bandia ~ IND 142-143 B 6
Bandiagara o••• RMM 202-203 J 2
Bandiagara, Falaise de ▲ RMM 202-203 J 2
Banding o RI 162-163 F 7
Bandipur National Park ⊥• IND 140-141 G 5
Bandırma ☆ TR 128-129 B 2
Bandjoukri o CAM 204-205 K 4
Bandjoun o CAM 204-205 J 6
Bandon o USA (OR) 244-245 A 7
Ba'n Đôn o VN 158-159 J 4
Bandon = Droichead na Bandan o IRL 90-91 C 6
Bandua o MOC 218-219 H 4
Bandula o MOC 218-219 G 4
Bandundu ▫ ZRE 210-211 F 5
Bandundu ☆ ZRE (Ban) 210-211 F 5
Bandung ☆ RI 168 B 3
Ban Dung o THA 158-159 G 2
Bandungan o•• RI 168 D 3
Bandur o ZA 218-219 E 6
Bandurrias, Caleta ≈ 76-77 B 3
Bandya o AUS 176-177 G 3
Bāne o IR 128-129 L 4
Băneasa o RO 102-103 E 5
Ba'n E. Klôp o VN 158-159 K 4
Banes o C 54-55 H 4
Banes, Bahía de ≈ 54-55 H 4
Banfèlè o RG 202-203 E 4
Banff o CDN (ALB) 232-233 C 4
Banff o• GB 90-91 F 3
Banff National Park ⊥ CDN (ALB) 232-233 B 4
Banfora o• BF 202-203 H 4
Banfora, Falaise de ▲ BF 202-203 H 4
Bang o RCA 206-207 B 5
Banga o ANG 216-217 C 4
Banga o BD 142-143 G 4
Banga o RCA (Kem) 206-207 D 6
Banga ~ RCA 206-207 F 5
Banga o RP 160-161 F 9
Banga o ZRE (BAN) 210-211 G 6
Banga o ZRE (KOC) 210-211 H 6
Bangabong o RP 160-161 D 6
Bangala, Lake o ZW 218-219 F 5
Bangalore ☆• IND 140-141 G 4
Banga Melo ~ ZRE 210-211 H 2
Bangana o RCA 206-207 E 5
Banganapalle o IND 140-141 H 3
Bangangté o CAM 204-205 J 6
Bangaon o IND 142-143 G 2
Bangar o RP 160-161 D 4
Bangaré o RN 202-203 L 3
Bangarpet o IND 140-141 H 4
Bangassoko o BF 202-203 J 3
Bangassou ☆ RCA 206-207 F 6
Bangba o RCA 206-207 C 5
Bangbagatome o ZRE 210-211 K 2
Bangbali o RCA 206-207 E 4
Bangbong o RI 164-165 H 6
Bangda o VRC 144-145 L 5
Bangem o CAM 204-205 H 6
Banggai o RI 164-165 H 4
Banggai, Kepulauan ⌒ RI 164-165 H 4
Banggai, Pulau ⌒ RI 164-165 H 4
Banggi, Pulau ⌒ MAL 160-161 B 9
Banggo o RI 168 D 7
Ban Ghanimah, Jabal ▲ LAR 192-193 F 5
Banghāzī ▫ LAR 192-193 J 2
Banghāzī ☆ LAR 192-193 J 1
Banghiang ~ LAO 158-159 J 2
Bangil o RI 168 E 3
Bangka, Pulau ⌒ RI (SLU) 164-165 J 3
Bangka, Pulau ⌒ RI (SUS) 162-163 G 6
Bangka, Selat ≈ 162-163 F 6
Bangkai, Tanjung ▲ RI 162-163 H 4
Bangkalan o RI 168 E 3
Bangkaru, Pulau ⌒ RI 162-163 B 3
Bangkdulis, Pulau ⌒ RI 164-165 E 2
Bangkinang o RI 162-163 D 4
Bangkir o RI 164-165 G 3
Bangko o RI 162-163 E 6
Bangkoa o RI 164-165 F 6
Bangkok ☆ THA 158-159 F 4
Bangkok, Bight of ≈ 158-159 F 4
Bangkulu, Pulau ⌒ RI 164-165 H 4
Bangladesh ■ BD 142-143 F 3
Bang Lamung o THA 158-159 F 4
Bang Len o THA 158-159 F 3
Bangli o• RI 168 B 7
Bang O o THA 158-159 E 6
Bangolo o CI 202-203 G 6
Bangong Co ⊙ IND 138-139 G 3
Bangong Co ⊙ VRC (XIZ) 144-145 B 4
Bangong Co • VRC (XIZ) 144-145 B 4
Bangor o CDN (SAS) 232-233 Q 5
Bangor o• GB (NIR) 90-91 E 4
Bangor o• GB (WAL) 90-91 E 5
Bangor o USA (IA) 274-275 E 2
Bangor o USA (ME) 278-279 N 4
Bangor o USA (MI) 272-273 C 5
Bangor o USA (PA) 280-281 L 3
Bangoran o RCA 206-207 D 4
Bangoran o RCA (Bam) 206-207 E 4
Bangoran ~ RCA 206-207 D 4
Bangou o RCB 210-211 E 5
Bangourèn o CAM 204-205 J 6
Bang Pakong o THA 158-159 F 4
Bangs o USA (TX) 266-267 H 2
Bangsalsembera o RI 164-165 E 4
Bang Saphan o THA 158-159 E 5
Bangsi, Tanjung ▲ RI 162-163 D 3
Bangsund o N 86-87 E 4
Bangu o ZRE (BAN) 216-217 E 3
Bangu o ZRE (SHA) 214-215 B 5
Bangu, Chute ~ ZRE 210-211 L 2
Bangué o CAM 210-211 E 2
Bangued ☆ RP 160-161 D 4
Banguey Barat Parit ≈ 160-161 B 9
Bangui ★• RCA 206-207 D 6
Bangui o RN 198-199 C 6
Bangui Bay ≈ 160-161 D 3
Bangui Kété ~ RCA 206-207 E 6
Bangui-Motaba o RCB 210-211 F 2
Bangula o MW 218-219 H 3
Bangun o VRC 156-157 E 5
Bangunpurba o RI 162-163 C 3
Bangweulu, Lake ⊙ Z 214-215 E 6
Bangweulu Swamps ⩙ Z 214-215 E 6
Banhā ☆ ET 194-195 E 2
Ban Haew Ta Bua o THA 158-159 F 3
Ban Hat Lek o THA 158-159 G 5
Banhine, Parque Nacional de ⊥ MOC 218-219 G 6
Ban Hinkhan o LAO 158-159 H 2
Ban Houayxay ☆ LAO 142-143 M 5
Bani o BF 202-203 K 3
Bani o CI 202-203 G 5
Baní ☆ DOM 54-55 K 5
Bani o RCA 206-207 F 5
Bani ~ RMM 202-203 H 3
Bani, Ibel ▲ MA 188-189 G 6
Bani, Playa ⩙• DOM 54-55 K 5
Bania o RCA 206-207 C 6
Bani 'Āmir o KSA 132-133 C 4
Bani 'Atiya ⩙ KSA 130-131 E 3
Bani-Bangou o RN 204-205 E 1
Bānica o DOM 54-55 K 5
Banifing ~ RMM 202-203 G 4
Banifing ~ RMM 202-203 H 3
Bani Hasan ∴• ET 194-195 E 4
Bani Hašbal, Wādī o KSA 132-133 C 4
Bani Island ⌒ RP 160-161 F 6
Banija ▲ BIH 100-101 E 2
Banikoara o DY 204-205 E 3
Banima o RCA 206-207 F 6
Bani-Mallāl = Beni-Mellal ☆ MA 188-189 H 4
Bani Mazar o ET 194-195 E 3
Baninah o LAR 192-193 J 1
Bani Rikāb ⩙ IRQ 128-129 L 7
Banir River ~ PNG 183 D 4
Bani Sa'id ⩙ IRQ 128-129 M 7
Banissa o EAK 212-213 H 2
Banister River ~ USA (VA) 280-281 G 7
Bani Suwaif ☆ ET 194-195 E 3
Baní Walid ☆ LAR 192-193 E 2
Bāniyās o• IRQ 128-129 F 5
Banja Luka o• BIH 100-101 F 2
Banjar o RI 168 C 3
Banjaran Bintang ▲ MAL 162-163 D 2
Banjaran Brassey ▲ MAL 160-161 B 10
Banjaran Timur ▲ MAL 162-163 E 2
Banjaran Titiwangsa ▲ MAL 162-163 D 3
Banjarbaru o RI 164-165 D 5
Banjarkasang o RI 162-163 D 5
Banjarmasin ☆ RI 164-165 D 5
Banjarnegara o RI 168 C 3
Banjia o VRC 142-143 L 4
Banjul ★• WAG 202-203 B 3
Bank o AZ 128-129 N 3
Bānka o IND 142-143 E 3
Banka Banka o AUS 174-175 C 6
Bankapur o IND 140-141 F 3
Bankas o RMM 202-203 J 2
Bankberg ▲ ZA 220-221 G 6
Bankend o CDN (SAS) 232-233 P 4
Banket o ZW 218-219 F 3
Ban Khamphô o LAO 158-159 J 3
Bankilaré o RN 202-203 L 2
Bankim o CAM 204-205 J 5
Banko o RG 202-203 E 4
Banko o RMM 202-203 G 3
Bankon o RG 202-203 E 4
Bankoumana o RMM 202-203 F 3
Banks o USA (AR) 276-277 C 7
Banks o USA (ID) 252-253 B 2
Banks, Cape ▲ AUS 180-181 F 4
Banks, Îles = Banks Island ⌒ VAN 184 II a 2
Banks, Point ▲ USA 22-23 U 3
Banks/ Torres ▫ VAN 184 II b 1
Banks Island ⌒ CDN (BC) 228-229 D 3
Banks Island ⌒ CDN (NWT) 24-25 L 4
Banks Islands = Îles Banks ⌒ VAN 184 II a 2
Banks Lake ⊙ CDN 30-31 W 4
Banks Lake ⊙ USA (GA) 284-285 G 6
Banks Lake ⊙ USA (WA) 244-245 F 3
Banks Peninsula ⩙ CDN 30-31 P 2
Banks Peninsula ⩙ NZ 182 D 5
Banks Strait ≈ 180-181 J 6
Bānkura o IND 142-143 E 4
Ban Lam Narai o THA 158-159 F 3
Ban La Pha o LAO 158-159 H 2
Banli o VRC 156-157 E 5
Banmankhi o IND 142-143 E 3
Banmauk o MYA 142-143 J 3
Ban Mouang o LAO 156-157 B 7
Ban Na Inh Noi o LAO 156-157 D 7
Bannaja ~ RUS 112-113 L 3
Ban Nakala o LAO 158-159 H 2
Ban Na Mang o LAO 156-157 D 6
Ban Nambak o LAO 156-157 C 6
Ban Nang Sata o THA 158-159 F 7
Ban Napè o LAO 156-157 D 7
Ban Na Phao o LAO 158-159 H 2
Ban Na Sam o THA 158-159 E 6
Bannerman Town o BS 54-55 G 2
Banner Reef ⌒ JA 54-55 F 6
Bannikoppa o IND 140-141 F 3
Banning o USA (CA) 248-249 H 6
Bannockburn o CDN (ONT) 238-239 H 4
Bannock Pass ▲ USA (MT) 250-251 F 7
Bannock Range ▲ USA (ID) 252-253 F 4
Ban Nong Chaeng o THA 158-159 F 3
Ban Nong Phu o THA 158-159 H 3
Ban Nongsim o LAO 158-159 H 3
Bannu o• PK 138-139 C 3
Bannur o IND 140-141 G 4
Baños o EC 64-65 C 2
Banos o PE 64-65 D 7
Baños, Los o PE 70-71 B 6
Banos, Los o USA (CA) 248-249 D 2
Ban Pa Daeng o THA 142-143 M 6
Ban Pak Bat o THA 158-159 F 2
Ban Pakbông o LAO 158-159 J 3
Ban Phai o THA 158-159 G 2
Ban Phon o LAO 158-159 J 3
Ban Phu o THA 158-159 G 2
Ban Pong o THA 158-159 E 4
Banqiao o VRC 156-157 H 6
Ban Rai o THA 158-159 E 3
Ban San Chao Po o THA 158-159 F 3
Bansara o WAN 204-205 H 5
Ban Sênkhan o LAO 156-157 C 6
Banská Bystrica o SK 92-93 P 4
Banská Štiavnica o••• SK 92-93 P 4
Bānswāra o IND 138-139 E 8
Banta o SP 212-213 J 4
Banta, Pulau ⌒ RI 168 D 7
Ban Tabôk o LAO 156-157 C 7
Bantadjé o CAM 204-205 K 4
Bantaeng o RI 164-165 F 6
Bantakoto o RMM 202-203 E 3
Bantala ~ RG 202-203 D 4
Bantarbolang o RI 168 C 3
Bantarkawung o RI 168 C 3
Bantaya Island ⌒ RP 160-161 E 7
Bantayan o RP 160-161 E 7
Bantè o DY 202-203 L 5
Banten o• RI 168 B 3
Ban Tha Rae o THA 158-159 H 2
Ban Tha Song Yang o THA 158-159 D 2
Ban Thieng o LAO 156-157 C 7
Bantimurung o RI 164-165 F 6
Bantimurung Reserve ⊥• RI 164-165 F 6
Banting o MAL 162-163 D 3
Bantioli, Réserve Partielle de ⊥ BF 202-203 J 4
Bantola o RI 164-165 F 3
Banton Island ⌒ RP 160-161 E 6
Bantry = Beanntraí o IRL 90-91 C 6
Bantshamba o ZRE 210-211 G 6
Bantul o RI 168 D 3
Ban Tung o LAO 158-159 H 2
Banua o RP 160-161 B 8
Banvo o ANG 216-217 E 4
Ban Xang o VN 156-157 D 7
Ban Xésavang o LAO 158-159 H 2
Banyak, Kepulauau ⌒ RI 162-163 B 4
Banynasin ~ RI 162-163 F 6
Banyo o CAM 204-205 J 5
Banyoles o• E 98-99 J 3
Banyumas o RI 168 C 3
Banyuwangi o RI 168 B 7
Banyuwedang o RI 168 B 7
Banz o PNG 183 C 3
Banzana o RMM 202-203 G 4
Banzare Land ⩙ ARK 16 G 13
Banza Sanda o ZRE 210-211 E 6
Banza Sosso o ANG 216-217 C 2
Banzi o CI 202-203 G 5
Bao o RCA 206-207 F 6
Bao o TCH 206-207 C 4
Bao, Río ~ DOM 54-55 K 5
Baode o VRC 154-155 G 2
Baodi o VRC 154-155 K 2
Baoding o VRC 154-155 J 2
Baodingchan Temple o VRC 156-157 D 2
Baofatu o VAN 184 II b 3
Baofeng o VRC 154-155 H 5
Baoji o VRC 154-155 E 4
Baojing o VRC 156-157 F 2
Baojiqu o VRC 154-155 D 3
Baokang o VRC 154-155 G 6
Bao Khao Sai o THA 158-159 F 2
Baolo o SOL 184 I d 2
Bảo Lộc o VN 158-159 J 5
Baoqing o VRC 150-151 J 4
Baoro o RCA 206-207 B 6
Baoruco, Parque Nacional Sierra de ⊥ DOM 54-55 K 5
Baoruco, Sierra de ▲ DOM 54-55 K 5
Baoshan o VRC (SGH) 154-155 M 6
Baoshan o VRC (YUN) 142-143 L 3
Baota Shan o VRC 154-155 F 3
Baotianman Z.B. ⊥• VRC 154-155 G 5
Baoting o VRC 156-157 F 7
Baotou o VRC 154-155 F 1
Baoulé ~ RMM 202-203 F 3
Baoulé ~ RMM 202-203 G 4
Baoule, Collines ▲ CI 202-203 H 6
Baoxun o VRC 156-157 G 5
Bảo Yên o VN 156-157 D 5
Bảo Yên o VN 156-157 D 5
Baoying o VRC 154-155 L 5
Bāp o IND 138-139 D 6
Bāpatla o IND 140-141 J 3
Bapaume o CDN (SAS) 232-233 L 2
Bappagaj ~ RUS 118-119 M 4
Bapsfontein o ZA 220-221 J 2
Baptist o JA 54-55 G 5
Baptiste River ~ CDN (ALB) 232-233 C 3
Baq'ā' o KSA 130-131 H 4
Baqên o VRC 144-145 K 5
Bāqerābād o IR 134-135 D 1
Bāqir, Ǧabal ▲ JOR 130-131 D 3
Ba'qūba ☆ IRQ 128-129 L 6
Baquedano o RCH 76-77 C 2
Baquerizo o EC 64-65 C 2
Bar o YU 100-101 G 3
Bara o RG 202-203 D 3
Bara o RI 166-167 D 3
Bara o WAN 204-205 J 3
Baraawe o SP 212-213 K 3
Baraba, gora ▲ RUS 120-121 R 6
Barabai o RI 164-165 D 5
Barabaš o RUS 122-123 D 7
Barabaš-Levada o RUS 122-123 D 6
Barabinsk o RUS 114-115 P 7
Barabinskaja nizmenost' ⩙ RUS 124-125 J 1
Barabinskaya Step' = Barabinskaja nizmenost' ⩙ RUS 124-125 J 1
Bar Abir < ETH 208-209 F 6
Baraboo o USA (WI) 274-275 J 1
Barabouié o BF 202-203 J 2
Baracaju ou Maracaja, Rio ~ BR 72-73 E 2
Barachois o CDN (QUE) 240-241 L 2
Barachois Pond Provincial Park ⊥ CDN (NFL) 242-243 K 4
Baracoa o C 54-55 H 4
Barādar-e Šāh, Kūh-e ▲ IR 128-129 M 4
Baradères o RH 54-55 J 5
Baradero o RA 78-79 K 2
Baradine o AUS 178-179 K 6
Baradine Creek ~ AUS 178-179 K 6
Baraga o USA (MI) 270-271 K 4
Baragoi o EAK 212-213 F 3
Bārah o SUD 200-201 E 6
Barahan o RP 160-161 D 6
Barāhanagar o IND 142-143 F 4
Barahona ☆ DOM 54-55 K 5
Barahona, Paso de ▲ RA 76-77 B 6
Barail Range ▲ IND 142-143 H 3
Bara-Issa ~ RMM 202-203 H 2
Barajy ~ RUS 120-121 E 2
Baraka ~ ER 200-201 H 5
Baraka o ZRE 212-213 B 6
Baraka, Khor ~ SUD 200-201 H 4
Barakaldo o E 98-99 F 3
Barakan o RI 166-167 H 5
Barakāt Sharīf Ya'qūb o SUD 200-201 F 5
Baraki o AFG 138-139 B 3
Baral ~ BD 142-143 F 3
Baralzon Lake ⊙ CDN 30-31 V 5
Baram ~ MAL 164-165 D 1
Baram, Tanjung ▲ MAL 162-163 K 2
Baramani o GUY 62-63 E 2
Baramata o PNG 183 E 6
Bārāmati o IND 138-139 E 10
Barambah Creek ~ AUS 178-179 L 4
Baramula o IND 138-139 E 2
Bārān o IND 138-139 F 7
Barān o IR 128-129 M 3
Bārān, Kūh-e ▲ IR 134-135 H 2
Baranavichy = Baranavičy ☆ BY 94-95 K 5
Baranavičy ☆ BY 94-95 K 5
Baranga o ZRE 210-211 L 2
Barangbarang o RI 168 E 6
Barani o BF 202-203 J 3
Baraniha o RUS 112-113 P 2
Barankol o KA 124-125 E 3
Baranoa o CO 60-61 D 2
Baranof o USA 32-33 C 3
Baranof Island ⌒ USA 32-33 C 3
Baranoviči = Baranavičy ☆ BY 94-95 K 5
Barão de Grajau o BR 68-69 G 5
Barão de Melgaço o BR 70-71 G 2
Barão do Melgaço o BR 70-71 K 5
Barão do Triunfo o BR 74-75 E 8
Baraouéli o RMM 202-203 G 3
Baraqish ∴• Y 132-133 D 6
Barāra o KSA 132-133 B 3
Bararati, Rio ~ BR 66-67 H 6
Bararis, togga ~ SP 208-209 G 3
Barataria Bay ≈ 48-49 D 5
Barataria Bay ≈ USA 268-269 L 7
Barat Bali National Park ⊥ RI 168 B 7
Barauli o IND 142-143 D 2
Baraúna, Rio ~ BR 62-63 D 5
Baraya o CO 60-61 D 6
Barbacena o BR 72-73 J 6
Barbacoas o CO 64-65 C 1
Barbadan o SP 212-213 J 2
Barbado o BR 66-67 D 7
Barbado, Rio ~ BR 70-71 H 4
Barbados ■ BDS 56 F 5
Barbágia Belvì ⩙• I 100-101 B 5
Barbalha o BR 68-69 J 5
Barbar o SUD 200-201 G 3
Barbara Lake ⊙ CDN (ONT) 234-235 Q 5
Barbastro o E 98-99 H 3
Barbate de Franco o E 98-99 E 6
Barbaza o RP 160-161 E 7
Bârbele o LV 94-95 J 3
Barberton o ZA 220-221 K 2
Barberville o USA (FL) 286-287 H 2
Barbes, Cap ▲ MA 196-197 B 3
Barbitaj ~ RUS 116-117 J 9
Barbosa o CO 60-61 E 5
Barbour Bay ≈ 30-31 X 4
Barbourville o USA (KY) 276-277 M 4
Barbuda Island ⌒ AG 56 E 3
Barbwire Range ▲ AUS 172-173 G 5
Barca = Al Marj ☆•• LAR 192-193 J 1
Barca, La o MEX 52-53 C 1
Barcaldine o AUS 178-179 H 2
Barcarena o BR 62-63 K 6
Barcarrota o E 98-99 D 5
Barcelona o BR 68-69 L 4
Barcelona ☆••• E 98-99 J 4
Barcelona o PE 70-71 C 2
Barcelona ☆ YV 60-61 J 2
Barcelonnette o• F 90-91 L 9
Barcelos o BR 66-67 F 3
Barciany o PL 92-93 Q 1
Barclay o USA (TX) 266-267 K 2
Barclay, Kap ▲ GRØ 28-29 c 2
Barclay Bugt ≈ 28-29 c 2
Barco o USA (NC) 282-283 M 4
Barcoo River ~ AUS 178-179 G 3
Barcs o H 92-93 O 6
Barcyn ☆ KA 124-125 F 4
Barda ☆ RUS 96-97 J 5
Barda, Arroyo de la ~ RA 78-79 F 4
Barda = Barda o AZ 128-129 M 2
Bardaale o SP 208-209 H 5
Barda del Medio o RA 78-79 E 5
Bardagué ~ TCH 198-199 H 2
Bardaï o TCH 198-199 H 2
Bardārāš o IRQ 128-129 K 4
Bárðarbunga ▲ IS 86-87 e 2
Bardas Blancas o RA 78-79 E 3
Barddhamān o IND 142-143 E 4
Bardejov o SK 92-93 Q 4
Bardeskan o IR 136-137 E 7
Bardoli o IND 138-139 D 9
Bardsir o IR 134-135 G 4
Bardstown o USA (KY) 276-277 K 3
Barduelva ~ N 86-87 J 2
Bardula o IND 142-143 C 5
Bardwell o USA (KY) 276-277 F 4
Bardymskij hrebet ▲ RUS 96-97 L 5
Barē o ETH 208-209 F 6
Bāre o IND 140-141 F 3
Bareilly o IND 138-139 G 5
Bareli o IND 138-139 G 8
Barentsburg o N 84-85 J 3
Barentsøya ⌒ N 84-85 N 3
Barents Sea ≈ 84-85 O 6
Barentu o ER 200-201 H 5
Bareo o MAL 164-165 D 2
Bare Rock ▲ AUS 178-179 M 4
Barfolomeevsk o RUS 122-123 E 6
Bārgā o IR 134-135 G 5
Barga o• VRC 144-145 C 5
Bargaal o SP 208-209 K 3
Bargarh o IND 142-143 C 5
Barge Bay o CDN (NFL) 242-243 M 1
Bargersville o USA (IN) 274-275 M 5
Barğovein, Kūh-e ▲ IR 136-137 E 6
Barguzin ☆ RUS 118-119 D 9
Barguzin ~ RUS 118-119 E 8
Barguzin, Ust'- o RUS 116-117 O 9
Barguzinskij, zapovednik ⊥ RUS 118-119 D 8
Barguzinskij hrebet ▲ RUS 118-119 D 9
Bārh o IND 142-143 D 3
Bar Harbor o USA (ME) 278-279 N 4
Barhi o IND 142-143 D 3
Bari ☆• I 100-101 F 4
Bāri o IND 138-139 F 6
Bari ▫ SP 208-209 K 3
Bari o WAN 204-205 F 3
Bari, Kūh-e ▲ IR 134-135 E 4
Bariadi o EAT 212-213 D 5
Baricho o EAK 212-213 G 5
Barik, al- o KSA 132-133 B 3
Barika o DZ 190-191 E 3
Barika ~ DZ 190-191 E 3
Barikōt o AFG 136-137 M 7
Barillas o GCA 52-53 J 4
Baril Station, Pointe au o CDN (ONT) 238-239 E 3
Barim, Ǧazīrat ⌒ Y 132-133 C 7
Barinas ☆ YV 60-61 F 3
Baring o CDN (SAS) 232-233 P 5
Baring o USA (MO) 274-275 F 4
Baring, Cape ▲ CDN 24-25 N 5
Baringa o ZRE 210-211 H 3
Baring Channel ≈ 24-25 W 4
Baringo, Lake ⊙ EAK 212-213 F 3
Baripāda o IND 142-143 E 5
Bariri o BR 72-73 F 7
Bariri, Represa < BR 72-73 F 7
Bāris o ET 194-195 E 5
Bari Sādri o IND 138-139 E 7
Barisal o BD 142-143 G 4
Barisan, Pegunungan ▲ RI 162-163 D 5
Barit, al- o IRQ 128-129 K 7
Barito ~ RI 164-165 D 4
Baritu, Parque Nacional ⊥ RA 76-77 E 2
Bariya < IRQ 128-129 K 5
Barjūj, Wādī ~ LAR 192-193 E 5
Barkā' o OM 132-133 K 2
Barkal, Ǧabal • SUD 200-201 E 3
Barkam o VRC 154-155 C 6
Barkan, Ra's-e ▲ IR 134-135 C 4
Barkava o LV 94-95 K 3
Barkédji o SN 202-203 C 2
Barkerville o• CDN (BC) 228-229 N 3
Barkerville Historic Town • CDN (BC) 228-229 N 3
Barkéwol Abiod o RIM 196-197 D 6
Barkhān o PK 138-139 B 5
Barkley, Lake ⊙ USA (KY) 276-277 H 4
Barkley Sound ≈ 32-33 H 7
Barkley Sound ≈ CDN 230-231 D 5
Barkly Downs o AUS 174-175 E 7
Barkly East o ZA 220-221 H 5
Barkly Highway II AUS 174-175 D 6
Barkly Homestead Roadhouse o AUS 174-175 C 6
Barkly Pass o ZA 220-221 H 5
Barkly Tableland ▲ AUS 174-175 C 5
Barkly West o ZA 220-221 G 4
Barkol o VRC 146-147 L 4
Barkol, Wādī ~ SUD 200-201 E 4
Barkol Hu ⊙ VRC 146-147 L 4
Bark River o USA (MI) 270-271 L 5
Barksdale o USA (TX) 266-267 G 4
Barkway o CDN (ONT) 238-239 F 4
Barlavento, Ilhas de ⌒ CV 202-203 B 5
Bar-le-Duc ☆• F 90-91 K 7
Barlee, Lake ⊙ AUS 176-177 E 4
Barlee Range ▲ AUS 176-177 D 1
Barletta o• I 100-101 F 4
Barlett Reservoir ⊙ USA (AZ) 256-257 D 5
Barling o USA (AR) 276-277 A 5
Barlow o USA (OH) 280-281 E 4
Barlo Warf o WAL 202-203 D 5
Barloweerie, Mount ▲ AUS 176-177 D 3
Barlyk ~ RUS 116-117 E 10
Barma o RI 166-167 G 2
Barmedman o AUS 180-181 J 3
Barmer o IND 138-139 C 7
Barmera o AUS 180-181 F 3
Barm Firuz, Kūh-e ▲ IR 134-135 D 3
Barnaby River o CDN (NB) 240-241 K 4
Barnāla o IND 138-139 E 4
Barnard o USA (SD) 260-261 H 1
Barnard Castle o• GB 90-91 G 4
Barnard Point ▲ CDN 24-25 P 4
Barnard River ~ AUS 178-179 L 6
Barnato o AUS 178-179 H 6
Barnaul ☆ RUS 124-125 N 2
Barnaulka ~ RUS 124-125 N 2
Barnegat Light o USA (NJ) 280-281 M 4
Barne Glacier ⊂ ARK 16 E 0
Barnes Ice Cap ⊂ CDN 26-27 O 8
Barnes Sound ≈ USA 286-287 J 6
Barnesville o USA (GA) 284-285 F 3
Barnesville o USA (MN) 270-271 B 4
Barnesville o USA (OH) 280-281 E 4
Barneys Brook ~ CDN (NFL) 242-243 M 3
Barneys Lake ⊙ AUS 180-181 H 2
Barnhart o USA (TX) 266-267 F 2
Barnsdall o USA (OK) 264-265 H 2
Barnstable o USA (MA) 278-279 L 7
Barnstaple o• GB 90-91 E 6
Barnum o USA (WY) 252-253 M 3
Barnwell o CDN (ALB) 232-233 F 6
Barnwell o USA (SC) 284-285 J 3
Baro o TCH 198-199 J 6
Baro o WAN 204-205 G 4
Baroe o ZA 220-221 G 6
Barōġil o AFG 136-137 N 6
Baron o RI (JTI) 168 E 3
Baron o RI (YOG) 168 D 4
Barons o CDN (ALB) 232-233 E 5
Barora Island ⌒ SOL 184 I d 2
Barora Ite Island ⌒ SOL 184 I d 2
Barossa Valley ⩙ AUS 180-181 E 3
Barotac Nuevo o RP 160-161 E 7
Barotske Floot Plain ⩙ Z 218-219 B 2
Baroua o RCA 206-207 G 6
Barouda, Hassi < DZ 190-191 C 6
Baro Wenz ~ ETH 208-209 B 4
Barpeta o IND 142-143 G 2
Barqah ⩙ LAR 192-193 J 2
Barquisimeto ☆ YV 60-61 G 2
Barra o BR (BAH) 68-69 G 7
Barra o BR (CAT) 74-75 F 7
Barra ⌒ GB 90-91 D 3
Barra o WAG 202-203 B 3
Barra, Ponta da ▲ BR 74-75 G 5
Barraba o AUS 178-179 L 6
Barra Bonita o BR 72-73 F 7
Barra Bonita, Represa de < BR 72-73 F 7
Barraca da Boca o BR 62-63 H 6
Barraca de A. Lopes o BR 66-67 H 6
Barracão o BR 74-75 E 6
Barracão do Barreto o BR 66-67 H 7
Barracas o E 98-99 G 4
Barracouta Shoal ⌒ AUS 172-173 G 2
Barra da Estiva o BR 72-73 K 2
Barradale Roadhouse o AUS 172-173 B 7
Barra del Chuy o ROU 74-75 D 9
Barra de Mamanguape o BR 68-69 L 5
Barra de Santa Rosa o BR 68-69 K 5
Barra de São Francisco o BR 72-73 K 5
Barra de São Manuel o BR 66-67 H 6
Barra de São Miguel o BR (ALA) 68-69 L 6
Barra de São Miguel o BR (PA) 68-69 K 5
Barra de Tuxpan o MEX 52-53 F 1
Barra do Bugres o BR 70-71 J 4
Barra do Corda o BR 68-69 F 4
Barra do Cuanza o ANG 216-217 B 4
Barra do Dande o ANG 216-217 B 4
Barra do Garças o BR 72-73 D 3
Barra do Mendes o BR 68-69 G 7
Barra do Ouro o BR 74-75 E 7
Barra do Piraí o BR 72-73 J 7
Barra do Quaraí o BR 76-77 J 6
Barrage Mercier • CDN (QUE) 238-239 K 2
Barra Longa o BR 72-73 J 6
Barra Mansa o BR 72-73 H 7
Barrāmiya o ET 194-195 F 5
Barranca o PE (LIM) 64-65 D 7
Barranca o PE (LOR) 64-65 D 4
Barrancabermeja o CO 60-61 E 4
Barranca del Cobre, Parque Natural ⊥ MEX 50-51 F 4
Barranca de Upía = Cumaral o CO 60-61 E 5
Barrancas o YV (BOL) 60-61 J 4
Barrancas o YV (MON) 60-61 K 3
Barrancas, Arroyo ~ RA 76-77 H 5
Barrancas, Río ~ RA 78-79 D 4
Barranco Alto o BR 70-71 G 3
Barranco de Guadalupe o MEX 50-51 G 2
Barranco de Loba o CO 60-61 D 3
Barranco Picure o CO 60-61 G 6
Barrancos o P 98-99 D 5
Barrancos, Los o YV 60-61 K 3
Barrancoso, Arroyo ~ RA 78-79 J 2
Barranco Vermelho, Corredeira ~ BR 70-71 G 3
Barranqueras o RA 76-77 H 4
Barranquilla ☆ CO 60-61 D 2
Barranquilla o RCH 76-77 B 4
Barranquitas o USA (PR) 286-287 P 2
Barranquitas o YV 60-61 E 2
Barras o BR 66-67 E 7
Barra Seca o BR 72-73 K 6
Barraute o CDN (QUE) 236-237 L 4
Barr'd Harbour o CDN (NFL) 242-243 L 2
Barre o USA (MA) 278-279 J 6
Barre o USA (VT) 278-279 J 4
Barre, Port o USA (LA) 268-269 J 6
Barreal o RA 76-77 C 6
Barreal, El o MEX 50-51 F 2
Barreal, El o RA 76-77 D 5
Barreira Branca o BR 68-69 C 6
Barreira da Cruz o BR 68-69 D 7
Barreira do Peiqui o BR 72-73 F 2
Barreiras o BR 72-73 H 2
Barreiras, Rio das ~ BR 68-69 D 6
Barreirinha o BR 66-67 J 4
Barreirinhas o BR 68-69 G 3
Barreiro o P 98-99 C 5
Barreiros o BR 68-69 L 6
Barrelville o USA (SC) 284-285 K 4
Barrême o F 90-91 L 10
Barren, Nosy ⌒ RM 222-223 C 7
Barren Grounds ⩙ CDN 30-31 O 2
Barren Island ⌒ IND 140-141 L 3
Barren Island, Cape ▲ AUS 180-181 K 6
Barren Islands ⌒ USA 22-23 U 3

302 Bam Island — Barren Islands

Bediani ○ GE 126-127 F 7
Bedias ~ USA (TX) 268-269 E 6
Bedi Dat ○ PK 134-135 L 5
Bediondo ○ TCH 206-207 C 4
Bedjedjene, Hassi ‹ DZ 190-191 K 4
Bednesti ○ CDN (BC) 228-229 L 3
Bednodem'janovsk ○ RUS 94-95 S 5
Bédo ‹ TCH 198-199 J 3
Bedoba ○ RUS 116-117 H 6
Bédouaram ‹ RN 198-199 F 5
Bedoud, Hassi ‹ MA 188-189 K 4
Bee ○ USA (NE) 262-263 J 4
Beebe ○ USA (AR) 276-277 D 6
Beechal River ~ AUS 178-179 H 4
Beecher ○ USA (IL) 274-275 L 3
Beechey Lake ○ CDN 30-31 Q 3
Beechey Point ○ USA 20-21 Q 1
Beech Fork Lake ‹ USA (WV) 280-281 D 5
Beech Grove ○ USA (IN) 274-275 M 5
Beechgrove ○ USA (TN) 276-277 J 2
Beech Island ○ USA (SC) 284-285 J 3
Beechwood ○ USA (MI) 272-273 C 5
Beechworth ○ AUS 180-181 J 4
Beecroft ○ CDN (SAS) 232-233 L 5
Beekman Peninsula ‹ CDN 36-37 R 3
Beeler ○ USA (KS) 262-263 F 6
Beenčíme ~ RUS 110-111 N 4
Beenleigh ○ AUS 178-179 M 4
Beeskow ○ D 92-93 N 2
Beestekraal ○ ZA 220-221 H 2
Beetaloo ○ AUS 174-175 B 5
Beeville ○ USA (TX) 266-267 K 5
Befale ○ ZRE 210-211 H 3
Befandefa ○ RM 222-223 C 9
Befandriana Atsimo ○ RM 222-223 C 9
Befandriana Avaratra ○ RM 222-223 F 5
Befasy ○ RM 222-223 D 8
Beffa ~ DY 204-205 E 4
Befori ○ RM 210-211 J 3
Beforona ○ RM 222-223 F 7
Befotakra ~ RM 222-223 E 9
Bega ○ AUS 180-181 K 4
Beggs ○ USA (OK) 264-265 H 3
Begičeva, grjada ▲ RUS 108-109 X 5
Begidžan ~ RUS 110-111 P 6
Bégin ○ CDN (QUE) 240-241 D 2
Begna ~ N 86-87 D 6
Begogo ○ RM 222-223 E 9
Bégon ○ RCA 206-207 D 4
Begoro ○ GH 202-203 K 6
Begunicy ○ RUS 94-95 L 2
Begusarai ○ IND 142-143 E 3
Beh ~ RI 168 C 7
Behábád ○ IR 134-135 G 3
Béhague, Pointe ▲ F 62-63 J 3
Behara ○ RM 222-223 E 10
Beheloka ○ RM 222-223 C 9
Behenjiy ○ RM 222-223 E 7
Béhili ○ RCA 206-207 D 5
Behm Canal ≈ 32-33 E 4
Behring Point ○ BS 54-55 G 2
Behšahr ○ IR 136-137 C 6
Bei'an ○ VRC 150-151 F 3
Beibu Wan ≈ 156-157 E 6
Beichuan ○ VRC 154-155 D 6
Beida = Goz ○ TCH 198-199 H 4
Beidaihe ○ VRC 154-155 L 2
Beidaneikechuke ○ VRC 144-145 F 5
Beidou ○ VRC 156-157 H 4
Beigi ○ ETH 208-209 B 4
Beihai ○ VRC 156-157 F 6
Bei Jiang ~ VRC 158-159 L 2
Bei Jiao ~ VRC 158-159 L 2
Beijing ★ • • • VRC 154-155 K 2
Beijing Gang ~ VRC 156-157 H 6
Beijin Shi ○ VRC 154-155 K 2
Bei Ling • VRC 150-151 D 7
Beiliu ○ VRC 156-157 G 5
Béinamar ○ TCH 206-207 B 4
Beipan Jiang ~ VRC 156-157 D 4
Beipiao ○ VRC 150-151 C 7
Beira ★ MOC 218-219 H 4
Beira Alta ○ ANG 216-217 C 4
Beirabad ○ IR 62-63 N 6
Beirut = Bairut ★ RL 128-129 F 6
Beiseker ○ CDN (ALB) 232-233 E 4
Bei Shan ▲ VRC 146-147 M 5
Beishan ○ VRC (JIL) 150-151 F 6
Beishan ○ VRC (ZHE) 156-157 L 2
Beitan ○ VRC 156-157 F 6
Beitau ○ VRC 156-157 F 6
Beitbridge ○ ZW 218-219 F 6
Beitstadfjorden ≈ 86-87 E 5
Beitun ○ VRC 146-147 H 2
Beizhangdian ○ VRC 154-155 H 3
Beizhen ○ VRC 150-151 C 7
Beja ○ • P 98-99 D 5
Béja ○ TN 190-191 G 2
Bejaia ☆ DZ 190-191 E 2
Béjar ○ E 98-99 E 4
Bejarm ○ RN 86-87 J 6
Beji ○ WAN 204-205 H 4
Bejlagan = Beylagan ○ AZ 128-129 M 3
B.E. Jordan Lake ‹ USA (NC) 282-283 H 5
Bejsug ~ RUS 102-103 L 5
Bejsugskij liman ≈ 102-103 L 4
Bejucal ○ C 54-55 D 3
Bek ~ CAM 210-211 E 2
Béka ○ CAM (ADA) 204-205 K 5
Béka ○ CAM (ADA) 206-207 C 4
Béka ○ CAM (NOR) 204-205 K 4
Bekabad ○ US 136-137 L 4
Békamba ○ TCH 206-207 C 4
Bekasi ○ RI 168 B 3
Bekati ○ US 136-137 N 4
Bekbeket ○ KA 96-97 H 10
Bekdaš ○ TM 136-137 N 4
Bek-Džar ○ KS 136-137 N 4
Beke ○ RI 168 E 7
Bèkè ~ RUS 110-111 K 6
Beke ○ ZRE 214-215 H 7

Bekenu ○ MAL 162-163 K 2
Békés ☆ H 92-93 Q 5
Békéscsaba ○ H 92-93 Q 5
Bekily ○ RM (TLA) 222-223 D 10
Bekipay ○ RM 222-223 E 6
Bekitro ○ RM 222-223 D 10
Bekkai ○ J 152-153 L 3
Bekmurat, gora ▲ TM 136-137 D 4
Bekodoka ○ RM 222-223 D 6
Bek'oji ○ ETH 208-209 D 5
Bekopa ○ RM 222-223 D 7
Bekwai ○ GH 202-203 J 6
Bekyem ○ GH 202-203 J 6
Bela ~ RUS 96-97 L 6
Bela ○ IND 142-143 C 3
Bela ○ PK 134-135 L 5
Bélabirim ‹ RN 198-199 F 5
Bélabo ○ CAM 204-205 K 6
Belaga ○ MAL 162-163 K 2
Belair ○ CDN (MAN) 234-235 G 4
Bel Air ○ USA (MI) 280-281 K 4
Belaja ~ RUS 96-97 L 6
Belaja ~ RUS 112-113 O 5
Belaja ~ RUS 112-113 R 4
Belaja ~ RUS 116-117 L 9
Belaja ~ RUS 122-123 D 3
Belaja ~ RUS 126-127 D 5
Belaja, gora ▲ RUS 112-113 S 4
Belaja Berëzka ○ RUS 102-103 M 3
Belaja, Ust'- ○ RUS 112-113 R 4
Belaja Cerkov' = Bila Cerkva ☆ UA 102-103 G 3
Belaja Gora ○ RUS 110-111 a 5
Belaja Holunica ☆ RUS 96-97 L 6
Belaja Kalitva ○ RUS 102-103 M 3
Belaja Skola ○ KA 124-125 N 5
Belajau, Danau ‹ RI 162-163 K 6
Belaja Zemlja, ostrova ‹ RUS 84-85 g 2
Belalcázar ○ E 98-99 E 5
Bela Lorena ○ BR 72-73 G 7
Belamoty ○ RM 222-223 D 10
Belang ○ RI 164-165 J 3
Belangbelang, Pulau ‹ RI (MAL) 164-165 K 4
Belangbelang, Pulau ‹ RI (SSE) 168 E 6
Belanger Island ‹ CDN 36-37 L 6
Belanger ○ CDN 34-35 H 4
Belanger River ~ CDN 34-35 H 4
Bela Palanka ○ YU 100-101 J 3
Belarus' = Belarus' ■ BY 94-95 K 5
Belas ○ ANG 216-217 B 4
Belâti ○ IND 142-143 F 2
Bela Vista ○ ANG (BGO) 216-217 B 3
Bela Vista ○ ANG (HBO) 216-217 D 6
Bela Vista ○ BR (APA) 62-63 J 4
Bela Vista ○ BR (GSU) 76-77 J 2
Bela Vista ○ BR (RSU) 74-75 D 7
Bela Vista ○ MOC 220-221 L 3
Bela Vista, Cachoeira ~ BR 68-69 C 3
Belawan ○ RI 162-163 C 3
Belayan ~ RI 164-165 E 3
Bélbéji ○ RN 198-199 C 5
Belbela, Sebkha Aïn ○ DZ 188-189 J 7
Belbutte ○ CDN (SAS) 232-233 L 2
Belc'c = Bălți ○ MD 102-103 E 4
Belčatów ○ PL 92-93 P 3
Belcher Channel ≈ 24-25 X 2
Belcher Islands ‹ CDN (NWT) 36-37 K 6
Belcher Islands ‹ CDN (NWT) 36-37 K 6
Belcher Point ○ CDN 24-25 g 3
Belchite ○ E 98-99 G 4
Belcourt Creek ~ CDN (BC) 228-229 O 2
Bel'cy = Bălți ○ MD 102-103 E 4
Belda ○ IND 142-143 E 4
Belden ○ USA (CA) 246-247 D 3
Belden ○ USA (NB) 258-259 E 3
Belding ○ USA (OH) 280-281 D 2
Belding ○ USA (MI) 272-273 D 4
Befdir, Us ~ RUS 116-117 J 10
Befdunčana, ozero ‹ RUS 116-117 E 8
Bele, ozero ‹ RUS 116-117 E 8
Belebej ★ RUS 96-97 J 6
Belebelka ○ RUS 94-95 M 3
Beledweyne ~ SP 208-209 G 6
Bélénbédjé ○ BF 202-203 K 2
Beléko-Soba ○ RMM 202-203 G 3
Bélel ○ CAM 206-207 B 5
Belel ○ WAN 204-205 K 4
Belele ○ AUS 176-177 D 4
Belém ○ BR (AMA) 66-67 C 5
Belém ○ BR • PE 62-63 K 6
Belém ○ PE 70-71 C 4
Belem de São Francisco ○ BR 68-69 G 4
Belen ○ CO 60-61 E 4
Belén ~ PA 52-53 D 7
Belén ○ RCH 70-71 C 6
Belen ○ USA (NM) 256-257 J 4
Belén, Río ~ RA 76-77 D 4
Belen'kaja ○ RUS 118-119 M 8
Belesc Cogani ○ SP 212-213 H 3
Belet Weyne = Beledweyne ~ SP 208-209 G 6
Beleuli ∴ • US 136-137 E 2
Belev ☆ RUS 94-95 P 4
Bèlèya Terara ▲ ETH 208-209 C 3
Beleza, Ribeiro ~ BR 68-69 C 6
Belezma, Monts de ▲ DZ 190-191 E 3
Belfast ☆ • GB 90-91 E 4
Belfast ○ USA (AR) 278-279 M 4
Belfast ○ USA (OH) 280-281 C 4
Belfield ○ USA (ND) 258-259 D 5
Bélfodiyo ○ ETH 208-209 B 3
Belfort ☆ F 90-91 M 4
Belfry ○ USA (MT) 250-251 N 6
Belgaum ○ IND 140-141 F 3
Belgica, La ○ BOL 70-71 F 5
Belgica Bank ≈ 26-27 s 4
Belgica Mountains ▲ ARK 16 F 31
Belgium = België = Belgique ■ B 92-93 G 3

Befgo ~ RUS 122-123 G 3
Belgo ○ SUD 206-207 L 3
Belgorod ○ RUS 102-103 K 2
Belgorod-Dnestrovskij ☆ UA 102-103 G 4
Belgrade (ME) 278-279 M 4
Belgrade ○ USA (MN) 270-271 C 5
Belgrade ○ USA (MT) 250-251 H 6
Belgrade = Beograd ★ • • YU 100-101 J 2
Belgrano ○ RA 76-77 F 3
Belgrano, Cerro ▲ RA 80 E 3
Belgreen ○ USA (AL) 284-285 D 5
Bel Guerdâne, Bir ○ RIM 196-197 E 2
Belic ○ RA 78-79 G 7
Belicoq ○ RA 78-79 D 7
Beliči, ostrov ‹ RUS 110-121 G 6
Belidži ○ RUS 126-127 H 7
Belifang ○ RM (LAM) 162-163 F 7
Beli Hill ▲ WAN 204-205 J 5
Belimbing ○ RI (LAM) 162-163 F 7
Belimbing ○ RI (SUS) 162-163 F 6
Belimbing, Tanjung ▲ RI 162-163 F 7
Belimbing, Teluk ≈ RI 162-163 F 7
Bélinga ○ G 210-211 D 3
Belinskij ○ RUS 94-95 R 5
Belinskoe ○ RUS 122-123 K 4
Belinyu ○ RI 162-163 F 5
Belitung, Pulau ‹ RI 162-163 H 6
Belize ○ ANG 210-211 D 6
Belize ○ BH 52-53 K 3
Belize City ○ BH 52-53 K 3
Belize River ~ BH 52-53 K 3
Bélizon ○ F 62-63 H 3
Beljacëvka ○ RUS 96-97 K 8
Beljaka, kosa ‹ RUS 112-113 X 3
Beljanica ▲ YU 100-101 J 2
Beljanka ○ RUS 118-119 O 4
Bel Kacem, Bir ○ TN 190-191 H 4
Beľkači ○ RUS 120-121 D 4
Beľkačil ~ RUS 120-121 D 4
Belkar ○ IND 140-141 F 5
Belknap Springs ○ USA (OR) 244-245 C 6
Beľkovskij, proliv ≈ 108-109 Z 1
Beľkovskij Nos, mys ▲ RUS 108-109 J 7
Bell ○ USA (FL) 286-287 G 2
Bell ○ ZA 220-221 H 6
Bell, Rivière ~ CDN (QUE) 236-237 L 3
Bell ○ CAM 210-211 C 2
Bella, Laguna ‹ RA 76-77 G 3
Bella Bella ○ CDN (BC) 228-229 F 4
Bella Coola ○ CDN (BC) 228-229 H 4
Bella Coola River ~ CDN (BC) 228-229 H 4
Belladère ○ RH 54-55 J 5
Bella Flor ○ BOL 70-71 D 2
Bellaire ○ USA (MI) 272-273 D 3
Bellaire ○ USA (OH) 280-281 F 3
Bellary ○ IND 140-141 G 4
Bellata ○ AUS 178-179 K 5
Bellavista ○ EC 64-65 B 10
Bellavista ○ PE (CAJ) 64-65 C 4
Bellavista ○ PE (MAR) 64-65 D 5
Bella Vista ○ PY 76-77 K 4
Bella Vista ○ RA 76-77 H 3
Belle ○ USA (WV) 280-281 F 4
Belledonne ▲ F 90-91 L 5
Bellefontaine ○ USA (OH) 280-281 C 3
Bellefonte ○ USA (PA) 280-281 J 3
Belle Fourche ○ USA (SD) 260-261 C 2
Belle Fourche Reservoir ‹ USA (SD) 260-261 C 2
Belle Fourche River ~ USA (WY) 252-253 N 3
Belle Glade ○ USA (FL) 286-287 J 5
Belle-Ile ‹ F 90-91 F 4
Belle Isle ○ CDN (NFL) 242-243 N 1
Belle Isle ○ CDN 38-39 R 3
Belle Isle, Strait of ≈ 38-39 Q 3
Belle Isle, Strait of ≈ CDN 242-243 M 1
Bellemont ○ USA (AZ) 256-257 D 3
Bellenden Ker ○ AUS 174-175 H 5
Bellenden Ker National Park ⊥ AUS 174-175 H 5
Belleoram ○ CDN (NFL) 242-243 N 5
Belle Plaine ○ CDN (SAS) 232-233 N 5
Belle Plaine ○ USA (KS) 262-263 J 7
Belle Plaine ○ USA (MN) 270-271 E 6
Belle River ○ CDN (ONT) 238-239 D 8
Belle River ○ CDN (PEI) 240-241 N 4
Belleterre ○ CDN (QUE) 236-237 K 5
Belleview ○ USA (FL) 286-287 H 3
Belleville ○ CDN (NS) 240-241 O 4
Belleville ○ CDN (ONT) 238-239 H 4
Belleville ○ USA (IL) 274-275 D 4
Belleville ○ USA (KS) 262-263 J 5
Belleville ○ USA (TX) 266-267 K 4
Bellevue ○ AUS 174-175 H 5
Bellevue ○ CDN (ALB) 232-233 D 6
Bellevue ○ USA (IA) 274-275 D 2
Bellevue ○ USA (MI) 272-273 D 5
Bellevue ○ USA (NE) 262-263 L 3
Bellevue ○ USA (TX) 264-265 F 5
Bellevue de--Inini, Mont ▲ F 62-63 H 4
Bellin ○ USA (WA) 244-245 C 2
Bellinger, Lac ‹ CDN 38-39 M 6
Bellingham ○ USA (WA) 244-245 C 2
Bellingshausen Abyssal Plain ≈ ARK 16 G 27

Bellingshausen Sea ≈ ARK 16 G 28
Bellinzona ☆ CH 92-93 K 5
Bell-Irving River ~ CDN 32-33 H 3
Bell Irving River ~ CDN 32-33 H 3
Bell Island ‹ CDN (NFL) 242-243 P 5
Bell Island ‹ CDN (NFL) 242-243 N 1
Bell Island Hot Springs ○ USA 32-33 E 4
Bellmead ○ USA (TX) 266-267 K 4
Bellmore ○ USA (IN) 274-275 L 5
Bell National Historic Park, Alexander Graham • CDN (NS) 240-241 P 4
Bello ○ CO 60-61 D 4
Bellona Island ‹ SOL 184 I d 4
Bellows Falls ○ USA (NH) 278-279 J 5
Bellpat ○ PK 138-139 B 5
Bell Peninsula ‹ CDN 36-37 H 3
Bell River ~ AUS 180-181 J 4
Bell River ~ CDN 20-21 W 3
Bells ○ USA (TX) 264-265 H 5
Bellsund ≈ N (SVA) 84-85 k 5
Belltown ○ USA (WV) 280-281 F 4
Belluno ○ I 100-101 D 1
Bellview ○ USA (NM) 256-257 M 4
Bell Ville ○ RA 78-79 H 2
Bellvue ○ USA (IA) 274-275 E 2
Belly River ~ CDN (ALB) 232-233 E 6
Belmond ○ USA (IA) 274-275 E 2
Belmont ○ USA (IL) 284-285 D 5
Belmont ○ USA (MAN) 234-235 D 5
Belmont ○ USA (MS) 268-269 M 2
Belmont ○ USA (NE) 262-263 C 2
Belmont ○ USA (NY) 278-279 J 5
Belmont ○ USA (TX) 266-267 K 4
Belmont ○ ZA 220-221 G 4
Belmonte ○ BR 72-73 L 3
Belmonte ○ USA (MN) 270-271 G 7
Belmopan ★ BH 52-53 K 3
Belmore Creek ~ AUS 174-175 J 6
Belmullet = Béal an Mhuirthead ○ IRL 90-91 C 4
Belo ○ RM 222-223 D 7
Belobaka ○ RM 222-223 D 7
Belo Campo ○ BR 72-73 K 3
Beloe, ozero ‹ RUS 94-95 P 3
Beloe, ozero ‹ RUS 114-115 U 7
Belogolovaja ~ RUS 110-121 U 2
Belogorsk ○ RUS (AMR) 122-123 C 3
Belogorsk ○ RUS (KMR) 114-115 J 3
Belogorskij materik ‹ RUS 114-115 J 3
Belogorskij materik, vozvyšennosť ▲ RUS 114-115 J 3
Beloha ○ RM 222-223 D 10
Belo Horizonte ★ BR 72-73 J 5
Beloit ○ USA (KS) 262-263 H 5
Beloit ○ USA (WI) 274-275 J 2
Belo Jardim ○ BR 68-69 K 6
Belo Monte ○ BR (ALA) 68-69 K 6
Belo Monte ○ BR (AMA) 66-67 E 5
Belo Monte do Pontal ○ BR 68-69 C 3
Belomorsk ○ RUS 88-89 N 4
Belomorsko-Baltijskij kanal ‹ RUS 88-89 N 4
Belonge ○ ZRE 210-211 H 5
Belopa ○ RI 164-165 G 5
Belorečensk ○ RUS 126-127 C 5
Beloreck ○ RUS 96-97 L 7
Belot, Lac ‹ CDN 30-31 G 2
Belo Tsiribihina ○ RM 222-223 D 7
Belousovka ○ KA 124-125 N 3
Belovo ○ RUS 114-115 T 7
Belovodskoe ○ KS 146-147 B 4
Beloye Ozero = Beloe, ozero ‹ RUS 94-95 P 1
Belozersk ○ RUS 94-95 P 3
Belozerskoe ○ RUS 114-115 M 7
Belozersko-Kirillovskie grjady ▲ RUS 94-95 P 1
Belpre ○ USA (KS) 262-263 G 7
Belpre ○ USA (OH) 280-281 E 4
Belrem, Hassi el ○ DZ 188-189 L 7
Belterra ○ BR 66-67 E 4
Belton ○ USA (MO) 274-275 D 6
Belton ○ USA (SC) 284-285 H 2
Belton ○ USA (TX) 266-267 K 4
Belton Lake ‹ USA (TX) 266-267 K 2
Beltov tepalik ~ US 136-137 G 3
Belubula River ~ AUS 180-181 K 3
Beluga Lake ‹ USA (AZ) 256-257 D 3
Beluha, gora ▲ KA 124-125 P 4
Beluran ○ MAL 160-161 B 10
Beluru ○ MAL 164-165 H 5
Beluš'e ○ RUS 88-89 T 3
Belušja Guba ○ RUS 108-109 G 6
Belužji Nos, mys ▲ RUS 108-109 M 6
Belvedere Marittimo ○ I 100-101 F 5
Belvidere ○ USA (IL) 274-275 K 2
Belvidere ○ USA (KS) 262-263 G 7
Belvidere ○ USA (SD) 260-261 G 3
Belwa, River ~ WAN 204-205 J 4
Belwali ○ LB 202-203 F 6
Belyando River ~ AUS 178-179 J 2
Belyj ~ RUS 94-95 N 4
Belyj, Ostrov = Belyj, ostrov ‹ RUS 108-109 O 5
Belzec ○ PL 92-93 R 3

Belzoni ○ USA (MS) 268-269 K 3
Béma ○ RMM 202-203 F 2
Bémal ○ RCA 206-207 C 5
Bemanevika ○ RM 222-223 G 5
Bemaraha ▲ RM 222-223 D 7
Bemarivo ~ RM 222-223 E 6
Bembe ○ ANG 216-217 C 3
Bembeche ⊥ TCH 198-199 J 3
Bembési ○ ZW 218-219 F 5
Bembetária ○ IND 142-143 B 5
Bemidji ○ USA (MN) 270-271 D 3
Bemis ○ USA (SD) 260-261 K 2
Bemonto ○ RM 222-223 D 7
Bemu ○ RI 166-167 E 3
Ben ○ BF 202-203 H 3
Bena ○ WAN 204-205 H 3
Benabarre ○ E 98-99 H 3
Benada ○ IND 138-139 G 9
Benagerie ○ AUS 178-179 H 5
Benahmed ○ MA 188-189 H 4
Benahouin ○ DZ 202-203 J 6
Benain ○ RI 166-167 C 6
Bena-Kamba ○ ZRE 210-211 K 5
Benalla ○ AUS 180-181 H 4
Ben-Ash Monument • USA (SD) 260-261 D 1
Benato-Toby ○ RM 222-223 D 9
Bena-Tshadi ○ ZRE 210-211 J 6
Benaule ▲ RM 222-223 D 7
Benavente ○ E 98-99 E 3
Benavides ○ USA (TX) 266-267 J 6
Ben Boït ○ USA (TX) 264-265 H 4
Benbonyathe Hill ▲ AUS 178-179 E 6
Benbrook Lake ‹ USA (TX) 264-265 G 6
Bencubbin ○ AUS 176-177 D 5
Bend ○ USA (OR) 244-245 D 6
Bend ○ USA (TX) 266-267 J 2
Bendándi ○ IND 140-141 E 2
Benda Range ▲ AUS 180-181 E 2
Bendel □ WAN 204-205 F 5
Bendeleben Mountains ▲ USA 20-21 H 4
Bendemeer ○ AUS 178-179 L 6
Bender = Tighina ○ MD 102-103 F 4
Bender Cassim = Boosaaso = Bender Qaasim ☆ SP 208-209 J 3
Bender Qaasim = Boosaaso ☆ SP 208-209 J 3
Bendery = Tighina ○ MD 102-103 F 4
Bendieuta Creek ~ AUS 178-179 E 6
Bendigo ○ AUS 180-181 H 4
Band of the Boyne • • • IRL 90-91 D 5
Bendugu ○ WAL 202-203 E 5
Bene ○ MOC 218-219 G 3
Benedict, Mount ▲ CDN 36-37 U 7
Benedict Fjord ≈ 26-27 r 2
Benedictine Monastery • AUS 176-177 D 5
Benedito Leite ○ BR 68-69 G 5
Bénéna ○ RMM 202-203 H 3
Benenitra ○ RM 222-223 D 9
Beneŝov ○ CZ 92-93 N 4
Benevento ○ I 100-101 F 4
Benevides ○ BR 62-63 K 6
Benewah ○ USA (ID) 250-251 C 4
Benfica ○ BR 72-73 J 6
Benga ○ MOC 218-219 G 3
Benga ○ WAN 204-205 H 2
Bengábád ○ IND 142-143 E 3
Bengal, Bay of ≈ 12 G 3
Bengala ○ CO 60-61 G 5
Bengalun, Tanjung ▲ RI 164-165 E 3
Bengamisa ○ ZRE 210-211 H 4
Bengawan ~ RI 168 E 3
Bengbis ○ CAM 206-207 C 4
Bengbu ○ VRC 154-155 K 5
Benge ○ USA (WA) 244-245 G 4
Benghazi = Banghází ★ LAR 192-193 J 4
Bengkalis ○ RI 162-163 E 4
Bengkalis, Pulau ‹ RI 162-163 E 4
Bengkayang ○ RI 162-163 H 4
Bengkulu ○ RI 162-163 E 6
Bengkulu, Teluk ≈ 162-163 E 7
Bengkunat, Teluk ≈ RI 162-163 F 7
Bengo ~ ANG 216-217 B 4
Bengo, Baia do ≈ ANG 216-217 B 4
Bengonça ○ CDN (SAS) 232-233 N 6
Bengou ○ ANG 216-217 E 6
Benguela ○ ANG (BGU) 216-217 B 6
Benguerir ○ MA 188-189 H 4
Beni ○ ZRE 212-213 B 3
Beni, Rio ~ BOL 70-71 E 3
Beni-Abbès ○ DZ 188-189 K 5
Beniah Lake ‹ CDN 30-31 N 4
Beni-Boufrah ○ MA 188-189 J 3
Benicarló ○ E 98-99 H 4
Benicia ○ USA (CA) 246-247 C 5
Benicito, Rio ~ BOL 70-71 E 2
Benidorm ○ E 98-99 G 5
Beni Haoua ○ DZ 190-191 D 2
Benihlef ○ DZ 188-189 L 5
Beni Kheddache ○ TN 190-191 H 4
Beni-Mellal ○ MA 188-189 H 4
Benin ■ DY 204-205 D 4
Benin, Bight of ≈ 204-205 D 5
Benin, River ~ WAN 204-205 F 6
Benin City ○ WAN 204-205 F 6
Beni Ounif ○ DZ 188-189 L 4
Beni Saf ○ DZ 188-189 K 3
Benisheikh ○ WAN 204-205 K 3
Beni Slimane ○ DZ 190-191 D 2
Beni-Smir ○ DZ 188-189 L 4
Beni-Snassen, Monts des ▲ MA 188-189 K 4
Beni Tajjite ○ MA 188-189 K 4
Benito ○ CDN (MAN) 234-235 B 3

Benito Juárez ○ MEX 50-51 F 3
Benito Juárez ○ RA 78-79 K 3
Benito Juárez, Parque Nacional ⊥ MEX 52-53 F 3
Benjamin ○ USA (TX) 264-265 G 5
Benjamin ○ USA (UT) 254-255 D 5
Benjamin, Isla ‹ RCH 80 C 2
Benjamin Aceval ○ PY 76-77 J 3
Benjamin Constant ○ BR 66-67 D 5
Benjamin River ~ CDN (NB) 240-241 J 4
Benjina ○ RI 166-167 H 5
Benkelman ○ USA (NE) 262-263 E 4
Ben Lawers ▲ GB 90-91 E 3
Ben Loganbil ○ LB 202-203 F 6
Ben Macdui ▲ GB 90-91 F 3
Ben Mehidi ○ DZ 190-191 F 2
Ben More ▲ GB 90-91 E 3
Benmore, Lake ‹ NZ 182 C 6
Benndale ○ USA (MS) 268-269 M 6
Bennett ○ CDN (SAS) 232-233 P 6
Bennett ○ USA (CO) 254-255 L 4
Bennett ○ USA (NC) 282-283 H 5
Bennett ○ USA (NM) 256-257 M 6
Bennett, Lake ‹ AUS 172-173 K 7
Bennett, Lake ‹ CDN 32-33 D 1
Bennett, Mount ▲ AUS 172-173 K 5
Bennetta, ostrov ‹ RUS 108-109 h 1
Bennett Lake ‹ CDN 20-21 X 6
Bennettsville ○ USA (SC) 284-285 L 2
Ben Nevis ▲ GB 90-91 E 3
Bennichâb ○ RIM 196-197 C 5
Bennington ○ USA (KS) 262-263 J 6
Bennington ○ USA (OK) 264-265 H 4
Bennington ○ USA (VT) 278-279 H 6
Benny ○ CDN (ONT) 238-239 D 2
Benoit ○ USA (WI) 270-271 G 4
Benoit's Cove ○ CDN (NFL) 242-243 N 4
Benoni ○ ZA 220-221 J 3
Benoud ○ DZ 188-189 L 4
Bénoué ~ CAM 204-205 K 5
Bénoué, Cuvette de la ⊥ CAM 204-205 K 4
Bénoué, Parc National de la ⊥ CAM 204-205 K 4
Bénoye ○ TCH 206-207 C 4
Ben Quang ○ VN 158-159 J 2
Bên Quang ○ VN 158-159 J 2
Ben Rinnes ▲ GB 90-91 F 3
Bensbach River ~ PNG 183 A 5
Bensèkou ○ DY 204-205 E 3
Ben-Slimane ○ MA 188-189 H 4
Benson ○ CDN (SAS) 232-233 P 6
Benson ○ USA (AZ) 256-257 F 7
Benson ○ USA (MN) 270-271 C 5
Ben S'Rour ○ DZ 190-191 E 3
Bent ○ IR 134-135 H 5
Bent, Rûḍẖâne-ye ~ IR 134-135 H 5
Ben Tadjine, Djebel ▲ DZ 188-189 K 6
Benta Seberang ○ MAL 162-163 D 2
Bentenan ○ RI 164-165 J 3
Benteng ○ RI (SLT) 164-165 G 4
Benteng ○ RI (SSE) 168 G 4
Benteng Tanahjampea ○ RI 168 E 6
Bentiaba ~ ANG 216-217 B 6
Bentick Island ‹ MYA 158-159 E 5
Bentinck Island ‹ AUS 174-175 E 5
Bentinck Sound ≈ 158-159 D 3
Bentiu ○ SUD 206-207 L 3
Bentley ○ CDN (ALB) 232-233 D 4
Bent Mountain ○ USA (VA) 280-281 G 6
Bento Gomes, Rio ~ BR 70-71 J 5
Bento Gonçalves ○ BR 74-75 E 7
Benton ○ USA (AL) 284-285 D 4
Benton ○ USA (CA) 248-249 G 4
Benton ○ USA (IL) 276-277 G 3
Benton ○ USA (LA) 276-277 C 4
Benton ○ USA (MO) 276-277 F 3
Benton ○ USA (MS) 268-269 K 4
Benton City ○ USA (WA) 244-245 F 4
Bentong ○ MAL 162-163 D 2
Benton Harbor ○ USA (MI) 272-273 C 5
Bentonia ○ USA (MS) 268-269 K 4
Bentonsport ○ USA (IA) 274-275 G 4
Bentonville ○ USA (AR) 276-277 B 4
Bentonville ○ USA (NC) 282-283 J 5
Bentota ○ CL 140-141 H 7
Bên Tre ○ VN 158-159 J 5
Bênxi ○ VRC 150-151 D 7
Benxi Shuidong • VRC 150-151 E 7
Benye ○ ZRE 210-211 H 4
Benz ○ RI 164-165 K 1
Beo ○ RI 166-167 J 3
Beoga ○ RI 166-167 J 3
Béograd = Beograd ★ • • YU 100-101 J 2
Beoumi ○ CI 202-203 H 6
Béowawe ○ USA (NV) 246-247 J 3
Bepondi, Pulau ‹ RI 166-167 H 2
Beppu ○ J 152-153 D 8
Bequa ‹ FJI 184 III b 3
Bequia Island ‹ WV 56 E 5
Ber ○ RMM 196-197 J 6
Berabevû ○ RA 78-79 J 2
Berafia, Nosy ‹ RM 222-223 E 6
Berahlê ○ ETH 200-201 H 4
Beramanja ○ RM 222-223 F 4
Bérandjokou ○ RCB 210-211 F 2

Berangas ○ RI 164-165 E 5
Berâni ○ PK 138-139 B 7
Berat ☆ AL 100-101 G 4
Berau ○ RI 164-165 E 3
Berau, Teluk ≈ 166-167 H 3
Beraun = Beroun ○ CZ 92-93 N 4
Beravina ○ RM 222-223 D 7
Beravy ○ RM 222-223 D 8
Berazino ☆ BY 94-95 L 5
Berbera ○ SP 208-209 H 3
Berbérati ☆ RCA 206-207 B 6
Berbia ○ RCA 206-207 D 6
Berbice ~ GUY 62-63 E 4
Berchtesgaden ○ D 92-93 M 5
Berclair ○ USA (TX) 266-267 K 5
Bercogoyi ○ KA 126-127 N 3
Berd° ~ RUS 114-115 P 7
Berdaale ○ SP 212-213 J 2
Berd'ans'ka kosa ‹ UA 102-103 K 4
Berdensar, köl ‹ KA 126-127 N 4
Berdičev = Berdyčiv ☆ UA 102-103 F 3
Berdigestjah ☆ RUS 118-119 N 4
Berdjans'k ○ UA 102-103 K 3
Berdsk ○ RUS 124-125 N 1
Berdyčiv ☆ UA 102-103 F 3
Béré ○ TCH 206-207 C 4
Berea ○ USA (KY) 276-277 L 3
Berea ○ USA (NC) 282-283 J 4
Béréba ○ BF 202-203 J 4
Berebere ○ RI 164-165 K 3
Bereeda ○ SP 208-209 K 3
Bereg Djogos Jar ‹ RUS 110-111 X 3
Bereg Haritona Lapteva ‹ RUS 108-109 W 4
Beregovoe ○ RUS 124-125 M 2
Beregovoj ○ RUS 118-119 N 8
Berehove ○ UA 102-103 C 3
Bereina ○ PNG 183 E 4
Bereja ~ RUS 122-123 B 3
Bereku ○ EAT (DOD) 212-213 E 6
Berekuna ○ WD 56 E 4
Berekum ○ GH 202-203 J 6
Bérélêh ~ RUS 110-111 b 4
Bérélêh ~ RUS 120-121 M 2
Berembang ○ RI 162-163 F 5
Berenda ○ USA (CA) 248-249 D 2
Berendi ○ TR 128-129 F 4
Berenike ○ ET 194-195 G 6
Berens Island ‹ CDN (MAN) 234-235 F 3
Berens River ○ CDN (MAN) 234-235 F 2
Berens River ~ CDN (MAN) 234-235 F 2
Berens River ~ CDN (ONT) 234-235 K 3
Bereš ~ RUS 114-115 S 7
Beresford ○ CDN (NB) 240-241 K 3
Beresford ○ USA (SD) 260-261 K 3
Beresford Lake ‹ CDN (MAN) 234-235 H 4
Berettyóújfalu ○ H 92-93 Q 5
Bereza = Biaroza ○ UA 102-103 G 4
Berežnaja ○ RUS 88-89 R 6
Bereznehuvate ○ UA 102-103 H 4
Bereznik ○ RUS 88-89 P 6
Berezniki ○ RUS 114-115 D 5
Berežnyh, mys ▲ RUS 110-111 X 1
Berezova ○ RUS 116-117 F 8
Berezovaja ~ RUS 112-113 H 5
Berežovka ~ RUS (KRN) 116-117 F 7
Berezovka ~ RUS (PRM) 96-97 L 6
Berezovka ~ RUS 112-113 H 3
Berezovka ~ RUS 114-115 R 5
Berezovo ☆ RUS 114-115 H 3
Berezovskij ☆ RUS 96-97 M 7
Berg ○ N 86-87 H 2
Berga, mys ▲ RUS 108-109 c 1
Bergama ○ TR 128-129 B 3
Bérgamo ○ I 100-101 B 2
Bergen ★ • N 86-87 B 6
Bergen ○ NL 92-93 H 2
Bergen ○ USA (MN) 270-271 D 7
Bergen (Rügen) ○ D 92-93 M 1
Berg en Dal ○ SME 62-63 G 3
Bergerac ○ F 90-91 H 4
Bergland ○ CDN (ONT) 234-235 J 6
Bergland ○ USA (MI) 272-273 C 4
Bergsig ○ NAM 216-217 C 10
Bergville ○ ZA 220-221 J 4
Berhait ○ IND 142-143 E 3
Berhala, Selat ≈ 162-163 E 5
Berhampur = Brahmapur ○ IND 142-143 D 5
Berikat, Tanjung ▲ RI 162-163 G 6
Berilo ○ BR 72-73 J 4
Beringa, mogila ‹ RUS 120-121 V 6
Beringa, ostrov ‹ RUS 112-113 X 4
Beringa, ostrov ~ RUS 120-121 W 6
Beringarra ○ AUS 176-177 D 3
Bering Glacier ‹ USA 20-21 T 6
Bering Land Bridge Nature Reserve ⊥ USA 20-21 G 4
Bering Sea = Beringovo more ≈ 22-23 J 4
Bering Strait = Beringov proliv ≈ 112-113 a 4
Beripeta ○ IND 140-141 J 4
Beris ~ RUS 110-111 Q 4
Berisso ○ RA 78-79 L 3
Beriza ○ BR 72-73 J 3
Berja ○ E 98-99 F 6
Berkåk ○ N 86-87 E 5
Berkane ○ MA 188-189 K 3
Berkeley, Cape ▲ CDN 24-25 V 4
Berkeley Point ▲ CDN 24-25 M 5
Berkeley River ~ AUS 172-173 H 3
Berkeley Sound ≈ 78-79 M 6
Berkley Group ‹ CDN 24-25 V 4

Berkner Island ⌒ ARK 16 F 30
Berkovica ○ BG 102-103 C 6
Berland River ~ CDN (ALB) 228-229 R 3
Berlengas, Rio ~ BR 68-69 G 5
Berlevåg ○ N 86-87 O 1
Berliet, Point ▲ RN 198-199 D 2
Berlin ★··· D 92-93 M 2
Berlin ○ USA (MD) 280-281 L 5
Berlin ○ USA (ND) 258-259 J 5
Berlin ○ USA (NH) 278-279 K 4
Berlin ○ USA (NJ) 280-281 M 4
Berlin ○ USA (OK) 264-265 E 3
Berlin ○ USA (PA) 280-281 H 4
Berlin ○ USA (WI) 270-271 K 7
Berlin, Mount ▲ ARK 16 F 23
Berlinguet Inlet ≈ 24-25 d 5
Berlin Reservoir < USA (OH) 280-281 E 3
Bermagui ○ AUS 180-181 L 4
Bermego, Río ~ RA 76-77 C 5
Bermeja, Sierra ▲ E 98-99 E 6
Bermejillo ○ MEX 50-51 H 5
Bermejo, Isla ⌒ RA 78-79 J 5
Bermejo, Río ~ RA 76-77 D 6
Bermejo, Río ~ RA 76-77 F 2
Bermuda Island ⌒ GB 54-55 L 1
Bermuda Islands ⌒ GB 54-55 L 2
Bermuda Rise ≃ 6-7 C 5
Bern ★··· CH 90-91 J 5
Bernabe Rivera ○ ROU 76-77 J 6
Bernalillo ○ USA (NM) 256-257 J 3
Bernam ~ MAL 162-163 D 3
Bernard Island ⌒ CDN 24-25 J 4
Bernardo ○ USA (NM) 256-257 J 4
Bernardo de Irigoyen ○ RA 74-75 D 6
Bernardo O'Higgins, Parque Nacional ⊥ RCH 80 C 5
Bernardo Sacuita, Ponta do ▲ BR 68-69 F 2
Bernard River ~ CDN 24-25 K 4
Bernay ○ F 90-91 H 7
Bernburg (Saale) ○• D 92-93 L 3
Berne ○ USA (IN) 274-275 O 4
Berne ○ USA (WA) 244-245 D 3
Berner ○ USA (GA) 284-285 G 3
Berner Alpen ▲ CH 92-93 J 5
Bernice ○ USA (LA) 268-269 H 4
Bernier, Cape ▲ AUS 172-173 H 3
Bernier Bay ≈ 24-25 b 5
Bernier Island ⌒ AUS 176-177 B 2
Bernina, Piz ▲ CH 92-93 K 5
Berninapass ▲ CH 92-93 K 5
Bernstorffs Isfjord ≈ 28-29 U 5
Bero ~ ANG 216-217 B 7
Beroroha ○ RM 222-223 D 8
Beroun ○ CZ 92-93 N 4
Berounka ~ CZ 92-93 M 4
Berrahal ○ DZ 190-191 F 2
Berrechid ○ MA 188-189 H 4
Berrekhem, Hassi < DZ 190-191 E 4
Berri ○ AUS 180-181 F 3
Berriane ○ DZ 190-191 D 3
Berridale ○ AUS 180-181 K 4
Berrigan ○ AUS 180-181 H 3
Berriwillock ○ AUS 180-181 G 3
Berrouaghia ○ DZ 190-191 D 2
Berrugas ○ CO 60-61 D 3
Berry ▲ F 90-91 H 8
Berry ○ USA (AL) 284-285 C 3
Berry, De ○ USA (TX) 264-265 K 6
Berry Creek ~ CDN (ALB) 232-233 G 4
Berrydale ○ USA (FL) 286-287 B 1
Berryessa, Lake ⊂ USA (CA) 246-247 C 5
Berry Head ○ CDN (NFL) 242-243 K 4
Berry Islands ⌒ BS 54-55 F 2
Berrymoor ○ CDN (ALB) 232-233 D 2
Berryville ○ USA (AR) 276-277 B 4
Berryville ○ USA (VA) 280-281 J 4
Berseba ○ NAM 220-221 C 3
Berté, Lac ⊂ CDN 38-39 K 3
Berthierville ○ CDN (QUE) 238-239 M 2
Berthold ○ USA (ND) 258-259 F 3
Bertiehaugh ○ AUS 174-175 G 3
Bertinho ○ BR 68-69 C 3
Bertolínia ○ BR 68-69 G 5
Bertoua ☆ CAM 204-205 K 6
Bertram ○ CDN (ONT) 236-237 D 3
Bertram ○ USA (TX) 266-267 J 3
Bertrand ○ CDN (NB) 240-241 K 3
Bertrandville ○ USA (LA) 268-269 L 7
Bertwell ○ CDN (SAS) 232-233 Q 3
Beruniј ☆ US 136-137 G 4
Beruri ○ BR 66-67 G 4
Beruwala ○ CL 140-141 H 7
Berwick ○ CDN (NB) 240-241 K 5
Berwick ○ CDN (NS) 240-241 L 5
Berwick ○ USA (PA) 280-281 K 2
Berwick-upon-Tweed ○• GB 90-91 F 4
Beryl ○ USA (UT) 254-255 B 6
Beryl Junction ○ USA (UT) 254-255 B 6
Beryslav ○ UA 102-103 H 4
Besa ○ RI 164-165 K 3
Besal ○ PK 138-139 D 2
Besalampy ○ RM 222-223 D 6
Besançon ☆·· F 90-91 L 8
Bešankovičy ☆ BY 94-95 L 4
Besar, Gunung ▲ MAL 162-163 E 3
Besar, Gunung ▲ RI 164-165 D 5
Besar, Pulau ⌒ RI 166-167 B 6
Besarabca ○ MD 102-103 F 4
Besarabjaska = Besarabca ○ MD 102-103 F 4
Besar Hantu, Gunung ▲ MAL (SEL) 162-163 D 3
Besa River ~ CDN 32-33 J 3
Bešaryk ○ US 136-137 M 4
Besbes, Oued ~ DZ 190-191 E 3
Besboro Island ⌒ USA 20-21 K 4
Bescoky, tau ▲ KA 126-127 K 5
Besedz' ~ BY 94-95 M 5
Besham ○ PK 138-139 D 2
Beshlo ~ ETH 208-209 D 3
Besi, Tanjung ▲ RI 168 E 7
Besikama ○ RI 166-167 C 6
Besima ○ PK 134-135 L 5
Besir ○ RI 166-167 F 2
Bėsjuke ~ RUS 110-111 Q 4
Beskid Mountains = Beskidy ▲ PL 92-93 P 4
Beskidy Zachodnie ▲ PL 92-93 P 4
Beslan ○ RUS 126-127 F 6
Besnard Lake ⊂ CDN 34-35 D 3
Besne ○ IR 134-135 F 4
Besni ☆ TR 128-129 G 4
Bessa Monteiro ○ ANG 216-217 B 3
Bessao ○ TCH 206-207 B 5
Bessarabia = Bessarabija ⩡ MD 102-103 E 3
Bessarabka = Aul Sarykobda ○ KA 126-127 M 3
Bessarabka = Besarabca ○ MD 102-103 F 4
Bessaz, gora ▲ KA 136-137 L 3
Bessaz, togi ▲ KA 136-137 L 3
Besselfjord ≈ 26-27 p 6
Bessemer ○ USA (AL) 284-285 D 3
Bessemer ○ USA (MI) 270-271 H 4
Bessmay ○ USA (TX) 268-269 G 6
Bessoung Kang ○ CAM 204-205 H 6
Best ○ USA (TX) 266-267 F 2
Bestám ○• IR 136-137 D 6
Bestam ∴• KA 136-137 H 3
Bestamak ○ KA 126-127 L 3
Bestjah ○ RUS (SAH) 110-111 P 7
Bestjah ○ RUS (SAH) 118-119 O 5
Beswick ○ AUS 174-175 B 4
Beswick Aboriginal Land Ⅹ AUS 172-173 L 3
Betafo ○ RM 222-223 E 7
Betalevana ○ RM 222-223 F 6
Betanantanana ○ RM 222-223 D 7
Betânia ○ BR (MAT) 70-71 G 4
Betânia ○ BR (PER) 68-69 J 6
Betânia, Área Indígena Ⅹ BR 66-67 C 4
Betanty ○ RM 222-223 D 10
Betanzos ○ BOL 70-71 E 6
Betanzos ○ E 98-99 C 3
Betarara ○ VAN 184 II b 2
Bétaré Oya ○ CAM 206-207 B 6
Betbakdala ⩡ KA 124-125 E 6
Betbulak ○ KA 124-125 F 4
Bete Grise Bay ≈ USA 270-271 L 3
Bete Hor ○ ETH 208-209 D 3
Betein ○ WAN 204-205 H 6
Betenkës ○ RUS 110-111 U 6
Bétérou ○ DY 204-205 E 4
Bethal ○ ZA 220-221 J 3
Bethanie ☆ NAM 220-221 C 3
Bethany ○ USA (IL) 274-275 K 5
Bethany ○ USA (MO) 274-275 D 4
Bethany ○ USA (OK) 264-265 G 3
Bethany Beach ○ USA (DE) 280-281 L 5
Bethel ○ USA (AK) 20-21 K 6
Bethel ○ USA (ME) 278-279 L 4
Bethel ○ USA (NC) 282-283 K 5
Bethel ○ USA (OH) 280-281 B 5
Bethel ○ USA (OK) 264-265 K 4
Bethel ○ USA (VT) 278-279 J 5
Bethel Park ○ USA (PA) 280-281 F 3
Bethesdaweg ○ ZA 220-221 G 5
Bethlehem ○ SME 62-63 G 3
Bethlehem ○ USA (PA) 280-281 L 3
Bethlehem ○ ZA 220-221 J 4
Bethlehem = Bet Leḥem ☆·· IL 130-131 D 2
Bethulie ○ ZA 220-221 G 5
Bethune ○ USA (SC) 284-285 K 2
Betinče ~ RUS 118-119 G 5
Betioky ○ RM 222-223 D 9
Bet Leḥem ☆·· WB 130-131 D 2
Betong ○ MAL 162-163 J 4
Betong ○ THA 158-159 F 8
Betongwe ○ ZRE 212-213 B 2
Betoota ○ AUS 178-179 F 3
Bétou ○ RCB 210-211 G 2
Be Town ○ LB 202-203 F 6
Betpak Dala = Betbakdala ⩡ KA 124-125 E 6
Betrandraka ○ RM 222-223 E 6
Betroka ○ RM 222-223 E 9
Bet She'an ○ IL 130-131 D 1
Betsiaka ○ RM 222-223 F 4
Betsiamites ○ CDN (QUE) 240-241 G 2
Betsiamites, Rivière ~ CDN 38-39 J 3
Betsiamites Indian Réserve Ⅹ CDN 38-39 K 4
Betsiboka ~ RM 222-223 E 6
Betsjoeanaland ⩡ ZA 220-221 E 3
Betsy Bay ○ BS 54-55 J 3
Bettiah ○ IND 142-143 D 2
Bettié ○ CI 202-203 J 6
Bettiesdam ○ ZA 220-221 J 3
Bettioua ○ DZ 188-189 L 3
Bettles ○ USA 20-21 P 3
Bet Touadjine, Hamadet ⩡ DZ 190-191 C 5
Betty, Lake ⊂ AUS 172-173 H 5
Betül ○ IND 138-139 F 9
Betulia ○ CO (ANT) 60-61 D 4
Betulia ○ CO (SAN) 60-61 E 4
Betun ○ RI 166-167 C 6
Betuwe ~ RI 164-165 F 5
Betwa ~ IND 138-139 G 7
Betwa ~ IND 142-143 B 3
Béu ○ ANG 216-217 C 3
Beu, Serranía del ▲ BOL 70-71 C 4
Beulah ○ AUS 180-181 G 3
Beulah ○ CDN (MAN) 234-235 B 4
Beulah ○ USA (MI) 272-273 C 3
Beulah ○ USA (ND) 258-259 F 4
Beulaville ○ USA (NC) 282-283 K 6
Beurfou < TCH 198-199 G 5
Beurkia ○ TCH 198-199 H 5
B. Everette Jordan Lake ⊂ USA (NC) 282-283 J 5
Bever Lake Indian Reserve Ⅹ CDN 32-33 P 4
Beverley ○ AUS 176-177 D 6
Beverley ○ CDN (SAS) 232-233 L 5
Beverley ○• GB 90-91 G 5
Beverley, Lake ⊂ USA 22-23 R 3
Beverley Springs ○ AUS 172-173 G 4
Beverly ○ USA (FL) 286-287 E 2
Beverly ○ USA (MA) 278-279 L 6
Beverly ○ USA (OH) 280-281 E 4
Beverly ○ USA (WA) 244-245 F 4
Beverly ○ USA (WV) 280-281 G 5
Beverly Beach ○ USA (MD) 280-281 K 5
Beverly Lake ⊂ CDN 30-31 T 3
Beveromay ▲ RM 222-223 E 6
Beveromay, Tampoketsan'i ▲ RM 222-223 E 6
Bevoalava Andrefana ○ RM 222-223 D 10
Bevoay ○ RM 222-223 C 8
Bewani ○ PNG 183 A 2
Bewani Mountains ▲ PNG 183 A 2
Bewar ○ IND 138-139 G 6
Bewdley ○ CDN (ONT) 238-239 G 4
Bewick Lake ⊂ CDN 30-31 R 4
Bexley ○ USA (OH) 280-281 D 3
Bey Dağ ▲ TR 128-129 G 3
Bey Dağları ▲ TR 128-129 D 4
Beyla ○ RG 202-203 F 5
Beylul ○ ER 200-201 L 6
Beylul Bahire Sekat'e ≈ 200-201 L 6
Beynon ○ CDN (ALB) 232-233 F 4
Beypazarı ○• TR 128-129 D 2
Beyra ○ SP 208-209 H 5
Beyşehir ☆ TR 128-129 D 4
Beyşehir Gölü ⊂ TR 128-129 D 4
Beytüşşebap ☆ TR 128-129 K 4
Bezaha ○ RM 222-223 D 9
Bežanicy ☆ RUS 94-95 L 3
Bežeck ☆ RUS 94-95 P 3
Bežeckij verh ▲ RUS 94-95 P 3
Bezenčuk ☆ RUS 96-97 F 7
Bezergen ○ US 136-137 G 4
Bezerra ou Montes Claros, Rio ~ BR 72-73 G 2
Béziers ○• F 90-91 J 10
Bezmein ○ TM 136-137 F 5
Bezymjannaja, guba ⊂ RUS 108-109 E 5
Bhābhar ○ IND 138-139 C 7
Bhadgaon ○ IND 138-139 E 9
Bhador ~ IND 138-139 C 9
Bhadrāchalam ○ IND 142-143 B 7
Bhadrak ○ IND 142-143 E 5
Bhadra Reservoir ⊂ IND 140-141 F 4
Bhadrāvati ○ IND 140-141 F 4
Bhadwan ○ IND 140-141 F 2
Bhāg ○ PK 134-135 M 4
Bhāgalpur ○ IND 142-143 E 3
Bhāgirathi ~ IND 138-139 G 4
Bhāgirathi ~ IND 142-143 F 3
Bhagirathi ~ VRC 144-145 B 5
Bhāgvati ○ IND 140-141 F 3
Bhagwanpur ○ NEP 144-145 D 7
Bhagyakul ○ BD 142-143 G 4
Bhainsrorgarh ○ IND 138-139 E 7
Bhāi Pheru ○ PK 138-139 D 4
Bhairab Bazar ○ BD 142-143 G 3
Bhairahawa ○ NEP 144-145 D 7
Bhairi Hol ▲ PK 134-135 L 6
Bhairowāl ○ PK 138-139 D 3
Bhaisa ○ IND 138-139 F 10
Bhakkar ○ PK 138-139 C 4
Bhaktapur ○• NEP 144-145 E 7
Bhālki ○ IND 138-139 F 10
Bhaluka ○ BD 142-143 G 3
Bhalukpong ○ IND 142-143 H 2
Bhalwāl ○ PK 138-139 D 3
Bhamo ○ MYA 142-143 K 3
Bhanas ○ IND 138-139 E 10
Bhanbore ∴• PK 134-135 M 6
Bhandāra ○ IND 138-139 G 9
Bhanjanagar ○ IND 142-143 D 6
Bhānpura ○ IND 138-139 E 7
Bharatpur ○ IND 140-141 L 3
Bharatpur ○• IND 138-139 F 6
Bhareli ~ IND 142-143 H 2
Bharūch ○ IND 138-139 D 9
Bhata ○ NEP 144-145 E 7
Bhatiapara ○ BD 142-143 F 4
Bhatkal ○ IND 140-141 F 3
Bhātpāra ○ IND 142-143 F 4
Bhaun ○ PK 138-139 D 3
Bhavāni ○ IND 140-141 G 5
Bhavnagar ○• IND 138-139 D 9
Bhawāna ○ PK 138-139 D 4
Bhawānipatna ○ IND 142-143 C 6
Bhera ○ PK 138-139 D 3
Bheri ~ NEP 144-145 C 6
Bhiavan ○ IND 138-139 E 10
Bhilainagar ○• IND 142-143 B 5
Bhilwāra ○ IND 138-139 E 7
Bhima ~ IND 138-139 D 10
Bhima ~ IND 140-141 F 2
Bhimāshankar ○ IND 138-139 D 10
Bhimavaram ○ IND 140-141 J 2
Bhimunipatnam ○ IND 142-143 C 7
Bhind ○ IND 138-139 G 6
Bhinmāl ○ IND 138-139 D 7
Bhit Shāh ○ PK 138-139 B 7
Bhiwandi ○ IND 138-139 D 10
Bhognipur ○ IND 138-139 G 6
Bhokar ○ IND 138-139 F 10
Bhol Aha ○ BD 142-143 F 3
Bhongaon ○ IND 138-139 G 6
Bhongir ○ IND 140-141 H 2
Bhopāl ☆·· IND 138-139 F 8
Bhopālpatnam ○ IND 142-143 B 6
Bhowali ○ IND 138-139 G 5
Bhuban ○ IND 142-143 D 5
Bhubaneshwar ☆·· IND 142-143 D 5
Bhuj ○ IND 138-139 B 8
Bhusāwal ○ IND 138-139 E 9
Bhutan ■ BHT 142-143 F 2
Bia, Rio ~ BR 66-67 D 5
Biafra ⩡ WAN 204-205 H 6
Biak ○ RI (IRJ) 166-167 J 2
Biak ○ RI (SLT) 164-165 H 4
Biak, Pulau ⌒ RI 166-167 J 2
Biała, Bielsko- ☆ PL 92-93 P 4
Biała Podlaska ☆ PL 92-93 R 2
Białogard ○ PL 92-93 N 1
Białowieski Park Narodowy ⊥··· PL 92-93 R 2
Biały Bór ○• PL 92-93 O 2
Białystok ☆• PL 92-93 R 2
Bian ~ RI 166-167 L 5
Biang ○ RI 164-165 K 3
Bianga ○ RCA 206-207 E 6
Biankouma ☆ CI 202-203 G 6
Biaora ○ IND 138-139 F 8
Biar ○ PK 138-139 D 2
Bī'ār, al- ○ KSA 130-131 F 6
Biaranga ○ ZRE 210-211 G 4
Biārğmand ○ IR 136-137 D 6
Biaro ○ ZRE 210-211 K 3
Biaro, Pulau ⌒ RI 164-165 J 2
Biarritz ○• F 90-91 G 10
Bias Fortes ○ BR 72-73 J 6
Biasi ~ ZRE 212-213 A 4
Biassini ○ ROU 76-77 J 6
Biata, Río ~ BOL 70-71 D 2
Bia-Tawya Game Production Reserve ⊥ GH 202-203 J 6
Biau ~ RI 166-167 K 6
Biaza ○ RUS 114-115 P 6
Bibā ○ ET 194-195 E 3
Bibai ○ J 152-153 J 3
Bibala ○ ANG 216-217 B 7
Biban, Chaîne de ▲ DZ 190-191 E 2
Bibas ○ G 210-211 C 3
Bibbiena ○ I 100-101 C 3
Bibby Island ⌒ CDN 30-31 X 5
Bibé ○ CAM 204-205 H 6
Bibémi ○ CAM 204-205 K 4
Biberach an der Riß ○ D 92-93 K 4
Bibiani ○ GH 202-203 J 6
Bibikovo ○ RUS 122-123 B 3
Bibirevo ○ RUS 94-95 N 3
Biblian ○ EC 64-65 C 3
Biboohra ○ AUS 174-175 H 5
Bibundi ○ CAM 204-205 H 6
Bičanekskij, pereval ▲ AZ 128-129 L 3
Bicas ○ BR 72-73 J 6
Bičevaja ○ RUS 122-123 F 5
Biche, Lac la ⊂ CDN 32-33 O 4
Bichena ○ ETH 208-209 D 3
Bicheno ○ AUS 180-181 K 6
Biche Range, La ▲ CDN 30-31 G 5
Biche River, La ~ CDN 30-31 G 5
Bichhua ○ IND 138-139 G 9
Bichi ○ WAN 198-199 D 6
Biči ~ RUS 122-123 G 3
Bickerton Island ⌒ AUS 174-175 D 3
Bickle Knob ▲ USA (WV) 280-281 G 5
Bickleton ○ USA (WA) 244-245 E 4
Bicknell ○ USA (IN) 274-275 L 6
Bicuari, Parque Nacional do ⊥ ANG 216-217 C 7
Bičura ☆ RUS 116-117 N 10
Bida ○ WAN 204-205 G 4
Bidadari, Tanjung ▲ MAL 160-161 C 10
Bidal ○• IND 140-141 G 2
Bidbid ○ OM 132-133 L 2
Bidde ○ SP 212-213 J 3
Biddeford ○ USA (ME) 278-279 L 5
Biddle ○ USA (MT) 250-251 O 6
Bide Arm ○ CDN (NFL) 242-243 M 2
Bideford ○• GB 90-91 E 6
Bidek, Anou-n- < DZ 198-199 B 3
Bidjovagge ○ N 86-87 L 2
Bidoḥt ○ IR 134-135 H 1
Bidon V ○ DZ 190-191 C 9
Bidor ○ MAL 162-163 D 2
Bidukbiduk ○ RI 164-165 F 3
Bidžan ○ RUS 122-123 D 5
Bié ▫ ANG 216-217 D 6
Bieber ○ USA (CA) 246-247 D 2
Biéha ○ BF 202-203 K 4
Biei ○ J 152-153 K 3
Biel ○• CH 92-93 J 5
Bield ○ CDN (MAN) 234-235 B 3
Bielefeld ○ D 92-93 K 2
Bieler Lake ⊂ CDN 26-27 O 8
Biella ☆• I 100-101 B 2
Biélou ○ CI 202-203 G 5
Bielsa ○ E 98-99 H 3
Bielsko-Biała ☆ PL 92-93 P 4
Bielsk Podlaski ○ PL 92-93 R 2
Biên Đông ≈ 158-159 J 7
Bienfait ○ CDN (SAS) 232-233 Q 6
Bienge ○ ZRE 210-211 G 6
Biên Hòa ☆• VN 158-159 J 5
Bienne = Biel ○• CH 92-93 J 5
Bienville ○ USA (LA) 268-269 H 4
Bienville, Lac ⊂ CDN 36-37 N 7
Bierdnačokka ▲ N 86-87 G 3
Biertan ○··· RO 102-103 D 4
Biesiesvlei ○ ZA 220-221 G 3
Bieszczadzki Park Narodowy ⊥ PL 92-93 R 4
Bifoulé ○ CAM 204-205 K 6
Bifuka ○ J 152-153 K 2
Biga ☆ TR 128-129 B 2
Bigadiç ☆ TR 128-129 C 3
Biğādiya, al- ○ KSA 130-131 H 5
Big Ambergris Cay ⌒ GB 54-55 K 4
Bigand ○ RA 78-79 J 2
Biga Yarımadası ⌒ TR 128-129 B 3
Big Arm ○ USA (MT) 250-251 E 4
Big Bald Mountain ▲ CDN (NB) 240-241 J 3
Big Baldy ▲ USA (ID) 252-253 C 2
Big Bar ○ USA (CA) 246-247 B 3
Big Bar Creek ○ CDN (BC) 230-231 G 2
Big Bay ≈ 36-37 T 7
Big Bay ≈ 184 II a 2
Big Bay ○ CDN (ONT) 238-239 E 4
Big Bay ○ USA (MI) 270-271 L 4
Big Bay de Noc ≈ USA 270-271 M 5
Big Bay Point ○ CDN (ONT) 238-239 F 4
Big Bear City ○ USA (CA) 248-249 H 5
Big Bear Creek ~ USA (MS) 268-269 M 2
Big Bear Lake ○ USA (CA) 248-249 H 5
Big Beaver ○ CDN (SAS) 232-233 N 6
Big Beaver Falls ~ CDN (ONT) 236-237 F 3
Big Beaver House ○ CDN (ONT) 234-235 O 2
Bigbee Valley ○ USA (MS) 268-269 M 3
Bigbé I ○ CI 202-203 H 6
Big Bell ○ AUS 176-177 D 3
Big Belt Mountains ▲ USA (MT) 250-251 H 5
Big Bend ○ SD 220-221 K 3
Big Bend ○ USA (CA) 246-247 D 2
Big Bend ○ USA (LA) 268-269 J 5
Big Bend National Park ⊥ USA (TX) 266-267 D 4
Big Black River ~ USA (MS) 268-269 L 3
Big Blue River ~ USA (IN) 274-275 N 5
Big Blue River ~ USA (KS) 262-263 J 3
Big Brook ○ CDN (NFL) 242-243 M 1
Big Brush Creek ~ USA (AL) 284-285 C 4
Big Butt ▲ USA (TN) 282-283 E 4
Big Canyon River ~ USA (TX) 266-267 E 3
Bigcedar Creek ~ CDN (ONT) 236-237 G 2
Big Creak Lake < USA (AL) 284-285 B 6
Big Creek ○ CDN (BC) 230-231 H 2
Big Creek ~ CDN (BC) 230-231 F 2
Big Creek ○ USA (ID) 250-251 D 6
Big Creek ~ USA (AL) 284-285 D 5
Big Creek ~ USA (AR) 276-277 D 6
Big Creek ~ USA (LA) 268-269 J 4
Big Cypress Seminole Indian Reservation Ⅹ USA (FL) 286-287 H 5
Big Cypress Swamp ⊂ USA (FL) 286-287 H 5
Big Desert ⩡ AUS 180-181 F 3
Big Desert Wilderness ⊥ AUS 180-181 F 3
Big Dry Creek, The ~ USA (MT) 250-251 M 4
Big Eau Plaine Reservoir < USA (WI) 270-271 J 6
Bigelow ○ USA (MN) 270-271 C 7
Bigene ○ GNB 202-203 C 3
Big Escambia Creek ~ USA (AL) 284-285 C 5
Big Falls ○ USA (MN) 270-271 E 2
Big Falls ○ USA (WI) 270-271 J 6
Big Field ○ USA (AZ) 256-257 C 7
Bigfork ○ USA (MT) 250-251 E 3
Big Fork River ~ USA (MN) 270-271 E 2
Big Frog Mountain ▲ USA (TN) 282-283 C 6
Biggar ○ CDN (SAS) 232-233 L 3
Bigge Island ⌒ AUS 172-173 G 3
Biggenden ○ AUS 178-179 M 3
Biggs ○ USA (KY) 276-277 N 3
Biggs ○ USA (OR) 244-245 E 5
Big Hips Island ⌒ CDN 30-31 W 3
Big Hole • ZA 220-221 G 4
Big Hole National Battlefield • USA (MT) 250-251 F 6
Big Hole River ~ USA (MT) 250-251 F 6
Big Hole Tract Indian Reserve Ⅹ• CDN (NB) 240-241 K 3
Bighorn ○ USA (MT) 250-251 M 5
Big Horn ○ USA (WY) 252-253 M 2
Bighorn Basin ⩡ USA (WY) 252-253 K 2
Bighorn Canyon National Recreation Area ⊥ USA (MT) 250-251 L 6
Bighorn Creek ~ CDN (BC) 230-231 L 2
Bighorn Lake ⊂ USA (MT) 250-251 L 6
Big Horn Mountains ▲ USA (AZ) 256-257 B 5
Bighorn Mountains ▲ USA (WY) 252-253 L 2
Bighorn River ~ USA (MT) 250-251 M 6
Bighorn Wildland Recreation Area ⊥ CDN (ALB) 232-233 B 3
Bight, The ○ BS 54-55 H 2
Big Island ⌒ CDN (ALB) 30-31 N 6
Big Island ⌒ CDN (NFL) 36-37 S 5
Big Island ⌒ CDN (NWT) 30-31 L 4
Big Island ⌒ CDN (NWT) 30-31 L 5
Big Island ⌒ CDN (NWT) 36-37 O 3
Big Island ⌒ CDN (ONT) 234-235 J 5
Big Island ⌒ CDN (QUE) 36-37 Q 5
Big Island ○ USA (VA) 280-281 G 6
Big John Creek ~ USA (KS) 262-263 K 6
Big Kalzas Lake ⊂ CDN 20-21 X 5
Big Koniuji Island ⌒ USA 22-23 R 5
Big Lake ⊂ CDN 30-31 N 3
Big Lake ○ USA (TX) 266-267 F 2
Big Lake ⊂ USA (ME) 278-279 O 3
Big Lake Ranch ○ CDN (BC) 228-229 N 4
Big Lost River ~ USA (ID) 252-253 E 3
Big Mossy Point ▲ CDN 34-35 G 4
Big Mountain Creek ~ CDN (ALB) 228-229 Q 2
Big Muddy Badlands ⩡ CDN (SAS) 232-233 N 6
Big Muddy Creek ~ USA (MT) 250-251 O 3
Big Muddy Lake ⊂ CDN (SAS) 232-233 O 6
Big Muddy River ~ USA (IL) 276-277 F 3
Big Nemaha River ~ USA (NE) 262-263 L 4
Bignona ○ SN 202-203 B 3
Bigoray River ~ CDN (ALB) 232-233 C 2
Bigori ○ SUD 208-209 B 3
Big Pine ○ USA (CA) 248-249 F 2
Big Pine ○ USA (FL) 286-287 H 7
Big Pine Mountain ▲ USA (CA) 248-249 E 5
Big Piney ○ USA (WY) 252-253 H 4
Big Piney River ~ USA (MO) 276-277 C 3
Big Piskwanish Point ▲ CDN 34-35 Q 5
Big Pond ○ CDN (NS) 240-241 P 5
Big Quill Lake ⊂ CDN (SAS) 232-233 O 4
Big Rapids ○ USA (MI) 272-273 D 4
Big River ○ CDN (SAS) 232-233 L 2
Big River ~ CDN 24-25 K 4
Big River ~ CDN 36-37 U 7
Big River ~ CDN (SAS) 232-233 L 2
Big River ○ USA (CA) 248-249 K 5
Big River ~ USA (MO) 274-275 H 6
Big River Indian Reserve Ⅹ CDN (SAS) 232-233 L 2
Big Sable Point ▲ USA (MI) 272-273 C 3
Big Salmon Range ▲ CDN 20-21 Y 6
Big Salmon River ~ CDN 20-21 X 6
Big Sand Lake ⊂ CDN 34-35 G 2
Big Sandy ○ USA (MT) 250-251 J 3
Big Sandy ○ USA (TN) 276-277 G 4
Big Sandy ○ USA (TX) 264-265 J 6
Big Sandy ○ USA (WY) 252-253 J 4
Big Sandy Creek ~ USA (CO) 254-255 M 5
Big Sandy River ~ USA (TX) 264-265 G 5
Big Sandy Lake ⊂ CDN 34-35 D 3
Big Sandy River ~ USA (AZ) 256-257 B 4
Big Sandy River ~ USA (KY) 276-277 N 2
Big Sandy River ~ USA (WY) 252-253 J 5
Big Satilla Creek ~ USA (GA) 284-285 H 5
Big Sky ○ USA (MT) 250-251 H 6
Big Slough Creek ~ USA (GA) 284-285 F 5
Big Smoky Valley ⌣ USA (NV) 246-247 H 6
Big Snow Mountain ▲ USA (MT) 250-251 K 5
Big South Fork National River and Recreation Area ⊥ USA (TN) 276-277 K 4
Big South Fork National River and Recreation Area ⊥ USA (TN) 282-283 C 4
Big Spring ○ USA (TN) 282-283 C 5
Big Spring ○ USA (TX) 264-265 C 6
Big Springs ○ USA (ID) 252-253 G 2
Bigstick Lake ⊂ CDN (SAS) 232-233 J 5
Big Stone ○ CDN (ALB) 232-233 G 4
Big Stone City ○ USA (SD) 260-261 K 1
Bigstone Lake ⊂ CDN 34-35 H 4
Big Stone Lake ⊂ USA (MN) 270-271 B 5
Bigstone River ~ CDN 34-35 J 3
Big Suehn ○ LB 202-203 F 7
Big Sur ○ USA (CA) 248-249 C 3
Big Timber ○ USA (MT) 250-251 K 6
Big Trout Lake ⊂ CDN (ONT) 34-35 M 4
Big Trout Lake ○ CDN (ONT) 34-35 L 4
Big Trout Lake Indian Reservation Ⅹ CDN 34-35 M 4
Big Valley ○ CDN (ALB) 232-233 F 3
Big Warrambool River ~ AUS 178-179 K 5
Big Water ○ USA (UT) 254-255 D 6
Big White Mountain ▲ CDN (BC) 230-231 L 4
Big White River ~ USA (SD) 260-261 D 3
Big Willow River ~ CDN 34-35 P 4
Big Wood Cay ⌒ BS 54-55 G 2
Big Wood River ~ USA (ID) 252-253 D 3
Bihać ○• BIH 100-101 E 2
Bihar ▫ IND 142-143 C 3
Biharamulo ○ EAT 212-213 C 5
Biharamulo Game Reservat ⊥ EAT 212-213 C 5
Bihār Sharīf ○• IND 142-143 D 3
Bihoro ○ J 152-153 L 3
Bihorului, Muntii ▲ RO 102-103 C 4
Bihta ○ IND 142-143 D 3
Bija ~ RUS 124-125 O 2
Bija ~ RUS 124-125 P 3
Bijagos, Arquipélago dos ⌒ GNB 202-203 B 4
Bijāpur ○•• IND 140-141 F 2
Bijbehara ○ IND 138-139 E 3
Bijelo Polje ○ YU 100-101 G 3
Bijie ○ VRC 156-157 D 3
Bijlikol', ozero ⊂ KA 136-137 M 3
Bijnor ○ IND 138-139 G 5
Bijou Creek ~ USA (CO) 254-255 L 4
Bijoutier Island ⌒ SY 224 C 3
Bijsk ☆ RUS 124-125 O 2
Bijskaja Griva, hrebet ▲ RUS 124-125 P 2
Bikāner ○• IND 138-139 D 5
Bikin ○ RUS 122-123 F 5
Bikin ~ RUS 122-123 G 5
Bikita ○ ZW 218-219 F 5
Bikok ○ CAM 210-211 C 2
Bikoro ○ ZRE 210-211 G 4
Bikou ○ VRC 154-155 D 5
Bikramganj ○ IND 142-143 D 3
Bikubiti ▲ LAR 198-199 J 2
Bilā ○ ET 194-195 E 2
Bila ~ RI 162-163 C 3
Bilaat Point ▲ RP 160-161 F 8
Bilac ○ BR 72-73 E 6
Bila Cerkva ☆ UA 102-103 G 3
Bilād Banī Bū Ḥasan ○ OM 132-133 L 2
Bilala ○ RCB 210-211 D 6
Bilang, Teluk ≈ 164-165 G 3
Bilanga ○ BF 202-203 K 3
Bilap Bay ≈ 140-141 L 4
Bilāsipāra ○ IND 142-143 G 2
Bilāspur ○ IND (MAP) 142-143 C 4
Bilāspur ○ IND (UTP) 138-139 G 5
Bilassana ○ RG 202-203 F 5
Bilatē Shet' ~ ETH 208-209 D 5
Bilati ~ ZRE 212-213 B 4
Bila Tserkva = Bila Cerkva ☆ UA 102-103 G 3
Bilauri ○ NEP 144-145 C 6
Bilāwal ○ PK 138-139 C 3
Bilbao = Bilbo ○• E 98-99 F 3
Bilberatha Hill ▲ AUS 176-177 D 4
Bilbo = Bilbao ○• E 98-99 F 3
Bilecik ☆ TR 128-129 C 2
Bilehsawār ○ IR 128-129 N 3
Bilēngui ○ G 210-211 C 4
Bilesha Plain ⩡ EAK 212-213 H 3
Biłgoraj ○• PL 92-93 R 3
Bilgram ○ IND 142-143 B 2
Bilhorod-Dnistrovs'kyj ☆ UA 102-103 G 4
Bili ○ ZRE 206-207 D 6
Bili ○ ZRE (Hau) 206-207 G 6
Bili ~ ZRE 206-207 F 6
Bilibili ○ RI 164-165 F 6
Bilibino ☆ RUS 112-113 O 2
Bilikköl ⊂ KA 136-137 M 3
Bilimora ○ IND 138-139 D 9
Bilin ○ MYA 158-159 D 2
Biling La ▲ NEP 144-145 C 5
Biliran Island ⌒ RP 160-161 F 7
Biliri ○ WAN 204-205 J 4
Biljasuvar = Bilasuvar ○ AZ 128-129 N 3
Bill ○ USA (WY) 252-253 N 3
Billabong Creek ~ AUS 180-181 H 3
Billefjorden ≈ 84-85 K 3
Billenbach ○ AUS 178-179 K 4
Billete, Cerro El ▲ MEX 52-53 D 2
Billiat Conservation Park ⊥ AUS 180-181 F 3
Billiluna ○ AUS 172-173 H 5
Billings ○ RUS 112-113 S 2
Billings ○ USA (MT) 250-251 L 6
Billings ○ USA (NY) 280-281 N 2
Billingsa, mys ▲ RUS 112-113 T 2
Billjah ~ RUS 110-111 S 6
Billsburg ○ USA (SD) 260-261 E 2
Billund ○ DK 86-87 D 9
Bill Williams Mountain ▲ USA (AZ) 256-257 C 3
Bill Williams River ~ USA (AZ) 256-257 B 4
Billy, Chutes de ~• RMM 202-203 F 3
Bilma ○ RN 198-199 F 3
Bilma, Grand Erg de ⩡ RN 198-199 F 4
Bilo ○ ETH 208-209 C 4
Biloela ○ AUS 178-179 L 3
Bilohors'k ☆• UA 102-103 J 5
Biloo ○ SP 212-213 J 3
Bilopil'a ○ UA 102-103 J 2
Bilou ○ CI 202-203 G 5
Bilovods'k ○ UA 102-103 L 3
Biloxi ○ USA (MS) 268-269 M 6
Bilpa Morea Claypan ⊂ AUS 178-179 E 3
Bilqās ○ ET 194-195 E 2
Bilthara ○ IND 142-143 C 2
Biltine ▫ TCH 198-199 K 5
Biltine ☆ TCH 198-199 K 5
Bilugyun ⌒ MYA 158-159 D 2
Bilungala ○ RI 164-165 H 3
Biluo Xueshan ▲ VRC 142-143 L 2
Bilverdi ○ IR 128-129 M 3
Bilyj Čeremoš ~ UA 102-103 D 4
Bima ○ RI 168 D 7
Bima ~ ZRE 210-211 L 2
Bimba ○ CAM 206-207 B 6
Bimbe ○ ANG 216-217 C 5
Bimberi Peak ▲ AUS 180-181 K 3
Bimbijy ○ AUS 176-177 E 4
Bimbila ○ GH 202-203 L 5
Bimbo ☆ RCA 206-207 D 6
Bimi, Sabon- ○ WAN 198-199 C 6
Bimini Islands ⌒ BS 54-55 F 2
Bina ○ IND 138-139 G 7
Binaluan ○ RP 160-161 C 7
Biname Lake ⊂ CDN 24-25 K 6
Binanga ○ RI 162-163 C 4
Binbee ○ AUS 174-175 J 7
Binbrook ○ CDN (ONT) 238-239 F 5
Bindé ○ BF 202-203 K 4
Bindegolly, Lake ⊂ AUS 178-179 H 5
Binder ○ TCH 206-207 B 4
Bindi Bindi ○ AUS 176-177 D 5
Bindu ○ ZRE 216-217 E 3
Bindura ☆ ZW 218-219 F 3
Bin-el-Ouidane ○ MA 188-189 H 4
Binga ○ ZW 218-219 D 3
Binga, Monte ▲ MOC 218-219 G 4
Binga, Quedas de Agua ~ ANG 216-217 C 5
Bingara ○ AUS 178-179 L 5
Bingassi ○ RMM 202-203 E 3
Bing Bong ○ AUS 174-175 D 4
Binger ○ USA (OK) 264-265 F 3
Bingerville ○ CI 202-203 J 7
Bingham ○ USA (ME) 278-279 M 3
Bingham ○ USA (NM) 256-257 J 5
Binghamton ○ USA (NY) 278-279 F 6
Bin Ghashir ○ LAR 192-193 E 1
Binginteiok ○ RI 162-163 E 6
Bingley ○ CDN (ALB) 232-233 D 3
Binglingsi Shankou • VRC 154-155 C 4
Bingöl ☆ TR 128-129 J 3
Bingöl Dağları ▲ TR 128-129 J 3
Binhai ○ VRC 154-155 L 4
Binh Chánh ○ VN 158-159 J 5
Binh Châu ○ VN 158-159 J 5
Binh Định ○ VN 158-159 K 4
Binh Giả ○ VN 158-159 J 5
Binh Gia ☆ VN 156-157 E 6
Binh Lâm ○ VN 158-159 K 3
Binh Long ○ VN 158-159 J 5
Bin-Hoyé ○ CI 202-203 F 6
Binibihali ○ PNG 183 F 6
Bini Drosso < TCH 198-199 J 3
Bini Erde < TCH 198-199 J 2
Bin 'Isa, Bi'r < LAR 192-193 F 2
Binjai ○ RI 162-163 C 3
Bin Jawwad ○ LAR 192-193 H 2
Binjuda ~ RUS 108-109 X 5
Binkolo ○ WAL 202-203 E 5
Binnaway ○ AUS 178-179 K 6
Binongko ○ RI 164-165 K 3
Binongko, Pulau ⌒ RI 164-165 H 6
Binscarth ○ CDN (MAN) 234-235 B 4
Bintagoungou ○ RMM 196-197 J 6
Bintan, Pulau ⌒ RI 162-163 F 4
Bintang, Banjaran ▲ MAL 162-163 D 2
Bint Ǧubail ☆ RL 128-129 F 6
Binthalya ○ AUS 176-177 C 2
Bintuan ○ RI 162-163 F 7
Bintulu ○ MAL 162-163 K 3
Bintuni ○ RI 166-167 G 3
Bintuni, Teluk ≈ 166-167 G 3
Binuang ○ RI 164-165 D 5
Bin Xian ○ VRC 150-151 F 5
Binyang ○ VRC 156-157 F 5
Binz, Ostseebad ○ D 92-93 M 1
Binzhou ○ VRC 154-155 K 3
Biobío, Río ~ RCH 78-79 C 4
Bio Caddo ○ SP 212-213 K 2
Bioco, Isla de ⌒ GQ 210-211 B 2
Biograd na Moru ○ HR 100-101 E 3
Biokovo ▲ HR 100-101 F 3
Biorra = Birr ○ IRL 90-91 D 5
Biosphere II •• USA (AZ) 256-257 E 6
Biot, Kap ▲ GRØ 26-27 o 8
Biougra ○ MA 188-189 G 5
Bipi Island ⌒ PNG 183 D 2
Bipindi ○ CAM 210-211 C 2
Bipok ○ CAM 204-205 J 6
Biquele ○ RI 166-167 C 6

Berkner Island — Biquele 305

Bir o IND 138-139 E 10
Bir, Ras ▲ DJI 200-201 L 6
Bira o RI 164-165 G 6
Bira o RUS 122-123 E 4
Bi'r Abū Ġulūd o SYR 128-129 H 4
Birāk o LAR 192-193 F 4
Birāk, Tall o SYR 128-129 J 4
Birak, Umm al- o KSA 130-131 F 6
Bir al Ghanam o LAR 192-193 E 1
Bir Ali Ben Khelifa o TN 190-191 H 3
Bi'r Allāq o LAR 192-193 D 2
Bir-Anzarane o MA 196-197 C 3
Birao ☆ • RCA 206-207 F 3
Biratnagar o NEP 144-145 F 7
Biratori o J 152-153 K 3
Bi'r A'yād o LAR 192-193 E 1
Bi'r Ben Ghimah o LAR 192-193 J 2
Bîrca o RO 102-103 C 6
Birch Bay o CDN (MAN) 234-235 E 3
Birch Creek o USA 20-21 S 3
Birch Creek ~ USA 20-21 S 3
Birch Creek ~ USA 20-21 P 5
Birch Creek ~ USA (OR) 244-245 F 5
Birchdale o USA (MN) 270-271 D 2
Birchenough Bridge o ZW 218-219 G 4
Birches o USA 20-21 O 4
Birch Harbor o USA (ME) 278-279 N 4
Birch Hills o CDN (SAS) 232-233 N 3
Birchi o WAN 198-199 C 6
Birchip o AUS 180-181 G 3
Birch Island o CDN (BC) 230-231 K 2
Birch Island ⌒ CDN (MAN) 234-235 D 2
Birch Lake o CDN (ALB) 232-233 G 2
Birch Lake o CDN (NWT) 30-31 L 4
Birch Lake o CDN (ONT) 234-235 L 3
Birch Lake o USA (OK) 264-265 H 2
Birch Mountains ▲ CDN 32-33 N 3
Birch River o CDN (MAN) 234-235 B 2
Birch River ~ CDN 32-33 O 3
Birchwood o USA (WI) 270-271 G 5
Bircot o ETH 208-209 F 5
Bird Cape ▲ USA 22-23 F 7
Bird City o USA (KS) 262-263 E 5
Bird Creek ~ USA (OK) 264-265 H 2
Bi'r Dhu'fān o LAR 192-193 F 2
Bi'r Di o SUD 206-207 J 5
Bird Island ⌒ GB 78-79 N 7
Bird Island ⌒ SY 224 D 1
Bird Island ⌒ USA 22-23 R 5
Bird Rock Lighthouse • BS 54-55 H 3
Birdseye o USA (IN) 274-275 M 6
Birdseye o USA (UT) 254-255 D 4
Birds Hill o CDN (MAN) 234-235 F 5
Birdsville o AUS 178-179 E 3
Birdsville Track • AUS 178-179 E 5
Birdtail o CDN (MAN) 234-235 C 4
Birdum o AUS 174-175 B 4
Birdum Creek ~ AUS 172-173 L 3
Bi'r Durb o KSA 130-131 G 4
Birecik ☆ • TR 128-129 G 4
Bire Kpatua Game Reserve ⊥ SUD 206-207 J 6
Birekte ~ RUS 110-111 L 5
Bir El Ater o DZ 190-191 G 3
Bireuen o RI 162-163 B 2
Bi'r Falaq < IRQ 128-129 J 5
Bi'r Fātima < IRQ 128-129 K 5
Birğand o • IR 134-135 H 2
Bir-Gandouz o MA 196-197 B 4
Birganj o NEP 144-145 E 7
Bi'r Ġuraibi'āt o IRQ 130-131 J 3
Bi'r Haġal < SYR 128-129 H 5
Bi'r Ḥamrān < IRQ 128-129 K 5
Bi'r Hasana o ET 194-195 F 2
Birhat al-Khuraba Pool • KSA 130-131 G 6
Biri o SUD (SR) 206-207 H 5
Biri ~ SUD 206-207 H 5
Biri Island ⌒ RP 160-161 F 6
Birilijussy o RUS 116-117 E 7
Birini o RCA 206-207 F 5
Biritinga o BR 68-69 J 7
Birjuk ~ RUS 118-119 J 5
Birjusa ~ RUS 116-117 H 7
Birjusa = Ona ~ RUS 116-117 G 7
Birjusinsk o RUS 116-117 H 8
Birjusinskoe plato ⊥ RUS 116-117 J 7
Birk, al- o KSA 132-133 B 4
Birka ••• S 86-87 H 7
Birkat al-'Amyā' o IRQ 130-131 H 3
Birkat Saira o SUD 198-199 L 6
Birkelane o SN 202-203 C 2
Birken o CDN (BC) 230-231 G 3
Birkenhead o AUS 178-179 J 3
Birkenhead o GB 90-91 F 5
Birkenhead Lake Provincial Park ⊥ CDN (BC) 230-231 G 3
Bi'r Khadijah o LAR 192-193 J 2
Birlad o RO 102-103 E 4
Birlad ~ RO 102-103 E 4
Birlik o KA 124-125 H 6
Birlik o KA (JUK) 136-137 L 4
Birma ~ RUS 122-123 C 3
Birma = Myanmar ■ MYA 142-143 J 4
Birmaj o AZ 128-129 M 3
Birmingham o CDN (SAS) 232-233 P 5
Birmingham o GB 90-91 G 5
Birmingham o USA (AL) 284-285 D 3
Bir Mogreïn o RIM 196-197 E 2
Birnagar o IND 142-143 F 4
Birney o USA (MT) 250-251 N 6
Birni o DY 202-203 L 5
Birnie o CDN (MAN) 234-235 D 4
Birni Gwari o WAN 204-205 G 3
Birnin ~ RN 198-199 D 5
Birnin-Gaouré o RN 204-205 E 2
Birnin-Kebbi o WAN 198-199 B 6
Birnin Konni o RN 198-199 B 6
Birnin Kudu o WAN 204-205 H 3
Birnin-Yauri o WAN 204-205 F 3
Birniwa o WAN 198-199 E 6
Biro o DY 204-205 E 4
Birobidžan o RUS 122-123 E 4
Birofel'd o RUS 122-123 E 4
Biromba ~ RUS 116-117 G 4
Biron o CDN (QUE) 240-241 J 2
Birougou, Mont ▲ G 210-211 D 4
Biroun o G 210-211 C 4
Birqin o LAR 192-193 E 4
Birr = Biorra o IRL 90-91 D 5
Birricannia o AUS 178-179 H 1
Birrim, Ğazirat ⌒ KSA 130-131 E 5
Birrindudu Out Station o AUS 172-173 L 3
Birrindudu o AUS 172-173 J 5
Birsay o CDN (SAS) 232-233 M 4
Birsilpur o IND 138-139 D 5
Birsk ☆ RUS 96-97 J 6
Birsuat ~ RUS 124-125 B 2
Birtam-Tam o MA 188-189 J 4
Bi'r Ṭarfāwi < IRQ 128-129 K 6
Birti o SUD 200-201 F 3
Birtle o CDN (SAS) 232-233 R 5
Biruaca o YV 60-61 H 4
Birufu o RI 166-167 K 4
Birūr o IND 140-141 F 4
Biržai ☆ •• LT 94-95 J 3
Bir Zar o TN 190-191 H 5
Biša o KSA 132-133 C 3
Bisa, Pulau ⌒ RI 164-165 K 4
Biša, Wādi ~ KSA 132-133 C 3
Bisagana o WAN 198-199 F 6
Bisalpur o IND 138-139 G 5
Bisanadi National Reserve ⊥ EAK 212-213 G 3
Bisbee o USA (AZ) 256-257 F 7
Biscarrosse o F 90-91 G 9
Biscay, Bay of ≈ 90-91 E 9
Biscay Abyssal Plain ≃ 6-7 J 4
Biscayne Bay ≈ 48-49 H 7
Biscayne Bay ≈ USA 286-287 J 6
Biscayne National Park ⊥ USA (FL) 286-287 J 6
Bischofshofen o A 92-93 M 5
Biscoe o USA (NC) 282-283 H 5
Biscoe Islands ⌒ ARK 16 G 30
Biscucuy o YV 60-61 G 3
Bisellia o SUD 206-207 H 5
Bisen o KA 96-97 E 9
Bisert' o RUS 96-97 L 5
Bisha o ER 200-201 H 5
Bishaltar o NEP 144-145 E 7
Bishan o VRC 156-157 E 2
Bishkek = Biškek ★ KS 146-147 B 4
Bishkhali ~ BD 142-143 G 4
Bishnupur o IND 142-143 E 4
Bisho o ZA 220-221 H 6
Bishop o USA (CA) 248-249 F 2
Bishop o USA (TX) 266-267 K 6
Bishop Hill State Historic Park • USA (IL) 274-275 H 3
Bishop Range ▲ AUS 172-173 H 6
Bishop's Falls o CDN (NFL) 242-243 N 3
Bishopville o USA (SC) 284-285 K 2
Bişhr o LAR 192-193 H 2
Bishushanzhang • VRC 148-149 N 7
Biscotasi Lake o CDN (ONT) 236-237 G 5
Biskra ☆ • DZ 190-191 E 3
Biskupiec o PL 92-93 Q 2
Bismarck o CDN (ONT) 238-239 F 5
Bismarck o USA (AR) 276-277 B 6
Bismarck o USA (MO) 276-277 E 3
Bismarck ★ USA (ND) 258-259 G 5
Bismarck Archipelago ⌒ PNG 183 E 2
Bismarck Range ▲ PNG 183 C 3
Bismarck Sea ≈ 183 D 2
Bismarckstraße ≈ 16 G 30
Bismil ☆ TR 128-129 J 4
Biso o EAU 212-213 C 3
Bison o USA (SD) 260-261 D 1
Bisonó o DOM 54-55 K 5
Bisotūn o IR 134-135 B 1
Bispgården o S 86-87 H 5
Bissame o RMM 196-197 K 6
Bissau ★ GNB 202-203 C 4
Bisset Lake o CDN 30-31 W 4
Bissikrima o RG 202-203 E 4
Bissingou II o RCA 206-207 E 4
Bissora ☆ GNB 202-203 C 3
Bistcho Lake o CDN 30-31 K 6
Bistineau, Lake o USA (LA) 268-269 G 4
Bistriţa ☆ • RO 102-103 D 4
Biswān o IND 142-143 B 2
Bita ~ RCA 206-207 G 5
Bita, Río ~ CO 60-61 G 4
Bitam o G 210-211 C 2
Bitangor o MAL 162-163 J 4
Bitata o ETH 208-209 D 6
Bitencourt o BR 66-67 C 3
Bitian Bank ≃ 168 E 2
Bitik o ETH 208-209 E 4
Bitik o KA 96-97 G 8
Bitilifondi o RCA 206-207 H 6
Bitjug ~ RUS 94-95 R 5
Bitjug ~ RUS 102-103 M 2
Bitkine o TCH 206-207 D 3
Bitlis ☆ • TR 128-129 K 3
Bitola o •• MK 100-101 H 4
Bitou o BF 202-203 K 4
Bitoutouk o CAM 210-211 C 2
Bitter Creek o USA (WY) 252-253 K 5
Bitter Creek ~ USA (WY) 252-253 J 5
Bitterfeld o D 92-93 M 3
Bitterfontein o ZA 220-221 D 5
Bitter Lake o CDN (SAS) 232-233 J 5
Bittern Lake o CDN (ALB) 232-233 E 3
Bittern Lake Indian Reservation ✗ CDN (SAS) 232-233 N 2
Bitterroot Range ▲ USA (ID) 250-251 D 4
Bitterroot River ~ USA (MT) 250-251 E 5
Bitui River ~ PNG 183 B 5
Bitumount o CDN 32-33 P 3
Bitung o RI 164-165 J 3
Biturna o BR 74-75 E 6
Bitzshtini Mount ▲ USA 20-21 P 4
Biu o WAN 204-205 K 3
Biuka-tōge ▲ J 152-153 K 2
Biu Plateau ▲ WAN 204-205 K 3
Biwabik o USA (MN) 270-271 F 3
Biwai, Mount ▲ PNG 183 B 4
Biwa-ko o J 152-153 G 7
Biwako Quasi National Park ⊥ J 152-153 F 7
Biwat o PNG 183 B 3
Bixby o USA (MN) 270-271 E 7
Bixby o USA (MO) 276-277 D 3
Biyagundi o ER 200-201 H 5
Biyang o VRC 154-155 H 5
Biyo K'obē o ETH 208-209 F 3
Biysk = Bijsk ☆ RUS 124-125 O 2
Bizana o ZA 220-221 J 5
Bīzanābād o IR 134-135 H 5
Bižbuljak ☆ RUS 96-97 J 7
Bize ~ KA 124-125 K 6
Bizen o J 152-153 F 7
Bizerte ☆ • TN 190-191 G 2
Bizigui ~ BF 202-203 K 3
Bjahoml' o BY 94-95 L 4
Bjala o BG 102-103 D 6
Bjala Slatina o BG 102-103 C 6
Bjarèzina ~ BY 94-95 L 5
Bjarezinski zapavednik ⊥ BY 94-95 L 4
Bjargtangar ▲ IS 86-87 a 2
Bjaroza o BY 94-95 J 5
Bjas'-Kjuel' o RUS (SAH) 118-119 J 6
Bjas'-Kjuel' o RUS (SAH) 118-119 N 4
Bjästa o S 86-87 J 5
Bjelašnica ▲ BIH 100-101 G 3
Bjelovar o HR 100-101 F 2
Bjerkvik o N 86-87 H 2
Bjorkdale o CDN (SAS) 232-233 P 3
Björna o S 86-87 J 5
Bjørnafjorden ≈ 86-87 B 6
Bjørne Øer ⌒ GRØ 26-27 n 8
Bjorne Peninsula ⌒ CDN 24-25 c 2
Bjørnesk Ø ⌒ GRØ 26-27 q 5
Bjørnøya ⌒ N 84-85 L 5
Bjørnøya Bank ≃ 84-85 M 5
Bjørnøy Radio o N 84-85 L 5
Bjurholm o • S 86-87 J 5
Bjutejdjah o • RUS 120-121 D 3
Bla o RMM 202-203 H 3
Blachly o USA (OR) 244-245 B 6
Black o USA 20-21 H 5
Blackall o AUS 178-179 H 3
Black Bay o CDN (ONT) 234-235 P 6
Black Bear Creek ~ USA (OK) 264-265 G 2
Black Bear River ~ CDN 34-35 L 3
Blackbear River ~ CDN 34-35 M 3
Black Bear River ~ CDN 38-39 Q 2
Black Birch Lake o CDN 34-35 C 2
Black Braes o AUS 174-175 H 6
Blackbull o AUS 174-175 F 5
Blackburn, Mount ▲ USA 20-21 T 6
Black Canyon City o USA (AZ) 256-257 C 4
Black Canyon of the Gunnison National Monument ∴ USA (CO) 254-255 H 5
Black Cape ▲ USA 22-23 U 3
Black Creek o CDN (BC) 230-231 D 4
Black Creek o USA (WI) 270-271 K 6
Black Creek ~ USA (MS) 268-269 L 5
Black Diamond o CDN (ALB) 232-233 D 5
Blackdown o AUS 174-175 G 5
Blackdown Tableland National Park ⊥ AUS 178-179 K 2
Blackfalds o CDN (ALB) 232-233 E 3
Blackfeet Indian Reservation ✗ USA (MT) 250-251 F 3
Blackfoot o CDN (ALB) 232-233 H 2
Blackfoot o USA (ID) 252-253 F 3
Blackfoot o USA (MT) 250-251 G 3
Blackfoot Indian Reserve ✗ CDN (ALB) 232-233 F 5
Blackfoot Reservoir o USA (ID) 252-253 G 4
Blackfoot River ~ USA (MT) 250-251 F 5
Black Forest = Schwarzwald ▲ D 92-93 K 4
Black Hawk o CDN (ONT) 234-235 K 6
Black Hills ▲ USA (SD) 260-261 B 2
Blackie o CDN (ALB) 232-233 E 5
Black Island ⌒ • CDN (MAN) 234-235 G 3
Black Lake o CDN (QUE) 238-239 O 2
Black Lake o CDN (SAS) 30-31 R 6
Black Lake o USA 22-23 R 4
Black Mesa ▲ USA (OK) 264-265 B 2
Black Mesa ⊥ USA (AZ) 256-257 E 2
Black Mountain ▲ AUS 178-179 E 1
Black Mountain ▲ CDN 26-27 G 3
Black Mountain ▲ USA (VA) 280-281 D 7
Black Mountains ▲ USA (AZ) 256-257 A 3
Black Nossob ~ NAM 216-217 E 10
Black Pines o CDN (BC) 230-231 K 3
Black Point o BS 54-55 G 2
Black Point ▲ USA 22-23 U 4
Blackpool o CDN (BC) 230-231 J 2
Blackpool o • GB 90-91 F 5
Black Range ▲ USA (NM) 256-257 H 5
Black River o CDN (NS) 240-241 O 4
Black River ~ CDN 20-21 X 6
Black River ~ CDN (MAN) 234-235 G 4
Black River ~ CDN (ONT) 238-239 F 4
Black River ~ •• JA 54-55 G 5
Black River ~ USA 20-21 T 3
Black River ~ USA (AR) 276-277 D 5
Black River ~ USA (AZ) 256-257 E 5
Black River ~ USA (FL) 286-287 H 1
Black River ~ USA (MI) 272-273 E 2
Black River ~ USA (MI) 272-273 G 4
Black River ~ USA (MO) 276-277 E 4
Black River ~ USA (NC) 282-283 J 6
Black River ~ USA (NM) 256-257 L 6
Black River ~ USA (NY) 278-279 F 5
Black River ~ USA (OH) 280-281 D 2
Black River ~ USA (SC) 284-285 L 3
Black River ~ USA (SC) 284-285 K 3
Black River ~ USA (WI) 270-271 H 6
Black River Falls o USA (WI) 270-271 H 6
Black Rock o USA (AR) 276-277 D 4
Black Rock o USA (UT) 254-255 C 5
Black Rock Desert ⊥ USA (NV) 246-247 F 3
Black Rock Point ▲ CDN 36-37 R 4
Black Rocks ▲ • WAN 204-205 H 4
Black Rocks Landing o AUS 174-175 D 4
Black Rock Summit ▲ USA (NV) 246-247 J 5
Blackrun o USA (OH) 280-281 D 3
Blacksburg o USA (VA) 280-281 F 6
Black Sea ≈ 102-103 G 6
Blacks Fork ~ USA (UT) 254-255 E 3
Blacks Harbour o CDN (NB) 240-241 J 5
Blackshear o USA (GA) 284-285 H 5
Blackshear, Lake < USA (GA) 284-285 G 5
Black Squirrel Creek ~ USA (CO) 254-255 L 5
Blackstone o USA (VA) 280-281 H 6
Blackstone River ~ CDN 20-21 V 4
Blackstone River ~ CDN 30-31 H 5
Blackstone River ~ CDN (ALB) 232-233 B 3
Black Sturgeon Lake o CDN (ONT) 234-235 P 5
Blackville o AUS 178-179 L 6
Blackville o CDN (NB) 240-241 K 4
Blackville o USA (SC) 284-285 J 3
Black Volta ~ GH 202-203 J 5
Black Warrior River ~ USA (AL) 284-285 C 4
Blackwater o AUS 178-179 K 2
Blackwater ~ USA (FL) 286-287 C 1
Blackwater Creek ~ AUS 178-179 H 3
Blackwater Creek ~ AUS 180-181 L 2
Blackwater Lake o CDN 30-31 H 3
Blackwater National Wildlife Refuge ✗ USA (MD) 280-281 K 5
Blackwater River ~ CDN 30-31 H 4
Blackwater River ~ USA (MO) 274-275 E 6
Blackwell o USA (OK) 264-265 G 2
Blackwell o USA (TX) 264-265 D 6
Blackwells Corner o USA (CA) 248-249 E 4
Blackwood River ~ AUS 176-177 D 6
Bladenboro o USA (NC) 282-283 J 6
Bladensburg National Park ⊥ AUS 178-179 G 2
Bladgrond o ZA 220-221 D 4
Bladon Springs State Park ⊥ • USA (AL) 284-285 B 5
Bladworth o CDN (SAS) 232-233 M 4
Blaeberry River ~ CDN (BC) 230-231 N 2
Blåfjellet ▲ N 86-87 F 4
Blagodarnyj o RUS 102-103 N 5
Blagoevgrad o BG 102-103 C 6
Blagoevo o RUS 88-89 T 5
Blagopolučija, zaliv o RUS 108-109 K 4
Blagoveščenka o KA 146-147 B 4
Blagoveščenka ☆ RUS 124-125 L 2
Blagoveščensk o • RUS 122-123 B 3
Blagoveščensk ☆ RUS (BAS) 96-97 J 6
Blagoveščenskij proliv ≈ 110-111 Z 2
Blagoveshchensk = Blagoveščensk ☆ RUS 118-119 N 10
Blaine o USA (KS) 262-263 K 5
Blaine o USA (KY) 276-277 N 2
Blaine o USA (MN) 270-271 E 5
Blaine o USA (TN) 282-283 D 4
Blaine o USA (WA) 244-245 C 2
Blaine Lake o CDN (SAS) 232-233 M 3
Blainville o CDN (QUE) 238-239 M 3
Blair o USA (NE) 262-263 K 3
Blair o USA (OK) 264-265 E 4
Blair o USA (WI) 270-271 G 6
Blair Athol o AUS 178-179 J 2
Blairbeth o ZA 220-221 H 2
Blairgowrie o GB 90-91 F 3
Blairmore o CDN (ALB) 232-233 D 6
Blairsden o USA (CA) 246-247 E 4
Blairsville o USA (GA) 284-285 G 2
Blairsville o USA (PA) 280-281 G 3
Blaka ~ RN 198-199 F 2
Blaka Laodemi < RN 198-199 F 2
Blake Bay ≈ 24-25 e 7
Blakely o USA (GA) 284-285 F 5
Blake Plateau ≃ 48-49 J 4
Blake Plateau ≃ 286-287 K 1
Blake Point ▲ USA (MI) 270-271 K 2
Blama o WAL 202-203 E 6
Blanc, Lac o CDN (QUE) 236-237 P 5
Blanc, le o F 90-91 H 8
Blanca, Bahía ≈ 78-79 H 5
Blanca, Cordillera ▲ PE 64-65 D 6
Blanca, Lago o RCH 70-71 C 5
Blanca, Laguna o RCH 80 E 6
Blanca, Punta ▲ MEX 50-51 B 3
Blanca, Rio ~ BOL 70-71 D 7
Blanca, Sierra ▲ USA (NM) 256-257 K 5
Blanca Grande, Laguna la o RA 78-79 H 5
Blanca Peak ▲ USA (CO) 254-255 K 6
Blancas, Sierras ▲ RA 78-79 F 6
Blancester o USA (OH) 280-281 C 4
Blanchard o USA (ID) 250-251 C 3
Blanchard o USA (ND) 258-259 K 4
Blanchard o USA (OK) 264-265 G 3
Blanchard River ~ USA (OH) 280-281 C 2
Blanchard Springs Caverns ∴ USA (AR) 276-277 C 5
Blanche, Lake o AUS (SA) 178-179 E 5
Blanche, Lake o AUS (WA) 172-173 F 7
Blanche Channel ≈ 184 I c 3
Blanche-Marievallen o SME 62-63 F 3
Blanchet Island ⌒ CDN 30-31 N 4
Blanchetown o AUS 180-181 E 3
Blanchisseuse o TT 60-61 L 2
Blanco o USA (NM) 256-257 H 2
Blanco o USA (TX) 266-267 J 3
Blanco, Cabo ▲ CR 52-53 B 7
Blanco, Cape ▲ USA (OR) 244-245 A 8
Blanco, Cerro ▲ RA 78-79 D 6
Blanco, Lago o RA 80 E 3
Blanco, Lago o RCH 80 F 7
Blanco, Río ~ BOL 70-71 E 3
Blanco, Río ~ PE 64-65 F 4
Blanco, Río ~ RA 76-77 C 6
Blanco, Río ~ RA 76-77 C 6
Blanco, Río ~ RA 76-77 B 6
Blanco, Río ~ RA 78-79 D 2
Blanco, Río ~ RA 80 E 3
Blanco, Río ~ RCH 80 D 2
Blanco Creek ~ USA (TX) 266-267 K 5
Blanco River ~ USA (TX) 266-267 J 3
Blancos, Los o RA 76-77 F 2
Blancos del Sur, Cayos ⌒ C 54-55 E 3
Blanc Sablon o CDN 38-39 Q 3
Bland o USA (VA) 280-281 E 6
Blandá ~ IS 86-87 d 2
Bland Creek ~ AUS 180-181 J 2
Blandford o CDN (NS) 240-241 L 6
Blanding o USA (IL) 274-275 H 2
Blanding o USA (UT) 254-255 F 6
Blanes o E 98-99 J 4
Blaney Park o USA (MI) 270-271 N 4
Blanfla o CI 202-203 H 6
Blangkejeren o RI 162-163 B 2
Blangpidie o RI 162-163 B 3
Blanket o USA (TX) 266-267 J 2
Blanquero, El o YV 60-61 K 3
Blanquilla, Isla ⌒ YV 60-61 J 2
Blanquillo o ROU 78-79 M 2
Blantyre ☆ • MW 218-219 H 2
Blåsjøen o N 86-87 C 7
Blau o RI 164-165 H 3
Blåvands Huk ⌒ DK 86-87 D 9
Blaye o F 90-91 G 9
Blayney o AUS 180-181 K 2
Bleaker Island ⌒ GB 78-79 L 7
Blebo o LB 202-203 G 7
Blednaja, gory ▲ RUS 108-109 L 3
Bledsoe o USA (TX) 264-265 A 5
Bled Tisseras o DZ 190-191 E 7
Blega o RI 168 E 3
Bleikvassli o N 86-87 F 4
Blendio o RMM 202-203 G 4
Blenheim o CDN (ONT) 238-239 D 6
Blenheim o NZ 182 D 4
Blenheim o USA (SC) 284-285 L 2
Blenheim Palace ••• GB 90-91 G 6
Blesmanspos o ZA 220-221 G 3
Blessing o USA (TX) 266-267 L 5
Bleu, Lac o CDN (QUE) 238-239 G 2
Bleus, Monts ▲ ZRE 212-213 C 3
Blewett o USA (WA) 244-245 E 3
Blicade o F 62-63 H 4
Blida ☆ DZ 190-191 D 2
Bligh Island ⌒ USA 20-21 R 6
Bligh Water ≈ 184 III a 2
Blikadi o CI 202-203 J 5
Blina o AUS 172-173 G 4
Blina Oil Field • AUS 172-173 G 4
Blind Channel o CDN (BC) 230-231 D 3
Blindman River ~ CDN (ALB) 232-233 D 3
Blind River o CDN (ONT) 238-239 C 2
Blinisht o AL 100-101 G 4
Blipi o LB 202-203 F 6
Bliss o USA (ID) 252-253 D 4
Bliss Bugt ≈ 26-27 l 2
Blissfield o USA (MI) 272-273 F 6
Bliss Landing o CDN (BC) 230-231 E 3
Blissville o CDN (NB) 240-241 J 5
Blitchton o USA (GA) 284-285 J 4
Blitta o RT 202-203 L 5
Blizzard Gap ▲ USA (OR) 244-245 F 8
Bloedel o CDN (BC) 230-231 D 3
Bloemfontein ☆ ZA 220-221 H 4
Bloemhof o ZA 220-221 G 3
Bloemhof Dam < ZA 220-221 G 3
Blois ☆ • F 90-91 H 8
Blolékin o CI 202-203 G 6
Blomkest o USA (MN) 270-271 C 6
Blommesteinmeer, W.J. van o SME 62-63 G 3
Blöndósbær ☆ IS 86-87 c 2
Blood Indian Creek ~ CDN (ALB) 232-233 G 4
Blood Indian Reserve ✗ CDN (ALB) 232-233 E 6
Blood River Monument • ZA 220-221 K 4
Bloodvein River ~ CDN (MAN) 234-235 G 3
Bloody Falls ~ CDN 30-31 M 2
Bloomer o USA (WI) 270-271 G 5
Bloomfield o CDN (ONT) 238-239 H 5
Bloomfield o USA (IA) 274-275 F 4
Bloomfield o USA (IN) 274-275 M 5
Bloomfield o USA (MO) 276-277 F 4
Bloomfield o USA (MT) 250-251 P 4
Bloomfield o USA (NE) 262-263 J 2
Bloomfield o USA (NM) 256-257 H 2
Bloomfield o USA (OH) 280-281 E 4
Bloomfield River ✗ AUS 174-175 H 4
Blooming Grove o USA (TX) 264-265 H 6
Blooming Prairie o USA (MN) 270-271 E 7
Bloomington o USA (IL) 274-275 J 4
Bloomington o USA (IN) 274-275 M 5
Bloomington o USA (MN) 270-271 E 6
Bloomington o USA (TX) 266-267 L 5
Bloomington o USA (WI) 274-275 H 2
Bloomington, Lake o USA (IL) 274-275 K 4
Bloomsburg o USA (PA) 280-281 K 2
Bloomsbury o AUS 174-175 K 7
Bloomsdale o USA (MO) 274-275 H 6
Blora o RI 168 D 3
Blosseville Kyst ⊥ GRØ 28-29 a 2
Blossom o USA (TX) 264-265 J 5
Blossom, mys ▲ RUS 112-113 U 1
Bloukranspas ▲ ZA 220-221 D 5
Blount Mountains ▲ USA (AL) 284-285 D 3
Blountstown o USA (FL) 286-287 D 1
Blountsville o USA (AL) 284-285 D 2
Blowering Reservoir < AUS 180-181 K 3
Blower Rock ⌒ JA 54-55 G 6
Blow River ~ CDN 20-21 W 2
Bloxsome Bay ≈ 24-25 K 2
Blubber Bay o CDN (BC) 230-231 E 4
Blucher o CDN (SAS) 232-233 M 3
Blucher Range ▲ PNG 183 A 3
Bludnaja ~ RUS 110-111 F 3
Bludnaja ~ RUS 118-119 E 10
Blue Ball o USA (AR) 276-277 B 6
Blue Bell Knoll ▲ USA (UT) 254-255 D 5
Blueberry River ~ CDN 32-33 K 3
Bluecreek o USA (WA) 244-245 H 2
Blue Cypress Lake o USA (FL) 286-287 J 4
Blue Earth o USA (MN) 270-271 D 7
Bluefield o USA (WV) 280-281 E 6
Bluefields ☆ NIC 52-53 C 5
Bluefields, Bahía de ≈ 52-53 C 6
Bluefish River ~ CDN 30-31 F 2
Bluegoose Prairie ⊥ CDN 36-37 N 2
Bluegoose River ~ CDN 36-37 N 2
Blue Grass Parkway II USA (KY) 276-277 L 3
Blue Hill o USA (ME) 278-279 N 4
Blue Hill o USA (NE) 262-263 H 4
Blue Hills ▲ CDN 24-25 O 3
Blue Hills of Couteau ▲ CDN (NFL) 242-243 L 5
Blue Hole National Park ⊥ BH 52-53 K 3
Blue Jay o USA (NV) 246-247 J 5
Blue Knob ▲ AUS 178-179 M 6
Blue Lagoon National Park ⊥ Z 218-219 D 2
Blue Lake o USA (CA) 246-247 B 3
Blue Licks Spring o USA (KY) 276-277 L 2
Blue Mesa ▲ USA (CO) 254-255 H 5
Blue Mesa Reservoir o USA (CO) 254-255 H 5
Blue Mound o USA (IL) 274-275 J 5
Blue Mountain ▲ IND 142-143 H 4
Blue Mountain ▲ USA (AR) 276-277 A 6
Blue Mountain ▲ USA (NH) 278-279 K 4
Blue Mountain ▲ USA (NV) 246-247 G 3
Blue Mountain Lake o USA (NY) 278-279 G 5
Blue Mountain Lake < USA (AR) 276-277 B 5
Blue Mountains ▲ JA 54-55 G 5
Blue Mountains ▲ USA (OR) 244-245 G 6
Blue Mountains ▲ USA (PA) 280-281 J 3
Blue Mountains ▲ USA (TX) 266-267 H 3
Blue Mountains National Park ⊥ •• AUS 180-181 L 2
Blue Mount Pass ▲ USA (OR) 244-245 H 8
Blue Mud Bay ≈ 174-175 C 3
Blue Mud Hills ▲ USA (MT) 250-251 P 6
Blue Nile = Abay Wenz ~ ETH 208-209 C 3
Blue Nile Falls = T'is Isat Fwafwatē ~ •• ETH 208-209 C 3
Bluenose Lake o CDN 24-25 M 6
Blue Rapids o USA (KS) 262-263 K 5
Blue Ridge o USA (GA) 284-285 F 2
Blue Ridge o USA (TX) 264-265 H 5
Blue Ridge ▲ USA (NY) 278-279 G 5
Blue Ridge Lake < USA (GA) 284-285 F 2
Blue Ridge Parkway II USA (NC) 282-283 F 4
Blue Ridge Parkway II USA (VA) 280-281 F 7
Blue River o CDN (BC) 228-229 P 4
Blue River ~ USA (AZ) 256-257 F 5
Blue River ~ USA (IN) 274-275 M 6
Blue River ~ USA (TX) 264-265 H 5
Blue Robin Hill ▲ AUS 176-177 H 4
Blueslide o USA (WA) 244-245 H 2
Blue Springs ∴ USA (FL) 286-287 D 1
Blue Springs Caverns • USA (IN) 274-275 M 6
Bluestone Reservoir < USA (WV) 280-281 F 6
Bluewater o AUS 174-175 J 6
Bluewater o USA (NM) 256-257 H 3
Bluff o AUS 178-179 K 2
Bluff o NZ 182 B 7
Bluff o USA (AK) 20-21 J 4
Bluff o USA (UT) 254-255 F 6
Bluff, Cape ▲ CDN 38-39 R 2
Bluff, The o BS 54-55 G 2
Bluff Dale o USA (TX) 264-265 F 6
Bluff Face Range ▲ AUS 172-173 H 4
Bluff Point ▲ AUS 176-177 C 3
Bluff Point ▲ USA (NC) 282-283 L 5
Bluffs of Llano Estacado ⊥ USA (NM) 256-257 M 4
Bluffton o USA (IN) 274-275 N 4
Blukwa o ZRE 212-213 C 3
Blum o USA (TX) 264-265 G 6
Blumenau o • BR 74-75 F 6
Blumenhof o CDN (SAS) 232-233 L 5
Blumenort o CDN (MAN) 234-235 G 5
Blunt o USA (SD) 260-261 G 2
Blunt Peninsula ⌒ CDN 36-37 R 3
Blup Blup Island ⌒ PNG 183 C 2
Bly o USA (OR) 244-245 D 8
Blyde River Canyon Nature Reserve ⊥ ZA 220-221 K 2
Bly Mountain Pass ▲ USA (OR) 244-245 D 8
Blyth o CDN (ONT) 238-239 D 5
Blythe o USA (CA) 248-249 K 6
Blytheville o USA (AR) 276-277 F 5
Blyth Lagoon o AUS 176-177 H 2
Blyth River ~ AUS 174-175 C 3
Bnagola o ZRE 210-211 H 5
B'Nom So'Ro'Long ▲ VN 158-159 J 5
Bø ☆ N 86-87 D 7
Bo ☆ WAL 202-203 E 6
Boa ~ CI 202-203 G 5
Boac ☆ RP 160-161 D 6
Boaco ☆ NIC 52-53 B 5
Boa Esperança o BR (AMA) 66-67 E 6
Boa Esperança o BR (RR) 72-73 H 6
Boa Esperança o BR (ROR) 62-63 D 4
Boa Esperança do Sul o BR 72-73 F 6
Boa Fé o BR 66-67 F 4
Boagis o PNG 183 G 5
Boalemo o RI 164-165 H 4
Boali o RCA 206-207 D 6
Boali, Chutes de ~ RCA 206-207 D 6
Boanamary o RM 222-223 E 5
Boanda o CAM 204-205 K 6
Boane o MOC 220-221 L 3
Boangi o ZRE 210-211 H 4
Boang Island ⌒ PNG 183 G 2
Boano, Pulau ⌒ RI 166-167 D 3
Boano, Selat ≈ 166-167 D 3
Boa Nova o BR (P) 68-69 E 2
Boa Nova o BR (RON) 66-67 F 7
Boardman o USA (OH) 280-281 F 2
Boardman o USA (OR) 244-245 F 5
Boas River ~ CDN 36-37 G 3
Boat Basin o CDN (BC) 230-231 C 4
Boatman o AUS 178-179 J 4
Boat of Garten o • GB 90-91 F 3
Boatswain, Baie ≈ 38-39 E 3
Boa Viagem o BR 68-69 J 4
Boa Vista o BR (AMA) 66-67 E 5
Boa Vista o BR (AMA) 66-67 C 6
Boa Vista o BR (AMA) 66-67 E 3
Boa Vista o BR (GSU) 76-77 J 2
Boa Vista o BR (P) 62-63 K 6
Boa Vista o BR (P) 68-69 C 3
Boa Vista o BR (RSU) 74-75 D 9
Boa Vista ☆ BR (ROR) 62-63 D 4
Boa Vista, Ilha de ⌒ CV 202-203 C 5
Boa Vista da Ramos o BR 66-67 J 4
Boa Vista das Palmas o BR 72-73 H 2
Boa Vista do Tupim o BR 72-73 K 2
Boawae o RI 168 E 7
Boaz o USA (AL) 284-285 D 2
Bobadah o AUS 180-181 J 2
Bobai o VRC 156-157 F 5
Bobandana o ZRE 212-213 B 4
Bobasakoa o RM 222-223 F 4
Bobbie Burns Creek ~ CDN (BC) 230-231 N 3
Bobbili o IND 142-143 C 6
Bobcaygeon o CDN (ONT) 238-239 G 4
Bobila o ZRE 210-211 H 2
Bob Marshall Wilderness Area ⊥ USA (MT) 250-251 F 4
Bob Marshall Wilderness Area ⊥ USA (MT) 250-251 F 3
Bobo ~ RCA 206-207 C 5
Bobo-Dioulasso ☆ BF 202-203 H 4
Bobolice o PL 92-93 O 2
Bobonaza, Río ~ EC 64-65 D 2
Bobonong o RB 218-219 E 5
Bobopayo o RI 164-165 K 3
Bobr ~ BY 94-95 L 4
Bóbr ~ PL 92-93 N 3
Bobrof Island ⌒ USA 22-23 H 7
Bobrov o RUS 102-103 L 2
Bobrujsk = Babrujsk ☆ BY 94-95 L 5
Bobrynec' o UA 102-103 H 3
Bobuk o SUD 208-209 B 3
Bobures o YV 60-61 F 3
Boby ▲ RM 222-223 E 9
Boca, Cachoeira da ~ BR 66-67 K 5
Boca, La o BOL 70-71 E 4
Boca Arenal o CR 52-53 B 6
Boca Candelaria ⌒ CO 60-61 C 6
Boca Caragual ⌒ CO 60-61 C 5
Boca Chica o • DOM 54-55 L 5
Boca de Anaro o YV 60-61 F 4
Boca de Arguaca o YV 60-61 H 4
Boca de la Serpiente ≈ 60-61 L 3
Boca del Pao o YV 60-61 J 4
Boca del Río o MEX 52-53 F 2
Boca del Río o YV 60-61 J 2
Boca del Río Indio o PA 52-53 D 7
Boca del Tocuyo o YV 60-61 G 2
Boca de Pozo o YV 60-61 J 2
Boca de Sábalo o PA 52-53 E 7
Boca de Uchire o YV 60-61 J 2
Boca de Yuma o DOM 54-55 L 5
Boca do Acará o BR 66-67 F 6
Boca do Acre o BR 66-67 D 7
Boca do Capanã o BR 66-67 G 5
Boca do Carapanatuba o BR 66-67 F 6
Boca do Jaco o BR 66-67 C 7
Boca do Jari o BR 62-63 J 6
Bocaina de Minas o BR 72-73 H 7
Bocaino do Sul o BR 74-75 F 6
Bocaiúva o BR 72-73 J 4
Bocaiúva do Sul o BR 74-75 F 5
Bocana, La o MEX 50-51 B 3
Bocanda o CI 202-203 H 6
Bocaranga o RCA 206-207 B 5
Bocas del Toro ☆ PA 52-53 C 7
Bocas del Toro, Archipiélago de ⌒ PA 52-53 C 7
Bocay, Río ~ NIC 52-53 B 4
Bochart o CDN (QUE) 236-237 P 3
Bochinche o YV 62-63 D 2
Bocholt o D 92-93 J 3
Bocoio o ANG 216-217 C 6
Bocón o YV 60-61 K 4
Bocon, Caño ~ CO 60-61 G 6
Bocono o YV 60-61 F 3
Boçoroca o BR 76-77 K 5
Bocoyna o MEX 50-51 F 4
Boda o RCA 206-207 C 6
Böda o S 86-87 H 8
Bodajbo ☆ RUS 118-119 G 7
Bodalangi o ZRE 210-211 J 2
Bodalla o AUS 180-181 L 4
Bodallin o AUS 176-177 E 5
Bodangora, Mount ▲ AUS 180-181 K 2
Boddington o AUS 176-177 D 6
Bodega Bay o USA (CA) 246-247 B 5
Bodélé ⊥ TCH 198-199 H 4
Boden o • S 86-87 K 4
Bodensee o CH 92-93 K 5
Bode-Shadu o WAN 204-205 F 4
Bodfish o USA (CA) 248-249 F 4
Bodhan o IND (ANP) 138-139 F 10
Bodhan o IND (KAR) 140-141 G 2
Bodhei o EAK 212-213 H 4
Bodh Gayā o IND 142-143 D 3
Bodi o DY 202-203 L 5
Bodi o GH 202-203 J 6
Bodie o USA (CA) 246-247 F 5
Bodinguė ~ RCA 210-211 F 2
Boditi o ETH 208-209 C 5
Bod'ja, Jaškur- ☆ RUS 96-97 H 5
Bodjokola o ZRE 210-211 H 2
Bodmin o CDN (SAS) 232-233 M 2
Bodmin o GB 90-91 E 6
Bodo o CDN (ALB) 232-233 H 3
Bodo o CI 202-203 H 7

Bodø ☆ N 86-87 G 3
Bodoco o BR 66-67 G 7
Bodocó o BR 68-69 J 5
Bodokro o CI 202-203 H 6
Bodoquena o BR 70-71 J 7
Bodoukpa o RCA 206-207 C 6
Bodrum ☆• TR 128-129 B 4
Bodum o S 86-87 H 5
Boduna o RCA 206-207 D 6
Boé o• GNB 202-203 C 4
Boëkovo ~ RUS 112-113 L 2
Boende o ZRE 210-211 H 4
Boenze o ZRE 210-211 E 6
Boerne o USA (TX) 266-267 J 4
Boesmansrivier ~ ZA 220-221 H 6
Boesmansriviermond o ZA 220-221 H 6
Boeuf River ~ USA (LA) 268-269 J 4
Boevaja gora • RUS 96-97 J 8
Bofete o BR 72-73 F 7
Boffa o RG 202-203 C 4
Bofossou o RG 202-203 F 5
Boga o ZRE 212-213 B 3
Bogal, Lagh ~ EAK 212-213 H 3
Bogale o MYA 158-159 C 2
Bogalusa o USA (LA) 268-269 L 6
Bogamangon o RCA 206-207 C 6
Bogandé o BF 202-203 K 3
Bogan Gate o AUS 180-181 J 2
Bogangolo o RCA 206-207 D 6
Boganida ~ RUS 108-109 c 5
Bogan River ~ AUS 178-179 J 6
Bogantungan o AUS 178-179 J 2
Bogaševo o RUS 114-115 S 6
Bogata o USA (TX) 264-265 J 5
Bogatoe ☆ RUS 96-97 G 7
Bogatye Saby ☆ RUS 96-97 G 6
Boğazkale ☆• TR 128-129 F 2
Boğazlıyan ☆ TR 128-129 F 3
Bogbonga o ZRE 210-211 G 3
Bogcang Zangbo ~ VRC 144-145 F 5
Bogd = Hovd o MAU 148-149 F 5
Bogda Feng ▲ VRC 146-147 J 4
Bogdanovič ☆ RUS 114-115 G 6
Bogdanovka o RUS 96-97 G 7
Bogda Shan ▲ VRC 146-147 J 4
Bogdoo o GH 202-203 K 4
Böget o KA 96-97 G 10
Bogetsaj o KA 126-127 N 2
Boggabilla o AUS 178-179 L 5
Boggabri o AUS 178-179 L 6
Boggola, Mount ▲ AUS 176-177 D 1
Boggy Creek o CDN (MAN) 234-235 B 3
Bogia o PNG 183 C 3
Bogilima o ZRE 210-211 G 2
Boğnürd o• IR 136-137 E 6
Bogo o CAM 206-207 B 3
Bogo o RP 160-161 F 7
Bogoin o RCA 206-207 D 6
Bogoladza, hrebet ▲ RUS 122-123 F 5
Bogol Manyo o ETH 208-209 E 6
Bogong, Mount ▲ AUS 180-181 J 4
Bogong National Park ⊥ AUS 180-181 J 4
Bogor (Buitenzorg) o RI 168 B 3
Bogoria, Lake o• EAK 212-213 F 3
Bogorodick ☆• RUS 94-95 Q 5
Bogorodsk o RUS 94-95 S 3
Bogorodsk o RUS (PRM) 96-97 K 5
Bogorodskoe ☆ RUS (KIR) 96-97 G 5
Bogorodskoe ☆• RUS 122-123 J 2
Bogoroud < TCH 198-199 G 5
Bogose-Mubea o ZRE 210-211 G 2
Bogoslof Island ʌ USA 22-23 N 6
Bogoso o GH 202-203 J 7
Bogotá ☆• CO 60-61 D 5
Bogotol ☆ RUS 114-115 U 6
Bogra o BD 142-143 F 3
Bogučany ☆ RUS 116-117 H 6
Bogučar o RUS 102-103 M 3
Bogué o RIM 196-197 C 6
Bogue o USA (KS) 262-263 G 5
Bogue Banks ≃ 282-283 L 6
Bogue Chitto o USA (MS) 268-269 K 5
Bogue Chitto River ~ USA (LA) 268-269 K 6
Boguédia o CI 202-203 G 6
Bogue Homo ~ USA (MS) 268-269 L 5
Bogueloosa Creek ~ USA (AL) 284-285 B 5
Boguila Kota o RCA 206-207 C 5
Bogunda o AUS 178-179 H 1
Bo Hai ≈ 154-155 L 2
Bohai Haixia ≈ 150-151 C 8
Bohai Wan ≈ 154-155 K 2
Boharm o CDN (SAS) 232-233 N 5
Bohemia o USA (LA) 268-269 L 7
Bohemia Downs o AUS 172-173 H 5
Bohena Creek ~ AUS 178-179 K 6
Bohicon o DY 204-205 E 5
Böhmisch-Trübau = Česká Třebová o• CZ 92-93 O 4
Bohobé o TCH 206-207 D 4
Bohodou o RG 202-203 F 5
Bohoduchiv o UA 102-103 J 2
Bohol ʌ RP 160-161 F 8
Bohol Sea ≈ 160-161 F 8
Bohol Strait ≈ 160-161 E 8
Bohong o RCA 206-207 B 5
Bohongou o BF 202-203 L 3
Böhönye o H 92-93 O 5
Bohorods'kyj Kostel • UA 102-103 D 2
Böhöt o MAU 148-149 J 5
Boi o WAN 204-205 H 4
Boi, Ponta do ▲ BR 72-73 H 7
Bóia, Rio ~ BR 66-67 C 5
Boiaçu o BR 62-63 D 6
Boiekevie Hill ▲ AUS 180-181 E 2
Boiestown o CDN (NB) 240-241 J 4
Boigu Island ʌ AUS 183 B 5
Boiken o PNG 183 B 2
Boila o MOC 218-219 K 3
Boilleau o CDN (QUE) 240-241 E 2
Boina ⚍ RM 222-223 E 6
Boipárigüda o IND 142-143 C 6
Boipeba, Ilha de ʌ BR 72-73 L 2
Bois, Lac des ⊖ CDN 30-31 G 2
Bois, Ribeiro dos ~ BR 68-69 D 6
Bois, Rio dos ~ BR 72-73 F 2
Bois, Rio dos ~ BR 72-73 F 4
Bois-Blanc o F 224 B 7
Bois Blanc o USA (MI) 272-273 E 2
Bois Blanc Island ʌ USA (MI) 272-273 E 2
Bois d'Arc Creek ~ USA (TX) 264-265 H 5
Boise ☆• USA (ID) 252-253 B 3
Boise City o USA (OK) 264-265 B 2
Boissevain o CDN (MAN) 234-235 C 5
Boituva o BR 72-73 G 7
Boja o RI 168 D 3
Bojano o I 100-101 E 4
Bojarka ~ RUS 108-109 b 6
Bojarsk o RUS 116-117 N 7
Bojčinovci o BG 102-103 C 6
Bojkov, liman ≈ 102-103 K 5
Bojmurot o US 136-137 K 4
Bojonegoro o RI 168 D 3
Boju o WAN 204-205 G 5
Boju-Ega o WAN 204-205 H 5
Bojuru o BR 74-75 E 8
Bojuru, Ponta do ▲ BR 74-75 E 8
Bokada o ZRE 206-207 D 6
Bokākhāt o IND 142-143 H 2
Boka Kotorska ≈••• 100-101 G 3
Bokala o ZRE 210-211 F 5
Bokata o ZRE 210-211 J 2
Bokatola o ZRE 210-211 G 4
Bokayanga o RCA 206-207 D 5
Boké ⊡ RG 202-203 C 4
Boké ☆ RG 202-203 C 4
Bokele o ZRE 210-211 H 4
Bokhara River ~ AUS 178-179 J 5
Bokh el Mâ < RIM 196-197 E 5
Bokhol Plain ⚍ EAK 212-213 G 2
Boki o CAM 204-205 K 4
Bokin o BF 202-203 K 3
Boki Saboudo o RIM 196-197 D 7
Bokito o CAM 204-205 J 6
Bokkeveldberge ▲ ZA 220-221 D 5
Boknafjorden ≈ 86-87 B 7
Boko o RCB 210-211 E 6
Bokode o ZRE 210-211 G 2
Bokoko o ZRE 206-207 H 6
Bokolako o SN 202-203 D 3
Bokolango o ZRE 210-211 H 3
Bokolo o CI 202-203 G 5
Bokonbaevckoe o KS 146-147 C 4
Bokondo o ZRE 210-211 G 3
Bokoro o TCH 198-199 H 6
Boko-Songho o RCB 210-211 D 6
Bokota o ZRE 210-211 J 4
Bokote o ZRE 210-211 H 4
Boksburg o ZA 220-221 J 3
Boksitogorsk ☆ RUS 94-95 N 2
Bokter Müzbel ▲ KA 126-127 L 6
Boktor ~ RUS 122-123 G 3
Boku o PNG 184 I b 2
Boku o ZRE 210-211 F 5
Bokuma o ZRE 210-211 G 4
Bokungu o ZRE 210-211 J 4
Bol ☆ TCH 198-199 G 6
Bola o RI 166-167 B 6
Bola, Bahr ~ TCH 206-207 D 3
Bolafa o ZRE 210-211 J 3
Bolaiti o ZRE 210-211 K 5
Bolama ☆• GNB 202-203 C 4
Bolama o ZRE 210-211 J 3
Bolān ~ PK 134-135 M 4
Boland Lake ⊖ CDN 30-31 U 5
Bolangitang o RI 164-165 H 3
Bolaños, Río ~ MEX 50-51 H 7
Bolan Pass ▲ PK 134-135 M 4
Bolbec o F 90-91 H 7
Bolbolo o RP 160-161 D 4
Bolčiha o RUS 124-125 M 2
Bold Point ▲ RP 160-161 C 7
Bold Spring o USA (TN) 276-277 H 5
Boldyr o US 136-137 K 6
Bole o ETH 208-209 C 5
Bole o GH 202-203 J 5
Bole o VRC 146-147 F 3
Boleko o ZRE 210-211 G 4
Bolena o ZRE 210-211 G 3
Bolesławiec o• PL 92-93 N 3
Bolgart o AUS 176-177 D 5
Bolgatanga ☆• GH 202-203 K 4
Bolger o CDN (QUE) 236-237 M 4
Bolhov ☆• RUS 94-95 O 5
Bolhrad ☆ UA 102-103 F 5
Boli o SUD 206-207 J 5
Boli o VRC 150-151 H 5
Boli o ZRE 210-211 L 4
Bolia o IND 138-139 E 7
Bolia o ZRE 210-211 G 4
Boliche = Pedro J. Montero o EC 64-65 C 3
Boliden o S 86-87 K 4
Bolifar o RI 166-167 F 3
Bolinha, Cachoeira da ~ BR 62-63 D 6
Bolintin-Vale o RO 102-103 D 5
Boliohutu, Gunung ▲ RI 164-165 H 3
Bolivar o BOL (COC) 70-71 D 5
Bolivar o BOL (PAN) 70-71 D 3
Bolivar o CO 60-61 C 7
Bolivar o PE 64-65 D 5
Bolivar o USA (MO) 276-277 B 3
Bolivar o USA (NY) 278-279 C 6
Bolivar o USA (TN) 276-277 G 5
Bolívar, Pico ▲•• YV 60-61 F 3
Bolivar Peninsula ⌣ USA (TX) 268-269 F 7
Bolivia ■ BOL 70-71 D 5
Bolivia o C 54-55 F 3
Boljevac o YU 100-101 H 3
Boljoon o RP 160-161 E 8
Bolkar Dağları ▲ TR 128-129 F 4
Bolléne o F 90-91 K 9
Bollnäs o S 86-87 H 6
Bollock, Mount ▲ CDN 24-25 W 3
Bollon o AUS 178-179 J 5
Bollons Seamount ≃ 14-15 L 13
Bolmen ⊖ S 86-87 F 8
Bolnisi o GE 126-127 F 7
Bolobo o ZRE 210-211 F 5
Boločaevka 2-ja o RUS 122-123 F 4
Bolodek o RUS 122-123 E 2
Bologna ☆•• I 100-101 C 2
Bolognesi o PE 64-65 E 7
Bologoe ☆ RUS 94-95 O 3
Bololedi ~ EAT 212-213 E 5
Bolomba o ZRE 210-211 G 3
Bolombo ~ ZRE 210-211 H 3
Bolon' o RUS 122-123 G 4
Bolon', ozero ⊖ RUS 122-123 G 4
Bolona o BF 202-203 G 4
Bolonchén ∴• MEX 52-53 K 2
Bolonchén de Rejón o• MEX 52-53 K 1
Bolondo o GQ 210-211 B 3
Bolongongo o ANG 216-217 C 4
Bolonguera o ANG 216-217 B 6
Bolontio o RI 164-165 H 3
Bolotnoe ☆ RUS 114-115 S 7
Bolovens, Plateau des ▲ LAO 158-159 J 3
Bol'šaja ~ RUS 110-111 a 2
Bol'šaja ~ RUS 122-123 K 2
Bol'šaja ~ RUS 122-123 R 2
Bol'šaja, guba ≈ 110-111 X 2
Bol'šaja Belaja ~ RUS 116-117 K 9
Bol'šaja Bi'ca ~ RUS 114-115 L 6
Bol'šaja Birjusa ~ RUS 116-117 H 8
Bol'šaja Bootankaga ~ RUS 108-109 b 4
Bol'šaja Černaja ~ RUS 116-117 E 5
Bol'šaja Černigovka ☆ RUS 96-97 G 7
Bol'šaja Erëma ~ RUS 116-117 N 5
Bol'šaja Glušica ☆ RUS 96-97 G 7
Bol'šaja Horga, ozero ⊖ RUS 118-119 E 9
Bol'šaja Ket' ~ RUS 116-117 E 7
Bol'šaja Kol'-Tajga, gora ▲ RUS 124-125 Q 2
Bol'šaja Kuropatočja ~ RUS 112-113 J 1
Bol'šaja Lebjaž'ja ~ RUS 116-117 E 5
Bol'šaja Martynovka = S'loboda Bol'šaja Martynovka ☆ RUS 102-103 M 4
Bol'šaja Murata ☆ RUS 116-117 F 7
Bol'šaja Mutnaja ~ RUS 88-89 X 3
Bol'šaja Nisogora o RUS 88-89 S 4
Bol'šaja Orlovka o RUS 102-103 M 4
Bol'šaja Padeja, gora ▲ RUS 108-109 J 7
Bol'šaja Pera ~ RUS 122-123 C 3
Bol'šaja Pula ~ RUS 88-89 V 3
Bol'šaja Rečka o RUS 96-97 E 4
Bol'šaja Saga, ozero ⊖ RUS 96-97 D 10
Bol'šaja Sosnovka ☆ RUS 96-97 J 5
Bol'šaja Tira ~ RUS 116-117 M 7
Bol'šaja Usa o RUS 96-97 J 5
Bol'šaja Ussurka ~ RUS 122-123 F 6
Bol'šaja Uzen' ~ RUS 96-97 F 8
Bol'šaja Vladimirovka o KA 124-125 L 3
Bol'šakovo o RUS 94-95 G 4
Bolsena, Lago di ⊖ I 100-101 C 3
Bol'šenarymskoe o KA 124-125 O 4
Bol'šerec'e ☆ RUS 114-115 N 6
Bol'šereck o RUS 122-123 R 2
Bol'šereck, Ust'- ☆ RUS 122-123 R 2
Bol'šereckij Sovhoz o RUS 122-123 R 2
Bol'šeustinskoe ☆ RUS 96-97 L 6
Bol'ševik o RUS 120-121 M 2
Bol'ševik, ostrov ʌ RUS 108-109 d 2
Bol'šezemel'skaja tundra ⚍ RUS 88-89 W 3
Bolsi o RN 202-203 L 3
Bolsico o RCH 76-77 B 2
Bol'šie Čukkuri, gora ▲ RUS 88-89 M 4
Bol'šie Hatymi o RUS 118-119 M 7
Bol'šoe Eravnoe, ozero ⊖ RUS 118-119 E 9
Bol'šoe Jarovoe ozero ⊖ RUS 124-125 L 2
Bol'šoe Jasavèjto, ozero ⊖ RUS 108-109 M 7
Bol'šoe Kizi, ozero ⊖ RUS 122-123 J 3
Bol'šoe Morskoe, ozero ⊖ RUS 112-113 K 1
Bol'šoe Nagatkino ☆ RUS 96-97 F 6
Bol'šoe Sorokino ☆ RUS 114-115 K 6
Bol'šoe Toko, ozero ⊖ RUS 120-121 D 6
Bol'šoe Topol'noe ozero ⊖ RUS 124-125 K 2
Bol'šoe Zaborov'e o RUS 94-95 N 2
Bol'šoj, ostrov ʌ RUS 108-109 U 4
Bol'šoj Abakan ~ RUS 124-125 Q 2
Bol'šoj Abakan ~ RUS 124-125 Q 3
Bol'šoj Aim ~ RUS 120-121 E 5
Bol'šoj Akzar o KA 124-125 L 3
Bol'šoj Amalat ~ RUS 118-119 F 9
Bol'šoj Anjuj ~ RUS 112-113 L 2
Bol'šoj Atlym ~ RUS 114-115 J 3
Bol'šoj Avam ~ RUS 108-109 Z 6
Bol'šoj Balhan, hrebet ▲ TM 136-137 D 5
Bol'šoj Baranov, mys ▲ RUS 112-113 M 2
Bol'šoj Begičev, ostrov ʌ RUS 110-111 J 2
Bol'šoj Čeremšan ~ RUS 96-97 G 6
Bol'šoj Čurki o RUS 88-89 T 5
Bol'šoj Dubčes ~ RUS 114-115 T 4
Bol'šoj Enisej ~ RUS 116-117 G 10
Bol'šoj Homus Jurjah ~ RUS 110-111 d 4
Bol'šoj Ik ~ RUS 96-97 K 7
Bol'šoj Ik ~ RUS 96-97 L 6
Bol'šoj Irakan ~ RUS 120-121 C 6
Bol'šoj Iremel', gora ▲ RUS 96-97 L 6
Bol'šoj Irgiz ~ RUS 96-97 F 8
Bol'šoj Jarhodon ~ RUS 112-113 H 4
Bol'šoj Jarudej ~ RUS 108-109 P 8
Bol'šoj Jugan ~ RUS 114-115 M 4
Bol'šoj Kamen' o RUS 122-123 E 7
Bol'šoj Karaman ~ RUS 96-97 E 8
Bol'šoj Kas ~ RUS 116-117 E 6
Bol'šoj Kazymskij Sor, ozero ⊖ RUS 114-115 J 3
Bol'šoj Kemčug ~ RUS 116-117 F 7
Bol'šoj Kèpèrveem ~ RUS 112-113 O 2
Bol'šoj Kinel' ~ RUS 96-97 H 7
Bol'šoj Kujbiveem ~ RUS 112-113 P 5
Bol'šoj Kumak ~ RUS 96-97 L 8
Bol'šoj Kun'jak ~ RUS 114-115 L 5
Bol'šoj Ljahovskij, ostrov ʌ RUS 110-111 X 3
Bol'šoj Ljamčin Nos, mys ▲ RUS 108-109 H 7
Bol'šoj Loptjuga ~ RUS 88-89 U 5
Bol'šoj Megtyg"egan ~ RUS 114-115 R 4
Bol'šoj Nimnyr o RUS 118-119 M 6
Bol'šoj Nimnyr ~ RUS 118-119 M 6
Bol'šoj Oju ~ RUS 108-109 J 7
Bol'šoj Oldoj ~ RUS 118-119 L 8
Bol'šoj On o RUS 124-125 Q 2
Bol'šoj On o RUS 124-125 Q 2
Bol'šoj Ous ~ RUS 114-115 F 4
Bol'šoj Patom ~ RUS 118-119 G 5
Bol'šoj Peledon ~ RUS 112-113 O 3
Bol'šoj Pit ~ RUS 116-117 F 6
Bol'šoj Pykarvaam ~ RUS 112-113 S 3
Bol'šoj Rautan, ostrov ʌ RUS 112-113 Q 2
Bol'šoj Sajan ▲ RUS 116-117 J 9
Bol'šoj Salym ~ RUS 114-115 L 4
Bol'šoj Šantar o RUS 120-121 G 6
Bol'šoj Šantar, ostrov ʌ RUS 120-121 G 6
Bol'šoj Selerikan ~ RUS 110-111 X 7
Bol'šoj Setnoj, ostrov ʌ RUS 126-127 H 5
Bol'šoj Šiskarym ozero ⊖ RUS 114-115 K 6
Bol'šoj Šor ⊖ KA 126-127 J 5
Bol'šoj Tap ~ RUS 114-115 H 4
Bol'šoj Turtas ~ RUS 114-115 L 5
Bol'šoj Tyrkan ~ RUS 120-121 E 5
Bol'šoj Uluj ☆ RUS 116-117 E 7
Bol'šoj Urkan ~ RUS 118-119 M 8
Bol'šoj Uvat ozero ⊖ RUS 114-115 L 6
Bol'šoj Uzen' ~ RUS 96-97 F 8
Bol'šoj Yllymah ~ RUS 118-119 N 6
Bol'šoj Zelenec, ostrov ʌ RUS 108-109 H 7
Bol'šoj Zelenzuk ~ RUS 126-127 D 5
Bol'šoj Zjudostinskij, ostrov ʌ RUS 126-127 H 5
Bol'šoj Žužmuj, ostrov ʌ RUS 88-89 N 4
Bolsón de Mapimí ⚍ MEX 50-51 G 3
Boltodden ▲ N 84-85 L 4
Bolton o GB 90-91 F 5
Bolton o USA (NC) 282-283 J 6
Bolu ☆ TR 128-129 D 2
Bolubolu o PNG 183 F 5
Bolvaninka ~ RUS 116-117 N 6
Bolvanskij Nos ▲ RUS 108-109 H 6
Bolyston o CDN (NS) 240-241 O 5
Bolzano = Bozen ☆ I 100-101 C 1
Boma o ZRE 210-211 D 6
Bomaderry, Nowra- o AUS 180-181 L 3
Bomadi o WAN 204-205 F 6
Bomarton o USA (TX) 264-265 E 5
Bomassa o RCB 210-211 F 2
Bombabasua o RI 164-165 F 4
Bombala o AUS 180-181 K 4
Bombay ☆•• IND 138-139 D 10
Bombay Beach o USA (CA) 248-249 J 6
Bomberai ~ RI 166-167 G 3
Bomberai Peninsula ⌣ RI 166-167 G 3
Bombo ☆ EAU 212-213 D 3
Bombo ~ ZRE 210-211 E 6
Bömbögör = Zadgaj o MAU 148-149 D 4
Bombo-Makuka o ZRE 210-211 F 6
Bombonal o CO 64-65 F 1
Bomboyo o TCH 198-199 G 6
Bombura o ZRE 210-211 G 2
Bom Comercio o BR 66-67 E 7
Bom Conselho o BR 68-69 K 6
Bom Despacho o BR 72-73 H 5
Bomdila o• IND 142-143 H 2
Bomet o EAK 212-213 E 4
Bomi o AUS 178-179 K 5
Bomi o VRC 144-145 K 6
Bomili o ZRE 212-213 A 3
Bom Intento o BR 66-67 F 5
Bom Jardim o BR (MAR) 68-69 F 3
Bom Jardim o BR (P) 62-63 J 6
Bom Jardim o BR (RIO) 72-73 J 7
Bom Jardim de Minas o BR 72-73 H 6
Bom Jardim ou Bacabal, Igarapé ~ BR 66-67 J 5
Bom Jesus o ANG 216-217 B 4
Bom Jesus o BR (CAT) 74-75 D 6
Bom Jesus o BR (PIA) 68-69 F 6
Bom Jesus o BR (RSU) 74-75 E 7
Bom Jesus, Rio ~ BR 68-69 F 7
Bom Jesus da Gurguéira, Serra ▲ BR 68-69 G 6
Bom Jesus da Lapa o BR 72-73 J 2
Bom Jesus da Penha o BR 72-73 G 6
Bom Jesus de Goiás o BR 72-73 F 5
Bom Jesus do Amparo o BR 72-73 J 5
Bom Jesus do Galho o BR 72-73 J 5
Bom Jesus do Itabapoana o BR 72-73 K 6
Bømlo ʌ N 86-87 B 7
Bom Lugar o BR 66-67 H 6
Bomnak o RUS 118-119 O 8
Bomokandi ~ ZRE 210-211 L 2
Bomongo o ZRE 210-211 G 3
Bomotu o ZRE 210-211 G 2
Bom Princípio o BR 68-69 E 6
Bomsucesso o BR 68-69 B 5
Bom Sucesso o BR (MIN) 72-73 H 6
Bom Sucesso o BR (P) 66-67 K 4
Bom Sucesso o BR (PA) 68-69 K 5
Bomu ~ ZRE 206-207 F 6
Bomu Occidentale, Réserve de faune ⊥ ZRE 206-207 G 6
Bomu Orientale, Réserve de faune ⊥ ZRE 206-207 G 6
Bom Viver o BR 68-69 F 3
Bon, Cap ▲ TN 190-191 H 2
Bona, Mount ▲ USA 20-21 U 6
Bonabaeri o CAM 204-205 H 6
Bonabo o IR 128-129 M 4
Bona Bona Island ʌ PNG 183 E 6
Bon Accord o CDN (ALB) 232-233 E 2
Bonaire ʌ NL 60-61 G 1
Bonam o BF 202-203 K 3
Bonampak ∴• MEX 52-53 J 3
Bonang o AUS 180-181 K 4
Bonang o RI 168 E 7
Bonanza o NIC 52-53 B 4
Bonanza o USA (ID) 252-253 D 2
Bonanza o USA (OR) 244-245 D 8
Bonanza o USA (UT) 254-255 F 3
Bonao ☆ DOM 54-55 K 5
Bonapabli o LB 202-203 F 6
Bonaparte, Mount ▲ USA (WA) 244-245 F 2
Bonaparte Archipelago ʌ AUS 172-173 G 3
Bonaparte Lake ⊖ CDN (BC) 230-231 J 2
Bonaparte River ~ CDN (BC) 230-231 H 2
Boñar o E 98-99 E 3
Bonara (Naulu Village) ⊥•• RI 166-167 E 3
Bonaventure o CDN (QUE) 240-241 K 2
Bonaventure, Rivière ~ CDN (QUE) 240-241 K 2
Bonavista o CDN (NFL) 242-243 P 4
Bonavista, Cape ▲•• CDN (NFL) 242-243 P 4
Bonavista Bay ≈ 38-39 S 4
Bonavista Bay ≈ CDN 242-243 P 4
Bonavista Peninsula ⌣•• CDN (NFL) 242-243 P 4
Boncuk Dağı ▲ TR 128-129 C 4
Bondari o RUS 94-95 S 5
Bond Lake, Governor ⊖ USA (IL) 274-275 J 6
Bondo o ZRE (EQU) 210-211 G 3
Bondo o ZRE (Hau) 210-211 J 2
Bondoc Peninsula ⌣ RP 160-161 E 6
Bondokodi o RI 168 D 7
Bondoukou ☆• CI 202-203 J 5
Bondoukui o BF 202-203 J 4
Bondowoso o RI 168 E 3
Bonds Cay ʌ BS 54-55 G 2
Bonduel o USA (WI) 270-271 K 6
Bondurant o USA (WY) 252-253 H 3
Boné o RG 202-203 E 4
Bone ~ RI 164-165 H 3
Bone = Watampone o RI 164-165 G 6
Bonebone o•• RI 164-165 G 5
Bon Echo Provincial Park ⊥ CDN (ONT) 238-239 H 4
Bone Creek ~ CDN (SAS) 232-233 K 6
Bone-Dumoga National Park ⊥•• RI 164-165 H 3
Bonelambere o RI 168 E 6
Bonelipu o RI 164-165 H 6
Bonelohe o RI 164-165 G 6
Bonépoupa o CAM 204-205 J 6
Bonerate o RI 168 E 6
Bonerate, Kepulauan ʌ RI 168 E 6
Bonerate, Pulau ʌ RI 168 E 6
Bonesteel o USA (SD) 260-261 H 3
Bonete, Cerro ▲ RA 76-77 C 4
Bonete, Río ~ RA 76-77 C 5
Bone Teluk ≈ 164-165 G 5
Bonfield o CDN (ONT) 238-239 F 2
Bonfim o BR (AMA) 66-67 D 6
Bonfim o BR (MAT) 70-71 K 5
Bonfim o BR (P) 66-67 K 5
Bonfim o BR (ROR) 62-63 E 4
Bonfinópolis de Minas o BR 72-73 H 4
Bonga o ETH 208-209 C 5
Bonga o PNG 183 D 4
Bongabon o RP 160-161 D 5
Bongandanga o ZRE 210-211 H 3
Bongaon o IND 142-143 F 4
Bongăr o IR 134-135 J 3
Bông Hu'ng ☆ VN 156-157 E 6
Bongka ~ RI 164-165 G 4
Bongo o RI 164-165 H 3
Bongo, Massif des ▲ RCA 206-207 F 4
Bongolava ⚍ RM 222-223 D 7
Bongolo, Grottes de • G 210-211 C 5
Bongor ☆ TCH 206-207 B 3
Bongouanou ☆ CI 202-203 H 6
Bongouanou, Collines de ▲ CI 202-203 H 6
Bonguélé o RCA 206-207 D 6
Bonham o USA (TX) 264-265 H 5
Boni o BF 202-203 J 4
Boni o RMM 202-203 J 2
Boniérdougou o CI 202-203 H 5
Bonifacio o• F 98-99 M 4
Bonifacio o RP 160-161 E 8
Bonifacio, Bocche di ≈ 100-101 B 4
Bonifacio, Bouches de ≈ 98-99 M 4
Bonifay o USA (FL) 286-287 D 1
Boninal o BR 72-73 K 2
Boni National Reserve ⊥ EAK 212-213 H 4
Boninin National Park ⊥ GH 202-203 J 7
Bonin Trench ≃ 14-15 G 4
Bonita o USA (AZ) 256-257 F 6
Bonita, La o EC 64-65 D 1
Bonitas, Las o YV 60-61 J 4
Bonita Springs o USA (FL) 286-287 H 5
Bonito o BR (BAH) 68-69 H 7
Bonito o BR (GSU) 76-77 J 1
Bonito o BR (MIN) 72-73 H 3
Bonito o BR (P) 68-69 E 2
Bonito o BR (PER) 68-69 L 6
Bonito, Big ~ USA (AZ) 256-257 F 5
Bonito, Pico ▲ HN 52-53 L 4
Bonito, Río ~ BR 72-73 E 4
Bonito Pico, Parque Nacional ⊥ HN 52-53 L 4
Bonjol o RI 162-163 D 4
Bonkahar, Küh-e ▲ IR 134-135 E 3
Bonkoukou o RN 204-205 E 1
Bonn o• D 92-93 J 3
Bonneau o USA (SC) 284-285 L 3
Bonne Bay ≈ 38-39 P 4
Bonne Bay ≈ CDN 242-243 K 3
Bonnechere Caves •• CDN (ONT) 238-239 H 3
Bonners Ferry o USA (ID) 250-251 C 3
Bonner Springs o USA (KS) 262-263 M 5
Bonnet, Cachoeira do ~ BR 66-67 H 6
Bonne Terre o USA (MO) 276-277 E 3
Bonnet Plume River ~ CDN 20-21 Y 4
Bonneville o USA (OR) 244-245 D 5
Bonneville o USA (WY) 252-253 K 3
Bonneville Salt Flats ⚍ USA (UT) 254-255 B 3
Bonney, Lake ⊖ AUS 180-181 F 4
Bonney Downs o AUS 172-173 D 7
Bonnie Rock o AUS 176-177 E 5
Bonnissant, Pointe ▲ CDN 36-37 K 5
Bonny o WAN 204-205 G 6
Bonny, Bight of ≈ 204-205 G 6
Bonnyville o CDN 32-33 P 4
Bono o USA (AR) 276-277 E 5
Bonoi o RI 166-167 J 2
Bonou o DY 204-205 E 5
Bonoua o CI 202-203 J 7
Bonsall o USA (CA) 248-249 G 6
Bon Secour Bay ≈ USA 284-285 C 6
Bonshaw o AUS 178-179 L 5
Bonshaw o CDN (PEI) 240-241 M 4
Bonsoaga ~ BF 202-203 L 3
Bontang o RI 164-165 E 3
Bontekoe Ø ʌ GRØ 26-27 p 7
Bonthe o WAL 202-203 D 6
Bontoc ☆ RP 160-161 D 4
Bontoc Point ▲ RP 160-161 E 6
Bontosunggu o RI 164-165 F 6
Bontosunggu-Jeneponto o RI 164-165 F 6
Bonvouloir Islands ʌ PNG 183 F 6
Bon Wier o USA (TX) 268-269 G 6
Bonyere o GH 202-203 J 7
Bonyhád o H 92-93 P 5
Bonzan o BF 202-203 J 4
Boo, Kepulauan ʌ RI 166-167 E 2
Boobare o AUS 178-179 H 4
Boodi Boodi Range ▲ AUS 176-177 G 2
Bookaloo o AUS 178-179 D 6
Booker o USA (TX) 264-265 D 2
Booko o CI 202-203 G 5
Boola o RG 202-203 F 5
Boolardy o AUS 176-177 D 3
Boolba o AUS 178-179 K 4
Booligal o AUS 180-181 H 2
Boolitharda Hill ▲ AUS 176-177 D 3
Boomarra o AUS 174-175 F 6
Boomi River ~ AUS 178-179 K 5
Boonah o AUS 178-179 M 5
Bööncagaan nuur ⊖ MAU 148-149 D 5
Boondooma Reservoir ⊖ AUS 178-179 L 4
Boone o USA (CO) 254-255 L 5
Boone o USA (IA) 274-275 E 2
Boone o USA (NC) 282-283 F 4
Boone Reservoir ⊖ USA (TN) 282-283 E 4
Boone River ~ USA (IA) 274-275 E 2
Booneville o USA (AR) 276-277 B 5
Booneville o USA (KY) 276-277 M 3
Booneville o USA (MS) 268-269 M 2
Boongaree Island ʌ AUS 172-173 G 3
Boonsboro o USA (MD) 280-281 J 4
Boonville o USA (CA) 246-247 B 4
Boonville o USA (IN) 274-275 L 6
Boonville o USA (MO) 274-275 F 6
Boonville o USA (NY) 278-279 F 5
Boopi, Río ~ BOL 70-71 D 4
Boorabbin o AUS 176-177 F 5
Boorabbin National Park ⊥ AUS 176-177 F 5
Boorama o SP 208-209 F 4
Bööröģ Dèlijn Èls ⚍ MAU 116-117 F 10
Booroondara, Mount ▲ AUS 178-179 H 6
Boorowa o AUS 180-181 K 3
Boort o AUS 180-181 G 4
Boosaaso = Bender Qaasim ☆ SP 208-209 J 3
Boothbay Harbor o USA (ME) 278-279 M 5
Boothby, Cape ▲ ARK 16 G 6
Boothby, Mount ▲ AUS 180-181 E 3
Boothia, Gulf of ≈ 24-25 a 5
Boothia Isthmus ⌣ CDN 24-25 Z 6
Boothia Peninsula ⌣ CDN 24-25 Y 5
Booth Islands ʌ CDN 24-25 J 5
Booth's River ~ BH 52-53 K 3
Boothulla o AUS 178-179 H 4
Booti Booti National Park ⊥ AUS 180-181 M 2
Boot Key ʌ USA (FL) 286-287 H 7
Booué o G 210-211 C 4
Booylgoo Spring o AUS 176-177 E 3
Bopa o DY 202-203 L 6
Bopako o ZRE 210-211 H 3
Bophuthatswana (former Homel., now part of North-West) ⊡ ZA 220-221 F 3
Bopo o WAN 204-205 G 5
Boqên o VRC 144-145 K 5
Boqueirão o BR (ACR) 64-65 F 5
Boqueirão o BR (BAH) 68-69 G 7
Boqueirão o BR (GSU) 76-77 J 1
Boqueirão o BR (PA) 68-69 K 5
Boqueirão, Serra do ▲ BR 68-69 G 7
Boqueirão, Serra do ▲ BR 72-73 H 2
Boqueirão, Serra do ▲ BR 76-77 K 5
Boqueirão Cesário o BR 68-69 J 4
Boquerón o C 54-55 H 5
Boquerón o USA (PR) 286-287 O 2
Boqueron o YV 60-61 G 3
Boquerón, Playa ⚍ USA (PR) 286-287 O 2
Boquete, Cerro ▲ RA 78-79 E 7
Boquilla, Presa de la < MEX 50-51 G 4
Boquilla del Conchos, La o MEX 50-51 G 4
Boquillas o USA (TX) 266-267 E 4
Boquillas del Carmen o MEX 50-51 H 3
Boquira o BR 72-73 J 2
Bor o RUS 116-117 E 5
Bor o RUS (GOR) 96-97 D 5
Bor o SUD 206-207 K 5
Bor ☆• TR 128-129 F 4
Bor, Lagh ~ EAK 212-213 G 2
Bora ▲ ETH 200-201 J 6
Bora o PNG 183 B 4
Bora o SUD 206-207 H 6
Borabu o THA 158-159 G 2
Borabu Park ⊥• THA 158-159 G 2
Boracho Peak ▲ USA (TX) 266-267 C 3
Borah Peak ▲ USA (ID) 252-253 E 2
Boraldaj ~ KA 136-137 L 3
Boraldaj, žota ▲ KA 136-137 L 3
Borang, Tanjung ▲ RI 166-167 G 4
Borås ☆ S 86-87 F 8
Borāzğān o IR 134-135 D 4
Borba o BR 66-67 H 5
Borbon o RP 160-161 F 7
Borbón o YV 60-61 J 4
Borborema, Planalto da ⚍ BR 68-69 K 5
Borçka ☆ TR 128-129 J 2
Borde Alto del Payún ▲ RA 78-79 E 4
Bordeaux ☆• F 90-91 G 9
Bordëbë o KS 136-137 N 5
Borden o AUS 176-177 E 7
Borden o CDN (PEI) 240-241 M 4
Borden o CDN (SAS) 232-233 L 3
Borden Island ʌ CDN 24-25 Q 1
Borden Peninsula ⌣ CDN 24-25 e 4
Borden River ~ CDN 30-31 Z 3
Border o USA (WY) 252-253 H 4
Border, Pegunungan ▲ RI 166-167 L 3
Border City Lodge o USA 20-21 U 5
Bordertown o AUS 180-181 F 4
Borðeyri o IS 86-87 c 2
Bord Hûn-e Nou o IR 134-135 D 4
Bordighera o I 100-101 A 3
Bordj Bou Arreridj ☆ DZ 190-191 E 2
Bordj Bounaama o DZ 190-191 C 3
Bordj Flye Sante Marie o DZ 188-189 K 7
Bordj Messouda o DZ 190-191 G 5
Bordj Mokhtar o DZ 196-197 L 4
Bordj Omar Driss o DZ 190-191 F 6
Bordo, El = Patía o CO 60-61 C 6
Bordoloni o IND 142-143 J 2
Borë o ETH 208-209 D 5
Boré o RMM 202-203 J 2
Boreda o ETH 208-209 C 5
Borensberg o S 86-87 G 7
Boren Xuanguan ∴• VRC 156-157 D 2
Borgå = Porvoo o FIN 88-89 H 6
Borgampād o IND 142-143 B 7
Borgarfjörður o IS 86-87 g 2
Borgarnes ☆ IS 86-87 c 2
Børgefjellet ▲ N 86-87 F 4
Børgefjell nasjonalpark ⊥ N 86-87 F 4
Børgen, Kap ▲ GRØ 26-27 q 6
Borger o USA (TX) 264-265 C 3
Borgholm ☆• S 86-87 H 8
Borgi o IND 142-143 B 6
Borgia, De o USA (MT) 250-251 D 4
Borg Jøkel Bræ ⊂ GRØ 26-27 n 5
Borg Massif = Borgmassivet ▲ ARK 16 F 36
Borgne, Lake ⊖ USA (MS) 268-269 L 6
Borgne, Le o RH 54-55 J 5
Borgomanero o I 100-101 B 2
Borgo San Lorenzo o I 100-101 C 3
Borgou o RT 202-203 L 4
Borgu ⚍ DY 204-205 E 4
Borgu Game Reserve ⊥ WAN 204-205 E 3
Borgund o N 86-87 C 6
Borgund stavkirke •• N 86-87 C 6
Borhojn-Tal o MAU 148-149 K 6
Bori o DY 204-205 E 4
Bori o IND 138-139 G 9
Bori o WAN 204-205 G 6
Boria Tibhu o IND 142-143 B 5
Borigumma o IND 142-143 C 6
Börili o KA 96-97 H 8
Borisoglebsk o RUS 102-103 N 2
Borisov = Barysav ☆ BY 94-95 L 4
Borisova, mys ▲ RUS 120-121 G 6
Borisovka o RUS 102-103 K 2
Borisovo-Sudskoe o RUS 94-95 P 2
Boriziny o RM 222-223 E 5
Borja o PE 64-65 D 4
Borj Bourguiba o TN 190-191 G 4
Borjhar o IND 138-139 E 8
Borj Jenein o TN 190-191 H 5
Borj Machened Salah o TN 190-191 H 4
Borj M'Chiguig o TN 190-191 H 5
Borj Slougui < TN 190-191 H 4
Borke o AFG 136-137 L 6
Borkou ⚍ TCH 198-199 H 3
Borkou-Ennedi-Tibesti ⊡ TCH 198-199 H 4
Borkum ʌ D 92-93 J 2
Borlänge ☆ S 86-87 G 6
Borne o DZ 190-191 F 8
Borneo = Kalimantan ʌ 164-165 B 4
Bornholm ʌ• DK 86-87 G 9
Bornholmsgattet ≈ 86-87 G 9
Borno ⊡ WAN 198-199 E 6
Boro ~ RB 218-219 B 4
Boro ~ SUD 206-207 G 4
Borobudur ••• RI 168 D 3
Borodale Creek ~ AUS 176-177 G 4
Borodino o RUS 116-117 G 8
Borogoncy ☆• RUS 118-119 P 4
Borohoro Shan ▲ VRC 146-147 E 3
Borojó o YV 60-61 F 2
Boroko o RI 164-165 H 3
Borol ~ TCH 206-207 C 3
Borom o TCH 206-207 C 4
Boromata o RCA 206-207 E 3
Boromo o• BF 202-203 J 4
Boron o CI 202-203 H 5
Boron o RMM 202-203 G 2
Boron o USA (CA) 248-249 G 5
Bor-Öndör = Herlen o MAU 148-149 J 4
Borong, hrebet ▲ RUS 110-111 V 6
Boronono o RM 222-223 E 5
Boronuk o RUS 110-111 T 6
Bororé o BR 76-77 K 5
Borovič o RUS (PSK) 94-95 L 3
Boroviči ☆ RUS (NVG) 94-95 N 2
Borovo o RUS 88-89 U 5
Borovoj o RUS 88-89 M 4
Borovsk o• RUS 94-95 P 4
Borovskoj ☆ KA 124-125 D 2
Borradaile o CDN (ALB) 232-233 H 2
Borrego Springs o USA (CA) 248-249 H 6
Borrero o EC 64-65 C 3
Borroloola Ẍ AUS 174-175 D 5
Borroloola Aboriginal Land Ẍ AUS 174-175 C 4
Borşa o RO 102-103 D 4
Borsad o IND 138-139 D 8
Borsa-kelmas šuri ⊖ US 136-137 E 3
Borščevočnyj, hrebet ▲ RUS 118-119 H 10
Borskoe ☆ RUS 96-97 G 7

Bodø — Borskoe 307

Bort-les-Orgues ○ F 90-91 J 9
Börtnan ○ S 86-87 F 5
Boru ○ RI 166-167 B 6
Boruambe ∼ ZRE 210-211 F 5
Borūǧen ○• IR 134-135 D 3
Borūǧerd ○• IR 134-135 C 2
Borulah ∼ RUS 110-111 U 6
Borulah ∼ RUS 118-119 O 5
Borups Corners ○ CDN (ONT) 234-235 L 5
Bor-Uzuur ○ MAU 146-147 L 3
Bory, Tianguel- ○ RG 202-203 D 4
Boryspil' ○ UA 102-103 G 2
Borzja ☆ RUS 118-119 H 10
Borzja ∼ RUS 118-119 G 10
Borzna ○ UA 102-103 H 2
Boržomi ○• GE 126-127 E 7
Borzongijn Gov' ⊥ MAU 148-149 G 6
Borzova, zaliv ○ RUS 108-109 J 3
Bosa ○• I 100-101 B 4
Bosaga ○ KA 124-125 H 5
Bosanska Brod ○ BIH 100-101 G 2
Bosanska Krupa ○ BIH 100-101 F 2
Bosanski Novi ○ BIH 100-101 F 2
Bosanski Petrovac ○ BIH 100-101 F 2
Bosanski Šamac ○ BIH 100-101 G 2
Bosavi, Mount ▲ PNG 183 B 4
Boscobel ○ USA (WI) 274-275 H 1
Bosconia ○ CO 60-61 E 2
Bose ○ VRC 156-157 E 5
Bosencheve, Parque Nacional ⊥ MEX 52-53 D 2
Boset Terara ▲ ETH 208-209 D 4
Boshoek ○ ZA 220-221 H 2
Boshof ○ ZA 220-221 G 4
Bó Sinh ○ VN 156-157 C 6
Boskamp ○ SME 62-63 G 3
Boslanti ○ SME 62-63 G 3
Bosler ○ USA (WY) 252-253 N 5
Bosmediano ○ PE 64-65 F 4
Bosna ∼ BIH 100-101 G 2
Bosnia and Herzegovina = Bosna i Hercegovina ■ BIH 100-101 F 2
Bosnik ○ RI 166-167 J 2
Bošnjakovo ○ RUS 122-123 K 4
Boso ○ ZRE 210-211 J 2
Bosobolo ○ ZRE 206-207 D 6
Bōsō-hantō ∪ J 152-153 H 7
Bososama ○ ZRE 206-207 E 6
Bosporus = İstanbul Boğazi ≈ 128-129 C 2
Bosporus = Karadeniz Boğazi ≈ 128-129 C 2
Bosque ○ USA (NM) 256-257 J 4
Bosque del Apache National Wildlife Refuge ⊥• USA (NM) 256-257 H 5
Bošrūye ○ IR 134-135 G 2
Bossaga ○ TM 136-137 J 6
Bossangoa ☆ RCA 206-207 C 5
Bossembélé ○ RCA 206-207 C 6
Bossentélé ○ RCA 206-207 B 6
Bossiekom ○ ZA 220-221 E 4
Bossier City ○ USA (LA) 268-269 G 4
Bossiesvlei ○ NAM 220-221 C 2
Bosso ○ RN 198-199 F 6
Bosso ∼ RN 204-205 E 1
Bosso, Dallol ∼ BF 204-205 E 2
Bossut, Cape ▲ AUS 172-173 E 5
Bostān ○ IR 134-135 B 3
Bostan ○ VRC 144-145 E 2
Bostānābād ○ IR 128-129 M 4
Bostankum ∴ KA 126-127 K 6
Bosten Hu • VRC 146-147 H 5
Boston ○ GB 90-91 G 5
Boston ○ USA (GA) 284-285 G 6
Boston ☆• USA (MA) 278-279 K 6
Boston Bar ○ CDN (BC) 230-231 H 4
Boston Mountains ▲ USA (AR) 276-277 A 5
Bostonnais, Rivière ∼ CDN (QUE) 240-241 C 3
Bosumba ∼ ZRE 210-211 G 3
Bosumtwi, Lake ○ GH 202-203 K 6
Boswell ○ CDN (BC) 230-231 N 4
Boswell ○ USA (OK) 264-265 J 4
Botād ○ IND 138-139 C 8
Botafogo ○ BR 66-67 B 5
Botalón, El ○ YV 60-61 F 2
Botan Çayı ∼ TR 128-129 K 4
Botany Bay ≈ 180-181 L 2
Botare ○ RI 166-167 G 3
Botata ○ LB 202-203 F 6
Bote ○ IND 138-139 E 10
Boteka ○ ZRE 210-211 G 4
Botemola ○ ZRE 210-211 G 5
Boteti ∼ RB 218-219 B 5
Botev ▲ BG 102-103 D 6
Botha ○ CDN (ALB) 232-233 F 3
Bothasberg ▲ ZA 220-221 J 3
Bothaville ○ ZA 220-221 H 3
Bothell ○ USA (WA) 244-245 C 3
Bothwell ○ AUS 180-181 J 7
Botija, Ilha da ∩ BR 66-67 F 4
Botijón ○ YV 60-61 J 3
Botín, El ○ YV 60-61 F 4
Botitembongo ○ ZRE 210-211 G 4
Botkul', ozero ○ RUS 96-97 E 9
Botlih ○ RUS 126-127 G 6
Bot Makak ○ CAM 210-211 C 2
Botolan ○ RP 160-161 D 5
Botomoju ∼ RUS 118-119 J 4
Botopasi ○ SME 62-63 G 3
Botoşani ☆• RO 102-103 E 4
Botou ○ BF (EST) 202-203 L 3
Botou ○ BF (EST) 204-205 E 2
Botou ○ VRC 154-155 K 2
Botro ○ CI 202-203 H 6
Botswana ■ RB 218-219 B 6
Bottenhavet ≈ 86-87 J 6
Bottenviken ≈ 86-87 L 4
Botterkloof ▲ ZA 220-221 D 5
Bottineau ○ USA (ND) 258-259 G 3
Bottle Creek ○ GB 54-55 K 4
Botuali ○ ZRE 210-211 F 4
Botucatu ○ BR 72-73 F 7
Botulu ○• RUS 118-119 J 3
Botumirim ○ BR 72-73 J 4
Botuobuja, Ulahan ∼ RUS 118-119 E 5
Botwood ○ CDN (NFL) 242-243 N 3
Bou ∼ CI 202-203 H 5
Bou ○ RI 164-165 G 3
Bouaflé ☆ CI 202-203 H 6
Bou Akba ⟨ DZ 188-189 H 6
Bouaké ☆• CI 202-203 H 6
Boû Aleb ⟨ RIM 196-197 F 6
Boualem ○ DZ 190-191 C 4
Bou Ali ○ DZ 188-189 L 7
Bou Ali, Oued ∼ DZ 190-191 D 5
Bou-Allala, Hassi ⟨ DZ 188-189 K 5
Bouam ○ CAM 204-205 K 6
Bouânane ○ MA 188-189 K 4
Bouandougou ∪ CI 202-203 H 5
Bouanri ○ DY 204-205 E 3
Bouansa ○ RCB 210-211 D 6
Bouar ☆• RCA 206-207 B 6
Bouârfa ○ MA 188-189 L 4
Bouârfa, Jbel ▲ MA 188-189 L 4
Bouba Ndjida, Parc National de ⊥ CAM 206-207 B 4
Boubela ○ CI 202-203 G 7
Bou Bernous, Hassi ⟨ DZ 188-189 K 7
Boubon ○ RN 202-203 L 3
Boubouri ○ CI 202-203 H 7
Bouca ○ RCA 206-207 D 5
Boucaut Bay ≈ 174-175 C 2
Bouchard ○ RA 78-79 H 3
Bouchette, Lac- ○ CDN (QUE) 240-241 C 2
Bouchie Lake ○ CDN (BC) 228-229 M 3
Bouchouaymiy ○ MA 196-197 B 2
Boucle du Baoulé, Parc National de la ⊥ RMM 202-203 F 2
Boû Çtaila ○ RIM 196-197 F 7
Boudamassa ○ TCH 206-207 C 3
Boudbouda ⟨ RIM 196-197 C 5
Boudenib ○ MA 188-189 K 5
Boudeuse Cay ∩ SY 224 C 3
Boû Dîb ○ RIM 196-197 F 5
Boudiéri ○ BF 202-203 L 3
Boû Djébéha ⟨ RMM 196-197 J 5
Boudo ○ ANG 216-217 E 8
Boudoua ○ RCA 206-207 C 6
Boudtenga ○ BF 202-203 K 3
Bouénguidi ∼ G 210-211 D 4
Bouenza ◘ RCB 210-211 D 6
Bouenza ∼ RCB 210-211 D 5
Boufarik ○ DZ 190-191 E 2
Boû Gâdoûm ○ RIM (HCH) 196-197 G 7
Boû Gâdoûm ○ RIM (HCH) 202-203 G 2
Bougainville, Cape ▲ AUS 172-173 H 2
Bougainville, Cape ▲ GB 78-79 L 6
Bougainville Island ∩ PNG 184 I b 2
Bougainville Reef ∩ AUS 174-175 J 4
Bougainville Strait ≈ 184 I c 2
Bougainville Trench ≃ 183 G 3
Bougaroun, Cap ▲ DZ 190-191 F 2
Boughessa ○ RMM 196-197 M 4
Bougoui ○ RCA 206-207 B 5
Bougouni ○ RMM 202-203 G 4
Bougouriba ∼ BF 202-203 J 4
Bougouso ○ CI 202-203 G 5
Bougtob ○ DZ 190-191 C 3
Bouguer, Cape ▲ AUS 180-181 D 4
Boû Guettâra ⟨ RIM 196-197 C 5
Bou Hadjar ○ DZ 190-191 G 2
Bou Iblane, Jbel ▲ MA 188-189 J 4
Bou-Izakarn ○ MA 188-189 G 6
Boujad ○ MA 188-189 H 4
Boujdour ○ MA 188-189 D 7
Boujdour, Cap ▲ MA 188-189 D 7
Bou Kadir ○ DZ 190-191 C 2
Bou Kahil, Djebel ▲ DZ 190-191 D 3
Boukân ○ IR 128-129 M 4
Bou Kettoum, Jbel ▲ MA 188-189 K 3
Boukoko ○ RCA 210-211 F 2
Boukoula ○ CAM 204-205 K 3
Boukoumbé ○ DY 202-203 L 4
Boukra ○ MA 188-189 E 7
Bou Ladiab, Jebel ▲ TN 190-191 H 4
Boula-Ibib ○ CAM 204-205 K 4
Boulal ○ RMM 202-203 F 2
Boulal ○ SN 202-203 C 2
Boû Lanouâr ○ RIM 196-197 B 4
Boulâouane • MA 188-189 G 4
Boulder ○• USA (CO) 254-255 K 3
Boulder ○ USA (MT) 250-251 G 5
Boulder ○ USA (UT) 254-255 D 6
Boulder ○ USA (WY) 252-253 J 4
Boulder, Kalgoorli- ○ AUS 176-177 F 5
Boulder City ○ USA (NV) 248-249 K 4
Boulder Creek ○ USA (CA) 248-249 B 2
Boulel ○ RMM 202-203 H 2
Boulél ○ SN 202-203 C 2
Boulemane ○ MA 188-189 J 4
Boulgou ○ BF 202-203 L 3
Bouli ∼ DY 204-205 E 3
Bouli ○ RIM 196-197 E 7
Boulia ○ AUS 178-179 E 2
Boulogne-sur-Mer ○• F 90-91 H 6
Bouloub ○ RCA 206-207 E 5
Bouloupari ○ F 13 F 5
Boulouli ○ RMM 202-203 F 3
Boulsa ○ BF 202-203 K 3
Boulsmail ○ DZ 190-191 D 2
Boultoum ○ RN 198-199 E 5
Boumaine-du-Dadès ○ MA 188-189 J 5
Boumango ○ G 210-211 D 5
Boumba ∼ CAM 210-211 E 2
Boumbé I ∼ RCA 206-207 B 6
Boumbé II ∼ CAM 206-207 B 6
Boumboum ○ RMM 202-203 K 2
Boumda National Park ⊥ AUS 180-181 K 4
Boûmdeid ○ RIM 196-197 E 6
Boumerdes ☆ DZ 190-191 D 2
Bou Mertala ⟨ RIM 196-197 F 4
Boumia ○ MA 188-189 J 4
Boum Kabir ○ TCH 206-207 D 3
Bou Mréga ⟨ RIM 196-197 E 6
Bouna ☆ CI 202-203 J 5
Bou Naceur, Ibel ▲ MA 188-189 K 4
Boû Nâga ○ RIM 196-197 D 5
Boû Nâga ⟨ RMM 196-197 J 5
Boundary ○ CDN 32-33 E 3
Boundary ○ USA (WA) 244-245 H 2
Boundary Mountains ▲ USA (ME) 278-279 L 3
Boundary Peak ▲ USA (CA) 248-249 F 2
Boundary Plateau ▲ CDN (SAS) 232-233 J 6
Boundary Ranges ▲ CDN 32-33 E 3
Boundiali ☆ CI 202-203 G 5
Boundji ○ G 210-211 D 4
Boundji ○ RCB 210-211 E 4
Boungo ∼ RCA 206-207 F 4
Boungou ∼ RCA 206-207 E 5
Boungou ○ RCA 206-207 F 5
Bouniandjé ∼ G 210-211 D 3
Bounkiling ○ SN 202-203 C 3
Bounoum ∼ SN 202-203 C 2
Bountiful ○ USA (UT) 254-255 D 3
Bountiful Islands ∩ AUS 174-175 E 5
Bounty Islands ∩ NZ 13 J 7
Bounty Plateau ≃ 13 J 7
Bounty Trough ≃ 13 J 7
Bouquet ○ RA 78-79 J 2
Boura ○ BF 202-203 J 4
Bourarhet, Erg ∴ DZ 190-191 G 7
Bourbeuse River ∼ USA (MO) 274-275 G 6
Bourbonnais ∴ F 90-91 J 8
Bourdel, Lac ○ CDN 36-37 M 6
Bourem ○ RMM 196-197 K 6
Bourg, Lac ○ CDN 36-37 N 6
Bourg-en-Bresse ☆• F 90-91 K 8
Bourges ☆••• F 90-91 J 8
Bourgogne ◘ F 90-91 J 8
Bourgogne ∴ F 90-91 K 8
Bourgoin-Jallieu ○ F 90-91 K 9
Bouria ☆ DZ 190-191 D 2
Boû Rjeimât ⟨ RIM 196-197 C 5
Bourke ○ AUS 178-179 H 6
Bournemouth ○ GB 90-91 G 6
Bourou ○ TCH 206-207 C 4
Bouroum ○ BF 202-203 K 3
Bourrah ○ CAM 204-205 K 3
Bourzanga ○ BF 202-203 K 3
Bous, Adrar ▲ RN 198-199 D 2
Bou Saada ○• DZ 190-191 E 3
Bouse ○ USA (AZ) 256-257 B 5
Bou Sellam ∼ DZ 190-191 E 2
Bou Sfer ○ DZ 188-189 L 3
Boussé ○ BF 202-203 K 3
Boussemghoun ○ DZ 190-191 C 4
Bousso ○ TCH 206-207 C 3
Bousso River ∼ CDN 30-31 M 4
Boussouma ○ BF 202-203 K 3
Boutilimit ○ RIM 196-197 C 6
Boutougou Fara ○ SN 202-203 D 3
Boutourou, Monts ▲ CI 202-203 J 5
Bouza ○ RN 198-199 C 5
Bouzghaïa ☆ DZ 190-191 C 2
Bovill ○ USA (ID) 250-251 C 5
Bovina ○ USA (TX) 264-265 B 4
Bowbells ○ USA (ND) 258-259 E 3
Bow City ○ CDN (ALB) 232-233 F 5
Bowden ○ CDN (ALB) 232-233 D 4
Bowdle ○ USA (SD) 260-261 G 1
Bowdon ○ USA (GA) 284-285 E 3
Bowdon ○ USA (ND) 258-259 H 4
Bowell ○ CDN (ALB) 232-233 H 5
Bowell Islands ∩ CDN 30-31 W 3
Bowen ○ AUS 174-175 K 7
Bowen ○ RA 78-79 F 3
Bowen ○ USA (IL) 274-275 G 4
Bowen, Cape ▲ AUS 174-175 H 4
Bowen Island ○ CDN (BC) 230-231 F 4
Bowens Hill ○ USA (GA) 284-285 G 5
Bowenville ○ AUS 178-179 L 4
Bowers Basin ≃ 22-23 E 5
Bowers Ridge ≃ 22-23 E 5
Bowie ○ USA (AZ) 256-257 F 6
Bowie ○ USA (MD) 280-281 K 5
Bowie ○ USA (TX) 264-265 G 5
Bowie National Historic Site, Fort • USA (AZ) 256-257 F 6
Bow Island ○ CDN (ALB) 232-233 G 6
Bowler ○ USA (WI) 270-271 K 6
Bowling Green ○ USA (FL) 286-287 H 4
Bowling Green ○ USA (KY) 276-277 J 4
Bowling Green ○ USA (MO) 274-275 G 5
Bowling Green ○ USA (OH) 280-281 C 2
Bowling Green ○ USA (VA) 280-281 J 5
Bowling Green Bay ≈ 174-175 J 6
Bowling Green Bay National Park ⊥ AUS 174-175 J 6
Bowman ○ USA (GA) 284-285 G 2
Bowman ○ USA (ND) 258-259 D 5
Bowman Bay ≈ 36-37 N 2
Bowman Island ∩ ARK 16 G 11
Bowmans Corner ○ USA (MT) 250-251 G 4
Bowmanville ○ CDN (ONT) 238-239 G 5
Bowokan, Kepulauan ∩ RI 164-165 H 5
Bowral ○ AUS 180-181 L 3
Bow River ∼ AUS 172-173 J 4
Bow River ∼ CDN (ALB) 232-233 E 5
Bowron Lake Provincial Park ⊥ CDN (BC) 228-229 N 3
Bowron Lake Provincial Park ⊥ CDN (BC) 228-229 O 3
Bowron River ∼ CDN (BC) 228-229 N 3
Bowser ○ CDN (BC) 230-231 E 4
Bowsman ○ CDN (MAN) 234-235 B 2
Bowutu Mountains ▲ PNG 183 D 4
Bow Valley Provincial Park ⊥ CDN (ALB) 232-233 C 4
Bowwood ○ Z 218-219 D 3
Boxborough ○ USA (MA) 278-279 K 6
Boxelder ○ USA (TX) 264-265 K 5
Box Elder Creek ∼ USA (MT) 250-251 L 4
Box Elder Creek ∼ USA (MT) 250-251 P 6
Box Lake ○ CDN 30-31 Q 6
Boxwood Hill ○ AUS 176-177 E 7
Boyabat ○ TR 128-129 F 2
Boyabo ○ ZRE 210-211 G 2
Boyacá ○ CO (BOL) 60-61 D 3
Boyacá ○ CO (BOY) 60-61 E 5
Boyang ○ VRC 156-157 K 2
Boyce ○ USA (LA) 268-269 H 5
Boyce Thompson Arboretum • USA (AZ) 256-257 D 5
Boyd ○ CDN 34-35 H 3
Boyd ○ USA (MT) 250-251 K 6
Boyd, Lac ○ CDN 38-39 F 2
Boyd Lake ○ CDN 30-31 S 5
Boyd River ∼ AUS 178-179 M 5
Boyds ○ USA (WA) 244-245 G 2
Boyellé ○ RCB 210-211 G 2
Boyero ○ USA (CO) 254-255 M 5
Boyer River ∼ CDN 30-31 L 6
Boyer River ∼ USA (IA) 274-275 C 3
Boykin ○ USA (AL) 284-285 C 4
Boykins ○ USA (VA) 280-281 J 7
Boyle ○ CDN 32-33 O 4
Boyle = Mainistir na Búille ○ IRL 90-91 C 5
Boylston ○ CDN (NS) 240-241 O 5
Boyne ○ ZA 218-219 E 6
Boyne City ○ USA (MI) 272-273 E 2
Boyne Valley ••• IRL 90-91 D 5
Boynton Beach ○ USA (FL) 286-287 J 5
Boyolali ○ RI 168 D 3
Boy River ○ USA (MN) 270-271 D 3
Boysen Reservoir ○ USA (WY) 252-253 K 3
Boys Ranch ○ USA (TX) 264-265 B 3
Boyte ○ CDN 32-33 O 4
Boyuibe ○ BOL 70-71 F 7
Boyup Brook ○ AUS 176-177 D 6
Bozburun ○ TR 128-129 C 4
Bozcaada ∩ TR 128-129 B 3
Bozdağlar ▲ TR 128-129 B 3
Boždomova, mys ▲ RUS 120-121 T 3
Bozeman ○ USA (MT) 250-251 H 6
Bozeman Pass ▲ USA (MT) 250-251 J 6
Bozen = Bolzano ☆ I 100-101 C 1
Bozene ○ ZRE 210-211 G 2
Bożgān ○ IR 136-137 F 6
Bozhou ○ VRC 154-155 J 5
Bozkır ☆ TR 128-129 E 4
Bozköl ○ KA 126-127 O 5
Bozok Yaylâsı ▲ TR 128-129 F 3
Bozoum ☆• RCA 206-207 C 5
Bozova ☆ TR 128-129 H 4
Bozüyük ☆ TR 128-129 D 3
Bozyazı ☆ TR 128-129 E 4
Brabant, Île ∩ ARK 16 G 30
Brač ∩ HR 100-101 F 3
Bracciano, Lago di ○ I 100-101 D 3
Bracebridge ○ CDN (ONT) 238-239 F 3
Bräcke ○ S 86-87 G 5
Bracken ○ CDN (SAS) 232-233 K 6
Brackendale ○ CDN (BC) 230-231 F 4
Brackett Lake ○ CDN 30-31 G 3
Brackettville ○ USA (TX) 266-267 G 4
Bracknell ○ GB 90-91 G 6
Braclavka ○ RUS 124-125 B 3
Braço de Lontra ∼ BR 68-69 C 4
Braço do Norte ○ BR 74-75 F 7
Braço Menor do Araguaia ou Jauaés ∼ BR 68-69 D 7
Brad ○ RO 102-103 C 4
Brad ○ USA (TX) 264-265 F 6
Brádano ∼ I 100-101 E 4
Braddock ○ USA (ND) 258-259 G 5
Braddyville ○ USA (IA) 274-275 C 4
Bradenton ○ USA (FL) 286-287 G 4
Bradford ○ CDN (ONT) 238-239 F 4
Bradford ○ GB 90-91 G 5
Bradford ○ USA (AR) 276-277 D 5
Bradford ○ USA (IL) 274-275 J 3
Bradford ○ USA (PA) 280-281 H 2
Bradford ○ USA (VT) 278-279 J 4
Bradley ○ USA (AR) 276-277 B 7
Bradley ○ USA (CA) 248-249 D 4
Bradley ○ USA (SC) 284-285 H 2
Bradleyville ○ USA (MO) 276-277 C 4
Bradore, Baie ≈ 38-39 Q 3
Bradshaw ○ USA (NE) 262-263 J 4
Bradshaw ○ USA (TX) 264-265 E 6
Bradwardine ○ CDN (MAN) 234-235 C 5
Bradwell ○ CDN (SAS) 232-233 M 4
Brady ○ USA (MT) 250-251 H 3
Brady ○ USA (TX) 266-267 H 2
Brady Creek ∼ USA (TX) 266-267 H 2
Brady Glacier ⊂ USA 32-33 B 2
Brady Reservoir ⟨ USA (TX) 266-267 H 2
Braemar ○ AUS 180-181 E 2
Braemar ○ GB 90-91 F 3
Braga ○• P 98-99 C 4
Bragado ○ RA 78-79 J 3
Bragança ○ BR 68-69 E 2
Bragança ○ P 98-99 D 4
Bragança Paulista ○ BR 72-73 G 7
Bragg, Fort ○ USA (CA) 246-247 B 4
Bragg Creek ○ CDN (ALB) 232-233 D 5
Braham ○ USA (MN) 270-271 E 5
Brahestad ○ FIN 88-89 H 4
Brahim, Hassi ⟨ MA 188-189 G 6
Brahmani ∼ IND 142-143 D 5
Brahmapur ○ IND 142-143 D 6
Brahmaputra ∼ 142-143 H 2
Braidwood ○ AUS 180-181 K 3
Brăila ☆• RO 102-103 E 5
Brainard ○ CDN 32-33 L 4
Brainerd ○ USA (MN) 270-271 D 4
Braintree ○ GB 90-91 H 6
Brajarājnagar ○ IND 142-143 C 5
Brakna ◘ RIM 196-197 D 6
Brakpan ○ NAM 220-221 D 2
Brakpan ○ ZA 220-221 J 3
Brakspruit ○ ZA 220-221 H 3
Brakwater ○ NAM 216-217 D 11
Bralorne ○ CDN (BC) 230-231 G 3
Brálos ○ GR 100-101 J 5
Bramhapuri ○ IND 138-139 G 9
Brampton ○ CDN (ONT) 238-239 F 5
Brampton Islands ∩ AUS 174-175 K 7
Bramwell ○ AUS 174-175 G 3
Branca, Serra ▲ BR 68-69 F 5
Brancepeth ○ CDN (SAS) 232-233 N 2
Branch ○ CDN (NFL) 242-243 P 6
Branch Creek ∼ AUS 174-175 E 5
Branchville ○ USA (SC) 284-285 K 3
Branco, Ilhéu ∩ CV 202-203 B 5
Branco, Rio ∼ BR 62-63 D 4
Branco, Rio ∼ BR 66-67 D 5
Branco, Rio ∼ BR 66-67 B 5
Branco, Rio ∼ BR 66-67 G 7
Branco, Rio ∼ BR 66-67 E 7
Branco, Rio ∼ BR 68-69 F 7
Branco, Rio ∼ BR 70-71 F 3
Branco, Rio ∼ BR 70-71 G 2
Branco, Rio ∼ BR 70-71 H 2
Branco ou Cabixi, Rio ∼ BR 70-71 G 3
Brandberg •• NAM 216-217 C 10
Brandberg Wes ○ NAM 216-217 C 10
Brandbu ☆ N 86-87 E 6
Brande ○ DK 86-87 D 9
Brandenburg ◘ D 92-93 M 3
Brandenburg ○ USA (KY) 276-277 J 3
Brandenburg an der Havel ○• D 92-93 M 2
Brandenton Beach ○ USA (FL) 286-287 G 4
Brandfort ○ ZA 220-221 H 4
Brandon ○ CDN (MAN) 234-235 D 5
Brandon ○ USA (FL) 286-287 G 4
Brandon ○ USA (MN) 270-271 C 5
Brandon ○ USA (MS) 268-269 L 4
Brandon ○ USA (SD) 260-261 K 3
Brandon ○ USA (VT) 278-279 H 5
Brandsen ○ RA 78-79 K 3
Brandvlei ○ ZA 220-221 E 5
Brandýs nad Labem-Stará Boleslav ○ CZ 92-93 N 3
Brandywine ○ USA (MD) 280-281 K 5
Branford ○ USA (FL) 286-287 G 2
Brang, Kuala ○ MAL 162-163 E 2
Braniewo ○• PL 92-93 P 1
Br'anka ○ UA 102-103 L 3
Branqueada do Salto ○ BR 74-75 D 9
Bransan ○ SN 202-203 D 3
Bransfield Strait ≈ 16 G 30
Branson ○ USA (CO) 254-255 M 6
Branson ○ USA (MO) 276-277 B 4
Brant ○ CDN (ALB) 232-233 E 5
Brantford ○ CDN (ONT) 238-239 E 5
Brantley ○ USA (AL) 284-285 D 5
Brantôme ○ F 90-91 H 9
Brantville ○ CDN (NB) 240-241 L 3
Brás ○ BR 66-67 H 4
Bras d'Or Lake ○ CDN (NS) 240-241 P 5
Brasil ○ C 54-55 G 4
Brasilândia ○ BR 72-73 D 6
Brasiléia ○ BR 70-71 C 2
Brasília ★••• BR 72-73 G 3
Brasília, Lago de ○ BR 72-73 G 3
Brasília de Minas ○ BR 72-73 H 4
Braslândia ○ BR 72-73 F 3
Braslav ○ BY 94-95 K 4
Brasnorte ○ BR 70-71 H 2
Brașov ☆• RO 102-103 D 5
Brass ○ WAN 204-205 G 6
Brasschaat ○ B 92-93 H 3
Brassey, Banjaran ▲ MAL 160-161 B 10
Brassey, Mount ▲ AUS 178-179 C 2
Brassey Range ▲ AUS 176-177 G 2
Brasstown Bald ▲ USA (GA) 284-285 G 2
Brastagi ○• RI 162-163 C 3
Bratislava ★•• SK 92-93 O 4
Bratovoești ○ RO 102-103 C 5
Bratsk ☆ RUS 116-117 K 7
Bratskoe vodohranilišče ⟨ RUS 116-117 K 8
Bratskoye Vodokhranilishche = Bratskoe vodohranilišče ⟨ RUS 116-117 K 8
Brattleboro ○ USA (VT) 278-279 J 6
Braulio Carrillo, Parque Nacional ⊥ CR 52-53 C 6
Braúnas ○ BR 72-73 J 5
Braunau am Inn ○ A 92-93 M 4
Braunlage ○ D 92-93 L 3
Braunschweig ○•• D 92-93 L 2
Brava, Ilha ∩ CV 202-203 B 6
Brava, La ○ RA 76-77 G 6
Brava, Laguna la ○ RA 78-79 H 2
Bravo, Cerro ▲ BOL (COC) 70-71 E 5
Bravo, Cerro ▲ BOL (POT) 76-77 D 2
Bravo, Cerro ▲ RCH 76-77 C 4
Bravo, El ○ RA 76-77 F 4
Bravo del Norte, Río ∼ MEX 50-51 J 3
Bravo River ∼ BH 52-53 K 3
Brawley ○ USA (CA) 248-249 J 7
Bray ○ USA (CA) 246-247 D 2
Bray ○ ZA 220-221 F 2
Bray = Bré ○ IRL 90-91 D 5
Bray Island ∩ CDN 24-25 h 6
Bray-sur-Seine ○ F 90-91 J 7
Brazeau, Mount ▲ CDN (ALB) 228-229 R 4
Brazeau Reservoir ⟨ CDN (ALB) 232-233 C 3
Brazeau River ∼ CDN (ALB) 228-229 R 4
Brazeau River ∼ CDN (ALB) 232-233 C 3
Brazil ○ USA (IN) 274-275 L 5
Brazil = Brasil ■ BR 74-75 C 2
Brazil Basin = Brasil Basin ≃ 6-7 G 10
Brazilian Highlands = Brasileiro, Planalto ∴ BR 72-73 G 3
Brazo Aná Cuá ∼ PY 76-77 J 4
Brazo de Loba ∼ CO 60-61 D 3
Brazos ○ USA (NM) 256-257 J 2
Brazos River ∼ USA (TX) 264-265 E 5
Brazos River ∼ USA (TX) 266-267 L 3
Brazo Sur del Río Coig ∼ RA 80 E 5
Brazzaville ★• RCB 210-211 E 6
Brčko ○ BIH 100-101 G 2
Brdy ▲ CZ 92-93 M 4
Bré = Bray ○ IRL 90-91 D 5
Brea, Cordillera de la ▲ RA 76-77 C 5
Brea, La ○ TT 60-61 L 2
Breaden, Lake ○ AUS 176-177 H 2
Breaksea Sound ≈ 182 A 6
Brea Pozo ○ RA 76-77 F 5
Breas, Las ○ RCH 76-77 B 5
Breaux Bridge ○ USA (LA) 268-269 J 6
Brebes ○ RI 168 C 3
Brechin ○ CDN (ONT) 238-239 F 4
Breckenridge ○ USA (CO) 254-255 J 4
Breckenridge ○ USA (MN) 270-271 B 4
Breckenridge ○ USA (TX) 264-265 F 6
Breckinridge Mountain ▲ USA (CA) 248-249 F 4
Brecknock, Península ∪ RCH 80 E 7
Brecon ○• GB 90-91 F 6
Brecon Beacons National Park ⊥ GB 90-91 F 6
Breda ○• NL 92-93 H 3
Bredasdorp ○ ZA 220-221 E 7
Bredbo ○ AUS 180-181 K 3
Bredbyn ○ S 86-87 J 5
Bredenbury ○ CDN (SAS) 232-233 Q 5
Brédi, ostrov ∩ RUS 84-85 d 2
Bredsel ○ S 86-87 K 4
Bredy ☆ RUS 124-125 B 2
Breede ∼ ZA 220-221 E 7
Breeza Plains Out Station ○ AUS 174-175 H 4
Bregalnica ∼ MK 100-101 J 4
Bregenz ☆ A 92-93 K 5
Bregovo ○ BG 102-103 C 5
Bréhal ○ F 90-91 G 7
Brehat ○ CDN (NFL) 242-243 N 1
Brehovskie ostrova ∩ RUS 108-109 U 6
Breiðafjörður ≈ 86-87 b 2
Breien ○ USA (ND) 258-259 G 5
Breivikbotn ○ N 86-87 L 1
Brejão da Caatinga ○ BR 68-69 H 7
Brejo ○ BR 68-69 G 3
Brejo, Riachão do ∼ BR 68-69 G 6
Brejo da Madre de Deus ○ BR 68-69 K 6
Brejo de São Félix ○ BR 68-69 G 4
Brejo do Cruz ○ BR 68-69 K 5
Brejo do Serra ○ BR 68-69 G 7
Brejo Grande ○ BR (CEA) 68-69 J 5
Brejo Grande ○ BR (SER) 68-69 K 7
Brejolândia ○ BR 72-73 J 2
Brejo Velho, Riachão ∼ BR 72-73 J 2
Brekken ○ N 86-87 E 5
Brekstad ○ N 86-87 D 5
Brelen ○ USA (ND) 258-259 G 5
Bremangerlandet ∩ N 86-87 B 6
Bremen ☆• D 92-93 K 2
Bremen ○ USA (AL) 284-285 D 3
Bremen ○ USA (GA) 284-285 E 3
Bremen ○ USA (IN) 274-275 M 3
Bremen ○ USA (ND) 258-259 H 4
Bremer Bay ≈ 176-177 E 7
Bremer Bay ○ AUS 176-177 E 7
Bremerhaven ○ D 92-93 K 2
Bremer Island ∩ AUS 174-175 D 3
Bremer Range ▲ AUS 176-177 F 6
Bremerton ○ USA (WA) 244-245 C 3
Bremervörde ○ D 92-93 K 2
Bremner ○ CDN (ALB) 232-233 E 2
Bremond ○ USA (TX) 266-267 L 2
Brenãs, Las ○ RA 76-77 G 4
Brenham ○ USA (TX) 266-267 L 3
Brennerpaß = Passo del Brennero ▲ A 92-93 L 5
Brennevinsfjorden ≈ 84-85 L 2
Brent ○ USA (AL) 284-285 C 4
Brenta ∼ I 100-101 C 2
Brentford Bay ≈ 24-25 Z 5
Brentwood ○ USA (TN) 276-277 J 4
Brenzina ○ DZ 190-191 C 4
Brep ○ PK 138-139 D 1
Bresaylor ○ CDN (SAS) 232-233 K 3
Bréscia ○• I 100-101 C 2
Bresnahan, Mount ▲ AUS 176-177 D 1
Bressanone = Brixen ○ I 100-101 C 1
Bressuire ○ F 90-91 G 8
Brèst ○ BY 94-95 H 5
Brest ○ F 90-91 E 7
Brest = Brèst ○ BY 94-95 H 5
Bretagne ◘ F 90-91 E 7
Bretaña ○ PE 64-65 E 4
Breteuil ○ F 90-91 J 7
Breton, Cape ▲ CDN (NS) 240-241 Q 5
Breton, Playa El ∴• DOM 54-55 L 5
Breton Cove ○ CDN (NS) 240-241 P 4
Breton Island ∩ USA (LA) 268-269 L 7
Breton National Wildlife Refuge ⊥ USA (LA) 268-269 M 7
Breton N. W. R. ⊥ USA (LA) 268-269 L 7
Breton Sound ≈ 48-49 D 5
Breton Sound ≈ USA 268-269 L 7
Brett, Cape ▲ NZ 182 E 1
Breueh, Pulau ∩ RI 162-163 A 2
Brevard ○ USA (NC) 282-283 E 5
Breverville ○ LB 202-203 E 6
Breves ○ BR 62-63 J 6
Brevoort, Kap ▲ GRØ 26-27 U 3
Brevoort Island ∩ CDN 36-37 R 3
Brevort ○ USA (MI) 270-271 N 4
Brewaniase ○ GH 202-203 L 5
Brewarrina ○ AUS 178-179 J 5
Brewer ○ CDN (SAS) 232-233 Q 4
Brewer ○ USA (ME) 278-279 N 4
Brewster ○ USA (KS) 262-263 E 5
Brewster ○ USA (NE) 262-263 G 3
Brewster ○ USA (NY) 280-281 N 2
Brewster ○ USA (WA) 244-245 F 2
Brewster, Lake ○ AUS 180-181 J 2
Brewton ○ USA (AL) 284-285 C 5
Breynat ○ CDN 32-33 O 4
Breyten ○ ZA 220-221 J 3
Brezina ○ DZ 190-191 C 4
Brežnev = Naberežnye Čelny ☆ RUS 96-97 H 6
Brezovo Polje ▲ HR 100-101 F 2
Bria ☆ RCA 206-207 E 5
Briakan ○ RUS 122-123 F 2
Briançon ○• F 90-91 L 9
Brian Head ▲ USA (UT) 254-255 C 6
Briarton ○ USA (WI) 270-271 K 6
Bribie Island ∩ AUS 178-179 M 4
Bribri ○ CR 52-53 C 7
Bričany = Briceni ☆ MD 102-103 E 3
Bričen' = Briceni ☆ MD 102-103 E 3
Briceni ☆ MD 102-103 E 3
Brices Cross Roads National Battlefield Site ∴ USA (MS) 268-269 M 2
Briconnet, Lac ○ CDN 38-39 O 3
Bridal Cave ∴ USA (MO) 274-275 F 6
Bridesville ○ CDN (BC) 230-231 K 4
Bridge City ○ USA (TX) 268-269 G 6
Bridgeford ○ CDN (SAS) 232-233 M 5
Bridge Lake ○ CDN (BC) 230-231 J 2
Bridgenorth ○ CDN (ONT) 238-239 G 4
Bridge over the River Kwai • THA 158-159 E 3
Bridge Point ▲ BS 54-55 G 2
Bridgeport ○ USA (AL) 284-285 E 2
Bridgeport ○ USA (CA) 246-247 F 5
Bridgeport ○ USA (CT) 280-281 N 2
Bridgeport ○ USA (NE) 262-263 C 3
Bridgeport ○ USA (OH) 280-281 F 3
Bridgeport ○ USA (OR) 244-245 H 6
Bridgeport ○ USA (TX) 264-265 G 5
Bridgeport ○ USA (WA) 244-245 F 2
Bridgeport, Lake ⊂ USA (TX) 264-265 G 5
Bridger ○ USA (MT) 250-251 L 6
Bridge River ∼ CDN (BC) 230-231 G 3
Bridge River Indian Reservation ⅄ CDN (BC) 230-231 G 3
Bridger Peak ▲ USA (WY) 252-253 L 5
Bridger State Historic Site, Fort • USA (WY) 252-253 H 5
Bridger Wilderness Area ⊥ USA (WY) 252-253 J 4
Bridgeton ○ USA (NJ) 280-281 L 4
Bridgetown ○ AUS 176-177 D 6
Bridgetown ★ BDS 56 F 5
Bridgetown ○ CDN (NS) 240-241 K 6
Bridgeville ○ CDN (QUE) 240-241 L 2
Bridgeville ○ USA (CA) 246-247 B 3
Bridgewater ○ AUS (TAS) 180-181 J 7
Bridgewater ○ AUS (VIC) 180-181 G 4
Bridgewater ○ CDN (NS) 240-241 L 6
Bridgewater ○ USA (NY) 278-279 F 6
Bridgewater ○ USA (SD) 260-261 J 3
Bridgewater ○ USA (VA) 280-281 H 5
Bridgewater ○ ZA 218-219 E 6
Bridgewater, Cape ▲ AUS 180-181 F 5
Bridgman, Kap ▲ GRØ 26-27 m 2
Bridgton ○ USA (ME) 278-279 L 4
Bridlington ○ GB 90-91 G 4
Bridport ○ AUS 180-181 J 6
Bridport ○ GB 90-91 F 6
Bridport Inlet ≈ 24-25 R 3
Brie ∴• F 90-91 J 7
Brieg = Brzeg ○• PL 92-93 O 3
Brier Creek ∼ USA (GA) 284-285 H 3
Briercrest ○ CDN (SAS) 232-233 N 5
Brier Island ∩ CDN (NS) 240-241 J 6
Brig ○• CH 92-93 J 5
Brig Bay ○ CDN (NFL) 242-243 M 1
Briggs ○ USA (TX) 266-267 K 3
Briggs, Cape ▲ CDN 24-25 Y 4
Briggsdale ○ USA (CO) 254-255 L 3
Brigham City ○ USA (UT) 254-255 C 2
Bright ○• AUS 180-181 J 4
Brighton ○ CDN (ONT) 238-239 H 4
Brighton ○ GB 90-91 G 6
Brighton ○ USA (AL) 284-285 C 3
Brighton ○ USA (CO) 254-255 L 4
Brighton ○ USA (FL) 286-287 H 4
Brighton ○ USA (IA) 274-275 G 3
Brighton ○ USA (IL) 274-275 H 5
Brighton ○ USA (IN) 274-275 N 3
Brighton ○ USA (MI) 272-273 F 5
Brighton Downs ○ AUS 178-179 F 2
Brighton Seminole Indian Reservation ⅄ USA (FL) 286-287 H 4
Brightsand Lake ○ CDN (SAS) 232-233 K 2
Brightstar ○ USA (AR) 276-277 B 7
Brígida, Riachão ou ∼ BR 68-69 J 6
Brignan ∪ CI 202-203 H 7
Brignoles ○ F 90-91 L 10
Brikama ○ WAG 202-203 B 3
Brilhante, Rio ∼ BR 76-77 K 1
Brilon ○ D 92-93 K 3
Brimley ○ USA (MI) 270-271 O 4
Brimstone Hill Fortress ∴ KAN 56 D 3
Brinckheuvel, National Reservaat ⊥ SME 62-63 G 3
Brindakit ○ RUS 120-121 G 3
Brindisi ☆• I 100-101 F 4
Brinkley ○ USA (AR) 276-277 D 6
Brinkleyville ○ USA (NC) 282-283 K 4
Brin-Navolok ○ RUS 88-89 Q 5
Brinnon ○ USA (WA) 244-245 C 3
Brion, Île ∩ CDN (QUE) 242-243 G 5
Brisbane ☆• AUS 178-179 M 4
Brisbane ○ CDN (ONT) 238-239 E 5
Brisbane River ∼ AUS 178-179 M 4
Brisco ○ CDN (BC) 230-231 N 3
Briscoe ○ USA (TX) 264-265 D 3
Brisson, Lac ○ CDN 36-37 R 6
Bristol ○ CDN (NB) 240-241 H 4
Bristol ○• GB 90-91 F 6
Bristol ○ USA (CO) 254-255 N 5
Bristol ○ USA (CT) 280-281 O 2
Bristol ○ USA (FL) 286-287 E 1
Bristol ○ USA (GA) 284-285 H 5
Bristol ○ USA (IN) 274-275 N 3
Bristol ○ USA (SD) 260-261 J 1
Bristol ○ USA (TN) 282-283 E 4
Bristol ○ USA (VA) 280-281 D 7
Bristol ○ USA (VT) 278-279 H 4
Bristol Bay ≈ 22-23 Q 4
Bristol Channel ≈ 90-91 E 6
Bristol Lake ○ USA (CA) 248-249 J 5
Bristow ○ USA (OK) 264-265 H 3
Britânia ○ BR 72-73 E 3
Britannia ○ CDN (NFL) 242-243 P 4
Britannia, Mount ▲ CDN 24-25 Y 2
Britannia Beach ○ CDN (BC) 230-231 F 4
Britannia Range ▲ ARK 16 E 0
Britanskij kanal ≈ 84-85 b 2
British Columbia ◘ CDN 32-33 F 3
British Empire Range ▲ CDN 26-27 K 2
British Mountains ▲ USA 20-21 U 2
British Virgin Islands ◘ GB 56 C 2
Brito Godins ○ ANG 216-217 D 4
Brits ○ ZA 220-221 H 2
Britstown ○ ZA 220-221 F 5
Britt ○ USA (IA) 274-275 E 1
Britton ○ USA (SD) 260-261 J 1
Britvin, mys ▲ RUS 108-109 F 5
Brive-la-Gaillarde ○ F 90-91 H 9
Brixen = Bressanone ○ I 100-101 C 1
Brjanka = Br'anka ○ UA 102-103 L 3
Brjansk ○ RUS 94-95 O 5
Brjansk ○ RUS 126-127 G 5
Brjanskaja Kosa, mys ▲ RUS 126-127 G 5
Brjanskoe ○ RUS 122-123 K 5
Brjanta ∼ RUS 118-119 N 8

308 Bort-les-Orgues — Brjanta

Brjungjade ~ RUS 120-121 J 2
Brjusa, ostrov ⌒ RUS 84-85 b 2
Brno o CZ 92-93 0 4
Broa, Ensenada de la ≈ 54-55 D 3
Broadacres o CDN (SAS) 232-233 K 3
Broadalbin o USA (NY) 278-279 G 5
Broad Arrow ∴ AUS 176-177 F 5
Broadback Rivière ~ CDN (QUE) 236-237 M 2
Broadford o AUS 180-181 H 4
Broad Peak ▲ IND 138-139 F 2
Broad River ~ USA (GA) 284-285 H 3
Broad River ~ USA (GA) 284-285 G 2
Broad River ~ USA (SC) 284-285 J 2
Broad Sound ≈ 178-179 K 2
Broadsound Range ▲ AUS 178-179 K 2
Broadus o USA (MT) 250-251 0 6
Broadview o CDN (SAS) 232-233 Q 5
Broadview o USA (MT) 250-251 L 5
Broadview o USA (NM) 256-257 M 4
Broadview Acton o USA (MT) 250-251 L 5
Broadwater o USA (NE) 262-263 D 3
Broadway o USA (VA) 280-281 H 5
Brobo o CI 202-203 H 6
Brochant, Rivière ~ CDN 36-37 0 5
Brochet o CDN 34-35 F 2
Brochet, Lac o CDN 30-31 T 6
Brochet, Lac du ⊖ CDN 38-39 K 4
Brock o CDN (SAS) 232-233 K 4
Brocken ▲ D 92-93 L 3
Brocket o CDN (ALB) 232-233 E 6
Brocket o USA (ND) 258-259 J 3
Brock Island ⌒ CDN 24-25 0 2
Brockman, Mount ▲ AUS 172-173 C 7
Brockport o USA (NY) 278-279 D 5
Brock River ~ CDN 24-25 L 6
Brockton o USA (MA) 278-279 K 6
Brockton o USA (MT) 250-251 P 3
Brockville o CDN (ONT) 238-239 K 4
Brockway o USA (MT) 250-251 0 4
Brockway o USA (PA) 280-281 H 2
Broco o USA (FL) 286-287 G 3
Brodec'ke o UA 102-103 F 3
Broderick o CDN (SAS) 232-233 M 4
Brodeur Peninsula ⌣ CDN 24-25 b 4
Brodeur River ~ CDN 24-25 b 4
Brodick o GB 90-91 E 4
Brodie Bay ≈ 28-29 G 2
Brodnica o· PL 92-93 P 2
Brodokalmak o RUS 114-115 G 7
Brody o UA 102-103 D 2
Broer Ruys, Kap ▲ GRØ 26-27 p 7
Brogan o USA (OR) 244-245 H 6
Broke Inlet ≈ 176-177 D 7
Broken Arrow o USA (OK) 264-265 J 2
Broken Bay ≈ 180-181 L 2
Broken Bow o USA (NE) 262-263 G 3
Broken Bow o USA (OK) 264-265 K 4
Broken Bow Lake ⊖ USA (OK) 264-265 K 4
Brokenburg o USA (VA) 280-281 J 5
Brokenhead o CDN (MAN) 234-235 G 4
Broken Hill o· AUS 178-179 F 6
Broken Ridge ≃ 12 H 7
Broken River ~ AUS 180-181 H 4
Broken Skull River ~ CDN 30-31 E 4
Broken Water Bay ≈ 183 C 2
Brokopondo ☆ SME 62-63 G 3
Bromby Islands ⌒ AUS 174-175 D 2
Bromley o ZW 218-219 F 3
Bromo, Gunung ▲ RI 168 E 3
Bromo-Tengger-Semeru National Park ⊥ RI 168 E 3
Bromsi, Pulau ⌒ RI 166-167 J 2
Brønderslev o DK 86-87 D 8
Brong-Ahafo Region ◻ GH 202-203 J 6
Bronkhorstspruit o ZA 220-221 J 2
Bronnicy o· RUS 94-95 Q 4
Brønnøysund o N 86-87 F 4
Bronson o USA (FL) 286-287 G 2
Bronson o USA (MI) 272-273 D 6
Bronson o USA (TX) 268-269 F 5
Bronte o USA (TX) 266-267 G 2
Brook, Lake ~ CDN 36-37 J 3
Brookeland o USA (TX) 268-269 G 5
Brookesmith o USA (TX) 266-267 H 2
Brooke's Point o RP 160-161 B 8
Brookfield o USA (MO) 274-275 E 5
Brookgreen Gardens · USA (SC) 284-285 L 3
Brookhaven o USA (MS) 268-269 K 5
Brookings o USA (OR) 244-245 A 8
Brookings o USA (SD) 260-261 K 2
Brooklet o USA (GA) 284-285 J 4
Brooklyn o CDN (NS) 240-241 L 5
Brooklyn o USA (AL) 284-285 D 5
Brooklyn o USA (IA) 274-275 F 3
Brooklyn o USA (MS) 268-269 L 5
Brooklyn (River cruises) · AUS 180-181 L 2
Brookneal o USA (VA) 280-281 H 6
Brooks o CDN (ALB) 232-233 G 5
Booksburg o USA (NY) 278-279 G 6
Brooksby o CDN (SAS) 232-233 O 3
Brooks Mount ▲ USA 20-21 G 4
Brooks Nek o ZA 220-221 J 5
Brooks Peninsula Provincial Recreation Area ⊥ CDN (BC) 230-231 B 3
Brooks Range ▲ USA 20-21 K 2
Brookston o USA (MN) 270-271 F 4
Brookstone o USA (IN) 274-275 M 4
Brooksville o USA (FL) 286-287 G 3
Brooksville o USA (MS) 268-269 M 3
Brookton o AUS 176-177 D 6
Brookville o AUS 174-175 J 7
Brookville o USA (IN) 274-275 N 5
Brookville o USA (PA) 280-281 G 2
Brookville Reservoir < USA (IN) 274-275 O 5
Broome o· AUS 172-173 F 4
Broomhill o CDN (MAN) 234-235 B 5
Brooms Head o AUS 178-179 M 5
Brotas o BR 72-73 F 7
Brotas de Macaúbas o BR 68-69 G 7
Brother John Gletscher ⊂ GRØ 26-27 0 4
Brothers o USA (OR) 244-245 E 7
Brothers, The ⌒ Y 132-133 H 7
Broughton Island ⌒ CDN (NWT) 28-29 J 3
Broughton Island ⌒ CDN (NWT) 36-37 L 6
Broulkou < TCH 198-199 J 4
Brouse o CDN (BC) 230-231 M 3
Brovary o UA 102-103 G 2
Brovinia o AUS 178-179 L 3
Browder o USA (KY) 276-277 H 3
Browerville o USA (MN) 270-271 D 4
Brown o CDN (MAN) 234-235 E 5
Brown, Mount ▲ ARK 16 F 9
Brown, Mount ▲ USA (MT) 250-251 H 3
Brown, Point ▲ AUS 176-177 M 6
Brown Bank ≃ 160-161 B 7
Brown City o USA (MI) 272-273 G 4
Brown Co. State Park ⊥ USA (IN) 274-275 M 5
Browne o USA 20-21 Q 4
Browne Bay ≈ 24-25 X 4
Browne Range ▲ AUS 176-177 H 2
Brownfield o CDN (ALB) 232-233 G 3
Brownfield o USA (TX) 264-265 B 5
Browning o CDN (SAS) 232-233 Q 6
Browning o USA (MT) 250-251 F 3
Brown Lake ⊖ CDN 30-31 Y 3
Brownlee o CDN (SAS) 232-233 N 5
Brownlow Point ▲ USA 20-21 S 1
Brownrigg o CDN (ONT) 236-237 G 3
Brown River ~ AUS 178-179 K 3
Brown River ~ PNG 183 D 5
Browns o USA (AL) 284-285 C 4
Brownsberg, National Reservaat ⊥ SME 62-63 G 3
Brownsboro o USA (OR) 244-245 C 8
Brownsburg o CDN (QUE) 238-239 L 3
Brownsburg o USA (IN) 274-275 M 5
Brown's Cay ⌒ BS 54-55 F 2
Brown's Cove o CDN (NFL) 242-243 M 3
Browns Town o JA 54-55 G 5
Brownstown o USA (IN) 274-275 M 6
Browns Valley o USA (MN) 270-271 B 5
Brownsville o USA (KY) 276-277 J 3
Brownsville o USA (TN) 276-277 F 5
Brownsville o USA (TX) 266-267 K 8
Brownsweg o SME 62-63 G 3
Brownton o USA (GA) 284-285 J 5
Brownwood o USA (TX) 266-267 J 2
Brownwood, Lake < USA (TX) 266-267 H 2
Browse Island ⌒ AUS 172-173 F 3
Broxton o USA (GA) 284-285 H 5
Broytona, ostrov ⌒ RUS 122-123 O 5
Bruce o CDN (ALB) 232-233 F 3
Bruce o USA (MS) 268-269 L 3
Bruce o USA (WI) 270-271 G 5
Bruce, Mount ▲ AUS 172-173 D 7
Bruce Crossing o USA (MI) 270-271 J 4
Bruce Highway II AUS 178-179 K 2
Bruce Lake ⊖ CDN (ONT) 234-235 L 4
Bruce Mines o CDN (ONT) 238-239 B 2
Bruce Peninsula ⌣ CDN (ONT) 238-239 D 3
Bruce Peninsula National Park ⊥ CDN (ONT) 238-239 D 3
Bruce Rock o AUS 176-177 E 5
Bruceton o USA (TN) 276-277 G 4
Bruceville-Eddy o USA (TX) 266-267 K 2
Bruck an der Leitha o A 92-93 O 5
Bruck an der Mur o A 92-93 N 5
Brudenell o CDN (ONT) 238-239 H 3
Bruderheim o CDN (ALB) 232-233 F 2
Brug, De o ZA 220-221 G 4
Bruges = Brugge ☆·· B 92-93 G 3
Brugge ☆·· B 92-93 G 3
Brühl o·· D 92-93 J 3
Bruini o IND 144-145 L 6
Bruit, Pulau ⌒ MAL 162-163 J 3
Brujas o CO 60-61 G 6
Brujas, Cueva de las · RA 78-79 E 3
Brujas, Las ▲ MEX 50-51 K 6
Brukkaros ▲ NAM 220-221 C 2
Brûlé o CDN (ALB) 228-229 R 3
Brule o USA (WI) 270-271 G 4
Brûle, Lac = Burnt Lake ⊖ CDN 38-39 N 2
Brumadinho o BR 72-73 H 6
Brumado o BR 72-73 K 3
Brumunddal ☆ N 86-87 E 6
Brunchilly o AUS 174-175 C 6
Brundage o USA (TX) 266-267 H 5
Brundidge o USA (AL) 284-285 E 5
Bruneau o USA (ID) 252-253 C 4
Bruneau River ~ USA (ID) 252-253 C 4
Brunei ■ BRU 164-165 D 1
Brunei = Bandar Seri Begawan ★·· BRU 164-165 D 1
Brunei, Teluk ≈ 160-161 A 10
Brunette Downs o AUS 174-175 C 6
Brunette Island ⌒ CDN (NFL) 242-243 M 5
Brunflo o S 86-87 G 5
Bruni o USA (TX) 266-267 J 6
Bruning o USA (NE) 262-263 J 4
Brunkild o CDN (MAN) 234-235 F 5
Brünn = Brno o CZ 92-93 O 4
Bruno o CDN (SAS) 232-233 N 3
Bruno o USA (MN) 270-271 F 4
Bruno o USA (NE) 262-263 K 3
Brunswick o USA (GA) 284-285 J 5
Brunswick o USA (MD) 280-281 J 4
Brunswick o USA (ME) 278-279 M 5
Brunswick o USA (MN) 270-271 E 5
Brunswick o USA (MO) 274-275 E 5
Brunswick o USA (NE) 262-263 J 2
Brunswick = Braunschweig o·· D 92-93 L 2
Brunswick, Peninsula ⌣ RCH 80 E 6
Brunswick Bay ≈ 172-173 G 3
Brunswick Heads o AUS 178-179 M 5
Brunswick Lake ⊖ CDN (ONT) 236-237 E 4
Bruntál o CZ 92-93 O 4
Bruny Island ⌒ AUS 180-181 J 7
Brus o YU 100-101 H 3
Brusett o USA (MT) 250-251 M 4
Brush o USA (CO) 254-255 M 3
Brus-Kamen' ▲ RUS 108-109 X 8
Brusque o BR 74-75 F 6
Brussel = Bruxelles ★·· B 92-93 H 3
Brussels = Bruxelles = Brussel ★·· B 92-93 H 3
Brüx = Most o CZ 92-93 M 3
Bruzual o YV 60-61 G 3
Bryan o USA (OH) 280-281 B 2
Bryan o USA (TX) 266-267 L 3
Bryan, Mount ▲ AUS 180-181 E 2
Bryansk = Brjansk o RUS 94-95 O 5
Bryant o CDN (SAS) 232-233 P 6
Bryant o USA (AR) 276-277 C 6
Bryant o USA (SD) 260-261 J 2
Bryant Creek ~ USA (MO) 276-277 C 4
Bryce Canyon National Park ∴ USA (UT) 254-255 C 6
Bryden, Mount ▲ AUS 178-179 K 1
Brylivka o UA 102-103 H 4
Bryne ☆ N 86-87 B 7
Bryson o USA (TX) 264-265 F 5
Bryson City o USA (NC) 282-283 D 5
Brzeg o· PL 92-93 O 3
Brześć Kujawski o PL 92-93 P 2
Brzesko o PL 92-93 Q 4
Bširri ☆ RL 128-129 G 5
Bua o FJI 184 III b 2
Bua ~ MW 218-219 G 1
Bua < SUD 206-207 G 3
Bua Bay ≈ 184 III b 2
Buabuang o RI 164-165 H 4
Buafri o GH 202-203 K 5
Buaka o GH 202-203 J 6
Buala o SOL 184 I d 3
Bū al Ghurāb, Bi'r < LAR 192-193 E 2
Bū al Hidān, Wādi ~ LAR 192-193 H 4
Buan, Pulau ⌒ RI 162-163 H 5
Buatan o RI 162-163 D 4
Bū Athlah < LAR 192-193 J 3
Buaya, Pulau ⌒ RI 162-163 F 4
Buaya Channel ≈ 166-167 K 6
Bu'ayrat al Hasun o LAR 192-193 F 2
Buba o GNB 202-203 C 4
Buba, Rio Grande de ~ GNB 202-203 C 4
Bubanda o ZRE 206-207 D 6
Bubanza o BU 212-213 C 5
Bubaque o· GNB 202-203 C 4
Bubi o ZW (Mvi) 218-219 F 5
Bubi ~ ZW 218-219 E 4
Bubi ~ ZW 218-219 F 5
Bubiai o·· LT 94-95 H 4
Bubiki o EAT 212-213 D 5
Būbiyān, Ğazirat ⌒ KWT 130-131 L 3
Bublitz = Bobolice o PL 92-93 O 2
Bublos ∴·· RL 128-129 F 5
Bubu ~ EAT 214-215 H 4
Bubu o PNG 183 F 3
Bubudu ~ ZRE 210-211 K 6
Buburu o ZRE 210-211 G 3
Buca o FJI 184 III b 2
Buçaco o ANG 216-217 F 5
Bucak ☆ TR 128-129 D 4
Bucalemu o RCH 78-79 C 3
Bucaramanga ☆ CO 60-61 E 4
Bucareli Bay ≈ 32-33 D 4
Bucas Grande Island ⌒ RP 160-161 F 8
Buccaneer Archipelago ⌒ AUS 172-173 F 3
Buccaneer Beach ⌣ USA (VI) 286-287 R 3
Buchan o AUS 180-181 K 4
Buchanan o CDN (SAS) 232-233 Q 4
Buchanan ☆ LB 202-203 E 7
Buchanan o USA (GA) 284-285 E 3
Buchanan o USA (MI) 272-273 C 6
Buchanan o USA (ND) 258-259 J 4
Buchanan o USA (OR) 244-245 G 7
Buchanan o USA (VA) 280-281 G 6
Buchanan, Lake ⊖ AUS 178-179 H 1
Buchanan, Lake < USA (TX) 266-267 J 3
Buchanan Bay ≈ 26-27 N 4
Buchanan Highway II AUS 172-173 J 4
Buchan Caves · AUS 180-181 K 4
Buchan Gulf ≈ 26-27 O 8
Buchans o CDN (NFL) 242-243 M 4
Buchans Junction o CDN (NFL) 242-243 M 4
Bucharest = București ★· RO 102-103 D 5
Bucheke o PK 138-139 D 4
Buchenwald o· D 92-93 L 3
Buch'isi o ETH 208-209 C 5
Buchon, Point ▲ USA (CA) 248-249 D 4
Buchwa o ZW 218-219 F 5
Buck, Lake ⊖ AUS 172-173 K 5
Buckambool Mountain ▲ AUS 178-179 H 6
Buckatunna Creek ~ USA (MS) 268-269 M 5
Buck Creek ~ CDN (BC) 228-229 H 2
Buck Creek ~ USA (KY) 276-277 L 3
Buck Creek ~ USA (TX) 264-265 D 4
Buckeye o USA (AZ) 256-257 C 5
Buckeye o USA (NM) 256-257 M 6
Buckeye Lake ⊖ USA (OH) 280-281 D 4
Buckhannon o USA (WV) 280-281 F 4
Buckhorn o USA (NM) 256-257 G 5
Buckhorn Draw ~ USA (TX) 266-267 G 3
Buckhorn Lake ⊖ CDN (ONT) 238-239 G 4
Buckhorn Reservoir < USA (KY) 276-277 M 3
Buckingham o CDN (QUE) 238-239 K 3
Buckingham Bay ≈ 174-175 C 3
Buckingham Downs o AUS 178-179 E 2
Buckingham Island ⌒ CDN 24-25 a 2
Buck Lake ⊖ CDN (ALB) 232-233 D 2
Buckland o USA 20-21 K 4
Buckland, Monte ▲ RA 80 H 7
Buckland River ~ USA 20-21 K 4
Buckley o USA (WA) 244-245 C 3
Buckley Bay ≈ 16 G 15
Buckley Bay o CDN (BC) 230-231 E 4
Buckley River ~ AUS 174-175 E 7
Bucklin o USA (KS) 262-263 G 7
Buckmuische = Ezernieki o LV 94-95 K 3
Buckner Creek ~ USA (KS) 262-263 F 7
Buck Ridge o CDN (BC) 228-229 M 4
Bucksport o USA (ME) 278-279 N 4
Buck Valley o USA (PA) 280-281 H 4
Buco Zau o ANG 210-211 D 6
Buctouche o CDN (NB) 240-241 L 4
București ★· RO 102-103 E 5
Bucyrus o USA (OH) 280-281 D 3
Buda o USA (TX) 266-267 K 3
Budaka o EAU 212-213 D 3
Budalin o MYA 142-143 J 4
Bù Đăngo o VN 158-159 J 5
Budapest ★··· H 92-93 P 5
Búðardalur ☆ IS 86-87 c 2
Budarino o KA 96-97 G 8
Budaun o IND 138-139 G 5
Budawang Range ▲ AUS 180-181 L 3
Bud Bud o SP 208-209 H 6
Budd, Pulau ⌒ RI 166-167 F 1
Buddabadah o AUS 178-179 J 6
Buddha Park · THA 158-159 H 3
Budd Land ⌣ ARK 16 G 12
Bude o USA (MS) 268-269 K 5
Budënnovsk o RUS 126-127 F 5
Budennovsk o RUS 126-127 F 5
Budhi Gandaki ~ NEP 144-145 E 6
Budi, Lago ⊖ RCH 78-79 C 5
Budibudi Islands ⌒ PNG 183 G 5
Buding o RI 162-163 G 6
Búðir o IS 86-87 b 2
Budjala o ZRE 210-211 G 2
Budogošč' o RUS 94-95 N 2
Budongquan o VRC 144-145 J 3
Budu o MAL 162-163 J 4
Budu, Tanjung ▲ MAL 162-163 J 3
Budungbudung ~ RI 164-165 F 5
Budva o· YU 100-101 G 3
Budweis = České Budějovice o CZ 92-93 N 4
Buéa ☆· CAM 204-205 H 6
Buedu o WAL 202-203 E 5
Buefjorden ≈ 86-87 B 6
Buela o ANG 216-217 C 2
Buena o USA (WA) 244-245 E 4
Buena Esperanza o RA 78-79 G 3
Buena Hora o BOL 70-71 D 3
Buenaventura o C 54-55 G 4
Buenaventura o CO 60-61 C 6
Buenaventura o MEX (CHA) 50-51 F 3
Buenaventura o MEX (YUC) 52-53 L 1
Buenaventura, Bahía de ≈ 60-61 C 6
Buena Vista ∴· BH 52-53 K 3
Buena Vista o BOL (PAN) 70-71 D 2
Buena Vista o BOL (SAC) 70-71 F 5
Buenavista o CO 60-61 E 5
Buena-vista o CO 60-61 D 3
Buenavista o MEX (CHI) 52-53 H 3
Buenavista o MEX (SIN) 50-51 E 5
Buena Vista o PY 76-77 J 4
Buena Vista o RA 76-77 D 4
Buenavista o RP (MAR) 160-161 D 6
Buenavista o RP (ZAS) 160-161 E 9
Buena Vista o USA (CO) 254-255 J 5
Buena Vista o USA (GA) 284-285 F 4
Buena Vista o USA (VA) 280-281 G 6
Buena Vista o YV 60-61 G 4
Buena Vista, Bahía ≈ 54-55 F 3
Buena Vista Alta o PE 64-65 C 6
Buena Vista Island = Vatilau Island ⌒ SOL 184 I d 3
Buena Vista Lake ⊖ USA (CA) 248-249 E 4
Buenavista Tomatlán o MEX 52-53 C 2
Buendía, Embalse de < E 98-99 F 4
Buenga ~ ANG 216-217 C 3
Bueno, Río ~ RCH 78-79 C 6
Bueno Brandão o BR 72-73 G 7
Buenópolis o BR 72-73 H 4
Buenos Aires o CO (AMA) 66-67 B 4
Buenos Aires o CO (MET) 60-61 E 6
Buenos Aires o CO (TOL) 60-61 D 5
Buenos Aires o CO (VAU) 64-65 F 1
Buenos Aires o CR 52-53 C 7
Buenos Aires ◻ RA 78-79 H 3
Buenos Aires ★· RA 78-79 K 3
Buenos Aires, Lago ⊖ RA 80 E 3
Buenos Aires Lérida o CO 66-67 B 2
Buen Pasto o RA 80 F 2
Buesaco o CO 64-65 D 1
Buet, Rivière ~ CDN 36-37 O 4
Buey o CO 60-61 C 4
Buey Arriba o C 54-55 G 4
Bueyeros o USA (NM) 256-257 M 3
Bueyes, Cerro de los ▲ RA 78-79 D 4
Búfalo o MEX 50-51 G 4
Bufalo, Reserva Parcial do ⊥ ANG 216-217 B 6
Bufareh o RI 166-167 K 3
Buffalo o CDN (ALB) 232-233 H 5
Buffalo o CDN (SAS) 232-233 N 6
Buffalo o USA (IA) 274-275 H 3
Buffalo o USA (MN) 270-271 E 5
Buffalo o USA (MO) 276-277 B 3
Buffalo o USA (ND) 258-259 K 5
Buffalo o USA (OK) 264-265 E 2
Buffalo o USA (SD) 260-261 C 1
Buffalo o USA (TN) 276-277 G 5
Buffalo o USA (TX) 266-267 L 2
Buffalo o USA (WV) 280-281 E 5
Buffalo o USA (WY) 252-253 M 2
Buffalo o· USA (NY) 278-279 C 6
Buffalo Bill Ranch State Historic Park ∴ USA (NE) 262-263 F 3
Buffalo Bill Reservoir ⊖ USA (WY) 252-253 J 2
Buffalo Center o USA (IA) 274-275 E 1
Buffalo City o USA (AR) 276-277 C 4
Buffalo Creek ~ CDN 32-33 O 3
Buffalo Gap National Grassland ⊥ USA (SD) 260-261 D 3
Buffalo Head Hills ▲ CDN 32-33 M 3
Buffalo Hump ▲ USA (ID) 250-251 D 6
Buffalo Lake ⊖ CDN (ALB) 232-233 F 3
Buffalo Lake ⊖ CDN (NWT) 30-31 M 5
Buffalo Lake ⊖ USA (TX) 264-265 B 4
Buffalo Mountain ▲ USA (NV) 246-247 G 3
Buffalo Narrows o CDN 32-33 Q 4
Buffalo National River ⊥ USA (AR) 276-277 C 5
Buffalo Pound Provincial Park ⊥ CDN (SAS) 232-233 N 5
Buffalo River ~ CDN 30-31 M 6
Buffalo River ~ CDN 32-33 M 3
Buffalo River ~ USA (AR) 276-277 C 4
Buffalo River ~ USA (MS) 268-269 J 5
Buffalo River ~ USA (TN) 276-277 G 5
Buffalo River ~ USA (WI) 270-271 G 6
Buffalo Springs National Reserve ⊥ EAK 212-213 F 3
Buff Bay o JA 54-55 G 5
Buffels Drift o ZA 218-219 D 6
Buffelsrivier ~ ZA 220-221 K 4
Buffelsrivier ~ ZA 220-221 C 4
Bufflé Noir o CAM 204-205 K 4
Buford o USA (CO) 254-255 H 4
Buford o USA (GA) 284-285 F 2
Buford o USA (ND) 258-259 D 4
Buford o USA (OH) 280-281 C 4
Buford o USA (WY) 252-253 N 5
Buftea o RO 102-103 D 5
Bug ~ PL 92-93 R 2
Buga o CO 60-61 C 6
Buga o MAU 146-147 M 2
Buga o WAN 204-205 G 4
Bugaboo Alpine Provincial Recreation Area ⊥ CDN (BC) 230-231 N 3
Bugadi o EAU 212-213 D 3
Bugala Island ⌒ EAU 212-213 D 4
Bugana o WAN 204-205 G 5
Bugant o MAU 148-149 H 3
Bugdajly o TM 136-137 D 5
Buge o VRC 144-145 M 5
Bugembe o EAU 212-213 D 3
Bugene o EAT 212-213 C 4
Buggs Island Lake ⊖ USA (VA) 280-281 H 7
Bugi o· RI 166-167 K 3
Bugingkalo o RI 164-165 G 6
Bugiri o EAU 212-213 D 3
Bugojno o BIH 100-101 F 2
Bugrino o RUS 88-89 U 2
Bugsuk Island ⌒ RP 160-161 B 8
Bugt o VRC 150-151 C 3
Buguey o RP 160-161 D 3
Bugui Point ▲ RP 160-161 E 6
Buguľma ☆ RUS 96-97 H 6
Buguľminsko-Belebeevskaja vozvyšennosť ▲ RUS 96-97 H 6
Bugunda o RUS 118-119 G 9
Buguruslan ☆ RUS 96-97 H 7
Buhara = Buharo ☆·· US 136-137 J 5
Buharskaja oblast' ◻ US 136-137 H 4
Bu He ~ VRC 144-145 M 2
Buhera o ZW 218-219 F 4
Buhl o USA (ID) 252-253 D 4
Buhlandshahr o IND 138-139 F 5
Buhoro ☆·· US 136-137 J 5
Buhtarma ~ KA 124-125 O 4
Buhtarminskoe sukojmasy < KA 124-125 N 4
Buhta Sytygan-Tala ≈ 110-111 S 4
Buhu ~ EAT 212-213 E 6
Buick o CDN 32-33 K 3
Buiko o EAT 212-213 G 6
Builth Wells o GB 90-91 F 5
Bū'in o IR 136-137 B 7
Buin o PNG 184 I b 2
Bui National Park ⊥ GH 202-203 J 5
Buinsk ☆ RUS 96-97 F 6
Buir Nur ⊖ VRC 148-149 N 4
Buitenzorg = Bogor o RI 168 B 3
Buitepos o NAM 216-217 E 11
Buiucu o BR 66-67 J 5
Buj o RUS 94-95 R 2
Buj ~ RUS 96-97 J 5
Bujanovac o YU 100-101 H 3
Bujant o MAU 148-149 K 4
Bujant gol ~ MAU 148-149 C 4
Bujaraloz o E 98-99 G 4
Bujaru o BR 62-63 K 6
Bujaru, Rio ~ BR 68-69 E 2
Bujnaksk o RUS 126-127 G 6
Bujukly o RUS 122-123 K 4
Bujumbura ★ BU 212-213 B 5
Bujunda ~ RUS 120-121 P 3
Buk o PNG 183 B 5
Buka o US 136-137 L 4
Bukaan o RI 164-165 G 3
Bukačača o RUS 118-119 H 9
Bukadaban Feng ▲ VRC 144-145 H 2
Bukairiya, al- o KSA 130-131 H 4
Buka Island ⌒ PNG 184 I b 1
Bukama o ZRE 214-215 C 5
Bu Kammāsh o LAR 192-193 D 1
Bukantov toglari ▲ US 136-137 H 3
Bukasa Island ⌒ EAU 212-213 D 4
Bukat, Pulau ⌒ RI 164-165 E 2
Bukaua o PNG 183 D 4
Bukavu ☆ ZRE 212-213 B 5
Bukedea o EAU 212-213 E 3
Bukene o EAT 212-213 D 6
Bukeya o ZRE 214-215 D 6
Bukhit o SUD 206-207 H 3
Bukhoro = Buhoro ☆·· US 136-137 J 5
Bukima o EAT 212-213 D 4
Bukitkemuning o RI 162-163 F 7
Bukit Lata Papalang ▲ MAL 162-163 D 2
Bukittinggi ·· RI 162-163 D 5
Bükk ▲ H 92-93 Q 4
Bukkāpatna o IND 140-141 G 4
Bukken Fiord ≈ 26-27 C 3
Bükki Nemzeti Park ⊥ H 92-93 Q 4
Bukoba ☆ EAT 212-213 C 4
Bukoloto o EAU 212-213 D 3
Bukombe o EAT 212-213 D 5
Bukrane o RI 166-167 F 5
Bukuru o WAN 204-205 H 4
Būl, Kūh-e ▲ IR 134-135 E 3
Bula o GNB 202-203 C 3
Bula o PNG 183 A 5
Bula o ZRE 212-213 B 3
Bula, Cachoeira ~ BR 66-67 C 2
Bula Atumba o ANG 216-217 C 4
Bulacaue Point ▲ RP 160-161 E 7
Bulacle o SP 208-209 H 6
Bulaevo ☆ KA 124-125 G 1
Bulag o MAU 148-149 J 3
Bulagansk o RUS 118-119 E 9
Bulagi o RI 164-165 H 4
Bulahdelah o AUS 180-181 M 2
Bulaka ~ RI 166-167 K 5
Bulalacao Island ⌒ RP 160-161 D 7
Bulalakao o RP 160-161 D 6
Bulan o RP 160-161 E 6
Bulanaš o RUS 96-97 M 5
Bulancak ☆ TR 128-129 H 2
Bulanghe o VRC 154-155 F 2
Bulangu o WAN 198-199 E 6
Bulanik ☆ TR 128-129 K 3
Bŭlăq o ET 194-195 E 5
Bulava o RUS 122-123 J 3
Bulawa, Gunung ▲ RI 164-165 H 3
Bulawayo ☆ ZW 218-219 E 5
Bulaya o Z 214-215 F 5
Bulbodney Creek ~ AUS 180-181 J 2
Bulbuhta o RUS 118-119 H 6
Bulbula o ETH 208-209 D 5
Buldan ☆ TR 128-129 C 3
Buldāna o IND 138-139 F 9
Buldibuyo o PE 64-65 D 6
Buldir Island ⌒ USA 22-23 D 6
Bŭldyrtty ~ KA 96-97 H 9
Buleleng o RI 164-165 H 5
Bulenga o GH 202-203 J 5
Bulga Downs o AUS 176-177 E 4
Bulgan o MAU 146-147 J 4
Bulgan o MAU (ÖMN) 148-149 F 5
Bulgan ◻ MAU 148-149 F 3
Bulgan ☆ MAU (BUL) 148-149 F 3
Bulgan = Burènhajrhan o MAU 146-147 K 2
Bulgan = Šargalant o MAU 146-147 K 2
Bulgan gol ~ MAU 146-147 K 2
Bulgar ☆ RUS 96-97 F 6
Bulgaria = Bălgarija ■ BG 102-103 C 6
Bulgnéville o F 90-91 K 7
Buli o RI 164-165 L 3
Bū Lifiyat o UAE 134-135 E 6
Buliluyan, Cape ▲ RP 160-161 B 8
Bulimba o AUS 174-175 G 5
Bulisa o EAU 212-213 C 2
Buliya ⌒ FJI 184 III b 3
Bulkley Ranges ▲ CDN (BC) 228-229 G 2
Bulkley River ~ CDN 32-33 G 4
Bullabulling o AUS 176-177 F 5
Bullara o AUS 172-173 B 7
Bullard o USA (TX) 264-265 J 6
Bulla Regia ∴·· TN 190-191 G 2
Bullaxaar o SP 208-209 G 3
Bull Bay o JA 54-55 G 6
Bull Creek ~ CDN (SAS) 232-233 L 6
Bullecourt o AUS 174-175 E 7
Bullen, Cape ▲ CDN 24-25 d 3
Bullen River ~ CDN 30-31 S 3
Buller, Mount ▲ AUS 180-181 J 4
Bullfinch o AUS 176-177 E 5
Bull Harbour o CDN (BC) 230-231 B 3
Bullhead City o USA (AZ) 256-257 A 3
Bulli o AUS 180-181 L 3
Bull Island ⌒ USA (SC) 284-285 L 4
Bullita Out Station o AUS 172-173 K 4
Bull Lake ⊖ CDN 30-31 R 5
Bullmoose Creek ~ CDN 32-33 K 4
Bull Mountains ▲ USA (MT) 250-251 L 5
Bullock o USA (NC) 282-283 J 4
Bullock's Harbour o BS 54-55 G 2
Bulloo Downs o AUS 176-177 E 2
Bulloo River ~ AUS 178-179 H 4
Bullo River o AUS 172-173 J 3
Bullpound Creek ~ CDN (ALB) 232-233 G 4
Bull River ~ CDN (BC) 230-231 O 4
Bulls o NZ 182 E 4
Bulls Bay ≈ 48-49 J 3
Bulls Bay ≈ USA 284-285 L 4
Bull Shoals Lake ⊖ USA (AR) 276-277 C 4
Büllsport o NAM 220-221 C 2
Bulmer Lake ⊖ CDN 30-31 J 4
Bulnajn Nuruu ▲ MAU 148-149 C 3
Bulnes o RCH 78-79 C 4
Bulo Balamal o SP 212-213 J 2
Buloke, Lake ⊖ AUS 180-181 G 4
Bulolo o PNG 183 D 4
Bulolo River ~ PNG 183 D 4
Bulongo o ZRE 210-211 H 6
Buloo River ~ AUS 178-179 H 3
Bulqizë o· AL 100-101 H 4
Bultfontein o ZA 220-221 H 4
Bulu o RI 168 D 3
Buluan o RP 160-161 F 9
Buluan ~ RP 160-161 F 9
Buluan Lake ⊖ RP 160-161 F 9
Bulukumba o RI 164-165 G 6
Bulukutu o ZRE 210-211 H 4
Bulula o ZRE 212-213 A 6
Bulumuri o PNG 183 F 3
Bulun o RUS (SAH) 120-121 E 2
Bulun ~ RUS 112-113 H 4
Bulungu o ZRE (Ban) 210-211 G 6
Bulungu o ZRE (KOC) 216-217 F 3
Bulupulu, Tanjung ▲ RI 164-165 G 5
Bulus o RUS 118-119 O 4
Bulusan o RP 160-161 F 6
Bulusan Vulcano ▲ RP 160-161 F 6
Bulwark o CDN (ALB) 232-233 G 3
Bulwer o ZA 220-221 J 4
Bulyea o CDN (SAS) 232-233 O 4
Buma ~ ZRE 210-211 F 5
Bū Marim o LAR 192-193 J 1
Bumba o ZRE 210-211 J 2
Bümbah o LAR 192-193 K 1
Bumbat o MAU 148-149 G 4
Bumbire Island ⌒ EAT 212-213 C 4
Bumble Bee o USA (AZ) 256-257 C 4
Bum Bum, Pulau ⌒ MAL 160-161 C 10
Bumbuna o WAL 202-203 E 5
Bumi Hills o ZW 218-219 E 3
Bumijawa o RI 168 C 3
Bumpus, Mount ▲ CDN 24-25 P 6
Buna o EAK 212-213 G 2
Buna o ZRE 210-211 G 5
Bunabun o PNG 183 C 3
Bunam o PNG 183 C 3
Bunapas o PNG 183 C 3
Bunbury o AUS 176-177 C 6
Bunda o EAT 212-213 D 5
Bundaberg o AUS 178-179 M 3
Bunda Bunda o AUS 174-175 G 7
Bundarra o AUS 178-179 L 6
Bundeena o AUS 178-179 G 4
Bundey, Mount ▲ AUS 172-173 K 2
Bundey River ~ AUS 178-179 C 1
Būndi o IND 138-139 E 7
Bundi o PNG 183 C 3
Bundibugyo o EAU 212-213 C 3
Bundick Creek ~ USA (LA) 268-269 G 6
Bundjalung National Park ⊥ AUS 178-179 M 5
Bunduqiya o SUD 206-207 K 6
Bunga ~ ZRE 210-211 K 3
Bunga, River ~ WAN 204-205 H 3
Bungadi o ZRE 206-207 H 6
Bungalaut, Selat ≈ 162-163 C 6
Bungamas o RI 162-163 E 6
Bungbulang o RI 168 B 3
Bunger Oasis ⌣ ARK 16 G 11
Bungi o RI 164-165 H 6
Bungikamasi, Pulau ⌒ RI 168 E 6
Bungil Creek ~ AUS 178-179 K 4
Bungku o RI 164-165 G 5
Bungle Bungle National Park ⊥ AUS 172-173 J 4
Bungle Bungle Range ▲ AUS 172-173 J 4
Bungo o ANG 216-217 C 3
Bungoma o EAK 212-213 E 3
Bungo-suido ≈ 152-153 E 8
Bungo-takada ⌣ J 152-153 D 8
Bung Sam Phan o THA 158-159 F 3
Bungtlang o IND 142-143 H 4
Bungudu o WAN 198-199 C 6
Bungunya o AUS 178-179 K 5
Bunguran, Pulau ⌒ RI 162-163 G 2
Buni o WAN 204-205 K 3
Bunia o ZRE 212-213 C 3
Bunie o ZRE 212-213 A 2
Buninyong o AUS 180-181 G 4
Bunji o IND 138-139 E 2
Bunker o USA (MO) 276-277 D 3
Bunker Group ⌒ AUS 178-179 M 2
Bunker Hill o USA 20-21 H 4
Bunkerville o USA (NV) 248-249 K 3
Bunkie o USA (LA) 268-269 H 6
Bunnell o USA (FL) 286-287 H 2
Bunneringee o AUS 180-181 F 2
Bunsuru ~ WAN 198-199 C 6
Bunta o RI 164-165 H 4
Bunthariq o THA 158-159 H 3
Buntu o RI 168 C 3
Bununu o WAN 204-205 H 4
Bunut o BRU 164-165 D 1
Bunyakiri o ZRE 212-213 B 5
Bünyan ☆ TR 128-129 F 3
Bunyan, Paul & Blue Ox Statue · USA (MN) 270-271 D 3
Bunyanyi, Lake ⊖ EAU 212-213 B 4
Bunyu, Pulau ⌒ RI 164-165 E 2
Bunza o WAN 204-205 E 2
Buolkalah ~ RUS 110-111 M 3
Buôn Ma Thuột ☆· VN 158-159 K 4
Buor-Ěekit ~ RUS 110-111 P 4
Buor-Haja, guba ≈ RUS 110-111 R 4
Buor-Haja, mys ▲ RUS 110-111 T 4
Buor-Jurjah ~ RUS 110-111 Z 6
Buotama ~ RUS 118-119 N 5
Buptgang Zangpo ~ VRC 144-145 E 5
Bupul o RI 166-167 L 5
Buqa', al- o KSA 132-133 D 5
Buqda Caqable o SP 208-209 G 6
Bur o RUS (IRK) 116-117 N 6
Bur ~ RUS 110-111 O 4
Bura o EAK 212-213 G 4
Buraan o SP 208-209 J 3
Buraatyn davaa ▲ MAU 146-147 K 1
Buraevo ☆ RUS 96-97 J 6
Buraida ☆ KSA 130-131 J 4
Buraika, al- o KSA 132-133 A 3
Buraimi, al- o OM 134-135 F 6
Burakin o AUS 176-177 D 5
Burālān o IR 128-129 L 5
Buram o SUD 206-207 G 3
Burang o VRC 144-145 C 5
Buranhem, Rio ~ BR 72-73 L 4
Burannoe o RUS 96-97 J 8
Buras o USA (LA) 268-269 L 7
Bū Rashādah, Wādi < LAR 192-193 G 4
Burauen o RP 160-161 F 7
Burayqah < SUD 200-201 E 4
Burbank o USA (CA) 248-249 F 5
Burbank o USA (WA) 244-245 G 4
Burchard o USA (NE) 262-263 K 4
Burcher o AUS 180-181 J 2
Burco ☆ SP 208-209 G 4
Burdalyk o TM 136-137 J 5
Burdekin Dam < AUS 174-175 J 7
Burden o USA (KS) 262-263 K 7
Burdulba o AUS 172-173 L 2
Burdur ☆· TR 128-129 D 4
Burdur Gölü ⊖ TR 128-129 D 4
Burdwood Bank ≃ 5 E 10
Burē o ETH (Ilu) 208-209 B 4
Burē o ETH (Wel) 208-209 C 3
Bureau, Lac ⊖ CDN (QUE) 236-237 N 4
Bureimi o RN 204-205 E 2
Bureinskiy hrebet ▲ RUS 122-123 E 4
Bureinskiy Khrebet = Bureinskij hrebet ▲ RUS 122-123 E 4
Bureiqa < SUD 200-201 E 4
Bureja ~ RUS 122-123 C 4
Burejnskij zapovednik ⊥ RUS 122-123 F 3
Burejnskoe vodohranilišče < RUS 122-123 D 3
Burengapara o IND 142-143 G 3
Burènhajrhan o MAU 146-147 K 2
Bureo, Río ~ RCH 78-79 C 4
Burera, Lac o RWA 212-213 B 4
Burevestnik o RUS 122-123 M 6
Búrfell o IS 86-87 d 2
Būr Fu'ād o ET 194-195 F 2
Burğ o OM 132-133 H 5
Burgagylkan ~ RUS 120-121 M 3
Burgal-'Arab o ET 194-195 D 2
Burgas o BG 102-103 E 6

Brjungjade — Burgas 309

C

Calandula o ANG 216-217 C 4
Calandula, Quedas do ~•• ANG 216-217 D 4
Calang o RI 162-163 A 2
Calanga o PE 64-65 D 8
Calanus Bay ≈ 36-37 H 3
Calapan ☆ RP 160-161 D 6
Cala Rajada o E 98-99 J 5
Călărași ☆ MD 102-103 F 4
Călărași ☆ RO 102-103 E 5
Calarca o CO 60-61 D 5
Calatambo o RCH 70-71 C 6
Calatayud o E 98-99 G 4
Calatrava o RP 160-161 E 7
Calavite Passage ≈ 160-161 D 6
Calayan Island ⌒ RP 160-161 D 3
Calbayog o RP 160-161 F 6
Calbore o PA 52-53 D 7
Calbuco o RCH 78-79 C 6
Calbuco, Volcán ▲ RCH 78-79 C 6
Calca o PE 70-71 B 3
Calcasieu Lake o USA (LA) 268-269 G 7
Calcasieu River ~ USA (LA) 268-269 H 6
Calceta o EC 64-65 B 2
Calchaquí o RA 76-77 G 5
Calchaquí, Río ~ RA 76-77 G 6
Calchaquí, Río ~ RA 76-77 D 3
Calchaquí las Aves, Laguna o RA 76-77 G 5
Calçoene o BR 62-63 J 4
Calçoene, Rio ~ BR 62-63 J 4
Calcutta ☆•• IND 142-143 F 4
Caldas o CO 60-61 D 4
Caldas Novas o BR 72-73 F 4
Caldeiras o BR 72-73 J 2
Calder o CDN (SAS) 232-233 R 4
Caldera o CR 52-53 B 7
Caldera o RCH 76-77 B 4
Caldera de Taburiente, Parque Nacional de la ⊥ E 188-189 C 6
Calderon, Cerro ▲ RA 78-79 E 6
Calder River ~ CDN 30-31 M 3
Calders Dock o CDN (MAN) 234-235 G 3
Çaldıran ☆ TR 128-129 K 3
Caldonia o USA (MN) 270-271 G 7
Caldwell o USA (ID) 252-253 B 3
Caldwell o USA (KS) 262-263 J 7
Caldwell o USA (NC) 282-283 H 4
Caldwell o USA (OH) 280-281 E 4
Caldwell o USA (TX) 266-267 L 3
Calebee Creek ~ USA (AL) 284-285 E 4
Caledon o ZA 220-221 D 7
Caledon Bay ≈ 174-175 D 3
Caledonia o CDN (NS) 240-241 N 5
Caledonia o CDN (ONT) 238-239 F 5
Caledonia o USA (MN) 270-271 G 7
Caledonia Hills ▲ CDN (NB) 240-241 K 5
Caledonrivier ~ ZA 220-221 H 4
Calen o AUS 174-175 K 7
Calepuisse o GNB 202-203 B 3
Calera o USA (AL) 284-285 D 3
Calera o USA (OK) 264-265 H 5
Calera, La o RCH 78-79 D 2
Caleta Josefina o RCH 80 F 6
Caleta Olivia o RA 80 G 3
Caleta Vitor o RCH 70-71 B 6
Caleufú o RA 78-79 G 3
Caleufú, Río ~ RA 78-79 D 6
Calexico o USA (CA) 248-249 J 7
Calfpen Swamp o USA (SC) 284-285 K 4
Calgary o• CDN (ALB) 232-233 D 4
Calhan o USA (CO) 254-255 L 4
Calhoun o USA (GA) 284-285 F 2
Calhoun o USA (KY) 276-277 H 3
Calhoun o USA (LA) 268-269 H 4
Calhoun City o USA (MS) 268-269 L 3
Calhoun Falls o USA (SC) 284-285 H 2
Calhua o PE 64-65 F 9
Cali ☆ CO 60-61 C 6
Calicoan Island ⌒ RP 160-161 F 7
Calico Ghost Town • USA (CA) 248-249 H 5
Calico Rock o USA (AR) 276-277 C 4
Calicut o• IND 140-141 F 5
Caliente o USA (CA) 248-249 F 4
Caliente o USA (NV) 248-249 K 2
California o BR 66-67 B 7
California o CO 60-61 E 4
California o USA (MO) 274-275 F 6
California ◘ USA (CA) 246-247 D 3
California, Gulf of = California, Golfo de ≈ MEX 50-51 B 2
California Aqueduct < USA (CA) 248-249 C 2
California City o USA (CA) 248-249 G 4
Calik ~ RI 162-163 F 6
Calilegua, Parque Nacional ⊥ RA 76-77 E 2
Calima = Darien o CO 60-61 C 6
Călimani, Munții ▲ RO 102-103 D 4
Calingasta o RA 76-77 C 6
Calingasta, Valle de ⌣ RA 76-77 C 6
Calingiri o AUS 176-177 D 5
Calintaan o RP 160-161 D 6
Calion o USA (AR) 276-277 C 7
Calipatria o USA (CA) 248-249 J 6
Caliper Lake o CDN (ONT) 234-235 K 5
Calipuy, Reserva Nacional ⊥ PE 64-65 C 6
Calispell Peak ▲ USA (WA) 244-245 H 2
Calistoga o USA (CA) 246-247 C 5
Calitzdorp o ZA 220-221 E 6
Calkar köl o KA 96-97 G 8
Calkarteniz, sor o KA 126-127 P 3
Calkiní o MEX 52-53 J 1
Callabonna o AUS 178-179 F 5
Callabonna, Lake o AUS 178-179 F 5
Callabonna Creek ~ AUS 178-179 F 5
Callaghan o USA (TX) 266-267 H 6
Callagiddy o AUS 176-177 C 2
Callahan o USA (CA) 246-247 C 2
Callahan o USA (FL) 286-287 H 1
Callahan, Mount ▲ USA (NV) 246-247 J 4
Callama ó Quirce, Río ~ BOL 70-71 D 7
Callana, Río ~ PE 64-65 E 5
Callander o CDN (ONT) 238-239 F 2
Callands o USA (VA) 280-281 G 7
Callanish o GB 90-91 D 2
Callao o PE 64-65 D 8
Callao o USA (UT) 254-255 B 4
Callao o USA (VA) 280-281 K 6
Callao, El o YV 62-63 D 2
Callaqui, Volcán ▲ RCH 78-79 D 4
Callara, Lake o AUS 178-179 D 5
Callatharra Springs o AUS 176-177 C 2
Callawa o AUS 172-173 E 6
Callaway o USA (FL) 286-287 D 1
Callaway o USA (MN) 270-271 C 4
Callaway o USA (NE) 262-263 G 3
Callaway Gardens • USA (GA) 284-285 F 4
Calle Calle, Río ~ RCH 78-79 C 5
Calles o MEX 50-51 K 6
Calling Lake o CDN 32-33 O 4
Calling River ~ CDN 32-33 O 4
Calliope o AUS 178-179 L 3
Callon o USA (WI) 270-271 J 6
Cal Madow, Buuraha ▲ SP 208-209 J 3
Calmar o CDN (ALB) 232-233 E 2
Calmar o USA (IA) 274-275 G 1
Cal Miskaat, Buuraha ▲ SP 208-209 J 3
Calm Point ▲ USA 22-23 Q 3
Čalna o RUS 88-89 N 6
Cal-Nev-Ari o USA (NV) 248-249 K 4
Calombo o ANG 216-217 C 6
Calonda o ANG 216-217 F 4
Calonga ~ ANG 216-217 C 7
Caloosahatchee River ~ USA (FL) 286-287 H 5
Caloto o CO 60-61 C 6
Caloundra o AUS 178-179 M 4
Calpet o USA (WY) 252-253 H 4
Calpon, Cerro ▲ PE 64-65 C 5
Calpulalpan o MEX 52-53 E 1
Calstock o CDN (ONT) 236-237 D 3
Caltagirone o I 100-101 E 6
Caltama, Cerro ▲ BOL 70-71 C 7
Caltanissetta o I 100-101 E 6
Calton Hills o AUS 174-175 E 7
Ca Lu o VN 158-159 J 2
Caluango o ANG 216-217 E 4
Calucinga o ANG 216-217 D 5
Calulo o ANG 216-217 C 4
Calumet o USA (OK) 264-265 F 3
Calunda o ANG 214-215 B 7
Caluquembe o ANG 216-217 C 6
Čalūs o• IR 136-137 B 6
Caluula o SP 208-209 K 3
Calvert o USA (AL) 284-285 B 5
Calvert o USA (TX) 266-267 L 2
Calvert, Cape ▲ CDN (BC) 230-231 B 2
Calvert Hills o AUS 174-175 D 5
Calvert Island ⌒ CDN (BC) 230-231 A 2
Calvi o•• F 98-99 M 3
Calvillo o MEX 50-51 H 7
Calvin o USA (OK) 264-265 H 4
Calvinia o ZA 220-221 D 5
Calwa o USA (CA) 248-249 E 3
Calzada de Calatrava o E 98-99 F 5
Camabatela o ANG 216-217 C 4
Camacã o BR 72-73 L 3
Camaçã, Rio ~ BR 66-67 D 6
Camaçari o BR 68-69 K 7
Camachi, Lac o CDN (QUE) 236-237 M 5
Camacupa o ANG 216-217 D 6
Camaguan o YV 60-61 H 3
Camagüey ☆• C 54-55 G 4
Camagüey, Archipiélago de ⌒ C 54-55 F 3
Camaipi o BR 62-63 J 5
Camaiú, Rio ~ BR 66-67 H 5
Camalote o C 54-55 G 4
Camamu o BR 72-73 L 2
Camana o PE 70-71 A 5
Camanābād o IR 134-135 H 1
Camanaú, Rio ~ BR 62-63 D 6
Čaman Bīd o IR 136-137 E 6
Camandog Island ⌒ RP 160-161 F 7
Čaman Soltān o IR 134-135 C 2
Camapuã o BR 70-71 K 6
Camaquã o BR 74-75 E 8
Camará o BR (AMA) 66-67 F 4
Camará o BR (P) 66-67 K 4
Camaragibe o BR 68-69 L 6
Camaraipi, Rio ~ BR 68-69 C 3
Camararé, Rio ~ BR 70-71 H 3
Camarata o YV 60-61 K 5
Camargo o MEX 50-51 K 4
Camargo o USA (OK) 264-265 E 2
Camaron o BOL 76-77 E 1
Camarón, Cabo ▲ HN 54-55 C 7
Camarones o RA 80 H 2
Camarones, Bahía ≈ 80 H 2
Camarones, Río ~ RCH 70-71 C 6
Camaruã o BR 66-67 E 5
Camarvik Creek ~ CDN 30-31 Z 3
Camas o USA (MT) 250-251 E 4
Camas o USA (WA) 244-245 C 5
Camas Valley o USA (OR) 244-245 B 7
Camata, Río ~ BOL 70-71 C 4
Camatambo o ANG 216-217 C 3
Cà Mau o VN 158-159 H 6
Camaxilo o ANG 216-217 E 4
Camba o RI 164-165 F 6
Čamba ~ RUS 116-117 L 5
Cambahee River ~ USA (SC) 284-285 K 4
Cambaju o GNB 202-203 C 3
Camballin o AUS 172-173 G 4
Cambândua o ANG 216-217 D 6
Cambange o ANG 216-217 F 4
Cambao o CO 60-61 D 5
Cambará do Sul o BR 74-75 E 7
Cambaxi o ANG 216-217 E 4
Cambellford o CDN (ONT) 238-239 H 4
Cambo ~ ANG 216-217 D 4
Cambodia = Kâmpŭchéa ■ K 158-159 G 4
Camboeiro, Riachão do ~ BR 68-69 F 7
Cambombo o ANG 216-217 C 5
Camboon P.O. o AUS 178-179 L 3
Camboriú, Ponta ▲ BR 74-75 G 5
Camborne o CDN (BC) 230-231 M 3
Cambrai o• F 90-91 J 6
Cambria o USA (CA) 248-249 C 4
Cambrian Mountains ▲ GB 90-91 F 5
Cambridge o CDN (NS) 240-241 N 4
Cambridge o CDN (ONT) 238-239 E 5
Cambridge o•• GB 90-91 H 5
Cambridge o JA 54-55 G 5
Cambridge o NZ 182 E 2
Cambridge o USA (ID) 252-253 B 2
Cambridge o USA (IL) 274-275 H 3
Cambridge o USA (MA) 278-279 K 6
Cambridge o USA (MD) 280-281 K 5
Cambridge o USA (MN) 270-271 E 5
Cambridge o USA (NE) 262-263 F 4
Cambridge o USA (OH) 280-281 E 3
Cambridge Bay ≈ 24-25 T 6
Cambridge Bay o CDN 24-25 U 6
Cambridge City o USA (IN) 274-275 N 5
Cambridge Gulf ≈ 172-173 J 3
Cambridge Junction o USA (MI) 272-273 E 5
Cambridge Point ▲ CDN 24-25 g 3
Cambridge Springs o USA (PA) 280-281 F 2
Cambrils o E 98-99 H 4
Cambu, Rio ~ BR 62-63 K 6
Cambuí o BR 72-73 G 7
Cambulo o ANG 216-217 F 3
Camburinga ☓ AUS 174-175 D 3
Cambutal o PA 52-53 D 8
Camden o USA (AL) 284-285 C 5
Camden o USA (AR) 276-277 C 7
Camden o USA (ME) 278-279 M 4
Camden o USA (MS) 268-269 L 4
Camden o USA (NC) 282-283 L 4
Camden o USA (NJ) 280-281 L 4
Camden o USA (NY) 278-279 F 5
Camden o USA (OH) 280-281 B 4
Camden o USA (TN) 276-277 G 4
Camden o• USA (SC) 284-285 K 2
Camden Bay ≈ 20-21 S 1
Camdenton o USA (MO) 274-275 F 6
Cameia, Parque Nacional da ⊥ ANG 216-217 F 5
Camel Back Mountain ▲ CDN (NB) 240-241 J 3
Camel Creek o AUS 174-175 H 6
Çameli o TR 128-129 C 4
Camel Race Course • KSA 130-131 K 5
Camelsfoot Range ▲ CDN (BC) 230-231 G 2
Cameo o CDN (SAS) 232-233 M 2
Cameron o USA (AZ) 256-257 D 3
Cameron o USA (LA) 268-269 G 7
Cameron o USA (MO) 274-275 D 5
Cameron o USA (SC) 284-285 K 3
Cameron o USA (TX) 266-267 L 3
Cameron Corner • AUS 178-179 F 5
Cameron Island ⌒ CDN 24-25 U 2
Cameron River ~ CDN 30-31 N 4
Cameroon = Cameroun ■ CAM 204-205 J 6
Cameroon, Mount = Mont Cameroun ▲•• CAM 204-205 H 6
Cameroun, Estuaire du ≈ 210-211 B 2
Cameroun, Mont = Mount Cameroon ▲•• CAM 204-205 H 6
Cametá o BR 68-69 D 3
Camfield o AUS 172-173 K 4
Camiaco o BOL 70-71 E 4
Camiguin Island ⌒ RP (CAG) 160-161 D 3
Camiguin Island ⌒ RP (MSO) 160-161 F 8
Camiling o RP 160-161 D 5
Camilla o USA (GA) 284-285 F 5
Camiña o RCH 70-71 C 6
Caming o RI 164-165 G 6
Caminha o P 98-99 C 4
Camino de Santiago ••• E 98-99 D 3
Caminos, Dos o YV 60-61 J 3
Camisea o PE 64-65 F 7
Camissombo o ANG 216-217 F 4
Čamkani o AFG 138-139 B 3
Çamlıdere ☆ TR 128-129 E 2
Cammarata, Monte ▲ I 100-101 D 6
Cammoo Caves • AUS 178-179 L 2
Camocim o BR 68-69 H 3
Camocim de São Felix o BR 68-69 L 6
Camogton o RP 160-161 E 6
Camongua o ANG 216-217 D 5
Camooweal o AUS 174-175 E 6
Camooweal Caves National Park ⊥ AUS 174-175 E 6
Camopi o F 62-63 H 4
Camopi ~ F 62-63 H 4
Camorta Island ⌒ IND 140-141 L 5
Camotes Islands ⌒ RP 160-161 F 7
Camotes Sea ≈ 160-161 F 7
Čamp, ostrov ⌒ RUS 84-85 e 2
Campamento o HN 52-53 L 4
Campamento Río Grande o YV 60-61 L 3
Campana, Cerro la ▲ RCH 80 D 5
Campana, Isla ⌒ RCH 80 C 4
Campana, Monte ▲ RA 80 H 7
Campana, Parque Nacional la ⊥ RCH 78-79 D 2
Campanario o BR 72-73 K 5
Campanario, Cerro ▲ RA 78-79 D 3
Campanas o RA 76-77 D 5
Campania ◘ I 100-101 E 4
Campania Island ⌒ CDN (BC) 228-229 E 3
Campanilla o PE 64-65 D 5
Campanquiz, Cerros ▲ PE 64-65 D 4
Campaspe o AUS 174-175 J 7
Campbell o USA (AL) 284-285 C 5
Campbell o USA (MO) 276-277 E 4
Campbell o USA (NE) 262-263 H 4
Campbell o ZA 220-221 F 4
Campbell, Cape ▲ NZ 182 E 4
Campbell Bay ≈ 24-25 U 6
Campbell Hill ▲ USA (OH) 280-281 C 3
Campbell Island ⌒ CDN 24-25 G 6
Campbell Lake o CDN (NWT) 20-21 Y 2
Campbell Lake o CDN (NWT) 30-31 Q 4
Campbell Plateau ≃ 13 H 7
Campbell River o CDN (BC) 230-231 D 3
Campbell's Bay o CDN (QUE) 238-239 J 3
Campbellsville o USA (KY) 276-277 K 3
Campbellton o CDN (NB) 240-241 J 3
Campbellton o CDN (PEI) 240-241 L 4
Campbellton o USA (FL) 286-287 D 1
Campbellton o USA (TX) 266-267 J 5
Campbell Town o AUS 180-181 J 6
Campbeltown o GB 90-91 E 4
Camp Century o GRØ 26-27 U 5
Camp Crook o USA (SD) 260-261 C 1
Campeana o GNB 202-203 C 4
Campeche ◘ MEX 52-53 J 2
Campeche ☆• MEX 52-53 J 2
Campeche, Bahía de ≈ 52-53 G 2
Campechuela o C 54-55 G 4
Camper o CDN (MAN) 234-235 E 3
Camperdown o AUS 180-181 G 5
Camperdown o ZA 220-221 K 4
Camperville o CDN (MAN) 234-235 C 3
Camp Gagetown xx CDN (NB) 240-241 J 5
Căm Phả ☆ VN 156-157 E 6
Camp Hill o USA (AL) 284-285 E 4
Campidano ⌣ I 100-101 B 5
Campillos o E 98-99 E 6
Campín, El o CO 60-61 F 5
Campina o BR 66-67 J 5
Campina da Lagoa o BR 74-75 D 5
Campina do Simão o BR 74-75 E 5
Campina Grande o BR 68-69 L 5
Campinas o BR (BAH) 72-73 J 2
Campinas o BR (PAU) 72-73 G 7
Campinas, Área Indígena ☓ BR 64-65 F 5
Campina Verde o BR 72-73 F 5
Camping Island ⌒ CDN 24-25 P 6
Campinho o BR (BAH) 72-73 J 2
Campinho o BR (BAH) 72-73 L 2
Camp Lloyd o GRØ 28-29 P 3
Camplong o RI 166-167 B 7
Campo o• CAM 210-211 B 2
Campo o MOC 218-219 J 3
Campo o USA (CA) 248-249 H 7
Campo o USA (CO) 254-255 N 6
Campo, El o USA (TX) 266-267 L 4
Campo, Réserve de = Campo Reserve ⊥ CAM 210-211 B 2
Campo Alegre o BR (ALA) 68-69 K 6
Campo Alegre o BR (PIA) 68-69 H 6
Campo Alegre o BR (TOC) 68-69 D 5
Campoalegre o CO 60-61 D 6
Campo Alegre o YV 60-61 K 3
Campo Alegre de Goiás o BR 72-73 G 4
Campo Alegre de Lourdes o BR 68-69 G 6
Campobasso ☆ I 100-101 E 4
Campo Belo o BR 72-73 H 6
Campo Bernal o YV 60-61 E 3
Campo Camalajue o MEX 50-51 B 3
Campo de Carabobo, Parque • YV 60-61 G 2
Campo de Talampaya • RA 76-77 D 5
Campo do Padre, Morro ▲ BR 74-75 F 6
Campo Erê o BR 74-75 D 6
Campo Esperanza o PY 76-77 H 2
Campo Gallo o RA 76-77 F 4
Campo Garay o RA 76-77 G 5
Campo Grande ☆ BR 70-71 K 7
Campo Grande o RA 76-77 K 4
Campo Grande, Cachoeira ~ BR 70-71 F 2
Campo Grayling Artillery Range xx USA (MI) 272-273 E 3
Campo Largo o BR 74-75 F 5
Campo Maior o BR 68-69 G 4
Campo Maior o P 98-99 D 5
Campomento o PY 76-77 H 1
Campo Mourão o BR 74-75 D 5
Campo Novo do Parecis o BR 70-71 J 3
Campo Nuevo o MEX 50-51 B 3
Campo Reserve = Réserve de Campo ⊥ CAM 210-211 B 2
Campos o BR 72-73 K 6
Campos ⩡ BR 68-69 G 7
Campos, Laguna o PY 70-71 G 7
Campos, Tierra de ▲ E 98-99 E 4
Campos Belos o BR 72-73 G 2
Campos do Jordão o BR 72-73 H 7
Campos dos Parecis ⩡ BR 70-71 H 3
Campo Seco o BR 76-77 K 6
Campos Eliseos o BR 72-73 D 6
Campo Serio o PE 64-65 E 2
Campos Gerais o BR 72-73 H 6
Campos Novos o BR 74-75 E 6
Campos Sales o BR 68-69 H 5
Camp Peary xx USA (VA) 280-281 K 6
Camp Pendleton Marine Corps Base • USA (CA) 248-249 G 6
Camp Point o USA (IL) 274-275 G 4
Camp Ripley Military Reservation xx USA (MN) 270-271 D 4
Camp Roberts Military Reservation xx USA (CA) 248-249 D 4
Camp Scenic o USA (TX) 266-267 H 3
Camp Sherman o USA (OR) 244-245 D 6
Campti o USA (LA) 268-269 G 5
Camp Verde o USA (AZ) 256-257 D 4
Camp Wood o USA (TX) 266-267 H 4
Cam Ranh o VN 158-159 K 5
Camrose o CDN (ALB) 232-233 F 2
Camsell Bay o CDN 28-29 F 3
Camsell Lake o CDN 30-31 Q 4
Camú, Río ~ DOM 54-55 K 5
Camucio o ANG 216-217 B 7
Camulemba, Capenda- o ANG 216-217 E 4
Camuy o USA (PR) 286-287 P 2
Camuya, Rio ~ CO 64-65 F 1
Čamzinka o RUS 96-97 D 6
Čamzinka o RUS 96-97 D 6
Can ☆ TR 128-129 B 2
Cana o BOL 70-71 C 7
Caña, La o CO 60-61 C 3
Canaã o BR 68-69 F 5
Canaã, Rio ~ BR 70-71 F 2
Canaan o USA (NH) 278-279 J 5
Canaan River ~ CDN (NB) 240-241 K 4
Canaan Station o CDN (NB) 240-241 K 4
Canabal o E 98-99 D 3
Cana-Brava o BR 72-73 H 4
Cana Brava, Rio ~ BR 72-73 F 2
Cana-Brava, Serra da ▲ BR 72-73 K 4
Canadá o BR 68-69 F 2
Canada ■ CDN 38-39 D 3
Cañada, La o RA (COD) 76-77 F 6
Cañada, La o RA (SAE) 76-77 F 4
Canada Basin ≃ 16 B 33
Canada Bay ≈ 38-39 Q 3
Canada Bay ≈ CDN 242-243 M 2
Cañada de Gómez o RA 78-79 J 2
Cañada de Luque o RA 76-77 F 6
Canada Harbour o CDN (NFL) 242-243 M 2
Canada Lake o USA (NY) 278-279 G 5
Cañada Rosquín o RA 78-79 J 2
Cañada Seca o RA 78-79 H 3
Canadian o USA (TX) 264-265 D 3
Canadian-Pacific-Railway II CDN 232-233 K 3
Canadian River ~ USA (NM) 256-257 M 3
Canadian River ~ USA (OK) 264-265 J 3
Canadian River ~ USA (TX) 264-265 D 3
Cañadón El Pluma ~ RA 80 F 3
Cañadón Lagarto o RA 80 F 2
Cañadón Sacho ~ RA 80 E 2
Cañadón Seco ~ RA 80 E 2
Canadys o USA (SC) 284-285 K 3
Canagu, Río ~ YV 60-61 F 3
Canaima o YV 60-61 K 4
Canaima, Parque Nacional ⊥ YV 60-61 K 5
Çanakkale ☆• TR 128-129 B 2
Çanakkale Boğazı ≈ 128-129 B 2
Canal de Tūnis ≃ 100-101 C 6
Canale di Sicilia ≃ 100-101 C 6
Canal Flats o CDN (BC) 230-231 O 3
Canalí o MEX 52-53 E 1
Canal P.O. o AUS 178-179 K 3
Canals o RA 78-79 H 2
Canal Winchester o USA (OH) 280-281 D 4
Canamã, Rio ~ BR 70-71 H 2
Cananari, Rio ~ CO 66-67 B 2
Canandaigua o USA (NY) 278-279 D 6
Cananea o MEX 50-51 D 2
Cananéia o BR 74-75 G 5
Canar o EC 64-65 C 3
Canarana o BR (BAH) 68-69 H 7
Canarana o BR (MAT) 72-73 D 2
Canárias, Ilha das ⌒ BR 68-69 H 3
Canarreos, Archipiélago de los ⌒ C 54-55 D 4
Canary o AUS 178-179 F 2
Canary Islands = Canarias, Islas ⌒ E 188-189 C 6
Cañas o MEX 52-53 D 2
Cañas, Bahía las ≈ 78-79 C 3
Cañas, Las o CR 52-53 B 6
Cañas, Playa las o C 54-55 D 3
Cañas, Río ~ RA 76-77 E 2
Cañasgordas o CO 60-61 C 4
Canastra, Rio ~ BR 68-69 D 7
Canastra, Serra da ▲ BR 68-69 J 7
Canastra, Serra da ▲ BR 72-73 G 6
Canatián o MEX 50-51 G 5
Canatiba o BR 72-73 J 2
Canaveral o EC 64-65 B 3
Canaveral, Cape ▲ USA (FL) 286-287 J 3
Canaveral National Seashore ⊥ USA (FL) 286-287 J 3
Cañaveras o E 98-99 F 4
Canavieiras o BR 72-73 L 3
Canayan o RP 160-161 E 8
Cañazas o PA (Pan) 52-53 E 7
Cañazas o PA (Ver) 52-53 D 7
Canberra ★• AUS 180-181 K 3
Canberra Space Centre • AUS 180-181 K 3
Canby o USA (CA) 246-247 E 2
Canby o USA (MN) 270-271 B 6
Canby o USA (OR) 244-245 C 5
Cancela o BR 68-69 G 3
Cancelão o BR 74-75 D 8
Canchayllo o PE 64-65 E 7
Canchungo o GNB 202-203 B 3
Canconga o ANG 216-217 E 6
Cancosa o RCH 70-71 C 6
Cancuc o MEX 52-53 H 3
Cancuén ∴• GCA 52-53 J 3
Cancún o• MEX 52-53 L 1
Cancún, Isla ⌒ MEX 52-53 L 1
Candarave o PE 70-71 B 5
Çandarlı Körfezi ≈ 128-129 B 3
Candeado o MOC 218-219 G 4
Candeias o BR 72-73 L 2
Candeias, Rio ~ BR 66-67 F 7
Candela o MEX 50-51 J 4
Candelaria o MEX 52-53 J 2
Candelaria o USA (TX) 266-267 C 3
Candelaria, La o CO 60-61 F 5
Candelaria, La o YV 60-61 H 2
Candelaria, Río ~ BOL 70-71 H 5
Candelaria, Río ~ MEX 52-53 J 2
Candeleda o E 98-99 E 4
Candelwood, Lake o USA (CT) 280-281 N 2
Candi • RI (LAM) 162-163 E 7
Candi • RI (RIA) 162-163 D 4
Candiac o CDN (SAS) 232-233 P 5
Candi Besakih • RI 168 B 7
Cândido de Abreu o BR 74-75 E 5
Cándido González o C 54-55 F 4
Cândido Mendes o BR 68-69 F 2
Cândido Rondon o BR 76-77 K 3
Cândido Sales o BR 72-73 K 3
Candi Mendut • RI 168 D 3
Candi Pura • RI 168 E 3
Candi Sukuh • RI 168 D 3
Candle o USA 20-21 K 4
Candle Lake o CDN (SAS) 232-233 N 2
Candle Lake o CDN (SAS) 232-233 N 2
Čandman' = Talšand o MAU 148-149 C 5
Cando o CDN (SAS) 232-233 K 3
Cando o USA (ND) 258-259 H 3
Candon o RP 160-161 D 4
Candover o ZA 220-221 K 3
Candulo o MOC 214-215 J 6
Cần Đước o VN 158-159 J 5
Cần Đước o VN 158-159 J 5
Candy Reservoir o USA (OK) 264-265 H 2
Canea o BR 62-63 G 5
Caneapo o BR 62-63 G 5
Canegrass o AUS 180-181 F 2
Cane Grove o GUY 62-63 F 2
Canela, La o C 54-55 H 4
Canela Baja o RCH 76-77 B 6
Canelo o USA (AZ) 256-257 E 7
Canelones ☆ ROU 78-79 L 3
Canelos o EC 64-65 D 2
Canelos, Los o RCH 80 E 6
Cane River o AUS 172-173 B 7
Cane River o AUS 172-173 B 7
Cañete o E 98-99 G 4
Cañete o• RCH 78-79 C 4
Cañete, Río de ~ PE 64-65 D 8
Caney o USA (KS) 262-263 L 7
Caney Fork ~ USA (TN) 276-277 K 5
Caney River ~ USA (KS) 262-263 K 7
Caney River ~ USA (OK) 264-265 J 2
Caneyville o USA (KY) 276-277 J 3
Canford o CDN (BC) 230-231 J 3
Čangada ~ RUS 108-109 c 7
Cangaime, Río ~ EC 64-65 D 3
Cangala o ANG 216-217 D 6
Cangallo o PE 64-65 E 8
Cangalo o ANG 216-217 D 5
Cangandala o ANG 216-217 D 4
Cangandala, Parque Nacional de ⊥ ANG 216-217 D 4
Cangas o E 98-99 C 3
Cangas del Narcea o E 98-99 D 3
Cangjie Temple • VRC 154-155 F 4
Cangoa o ANG 216-217 E 6
Cango Caves • ZA 220-221 E 6
Cangombe o ANG 216-217 F 7
Cangrejo, Cerro ▲ RA 80 D 4
Cangshan o VRC 154-155 L 4
Canguaretama o BR 68-69 L 5
Canguçu o BR 74-75 D 8
Čangūle, Rūdḫāne-ye ~ IRQ 128-129 M 6
Cangumbe o ANG 216-217 E 5
Cangxi o VRC 154-155 D 6
Cangyanshan • VRC 154-155 J 3
Cangyuan o VRC 142-143 L 4
Cangzhou o VRC 154-155 K 2
Can Hasan Höyüğü ∴• TR 128-129 E 4
Canhotinho o BR 68-69 K 6
Caniapiscau, Lac o CDN 36-37 P 7
Caniapiscau, Réservoir de < CDN 36-37 P 7
Caniapiscau, Rivière ~ CDN 36-37 P 7
Canicattì o I 100-101 D 6
Canigao Channel ≈ 160-161 F 7
Canik Dağları ▲ TR 128-129 G 2
Canim Lake o CDN (BC) 230-231 J 2
Canim Lake o CDN (BC) 230-231 J 2
Canindé o BR 68-69 J 4
Canindé, Rio ~ BR 68-69 G 5
Caninde de São Francisco o BR 68-69 K 6
Canipo Island ⌒ RP 160-161 D 7
Canisteo o USA (NY) 278-279 D 6
Canisteo River ~ USA (NY) 278-279 D 6
Canister Fall ~ GUY 62-63 E 3
Canit Point ▲ RP 160-161 E 6
Canjime o ANG 216-217 E 8
Çankırı ☆• TR 128-129 E 2
Cankuzo o BU 212-213 C 5
Canlaon, Mount ▲ RP 160-161 E 7
Canmang o VRC 156-157 G 2
Canmore o CDN (ALB) 232-233 C 4
Cann, Mount ▲ AUS 180-181 K 4
Cannac Island ⌒ PNG 183 G 5
Cannanore o• IND 140-141 F 5
Cannanore Islands ⌒ IND 140-141 E 5
Cannelton o USA (IN) 274-275 M 7
Cannes o• F 90-91 L 10
Canning Hill ▲ AUS 176-177 D 4
Canning River ~ USA 20-21 R 2
Canning Stock Route II AUS 172-173 G 7
Cannon Ball o USA (ND) 258-259 G 5
Cannonball River ~ USA (ND) 258-259 F 5
Cannon Beach o USA (OR) 244-245 B 5
Cannondale Mount ▲ AUS 178-179 K 3
Cannon Falls o USA (MN) 270-271 F 6
Cannonville o USA (UT) 254-255 C 6
Cann River o AUS (VIC) 180-181 K 4
Cann River ~ AUS 180-181 K 4
Caño, El o PA 52-53 D 7
Caño, Isla de ⌒ CR 52-53 C 7
Cano, Pico do ▲ CV 202-203 B 6
Canoa o HN 52-53 K 4
Canoas o BR 74-75 E 7
Canoas o MEX 50-51 K 6
Canoas, Punta ▲ MEX 50-51 B 3
Canobie o AUS 174-175 F 6
Canobolas, Mount ▲ AUS 180-181 K 2
Canochee River ~ USA (GA) 284-285 J 4
Canoe o CDN (BC) 230-231 K 3
Canoe Creek Indian Reserve ☓ CDN (BC) 230-231 G 2
Canoe Lake o CDN 32-33 Q 4
Canoe Reach ~ CDN (BC) 228-229 Q 4
Canoe River o CDN (BC) 228-229 P 4
Canoe River ~ CDN (BC) 228-229 P 4
Caño Hondo, Cuevas de ∴• DOM 54-55 L 5
Canoinhas o BR 74-75 E 6
Cañon • DZ 190-191 F 3
Canonaco, Río ~ EC 64-65 D 2
Canonba o AUS 178-179 J 6
Cañoncito Indian Reservation ☓ USA (NM) 256-257 H 3
Canon City o USA (CO) 254-255 K 5
Cañon del Sumidero, Parque Nacional ⊥ MEX 52-53 H 3
Cañon de Río Blanco, Parque Nacional ⊥ MEX 52-53 F 2
Cañon Fiord ≈ 26-27 J 3
Cañon Plaza o USA (NM) 256-257 J 2
Canonsburg o USA (PA) 280-281 F 3
Canoochee o USA (GA) 284-285 H 4
Canopus o CDN (SAS) 232-233 M 6
Canora o CDN (SAS) 232-233 Q 4
Canosa di Púglia o• I 100-101 F 4
Canouan Island ⌒ WV 56 E 5
Canowindra o AUS 180-181 K 2
Canquel, Meseta del ⩡ RA 80 F 2
Canrober Hills ▲ CDN 24-25 N 2
Canso o CDN (NS) 240-241 O 5
Canso, Strait of ≈ 38-39 O 6
Canso, Strait of ≈ CDN 240-241 O 5
Canso Channel ≈ 28-29 J 3
Canta o PE 64-65 D 7
Cantabria ◘ E 98-99 E 3
Cantábrica, Cordillera ▲ E 98-99 D 3
Cantador, Cerro el ▲ MEX 52-53 C 2
Cantagalo, Ponta ▲ BR 74-75 F 6
Cantalejo o E 98-99 F 4
Cantalpino o E 98-99 E 4
Čantal'skij hrebet ▲ RUS 112-113 T 3
Čantalvèrgyrgyn ~ RUS 112-113 U 3
Cantamar o MEX 50-51 A 1
Cantanal, Sierra de ▲ RA 76-77 D 6
Cantário, Rio ~ BR 70-71 F 2
Cantaura o YV 60-61 J 3
Canterbury o•• GB 90-91 H 6
Canterbury Bight ≈ 182 D 5
Cần Thơ' o• VN 158-159 H 5
Canthyuaya, Cerros de ▲ PE 64-65 E 5
Cantil o USA (CA) 248-249 G 4
Cantilan o RP 160-161 F 8
Cantiles, Cayo ⌒ C 54-55 D 4
Canto del Agua o RCH 76-77 B 5
Canto do Buriti o BR 68-69 G 6
Canton o USA (GA) 284-285 F 2
Canton o USA (IL) 274-275 J 4
Canton o USA (MO) 274-275 G 4
Canton o USA (MS) 268-269 K 4
Canton o USA (NC) 282-283 E 5
Canton o USA (NY) 278-279 F 4
Canton o USA (OK) 264-265 F 2
Canton o USA (PA) 280-281 K 2
Canton o USA (SD) 260-261 K 3
Canton o USA (TX) 264-265 J 6
Canton o• USA (OH) 280-281 E 3
Canton, El o YV 60-61 F 4
Canton = Guangzhou ☆•• VRC 156-157 H 5
Canton Lake o USA (OK) 264-265 F 2
Cantuar o CDN (SAS) 232-233 K 5
Cantwell o USA 20-21 Q 5
Canudos o BR 68-69 J 6
Cañuelas o RA 78-79 K 3
Canumã, Rio ~ BR 66-67 H 5
Canunda National Park ⊥ AUS 180-181 F 4
Canutama o BR 66-67 E 6
Canutillo o USA (TX) 266-267 A 2
Canwood o CDN (SAS) 232-233 M 2
Canxixe o MOC 218-219 H 3
Čany ☆ RUS 114-115 O 7
Čany, ozero o RUS 124-125 K 1
Canyon o CDN (ONT) 234-235 K 5
Canyon o CDN (ONT) 236-237 D 5
Canyon ⩡•• RI 166-167 K 4
Canyon o USA (TX) 264-265 C 4
Canyon o USA (WY) 252-253 H 2
Canyon Creek o USA (MT) 250-251 G 5
Canyon de Chelly National Monument ∴• USA (AZ) 256-257 F 2
Canyon Ferry o USA (MT) 250-251 H 5
Canyon Ferry Lake o USA (MT) 250-251 H 5
Canyon Lake o USA (TX) 266-267 J 4
Canyonlands National Park ⊥ USA (UT) 254-255 F 5
Canyon Largo River ~ USA (NM) 256-257 H 2
Canyon Ranges ▲ CDN 30-31 G 4
Canyon River ~ CDN 36-37 G 2
Canyonville o USA (OR) 244-245 B 8
Canzar o ANG 216-217 F 3
Cao Bằng ☆• VN 156-157 E 5
Caohekou o VRC 150-151 D 7
Caojian o VRC 142-143 L 3
Cao Lãnh o VN 158-159 H 5
Caombo o ANG 216-217 D 4
Caonao ~ C 54-55 F 4
Caoqiao o VRC 154-155 L 6
Cáorle o I 100-101 D 2
Cao Xian o VRC 154-155 J 4
Čapa ~ RUS 116-117 F 5
Capachica o PE 70-71 C 4
Čapaev = Čapaevo ☆ KA 96-97 G 8
Čapaevka ~ RUS 96-97 G 7
Čapaevo ☆ KA 96-97 G 8
Čapaevo o RUS 118-119 H 5
Čapaevskoe o KA 124-125 H 2
Capahuari, Río ~ EC 64-65 D 3
Capaias o RP 160-161 C 7
Capalonga o RP 160-161 E 5
Capalulu o RI 164-165 J 4
Capana o BR 66-67 C 3
Capana, Punta ▲ YV 60-61 F 2
Capanema o BR 68-69 E 2
Capão Alto o BR 74-75 E 6
Capão Bonito o BR 72-73 F 7
Capão Branco o BR 74-75 D 7
Capão da Canoa o BR 74-75 E 7
Capão Doce, Morro do ▲ BR 74-75 E 6
Caparaó, Parque Nacional do ⊥ BR 72-73 K 6
Čaparhār o AFG 138-139 C 2
Capas o RP 160-161 D 5
Capauari, Rio ~ BR 66-67 C 3
Capauari, Serra do ▲ BR 66-67 C 3
Cap-aux-Meules o CDN (QUE) 242-243 G 5
Capay o RP 160-161 E 6
Capbreton o F 90-91 G 10
Cap-Chat o CDN (QUE) 242-243 B 3
Cap-de-la-Madeleine o CDN (QUE) 238-239 N 2

Calandula — Cap-de-la-Madeleine 311

Cap-de-Rabast ○ CDN (QUE) 242-243 D 3
Cap-d'Espoir ○ CDN (QUE) 240-241 L 2
Cape Abyssal Plain ≃ 6-7 L 12
Cape Adare ▲ ARK 16 F 18
Cape Alexander ▲ SOL 184 I c 2
Cape Anguille ○ CDN (NFL) 242-243 J 5
Cape Arid National Park ⊥ AUS 176-177 G 6
Cape Basin ≃ ZA 6-7 K 12
Cape Bertholet Wildlife Sanctuary ⊥ AUS 172-173 F 4
Cape Borda ○ AUS 180-181 D 3
Cape Breton Highlands National Park ⊥ CDN (NS) 240-241 O 4
Cape Breton Island ⌒ CDN (NS) 240-241 P 4
Cape Bryd ▲ ARK 16 G 8
Cape Canaveral ○ USA (FL) 286-287 J 3
Cape Canaveral Air Force Station xx USA (FL) 286-287 J 3
Cape Charles ○ USA (VA) 280-281 K 6
Cape Chidley Islands ⌒ CDN 36-37 R 4
Cape Coast ☆• GH 202-203 K 7
Cape Cod Bay ≈ 46-47 N 5
Cape Cod Bay ≈ USA 278-279 L 7
Cape Cod Peninsula ⊥ USA (MA) 278-279 M 7
Cape Colbeck ▲ ARK 16 F 21
Cape Coral ○ USA (FL) 286-287 H 5
Cape Crawford ○ AUS 174-175 C 5
Cape Croker ○ CDN (ONT) 238-239 D 4
Cape Croker Indian Reserve ✗ CDN (ONT) 238-239 E 4
Cape Dart ▲ ARK 16 F 24
Cape Dorset ○ CDN 36-37 L 2
Cape Elizabeth ○ USA (ME) 278-279 L 5
Cape Fear River ∼ USA (NC) 282-283 J 6
Cape Fear River ∼ USA (NC) 282-283 J 5
Cape Flying Fish ▲ ARK 16 F 26
Cape Freshfield ▲ ARK 16 G 16
Cape Gantheaume Conservation Park ⊥ AUS 180-181 D 4
Cape George ○ CDN (NS) 240-241 O 5
Cape Girardeau ○ USA (MO) 276-277 F 3
Cape Girgir ▲ PNG 183 C 2
Cape Hope Islands ⌒ CDN 38-39 E 2
Cape Horn ○ USA (ID) 252-253 C 2
Cape Horn = Hornos, Cabo de ▲ RCH 80 G 8
Cape Island ⌒ USA (SC) 284-285 L 3
Cape Jeruis ○ AUS 180-181 E 3
Cape Krusenstern National Monument ⊥ USA 20-21 H 3
Capel ○ AUS 176-177 C 6
Capel, Cape ▲ CDN 24-25 X 3
Capela do Mato Verde ○ BR 72-73 H 4
Cape Le Grand National Park ⊥ AUS 176-177 G 6
Capelinha ○ BR 72-73 J 4
Capel'ka ○ RUS 94-95 L 2
Capella ○ AUS 178-179 K 2
Capelle, la ○ F 90-91 J 7
Cape Lookout National Seashore ⊥ USA (NC) 282-283 L 6
Cape May ○ USA (NJ) 280-281 M 5
Capembe ∼ ANG 216-217 F 8
Cape Melville National Park ⊥ AUS 174-175 H 4
Cape Monze = Rās Muari ▲ PK 134-135 M 6
Cape Moore ▲ ARK 16 F 17
Capenda-Camulemba ○ ANG 216-217 E 4
Cape of Good Hope ▲• ZA 220-221 D 7
Cape of Good Hope = Kaap die Goeie Hoop ▲• ZA 220-221 D 7
Cape Palmer ▲ ARK 16 F 27
Cape Parry ○ CDN 24-25 K 5
Cape-Pele ○ CDN (NB) 240-241 L 4
Cape Peninsula ⊥ ZA 220-221 D 7
Cape Pole ○ USA 32-33 D 3
Cape Race ○ CDN (NFL) 242-243 P 6
Cape Rama ○ IND 140-141 E 3
Cape Range ▲ AUS 172-173 A 7
Cape Range National Park ⊥ AUS 172-173 A 7
Cape Ray ○ CDN (NFL) 242-243 J 5
Cape River ∼ AUS 174-175 H 7
Cape Romain National Wildlife Refuge ⊥ USA (SC) 284-285 L 4
Cape Sable Island ⌒ CDN (NS) 240-241 K 7
Cape Saint Francis ▲ CDN (NFL) 242-243 Q 5
Cape Saint Francis ○ ZA 220-221 G 7
Cape Saint John ▲ CDN (NFL) 242-243 N 2
Cape Scott Provincial Park ⊥ CDN (BC) 230-231 A 3
Čāpešlū ○ IR 136-137 F 6
Cape Smiley ▲ ARK 16 F 29
Capesterre-Belle-Eau ○ F 56 E 3
Cape Surville ▲ SOL 184 I f 4
Cape Tormentine ○ CDN (NB) 240-241 M 4
Cape Town ☆•• ZA 220-221 D 6
Cape Town = Cape Town = Kaapstad ☆•• ZA 220-221 D 7
Cape Tribulation National Park ⊥ AUS 174-175 H 5
Cape Upstart National Park ⊥ AUS 174-175 J 6
Cape Verde = Cabo Verde ■ CV 202-203 B 6
Cape Verde Islands = Cabo Verde, Arquipélago de ⌒ CV 202-203 B 6
Cape Verde Plateau ≃ 6-7 G 7
Cape Vincent ○ USA (NY) 278-279 E 4
Cape Washington ▲ FJI 184 III a 3
Cape York Peninsula ⊥ AUS 174-175 G 3
Cape Young ○ CDN 24-25 O 6
Cape Zele'e = Nialaha'u Point ▲ SOL 184 I e 3
Cap-Haïtien ☆ RH 54-55 J 5
Capiá, Rio ∼ BR 68-69 K 6
Capibaribe, Rio ∼ BR 68-69 L 5
Capilla del Monte ○ RA 76-77 E 6
Capim, Rio ∼ BR 62-63 K 6
Capim Grosso ○ BR 68-69 H 7
Capinópolis ○ BR 72-73 F 5
Capinzal ○ BR 74-75 E 6
Capirenda ○ BOL 76-77 F 1
Cap Island ⌒ RP 160-161 D 10
Capissayan ○ RP 160-161 D 3
Capistrano ○ BR 68-69 J 4
Capitachouane, Rivière ∼ CDN (QUE) 236-237 M 5
Capitan ○ USA (NM) 256-257 K 5
Capitán Aracena, Isla ⌒ RCH 80 E 7
Capitán Baldo ○ PY 76-77 K 2
Capitan Grande Indian Reservation ✗ USA (CA) 248-249 H 7
Capitán Pablo Lagerenza ☆ PY 70-71 G 6
Capitán Porto Alegro ○ BR 76-77 K 5
Capitán Sarmiente ○ RA 78-79 K 3
Capitán Ustares, Cerro ▲ BOL 70-71 G 6
Capitão, Igarapé ∼ BR 66-67 E 6
Capitão Cardoso, Rio ∼ BR 70-71 G 2
Capitão de Campos ○ BR 68-69 H 4
Capitão Enéas ○ BR 72-73 J 4
Capitão Leônidas Marques ○ BR 74-75 D 5
Capitão Poço ○ BR 68-69 E 2
Capitán Rivadenaira ○ EC 64-65 E 2
Capitol ○ USA (MT) 250-251 P 6
Capitol Peak ▲ USA (CO) 254-255 H 4
Capitol Peak ▲ USA (NV) 246-247 H 2
Capitol Reef National Park ⊥ USA (UT) 254-255 D 5
Capivara, Represa < BR 72-73 E 7
Capivara, Rio ∼ BR 68-69 D 6
Capivaras, Cachoeira das ∼ BR 66-67 K 6
Capivaras, Salto das ∼ BR 70-71 K 3
Capivari ○ BR 72-73 G 7
Capivari, Rio ∼ BR 70-71 J 6
Capixaba ○ BR 68-69 G 7
Čaplanovo ○ RUS 122-123 K 5
Čaplino ○ RUS 112-113 Y 4
Čaplino, Novoe ○ RUS 112-113 Y 4
Čapljina ○ BIH 100-101 F 3
Čaplygin ○ RUS 94-95 Q 5
Čaplynka ○ UA 102-103 H 4
Cap Marcos, Área Indígena ✗ BR 70-71 H 4
Cap Mountain ▲ CDN 30-31 H 4
Capoche ∼ MOC 218-219 G 2
Capoeira do Rei ○ BR 62-63 J 5
Capolo ○ ANG 216-217 B 5
Čapoma ∼ RUS 88-89 P 3
Caponda ○ MOC 218-219 F 2
Čapo-Ologo ○ RUS 118-119 J 7
Capo Rizzuto ○ I 100-101 F 5
Capot Blanc, Lac ○ CDN 30-31 O 4
Capoto, Área Indígena ✗ BR 68-69 B 6
Capotoah, Mount ▲ RP 160-161 F 6
Cappadocia = Capadocia ⊥ TR 128-129 F 3
Cappahayden ○ CDN (NFL) 242-243 Q 6
Capps ○ USA (FL) 286-287 F 1
Caprája, Ísola di ⌒ I 100-101 B 3
Capreol ○ CDN (ONT) 238-239 E 2
Capri, Ísola di ⌒• I 100-101 E 4
Capricorn, Cape ▲ AUS 178-179 L 2
Capricorn Group ⌒ AUS 178-179 L 2
Capricorn Highway II AUS 178-179 H 2
Capricorn Section ⊥ AUS 178-179 M 2
Caprivi Game Park ⊥ NAM 218-219 B 4
Caprivi Strip = Caprivistrook ⊥ NAM 218-219 B 3
Caprock ○ USA (NM) 256-257 M 5
Caprock Canyons State Park ⊥• USA (TX) 264-265 C 4
Capron ○ USA (VA) 280-281 J 7
Cap Seize ○ CDN (QUE) 242-243 B 3
Captain Cook ○ USA (HI) 288 K 5
Captains Flat ○ AUS 180-181 K 3
Captiva ○ USA (FL) 286-287 G 5
Captiva Island ⌒ USA (FL) 286-287 G 5
Capua ○ ANG 216-217 E 7
Capucapu, Rio ∼ BR 62-63 E 6
Capulin ○ USA (NM) 256-257 M 2
Capulin Mountain National Monument • USA (NM) 256-257 L 2
Capul Island ⌒ RP 160-161 F 6
Capunda ○ ANG 216-217 D 5
Cap Worn National Park ⊥ PNG 183 B 2
Čaqlāve, Čam-e ∼ IRQ 128-129 L 5
Caqua ○ YV 60-61 K 4
Caquena ○ RCH 70-71 C 6
Caquetá, Rio ∼ CO 64-65 F 2
Caqueza ○ CO 60-61 E 5
Car ∼ KA 124-125 M 4
Čara ☆ RUS (CTN) 118-119 J 7
Čara ∼ RUS 118-119 H 7
Čara ∼ RUS 118-119 K 5
Čara ∼ RUS 118-119 J 6
Carabao Island ⌒ RP 160-161 D 6
Carabaya, Cordillera de ▲ PE 70-71 B 3
Carabaya, Rio ∼ PE 70-71 C 4
Carabayllo ○ PE 64-65 D 7
Carabinani, Rio ∼ BR 66-67 G 4
Carabobo ○ YV 62-63 D 2
Caracal ○ RO 102-103 D 5
Caracal, Rio ∼ BR 68-69 E 6
Caracara, Estação Ecológica ⊥ BR 62-63 D 5
Caracarai ○ BR 62-63 D 5
Caracas ★• YV 60-61 H 2
Caracol ∴• BH 52-53 K 3
Caracol ○ BR 68-69 G 6
Caracol ○ BR 76-77 J 2
Caracol ∼ MEX 50-51 D 5
Caracoli ○ CO 60-61 E 2
Caracuja Falls ∼ CDN 30-31 F 3
Caraculo ○ ANG 216-217 B 7
Carad ○ RH 54-55 J 5
Caraguatá, Arroyo ∼ ROU 78-79 M 2
Carai ○ BR 72-73 K 4
Caraiari, Rio ∼ BR 68-69 B 4
Caraíva ○ BR 72-73 L 4
Carajas ○ BR 68-69 C 5
Carajás, Serra dos ▲ BR 68-69 C 5
Čarak, Bandar-e ○ IR 134-135 F 5
Caramat ○ CDN (ONT) 236-237 B 3
Caramelo ○ CO 60-61 D 3
Caramoan ○ RP 160-161 E 6
Caramoan Peninsula ⊥ RP 160-161 E 6
Caraná, Rio ∼ BR 70-71 H 3
Caranavi ○ BOL 70-71 D 4
Carandaí ○ BR 72-73 J 6
Carandazinho ○ BR 70-71 J 5
Carandotta ○ AUS 178-179 E 1
Carangola ○ BR 72-73 J 6
Caransebeş ○ RO 102-103 C 5
Carapa ○ YV 60-61 K 3
Carapajó ○ BR 68-69 D 3
Carapán ○ MEX 52-53 C 2
Cara-Paraná, Rio ∼ CO 64-65 F 2
Carapé, Sierra de ▲ ROU 78-79 M 3
Carapebus ○ BR 72-73 K 7
Carapo ○ YV 60-61 K 5
Caraquet ○• CDN (NB) 240-241 L 3
Carara Puca ○ BR 66-67 D 2
Carat, Tanjung ▲ RI 162-163 F 6
Caratasca, Cayo ⌒ HN 54-55 D 6
Caratasca, Laguna de ≈ 54-55 C 7
Caratateua ○ BR 68-69 E 2
Caratinga ○ BR 72-73 J 5
Carauari ○ BR 66-67 D 5
Caraúbas ○ BR 68-69 K 4
Caravaca de la Cruz ○ E 98-99 G 5
Caravela ○ GNB 202-203 B 4
Caravelas ○ BR 72-73 L 4
Caraveli ○ PE 64-65 F 9
Caravelle ⊥ F 56 E 3
Caraz ○ PE 64-65 D 6
Carazinho ○ BR (CAT) 74-75 E 7
Carazinho ○ BR (RSU) 74-75 D 7
Carballino, O ○ E 98-99 C 3
Carballo ○ E 98-99 C 3
Carberry ○ CDN (MAN) 234-235 D 5
Carbet, Chutes du ∼• F 56 E 3
Carbine ○ AUS 176-177 F 5
Carbó ○ MEX 50-51 D 3
Carbon ○ CDN (ALB) 232-233 E 4
Carbon ○ USA (TX) 264-265 F 6
Carbonado ○ USA (WA) 244-245 C 3
Carbonara, Capo ▲ I 100-101 B 5
Carbondale ○ USA (CO) 254-255 H 4
Carbondale ○ USA (IL) 276-277 F 3
Carbondale ○ USA (KS) 262-263 L 6
Carbondale ○ USA (MI) 270-271 L 5
Carbondale ○ USA (PA) 280-281 L 2
Carbonear ○ CDN (NFL) 242-243 P 5
Carbonera, La ○ MEX 50-51 L 5
Carboneras ○ E 98-99 G 6
Carbon Hill ○ USA (AL) 284-285 C 3
Carbónia ○ I 100-101 B 5
Carbonita ○ BR 72-73 J 4
Carcajou Lake ○ CDN 30-31 F 2
Carcajou River ∼ CDN 30-31 F 3
Carcar ○ RP 160-161 E 7
Carcaraña, Río ∼ RA 78-79 J 2
Carcassonne ☆•• F 90-91 J 10
Carcross ○ CDN 20-21 X 6
Čardak ☆ TR 128-129 C 4
Cardale ○ CDN (MAN) 234-235 C 4
Cardamon Hills ▲ IND 140-141 G 5
Cardamum Island ⌒ IND 140-141 E 5
Cardeña ○ E 98-99 E 5
Cárdenas ○ C 54-55 E 3
Cárdenas ○ MEX (SLP) 50-51 K 6
Cárdenas ○• MEX (TAB) 52-53 H 2
Cardenyabba Creek ∼ AUS 178-179 G 5
Cardiel, Lago ○ RA 80 E 4
Cardiff ○ GB 90-91 F 6
Cardiff Hall ⊥• JA 54-55 G 5
Cardigan ○ CDN (NS) 240-241 N 4
Cardigan ○ GB 90-91 E 5
Cardigan Bay ≈ 90-91 E 5
Cardigan Strait ≈ 24-25 a 2
Cardinal ○ CDN (MAN) 234-235 E 5
Cardona ○ E 98-99 H 4
Cardona ○ ROU 78-79 L 3
Cardón del Plata ▲ RA 78-79 E 2
Cardoso ○ BR 72-73 F 6
Cardoso, Ilha do ⌒ BR 74-75 G 5
Cardston ○ CDN (ALB) 232-233 E 6
Cardwell ○ AUS 174-175 J 6
Cardwell ○ USA (MT) 250-251 H 6
Cardwell, Cape ▲ CDN 24-25 L 5
Cardwell Range ▲ AUS 174-175 H 6
Čardzouskaja oblast' ○ TM 136-137 G 4
Careen Lake ○ CDN 32-33 Q 3
Carefree ○ USA (IN) 274-275 M 6
Carei ○ RO 102-103 C 4
Careiro ○ BR 66-67 G 4
Careiro da Várzea ○ BR 66-67 H 4
Carén ○ RCH 76-77 B 6
Čarencavan ○ AR 128-129 L 2
Carentan ○ F 90-91 G 7
Carevo ○ BG 102-103 E 6
Carey ○ USA (ID) 252-253 E 3
Carey ○ USA (OH) 280-281 C 3
Carey, Lake ○ AUS 176-177 G 4
Carey Downs ○ AUS 176-177 C 2
Carey Lake ○ CDN 30-31 S 4
Carey Øer ⌒ GRØ 26-27 O 5
Careysburg ○ LB 202-203 E 6
Careys Cave • AUS 180-181 K 3
Cargados Carajos Islands ⊥ MS 12 D 6
Čarh ○ AFG 138-139 B 3
Carhaix-Plouguer ○ F 90-91 F 7
Carhuamayo ○ PE 64-65 D 7
Carhuanca ○ PE 64-65 F 8
Carhuaz ○ PE 64-65 D 6
Carhué ○ RA 78-79 H 4
Cariaco, Golfo de ≈ 60-61 J 2
Cariamanga ○ EC 64-65 C 4
Cariango ○ ANG 216-217 C 5
Cariati ○ I 100-101 F 5
Caribaná, Punta ▲ CO 60-61 C 3
Caribbean Basin ≃ 56 A 4
Caribbean Marine Research Centre Lee Stocking Island ∴• BS 54-55 G 3
Caribbean Sea ≈ 5 J 4
Caribe, Río ∼ MEX 52-53 J 2
Caribes, Los ○ YV 62-63 D 3
Caribia ○ CO 60-61 C 3
Cariboo Highway • CDN (BC) 230-231 H 2
Cariboo Mountains ▲ CDN (BC) 228-229 N 3
Caribou ○ CDN 30-31 V 6
Caribou ○ USA (ME) 278-279 O 2
Caribou Depot ○ CDN (NB) 240-241 J 3
Caribou Island ⌒ CDN 36-37 J 2
Caribou Lake ○ CDN (MAN) 30-31 W 6
Caribou Lake ○ CDN (NWT) 20-21 Y 2
Caribou Lake ○ CDN (ONT) 234-235 O 4
Caribou Mount ▲ USA 20-21 P 3
Caribou Mountains ▲ CDN 30-31 M 6
Caribou River ∼ CDN 20-21 X 3
Caribou River ∼ CDN 30-31 W 6
Caribou River ∼ CDN 30-31 F 5
Caribou River ∼ CDN (BC) 228-229 N 4
Caribou River ∼ USA 22-23 Q 5
Caricaca, Rio ∼ BR 68-69 E 5
Carié ○ BR 68-69 K 6
Carievale ○ CDN (SAS) 232-233 R 6
Carigara ○ RP 160-161 F 7
Čārīkār ☆ AFG 138-139 B 2
Cari Laufquen, Bajo de ⊥ RA 78-79 E 6
Cari Laufquen Grande, Laguna ○ RA 78-79 E 6
Carinda ○ AUS 178-179 J 6
Cariñena ○ E 98-99 G 4
Carinhanha ○ BR 72-73 J 3
Carinhanha, Rio ∼ BR 72-73 H 3
Caripande ○ ANG 214-215 B 7
Caripare ○ BR 68-69 F 7
Caripé, Rio ∼ BR 68-69 D 3
Caripira ○ BR 66-67 E 3
Caripito ○ YV 60-61 K 2
Cariquima ○ RCH 70-71 C 6
Carira ○ BR 68-69 K 7
Cariré ○ BR 68-69 H 3
Cariris Novos, Serra dos ▲ BR 68-69 H 5
Caritaya, Embalse de < RCH 70-71 C 6
Caritianas ○ BR 66-67 F 7
Carito, El ○ YV 60-61 J 3
Carius ○ BR 68-69 J 5
Čarky (Muolakan) ∼ RUS 110-111 V 6
Carl Blackwell, Lake ○ USA (OK) 264-265 G 2
Carleton ○ CDN (NS) 240-241 K 6
Carleton, Mount ▲ CDN (NB) 240-241 J 3
Carleton Place ○ CDN (ONT) 238-239 J 3
Carletonville ○ ZA 220-221 H 3
Carlin ○ USA (NV) 246-247 J 3
Carlindi ○ AUS 172-173 D 6
Carlin Gold Mine ○ USA (NV) 246-247 J 3
Carlinville ○ USA (IL) 274-275 J 5
Carlisle ○ GB 90-91 F 4
Carlisle ○ USA (IA) 274-275 E 3
Carlisle ○ USA (IN) 274-275 L 6
Carlisle ○ USA (PA) 280-281 J 3
Carlisle ○ USA (SC) 284-285 J 2
Carlisle ○ USA (TX) 268-269 E 6
Carlisle Island ⌒ USA 22-23 L 6
Carlisle Lakes ○ AUS 176-177 J 4
Carlo ○ AUS 178-179 E 2
Carloforte ○ I 100-101 B 5
Carlópolis ○ BR 72-73 F 7
Carlos ○ CDN (ALB) 232-233 D 3
Carlos ○ USA (TX) 266-267 L 4
Carlos Casares ○ RA 78-79 J 3
Carlos Chagas ○ BR 72-73 K 4
Carlos Tejedor ○ RA 78-79 H 3
Carlota, La ○ RA 78-79 H 2
Carlow = Ceatharlach ○ IRL 90-91 D 5
Carlowrie ○ CDN (MAN) 234-235 G 5
Carlsbad ○ USA (CA) 248-249 G 6
Carlsbad ○ USA (NM) 256-257 L 6
Carlsbad ○ USA (TX) 266-267 G 2
Carlsbad Caverns National Park ⊥ USA (NM) 256-257 L 6
Carlsberg Fjord ≈ 26-27 o 8
Carlsbergfondet Land ⊥ GRØ 26-27 n 5
Carlsberg Ridge ≃ 12 D 4
Carlton ○ CDN (SAS) 232-233 M 3
Carlton ○ USA (AL) 284-285 C 5
Carlton ○ USA (GA) 284-285 G 2
Carlton ○ USA (OR) 244-245 B 5
Carlton ○ USA (WA) 244-245 E 2
Carlyle ○ CDN (SAS) 232-233 Q 6
Carlyle ○ USA (IL) 274-275 J 6
Carlyle ○ USA (MT) 250-251 P 5
Carlyle Lake ○ CDN (SAS) 232-233 Q 6
Carlyle Lake ○ USA (IL) 274-275 J 6
Carmacks ○ CDN 20-21 W 5
Carmagnola ○ I 100-101 A 2
Carman ○ CDN (MAN) 234-235 E 5
Carmangay ○ CDN (ALB) 232-233 E 5
Carmanville ○ CDN (NFL) 242-243 O 3
Carmarthen ○ GB 90-91 E 6
Carmaux ○ F 90-91 J 9
Carmel ○ USA (IN) 274-275 M 5
Carmelita ○ GCA 52-53 J 3
Carmelo ○ ROU 78-79 K 3
Carmen ○ RP 160-161 F 8
Carmen ○ USA (OK) 264-265 F 2
Carmen, El ○ BOL 70-71 F 3
Carmen, El ○ CO 60-61 B 6
Carmen, El ○ EC 64-65 C 2
Carmen, El ○ GCA 52-53 H 4
Carmen, El ○ RA 76-77 E 3
Carmen, Isla del ⌒ MEX 52-53 J 2
Carmen, Isla El ⌒ MEX 50-51 D 5
Carmen, Laguna del ≈ 52-53 H 2
Carmen, Río del ∼ RCH 76-77 B 5
Carmen de Areco ○ RA 78-79 K 3
Carmen de Bolivar, El ○ CO 60-61 D 3
Carmen de Patagones ○ RA 78-79 H 6
Carmen Silva, Sierra de ▲ RCH 80 F 6
Carmi ○ CDN (BC) 230-231 K 4
Carmi ○ USA (IL) 274-275 K 6
Carmichael ○ AUS 178-179 J 1
Carmichael ○ USA (CA) 246-247 D 5
Carmichael ○ USA (MS) 268-269 M 5
Carmichael Craq ▲ AUS 176-177 L 2
Carmichael River ∼ AUS 178-179 J 2
Carmila ○ AUS 178-179 K 1
Carmo ○ BR 68-69 D 4
Carmo de Mata ○ BR 72-73 H 6
Carmo de Minas ○ BR 72-73 H 7
Carmo do Paranaíba ○ BR 72-73 G 5
Carmody, Lake ○ AUS 176-177 E 6
Carmona ○ CR 52-53 B 7
Carmona ○•• E 98-99 E 6
Carnage, Mount ▲ AUS 176-177 F 5
Carnaíba ○ BR 68-69 K 5
Carnamah ○ AUS 176-177 C 4
Carnarvon ○ AUS (QLD) 178-179 J 3
Carnarvon ○ AUS (WA) 176-177 B 2
Carnarvon ○ CDN (ONT) 238-239 G 3
Carnarvon ○ ZA 220-221 F 5
Carnarvon National Park ⊥ AUS 178-179 J 3
Carnarvon Range ▲ AUS 176-177 F 2
Carnarvon Range ▲ AUS 178-179 K 3
Carnatic Shoal ≃ 160-161 B 7
Carndonagh ○ IRL 90-91 D 4
Carnduff ○ CDN (SAS) 232-233 R 6
Carnegie ○ AUS 176-177 G 2
Carnegie ○ USA (OK) 264-265 F 3
Carnegie ○ USA (PA) 280-281 G 3
Carnegie ○ USA (PA) 280-281 F 3
Carnegie, Lake ○ AUS 176-177 G 3
Carn Eige ▲ GB 90-91 E 3
Carneiro ○ USA (KS) 262-263 H 6
Carnera, Punta ▲ EC 64-65 B 3
Carnes ○ AUS 178-179 C 6
Carnesville ○ USA (GA) 284-285 G 2
Carney ○ USA (MI) 270-271 L 5
Car Nicobar Island ⌒ IND 140-141 L 5
Carnikava ○ LV 94-95 J 3
Carnot ○• RCA 206-207 B 6
Carnot, Cape ▲ AUS 180-181 C 3
Carnot Bay ≈ 172-173 F 4
Carnsore Point ▲ IRL 90-91 D 5
Carnwath River ∼ CDN 30-31 F 2
Carnwood ○ CDN (ALB) 232-233 D 2
Caro ○ USA (MI) 272-273 F 4
Caro, El ○ YV 60-61 J 3
Caro de La Negra, El ○ YV 60-61 J 3
Carol City ○ USA (FL) 286-287 J 6
Carolina ○ BR 68-69 E 5
Carolina ○ CO 60-61 D 4
Carolina ○ E 98-99 F 5
Carolina ○ RCH 76-77 B 2
Carolina ○ USA (PR) 286-287 Q 2
Carolina ○ ZA 220-221 K 3
Carolina Sandhills National Wildlife Refuge ⊥ USA (SC) 284-285 K 2
Caroline ○ CDN (ALB) 232-233 D 3
Caroline, Lake ○ AUS 178-179 D 3
Caroline Beach ○ USA (NC) 282-283 K 6
Caroline Island ⌒ KIB 13 M 3
Caroline Islands ⌒ FSM 13 M 3
Caroline National Memorial, Fort • USA (FL) 286-287 H 1
Caroline Seamounts ≃ 13 F 2
Carolside ○ CDN (ALB) 232-233 G 4
Caron ○ AUS 176-177 D 4
Caron Brook ○ CDN (NB) 240-241 G 3
Caroni, Río ∼ YV 60-61 K 5
Carora ○ YV 60-61 F 2
Carp ○ USA (NV) 248-249 K 2
Carpathian Mountains = Karpaty ▲ 102-103 B 3
Carpații Orientali ▲ RO 102-103 D 4
Carpentaria, Gulf of ≈ AUS 174-175 D 3
Carpentaria Highway II AUS 174-175 B 5
Carpenter ○ USA (SD) 260-261 J 2
Carpenter ○ USA (WY) 252-253 O 5
Carpenter Lake ○ CDN (BC) 230-231 G 3
Carpentras ○ F 90-91 K 9
Carpi ○ I 100-101 C 2
Carpina ○ BR 68-69 L 5
Carpincho, Riacho ∼ PY 76-77 H 2
Carpinteria ○ USA (CA) 248-249 E 5
Carpio ○ USA (ND) 258-259 F 3
Carp Lake ○ CDN (BC) 228-229 L 2
Carp Lake ○ USA (MI) 272-273 E 2
Carp Lake Provincial Park ⊥ CDN (BC) 228-229 L 2
Carpolac ○ AUS 180-181 F 4
Carr ○ USA (CO) 254-255 L 3
Carrabelle ○ USA (FL) 286-287 E 2
Carracollo ○ BOL 70-71 D 5
Carragana ○ CDN (SAS) 232-233 P 3
Čār Rāh ○ AFG 134-135 K 2
Carraipia ○ CO 60-61 E 2
Carranya ○ AUS 172-173 H 5
Carrapatal ○ BR 68-69 G 3
Carrapatal, Ilha ⌒ BR 68-69 G 3
Carrara ○ I 100-101 C 2
Carrasquero ○ YV 60-61 E 2
Carr Boyd Ranges ▲ AUS 172-173 J 4
Carreira Comprida, Cachoeira ∼ BR 68-69 D 7
Carrere, Cerro ▲ RA 78-79 E 4
Carreta, Punta ▲ PE 64-65 D 9
Carretera Interamericana II MEX 50-51 F 2
Carretero, Puerto de ▲ E 98-99 F 6
Carr Fork Lake ○ USA (KY) 276-277 M 3
Carriacou Island ⌒ WG 56 E 5
Carrical ○ CV 202-203 B 5
Carrick ○ IRL 90-91 C 4
Carriere ○ USA (MS) 268-269 L 6
Carrieton ○ AUS 180-181 E 2
Carril, El ○ RA 76-77 E 3
Carrington ○ USA (ND) 258-259 H 4
Carrington Island ⌒ USA (UT) 254-255 C 3
Carrión, Río ∼ E 98-99 E 3
Carriringue ○ RCH 78-79 D 5
Carrizal ○ CO 60-61 E 1
Carrizal ○ RA 76-77 D 5
Carrizal ○ YV 62-63 D 2
Carrizal, El ○ MEX 50-51 F 2
Carrizal, Punta ▲ RCH 76-77 B 5
Carrizal, Quebrada ∼ RCH 76-77 B 5
Carrizal Bajo ○ RCH 76-77 B 5
Carrizo ○ USA (AZ) 256-257 E 5
Carrizo, Quebrada del ∼ RCH 76-77 C 3
Carrizo Creek ∼ USA (NM) 256-257 M 2
Carrizo Springs ○ USA (TX) 266-267 H 5
Carrizozo ○ USA (NM) 256-257 K 5
Carroll ○ CDN (MAN) 234-235 C 5
Carroll ○ USA (IA) 274-275 D 2
Carrollton ○ USA (AL) 284-285 B 3
Carrollton ○ USA (GA) 284-285 E 3
Carrollton ○ USA (IL) 274-275 H 5
Carrollton ○ USA (KY) 276-277 K 2
Carrollton ○ USA (MI) 272-273 F 4
Carrollton ○ USA (MO) 274-275 E 5
Carrollton ○ USA (MS) 268-269 L 3
Carrollton ○ USA (OH) 280-281 E 3
Carrol Summit ▲ USA (NV) 246-247 H 4
Carrot Creek ○ CDN (ALB) 232-233 C 2
Carrot River ○ CDN (SAS) 232-233 P 2
Carrot River ∼ CDN (SAS) 232-233 Q 2
Carrozas ○ CO 60-61 E 6
Čarrūd ○ IR 134-135 G 3
Carruthers ○ CDN (SAS) 232-233 J 3
Çarşamba ☆ TR 128-129 G 2
Čaršanga ○ TM 136-137 K 6
Carseland ○ CDN (ALB) 232-233 E 5
Carsk ○ KA 124-125 M 4
Carson ○ USA (ND) 258-259 F 5
Carson, Fort • USA (CO) 254-255 L 5
Carson City ○ USA (MI) 272-273 E 4
Carson City ☆ USA (NV) 246-247 F 4
Carson River ∼ USA 172-173 H 3
Carson Sink ○ USA (NV) 246-247 G 4
Carstairs ○ CDN (ALB) 232-233 D 4
Cartagena ☆••• CO 60-61 D 2
Cartagena ○ E 98-99 G 6
Cartagena del Chaira ○ CO 64-65 E 1
Cartago ○ CO 60-61 D 5
Cartago ☆ CR 52-53 C 7
Cartago ○ USA (CA) 248-249 F 3
Carta Valley ○ USA (TX) 266-267 G 4
Carter ○ USA (MT) 250-251 J 4
Carter ○ USA (OK) 264-265 E 3
Carter ○ USA (WY) 252-253 H 5
Carter, Mount ▲ AUS 174-175 G 3
Carters Lake < USA (GA) 284-285 F 2
Carter Spit ▲ USA 22-23 P 3
Carters Range ▲ AUS 178-179 F 2
Cartersville ○ USA (GA) 284-285 F 2
Cartersville ○ USA (IA) 274-275 E 2
Cartersville ○ USA (MT) 250-251 N 5
Carthage ∴••• TN 190-191 H 2
Carthage ○ USA (AR) 276-277 C 6
Carthage ○ USA (IL) 274-275 G 4
Carthage ○ USA (MO) 276-277 A 3
Carthage ○ USA (MS) 268-269 L 4
Carthage ○ USA (NC) 282-283 H 5
Carthage ○ USA (NY) 278-279 F 5
Carthage ○ USA (SD) 260-261 J 2
Carthage ○ USA (TN) 276-277 K 4
Carthage ○ USA (TX) 264-265 K 6
Cartier ○ CDN (ONT) 238-239 D 2
Cartier, Port- ○ CDN (QUE) 242-243 B 2
Cartier Islet ⌒ AUS 172-173 F 2
Carti Suitupo ○ PA 52-53 E 7
Cartridge Mount ▲ CDN 30-31 K 4
Cartwright ○ CDN (MAN) 234-235 D 5
Cartwright ○ USA (KY) 276-277 K 4
Carú, Área Indígena ✗ BR 68-69 F 3
Caru, Rio ∼ BR 68-69 E 3
Caruachi ○ YV 60-61 K 3
Caruaru ○ BR 68-69 L 6
Caruban ○ RI 168 D 3
Carún, Río ∼ YV 60-61 K 5
Carunantabari ○ YV 60-61 K 5
Carúpano ○ YV 60-61 K 2
Carurai ○ RP 160-161 C 7
Caruthersville ○ USA (MO) 276-277 F 4
Čarvakskoe vodohranilišče < US 136-137 M 4
Carvel ○ CDN (ALB) 232-233 D 2
Carver ○ USA (NV) 246-247 H 5
Carvinas ○ BOL 70-71 D 3
Carvoal ○ BR 70-71 J 5
Carvoeiro ○ BR 62-63 D 6
Carway ○ CDN (ALB) 232-233 E 6
Cary ○ USA (MS) 268-269 K 4
Cary ○ USA (NC) 282-283 J 5
Carycanka ○ UA 102-103 J 3
Caryš ∼ RUS 124-125 O 3
Caryš ∼ RUS 124-125 N 2
Carysfort, Cape ▲ GB 78-79 M 6
Caryškoe ○ RUS 124-125 N 3
Carysville ○ USA (OH) 280-281 C 3
Caryville ○ USA (TN) 282-283 C 4
Čaš ○ US 136-137 K 5
Casabe, El ○ YV 60-61 K 4
Casabindo ○ RA 76-77 D 2
Casablanca ○ RCH 78-79 D 2
Casablanca = Ad-Dār-al-Bayda ☆• MA 188-189 H 4
Casa Branca ○ BR 72-73 G 6
Casa da Pedra • BR 70-71 K 4
Casadepaga ○ USA 20-21 H 4
Casa de Piedra ○ RA 78-79 F 5
Casa Grande ○ USA (AZ) 256-257 D 6
Casa Grandes Ruins National Monument • USA (AZ) 256-257 D 5
Casale Monferrato ○• I 100-101 B 2
Casalins ○ RA 78-79 K 4
Casamance ⊥ SN 202-203 B 3
Casamance ∼ SN 202-203 C 3
Casamento, Lagoa do ○ BR 74-75 E 8
Casamozza ○ F 98-99 M 3
Casanare ○ CO 60-61 G 5
Casanare, Río ∼ CO 60-61 F 4
Casanay ○ YV 60-61 K 2
Casa Nova ○ BR 68-69 H 6
Casa Piedra ○ USA (TX) 266-267 C 4
Casarabi ○ BOL 70-71 E 4
Casares ○ NIC 52-53 L 6
Casas ○ MEX 50-51 K 6
Casas Adobes ○ USA (AZ) 256-257 E 6
Casas Grandes ∴ MEX 50-51 F 2
Casas Grandes, Río ∼ MEX 50-51 F 2
Casa Verde ○ BR 72-73 D 6
Casavieja ○• E 98-99 E 4
Casazinc ○ CO 60-61 E 6
Casca ○ BR (RSU) 74-75 E 8
Casca ○ BR (RSU) 74-75 E 7
Cascade ○ CDN (BC) 230-231 L 4
Cascade ○ USA (IA) 274-275 G 2
Cascade ○ USA (ID) 252-253 B 2
Cascade ○ USA (MT) 250-251 H 4
Cascade Caverns ∴• USA (TX) 266-267 J 4
Cascade Mountain Ski Area • USA (WI) 274-275 J 1
Cascade Range ▲ USA (CA) 246-247 C 2
Cascade Reservoir ○ USA (ID) 252-253 B 2
Cascade River ∼ CDN (ALB) 232-233 C 4
Cascades ○ AUS 176-177 F 6
Cascais ○ P 98-99 C 5
Cascajal ○ C 54-55 E 3
Cascajal, Río ∼ PE 64-65 B 4
Cascapédia, Rivière ∼ CDN (QUE) 240-241 J 2
Cascas ○ PE 64-65 C 5
Cascavel ○ BR (CEA) 68-69 J 4
Cascavel ○ BR (PAR) 74-75 D 5
Casco, El ○ MEX 50-51 G 5
Casco Bay ≈ USA 278-279 L 5
Cascorro ○ C 54-55 G 4
Cascumpeque Bay ≈ 38-39 N 5
Cascumpeque Bay ≈ CDN 240-241 M 4
Časeľka ∼ RUS 114-115 Q 2
Časeľskoe, ozero ○ RUS 114-115 P 2
Caselton ○ USA (NV) 248-249 K 2
Caserta ☆ I 100-101 E 4
Caseville ○ USA (MI) 272-273 F 4
Casey ○ USA (IL) 274-275 L 5
Caseyr, Raas = Gwardafuy ▲ SP 208-209 K 3
Cashel ○ ZW 218-219 G 4
Cashel = Caiseal ○• IRL 90-91 D 5
Cashmere Downs ○ AUS 176-177 E 4
Cashton ○ USA (WI) 270-271 H 7
Casian Island ⌒ RP 160-161 C 7
Casigua ○ YV 60-61 F 2
Casiguran ○ RP 160-161 E 4
Casilda ○ RA 78-79 J 2
Casimiro de Abreu ○ BR 72-73 J 7
Casino ○ AUS 178-179 M 5
Casinos ○ E 98-99 G 5
Casiquiare, Río ∼ YV 60-61 H 6
Casma ○ PE 64-65 C 6
Časniki ☆ BY 94-95 L 4
Časovaja ○ RUS 118-119 J 9
Časovo ○ RUS 88-89 V 5
Caspana ○ RCH 76-77 C 2
Caspe ○ E 98-99 G 4
Casper ○ USA (WY) 252-253 M 4
Caspian ○ USA (MI) 270-271 K 4
Caspian Depression = Prikaspijskaja nizmennost' ⊥ 126-127 F 5
Caspian Sea ≈ 10-11 D 4
Cass ○ RCH 76-77 D 2
Cass ○ USA (AR) 276-277 B 5
Cassacatiza ○ MOC 218-219 G 2
Cassai ○ ANG 216-217 F 5
Cassai ∼ ANG 216-217 F 5
Cassamba ○ ANG 216-217 E 6
Cassange, Rio ∼ BR 70-71 J 5
Cassango ○ ANG 216-217 D 4
Cassasala ○ ANG 216-217 E 5
Cass City ○ USA (MI) 272-273 F 4
Casselman ○ CDN (ONT) 238-239 K 3
Casselton ○ USA (ND) 258-259 K 5
Cass Fjord ≈ 26-27 S 3
Cássia ○ BR 72-73 G 6
Cassiar ○ CDN 30-31 E 6
Cassiar Mountains ▲ CDN 30-31 D 5
Cassiar-Stewart Highway II CDN 32-33 E 3
Cassidy ○ CDN (BC) 230-231 F 4
Cassilândia ○ BR 72-73 E 5
Cassilis ○ AUS 180-181 K 2
Cassinga ○ ANG 216-217 D 7
Cassino ○ I 100-101 D 4
Cass Lake ○ USA (MN) 270-271 D 3
Cassoday ○ USA (KS) 262-263 K 6
Cassongue ○ ANG 216-217 C 5
Cassopolis ○ USA (MI) 272-273 C 6
Cass River ∼ USA (MI) 272-273 F 4
Cassville ○ USA (MO) 276-277 B 4
Cassville ○ USA (WI) 274-275 H 2
Cast ▲ MAU 146-147 K 1
Castaic ○ USA (CA) 248-249 F 5
Castaña ○ YV 60-61 J 5
Castanhal ○ BR (AMA) 66-67 F 6
Castanhal ○ BR (P) 68-69 E 2
Castanheira ○ BR 70-71 H 2
Castaños ○ MEX 50-51 J 4
Castaño Viejo ○ RA 76-77 C 6
Castèl del Monte •• I 100-101 F 4
Castelhanos, Ponta dos ▲ BR (ESP) 72-73 K 6
Castelhanos, Ponta dos ▲ BR (RIO) 72-73 H 7
Casteljaloux ○ F 90-91 H 9
Castella ○ USA (CA) 246-247 C 2
Castellana, Grotte di •• I 100-101 F 4
Castellana, La ○ RP 160-161 E 7
Castellar de Santisteban ○ E 98-99 F 5
Castelldefels ○ E 98-99 H 4
Castelli ○ RA (BUA) 78-79 L 4
Castelli ○ RA (CHA) 76-77 G 3
Castelló de la Plana ○ E 98-99 G 5
Castellón de la Plana = Castelló de la Plana ○ E 98-99 G 5
Castelnaudary ○• F 90-91 H 10
Castelnau-Magnoac ○ F 90-91 H 10
Castelo ○ BR 72-73 K 6
Castelo Branco ☆• P 98-99 D 5
Castelo do Piauí ○ BR 68-69 H 4
Castelsardo ○• I 100-101 B 4
Castelsarrasin ○ F 90-91 H 9
Castelvetrano ○ I 100-101 D 6
Casterton ○ AUS 180-181 F 4
Castilla ○ PE 64-65 B 4
Castilla ○ RA 78-79 K 3
Castilla la Mancha ◻ E 98-99 F 5
Castilla y León ◻ E 98-99 D 3
Castilletes ○ CO 60-61 F 2
Castillo, El ∴• NIC 52-53 B 6
Castillo, Pampa del ⊥ RA 80 F 2
Castillo de Bayuela ○ E 98-99 E 4
Castillo de San Marcos National Monument • USA (FL) 286-287 H 2
Castillos ○ ROU 74-75 D 10

312 Cap-de-Rabast — Castillos

Castillos, Laguna de ⊂⊃ ROU 74-75 D 10
Castle o USA (MT) 250-251 J 5
Castlebar = Caisleán an Bharraigh o IRL 90-91 C 5
Castleberry o USA (AL) 284-285 C 5
Castle Cape ▲ USA 22-23 R 4
Castle Creek ~ CDN (BC) 228-229 O 3
Castledale o CDN (BC) 230-231 N 2
Castle Dale o USA (UT) 254-255 E 4
Castleford o USA (ID) 252-253 D 4
Castlegar o CDN (BC) 230-231 M 4
Castle Island ∩ BS 54-55 H 3
Castle Island o CDN (NFL) 38-39 R 3
Castle Island o CDN (NFL) 242-243 N 1
Castle Island ∩ CDN (NWT) 36-37 L 7
Castlemaine o• AUS 180-181 H 4
Castle Mountain ▲ USA (CA) 248-249 D 4
Castle Peak ▲ USA (ID) 252-253 D 2
Castlepoint o NZ 182 F 4
Castlereagh Bay ≈ 174-175 C 3
Castlereagh River ~ AUS 178-179 K 6
Castle Rock o CDN (BC) 228-229 M 4
Castle Rock o USA (CO) 254-255 L 4
Castle Rock o USA (SD) 260-261 C 2
Castle Rock o USA (WA) 244-245 C 4
Castleton o• JA 54-55 G 5
Castletown o GBM 90-91 E 4
Castletown Bearhaven = Baile Chaisleáin Bhéarra o IRL 90-91 C 6
Castle Windsor •• GB 90-91 G 6
Castlewood o USA (SD) 260-261 J 2
Castolon o USA (TX) 266-267 D 4
Castor o CDN (ALB) 232-233 G 3
Castor o USA (LA) 268-269 G 4
Castor Creek ~ USA (LA) 268-269 H 4
Castor River ~ USA (MO) 276-277 E 3
Castres o F 90-91 J 10
Castries ★ WL 56 E 4
Castro o BR (BAH) 72-73 L 2
Castro o BR (PAR) 74-75 E 5
Castro o RCH 78-79 C 7
Castro, Canal ≈ 80 C 5
Castro, Punta ▲ RA 78-79 G 7
Castro Barras o RA 76-77 E 6
Castro Daire o P 98-99 D 4
Castrovillari o I 100-101 F 5
Castroville o USA (TX) 266-267 J 4
Castrovirreyna o PE 64-65 E 8
Castuera o E 98-99 E 5
Čaštye ☆ RUS 96-97 J 5
Častyh o RUS 118-119 E 6
Casuarina Coast ∪ RI 166-167 J 4
Casummit Lake o CDN (ONT) 234-235 L 3
Caswell o USA 20-21 Q 6
Çat ☆ TR 128-129 J 3
Catabola o ANG (BIE) 216-217 D 6
Catabola o ANG (HBO) 216-217 C 6
Cataby Roadhouse o AUS 176-177 C 5
Catacamas o HN 52-53 B 4
Catacaos o PE 64-65 B 4
Catache o PE 64-65 C 5
Catacocha o EC 64-65 C 4
Cataguases o BR 72-73 J 6
Catahoula Lake ⊂⊃ USA (LA) 268-269 H 5
Catahoula National Wildlife Refuge ⊥ USA (LA) 268-269 H 5
Catahuasi o PE 64-65 E 8
Cataingan o RP 160-161 E 6
Çatak ☆ TR 128-129 K 3
Çatak Çayı ~ TR 128-129 K 3
Catalão o BR 72-73 G 5
Çatalhöyük ∴• TR 128-129 E 4
Catalina o CDN (NFL) 242-243 P 4
Catalina o RCH 76-77 C 3
Catalina, Punta ▲ RCH 80 F 6
Catalunya □ E 98-99 J 4
Catama o SP 212-213 H 2
Catamarca □ RA 76-77 D 4
Catamarca = San Fernando del Valle de Catamarca ☆• RA 76-77 E 5
Catamayo o EC 64-65 C 3
Catambué o ANG 216-217 E 8
Catanacuname o CO 60-61 H 6
Catandica o MOC 218-219 G 4
Catanduanes ∩ RP 160-161 F 6
Catanduva o BR 72-73 F 6
Catanduvas o BR 74-75 D 5
Catânia o I 100-101 E 6
Catán Lil o RA 78-79 D 5
Cataño o USA (PR) 286-287 P 2
Catanzaro o I 100-101 F 5
Cataract o USA (WI) 270-271 H 6
Cataract, 1st ~ ET 194-195 F 5
Cataract, 3rd = ash-Shallāl ath-Thālith ~ SUD 200-201 E 3
Cataract, 4th = ash Shallāl ar-Rābi' ~ SUD 200-201 F 3
Cataract, 5th = ash-Shallāl al-Khāmis ~ SUD 200-201 F 3
Cataract, 6th = Shallal as-Sablūkah ~ SUD 200-201 F 4
Cataract Canyon ∪ USA (UT) 254-255 E 6
Cataractes • RM 222-223 F 7
Cataraugus Creek ~ USA (NY) 278-279 C 6
Catarina o USA (TX) 266-267 H 5
Catarman ☆ RP 160-161 F 6
Catastrophe, Cape ▲ AUS 180-181 D 3
Catata-a-Nova o ANG 216-217 C 6
Catatumbo, Río ~ YV 60-61 E 3
Cataula o USA (GA) 284-285 F 4
Cataviña o MEX 50-51 B 3
Catawba o USA (WI) 270-271 H 5
Catawba Island o USA (OH) 280-281 D 2
Catawba Lake < USA (NC) 282-283 F 5
Catawba River ~ USA (SC) 284-285 K 2
Cataxa o MOC 218-219 G 2
Catazaja o MEX 52-53 H 3
Catbalogan ☆ RP 160-161 F 7
Čat-Bazar o KS 136-137 N 3
Cat Cays ∩ BS 54-55 F 2
Cateau-Cambrésis, le o F 92-93 G 3
Cateco Cangola o ANG 216-217 C 4
Catemaco o MEX 52-53 G 2
Catemaco, Laguna de ⊂⊃• MEX 52-53 G 2
Catembe o MOC 220-221 L 3
Catende o BR 68-69 L 6
Catengue o ANG 216-217 B 6
Cater o CDN (SAS) 232-233 K 2
Catete o ANG 216-217 B 4
Catete, Área Indígena ✗ BR 68-69 C 5
Catete, Rio ~ BR 66-67 K 6
Cathair na Mart = Westport o• IRL 90-91 C 5
Cathay o USA (ND) 258-259 H 4
Cathcart o ZA 220-221 H 6
Cathedral Gorge State Park • USA (NV) 248-249 K 2
Cathedral Mountain ▲ USA (TX) 266-267 D 3
Cathedral Peak o ZA 220-221 J 4
Cathedral Provincial Park ⊥ CDN (BC) 230-231 J 4
Cathedral Valley ∴ USA (UT) 254-255 D 5
Catherine o USA (AL) 284-285 C 4
Catherine, Mount ▲ AUS 178-179 K 3
Cathlamet o USA (WA) 244-245 B 4
Catia la Mar o YV 60-61 H 2
Catió ☆ GNB 202-203 C 4
Catire, Sierra el ▲ YV 60-61 K 4
Cat Island ∩ BS 54-55 H 2
Cat Island ∩ USA (MS) 268-269 L 6
Čatkal'skij hrebet ▲ US 136-137 M 4
Čatkaly Kamyclovskij Log ⊥ KA 124-125 F 1
Cat Lake o CDN (ONT) 234-235 M 3
Cat Lake ⊂⊃ CDN (ONT) 234-235 M 3
Catlettsburg o USA (KY) 276-277 N 2
Catlow Valley ∪ USA (OR) 244-245 F 7
Cato o USA (AR) 276-277 C 6
Catoche, Cabo ▲ MEX 52-53 L 1
Catolândia o BR 72-73 H 2
Catolé do Rocha o BR 68-69 K 5
Catolo o ANG 216-217 D 4
Caton Island ∩ USA 22-23 P 5
Catoute ▲ E 98-99 D 3
Cátria, Monte ▲ I 100-101 D 3
Catriel o RA 78-79 F 4
Catrilo o RA 78-79 H 4
Catrimani o BR (ROR) 62-63 D 5
Catrimani o BR (ROR) 66-67 F 2
Catrimani, Rio ~ BR 60-61 K 6
Catskill o USA (NY) 278-279 H 6
Catskill Mountains ▲ USA (NY) 278-279 G 6
Cattaraugus Indian Reservation ✗ USA (NY) 278-279 C 6
Cattle Creek ~ AUS 172-173 K 4
Cattle Creek Out Station o AUS 172-173 K 4
Catuane o MOC 220-221 L 3
Catumbela ~ ANG 216-217 C 6
Caturiá, Ilha ∩ BR 66-67 C 4
Catyr-Kël, ozero ⊂⊃ KS 146-147 B 5
Čatyrtaš o KS 146-147 C 5
Cauaburi, Rio ~ BR 66-67 D 2
Cauale ~ ANG 216-217 D 3
Cauayan o RP 160-161 E 7
Cauca o ANG 216-217 C 4
Cauca, Río ~ CO 60-61 D 3
Caucagua o YV 60-61 H 2
Caucaia o BR 68-69 J 3
Caucas o BOL 70-71 H 5
Caucasia o CO 60-61 D 3
Caucasus = Bol'šoj Kavkaz ▲ RUS 126-127 C 5
Cauce Seco del Río Pilcomayo ~ RA 76-77 G 2
Caucete o RA 76-77 C 6
Cauchari o RA 76-77 D 3
Cauchari, Salar de ⊂⊃ RA 76-77 D 2
Caucomgiomoc Lake ⊂⊃ USA (ME) 278-279 M 2
Caulfield o USA (MO) 276-277 C 4
Caumbue o ANG 216-217 F 4
Čaun ~ RUS 112-113 Q 2
Čauns kaja guba ≈ 112-113 P 2
Caupolican ⊥ BOL 70-71 C 4
Cauquenes o RCH 78-79 C 3
Caurés, Rio ~ BR 66-67 F 3
Causabiscau, Lac ⊂⊃ CDN 38-39 F 2
Causapscal o CDN (QUE) 240-241 H 2
Causapscal, Parc Provincial ⊥ CDN (QUE) 240-241 H 2
Čaušeni ☆ MD 102-103 F 4
Causey o USA (NM) 256-257 M 5
Cautário, Rio ~ BR 70-71 E 3
Cautin, Río ~ RCH 78-79 C 5
Caution, Cape ▲ CDN (BC) 230-231 B 2
Caution Point ▲ AUS 172-173 K 1
Cauto ~ C 54-55 G 4
Cauto Cristo o C 54-55 G 4
Cauto Embarcadero o C 54-55 G 4
Cauvery ~ IND 140-141 F 4
Cauvery ~ IND 140-141 G 5
Cavalier o USA (ND) 258-259 K 3
Cavalla River ~ LB 202-203 G 7
Cavallo Passage ≈ USA 266-267 L 5
Cavalonga, Sierra ▲ RA 76-77 D 2
Cavan = An Cabhán ☆ IRL 90-91 D 5
Cavdan o MAU 148-149 C 3
Çavdarhisar ☆ TR 128-129 C 3
Cave o NZ 182 C 6
Cave City o USA (AR) 276-277 D 5
Cave Junction o USA (OR) 244-245 B 8
Cavendish o AUS 180-181 G 4
Cavendish o CDN (ALB) 232-233 H 5
Cavendish o CDN (PEI) 240-241 M 4
Caverns of Sonora ∴• USA (TX) 266-267 G 3
Caves, The o AUS 178-179 L 2
Cave Spring o USA (GA) 284-285 E 2
Caviana de Dentro, Ilha ∩ BR 62-63 J 5
Caviana de Fora, Ilha ∩ BR 62-63 J 5
Cavite o RP 160-161 D 5
Čavki o AFG 138-139 C 2
Cawayan o RP 160-161 E 7
Caxambu o BR 72-73 H 6
Caxias o BR 68-69 G 4
Caxias do Sul o BR 74-75 E 7
Caxito ☆ ANG 216-217 B 4
Caxiuanã, Baía de ⊂⊃ BR 62-63 J 6
Caxiuanã, Reserva Florestal de ⊥ BR 62-63 J 6
Caxuxa o BR 68-69 F 4
Çay ☆• TR 128-129 D 3
Cayajabos o C 54-55 D 3
Cayambe o EC 64-65 C 1
Cayambe, Volcán ▲ EC 64-65 D 1
Cayambre, Isla ∩ CO 60-61 C 6
Cayara o PE 64-65 F 8
Cayastá, Ruinas • RA 76-77 G 6
Cayce o USA (SC) 284-285 J 3
Cây Du'o'ng, Vũng ≈ 158-159 H 5
Cayenne ☆ F 62-63 H 3
Cayes, Les ☆• RH 54-55 J 5
Cayley o CDN (ALB) 232-233 E 5
Cayman Brac ∩ GB 54-55 F 5
Cayman Ridge ≃ 54-55 D 5
Cayman Trench ≃ 54-55 D 5
Caynabo o SP 208-209 H 4
Cayo, El ∴• MEX 52-53 J 3
Cayo Guillerme o•• C 54-55 F 3
Cayo Güin o C 54-55 H 4
Cayo Largo o•• C 54-55 E 4
Cayo Mambi o C 54-55 H 4
Cayo Ramona o C 54-55 E 3
Cayos Arcas, Isla ∩ MEX 52-53 J 1
Cay Sal Bank ∩ BS 54-55 E 3
Cayucos o USA (CA) 248-249 D 4
Cayuga o CDN (ONT) 238-239 F 6
Cayuga o USA (IN) 274-275 L 5
Cayuga o USA (ND) 258-259 K 5
Cayuga o USA (TX) 268-269 E 5
Cayuga Lake ⊂⊃ USA (NY) 278-279 E 6
Cayuse Pass ▲ USA (WA) 244-245 D 4
Cazage o ANG 216-217 F 5
Cazalla de la Sierra o E 98-99 E 6
Čažma, mys ▲ RUS 120-121 T 6
Cazombo o ANG 214-215 B 6
Cazones, Golfo de ≈ 54-55 E 4
Cazorla o E 98-99 F 6
Cazorla o YV 60-61 H 3
Cazorla, Segura y Las Villas Parque Nacional de ⊥ E 98-99 F 5
Cazula o MOC 218-219 G 2
Ccatca o PE 70-71 B 3
Cea, Río ~ E 98-99 E 3
Ceará □ BR 68-69 H 4
Ceara Abyssal Plain = Ceará Abyssal Plain ≃ 6-7 H 8
Ceará-Mirim o BR 68-69 L 4
Ceatharlach = Carlow o IRL 90-91 D 5
Ceba o CDN (SAS) 232-233 Q 2
Ceballos o MEX 50-51 G 4
Čebarkul' ☆ RUS 96-97 M 6
Čeboksarskoe vodohranilišče < RUS 96-97 E 5
Čeboksary ☆ RUS 96-97 E 5
Cebollati o ROU 74-75 D 9
Ceboruco, Cerro ▲ MEX 52-53 B 2
Cebu ∩ RP 160-161 E 8
Cebu City ☆•• RP 160-161 E 7
Čečeljugjun ~ RUS 110-111 a 6
Čečen, ostrov ∩ RUS 126-127 G 5
Cècèrlèg ☆ MAU 148-149 E 4
Čechy ⊥ CZ 92-93 N 4
Cecil o USA (AL) 284-285 E 4
Cecil o USA (AR) 276-277 B 5
Cecil o USA (OR) 244-245 E 5
Cecil, Mount ▲ AUS 176-177 M 2
Cecil Goodman o AUS 172-173 K 2
Cecil Plains o AUS 178-179 L 4
Cecil Rhodes, Mount ▲ AUS 176-177 F 2
Cecilville o USA (CA) 246-247 B 2
Cecina o I 100-101 C 3
Čečuj ~ RUS 118-119 D 7
Čečujsk o RUS 116-117 O 6
Cedar o CDN (BC) 230-231 F 4
Cedar o USA (KS) 262-263 H 5
Cedar Bluff o USA (IA) 274-275 G 3
Cedar Bluff Reservoir ∪ USA (KS) 262-263 G 6
Cedar Bluffs o USA (KS) 262-263 F 5
Cedar Breaks National Monument ∴ USA (UT) 254-255 C 6
Cedar Butte o USA (SD) 260-261 E 3
Cedar City o USA (UT) 254-255 B 6
Cedar Creek ~ USA (TX) 266-267 K 3
Cedar Creek ~ USA (AL) 284-285 B 2
Cedar Creek ~ USA (AL) 284-285 D 4
Cedar Creek ~ USA (IA) 274-275 G 4
Cedar Creek ~ USA (ND) 258-259 F 5
Cedar Creek Reservoir o USA (TX) 264-265 H 6
Cedaredge o USA (CO) 254-255 H 5
Cedar Falls o USA (IA) 274-275 F 2
Cedar Grove o USA (TN) 276-277 G 5
Cedar Grove o USA (WI) 274-275 L 1
Cedar Hill o USA (MO) 274-275 H 6
Cedar Hill o USA (TX) 264-265 H 6
Cedar Island ∩ USA (NC) 282-283 L 6
Cedar Island National Wildlife Refuge ⊥ USA (NC) 282-283 L 6
Cedar Key o USA (FL) 286-287 F 2
Cedar Lake o CDN 34-35 F 4
Cedar Lake o CDN (QUE) 238-239 G 2
Cedar Lake o USA (IL) 276-277 F 3
Cedar Lake o USA (TX) 264-265 B 6
Cedar Mills o USA (MN) 270-271 D 6
Cedar Mountain ▲ USA (MT) 250-251 D 4
Cedar Park o USA (TX) 266-267 K 3
Cedar Pass ▲ USA (CA) 246-247 E 2
Cedar Point o CDN (ONT) 238-239 E 4
Cedar Point ▲ USA (CO) 254-255 M 4
Cedar Rapids o USA (IA) 274-275 G 3
Cedar Rapids o USA (NE) 262-263 H 3
Cedar River ~ CDN (BC) 228-229 F 2
Cedar River ~ USA (MI) 270-271 L 5
Cedar River ~ USA (IA) 274-275 G 3
Cedar River ~ USA (NE) 262-263 H 3
Cedar River National Grassland ⊥ USA (ND) 258-259 F 5
Cedars of Lebanon State Park ⊥ USA (TN) 276-277 J 4
Cedar Springs o USA (MI) 272-273 D 4
Cedartown o USA (GA) 284-285 E 2
Cedar Vale o USA (KS) 262-263 K 5
Cedarvale o USA (NM) 256-257 K 4
Cedarville o USA (AR) 276-277 A 5
Cedarville o USA (CA) 246-247 E 2
Cedarville o USA (MI) 270-271 O 4
Cedarville o ZA 220-221 J 5
Cedeño o HN 52-53 L 5
Cedoux o CDN (SAS) 232-233 P 6
Cedral o BR 68-69 F 3
Cedral o MEX (SLP) 50-51 J 6
Cedral ∴• MEX (QR) 52-53 L 1
Cèdres, Parque National des ⊥ DZ 190-191 C 3
Cedro o BR 68-69 J 5
Cedros o MEX (DGO) 50-51 J 5
Cedros o MEX (SON) 50-51 E 4
Cedros, Isla ∩ MEX 50-51 B 3
Ceduna o AUS 176-177 M 6
Ceek o SP 208-209 G 4
Ceel Afweyn o SP 208-209 H 4
Ceelayo o SP 208-209 J 3
Ceelbuur o SP 208-209 H 6
Ceel Dheere o SP 208-209 H 6
Ceel Duubo o SP 212-213 K 2
Ceel Gaal o SP 208-209 K 3
Ceel Garas o SP 208-209 G 6
Ceel Huur o SP 208-209 J 6
Ceel Madoobe, togga ~ SP 208-209 J 4
Ceepeecee o CDN (BC) 230-231 C 4
Ceerigaabo ☆ SP 208-209 H 3
Cefalù o I 100-101 E 5
Cega, Río ~ E 98-99 E 4
Čegdomyn o RUS 122-123 E 3
Čegitun ~ RUS 112-113 Z 3
Cegléd o H 92-93 P 5
Cegonha, Corredeira da ~ BR 72-73 E 7
Čehel Abdālān, Kūh-e ▲ AFG 134-135 K 2
Ceheng o VRC 156-157 D 4
Čehov o RUS 122-123 K 5
Čehov ☆• RUS (Mos) 94-95 P 4
Čehova, gora ▲ RUS 122-123 K 5
Ceiba, La ☆ HN 52-53 L 4
Ceiba, La o YV (ANZ) 60-61 J 3
Ceiba, La o YV (TRU) 60-61 F 3
Ceibal, El ∴• GCA 52-53 J 3
Ceibalito o RA 76-77 E 3
Ceibas o RA 78-79 K 2
Ceja, La o CO 60-61 D 4
Cejas, Las o RA 76-77 E 4
Čeka ~ RUS 114-115 O 6
Čekanovskij o RUS 116-117 K 7
Čekanovskogo, krjaž ▲ RUS 110-111 N 3
Çekerek ☆ TR 128-129 F 2
Çekerek Irmağı ~ TR 128-129 G 2
Çekerek Irmağı ~ TR 128-129 F 2
Čekmaguš ☆ RUS 96-97 J 6
Čekunda o RUS 122-123 E 3
Čekurdah o RUS 110-111 a 4
Čekurovka o RUS 110-111 Q 4
Celaque, Parque Nacional ⊥ HN 52-53 K 4
Celarain, Punta ▲ MEX 52-53 L 1
Čelasin ~ RUS 120-121 G 5
Celaya o MEX 52-53 D 1
Čelbas ~ RUS 102-103 M 5
Čeldonka o RUS 118-119 J 9
Celebes Basin ≃ 14-15 E 7
Celebes Sea ≈ 164-165 G 2
Celeiro Murta o BR 72-73 J 4
Čeleken o TM 136-137 C 5
Celendín o PE 64-65 C 5
Celeste, Río ~ BR 70-71 K 3
Celestún o• MEX 52-53 J 1
Celica o EC 64-65 C 4
Celina o RUS 102-103 M 4
Celina o USA (OH) 280-281 B 3
Celina o USA (TN) 276-277 K 4
Celina o USA (TX) 264-265 H 5
Celinnoe o KA 136-137 L 4
Celinnoe ☆ RUS (ALT) 124-125 O 2
Celinnoe ☆ RUS (KRG) 114-115 G 7
Celinograd = Akmola ☆ KA 124-125 G 3
Celista o CDN (BC) 230-231 K 3
Čeljabinsk ☆ RUS 96-97 M 6
Celje o SLO 100-101 E 1
Čeljuskin, mys ▲ RUS 108-109 f 3
Čeljuskin, poluostrov ∩ RUS 108-109 e 3
Celle o• D 92-93 L 2
Čel'mana, ostrova ∩ RUS 108-109 V 4
Čelno-Veršiny ☆ RUS 96-97 G 6
Čelomdža ~ RUS 120-121 M 3
Čelončěn ~ RUS 118-119 G 6
Celorico da Beira o P 98-99 D 4
Celtic Shelf ≃ 8 B 3
Çeltik ☆ TR 128-129 D 3
Celuk o RI 168 B 7
Čema ~ RUS 88-89 T 4
Čemal o RUS 124-125 P 3
Cemara ~ RI 166-167 J 4
Čemdal'sk o RUS 116-117 L 6
Cemoltan o KA 146-147 C 4
Cempi, Teluk ≈ 168 D 7
Cenajo, Embalse del < E 98-99 G 5
Čenārān o IR 136-137 F 6
Čenāreh o IR 128-129 M 5
Cenderawasih, Teluk ≈ 166-167 H 3
Cenderawasih Marine Reserve ⊥• RI 166-167 H 3
Cenepa, Río ~ PE 64-65 C 4
Cengel = Hösööt o MAU 146-147 J 1
Cenghis Khan Ling • VRC 154-155 F 2
Čenhèr = Altan Ovoo o MAU 148-149 E 4
Čenhèrmandal = Modot o MAU 148-149 J 4
Cennet ve Cehennem • TR 128-129 F 4
Cenotillo o MEX 52-53 K 1
Centani o ZA 220-221 J 6
Centenario, El o MEX 50-51 D 5
Centenário do Sul o BR 72-73 E 7
Centenary o USA (SC) 284-285 L 2
Centenary o ZW 218-219 F 3
Centennial o USA (WY) 252-253 M 5
Center o USA (CO) 254-255 J 6
Center o USA (NE) 262-263 J 2
Center o USA (TX) 268-269 F 5
Center, Le o USA (MN) 270-271 E 6
Centerburg o USA (OH) 280-281 D 3
Center Hill o USA (AR) 276-277 D 5
Center Hill Lake ⊂⊃ USA (TN) 276-277 K 4
Center Ossipee o USA (NH) 278-279 K 5
Center Point o USA (AL) 284-285 D 3
Centerville o USA (IA) 274-275 F 4
Centerville o USA (MO) 276-277 E 3
Centerville o USA (NC) 282-283 J 4
Centerville o USA (TN) 276-277 H 5
Centerville o USA (TX) 268-269 E 5
Centerville o USA (WI) 270-271 G 6
Centinela, Cerro ▲ RA 78-79 D 4
Centinela, Picacho del ▲ MEX 50-51 H 3
Centinela, Sierra del ▲ RA 76-77 E 3
Central o BR 68-69 G 7
Central □ EAK 212-213 F 4
Central □ MW 218-219 G 1
Central □ RB 218-219 C 5
Central o USA (AL) 284-285 E 2
Central o USA (NM) 256-257 G 6
Central □ Z 218-219 D 2
Central = Centre □ CAM 204-205 J 6
Central, Cordillera ▲ BOL 70-71 D 6
Central, Cordillera ▲ CO 60-61 C 6
Central, Cordillera ▲ CR 52-53 B 6
Central, Cordillera ▲ DOM 54-55 K 5
Central, Cordillera ▲ PE 64-65 C 5
Central, Cordillera ▲ USA (PR) 286-287 P 2
Central African Republic = Centrafricaine, République ■ RCA 206-207 C 5
Central Australia Aboriginal Land ✗ AUS 172-173 J 6
Central Bedeque o CDN (PEI) 240-241 M 4
Central Brāhui Range ▲ PK 134-135 M 4
Central Butte o CDN (SAS) 232-233 M 5
Central City o USA (CO) 254-255 K 4
Central City o USA (IA) 274-275 G 2
Central City o USA (KY) 276-277 H 3
Central City o USA (NE) 262-263 J 3
Central de Minas o BR 72-73 K 5
Central Desert Aboriginal Land ✗ AUS 172-173 K 5
Central Eastern Australian Rainforest ⊥••• AUS 178-179 M 5
Central Ferry o USA (WA) 244-245 H 4
Centralia o USA (IL) 274-275 J 6
Centralia o USA (MO) 274-275 F 5
Centralia o USA (WA) 244-245 C 4
Central Island ∩ EAK 212-213 F 2
Central Island National Park ⊥ EAK 212-213 F 2
Central Kalahari Game Reserve ⊥ RB 218-219 B 5
Central los Molles o RCH 76-77 B 6
Central Makrān Range ▲ PK 134-135 J 5
Central Mount Stuart ▲ AUS 178-179 B 1
Central Mount Wedge ▲ AUS 172-173 K 7
Central'naja, gora ▲ RUS 108-109 e 4
Central'nojakutskaja ravnina ∪ RUS 118-119 J 3
Central'nolesnoj zapovednik ⊥ RUS 94-95 N 3
Central'nosibirskij zapovednik ⊥ RUS (KRN) 114-115 U 3
Central'nosibirskij zapovednik ⊥ RUS (KRN) 114-115 S 4
Central'no-Tungusskoe, plato ⊥ RUS 116-117 K 5
Central'nye Karakumy ⊥ TM 136-137 E 5
Central'nyj o RUS 114-115 T 7
Central Pacific Basin ≃ 14-15 K 6
Central Patricia o CDN (ONT) 234-235 N 3
Central Point o USA (OR) 244-245 C 8
Central Range ▲ LS 220-221 J 4
Central Range ▲ PNG 183 B 3
Central Region □ GH 202-203 K 7
Central Saanich o CDN (BC) 230-231 F 5
Central Siberian Plateau = Srednesibirskoe ploskogor'e ⊥ RUS 10-11 J 2
Central Valley o USA (CA) 246-247 C 3
Central West Goldfields • AUS 180-181 K 2
Central West River o CDN (NS) 240-241 N 5
Centre □ F 90-91 H 8
Centre o USA (AL) 284-285 E 2
Centre = Central □ CAM 204-205 J 6
Centre de Flacq o MS 224 C 7
Centre Island ∩ AUS 174-175 D 4
Centre Mountain ▲ USA (ID) 250-251 D 6
Centre Spatial Guyanais • F 62-63 H 3
Centreville o CDN (NB) 240-241 H 4
Centreville o CDN (NFL) 242-243 P 4
Centreville o USA (AL) 284-285 C 4
Centreville o USA (MD) 280-281 K 4
Centreville o USA (MS) 268-269 J 5
Centro, Cayo ∩ MEX 52-53 L 2
Centro, El o USA (CA) 248-249 J 7
Centro do Vieira o BR 68-69 F 3
Centurion o ROU 74-75 D 9
Century o USA (FL) 286-287 B 4
Cenxi o VRC 156-157 G 5
Cenzontle o MEX 50-51 H 4
Čepca ~ RUS 96-97 J 5
Čepeck, Kirovo- ☆ RUS 96-97 G 4
Cepiring o RI 168 D 3
Cepu o RI 168 D 3
Ceram = Pulau Seram ∩ RI 166-167 E 3
Ceram Sea = Seram, Laut ≈ RI 166-167 D 3
Cerbatana, Serrania de la ▲ YV 60-61 H 4
Cercado, El o DOM 54-55 K 5
Čerdakly ☆ RUS 96-97 F 6
Čerdyn' ☆ RUS 114-115 D 4
Cereal o CDN (ALB) 232-233 H 4
Cerejeiras o BR 70-71 G 3
Čeremhovo ☆ RUS 116-117 L 9
Čeremhovskaja, Irkutsko, ravnina ∪ RUS 116-117 K 8
Čeremšan ☆ RUS 96-97 G 6
Čeremuhovo o RUS 114-115 F 4
Čerëmuški o RUS 116-117 E 9
Čerendej ~ RUS 118-119 J 5
Čerepanovo ☆ RUS 124-125 N 1
Čerepovec ☆ RUS 94-95 P 2
Ceres o BR 72-73 F 3
Ceres o RA 76-77 G 5
Ceres o ZA 220-221 D 6
Ceresco o USA (NE) 262-263 K 3
Cerete o CO 60-61 D 3
Cerezo de Abajo o E 98-99 F 4
Čerga o RUS 124-125 O 3
Cerignola o I 100-101 E 4
Čeriktej o RUS 118-119 P 4
Čerkasskoe o RUS 96-97 E 7
Čerkassy = Čerkasy ☆ UA 102-103 H 3
Čerkasy ☆ UA 102-103 H 3
Çerkeş ☆ TR 128-129 E 2
Čerkessk ☆ RUS 126-127 E 5
cerkva Česnoho chresta • UA 102-103 C 3
Čerlak ☆ RUS 124-125 J 1
Çermik ☆ TR 128-129 H 3
Cerna o RO 102-103 F 5
Černaja ~ RUS 112-113 L 5
Černaja ~ RUS 112-113 P 5
Černaja ~ RUS 118-119 J 9
Černaja, gora ▲ RUS 122-123 F 7
Cernavodă o RO 102-103 F 5
Černenko = Šarypovo o RUS 114-115 U 7
Černigov = Černihiv o• UA 102-103 G 2
Černihiv o• UA 102-103 G 2
Černihivs'ke polissja ⊥ UA 102-103 G 2
Černivci ☆ UA 102-103 D 3
Černjachiv o UA 102-103 F 2
Černjaevo o RUS 118-119 N 9
Černjahovsk ☆•• RUS 94-95 G 4
Černjanka o RUS 102-103 K 2
Černogorsk o RUS 116-117 E 9
Černorečenskij o RUS 96-97 H 3
Černovcy = Černivci ☆ UA 102-103 D 3
Černovka o RUS 124-125 M 1
Černozemel'skij kanal ~ RUS 126-127 F 5
Černuška ☆ RUS 96-97 K 5
Černut'evo o RUS 88-89 U 5
Černycev cyganak ≈ 126-127 N 5
Černye Brat'ja, ostrova ∩ RUS 122-123 O 5
Černye zemli ⊥ RUS 96-97 D 10
Černyj Čulym ~ RUS 116-117 U 7
Černyj Irtyš = Qara Ertis ~ KA 124-125 O 5
Čërnyj Urjum ~ RUS 118-119 J 9
Černyševa, grjada ▲ RUS 108-109 H 9
Černyševskij o RUS 118-119 F 4
Černyškovskij o RUS 102-103 N 3
Černyšova, hrebet ▲ RUS 118-119 L 8
Cero, Corredeira ~ BR 70-71 J 5
Cerqueira César o BR 72-73 F 7
Cerralvo o MEX 50-51 K 4
Cerralvo, Isla ∩ MEX 50-51 E 5
Cërrik o• AL 100-101 G 4
Cerrillada o ROU 76-77 K 6
Cerrillos o RCH 76-77 C 2
Cerrito o PY 76-77 J 4
Cerrito, El o CO 60-61 C 6
Cerritos o MEX 50-51 J 6
Cerro, El o BOL 70-71 G 5
Cerro Azul o BR 74-75 F 5
Cerro Blanco o RA 80 G 3
Cerro Blanco o RCH 76-77 B 5
Cerro Chato o ROU 78-79 M 2
Cerro Chovoreca ⊥ PY 70-71 H 6
Cerro Colorado o ROU 78-79 M 2
Cerro-Cora o BR 68-69 K 5
Cerro Cora, Parque Nacional del ⊥ PY 76-77 J 2
Cerro de Pasco ☆ PE 64-65 D 7
Cerro Gordo o USA (IL) 274-275 K 5
Cerro Largo o BR 76-77 K 5
Cerro Mangote ∴• PA 52-53 D 7
Cerrón, Cerro ▲ YV 60-61 F 2
Cerro Pintado • YV 60-61 H 5
Cerro Policia o RA 78-79 E 5
Cerro Punta o PA 52-53 C 7
Cerro Rico o RA 76-77 E 5
Cerros Colorados, Embalse < RA 78-79 E 5
Cerros de Amotape, Parque Nacional ⊥ PE 64-65 B 3
Cerro Vera o ROU 78-79 L 2
Cerrudo Cué o RA 76-77 J 4
Čerskij o RUS 112-113 L 2
Čerskogo, hrebet ▲ RUS 110-111 W 5
Čerskogo, hrebet ▲ RUS 118-119 E 10
Čertala ~ RUS 114-115 O 6
Certaldo o I 100-101 C 3
Cértegui o CO 60-61 C 5
Čertkovo o RUS 102-103 M 3
Čërtov, porog ~ RUS 110-111 H 5
Čertovo, ozero ⊂⊃ RUS 114-115 Q 2
Cervantes o AUS 176-177 C 5
Cervati, Monte ▲ I 100-101 E 4
Červen' ☆ BY 94-95 L 5
Cervera o E 98-99 H 4
Cervera de Pisuerga o E 98-99 E 3
Cervéteri o• I 100-101 D 4
Cérvia o I 100-101 D 2
Cervino, Monte = Matterhorn ▲•• I 100-101 A 1
Červjanka o RUS 116-117 J 7
Červonograd = Červonohrad o UA 102-103 D 2
Červonohrad o UA 102-103 D 2
Červonoznam'janka o UA 102-103 G 4
Cerwa o VRC 144-145 M 3
Čeryševsk o RUS 118-119 H 9
César, Río ~ CO 60-61 E 3
Césares, Isla de los ∩ RA 78-79 H 6
Cesário Lange o BR 72-73 G 7
Cesena o I 100-101 D 2
Cēsis ☆•• LV 94-95 J 3
Česká Třebová o CZ 92-93 O 4
České Budějovice o CZ 92-93 N 4
Českomoravská vrchovina ▲ CZ 92-93 N 4
Český Krumlov o••• CZ 92-93 N 4
Český Šternberk •• CZ 92-93 N 4
Český Těšín o CZ 92-93 P 4
Česma ☆ RUS 124-125 B 2
Çeşme ☆ TR 128-129 B 3
Češme Bīğār o IR 128-129 M 5
Češme Kabūd o IR 134-135 B 2
Cess, River ~ LB 202-203 F 7
Cessford o CDN (ALB) 232-233 G 5
Čëšskaja guba ≈ 88-89 S 3
Cessnock o AUS 180-181 L 2
Češt-e Šarif o• AFG 134-135 K 1
Cestos Bay ≈ 202-203 F 7
Cestos River ~ LB 202-203 F 7
Cesvaine ☆•• LV 94-95 K 3
Čet' ~ RUS 114-115 T 6
Cetaceo, Mount ▲ RP 160-161 E 4
Četar o VRC 154-155 B 3
Četlasskij Kamen' ▲ RUS 88-89 U 4
Cetraro o I 100-101 E 5
Četvërtyj Kuril'skij proliv ≈ RUS 122-123 Q 3
Četyrëhstolbovoj, ostrov ∩ RUS 112-113 M 1
Céu Azul o BR 74-75 D 5
Čeugda o RUS 122-123 D 3
Ceuta o E 98-99 E 7
Ceuta o YV 60-61 F 3
Cevcenko, cyganak ≈ 126-127 O 4
Cévennes ⊥ F 90-91 J 9
Cévennes, Parc National des ⊥• F 90-91 J 9
Ceyhan ☆ TR 128-129 F 4
Ceyhan Nehri ~ TR 128-129 F 4
Ceylanpınar ☆ TR 128-129 J 4
Ceylon o CDN (SAS) 232-233 O 6
Ceylon o USA (MN) 270-271 D 7
Chaah o MAL 162-163 E 3
Cha-am o THA 158-159 E 4
Cha'anpu o VRC 156-157 G 2
Chabbie Lake ⊂⊃ CDN (ONT) 236-237 J 3
Chabet El Akra • DZ 190-191 E 2
Chablé o MEX 52-53 J 3
Chabyër Caka ⊂⊃ VRC 144-145 E 5
Chacabuco o RA 78-79 J 3
Chacahua, Laguna de ⊂⊃• 52-53 F 4
Chacala o BOL 70-71 D 5
Chacane o MOC 218-219 H 7
Chacao o RCH 78-79 C 6
Chacao, Canal de ≈ 78-79 C 6
Chacarilla, Quebrada de ~ RCH 70-71 C 7
Chacarrão, Cachoeira do ~ BR 66-67 H 6
Chacas o PE 64-65 D 6
Chacay, Arroyo el ~ RA 78-79 E 3
Chacay Alto o RCH 76-77 B 5
Chacayan o PE 64-65 D 7
Chachani, Volcán ▲ PE 70-71 B 5
Chachapoyas ☆ PE 64-65 D 5
Cháchar ~ PK 138-139 C 5
Chacharramendi o RA 78-79 G 4
Chache o GH 202-203 J 5
Chacho, El o RA 76-77 E 6
Chachoengsao o THA 158-159 F 4
Chāchro o• PK 138-139 C 7
Chacmool ∴• MEX 52-53 L 2
Chaco □ RA 76-77 G 3
Chaco, Quebrada de ~ RCH 76-77 C 3
Chaco Austral ⊥ RA 76-77 G 3
Chaco Boreal ⊥ PY 70-71 G 7
Chaco Central ⊥ PY 76-77 G 3
Chaco Culture National Historic Park ⊥••• USA (NM) 256-257 H 2
Chacon, Cape ▲ USA 32-33 E 4
Chacopaya o BOL 70-71 C 4
Chaco River ~ USA (NM) 256-257 G 2
Chacras, Cerro ▲ EC 64-65 B 10
Chad, Lake = Tchad, Lac ⊂⊃ 198-199 F 6
Chad = Tchad ■ TCH 198-199 G 5
Chadaouanka o RN 198-199 C 5
Chadayang o VRC 156-157 K 5
Chadbourn o USA (NC) 282-283 J 6
Chadin o PE 64-65 C 5
Chadiza o Z 218-219 G 2
Chadron o USA (NE) 262-263 D 2
Chafarinas, Islas ∩ E 98-99 F 7
Chafe o WAN 204-205 G 3
Chaffee Military Reservation, Fort ✗✗• USA (AR) 276-277 A 5
Chaffers, Isla ∩ RCH 80 C 2
Chafo o WAN 204-205 F 3
Chafurray o CO 60-61 E 6
Chágai o PK 134-135 L 4
Chágai Hills ▲ PK 134-135 K 4
Chāgalamarri o IND 140-141 H 3
Chaghat ~ BD 142-143 F 3
Chagne o ETH 208-209 C 3
Chagoness o CDN (SAS) 232-233 O 3
Chagos Archipel ~ GB 12 F 5
Chagos Archipelago ~ GB 12 F 5
Chagos-Laccadive Ridge ≃ 12 F 5
Chagos Trench ≃ 12 F 5
Chaguanas o TT 60-61 L 2
Chaguaramal o YV 60-61 K 3
Chaguaramas o TT 60-61 L 2
Chaguaramas o YV (GUA) 60-61 H 3
Chaguaramas o YV (MON) 60-61 K 3
Chaguarpambo o EC 64-65 C 3
Chagulak Island ∩ USA 22-23 L 6
Chagyümgoinba o VRC 144-145 H 5
Chahbounia o DZ 190-191 D 3
Chāh Sandan o PK 134-135 K 4
Chai o MOC 214-215 L 6
Chaïba, Col de ▲ DZ 190-191 E 3
Chaibāsa o IND 142-143 D 4
Chaigneau, Islas ∩ RCH 80 C 6
Chaillu, Massif du ▲ G 210-211 C 4
Chai Nat o THA 158-159 F 3
Chain Fracture Zone ≃ 6-7 H 9
Chaira, La ⊂⊃ CO 64-65 E 1
Chaitén o RCH 78-79 C 7
Chaitén, Ensenada ≈ 78-79 C 7
Chaiwopu o VRC 146-147 H 4
Chaiya o THA 158-159 E 6
Chaiyaphum o THA 158-159 G 3
Chajarí o RA 76-77 K 4

Castillos, Laguna de — Chajarí 313

Chak o PK 138-139 D 5
Chakachamna Lake ⊂ USA 20-21 O 6
Chakachatna River ~ USA 20-21 O 6
Chākāi o IND 142-143 E 3
Chakaktolik o USA 20-21 J 6
Chākar ~ PK 138-139 B 5
Chakari o ZW 218-219 E 4
Chakdara o• PK 138-139 D 2
Chake Chake o EAT 212-213 G 6
Chakia o IND 142-143 C 3
Chak Jhumra o PK 138-139 D 4
Chakkrarat o THA 158-159 G 3
Chakonipau, Lac ⊂ CDN 36-37 P 6
Chakri o PK 138-139 D 3
Chak Swari o IND 138-139 D 3
Chakwāl o PK 138-139 D 3
Chakwenga o Z 218-219 E 2
Chala o EAT 214-215 F 4
Chala o PE 64-65 E 9
Chalaco o PE 64-65 C 4
Chalais o F 90-91 H 9
Chalalou o PNG 183 D 2
Chalanta o RA 78-79 G 2
Chalatenango ☆ ES 52-53 K 4
Chalaua o MOC 218-219 K 3
Chalawa, River ~ WAN 204-205 H 3
Chalbi Desert ⊥ EAK 212-213 F 2
Chalchuapa o ES 52-53 K 5
Chalengkou o VRC 146-147 L 6
Chaleur Bay ≈ 38-39 M 4
Chaleur Bay ≈ CDN 240-241 K 3
Chaleurs, Baie des ≈ 38-39 M 4
Chaleurs, Baie des ≈ CDN 240-241 K 3
Chalhuanca o PE 64-65 F 9
Chalía o Shehuen, Río ~ RA 80 E 4
Chaling o VRC 156-157 H 3
Chalinze o EAT 214-215 K 4
Chālisgaon o IND 138-139 E 9
Chalk River o CDN (ONT) 238-239 H 2
Chalky Inlet ≈ 182 A 7
Chalkyitsik o USA 20-21 T 3
Challakere o IND 140-141 G 3
Challans o F 90-91 G 8
Challa-Ogoyi o DY 204-205 E 4
Challapata o BOL 70-71 D 6
Challenger Deep ≃ 14-15 G 6
Challenger Plateau ≃ 182 B 3
Challis o USA (ID) 252-253 D 2
Chalmette o USA (LA) 268-269 L 7
Châlons-sur-Marne ☆• F 90-91 K 7
Chalon-sur-Saône o F 90-91 K 8
Chalouba = Oum o TCH 198-199 K 5
Chaltel o Fitz Roy, Cerro ▲ RA 80 D 4
Chaltubo o• GE 126-127 E 6
Chá Lugela o MOC 218-219 J 3
Cham o D 92-93 M 4
Châm ⌒ VN 158-159 K 3
Chama o USA (NM) 256-257 J 2
Chama o Z 214-215 G 6
Chama, Rio ~ USA (NM) 256-257 J 2
Chamah, Gunung ▲ MAL (PEK) 162-163 D 2
Chamais < NAM 220-221 B 3
Chaman o PK 134-135 M 3
Chamax ∴• MEX 52-53 L 2
Chamaya, Río ~ PE 64-65 C 5
Chamba o EAT 214-215 J 6
Chamba o•• IND 138-139 F 3
Chambal ~ IND 138-139 G 6
Chambas o C 54-55 F 3
Chamberlain o CDN (SAS) 232-233 N 5
Chamberlain o USA (SD) 260-261 G 3
Chamberlain Island ⌒ CDN 36-37 M 2
Chamberlain Lake ⊂ USA (ME) 278-279 M 2
Chamberlain River ~ AUS 172-173 H 4
Chambers o USA (NE) 262-263 H 2
Chambers Bay ≈ 172-173 K 2
Chambersburg o USA (PA) 280-281 J 4
Chambers Cois o CDN (ONT) 238-239 F 6
Chambers Creek ~ USA (TX) 264-265 H 6
Chambers Island ⌒ USA (WI) 270-271 L 5
Chambéry ☆• F 90-91 K 9
Chambeshi ~ Z 214-215 F 6
Chambi, Jebel ▲ TN 190-191 G 3
Chambira, Río ~ PE 64-65 E 4
Chambishi o Z 214-215 E 7
Chambo o EC 64-65 C 2
Chambord o CDN (QUE) 240-241 C 2
Chambord, Château ••• F 90-91 H 8
Chambrey o RP 160-161 E 7
Chambri Lakes ⊂ PNG 183 B 3
Chame o PA 52-53 E 7
Chamelecón, Río ~ HN 52-53 K 4
Chametengo o MOC 218-219 H 3
Chameza o CO 60-61 E 5
Chāmi < RIM 196-197 C 4
Chamical o RA 76-77 D 6
Chamiss Bay o CDN (BC) 230-231 B 3
Cham Kha o THA 142-143 L 6
Chamlang ▲ NEP 144-145 F 7
Ch'amo Hāyk' ⊂ ETH 208-209 C 6
Chamois o USA (MO) 274-275 G 6
Chamouchouane, Rivière ~ CDN (QUE) 236-237 P 3
Champ, Lac ⊂ CDN 36-37 R 7
Champagne o CDN 20-21 W 6
Champagne ⊥• F 90-91 K 7
Champagne-Ardenne ◘ F 90-91 K 8
Champaign o USA (IL) 274-275 K 4
Champaqui, Cerro ▲ RA 76-77 E 6
Champasak o LAO 158-159 H 3
Champerico o GCA 52-53 J 4
Champhai o IND 142-143 H 4
Champion o CDN (ALB) 232-233 E 5
Champion o USA (MI) 270-271 L 4
Champlain o USA (NY) 278-279 H 4
Champlain, Lake ⊂ USA (NY) 278-279 H 4
Champotón o• MEX 52-53 J 2
Chāmrājnagar o IND 140-141 G 5
Chana, Kafin- o WAN 198-199 B 6
Chanachane, Oued ~ DZ 196-197 H 2
Chañaral o RCH 76-77 B 4
Chañaral, Isla ⌒ RCH 76-77 B 5
Chança, Rio ~ P 98-99 D 6
Chancani o RA 76-77 E 6
Chancay o PE 64-65 D 7
Chancay, Río ~ PE 64-65 C 5
Chancaybaños o PE 64-65 C 5
Chancellor o CDN (ALB) 232-233 F 4
Chan-Chan ••• PE 64-65 C 6
Ch'anch'o o ETH 208-209 D 4
Chanco o RCH 78-79 C 3
Chanco, Bahía ≈ 78-79 C 3
Chanda o IND 142-143 C 2
Chandalar River ~ USA 20-21 Q 3
Chandaler o USA 20-21 Q 3
Chandannagar o IND 142-143 F 4
Chandarpur o IND 142-143 C 5
Chandausi o IND 138-139 G 5
Chāndbāli o IND 142-143 E 5
Chandeleur Islands ⌒ USA (LA) 268-269 M 7
Chandeleur Sound ≈ 48-49 D 5
Chandeleur Sound ≈ USA 268-269 L 7
Chandeliers, Col des ▲ RN 198-199 F 2
Chanderi o IND 138-139 G 7
Chandgad o IND 140-141 F 3
Chandigarh ☆•• IND 138-139 F 4
Chandipur o IND 142-143 E 5
Chandla o IND 142-143 B 3
Chandler o CDN (QUE) 240-241 L 2
Chandler o USA (AZ) 256-257 D 5
Chandler o USA (OK) 264-265 H 3
Chandler o USA (TX) 264-265 J 6
Chandler, Mount ▲ AUS 176-177 M 3
Chandler Lake ⊂ USA 20-21 O 2
Chandler River ~ USA 20-21 P 2
Chandless, Rio ~ BR 66-67 C 7
Chandless, Rio ~ BR 70-71 J 2
Chandpur o BD 142-143 G 4
Chandrabhāga ~ IND 138-139 F 3
Chandragadi o NEP 144-145 G 7
Chandrapur o IND 138-139 G 10
Chandrasekharapuram o IND 140-141 H 3
Chanduy o EC 64-65 B 3
Chandvad o IND 138-139 E 9
Chandwa o IND 142-143 D 4
Chang o PK 138-139 B 6
Changa o Z 218-219 E 3
Changadae Dan ▲ DVR 150-151 G 8
Changamba o ANG 216-217 E 6
Changamwe o EAK 212-213 G 6
Changanācheri o IND 140-141 G 6
Changane, Rio ~ MOC 218-219 G 6
Changara o MOC 218-219 G 3
Changar Char o BD 142-143 G 4
Changbai o VRC 150-151 G 7
Changbai Shan ▲ VRC 150-151 F 7
Changbaishan • VRC 150-151 G 6
Changbaishan Z.B. ⊥• VRC 150-151 F 6
Changcheng o VRC 156-157 F 7
Chang Chenmo ~ IND 138-139 G 2
Changchun ☆ VRC 150-151 E 6
Changdao o VRC 154-155 M 3
Changde o VRC 156-157 G 2
Changdianhekou o VRC 150-151 E 7
Changfeng o VRC 154-155 K 5
Changgi Gap ▲ ROK 150-151 G 9
Changhang o ROK 150-151 F 9
Changhua o RC 156-157 M 4
Changji o VRC 146-147 H 3
Changjiang o VRC 156-157 F 7
Chang Jiang ~ VRC 154-155 L 6
Changjiang Kou ≈ 154-155 N 6
Changjiang Sanxia ~•• VRC 154-155 F 6
Changjin o DVR 150-151 F 7
Changjin Gang ~ DVR 150-151 F 7
Changjin Ho ⊂ DVR 150-151 F 7
Changkat Jering o MAL 162-163 D 2
Changle o VRC (FUJ) 156-157 L 4
Changle o VRC (SIC) 154-155 E 6
Changli o VRC 154-155 L 2
Changling o VRC (HUB) 154-155 H 6
Changling o VRC (JIL) 150-151 E 5
Changlun o MAL 162-163 D 2
Changma He ~ VRC 146-147 N 6
Changmar o VRC 144-145 C 3
Changning o VRC (HUN) 156-157 H 3
Changning o VRC (SIC) 156-157 D 2
Changning o VRC (YUN) 142-143 L 3
Chango o IND 138-139 G 4
Changoti o IND 138-139 E 5
Changpin o RC 156-157 M 5
Changping o VRC 154-155 K 1
Changsan Got ▲ DVR 150-151 E 8
Changsha ☆• VRC 156-157 H 2
Changshan o VRC 156-157 L 2
Changshan Qundao ⌒ VRC 150-151 D 8
Changshou o VRC 156-157 E 2
Changshu o VRC 154-155 M 6
Changshun o VRC 156-157 E 3
Changsong o DVR 150-151 E 7
Changsŏng o ROK 150-151 F 10
Changtai o VRC 156-157 K 4
Changting o VRC 156-157 K 4
Changtu o VRC 150-151 E 6
Changuillo o PE 64-65 E 9
Ch'angwon o ROK 150-151 G 10
Changwu o VRC 156-157 G 5
Changxing o VRC 154-155 L 6
Changyang o VRC 156-157 D 3
Changyon o DVR 150-151 E 8
Changyuan o VRC 154-155 J 4
Changzhi o VRC 154-155 H 3
Changzhou o VRC 154-155 L 6
Chankanai o CL 140-141 H 6
Chanler's Falls ~ EAK 212-213 G 3
Channapatna o IND 140-141 G 4
Channarāyapatna o IND 140-141 G 4
Channel Country, The ⌣ AUS 178-179 E 3
Channel Islands ◘ GB 90-91 F 7
Channel Islands ⌒ USA (CA) 248-249 D 6
Channel Islands National Park ∴ USA (CA) 248-249 D 6
Channel-Port-aux-Basques o CDN (NFL) 242-243 J 5
Channel Rock ⌒ BS 54-55 G 3
Channing o USA (TX) 264-265 B 3
Chantada o E 98-99 D 3
Chanthaburi o THA 158-159 G 4
Chantrey Inlet ≈ 30-31 W 2
Chanu Daro ∴• PK 138-139 B 6
Chanute o USA (KS) 262-263 L 7
Chany, Ozero = Čany, ozero ⊂ RUS 124-125 K 1
Chao, Isla ⌒ PE 64-65 C 6
Chaohu o VRC 154-155 K 6
Chao Hu • VRC 154-155 K 6
Chaouia ⊥ MA 188-189 H 4
Chaoyang o VRC 150-151 C 7
Chaozhou o VRC 156-157 K 5
Chapacura, Cachoeira ~ BOL 70-71 F 4
Chapada o BR 74-75 D 7
Chapada Diamantina ▲ BR 72-73 J 2
Chapada Diamantina, Parque Nacional ⊥ BR 72-73 K 2
Chapada do Araripe ▲ BR 68-69 H 5
Chapada dos Guimarães o BR 70-71 K 4
Chapada dos Veadeiros, Parque Nacional da ⊥ BR 72-73 G 3
Chapada Grande ▲ BR 68-69 G 5
Chapadinha o BR 68-69 G 3
Chapais o CDN (QUE) 236-237 O 3
Chapala o MEX 52-53 C 1
Chapala, Lago de ⊂ MEX 52-53 C 1
Chapalcó, Valle de ⌣ RA 78-79 G 4
Chaparaó, Serra do ▲ BR 72-73 J 6
Chapare, Río ~ BOL 70-71 E 5
Chaparra o PE 64-65 F 9
Chaparral o CO 60-61 D 6
Chaparrito o CO 60-61 F 5
Chaparro, El o YV 60-61 J 3
Chapas, Las o RA 78-79 F 7
Chapeco o BR 74-75 D 6
Chapel Hill o USA (NC) 282-283 H 5
Chapel Hill o USA (TN) 276-277 J 5
Chapel Island Indian Reserve ✕ • CDN (NS) 240-241 P 5
Chapelle, La o RH 54-55 J 5
Chapelton o JA 54-55 G 5
Chaperito o USA (NM) 256-257 L 3
Chapin o USA (MI) 272-273 E 4
Chapleau o CDN (ONT) 236-237 E 5
Chapleau-Nemegosenda Provincial Park ⊥ CDN (ONT) 236-237 F 4
Chapleau River ~ CDN (ONT) 236-237 E 4
Chaplin o CDN (SAS) 232-233 M 5
Chaplin o USA (KY) 276-277 K 3
Chaplin Lake ⊂ CDN (SAS) 232-233 M 5
Chapman, Cape ▲ CDN 24-25 b 6
Chapman, Lac ⊂ CDN (QUE) 236-237 O 4
Chapman Ranch o USA (TX) 266-267 K 6
Chapmanville o USA (WV) 280-281 D 6
Chapo, Lago ⊂ RCH 78-79 C 6
Chappell o USA (NE) 262-263 D 3
Chappells o USA (SC) 284-285 J 2
Chapra o IND (BIH) 142-143 D 3
Chapra o IND (MAP) 138-139 F 8
Chā Preta o BR 68-69 K 6
Chaptico o USA (MD) 280-281 K 5
Chapuru o• SOL 184 I d 3
Chapuy o RA 78-79 J 2
Chār < RIM 196-197 D 4
Charache o YV 60-61 F 3
Charadai o RA 76-77 H 4
Charagua o BOL 70-71 F 6
Charala o CO 60-61 E 4
Charancho, El o RA 78-79 G 4
Charara Safari Area ⊥ ZW 218-219 E 3
Charcas o MEX 50-51 J 6
Charco o USA (TX) 266-267 K 5
Charco, El o RA 76-77 E 4
Charco de la Peña o MEX 50-51 G 3
Charcot, Île ⌒ ARK 16 G 23
Charcot Land ⊥ GRØ 26-27 l 7
Chardon o USA (OH) 280-281 E 2
Chardzhev ☆ TM 136-137 H 5
Charef, Oued ~ MA 188-189 K 4
Charente ~ F 90-91 H 8
Charentes ~ F 90-91 G 9
Chari ~ TCH 206-207 C 3
Chari-Baguirmi ◘ TCH 206-207 C 3
Charité-sur-Loire, la o F 90-91 J 8
Chariton o USA (IA) 274-275 E 3
Chariton River ~ USA (MO) 274-275 F 4
Charity o GUY 62-63 E 2
Charkhi Dādri o IND 138-139 F 5
Charkiv o UA 102-103 K 3
Charleroi o B 92-93 H 3
Charles o CDN 34-35 F 3
Charles, Cape ▲ USA (VA) 280-281 L 6
Charles, Mount ▲ AUS (WA) 176-177 J 2
Charles, Mount ▲ AUS (WA) 176-177 D 3
Charles, Peak ▲ AUS 176-177 F 6
Charles Bay ≈ 36-37 M 3
Charlesbourg o CDN (QUE) 238-239 O 2
Charles City o USA (IA) 274-275 F 1
Charles City o USA (VA) 280-281 J 6
Charles Dickens Point ▲ CDN 24-25 X 5
Charles Fuhr o RA 80 E 5
Charles Island ⌒ CDN 36-37 M 3
Charles Knob ▲ AUS 176-177 H 2
Charles Lake ⊂ CDN 30-31 O 6
Charles Lighthouse, Cape • USA (VA) 280-281 L 6
Charles Mound ▲ USA (IL) 274-275 H 2
Charles M. Russell National Wildlife Refuge ⊥ USA (MT) 250-251 M 4
Charleston o• NZ 182 C 4
Charleston o USA (AR) 276-277 A 5
Charleston o USA (IL) 274-275 K 5
Charleston o USA (MO) 276-277 F 4
Charleston o USA (MS) 268-269 K 2
Charleston o• USA (SC) 284-285 L 4
Charleston ☆ USA (WV) 280-281 E 5
Charleston, Lake ⊂ USA (IL) 274-275 L 5
Charleston Peak ▲ USA (NV) 248-249 J 3
Charlestown o•• KAN 56 D 3
Charlestown o USA (IN) 274-275 N 6
Charles Town o USA (WV) 280-281 J 4
Charlestown = Baile Chathail o IRL 90-91 C 5
Charles Yorke, Cape ▲ CDN 24-25 f 4
Charleville o AUS 178-179 J 4
Charleville-Mézières ☆ F 90-91 K 7
Charlevoix o USA (MI) 272-273 D 2
Charlevoix, Lake ⊂ USA (MI) 272-273 D 2
Charlie Gibbs Fracture Zone ≃ 6-7 E 3
Charlo o CDN (NB) 240-241 J 3
Charlot, Lac de ⊂ CDN 30-31 Q 4
Charlotte o USA (MI) 272-273 E 5
Charlotte o USA (NC) 282-283 G 5
Charlotte o USA (TN) 276-277 H 4
Charlotte o USA (TX) 266-267 J 5
Charlotte, Lake ⊂ CDN (NS) 240-241 M 6
Charlotte Amalie ☆• USA (VI) 286-287 R 2
Charlotte Bank ≃ 158-159 J 7
Charlotte Court House o USA (VA) 280-281 H 6
Charlotte Harbor ≈ 48-49 G 6
Charlotte Harbor ≈ USA 286-287 G 5
Charlotte Lake ⊂ CDN (BC) 228-229 J 4
Charlottesville o••• USA (VA) 280-281 H 5
Charlottetown ☆• CDN (PEI) 240-241 M 4
Charlotteville o TT 60-61 L 2
Charlson o USA (ND) 258-259 E 3
Charlton o AUS 180-181 G 4
Charlton o CDN (ONT) 236-237 J 5
Charlton Island ⌒ CDN 38-39 E 2
Charnley River ~ AUS 172-173 G 4
Charouine o DZ 188-189 L 6
Charron Lake ⊂ CDN (MAN) 234-235 H 2
Chārsadda o• PK 138-139 C 2
Charters Towers o• AUS 174-175 J 7
Chartres ☆••• F 90-91 H 7
Chās o IND 142-143 E 4
Chaschuil o RA 76-77 C 4
Chaschuil, Valle de ⌣ RA 76-77 C 4
Chaschuil o Guanchín, Río ~ RA 76-77 C 4
Chascomús o RA 78-79 K 3
Chase o CDN (BC) 230-231 K 3
Chase City o USA (VA) 280-281 H 7
Chasicó o RA (BUA) 78-79 H 5
Chasicó o RA (RIN) 78-79 E 6
Chasicó, Arroyo ~ RA 78-79 H 5
Chasicó, Laguna ⊂ RA 78-79 H 5
Chasm o CDN (BC) 230-231 H 2
Chasong o DVR 150-151 F 7
Chasquitambo o PE 64-65 D 7
Chassahowitzka o USA (FL) 286-287 G 3
Chassahowitzka Bay ≈ USA 286-287 G 3
Chassahowitzka National Wildlife Refuge ⊥ USA (FL) 286-287 G 3
Chasse, Réserve de ⊥ MA 188-189 J 3
Châtaigneraie, la o F 90-91 G 8
Chatanika River ~ USA 20-21 R 4
Chateau o CDN (NFL) 242-243 N 1
Châteaubriant o F 90-91 G 8
Château Chambord ••• F 90-91 H 8
Château-d'Oex o CH 92-93 J 5
Châteaudun o F 90-91 H 7
Chateaugay o USA (NY) 278-279 G 4
Château-Gontier o F 90-91 G 8
Châteauguay o CDN (QUE) 238-239 M 3
Châteauguay, Lac ⊂ CDN 36-37 P 6
Châteaulin o F 90-91 E 7
Châteauneuf-sur-Charente o F 90-91 G 9
Châteauneuf-sur-Loire o F 90-91 J 8
Château-Renault o F 90-91 H 8
Château-Richer o CDN (QUE) 238-239 O 2
Châteauroux ☆ F 90-91 H 8
Château-Thierry o F 90-91 J 7
Châtellerault o F 90-91 H 8
Chater o CDN (MAN) 234-235 D 5
Chatfield o CDN (MAN) 234-235 F 4
Chatfield o USA (MN) 270-271 F 7
Chatham o CDN (NB) 240-241 K 3
Chatham o CDN (ONT) 238-239 C 6
Chatham o USA (AK) 32-33 C 3
Chatham o USA (IL) 274-275 J 5
Chatham o USA (LA) 268-269 H 4
Chatham o USA (MI) 270-271 M 4
Chatham o USA (VA) 280-281 G 7
Chatham, Isla ⌒ RCH 80 C 5
Chatham Hill o USA (VA) 280-281 E 7
Chatham Island ⌒ AUS 176-177 D 7
Chatham Islands ⌒ NZ 13 K 7
Chatham Rise ≃ 182 F 5
Chatham Sound ≈ 32-33 E 4
Chatham Sound ≈ CDN 228-229 D 2
Chatham Strait ≈ 32-33 C 3
Châtillon o I 100-101 A 2
Châtillon-sur-Seine o• F 90-91 K 8
Chato, Cerro ▲ RA 78-79 C 7
Chatom o USA (AL) 284-285 B 5
Chatra o IND 142-143 D 3
Chatrapur o IND 142-143 D 6
Chatsworth o AUS 178-179 F 1
Chatsworth o CDN (ONT) 238-239 E 4
Chatsworth o USA (GA) 284-285 F 2
Chattahoochee o USA (FL) 286-287 E 1
Chattahoochee River ~ USA (AL) 284-285 E 5
Chattahoochee River ~ USA (GA) 284-285 E 3
Chattanooga o USA (OK) 264-265 F 4
Chattanooga o• USA (TN) 276-277 K 5
Chattaroy o USA (WA) 244-245 H 3
Chattoga River ~ USA (GA) 284-285 E 2
Chattooga River ~ USA (GA) 284-285 G 2
Chatuge Lake < USA (GA) 284-285 G 2
Chaua o ANG 216-217 E 4
Chaubara o PK 138-139 C 4
Chaudepalle o IND 140-141 H 4
Chaudière, Rivière ~ CDN (QUE) 238-239 O 2
Châu Đốc o• VN 158-159 H 5
Chauk o MYA 142-143 J 5
Chaukundi ∴• PK 134-135 M 6
Chaumont o F 90-91 K 7
Chaumont o F 90-91 H 8
Chauncey o USA (GA) 284-285 G 4
Chauques, Islas ⌒ RCH 78-79 C 7
Chaura Island ⌒ IND 140-141 L 5
Chauri o• IND 140-141 F 3
Chautara o NEP 144-145 E 7
Chautauqua Lake ⊂ USA (IL) 274-275 J 4
Chautauqua Lake ⊂ USA (NY) 278-279 B 6
Chauvin o USA (LA) 268-269 K 7
Chavakachcheri o CL 140-141 J 6
Chāvakkād o IND 140-141 G 5
Chaval o BR 68-69 H 3
Chavarría o RA 76-77 H 5
Cha-Vat o THA 158-159 F 7
Chaves o BR 62-63 K 6
Chaves o• P 98-99 D 4
Chaveslândia o BR 72-73 E 5
Chavez, Los o USA (NM) 256-257 J 4
Chavigny, Lac ⊂ CDN 36-37 M 5
Chavín de Huántar ••• PE 64-65 D 6
Chavinillo o PE 64-65 D 6
Chavón, Río ~ DOM 54-55 L 5
Chavuma o Z 218-219 B 1
Chavuma Falls ~ Z 218-219 B 1
Chavuna o EAT 214-215 D 6
Chayanta, Río ~ BOL 70-71 D 6
Chazón o RA 78-79 H 2
Chazón, Arroyo ~ RA 78-79 H 2
Cheadle o CDN (ALB) 232-233 E 4
Cheaha Mountain ▲ USA (AL) 284-285 E 3
Cheakamus Indian Reserve ✕ CDN (BC) 230-231 F 4
Cheat Lake ⊂ USA (WV) 280-281 G 4
Cheat Mountain ▲ USA (WV) 280-281 G 5
Cheat River ~ USA (WV) 280-281 G 4
Cheb o CZ 92-93 M 3
Chebaba, Hassi < DZ 190-191 D 6
Chebba o TN 190-191 H 3
Chebbi, Erg ⊥ MA 188-189 K 5
Chebogue Point o CDN (NS) 240-241 J 7
Cheboksary = Čeboksary ☆ RUS 96-97 E 5
Cheboygan o USA (MI) 272-273 E 2
Checa o E 98-99 G 4
Chech, Erg ⊥ DZ 196-197 J 2
Chech, Erg ⊥ RIM 196-197 G 3
Ché Ché o GNB 202-203 C 4
Checheng o RC 156-157 M 5
Chechenia = Nohčijčo' Respublika ◘ RUS 126-127 F 6
Cheche Pass ▲ LS 220-221 J 4
Chech'ŏn o ROK 150-151 G 9
Checotah o USA (OK) 264-265 J 3
Chedabucto Bay ≈ 38-39 O 6
Chedabucto Bay ≈ CDN 240-241 O 5
Chéddra o TCH 198-199 H 6
Cheding o VRC 144-145 G 6
Cheduba = Man'aung o MYA 142-143 H 6
Cheduba Island = Man'aung Kyun ⌒ MYA 142-143 H 6
Cheduba Strait ≈ 142-143 H 6
Cheecham o CDN 32-33 P 3
Cheektowaga o USA (NY) 278-279 C 6
Cheepash River ~ CDN (ONT) 236-237 G 2
Cheepie o AUS 178-179 H 4
Cheesman Peak ▲ AUS 176-177 L 3
Chefchaouene ☆ MA 188-189 J 3
Chefornak o USA 20-21 H 6
Chéfu, Rio ~ MOC 194-195 F 6
Chegga o DZ 190-191 E 4
Chegga o RIM 196-197 H 2
Chegge < RIM 196-197 E 5
Chegutu o ZW 218-219 F 4
Chehalis o USA (WA) 244-245 C 4
Chehalis River ~ USA (WA) 244-245 B 4
Chehaw Indian Monument • USA (GA) 284-285 F 5
Chehong Jiang ~ VRC 156-157 C 3
Chejchila, La o RA 76-77 E 4
Cheju o ROK 150-151 F 11
Cheju Do ⌒ ROK 150-151 F 11
Cheju Haehyŏp ≈ 150-151 F 11
Chela, Serra da ▲ ANG 216-217 B 8
Chelan o CDN (SAS) 232-233 P 3
Chelan o USA (WA) 244-245 E 3
Chelan, Lake ⊂ USA (WA) 244-245 E 2
Chelaslie River ~ CDN (BC) 228-229 H 3
Chelatna Lake ⊂ USA 20-21 P 5
Ch'elenk'o o ETH 208-209 E 4
Chelforó o RA 78-79 F 5
Chelforo, Arroyo ~ RA 78-79 K 4
Chelghoum El Aïd o DZ 190-191 F 2
Chelia, Djebel ▲ DZ 190-191 F 3
Chelif, Oued ~ DZ 190-191 C 3
Chelinda o MW 214-215 G 6
Cheline o MOC 218-219 H 6
Chellal o DZ 190-191 E 3
Chełm ☆ PL 92-93 R 3
Chełmno o• PL 92-93 P 2
Chelmsford o CDN (ONT) 238-239 D 2
Chelmsford Dam < ZA 220-221 J 4
Chełmża o• PL 92-93 P 2
Chelsea o USA (OK) 264-265 J 2
Chelsea o USA (VT) 278-279 J 5
Cheltenham o• GB 90-91 F 6
Chelvai o IND 142-143 B 6
Chelyabinsk = Čeljabinsk ☆ RUS 96-97 M 6
Chemaïa o MA 188-189 G 4
Chemainus o CDN (BC) 230-231 F 5
Chemax o MEX 52-53 L 1
Chemba o MOC 218-219 H 3
Chembe o Z 214-215 E 6
Chemchâm, Sebkhet ⊂ RIM 196-197 D 4
Chemehuevi Valley Indian Reservation ✕ USA (CA) 248-249 K 5
Chemillé o F 90-91 G 8
Chemnitz o D 92-93 M 3
Chemong o CDN (SAS) 232-233 Q 2
Chemult o USA (OR) 244-245 D 7
Chemung River ~ USA (NY) 278-279 E 6
Chenab ~ IND 138-139 E 3
Chenāb ~ PK 138-139 D 3
Chenachen < DZ 188-189 J 7
Chena Hot Springs o USA 20-21 R 4
Chenango River ~ USA (NY) 278-279 F 6
Chena River ~ USA 20-21 R 4
Chen Barag Qi o VRC 150-151 B 3
Ch'ench'a o ETH 208-209 C 5
Chencoyi o MEX 52-53 J 2
Chenereh, Kampung o MAL 162-163 E 2
Chénéville o CDN (QUE) 238-239 K 3
Cheney o USA (KS) 262-263 J 7
Cheney o USA (WA) 244-245 H 3
Cheney Reservoir ⊂ USA (KS) 262-263 J 7
Chengalpattu o IND 140-141 H 4
Chengam o IND 140-141 H 4
Chengannūr o IND 140-141 G 6
Chengbu o VRC 156-157 F 3
Chengcheng o VRC 154-155 F 4
Chengde o VRC 154-155 K 1
Chengdu ☆ VRC 154-155 D 6
Chenggu o VRC 154-155 E 5
Chenghai o VRC 156-157 K 5
Cheng Hai ⊂ VRC 142-143 M 2
Chengkung o RC 156-157 M 5
Chengmai o VRC 156-157 G 7
Chengqian o VRC 154-155 K 4
Chengshan Jiao ▲ VRC 154-155 N 3
Chengwu o VRC 154-155 J 4
Cheng Xian o VRC 154-155 D 5
Cheniere Lake < USA (LA) 268-269 H 4
Chenik o USA 22-23 T 3
Chenini o• TN 190-191 H 4
Chenjiagang o VRC 154-155 L 4
Chenoa o USA (IL) 274-275 K 4
Chenpur o NEP 144-145 C 6
Chenque, Cerro ▲ RA 80 G 2
Chenxi o VRC (HUN) 156-157 G 2
Chenxi o VRC (SIC) 154-155 E 6
Chenzhou o VRC 156-157 H 4
Cheo Reo o VN 158-159 K 4
Chepachet o USA (RI) 278-279 K 7
Chepen o PE 64-65 C 5
Chepes o RA 76-77 D 6
Chepes, Sierra de ▲ RA 76-77 D 6
Chepo o• PA 52-53 E 7
Chepstow o GB 90-91 F 6
Chequamegon Bay o USA (WI) 270-271 H 4
Cheran o MEX 52-53 D 2
Cheranchi o WAN 198-199 C 6
Cherangany Hills ▲ EAK 212-213 E 3
Cheraw o USA (CO) 254-255 M 5
Cheraw o USA (SC) 284-285 L 2
Cherbourg o F 90-91 G 7
Cherchell o• DZ 190-191 D 2
Cherepani o GH 202-203 L 4
Cherepovets = Čerepovec ☆ RUS 94-95 P 2
Cherful, Cape ▲ USA 22-23 N 5
Chergui, Aftoût ech ⊥ RIM 196-197 C 6
Chergui, Zahrez ⊂ DZ 190-191 D 3
Cherhill o CDN (ALB) 232-233 D 2
Chéri o RN 198-199 E 6
Cheria o DZ 190-191 F 3
Cheriāl o IND 140-141 H 2
Cherkasy = Čerkasy ☆ UA 102-103 H 3
Chernabura Island ⌒ USA 22-23 R 5
Chernihiv = Černihiv o• UA 102-103 G 2
Cherni Island ⌒ USA 22-23 P 5
Chernivtsi = Černivci ☆ UA 102-103 D 3
Chernobyl = Čornobyl' o UA 102-103 G 2
Chernyakhovsk = Černjahovsk ☆•• RUS 94-95 G 4
Cherokee o BS 54-55 G 1
Cherokee o USA (AL) 284-285 B 2
Cherokee o USA (IA) 274-275 C 2
Cherokee o USA (NC) 282-283 D 5
Cherokee o USA (OK) 264-265 F 2
Cherokee o USA (TX) 266-267 J 2
Cherokee Indian Reservation ✕ USA (NC) 282-283 D 5
Cherokee Lake ⊂ USA (TN) 282-283 D 4
Cherokee Sound o BS 54-55 G 1
Cherokee Village o USA (AR) 276-277 D 4
Cherraboun o AUS 172-173 G 5
Chérrepe, Punta de ▲ PE 64-65 C 5
Cherry Creek ~ CDN (BC) 230-231 L 3
Cherry Creek ~ USA (NV) 246-247 L 4
Cherry Creek ~ USA (SD) 260-261 E 2
Cherry Creek ~ USA (CO) 254-255 L 4
Cherryfield o USA (ME) 278-279 O 4
Cherry Hill o USA (VA) 280-281 J 7
Cherryspring o USA (TX) 266-267 J 3
Cherryvale o USA (KS) 262-263 L 7
Cherry Valley o USA (AR) 276-277 E 5
Cherryville o CDN (BC) 230-231 L 3
Cherryville o USA (MO) 276-277 D 3
Cherskogo, Khrebet = Čerskogo, hrebet ▲ RUS 110-111 W 5
Cherson ☆• UA 102-103 H 4
Chesaning o USA (MI) 272-273 E 4
Chesapeake Bay Bridge Tunnel II USA (VA) 280-281 L 6
Chesapeake o USA (VA) 280-281 K 7
Chesapeake Bay ≈ 46-47 K 6
Chesapeake Bay ≈ USA 280-281 K 5
Chesapeake Beach o USA (MD) 280-281 K 5
Chesea, Río ~ PE 64-65 F 6
Cheshire o USA (OR) 244-245 B 6
Chëshskaya Guba = Čëšskaja guba ≈ RUS 88-89 S 3
Cheslatta Lake ⊂ CDN (BC) 228-229 J 3
Chesley o CDN (ONT) 238-239 D 4
Chesnee o USA (SC) 284-285 J 1
Chester o CDN (NS) 240-241 L 6
Chester o•• GB 90-91 F 5
Chester o USA (IA) 274-275 F 1
Chester o USA (ID) 252-253 G 3
Chester o USA (IL) 276-277 F 3
Chester o USA (MT) 250-251 J 3
Chester o USA (NE) 262-263 J 4
Chester o USA (OH) 280-281 F 3
Chester o USA (OK) 264-265 F 2
Chester o USA (PA) 280-281 L 4
Chester o USA (SC) 284-285 J 2
Chester o USA (TX) 268-269 F 6
Chester o USA (VA) 280-281 J 6
Chesterfield o GB 90-91 G 5
Chesterfield o USA (SC) 284-285 K 2
Chesterfield Inlet ≈ 30-31 X 4
Chesterfield Inlet o CDN 30-31 Y 4
Chesterton o USA (IN) 274-275 L 3
Chesterton Range ▲ AUS 178-179 J 3
Chestertown o USA (MD) 280-281 K 4
Chesterville o CDN (ONT) 238-239 K 3
Chestnut o USA (IL) 274-275 J 4
Chesuncook Lake ⊂ USA (ME) 278-279 M 3
Chetaïbi o• DZ 190-191 F 2
Chetek o USA (WI) 270-271 G 5
Chéticamp o CDN (NS) 240-241 P 4
Cheticamp River ~ CDN (NS) 240-241 P 4
Chetimacha Indian Reservation ✕ USA 268-269 J 7
Chet Korkora < RMM 196-197 H 6
Chetlat Island ⌒ IND 140-141 E 5
Chetopa o USA (KS) 262-263 L 7
Chetumal ☆• MEX 52-53 K 2
Chetumal, Bahía de ≈ 52-53 K 2
Chetwynd o CDN 32-33 K 4
Chevak o USA 20-21 H 6
Chevejecure, Río ~ BOL 70-71 D 4
Cheviot o CDN (SAS) 232-233 M 3
Cheviot Hills, The ▲ GB 90-91 F 4
Cheviot Range ▲ AUS 178-179 G 3
Chewack River ~ USA (WA) 244-245 E 2
Chewelah o USA (WA) 244-245 H 2
Chewore Safari Area ⊥ ZW 218-219 E 3
Cheyenne o USA (OK) 264-265 E 3
Cheyenne ☆ USA (WY) 252-253 O 5
Cheyenne Bottoms ⊂ USA (KS) 262-263 H 6
Cheyenne River ~ USA (SD) 260-261 D 2
Cheyenne River ~ USA (WY) 252-253 O 3
Cheyenne River Indian Reservation ✕ USA (SD) 260-261 E 1
Cheyenne Wells o USA (CO) 254-255 N 5
Cheyūr o IND 140-141 J 4
Chezacut o CDN (BC) 228-229 L 4
Chhāpar o IND 138-139 E 6
Chhatak o BD 142-143 G 3
Chhatarpur o IND 138-139 G 7
Chhattisgarh ⊥ IND 142-143 B 5
Chhaygaon o IND 142-143 G 2
Chheharta o IND 138-139 E 4
Chhindwāra o IND 138-139 G 8
Chhota Udepur o IND 138-139 E 8
Chhukha o BHT 142-143 F 2
Chhura o IND 142-143 C 5
Chiachi Island ⌒ USA 22-23 R 5
Ch'iaksan National Park ⊥ ROK 150-151 G 9
Chiamboni o SP 212-213 H 4
Chiangchūn o RC 156-157 M 5
Chiang Dao o THA 142-143 L 6
Chiang Kan o THA 158-159 F 2
Chiang Kham o THA 142-143 M 6
Chiang Khong o THA 142-143 M 5
Chiang Mai ☆ THA 142-143 L 6
Chiang Rai o THA 142-143 L 6
Chian Muan o THA 142-143 M 6
Chiapa, Río ~ MEX 52-53 H 3
Chiapa de Corzo o• MEX 52-53 H 3
Chiapas ◘ MEX 52-53 H 3
Chiari o I 100-101 B 2
Chiasien o RC 156-157 M 5
Chiautla o MEX 52-53 E 2
Chiávari o• I 100-101 B 2
Chiavenna o I 100-101 B 1
Chiawa o Z 218-219 E 2
Chiayi o RC 156-157 M 5
Chiba ☆ J 152-153 J 7
Chibabava o MOC 218-219 G 5
Chibembe o Z 218-219 G 1
Chibia o ANG 216-217 B 7
Chibiaparú o YV 62-63 D 3
Chibi Moya • VRC 156-157 H 2
Chibougamau o CDN (QUE) 236-237 O 3
Chibougamau, Lac ⊂ CDN (QUE) 236-237 O 3
Chibougamau, Rivière ~ CDN (QUE) 236-237 N 3
Chibuto o MOC 220-221 L 2
Chibuzhanghu ⊂ VRC 144-145 H 4
Chibwika o Z 214-215 C 7
Chica, Sierra ▲ RA 78-77 E 6
Chicago o• USA (IL) 274-275 L 3
Chicago Heights o USA (IL) 274-275 L 3
Chicala o ANG (BIE) 216-217 D 6
Chicala o ANG (MOX) 216-217 E 5
Chicamba o MOC 218-219 G 4
Chicamba Real, Barragem de < MOC 218-219 G 4
Chicambi o ANG 216-217 B 6
Chicaná ∴• MEX 52-53 K 2
Chicapa ~ ANG 216-217 F 3
Chicas, Salinas ⊂ RA 78-79 H 5
Chicbul o MEX 52-53 J 2
Chic-Choc, Parc Provincial ⊥ CDN (QUE) 240-241 K 2
Chic-Chocs, Monts ▲ CDN (QUE) 240-241 H 2
Chicha < TCH 198-199 J 4
Chichagof o USA 32-33 B 3
Chichagof Island ⌒ USA 32-33 B 3
Chichancanab, Laguna ⊂• MEX 52-53 K 2
Chichaoua o MA 188-189 G 5
Chicharrona, La o MEX 50-51 H 6
Chichāwatni o PK 138-139 D 4
Chiché, Río ~ BR 68-69 B 6
Chicheng o VRC 154-155 J 1
Chichén Itzá ∴••• MEX 52-53 K 1
Chichester Range ▲ AUS 172-173 D 7

314 Chak — Chichester Range

Chichibu o J 152-153 H 6
Chichibu-Tama National Park ⊥ J 152-153 H 7
Chichigalpa o NIC 52-53 L 5
Chichirate o EC 64-65 D 3
Chichón, Volcan ▲ MEX 52-53 H 3
Chickaloon o USA 20-21 Q 6
Chickamauga & Chattanooga National Military Park • USA (GA) 284-285 E 2
Chickamauga Lake < USA (TN) 282-283 C 5
Chickasaw o USA (AL) 284-285 B 6
Chickasaw Bogue ~ USA (AL) 284-285 C 4
Chickasawhatchee Creek ~ USA (GA) 284-285 F 5
Chickasawhay River ~ USA (MS) 268-269 M 5
Chickasaw National Recreation Area ⊥ • USA (OK) 264-265 H 4
Chickasha o USA (OK) 264-265 G 3
Chickasha, Lake < USA (OK) 264-265 F 3
Chic Kata o RH 54-55 J 5
Chicken o USA 20-21 U 4
Chicken Creek Summit ▲ USA (NV) 246-247 J 2
Chick Lake o CDN 30-31 F 3
Chiclayo ☆ PE 64-65 C 5
Chico o MOC 218-219 G 5
Chico o USA (CA) 246-247 D 4
Chico, Arroyo ~ RA 78-79 L 4
Chico, Río ~ RA 76-77 E 4
Chico, Río ~ RA 78-79 D 7
Chico, Río ~ RA 80 F 5
Chico, Río ~ RA 80 F 4
Chico, Río ~ RA 80 G 2
Chicoa o MOC 218-219 G 2
Chico Arroyo ~ USA (NM) 256-257 H 3
Chicoasén o MEX 52-53 H 3
Chicoasén, Presa <• MEX 52-53 H 3
Chicoca o ANG 216-217 F 7
Chicomba o ANG 216-217 C 7
Chicomo o MOC 220-221 M 2
Chicomoztoc ∴• MEX 50-51 H 6
Chicomuselo o MEX 52-53 H 4
Chicondua ~ ANG 216-217 B 7
Chicontepec de Tejeda o MEX 52-53 E 1
Chicopee o USA (MA) 278-279 J 6
Chicoral o CO 60-61 D 5
Chicot State Park ⊥ USA (LA) 268-269 H 6
Chicotte o CDN (QUE) 242-243 E 3
Chicoutimi o CDN (QUE) 240-241 D 2
Chicualacuala o MOC 218-219 F 6
Chicuma o ANG 216-217 C 6
Chicundo o ANG 216-217 D 6
Chicupa o ANG 216-217 E 7
Ch'ida o ETH 208-209 C 5
Chidambaram o•• IND 140-141 H 5
Chidenguele o MOC 220-221 M 2
Chidester o USA (AR) 276-277 B 7
Chido o ROK 150-151 F 10
Chiede o ANG 216-217 C 8
Chief Joseph Pass ▲ USA (MT) 250-251 F 6
Chiefland o USA (FL) 286-287 G 2
Chief Menominee Monument • USA (IN) 274-275 M 3
Chiefs Island ⌒ RB 218-219 B 4
Chief's Point Indian Reservation Ⅹ CDN (ONT) 238-239 D 4
Chiemsee o D 92-93 M 5
Chiengi o Z 214-215 E 5
Chiềng Khu'o'ng o VN 156-157 C 6
Chiengo o ANG 216-217 D 7
Chieo Lan Reservoir < THA 158-159 E 6
Chiese ~ I 100-101 C 2
Chieti ☆ I 100-101 E 3
Chifango o ANG 216-217 D 7
Chifeng o VRC 148-149 O 6
Chifre, Serra do ▲ BR 72-73 K 4
Chifu o WAN 204-205 F 3
Chifukunya Hills ▲ Z 218-219 E 2
Chifumage ~ ANG 216-217 F 5
Chifunda o Z 214-215 G 6
Chifunde o MOC 218-219 G 2
Chig < RIM 196-197 D 5
Chigamane o MOC 218-219 G 5
Chiginagak, Mount ▲ USA 22-23 S 4
Chiginagak Bay ≈ 22-23 S 4
Chigmit Mountains ▲ USA 22-23 U 3
Chignecto, Cape ▲ CDN (NB) 240-241 K 5
Chignecto Bay ≈ 38-39 M 6
Chignecto Bay ≈ CDN 240-241 L 5
Chignecto Game Sanctuary ⊥ CDN (NS) 240-241 L 5
Chignik o USA 22-23 R 4
Chignik Bay ≈ 22-23 R 4
Chigombe, Rio ~ MOC 218-219 G 6
Chigorodo o CO 60-61 C 4
Chigoubiche, Lac o CDN (QUE) 236-237 P 3
Chiguana o BOL 70-71 D 7
Chigubo o MOC 218-219 G 6
Chihli, Gulf of = Bo Hai ≈ VRC 154-155 L 2
Chihsing Yen ⌒ RC 156-157 M 6
Chihuahua □ MEX 50-51 F 3
Chihuahua ☆ MEX (CHA) 50-51 F 3
Chihuido de Medio, Cerro ▲ RA 78-79 E 5
Chijmuni o BOL 70-71 D 5
Chikanda o WAN 204-205 E 4
Chikaskia River ~ USA (KS) 262-263 J 7
Chik Ballāpur o IND 140-141 G 4
Chikhli o IND (GUJ) 138-139 D 9
Chikhli o IND (MAH) 138-139 F 9
Chikhli o IND (MAP) 138-139 G 8
Chikjajur o IND 140-141 G 3
Chikmagalūr o IND 140-141 F 4
Chiknāyakanhalli o IND 140-141 G 4
Chikodi o IND 140-141 F 2
Chikombedzi o ZW 218-219 F 5
Chikonkomene o Z 218-219 E 2
Chikuma-gawa ~ J 152-153 H 6
Chikuminuk Lake o USA 20-21 L 6
Chikwa o Z 214-215 G 6
Chikwawa o MW 218-219 H 3
Chikwina o MW 214-215 H 6
Chikyu-misaki ▲ J 152-153 J 3
Chila o ANG 216-217 C 6
Chila o MEX 52-53 F 3
Chila, Laguna o MEX 50-51 K 6
Chilakalūrupet o IND 140-141 J 2
Chilako River ~ CDN (BC) 228-229 L 3
Chilan o RC 156-157 M 4
Chi Lăng o VN 156-157 E 6
Chilanga o Z 218-219 E 2
Chilanko Forks o CDN (BC) 228-229 K 4
Chilanko River ~ CDN (BC) 228-229 K 4
Chilapa o MEX 52-53 E 3
Chilapa de Díaz o MEX 52-53 F 3
Chilas o• IND 138-139 E 2
Chilaw o CL 140-141 H 7
Chilca o PE 64-65 D 8
Chilca, Punta ▲ PE 64-65 D 8
Chilcas o RA 76-77 E 4
Chilcaya o RCH 70-71 C 6
Chilcoot o USA (CA) 246-247 E 4
Chilcotin Ranges ▲ CDN (BC) 230-231 F 2
Chilcotin River ~ CDN (BC) 230-231 G 2
Chilcott Island ⌒ AUS 174-175 L 5
Childers o AUS 178-179 M 3
Childersburg o USA (AL) 284-285 D 3
Childress o USA (TX) 264-265 D 4
Chile ■ RCH 78-79 C 5
Chile Basin ≃ 5 D 7
Chile Chico o RCH 80 E 3
Chilecito o• RA 76-77 D 5
Chileka o MW 218-219 H 2
Chilembwe o Z 218-219 F 1
Chilena, Cordillera ▲ RCH 80 D 6
Chilengue, Serra do ▲ ANG 216-217 C 6
Chile Rise ≃ 5 B 8
Chiles, Los o CR 52-53 B 6
Chilesburg o USA (VA) 280-281 J 5
Chilete o PE 64-65 C 5
Chili, Gulf of = Bo Hai ≈ 154-155 L 2
Chilikadrotna River ~ USA 20-21 N 6
Chililabombwe o Z 214-215 D 7
Chilili o USA (NM) 256-257 J 4
Chilkat o USA 20-21 S 6
Chilkat Bald Eagle Preserve ⊥ USA 20-21 W 7
Chilkat Inlet ≈ 20-21 X 7
Chilko Lake o CDN (BC) 230-231 E 2
Chilkoot Pass ▲ USA 20-21 X 7
Chilko River ~ CDN (BC) 230-231 E 2
Chilla o EC 64-65 C 3
Chillagoe o AUS 174-175 H 5
Chillajara o BOL 70-71 E 7
Chillán o RCH 78-79 C 4
Chillán, Río ~ RCH 78-79 D 4
Chillán, Volcán ▲ RCH 78-79 D 4
Chillar o RA 78-79 J 4
Chilla Well o AUS 172-173 K 6
Chillicothe o USA (IL) 274-275 J 4
Chillicothe o USA (MO) 274-275 E 5
Chillicothe o USA (OH) 280-281 D 4
Chillicothe o USA (TX) 264-265 E 4
Chillinji o IND 138-139 E 1
Chilliwack o CDN (BC) 230-231 H 4
Chillūa Tāl o IND 142-143 C 2
Chillūpar o IND 142-143 C 2
Chilmari o BD 142-143 F 3
Chilmark o USA (MA) 278-279 L 7
Chiloango ~ ANG 210-211 D 6
Chilobwe o MW 218-219 G 1
Chiloé, Isla de ⌒ RCH 78-79 C 7
Chiloé, Parque Nacional ⊥ RCH 78-79 B 7
Chilombo o ANG 214-215 B 7
Chilongozi o Z 218-219 F 1
Chiloquin o USA (OR) 244-245 D 8
Chilpancingo de los Bravos ☆ MEX 52-53 E 3
Chilpi o IND 142-143 B 4
Chiltepec o MEX 52-53 H 2
Chilticothe o USA (IL) 274-275 J 4
Chilton o USA (TX) 266-267 K 2
Chilton o USA (WI) 270-271 K 6
Chiluage o ANG 216-217 F 4
Chilubula o Z 214-215 F 6
Chilumba o MW 214-215 H 6
Chilumbulwa o Z 214-215 D 7
Chilwa, Lake o MW 218-219 H 2
Chimala o EAT 214-215 H 5
Chimaliro ▲ MW 214-215 H 6
Chimaltenango ☆ GCA 52-53 J 4
Chimán o PA 52-53 E 7
Chimanimani o• ZW 218-219 G 4
Chimanimani National Park ⊥ ZW 218-219 G 4
Chimasula o Z 218-219 F 2
Chimban o PE 64-65 C 5
Chimbangombe o ANG 216-217 D 6
Chimbaronga o RCH 78-79 D 3
Chimbinde o ANG 216-217 E 6
Chimbo, Río ~ EC 64-65 C 3
Chimborazo, Volcán ▲ EC 64-65 C 2
Chimbote o PE 64-65 C 6
Chimbwingombi ▲ Z 218-219 F 1
Chiméal o K 158-159 G 5
Chimney Rock • USA (NC) 282-283 E 5
Chimney Rock National Historic Site ∴ USA (NE) 262-263 C 3
Chimoio ☆ MOC 218-219 G 4
Chimumo ~ ANG 216-217 D 8
China o MEX 50-51 K 5
China o USA (TX) 268-269 F 6
China = Zhongguo ■ VRC 144-145 E 6
Chinach, Ḥn- < RMM 196-197 K 6
Chinacota o CO 60-61 E 4
Chinake o IND 140-141 F 2
China Lake o USA (CA) 248-249 G 4
China Lake Naval Weapons Center xx USA (CA) 248-249 G 4
Chinampas o MEX 50-51 J 7
China Muerte, Arroyo ~ RA 78-79 E 5
Chinandega ☆ NIC 52-53 L 5
China Point ≃ 248-249 F 7
Chinati Peak ▲ USA (TX) 266-267 C 4
Chincha, Islas de ⌒ PE 64-65 D 8
Chincha Alta o PE 64-65 D 8
Chinchaga River ~ CDN 30-31 K 6
Chinchilla o AUS 178-179 L 4
Chinchilla de Monte Aragón o E 98-99 G 5
Chinchina o CO 60-61 D 5
Chinchin Straits ≈ 162-163 C 2
Chinchorro, Banco ⌒ MEX 52-53 L 2
Chincolco o RCH 78-79 D 2
Chincoteague o USA (VA) 280-281 L 6
Chincoteague Bay ≈ 46-47 L 6
Chincoteague Bay ≈ USA 280-281 L 5
Chincultic ∴• MEX 52-53 J 3
Chinde o MOC 218-219 J 4
Chindo o ROK 150-151 F 10
Chin Do ⌒ ROK 150-151 F 10
Chindwin Myit ~ MYA 142-143 J 3
Chinengue o MOC 218-219 H 1
Chinero, El o MEX 50-51 B 2
Chingaza, Parque Nacional ⊥ CO 60-61 E 5
Chingo o ANG 216-217 B 7
Chingola o Z 214-215 D 7
Chingombe o Z 218-219 F 2
Chinguar o ANG 216-217 D 6
Chingueia o ANG 216-217 D 6
Chinguetti o• RIM 196-197 D 4
Chinguil o TCH 206-207 D 3
Chingwin Bum ▲ MYA 142-143 L 3
Chinhama o ANG 216-217 D 6
Chinhanda o MOC 218-219 G 2
Chinhanguanine o MOC 220-221 L 2
Chin Hills ▲ MYA 142-143 H 4
Chinhoyi ☆• ZW 218-219 F 3
Chiniak, Cape ▲ USA 22-23 U 4
Chiniak Bay ≈ 22-23 U 4
Chiniot o• PK 138-139 D 4
Chinitna Point ▲ USA 22-23 U 3
Chinjan o PK 134-135 M 3
Chinkapook o AUS 180-181 G 3
Chinko ~ RCA 206-207 G 6
Chinle o USA (AZ) 256-257 F 2
Chinle Wash ~ USA (AZ) 256-257 F 2
Chinmen o RC 156-157 L 4
Chinmen Tao ⌒ RC 156-157 L 4
Chinnūr o IND 138-139 G 10
Chino o USA (CA) 248-249 G 5
Chino Creek ~ USA (AZ) 256-257 C 3
Chinon o F 90-91 H 8
Chinook o CDN (ALB) 232-233 H 4
Chinook o USA (MT) 250-251 K 3
Chinook o USA (WA) 244-245 B 4
Chinook Trough ≃ 14-15 L 3
Chinook Valley o CDN 32-33 M 3
Chino Valley o USA (AZ) 256-257 C 4
Chinpurtar o NEP 144-145 E 7
Chinquite o ANG 216-217 B 6
Chinsali o Z 214-215 G 6
Chintāmani o IND 140-141 H 4
Chinteche o MW 214-215 H 6
Chinturu o IND 142-143 B 7
Chinvali o GE 126-127 F 6
Chinyama Litapi o Z 218-219 B 1
Chioa, Lago o PE 64-65 E 6
Chioco o MOC 218-219 G 3
Chióggia o• I 100-101 D 2
Chipai Lake o CDN 34-35 N 4
Chipanga o MOC 218-219 H 3
Chipasanse o Z 214-215 F 5
Chipata ☆ Z 218-219 G 1
Chipepo o Z 218-219 D 3
Chiperone, Monte ▲ MOC 218-219 H 3
Chipewyan Indian Reserve Ⅹ CDN 30-31 O 6
Chipewyan River ~ CDN 32-33 O 3
Chipili o Z 214-215 E 6
Chipinda Pools o ZW 218-219 F 5
Chipindo o ANG 216-217 C 6
Chipinga Safari Area ⊥ ZW 218-219 G 5
Chipinge o ZW 218-219 G 5
Chipiona o E 98-99 D 6
Chipipa o ANG 216-217 C 6
Chipiriri, Río ~ BOL 70-71 E 5
Chip Lake o CDN (ALB) 232-233 C 2
Chip Lake o CDN (ALB) 232-233 C 2
Chipley o USA (FL) 286-287 D 1
Chiplūn o IND 140-141 E 2
Chipman o CDN (ALB) 232-233 F 2
Chipman o CDN (NB) 240-241 K 4
Chipman Lake o CDN (ONT) 236-237 B 3
Chipman River ~ CDN 30-31 R 6
Chipogolo o EAT 214-215 J 4
Chipoia o ANG 216-217 E 6
Chipoka o MW 218-219 H 1
Chipola River ~ USA (FL) 286-287 D 1
Chippenham o GB 90-91 F 6
Chippewa, Lake o USA (WI) 270-271 G 5
Chippewa Falls o USA (WI) 270-271 G 6
Chippewa River ~ USA (WI) 270-271 G 5
Chipungo o Z 218-219 F 1
Chiputneticook Lakes ~ USA (ME) 278-279 O 3
Chiputo o MOC 218-219 G 2
Chiquian o PE 64-65 D 7
Chiquilá o MEX 52-53 L 1
Chiquimula ☆ GCA 52-53 K 4
Chiquimulilla o GCA 52-53 J 4
Chiquinata, Bahía ≈ 70-71 B 7
Chiquinquirá o CO 60-61 E 5
Chiquitina, Isla ⌒ PE 64-65 D 7
Chiquitos, Llanos de ∸ BOL 70-71 F 6
Ch'ira o ETH 208-209 C 5
Chira, Río ~ PE 64-65 B 4
Chirāla o IND 140-141 J 3
Chiramba o MOC 218-219 H 3
Chiredzi o ZW 218-219 F 5
Chireno o USA (TX) 268-269 F 5
Chirfa o RN 198-199 F 2
Chiriacu o PE 64-65 C 4
Chiribiquete, Raudal ~ CO 64-65 F 1
Chiricahua Peak ▲ USA (AZ) 256-257 F 7
Chiriguare, Reserva Faunística ⊥ YV 60-61 G 3
Chirikof Island ⌒ USA 22-23 T 5
Chirikof Point ▲ USA 22-23 C 6
Chirimena o YV 60-61 H 2
Chiriquí, Golfo de ≈ 52-53 C 7
Chiriqui, Laguna de ≈ 52-53 C 7
Chiriqui Grande o PA 52-53 C 7
Chiris, Río ~ PE 64-65 E 8
Chiri San ▲ ROK 150-151 F 10
Chirisan National Park ⊥• ROK 150-151 F 10
Chirisa Safari Area ⊥ ZW 218-219 E 3
Chirma River ~ PNG 183 D 5
Chiromo o MW 218-219 H 3
Chirripó, Río ~ CR 52-53 C 6
Chirripó del Atlántico, Río ~ CR 52-53 C 7
Chirripó Grande, Cerro ▲ CR 52-53 C 7
Chirumanzu o ZW 218-219 F 4
Chirundu o Z 218-219 E 3
Chirundu o ZW 218-219 E 3
Chisamba o Z 218-219 E 2
Chisana o USA 20-21 U 5
Chisana River ~ USA 20-21 U 5
Chisasa o Z 214-215 C 7
Chisasibi o CDN 38-39 E 2
Chisec o GCA 52-53 J 4
Chisekesi o Z 218-219 D 3
Chisenga o MW 214-215 G 5
Chishan o RC 156-157 M 5
Chishang o RC 156-157 M 5
Chisholm o USA (MN) 270-271 F 3
Chishui o VRC 156-157 D 2
Chishuihe o VRC 156-157 D 3
Chishui He ~ VRC 156-157 D 2
Chisik Island ⌒ USA 20-21 O 6
Chisimba Falls ~ Z 214-215 F 6
Chişinău ★ MD 102-103 F 4
Chişineu-Criş o RO 102-103 B 4
Chisos Mountains ▲ USA (TX) 266-267 D 4
Chissano o MOC 220-221 L 2
Chissibuca o MOC 220-221 M 2
Chissinguane o MOC 218-219 H 5
Chistiān Mandy o PK 138-139 D 5
Chisumbanje o ZW 218-219 G 5
Chita o BOL 70-71 D 6
Chita o EAT 214-215 H 5
Chita = Čita ☆• RUS 118-119 F 9
Chitado o ANG 216-217 B 8
Chitaga o CO 60-61 E 4
Chitāpur o IND 140-141 G 2
Chitek o CDN (SAS) 232-233 L 2
Chitek Lake o CDN (SAS) 232-233 L 2
Chitek Lake o CDN (MAN) 234-235 D 2
Chitek Lake Indian Reservation Ⅹ CDN (SAS) 232-233 L 2
Chitembo o ANG 216-217 D 6
Chí Thanh o VN 158-159 K 4
Chitina o USA 20-21 S 6
Chitina River ~ USA 20-21 T 6
Chitipa o MW 214-215 G 5
Chito o EC 64-65 C 4
Chitobe o MOC 218-219 G 5
Chitongo o Z 218-219 D 3
Chitose o J 152-153 J 3
Chitowe o EAT 214-215 K 6
Chitradurga o• IND 140-141 G 3
Chitrakūt o IND 142-143 B 3
Chitré ☆ PA 52-53 D 8
Chittagong o• BD 142-143 G 4
Chittaurgarh o• IND 138-139 E 7
Chittivalasa o IND 142-143 C 7
Chittoor o IND 140-141 H 4
Chitungwiza o ZW 218-219 F 3
Chitwood o USA (OR) 244-245 B 6
Chityal o IND 140-141 H 2
Chiu Chiu o RCH 76-77 C 2
Chiulezi, Rio ~ MOC 214-215 J 6
Chiumbe ~ ANG 216-217 F 4
Chiumbo o ANG 216-217 D 6
Chiume o ANG 216-217 F 7
Chiúre Novo o MOC 218-219 K 1
Chivacoa o YV 60-61 G 2
Chivasing o PNG 183 D 4
Chivasso o I 100-101 A 2
Chivato o RCH 76-77 B 4
Chivay o PE 70-71 B 4
Chivé o BOL 70-71 C 3
Chivhu o ZW 218-219 F 4
Chivicahua National Monument ∴ USA (AZ) 256-257 F 6
Chivilcoy o RA 78-79 K 3
Chivirico o C 54-55 G 5
Chiviriga Falls ~ ZW 218-219 F 5
Chivuna o Z 218-219 D 3
Chiweta o MW 214-215 H 6
Chixoy o Negro, Río ~ GCA 52-53 J 4
Chizarira Hills ▲ ZW 218-219 D 3
Chizarira National Park ⊥ ZW 218-219 D 3
Chizela o Z 218-219 C 1
Chizu o J 152-153 F 7
Chizwina o RB 218-219 D 5
Chlef ☆ DZ 190-191 C 2
Chloride o USA (AZ) 256-257 A 3
Chmel'nyc'kyj ☆ UA 102-103 E 3
Chmel'nyc'kyj, Perejaslav- o UA 102-103 G 2
Chnattisgarh ∸ IND 142-143 B 5
Chŏâm Khsant o K 158-159 H 3
Choapa, Río ~ RCH 76-77 B 6
Choapan o MEX 52-53 G 3
Choapas, Las o MEX 52-53 G 3
Choate o CDN (BC) 230-231 H 4
Chobe ~ NAM 218-219 C 3
Chobe □ RB 218-219 C 4
Chobe National Park ⊥ RB 218-219 C 4
Chocca, Cerro ▲ PE 64-65 E 8
Chocolate Hills ⊥•• RP 160-161 F 8
Chocolate Mountain Gunnery Range • USA (CA) 248-249 J 6
Chocolate Mountains ▲ USA (CA) 248-249 J 6
Choconta o CO 60-61 E 5
Chocope o PE 64-65 C 5
Chocowinity o USA (NC) 282-283 K 5
Choctawhatchee Bay ≈ 48-49 E 4
Choctawhatchee Bay ≈ USA 286-287 C 1
Choctawhatchee River ~ USA (FL) 286-287 C 1
Choctawhatchee River, East Fork ~ USA (AL) 284-285 E 5
Choctawhatchee River, West Fork ~ USA (AL) 284-285 E 5
Choctaw Indian Reservation Ⅹ USA (MS) 268-269 L 4
Chodavaram o IND 142-143 C 7
Cho Do ⌒ DVR 150-151 E 8
Chodzież o• PL 92-93 O 2
Choele Choel o RA 78-79 G 5
Chofombo o MOC 218-219 F 2
Choice o USA (MN) 270-271 G 7
Choichuff, Lagh ~ EAK 212-213 F 2
Choiseland o CDN (SAS) 232-233 O 2
Choiseul ⌒ SOL 184 I c 2
Choiseul Sound ≈ 78-79 L 6
Choix o MEX 50-51 E 4
Choix, Port aux o CDN (NFL) 242-243 L 2
Chojnice o PL 92-93 O 2
Chojniki o BY 94-95 M 6
Chōkai Quasi National Park ⊥ J 152-153 J 5
Chōkai-san ▲ J 152-153 J 5
Chok Chai o THA 158-159 G 3
Choke Canyon Lake < USA (TX) 266-267 J 5
Ch'ok'ē Terara ▲ ETH 208-209 C 3
Chokio o USA (MN) 270-271 B 5
Chókué o MOC 220-221 L 2
Cholame o USA (CA) 248-249 D 4
Chola Shan ▲ VRC 144-145 M 4
Chola Shankou ▲ VRC 144-145 M 5
Cholay o MEX 50-51 D 3
Cholchol, Río ~ RCH 78-79 C 5
Chole • EAT 214-215 K 4
Cholet o F 90-91 G 8
Choluteca ☆ HN 52-53 L 5
Choluteca, Río ~ HN 52-53 L 5
Ch'ŏlwŏn o ROK 150-151 F 8
Choma o Z 218-219 D 3
Chom Bung o THA 158-159 E 4
Chom Phra o THA 158-159 G 3
Chom Tong o THA 142-143 L 6
Chomūn o IND 138-139 E 6
Chona ~ EAT 212-213 D 6
Ch'ŏnan o ROK 150-151 F 9
Chonarwa o NEP 144-145 F 7
Chon Buri o THA 158-159 F 4
Chonchi o RCH 78-79 C 7
Chonchon o DVR 150-151 F 7
Chone o EC 64-65 B 2
Chongchon Gang ~ DVR 150-151 E 8
Chongjin ☆ DVR 150-151 G 7
Chŏngju o ROK 150-151 F 10
Chongming o VRC 154-155 M 6
Chongoene o MOC 220-221 L 2
Chongorói o ANG 216-217 B 6
Chongoyape o PE 64-65 C 5
Chong Phan ≈ 158-159 E 6
Chongpyong o DVR 150-151 F 8
Chongqing o VRC (SIC) 154-155 C 6
Chongqing o• VRC (SIC) 156-157 E 2
Chongren o VRC 156-157 K 3
Chong Samui ≈ 158-159 E 6
Ch'ŏngsan Do ⌒ ROK 150-151 F 10
Chong Tao ≈ 158-159 E 6
Chongwe o Z 218-219 E 2
Chongwe ~ Z 218-219 E 2
Chongyang o VRC 156-157 J 2
Chongyi o VRC 156-157 J 4
Chŏnju o ROK 150-151 F 10
Chonos, Archipiélago de los ⌒ RCH 80 C 2
Chontaleña, Cordillera ▲ NIC 52-53 B 6
Chontali o PE 64-65 C 4
Chontalpa o MEX 52-53 H 3
Cho'n Thành o VN 158-159 J 5
Cho Oyu ▲ NEP 144-145 F 6
Chopda o IND 138-139 E 9
Chopinzinho o BR 74-75 D 5
Choptank River ~ USA (MD) 280-281 L 5
Choqā Zanbil ∴••• IR 134-135 C 2
Choras, Isla ⌒ RCH 76-77 B 5
Choreti o BOL 70-71 F 7
Chorkbak Inlet ≈ 36-37 M 2
Choró o BR 68-69 J 4
Choro, Río ~ BOL 70-71 E 5
Choro, Rio ~ BR 68-69 J 4
Chorol o UA 102-103 H 3
Chorolque ▲ BOL 70-71 E 7
Choromoro o RA 76-77 E 4
Choroní o YV 60-61 H 2
Chorregon o AUS 178-179 G 2
Chorrera, La o CO 64-65 F 2
Chorrera, La o PA 52-53 E 7
Chorrillos o PE 64-65 D 8
Chorro, El o RA 76-77 E 5
Chorro la Libertad ~ CO 66-67 C 3
Chorzung o VRC 144-145 L 5
Chosan o DVR 150-151 E 7
Chōshi o J 152-153 J 7
Chosica o PE 64-65 D 7
Chos Malal o RA 78-79 D 4
C. H. Ostenfeld Gletscher ⊂ GRØ 26-27 c 3
C. H. Ostenfeld Land ∸ GRØ 26-27 o 6
Chota o PE 64-65 C 5
Choteau o USA (MT) 250-251 G 4
Choûm o RIM 196-197 D 4
Chouteau o USA (OK) 264-265 J 2
Chowan River ~ USA (NC) 282-283 L 4
Chowchilla o USA (CA) 248-249 D 2
Chowduār o IND 142-143 D 5
Chowiet Island ⌒ USA 22-23 S 4
Chozi ~ Z 214-215 G 5
Chreïrîk < RIM 196-197 D 4
Chrisman o USA (IL) 274-275 L 5
Chrissiesmeer o ZA 220-221 K 3
Christchurch o•• NZ 182 D 5
Christiana o ZA 220-221 G 3
Christian Island ⌒ CDN (ONT) 238-239 E 4
Christian Island Indian Reservation Ⅹ CDN (ONT) 238-239 E 4
Christian IV, Kap ▲ GRØ 26-27 h 2
Christian IV Gletscher ⊂ GRØ 28-29 Z 2
Christian River ~ USA 20-21 S 3
Christiansburg o USA (VA) 280-281 F 6
Christianshåb = Qasigiannguit o GRØ 28-29 P 2
Christian Sound ≈ 32-33 C 3
Christiansted o USA (VI) 286-287 R 3
Christie Bay o CDN 30-31 O 4
Christie Lake o CDN 24-25 c 7
Christina Lake o CDN (BC) 230-231 L 4
Christina River ~ CDN 32-33 P 3
Christino Castro o BR 68-69 F 6
Christmas, Islas ⌒ RCH 80 E 7
Christmas Creek o AUS 172-173 G 5
Christmas Creek ~ AUS 172-173 H 5
Christmas Island ⌒ AUS 13 B 4
Christmas Island o CDN (NS) 240-241 P 5
Christmas Valley o USA (OR) 244-245 E 7
Christopher Falls ~ CDN (ONT) 236-237 F 2
Christopher Lake o AUS 176-177 J 2
Christoval o USA (TX) 266-267 G 2
Chrome o USA (CA) 246-247 C 4
Chromer o• GB 90-91 H 5
Chromo o USA (CO) 254-255 J 6
Chrysler o USA (AL) 284-285 C 5
Chuali, Lagoa o MOC 220-221 L 2
Chuave o PNG 183 C 4
Chub Cay o BS 54-55 G 2
Chubu-Sangaku National Park ⊥ J 152-153 G 6
Chubut □ RA 78-79 D 7
Chubut, Río ~ RA 78-79 E 7
Chuchi Lake o CDN 32-33 H 4
Chuchiliga o GH 202-203 K 4
Chu Chua o CDN (BC) 230-231 J 2
Chuckery o USA (OH) 280-281 C 3
Chucuma o RA 76-77 D 6
Chucunaque ~ PA 52-53 E 7
Chu Dang Sin ▲ VN 158-159 K 4
Chudleigh o CDN (ONT) 238-239 E 2
Chudskoye Ozero = Čudskoe ozero o RUS 94-95 K 2
Chugach Islands ⌒ USA 22-23 V 3
Chugach Mountains ▲ USA 20-21 R 6
Chugchug, Cerros de ▲ RCH 76-77 C 2
Chugchug, Quebrada ~ RCH 76-77 C 2
Chugiak o USA 20-21 Q 6
Chuginadak Island ⌒ USA 22-23 L 6
Chugoku-sanchi ▲ J 152-153 E 7
Chugul Island ⌒ USA 22-23 J 7
Chugwater o USA (WY) 252-253 O 5
Chuhar Jamāli o PK 134-135 M 6
Chuhar Kāna o PK 138-139 D 4
Ch'uja Do ⌒ ROK 150-151 F 11
Chuka o EAK 212-213 F 4
Chukai o MAL 162-163 E 2
Chukchi Autonomous District = Čukotskij avtonomnyj okrug □ RUS 112-113 N 3
Chukchi Plateau ≃ 16 B 35
Chukchi Sea ≈ 112-113 X 1
Chukotat, Rivière ~ CDN 36-37 L 4
Chukotskiy Poluostrov = Čukotskij poluostrov ⌣ RUS 112-113 W 3
Chula o USA (GA) 284-285 G 5
Chulahuma o USA (MS) 268-269 L 2
Chulas, Raudal las ~ CO 60-61 F 6
Chula Vista o USA (CA) 248-249 G 7
Chulitna River ~ USA 20-21 Q 5
Chulucanas o PE 64-65 B 4
Chuma o BOL 70-71 C 4
Chuma Shankou ▲ VRC 144-145 L 5
Chumba o ETH 208-209 D 6
Chumbicha o RA 76-77 D 5
Chumbo o BR 72-73 G 5
Chumikgiarsa o IND 138-139 F 3
Chumphae o THA 158-159 G 2
Chumphon o THA 158-159 E 5
Chumpi o PE 64-65 F 9
Chumpón o MEX 52-53 L 2
Chumsaeng o THA 158-159 F 3
Chumul ∴• MEX (YUC) 52-53 K 2
Chumul ∴• MEX (YUC) 52-53 K 1
Chun o THA 142-143 M 6
Chuna o PK 138-139 D 4
Chunăn o VRC 156-157 L 2
Chuncar o PE 64-65 B 4
Chunchanga, Pampa de ∸ PE 64-65 E 9
Chunchi o EC 64-65 C 3
Ch'unch'ŏn o ROK 150-151 F 9
Chunchura o IND 142-143 F 4
Chundela o ANG 216-217 F 7
Chunga o Z 218-219 D 2
Chungara o RCH 70-71 C 6
Chungara, Lago o RCH 70-71 C 6
Chunggang o DVR 150-151 F 7
Ch'ungju o ROK 150-151 F 9
Ch'ungmu o ROK 150-151 G 10
Chungu o Z 214-215 G 6
Chungui o PE 64-65 F 8
Chungyang Shanmo ▲ RC 156-157 M 5
Chūniān o PK 138-139 D 4
Chuniespoort o ZA 220-221 J 2
Chunky River ~ USA (MS) 268-269 M 4
Chunshui o VRC 154-155 H 5
Chunu, Cape ▲ USA 22-23 H 7
Chunwan o VRC 156-157 G 5
Chunya o EAT 214-215 G 5
Chuŏr Phnum Dângrek ▲ K 158-159 G 3
Chuŏr Phnum Krvanh ▲ K 158-159 G 4
Chupabe, Caño ~ CO 60-61 G 6
Chupadero de Caballo o MEX 50-51 J 3
Chupadero Springs o USA (TX) 266-267 G 5
Chu' Pha o VN 158-159 J 4
Chu' Prông o VN 158-159 J 4
Chuquatonchee Creek ~ USA (MS) 268-269 M 3
Chuquibamba o PE 64-65 F 9
Chuquibambilla o PE 64-65 F 9
Chuquicamata o RCH 76-77 C 2
Chuquicara o PE 64-65 C 6
Chuquiribamba o EC 64-65 C 3
Chuquis o PE 64-65 D 6
Chur ☆• CH 92-93 K 5
Churachāndpur o IND 142-143 H 3
Churcampa o PE 64-65 E 8
Church o USA (VA) 280-281 J 6
Churchbridge o CDN (SAS) 232-233 R 5
Church Hill o USA (TN) 282-283 E 4
Churchill o• CDN 30-31 W 6
Churchill, Cap ▲ CDN 30-31 X 6
Churchill Falls o CDN 38-39 M 2
Churchill Lake o CDN 32-33 Q 3
Churchill Lake o USA (ME) 278-279 M 2
Churchill Reef ⌒ AUS 172-173 F 3
Churchill River ~ CDN 32-33 Q 4
Churchill River ~ CDN 34-35 E 3
Churchill River ~ CDN 34-35 J 2
Churchill River ~ CDN 38-39 N 2
Churchill Sound ≈ 36-37 J 7
Church Point o USA (LA) 268-269 H 6
Churchs Ferry o USA (ND) 258-259 H 3
Churchville o USA (VA) 280-281 G 5
Churdan o USA (IA) 274-275 D 2
Chureo o Deshecho, Paso ▲ RA 78-79 D 4
Churia Range ▲ NEP 144-145 E 7
Churin o PE 64-65 D 7
Churobusco o USA (IN) 274-275 N 3
Churu o IND 138-139 E 5
Churuguara o YV 60-61 G 2
Chu' Sê o VN 158-159 K 4
Chuska Mountains ▲ USA (AZ) 256-257 F 2
Chusmisa o RCH 70-71 C 6
Chūsonji • J 152-153 J 5
Chust ☆ UA 102-103 C 3
Chute-des-Passes o CDN 38-39 J 4
Chute Lake o CDN (BC) 230-231 K 4
Chutine Landing o CDN 32-33 E 3
Chuvashia = Čavaš respubliki □ RUS 96-97 E 6
Chuwangsan National Park ⊥• ROK 150-151 G 9
Chuxiong o VRC 156-157 B 4
Chuy o ROU 74-75 D 9
Chuzhou o VRC 154-155 L 5
Chwaka o EAT 214-215 K 4
Chyulu Hills ▲ EAK 212-213 F 5
Ciágola, Monte ▲ I 100-101 E 5
Ciamis o RI 168 C 3
Ciandur o RI 168 A 3
Cianjur o RI 168 B 3
Ciano o EC 64-65 C 3
Cianorte o BR 72-73 D 7
Čiatura o GE 126-127 E 6
Cibadak o RI 168 B 3
Čibagalah ~ RUS 110-111 Y 6
Čibagalahskij hrebet ▲ RUS 110-111 W 6
Cibatu o RI 168 B 3
Cibit o RUS 124-125 P 3
Čibit o RUS 124-125 P 3
Cibitoke o BU 212-213 B 5
Cibu ▲ MEX 50-51 D 2
Cicalengka o RI 168 B 3
Čičatka, Bol'šaja ~ RUS 118-119 K 8
Cícero Dantas o BR 68-69 J 7
Cicia ⌒ FJI 184 III c 2
Čičkajul ~ RUS 114-115 T 6
Cicurug o RI 168 B 3
Cidade Gaúcha o BR 72-73 D 7
Cide ☆ TR 128-129 E 2
Ciechanów ☆• PL 92-93 Q 2
Ciego, El o C 54-55 G 4
Ciego de Ávila ☆ C 54-55 F 4
Ciempozuelos o E 98-99 F 4
Ciénaga o CO 60-61 D 2
Cienaga, La o RA 76-77 C 5
Ciénaga Grande de Santa Marta ≈ 60-61 D 2
Cieneguillas o RA 76-77 E 2
Cienfuegos ☆ C 54-55 E 3
Cieszanów o PL 92-93 R 3
Cieza o E 98-99 G 5
Çifteler ☆ TR 128-129 D 3
Cifuentes o C 54-55 E 3
Cifuentes o E 98-99 F 4
Cifuncho o RCH 76-77 B 3
Cigarette Spring Cave ∴ USA (UT) 254-255 F 6
Cigarro o BR 66-67 F 4
Ciglera, ostrov ⌒ RUS 84-85 e 2
Cihanbeyli ☆ TR 128-129 E 3
Cihanbeylı Yaylâsı ▲ TR 128-129 E 3
Cihuatlán o MEX 52-53 B 2
Čiili o KA 124-125 E 6
Cíjara, Reserva Nacional de ⊥ E 98-99 E 5
Cijulang o RI 168 C 3
Cikajang o RI 168 B 3
Cikalongkulon o RI 168 B 3
Cikalongwetan o RI 168 B 3
Cikampek o RI 168 B 3
Čikoj o RUS 116-117 N 10
Čikoj ~ RUS 116-117 O 10
Čikoj ~ RUS 116-117 N 10
Čikoj ~ RUS 118-119 E 11
Čikoj ~ RUS 118-119 E 10
Čikokon ~ RUS 118-119 E 10
Čikokonskij, hrebet ▲ RUS 118-119 D 11
Cikotok o• RI 168 B 3
Čikšina ~ RUS 88-89 Y 4
Čikšina ~ RUS 114-115 D 2
Cilacap o RI 168 C 3
Cilamaya o RI 168 B 3
Cilaos o F 224 B 7
Cilaos, Cirque de • F 224 B 7
Čilat o IRQ 128-129 M 6
Čil'či o RUS 118-119 L 7
Çıldır o TR 128-129 K 2
Çıldır Gölü o TR 128-129 K 2
Ciledug o RI 168 C 3
Cileungsi o RI 168 B 3
Cili o VRC 156-157 G 2
Cilibia o RO 102-103 E 5
Cilik o KA 146-147 D 4
Čilik ~ KA 146-147 C 4
Ćilipi o HR 100-101 G 3
Cill Airne = Killarney o• IRL 90-91 C 5
Cill Bheagáin = Kilbeggan o IRL 90-91 D 5
Cill Chainnigh = Kilkenny ☆• IRL 90-91 D 5
Cill Chaoi = Kilkee o IRL 90-91 C 5
Cill Dara = Kildare o IRL 90-91 D 5

Chichibu — Cill Dara 315

Čilli ~ RUS 118-119 J 3
Cill Mhantáin = Wicklow ☆ IRL 90-91 D 5
Cill Orglan = Killorglin o IRL 90-91 C 5
Cill Rois = Kilrush o IRL 90-91 C 5
Cil'ma ~ RUS 88-89 U 4
Cil'ma ~ RUS 88-89 V 4
Čil'mamedkum ∸ TM 136-137 D 4
Cima o USA (CA) 248-249 J 4
Cimahi o RI 168 B 3
Cimanggu o RI 168 A 3
Cimanuk, Tanjung ▲ RI 168 C 3
Cimarron o USA (CO) 254-255 H 5
Cimarron o USA (KS) 262-263 F 7
Cimarron o USA (NM) 256-257 L 2
Cimarron National Grassland ⊥ USA (KS) 262-263 E 7
Cimarron River ~ USA (CO) 254-255 N 6
Cimarron River ~ USA (NM) 256-257 M 2
Cimarron River ~ USA (OK) 264-265 G 3
Čimbaj o US 136-137 F 3
Čimboj ☆ US 136-137 F 3
Cimbur o RI 166-167 C 6
Čimčememel' ~ RUS 112-113 O 3
Čimidikjan ~ RUS 110-111 M 6
Cimişlia ☆ MD 102-103 F 4
Cimitarra o CO 60-61 E 4
Cimljansk o RUS 102-103 N 4
Cimljanskoe vodohranilišče < RUS 102-103 N 4
Cimmermanovka o RUS 122-123 H 3
Cimpeni o RO 102-103 C 4
Cimpina o• RO 102-103 D 5
Cimpu o RI 164-165 G 5
Cîmpulung o• RO 102-103 D 5
Cîmpulung Moldovenesc o• RO 102-103 D 4
Čina ~ RUS 116-117 L 3
Čina ~ RUS 118-119 F 8
Cina, Tanjung ▲ RI 162-163 F 7
Çınar ☆ TR 128-129 J 4
Cinaruco, Río ~ YV 60-61 H 4
Cincel, Río ~ RA 76-77 D 2
Cincinnati o USA (OH) 280-281 B 4
Cinco Balas, Cayos ⌒ C 54-55 F 4
Cinco de Maio, Cachoeira ~ BR 70-71 K 3
Çine ☆• TR 128-129 C 4
Činejveem ~ RUS 112-113 Q 3
Cinema o CDN (BC) 228-229 M 3
Cingaly o RUS 114-115 K 4
Čingandža, gora ▲ RUS 112-113 H 4
Čingirea, mys ▲ RUS 108-109 f 2
Cingildi o US 136-137 J 4
Cingirlau o KA 96-97 H 8
Cingis Chaan Cherem ∴• MAU 148-149 L 3
Cinnabar Mountain ▲ USA (ID) 252-253 B 4
Činoz ☆ US 136-137 L 4
Činozero, ozero ⊖ RUS 88-89 M 5
Cinque Island ⌒ IND 140-141 L 4
Cinta, Serra da ⛰ BR 68-69 E 5
Cintalapa de Figueroa o MEX 52-53 H 3
Cinto, Monte ▲ F 98-99 M 3
Cintra o RA 78-79 H 2
Cintra, Golfe de ≈ 196-197 B 3
Cinuelos, Los o DOM 54-55 K 5
Cinzas, Rio das ~ BR 72-73 E 7
Ciotat, la o F 90-91 K 10
Cipa ~ RUS 118-119 G 8
Cipanda o RUS 120-121 F 4
Cipatujah o RI 168 C 3
Cipikan o RUS 118-119 F 8
Cipikan ~ RUS 118-119 E 8
Cipo, Rio ~ BR 72-73 J 5
Cipoal o BR 66-67 E 3
Cipolândia o BR 70-71 K 7
Cipolletti o RA 78-79 F 5
Cipotuba, Ilha ⌒ BR 66-67 F 4
Čir ~ RUS 102-103 N 3
Circa o PE 64-65 F 8
Čirčik o US 136-137 L 4
Čirčik ~ US 136-137 L 4
Circle o USA (AK) 20-21 S 4
Circle o USA (MT) 250-251 O 4
Circleville o USA (OH) 280-281 D 4
Circular Head ▲ AUS 180-181 H 6
Circular Reef ⌒ PNG 183 D 2
Cirebon o RI 168 C 3
Čirikovo o RUS 94-95 P 4
Čirin, vulkan ▲ RUS 122-123 M 6
Čirinda o RUS 116-117 K 2
Ciriquiri, Rio ~ BR 66-67 E 7
Čirka Kem' ~ RUS 88-89 M 5
Cir Kud o SP 212-213 J 2
Čirkuo ~ RUS 118-119 D 4
Cirò o I 100-101 F 5
Čirokči o US 136-137 K 5
Čirpan o BG 102-103 D 6
Cirque, Cerro ▲ BOL 70-71 C 5
Cirque Mountain ⛰ CDN 36-37 S 5
Ciruelo, El o MEX 50-51 D 5
Cisarua o RI 168 B 3
Cisco o USA (GA) 284-285 F 2
Cisco o USA (TX) 264-265 F 6
Cisco o USA (UT) 254-255 F 5
Ciskei (former Homeland, now part of East-Cape) □ ZA 220-221 H 5
Čiskova ~ RUS 116-117 G 3
Čišmy ☆ RUS 96-97 J 6
Cisne, Islas del = Islas Santanilla ⌒ HN 54-55 D 6
Cisne, Laguna del ⊖ RA 76-77 F 5
Cisne, Santuario del • EC 64-65 C 3
Cisnes, Río ~ RCH 80 E 2
Cisnes Medio o RCH 80 D 2
Cisolok o RI 168 B 3
Cisséla o RG 202-203 E 4
Cistern o USA (TX) 266-267 K 4
Cistern Point ▲ BS 54-55 G 3
Cistierna o E 98-99 E 3
Čistoe, ozero ⊖ RUS 120-121 O 4
Čistopol' ☆ RUS 96-97 G 6
Čistopol'e ☆ KA 124-125 E 2
Čita ☆• RUS 118-119 F 9
Čita ~ RUS 118-119 F 9
Citadelle, La ∴• RH 54-55 J 5
Čita Kandaw, Kōtal-e ▲ AFG 138-139 B 3
Citaré, Rio ~ BR 62-63 G 5
Citiari, Igarapé ~ BR 66-67 E 6
Citico Beach o USA (TN) 282-283 C 5
Citra o USA (FL) 286-287 G 2
Citra o USA (OK) 264-265 H 4
Citronelle o USA (AL) 284-285 B 5
Citrusdal o ZA 220-221 D 6
Citrus Heights o USA (CA) 246-247 D 5
Città del Vaticano ★••• SCV 100-101 D 4
Cittanova o I 100-101 F 5
Ciu o RI 164-165 L 2
Ciudad o MEX 50-51 G 6
Ciudad Acuña o MEX 50-51 J 3
Ciudad Altamirano o MEX 52-53 D 2
Ciudad Bolívar ☆• YV 60-61 K 3
Ciudad Camargo o• MEX 50-51 G 4
Ciudad Colon o CR 52-53 B 7
Ciudad Constitución o• MEX 50-51 D 5
Ciudad Cortes o CR 52-53 C 7
Ciudad Cuauhtémoc o MEX 52-53 J 4
Ciudad Darío o• NIC 52-53 L 5
Ciudad de Guatemala = Guatemala ★•• GCA 52-53 J 4
Ciudad del Carmen o• MEX 52-53 J 2
Ciudad del Este ☆ PY 76-77 K 3
Ciudad del Maíz o MEX 50-51 K 6
Ciudad de México = México ★••• MEX 52-53 E 2
Ciudad de Nutria o YV 60-61 G 3
Ciudad Guayana o• YV 60-61 K 3
Ciudad Guzman o• MEX 52-53 C 2
Ciudad Hidalgo o MEX 52-53 D 2
Ciudad Ixtepec o MEX 52-53 G 3
Ciudad Juárez o• MEX 50-51 F 2
Ciudad Lerdo o MEX 50-51 H 5
Ciudad López Mateos o MEX 52-53 E 2
Ciudad Madero o MEX 50-51 L 6
Ciudad Mante o MEX 50-51 K 6
Ciudad Melchor de Mentos o GCA 52-53 K 3
Ciudad Mutis = Bahía Solano o CO 60-61 C 4
Ciudad Neily o CR 52-53 C 7
Ciudad Nezahualcóyotl o MEX 52-53 E 2
Ciudad Obregón o MEX 50-51 E 4
Ciudad Ojeda o YV 60-61 F 2
Ciudad Pemex o MEX 52-53 H 3
Ciudad Piar o YV 60-61 K 4
Ciudad Quesada o CR 52-53 B 6
Ciudad Real o• E 98-99 F 5
Ciudad-Rodrigo o•• E 98-99 D 4
Ciudad Sahagún o MEX 52-53 E 2
Ciudad Serdán o MEX 52-53 F 2
Ciudad Valles o MEX 50-51 K 7
Ciudad Victoria ☆• MEX 50-51 K 6
Ciutadella o E 98-99 J 5
Civil'sk o RUS 96-97 E 6
Civita Castellana o• I 100-101 D 3
Civitanova Marche o I 100-101 D 3
Civitavécchia o I 100-101 C 3
Civol'ki, zaliv ≈ RUS 108-109 H 4
Çivril ☆ TR 128-129 C 3
Ciwidey o RI 168 B 3
Cixi o VRC 154-155 M 6
Čiža o RUS 88-89 S 3
Čižapka ~ RUS 114-115 P 5
Čižinskij taskyn cu ⊖ KA 96-97 F 8
Cizre ☆ TR 128-129 K 4
C.J. Strike Reservoir ⊖ USA (ID) 252-253 C 4
Cjurupyns'k o UA 102-103 H 4
Čkalov o RUS 110-111 Z 4
Čkalovsk o RUS 94-95 S 3
Clacton-on-Sea o GB 90-91 H 6
Clagstone o USA (ID) 250-251 C 3
Claiborne o USA (AL) 284-285 C 5
Claiborne, Lake < USA (LA) 268-269 H 4
Clain ~ F 90-91 H 8
Clair o CDN (SAS) 232-233 O 3
Claire, Lake ⊖ CDN 30-31 N 6
Claire City o USA (SD) 260-261 J 1
Clairemont o USA (TX) 264-265 D 5
Clair Engle Lake ⊖ USA (CA) 246-247 C 3
Clair Falls ~ CDN 30-31 X 3
Clairview o AUS 178-179 K 2
Clallam Bay o USA (WA) 244-245 A 2
Clamecy o F 90-91 J 8
Clam Lake o USA (WI) 270-271 H 4
Clandonald o CDN (ALB) 232-233 H 2
Clanton o USA (AL) 284-285 D 4
Clanville o ZA 220-221 H 5
Clanwilliam o CDN (BC) 230-231 L 3
Clanwilliam o CDN (MAN) 234-235 D 4
Clanwilliam o ZA 220-221 D 6
Clapperton o CDN (BC) 230-231 H 3
Claquato Church • USA (WA) 244-245 B 4
Clara o USA (MS) 268-269 M 5
Clara, Punta ▲ RA 78-79 G 7
Clara City o USA (MN) 270-271 C 6
Clarafield o AUS 178-179 G 1
Clara Island ⌒ MYA 158-159 D 5
Claravale o AUS 172-173 K 3
Claraville o AUS (NT) 178-179 C 2
Claraville o AUS (QLD) 174-175 F 6
Clare o AUS (QLD) 174-175 J 6
Clare o AUS (QLD) 178-179 H 2
Clare o AUS (SA) 180-181 E 2
Clare o USA (MI) 272-273 E 4
Claremont o USA (NH) 278-279 J 5
Claremore o USA (OK) 264-265 J 2
Clarence o NZ 182 D 5
Clarence o USA (LA) 268-269 G 5
Clarence o USA (MO) 274-275 F 5
Clarence, Cape ▲ CDN 24-25 b 4
Clarence, Isla ⌒ RCH 80 E 6
Clarence, Port ≈ 20-21 G 4
Clarence Cannon National Wildlife Refuge ⊥ USA (IL) 274-275 H 5
Clarence Island ⌒ ARK 16 G 31
Clarence River ~ AUS 178-179 M 5
Clarence Strait ≈ 32-33 D 3
Clarence Strait ≈ 172-173 K 2
Clarence Town o• BS 54-55 H 3
Clarendon o USA (AR) 276-277 D 6
Clarendon o USA (TX) 264-265 D 4
Clarens o ZA 220-221 J 4
Clarenville o CDN (NFL) 242-243 O 4
Claresholm o CDN (ALB) 232-233 E 5
Clareton o USA (WY) 252-253 O 3
Clareville o USA (TX) 266-267 K 5
Clarie, Terre ∸ ARK 16 G 14
Clarinda o USA (IA) 274-275 C 4
Clarines o• YV 60-61 J 3
Clarion o USA (IA) 274-275 E 2
Clarion o USA (PA) 280-281 G 2
Clarión, Isla ⌒ MEX 50-51 A 7
Clarion Fracture Zone ≃ 14-15 O 6
Clarion River ~ USA (PA) 280-281 G 2
Clark o USA (SD) 260-261 J 2
Clark o USA (WY) 252-253 J 2
Clark, Lake ⊖ USA 20-21 N 6
Clark, Point ▲ CDN (ONT) 238-239 D 4
Clark Canyon Reservoir < USA (MT) 250-251 G 7
Clarkdale o USA (AZ) 256-257 C 4
Clarkdon o CDN (ONT) 234-235 M 5
Clarke, Cape ▲ CDN 24-25 d 7
Clarke City o CDN (QUE) 242-243 B 2
Clarke Island ⌒ AUS 180-181 K 6
Clarke Lake ⊖ CDN 34-35 C 3
Clarke Range ⛰ AUS 174-175 J 7
Clarke River ~ AUS 174-175 H 6
Clarke River ~ CDN 30-31 S 4
Clarke River P.O. o AUS 174-175 H 6
Clarkfield o USA (MN) 270-271 C 6
Clark Fork o USA (ID) 250-251 C 3
Clark Fork River ~ USA (MT) 250-251 D 4
Clark Fork River ~ USA (MT) 250-251 F 5
Clarkia o USA (ID) 250-251 C 4
Clarkleigh o CDN (MAN) 234-235 E 4
Clark Mountain ▲ USA (CA) 248-249 J 4
Clarkrange o USA (TN) 276-277 K 4
Clarks o USA (NE) 262-263 J 3
Clarksburg o USA (OH) 280-281 C 4
Clarksburg o USA (TN) 276-277 G 5
Clarksburg o USA (WV) 280-281 F 4
Clarksdale o USA (MS) 268-269 K 2
Clarks Fork River ~ USA (WY) 252-253 J 2
Clark's Harbour o CDN (NS) 240-241 K 7
Clarks Hill o USA (SC) 284-285 H 3
Clarks Hill Lake < USA (GA) 284-285 H 3
Clarks Junction o NZ 182 C 6
Clarkson o ZA 220-221 G 6
Clarks Point o USA 22-23 R 3
Clarks Summit o USA (PA) 280-281 L 2
Clarkston o USA (UT) 254-255 C 2
Clarkston o USA (WA) 244-245 H 4
Clarkstone o USA (MI) 272-273 F 5
Clarksville o USA (AR) 276-277 B 5
Clarksville o USA (FL) 286-287 D 1
Clarksville o USA (GA) 284-285 G 2
Clarksville o USA (TN) 276-277 H 4
Clarksville o USA (TX) 264-265 J 5
Clarksville o USA (VA) 280-281 H 7
Clarkton o USA (NC) 282-283 J 6
Clarkville o USA (CO) 254-255 N 3
Clarno o USA (OR) 244-245 E 6
Claro, Rio ~ BR 66-67 K 6
Claro, Rio ~ BR 72-73 D 4
Claro, Rio ~ BR 72-73 E 4
Claromecó o RA 78-79 J 5
Claros, Los o YV 60-61 F 2
Clatskanie o USA (OR) 244-245 B 4
Clatsop National Memorial, Fort • USA (OR) 244-245 B 4
Claude o USA (TX) 264-265 C 3
Cláudia o BR 70-71 K 2
Claudio Gay, Cordillera ⛰ RCH 76-77 C 4
Claunch o USA (NM) 256-257 K 4
Clausharn = Ilimanaq o GRØ 28-29 P 2
Claveria o RP (CAG) 160-161 D 3
Claveria o RP (MAS) 160-161 E 6
Clavet o CDN (SAS) 232-233 M 3
Claxton o USA (GA) 284-285 J 4
Clay o USA (CA) 246-247 D 5
Clay o USA (TX) 266-267 L 3
Claybank o CDN (SAS) 232-233 N 5
Clay Belt ∸ CDN (ONT) 236-237 B 2
Clay Center o USA (KS) 262-263 J 5
Clay Center o USA (NE) 262-263 H 4
Clay City o USA (IN) 274-275 L 5
Clay City o USA (KY) 276-277 M 3
Claydon o CDN (SAS) 232-233 J 6
Clayoquot Sound ≈ 32-33 G 7
Clayoquot Sound ≈ CDN 230-231 C 4
Claypool o USA (AZ) 256-257 E 5
Clay River ~ PNG 183 C 3
Clay Springs o USA (AZ) 256-257 E 4
Claysville o USA (KY) 276-277 L 2
Clayton o USA (AL) 284-285 E 5
Clayton o USA (GA) 284-285 G 2
Clayton o USA (ID) 252-253 D 2
Clayton o USA (LA) 268-269 J 5
Clayton o USA (MO) 274-275 H 6
Clayton o USA (NM) 256-257 M 2
Clayton o USA (NY) 278-279 E 4
Clayton o USA (OK) 264-265 J 4
Clayton o USA (TX) 264-265 K 6
Claytor Lake ⊖ USA (VA) 280-281 F 6
Clear Boggy Creek ~ USA (OK) 264-265 H 4
Clearbrook o USA (MN) 270-271 C 3
Clear Creek o USA (CA) 246-247 B 2
Clear Creek ~ USA 20-21 R 4
Clear Creek ~ USA (AL) 284-285 C 2
Clear Creek ~ USA (AZ) 256-257 E 4
Clear Creek ~ USA (TX) 264-265 G 5
Cleardale o CDN 32-33 L 3
Cleare, Cape ▲ USA 20-21 R 7
Clearfield o USA (PA) 280-281 H 2
Clearfield o USA (SD) 260-261 F 3
Clearfield o USA (UT) 254-255 C 2
Clear Fork ~ USA (TX) 264-265 G 6
Clear Fork Brazos ~ USA (TX) 264-265 E 6
Clear Hills ⛰ CDN 32-33 L 3
Clearlake o USA (CA) 246-247 C 4
Clear Lake o USA (IA) 274-275 E 1
Clear Lake o USA (MN) 270-271 D 5
Clear Lake o USA (SD) 260-261 K 2
Clear Lake o USA (WI) 270-271 F 5
Clear Lake ⊖ USA (CA) 246-247 C 4
Clear Lake ⊖ USA (LA) 268-269 G 4
Clear Lake National Wildlife Refuge ⊥ USA (CA) 246-247 D 2
Clear Lake Reservoir ⊖ USA (CA) 246-247 D 2
Clear Prairie o CDN 32-33 L 3
Clearwater o CDN (BC) 230-231 J 2
Clearwater o USA (FL) 286-287 G 4
Clearwater o USA (MT) 250-251 F 4
Clearwater o USA (NE) 262-263 H 2
Clearwater Creek ~ CDN 30-31 F 4
Clearwater Lake ⊖ CDN 34-35 F 3
Clearwater Lake ⊖ CDN (BC) 228-229 O 4
Clearwater Lake ⊖ USA (MO) 276-277 E 3
Clearwater Mountains ⛰ USA (ID) 250-251 D 5
Clearwater Provincial Park ⊥ CDN 34-35 F 3
Clearwater River ~ CDN 32-33 P 3
Clearwater River ~ CDN (ALB) 232-233 C 4
Clearwater River ~ CDN (BC) 230-231 J 2
Clearwater River ~ USA (ID) 250-251 C 5
Cleburne o USA (TX) 264-265 G 6
Cle Elum o USA (WA) 244-245 E 3
Clegg o USA (TX) 266-267 J 5
Clematis Creek ~ AUS 178-179 K 3
Clemenceau Icefield ⊂ CDN (BC) 228-229 R 4
Clements, Port o CDN (BC) 228-229 B 3
Clements Markham Inlet ≈ 26-27 R 2
Clementson o USA (MN) 270-271 D 2
Clemesi, Pampa de la ∸ PE 70-71 B 5
Clemson o USA (SC) 284-285 G 2
Clendenin o USA (WV) 280-281 E 5
Cleo o USA (TX) 266-267 H 3
Cleopatra Needle ▲ RP 160-161 C 7
Cleo Springs o USA (OK) 264-265 F 2
Clephane Bay ≈ 28-29 J 3
Clerke Reef ⌒ AUS 172-173 D 4
Clerke Rocks ⌒ GB 78-79 P 7
Clermont o AUS 178-179 J 2
Clermont o CDN (QUE) 240-241 E 3
Clermont o F 90-91 J 7
Clermont o USA (FL) 286-287 H 3
Clermont-Ferrand ☆• F 90-91 J 9
Clermont-l'Hérault o F 90-91 J 10
Clerval o CDN (QUE) 236-237 J 4
Cleugh Passage ≈ 140-141 L 3
Cleve o AUS 180-181 D 2
Cleveland o USA (AR) 276-277 C 5
Cleveland o USA (GA) 284-285 G 2
Cleveland o USA (MS) 268-269 K 3
Cleveland o USA (MT) 250-251 K 3
Cleveland o USA (ND) 258-259 H 5
Cleveland o USA (OK) 264-265 H 2
Cleveland o USA (TN) 282-283 C 5
Cleveland o USA (TX) 268-269 E 6
Cleveland o USA (UT) 254-255 E 4
Cleveland o• USA (OH) 280-281 E 2
Cleveland, Kap ▲ GRØ 26-27 P 5
Cleveland, Mount ▲ USA (AK) 22-23 M 6
Cleveland, Mount ▲ USA (MT) 250-251 F 3
Cleveland Heights o USA (OH) 280-281 E 2
Clevelândia o BR 74-75 D 6
Cleveland Peninsula ⌣ USA 32-33 D 4
Cleveland River ~ CDN 36-37 G 2
Clewiston o USA (FL) 286-287 J 5
Clifden o NZ 182 A 7
Clifden = An Clochán o• IRL 90-91 B 5
Cliff o USA (NM) 256-257 G 6
Cliff o USA (NM) 256-257 G 5
Cliffdell o USA (WA) 244-245 D 4
Clifford o CDN (ONT) 238-239 E 5
Cliffs of Moher •• IRL 90-91 C 5
Clifton o USA (AZ) 256-257 F 5
Clifton o USA (IL) 274-275 K 4
Clifton o USA (KS) 262-263 J 5
Clifton o USA (LA) 268-269 K 6
Clifton o USA (TN) 276-277 G 5
Clifton o USA (TX) 266-267 K 2
Clifton Forge o USA (VA) 280-281 G 6
Clifton Hills o AUS 178-179 E 4
Clifton Point ▲ CDN 24-25 N 6
Clifty o USA (KY) 276-277 H 3
Cli Lake ⊖ CDN 30-31 H 4
Climax o CDN (SAS) 232-233 K 6
Climax o USA (CO) 254-255 J 4
Climax o USA (GA) 284-285 F 6
Climax o USA (MI) 272-273 D 5
Climax o USA (MN) 270-271 B 3
Clinch Mountains ⛰ USA (TN) 282-283 D 4
Clinchport o USA (VA) 280-281 D 7
Clinch River ~ USA (TN) 282-283 D 4
Clinch River ~ USA (TN) 282-283 C 5
Clinch River ~ USA (VA) 280-281 D 7
Cline o USA (TX) 266-267 G 4
Cline River o CDN (ALB) 232-233 B 3
Cline River ~ CDN (ALB) 232-233 B 3
Clines Corners o USA (NM) 256-257 K 3
Clingmans Dome ▲ USA (NC) 282-283 D 5
Clint o USA (TX) 266-267 A 2
Clinton o CDN (BC) 230-231 H 2
Clinton o CDN (ONT) 238-239 D 5
Clinton o NZ 182 B 7
Clinton o USA (AL) 284-285 C 4
Clinton o USA (AR) 276-277 C 5
Clinton o USA (CT) 280-281 O 2
Clinton o USA (IA) 274-275 H 3
Clinton o USA (IL) 274-275 K 4
Clinton o USA (IN) 274-275 L 5
Clinton o USA (KY) 276-277 G 4
Clinton o USA (LA) 268-269 J 6
Clinton o USA (MI) 272-273 F 5
Clinton o USA (MO) 274-275 E 6
Clinton o USA (MS) 268-269 K 4
Clinton o USA (MT) 250-251 F 5
Clinton o USA (NC) 282-283 J 6
Clinton o USA (OK) 264-265 F 3
Clinton o USA (SC) 284-285 J 2
Clinton o USA (TN) 282-283 C 4
Clinton, Cape ▲ AUS 178-179 L 2
Clinton, Port ≈ 178-179 L 2
Clinton-Colden Lake ⊖ CDN 30-31 Q 3
Clinton Lake ⊖ USA (IL) 274-275 K 4
Clinton Lake ⊖ USA (KS) 262-263 L 6
Clinton Point ▲ CDN 24-25 M 6
Clintonville o USA (WI) 270-271 K 6
Clio o USA (AL) 284-285 E 5
Clio o USA (MI) 272-273 F 4
Clio o USA (SC) 284-285 L 2
Cliong Karik Tagh ▲ VRC 144-145 H 2
Clipperton Fracture Zone ≃ 14-15 O 7
Clisbako River ~ CDN (BC) 228-229 L 4
Clive Lake ⊖ CDN 30-31 K 4
Čija o RUS 122-123 J 2
Čija, ozero ⊖ RUS 122-123 J 2
Cloan o CDN (SAS) 232-233 K 3
Clocolan o ZA 220-221 H 4
Clodomira o RA 76-77 E 4
Clonagh o AUS 174-175 F 7
Clonbrook o GUY 62-63 F 2
Cloncurry o AUS 174-175 F 7
Cloncurry Plateau ∸ AUS 178-179 E 1
Cloncurry River ~ AUS 174-175 F 6
Clonmacnoise o•• IRL 90-91 D 5
Clonmel = Cluain Meala o IRL 90-91 D 5
Clo-oose o CDN (BC) 230-231 E 5
Cloppenburg o D 92-93 K 2
Cloquet o USA (MN) 270-271 F 4
Cloquet River ~ USA (MN) 270-271 F 3
Clore River ~ CDN (BC) 228-229 G 2
Cloridorme o CDN (QUE) 242-243 D 3
Clorinda o RA 76-77 J 3
Cloudcroft o USA (NM) 256-257 K 6
Cloud Peak ▲ USA (WY) 252-253 L 2
Clouds Creek o AUS 178-179 M 6
Cloudy Mountain ▲ USA 20-21 M 5
Clover o USA (SC) 284-285 J 1
Clover o USA (VA) 280-281 H 7
Cloverdale o USA (CA) 246-247 B 5
Cloverdale o USA (IN) 274-275 M 5
Cloverdale o USA (MN) 270-271 F 4
Cloverport o USA (KY) 276-277 J 3
Cloverton o USA (MN) 270-271 F 4
Clovis o USA (CA) 248-249 E 3
Clovis o USA (NM) 256-257 M 4
Cloyne o CDN (ONT) 238-239 H 4
Cluain Meala = Clonmel o IRL 90-91 D 5
Club Mayanabo o C 54-55 G 4
Cluj-Napoca ☆• RO 102-103 C 4
Cluny o CDN (ALB) 232-233 F 5
Clute o CDN (ONT) 236-237 G 3
Clute o USA (TX) 268-269 E 7
Clyde o CDN (ALB) 32-33 O 4
Clyde o CDN (NWT) 26-27 Q 8
Clyde ~ GB 90-91 F 4
Clyde o USA (ND) 258-259 J 3
Clyde o USA (NY) 278-279 E 5
Clyde o USA (OH) 280-281 D 2
Clyde o USA (TX) 264-265 E 6
Clyde Inlet ≈ 26-27 Q 8
Clyde Park o USA (MT) 250-251 J 6
Clyde River o CDN (NS) 240-241 K 7
Clyde River ~ CDN (NS) 240-241 K 7
Clyo o USA (GA) 284-285 J 4
Cna ~ RUS 94-95 R 5
Cnori o GE 126-127 F 7
Coachella o USA (CA) 248-249 H 6
Coachella Canal < USA (CA) 248-249 J 7
Coachman's Cove o CDN (NFL) 242-243 M 2
Coahoma o USA (TX) 264-265 C 6
Coahuayana o MEX 52-53 C 2
Coahuayutla o MEX 52-53 D 2
Coahuila □ MEX 50-51 H 4
Coalcomán, Río ~ MEX 52-53 C 2
Coalcomán de Matamoros o MEX 52-53 C 2
Coal Creek o CDN (BC) 230-231 P 4
Coal Creek o USA 20-21 T 4
Coaldale o CDN (ALB) 232-233 F 6
Coaldale o USA (NV) 246-247 H 5
Coalgate o USA (OK) 264-265 H 4
Coal Harbour o CDN (BC) 230-231 B 3
Coal Hill o USA (AR) 276-277 B 5
Coalhurst o CDN (ALB) 232-233 E 6
Coalinga o USA (CA) 248-249 D 3
Coal Mine • AUS 178-179 E 6
Coalmont o CDN (BC) 230-231 J 4
Coalridge o USA (MT) 250-251 P 3
Coal River o CDN (BC) 30-31 F 6
Coal River ~ CDN 30-31 F 5
Coal River ~ USA (WV) 280-281 E 5
Coalspur o CDN (ALB) 228-229 R 3
Coal Valley o CDN (ALB) 232-233 B 2
Coalville o USA (UT) 254-255 D 3
Coamo o USA (PR) 286-287 P 2
Coaraci o BR 72-73 L 3
Coari o BR 66-67 F 5
Coari, Lago de ⊖ BR 66-67 F 5
Coari, Rio ~ BR 66-67 F 5
Coasa o PE 70-71 B 4
Coast □ EAK 212-213 G 5
Coastal Plains Research Station o AUS 172-173 K 2
Coast Mountains ⛰ CDN 32-33 D 2
Coast of Labrador ∸ CDN 36-37 R 5
Coast Range ⛰ AUS 178-179 L 2
Coast Range ⛰ AUS 178-179 L 3
Coast Range ⛰ USA 40-41 C 3
Coata o PE 70-71 C 4
Coatá, Cachoeira ~ BR 66-67 G 6
Coatá, Cachoeira do ~ BR 66-67 F 7
Coatá Laranjal, Área Indígena ✕ BR 66-67 H 5
Coatbridge o GB 90-91 E 4
Coatepec o MEX 52-53 F 2
Coatepeque o GCA 52-53 J 4
Coatesville o USA (PA) 280-281 L 4
Coaticook o CDN (QUE) 238-239 O 3
Coats Bay ≈ 36-37 K 6
Coats Island ⌒ CDN 36-37 H 3
Coats Land ∸ ARK 16 F 34
Coatzacoalcos o MEX 52-53 G 2
Coatzacoalcos, Río ~ MEX 52-53 G 3
Coba ∴• MEX 52-53 L 1
Cobadin o RO 102-103 F 5
Cobalt o CDN (ONT) 236-237 J 5
Cobalt o USA (ID) 250-251 E 6
Cobán ☆ GCA 52-53 J 4
Cobar o AUS 180-181 H 2
Cobargo o AUS 180-181 K 4
Cobb, Lake ⊖ AUS 176-177 J 2
Cobberas, Mount ▲ AUS 180-181 K 4
Cobb Highway II AUS 180-181 G 2
Cobb Island ⌒ USA (VA) 280-281 L 6
Cobbs Arm o CDN (NFL) 242-243 O 3
Cobden o AUS 180-181 G 5
Cobden o CDN (ONT) 238-239 J 3
Cobequid Mountains ⛰ CDN (NS) 240-241 L 5
Cobh = An Cóbh o IRL 90-91 C 6
Cobham River ~ CDN 34-35 J 4
Cobija ☆ BOL 70-71 C 2
Cobija, Punta ▲ RCH 76-77 B 2
Cobleskill o USA (NY) 278-279 G 6
Cobocork o CDN (ONT) 238-239 G 4
Cobourg o CDN (ONT) 238-239 G 5
Cobourg Peninsula ⌣ AUS 172-173 K 1
Cobquecura o RCH 78-79 C 4
Cobra o AUS 176-177 D 2
Cobre o USA (NV) 246-247 L 2
Cobre, El o RCH 76-77 B 3
Cobre, Sierra del ⛰ RA 76-77 D 2
Cobuè o MOC 214-215 H 7
Coburg o• D 92-93 L 3
Coburg Island ⌒ CDN 24-25 h 2
Coburg Marine Park ⊥ AUS 172-173 K 1
Coburn o AUS 176-177 C 3
Coburn Mount ▲ USA (ME) 278-279 L 3
Coca = Puerto Francisco de Orellana o EC 64-65 D 2
Coca, Río ~ EC 64-65 D 2
Cocachacra o PE 64-65 D 7
Cocagne o CDN (NB) 240-241 L 4
Cocal o BR 68-69 H 3
Cocalinho o BR (MAR) 68-69 F 3
Cocalinho o BR (MAT) 72-73 E 3
Cocha, La o RA 76-77 E 4
Cochabamba ☆ BOL 70-71 D 5
Cochabamba o PE 64-65 C 5
Cochagne o CDN (NB) 240-241 L 4
Cochagón, Cerro ▲ NIC 52-53 B 5
Cochamarca o PE 64-65 D 7
Cochamó o RCH 78-79 C 6
Cochaquingu o EC 64-65 D 2
Coche, Isla ⌒ YV 60-61 K 2
Cochem o• D 92-93 J 3
Cochenour o CDN (ONT) 234-235 K 3
Cochetopa Hills ⛰ USA (CO) 254-255 J 6
Cochico, Sierra de ⛰ RA 78-79 D 4
Cochiguas, Río ~ RCH 76-77 B 6
Cochin o CDN (SAS) 232-233 K 2
Cochin o•• IND 140-141 G 6
Cochinos, Bahía de ≈ 54-55 E 3
Cochise o USA (AZ) 256-257 F 6
Cochran o USA (GA) 284-285 G 4
Cochrane o CDN (ALB) 232-233 D 4
Cochrane o CDN (ONT) 236-237 H 3
Cochrane o RCH 80 D 3
Cochrane, Cerro ▲ RCH 80 D 3
Cochrane, Lago ≈ 80 D 3
Cockakol' o KA 124-125 G 4
Cockakol' kyrkasy ⛰ KA 126-127 N 4
Cockburn o AUS 180-181 F 2
Cockburn, Canal ≈ 80 E 7
Cockburn, Cape ▲ CDN 24-25 V 3
Cockburn, Mount ▲ AUS (NT) 172-173 K 7
Cockburn, Mount ▲ AUS (NT) 176-177 K 2
Cockburn Harbor o GB 54-55 K 4
Cockburn Island ⌒ CDN (ONT) 238-239 B 3
Cockburn Islands ⌒ CDN 24-25 R 6
Cockburn North, Mount ▲ AUS 172-173 J 3
Cockburn Town o BS 54-55 H 2
Cockburn Town ☆• GB 54-55 K 4
Cocklebiddy Cave • AUS 176-177 H 5
Cocklebiddy Motel o AUS 176-177 J 6
Cockram Strait ≈ 28-29 C 3
Cockrum o USA (MS) 268-269 L 2
Coco, Cayo ⌒ C 54-55 F 3
Coco, El o CR 52-53 B 6
Coco, Punta ▲ CO 60-61 C 6
Coco, Río ~ NIC 52-53 L 5
Côco, Rio do ~ BR 68-69 D 6
Cocoa o USA (FL) 286-287 J 3
Cocoa Beach o USA (FL) 286-287 J 3
Cocobeach o G 210-211 B 3
Coco Channel ≈ 140-141 L 3
Cococi o BR 68-69 H 5
Cocodrie o USA (LA) 268-269 K 7
Cocolalla o USA (ID) 250-251 C 3
Coconho, Ponta ▲ BR 68-69 L 4
Coconino Plateau ⛰ USA (AZ) 256-257 C 3
Coco o Segovia = Río Wangkí ~ HN 52-53 B 4
Cocoparra National Park ⊥ AUS 180-181 J 3
Cocorna o CO 60-61 D 4
Cocorocuma, Cayos ⌒ NIC 54-55 D 7
Côcos o BR 72-73 H 2
Cocos o BR (BAH) 72-73 H 3
Cocos o BR (MAR) 68-69 G 4
Cocos Basin ≃ 12 H 4
Cocos Island ⌒ AUS 12 H 6
Cocos Ridge ≃ 5 C 4
Cocotier Beach = Cocotier Plage ∸• CAM 210-211 B 2
Cocotier Plage = Cocotier Beach ∸• CAM 210-211 B 2
Cocuí, Parque Nacional el ⊥ CO 60-61 E 4
Cocuizas, Las o YV 62-63 D 2
Cocula o MEX 52-53 C 1
Cod, Cape ▲ USA (MA) 278-279 L 6
Codajás o BR 66-67 F 4
Codeagro o BR 66-67 G 4
Codera, Cabo ▲ YV 60-61 H 2
Codette o CDN (SAS) 232-233 O 2
Cod Island ⌒ CDN 36-37 T 6
Cod National Seashore, Cape ⊥ USA (MA) 278-279 M 6
Codó o BR 68-69 G 4
Codo de Pozuzo o PE 64-65 E 6
Codora o USA (CA) 246-247 C 4
Codorniz, Paso ▲ RCH 80 D 3
Codozinho o BR 68-69 F 4
Codpa o RCH 70-71 C 6
Codrii ⛰ MD 102-103 E 3
Codrington o AG 56 E 3
Codru-Moma, Munții ⛰ RO 102-103 C 4
Cody o USA (NE) 262-263 E 2
Cody o USA (WY) 252-253 J 2
Coeburn o USA (VA) 280-281 D 7
Coelemu o RCH 78-79 C 4
Coelho Neto o BR 68-69 G 4
Coen o AUS 174-175 G 3
Coerney o ZA 220-221 G 6
Coeroeni o SME 62-63 F 4
Coesfeld o• D 92-93 J 3
Coëtivy Island ⌒ SY 224 E 3
Coeur d'Alene o USA (ID) 250-251 C 4
Coeur d'Alene Indian Reservation ✕ USA (ID) 250-251 C 4
Coeur d'Alene Lake ⊖ USA (ID) 250-251 C 4
Coeur d'Alene Mountains ⛰ USA (ID) 250-251 C 4
Coeur d'Alene River ~ USA (ID) 250-251 C 4
Coevorden o NL 92-93 J 2
Coffee Bay o ZA 220-221 J 5
Coffee Creek o CDN 20-21 V 5
Coffeen Lake ⊖ USA (IL) 274-275 J 5
Coffeeville o USA (AL) 284-285 B 5
Coffeeville o USA (MS) 268-269 L 3
Coffeyville o USA (KS) 262-263 L 7
Coffin Bay ≈ 180-181 C 3
Coffin Bay National Park ⊥ AUS 180-181 C 3
Coffs Harbour o AUS 178-179 M 6
Cofimvaba o ZA 220-221 H 6
Čogádäk o IR 134-135 D 4
Čogar ~ RUS 120-121 E 6
Cogar o USA (OK) 264-265 F 3
Cogatí, Embalse < RCH 76-77 B 6
Coghlan o ZA 220-221 J 5
Cognac o• F 90-91 G 9
Cogo o GQ 210-211 B 3
Cogollal, El o YV 60-61 K 4
Cogotí, Río ~ RCH 76-77 B 6
Čograjskoe vodohranilišče ⊖ RUS 126-127 F 5
Cogswell o USA (ND) 258-259 K 5
Cogt = Tahilt o MAU 148-149 C 5
Cogt-Ovoo = Doloon o MAU 148-149 G 5
Coguno o MOC 220-221 M 2
Cohade, Rivière ~ CDN 36-37 N 5
Cohagen o USA (MT) 250-251 N 4
Cohocton River ~ USA (NY) 278-279 D 6
Cohoes o USA (NY) 278-279 H 6
Cohutta Mountain ▲ USA (GA) 284-285 F 2
Coiba, Isla de ⌒ PA 52-53 D 8
Coig, Río ~ RA 80 E 5
Coihaique ☆ RCH 80 D 2
Coihaique Alto o RCH 80 E 2
Coihué o RCH 78-79 C 4
Coihueco o RCH 78-79 D 4
Coimbatore o IND 140-141 G 5
Coimbra o BR 72-73 J 6
Coimbra ☆•• P 98-99 C 4
Coín o E 98-99 E 6
Coin de Mire ⌒ MS 224 C 6
Coipasa, Cerro ▲ BOL 70-71 C 6
Coipasa, Salar de ⊖ BOL 70-71 C 6
Coiposa, Lago de ⊖ BOL 70-71 C 6
Čojbalsan ☆ MAU 148-149 M 3
Cojedes, Río ~ YV 60-61 G 3
Cojimíes o EC 64-65 B 1
Cojoida o YV 60-61 L 3
Čojr o MAU 148-149 J 4
Cojúa o YV 60-61 F 2
Cojudo Blanco, Cerro ▲ RA 80 F 3
Cojutepeque ☆ ES 52-53 K 5
Cojyndykól ⊖ KA 124-125 E 3
Coker Creek o USA (TN) 282-283 C 5
Cokeville o USA (WY) 252-253 H 4
Čokrakbejik, Gora ▲ TM 136-137 F 5
Čokurdah-Kerike, gora ▲ RUS 110-111 F 3
Colac o AUS 180-181 G 5
Colakşor, köli ⊖ KA 124-125 J 2
Colan, Cape ▲ CDN 26-27 R 2
Colán Conhué o RA 78-79 E 7
Colangüil, Cordillera de ⛰ RA 76-77 C 5
Colares o BR 62-63 K 6
Colasi Point ▲ RP 160-161 F 7
Colatina o BR 72-73 K 5
Colazo o RA 76-77 F 6
Colbert o USA (WA) 244-245 H 3
Čolbon o RUS 110-111 U 6
Colborne o CDN (ONT) 238-239 H 4
Colborne, Port o CDN (ONT) 238-239 F 6
Colby o USA (KS) 262-263 E 5
Colca, Río ~ PE 64-65 F 9
Colcabamba o PE 64-65 F 9
Colchester o• GB 90-91 H 6
Colchester o USA (VT) 278-279 H 4
Colchester o ZA 220-221 G 6
Cold Bay o USA 22-23 P 5
Cold Lake ⊖ CDN 32-33 Q 4
Cold Spring o USA (NV) 246-247 H 4
Coldspring o USA (TX) 268-269 E 6
Coldspring Mountain ▲ CDN 20-21 W 5
Coldstream o CDN (BC) 230-231 K 3
Coldstream o GB 90-91 F 4
Coldwater o USA (KS) 262-263 G 7
Coldwater o USA (MI) 272-273 D 6
Coldwater o USA (MS) 268-269 L 2
Coldwater Creek ~ USA (TX) 264-265 B 2
Coldwater River ~ USA (MS) 268-269 K 2
Coleambally o AUS 180-181 H 3
Coleambally Creek ~ AUS 180-181 H 3
Cole Bay o CDN 32-33 Q 4
Colebrook o USA (NH) 278-279 K 4
Cole Camp o USA (MO) 274-275 E 6

Coleen River ~ USA 20-21 T 3
Colekeplaas o ZA 220-221 G 6
Coleman o CDN (ALB) 232-233 D 6
Coleman o USA (MI) 272-273 E 4
Coleman o USA (TX) 266-267 H 2
Coleman, Lake < USA (TX) 264-265 E 6
Coleman Lake o CDN (ALB) 232-233 G 4
Coleman River ~ AUS 174-175 F 4
Colenso o ZA 220-221 J 4
Colerain o USA (NC) 282-283 L 4
Coleraine o AUS 180-181 F 4
Coleraine o GB 90-91 D 4
Coleraine o USA (MN) 270-271 E 3
Coleridge, Lake o NZ 182 C 5
Coleroon ~ IND 140-141 H 5
Coles, Punta ▲ PE 70-71 B 5
Colesberg o ZA 220-221 G 5
Coles Island o CDN (NB) 240-241 K 5
Coleto Creek ~ USA (TX) 266-267 K 5
Coleville o CDN (SAS) 232-233 J 4
Colfax o USA (CA) 246-247 E 4
Colfax o USA (IA) 274-275 E 3
Colfax o USA (IL) 274-275 K 4
Colfax o USA (LA) 268-269 H 5
Colfax o USA (ND) 258-259 L 5
Colfax o USA (WA) 244-245 H 4
Colfax o USA (WI) 270-271 G 6
Colga Downs o AUS 176-177 E 3
Colgate o CDN (SAS) 232-233 P 6
Colguula o SP 208-209 H 5
Colhué Huapi, Lago o RA 80 F 2
Colídor o BR 70-71 K 2
Colignan o AUS 180-181 G 3
Coligny o ZA 220-221 H 3
Colima ■ MEX 52-53 B 2
Colima ☆ • MEX (COL) 52-53 C 2
Colina o BR 72-73 F 6
Colin Archer Peninsula ∪ CDN 24-25 a 2
Colinas o BR 68-69 F 5
Colinas do Tocantins o BR 68-69 D 6
Colindina, Mount ▲ AUS 176-177 G 4
Colinet o CDN (NFL) 242-243 P 5
Coliseo o C 54-55 E 3
Coll ⌒ GB 90-91 D 3
Collacagua o RCH 70-71 C 7
Colladere o RH 54-55 J 5
Collado-Villalba o E 98-99 F 4
Collarenebri o AUS 178-179 K 5
Collaroy o AUS 178-179 K 2
Collbran o USA (CO) 254-255 H 4
Collector o AUS 180-181 K 3
College Park o USA (GA) 284-285 F 3
College Place o USA (WA) 244-245 G 4
College Station o USA (TX) 266-267 L 3
Collerina o AUS 178-179 J 5
Colleymount o CDN (BC) 228-229 H 2
Collie o AUS 176-177 D 6
Collier Bay ≈ 172-173 G 4
Collier Bay Aboriginal Land X AUS 172-173 F 4
Collier Range ▲ AUS 176-177 E 2
Collier Range National Park ⊥ AUS 176-177 E 2
Collier Tunnel II USA (CA) 246-247 B 2
Collierville o USA (TN) 276-277 F 5
Collingwood o CDN (ONT) 238-239 E 4
Collingwood o NZ 182 D 4
Collingwood Bay ≈ 183 E 5
Collins o CDN (ONT) 234-235 O 4
Collins o USA (AR) 276-277 D 7
Collins o USA (IA) 274-275 E 3
Collins o USA (MO) 276-277 B 3
Collins o USA (MS) 268-269 L 5
Collins o USA (MT) 250-251 H 4
Collins, Mount ▲ AUS 178-179 F 3
Collinson, Cape ▲ CDN 26-27 P 3
Collinson Peninsula ∪ CDN 24-25 V 5
Collins River ~ USA (TN) 276-277 K 5
Collinsville o AUS 174-175 J 7
Collinsville o USA (AL) 284-285 E 2
Collinsville o USA (CA) 246-247 D 5
Collinsville o USA (IL) 274-275 J 6
Collinsville o USA (OK) 264-265 J 2
Collinwood o USA (TN) 276-277 G 5
Collipulli o RCH 78-79 C 4
Collo o DZ 190-191 F 2
Collón Curá, Río ~ RA 78-79 D 6
Colly Creek ~ USA (NC) 282-283 J 6
Colmar ☆ • F 90-91 L 7
Colméia o BR 68-69 D 6
Colmena o RA 76-77 G 5
Colmenar Viejo o E 98-99 F 4
Colnett o MEX 50-51 A 2
Colnett, Cabo ▲ MEX 50-51 A 2
Cologne = Köln o •• D 92-93 J 3
Cololo, Arroyo ~ ROU 78-79 L 2
Coloma o USA (WI) 270-271 J 6
Colombia o C 54-55 G 4
Colombia o CO 60-61 D 6
Colombia ■ CO 60-61 D 6
Colombia o MEX 50-51 K 4
Colombia Basin ≃ 5 D 3
Colombier o CDN (QUE) 240-241 G 2
Colombo o BR 68-69 F 3
Colombo ★ CL 140-141 H 7
Colome o USA (SD) 260-261 G 3
Colomiers o F 90-91 H 10
Colón o C 54-55 E 3
Colón ☆ PA 52-53 E 7
Colón o RA (BUA) 78-79 J 2
Colón o RA (ERI) 78-79 K 2
Colón, Archipiélago de = Islas Galápagos ⌒ EC 64-65 B 9
Colonelganj o IND 142-143 B 2
Colonel Hill o BS 54-55 H 3
Colonia 10 de Julio o RA 76-77 F 6
Colonia Angamos o PE 64-65 F 4
Colonia Carlos Pellegrini o RA 76-77 J 5
Colonia del Sacramento ☆ • ROU 78-79 L 3
Colonia Dora o RA 76-77 F 5
Colonial Beach o USA (MD) 280-281 K 5
Colônia Leopoldina o BR 68-69 L 6
Colonial Heights o USA (VA) 280-281 J 6
Colonial National Historic Park • USA (VA) 280-281 K 6
Colônia Osório o BR 68-69 E 2
Colonia piel foca • EC 64-65 B 10
Colonia Prosperidad o RA 76-77 F 6
Colonias o USA (NM) 256-257 L 3
Colonias Unidas o RA 76-77 H 4
Colonia Teresa o RA 76-77 H 6
Colonia Vicente Guerrero o MEX 50-51 B 2
Colon Ridge ≃ 5 B 4
Colonsay o CDN (SAS) 232-233 N 4
Colony o USA (KS) 262-263 L 6
Colony o USA (WY) 252-253 O 2
Colorada, Laguna o BOL 76-77 D 2
Colorada, Sierra ▲ RA 76-77 E 3
Colorado o BR 72-73 E 7
Colorado o C 54-55 F 4
Colorado o CR 52-53 B 6
Colorado ■ USA (CO) 254-255 H 4
Colorado, Caño o YV 60-61 K 3
Colorado, Cerro ▲ MEX 50-51 B 2
Colorado, Cerro ▲ RA (CHU) 80 F 2
Colorado, Cerro ▲ RA (LAR) 76-77 D 5
Colorado, Cerro ▲ RCH 80 E 2
Colorado, El o RA 76-77 F 4
Colorado, Punta ▲ MEX 50-51 C 3
Colorado, Río ~ BR 70-71 F 3
Colorado, Río ~ RA 76-77 D 4
Colorado, Río ~ RA 76-77 D 6
Colorado, Río ~ RA 76-77 E 2
Colorado, Río ~ RA 78-79 F 5
Colorado, Río ~ RCH 78-79 D 2
Colorado City o USA (AZ) 256-257 C 2
Colorado City o USA (CO) 254-255 L 6
Colorado City o USA (TX) 264-265 D 6
Colorado Desert ∸ USA (CA) 248-249 H 6
Colorado d'Oeste o BR 70-71 G 3
Colorado National Monument • USA (CO) 254-255 G 4
Colorado Plateau ▲ USA (AZ) 256-257 D 2
Colorado River ~ USA (AZ) 256-257 B 2
Colorado River ~ USA (CA) 248-249 K 6
Colorado River ~ USA (CO) 254-255 G 4
Colorado River ~ USA (TX) 264-265 D 6
Colorado River ~ USA (TX) 266-267 J 2
Colorado River ~ USA (UT) 254-255 E 5
Colorado River Aqueduct < USA (CA) 248-249 K 5
Colorado River Indian Reservation X USA (AZ) 256-257 A 5
Colorados, Archipiélago de los ⌒ C 54-55 C 3
Colorados, Cerros ▲ RA 78-79 E 6
Colorado Springs o • USA (CO) 254-255 L 5
Colotlán o MEX 50-51 H 6
Colotlipa o MEX 52-53 E 3
Colpitts Creek ~ CDN (ONT) 236-237 B 2
Colpon-Ata o KS 146-147 C 4
Colquechaca o BOL 70-71 D 6
Colquen, Cerro ▲ RCH 78-79 C 4
Colquiri o BOL 70-71 D 5
Colquitt o USA (GA) 284-285 F 5
Colrain o USA (MA) 278-279 J 6
Colson Track II USA 178-179 D 3
Colston Park o AUS 178-179 K 1
Colstrip o USA (MT) 250-251 N 6
Colter Pass ▲ USA (MT) 250-251 K 6
Colton o USA (SD) 260-261 K 3
Colton o USA (UT) 254-255 E 4
Colton o USA (WA) 244-245 H 4
Coltons Point o USA (MD) 280-281 K 5
Coltwater o USA (AR) 276-277 E 5
Columbia o USA (AL) 284-285 E 5
Columbia o USA (KY) 276-277 K 3
Columbia o USA (LA) 268-269 H 4
Columbia o USA (MD) 280-281 K 4
Columbia o USA (MO) 274-275 F 6
Columbia o USA (MS) 268-269 L 5
Columbia o USA (NC) 282-283 L 5
Columbia o USA (PA) 280-281 K 3
Columbia o USA (SD) 260-261 H 1
Columbia o USA (TN) 276-277 H 5
Columbia ☆ USA (SC) 284-285 J 3
Columbia, Mount ▲ CDN (BC) 228-229 R 4
Columbia Beach o USA (WA) 244-245 C 3
Columbia Center o USA (WA) 244-245 H 4
Columbia City o USA (FL) 286-287 G 1
Columbia City o USA (IN) 274-275 N 3
Columbia Falls o USA (ME) 278-279 O 4
Columbia Falls o USA (MT) 250-251 E 3
Columbia Glacier ⊂ USA 20-21 R 6
Columbia Icefield ⊂ CDN (ALB) 228-229 R 4
Columbia Mountains ▲ CDN (BC) 228-229 M 3
Columbiana o USA (AL) 284-285 D 3
Columbia National Wildlife Refuge ⊥ USA (WA) 244-245 F 4
Columbia Plateau ▲ USA (OR) 40-41 E 3
Columbia Reach ~ CDN (BC) 230-231 M 2
Columbia River ~ CDN (BC) 230-231 L 2
Columbia River ~ USA (WA) 244-245 D 5
Columbine o USA (CO) 254-255 J 3
Columbus o USA (GA) 284-285 F 4
Columbus o USA (IN) 274-275 N 5
Columbus o USA (KS) 262-263 M 7
Columbus o USA (KY) 276-277 F 4
Columbus o USA (MS) 268-269 M 3
Columbus o USA (MT) 250-251 K 6
Columbus o USA (NC) 282-283 E 5
Columbus o USA (ND) 258-259 E 3
Columbus o USA (NE) 262-263 J 3
Columbus o USA (NM) 256-257 H 7
Columbus o USA (PA) 280-281 G 2
Columbus o USA (TX) 266-267 L 4
Columbus o USA (WI) 274-275 J 1
Columbus ☆ USA (OH) 280-281 D 4
Columbus Cay ⌒ BH 52-53 L 3
Columbus City o USA (AL) 284-285 D 2
Columbus Grove o USA (OH) 280-281 B 3
Columbus Junction o USA (IA) 274-275 G 3
Columbus Lake < USA (MS) 268-269 M 3
Columbus Landing 5/ 4th./ 1494 • JA 54-55 G 5
Columbus Monument • BS 54-55 H 2
Columbus Point ▲ BS 54-55 H 2
Columna, Pico ▲ PA 52-53 E 7
Coluna o BR 72-73 J 5
Colup, Cerro ▲ RCH 76-77 C 2
Colusa o USA (CA) 246-247 C 4
Colville o USA (WA) 244-245 H 2
Colville Channel ≈ 182 E 2
Colville Indian Reservation X USA (WA) 244-245 F 2
Colville Lake o CDN (NWT) 30-31 F 2
Colville Lake o CDN (NWT) 30-31 G 2
Colville River ~ USA 20-21 L 2
Coma, La o MEX 50-51 K 5
Comácchio o I 100-101 D 2
Comácha o MOC 218-219 G 3
Comalcalco o MEX (TAB) 52-53 H 2
Comalcalco ∴ • MEX (TAB) 52-53 H 2
Comallo o RA 78-79 D 6
Comallo, Arroyo ~ RA 78-79 D 6
Comanche o USA (OK) 264-265 G 4
Comanche o USA (TX) 266-267 J 2
Comandante Fontana o RA 76-77 H 3
Comandante Giribone o RA 78-79 L 3
Comandante Luis Piedra Buena o RA 80 F 4
Comănești o RO 102-103 E 4
Comarapa o BOL 70-71 E 5
Comas o PE 64-65 E 7
Comau, Fiordo ≈ 78-79 C 7
Comayagua ☆ • HN 52-53 L 4
Comayagua, Montañas de ▲ HN 52-53 L 4
Comayagüela o HN 52-53 L 4
Combapata o PE 70-71 B 4
Combarbala o RCH 76-77 B 6
Combermere o CDN (ONT) 238-239 H 3
Combermere, Cape ▲ CDN 24-25 g 2
Combermere Bay ≈ 142-143 H 6
Combo, Selat ≈ 162-163 F 4
Combol, Pulau ⌒ RI 162-163 E 4
Combomune o MOC 218-219 G 6
Combs o USA (AR) 276-277 B 5
Comè o DY 202-203 L 6
Come by Chance o AUS 178-179 K 6
Comechingones, Sierra de ▲ RA 78-79 G 2
Comedero o MEX 50-51 F 5
Comemoração, Rio ~ BR 70-71 G 2
Comer o USA (GA) 284-285 G 2
Comerío o USA (PR) 286-287 P 2
Comer Strait ≈ 36-37 G 2
Comerzinho o BR 72-73 K 4
Comet Downs o AUS 178-179 K 2
Cometela o MOC 218-219 H 5
Comet Outstation o AUS 178-179 C 5
Comet River ~ AUS 178-179 K 3
Comfort o USA (TX) 266-267 J 4
Comfort, Cape ▲ CDN 36-37 H 2
Comfort, Point o USA (TX) 266-267 L 5
Comfort Bight o CDN 38-39 R 2
Comicó, Arroyo ~ RA 78-79 F 6
Comilla o BD 142-143 G 4
Comino, Capo ▲ I 100-101 B 4
Comitán de Domínguez o MEX 52-53 H 3
Comite River ~ USA (LA) 268-269 J 6
Commander Islands = Komandorskie ostrova ⌒ RUS 120-121 W 6
Commee o CDN (ONT) 234-235 O 6
Commerce o USA (GA) 284-285 G 2
Commerce o USA (MS) 268-269 K 2
Commerce o USA (TX) 264-265 J 5
Commissioner Island ⌒ CDN (MAN) 234-235 F 2
Committee Bay ≈ 24-25 c 6
Commodore Reef ⌒ 160-161 A 8
Commonwealth Meteorological Station • AUS 178-179 H 6
Commonwealth Range ▲ ARK 16 E 0
Commoron Creek ~ AUS 178-179 L 5
Como ☆ • I 100-101 B 2
Como ~ RCB 210-211 E 3
Como o USA (MS) 268-269 L 2
Como o USA (TX) 264-265 J 5
Como, Lago di o I 100-101 B 2
Comoapa o NIC 52-53 B 5
Como Bluff Fossil Beds ∴ USA (WY) 252-253 N 5
Comodo o ETH 208-209 E 6
Comodoro o BR 70-71 H 3
Comodoro Rivadavia o RA 80 G 2
Comoé ~ CI 202-203 J 6
Comoé, Parc National de la ⊥ ••• CI 202-203 H 5
Comonfort o MEX 52-53 D 1
Comorin, Cape ▲ IND 140-141 G 6
Comoros = Comores ■ COM 222-223 C 3
Comoros = Comores, Archipel des ⌒ COM 222-223 C 3
Comox o CDN (BC) 230-231 E 4
Compass Lake o USA (FL) 286-287 D 1
Compeer o CDN (ALB) 232-233 H 4
Compiègne o • F 90-91 J 7
Complejo Ferrovial Zárate-Brazo Largo • RA 78-79 K 2
Čompolo ~ RUS 118-119 L 6
Compostela o MEX 50-51 G 7
Comprida, Ilha ⌒ BR 74-75 G 5
Compton o USA (CA) 248-249 F 6
Compton Névé ~ CDN (BC) 230-231 E 3
Comrat o MD 102-103 F 4
Comstock o USA (MI) 272-273 D 5
Comstock o USA (TX) 266-267 F 4
Côm Thiêu, Műi ▲ VN 158-159 J 5
Comunidad o CR 52-53 B 6
Comunidad o YV (AMA) 60-61 H 6
Comunidad o YV (BOL) 60-61 K 4
Comunidad de Madrid ■ E 98-99 F 4
Čona ~ RUS 118-119 D 5
Cona o VRC 144-145 H 7
Conakry ■ RG 202-203 D 5
Conakry ★ • RG 202-203 D 5
Conambo, Río ~ EC 64-65 D 3
Conasauga River ~ USA (GA) 284-285 F 2
Conay o RCH 76-77 B 5
Conay, Río ~ RCH 76-77 B 5
Concan o USA (TX) 266-267 H 4
Concarán o RA 78-79 G 2
Concarneau o • F 90-91 F 8
Conceição o BR (AMA) 66-67 G 4
Conceição o BR (PA) 68-69 J 5
Conceiçao, Riachão ~ BR 68-69 H 5
Conceição da Barra o BR 72-73 L 5
Conceição das Alagoas o BR 72-73 F 5
Conceição de Macabu o BR 72-73 K 7
Conceição do Araguaia o BR 68-69 D 6
Conceição do Canindé o BR 68-69 H 5
Conceição do Coité o BR 68-69 J 7
Conceição do Mato Dentro o BR 72-73 J 5
Conceicão do Mau o BR 62-63 E 4
Conceicão do Norte o BR 72-73 G 2
Concepción o BOL 70-71 F 5
Concepcion o CO 64-65 F 2
Concepcion o PE 64-65 E 7
Concepción ☆ PY 76-77 J 2
Concepción o RA 76-77 E 4
Concepción ☆ RCH 78-79 C 4
Concepcion, Canal ≈ 80 C 5
Concepcion, La o EC 64-65 C 1
Concepcion, La o PA 52-53 C 7
Concepcion, La o YV 60-61 F 2
Concepcion, Lago o BOL 70-71 G 5
Concepción, Punta ▲ MEX 50-51 D 4
Concepción, Volcán ▲ NIC 52-53 B 6
Concepcion de Buenos Aires o MEX 52-53 C 2
Concepción del Oro o MEX 50-51 J 5
Concepción del Uruguay o RA 78-79 K 2
Concepción Island ⌒ BS 54-55 H 3
Conception o RP 160-161 D 5
Conception, Lago o BOL 70-71 F 4
Conception, Point ▲ USA (CA) 248-249 D 5
Conception Bay ≈ 38-39 S 5
Conception Bay ≈ CDN 242-243 P 5
Conch o IND 138-139 G 7
Conchal o BR 72-73 G 7
Conchalí, Bahía ≈ 76-77 B 6
Conchas o BR 72-73 G 7
Conchas o USA (NM) 256-257 L 3
Conchas, Las o BOL 70-71 H 5
Conchas Lake o USA (NM) 256-257 L 3
Conchas River ~ USA (NM) 256-257 L 3
Conch Bar o GB 54-55 K 4
Conche o CDN (NFL) 242-243 N 2
Conchi o RCH 76-77 C 2
Concho o USA (AZ) 256-257 F 4
Concho River ~ USA (TX) 266-267 G 2
Concho River, Middle ~ USA (TX) 266-267 F 2
Concho River, North ~ USA (TX) 266-267 G 2
Conchos, Río ~ MEX 50-51 K 5
Conchos, Río ~ MEX 50-51 F 4
Concón o RCH 78-79 D 2
Concón, Punta de ▲ RCH 78-79 D 2
Conconully o USA (WA) 244-245 F 2
Concord o USA (CA) 248-249 C 2
Concord o USA (KY) 276-277 M 2
Concord o USA (NC) 282-283 G 5
Concord o USA (NE) 262-263 K 2
Concord ☆ USA (NH) 278-279 K 5
Concórdia o BR 74-75 D 6
Concordia o MEX 50-51 F 6
Concordia o PE 64-65 E 4
Concordia o RA 76-77 H 6
Concordia o USA (KS) 262-263 J 5
Concordia o USA (MO) 274-275 E 6
Concordia o ZA 220-221 C 4
Concordia, La o MEX 52-53 H 3
Concórdia do Para o BR 68-69 E 2
Concord Point ▲ USA 22-23 M 6
Con Cuông ☆ VN 156-157 D 7
Conda o ANG 216-217 C 5
Conda o USA (ID) 252-253 G 4
Condal, Cañada ~ RA 76-77 F 2
Condamine o AUS 178-179 L 4
Condamine River ~ AUS 178-179 L 4
Côn Đảo ⌒ VN (Con) 158-159 J 6
Côn Đảo ⌒ VN (Con) 158-159 J 6
Condé o ANG 216-217 C 5
Conde o BR 68-69 K 7
Conde o USA (SD) 260-261 H 1
Condédezi, Rio ~ MOC 218-219 G 2
Condega o NIC 52-53 L 5
Condeixas o BR 62-63 K 6
Conde Loca o ANG 216-217 B 4
Conde Matarazzo o BR 74-75 D 9
Condeúba o BR 72-73 K 3
Condingup o AUS 176-177 G 6
Condobolin o AUS 180-181 J 2
Condom o F 90-91 H 10
Čondon ~ RUS 110-111 V 4
Condon o USA (OR) 244-245 E 5
Condor o CDN (ALB) 232-233 D 3
Cóndor, Cerro el ▲ RA 76-77 C 4
Cóndor, Cordillera del ▲ PE 64-65 C 4
Cone o USA (TX) 264-265 C 5
Conecuh River ~ USA (AL) 284-285 E 5
Conecuh River ~ USA (AL) 284-285 E 5
Conejo, El o MEX 50-51 D 5
Conejos o USA (CO) 254-255 J 6
Cone Peak ▲ AUS 174-175 G 3
Conesa o RA 78-79 J 2
Conestogo River ~ CDN (ONT) 238-239 E 5
Confluencia o RA 78-79 D 6
Confolens o F 90-91 H 8
Confusion Bay ≈ 38-39 R 3
Confusion Bay ≈ CDN 242-243 N 2
Confuso, Río ~ PY 76-77 H 3
Congaree River ~ USA (SC) 284-285 K 3
Congaree Swamp National Monument ⊥ USA (SC) 284-285 K 3
Congaz o MD 102-103 F 4
Congerenge o MOC 218-219 H 2
Conger Range ▲ CDN 26-27 J 3
Conghua o VRC 156-157 H 5
Congjiang o VRC 156-157 F 4
Congnarauya, Pointe ▲ CDN 36-37 Q 5
Congo o BR 68-69 K 5
Congo ■ RCB 210-211 D 5
Congo ~ RCB 210-211 F 5
Congo Basin = Grande Dépression Centrale ∸ ZRE 210-211 F 5
Congo Fan ≃ 6-7 K 9
Congonhas o ••• BR 72-73 H 6
Congonhas do Norte o BR 72-73 J 5
Congo Town o • BS 54-55 G 2
Congress o CDN (SAS) 232-233 N 6
Congress o USA (AZ) 256-257 C 4
Conguillo los Paraguas, Parque Nacional ⊥ RCH 78-79 D 5
Conhello o RA 78-79 G 4
Conifer o USA (CO) 254-255 K 4
Coniston o AUS 172-173 L 7
Coniston o CDN (ONT) 238-239 E 2
Conitaca o MEX 50-51 F 5
Conjo ~ ANG 216-217 D 5
Conjuboy o AUS 174-175 H 6
Conjuror Bay o CDN 30-31 K 3
Conkal o MEX 52-53 K 1
Conklin o CDN 32-33 P 4
Conlara, Río ~ RA 78-79 G 2
Conmee o CDN (ONT) 234-235 O 6
Conn o USA (MS) 268-269 K 5
Connaughton, Mount ▲ AUS 172-173 F 7
Conneaut o USA (OH) 280-281 F 2
Conneaut Lake o USA (PA) 280-281 F 2
Conneautville o USA (PA) 280-281 F 2
Connecticut ■ USA (CT) 280-281 N 2
Connecticut River ~ USA 278-279 J 5
Connecticut River ~ USA (CT) 280-281 O 2
Connell o USA (WA) 244-245 G 4
Connellsville o USA (PA) 280-281 G 3
Connelly, Mount ▲ AUS 172-173 H 3
Connels Lagoon Conservation Reserve ⊥ AUS 174-175 D 6
Conner o RP 160-161 D 4
Conner, Mount ▲ AUS 176-177 L 2
Conne River o CDN (NFL) 242-243 N 5
Conner Prairie • USA (IN) 274-275 N 4
Connersville o USA (IN) 274-275 N 5
Connerville o USA (OK) 264-265 H 4
Conn Lake o CDN 26-27 O 8
Connor, Mount ▲ AUS 172-173 H 3
Connors o CDN (NB) 240-241 G 3
Connors Pass ▲ USA (NV) 246-247 L 4
Connors Range ▲ AUS 178-179 K 1
Connors River ~ AUS 178-179 K 2
Connorsville o USA (WI) 270-271 F 5
Conoble Lake o AUS 180-181 H 2
Conodoguinet Creek ~ USA (PA) 280-281 J 3
Čonogol o MAU 148-149 M 5
Cononaco o EC 64-65 E 2
Conover o USA (MI) 270-271 J 4
Conquest o CDN (SAS) 232-233 L 4
Conquet o F 90-91 E 7
Conquista o BOL 70-71 D 2
Conrad o USA (MT) 250-251 H 3
Conrad Rise ≃ 12 B 10
Conran, Cape ▲ AUS 180-181 K 4
Conrana ~ RI 164-165 G 6
Conrich o CDN (ALB) 232-233 E 4
Conroe o USA (TX) 268-269 E 6
Conroe, Lake < USA (TX) 268-269 E 6
Consata, Río ~ BOL 70-71 C 4
Conselheiro Lafaiete o BR 72-73 J 6
Conselho, Ponta do ▲ BR 72-73 L 2
Consett o GB 90-91 G 4
Consolación del Sur o C 54-55 D 3
Consort o CDN (ALB) 232-233 H 4
Constance, Lac de = Bodensee o CH 92-93 K 5
Constance Bay ≈ 140-141 L 4
Constance Headland ▲ AUS 176-177 G 2
Constance Lake o CDN (ONT) 236-237 D 3
Constancia, Cerro ▲ RCH 70-71 C 7
Constanța ☆ • RO 102-103 F 5
Constantina o BR 74-75 D 6
Constantina o • E 98-99 E 6
Constantine ☆ •• DZ 190-191 F 2
Constantine, Cape ▲ USA 22-23 R 3
Constantine, Mount ▲ CDN 20-21 U 6
Constanza o •• DOM 54-55 K 5
Constitución o RCH 78-79 C 3
Constitución de 1857, Parque Nacional ⊥ MEX 50-51 B 1
Consuelo Peak ▲ AUS 178-179 K 3
Consul o BR 70-71 K 3
Consul o CDN (SAS) 232-233 J 6
Consul River ~ CDN 30-31 T 3
Contact o USA (NV) 246-247 L 2
Contagem o BR 72-73 H 5
Contamana o PE 64-65 E 5
Contamana, Sierra ▲ PE 64-65 F 6
Contão o BR 62-63 D 4
Contas, Rio de ~ BR 72-73 L 3
Contendas do Sincorá o BR 72-73 K 2
Continental o USA (AZ) 256-257 E 7
Continental o USA (OH) 280-281 B 2
Contoy, Isla ⌒ MEX 52-53 L 1
Contramaestre o C 54-55 G 4
Contrato, Rio ~ BR 68-69 F 6
Con Trau, Hòn ⌒ VN 158-159 K 4
Contreras, Isla ⌒ RCH 80 C 6
Contuboel o GNB 202-203 C 3
Contumaza o PE 64-65 C 5
Contwoyto Lake o CDN 30-31 O 3
Conucos, Los o YV 60-61 E 3
Convencion o CO 60-61 E 3
Convento, Cerro ▲ RA 80 F 5
Convento, Montañas de ▲ EC 64-65 C 2
Converse o USA (IN) 274-275 N 4
Converse o USA (LA) 268-269 G 5
Conway o USA (AR) 276-277 C 5
Conway o USA (NH) 278-279 K 5
Conway o USA (SC) 284-285 L 3
Conway o USA (TX) 264-265 C 3
Conway o ZA 220-221 G 5
Conway, Lake o AUS 178-179 C 5
Conway, Lake < USA (AR) 276-277 C 5
Conway National Park ⊥ AUS 174-175 K 7
Coober Pedy o • AUS 178-179 C 5
Coocoran Lake o AUS 178-179 J 5
Cooinda Motel o AUS 172-173 L 2
Cook o AUS 176-177 L 5
Cook o USA (MN) 270-271 F 3
Cook, Cape ▲ CDN (BC) 230-231 A 3
Cook, Mount ▲ NZ 182 C 5
Cook, Mount ▲ USA 20-21 U 6
Cook Bay ≈ 16 G 16
Cook Bay ≈ 184 II b 4
Cooke, Mount ▲ AUS (WA) 172-173 E 7
Cooke, Mount ▲ AUS (WA) 176-177 D 6
Cooke City o USA (MT) 250-251 K 6
Cookeville o USA (TN) 276-277 K 4
Cook Forest State Park ⊥ USA (PA) 280-281 G 2
Cookhouse o ZA 220-221 G 6
Cooking Lake o CDN (ALB) 232-233 E 2
Cook Inlet ≈ 22-23 U 3
Cook Islands ⌒ NZ 13 L 4
Cook Lake o CDN 30-31 P 4
Cook Peninsula ∪ CDN 26-27 M 4
Cooks o USA (MI) 270-271 M 5
Cooksburg o USA (NY) 278-279 G 6
Cooks Harbour o CDN (NFL) 242-243 N 1
Cookshire o CDN (QUE) 238-239 O 3
Cookstown o CDN (ONT) 238-239 F 4
Cookstown o GB 90-91 D 4
Cook Strait ≈ 182 E 4
Cooktown o •• AUS 174-175 H 4
Cool, Tanjung ▲ RI 166-167 K 6
Coolabah o AUS 178-179 J 6
Cooladdi o AUS 178-179 H 4
Coolah o AUS 178-179 K 6
Coolamon o AUS 180-181 J 3
Coolangatta o AUS 178-179 M 5
Coolgardie o AUS 176-177 F 5
Coolidge o USA (AZ) 256-257 D 6
Coolidge o USA (TX) 266-267 L 2
Coolin o USA (ID) 250-251 C 3
Coolmunda Reservoir < AUS 178-179 L 5
Cooloola National Park ⊥ AUS 178-179 M 4
Coolville o USA (OH) 280-281 E 4
Cooma o AUS 180-181 K 4
Coombes Cove o CDN (NFL) 242-243 N 5
Coonabarabran o AUS 178-179 M 4
Coonabarabran o AUS 178-179 K 6
Coonalpyn o AUS 180-181 E 3
Coonamble o AUS 178-179 K 6
Coonawarra o • AUS 180-181 F 4
Coondapoor o IND 140-141 F 4
Coongan River ~ AUS 172-173 D 6
Coongoola o AUS 178-179 H 4
Coon Rapids o USA (IA) 274-275 D 3
Coon Rapids o USA (MN) 270-271 E 5
Cooper o USA (ME) 278-279 O 4
Cooper o USA (NM) 256-257 M 6
Cooper o USA (TX) 264-265 J 5
Cooper Creek ~ AUS 178-179 F 4
Cooper Creek ~ AUS 178-179 E 5
Cooperfield o USA (OR) 244-245 J 6
Cooper River ~ USA (SC) 284-285 L 3
Coopers Island ⌒ CDN 36-37 T 6
Coopers Mills o USA (ME) 278-279 M 4
Cooper's Town o BS 54-55 G 1
Cooperstown o USA (ND) 258-259 J 4
Cooperstown o USA (NY) 278-279 G 6
Coop Lake o CDN 30-31 M 5
Coorabie o AUS 176-177 M 5
Coorabulka o AUS 178-179 F 2
Coorada o AUS 178-179 K 3
Coordewandy ▲ AUS 176-177 D 2
Coorong National Park ⊥ AUS 180-181 E 4
Coorow o AUS 176-177 D 4
Cooroy o AUS 178-179 M 4
Coosa o USA (GA) 284-285 E 2
Coosa River ~ USA (AL) 284-285 D 3
Coosawattee River ~ USA (GA) 284-285 F 2
Coosawhatchie River ~ USA (SC) 284-285 J 4
Coos Bay ≈ 40-41 B 4
Coos Bay o USA (OR) 244-245 A 7
Coos Bay ≈ USA 244-245 A 7
Cootamundra o AUS 180-181 K 3
Coover Creek ~ USA (VA) 280-281 D 7
Čop o UA 102-103 C 3
Copa, Cerro ▲ BOL 70-71 C 7
Copacabana o BOL (PAZ) 70-71 C 5
Copacabana o BOL (SAC) 70-71 G 4
Copacabana o CO 60-61 D 4
Copacabana, Península de ∪ BOL 70-71 C 5
Copahué o RA 78-79 D 4
Copahué, Paso ▲ RCH 78-79 D 4
Copahué, Volcán ▲ RCH 78-79 D 4
Copal Urco o PE 64-65 F 3
Copán ∴ ••• HN 52-53 K 4
Copan o USA (OK) 264-265 J 2
Copan Lake o USA (OK) 264-265 J 2
Copano Bay ≈ 44-45 J 5
Copano Bay ≈ USA 266-267 K 5
Copán Ruinas o HN 52-53 K 4
Copas o USA (MN) 270-271 F 5
Cope o USA (CO) 254-255 N 4
Copé, El o PA 52-53 D 7
Copeland o USA (ID) 250-251 C 3
Copeland o USA (KS) 262-263 F 7
Copemish o USA (MI) 272-273 D 3
Copenhagen = København ☆ •• DK 86-87 F 9
Copere o BOL 70-71 F 6
Copeton Reservoir < AUS 178-179 L 5
Copeyal o YV 60-61 G 2
Copiapó ☆ RCH 76-77 B 4
Copiapó, Río ~ RCH 76-77 B 4
Čopko ~ RUS 108-109 f 7
Čopko ~ RUS 108-109 Z 6
Coporito o YV 60-61 L 3
Coporolo ~ ANG 216-217 B 6
Coposa, Cerro ▲ RCH 70-71 C 7
Coppabella o AUS 178-179 K 1
Coppename Monding, National Reservaat ⊥ SME 62-63 G 2
Coppenamerivier ~ SME 62-63 F 3
Copper o USA (OR) 244-245 B 8
Copperas Cove o USA (TX) 266-267 K 2
Copperbelt ■ Z 218-219 D 1
Copper Breaks State Park ⊥ • USA (TX) 264-265 E 4
Copper Creek o CDN (BC) 230-231 J 3
Copper Harbor o USA (WI) 270-271 L 3
Coppermine o CDN 30-31 M 2
Coppermine Point ▲ CDN (ONT) 236-237 D 5
Coppermine River ~ CDN 30-31 M 2
Copper Mines • AUS 180-181 H 7
Copperneedle River ~ CDN 30-31 W 4
Copper River ~ USA 20-21 S 5
Copperstown o USA (PA) 280-281 G 3
Coppersville o USA (MI) 272-273 D 4
Copperton o ZA 220-221 F 4
Copton Creek ~ CDN (ALB) 228-229 P 2
Coqên o VRC 144-145 E 5
Coqueiro, Ribeiro ~ BR 70-71 J 5
Coqueiros, Ponta dos ▲ BR 68-69 L 5
Coquí o BR 66-67 E 3
Coquí o CO 60-61 C 5
Coquilhatville = Mbandaka ☆ ZRE 210-211 G 3
Coquille o USA (OR) 244-245 A 7
Coquimatlán o MEX 52-53 C 2
Coquimbo o RCH 76-77 B 5
Coquimbo, Bahía ≈ 76-77 B 5
Corabia o RO 102-103 D 6
Coração de Jesus o BR 72-73 H 4
Coraci-Paraná, Rio ~ BR 68-69 E 3
Coracora o PE 64-65 F 9
Corail o RH 54-55 J 5
Corais, Ilha dos ⌒ BR 74-75 F 5
Coral o CDN (ONT) 236-237 G 2
Coralaque, Río ~ PE 70-71 B 5
Coral Basin ≃ 13 F 4
Coral Bay ≈ 160-161 B 8
Coral Gables o USA (FL) 286-287 J 6
Coral Harbour o CDN 36-37 H 2
Coral Heights o BS 54-55 G 2
Coral Sea ≈ 13 G 4
Coral Springs o USA (FL) 286-287 J 5
Corangamite, Lake o AUS 180-181 G 5
Coranzuli o RA 76-77 D 2
Corapeake o USA (NC) 282-283 L 4
Cora Trepadeira ~ BR 70-71 K 3
Corazón, El o EC 64-65 C 2
Corberrie o CDN (NS) 240-241 K 6
Corbett Inlet ≈ 30-31 X 4
Corbett National Park ⊥ • IND 138-139 G 5
Corbin o USA (KY) 276-277 L 4
Corby o GB 90-91 G 5
Corcaigh = Cork ☆ IRL 90-91 C 6
Corcoran o USA (CA) 248-249 E 3
Corcovada, Park Nacional ⊥ CR 52-53 C 7
Corcovado o RA 78-79 D 7
Corcovado, Golfo ≈ 78-79 C 7
Corcovado, Volcán ▲ RCH 78-79 C 7
Corcubión o E 98-99 C 3
Corda, Ribeiro ~ BR 68-69 D 5
Corda, Rio ~ BR 68-69 F 5
Cordeiro o BR 72-73 J 7
Cordeiro, Rio ~ BR 68-69 K 6
Cordele o USA (GA) 284-285 G 5
Cordell o USA (OK) 264-265 F 3
Cordilheira o BR 74-75 D 8
Cordilheiras, Serra das ▲ BR 68-69 D 5
Cordillera Cantábrica ▲ E 98-99 D 3
Cordillera Central ▲ E 98-99 E 4
Cordillera Central ▲ RP 160-161 D 4
Cordillera de la Costa ▲ YV 60-61 H 2
Cordillera de los Picachos, Parque Nacional ⊥ CO 60-61 D 6
Cordilleras Range ▲ RP 160-161 E 7
Cordisburgo o BR 72-73 H 5
Córdoba o ••• E 98-99 E 6
Córdoba o MEX 52-53 F 2
Córdoba ■ RA 78-79 G 2
Córdoba ☆ • RA 76-77 E 6
Córdoba, Sierra de ▲ RA 78-79 G 2
Cordobés, Arroyo del ~ ROU 78-79 M 2
Cordobés, Cerro ▲ RA 76-77 C 5
Cordón Alto ∸ RA 80 F 4
Cordón de las Llarretas ▲ RA 78-79 E 3
Cordon de Puntas Negras ▲ RCH 76-77 D 2
Cordón Seler ▲ RCH 80 D 3
Cordova o USA 20-21 S 6
Cordova o USA (AL) 284-285 C 3
Cordova o USA (IA) 274-275 H 3
Córdova, Península ∪ RCH 80 D 6
Cordova Bay ≈ 32-33 D 4
Cordova Peak ▲ USA 20-21 S 6
Coreaú, Rio ~ BR 68-69 H 3
Coremas o BR 68-69 K 5
Corey, La o CDN 32-33 P 4
Corfield o AUS 178-179 G 1
Corfu = Kérkira ⌒ GR 100-101 G 5
Corguinho o BR 70-71 K 6
Coria o • E 98-99 D 5
Coriabo o GUY 62-63 E 2
Coria del Río o E 98-99 D 6
Coribe o BR 72-73 H 2
Corico, Lago o RCH 78-79 C 5
Coricó, Laguna o RA 78-79 F 6
Coricudgy, Mount ▲ AUS 180-181 L 2
Co' Rinh, Ngoc ▲ VN 158-159 K 3
Corinna o AUS 180-181 H 6
Corinna o USA (ME) 278-279 M 4
Corinne o CDN (SAS) 232-233 O 5
Corinne o USA (MI) 270-271 N 4
Corinne o USA (UT) 254-255 C 2
Corinth o USA (KY) 276-277 L 2
Corinth o USA (ME) 278-279 N 3
Corinth o USA (MS) 268-269 M 2
Corinto o BR 72-73 H 5
Corinto o CO 60-61 C 6
Corinto o HN 52-53 K 4
Corinto o NIC 52-53 L 5
Corio Bay ≈ 178-179 L 2
Corisco, Baie de ≈ 210-211 B 3

Coleen River — Corisco, Baie de 317

Corisco o Mandyi, Isla de ~ GQ 210-211 B 3
Corixa Grande ~ BR 70-71 J 5
Corixão, Rio ~ BR 70-71 J 6
Cork ★ IRL 178-179 G 2
Cork o IRL 90-91 C 6
Corleone o I 100-101 D 6
Corme e Laxe, Ría de ≈ 98-99 C 3
Cormorant o CDN 34-35 F 3
Cormorant Forest Reserve ⊥ CDN 34-35 F 3
Cormorant Lake o CDN 34-35 F 3
Čornae, vozero o RUS 88-89 J 5
Čornaja ~ RUS 88-89 Y 2
Čornaja ~ RUS 88-89 Y 2
Cornate, le ▲ I 100-101 C 3
Corn Creek ~ USA (AZ) 256-257 E 3
Cornelia o USA (GA) 284-285 G 2
Cornelia ~ ZA 220-221 J 3
Cornelio o MEX 50-51 D 3
Cornélio Procópio o BR 72-73 E 7
Cornelius o USA (NC) 282-283 G 5
Cornelius Grinnell Bay ≈ 36-37 R 3
Cornell o USA (WI) 270-271 L 5
Cornell o USA (MI) 270-271 G 5
Cornell Gletscher ⊏ GRØ 26-27 W 6
Čorne more o 102-103 G 5
Corner Brook o CDN (NFL) 242-243 L 4
Corner Inlet ≈ 180-181 J 5
Corner River ~ CDN (ONT) 236-237 J 2
Corney Bayou ~ USA (TX) 268-269 F 5
Corning o USA (AR) 276-277 E 4
Corning o USA (CA) 246-247 C 4
Corning o USA (IA) 274-275 D 4
Corning o USA (KS) 262-263 K 5
Corning o USA (NY) 278-279 D 6
Cornish, Mount ▲ AUS 172-173 H 6
Cornish Creek ~ AUS 178-179 J 4
Corn Islands = Islas del Maíz ~ NIC 52-53 C 5
Čomobyľ o UA 102-103 G 2
Čomomors'ke ~ UA 102-103 H 5
Cornouaille ⊥ F 90-91 E 7
Comudas o USA (TX) 266-267 B 2
Cornwall o CDN (ONT) 238-239 L 3
Cornwall ⊢ GB 90-91 D 6
Cornwall Coast ⊾ GB 90-91 E 6
Cornwallis Island ~ CDN 24-25 Y 3
Cornwall Island ~ CDN 24-25 X 4
Čornyj Čeremoš ~ UA 102-103 D 3
Coro ★ YV 60-61 F 2
Coro, Golfete de ≈ 60-61 F 2
Coro, Ilha do ~ BR 66-67 F 4
Coro, Raudal ~ CO 66-67 B 3
Coroa, Cachoeira de ~ BR 68-69 E 5
Coroatá o BR 68-69 F 4
Corocoro o BOL 70-71 C 5
Coroico o BOL 70-71 D 5
Coroico, Rio ~ BOL 70-71 D 4
Corojal, El o C 54-55 E 3
Corolla o USA (NC) 282-283 M 4
Coromandel o BR 72-73 G 5
Coromandel o NZ 182 E 2
Coromandel Coast ⊾ IND 140-141 J 6
Coromandel Peninsula ⊶ NZ 182 E 2
Coron o RP 160-161 D 7
Corona o USA (CA) 248-249 G 6
Corona o USA (NM) 256-257 K 4
Corona, Cerro ▲ RA 78-79 D 4
Corona, Rio ~ MEX 50-51 K 5
Coronach o CDN (SAS) 232-233 N 6
Coronado, Bahía de ≈ 52-53 C 7
Coronado National Monument • USA (AZ) 256-257 E 7
Coronation o CDN (ALB) 232-233 G 3
Coronation Gulf ≈ 24-25 O 6
Coronation Island ~ ARK 16 G 32
Coronation Island ~ AUS 172-173 G 3
Coronation Island Wilderness ⊥ USA 32-33 C 4
Coron Bay ≈ 160-161 D 7
Coronda o RA 76-77 G 6
Coronel o RCH 78-79 C 4
Coronel Bogado o PY 76-77 J 4
Coronel Dorrego o RA 78-79 J 5
Coronel Martinez o PY 76-77 J 3
Coronel Moldes o RA 78-79 G 2
Coronel Oviedo ★ PY 76-77 J 3
Coronel Pringles o RA 78-79 J 4
Coronel Rodolfo Bunge o RA 78-79 J 4
Coronel Sapucaia o BR 76-77 K 2
Coronel Suárez o RA 78-79 J 4
Coronel Vidal o RA 78-79 K 4
Coronel Vivida o BR 74-75 D 5
Coroni Bird Sanctuary ⊥ TT 60-61 L 2
Corowa-Wahgunyah o AUS 180-181 J 4
Corozal o BH 52-53 K 2
Corozo, El o YV 60-61 K 4
Corpus Christi o USA (TX) 266-267 K 6
Corpus Christi, Lake o USA (TX) 266-267 K 5
Corpus Christi Bay ≈ 44-45 J 6
Corque o BOL 70-71 D 6
Corral o USA (ID) 252-253 D 3
Corral de Bustos o RA 78-79 H 2
Corralejo o E 188-189 E 6
Corrales o CO 60-61 E 5
Corrales, Los (Los Corrales de Buelna) o E 98-99 E 3
Corralillo o C 54-55 E 4
Corrane o MOC 218-219 K 2
Correctionville o USA (IA) 274-275 C 2
Corregidor Island ~ RP 160-161 D 7
Córrego do Ouro o BR 72-73 E 4
Córrego Novo o BR 72-73 J 5
Correia Pinto o BR 74-75 E 6
Corrente o BR 68-69 F 7
Corrente, Rio ~ BR 68-69 F 5
Corrente, Rio ~ BR 68-69 G 4
Corrente, Rio ~ BR 72-73 J 2

Correntes o BR 68-69 K 6
Correntes, Riachão ~ BR 68-69 H 4
Correntina o BR 72-73 H 2
Correntinho o BR 68-69 F 4
Corretoso o BR 78-79 D 6
Corrib, Lough ≈ IRL 90-91 C 5
Corrida de Cori ▲ RA 76-77 C 3
Corrientes o RA 76-77 H 4
Corrientes ★ RA 76-77 H 4
Corrientes, Cabo ▲ C 54-55 C 4
Corrientes, Cabo ▲ CO 60-61 C 5
Corrientes, Cabo ▲ MEX 52-53 B 1
Corrientes, Rio ~ PE 64-65 E 3
Corrientes, Rio ~ RA 76-77 H 5
Corrientes, Rio ~ RA 78-79 F 4
Corrigan o USA (TX) 268-269 F 5
Corryong o AUS 180-181 J 4
Corse ▫ F 98-99 M 3
Corse, Cap ▲ F 98-99 M 3
Corsica = Corse ⊐ F 98-99 M 4
Corsica ~ USA (TX) 264-265 H 6
Corsicana o USA (TX) 268-269 F 2
Cortadera, La o RA 78-79 E 4
Cortaderal, Cerro ▲ RCH 76-77 C 3
Cortaderas, Pampa de ⊾ PE 70-71 A 5
Cortaro o USA (AZ) 256-257 D 6
Corte o F 98-99 M 3
Cortegana o E 98-99 D 6
Cortez o USA (CO) 254-255 G 6
Cortez Gold Mine o USA (NV) 246-247 J 3
Cortina d' Ampezzo o I 100-101 D 1
Čortkiv ~ UA 102-103 D 3
Cortland o USA (NE) 262-263 K 4
Cortland o USA (NY) 278-279 D 6
Cortona o I 100-101 C 3
Conuage, Cachoeira ~ BR 68-69 B 4
Corubal, Rio ~ GNB 202-203 C 4
Coruche o P 98-99 C 5
Çoruh Nehri ~ TR 128-129 J 2
Çoruh Neri ~ TR 128-129 J 2
Çorum ★ TR 128-129 F 2
Coruma o BR 70-71 J 6
Corumbá o BR 70-71 J 6
Corumba, Rio ~ BR 72-73 G 4
Corumbá de Goiás o BR 72-73 F 3
Corumbaíba o BR 72-73 F 5
Corumbiara, Ponta de ▲ BR 72-73 L 4
Corumbiara Antigo, Rio ~ BR 70-71 G 3
Coruña, A ★ E 98-99 C 3
Corunna o CDN 238-239 C 6
Corunna North ▲ AUS 180-181 D 2
Čoruoda ~ RUS 118-119 K 7
Corupá o BR 74-75 F 6
Coruto, Laguna o BOL 76-77 E 2
Corutuba o BR 72-73 J 3
Corvallis o USA (OR) 244-245 B 6
Corvette, Rivière ~ CDN 38-39 G 2
Corwen o GB 90-91 F 5
Corwin o USA 20-21 H 2
Corwin, Cape ▲ USA 22-23 O 3
Cory Bay ≈ 36-37 M 2
Corydon o USA (IA) 274-275 E 4
Corydon o USA (IN) 274-275 M 6
Cosa • I 100-101 C 3
Cosamaloapan o MEX 52-53 G 2
Cosapa o BOL 70-71 C 6
Cosapilla o RCH 70-71 C 6
Coscaya o RCH 70-71 C 6
Cosenza o I 100-101 F 5
Coshocton o USA (OH) 280-281 E 3
Cosigüina, Punta ▲ NIC 52-53 L 5
Cosigüina, Volcán ▲ NIC 52-53 L 5
Cosmoledo Atoll ~ SY 222-223 E 2
Cosmo Newberry Aboriginal Land X AUS 176-177 G 4
Cosmo Newberry Mission X AUS 176-177 G 4
Cosmópolis o BR 72-73 G 7
Cosne-Cours-sur-Loire o F 90-91 J 8
Cosoleacaque o MEX 52-53 G 2
Costa, Cordillera de la ⊾ RCH 78-79 C 4
Costa, La o MEX 52-53 J 1
Costa, Punta de la ▲ BR 62-63 J 3
Costa Blanca ⊾ E 98-99 G 6
Costa Brava ⊾ E 98-99 J 4
Costa da Cadeia ⊾ BR 74-75 E 7
Costa Daurada ⊾ E 98-99 H 4
Costa de Araujo o RA 78-79 D 6
Costa de la Luz ⊾ E 98-99 D 6
Costa del Sol ⊾ E 98-99 E 7
Costa de Prata ⊾ P 98-99 C 5
Costa Island, La ~ USA (FL) 286-287 D 5
Costa Marques o BR 70-71 G 3
Costa Rica o BR 72-73 D 5
Costa Rica ■ CR 52-53 B 7
Costa Rica ~ USA 54-55 H 4
Costa Vasca ⊾ E 98-99 F 3
Costa Verde ⊾ E 98-99 D 3
Costera del Golfo, Llanura ⊾ MEX 50-51 K 5
Costera del Pacífico, Llanura ⊾ MEX 50-51 D 3
Costegti o MD 102-103 E 4
Costegti o RO 102-103 E 4
Costilla o USA (NM) 256-257 K 2
Cota o CO 60-61 D 5
Cotabambas o PE 64-65 E 7
Cotabato City o RP 160-161 F 9
Cotacachi, Cerro ▲ EC 64-65 C 1
Cotacachi-Cayapas, Reserva Ecológica ⊥ EC 64-65 C 1
Cotacajes, Rio ~ BOL 70-71 D 5
Cotagaita o BOL 70-71 E 7
Cotahuasi o PE 64-65 E 8
Cotaxe, Rio ~ BR 72-73 K 5
Cotazar o MEX 52-53 D 1
Coteau des Prairies ⊾ USA (SD) 260-261 J 1
Coteau du Missouri ⊾ USA (ND) 258-259 F 2
Coteau Hills ⊾ CDN (SAS) 232-233 L 4

Côteaux o RH 54-55 H 5
Côte d'Azur ⊾ F 90-91 L 10
Côte d'Ivoire = Côte-d'Ivoire ■ CI 202-203 G 5
Cotejipe o BR 72-73 H 2
Côte Nord ⊾ CDN 38-39 L 3
Cotentin ⊾ F 90-91 G 7
Côtes de Fer o RH 54-55 H 5
Coti, Rio ~ BR 66-67 C 3
Cotia, Rio ~ BR 66-67 E 7
Cotija de la Paz o MEX 52-53 C 2
Cotingo, Rio ~ BR 66-67 F 3
Coto de Doñana, Parque Nacional ⊥ E 98-99 D 6
Cotonou ★ DY 204-205 E 5
Cotopaxi o USA (CO) 254-255 K 5
Cotopaxi, Volcán ▲ EC 64-65 C 2
Cotorro o C 54-55 D 3
Cotoveio, Corredeira do ~ BR 66-67 H 6
Cotronei o I 100-101 F 5
Cottage Grove o USA (MN) 270-271 F 6
Cottage Grove o USA (OR) 244-245 C 6
Cottageville o USA (SC) 284-285 K 4
Cottar's Mara Camp o EAK 212-213 E 4
Cottbus o D 92-93 N 3
Cotter o USA (AR) 276-277 C 4
Cottonbush Creek ~ AUS 178-179 E 2
Cottondale o USA (FL) 286-287 D 1
Cotton Draw ~ USA (TX) 266-267 C 2
Cotton Plant o USA (AR) 276-277 D 5
Cottonport o USA (LA) 268-269 H 6
Cotton Valley o USA (LA) 268-269 F 3
Cottonwood o CDN 228-229 M 3
Cottonwood o USA (AL) 284-285 E 5
Cottonwood o USA (AZ) 256-257 C 4
Cottonwood o USA (ID) 250-251 C 5
Cottonwood o USA (SD) 260-261 E 3
Cottonwood Cove ~ USA (NV) 248-249 K 4
Cottonwood Creek ~ USA (MT) 250-251 H 3
Cottonwood Creek ~ USA (UT) 254-255 F 6
Cottonwood Falls o USA (KS) 262-263 K 6
Cottonwood River ~ USA (KS) 262-263 K 6
Cottonwood River ~ USA (MN) 270-271 C 6
Cottonwood Wash ~ USA (AZ) 256-257 F 3
Cotuhe, Rio ~ PE 66-67 B 4
Cotui ★ DOM 54-55 K 5
Cotulla o USA (TX) 266-267 H 5
Couchman Range ⊾ AUS 172-173 H 3
Coudersport o USA (PA) 280-281 H 2
Coudres, Île aux ~ CDN (QUE) 240-241 J 4
Couëron o F 90-91 G 8
Cougar o USA (CA) 246-247 C 2
Couhé o F 90-91 H 8
Coulee o USA (ND) 258-259 F 3
Coulee City o USA (WA) 244-245 F 3
Coulee Dam o USA (WA) 244-245 G 3
Coulman Island ▲ ARK 16 F 18
Couloir 1 ⊾ DZ 190-191 J 7
Coulomb Point ▲ AUS 172-173 F 4
Coulommiers o F 90-91 J 7
Coulonge, Rivière ~ CDN (QUE) 238-239 J 2
Coulta o AUS 180-181 C 3
Coulterville o USA (CA) 248-249 D 2
Coulterville o USA (IL) 274-275 J 6
Council o USA (AK) 20-21 J 4
Council o USA (ID) 252-253 D 2
Council Bluffs o USA (IA) 274-275 C 3
Council Grove o USA (KS) 262-263 K 6
Council Grove Lake o USA (KS) 262-263 K 6
Council Hill o USA (OK) 264-265 J 3
Counselors o USA (NM) 256-257 H 2
Countess o USA 280-281 F 6
Country Force Base Suffield xx CDN (ALB) 232-233 H 5
Country Harbour o CDN 240-241 O 5
Coupeville o USA (WA) 244-245 C 2
Coupland o USA (TX) 266-267 K 3
Courageous Lake o CDN 30-31 O 3
Courantyne ~ GUY 62-63 H 3
Cours, Cours-sur-Loire- o F 90-91 J 8
Court o USA (SAS) 232-233 J 4
Courtenay o CDN (BC) 230-231 E 4
Courtenay o USA (ND) 258-259 J 4
Courtis River ~ CDN 24-25 X 4
Courtright o CDN (ONT) 238-239 C 6
Courval o CDN (SAS) 232-233 M 5
Coushatta o USA (LA) 268-269 G 4
Coushatta Indian Reservation, & Alabama X USA (TX) 268-269 F 6
Coutances o F 90-91 G 7
Couto de Magalhães, Rio ~ BR 72-73 D 2
Couto de Magelhães de Minas o BR 72-73 J 5
Coutras o F 90-91 G 9
Coutts o CDN (ALB) 232-233 G 6
Couture, Lac o CDN 38-39 L 1
Cova Figueira o CV 202-203 B 6
Covè o DY 204-205 E 5
Cove Fort o USA (UT) 254-255 C 5
Cove Island ~ CDN (ONT) 238-239 D 3
Covelo o USA (CA) 246-247 B 4
Coventry o GB 90-91 G 5
Coventry Lake o CDN 30-31 R 5
Cove Palisades State Park, The ⊥ • USA (OR) 244-245 D 6
Covered Wells o USA (AZ) 256-257 C 6
Covilhã o P 98-99 D 4
Covington o USA (GA) 284-285 G 3
Covington o USA (IN) 274-275 L 4
Covington o USA (KY) 276-277 L 1
Covington o USA (LA) 268-269 K 6
Covington o USA (MI) 270-271 K 4

Covington o USA (OH) 280-281 B 3
Covington o USA (OK) 264-265 G 2
Covington o USA (TN) 276-277 F 5
Covington o USA (VA) 280-281 F 6
Covunco, Arroyo ~ RA 78-79 D 5
Cowal, Lake o AUS 180-181 J 2
Cowan o USA 174-175 G 4
Cowan o USA (TN) 276-277 F 5
Cowan, Cerro ▲ EC 64-65 B 10
Cowan, Lake o AUS 176-177 G 5
Cowan Downs o AUS 174-175 F 6
Cowan Hill ▲ AUS 174-175 F 6
Coward o USA (SC) 284-285 L 3
Cowansville o CDN (QUE) 238-239 N 3
Coward Springs o AUS 178-179 D 5
Cow Bay o CDN (NS) 240-241 M 6
Cowboy Pass ▲ USA (UT) 254-255 B 4
Cowcowing Lakes o AUS 176-177 D 5
Cow Creek ~ USA (WY) 252-253 M 3
Cow Creek ~ USA (OR) 244-245 C 7
Cowden o USA (IL) 274-275 K 5
Cowdrey o USA (CO) 254-255 J 3
Cowell o AUS 180-181 D 2
Cow Head o CDN (NFL) 242-243 L 3
Cowhouse Creek ~ USA (TX) 266-267 J 2
Cowichan Lake o CDN (BC) 230-231 E 5
Cowie Point ▲ CDN 24-25 P 4
Cowles o USA (NM) 256-257 K 3
Cowley o CDN (ALB) 232-233 G 6
Cowlic o USA (AZ) 256-257 C 7
Cowlitz River ~ USA (WA) 244-245 C 4
Cowpasture River ~ USA (VA) 280-281 G 6
Cowpens o USA (SC) 284-285 J 1
Cowra o AUS 180-181 K 2
Cowwal ~ GUY 62-63 F 3
Cox o USA (OH) 280-281 D 4
Coxilha de Santana ⊾ BR 76-77 J 6
Coxim o BR 70-71 K 6
Cox Island o AUS 36-37 K 5
Cox River ~ AUS 174-175 G 4
Cox's Bazar o BD 142-143 H 5
Cox's Cove o CDN (NFL) 242-243 L 3
Coxs Creek ~ USA 178-179 K 6
Coyaguaima, Cerro ▲ RA 76-77 D 2
Coyah o RG 202-203 D 5
Coyame o MEX 50-51 G 3
Coyanosa Draw ~ USA (TX) 266-267 D 2
Coy City o USA (TX) 266-267 J 5
Coyoacan o MEX 52-53 J 6
Coyolate ~ GCA 52-53 J 4
Coyolito o HN 52-53 L 5
Coyote o USA (NM) 256-257 K 5
Coyote o USA (NM) 256-257 J 2
Coyote, Bahía ≈ 50-51 D 5
Coyote, Rio ~ MEX 50-51 J 2
Coyotitán o MEX 50-51 F 6
Coyte, El o RA 80 E 2
Coyuca de Benitez o MEX 52-53 D 3
Cozad o USA (NE) 262-263 G 4
Cozes o F 90-91 G 9
Cozumel o MEX 52-53 L 1
Cozumel, Isla del ~ ▪▪ MEX 52-53 L 1
Crab Orchard o USA (TN) 282-283 C 5
Crab Orchard Lake o USA (IL) 276-277 F 7
Crabwood Creek o GUY 62-63 F 3
Cracow o AUS 178-179 L 3
Cracroft Island ~ CDN (BC) 230-231 D 3
Craddock o CDN (SAS) 232-233 O 5
Cradle Mountain Lake St. Clair National Park ⊥ AUS 180-181 H 6
Cradle Valley o AUS 180-181 H 6
Cradock o ZA 220-221 G 6
Craig o USA (AK) 32-33 D 4
Craig o USA (CO) 254-255 H 3
Craig o USA (FL) 286-287 J 7
Craig o USA (MS) 268-269 K 4
Craig o AUS 174-175 H 4
Craig Harbour o CDN 24-25 f 3
Craigellachie o CDN (BC) 230-231 L 3
Craigend o CDN 32-33 P 4
Craigieburn o AUS 180-181 H 4
Craigmore o CDN (SAS) 240-241 O 5
Craigmyle o CDN (ALB) 232-233 F 4
Craignure o GB 90-91 E 3
Craig Pass ▲ USA (WY) 252-253 H 2
Craigsville o USA (WV) 280-281 F 5
Craik o CDN (SAS) 232-233 N 4
Craiova ★ RO 102-103 D 5
Cramond o ZA 220-221 E 3
Cranberry Junction o CDN 32-33 F 4
Cranberry Lake o USA (NY) 278-279 G 4
Cranberry Portage o CDN 34-35 F 3
Cranbourne o AUS 180-181 H 5
Cranbrook o AUS 176-177 D 7
Cranbrook o CDN (BC) 230-231 O 4
Crandall o CDN (MAN) 234-235 C 3
Crandon o USA (WI) 270-271 K 5
Crane o USA (MO) 276-277 B 7
Crane o USA (OR) 244-245 G 7
Crane o USA (TX) 266-267 D 2
Crane Creek State Park ⊥ USA (OH) 280-281 C 2
Crane Lake o CDN (SAS) 232-233 J 5
Crane Lake o USA (MN) 270-271 F 2
Crane Lake o USA (MN) 270-271 F 2
Crane River o CDN (MAN) 234-235 D 3
Crane Valley o CDN (SAS) 232-233 N 6
Cranfills Gap o USA (TX) 266-267 J 2
Cranford o CDN (ALB) 232-233 G 6
Cranston o USA (RI) 278-279 K 7
Cranswick River ~ CDN 24-25 X 4
Crapaud o CDN (PEI) 240-241 N 5
Crary Mountains ⊾ ARK 16 F 25
Crasna ~ RO 102-103 C 4
Crater Lake ⊥ WAN 204-205 K 3

Crater Lake National Monument ∴ USA (OR) 244-245 C 8
Crater Lake National Park ⊥ USA (OR) 244-245 C 8
Crater Mountain ▲ USA 20-21 M 5
Crater of Diamonds State Park ∴ USA (AR) 276-277 C 6
Craters of the Moon National Monument ∴ USA (ID) 252-253 E 3
Cratéus o BR 68-69 H 4
Crati ~ I 100-101 F 5
Crato o BR 68-69 J 5
Craven o CDN (SAS) 232-233 O 5
Cravo Norte o CO 60-61 F 4
Cravari ou Curucuinazá, Rio ~ BR 70-71 J 3
Crawford o CDN (SAS) 232-233 O 5
Crawford o USA (GA) 284-285 G 3
Crawford o USA (NE) 262-263 D 2
Crawford o USA (TX) 266-267 K 2
Crawford Bay o CDN (BC) 230-231 N 4
Crawfordsville o USA (IN) 274-275 M 4
Crawley o USA (WV) 280-281 F 6
Crazy Peak ▲ USA (MT) 250-251 J 5
Creede o USA (CO) 254-255 J 5
Creedmoor o USA (NC) 282-283 J 4
Creek Town o WAN 204-205 H 6
Creel o MEX 50-51 F 4
Cree Lake o CDN 34-35 C 3
Creelman o CDN (SAS) 232-233 P 6
Creighton o CDN (SAS) 34-35 F 3
Creighton o USA (NE) 262-263 J 2
Creighton o USA (SD) 260-261 D 2
Creil o F 90-91 J 7
Cremona o CDN (ALB) 232-233 E 4
Cremona o I 100-101 C 2
Crenshaw o USA (MS) 268-269 K 2
Creola o USA (AL) 284-285 C 5
Creole o USA (LA) 268-269 G 7
Crepori, Rio ~ BR 66-67 J 6
Cres ~ HR 100-101 E 2
Cres ▲ HR 100-101 E 2
Cresbard o USA (SD) 260-261 H 1
Crescent o USA (OK) 264-265 G 2
Crescent o USA (OR) 244-245 D 7
Crescent, La o USA (MN) 270-271 G 7
Crescent City o USA (CA) 246-247 A 1
Crescent City o USA (FL) 286-287 H 2
Crescent Group = Yongle Qundao ~ VRC 158-159 L 2
Crescent Head o AUS 178-179 M 6
Crescent Junction o USA (UT) 254-255 F 5
Crescent Lake o CDN (SAS) 232-233 O 3
Crescent Lake o USA (OR) 244-245 D 7
Crescent Lake National Wildlife Refuge ⊥ USA (NE) 262-263 D 3
Crescent Valley o USA (NV) 246-247 J 3
Cresco o USA (IA) 274-275 F 1
Crespo o RA 78-79 J 2
Cresson o USA (TX) 264-265 G 6
Crest o F 90-91 K 9
Crested Butte o USA (CO) 254-255 J 5
Crestline o USA (OH) 280-281 D 3
Crestmore o CDN (ALB) 232-233 E 3
Creston o CDN (BC) 230-231 N 4
Creston o USA (CA) 248-249 D 4
Creston o USA (IA) 274-275 D 3
Creston o USA (MT) 250-251 G 3
Creston o USA (WY) 252-253 L 5
Crestón, Cerro ▲ RA 76-77 B 4
Crestview o USA (FL) 286-287 C 1
Crestwynd o CDN (SAS) 232-233 N 5
Creswell o CDN (ALB) 232-233 J 4
Creswell Bay ≈ 24-25 Z 4
Creswell Downs o AUS 174-175 D 3
Crete o AUS 180-181 H 4
Crete = Kriti ⊐ GR 100-101 K 7
Crete, Sea of = Kritiko Pélagos ≈ GR 100-101 K 6
Creus, Cap de ▲ E 98-99 J 3
Creuse ~ F 90-91 J 8
Crewe o GB 90-91 F 5
Crewe o USA (VA) 280-281 H 6
Criba, Rio ~ BR 70-71 J 4
Crichton o CDN (SAS) 232-233 L 6
Criciúma o BR 74-75 F 7
Crieff o GB 90-91 F 3
Crikvenica o HR 100-101 E 2
Crilly o CDN 234-235 J 6
Crimea = Krym, Respublika ▫ UA 102-103 H 5
Crimea = Kryms'kyj pivostriv ⊶ UA 102-103 H 5
Criminosa, Cachoeira ~ BR 62-63 D 6
Criminosa, Cachoeira ~ BR 62-63 D 6
Crimson Cliffs ▲ GRØ 26-27 R 5
Crimson Lake Provincial Park ⊥ CDN (ALB) 232-233 E 3
Criolla, Cerro la ▲ RA 80 E 5
Cripple o USA 20-21 M 5
Cripple Creek o USA (CO) 254-255 K 5
Cris, Chișineu- o RO 102-103 B 4
Crisfield o USA (MD) 280-281 K 5
Crisostomo, Ribeiro ~ BR 68-69 G 7
Crispín, El o RA 76-77 F 6
Cristais, Serra dos ▲ BR 72-73 G 4
Cristal, Monts de ▲ G 210-211 J 3
Cristalândia o BR 68-69 D 7
Cristalina o BR 72-73 G 4
Cristiano Muerto, Arroyo ~ RA 78-79 K 5
Cristianópolis o BR 72-73 F 4
Cristianos, Los o E 188-189 D 6
Cristóbal, Punta ▲ EC 64-65 B 10
Cristóbal Colón, Pico ▲ CO 60-61 E 2
Cristoffel, National Reservaat ⊥ NL 60-61 G 1
Cristópolis o BR 72-73 H 3
Cristovão Pereira, Ponta ▲ BR 74-75 E 8
Criterion o USA (OR) 244-245 D 5
Criterion Pass ▲ USA (OR) 244-245 D 5
Crixás o BR 72-73 E 2
Crixás, Rio ~ BR 68-69 D 7

Crixás Açu, Rio ~ BR 72-73 E 2
Crixás Mirim, Rio ~ BR 72-73 E 2
Crna gora ⊾ MK 100-101 H 3
Cmi vrh ▲ BIH 100-101 F 3
Croajingolong National Park ⊥ AUS 180-181 K 5
Croatá o BR 68-69 H 4
Croatan Sound ≈ USA 282-283 M 5
Croatia = Hrvatska ■ HR 100-101 E 2
Croche, Rivière ~ CDN (QUE) 240-241 C 3
Crocker o USA (SD) 260-261 J 1
Crocker, Banjaran ▲ MAL 160-161 A 10
Crocker Range National Park ⊥ MAL 160-161 B 10
Crockett o USA (TX) 268-269 F 4
Crocodile Camp o EAK 212-213 K 2
Crocodile Farm • AUS 172-173 K 2
Crocodiles ⊾ BF 202-203 J 3
Crofton o CDN (NE) 262-263 J 1
Croher River o CDN 24-25 M 6
Croix, La o USA 174-175 G 2
Croix des Bouquets o RH 54-55 J 5
Croix-de-Vie, Saint-Gilles- o F 90-91 G 8
Croker, Cape ▲ AUS 172-173 L 1
Croker Bay ≈ 24-25 e 3
Croker Island ~ AUS 172-173 L 1
Cromer o CDN (MAN) 234-235 B 5
Cromwell o CDN (MAN) 234-235 G 4
Cromwell o NZ 182 B 6
Cromwell o USA (MN) 270-271 F 4
Crăng Kno ~ VN 158-159 K 4
Cronin, Mount ▲ CDN (BC) 228-229 H 2
Crook o USA (CO) 254-255 N 3
Crooked Creek o USA 20-21 L 6
Crooked Creek ~ USA (KS) 262-263 F 7
Crooked Island ~ BS 54-55 H 3
Crooked Island ~ USA 22-23 Q 3
Crooked Island ~ USA (FL) 286-287 D 2
Crooked Island Passage ≈ 54-55 H 3
Crooked Lake o CDN 24-25 X 4
Crooked River ~ CDN (SAS) 232-233 P 3
Crooked River o CDN (BC) 228-229 M 2
Crooked River ~ USA 244-245 D 6
Crooks Inlet ≈ 36-37 O 3
Crookston o USA (MN) 270-271 B 3
Crookston o USA (NE) 262-263 G 2
Crooksville o USA (OH) 280-281 D 4
Crookwell o AUS 180-181 K 3
Croppa Creek o AUS 178-179 L 5
Croque o CDN (NFL) 242-243 N 1
Crosby o CDN (ONT) 238-239 J 4
Crosby o USA (MN) 270-271 E 4
Crosby o USA (ND) 258-259 D 3
Crosby o USA (TX) 268-269 F 5
Crosbyton o USA (TX) 264-265 D 4
Crosia o USA (SC) 284-285 K 3
Cross o USA (TX) 266-267 J 5
Cross, Cape = Kaap Kruis ▲ NAM 216-217 B 10
Cross Anchor o USA (SC) 284-285 J 2
Cross City o USA (FL) 286-287 F 2
Crosse, La o USA 244-245 H 5
Crossett o USA (AR) 276-277 D 6
Crossfield o CDN (ALB) 232-233 E 4
Crosshill o CDN (ONT) 238-239 E 6
Cross Lake o CDN (MAN) 34-35 H 3
Cross Lake o CDN (MAN) 34-35 H 3
Cross Lake o USA (MN) 270-271 D 4
Cross Lake o USA (TX) 268-269 G 4
Cross Lake < USA (LA) 268-269 G 4
Crossley Lakes o CDN 20-21 S 5
Crossman Peak ▲ USA (AZ) 256-257 A 4
Cross Plains o USA (TX) 264-265 F 6
Cross River ~ WAN 204-205 H 6
Cross River o WAN 204-205 H 6
Crossroads o USA (NM) 256-257 M 5
Cross Roads o USA (TX) 264-265 J 2
Cross Sound ≈ 32-33 B 4
Cross Village o USA (MI) 272-273 D 2
Crosswell Lake o USA 20-21 S 5
Croswell o USA (MI) 272-273 G 4
Croton Creek ~ USA (TX) 264-265 D 5
Crotone o I 100-101 F 5
Crouch o USA (ID) 252-253 D 2
Crouse o CDN (NFL) 242-243 N 2
Crow Agency o USA (MT) 250-251 M 6
Crow Creek ~ USA (CO) 254-255 L 3
Crow Creek Indian Reservation X USA (SD) 260-261 G 2
Crowder Lake State Park ⊥ USA (OK) 264-265 F 3
Crowdy Bay National Park ⊥ AUS 178-179 M 6
Crowell o USA (TX) 264-265 E 5
Crow River ~ USA (ONT) 238-239 H 4
Crowfoot o USA (ALB) 232-233 F 5
Crowfoot Creek ~ CDN (ALB) 232-233 F 5
Crowheart o USA (WY) 252-253 J 4
Crowl Creek ~ AUS 180-181 H 2
Crowley o USA (CO) 254-255 M 5
Crowley o USA (LA) 268-269 H 6
Crowley, Lake o USA (CA) 248-249 F 2
Crowley Ranch o USA (AZ) 256-257 H 4
Crowleys Ridge ▲ USA (AR) 276-277 E 5
Crown Island ~ PNG 183 D 3
Crown Point o USA (IN) 274-275 L 4
Crownpoint o USA (NM) 256-257 G 3
Crown Prince Christian Land = Kronprins Christian Land ⊾ GRØ 26-27 u 3
Crown Prince Frederik Island ~ CDN 24-25 c 6
Crown Prince Range ▲ PNG 184 I b 2
Crows o USA 276-277 C 6
Crows Nest o AUS 178-179 M 4
Crowsnest Pass ▲ CDN (BC) 230-231 P 4
Croydon o SD 220-221 K 3
Croydon o AUS 174-175 G 6
Crozet, Îles ⊏ F 9 J 11
Crozier Channel ≈ 24-25 M 3

Crozon o F 90-91 E 7
Cruce, El o GCA 52-53 K 3
Cruce de la Jagua o DOM 54-55 L 5
Crucero o PE 70-71 B 4
Crucero, El o MEX 50-51 D 3
Crucero, El o YV 60-61 J 3
Cruces o C 54-55 E 3
Cruces, Las o MEX 52-53 H 3
Cruces, Las o MEX (SIN) 50-51 F 6
Cruces, Las o MEX (TAM) 50-51 L 6
Cruces, Punta ▲ CO 60-61 C 4
Crucetillas, Puerto de las ▲ E 98-99 F 5
Crucita o C 64-65 B 2
Cruger o USA (MS) 268-269 K 3
Cruïlas o MEX 50-51 K 5
Crump o USA (MI) 272-273 E 4
Crump Lake o USA (OR) 244-245 E 8
Cruz, Bahía ≈ 80 H 2
Cruz, Cabo ▲ C 54-55 G 5
Cruz, Ilha ~ BR 72-73 L 3
Cruz, La o BOL (LPZ) 70-71 F 5
Cruz, La o BOL (SAC) 70-71 F 5
Cruz, La o CR 52-53 B 6
Cruz, La o MEX (SIN) 50-51 F 6
Cruz, La o MEX (TAM) 50-51 L 6
Cruz, La o RA 78-79 G 2
Cruz Alta o BR 74-75 D 7
Cruz Bay o USA (VI) 286-287 R 2
Cruz de Elorza o MEX 50-51 J 6
Cruz del Eje o RA 76-77 E 6
Cruz de Taratara, La o YV 60-61 G 2
Cruzeiro o BR 72-73 H 7
Cruzeiro o MOC 218-219 H 5
Cruzeiro do Nordeste o BR 68-69 K 6
Cruzeiro do Sul o BR 64-65 F 6
Cruzen Island ▲ ARK 16 F 22
Cruzes, Corredeira das ~ BR 70-71 J 4
Cruz Grande o MEX 52-53 E 3
Cruzinha da Garca o CV 202-203 B 5
Cruz Machado o BR 74-75 E 6
Crysdale, Mount ▲ CDN 32-33 J 4
Crystal o USA (ND) 264-265 J 2
Crystal Bay ≈ 48-49 G 5
Crystal Bay ≈ USA 286-287 G 3
Crystal Brook o AUS 180-181 D 2
Crystal Cave ∴ USA (WI) 270-271 F 6
Crystal City o CDN (MAN) 234-235 D 5
Crystal City o USA (TX) 266-267 H 5
Crystal Creek National Park ⊥ AUS 174-175 J 4
Crystal Falls o USA (MI) 270-271 K 4
Crystal Lake o USA (IL) 274-275 L 3
Crystal Lake Cave ∴ USA (IA) 274-275 G 3
Crystal River o USA (FL) 286-287 G 3
Crystal River ~ USA (CO) 254-255 H 4
Crystal River State Archaeological Site • USA (FL) 286-287 G 3
Crystal Springs o CDN (SAS) 232-233 N 3
Crystal Springs o USA (MS) 268-269 K 5
Cserhát ⊥ H 92-93 P 5
C. Silverberge ∅ ▲ GRØ 26-27 p 5
Csorna o H 92-93 O 5
Cu ~ KA 124-125 H 6
Cù ~ KS 146-147 B 4
Cúa o YV 60-61 H 2
Cù'a Bày Háp ≈ 158-159 H 6
Cuacaña o YV 60-61 H 2
Cù'a Cung Háu ≈ 158-159 J 6
Cuaio ~ ANG 216-217 D 4
Cuajiniculapa o MEX 52-53 E 3
Cuale o ANG 216-217 D 4
Cuamato o ANG 216-217 C 8
Cuamba o MOC 218-219 J 2
Cuanavale ~ ANG 216-217 E 7
Cuando ~ ANG 216-217 F 7
Cuando-Cubango ▫ ANG 216-217 E 7
Cuangar o ANG 216-217 D 8
Cuango o ANG (LUN) 216-217 E 4
Cuango o ANG (BIE) 216-217 D 5
Cuanza ~ ANG 216-217 D 5
Cuanza Norte ▫ ANG 216-217 C 4
Cuanza Sul ▫ ANG 216-217 C 5
Cuao, Rio ~ YV 60-61 H 5
Cuareim, Rio ~ ROU 76-77 J 6
Cuarinuma o CO 60-61 G 4
Cuaró Grande, Arroyo ~ ROU 76-77 J 6
Cù'a Soi Rap ≈ 158-159 J 6
Cuatir ~ ANG 216-217 E 8
Cuatro Bocas, Las o YV 60-61 F 2
Cuatro Caminos o C 54-55 G 4
Cuatrocienegas de Carranza o MEX 50-51 H 4
Cuauhtémoc o MEX (CHA) 50-51 F 3
Cuauhtémoc o MEX (TAM) 50-51 K 5
Cuautitlán o MEX 52-53 D 2
Cuautla de Morelos o MEX 52-53 E 2
Cuba ⊏ C 54-55 E 4
Cuba o USA (AL) 284-285 B 4
Cuba o USA (IL) 274-275 H 4
Cuba o USA (NM) 256-257 J 2
Cuba o USA (NY) 278-279 C 6
Cù Bai o VN 158-159 J 3
Cubal o ANG (BGU) 216-217 C 6
Cubal ~ ANG 216-217 B 7
Cubal ~ ANG 216-217 C 6
Cubango ~ ANG 216-217 D 7
Cubango ▫ ANG 216-217 D 7
Cubaté, Rio ~ BR 66-67 D 7
Cubati ▫ ANG 216-217 D 7
Cubero o USA (NM) 256-257 H 3
Cubillas o C 64-65 E 2
Cubitas o C 54-55 G 4
Čubuk ★ TR 128-129 E 2
Čubuka-Tala, gora ▲ RUS 110-111 a 7
Čubukulah ▲ RUS 110-111 d 6
Čubukulah, krjaž ▲ RUS 110-111 d 7

Cubulco ○ GCA 52-53 J 4
Cuchara ○ USA (CO) 254-255 K 6
Cuchi ○ ANG (CUA) 216-217 D 7
Cuchi ~ ANG 216-217 D 6
Cuchilla, La ○ RA 76-77 G 4
Cuchillo ○ USA (NM) 256-257 H 5
Cuchillo-Co ○ RA 78-79 G 5
Cuchivero ○ YV 60-61 J 4
Cuchivero, Río ~ YV 60-61 J 4
Cucho Ingenio ○ BOL 70-71 E 6
Cuchumatanas, Parque Nacional Los ⊥ • GCA 52-53 J 4
Cuchumatanas, Sierra de los ▲ GCA 52-53 J 4
Cuckadoo ○ AUS 178-179 F 1
Cuckoo ○ USA (VA) 280-281 J 6
Cucuí ○ BR 66-67 D 2
Cucumbi ~ ANG 216-217 E 4
Cucuri, Cachoeira ~ BR 72-73 D 2
Cucurital ○ YV 60-61 J 5
Cucuta ☆ CO 60-61 E 4
Cudahy ○ USA (WI) 274-275 L 2
Cuddalore ○ IND 140-141 H 5
Cuddapah ○ IND 140-141 H 3
Čudovo ☆ RUS 94-95 M 2
Čudskoe ozero ○ RUS 94-95 K 2
Cudworth ○ CDN (SAS) 232-233 N 3
Čudzjavr, ozero ○ RUS 88-89 N 2
Cue ○ AUS 176-177 D 3
Cuebe ~ ANG 216-217 D 7
Cueio ~ ANG 216-217 D 7
Cueiras, Rio ~ BR 66-67 G 4
Cuélab • PE 64-65 D 5
Cuelei ~ ANG 216-217 D 7
Cuéllar ○ E 98-99 E 4
Cuemba ○ ANG 216-217 E 6
Cuenca ○ E 98-99 F 4
Cuenca ☆ •• EC 64-65 C 3
Cuenca, Serranía de ▲ E 98-99 F 4
Cuenca del Añelo ⊥ RA 78-79 E 5
Cuencamé ○ MEX 50-51 H 5
Cuengo ~ ANG 216-217 E 4
Cueramaro ○ MEX 52-53 D 1
Cuernavaca ☆ • MEX 52-53 E 2
Cuero ○ C 54-55 H 5
Cuero ○ USA (TX) 266-267 K 4
Cuervo ○ USA (NM) 256-257 L 3
Cueto ○ C 54-55 H 4
Cuetzalń ○ • MEX 52-53 F 1
Cueva de la Quebrada del Toro, Parque Nacional ⊥ YV 60-61 G 2
Cuevas, Las ○ RA 78-79 D 2
Cuevas o de las Cañas, Río ~ RA 76-77 E 3
Cuevo ○ BOL 70-71 F 7
Cuevo, Quebrada de ~ BOL 70-71 F 7
Čuga ~ RUS 118-119 L 7
Čuginskoe ploskogor'e ▲ RUS 118-119 K 7
Cugo ~ ANG 216-217 D 3
Čugor', mys ▲ RUS 108-109 Q 7
Čugor'jaha ~ RUS 108-109 Q 7
Čuguš, gora ▲ RUS 126-127 D 6
Čuhloma ○ RUS 94-95 S 2
Čuhujiv ○ UA 102-103 K 3
Cuiabá ○ BR (AMA) 66-67 C 4
Cuiabá ☆ BR (MAT) 70-71 J 4
Cuiabá, Rio ~ BR 70-71 J 5
Cuije ~ ANG 216-217 D 4
Cuilapa ☆ GCA 52-53 J 4
Cuilo ○ ANG 216-217 E 4
Cuilo ~ ANG 216-217 C 3
Cuilo ~ ANG 216-217 E 4
Cuilo ~ ANG 216-217 E 5
Cuilo-Futa ○ ANG 216-217 C 3
Cuilo Pombo ○ ANG 216-217 C 3
Cuima ○ ANG 216-217 C 6
Cuimba ○ ANG 216-217 C 3
Cuio ○ ANG 216-217 B 6
Cuira o Monos ○ CO 64-65 F 2
Cuiriri ~ ANG 216-217 E 7
Cuito ~ ANG 216-217 E 8
Cuito Cuanavale ○ ANG 216-217 E 7
Cuiubi ○ BR 66-67 C 2
Cuiuni, Rio ~ BR 66-67 F 3
Cuivre River ~ USA (IL) 274-275 H 5
Cuiyun Lang • VRC 154-155 D 5
Čuja ~ RUS 118-119 F 6
Čuja ~ RUS 124-125 Q 3
Čuja ~ RUS 124-125 P 3
Čuja, Bol'šaja ~ RUS 118-119 E 7
Cujar, Río ~ PE 64-65 F 7
Čujskij, Gorno ○ RUS 118-119 E 7
Cujubim ○ BR 66-67 G 7
Čukar ○ RUS 118-119 H 4
Cukas, Pulau ⌒ RI 162-163 F 5
Čukča ~ RUS 110-111 Z 6
Čukčagirskoe, ozero ○ RUS 122-123 G 3
Čukoč'e, ozero ○ RUS 112-113 L 2
Čukočja, Bol'šaja ~ RUS 112-113 K 2
Čukotskij, mys ▲ RUS 112-113 Y 4
Čukotskij poluostrov ⌣ RUS 112-113 W 3
Čukotskoe more ≈ 112-113 V 1
Čukša ~ RUS 116-117 J 7
Çukurca ☆ TR 128-129 K 4
Cula ~ MD 102-103 F 4
Čulakan ~ RUS 116-117 M 6
Čulakkurgan ○ KA 136-137 L 3
Culamagia ○ ANG 216-217 C 6
Cu Lao Thu ⌒ VN 158-159 K 5
Cù Lao Thu = Phù Qùy ⌒ VN 158-159 K 5
Čulas ~ RUS 88-89 T 4
Čulasa ○ RUS 88-89 T 4
Culasi ○ RP 160-161 E 7
Culbertson ○ USA (MT) 250-251 P 3
Culbertson ○ USA (NE) 262-263 F 4
Culdesac ○ USA (ID) 250-251 C 5
Culebra, Isla de ⌒ USA (PR) 286-287 Q 2
Culebra, La ○ YV 60-61 H 3
Culebras ○ PE 64-65 C 6
Culebras, Punta ▲ PE 64-65 C 6
Culgoa River ~ AUS 178-179 J 5
Culiacán Rosales ☆ MEX 50-51 F 5
Culion ○ RP 160-161 D 7
Culion Island ⌒ RP 160-161 C 7
Culiseu, Rio ~ BR 72-73 D 2
Cullen Garden • CDN (ONT) 238-239 F 5
Cullera ○ E 98-99 G 5
Cullinan ○ ZA 220-221 J 2
Cullison ○ USA (KS) 262-263 H 7
Cullmann ○ USA (AL) 284-285 D 2
Cullulleraine ○ AUS 180-181 F 3
Čul'man ○ RUS 118-119 M 7
Čul'man ~ RUS 118-119 M 7
Culpeper ○ USA (VA) 280-281 J 5
Culpina ○ BOL 70-71 E 7
Culross Island ⌒ USA 20-21 R 6
Culuene, Rio ~ BR 72-73 D 2
Čuluunhoroom = Érèèncav ○ MAU 148-149 M 3
Čuluut gol ~ MAU 148-149 E 3
Culver ○ USA (IN) 274-275 M 3
Culver, Point ▲ AUS 176-177 H 6
Culverden ○ NZ 182 D 5
Čulym ☆ RUS (NVS) 114-115 Q 7
Čulym ~ RUS 114-115 U 6
Čulym ~ RUS 116-117 E 8
Čulym ~ RUS 124-125 L 1
Čulymskaja, ravnina ⌣ RUS 114-115 T 6
Čulyšman ~ RUS 124-125 Q 3
Čulyšman ~ RUS 124-125 P 3
Čulyšmanskoe, nagor'e ⩩ •• RUS 124-125 Q 3
Čulyšmanskoe nagorie ▲ RUS 124-125 P 3
Cuma ○ ANG 216-217 C 6
Cumã, Baía do ≈ 68-69 F 3
Cuma, Cachoeira ~ BR 66-67 C 2
Cumana ☆ • YV 60-61 J 2
Cumanacoa ○ YV 60-61 K 2
Cumanayagua ○ C 54-55 E 3
Cumanda ○ EC 64-65 C 3
Cumaral ○ CO 60-61 E 5
Cumaral = Barranca de Upía ○ CO 60-61 E 5
Cumaral, Raudal ~ CO 60-61 F 6
Cumaribo ○ CO 60-61 G 5
Cumaru, Cachoeira ~ BR 62-63 G 6
Cumbe ○ EC 64-65 C 3
Cumberland ○ CDN (BC) 230-231 D 4
Cumberland ○ USA (IA) 274-275 D 3
Cumberland ○ USA (IN) 274-275 N 5
Cumberland ○ USA (KY) 276-277 N 4
Cumberland ○ USA (MD) 280-281 H 4
Cumberland ○ USA (MS) 268-269 L 3
Cumberland ○ USA (OH) 280-281 E 4
Cumberland ○ USA (VA) 280-281 H 6
Cumberland ○ USA (WI) 270-271 F 5
Cumberland, Cape = Cape Nahoi ▲ VAN 184 II a 2
Cumberland, Lake < USA (KY) 276-277 K 4
Cumberland Bay ≈ 78-79 O 7
Cumberland Caverns Park ⩙ USA (TN) 276-277 K 5
Cumberland City Reservoir < USA (PA) 280-281 H 4
Cumberland Downs ○ AUS 178-179 J 2
Cumberland Falls ~ USA (KY) 276-277 L 4
Cumberland Gap ▲ USA (TN) 282-283 D 4
Cumberland Gap National Historic Park ∴ USA (KY) 276-277 M 4
Cumberland House ○ CDN (SAS) 232-233 Q 2
Cumberland Island ⌒ USA (GA) 284-285 J 6
Cumberland Island National Seashore ⊥ USA (GA) 284-285 J 6
Cumberland Islands ⌒ AUS 174-175 K 7
Cumberland Lake ○ CDN 34-35 E 3
Cumberland Mountains ▲ USA (TN) 282-283 D 4
Cumberland Parkway II USA (KY) 276-277 K 3
Cumberland Peninsula ⌣ CDN 28-29 G 3
Cumberland River ~ USA (KY) 276-277 M 4
Cumberland River ~ USA (TN) 276-277 K 4
Cumberland Sound ≈ 36-37 R 2
Cumbi ○ ANG 216-217 B 3
Cumborah ○ AUS 178-179 J 5
Cumbre, Paso de la ▲ RA 78-79 E 2
Cumbre, Volcán La ▲ EC 64-65 B 10
Cumbrera, Cerro ▲ RCH 80 D 4
Cumbres and Toltec Scenic Railroad • USA (CO) 254-255 J 6
Cumbres de Majalca ○ MEX 50-51 F 3
Cumbres de Majalca, Parque Nacional ⊥ MEX 50-51 F 3
Cumbrian Mountains ▲ GB 90-91 F 4
Cumbum ○ IND 140-141 H 3
Cumburão ○ BR 62-63 G 6
Cumby ○ USA (TX) 264-265 J 5
Čumikan ☆ RUS 120-121 F 6
Čumikan ~ RUS 120-121 F 5
Cuminá ○ BR 62-63 F 6
Cuminá, Rio ~ BR 62-63 F 5
Cuminapanema, Rio ~ BR 62-63 G 6
Cumming ○ USA (GA) 284-285 F 2
Cummings ○ USA (CA) 246-247 B 4
Cummins ○ AUS 180-181 C 3
Cummins Range ▲ AUS 172-173 H 5
Cumnock ○ GB 90-91 E 4
Čumpu-Kytyl ○ RUS 110-111 Y 7
Çumra ☆ TR 128-129 E 4
Cumshewa Head ▲ CDN (BC) 228-229 C 3
Cumshewa Inlet ≈ CDN 228-229 C 3
Cumueté, Rio ~ BR 68-69 C 6
Čumyš ~ RUS 124-125 P 2
Čumyš ~ RUS 124-125 N 2
Čuna ~ RUS 116-117 H 7
Cunaguaro ○ YV 60-61 J 3
Cunani ○ BR 62-63 J 4
Cuñare ○ CO 64-65 F 1
Cunarno ○ RCH 78-79 C 6
Cunauaru, Rio ~ BR 66-67 F 4
Cund ~ ANG 216-217 D 6
Cunday ○ CO 60-61 D 5
Cundeelee ⩙ AUS 176-177 G 5
Cundeelee Aboriginal Land ⩙ AUS 176-177 G 5
Cunderdin ○ AUS 176-177 D 5
Cunduacán ○ MEX 52-53 H 2
Cundza ○ KA 146-147 D 4
Cunene ○ ANG 216-217 C 7
Cunene ▫ ANG 216-217 C 8
Cunene ~ ANG 216-217 C 8
Cunene ~ ANG 216-217 D 7
Cúneo ☆ I 100-101 A 2
Cung Hầu, Cử'a ≈ 158-159 J 6
Cunha ○ BR 72-73 H 7
Cunhãs, Rio das ~ BR 68-69 D 5
Cunhinga ~ ANG 216-217 D 5
Cunia, Estação Ecológica ⊥ BR 66-67 F 7
Cuniuá, Rio ~ BR 66-67 D 6
Čunja ~ RUS 116-117 K 5
Čunja, Strelka ○ RUS 116-117 L 5
Cunjamba ○ ANG 216-217 F 7
Cunnamulla ○ • AUS 178-179 H 5
Cunningham ○ USA (KY) 276-277 G 4
Cunningham ○ USA (TN) 276-277 H 4
Cunningham ○ USA (TX) 264-265 J 5
Cunningham, Lake ○ ZW 218-219 E 5
Cunningham Islands ⌒ AUS 174-175 D 2
Cunningham Lake ○ CDN (BC) 228-229 J 2
Čunskij ○ RUS 116-117 H 7
Čun'skij ☆ RUS 116-117 J 7
Cuntima ○ GNB 202-203 C 3
Čuokkarašša ▲ N 86-87 M 2
Čupa ○ RUS 88-89 M 3
Čūpānān ○ IR 134-135 F 2
Cupar ○ CDN (SAS) 232-233 O 5
Cupari, Rio ~ BR 66-67 K 4
Cupertino ○ USA (CA) 248-249 B 2
Cupica ○ CO 60-61 C 4
Cupica, Golfo de ≈ 60-61 C 4
Cupisnique, Cerro ▲ PE 64-65 C 5
Cupixi ○ BR 62-63 J 5
Čuprovo ○ RUS 88-89 T 4
Cuprum ○ USA (ID) 250-251 C 6
Cuptano, Isla ⌒ RCH 80 D 2
Curaça ○ BR 68-69 J 6
Curaça, Rio ~ BR 68-69 J 6
Curaçao ⌒ NL 60-61 G 1
Curacautín ○ RCH 78-79 D 5
Curacaví ○ RCH 78-79 D 2
Curachi ○ GUY 62-63 D 2
Curácuaro de Morelos ○ MEX 52-53 D 2
Curahuara de Carangas ○ BOL 70-71 C 5
Curale ○ ETH 208-209 G 5
Cura Malal, Sierra de ▲ RA 78-79 H 4
Curanilahué ○ RCH 78-79 C 4
Curanja ○ BR 66-67 B 7
Curanja, Río ~ PE 70-71 B 2
Čurapča ☆ • RUS 120-121 E 3
Curaray ○ EC 64-65 D 2
Curaray ○ PE 64-65 E 3
Curaray, Río ~ PE 64-65 E 3
Curari, Ilha de ⌒ BR 66-67 G 4
Curaru ○ RA 78-79 H 3
Curauai, Rio ~ BR 66-67 H 5
Čurbuka, gora ▲ RUS 110-111 Q 4
Čurbukan ~ RUS 116-117 H 2
Curdimurka ○ AUS 178-179 D 5
Čūre ○ AFG 134-135 M 2
Curecanti National Recreation Area ⊥ • USA (CO) 254-255 H 5
Curepipe ○ MS 224 C 7
Curepto ○ RCH 78-79 C 3
Curib ○ RUS 126-127 G 6
Curibaya ○ PE 70-71 B 5
Curiche Liverpool ○ BOL 70-71 F 4
Curichi de Oquiriquia ~ BOL 70-71 G 5
Curichi Tunas ~ BOL 70-71 G 5
Curico ○ RCH 78-79 D 3
Curicuriari, Rio ~ BR 66-67 C 3
Curieuse Marine National Park ⊥ SY 224 D 2
Curi Leuvú, Arroyo ~ RA 78-79 D 4
Curimatá ○ BR 68-69 F 7
Curimatá, Rio ~ BR 68-69 F 6
Curimatá de Baixo, Rio ~ BR 66-67 E 5
Curimávida, Cerro de ▲ RCH 76-77 B 6
Curionópolis ○ BR 68-69 D 5
Curitiba ○ BR (ACR) 70-71 C 2
Curitiba ☆ • BR (PAR) 74-75 F 5
Curitibanos ○ BR 74-75 E 6
Curiúva ○ BR 74-75 E 5
Čurkin, mys ▲ RUS 110-111 W 3
Curlew ○ USA (WA) 244-245 G 2
Curly Cut Cays ⌒ BS 54-55 G 3
Curnamona ○ AUS 178-179 E 6
Čuro ~ RUS 118-119 F 7
Curoca ~ ANG 216-217 B 8
Curoca, Cachoeira da ~ BR 66-67 G 7
Currais Novos ○ BR 68-69 K 5
Curral Alto ○ BR 74-75 D 9
Curral Falso ○ BR 74-75 E 8
Curralinho ○ BR 62-63 K 6
Curral Novo ○ BR 68-69 H 6
Curral Velho ○ BR 72-73 H 2
Curral Velho ○ CV 202-203 C 5
Curran ○ CDN (ONT) 238-239 L 3
Currant ○ USA (NV) 246-247 K 5
Currarehue ○ RCH 78-79 D 5
Currawinya ○ AUS 178-179 H 5
Currawinya National Park ⊥ AUS 178-179 H 5
Current Island ⌒ BS 54-55 G 2
Current River ~ USA (MO) 276-277 D 3
Currie ○ AUS 180-181 G 5
Currie ○ USA (MN) 270-271 C 6
Currie ○ USA (NV) 246-247 L 3
Currie Indian Reserve, Mount ⩙ CDN (BC) 230-231 G 3
Currituch Sound ≈ 46-47 L 7
Currituck ○ USA (NC) 282-283 L 4
Currituck Sound ≈ USA 280-281 L 7
Curtea de Argeş ○ • RO 102-103 D 5
Čūrti ○ IR 136-137 B 6
Curtin ○ AUS 176-177 G 5
Curtin Springs ○ AUS 176-177 L 2
Curtis ○ USA (NE) 262-263 F 4
Curtis Island ⌒ AUS 178-179 L 2
Curtis Lake ○ CDN 30-31 Z 2
Curtis River ~ CDN 30-31 Z 2
Curu, Rio ~ BR 68-69 J 3
Curuá ○ BR 62-63 G 6
Curuá, Ilha do ⌒ BR 62-63 J 5
Curuá, Rio ~ BR 62-63 G 6
Curuá, Rio ~ BR 66-67 K 7
Curuaés, Rio ~ BR 66-67 K 7
Curuai ○ BR 66-67 K 4
Curuá ou Cururu, Rio ~ BR 72-73 D 3
Curuà-Una, Rio ~ BR 66-67 K 4
Curuá-Una, Rio ~ BR 66-67 K 4
Curuça ○ BR 68-69 E 2
Curuçá, Ponta ▲ BR 68-69 E 2
Curuça, Rio ~ BR 64-65 F 4
Cururduri, Rio ~ BR 66-67 F 2
Curuguaty ○ PY 76-77 K 3
Curuma la Grande, Cerro ▲ RA 78-79 H 4
Curumutopo ○ YV 60-61 J 4
Curup ○ RI 162-163 E 6
Curupá ○ BR 68-69 F 6
Curupaiti ○ BR 68-69 E 3
Curupira ○ BR 68-69 J 4
Curuquetê, Rio ~ BR 66-67 E 7
Cururu, Raudal ~ CO 66-67 B 2
Cururu-Açu, Rio ~ BR 66-67 J 7
Cururu ou Cururuí, Rio ~ BR 66-67 J 7
Cururupu ○ BR 68-69 F 2
Curuzú Cuatiá ○ RA 76-77 H 5
Curva del Turco ○ RA 76-77 E 3
Curva Grande ○ BR 68-69 F 3
Curvelo ○ BR 72-73 H 5
Curwood, Mount ▲ USA (MI) 270-271 K 4
Cushabatay, Río ~ PE 64-65 E 5
Cushamen ○ RA 78-79 D 7
Cushing ○ USA (MN) 270-271 D 4
Cushing ○ USA (OK) 264-265 H 3
Cushing ○ USA (TX) 268-269 F 5
Cushing ○ USA (WI) 270-271 F 5
Cusick ○ USA (WA) 244-245 H 2
Cusime ○ YV 60-61 J 5
Cusipata ○ PE 70-71 B 3
Cusis, Río ~ BOL 70-71 H 5
Čusovaja ~ RUS 96-97 L 5
Čusovoj ☆ RUS 96-97 K 4
Čusovskoe, ozero ○ RUS 114-115 D 4
Cusseta ○ USA (GA) 284-285 F 4
Cussivi ~ ANG 216-217 F 7
Cusso ~ ANG 216-217 C 7
Cusson, Pointe ▲ CDN 36-37 K 4
Čust ○ US 136-137 M 4
Custer ○ USA (MT) 250-251 M 5
Custer ○ USA (SD) 260-261 C 3
Custer Battlefield National Monument ∴ USA (MT) 250-251 M 6
Custer State Park ⊥ USA (SD) 260-261 C 3
Custódia ○ BR 68-69 K 6
Cusuco, Parque Nacional ⊥ HN 52-53 K 4
Cutato ○ ANG (BIE) 216-217 D 6
Cutato ○ ANG (CUA) 216-217 D 7
Cutato ~ ANG 216-217 D 5
Cutato ~ ANG 216-217 D 7
Cutbank ○ CDN (SAS) 232-233 M 4
Cut Bank ○ USA (MT) 250-251 G 3
Cut Bank Creek ~ USA (MT) 250-251 G 3
Cutbank River ~ CDN (ALB) 228-229 P 2
Cutenda ○ ANG 216-217 C 7
Cutervo ○ PE 64-65 C 5
Cutervo, Parque Nacional de ⊥ PE 64-65 C 5
Cuthbert ○ USA (GA) 284-285 F 5
Cutknife ○ CDN (SAS) 232-233 K 3
Cutler ○ USA (ME) 278-279 O 4
Čutove ○ UA 102-103 J 3
Cuttaburra Creek ~ AUS 178-179 H 5
Cutta Cutta Caves • AUS 172-173 L 3
Cuttak=Kataka ○ IND 142-143 D 5
Cutzamala de Pinzón ○ MEX 52-53 D 2
Cử'u Long, Cử'a Sông ⩩ VN 158-159 J 6
Čuvanajskie gory ▲ RUS 112-113 O 3
Čuvanskij hrebet ▲ RUS 112-113 O 4
Čuvanskoe ○ RUS 112-113 O 4
Cuvelai ○ ANG 216-217 C 7
Cuvelai ~ ANG 216-217 D 7
Cuvette ▫ RCB 210-211 E 4
Cuvo ~ ANG 216-217 C 5
Cuxhaven ○ D 92-93 K 2
Cuxiuara, Ilha ⌒ BR 66-67 G 4
Cuy, El ○ RA 78-79 E 5
Cuyabeno, Reserva Faunística ⊥ EC 64-65 E 2
Cuyahoga Valley National Recreation Area ⊥ USA (OH) 280-281 E 2
Cuyama ○ USA (CA) 248-249 E 5
Cuyo, El ○ MEX 52-53 L 1
Cuyo East Pass ≈ 160-161 D 7
Cuyo 'English Game' Subterranean National Park ⊥ RP 160-161 D 7
Cuyo Island ⌒ RP 160-161 D 7
Cuyo Islands ⌒ RP 160-161 D 7
Cuyo West Pass ≈ 160-161 D 7
Cuyuni, Río ~ YV 62-63 D 2
Cuzco ☆ ••• PE 70-71 B 3
Čuzik ~ RUS 114-115 P 6
Čvrisnica ▲ BIH 100-101 F 3
Cyama River ~ USA (CA) 248-249 E 4
Cyangugu ○ RWA 212-213 B 5
Čyappara ○ RUS 118-119 P 4
Čyb ~ RUS 88-89 V 5
Čybyda ~ RUS 118-119 K 4
Cyclades = Kiklådes ⌒ GR 100-101 K 6
Cycloop, Pegunungan ▲ RI 166-167 L 3
Cyclop Mountains Reserve ⊥ • RI 166-167 L 3
Čyhyryn ○ UA 102-103 H 3
Čyjyrčyk, pereval ▲ KS 136-137 N 4
Čym ○ RUS 108-109 K 8
Cymric ○ CDN (SAS) 232-233 O 4
Čyna ~ RUS 118-119 M 5
Cynthia ○ AUS 178-179 L 3
Cynthia ○ CDN (ALB) 232-233 C 2
Cynthiana ○ USA (KY) 276-277 L 2
Cyohoha Sud, Lac ○ BU 212-213 C 5
Cypnavolok, mys ▲ RUS 88-89 M 2
Cypress ○ USA (LA) 268-269 G 5
Cypress Bayou ~ USA (AR) 276-277 D 5
Cypress Creek ~ USA (TX) 268-269 E 7
Cypress Gardens ∴ • USA (FL) 286-287 H 4
Cypress Hills ▲ CDN (SAS) 232-233 H 6
Cypress Hills Provincial Park ⊥ CDN (ALB) 232-233 H 6
Cypress Hills Provincial Park ⊥ CDN (SAS) 232-233 J 6
Cypress Provincial Park ⊥ CDN (BC) 230-231 F 4
Cypress River ○ CDN (MAN) 234-235 D 5
Cypress Springs, Lake < USA (TX) 264-265 J 5
Cyprus = Kypros ■ CY 128-129 E 5
Čyra ~ RUS 118-119 M 5
Cyrene ○ ZW 218-219 E 5
Cyrene = Shahhāt ∴ ••• LAR 192-193 J 1
Cyril ○ USA (OK) 264-265 F 4
Cyrus Field Bay ≈ 36-37 R 3
Čyrvonae, vozero ○ BY 94-95 L 5
Cytherea ○ AUS 178-179 J 4
Czaplinek ○ • PL 92-93 O 2
Czar ○ CDN (ALB) 232-233 H 3
Czarnków ○ PL 92-93 O 2
Czech Republic = Česká Republika ■ CZ 92-93 M 4
Czersk ○ PL 92-93 O 2
Częstochowa ☆ •• PL 92-93 P 3
Człuchów ○ • 92-93 O 2

D

Da'an ○ VRC 150-151 E 5
Daanbantayan ○ RP 160-161 F 7
Daan Viljoen Game Park ⊥ NAM 216-217 D 11
Daaquam ○ CDN (QUE) 240-241 E 4
Dab'a, Maḥaṭṭat ○ JOR 130-131 E 2
Dabadougou ○ CI 202-203 G 5
Dabaga ○ EAT 214-215 H 5
Dabai ○ WAN 204-205 F 3
Dabajuro ○ YV 60-61 F 2
Dabakala ☆ CI 202-203 H 5
Dabancheng ○ VRC 146-147 J 4
Dabaray ○ AFG 134-135 M 3
Dabaro ○ SP 208-209 J 5
Daba Shan ▲ VRC 154-155 F 5
Dabassi ○ RG 202-203 C 4
Dabat ○ ETH 200-201 H 6
Dabatou ○ RG 202-203 E 4
Dabeiba ○ CO 60-61 C 4
Daben ○ VRC 156-157 F 7
Dābhāde ○ IND 138-139 D 10
Dabhoi ○ IND 138-139 D 8
Dābhol ○ IND 140-141 E 2
Dabie Shan ▲ VRC 154-155 J 6
Dablo ○ BF 202-203 K 3
Dabnou ○ RN 198-199 B 5
Dabo ○ SN 202-203 C 3
Dabola ○ RG 202-203 E 4
Dabou ○ CI 202-203 H 7
Daboya ○ GH 202-203 K 5
Dabra ○ IND 138-139 G 7
Dabsan Hu ○ VRC 144-145 K 2
Dabuk ○ RI 162-163 E 6
Dabus Wenz ~ ETH 208-209 B 3
Dabwa ○ TCH 198-199 F 5
Dacca = Dhaka ★ BD 142-143 G 4
Đắc Glei ○ VN 158-159 J 3
Dachau ○ D 92-93 L 4
Dacheng ○ VRC 156-157 J 2
Dachenzhuang ○ VRC 154-155 K 2
Dachigam National Park ⊥ IND 138-139 E 2
Dachsteingruppe ▲ A 92-93 M 5
Dachung Yogma ○ IND 138-139 G 3
Dacia Seamount ⩩ 188-189 E 5
Đắc Mil ○ VN 158-159 J 4
Dacre ○ CDN (ONT) 238-239 J 3
Đắc Song ○ VN 158-159 J 4
Đắc Tô ○ VN 158-159 J 3
Dadanawa ○ GUY 62-63 E 4
Dade City ○ USA (FL) 286-287 G 3
Dades, Gorges du •• MA 188-189 J 5
Dades, Oued ~ MA 188-189 J 5
Dadès, Vallée du ⩩ MA 188-189 H 5
Dadeville ○ USA (AL) 284-285 E 4
Dādhar ○ PK 134-135 M 4
Dadi, Tanjung ▲ RI 166-167 F 2
Dadong ○ VRC 156-157 F 5
Dadonghai • VRC 156-157 F 7
Dadra and Nagar Haveli ▫ IND 138-139 D 9
Dādu ○ PK 134-135 M 5
Daduan ○ VRC 156-157 J 2
Dādu Canal ~ PK 134-135 M 5
Dadu He ~ VRC 154-155 C 6
Dadukou ○ VRC 154-155 K 6
Dadynskoe, ozero ○ RUS 126-127 F 5
Daerah Istimewa Aceh ▫ RI 162-163 A 2
Daerah Istimewa Yogyakarta ▫ RI 168 C 4
Daet ☆ RP 160-161 E 5
Dafang ○ VRC 156-157 D 3
Dafanpu ○ VRC 154-155 G 2
Dafeng ○ VRC 154-155 M 5
Dafengding Natural Biosystem Reserves ⊥ VRC 156-157 C 2
Daffat ad Dabāb ⩩ LAR 192-193 J 2
Dafina, ad- ○ KSA 130-131 H 6
Dafoe ○ CDN (SAS) 232-233 O 4
Dafoe River ~ CDN 34-35 J 3
Dafor ○ GH 202-203 L 6
Dafra ○ TCH 206-207 D 3
Dafter ○ USA (MI) 270-271 O 4
Daga ○ BHT 142-143 F 2
Daga ⌒ ETH 208-209 C 3
Daga ~ SUD 208-209 A 4
Dagaari ○ SP 208-209 H 5
Dagaldyn ~ RUS 108-109 c 7
Dagami ○ RP 160-161 F 7
Dagana ○ • SN 196-197 C 6
Dagandely ~ KA 124-125 K 4
Dagasuli, Pulau ⌒ RI 164-165 K 2
Dagda ○ LV 94-95 K 3
Dages Range ▲ PNG 183 F 3
Dagestan = Dagestan, Respublika ▫ RUS 126-127 G 5
Dagestan, Respublika ▫ RUS 126-127 G 5
Dagestanskie Ogni ○ RUS 126-127 H 6
Dagestanskij zapovednik ⊥ RUS 126-127 G 5
Daggaboersnek ▲ ZA 220-221 G 6
Daggett ○ USA (CA) 248-249 H 5
Daggyai Co ○ VRC 144-145 E 6
Dagida Game Reserve ⊥ WAN 204-205 F 4
Dagingou ⊥ • VRC 150-151 C 6
Daglung ○ VRC 144-145 H 6
Dagmar ○ OM 132-133 L 2
Dagmar ○ USA (MT) 250-251 P 3
Dagö = Hiiumaa saar ⩩ EST 94-95 H 2
Dagomys ○ RUS 126-127 C 6
Dagoudane-Pickine ○ SN 202-203 B 2
Dagua ○ CO 60-61 C 6
Daguan ○ VRC (SIC) 156-157 C 2
Daguan ○ VRC (YUN) 156-157 C 3
D'Aguilar Range ▲ AUS 178-179 M 4
Daguit ○ RP 160-161 E 5
Daguragu-Kurintji Aboriginal Land ⩙ AUS 172-173 K 4
Dagushan ○ VRC 150-151 D 8
Dagu Shan ⌒ VRC 154-155 N 6
Dagworth ○ AUS (QLD) 174-175 G 5
Dagworth ○ AUS (QLD) 178-179 G 1
Dagzhuka ○ VRC 144-145 G 6
Dah ○ RI 166-167 K 5
Dahab ○ ET 194-195 G 3
Ḍahabān ○ KSA 132-133 A 3
Dahadinni River ~ CDN 30-31 G 4
Dahānib, Ǧabal ▲ ET 194-195 G 6
Dahbed ○ US 136-137 K 5
Daheba ○ VRC 144-145 M 3
Dahequ ○ VRC 154-155 C 3
Dahi, ad- ○ Y 132-133 C 6
Dahinda ○ CDN (SAS) 232-233 N 6
Dahiri ○ CI 202-203 H 7
Dahlak Archipelago ⌒ ER 200-201 K 5
Dahle ○ AFG 134-135 L 3
Dahle, Band-e < AFG 134-135 M 3
Dahlonega ○ USA (GA) 284-285 G 2
Dahmani ○ TN 190-191 G 3
Dahnā', ad- ▲ KSA 130-131 H 3
Dahnā', ad- ⩩ KSA 130-131 J 4
Dāhod ○ IND 138-139 E 8
Dahongliutan ○ VRC 144-145 B 3
Dahra, Corniche des ⌣ DZ 190-191 C 2
Dahra, Massif de ▲ DZ 190-191 C 2
Dahra Oil Field ⩩ LAR 192-193 G 2
Dahsa, Wādī d- ~ ET 194-195 E 4
Dahšūr ○ ET 194-195 E 3
Dahšūr, Pyramids of ∴ ••• ET 194-195 E 3
Dahūk ○ IRQ 128-129 K 4
Dahūk ☆ IRQ (DAH) 128-129 K 4
Đại, Cử'a ≈ 158-159 J 5
Dai, Pulau ⌒ RI 166-167 E 5
Daïa, Monts de ▲ DZ 188-189 L 3
Ḍaid, ad- ○ UAE 134-135 F 6
Dai Hai ○ VRC 154-155 H 1
Dai Island ⌒ SOL 184 I e 2
Dailing • VRC 150-151 G 4
Đại Lộ'i ○ VN 156-157 D 7
Daimāniyāt, ad- ⌒ OM 132-133 K 2
Daimiel ○ E 98-99 F 5
Daingerfield ○ USA (TX) 264-265 K 5
Daintree ○ AUS 174-175 H 5
Daintree National Park ⊥ AUS 174-175 H 5
Dair, ad- ○ ET 194-195 F 5
Dair, Ǧabal ad- ▲ SUD 200-201 E 6
Dairana ○ RM 222-223 F 4
Dā'irat ar-Riyy ○ IRQ 128-129 L 6
Dair az-Zaur ☆ SYR 128-129 J 5
Daireaux ○ RA 78-79 J 4
Dairen = Dalian ○ VRC 150-151 C 8
Dair Ḥāfir ○ SYR 128-129 G 4
Dair Mawās ○ ET 194-195 E 4
Dairūṭ ○ ET 194-195 E 4
Dairy ○ USA (OR) 244-245 D 8
Dairy Creek ○ AUS 176-177 C 2
Dairyland ○ USA (WI) 270-271 F 4
Dai-sen ▲ J 152-153 E 7
Daisengen-dake ▲ J 152-153 J 4
Daisen-Oki National Park ⊥ J 152-153 E 6
Daisetsuzan National Park ⊥ J 152-153 K 3
Dai Shan ⌒ VRC 154-155 M 6
Daisy ○ USA (OK) 264-265 J 4
Đại Tù ☆ VN 156-157 D 6
Dai Xian ○ VRC 154-155 H 2
Daiyun Shan ▲ VRC 156-157 K 4
Dajabón ☆ DOM 54-55 K 5
Dājal ○ PK 138-139 C 5
Dajan nuur ○ MAU 146-147 J 1
Dajarra ○ AUS 178-179 E 1
Dajiuba ○ VRC 144-145 G 2
Daka ~ GH 202-203 K 5
Dakar ★ • SN 202-203 B 2
Dakataua, Lake ○ PNG 183 F 3
Dakawa ○ EAT 214-215 J 4
Dakelangsi ○ VRC 144-145 G 6
Dakeshi ○ VRC 144-145 G 6
Daketa Shet' ~ ETH 208-209 F 5
Dakhla < RIM 196-197 E 6
Dakhlet Nouâdhibou ≈ 196-197 B 4
Dakhlet Nouâdhibou ▫ RIM 196-197 B 4
Dakingari ○ WAN 204-205 F 3
Daki Takwas ○ WAN 204-205 F 3
Đắk Nông ○ VN 158-159 J 4
Dako, Gunung ▲ RI 164-165 G 3
Dākoānk ○ IND 140-141 L 6
Dakoro ○ RN 198-199 C 5
Dakota ○ USA (MN) 270-271 G 7
Dakota City ○ USA (IA) 274-275 D 2
Dakota City ○ USA (NE) 262-263 K 2
Dakovica ○ YU 100-101 H 3
Đakovo ○ • HR 100-101 G 2
Daksum ○ IND 138-139 E 3
Dala ○ ANG (LUS) 216-217 F 4
Dala ○ ANG (LUS) 216-217 F 5
Dala ○ SOL 184 I e 3
Dalaba ○ • RG 202-203 D 4
Dalaba ○ SN 202-203 D 3
Dalad Qi ○ VRC 154-155 G 1
Dalahaj ○ RUS 116-117 L 10
Dālāhāni, Kūh-e ▲ IR 134-135 B 1
Dalai Nur ○ VRC 148-149 N 6
Dālaki ○ IR 134-135 D 4
Dālaki, Rūdhāne-ye ~ IR 134-135 D 4
Dalälven ~ S 86-87 H 6
Dalaman Çayı ~ TR 128-129 C 4
D'Alambert ○ CDN (QUE) 236-237 J 4
Dalāmi ○ SUD 206-207 K 3
Dalandole < SP 212-213 K 2
Dalangyun ○ MYA 142-143 J 6
Dalanzadgad ☆ MAU 148-149 G 6
Dala River ~ CDN (BC) 228-229 F 3
Dalark ○ USA (AR) 276-277 C 6
Dalarna ⩩ S 86-87 F 6
Dalat ○ MAL 162-163 J 3
Đà Lat ☆ •• VN 158-159 K 5
Dal'at Rašid 'Abbās ○ IRQ 128-129 L 6
Dālbandin ○ PK 134-135 L 4
Dalbeg ○ AUS 174-175 J 7
Dalbo ○ USA (MN) 270-271 E 5
Dalby ○ AUS 178-179 L 4
Dalcahue ○ RCH 78-79 C 7
Dale ○ N (HOR) 86-87 B 6
Dale ☆ N (FJO) 86-87 B 6
Dale ○ USA (IN) 274-275 M 6
Dale ○ USA (OR) 244-245 G 6
Dale Hollow Lake ○ USA (TN) 276-277 K 4
Dalei Shan ▲ VRC 146-147 N 6
Dalemead ○ CDN (ALB) 232-233 E 5
Daletme ○ MYA 142-143 H 5
Daleville ○ USA (AL) 284-285 E 5
Dalǧā' ○ ET 194-195 E 4
Dalgān ○ IR 134-135 H 5
Dalgaranga Hill ▲ AUS 176-177 D 3
Dalgety Brook ~ AUS 176-177 D 2
Dalgonally ○ AUS 174-175 F 7
Dălgopol ○ BG 102-103 E 6
Dalgyn ~ RUS 110-111 J 6
Dalhart ○ USA (TX) 264-265 B 2
Dalhousie ○ CDN (NB) 240-241 J 2
Dalhousie ○ IND 138-139 F 3
Dalhousie, Cape ▲ CDN 24-25 G 5
Dalhousie Road ○ CDN (NS) 240-241 L 6
Dalhousie West ○ CDN (NS) 240-241 K 6
Dali ○ RMM 202-203 G 2
Dali ○ VRC (SXI) 154-155 F 4
Dali ○ • VRC (YUN) 142-143 M 3
Ḍāli', aḍ- ○ • Y 132-133 D 7
Dalian ○ VRC 150-151 C 8
Daliang Shan ▲ VRC 156-157 C 2
Dālimb ○ IND 140-141 G 2
Dali Sharafat ○ SUD 200-201 F 6
Dalkola ○ IND 142-143 E 3
Dall, Mount ▲ USA 20-21 O 5
Dallas ○ CDN (MAN) 234-235 F 3
Dallas ○ USA (GA) 284-285 F 3
Dallas ○ USA (OR) 244-245 B 6
Dallas ○ • USA (TX) 264-265 H 6
Dallas City ○ USA (IL) 274-275 G 4
Dalles, The ○ USA (OR) 244-245 D 5
Dalli ○ WAN 204-205 J 4
Dall Island ⌒ USA 32-33 D 4
Dall Lake ○ USA 20-21 J 6
Dalmā ⌒ UAE 134-135 E 6
Dalmacija ⩩ HR 100-101 E 3
Dalmacio Vélez Sarsfield ○ RA 78-79 H 2
Dalmas, Lac ○ CDN 38-39 J 2
Dalmatia = Dalmacija ⩩ HR 100-101 E 3
Dalmatovo ☆ RUS 114-115 G 6
Dalmeny ○ CDN (SAS) 232-233 M 3
Dalmǧ, Haur ○ IRQ 128-129 L 6
Dal'nee ○ RUS 122-123 K 5
Dal'negorsk ☆ RUS 122-123 F 6
Dal'nerečensk ○ RUS 122-123 E 6
Dal'nij ○ RUS 120-121 R 7
Dal'nije Zelency ○ RUS 88-89 O 2
Dal'noe ○ KA 124-125 E 2
Dalny ○ CDN (MAN) 234-235 C 5
Daloa ☆ CI 202-203 G 6
Dalong ○ VRC 156-157 F 5
Dalrymple, Mount ▲ AUS 178-179 K 1
Dalrymple Lake < AUS 174-175 J 7
Dalsland ⩩ S 86-87 F 7
Dalsmynni ○ IS 86-87 c 2
Dāltenganj ○ IND 142-143 D 3
Dalton ○ CDN (ONT) 236-237 D 4
Dalton ○ USA (GA) 284-285 F 2
Dalton ○ USA (NE) 262-263 D 3
Dalton Gardens ○ USA (ID) 250-251 C 4
Dalton Ice Tongue ⊂ ARK 16 G 13
Daltro Filho ○ BR 74-75 D 6
Dalu ○ VRC 154-155 D 3
Daludalu ○ RI 162-163 D 4
Dalugama ○ CL 140-141 H 7
Dalupiri Island ⌒ RP (CAG) 160-161 D 3
Dalupiri Island ⌒ RP (NSA) 160-161 F 6
Dalu Shan ▲ VRC 156-157 E 2
Dalvík ○ IS 86-87 d 2
Dalwallinu ○ AUS 176-177 D 5
Dalwhinnie ○ GB 90-91 E 3
Daly Bay ≈ 30-31 Z 4
Dalyr ○ RUS 118-119 K 4
Daly River ⩙ AUS (NT) 172-173 K 2
Daly River ~ AUS 172-173 K 2
Daly River Aboriginal Land ⩙ AUS 172-173 J 2
Daly River Wildlife Sanctuary ⊥ AUS 172-173 J 2
Daly Waters ○ AUS 174-175 B 5
Dal'ža, ozero ○ RUS 122-123 H 2
Dalzell ○ CDN (SAS) 232-233 Q 5
Damā, Wādī ~ KSA 130-131 E 4
Ḍamad ○ KSA 132-133 C 5
Damagaram-Takaya ○ RN 198-199 D 5
Damaguete ☆ RP 160-161 E 8
Damamgani ○ PK 138-139 B 5
Dāmān ○ AFG 134-135 L 3
Damān ☆ IND 138-139 D 9
Damān and Diu ▫ IND 138-139 D 9
Dāmane ○ IR 134-135 D 2
Damanhūr ☆ ET 194-195 E 2
Damant Lake ○ CDN 30-31 R 5

Cubulco — Damant Lake 319

Damaqun Shan ▲ VRC 148-149 M 7
Damār o Y 132-133 D 6
Damar, Kepulauan ⌒ RI 166-167 E 5
Damar, Pulau ⌒ RI (MAL) 164-165 L 4
Damar, Pulau ⌒ RI (MAL) 166-167 E 5
Damara o RCA 206-207 D 6
Damaraland ⊥ NAM 216-217 B 9
Damariscotta o USA (ME) 278-279 M 4
Damasak o WAN 198-199 F 6
Damas Cays ⌒ BS 54-55 F 3
Damascus o USA 276-277 C 5
Damascus o USA (GA) 284-285 F 5
Damascus o USA 280-281 E 7
Damascus = Dimašq ☆ ••• SYR
128-129 G 6
Damaturu o WAN 204-205 J 3
Damauli o NEP 144-145 E 7
Dámávand o IR 136-137 E 7
Dámávand, Küh-e ▲ •• IR 136-137 C 7
Damazine o SUD 200-201 A 3
Damba o ANG 216-217 C 3
Dambai o GH 202-203 L 5
Dambam o WAN 204-205 J 3
Damboa o WAN 204-205 K 3
Dambulla o ••• CL 140-141 J 7
Dam Creek o USA (TX) 264-265 K 6
Dãm Do'i o VN 158-159 H 6
Dame Marie o RH 54-55 H 5
Dame Marie, Cape ⌃ RH 54-55 H 5
Dámgán o IR 136-137 D 6
Damietta = Dumyất ☆ ET 194-195 E 2
Dámini, Rüdhạne-ye o IR 134-135 J 5
Damji o BHT 142-143 F 2
Dammām, ad- o KSA 134-135 D 5
Dámnagar o IND 138-139 C 9
Dámodar ~ IND 142-143 E 4
Damo Debir, Debre • ETH 200-201 J 5
Damoh o IND 138-139 D 4
Damongo o GH 202-203 K 5
Damortis o RP 160-161 D 4
Dampar o WAR 204-205 J 2
Dampelas, Tanjung ▲ RI 164-165 F 3
Damphu o BHT 142-143 G 2
Dampier o AUS 172-173 C 6
Dampier Archipelago ⌒ AUS
172-173 C 6
Dampier Downs o AUS 172-173 F 5
Dampier Land ⊥ AUS 172-173 F 4
Dampier Strait ≈ 183 E 4
Dampir, Selat ≈ 166-167 F 2
Damqaut o Y 132-133 H 5
Dam Qu ~ VRC 144-145 J 4
Damrür o KSA 132-133 A 3
Damt o Y 132-133 D 6
Damtang o VRC 144-145 D 4
Damwal o BHT 142-143 G 2
Damxung o VRC 144-145 H 5
Dana o CDN (SAS) 232-233 N 3
Dana, Lac o CDN (QUE) 236-237 L 2
Dana-Barat, Kepulauan ⌒ RI 166-167 C 5
Danané o CI 202-203 H 6
Đà Nẵng o ∴ VN 158-159 K 2
Danao o RP 160-161 F 7
Danas Banke ≈ 28-29 P 5
Danau Rombebai o RI 166-167 J 2
Danau Toba o RI 162-163 C 3
Danba o VRC 154-155 B 6
Danbatta o WAN 198-199 H 6
Danbury o USA (CT) 280-281 N 2
Danbury o USA (WI) 270-271 F 4
Danby Lake o USA (CA) 248-249 J 6
Dan Chang o THA 158-159 F 3
Dancheng o VRC 154-155 J 5
Dandara o ET (QIN) 194-195 F 4
Dandara ∴•• ET (QIN) 194-195 F 4
Dandaragan o AUS 176-177 C 5
Dandau o ANG 216-217 D 5
Dande o ETH 208-209 D 4
Dandeli o IND 140-141 F 3
Dandenong o AUS 180-181 H 4
Dandenong Park o AUS 174-175 C 3
Dandenong Range National Park ⊥ AUS
180-181 H 4
Dando o ANG 216-217 D 5
Dandong o VRC 150-151 E 7
Daneborg o GRØ 26-27 s 6
Danesfahan o IR 128-129 N 5
Danfeng o VRC 154-155 G 4
Danforth o USA (ME) 278-279 O 3
Dang o CAM 204-205 L 6
Danga o RMM 196-197 J 6
Dangara o TJ 136-137 L 5
Dangar Falls ⌃ AUS 178-179 L 6
Dangchang o VRC 154-155 E 4
Dange o ANG 216-217 C 4
Dange o WAN 198-199 B 6
Danger Area xx USA (NV) 246-247 G 4
Dangerous Cape ⌃ USA 22-23 J 4
Danggali Conservation Park ⊥ AUS
180-181 F 2
Dangila o ETH 208-209 C 3
Danglin Shankou ▲ VRC 146-147 M 6
Dangoura, Mont ▲ RCA 206-207 H 5
Dangriga o BH 52-53 K 3
Dangshan o VRC 154-155 K 4
Dangtu o VRC 154-155 L 6
Dan-Gulbi o WAN 204-205 G 3
Dangur o ETH 200-201 G 6
Dangur ▲ ETH 208-209 B 3
Dangyang o VRC 154-155 G 6
Daniel o USA (WY) 252-253 H 4
Daniel's Harbour o CDN (NFL)
242-243 J 4
Danielskuil o ZA 220-221 F 4
Danielson o USA (CT) 278-279 K 7
Danielson Provincial Park ⊥ CDN (SAS)
232-233 M 4
Danilov o RUS 94-95 O 2
Danilovka o RUS 96-97 R 8
Danilovskaja vozvýšennost' ▲ RUS
94-95 Q 2
Daning o VRC 154-155 G 3
Daninghe • VRC 154-155 F 6
Dan-Issa o RN 198-199 C 6

Danja o WAN 204-205 G 3
Danjiangkou o VRC 154-155 G 5
Danjiankou Sk ~ VRC 154-155 G 5
Danjo-guntō ⌒ J 152-153 C 8
Dank o OM 132-133 K 2
Dankov o RUS 94-95 Q 5
Dankova, pik ▲ KS 146-147 C 5
Danli o HN 52-53 L 4
Danmark Fjord ≈ 26-27 o 3
Danmark Ø o GRØ 26-27 q 5
Danmarkshavn o GRØ 26-27 s 6
Danmarkshavn o GRØ 28-29 V 4
Dannemora o USA (NY) 278-279 M 4
Dannenberg (Elbe) o D 92-93 L 2
Dannevirke o NZ 182 F 5
Danot o ETH 208-209 G 5
Danridge o USA (TN) 282-283 D 4
Dan River ~ USA (NC) 282-283 H 4
Dan Sadau o WAN 204-205 G 3
Dansary, köl o KA 124-125 D 4
Danskøya ⌒ N 84-85 G 3
Dansville o USA (NY) 278-279 D 6
Dánta o IND 138-139 D 7
Dantapalli o IND 142-143 H 2
Dantcho o RT 202-203 L 5
Danube = Donau ~ D 92-93 L 4
Danubyu o MYA 158-159 C 2
Danum Valley Conservation Area ⊥ MAL
160-161 B 10
Danville o CDN (QUE) 238-239 N 3
Danville o USA (AR) 276-277 B 5
Danville o USA (GA) 284-285 G 4
Danville o USA (IL) 274-275 L 5
Danville o USA (IN) 274-275 M 5
Danville o USA (KY) 276-277 L 3
Danville o USA (PA) 280-281 H 5
Danville o USA (VA) 280-281 G 7
Danville o USA (WA) 244-245 G 2
Dan Xian o VRC 156-157 F 7
Danxiashan • VRC 156-157 H 5
Danyang o VRC 154-155 L 5
Danyí-Apéyémé o RT 202-203 L 6
Danzhai o VRC 156-157 E 3
Danzhou o VRC 156-157 E 3
Dao Lý So'n ⌒ VN 158-159 K 3
Dao Xian o VRC 156-157 G 4
Daozhen o VRC 156-157 E 2
Dapaong o RT 202-203 L 4
Dapchi o WAN 198-199 E 6
Dapélogo o BD 202-203 K 3
Đa Phúc ≈ VN 158-159 D 6
Dapitan o RP 160-161 E 8
Dápoli o IND 140-141 E 2
Dapsang = K2 ▲ PK 138-139 F 2
Dapuchaihe o VRC 150-151 G 6
Da Qaidam o VRC 144-145 K 2
Daqiao o VRC 156-157 C 3
Daqing o VRC 150-151 E 4
Daqinggou ⊥• VRC 150-151 D 6
Daqing Shan ▲ VRC 154-155 G 1
Dara o SN 202-203 C 2
Dar'a o SYR 128-129 G 6
Dáráb o IR 134-135 F 4
Darab o SP 212-213 H 3
Dárában o IR 138-139 C 4
Daradou o RCA 206-207 G 6
Daraj o LAR 190-191 H 3
Dár al-Hamrá', ad- o KSA 132-133 B 3
Dárán o IR 134-135 D 2
Darapap o PNG 183 C 2
Darasun o RUS 118-119 F 10
Darasun, Kurort o RUS 118-119 F 10
Darasunskij, Veršino o RUS 118-119 Q 9
Daráu o IND 142-143 D 2
Darãw o ET 194-195 F 5
Darazo o WAN 204-205 J 3
Darb, ad- o KSA 132-133 C 5
Darband o IR 134-135 G 3
Darband, Küh-e ▲ IR 134-135 G 3
Darband-e Hàn o IRQ 128-129 M 5
Darband Sar ▲ IR 136-137 B 6
Dárbhanga o IND 142-143 D 2
Daryáče-ye Tašk o IR 134-135 F 4
Darvoza o IS 136-137 K 4
Darwaz o AFG 136-137 M 3
Darwązagai o AFG 134-135 A 3
Darwell o CDN (ALB) 232-233 D 2
Darwendale o ZW 218-219 F 3
Dárwha o IND 138-139 F 4
Darwin o GB 78-79 L 6
Darwin o AUS 172-173 K 2
Darwin o USA (OH) 280-281 D 7
Darwin, Bahia ≈ 80 C 2
Darwin, Canal ≈ 80 C 2
Darwin, Cordillera ▲ RCH 80 D 4
Darwin, Cordillera de ▲ RCH 76-77 C 4
Darwin, Isla ⌒ EC 64-65 B 4
Darwin, Volcán ▲ EC 64-65 B 4
Daryá o USA 172-173 K 2
Darya Chán o PK 138-139 C 4
Daryaleh o SP 208-209 G 4
Daryápur o IND 138-139 F 9
Daryá-ye Hazar ~ IR 128-129 N 3
Darya-ye Váhján ~ AFG 136-137 N 6
Darza ~ Y 132-133 H 7
Dárzin o IR 134-135 H 4
Dás o UAE 134-135 E 6
Dasáda o IND 138-139 K 2
Dashan o VRC 156-157 K 2
Dashapalla o IND 142-143 D 5
Dashennongjia ▲ VRC 154-155 G 6
Dashennongjia o VRC 154-155 G 6
Dashen Terara, Ras ▲ ETH 200-201 J 6
Dashhowuz = Dažhovuz o TM
136-137 F 4
Dashuikeng o VRC 154-155 E 3
Dashwood o CDN (BC) 230-231 L 4
Dásing o TR 128-129 J 3
Da'sü o PK 138-139 D 2

Darién ⊥ PA 60-61 C 4
Darien o USA 284-285 J 5
Darien = Calima o CO 60-61 C 6
Darien, El o CO 60-61 E 4
Darién, Golfo del ≈ 60-61 C 3
Darién, Parque Nacional de ⊥ ••• PA
52-53 F 8
Darien Center o USA 278-279 C 6
Daríha, Abú ~ SYR 128-129 G 5
Dárin o KSA 134-135 D 5
Dario Meira o BR 72-73 L 3
Dárjüling o IND 142-143 F 2
Dárjüng o IND 142-143 D 5
Darkan o AUS 176-177 D 6
Darke Peak o AUS 180-181 D 2
Darkylah o RUS 120-121 D 3
Darling, Mount ▲ AUS 180-181 K 3
Darling Downs ⊥ AUS 178-179 L 4
Darlingford o CDN (MAN) 234-235 E 5
Darling Peninsula ⊥ CDN 26-27 O 4
Darling Range ▲ AUS 176-177 D 5
Darling River ~ AUS 178-179 H 6
Darling River ~ AUS 180-181 G 2
Darlington o GB 90-91 G 4
Darlington o USA (FL) 286-287 D 1
Darlington o USA (SC) 284-285 L 2
Darlington o USA (WI) 274-275 H 2
Darlington Point o AUS 180-181 H 3
Darlot, Lake o AUS 176-177 F 3
Darlowo ⌒ PL 92-93 O 1
Darmazár o IR 134-135 G 4
Darmiyán o IR 134-135 H 3
Darmody o CDN (SAS) 232-233 M 5
Darmstadt o D 92-93 K 4
Darnah o LAR 192-193 K 1
Darnah ☆ LAR 192-193 L 1
Darnétal o F 90-91 H 7
Darnick o AUS 180-181 G 2
Darnis = Darnah o LAR 192-193 K 1
Darnley, Cape ▲ ARK 16 G 7
Darnley Bay ≈ 24-25 K 6
Darnley Island o AUS 183 B 5
Daro o MAL 162-163 J 3
Daroca o E 98-99 G 4
Darouma o RMM 202-203 P 2
Darou-Mousti o SN 202-203 C 2
Darovskoe o RUS 96-97 E 4
Darre Angir, Kavir-e o IR 134-135 F 2
Darregueira o RA 78-79 H 4
Darre Qeyád ~ IR 134-135 C 2
Darre Šahr o IR 134-135 C 2
Darre-ye Büm o AFG 136-137 H 7
Darre-ye Šüf o AFG 136-137 K 7
Darrington o USA (WA) 244-245 D 2
Darr River ~ AUS 178-179 G 3
Darrüd o IR 136-137 F 6
Darsana o BD 142-143 F 4
Dartford o GB 90-91 H 6
Dartmoor o AUS 180-181 F 4
Dartmoor National Park ⊥ GB 90-91 F 6
Dartmouth o CDN (NS) 240-241 M 6
Dartmouth, Lake o AUS 178-179 H 4
Dartmouth Reservoir < AUS 180-181 J 4
Daru o PNG 183 B 5
Daru o WAL 202-203 E 6
Daruba o RI 164-165 L 2
Darubia o PNG 183 B 5
Daru Island ⌒ PNG 183 B 5
Daruvar o HR 100-101 F 2
Darvel, Teluk ≈ 160-161 C 10
Darvi = Bulgan o MAU 146-147 L 2
Darvills o USA 280-281 J 6
Darvinskij zapovednik ⊥ RUS 94-95 P 2
Darvoza o IS 136-137 K 4
Darwaz o AFG 136-137 M 3
Darwázagai o AFG 134-135 A 3
Darwell o CDN (ALB) 232-233 D 2
Darwin o GB 78-79 L 6
Darwin o AUS 172-173 K 2
Dasáda o IND 138-139 K 2
Dashan o VRC 156-157 K 2
Dasol Bay ≈ 160-161 C 5
Dass o WAN 204-205 H 3
Dassa o DY 204-205 L 7
Dassari o DY 202-203 L 4
Dassel o USA (MN) 270-271 C 4
Dasseneiland ⌒ ZA 220-221 C 5
Dastak o IR 134-135 D 3
Dašt-e 'Abbás o IR 134-135 C 2
Dašte Palang, Rüd-e ~ IR 134-135 E 4
Dašt-e Qal'e o AFG 136-137 L 6
Dásü o PK 138-139 D 2

Datang o VRC (GXI) 156-157 F 4
Datang o VRC (GXI) 156-157 F 4
Data Temple • VRC 154-155 F 4
Datça o TR 128-129 B 4
Date o J 152-153 J 3
Datian o VRC 156-157 K 4
Datian Ding ▲ VRC 156-157 G 5
Datian Z.B. ⊥• VRC 156-157 G 5
Datil o USA (NM) 256-257 H 4
Dating o VRC 144-145 M 2
Datkan o MYA 142-143 J 6
Datong o VRC (QIN) 154-155 D 8
Datong o VRC (SHA) 154-155 H 1
Datong o VRC (XUZ) 146-147 C 2
Datong He ~ VRC 154-155 D 7
Datong Shan ▲ VRC 144-145 M 2
Datori o DY 202-203 L 4
Dato Temple o VRC (SIC) 156-157 D 2
Datong o VRC (SIC) 156-157 D 2
Datta o CI 202-203 H 7
Datta o VRC (SIC) 154-155 J 6
Datton, Kap ▲ GRØ 28-29 e 2
Datu, Tanjung ▲ RI 162-163 E 4
Datuk, Tanjung ▲ RI 162-163 E 4
Datu Piang o RP 160-161 F 9
Dau o RP 160-161 D 5
Daub o RI 166-167 L 6
Dáúd Khel o PK 138-139 D 3
Daudkandi o BD 142-143 G 4
Daudnagar o IND 142-143 D 3
Daudmannsodden ▲ N 84-85 H 3
Daugaard Jensen Land ⊥ GRØ
26-27 T 3
Daugava ~ LV 94-95 K 4
Daugavpils o ∴ LV 94-95 K 4
Dauha, ad- o Q 134-135 D 6
Dauka o OM 132-133 J 4
Daule o EC 64-65 C 2
Daule ~ EC 64-65 B 2
Daule o WAN 204-205 G 3
Daund o IND 138-139 E 4
Daung Kyun ⌒ MYA 158-159 E 4
Dáún o IND 138-139 D 6
Daura o WAN 198-199 D 6
Daurán, Ǧabal ▲ Y 132-133 D 6
Daur'an, Wádí ~ Y 132-133 D 6
Daurkina, poluostrov ⌃ RUS 112-113 Y 3
Dausa o KSA 132-133 B 3
Dausa o IND 138-139 E 3
Dáú Tiêng o VN 158-159 J 5
Da Yunhe ~ VRC 154-155 J 3
Dayville o USA (OR) 244-245 F 6
Dazey o USA (ND) 258-259 J 4
Dazhou Dao ⌒ VRC 156-157 G 7
Dazhu o VRC 154-155 E 6
Dazkin ▲ IR 134-135 H 3
Dazu o VRC 156-157 D 2
Dazu Shike • VRC 156-157 D 2
Dchira o MA 188-189 C 4
Dead Horse Point State Park • USA (UT)
254-255 F 6
Dead Indian Peak ▲ USA (WY)
252-253 J 4
Dead Lake o USA (MN) 270-271 C 4
Deadman Bay ≈ 48-49 G 5
Deadman's Bay o USA (FL) 286-287 F 2
Deadman's Bay o CDN (NFL)
242-243 P 3
Deadman's Cay o BS 54-55 H 3
Deadmans Cove o CDN (NFL)
242-243 M 1
Deadman's Creek Indian Reserve X CDN
(BC) 230-231 J 4
Deadman Summit ▲ USA (CA)
248-249 F 4
Dead Sea = Yam Hamelah = Bahret Lut o
JOR 130-131 D 2
Deadwood o USA (SD) 260-261 C 2
Deakin o AUS 177-177 K 5
Dealesville o ZA 220-221 G 4
Déali o SN 202-203 C 2
De'an o VRC 156-157 J 2
Dean Channel ≈ 32-33 G 5
Dean Channel ≈ CDN 228-229 G 4
Deán Funes o RA 76-77 E 4
Deans Dundas Bay ≈ 24-25 N 4
Deatsville o USA (AL) 284-285 D 4
Deauville o •• F 90-91 H 7
Deaver o USA (WY) 252-253 K 2
Debak o MAL 162-163 J 4
Debal, Cerro ▲ RA 80 E 5
Debaltceve o UA 102-103 L 3
Debao o VRC 156-157 D 4
Debar o MK 100-101 H 4
Debark o ETH 200-201 H 6
Debauch Mountain ▲ USA 20-21 L 4
Debayisma o ER 200-201 K 5
Debden o CDN (SAS) 232-233 M 2

Dawn o USA (VA) 280-281 J 6
Dawson o CDN 20-21 V 4
Dawson o USA (GA) 284-285 F 5
Dawson o USA (MN) 270-271 B 4
Dawson o USA (ND) 258-259 H 5
Dawson, Isla ⌒ RCH 80 E 4
Dawson, Mount ▲ CDN (BC)
230-231 M 2
Dawson Bay Indian Reserve X CDN
(MAN) 234-235 C 2
Dawson Creek o CDN 32-33 K 4
Dawson Highway II AUS 178-179 K 3
Dawson-Lambton Glacier ◁ ARK 16 F 33
Dawson Range ▲ AUS 176-177 E 5
Dawson Range o CDN 20-21 V 5
Dawson River ~ AUS 178-179 K 3
Dawsons Landing o CDN (BC)
230-231 B 2
Dawson Springs o USA (KY)
276-277 H 3
Dawsonville o USA (GA) 284-285 F 3
Dawu o VRC (HUB) 154-155 J 6
Dawu o VRC (SIC) 154-155 B 6
Daww, ad- ~ SYR 128-129 G 5
Dax o F 90-91 G 10
Daxi o VRC 156-157 M 2
Da Xian o VRC 154-155 E 6
Daxin o VRC 156-157 E 5
Daxue Shan ▲ VRC 154-155 B 6
Day o USA (CA) 246-247 D 2
Daya o RIM 196-197 E 5
Daya Wan ≈ 156-157 J 6
Dayang Bunting, Pulau ⌒ MAL (KED)
162-163 C 2
Dayangshu o VRC 150-151 E 4
Dayao o VRC 156-157 B 4
Daylesford o AUS 180-181 H 4
Daylight Pass ▲ USA (CA) 248-249 H 3
Daymán, Cuchilla del ▲ ROU 76-77 J 6
Daymán, Río ~ ROU 76-77 J 6
Daymán, Termas del ~ ROU 76-77 J 6
Dayong o VRC 156-157 G 2
Dayton o USA (NV) 246-247 E 4
Dayton o USA (OH) 280-281 B 6
Dayton o USA (OR) 244-245 B 5
Dayton o USA (TX) 268-269 J 4
Dayton o USA (WA) 252-253 L 2
Daytona Beach o USA (FL) 286-287 H 2
Dayu o RI 164-165 D 4
Dayu o VRC 156-157 J 4
Dazey o USA (ND) 258-259 J 4

Debdirge o RUS 120-121 E 2
Debdou o RM 188-189 K 4
Debed ~ AR 128-129 L 2
Debepare o PNG 183 A 4
Débéré o BF 202-203 J 3
Debesa o RUS 172-173 G 4
Debesy ☆ RUS 96-97 H 5
Debin o RUS 120-121 O 2
Debin o CDN (QUE) 240-241 F 2
Debo, Lac o RMM 202-203 H 2
Debolt o CDN 32-33 M 4
Deborah East, Lake o AUS 176-177 D 5
Deborah West, Lake o AUS 176-177 E 5
Débougou o RMM 202-203 H 3
Debre Birhan o ETH 208-209 D 3
Debre Markos o ETH 208-209 C 3
Debre May o ETH 208-209 D 4
Debre Tabor o ETH 208-209 D 3
Debre Work' o ETH 208-209 D 3
Debre Zebit o ETH 208-209 D 3
Debre Zeyit o ETH (Goj) 208-209 D 3
Debre Zeyit o ETH (She) 208-209 D 4
Decatur o USA (AL) 284-285 D 2
Decatur o USA (GA) 284-285 F 3
Decatur o USA (IL) 274-275 K 5
Decatur o USA (IN) 274-275 O 4
Decatur o USA (MI) 272-273 D 5
Decatur o USA (NE) 262-263 K 3
Decatur o USA (TX) 264-265 G 5
Decaturville o USA (TN) 276-277 D 5
Deccan ⊥ IND 10-11 G 7
Decelles, Lac o CDN (QUE) 236-237 O 4
Decelles, Réservoir o CDN (QUE)
236-237 L 5
Deception o CDN 34-35 D 2
Déception, Rivière ~ CDN 36-37 M 3
Déception Bay ≈ 36-37 M 3
Deception Bay o 183 C 4
Deception Lake o CDN (SAS) 232-233 J 2
Deception Point o AUS 172-173 K 1
Dechang o VRC 156-157 B 4
Decherd o USA (TN) 276-277 J 5
Dechu o IND 138-139 D 6
Décin o CZ 92-93 N 3
Deciolândia o BR 70-71 J 4
Decize o F 90-91 J 8
Decker o CDN (MAN) 234-235 C 4
Decker o USA (MT) 250-251 N 6
Decker Field o USA 176-177 H 2
Decker Lake o CDN (BC) 228-229 J 2
Deckers o USA (CO) 254-255 K 4
Declo o USA (ID) 252-253 F 4
Decoigne o CDN (ALB) 228-229 Q 4
Decorah o USA (IA) 274-275 G 1
Dedegöl Dağları ▲ TR 128-129 D 4
Dedham o USA (MA) 244-245 H 4
Dedougou o BF 202-203 J 3
Dédougou ☆ BF 202-203 J 3
Dedovichi o RUS 94-95 L 3
Dedza o MW 218-219 H 2
Dee ~ GB 90-91 F 5
Dee ~ GB 90-91 F 3
Deep Bay o NZ 30-31 L 5
Deep Cove o NZ 182 A 6
Deep Creek, North Fork ~ USA (WA)
244-245 H 3
Deep Creek, South Fork ~ USA (WA)
244-245 H 2
Deep Creek Lake < USA (MD)
280-281 G 4
Deep Fork ~ USA (OK) 264-265 H 3
Deep River o CDN (ONT) 238-239 H 2
Deep River ~ USA (NC) 282-283 H 5
Deep Rose Lake o CDN 30-31 M 3
Deep Valley Creek ~ USA (ALB)
228-229 P 4
Deepwater o AUS 178-179 L 5
Deepwater o USA (MO) 274-275 D 4
Deep Well o AUS 178-179 D 3
Deer o USA (AR) 276-277 B 5
Deer Bay ≈ 24-25 T 1
Deer Creek o USA (MS) 268-269 K 4
Deer Creek Lake o USA (OH)
280-281 C 4
Deerfield o USA (SD) 260-261 C 2
Deerfield Beach o USA (FL) 286-287 J 5
Deerfield River ~ USA (MA) 278-279 J 6
Deer Fork ~ USA (TN) 276-277 F 5
Deerhorn o CDN (MAN) 234-235 E 4
Deering o USA 20-21 J 3
Deering, Mount ▲ AUS 176-177 J 4
Deer Island o CDN (MAN) 234-235 D 3
Deer Island o USA (ME) 278-279 N 4
Deer Isle o USA (ME) 278-279 N 4
Deer Lake o CDN (NFL) 242-243 L 4
Deer Lake o CDN (ONT) 234-235 J 2
Deer Lake o CDN (NFL) 242-243 L 3
Deer Lake o USA (LA) 268-269 J 5
Deer Lodge Pass ▲ USA (MT)
250-251 G 6
Deer Park o CDN (BC) 230-231 L 4
Deer Park o USA (WA) 244-245 H 4
Deer Park o USA (AL) 268-269 L 4
Deerpass Bay ≈ CDN 30-31 J 3
Deer Pond o CDN (NFL) 242-243 O 4
Deer River o CDN 34-35 G 2
Deer River o USA (MN) 270-271 D 2
Deer River o USA (MI) 270-271 L 4
Deer Trail o USA (CO) 254-255 M 4
Deer Trail Creek ~ USA (CO)
254-255 M 4
Deerwood o USA (MN) 270-271 D 3
Deeth o USA (NV) 246-247 J 1
Defensores del Chaco, Parque Nacional ⊥
PY 70-71 G 7
Defferrari o RA 78-79 K 5
Defia, Hassi < MA 188-189 K 4
Defiance o USA (OH) 280-281 B 5
Défilé de Tosaye ⊥ RMM 196-197 K 6

Degache o TN 190-191 G 4
Degali ~ RUS 116-117 F 4
Degayé, Ra's ▲ ER 200-201 L 6
Dêgê o VRC 144-145 M 5
Degeh Bur o ETH 208-209 F 4
Degeh Medo o ETH 208-209 F 5
Dégelis o CDN (QUE) 240-241 G 3
Degema o WAN 204-205 G 6
Deggendorf o D 92-93 M 4
Degoma o ETH 200-201 H 6
Dégrad Claude o F 62-63 H 4
Dégrad des Emerillon = Dégrad Claude o
F 62-63 H 4
Dégrad Haut Camopi o F 62-63 H 4
Dégrad Saint-Léon o F 62-63 H 4
Dégrad Vitalo o F 62-63 H 4
De Grau o USA (NFL) 242-243 H 3
De Grey River ~ AUS 172-173 D 6
Dehalak Desêt ~ ER 200-201 K 5
Dehãqãn o IR 134-135 D 3
Dehbárez o IR 134-135 H 4
Dehbid o IR 134-135 E 3
Deh Dašt o IR 134-135 D 3
Dehdez o IR 134-135 D 3
Dehej o IR 134-135 D 3
Deh-e Kohne o IR 134-135 G 3
Dehekolano, Tanjung ▲ RI 164-165 K 4
Dehepodo o RI 164-165 K 3
Deh Heir o IR 134-135 F 4
Dehibai o TN 190-191 H 4
Dehkanabad o US 136-137 K 4
Dehlorán o IR 134-135 C 2
Dehnow o IR 134-135 G 3
Dehra Dun o •• IND 138-139 G 4
Deh Rávüd o AFG 134-135 L 2
Dehri o IND 142-143 D 3
Dehšir o IR 134-135 E 3
Deh Šü o AFG 134-135 K 3
Dehua o VRC 156-157 L 4
Dehui o VRC 150-151 F 5
Deilam, Bandar-e o IR 134-135 D 3
Deim Bükhit o SUD 206-207 H 5
Deira o UAE 134-135 F 6
Dej o RO 102-103 J 4
Dejen o ETH 208-209 D 3
Dejiang o VRC 156-157 F 2
Dejnau o TM 136-137 H 4
De Jongs, Tanjung ▲ RI 166-167 K 5
De-Kastri o RUS 122-123 J 3
Dek'emhare o ER 200-201 J 5
Dekese o ZRE 210-211 H 5
Dekina o WAN 204-205 G 4
Dekoa o RCA 206-207 D 5
Delaa o DZ 190-191 D 4
Delacour o CDN (ALB) 232-233 E 4
Delacroix o USA (LA) 268-269 L 7
Delaki o RI 166-167 E 6
Delancey o USA (NY) 278-279 L 6
Delang o RI 168 D 3
Delano o USA (CA) 248-249 F 6
Delárám o AFG 134-135 K 2
Delareyville o ZA 220-221 G 3
Delaronde Lake o CDN 34-35 D 2
Delavan o USA (IL) 274-275 J 4
Delavan o USA (WI) 274-275 K 2
Delaware o USA (OH) 280-281 C 5
Delaware □ USA 276-277 B 5
Delaware Lake o USA (OH) 280-281 C 3
Delaware River ~ USA (KS) 262-263 L 5
Delaware River ~ USA (NY) 278-279 L 6
Delaware River ~ USA (PA)
280-281 M 2
Delaware Bay ≈ 46-47 L 6
Delaware Bay ≈ USA 280-281 L 5
Delaware Creek ~ USA (TX)
266-267 C 2
Delbi o SN 202-203 C 2
Del Bonita o CDN (ALB) 232-233 F 6
Delburne o CDN (ALB) 232-233 E 3
Delcambre o USA (LA) 268-269 J 7
Del Cano Rise ≈ 9 H 10
Delčevo o MK 100-101 J 3
Delco o USA (NC) 282-283 J 6
Deleau o CDN (MAN) 234-235 C 5
Deleg o EC 64-65 C 3
Delegate River o AUS 180-181 K 4
Délembé o CDN 206-207 F 4
Délépo o TCH 198-199 J 8
Delfino o BR 68-69 H 7
Delfinópolis o BR 72-73 G 6
Delft o NL 92-93 H 2
Delfus o PE 64-65 C 4
Delfzijl o NL 92-93 J 2
Dèlgèr = Tajgan o MAU 148-149 E 3
Dèlgèrèh = Hongor o MAU 148-149 K 5
Dèlgèrhangaj = Hašaat o MAU
148-149 G 5
Dèlgèr mörön ~ MAU 148-149 D 3
Delgo o SUD 200-201 E 2
Delhi o CDN (ONT) 238-239 E 6
Delhi o •• IND 138-139 F 9
Delhi o USA (CA) 254-255 L 6
Delhi o USA (LA) 268-269 J 4
Delhi o USA (NY) 278-279 O 6
Déli o TCH 206-207 B 4
Deli, Pulau ⌒ RI 168 A 3
Delia o CDN (ALB) 232-233 F 4
Delicias o CO 60-61 F 5
Delicias o MEX 50-51 G 3
Delicias, Las o CO 60-61 F 7
Delight o USA (AR) 276-277 B 6
Délimane, I-n- < RMM 196-197 L 5
Delingdè o RUS 110-111 O 7
Delingha o VRC 144-145 L 2
Delisle o CDN (QUE) 240-241 D 2
Delisle o CDN (SAS) 232-233 L 4
Delissaville X AUS 172-173 K 2
Delitič o RI 162-163 G 4
Deljankir o RUS 110-111 a 7

Del'kju-Ohotskaja ~ RUS 120-121 J 3
Del'ku ~ RUS 110-111 a 6
Dell o USA (MT) 250-251 G 7
Dell City o USA (TX) 266-267 B 2
Delle o USA (UT) 254-255 C 3
Dell Rapids o USA (SD) 260-261 K 3
Dellys o DZ 190-191 D 2
Delmar Lake o USA (NV) 248-249 K 2
Delmarva Peninsula ⌣ USA (MD) 280-281 L 4
Delmas o CDN (SAS) 232-233 K 3
Delmas o ZA 220-221 J 3
Delmenhorst o D 92-93 K 2
Delmont o USA (NJ) 280-281 M 4
Delmore Downs o AUS 178-179 C 2
Del Norte o USA (CO) 254-255 J 6
De-Longa, ostrova ⌒ RUS 110-111 b 1
Deloraine o AUS 180-181 J 6
Deloraine o CDN (MAN) 234-235 C 5
Delos ∴ GR 100-101 K 6
Delphi ∴ GR 100-101 J 5
Delphi o USA (IN) 274-275 M 4
Delphos o USA (OH) 280-281 B 3
Delportshoop o ZA 220-221 G 4
Delray Beach o USA (FL) 286-287 J 5
Del Rio o USA (TX) 266-267 G 4
Delsbo o S 86-87 H 6
Del Sur o USA (CA) 248-249 F 5
Delta o CDN (BC) 230-231 G 4
Delta o CDN (MAN) 234-235 E 4
Delta o USA (CO) 254-255 G 5
Delta o USA (OH) 280-281 B 2
Delta o USA (UT) 254-255 C 4
Delta Camp < RB 218-219 B 4
Delta del Tigre o ROU 78-79 L 3
Delta Downs o AUS 174-175 F 5
Delta Dunării ∴ RO 102-103 F 5
Delta Junction o USA 20-21 S 4
Delta Mendota Canal < USA (CA) 248-249 D 3
Delta National Wildlife Refuge ⊥ USA (LA) 268-269 L 7
Delthore Mountain ▲ CDN 30-31 F 4
Deltona o USA (FL) 286-287 H 3
Del'tula ~ RUS 116-117 E 3
Delungra o AUS 178-179 L 5
Dèluun = Rašaant o MAU 146-147 K 2
Del Verme Falls ~ ETH 208-209 E 6
Dèm, Lac de o • BF 202-203 K 3
Dema ~ RUS 96-97 J 6
Demagiri o IND 142-143 H 4
Demaine o CDN (SAS) 232-233 L 5
Demak o RI 168 D 3
Demalisques de Leshwe ⊥ ZRE 214-215 E 7
Demaraisville o CDN (ONT) 236-237 M 3
Demarcation Point ▲ USA 20-21 U 2
Demba o ZRE 210-211 J 6
Demba Koli o SN 202-203 D 3
Dembecha o ETH 208-209 C 3
Dembi o ETH 208-209 C 4
Dembia o RCA 206-207 G 6
Dembi Dolo o • ETH 208-209 B 4
Dembo o CAM 204-205 K 4
Dembo o TCH 206-207 C 4
Demensk, Spas- o RUS 94-95 O 4
Demerara Abyssal Plain ≃ 6-7 D 7
Demers, Pointe ▲ CDN 36-37 K 4
Demers Centre o CDN (QUE) 238-239 H 3
Demidov ☆ RUS 94-95 M 4
Deming o USA (NM) 256-257 H 6
Deming o USA (WA) 244-245 C 2
Demini, Rio ~ BR 66-67 F 3
Demirci o TR 128-129 C 3
Dem'janka ~ RUS 114-115 K 5
Dem'janka ~ RUS 114-115 N 5
Dem'janovo o RUS 96-97 E 3
Demjansk ☆ RUS 94-95 N 3
Dem'janskoe o RUS 114-115 K 5
Demmin o D 92-93 M 2
Demnate o MA 188-189 H 5
Demopolis o USA (AL) 284-285 C 4
Demotte o USA (IN) 274-275 L 3
Dempo, Gunung ▲ RI 162-163 E 6
Dempo, Selat ≈ 162-163 F 4
Dempseys o AUS 174-175 C 7
Dempster Highway II CDN 20-21 V 4
Dempta o RI 166-167 L 3
Dêmqog o IND 138-139 G 3
Demsa o CAM 204-205 K 4
Denakil ∴ ETH 200-201 K 5
Denali Highway II USA 20-21 Q 5
Denali National Park o USA 20-21 Q 5
Denali National Park and Preserve ⊥ USA 20-21 P 5
Denan o ETH 208-209 F 5
Denau o US 136-137 K 5
Denbigh o CDN (ONT) 238-239 H 3
Denbigh, Cape ▲ USA 20-21 K 4
Denbigh Downs o AUS 178-179 F 2
Den Chai o THA 158-159 F 2
Dendang o RI 162-163 G 6
Dendâra o RIM 196-197 G 6
Déndoudi o SN 202-203 D 2
Deneba o ETH 208-209 D 4
Denežkin Kamen', gora ▲ RUS 114-115 E 4
Dengfeng o VRC 154-155 H 4
Dengi o WAN 204-205 H 4
Dengkou o VRC 154-155 E 1
Dêngqên o VRC 144-145 K 5
Denguiro o RCA 206-207 F 6
Dengyuan o VRC 156-157 D 2
Dengzhou o VRC 154-155 H 5
Den Haag = 's-Gravenhage ☆ • NL 92-93 H 2
Denham o AUS 176-177 B 2
Denham, Mount ▲ JA 54-55 G 5
Denham Island ⌒ AUS 174-175 E 5
Denham Range ▲ AUS 178-179 J 2
Denham Sound ≈ 176-177 B 2
Denham Springs o USA (LA) 268-269 K 6
Denhart o CDN (ALB) 232-233 G 5
Den Helder o NL 92-93 H 2
Denholm o CDN (SAS) 232-233 L 3
Deni, Área Indígena ⊼ BR 66-67 C 6
Denia o E 98-99 H 5
Denial Bay ≈ 176-177 M 6
Denikourola o RMM 202-203 H 4
Deniliquin o AUS 180-181 H 3
Denio o USA (NV) 246-247 G 2
Denio Junction o USA (NV) 246-247 G 2
Denio Summit ▲ USA (NV) 246-247 G 2
Denise Island ⌒ SY 224 D 1
Denison o USA (IA) 274-275 C 2
Denison o USA (TX) 264-265 H 5
Denison Range ▲ AUS 172-173 J 5
Denizli ☆ TR 128-129 C 4
Denkanikota o IND 140-141 G 4
Denkola ∴ • TM 136-137 E 4
Denman o • AUS 180-181 L 2
Denman o USA (NE) 262-263 H 4
Denman Glacier ⊂ ARK 16 G 10
Denman Island o CDN (BC) 230-231 E 4
Denmark o AUS 176-177 D 7
Denmark o USA (SC) 284-285 J 3
Denmark o USA (WI) 270-271 L 6
Denmark = Danmark ■ DK 86-87 C 9
Denmark Strait ≈ 6-7 F 2
Denmark Strait ≈ 6-7 G 2
Denniel Creek ~ CDN (SAS) 232-233 L 6
Dennis, Lake o AUS 172-173 J 6
Dennysville o USA (ME) 278-279 O 4
Den Oever o NL 92-93 H 2
Denpasar ☆ RI 168 B 7
Dent, La ▲ CI 202-203 G 6
Denton o USA (GA) 284-285 H 5
Denton o USA (MD) 280-281 L 5
Denton o USA (MT) 250-251 K 4
Denton o USA (NC) 282-283 G 5
Denton o USA (TX) 264-265 G 5
Denton Creek ~ USA (TX) 264-265 G 5
Dentons Corner o USA (VA) 280-281 H 6
D'Entrecasteaux, Point ▲ AUS 176-177 D 7
D'Entrecasteaux Islands ⌒ PNG 183 F 5
D'Entrecasteaux National Park ⊥ AUS 176-177 C 7
Denu o GH 202-203 L 6
Denver o USA (IA) 274-275 F 2
Denver ☆ • USA (CO) 254-255 L 4
Denver City o USA (TX) 264-265 B 6
Denzil o CDN (SAS) 232-233 J 3
Déo o RCA 206-207 E 4
Déo, Mayo ~ CAM 204-205 K 5
Deoband o IND 138-139 F 5
Deodápolis o BR 76-77 K 2
Deogarh o IND 142-143 D 5
Deogarh Peak ▲ IND 142-143 C 4
Deoghar o • IND 142-143 E 3
Deolāli o IND 138-139 D 10
Deoli o IND 138-139 G 9
Deolia o IND 138-139 E 7
Deora o USA (CO) 254-255 N 6
Deori o IND 142-143 B 5
Déou o BF 202-203 K 2
Dep ~ RUS 118-119 N 9
Dep ~ RUS 122-123 C 2
Dep, River ~ WAN 204-205 H 4
Depālpur o IND 138-139 E 8
De Panne o B 92-93 G 3
Depapre o RI 166-167 L 3
Departure Bay o CDN (BC) 230-231 F 4
Departure Lake o CDN (ONT) 236-237 G 3
Depew o USA (NY) 278-279 C 6
Depew o USA (OK) 264-265 H 3
Deposit o USA (NY) 278-279 F 6
Depot d'Aigle o CDN (QUE) 238-239 J 2
Dépôt-de-la-Lièvre o CDN (QUE) 240-241 C 2
Dépôt Lézard Rnes o F 62-63 H 3
Deptumala ~ RUS 108-109 a 5
Deputatskij ☆ RUS 110-111 W 5
Dêqên o VRC (XIZ) 144-145 H 5
Dêqên o VRC (YUN) 144-145 M 6
Deqing o VRC 156-157 G 5
Dera o ETH 208-209 D 4
Dera ~ SP 212-213 J 3
Dera Bugti o PK 138-139 B 5
Dera Ghāzi Khān o • PK 138-139 C 4
Dera Ismāīl Khān o PK 138-139 C 4
Derale ▲ AUS 180-181 K 2
Dera Murād Jamali o PK 138-139 B 5
Dera Nānak o IND 138-139 E 3
Dera Nawāb Sahib o PK 138-139 C 5
Đeravica ▲ • YU 100-101 H 3
Derāwar Fort o • PK 138-139 C 5
Derbeikan, Wādi ~ SUD 200-201 G 3
Derbeke ~ RUS 110-111 U 7
Derbekinskaja vpadina ⌣ RUS 110-111 U 7
Derbent o RUS 126-127 H 6
Derbissaka o RCA 206-207 G 6
Derby o AUS (TAS) 180-181 J 6
Derby o AUS (WA) 172-173 F 4
Derby o CDN (PEI) 240-241 L 4
Derby o GB 90-91 G 5
Derby o USA (IN) 274-275 M 6
Derby o USA (KS) 262-263 J 7
Derby o ZA 220-221 H 2
Derby Lake o CDN 30-31 X 2
Derby Shelton o USA (CT) 280-281 N 2
Derdepoort o ZA 220-221 H 2
Dereli ☆ TR 128-129 H 2
Deren, Adrar-n- ▲ MA 188-189 G 5
Derésa o TCH 198-199 K 6
Derewo ~ RI 166-167 J 3
Derg, Lough o IRL 90-91 C 5
Dergači ☆ RUS 96-97 F 8
Derhačy o UA 102-103 K 2
Derickson Seamount ≃ 22-23 Q 6
Derik ☆ TR 128-129 J 4
Derjugina, vpadina ≃ 122-123 L 2
Derkül ~ KA 96-97 G 8
Derm o NAM 220-221 D 1
Dermitt o USA (TX) 264-265 C 6
Dermott o USA (AR) 276-277 D 7
Dernieres, Isles ⌒ USA (LA) 268-269 K 7
Deroche o CDN (BC) 230-231 G 4
Derramadero o C 54-55 F 4
Derre o MOC 218-219 J 3
Derri o SP 208-209 H 6
Derry o USA (NH) 278-279 K 6
Derry Doire = Londonderry ☆ • GB 90-91 D 4
Derry Downs o AUS 178-179 C 2
Derudeb o SUD 200-201 H 4
Derval o F 90-91 G 8
Derville, Rivière ~ CDN 36-37 L 3
Derwent o AUS 176-177 M 1
Derwent o CDN (ALB) 232-233 H 2
Derwent, River ~ AUS 180-181 J 7
Deržavinsk ☆ KA 124-125 E 3
Deržavnyj zapovednyk Dunajskie plavni • UA 102-103 F 5
Desaguadero, Río ~ BOL 70-71 D 5
Desaguadero, Río ~ RA 78-79 F 2
Desagües de los Colorados o RA 76-77 D 5
Desaru o MAL 162-163 F 4
Desbarats o CDN (ONT) 238-239 B 2
Desbarats Strait ≈ 24-25 T 2
Descabezado Grande, Volcán ▲ RCH 78-79 D 3
Descanso o USA (CA) 248-249 H 7
Descanso, El o PE 70-71 B 4
Deschaillons o CDN (QUE) 238-239 N 2
Deschambault Lake o CDN 34-35 D 3
Descharme River ~ CDN 32-33 Q 3
Deschutes River ~ USA (OR) 244-245 E 5
Deschutes River ~ USA (OR) 244-245 D 6
Descoberto o BR 72-73 H 2
Descubierta, La o DOM 54-55 K 5
Desē ☆ ETH 208-209 D 3
Deseado, Cabo ▲ RCH 80 C 6
Deseado, Río ~ RA 80 G 3
Desecheo, Isla ⌒ USA (PR) 286-287 O 2
Desecho o YV 60-61 H 6
Desemboque, El o MEX 50-51 C 2
Desengaño, Punta ▲ RA 80 G 4
Desenzano del Garda o I 100-101 C 2
Deseret o USA (UT) 254-255 C 4
Deseret Peak ▲ USA (UT) 254-255 C 3
Desertas, Ilhas ⌒ P 188-189 C 4
Desertas, Ponta das ▲ BR 74-75 E 8
Desert Center o USA (CA) 248-249 J 6
Desert Hot Springs o USA (CA) 248-249 H 6
Desert National Park ⊥ IND 138-139 C 6
Desert National Wildlife Refuge ⊥ USA (NV) 248-249 J 3
Desert Peak ▲ USA (UT) 254-255 B 2
Desert Range ▲ USA (NV) 248-249 J 3
Desert Range xx USA (UT) 254-255 B 5
Desert Test Center xx USA (UT) 254-255 B 3
Desert View o USA (AZ) 256-257 D 2
Deshler o USA (OH) 280-281 C 2
Desiderio Tello o RA 76-77 D 6
Desierto, Canal al < RA 76-77 F 4
Desierto Central de Baja California, Parque Nacional del ⊥ MEX 50-51 B 3
Desirade, La ⌒ F 56 E 3
Des Lacs o USA (ND) 258-259 F 3
Des Lacs National Wildlife Refuge ⊥ USA (ND) 258-259 E 3
Desmarais Lake o CDN 30-31 R 5
Des Moines o USA (WA) 244-245 C 3
Des Moines ☆ • USA (IA) 274-275 E 3
Des Moines River ~ USA (IA) 274-275 F 4
Desna ~ RUS 94-95 N 4
Desna ~ UA 102-103 G 2
Desna ~ UA 102-103 H 2
Desnățui ~ RO 102-103 C 5
Desolación, Isla ⌒ RCH 80 C 6
Desolation Canyon ⌣ USA (UT) 254-255 E 4
Desolation Point ▲ RP 160-161 F 7
Desolation Sound Provincial Marine Park ⊥ CDN (BC) 230-231 E 3
Desoronto o CDN (ONT) 238-239 H 4
De Soto National Monument • USA (FL) 286-287 G 4
Despatch o ZA 220-221 G 6
Despeñaderos o RA 76-77 E 6
Despotovac o YU 100-101 H 2
Des Roches o CDN (QUE) 240-241 D 3
Desroches, Île ⌒ SY 224 C 2
Dessau o • D 92-93 M 3
Destacado Island ⌒ RP 160-161 F 6
Destacamento São Simão o BR 70-71 G 4
Desterro o BR 66-67 C 6
Destin o USA (FL) 286-287 C 1
D'Estrees Bay ≈ 180-181 D 3
Destruction Bay o CDN 20-21 V 6
Desvelos, Bahía ≈ 80 G 4
Dete o ZW 218-219 D 4
Detmold o • D 92-93 K 3
Detour, Point ▲ USA (MI) 270-271 M 5
Detpa o AUS 180-181 F 4
Detrin ~ RUS 120-121 N 3
Detroit o USA (AL) 284-285 B 2
Detroit o USA (OR) 244-245 C 6
Detroit o USA (TX) 264-265 J 5
Detroit o • USA (MI) 272-273 F 5
Detroit, Fort ∴ USA (MN) 270-271 C 4
Détroit de Bougainville ≈ 184 II a 2
Détroit de Jaques-Cartier ≈ 38-39 N 4
Détroit d'Honguedo ≈ 38-39 M 4
Detroit Lake o USA (OR) 244-245 C 6
Detroit Lakes o USA (MN) 270-271 C 4
Dettifoss ~ IS 86-87 e 2
Det Udom o THA 158-159 H 3
Detuo o VRC 156-157 C 2
Deua National Park ⊥ AUS 180-181 K 3
Deukeskenkala ∴ • TM 136-137 F 3
Deustua o PE 70-71 B 4
Deutsch Brod = Havlíčkův Brod o • CZ 92-93 N 4
Deutsche Bucht ≈ D 92-93 J 1
Deutschheim State Historic Site • USA (MO) 274-275 G 6
Deux Balé, Forêt des ⊥ BF 202-203 J 4
Deux Bassins, Col de ▲ DZ 190-191 D 2
Deux Pietons • WL 56 E 5
Deva ☆ • RO 102-103 C 5
Devadurg o IND 140-141 G 2
Devakottai o IND 140-141 H 6
Devanhalli o IND 140-141 G 4
Devar Hippargi o IND 140-141 G 2
Devarkonda o IND 140-141 H 2
Devarshola o IND 140-141 G 5
De Veber, Mount ▲ CDN (ALB) 228-229 P 3
Devechi = Davaçi o AZ 128-129 N 2
Deveci Dağı ▲ TR 128-129 F 2
Develi ☆ TR 128-129 F 3
Deveril o AUS 178-179 K 2
Devers o USA (TX) 268-269 F 6
Devgarh o IND 138-139 D 7
Deviation Peak ▲ USA 20-21 K 3
Devica ~ RUS 102-103 L 2
Deville o CDN (ALB) 232-233 F 2
Deville Névé ~ CDN (BC) 230-231 M 2
Devil Mountain ▲ USA 20-21 H 3
Devil Mountain Lake o USA 20-21 H 3
Devils Bridge ∴ AG 56 E 3
Devils Den o USA (CA) 248-249 E 4
Devils Den State Parks ⊥ USA (AR) 276-277 A 5
Devils Gate ▲ USA (CA) 246-247 F 5
Devil's Hole ≈ 90-91 H 3
Devil's Hole National Monument ∴ USA (NV) 248-249 H 3
Devil's Island = Diable, Île du ⌒ F 62-63 H 3
Devils Kitchen Lake o USA (IL) 276-277 F 3
Devils Lake o USA (ND) 258-259 J 3
Devils Lake Sioux Indian Reservation ⊼ USA (ND) 258-259 J 4
Devils Marbles Scenic Reserve • AUS 174-175 C 7
Devil's Playground ∴ USA (CA) 248-249 H 4
Devil's Point ▲ BS 54-55 J 3
Devils Postpile National Monument ∴ USA (CA) 248-249 E 2
Devils River ~ USA (TX) 266-267 F 3
Devils Tower Junction o USA (WY) 252-253 O 2
Devils Tower National Monument ∴ USA (WY) 252-253 O 2
Devin o BG 102-103 D 7
Devine o USA (TX) 266-267 J 4
Devipattinam o IND 140-141 H 6
Devli o IND 138-139 E 7
Devlin o CDN (ONT) 234-235 K 6
Devnja o BG 102-103 E 6
Devoll, Lumi ~ AL 100-101 H 4
Devon o CDN (ALB) 232-233 E 2
Devon ∴ GB 90-91 E 6
Devon o USA (MT) 250-251 H 3
Devon o ZA 220-221 J 3
Devon 30 Indian Reserve ⊼ • CDN (NB) 240-241 J 4
Devon Island ⌒ CDN 24-25 b 3
Devonport o AUS 180-181 H 6
Devonshire o AUS 178-179 H 2
Devrek ☆ TR 128-129 D 2
Devure ~ ZW 218-219 F 4
Dewa, Tanjung ▲ RI (ACE) 162-163 A 3
Dewa, Tanjung ▲ RI (KSE) 164-165 E 5
Dewar o USA (OK) 264-265 J 3
Dewās o IND 138-139 F 8
Dewatto o USA (WA) 244-245 C 3
Dewberry o CDN (ALB) 232-233 H 2
Dewdney o CDN (BC) 230-231 G 4
Dewelē o ETH 208-209 F 3
Dewetsdorp o ZA 220-221 H 4
Dewey o USA (AZ) 256-257 C 4
Dewey o USA (SD) 260-261 B 3
Dewey o • USA (PR) 286-287 Q 2
Dewey Lake o USA (KY) 276-277 N 3
Dexing o VRC 156-157 K 2
Dexter o USA (ME) 278-279 M 3
Dexter o USA (MO) 276-277 F 4
Dexter o USA (MS) 268-269 L 5
Dexter o USA (NM) 256-257 L 5
Dexterity Island ⌒ CDN 26-27 O 8
Deyang o VRC 154-155 D 6
Dey-Dey, Lake o AUS 176-177 L 4
Deyhūk o IR 134-135 G 2
Deyyer o IR 134-135 D 5
Dez, Rūd-e ~ IR 134-135 C 2
Dezadeash o CDN 20-21 W 6
Dezadeash Lake o CDN 20-21 W 6
Dezfūl o • IR 134-135 C 2
Dežgān o IR 134-135 F 5
Dežneva, Mys = Dežneva, mys ▲ RUS 112-113 a 3
Dezhou o VRC 154-155 K 3
Dežneva, buhta o RUS 112-113 R 6
Dežneva, mys ▲ RUS 112-113 a 3
Dezong o VRC 144-145 H 4
Dhahran = az-Ẓahrān o KSA 134-135 D 5
Dhahran = Ẓahrān, az- o KSA 134-135 D 5
Dhaka ★ • BD 142-143 G 4
Dhakia o IND 144-145 C 6
Dhaleswari ~ BD 142-143 F 3
Dhanāna o IND 138-139 C 6
Dhanasar o PK 138-139 B 4
Dhanaura o IND 138-139 G 5
Dhanbād o IND 142-143 E 4
Dhandelhura o NEP 144-145 C 6
Dhandhuka o IND 138-139 C 8
Dhangarhi o NEP 144-145 C 6
D'Hanis o USA (TX) 266-267 H 4
Dhankuta o NEP 144-145 F 7
Dhanpuri o IND 142-143 B 4
Dhanushkodi o IND 140-141 H 6
Dhār o IND 138-139 E 8
Dharampur o IND 138-139 D 9
Dharan Bazar o NEP 144-145 F 7
Dhārapuram o IND 140-141 G 5
Dhāri o IND 138-139 C 9
Dhāriwal o IND 138-139 E 4
Dharla ~ BD 142-143 F 3
Dharmapuri o IND 140-141 H 4
Dharmastala o IND 140-141 F 4
Dharmavaram o IND 140-141 G 3
Dharmsala o IND 138-139 F 3
Dhārni o IND 138-139 F 9
Dharwad o IND 140-141 F 3
Dhasān ~ IND 138-139 G 7
Dhaulagiri ▲ NEP 144-145 D 6
Dhaulagiri Himal ▲ NEP 144-145 D 6
Dhauliganga ~ IND 138-139 G 4
Dhaulpur o IND 138-139 F 6
Dhaya o DZ 188-189 L 3
Dhaym-al-Khayl o MA 196-197 D 2
Dhebar Lake o IND 138-139 D 7
Dhekelia Sovereign Base Area (GB) xx CY 128-129 E 5
Dhenkānāl o IND 142-143 D 5
Dhiinsoor o SP 212-213 J 2
Dhing o IND 142-143 H 2
Dhlo Dhlo Ruins ∴ • ZW 218-219 E 4
Dholera o IND 138-139 D 8
Dhone o IND 140-141 G 3
Dhoodi, Bannaanka ∴ SP 208-209 H 4
Dhorpatan o NEP 144-145 D 6
Dhrāngadhra o IND 138-139 C 8
Dhubbato o SP 208-209 G 4
Dhuburi o IND 142-143 F 2
Dhud, togga ~ SP 208-209 J 3
Dhule o IND 138-139 E 9
Dhulian o BD 142-143 F 3
Dhull o IND 138-139 D 3
Dhunat o BD 142-143 F 3
Dhunche o NEP 144-145 E 6
Dhūndār ∴ IND 138-139 E 7
Dhurbo o SP 208-209 K 3
Dhuudo o SP 208-209 K 4
Dhuudo, togga ~ SP 208-209 K 4
Dhuusa Mareeb ☆ SP 208-209 H 6
Di o BF 202-203 J 3
Dia o LB 202-203 E 6
Diaba < RMM 196-197 H 6
Diabakania o RG 202-203 E 4
Diabali o RMM 202-203 G 2
Diable, Île du ⌒ F 62-63 H 3
Diablo, Punta del ▲ ROU 74-75 D 10
Diablo Range ▲ USA (CA) 248-249 C 2
Diablotins, Morne ▲ WD 56 E 4
Diabo o BF 202-203 K 3
Diabo, Caverna do • BR 74-75 F 5
Diabugu o WAG 202-203 C 3
Diaca o MOC 214-215 K 6
Diadema o BR 72-73 G 7
Diadi o RP 160-161 D 4
Diadioumbéra o RMM 202-203 E 2
Diafarabé o RMM 202-203 H 2
Diaka ~ RMM 202-203 H 2
Diakon o RMM 202-203 E 2
Dialafara o RMM 202-203 E 3
Dialakoto o SN 202-203 D 3
Diallassagou o RMM 202-203 J 3
Dialloubé o RMM 202-203 H 2
Diamante o RA 78-79 J 2
Diamante, Pampa del ∴ RA 78-79 E 3
Diamante, Río ~ RA 78-79 F 3
Diamante, Río ~ RA 78-79 E 3
Diamantina o • BR 72-73 J 5
Diamantina, Chapada da ▲ BR 68-69 H 7
Diamantina Development Road II AUS 178-179 E 2
Diamantina Fracture Zone ≃ 12 J 8
Diamantina Lakes o AUS 178-179 F 2
Diamantina River ~ AUS 178-179 E 3
Diamantino o BR (MAT) 70-71 J 4
Diamantino o BR (MAT) 72-73 D 4
Diamantino, Rio ~ BR 72-73 D 4
Diamarakro o CI 202-203 J 6
Diamare ∴ CAM 206-207 B 3
Diambala o RCB 210-211 E 4
Diamond Area Restricted xx NAM 220-221 B 3
Diamond Cave • USA (AR) 276-277 B 5
Diamond Diggings • ZA 220-221 F 4
Diamond Islands ⌒ CDN 36-37 M 2
Diamond Jennes Peninsula ⌣ CDN 24-25 N 5
Diamond Lake o USA (OR) 244-245 C 7
Diamond Peak ▲ USA (NV) 246-247 K 4
Diamondville o USA (WY) 252-253 H 5
Diamou o RMM 202-203 E 2
Diamounguél o SN 202-203 D 2
Diana o SN 202-203 D 3
Diana Bay ≈ 36-37 P 4
Dianbai o VRC 156-157 G 6
Dianbé o RMM 202-203 H 2
Diancang Shan ▲ VRC 142-143 M 3
Dian Chi o VRC 156-157 C 4
Dianda, Kabondo- o ZRE 214-215 C 5
Diandian o RG 202-203 D 4
Diandioumé o RMM 202-203 F 2
Diangouté Kamara o RMM 202-203 F 2
Dianké Makam o SN 202-203 D 3
Dianópolis o BR 68-69 E 7
Dianra o CI 202-203 G 5
Diapaga o BF 202-203 L 3
Diaramana o RMM 202-203 H 3
Dias o MOC 218-219 H 1
Diassa = Madina o RMM 202-203 G 4
Diatas, Danau o RI 162-163 D 5
Diavlos Zakinthou ≈ 100-101 H 6
Diawala o CI 202-203 H 4
Díaz Ordaz o MEX 50-51 C 4
Diaz Point ▲ • NAM 220-221 B 3
Dibā o UAE 134-135 G 6
Dibage o IRQ 128-129 K 5
Ḍibān o JOR 130-131 D 2
Dibaru, Danau o RI 162-163 D 5
Dibaya o ZRE 214-215 B 4
Dibaya-Lubue o ZRE 210-211 G 6
Dibble Ice Tongue ⊂ ARK 16 G 14
Dib Dabiib < SP 212-213 J 2
Dibdiba, ad- ▲ KSA 130-131 K 3
Dibella < RN 198-199 F 4
Dibeng o ZA 220-221 F 3
Dibia o WAL 202-203 E 6
Di Bin o Y 132-133 D 6
Ḍī Bin ∴ • Y 132-133 D 5
Dibin, ad- o Y 132-133 G 5
Dibiri Island ⌒ PNG 183 B 5
Dibni o NEP 144-145 D 6
Diboll o USA (TX) 268-269 F 5
Dibombari o CAM 204-205 H 6
Dibrugarh o IND 142-143 J 2
Dibs o SUD 200-201 B 6
Dibs, Bi'r < ET 194-195 D 6
Dick, Mount ▲ AUS 174-175 H 7
Dickens o USA (TX) 264-265 D 5
Dickey o USA (ND) 258-259 J 5
Dickeyville o USA (WI) 274-275 H 2
Dickinson o USA (ND) 258-259 E 5
Dickinson o USA (TX) 268-269 E 7
Dicks Creek Gap ▲ USA (GA) 284-285 G 2
Dickson o USA (AK) 20-21 H 4
Dickson o USA (TN) 276-277 H 4
Dickson Land ∴ N 84-85 J 3
Dickson Mounds Museum • USA (IL) 274-275 H 4
Dicle Nehri ~ TR 128-129 J 3
Dicle Nehri ~ TR 128-129 J 4
Dico Leopoldino o BR 68-69 H 4
Dida Galgalu Desert ∴ EAK 212-213 G 2
Didah o KSA 130-131 H 4
Didēsa Wenz ~ ETH 208-209 B 4
Didiéni o RMM 202-203 F 3
Didiévi o CI 202-203 H 6
Didig Sala o ETH 200-201 K 6
Didimótiho o GR 100-101 L 4
Didsbury o CDN (ALB) 232-233 D 4
Didwāna o IND 138-139 E 6
Didy o RM 222-223 F 7
Didyma ∴ • TR 128-129 B 4
Didyr o BF 202-203 J 3
Die Bos o ZA 220-221 D 5
Diébougou o BF 202-203 J 4
Dieciocho de Marco o MEX 50-51 L 5
Dieciocho de Marzo o MEX 52-53 J 2
Diecké o RG 202-203 F 6
Diefenbaker, Lake o CDN (SAS) 232-233 L 5
Diego de Almagro o RCH 76-77 B 4
Diego de Almagro, Isla ⌒ RCH 80 C 5
Diego de Alvear o RA 78-79 H 3
Diego Garcia, Archipelago ⌒ GB 12 F 5
Diego Lamas o ROU 76-77 J 6
Diégo Suarez = Antsiranana ☆ RM 222-223 F 4
Diéli o RMM 202-203 H 3
Diéma o RMM 202-203 F 2
Diemals o AUS 176-177 E 4
Diemansputs o ZA 220-221 E 4
Điên Biên ☆ • VN 156-157 C 6
Diễn Châu ☆ VN 156-157 D 7
Dieng Plateau • RI 168 C 3
Diên Khánh o VN 158-159 K 4
Dienné o • RMM 202-203 H 3
Diepholz o D 92-93 K 2
Dieppe o • F 90-91 H 7
Dierks o USA (AR) 276-277 A 6
Dieterich o USA (IL) 274-275 K 5
Dietrich o USA (ID) 252-253 D 4
Die Venster ▲ ZA 220-221 D 6
Dif o EAK 212-213 H 3
Diffa ◘ RN 198-199 F 4
Diffa ☆ RN (DIF) 198-199 F 6
Difounda o G 210-211 C 5
Difuma o ZRE 210-211 K 5
Dig o IND 138-139 F 6
Digba o ZRE 206-207 G 6
Digboi o IND 142-143 J 2
Digby o CDN (NS) 240-241 K 6
Digges o CDN 30-31 W 6
Digges Islands ⌒ CDN 36-37 K 3
Digges Sound ⌒ CDN 36-37 K 3
Dighanchi o IND 140-141 F 2
Dighton o USA (KS) 262-263 F 6
Diğla ~ IRQ 128-129 M 6
Diglūr o IND 138-139 F 10
Digne-les-Bains o • F 90-91 L 9
Digoin o F 90-91 K 8
Digor ☆ TR 128-129 K 2
Digora o RUS 126-127 F 6
Digos ☆ RP 160-161 F 9
Digri o PK 138-139 B 7
Digsa • ER 200-201 J 5
Digua o RCH 78-79 D 4
Digue Island, La ⌒ SY 224 D 2
Diguillín, Río ~ RCH 78-79 D 4
Digul ~ RI 166-167 L 5
Digya National Park ⊥ GH 202-203 K 6
Dihang or Siang ~ IND 142-143 J 1
Diibao o CAM 206-207 B 4
Dijar o KA 126-127 M 4
Dijmphna Sund ≈ 26-27 p 4
Dijon ☆ • F 90-91 K 8
Dijon ~ RG 202-203 F 5
Dijur o RUS 88-89 W 4
Dik o TCH 206-207 C 4
Dika, mys ▲ RUS 108-109 k 3
Dikāka, ad- ∴ KSA 132-133 G 4
Dikanās o S 86-87 G 4
Dikhil o DJI 208-209 F 3
Dikhu ~ IND 142-143 J 2
Dikili ☆ TR 128-129 B 3
Dikimdja o RUS 118-119 K 6
Dikimis o ET 194-195 E 2
Dikodougou o CI 202-203 H 5
Dikson ☆ RUS 108-109 T 5
Dikson, ostrov ⌒ RUS 108-109 T 5
Dikulwe ~ ZRE 214-215 D 6
Dikwa o WAN 198-199 F 6
Ḍila o AFG 138-139 B 3
Dila o ETH 208-209 D 5
Dilam, ad- o KSA 130-131 K 6
Dilezi Geçidi ▲ TR 128-129 L 4
Dili ☆ RI 166-167 C 6
Dili o ZRE 210-211 L 2
Dilia ~ RN 198-199 F 5
Dilia o USA (NM) 256-257 K 3
Di Linh o • VN 158-159 K 5
Diližan o AR 128-129 L 2
Diližanskij zapovednik ⊥ AR 128-129 L 2
Dilj ▲ HR 100-101 F 2
Dilke o CDN (SAS) 232-233 N 5
Dilkon o USA (AZ) 256-257 E 3
Dilley o USA (TX) 266-267 H 5
Dilli o RMM 202-203 G 2
Dillikot o NEP 144-145 C 6
Dilling o SUD 200-201 D 6
Dillingham o USA 22-23 R 3
Dillon o USA (CO) 254-255 J 4
Dillon o USA (MT) 250-251 G 6
Dillon o USA (SC) 284-285 L 2
Dillon Lake o USA (OH) 280-281 E 3
Dillon River ~ CDN 32-33 P 4
Dillsboro o USA (IN) 274-275 N 5
Dillsburg o USA (PA) 280-281 J 3
Dilo = Djidji ~ G 210-211 D 4
Dilolo o ZRE 214-215 B 6
Dilts Historic Site, Fort ∴ USA (ND) 258-259 D 5
Dima o ETH 208-209 D 3
Dimako o CAM 204-205 K 6
Dimalla < RIM 196-197 E 6
Dimāpur o IND 142-143 H 3
Dimašq ★ • SYR 128-129 G 6
Dimbaza o ZA 220-221 H 6
Dimbelenge o ZRE 210-211 J 6
Dimbokro ☆ CI 202-203 H 6
Dimboola o AUS 180-181 G 4
Dimbulah o AUS 174-175 H 5
Dimissi o PNG 183 B 5
Dimitrievka o RUS 94-95 R 5
Dimitrovgrad o BG 102-103 D 6
Dimitrovgrad ☆ RUS 96-97 F 6
Dimitrovgrad o • YU 100-101 J 3
Dimlang ▲ WAN 204-205 J 4
Dimlao o RP 160-161 F 8
Dimlik ~ TCH 206-207 C 4
Dimma Lake o CDN 30-31 T 5
Dimmitt o USA (TX) 264-265 B 4
Dimona ☆ IL 130-131 D 2
Dimora o AUS 178-179 G 1
Dimovo o BG 102-103 C 6
Dimpam o CAM 210-211 D 2
Dina o PK 138-139 D 3
Dinagat o RP 160-161 F 8
Dinagat Island ⌒ RP 160-161 F 7
Dinajpur o BD 142-143 F 3
Dinalongan o RP 160-161 D 4
Dinan o • F 90-91 F 7
Dinangourou o RMM 202-203 J 2
Dinant o • B 92-93 H 3
Dinapigui o RP 160-161 E 4
Dinar ☆ TR 128-129 D 3
Dinār, Kūh-e ▲ IR 134-135 D 3
Dinara ▲ YU 100-101 F 2
Dinchiya Shet' ~ ETH 208-209 C 5
Dindar ~ SUD 200-201 F 6
Dindar National Park ⊥ SUD 200-201 G 6
Dinder Wenz ~ ETH 208-209 B 3
Dindi o ZW 218-219 G 3
Dindigul o IND 140-141 G 5
Dindima o WAN 204-205 J 3
Dindori o IND 142-143 B 4
Dindoudi Séydi o SN 202-203 D 2
Dinga o PK 138-139 D 3
Dinga o ZRE 210-211 F 6
Dingalan Bay ≈ 160-161 D 5
Ding'an o VRC 156-157 D 4
Dingbian o VRC 154-155 E 3
Ding Ding o SUD 206-207 L 4
Dinge o ANG 216-217 B 7
Dinggye o VRC 144-145 F 6
Dinghushan • VRC 156-157 H 5
Dinghushan Z.B. ⊥ • VRC 156-157 H 5
Dingila o ZRE 210-211 L 2
Dingjie o VRC 144-145 G 6
Dingle = An Daingean o IRL 90-91 B 5
Dingle Bay ≈ 90-91 B 5
Dingley Dell Cons. P. • AUS 180-181 F 5
Dingnan o VRC 156-157 J 4
Dingo o ANG 216-217 F 8
Dingo o AUS 178-179 K 2
Dingtao o VRC 154-155 J 4
Dinguirayé o RG 202-203 E 4
Dingwall o CDN (NS) 240-241 P 4
Dingwall o GB 90-91 E 3
Dingwells Mills o CDN (NS) 240-241 N 4
Dingxi o VRC 154-155 D 4
Dingxiang o VRC 154-155 H 2
Dingyuan o VRC 154-155 K 5
Dingzhou o VRC 154-155 J 2
Dingzikou o VRC 146-147 L 6
Dinhata o IND 142-143 F 2
Đinh Lap ☆ VN 156-157 E 6
Dinnebito Wash ~ USA (AZ) 256-257 E 2
Dinnik, Plateau de ▲ RN 204-205 E 1
Dinokwe o RB 218-219 D 6
Dinorwic o CDN (ONT) 234-235 L 5
Dinosaur o USA (CO) 254-255 G 3
Dinosaur National Monument ∴ USA (CO) 254-255 G 3
Dinosaur Provincial Park ⊥ • CDN (ALB) 232-233 G 5
Dinosaurusspore • NAM 216-217 D 10
Dinsmore o CDN (SAS) 232-233 L 4
Dintiteladas o RI 162-163 F 7
Dinuba o USA (CA) 248-249 E 3
d'In Ziza, Gueltas < DZ 190-191 D 9
Dioila o RMM 202-203 G 3
Diokana o TCH 198-199 H 6
Diomandou o RG 202-203 F 5
Diona o BF 202-203 J 4
Diona < TCH 198-199 L 4
Diongoï o RMM 202-203 F 2
Dionisio o BR 72-73 J 5
Dionisio Cerqueira o BR 74-75 D 6
Dionouga o BF 202-203 K 2
Diorama o BR 72-73 E 4
Dios, Canal de < RA 76-77 F 3
Diosso o RCB 210-211 C 6
Diou o F 90-91 J 8
Dioulatiédougou o CI 202-203 G 5
Dioulouiou o SN 202-203 B 3
Dioumara o RMM 202-203 F 2
Dioundiou o RN 204-205 E 2
Dioura o RMM 202-203 H 2
Diourbel ☆ • SN 202-203 B 2
Diourou o RMM 202-203 H 3
Dipālpur o PK 138-139 D 4
Dipchari o WAN 204-205 K 3
Diphu o IND 142-143 H 3
Dipkun o RUS 118-119 N 8
Diplo o PK 138-139 B 7
Dipolog ☆ RP 160-161 E 8
Dippa ~ RUS 118-119 K 3
Dipper Lake o CDN 34-35 C 3
Dipperu National Park ⊥ AUS 178-179 K 1
Ḍī Qār ◘ IRQ 128-129 M 7

Del'kju-Ohotskaja — Ḍī Qār 321

Diqdāqa o **UAE** 134-135 F 6
Dira < **TCH** 198-199 G 5
Dirat at-Tulūl o **SYR** 128-129 G 6
Dire o **IRQ** 128-129 L 4
Diré o **RMM** 196-197 J 6
Direction, Cape ▲ **AUS** 174-175 G 3
Dirê Dawa o **ETH** 208-209 E 4
Dirgi Shabozai o **PK** 138-139 B 4
Diriamba o **NIC** 52-53 L 6
Dirico o **ANG** 216-217 F 8
Dir'iya, ad- o **KSA** (QAS) 130-131 K 5
Dir'iya, ad- • **KSA** (RIY) 130-131 K 5
Dirk Hartog Island ∩ **AUS** 176-177 B 2
Dirkou o **RN** 198-199 F 3
Dirrah o **SUD** 200-201 C 6
Dirranbandi o **AUS** 178-179 K 5
Dirty Devil River ~ **USA** (UT) 254-255 E 5
Disa o **IND** 138-139 D 7
Disang ~ **IND** 142-143 J 2
Disappointment, Cape ▲ **GB** 78-79 O 7
Disappointment, Cape ▲ **USA** (WA) 244-245 A 4
Disappointment, Lake o **AUS** 176-177 G 1
Disautel o **USA** (WA) 244-245 F 2
Discovery, Cape ▲ **CDN** 26-27 M 2
Discovery Bay ≈ 180-181 H 4
Discovery Bay ≈ **USA** (WA) 244-245 C 3
Discovery Reef = Huaguang Jiao ∩ **VRC** 158-159 L 2
Discovery Seamounts ≅ 6-7 K 13
Dishkakat o **USA** 20-21 M 5
Dishna River ~ **USA** 20-21 M 5
Disko Banke ≈ 28-29 M 2
Disko Fjord ≈ 28-29 N 2
Disko Ø ~ **GRØ** 28-29 N 2
Diskofjord = Kangerluk o **GRØ** 28-29 N 2
Disley o **CDN** (SAS) 232-233 N 5
Dismal Creek ~ **CDN** (ALB) 232-233 B 2
Dismal Lakes o **CDN** 30-31 L 2
Dišnä o **ET** 194-195 E 2
Disney o **AUS** 178-179 J 1
Disneyland •• **USA** (CA) 248-249 G 6
Disney World, Walt • **USA** (FL) 286-287 H 3
Dispur o **IND** 142-143 G 2
Disputada, La o **RCH** 78-79 D 2
Disraeli o **CDN** (QUE) 238-239 O 3
Disraeli Fiord ≈ 26-27 O 2
Diss o **GB** 90-91 H 5
Dissain, Ğazirat ∩ **KSA** 132-133 B 5
Disteghil Sar ▲ **IND** 138-139 F 1
District of Columbia = D.C., Washington □ **USA** (DC) 280-281 J 5
Disûq o **ET** 194-195 E 2
Ditang o **VRC** 156-157 F 2
Ditinn o **RG** 202-203 D 4
Ditsinane o **RB** 218-219 C 5
Ditu, Mwene- o **ZRE** 214-215 D 4
Diu o **IND** 138-139 C 9
Divândarre o **IR** 128-129 M 5
Divénié o **RCB** 210-211 D 5
Diverson Lake ~ **USA** (TX) 264-265 F 5
Divide o **CDN** (SAS) 232-233 J 6
Divide o **USA** (CO) 254-255 K 5
Divide o **USA** (MT) 250-251 G 6
Divilican o **RP** 160-161 E 4
Divilican Bay ≈ **RP** 160-161 E 4
Divinhe o **MOC** 218-219 H 5
Divinolândia de Minas o **BR** 72-73 J 5
Divinópolis o **BR** 72-73 K 3
Divisa o **PA** 52-53 D 7
Divisadero, El o **MEX** 50-51 G 5
Divisões ou de Santa Marta, Serra das ▲ **BR** 72-73 D 4
Divisópolis o **BR** 72-73 K 3
Divisor, Serra de ▲ **BR** 64-65 F 5
Divisoria o **RP** 160-161 F 7
Divisorio, El o **RA** 78-79 H 3
Divnogorsk o **RUS** 116-117 F 8
Divo o **CI** 202-203 H 7
Divor, Ribeira do ~ **P** 98-99 C 5
Divot o **USA** (TX) 266-267 H 5
Diwiğî o **TR** 128-129 H 3
Diwma o **ZRE** 214-215 B 6
Diwâniya, ad- = ad-Dīwānīyah o **IRQ** 128-129 L 7
Diwopu J. II **VRC** 146-147 H 4
Diwouni, Mare o **DY** 202-203 L 4
Dixcove o **GH** 202-203 K 7
Dixfield o **USA** (ME) 278-279 L 4
Dixianšenlin • **VRC** 150-151 G 5
Dixie o **USA** (ID) 250-251 D 6
Dixie o **USA** (WA) 244-245 G 4
Dixie Valley o **USA** (NV) 246-247 G 4
Dix-Milles, Lac o **CDN** (QUE) 238-239 H 2
Dixmont o **USA** (ME) 278-279 M 4
Dixon o **USA** (CA) 246-247 D 5
Dixon o **USA** (IL) 274-275 J 3
Dixon o **USA** (KY) 276-277 C 3
Dixon o **USA** (MO) 276-277 D 2
Dixon o **USA** (MS) 268-269 L 4
Dixon o **USA** (MT) 250-251 E 4
Dixon o **USA** (WY) 252-253 L 5
Dixon Entrance ≈ 32-33 D 4
Dixon Entrance o **CDN** 228-229 D 4
Dixonville o **RA** 78-79 G 3
Diyadin ☆ **TR** 128-129 K 3
Diyālā □ **IRQ** 128-129 L 6
Diyarbakır o- **TR** 128-129 J 4
Dize o **IR** 128-129 L 4
Dizhipoumian J. • **VRC** 154-155 K 1
Dja ~ **CAM** 210-211 D 4
Dja Reserve = Réserve du Dja ⊥••• **CAM** 210-211 D 4
Djado o **RN** 198-199 F 2
Djado, Plateau du ▲ **RN** 198-199 F 1
Djakarta = Jakarta ☆ **RI** 168 B 3
Djakotomè o **DY** 202-203 L 6
Djalasiga o **ZRE** 212-213 C 2
Djale ~ **ZRE** 210-211 J 5
Djalon, Fouta ▲ **RG** 202-203 D 4

Djaluwon Creek ~ **AUS** 172-173 H 6
Djamâa o **DZ** 190-191 E 4
Djamandjary o **RM** 222-223 F 4
Djamba o **ZRE** (HAU) 210-211 K 2
Djamba o **ZRE** (SHA) 214-215 B 5
Djambala o **RCB** 210-211 D 5
Djampiel o **CAM** 206-207 B 6
Djanet ☆ **DZ** 190-191 G 8
Djangylah, ostrov ∩ **RUS** 110-111 N 3
Djanyška o **RUS** 110-111 Q 7
Djara ~ **RUS** 110-111 T 5
Djaret, Oued ~ **DZ** 190-191 C 7
Djarua ~ **RUS** 94-95 O 5
Djat'kovo o **RUS** 94-95 O 5
Djeboho ▲ **DZ** 190-191 E 4
Djébrène o **TCH** 206-207 D 3
Djédaa o **TCH** 198-199 J 6
Djeddars o **DZ** 190-191 D 3
Djedi, Oued ~ **DZ** 190-191 E 4
Djedid, Bir < **DZ** 190-191 F 4
Djelfa ☆ **DZ** 190-191 D 3
Djéma o **RCA** 206-207 H 6
Djemadja, Pulau ∩ **RI** 162-163 F 3
Djember o **TCH** 206-207 C 3
Djems Bank ≈ 162-163 K 3
Djerem ~ **CAM** 204-205 K 6
Djérem o **CAM** 204-205 K 5
Djermaya o **TCH** 198-199 G 6
Djibasso o **BF** 202-203 H 3
Djibo o **BF** 202-203 J 3
Djiborosso o **CI** 202-203 G 5
Djibouti ■ **DJI** 208-209 F 3
Djibouti ☆ **DJI** 208-209 F 3
Djidja o **DY** 202-203 L 6
Djidji = Dilo ~ **G** 210-211 D 4
Djigoué o **BF** 202-203 J 4
Djigouéra o **BF** 202-203 H 4
Djiguéni o **RIM** 196-197 F 7
Djilbe o **CAM** 204-205 M 4
Djillali Ben Amar o **DZ** 190-191 C 3
Djiroutou o **CI** 202-203 G 7
Djohong o **CAM** 206-207 B 5
Djoku-Punda o **ZRE** 210-211 H 6
Djolu o **ZRE** 210-211 J 3
Djombo o **ZRE** 210-211 H 3
Djombo = Haraz o **TCH** 198-199 J 6
Djombo Kibbit o **TCH** 198-199 J 6
Djona, Zone Cynégétique de ⊥ **DY** 204-205 K 5
Djonâba o **RIM** 196-197 D 6
Djorf Torba o **DZ** 188-189 K 5
Djorf-Torba, Barrage < **DZ** 188-189 K 5
Djoua ~ **G** 210-211 E 3
Djoubissi o **RCA** 206-207 E 5
Djoudj, Parc National des oiseaux du ⊥••• **SN** 196-197 B 6
Djoué o **RCB** 210-211 D 5
Djougou o **DY** 202-203 L 5
Djoûk, Passe de ▲ **RIM** 196-197 D 6
Djoum o **CAM** 204-205 K 6
Djoumbouli o **CAM** 204-205 K 5
Djourab, Erg du ▲ **TCH** 198-199 H 4
Djoutou-Pétel o **RG** 202-203 D 4
Djugadjak ~ **RUS** 112-113 K 4
Djugu o **ZRE** 212-213 C 3
Djuiljukju o **RUS** 118-119 G 7
Djukta, gora ▲ **RUS** 126-127 G 7
Djúpivogur o **IS** 86-87 J 2
Djupkun, ozero o **RUS** (EVN) 108-109 c 7
Djupkun, ozero o **RUS** (EVN) 116-117 F 2
Djura, Kytyl- o **RUS** 118-119 M 5
Djurdjura, Djebel ▲ **DZ** 190-191 G 2
Djurtjuli o **RUS** 96-97 J 6
D'kar o **RB** 216-217 F 10
Dla ~ **RMM** 202-203 F 5
Dlinnyj, ostrov ∩ **RUS** 108-109 Y 2
Dlolwana o **ZA** 220-221 K 4
Dmitrievka o **KA** 124-125 J 5
Dmitriev-L'govskij o **RUS** 94-95 O 5
Dmitrija Lapteva, proliv ≈ 110-111 W 3
Dmitrov ☆ **RUS** 94-95 P 3
Dmytrivka o **UA** 102-103 J 4
Dnepr ~ **RUS** 94-95 N 5
Dneprodzeržinsk = Dniprodzeržyns'k o **UA** 102-103 J 3
Dnepropetrovsk = Dnipropetrovs'k ☆ **UA** 102-103 J 3
Dnestr = Dnister ~ **UA** 102-103 F 4
Dnestr = Nistru ~ **MD** 102-103 F 4
Dnipro ~ **UA** 102-103 G 2
Dnipro ~ **UA** 102-103 G 2
Dniprodzeržyns'k o **UA** 102-103 J 3
Dniprodzeržyns'k = Dniprodzeržyns'k o **UA** 102-103 J 3
Dnipropetrovs'k ☆ **UA** 102-103 J 3
Dniprovs'kyj lyman ≈ **UA** 102-103 G 4
Dniprovs'kyj lyman ≈ **UA** 102-103 H 4
Dnister = Dnister ~ **UA** 102-103 G 4
Dnistrovs'kyj lyman ≈ **UA** 102-103 G 4
Dnjapro ~ **BY** 94-95 M 5
Dnjaprovska-Buhski, Kanal < **BY** 94-95 J 5
Dno o **RUS** 94-95 L 3
Doa o **MOC** 218-219 H 3
Doäba o **PK** 138-139 C 4
Doaktown o **CDN** (NB) 240-241 J 4
Doang-Doangan Besar, Pulau ∩ **RI** 164-165 G 6
Doany o **RM** 222-223 F 5
Doba ☆ **TCH** 206-207 C 4
Dobaninnsuk ~ **RUS** 154-155 K 1
Dobbiaco = Toblach o **I** 100-101 D 1
Dobbin o **USA** (TX) 268-269 E 6
Dobbin Bay ≈ 26-27 N 4
Dobbs, Cape ▲ **CDN** 36-37 T 6
Dobbspelt o **IND** 140-141 G 4
Dobbyn o **AUS** 174-175 F 6
Dobele o **LV** 94-95 H 3
Doberai Peninsula ∩ **RI** 166-167 H 4

Dobie River ~ **CDN** (ONT) 234-235 N 3
Dobinga o **CAM** 204-205 K 4
Doblas o **RA** 78-79 G 4
Dobo o •• **IND** 166-167 H 4
Doboj o **BIH** 100-101 H 3
Doboy Sound ≈ **USA** 284-285 J 5
Dobre Miasto o **PL** 92-93 Q 2
Dobrič = Dobrič o **BG** 102-103 E 6
Dobrinka o **RUS** 94-95 R 5
Dobrjanka ☆ **RUS** 96-97 K 4
Dobromyl' o **UA** 102-103 C 3
Dobron' o **UA** 102-103 C 3
Dobroteşti o **RO** 102-103 D 5
Dobruč o **RUS** 94-95 L 3
Dobruš o **BY** 94-95 M 5
Dobrzańskogo, ostrov ∩ **RUS** 112-113 E 2
Dobzha o **VRC** 144-145 G 4
Docas, Cachoeira das ~ **BR** 72-73 J 1
Doc Can Island ∩ **RP** 160-161 C 10
Doce, Rio ~ **BR** 72-73 K 5
Doce, Rio ~ **BR** 72-73 E 4
Dochigam National Park ⊥ **IND** 138-139 E 2
Docker River X **AUS** (NT) 176-177 K 2
Docker River ~ **AUS** 176-177 K 2
Docking o **GB** 90-91 H 5
Dock Junction o **USA** (GA) 284-285 J 5
Dockrell, Mount ▲ **AUS** 172-173 H 5
Dockyard, The ~ **AG** 56 E 3
Doctor Arroyo o **MEX** 50-51 J 5
Doctor González o **MEX** 50-51 K 5
Doctor Mora o **MEX** 50-51 J 7
Doctor Pedro P. Peña o **PY** 76-77 J 2
Doda o **EAT** 212-213 G 6
Doda o **RI** 164-165 G 4
Dodaga o **RI** 164-165 L 3
Dod Ballapur o **IND** 140-141 G 4
Dodecanese = Dodekanisa ∩ **GR** 100-101 L 6
Dodge o **USA** (ND) 258-259 E 4
Dodge Center o **USA** (MN) 270-271 F 4
Dodge City • **USA** (KS) 262-263 F 7
Dodge Lake o **CDN** 30-31 R 6
Dodge River ~ **CDN** (SAS) 30-31 S 6
Dodinga o **RI** 164-165 K 3
Dodji o **SN** 202-203 C 2
Dodola o **ETH** 208-209 D 5
Dodoma ★ **EAT** 212-213 G 6
Dodori o **EAK** 212-213 H 4
Dodori National Reserve ⊥ **EAK** 212-213 H 4
Dodowa o **GH** 202-203 K 7
Dodsland o **CDN** (SAS) 232-233 K 4
Dodson o **USA** (LA) 268-269 H 4
Dodson o **USA** (TX) 264-265 D 4
Dodson Peninsula ∩ **ARK** 16 F 30
Doege o **ANG** 216-217 E 4
Doembang Nangbuat o **THA** 158-159 F 3
Doerun o **USA** (GA) 284-285 G 5
Dofa o **RI** 164-165 J 4
Dôgā'i o **IR** 136-137 H 6
Dogai Coring o **VRC** 144-145 G 3
Dogal'dyn ~ **RUS** 108-109 a 7
Doğansehir o **TR** 128-129 G 3
Doğansu o **TR** 128-129 K 3
Dogbo-Tota o **DY** 202-203 L 6
Dogdo ~ **RUS** 110-111 Y 5
Dog Island ∩ **USA** (FL) 286-287 E 2
Dog Lake o **CDN** (MAN) 234-235 E 4
Dog Lake o **CDN** (ONT) 234-235 O 6
Dog Lake o **CDN** (ONT) 236-237 O 4
Dôgo o **J** 152-153 E 6
Dôgo ~ **RMM** 202-203 G 4
Dogo o **RMM** 202-203 G 4
Dogoba o **SUD** 206-207 J 5
Dö Gonbadân o **IR** 134-135 D 3
Dogondoutchi o **RN** 198-199 D 6
Dogoumbo o **TCH** 206-207 C 3
Dôgo-yama ▲ **J** 152-153 E 7
Dogpatch U.S.A. • **USA** 276-277 D 4
Dogratch Creek ~ **CDN** (ALB) 232-233 H 4
Dog Salmon River ~ **USA** 22-23 S 4
Doğubayazıt ☆ **TR** 128-129 L 3
Dogwal o **WAN** 204-205 H 4
Dogwood Creek ~ **AUS** 178-179 K 4
Dogyaling o **VRC** 144-145 G 5
Dogyolo o **RUS** 114-115 U 4
Doha = ad-Dauha ★ **Q** 134-135 D 6
Doha = Dauha, ad- ★ **Q** 134-135 D 6
Doi ~ **RI** 164-165 K 2
Doigan o **EAK** 212-213 F 3
Doig River ~ **CDN** 32-33 K 3
Doi Inthanon ▲ **THA** 142-143 L 6
Doi Inthanon National Park ⊥ **THA** 142-143 L 6
Dois Corregos o **BR** 72-73 F 7
Dois de Novembro, Cachoeira ~ **BR** 66-67 F 7
Dois Irmãos ▲ **BR** 72-73 F 3
Dois Irmãos, Cachoeira ~ **BR** 66-67 H 7
Dois Riachos, Rio ~ **BR** 68-69 K 6
Doi Suthep-Poi National Park ⊥ **THA** 142-143 L 6
Dois Vizinhos o **BR** 74-75 D 5
Doi Tachi ▲ **THA** 158-159 E 2
Doka o **RI** 166-167 H 5
Doka o **SUD** 200-201 G 5
Dokhara, Dunes de ▲ **DZ** 190-191 E 4
Dokis Indian Reserve X **CDN** (ONT) 238-239 F 2
Doko o **RG** 202-203 F 4
Doko o **WAN** 198-199 D 6
Dokpam o **GH** 202-203 K 5

Doktorskij, mys ▲ **RUS** 110-111 Q 3
Dokučaevs'k o **UA** 102-103 K 4
Dokui o **SME** 62-63 F 3
Dolak, Pulau ∩ **RI** 166-167 K 5
Dolak Pulau Reserve ⊥ **RI** 166-167 J 5
Doland o **USA** (SD) 260-261 H 2
Dolan Springs o **USA** (AZ) 256-257 A 3
Dolavon o **RA** 78-79 G 2
Dolbeau o **RN** 202-203 L 2
Dolby Lake o **CDN** 30-31 R 5
Dole o **F** 90-91 K 8
Doleib Hill o **SUD** 108-109 H 7
Dolenci o **MK** 100-101 H 4
Dolgellau o **GB** 90-91 F 5
Dolgi, ostrov ∩ **RUS** 108-109 H 7
Dolgi, ostrov ∩ **RUS** (NAO) 88-89 X 2
Dolgij Most o **RUS** 116-117 H 7
Dolgoderevenskoe o **RUS** 96-97 M 6
Dolgoi Island ∩ **USA** 22-23 Q 5
Dolia ~ **IND** 138-139 C 8
Dolina gejzerov ~ **RUS** 120-121 S 6
Dolinka o **KS** 146-147 J 5
Dolinsk o **RUS** 122-123 K 5
Dolit ~ **RI** 164-165 K 4
Dolleman Island ∩ **ARK** 16 F 30
Dollo Odo o **ETH** 208-209 E 5
Dolni Lom o **BG** 102-103 C 6
Dolný Kubín o **SK** 92-93 P 4
Dolo o **RI** 164-165 J 4
Dolokmerawan o **RI** 162-163 C 3
Dolok Pinapan ▲ **RI** 162-163 C 3
Dolong o **RI** 164-165 H 4
Dolores o **CO** 60-61 D 5
Dolores o **GCA** 52-53 K 3
Dolores o **RA** 78-79 J 4
Dolores o **ROU** 78-79 J 4
Dolores o **RP** 160-161 F 6
Dolores o **USA** (CO) 254-255 G 6
Dolores Hidalgo o **MEX** 50-51 J 7
Dolores River ~ **USA** (CO) 254-255 G 5
Doloroso o **USA** (MS) 268-269 J 5
Dolphin, Cape ▲ **USA** 180-181 J 8
Dolphin and Union Strait ≈ 24-25 O 6
Dolyna o **UA** 102-103 H 3
Dolyns'ka o **UA** 102-103 H 3
Dom, Gunung ▲ **RI** 166-167 J 4
Doma o **ZW** 218-219 F 3
Domain o **CDN** (MAN) 234-235 F 5
Domaine de chasse d'Iguéla ⊥ **G** 210-211 B 5
Dom Aquino o **BR** 70-71 K 4
Domar o **VRC** 144-145 C 4
Doma Safari Area ⊥ **ZW** 218-219 F 3
Domažlice o **CZ** 92-93 M 4
Dombaj Ufgen, gora ▲ **RUS** 126-127 D 6
Dombarovskij o **RUS** 126-127 N 2
Dombás o **N** 86-87 D 5
Dombe o **ANG** 216-217 B 6
Dombe Grande o **ANG** 216-217 B 6
Dombey, Cape ▲ **AUS** 180-181 J 4
Dombo o **RI** 166-167 J 2
Domboshawa o **ZW** 218-219 F 3
Domboshawa ▲ **ZW** (Mle) 218-219 F 3
Dombóvár o **H** 92-93 P 5
Dom Cavat o **BR** 72-73 J 5
Dome Bay ≈ 24-25 U 1
Dome Creek o **CDN** (BC) 228-229 N 3
Domel ▲ **IND** 138-139 E 3
Domeyko o **RCH** 76-77 B 5
Domeyko, Cordillera de ▲ **RCH** 76-77 C 3
Domfront o **F** 90-91 G 7
Dominase o **GH** 202-203 K 6
Domingos Martins o **BR** 72-73 K 6
Domingos Mourão o **BR** 68-69 H 4
Dominica ■ **WD** 56 E 4
Dominical o **CR** 52-53 C 7
Dominican Republic = Republica Dominicana ■ **DOM** 54-55 K 6
Dominica Passage ≈ 56 E 4
Dominican City o **CDN** 234-235 P 3
Dominion Range ▲ **ARK** 16 A 24
Domingo o **ZRE** 210-211 H 6
Domkonda o **IND** 138-139 G 10
Domo o **ETH** 208-209 H 5
Domodedovo o **RUS** 94-95 P 4
Domodóssola o **I** 100-101 B 1
Domoni o **COM** 222-223 H 4
Dom Pedrito o **BR** 76-77 K 6
Dom Pedro o **BR** 68-69 F 4
Dompem o **BR** 202-203 J 7
Dompu o **RI** 168 D 7
Domrermy o **CDN** (SAS) 232-233 N 3
Dom Silvério o **BR** 72-73 J 6
Domuyo, Volcán ▲ **RA** 78-79 D 4
Don ~ **GB** 90-91 F 3
Don ~ **RUS** 94-95 Q 5
Don ~ **USA** 102-103 L 2
Doña Ana o **USA** (NM) 256-257 G 4
Doña Ana, Cerro ▲ **RCH** 76-77 B 5
Doña Inés, Cerro ▲ **RCH** 76-77 C 3
Doña Juana, Volcán ▲ **CO** 64-65 D 1
Donald o **AUS** 180-181 G 4
Donald o **CDN** 230-231 M 2
Donalda o **CDN** (ALB) 232-233 F 3
Donald Landing o **CDN** (BC) 228-229 J 4
Donaldsonville o **USA** (LA) 268-269 J 5
Donalsonville o **USA** (GA) 284-285 F 5
Doña Rosa, Cordillera ▲ **RCH** 76-77 C 4
Donau ~ 8 E 4
Donau ~ **D** 92-93 L 4
Donauwörth o **D** 92-93 L 4
Don Benito o **E** 98-99 E 5
Doncaster o **GB** 90-91 G 5
Doncaster Indian Réserve X **CDN** (QUE) 238-239 L 2

Doncello, El o **CO** 64-65 E 1
Dondaicha o **IND** 138-139 J 2
Donderkamp o **SME** 62-63 F 3
Don Diego o **CO** 60-61 E 2
Dondo o **ANG** 216-217 C 5
Dondo o **MOC** 218-219 H 4
Dondo o **RI** (NTI) 168 E 7
Dondo o **RI** (SLT) 164-165 H 4
Dondo, Teluk ≈ 164-165 G 3
Dondon o **RH** 54-55 J 5
Ðon'n Du'o'ng o **VN** 158-159 K 5
Dondra, El o **YV** 62-63 F 4
Dondra, Rio ~ **BR** 72-73 K 6
Dörähäk o **IR** 134-135 D 5
Doraga o **CDN** (ONT) 238-239 J 2
Doran Lake o **CDN** 30-31 Q 5
Dorbod o **VRC** 150-151 E 4
Dorchester o **CDN** (NB) 240-241 L 5
Dorchester, Cape ▲ **CDN** 36-37 L 2
Dordabis o **NAM** 216-217 D 11
Dordogne ~ **F** 90-91 H 9
Dordrecht o **NL** 92-93 H 3
Dordrecht o **ZA** 220-221 H 5
Doreen, Mount ▲ **AUS** 172-173 K 7
Doré Lake o **CDN** (SAS) 34-35 C 3
Doré Lake o **CDN** (SAS) 34-35 C 3
Dores do Indaiá o **BR** 72-73 H 5
Dores do Rio Preto o **BR** 72-73 K 6
Dores Turvo o **BR** 72-73 J 6
Dörgön = Seer o **MAU** 146-147 L 1
Dori ☆ **BF** 202-203 K 3
Doringbaai o **ZA** 220-221 D 5
Doringrivier ~ **ZA** 220-221 D 6
Dorintosh o **CDN** (SAS) 232-233 K 3
Dorion o **CDN** (ONT) 234-235 P 6
Dorion o **CDN** (QUE) 238-239 L 3
Dorisvale o **AUS** 172-173 K 3
Dorlin o **F** 62-63 H 4
Dormansville o **USA** (NY) 278-279 K 4
Dormentes o **BR** 68-69 H 6
Dornakal o **IND** 142-143 B 7
Dornoch o **GB** 90-91 E 3
Dornod o **MAU** 148-149 L 4
Dorno Djoutougué o **TCH** 198-199 L 6
Domogov' o **MAU** 148-149 J 5
Doro o **RMM** 196-197 J 5
Dorogobuž o **RUS** 94-95 N 4
Doroh o **IR** 134-135 J 2
Dorohoi o **RO** 102-103 E 4
Dorohovo o **RUS** 94-95 P 4
Dorolamo o **RI** 164-165 L 3
Doroninskoe o **RUS** 118-119 F 10
Dorothy o **CDN** 232-233 F 4
Dorowa o **ZW** 218-219 G 3
Dorožnyj o **RUS** 118-119 G 5
Dorra o **DJI** 208-209 F 3
Dorrance o **USA** (KS) 262-263 H 6
Dorreen o **CDN** (BC) 228-229 F 2
Dorre Island ∩ **AUS** 176-177 B 2
Dorrigo o **AUS** 178-179 M 6
Dorrigo National Park ⊥ **AUS** 178-179 M 6
Dorris o **USA** (CA) 246-247 D 2
Dorsale Camerounaise ▲ **CAM** 204-205 J 5
Dorset o **CDN** (ONT) 238-239 J 3
Dorset o **CDN** (ONT) 238-239 G 3
Dorset Island ∩ **CDN** 36-37 L 2
Dört Kilise ∴ **TR** 128-129 J 4
Dörtmund o **D** 92-93 J 3
Dörtyol ☆ **TR** 128-129 G 4
Dorucha o **RUS** 110-111 J 3
Dorüd o **IR** 134-135 L 1
Doruma o **ZRE** 206-207 H 6
Dörvöžin = Buga o **MAU** 146-147 M 2
Dos, El • **MEX** 52-53 L 1
Dos Bocas o **USA** (PR) 286-287 O 2
Dos Cabezas o **USA** (AZ) 256-257 G 6
Dos Cabezas Peak ▲ **USA** (AZ) 256-257 F 6
Dos Caminos o **C** 54-55 H 4
Dos Caminos o **YV** 60-61 H 3
Dos de Mayo o **PE** 64-65 E 5
Doseo, Bahr ~ **TCH** 206-207 D 4
Dos Hermanas o **E** 98-99 E 6
Douro ~ **RMM** 202-203 J 2
Douro, Rio ~ **P** 98-99 D 3
Ðô So'n o **VN** 156-157 E 6
Dos Lagunas o **GCA** 52-53 K 3
Dos Lagunas, Parque Nacional ⊥ **RCH** 80 C 2
Doussala o **G** 210-211 C 5
Doutouchok o **RN** 198-199 D 6
Douz o **TN** 190-191 G 4
Dove o **PNG** 183 E 5
Dove Bugt ≈ 26-27 q 5
Dove Creek o **USA** (CO) 254-255 G 6
Dover o **AUS** 180-181 J 7
Dover o **GB** 90-91 H 6
Dover o- **GB** 90-91 H 6
Dover o **USA** (AR) 276-277 D 2
Dover o **USA** (DE) 280-281 L 5
Dover o **USA** (NJ) 280-281 M 3
Dover o **USA** (OH) 280-281 E 3
Dover o **USA** (TN) 276-277 H 4
Dover o **USA** (DE) 280-281 L 5
Dover, Point ▲ **AUS** 176-177 H 6
Dover, Strait of ≈ 90-91 H 6
Dovercourt o **CDN** (ALB) 232-233 D 3
Dover-Foxcroft o **CDN** (ME) 278-279 M 3
Dover River ~ **CDN** 32-33 O 3
Dovrefjell ▲ **N** 84-85 H 3
Dovsk o **BY** 94-95 M 5
Dowa o **MW** 218-219 G 1
Dowagiac o **USA** (MI) 272-273 C 6
Dowd, Mount ▲ **PNG** 183 D 3
Dowerin o **AUS** 176-177 D 6
Dowling Lake o **CDN** (ALB) 232-233 F 4
Downey o **USA** (ID) 252-253 K 4
Downie Creek o **CDN** (BC) 230-231 L 2
Downie Creek ~ **CDN** 230-231 L 2
Downieville o **USA** (CA) 246-247 E 4
Downs o **USA** (KS) 262-263 H 5
Downsville o **USA** (NY) 278-279 K 4

Downton, Mount ▲ CDN (BC) 228-229 K 4
Doyle o USA (CA) 246-247 E 3
Doylestown o USA (PA) 280-281 L 3
Doyleville o USA (CO) 254-255 J 5
Doyon o USA (ND) 258-259 J 3
Doze de Outubro, Rio ~ BR 70-71 H 3
Dozgah, Rūdḫāne-ye ~ IR 134-135 E 4
Dozois, Réservoir o CDN (QUE) 236-237 L 5
Drâa, Cap ▲ MA 188-189 F 6
Drâa, Hamada du ⩦ DZ 188-189 G 6
Drâa, Oued ~ MA 188-189 G 6
Drâa, Vallée du ⩡ •• MA 188-189 H 5
Dra Afratir ⩦ MA 196-197 D 2
Drabonso o GH 202-203 K 6
Dracena o BR 72-73 E 6
Drachten o NL 92-93 J 2
Drăgănești-Olt o RO 102-103 D 5
Drăgănești-Vlașca o RO 102-103 D 5
Drăgășani o RO 102-103 D 5
Draghoender o ZA 220-221 F 4
Dragocennaja, guba ≈ 110-111 W 1
Dragon, Kap ▲ GRØ 26-27 Y 2
Dragoon o USA (AZ) 256-257 E 6
Draguignan o F 90-91 L 10
Drahičyn o BY 94-95 J 5
Drain o USA (OR) 244-245 B 7
Drake o CDN (SAS) 232-233 N 4
Drake o USA (MO) 274-275 G 6
Drake o USA (ND) 258-259 G 4
Drakensberge ▲ ZA 220-221 J 4
Drake Passage ≈ 9 E 10
Drake Peak ▲ USA (OR) 244-245 E 8
Drakes Bay ≈ 40-41 C 7
Drakes Bay ≈ USA 248-249 B 2
Dráma o GR 100-101 K 4
Drammen ☆ N 86-87 E 7
Drangajökull ⊂ IS 86-87 b 1
Dranoz ▲ TR 128-129 F 2
Draper, Mount ▲ USA 20-21 V 7
Drar Souttouf ⩦ MA 196-197 C 4
Drāsan o PK 138-139 D 1
Drasco o USA (AR) 276-277 C 5
Drava ~ HR 100-101 F 2
Drawa ~ PL 92-93 N 2
Drawsko Pomorskie o PL 92-93 N 2
Drayton o USA (ND) 258-259 K 3
Drayton Valley o CDN (ALB) 232-233 D 2
Dreamworld • AUS 178-179 M 4
Dréan o DZ 190-191 F 2
Dreikikir o PNG 183 B 2
Dremsel, Mount ▲ PNG 183 D 2
Drennan o ZA 220-221 G 6
Dresden o CDN (ONT) 238-239 C 6
Dresden ☆ •• D 92-93 M 3
Dresden o USA (KS) 262-263 F 5
Dresden o USA (OH) 280-281 D 3
Dresden o USA (TN) 276-277 G 4
Dreux o F 90-91 H 7
Drevsjø o N 86-87 F 6
Drew o USA (MS) 268-269 K 3
Drewsey o USA (OR) 244-245 G 7
Drew's Gap ▲ USA (OR) 244-245 E 8
Drews Reservoir o USA (OR) 244-245 E 8
Drexel o USA (MO) 274-275 D 6
Drezdenko o PL 92-93 N 2
Driffield o GB 90-91 G 4
Drifton o USA (FL) 286-287 F 1
Driftpile River ~ CDN 32-33 N 4
Driftpile River Indian Reserve ⩙ CDN 32-33 N 4
Driftwood o CDN 32-33 G 4
Driftwood o USA (PA) 280-281 H 2
Driftwood Creek ~ CDN (BC) 228-229 G 2
Driftwood River ~ CDN 32-33 N 4
Driftwood River ~ CDN (ONT) 236-237 G 3
Driggs o USA (ID) 252-253 G 3
Drimiopsis o NAM 216-217 E 11
Drin, Lumi ~ AL 100-101 G 3
Drina ~ YU 100-101 G 3
Drinkwater o CDN (SAS) 232-233 N 5
Drinkwater Pass ▲ USA (OR) 244-245 G 7
Dripping Springs o USA (TX) 266-267 J 3
Driscoll o USA (TX) 266-267 K 6
Drjanovo o BG 102-103 D 6
Drniš o HR 100-101 F 3
Drobeta-Turnu Severin o • RO 102-103 C 5
Drobin o PL 92-93 P 2
Droërivier o ZA 220-221 E 6
Drogheda = Droichead Átha o IRL 90-91 D 5
Drogobyč = Drohobyč ☆ UA 102-103 C 3
Drohobyč ☆ UA 102-103 C 3
Droichead Átha = Drogheda o IRL 90-91 D 5
Droichead na Bandan = Bandan o IRL 90-91 C 6
Drôme ~ F 90-91 K 9
Drome o PNG 183 B 2
Dromedary, Cape ▲ AUS 180-181 L 4
Dronne ~ F 90-91 H 9
Dronning Ingrid Land ⩦ GRØ 28-29 P 4
Dronning Louise Land ⩦ GRØ 26-27 n 5
Dronning Maud fjellkjede ▲ ARK 16 E 0
Dronning Maud land ⩦ ARK 16 F 36
Dronten o NL 92-93 H 2
Dropmore o CDN (MAN) 234-235 B 3
Drossopigí o GR 100-101 H 5
Dro Station o CDN (ONT) 238-239 F 4
Drottningholm ••• S 86-87 H 7
Drovers Cave National Park ⊥ AUS 176-177 C 5
Drovjanoj o RUS 108-109 P 5
Drowned Cays ⩎ BH 52-53 K 3
Drowning River ~ CDN (ONT) 236-237 C 2
Dr. Petru Groza = Ștei o RO 102-103 C 4
Druid o CDN (SAS) 232-233 K 4
Drumduff o AUS 174-175 G 5
Drume o YU 100-101 G 3
Drumheller o CDN (ALB) 232-233 F 4
Drummond o USA (MI) 270-271 P 4
Drummond o USA (MT) 250-251 F 5
Drummond o USA (WI) 270-271 G 4
Drummond Island ⩎ USA (MI) 272-273 F 2
Drummond Range ▲ AUS 178-179 J 2
Drummondville o CDN (QUE) 238-239 N 3
Drumochter, Pass of ▲ GB 90-91 E 3
Drumright o USA (OK) 264-265 H 3
Druskininkai o •• LT 94-95 H 4
Druza, gora ▲ RUS 120-121 K 3
Druzba o KA 146-147 F 3
Družina o RUS 110-111 Z 5
Družkivka o UA 102-103 K 3
Družkovka = Družkivka o UA 102-103 K 3
Družnyj o RUS 114-115 T 5
Dry Bay ≈ 20-21 V 7
Dryberry Lake o CDN (ONT) 234-235 K 5
Drybrough o CDN 34-35 F 2
Dry Creek o USA (LA) 268-269 G 6
Dry Creek ~ USA (WY) 252-253 J 3
Dryden o CDN (ONT) 234-235 L 5
Dryden o USA (NY) 278-279 E 6
Dryden o USA (TX) 266-267 E 3
Dry Fork ~ USA (WY) 252-253 N 3
Drygalski Glacier ⊂ ARK 16 F 17
Drygalski-Island ⩎ ARK 16 G 10
Drygalskis Halvø ⩡ GRØ 28-29 P 1
Dry Hartsrivier ~ ZA 220-221 G 3
Dry Island Buffalo Jump Provincial Park ⊥ CDN (ALB) 232-233 F 4
Dry Prong o USA (LA) 268-269 H 5
Dry River ~ AUS 172-173 L 3
Drysdale Island ⩎ AUS 174-175 C 2
Drysdale River o AUS (WA) 172-173 H 3
Drysdale River ~ AUS 172-173 H 3
Drysdale River National Park ⊥ AUS 172-173 H 3
Dry Tortugas ⩎ USA (FL) 286-287 G 7
Drytown o USA (CA) 246-247 E 5
Dschang o CAM 204-205 J 6
Dtscord, Kap ▲ GRØ 28-29 T 6
Dua ~ ZRE 210-211 J 2
Duaca o YV 60-61 G 2
Duale ~ ZRE 210-211 J 3
Ḍū al-Faif, Ġazirat ⩎ KSA 132-133 B 5
Dualla o CI 202-203 G 5
Du'an o VRC 156-157 F 5
Duane Center o USA (NY) 278-279 G 4
Duangua, Rio ~ MOC 218-219 F 2
Duanshan o VRC 156-157 E 4
Duaringa o AUS 178-179 K 2
Duart o CDN (ONT) 238-239 D 6
Duarte o MEX 50-51 J 7
Duas Barras do Morro o BR 68-69 H 7
Duau, Mount ▲ PNG 183 C 4
Dubā o KSA 130-131 D 4
Duba o WAN 204-205 F 4
Ḍubāb o Y 132-133 C 7
Dubach o USA (LA) 268-269 H 4
Dubai'a, ad- o KSA 130-131 K 5
Dubai'a, ad- o UAE 134-135 F 6
Dubăsari ☆ MD 102-103 F 4
Dubawnt Lake o CDN 30-31 S 4
Dubawnt River ~ CDN 30-31 T 3
Dubayy = Dubai o • UAE 134-135 F 6
Dubbo o AUS 180-181 K 2
Dubčes ~ RUS 114-115 U 4
Dubec o RUS 94-95 Q 2
Dubela o ZRE 212-213 B 2
Dubėsar' = Dubăsari ☆ MD 102-103 F 4
Dubie o ZRE 214-215 E 5
Dublikan ~ RUS 122-123 E 3
Dublin o USA (GA) 284-285 H 4
Dublin o USA (TX) 264-265 F 6
Dublin o USA (VA) 280-281 F 6
Dublin = Baile Átha Cliath ★ •• IRL 90-91 D 5
Dubli River ~ USA 20-21 N 4
Dubna o RUS 94-95 P 3
Dubno o UA 102-103 D 2
Dubois o USA (ID) 252-253 F 2
Du Bois o USA (PA) 280-281 H 2
Dubois o USA (WY) 252-253 J 3
Du Bose o CDN (BC) 228-229 F 2
Dubossary = Dubăsari ☆ MD 102-103 F 4
Dubovka o RUS 96-97 D 9
Dubréka o RG 202-203 D 5
Dubreuilville o CDN (ONT) 236-237 D 4
Dubrovnik o ••• HR 100-101 G 3
Dubrovycja o UA 102-103 E 2
Dubulu o ZRE 206-207 E 6
Dubuque o • USA (IA) 274-275 H 2
Dubwe o LB 202-203 G 7
Đu'c Hanh o VN 158-159 J 5
Duchener, Réserve de ⊥ CDN (QUE) 240-241 G 2
Duchesne o USA (UT) 254-255 E 3
Duchesne River ~ USA (UT) 254-255 E 3
Duchess o AUS 178-179 E 1
Duchess o CDN (ALB) 232-233 G 5
Duck Bay o CDN (MAN) 234-235 C 2
Duck Creek ~ AUS 172-173 C 7
Duck Hill o USA (MS) 268-269 L 3
Duck Islands ⩎ CDN (NWT) 28-29 J 3
Duck Islands ⩎ CDN (ONT) 238-239 C 3
Duck Lake o CDN (SAS) 232-233 M 3
Duck Mountain ▲ CDN (MAN) 234-235 B 3
Duck Mountain Forest Reserve ⊥ CDN (MAN) 234-235 B 3
Duck Mountain Provincial Park ⊥ CDN (MAN) 234-235 B 3
Duck River o USA (TN) 276-277 H 5
Duck River ~ USA (TN) 276-277 H 5
Ducktown o USA (TN) 282-283 C 5
Duck Valley Indian Reservation ⩙ USA (NV) 246-247 J 1
Duckwater o USA (NV) 246-247 K 5
Duckwater Point ▲ USA (NV) 246-247 K 5
Duc Lập ☆ VN 158-159 J 2
Đu'c Liêu o VN 158-159 J 5
Dục Myo o VN 158-159 K 4
Ducor o USA (CA) 248-249 E 4
Du Couedic, Cape ▲ AUS 180-181 D 4
Đu'c Phổ o VN 158-159 K 3
Đu'c Phổ o VN 158-159 K 3
Đu'c Tho ☆ VN 156-157 D 7
Đu'c Trọng o VN 158-159 K 5
Duda, Río ~ CO 60-61 D 6
Dudduumo o SP 212-213 J 3
Düdensuyu Mağarası •• TR 128-129 D 4
Dudhani o IND 140-141 G 2
Dūdhi o IND 142-143 C 3
Dudh Kosi ~ NEP 144-145 F 7
Dudhwa National Park ⊥ IND 144-145 C 6
Dudignac o RA 78-79 J 3
Dudinka ☆ RUS 108-109 W 7
Dudinka ~ RUS 108-109 W 7
Dudley o GB 90-91 F 5
Dudorovskij o RUS 94-95 O 5
Dūdu o IND 138-139 E 6
Dudub o ETH 208-209 H 5
Dudypta ~ RUS 108-109 b 5
Due o ZRE 210-211 G 6
Duékoué o CI 202-203 G 6
Duere, Rio ~ BR 68-69 D 7
Duero, Río ~ E 98-99 F 4
Duette o USA (FL) 286-287 G 4
Due West o USA (SC) 284-285 H 2
Duff o CDN (SAS) 232-233 P 5
Dufreboy, Lac o CDN 36-37 O 5
Dufrost, Pointe ▲ CDN 36-37 L 4
Dufur o USA (OR) 244-245 D 5
Duġail, ad- o IRQ 128-129 L 6
Dugaimiya o KSA 130-131 L 5
Dugal o CDN (QUE) 240-241 J 2
Dugald o CDN (MAN) 234-235 G 5
Dugbia o ZRE 210-211 K 2
Dugda o RUS 122-123 C 2
Dugda ~ RUS 122-123 D 2
Dugdemona River ~ USA (LA) 268-269 H 4
Dugdug o SUD 206-207 J 4
Duge o LB 202-203 F 6
Dugi Otok ⩎ HR 100-101 E 2
Dugum o ETH 200-201 J 6
Dugway o USA (UT) 254-255 C 3
Dugwaya o SUD 200-201 G 4
Dugway Proving Ground xx USA (UT) 254-255 B 3
Duhamel o CDN (QUE) 238-239 K 2
Duḫān o Q 134-135 D 6
Duhau o RA 78-79 H 4
Du He ~ VRC 154-155 G 5
Duḫna o KSA 130-131 H 5
Duhovnickoe ☆ RUS 96-97 F 7
Duhovščina ☆ RUS 94-95 N 4
Duhubi o NEP 144-145 F 7
Duḥūr, Abū d- o SYR 128-129 G 5
Duida, Cerro ▲ YV 60-61 J 6
Duifken Point ▲ AUS 174-175 F 3
Duisburg o D 92-93 J 3
Duitama o CO 60-61 E 5
Duiwelskloof o ZA 218-219 F 6
Dujiangyan o VRC 154-155 C 6
Dujiang Yan • VRC 154-155 C 6
Dukambiya o ER 200-201 H 5
Dūkān o IRQ 128-129 L 5
Dūkān Buhairat < IRQ 128-129 L 4
Duke o USA (OK) 264-265 E 4
Duke Island ⩎ USA 32-33 E 4
Duken o KA 126-127 O 3
Duke of York Archipelago ⩎ CDN 24-25 P 6
Duke of York Bay ≈ 36-37 G 2
Duke of York Island ⩎ PNG 183 G 3
Dūk Fadiat o SUD 206-207 K 5
Dūk Faiwil o SUD 206-207 K 5
Duki o RUS 122-123 F 3
Duki ~ RUS 122-123 F 3
Dukkālah ⩦ MA 188-189 G 4
Dukku o WAN 204-205 F 3
Dukoa, ozero o RUS 112-113 J 2
Dūkštas o LT 94-95 K 4
Duku o WAN 204-205 J 3
Dulac o USA (LA) 268-269 K 7
Dulaiḥān o KSA 130-131 G 4
Dulaimiya, ad- o KSA 130-131 H 4
Dulai' Rasid o KSA 130-131 H 5
Dulala o ZRE 214-215 C 6
Dulamaya o RI 164-165 H 3
Dulan o VRC 144-145 M 2
Dulayb, Khor ~ SUD 208-209 A 3
Dulce o USA (NM) 256-257 J 2
Dulce, Arroyo ~ RA 78-79 L 4
Dulce, Golfo ≈ 52-53 C 7
Dulce, Laguna la o RA 78-79 F 4
Dulce, Río ~ GCA 52-53 K 4
Dulce, Río ~ RA 76-77 F 5
Dulce Nombre de Culmí o HN 54-55 C 7
Dul'durga ☆ RUS 118-119 F 10
Dulgalah ~ RUS 110-111 S 6
Dulgalah ~ RUS 118-119 P 3
Dulhunty River ~ AUS 174-175 G 2
Dulia o ZRE (HAU) 210-211 K 2
Dulia o ZRE (KIV) 212-213 B 3
Dulkaninna o AUS 178-179 E 5
Dullewāla o PK 138-139 C 4
Dullingari Gas and Oil Field • AUS 178-179 F 5
Dulovo o BG 102-103 E 6
Duluth o USA (MN) 270-271 F 4
Dulzura o USA (CA) 248-249 H 7
Duma ~ EAT 212-213 D 5
Duma o RB 218-219 B 4
Dūmā ☆ SYR 128-129 G 6
Duma o ZRE (Equ) 210-211 G 2
Duma ~ ZRE 206-207 H 6
Dumai o RI 162-163 D 4
Dumalag o RP 160-161 E 7
Dumaran Island ⩎ RP 160-161 C 7
Dumaresq River ~ AUS 178-179 L 5
Dumas o USA (AR) 276-277 D 7
Dumas o USA (TX) 264-265 C 3
Dumas, Península ⩡ RCH 80 F 7
Dūmat al-Ǧandal o • KSA 130-131 F 3
Dumba Cambango o ANG 216-217 D 5
Dumbleyung o AUS 176-177 D 6
Dumbleyung Lake o AUS 176-177 D 6
Dumbo o CAM 204-205 J 5
Dum Duma o IND 142-143 J 2
Dume, Point ▲ USA (CA) 248-249 F 5
Dumfries o • GB 90-91 F 4
Dumfries o USA (VA) 280-281 J 5
Dumjala o NEP 144-145 D 6
Dummer o CDN (SAS) 232-233 O 6
Dumogabesar o RI 164-165 J 3
Dumoine, Lac o CDN (QUE) 238-239 H 2
Dumoine, Rivière ~ CDN (QUE) 238-239 H 2
Dumond River ~ CDN (ONT) 234-235 O 2
Dumont o USA (TX) 264-265 D 5
Dumont d'Urville o ARK 16 G 15
Dumore o USA (PA) 280-281 L 2
Dumpu o PNG 183 C 3
Dumrān, Wādī ad ~ LAR 192-193 F 4
Dumri o IND 142-143 E 4
Dumsuk, Ġazirat ⩎ KSA 132-133 C 5
Dumyāṭ ☆ ET 194-195 E 2
Dumyāṭ, Maṣabb ~ ET 194-195 E 2
Duna o ANG 216-217 F 6
Dunaföldvár o H 92-93 P 5
Dunai o NEP 144-145 D 6
Dunaj ~ UA 102-103 F 5
Dunajivci ☆ UA 102-103 E 3
Dunajská Streda o SK 92-93 O 5
Dunalley o AUS 180-181 J 7
Dunărea ~ RO 102-103 C 5
Dunaújváros o H 92-93 P 5
Dunav ~ BG 102-103 D 6
Dunav ~ YU 100-101 G 2
Dunbar o AUS 174-175 G 5
Dunbar o GB 90-91 F 4
Dunbrody Abbey •• IRL 90-91 D 5
Duncairn o CDN (SAS) 232-233 K 5
Duncan o CDN (BC) 230-231 F 5
Duncan o USA (AZ) 256-257 F 6
Duncan o USA (OK) 264-265 G 4
Duncan, Cape ▲ CDN 34-35 Q 4
Duncan, Lac o CDN 38-39 E 2
Duncanby Landing o CDN (BC) 230-231 B 2
Duncan Highway II AUS 172-173 H 5
Duncan Lake o CDN 30-31 N 4
Duncan Lake o CDN (BC) 230-231 N 3
Duncan Passage ≈ 140-141 L 4
Duncan River ~ CDN (BC) 230-231 M 3
Duncansby Head ▲ GB 90-91 F 2
Duncan Town o BS 54-55 H 3
Dundaga o • LV 94-95 H 3
Dundalk o CDN (ONT) 238-239 E 4
Dundalk o • IRL 90-91 D 4
Dundalk o USA (MD) 280-281 K 4
Dundangan Island ⩎ RP 160-161 D 10
Dundas o CDN (ONT) 238-239 F 5
Dundas o GRØ 26-27 Q 5
Dundas o USA (IL) 274-275 K 6
Dundas, Lake o AUS 176-177 F 6
Dundas Harbour o CDN 24-25 f 3
Dundas Island ⩎ CDN (BC) 228-229 D 2
Dundas Peninsula ⩡ CDN 24-25 P 3
Dundas Strait ≈ 172-173 K 1
Dundburd o MAU 148-149 K 4
Dún Dealgan = Dundalk o • IRL 90-91 D 4
Dundee o AUS 178-179 G 1
Dundee o GB 90-91 F 3
Dundee o USA (MI) 272-273 F 6
Dundee o USA (TX) 264-265 F 5
Dundee o ZA 220-221 K 4
Dundgov' ⊡ MAU 148-149 G 5
Dundo o ANG 216-217 F 3
Dundooboo Range ▲ AUS 180-181 H 2
Dundret ▲ •• S 86-87 K 3
Dundurn o CDN (SAS) 232-233 M 4
Dunedin o NZ 182 C 6
Dunedin o USA (FL) 286-287 G 3
Dunedin River ~ CDN 30-31 G 6
Dunedoo o AUS 180-181 K 2
Dunes City o USA (OR) 244-245 A 7
Dunfermline o GB 90-91 F 3
Dūnga Būnga o PK 138-139 D 5
Dungan, Kuala o • MAL 162-163 E 2
Dungannon o GB 90-91 D 4
Dún Garbhán = Dungarvan o IRL 90-91 D 5
Dūngarpur o IND 138-139 D 8
Dungarvan = Dún Garbhán o IRL 90-91 D 5
Dungas o RN 198-199 D 6
Dungeness, Punta ▲ RA 80 F 6
Dungeness Spit ▲ USA (WA) 244-245 B 2
Dungog o AUS 180-181 L 2
Dungu o ZRE 212-213 B 2
Dungu ~ ZRE 212-213 B 2
Dungunāb o SUD 200-201 H 2
Dungunāb, Ġazirat ⩊ SUD 200-201 H 2
Dunham o CDN (QUE) 238-239 N 3
Dunham River ~ AUS (WA) 172-173 J 4
Dunham River ~ AUS 172-173 J 4
Dunhua o VRC 150-151 G 6
Dunhuang = Minghoshan o • VRC 146-147 M 5
Dunière, Parc Provincial de ⊥ CDN (QUE) 240-241 J 2
Dunkeld o AUS 180-181 G 4
Dunken o USA (NM) 256-257 K 6
Dunkerque o F 90-91 J 6
Dunkirk o USA (NY) 278-279 B 6
Dunk Island ⩎ AUS 174-175 J 5
Dunkwa o GH 202-203 K 7
Dun Laoghaire o IRL 90-91 D 5
Dunlap o USA (IA) 274-275 C 3
Dunlap o USA (NM) 256-257 L 4
Dunlap o USA (TN) 276-277 K 5
Dunlap o USA (TX) 264-265 D 4
Dunleath o CDN (SAS) 232-233 Q 4
Dunmarra o AUS 174-175 B 5
Dunmore o CDN (ALB) 232-233 H 6
Dunmore o USA (PA) 280-281 L 2
Dunmore Town o BS 54-55 G 2
Dunn o USA (NC) 282-283 J 5
Dunn o USA (TX) 264-265 D 6
Dún na Séad = Baltimore o IRL 90-91 C 6
Dunnellon o USA (FL) 286-287 G 2
Dunne River ~ CDN 36-37 L 2
Dunnigan o USA (CA) 246-247 C 5
Dunning o USA (NE) 262-263 F 3
Dunns River Falls ~ • JA 54-55 G 5
Dunnville o CDN (ONT) 238-239 F 6
Dunolly o AUS 180-181 G 4
Dunqul < ET 194-195 E 6
Dunraven o USA (NY) 278-279 G 6
Dunrea o CDN (MAN) 234-235 D 5
Dunrobin o AUS 178-179 J 2
Dunsborough o AUS 176-177 C 6
Dunseith o USA (ND) 258-259 G 3
Dunster o CDN (BC) 228-229 P 3
Dunvegan o CDN 32-33 L 4
Dunvegan o CDN (NS) 240-241 O 4
Dunvegan Historic Site ∴ CDN 32-33 L 4
Dunvegan Lake o CDN 30-31 Q 5
Dunville o CDN (NFL) 242-243 P 5
Dunyāpur o PK 138-139 C 5
Duolun o VRC 148-149 N 6
Du'o'ng Đông o • VN 158-159 G 5
Duparquet o CDN (QUE) 236-237 J 4
Duparquet, Lac o CDN (QUE) 236-237 J 4
Dupnica o BG 102-103 C 6
Du Pont o USA (GA) 284-285 H 6
Dupree o USA (SD) 260-261 E 1
Dupuy, Cape ▲ AUS 172-173 B 6
Dupuyer o USA (MT) 250-251 G 3
Duqaila, Ġazirat ⩎ KSA 132-133 C 5
Duqm o OM 132-133 K 4
Duque de York, Isla ⩎ RCH 80 C 5
Duquesne o USA (AZ) 256-257 E 7
Dura, La o MEX 50-51 E 3
Dūr Abū Arhlah o LAR 192-193 F 2
Durack Range ▲ AUS 172-173 H 4
Durack River ~ AUS 172-173 H 4
Dūrāğ o AFG 136-137 M 6
Durağan ☆ TR 128-129 F 2
Dur al Fawākhir ⩦ LAR 192-193 J 3
Dūr al Ġhānī ⩦ LAR 192-193 F 4
Duran o USA (NM) 256-257 K 4
Durán = Eloy Alfaro o EC 64-65 C 3
Durance ~ F 90-91 L 9
Durand o USA (IL) 274-275 J 2
Durand o USA (MI) 272-273 F 5
Durand o USA (WI) 270-271 G 6
Durango o • E 98-99 F 3
Durango o • HN 54-55 C 7
Durango ⊡ MEX 50-51 G 5
Durango ☆ • MEX 50-51 G 5
Durango o USA (CO) 254-255 H 6
Durango, Victoria de = Durango ☆ • MEX 50-51 G 5
Durañona o RA 78-79 J 4
Durant o USA (MS) 268-269 L 3
Durant o USA (OK) 264-265 H 5
Durazno ☆ ROU 78-79 L 2
Durban o CDN (MAN) 234-235 B 3
Durban o ☆ ZA 220-221 K 4
Durban Island ⩎ CDN 28-29 J 3
Durbanville o ZA 220-221 D 6
Durbet-Daba, pereval ▲ MAU 146-147 J 1
Durdur ~ SP 208-209 F 3
Dureji o PK 134-135 M 6
Durenan o RI 168 D 4
Durg o IND 142-143 B 5
Durgāpur o • IND 142-143 E 4
Durgarajupatnam o IND 140-141 J 4
Durham o CDN (ONT) 238-239 E 4
Durham ☆ ••• GB 90-91 G 4
Durham o USA (KS) 262-263 J 6
Durham o USA (NC) 282-283 J 4
Durham Downs o AUS 178-179 F 4
Duri o RI 162-163 D 4
Durian, Selat ≈ 162-163 E 4
Durika, Cerro ▲ CR 52-53 C 7
Durjela o RI 166-167 H 4
Durkee o USA (OR) 244-245 H 6
Durkin Outstation o AUS 176-177 M 5
Durlas = Thurles o IRL 90-91 D 5
Ḍurma o KSA 130-131 K 5
Durmitor ▲ YU 100-101 G 3
Durmitor Nacionalni park ⊥ ••• YU 100-101 G 3
Durness o GB 90-91 E 2
Durnev, aral ⩎ KA 96-97 H 10
Duro ▲ ETH 208-209 C 6
Duroa o RI 166-167 G 4
Durong South o AUS 178-179 L 4
Durra o ETH 208-209 C 5
Durrandella o AUS 178-179 J 3
Durrës ☆ •• AL 100-101 G 4
Duru o ZRE 206-207 J 6
Duru ~ ZRE 212-213 B 2
Durubu o ZRE 206-207 J 6
Durūz, Ġabal ad ▲ SYR 128-129 G 6
D'Urville, Tanjung ▲ RI 166-167 J 2
D'Urville Island ⩎ NZ 182 D 4
Duryu San ▲ DVR 150-151 G 7
Dūš, 'Izbat o ET 194-195 E 5
Ḍū Šaiḥ o IRQ 128-129 L 6
Dušak o TM 136-137 G 6
Dušanbe ☆ • TJ 136-137 L 5
Dusey River ~ CDN (ONT) 234-235 Q 3
Dushan o VRC 156-157 E 4
Dushanbe = Dušanbe ☆ • TJ 136-137 L 5
Dushore o USA (PA) 280-281 K 2
Dusin o PNG 183 C 3
Dusky Sound ≈ 182 A 6
Dussejour, Cape ▲ AUS 172-173 J 3
Düsseldorf ☆ • D 92-93 J 3
Dussoumbidiagna o RMM 202-203 E 2
Dustin o USA (OK) 264-265 H 3
Düstlik ☆ US 136-137 L 4
Düst Moḥammad Ḫān o IR 134-135 J 3
Dusty o USA (WA) 244-245 H 4
Dusunmudo o RI 162-163 E 5
Dusunpasirmayang o RI 162-163 E 5
Dusuntuo o RI 162-163 D 6
Duta o Z 214-215 F 6
Dutch Creek ~ CDN (BC) 230-231 N 3
Dutch Fort ∴ • RI (MAL) 166-167 E 3
Dutch Fort ∴ • RI (SLT) 164-165 G 3
Dutch Harbour o USA 22-23 N 6
Dutch Village • USA (MI) 272-273 C 5
Dutsan Wai o WAN 204-205 H 3
Dutse o WAN 204-205 H 3
Dutsin-Ma o WAN 198-199 C 6
Duttaluru o IND 140-141 H 3
Dutton o USA (MT) 250-251 H 4
Dutton, Lake o AUS 178-179 D 6
Dutton, Mount ▲ USA (UT) 254-255 C 5
Dutzow o USA (MO) 274-275 H 6
Duvall o USA (WA) 244-245 D 3
Duvefjorden ≈ 84-85 N 2
Duvernay o CDN (ALB) 232-233 G 2
Duvno o BIH 100-101 F 3
Duwisib Castle • NAM 220-221 C 2
Duwwa o OM 132-133 L 3
Duxbury, Lac o CDN 38-39 F 2
Duye ~ ZRE 212-213 B 3
Duyun o VRC 156-157 E 3
Düzce ☆ TR 128-129 D 2
Düzdüzān o IR 128-129 M 4
Düziçi o TR 128-129 G 4
Duziguo Gang ▲ VRC 156-157 C 2
Dvinskaja guba ≈ 88-89 P 4
Dvinskaya Guba = Dvinskaja guba ≈ RUS 88-89 P 4
Dwarsberg o ZA 220-221 H 2
Dwellingup o AUS 176-177 D 6
Dwesa-naturreservaat ⊥ ZA 220-221 J 6
Dwight o CDN (ONT) 238-239 G 3
Dwight o USA (IL) 274-275 K 3
Dwokwa o GH 202-203 K 7
Dworshak Reservoir o USA (ID) 250-251 C 5
Dwyer o USA (NM) 256-257 H 6
Dwyer Hill o CDN (ONT) 238-239 K 3
Dwyka ~ ZA 220-221 E 6
Dyaul Island ⩎ PNG 183 F 2
Dyer o USA (NV) 248-249 F 2
Dyer, Cabo ▲ RCH 80 C 4
Dyer, Cape ▲ CDN 28-29 K 3
Dyer Bay ≈ 24-25 L 3
Dyer Plateau ▲ ARK 16 G 30
Dyer's Bay o CDN (ONT) 238-239 D 3
Dyersburg o USA (TN) 276-277 F 4
Dyersville o USA (IA) 274-275 G 2
Dygdal o RUS 118-119 P 4
Dyh-Tau, gora ▲ RUS 126-127 E 6
Dyje ~ CZ 92-93 N 4
Dyjsembaj ~ KA 124-125 E 5
Dyke Ackland Bay ≈ 183 E 5
Dymond Lake o CDN 30-31 Q 5
Dynaj, ostrova ⩎ RUS 110-111 P 3
Dyrhóley ▲ IS 86-87 d 3
Dyryn-Jurjah ~ RUS 118-119 K 7
Dysart o AUS 178-179 K 2
Dysart o CDN (SAS) 232-233 O 5
Dysart o USA (IA) 274-275 F 2
Dytikí ⊡ GR 100-101 H 5
Dytikí Macedonía ⊡ GR 100-101 H 4
Džagdy, hrebet ▲ RUS 122-123 C 2
Džagyn ~ RUS 112-113 H 5
Džalal-Abad = Jalal-Abad o KS 136-137 N 4
Džalilabad = Çəlilabad o AZ 128-129 N 3
Džambul o KA 124-125 G 5
Džambul ☆ KA 136-137 M 3
Džana ~ RUS 120-121 F 6
Džanda ~ RUS 120-121 D 4
Džanga o TM 136-137 C 4
Džangylah, ostrov ⩎ RUS 110-111 N 3
Džankoj ☆ UA 102-103 J 5
Dzaoudzi o COM 222-223 D 4
Džapi ~ RUS 122-123 H 2
Džardžan o RUS 110-111 P 5
Džardžan ~ RUS 110-111 P 5
Džargalah o RUS 110-111 S 6
Džarkurgan = Jarqurghon o US 136-137 K 6
Džartyrabot o TJ 136-137 N 6
Dzata Ruins ∴ • ZA 218-219 F 6
Džaur ~ RUS 122-123 H 4
Džebariki-Haja o RUS 120-121 F 2
Džebel = Ġebel o TM 136-137 D 5
Džebrail o AZ 128-129 M 3
Džejhun o TM 136-137 H 5
Džejnau o US 136-137 J 5
Džekson, ostrov ⩎ RUS 84-85 d 2
Dželandy o TJ 136-137 N 6
Dželgala o RUS 120-121 N 2
Dželonda o RUS 118-119 J 9
Dželtulah ~ RUS 118-119 N 6
Dželtulinskij stanovik ▲ RUS 118-119 L 8
Dzeng o CAM 210-211 C 2
Džerba ~ RUS 118-119 H 5
Džermuk o AR 128-129 L 3
Džėrnjur, boloto ⩦ RUS 88-89 X 5
Dzerzhinsk = Dzeržinsk o RUS 94-95 S 3
Dzeržinsk o RUS 94-95 S 3
Dzeržyns'k o UA 102-103 K 3
Dževdaha, ozero o RUS 122-123 H 2
Dzhugdzhur, Khrebet = Džug-Džur, hrebet ▲ RUS 120-121 F 6
Działdowo o • PL 92-93 Q 2
Dzibalchén o MEX 52-53 K 2
Dzibilchaltún ∴ • MEX 52-53 K 1
Džida o RUS 116-117 N 10
Džida ~ RUS 116-117 L 10
Džidinskij hrebet ▲ MAU 148-149 F 2
Dzierżoniów o • PL 92-93 O 3
Džigda o RUS 120-121 F 5
Džila ~ RUS 118-119 F 10
Dzilam de Bravo o MEX 52-53 K 1
Džilinda, Ust'- o RUS 118-119 E 9
Dzioua o DZ 190-191 E 4
Džirgatal' o TJ 136-137 M 5
Dzisna ~ BY (VTB) 94-95 L 4
Dzisna ~ BY 94-95 K 4
Dzita o GH 202-203 L 7
Dzitás o MEX 52-53 K 1
Džizakskaja oblast' ⊡ US 136-137 K 4
Džjaržynsk ☆ BY 94-95 K 5
Džjunekjan ~ RUS 120-121 F 3
Dzodze o GH 202-203 L 6
Džogdžo ~ RUS 108-109 e 6
Džubga o RUS 126-127 C 5
Džug-Džur, hrebet ▲ RUS 120-121 F 6
Džugdžurskij zapovednik ⊥ RUS 120-121 F 6
Džuk ~ RUS 122-123 H 2
Džul'fa = Culfa o AZ (NAH) 128-129 L 3
Dzungarian Basin = Junggar Pendi ⩦ VRC 146-147 H 3
Džungarskij Alatau, žota ▲ KA 124-125 L 6
Dzungarskije voroda ▲ KA 146-147 F 3
Džurak-Sal ~ RUS 102-103 N 4
Džuryn o UA 102-103 F 3
Dzvari o GE 126-127 E 6
Dźwierzuty o PL 92-93 Q 2

E

Ea A Dun ~ VN 158-159 K 3
Eabamet Lake o CDN (ONT) 234-235 Q 3
Eades o CDN (ONT) 236-237 J 4
Eads o USA (CO) 254-255 N 5
Eadytown o USA (SC) 284-285 K 3
Eagar o USA (AZ) 256-257 F 4
Eagle o USA (AK) 20-21 U 4
Eagle o USA (CO) 254-255 J 4
Eagle o USA (ID) 252-253 B 3
Eagle o USA (NE) 262-263 K 4
Eagle o USA (WI) 274-275 K 2
Eagle Bend o USA (MN) 270-271 C 4
Eagle Butte o USA (SD) 260-261 E 2
Eagle Cape Wilderness Area ⊥ USA (OR) 244-245 H 5
Eagle Cap Wilderness Area • USA (OR) 244-245 H 5
Eagle Cave ∴ USA (WI) 274-275 H 1
Eagle Creek o CDN (BC) 230-231 J 2
Eagle Creek ~ CDN (BC) 228-229 N 4
Eagle Creek ~ CDN (SAS) 232-233 L 4
Eagle Creek ~ USA (OR) 244-245 C 5
Eagle Creek ~ USA (KY) 276-277 L 2
Eagle Grove o USA (IA) 274-275 E 2
Eagle Harbor o USA (MI) 270-271 K 3
Eagle Hills ▲ CDN (SAS) 232-233 K 3
Eagle Island ⩎ CDN 34-35 G 4
Eagle Island ⩎ SY 224 C 2
Eagle Lake o CDN (ONT) 234-235 K 5
Eagle Lake o USA (ME) 278-279 N 1
Eagle Lake o USA (TX) 266-267 L 4
Eagle Lake o USA (CA) 246-247 E 3
Eagle Mountain o USA (CA) 248-249 J 6
Eagle Mountain Lake < USA (TX) 264-265 G 6
Eagle Mountains ▲ USA (TX) 266-267 B 3
Eagle Nest o USA (NM) 256-257 K 2
Eagle Pass o USA (TX) 266-267 G 5
Eagle Passage ≈ 78-79 L 7
Eagle Picher Mine o USA (NV) 246-247 G 3
Eagle Plains o CDN 20-21 W 3
Eagle Point ▲ PNG 183 E 6
Eagle Point o USA (OR) 244-245 C 8
Eagle River o CDN (ONT) 234-235 K 5
Eagle River ~ CDN 20-21 W 3
Eagle River ~ CDN 38-39 P 2
Eagle River ~ CDN (BC) 230-231 L 3
Eagle River o USA (WI) 270-271 J 5
Eagle River ~ USA (CO) 254-255 H 4
Eagle Summit ▲ USA 20-21 S 4
Eagleton o USA (AR) 276-277 A 6
Eagleville o USA (CA) 246-247 E 2
Eagleville o USA (MO) 274-275 E 4
Eagleville o USA (TN) 276-277 J 5
Ea H'leo o VN 158-159 K 4
Eandja o ZRE 210-211 H 4
Earaheedy o AUS 176-177 F 2
Ear Falls o CDN (ONT) 234-235 K 4
Earle o USA (AR) 276-277 E 5
Earl Grey o CDN (SAS) 232-233 O 5
Earling o USA (IA) 274-275 C 3
Earls Cove o CDN (BC) 230-231 F 4
Earlton o CDN (ONT) 236-237 J 5
Earltown o CDN (NS) 240-241 M 5
Earlville o USA (IL) 274-275 K 3
Early o USA (IA) 274-275 C 2
Early o USA (TX) 266-267 J 2
Earn ~ GB 90-91 F 3
Earn Lake o CDN 20-21 X 5
Earp o USA (CA) 248-249 K 5
Easley o USA (SC) 284-285 H 2
East = Est ⊡ CAM 210-211 D 2
East, Mount ▲ AUS 176-177 G 4
East Alligator River ~ AUS 174-175 B 3
East Amatuli Island ⩎ USA 22-23 V 3
East Angus o CDN (QUE) 238-239 O 3
East Arm o CDN 30-31 E 5
East Arrow Park o CDN (BC) 230-231 M 3
East Aurora o USA (NY) 278-279 C 6
East Bay ≈ 36-37 J 2
East Bay o CDN (ONT) 234-235 P 5
East Bay ≈ USA 268-269 L 7
East Bay ≈ USA 268-269 F 7
East Bethel o USA (MN) 270-271 E 5
East Bijou Creek ~ USA (CO) 254-255 L 4
East Bluff ▲ CDN 36-37 R 4
Eastbourne o GB 90-91 H 6
East Brady o USA (PA) 280-281 G 3
East Broughton o CDN (QUE) 238-239 O 2
East Caicos ⩎ GB 54-55 K 4
East Cape ▲ NZ 182 G 2
East Cape ▲ USA (AK) 22-23 F 7
East Cape ▲ USA (FL) 286-287 H 6
East-Cape Province ⊡ ZA 220-221 H 5
East Carbon City o USA (UT) 254-255 E 4
East Cay ⩎ AUS 183 C 5
East Channel ~ CDN 20-21 Y 3
East China Sea ≈ 10-11 M 5
East Chugach Island ⩎ USA 22-23 V 3
East Coulee o CDN (ALB) 232-233 F 4
East Dereham o GB 90-91 H 5
Eastend o CDN (SAS) 232-233 K 6
East End Point ▲ BS 54-55 G 2
East Enterprise o USA (IN) 274-275 O 6

Downton, Mount — East Enterprise 323

Elk Lakes Provincial Park ⊥ CDN (BC) 230-231 O 3
Elk Mountain ▲ USA (NM) 256-257 G 5
Elk Mountains ▲ USA (CO) 254-255 H 4
Elko o CDN (BC) 230-231 O 4
Elko o • USA (NV) 246-247 K 3
Ėl'konka o RUS 118-119 N 6
Ėl K'oran o ETH 208-209 G 6
Elk Point o CDN (ALB) 232-233 H 2
Elk Point o USA (SD) 260-261 K 4
Elk Rapids o USA (MI) 272-273 D 3
El Krebs, Erg ∴ DZ 188-189 L 7
El Krenig, Hassi < DZ 190-191 D 7
Elk River ∼ CDN (ALB) 232-233 C 3
Elk River ∼ CDN (BC) 230-231 O 4
Elk River o USA (ID) 250-251 C 5
Elk River o USA (MN) 270-271 E 5
Elk River ∼ USA (AL) 284-285 C 2
Elk River ∼ USA (KS) 262-263 K 7
Elk River ∼ USA (MO) 276-277 A 4
Elk River ∼ USA (TN) 276-277 J 5
Elk River ∼ USA (WV) 280-281 F 5
Elk River ∼ USA (WV) 280-281 E 5
El Ksar el Kbir o MA 188-189 J 3
EL Kseur o DZ 190-191 E 2
El Ksiba o MA 188-189 J 4
Elk Springs o USA (CO) 254-255 G 3
Elkton o USA (KY) 276-277 H 4
Elkton o USA (MD) 280-281 L 4
Elkton o USA (OR) 244-245 B 7
Elkton o USA (TN) 276-277 J 5
Elkton o USA (VA) 280-281 H 5
Elkwater o CDN (ALB) 232-233 H 6
Ella o USA (KY) 276-277 K 3
Ella Ø ⌒ GRØ 26-27 n 7
Ellaville o USA (FL) 286-287 F 1
Ellaville o USA (GA) 284-285 F 4
Ell Bay ≈ 36-37 F 2
Elléba Fonfou < RN 198-199 B 4
Ellef Ringnes Island ⌒ CDN 24-25 U 1
Ėl Lėh o ETH 208-209 D 7
El Lein < EAK 212-213 H 4
Ellėloyė o TCH 198-199 J 4
Ellen, Mount ▲ USA (UT) 254-255 E 5
Ellenboro o USA (WV) 280-281 E 4
Ellenburg o USA (NY) 278-279 H 4
Ellendale o USA (ND) 258-259 J 5
Ellensburg o USA (WA) 244-245 E 3
Ellenville o USA (NY) 280-281 M 2
Ėllepugol-Ėmtor, ozero ⊂⊃ RUS 114-115 Q 4
Ellerbe o USA (NC) 282-283 H 5
Ellery, Mount ▲ AUS 180-181 K 4
Ellesby o CDN (BC) 228-229 L 2
Ellesmere Island ⌒ CDN 24-25 e 2
Ellice Islands ⌒ TUV 13 J 3
Ellice River ∼ CDN 30-31 R 2
Ellicott City o USA (MD) 280-281 K 4
Ellicottville o USA (NY) 278-279 C 6
Ellijay o USA (GA) 284-285 F 2
Ellinger o USA (TX) 266-267 L 4
Ellington o USA (MO) 276-277 E 3
Ellinwood o USA (KS) 262-263 H 6
Elliot o ZA 220-221 H 5
Elliot, Mount ▲ AUS 174-175 J 6
Elliot Lake o CDN (ONT) 238-239 C 2
Elliot Price Conservation Park ⊥ AUS 178-179 D 5
Elliott o AUS 174-175 B 5
Elliott o USA (MD) 280-281 L 5
Elliott, Mount ▲ AUS 172-173 H 6
Elliott Key ⌒ USA (FL) 286-287 J 6
Ellis o USA (ID) 252-253 D 2
Ellis o USA (KS) 262-263 G 6
Ellisforde o USA (WA) 244-245 F 2
Ellisras o ZA 218-219 D 6
Elliston o AUS 180-181 C 2
Elliston o CDN (NFL) 242-243 P 4
Elliston o USA (MT) 250-251 G 5
Ellisville o USA (AL) 284-285 E 2
Ellisville o USA (MS) 268-269 L 5
Ellora o ••• IND 138-139 E 9
Ellora Caves ••• IND 138-139 E 9
Ellsberry o USA (MO) 274-275 H 5
Ellsworth o USA (KS) 262-263 H 6
Ellsworth o USA (ME) 278-279 N 4
Ellsworth o USA (MN) 270-271 B 7
Ellsworth o USA (NE) 262-263 E 2
Ellsworth o USA (WI) 270-271 F 6
Ellsworth Highland ▲ ARK 16 F 28
Ellwood City o USA (PA) 280-281 F 3
Elma o CDN (MAN) 234-235 H 5
Elma o USA (IA) 274-275 F 1
Elma o USA (WA) 244-245 B 3
El Ma, Oued ∼ RIM 196-197 F 2
El Maad o DZ 190-191 E 2
El Mabrouk < RIM 196-197 C 6
Elmadağ o TR 128-129 E 3
Elma Dağı ▲ TR 128-129 E 3
El Mahbas o MA 188-189 G 7
Elma Labiod o DZ 190-191 G 3
El Malah o DZ 188-189 L 3
El Malah, Chott ⊂⊃ DZ 190-191 E 4
Elmalı ☆ • TR 128-129 C 4
El Mallaile o ETH 208-209 F 6
El Mamouel < RMM 196-197 J 5
El Mâmoûn < RMM 196-197 K 5
El Mamour < RMM 196-197 J 5
El Mannsour o DZ 188-189 L 7
el-Mansour-Eddahbi, Barrage < MA 188-189 H 5
El Marsa o DZ 190-191 C 2
El Maya o DZ 190-191 D 4
Elm Creek o CDN (MAN) 234-235 F 5
Elm Creek o USA (NE) 262-263 G 4
El Medo o ETH 208-209 E 6
El Meghaier o DZ 190-191 E 4
Elmeki o RN 198-199 D 4
El Melah, Oued < DZ 190-191 E 6
El Melhes < RIM 196-197 D 5
El Mellah, Sebkha ⊂⊃ DZ 188-189 L 6
El Menabba o DZ 188-189 K 5
el-Menzel o MA 188-189 J 4
Elmer o USA (OK) 264-265 E 4
Elmer City o USA (WA) 244-245 G 2
Elmerson Peninsula ∪ CDN 26-27 J 3
Elm Fork ∼ USA (TX) 264-265 G 5
Elm Fork Red River ∼ USA (TX) 264-265 D 3
Elm Grove o USA (LA) 268-269 G 4
El Mhaijrât o RIM 196-197 B 5
El Milia o DZ 190-191 F 2
Elmina o • GH 202-203 K 7
Elmira o CDN (ONT) 238-239 E 5
Elmira o CDN (PEI) 240-241 N 4
Elmira o USA (ID) 250-251 C 3
Elmira o USA (NY) 278-279 E 6
Elmo o USA (KS) 262-263 J 6
Elmodel o USA (GA) 284-285 F 5
El Moinâne < RIM 196-197 E 5
Elmore o AUS 180-181 H 4
Elmore o CDN (SAS) 232-233 R 6
Elmore o USA (MN) 270-271 D 7
El Morro National Monument ∴ USA (NM) 256-257 G 3
El Mounir, Hassi < DZ 188-189 H 6
El Mraïti < RMM 196-197 J 5
El Mreïti < RIM 196-197 G 3
Elmvale o CDN (ONT) 238-239 F 4
Elmwood o USA (IL) 274-275 J 4
Elmwood o USA (MI) 270-271 K 4
Elmwood o USA (OK) 264-265 D 2
Elmwood o USA (WI) 270-271 F 6
El Nido o •• RP 160-161 C 7
Elnja o RUS 94-95 N 4
Elnora o CDN (ALB) 232-233 E 4
El Obeid = al-Ubayyid ☆ • SUD 200-201 E 6
El Obeid = Ubayyid, al- ☆ • SUD 200-201 E 6
Elogbatindi o CAM 210-211 C 2
El Ogla o DZ 190-191 F 4
El Ogla Gasses o DZ 190-191 F 3
Elogo o RCB 210-211 E 3
Eloguj ∼ RUS 114-115 S 3
Eloguiskij, učastok ⊥ RUS 114-115 S 4
Elojaha ∼ RUS 108-109 R 8
Elopada o RI 168 D 7
Elora o USA (TN) 276-277 J 5
Elorza o YV 60-61 G 4
Elota o MEX 50-51 F 6
El Ouadey ∼ TCH 198-199 J 6
el-Oualidia o MA 188-189 G 4
El Ouar, Erg ∴ DZ 190-191 F 6
El Ouass'ât ∴ RIM 196-197 E 3
El Oued ☆ • DZ 190-191 F 4
Elovaja, Bol'šaja (Tet) ∼ RUS 114-115 U 5
Elovka ∼ RUS 120-121 T 5
Elovo ☆ RUS 96-97 J 5
Eloy o USA (AZ) 256-257 D 6
Eloy Alfaro o EC (GUA) 64-65 C 3
Eloy Alfaro o EC (MAN) 64-65 B 2
El Paso o • USA (TX) 266-267 A 2
El Paso Gap o USA (NM) 256-257 L 6
El Paso Mountains ▲ USA (CA) 248-249 G 4
Elphant, Rapides de l' ∼ ZRE 206-207 D 6
Elphinstone o AUS 178-179 K 1
Elphinstone o CDN (MAN) 234-235 C 4
Elpitiya o CL 140-141 J 7
El Portal o USA (CA) 248-249 E 2
El Porvenir o USA (NM) 256-257 K 3
Elquí, Río ∼ RCH 76-77 B 6
El Rharbi, Oued ∼ DZ 190-191 C 4
Elrosa o USA (MN) 270-271 D 5
Elrose o CDN (SAS) 232-233 K 4
Elroy o USA (WI) 270-271 H 7
El Salvador ■ ES 52-53 K 5
Elsamere National Park ⊥ EAK 212-213 F 4
Elsberry o USA (MO) 274-275 H 5
Elsey o AUS 174-175 B 4
Elsey Cemetery • AUS 174-175 B 4
Elsey National Park ⊥ AUS 174-175 B 4
El Sharana Mine • AUS 172-173 L 2
Elsie Hills o AUS 178-179 J 3
Elsie Island ⌒ CDN 36-37 K 5
Elsinore, Lake ⊂⊃ USA (CA) 248-249 G 6
Elstad o N 86-87 E 6
Elstow o CDN (SAS) 232-233 M 3
Eltanin Fracture Zone System ≃ 14-15 O 13
El Tarf o TN 190-191 G 2
Eltice Island ⌒ CDN 20-21 X 2
El Tichlitt < RIM 196-197 D 6
Elton o RUS 96-97 E 9
Elton o USA (LA) 268-269 H 6
Elton, ozero ⊂⊃ RUS 96-97 E 9
Eltopia o USA (WA) 244-245 F 4
El Tuparro, Parque Nacional ⊥ CO 60-61 G 5
Eltyreva ∼ RUS 114-115 R 5
Elu o RI 166-167 E 6
Elubo o GH 202-203 J 7
Elu Inlet ≈ 24-25 T 6
El Ure < SP 212-213 J 2
Elūru o IND 140-141 J 2
Elva o •• EST 94-95 K 2
Ėlva ∼ RUS 88-89 V 5
Elvas o • P 98-99 D 5
Elverum ☆ N 86-87 E 6
Elvira o RA 78-79 K 3
Elvira, Cape ▲ CDN 24-25 S 4
Elvira Island ⌒ CDN 24-25 S 4
Elvire, Mount ▲ AUS 172-173 C 6
Elvire River ∼ AUS 172-173 J 5
Elvita, Río ∼ CO 60-61 F 5
El Wak o EAK 212-213 H 2
El Warsesa < EAK 212-213 G 2
Elwell, Lake ⊂⊃ USA (MT) 250-251 H 3
Elwood o USA (IN) 274-275 N 4
Elwood o USA (NE) 262-263 G 4
Elx o E 98-99 G 5
Ely o • GB 90-91 H 5
Ely o USA (MN) 270-271 G 3
Ely o USA (NV) 246-247 L 4
Elyria o USA (OH) 280-281 D 2
Emae = Île Mai ⌒ VAN 184 II b 3
Emali o EAK 212-213 F 5
Emām 'Abbās o IR 134-135 A 1
Emām Ḥasan o IR 134-135 D 4
Emām Ḥomeini, Bandar-e o IR 134-135 C 3
Emām Tāqī o IR 136-137 F 7
Emån ∼ S 86-87 G 8
Ėmanda, ozero ⊂⊃ RUS 110-111 U 7
Emanželinsk o RUS 96-97 M 6
Emas, Parque Nacional das ⊥ BR 72-73 D 5
Embarcación o RA 76-77 E 2
Embarras River ∼ CDN (ALB) 228-229 R 3
Embarrass River ∼ USA (IL) 274-275 K 5
Embarrass River ∼ USA (WI) 270-271 K 6
Ėmbenčimė ∼ RUS 116-117 J 3
Embetsu o J 152-153 J 2
Embi ☆ KA 126-127 N 3
Embi ∼ KA 156-157 L 3
Embi ∼ RUS 96-97 H 10
Embi, Mount ▲ PNG 183 B 3
Embilipitiya o CL 140-141 J 7
Embira o BR 68-69 F 5
Embira, Rio ∼ BR 66-67 B 6
Emblem o USA (WY) 252-253 K 2
Embocada o BOL 70-71 F 4
Embondo o ZRE 210-211 G 3
Embracação, Represa < BR 72-73 G 5
Emboraí, Baía do ≈ 68-69 E 2
Emboscada o BOL 70-71 E 2
Emboscada, La o BOL 70-71 D 2
Emboscada Nueva o PY 76-77 J 3
Embreeville o USA (TN) 282-283 E 4
Embrun o CDN (ONT) 238-239 K 3
Embu ☆ EAK 212-213 F 4
Embudo, Raudal del ∼ CO 64-65 F 1
Embundo o ANG 216-217 D 8
Emca o RUS 88-89 Q 5
Emca ∼ RUS 88-89 Q 5
Emcisweni o MW 214-215 G 6
Emden o • D 92-93 J 2
Emeck o RUS 88-89 Q 5
Emeishan o VRC (SIC) 156-157 C 2
Emeishan •• VRC (SIC) 156-157 C 2
Emel' ∼ KA 124-125 N 5
Emel'janovskaja o RUS 88-89 Q 4
Emelle o USA (AL) 284-285 B 4
Emerald o AUS 178-179 K 2
Emerald o USA (NE) 262-263 K 4
Emerald Bank ≃ 38-39 N 7
Emerald Isle ⌒ CDN 24-25 P 2
Emeriau Point ▲ AUS 172-173 F 4
Emerillon o F 62-63 H 4
Emersen o CDN (MAN) 234-235 F 5
Emerson o USA (AR) 276-277 B 7
Emery o USA (UT) 254-255 D 5
Emery Range ▲ AUS 178-179 C 4
Emet ☆ TR 128-129 C 3
Emeti o PNG 183 B 4
Emigrant o USA (MT) 250-251 J 6
Emigrant Gap o USA (CA) 246-247 E 4
Emigrant Pass ▲ USA (NV) 246-247 J 3
Emilia, La o YV 60-61 H 4
Emiliano Zapata o MEX (CHI) 52-53 J 3
Emiliano Zapata o MEX (COA) 50-51 H 5
Emiliano Zapata o MEX (SON) 50-51 D 3
Emilia-Romagna □ I 100-101 B 2
Emin o VRC 146-147 F 2
Eminābād o PK 138-139 E 3
Eminee o RI 166-167 K 5
Eminence o USA (IN) 274-275 M 5
Eminence o USA (KY) 276-277 K 2
Eminence o USA (MO) 276-277 D 3
Emin He ∼ VRC 146-147 F 2
Emini o CAM 210-211 D 2
Emin Pasha Gulf ⊂⊃ EAT 212-213 C 5
Emirdağ ☆ TR 128-129 D 3
Emirgazi ☆ TR 128-129 E 4
Emlinskaja, buhta ⊂⊃ RUS 120-121 Q 3
Emma, Mount ▲ CDN 24-25 g 4
Emmaboda ☆ S 86-87 G 8
Emma Fiord ≈ 26-27 E 3
Emmen o NL 92-93 J 2
Emmet o AUS 178-179 H 3
Emmetsburg o USA (IA) 274-275 D 1
Emmett o USA (ID) 252-253 B 3
Emmett o USA (MI) 272-273 G 5
Emmiganuru o IND 140-141 G 3
Emmitsburg o USA (MD) 280-281 J 4
Emmonak o USA 20-21 H 5
Ėmmy, mys ▲ RUS 110-111 a 1
Emo o CDN (ONT) 234-235 K 6
Emory o USA (TX) 264-265 J 6
Emory Pass ▲ USA (NM) 256-257 H 6
Emory Peak ▲ USA (TX) 266-267 D 4
Emoulas < RN 198-199 C 5
Empalme o MEX 50-51 D 4
Empalme, El = Velasco Ibarra o EC 64-65 C 2
Empangeni o ZA 220-221 K 4
Empedrado o RCH 78-79 C 3
Emperado, El o YV 60-61 F 3
Emperor Range ▲ PNG 184 I b 1
Emperor Seamount Chain ≃ 14-15 K 3
Emperor Trough ≃ 14-15 K 3
Empexa, Salar de ⊂⊃ BOL 70-71 C 7
Empire o USA (AR) 276-277 D 7
Empire o USA (CA) 248-249 D 2
Empire o USA (CO) 254-255 K 4
Empire o USA (MI) 272-273 C 3
Emporia o USA (KS) 262-263 K 6
Emporia o USA (VA) 280-281 J 7
Emporium o USA (PA) 280-281 H 2
Empress o CDN (ALB) 232-233 H 5
Empress Augusta Bay ≈ 184 I b 2
Empress Mine o ZW 218-219 E 4
Ems ∼ D 92-93 J 2
Emu Park o • AUS 178-179 L 2
Emure o WAN 204-205 F 5
Emva o RUS 88-89 V 5
Emvan o CAM 204-205 K 6
Ena o J 152-153 G 7
Enakievo = Jenakijeve o UA 102-103 L 3
Enangiperi o EAK 212-213 E 4
Enarotali o RI 166-167 J 3
Enašimo ∼ RUS 116-117 F 5
Encantado o BR 68-69 J 4
Encantado, Valle ∴ RA 78-79 D 6
Encanto, Cape ▲ RP 160-161 D 5
Encanto, El o CO 64-65 F 2
Encarnación ☆ PY 76-77 K 4
Encarnacion de Díaz o MEX 50-51 H 7
Enchant o CDN (ALB) 232-233 F 5
Encinal o USA (TX) 266-267 H 5
Encinal, El o MEX 50-51 K 5
Encinitas o USA (CA) 248-249 G 7
Encino o CO 60-61 E 4
Encino o USA (NM) 256-257 K 4
Encino o USA (TX) 266-267 J 7
Encoje o ANG 216-217 C 3
Encon o RA 78-79 F 2
Encontrados o YV 60-61 E 3
Encounter Bay ≈ 180-181 E 3
Encrucijada, La o YV 60-61 J 3
Encruzilhada o BR 72-73 K 3
Encruzilhada do Sul o BR 74-75 D 8
Encucijada, La o YV 60-61 H 3
Enda o VRC 144-145 L 5
Endako o CDN (BC) 228-229 J 2
Endau o EAK (EAS) 212-213 G 4
Endau ▲ EAK (EAS) 212-213 G 4
Ėndė ∼ RUS 116-117 E 2
Ende, Pulau ⌒ RI 168 E 7
Endeavor o CDN (SAS) 232-233 Q 3
Endeavour Strait ≈ 174-175 G 2
Endebes o EAK 212-213 E 3
Endeh o RI 168 E 7
Endengue o CAM 210-211 D 2
Enderby o CDN (BC) 230-231 K 3
Enderby Abyssal Plain ≃ 12 B 10
Enderby Land ∴ ARK 16 G 6
Enderlin o USA (ND) 258-259 K 5
Endiang o CDN (ALB) 232-233 F 4
Endicott o USA (NY) 278-279 E 6
Endicott o USA (WA) 244-245 H 4
Endicott Arm ≈ 32-33 D 3
Endicott Mountains ▲ USA 20-21 N 3
Endicott Mountains Range ▲ USA 20-21 N 3
Endikė o RCB 210-211 E 4
Endimari, Rio ∼ BR 66-67 D 7
Endom o CAM 210-211 D 2
Endra, ozero ⊂⊃ RUS 114-115 J 4
Endyalgout Island ⌒ AUS 172-173 L 1
Ene, Río ∼ PE 64-65 E 7
Eneabba o AUS 176-177 C 4
Enemawira o RI 164-165 J 2
Enemy, Lake of the ⊂⊃ CDN 30-31 O 4
Énéné Patatpe o F 62-63 G 4
Energia o RA 78-79 K 5
Enerucijada, La o YV 60-61 K 3
Enez ☆ TR 128-129 B 2
Enfer, Portes de l' ∼ • ZRE 212-213 A 6
Enfield o CDN (NS) 240-241 M 6
Enfield o USA (CT) 280-281 O 2
Enfield o USA (NC) 282-283 K 4
Enfok o IND 140-141 L 6
Engadin ∴ CH 92-93 K 5
Engadine o USA (MI) 270-271 N 4
Engaño, Cabo ▲ DOM 54-55 L 5
Engaru o J 152-153 K 2
Engaruka o EAT (ARV) 212-213 E 5
Engaruka ∴ • EAT (MA) 212-213 E 5
Engaruka Basin ∴ EAT 212-213 F 5
Engcobo o ZA 220-221 H 5
En Gedi • IL 130-131 D 2
Engelhard o USA (NC) 282-283 M 5
Engelmine o USA (CA) 246-247 E 3
Ėngel's o RUS 96-97 E 8
Engels = Ėngel's o RUS 96-97 E 8
Engelsbergs bruk ••• S 86-87 H 7
Engen o CDN (BC) 228-229 K 2
Engenheiro Navarro o BR 72-73 J 4
Engenio, El o PE 64-65 E 9
Engerina Creek ∼ AUS 178-179 C 5
Enggano, Pulau ⌒ RI 162-163 E 7
Engh o VRC 150-151 B 2
Engida ∼ RUS 116-117 G 5
Engineer o CDN 20-21 X 7
Engineer Group ⌒ PNG 183 F 6
Engkilili o MAL 162-163 J 4
England □ GB 90-91 F 5
England o USA (AR) 276-277 D 6
Engle o USA (NM) 256-257 H 5
Englee o CDN (NFL) 242-243 M 2
Englefeld o CDN (SAS) 232-233 O 3
Englefield, Cape ▲ CDN 24-25 d 6
Englefield Bay ≈ CDN 228-229 B 4
Englehart o CDN (ONT) 236-237 J 5
Englevale o USA (ND) 258-259 K 5
Englewood o USA (FL) 286-287 G 5
Englewood o USA (KS) 262-263 G 7
Englewood o USA (OH) 280-281 B 4
Englewood o USA (TN) 282-283 C 5
English o USA (TX) 264-265 K 5
English Channel = English Channel = La Manche ≈ 90-91 G 6
English Coast ∪ ARK 16 F 29
English Company's Islands, The ⌒ AUS 174-175 D 3
English Harbour East o CDN (NFL) 242-243 O 5
English Harbour Town o AG 56 E 3
English Harbour West o CDN (NFL) 242-243 N 5
English River o CDN (ONT) 234-235 N 5
Engoordina o AUS 178-179 C 3
Engozero o RUS 88-89 M 4
Engure o LV 94-95 H 3
Enid o USA (OK) 264-265 G 2
Enid Creek ∼ CDN (ONT) 236-237 G 4
Enid Lake ⊂⊃ USA (MS) 268-269 L 2
Enid Mining Area, Mount • AUS 172-173 C 6
Enisej ⌒ 10-11 H 2
Enisej ∼ RUS 10-11 H 2
Enisejsk ☆ RUS 116-117 F 6
Enisejskij zaliv ≈ 108-109 S 5
Enisejsko-Stolbovoj, učastok ⊥ RUS 114-115 U 3
Eniwa o J 152-153 J 3
Enjil o MA 188-189 J 4
Enjukovo o RUS 94-95 P 2
Ėnkėn, mys ▲ RUS 120-121 J 5
Enkhuizen o • NL 92-93 H 2
Enköping ☆ S 86-87 H 7
Ėnmelen o RUS 112-113 T 4
Ėnmelen o RUS 112-113 X 4
Ėnmyvaam ∼ RUS 112-113 R 3
Enna o I 100-101 E 6
Ennadai o CDN 30-31 T 5
Ennadai Lake ⊂⊃ CDN 30-31 T 5
En Naga, Oued ∼ DZ 188-189 H 6
En Nahüd o SUD 200-201 D 6
Enné, Ouadi ∼ TCH 198-199 J 5
Ennedi ▲ TCH 198-199 K 4
Ennery o RH 54-55 J 5
Enngonia o AUS 178-179 H 5
Ennis o USA (MT) 250-251 H 6
Ennis o USA (TX) 264-265 H 6
Ennis = Inis ☆ • IRL 90-91 C 5
Enniscorthy = Inis Córthaidh o IRL 90-91 D 5
Enniskillen o CDN (ONT) 238-239 G 4
Enniskillen ☆ • GB 90-91 D 4
En Noual, Sebkhet ⊂⊃ TN 190-191 G 3
Enns ∼ A 92-93 N 5
En Nsa, Oued ∼ DZ 190-191 E 4
Enoch o USA (UT) 254-255 B 6
Enochs o USA (TX) 264-265 B 5
Enontekiö o FIN 88-89 G 2
Enoree River ∼ USA (SC) 284-285 J 2
Enosburg Falls o USA (VT) 278-279 J 4
Enotaevka ☆ RUS 96-97 E 10
Enozero ⊂⊃ RUS 88-89 O 2
Enping o VRC 156-157 H 5
Enrekang o RI 164-165 F 5
Enridaville o TN 190-191 H 2
Enrile o RP 160-161 D 4
Enriquillo, Lago ⊂⊃ DOM 54-55 K 5
Enschede o NL 92-93 J 2
Ensenada o • MEX 50-51 A 2
Ensenada o RCH 78-79 C 6
Enshi o VRC 154-155 F 6
Enshū-nada ≈ 152-153 G 7
Ensign o USA (KS) 262-263 F 7
Ensley o USA (FL) 286-287 B 1
Ėnstor, ozero ⊂⊃ RUS 114-115 K 4
Entebang, Rumah o MAL 162-163 K 3
Entebbe o EAU 212-213 D 3
Enterprise o CDN 30-31 L 5
Enterprise o USA (AL) 284-285 E 5
Enterprise o USA (MS) 268-269 M 4
Enterprise o USA (OR) 244-245 H 5
Enterprise o USA (UT) 254-255 B 6
Enterprise Point ▲ RP 160-161 C 7
Entiako River ∼ CDN (BC) 228-229 J 3
Entiat o USA (WA) 244-245 E 3
Ėntl'-Imiagun ∼ RUS 114-115 M 3
En Tmadé < RIM 196-197 E 5
Entrada, Punta ▲ RA 80 F 5
Entrance o CDN (ALB) 228-229 R 3
Entre Lagos o RCH 78-79 C 6
Entre Rios o BOL 76-77 E 1
Entre Rios o BR 66-67 K 5
Entre-Rios o BR 68-69 J 7
Entre Ríos □ RA 76-77 H 6
Entre Ríos, Cordillera ▲ HN 52-53 B 4
Entriken o USA (PA) 280-281 H 3
Entrocamento o BR 68-69 F 5
Entrocamento o BR 68-69 E 4
Entronque La Cuchilla o MEX 50-51 H 5
Entrop o RI 166-167 L 3
Entumeni o ZA 220-221 K 4
Ėntuziastov o RUS 110-111 U 4
Entwistle o CDN (ALB) 232-233 D 2
Enu, Pulau ⌒ RI 166-167 H 5
Enugu ☆ WAN 204-205 G 5
Enugu Ezike o WAN 204-205 G 5
Enumclaw o USA (WA) 244-245 D 3
Ėnurmino o RUS 112-113 Z 3
Envigado o CO 60-61 D 4
Envira o BR 66-67 B 6
Environ o CDN (SAS) 232-233 L 3
Enxudé o GNB 202-203 C 4
Enyamba o ZRE 210-211 K 5
Enyčavajam ∼ RUS 112-113 O 6
Enyellé o RCB 210-211 G 2
Ėnyngvajam ∼ RUS 120-121 V 3
Eo, Río ∼ E 98-99 D 3
Eochaill = Youghal o IRL 90-91 D 6
Eola o USA (TX) 266-267 G 2
Eolie o Lípari, Isole ⌒ I 100-101 E 5
Epako o NAM 216-217 D 10
Epanomí o GR 100-101 J 4
Epatlán o MEX 52-53 E 2
Epe o WAN 204-205 E 5
Epecuén, Laguna ⊂⊃ RA 78-79 H 4
Epembe o NAM 216-217 B 8
Epéna o RCB 210-211 F 3
Epenarra o AUS 174-175 C 7
Épernay o • F 90-91 J 7
Ephesus = Efes ∴ •• TR 128-129 B 3
Ephraim o USA (UT) 254-255 D 4
Ephrata o USA (WA) 244-245 F 3
Ephrata o • USA (PA) 280-281 K 3
Epi □ VAN 184 II b 3
Epi ⌒ VAN (EPI) 184 II b 3
Epi o ZRE 210-211 L 2
Epidauros ••• GR 100-101 J 6
Épinal ☆ • F 90-91 L 7
Epini o ZRE 212-213 B 3
Epiphany o USA (SD) 260-261 J 3
Epizana o BOL 70-71 E 5
Epokenkoso o ZRE 210-211 F 5
Epoma o RCB 210-211 E 3
Epping o USA (ND) 258-259 D 3
Epping o USA (NH) 278-279 L 5
Epping Forest o AUS 178-179 J 2
Epping Forest National Park ⊥ AUS 178-179 J 2
Epps o USA (LA) 268-269 J 4
Epsom o AUS 178-179 K 1
Epu, River ∼ WAN 204-205 G 5
Epukiro o NAM 216-217 E 10
Epukiro ∼ NAM 216-217 F 10
Epulu ∼ ZRE 212-213 B 3
Epulu, Station de capture d' • ZRE 212-213 B 3
Epupa Falls ∼ NAM 216-217 B 8
Epuyén o RA 78-79 D 7
Eqlid o IR 134-135 E 3
Equateur □ ZRE 210-211 G 3
Equator 14-15 Q 7
Equatorial Guinea = Guinea Ecuatorial ■ GQ 210-211 B 2
Eračimo ∼ RUS 116-117 E 3
Erahtur o RUS 94-95 R 4
Eralé o BR 62-63 H 5
Eram o PNG 183 B 3
Eran Bay ≈ 160-161 B 8
Era River ∼ PNG 183 C 4
Erátini o GR 100-101 J 5
Erave o PNG 183 B 4
Erave River ∼ PNG 183 B 4
Eravur o CL 140-141 J 7
Erāwadi Myit ∼ MYA 142-143 J 5
Erāwadi Myitwanyā ∼ MYA 158-159 C 3
Erawan National Park ⊥ • THA 158-159 E 3
Erba, Ǧabal ▲ SUD (Ahm) 200-201 H 2
Erba, Ǧabal ▲ SUD (Ahm) 200-201 G 3
Erbaa ☆ TR 128-129 G 2
Erbogačen ☆ RUS 116-117 N 5
Ėrča, Bol'šaja ∼ RUS 110-111 b 5
Erçek Gölü ⊂⊃ TR 128-129 K 3
Erciş ☆ TR 128-129 K 3
Erciyes Dağı ▲ TR 128-129 F 3
Erdaobaihe o VRC 150-151 G 6
Erdek ☆ • TR 128-129 B 2
Erdemli ☆ TR 128-129 F 4
Ėrdėnėcagaan = Čonogol o MAU 148-149 M 5
Ėrdėnėcogt o MAU 148-149 E 4
Ėrdėnėdalaj = Sangijn Dalaj o MAU 148-149 G 4
Ėrdėnėmandal = Ölzijm o MAU 148-149 E 3
Ėrdėnėsant = Ulaanhudag o MAU 148-149 J 4
Ėrdėnėt o MAU 148-149 G 3
Ėrdėni Cu • MAU 148-149 F 4
Erdi ∴ TCH 198-199 L 3
Eré o TCH 206-207 B 4
Erebus, Mount ▲ ARK 16 F 17
Erebus and Terror Gulf ≈ 16 G 31
Erebus Bay ≈ 24-25 W 6
Erech ∴ • IRQ 128-129 L 7
Erechim o BR 74-75 D 6
Ėrėėncav o MAU 148-149 M 3
Ereğli ☆ TR 128-129 D 2
Ereğli ☆ TR 128-129 F 4
Eréké ∼ RCA 206-207 C 5
Erëma o RUS 116-117 N 5
Erëma, Bol'šaja ∼ RUS 116-117 M 5
Erenhot o VRC 148-149 K 6
Erepecuru, Lago de ⊂⊃ BR 62-63 F 6
Ereré o BR 68-69 J 5
Ėrer Wenz ∼ ETH 208-209 F 5
Erevan ☆ AR 128-129 L 2
Erfenisdam < ZA 220-221 H 4
Erfoud o MA 188-189 J 5
Erfurt ☆ •• D 92-93 L 3
Ergani ☆ TR 128-129 H 3
Ėrgėl o MAU 148-149 J 6
Ergëlėh o RUS 118-119 O 4
Ergene Çayı ∼ TR 128-129 B 2
Ergene Nehri ∼ TR 128-129 B 2
Ergeni ▲ RUS 96-97 D 9
Ērgļi o LV 94-95 J 3
Erguig, Bahr ∼ TCH 206-207 C 3
Ergun He ∼ VRC 150-151 C 1
Ergun Youqi o VRC 150-151 C 2
Ergun Zuoqi o VRC 150-151 C 2
Ėrguveem ∼ RUS 112-113 X 4
Er Hai ⊂⊃ VRC 142-143 M 3
Eri, River ∼ WAN 204-205 E 4
Eria, Río ∼ E 98-99 D 3
Eriba o SUD 200-201 H 4
Eric o CDN 38-39 M 3
Erica o AUS 180-181 J 5
Erichsen Lake ⊂⊃ CDN 24-25 f 5
Erick o USA (OK) 264-265 E 3
Erickson o CDN (MAN) 234-235 D 4
Ericson o USA (NE) 262-263 H 3
Eridu = Abū Šahrain ∴ • IRQ 130-131 J 2
Erie o USA (IA) 274-275 H 3
Erie o USA (KS) 262-263 L 7
Erie o USA (PA) 280-281 F 1
Erie, Lake ⊂⊃ 46-47 G 5
Erie, Lake ⊂⊃ 280-281 D 2
Erieau o CDN (ONT) 238-239 D 6
Erie Canal ∼ USA (NY) 278-279 C 5
Erie Canal < USA (NY) 278-279 F 5
Ėriečka ∼ RUS 108-109 e 6
Erie National Wildlife Refuge ⊥ USA (PA) 280-281 G 2
'Erîgât ∴ RMM 196-197 H 5
Erik den Rødes Ø ⌒ GRØ 28-29 W 4
Erik Eriksenstredet ≈ 84-85 O 3
Ėrikit ∼ RUS 110-111 Z 7
Erik Point ▲ CDN 26-27 Q 8
Eriksdale o CDN (MAN) 234-235 E 4
Eriksmåla o S 86-87 G 8
Erimo o J 152-153 K 3
Erimo-misaki ▲ J 152-153 K 4
Erimo Seamount ≃ 152-153 L 4
Erin o USA (TN) 276-277 H 4
Erinferry o CDN (SAS) 232-233 M 2
Erith River ∼ CDN (ALB) 232-233 B 2
Eritrea ■ ER 200-201 H 5
Erkalnadeįpur ∼ RUS 114-115 P 3
Erkovcy o RUS 122-123 C 3
Erkowit o SUD 200-201 H 3
Erlangen o D 92-93 L 4
Erlang Shan ▲ VRC 156-157 C 2
Erldunda o AUS 176-177 M 2
Erling, Lake ⊂⊃ USA (AR) 276-277 B 7
Erlistoun Creek ∼ AUS 176-177 F 3
Erlongshan • VRC 150-151 F 5
Ermaki o RUS 116-117 N 7
Ermao = Île Mau ⌒ VAN 184 II b 3
Ermelo o ZA 220-221 J 3
Ermeneevo ☆ RUS 96-97 H 6
Ermenek ☆ TR 128-129 E 4
Ermentau ☆ KA 124-125 H 3
Ermera o RI 166-167 C 6
Ermil Post o SUD 200-201 C 6
Ermineskin Indian Reservation ⚔ CDN (ALB) 232-233 E 3
Ermoúpoli o • GR 100-101 K 6
Ernakulam o IND 140-141 G 6
Ernée o F 90-91 G 7
Ernest Giles Range ▲ AUS 176-177 G 3
Ernest Sound ≈ 32-33 D 4
Ernestville o USA (TN) 282-283 E 4
Ernul o USA (NC) 282-283 K 5
Erode o IND 140-141 G 5
Erofej Pavlovič o RUS 118-119 L 8
Eromalido, Tanjung ▲ RI 166-167 C 6
Eromanga o AUS 178-179 G 4
Eromanga Island = Île Erromango ⌒ VAN 184 II b 4
Eromohon ∼ RUS 116-117 L 2
Erongoberg ▲ NAM 216-217 C 10
Erong Springs o AUS 176-177 D 2
Eröö = Bugant o MAU 148-149 H 3
Eröö gol ∼ MAU 148-149 H 3
Eropol ∼ RUS 112-113 O 4
Eroro o PNG 183 E 5
Errabiddy o AUS 176-177 D 2
Erragondapa'em o IND 140-141 H 2
Er Raoui, Erg ∴ DZ 188-189 K 6
Errego o MOC 218-219 J 3
er-Remla o TN 190-191 H 3
Er Rîchât, Guelb ▲ RIM 196-197 E 4
Errigal Mountain ▲ IRL 90-91 C 4
Errington o CDN (BC) 230-231 E 4
Erris Head ▲ IRL 90-91 B 4
Errittau o PNG 183 C 4
Errol o USA (NH) 278-279 K 4
Erromango, Île = Eromanga Island ⌒ VAN 184 II b 4
Erronan, Île = Futuna Island ⌒ VAN 184 II c 4
Ersa ∼ RUS 88-89 W 3
Ersekë ☆ • AL 100-101 H 4
Erši o RUS 94-95 O 4
Erskine o CDN (ALB) 232-233 F 3
Erskine o USA (MN) 270-271 B 3
Erskine Inlet ≈ 24-25 V 2
Eršov ☆ RUS 96-97 F 8
Eršova o RUS 116-117 L 7
Ert o RUS 118-119 M 4
Ertai o VRC 146-147 K 2
Ertil' o RUS 102-103 M 2
Ertis ∼ KA 124-125 L 3
Ertis-Karaganda kanal < KA 124-125 H 3
Ertix He ∼ VRC 146-147 G 2
Ërtom ∼ RUS 88-89 T 5
Ërtoma o RUS 88-89 T 5
Ertwa, Mount ▲ AUS 176-177 M 1
Erua ⌒ ER 200-201 K 5
Erufa o WAN 204-205 F 4
Eruh ☆ TR 128-129 K 4
Eruki, Mount ▲ PNG 183 C 4
Erundu o NAM 216-217 D 10
Eruslan ∼ RUS 96-97 E 8
Eruwa o WAN 204-205 E 5
Erval o BR 74-75 D 9
Ervay o USA (WY) 252-253 L 4
Erveiras o BR 74-75 D 7
Ervent o TM 136-137 F 5
Erwin o USA (MS) 268-269 J 3
Erwin o USA (NC) 282-283 J 5
Erwood o CDN (SAS) 232-233 Q 3
Erzgebirge ▲ D 92-93 M 3
Ėrzin ☆ RUS 116-117 G 10
Ėrzin ∼ RUS 116-117 G 10
Erzincan ☆ TR 128-129 H 3
Erzurum ☆ • TR 128-129 J 3
Eržvilkas o LT 94-95 H 4
Esa, Isanlu- o WAN 204-205 F 4
Esa'ala o PNG 183 F 5
Esan o J 152-153 J 4
Esang o RI 164-165 K 1
Esashi o J (HOK) 152-153 K 2
Esashi o J (HOK) 152-153 J 4
Esayoo Bay ≈ 26-27 J 3
Esbjerg o • DK 86-87 D 9
Esbo = Espoo o FIN 88-89 H 6
Escada o BR 68-69 L 6
Escala, La o BOL 70-71 E 4
Escalante o RP 160-161 E 7
Escalante o USA (UT) 254-255 D 6
Escalante Canyons • USA (UT) 254-255 D 6
Escalante Desert ∴ USA (UT) 254-255 B 6
Escalante River ∼ USA (UT) 254-255 D 6
Escalante Valley ∪ USA (UT) 254-255 B 5
Escalerilla o RCH 76-77 C 1
Escalón o MEX 50-51 G 4
Escalon o USA (CA) 248-249 D 2
Escambia River ∼ USA (FL) 286-287 B 1
Escanaba o USA (MI) 270-271 L 5
Escanaba River ∼ USA (MI) 270-271 L 4
Escara o BOL 70-71 C 6
Escárcega o • MEX 52-53 J 2
Escarpada Point ▲ RP 160-161 E 3
Escatawpa River ∼ USA (AL) 284-285 B 6
Eschscholtz Bay ≈ 20-21 K 3
Eschwege o • D 92-93 L 3
Escobas o USA (TX) 266-267 J 6
Escocesa, Bahía ≈ 54-55 L 5
Escola o BOL 70-71 E 5
Escondida, La o MEX 50-51 K 5
Escondida, Punta ▲ MEX 52-53 F 4
Escondido o USA (CA) 248-249 G 6
Escondido, Área Indígena ⚔ BR 66-67 H 7
Escondido, Río ∼ MEX 52-53 K 2
Escondido, Río ∼ NIC 52-53 B 5
Escoporanga o BR 72-73 K 5
Escorial, El o ••• E 98-99 E 4
Escott o AUS 174-175 E 5
Escoumins, Les o CDN (QUE) 240-241 F 2
Escravos o WAN 204-205 F 6
Escudilla Mountain ▲ USA (AZ) 256-257 F 5
Escuinapa de Hidalgo o MEX 50-51 G 6
Escuintla ☆ GCA 52-53 J 4
Escuminac o • CDN (NB) 240-241 L 3
Escuminac, Point ▲ CDN (NB) 240-241 L 3
Ese o ZRE 206-207 H 6
Esė-Hajja o RUS 110-111 U 6
Eséka o CAM 210-211 C 2
Eseli o PNG 183 E 4
Esenanhaty ∼ KA 96-97 H 8
Eşen Çayı ∼ TR 128-129 C 4
Esence Dağları ▲ TR 128-129 H 3
Esensaj o KA 96-97 G 9
Esenyurt o TR 128-129 G 3
Eşfahān □ IR 134-135 D 2
Eşfahān ☆ ••• IR (ESF) 134-135 D 2
Esfarāyen o IR 136-137 E 6

Elk Lakes Provincial Park — Esfarāyen 325

Esfolado, Rio ~ **BR** 68-69 G 5
Eşger, Küh-e ▲ **IR** 134-135 H 1
Eshan o **VRC** 156-157 C 4
Eshimba o **ZRE** 210-211 K 6
Eshowe o **ZA** 220-221 K 4
Esigodini o **ZW** 218-219 E 5
Esik o **KA** 146-147 C 4
Esil ☆ **KA** 124-125 E 3
Esim o **KA** 124-125 F 1
Esinskaja o **RUS** 94-95 R 1
Esira o **RM** 222-223 E 10
Esjajaha o **RUS** 108-109 S 6
Esk o **AUS** 178-179 M 4
Esk o **CDN** (SAS) 232-233 O 4
Eškameš o **AFG** 136-137 L 6
Eškašem o **AFG** 136-137 M 6
Eskdale o **AUS** 180-181 J 4
Esker o **CDN** 38-39 L 2
Eskifjörður o **IS** 86-87 f 2
Eskil ☆ **TR** 128-129 E 3
Eskilstuna ☆ **S** 86-87 H 7
Eskimo Lakes o **CDN** 20-21 Y 2
Eskimonæsset ▲ **GRØ** 26-27 s 3
Eskimo Point o **CDN** (NWT) 30-31 W 5
Eskimo Point o **CDN** (NWT) 30-31 W 6
Éski-Nookat o **KS** 136-137 N 4
Eskişehir ☆ **TR** 128-129 C 3
Eskridge o **USA** (KS) 262-263 K 6
Esla, Río ~ ▲ **E** 98-99 D 3
Eslämäbäd-e Garb o **IR** 134-135 B 1
Eslām Qal'e o **AFG** 134-135 J 1
Eslām Qal'e o **IR** 136-137 F 7
Eslämäbähr o **IR** 136-137 B 7
Eslöv o **S** 86-87 F 9
Eşme o **TR** 128-129 C 3
Esmeralda o **AUS** 174-175 G 6
Esmeralda o **C** 54-55 F 4
Esmeralda, Isla ▲ **RCH** 80 C 4
Esmeralda, La o **YV** (AMA) 60-61 J 6
Esmeralda, La o **YV** (BAR) 60-61 F 3
Esmeralda, Río o **BOL** 70-71 D 3
Esmeraldas o **EC** 64-65 C 1
Esmeraldas ☆ **EC** 64-65 C 1
Esmeraldas, Río ~ **EC** 64-65 C 1
Esmond o **USA** (ND) 258-259 H 3
Esnagami Lake o **CDN** (ONT) 236-237 D 2
Esnagi Lake o **CDN** (ONT) 236-237 D 4
Espadim Paranhos o **BR** 76-77 K 2
Espake o **IR** 134-135 J 5
Espalion o **F** (90-91) J 9
España o **RP** 160-161 G 6
Espanola o **CDN** (ONT) 238-239 D 2
Espanola, Isla ▲ **EC** 64-65 C 10
Española, Isla ▲ **EC** 64-65 C 10
Esparto o **USA** (CA) 246-247 C 5
Espavelta o **PA** 52-53 D 8
Espenberg, Cape ▲ **USA** 20-21 J 3
Espenberg o **USA** 20-21 J 3
Esperanca o **BR** (P) 62-63 H 6
Esperança o **BR** (PA) 68-69 L 5
Esperança, Serra da ▲ **BR** 74-75 E 5
Esperança dos Indios o **BR** 70-71 J 7
Esperance o **AUS** 176-177 F 6
Esperance Bay ≋ **AUS** 176-177 F 6
Esperantina o **BR** 68-69 G 3
Esperantónpolis o **BR** 68-69 F 4
Esperanza o **BR** (AMA) 66-67 C 5
Esperanza o **BR** (UCA) 66-67 D 5
Esperanza o **C** 54-55 E 3
Esperanza o **MEX** 50-51 E 4
Esperanza o **RA** (SAC) 80 E 5
Esperanza o **RA** (SAF) 76-77 G 6
Esperanza o **USA** (TX) 266-267 B 2
Esperanza, La o **C** 54-55 D 3
Esperanza, La ☆ **HN** 52-53 K 4
Esperanza, La o **RA** 78-79 E 8
Esperanza, La o **YV** 60-61 J 4
Esperanza, Sierra la ▲ **HN** 54-55 C 7
Esperanza Inlet ≋ **CDN** 230-231 B 4
Espichel, Cabo ▲ **P** 98-99 C 5
Espiel o **E** 98-99 E 6
Espigão, Serra do ▲ **BR** 74-75 E 5
Espigão do Oeste o **BR** 70-71 G 2
Espigão Mestre ▲ **BR** 68-69 E 7
Espinal o **BOL** 70-71 H 5
Espinal o **CO** 60-61 D 5
Espinal, El o **RA** 52-53 D 8
Espinero o **YV** 60-61 N 4
Espinhaço, Serra da ▲ **BR** 72-73 J 6
Espinheira o **ANG** 216-217 B 8
Espinho o **P** 98-99 C 4
Espinilho, Serra do ▲ **BR** 76-77 K 5
Espinillo o **RA** 76-77 H 4
Espino o **YV** 60-61 J 4
Espino, o **BOL** 70-71 F 6
Espino, El o **PA** 52-53 E 7
Espinosa o **BR** 72-73 J 3
Espírito Santo o **BR** 66-67 C 4
Espírito Santo □ **BR** 72-73 K 5
Espírito Santo do Turvo o **BR** 72-73 F 7
Espíritu Santo o **MEX** 50-51 C 3
Espíritu Santo ~ **VAN** 184 II a 2
Espíritu Santo, Bahía del ≋ **MEX** 52-53 L 2
Espíritu Santo, Isla ▲ **MEX** 50-51 D 3
Espíritu Santo do Pinhal o **BR** 72-73 G 7
Espita o **MEX** 52-53 K 1
Esplanada o **BR** 68-69 K 7
Espoo o **FIN** 88-89 H 6
Espungabera o **MOC** 218-219 G 5
Esqâbôd o **IR** 134-135 G 1
Esquel o **RA** 78-79 D 7
Esquibel, Gulf of ≋ 32-33 D 4
Esquimalt o **CDN** 230-231 F 5
Esquina o **RA** 76-77 H 6
Esquina o **RCH** 70-71 C 6
Esquiú o **RA** 76-77 E 5
Ess ~ **USA** 114-115 Q 4
Essaouira o = As-Şawîrah ☆ • **MA** 188-189 G 3
Essé o **CAM** 204-205 J 6
Es-Sed, Oued ~ **TN** 190-191 H 4
Essedakana, In- o **RMM** 196-197 K 4
Es Seggeur, Oued ~ **DZ** 190-191 C 4

Essej o **RUS** 108-109 e 7
Essej, ozero o **RUS** 108-109 e 7
Essen ▲ **D** 92-93 H 3
Essen o **D** 92-93 J 3
Essendon, Mount ▲ **AUS** 176-177 F 2
Essentuki o **RUS** 126-127 E 5
Essequibo ▲ **GUY** 62-63 E 5
Essequibo River ~ **GUY** 62-63 E 2
Essex o **CDN** 238-239 C 8
Essex o **CA** (CA) 248-249 J 5
Essex o **USA** (CA) 274-275 C 4
Essex o **USA** (MD) 280-281 K 4
Essex o **USA** (MS) 268-269 K 2
Essex o **USA** 250-251 P 5
Essex Junction o **USA** 278-279 H 4
Essexville o **USA** (MI) 272-273 F 4
Essiama o **GH** 202-203 J 7
Essington, Port ≋ 172-173 K 1
Esslingen am Neckar ▲ • **D** 92-93 K 4
Êsso o **RUS** 120-121 S 6
Est = East □ **CAM** 210-211 C 4
Est, Pointe de l' ▲ **CDN** (QUE) 242-243 Q 3
Estabrook Lake o **CDN** 24-25 K 6
Estacada o **USA** (OR) 244-245 C 5
Estaca de Bares, Punta o ▲ **E** 98-99 D 3
Estação Catur o **MOC** 218-219 H 1
Estacia Camacho o **MEX** 50-51 H 5
Estación 14 de Mayo o **PY** 76-77 H 2
Estación Alianza o **RA** 76-77 F 5
Estacion biologica o **EC** 64-65 B 10
Estación Buena Suerte o **PY** 76-77 H 2
Estación Candela o **MEX** 50-51 J 4
Estación Careros Cué o **PY** 76-77 H 2
Estacione Don o **MEX** 50-51 E 4
Estación Km. 329 o **ROU** 78-79 M 2
Estación la Concepción o **PY** 76-77 H 3
Estación Pozo Blanco o **PY** 76-77 J 2
Estación Salto Cué o **PY** 76-77 J 4
Estación Santa Clara • **BR** 74-75 C 5
Estación Simón o **MEX** 50-51 H 5
Estación Vanegas o **MEX** 50-51 J 6
Estación Victoria o **PY** 76-77 H 2
Estado Cañitas de Felipe Pescador o **MEX** 50-51 H 5
Estado de Guerrero, Parque Natural del ⊥ **MEX** 52-53 E 3
Estado la Calle o **MEX** 52-53 D 1
Estado Las Tablas o **MEX** 50-51 H 5
Estado Pabellones o **MEX** 50-51 H 6
Estados, Isla de los ▲ **RA** 80 H 7
Estados, Parque Nacional de los ⊥ **RA** 80 H 7
Estahbänät o **IR** 134-135 F 4
Estambul o **BOL** 70-71 D 4
Estância o **BR** 68-69 K 7
Estancia Camerón o **RCH** 80 F 7
Estancia Carmen o **RA** 80 F 7
Estancia el Durazno o **RA** 76-77 C 6
Estancia Invierno o **RCH** 80 E 6
Estancia la Federica o **RA** 80 D 5
Estancia la Jerónima o **RA** 80 D 5
Estancia la Julia o **RA** 80 F 4
Estancia la Oriental o **RA** 80 D 3
Estancia las Cumbres o **RCH** 80 E 7
Estancia Maria Esther o **RA** 80 F 6
Estancia María Luisa o **RA** 80 G 7
Estancia Marina o **RA** 80 F 7
Estancia Moat o **RA** 80 G 7
Estancia Monte Dinero o **RA** 80 F 6
Estancia Policarpo o **RA** 80 H 7
Estancia Rocallosa o **RCH** 80 E 6
Estancia Rosalía o **PY** 76-77 J 2
Estancia San Justo o **RA** 80 F 7
Estand, Küh-e ▲ **IR** 134-135 J 3
Estandarte o **BR** 68-69 F 2
Estanica o **USA** (NM) 256-257 J 4
Estanques o **YV** 60-61 F 3
Estarca, Río o **BOL** 76-77 D 1
Estcourt o **ZA** 220-221 J 4
Estcourt, Réserve ⊥ **CDN** (QUE) 240-241 F 3
Este, Laguna del ≋ 52-53 J 2
Este, Parque nacional del ⊥ **DOM** 54-55 L 5
Este, Punta del ▲ **ROU** 78-79 M 3
Esteban, Canal ≋ **RCH** 80 C 4
Êstéhärd o **IR** 136-137 B 7
Esteio o **BR** 74-75 E 4
Estelí ☆ **NIC** 52-53 L 5
Estella o **E** 98-99 F 3
Estelline o **USA** (SD) 260-261 K 2
Estelline o **USA** (TX) 264-265 D 4
Estépar o **E** 98-99 E 3
Êstepïktjah ~ **RUS** 110-111 Y 5
Estepona o **E** 98-99 E 6
Ester o **USA** 20-21 N 4
Esterbrook o **USA** (WY) 252-253 N 4
Esterhazy o **CDN** (SAS) 232-233 Q 5
Esteríktjah-Tas, hrebet ▲ **RUS** 110-111 X 5
Estero o **USA** (FL) 286-287 H 5
Estero Bay ≋ 40-41 D 8
Estero Bay ≋ **USA** 248-249 D 4
Estero Blanco o **RCH** 76-77 B 4
Estero de Boca o **RA** 76-77 F 5
Esterwood o **USA** (LA) 268-269 H 6
Estes Park o **USA** (CO) 254-255 K 3
Estevan o **CDN** (SAS) 232-233 Q 6
Estevan Group o **CDN** 228-229 D 3
Estevan Point o **CDN** (BC) 230-231 C 4
Estey o **USA** (MI) 272-273 C 4
Esther o **CDN** (ALB) 232-233 H 4
Esther o **USA** (LA) 268-269 H 7
Esther Lac o **CDN** (ONT) 236-237 K 2
Estherville o **USA** (IA) 260-261 L 5
Estill o **USA** (SC) 284-285 J 4
Estima o **MOC** 218-219 G 2
Estique o **PE** 70-71 E 5
Estirão do Equador o **BR** 66-67 B 5
Estiva o **BR** 68-69 F 7
Estiva, Riachão da ~ **BR** 68-69 F 5
Estlin o **CDN** (SAS) 232-233 O 5
Esto o **USA** (LA) 268-269 G 5
Estonia o **CDN** (SAS) 232-233 M 4
Estonia = Eesti ■ **EST** 94-95 J 2

Estor, El o **GCA** 52-53 K 4
Estrecho, El o **CO** 60-61 C 7
Estreito o **BR** 68-69 E 5
Estrela, Serra da ▲ **P** 98-99 C 4
Estrela do Sul o **BR** 72-73 G 5
Estrela, La o **BOL** 70-71 F 5
Estrela, La o **RA** 76-77 F 5
Estrella, Punta ▲ **MEX** 50-51 B 2
Estretto, Serra do ▲ **BR** 68-69 G 7
Estremadura ∴ **P** 98-99 C 5
Estremo o **P** 98-99 D 5
Estrondo, Serra do ▲ **BR** 68-69 D 6
Estuary o **CDN** (SAS) 232-233 J 5
Esumba, Île- ▲ **ZRE** 210-211 H 3
Esztergom o **H** 92-93 P 5
Etacho Point o **AUS** 30-31 J 2
Etah o **GRØ** 26-27 O 4
Etah o **IND** 138-139 F 3
Etaka o **NAM** 216-217 C 9
Étampes o **F** 90-91 J 7
Etamunbanie, Lake o **AUS** 178-179 E 4
Etawah o **IND** 138-139 G 3
Etchojoa o **MEX** 50-51 E 4
Etchoropo o **MEX** 50-51 E 4
Étéké o **G** 210-211 C 4
Êterikan, proliv ≋ 110-111 X 3
Eternity Range ▲ **ARK** 16 G 30
Ethel o **USA** (MS) 268-269 L 3
Ethelbert o **CDN** (MAN) 234-235 C 3
Ethel Creek o **AUS** 172-173 F 2
Etheldale o **AUS** 174-175 G 6
Ethel Lake o **CDN** 20-21 W 5
Ethel River o **AUS** 176-177 E 2
Ethiopia = Ityopya ■ **ETH** 208-209 C 3
Ethridge o **USA** (MT) 250-251 G 3
Etïvluk River ~ **USA** 20-21 M 2
Etler Rasmussen, Kap ▲ **GRØ** 26-27 p 2
Etna, Monte ▲ l 100-101 E 6
Etna o **USA** 30-31 K 3
Etoile o **USA** (TX) 268-269 F 5
Etoile Cay ▲ **SY** 224 C 2
Etolin, Cape ▲ **USA** 20-21 G 6
Etolin Island ▲ **USA** 32-33 D 3
Etolin Point ▲ **USA** 22-23 R 3
Etolin Strait ≋ 20-21 H 6
Eton o **AUS** 178-179 K 1
Etorohaberge ▲ **NAM** 216-217 B 8
Etosha Lookout o **NAM** 216-217 D 9
Etosha National Park ⊥ **NAM** 216-217 C 9
Etosha Pan ≋ **NAM** 216-217 D 9
Etou o **CAM** 204-205 J 6
Etoumbi o **RCB** 210-211 E 3
Etowah o **USA** (TN) 282-283 C 5
Etowah Mounds State Historic Site ∴ **USA** (GA) 284-285 F 2
Etowah River ~ **USA** (GA) 284-285 F 2
Etropole o **BG** 102-103 D 6
Etta Plains o **AUS** 174-175 F 6
Et Tarf, Garaet o **DZ** 190-191 F 3
Etten Island ▲ **CDN** 30-31 O 4
Ettington o **CDN** (MAN) 234-235 C 3
et-Tleta-de-Oved-Laov o **MA** 188-189 J 3
et-Tnine o **MA** 188-189 G 5
Ettumanur o **IND** 140-141 G 6
Êturem ~ **RUS** 116-117 M 2
Eturnagaram o **IND** 142-143 G 4
Êtyrkën o **RUS** 122-123 D 3
'Eua ▲ **TON** 184 IV a 2
Euabalong o **AUS** 180-181 J 2
Euaiki ▲ **TON** 184 IV a 2
Euca o **BR** 62-63 J 4
Eucaliptó, El o **ROU** 76-77 J 6
Euchiniko River ~ **CDN** (BC) 228-229 K 3
Eucla Basin ⊥ **AUS** 176-177 H 6
Eucla Motels o **AUS** 176-177 K 5
Euclid o **USA** (MN) 270-271 E 3
Euclid o **USA** (OH) 280-281 E 2
Euclides da Cunha o **BR** 68-69 J 7
Eucumbene, Lake o **AUS** 180-181 K 4
Eudistes, Lac des o **CDN** (QUE) 242-243 J 2
Eudora o **USA** (AR) 276-277 D 7
Eudora o **USA** (GA) 284-285 G 3
Eudunda o **AUS** 180-181 E 3
Eufaula o **USA** (AL) 284-285 E 4
Eufaula o **USA** (OK) 266-267 J 3
Eufaula Lake o **USA** (OK) 264-265 J 3
Eufrasio Loza o **RA** 76-77 F 5
Eugene o **USA** (OR) 244-245 B 6
Eugene McDermott Shoal ≈ **AUS** 172-173 G 2
Eugênia, Rio da ~ **BR** 70-71 H 2
Eugowra o **AUS** 180-181 K 2
Euless o **USA** (TX) 264-265 G 6
Eulo o **AUS** 178-179 H 5
Eulogy o **USA** (TX) 264-265 G 6
Eumara Springs o **AUS** 174-175 H 6
Eunápolis o **BR** 72-73 L 4
Eungella o **AUS** 178-179 K 1
Eungella National Park ⊥ **AUS** 174-175 K 7
Eunice o **USA** (LA) 268-269 H 6
Eunice o **USA** (NM) 256-257 M 6
Eupen o **B** 92-93 J 3
Euphrates ~ 128-129 L 7
Euphrates = Furât, al- ~ **SYR** 128-129 J 5
Eupora o **USA** (MS) 268-269 L 3
Eura o **FIN** 88-89 G 6
Eurambie o **AUS** 174-175 H 5
Euratsminde o **FIN** 88-89 G 6
Eureka o **CDN** 26-27 P 2
Eureka o **USA** (CA) 254-255 H 4
Eureka o **USA** (CA) 248-249 E 3
Eureka o **USA** (KS) 262-263 K 7
Eureka o **USA** (NV) 246-247 K 4
Eureka o **USA** (SD) 260-261 G 1
Eureka o **USA** (UT) 254-255 C 4
Eureka o **USA** (WA) 244-245 G 4
Eureka o **USA** (CA) 246-247 A 3

Eureka Sound ≈ 26-27 N 3
Eureka Springs o **USA** (AR) 276-277 D 3
Eurimbula National Park ⊥ **AUS** 178-179 L 3
Eurinilla Creek ~ **AUS** 178-179 F 6
Euriowie o **AUS** 178-179 F 6
Euroa o **AUS** 180-181 H 4
Euromsos • **TR** 128-129 B 3
Europa, Île ~ **F** 218-219 H 6
Europa, Picos de ▲ **E** 98-99 D 3
Europa, Punta ▲ **GO** 210-211 B 2
Europoort ⊥ **NL** 92-93 H 3
Eurotunnel II• 90-91 H 6
Euskadi □ **E** 98-99 F 3
Euskadi Pis -Vasco→ **E** 98-99 F 3
Eustis o **FL** 286-287 H 5
Eutaw o **USA** (AL) 284-285 C 4
Euthini o **MW** 214-215 G 6
Eutsuk Lake o **CDN** (BC) 228-229 H 3
Eva o **USA** (AL) 284-285 D 2
Eva o **USA** (AL) 284-285 D 2
Eva o **USA** (OK) 264-265 C 2
Eva o **USA** 172-173 F 7
Eva Downs o **AUS** 174-175 C 4
Eva-Liv, ostrov ~ **RUS** 84-85 h 2
Evale o **ANG** 216-217 C 8
Evandale o **USA** (NB) 240-241 J 5
Evander o **ZA** (CO) 254-255 J 3
Evans o **USA** (WA) 244-245 H 2
Evans, Lac o **CDN** (QUE) 236-237 G 2
Evans, Mount ▲ **USA** (MT) 250-251 J 5
Evansburg o **CDN** (ALB) 232-233 C 2
Evans Island ▲ **USA** 20-21 Q 7
Evans Shoal ≈ 166-167 E 6
Evans Strait ≈ 36-37 H 4
Evanston o **USA** (IL) 274-275 L 2
Evanston o **USA** (WY) 252-253 H 5
Evansville o **CDN** (ONT) 238-239 C 2
Evansville o **USA** (IN) 274-275 L 7
Evansville o **USA** (WY) 252-253 M 4
Evant o **USA** (TX) 266-267 G 4
Evaro o **USA** (MT) 250-251 F 4
Evart o **USA** (MI) 272-273 D 4
Evaton o **ZA** 220-221 H 3
Eva Valley o **USA** 172-173 L 3
Evaz o **IR** 134-135 G 5
Eveleth o **USA** (MN) 270-271 F 3
Evelyn o **CDN** (BC) 228-229 G 2
Evelyn, Mount ▲ **USA** 172-173 L 2
Evenk Autonomous District = **RUS**
Evenkijskij avtonomnyj okrug □ **RUS** 116-117 Q 3
Êvensk ☆ **RUS** 120-121 S 5
Everard, Lake o **USA** 178-179 C 6
Everard Junction o **AUS** 176-177 H 2
Everard Ranges ≈ 176-177 M 5
Everest, Mount ▲ **NEP** 144-145 F 7
Everett o **CDN** (NB) 240-241 H 5
Everett o **USA** (GA) 284-285 J 5
Everett o **USA** (WA) 244-245 C 3
Everett, Mount ▲ **USA** (MA) 278-279 H 6
Everett Mountains ▲ **CDN** 36-37 O 5
Everglades, The ⊥ **USA** (FL) 286-287 J 6
Everglades City o **USA** (FL) 286-287 H 6
Everglades National Park ⊥ • • • **USA** (FL) 286-287 J 6
Everglades Reclamation State Historic Site • **USA** (FL) 286-287 J 5
Evergreen o **USA** (AL) 284-285 D 5
Evergreen o **USA** (MN) 270-271 D 3
Evergreen Lake o **USA** (IL) 274-275 J 4
Evesham o **AUS** 178-179 G 2
Evesham o **CDN** (SAS) 232-233 J 3
Evgen'evka o **KA** 146-147 C 4
Évia ~ **GR** 100-101 J 5
Evijärvi o **FIN** 88-89 G 5
Evinayong o **GO** 210-211 C 3
Evje o **N** 86-87 C 7
Evodoula o **CAM** 204-205 J 6
Êvöğli o **IR** 128-129 L 2
Évora o **P** 98-99 D 5
Évora ❋ • • • **P** 98-99 D 5
Évoron, ozero o **RUS** 122-123 G 3
Êvota, gora ▲ **RUS** 118-119 M 7
Evpatorija = Jevpatorija ☆ • **UA** 102-103 J 5
Evreinova, Mys ~ **RUS** 120-121 P 4
Evreinova, proliv ≋ **RUS** 122-123 Q 4
Évreux • **F** 90-91 H 7
Evron o **F** 90-91 G 7
Êvur ~ **RUS** 122-123 G 3
Êwa o **USA** 88-89 U 5
Ewan o **USA** (WA) 244-245 H 3
Ewango o **WAN** 204-205 H 5
Ewarton o **JA** 54-55 G 5
Ewaso Ngiro ~ **EAK** (RIF) 212-213 E 4
Ewaso Ngiro ~ **EAK** 212-213 F 3
Ewasse o **PNG** 183 F 3
Ewell o **USA** (MD) 280-281 K 4
Ewing o **USA** (MO) 274-275 G 4
Ewing o **USA** (NE) 262-263 H 3
Ewing o **USA** (NJ) 280-281 M 4
Ewo o **RCB** 210-211 E 4
Exaltación o **BOL** (BEN) 70-71 F 3
Exaltación o **BOL** (PAN) 70-71 D 2
Excel o **USA** (TX) 264-265 C 2
Excello o **USA** (MO) 274-275 F 5
Excelsior o **ZA** 220-221 H 4
Excelsior Springs o **USA** (MO) 274-275 D 5
Exchamsiks River ~ **CDN** (BC) 228-229 E 2
Executive Committee Range ▲ **ARK** 16 F 24
Exeter o **CDN** (ONT) 238-239 D 5
Exeter ☆ • **GB** 90-91 H 6
Exeter o **USA** (CA) 248-249 E 3
Exeter o **USA** (NH) 278-279 H 6
Exeter Bay ≈ 28-29 K 3
Exeter Sound ≈ 28-29 K 3
Exira o **USA** (IA) 260-261 L 6
Exmoor National Park ⊥ **GB** 90-91 H 6
Exmore o **USA** (VA) 280-281 L 6

Exmouth o **AUS** 172-173 B 6
Exmouth Gulf ≈ 172-173 B 7
Exmouth, Lake o **USA** 30-31 M 3
Exmouth Plateau ≈ 13 C 4
Expedition National Park ⊥ **AUS** 178-179 K 3
Expedition Range ▲ **AUS** 178-179 K 3
Expedito Lopes Francisco Santos, D. o **BR** 68-69 H 5
Exploits, Bay of ≈ 38-39 R 4
Exploits, Bay of ≈ 38-39 R 4
Exploits Islands ~ **CDN** (NFL) 242-243 N 3
Exploits River ~ **CDN** (NFL) 242-243 M 4
Explorer Mountain ▲ **AUS** 32-33 Q 3
Exshaw o **CDN** (ALB) 232-233 C 4
Exstew o **CDN** 228-229 E 2
Extremadura ∴ **E** 98-99 D 5
Extrême Nord = Extreme North □ **CAM** 206-207 J 4
Extreme North = Extrême Nord □ **CAM** 206-207 J 4
Exu o **BR** 68-69 J 5
Exuma Cays ~ **BS** 54-55 G 2
Exuma Cays Land and Sea Park • **BS** 54-55 G 2
Exuma Sound ≈ 54-55 F 2
Eyasi, Lake o **EAT** 212-213 E 5
Eyeberry Lake o **CDN** 30-31 R 4
Eyebrow o **CDN** (SAS) 232-233 N 5
Eyehill Creek ~ **CDN** (SAS) 232-233 J 3
Eye of Kuruman • **ZA** 220-221 F 3
Eyl o **SP** 208-209 G 3
Eyota o **USA** (MN) 270-271 F 7
Eyre o **CDN** (SAS) 232-233 J 4
Eyre, Seno ≈ **RCH** 80 C 4
Eyre Creek ~ **AUS** 178-179 E 3
Eyre Highway II **AUS** 176-177 H 6
Eyre Mountains ▲ **NZ** 182 A 7
Eyre North, Lake o **AUS** 178-179 D 5
Eyre Peninsula ~ **AUS** 180-181 C 2
Eyre South, Lake o **AUS** 178-179 D 5
Eyumojok o **CAM** 204-205 H 6
Ezequiel Montes o **MEX** 52-53 E 1
Ezequiel Ramos Mexia, Embalse < **RA** 78-79 E 6
Ezere o **LV** 94-95 H 3
Êzernieki o **LV** 94-95 K 3
Ezgueret o **RMM** 196-197 M 6
Ezhou o **VRC** 154-155 M 4
Ezibeleni o **ZA** 220-221 H 5
Ezike, Enugu o **WAN** 204-205 G 5
Ezine ☆ **TR** 128-129 B 3
Ezo o **SUD** 206-207 H 6
Êzop, gora ▲ **RUS** 120-121 O 7
Êžuga ~ **RUS** 88-89 S 4
Ezzane, In **DZ** 192-193 D 6
Ezzango o **WAN** 204-205 H 5
ez-Zhiliga o **MA** 188-189 H 4

F

Fabens o **USA** (TX) 266-267 A 2
Faber Lake o **CDN** 30-31 L 4
Fåborg o **DK** 86-87 E 9
Fabriano o I 100-101 D 3
Fabyan o **CDN** (ALB) 232-233 H 3
Facatativá o **CO** 60-61 D 5
Fachi o **RN** 198-199 E 3
Fâchûd o **IND** 138-139 E 10
Facundo o **RA** 80 F 2
Fada o **TCH** 198-199 K 5
Fada-Ngourma o **BF** 202-203 L 3
Faddeevskij, ostrov ~ **RUS** 110-111 Y 2
Faddeja, ostrov ~ **RUS** 108-109 g 3
Faddeja, zaliv ≈ **RUS** 108-109 g 3
Faddoi o **SUD** 206-207 L 4
Faden o **CDN** 36-37 Q 7
Fadiadougou o **CI** 202-203 G 5
Fadiffolu Atoll ~ **MV** 140-141 B 5
Fadnoun, Plateau du ▲ **DZ** 190-191 G 7
Fadugu o **WAL** 202-203 E 6
Fa'er o **VRC** 156-157 E 3
Faërina, Wâdi ~ **ET** 194-195 F 3
Fagagha o **SOL** 184 I a 3
Fagan o **PY** 286-287 Q 2
Faje o **WAN** 204-205 F 6
Fakenham o **GB** 90-91 H 5
Fakfak o **RI** 166-167 G 3
Fakfak, Pegunungan ▲ **RI** 166-167 G 3
Fako o **CAM** 204-205 H 6
Fakse o **DK** 86-87 F 9
Fakse Bugt ≈ 86-87 F 9
Fak Tha o **THA** 158-159 F 2
Faku o **VRC** 150-151 D 6
Fala o **RMM** 202-203 F 3
Falaba o **WAL** 202-203 E 5
Falagountou o **BF** 202-203 L 2
Falaise o **F** 90-91 G 7
Falaise Lake o **CDN** 30-31 L 4
Falam o **MYA** 142-143 H 4
Falaq, Bi'r o **ET** 128-129 J 5
Falavarğân o **IR** 134-135 D 2
Falcon, Cape ▲ **AUS** 174-175 G 3
Falcon o **USA** (TX) 266-267 G 4
Falcón, Fiordo ≈ **RCH** 80 C 4
Falcón, Presa < **MEX** 50-51 K 4
Falcon Lake o **CDN** (MAN) 234-235 H 5
Falda, La o **RA** 76-77 F 5
Faléa o **RMM** 202-203 E 3
Faléapuna o **WS** 184 V a 1
Faleäipuna o **WS** 184 V b 1
Falémé ~ **SN** 202-203 E 3
Falenki o **RUS** 96-97 G 4
Falfurrias o **USA** (TX) 266-267 G 6
Falima o **WAL** 202-203 E 5
Fali Mountains ▲ **WAN** 204-205 J 5
Falkat o **ER** 200-201 J 4
Falken, In- o **S** 86-87 F 8
Falkenberg (Elster) o **D** 92-93 M 3
Fağr, Wâdi ~ **KSA** 130-131 K 7
Fagnikotti o **SUD** 200-201 E 3
Fagudu o **RI** 164-165 K 4
Faguibine, Lac o **RMM** 196-197 H 6
Fagurhólsmýri o **IS** 86-87 e 3
Fahl, Hassi ~ **DZ** 190-191 D 5
Fahliyän, Rüd-e ~ **IR** 134-135 D 3
Fahreĝ o **IR** 134-135 H 4
Fâ'id o **ET** 194-195 F 2
Fäid o **TN** 190-191 G 3
Failaka, Ğazirat ~ **KWT** 130-131 K 7
Faillon, Lac o **CDN** (QUE) 236-237 M 4
Fain o **SUD** 200-201 E 5
Fairbairn Reservoir < **AUS** 178-179 K 2
Fairbank o **USA** (MD) 280-281 K 4
Fairbanks o • **USA** 20-21 N 4
Fair Bluff o **USA** (NC) 282-283 K 3
Fairborn o **USA** (OH) 280-281 B 4
Fairbury o **USA** (NE) 262-263 J 4
Fairchild o **USA** (WI) 270-271 H 6

Fairfax o **CDN** (BC) 230-231 H 3
Fairfax o **USA** (MN) 270-271 D 6
Fairfax o **USA** (OK) 264-265 H 2
Fairfax o **USA** (SC) 284-285 J 4
Fairfax o **USA** (SD) 260-261 H 3
Fairfield o **USA** (AL) 284-285 D 3
Fairfield o **USA** (IA) 274-275 G 4
Fairfield o **USA** (ID) 252-253 D 3
Fairfield o **USA** (ME) 278-279 L 7
Fairfield o **USA** (MT) 250-251 H 4
Fairfield o **USA** (NC) 282-283 L 5
Fairfield o **USA** (OH) 280-281 B 5
Fairfield o **USA** (TX) 266-267 L 2
Fairfield o **USA** (TX) 278-279 H 6
Fairfield Lake < **USA** (TX) 266-267 L 2
Fairford o **CDN** (MAN) 234-235 E 3
Fairholme o **CDN** (SAS) 232-233 K 2
Fairhope o **USA** (AL) 284-285 C 6
Fairhill o **AUS** 178-179 K 2
Fairlight o **CDN** (SAS) 232-233 R 6
Fairmont o **CDN** (MN) 270-271 D 7
Fairmont o **USA** (MN) 270-271 D 7
Fairmont o **USA** (NE) 262-263 J 4
Fairmont o **USA** (WV) 280-281 F 4
Fairmount o **USA** (GA) 284-285 F 2
Fairmount o **USA** (ND) 258-259 K 4
Fair Ness ▲ **CDN** 36-37 N 3
Fairo o **WAL** 202-203 E 6
Fair Oaks o **USA** (AR) 276-277 D 5
Fairoaks o **USA** (AR) 280-281 E 4
Fairplay o **USA** (CO) 254-255 J 4
Fair Play o **USA** (MO) 276-277 B 3
Fairplay, Mount ▲ **USA** 20-21 T 5
Fairview o **USA** 174-175 H 4
Fairview o **CDN** 32-33 L 3
Fairview o **USA** (AL) 284-285 D 5
Fairview o **USA** (CA) 248-249 F 4
Fairview o **USA** (KS) 262-263 L 5
Fairview o **USA** (MT) 250-251 P 4
Fairview o **USA** (OK) 264-265 G 2
Fairview o **USA** (TN) 276-277 H 5
Fairview o **USA** (UT) 254-255 D 4
Fairview o **USA** (WY) 252-253 H 5
Fairview Peak ▲ **USA** (OR) 244-245 C 7
Fairweather, Cape ▲ **USA** 32-33 A 2
Fairweather, Mount ▲ **USA** 32-33 A 2
Fairy o **USA** (TX) 266-267 K 2
Fairy Glen o **CDN** (SAS) 232-233 O 2
Faisalabad ☆ • **PAK** 138-139 D 2
Faişäliya, al- o **KSA** 132-133 B 3
Faith o **USA** (SD) 260-261 D 1
Faiyiba o **SUD** 200-201 E 5
Faizabad o **AFG** 136-137 M 6
Faizäbäd o **IND** 142-143 C 2
Fajardo o **PY** (R) 286-287 Q 2
Fakao o **WAN** 204-205 F 6
Fakenham o **GB** 90-91 H 5
Fakfak o **RI** 166-167 G 3
Fakfak, Pegunungan ▲ **RI** 166-167 G 3
Fako o **CAM** 204-205 H 6
Fakse o **DK** 86-87 F 9
Fala o **RMM** 202-203 F 3
Falam o **MYA** 142-143 H 4
Falealupo o **WS** 184 V a 1

Falls Creek o **CDN** (BC) 230-231 H 3
Falls Lake Reservoir < **USA** (NC) 282-283 J 4
Fallüğa, al- o **IRQ** 128-129 K 6
Falmey o **RN** 204-205 E 2
Falmouth o **GB** 90-91 G 6
Falmouth o **JA** 54-55 G 5
Falmouth o **USA** (KY) 276-277 L 2
Falmouth o **USA** (MA) 278-279 L 7
Falou o **RMM** (BAM) 202-203 G 2
Falou o **RMM** (KAY) 202-203 F 3
Falsa, Bahía ≈ 78-79 H 5
Falsa Calera, Punta ▲ **DOM** 54-55 K 6
False, Rivière ~ **CDN** 36-37 P 6
False Bay ≈ 220-221 D 7
False Bay ≈ **CDN** (BC) 230-231 E 4
False Bay ≈ **ZA** 220-221 D 7
False Cabo ▲ **HN** 54-55 D 7
False Pass o **USA** 22-23 P 5
False Point ▲ **IND** 142-143 E 5
Falsinio, Rio ~ **BR** 62-63 J 5
Falso, Cabo ▲ **HN** 54-55 D 7
Falso Cabo de Hornos ▲ **RCH** 80 F 7
Falso ÓP. Aguja, Cabo ▲ **DOM** 54-55 K 6
Falster ▲ **DK** 86-87 E 9
Falsterselv ~ **GRØ** 26-27 n 8
Falterona, Monte ▲ I 100-101 C 3
Falun o **CDN** (ALB) 232-233 E 3
Falun o **S** 86-87 G 6
Fam = Fafa ~ **RCA** 206-207 D 5
Fam, Kepulauan ~ **RI** 166-167 F 2
Fama o **SUD** 206-207 K 3
Famaillá o **RA** 76-77 E 4
Famalé o **RN** 202-203 L 2
Fámanin o **IR** 128-129 N 5
Fámarin o **IR** 134-135 C 1
Famatina, Sierra de ▲ **RA** 76-77 D 5
Fambusi o **GH** 202-203 K 4
Famen Si • **VRC** 154-155 E 4
Fame Range ▲ **AUS** 176-177 G 2
Family Lake o **CDN** (MAN) 234-235 G 3
Fana o **RMM** 202-203 G 3
Fanado, Rio ~ **BR** 72-73 J 4
Fanamambana o **RM** 222-223 F 4
Fanambana ~ **RM** 222-223 F 4
Fanär Qaşr Ahmad o **LAR** 192-193 F 1
Fanchang o **VRC** 154-155 L 6
Fandango Pass ≈ **USA** (CA) 246-247 E 2
Fandriana o **RM** 222-223 E 8
Fang o **THA** 142-143 I 5
Fangak o **SUD** 206-207 K 4
Fangamadou o **RG** 202-203 F 5
Fangcheng o **VRC** (GXI) 156-157 F 3
Fangcheng o **VRC** (HEN) 154-155 H 5
Fangliao o **RC** 156-157 M 5
Fang Xian o **VRC** 154-155 G 5
Fangzheng o **VRC** 150-151 G 5
Fanjingshan z.B. ⊥ **VRC** 156-157 F 3
Fannin o **USA** (TX) 266-267 K 2
Fannin ~ **USA** (TX) 266-267 K 5
Fanning River o **AUS** 174-175 J 6
Fanny Bay o **CDN** (BC) 230-231 E 4
Fannystelle o **CDN** (MAN) 234-235 F 5
Fana ~ **DK** 86-87 E 8
Fano o I 100-101 D 3
Fanshi o **VRC** 154-155 H 2
Fantome, Trou des = Phantoms Cave • **CAM** 210-211 C 2
Fanug o **IR** 134-135 H 5
Fan Xian o **VRC** 154-155 J 3
Fanxue o **VRC** 154-155 E 3
Fão o **BR** 74-75 D 7
Fao, Koun- o **CI** 202-203 J 6
Faouët, le o **F** 90-91 F 7
Faqih Soleimän o **IR** 128-129 N 4
Fâgüs o **ET** 194-195 F 2
Faraba o **RMM** 202-203 F 3
Farab-Pristan' = Dżejhun o **TM** 136-137 H 5
Faraday Fracture Zone ≈ 6-7 F 4
Faradje o **ZRE** 212-213 D 2
Farafangana o **RM** 222-223 E 9
Farafara Oasis = Farâfira, al-Wâhât al- ⊥ **ET** 194-195 D 3
Farafenni o **WAG** 202-203 D 3
Farâfira, al-Wâhât al- ⊥ **ET** 194-195 D 3
Faraguaran o **RMM** 202-203 G 4
Farah ☆ **AFG** (FA) 134-135 J 2
Farähäbäd o **IND** 140-141 H 2
Farahalana o **RM** 222-223 G 5
Farahnāze, Bandar-e o **IR** 128-129 N 4
Farährüd o **AFG** 134-135 K 2
Farakaraina, Corniche de • **RM** 222-223 F 5
Farako o **RMM** 202-203 G 4
Farallones de Cali, Parque Nacional ⊥ **CO** 60-61 C 6
Faramana o **BF** 202-203 H 3
Faramuti o **SUD** 206-207 K 3
Farangal o **USA** 30-31 A 4
Faranah o **RG** 202-203 E 4
Farany ~ **RM** 222-223 E 8
Far'aoun o **ET** 194-195 F 3
Farasan o **KSA** 132-133 C 5
Farasän, Ğazâ'ir ~ **KSA** 132-133 B 5
Farasän, Ğazîrat ~ **KSA** 132-133 B 5
Faratsiho o **RM** 222-223 E 7
Farda, al- o **Y** 132-133 G 6
Farda, Naqil al- ~ **Y** 132-133 D 6
Farewell o **USA** 20-21 O 5
Farewell, Cape ▲ **NZ** 182 D 4
Farewell ~ **SUD** 200-201 G 6
Fargo o **USA** 284-285 G 6
Fargo o **USA** (ND) 258-259 L 4
Fargo o **USA** (OK) 264-265 E 2
Fari o **USA** 136-137 L 6
Faria ~ **RMM** 202-203 G 2
Farias Brito o **BR** 68-69 J 5
Faribault o **USA** (MN) 270-271 E 6
Faribault, Lac o **CDN** 36-37 O 5
Faridäbäd o **IND** 138-139 F 3
Faridkot o **IND** 138-139 E 2
Faridpur o **BD** 142-143 F 4

Foggaret el 'Arab ○ DZ 190-191 D 7
Foggaret ez Zoua ○ DZ 190-191 D 7
Fóggia ☆ I 100-101 E 4
Foggy Cape ▲ USA 22-23 S 4
Fogi ○ RI 166-167 D 3
Fogo ○ CDN (NFL) 242-243 O 3
Fogo, Ilha de ⌒ CV 202-203 B 6
Fogo Island ⌒ CDN (NFL) 242-243 O 3
Føhn Fjord ≈ 26-27 m 8
Föhr ⌒ D 92-93 K 1
Fóia ▲ P 98-99 C 6
Foisy ○ CDN (ALB) 232-233 G 2
Foix ○ F 90-91 H 10
Foja, Pegunungan ▲ RI 166-167 K 3
Fokina ~ RUS 108-109 W 7
Fokino ○ RUS 94-95 O 5
Fokku ○ WAN 204-205 F 3
Folda ≈ 86-87 G 3
Foldereid ○ N 86-87 F 4
Foley ○ RB 218-219 D 5
Foley ○ USA (AL) 284-285 C 6
Foley ○ USA (MN) 270-271 E 5
Foleyet ○ CDN (ONT) 236-237 F 4
Foley Island ⌒ CDN 24-25 j 6
Folgares ○ ANG 216-217 C 7
Folgefonni ⊂ N 86-87 C 7
Foligno ○ I 100-101 D 3
Folkestone ○• GB 90-91 H 6
Folkston ○ USA (GA) 284-285 H 6
Folkstone ○ USA (NC) 282-283 K 6
Folldal ☆ N 86-87 D 5
Follett ○ USA (TX) 264-265 D 2
Follette, La ○ USA (TN) 282-283 C 4
Föllinge ○ S 86-87 G 5
Follónica ○ I 100-101 C 3
Folly Beach ○ USA (SC) 284-285 L 4
Folly Island ⌒ USA (SC) 284-285 L 4
Folsom ○ USA (LA) 268-269 K 6
Folsom ○ USA (NM) 256-257 M 2
Fomboni ○ COM 222-223 C 4
Fome, Rio da ~ BR 68-69 G 3
Fomena ○ GH 202-203 K 6
Fomento ○ C 54-55 F 3
Fomič ~ RUS 110-111 F 4
Fona ○ VAN 184 II b 3
Fonda ○ USA (IA) 274-275 D 2
Fondale ○ USA (LA) 268-269 H 4
Fond-du-Lac ○ CDN 30-31 Q 6
Fond du Lac ○ CDN 30-31 Q 6
Fond du Lac ○ USA (WI) 270-271 K 7
Fond du Lac Indian Reservation ✗ USA (MN) 270-271 F 4
Fond du Lac River ~ CDN 30-31 R 6
Fonehill ○ CDN (SAS) 232-233 Q 4
Fonéko ○ RN 202-203 L 2
Fongolembi ○ SN 202-203 D 3
Fonni ○ I 100-101 B 4
Fonoifua ⌒ TON 184 IV a 2
Fonsagrada, A ○ E 98-99 D 3
Fonseca ○ CO 60-61 E 2
Fonseca, Golfo de ≈ 52-53 L 5
Fonsecas, Serra dos ▲ BR 72-73 H 4
Fontaine Lake ⊂ CDN 30-31 Q 6
Fontana, Lago ⊂ RA 80 E 2
Fontana Lake < USA (NC) 282-283 D 5
Fontanelle ○ USA (NE) 262-263 K 3
Fontanina ○ ETH 208-209 D 3
Fontas ○ CDN 30-31 J 6
Fontas River ~ CDN 30-31 J 6
Fonte Boa ○ BR 66-67 D 4
Fontenay, Abbaye de ••• F 90-91 K 8
Fontenay-le-Comte ○ F 90-91 G 8
Fonteneau, Lac ⊂ CDN 38-39 O 3
Fontenelle ○ CDN (QUE) 240-241 L 2
Fontenelle ○ USA (WY) 252-253 H 5
Fontenelle Reservoir ⊂ USA (WY) 252-253 H 4
Fontibón ○ CO 60-61 D 5
Fontur ▲ IS 86-87 f 1
Fonuafo'ou ⌒ TON 184 IV a 2
Fonualei ⌒ TON 184 IV a 1
Fo'ondo ○ SOL 184 I e 3
Foping ○ VRC 154-155 E 5
Foping Z.B. ⊥• VRC 154-155 E 5
Forage Christine eau potable < BF 202-203 K 2
Forari ○ VAN 184 II b 3
Forbes ○ AUS 180-181 K 2
Forbes ○ USA (ND) 258-259 J 6
Forbes, Kap ▲ GRØ 26-27 R 4
Forbus ○ USA (TN) 276-277 K 4
Forcados ○ WAN 204-205 F 6
Ford ○ USA (ID) 250-251 B 4
Ford ○ USA (KS) 262-263 G 7
Ford, Cape ▲ AUS 172-173 J 2
Ford, Cerro el ▲ RCH 80 E 6
Fordate, Pulau ⌒ RI 166-167 F 5
Ford Costantine ○ AUS 174-175 F 7
Førde ☆ N 86-87 B 6
Ford Falls ~ CDN 30-31 R 4
Fording River ~ CDN (BC) 230-231 P 4
Ford River ~ CDN 36-37 H 2
Ford River ~ USA (MI) 270-271 L 5
Fordsville ○ USA (KY) 276-277 J 3
Fordyce ○ USA (AR) 276-277 C 7
Forécariah ○ RG 202-203 D 5
Foreman ○ USA (AR) 276-277 A 7
Foremost ○ CDN (ALB) 232-233 G 6
Foresman ○ USA (IN) 274-275 L 4
Forest ○ CDN (ONT) 238-239 D 5
Forest ○ USA (MS) 268-269 L 4
Forest, Lac la ⊂ CDN 36-37 O 7
Forest Acres ○ USA (SC) 284-285 K 2
Forestburg ○ CDN (ALB) 232-233 F 3
Forestburg ○ USA (TX) 264-265 G 5
Forest City ○ USA (IA) 274-275 E 1
Forest City ○ USA (NC) 282-283 F 5
Forestdale ○ CDN (BC) 228-229 H 2
Forest Glen ○ USA (CA) 246-247 B 3
Forest Grove ○ CDN (BC) 230-231 H 2
Forestgrove ○ USA (MT) 250-251 K 4
Forest Grove ○ USA (OR) 244-245 B 5
Forest Home ○ AUS 174-175 G 6
Forestier, Cape ▲ AUS 180-181 K 7
Forest Lake ○ USA (MN) 270-271 F 5
Forest Park ○ USA (GA) 284-285 F 3
Forest River ○ USA (ND) 258-259 K 3
Forest Strait ≈ 158-159 E 5
Forestville ○ CDN (QUE) 240-241 F 2
Forestville ○ USA (MI) 272-273 G 4
Forestville ○ USA (WI) 270-271 L 6
Forfar ○ GB 90-91 F 3
Forgan ○ CDN (SAS) 232-233 L 4
Forgan ○ USA (OK) 264-265 D 2
Forges-les-Eaux ○ F 90-91 H 7
Forget ○ CDN (SAS) 232-233 Q 6
Forillon, Parc National de ⊥ CDN (QUE) 240-241 L 2
Fork ○ USA (SC) 284-285 L 2
Forked Island ○ USA (LA) 268-269 H 7
Fork Lake ○ CDN 32-33 P 4
Forkland ○ USA (AL) 284-285 C 4
Fork Reservoir, Lake ⊂ USA (TX) 264-265 J 6
Forks ○ USA (WA) 244-245 A 3
Forks of Cacapon ○ USA (WV) 280-281 H 4
Forks of Salmon ○ USA (CA) 246-247 B 2
Fork Union ○ USA (VA) 280-281 H 6
Forlandet nasjonalpark ⊥ N 84-85 G 3
Forlandsundet ≈ 84-85 G 3
Forlì ○ I 100-101 D 2
Forman ○ USA (ND) 258-259 K 5
Formation Cave ∴ USA (ID) 252-253 G 4
Formby Bay ≈ 180-181 D 3
Formentera, Illa de ⌒ E 98-99 H 5
Formentor, Cap de ▲• E 98-99 J 5
Formia ○ I 100-101 D 4
Formiga ○ BR (MAR) 68-69 F 3
Formiga ○ BR (MIN) 72-73 H 6
Formosa ○ BR 72-73 G 3
Formosa ▫ RA 76-77 G 3
Formosa ☆ RA (FOR) 76-77 H 4
Formosa, Cachoeira da ~ BR 72-73 D 2
Formosa, Ilha ⌒ GNB 202-203 B 4
Formosa, La ○ BR 72-73 G 5
Formosa, Serra ▲ BR 70-71 K 3
Formosa do Rio Preto ○ BR 68-69 F 7
Formoso ○ BR (GOI) 72-73 F 2
Formoso ○ BR (GSU) 72-73 D 6
Formoso ○ BR (MIN) 72-73 G 3
Formoso, Cape ▲ WAN 204-205 G 6
Formoso, Rio ~ BR 68-69 D 7
Formoso, Rio ~ BR 72-73 H 2
Formoso, Rio ~ BR 72-73 H 4
Formoso, Rio ~ BR 72-73 D 5
Fornæs ▲ DK 86-87 E 8
Fornells ○ E 98-99 K 4
Fornos ○ MOC 218-219 H 6
Foro Burunga ○ SUD 198-199 L 6
Foroko ○ PNG 183 C 3
Forolshogna ▲ N 86-87 E 5
Foropaugh ○ USA (AZ) 256-257 B 5
Foros ○• UA 102-103 H 5
Forpost-Kargat ○ RUS 114-115 Q 7
Forres ○ RA 76-77 F 4
Forrest ○ AUS (VIC) 180-181 G 5
Forrest ○ AUS (WA) 176-177 K 5
Forrest ○ USA (IL) 274-275 K 4
Forrest, Mount ▲ AUS 176-177 E 4
Forrest City ○ USA (AR) 276-277 E 5
Forrest Lakes ⊂ AUS 176-177 K 4
Forreston ○ USA (IL) 274-275 J 2
Forrest River Aboriginal Land ✗ AUS 172-173 H 3
Forrest Station ○ CDN (MAN) 234-235 D 5
Forsayth ○ AUS 174-175 G 6
Forshaga ☆ S 86-87 F 7
Forsnes ○ N 86-87 D 5
Forssa ○ FIN 88-89 G 6
Forsyth ○ USA (GA) 284-285 G 3
Forsyth ○ USA (MO) 276-277 B 4
Forsyth ○ USA (MT) 250-251 N 5
Forsyth Island ⌒ AUS 174-175 E 5
Forsyth Range ▲ AUS 178-179 G 2
Fort (Dutch) ∴• RI 164-165 J 5
Fort Abbás ○ PK 138-139 D 5
Fort Abercrombie • USA (ND) 258-259 L 5
Fort Albany ○ CDN 34-35 Q 4
Fort Albercrombie State Historical Park • USA 22-23 U 4
Fortale, Caño la ~ CO 60-61 F 5
Fort Alexander ○ CDN (MAN) 234-235 G 4
Fortaleza ○ BOL 70-71 D 3
Fortaleza ○ BR (ACR) 66-67 B 7
Fortaleza ○ BR (AMA) 66-67 C 6
Fortaleza ○ BR (AMA) 66-67 H 4
Fortaleza ○ BR (RON) 66-67 F 7
Fortaleza ☆• BR (CEA) 68-69 J 3
Fortaleza, La ○ YV 60-61 J 3
Fortaleza dos Nogueiras ○ BR 68-69 E 5
Fort Amanda State Memorial • USA (OH) 280-281 B 3
Fort Amherst National Historic Park • CDN (PEI) 240-241 M 4
Fort Anne National Historic Park • CDN (NS) 240-241 K 6
Fort Apache Indian Reservation ✗ USA (AZ) 256-257 E 4
Fort Atkinson ○ USA (WI) 274-275 K 2
Fort Augustus ○• GB 90-91 E 3
Fort Battleford National Historic Park • CDN (SAS) 232-233 K 3
Fort Beaufort ○ ZA 220-221 H 6
Fort Belknap Agency ○ USA (MT) 250-251 L 3
Fort Belknap Indian Reservation ✗ USA (MT) 250-251 L 3
Fort Belmont • USA (MN) 270-271 C 7
Fort Belvoir ✗✗ USA (VA) 280-281 J 5
Fort Benning ○ USA (GA) 284-285 F 4
Fort Benning ✗✗ USA (GA) 284-285 F 4
Fort Benton ○ USA (MT) 250-251 J 4
Fort Benton Ruins • USA (MT) 250-251 J 4
Fort Berthold Indian Reservation ✗ USA (ND) 258-259 E 4
Fort Black ○ CDN 34-35 C 3
Fort Bliss Military Reservation ✗✗ USA (NM) 256-257 J 6
Fort Bragg ○ USA (NC) 282-283 J 5
Fort Bragg Military Reservation ✗✗ USA (NC) 282-283 H 5
Fort Branch ○ USA (IN) 274-275 L 6
Fort Bridger ○ USA (WY) 252-253 H 5
Fort-Chimo = Kuujjuaq ○ CDN 36-37 P 5
Fort Chipewyan ○ CDN 30-31 O 6
Fort Churchill ○ CDN 30-31 X 6
Fort Clark ○ USA (ND) 258-259 F 4
Fort Cobb ○ USA (OK) 264-265 F 3
Fort Cobb Reservoir < USA (OK) 264-265 F 3
Fort Cobb State Park ⊥• USA (OK) 264-265 F 3
Fort Collins ○ USA (CO) 254-255 K 3
Fort Collinson ○ CDN 24-25 N 5
Fort Coulonge ○ CDN (QUE) 238-239 J 3
Fort Craig, Ruins of • USA (NM) 256-257 H 5
Fort-Dauphin = Tôlanaro ○• RM 222-223 E 10
Fort Davis ○ USA (AL) 284-285 E 4
Fort de Cock • RI 162-163 D 5
Fort-de-France ☆ F 56 E 4
Fort Deposit ○ USA (AL) 284-285 D 5
Fort Dodge ○ USA (IA) 274-275 D 2
Fort Drum • USA (NY) 278-279 F 4
Forteau ○ CDN (NFL) 242-243 M 1
Fort Edward National Historic Site • CDN (NS) 240-241 L 6
Fort Egbert National Historic Site • USA 20-21 U 4
Fort Erie ○ CDN (ONT) 238-239 G 6
Fortescue River ~ AUS 172-173 C 6
Fortescue River Roadhouse ○ AUS 172-173 C 6
Fort Eustis ✗✗ USA (VA) 280-281 K 6
Fort Fisher • USA (NC) 282-283 K 7
Fort Frances ○ CDN (ONT) 234-235 K 6
Fort Franklin ○ CDN 30-31 H 3
Fort Fraser ○ CDN (BC) 228-229 K 2
Fort Fred Steele ○ USA (WY) 252-253 M 5
Fort Gadsden State Historical Site • USA (FL) 286-287 E 2
Fort Gaines ○ USA (GA) 284-285 E 5
Fort Garland ○ USA (CO) 254-255 K 6
Fort George ○ CDN 38-39 E 2
Fort George National Historic Park • CDN (ONT) 238-239 F 5
Fort George River = La Grande Rivière ~ CDN 38-39 G 2
Fort Gibson ○ USA (OK) 264-265 J 3
Fort Gibson Lake ⊂ USA (OK) 264-265 J 2
Fort Glenn ○ USA 22-23 N 6
Fort Good Hope ○ CDN 30-31 E 2
Fort Gordon ✗✗ USA (GA) 284-285 H 3
Fort Griffin State Historic Park ⊥ USA (TX) 264-265 E 6
Fort Hall ○ CDN 30-31 T 6
Fort Hall ○ USA (ID) 252-253 F 3
Fort Hall Indian Reservation ✗ USA (ID) 252-253 F 3
Fort Hancock ○ USA (TX) 266-267 B 2
Forthassa Gharbia ○ DZ 188-189 L 4
Fort Hope ○ CDN (ONT) 234-235 P 3
Fort Hope Indian Reserve ✗ CDN (ONT) 234-235 Q 3
Fort Huachuca • USA (AZ) 256-257 E 7
Fort Hunter Liggett Military Reservation ✗✗ USA (CA) 248-249 C 3
Fortierville ○ CDN (QUE) 238-239 N 2
Fortín 1° de Mayo ○ RA 78-79 D 5
Fortín, El ○ RA 76-77 F 6
Fortín Avalos Sanchez ○ PY 76-77 G 2
Fortín Boquerón ○ PY 76-77 H 2
Fortín Cabo 1° Cano ○ PY 76-77 H 3
Fortín Cadete Pastor Pando ○ PY 76-77 H 3
Fortín Carlos A. Lopez ○ PY 76-77 H 1
Fortín Charrúa ○ RA 76-77 G 5
Fortín Crnate Nowak ○ PY 76-77 H 3
Fortín Colonel Bogado ○ PY 70-71 H 7
Fortín de las Flores ○ MEX 52-53 F 2
Fort Independence Indian Reservation ✗ USA (CA) 248-249 F 3
Fortín Gaspar de Francia ○ PY 76-77 H 2
Fortín General Díaz ○ PY 76-77 G 2
Fortín Guanacos • RA 78-79 D 4
Fortín Hernandarias ○ PY 76-77 G 1
Fortín Infante Rivarola ○ PY 76-77 F 1
Fortín Lagerenza ○ PY 70-71 G 7
Fortín Lavalle ○ RA 76-77 G 3
Fortín Leonida Escobar ○ PY 76-77 G 2
Fortín Madrejon ○ PY 70-71 H 7
Fortín Malargüe • RA 78-79 E 3
Fortín Nueva Asunción ○ PY 70-71 G 7
Fortín Olmos ○ RA 76-77 G 5
Fortín Pilcomayo ○ RA 76-77 G 2
Fortín Pozo Hondo ○ PY 76-77 F 2
Fortín Ravelo ○ BOL 70-71 G 6
Fortín Teniente Américo Picco ○ PY 70-71 H 6
Fortín Teniente Montanía ○ PY 76-77 H 2
Fortín Teniente Rojas Silva ○ PY 76-77 G 2
Fortín Toledo ○ PY 76-77 G 2
Fortín Torres ○ PY 76-77 H 1
Fortín Zalazar ○ PY 76-77 H 2
Fort Irwin ○ USA (CA) 248-249 G 4
Fortin ○ CDN (ONT) 238-239 G 3
Fort Jackson ∴ USA (SC) 284-285 K 2
Fort Jones ○ USA (CA) 246-247 C 2
Fort Kearney State Historic Park ∴• USA (NE) 262-263 G 4
Fort Kent ○ USA (ME) 278-279 N 1
Fort Kent Historic Site • USA (ME) 278-279 N 1
Fort Kissimmee ○ USA (FL) 286-287 H 4
Fort Klamath ○ USA (OR) 244-245 C 8
Fort Knox ✗✗ USA (KY) 276-277 K 3
Fort Langley National Historic Park • CDN (BC) 230-231 G 4
Fort Laramie ○ USA (WY) 252-253 O 4
Fort la Reine • CDN (MAN) 234-235 E 5
Fort Lauderdale ○ USA (FL) 286-287 J 5
Fort Lemhi Monument • USA (ID) 252-253 E 2
Fort Lewis • USA (WA) 244-245 C 4
Fort Liard ○ CDN 30-31 H 5
Fort Liberté ☆ RH 54-55 K 5
Fort MacKavett ○ USA (TX) 266-267 G 3
Fort MacKay ○ CDN 32-33 P 3
Fort Mackinac • USA (MI) 272-273 E 2
Fort Madison ○ USA (IA) 274-275 G 4
Fort Matanzas National Monument • USA (FL) 286-287 H 2
Fort Maurepas • CDN (MAN) 234-235 G 4
Fort McClellan ✗✗ USA (AL) 284-285 E 3
Fort McCoy Military Reservation ✗✗ USA (WI) 270-271 H 6
Fort McHenry • USA (MD) 280-281 K 4
Fort McKavett State Historic Site • USA (TX) 266-267 G 3
Fort McMurray ○• CDN 32-33 P 3
Fort McPherson ○ CDN 20-21 Y 3
Fort Meade ○ USA (FL) 286-287 H 4
Fort Mill ○ USA (SC) 284-285 K 1
Fort Mohave Indian Reservation ✗ USA (AZ) 256-257 A 4
Fort Morgan ○ USA (CO) 254-255 M 3
Fort Morgan • USA (AL) 284-285 B 6
Fort Mtobeni ○ ZA 220-221 K 4
Fort Munro ○• PK 138-139 B 5
Fort Myers ○ USA (FL) 286-287 H 5
Fort Nelson ○ CDN 30-31 H 6
Fort Nelson Indian Reserve ✗ CDN 30-31 H 6
Fort Nelson River ~ CDN 30-31 H 6
Fort Norman ○ CDN 30-31 G 3
Fort Oglethorpe ○ USA (GA) 284-285 E 2
Fort Payne ○ USA (AL) 284-285 E 2
Fort Peck ○ USA (MT) 250-251 N 3
Fort Peck Indian Reservation ✗ USA (MT) 250-251 O 3
Fort Pickett ✗✗ USA (VA) 280-281 J 6
Fort Pierce ○ USA (FL) 286-287 J 4
Fort Pierre ○ USA (SD) 260-261 F 2
Fort Pierre National Grassland ⊥ USA (SD) 260-261 F 2
Fort Pierre Verendrye Monument • USA (SD) 260-261 F 2
Fort Pitt Historic Park • CDN (SAS) 232-233 J 2
Fort Portal ☆ EAU 212-213 C 3
Fort Prince of Wales National Historic Park • CDN 30-31 W 6
Fort Providence ○ CDN 30-31 L 5
Fort Qu'Appelle ○ CDN (SAS) 232-233 P 5
Fort Ransom ○ USA (ND) 258-259 K 5
Fort Recovery ○ USA (OH) 280-281 B 3
Fort Resolution ○ CDN 30-31 N 5
Fortress • RI 162-163 C 3
Fortress of Louisbourg National History Park • CDN (NS) 240-241 P 5
Fort Rice ○ USA (ND) 258-259 G 5
Fort Rice Historic Site • USA (ND) 258-259 G 5
Fort Ripley ○ USA (MN) 270-271 D 4
Fort Rixon ○ ZW 218-219 E 5
Fort Rock ○ USA (OR) 244-245 D 7
Fortrose ○ NZ 182 B 7
Fort Rotterdam ∴• RI 166-167 D 3
Fort Rotterdam, Museum ∴• RI 164-165 F 6
Fort Rucker ✗✗ USA (AL) 284-285 E 5
Fort Rupert ○ CDN 38-39 E 3
Fort Rupert ○ CDN (BC) 230-231 B 3
Fort Saint James ○ CDN (BC) 228-229 K 2
Fort Saint James • CDN (BC) 228-229 K 2
Fort Saint James National Historic Park ∴• CDN (BC) 228-229 K 2
Fort Saint John ○ CDN 32-33 K 3
Fort San ○ CDN (SAS) 232-233 P 5
Fort Sandeman = Zhob ○ PK 138-139 B 4
Fort Saskatchewan ○ CDN (ALB) 232-233 E 2
Fort Scott ○ USA (KS) 262-263 M 7
Fort-Ševčenko ○ KA 126-127 J 5
Fort Severn ○ CDN 34-35 N 3
Fort Sheridan • USA (IL) 274-275 L 2
Fort Simpson ○ CDN 30-31 J 5
Fort Smith ○ CDN 30-31 O 5
Fort Smith ○ USA (AR) 276-277 A 5
Fort Smith ○ USA (MT) 250-251 M 6
Fort Steele Heritage Town • CDN (BC) 230-231 O 4
Fort Stewart ✗✗ USA (GA) 284-285 J 4
Fort Stockton ○ USA (TX) 266-267 E 3
Fort Supply ○ USA (OK) 264-265 E 2
Fort Supply Lake ⊂ USA (OK) 264-265 E 2
Fort Témiscamingue National Historic Park • CDN (QUE) 236-237 J 5
Fort Thomas ○ USA (AZ) 256-257 F 5
Fort Thompson ○ USA (SD) 260-261 G 2
Fort Totten ○ USA (ND) 258-259 J 4
Fort Towson ○ USA (OK) 264-265 J 4
Fort Trois Rivières • CDN (QUE) 238-239 N 2
Fortuna ○ BR 68-69 F 4
Fortuna ○ USA (CA) 246-247 A 3
Fortuna ○ USA (ND) 258-259 D 3
Fortuna, La ○ MEX 50-51 E 6
Fortuna, Rio ~ BR 70-71 G 2
Fortuna de Minas ○ BR 72-73 H 5
Fortuna de San Carlos ○ CR 52-53 B 6
Fortuna Ledge ○ USA 20-21 J 6
Fortune ○ CDN (NFL) 242-243 N 5
Fortune Bank ≃ 224 E 3
Fortune Bay ≈ 38-39 R 5
Fortune Bay ≈ CDN 242-243 N 5
Fortune Harbour ○ CDN (NFL) 242-243 N 3
Fort Union Trading Post National Historic Site ∴ USA (MT) 250-251 P 3
Fort Valley ○ USA (GA) 284-285 G 4
Fort Vasquez State Museum • USA (CO) 254-255 L 3
Fort Vermilion ○ CDN 30-31 M 6
Fort Victoria Historic Site ∴• CDN 32-33 O 4
Fortville ○ USA (IN) 274-275 N 5
Fort Walsh National Historic Park • CDN (SAS) 232-233 J 6
Fort Walton Beach ○ USA (FL) 286-287 C 1
Fort Washakie ○ USA (WY) 252-253 K 4
Fort Wayne ○ USA (IN) 274-275 N 3
Fort Wellington ○ GUY 62-63 F 2
Fort William ○ GB 90-91 E 3
Fort William Historic Park • CDN (ONT) 234-235 O 6
Fort Wingate ○ USA (NM) 256-257 G 3
Fort Worth ○ USA (TX) 264-265 G 6
Fort Yates ○ USA (ND) 258-259 G 5
Fortymile River ~ USA 20-21 U 4
Fort Yukon ○ USA 20-21 S 3
Fort Yuma Indian Reservation ✗ USA (CA) 248-249 K 7
Forūdgān ○ IR 134-135 D 2
Forūmad ○ IR 136-137 E 6
Forūr, Ğazīre-ye ⌒ IR 134-135 F 5
Forvik ○ N 86-87 F 4
Fosa de Cariaco ≈ 60-61 J 2
Fosca ○ CO 60-61 E 5
Foshan ○• VRC 156-157 H 5
Fosheim Peninsula ◡ CDN 26-27 H 4
Fosnavåg ☆ N 86-87 B 5
Foso ○ GH 202-203 K 7
Foss ○ USA (OK) 264-265 E 3
Fossa, Corredeira ~ BR 66-67 H 6
Fossil ○ USA (OR) 244-245 E 5
Fossil Butte National Monument ∴ USA (WY) 252-253 H 5
Fossil Downs ○• AUS 172-173 G 5
Foss Lake < USA (OK) 264-265 E 3
Fossong Fontem ○ CAM 204-205 H 6
Fosston ○ CDN (SAS) 232-233 P 3
Fosston ○ USA (MN) 270-271 C 3
Foster ○ AUS 180-181 J 5
Foster Bay ≈ 24-25 f 6
Foster Bugt ≈ 26-27 o 7
Fostoria ○ USA (OH) 280-281 C 2
Fostoria ○ USA (TX) 268-269 E 6
Fotadrevo ○ RM 222-223 D 10
Fotiná ○ GR 100-101 J 4
Fotokol ○ CAM 198-199 G 6
Fotuha'a ⌒ TON 184 IV a 1
Foucauld, Ermitage du P. de • DZ 190-191 E 9
Fouénan ○ CI 202-203 G 5
Fougamou ○ G 210-211 C 4
Fougani, Hassi < MA 188-189 J 5
Fougères ○• F 90-91 G 7
Foulni, Hâssi < RIM 196-197 G 6
Fouke ○ USA (AR) 276-277 B 7
Foula ⌒ GB 90-91 F 1
Foulabala ○ RMM 202-203 G 4
Foulamory ○ RG 202-203 D 3
Foul Bay ≈ 36-37 N 3
Foulenzem ○ G 210-211 B 4
Foulwind, Cape ▲ NZ 182 C 4
Fouman ○ IR 128-129 N 4
Foumbadou ○ RG 202-203 F 5
Foumban ○• CAM 204-205 J 6
Foumbot ○ CAM 204-205 J 6
Foumbouni ○ COM 222-223 C 3
Foum-el-Hassan • MA 188-189 G 6
Foum-Zguid ○ MA 188-189 H 5
Foundiougne ○ SN 202-203 B 2
Founougo ○ DY 204-205 E 3
Fountain ○ USA (CO) 254-255 L 5
Fountain Creek ~ USA (CO) 254-255 L 5
Fountain Hill ○ USA (AR) 276-277 D 7
Fountain Inn ○ USA (SC) 284-285 H 2
Fountains Abbey ••• GB 90-91 G 4
Fountain Valley ○ CDN (BC) 230-231 H 3
Fouquet ○ RH 54-55 J 5
Four Archers, The • AUS 174-175 C 4
Fourche La Fave River ~ USA (AR) 276-277 B 6
Fourche Maline River ~ USA (OK) 264-265 J 4
Fourche Mountain ▲ USA (AR) 276-277 B 6
Fourchu ○ CDN (NS) 240-241 P 5
Four Corners ○ USA (CA) 248-249 G 5
Four Corners ○ USA (WY) 252-253 O 2
Fourcroy, Cape ▲ AUS 172-173 K 1
Four Forks ○ USA (LA) 268-269 G 4
Fouriesburg ○ ZA 220-221 J 4
Four Mountains, Islands of the ⌒ USA 22-23 L 6
Fournaise, Piton de la ▲ F 224 B 7
Four North Fracture Zone ≃ 6-7 F 8
Fouroù ○ RMM 202-203 G 4
Fourteen Mile Point ▲ USA (MI) 270-271 J 3
Fourtown ○ USA (MN) 270-271 C 2
Foveaux Strait ≈ 182 A 7
Fowler ○ USA (CO) 254-255 L 5
Fowler ○ USA (IN) 274-275 L 4
Fowler ○ USA (KS) 262-263 F 7
Fowler ○ USA (MI) 272-273 E 4
Fowler ○ USA (SC) 284-285 L 3
Fowlers Bay ≈ 176-177 M 6
Fowlers Bay ○ AUS 176-177 M 5
Fowlers Gap ○ AUS 178-179 F 6
Fowlerton ○ USA (TX) 266-267 J 5
Fox ○ USA 20-21 R 4
Fox Cove ○ CDN (NFL) 242-243 N 5
Fox Creek ○ CDN 32-33 M 4
Foxe Basin ≈ 24-25 g 6
Foxe Channel ≈ 36-37 J 2
Foxe Peninsula ◡ CDN 36-37 L 2
Fox Glacier ○ NZ 182 C 5
Fox Islands ⌒ USA (AK) 22-23 M 6
Fox Islands ⌒ USA (MI) 272-273 D 2
Fox Lake ○ CDN 30-31 M 6
Fox Lake ○ USA (IL) 274-275 K 2
Fox Lake ○ USA (WI) 274-275 K 1
Fox Lake Indian Reserve ✗ CDN 30-31 M 6
Fox Point ▲ CDN 30-31 J 3
Fox Point ○ USA (WI) 274-275 L 1
Fox River ○ CDN (MAN) 234-235 C 3
Fox River ~ CDN 34-35 J 3
Fox River ~ USA (IL) 274-275 K 3
Fox River ~ USA (MO) 274-275 G 4
Fox River ~ USA (WI) 270-271 K 6
Foxton Beach ○ NZ 182 E 4
Fox Valley ○ CDN (SAS) 232-233 J 5
Foxvill ○ CDN (ONT) 236-237 G 2
Foxwarren ○ CDN (MAN) 234-235 B 4
Foxworth ○ USA (MS) 268-269 L 5
Foyle, Lough ≈ 90-91 D 4
Foyn, Cape ▲ ARK 16 G 30
Foynøya ⌒ N 84-85 P 2
Foz de Areala, Represa de < BR 74-75 E 5
Foz de Jaú ○ BR 62-63 D 6
Foz do Cunene ○ ANG 216-217 A 8
Foz do Iguaçu ○ BR 76-77 K 3
Foz do Jordão ○ BR 66-67 B 7
Foz do Mamoriá ○ BR 66-67 D 4
Foz Jurupari ○ BR 66-67 B 6
Frænkel Land ⊥ GRØ 26-27 m 7
Fraga ○ E 98-99 H 4
Fragoso, Cayo ⌒ C 54-55 F 3
Fraile Muerto ○ ROU 78-79 M 2
Frailes, Islas Los ⌒ YV 60-61 K 2
Frambo ○ CI 202-203 J 7
Framingham ○ USA (MA) 278-279 K 6
Frammesfjella ▲ ARK 16 G 7
Franca ○ BR 72-73 G 6
Francavilla Fontana ○ I 100-101 F 4
France ■ F 90-91 H 8
France, Glacier de ⊂ GRØ 28-29 X 3
France, Île de ⌒ 26-27 r 5
Francés, Caverna do • BR 70-71 K 4
Frances, Lake ⊂ USA (MT) 250-251 G 3
Franceses ○ GCA 52-53 K 4
Frances Lake ○ CDN 30-31 E 5
Frances River ~ CDN 30-31 E 5
Francés Viejo, Cabo ▲ DOM 54-55 L 5
Franceville ☆ G 210-211 D 4
Franche-Comté ▫ F 90-91 K 8
Francia, La ○ RA 76-77 F 6
Francis ○ CDN (SAS) 232-233 P 5
Francis Case, Lake ⊂ USA (SD) 260-261 G 3
Francisco Aires ○ BR 68-69 G 5
Francisco Beltrão ○ BR 74-75 D 6
Francisco de Vitoria ○ RA 78-79 H 3
Francisco Dumont ○ BR 72-73 H 4
Francisco Grande ○ USA (AZ) 256-257 D 6
Francisco I. Madero ○ MEX (COA) 50-51 H 5
Francisco I. Madero ○ MEX (DGO) 50-51 G 5
Francisco I. Madero, Presa < MEX 50-51 G 3
Francisco Perito Moreno, Parque Nacional ⊥ RA 80 D 3
Francisco Rueda ○ MEX 52-53 H 3
Francisco Sá ○ BR 72-73 J 4
Franciscusbaai ≈ 220-221 B 2
Francistown ☆ RB 218-219 D 5
Franco da Rocha ○ BR 72-73 G 7
Franco de Orellana ○ PE 64-65 F 3
François ○ CDN (NFL) 242-243 M 5
François, Le ○ F 56 E 4
Francois Lake ○ CDN (BC) 228-229 J 2
Francois Lake ⊂ CDN (BC) 228-229 J 3
Franconia Notch • USA (NH) 278-279 K 4
Francs Peak ▲ USA (WY) 252-253 J 3
Frankel City ○ USA (TX) 264-265 B 6
Frankfield ○ AUS 178-179 J 2
Frankfort ○ USA (IN) 274-275 M 4
Frankfort ○ USA (KS) 262-263 K 5
Frankfort ○ USA (MI) 272-273 C 3
Frankfort ○ USA (SD) 260-261 H 2
Frankfort ☆ USA (KY) 276-277 L 2
Frankfort ○ ZA 220-221 J 3
Frankfurt (Oder) ○• D 92-93 N 2
Frankfurt am Main ○ D 92-93 K 3
Frank Hann National Park ⊥ AUS 176-177 F 6
Fränkische Alb ▲ D 92-93 L 4
Fränkische Saale ~ D 92-93 K 3
Franklin ○ AUS 178-179 F 2
Franklin ○ CDN (MAN) 234-235 D 4
Franklin ○ USA (GA) 284-285 E 3
Franklin ○ USA (ID) 252-253 G 4
Franklin ○ USA (IN) 274-275 M 5
Franklin ○ USA (KY) 276-277 J 4
Franklin ○ USA (LA) 268-269 J 7
Franklin ○ USA (NC) 282-283 D 5
Franklin ○ USA (NE) 262-263 H 4
Franklin ○ USA (NH) 278-279 K 5
Franklin ○ USA (NM) 256-257 F 6
Franklin ○ USA (OH) 280-281 B 4
Franklin ○ USA (PA) 280-281 G 2
Franklin ○ USA (TN) 276-277 J 5
Franklin ○ USA (TX) 266-267 L 3
Franklin ○ USA (VA) 280-281 K 7
Franklin ○ USA (WV) 280-281 G 5
Franklin ○ ZA 220-221 J 5
Franklin, Kap ▲ GRØ 26-27 o 7
Franklin, Point ▲ USA 20-21 L 1
Franklin Bay ≈ 24-25 J 6
Franklin D. Roosevelt Lake ⊂ USA (WA) 244-245 G 2
Franklin Glacier ⊂ CDN (BC) 230-231 D 2
Franklin Harbour ≈ 180-181 D 2
Franklin Island ⌒ ARK 16 F 17
Franklin Island ⌒ CDN (ONT) 238-239 E 3
Franklin Lake ⊂ CDN (NWT) 30-31 V 2
Franklin Lake ⊂ CDN (SAS) 30-31 S 6
Franklin Lake ⊂ USA (NV) 246-247 K 3
Franklin Lower Gordon Wild Rivers Nationalpark ⊥ AUS 180-181 H 7
Franklin Mountains ▲ CDN 30-31 F 3
Franklin Mountains ▲ USA 20-21 S 2
Franklin Ø ⌒ GRØ 26-27 R 3
Franklin Point ▲ CDN 24-25 W 6
Franklin Strait ≈ 24-25 X 5
Franklinton ○ USA (LA) 268-269 K 6
Franklinton ○ USA (NC) 282-283 J 4
Franklinville ○ USA (NY) 278-279 C 6
Frankston ○ USA (TX) 264-265 J 6
Frankton ○ NZ 182 B 6
Franktown ○ USA (CO) 254-255 L 4
Frannie ○ USA (WY) 252-253 K 2
Franquelin ○ CDN (QUE) 242-243 A 3
Fransfontein ○ NAM 216-217 C 10
Fransfonteinberge ▲ NAM 216-217 C 10
Franske Øer ⌒ GRØ 26-27 q 4
Fränsta ○ S 86-87 H 5
Franz ○ CDN (ONT) 236-237 D 4
Franz Josef Glacier ○ NZ 182 C 5
Franz Josef Land = Franca-Iosifa, Zemlja ⌒ RUS 84-85 Y 2
Frascati ○ I 100-101 D 4
Fraser, Mount ▲ AUS 176-177 E 2
Fraser Basin ◡ CDN (BC) 228-229 K 2
Fraserburg ○ ZA 220-221 E 5
Fraserburgh ○ GB 90-91 F 3
Fraserdale ○ CDN (ONT) 236-237 G 3
Fraser Island ⌒••• AUS 178-179 M 3
Fraser Island National Park ⊥ AUS 178-179 M 3
Fraser Lake ○ CDN (BC) 228-229 K 2
Fraser Lake ⊂ CDN (BC) 228-229 K 2
Fraser Lake ⊂ CDN (NFL) 36-37 S 7
Fraser National Park ⊥ AUS 180-181 H 4
Fraser Plateau ▲ CDN (BC) 228-229 J 4
Fraser Range ○ AUS 176-177 G 6
Fraser River ~ CDN 36-37 S 6
Fraser River ~ CDN (BC) 228-229 Q 4
Fraser River ~ CDN (BC) 228-229 M 3
Fraser River ~ CDN (BC) 230-231 H 4
Frater ○ CDN (ONT) 236-237 D 5
Fraustro ○ MEX 50-51 J 5
Fray Bentos ☆ ROU 78-79 K 2
Fray Jorge ○ RCH 76-77 B 6
Fray Jorge, Parque Nacional ⊥ RCH 76-77 B 6
Fray Marcos ○ ROU 78-79 M 3
Frazee ○ USA (MN) 270-271 C 4
Frazer ○ USA (MT) 250-251 N 3
Frazier Park ○ USA (CA) 248-249 F 5
Freakly Point ▲ CDN 36-37 K 7
Frebag River ~ CDN 32-33 Q 3
Fred ○ USA (TX) 268-269 F 6
Freden, ostrov ⌒ RUS 84-85 g 2
Frederica National Monument, Fort • USA (GA) 284-285 J 5
Fredericia ○• DK 86-87 D 9
Frederick ○ USA (MD) 280-281 J 4
Frederick ○ USA (OK) 264-265 E 4
Frederick ○ USA (SD) 260-261 H 1
Frederick, Mount ▲ AUS (NT) 172-173 J 5
Frederick, Mount ▲ AUS (WA) 172-173 D 7
Frederick E. Hyde Fjord ≈ 26-27 j 2
Fredericksburg ○ USA (IA) 274-275 F 2
Fredericksburg ○ USA (TX) 266-267 J 3
Fredericksburg ○ USA (VA) 280-281 J 5
Frederick Sound ≈ 32-33 C 3
Fredericton ○ CDN (NFL) 242-243 O 3
Fredericktown ○ USA (MD) 280-281 L 4
Fredericktown ○ USA (MO) 276-277 E 3
Fredericktown ○ USA (OH) 280-281 D 3
Frederico Westphalen ○ BR 74-75 D 6
Fredericton ☆ CDN (NB) 240-241 J 5
Frederik Henrik Island = Pulau Dolak ⌒ RI 166-167 K 5
Frederiksdal = Narsaq Kujalleg ○ GRØ 28-29 S 6
Frederikshåb = Paamiut ○ GRØ 28-29 Q 5
Frederikshåbs Banke ≃ 28-29 P 5
Frederikshavn ○ DK 86-87 E 8
Frederiksted ○• USA (VI) 286-287 R 3
Fredonia ○ CO 60-61 D 5
Fredonia ○ USA (AZ) 256-257 C 2
Fredonia ○ USA (KS) 262-263 L 7
Fredonia ○ USA (NY) 278-279 B 6
Fredonyer Summit ▲ USA (CA) 246-247 E 3
Fredrika ○ S 86-87 J 4
Fredriksberg ○ S 86-87 G 6
Fredrikstad ☆ N 86-87 E 7
Freeborn ○ USA (MN) 270-271 E 7
Freeburg ○ USA (MO) 274-275 G 6
Freedom ○ USA (CA) 248-249 C 3
Freedom ○ USA (KY) 276-277 K 4
Freedom ○ USA (OK) 264-265 E 2
Freedom ○ USA (WY) 252-253 H 4
Freehold ○ USA (NJ) 280-281 M 3
Free Home ○ USA (GA) 284-285 F 2
Freeland ○ USA (WA) 244-245 C 2
Freelandville ○ USA (IN) 274-275 L 6
Freeling Heights ▲ AUS 178-179 E 6
Freels, Cape ▲ CDN (NFL) 242-243 P 3
Freeman ○ USA (SD) 260-261 J 3
Freeman ○ USA (WA) 244-245 H 3
Freeman River ~ CDN 32-33 N 4
Freemansundet ≈ 84-85 M 3
Freemont ○ CDN (SAS) 232-233 J 3
Freeport ○ BS 54-55 F 1
Freeport ○ CDN (NS) 240-241 J 6
Freeport ○ USA (FL) 286-287 C 1
Freeport ○ USA (IL) 274-275 J 2
Freeport ○ USA (PA) 280-281 G 3
Freeport ○ USA (TX) 266-267 M 5
Freer ○ USA (TX) 266-267 J 6
Freesoil ○ USA (MI) 272-273 C 3
Freetown ○ USA (IN) 274-275 M 6
Freetown ★• WAL 202-203 D 5
Freezeout Mountain ▲ USA (OR) 244-245 H 7
Frégate Island ⌒ SY 224 D 2
Fregenal de la Sierra ○• E 98-99 D 5
Fregon ✗ AUS 176-177 M 3
Freiberg ○• D 92-93 M 3
Freiburg im Breisgau ○• D 92-93 J 5
Frei Inocêncio ○ BR 72-73 K 5
Frei Orlando ○ BR 72-73 H 5
Freire ○ RCH 78-79 C 5
Freirina ○ RCH 76-77 B 5
Freising ○ D 92-93 L 4
Freiwaldau = Jeseník ○ CZ 92-93 O 3
Fréjus ○ F 90-91 L 10
Fremantle ○ AUS 176-177 C 6
Fremont ○ USA (CA) 248-249 C 2
Fremont ○ USA (MI) 272-273 D 4
Fremont ○ USA (NC) 282-283 K 5
Fremont ○ USA (NE) 262-263 K 3
Fremont ○ USA (OH) 280-281 C 2
Fremont ○ USA (WI) 270-271 K 6
Fremont Lake ⊂ USA (WY) 252-253 J 3
Fremont Mountains ▲ USA (OR) 244-245 D 7

French River — Garber

Fremont River ~ USA (UT) 254-255 D 5
French Bay ≥ • BS 54-55 H 3
French Cove ○ CDN (NFL) 242-243 N 5
French Creek ~ USA (PA) 280-281 F 2
Frenchglen ○ USA (OR) 244-245 G 8
French Guiana = Guyane Française ▫ F 62-63 H 3
French Hills ▲ AUS 172-173 H 6
French Lick ○ USA (IN) 274-275 M 6
Frenchman Butte ○ CDN (SAS) 232-233 J 2
Frenchman Creek ~ CDN (SAS) 232-233 L 6
Frenchman Creek ~ USA (NE) 262-263 D 4
Frenchman's Bay ≈ • 54-55 G 6
Frenchman's Cove Provincial Park ⊥ CDN (NFL) 242-243 N 5
French Pass ○ NZ 182 D 4
French River ○ CDN (ONT) 238-239 E 2
French River ~ CDN (ONT) 238-239 E 2
Frenchtown ○ USA (MT) 250-251 E 4
Frenchville ○ USA (ME) 278-279 N 1
Frenda ○ DZ 190-191 C 3
Frere ○ ZA 220-221 J 4
Fresco ○ CI 202-203 H 7
Fresco, Rio ~ BR 68-69 C 5
Freshfield Icefield ⊂ CDN (ALB) 232-233 B 4
Freshwater ○ CDN (NFL) 242-243 P 5
Freshwater Point ▲ USA (TX) 266-277 C 4
Fresia ○ RCH 78-79 C 6
Fresnal Canyon ~ USA (AZ) 256-257 D 7
Fresnillo de González Echeverría ○ MEX 50-51 H 6
Fresno ○ USA (CA) 248-249 E 3
Fresno Reservoir ○ USA (MT) 250-251 J 3
Freuchen Bay ≈ 24-25 f 7
Freuchen Land ⊥ GRØ 26-27 c 2
Freudenthal = Bruntál ○ CZ 92-93 O 4
Freundschaftsinseln = Tonga ~ TON 184 IV a 2
Frewena ○ AUS 174-175 C 6
Freycinet Estuary ⊵ 176-177 B 3
Freycinet National Park ⊥ AUS 180-181 K 7
Freycinet Peninsula ⊻ AUS 180-181 J 7
Fria ○ RG 202-203 D 4
Fria, Kaap ▲ NAM 216-217 A 9
Fria, La ○ YV 60-61 E 3
Friant ○ USA (CA) 248-249 E 3
Friars Point ○ USA (MS) 268-269 K 2
Frías ○ RA 76-77 D 5
Friday Creek ~ CDN (ONT) 236-237 F 2
Friday Harbour ○ USA (WA) 244-245 B 2
Friedberg (Hessen) ○ D 92-93 K 3
Friedrichshafen ○ D 92-93 K 5
Friend ○ USA (NE) 262-263 J 4
Friendship ○ USA (AR) 276-277 B 6
Friendship ○ USA (WI) 280-281 C 5
Friendship Hill National Historic Site • USA (PA) 280-281 G 4
Friendship Shoal ≂ 162-163 K 2
Friesach ○ A 92-93 N 5
Frigate, Lac ○ CDN 38-39 G 2
Frigate Bay Beach ⊥ KAN 56 D 3
Friggesund ○ S 86-87 H 6
Frindisburg Reef ≂ SOL 184 I d 1
Frio, Cabo ▲ BR 72-73 K 7
Frio Draw ~ USA (NM) 256-257 M 4
Friona ○ USA (TX) 264-265 B 4
Frio River ~ USA (TX) 266-267 J 5
Frisco ○ USA (CO) 254-255 J 4
Frisco City ○ USA (AL) 284-285 C 5
Fritch ○ USA (TX) 264-265 C 3
Fritz Hugh Sound ○ 32-33 G 6
Fritz Hugh Sound ≈ CDN 230-231 D 2
Friuli-Venézia Giùlia ▪ I 100-101 D 1
Friza, proliv ≈ RUS 122-123 N 6
Frome, Lake ○ AUS 178-179 E 6
Frome Downs ○ AUS 178-179 E 6
Fronteiro, Cachoeira da ⊲ BR 68-69 B 6
Frontenac ○ USA (KS) 262-263 M 7
Frontera ○ E 188-189 C 7
Frontera ○ • MEX 52-53 H 2
Frontera, Punta ▲ MEX 52-53 H 2
Frontera Comalapa ○ MEX 52-53 H 4
Fronteras ○ MEX 50-51 E 2
Frontier ○ USA (SAS) 232-233 K 6
Front Range ▲ USA (CO) 254-255 K 3
Front Royal ○ USA (VA) 280-281 H 5
Frosinone ○ I 100-101 D 4
Frostburg ○ USA (MD) 280-281 H 4
Frostproof ○ USA (FL) 286-287 H 4
Froude ○ CDN (SAS) 232-233 P 6
Frøya ~ N 86-87 D 5
Frozen Strait ≈ 24-25 d 7
Fruita ○ USA (CO) 254-255 G 4
Fruitland ○ USA (ID) 252-253 B 3
Fruitland ○ USA (MD) 276-277 L 7
Fruitland ○ USA (NM) 254-255 J 5
Frunze = Biškek ★ KS 146-147 B 4
Frunze, mys ▲ RUS 108-109 Y 1
Fruta de Leite ○ BR 72-73 J 4
Frutal ○ BR 72-73 F 6
Frutillar ○ RCH 78-79 C 6
Fryatt, Mount ▲ CDN (ALB) 228-229 R 4
Fryeburg ○ USA (ME) 278-279 L 4
Fryeburg ○ USA (ME) 278-279 L 4
Frymire ○ USA (KY) 276-277 J 3
Frys ○ CDN (SAS) 232-233 R 6
Fua'amotu ○ TON 184 IV a 2

Fucheng ○ VRC 154-155 K 3
Fuding ○ VRC 156-157 M 3
Fududa ◁ EAK 212-213 G 5
Fuego, Tierra del ⊥ RA/RCH 80 E 7
Fuencaliente ○ E 188-189 C 6
Fuencaliente de la Palma ○ E 188-189 C 6
Fuengirola ○ E 98-99 E 6
Fuente del Fresno ○ E 98-99 F 5
Fuente de San Esteban, La ○ E 98-99 D 4
Fuente Obejuna ○ E 98-99 E 5
Fuentesaúco ○ E 98-99 E 4
Fuerte ○ BOL 70-71 E 7
Fuerte, El ○ MEX 50-51 E 4
Fuerte, El ~ MEX 50-51 E 4
Fuerte Bulnes ○ RCH 80 E 6
Fuerte Olimpo ☆ PY 76-77 J 1
Fuerte Quemado ○ RA 76-77 D 4
Fuerte San Lorenzo ∴ •• PA 52-53 E 7
Fuerte San Rafael • RA 78-79 F 3
Fuerteventura ~ E 188-189 D 6
Fufeng ○ VRC 154-155 E 4
Fufulsu ○ GH 202-203 K 5
Fuga Island ~ RP 160-161 D 3
Fuglasker ~ IS 86-87 b 3
Fugløy Bank ≂ 86-87 J 1
Fugong ○ VRC 142-143 L 2
Fugou ○ VRC 154-155 J 4
Fugu ○ VRC 154-155 G 2
Fuhai ○ VRC 146-147 H 2
Fuhaihil, al- ○ KWT 130-131 L 3
Fuji ○ J 152-153 H 7
Fujian ○ VRC 156-157 K 3
Fu Jiang ~ VRC 154-155 D 6
Fujieda ○ J 152-153 H 7
Fuji-gawa ~ J 152-153 H 7
Fuji-Hakone-Izu National Park ⊥ J 152-153 H 7
Fujin ○ VRC 150-151 J 4
Fuji-san ▲ J 152-153 H 7
Fujisawa ○ J 152-153 H 7
Fujiyoshida ○ J 152-153 H 7
Fūka ○ ET 194-195 C 2
Fukagawa ○ J 152-153 K 3
Fukang ○ VRC 146-147 H 3
Fukuchiyama ○ J 152-153 F 7
Fukue ○ J 152-153 C 8
Fukuei Chiao ▲ RC 156-157 N 4
Fukue-shima ~ J 152-153 C 8
Fukui ○ J 152-153 G 6
Fukuoka ★ J 152-153 D 8
Fukushima ○ J (HOK) 152-153 J 4
Fukushima ○ J (FUK) 152-153 J 6
Fukuyama ○ J 152-153 E 7
Fulacunda ○ GNB 202-203 C 4
Fulaga ~ FIJI 184 III c 3
Fulda ○ CDN (SAS) 232-233 N 3
Fulda ○• S 86-87 N 4
Fulda ○ D 92-93 K 3
Fulda ○ USA (MN) 270-271 C 7
Fulford Harbour ○ CDN (BC) 230-231 F 5
Fuli ○ RC 156-157 M 5
Fuling ○ VRC 156-157 E 2
Fullarton ○ TT 60-61 L 2
Fullerton ○ USA (CA) 248-249 F 5
Fullerton ○ USA (ND) 258-259 J 5
Fullerton ○ USA (NE) 262-263 J 3
Fulton ○ USA (AR) 276-277 B 7
Fulton ○ USA (IL) 274-275 K 3
Fulton ○ USA (KY) 276-277 G 4
Fulton ○ USA (MO) 274-275 G 6
Fulton ○ USA (MS) 268-269 M 2
Fulton ○ USA (NY) 278-279 E 5
Fultondale ○ USA (AL) 284-285 D 3
Fulton River ~ CDN (BC) 228-229 H 2
Futoro ○ RI 166-167 G 6
Fulula ○ ZRE 210-211 F 6
Fulunäs ○ S 86-87 F 6
Fumbelo ○ ANG 216-217 E 5
Fumel ○ F 90-91 H 9
Fumiela ○ ANG 216-217 D 3
Funabashi ○ J 152-153 H 7
Funadomari ○ J 152-153 J 2
Funafuti Atoll ~ TUV 13 J 3
Funan ○ VRC 154-155 J 5
Funäsdalen ○ S 86-87 F 5
Funchal ○ P 188-189 C 4
Fundação Eclética ○ BR 72-73 F 3
Fundão ○ BR 72-73 K 5
Fundão ○ P 98-99 D 4
Fundición ○ MEX 50-51 E 4
Fundo, Rio ~ BR 68-69 G 6
Fundo das Figueiras ○ CV 202-203 C 5
Fundong ○ CAM 204-205 J 5
Fundy, Bay of ≈ 38-39 L 6
Fundy, Bay of ≈ CDN 240-241 J 2
Fundy National Park ⊥ CDN (NB) 240-241 K 5
Fungom ○ CAM 204-205 H 5
Funhalouro ○ MOC 218-219 H 6
Funiak Springs, De ○ USA (FL) 286-287 C 1
Funing ○ VRC (JIA) 154-155 L 5
Funing ○ VRC (YUN) 156-157 D 5
Funkley ○ USA (MN) 270-271 D 3
Funsi ○ GH 202-203 K 4
Funtua ○ WAN 204-205 G 5
Funzi Island ~ EAK 212-213 G 6
Fuping ○ VRC (HEB) 154-155 J 2
Fuping ○ VRC (SXI) 154-155 F 4
Fuquan ○ VRC 156-157 E 4
Fuquay Varina ○ USA (NC) 282-283 H 5
Fura Braço, Corredeira ⊲ BR 66-67 H 6
Furaiši, al- ○ JOR 130-131 D 2
Furancungo ○ MOC 218-219 G 2
Furano ○ J 152-153 K 3
Furano, Kami- ○ J 152-153 K 3
Furät, al- ~ IRQ 128-129 L 7
Furāwiya, Bi'r ⥁ SUD 188-189 L 5
Furdale ○ CDN (SAS) 232-233 M 3
Fürg ○ IR 134-135 G 4

Furkwa ○ EAT (DOD) 212-213 E 6
Furman ○ USA (AL) 284-285 D 5
Furmanov ☆ RUS 94-95 R 3
Furnace Creek ○ USA (CA) 248-249 H 3
Furnas, Represa de ○ BR 72-73 G 6
Furneaux Group ~ AUS 180-181 K 6
Furness ○ VRC 154-155 G 2
Furo Carandazinho ~ BR 70-71 J 5
Furo do Jurupari ~ BR 68-69 D 3
Furo do Tajapuru ~ BR 62-63 J 4
Furqlūs ○ SYR 128-129 G 5
Furrial, El ○ YV 60-61 K 3
Furroli ▲ ETH 208-209 D 7
Fürstenfeld ○ A 92-93 O 5
Fürstenwalde (Spree) ○ • D 92-93 N 2
Fürth ○ D 92-93 L 4
Furubira ○ J 152-153 J 3
Fury Point ▲ USA (AK) 24-25 a 4
Fury and Hecla Strait ≈ 24-25 f 6
Fusagasuga ○ CO 60-61 D 5
Fushimi Lake Provincial Park ⊥ CDN (ONT) 236-237 E 3
Fushui ○ VRC 154-155 F 6
Fushun ○ VRC 150-151 D 7
Fusilier ○ CDN (SAS) 232-233 J 4
Fuskam Mata ○ WAN 204-205 H 3
Fusong ○ VRC 150-151 F 6
Fussa, vulkan ▲ RUS 122-123 Q 3
Füssen ○ D 92-93 L 5
Fusui ○ VRC 156-157 E 5
Futa, Cuilo ~ ANG 216-217 C 3
Futalaufquen, Lago ○ RA 78-79 D 7
Futaleufú ○ RCH 78-79 D 7
Futaleufú, Rio ~ RA 78-79 D 7
Futrono ○ RCH 78-79 C 6
Futuna Island = Île Erronan ~ VAN 184 II c 4
Fu Xian ○ VRC 154-155 F 4
Fuxian Hu ○ VRC 156-157 C 4
Fuxin ○ VRC 150-151 C 6
Fuxing ○ VRC 156-157 J 2
Fuyang ○ VRC 154-155 J 5
Fuyu ○ VRC (HEI) 150-151 E 4
Fuyu ○ VRC (JIL) 150-151 D 4
Fuyuan ○ VRC (HEI) 150-151 K 3
Fuyuan ○ VRC (YUN) 156-157 D 4
Fuyun ○ VRC 146-147 J 2
Fuzhou ○ VRC 156-157 L 3
Fuzhouzhen ○ VRC 150-151 C 8
Fwa, Lac ○ ZRE 210-211 J 6
Fyllas Banke ≂ 28-29 O 5
Fyn ~ DK 86-87 E 9
Fyresvatn ○ N 86-87 D 7

G

Ga ○ GH 202-203 J 5
Gaalkacyo ☆ SP 208-209 H 5
Gaamodebli ○ LB 202-203 F 6
Gaasefjord ○ 26-27 m 8
Gaaseland ⊥ GRØ 26-27 m 8
Gaase Pynt ▲ GRØ 26-27 m 8
Gåb, al- ⊻ SYR 128-129 G 5
Gaba ○ ETH 208-209 D 7
Gabagaba ○ PNG 183 D 5
Ĝabal, al-al-Aḫḍar ▲ OM 132-133 K 2
Ĝabala ○• SYR 128-129 F 5
Gabalatud ○ LB 202-203 F 6
Ĝabal 'Abdal'aziz ▲ SYR 128-129 J 4
Gabalutud ○ LB 202-203 F 6
Ĝabal Auliyá ○ SUD 200-201 F 5
Ĝabal Bozi ○ SUD 200-201 F 6
Gabaldon ○ RP 160-161 D 3
Ĝabal Mazmum ○ SUD 200-201 F 6
Ĝabal os Saráğ ○ AFG 136-137 L 7
Gabargaron ○ BD 142-143 F 3
Gabarouse ○ CDN (NS) 240-241 P 5
Ĝabarka, Raas ▲ SP 208-209 K 4
Gabba Island ~ AUS 183 B 5
Gabbro Lake ○ CDN 38-39 M 2
Gabela ○ ANG 216-217 C 5
Gabensis ○ PNG 183 D 4
Gabes = Gabès ☆ TN 190-191 H 4
Gabes, Golfe de ≈ TN 190-191 H 3
Gabès, Gulf of = Gabès, Golfe de ≈ TN 190-191 H 3
Gabèt al-Ma'ādin ○ SUD 200-201 H 2
Gabgaba, Wâdi ~ SUD 200-201 F 2
Gabi ○ RN 198-199 G 5
Gabia ○ ZRE 210-211 F 6
Gabiane ○ TCH 206-207 H 2
Gabir ○ SUD 206-207 J 4
Ĝabir, Qal'at • SYR 128-129 G 4
Gabiro ○ RWA 212-213 C 4
Gabo Island ~ AUS 180-181 K 4
Gabon ▫ G 210-211 D 4
Gabon, Estuaire de ≈ 210-211 B 3
Gaborone ★ RB 220-221 G 2
Gabras ○ SUD 206-207 H 3
Gabrešević ○ BG 102-103 C 6
Gabriel, Lac ○ CDN 36-37 P 5
Gabriel Strait ≈ 36-37 R 4
Gabriel Vera ○ BOL 70-71 E 6
Gabriel Zamora ○ MEX 52-53 C 2
Gâbrik, Rüd-e ~ IR 134-135 H 5
Ĝabrīn, Ĝazīre-ye ~ IR 134-135 H 5
Gabriola ○ CDN (BC) 230-231 F 4
Gabrovo ○ BG 102-103 D 6
Gabú ☆ GNB 202-203 C 3
Gabu ○ ZRE 212-213 A 2
Gacheta ○ CO 60-61 S E 5
Gacko ○ BIH 100-101 J 3
Gadabeji ○ RN 198-199 G 5
Ĝadat, Wâdi I- ~ JOR 130-131 D 2
Gadag ○ IND 140-141 F 7
Gadamai ○ SUD 200-201 H 4
Gada-Oundou ○ RG 202-203 D 4
Gäddede ○ S 86-87 G 4
Gadein ○ SUD 206-207 J 4
Gado Bravo, Serra do ▲ BR 68-69 E 6

Gädra ○ PK 138-139 C 7
Ĝadrân ○ AFG 138-139 B 3
Gadsby ○ CDN (ALB) 232-233 F 3
Gadsden ○ USA (AL) 284-285 E 3
Gadsden ○ USA (SC) 284-285 D 5
Gadûn, Wâdi ~ OM 132-133 H 4
Gadwàl ○ IND 140-141 G 7
Gadzi ○ RCA 206-207 C 6
Gael Hamke Bugt ≈ 26-27 p 6
Gãešti ○ RO 102-103 D 5
Gaeta, Golfo di ≈ 100-101 D 4
Gael Hamke Bugt ≈ 26-27 p 6
Gafargarh ○ IND 142-143 C 2
Gagarin ○ RUS 94-95 O 4
Gagarin ○ US 136-137 L 4
Ĝâğarm ○ IR 136-137 E 6
Ĝâğati ○ AFG 138-139 B 3
Ĝâleq ○ IR 134-135 M 3
Gagau, Gunung ▲ MAL (PAH) 162-163 E 2
Gage ○ USA (NM) 256-257 G 6
Gage ○ USA (OK) 264-265 E 2
Gagera ~ 198-199 C 6
Ĝâğgâga, Nahr ~ SYR 128-129 J 4
Gaghamni ○ SUD 206-207 J 3
Ĝâği ○ AFG 138-139 B 3
Ĝâği Meidân ○ AFG 138-139 C 3
Ĝâğin, Rüd-e ~ IR 134-135 G 6
Gagnoa ☆ CI 202-203 H 7
Gagnon ○ 38-39 K 3
Gagnon, Lac ○ CDN (QUE) 238-239 K 2
Ĝâğôri ○ AFG 134-135 M 2
Gahnpa = Ganta ○ LB 202-203 G 7
Gahkom ○ IR 134-135 F 4
Ĝahnin ○ OM 132-133 J 5
Ĝahra, al- ○ KWT 130-131 L 3
Ĝahrom ○ IR 134-135 F 4
Gaiba, Lago ○ BOL 70-71 J 5
Gaibanda ○ BD 142-143 F 3
Ĝâiđa, al- ○ Y 132-133 H 5
Gaigou ○ BF 202-203 K 2
Gail ~ A 92-93 M 5
Gail USA (TX) 264-265 C 5
Gail Bäwazir ○ Y 132-133 F 6
Gaillac ○ F 90-91 J 9
Gaillimh = Galway ☆ IRL 90-91 C 5
Gaiman ○ RA 78-79 G 7
Gaimonaki ○ PNG 183 E 5
Gaines, Fort • USA (AL) 284-285 B 6
Gainesboro ○ USA (TN) 276-277 K 4
Gainesville ○ USA (FL) 286-287 G 2
Gainesville ○ USA (GA) 284-285 G 2
Gainesville ○ USA (MO) 276-277 C 4
Gainesville ○ USA (TX) 264-265 H 5
Gainford ○ CDN (ALB) 232-233 D 2
Gainsborough ○ CDN (SAS) 232-233 R 6
Gairdner, Lake ○ AUS 178-179 C 6
Gairdner River ~ AUS 176-177 E 7
Gaire ○ PNG 183 D 5
Gairesi ~ ZW 218-219 G 3
Gairo ○ EAT (MOR) 212-213 F 6
Gaital, Cerro ▲ PA 52-53 D 7
Gaithersburg ○ USA (MD) 280-281 J 4
Gaivota ○ BR 62-63 J 5
Gai Xian ○ VRC 150-151 D 7
Gaja, Pulau ~ MAL 160-161 C 10
Gajah, Kampung ○ MAL 162-163 D 2
Gajahmunggur, Danau ○ RI (KDB) 168 D 3
Gajčaveem ○ RUS 112-113 O 5
Gajendragarh ○ IND 140-141 F 3
Gaji, River ~ WAN 204-205 J 3
Gajiram ○ WAN 198-199 F 6
Gajny ☆ RUS 96-97 J 3
Gajwel ○ IND 140-141 H 6
Gakarosa ▲ ZA 220-221 F 3
Gakem ○ WAN 204-205 H 5
Gakona ○ USA 20-21 S 5
Gakona River ~ USA 20-21 S 5
Gakou ○ RMM 202-203 F 3
Gal ○ VRC 144-145 G 6
Galachipa ○ BD 142-143 G 4
Gal Adhale ○ SP 208-209 H 5
Ĝâlaĝil ○ KSA 130-131 J 5
Galahad ○ CDN (ALB) 232-233 G 3
Galal, togga ~ SP 208-209 K 3
Ĝâlâlâbâd = AFG 138-139 C 2
Galam, Selat ≈ 162-163 E 4
Ĝâlâmid, al- ○ KSA 130-131 G 2
Galán, Cerro ▲ RA 76-77 D 3
Galana ~ EAK 212-213 G 5
Galandük ○ IR 136-137 J 3
Galanga ○ ANG 216-217 C 6
Galangachi ○ RT 202-203 L 4
Galangue ○ ANG 216-217 D 6
Galaosié ○ US 136-137 J 6
Galápagos, Islas = Archipiélago de Colón ~ EC 64-65 B 9
Galápagos, Parque Nacional de ⊥ •• EC 64-65 B 9
Galápagos Fracture Zone = Galápagos Fracture Zone ≂ 14-15 P 8
Galápagos Islands = Islas Galápagos ~ EC 64-65 B 9
Galápagos Rise = Galápagos Rise ≂ 5 B 4
Galarza ○ RA 76-77 J 5

Galarza, Laguna ○ RA 76-77 J 5
Galas ○ MAL 162-163 D 2
Galashiels ○ GB 90-91 F 4
Galata ○ CY 128-129 E 5
Galata ○ USA (MT) 250-251 H 3
Galaţi ☆ • RO 102-103 F 5
Galatia ○ USA (IL) 276-277 G 3
Galax ○ USA (VA) 280-281 F 7
Galbraith ○ AUS 174-175 F 5
Galbraith ○ CDN (BC) 230-231 O 4
Galbyn Gov' ⊵ MAU 148-149 H 6
Ĝâldak ○ AFG 134-135 M 3
Ĝáldar ○ E 188-189 D 6
Galdhøpiggen ▲ • N 86-87 D 6
Ĝáldiyan ○ IR 128-129 M 3
Galé ○ RMM 202-203 F 3
Galeana ○ MEX (CHA) 50-51 F 2
Galeana ○ MEX (NL) 50-51 J 5
Galečnyj, mys ▲ RUS 110-111 d 1
Galegu ○ SUD (Naz) 200-201 G 6
Galegu ~ SUD 200-201 G 5
Galela ○ RI 164-165 K 3
Galela, Teluk ≈ 164-165 K 3
Galena ○ USA (AK) 20-21 M 4
Galena ○ USA (IL) 274-275 K 3
Galena ○ USA (MO) 276-277 B 4
Galena Bay ○ CDN (BC) 230-231 M 3
Galenbindunuwewa ○ CL 140-141 J 6
Galeo ○ LB 202-203 G 7
Ĝáleq ○ IR 134-135 M 3
Galera ○ EC 64-65 B 1
Galera, Punta ▲ EC 64-65 B 1
Galera, Rio ~ BR 70-71 H 4
Galesburg ○ USA (IL) 274-275 H 4
Galesburg ○ USA (ND) 258-259 K 4
Galesong ○ RI 164-165 F 6
Galesville ○ USA (WI) 270-271 G 6
Galeta ○ USA (NM) 256-257 G 6
Galeton ○ USA (PA) 280-281 J 2
Galgamuwa ○ CL 140-141 J 7
Ĝálgâsan, Kûh-e ▲ IR 134-135 J 4
Galgudud ○ SP 208-209 H 6
Gal Harreri ○ SP 208-209 H 6
Galheirão, Rio ~ BR 72-73 G 2
Galheiros ○ BR 72-73 G 2
Gali ○ GE 126-127 G 6
Galia ○ BR 72-73 F 7
Galiano ○ CDN (BC) 230-231 F 5
Ĝáliba ○ IRQ 130-131 J 4
Galibi ○ SME 62-63 G 3
Galibi, National Reservaat ⊥ SME 62-63 G 3
Galič ○ RUS 94-95 S 2
Galice ○ USA (OR) 244-245 B 8
Galicia ○ E 98-99 C 3
Galičskaja vozvyšennost' ▲ RUS 94-95 R 3
Galilee ○ CDN (SAS) 232-233 N 6
Galilee, Lake ○ AUS 178-179 J 4
Galiléia ○ BR 72-73 K 5
Galilio ○ PNG 183 F 3
Galim ○ CAM (ADA) 204-205 K 5
Galim ○ CAM (OUE) 204-205 J 6
Galimovskij hrebet ▲ RUS 112-113 H 5
Galimyj ○ RUS 112-113 H 5
Galina • JA 54-55 G 5
Galinda ○ ANG 216-217 B 4
Galinhas, Ilha das ~ GNB 202-203 C 4
Galion ○ USA (OH) 280-281 D 3
Galite, La ~ TN 190-191 G 3
Galiuro Mountains ▲ USA (AZ) 256-257 E 6
Galivedu ○ IND 140-141 H 4
Galiwinku ○ AUS 174-175 C 3
Ĝállábát ○ SUD 200-201 H 5
Gallants ○ CDN (NFL) 242-243 K 4
Gallarol ○ US 136-137 K 5
Gallatin ○ USA (MO) 274-275 C 4
Gallatin ○ USA (TN) 276-277 J 4
Gallatin Peak ▲ USA (MT) 250-251 H 6
Gallatin River ~ USA (MT) 250-251 H 6
Galle ○ • CL 140-141 J 7
Gállego, Rio ~ E 98-99 G 3
Gallego Rise ≂ 14-15 R 8
Gallegos, Rio ~ RA 80 D 7
Gallegos, Río ~ RA 80 F 5
Galleguillos ○ RCH 76-77 B 4
Gallia, ostrov ~ RUS 84-85 e 2
Galljaarat ○ US 136-137 K 5
Gallo Arroyo ~ USA (NM) 256-257 K 4
Gallo Mountains ▲ USA (NM) 256-257 G 4
Galloo Island ~ USA (NY) 278-279 E 5
Galloway ○ CDN (BC) 230-231 O 4
Galloway ⊵ GB 90-91 E 4
Gallup ○ USA (NM) 256-257 H 4
Galma, River ~ WAN 204-205 H 3
Galma Galla ○ EAK 212-213 H 4
Galmi ○ RN 198-199 B 6
Gal Oya National Park ⊥ CL 140-141 J 7
Galpón, El ○ RA 76-77 E 3
Ĝálrëz ○ AFG 138-139 B 2
Galt ○ USA (MO) 274-275 E 4
Galtaţ-Zemmour ○ MA 196-197 D 3
Gálüĝâh ○ IR 136-137 C 6
Ĝálülâf ○ IR 128-129 L 5
Galva ○ USA (IL) 274-275 H 4
Galvão ○ BR 74-75 D 6
Galveás ○ BR 78-79 J 2
Galveston ○ USA (TX) 268-269 F 7

Galveston Bay ≈ USA 268-269 F 7
Galvestone ○ USA (IN) 274-275 M 4
Galveston Island ~ USA (TX) 268-269 F 7
Galvez, Rio ~ PE 64-65 F 4
Galway = Gaillimh ☆ IRL 90-91 C 5
Galway Bay ≈ 90-91 C 5
Galway's Soufrière ⊥ BR 56 D 3
Gam, Pulau ~ RI 166-167 F 2
Gama ○ RG 202-203 D 4
Gama, Isla ~ RA 78-79 H 6
Gamaches ○ F 90-91 H 7
Ĝamai, Umm al- ○ KSA 130-131 J 4
Gamana River ~ PNG 183 E 4
Gámásáb, al- ⊻ KSA 130-131 K 6
Gamawa ○ WAN 198-199 E 6
Gamba ○ G 210-211 C 5
Gamba ○ VRC 144-145 G 6
Gamba ○ ZRE 210-211 K 6
Gambaga ○ GH 202-203 K 4
Gambang ○ MAL 162-163 E 3
Gambara ○ MEX 52-53 C 2
Gambéla ○ ETH 208-209 B 4
Gambela National Park ⊥ ETH 208-209 A 4
Gambell ○ USA 20-21 E 5
Gambia ■ WAG 202-203 B 3
Gambia, River ~ WAG 202-203 B 3
Gambia No.1 ○ GH 202-203 J 6
Gambier ○ SN 202-203 D 3
Gambier Islands ~ AUS 180-181 D 3
Gambo ○ ANG 216-217 F 6
Gambo ○ CDN (NFL) 242-243 O 4
Gambo ○ RCA 206-207 F 6
Gamboa ○ PA 52-53 E 7
Gambома ○ RCB 210-211 E 4
Gamboula ○ RCA 206-207 B 6
Gamčen, hrebet ▲ RUS 120-121 T 6
Gamčen, vulkan ▲ RUS 120-121 T 6
Gamdou ○ RN 198-199 D 6
Gameleir, Ribeiro ~ BR 68-69 C 7
Gameleira, Serra da ▲ BR 68-69 G 5
Gameleira da Lapa ○ BR 72-73 J 2
Gameleiras ○ BR 72-73 J 3
Gameteira, Riachão ~ BR 68-69 H 6
Ĝámğamâl ○ IR 128-129 L 5
Gamia ○ DY 204-205 E 3
Ĝâmid az-Zinâd ○ KSA 132-133 B 4
Ĝâmil al-'Imrân ○ IRQ 128-129 L 5
Gamis ○ NAM 220-221 C 2
Gamkab ○ NAM 220-221 C 4
Gamkahe ○ RI 164-165 K 3
Gamkarivier ~ ZA 220-221 D 7
Gamlakarleby = Kokkola ○ FIN 86-87 L 5
Gamleby ○ S 86-87 G 8
Gammelstaden ○• S 86-87 L 4
Gammel Sukkertoppen = Kangaamiut ○ GRØ 28-29 O 4
Gammon Ranges National Park ⊥ AUS 178-179 E 6
Gammouda = Sidi Bouzid ☆ TN 190-191 G 3
Gamoep ○ ZA 220-221 D 4
Gamo-Gofa ⊵ ETH 208-209 C 4
Gamova, mys ▲ RUS 122-123 D 7
Gamperê ▲ CAM 206-207 B 5
Gamping ○ RI 168 D 3
Gamra ○ RIM 196-197 D 6
Ĝâmsa, Ra's ▲ ET 194-195 F 4
Gamsberg ▲ NAM 220-221 C 1
Gamsby River ~ CDN (BC) 228-229 G 3
Ĝâmsídzái, Kûh-e ▲ IR 134-135 J 4
Gamûd ▲ ETH 208-209 D 5
Gamvik ○ N 86-87 O 1
G'amys, gora ▲ AZ 128-129 M 4
Gana, Komadougou ~ WAN 198-199 E 6
Ĝanad, al- ○ Y 132-133 D 7
Ganado ○ USA (AZ) 256-257 G 4
Ganado ○ USA (TX) 266-267 L 4
Ganai ○ PNG 183 E 5
Ganafskij hrebet ▲ RUS 120-121 R 7
Ganaly ○ RUS 120-121 R 7
Ĝânamiya, al- ○ KSA 130-131 K 5
Ĝânâna ~ UAE 134-135 G 5
Gananoque ○ CDN (ONT) 238-239 J 4
Ganâve, Bandar-e ○ IR 134-135 D 4
Gancheng ○ VRC 156-157 F 7
Gand = Gent ☆• B 92-93 G 3
Ganda ○ ANG 216-217 C 5
Gandadiwata, Gunung ▲ RI 164-165 F 5
Gandajika ○ ZRE 214-215 B 4
Gandak ~ IND 142-143 D 2
Ĝandaq ○ IR 134-135 F 1
Gandar, Pir ▲ PK 138-139 C 8
Gandava ○ PK 134-135 M 4
Gande ○ VRC 144-145 H 6
Ganden • VRC 144-145 H 6
Gander ○ CDN (NFL) 242-243 O 4
Gander Bay ○ CDN (NFL) 242-243 O 3
Gander Lake ○ CDN (NFL) 242-243 O 3
Gander River ~ CDN (NFL) 242-243 O 3
Gândhi Dham ○ IND 138-139 C 8
Gândhinagar ☆ IND 138-139 E 7
Gândhi Sâgar ○ IND 138-139 E 7
Gandia ○ E 98-99 G 5
Gandiaye ○ SN 202-203 B 2
Gandomak ○ AFG 138-139 C 2
Gandomán ○ IR 134-135 E 3
Gandu ○ BR 72-73 L 2
Ganedidâlam ○ CL 140-141 J 7
Ĝâneb ⊲ RIM 196-197 E 5
Ganespur ○ IND 142-143 B 2
Ganga, Mouths of the ≈ 142-143 F 5
Gangala na Bodio ○ ZRE 212-213 B 2
Gan Gan ○ RA 78-79 F 6
Gangán ▲ RG 202-203 D 4
Gángápur ○ IND (RAJ) 138-139 F 6
Gángápur ○ IND (RAJ) 138-139 E 7

Gangara ○ RN 198-199 D 5
Gangaw ○ MYA 142-143 J 4
Gangca ○ VRC 154-155 B 3
Gangchang ○ VRC 154-155 D 3
Ganges ○ CDN (BC) 230-231 F 5
Ganges ○ F 90-91 J 10
Ganges ~ IND 10-11 H 6
Ganges = Ganga ~ IND 10-11 H 6
Ganges, Mouths of the ≈ 142-143 F 5
Ganges Fan = Bengal Fan ≂ 12 G 3
Ganges River Delta = Ganga Delta ⊥ IND 142-143 F 4
Gangir, Rüdhâne-ye ~ IR 134-135 A 2
Gangkha ○ BHT 142-143 F 2
Gango ○ ANG 216-217 C 5
Gangoli ○ IND 140-141 F 4
Gangotri ○ IND 138-139 G 4
Gangtok ○ • IND 142-143 F 2
Gangu ○ VRC 154-155 D 3
Gangui ○ CAM 206-207 B 5
Gangula ○ ANG 216-217 B 5
Ganhe ○ VRC 150-151 D 2
Gani ○ RI 164-165 L 4
Gâni Hêl ○ AFG 138-139 B 3
Gan Jiang ~ VRC 156-157 J 3
Ganjuškino ○ KA 96-97 F 10
Ganlanba • VRC 156-157 B 6
Ganluo ○ VRC 156-157 C 2
Gannan ○ VRC 150-151 D 4
Gannat ○ F 90-91 J 8
Gannett Peak ▲ USA (WY) 252-253 J 3
Ganquan ○ VRC 154-155 F 3
Gansbaai ○ ZA 220-221 D 7
Gansé ○ CI 202-203 J 4
Gansen ○ VRC 144-145 J 2
Gansu ▫ VRC 148-149 J 7
Ganta ○ LB 202-203 F 6
Gantang ○ VRC 154-155 D 3
Gantas, La ○ RA 76-77 G 5
Gantheaume, Cape ▲ AUS 180-181 D 4
Gantheaume Bay ≈ 176-177 C 3
Gantheaume Point ▲ AUS 172-173 F 4
Ganti ○ RI 168 C 7
Gantira ○ RI 164-165 G 5
Gantisan ○ MAL 160-161 C 9
Gantt ○ USA (AL) 284-285 D 5
Gantt Lake < USA (AL) 284-285 D 5
Ĝânûbiya, al-Bâdiya I- ⊵ IRQ 130-131 K 2
Ganxi ○ VRC 156-157 F 1
Ganye ○ WAN 204-205 K 4
Ganyesa ○ ZA 220-221 G 3
Ganyh ~ AZ 128-129 M 2
Ganyu ○ VRC 154-155 L 4
Ganža ○ AZ 128-129 M 2
Ganzhou ○ VRC 156-157 J 4
Gao ○ BF 202-203 J 4
Gao ☆ RMM 196-197 J 5
Gao •• RMM (GAO) 196-197 K 6
Gao ○ ZRE 212-213 B 2
Gao'an ○ VRC 156-157 J 2
Gaochang Gucheng ∴ • VRC 146-147 J 4
Gaochun ○ VRC 154-155 L 6
Gaofengtao ○ VRC 154-155 L 4
Gaogou ○ VRC 154-155 L 4
Gaohezhen ○ VRC 154-155 K 6
Gaojiabu ○ VRC 154-155 F 3
Gaolan • VRC (GAN) 154-155 C 3
Gaoligong Shan ▲ VRC 142-143 L 2
Gaomi ○ VRC 154-155 L 3
Gaoping ○ VRC 154-155 H 4
Gaotai ○ VRC 154-155 A 2
Gaotang ○ VRC 154-155 K 3
Gaotou ○ VRC 154-155 K 2
Gaoua ○ BF 202-203 J 4
Gaoual ○ RG 202-203 D 4
Gaoun, Mont ▲ RCA 206-207 B 5
Gao Xian ○ VRC 156-157 D 2
Gaoyi ○ VRC 154-155 J 3
Gaozhou ○ VRC 156-157 G 5
Gap ○ F 90-91 L 9
Gap, Pico ▲ RCH 80 F 6
Gapi ○ ZRE 206-207 F 6
Gapuwiyak ▲ AUS 174-175 C 3
Gar' ~ RUS 122-123 C 2
Garaa Tebourt ⊂ TN 190-191 H 5
Garabinzam ○ RCB 210-211 E 3
Ĝárablus ★ SYR 128-129 H 4
Garabogazköl = TM (KRS) 136-137 C 4
Gara Brune ○ DZ 190-191 E 6
Garacad ○ SP 208-209 J 5
Garada ○ SUD 200-201 E 3
Garadag ○ SP 208-209 H 4
Gara Dragoman ○ BG 102-103 C 6
Ĝarâğir, Wâdi al- ~ KSA 130-131 H 4
Garagoa ○ CO 60-61 E 5
Garanhuns ○ BR 68-69 K 6
Ga-Rankuwa ○ ZA 220-221 H 2
Garapa, Serra do ▲ BR 72-73 J 2
Garapu ○ BR 72-73 D 2
Garapuava ○ BR 72-73 G 4
Ĝárarâ ○ KSA 130-131 K 4
Ĝârarâ ○ LB 202-203 G 7
Garawe ○ LB 202-203 G 7
Ĝarâw, al- ⊲ JOR 130-131 D 1
Garayalde ○ RA 80 G 2
Garba ○ RCA 206-207 E 6
Garbaharrey ☆ SP 212-213 J 2
Garba Tula ○ EAK 212-213 G 3
Garber ○ USA (OK) 264-265 G 2

Garberville ○ USA (CA) 246-247 B 3
Garbi, 'Ali al- ☆ IRQ 128-129 M 6
Gārboš, Kūh-e ▲ IR 134-135 D 2
Garças, Cachoeira das ~ BR 70-71 K 4
Garças, Cachoeira das ~ BR 70-71 H 2
Garças ou Jacaréguéau, Rio das ~ BR 72-73 D 3
Garchitorena ○ RP 160-161 E 6
Garciasville ○ USA (TX) 266-267 J 7
Garcitas, Las ○ RA 76-77 H 4
Garco ○ VRC 144-145 G 4
Garda ○ I 100-101 C 2
Gardabani ○ GE 126-127 F 7
Gardandēwāl ○ AFG 138-139 B 2
Garde Lake ○ CDN 30-31 Q 4
Gardelegen ○• D 92-93 L 2
Garden City ○ USA (AL) 284-285 D 2
Garden City ○ USA (GA) 284-285 J 4
Garden City ○ USA (KS) 262-263 F 7
Garden City ○ USA (TX) 266-267 F 2
Garden City ○ USA (UT) 254-255 D 2
Garden Cove ○ CDN (NFL) 242-243 O 5
Gardendale ○ USA (TX) 264-265 B 6
Gardenia Lake ○ CDN 30-31 R 4
Garden Island ⌒ USA (MI) 272-273 D 2
Garden Peninsula ⌣ USA (MI) 270-271 M 5
Garden River ○ CDN (ONT) 236-237 D 6
Garden River ~ CDN (ONT) 238-239 B 2
Garden River Indian Reserve ⚔ CDN (ONT) 236-237 D 6
Gardens Corner ○ USA (SC) 284-285 K 4
Garden State Parkway II USA (NJ) 280-281 M 4
Gardenton ○ CDN (MAN) 234-235 G 5
Garden Valley ○ USA (TX) 264-265 D 4
Gardēz ☆ AFG 138-139 B 3
Gardi ○ USA (GA) 284-285 J 5
Gardiner ○ CDN (ONT) 236-237 G 3
Gardiner ○ USA (ME) 278-279 M 4
Gardiner ○ USA (MT) 250-251 J 6
Gardiner, Mount ▲ AUS 178-179 K 2
Gardiners Island ⌒ USA (NY) 280-281 O 2
Gardner ⌒ KIB 13 K 3
Gardner ○ USA (CO) 254-255 K 6
Gardner ○ USA (FL) 286-287 H 4
Gardner ○ USA (IL) 274-275 K 3
Gardner ○ USA (KS) 262-263 M 6
Gardner ○ USA (LA) 268-269 H 5
Gardner ○ USA (ND) 258-259 L 4
Gardner Canal < CDN (BC) 228-229 F 3
Gardner Pinnacles ⌒ USA 14-15 M 5
Gardner Plateau ⩳ AUS 172-173 G 3
Gardner Range ▲ AUS 172-173 J 5
Gardnerville ○ USA (NV) 246-247 F 5
Gardunha, Serra da ▲ P 98-99 D 4
Garei ~ BD 142-143 F 4
Gareloi Island ⌒ USA 22-23 G 7
Gare Tigre ○ F 62-63 H 3
Garfa, Oued ~ RIM 196-197 D 7
Garfield ○ AUS 178-179 H 2
Garfield ○ USA (KS) 262-263 G 6
Garfield ○ USA (NM) 256-257 H 6
Garfield ○ USA (WA) 244-245 H 3
Garfield Mountain ▲ USA (MT) 250-251 G 7
Garford ○ AUS 176-177 M 4
Gargamelle ○ CDN (NFL) 242-243 L 2
Gargando ○ RMM 196-197 H 6
Gargano, Promontorio del ▲ I 100-101 E 4
Gargantua, Cape ▲ CDN (ONT) 236-237 C 5
Gargaris ○ PNG 183 G 2
Gargnäs ○ S 86-87 H 4
Gargouna ○ RMM 202-203 L 2
Gargždai ☆• LT 94-95 G 4
Garhjāt Hills ▲ IND 142-143 D 5
Garhshankar ○ IND 138-139 F 4
Gari ☆ RUS 114-115 G 5
Gariāband ○ IND 142-143 C 5
Gariau ○ RI 166-167 H 3
Gārīb, Ra's ▲ ET 194-195 F 3
Garibaldi ○ BR 74-75 E 7
Garibaldi ○ CDN (BC) 230-231 F 4
Garibaldi ○ USA (OR) 244-245 B 5
Garibaldi, Mount ▲ CDN (BC) 230-231 F 4
Garibaldi Provincial Park ⊥ CDN (BC) 230-231 G 4
Garies ○ ZA 220-221 C 5
Ġarīf, al- ○ KSA 130-131 F 6
Gariganus ○ NAM 220-221 D 3
Garimpinho ○ BR 68-69 D 5
Garīn, Kūh-e ▲ IR 134-135 C 2
Garin Shehu ○ WAN 204-205 J 4
Garin Yerima ○ WAN 204-205 J 4
Ġarīr, Wādī al- ~ KSA 130-131 H 5
Garissa ☆ EAK 212-213 G 4
Garkem ○ WAN 204-205 H 5
Garki ○ WAN 198-199 D 6
Garkida ○ WAN 204-205 K 3
Garladinne ○ IND 140-141 G 3
Garland ○ CDN (MAN) 234-235 C 3
Garland ○ USA (AR) 276-277 B 7
Garland ○ USA (MT) 250-251 O 5
Garland ○ USA (NC) 282-283 J 6
Garland ○ USA (TX) 264-265 H 6
Garland ○ USA (UT) 254-255 C 2
Garland ○ USA (WY) 252-253 K 2
Garm ○ TJ 136-137 M 5
Garmāb ○ IR 128-129 N 5
Garmabe ○ SUD 206-207 K 6
Garmanda ○ RUS 112-113 K 5
Garmanda, Bol'šaja ~ RUS 112-113 K 5
Garm Bīt ○ IR 134-135 J 6
Garme ○ IR 136-137 E 6
Garmisch-Partenkirchen ○• D 92-93 L 5
Garmsār ○ AFG 134-135 L 3
Garmsār ⩳ AFG 134-135 K 3
Garmsār ○ IR 136-137 C 7
Garner ○ USA (IA) 274-275 E 1
Garner ○ USA (NC) 282-283 J 5
Garnet ○ USA (MI) 270-271 N 4
Garnet Bank ⩳ 74-75 F 9
Garnet Bay ≈ 36-37 M 2
Garnett ○ USA (KS) 262-263 L 6
Garnett ○ USA (SC) 284-285 J 4
Garnish ○ CDN (NFL) 242-243 N 5
Garnpung, Lake ○ AUS 180-181 G 2
Garonne ~ F 90-91 H 9
Garoowe ☆ SP 208-209 J 4
Garou ○ DY 204-205 E 3
Garou, Lac ○ RMM 196-197 J 6
Garoua ☆ CAM 204-205 K 4
Garoua Boulaï ○ CAM 206-207 B 6
Garove Island ⌒ PNG 183 E 3
Garré ○ RA 78-79 H 4
Garretson ○ USA (SD) 260-261 K 3
Garrett ○ USA (WY) 252-253 N 4
Garrett Fracture Zone ⩳ 14-15 R 9
Garrick ○ CDN (SAS) 232-233 O 2
Garrido, Isla ⌒ RCH 80 C 2
Garrington ○ CDN (ALB) 232-233 D 4
Garrison ○ USA (MN) 270-271 E 4
Garrison ○ USA (MT) 250-251 G 5
Garrison ○ USA (ND) 258-259 F 4
Garrison ○ USA (NV) 246-247 M 5
Garrison ○ USA (TX) 268-269 F 5
Garro ○ MEX 52-53 G 2
Garrobo, El ○ NIC 52-53 B 5
Garruchos ○ BR 76-77 K 5
Garry, Cape ▲ CDN 24-25 Z 4
Garry Bay ≈ 24-25 d 6
Garry Lake ○ CDN 30-31 T 3
Garsala ○ SP 212-213 K 2
Garsen ○ EAK 212-213 H 5
Garsila ○ SUD 198-199 L 6
Garson Lake ○ CDN 32-33 Q 3
Gartempe ~ F 90-91 H 8
Gartok = Garyarsa ○ VRC 144-145 C 5
Garu ○ PNG 183 E 3
Garuahi ○ PNG 183 F 6
Garub ○ NAM 220-221 C 3
Ġarūb ○ Y 132-133 H 5
Garuma ○ RCH 76-77 C 2
Garupá, Rio ~ BR 76-77 J 6
Garut ○• RI 168 B 3
Garuva ○ BR 74-75 F 6
Garwa ○ IND 142-143 C 3
Garwolin ○ PL 92-93 Q 3
Gar Xincun ○ VRC 144-145 C 4
Gary ○ USA (IN) 274-275 L 3
Garyarsa ○ VRC 144-145 C 5
Garysburg ○ USA (NC) 282-283 K 4
Garza ○ RA 76-77 F 5
Garzas, Las ○ RA 76-77 H 5
Garzê ○ VRC 144-145 M 5
Garzon ○ CO 60-61 D 6
Gasan Kuli ○ TM 136-137 C 6
Gasan-Kulijskijučastok Krasnovodskogo zapovednik ⊥ TM 136-137 C 6
Gaschiga ○ CAM 204-205 K 4
Gas City ○ USA (IN) 274-275 N 4
Gascogne ⩳ F 90-91 G 10
Gascoigne ○ CDN (SAS) 232-233 J 5
Gasconade River ~ USA (MO) 274-275 G 6
Gasconade River ~ USA (MO) 276-277 C 3
Gascoyne, Mount ▲ AUS 176-177 D 2
Gascoyne Junction ○ AUS 176-177 C 2
Gascoyne River ~ AUS 176-177 C 2
Gasera ○ ETH 208-209 E 5
Gash ~ ER 200-201 H 5
Gashaka ○ WAN 204-205 J 5
Gasherbrum I ▲ PK 138-139 F 2
Gasherbrum II ▲ PK 138-139 F 2
Gas Hu ○ VRC 146-147 K 6
Gashua ○ WAN 198-199 E 6
Gashunchaka ○ VRC 144-145 K 2
Gasim ○ RI 166-167 F 2
Ġāsk ○ IR 134-135 G 6
Ġāsk, Ḫaliğ-e ≈ 134-135 G 6
Gaskačokka ▲ N 86-87 H 3
Gasmata ○ PNG 183 F 4
Gaspar, Selat ≈ 162-163 G 6
Gaspar Hernández ○ DOM 54-55 K 5
Gasparilla Island ⌒ USA (FL) 286-287 G 5
Gaspé ○ CDN (QUE) 240-241 L 2
Gaspé, Baie de ≈ 38-39 M 4
Gaspé, Baie de ≈ CDN 240-241 L 2
Gaspé, Cape ▲ CDN (QUE) 240-241 L 2
Gaspé, Péninsule de ⌣ CDN (QUE) 240-241 J 2
Gaspereau Forks ○ CDN (NB) 240-241 K 4
Gaspésie, Parc de la ⊥ CDN (QUE) 240-241 J 2
Gasquet ○ USA (CA) 246-247 B 2
Gassan ○ BF 202-203 J 3
Ġassān ○ IRQ 128-129 L 6
Gassan ▲ J 152-153 H 5
Gassane ○ SN 202-203 C 2
Gassaway ○ USA (WV) 280-281 F 5
Gassend Lake ○ CDN 24-25 J 6
Gassi Touil ⩳ DZ 190-191 F 6
Gassol ○ WAN 204-205 J 4
Gass Peak ▲ USA (NV) 248-249 J 3
Gašt ○ IR 134-135 J 5
Gastello ○ RUS 122-123 K 4
Gastón ○ C 54-55 G 4
Gastona, Río ~ RA 76-77 E 4
Gastonia ○ USA (NC) 282-283 F 5
Gastre ○ RA 78-79 E 7
Ġāṭ, al- ○ KSA 130-131 J 4
Gata ○ CV 202-203 C 5
Gata, Cabo de ▲ E 98-99 F 6
Gata, Sierra de ▲ E 98-99 D 4
Gataga River ~ CDN 30-31 F 6
Gatanga ○ SUD 206-207 H 5
Gatčina ☆ RUS 94-95 M 2
Gate ○ USA (OK) 264-265 D 2
Gate City ○ USA (VA) 280-281 D 7
Gatehouse of Fleet ○ GB 90-91 E 4
Gatentiri ○ RI 166-167 L 5
Gates ○ USA (NC) 282-283 L 4
Gateshead Island ⌒ CDN 24-25 W 5
Gates of the Artic National Park and Preserve ⊥ USA 20-21 N 2
Gatesville ○ USA (TX) 266-267 K 2
Gateview ○ USA (CO) 254-255 H 5
Gateway ○ USA (CO) 254-255 G 5
Gateway National Recreation Area • USA (NY) 280-281 N 3
Gathto Creek ~ CDN 30-31 G 6
Gati-Loumo ○ RMM 202-203 H 2
Gatin, Rivière ~ CDN 36-37 M 4
Gatineau ○ CDN (QUE) 238-239 K 3
Gatineau, Rivière ~ CDN (QUE) 236-237 N 5
Gatineau, Rivière ~ CDN (QUE) 238-239 K 3
Gatlinburg ○ USA (TN) 282-283 D 5
Gatos, Los ○ USA (CA) 248-249 C 2
Ġaṭṭi ○ KSA 130-131 E 2
Gatton ○ AUS 178-179 M 4
Gatún, Lago ○• PA 52-53 E 7
Gatuncito ○ PA 52-53 D 7
Gatvand ○ IR 134-135 C 2
Gau ⌒ FJI 184 III b 3
Gaua, Île = Santa Maria Island ⌒ VAN 184 II a 2
Gaudan ○ TM 136-137 F 6
Gaudan, pereval ▲ TM 136-137 F 6
Gauer Lake ○ CDN 34-35 H 2
Ġauf, al- ◘ KSA 130-131 F 2
Ġauf, Wādī al- ~ Y 132-133 D 5
Ġaufa, al- ○ KSA 132-133 B 3
Gaujas nacionālais parks ⊥ LV 94-95 J 3
Gaula ~ N 86-87 E 5
Gaulay River ~ USA (WV) 280-281 F 5
Gauley Mountain ▲ USA (WV) 280-281 F 5
Gaulim ○ PNG 183 G 3
Gaulle, De ○ RCA 206-207 B 5
Gaultois ○ CDN (NFL) 242-243 N 5
Gaurdak ○ TM 136-137 K 6
Gauribidanur ○ IND 140-141 G 4
Gauss Halvø ⩳ GRØ 26-27 o 7
Gausta ▲ N 86-87 D 7
Gauthiot, Chutes ~• TCH 206-207 B 4
Gauttier, Pegunungan ▲ RI 166-167 K 3
Ġavāher Deh ○ IR 136-137 B 6
Ġavand ○ AFG 136-137 J 7
Ġavānrūd ○ IR 134-135 B 1
Gāvbandi ○ IR 134-135 E 5
Gāvbast, Kūh-e ▲ IR 134-135 E 5
Gávdos ⌒ GR 100-101 K 7
Gave de Pau ~ F 90-91 G 10
Gäve Rūd ~ IR 134-135 B 1
Gāvgān ○ IR 128-129 L 4
Gavião ○ BR 68-69 J 7
Gavião ○ P 98-99 D 5
Gavião, Rio ~ BR 72-73 K 3
Gavien ○ PNG 183 C 3
Gaviota ○ USA (CA) 248-249 D 5
Gaviota Beach • USA (CA) 248-249 D 5
Gaviota Pass ▲ USA (CA) 248-249 D 5
Gaviotas, Las ○ YV 60-61 K 3
Gävle ☆ S 86-87 H 6
Gavrilla, guba ○ RUS 112-113 U 5
Gavrilov -Jam ☆ RUS 94-95 Q 3
Gávrio ○ GR 100-101 K 6
Gavriša-Tas, gora ▲ RUS 110-111 X 3
Gavunipalli ○ IND 140-141 H 4
Gawachab ○ NAM 220-221 C 3
Gawa Island ⌒ PNG 183 F 5
Gawalisi, Gunung ▲ RI 164-165 F 4
Gawa Obo ○ VRC 144-145 M 3
Ġawār,al- ⩳ UAE 130-131 L 5
Gāwilgarh Hills ▲ IND 138-139 F 9
Gawler ○ AUS 180-181 E 3
Gawler Ranges ▲ AUS 180-181 C 2
Gawu ○ WAN 204-205 G 4
Gawwār, Ġazirat ⌒ KSA 130-131 E 5
Gaxun Nur ○ VRC 148-149 E 6
Gay ○ USA (GA) 284-285 F 3
Gay ○ USA (OK) 264-265 J 5
Gaya ○•• IND 142-143 D 3
Gaya ○ MAL 160-161 B 9
Gaya ○ RN 204-205 E 3
Gaya ○ WAN 204-205 H 3
Gaya, Pulau ⌒ MAL 160-161 B 9
Gayam ○ TCH 206-207 C 4
Gayamcam ○ RP 160-161 E 9
Gayaza ○ EAU 212-213 C 4
G'Aydat Al Ihoucha ⩳ MA 188-189 F 7
Gayéri ○ BF 202-203 L 3
Gay Head ▲ USA (MA) 278-279 L 7
Gaylord ○ USA (MI) 272-273 E 2
Gaylord ○ USA (MN) 270-271 D 6
Gaylord ○ USA (VA) 280-281 J 4
Gayna River ~ CDN 30-31 E 3
Gays River ○ CDN (NS) 240-241 M 5
Gayville ○ USA (SD) 260-261 J 4
Ġayyāda, Šu'aib ~ IRQ 128-129 J 6
Gaz, Rūd-e ~ AFG 134-135 K 2
Gaza ◘ MOC 218-219 G 6
Gaza/ Ġazza ☆ AUT 130-131 C 2
Gazačak ○ TM 136-137 G 4
Gaz-Ačak = Gazačak ○ TM 136-137 G 4
Gazakh = Qazax ○• AZ 128-129 L 2
Ġazala, al- ○ KSA 130-131 G 4
Gazalkent ○ US 136-137 L 4
Gazanak ○ IR 136-137 C 7
Gazankulu (former Homel., now part of North-Transvaal) ⊥ ZA 218-219 D 6
Gazaoua ○ RN 198-199 C 6
Gazara ○ TJ 136-137 L 5
Gazelle ○ USA (CA) 246-247 C 2
Gazelle Channel ≈ 183 F 2
Gazelle Peninsula ⌣ PNG 183 F 3
Gazerān ○ IR 134-135 D 1
Gāzergāh ○• AFG 134-135 K 1
Gazi ○ EAK 212-213 G 6
Gazi Antep ☆ TR 128-129 G 4
Gazik ○ IR 134-135 J 2
Gazimur ~ RUS 118-119 J 9
Gazimurskij Zavod ☆ RUS 118-119 J 10
Gazipaşa ☆ TR 128-129 E 4
Gazipur ○ BD 142-143 G 4
Gazli ○ US 136-137 H 4
Ġaz Mūrīān, Hāmūn-e ○ IR 134-135 H 5
Gazni ◘ AFG 134-135 M 2
Gazni ☆• AFG 138-139 B 3
Gazni, Daryā-ye ~ AFG 138-139 B 3
Gbabam ○ CI 202-203 H 7
Gbaboua ○ CAM 206-207 B 5
Gbadolite ○ ZRE 206-207 E 6
Gbagba ○ RCA 206-207 E 6
Gbaizera ○ RCA 206-207 D 5
Gbako, River ~ WAN 204-205 G 4
Gbananmè ○ DY 204-205 E 5
Gbanendji ○ RCA 206-207 E 5
Gbanga ☆ LB 202-203 F 6
Gbanga ○ WAN 204-205 G 4
Gbangbatok ○ WAL 202-203 D 6
Gbanhala ~ RG 202-203 F 5
Gbapleu ○ CI 202-203 F 6
Gbassa ○ DY 204-205 E 3
Gbassigbiri ○ RCA 206-207 H 6
Gbatala ○ LB 202-203 F 6
Gbele Game Production Reserve ⊥ GH 202-203 J 4
Gbengué ○ BF 202-203 J 4
Gbentu ○ WAL 202-203 E 5
Gberia Timbako ○ WAL 202-203 E 5
Gbéroubouè ○ DY 204-205 E 3
Gbibo ○ LB 202-203 F 7
Gbodonon ○ CI 202-203 H 5
Gboko ○ WAN 204-205 H 5
Gbongaa ○ CI 202-203 G 5
Gbongan ○ WAN 204-205 F 5
Gbung ○ GH 202-203 K 5
Gbwado ○ ZRE 210-211 H 2
Gdańsk ☆•• PL 92-93 P 1
Gdańsk, Gulf of = Gdańska, Zatoka ≈ PL 92-93 P 1
Gdańska, Zatoka ≈ 92-93 P 1
Gdov ☆ RUS 94-95 K 2
Gdyel ○ DZ 188-189 L 3
Gdynia ○•• PL 92-93 P 1
Geary ○ CDN (NB) 240-241 J 5
Geary ○ USA (OK) 264-265 F 3
Gêba, Canal do ≈ 202-203 B 4
Geba, Rio ~ GNB 202-203 C 3
Gebä Bärez, Kūh-e ▲ IR 134-135 G 4
Gebasawa ○ WAN 198-199 D 6
Geba Wenz ~ ETH 208-209 B 4
Gebe, Pulau ⌒ RI 166-167 E 2
Gebeit ○ SUD 200-201 H 3
Gebeledan ○ CI 202-203 F 5
Gebituolatuo ○ VRC 146-147 L 6
Gebo ○ USA (WY) 252-253 K 3
Gebre Guracha ○ ETH 208-209 D 4
Gebze ☆ TR 128-129 C 2
Gech'a ○ ETH 208-209 B 5
Gedabiet ○ ETH 200-201 H 6
Geddes ○ USA (SD) 260-261 H 3
Gedenštroma, zaliv ≈ 110-111 Y 2
Gedi ○ EAK 212-213 H 5
Gedi National Monument • EAK 212-213 H 5
Gediz ☆ TR 128-129 C 3
Gediz Nehri ~ TR 128-129 C 3
Gedlegube ○ ETH 208-209 G 5
Gēdo ○ ETH 208-209 C 4
Gedo ◘ SP 212-213 H 2
Gedongratu ○ RI 162-163 F 7
Gedser ○ DK 86-87 E 9
Geegully Creek ~ AUS 172-173 F 5
Geel ○ B 92-93 H 3
Geelong ○• AUS 180-181 H 5
Geelvink Channel ≈ 176-177 B 4
Geesaley ○ SP 208-209 K 3
Geese Islands ⌒ USA 22-23 U 4
Geeveston ○ AUS 180-181 J 7
Gēga Shet' ~ ETH 208-209 E 3
Gegbwema ○ WAL 202-203 E 6
Gegentala Caoyuan • VRC 148-149 K 7
Gē'gyai ○ VRC 144-145 C 4
Geidam ○ WAN 198-199 E 6
Geifil ○ SUD 200-201 E 6
Geikie Island ⌒ CDN (ONT) 234-235 P 4
Geikie River ~ CDN 34-35 D 2
Geiki Gorge National Park ⊥ AUS 172-173 G 5
Geillini Lake ○ CDN 30-31 W 5
Geillini River ~ CDN 30-31 W 5
Geilo ○ N 86-87 D 6
Geirangerfjorden ≈•• 86-87 C 5
Geiser del Tatio ○• RCH 76-77 C 2
Geita ○ EAT 212-213 D 5
Gejbenga, ostrova ⌒ RUS 108-109 c 3
Gejiu ○ VRC 156-157 C 5
Geka, mys ▲ RUS 112-113 U 4
Gel ~ SUD 206-207 J 5
Gela ○ I 100-101 E 6
Geladangong ▲ VRC 144-145 H 4
Geladi ○ ETH 208-209 H 5
Gelai ▲ EAT 212-213 F 5
Gelam, Pulau ⌒ RI 162-163 J 6
Gele ○ ZRE 206-207 E 6
Gelemso ○ ETH 208-209 E 4
Gelendžik ○ RUS 126-127 C 5
Gel Gulbis < EAK 212-213 G 2
Gelibolu ☆• TR 128-129 B 2
Gelila ○ ETH 208-209 C 4
Gellāb ○ SUD 206-207 G 4
Gellinsor ○ SP 208-209 H 5
Geloketapang ○ RI 162-163 A 3
Gelot' ○ RUS 116-117 L 7
Gelsenkirchen ○ D 92-93 J 3
Gelumbang ○ RI 162-163 F 6
Gemaliel ○ USA (KY) 276-277 K 4
Gemas ○ MAL 162-163 E 3
Gembele, Rapides ~ ZRE 210-211 J 2
Gembogl ○ PNG 183 C 3
Gembu ○ WAN 204-205 J 5
Geme ○ RI 164-165 K 1
Gemena ○ ZRE 210-211 G 2
Gemerek ☆ TR 128-129 G 3
Gemeri Häyk' ○ ETH 208-209 E 3
Gemi ▲ ETH 208-209 B 4
Gemlik ☆ TR 128-129 C 2
Gemlik Körfezi ≈ 128-129 C 2
Gemmeiza ○ SUD 200-201 G 4
Gemmell ○ USA (MN) 270-271 D 3
Gemona del Friuli ○ I 100-101 D 1
Gempol ○ RI 168 E 3
Gemsbok National Park ⊥ RB 220-221 E 2
Gemsbokvlakte ○ ZA 220-221 G 2
Genalē Wenz ~ ETH 208-209 E 6
Genali, Danau ○ RI 162-163 K 4
Gendarān Bāshī ▲ IR 128-129 M 3
Genémasson ○ DY 204-205 E 3
General Acha ○ RA 78-79 G 4
General A. Darnes ○ BR 74-75 E 7
General Alvear ○ RA (BUA) 78-79 J 4
General Alvear ○ RA (MEN) 78-79 F 3
General Arenales ○ RA 78-79 J 3
General Arnulfo R. Gómez ○ MEX 50-51 G 5
General Ballivián ○ RA 76-77 F 2
General Belgrano ○ RA 78-79 K 3
General Bravo ○ MEX 50-51 K 5
General Cabrera ○ RA 78-79 H 2
General Camacho ○ BOL 70-71 C 5
General Carrera, Lago ○ RCH 80 D 3
General Cepeda ○ MEX 50-51 J 5
General Conesa ○ RA (BUA) 78-79 L 4
General Conesa ○ RA (RIN) 78-79 G 6
General Elizardo Aquino ○ PY 76-77 J 3
General Enrique Martínez ○ ROU 74-75 D 9
General Enrique Mosconi ○ RA 76-77 F 2
General Eugenio a Garay ☆ PY 70-71 F 7
General Francisco Murguía ○ MEX 50-51 H 5
General Güemes ○ RA 76-77 E 3
General Ignacio Zaragoza ○ MEX 50-51 K 6
General José de San Martín ○ RA 76-77 H 4
General Juan Madariaga ○ RA 78-79 L 4
General la Madrid ○ RA 78-79 J 4
General Levalle ○ RA 78-79 H 3
General L. Plaza Gutiérrez ○ EC 64-65 C 3
General Luz ○ BR 74-75 E 7
General Mansilla ○ RA 78-79 L 3
General M. Belgrano ○ RA 76-77 H 3
General Mosconi ○ RA 76-77 F 2
General Obligado ○ RA 76-77 H 4
General Pico ○ RA 78-79 H 3
General Pinedo ○ RA 76-77 G 4
General Roca ○ RA 78-79 F 5
General Sampaio ○ BR 68-69 J 4
General San Martín ○ RA 78-79 H 4
General Santos ☆ RP 160-161 F 9
General Simón Bolívar ○ MEX 50-51 H 5
General Terán ○ MEX 50-51 K 5
General Tiburcio ○ BR 68-69 H 3
General Toševo ○ BG 102-103 F 6
General Treviño ○ MEX 50-51 K 4
General Trías ○ MEX 50-51 F 3
General Villegas ○ RA 78-79 H 3
General Vintter, Lago ○ RA 78-79 D 7
Genesee ○ CDN (ALB) 232-233 D 2
Geneseo ○ USA (IL) 274-275 H 3
Geneseo ○ USA (KS) 262-263 H 6
Geneseo ○ USA (NY) 278-279 D 6
Genet ○ ETH 208-209 D 4
Geneva ○ USA (AL) 284-285 E 5
Geneva ○ USA (GA) 284-285 F 4
Geneva ○ USA (ID) 252-253 G 4
Geneva ○ USA (NE) 262-263 J 4
Geneva ○ USA (NY) 278-279 E 6
Geneva ○ USA (OH) 280-281 F 2
Geneva = Genève ☆•• CH 92-93 J 4
Geneva, Lake = Léman, Lac ○ CH 92-93 J 5
Genève ☆•• CH 92-93 J 5
Genévriers, Île des ⌒ CDN 38-39 P 3
Genf = Genève ☆•• CH 92-93 J 5
Genfer See = Lac Léman ○ CH 92-93 J 5
Gengma ○ VRC 142-143 L 4
Gengwa ○ ZRE 210-211 J 5
Genil, Río ~ E 98-99 E 6
Genk ○ B 92-93 H 3
Genkai-nada ≈ 152-153 D 8
Genkanyj, hrebet ▲ RUS 112-113 Y 3
Gennargentu, Monti del ▲ I 100-101 B 4
Genoa ○ AUS 180-181 K 4
Genoa ○ USA (CO) 254-255 M 4
Genoa ○ USA (NE) 262-263 J 3
Genoa ○ USA (NV) 246-247 F 4
Genoa ○ USA (WI) 270-271 G 7
Genoa = Génova ☆•• I 100-101 B 2
Genoa City ○ USA (WI) 274-275 K 2
Génova ☆• I 100-101 B 2
Genova, Golfo di ≈ 100-101 B 2
Genovesa, Isla ⌒ EC 64-65 C 9
Gens-de-Terre, Rivière ~ CDN (QUE) 236-237 M 5
Gent ☆•• B 92-93 G 3
Genteng ○ RI 168 B 3
Genteng, Pulau ⌒ RI 168 E 3
Genteng, Ujung ▲ RI 168 B 3
Genteng Game Park ⊥ RI 168 B 3
Genting ○ RI 162-163 C 3
Gentios, Isla dos ⌒ BR 70-71 E 3
Gentryville ○ USA (MO) 276-277 C 4
Genyem ○ RI 166-167 L 3
Geographe Bay ≈ 176-177 C 6
Geographe Channel ≈ 176-177 B 2
Geographical Center of Conterminous United States • USA (KS) 262-263 H 5
Geographical Center of North American Continent ∴ USA (ND) 258-259 H 3
Geographical Center of the United States ∴ USA (SD) 260-261 C 1
Geographical Society Ø ⌒ GRØ 26-27 o 7
Geok-Tepe ○ TM 136-137 E 5
Geologičeskaja, grjada ▲ RUS 108-109 Z 4
Geologičeskij ○ RUS 112-113 V 3
George, Zemlja ⌒ RUS 84-85 a 2
George ○ USA (IA) 274-275 C 1
George ○ USA (WA) 244-245 F 3
George ○ ZA 220-221 F 6
George, Cape ▲ CDN (BC) 228-229 D 3
George, Cape ▲ CDN (NS) 240-241 N 5
George, Lake ○ AUS (NSW) 180-181 K 3
George, Lake ○ AUS (SA) 180-181 E 4
George, Lake ○ AUS (WA) 172-173 F 7
George, Lake ○ EAU 212-213 C 3
George, Lake ○ USA (FL) 286-287 H 2
George, Lake ○ USA (NY) 278-279 H 5
George, Mount ▲ AUS 172-173 D 7
George, Mount ▲ CDN 24-25 S 6
George, Rivière ~ CDN 36-37 R 6
George Gill Range ▲ AUS 176-177 L 2
George Island ⌒ CDN 36-37 V 7
George Island ⌒ GB 78-79 L 7
George National Historic Park, Fort • CDN (ONT) 238-239 F 5
George Reservoir, Walter F. < USA (AL) 284-285 E 5
George Richards, Cape ▲ CDN 24-25 R 2
George River ~ USA 20-21 M 5
George R. Parks Highway II USA 20-21 P 5
Georges Bank ⩳ 46-47 P 5
Georges Bank ⩳ 278-279 O 7
Georges de l'Oudingueur • TCH 198-199 H 2
George Sound ≈ 182 A 6
Georges Tavern ○ USA (VA) 280-281 H 6
Georgetown ○ AUS 174-175 G 6
George Town ○ AUS 180-181 J 6
George Town ○• BS 54-55 H 3
Georgetown ○ CDN (NS) 240-241 N 4
Georgetown ○ CDN (ONT) 238-239 F 5
Georgetown ○ GB (STH) 202-203 B 7
Georgetown ☆ GB 54-55 E 5
Georgetown ★ GUY 62-63 E 2
Georgetown ○ USA (CA) 246-247 E 5
Georgetown ○ USA (DE) 280-281 L 5
Georgetown ○ USA (GA) 284-285 E 5
Georgetown ○ USA (KY) 276-277 L 2
Georgetown ○ USA (MS) 268-269 K 5
Georgetown ○ USA (OH) 280-281 C 5
Georgetown ○ USA (TX) 266-267 K 3
Georgetown ○• USA (SC) 284-285 L 3
Georgetown ☆• WAG 202-203 C 3
Georgetown ○ WV 56 E 5
Georgetown, Lake < USA (TX) 266-267 K 3
Georgeville ○ CDN (QUE) 238-239 N 3
George Washington Carver National Monument ∴ USA (MO) 276-277 A 3
George West ○ USA (TX) 266-267 J 5
Georgia ◘ USA (GA) 284-285 F 4
Georgia = Gruzija ■ GE 126-127 E 7
Georgia, Strait of ≈ CDN 230-231 E 4
Georgia Basin ⩳ 6-7 F 14
Georgiana ○ USA (AL) 284-285 D 5
Georgian Bay ○ CDN (ONT) 238-239 D 3
Georgian Bay Island National Park ⊥ CDN (ONT) 238-239 F 4
Georgian Bay Islands National Park ⊥ CDN (ONT) 238-239 F 4
Georgievka ○ KA 124-125 M 4
Georgievka ○ KA 146-147 B 4
Georgievsk ○ RUS 126-127 E 5
Georgina Downs ○ AUS 178-179 D 1
Georgina River ~ AUS 178-179 E 2
Georgiu-Dež = Liski ○ RUS 102-103 L 2
Georg von Neumayer ○ ARK 16 F 36
Gera ○• D 92-93 M 3
Gerace ○ I 100-101 F 5
Geraché ○ PA 52-53 E 7
Geráki ○ GR 100-101 J 6
Geral, Serra ▲ BR 72-73 K 2
Geral, Serra ▲ BR 74-75 E 5
Gerald ○ CDN (SAS) 232-233 R 5
Gerald, ostrov ⌒ RUS 112-113 X 1
Geral de Goiás, Serra ▲ BR 72-73 G 2
Geraldine ○ NZ 182 C 6
Geraldine ○ USA (MT) 250-251 J 4
Geraldo, Furo do ~ BR 66-67 F 5
Geral do Paraná ou do Veadeiros, Serra ▲ BR 72-73 G 3
Geraldton ○ AUS 176-177 C 4
Geraldton ○ CDN (ONT) 236-237 B 3
Geralton ○ CDN (ONT) 236-237 B 3
Geralton East ○ CDN (ONT) 236-237 B 3
Geralzinho ○ BR 72-73 K 3
Gerampi ○ RI 168 D 7
Geranium ○ AUS 180-181 F 3
Gerāš ○ IR 134-135 F 5
Geraumele ∴ RN 198-199 F 5
Gērbiči, gora ▲ RUS 116-117 M 2
Gerdau ○ ZA 220-221 H 3
Gerdine, Mount ▲ USA 20-21 O 6
Gerede ☆ TR 128-129 E 2
Gerede Çayı ~ TR 128-129 E 2
Gērel'de ○ US 136-137 H 4
Gereśk ○ AFG 134-135 L 3
Gerger ☆ TR 128-129 H 3
Gerihun ○ WAL 202-203 E 6
Gerik ○• MAL 162-163 D 2
Gering ○ USA (NE) 262-263 C 3
Gerisa ○ SP 208-209 F 3
Gerlach ○ USA (NV) 246-247 F 3
Germakolo ○ RI 166-167 G 2
German Busch, Reserva Busch ⊥ BOL 70-71 F 5
German Creek ○ AUS 178-179 K 2
Germania ○ RA 78-79 H 3
Germania Land ⩳ GRØ 26-27 p 5
Germansen Landing ○ CDN 32-33 H 4
Germantown ○ USA (TN) 276-277 F 5
Germany = Deutschland ■ D 92-93 J 4
Germencik ☆ TR 128-129 B 4
Germi ○ IR 128-129 N 3
Germiston ○ ZA 220-221 J 3
Gernika-Lumo ○ E 98-99 F 3
Gero ○ J 152-153 G 7
Gerolimēnas ○ GR 100-101 J 6
Gerona ○ RP 160-161 D 5
Gerona = Girona ○ E 98-99 J 4
Gerrard ○ CDN (BC) 230-231 M 3
Gers ~ F 90-91 H 10
Ġerūf ○ JOR 130-131 D 2
Gerung ○ RI 168 C 7
Gerze ☆ TR 128-129 F 2
Gērzê ○ VRC 144-145 E 4
Gesa ~ RI 166-167 J 3
Gesellschafts-Inseln ⌒ F 13 M 4
Gestro, Wabē ~ ETH 208-209 E 5
Getafe ○ E 98-99 F 4
Geti ○ ZRE 212-213 C 3
Getkan ~ RUS 118-119 L 8
Gětljangěn, laguna ≈ 112-113 Y 4
Getta ○ BHT 142-143 F 2
Gettysburg ○ USA (PA) 280-281 J 4
Gettysburg ○ USA (SD) 260-261 G 1
Gettysburg National Military Park • USA (PA) 280-281 J 4
Gettysburg Seamount ⩳ 188-189 F 2
Getúlio Vargas ○ BR 74-75 D 6
Getz Ice Shelf ⊂ ARK 16 F 24
Gevaş ☆ TR 128-129 K 3
Gevgelija ○ MK 100-101 J 4
Gevrai ○ IND 138-139 E 10
Gewanē ○ ETH 208-209 E 3
Geychay = Göyçay ○ AZ 128-129 M 2
Geyik Dağları ▲ TR 128-129 D 4
Geylegphug ○ BHT 142-143 G 2
Geyser ○ USA (MT) 250-251 J 4
Geyser, Banc du ⌒ RM 222-223 E 4
Geyserville ○ USA (CA) 246-247 C 5
Geyve ☆ TR 128-129 D 2
Gezāb ○ AFG 134-135 M 2
Gezhou Ba • VRC 154-155 G 6
Ghābat al-'Arab ○ SUD 206-207 J 4
Ghadāmis ◘ LAR 190-191 H 5
Ghadāmis ☆•• LAR 190-191 G 5
Ghaddūwah ○ LAR 192-193 F 4
Ghaghara ~ IND 142-143 C 2
Ghaghat ~ BD 142-143 F 3
Ghaghe Island ⌒ SOL 184 I d 2
Ghāghra ○ IND 142-143 D 4
Ghaibi Dero ○ PK 134-135 M 5
Ghallamane ⩳ RIM 196-197 E 3
Ghallamane, Sebkhet ○ RIM 196-197 F 3
Ghana ■ GH 204-205 B 5
Ghangmi ○ RI 166-167 K 4
Ghansali ○ IND 138-139 G 4
Ghanzi ◘ RB 216-217 F 11
Ghanzi ☆ RB 216-217 F 10
Ghanzi Farms ⩳ RB 216-217 F 10
Ghaoua, Goûr ▲ DZ 190-191 D 9
Gharb Binna ○ SUD 200-201 E 3
Gharbi, Chott el ○ DZ 188-189 L 4
Gharbi, Zahrez ○ DZ 190-191 D 3
Ghardaïa ☆• DZ 190-191 D 4
Ghardimaou ○ TN 190-191 G 2
Gharig ○ SUD 206-207 H 3
Ghāro ○ PK 134-135 M 6
Gharyān ◘ LAR 192-193 E 2
Gharyān ☆ LAR 192-193 E 1
Ghāt ○ LAR 190-191 H 8
Ghātāl ○ IND 142-143 E 4
Ghātampur ○ IND 142-143 B 2
Ghātsila ○ IND 142-143 E 4
Ghauspur ○ PK 138-139 B 5
Ghawdex = Gozo ⌒ M 100-101 E 6
Ghazaouet ○ DZ 188-189 L 3
Ghāziābād ○ IND 138-139 F 5
Ghāzīpur ○ IND 142-143 C 3
Ghazluna ○ PK 134-135 M 3
Gheorghe Gheorghiu-Dej = Onești ○ RO 102-103 E 4
Gheorgheni ○ RO 102-103 D 4
Gherdi ○ IND 140-141 F 2
Gherla ○ RO 102-103 C 4
Ghilarza ○ I 100-101 B 4
Ghimpați ○ RO 102-103 D 5
Ghio, Lago ○ RA 80 E 3
Ghizar ○ IND 138-139 D 1
Ghizar ~ IND 138-139 D 1
Gho Đôn ○ VN 156-157 D 5
Ghogha ○ IND 138-139 D 9
Ghomrassen ○ TN 190-191 H 4
Ghorahi ○ NEP 144-145 D 6
Ghosla ○ IND 138-139 E 8
Ghost Lake ○ CDN (ALB) 232-233 D 4
Ghost Lake ○ CDN 30-31 M 4
Ghost River ○ CDN (ONT) 234-235 M 4
Ghost River Wilderness ⊥ CDN (ALB) 232-233 C 4
Ghost Town • USA (ID) 252-253 C 3
Ghot ○ IND 142-143 B 6
Ghotanu ○ IND 138-139 C 6
Ghotki ○• PK 138-139 B 6
Ghoveo ○ SOL 184 I d 3
Ghriss ○ DZ 190-191 C 3
Ghuar ○ IND 138-139 B 8
Ghubaysh ○ SUD 200-201 C 6
Ghugri ~ IND 142-143 E 3
Ghutkel ○ IND 142-143 B 5
Ghuzayyil, Sabkhat ○ LAR 192-193 H 3
Ghwarriepoort ▲ ZA 220-221 F 6
Gialalassi ○ SP 212-213 K 2
Giang ○ VN 158-159 J 4
Giang Trung ○ VN 158-159 K 4
Giannitsá ○ GR 100-101 J 4
Giant Forest ○ USA (CA) 248-249 F 3
Giants Castle ▲ ZA 220-221 J 4
Giants Castle Game Reserve ⊥ ZA 220-221 J 4
Giant's Causeway ••• GB 90-91 D 4
Giants Tomb Island ⌒ CDN (ONT) 238-239 E 4
Giant Yellowknife Mine • CDN 30-31 M 4
Gianyar ○ RI 168 B 7
Giá Rai ○ VN 158-159 H 6
Giarre ○ I 100-101 E 6
Gia Vực ○ VN 158-159 K 3
Giba ○ I 100-101 B 5
Gibara ○ C 54-55 G 4
Gibbon ○ USA (NE) 262-263 H 4
Gibbon ○ USA (OR) 244-245 G 5
Gibbons ○ CDN (ALB) 232-233 E 2
Gibbonsville ○ USA (ID) 250-251 F 6
Gibb River ○ AUS (WA) 172-173 H 4
Gibb River ~ AUS 172-173 H 3
Gibbs ○ CDN (SAS) 232-233 O 5
Gibbs City ○ USA (MI) 270-271 K 4
Gibeon ○ NAM 220-221 C 2
Gibeon Station ○ NAM 220-221 C 2
Gibe Shet' ~ ETH 208-209 C 5
Gibē Wenz ~ ETH 208-209 C 4
Ġibla, Ḏū ○• Y 132-133 D 7
Gibraltar ○ CDN (NS) 240-241 M 6
Gibraltar ○ GBZ 98-99 E 6
Gibraltar, Estrecho de ≈ 188-189 J 3
Gibraltar Range National Park ⊥ AUS 178-179 M 5
Gibsland ○ USA (LA) 268-269 G 4
Gibson ○ USA (LA) 268-269 K 7
Gibson City ○ USA (IL) 274-275 K 4
Gibson Desert ⩳ AUS 172-173 G 7
Gibson Desert Nature Reserve ⊥ AUS 176-177 H 2
Gibson Island ○ USA (MD) 280-281 K 4

330 Garberville — Gibson Island

Gibson Lake ⊙ CDN 30-31 X 4
Gibsons o CDN (BC) 230-231 F 4
Gibsonville o USA (NC) 282-283 H 4
Gida o WAN 204-205 J 5
Gidalo o ETH 208-209 B 4
Gidami o ETH 208-209 B 4
Gidar o PK 134-135 M 4
Gidar Dhor ~ PK 134-135 M 4
Ġidda o • KSA 132-133 A 3
Giddalur o IND 140-141 H 3
Ġiddat al-Harāsis ⊥ OM 132-133 K 4
Giddings o USA (TX) 266-267 L 3
Gideån ~ S 86-87 J 5
Gidgealpa Gas Field • AUS 178-179 F 4
Gidgee o AUS 176-177 E 3
Gidgi, Lake ⊙ AUS 176-177 H 4
Gidolē o ETH 208-209 C 6
Gielnaga del Coro o RA 76-77 E 6
Gien o F 90-91 J 8
Gieseckes Isfjord ≈ 26-27 X 7
Gießen o D 92-93 K 3
Gifford o USA (FL) 286-287 J 4
Gifford o USA (WA) 244-245 G 2
Gifford Creek o AUS 176-177 D 2
Gifford Fiord ≈ 24-25 f 5
Gifford River ~ CDN 24-25 f 5
Ġifġāfa, Bi'r o ET (SIN) 194-195 F 2
Gift Lake o CDN 32-33 N 4
Giftūn al-Kabīr, Ġazīrat ⌒ ET 194-195 F 4
Gifu ☆ J 152-153 G 7
Gigant o RUS 102-103 M 4
Giganta, Cerro ▲ MEX 50-51 D 4
Giganta, Sierra de la ▲ MEX 50-51 D 4
Gigante o CO 60-61 D 6
Gig Harbor o USA (WA) 244-245 C 3
Gigi, Danau o RI 166-167 G 2
Giglio, Ísola del ⌒ I 100-101 C 3
Gigüela, Río ~ E 98-99 F 5
Ġiḥāna o Y 132-133 D 6
Gihofi o BU 212-213 C 5
Giir Forest National Park ⊥ IND 138-139 C 9
Giir Hills ▲ IND 138-139 C 9
Gijón = Xixón o • E 98-99 E 3
Gikongoro o RWA 212-213 B 5
Gila o USA (NM) 256-257 G 6
Gila, Tanjung ▲ RI 164-165 L 3
Gila Bend o USA (AZ) 256-257 C 6
Gila Cliff Dwellings National Monument • USA (NM) 256-257 G 5
Gila Mountains ▲ USA (AZ) 256-257 E 5
Gilān o AFG 134-135 M 2
Gilān o IR 136-137 D 6
Gilān ◘ IR 128-129 N 3
Gilan-e Garb o IR 134-135 A 1
Gila River ~ USA (AZ) 256-257 D 5
Gila River ~ USA (NM) 256-257 G 6
Gila River Indian Reservation ✕ USA (AZ) 256-257 C 5
Gilbert o USA (MN) 270-271 F 3
Gilbert, Islas ⌒ RCH 80 E 7
Gilbert, Mount ▲ CDN (BC) 230-231 E 3
Gilbert Islands ⌒ KIB 13 J 2
Gilbert Lake ⊙ CDN 38-39 Q 2
Gilberton o AUS 174-175 G 6
Gilbert Plains o CDN (MAN) 234-235 C 3
Gilbert River o AUS (QLD) 174-175 G 6
Gilbert River ~ AUS 174-175 F 5
Gilberts Dome ▲ AUS 178-179 J 2
Gilbués o BR 68-69 F 6
Gilby o USA (ND) 258-259 K 3
Gildford o USA (MT) 250-251 J 3
Gilé o MOC 218-219 K 3
Giles, Lake ⊙ AUS 176-177 E 4
Giles Meteorological Station o AUS 176-177 K 2
Ġilf al-Kabīr, Haḍbat al- ▲ ET 192-193 L 6
Gilford Island ⌒ CDN (BC) 230-231 C 3
Gilgandra o AUS 178-179 K 6
Gilgil o EAK 212-213 F 4
Gil Gil Creek ~ AUS 178-179 K 5
Gilgit o IND 138-139 E 2
Gilgit ~ IND 138-139 E 2
Gilgit Mountains ▲ IND 138-139 D 1
Gilgunnia o AUS 180-181 J 2
Gilgunnia Range ▲ AUS 180-181 H 2
Gili, Reserva do ⊥ MOC 218-219 K 3
Gilimanuk o RI 168 B 7
Gil Island ⌒ CDN (BC) 228-229 E 3
Giljuj ~ RUS 118-119 M 8
Gillam o AUS 172-173 D 6
Gillam o CDN 34-35 J 2
Gillams o CDN (NFL) 242-243 K 3
Gilleleje o DK 86-87 F 8
Gillen, Lake ⊙ AUS 176-177 H 3
Gilles, Lake ⊙ AUS 180-181 D 2
Gillespie o USA (IL) 274-275 J 5
Gillet o USA (AR) 276-277 D 6
Gillett o USA (WI) 270-271 K 6
Gillett o USA (TX) 266-267 K 4
Gillette o USA (WY) 252-253 N 2
Gillham o USA (AR) 276-277 A 6
Gillian Lake ⊙ CDN 24-25 j 6
Gilliat o AUS 174-175 F 7
Gilliat River ~ AUS 174-175 F 7
Gillies Bay o CDN (BC) 230-231 E 4
Gillies Island ⌒ CDN 36-37 L 6
Gillingham o GB 90-91 H 6
Gillon Point ▲ USA 22-23 C 6
Gills Rock o USA (WI) 270-271 L 5
Gilman o USA (IL) 274-275 L 4
Gilman o USA (WI) 270-271 H 5
Gilmanton o USA (WI) 270-271 G 6
Gilmer o USA (TX) 264-265 K 6
Gil'mitka ~ RUS 112-113 O 5
Gilmore, Lake ⊙ AUS 176-177 F 6
Gilmour o CDN (ONT) 238-239 H 4
Gilmour Island ⌒ CDN 36-37 J 5
Gilo Wenz ~ ETH 208-209 A 5
Gilpo o LB 202-203 G 6
Gilroy o CDN (SAS) 232-233 M 5
Gilroy o USA (CA) 248-249 C 2
Gilruth, Mount ▲ AUS 174-175 B 3
Giltner o USA (NE) 262-263 H 4
Giluwe, Mount ▲ PNG 183 B 4
Gima o EC 64-65 C 3
Ġimāl, Umm al ∴• JOR 130-131 E 1
Gimbi o ETH 208-209 B 4
Gimi o WAN 204-205 H 4
Gimli o CDN (MAN) 234-235 G 4
Gimo o S 86-87 J 6
Gimpu o RI 164-165 G 4
Ġina, Wādī al- ~ KSA 130-131 F 2
Ġināh o ET 194-195 E 5
Ginchi o ETH 208-209 D 4
Ginda o ER 200-201 J 5
Gineta, La o E 98-99 G 5
Ginevrabotnen ≈ 84-85 L 3
Gingin o AUS 176-177 C 5
Gin Gin o AUS 178-179 L 3
Gingindlovu o ZA 220-221 K 4
Gingko Petrified Forest State Park • USA (WA) 244-245 E 4
Gingoog o RP 160-161 F 8
Gingoog Bay ≈ 160-161 F 8
Ginir o ETH 208-209 E 5
Giòia del Colle o I 100-101 F 4
Giòia Táuro o I 100-101 E 5
Giralia o AUS 172-173 B 7
Giralia Range ▲ AUS 176-177 C 1
Girān Rig, Kūh-e ▲ IR 134-135 H 4
Girard o USA (KS) 262-263 M 7
Girard o USA (TX) 264-265 D 5
Girardot o CO 60-61 D 5
Girardville o CDN (QUE) 240-241 C 2
Gira River ~ PNG 183 D 5
Girau o IRQ 128-129 K 5
Giraul ~ ANG 216-217 B 7
Gir Deh o IR 128-129 N 4
Girdwood o USA 20-21 Q 6
Giresun ☆ TR 128-129 H 2
Giresun Dağları ▲ TR 128-129 H 2
Ġirġā o ET 194-195 E 4
Giri ~ ZRE 210-211 G 2
Giridih o IND 142-143 E 3
Girilambone o AUS 178-179 J 6
Giro o WAN 204-205 F 3
Giron o EC 64-65 C 3
Girona o • E 98-99 J 4
Gironde ~ F 90-91 G 9
Giroux o CDN (MAN) 234-235 G 5
Girū o AFG 138-139 B 3
Giru o AUS 174-175 J 6
Girvan o GB 90-91 E 4
Girvin o CDN (SAS) 232-233 N 4
Girvin o USA (TX) 266-267 E 2
Girza o ET 194-195 E 3
Ġīšā, al- o KSA 130-131 L 5
Gisasa River ~ USA 20-21 L 4
Gisborne o AUS 180-181 H 4
Gisborne o NZ 182 G 3
Gisborne Lake ⊙ CDN (NFL) 242-243 O 5
Giscome o CDN (BC) 228-229 M 2
Gisenyi o • RWA 212-213 B 4
Gisi o RI 164-165 K 2
Gislaved ☆ S 86-87 F 8
Gisors o F 90-91 H 7
Ġisr aš-Šuġūr o SYR 128-129 G 5
Gissar o TJ 136-137 L 5
Gissarskij hrebet ▲ US 136-137 K 5
Gisuru o BU 212-213 C 5
Gita, Danau o RI 166-167 G 2
Gitagum o RP 160-161 F 8
Gitarama o RWA 212-213 B 5
Gitata o WAN 204-205 G 4
Gitega o BU 212-213 B 5
Githi • TN 190-191 H 4
Githio o GR 100-101 J 6
Gitnadoix River Provincial Recreation Area ⊥ CDN (BC) 228-229 E 2
Giulianova o I 100-101 D 3
Giurgiu ☆ • RO 102-103 D 6
Giv o IR 134-135 H 2
Givet o F 90-91 K 6
Giwa o WAN 204-205 G 3
Ġiyān o IR 134-135 E 3
Giyani ☆ ZA 218-219 F 6
Ġiyati o UAE 132-133 H 2
Ġiylana, al- o KSA 130-131 K 5
Giyon o ETH 208-209 C 4
Ġiz', Wādī al- ~ Y 132-133 G 5
Ġiza, al- ☆ •• ET 194-195 E 2
Giza = Ġiza, al- ☆ •• ET 194-195 E 2
Ġiza, Pyramids of ∴•• ET 194-195 E 3
Ġizān ◘ KSA 132-133 C 5
Ġizān ☆ KSA 132-133 C 5
Gižduvon ☆ US 136-137 J 4
Gize, Pyramids of ∴•• ET 194-195 E 3
Gižiga o RUS (MAG) 120-121 T 3
Gižiga ~ RUS 112-113 L 5
Gižiginskaja guba ≈ 120-121 R 3
Gižiginskaja ravina ~ RUS 112-113 L 5
Ġizl, Wādī al- ~ KSA 130-131 E 4
Gizo ☆ SOL (Wes) 184 I c 3
Gizo ⌒ SOL (Wes) 184 I c 3
Giżycko o • PL 92-93 Q 1
Ġizzin ☆ RL 128-129 F 6
Gjandža = Ganža o • AZ 128-129 M 2
Gjiri i Drinit ≈ 100-101 G 4
Gjirokastër ☆ •• AL 100-101 H 4
Gjoa Haven o CDN 24-25 Y 6
Gjøgur ▲ IS 86-87 c 1
Gjoklenkui, Solončak ⊙ TM 136-137 E 4
Gjøvik ☆ N 86-87 E 6
Gjuhëzës, Kepi i ▲ AL 100-101 G 4
Gjumri o AR 128-129 K 2
Glace, La o CDN 32-33 L 4
Glace Bay o CDN (NS) 240-241 Q 4
Glaciares, Parque Nacional los ⊥ ••• RA 80 D 4
Glaciar Perito Moreno •• RA 80 D 5
Glaciar Upsala • RCH 80 D 4
Glacier o CDN (BC) 230-231 M 2
Glacier o USA (WA) 244-245 D 2
Glacier Bay ≈ 32-33 B 2
Glacier Bay National Park and Preserve ⊥ USA 32-33 B 2
Glacier Island ⌒ USA 20-21 R 6
Glacier Mount ▲ USA 20-21 U 4
Glacier National Park ⊥ CDN (BC) 230-231 M 2
Glacier National Park ⊥ USA (MT) 250-251 F 3
Glacier Peak ▲ USA (WA) 244-245 D 2
Glacier Peak Wilderness Area ⊥ USA (WA) 244-245 D 2
Glacier Strait ≈ 24-25 g 2
Gladewater o USA (TX) 264-265 K 6
Gladstad o N 86-87 E 4
Gladstone o AUS (QLD) 178-179 L 2
Gladstone o AUS (SA) 180-181 E 2
Gladstone o AUS (TAS) 180-181 J 6
Gladstone o CDN (MAN) 234-235 E 4
Gladstone o USA (MI) 270-271 L 5
Gladstone o USA (MO) 274-275 D 5
Gladstone o USA (OR) 244-245 C 5
Glad Valley o USA (SD) 260-261 E 1
Gladwin o USA (MI) 272-273 E 4
Gladys Lake ⊙ CDN 20-21 Y 7
Glåma ▲ IS 86-87 b 2
Glåma ~ N 86-87 E 6
Glamis o USA (CA) 248-249 J 6
Glamoč o BIH 100-101 F 2
Glan o RP 160-161 F 10
Glarner Alpen ▲ CH 92-93 K 5
Glasco o USA (KS) 262-263 J 5
Glasgow ☆ • GB 90-91 E 4
Glasgow o USA (KY) 276-277 K 3
Glasgow o USA (MO) 274-275 F 5
Glasgow o USA (MT) 250-251 N 3
Glaslyn o CDN (SAS) 232-233 K 2
Glasnevin o CDN (SAS) 232-233 N 6
Glassboro o USA (NJ) 280-281 L 4
Glass Mountains ▲ USA (TX) 266-267 D 3
Glass Window • BS 54-55 G 2
Glavering Ø ⌒ GRØ 26-27 p 6
Glavinica o BG 102-103 E 6
Glavnaja, grjada ▲ RUS 108-109 Z 5
Glavnij Survanskij kanal < AZ 128-129 M 2
Glazaniha o RUS 88-89 P 5
Glazier o USA (TX) 264-265 D 2
Glazoué o DY 204-205 E 5
Glazov ☆ RUS 96-97 H 4
Glazova, guba ⊙ RUS 108-109 G 4
Gleeson o USA (AZ) 256-257 F 7
Gleibat Boukenni o RIM 202-203 F 2
Gleichen o CDN (ALB) 232-233 E 5
Gleisdorf o A 92-93 N 5
Glélé o CI 202-203 G 7
Glen o AUS 176-177 D 3
Glen o USA (NH) 278-279 K 4
Glen o ZA 220-221 H 4
Glen Alda o CDN (ONT) 238-239 H 4
Glénan, Îles de ⌒ F 90-91 F 8
Glenannan o CDN (BC) 228-229 K 2
Glenavon o CDN (SAS) 232-233 P 5
Glenayle o AUS 176-177 G 2
Glenboro o CDN (MAN) 234-235 D 5
Glenboyle o CDN 20-21 V 5
Glenbrook o USA (NV) 246-247 F 4
Glenburgh o AUS 176-177 D 2
Glenburn o USA (ND) 258-259 F 3
Glencairn o CDN (MAN) 234-235 D 4
Glen Canyon ∪ USA (UT) 254-255 E 6
Glen Canyon National Recreation Area ∴ USA (UT) 254-255 E 6
Glen Canyon Reservoir < USA (UT) 254-255 E 6
Glencoe o CDN (NB) 240-241 J 3
Glencoe o CDN (ONT) 238-239 D 6
Glencoe o USA (AL) 284-285 E 3
Glencoe o USA (MN) 270-271 D 6
Glencoe o USA (NM) 256-257 K 5
Glencoe o ZA 220-221 K 4
Glen Cove o USA (NY) 280-281 N 3
Glendale o USA (AZ) 256-257 C 5
Glendale o USA (CA) 248-249 F 5
Glendale o USA (IL) 276-277 G 3
Glendale o USA (TN) 282-283 C 5
Glendale o USA (TX) 268-269 E 5
Glendale o ZW 218-219 F 3
Glendale Cove o CDN (BC) 230-231 D 3
Glendale Lake ⊙ USA (PA) 280-281 H 3
Glendambo o AUS 178-179 C 6
Glen Daniel o USA (WV) 280-281 E 6
Glenden o AUS 178-179 K 1
Glendive o USA (MT) 250-251 P 4
Glendo o USA (WY) 252-253 N 4
Glendora o USA (CA) 248-249 G 5
Glendo Reservoir < USA (WY) 252-253 O 4
Glenelg River ~ AUS 180-181 F 4
Glenella o CDN (MAN) 234-235 D 4
Glenfield o USA (ND) 258-259 J 4
Glengyle o AUS 178-179 E 3
Glen Helen o AUS 176-177 M 1
Glenholme o CDN (NS) 240-241 M 5
Glen Hope o USA (PA) 280-281 H 3
Glenifter Lake ⊙ CDN (ALB) 232-233 D 3
Glen Innes o AUS 178-179 L 5
Glen Kerr o CDN (SAS) 232-233 L 5
Glenlivet < ZW 218-219 F 5
Glenlyon Dam < AUS 178-179 L 5
Glenmire o AUS 178-179 H 3
Glen Mor ⊥ GB 90-91 E 3
Glenmora o USA (LA) 268-269 H 6
Glen More ∪ GB 90-91 E 3
Glenmorgan o AUS 178-179 K 4
Glennallen o USA 20-21 S 5
Glenn Highway II USA 20-21 R 6
Glennie o USA (MI) 272-273 F 3
Glenns o USA (VA) 280-281 K 6
Glenns Ferry o USA (ID) 252-253 C 4
Glennville o USA (CA) 248-249 F 4
Glennville o USA (GA) 284-285 J 5
Glenora o AUS 174-175 G 6
Glenora o CDN (MAN) 234-235 D 5
Glen Orchard o CDN (ONT) 238-239 F 3
Glenorchy o AUS 180-181 J 7
Glenorchy o NZ 182 B 6
Glenore o AUS 174-175 F 5
Glenormiston o AUS 178-179 E 2
Glen Raven o USA (NC) 282-283 H 4
Glenrio o USA (NM) 256-257 M 3
Glenrock o USA (WY) 252-253 N 4
Glen Rose o USA (TX) 264-265 G 6
Glensboro o USA (KY) 276-277 K 2
Glens Falls o USA (NY) 278-279 H 5
Glenside o CDN (SAS) 232-233 M 4
Glenties o IRL 90-91 C 4
Glentworth o CDN (SAS) 232-233 M 6
Glenville o USA (MN) 270-271 E 7
Glenville o USA (WV) 280-281 F 5
Glenwood o CDN (ALB) 232-233 E 6
Glenwood o CDN (NFL) 242-243 O 4
Glenwood o USA (AR) 276-277 B 6
Glenwood o USA (HI) 288 K 5
Glenwood o USA (IA) 274-275 C 3
Glenwood o USA (MN) 270-271 C 5
Glenwood o USA (NM) 256-257 G 5
Glenwood o USA (OR) 244-245 C 5
Glenwood City o USA (WI) 270-271 F 5
Glenwood Springs o • USA (CO) 254-255 H 4
Glidden o CDN (SAS) 232-233 J 4
Glidden o USA (WI) 270-271 H 4
Glide o USA (OR) 244-245 B 7
Glina o HR 100-101 F 2
Glittertinden ▲ N 86-87 D 6
Gliwice o • PL 92-93 P 3
Gljaden' o RUS 116-117 E 8
Gljadjanskoe ☆ RUS 114-115 H 7
Globe o • USA (AZ) 256-257 E 5
Głogów o • PL 92-93 O 3
Gloie o LB 202-203 F 6
Glomfjord o N 86-87 F 3
Glommersträsk o S 86-87 J 4
Gloria o MEX 50-51 J 4
Gloria, Bahía de la ≈ 54-55 G 4
Glória, Cachoeira da ~ BR 66-67 G 7
Gloria, La o CO 60-61 E 3
Gloria, La o MEX 50-51 K 4
Gloria, Sierra de la ▲ RCH 76-77 B 4
Glorias, Las o MEX 50-51 E 5
Glorieta o USA (NM) 256-257 K 3
Glorieuses, Îles ⌒ F 222-223 E 3
Gloster o USA (MS) 268-269 J 5
Gloucester o AUS 180-181 L 2
Gloucester o GB 90-91 F 6
Gloucester o PNG 183 E 3
Gloucester o USA (MA) 278-279 L 6
Gloucester o USA (VA) 280-281 K 6
Gloucester Island ⌒ AUS 174-175 K 7
Gloucester Point o USA (VA) 280-281 K 6
Glouster o USA (OH) 280-281 D 4
Glover Island ⌒ CDN (NFL) 242-243 L 4
Glovers Reef ⌒ BH 52-53 L 3
Gloversville o USA (NY) 278-279 G 5
Glovertown o CDN (NFL) 242-243 O 4
Glubczyce o • PL 92-93 O 3
Glubokaja, buhta o RUS 112-113 R 6
Glubokaja, laguna ⊙ RUS 112-113 U 5
Glubokij o RUS 102-103 M 3
Glubokij Poluj ~ RUS 114-115 K 2
Glubokij Sabun ~ RUS 114-115 Q 3
Glubokoe, ozero ⊙ RUS 108-109 Y 7
Gluharinyj o RUS 110-111 d 7
Glumpangdua o RI 162-163 B 2
Glymur ~ IS 86-87 c 2
Glyndon o USA (MN) 270-271 B 4
Gmünd o • A 92-93 N 4
Gmunden o A 92-93 M 5
Gnadenthal o CDN (MAN) 234-235 F 5
Gnaraloo o AUS 176-177 B 1
Gnarp o S 86-87 H 5
Gnibi o SN 202-203 C 2
Gniezno o •• PL 92-93 O 2
Gnit o SN 196-197 C 6
Gnjilane o YU 100-101 H 3
Gnowangerup o AUS 176-177 D 6
Gnows Nest Range ▲ AUS 176-177 D 4
Goa ◘ IND 140-141 E 3
Goageb o NAM 220-221 C 3
Goal Mountain ▲ USA (MT) 250-251 F 4
Goālpāra o IND 142-143 G 2
Goaltor o IND 142-143 E 4
Goa Mampu Caves • RI 164-165 G 6
Goan o RMM 202-203 H 3
Goari o PNG 183 C 4
Goaso o GH 202-203 J 6
Goat River ~ CDN (BC) 228-229 O 3
Goat River ~ CDN (BC) 230-231 N 4
Goat Rocks Wilderness ⊥ USA (WA) 244-245 D 4
Goba ☆ ETH 208-209 D 5
Goba o MOC 220-221 L 3
Gobabed o NAM 220-221 B 1
Gobabis ☆ NAM 216-217 E 11
Goba Fronteira o MOC 220-221 L 3
Gobālpur o IND 142-143 E 3
Gobari ~ ZRE 210-211 G 6
Gobe o PNG 183 E 5
Gobēlē Wenz ~ ETH 208-209 E 4
Gobernador Crespo o RA 76-77 G 6
Gobernador Gregores o RA 80 E 4
Gobernador Ingeniero Valentín Virasoro o RA 76-77 J 5
Gobernador Moyano o RA 80 F 3
Gobernador Piedrabuena o RA 76-77 E 4
Gobernador Solá o RA 78-79 K 2
Gobi = Gov' ⊥ MAU 148-149 F 6
Gobles o USA (MI) 272-273 D 5
Gobnangou, Falaises du ▲•• BF 202-203 L 4
Gobō o J 152-153 F 8
Gobo, Col de ▲ RN 198-199 G 2
Goboumo ~ RCA 210-211 F 2
Gobur o SUD 206-207 K 6
Gobustan o AZ 128-129 N 2
Gobustan ⊥ AZ 128-129 N 2
Goce Delčev o BG 102-103 C 7
Gochas o NAM 220-221 D 2
Gōchi o J 152-153 E 7
Gò Công Đông o VN 158-159 J 5
Godafoss ~ 86-87 e 2
Godahl o USA (MN) 270-271 D 6
Godatair o SUD 206-207 H 4
Godāvari ~ IND 138-139 E 10
Godāvari ~ IND 142-143 B 7
Godāwari o NEP 144-145 C 6
Godbout o CDN (QUE) 242-243 A 3
Godbout, Rivière ~ CDN (QUE) 242-243 A 3
Godda o IND 142-143 E 3
Godē o ETH 208-209 F 6
Godé o RMM 202-203 J 3
Gode, Hosséré ▲ CAM 204-205 K 4
Godegode o EAT 214-215 J 4
Goderich o CDN (ONT) 238-239 D 5
Godfreys Tank < AUS 172-173 H 6
Godfried Hansen Ø ⌒ GRØ 26-27 p 5
Godhavn = Qeqertarsuaq o GRØ 28-29 O 2
Godhra o IND 138-139 D 8
Godhyogol o SP 208-209 F 4
Godi, Mayo ~ CAM 206-207 B 4
Göding = Hodonín o CZ 92-93 O 4
Godinlabe o SP 208-209 H 6
Godofredo Viana o BR 68-69 F 2
Godong o RI 168 D 3
Godong Kangri ▲ VRC 144-145 D 5
Godoy Cruz o RA 78-79 E 2
Gods Lake ⊙ CDN 34-35 J 3
Gods Lake Indian Reserve ✕ CDN 34-35 J 3
Gods Lake Narrows o CDN 34-35 J 3
Gods Mercy, Bay of ≈ 36-37 F 3
Gods River ~ CDN 34-35 K 2
Godthåb = Nuuk ☆ GRØ 28-29 P 4
Godwin Austen, Mount = K2 ▲ PK 138-139 F 2
Goe o PNG 183 A 5
Goeie Hoop, Kaap die = Cape of Good Hope ▲ • ZA 220-221 D 7
Goejegebergte, De ▲ SME 62-63 G 4
Goéland, Lac ⊙ CDN (QUE) 236-237 M 3
Goëlettes ⌒ SY 224 B 5
Goeree ⊥ NL 92-93 G 3
Goes o NL 92-93 G 3
Goeygina ~ RUS 122-123 R 3
Gofar Fracture Zone ≃ 14-15 S 8
Goffs o USA (CA) 248-249 J 5
Gofmana, ostrov ⌒ RUS 84-85 g 2
Goft'ima Sebeka o ETH 208-209 C 3
Gog o ETH 208-209 B 5
Gogama o CDN (ONT) 236-237 G 5
Gogango o AUS 178-179 L 2
Ġogardan, Kōtal-e ▲ AFG 134-135 M 1
Gō-gawa ~ J 152-153 E 7
Gogebic, Lake ⊙ USA (MI) 270-271 J 4
Gogland, ostrov ⌒ RUS 94-95 K 1
Gogo o AUS 172-173 G 5
Gogo o WAN 204-205 H 4
Gogogogo o RM 222-223 D 10
Gogói o MOC 218-219 G 5
Gogorrón, Parque Natural ⊥ MEX 50-51 J 7
Gogounou o DY 204-205 E 3
Gogrial o SUD 206-207 J 4
Goguí o RMM 196-197 F 7
Goh o IND 142-143 D 3
Goha Ts'iyon o ETH 208-209 D 3
Goiana o BR 68-69 L 5
Goiandira o BR 72-73 F 5
Goianésia o BR 72-73 F 3
Goianésia do Pará o BR 68-69 D 3
Goiânia ☆ BR 72-73 F 4
Goianinha o BR 68-69 L 5
Goianorte o BR 68-69 D 6
Goiás o • BR 72-73 E 3
Goiás ◘ BR 72-73 D 4
Goiatins o BR 68-69 E 5
Goiatuba o BR 72-73 F 5
Goio, Rio ~ BR 72-73 D 7
Goio-Erê o BR 74-75 D 5
Goi-Pula o ZRE 214-215 D 4
Gojeb Wenz ~ ETH 208-209 C 5
Gojo o ETH 208-209 D 4
Gojra o PK 138-139 D 4
Gojyō o J 152-153 F 7
Gökçeada ⌒ TR 128-129 A 2
Gökırmak ~ TR 128-129 F 2
Gökova o TR 128-129 C 4
Gökova Körfezi ≈ 128-129 B 4
Gokprosh Range ▲ PK 134-135 K 5
Göksu Çayı ~ TR 128-129 G 3
Göksun ☆ TR 128-129 G 3
Göksu Nehri ~ TR 128-129 E 4
Gokteik Viaduct • MYA 142-143 K 4
Gokwe o ZW 218-219 E 4
Gol ☆ N 86-87 D 6
Golaghāt o IND 142-143 H 2
Gola Hills ▲ WAL 202-203 E 6
Golaja, gora ▲ RUS 112-113 K 4
Golan ▲ SYR 128-129 F 6
Golana Gof ~ EAK 212-213 G 3
Golbāf o IR 134-135 G 4
Gölbaşı o TR 128-129 E 3
Gölbaşı ☆ TR 128-129 G 4
Golconda o USA (IL) 276-277 G 3
Golconda o USA (NV) 246-247 H 3
Golconda Summit ▲ USA (NV) 246-247 H 3
Gol'covaja ~ RUS 108-109 f 3
Gölcük o TR 128-129 H 4
Gölcük ☆ TR 128-129 C 2
Goldap o PL 92-93 R 1
Gold Bar o CDN 32-33 J 3
Gold Beach o USA (OR) 244-245 A 8
Gold Bridge o CDN (BC) 230-231 G 3
Gold Coast o AUS 178-179 N 4
Gold Coast ∪ GH 202-203 K 7
Golddust o USA (TN) 276-277 F 5
Golden o CDN (BC) 230-231 N 2
Golden o USA (CO) 254-255 K 4
Golden Bay ≈ 182 D 4
Golden City o USA (MO) 276-277 A 3
Goldendale o USA (WA) 244-245 E 5
Golden Ears Provincial Park ⊥ CDN (BC) 230-231 G 4
Golden Gate o USA (FL) 286-287 H 5
Golden Gate Bridge •• USA (CA) 248-249 B 2
Golden Grove o JA 54-55 G 6
Golden Hinde ▲ CDN (BC) 230-231 D 4
Golden Lake ⊙ CDN (ONT) 238-239 H 3
Golden Meadow o USA (LA) 268-269 K 7
Golden Prairie o CDN (SAS) 232-233 J 5
Golden Spike National Historic Site ∴ USA (UT) 254-255 C 2
Golden Valley o USA (ND) 258-259 E 4
Golden Valley o ZW 218-219 E 4
Goldereck o USA 250-251 F 5
Goldfield o USA (NV) 248-249 G 2
Gold Hill o USA (UT) 254-255 B 3
Goldoikta ~ RUS 116-117 F 4
Gold Pines o CDN (ONT) 234-235 K 4
Gold River o CDN (BC) 230-231 C 4
Gold Rock o CDN (ONT) 234-235 L 5
Goldsand Lake ⊙ CDN 34-35 F 2
Goldsboro o USA (MD) 280-281 L 4
Goldsboro o USA (NC) 282-283 K 5
Goldsmith Channel ≈ 24-25 T 4
Goldstream River ~ CDN (BC) 230-231 L 2
Goldsworthy o AUS 172-173 D 6
Goldsworthy, Mount ▲ AUS 172-173 D 6
Goldthwaite o USA (TX) 266-267 J 2
Goldwater o USA (LA) 268-269 H 5
Goldyrevskij o RUS 96-97 K 5
Göle o IRQ 128-129 L 5
Göle ☆ TR 128-129 K 2
Goleniów o PL 92-93 N 2
Goleniščeva, mys ▲ RUS 120-121 V 4
Golestān o AFG 134-135 K 2
Ġolfa o • IR 128-129 L 3
Golfete, El o GCA 52-53 K 4
Golfito o • CR 52-53 C 7
Golfo Aranci o I 100-101 B 4
Golfo de Santa Clara, El o MEX 50-51 B 2
Golfo Nuevo ≈ 78-79 G 7
Gölgeli Dağları ▲ TR 128-129 C 4
Gol Gol o AUS 180-181 G 2
Gölhisar ☆ TR 128-129 C 4
Goli o EAU 212-213 C 2
Goliad o USA (TX) 266-267 K 5
Golija ▲ • YU 100-101 H 3
Goliševa o LV 94-95 K 3
Gölköy ☆ TR 128-129 G 2
Golmānḫāne, Bandar-e o IR 128-129 L 4
Gölmarmara ☆ TR 128-129 B 3
Golmud o VRC 144-145 K 2
Golodnaja Guba, ozero ⊙ RUS 88-89 W 3
Golog Shan ▲ VRC 154-155 B 5
Golo Island ⌒ RP 160-161 D 6
Golokuati o GH 202-203 L 6
Golol o SP 212-213 J 2
Gololcha o ETH 208-209 E 4
Golomoti o MW 218-219 H 2
Golongosso o RCA 206-207 D 4
Goloustnaja ~ RUS 116-117 M 9
Golovin o USA 20-21 J 4
Golovin Bay ≈ 20-21 J 4
Golovin Mission o USA 20-21 J 4
Golovino o RUS 122-123 E 4
Golovnino o RUS 122-123 L 7
Golpāyegān o • IR 134-135 D 2
Gol Tappe o IR (AZG) 128-129 L 4
Gol Tappe o IR (HAM) 128-129 N 5
Gol'tjavino o RUS 116-117 J 6
Goltry o USA (OK) 264-265 F 2
Golū, Rūdḫāne-ye ~ IR 136-137 B 7
Golungo o ANG 216-217 C 4
Golva o USA (ND) 258-259 D 5
Golweyn o SP 212-213 K 3
Golyšmanovo ☆ RUS 114-115 K 6
Goma o ZRE 212-213 B 4
Goma-Gofa ◘ ETH 208-209 C 6
Gomati ~ IND 142-143 C 3
Gomati ~ IND 144-145 C 6
Gombari o ZRE 212-213 B 2
Gombe o WAN 204-205 J 3
Gombe-Matadi o ZRE 210-211 E 6
Gombi o WAN 204-205 K 3
Gombi Fulani o WAN 204-205 K 3
Gombo ~ RG 202-203 E 4
Gomboro o BF 202-203 J 3
Gomboussougou o BF 202-203 K 4
Gomel' = Homel' ☆ BY 94-95 M 5
Gomera, La ⌒ E 188-189 C 6
Gomes Carneiro, Área Indígena ✕ BR 70-71 K 5
Gómez, Laguna de ⊙ RA 78-79 J 3
Gómez Farías o MEX (CHA) 50-51 F 3
Gómez Farías o MEX (TAM) 50-51 K 6
Gómez Palacio o MEX 50-51 H 5
Gómez Rendón o EC 64-65 B 3
Ġomišān o IR 136-137 D 6
Gomon o • CI 202-203 H 7
Gomontang Caves • MAL 160-161 C 10
Gomorovići o RUS 94-95 O 1
Gomumu, Pulau ⌒ RI 164-165 K 4
Gona o CI 202-203 G 5
Gonābād o • IR 134-135 H 1
Gonaïves ☆ RH 54-55 J 5
Gonam ~ RUS 118-119 M 8
Gonam ~ RUS 120-121 D 5
Gonamskij, Sutamo-hrebet ▲ RUS 118-119 N 7
Gonarezhou National Park ⊥ ZW 218-219 F 5
Gonaté o CI 202-203 G 6
Gonâve, Canal de la ≈ 54-55 J 5
Gonâve, Golfe de la ≈ 54-55 J 5
Gonâve, Ile de la ⌒ RH 54-55 J 5
Gonbad-e Kabūd o IR 136-137 F 6
Gonbad-e Qābūs o • IR 136-137 D 6
Gonçalo, Canal de < BR 74-75 D 9
Gonçalves Dias o BR 68-69 F 4
Gonda o IND 142-143 B 2
Gondal o IND 138-139 C 9
Gondē o ETH 208-209 D 4
Gonder ◘ ETH 200-201 H 6
Gonder ☆ • ETH 200-201 H 6
Gondey o TCH 206-207 D 4
Gondia o IND 142-143 B 5
Gondola o MOC 218-219 G 4
Gondolahun o LB 202-203 E 6
Gondomar o • P 98-99 C 4
Gönen ☆ TR 128-129 B 2
Gonga o CAM 204-205 K 6
Gong'an o VRC 154-155 H 6
Gongbo'gyamda o VRC 144-145 J 6
Gongchen o VRC 156-157 G 4
Gongda ~ RUS 108-109 b 7
Gonggar o VRC 144-145 H 6
Gongga Shan ▲ VRC 156-157 B 2
Gongguan o VRC 156-157 F 6
Gonghe o VRC 154-155 B 3
Gongliu o VRC 146-147 F 4
Gongo o TCH 206-207 D 4
Gongola ◘ WAN 204-205 J 4
Gongola, River ~ WAN 204-205 K 4
Gongolgon o AUS 178-179 J 6
Gongoué o G 210-211 B 4
Gongpoquan o VRC 148-149 C 7
Gongshan o VRC 142-143 L 2
Gong Xian o VRC (HEN) 154-155 H 4
Gong Xian o VRC (SIC) 156-157 D 2
Gongzhuling o VRC 150-151 E 6
Gonikoppla o IND 140-141 F 4
Gono, togga ~ SP 208-209 K 4
Gonoa • TCH 198-199 H 2
Gonohe o J 152-153 J 4
Gonoruwa o CL 140-141 J 7
Gōnoura o J 152-153 C 8
Gonža o RUS 118-119 M 9
Gonzales o USA (CA) 248-249 C 3
Gonzales o USA (FL) 286-287 B 1
Gonzales o USA (LA) 268-269 K 6
Gonzales o USA (TX) 266-267 K 4
González, Río ~ PY 76-77 H 2
Gonzáles Moreno o RA 78-79 H 3
Gonzales Suares o PE 64-65 E 3
González o MEX 50-51 K 6
Gonzanamá o EC 64-65 C 4
Goobang Creek ~ AUS 180-181 J 2
Goobies o CDN (NFL) 242-243 P 5
Gooch Range ▲ AUS 176-177 C 1
Goode, Mount ▲ AUS 176-177 F 3
Goodenough, Cape ▲ ARK 16 G 13
Goodenough Bay ≈ 183 E 5
Goodenough Island ⌒ PNG 183 F 5
Goodenough Land ⊥ GRØ 26-27 l 7
Gooderham o CDN (ONT) 238-239 G 4
Goodeve o CDN (SAS) 232-233 P 4
Good Hope, Cape of ▲ • ZA 220-221 D 7
Good Hope Mountain ▲ CDN (BC) 230-231 E 2
Good Hope Plantation •• JA 54-55 G 5
Goodhouse o ZA 220-221 D 4
Gooding o USA (ID) 252-253 D 4
Goodland o USA (KS) 262-263 E 5
Goodland o USA (MN) 270-271 E 3
Goodland o USA (TX) 264-265 B 5
Goodlands o CDN (MAN) 234-235 C 5
Goodlands o MS 224 C 7
Goodlett o USA (TX) 264-265 E 4
Goodlettsville o USA (TN) 276-277 J 4
Goodman o USA (MS) 268-269 L 4
Goodnews Mining Camp o USA 22-23 Q 3
Goodnight o USA (TX) 264-265 C 3
Goodnoe Hills o USA (WA) 244-245 E 5
Goodooga o AUS 178-179 J 5
Goodparla o AUS 172-173 L 2
Goodpaster River ~ USA 20-21 S 4
Goodrich o USA (CO) 254-255 L 3
Goodrich Bank ≃ 166-167 F 7
Goodridge o USA (MN) 270-271 C 2
Goodsir, Mount ▲ CDN (BC) 230-231 N 2
Goodsoil o CDN 32-33 Q 4
Good Spirit Lake ⊙ CDN (SAS) 232-233 Q 4
Good Spirit Lake Provincial Park ⊥ CDN (SAS) 232-233 Q 4
Goodsprings o USA (NV) 248-249 J 4
Goodview o USA (MN) 270-271 G 6
Goodwater o USA (AL) 284-285 D 3
Goodwell o USA (OK) 264-265 C 2
Goodwin o CDN 32-33 L 4
Goodyear o USA (AZ) 256-257 C 5
Goold Island ⌒ AUS 174-175 J 6
Goole o GB 90-91 G 5
Goolgowi o AUS 180-181 H 2
Goolwa o AUS 180-181 E 3
Goomader River ~ AUS 174-175 B 3
Goomalling o AUS 176-177 D 5
Goomeri o AUS 178-179 M 4
Goomny, gora ▲ RUS 116-117 H 5
Goondiwindi o AUS 178-179 L 5
Goongarrie, National Park ⊥ AUS 176-177 F 4
Goonyella Mine o AUS 178-179 K 1
Goorly, Lake ⊙ AUS 176-177 D 5
Goornong o AUS 180-181 H 4
Goose Bay o CDN (BC) 230-231 B 2
Goose Bay o CDN (NFL) 38-39 O 2
Goose Bay ⊙ CDN (NFL) 38-39 O 2
Gooseberry River ~ USA (WY) 252-253 K 2
Goose Cove o CDN (NFL) 242-243 N 1
Goose Creek ~ CDN 34-35 N 3
Goose Creek o USA (SC) 284-285 K 4
Goose Creek ~ USA (ID) 252-253 E 4
Goose Island ⌒ CDN (NS) 240-241 O 5
Goose Lake ⊙ CDN (SAS) 232-233 L 4
Goose Lake o USA (IA) 274-275 H 3
Goose Lake ⊙ USA (CA) 246-247 E 2
Goose River ~ CDN 32-33 M 4
Goose River ~ CDN 38-39 O 2
Goosport o USA (LA) 268-269 G 6
Gooty o IND 140-141 G 3
Gopalganj o IND 142-143 D 2
Gopichettipalaiyam o IND 140-141 G 5
Goplo, Jezioro ⊙ PL 92-93 P 2
Goppe Bazar o MYA 142-143 H 5
Gò Quao o VN 158-159 H 6
Gōr ◘ AFG 134-135 K 1
Goradiz o AZ 128-129 M 3
Goragorskij o RUS 126-127 F 6
Gorahun o WAL 202-203 E 6
Goraici, Kepulauan ⌒ RI 164-165 K 4
Góra Kalwaria o PL 92-93 Q 3
Gorakhpur o IND 142-143 C 2
Goram, Tanjung ▲ RI 164-165 H 6
Goran, Lake ⊙ AUS 178-179 L 6
Goranlega ~ SP 212-213 H 4
Gorantla o IND 140-141 G 4
Goražde o BIH 100-101 G 3
Görband o AFG 138-139 B 2
Gorbea o RCH 78-79 C 5
Gorbi ~ RUS 120-121 G 4
Gorbiačin ~ RUS 108-109 X 8
Gorbica o RUS 118-119 J 9
Gorbilok ~ RUS 116-117 G 6
Gorbita ~ RUS 108-109 a 5
Gorbovy, ostrova ⌒ RUS 108-109 H 4
Gorbyl' ~ RUS 122-123 C 3
Gorda, Punta ▲ NIC 52-53 C 4
Gorda, Punta ▲ RCH 70-71 B 6
Gorda Cay o BS 54-55 G 1
Gördes ☆ TR 128-129 C 3

Gibson Lake — Gördes 331

Guiri o **CAM** 206-207 B 3
Güiria o **YV** 60-61 K 2
Guirripa, Caño ~ **CO** 60-61 F 5
Guirvas o **SN** 196-197 C 7
Guisa o **C** 54-55 G 4
Guishanfeng • **VRC** 154-155 J 6
Guishi SK ~ **VRC** 156-157 G 4
Guissat < **RN** 198-199 D 4
Guissèr o **MA** 188-189 H 4
Guissoumalé o **RMM** 202-203 F 3
Guitri o **CI** 202-203 H 7
Guiuan o **RP** 160-161 F 7
Guixi o **VRC** 156-157 K 2
Guiyang o **VRC** (HUN) 156-157 H 4
Guiyang ☆ **VRC** (GZH) 156-157 E 3
Guizhou ◘ **VRC** 156-157 D 3
Gujarat ◘ **IND** 138-139 C 8
Gūjar Khān o **PK** 138-139 D 3
Gujba o **WAN** 204-205 J 3
Gujiao o **VRC** 154-155 H 3
Gujrānwāla o **PK** 138-139 E 3
Gujrāt o **PK** 138-139 E 3
Gujri o **IND** 138-139 E 8
Gukera, ostrov ∩ **RUS** 84-85 c 2
Gulang o **VRC** 154-155 C 3
Gulargambone o **AUS** 178-179 K 6
Gulbarga o• **IND** 140-141 G 2
Gulbene ☆ **LV** 94-95 K 3
Gulbin Ka, River ~ **WAN** 204-205 F 3
Gul'ča o **KS** 136-137 N 4
Gul'ča ~ **KS** 136-137 N 5
Guledagudda o **IND** 140-141 F 2
Gulf Breeze o **USA** (FL) 286-287 B 1
Gulf Development Road II **AUS** 174-175 G 6
Gulf Islands National Seashore ⊥ **USA** (MS) 268-269 M 6
Gulflander (Historical Railway) • **AUS** 174-175 F 5
Gulf of Bothnia = Bothnia, Gulf of ≈ 86-87 J 6
Gulf of Finland ≃ **FIN** 86-87 M 7
Gulfport o **USA** (FL) 286-287 G 4
Gulfport o **USA** (MS) 268-269 L 6
Gulf Shores o **USA** (AL) 284-285 C 6
Gulgong o **AUS** 180-181 K 2
Gulir o **RI** 166-167 F 4
Gulistan = Guliston ☆ **US** 136-137 L 4
Guliston ☆ **US** 136-137 L 4
Guliya Shan ▲ **VRC** 150-151 D 3
Gulja o **RUS** 118-119 K 8
Guljaevskie Koški, ostrova ∩ **RUS** 88-89 X 2
Guljanci o **BG** 102-103 D 6
Gul Kach o **PK** 138-139 B 4
Gulkana River ~ **USA** 20-21 S 5
Gul'kevići o **RUS** 102-103 M 5
Güllab Dere ~ **TR** 128-129 H 4
Gull Bay o **CDN** (ONT) 234-235 O 5
Gullfoss •• **IS** 86-87 c 2
Gull Lake o **CDN** (SAS) 232-233 K 5
Gull Lake ⬭ **CDN** (ALB) 232-233 E 3
Gull Lake ⬭ **USA** (MN) 270-271 D 4
Gull Pond ⬭ **CDN** (NFL) 242-243 M 3
Gullrock Lake ⬭ **CDN** (ONT) 234-235 K 4
Güllük Körfezi ≈ 128-129 B 4
Gully, The ≃ 38-39 P 6
Gulmarg o• **IND** 138-139 E 2
Gulmar Kale ∴•• **TR** 128-129 K 4
Gulmit o **PK** 138-139 E 1
Gul Muhammad o **PK** 134-135 M 5
Gülnar ☆ **TR** 128-129 E 4
Gülpınar ☆ **TR** 128-129 B 3
Gul'rips o **GE** 126-127 D 6
Gülşehir ☆ **TR** 128-129 F 3
Gulu ☆ **EAU** 212-213 D 2
Gulumba Gana o **WAN** 206-207 B 3
Gulūr o **IND** 140-141 G 4
Guluwuru Island ∩ **AUS** 174-175 D 2
Gulwe o **EAT** 214-215 J 4
Ğumaira o **UAE** 134-135 F 6
Gumal ~ **PK** 138-139 B 3
Gumal ~ **PK** 138-139 C 4
Gumani Hurasagar ~ **BD** 142-143 F 3
Gumare o **RB** 218-219 B 4
Gumawana Island ∩ **PNG** 183 F 5
Gumba o **ANG** 216-217 C 5
Gumba o **ZRE** 210-211 H 2
Gumbiri, Ğabal ▲ **SUD** 206-207 K 6
Gumbiro o **EAT** 214-215 H 6
Gumbo Gumbo Creek ~ **AUS** 178-179 G 4
Gumel o **WAN** 198-199 D 6
Gumgarhi o **NEP** 144-145 D 6
Gumi o **RI** 164-165 K 3
Gumine o **PNG** 183 C 4
Gumla o **IND** 142-143 D 4
Gumlu o **AUS** 174-175 J 6
Gummersbach o **D** 92-93 J 3
Gummi o **WAN** 198-199 B 6
Gumpolds = Humpolec o **CZ** 92-93 N 4
Gums, The o **AUS** 178-179 L 4
Gumsi o **WAN** 198-199 E 6
Gum Swamp Creek ~ **USA** (GA) 284-285 G 4
Gümüşhane ☆ **TR** 128-129 H 2
Gumu Uen, Uar < **SP** 212-213 J 3
Gumzai o **RI** 166-167 H 4
Gūnābād o **IR** 134-135 J 4
Guna Terara ▲ **ETH** 208-209 D 3
Gunbar o **AUS** 180-181 H 3
Gundagai o• **AUS** 180-181 K 3
Gundāla o **IND** 142-143 B 7
Gundji o **ZRE** 210-211 H 2
Gundlupet o **IND** 140-141 G 5
Gündoğmuş ☆ **TR** 128-129 E 4
Güneydoğu Toroslar ▲▲ **TR** 128-129 G 4
Gunga o **ANG** 216-217 E 7
Gungi o **ZRE** 216-217 E 3
Gungo o **ANG** 216-217 C 5
Gungu o **ZRE** 210-211 G 6
Gungure o **MOC** 214-215 K 6
Gunisao Lake ⬭ **CDN** 34-35 H 4
Gunisao River ~ **CDN** 34-35 H 4
Guniujiang Z.B. ⊥• **VRC** 156-157 K 2
Ğūniya ☆ **RL** 128-129 F 6
Gunn o **CDN** (ALB) 232-233 D 2
Gunna o **SUD** 206-207 H 5
Gunnaramby Swamp ⬭ **AUS** 180-181 G 2
Gunnarn o **S** 86-87 H 4
Gunnawarra o **AUS** 174-175 H 5
Gunnbjørn Fjeld ▲▲ **GRØ** 28-29 Y 2
Gunnedah o **AUS** 178-179 L 6
Gunning o **AUS** 180-181 K 3
Gunningbar Creek ~ **AUS** 178-179 J 6
Gunnison o **USA** (CO) 254-255 J 5
Gunnison o **USA** (UT) 254-255 D 4
Gunnison, Mount ▲ **USA** (CO) 254-255 H 5
Gunnison River ~ **USA** (CO) 254-255 G 5
Gunpowder o **AUS** 174-175 E 6
Günsang o **VRC** 144-145 D 5
Gunsight o **USA** (AZ) 256-257 C 6
Gunt ~ **TJ** 136-137 N 6
Gunta o **WAN** 204-205 H 3
Guntakal o **IND** 140-141 G 3
Guntersville o **USA** (AL) 284-285 D 2
Guntersville Lake < **USA** (AL) 284-285 D 2
Gunton o **CDN** (MAN) 234-235 F 4
Guntur o **IND** 140-141 J 2
Gununa o **AUS** 174-175 E 5
Gunung, Tanjung ▲ **RI** 162-163 H 4
Gunungapi, Pulau ∩ **RI** 166-167 D 5
Gunung Gading National Park ⊥ **MAL** 162-163 H 4
Gununghalum o **RI** 168 B 3
Gunung-Leuser, National-Reservation- ⊥ **RI** 162-163 C 3
Gunung Leuser Nature Reserve ⊥ **RI** 162-163 B 3
Gunung Lompobatang Reserve ⊥• **RI** 164-165 G 6
Gunung Meja Reserve ⊥• **RI** 166-167 G 2
Gunung Mulu National Park ⊥• **MAL** 164-165 D 1
Gunung Rinjani Reserve ⊥• **RI** 168 C 7
Gunungsitoli o **RI** 162-163 B 4
Gunungtua o **RI** 162-163 C 4
Gunupur o **IND** 142-143 C 6
Gunyan, Mount ▲ **AUS** 178-179 L 5
Gunzenhausen o **D** 92-93 L 4
Guocheng o **VRC** 154-155 D 3
Guocun o **VRC** 154-155 B 5
Guodao o **VRC** 154-155 H 3
Guoguo Wenwu • **VRC** 154-155 G 4
Guo He ~ **VRC** 154-155 K 5
Guoju o **VRC** 156-157 N 2
Guoquanyan ▲ **VRC** 154-155 C 6
Guoyang o **VRC** 154-155 K 5
Gur ~ **RUS** 122-123 H 4
Ġurābī, Ğabal ▲ **ET** 194-195 D 3
Gurabo o **USA** (PR) 286-287 Q 2
Guragē ▲ **ETH** 208-209 D 4
Gurān o• **IR** 134-135 F 5
Gurara, River ~ **WAN** 204-205 G 4
Gurba ~ **ZRE** 206-207 H 6
Gurbantünggut Shamo ∸ **VRC** 146-147 H 3
Gurdāspur o **IND** 138-139 E 3
Gurdon o **USA** (AR) 276-277 B 7
Gurdzaani o• **GE** 126-127 F 7
Gurē o **ETH** 208-209 D 5
Gur'ev = Atyrau ☆ **KA** 96-97 H 10
Gur'evsk ☆ **RUS** 114-115 S 7
Gurgaon o **IND** 138-139 F 5
Gurgei, Ğabal ▲ **SUD** 200-201 B 6
Gurguéia, Rio ~ **BR** 68-69 G 5
Gurguéira, Rio ~ **BR** 68-69 F 6
Guri, Embalse de < **YV** 60-61 K 4
Gurib ~ **NAM** 220-221 C 3
Gurig National Park ⊥ **AUS** 172-173 K 1
Gurijuba, Canal do ~ **BR** 62-63 J 5
Ğūrīn o **IRQ** 128-129 K 4
Gurin o **WAN** 204-205 K 4
Gurinhatã o **BR** 72-73 F 5
Gurlan o **US** 136-137 G 4
Ğurm o **AFG** 136-137 M 6
Gurner o **AUS** 172-173 K 7
Guro o **MOC** 218-219 G 3
Güroymak ☆ **TR** 128-129 K 3
Gurri o **SUD** 198-199 L 6
Gurskoe o **RUS** 122-123 G 3
Guru o **VRC** 144-145 G 6
Gurué o **MOC** 218-219 J 2
Gurumeti ~ **EAT** (MA) 212-213 E 5
Gurun o **MAL** 162-163 D 2
Gürün ☆ **TR** 128-129 G 3
Gurupa o **BR** 62-63 J 6
Gurupi o **BR** 68-69 D 7
Gurupi, Baía do ≈ 68-69 E 2
Gurupi, Cabo ▲ **BR** 68-69 E 2
Gurupi, Rio ~ **BR** 68-69 E 3
Gurupi, Serra do ▲▲ **BR** 68-69 D 4
Gurupizinho o **BR** 68-69 E 3
Guru Sikhar ▲ **IND** 138-139 D 7
Guruve o **ZW** 218-219 F 3
Guruzāla o **IND** 140-141 H 2
Gurvan Sajchan ▲▲ **MAU** 148-149 F 6
Gurvansajhan = Suugaant o **MAU** 148-149 H 5
Gurvantès = Urt o **MAU** 148-149 E 6
Gurydangdan, peski ∸ **TM** 136-137 F 6
Gusar = Qusar o **AZ** 128-129 N 2
Gusau o **WAN** 198-199 C 6
Gusev o **RUS** 94-95 H 4
Gushan • **VRC** 156-157 L 3
Gusher o **USA** (UT) 254-255 F 3
Gushgy o **TM** 136-137 H 7
Gushgy ~ **TM** 136-137 H 7
Gushi o **VRC** (HEN) 154-155 J 5
Gushi o **VRC** (QIN) 144-145 L 5
Gushiegu o **GH** 202-203 K 5
Gushie Point ▲ **CDN** 36-37 K 6
Gushikawa o **J** 152-153 B 11
Gus'-Hrustal'nyj ☆•• **RUS** 94-95 R 4
Gusi o **RI** 166-167 G 3
Gusika ~ **RUS** 110-111 F 3
Gusinaja ~ **RUS** 110-111 a 4
Gusinaja, guba ≈ 110-111 b 4
Gusinaja Vadega ~ **RUS** 108-109 E 5
Gusinaja Zemlja, poluostrov ⌣ **RUS** 108-109 D 6
Gusinoe, ozero ⬭•• **RUS** 116-117 M 10
Gusinoozërsk ☆ **RUS** 116-117 N 10
Gūš Lāġar o **IR** 136-137 G 7
Gusmp, ostrov ∩ **RUS** 112-113 L 2
Gúspini o **I** 100-101 B 5
Gustav Adolf Land ∩ **N** 84-85 M 3
Gustavfjellet ▲ **N** 84-85 K 4
Gustav Holm, Kap ▲ **GRØ** 28-29 X 3
Gustavia ☆ **F** 56 D 3
Gustavo A. Madero o **MEX** 52-53 E 2
Gustavsberg ☆ **S** 86-87 J 7
Gustavus o **USA** 32-33 C 2
Gustav V land ≈ 84-85 L 2
Gustine o **USA** (CA) 248-249 D 2
Güstrow o• **D** 92-93 M 2
Gutah o **CDN** 32-33 K 3
Gutara ~ **RUS** 116-117 H 8
Gutarskij hrebet ▲▲ **RUS** 116-117 H 8
Gutenko Mountains ▲▲ **ARK** 16 F 30
Gütersloh o **D** 92-93 K 3
Guthalungra o **AUS** 174-175 J 6
Guthrie o **USA** (AZ) 256-257 F 6
Guthrie o **USA** (OK) 264-265 G 3
Guthrie o **USA** (TX) 264-265 D 5
Guthrie Center o **USA** (IA) 274-275 D 3
Gutian o **VRC** 156-157 L 3
Gutiérrez Zamora o **MEX** 52-53 F 1
Gut River o **JA** 54-55 G 6
Gutsuo o **VRC** 144-145 F 6
Guttaiyūr o **IND** 140-141 G 5
Guttenberg o **USA** (IA) 274-275 G 2
Guttstadt = Dobre Miasto o• **PL** 92-93 Q 2
Gutu o **ZW** 218-219 F 4
Gu Vo o **USA** (AZ) 256-257 C 6
Guwahati ☆ **IND** 142-143 G 2
Ġuwaifāt o **UAE** 134-135 D 6
Ğuwaiza o **UAE** 134-135 F 6
Guwayr o **SUD** 200-201 F 4
Guy o **CDN** 32-33 M 4
Guyana ■ **GUY** 62-63 E 3
Guyandot River ~ **USA** (WV) 280-281 D 5
Guyang o **VRC** 148-149 J 7
Guyenne ∸ **F** 90-91 G 9
Guy Fawkes River National Park ⊥ **AUS** 178-179 M 6
Guyī o **ETH** 208-209 B 4
Guymon o **USA** (OK) 264-265 C 2
Ğūyom o **IR** 134-135 E 4
Guyot Glacier ⊂ **USA** 20-21 U 6
Guyra o **AUS** 178-179 L 6
Guyton o **USA** (GA) 284-285 J 4
Guyuan o **VRC** (HEB) 148-149 M 7
Guyuan o **VRC** (NIN) 154-155 E 4
Guzar o **US** 136-137 K 5
Güzeloluk o **TR** 128-129 F 4
Güzelsu o **TR** 128-129 K 3
Guzhen o **VRC** (ANH) 154-155 K 5
Guzhen o **VRC** (FUJ) 156-157 M 3
Guzmán o **MEX** 50-51 F 2
Guzmán, Laguna de ⬭ **MEX** 50-51 F 2
Gvādar o **IR** 134-135 J 6
Gvardejsk ☆ **RUS** 94-95 G 4
Gvardeysk = Gvardejsk ☆ **RUS** 94-95 G 4
Gvasjugi o **RUS** 122-123 G 5
Gwa o **MYA** 158-159 C 2
Gwaai o **ZW** 218-219 D 4
Gwabegar o **AUS** 178-179 K 6
Gwada o **WAN** 204-205 G 4
Gwadabawa o **WAN** 198-199 B 6
Gwādar o **PK** 134-135 K 6
Gwagwalada o **WAN** 204-205 G 4
Gwalia ∴ **AUS** 176-177 F 4
Gwalior o• **IND** 138-139 G 6
Gwalishtap o **PK** 134-135 K 4
Gwamba o **WAN** 204-205 F 3
Gwambara o **WAN** 198-199 B 6
Gwanda ☆ **ZW** 218-219 E 5
Gwane o **ZRE** 206-207 G 6
Gwaram o **WAN** 204-205 H 3
Gwardafuy = Raas Caseyr ▲ **SP** 208-209 K 3
Gwarif o **RI** 166-167 K 3
Gwarzo o **WAN** 204-205 G 3
Gwasero o **WAN** 204-205 E 4
Gwayi ~ **ZW** 218-219 D 4
Gwayi River o **ZW** 218-219 D 4
Gweedore o **IRL** 90-91 C 4
Gwembe o **Z** 218-219 D 3
Gweru ☆ **ZW** (Mid) 218-219 E 4
Gweru ~ **ZW** 218-219 E 4
Gweta o **RB** 218-219 C 5
Gwi o **WAN** 204-205 G 4
Gwillim River ~ **CDN** 34-35 C 2
Gwinn o **USA** (MI) 270-271 L 4
Gwinner o **USA** (ND) 258-259 K 5
Gwoza o **WAN** 204-205 K 3
Gwydir Highway II **AUS** 178-179 K 5
Gwydir River ~ **AUS** 178-179 L 6
Gwynne o **CDN** (ALB) 232-233 E 2
Gwynn Island ∩ **USA** (VA) 280-281 K 6
Gyaca o **VRC** 144-145 J 6
Gya'gya = Saga o **VRC** 144-145 E 6
Gyalshing o **IND** 142-143 F 2
Gyandzha = Ganca o• **AZ** 128-129 M 2
Gyangzê o• **VRC** 144-145 G 6
Gyaring Co ⬭ **VRC** 144-145 G 5
Gyaring Hu ⬭ **VRC** 144-145 L 3
Gyda o **RUS** 108-109 S 6
Gydanskaja grjada ▲▲ **RUS** 108-109 Q 7
Gydanskaja guba ≈ 108-109 R 5
Gydanskij poluostrov ⌣ **RUS** 108-109 Q 6
Gydanskij proliv ⬭ **RUS** 108-109 Q 5
Gydanskiy Poluostrov = Gydanskij poluostrov ⌣ **RUS** 108-109 Q 6
Gyêsar Co ⬭ **VRC** 144-145 E 5
Gyirong o **VRC** 144-145 E 6
Gyitang o **VRC** 144-145 L 5
Gyldenløves Fjord ≈ 28-29 U 4
Gympie o• **AUS** 178-179 M 4
Gynym ~ **RUS** 118-119 O 7
Gynym ~ **RUS** 120-121 D 5
Gyobinchan o **MYA** 142-143 J 6
Gyokusendo • **J** 152-153 B 11
Gyöngyös o **H** 92-93 P 5
Győr o **H** 92-93 O 5
Gypsum Palace o **AUS** 180-181 H 2
Gypsum Point ▲ **CDN** 30-31 M 5
Gypsumville o **CDN** (MAN) 234-235 E 3
Gyrfalcon Islands ∩ **CDN** 36-37 P 5
Gyrgyčan o **RUS** 112-113 Q 2

H

H1 o **IRQ** 128-129 J 6
H3 o **IRQ** 128-129 H 6
Häädemeeste o **EST** 94-95 J 2
Ha'afeva ∩ **TON** 184 IV a 1
Haag, Den = 's-Gravenhage ☆•• **NL** 92-93 H 2
Haakon VII Land ∸ **N** 84-85 H 3
Haalenberg o **NAM** 220-221 B 3
Ha'amonga Trilithon • **TON** 184 IV a 2
Ha'ano ∩ **TON** 184 IV a 1
Ha'apai Group ∩ **TON** 184 IV a 1
Haapajärvi o **FIN** 88-89 H 5
Haapsalu ☆ **EST** 94-95 H 2
Haarlem ☆•• **NL** 92-93 H 2
Haarlem o **ZA** 220-221 F 6
Haast o **NZ** 182 B 5
Haastberget ▲ **N** 84-85 M 3
Haast Bluff X **AUS** 176-177 L 1
Haast Pass ▲ **NZ** 182 B 6
Haasts Bluff Aboriginal Land X **AUS** 176-177 K 1
Hab ~ **PK** 134-135 M 6
Haba, al- o **UAE** 134-135 F 6
Habadra, Hassi < **DZ** 190-191 E 7
Habahe o **VRC** 146-147 H 1
Habana, La ★••• **C** 54-55 D 3
Habarane o **CL** 140-141 J 6
Habar Cirir o **SP** 208-209 H 6
Habarovsk o **RUS** 122-123 F 4
Ḥabarūt o **OM** 132-133 H 5
Habaswein o **EAK** 212-213 G 3
Ḥabauna, Wādī ~ **KSA** 132-133 D 5
Habay o **SP** 212-213 J 3
Ḥabbā, al- o **KSA** 130-131 G 4
Ḥabbān o **Y** 132-133 E 6
Ḥabbānīya, al- o **IRQ** 128-129 K 6
Ḥabbārīya, al- o **IRQ** 128-129 K 6
Habejjaha ~ **RUS** 108-109 O 5
Ḥabībābād o **IR** 134-135 D 2
Habirag o **VRC** 148-149 M 6
Ḥable Rūd, Rūdḫāne-ye ~ **IR** 136-137 C 7
Habob ~ **SUD** 200-201 G 3
Habraykhoun o **LAO** 158-159 H 3
Ḥabšān o **UAE** 132-133 H 2
Ḥabūr o **Y** 132-133 C 5
Ḫābūr, al- ~ **SYR** 128-129 J 5
Ḫābūr, Nahr al- ~ **SYR** 128-129 J 4
Ḫābūra, al- o **OM** 132-133 K 2
Hacari o **CO** 60-61 E 3
Hacha, Raudal ~ **CO** 64-65 F 1
Hachinohe o **J** 152-153 J 4
Hachiōji o **J** 152-153 H 7
Hachirōgata-ko ⬭ **J** 152-153 J 5
Hachita o **USA** (NM) 256-257 G 7
Hack, Mount ▲ **AUS** 178-179 E 6
Hackberry o **USA** (AZ) 256-257 B 3
Hackberry o **USA** (LA) 268-269 G 7
Hackberry Creek ~ **USA** (KS) 262-263 F 6
Hackensack o **USA** (MN) 270-271 D 4
Hackett o **CDN** (ALB) 232-233 F 3
Hackettstown o **USA** (NJ) 280-281 M 3
Hackleburg o **USA** (AL) 284-285 B 2
Hackney o **GUY** 62-63 E 2
Hačmas = Xaçmaz o **AZ** 128-129 N 2
Haco o **ANG** 216-217 C 5
Hacufera o **MOC** 218-219 G 5
Hadaaftimo o **SP** 208-209 J 3
Hadagalli o **IND** 140-141 F 3
Hadakta o **RUS** 118-119 F 10
Hadaliya o **SUD** 200-201 H 4
Hadama o **RUS** 116-117 J 9
Ḥadar, al- ☆ **IRQ** 128-129 K 5
Hadaran'ja, hrebet ▲▲ **RUS** 110-111 V 5
Hadashville o **CDN** (MAN) 234-235 H 5
Ḥaḏbaram o **OM** 132-133 J 5
Ḥadd, al- o **OM** 132-133 L 2
Ḥadd, Ra's al- ▲ **OM** 132-133 L 2
Hadda ∴• **AFG** 138-139 C 2
Ḥaddā' o **KSA** 132-133 A 3
Ḥaddād Banī Malik o **KSA** 132-133 B 3
Ḥaddār, al- o **KSA** 132-133 D 3
Haddington • **GB** 90-91 F 4
Haddon Corner • **AUS** 178-179 F 4
Haddummati Atoll ∩ **MV** 140-141 B 7
Hadejia o **WAN** (KAN) 198-199 E 6
Hadejia ~ **WAN** 198-199 D 6
Hadera ☆ **IL** 130-131 D 1
Haderslev o• **DK** 86-87 D 9
Hadhf o **NZ** 134-135 F 6
Hadhour, Hassi < **DZ** 188-189 L 5
Hadibū o **Y** 132-133 H 7
Hadīga o **SUD** 200-201 G 4
Hadilik o **VRC** 144-145 F 2
Hadım ☆ **TR** 128-129 E 4
Ḥadīta, al- o **KSA** 130-131 E 2
Hadjač o **UA** 102-103 H 2
Hadjadj, Oued el ~ **DZ** 190-191 E 6
Hadjer = Oum o **TCH** 198-199 J 6
Hadjer Bandala o **TCH** 206-207 E 3
Hadjer el Hamis o **TCH** 198-199 G 6
Hadley o **USA** (WA) 244-245 G 4
Hadley Bay ≈ 24-25 R 4
Ḥadnān o **IRQ** 128-129 K 4
Hà Đông ☆ **VN** 156-157 D 6
Ḥaḏrā', al- o **KSA** 130-131 H 3
Ḥaḍramaut ∸ **Y** 132-133 E 6
Ḥaḍramaut, Wādī ~ **Y** 132-133 F 5
Hadrametum = Sousse ☆• **TN** 190-191 H 3
Ḥadrānīya o **IRQ** 128-129 K 5
Hadrian's Wall ••• **GB** 90-91 F 4
Hadseløya ∩ **N** 86-87 G 2
Hadsund o **DK** 86-87 E 8
Hadudejpur ~ **RUS** 114-115 P 3
Haduttè ~ **RUS** 108-109 R 8
Hadweenzie River ~ **USA** 20-21 Q 3
Hadyjah ~ **RUS** 114-115 K 2
Hadyr'jaha, Bol'šaja ~ **RUS** 114-115 P 2
Hadytajha ~ **RUS** 108-109 N 8
Hadyžensk o **RUS** 126-127 C 5
Hae o **THA** 142-143 M 6
Haedo, Cuchilla de ▲▲ **ROU** 78-79 L 2
Haeju o **DVR** 150-151 E 8
Haena o **USA** (HI) 288 F 2
Haenam o **ROK** 150-151 F 10
Haenertsburg o **ZA** 218-219 E 6
Ḥafar al-Bāṭin o **KSA** 130-131 J 3
Haffa, al- o **SYR** 128-129 G 5
Haffner Bjerg ▲ **GRØ** 26-27 T 5
Hafford o **CDN** (SAS) 232-233 L 3
Haffouz o **TN** 190-191 G 3
Ḫafǧī, Ra's al- o **KSA** 130-131 L 3
Hafik ☆ **TR** 128-129 G 3
Ḥāfirat Nisāḥ o **KSA** 130-131 K 5
Hāfizābād o **PK** 138-139 D 3
Hafnarfjörður ☆ **IS** 86-87 c 2
Haftgel o **IR** 134-135 C 3
Haft Tappe o **IR** 134-135 C 2
Hagadera o **EAK** 212-213 H 3
Ḥaǧal Bi'r < **SYR** 128-129 H 5
Hagar o **CDN** (ONT) 238-239 E 2
Ḥaǧar, al- ▲▲ **OM** 132-133 K 2
Ḥaǧara, al ∸ **IRQ** 128-129 K 6
Ḥaǧara, al- ▲▲ **KSA** 130-131 H 3
Ḥaǧarain, al- o **Y** 132-133 F 6
Ḥaǧar aš-Šarqī ▲▲ **OM** 132-133 L 2
Hagar Banga o **SUD** 206-207 F 3
Hagari ~ **IND** 140-141 G 3
Ḥaǧda o **Y** 132-133 C 7
Hagemeister Island ∩ **USA** 22-23 Q 3
Hagemeister Strait ≈ 22-23 Q 3
Hagen o **CDN** (SAS) 232-233 N 3
Hagen o **D** 92-93 J 3
Hagen, Mount ▲ **PNG** 183 C 3
Hagen Fjord ≈ 26-27 m 3
Hagensborg o **CDN** (BC) 228-229 H 4
Hāgere Hiywet o• **ETH** 208-209 C 4
Hāgere Selam o **ETH** 208-209 D 5
Hagerman o **USA** (ID) 252-253 D 4
Hagerman o **USA** (NM) 256-257 L 5
Hagerman National Wildlife Refuge ⊥ **USA** (TX) 264-265 H 5
Hagerstown o **USA** (IN) 274-275 N 5
Hagerstown o **USA** (MD) 280-281 J 4
Ḥaǧǧa o• **Y** 132-133 C 6
Ḥāǧǧ 'Alī Qolī, Kavīr-e ⬭ **IR** 136-137 D 7
Ḥaǧǧīābād o **IR** 134-135 F 4
Hagi o **J** 152-153 D 7
Hà Giang ☆ **VN** 156-157 D 5
Ḥaǧr, al- o **KSA** 130-131 K 5
Hague o **CDN** (SAS) 232-233 M 3
Hague, Cap de la ▲ **F** 90-91 G 7
Hague, Hasy < **LAR** 190-191 H 7
Haguenau o• **F** 90-91 L 7
Hahan ~ **RUS** 120-121 D 4
Hahčan ~ **RUS** 110-111 N 6
Hahira o **USA** (GA) 284-285 G 6
Hahndorf o **AUS** 180-181 E 3
Hahnville o **USA** (LA) 268-269 K 7
Haho o **BF** 202-203 J 4
Haho ~ **RT** 202-203 L 6
Haia o **PNG** 183 C 4
Hai'an o **VRC** (GDG) 156-157 G 6
Hai'an o **VRC** (JIA) 154-155 M 5
Haib o **NAM** 220-221 D 4
Haib ~ **NAM** 220-221 C 4
Ḫaibar o **KSA** 130-131 F 5
Ḫaibar al-Ǧanūb o **KSA** 132-133 C 4
Haicheng o **VRC** 150-151 D 7
Haida o• **CDN** (BC) 228-229 B 2
Haida = Nový Bor o **CZ** 92-93 N 3
Haïdra • **TN** 190-191 G 3
Hải Du'o'ng ☆ **VN** 156-157 E 6
Haifa = Hefa ☆• **IL** 130-131 D 1
Ḥaifān o **Y** 132-133 D 7
Haifeng o **VRC** 156-157 J 5
Haig o **AUS** 176-177 J 5
Haigler o **USA** (NE) 262-263 E 4
Haikang o **VRC** 156-157 G 6
Haikou ☆• **VRC** 156-157 G 6
Ḥā'il ◘ **KSA** 130-131 G 4
Ḥā'il ☆• **KSA** (HAI) 130-131 G 4
Ḥā'il, Wādī ~ **KSA** 130-131 G 4
Hailalua o **SOL** 184 I e 3
Hailar o **VRC** 150-151 B 3
Hailar He ~ **VRC** 150-151 C 3
Hailey o **USA** (ID) 252-253 D 3
Haileybury o **CDN** (ONT) 236-237 J 5
Hailin o **VRC** 150-151 G 5
Hailino o **RUS** 112-113 O 6
Hailun o **VRC** 150-151 F 4
Hailuogou • **VRC** 156-157 B 2
Hailuoto (Karlö) ∩ **FIN** 88-89 H 4
Ḫaima, Ra's al- o **UAE** 134-135 F 6
Haimen o **VRC** 154-155 M 6
Hainan ◘ **VRC** 156-157 F 7
Hainan Dao ∩ **VRC** 156-157 G 7
Hainan Strait = Qiongzhou Haixia ≈ **VRC** 156-157 F 6
Hainault Tourist Mine • **AUS** 176-177 F 5
Haindi o **LB** 202-203 E 6
Haines o **USA** (AK) 20-21 X 7
Haines o **USA** (OR) 244-245 H 6
Haines City o **USA** (FL) 286-287 H 3
Haines Highway II **CDN** 20-21 W 6
Haines Junction o **CDN** 20-21 W 6
Haingsisi o **RI** 166-167 B 7
Hainin o **Y** 132-133 F 6
Haining o **VRC** 154-155 M 6
Hải Ninh ☆ **VN** 156-157 E 6
Hải Phong ☆• **VN** 156-157 E 6
Ḥair, Qaṣr al- • **SYR** 128-129 H 5
Ḥair al-Ġarbī, Qaṣr al- ∴• **SYR** 128-129 G 5
Haïré Lao o **SN** 196-197 C 6
Hairjuzova ~ **RUS** 120-121 R 5
Hairy Hill o **CDN** (ALB) 232-233 G 2
Ḥais o **Y** 132-133 C 7
Ḫaiṣat an-Naum, Ra's ▲ **Y** 132-133 H 7
Haishiwan o **VRC** 154-155 C 3
Ḥā'iṭ, al- o **KSA** 130-131 G 5
Haitan Dao ∩ **VRC** 156-157 L 4
Haiti = Haïti ■ **RH** 54-55 J 5
Haitou o **VRC** 156-157 F 7
Haiwee Reservoir ⬭ **USA** (CA) 248-249 G 3
Haiyan o **VRC** (QIN) 154-155 B 3
Haiyan o **VRC** (ZHE) 154-155 M 6
Haiyang o **VRC** 154-155 M 3
Haiyuan o **VRC** 154-155 D 3
Haizhou Wan ~ **VRC** 154-155 L 4
Haja, Džebariki- o **RUS** 120-121 F 2
Haja, Jurjung- o **RUS** 110-111 J 3
Hajata, Suntar-hrebet ▲▲ **RUS** 110-111 V 7
Hajdarkan o **KS** 136-137 M 5
Hajeb El Ayoun o **TN** 190-191 G 3
Hajiki-saki ▲ **J** 152-153 H 5
Hajja, Èjè- o **RUS** 110-111 U 6
Hajljulja ~ **RUS** 120-121 T 4
Hajnówka o **PL** 92-93 R 2
Hajo Do ∩ **ROK** 150-151 F 10
Hajpudyrskaja, guba ⬭ **RUS** 108-109 H 7
Hajrjuzovo o **RUS** 120-121 R 5
Hajrjuzovo, Ust'- o **RUS** 120-121 R 5
Hajsyn ☆ **UA** 102-103 F 3
Hajyr o **RUS** 110-111 T 4
Hajysardah o **RUS** 118-119 O 5
Haka o **MYA** 142-143 H 4
Hakai Recreation Area ⊥ **CDN** (BC) 230-231 A 2
Hakalau o **USA** (HI) 288 K 5
Hakanëa ~ 108-109 T 7
Hakčan, Ust'- o **RUS** 120-121 M 2
Hakkari ☆ **TR** 128-129 K 4
Hakkâri Dağları ▲▲ **TR** 128-129 K 4
Hakken-san ▲ **J** 152-153 F 7
Hakkoda-san ▲ **J** 152-153 J 4
Hakkulabad o **US** 136-137 N 4
Hakodate o **J** 152-153 J 4
Hakoma ~ **RUS** 116-117 J 2
Hakskeenpan ⬭ **ZA** 220-221 E 3
Hakui o **J** 152-153 G 6
Haku-san ▲ **J** 152-153 G 6
Hakusan National Park ⊥ **J** 152-153 G 6
Hāla o• **PK** 138-139 B 7
Halab (Aleppo) ☆••• **SYR** 128-129 G 4
Halaban o **RI** 162-163 B 3
Halabǧa ☆ **IRQ** 128-129 M 5
Halač o **TM** 136-137 J 5
Ḥalā'ib o **ET** 194-195 H 6
Halali o **NAM** 216-217 D 9
Halali Reservoir < **IND** 138-139 F 8
Ḥālat 'Ammār o **KSA** 130-131 E 3
Halawa o **USA** (HI) 288 J 3
Halberstadt o•• **D** 92-93 L 3
Halbrite o **CDN** (SAS) 232-233 P 6
Halčaganahta, krjaž ▲▲ **RUS** 110-111 G 4
Halcon, Mount ▲ **RP** 160-161 D 6
Haldane River ~ **CDN** 30-31 J 2
Halden ☆ **N** 86-87 E 7
Haldia o **IND** 142-143 F 4
Hal'džaj, Krest- o **RUS** 120-121 F 2
Hale, Mount ▲ **AUS** 176-177 D 3
Haleakala Crater ▲ **USA** (HI) 288 J 4
Haleakala National Park ⊥• **USA** (HI) 288 J 4
Halebid o• **IND** 140-141 F 4
Hale Center o **USA** (TX) 264-265 C 4
Haleiwa o **USA** (HI) 288 G 3
Hale River ~ **AUS** 178-179 C 2
Haley Dome o **USA** (UT) 254-255 F 4
Haleyville o **USA** (AL) 284-285 C 2
Ḥalfain, Wādī ~ **OM** 132-133 K 2
Half Assini o **GH** 202-203 J 7
Halfāyat al-Mulūk o **SUD** 200-201 F 5
Hal Flood Range ▲▲ **ARK** 16 F 23
Halfmoon Bay o **CDN** (BC) 230-231 F 4
Halfmoon Bay o **NZ** 182 B 7
Half Moon Bay o **USA** (CA) 248-249 B 2
Half Moon Lake ⬭ **AUS** 176-177 M 4
Halfway o **USA** (OR) 244-245 H 6
Half Way Hills ▲ **CDN** 30-31 V 3
Halfway Point ▲ **CDN** 34-35 Q 5
Halfway River ~ **CDN** 32-33 J 3
Halgen o **SP** 208-209 G 6
Ḥalḥāl o **IR** 128-129 N 4
Halhgol o **MAU** 148-149 O 4
Ḥalibān o **KSA** 130-131 J 6
Haliburton o **CDN** (ONT) 238-239 G 3
Haliburton Highlands ▲▲ **CDN** (ONT) 238-239 G 3
Ḫālid o **IRQ** 128-129 L 6
Ḫālida, Bi'r < **ET** 194-195 C 2
Halifax o **AUS** 174-175 J 6
Halifax ☆ **CDN** (NS) 240-241 M 6
Halifax o **USA** (NC) 282-283 K 4
Halifax, Mount ▲ **AUS** 174-175 J 6
Halifax Bay ≈ 174-175 J 6
Ḫalīǧ-e Fārs • **IR** 134-135 C 4
Halikarnassos ∴•• **TR** 128-129 B 4
Ḫalīl, al-= Hevron ☆ **WB** 130-131 D 2
Ḫalīlābād o **IR** 136-137 F 7
Halīle, Ra's-e ▲ **IR** 134-135 D 4
Halilovo o **RUS** 96-97 L 8
Halīl Rūd ~ **IR** 134-135 H 5
Halilulik o **RI** 166-167 C 6
Halin, Ruins of • **MYA** 142-143 J 4
Ḫālis, al- o **IRQ** 128-129 L 6
Haliyāl o **IND** 140-141 F 3
Haljala o **EST** 94-95 K 2
Haljango, ostrov ∩ **RUS** 108-109 P 5
Halkanskij hrebet ▲ **RUS** 120-121 L 3
Halke Shan ▲▲ **VRC** 146-147 E 4
Halkett, Cape ▲ **USA** 20-21 O 1
Hálki ∩ **GR** 100-101 L 6
Halkída o **GR** 100-101 J 5
Halkidiki ∸ **GR** 100-101 J 4
Halkirk o **CDN** (ALB) 232-233 F 3
Hallam Peak ▲ **CDN** (BC) 228-229 Q 4
Halland ∸ **S** 86-87 F 8
Hallandale o **USA** (FL) 286-287 J 6
Ḥallāniyāt, al- ∩ **Y** 132-133 K 5
Hallasan ▲ **ROK** 150-151 F 11
Hallasan National Park ⊥• **ROK** 150-151 F 11
Hall Bassin ≈ 26-27 T 3
Hall Beach o **CDN** 24-25 f 6
Hallboro o **CDN** (MAN) 234-235 D 4
Hall Bredning ≈ 26-27 n 8
Hall Creek ~ **USA** (UT) 254-255 D 6
Halle (Saale) o• **D** 92-93 L 3
Hallebourg o **CDN** (ONT) 236-237 E 3
Halleck o **USA** (NV) 246-247 K 3
Hallein o **A** 92-93 M 5
Hallen o **S** 86-87 G 5
Hallersville o **USA** 22-23 S 3
Hallett o **AUS** 180-181 E 2
Hallettsville o **USA** (TX) 266-267 L 4
Halley Bay o **ARK** 16 F 34
Halliday o **USA** (ND) 258-259 E 4
Halliday Lake ⬭ **CDN** 30-31 P 5
Hall Indian Reservation, Fort X **USA** (ID) 252-253 F 3
Hallingdal ⌣ **N** 86-87 D 6
Hallingdalselvi ~ **N** 86-87 D 6
Hallingskarvet ▲▲ **N** 86-87 C 6
Hall in Tirol o **A** 92-93 L 5
Hall Island ∩ **FSM** 13 G 2
Hall Island ∩ **USA** 112-113 Y 6
Hall Lake ⬭ **CDN** 24-25 f 6
Hall Land ∸ **GRØ** 26-27 U 3
Hällnäs o **S** 86-87 J 4
Hallock o **USA** (MN) 270-271 B 2
Hallonquist o **CDN** (SAS) 232-233 N 5
Hallowell, Cape ▲ **CDN** 24-25 d 6
Hall Peninsula ⌣ **CDN** 36-37 Q 3
Hall Point ▲ **AUS** 174-175 B 2
Halls o **USA** (TN) 276-277 F 5
Halls Creek o• **AUS** 172-173 H 5
Halls Crossroads o **USA** (TN) 282-283 D 4
Halls Gap o• **AUS** 180-181 G 4
Hallson o **USA** (ND) 258-259 K 3
Hallsville o **USA** (TX) 264-265 K 6
Hallville o **CDN** (ONT) 238-239 K 3
Hallyŏ Haesang National Park ⊥• **ROK** 150-151 G 10
Halmahera, Pulau ∩ **RI** 164-165 L 3
Halmahera Sea = Halmahera, Laut ≈ **RI** 166-167 E 1
Hal'merto, ozero ⬭ **RUS** 108-109 N 7
Halmstad o **S** 86-87 F 8
Hālol o **IND** 138-139 D 8
Halong o **RI** 166-167 E 3
Hal'šany o **BY** 94-95 K 4
Halstad o **USA** (MN) 270-271 B 3
Halstead o **USA** (KS) 262-263 J 7
Haltom City o **USA** (TX) 264-265 G 6
Halturin o **RUS** 96-97 F 4
Halura, Pulau ∩ **RI** 168 E 8
Halvad o **IND** 138-139 C 8
Halverson Ridge ▲▲ **CDN** 32-33 L 3
Halvmåneøya ∩ **N** 84-85 N 4
Halvorgate o **CDN** (SAS) 232-233 M 5
Ḥalwān al-Ḫunfa ▲ **KSA** 130-131 F 3
Halyja ~ **RUS** 120-121 H 2
Halzan Sogootyn davaa ▲ **MAU** 148-149 D 3
Ham ~ **NAM** 220-221 D 4
Ham o **TCH** 206-207 B 3
Hamab o **NAM** 220-221 D 4
Ḥamād, al- ∸ **KSA** 130-131 F 2
Hamada o **J** 152-153 E 7
Hamadān o• **IR** 134-135 C 1
Hamadān ◘ **IR** 134-135 C 1
Hamaguir o **DZ** 188-189 K 5
Hamāh ☆•• **SYR** 128-129 G 5
Hamakua Coast ⌣ **USA** (HI) 288 K 4
Hamamah o **LAR** 192-193 J 1
Hamamasu o **J** 152-153 J 3
Hamamatsu o **J** 152-153 G 7
Haman o **CAM** 204-205 K 6
Hamar ☆• **N** 86-87 E 6
Hamar o **USA** (ND) 258-259 J 4
Ḥamar, al- o **KSA** 130-131 K 6
Hamar-Daban, hrebet ▲▲ **RUS** 116-117 L 10
Hamasaka o **J** 152-153 F 7
Ḥamāsīn, al- o **KSA** 132-133 D 3
Ḥamāṭa, Ğabal ▲ **ET** 194-195 G 5
Hama-Tombetsu o **J** 152-153 K 2
Hamba o **COM** 222-223 C 4
Hambantota o **CL** 140-141 J 7
Hambaparoing o **RI** 168 E 7
Hamberg o **USA** (ND) 258-259 H 4
Hamber Provincial Park ⊥ **CDN** (BC) 228-229 R 4
Hambidge Conservation Park ⊥ **AUS** 180-181 C 2
Hamborgerland ∩ **GRØ** 28-29 O 4
Hamburg ☆•• **D** 92-93 L 2
Hamburg o **SME** 62-63 G 3
Hamburg o **USA** (AR) 276-277 D 7
Hamburg o **USA** (CA) 246-247 B 2
Hamburg o **USA** (IA) 274-275 C 4
Hamburg o **USA** (NY) 278-279 C 6
Hamburg o **ZA** 220-221 H 6
Hamchang o **VRC** 144-145 B 4
Hamḍ, Wādī al- ~ **KSA** 130-131 E 5
Hämeenlinna ☆ **FIN** 88-89 H 6
Hamelin o **AUS** 176-177 C 3
Hamelin, Mount ▲ **CDN** 24-25 P 3
Hamelin Pool ≈ 176-177 B 3
Hameln o• **D** 92-93 K 2
Hamen Wan ~ **VRC** 156-157 K 5
Hamer o **USA** (ID) 252-253 F 3
Hamer Koke o **ETH** 208-209 C 6
Hamero Hadad o **ETH** 208-209 F 5
Hamersley o **AUS** 172-173 C 7
Hamersley Lakes ⬭ **AUS** 176-177 E 5
Hamersley Range ▲▲ **AUS** 172-173 C 6
Hamersley Range National Park ⊥•• **AUS** 172-173 C 7
Hamǧā, al- o **KSA** 130-131 H 5
Hamhung o **DVR** 150-151 F 8
Hami o **VRC** 146-147 L 4
Ḥāmī, al- o **Y** 132-133 F 6
Hamīd o **SUD** 200-201 E 2
Ḥamīdī, Qal'at o **IRQ** 128-129 L 6
Ḥamīdīya o **SYR** 128-129 F 5
Ḥamīdīye o **IR** 134-135 C 3
Hamill Creek ~ **CDN** (BC) 230-231 N 3
Hamilton o **AUS** (TAS) 180-181 J 7
Hamilton o• **AUS** (VIC) 180-181 G 4
Hamilton o **CDN** (ONT) 238-239 F 5
Hamilton ☆ **GB** 54-55 L 1
Hamilton o **NZ** 182 E 2
Hamilton o **USA** (AK) 20-21 J 5
Hamilton o **USA** (AL) 284-285 C 2
Hamilton o **USA** (CO) 254-255 H 3
Hamilton o **USA** (IL) 274-275 G 4
Hamilton o **USA** (IN) 274-275 O 3
Hamilton o **USA** (KS) 262-263 K 7
Hamilton o **USA** (MO) 274-275 D 5
Hamilton o **USA** (MT) 250-251 E 5

334 Guiri — Hamilton

Hindiktig-Hol', ozero ⊖ RUS 124-125 Q 3
Hindiya, al- ☆ IRQ 128-129 L 6
Hindmarsh, Lake ⊖ AUS 180-181 F 4
Hinds Lake ⊖ CDN (NFL) 242-243 M 4
Hindubaāgh o PK 134-135 M 3
Hindukusch ▲ 138-139 B 2
Hindu Kush = Hendūkoš ▲ 10-11 G 5
Hindupur o IND 140-141 G 4
Hindustan ∪ IND 142-143 B 2
Hines o USA (FL) 286-287 F 2
Hines o USA (OR) 244-245 F 7
Hines Creek o CDN 32-33 L 3
Hinesville o USA (GA) 284-285 J 5
Hinganghāt o IND 138-139 G 9
Hinganskij zapovednik ⊥ RUS 122-123 C 4
Hingham o USA (MT) 250-251 J 3
Hinglaj o PK (BEL) 134-135 L 6
Hinglaj o • PK (BEL) 138-139 E 7
Hingol ∼ PK 134-135 L 6
Hingoli o IND 138-139 F 10
Hingoraja o PK 138-139 B 6
Hinidān o PK 134-135 M 6
Hinike ∼ RUS 120-121 L 2
Hınıs ☆ TR 128-129 J 3
Hink Land ⊥ GRØ 26-27 l 8
Hinkleville o USA (KY) 276-277 G 3
Hinlopenrenna ≃ 84-85 J 2
Hinlopenstretet ≈ 84-85 K 2
Hinnøya ⌒ N 86-87 G 2
Hinoba-an o RP 160-161 E 8
Hino-gawa ∼ J 152-153 E 7
Hinogyaung o MYA 158-159 C 2
Hinojo o RA 78-79 J 4
Hinojosa del Duque o •• E 98-99 E 5
Hinomi-saki ▲ J 152-153 E 7
Hinsdale o USA (MT) 250-251 M 3
Hinsdale o USA (NY) 278-279 C 6
Hinton o CDN (ALB) 228-229 R 3
Hinton o USA (OK) 264-265 F 3
Hinton o USA (WV) 280-281 F 6
Híos ⊙ GR 100-101 L 5
Híos ⌒ GR 100-101 L 5
Hipólito o MEX 50-51 J 5
Hipuapua Falls ∼ • USA (HI) 288 J 3
Hir o IR 136-137 B 6
Hira o IND 140-141 G 2
Hirado o • J 152-153 C 8
Hirado-shima ⌒ J 152-153 C 8
Hirafok o DZ 190-191 E 9
Hirākūd Reservoir < IND 142-143 C 5
Hiram o USA (ME) 278-279 L 5
Hiraman ∼ EAK 212-213 G 4
Hiranai o J 152-153 J 4
Hiratsuka o J 152-153 H 7
Ḫirbat al-Umbāšī ∴ • SYR 128-129 G 6
Hirbat Isriya o SYR 128-129 G 5
Hirehadagalli o IND 140-141 F 3
Hiré-Watta o CI 202-203 H 6
Hirfanlı Barajı < TR 128-129 E 3
Hiripitiya o CL 140-141 J 7
Hiriyur o IND 140-141 G 4
Hirmās, Bi'r Ibn o KSA 130-131 E 3
Hirmil, al- ☆ RL 128-129 G 5
Hirna o ETH 208-209 E 4
Hiroo o J 152-153 K 3
Hirosaki o • J 152-153 J 4
Hiroshima o J (HOK) 152-153 J 3
Hiroshima ☆ • J (HIR) 152-153 E 7
Ḫirr, Wādī l- ∼ IRQ 128-129 K 7
hirs'ka miscevisc' • UA 102-103 G 3
Hirs'kyj Tikyč ∼ UA 102-103 F 3
Hirson o F 90-91 K 7
Hirşova o • RO 102-103 F 5
Hirtshals o DK 86-87 D 8
Hisaka-shima ⌒ J 152-153 C 8
Hisān, al- o KSA 132-133 B 3
Hisār o IND 138-139 E 5
Ḥisb, Ša'īb ∼ IRQ 128-129 K 7
Hišig-Öndör = Maan't o MAU 148-149 F 3
Hisiu o PNG 183 D 5
Hislaviči o RUS 94-95 N 4
Hisle o USA (SD) 260-261 E 3
Ḥisn, Qal'at al- •• SYR 128-129 G 5
Ḥişn aş Şahābī o LAR 192-193 J 2
Hispaniola ⌒ 54-55 K 6
Historic Fort Delaware • USA (NY) 280-281 M 2
Historic Remains ∴ • RI 164-165 K 3
Historic Remains, Forts ∴ • RI 164-165 K 3
Historyland ∴ • USA (WI) 270-271 G 5
Ḥisw, al- o KSA 130-131 G 5
Hīt o IRQ 128-129 K 6
Hitachi o J 152-153 J 6
Hitia Sand Hills o GUY 62-63 F 3
Hitoyoshi o J 152-153 D 8
Hitra ∼ N 86-87 D 5
Hiu = Île Hiu ⌒ VAN 184 II a 1
Hiu, Île = Hiu ⌒ VAN 184 II a 1
Hiuchi-nada ≈ 152-153 E 7
Hiva-Oa ⌒ F 13 O 3
Hivaro o PNG 183 B 4
Hiw o ET 194-195 F 4
Hiwarkhed o IND 138-139 F 9
Hiwassee Lake < USA (NC) 282-283 C 5
Hiwassee River ∼ USA (TN) 282-283 C 5
Hixon o CDN (BC) 228-229 M 3
Hiyoshi o J 152-153 E 8
Hiyyon, Nāal ∼ IL 130-131 D 2
Hizan ☆ TR 128-129 K 3
Hjälmaren ⊖ S 86-87 G 7
Hjalmar Lake ⊖ CDN 30-31 P 5
Hjargas nuur ⊖ MAU 116-117 F 11
Hjellset o N 86-87 C 5
Hjerkinn o N 86-87 D 5
Hjørring o DK 86-87 E 8
Hkākabo Rāzi ▲ MYA 142-143 K 1
Hkqingzi o MYA 142-143 H 5
Hkyenhpa o MYA 142-143 K 2
Hlabisa o ZA 220-221 K 4
Hlebarovo = Car Kalojan o BG 102-103 E 6
Hlegu o MYA 158-159 D 2
Hlobyne o UA 102-103 H 3
Hlotse o LS 220-221 J 4
Hluchiv o UA 102-103 H 2
Hluhluwe o ZA 220-221 L 4
Hluhluwe Game Reserve ⊥ ZA 220-221 L 4
Hluthi o SD 220-221 K 3
Hlybokae o BY 94-95 K 4
Hmel'nickij = Chmel'nyc'kyj ☆ UA 102-103 E 3
Hmitevskogo, poluostrov ∪ RUS 120-121 N 4
Hnalān o IND 142-143 H 4
H. N. Andersen, Kap ▲ GRØ 26-27 r 3
Hnausa o CDN (MAN) 234-235 G 4
Hnilij Tikič ∼ UA 102-103 G 3
Ho ☆ GH 202-203 L 6
Hòa Binh o VN 158-159 J 2
Hòa Binh ☆ VN 156-157 D 6
Hoadley o CDN (ALB) 232-233 D 3
Hoài Nho'n o VN 158-159 K 3
Hoanib ∼ NAM 216-217 B 9
Hoar, Lake ⊖ AUS 176-177 G 2
Hoare Bay ≈ 36-37 S 2
Hoarusib ∼ NAM 216-217 B 9
Hoback Junction o USA (WY) 252-253 H 3
Hoba Meteorite •• NAM 216-217 D 9
Hoban o DVR 150-151 F 7
Hobart ☆ • AUS 180-181 J 7
Hobart o USA (IN) 274-275 L 3
Hobart o USA (OK) 264-265 E 3
Hobart Island ⌒ CDN 36-37 N 2
Hobbema o CDN (ALB) 232-233 E 3
Hobbs o USA (NM) 256-257 M 6
Hobbs Coast ∪ ARK 16 F 23
Hobetsu o J 152-153 K 3
Hobhouse o ZA 220-221 H 4
Hobo o CO 60-61 D 6
Hoboken o USA (GA) 284-285 H 5
Hoboksar o VRC 146-147 G 2
Hobol ∼ RUS 110-111 R 6
Hobro o DK 86-87 D 8
Hobson, Cape ▲ CDN 24-25 X 5
Hobson Lake ⊖ CDN (BC) 228-229 O 4
Hobucken o USA (NC) 282-283 L 5
Hobyo o SP 208-209 J 6
Hoceima, Al ☆ MA 188-189 K 3
Hochalmspitze ▲ A 92-93 M 5
Hochberry Draw ∼ USA (TX) 266-267 D 2
Hochfeld o NAM 216-217 D 10
Hochfield o CDN (MAN) 234-235 F 5
Hochheim o USA (TX) 266-267 K 4
Hô Chí Minh, Thành Phô = Thành Phô Hô Chí Minh ☆ •• VN 158-159 J 5
Hochstetterbugten ≈ 26-27 q 6
Hochstetter Forland ⊥ GRØ 26-27 p 6
Hockin o CDN 34-35 H 3
Hocking River ∼ USA (OH) 280-281 D 4
Hockley o USA (TX) 268-269 E 6
Hóc Môn o VN 158-159 J 5
Hočo o RUS 120-121 D 3
Hočo, Ystannah- o RUS 110-111 N 3
Hoctún o MEX 52-53 K 1
Ḥodā Āfarīn o IR 128-129 M 3
Hodal o IND 138-139 F 6
Hodar, utes • RUS 122-123 H 3
Hodgenville o USA (KY) 276-277 K 3
Hodges Gardens ∴ • USA (LA) 268-269 G 5
Hodges Hill ▲ CDN (NFL) 242-243 N 3
Hodgeville o CDN (SAS) 232-233 M 5
Hodgkins Ridge ≃ 32-33 B 5
Hodgson o CDN (MAN) 234-235 F 3
Hodgson Downs o AUS 174-175 C 4
Hodgson River ∼ AUS 174-175 C 4
Hodh ∴ RIM 196-197 F 6
Hodh ech-Chargui ◘ RIM 196-197 G 5
Hodh el-Gharbi ◘ RIM 196-197 E 6
Hodigere o IND 140-141 G 4
Hodma ∼ SP 208-209 J 4
Hódmezővásárhely o H 92-93 Q 5
Hodna, Plaine du ⊥ DZ 190-191 E 3
Hodo Dan ▲ DVR 150-151 F 8
Hō Đo'n Du'o'ng ⊖ VN 158-159 K 5
Hodonín o CZ 92-93 O 4
Hodq Shamo ∴ VRC 154-155 E 1
Hodutka, gora ▲ RUS 122-123 R 2
Hodžambas o TM 136-137 J 5
Hodzana River ∼ USA 20-21 Q 3
Hodža-Obigarm o TJ 136-137 L 5
Hodžejli = Hūdžajli ☆ • US 136-137 F 3
Hoè o RUS 122-123 K 3
Hoedspruit o ZA 220-221 K 2
Hoehne o USA (CO) 254-255 L 6
Hoë Karoo = Upper Karoo ⊥ ZA 220-221 D 5
Hoek van Holland o NL 92-93 H 3
Hoeryong o DVR 150-151 G 6
Hoëveld ⊥ ZA 220-221 J 3
Hoey o CDN (SAS) 232-233 N 3
Hoeyang o DVR 150-151 F 8
Hof o D 92-93 L 3
Höfðakaupstaður = Skagaströnd o IS 86-87 c 2
Hoffmans Cay ⌒ BS 54-55 G 2
Hofmarkt = Odorheiu Secuiesc o RO 102-103 D 4
Hofmeyr o ZA 220-221 G 5
Höfn o IS 86-87 f 2
Hofsjökull ⊂ IS 86-87 d 2
Hofsós o IS 86-87 d 2
Hōfu o J 152-153 D 7
Hōğalāk, Kūh-e ▲ IR 128-129 M 5
Höganäs o S 86-87 F 8
Hogan Group ⌒ AUS 180-181 J 5
Hogansville o USA (GA) 284-285 F 3
Hogart, Mount ▲ AUS 178-179 D 1
Hogatza River ∼ USA 20-21 N 3
Hogback Mountain ▲ USA (NE) 262-263 C 3
Hog Cay ⌒ BS 54-55 H 3
Hogeland o USA (MT) 250-251 L 3
Høgeloft ▲ N 86-87 D 6
Hogem Range ▲ CDN 32-33 G 3
Hogem Ranges ▲ CDN 32-33 G 4
Hoggar ▲ DZ 190-191 E 9
Hoggar, Tassili du ▲ DZ 190-191 E 10
Høggia ▲ N 86-87 E 5
Hog Harbor o VAN 184 II a 2
Hog Island ⌒ USA (MI) 272-273 D 2
Hog Island ⌒ USA (VA) 280-281 L 6
Hog Landing o USA 20-21 N 4
Hogsback o ZA 220-221 H 6
Högsby ☆ S 86-87 H 8
Høgtuvbreen ▲ N 86-87 F 3
Hohenstein = Olsztynek o PL 92-93 Q 2
Hohenwald o USA (TN) 276-277 H 5
Hohe Tatra = Tatry ▲ SK 92-93 P 4
Hohe Tauern ▲ A 92-93 M 5
Hohhot ☆ VRC 154-155 G 1
Hoh Indian Reservation ✕ USA (WA) 244-245 A 3
Hohoe o GH 202-203 L 6
Hoholitna River ∼ USA 20-21 M 6
Hoh Sai Hu ⊖ VRC 144-145 J 3
Hōhuku o J 152-153 D 7
Hoh Xil Hu ⊖ VRC 144-145 H 3
Hoh Xil Shan ▲ VRC 144-145 F 3
Hôi An o •• VN 158-159 K 3
Hoima o EAU 212-213 C 3
Hoisington o USA (KS) 262-263 H 6
Hoj, vozvyšennost' ▲ RUS 108-109 O 7
Hoja Wajeer o SP 212-213 H 4
Hojd Tamir gol ∼ MAU 148-149 E 4
Hoka o RI 166-167 E 5
Hokitika o NZ 182 C 5
Hokkaidō ⌒ J 152-153 K 3
Hokksund ☆ N 86-87 D 7
Hokmābād o IR 136-137 E 6
Hokua o VAN 184 II a 2
Hola o EAK 212-213 H 4
Holalagondi o IND 140-141 G 3
Holanda Rous, Reserva Florestal ⊥ RCH 80 F 7
Hola Prystan' o UA 102-103 H 4
Holbæk o DK 86-87 E 9
Holbein o CDN (SAS) 232-233 M 2
Holberg o CDN (BC) 230-231 A 3
Holberg Inlet ≈ CDN 230-231 B 3
Holbox, Isla ⌒ MEX 52-53 L 1
Holbrook o AUS 180-181 J 3
Holbrook o USA (AZ) 256-257 E 4
Holbrook o USA (ID) 252-253 F 4
Holchit, Punta ▲ MEX 52-53 K 1
Holcomb o USA (MS) 268-269 L 3
Holden o CDN (ALB) 232-233 F 2
Holden o USA (MO) 274-275 E 6
Holden o USA (UT) 254-255 C 4
Holdenville o USA (OK) 264-265 H 3
Holdfast o CDN (SAS) 232-233 N 5
Holdingford o USA (MN) 270-271 D 5
Holdman o USA (OR) 244-245 G 5
Holdrege o USA (NE) 262-263 G 4
Hold with Hope Halvø ∪ GRØ 26-27 p 7
Hole in the Wall ∴ • BS 54-55 G 2
Holejaha ∼ RUS 108-109 O 5
Holešov o CZ 92-93 O 4
Holger Danskes Tinde ▲ GRØ 26-27 n 6
Holguín ☆ C 54-55 G 4
Holhol o DJI 208-209 F 3
Holiday o USA (FL) 286-287 G 3
Holiday Resort • AUS 176-177 E 7
Holitna River ∼ USA 20-21 M 6
Hollabrunn o A 92-93 O 4
Holland o CDN (MAN) 234-235 E 5
Holland o • USA (MI) 272-273 C 5
Hollandale o USA (MS) 268-269 K 3
Hollandale o USA (WI) 274-275 J 2
Holland Bay ≈ 54-55 G 6
Hollat o RI 166-167 G 4
Holleschau = Holešov o CZ 92-93 O 4
Hollick-Kenyon Plateau ▲ ARK 16 F 26
Holliday o USA (TX) 264-265 F 5
Hollidaysburg o USA (PA) 280-281 H 3
Hollis o USA (AK) 32-33 D 4
Hollis o USA (AR) 276-277 B 6
Hollis o USA (OK) 264-265 E 4
Hollister o USA (CA) 248-249 C 3
Hollister o USA (ID) 252-253 D 4
Hollister o USA (MO) 276-277 B 4
Hollister o USA (OK) 264-265 F 4
Hollister, Mount ▲ AUS 172-173 B 7
Hollōkō o •• H 92-93 P 4
Hollow Water o CDN (MAN) 234-235 G 3
Hollow Water Indian Reserve ✕ CDN (MAN) 234-235 G 3
Holly o USA (CO) 254-255 N 5
Holly Beach o USA (LA) 268-269 G 7
Holly Bluff o USA (MS) 268-269 K 4
Holly Hill o USA (SC) 284-285 K 3
Holly Hove o USA (AR) 276-277 D 6
Holly Ridge o USA (NC) 282-283 K 6
Holly Springs o USA (AR) 276-277 C 7
Holly Springs o USA (MS) 268-269 L 2
Hollywood o USA (AR) 276-277 B 6
Hollywood o USA (FL) 286-287 J 5
Hollywood, Los Angeles- •• USA (CA) 248-249 F 5
Holm ☆ RUS 94-95 M 3
Holma o WAN 204-205 K 4
Holman Island o CDN 24-25 N 5
Hólmavík ☆ IS 86-87 c 2
Holme Park o ZA 220-221 J 2
Holmes Creek ∼ USA (FL) 286-287 D 1
Holmes Reef ⌒ AUS 174-175 J 5
Holmes River ∼ CDN (BC) 228-229 P 3
Holmfield o CDN (MAN) 234-235 D 5
Holmia o GUY 62-63 E 3
Holm Land ⊥ GRØ 26-27 q 3
Holmogorskaja o RUS 88-89 Q 5
Holmogory o RUS 88-89 Q 4
Holmsk o RUS 122-123 K 5
Holmskij o RUS 126-127 C 5
Holms Ø ⌒ GRØ 26-27 W 6
Holmsund o S 86-87 K 5
Holm-Žirkovskij o RUS 94-95 N 4
Holnicote Bay ≈ 183 E 5
Holohovčan ∼ RUS 112-113 N 5
Holoj ∼ RUS 118-119 F 9
Holokit ∼ RUS 108-109 a 7
Holomoloh-Jurjah ∼ RUS 118-119 G 4
Holoog o NAM 220-221 C 3
Holroyd River ∼ AUS 174-175 F 4
Holstebro o •• DK 86-87 D 8
Holstein o USA (IA) 274-275 C 2
Holsteinsborg = Sisimiut o GRØ 28-29 O 3
Holston Lake ⊖ USA (TN) 282-283 E 4
Holston River ∼ USA (TN) 282-283 D 4
Holston River ∼ USA (VA) 280-281 D 7
Holt o USA (AL) 284-285 C 3
Holt o USA (FL) 286-287 C 1
Holt o USA (MI) 272-273 E 5
Holter Lake ⊖ USA (MT) 250-251 H 5
Holt Lake < USA (AL) 284-285 C 3
Holton o CDN 36-37 V 7
Holton o USA (KS) 262-263 L 5
Holt Rock o AUS 176-177 E 6
Holtville o USA (CA) 248-249 J 7
Holualoa o USA (HI) 288 K 5
Holub o USA (AR) 276-277 E 6
Holuwon o RI 166-167 K 4
Holyhead o GB 90-91 E 5
Holy Island o GB 90-91 G 4
Holyoke o USA (CO) 254-255 N 3
Holyoke o USA (MA) 278-279 J 6
Holyrood o CDN (NFL) 242-243 P 5
Holyrood o USA (KS) 262-263 H 6
Holy Trinity o USA (AL) 284-285 E 4
Hom ∼ NAM 220-221 D 4
Homa Bay o EAK 212-213 E 4
Ḥomām o IR 128-129 N 4
Homand o IR 134-135 H 2
Hománe o MOC 218-219 H 6
Homathko Icefield ⊂ CDN (BC) 230-231 E 2
Homathko River ∼ CDN (BC) 230-231 E 2
Hombetsu o J 152-153 K 3
Hombori o RMM 202-203 K 2
Hombori, Monts du ▲ RMM 202-203 J 2
Hombre Muerto, Salar del ⊖ RA 76-77 D 3
Home Bay ≈ 28-29 G 2
Homedale o USA (ID) 252-253 B 3
Homefield o CDN (SAS) 232-233 P 4
Home Hill o AUS 174-175 J 6
Ḥomein o IR 134-135 D 2
Homel' ☆ BY 94-95 M 5
Home of Bullion Mine • AUS 178-179 C 1
Homer o USA (AK) 22-23 V 3
Homer o USA (IA) 274-275 E 2
Homer o USA (IL) 274-275 L 4
Homer o USA (LA) 268-269 G 4
Homer Tunnel ▲ NZ 182 A 6
Homerville o USA (GA) 284-285 H 5
Homestead o AUS 174-175 H 7
Homestead o USA (FL) 286-287 J 6
Homestead National Monument ∴ USA (NE) 262-263 K 4
Homewood o USA (AL) 284-285 D 3
Homi, hrebet ▲ RUS 122-123 H 3
Hominy o USA (OK) 264-265 H 2
Homnābād o IND 140-141 G 2
Homo, Cerro el ▲ HN 52-53 L 4
Homochitto River ∼ USA (MS) 268-269 J 5
Homodji < RN 198-199 F 4
Homolha o RUS 118-119 G 6
Homolho ∼ RUS 118-119 H 6
Homonhon Island ⌒ RP 160-161 F 7
Homosassa Springs o USA (FL) 286-287 G 3
Homot Tohadar, Ğabal ▲ SUD 200-201 H 3
Homutah o RUS 118-119 P 4
Homyel' = Homel' ☆ BY 94-95 M 5
Honaunau o USA (HI) 288 K 5
Honāvar o IND 140-141 F 3
Honaz Dağ ▲ TR 128-129 C 4
Honda o CO 60-61 D 5
Honda, Chott El ⊖ DZ 190-191 E 3
Honda, Monts du ▲ DZ 190-191 E 3
Honda Bay ≈ 160-161 C 8
Hòn Đất o VN 158-159 H 5
Hondeklipbaai o ZA 220-221 C 5
Hondo ∼ C 54-55 D 3
Hondo o J 152-153 D 8
Hondo o USA (NM) 256-257 K 5
Hondo o USA (TX) 266-267 H 4
Hondo, Rio ∼ USA (NM) 256-257 K 5
Hondo Creek ∼ USA (TX) 266-267 H 4
Hondo River ∼ BH 52-53 K 3
Honduras ■ HN 52-53 K 4
Honduras, Cabo de ▲ HN 52-53 L 3
Hone o CDN 34-35 F 2
Honea Path o USA (SC) 284-285 H 2
Hønefoss ☆ N 86-87 E 6
Honey Harbour o CDN 36-37 O 2
Honesdale o USA (PA) 280-281 L 2
Honey Grove o USA (TX) 264-265 J 5
Honey Lake ⊖ USA (CA) 246-247 E 3
Honeymoon Bay o CDN (BC) 230-231 E 5
Ḥonğ o IR 134-135 E 5
Hong'an o VRC 154-155 J 6
Hongch'ŏn o ROK 150-151 F 9
Hongde o VRC 154-155 E 3
Hong Do ⌒ ROK 150-151 E 10
Hongdong o VRC 154-155 G 3
Hongfeng Hu ⊖ VRC 156-157 E 3
Hong Gai ☆ VN 156-157 E 6
Honggun-ri o DVR 150-151 G 7
Hongguqu o VRC 154-155 C 3
Honghu o VRC 156-157 H 2
Hong Hu ⊖ VRC 156-157 H 2
Hongjiang o VRC 156-157 F 3
Hong Kong = Xianggang ◘ HK 156-157 J 5
Hongliuyuan o VRC (GAN) 146-147 M 5
Hongliuyuan o VRC (GAN) 154-155 B 2
Hongmen o VRC 156-157 K 2
Hongmenhe o VRC 154-155 F 5
Hông Ngu' o VN 158-159 H 5
Hòn Gŏm, B. D. ⌒ VN 158-159 K 4
Hongor o MAU (DOG) 148-149 K 5
Hongor o MAU (SUH) 148-149 L 5
Hongshan o VRC 154-155 H 6
Hongshishan o VRC 148-149 C 6
Hongshui He ∼ VRC 156-157 E 5
Hongū o J 152-153 F 8
Honguedo, Détroit d' ≈ CDN 242-243 D 3
Hongwei o VRC 156-157 K 2
Hongwon o DVR 150-151 F 7
Hongya o VRC 156-157 C 2
Hongyuan o VRC 154-155 C 5
Hongze o VRC 154-155 L 5
Hongze Hu ⊖ VRC 154-155 L 5
Hongzhi Liang ▲ VRC 154-155 F 4
Honi o GE 126-127 E 6
Honiara ★ • SOL 184 I d 3
Honiton o GB 90-91 F 6
Honjō o J 152-153 J 5
Honkawane o J 152-153 H 7
Hon Minh Hoa ⌒ VN 158-159 J 5
Honnali o IND 140-141 F 3
Honningsvåg o N 86-87 M 1
Honobia o USA (OK) 264-265 K 4
Honohina o USA (HI) 288 K 5
Honokaa o USA (HI) 288 K 4
Honokahua o USA (HI) 288 J 4
Honolulu ☆ • USA (HI) 288 H 3
Honoria o PE 64-65 E 6
Hon Rái ⌒ VN 158-159 H 6
Honshū ⌒ J 152-153 E 7
Hòn Thị, Mũi ▲ VN 158-159 K 4
Hontorbé o SN 202-203 D 2
Honuu ☆ RUS 110-111 Y 6
Hood, Fort ✕✕ USA (TX) 266-267 K 2
Hood, Mount ▲ USA 244-245 D 5
Hood Bay ≈ 183 D 6
Hood Canal ∼ USA (WA) 244-245 B 3
Hood Point ▲ AUS 176-177 E 7
Hood River ∼ CDN 30-31 P 2
Hood River o USA (OR) 244-245 D 5
Hoodsport o USA (WA) 244-245 B 3
Hoogeveen o NL 92-93 J 2
Hooker o USA (OK) 264-265 C 2
Hooker Creek Aboriginal Land ✕ AUS 172-173 K 5
Hook Island ⌒ AUS 174-175 K 7
Hook Point ▲ CDN 34-35 P 3
Hool o MEX 52-53 J 2
Hoonah o USA 32-33 C 2
Hoopa o USA (CA) 246-247 B 2
Hoopa Valley Indian Reservation ✕ USA (CA) 246-247 B 2
Hooper o USA (CO) 254-255 K 6
Hooper o USA (NE) 262-263 K 3
Hooper o USA (WA) 244-245 G 4
Hooper, Cape ▲ CDN 28-29 G 2
Hooper Bay ≈ 20-21 G 6
Hooper Bay o USA 20-21 G 6
Hooper Inlet ≈ 24-25 f 6
Hooper Point ▲ CDN (BC) 228-229 D 2
Hooper Strait ≈ USA 280-281 K 5
Hopeston o USA (IL) 274-275 L 4
Hooping Harbour o CDN (NFL) 242-243 M 2
Hoople o USA (ND) 258-259 K 3
Hoop Nature Reserve, De ⊥ ZA 220-221 E 7
Hoopstad o ZA 220-221 G 3
Hoosick Falls o USA (NY) 278-279 H 6
Hoosier o CDN (SAS) 232-233 J 4
Hoover o USA (TX) 264-265 D 3
Hoover Dam < • USA (NV) 248-249 K 3
Hoover Reservoir ⊖ USA (OH) 280-281 D 3
Hopa ☆ TR 128-129 J 2
Ho-pang o MYA 142-143 L 4
Hope o CDN (BC) 230-231 H 4
Hope < NAM 220-221 C 3
Hope o USA (AK) 20-21 Q 6
Hope o USA (AR) 276-277 B 7
Hope o USA (ID) 250-251 C 3
Hope o USA (IN) 274-275 N 5
Hope o USA (ND) 258-259 K 4
Hope o USA (NM) 256-257 L 6
Hope, Cape ▲ CDN 24-25 O 6
Hope, Kap = Ittaajimmiit o GRØ 26-27 o 8
Hope, Lake ⊖ AUS 176-177 F 6
Hope, Mount o AUS 180-181 H 2
Hope Campbell Lake ⊖ AUS 176-177 G 4
Hopefield o ZA 220-221 D 6
Hopeful o USA (GA) 284-285 F 5
Hope Island ⌒ CDN (ONT) 238-239 E 4
Hopelchén o • MEX 52-53 K 2
Hopeless, Mount ▲ AUS 178-179 E 5
Hope Mills o USA (NC) 282-283 J 6
Hopen o N (ROM) 86-87 D 5
Hopen ⌒ N (SVA) 84-85 O 4
Hopenbanken ≃ 84-85 P 4
Hopen Radio o N 84-85 O 4
Hope or Panda, Lake ⊖ AUS 178-179 E 5
Hoper ∼ RUS 94-95 S 5
Hoper ∼ RUS 102-103 N 2
Hope River ∼ AUS 176-177 E 3
Hopes Advance Bay ≈ 36-37 P 5
Hopeton o USA (OK) 264-265 E 2
Hopetoun o AUS (VIC) 180-181 G 3
Hopetoun o AUS (WA) 176-177 F 6
Hopetown o CDN (ONT) 238-239 J 3
Hopetown o ZA 220-221 G 4
Hope Vale ✕ AUS 174-175 H 4
Hope Vale Aboriginal Land ✕ AUS 174-175 H 4
Hopewell o USA (VA) 280-281 J 6
Hopewell Cape o CDN (NB) 240-241 L 5
Hopewell Islands ⌒ CDN 36-37 K 5
Hô Phú Ninh ⊖ VN 158-159 K 3
Hopi Buttes ▲ USA (AZ) 256-257 E 3
Hopi Indian Reservation ✕ USA (AZ) 256-257 E 2
Hopin o MYA 142-143 K 3
Hopkins o USA (MO) 274-275 D 4
Hopkins, Lake ⊖ AUS 176-177 K 2
Hopkinsville o USA (KY) 276-277 H 4
Hopland o USA (CA) 246-247 B 5
Ho-pong o MYA 142-143 K 5
Hoppner Inlet ≈ 24-25 e 7
Hopton Lake ⊖ CDN 30-31 V 5
Hoque o ANG 216-217 B 7
Hoquiam o USA (WA) 244-245 B 4
Hor ∼ RUS 122-123 F 5
Horace Mount ▲ USA 20-21 Q 3
Horana o CL 140-141 J 7
Ḥorāsān ◘ IR 134-135 G 2
Horasan ☆ TR 128-129 K 2
Horatio o USA (AR) 276-277 A 7
Horbusuonka ∼ RUS 110-111 P 4
Hörby o S 86-87 F 9
Horcajo de los Montes o E 98-99 E 5
Horcones, Río ∼ RA 76-77 E 3
Horden, Lac ⊖ CDN (ONT) 236-237 L 2
Horden River ∼ PNG 183 A 2
Hor'dil Sar'dag ▲ MAU 148-149 D 2
Hordogoj o RUS 118-119 G 4
Horej-Ver o RUS 88-89 Y 3
Horezmskaja oblast' ◘ US 136-137 G 4
Horezu • RO 102-103 C 5
Horgo o MAU 148-149 D 3
Horgoččuma ∼ RUS 110-111 N 7
Horicon o USA (WI) 274-275 K 1
Horicon National Wildlife Refuge ⊥ USA (WI) 274-275 K 1
Horincy o RUS 118-119 K 5
Horinger o VRC 154-155 G 1
Horinsk ☆ RUS 118-119 D 9
Horizontina o BR 76-77 K 4
Horki ☆ BY 94-95 M 4
Horlick Mountains ▲ ARK 16 E 0
Horlivka o UA 102-103 L 3
Horlog Hu ∼ VRC 144-145 L 2
Hormigas, Las o PE 70-71 C 3
Hormoz o IR 134-135 F 5
Hormoz, Ğazire-ye ⌒ IR 134-135 G 5
Hormoz, Kūh-e ▲ IR 134-135 F 5
Hormozgān ◘ IR 134-135 F 5
Hormūd o IR 134-135 F 5
Hormuz, Strait of = Hormoz, Tange-ye ≈ 134-135 G 5
Horn, The ▲ AUS 180-181 J 4
Horn, Van o USA (TX) 266-267 C 2
Horna o RI 166-167 G 2
Hornachos o E 98-99 D 5
Hornaday River ∼ CDN 24-25 K 6
Hornavan ⊖ S 86-87 H 3
Hornbjarg ▲ IS 86-87 b 1
Hornby Bay ⊖ CDN 30-31 L 2
Hornby Island o CDN (BC) 230-231 E 4
Horncocitos o PA 52-53 C 7
Horndal o S 86-87 H 6
Horndean o CDN (MAN) 234-235 F 5
Hornell o USA (NY) 278-279 D 6
Hornell Lake ⊖ CDN 30-31 K 4
Hornepayne o CDN (ONT) 236-237 D 3
Hornillos, Punta ▲ PE 70-71 A 5
Horn Island ⌒ AUS 174-175 G 2
Horn Island ⌒ USA (MS) 268-269 M 6
Horn Mountains ▲ USA 20-21 L 6
Horno Islands ⌒ PNG 183 D 2
Hornos, Caleta los ≈ 76-77 B 5
Horn Plateau ▲ CDN 30-31 J 4
Horn River ∼ CDN 30-31 K 4
Hornsby o AUS 180-181 L 2
Hornslandet ⊥ S 86-87 H 6
Hornsund ≈ 84-85 J 4
Hornsundtind ▲ N 84-85 K 4
Horodnja o UA 102-103 G 2
Horodok ☆ UA 102-103 C 3
Horog ☆ TJ 136-137 M 6
Horol' o RUS 122-123 E 6
Horombe ▲ RM 222-223 D 9
Horošee ozero ⊖ RUS 124-125 L 2
Horoshiri-dake ▲ J 152-153 K 3
Horowupotana o CL 140-141 J 6
Horqin Youji Zhongqi o VRC 150-151 C 5
Horqin Zuoyi Houqi o VRC 150-151 D 6
Horqueta o PY 76-77 J 2
Horqueta, La o YV (BOL) 62-63 D 2
Horqueta, La o YV (DAM) 60-61 K 3
Horquetas, Las o CR 52-53 C 6
Ḥorramābād ☆ • IR 134-135 C 2
Ḥorram Darre o IR 128-129 N 4
Ḥorramšahr o • IR 134-135 C 3
Horrocks o AUS 176-177 C 4
Horru o VRC 144-145 J 5
Horsburgh Atoll ⌒ MV 140-141 B 5
Horse (Saint Barbe) Islands ⌒ CDN (NFL) 242-243 N 2
Horse Creek o USA (WY) 252-253 N 5
Horse Creek ∼ USA (CO) 254-255 M 5
Horse Creek ∼ USA (FL) 286-287 H 4
Horse Creek ∼ USA (GA) 284-285 G 5
Horse Creek ∼ USA (MO) 276-277 A 3
Horse Creek ∼ USA (WY) 252-253 O 5
Horsefly o CDN (BC) 228-229 N 4
Horsefly Lake ⊖ CDN (BC) 228-229 N 4
Horsefly River ∼ CDN (BC) 228-229 N 4
Horse Gap ▲ USA (NC) 282-283 F 4
Horsens o DK 86-87 D 9
Horse River ∼ CDN 32-33 P 3
Horseshoe Bay o CDN (ALB) 32-33 P 4
Horseshoe Bay o CDN (BC) 230-231 F 4
Horseshoe Bay ≈ USA 286-287 F 2
Horseshoe Beach o USA (FL) 286-287 F 2
Horseshoe Bend o USA (ID) 252-253 B 3
Horseshoe Bend National Military Park • USA (AL) 284-285 E 4
Horsham o • AUS 180-181 G 4
Horsham o CDN (SAS) 232-233 J 5
Horten ☆ N 86-87 E 7
Hortense o USA (GA) 284-285 J 5
Hortensias, Las o RCH 78-79 C 5
Horti o IND 140-141 F 2
Hortobágy o H 92-93 Q 5
Hortobágyi Nemzeti Park ⊥ H 92-93 Q 5
Horton o USA (KS) 262-263 L 5
Horton Bay o USA (MI) 272-273 D 2
Horton Lake ⊖ CDN 30-31 H 2
Horton River ∼ CDN 24-25 K 6
Horumnug-Tajga, hrebet ▲ RUS 116-117 G 10
Horuongka ∼ RUS 110-111 O 6
Horus, Temple of ∴ • ET 194-195 F 5
Horwood Lake ⊖ CDN (ONT) 236-237 F 5
Horyn' ∼ UA 102-103 D 3
Horyn' ∼ UA 102-103 E 2
Horyuji ••• J 152-153 F 7
Hosab Kalesi • TR 128-129 K 3
Hoşab Kalesi • TR 128-129 K 3
Hosahalli o IND 140-141 F 4
Hosa'ina o ETH 208-209 C 5
Hosakote o IND 140-141 G 3
Hos-Alas o RUS 110-111 S 6
Ḥosāmand o AFG 138-139 B 3
Hosanagara o IND 140-141 F 4
Hosato, ozero ⊖ RUS 108-109 T 6
Hosdrug o IND 140-141 F 4
Hosdurga o IND 140-141 G 4
Hose, Pegunungan ▲ MAL 162-163 K 3
Hosedaju ∼ RUS 108-109 H 8
Hoseinābād o IR 128-129 M 5
Hoseinābād o IR 134-135 J 3
Hoseinābād, Rūdḫāne-ye ∼ IR 134-135 J 3
Hoseiniye-ye Ḥoda Dād o IR 134-135 C 2
Hoselaw o CDN 32-33 P 4
Hošeutovo o RUS 96-97 E 10
Hosford o USA (FL) 286-287 E 1
Hoshāb o PK 134-135 K 5
Hoshangābād o IND 138-139 F 8
Hoshiārpur o IND 138-139 E 4
Hoshib ∼ SUD 200-201 G 3
Ḥōsī o AFG 138-139 B 2
Hoska ∼ RUS 110-111 c 6
Hoskins o PNG 183 F 3
Hoskins o USA (NE) 262-263 J 2
Hoskote o IND 140-141 G 4
Hosmer o CDN (BC) 230-231 P 4
Hōšōōt o MAU 146-147 J 1
Hospah o USA (NM) 256-257 H 3
Ḥospās Rūd ∼ AFG 134-135 K 3
Hospet o IND 140-141 G 3
Hospicia o PE 70-71 B 6
Hospicio o PE 70-71 B 5
Hospital, Cuchilla del ▲ ROU 78-79 M 2
Ḥosrovī o IR 134-135 A 1
Hosrovskij zapovednik ⊥ AR 128-129 L 2
Ḥōst o AFG 138-139 B 3
Hoste, Isla ⌒ RCH 80 F 7
Hostomel' o UA 102-103 G 2
Hosūr o IND 140-141 G 4
Ḥōš Yeilāg o IR 136-137 D 6
Hot o THA 142-143 L 6
Hotaka-dake ▲ J 152-153 G 6
Hotamış Gölü ⊖ TR 128-129 E 4
Hotan o VRC 144-145 B 2
Hotan He ∼ VRC 146-147 E 6
Hotazel o ZA 220-221 F 3
Ḥotbe Sarā o IR 128-129 N 3
Hotchkiss o CDN 32-33 M 3
Hotchkiss o USA (CO) 254-255 H 5
Hotchkiss River ∼ CDN 32-33 M 3
Hotel dos Manantiales o RA 80 F 4
Hotel el Cerrito o RA 80 E 5
Hotel las Horquetas o RA 80 E 4
Hotel Río Negro o PY 76-77 H 3
Hotevilla o USA (AZ) 256-257 E 3
Hô Thác Bà < VN 156-157 D 6
Hotham, Cape ▲ AUS 172-173 K 2
Hotham, Cape ▲ CDN 24-25 Z 3
Hotham Inlet ≈ 20-21 J 3
Hotham River ∼ AUS 176-177 D 6
Hotmin Mission o PNG 183 A 3
Hotoho ∼ RUS 118-119 F 5
Hotpaas o RI 166-167 D 5
Hot Springs o USA (NC) 282-283 E 5
Hot Springs o USA (SD) 260-261 C 3
Hot Springs o • USA (AR) 276-277 B 6
Hot Springs • USA (CA) 246-247 E 6
Hot Springs • USA (OR) 244-245 E 8
Hot Springs o ZW 218-219 G 4
Hot Springs, Cove • USA (OR) 244-245 H 5
Hot Springs Cove o CDN (BC) 230-231 C 4
Hot Springs National Park ⊥ USA (AR) 276-277 B 6
Hot Springs Village o USA (AR) 276-277 B 6
Hotspur Seamount ≃ 72-73 M 4
Hot Sulphur Springs o USA (CO) 254-255 J 3
Hottah Lake ⊖ CDN 30-31 K 3
Hottentotsbaai ≈ 220-221 B 3
Hottentotskloof o ZA 220-221 D 6
Hot Water Beach • NZ 182 E 2
Hot Wells o USA (TX) 266-267 C 3
Houègbo o DY 204-205 E 5
Houeïriye o RIM 196-197 G 6
Houghton o USA (NY) 278-279 C 6
Houghton o USA (WI) 270-271 K 3
Houghton Lake o USA (MI) 272-273 E 3
Houghton Lake ⊖ USA (MI) 272-273 E 3
Houhai o VRC 156-157 G 6
Houhora o NZ 182 D 1
Houhu o VRC 156-157 G 6
Houlton o USA (ME) 278-279 O 2
Houma o TON 184 IV a 2
Houma o USA (LA) 268-269 K 7
Houma o VRC 154-155 G 4
Houmt Souk o TN 190-191 H 4
Houndé o • BF 202-203 J 4
Hounien, Zorus- o CI 202-203 F 6
Hourtin et de Carcans, Lac d' ⊖ F 90-91 G 9
Housatonic River ∼ USA (CT) 280-281 N 2
House o USA (NM) 256-257 M 4
Housholder Pass ▲ USA (AZ) 256-257 A 3
Houshui Wan ≈ 156-157 F 7
Houston o CDN (BC) 228-229 H 2
Houston o USA (AK) 20-21 Q 6
Houston o USA (MN) 270-271 G 7
Houston o USA (MO) 276-277 D 3
Houston o USA (MS) 268-269 M 3
Houston o • USA (TX) 268-269 E 7
Houston, Lake < USA (TX) 268-269 E 6
Houston Co. Lake < USA (TX) 268-269 E 5
Houston Point ▲ CDN 34-35 Q 4
Houston River ∼ USA (LA) 268-269 G 6
Houtman Abrolhos ⌒ AUS 176-177 B 4
Houton Island ⌒ CDN (NS) 240-241 L 7
Houxia o VRC 146-147 H 4
Houz-e Soltān o IR 134-135 D 1
Hova o S 86-87 G 7
Hovd o MAU (ÖVÖ) 148-149 F 5
Hovd ◘ MAU 146-147 L 2

Hindiktig-Hol', ozero — Hovd 337

Hovd ☆ MAU 146-147 K 1
Hovden o N 86-87 C 7
Hovd gol ~ MAU 146-147 K 1
Hoveize o IR 134-135 C 3
Hoven o USA (SD) 260-261 G 1
Hovenweep National Monument ∴ USA (UT) 254-255 F 6
Hoverla, hora ▲ UA 102-103 D 3
Hovgaards Ø ⌒ GRØ 26-27 q 4
Hovland o USA (MN) 270-271 H 3
Hovoro o SOL 184 I c 3
Hövsgöl □ MAU 148-149 D 3
Hövsgöl nuur ⊖ MAU 148-149 E 2
Hovu-Aksy o RUS 116-117 F 10
Howakil ⌒ ER 200-201 K 5
Howakil Bay ≈ 200-201 K 5
Howard o USA (KS) 262-263 K 7
Howard o USA (SD) 260-261 J 2
Howard o USA (WI) 270-271 K 6
Howard City o USA (MI) 272-273 D 4
Howard Island ⌒ AUS 174-175 C 3
Howard Junction o NZ 182 D 4
Howard Lake ⊖ CDN 30-31 Q 4
Howard Lake o USA (MN) 270-271 D 5
Howards Creek ~ USA (TX) 266-267 F 3
Howard Springs o • AUS 172-173 K 2
Howe o USA (ID) 252-253 F 3
Howe, Cape ▲ AUS 180-181 K 6
Howell o USA (MI) 272-273 F 5
Howell o USA (UT) 254-255 C 2
Howells o USA (NE) 262-263 K 3
Howes o USA (SD) 260-261 D 2
Howe Sound ≈ 32-33 J 7
Howe Sound ≈ CDN 230-231 F 4
Howick o ZA 220-221 K 4
Howick Group ⌒ AUS 174-175 H 4
Howitt, Lake ⊖ AUS 178-179 E 4
Howland o USA (ME) 278-279 N 3
Howley o CDN (NFL) 242-243 L 3
Howlong o AUS 180-181 J 3
Howser o CDN (BC) 230-231 N 3
Howship, Mount ▲ AUS 174-175 B 3
Hoxie o USA (AR) 276-277 E 4
Hoxie o USA (KS) 262-263 F 5
Hoxtolgay o VRC 146-147 H 2
Hoxud o VRC 146-147 H 4
Höy o • IR 128-129 L 3
Høyanger ☆ N 86-87 C 6
Hoyé, Bin- o CI 202-203 F 6
Hoyerswerda o D 92-93 N 3
Høylandet o N 86-87 F 4
Hoyo, Mont ▲ ZRE 212-213 C 3
Hoyt o USA (CO) 254-255 L 4
Hoyt Lakes o USA (MN) 270-271 F 3
Hozier Islands ⌒ CDN 36-37 R 2
Hpangpai o MYA 142-143 L 4
Hpawngtut o MYA 142-143 K 3
Hradec Králové o CZ 92-93 N 3
Hradyz'k o UA 102-103 H 3
Hrami ~ GE 126-127 F 7
Hrebinka o UA 102-103 H 2
Hrebtovaja gora ▲ RUS 122-123 R 2
Hristais o BR 68-69 J 4
Hrodna ☆ BY 94-95 H 5
Hroma ~ RUS 110-111 Z 4
Hromskaja guba ≈ 110-111 Z 4
Hromtau ☆ KA 126-127 N 2
Hron ~ SK 92-93 P 4
Hrubieszów o PL 92-93 R 3
Hsenwi o MYA 142-143 K 4
Hsinchu o RC 156-157 M 4
Hsingying o RC 156-157 M 5
Hsipaw o MYA 142-143 K 4
Hsuen Shan ▲ RC 156-157 M 4
Htingu o MYA 142-143 K 3
Hua'an o VRC 156-157 K 4
Huab ~ NAM 216-217 C 9
Huabuzhen o VRC 156-157 L 2
Huaca o EC 64-65 D 1
Huacalera o RA 76-77 E 2
Huacaña o PE 64-65 E 9
Huacas, Las ∴ CR 52-53 B 6
Huacaya o BOL 70-71 F 7
Huacaya, Río ~ BOL 76-77 F 1
Huacaybamba o PE 64-65 D 6
Huachacalla o BOL 70-71 C 6
Huachi o VRC 154-155 E 3
Huachi, Lago ⊖ BOL 70-71 F 4
Huacho o PE 64-65 D 7
Huachos o PE 64-65 E 8
Huachuca City o USA (AZ) 256-257 E 7
Huacrachuco o PE 64-65 D 6
Huacullani o PE 70-71 C 5
Huade o VRC 148-149 M 7
Huadian o VRC 150-151 F 6
Huaguang Jiao ⌒ VRC 158-159 L 2
Huahaizi o VRC 146-147 M 6
Hua Hin o THA 158-159 E 4
Huahua, Río = Río Wawa ~ NIC 52-53 B 4
Huaiá-Miçu, Rio ~ BR 68-69 B 7
Huai'an o VRC (HEB) 154-155 J 1
Huai'an o VRC (JIA) 154-155 L 5
Huaibei o VRC 154-155 K 5
Huaibin o VRC 154-155 J 5
Huai He ~ VRC 154-155 K 5
Huaihua o VRC 156-157 F 3
Huaiji o VRC 156-157 H 5
Huailai o VRC 154-155 J 1
Huaillas, Cerro ▲ BOL 70-71 D 5
Huai Na o THA 158-159 F 2
Huainan o VRC 154-155 K 5
Huairen o VRC 154-155 H 2
Huaiyang o VRC 154-155 J 5
Huaiyin o VRC 154-155 L 5
Huai Yot o THA 158-159 E 7
Huaiyuan o VRC 154-155 K 5
Huajialing o VRC 154-155 D 4
Huajianzi o VRC 150-151 E 7
Huajuapan o MEX 50-51 G 5
Huajuapan de León o • MEX 52-53 F 3
Huaki o • RI 166-167 D 5
Hualalai ▲ USA (HI) 288 K 5
Hualapai Indian Reservation ⅄ USA (AZ) 256-257 B 3
Hualapai Mountain Park ⊥ • USA (AZ) 256-257 B 3
Hualapai Mountains ▲ USA (AZ) 256-257 B 4
Hualiangting SK ~ VRC 154-155 J 6
Hualien o RC 156-157 M 5
Huallaga, Río ~ PE 64-65 D 6
Huallanca o PE 64-65 D 6
Hualong o VRC 154-155 C 3
Huamachuco o PE 64-65 C 5
Huamali o PE 64-65 E 7
Huamani o PE 64-65 E 8
Huamantla o MEX 52-53 F 2
Huambo □ ANG 216-217 C 6
Huambo ☆ ANG (HBO) 216-217 C 6
Huambo o PE 64-65 F 9
Huamboya o EC 64-65 C 2
Huampami o PE 64-65 C 4
Huamuxtitlán o MEX 52-53 E 3
Huañamarca o PE 70-71 A 5
Huanan o VRC 150-151 H 4
Huancabamba o PE 64-65 C 4
Huancabamba, Río ~ PE 64-65 C 4
Huancacho, Sierra ▲ RA 78-79 D 7
Huancane o PE 70-71 C 4
Huancano o PE 64-65 E 8
Huancapallac o PE 64-65 D 6
Huanca Sancos o PE 64-65 E 8
Huancavelica ☆ PE 64-65 E 8
Huancayo ☆ • PE 64-65 E 8
Huanchaca, Cerro ▲ BOL 70-71 D 7
Huanchaca, Parque Nacional ⊥ BOL 70-71 G 4
Huanchon o PE 64-65 E 7
Huangcangyu • VRC 154-155 K 5
Huangchuan o VRC 154-155 J 5
Huangda Yang ~ VRC 154-155 N 6
Huangdi Ling • VRC 154-155 F 4
Huanggang o VRC 154-155 J 6
Huanggangliang ▲ VRC 148-149 N 6
Huanggang Shan ▲ VRC 156-157 K 3
Huangguoshu Pubu • VRC 156-157 D 3
Huang He ~ VRC 154-155 G 3
Huanghe Kou ≈ 154-155 L 3
Huanghua o VRC 154-155 K 2
Huanglianyu ▲ VRC 156-157 K 4
Huangling o VRC 154-155 F 4
Huanglong o VRC 154-155 F 4
Huanglonggong ••• VRC 154-155 M 6
Huanglong Si • VRC 154-155 C 5
Huangmei o VRC 154-155 J 6
Huangpi o VRC 154-155 J 6
Huangping o VRC 156-157 E 3
Huangqi Hai ⊖ VRC 154-155 H 1
Huangsha o VRC 156-157 L 3
Huangshan o • VRC (ANH) 156-157 L 2
Huangshan ••• VRC (ANH) 154-155 L 6
Huangshi o VRC 154-155 J 6
Huang Shui ~ VRC 154-155 C 3
Huangtu Gaoyuan ⌒ VRC 154-155 E 3
Huangyaguan • VRC 154-155 K 1
Huangyan o VRC 156-157 M 2
Huangyuan o VRC 154-155 B 3
Huangzhong o VRC 154-155 B 3
Huaninaoyuan o VRC 156-157 G 3
Huaning o VRC 156-157 C 4
Huaniqueo o MEX 52-53 D 2
Huanquelén o RA 78-79 J 4
Huanquer o RA 76-77 G 6
Huanren o VRC 150-151 E 7
Huanta o PE 64-65 E 8
Huantacareo o MEX 52-53 D 2
Huantraico, Sierra del ▲ RA 78-79 E 4
Huanuco ☆ PE 64-65 D 6
Huanuni o BOL 70-71 D 6
Huanusco o MEX 50-51 H 7
Huan Xian o VRC 154-155 E 3
Huanza o PE 64-65 D 7
Huanzo, Cordillera de ▲ PE 64-65 F 9
Huapí, Serranías ▲ NIC 52-53 B 5
Huaping o VRC 156-157 B 3
Huaping Yü ⌒ RC 156-157 M 4
Huaping Z.B. ⊥ • VRC 156-157 F 4
Huaqiao o VRC 154-155 E 6
Huaqingchi • VRC 154-155 F 4
Huaquén o RCH 78-79 D 2
Huaquillas o EC 64-65 B 3
Huara o RCH 70-71 C 7
Huaral o PE 64-65 D 7
Huaraz ☆ PE 64-65 D 6
Huari o PE 64-65 D 6
Huarina o BOL 70-71 C 5
Huarmey o PE 64-65 C 7
Huarochirí o PE 64-65 D 8
Huarocondo o PE 64-65 F 8
Huarong o VRC 156-157 H 2
Huarquehue, Parque Nacional ⊥ RCH 78-79 D 5
Huasabas o MEX 50-51 E 3
Huasaga o EC 64-65 D 3
Huasago, Río ~ PE 64-65 D 3
Hua Sai o THA 158-159 F 6
Huascarán, Parque Nacional ⊥ ••• PE 64-65 D 6
Huasco o RCH 76-77 B 5
Huasco, Río ~ RCH 76-77 B 5
Huasco, Salar de ⊖ RCH 70-71 C 7
Huashan o VRC (GXI) 156-157 F 4
Huashan • VRC (SXI) 154-155 G 4
Huashan-Yabihua • VRC 156-157 E 6
Huashaoying o VRC 154-155 J 1
Huashixia o VRC 144-145 M 3
Huata, Península de ⌒ BOL 70-71 C 5
Huatabampo o MEX 50-51 E 4
Huatugou o VRC 146-147 K 6
Huatunas, Lago ⊖ BOL 70-71 E 3
Huatusco de Chicuellar o MEX 52-53 F 2
Huaura, Río ~ PE 64-65 D 7
Huautla o MEX 50-51 K 7
Huautla de Jiménez o MEX 52-53 F 2
Huaxi • VRC 156-157 E 3
Hua Xian o VRC (GDG) 156-157 H 5
Hua Xian o VRC (HEN) 154-155 J 4
Huayabamba, Río ~ PE 64-65 D 5
Huayacocotla o MEX 52-53 E 1
Huaying o VRC (SIC) 154-155 E 6
Huaying o VRC (SXI) 154-155 F 4
Huayllacayan o PE 64-65 D 7
Huayllay o PE 64-65 D 7
Huaynamota, Río ~ MEX 50-51 G 6
Huaytiquina o RA 76-77 D 2
Huayuan o VRC 156-157 F 2
Huayucachi o PE 64-65 E 8
Huayuri, Pampa de ⌒ PE 64-65 E 9
Huazhou o VRC 156-157 G 6
Hubar, al- o KSA 134-135 D 5
Hubayah, Bi'r < LAR 192-193 K 2
Huib-Hochplato ⌒ NAM 220-221 C 3
Hubbard o CDN (SAS) 232-233 P 4
Hubbard o USA (IA) 274-275 E 2
Hubbard o USA (TX) 266-267 L 2
Hubbard, Mount ▲ CDN 20-21 V 6
Hubbard, Pointe ▲ CDN 36-37 Q 5
Hubbard Creek Reservoir ⊖ USA (TX) 264-265 E 6
Hubbard Glacier ⊂ CDN 20-21 V 6
Hubbard Lake o USA (MI) 272-273 F 3
Hubbard Lake ⊖ USA (MI) 272-273 F 3
Hubbards o CDN (NS) 240-241 L 6
Hub Chauki o PK 134-135 M 6
Hub City o USA (WI) 274-275 H 1
Hubei □ VRC 154-155 G 6
Hubli o IND 140-141 F 3
Hubynycha o UA 102-103 J 3
Hucal o RA 78-79 G 4
Hucal, Valle de ⌒ RA 78-79 G 4
Hučeto, ozero ⊖ RUS 108-109 S 6
Huckitta o AUS 178-179 C 2
Huckitta Creek ~ AUS 178-179 C 2
Huckitta Out Station o AUS 178-179 C 2
Hudaida, al- o Y 132-133 C 6
Hudan, Wādī ~ ET 194-195 G 6
Hudan ~ RUS 118-119 E 10
Hudat = Xudat o AZ 128-129 N 2
Huddersfield o GB 90-91 G 5
Hudgin Creek ~ USA (AR) 276-277 D 7
Hūdi o SUD 200-201 G 4
Hudie Quan • VRC 142-143 M 2
Hudiksvall o S 86-87 H 6
Hud Mount ▲ USA 20-21 T 3
Hudosej ~ RUS 114-115 S 2
Hudra, Wādī ~ Y 132-133 F 5
Hudson o CDN (ONT) 234-235 L 4
Hudson o USA (CO) 254-255 L 3
Hudson o USA (FL) 286-287 G 3
Hudson o USA (IA) 274-275 F 2
Hudson o USA (MD) 280-281 K 5
Hudson o USA (MI) 272-273 E 6
Hudson o USA (NY) 278-279 H 6
Hudson o USA (TX) 268-269 F 5
Hudson o USA (WI) 270-271 F 6
Hudson, Cerro ▲ RCH 80 D 3
Hudson, Lake ⊖ USA (OK) 264-265 J 2
Hudson Bay ≈ 34-35 N 2
Hudson Bay o CDN (SAS) 232-233 Q 3
Hudson Canyon ≃ 46-47 M 6
Hudson Falls o USA (NY) 278-279 H 5
Hudson Land ⌒ GRØ 26-27 o 7
Hudson Mountains ▲ ARK 16 F 27
Hudson River ~ USA (GA) 284-285 G 2
Hudson's Hope o CDN 32-33 K 3
Hudson Strait ≈ CDN 36-37 M 3
Huduk, Naryn- o RUS 126-127 G 5
Hudwin Lake ⊖ CDN 34-35 J 4
Hudžah ~ RUS 120-121 M 2
Hüdžajli ☆ • US 136-137 F 3
Huē ☆ ••• VN 158-159 J 2
Huechulafquén, Lago ⊖ RA 78-79 D 5
Hueco o USA (TX) 266-267 B 2
Huecu, El o RA 78-79 D 4
Huedin o RO 102-103 C 4
Huehuetenango ☆ GCA 52-53 J 4
Huehuetla o MEX 52-53 E 1
Huejotzingo o MEX 52-53 E 2
Huejúcar o MEX 50-51 H 6
Huejuquilla El Alto o MEX 50-51 H 6
Huejutla de Reyes o MEX 50-51 K 7
Huelma o E 98-99 F 6
Huelva o • E 98-99 D 6
Huencuecho Sur o RCH 78-79 D 3
Huéneja o E 98-99 F 6
Huenque, Río ~ PE 70-71 C 5
Huepil o RCH 78-79 D 4
Hueque, Río ~ YV 60-61 G 2
Huequi, Península ⌒ RCH 78-79 C 7
Huequi, Volcán ▲ RCH 78-79 C 7
Huércal-Overa o E 98-99 G 6
Huerfano River ~ USA (CO) 254-255 L 6
Huerfano Trading Post o USA (NM) 256-257 H 2
Huerta, La o MEX 52-53 B 2
Huerta, La o RCH 78-79 D 3
Huerta, Sierra de la ▲ RA 76-77 D 6
Huertecillas o MEX 50-51 J 5
Huesca o • E 98-99 G 3
Huéscar o E 98-99 F 6
Huesos, Arroyo de los ~ RA 78-79 K 4
Huetamo de Nuñez o MEX 52-53 D 2
Huey Yang Waterfall ⊥ • THA 158-159 E 5
Hufayyira, al- o KSA 130-131 J 5
Hufra, al- ⌒ KSA 130-131 F 3
Huftarøy ⌒ N 86-87 B 6
Hufūf, al- o KSA 130-131 L 5
Hufuma o RI 166-167 G 2
Hugand ☆ TJ 136-137 L 4
Hugdjakit ~ RUS 108-109 b 7
Hugdjungda, hrebet ▲ RUS 116-117 H 2
Huger o USA (SC) 284-285 L 3
Hugh Butler Lake ⊖ USA (NE) 262-263 F 4
Hughenden o AUS 174-175 H 7
Hughenden o CDN (ALB) 232-233 H 3
Hughes o RA 78-79 J 2
Hughes o USA 20-21 N 3
Hughes o USA (AR) 276-277 E 6
Hughes Springs o USA (TX) 264-265 K 6
Hughesville o USA (MD) 280-281 K 5
Hughesville o USA (PA) 280-281 K 2
Hugh Glass Monument • USA (SD) 260-261 D 1
Hugh River ~ AUS 176-177 M 2
Hugh White State Recreational Park • USA (MS) 268-269 L 3
Hugli ~ IND 142-143 E 5
Hugo o USA (OK) 264-265 J 4
Hugo Reservoir ⊖ USA (OK) 264-265 J 4
Hugoton o USA (KS) 262-263 E 7
Huguangyan • VRC 156-157 G 6
Huguenot Memorial • ZA 220-221 D 6
Huguo o VRC 156-157 D 2
Huia o NZ 182 E 2
Hui'an o VRC 156-157 L 4
Hui'anpu o VRC 154-155 E 3
Huichang o VRC 156-157 J 4
Huichapan o MEX 52-53 E 1
Huichon o DVR 150-151 F 7
Huichuan o VRC 154-155 C 4
Huidong o VRC (GDG) 156-157 J 5
Huidong o VRC (SIC) 156-157 C 3
Huíla □ ANG 216-217 C 7
Huilai o VRC 156-157 K 5
Huíla Plateau ▲ ANG 216-217 C 7
Huili o VRC 156-157 C 3
Huillapima o RA 76-77 E 5
Huilong o VRC 156-157 G 3
Huimbayoc o PE 64-65 E 5
Huimilpan o MEX 52-53 D 1
Huimin o VRC 154-155 K 3
Huiñaimarca, Lago ⊖ PE 70-71 C 5
Huinan o VRC 150-151 F 6
Huinca Renancó o RA 78-79 G 3
Huining o VRC 154-155 D 4
Huishui o VRC 156-157 E 3
Huisne ~ F 90-91 H 7
Huitimbo o GH 202-203 J 7
Huitong o VRC 156-157 F 3
Huitoto, Raudal ~ CO 64-65 F 1
Huitoyacu, Río ~ PE 64-65 D 3
Huittinen o FIN 88-89 G 6
Huitzo o MEX 52-53 F 3
Huivulai o MEX 50-51 E 4
Huixtepec o MEX 52-53 F 3
Huixtla o MEX 52-53 H 4
Huiyang o VRC 156-157 J 5
Huize o VRC 156-157 C 3
Huizhou o VRC 156-157 J 5
Huji o VRC 154-155 H 6
Hujra Shāh Meqeem o PK 138-139 D 4
Hukeri o IND 140-141 F 2
Hukou o VRC 156-157 K 2
Hukou Pubu • VRC 154-155 G 4
Hukovo o UA 102-103 L 3
Hukuntsi o RB 220-221 E 1
Hula o PNG 183 D 6
Hulah Lake ⊖ USA (OK) 264-265 H 2
Hulaiba o KWT 130-131 K 2
Hulaifa as-Sufla, al- o KSA 130-131 G 5
Hulais o KSA 130-131 F 6
Hulajpole o UA 102-103 K 4
Hulan o VRC 150-151 F 5
Hulane o RI 166-167 D 3
Hulekal o IND 140-141 F 3
Hulett o USA (WY) 252-253 O 2
Hulga ~ RUS 114-115 G 2
Hulhuta o RUS 96-97 E 10
Hulin o VRC 150-151 J 5
Huliyar o IND 140-141 G 4
Hull o CDN (QUE) 238-239 K 3
Hull o USA (IA) 274-275 B 1
Hull o USA (IL) 274-275 G 5
Hull o USA (TX) 268-269 F 6
Hullehgush o IND 138-139 E 1
Hülm o • AFG 136-137 K 6
Hulo o GE 126-127 E 7
Hultsfred ☆ S 86-87 G 8
Hulun Nur ⊖ VRC (NMZ) 148-149 N 3
Hulun Nur • VRC (NMZ) 148-149 N 3
Hulwa, al- o KSA 130-131 K 6
Hulwān o • ET 194-195 E 3
Huma o VRC 150-151 F 2
Humā' aš-Šimāliya, al- o KSA 130-131 J 5
Humacao o USA (PR) 286-287 Q 2
Humahuaca o RA 76-77 E 2
Humaid, al- o KSA 132-133 B 4
Humaitá o BOL 70-71 D 2
Humaitá o BR 66-67 F 6
Humansdorp o ZA 220-221 G 7
Humari o SUD 200-201 G 4
Humay o PE 64-65 E 8
Humbe o ANG 216-217 C 8
Humber ≈ 90-91 G 5
Humberto 1 o RA 76-77 G 6
Humberto de Campos o BR 68-69 G 3
Humbert River o AUS 172-173 K 4
Humble o USA (TX) 268-269 E 7
Humble City o USA (NM) 256-257 M 6
Humboldt o CDN (SAS) 232-233 N 3
Humboldt o USA (IA) 274-275 D 2
Humboldt o USA (KS) 262-263 L 7
Humboldt o USA (NE) 262-263 L 4
Humboldt o USA (NV) 246-247 G 3
Humboldt o USA (SD) 260-261 J 3
Humboldt o USA (TN) 276-277 G 5
Humboldt Bay ≈ 40-41 B 5
Humboldt Bay ⊖ CDN (ONT) 234-235 P 5
Humboldt Bay ≈ USA 246-247 A 3
Humboldt Gletscher ⊂ GRØ 26-27 S 4
Humboldt Redwoods State Park ⊥ USA (CA) 246-247 B 3
Humboldt River ~ USA (NV) 246-247 G 3
Humboldt Salt Marsh ⊖ USA (NV) 246-247 H 4
Hume, Lake < AUS 180-181 J 4
Hume Highway II AUS 180-181 J 3
Humeida, al- o KSA 130-131 D 3
Humenné o SK 92-93 Q 4
Hume River ~ CDN 30-31 E 3
Humeston o USA (IA) 274-275 E 4
Hummi, ozero ⊖ RUS 122-123 G 3
Humocaro Bajo o YV 60-61 G 3
Humos, Cabo ▲ RCH 78-79 C 3
Humos, Isla ⌒ RCH 80 C 2
Humpata o ANG 216-217 B 7
Humphrey o USA (AR) 276-277 D 6
Humphrey o USA (ID) 252-253 F 2
Humphrey o USA (NE) 262-263 J 3
Humphreys Peak ▲ USA (AZ) 256-257 D 3
Humpolec o CZ 92-93 N 4
Humptulips o USA (WA) 244-245 B 3
Humpty Doo o AUS 172-173 K 2
Humuula o USA (HI) 288 K 5
Hün ☆ • LAR 192-193 F 3
Húnaflói ≈ 86-87 c 2
Hunan □ VRC 156-157 G 3
Hunchun o VRC 150-151 H 6
Hundested o DK 86-87 E 9
Hundred and Two River ~ USA (MO) 274-275 D 4
Hundred Islands National Park • RP 160-161 D 4
Hunedoara o • RO 102-103 C 5
Hunga ⌒ TON 184 IV a 1
Hunga Ha'apai ⌒ TON 184 IV a 2
Hungary = Magyarország ■ H 92-93 O 5
Hunga Tonga ⌒ TON 184 IV a 2
Hungerford o AUS 178-179 H 5
Hungiy o MAU 146-147 M 1
Hungnam o DVR 150-151 F 8
Hungry Horse o USA (MT) 250-251 E 3
Hungry Horse Reservoir ⊖ USA (MT) 250-251 F 3
Hunguj gol ~ MAU 146-147 L 1
Hungund o IND 140-141 G 2
Hu'ng Yên ☆ VN 156-157 E 6
Hunhada ~ RUS 110-111 U 7
Hūnik o IR 134-135 J 3
Huni Valley o GH 202-203 K 7
Hunjiang o VRC 150-151 F 7
Hunkurāb, Ra's ▲ ET 194-195 G 5
Hunkuyi o WAN 204-205 G 3
Hūnsār o • IR 134-135 D 2
Hunsberge ▲ NAM 220-221 C 3
Hunsrück ▲ D 92-93 J 4
Hunstein Range ▲ PNG 183 B 3
Hunsūr o IND 140-141 G 4
Hunt o USA (AZ) 256-257 F 4
Hunte ~ D 92-93 K 2
Hunter o USA (AR) 276-277 D 5
Hunter o USA (KS) 262-263 H 5
Hunter o USA (ND) 258-259 K 4
Hunter Island ⌒ AUS 180-181 H 6
Hunter Island ⌒ CDN (BC) 230-231 A 2
Hunter Liggett Military Reservation, Fort xx USA (CA) 248-249 C 4
Hunter River ~ AUS 180-181 L 2
Hunter River o CDN (PEI) 240-241 M 4
Hunters o USA (WA) 244-245 G 2
Hunter's Lodge o EAK 212-213 F 5
Huntingburg o USA (IN) 274-275 M 6
Huntingdon o CDN (QUE) 238-239 L 3
Huntingdon o USA (TN) 276-277 G 5
Hunting Island ⌒ USA (SC) 284-285 K 4
Huntington o USA (IN) 274-275 N 3
Huntington o USA (MA) 278-279 J 6
Huntington o USA (NY) 280-281 N 3
Huntington o USA (OR) 244-245 H 6
Huntington o USA (PA) 280-281 J 3
Huntington o USA (TX) 268-269 F 5
Huntington o USA (UT) 254-255 E 4
Huntington o USA (WV) 280-281 D 5
Huntington Beach o USA (CA) 248-249 G 6
Huntland o USA (TN) 276-277 J 5
Huntly o GB 90-91 F 3
Huntly o NZ 182 E 2
Huntoon o CDN (SAS) 232-233 P 6
Hunts Inlet o CDN (BC) 228-229 D 2
Huntsville o CDN (ONT) 238-239 F 3
Huntsville o USA (AR) 276-277 B 4
Huntsville o USA (MO) 274-275 F 5
Huntsville o USA (TX) 268-269 E 6
Huntsville o USA (UT) 254-255 D 2
Huntsville o • USA (AL) 284-285 D 2
Hunucma o MEX 52-53 K 1
Hunyuan o VRC 154-155 H 2
Hunza ~ PK 138-139 E 1
Huocheng o VRC 146-147 E 3
Huolingol o VRC 148-149 O 5
Huonfels o AUS 174-175 G 6
Hu'o'ng Diên o VN 158-159 J 2
Hu'o'ng Khê ☆ VN 156-157 D 7
Hu'o'ng So'n ☆ VN 156-157 D 7
Huon Gulf ≈ 183 D 4
Huon Peninsula ⌒ PNG 183 D 4
Hùon Rái ⌒ VN 158-159 H 6
Huonville-Ranelagh o AUS 180-181 J 7
Huoqiu o VRC 154-155 K 5
Huoshan o VRC 154-155 K 6
Huoshou o VRC 154-155 G 3
Hupel o CDN (BC) 230-231 K 3
Huqf, al- ⌒ OM 132-133 K 4
Huqna, Tall o IRQ 128-129 K 4
Huqui, Ilha do ⌒ BR 66-67 K 4
Hūr o IR (ESF) 134-135 F 2
Hūr o IR (HOR) 134-135 H 2
Huraba o RI 162-163 C 4
Huraiba, al- o Y 132-133 F 6
Huraimilā o KSA 130-131 K 5
Hurais o KSA (EPR) 130-131 L 5
Hurais o KSA (EPR) 130-131 K 5
Hūran ≈ 134-135 F 5
Hurd, Cape ▲ CDN (ONT) 238-239 D 3
Hurdiyo o SP 208-209 K 3
Hurdsfield o USA (ND) 258-259 H 4
Hurėn ~ RUS 120-121 M 3
Hure Qi o VRC 150-151 C 6
Hurghada = al-Ġurdaqa ☆ • ET 194-195 F 4
Huri Hills ▲ EAK 212-213 F 2
Huringda ~ RUS 114-115 U 2
Huringda ~ RUS 116-117 F 2
Hurīyā Murīyā, Ğazā'ir ⌒ Y 132-133 J 5
Hurki o BY 94-95 M 4
Hurley o USA (NM) 256-257 G 6
Hurley o USA (WI) 270-271 H 4
Hurma, al- o KSA 132-133 C 3
Hurman Çayı ~ TR 128-129 G 3
Hurmuli o RUS 122-123 G 3
Huron o USA (CA) 248-249 D 3
Huron o USA (SD) 260-261 H 2
Huron, Lake ⊖ 46-47 G 3
Huron, Lake ⊖ 272-273 F 2
Huron Islands ⌒ USA (MI) 270-271 L 4
Hurr, Wādī al- ~ KSA 130-131 H 2
Hurricane o USA (AK) 20-21 Q 5
Hurricane o USA (UT) 254-255 B 6
Hurricane o USA (WV) 280-281 D 5
Hurricane Creek ~ USA (GA) 284-285 H 5
Hurry Fjord ≈ 26-27 o 8
Hurso o ETH 208-209 E 4
Hurstown o USA (TX) 268-269 F 5
Hurtado o RCH 76-77 B 6
Hurtado, Río ~ RCH 76-77 B 6
Hurtsboro o USA (AL) 284-285 E 4
Hurwitz Lake ⊖ CDN 30-31 V 5
Huš'a, al- o KSA 132-133 C 5
Hušaibi, al- o KSA 130-131 H 5
Husainābād o IND 142-143 D 4
Husain al-Ġāfūs o IRQ 128-129 L 6
Husana ~ RUS 108-109 b 7
Húsavík ☆ IS 86-87 e 1
Hūsf o IR 134-135 H 2
Husheib o SUD 200-201 G 5
Huşi o RO 102-103 F 4
Hūš Īsā o ET 194-195 E 2
Huskisson o AUS 180-181 L 3
Huskvarna o S 86-87 G 8
Huslia o USA 20-21 M 4
Huslia River ~ USA 20-21 M 4
Husmund ~ RUS 116-117 K 2
Hussar o CDN (ALB) 232-233 F 4
Hustisford o USA (WI) 274-275 K 1
Hustonville o USA (KY) 276-277 L 3
Husum o D 92-93 K 1
Husum o USA (WA) 244-245 D 5
Hūt o Y 132-133 C 5
Hutag o MAU 148-149 F 3
Hutan Melintang o MAL 162-163 D 3
Hutchinson o USA (KS) 262-263 J 6
Hutchinson o USA (MN) 270-271 D 6
Hutchinson o ZA 220-221 F 5
Hutchinson Island ⌒ USA (FL) 286-287 J 4
Hutch Mountain ▲ USA (AZ) 256-257 D 4
Hutjena o PNG 184 I b 1
Hutou o VRC 150-151 J 5
Hutta, al- o KSA 130-131 G 3
Hutton Range ▲ AUS 176-177 G 2
Huttonsville o USA (WV) 280-281 G 5
Hutubi o VRC 146-147 H 3
Hutudabiga ~ RUS 108-109 W 4
Huu o RI 168 D 7
Hữu Lũng ☆ VN 156-157 E 6
Huvin Hippargi o IND 140-141 G 2
Huwair, al- o KSA 130-131 H 4
Huwairah, Wādī ~ Y 132-133 F 6
Huwār, Wādī ~ SUD 200-201 B 4
Huwaymī, al- o Y 132-133 E 6
Huwayt, Wādī ~ SUD 200-201 F 2
Huxi Xincun o VRC 148-149 E 7
Huxley o CDN (ALB) 232-233 E 4
Huxley, Mount ▲ USA 20-21 U 6
Huyuyun He ~ VRC 144-145 M 2
Hūzestān □ IR 134-135 C 3
Huzhong Z.B. II VRC (HEI) 150-151 D 2
Huzhong Z.B. ⊥ • VRC (HEI) 150-151 D 2
Huzhou o VRC 154-155 M 6
Huzhu Tuzu Zizhixian o VRC 154-155 B 3
Hužir o RUS 116-117 N 9
Hužirt o MAU 148-149 F 4
Huzūrābād o IND 138-139 G 10
Hvāğe o IR 128-129 M 3
Hvāğe Moḥammad, Kūh-e ▲ AFG 136-137 M 7
Hvalynsk ☆ RUS 96-97 F 7
Hvammstangi o IS 86-87 c 2
Hvar o • HR 100-101 F 3
Hvar ⌒ HR 100-101 F 3
Hvitfeldt, Kap ▲ GRØ 28-29 T 6
Hvojnaja o RUS 94-95 O 2
Hvolsvöllur ☆ IS 86-87 c 3
Hvormūğ o IR 134-135 D 4
Hvorostjanka ☆ RUS 96-97 F 7
Hvostovo o RUS 122-123 K 5
Hwali o ZW 218-219 E 5
Hwange o ZW 218-219 D 4
Hwange National Park ⊥ ZW 218-219 D 4
Hwedza o ZW 218-219 F 4
Hyades, Cerro ▲ RCH 80 D 3
Hyak o USA (WA) 244-245 D 3
Hyannis o USA (MA) 278-279 L 7
Hyannis o USA (NE) 262-263 E 3
Hyas o CDN (SAS) 232-233 Q 4
Hyattsville o USA (MD) 280-281 K 5
Hyattville o USA (WY) 252-253 L 2
Hybart o USA (AL) 284-285 C 5
Hyco Reservoir ⊖ USA (NC) 282-283 H 4
Hyco River ~ USA (VA) 280-281 G 7
Hydaburg o USA 32-33 D 4
Hyde Inlet ≈ 24-25 g 3
Hyde Lake ⊖ CDN 30-31 W 5
Hyden o AUS 176-177 E 6
Hyden o USA (KY) 276-277 M 3
Hyde Park o GUY 62-63 E 2
Hyder o USA (AK) 32-33 E 4
Hyder o USA (AZ) 256-257 B 5
Hyderābād ☆ •• IND 140-141 H 2
Hyderābād o • PK 138-139 B 7
Hydraulic o CDN (BC) 228-229 N 4
Hyen o N 86-87 B 6
Hyères o F 90-91 L 10
Hyères, Îles d' ⌒ • F 90-91 L 10
Hyesan ☆ DVR 150-151 G 7
Hyland Bay ≈ 172-173 J 2
Hyland Plateau ▲ CDN 30-31 E 5
Hyland River ~ CDN 30-31 E 5
Hyľčuju ~ RUS 88-89 X 2
Hylly o AZ 128-129 N 3
Hymera o USA (IN) 274-275 L 5
Hynčešť = Hînceşti ☆ MD 102-103 F 4
Hyndman Peak ▲ USA (ID) 252-253 D 3
Hyono-sen ▲ J 152-153 F 7
Hyrax Hill ∴ • EAK 212-213 F 4
Hyrdalan = Xirdalan o AZ 128-129 N 2
Hyrynsalmi o FIN 88-89 K 4
Hysham o USA (MT) 250-251 M 5
Hythe o CDN 32-33 L 4
Hyuga o J 152-153 D 8
Hyūga-nada ≈ 152-153 D 8

I

Iá, Rio ~ BR 66-67 D 3
Iabes, Erg ⌒ DZ 188-189 K 7
Iaciara o BR 72-73 G 3
Iaco, Rio ~ BR 66-67 C 7
Iaco, Río ~ PE 70-71 B 2
Iaçu o BR 72-73 K 2
Iakora o RM 222-223 E 9
Ia Krăng Po' Cô ~ VN 158-159 J 3
Ialibu o PNG 183 B 4
Ialomiţa ~ RO 102-103 E 5
Ialpug ~ MD 102-103 F 4
Iamara o PNG 183 B 5
Iamonia, Lake ⊖ USA (FL) 286-287 E 1
Ianabinda o RM 222-223 D 9
Ianca o RO 102-103 E 5
Ian Lake ⊖ CDN (BC) 228-229 B 3
Iao Valley ⌣ • USA (HI) 288 J 4
Iaripo o BR 62-63 G 5
Iaşi ☆ • RO 102-103 E 4
Iauaretê o BR 66-67 C 2
Iauaretê, Cachoeira ~ BR 66-67 D 3
Iauiari, Igarapé ~ BR 66-67 C 2
Iba ☆ RP 160-161 C 5
Ibadan ☆ WAN 204-205 E 5
Ibagué ☆ CO 60-61 D 5
Ibaiti o BR 72-73 E 7
Ibanabuiú o BR 68-69 J 4
Ibanda o EAU 212-213 C 4
Ibáñez, Río ~ RCH 80 D 3
Ibanga o ZRE 212-213 A 5
Ibapah o USA (UT) 254-255 B 3
Ibar ~ YU 100-101 H 3
Ibarej, Río ~ BOL 70-71 E 4
Ibarra ☆ EC 64-65 C 1
Ibb o • Y 132-133 D 6
Ibba o SUD (SR) 206-207 J 6
Ibba ~ SUD 206-207 J 5
Ibembo o ZRE 210-211 J 2
Ibenga ~ RCB 210-211 F 2
Iberá, Esteros del ⊖ RA 76-77 J 5
Iberá, Laguna ⊖ RA 76-77 J 5
Iberia o PE (LOR) 64-65 E 4
Iberia o PE (MDI) 70-71 C 2
Iberia o USA (MO) 274-275 F 6
Iberville, Lac d' ⊖ CDN 36-37 N 7
Ibestad o N 86-87 H 2
Ibeto o WAN 204-205 F 3
Ibex Pass ▲ USA (CA) 248-249 H 4
Ibi o E 98-99 G 5
Ibi o WAN 204-205 H 4
Ibiá o BR 72-73 G 5
Ibiaí o BR 72-73 H 4
Ibiapaba, Serra da ▲ BR 68-69 H 3
Ibiapina o BR 68-69 H 3
Ibiara o BR 68-69 J 5
Ibib, Wādī ~ ET 194-195 G 6
Ibibobo o BOL 76-77 F 1
Ibicaraí o BR 72-73 L 3
Ibicuí, Rio ~ BR 76-77 J 5
Ibicuitinga o BR 68-69 J 4
Ibimirim o BR 68-69 K 6
Ibina ~ ZRE 212-213 B 3
Ibindy ▲ RM 222-223 E 8
Ibipeba o BR 68-69 G 7
Ibipira o BR 68-69 F 5
Ibipitanga o BR 72-73 J 2
Ibiporã o BR 72-73 E 7
Ibiquera o BR 72-73 K 2
Ibiraba o BR 68-69 G 7
Ibiraci o BR 72-73 G 6
Ibirama o BR 74-75 F 6
Ibirocaí, Rio ~ BR 76-77 J 5
Ibiruba o BR 74-75 D 7
Ibitiara o BR 72-73 J 2
Ibitinga o BR 72-73 F 6
Ibitinga, Represa < BR 72-73 F 6
Ibitira o BR 72-73 J 3
Ibitirama o BR 72-73 K 6
Ibó o BR 68-69 J 6
Ibo o MOC 214-215 L 7
Ibobobo, Serranía de ▲ BOL 76-77 F 1
Ibohamane o RN 198-199 C 5
Iboko o ZRE 210-211 G 4
Ibondo o ZRE 212-213 B 4
Ibonma o RI 166-167 G 3
Iboro o WAN 204-205 E 5
Ibotirama o BR 72-73 J 2
Iboundji, Mont ▲ G 210-211 C 4
Ibra o OM 132-133 L 2
Ibra o RI 166-167 G 4
Ibra, Wādī ~ SUD 206-207 G 3
'Ibrī o OM 132-133 K 2
Ibšawāy o ET 194-195 E 3
Ibstone o CDN (SAS) 232-233 K 3
Ibuaçu o BR 68-69 J 4
Ibuguaçu o BR 68-69 H 3
Ibusuki o • J 152-153 D 9
Ica o PE 64-65 E 9
Ica ~ RUS 114-115 P 6
Ica ~ RUS 120-121 R 6
Içá, Rio ~ BR 66-67 C 4
Ica, Río de ~ PE 64-65 E 9
Icabarú o YV 62-63 D 3
Icalma, Paso de ▲ RA 78-79 D 5
Içana o BR 66-67 D 2
Içana, Rio ~ BR 66-67 D 2
Icaño o RA 76-77 E 5
Icapuí o BR 68-69 K 4
Icaraí o BR 68-69 J 3
Icaraíma o BR 72-73 D 7
Icatu o BR 68-69 F 3
Iceberg Point ▲ CDN 26-27 G 3
Ice Caves ∴ USA (WA) 244-245 D 5
Icefields Parkway o CDN (ALB) 228-229 R 4
Iceland = Ísland ■ IS 86-87 c 2
Iceland Basin ≃ 6-7 G 3
Iceland-Faroe Rise ≃ 6-7 H 2
Icelandic Plateau ≃ 6-7 H 2
Icém o BR 72-73 F 6
Ice Mountain ▲ CDN (BC) 228-229 N 2
Ičera ~ RUS 118-119 D 6
Ichalkaranji o IND 140-141 F 2
Iche o MA 188-189 L 4
Icheu o WAN 204-205 G 5
Ichi-gawa ~ J 152-153 F 7
Ichilo, Río ~ BOL 70-71 E 5
Ichinomiya o J 152-153 G 7
Ichinoseki o J 152-153 J 5
Ichkeul, Parc national de l' ⊥ ••• TN 190-191 G 2
Ichmul o MEX 52-53 K 1

338 Hovd — Ichmul

Ichoa, Río ~ BOL 70-71 E 4
Ichocan o PE 64-65 C 5
Ich'ŏn o ROK 150-151 F 9
Ichuña o PE 70-71 B 5
Ičigemskij hrebet ▲ RUS 112-113 L 5
Ičinskaja Sopka, vulkan ▲ RUS 120-121 R 6
Ičinskij o RUS 120-121 Q 6
Icó o BR 68-69 J 5
Icoca o ANG 216-217 D 3
Ičoda ~ RUS 118-119 E 5
Ičuveem ~ RUS 112-113 Q 2
Icy Bay ≈ 20-21 U 7
Icy Cape ▲ USA 20-21 J 1
Icy Cape ▲ USA 20-21 T 7
Icy Reef ⌒ USA 20-21 U 2
Icy Strait ≈ 32-33 C 2
Ida ~ RUS 116-117 M 9
Ida o USA (LA) 268-269 G 4
Idabato o CAM 204-205 H 6
Idabel o USA (OK) 264-265 K 5
Idabo o ETH 208-209 E 5
Idaga Hamus o ETH 200-201 J 5
Ida Grove o USA (IA) 274-275 C 2
Idah o WAN 204-205 G 5
Idaho □ USA (ID) 252-253 B 2
Idaho Army National Guard Artillery Range xx USA (ID) 252-253 B 3
Idaho Falls o USA (ID) 252-253 F 3
Idaho National Engineering Laboratory • USA (ID) 252-253 F 3
Idaiatuba o BR 72-73 G 7
Idak, Cape ▲ USA 22-23 N 6
Idalia o USA (CO) 254-255 N 4
Idalia National Park ⊥ AUS 178-179 H 3
Idalina, Cachoeira ~ BR 70-71 G 2
Idalou o USA (TX) 264-265 C 5
Idanre o• WAN 204-205 F 5
Ida-Oumarkt o MA 188-189 G 6
Idäppädi o IND 140-141 G 5
Idar o IND 138-139 D 8
Idar-Oberstein o D 92-93 J 4
Ida Valley o AUS 176-177 F 4
'Idd al-Ghanam o SUD 206-207 G 3
Iddesleigh o CDN (ALB) 232-233 G 5
Ideal, El o MEX 52-53 L 1
Ideles o DZ 190-191 E 9
Idenao o CAM 204-205 H 6
Idèr gol ~ MAU 148-149 D 3
Idfū o• ET 194-195 F 5
Idhan' Awbāri ∴ LAR 192-193 D 4
Idi o RI 162-163 B 2
Idi-Iroko o WAN 204-205 E 5
Idil ★ TR 128-129 J 4
Idini o RIM 196-197 C 6
Idiofa o ZRE 210-211 G 6
Idiriya o MA 188-189 F 7
Idjiwi o ZRE 212-213 B 5
Idjiwi, Ile ⌒ ZRE 212-213 B 5
Idjum ~ RUS 120-121 D 6
Idkū o ET 194-195 E 2
Idlib ★ SYR 128-129 G 5
Idoani o WAN 204-205 F 5
Idodi o EAT 214-215 H 4
Idogo o WAN 204-205 E 5
Idoho < WAN 204-205 G 6
Idolo, Isla del ⌒ MEX 50-51 L 7
Idongo o RCA 206-207 E 5
Ídra ⌒ GR 100-101 J 6
Idre o S 86-87 F 6
Idrigill o GB 90-91 D 3
Idrija o SLO 100-101 D 2
Idrinskoe ★ RUS 116-117 F 8
Idriss 1., Barrage < MA 188-189 J 3
Idumbe o ZRE 210-211 H 5
Idutywa o ZA 220-221 J 6
Idwa, al- o KSA 130-131 H 4
Idževan o AR 128-129 L 2
Iecava o LV 94-95 J 3
Iengra ~ RUS 118-119 M 7
Iepê o BR 72-73 E 7
Ieper o• B 92-93 G 3
Ierápetra o GR 100-101 K 7
Ie-shima ⌒ J 152-153 B 11
Ievlevo o RUS 114-115 J 6
Ifakara o EAT 214-215 J 5
Ifaki o WAN 204-205 F 5
'Ifāl, Wādī ~ KSA 130-131 D 3
Ifanadiana o RM 222-223 E 8
Ifanirea o RM 222-223 E 9
Ifaty o RM 222-223 C 9
Ife o• WAN 204-205 F 5
Ifenat o TCH 198-199 J 6
Iferouâne o RN 198-199 D 3
Ifertas, Hassi < LAR 190-191 H 6
Ifetedo o WAN 204-205 F 5
Ifetesene ▲ DZ 190-191 E 8
Iffley o AUS 174-175 F 6
Iffley o CDN (SAS) 232-233 K 2
Ifjord o N 86-87 N 1
Ifon o WAN 204-205 F 5
Iforhas, Adrar des ▲ RMM 196-197 L 4
Ifould Lake ⬭ AUS 176-177 M 5
Ifrane ★ MA 188-189 J 4
Ifri, Imi-n- • MA 188-189 H 5
Ifunda o EAT 214-215 H 4
Iga ~ RUS 116-117 N 7
Iga ~ RUS 122-123 D 2
Igabi o WAN 204-205 G 3
Igaliku o GRØ 28-29 S 6
Igaliku Fjord ≈ 28-29 S 6
Igalula o EAT 212-213 D 6
Iganga o EAU 212-213 D 3
Igangan o WAN 204-205 E 5
Igapó o BR 68-69 K 6
Igapora o BR 72-73 J 2
Igara Paraná, Río ~ CO 64-65 F 2
Igarapava o BR 72-73 G 6
Igarapé-Açu o BR 68-69 E 2
Igarapé Grande o BR 68-69 F 4
Igarapé Lage, Area Indígena ⚔ BR 70-71 E 2
Igarapé Lourdes, Área Indígena ⚔ BR 70-71 G 2
Igarapé Mirim o BR 62-63 K 6
Igarite o BR 68-69 G 7
Igarka o RUS 108-109 W 8
Igarka-Lybangajaha ~ RUS 108-109 R 7
Igarra o WAN 204-205 G 5
Igawa o EAT 214-215 H 5
Igbeti o WAN 204-205 F 4
Igbogor o WAN 204-205 F 5
Igboho o WAN 204-205 E 4
Igbo-Ora o WAN 204-205 E 5
Igbor o WAN 204-205 H 5
Iğdır ★ TR 128-129 L 3
Igdlorssuit Sund ≈ 26-27 Y 8
Igdlulik o GRØ 26-27 W 6
Igèl'veem ~ RUS 112-113 Y 4
Igichuk Hills ▲ USA 20-21 J 3
Igirma o RUS 116-117 L 7
Igiugig o USA 22-23 T 3
Iglau = Jihlava o CZ 92-93 N 4
Igle, Cerro ▲ RA 80 D 5
Iglesia, Arroyo de la ~ RA 76-77 C 6
Iglesias o I 100-101 B 5
Iglesias, Cerro ▲ RA 80 G 3
Igli o DZ 188-189 K 5
Iglino ★ RUS 96-97 K 6
Igloolik o CDN 24-25 f 6
Igloolik Island ⌒ CDN 24-25 f 6
Igloolik Island Ideal Island ⌒ CDN 36-37 T 6
Ignace o CDN (ONT) 234-235 M 5
Ignacio o USA (CO) 254-255 H 6
Ignalina o LT 94-95 K 4
Ignašino o RUS 118-119 L 9
Ignatovo o RUS 94-95 P 1
Iğneada o TR 128-129 B 2
Ignit Fiord ≈ 36-37 T 2
Igolo o DY 204-205 E 5
Igom o RI 166-167 F 2
Igoma o EAT 214-215 G 4
Igombe ~ EAT 212-213 D 6
Igombe ~ EAT (TAB) 212-213 C 6
Igornachoix Bay ≈ 38-39 Q 3
Igornachoix Bay ≈ CDN 242-243 L 2
Igoumenitsa o GR 100-101 H 5
Igoumen o WAN 204-205 F 4
Igra ★ RUS 96-97 H 5
Igreja o CV 202-203 B 6
Igrim o RUS 114-115 H 3
Igrita o WAN 204-205 G 6
Iguache, Mesas de ∴ CO 64-65 F 1
Iguaçu, Parque Nacional do ⊥••• BR 74-75 D 5
Iguaçu, Rio ~ BR 74-75 D 5
Iguaí o BR 72-73 K 3
Iguala de la Independencia o MEX 52-53 E 2
Iguape o BR 74-75 G 5
Iguará, Rio ~ BR 68-69 G 3
Iguatemi o BR 76-77 K 2
Iguatemi, Rio ~ BR 76-77 K 2
Iguatu o BR 68-69 J 5
Iguazú, Cataratas del ~•• RA 76-77 K 3
Iguazú, Parque Nacional del ⊥••• RA 76-77 K 3
Iguéla o G 210-211 B 4
Iguetti < RIM 196-197 F 2
Iguetti, Sebkhet ⬭ RIM 196-197 F 2
Iguguno o EAT 212-213 E 6
Iguidi, Erg ∴ DZ 196-197 G 2
Iguidi Ouan Kasa ∴ LAR 190-191 H 8
Iguitu o BR 68-69 G 7
Igumnovskaja o RUS 94-95 S 1
Igunga o EAT 212-213 D 6
Igurubi o EAT (TAB) 212-213 D 5
Igžej o RUS 116-117 L 8
Iharana o RM 222-223 G 4
Ihavandiffulu Atoll ⌒ MV 140-141 B 4
Ihbulag o MAU 148-149 G 6
Ihema, Lac ⬭ RWA 212-213 C 4
Iherir o• DZ 190-191 G 8
Iheya o J 152-153 B 11
Iheya-shima ⌒ J 152-153 B 11
Ihhairhan o MAU 148-149 H 4
Ihiala o WAN 204-205 G 6
Ihitasa < LAR 192-193 E 5
Ihosy o RM 222-223 E 9
Ihotry, Fahiry ⬭ RM 222-223 C 8
Ih suuž o MAU 148-149 H 3
Ihtiman o BG 102-103 C 6
Ihtiyarşahap Dağları ▲ TR 128-129 K 3
Ihu o PNG 183 C 4
Ihuari o PE 64-65 D 7
Ihugh o WAN 204-205 H 5
Ihumri Tilaiya o IND 142-143 D 3
Ihuo o WAN 204-205 G 6
Ih-Uul = Selenge o MAU 148-149 E 3
Iida o J 152-153 G 7
Iidaan o SP 208-209 J 5
Iide-san ▲ J 152-153 H 6
Iijoki ~ FIN 88-89 J 4
Iisaku o EST 94-95 K 2
Iisalmi o FIN 88-89 J 5
Iiyama o J 152-153 H 6
Iizuka o J 152-153 D 8
Ij o IND 140-141 G 2
Ija ~ RUS 116-117 K 8
Ijâfene ∴ RIM 196-197 F 4
Ijaji o ETH 208-209 C 4
Ijebu-Igbo o WAN 204-205 E 5
Ijebu-Ode o WAN 204-205 E 5
Ijero o WAN 204-205 F 5
Ijkharrah o LAR 192-193 J 3
Ijoubban ∴ RIM 196-197 G 4
Ijoukak o MA 188-189 G 5
IJsselmeer ≈ NL 92-93 H 2
Ijuí o BR 74-75 D 7
Ik ~ RUS 96-97 H 7
Ik, ozero ⬭ RUS 114-115 L 6
Ika o RUS 116-117 N 6
Ikahavo ▲ RM 222-223 D 6
Ikalamavony o RM 222-223 E 8
Ikamiut o GRØ 28-29 O 4
Ikamiut = Qeersorfik o GRØ 28-29 P 2
Ikanbujimal o VRC 146-147 J 6
Ikanda o ZRE 210-211 H 5
Ikang o WAN 204-205 H 6
Ikanga o EAK 212-213 G 4
Ikare o WAN 204-205 F 5
Ikaría ⌒ GR 100-101 L 6
Ikatskij, hrebet ▲ RUS 118-119 E 9
Ikauna o IND 142-143 B 2
Ikebe o WAN 204-205 G 5
Ikeda o J 152-153 K 3
Ikej o RUS 116-117 K 8
Ikej ~ RUS 116-117 J 8
Ikeja ★ WAN 204-205 E 5
Ikela o ZRE 210-211 J 4
Ikelemba ~ ZRE 210-211 H 3
Ikelenge o Z 214-215 C 6
Ikem o WAN 204-205 G 5
Ikèn ~ RUS 108-109 X 6
Ikèngué o G 210-211 B 4
Ikeq Sund ≈ 28-29 T 6
Ikerasârssuk o GRØ 26-27 X 7
Ikere o WAN 204-205 F 5
Ikermiut ⌒ GRØ 28-29 U 5
Ikerssuaq ≈ 28-29 V 4
Ikertivaq ≈ 28-29 X 3
Iki ⌒ J 152-153 C 8
Ikimba Kamachumu, Lake ⬭ EAT (KAG) 212-213 C 4
Ikire o WAN 204-205 F 5
Ikirun o WAN 204-205 F 5
Iki-Tsushima Quasi National Park ⊥ J 152-153 C 7
Ikkatteq o GRØ 28-29 W 4
Ikobé o G 210-211 C 4
Ikohahoene, Adrar ▲ DZ 190-191 G 8
Ikola o EAT 214-215 F 4
Ikole o WAN 204-205 F 5
Ikolik, Cape ▲ USA 22-23 T 4
Ikom o WAN 204-205 H 6
Ikomu o WAN 204-205 E 4
Ikongo o RM 222-223 E 8
Ikonongo o ZRE 210-211 G 3
Ikoo o EAK 212-213 G 4
Ikopa ~ RM 222-223 E 7
Ikorodu o WAN 204-205 E 5
Ikot Ekpene o WAN 204-205 G 6
Ikoto o SUD 208-209 A 6
Ikoy ~ G 210-211 C 4
Ikpik Bay ≈ 24-25 j 6
Ikpikpuk River ~ USA 20-21 N 1
Ikrjanoe ★ RUS 96-97 E 10
Iksa ~ RUS 114-115 R 6
Ikutha o EAK 212-213 G 5
Ila o USA (GA) 284-285 G 2
Ilafergh, Oued ~ DZ 196-197 L 4
Ilaga o RI 166-167 J 4
Ilagan ★ RP 160-161 D 4
Ilaiyānkudi o IND 140-141 H 6
Ilaji o WAN 204-205 E 5
Ilaka Atsinanana o RM 222-223 F 7
Ilakaka o RM 222-223 D 9
Ilakana Patatpe o F 62-63 G 4
Īlām □ IR 134-135 B 2
Īlām ★• IR 134-135 B 2
Ilan o RC 156-157 M 4
Ilanskij ★ RUS 116-117 H 7
Ila-Orangun o WAN 204-205 F 4
Ilara o WAN 204-205 F 5
Ilaro o WAN 204-205 E 5
Ilaura o PNG 183 D 4
Ilave o PE 70-71 C 5
Ilave, Río ~ PE 70-71 C 5
Ilawe o WAN 204-205 F 5
Ilbenge o RUS 118-119 M 4
Ilbilbie o AUS 178-179 K 1
Île à la Crosse, Lac ⬭ CDN 34-35 C 3
Ilebgäne, Adrar ▲ RMM 196-197 L 5
Ilebo o ZRE 210-211 H 6
Ileck, Sol'- ★ RUS 96-97 J 8
Île-de-France □ F 90-91 J 7
Île-d'Entrée o CDN (QUE) 242-243 G 5
Ileg o PNG 183 C 3
Ilek ~ KA 126-127 M 3
Ilek ~ RUS (ORB) 96-97 H 8
Ilek ~ RUS 96-97 H 8
Ileksa ~ RUS 88-89 O 5
Ileret o EAK 212-213 F 1
Île-Rousse, L' o F 98-99 M 3
Iles, Lac des ⬭ CDN (QUE) 238-239 H 2
Ileśa ~ RUS 88-89 T 5
Ilesa o WAN (KWA) 204-205 E 4
Ilesa o WAN (OYO) 204-205 F 5
Ilford o CDN 34-35 J 2
Ilfracombe o AUS 178-179 H 2
Ilfracombe o• GB 90-91 E 6
Ilga ~ RUS 116-117 M 9
Ilgaz ★ TR 128-129 E 2
Ilgaz Dağları ▲ TR 128-129 E 2
Ilgın ★ TR 128-129 D 3
Ilha Grande, Baía da ≈ 72-73 H 7
Ilha Solteira o BR 72-73 E 6
Ilhéus o• BR 72-73 L 3
Ilhota da Maloca Arori o BR 62-63 F 5
Ili ~ KA 146-147 D 4
Ilia o RO 102-103 C 5
Ilia o USA (WA) 244-245 H 4
Iliamna Lake ⬭ USA 22-23 T 3
Iliamna Volcano ▲ USA 20-21 O 6
Ilič o KA 136-137 L 4
Iliç ★ TR 128-129 B 3
Ilica ★ TR 128-129 J 3
Ilicínia o BR 72-73 H 6
Ilidža o BIH 100-101 G 3
Ilig, Raas ▲ SP 208-209 J 5
Iligan ★ RP 160-161 F 8
Iligan ~ RP 160-161 F 8
Iligan Bay ≈ 160-161 E 8
Iligan Point ▲ RP 160-161 E 3
Ili He ~ VRC 146-147 E 4
Ilikok Island ⌒ CDN 36-37 S 2
Ilim ~ RUS 116-117 L 8
Ilimanaq = Claushavn o GRØ 28-29 P 2
Ilimo o PNG 183 D 5
Ilimpeja ~ RUS 116-117 M 4
Ilimsk o RUS 116-117 L 7
Ilin-Džerli ~ RUS 118-119 H 4
Ilingelyo, Tanjung ▲ RI 166-167 E 2
Ilin Island ⌒ RP 160-161 D 6
Ilin-Jurjah ~ RUS 110-111 c 5
Il'inka o RUS 96-97 K 8
Il'ino o RUS 94-95 M 4
Il'inovka o RUS 122-123 C 4
Il'inskaja Sopka, vulkan ▲ RUS 122-123 R 3
Il'inskij o RUS 96-97 J 4
Il'inskij o RUS 122-123 K 5
Iliomar o RI 166-167 D 6
Ilio Point ▲ USA (HI) 288 H 3
Ilir o RUS 116-117 K 8
Ilir ~ RUS 116-117 K 8
Ilirgytgyn, ozero ⬭ RUS 112-113 K 1
Ilirnej o RUS 112-113 P 3
Ilirnej, ozero ⬭ RUS 112-113 P 3
Ilirnejskij krjaž ▲ RUS 112-113 P 3
Ilistaja ~ RUS 122-123 E 6
Ilisu Barajı < TR 128-129 J 4
Il'ja ~ RUS 110-111 F 4
Ilja ~ RUS 118-119 F 10
Il'jak ~ RUS 114-115 O 4
Il'jali ★ TM 136-137 F 4
Iljalinskij kanal < TM 136-137 E 4
Iljara o EAK 212-213 H 4
Ilktugitak, Cape ▲ USA 22-23 T 3
Ill ~ F 90-91 L 7
Illampu, Nevado ▲ BOL 70-71 C 4
Illapel o RCH 76-77 B 6
Illapel, Río ~ RCH 76-77 B 6
Illara Creek ~ AUS 176-177 M 2
Illawarra, Lake ⬭ AUS 180-181 L 3
Illawong o AUS 176-177 C 4
Illbillee, Mount ▲ AUS 176-177 M 3
Illecillewaet Névé ~ CDN (BC) 230-231 M 2
Illéla o RN 198-199 B 5
Illela o WAN 198-199 B 6
Iller ~ D 92-93 L 4
Illes Balears ⌒ E 98-99 H 5
Illescas, Cerro ▲ PE 64-65 B 4
Illescas o MEX 50-51 H 6
Illgen City o USA (MN) 270-271 G 3
Illimo o PE 64-65 C 5
Illingworth o CDN (ALB) 232-233 G 5
Illiniza, Volcán ▲ EC 64-65 C 2
Illinois □ USA (IL) 274-275 H 4
Illinois City o USA (IL) 274-275 H 3
Illinois Point ▲ USA (MT) 250-251 D 4
Illinois River ~ USA (AR) 276-277 B 5
Illinois River ~ USA (IL) 274-275 H 5
Illinois River ~ USA (OK) 264-265 K 2
Illinois River ~ USA (OR) 244-245 B 8
Illiopolis o USA (IL) 274-275 J 5
Illiwa ~ GUY 62-63 E 4
Illizi o DZ 190-191 G 7
Illmo o USA (MO) 276-277 F 3
Illorsuit o GRØ 26-27 Y 8
Illueca o E 98-99 G 4
Illusion Lake ⬭ USA (TX) 264-265 B 5
Ilma, Lake ⬭ AUS 176-177 J 4
Ilmalianuk, Cape ▲ USA 22-23 M 6
Il'men', ozero ⬭ RUS 94-95 M 2
Il'menskij zapovednik ⊥ RUS 96-97 M 6
Ilnik o USA 22-23 R 4
Ilo o PE 70-71 B 5
Ilobasco o• ES 52-53 K 5
Ilobu ~ RCB 210-211 F 2
Ilobu o WAN 204-205 F 5
Iloca o RCH 78-79 C 3
Ilofa o WAN 204-205 F 4
Ilog ~ RP 160-161 E 8
Iloilo City ★•• RP 160-161 E 7
Ilomantsi o FIN 88-89 L 5
Ilonga o EAT 214-215 J 5
Ilorin ★ WAN 204-205 F 4
Ilovlja ~ RUS 96-97 D 8
Il'pinskij, mys ▲ RUS 120-121 V 4
Il'pinskij, poluostrov ⌒ RUS 120-121 V 4
Il'pyr, poluostrov ⌒ RUS 120-121 V 4
Il'pyrskij o RUS 120-121 V 4
Ilua Fjord ≈ 28-29 S 6
Ilubabor □ ETH 208-209 B 5
Ilugwa o RI 166-167 K 3
Iluileq ⌒ GRØ 28-29 T 6
Ilūkste o LV 94-95 K 4
Ilula o EAT 212-213 D 5
Ilulissat = Jakobshavn o GRØ 28-29 P 2
Ilur o RI 166-167 F 4
Ilushi o WAN 204-205 G 5
Ilwaco o USA (WA) 244-245 B 4
Ilwendo o Z 218-219 C 3
Ilyč ~ RUS 114-115 D 3
Im ~ RUS 122-123 H 2
Imabari o J 152-153 E 7
Imabetsu o J 152-153 J 4
Imaichi o J 152-153 H 6
Imajō o J 152-153 G 7
Imakane o J 152-153 H 3
Imala o MOC 218-219 K 2
Imām Ānas o IRQ 130-131 K 2
Imamoğlu ★ TR 128-129 F 4
Imanbūlak ~ KA 124-125 E 2
Imandi o RI 164-165 H 3
Imandra, ozero ⬭ RUS 88-89 M 3
Imangra ~ RUS 118-119 K 7
Imanombo o RM 222-223 D 10
Imantau, köli ⬭ KA 124-125 F 2
Imari o J 152-153 C 8
Imasa o SUD 200-201 H 3
Imassogo o BF 202-203 J 3
Imata o PE 70-71 B 4
Imata, Serrania de ▲ YV 62-63 D 2
Imataca, Reserva Forestal ⊥ YV 60-61 L 3
Imataca, Reserva Forestal ⊥ YV 62-63 D 2
Imatong Mountains ▲ SUD 206-207 L 6
Imatra o FIN 88-89 K 6
Imbāba o ET 194-195 E 2
Imbituba o BR 74-75 F 7
Imbituba, Ponta de ▲ BR 74-75 F 7
Imbituva o BR 74-75 E 5
Imbler o USA (OR) 244-245 H 5
Imboden o USA (AR) 276-277 D 4
Imborditure Creek ~ AUS 178-179 D 2
Imbrinis o PNG 183 A 2
Imbwae o Z 218-219 C 3
Iménas < RMM 196-197 L 6
Imerimandroso o RM 222-223 F 6
Imerina Imady o RM 222-223 E 8
Imerintsiatesika o RM 222-223 E 7
Imese o ZRE 210-211 G 2
Imessouane, Pointe ▲ MA 188-189 G 5
Imgyt ~ RUS 114-115 M 5
Imgytskoe, boloto ∴ RUS 114-115 L 5
Imi o ETH 208-209 F 5
Imi-n-Tanoute o MA 188-189 G 5
Imišly = Imişli o AZ 128-129 N 3
Imja Do ⌒ ROK 150-151 F 10
Imjin Gang ~ DVR 150-151 F 8
Imlan ~ RUS 112-113 P 5
Imlay o USA (NV) 246-247 G 3
Imlay City o USA (MI) 272-273 F 4
Imlily o MA 196-197 C 3
Immokalee o USA (FL) 286-287 H 5
Immouzzer-des-Ida-Outanane o MA 188-189 G 5
Imnaha o USA (OR) 244-245 J 5
Imnaha River ~ USA (OR) 244-245 J 5
Imnlor, ozero ⬭ RUS 114-115 N 4
Imo □ WAN 204-205 G 6
Imofossen ~ N 86-87 K 2
Ímola o I 100-101 C 2
Imonda o PNG 183 A 2
Imo River ~ WAN 204-205 G 6
Imotski o HR 100-101 F 3
Imoulaye, Hassi < DZ 190-191 G 6
Imouzèr-du-Kandar o MA 188-189 J 4
Impenvéem ~ RUS 112-113 P 5
Imperatriz o BR 68-69 E 4
Imperia o I 100-101 B 3
Imperial o CDN (SAS) 232-233 N 4
Imperial o USA (CA) 248-249 J 7
Imperial o USA (NE) 262-263 E 4
Imperial o USA (TX) 266-267 E 2
Imperial, Río ~ RCH 78-79 C 5
Imperial Mills o CDN 32-33 P 4
Imperieuse Reef ⌒ AUS 172-173 D 4
Impfondo ★ RCB 210-211 G 3
Imphāl ★• IND 142-143 H 3
Imposible, Parque Nacional El ⊥ GCA 52-53 J 5
Impulo o ANG (HUA) 216-217 B 6
Impulo ~ ANG 216-217 B 6
Imranlı ★ TR 128-129 H 3
İmroz o TR 128-129 A 2
Imtān o SYR 128-129 G 6
Imuris o MEX 50-51 D 2
Imuruan Bay ≈ 160-161 C 7
Imuruk Basin ⬭ USA 20-21 H 4
Imuruk Lake ⬭ USA 20-21 J 4
Imusho o Z 218-219 B 3
Ina ~ PL 92-93 N 2
Ina ~ RUS 118-119 E 9
Inaafmadow o SP 208-209 G 4
Inabu o J 152-153 G 7
Inácio Dias, Ponta ▲ BR 74-75 F 5
Inácio Martins o BR 74-75 E 5
Inadale o USA (TX) 264-265 D 6
I-n-Adiattafene o RMM 202-203 J 2
Inaja o BR 66-67 H 5
Inajá o BR 68-69 K 6
Inaja, Rio ~ BR 68-69 C 6
Inâl o RIM 196-197 C 4
Inalik o USA 20-21 F 4
Inambari o PE 70-71 C 3
Inambari, Río ~ PE 70-71 B 3
In Amenas o DZ 190-191 G 6
In Amguel o DZ 190-191 E 9
Inangahua o NZ 182 C 4
Inan'ja ~ RUS 120-121 N 2
Inanudak Bay ≈ 22-23 M 6
Inanwatan o RI 166-167 G 3
Iñapari o PE 70-71 C 2
Inari o• FIN 88-89 J 2
Inarigda o RUS 116-117 N 4
Inarijärvi ⬭•• FIN 88-89 J 2
Inaru River ~ USA 20-21 M 1
Inarwa o NEP 144-145 F 7
Inauini, Rio ~ BR 66-67 C 7
Inawashiro-ko ⬭ J 152-153 J 6
In-Azaoua o RN 198-199 C 2
In Azzene, Djebel ▲ DZ 190-191 C 7
In Belbel o DZ 190-191 C 7
Inca o E 98-99 J 5
Inca, Cerro del ▲ RCH 76-77 C 1
Inca, Río del ~ RA 76-77 C 5
Inca de Oro o RCH 76-77 C 4
Incahuasi o PE 64-65 C 5
Incahuasi o RA 76-77 D 3
İnč e Borūn o IR 136-137 D 6
İnce Burnu ▲ TR 128-129 F 2
İncesu ★• TR 128-129 F 3
Inchbonnie o NZ 182 C 5
Inchiri □ RIM 196-197 C 4
Inch'ŏn o ROK 150-151 F 9
Inchope o MOC 218-219 G 4
Inchul ~ UA 102-103 H 3
Inchulec' ~ UA 102-103 H 3
Incisioni Rupestri, Parco Nazionale ⊥••• I 100-101 C 1
Incomappleaux River ~ CDN (BC) 230-231 M 3
Incomati, Rio ~ MOC 220-221 L 2
Inčoun o RUS 112-113 Z 3
Increase o USA (MS) 268-269 M 4
Incudine, Monte ▲ F 98-99 M 4
Incuyo o PE 64-65 F 9
Indaial o BR 74-75 F 6
Indalsälven ~ S 86-87 H 5
Inda Medhani o ETH 200-201 J 6
Indapur o IND 138-139 E 10
Indara Point o IND 140-141 L 6
Indargarh o IND 138-139 F 7
Inda Silasē o ETH 200-201 J 5
Indaugyi Aing ⬭ MYA 142-143 K 2
Indaw o MYA 142-143 K 5
Indé o MEX 50-51 G 5
Independence o USA (CA) 248-249 F 3
Independence o USA (IA) 274-275 G 2
Independence o USA (KS) 262-263 L 7
Independence o USA (KY) 276-277 L 2
Independence o USA (LA) 268-269 K 6
Independence o USA (MN) 270-271 F 4
Independence o USA (MN) 270-271 E 5
Independence o USA (MO) 274-275 D 5
Independence o USA (OR) 244-245 B 6
Independence o USA (VA) 280-281 E 7
Independence Creek ~ USA (TX) 266-267 E 3
Independence Fjord ≈ 26-27 k 3
Independence Hall ••• USA (PA) 280-281 M 4
Independence Mine • USA 20-21 Q 6
Independence Rock State Historic Site ∴ USA (WY) 252-253 L 4
Independencia o BOL (COC) 70-71 D 5
Independencia o BOL (PAN) 70-71 D 2
Independência o BR 68-69 H 4
Independencia o YV 60-61 E 4
Independencia, Isla de la ⌒ PE 64-65 D 9
Independenţa o RO 102-103 F 5
Inder, köl ⬭ KA 96-97 H 9
Inderaba o SUD 200-201 F 6
Inderbor ★ KA 96-97 H 9
Index o USA (WA) 244-245 D 3
Indi o IND 140-141 F 2
India ■ IND 138-139 D 7
Indiana o AUS 178-179 C 2
Indiana o USA (PA) 280-281 G 3
Indiana □ USA (IN) 274-275 M 5
Indiana Dunes • USA (IN) 274-275 L 3
Indianapolis ★ USA (IN) 274-275 M 5
Indiana Trail Caverns • USA (OH) 280-281 C 3
Indian Bay o CDN (NFL) 242-243 P 3
Indian Bayou ~ USA (AR) 276-277 D 6
Indian Brook ~ CDN (NS) 240-241 P 4
Indian Cabins o CDN 30-31 L 6
Indian Community ∴• BS 54-55 J 3
Indian Creek ~ USA (UT) 254-255 F 5
Indian Falls o USA (CA) 246-247 E 3
Indian Gardens o CDN (NS) 240-241 K 6
Indian Grave Mount ▲ USA 20-21 U 4
Indian Harbour o CDN (NS) 240-241 M 6
Indian Head o CDN (SAS) 232-233 P 5
Indian Head o USA (MD) 280-281 J 5
Indian Heaven Wilderness ⊥ USA (WA) 244-245 D 4
Indian Lake o USA (NY) 278-279 G 5
Indian Lake ⬭ USA (MI) 270-271 M 4
Indian Lake ⬭ USA (OH) 280-281 C 3
Indian Lake Estates o USA (FL) 286-287 H 4
Indian Nation Turnpike II USA (OK) 264-265 J 4
Indian Ocean ≈ 12 F 6
Indianola o USA (IA) 274-275 E 3
Indianola o USA (MS) 268-269 K 3
Indianola o USA (NE) 262-263 F 4
Indianola o USA (OK) 264-265 J 3
Indianópolis o BR 72-73 G 5
Indian-Pacific II AUS 176-177 H 5
Indian Passage ≈ USA 286-287 D 2
Indian Pine o USA (AZ) 256-257 F 4
Indian Point ▲ USA (UT) 254-255 B 5
Indian Reservation ⚔ CDN (MAN) 234-235 G 5
Indian Reservation ⚔ CDN (MAN) 234-235 C 5
Indian Reservation ⚔ CDN (QUE) 236-237 P 2
Indian Reserve ⚔ CDN (MAN) 234-235 H 3
Indian Reserve ⚔ CDN (MAN) 234-235 C 5
Indian Reserve ⚔ CDN (ONT) 234-235 L 4
Indian Reserve ⚔ CDN (ONT) 234-235 J 4
Indian Reserve ⚔ CDN (ONT) 234-235 O 3
Indian Reserve ⚔ CDN (SAS) 232-233 K 3
Indian Reserve ⚔ CDN (SAS) 232-233 P 4
Indian Reserve ⚔ CDN (SAS) 232-233 R 4
Indian Reserve ⚔• CDN (ONT) 236-237 D 3
Indian Reserve 3 ⚔ CDN (MAN) 234-235 G 4
Indian Reserve 13 ⚔ CDN (MAN) 234-235 G 2
Indian Reserve 33 ⚔ CDN 34-35 G 4
Indian Reserve 159 ⚔ CDN (SAS) 232-233 K 2
Indian Reserve 194 ⚔ CDN 32-33 Q 4
Indian Reserve Birds Hill ⚔ CDN (MAN) 234-235 G 5
Indian Reserve Fort Albany ⚔ CDN 34-35 Q 4
Indian Reserve Nineteen ⚔ CDN 34-35 H 3
Indian Reserves ⚔ CDN (SAS) 232-233 Q 5
Indian Reserves 81-84 ⚔ CDN (SAS) 232-233 P 5
Indian Reserve Seventeen ⚔ CDN 34-35 H 3
Indian River ≈ 48-49 H 5
Indian River ~ CDN (NFL) 242-243 M 3
Indian River ~ CDN (ONT) 238-239 H 3
Indian River o USA (MI) 272-273 E 2
Indian River ≈ USA 286-287 J 3
Indian River Bay < USA (DE) 280-281 L 5
Indian Springs o USA (NV) 248-249 J 3
Indiantown o USA (FL) 286-287 J 4
Indian Township o USA (ME) 278-279 O 3
Indian Trail Caverns ∴ USA (OH) 280-281 C 2
Indian Wells o USA (AZ) 256-257 E 3
Indiara o BR 72-73 E 4
Indiaroba o BR 68-69 K 7
Indibir o ETH 208-209 C 4
Indiga o RUS 88-89 U 3
Indiga ~ RUS 88-89 U 3
Indígenas de Quilmes, Ruinas • RA 76-77 D 4
Indigirka ~ RUS 110-111 Y 6
Indigirka ~ RUS 120-121 K 2
Indik"jaha ~ RUS 108-109 S 7
Indin Lake ⬭ CDN 30-31 M 3
Indio o USA (CA) 248-249 H 6
Indio, El o USA (TX) 266-267 G 5
Indio, Río ~ NIC 52-53 B 6
Indio Rico o RA 78-79 J 5
Indio Rico, Arroyo ~ RA 78-79 J 5
Índios, Cachoeira dos ~ BR 66-67 F 2
Indios, Cayos los ⌒ C 54-55 D 4
Indios, Los o C 54-55 H 4
Indios, Rio dos ~ BR 72-73 D 7
Indiskaja guba ≈ 88-89 U 3
Indispensable Strait ≈ 184 I e 3
Indombo o G 210-211 D 3
Indonesia ■ RI 168 B 2
Indooroopilly Outstation o AUS 176-177 M 4
Indore o• IND 138-139 E 8
Indragiri ~ RI 162-163 E 5
Indralaya o RI 162-163 F 6
Indramayu o RI 168 C 3
Indrapura o RI 162-163 C 3
Indravati ~ IND 142-143 C 6
Indre ~ F 90-91 H 8
Indulkana ⚔ AUS 176-177 M 3
Indus = Sind ~ IND 138-139 F 7
Indus Fan ≃ 12 E 2
Industry o USA (IL) 274-275 H 4
Industry o USA (TX) 266-267 L 4
Indwe o ZA 220-221 H 5
Ine Abeg < RMM 196-197 K 4
İnebolu ★ TR 128-129 E 2
İnegöl ★ TR 128-129 C 2
Ineguha o ETH 208-209 G 4
Inékar o RMM 196-197 M 7
Inés, Monte ▲ RA 80 F 4
Inewari o ETH 208-209 D 4
Inez o USA (KY) 276-277 N 3
Inezgane o MA 188-189 G 5
Infanta o RP 160-161 D 5
I-n-Farba o RIM 196-197 E 7
Inferior, Laguna ≈ 52-53 G 3
Inferno, Cachoeira ~ BR 66-67 K 4
Inferno, Cachoeira do ~ BR 66-67 H 7
Infiernillo o MEX 52-53 C 2
Infiernillo, Presa del < MEX 52-53 D 2
Ingá o BR 68-69 L 5
Inga • ZRE 210-211 D 6
Ingaí, Rio ~ BR 72-73 H 6
Ingal o RN 198-199 C 4
Ingaliston o USA (MI) 270-271 L 5
Ingallan Creek ~ AUS 172-173 L 6
Ingalls Lake ⬭ CDN 30-31 R 5
Ingaly o RUS 114-115 N 7
Inğāna o IRQ 128-129 L 5
Inganda o ZRE 210-211 H 4
Ingapirca • EC 64-65 C 3
Ingavi o BOL 70-71 D 2
Ingawa o WAN 198-199 D 6
Ingende o ZRE 210-211 G 4
Ingeniero Chanourdie o RA 76-77 H 5
Ingeniero Giagnoni o RA 78-79 E 2
Ingeniero G. N. Juárez o RA 76-77 G 2
Ingeniero Jacobacci o RA 78-79 E 6
Ingeniero Moneta o RA 78-79 K 2
Ingenika River ~ CDN 32-33 H 3
Ingenio Mora o BOL 70-71 F 6
Ingenstrem Rocks ⌒ USA 22-23 D 6
Ingeqare, Küh-e ▲ IR 128-129 N 5
Ingersoll o CDN (ONT) 238-239 E 5
Ingham o AUS 174-175 J 6
Ingia Fjord ≈ 26-27 Y 8
Ingile < EAK 212-213 G 4
Ingili ~ RUS 120-121 F 4
Inginiyagala o CL 140-141 J 7
Inglefield, Kap ▲ GRØ 26-27 O 4
Inglefield Bredning ≈ 26-27 Q 5
Inglefield Land ∴ GRØ 26-27 P 4
Inglefield Mountains ▲ CDN 24-25 g 2
Inglesa, Bahía ≈ 76-77 B 4
Ingleses do Rio Vermelho o BR 74-75 F 6
Ingleside o CDN (ONT) 238-239 L 3
Ingleside o USA (TX) 266-267 K 6
Inglewood o AUS (QLD) 178-179 L 5
Inglewood o AUS (VIC) 180-181 G 4
Inglewood o USA (CA) 248-249 F 6
Inglewood o USA (NE) 262-263 K 3
Inglis o CDN (MAN) 234-235 B 4
Inglis o USA (FL) 286-287 G 2
Inglis, Mount ▲ AUS 178-179 K 3
Inglutalik River ~ USA 20-21 K 4
Ingnerit ≈ 26-27 Z 8
Ingnerit ⌒ GRØ 26-27 X 8
Ingoda ~ RUS 118-119 E 10
Ingo holiday resort • RI 164-165 G 5
Ingolf Fjord ≈ 26-27 q 3
Ingólfhöfði ▲ IS 86-87 e 3
Ingolo o RCB 210-211 D 5
Ingolstadt o D 92-93 L 4
Ingomar o USA (MT) 250-251 M 5
Ingonish o CDN (NS) 240-241 P 4
Ingonish Beach o CDN (NS) 240-241 P 4
Ingoré o GNB 202-203 C 3
Ingrāj Bāzār o IND 142-143 F 3
Ingray Lake ⬭ CDN 30-31 L 3
Ingrid Christensen land ∴ ARK 16 F 8
Ingujagun ~ RUS 114-115 N 3
Inguri ~ GE 126-127 E 6
Ingushetia = Galgaj Respublika □ RUS 126-127 F 6
Ingušskaja Respublika □ RUS 126-127 F 6
Ingwe o Z 218-219 D 1
Ingwempisi ~ ZA 220-221 K 3
Inhaca o MOC 220-221 L 3
Inhaca, Ilha da ⌒ MOC 220-221 L 2
Inhafenga o MOC 218-219 G 5
Inhagapi o BR 68-69 E 2
Inhaí o BR 72-73 J 4
Inhambane □ MOC 218-219 G 6
Inhambane ★ MOC (INH) 218-219 H 6
Inhambane, Baia de ≈ 218-219 H 6
Inhambupe o BR 68-69 J 7
Inhambupe, Rio ~ BR 68-69 J 7
Inhaminga o MOC 218-219 H 4
Inhamissiba, Rio ~ MOC 218-219 G 6
Inhamitanga o MOC 218-219 H 4
Inharrime o MOC 218-219 H 7
Inharrime, Rio ~ MOC 220-221 M 2
Inhassoro o MOC 218-219 H 5
Inhaúmas o BR 72-73 H 2
In Hihaou, Adrar ▲ DZ 190-191 D 9
In Hihaou, Oued ~ DZ 190-191 C 9
Inhuçu o BR 68-69 H 4
Inhul ~ UA 102-103 H 4
Inhulec' ~ UA 102-103 H 4
Inhúma o BR 68-69 H 5
Inhumas o BR 72-73 F 4
Inhuporanga o BR 68-69 J 4
Inifel, Hassi < DZ 190-191 D 6
Inin < WAN 204-205 G 6
Inirida, Río ~ CO 60-61 G 6
Inis = Ennis ★• IRL 90-91 C 5

Ichoa, Río — Inis 339

Inis Ceithleann = Enniskillen ☆ • GB 90-91 D 4
Inis Córthaidh = Enniscorthy o IRL 90-91 D 5
Iniu o SOL 184 I c 3
Inja o RUS 124-125 P 3
Inja ∼ RUS 114-115 S 7
Inja ∼ RUS 120-121 L 3
In'jali ∼ RUS 110-111 Y 7
Inje o ROK 150-151 G 8
Injibara o ETH 208-209 C 3
In-Jitane o RN 198-199 C 4
Injune o AUS 178-179 K 3
Inkanwaya • BOL 70-71 C 4
Inkerman o AUS 174-175 F 5
Inkisi ∼ ZRE 210-211 E 6
Inklin River ∼ CDN 32-33 D 2
Inkom o USA (ID) 252-253 F 4
Inkouéle o RCB 210-211 E 4
Inkster o USA (ND) 258-259 K 3
Inlander II AUS 174-175 G 7
Inland Kaikoura Range ▲▲ NZ 182 D 5
Inland Lake o USA 20-21 L 3
Inman o USA (KS) 262-263 J 6
Inman o USA (NE) 262-263 H 2
Inman o USA (SC) 284-285 H 1
Inman River ∼ CDN 24-25 N 6
Inn ∼ D 92-93 M 4
Innahas Chebbi ⊖ DZ 190-191 D 7
Innalik o GRØ 28-29 O 2
Innamincka o AUS 178-179 F 4
Innamincka Regional Reserve ⊥ AUS 178-179 F 4
Inndyr o N 86-87 G 3
Inner Mongolia = Nei Mongol Zizhiqu □ VRC 154-155 D 2
Innes National Park ⊥ AUS 180-181 D 3
Inneston o AUS 180-181 D 3
Innesvale o AUS 172-173 K 3
Innetalling Island ⌒ CDN 36-37 K 7
Innisfail o • AUS 174-175 J 5
Innisfail o CDN (ALB) 232-233 E 4
Innisfree o CDN (ALB) 232-233 G 2
Innjah o RUS 118-119 J 6
Innokent'evka o RUS 122-123 C 4
Innoko River ∼ USA 20-21 L 5
Innsbruck ☆ A 92-93 L 5
Innuksuac, Rivière ∼ CDN 36-37 L 5
Inobonto o RI 164-165 J 3
Inoca o BOL 70-71 C 5
Inocência o BR 72-73 E 5
Inocentes, Los o MEX 50-51 D 6
Inongo o ZRE 210-211 G 4
Inoni o RCB 210-211 E 5
Inostranceva, zaliv o RUS 108-109 L 3
Inowrocław o • PL 92-93 P 2
Inpynèkul' ∼ RUS 112-113 T 4
I-n-Quezzam o DZ 198-199 B 3
Inquisivi o BOL 70-71 D 5
In Rhar o DZ 190-191 C 7
Inriville o RA 78-79 H 2
I-n-Sâkâne, Erg ∸ RMM 196-197 K 4
In Salah o • DZ 190-191 D 7
Insar o RUS 96-97 D 7
Inscription, Cape ▲ AUS 176-177 B 2
Insculas o PE 64-65 C 4
Insein o MYA 158-159 D 2
Inskip Point ▲ AUS 178-179 M 3
In Sokki, Oued ∼ DZ 190-191 D 6
Inster o USA (ND) 258-259 K 3
Instow o CDN (SAS) 232-233 K 6
Însurăţei o RO 102-103 E 5
Inta o RUS 108-109 J 8
Intakareyen < RN 198-199 C 5
In Talak o RMM 196-197 M 6
I-n-Tebezas o RMM 196-197 L 6
Intendente Alvear o RA 78-79 H 3
Intercoastal Waterway ∼ USA (VA) 280-281 K 7
Interior o USA (SD) 260-261 E 3
Interlachen o USA (FL) 286-287 H 2
Interlaken o CDN (ONT) 238-239 G 3
Interlaken o • CH 92-93 J 5
Interlochen o USA (MI) 272-273 D 3
International Amistad Reservoir < USA (TX) 266-267 F 4
International Falcon Reservoir < USA (TX) 266-267 H 7
International Falls o USA (MN) 270-271 E 2
Intervew Island ⌒ IND 140-141 L 3
Intich'o o ETH 200-201 J 5
Intihuasi, Gruta de • RA 78-79 G 2
I-n-Tillit o RMM 202-203 K 2
Intracoastal Waterway < USA (FL) 286-287 H 1
Intracoastal Waterway < USA (LA) 268-269 K 7
Intracoastal Waterway < USA (SC) 284-285 M 3
Intracoastal Waterway < USA (TX) 268-269 F 7
Intrepid Inlet ≈ 24-25 M 2
Intutu o PE 64-65 E 3
Inuarfigssuaq o GRØ 26-27 Q 4
Inúbia o BR 72-73 K 2
Inubō-saki ▲ J 152-153 J 7
Inugsuin Fiord ≈ 28-29 F 2
Inukjuak o CDN 36-37 K 5
Inulik Lake o CDN 30-31 N 2
Inulterg Sø o GRØ 26-27 h 3
Inuo o PNG 183 B 4
Inuria, Lago o PE 64-65 E 6
Inutil, Bahía ≈ 80 E 6
Inuvik o • CDN 20-21 Y 2
Inuya, Río ∼ PE 64-65 F 7
In'va ∼ RUS 96-97 J 4
Inveraray o • GB 90-91 E 3
Invercargill o NZ 182 B 7
Inverell o AUS 178-179 L 5
Inverhuron o CDN (ONT) 238-239 D 4
Inverleigh o AUS (QLD) 174-175 F 6
Inverleigh o AUS (VIC) 180-181 H 5
Inverloch o AUS 180-181 H 5
Invermay o CDN (SAS) 232-233 P 4
Invermere o CDN (BC) 230-231 N 3
Inverness o AUS 178-179 H 2
Inverness o CDN (NS) 240-241 O 4
Inverness o CDN (QUE) 238-239 O 2
Inverness o • GB 90-91 E 3
Inverness o USA (FL) 286-287 G 3
Inverurie o GB 90-91 F 3
Inverway o AUS 172-173 J 4
Investigator Channel ≈ 158-159 E 5
Investigator Group ⌒ AUS 180-181 C 2
Investigator Passage ≈ 158-159 D 4
Investigator Ridge ≃ 12 H 5
Investigator Strait ≈ 180-181 D 3
Inwood o CDN (MAN) 234-235 F 4
Inwood o USA (IA) 274-275 B 1
Inyangani ▲ ZW 218-219 G 4
Inyarinyi (Kenmore Park) ✗ AUS 176-177 M 3
Inyathi o ZW 218-219 E 4
Inyokern o USA (CA) 248-249 G 4
Inyo Mountains ▲▲ USA (CA) 248-249 F 2
Inyonga o EAT (RUK) 214-215 G 4
Inza o RUS (ULN) 96-97 E 7
Inza ∼ RUS 96-97 D 7
Inzana Lake o CDN (BC) 228-229 K 2
Inžavino o RUS 94-95 S 5
Inzia ∼ ZRE 210-211 F 6
Ioánnina o • GR 100-101 H 5
Iokanga ∼ RUS 88-89 O 3
Iola o USA (KS) 262-263 L 7
Iola o USA (WI) 270-271 J 6
Iolgo, hrebet ▲▲ RUS 124-125 P 3
Iolotan o TM 136-137 H 6
Iomi, ozero o RUS 112-113 Y 4
Iona o ANG 216-217 B 8
Iona, Parque Nacional do ⊥ ANG 216-217 B 8
Ionava ☆ LT 94-95 J 4
Ione o USA (CA) 246-247 H 5
Ione o USA (CA) 246-247 E 5
Iones, Cap ▲ CDN 36-37 K 7
Ionesport o USA (ME) 278-279 O 4
Iongo o ANG 216-217 D 4
Ionia o USA (MI) 272-273 D 4
Ionian Islands = Iónioi Nísoi ⌒ GR 100-101 G 5
Ionian Sea ≈ 100-101 F 6
Ionian Sea = Iónio, Mare ≈ 100-101 F 6
Iónioi Nísoi □ GR 100-101 H 5
Iónio Pélagos ≈ 100-101 F 6
Ioniveem ∼ RUS 112-113 Y 4
Ión Nísoi ≈ 100-101 G 5
Iony, ostrov ⌒ RUS 120-121 K 5
Iori ∼ GE 126-127 F 6
Iori o PNG 183 C 4
Ios ⌒ GR 100-101 K 6
Iō-shima ⌒ J 152-153 D 9
Iota o USA (LA) 268-269 H 6
Iouê Juruena, Estação Ecológica ⊥ BR 70-71 H 3
Iouigharacène, Ibel ▲ MA 188-189 J 4
Iouîk o RIM 196-197 B 5
Iowa o USA (LA) 268-269 H 6
Iowa □ USA (IA) 274-275 D 2
Iowa City o USA (IA) 274-275 G 3
Iowa Falls o USA (IA) 274-275 E 2
Iowa Park o USA (TX) 264-265 F 5
Iowa River ∼ USA (IA) 274-275 G 3
Iowa River ∼ USA (IA) 274-275 E 1
Iowa Sac and Fox Indian Reservation ✗ USA (KS) 262-263 L 5
Ipadu, Cachoeira ∼ BR 66-67 D 2
Ipala o GCA 52-53 K 4
Ipameri o BR 72-73 F 4
Ipanema o BR 72-73 K 5
Ipao o VAN 184 II c 4
Iparia o PE 64-65 E 6
Ipatinga o BR 72-73 J 5
Ipatovo o RUS 102-103 N 5
Ipauçu o BR 72-73 F 7
Ipaumirim o BR 68-69 J 5
İpek Geçidi ▲ TR 128-129 K 3
Iperu o WAN 204-205 E 5
Ipetu-Ijesha o WAN 204-205 F 5
Ipewik River ∼ USA 20-21 H 2
Iphigenia Bay ≈ 32-33 C 4
Ipiaçava, Río ∼ BR 68-69 B 4
Ipiaçu o BR 72-73 F 5
Ipiales o CO 64-65 D 1
Ipiaú o BR 72-73 L 3
Ipil o RP 160-161 E 9
Ipirá o BR 72-73 L 2
Ipiranga, Rio ∼ BR 66-67 K 7
Ipiros □ GR 100-101 H 5
Ipita o BOL 70-71 F 6
Ipitinga, Rio ∼ BR 62-63 H 5
Ipixuma, Igarapé ∼ BR 66-67 D 5
Ipixuma, Rio ∼ BR 64-65 F 5
Ipixun o BR 62-63 J 6
Ipixuna o BR 66-67 B 6
Ipixuna, Área Indígena ✗ BR 66-67 F 5
Ipixuna, Igarapé ∼ BR 68-69 B 4
Ipixuna, Ilha ⌒ BR 66-67 F 4
Ipixuna, Rio ∼ BR 66-67 F 6
Ipixuna ou Paraná Pixuna, Rio ∼ BR 66-67 F 6
I pobutu • UA 102-103 G 2
Ipoh ☆ • MAL 162-163 D 2
Iporá o BR 72-73 E 4
Iporanga o BR 74-75 F 5
Ipota o VAN 184 II b 4
Ippy o RCA 206-207 E 5
Ipsári ▲ GR 100-101 K 4
Ipswich o AUS 178-179 M 4
Ipswich o GB 90-91 H 5
Ipswich o USA (MA) 278-279 L 6
Ipswich o USA (SD) 260-261 G 1
Ipu o BR 68-69 H 4
Ipumirim o BR 74-75 D 6
Ipun, Isla ⌒ RCH 80 C 2
Ipurupuro, Río ∼ BOL 70-71 E 4
Iqe o VRC 146-147 M 6
Iqlit o ET 194-195 F 5
Iquipi o PE 64-65 F 9
Iquique ☆ RCH 70-71 B 7
Iquitos ☆ • PE 64-65 F 3
Ira o USA (TX) 264-265 D 6
Irá, Igarapé ∼ BR 66-67 C 3
Iraan o USA (TX) 266-267 F 3
Ira Banda o RCA 206-207 F 6
Iracaja, Cachoeira do ∼ BR 70-71 E 2
Iracema o BR 68-69 J 4
Iracoubo o F 62-63 H 3
Iraël o RUS 88-89 X 4
Iraí de Minas o BR 72-73 G 5
Iraïfia < MA 196-197 C 2
Irajuba o BR 72-73 K 2
Iraka o WAN 204-205 H 3
Iráklio o GR 100-101 K 7
Iramaia o BR 72-73 K 2
Iran = Īrān ■ IR 134-135 D 2
Iranduba o BR 66-67 G 4
Īrānšahr o IR 134-135 J 5
Irantxé, Área Indígena ✗ BR 70-71 H 3
Irapuato o MEX 52-53 D 1
Iraq = 'Irāq ■ IRQ 128-129 J 6
Iraquara o BR 72-73 K 2
Irará o BR 72-73 L 2
Irarraren ∸ DZ 190-191 E 7
Irasville o USA (VT) 278-279 J 4
Irati o BR 74-75 E 5
Irau, Gunung ▲ RI 166-167 G 2
Iraučuba o BR 68-69 J 3
Irawan, Wādi < LAR 192-193 D 4
Irbejskoe ☆ RUS 116-117 G 8
Irbeni väin ≈ 94-95 G 3
Irbes Šaurums ≈ 94-95 G 3
Irbid ☆ JOR 130-131 D 1
Irbit ☆ RUS 114-115 G 6
Irebue o ZRE 210-211 F 4
Irecê o BR 68-69 H 7
Irech, I-n- < RMM 196-197 K 5
Iredell o USA (TX) 264-265 G 6
Ireland = Éire ■ IRL 90-91 C 5
Ireland = Éire ⌒ IRL 90-91 C 5
Irendyk hrebet ▲▲ RUS 96-97 L 7
Irène o F 62-63 H 3
Irene o RA 78-79 J 5
Irene o USA (SD) 260-261 J 3
Iretama o BR 74-75 D 5
Iretskij, mys ▲ RUS 120-121 Q 4
Iretskij liman o RUS 120-121 Q 3
Ireupuow o VAN 184 II b 4
Irgakly o RUS 126-127 F 5
Irgičan ∼ RUS 110-111 W 5
Irgičanskij hrebet ▲▲ RUS 110-111 V 5
Irharhar, Oued ∼ DZ 190-191 E 8
Irharrhar, Oued ∼ DZ 198-199 C 2
Irherm o MA 188-189 G 5
Irhil M'Goun ▲ MA 188-189 H 5
Irhil o ROK 150-151 F 10
Iriaki o RI 166-167 H 3
Irian Jaya □ RI 166-167 H 4
Iriba o TCH 198-199 L 5
Irié o RG 202-203 F 5
Iriji < RIM 196-197 D 5
Iriki o MA 188-189 H 6
Iriklinskoe vodohranilišče < RUS 96-97 L 8
Irimi o RI 166-167 G 3
Iringa □ EAT 214-215 H 4
Iringa ☆ EAT 214-215 H 4
Iriona o HN 54-55 C 7
Iriri, Rio ∼ BR 68-69 B 5
Iririmirim, Baía ≈ 68-69 F 2
Iriri Nôvo, Rio ∼ BR 68-69 B 6
Iritka ∼ RUS 116-117 M 4
Irituia o BR 68-69 E 2
Irkeštam o KS 136-137 N 5
Irkineeva ∼ RUS 116-117 J 6
Irkineevo o RUS 116-117 H 6
Irkut ∼ RUS 116-117 L 10
Irkutsk ☆ • RUS 116-117 M 9
Irkutsko-Čeremhovskaja ravnina ⌣ RUS 116-117 K 8
Irlir, togi ▲ US 136-137 H 3
Irma o CDN (ALB) 232-233 G 3
Irminger Basin ≃ 6-7 E 3
Irminger Sea ≈ 6-7 F 2
Irmo o USA (SC) 284-285 J 2
Irmogou ∼ CI 202-203 J 5
Iro, Lac o TCH 206-207 D 3
Irobo o CI 202-203 H 7
Iroise ≈ 90-91 E 7
Ironasiteri o YV 66-67 E 2
Iron Bridge o CDN (ONT) 238-239 B 2
Iron-Bridge o GB 90-91 F 5
Ironbridge ••• GB 90-91 F 5
Iron Creek ∼ CDN (ALB) 232-233 G 3
Iron Creek o USA 20-21 H 4
Irondequoit o USA (NY) 278-279 D 5
Irondo o EAT 214-215 J 4
Irondro o RM 222-223 E 8
Irong, Gunung ▲ MAL (PAH) 162-163 E 2
Iron Knob o AUS 180-181 D 2
Iron Mountain o USA (MI) 270-271 K 5
Iron Mountain o USA (WY) 252-253 N 5
Iron Mountains ▲▲ USA (TN) 282-283 E 4
Iron Range National Park ⊥ AUS 174-175 G 3
Iron River o USA (MI) 270-271 K 4
Iron River o USA (WI) 270-271 G 4
Ironside o USA (OR) 244-245 H 6
Iron Springs o USA (UT) 254-255 B 6
Ironton o USA (MO) 276-277 E 3
Ironton o USA (OH) 280-281 D 5
Ironwood o USA (MI) 270-271 H 4
Iroquois o CDN (ONT) 238-239 K 4
Iroquois o USA (SD) 260-261 J 2
Iroquois Falls o CDN (ONT) 236-237 H 4
Iroquois River ∼ CDN 30-31 E 2
Irō-saki ▲ J 152-153 H 7
'Irqa, al- o Y 132-133 E 7
Irrawaddy ∼ MYA 142-143 J 6
Irrua o WAN 204-205 G 5
'Irsāl o RL 128-129 G 5
Irsina o I 100-101 F 4
Irtjaš, ozero o RUS 96-97 M 6
Irtyš ∼ RUS 114-115 K 4
Irtyš ∼ RUS 124-125 J 1
Irtyš = Ertis ∼ KA 124-125 K 3
Irtyšsk ☆ KA 124-125 J 2
Irumu o ZRE 212-213 B 3
Irún o E 98-99 G 3
Irupana o BOL 70-71 D 5
Irurita o E 98-99 G 3
Irurzun o E 98-99 G 3
Iruya, Río ∼ RA 76-77 E 2
Irva ∼ RUS 88-89 U 5
Irvine o CDN (ALB) 232-233 H 6
Irvine o USA (CA) 248-249 G 6
Irvine o USA (KY) 276-277 M 3
Irvine Inlet ≈ 36-37 Q 2
Irvines Landing o CDN (BC) 230-231 F 4
Irving o USA (IA) 274-275 F 3
Irving o USA (TX) 264-265 H 6
Irvington o USA (KY) 276-277 J 3
Irwin o USA (IA) 274-275 C 3
Irwin o USA (ID) 252-253 G 3
Irwin Military Reservation, Fort • USA (CA) 248-249 H 4
Irwin River ∼ AUS 176-177 C 4
Irwinton o USA (GA) 284-285 G 4
Iryguarenda o BOL 76-77 F 1
'Is, al- o KSA 130-131 F 5
Is, Ğabal ▲ ET 194-195 G 6
Isa o RUS 122-123 D 3
Isa o WAN 198-199 C 6
'Īsā, 'Ain o SYR 128-129 H 4
Isaac River ∼ AUS 178-179 K 2
Isaaq Jilible ∼ SP 212-213 H 3
Isabel o USA (SD) 260-261 E 1
Isabel, Bahía ≈ 64-65 B 10
Isabela o RP 160-161 D 9
Isabela o USA (PR) 286-287 O 2
Isabela, Cabo ▲ DOM 54-55 K 5
Isabela, Canal ≈ 64-65 B 10
Isabela, Isla ⌒ EC 64-65 B 10
Isabela, La o C 54-55 E 3
Isabela, La o DOM 54-55 K 5
Isabela, Ruinas de la ∴ • DOM 54-55 K 5
Isabela de Sagua o C 54-55 E 3
Isabel II o USA (PR) 286-287 Q 2
Isabella o CDN (MAN) 234-235 C 4
Isabella o USA (MN) 270-271 G 3
Isabella, Bahía de la ≈ 54-55 K 5
Isabella, Cape ▲ CDN 26-27 N 4
Isabella, Cordillera ▲▲ NIC 52-53 B 5
Isabella Bay ≈ 28-29 G 2
Isabella Indian Reservation ✗ USA (MI) 272-273 E 4
Isabella Reservoir o USA (CA) 248-249 F 4
Isabelle Range ▲▲ AUS 172-173 E 6
Isabel Pass ▲ USA 20-21 S 5
Isabel Rubio o C 54-55 C 3
Isabis o NAM 220-221 C 1
Isaccea o RO 102-103 F 5
Isačenko, ostrov ⌒ RUS 108-109 Y 3
Isachsen o CDN 24-25 U 1
Isachsen, Cape ▲ CDN 24-25 T 1
Isachsen Peninsula ⌣ CDN 24-25 T 1
Ísafjörður ☆ IS 86-87 b 1
Isahaya o J 152-153 D 8
Isaka o ZRE 210-211 F 5
Isa Khel o PK 138-139 C 3
Isakly ☆ RUS 96-97 G 6
Isalo ▲▲ RM 222-223 D 9
Isalo Parc National de I ⊥ RM 222-223 D 9
Isambe o ZRE 210-211 L 4
Isandja o ZRE (EQU) 210-211 H 4
Isandja o ZRE (KOC) 210-211 H 5
Isanga o ZRE (Ban) 210-211 G 4
Isanga o ZRE (EQU) 210-211 J 4
Isangano National Park ⊥ Z 214-215 F 6
Isangi o ZRE 210-211 K 3
Isango o ZRE 212-213 B 4
Isanlu o WAN 204-205 F 4
Isanlu-Esa o WAN 204-205 F 4
Išan Šalib o IRQ 128-129 L 7
Isar ∼ D (BAY) 92-93 M 4
Isas o CDN (ONT) 236-237 F 4
'Išāš, al- o KSA 130-131 F 4
Isasa o ZRE 212-213 B 5
'Isāwiya, al- o KSA 130-131 F 2
Isbil, Ğabal ▲ Y 132-133 G 6
Isbjørn Strait ≈ 26-27 O 8
Iscayachi o BOL 76-77 E 1
Iscehisar ☆ TR 128-129 D 3
Ischia o I 100-101 C 1
Ischia o • I 100-101 D 4
Ischia, Isola d' ⌒ I 100-101 D 4
Ischigualasto y, Parque Natural Provincial ⊥ • • RA 76-77 C 6
Iscuande, Río ∼ CO 60-61 C 6
Isdell River ∼ AUS 172-173 G 4
Ise o J 152-153 G 7
Iseevka ☆ RUS 96-97 F 6
Iseke o EAT 214-215 H 4
Iseo, Lago d' ⊖ I 100-101 C 2
Isémia ☆ I 100-101 E 4
Ise-shima National Park ⊥ J 152-153 G 7
Iset' ∼ RUS 96-97 M 5
Iset' ∼ RUS 114-115 G 6
Isetskoe ☆ RUS 114-115 H 6
Ise-wan ≈ 152-153 G 7
Iseyin o WAN 204-205 E 5
Isfahan = Esfahān ☆ • • IR 134-135 D 2
Isfahan = Esfahān ☆ ••• IR 134-135 D 2
Isfara o TJ 136-137 M 4
Isfjordbanken ≃ 84-85 H 4
Isfjorden ≈ 84-85 J 3
Isfjord Radio o N 84-85 H 3
Isfjordrenna ≃ 84-85 G 3
Isha o PK 138-139 C 3
Ishak Paşa Sarayı •• TR 128-129 L 3
Isham o CDN (SAS) 232-233 K 4
Ishasha o EAU 212-213 B 4
Isherton o GUY 62-63 E 4
Ishiara o EAK 212-213 F 4
Ishikari o J 152-153 J 3
Ishikari-wan ≈ 152-153 J 3
Ishikawa o J 152-153 B 11
Ishimskaja Step' = Išimskaja ravnina ⌣ RUS 114-115 J 6
Ishinomaki o J 152-153 J 5
Ishioka o J 152-153 J 6
Ishizuchi-san ▲ J 152-153 E 8
Ishpeming o USA (MI) 270-271 L 4
Ishurdi o BD 142-143 F 3
Isiboro Sécure, Parque Nacional ⊥ BOL 70-71 D 5
Isikari-santi ▲ J 152-153 K 3
Isil'kul' o RUS 124-125 G 1
Išim o RUS 114-115 L 6
Išim ∼ RUS 114-115 L 6
Išim = Esim ∼ KA 124-125 E 2
Išim, Ust'- o RUS 114-115 L 6
Isimala • EAT 214-215 H 4
Išimbaj ☆ RUS 96-97 K 7
Isimbira o EAT 214-215 G 4
Išimskaja ravnina ⌣ RUS 114-115 J 6
Išimskaja ravnina ⌣ RUS 114-115 J 6
Isinga o RUS 118-119 E 9
Isiolo o EAK 212-213 F 3
Isiolo, Lagh ∼ EAK 212-213 F 3
Isiovo, Río ∼ BOL 70-71 E 5
Isipingo o ZA 220-221 K 5
Isiro o ZRE 212-213 A 2
Isisford o AUS 178-179 H 3
Isit o RUS 118-119 M 5
Isjangulovo ☆ RUS 96-97 K 7
Iska o RUS 114-115 H 6
Iskanawatu, Tanjung ▲ RI 166-167 D 5
Iskandarīya, al-= Alexandria ☆ •• ET 194-195 D 2
Iskăr ∼ BG 102-103 C 6
Iskašim o TJ 136-137 M 6
Iskaten', hrebet ▲▲ RUS 112-113 V 3
İskenderun ☆ TR 128-129 G 4
İskenderun Körfezi ≈ 128-129 F 4
İskilip ☆ TR 128-129 F 2
Iskitim ☆ RUS 124-125 N 1
Iskushuban o SP 208-209 K 3
Iskut River ∼ CDN 32-33 E 3
Isla o MEX 52-53 G 2
Isla, Salar de la ⊖ RCH 76-77 C 3
Isla Angel de la Guarda, Parque Natural ⊥ MEX 50-51 C 3
Isla de Aguada o MEX 52-53 J 2
Isla de Salamanca, Parque Nacional ⊥ •• CO 60-61 D 2
Isla de Taiamá, Estação Ecológica ⊥ BR 70-71 J 5
Isla Guamblin, Parque Nacional ⊥ RCH 80 C 2
Islahiye ☆ TR 128-129 G 4
Islamabad ★ • PK 138-139 D 3
Isla Magdalena, Parque Nacional ⊥ RCH 80 D 2
Islāmgarh o PK 138-139 C 6
Isla Mona ⌒ USA (PR) 286-287 O 2
Islamorada o USA (FL) 286-287 J 7
Islampur o BD 142-143 F 3
Islāmpur o IND 142-143 F 2
Islampur o IND 142-143 D 3
Island Bay ≈ 160-161 C 8
Island City o USA (OR) 244-245 G 5
Island Falls o CDN (ONT) 236-237 G 3
Island Falls o USA (ME) 278-279 N 2
Island Lagoon o AUS 178-179 D 6
Island Lake o CDN (ONT) 236-237 F 5
Island Lake o CDN 34-35 K 4
Island Lake o USA (MN) 270-271 F 3
Island Lake Indian Reserve ✗ CDN 34-35 J 4
Island Park Reservoir ∼ USA (ID) 252-253 G 2
Island Pond ⊖ CDN (NFL) 242-243 M 4
Island Pond o USA (VT) 278-279 K 4
Island River ∼ CDN 30-31 J 5
Islands, Bay of ≈ 36-37 U 7
Islands, Bay of ≈ 38-39 P 4
Islands, Bay of ≈ 182 E 1
Islands, Bay of ≈ CDN 242-243 K 3
Isla Riesco, Reserva Florestal ⊥ RCH 80 D 6
Islas Columbretes ⌒ E 98-99 H 5
Isla Umbú o PY 76-77 H 4
Islay o CDN (ALB) 232-233 H 2
Islay ⌒ GB 90-91 D 4
Islay o PE 70-71 A 5
Islaz o RO 102-103 D 6
Isle o USA (MN) 270-271 E 4
Isle aux Morts o CDN (NFL) 242-243 K 5
Isle Historic Site, Fort de L' • CDN (ALB) 232-233 G 2
Isle of Man □ GBM 90-91 E 4
Isle of Wight ⌒ GB 90-91 G 6
Isle Pierre o CDN (BC) 228-229 L 3
Isle Royale National Park ⊥ USA (MI) 270-271 K 2
Isles of Scilly ⌒ •• GB 90-91 D 7
Isleta o CO 60-61 H 6
Isleta o USA (NM) 256-257 J 4
Isleta Indian Reservation ✗ USA (NM) 256-257 J 4
Isle Woodah ⌒ AUS 174-175 D 3
Islington o CDN (NFL) 242-243 P 5
Isluga, Parque Nacional ⊥ RCH 70-71 C 6
Isly, Oued ∼ MA 188-189 K 3
Ismael Cortinas o ROU 78-79 L 2
Ismā'īlīya, al- ☆ ET 194-195 F 2
Ismailly = İsmayıllı o AZ 128-129 N 2
Ismaning o D 92-93 L 4
Isnā o • ET 194-195 F 5
Isoanala o RM 222-223 D 9
Isoka o Z 214-215 G 6
Isola o USA (MS) 268-269 K 3
Isola di Capo Rizzuto o I 100-101 F 5
Isom o USA (KY) 276-277 N 3
Isonga o PNG 183 F 3
Isopa o EAT 214-215 F 5
Isorana o RM 222-223 E 8
Isororo o GUY 62-63 E 3
Isortoq o GRØ (ØGR) 28-29 V 4
Isortoq o GRØ (VGR) 28-29 O 3
Iso-Vietonen ⊖ FIN 88-89 H 3
Isparta ☆ TR 128-129 D 4
Isperih o BG 102-103 E 6
Íspica o I 100-101 E 6
Ispir ☆ TR 128-129 J 2
Isquiliac, Isla ⌒ RCH 80 C 2
Israel = Yisrā'el ■ IL 130-131 D 2
Israelite Bay ≈ 176-177 G 6
Israelite Bay o AUS 176-177 G 6
Isra-tu ⌒ ER 200-201 J 4
Issa o RUS 96-97 D 7
Issaba o DY 204-205 E 5
Issangele o CAM 204-205 H 6
Issano o GUY 62-63 E 3
Issaouane, Erg ∸ DZ 190-191 F 7
Issaquah o USA (WA) 244-245 C 3
Isseke o EAT 214-215 H 4
Issia ☆ CI 202-203 G 6
Issimu o RI 164-165 H 3
Issinga o G 210-211 B 4
Issoire o F 90-91 J 9
Issoro o SUD 212-213 D 2
Issoudun o F 90-91 H 8
Issoulane Erarenine ∸ DZ 190-191 D 9
Issyk = Esik o KA 146-147 C 4
Issyk-Kul', ozero ⊖ KS 146-147 C 4
Issyk-Kul' = Ysyk-Köl o KS 146-147 C 4
İstanbul ☆ ••• TR 128-129 C 2
İstanbul Boğazı ≈ 128-129 C 2
Istgāh-e Nāin o IR 134-135 E 2
Isthmus of Kra ⌒ THA 158-159 E 5
Istiéa o GR 100-101 J 5
Istisu o • AZ 128-129 L 3
Istmina o CO 60-61 C 5
Istmo de Ofqui o RCH 80 C 3
Istmo Malagua ⌒ CO 60-61 C 5
Istokpoga, Lake o USA (FL) 286-287 H 4
Istra ☆ • RUS 94-95 P 4
Istra ∸ SLO 100-101 D 2
Istunmäki o FIN 88-89 J 5
Isumrud Strait ≈ 183 C 3
Isuna o EAT (SIN) 212-213 E 6
Iswepe o ZA 220-221 K 3
Itabaiana o BR (PA) 68-69 L 5
Itabaiana o BR (SER) 68-69 K 7
Itabaianinha o BR 68-69 K 7
Itabaiza o BR 68-69 E 7
Itabapoana o BR 72-73 K 6
Itabapoana, Rio ∼ BR 72-73 K 6
Itaberá o BR 72-73 F 7
Itaberaba o BR 72-73 K 2
Itaberaí o BR 72-73 F 4
Itabira o BR 72-73 J 5
Itabirinha de Mantena o BR 72-73 K 5
Itabirito o BR 72-73 J 6
Itaboca o BR 66-67 F 5
Itaboraí o BR 72-73 J 7
Itabuna o BR 72-73 L 3
Itacaiuna, Rio ∼ BR 68-69 C 4
Itacaiúna, Rio ∼ BR 68-69 D 4
Itacaja o BR 68-69 E 6
Itacambira o BR 72-73 J 4
Itacarambi o BR 72-73 H 3
Itacaré o BR 72-73 L 3
Itacaruaré o RA 76-77 K 4
Itacolomi, Ilha ⌒ BR 74-75 F 5
Itaetê o BR 72-73 K 2
Itaguaí o BR 72-73 J 7
Itaguajé o BR 72-73 E 7
Itaguara o BR 72-73 H 6
Itaguari, Rio ∼ BR 72-73 H 3
Itagüí o CO 60-61 D 4
Itah Lake o AUS 180-181 H 3
Ita Ibaté o RA 76-77 J 4
Itaim, Rio ∼ BR 68-69 H 5
Itainópolis o BR 68-69 H 5
Itainzinho, Rio ∼ BR 68-69 H 5
Itaiópolis o BR 74-75 F 6
Itaipu • BR 76-77 K 3
Itaipu, Represa de < BR 76-77 K 3
Itäisen Suomenlahden kansallispuisto ⊥ FIN 88-89 J 6
Itaitu o BR 68-69 H 7
Itaituba o BR (AMA) 66-67 F 5
Itaituba o BR (P) 66-67 K 5
Itajá o BR 72-73 E 5
Itajaí o BR 74-75 F 6
Itaji o BR 72-73 K 3
Itajubá o BR 72-73 H 7
Itajubaquara o BR 68-69 G 7
Itaju do Colônia o BR 72-73 L 3
Itakhola o BD 142-143 G 3
Itala Nature Reserve ⊥ ZA 220-221 K 3
Italy o USA (TX) 264-265 H 6
Italy = Italia ■ I 100-101 C 4
Itamaraju o BR 72-73 L 4
Itamarandiba o BR 72-73 J 4
Itamarati o BR 66-67 C 6
Itamataré o BR 68-69 E 3
Itambacuri o BR 72-73 K 5
Itambé o BR 72-73 K 3
Itamirim o BR 72-73 J 3
Itampolo o RM 222-223 D 10
Itanagar ☆ • IND 142-143 H 2
Itanagra o BR 72-73 L 2
Itanajé o BR 72-73 J 2
Itanari o NEP 144-145 F 7
Itang o ETH 208-209 B 4
Itangua o BR 68-69 H 3
Itanhaém o BR 74-75 G 5
Itanhauã, Rio ∼ BR 66-67 E 5
Itanhém o BR 72-73 K 4
Itanhém, Rio ∼ BR 72-73 L 4
Itanhoma o BR 72-73 K 5
Itaobim o BR 72-73 K 4
Itaocara o BR 72-73 J 6
Itapacurá, Rio ∼ BR 66-67 K 5
Itapaiúna o BR 70-71 J 2
Itapajé o BR 68-69 J 3
Itaparaná, Rio ∼ BR 66-67 F 6
Itaparica o BR 72-73 L 2
Itaparica, Ilha ⌒ •• BR 72-73 L 2
Itapebi o BR 72-73 L 3
Itapecerica o BR 72-73 H 6
Itapecerica da Serra o BR 72-73 G 7
Itapecurumirim o BR 68-69 F 3
Itapeipu o BR 68-69 H 7
Itapejara d'Oeste o BR 74-75 D 5
Itapemirim o BR 72-73 K 6
Itapemirim, Rio ∼ BR 72-73 K 6
Itapera o BR 68-69 G 3
Itapera, Lagoa ⊖ BR 74-75 F 7
Itaperuna o BR 72-73 K 6
Itapetinga o BR 72-73 K 3
Itapetininga o BR 72-73 F 7
Itapetininga, Rio ∼ BR 72-73 F 7
Itapeva o BR 72-73 F 7
Itapevi o BR 72-73 G 7
Itapicuru, Rio ∼ BR 68-69 J 7
Itapicuru, Rio ∼ BR 68-69 G 4
Itapicuru-Açu, Rio ∼ BR 68-69 H 7
Itapicuru-Mirim, Rio ∼ BR 68-69 H 7
Itapipoca o BR 68-69 J 3
Itapira o BR 72-73 G 7
Itapiranga o BR (AMA) 66-67 H 4
Itapiranga o BR (CAT) 74-75 D 6
Itapirapuã o BR 72-73 E 3
Itapirapuã, Pico ▲ BR 74-75 F 5
Itapiúna o BR 68-69 J 4
Itápolis o BR 72-73 F 6
Itapora o BR 76-77 K 2
Itaporanga o BR (PA) 68-69 J 5
Itaporanga o BR (PAU) 72-73 F 7
Itapuã o BR 74-75 E 8
Itapuã do Oeste o BR 66-67 F 7
Itapuranga o BR 72-73 F 3
Itaquai, Rio ∼ BR 66-67 B 5
Itaquaquecetuba o BR 72-73 G 7
Itaquatiara o BR 66-67 H 4
Itaqui o BR 76-77 J 5
Itaquyry o PY 76-77 K 3
Itarana o BR 72-73 K 5
Itarana, Ilha ⌒ BR 68-69 E 2
Itarare o BR 74-75 F 5
Itararé, Rio ∼ BR 72-73 F 7
Itarema o BR 68-69 J 3
Itārsi o IND 138-139 F 8
Itasca o USA (TX) 264-265 G 6
Itasca State Park ⊥ USA (MN) 270-271 C 3
Itasy, Farihy ⊖ RM 222-223 E 7
Itata, Río ∼ RCH 78-79 C 4
Itati o • RA 76-77 H 4
Itatiaia, Parque Nacional do ⊥ BR 72-73 H 7
Itatiba o BR 72-73 G 7
Itatinga o BR 72-73 F 7
Itatingui o BR 72-73 L 3
Itatira o BR 68-69 J 4
Itatupã o BR 62-63 J 6
Itaú o BR 68-69 K 4
Itaú, Río ∼ BOL 76-77 E 2
Itauba o BR 70-71 K 2
Itauçu o BR 72-73 F 4
Itaueira o BR 68-69 G 5
Itaueira, Rio ∼ BR 68-69 G 5
Itaum o BR 76-77 K 2
Itauna o BR 68-69 F 3
Itaúna o BR 72-73 H 6
Itaúnas o BR 72-73 L 5
Itaunja o IND 142-143 B 2
Itbayat Island ⌒ RP 160-161 D 2
Itbu Point ▲ RP 160-161 D 6
Itche Lake o CDN 30-31 N 3
Ite o PE 70-71 B 5
Itéa o GR 100-101 J 5
Itemgen, köli o KA 124-125 G 2
Iten o EAK 212-213 E 3
Itenecito, Río ∼ BOL 70-71 E 3
Itenes o Guaporé, Río ∼ BOL 70-71 F 3
Iterh, Oued ∼ DZ 196-197 M 4
Itete o EAT 214-215 J 5
Itezhi-Tezhi Dam o Z 218-219 D 2
Ithaca o USA (MI) 272-273 E 4
Ithaca o USA (NY) 278-279 E 6
Ithaca o USA (OH) 280-281 B 4
Itháki o GR 100-101 H 5
Itigi o EAT 212-213 E 6
Itiki o IND 140-141 G 3
Itilleq ⊖ GRØ 28-29 O 3
Itimbiri ∼ ZRE 210-211 J 2
Itinga, Rio ∼ BR 68-69 E 4
Itipo o ZRE 210-211 G 4
Itiquira o BR 70-71 K 5
Itiquira, Rio ∼ BR 70-71 K 5
Itiquira ou Piquiri ∼ BR 70-71 J 5
Itirapuão o BR 72-73 G 6
Itirr Plain ∸ EAK 212-213 G 2
Itiúba o BR 68-69 J 7
Itiyuro, Arroyo ∼ RA 76-77 F 2
Itkillik River ∼ USA 20-21 P 2
Itō o J 152-153 H 7
Ito, Paysage d' • MA 188-189 J 4
Itobe o WAN 204-205 G 5
Itobo o EAT 212-213 D 6
Itoculo o MOC 218-219 L 2
Itoigawa o J 152-153 G 6
Itoko o ZRE 210-211 H 4
Itomampy ∼ RM 222-223 E 9
Itonamas, Río ∼ BOL 70-71 E 3
Itoquois River ∼ USA (IL) 274-275 L 4
Itquiy o MA 188-189 J 4
Ittaajimmiit = Kap Hope o GRØ 26-27 o 8
Ittel, Oued ∼ DZ 190-191 E 3
Ittoqqortoormiit = Scoresbysund o GRØ 26-27 p 8
Itu o BR 72-73 G 7
Itu o WAN 204-205 G 6
Ituaçu o BR 72-73 K 2
Ituango o CO 60-61 D 4
Ituberá o BR 72-73 L 2
Itui, Rio ∼ BR 66-67 B 5
Ituiutaba o BR 72-73 F 5
Itula o ZRE 212-213 A 5
Itumba o EAT (MBE) 214-215 G 5
Itumba o EAT (SIN) 214-215 G 4
Itumbiara o BR 72-73 F 5
Ituna o CDN (SAS) 232-233 P 4
Itungi o EAT 214-215 G 5
Ituni o GUY 62-63 E 3
Ituporanga o BR 74-75 F 6
Iturama o BR 72-73 E 5
Iturbide o MEX (CAM) 52-53 K 2
Iturbide o MEX (NL) 50-51 K 5
Ituri ∼ ZRE 212-213 B 3
Iturup, ostrov ⌒ RUS 122-123 N 6
Itutinga o BR 72-73 H 6
Itutinga, Represa < BR 72-73 H 6
Ituverava o BR 72-73 G 6
Ituxi, Rio ∼ BR 66-67 E 6
Ituzaingo o RA 76-77 J 4
Itwangi o EAT 212-213 D 5
Itzamna ∴ • MEX 52-53 K 1
Itztapa o GCA 52-53 J 5
Iuka o USA (KS) 262-263 H 7
Iuka o USA (MS) 268-269 M 2
Iul'tin o RUS 112-113 V 3
Iulúti o MOC 218-219 K 2
Iva o USA (SC) 284-285 H 2
Ivacėvičy o BY 94-95 J 5
Ivaí o BR 74-75 E 5
Ivaí, Rio ∼ BR 72-73 D 7
Ivaiporã o BR 74-75 E 5
Ivakoany ▲ RM 222-223 E 9
Ivalo o FIN 88-89 J 2

340 Inis Ceithleann — Ivalo

Ivalojoki ○ FIN 88-89 J 2
Ivan ○ USA (FL) 286-287 E 1
Ivan ~ USA (LA) 268-269 G 4
Ivangorod ○ RUS 94-95 L 2
Ivangrad ○ YU 100-101 G 3
Ivanhoe ○ AUS 180-181 H 2
Ivanhoe ○ USA (MN) 270-271 B 6
Ivanhoe River ~ CDN (ONT) 236-237 F 4
Ivanivka ○ UA 102-103 C 3
Ivanjica ○• YU 100-101 H 3
Ivankiv ○ UA 102-103 F 2
Ivano-Frankivs'k ☆ UA 102-103 D 3
Ivano-Frankovsk = Ivano-Frankivs'k ☆ UA 102-103 D 3
Ivanovka ○ RUS (AMR) 122-123 B 3
Ivanovka ○ RUS (CTN) 118-119 J 10
Ivanovka ○ RUS (ORB) 96-97 H 7
Ivanovka ~ RUS 122-123 C 3
Ivanovo ○•• BG 102-103 D 6
Ivanovo ○ RUS (PSK) 94-95 M 3
Ivanovo ☆ RUS (IVN) 94-95 R 3
Ivanovsk, Katav- ○ RUS 96-97 L 6
Ivanteevka ☆ RUS 96-97 F 7
Ivaška ○ RUS 120-121 U 4
Ivato ○ RM 222-223 E 8
Ivdel' ○ RUS 114-115 F 4
Iveetok Camp ○ USA 20-21 E 5
Ivindo ~ RCB 210-211 D 3
Ivinheima, Rio ~ BR 76-77 K 1
Ivinhema ○ BR 72-73 D 7
Ivisan ○ RP 160-161 E 7
Ivisaruk River ~ USA 20-21 K 2
Ivittuut ○ GRØ 28-29 Q 6
Ivnanganek ○ GRØ 26-27 R 6
Ivnarssuit ○ GRØ 26-27 W 7
Ivohibe ○ RM 222-223 E 9
Ivolginsk ☆ RUS 116-117 N 10
Ivon, Río ~ BOL 70-71 D 2
Ivondro ~ RM 222-223 F 6
Ivongo, Soanierana- ○ RM 222-223 F 6
Ivori River ~ PNG 183 C 4
Ivorogbo ○ WAN 204-205 G 6
Ivory Coast ■ CI 202-203 H 7
Ivrea ○ I 100-101 A 2
Ivrindi ☆ TR 128-129 B 3
Ivujivik ○ CDN 36-37 L 3
Ivuna ○ EAT 214-215 G 5
Iwa Island ⌒ PNG 183 F 5
Iwaizumi ○ J 152-153 J 5
Iwaki ○ J 152-153 J 6
Iwaki-san ▲ J 152-153 J 4
Iwakuni ○ J 152-153 E 7
Iwala ○ ZRE 210-211 J 5
Iwamizawa ○ J 152-153 J 3
Iwanai ○ J 152-153 J 3
Iwanuma ○ J 152-153 J 5
Iwatebu ○ PNG 183 B 4
Iwate-san ▲ J 152-153 J 5
Iwe ○ ZRE 210-211 K 5
Iwo ○ WAN 204-205 F 5
Iwopin ○ WAN 204-205 F 5
Iwungu ○ ZRE 210-211 G 6
Iwupataka ⨯ AUS 176-177 M 1
Ixcún ∴• GCA 52-53 K 3
Ixiamas ○ BOL 70-71 C 3
Ixmiquilpan ○• MEX 52-53 E 1
Ixopo ○ ZA 220-221 K 5
Ixtapa ○ MEX (GRO) 52-53 D 3
Ixtapa ○ MEX (OAX) 52-53 F 3
Ixtapan de la Sal ○ MEX 52-53 E 2
Ixtlahuaca ○ MEX 52-53 F 2
Ixtlahuacan ○ MEX 52-53 C 2
Ixtlahuacán del Río ○ MEX 52-53 C 1
Ixtlán ∴ MEX 52-53 B 1
Ixtlán de Juárez ○• MEX 52-53 F 3
Ixtlán del Río ○ MEX 50-51 G 7
Ixu ○ BR 70-71 J 5
'Iyāl Bakhīt ○ SUD 200-201 D 6
Iyapa ○ WAN 204-205 F 5
Iyayi ○ EAT 214-215 H 5
Iyo ○ J 152-153 E 8
Iyo-nada ≈ 152-153 D 8
Iž ~ RUS 96-97 H 5
Izabal, Lago de ○ GCA 52-53 K 4
Izadḫvāst ○ IR 134-135 E 3
Izaguène < RIM 196-197 C 6
Izamal ○ MEX 52-53 K 1
Izapa ∴• MEX 52-53 H 4
'Izbat al-Ǧāǧa ○ ET 194-195 E 5
Izberbaš ○ RUS 126-127 G 6
Izborsk ○• RUS 94-95 K 3
Ize ○ IR 134-135 C 3
Izena-shima ⌒ J 152-153 B 11
Iževsk ☆ RUS 96-97 H 5
Izhevsk = Iževsk ☆ RUS 96-97 H 5
Izhma = Ižma ~ RUS 88-89 X 5
Izjum ○ UA 102-103 K 3
Izki ○ OM 132-133 K 2
Izlistan = Žizah ☆• US 136-137 K 4
Ižma ○ RUS 88-89 W 4
Ižma ~ RUS 88-89 W 4
Izmail = Izmajil ☆ UA 102-103 F 5
Izmajil ☆ UA 102-103 F 5
Izmir ☆•• TR 128-129 B 3
İzmit=Kocaeli ○ TR 128-129 C 2
Izmorskij ☆ RUS 114-115 T 6
İznik ☆ TR 128-129 C 2
İznik Gölü ○ TR 128-129 C 2
Izobil'noe ○ KA 124-125 H 2
Izobil'nyj ○ RUS 102-103 M 5
Izozog ○ BOL 70-71 F 6
Izozog, Bañados de ○ BOL 70-71 F 6
Izra' ☆ SYR 128-129 G 6
Izúcar de Matamoros ○ MEX 52-53 E 2
Izu-hanto ⌒ J 152-153 H 7
Izuhara ○ J 152-153 C 7
Izumi ○ J 152-153 J 5
Izumo ○ J 152-153 E 7
Izu-shotō ⌒ J 152-153 H 7
Izvestij CIK, ostrova ⌒ RUS 108-109 T 4
Izyestkovyj ○ RUS 122-123 D 4

J

Jaab Lake ○ CDN 34-35 P 5
Jaala ○ FIN 88-89 J 6
Jaba ○ PK 138-139 D 3
Jabali, Isla ⌒ RA 78-79 H 6
Jabalón, Río ~ E 98-99 F 5
Jabalpur ○ IND 138-139 G 8
Jabarona < SUD 200-201 C 4
Jabillo ○ CR 52-53 C 7
Jabiru ○ AUS 172-173 L 2
Jabitaca ○ BR 68-69 K 5
Jablanica ○ BG 102-103 D 6
Jablanica ○ BIH 100-101 F 3
Jablon ~ RUS 112-113 P 4
Jablonevyj ○ RUS 120-121 O 3
Jablonovyj hrebet ▲ RUS 118-119 D 10
Jabo ○ WAN 198-199 B 6
Jabon ○ RI 168 E 3
Jaboncillos Creek ~ USA (TX) 266-267 J 6
Jabotá, Rio ~ BR 70-71 K 3
Jabung, Tanjung ▲ RI 162-163 F 5
Jaburu, Rio ~ BR 68-69 C 7
Jabuticabal ○ BR 72-73 F 6
Jabuticatubas ○ BR 72-73 J 5
Jaca ○ E 98-99 G 3
Jacaf, Canal ≈ 80 D 2
Jacaí ○ SP 208-209 H 6
Jacala ○ MEX 50-51 K 7
Jacana ○ BR 68-69 K 5
Jacarai, Rio ~ BR 68-69 H 3
Jacaraú Estradas ○ BR 68-69 L 5
Jacaré ○ BR 66-67 C 6
Jacaré, Ilha ⌒ BR 66-67 H 5
Jacaré, Rio ~ BR 66-67 F 6
Jacaré, Rio ~ BR 72-73 H 6
Jacareacanga ○ BR 66-67 J 6
Jacaré Grande ○ BR 72-73 J 3
Jacaré Guaçu, Rio ~ BR 72-73 F 6
Jacareí ○ BR 72-73 H 7
Jacaré Pepira, Rio ~ BR 72-73 F 6
Jacaretinga ○ BR 66-67 H 7
Jacas Grande ○ PE 64-65 D 6
Jacaúna ○ BR 68-69 J 3
Jaceel, togga ~ SP 208-209 K 3
Jaceyl ~ SP 208-209 K 3
Jáchal, Río ~ RA 76-77 C 6
Jáchymov ○ CZ 92-93 M 3
Jaciara ○ BR 70-71 K 4
Jacinto ○ BR 72-73 K 4
Jacinto, San ○ USA (CA) 248-249 H 6
Jaci Paraná ○ BR 66-67 E 7
Jaciparaná, Rio ~ BR 66-67 E 7
Jacitara ○ BR 66-67 E 4
Jack ○ USA (AL) 284-285 D 5
Jack Creek ○ USA (NV) 246-247 J 2
Jack Daniels Distillery • USA (TN) 276-277 J 5
Jackfish Creek ~ CDN 30-31 N 6
Jackfork Mountain ▲ USA (OK) 264-265 J 4
Jackhead Harbour ○ CDN (MAN) 234-235 F 3
Jack Lee, Lake < USA (AR) 276-277 C 7
Jackman ○ USA (ME) 278-279 L 3
Jackpine River ~ CDN (ALB) 228-229 P 3
Jackpot ○ USA (NV) 246-247 L 2
Jacksboro ○ USA (TX) 264-265 F 5
Jacks Fork ~ USA (MO) 276-277 D 3
Jackson ○ AUS 178-179 K 4
Jackson ○ CDN (NS) 240-241 M 5
Jackson ○ USA (AL) 284-285 C 5
Jackson ○ USA (CA) 246-247 E 5
Jackson ○ USA (GA) 284-285 G 3
Jackson ○ USA (KY) 276-277 M 3
Jackson ○ USA (LA) 268-269 J 6
Jackson ○ USA (MI) 272-273 E 5
Jackson ○ USA (MN) 270-271 D 7
Jackson ○ USA (MO) 276-277 F 3
Jackson ○ USA (MT) 250-251 F 6
Jackson ○ USA (NC) 282-283 K 4
Jackson ○ USA (OH) 280-281 D 4
Jackson ○ USA (TN) 276-277 G 5
Jackson ○ USA (WY) 252-253 H 3
Jackson ☆ USA (MS) 268-269 K 4
Jackson, Fort ✕✕ USA (LA) 268-269 L 7
Jackson, Kap ▲ GRØ 26-27 R 3
Jackson, Lake ○ USA (FL) 286-287 E 1
Jackson, Mount ▲ AUS 176-177 E 4
Jackson Arm ○ CDN (NFL) 242-243 M 3
Jackson Bay ○ CDN (BC) 230-231 D 3
Jacksonboro ○ USA (SC) 284-285 K 4
Jackson Junction ○ USA (IA) 274-275 F 1
Jackson Lake ○ USA (OH) 280-281 D 5
Jackson Lake ○ USA (WY) 252-253 H 3
Jackson Lake < USA (GA) 284-285 G 3
Jackson Lake Lodge ○ USA (WY) 252-253 H 3
Jackson River ~ USA (VA) 280-281 G 6
Jacksonville ○ C 54-55 D 4
Jacksonville ○ USA (AL) 284-285 E 3
Jacksonville ○ USA (AR) 276-277 C 6
Jacksonville ○ USA (FL) 286-287 H 1
Jacksonville ○ USA (GA) 284-285 H 5
Jacksonville ○ USA (IL) 274-275 H 5
Jacksonville ○ USA (NC) 282-283 K 6
Jacksonville ○ USA (TX) 268-269 E 5
Jacksonville Beach ○ USA (FL) 286-287 H 1
Jacktown ○ USA (KY) 276-277 K 3
Jack Wade ○ USA 20-21 U 4
Jacmel ☆• RH 54-55 J 5
Jacó ○ CR 52-53 B 7
Jacobābād ○• PK 138-139 B 5
Jacob Island ⌒ USA 22-23 R 5
Jacob Lake ○ USA (AZ) 256-257 C 2
Jacobsdal ○ ZA 220-221 G 4
Jacobson ○ USA (MN) 270-271 E 4
Jacobsville ○ USA (MI) 270-271 K 4
Jacona ○ MEX 52-53 C 2
Jacques, Lac ○ CDN (QUE) 240-241 D 3
Jacques, Lac à ○ CDN 30-31 F 2
Jacques Cartier, Mont ▲ CDN (QUE) 240-241 K 2
Jacques Cartier, Parc de la ⊥ CDN (QUE) 240-241 D 3
Jacques Cartier, Rivière ~ CDN (QUE) 240-241 D 3
Jacqueville ○• CI 202-203 H 7
Jacquinot Bay ≈ 183 F 3
Jacu ○ BR 68-69 F 6
Jacuba, Rio ~ BR 72-73 D 5
Jacuí ○ BR 72-73 G 6
Jacuí, Rio ~ BR 74-75 D 7
Jacuípe ○ BR 72-73 L 2
Jacuípe, Rio ~ BR 68-69 J 7
Jacuizinho ○ BR 74-75 D 7
Jacumba ○ USA (CA) 248-249 H 7
Jacundá ○ BR 66-67 F 7
Jacundá, Rio ~ BR 66-67 F 7
Jacunda, Rio ~ BR 68-69 C 3
Jacup ○ AUS 176-177 E 6
Jacupiranga ○ BR 74-75 F 5
Jacurici, Açude < BR 68-69 J 7
Jacurici, Rio ~ BR 68-69 J 7
Jada ○ WAN 204-205 K 4
Jadajahodyjaha ~ RUS 108-109 O 8
Jaddi, Rās ▲ PK 134-135 K 6
Jadebusen ≈ D 92-93 K 2
Jadkal ○ IND 140-141 F 4
Jadranska magistrala II HR 100-101 F 3
Jadransko more ≈ 100-101 D 2
Jādū ○• LAR 192-193 E 2
Jaén ○ E 98-99 F 6
Jaen ○ PE 64-65 C 4
Jafarābād ○ IND 138-139 F 9
Jāfarābād ○ IND 138-139 C 9
Jafarah ⊥ TN 190-191 H 4
Jaffa, Cape ▲ AUS 180-181 E 4
Jaffa, Cirque de • MA 188-189 J 4
Jaffna ○• CL 140-141 J 6
Jagalūr ○ IND 140-141 G 3
Jagbahun ○ WAL 202-203 D 5
Jagdagi ○ VRC 150-151 E 2
Jagdalpur ○ IND 142-143 C 6
Jagdispur ○ IND 142-143 B 2
Jagdyg ○ RUS 118-119 E 8
Jagel'urta, gora ▲ RUS 88-89 P 3
Jagenetta ~ RUS 114-115 O 2
Jagersfontein ○ ZA 220-221 G 4
Jaggayyapeta ○ IND 140-141 J 2
Jagodnoe ☆ RUS 120-121 N 2
Jago River ~ USA 20-21 T 2
Jagtial ○ IND 138-139 G 10
Jagua ○• C 54-55 E 3
Jagua, La ○ C 54-55 F 4
Jaguapitã ○ BR 72-73 E 7
Jaguaquara ○ BR 72-73 L 2
Jaguarão ○ BR 74-75 D 9
Jaguarão, Rio ~ BR 74-75 D 9
Jaguarari ○ BR 68-69 H 7
Jaguaré ○ BR 72-73 K 5
Jaguarembé ○ BR 72-73 J 6
Jaguaretama ○ BR 68-69 J 4
Jaguari ○ BR 76-77 K 5
Jaguari, Rio ~ BR 72-73 G 7
Jaguariaíva ○ BR 74-75 F 5
Jaguaribe ○ BR 68-69 J 4
Jaguaribe, Rio ~ BR 68-69 J 5
Jaguaruana ○ BR 68-69 K 4
Jaguaruna ○ BR 74-75 F 7
Jagüé, Río ~ RA 76-77 C 5
Jagüey Grande ○ C 54-55 E 3
Jagvi ○ IND 140-141 F 3
Jagyl'ja ~ RUS 114-115 N 5
Jah, Pyt'- ○ RUS 114-115 M 4
Jahadyjaha ~ RUS 108-109 O 5
Jahānābād ○ IND 142-143 D 3
Jahangiraba ○ IND 138-139 G 5
Jahleel, Point ▲ AUS 172-173 K 1
Jahorina ▲ BIH 100-101 G 3
Jahuey Creek ~ USA (TX) 266-267 H 5
Jaicós ○ BR 68-69 H 5
Jailleu, Bourgoin- ○ F 90-91 K 9
Jailolo ○ RI 164-165 K 3
Jailolo, Selat ≈ 166-167 E 2
Jainagar ○ IND 142-143 C 4
Jainpur ○ IND 142-143 B 4
Jaintiapur ○ BD 142-143 H 3
Jainu ○ BR 66-67 C 6
Jaipur ○ IND (ASS) 142-143 J 2
Jaipur ☆•• IND (RAJ) 138-139 E 6
Jaisalmer ○• IND 138-139 C 6
Jaisinghnagar ○ IND 142-143 B 4
Jaj ~ RUS 122-123 H 3
Jaja ☆ RUS 114-115 T 6
Jaja ~ RUS 114-115 T 6
Jājapur ○ IND 142-143 E 5
Jājapur Road ○ IND 142-143 E 5
Jajarkot ○ NEP 144-145 D 6
Jajce ○ BIH 100-101 F 2
Jajpan ○ US 136-137 M 4
Jajva ○ RUS 114-115 D 5
Jākar ○ BHT 142-143 G 2
Jakarta ☆ RI 168 B 3
Jakarta, Teluk ≈ 168 B 3
Jaken ○ RI 168 D 3
Jakes Corner ○ USA (AZ) 256-257 D 4
Jakiri ○ CAM 204-205 J 5
Jäkkvik ○ S 86-87 H 3
Jako, Pulau ⌒ RI 166-167 D 6
Jakob Kjode Bjerg ▲ GRØ 26-27 m 6
Jakobshavn = Ilulissat ○ GRØ 28-29 P 2
Jakobshavns Isfjord ≈ 28-29 P 2
Jakob's Ladder Great Falls ~ GUY 62-63 E 4
Jakobstad ○ FIN 88-89 G 5
Jakokit ○ RUS 118-119 M 6
Jakokut ○ RUS 118-119 M 6
Jakovleva ~ RUS 108-109 U 6
Jakpa ○ WAN 204-205 F 6
Jakšino ○ RUS 88-89 W 3
Jaktali ~ RUS 116-117 H 2
Jaktali, plato ⊥ RUS 116-117 H 2
Jakutsk ☆•• RUS 118-119 O 4
Jal ○ USA (NM) 256-257 M 6
Jaladi Qi ○ VRC 150-151 D 4
Jalal-Abad ○ KS 136-137 N 4
Jalālpur ○ IND 142-143 C 2
Jalālpur ○ PK 138-139 E 3
Jalālpur Pirwāla ○ PK 138-139 C 5
Ja'lān ⊥ OM 132-133 L 2
Jalán, Río ~ HN 52-53 L 4
Jalang ○ RI 164-165 G 6
Jalapa ☆ GCA 52-53 K 4
Jalapa ○ MEX (TAB) 52-53 H 3
Jalapa ☆• MEX (VER) 52-53 F 2
Jalapa de Díaz ○ MEX 52-53 F 2
Jalapa Enríquez = Jalapa ☆• MEX 52-53 F 2
Jalasjärvi ○ FIN 88-89 G 5
Jalaté, Río ~ MEX 52-53 J 3
Jalaud ~ RP 160-161 E 7
Jalbyn'ja ~ RUS 114-115 G 3
Jales ○ BR 72-73 E 6
Jaleshwar ○ NEP 144-145 E 7
Jaleswar ○ IND 142-143 E 5
Jalgaon ○ IND 138-139 E 10
Jālgaon ○ IND (MAH) 138-139 F 9
Jālgaon ○•• IND (MAH) 138-139 E 9
Jalingo ○ WAN 204-205 J 4
Jalisco ◘ MEX 52-53 B 2
Jālna ○ IND 138-139 E 10
Jālor ○ IND 138-139 D 7
Jalostotitlan ○ MEX 50-51 H 7
Jalpa ○ MEX 50-51 H 7
Jalpa de Méndez ○ MEX 52-53 H 2
Jalpāiguri ○ IND 142-143 F 2
Jalpan ○ MEX 50-51 K 7
Jalpuh, ozero ○ UA 102-103 F 5
Jalta ☆•• UA 102-103 J 5
Jáltipan de Morelos ○ MEX 52-53 G 3
Jalu ○ LAR 192-193 J 3
Jalutorovsk ☆ RUS 114-115 J 6
Jama ○ EC 64-65 B 2
Jama ~ RUS 120-121 P 3
Jama, Paso de ▲ RA 76-77 D 2
Jamaame ○ SP 212-213 J 3
Jāmai ○ IND 138-139 G 8
Jamaica ■ JA 54-55 F 6
Jamaica ⌒ JA 54-55 G 5
Jamaica Channel ≈ 54-55 H 6
Jamal ○ C 54-55 H 4
Jamal, poluostrov ⌣ RUS 108-109 N 7
Jamalin', hrebet ▲ RUS 122-123 F 2
Jamalpur ○ BD 142-143 F 3
Jamalwal ○ PK 138-139 B 4
Jamantau, gora ▲ RUS 96-97 L 6
Jamanxim, Rio ~ BR 66-67 K 6
Jamari ○ WAN 204-205 J 3
Jamari, Rio ~ BR 66-67 F 7
Jamarovka ○ RUS 118-119 E 10
Jamb ○ IND 138-139 G 9
Jamba ○ ANG (HUA) 216-217 D 7
Jamba ~ ANG 216-217 E 4
Jambeli, Canal de ≈ 64-65 B 3
Jambi ◘ RI 162-163 E 5
Jambi ☆ RI 162-163 E 5
Jambi = Telanaipura ☆ RI 162-163 E 5
Jamboeye ~ RI 162-163 B 2
Jambol ○ BG 102-103 E 6
Jambon, Pointe ▲ CDN (QUE) 240-241 J 2
Jambongan, Pulau ⌒ MAL 160-161 B 9
Jambuair, Tanjung ▲ RI 162-163 B 2
Jambu Bongkok, Kampung ○ MAL 162-163 E 2
Jambukan ~ RUS 116-117 J 3
Jambusar ○ IND 138-139 D 8
Jambuto, ozero ○ RUS (JAN) 108-109 S 6
Jambuto, ozero ○ RUS (JAN) 108-109 O 6
Jambuto, ozero ○ RUS (JAN) 108-109 N 7
James ○ USA (MS) 268-269 J 3
James, Isla ⌒ RCH 80 C 2
James, Lake < USA (NC) 282-283 F 5
Jamesābād ○ PK 138-139 B 7
James A. Reed Memorial Wildlife Refuge ⊥ USA (MO) 274-275 D 6
James Bay ≈ 34-35 Q 4
James Beach, Fort • AG 56 E 3
James Cook Monument • AUS 174-175 H 4
James Creek ~ CDN 30-31 L 6
James Dalton Highway II USA 20-21 P 3
James Island ○ USA (SC) 284-285 L 4
Jameson, Cape ▲ CDN 24-25 j 4
Jameson Islands ⌒ CDN 24-25 R 6
Jameson Land ⊥ GRØ 26-27 o 8
James Ranges ▲ AUS 176-177 M 2
James River ~ CDN 30-31 P 2
James River ~ CDN (ALB) 232-233 C 4
James River ~ USA (MO) 276-277 B 4
James River ~ USA (ND) 258-259 H 4
James River ~ USA (SD) 260-261 J 3
James River ~ USA (VA) 280-281 H 6
James Ross, Cape ▲ CDN 24-25 O 3
James Ross Strait ≈ 24-25 Y 6
James Smith Indian Reservation ⨯ CDN (SAS) 232-233 O 2
Jamestown ○ AUS 180-181 E 2
Jamestown ☆ GB 202-203 C 7
Jamestown ○ USA (MO) 274-275 F 6
Jamestown ○ USA (NY) 278-279 B 6
Jamestown ○ USA (PA) 280-281 F 2
Jamestown ○ USA (SC) 284-285 L 3
Jamestown ○ USA (TN) 282-283 C 4
Jamestown ○ USA (ND) 258-259 J 5
Jamestown ○ ZA 220-221 H 5
Jamestown Reservoir ○ USA (ND) 258-259 J 4
Jamesville ○ USA (NC) 282-283 L 5
Jamieson ○• AUS 180-181 J 4
Jaminawá, Área Indígena ⨯ BR 64-65 F 6
Jaminawá Arara, Área Indígena ⨯ BR 64-65 F 6
Jämjö ○ S 86-87 G 8
Jam Jodhpur ○ IND 138-139 C 9
Jamkhandi ○ IND 140-141 F 2
Jāmkhed ○ IND 138-139 E 10
Jamkine, Verchnie ○ RUS 112-113 L 2
Jamliyah, al- ○ Q 134-135 D 6
Jamm ○ RUS 94-95 L 2
Jammalamadugu ○ IND 140-141 H 3
Jammerbugten ≈ 86-87 D 8
Jammersdrif ○ ZA 220-221 H 4
Jammu ○• IND 138-139 E 3
Jammu and Kashmir ◘ IND 138-139 E 2
Jāmnagar ○• IND 138-139 C 8
Jāmner ○ IND 138-139 E 9
Jamozero ○ RUS 88-89 V 4
Jampangkulon ○ RI 168 B 3
Jampil' ☆ UA 102-103 F 3
Jampue ○ RI 164-165 F 5
Jāmpur ○ PK 138-139 C 5
Jämsä ○ FIN 88-89 H 6
Jamsavėj ~ RUS 114-115 O 2
Jamshedpur ○•• IND 142-143 E 4
Jamsk ○ RUS 120-121 Q 4
Jamskaja, guba ○ RUS 120-121 Q 4
Jamskaja nizmenost' ⌣ RUS 120-121 P 3
Jamskie, ostrova ⌒ RUS 120-121 Q 4
Jamskoe lesničestvo ⊥ RUS 120-121 O 4
Jamtari ○ WAN 204-205 J 5
Jämtland ⊥ S 86-87 F 5
Jamu ○ ETH 208-209 B 5
Jamūi ○ IND 142-143 E 3
Jamul ○ USA (CA) 248-249 H 7
Jamuna ~ BD 142-143 F 3
Jamundí ○ CO 60-61 C 6
Jamutarida ~ RUS 108-109 e 4
Jana ○ RUS (MAG) 120-121 N 3
Jana ~ RUS 110-111 V 4
Janakpur ○• NEP 144-145 E 7
Janauacá, Lago ○ BR 66-67 G 4
Janaúba ○ BR 72-73 J 3
Janauçu, Ilha ⌒ BR 62-63 J 5
Janaul ☆ RUS 96-97 J 5
Jand ○ PK 138-139 D 3
Jandaia do Sul ○ BR 72-73 E 7
Jandaíra ○ BR 68-69 K 4
Jandía Playa ○ E 188-189 D 6
Jandiatuba, Rio ~ BR 66-67 C 5
Jandola ○ PK 138-139 C 3
Jandowae ○ AUS 178-179 L 4
Janeiro, 31 de ○ ANG 216-217 C 3
Janeiro, Área Indígena 9 de ⨯ BR 66-67 F 6
Janeiro, Rio de ~ BR 68-69 F 7
Janesville ○ USA (MN) 270-271 E 6
Janesville ○ USA (WI) 274-275 J 2
Janeville ○ CDN (NB) 240-241 K 3
Jang ○ GH 202-203 J 5
Jang ○ IND 142-143 G 2
Jang, plato ⊥ RUS 108-109 b 7
Jangada ○ BR 70-71 J 4
Jangamo ○ MOC 218-219 H 7
Jangaon ○ IND 140-141 H 2
Jangeto ~ RUS 116-117 G 3
Jangiabad ○ US 136-137 M 4
Jangier ○ US 136-137 L 4
Jangijul ○ US 136-137 L 4
Jangikišlok ○ US 136-137 K 4
Jangikurgan ○ US 136-137 M 4
Jangil', hrebet ▲ RUS 116-117 K 4
Jangipur ○ IND 142-143 F 3
Jangirabad ○ US 136-137 J 4
Jangngai Shan ▲ VRC 144-145 F 4
Jangoda ~ RUS 108-109 X 6
Jangozero, ozero ○ RUS 88-89 M 5
Janice ○ USA (MS) 268-269 L 5
Jāni Khel ○ PK 138-139 C 3
Janiopolis ○ BR 74-75 D 5
Janiševo ○ RUS 88-89 O 6
Janiuay ○ RP 160-161 E 7
Jankan, hrebet ▲ RUS 118-119 H 8
Jan Kempdorp ○ ZA 220-221 G 3
Jan Lake ○ CDN (SAS) 34-35 E 3
Jan Lake ○ CDN (SAS) 34-35 E 3
Jan Mayen ⌒ N 6-7 J 1
Jan Mayen Fracture Zone ≃ 6-7 J 1
Jannaye, Lac la ○ CDN 38-39 L 2
Jano-Indigirskaja nizmennost ⌣ RUS 110-111 U 4
Janos ○ MEX 50-51 E 2
Janów Lubelski ○ PL 92-93 R 3
Janrakynnot ○ RUS 112-113 Y 4
Janranaj ○ RUS 112-113 Q 2
Jansen ○ CDN (SAS) 232-233 O 4
Jansen ○ USA (CO) 254-255 L 6
Jansenville ○ ZA 220-221 G 6
Jansk, Ust'- ○ RUS 110-111 V 4
Janskie porogi ~ RUS 110-111 T 5
Janskij zaliv ≈ 110-111 U 4
Janskoe ploskogor'e ▲ RUS 110-111 T 6
Jantan ○ RI 166-167 H 3
Jantetelco ○ MEX 52-53 E 2
Janthoe ○ RI 162-163 A 2
Jantingue ○ MOC 220-221 L 2
Januária ○ BR 72-73 H 3
Januário Cicco ○ BR 68-69 L 5
Janus Ø ⌒ GRØ 26-27 p 8
Janykurgan ○ KA 136-137 K 3
Jaora ○ IND 138-139 E 8
Japan = Nippon ■ J 152-153 J 6
Japan, Sea of ≈ 10-11 N 4
Japan, Sea of = Nippon Kai = Sea of Japan = Japonskoe more ≈ 10-11 N 4
Japan Basin ≃ 10-11 N 4
Japanese War Cemetery • AUS 180-181 K 2
Japanese World War II Bunker ∴• RI 166-167 G 4
Japan Trench ≃ 152-153 K 7
Japaratinga ○ BR 68-69 L 6
Japaratuba ○ BR 68-69 K 7
Japerica ○ BR 68-69 E 2
Japerica, Baía do ≈ 68-69 E 2
Japim ○ BR 64-65 F 5
Japon, mys ▲ RUS 120-121 Q 4
Japtiksale ○ RUS 108-109 O 7
Japuíra, Área Indígena ⨯ BR 70-71 H 2
Japurá ○ BR 66-67 D 3
Japurá, Rio ~ BR 66-67 D 3
Jaqué ○ PA 52-53 E 8
Jaques-Cartier, Détroit de ≈ CDN 242-243 E 2
Jar ○ RUS 114-115 H 6
Jar ☆ RUS (UDM) 96-97 H 4
Jar, Krasnyj ○ RUS 114-115 T 7
Jara ~ RUS 108-109 T 7
Jara, La ○ USA (CO) 254-255 K 6
Jarabacoa ○• DOM 54-55 K 5
Jaraguá ○ BR 72-73 F 3
Jaraguá ○ C 54-55 E 3
Jaraguá do Sul ○ BR 74-75 F 6
Jaraguari ○ BR (GSU) 70-71 K 7
Jaraguari ○ BR (GSU) 70-71 K 6
Jarahueca ○ C 54-55 F 3
Jaram, La ⊥ MA 188-189 F 7
Jaraniyo ○ ETH 208-209 D 3
Jaransk ○ RUS 96-97 E 5
Jarānwāla ○ PK 138-139 D 4
Jarato, ozero ○ RUS 108-109 Q 6
Jarauçu, Rio ~ BR 68-69 B 3
Jarawara, Área Indígena ⨯ BR 66-67 E 6
Jarbidge ○ USA (NV) 246-247 K 2
Jarbo Pass ▲ USA (CA) 246-247 D 4
Jarcevo ○ RUS 116-117 E 5
Jarcevo ☆ RUS (SML) 94-95 N 4
Jarclas al Abid ○ LAR 192-193 J 1
Jardim ○ BR (CEA) 68-69 J 5
Jardim ○ BR (GSU) 76-77 J 1
Jardim do Seridó ○ BR 68-69 K 5
Jardín, Sierra del ▲ RCH 76-77 C 3
Jardín América ○ RA 76-77 K 4
Jardine River ~ AUS 174-175 G 2
Jardine River National Park ⊥ AUS 174-175 G 2
Jardines de la Reina, Archipiélago de los ⌒ C 54-55 F 4
Jardymly = Yardımlı ○ AZ 128-129 N 3
Jaredi ○ WAN 198-199 B 6
Jarega ○ RUS 88-89 W 5
Jarenga ○ RUS (ARH) 88-89 U 5
Jarenga ~ RUS 88-89 U 5
Jarensk ○ RUS 88-89 U 5
Jari ○ BR 76-77 K 5
Jari, Estação Ecológica do ⊥ BR 62-63 H 5
Jari, Lago ○ BR 66-67 F 5
Jari, Rio ~ BR 62-63 H 5
Jari, Rio ~ BR 66-67 F 5
Jaria-Jhanjail ○ BD 142-143 G 3
Jarif, Wādī ~ LAR 192-193 G 2
Jarina ou Juruna, Rio ~ BR 68-69 B 7
Jarkovo ☆ RUS 114-115 J 6
Jarnema ○ RUS 88-89 P 5
Jarny ○ F 90-91 K 7
Jarocin ○• PL 92-93 O 3
Jarok, ostrov ⌒ RUS 110-111 V 4
Jaroslavl' ☆•• RUS 94-95 Q 3
Jaroslavskij ○ RUS 118-119 F 5
Jarosław ○• PL 92-93 R 3
Jaroto pervoe, ozero ○ RUS 108-109 O 8
Jaroto vtoroe, ozero ○ RUS 108-109 O 7
Jarotschin = Jarocin ○• PL 92-93 O 3
Jarovaja ~ RUS 112-113 L 3
Jarovoe ○ RUS 124-125 L 2
Järpen ○ S 86-87 F 5
Jarqurghon ○ US 136-137 K 6
Jarrahdale ○ AUS 176-177 D 6
Jarrow ○ CDN (ALB) 232-233 G 3
Jar-Sale ○ RUS 108-109 O 8
Jarso ○ ETH 208-209 B 4
Jartai ○ VRC 154-155 D 2
Jartai Yanchi ○ VRC 154-155 D 2
Jaru ○ BR 70-71 F 2
Jaru, Reserva Biológica do ⊥ BR 66-67 G 7
Jaru, Rio ~ BR 70-71 F 2
Jarudej ~ RUS 114-115 L 2
Jarud Qi ○ VRC 150-151 C 5
Jaruma ○ BOL 70-71 C 5
Järva-Jaani ○ EST 94-95 J 2
Järvakandi ○ EST 94-95 J 2
Järvenpää ○ FIN 88-89 H 6
Jarvis ○ CDN (ONT) 238-239 E 6
Jarvis Island ⌒ USA 13 L 3
Järvsö ○ S 86-87 H 6
Jarwāli ○ IND 138-139 D 5
Jary ○ RUS 108-109 M 7
Jasaan ○ RP 160-161 F 8
Jasačnaja ~ RUS 110-111 c 7
Jasačnaja ~ RUS 120-121 Q 2
Jasavėjjaha ~ RUS 108-109 O 6
Jasavėjto, ozero ○ RUS 108-109 N 7
Jasel'da ~ BY 94-95 J 5
Jashpurnagar ○ IND 142-143 D 4
Jasiira ○ SP 212-213 K 3
Jasikan ○ GH 202-203 L 6
Jašil'kul', ozero ○ TJ 136-137 N 6
Jašiūnai ○•• LT 94-95 J 4
Jaškino ☆ RUS 114-115 S 7
Jaškul' ○ RUS 96-97 D 10
Jaškur-Bod'ja ☆ RUS 96-97 H 5
Jasło ○• PL 92-93 Q 4
Jasmin ○ CDN (SAS) 232-233 P 4
Jasnaja ○ RUS 118-119 G 10
Jasnoe ○ RUS 94-95 G 4
Jasnogorsk ☆• RUS 94-95 P 4
Jasnomorskí ○ RUS 122-123 J 5
Jasnyj ○ RUS (AMR) 122-123 C 2
Jasnyj ☆ RUS (ORB) 126-127 N 2
Jasonhalvøy ⊥ ARK 16 G 30
Jason Islands ⌒ GB 78-79 K 6
Jasper ○ CDN (ALB) 228-229 Q 4
Jasper ○ USA (AL) 284-285 C 3
Jasper ○ USA (AR) 276-277 B 4
Jasper ○ USA (FL) 286-287 G 1
Jasper ○ USA (GA) 284-285 F 2
Jasper ○ USA (IN) 274-275 M 6
Jasper ○ USA (MN) 270-271 B 7
Jasper ○ USA (NY) 278-279 D 6
Jasper ○ USA (TN) 276-277 K 5
Jasper ○ USA (TX) 268-269 G 6
Jasper Lake ○ CDN (ALB) 228-229 R 3
Jasper National Park ⊥••• CDN (ALB) 228-229 Q 3
Jasrāna ○ IND 138-139 G 6
Jastrow = Jastrowie ○ PL 92-93 O 2
Jastrowie ○ PL 92-93 O 2
Jasubibeteri ○ YV 60-61 J 6
Jataí ○ BR 72-73 E 4
Jatapu, Rio ~ BR 66-67 H 4
Jatapu, Serra do ▲ BR 62-63 E 6
Jatapuzinho, Rio ~ BR 62-63 E 5
Jatei ○ BR 76-77 K 2
Jath ○ IND 140-141 F 2
Jati ○ BR 68-69 J 5
Jati ○ PK 138-139 B 7
Jati ○ RI 168 D 3
Jatibarang ○ RI 168 C 3
Jatibonico ○ C 54-55 F 4
Jatiluhur, Danau ○ RI 168 B 3
Jatirogo ○ RI 168 D 3
Jatiwangi ○ RI 168 C 3
Jatobá ○ BR (MAT) 70-71 K 3
Jatobá ○ BR (PA) 68-69 B 4
Jaú ○ BR 72-73 F 7
Jaú, Parque Nacional do ⊥ BR 66-67 F 4
Jaú, Rio ~ BR 66-67 F 4
Jauaperí, Rio ~ BR 62-63 E 5
Jauaruá ○ BR 66-67 E 4
Jaucha, Arroyo de ~ RA 78-79 E 3
Jauharābād ○ PK 138-139 D 3
Jauja ○• PE 64-65 E 7
Jaumave ○ MEX 50-51 K 6
Jaunpiebalga ○•• LV 94-95 K 3
Jaunpur ○ IND 142-143 C 3
Jaupaci ○ BR 72-73 E 4
Jauquara, Rio ~ BR 70-71 J 4
Jaurdi ○ AUS 176-177 F 5
Jaurin ~ RUS 122-123 D 4
Jauru ○ BR (GSU) 70-71 K 6
Jauru ○ BR (MAT) 70-71 H 4
Jauru, Rio ~ BR 70-71 H 5
Java Barat ◘ RI 168 B 3
Java Center ○ USA (NY) 278-279 C 6
Javaj, poluostrov ⌣ RUS 108-109 Q 5
Javan ○ TJ 136-137 L 5
Javari, Rio ~ BR 62-63 H 6
Javari, Rio ~ BR 64-65 F 4
Java Sea = Java, Laut ≈ 13 C 3
Java Tengah ◘ RI 168 C 3
Java Timur ◘ RI 168 D 4
Java Trench ≃ 168 C 8
Javier, Isla ⌒ RCH 80 C 3
Javier de Viana ○ ROU 76-77 J 6
Javlenka ☆ KA 124-125 F 1
Jawa ⌒ RI 168 B 3
Jāwad ○ IND 138-139 E 7
Jawi ○ RI 162-163 H 5
Jawor ○• PL 92-93 O 3
Jaworzno ○ PL 92-93 P 3
Jay ○ USA (OK) 264-265 K 2
Jayamkondacholapuram ○ IND 140-141 H 5
Jayanca ○ PE 64-65 C 5
Jayapura ○ RI 166-167 L 3
Jayawijaya, Pegunungan ▲ RI 166-167 K 4
Jay Em ○ USA (WY) 252-253 O 4
Jayton ○ USA (TX) 264-265 D 5
Jazā'ir, Al ☆••• DZ 190-191 D 2
Jažełbicy ○ RUS 94-95 N 2
Jazevec ○ RUS 88-89 T 4
Jazira Tarut ○ KSA 134-135 D 5
Jazykovo ○ RUS (ULN) 96-97 E 6
Jazykovo ☆ RUS (BAS) 96-97 J 6
J. C. Jacobsen, Kap ▲ GRØ 28-29 Z 2
Jconha ○ BR 72-73 K 6
Jean ○ USA (NV) 248-249 J 4
Jean ○ USA (TX) 264-265 F 5
Jean de Baie ○ CDN (NFL) 242-243 N 5
Jeanerette ○ USA (LA) 268-269 J 7
Jeanette Bay ≈ 36-37 V 7
Jean Rabel ○ RH 54-55 J 5
Jeavons, Lake ○ AUS 172-173 J 6
Jebala ⊥ MA 188-189 J 3
Jebba ○ WAN 204-205 F 4
Jeberos ○ PE 64-65 D 4
Jebiniana ○ TN 190-191 H 3
Jebri ○ PK 134-135 L 5
Jedburgh ○ CDN (SAS) 232-233 P 4
Jeddah = Ǧidda ○ KSA 132-133 A 3
Jeddore Cape ▲ CDN (NS) 240-241 M 6
Jędrzejów ○• PL 92-93 Q 3
Jeedamya ○ AUS 176-177 F 4
Jefawa ○ SUD 206-207 F 3
Jefe, Cerro ▲ PA 52-53 E 7
Jeffara ⊥ TN 190-191 H 4
Jeffers ○ USA (MN) 270-271 C 6
Jefferson ○ USA (AR) 276-277 C 6
Jefferson ○ USA (CO) 254-255 K 4
Jefferson ○ USA (GA) 284-285 G 2
Jefferson ○ USA (IA) 274-275 D 2
Jefferson ○ USA (NC) 282-283 F 4
Jefferson ○ USA (OR) 244-245 B 6
Jefferson ○ USA (SC) 284-285 K 2
Jefferson ○ USA (SD) 260-261 K 4
Jefferson ○ USA (TX) 264-265 K 6
Jefferson, Fort • USA (OH) 280-281 B 4
Jefferson, Mount ▲ USA (NV) 246-247 J 5
Jefferson, Mount ▲ USA (OR) 244-245 D 6
Jefferson City ○ USA (MO) 274-275 F 6
Jefferson City ○ USA (MT) 250-251 G 5
Jefferson City ○ USA (TN) 282-283 D 4
Jefferson National Memorial, Fort ∴• USA (FL) 286-287 G 7
Jefferson Proving Ground ✕✕ USA (IN) 274-275 N 6
Jefferson State Memorial, Fort • USA (OH) 280-281 B 3
Jeffersontown ○ USA (KY) 276-277 K 2
Jeffersonville ○ USA (GA) 284-285 G 4
Jeffersonville ○ USA (IN) 274-275 N 6
Jeffersonville ○ USA (OH) 280-281 C 4
Jeffersonville ○ USA (VT) 278-279 J 4
Jeffrey City ○ USA (WY) 252-253 L 4
Jeffries, Lake ○ AUS 176-177 G 3
Jef-Jef el Kébir ⊥ TCH 198-199 K 2
Jega ○ WAN 198-199 B 6
Jege ○ WAN 204-205 F 4
Jeinemeni, Cerro ▲ RCH 80 D 3
Jejekangphu Kang ▲ BHT 142-143 F 1
Jejevo ○ SOL 184 I d 3
Jejuí-Guazú, Río ~ PY 76-77 J 3
Jēkabpils ○•• LV 94-95 J 3
Jekyll Island ⌒ USA (GA) 284-285 J 5
Jelai ~ RI 162-163 J 6
Jelap La ▲ BHT 142-143 F 2
Jelenia Góra ☆• PL 92-93 N 3
Jelgava ○•• LV 94-95 H 3
Jeli ○ MAL 162-163 D 2
Jellico ○ USA (TN) 282-283 C 4
Jellicoe ○ CDN (BC) 230-231 J 4
Jellicoe ○ CDN (ONT) 234-235 Q 5
Jelly Bean Crystals • AUS 178-179 L 5
Jelmusibak ○ RI 164-165 D 4
Jelsa ○ HR 100-101 F 3
Jema ○ GH 202-203 K 6
Jemâa-Ida-Oussemlat ○ MA 188-189 G 6
Jemaluang ○ MAL 162-163 E 3
Jema Shet' ~ ETH 208-209 D 4
Jembawan, Danau ○ RI 162-163 F 6
Jember ○ RI 168 E 4

Ivalojoki — Jember 341

Jemberam o **GNB** 202-203 C 4
Jemez Indian Reservation X **USA** (NM) 256-257 J 3
Jemez Pueblo o **USA** (NM) 256-257 J 3
Jemez Springs o **USA** (NM) 256-257 J 3
Jemil'čyne o **UA** 102-103 E 2
Jeminay o **VRC** 146-147 G 2
Jemison o **USA** (AL) 284-285 D 4
Jemma o **WAN** (BAU) 204-205 H 3
Jemma o **WAN** (KAD) 204-205 H 4
Jempang, Danau ⬭ **RI** 164-165 D 4
Jemseg o **CDN** (NB) 240-241 J 5
Jen o **WAN** 204-205 J 4
Jena o **D** 92-93 L 3
Jena o **USA** (LA) 268-269 H 5
Jenakijeve o **UA** 102-103 L 3
Jenda o **MW** 214-215 G 7
Jendouba ☆ **TN** 190-191 G 2
Jeneien, Oued ~ **TN** 190-191 G 5
Jenerhodar o **UA** 102-103 J 4
Jeneshuaya, Arroyo ~ **BOL** 70-71 D 3
Jenīn o•• **WB** 130-131 D 1
Jenipapo o **BR** (AMA) 66-67 G 5
Jenipapo o **BR** (P) 62-63 K 6
Jenipapo o **BR** (TOC) 68-69 D 5
Jenipapo, Ribeiro ~ **BR** 68-69 D 5
Jenipapo, Rio ~ **BR** 68-69 G 4
Jenissej = Enisej ⌒ 10-11 H 2
Jenissej = Enisej ~ **RUS** 10-11 H 2
Jenkins o **USA** (KY) 276-277 N 3
Jenkins o **USA** (NJ) 280-281 M 4
Jenner o **CDN** (ALB) 232-233 G 5
Jenner o **USA** (CA) 246-247 B 5
Jennings ~ **CDN** 20-21 Z 7
Jennings o **USA** (LA) 268-269 H 6
Jennings Randolph Lake ⬭ **USA** (MD) 280-281 G 4
Jenny o **SME** 62-63 G 3
Jenny Lind Island ⌒ **CDN** 24-25 V 6
Jenolan Caves • **AUS** 180-181 L 2
Jensen o **USA** (UT) 254-255 F 3
Jensen, Cape ▲ **CDN** 24-25 h 6
Jens Munk Island ⌒ **CDN** 24-25 g 6
Jens Munk Ø ⌒ **GRØ** 28-29 U 4
Jepara o **RI** 168 D 3
Jeparit o **AUS** 180-181 F 4
Jequié o **BR** 72-73 K 2
Jequintinhonha, Rio ~ **BR** 72-73 L 3
Jequiriçá o **BR** 72-73 L 2
Jequitaí o **BR** 72-73 H 4
Jequitai, Rio ~ **BR** 72-73 H 4
Jequitiba o **BR** 72-73 J 5
Jequitinhonha o **BR** 72-73 K 4
Jequitinhonha, Rio ~ **BR** 72-73 J 4
Jerada o **MA** 188-189 K 3
Jerangau, Kampung o **MAL** 162-163 E 2
Jerangle o **AUS** 180-181 K 3
Jerantut o **MAL** 162-163 E 3
Jerba, Île de ⌒ **TN** 190-191 G 4
Jerbar o **SUD** 206-207 K 6
Jerdera o **RI** 166-167 H 5
Jere o **RI** 164-165 K 4
Jerecuaro o **MEX** 52-53 D 1
Jérémie ☆•• **RH** 54-55 H 5
Jeremoabo o **BR** 68-69 J 7
Jerer Shet' ~ **ETH** 208-209 F 4
Jerez, Río ~ **MEX** 50-51 H 6
Jerez de García Salinas o• **MEX** 50-51 H 6
Jerez de la Frontera o **E** 98-99 D 6
Jerez de los Caballeros o•• **E** 98-99 D 5
Jericho o **AUS** 178-179 J 2
Jericho o **SOL** 184 I c 3
Jericho = Arīḥāl ☆•• **AUT** 130-131 D 2
Jericho Dam < **ZA** 220-221 K 3
Jericoacoara o **BR** 68-69 H 3
Jericoacoara, Ponta ▲ **BR** 68-69 H 3
Jerigu o **GH** 202-203 K 5
Jerilderie o **AUS** 180-181 H 3
Jerko La ▲ **VRC** 144-145 C 5
Jerome o **USA** (AZ) 256-257 C 4
Jerome o **USA** (FL) 286-287 H 6
Jerome o **USA** (ID) 252-253 D 4
Jerori o **BOL** 70-71 E 4
Jerramungup o **AUS** 176-177 E 6
Jersey ⌒ **GBJ** 90-91 F 7
Jersey City o **USA** (NJ) 280-281 M 3
Jersey Cove o **CDN** (QUE) 240-241 L 2
Jersey Shore o **USA** (PA) 280-281 J 2
Jerseyville o **USA** (IL) 274-275 H 5
Jertih o **MAL** 162-163 E 2
Jerumenha o **BR** 68-69 G 5
Jerusalem = Yĕrūshalayim ★••• **IL** 130-131 D 2
Jervis, Monte ▲ **RCH** 80 C 4
Jervis Bay • **AUS** 180-181 L 3
Jervis Inlet ≈ 32-33 J 7
Jervis Inlet ≈ **CDN** 230-231 F 4
Jervois o **AUS** 178-179 D 2
Jesenice o **SLO** 100-101 E 1
Jeseník o **CZ** 92-93 O 3
Jesi o **I** 100-101 D 3
Jesi, Monte ▲ **MOC** 214-215 H 7
Jesmond o **CDN** (BC) 230-231 H 2
Jessama o **USA** (NC) 282-283 L 5
Jessamine Creek ~ **AUS** 178-179 G 2
Jesseltown = Kota Kinabalu ☆• **MAL** 160-161 B 10
Jessheim ☆ **N** 86-87 E 6
Jessore o **BD** 142-143 F 4
Jester o **USA** (OK) 264-265 E 3
Jesup o **USA** (GA) 284-285 J 5
Jesup o **USA** (IA) 274-275 F 2
Jesus, Mount ▲ **USA** (KS) 262-263 G 7
Jesús Carranza o **MEX** 52-53 G 3
Jesus María o **RA** 76-77 E 6
Jesús Menéndez o **C** 54-55 G 4
Jet o **USA** (OK) 264-265 F 2
Jeta, Ilha de ⌒ **GNB** 202-203 B 4
Jetmore o **USA** (KS) 262-263 G 6
Jetpur o **IND** 138-139 C 9
Jeudin, Pulau ⌒ **RI** 166-167 H 5
Jevargi o **IND** 140-141 G 2
Jevnaker ☆ **N** 86-87 E 6
Jevpatorija ☆• **UA** 102-103 H 5
Jewel Cave National Monument ∴ **USA** (SD) 260-261 C 3
Jewell o **USA** (IA) 274-275 E 2
Jewell o **USA** (KS) 262-263 H 5
Jewell o **USA** (OR) 244-245 B 5
Jewett o **USA** (TX) 266-267 L 2
Jewish Autonomous Region = Evrejskaja avtonomnaja oblast' □ **RUS** 122-123 D 4
Jeypore o **IND** 142-143 C 6
Jezercës, maja e ▲ **AL** 100-101 G 3
Jgarassu o• **BR** 68-69 L 5
Jhābua o **IND** 138-139 E 8
Jhajjar o **IND** 138-139 F 5
Jhal o **PK** 134-135 M 4
Jhālawār o **IND** 138-139 F 7
Jhālāwār ∸ **IND** 138-139 C 8
Jhamat o **PK** 138-139 C 3
Jhang o **PK** 138-139 D 4
Jhang Branch < **PK** 138-139 D 4
Jhānsi o **IND** 138-139 G 7
Jharol o **IND** 138-139 D 7
Jhārsuguda o **IND** 142-143 D 5
Jhatpat o **PK** 138-139 B 5
Jheeruk o **PK** 138-139 B 7
Jhelum ~ **IND** 138-139 E 3
Jhelum o **PK** (PU) 138-139 D 3
Jhelum ~ **PK** 138-139 D 4
Jhenida o **BD** 142-143 F 4
Jhimpir o **PK** 138-139 B 7
Jhudo o **PK** 138-139 B 7
Jhunjhunūn o **IND** 138-139 E 5
Jiading o **VRC** 154-155 M 6
Jiahe o **VRC** 156-157 H 4
Jiajiang o **VRC** 156-157 C 2
Jialing Jiang ~ **VRC** 154-155 E 6
Jiamusi o **VRC** 150-151 H 4
Ji'an o **VRC** (JIL) 150-151 F 7
Ji'an o **VRC** (JXI) 156-157 J 3
Jianchang o **VRC** 154-155 L 1
Jianchuan o **VRC** 142-143 L 2
Jiande o **VRC** 156-157 L 2
Jiangaoshan ▲ **MYA** 142-143 L 3
Jiangbai o **VRC** 156-157 E 2
Jiangcheng o **VRC** 156-157 B 5
Jiangcheng Hanizu Yizu Zizhixian o **VRC** 156-157 B 5
Jiange o **VRC** 154-155 D 5
Jianghong o **VRC** 156-157 F 6
Jianghua o **VRC** 156-157 G 4
Jiangjin o **VRC** 156-157 E 2
Jiangjunmiao o **VRC** 146-147 J 3
Jiangkou o **VRC** (GZH) 156-157 F 3
Jiangkou o **VRC** (SIC) 154-155 F 6
Jiangle o **VRC** 156-157 K 3
Jiangling o **VRC** 154-155 H 6
Jiangluo o **VRC** 154-155 D 5
Jiangmen o **VRC** 156-157 H 5
Jiangshan o **VRC** 156-157 L 2
Jiang Shan ▲ **VRC** 154-155 G 6
Jiangsu □ **VRC** 154-155 L 5
Jiangxi □ **VRC** 156-157 J 3
Jiangyin o **VRC** 154-155 M 6
Jiangyong o **VRC** 156-157 G 4
Jiangyou o **VRC** 154-155 D 6
Jianhe o **VRC** 156-157 F 3
Jianhu o **VRC** 154-155 L 5
Jianli o **VRC** 156-157 H 2
Jianmen G. • **VRC** 154-155 D 5
Jianning o **VRC** 156-157 K 3
Jian'ou o **VRC** 156-157 L 3
Jianping o **VRC** 154-155 L 1
Jianshi o **VRC** 154-155 F 6
Jianshui o **VRC** 156-157 C 5
Jianyang o **VRC** (FUJ) 156-157 L 3
Jianyang o **VRC** (SIC) 154-155 D 6
Jiaohe o **VRC** 150-151 F 6
Jiaohe Gucheng ∴• **VRC** 146-147 J 4
Jiaojiang o **VRC** 156-157 M 2
Jiaokou o **VRC** 154-155 G 3
Jiaoling o **VRC** 156-157 K 4
Jiaonan o **VRC** 154-155 L 4
Jiaotelo o **VRC** 144-145 F 6
Jiaozhou o **VRC** 154-155 L 3
Jiaozuo o **VRC** 154-155 H 4
Jiashan o **VRC** 154-155 K 5
Jiashi o **VRC** 146-147 C 6
Jia Tsuo La ▲ **VRC** 144-145 F 6
Jia Xian o **VRC** (HEN) 154-155 H 5
Jia Xian o **VRC** (SHA) 154-155 G 2
Jiaxing o **VRC** 154-155 M 6
Jiayin o **VRC** 150-151 H 3
Jiayu o **VRC** 156-157 H 2
Jiayu G. • **VRC** 146-147 O 6
Jiayuguan o **VRC** 146-147 O 6
Jíbaro, El o **C** 54-55 F 4
Jiberu o **WAN** 204-205 K 4
Jibisa ▲ **EAK** 212-213 F 1
Jibiya o **WAN** 198-199 C 6
Jibóia o **BR** 66-67 C 2
Jibou o **RO** 102-103 C 4
Jicarilla Apache Indian Reservation X **USA** (NM) 256-257 H 2
Jicaro Galán o **HN** 52-53 L 5
Jichang o **VRC** 156-157 D 3
Jičín o **CZ** 92-93 N 3
Jidali, togga ~ **SP** 208-209 H 3
Jiddah = Ğidda o• **KSA** 132-133 A 3
Jidhi o **SP** 208-209 F 3
Jiekkevarrebreen ▲ **N** 86-87 J 2
Jieshi o **VRC** 156-157 J 5
Jieshi Wan ~ **VRC** 156-157 J 5
Jieshou o **VRC** 154-155 J 5
Jiexi o **VRC** 156-157 J 5
Jiexiu o **VRC** 154-155 G 3
Jieyang o **VRC** 156-157 K 5
Jieznas o **LT** 94-95 J 4
Jiga o **ETH** 208-209 C 3
Jiggalong X **AUS** 176-177 F 1
Jiggalong Aboriginal Land X **AUS** 176-177 F 1
Jiggs o **USA** (NV) 246-247 K 3
Jigongshan • **VRC** 154-155 J 6
Jiguaní o **C** 54-55 G 4
Jigzhi o **VRC** 154-155 B 5
Jihlava o **CZ** 92-93 N 4
Jihlava ~ **CZ** 92-93 N 4
Jihur o **ETH** 208-209 D 4
Jiiqley o **SP** 208-209 G 6
Jijel ☆ **DZ** 190-191 E 2
Jijie o **VRC** 156-157 C 5
Jijiga o **ETH** 208-209 F 4
Jijona = Xixona o **E** 98-99 G 5
Jilakin Lake ⬭ **AUS** 176-177 E 6
Jilamo o **HN** 52-53 L 4
Jilib ☆ **SP** 212-213 J 3
Jilin o **VRC** (JIL) 150-151 F 6
Jilin □ **VRC** 150-151 E 6
Jilin Hada Ling ▲ **VRC** 150-151 E 6
Jilotlán de los Dolores o **MEX** 52-53 C 2
Jima ☆ **ETH** 208-209 C 5
Jimani ☆ **DOM** 54-55 K 5
Jimata o **ETH** 208-209 C 4
Jimbe o **ANG** 214-215 B 6
Jimei o **VRC** 156-157 L 4
Jiménez o **MEX** (CHA) 50-51 G 4
Jiménez o **MEX** (COA) 50-51 J 3
Jimenez o **RP** 160-161 E 8
Jiménez de Teul o **MEX** 50-51 H 6
Jimeta o **WAN** 204-205 K 4
Jimi River ~ **PNG** 183 C 3
Jimkar o **BHT** 142-143 G 2
Jimna Range ▲ **AUS** 178-179 M 4
Jimo o **VRC** 154-155 M 3
Jimsar o **VRC** 146-147 J 4
Jimulco o **MEX** 50-51 H 5
Jin, Kepulauan ⌒ **RI** 166-167 H 5
Jinan ☆• **VRC** 154-155 K 3
Jinchang o **VRC** 154-155 C 2
Jincheng o **VRC** (SHA) 154-155 H 4
Jincheng o **VRC** (YUN) 156-157 C 4
Jinchuan o **VRC** 154-155 C 6
Jin Ci • **VRC** 154-155 H 3
Jind o **IND** 138-139 F 5
Jindabyne o **AUS** 180-181 K 4
Jindare o **AUS** 172-173 K 3
Jin Dian • **VRC** 156-157 C 4
Jindřichův Hradec o **CZ** 92-93 N 4
Jinfo Shan ▲ **VRC** 156-157 E 2
Jingbian o **VRC** 154-155 F 3
Jingchuan o **VRC** 154-155 E 4
Jingde o **VRC** 154-155 L 6
Jingdezhen o• **VRC** 156-157 K 2
Jingdong o **VRC** 142-143 M 3
Jingellic o **AUS** 180-181 J 3
Jingemarra o **AUS** 176-177 D 3
Jinggangshan o **VRC** (JXI) 156-157 J 3
Jinggangshan • **VRC** (JXI) 156-157 J 3
Jinggu o **VRC** 142-143 M 4
Jinghe o **VRC** 146-147 F 3
Jing He ~ **VRC** 154-155 F 4
Jinghong o **VRC** 142-143 M 5
Jingjiang o **VRC** 154-155 M 5
Jingle o **VRC** 154-155 G 2
Jingmen o **VRC** 154-155 H 6
Jingning o **VRC** 154-155 D 4
Jingpo o **VRC** 150-151 G 6
Jingpo Hu • **VRC** 150-151 G 6
Jingshan o **VRC** 154-155 H 6
Jingtai o **VRC** 154-155 D 3
Jingtieshan o **VRC** (GAN) 146-147 N 6
Jingtieshan o **VRC** (XUZ) 146-147 O 6
Jingtie Shan ▲ **VRC** 146-147 N 6
Jingxi o **VRC** 156-157 E 5
Jing Xian o **VRC** 154-155 L 6
Jingxing o **VRC** 154-155 J 3
Jingyan o **VRC** 156-157 D 2
Jingyu o **VRC** 150-151 F 6
Jingyuan o **VRC** 154-155 D 3
Jingyu Hu ~ **VRC** 144-145 G 2
Jingyu Nao ▲ **VRC** 154-155 F 5
Jingzhou o **VRC** 156-157 F 3
Jinhe o **VRC** 150-151 C 2
Jinhua o **VRC** 156-157 L 2
Jining o **VRC** (NMZ) 148-149 L 7
Jining o **VRC** (SHD) 154-155 K 4
Jinja ☆ **EAU** 212-213 D 3
Jinka o **AUS** 178-179 C 2
Jinka o **ETH** 208-209 C 6
Jinkou o **VRC** 154-155 J 6
Jinning o **VRC** 156-157 C 4
Jinniu o **VRC** 154-155 J 6
Jinotega ☆ **NIC** 52-53 B 5
Jinotepe ☆ **NIC** 52-53 L 6
Jinping o **VRC** (GZH) 156-157 F 3
Jinping o **VRC** (YUN) 156-157 C 5
Jinqian He ~ **VRC** 154-155 F 5
Jinsha o **VRC** 156-157 E 3
Jinsha Jiang ~ **VRC** 142-143 L 2
Jinsha Jiang ~ **VRC** 144-145 M 4
Jinsha Jiang ~ **VRC** 156-157 C 3
Jinshanlin • **VRC** 154-155 K 1
Jinshatan o **VRC** 154-155 H 2
Jinshi ☆ **VRC** 156-157 G 2
Jinshiqiao o **VRC** 156-157 G 3
Jinta o **VRC** 146-147 O 6
Jintan o **VRC** 154-155 L 6
Jintang o **VRC** 154-155 D 6
Jintotolo Channel ≈ 160-161 E 7
Jintur o **IND** 138-139 F 10
Jinxi o **VRC** (JXI) 156-157 K 3
Jinxi o **VRC** (LIA) 150-151 C 7
Jinxian o **VRC** 156-157 K 2
Jinxiang o **VRC** 154-155 K 4
Jinyin Dao ⌒ **VRC** 158-159 L 2
Jinyun o **VRC** 156-157 M 2
Jinyunshan • **VRC** 156-157 E 2
Jinzhai o **VRC** 154-155 J 6
Jinzhong Shan ▲ **VRC** 156-157 D 4
Jinzhou o **VRC** (LIA) 150-151 C 8
Jinzhou o **VRC** (LIA) 150-151 C 7
Jinzū-gawa ~ **J** 152-153 G 6
Ji-Paraná o **BR** 70-71 G 2
Jipe, Lake ⬭ **EAK** 212-213 F 5
Jipijapa o **EC** 64-65 B 2
Jiquí o **C** 54-55 F 4
Jiquilpan o **MEX** 52-53 C 1
Jiquiriçá, Rio ~ **BR** 72-73 L 2
Jirau, Salto do ~ **BR** 66-67 E 7
Jiri o **NEP** 144-145 F 7
Jirrliban o **SP** 208-209 J 5
Jishan o **VRC** 154-155 G 4
Jishou o **VRC** 156-157 F 2
Jishu o **VRC** 150-151 F 5
Jitang Gulou • **VRC** 156-157 F 3
Jitarning o **AUS** 176-177 E 6
Jitaúna o **BR** 72-73 L 3
Jitra o **MAL** 162-163 D 2
Jitschin = Jičín o **CZ** 92-93 N 3
Jiu ~ **RO** 102-103 C 6
Jiucai Ling ▲ **VRC** 156-157 G 4
Jiuchang o **VRC** 156-157 E 3
Jiuhuashan • **VRC** 154-155 K 6
Jiujiang o **VRC** 156-157 K 2
Jiulihu • **VRC** 156-157 L 4
Jiuling Shan ▲ **VRC** 156-157 J 2
Jiulong = Kowloon o **HK** 156-157 J 5
Jiulongpo o **VRC** 156-157 E 2
Jiulongshibatan • **VRC** 156-157 H 4
Jiuquan o **VRC** 146-147 O 6
Jiurongcheng o **VRC** 154-155 N 3
Jiusuo o **VRC** 156-157 F 7
Jiutai o **VRC** 150-151 E 5
Jiuxu o **VRC** 156-157 E 4
Jiuyishan • **VRC** 156-157 H 4
Jiuzhaigou ••• **VRC** 154-155 C 5
Jivundu o **Z** 218-219 C 1
Jiwā', al- ∸ **UAE** 132-133 H 2
Jiwani o **PK** 134-135 J 6
Jiwani, Rās ▲ **PK** 134-135 J 6
Jixi o **VRC** (ANH) 154-155 L 6
Jixi o **VRC** (HEI) 150-151 H 5
Jixian o **VRC** 150-151 H 4
Ji Xian o **VRC** (SXI) 154-155 G 3
Ji Xian o **VRC** (TIA) 154-155 K 1
Jiyang o **VRC** 154-155 K 3
Jiyuan o **VRC** 154-155 H 4
Jizan = Ğīzān ☆ **KSA** 132-133 C 5
Jlam o **NEP** 144-145 F 7
Jli ~ **KA** 124-125 K 6
Joaçaba o **BR** 74-75 E 6
Joachín o **MEX** 52-53 F 2
Joaíma o **BR** 72-73 K 4
Joal-Fadiout o• **SN** 202-203 B 2
Joana o **YV** 60-61 L 3
Joana Coeli o **BR** 62-63 K 6
Joanna o **USA** (SC) 284-285 J 2
João, Rio ~ **BR** 72-73 J 7
João Arregui o **BR** 76-77 J 5
João Cãmara o **BR** 68-69 L 4
João Chagas o **ANG** 214-215 B 6
João Fagundes o **BR** 76-77 J 6
João Farias o **BR** 62-63 E 6
João Lisboa o **BR** 68-69 E 4
João Monlevade o **BR** 72-73 J 5
João Neiva o **BR** 72-73 K 5
João Pessoa ☆• **BR** 68-69 L 5
João Pinheiro o **BR** 72-73 G 4
João Vaz o **BR** 72-73 K 2
Joaquim o **BR** 68-69 G 5
Joáquim Gomes o **BR** 68-69 L 6
Joaquim Rios, Salto ~ **BR** 70-71 H 3
Joaquin o **USA** (TX) 268-269 F 5
Jobabo o **C** 54-55 G 4
Jobele o **WAN** 204-205 E 5
Jobillos, Los o **DOM** 54-55 K 5
Jobos, Playa ∸ **USA** (PR) 286-287 O 2
Jócar o **E** 98-99 F 6
Jocoli o **RA** 78-79 E 2
Jocotepec o **MEX** 52-53 C 1
Jodensavanna o **SME** 62-63 G 3
Jodhpur o• **IND** 138-139 D 6
Joe Batts Arm o **CDN** (NFL) 242-243 O 3
Joensuu ☆ **FIN** 88-89 K 5
Joerg Plateau ▲ **ARK** 16 F 30
Jõetsu o **J** 152-153 H 6
Joe Wheeler State Park ⊥ **USA** (AL) 284-285 C 2
Jof o **TN** 190-191 H 4
Jofane o **MOC** 218-219 H 5
Joffre o **CDN** (ALB) 232-233 E 3
Joffre, Mount ▲ **CDN** (BC) 230-231 O 3
Jogana o **WAN** 198-199 D 6
Jogbani o **IND** 142-143 E 2
Jõgeva o **EST** 94-95 K 2
Jogg Falls ~•• **IND** 140-141 F 3
Jogighopa o **IND** 142-143 G 2
Jogindarnagar o **IND** 138-139 F 4
Jogipet o **IND** 140-141 H 2
Jog Lake ⬭ **CDN** (ONT) 236-237 C 2
Jogues o **CDN** (ONT) 236-237 E 3
Johān o **PK** 134-135 M 4
Johan en Margeretha o **SME** 62-63 G 3
Johannesburg o•• **ZA** 220-221 J 3
Johan Peninsula ⌣ **CDN** 26-27 N 4
Johi o **GUY** 62-63 E 5
Johi o **PK** 134-135 M 5
John Day o **USA** (OR) 244-245 G 6
John Day Fossil Beds National Monument ∴ **USA** (OR) 244-245 F 6
John Day Fossil Beds National Monument • **USA** (OR) 244-245 E 6
John Day River ~ **USA** (OR) 244-245 F 6
John D'Or Prairie o **CDN** 30-31 M 6
John D'Or Prairie Indian Reserve X **CDN** 30-31 M 6
John D. Rockefeller Junior Memorial Parkway ⊥ **USA** (WY) 252-253 H 2
John Dyer, Cape ▲ **CDN** 24-25 V 4
John Eyre Motel o **AUS** 176-177 H 6
John Eyre Telegraph Station ∴ **AUS** 176-177 J 6
John Flagler, Kap ▲ **GRØ** 26-27 n 2
John Flynn Memorial • **AUS** 174-175 C 6
John H. Kerr Reservoir ⬭ **USA** (NC) 282-283 J 4
John Martin Reservoir ⬭ **USA** (CO) 254-255 M 5
John Murray Ø ⌒ **GRØ** 26-27 a 2
Johnny Hoe River ~ **CDN** 30-31 J 3
John Redmond Reservoir ⬭ **USA** (KS) 262-263 L 6
John River ~ **USA** 20-21 O 3
John's Corner o **EAT** (IRI) 214-215 H 5
Johnson, Mount ▲ **AUS** 176-177 H 2
Johnson, Pico de ▲ **MEX** 50-51 C 3
Johnson City o **USA** (KS) 262-263 E 7
Johnson City o **USA** (TN) 282-283 E 4
Johnson City o **USA** (TX) 266-267 J 3
Johnson Dam, Daniel ∴ **CDN** 38-39 K 3
Johnson Draw ~ **USA** (TX) 266-267 F 3
Johnson Island ⌒ **CDN** 36-37 K 6
Johnson National Historic Park, Lyndon Baines ∴ **USA** (TX) 266-267 J 3
Johnson Pass ▲ **USA** (UT) 254-255 C 3
Johnson River ~ **CDN** 30-31 G 4
Johnsons o **USA** (CA) 246-247 B 2
Johnsons Crossing o **CDN** 20-21 Y 6
Johnsons Landing o **CDN** (BC) 230-231 N 3
Johnson Space Center, Lyndon Baines ∴ **USA** (TX) 268-269 E 7
Johnsonville o **USA** (SC) 284-285 L 3
Johnston o **USA** (SC) 284-285 J 3
Johnston, Chute ~• **ZRE** 214-215 E 6
Johnstone Hill ▲ **AUS** 176-177 L 1
Johnstone South o• **AUS** 174-175 J 5
Johnstone Strait ≈ 32-33 G 6
Johnstone Strait ≈ **CDN** 230-231 C 3
Johnston Islands ⌒ **PNG** 183 D 2
Johnston Lakes, The ⬭ **AUS** 176-177 F 6
Johnstown o **CDN** (NS) 240-241 P 5
Johnstown o **USA** (NE) 262-263 F 2
Johnstown o **USA** (OH) 280-281 D 3
Johnstown o **USA** (PA) 280-281 H 3
Johnstown Flood National Monument • **USA** (PA) 280-281 H 3
Johnsville o **USA** (AR) 276-277 C 7
Johntown o **USA** (GA) 284-285 F 2
John W. Kyle State Park ⊥• **USA** (MS) 268-269 L 2
Johor □ **MAL** 162-163 E 3
Johor Bahru ☆•• **MAL** 162-163 E 4
Jõhvi-Ahtme o **EST** 94-95 K 2
Joigny o **F** 90-91 J 8
Joinville o **BR** 74-75 F 6
Joinville, Île ⌒ **ARK** 16 G 31
Jojutla de Juárez o **MEX** 52-53 E 2
Jokau o **SUD** 208-209 A 4
Jokau ~ **SUD** 208-209 A 4
Jøkel-bugten ≈ 26-27 p 4
Jokkmokk o• **S** 86-87 J 3
Jökulsá á Brú ~ **IS** 86-87 f 2
Jökulsá á Fjöllum ~ **IS** 86-87 e 2
Joli, Mont- o **CDN** (QUE) 240-241 G 2
Joliet o **USA** (IL) 274-275 K 3
Joliette o **CDN** (QUE) 238-239 M 2
Jolly Lake ⬭ **CDN** 30-31 N 3
Jolo ☆ **RP** 160-161 D 9
Jolo o **USA** (WV) 280-281 E 6
Jolo Island ⌒ **RP** 160-161 D 9
Jomala o **FIN** 88-89 F 6
Jomalig Island ⌒ **RP** 160-161 E 5
Jombang o **RI** 168 E 3
Jombo ~ **ANG** 216-217 E 5
Jombo o **GH** 202-203 L 5
Jomda o **VRC** 144-145 M 5
Jommon o **RI** 166-167 H 5
Jomo Lhari ▲ **BHT** 142-143 F 2
Jomonkum kumligi ∸ **US** 136-137 H 4
Jomsom o **NEP** 144-145 D 6
Jomu o **EAT** 212-213 D 5
Jona o **USA** (SD) 260-261 G 3
Jonathan Dickinson State Park ⊥ **USA** (FL) 286-287 J 4
Jonava = Ionava ☆ **LT** 94-95 J 4
Jonê o **VRC** 154-155 C 4
Jones o **CDN** (ONT) 234-235 J 5
Jones, Cape ▲ **CDN** 30-31 Y 4
Jones, Kap ▲ **GRØ** 26-27 p 8
Jones, Lake ⬭ **AUS** (WA) 172-173 H 5
Jones, Lake ⬭ **AUS** (WA) 176-177 G 2
Jonesboro o **USA** (AR) 276-277 E 5
Jonesboro o **USA** (GA) 284-285 F 3
Jonesboro o **USA** (LA) 268-269 H 4
Jonesboro o **USA** (TX) 266-267 K 2
Jonesborough o **USA** (TN) 282-283 E 4
Jones Islands ⌒ **USA** 20-21 Q 1
Jones Sound ≈ 24-25 c 2
Jones Swamp ⬭ **USA** (SC) 284-285 K 4
Jonesville o **USA** (LA) 268-269 J 5
Jonesville o **USA** (SC) 284-285 J 2
Jonesville o **USA** (TN) 282-283 C 4
Jonesville o **USA** (VA) 280-281 C 7
Jonggol o **RI** 168 B 3
Jonglei Canal = Junqoley Canal < **SUD** 206-207 K 4
Joniškis ☆ **LT** 94-95 H 3
Jönköping ☆ **S** 86-87 G 8
Jonquière o **CDN** (QUE) 240-241 D 2
Jonuta o **MEX** 52-53 H 2
Joowhar ☆ **SP** 212-213 K 2
Jopalayo, Cerro ▲ **RA** 76-77 D 3
Joplin o **USA** (MO) 276-277 A 3
Joplin o **USA** (MT) 250-251 J 3
Jordan o **RP** 160-161 E 7
Jordan o **USA** (MN) 270-271 E 6
Jordan o **USA** (MT) 250-251 N 4
Jordán, El o **CO** 60-61 F 5
Jordan, Lake < **USA** (AL) 284-285 D 4
Jordan, River o **CDN** (BC) 230-231 E 5
Jordan = Urdunn ■ **JOR** 130-131 D 2
Jordan Bay ≈ **CDN** 240-241 K 7
Jordânia o **BR** 72-73 K 3
Jordan Lake ⬭ **CDN** (NS) 240-241 K 6
Jordan Valley o **USA** (OR) 244-245 H 8
Jorf o **MA** 188-189 J 5
Jorge, Cabo ▲ **RCH** 80 C 5
Jorge Montt, Isla ⌒ **RCH** 80 C 5
Jorgucat o• **AL** 100-101 H 5
Jorhāt o **IND** 142-143 J 2
Joriapani o **NEP** 144-145 C 6
Jörn o **S** 86-87 K 4
Jornada del Muerto ∸ **USA** (NM) 256-257 J 6
Jorong o **RI** 164-165 D 5
Joronga = Pulau Hasil ⌒ **RI** 164-165 L 4
Jorskoe ploskogor'e ▲ **GE** 126-127 F 7
Joru o **WAL** 202-203 E 6
Jos ☆• **WAN** 204-205 H 4
Jose Abad Santos o **RP** 160-161 F 10
José Batlley Ordoñez o **ROU** 78-79 M 2
José Cardel o **MEX** 52-53 F 2
José de la Costa o **YV** 60-61 G 2
José del Carmen Ramirez, Parque Nacional ⊥ **DOM** 54-55 K 5
José de San Martín o **RA** 80 E 2
José Diaz, Ponta ▲ **BR** 74-75 F 6
José E. Rodo o **ROU** 78-79 L 2
Josefa Ortiz de Dominguez Estacione, Presa < **MEX** 50-51 E 4
Josegun River ~ **CDN** 32-33 M 4
Joselândia o **BR** 70-71 J 5
José Pedro Varela o **ROU** 78-79 M 2
Joseph o **USA** (OR) 244-245 H 5
Joseph, Lake ⬭ **CDN** (NFL) 38-39 M 2
Joseph, Lake ⬭ **CDN** (ONT) 238-239 F 3
Joseph Bonaparte Gulf ≈ 172-173 J 3
Josephburg o **CDN** (ALB) 232-233 E 2
Joseph City o **USA** (AZ) 256-257 E 4
Joseph Henry, Cape ▲ **CDN** 26-27 T 2
Josephine River ~ **CDN** 30-31 Y 4
Josephstaal o **PNG** 183 C 3
José Rodrigues o **BR** 68-69 C 4
Joshīmath o **IND** 138-139 G 4
Jōshin Etsu Kōgen National Park ⊥ **J** 152-153 G 6
Joshkar Ola = Joškar-Ola ☆ **RUS** 96-97 E 5
Joshua o **USA** (TX) 264-265 G 6
Joshua Tree o **USA** (CA) 248-249 H 5
Joshua Tree National Monument ⊥ **USA** (CA) 248-249 J 6
Joškar-Ola ☆ **RUS** 96-97 E 5
Jos Plateau ▲ **WAN** 204-205 H 3
Jostedalsbreen ⊂ **N** 86-87 C 6
Jost van Dyke ⌒ **GB** (VI) 286-287 R 2
Jotajana o **YV** 60-61 L 3
Jotunheimen ▲ **N** 86-87 D 6
Jotunheimen nasjonalpark ⊥ **N** 86-87 D 6
Joubertberge ▲ **NAM** 216-217 B 9
Joubertina o **ZA** 220-221 F 6
Joulter Cays ⌒ **BS** 54-55 F 2
Jourdanton o **USA** (TX) 266-267 J 5
Joutel o **CDN** (QUE) 236-237 K 3
Joutsa o **FIN** 88-89 J 6
Joutsijärvi o **FIN** 88-89 J 3
Jovellanos o **C** 54-55 E 3
Joviânia o **BR** 72-73 F 4
Joy o **USA** (KY) 276-277 G 3
Joy, Mount ▲ **CDN** 20-21 Y 5
Joya de Ceren ∴••• **ES** 52-53 K 5
Joya de los Sachas, La o **EC** 64-65 D 2
Joy Bay ≈ 36-37 O 4
Joyce o **USA** (WA) 244-245 B 2
Jreïda o **RIM** 196-197 B 5
Jreïf < **RIM** 196-197 D 6
J. Richardson Bay ≈ 26-27 P 3
Juaben o **GH** 202-203 K 6
Juami, Rio ~ **BR** 66-67 D 3
Juami-Japura, Reserva Ecológica ⊥ **BR** 66-67 C 4
Juanacatlán o **MEX** 52-53 C 1
Juan Aldamo o **MEX** 50-51 H 5
Juan Antonio o **YV** 60-61 K 2
Juan B. Alberdi o **RA** 76-77 E 4
Juan Bautista Tuxtepec o• **MEX** 52-53 F 2
Juan de Fuca Strait ≈ 40-41 B 1
Juan de Fuca Strait ≈ **USA** 244-245 A 2
Juan de Guia, Cabo San ▲ **CO** 60-61 D 2
Juân de Nova, Île ⌒ **F** 222-223 C 6
Juan E. Barra o **RA** 78-79 J 4
Juan Fernández, Islas ⌒ **RCH** 78-79 B 1
Juangchen o **VRC** 154-155 J 4
Juangon o **RP** 160-161 F 7
Juan Guerra o **PE** 64-65 D 5
Juani Island ⌒ **EAT** 214-215 K 4
Juanita o **USA** (CO) 254-255 H 6
Juan Jorba o **RA** 78-79 G 2
Juán José Perez o **BOL** 70-71 C 4
Juanjui o **PE** 64-65 D 5
Juankoski o **FIN** 88-89 K 5
Juan L. Lacaze o **ROU** 78-79 L 3
Juan Perez Sound ≈ **CDN** 228-229 C 4
Juan R. Cháve o **PY** 76-77 J 3
Juan Sola o **RA** 76-77 F 2
Juan Stuben, Isla ⌒ **RCH** 80 C 3
Juan Vicente o **C** 54-55 H 4
Juan W. Gez o **RA** 78-79 F 2
Juapon o **GH** 202-203 L 6
Juara o **BR** 70-71 J 2
Juárez o **MEX** (CHA) 50-51 E 2
Juárez o **MEX** (CHI) 52-53 H 3
Juárez o **MEX** (COA) 50-51 J 4
Juárez, Ciudad o• **MEX** 50-51 F 2
Juarez, Sierra de ▲ **MEX** 50-51 B 1
Juari, Rio ~ **BR** 68-69 C 5
Juatinga, Ponta da ▲ **BR** 72-73 H 7
Juazeiro o• **BR** 68-69 H 6
Juázeiro, Riachão ~ **BR** 72-73 J 2
Juazeiro do Norte o• **BR** 68-69 J 5
Juazohn o **LB** 202-203 F 7
Jūbā ☆ **SUD** 206-207 K 6
Juba, Rio ~ **BR** 70-71 H 4
Jubaylah, al- ⌒ **Y** 132-133 K 5
Jubba, Webi ~ **SP** 212-213 J 2
Jubbada Dhexe □ **SP** 212-213 J 3
Jubbada Hoose □ **SP** 212-213 H 3
Juberina o **YV** 60-61 L 3
Jubilee Island ⌒ **CDN** 36-37 N 2
Jubilee Lake ⬭ **AUS** 176-177 J 4
Jubilee Lake ⬭ **CDN** (NFL) 242-243 N 4
Jubilee Pass ▲ **USA** (CA) 248-249 H 4
Jubnī, Bi'r < **LAR** 192-193 L 2
Jucá, Rio ~ **BR** 68-69 H 5
Júcar, Río ~ **E** 98-99 G 5
Juçara o **BR** (BAH) 68-69 H 7
Juçara o **BR** (GOI) 72-73 E 3
Jucás o **BR** 68-69 J 5
Juchipila o **MEX** 50-51 H 7
Juchitán o **MEX** 52-53 E 3
Juchitán de Zaragoza o• **MEX** 52-53 G 3
Juchusujahuira, Río ~ **BOL** 70-71 D 5
Juciape o **BR** 72-73 K 2
Jučjugej o **RUS** 120-121 K 2
Jucul o **PE** 64-65 D 7
Jucumarini, Lago ⬭ **PE** 70-71 B 5
Jucuri o **BR** 68-69 K 4
Jucurucu, Rio ~ **BR** 72-73 L 4
Jucurutu o **BR** 68-69 K 5
Judenburg o **A** 92-93 N 5
Judèto, ozero ⬭ **RUS** 108-109 O 8
Judge Daly Promontory ∸ **CDN** 26-27 Q 3
Judith Gap o **USA** (MT) 250-251 K 5
Judith River ~ **USA** (MT) 250-251 K 4
Judoma ~ **RUS** 120-121 J 2
Judoma ~ **RUS** 120-121 H 4
Judomskij, hrebet ▲ **RUS** 120-121 J 3
Judybaevo o **RUS** 96-97 K 7
Juelsminde o **DK** 86-87 E 9
Jufrah, Al □ **LAR** 192-193 G 3
Jug ~ **RUS** 96-97 D 4
Juganskij, zapovednik ⊥ **RUS** 114-115 N 5
Jugarskaja Ob' ~ **RUS** 114-115 M 4
Jugiong o **AUS** 180-181 K 3
Jugo-Kamskij o **RUS** 96-97 J 5
Jugorënok o **RUS** 120-121 G 4
Jugorskij poluostrov ⌣ **RUS** 108-109 J 7
Jugorskij Šar, proliv ⬭ **RUS** 108-109 H 7
Juh o **VRC** 154-155 F 3
Juhnov o **RUS** 94-95 O 4
Juhoviči o **RUS** 94-95 L 3
Juhua Dao • **VRC** 150-151 C 7
Jui ~ **RO** 102-103 C 5
Juigalpa ☆ **NIC** 52-53 B 5
Juína o **BR** 70-71 H 2
Juinamirim, Rio ~ **BR** 70-71 H 2
Juiná ou Zui-Uina, Rio ~ **BR** 70-71 H 3
Juist ⌒ **D** 92-93 J 2
Juiz de Fora o **BR** 72-73 J 6
Juizhou o **VRC** 156-157 D 4
Jujun o **RI** 162-163 D 6
Jujuy □ **RA** 76-77 D 2
Jukagirskoe ploskogor'e ▲ **RUS** 110-111 d 6
Jukamenskoe ☆ **RUS** 96-97 H 5
Jukkasjärvi o• **S** 86-87 K 3
Jukonda ~ **RUS** 114-115 J 4
Juksa, Bol'šaja ~ **RUS** 114-115 S 6
Jukseevo o **RUS** 96-97 J 4
Jukta o **RUS** 116-117 M 4
Juktali ~ **RUS** 116-117 O 5
Jula ~ **RUS** 88-89 S 5
Jula, Jasiira ⌒ **SP** 212-213 J 4
Julaca o **BOL** 70-71 D 7
Juldessa ▲ **ETH** 208-209 D 7
Julesburg o **USA** (CO) 254-255 N 3
Juli o **PE** 70-71 C 5
Júlia o **BR** 66-67 C 3
Juliaca o **PE** 70-71 B 4
Julia Creek o **AUS** 174-175 F 7
Julia-Mabay o **C** 54-55 G 4
Julian o **USA** (CA) 248-249 H 6
Julian o **USA** (NC) 282-283 H 5
Julian, Lac ⬭ **CDN** 36-37 L 7
Julianatop ▲ **SME** 62-63 F 4
Julianehab = Qaqortoq o **GRØ** 28-29 R 6
Julianehabsfjord ≈ 28-29 R 6
Juliasdale o **ZW** 218-219 G 4
Julijske Alpe ▲ **SLO** 100-101 D 1
Julio, 9 de o **RA** 78-79 J 3
Julio, 16 de o **RA** 78-79 J 4
Julio de Castilhos o **BR** 74-75 D 7
Jullundur o **IND** 138-139 E 4
Julong Shan ▲ **VRC** 154-155 G 6
Julpa, Río ~ **BOL** 70-71 E 6
Julwānia o **IND** 138-139 E 9
Juma o **RUS** 88-89 M 4
Juma, Rio ~ **BR** 66-67 G 4
Juma, Rio ~ **BR** 66-67 E 5
Jumandi, Cuevas de • **EC** 64-65 D 2
Jumbe Salim's o **EAT** 214-215 J 6
Jumbilla o **PE** 64-65 D 4
Jumboo o **SP** 212-213 J 4
Jumelles, Longué- o **F** 90-91 G 8
Jumentos Cays ⌒ **BS** 54-55 H 3
Jumilla o **E** 98-99 G 5
Jumi Pozo o **RA** 76-77 E 5
Jumla o **NEP** 144-145 D 6
Jummayza o **SUD** (SR) 206-207 J 5
Jummayza o **SUD** (SR) 206-207 K 6
Jumper Uajv, gora ▲ **RUS** 88-89 O 3
Jump River o **USA** (WI) 270-271 H 5
Jump River ~ **USA** (WI) 270-271 H 5
Jumurčen ~ **RUS** 118-119 G 9
Jun', Allah- o **RUS** 120-121 H 3
Juna o **BR** 72-73 K 6
Juna Downs o **AUS** 172-173 D 7
Jūnāgadh o• **IND** 138-139 C 9
Junāgarh o **IND** 142-143 C 6
Junan o **VRC** 154-155 L 4
Junari ~ **RUS** 116-117 J 4
Juncal, Quebrada ~ **RCH** 76-77 C 3
Juncos o **USA** (PR) 286-287 Q 2
Junction o **USA** (TX) 266-267 H 3
Junction o **USA** (UT) 254-255 C 5
Junction, Mount ▲ **AUS** 172-173 J 5
Junction Bay ≈ 36-37 J 3
Junction Bay ≈ 174-175 B 2
Junction City o **USA** (AR) 276-277 C 7
Junction City o **USA** (KS) 262-263 K 5
Junction City o **USA** (OR) 244-245 B 6
Junction City o **USA** (SD) 260-261 K 4
Jundah o **AUS** 178-179 G 3
Jundiaí o **BR** 72-73 G 7
Juneau ☆ **USA** 32-33 C 2
Junee o **AUS** (NSW) 180-181 J 3
Junee o **AUS** (QLD) 178-179 K 2
June in Winter, Lake ⬭ **USA** (FL) 286-287 H 4
Junèkèn ~ **RUS** 116-117 M 3
June Lake o **USA** (CA) 248-249 E 2
Jungar Qi o **VRC** 154-155 G 2
Jungbunzlau = Mladá Boleslav o•• **CZ** 92-93 N 3
Jungfrau ▲ **CH** 92-93 J 5
Jungue o **ANG** 216-217 C 5
Juniata o **CDN** (SAS) 232-233 L 3
Juniata River ~ **USA** (PA) 280-281 J 3
Junin o **CO** 64-65 C 1
Junin o **EC** 64-65 B 2
Junin o **PE** 64-65 E 7
Junín o **RA** 78-79 J 3
Junin o **RCH** 70-71 B 6
Junin, Lago de ⬭ **PE** 64-65 D 7
Junin, Parque Nacional ⊥ **PE** 64-65 E 7
Junín de los Andes o **RA** 78-79 D 5
Juniper o **CDN** (NB) 240-241 H 4
Juniper Dunes Wilderness ⊥ **USA** (WA) 244-245 G 4
Juniper Springs ∴• **USA** (FL) 286-287 H 2
Jun'jaga ~ **RUS** 108-109 K 8
Junkjur o **RUS** 110-111 T 6
Junleri o **WAN** 204-205 J 4
Junlian o **VRC** 156-157 D 2
Junnar o **IND** 138-139 D 10
Juno o **USA** (TX) 266-267 F 3
Juno, El ▲ **BOL** 70-71 E 5
Junosuando o **S** 86-87 L 3
Junqoley o **SUD** 206-207 K 5

342 Jemberam — Junqoley

Kamaši o **US** 136-137 K 5
Kamativi o **ZW** 218-219 D 4
Kamba o **WAN** 204-205 E 3
Kamba Kota o **RCA** 206-207 C 5
Kambal o **SUD** 208-209 B 3
Kambalda o· **AUS** 176-177 F 5
Kambal'naja Sopka, vulkan ▲ **RUS** 122-123 R 3
Kambal'nickie Koški, ostrova ⌒ **RUS** 88-89 T 2
Kambal'nyj, mys ▲ **RUS** 122-123 R 3
Kambang o **RI** 162-163 D 5
Kambarka ☆ **RUS** 96-97 J 5
Kamberatoro o **PNG** 183 A 2
Kambia o **WAL** 202-203 D 5
Kambing, Gunung ▲ **MAL** 162-163 E 2
Kambolé o **RT** 202-203 L 5
Kambot o **PNG** 183 C 3
Kambove o **ZRE** 214-215 D 6
Kambuku o **PNG** 183 G 3
Kambūt o **LAR** 192-193 L 2
Kamčatka ~ **RUS** 120-121 R 6
Kamčatkskij, mys ▲ **RUS** 120-121 U 5
Kamčatkskij poluostrov ⌣ **RUS** 120-121 U 5
Kamčatsk, Ust'- ☆ **RUS** 120-121 U 5
Kamčatskij, Petropavlovsk- ☆· **RUS** 120-121 S 7
Kamčatskij proliv ≈ 120-121 U 6
Kamčatskij zaliv ≈ 120-121 T 6
Kamchatka Peninsula = Kamčatka, poluostrov ⌣ **RUS** 120-121 Q 5
Kāmdēš o· **AFG** 136-137 M 7
Kameasi o **RI** 164-165 G 4
Kameel o **ZA** 220-221 G 3
Kamélé o **CI** 202-203 J 5
Kamelik ~ **RUS** 96-97 F 8
Kamen' o **BY** 94-95 L 4
Kamen', Serdce-mys ▲ **RUS** 112-113 Z 3
Kamende o **ZRE** 214-215 C 4
Kamenec-Podol'skij = Kam'janec'-Podil's'kyj ☆ **UA** 102-103 E 3
Kameng̃ o **AFG** 134-135 L 1
Kameng ~ **IND** 142-143 H 2
Kamenica o **BIH** 100-101 G 3
Kamenka ☆ **KA** 96-97 G 8
Kamenka o **RUS** (ARH) 88-89 S 4
Kamenka o **RUS** (HBR) 122-123 G 2
Kamenka o **RUS** (KRN) 116-117 G 6
Kamenka o **RUS** (PEN) 96-97 D 7
Kamenka o **RUS** (SML) 94-95 N 4
Kamenka ~ **RUS** 108-109 d 2
Kamenka ~ **RUS** 110-111 d 6
Kamenka ~ **RUS** 116-117 G 6
Kamenka ~ **RUS** 124-125 O 2
Kamennaja, kosa ∸ **RUS** 108-109 P 7
Kamennaja tundra ∸ **RUS** 108-109 a 7
Kamen'-na-Obi ☆ **RUS** 124-125 M 2
Kamennik, gora ▲ **RUS** 88-89 N 3
Kamennogorsk o **RUS** 94-95 L 1
Kamennyj, Mys- o **RUS** 108-109 P 7
Kamennyj, mys ▲ **RUS** 110-111 c 2
Kamennyj Dubčes ~ **RUS** 114-115 T 4
Kamennyj Stolb, mys ▲ **RUS** 110-111 S 4
Kameno o **BG** 102-103 E 6
Kamen'-Rybolov o **RUS** 122-123 E 6
Kamenskoe ☆ **RUS** 112-113 O 5
Kamensk-Šahtinskij o **RUS** 102-103 M 3
Kamensk-Ural'skij ☆ **RUS** 96-97 M 5
Kamensk Ural'skiy = Kamensk-Ural'skij ☆ **RUS** 96-97 M 5
Kamenz o **D** 92-93 N 3
Kameshia o **ZRE** 214-215 D 5
Kameškova ~ **RUS** 112-113 M 3
Kameškovo ☆ **RUS** 94-95 R 3
Kāmet ▲ **IND** 138-139 G 4
Kameur, Bahr ~ **RCA** 206-207 E 4
Kamiah o **USA** (ID) 250-251 C 5
Kamienna, Skarżysko- o **PL** 92-93 Q 3
Kamiesberge ▲ **ZA** 220-221 C 5
Kamieskroon o **ZA** 220-221 C 5
Kami-Furano o **J** 152-153 K 3
Kamiiso o **J** 152-153 J 4
Kamiji o **ZRE** 214-215 B 4
Kamikawa o **J** 152-153 K 3
Kami-koshiki-shima ⌒ **J** 152-153 C 9
Kāmil, al- o **KSA** 130-131 F 6
Kāmil, al- o **OM** 132-133 L 2
Kamileroi o **AUS** 174-175 F 6
Kamilukuak Lake o **CDN** 30-31 T 4
Kamilukuak River ~ **CDN** 30-31 S 5
Kamimbi Fuka, Chute ~ **ZRE** 214-215 C 5
Kamina o **PNG** 183 C 4
Kamina o **RT** 202-203 L 5
Kamina o **ZRE** (SHA) 210-211 L 6
Kamina o **ZRE** (SHA) 214-215 C 5
Kamina Base o **ZRE** 214-215 C 5
Kaminak Lake o **CDN** 30-31 W 4
Kamin'-Kašyrs'kyj o **UA** 102-103 D 2
Kaminokuni o **J** 152-153 J 4
Kamino-shima ⌒ **J** 152-153 C 7
Kaminuriak Lake o **CDN** 30-31 W 4
Kamioka o **J** 152-153 G 6
Kamishak Bay ≈ 22-23 T 3
Kamishak River ~ **USA** 22-23 T 3
Kami-Shihoro o **J** 152-153 K 3
Kami-shima ⌒ **J** 152-153 D 8
Kamitsushima o **J** 152-153 C 7
Kamituga o **ZRE** 212-213 B 5
Kami-Yaku o **J** 152-153 D 9
Kamjana mohyla · **UA** 102-103 J 4
Kam'janec'-Podil's'kyj ☆ **UA** 102-103 E 3
Kamjani Mohyly · **UA** 102-103 K 4
Kamjanka o **UA** 102-103 H 3
Kam'janka o **UA** 102-103 G 4
Kam'janske o **UA** 102-103 C 3
Kamjong o **IND** 142-143 J 3
Ḳamḳaly o **KA** 124-125 G 6
Kamloops o **CDN** (BC) 230-231 J 3
Kamloops Indian Reserve X **CDN** (BC) 230-231 J 3
Kamloops Plateau ▲ **CDN** (BC) 230-231 J 3
Kammanassieberge ▲ **ZA** 220-221 F 6
Kamo o **AR** 128-129 L 2
Kamo ~ **RUS** 116-117 G 6
Kāmoke o **PK** 138-139 E 4
Kamola o **ZRE** 214-215 D 4
Kamoro ▲ **RM** 222-223 E 6
Kamoro ~ **RM** 222-223 E 6
Kamoro, Tampoketsan'i ▲ **RM** 222-223 E 6
Kamoto o **Z** 218-219 G 1
Kamp 52 o **SME** 62-63 F 3
Kampa, Teluk ≈ 162-163 F 5
Kampa do Rio Amônea, Área Indígena X **BR** 64-65 F 6
Kampala ★ **EAU** 212-213 D 3
Kampala o **SUD** 206-207 G 4
Kampar o **MAL** 162-163 D 2
Kampar ~ **RI** 162-163 E 4
Kamparkanan ~ **RI** 162-163 D 4
Kamparkiri ~ **RI** 162-163 D 4
Kampene o **ZRE** 210-211 L 5
Kamphaeng Phet o **THA** 158-159 E 2
Kamphambale o **MW** 214-215 G 7
Kampi Katoto o **EAT** 214-215 G 4
Kampi Ya Moto o **EAK** 212-213 E 4
Kampli o **IND** 140-141 G 3
Kampolombo, Lake o **Z** 214-215 E 6
Kâmpóng Cham o **K** 158-159 H 4
Kâmpóng Chhnâng o **K** 158-159 H 4
Kâmpóng Saôm ≈ 158-159 G 5
Kâmpóng Saôm o **K** 158-159 G 5
Kâmpóng Spoe o **K** 158-159 H 5
Kâmpóng Trach o **K** 158-159 H 5
Kâmpôt o **K** 158-159 H 5
Kampsville o **USA** (IL) 274-275 H 5
Kampti o **BF** 202-203 J 4
Kampumbu o **Z** 214-215 G 6
Kampung ~ **RI** 166-167 K 4
Kampung Ayer Puteh o **MAL** 162-163 E 2
Kampung Balok o **MAL** 162-163 E 3
Kampung Berawan o **MAL** 164-165 D 1
Kampung Buloh o **MAL** 162-163 E 2
Kampung Chenereh o **MAL** 162-163 E 2
Kampung Cherating o **MAL** 162-163 E 2
Kampung Gajah o **MAL** 162-163 D 2
Kampung Jambu Bongkok o **MAL** 162-163 E 2
Kampung Jerangau o **MAL** 162-163 E 2
Kampung Kemara o **MAL** 162-163 E 2
Kampung Koh o **MAL** 162-163 D 2
Kampung Lamir o **MAL** 162-163 E 3
Kampung Laut o **MAL** 162-163 F 4
Kampung Leban Condong o **MAL** 162-163 E 3
Kampung Merang o **MAL** 162-163 E 2
Kampung Merting o **MAL** 162-163 E 2
Kampung Nibong o **MAL** 162-163 D 2
Kampung Penarik o **MAL** 162-163 E 2
Kampung Relok o **MAL** 162-163 E 2
Kampung Sekinchan o **MAL** 162-163 D 3
Kampung Sepat o **MAL** 162-163 E 3
Kampung Sook o **MAL** 160-161 B 10
Kampung Sungai Ayer Deras o **MAL** 162-163 E 2
Kampung Sungai Rengit o **MAL** 162-163 F 4
Kampung Tebingtinggi o **RI** 162-163 H 3
Kampung Tekek o· **MAL** 162-163 F 3
Kampung Tengah o **MAL** 162-163 F 4
Kampung Terolak o **MAL** 162-163 D 2
Kamrau, Teluk ≈ 166-167 G 3
Kamsack o **CDN** (SAS) 232-233 R 4
Kamsar o **RG** 202-203 C 4
Kamskoe Ust'e ☆ **RUS** 96-97 F 6
Kamskoe vodohranilišče < **RUS** 96-97 K 4
Kamskoye Vodokhranilishche = Kamskoe vodohranilišče < **RUS** 96-97 K 4
Kamsuuma o **SP** 212-213 J 3
Kāmthi o **IND** 138-139 G 9
Kamtsha ~ **ZRE** 210-211 G 6
Kamuchawi Lake o **CDN** 34-35 E 2
Kamudi o **IND** 140-141 H 6
Kamuela o **USA** (HI) 288 K 4
Kamuj, gora ▲ **RUS** 122-123 N 6
Kámuk, Cerro ▲ **CR** 52-53 C 7
Kamuli o **EAU** 212-213 D 3
Kamušnyj ☆ **KA** 124-125 B 3
Kamutambai ~ **ZRE** 214-215 B 4
Kam'yanets'-Podil's'kyy = Kam'janec'-Podil's'kyj ☆ **UA** 102-103 E 3
Kāmyārān o **IR** 134-135 B 1
Kamyšanovka o **KS** 146-147 B 4
Kamyšet o **RUS** 116-117 J 8
Kamyševatskaja o **RUS** 102-103 K 4
Kamyševka o **RUS** 114-115 H 6
Kamyshin = Kamyšin o **RUS** 96-97 D 8
Kamyšin o **RUS** 96-97 D 8
Ḳamysköl o **KA** 96-97 H 10
Kamyšlov ☆ **RUS** 114-115 G 6
Kamyšovyj, Južno-, hrebet ▲ **RUS** 122-123 K 5
Kamyšovyj hrebet ▲ **RUS** 122-123 K 3
Ḳamys-Samarkölinin ḳujmasy o **KA** 96-97 G 9
Ḳamysty-Ajat ~ **KA** 124-125 B 2
Ḳamystybas, köl o **KA** 126-127 O 4
Kamyzjak ☆ **RUS** (AST) 96-97 F 10
Kamyzjak ~ **RUS** 126-127 H 5
Kan ~ **RUS** 116-117 G 8
Kan o **US** 136-137 K 5
Kanaaupscow, Rivière ~ **CDN** 36-37 M 7
Kanab o **USA** (UT) 254-255 C 6
Kanab Creek ~ **USA** (AZ) 256-257 C 2
Kanacea ⌒ **FJI** 184 III c 2
Kanadej o **RUS** 96-97 E 7
Kanaga Pass ≈ 22-23 H 7
Kanagi o **J** 152-153 J 4
Kanaima Falls ~ **GUY** 62-63 D 2
Kanairiktok River ~ **CDN** 36-37 S 7
Kanaka o **RI** 166-167 G 3
Kanakakee River ~ **USA** (IN) 274-275 L 3
Kanakapura o **IND** 140-141 G 4
Kanakatte o **IND** 140-141 G 4
Kanakoro o **BF** 202-203 G 4
Kanaktok Mount ▲ **USA** 20-21 L 3
Kanamari do Rio Juruá, Área Indígena X **BR** 66-67 C 6
Kananaskis River ~ **CDN** (ALB) 232-233 C 5
Kananga ☆ **ZRE** (KOC) 210-211 J 6
Kananggar o **RI** 168 E 8
Kanangio, Mount ▲ **PNG** 183 C 3
Kanangra Boyd National Park ⊥ **AUS** 180-181 L 2
Kananto o **GH** 202-203 K 5
Kananyga ~ **RUS** 120-121 Q 3
Kanaraville o **USA** (UT) 254-255 B 6
Kanas o **IND** 138-139 E 8
Kanaš o **RUS** 96-97 E 6
Kanatak o **USA** 22-23 S 4
Kanawha o **USA** (IA) 274-275 E 2
Kanawha River ~ **USA** (WV) 280-281 D 5
Kanawi, Pulau ⌒ **MAL** 160-161 B 10
Kanazawa ☆· **J** 152-153 G 6
Kanazi o **EAT** 212-213 C 4
Kanbalu o **MYA** 142-143 J 4
Kanbe o **MYA** 158-159 D 2
Kanbi ~ **BF** 202-203 K 3
Kančalan o **RUS** 112-113 T 4
Kančalan ~ **RUS** 112-113 T 4
Kanchana Buri o **THA** 158-159 E 3
Kanchanadit o **THA** 158-159 E 6
Kanchanpur o **NEP** 144-145 F 7
Kanchenjunga ▲ **NEP** 144-145 G 7
Kanchibya ~ **Z** 214-215 F 6
Kānchipuram o·· **IND** 140-141 H 4
Kanci o **RI** 168 C 3
Kandahar o **CDN** (SAS) 232-233 O 4
Kandahār o **IND** 138-139 F 10
Kandahar = Qandahār ☆·· **AFG** 134-135 L 3
Kandahār = Qandahār ☆·· **AFG** 134-135 L 3
Kandalakša o **RUS** 88-89 M 3
Kandalakshskaya Guba = Kandalakšskaja guba ≈ **RUS** 88-89 M 3
Kandalakšskaja guba ≈ 88-89 M 3
Kandalakšskij bereg ⌣ **RUS** 88-89 M 3
Kandang o **RI** 162-163 B 3
Kandangan o **RI** 164-165 D 5
Kandanghaur o **RI** 168 C 3
Kandar o **RI** 166-167 F 6
Kandare o **WAN** 204-205 H 4
Kandarisa o **PNG** 183 A 5
Kandé o **RT** 202-203 L 5
Kandéko ~ **RCB** 210-211 F 3
Kandep o **PNG** 183 B 3
Kandero o **DY** 204-205 E 3
Kandi o **DY** 204-205 E 3
Kāndi o **IND** 142-143 F 4
Kandi, Tanjung ▲ **RI** 164-165 G 3
Kandiadiou o **SN** 202-203 B 3
Kandiāro o **PK** 138-139 B 6
Kandika o **RG** 202-203 D 3
Kandik River ~ **USA** 20-21 T 4
Kandil Bouzou < **RN** 198-199 E 5
Kandıra ☆ **TR** 128-129 D 2
Kandja o **RCA** 206-207 E 6
Kandkhot o **PK** 138-139 B 5
Kāndla o **IND** 138-139 C 8
Kando ~ **ZRE** 214-215 D 6
Kandos o **AUS** 180-181 K 2
Kandreho o **RM** 222-223 E 6
Kandrian o **PNG** 183 E 4
Kandry ☆ **RUS** 96-97 J 6
Kanduanam o **PNG** 183 B 3
Kandukūr o **IND** 140-141 H 3
Kandy o··· **CL** 140-141 J 7
Kane o **CDN** (MAN) 234-235 F 5
Kane, Kap ▲ **GRØ** 26-27 e 2
Kane Basin ≃ 26-27 P 4
Kane Bassin ≃ 26-27 P 4
Kane Fracture Zone ≃ 6-7 D 6
Kanektok River ~ **USA** 22-23 Q 3
Kanel o **SN** 202-203 D 2
Kanem □ **TCH** 198-199 G 5
Kaneohe o **USA** (HI) 288 H 3
Kaneohe Bay ≈ **USA** 288 H 3
Kanevka o **RUS** 88-89 P 3
Kanevskaja o **RUS** 102-103 L 4
Kanferandé o **RG** 202-203 C 4
Kang o **AFG** 134-135 J 3
Kang o **RB** 218-219 B 6
Kangaamiut = Gammel Sukkertoppen o **GRØ** 28-29 O 4
Kangaatsiaq o **GRØ** 28-29 O 2
Kangahun o **WAL** 202-203 D 5
Kangal ☆ **TR** 128-129 G 3
Kangalassy o **RUS** 118-119 O 4
Kangalas-Uèle ~ **RUS** 110-111 L 3
Kangān o **IR** 134-135 E 5
Kanğān Čam ~ **IR** 134-135 B 2
Kangar o **MAL** 162-163 D 2
Kangara o **RMM** 202-203 F 4
Kangaré o **RMM** 202-203 F 4
Kangaroo Island ⌒ **AUS** 180-181 D 3
Kangaroo Valley ⌣ **AUS** 180-181 L 3
Kangasniemi o **FIN** 88-89 J 6
Kangāvar o· **IR** 134-135 B 1
Kangding o **VRC** 154-155 B 6
Kangdong o **DVR** 150-151 F 8
Kangean, Kepulauau ⌒ **RI** 168 B 6
Kangean, Pulau ⌒ **RI** 168 B 6
Kangeeak Point ▲ **CDN** 28-29 H 3
Kangen ~ **SUD** 208-209 A 5
Kangeq ⌒ **GRØ** 26-27 X 7
Kangerdluarssuk ≈ 26-27 Z 8
Kangerdlugssuaq ≈ 26-27 Z 8
Kangerdluluk Fjord ≈ 28-29 T 6
Kangerluarsoruseq = Færingehavn o **GRØ** 28-29 P 5
Kangerluarsuk o **GRØ** 28-29 O 4
Kangerluk = Diskofjord o **GRØ** 28-29 N 2
Kangerlussuaq ≈ 26-27 Z 8
Kangerlussuaq ≈ 28-29 Y 2
Kangerlussuaq ≈ 28-29 O 3
Kangerlussuaq = Søndrestrømfjord o **GRØ** 28-29 P 3
Kangersuneq ≈ 28-29 P 4
Kangertitsivaq ≈ 28-29 X 3
Kangertittivag = Scoresby Sund ≈ 26-27 o 8
Kanghwa o **ROK** 150-151 F 9
Kanghwa Do ⌒ **ROK** 150-151 F 9
Kangi o **SUD** 206-207 H 4
Kangik o **USA** 20-21 L 1
Kangikajip Appalia = Brewster, Kap ▲ **GRØ** 26-27 p 8
Kangilinnguit = Grønnedal o **GRØ** 28-29 Q 6
Kangilo Fiord ≈ 28-29 G 3
Kangiqsujuak o **CDN** 36-37 O 4
Kangiwa o **WAN** 204-205 E 2
Kangkir o **VRC** 144-145 B 2
Kang Kra Chan National Park ⊥· **THA** 158-159 E 4
Kangmar o **VRC** 144-145 G 6
Kangnŭng o **ROK** 150-151 G 9
Kango o **G** 210-211 C 3
Kangole o **EAU** 212-213 E 2
Kangonde o **EAK** 212-213 F 4
Kangounadéni o **BF** 202-203 H 4
Kangping o **VRC** 150-151 D 6
Kangrinboqê Feng ▲ **VRC** 144-145 C 5
Kangro o **VRC** 144-145 E 4
Kangsar, Kuala o· **MAL** 162-163 D 2
Kangto ▲ **IND** 142-143 H 2
Kangye ☆ **DVR** 150-151 F 7
Kangz'gyai ▲ **VRC** 146-147 N 6
Kanha National Park ⊥· **IND** 142-143 B 4
Kanhar ~ **IND** 142-143 C 4
Kani o· **CI** 202-203 G 5
Kani o **J** 152-153 G 7
Kani o **MYA** 142-143 J 4
Kaniama o **ZRE** 214-215 C 4
Kaniasso o **CI** 202-203 G 5
Kanibadam o **TJ** 136-137 M 4
Kanibes ~ **NAM** 220-221 C 2
Kanigiri o **IND** 140-141 H 3
Kanimeh o **US** 136-137 J 4
Kanin, poluostrov ⌣ **RUS** 88-89 S 3
Kanin Kamen' ▲ **RUS** 88-89 R 2
Kanin Nos o **RUS** 88-89 R 2
Kanin Nos, mys ▲ **RUS** 88-89 R 2
Kaninskaja tundra ∸ **RUS** 88-89 S 3
Kanioumé o **RMM** 202-203 J 2
Kanisa o **SUD** 200-201 E 3
Kanita o **J** 152-153 J 4
Kaniva o **AUS** 180-181 F 4
Kanivs'ke vodoschovyšče < **UA** 102-103 G 2
Kaniya o **PNG** 183 B 4
Kanji-dong o **DVR** 150-151 G 7
Kanjirapalli o **IND** 140-141 G 6
Kanjiroba ▲ **NEP** 144-145 D 6
Kankaanpää o **FIN** 88-89 G 6
Kankai ~ **IND** 142-143 E 2
Kankakee o **USA** (IL) 274-275 L 3
Kankakee River ~ **USA** (IL) 274-275 K 3
Kankalabé o **RG** 202-203 E 4
Kankan □ **RG** 202-203 E 4
Kankan ☆ **RG** 202-203 F 4
Kankara o **WAN** 204-205 G 3
Kankelaba ~ **RMM** 202-203 G 4
Kankesanturai o **CL** 140-141 J 6
Kankiya o **WAN** 198-199 C 6
Kankossa o **RIM** 196-197 E 7
Kankunskij o **RUS** 118-119 N 7
Kanmaw Kyun ⌒ **MYA** 158-159 E 5
Kann o **IR** 136-137 B 7
Kanna o **MYA** 142-143 K 6
Kannad o **IND** 138-139 E 9
Kannapolis o **USA** (NC) 282-283 G 5
Kannata Valley o **CDN** (SAS) 232-233 O 5
Kannavam o **IND** 140-141 F 5
Kannoka = Sillamäe o **EST** 94-95 K 2
Kannonkoski o **FIN** 88-89 H 5
Kannonsaha o **FIN** 88-89 H 5
Kannus o **FIN** 88-89 G 5
Kano o **J** 152-153 D 7
Kano o **RMM** 202-203 F 3
Kano □ **WAN** 204-205 H 3
Kano ☆·· **WAN** 198-199 D 6
Kano, River ~ **WAN** 204-205 H 3
Kanobe, Pulau ⌒ **RI** 166-167 F 1
Kanona o **Z** 218-219 F 1
Kano Nak o **VN** 158-159 K 3
Kanoni o **ZRE** 214-215 D 6
Kanono o **NAM** 218-219 C 3
Kanopolis Lake o **USA** (KS) 262-263 H 6
Kanorado o **USA** (KS) 262-263 D 5
Kanoroba o **CI** 202-203 G 5
Kanosh o **USA** (UT) 254-255 C 5
Kanouri ∸ **RN** 198-199 F 5
Kanovlei o **NAM** 216-217 E 9
Kanowit o **MAL** 162-163 K 3
Kanowna ∴ **AUS** 176-177 F 5
Kanoya o **J** 152-153 D 9
Kanozero o **RUS** 88-89 N 3
Kanpur o **IND** 142-143 B 2
Kansanshi o **Z** 214-215 D 7
Kansas o **USA** (IL) 274-275 L 5
Kansas o **USA** (OK) 264-265 K 2
Kansas □ **USA** (KS) 262-263 F 6
Kansas City o **USA** (KS) 262-263 M 5
Kansas City o **USA** (MO) 274-275 D 5
Kansas River ~ **USA** (KS) 262-263 K 5
Kanšengel' o **KA** 124-125 J 6
Kansenia o **ZRE** 214-215 D 6
Kansk ☆ **RUS** 116-117 G 7
Kant o **KS** 146-147 B 4
Kantah o **CDN** 30-31 J 6
Kantah River ~ **CDN** 32-33 K 3
Kantalai o **CL** 140-141 J 6
Kantang o **THA** 158-159 E 7
Kantchari o **BF** 202-203 L 3
Kantche o **RN** 198-199 D 6
Kantegir ~ **RUS** 116-117 E 9
Kantemirovka o **RUS** 102-103 L 3
Kantharalak o **THA** 158-159 H 3
Kānthi o **IND** 142-143 E 5
Kantishna o **USA** 20-21 P 5
Kantishna River ~ **USA** 20-21 P 4
Kanto-sanchi ▲ **J** 152-153 H 6
Kantunil o **MEX** 52-53 K 1
Kanuku Mountains ▲ **GUY** 62-63 E 4
Kanur o **IND** 140-141 G 3
Kanus o **NAM** 220-221 D 3
Kanu Woralaksaburi o **THA** 158-159 E 2
Kanye ☆ **RB** 220-221 G 2
Kanyemba o **ZW** 218-219 F 2
Kanyilombi o **Z** 214-215 C 7
Kanym Bol'šoj, gora ▲ **RUS** 114-115 U 7
Kanyš-Kija o **KS** 136-137 M 4
Kanyu o **RB** 218-219 C 5
Kao o **RN** 198-199 B 5
Kaôh Kŏng ⌒ **K** 158-159 G 5
Kaôh Rŭng ⌒ **K** 158-159 G 5
Kaŏh Rŭng Sâmlŏem ⌒ **K** 158-159 G 5
Kaohsiung o **RC** 156-157 M 5
Kaôh Tang ⌒ **K** 158-159 G 5
Kaôh Thmei ⌒ **K** 158-159 G 5
Kaoka o **SOL** 184 I e 3
Kaokaona ☆ **SOL** 184 I e 4
Kaokoveld ∸ **NAM** 216-217 B 8
Kaolack ☆ **SN** 202-203 B 2
Kaolak River ~ **USA** 20-21 K 2
Kaolé < **RIM** 196-197 F 6
Kaoleni o **EAK** 212-213 G 5
Kaole Ruins · **EAT** 214-215 K 4
Kaolinovo o **BG** 102-103 E 6
Kaolo o **SOL** 184 I d 3
Kaoma o **Z** 218-219 C 2
Kaouadja o **RCA** (Kot) 206-207 F 5
Kaouadja ~ **RCA** 206-207 F 4
Kaouadja ~ **RCA** 206-207 G 5
Kap o **IND** 138-139 G 10
Kap o **PK** 134-135 K 5
Kapa o **MYA** 158-159 E 4
Kapaa o **USA** (HI) 288 F 2
Kapaahu o **USA** (HI) 288 K 5
Kapaau o **USA** (HI) 288 K 4
Kapadokya ∸ **TR** 128-129 F 4
Kapadvanj o **IND** 138-139 D 8
Kapaimeri o **PNG** 183 B 3
Kapalabuaya o **RI** 164-165 K 4
Kapalala o **Z** 214-215 E 7
Kapandae o **GH** 202-203 K 5
Kapande ~ **ZRE** 214-215 D 6
Kapanga o **ZRE** 214-215 B 5
Kapangan o **RP** 160-161 D 4
Kapapa o **ZRE** 214-215 E 5
Kapasia o **BD** 142-143 G 3
Kapatu ~ **EAT** 212-213 E 6
Kapatu o **Z** 214-215 F 5
Kapau River ~ **PNG** 183 D 4
Kapčagaj = Ḳapšagaj o **KA** 146-147 C 4
Kapchorwa o **EAU** 212-213 E 3
Kapčiamiėstis o **LT** 94-95 H 4
Kapedo o **EAK** 212-213 F 3
Kapema o **ZRE** 214-215 E 6
Kapenguria o **EAK** 212-213 E 3
Kapia o **ZRE** 210-211 G 6
Kapichira Falls ~ **MW** 218-219 H 2
Kapini o **LV** 94-95 K 3
Kapip o **PK** 138-139 B 4
Kapiri Mposhi o **Z** 218-219 E 1
Kāpisa □ **AFG** 138-139 B 2
Kapisillit o **GRØ** 28-29 P 4
Kapiskau River ~ **CDN** 34-35 O 4
Kapiskau River ~ **CDN** (ONT) 234-235 R 3
Kapiskong Lake o **CDN** (ONT) 236-237 G 5
Kapit o **MAL** 162-163 K 3
Kapiti Island ⌒ **NZ** 182 E 4
Kapiura River ~ **PNG** 183 F 3
Kapka, Massif du ▲ **TCH** 198-199 K 5
Kaplamada, Gunung ▲ **RI** 166-167 D 3
Kaplan o **USA** (LA) 268-269 H 7
Kaplankyr, plato ▲ **US** 136-137 E 4
Kaplankyrskij zapovednik ⊥ **TM** 136-137 E 4
Kapoe o **THA** 158-159 E 6
Kapoeta o **SUD** 208-209 A 6
Ka Poh National Park ⊥· **THA** 158-159 E 5
Kapoke o **Z** 214-215 F 5
Kapona o **ZRE** 214-215 E 4
Kapondai, Tanjung ▲ **RI** 166-167 B 6
Kaponde o **ZRE** 214-215 B 4
Kapong o **THA** 158-159 E 6
Kapoposang, Pulau ⌒ **RI** 164-165 F 6
Kaporo o **MW** 214-215 G 5
Kaposvár o **H** 92-93 O 5
Kapotakshi ~ **BD** 142-143 F 4
Kappar o **PK** 134-135 K 6
Kappellskär o **S** 86-87 J 7
Kappelshamn o **S** 86-87 J 8
Kapp Platen ▲ **N** 84-85 N 2
Kapps o **NAM** 216-217 D 11
Kapsabet o **EAK** 212-213 E 3
Ḳapšagaj o **KA** 146-147 C 4
Ḳapšagaj su ḳojmasy < **KA** 146-147 C 4
Kapsan o **DVR** 150-151 G 7
Kapsaouis, Rivière ~ **CDN** 36-37 K 7
Kāpsi o **IND** 140-141 F 2
Kapsiki ▲· **CAM** 204-205 K 3
Kaptai o **BD** 142-143 H 4
Kaptai Lake o **BD** 142-143 H 4
Kaptiau o **RI** 166-167 K 3
Kapuas ~ **RI** 162-163 H 5
Kapuas ~ **RI** 162-163 J 4
Kapuas ~ **RI** 164-165 D 4
Kapuas Hulu, Banjaran ▲ **MAL** 162-163 K 4
Kapur Utara, Pegunungan ▲ **RI** 168 D 3
Kapuskasing o **CDN** (ONT) 236-237 F 3
Kapuskasing River ~ **CDN** (ONT) 236-237 F 4
Kapuskasing River ~ **CDN** (ONT) 236-237 F 3
Kapustin Jar o **RUS** 96-97 D 9
Kaputa o **Z** 214-215 E 5
Kaputir o **EAK** 212-213 E 2
Kap Walløe Banke ≃ 28-29 T 6
Kapydžik, gora ▲ **AZ** 128-129 L 3
Kapyl'uši, ozero o **RUS** 118-119 F 8
Kara o **RI** 166-167 C 5
Kara ☆ **RT** (DLK) 202-203 L 5
Kara ~ **RT** 202-203 L 5
Kara ~ **RUS** 108-109 L 8
Kara, Ust'- o **RUS** 108-109 L 7
Karaba, Ra's ▲ **KSA** 130-131 E 5
Kara-Balta = Kara-Balty o **KS** 136-137 N 3
Kara-Balty o **KS** 136-137 N 3
Karabaš ☆ **RUS** 96-97 M 6
Karabastau o **KA** 136-137 M 3
Ḳarabau o **KA** 96-97 H 9
Karabaur, pastiligi ▲ **KA** 126-127 L 6
Karabekaul o **TM** 136-137 J 5
Karabil', vozvyšennost' ▲ **TM** 136-137 H 6
Karabinka o **RUS** 124-125 P 2
Kara-Bogaz-Gol = Garabogazköl ≈ **TM** (KRS) 136-137 C 4
Karabogazköl, zaliv ≈ 136-137 C 4
Karabuget o **KA** 124-125 H 6
Karabük ☆ **TR** 128-129 E 2
Karabula o **RUS** 116-117 H 6
Karabula ~ **RUS** 116-117 H 7
Ḳarabulaḳ o **KA** 136-137 L 3
Karaburun ☆ **TR** 128-129 B 3
Ḳarabūtaḳ ☆ **KA** 126-127 O 3
Karaca Dağ ▲ **TR** 128-129 H 4
Karačaevsk o **RUS** 126-127 D 6
Karacaköy o **TR** 128-129 C 2
Karacasu ☆ **TR** 128-129 C 4
Ḳaracek, köl o **KA** 126-127 L 6
Karačev o **RUS** 94-95 O 5
Karachay-Cherkessia = Karačaj-Čerkes Respublika □ **RUS** 126-127 D 6
Karāchi ☆· **PK** 134-135 M 6
Karaçoban ☆ **TR** 128-129 K 3
Karād o **IND** 140-141 F 2
Kara Deniz ≈ 128-129 D 1
Karadeniz Boğazi = Bosporus ≈ 128-129 C 2
Ḳaraespe ~ **KA** 124-125 E 5
Karağ o **IR** 136-137 B 7
Karaga o **GH** 202-203 K 5
Karaga ~ **RUS** 120-121 U 4
Karaga, buhta o **RUS** 120-121 U 4
Karagaj ☆ **RUS** 96-97 J 4
Karagajly o **KA** 124-125 J 4
Ḳaragajly o **KA** 124-125 J 4
Karagajly-Ajat ~ **RUS** 124-125 B 2
Karaganda = Ḳaraghandy o **KA** 124-125 H 4
Karagandysay o **KA** 126-127 L 2
Karagaz, hrebet ▲ **TM** 136-137 D 5
Ḳaraghandy ☆ **KA** 124-125 H 4
Karagije, vpadina ⌣ **KA** 126-127 J 6
Karaginskij, ostrov ⌒ **RUS** 120-121 V 4
Karaginskij zaliv ≈ 120-121 U 4
Karagoš, gora ▲ **RUS** 124-125 Q 3
Karagüney Dağı ▲ **TR** 128-129 E 2
Karahalı ☆ **TR** 128-129 C 3
Ḳara Hobda ~ **KA** 126-127 M 2
Karaiai o **PNG** 183 E 3
Karaidel' ☆ **RUS** 96-97 K 6
Karaisalı ☆ **TR** 128-129 F 4
Karaitem o **PNG** 183 B 2
Karajagi o **IND** 140-141 F 2
Karaja Masel'ga o **RUS** 88-89 N 5
Karak o **MAL** 162-163 E 3
Karak, al- ☆· **JOR** 130-131 D 2
Kara-Kabak o **KS** 136-137 N 5
Kara-Kala o **TM** 136-137 E 5
Ḳaraḳamys o **KA** 96-97 H 9
Karakax He ~ **VRC** 138-139 F 1
Karakax He ~ **VRC** 144-145 B 2
Karakaya Barajı < **TR** 128-129 H 3
Karakeçi o **TR** 128-129 H 4
Ḳarakeču ∸ **KA** 126-127 K 5
Karakelong, Kepulauan ⌒ **RI** 164-165 K 1
Ḳara-Kengir ~ **KA** 124-125 E 4
Karaketang, Pulau ⌒ **RI** 164-165 J 2
Karaklis o **AR** 128-129 L 2
Karakoçan ☆ **TR** 128-129 J 3
Ḳaraḳojyn, köl o **KA** 124-125 F 5
Ḳaraköl o **KA** (GUR) 96-97 H 9
Ḳaraköl o **KA** (KZL) 126-127 O 5
Ḳaraköl o **KA** (KZL) 124-125 D 6
Karakol o **KS** 146-147 C 5
Ḳaraköl, köl ~ **KA** 126-127 N 3
Karakoram ▲ **IND** 138-139 E 1
Kara K'orē o **ETH** 208-209 D 3
Karakoro ~ **RMM** 202-203 E 2
Karakorum Highway II **PK** 138-139 E 1
Karakovaja ~ **RUS** 120-121 S 6
Karaktau, gory ▲ **KA** 136-137 K 3
Kara-Kudzur ~ **KS** 146-147 C 5
Kara-Kul' o **KS** 136-137 N 4
Karakul' o **TJ** 136-137 N 5
Karakul' o **US** 136-137 H 5
Karakul', ozero o **TJ** 136-137 N 5
Kara-Kul'dža o **KS** 136-137 N 4
Karakulino o **RUS** 96-97 H 5
Ḳaraḳūm ∸ **KA** 96-97 H 10
Karakūm ∸ **KA** 96-97 H 10
Karaḳum ∸ **KA** 124-125 L 5
Kara Kum = Garagum ∸ **TM** 136-137 E 4
Karakumskij kanal < **TM** (ASH) 136-137 E 5
Karakumskij kanal < **TM** (MAR) 136-137 H 6
Karal o **TCH** 198-199 G 6
Karal'ka ~ **RUS** 114-115 R 3
Karalundi Mission o **AUS** 176-177 E 3
Karam o **RUS** 116-117 N 8
Karama ~ **RI** 164-165 F 5
Karamadai o **IND** 140-141 G 5
Karaman ☆· **TR** 128-129 E 4
Karamanbeyli Geçidi ▲ **TR** 128-129 D 4
Karamay o **VRC** 146-147 G 3
Karambu o **RI** 164-165 E 5
Karamea o **NZ** 182 D 4
Karamea Bight ≈ 182 C 4
Karamet-Nijaz o **TM** 136-137 J 6
Karami, River ~ **WAN** 204-205 H 3
Karamian, Pulau ⌒ **RI** 164-165 D 6
Karamiran o **VRC** 144-145 E 2
Karamiran He ~ **VRC** 144-145 E 2
Karamken o **RUS** 120-121 O 3
Karamoja □ **EAU** 208-209 B 6
Karamor, Pegunungan ▲ **RI** 166-167 C 3
Karamyk o **KS** 136-137 M 5
Karamyševo o **RUS** 116-117 K 7
Karān ⌒ **KSA** 130-131 E 5
Karang o **SN** 202-203 B 3
Karangampel o **RI** 168 C 3
Karanganyar o **RI** 168 D 3
Karangasem o· **RI** 168 B 7
Karangboto, Tanjung ▲ **RI** 168 C 3
Karanggede o **RI** 168 D 3
Karangjati o **RI** 168 D 3
Karangnunggal o **RI** 168 C 3
Karangoua ~ **RCB** 210-211 D 3
Karangpandan o **RI** 168 D 3
Karangua o **Z** 214-215 D 7
Karanguana o **RMM** 202-203 H 3
Karanji o **IND** 138-139 G 9
Karanpur o **IND** 138-139 D 5
Ḳaraoba o **KA** 126-127 M 4
Karaoj o **KA** 124-125 J 6
Karap o **PNG** 183 C 3
Karapınar ☆ **TR** 128-129 E 4
Karapuz ~ **RUS** 114-115 P 7
Karara o **AUS** 178-179 L 5
Kararaô, Área Indígena X **BR** 68-69 B 4
Karas, Pulau ⌒ **RI** 166-167 G 3
Kara-Saj o **KS** 146-147 C 5
Kara-Sal ~ **RUS** 102-103 N 4
Karasavvon o **FIN** 88-89 G 2
Karasburg ☆ **NAM** 220-221 D 4
Karas'e, ozero Bol'šoe o **RUS** 114-115 J 5
Kara Sea = Karskoe more ≈ **RUS** 10-11 F 1
Karašek, Ozero = köl Ḳaracek o **KA** 126-127 L 6
Karasjok o **N** 86-87 M 2
Karašjokka ~ **N** 86-87 M 2
Karasol', kölí o **KA** 124-125 K 3
Karasol', ozero = Kölí Karasor o **KA** 124-125 K 3
Karasor, kölí o **KA** 124-125 J 4
Ḳarasor, köli o **KA** 124-125 J 4
Karasor, ozero = köľı Karasor o **KA** 124-125 J 4
Karasu ☆ **TR** 128-129 D 2
Karasu ~ **TR** 128-129 K 3
Karasu-Aras Dağları ▲ **TR** 128-129 J 3
Karasu Çayı ~ **TR** 128-129 G 4
Karasuk ☆ **RUS** 124-125 L 2
Karasuk Hills ▲ **EAK** 212-213 E 2
Kara-Suu o **KS** 136-137 N 4
Karāt o **IR** 134-135 J 1
Karatajka o **RUS** 108-109 J 7
Karatal ~ **KA** 124-125 K 6
Karatas o **KA** 136-137 L 4
Ḳaratas o **KA** 136-137 L 4
Karataş ☆ **TR** 128-129 F 4
Karataš, gora ▲ **RUS** 96-97 L 7
Karatau o **KA** 136-137 M 3
Ḳaratau o **KA** (DZM) 136-137 M 3
Ḳaratau ▲ **KA** 126-127 J 5
Karatau, hrebet ▲ **KA** 124-125 E 6
Ḳaratau, žota ▲ **KA** 124-125 E 6
Karatau hrebet ▲ **RUS** 96-97 K 6
Karatina o **EAK** 212-213 F 4
Ḳaratöbe ☆ **KA** 96-97 H 9
Karatogaj o **KA** 124-125 O 4
Ḳaraton o **KA** 96-97 H 10
Ḳara-Torgaj ~ **KA** 124-125 E 4
Karats o **S** 86-87 J 3
Karatsu o **J** 152-153 C 8
Karatu o **EAT** 212-213 E 5
Ḳaratulej, sor ∸ **KA** 126-127 L 5
Karatung, Pulau ⌒ **RI** 164-165 K 1
Karaudanawa o **GUY** 62-63 E 4
Ḳaraul o **KA** 124-125 L 4
Karaul o **RUS** 108-109 U 6
Karaulbazar o **US** 136-137 J 5
Karauli o **IND** 138-139 F 6
Karaungir ∸ **KA** 124-125 J 5
Karauwi o **PNG** 183 C 4
Karavan o **KS** 136-137 M 4
Karavānsarāy-ye Šams o **IR** 134-135 F 3
Karavās o **GR** 100-101 J 6
Karawa o **ZRE** 210-211 H 2
Karawanella o **CL** 140-141 J 7
Karawang o **RI** 168 B 3
Karawang, Tanjung ▲ **RI** 168 B 2
Karawanken ▲ **A** 92-93 M 5
Karawari River ~ **PNG** 183 B 3
Karayazı ☆ **TR** 128-129 K 3
Karaye o **WAN** 204-205 H 3
Karayulgun o **VRC** 146-147 E 5
Karažal o **KA** 124-125 G 5
Ḳaražal ☆ **KA** 124-125 G 4
Karbalā' □ **IRQ** 128-129 J 6
Karbalā' ☆ **IRQ** (KAR) 128-129 L 6
Kårböle o **S** 86-87 G 6
Karbulik o **RUS** 116-117 O 9
Karchat o **PK** 134-135 M 6
Karda o **RUS** 116-117 L 8
Kardakāta o **GR** 100-101 H 5
Kardeljevo = Ploče o **HR** 100-101 F 3
Kardítsa o **GR** 100-101 H 5
Kardiva Channel ≈ 140-141 B 5
Kärdla ☆ **EST** 94-95 H 2
Kărdžali o **BG** 102-103 D 7
Kârdžali o **BG** 102-103 D 7
Karé, Monts ▲ **RCA** 206-207 C 5
Kareeberge ▲ **ZA** 220-221 F 5
Kareebospoort ▲ **ZA** 220-221 F 5
Karegari o **PNG** 183 B 3
Karelia = Karelija ∸ 94-95 L 1
Karelia = Karelija, Respublika □ **RUS** 88-89 M 5
Karelka ~ **RUS** 108-109 E 5
Karel'skij bereg ⌣ **RUS** 88-89 M 3
Karema o **EAT** 214-215 F 4
Karema o **PNG** 183 D 5
Karenga ~ **RUS** 118-119 H 8
Karenga, Ust'- o **RUS** 118-119 H 8
Karengi o **WAN** 204-205 E 3
Karera o **IND** 138-139 G 7
Karesuando o **S** 86-87 L 6
Kārevāndar o **IR** 134-135 J 5
Kargal o **IND** 140-141 F 3
Kargala o **RUS** 114-115 R 6
Kargala o **RUS** (ORB) 96-97 J 8
Kargalinskaja o **RUS** 126-127 G 6
Kargalytau ▲ **KA** 126-127 P 2
Kargapol'e ☆ **RUS** 114-115 H 6
Kargasok ☆ **RUS** 114-115 Q 5
Kargat ☆ **RUS** 114-115 Q 7
Kargat ~ **RUS** 114-115 Q 7
Kargat, Forpost- o **RUS** 114-115 Q 7
Kargı ☆ **TR** 128-129 F 2
Kargil o **IND** 138-139 F 2
Kargopol' ☆ **RUS** 88-89 P 6

344 Kamaši — Kargopol'

Karguéri o RN 198-199 E 6
Karђe, Rūd-e ~ IR 134-135 C 3
Karђe, Rūdђāne-ye ~ IR 134-135 D 3
Kari o WAN 204-205 J 3
Karia o PNG 183 F 2
Karianga o RM 222-223 E 9
Kariba o ZW 218-219 E 3
Kariba, Lake < Z 218-219 D 3
Kariba-yama ▲ J 152-153 H 3
Karibib ☆ NAM 216-217 C 10
Karie o SOL 184 I f 4
Kariega ~ ZA 220-221 F 6
Kariés o GR 100-101 K 4
Karigasniemi o FIN 88-89 H 2
Karikachi-tōge ▲ J 152-153 K 3
Kārikāl o IND 140-141 H 5
Karikari, Cape ▲ NZ 182 D 1
Karilatsi o EST 94-95 K 2
Karima o SUD 200-201 E 3
Karimabad o• IND 138-139 E 1
Karimama o DY 204-205 E 2
Karimata, Pulau ⌒ RI 162-163 H 5
Karimata Kepulauan ⌒ RI 162-163 H 5
Karimata Strait = Karimata, Selat ≈ 162-163 G 5
Karimbola ⊥ RM 222-223 D 10
Karimganj o IND 142-143 H 3
Karimnagar o IND 138-139 G 10
Karimui o PNG 183 C 4
Karimui, Mount ▲ PNG 183 C 4
Karimun, Pulau ⌒ RI 162-163 E 4
Karimunjawa, Kepulaua ⌒ RI 168 D 2
Karin o SP 208-209 G 3
Karina o WAL 202-203 E 5
Karipuna, Área Indígena ⅄ BR 66-67 E 7
Karisimbi, Mount ▲ RWA 212-213 B 4
Káristos o GR 100-101 K 5
Karitiana, Área Indígena ⅄ BR 66-67 E 7
Kariya o J 152-153 G 7
Kāriyāpatti o IND 140-141 H 6
Karjala ⊥ FIN 88-89 K 6
Karjat o IND 138-139 E 10
Karkabane, Hâssi < RMM 196-197 K 6
Kārkal o IND 140-141 F 4
Karkar o PNG 183 C 3
Karkaralinsk = Qarqaraly o KA 124-125 J 4
Karkaraly o KA 124-125 J 4
Karkar Island ⌒ PNG 183 D 3
Karkas, Kūh-e ▲ IR 134-135 D 2
Karkh o PK 134-135 M 5
Karkinits'ka zatoka ≈ 102-103 H 5
Karkonosze ▲ PL 92-93 N 3
Karksi-Nuia o•• EST 94-95 J 2
Karla-Aleksandra, ostrov ⌒ RUS 84-85 e 2
Karlaralong, Kepulauan ⌒ RI 164-165 J 1
Karleby = Kokkola o FIN 88-89 G 5
Karlik ▲ VRC 146-147 L 4
Karlıova ☆ TR 128-129 J 3
Karlivka o UA 102-103 J 3
Karl-Marx-Stadt = Chemnitz o D 92-93 M 3
Karlobag o HR 100-101 E 2
Karlo-Libknehtovsk = Soledar o UA 102-103 L 3
Karlovac o HR 100-101 E 2
Karlovássi o GR 100-101 L 6
Karlovo o BG 102-103 D 6
Karlovy Vary o CZ 92-93 M 3
Karlsbad = Karlovy Vary o CZ 92-93 M 3
Karlsborg ☆ S 86-87 G 7
Karlsena, mys ▲ RUS 108-109 M 3
Karlshamn ☆ S 86-87 G 8
Karlskoga ☆ S 86-87 G 7
Karlskrona ☆• S 86-87 G 8
Karlsruhe o• D 92-93 K 4
Karlsruhe o USA (ND) 258-259 G 3
Karlstad ☆•• S 86-87 F 7
Karlstad o USA (MN) 270-271 B 2
Karlstadt o• D 92-93 K 4
Karlštejn • CZ 92-93 O 4
Karluk o USA 22-23 T 4
Karma o RN 202-203 L 3
Karma ~ TCH 206-207 C 3
Karmah o• SUD 200-201 E 3
Karmāla o• IND 138-139 E 10
Karmaskaly ☆ RUS 96-97 K 6
Karmé o TCH 198-199 G 6
Karmelitskyj monastyr • UA 102-103 E 3
Karmina ☆ US 136-137 J 4
Karmøy ⌒ N 86-87 B 7
Karnak, al- o•• ET 194-195 F 5
Karnāl o IND 138-139 F 5
Karnali ~ NEP 144-145 C 6
Karnaou ▲ TCH 198-199 H 2
Karnaphuli ~ BD 142-143 G 4
Karnataka ▫ IND 140-141 F 3
Karnataka Plateau ▲ IND 140-141 F 2
Karnes City o USA (TX) 266-267 K 5
Karnobat o BG 102-103 E 6
Karnprayāg o IND 138-139 G 4
Kärnten ▫ A 92-93 M 5
Karo Batak House • RI 162-163 C 3
Karoi o ZW 218-219 E 3
Karo La ▲ VRC 144-145 H 6
Karolinen ⌒ FSM 13 F 2
Karoma, Mount ▲ PNG 183 B 3
Karonga o MW 214-215 G 5
Karoni, Gunung ▲ RI 164-165 G 5
Karonie o AUS 176-177 G 5
Karoo National Park ⊥ ZA 220-221 F 6
Karoonda o AUS 180-181 E 3
Karor o PK 138-139 C 4
Karora o SUD 200-201 J 4
Karosa o RI 164-165 F 4
Karoso, Tanjung ▲ RI 168 D 7
Karpathio Pélagos ≈ 100-101 L 6
Kárpathos o GR 100-101 L 7
Kárpathos ⌒ GR 100-101 L 7
Karpenissi o GR 100-101 H 5
Karpinsk o RUS 114-115 F 5
Karpinskogo, vulkan ▲ RUS 122-123 Q 3
Karpogory o RUS 88-89 S 4
Karpuzlu ☆ TR 128-129 B 4
Karpysak o RUS 114-115 R 7
Karratha o AUS 172-173 C 6
Karratha Roadhouse o AUS 172-173 C 6
Karrats Fjord ≈ 26-27 Y 8
Karredouw o ZA 220-221 G 6
Karridale o AUS 176-177 C 7
Kars ☆• TR 128-129 K 2
Karsakbaj o KA 124-125 E 5
Kārsämäki o FIN 88-89 H 5
Kārsava o LV 94-95 K 3
Karshi o WAN 204-205 G 4
Karši ☆ US 136-137 J 5
Karšinskaja step' ⊥ US 136-137 J 5
Karsk, Ust'- o RUS 118-119 J 9
Karskie Vorota, proliv ≈ 108-109 G 6
Karskiye Vorota, Proliv = Karskie Vorota, proliv ≈ RUS 108-109 G 6
Karsriviervlei o ZA 220-221 E 7
Kartabu o GUY 62-63 E 2
Kartabyz, ozero o RUS 114-115 G 7
Kartaèl' o RUS 88-89 W 4
Kartaly ☆ RUS 124-125 B 2
Karte Conservation Park ⊥ AUS 180-181 F 3
Karthala ▲ COM 222-223 C 3
Karti o IR 134-135 H 6
Kartosuro o RI 168 D 3
Kartuzy o• PL 92-93 P 1
Karu o PNG 183 G 2
Karubaga o RI 166-167 K 3
Karubeamsberge ▲ NAM 220-221 C 1
Karufa o RI 166-167 G 3
Karuђ o• AFG 134-135 K 1
Karumba o AUS 174-175 F 5
Kārumbhar Island ⌒ IND 138-139 B 8
Karumei o J 152-153 J 4
Karumwa o EAT 212-213 D 5
Kārūn, Kūh-e ▲ IR 134-135 D 3
Kārūn, Rūd-e ~ IR 134-135 C 3
Karungu o EAK 212-213 E 4
Karūr o IND 140-141 H 5
Karuzi o BU 212-213 C 5
Karval o USA (CO) 254-255 M 5
Karvinā o CZ 92-93 P 4
Karwai o RI 166-167 H 4
Kārwār o IND 140-141 F 3
Karwin = Karviná o CZ 92-93 P 4
Karymskoe ☆ RUS 118-119 G 10
Karyngūrly ⊥ KA 126-127 L 6
Karynžaryk ⊥ KA 126-127 K 6
Kas ~ RUS 116-117 E 6
Kas o SUD 200-201 B 6
Kaş ☆•• TR 128-129 C 4
Kasa o RP 160-161 D 3
Kasa o VRC 154-155 B 6
Kasa o ZRE 210-211 G 4
Kasaan Bay ≈ 32-33 D 4
Kasaba o Z 214-215 E 6
Kasabi o ZRE 214-215 E 5
Kasabonika o CDN 34-35 M 4
Kašaf Rūd ~ IR 136-137 G 6
Kasah ~ AR 128-129 L 2
Kasai o J 152-153 F 7
Kasai ~ ZRE 210-211 G 5
Kasai-Occidental ▫ ZRE 210-211 H 6
Kasai-Oriental ▫ ZRE 210-211 J 5
Kasaji o ZRE 214-215 B 6
Kāsa Khurd o IND 138-139 D 10
Kasāl o IND 140-141 E 2
Kasalu o Z 218-219 D 2
Kasama ☆ Z 214-215 F 6
Kāšān o• IR 134-135 D 2
Kašan ~ TM 136-137 H 7
Kasan o US 136-137 J 5
Kasane ☆ RB 218-219 C 3
Kasanga o EAT 214-215 F 5
Kasangulu o ZRE 210-211 E 6
Kasanka National Park ⊥ Z 214-215 F 7
Kasansaj o US 136-137 M 4
Kasanza o ZRE 214-215 B 4
Kāsaragod o IND 140-141 F 4
Kasari o J 152-153 C 10
Kasaro ~ SUD 200-201 F 6
Kasasi o WAL 202-203 E 5
Kasatochi Island ⌒ USA 22-23 J 6
Kasbahs, Route des • MA 188-189 H 5
Kasba Lake o CDN 30-31 S 5
Kasba-Tadla o MA 188-189 H 4
Kascjukoviči o BY 94-95 N 5
Kasdir < DZ 188-189 L 4
Kaseda o J 152-153 D 9
Kasegaluk Lagoon ≈ 20-21 J 2
Kasei ~ ZRE 216-217 F 3
Kasempa o Z 218-219 C 1
Kasenga o ZRE (SHA) 214-215 B 6
Kasenga o ZRE (SHA) 214-215 E 6
Kasenge o ZRE 210-211 G 4
Kasengu o ZRE 212-213 C 2
Kasenye o ZRE 212-213 C 3
Kasese o EAU 212-213 C 3
Kasese o ZRE 212-213 A 4
Kaset Wisai o THA 158-159 G 3
Kaseyville o USA (MO) 274-275 F 5
Kashabowie o CDN (ONT) 234-235 N 6
Kashechewan o CDN 34-35 Q 4
Kashega o USA 22-23 N 6
Kashi o• VRC 146-147 C 6
Kashileshi ~ ZRE 214-215 B 6
Kashima o J 152-153 J 7
Kashima-nada ≈ 152-153 J 6
Kashinatpur o BD 142-143 F 4
Kashipur o IND 138-139 G 5
Kashiwa o J 152-153 H 7
Kashiwazaki o J 152-153 H 6
Kāshmor o PK 138-139 B 5
Kashunuk River ~ USA 20-21 H 6
Kashwal o SUD 206-207 J 5
Kasi ~ RI 166-167 G 2
Kasidishi ~ ZRE 214-215 B 5
Kasigau ▲ EAK 212-213 G 5
Kasigluk o USA 20-21 J 6
Kasimbar o RI 164-165 G 4
Kasimov o RUS 94-95 R 4
Kašin ☆• RUS 94-95 P 3
Kasindi o ZRE 212-213 B 3
Kasinje o MW 218-219 H 2
Kašira ☆• RUS 94-95 Q 4
Kasiruta, Pulau ⌒ RI 164-165 K 4
Kasiui, Pulau ⌒ RI 166-167 F 4
Kaskabulak o KA 124-125 L 4
Kaskadar'inskaja oblast' ▫ US 136-137 J 5
Kaškadar'ja ~ US 136-137 J 5
Kaškān, Rūdђāne-ye ~ IR 134-135 B 2
Kaškarancy o RUS 88-89 O 3
Kaskas o SN 196-197 C 6
Kaskaskia River ~ USA (IL) 274-275 J 6
Kaskaskia River State Fish and Wildlife Area ⊥ USA (IL) 274-275 J 6
Kaskaskia State Historic Site, Fort • USA (IL) 274-275 J 6
Kaškasu o KS 146-147 B 5
Kaskattama River ~ CDN 34-35 L 2
Kaskeleŋ o KA 146-147 C 4
Kaskeleŋ ~ KA 146-147 C 4
Kaskelen = Kaskeleŋ o KA 146-147 C 4
Kaskelen = Kaskeleŋ ~ KA 146-147 C 4
Kaskinen o FIN 88-89 F 5
Kaskö = Kaskinen o FIN 88-89 F 5
Kasli ☆ RUS 96-97 M 6
Kaslo o CDN (BC) 230-231 N 4
Kāšmar o IR 136-137 F 7
Kasmere Lake o CDN 30-31 T 6
Kasompe o Z 218-219 C 1
Kasongo o ZRE 210-211 L 6
Kasongo-Lunda o ZRE 216-217 D 3
Kasongo-Lunda, Chutes ~ ZRE 216-217 D 3
Kasouga o ZA 220-221 H 6
Kaspi o GE 126-127 F 7
Kaspij many sineklizasy = Prikaspijskaja nizmennost' ⌣ RUS 126-127 F 5
Kaspijsk o RUS 126-127 G 6
Kaspijskij = Lagan' ☆ RUS 126-127 G 5
Kasr, Ra's ▲ SUD 200-201 J 3
Kassa o DY 204-205 E 3
Kassalā ☆• SUD 200-201 H 5
Kassama o RMM 202-203 E 3
Kassándra ~ GR 100-101 J 5
Kassándras, Kólpos ≈ 100-101 J 4
Kassándria o GR 100-101 J 4
Kassel o• D 92-93 K 3
Kasséré o CI 202-203 G 5
Kasserine ☆ TN 190-191 G 3
Kassipute o RI 164-165 H 6
Kassler o USA (CO) 254-255 K 4
Kássos ⌒ GR 100-101 L 7
Kassoum o BF 202-203 J 3
Kastamonu ☆• TR 128-129 E 2
Kastéli o GR 100-101 J 7
Kastoriá o GR 100-101 H 4
Kasuga o J (FKA) 152-153 D 8
Kasuga o J (HYO) 152-153 F 7
Kasuku ~ ZRE 210-211 K 4
Kasuku, Lac o ZRE 210-211 K 5
Kasulu o EAT 212-213 C 6
Kasumba o ZRE 214-215 D 7
Kasumi o J 152-153 F 7
Kasumigaura-ura o J 152-153 J 6
Kasumkent o RUS 126-127 H 7
Kasumpti o IND 138-139 F 4
Kasungu o MW 218-219 G 1
Kasungu National Park ⊥ MW 214-215 G 7
Kasūr o PK 138-139 E 4
Kat o IR 138-139 E 4
Kata ~ RUS 116-117 L 6
Kataba o Z 218-219 C 3
Katabaie o ZRE 214-215 B 4
Katagum o WAN 198-199 E 6
Katagum, River ~ WAN 204-205 H 3
Katahdin, Mount ▲ USA (ME) 278-279 N 3
Katajsk ☆ RUS 114-115 G 6
Kataka o IND 142-143 D 5
Katakakishi o ZRE 214-215 B 5
Katako-Kombe o ZRE 210-211 K 5
Kataku o RI 168 D 7
Katakwi o EAU 212-213 D 3
Katalah o RUS 118-119 N 6
Katamatite o AUS 180-181 H 4
Katana o RI 164-165 L 3
Katana o ZRE 212-213 B 5
Katanda o ZRE 214-215 B 4
Katanga ~ RUS 116-117 L 6
Katangi o IND 138-139 G 8
Katangi o IND 138-139 G 9
Katanning o AUS 176-177 D 6
Kataouâne o RIM 196-197 G 6
Kataramba ~ RUS 116-117 H 4
Katavi National Park ⊥ EAT 214-215 F 4
Katav-Ivanovsk ☆ RUS 96-97 L 6
Katcha o WAN 204-205 G 4
Katchall Island ⌒ IND 140-141 L 6
Katchamba o RT 202-203 L 5
Katchirga o BF 202-203 K 3
Kateel River ~ USA 20-21 L 4
Kateman, Pulau ⌒ RI 162-163 E 4
Katemcy o USA (TX) 266-267 H 3
Katende o ZRE 214-215 B 4
Katende, Chutes de ~ ZRE 214-215 B 4
Katenge o ZRE 214-215 B 4
Katengo o ZRE 212-213 B 6
Katepwa Beach o CDN (SAS) 232-233 P 5
Katere o NAM 216-217 F 9
Katerini o GR 100-101 J 4
Katesh o EAT 212-213 E 6
Katete o Z 218-219 G 2
Katha o MYA 142-143 K 3
Kathang o IND 142-143 K 2
Kathangor, Ğabal ▲ SUD 208-209 A 6
Kathawachaga Lake o CDN 30-31 O 2
Katherine o AUS 172-173 L 3
Katherine River ~ AUS 172-173 K 3
Kāthiāwār Peninsula ⌣ IND 138-139 B 8
Kathleen Lake o CDN (ONT) 236-237 E 5
Kathmandu ★••• NEP 144-145 E 7
Kathu o ZA 220-221 F 3
Kathua o IND 138-139 E 3
Kati ~ NEP 144-145 C 6
Kati o RMM 202-203 F 3
Katiali o CI 202-203 G 5
Katiati o PNG 183 C 3
Katīb, Ra's al- ▲ Y 132-133 C 6
Katiéna o RMM 202-203 H 3
Katihar o IND 142-143 E 3
Katima Mulilo ☆ NAM 218-219 C 3
Katimik Lake o CDN (MAN) 234-235 D 2
Katini o ZRE 216-217 E 3
Katiola ☆ CI 202-203 H 5
Katios, Parque Nacional los ⊥ CO 60-61 C 4
Katiti Aboriginal Land ⅄ AUS 176-177 L 2
Katla o SUD 206-207 J 3
Katlanovo o MK 100-101 H 4
Katmai, Mount ▲ USA 22-23 T 3
Katmai National Park and Preserve ⊥ USA 22-23 T 3
Katmay Bay ≈ 22-23 T 4
Kato o GUY 62-63 E 3
Katoa o TCH 206-207 B 3
Kātoda o IND 138-139 E 7
Káto Glikóvrisi o GR 100-101 J 6
Kātol o IND 138-139 G 9
Katombe o ZRE 210-211 H 6
Katompi o ZRE 214-215 D 4
Katonga ~ EAU 212-213 C 3
Katon-Karagaj o KA 124-125 O 4
Katoomba-Wentworth Falls o AUS 180-181 L 2
Katoposo, Gunung ▲ RI 164-165 G 4
Káto Soúnio o GR 100-101 K 6
Katoto o EAT 212-213 C 6
Katowice ☆•• PL 92-93 P 3
Katoya o IND 142-143 F 4
Katrancık Dağı ▲ TR 128-129 D 4
Katrina, Ğabal ▲ ET 194-195 F 3
Katrineholm ☆ S 86-87 H 7
Katse o EAK 212-213 G 4
Katséna ~ CAM 204-205 J 5
Katsepy o RM 222-223 E 5
Katsina o WAN 198-199 C 6
Katsina ▫ WAN 198-199 C 6
Katsina-Ala o WAN 204-205 H 5
Katsina-Ala, River ~ WAN 204-205 H 5
Katsumoto o J 152-153 C 8
Katsuta o J 152-153 J 6
Katsuura o J (CHI) 152-153 J 7
Katsuura o J (WAK) 152-153 F 8
Kattakišlok o US 136-137 K 5
Kattakurgan = Kattaķŭrgon o US 136-137 K 5
Kattaķŭrgon o US 136-137 K 5
Kattankudi o CL 140-141 J 7
Kattarakara o IND 140-141 G 6
Kattavia o GR 100-101 L 7
Kattawagami Lake o CDN (ONT) 236-237 H 3
Kattawagami River ~ CDN (ONT) 236-237 J 2
Kattegat ≈ 86-87 E 8
Katterjåkk o S 86-87 J 2
Kåttupputtūr o IND 140-141 H 5
Katumbi o MW 214-215 G 6
Katun' ~ RUS 124-125 P 3
Katundu o Z 218-219 C 3
Katunguru o EAU 212-213 C 4
Katunskij hrebet ▲ RUS 124-125 O 3
Katupa o RI 168 D 7
Katūria o IND 142-143 E 3
Katwe o EAU 212-213 B 4
Katwe o ZRE 214-215 D 6
Katy o USA (TX) 268-269 E 7
Katym ~ RUS 114-115 K 5
Kau o RI 164-165 K 3
Kau, Teluk ≈ 164-165 K 3
Kauai ⌒ USA (HI) 288 F 2
Kauai Channel ≈ 48-49 C 7
Kauai Channel ≈ USA 288 G 3
Kauara o CI 202-203 H 4
Kaubi o PNG 183 B 3
Kaudom o NAM 216-217 F 9
Kaudom ~ NAM 216-217 F 9
Kaudom Game Park ⊥ NAM 216-217 F 9
Kaufbeuren o• D 92-93 L 5
Kaufman o USA (TX) 264-265 H 6
Kaugel River ~ PNG 183 C 4
Kauhajoki o FIN 88-89 G 5
Kauhava o FIN 88-89 G 5
Kaukas o RI 164-165 H 3
Kaukauna o USA (WI) 270-271 K 6
Kaukauveld ⊥ NAM 216-217 F 9
Kauksi o• EST 94-95 K 2
Kaula ⌒ USA (HI) 288 E 3
Kaulakahi Channel ≈ 48-49 B 6
Kaulakahi Channel ≈ USA 288 E 2
Kaulžur ~ KA 126-127 N 3
Kaumalapau Harbor o USA (HI) 288 J 4
Kauman o RI 168 E 3
Kaunakakai o• USA (HI) 288 H 3
Kauna Point ▲ USA (HI) 288 K 5
Kaunas ☆•• LT 94-95 H 4
Kaundy, vpadina ⌣ KA 126-127 K 6
Kaunolu o• USA (HI) 288 J 4
Kaup o PNG 183 B 2
Kaupanger o N 86-87 C 6
Kaupena o PNG 183 C 4
Kaupo o USA (HI) 288 J 4
Kaurai o PNG 183 E 5
Kauro ~ EAK 212-213 F 3
Kaušany = Căuşeni ☆ MD 102-103 F 4
Kaustinen o FIN 88-89 G 5
Kautokeino o N 86-87 L 2
Kauur o WAG 202-203 C 3
Kauwa o WAN 198-199 F 6
Kau-Ye Kyun ⌒ MYA 158-159 E 5
Kava ~ RUS 120-121 M 4
Kavadarci o MK 100-101 J 4
Kavak ☆ TR 128-129 G 2
Kavála o GR 100-101 K 4
Kavalerovo o RUS 122-123 F 6
Kavalga Island ⌒ USA 22-23 G 7
Kāvali o IND 140-141 J 3
Kavār o IR 134-135 E 4
Kavaratti o IND 140-141 E 5
Kavendu ▲ RG 202-203 D 4
Kavi o IND 138-139 D 8
Kavieng ☆ PNG 183 F 2
Kavigyalik Lake o USA 20-21 J 6
Kavik River ~ USA 20-21 R 2
Kavinga o Z 214-215 G 7
Kavīr, Dašt-e ⊥ IR 134-135 E 1
Kavkazkij zapovednik ⊥ RUS 126-127 D 6
Kávos o GR 100-101 H 5
Kavrizhka, Cape ▲ USA 22-23 N 6
Kavuu ~ EAT 214-215 F 4
Kawa o CDN (ONT) 234-235 O 4
Kawa o RI 166-167 E 3
Kawa ~ RI 166-167 E 3
Kawa, Temple of • SUD 200-201 E 3
Kawagit o RI 166-167 L 4
Kawagoe o J 152-153 H 7
Kawaguchi o J 152-153 H 7
Kawai o IND 138-139 F 7
Kawaihae o• USA (HI) 288 K 4
Kawaihae Bay ≈ USA 288 L 4
Kawaihoa Point ▲ USA (HI) 288 E 3
Kawaikini ▲ USA (HI) 288 F 2
Kawajena o SUD 206-207 J 5
Kawakawa o NZ 182 E 1
Kawala o MYA 142-143 J 2
Kawali o RI 168 C 3
Kawambwa o Z 214-215 E 5
Kawana o Z 218-219 C 1
Kawanee o USA (MO) 276-277 F 4
Kawangko o RI 168 D 7
Kawangkoan o RI 164-165 J 3
Kawanoe o J 152-153 E 7
Kawant o IND 138-139 E 8
Kawardha o IND 142-143 B 4
Kawarga ~ RI 166-167 K 5
Kawartha Lakes o CDN (ONT) 238-239 G 4
Kawasa o ZRE 214-215 E 5
Kawasaki o J 152-153 H 7
Kawatipoli o MYA 142-143 K 6
Kawauchi o J 152-153 J 4
Kawau Island ⌒ NZ 182 E 2
Kawaya o ZRE 214-215 E 5
Kawayan o RP 160-161 F 7
Kawayu o J 152-153 L 3
Kawe, Pulau ⌒ RI 166-167 F 2
Kaweah, Lake o USA (CA) 248-249 F 3
Kaweka ▲ NZ 182 F 3
Kawembwe o Z 214-215 F 6
Kawene o CDN (ONT) 234-235 M 6
Kawentinkim o RI 166-167 L 4
Kawe Rapids ~ Z 218-219 F 2
Kawhia o NZ 182 E 3
Kawich Peak ▲ USA (NV) 246-247 J 5
Kawich Peak ▲ USA (NV) 248-249 H 2
Kawinaw Lake o CDN (MAN) 234-235 D 2
Kawkawlin o USA (MI) 272-273 F 4
Kawkpalut o MYA 158-159 E 2
Kawkwareik o MYA 158-159 E 2
Kawlin o MYA 142-143 J 4
Kawltang o MYA 142-143 J 3
Kaw Reservoir o USA (OK) 264-265 H 2
Kaxarari, Área Indígena ⅄ BR 66-67 D 7
Kaxgar He ~ VRC 146-147 C 6
Kax He ~ VRC 146-147 F 4
Kaxian D. ∴• VRC 150-151 D 2
Kaxinauá Nova Olinda, Área Indígena ⅄ BR 66-67 B 7
Kaxinawá do Rio Humaitá, Área Indígena ⅄ BR 66-67 B 7
Kaxinawá do Rio Jordão, Área Indígena ⅄ BR 64-65 F 6
Kaya ☆ BF 202-203 K 3
Kayaapu o RI 162-163 E 7
Kayabi, Área Indígena ⅄ BR 70-71 J 2
Kayak Island ⌒ USA 20-21 S 7
Kayambi o Z 214-215 G 5
Kayan ~ RI 164-165 E 3
Kayanga ~ SN 202-203 C 3
Kāyankulam o IND 140-141 G 6
Kayanza o BU 212-213 B 5
Kayapó, Área Indígena ⅄ BR 68-69 B 5
Kayar o SN 202-203 B 2
Kayasa o RI 164-165 K 3
Kayattār o IND 140-141 G 6
Kaycee o USA (WY) 252-253 M 3
Kaye, Mount ▲ AUS 180-181 K 4
Kayedon Lake o CDN (ONT) 236-237 B 2
Kayeli o RI 166-167 D 3
Kayembe-Mukulu o ZRE 214-215 B 5
Kayenta o USA (AZ) 256-257 E 2
Kayenzi o EAT 212-213 D 5
Kayes ▫ RMM 202-203 E 3
Kayes ☆ RMM 202-203 E 2
Kayima o WAL 202-203 E 5
Kaymor o SN 202-203 C 3
Kaynabayongo o ZRE 212-213 B 4
Kayoa, Pulau ⌒ RI 164-165 K 3
Kayokwe o BU 212-213 B 5
Kayonza o RWA 212-213 C 4
Kay Point ▲ CDN 20-21 W 2
Kayrunnera o AUS 178-179 G 6
Kayseri ☆•• TR 128-129 F 3
Kayuadi, Pulau ⌒ RI 168 E 6
Kayuagung o RI 162-163 F 6
Kayuku o RI 164-165 G 4
Kayupangang, Pulau ⌒ RI 168 D 6
Kayuyu o ZRE 210-211 L 5
Kayville o CDN (SAS) 232-233 N 6
Kazabazua o CDN (QUE) 238-239 J 3
Kazača Lopan' o UA 102-103 K 2
Kazač'e o RUS 110-111 V 4
Kazačinskoe ☆ RUS 116-117 F 7
Kazah o• AZ 128-129 L 2
Kazahdar'ja o US 136-137 F 3
Kazahskij zaliv ≈ 126-127 K 6
Kazakhstan = Kazakstan ■ KA 126-127 K 3
Kazakh Uplands = Saryarka ⊥ KA 124-125 G 4
Kazak'jaha ~ RUS 108-109 V 6
Kazamabika o G 210-211 C 4
Kazan' ☆•• RUS 96-97 F 6
Kazandžik = Gazanğyk o TM 136-137 D 5
Kazanlăk o•• BG 102-103 D 6
Kazan River ~ CDN 30-31 V 4
Kazanskoe ☆ RUS 114-115 K 7
Kazantips'ka zatoka ≈ 102-103 J 5
Kazarman o KS 146-147 B 5
Kazas ~ RUS 116-117 H 9
Kazaure o WAN 198-199 D 6
Kazbegi o GE 126-127 F 6
Kazbek, gora ▲ GE 126-127 F 6
Kaz Dağı ▲ TR 128-129 B 3
Kazer • TCH 198-199 J 3
Kazer, Pico ▲ RCH 80 G 7
Kāzerūn o IR 134-135 D 4
Kāzi Ahmad o PK 138-139 B 6
Kazibacna ~ BD 142-143 F 4
Kazıklı Çayı ~ TR 128-129 G 3
Kazil'skoe ☆ RUS 96-97 L 7
Kazi-Magomed o AZ 128-129 N 2
Kāzimiya, al- o IRQ 128-129 L 6
Kāzımkarabekir ☆• TR 128-129 E 4
Kaziranga National Park ⊥••• IND 142-143 H 2
Kaziza o ZRE 214-215 B 6
Kaznakovka o KA 124-125 N 4
Każtalovka ☆ KA 96-97 F 9
Kažukas = Marijampole ☆•• LT 94-95 H 4
Kazuma Pan National Park ⊥ ZW 218-219 C 4
Kazumba o ZRE 214-215 B 4
Kazungula o Z 218-219 C 3
Kazuno o J 152-153 J 4
Kazym ~ RUS 114-115 L 3
Kazyr ~ RUS 116-117 G 9
Kbombole o SN 202-203 B 2
Kbor Roumia • DZ 190-191 D 2
Ké o G 210-211 C 3
Ké, Enneri ~ TCH 198-199 H 3
Kéa ⌒ GR 100-101 K 6
Keaau o USA (HI) 288 K 5
Keahole Point ▲ USA (HI) 288 J 5
Kealaikahiki Channel ≈ USA 288 H 4
Kealakekua o USA (HI) 288 K 5
Kealia o USA (HI) 288 F 3
Keanae o USA (HI) 288 J 4
Keansburg o USA (NJ) 280-281 M 3
Kearney o USA (NE) 262-263 G 4
Kearns o USA (UT) 254-255 C 3
Kearny o USA (AZ) 256-257 E 5
Kearsarge Pass ▲ USA (CA) 248-249 F 3
Keating Point ▲ IND 140-141 L 5
Kébaly o RG 202-203 D 4
Keban ☆ TR 128-129 H 3
Keban Barajı < TR 128-129 H 3
Kebaowek Indian Reservation ⅄ CDN (QUE) 238-239 G 2
Kébara o RCB 210-211 E 5
Kebasen o RI 168 C 3
Kebbe o WAN 198-199 B 6
Kebbi, Mayo ~ TCH 206-207 B 4
Kébémer o SN 202-203 B 2
Kébi, Mayo ~ CAM 204-205 K 4
Kébila o RMM 202-203 G 4
Kebili ☆ TN 190-191 G 4
Kebnekaise ▲•• S 86-87 J 3
K'ebri Dehar o ETH 208-209 G 5
Kebumen o RI 168 C 3
Kech ~ PK 134-135 K 5
K'ech'a Terara ▲ ETH 208-209 D 5
Kéché o RCA 206-207 E 3
Kechika Ranges ▲ CDN 30-31 F 6
Kechika River ~ CDN 30-31 F 6
Kecskemét o H 92-93 P 5
Keda o GE 126-127 D 7
Kedah ▫ MAL 162-163 D 2
Kėdainiai ☆• LT 94-95 H 4
Kedawung o RI 168 C 3
Keddie o USA (CA) 246-247 E 3
Kédédéssé o TCH 206-207 B 3
Kedgwick o CDN (NB) 240-241 H 3
Kedgwick River o CDN (NB) 240-241 H 3
Kedgwick River ~ CDN (NB) 240-241 H 3
Kedi o IND 138-139 F 4
Kedi o RI 164-165 K 3
Kedir o RI 166-167 K 3
Kediri o RI 168 E 3
Kedon o RUS 112-113 K 4
Kedon ~ RUS 112-113 K 4
Kedonskij hrebet ▲ RUS 112-113 K 4
Kédougou o SN 202-203 D 3
Kedrovaja, gora ▲ RUS 122-123 D 6
Kedrovyj o RUS 114-115 P 6
Kedungwuni o RI 168 C 3
Kedva ~ RUS 88-89 W 5
Kędzierzyn o PL 92-93 P 3
Kędzierzyn-Koźle o• PL 92-93 P 3
Keefton o USA (OK) 264-265 J 3
Keekorok Lodge o EAK 212-213 E 4
Keel = An Caol o IRL 90-91 B 5
Keele Peak ▲ CDN 30-31 E 4
Keeler o USA (CA) 248-249 G 3
Keele River ~ CDN 30-31 F 3
Keeley Lake o CDN 32-33 Q 4
Keelinawi o USA (HI) 288 E 3
Keelung o• RC 156-157 M 4
Keene o USA (CA) 248-249 F 4
Keene o USA (NH) 278-279 J 6
Keene, Lake o AUS 176-177 G 2
Keenjhar Lake o•• PK 138-139 B 7
Keepit, Lake < AUS 178-179 L 6
Keep River ~ AUS 172-173 J 3
Keep River National Park ⊥ AUS 172-173 J 3
Keerweer, Cape ▲ AUS 174-175 F 3
Keeseville o USA (NY) 278-279 H 4
Keetmannshoop ☆ NAM 220-221 D 3
Keewatin o CDN (ONT) 234-235 J 5
Keewatin River ~ CDN 34-35 J 2
Keezhik Lake o CDN (ONT) 234-235 P 3
Kefa ▫ ETH 208-209 B 5
Kefalonia ⌒ GR 100-101 H 5
Kefamenanu o RI 166-167 C 6
Keffi o WAN 204-205 G 4
Keflavik o IS 86-87 b 2
K'eftya o ETH 200-201 H 6
Kegajli ☆ US 136-137 F 3
Kegali ~ RUS 112-113 L 4
Kēgart o KS 136-137 N 4
Kegaska o CDN (QUE) 242-243 G 2
Kegdal o IND 140-141 F 3
Kegen o KA 146-147 D 4
Kegworth o CDN (SAS) 232-233 P 5
Keihiwin Indian Reserve ⅄ CDN 32-33 P 4
Kehl o D 92-93 J 4
Keibul-Lamjoa National Park ⊥ IND 142-143 H 3
Keikakolo o RI 168 E 7
Keila o•• EST 94-95 J 2
Keila ⌒ SOL 184 I d 1
Keimoes o ZA 220-221 E 4
Kei Mouth o ZA 220-221 J 6
Keipene o LV 94-95 J 3
Kei Road o ZA 220-221 H 6
Keiskammarivier ~ ZA 220-221 H 6
Keïta o RN 198-199 B 5
Keïta ou Douka, Bahr ~ TCH 206-207 D 4
Keitele o FIN (KPN) 88-89 J 5
Keitele o FIN (KSS) 88-89 H 5
Keith o AUS 180-181 F 4
Keith, Cape ▲ AUS 172-173 K 1
Keith Arm o CDN 30-31 J 3
Keithley Creek o CDN (BC) 228-229 N 4
Keith Sebelius Lake o USA (KS) 262-263 G 5
Keithville o USA (LA) 268-269 G 4
Keiyasi o FJI 184 III a 2
Keizer o USA (OR) 244-245 C 5
Kejaman o MAL 162-163 K 3
Kejimkujik National Park ⊥ CDN (NS) 240-241 K 6
Kéjngypil'gyn, laguna o RUS 112-113 U 5
Kejobon o RI 168 C 3
Kejvy ▲ RUS 88-89 O 3
Kekaha o USA (HI) 288 F 3
Kékagyr o KS 146-147 B 6
Kék-Art o KS 146-147 B 5
Keke o PNG 183 D 5
Kékem o CAM 204-205 J 6
Kekertuk o CDN 28-29 J 3
Kekesu o PNG 184 I b 1
Kekirawa o CL 140-141 J 6
Kekneno, Gunung ▲ RI 166-167 C 6
Kekova Adası ⌒ TR 128-129 C 4
Kekovandasi ⌒ TR 128-129 C 4
Kekri o IND 138-139 E 7
Kekurnoi, Cape ▲ USA 22-23 T 4
Kekurnyj, zaliv o RUS 120-121 Q 4
Keku Strait ≈ 32-33 D 3
Kelabo o PNG 183 B 3
K'elafo o ETH 208-209 G 6
Kelag o VRC 154-155 B 6
Kelagay o AFG 136-137 L 7
Kelai ~ RI 164-165 E 3
Kélakam o RN 198-199 E 6
Kelambakkam o IND 140-141 J 4
Kelan o VRC 154-155 G 2
Kelandic Plateau ≃ 86-87 g 1
Kelang, Pulau ⌒ RI 166-167 D 3
Kelankyla o FIN 88-89 J 4
Kelanoa o PNG 183 D 4
Kelantan ▫ MAL 162-163 D 2
Kelapa o RI 162-163 F 5
Kélbo o BF 202-203 K 3
Kélcyrë o• AL 100-101 H 4
Keľda ~ RUS 88-89 R 4
Kele ~ RUS 118-119 P 4
Keleft o AFG 136-137 K 6
Kelem o ETH 208-209 B 6
Kelema o EAT 212-213 E 6
Kėlėraš' = Călăraşi ☆ MD 102-103 F 4
Keles ☆ US 136-137 L 4
Keléya o RMM 202-203 G 4
Kelež ~ RUS 116-117 F 9
Kelfield o CDN (SAS) 232-233 K 4
Kelford o USA (NC) 282-283 K 4
Kelgo Bay ≈ 36-37 R 5
Kelibia o TN 190-191 H 2
Kelifskij Uzboj ⊥ TM 136-137 H 6
Kelil'vun, gora ▲ RUS 112-113 O 2
Kelimjar ~ RUS 110-111 P 4
Keling o RI 168 D 3
Kelkit ☆ TR 128-129 H 2
Kelkit Çayı ~ TR 128-129 G 2
Kelkit Çayı ~ TR 128-129 H 2
Kéllé o RCB 210-211 E 4
Kellé o RN 198-199 E 5
Keller o USA (WA) 244-245 G 2
Kellerberrin o AUS 176-177 D 5
Keller Lake o CDN 30-31 J 3
Kellerville o USA (TX) 264-265 D 3
Kellet, Canal de ≈ 50-51 B 4
Kellet, Cape ▲ CDN 24-25 H 5
Kellet River ~ CDN 24-25 H 6
Kellett River ~ CDN 24-25 K 5
Kellett River ~ CDN 30-31 Y 2
Kellett Strait ≈ 24-25 M 3
Kelliher o CDN (SAS) 232-233 P 4
Kelliher o USA (MN) 270-271 D 3
Kelloe o CDN (MAN) 234-235 C 4
Kellog o RUS 114-115 T 3
Kellog ~ RUS 114-115 S 3
Kellogg o USA (ID) 250-251 C 4
Kellogg o USA (MN) 270-271 F 6
Kelloselkä o FIN 88-89 K 3
Kelly, Mount ▲ USA 20-21 J 2
Kelly Lake o CDN (BC) 230-231 H 2
Kelly Lake o CDN 30-31 G 3
Kelly Range ▲ AUS 176-177 F 2
Kelly River ~ USA 20-21 J 2
Kel'ma ~ RUS 114-115 U 5
Kelmė ☆ LT 94-95 H 4
Kelmet o ER 200-201 J 4
Kelo o TCH 206-207 B 4
Kelongwa o Z 218-219 D 1
Kelowna o CDN (BC) 230-231 K 4
Kelsey o CDN 34-35 H 2
Kelsey Bay o CDN (BC) 230-231 C 3
Kelso o CDN (SAS) 232-233 R 6
Kelso o• GB 90-91 F 4
Kelso o USA (CA) 248-249 J 4
Kelso o USA (WA) 244-245 C 4
Kelstern o CDN (SAS) 232-233 M 5
Keltie Bugt ≈ 26-27 Z 2
Kelton o USA (TX) 264-265 D 3
Kelton o USA (UT) 254-255 B 2
Kelu o VRC 156-157 G 6
Kelua o RI 164-165 D 5
Keluang, Tanjung ▲ RI 162-163 H 5
Kelume o RI 162-163 F 5
Kel'vat ~ RUS 114-115 N 5
Kelvin o USA (AZ) 256-257 E 5
Kelvington o CDN (SAS) 232-233 P 3
Kem' o RUS (KAR) 88-89 N 4

Karguéri — Kem' 345

Kem' ~ **RUS** 88-89 M 4
Kem' ~ **RUS** 116-117 E 6
Kemah ☆ **TR** 128-129 H 3
Kemal, Gunung ▲ **RI** 164-165 E 3
Kemäliye ☆ **TR** 128-129 H 3
Kemano ○ **CDN** (BC) 228-229
Kemano River ~ **CDN** (BC) 228-229 G 3
Kemara, Kampung ○ **MAL** 162-163 E 2
Kemasik ○ **MAL** 162-163 E 2
Kemata I ○ **TCH** 206-207 D 4
Kemba ○ **RCA** 206-207 F 4
Kembani ○ **RI** 164-165 H 4
Kembapi ○ **RI** 166-167 L 6
Kembé ○ **RCA** 206-207 D 4
Kembé, Chutes de ~ **RCA** 206-207 E 6
Kembéra ○ **RG** 202-203 D 4
Kembolcha ○ **ETH** (Wel) 208-209 C 4
Kembolcha ○ **ETH** (Weo) 208-209 D 4
Kemčug ~ **RUS** 116-117 E 7
Kemdéré ○ **TCH** 206-207 D 4
Kemenagi, Mount ▲ **PNG** 183 B 4
Kemer ○ **TR** 128-129 D 4
Kemer ☆ **TR** 128-129 D 4
Kemerhisar ○ **TR** 128-129 F 4
Kemerovo ☆ **RUS** 114-115 T 7
Kemi ○ **FIN** 88-89 H 4
Kemijärvi ○ **FIN** (LAP) 88-89 J 3
Kemijärvi ○ **FIN** (LAP) 88-89 J 3
Kemijoki ~ **FIN** 88-89 J 3
Kemkara ○ **RUS** 120-121 H 6
Kemlja ~ **RUS** 96-97 D 6
Kemmerer ○ **USA** (WY) 252-253 H 4
Kemnay ○ **CDN** (MAN) 234-235 C 5
Kémo ○ **RCA** 206-207 D 6
Kemp ○ **USA** (TX) 264-265 H 6
Kemp, Lake ⪡ **USA** (TX) 264-265 E 5
Kempaž ~ **RUS** 114-115 P 2
Kempe Fjord ≈ 26-27 m 7
Kempele ○ **FIN** 88-89 H 4
Kempendjai ~ **RUS** 118-119 J 4
Kempendjaji ~ **RUS** 118-119 J 4
Kemp Land ⊥ **ARK** 16 G 6
Kemp Peninsula ⤳ **ARK** 16 F 30
Kemps Bay ○ **BS** 54-55 G 2
Kempsey ○ **AUS** 178-179 M 6
Kempt, Lac ⪡ **CDN** (QUE) 236-237
Kempten (Allgäu) ○ **D** 92-93 L 5
Kempton ○ **AUS** 180-181 J 7
Kempton Park ○ **ZA** 220-221 J 2
Kemptown ○ **CDN** (NS) 240-241 M 5
Kemptville ○ **CDN** (ONT) 238-239 K 3
Kemujan ○ **MAL** 162-163
Ken ~ **IND** 142-143 H 3
Kenadsa ○ **DZ** 188-189 K 5
Kenai ○ **USA** 20-21 P 6
Kenai Fjords National Park ⊥ **USA** 22-23 V 3
Kenai Mountains ▲ **USA** 20-21 P 7
Kenai National Wildlife Refuge ⊥ **USA** 20-21 P 6
Kenai Peninsula ⤳ **USA** 20-21 P 6
Kenalia ○ **PNG** 183 B 5
Kenam ○ **NEP** 144-145 Q 4
Kenamuke Swamp ⪨ **SUD** 208-209 A 5
Kenamu River ~ **CDN** 38-39 P 2
Kenamu River ~ **CDN** 38-39 O 2
Kenansville ○ **USA** (FL) 286-287 J 4
Kenapuru Head ○ **NZ** 182 E 4
Kenär Daryä ○ **IR** 136-137 H 6
Kenari ○ **RI** 168 D 7
Kenaston ○ **CDN** (SAS) 232-233 M 4
Kenawa ○ **PNG** 183 B 5
Kenbridge ○ **USA** (VA) 280-281 H 7
Kencong ○ **RI** 168 E 4
Kendal ● **GB** 90-91 F 4
Kendal ○ **RI** 168 D 3
Kendal ○ **USA** (FL) 286-287 J 6
Kendall ○ **USA** (KS) 262-263 E 7
Kendall ○ **USA** (WA) 244-245 C 2
Kendall, Cape ▲ **CDN** (NWT) 24-25 O 6
Kendall, Mount ▲ **NZ** 182 D 4
Kendall, Point ▲ **CDN** 24-25 d 6
Kendall River ~ **AUS** 174-175 G 3
Kendallville ○ **USA** (IN) 274-275 N 3
Kendari ○ **RI** 164-165 H 5
Kendawangan ○ **RI** 162-163 J 6
Kéndégué ○ **TCH** 206-207 D 2
Kendeng, Pegunungan ▲ **RI** 168 D 3
Kendenup ○ **AUS** 176-179
Kendleton ○ **USA** (TX) 266-267 L 4
Kendräpära ○ **IND** 142-143 K 5
Kendrick ○ **USA** (ID) 250-251 C 5
Kendu Bay ○ **EAK** 212-213 E 4
Kenduijhar Plateau ▲ **IND** 142-143
Kendyrli-Kajasanskoe plato ▲ **KA** 126-127 K 4
Kenedy ○ **USA** (TX) 266-267 K 5
Kenel ○ **USA** (SD) 260-261 F 1
Kenema ○ **WAL** 202-203 E 6
Kenenikjan ○ **RUS** 118-119 J 5
Kenenkou ○ **RMM** 202-203 G 3
Kenevi, Mount ▲ **PNG** 183 B 5
Kénga ~ **RUS** 114-115 Q 6
Kéngdaj ~ **RUS** 110-111 Q 4
Kenge ○ **ZRE** 210-211 F 6
Kengirli sukojmasy ⪡ **KA** 124-125 E 5
Kengjade ~ **RUS** 110-111 P 4
Kengkeme ~ **RUS** 110-111 Q 4
Keng Tung ○ **MYA** 142-143 L 5
Kengué ○ **RCB** 210-211 D 5
Kenhardt ○ **ZA** 220-221 E 4
Kéniéba ○ **RMM** 202-203 E 3
Kénié'bandi ~ **RMM** 202-203 E 3
Kéniébaoulé, Reserve de ⊥ **RMM** 202-203 F 3
Keningau ○ **MAL** 160-161 K 9
Kénitra = Al-Q'nitra ○ **MA** 188-189 H 4
Kénitra = al-Q'nitra ○ **MA** 188-189 H 5
Kenli ○ **VRC** 154-155 L 2
Kenmare ○ **USA** (ND) 258-259 E 3
Kenmare River ~ ··· **IRL** 90-91 C 6
Kenmare = Neidín ○ **IRL** 90-91
Kenna ○ **USA** (NM) 256-257 M 5
Kenna ○ **USA** (WV) 280-281 E 5

Kennard ○ **USA** (TX) 268-269 E 5
Kennebec ○ **USA** (SD) 260-261 G 3
Kennebecasis River ~ **CDN** (NB) 240-241 K 5
Kennebunk ○ **USA** (ME) 278-279 L 5
Kennedy ○ **AUS** 174-175 H 6
Kennedy ○ **CDN** (SAS) 232-233 Q 6
Kennedy ○ **USA** (NE) 262-263 F 2
Kennedy ○ **USA** (NY) 278-279 B 6
Kennedy ○ **ZW** 218-219 D 4
Kennedy Channel ≈ 26-27 Q 3
Kennedy Development Road ∥ **AUS** 174-175 H 6
Kennedy Hill ▲ **AUS** 174-175 G 3
Kennedy Kanal ≈ 26-27 R 3
Kennedy Peak ▲ **MYA** 142-143 H 4
Kennedy Range ▲ **AUS** 176-179 C 2
Kennedy River ~ **AUS** 174-175 H 4
Kennedy Space Center, John Fitzgerald ×× **USA** (FL) 286-287 J 3
Kennedy's Vale ○ **ZA** 220-221 K 2
Kenner ○ **USA** (LA) 268-269 K 6
Kennesaw Mountain National Battlefield Park ⊥ **USA** (GA) 284-285 M 5
Kennetcook ○ **CDN** (NS) 240-241 M 5
Kenneth Range ▲ **AUS** 176-177 D 1
Kennett ○ **USA** (MO) 276-277 E 4
Kennewick ○ **USA** (WA) 244-245 F 4
Kenney Dam • **CDN** (BC) 228-229 K 3
Kennisis Lake ○ **CDN** (ONT) 238-239 G 3
Keno ○ **USA** (OR) 244-245 D 8
Keno City ○ **CDN** 20-21 X 5
Kenogami Lake ○ **CDN** (ONT) 236-237 H 4
Kenogami River ~ **CDN** (ONT) 236-237 D 2
Kenogami River ~ **CDN** (ONT) 236-237 C 2
Kenogamissi Lake ○ **CDN** (ONT) 236-237 G 5
Kenora ○ **CDN** (ONT) 234-235 J 5
Kenosee Park ○ **CDN** (SAS) 232-233 Q 6
Kenosha ○ **USA** (WI) 274-275 L 2
Kensal ○ **USA** (ND) 258-259 J 4
Kenscoff ○ **RH** 54-55 K 5
Kensett ○ **USA** (AR) 276-277 D 5
Kensington ○ **CDN** (PEI) 240-241 M 4
Kensington ○ **USA** (KS) 262-263 G 5
Kensington Downs ○ **AUS** 178-179 J 4
Kent ○ **USA** (MN) 270-271 B 4
Kent ○ **USA** (OH) 280-281 E 3
Kent ○ **USA** (TX) 266-267 C 2
Kent ○ **USA** (WA) 244-245 E 5
Kent City ○ **USA** (MI) 272-273 D 4
Kent Group ⊠ **AUS** 180-181 J 5
Ken Thao ○ **LAO** 158-159 F 2
Kenting National Park ⊥ **RC** 156-157 M 5
Kent Island ⊠ **USA** (MD) 280-281 K 5
Kent Junction ○ **CDN** (NB) 240-241 K 4
Kentland ○ **USA** (IN) 274-275 L 4
Kenton ○ **CDN** (MAN) 234-235 C 5
Kenton ○ **USA** (MI) 270-271 K 4
Kenton ○ **USA** (OH) 280-281 C 3
Kenton ○ **USA** (OK) 264-265 B 2
Kent Peninsula ⤳ **CDN** 24-25 S 6
Kentrikí Makedonía ◻ **GR** 100-101 J 4
Kentucky ◻ **USA** (KY) 276-277 H 3
Kentucky Lake ⪡ **USA** (KY) 276-277 F 4
Kentucky River ~ **USA** (KY) 276-277 L 3
Kentville ○ **CDN** (NS) 240-241 L 5
Kentwood ○ **USA** (LA) 268-269 K 5
Kenya ■ **EAK** 212-213 E 3
Kenya, Mount ▲ **EAK** 212-213 F 4
Kenya National Park, Mount ⊥ **EAK** 212-213 F 4
Kenyon ○ **USA** (MN) 270-271 E 6
Kenzou ○ **CAM** 206-207 B 6
Keokuk ○ **USA** (IA) 274-275 G 4
Keoladeo National Park ⊥ •••• **IND** 138-139 F 4
Keoma ○ **CDN** (ALB) 232-233 E 4
Keosauqua ○ **USA** (IA) 274-275 G 4
Keota ○ **USA** (IA) 274-275 G 3
Keowee, Lake ⪡ **USA** (SC) 284-285 H 2
Kepa ○ **RUS** 88-89 M 4
Kepahiang ○ **RI** 162-163 E 6
Kepanjen ○ **RI** 168 E 4
Kepelekese ~ **ZRE** 216-217 F 3
Keperveem ~ **RUS** 112-113 N 3
Kepi ○ **RI** 166-167 K 5
Kepina ~ **RUS** 88-89 Q 4
Kepino ○ **RUS** 88-89 Q 4
Keppno ○ **PL** 92-93 O 3
Keppe ○ **RI** 164-165 G 5
Keppel Bay ≈ 178-179 L 2
Keppel Island ⊠ **GB** 78-79 L 6
Kepsut ☆ **TR** 128-129 C 3
Kepteni ○ **RUS** 118-119 P 4
Keptin ○ **RUS** 118-119 M 4
Kepudori ○ **RI** 166-167 H 2
Kepuhi ○ **USA** (HI) 288 K 5
Kerai, Kuala ○ **MAL** 162-163 E 2
Kerala ○ **IND** 140-141 F 5
Kerama-rettō ⊠ **J** 152-153 B 11
Keram River ~ **PNG** 183 C 3
Keran ○ **IND** 138-139 D 2
Kéran ~ **RT** 202-203 L 4
Kéran, Gorges du ⊔• **RT** 202-203 L 5
Kéran, Parc National de la ⊥ **RT** 202-203 L 4
Kerang ○ **AUS** 180-181 G 3
Keranirhat ○ **BD** 142-143 H 4
Keraudren, Cape ▲ **AUS** 172-173 D 5
Keravat ○ **PNG** 183 G 3
Kerba, Col de ▲ **DZ** 190-191 D 3
Kerbau, Tanjung ▲ **RI** 162-163 G 6
Kerbi ~ **RUS** 122-123 F 4
Kerč ○ **UA** 102-103 K 5
Kerčenska Protoka ≈ 102-103 K 5

Kerch = Kerč ○ **UA** 102-103 K 5
Kerchouel ~ **RMM** 196-197 L 6
Kerdem ○ **RUS** 118-119 O 5
Kéré ○ **RCA** 206-207 G 6
Kéré ○ **RCA** 206-207 H 6
Kerec, mys ▲ **RUS** 88-89 P 4
Kerein Hills ○ **AUS** 180-181 J 2
Kerema ○ **PNG** 183 C 4
Keremeos ○ **CDN** (BC) 230-231 K 4
Keremeos Ranche Indian Reserve X **CDN** (BC) 230-231 K 4
Keremesit ~ **RUS** 110-111 b 4
Kérémou ○ **DY** 204-205 E 3
Kerempe Burnu ▲ **TR** 128-129 E 1
Keren ○ **ER** 200-201 J 5
Kerend ○ **IR** 134-135 J 5
Kerens ○ **USA** (TX) 264-265 H 6
Kereru Range ▲ **PNG** 183 C 4
Keret' ○ **RUS** 88-89 M 3
Kerewan ○ **WAG** 202-203 B 3
Kerguélen, Îles ⊠ **F** 12 E 9
Kerguelen Plateau ≃ 12 F 10
Keria Landing ○ **GUY** 62-63 F 4
Kericho ○ **EAK** 212-213 E 4
Keri Kera ○ **SUD** 200-201 F 6
Kerikeri ○ **NZ** 182 D 1
Kerimgaon ○ **IND** 142-143 J 2
Kerinci, Danau ○ **RI** 162-163 D 6
Kerinci, Gunung ▲ **RI** 162-163 D 5
Keriya ~ **VRC** 144-145 C 2
Kerkenah, Îles de ⊠ **TN** 190-191 H 3
Kerkertaluk Island ⊠ **CDN** 28-29 G 2
Kerki ○ **TM** 136-137 J 6
Kerkíci ○ **TM** 136-137 J 6
Kérkira ○ **GR** 100-101 G 5
Kérkira ⊠ **GR** 100-101 G 5
Kerkouane ∴ **TN** 190-191 H 2
Kermadec Islands ⊠ **NZ** 13 K 5
Kermadec Trench ≃ 14-15 L 11
Kermän ○ **IR** 134-135 F 4
Kermän ○ **IR** 134-135 G 3
Kermänšähan ○ **IR** 134-135 F 3
Kermit ○ **USA** (TX) 266-267 D 2
Kérmjukej, gora ▲ **AZ** 128-129 N 3
Kermū, Kôtal-e ▲ **AFG** 134-135 M 1
Kernay ∴ **TM** 136-137 F 3
Kernersville ○ **USA** (NC) 282-283 G 4
Kernnertut, Cap ▲ **CDN** 38-39 M 2
Kern National Wildlife Refuge ⊥ • **USA** (CA) 248-249 E 4
Kern River ~ **USA** (CA) 248-249 F 3
Kernville ○ **USA** (CA) 248-249 F 4
Kernville ○ **USA** (OR) 244-245 B 6
Kérou ○ **DY** 204-205 E 3
Kérouané ○ **RG** 202-203 F 5
Kerrick ○ **USA** (TX) 264-265 B 2
Kerriya Shankou ⪨ **VRC** 144-145 C 3
Kerr Lake, Robert S. ○ **USA** (OK) 264-265 J 3
Kerrobert ○ **CDN** (SAS) 232-233 J 4
Kerr Scott Reservoir, W. ○ **USA** (NC) 282-283 F 4
Kerrville ○ **USA** (TX) 266-267 H 3
K'ersa ○ **ETH** 208-209 E 4
Kersa Dek ○ **ETH** 208-209 D 6
Kershaw ○ **USA** (SC) 284-285 K 2
Kersinyané ○ **RMM** 202-203 M 4
Kersley ○ **CDN** (BC) 228-229 M 4
Kertamulia ○ **RI** 162-163 H 5
Kerteh ○ **MAL** 162-163 E 2
Kerteminde ○ **DK** 86-87 E 9
Kertosono ○ **RI** 168 E 4
Keruak ○ **RI** 168 C 7
Kerugoya ○ **EAK** 212-213 F 4
Kervansaray ∴ **TR** 128-129 E 3
Keryneia ○ **TR** 128-129 E 5
Kerzaz ○ **DZ** 188-189 L 6
Kesagami Lake ⪡ **CDN** (ONT) 236-237 H 2
Kesagami Lake Provincial Park ⊥ **CDN** (ONT) 236-237 H 2
Kesagami River ~ **CDN** (ONT) 236-237 H 2
Keşan ☆ **TR** 128-129 B 2
Keşem ○ **AFG** 136-137 M 6
Kesennuma ○ **J** 152-153 S 4
Keshena ○ **USA** (WI) 270-271 K 6
Keshod ○ **IND** 138-139 C 9
Kesiman ○ **RI** 168 B 7
Keskin ○ **TR** 128-129 F 3
Kestell ○ **ZA** 220-221 J 4
Kestenğa ○ **RUS** 88-89 L 4
Keswick ○ **GB** 90-91 F 4
Keszthely ○ **H** 92-93 O 5
Ket' ~ **RUS** 114-115 R 5
Ket' ~ **RUS** 116-117 E 6
Keta ○ **GH** 202-203 L 7
Keta, gory ▲ **RUS** 108-109 Y 7
Ketahun ○ **RI** 162-163 D 6
Keta Lagoon ○ **GH** 202-203 L 7
Ketama ○ **MA** 188-189 J 3
Ketanda ○ **RUS** 120-121 J 3
Ketanggungan ○ **RI** 168 C 3
Ketapang ○ **RI** (JTI) 168 E 4
Ketapang ○ **RI** (KBA) 162-163 H 5
Ketchary ~ **RUS** 96-97 D 10
Ketchen ○ **CDN** (SAS) 232-233 Q 4
Ketchikan ○ **USA** 32-33 E 4
Ketchum ○ **USA** (ID) 252-253 D 3
Kete-Krachi ○ **GH** 202-203 K 6
Ketesso ○ **CI** 202-203 J 7
Keti Bandar ○ **PK** 134-135 M 6
Ketlica, ostrov ⊠ **RUS** 84-85 c 2
Ketlik River ~ **USA** 20-21 N 2
Ketoj, ostrov ⊠ **RUS** 122-123 P 5
Ketok Mountain ▲ **USA** 22-23 S 3
Ketoria, Cape ▲ **CDN** 36-37 M 2
Kétou ○ **DY** 204-205 E 5
Ketovo ○ **RUS** 114-115 N 7
Ke Town ○ **LB** 202-203 H 7
Kętrzyn ○ **PL** 92-93 Q 1

Ketsko-Tymskaja, ravnina ⤳ **RUS** 114-115 S 4
Ketta ○ **RCB** 210-211 E 3
Kétté ○ **CAM** 206-207 B 6
Kettering ○ **USA** (OH) 280-281 B 4
Kettle Falls ○ **USA** (WA) 244-245 F 4
Kettleman City ○ **USA** (CA) 248-249 E 3
Kettleman Hills ▲ **USA** (CA) 248-249 D 3
Kettle Point ▲ **CDN** (ONT) 238-239 C 3
Kettle Range ▲ **USA** (WA) 244-245 G 2
Kettle River ~ **CDN** 34-35 M 2
Kettle River ~ **CDN** (MN) 270-271 F 4
Kettle River ~ **USA** (WA) 244-245 G 3
Kettle Valley ○ **CDN** (BC) 230-231 K 4
Keudeuteunom ○ **RI** 162-163 A 2
Keuka Lake ○ **USA** (NY) 278-279 C 6
Keuf ~ **RUS** 116-117 L 6
Keum ~ **RUS** 88-89 M 3
Keur Madiabel ○ **SN** 202-203 B 3
Keur Massène ○ **RIM** 196-197 K 6
Keur Momar Sar ○ **SN** 196-197 C 7
Keuruu ○ **FIN** 88-89 H 6
Keur ○ **RT** 202-203 L 6
Kévem ~ **RUS** 112-113 R 2
Kewanee ○ **USA** (IL) 274-275 J 3
Kewanna ○ **USA** (IN) 274-275 M 3
Kewapante ○ **RI** 166-167 B 6
Kewasasap ○ **PNG** 183 E 5
Kewaskum ○ **USA** (WI) 270-271 K 1
Kewaunee ○ **USA** (WI) 270-271 L 6
Keweenaw Bay ≈ **USA** (MI) 270-271 K 4
Keweenaw Bay ○ **USA** (MI) 270-271 K 4
Keweenaw Bay Indian Reservation X **USA** (MI) 270-271 K 4
Keweenaw Peninsula ⤳ **USA** (MI) 270-271 K 3
Keweenaw Point ▲ **USA** (MI) 270-271 L 4
Key ○ **USA** (TX) 264-265 C 6
K'ey Āfer ○ **ETH** 208-209 C 6
Keyalüvik ○ **USA** 20-21 H 6
Keyapaha ~ **USA** (SD) 260-261 F 3
Keyes ○ **CDN** (MAN) 234-235 D 4
Keyes ○ **USA** (OK) 264-265 B 2
Keyhole Reservoir ○ **USA** (WY) 252-253 O 2
Keyihe ○ **VRC** 150-151 R 3
Key Largo ○ **USA** (FL) 286-287 J 6
Key Largo ⊠ **USA** (FL) 286-287 J 6
Key Like Mine ○ **CDN** 34-35 D 2
Keyling Inlet ≈ 172-173 J 4
Keyser ○ **USA** (WV) 280-281 H 4
Keystone ○ **USA** (CA) 248-249 D 2
Keystone ○ **USA** (NE) 262-263 E 3
Keystone ○ **USA** (SD) 260-261 C 3
Keystone ○ **USA** (WA) 244-245 C 2
Keystone Heights ○ **USA** (FL) 286-287 G 2
Keystone Lake ○ **USA** (OK) 264-265 H 2
Keysville ○ **USA** (VA) 280-281 H 6
Keytesville ○ **USA** (MO) 274-275 F 6
Key West ○• **USA** (FL) 286-287 H 7
Kez ○ **RUS** 96-97 H 5
Kežar Falls ○ **USA** (ME) 278-279 L 5
Kezi ○ **ZW** 218-219 E 5
Kežma ○ **RUS** 116-117 K 6
Kežmarok ○ **SK** 92-93 Q 4
Kgalagadi ○ **RB** 220-221 E 2
Kgatleng ○ **RB** 220-221 H 2
Kgokgole ○ **ZA** 220-221 H 2
Kgun Lake ○ **USA** 20-21 H 6
Khabou ○ **RIM** 202-203 D 2
Khadki ○ **IND** 138-139 D 10
Khadwa ○ **IND** 138-139 F 9
Khagaria ○ **IND** 142-143 E 3
Khagia Sumna ○ **VRC** 144-145 C 5
Khairägarh ○ **IND** 142-143 H 5
Khairapa ○ **IND** 138-139 C 9
Khairpur ○ **PK** (PU) 138-139 C 3
Khairpur Näthan Shäh ○ **PK** 134-135 M 5
Khajurago ○ **IND** 138-139 G 7
Khajuri Kach ○ **PK** 138-139 C 2
Khakassia = Hakasija, Respublika ◻ **RUS** 116-117 D 9
Khakhea ○ **RB** 220-221 F 2
Khakurdi ○ **IND** 138-139 F 7
Khalaf Allāh, Bi'r ⪡ **LAR** 192-193 E 4
Khalaf Allāh, Qārat ▲ **LAR** 192-193 D 4
Khalfallah ○ **DZ** 190-191 D 2
Khaleh ○ **IR** 134-135 G 1
Khali al-Bahrain ⪡ **IND** 134-135 D 6
Khali al Bumbah ⪡ **LAR** 192-193 K 1
Khambhaliya ○ **IND** 138-139 B 8
Khambhat ○ **IND** 138-139 D 8
Khambhāt, Gulf of ≈ 138-139 C 9
Khāmgaon ○ **IND** 138-139 F 8
Khami Ruins ∴ **ZW** 218-219 E 5
Khamis Mushayt = Ḥamis Mušaiṭ ○ **KSA** 132-133 C 4
Kham Khuan Kaeo ○ **THA** 158-159 H 3
Khammam ○ **IND** 142-143 J 4
Khampat ○ **MYA** 142-143 J 4
Kham Ta Kla ○ **THA** 158-159 G 2
Khan ~ **NAM** 216-217 C 11
Khānäpur ○ **IND** 140-141 F 3
Khandala ○ **IND** 138-139 F 10
Khandala ○ **IND** 138-139 D 10
Khānewäl ○ **PK** 138-139 C 2
Khängäh Dogrän ○ **PK** 138-139 D 4
Khdadäbäd ○ **PK** 134-135 M 5
Khanda ○ **PK** 134-135 M 5
Khangar Sidi Nadji ○ **DZ** 190-191 F 3
Khanka, Ozero = Hanka, ozero ○ **RUS** 122-123 H 6
Khankendi = Xankandi ☆ **AZ** (NAG) 128-129 M 3
Khannanfoussa, Gara ▲ **DZ** 190-191 D 3
Khanom ○ **THA** 158-159 E 6
Khänpur ○ **PK** (SIN) 138-139 B 6
Khanty-Mansi Autonomous District=Hanty-Mans.avt.okrug ◻ **RUS** 114-115 N 5
Khao Chmao National Park ⊥ **THA** 158-159 F 4

Khao Kha Khaeng ▲ **THA** 158-159 E 2
Khao Kheaw National Park ⊥• **THA** 158-159 F 4
Khao Khieo Open Zoo • **THA** 158-159 F 4
Khao Laem Reservoir ⪡ **THA** 158-159 E 3
Khao Sok National Park ⊥ **THA** 158-159 D 6
Khapalu ○ **IND** 138-139 F 2
Khaptada National Park ⊥ **NEP** 144-145 Q 6
Khárán ○ **PK** 134-135 L 5
Kharar ○ **IND** 138-139 F 4
Khardung La ▲ **IND** 138-139 F 2
Kharepätan ○ **IND** 140-141 E 4
Khärga, El = Ḥārīḍa, al- ☆ **ET** 194-195 E 5
Khargon ○ **IND** 138-139 E 9
Khárián ○ **PK** 138-139 D 3
Khariär ○ **IND** 142-143 C 5
Kharikhola ○ **NEP** 144-145 F 7
Kharj, al = Ḥarǧ, al ○ **KSA** 130-131 A 5
Kharkiv = Charkiv ☆ **UA** 102-103 K 3
Khárroüb, Oued ~ **RIM** 196-197 F 3
Kharsia ○ **IND** 142-143 C 5
Khartaksho ○ **IND** 138-139 F 2
Khartoum = al-Ḥarṭūm ★ • **SUD** 200-201 F 5
Khartoum North = al-Ḥarṭūm Baḥrī ○ **SUD** 200-201 F 5
Khartoum North = Harṭūm Baḥrī, al- ○ **SUD** 200-201 F 5
Khashm al-Qirbah ○ **SUD** 200-201 G 5
Khasi Hills ▲ **IND** 142-143 G 3
Khási-Jaintia Hills ▲ **IND** 142-143 G 3
Khasm Elmi ○ **SUD** 200-201 C 6
Khatauli ○ **IND** 142-143 B 4
Khätegaon ○ **IND** 138-139 F 8
Khatima ○ **IND** 138-139 G 5
Khatoli ○ **IND** 138-139 F 7
Khatt Atoui ~ **RIM** 196-197 C 4
Khaur ○ **PK** 138-139 D 3
Khāvda ○ **IND** 138-139 B 8
Khazzän ar-Rusayri ⪡ **SUD** 208-209 A 3
Khed ○ **IND** 140-141 E 4
Khedive ○ **CDN** (SAS) 232-233 O 6
Kheis ○ **ZA** 220-221 E 4
Kherba ○ **DZ** 190-191 C 2
Kheri ○ **IND** 138-139 F 9
Kherir, Oued ~ **RIM** 196-197 F 2
Kherrata ○ **DZ** 190-191 E 2
Kherwära ○ **IND** 138-139 D 8
Khe Sanh ∴ **VN** 158-159 J 2
Khe Ve ○ **VN** 158-159 H 2
Khewra ~ **PK** 138-139 D 3
Khezmir ○ **RIM** 196-197 E 5
Khimki = Himki ○ **RUS** 94-95 P 4
Khipro ○ **PK** 138-139 B 7
Khiran, al- ○ **KWT** 130-131 L 3
Khiu ○ **PK** 138-139 C 4
Khlong Ngae ○ **THA** 158-159 F 7
Khlong Thom ○ **THA** 158-159 E 6
Khmel'nyts'kyy = Chmel'nyc'kyj ☆ **UA** 102-103 E 3
Khodzhavend = Xocavand ○ **AZ** (NAG) 128-129 M 3
Khogue Tobène ○ **SN** 202-203 C 2
Khojak Pass ▲ **PK** 134-135 M 3
Khokarmoho ○ **IND** 138-139 G 10
Khok Chang ○ **THA** 158-159 H 2
Khok Kloi ○ **THA** 158-159 D 6
Khok Phek ○ **THA** 158-159 G 3
Khok Pho ○ **THA** 158-159 F 7
Khok Samrong ○ **THA** 158-159 F 3
Khomas Hochland ▲ **NAM** 216-217 D 11
Khomeynishär = **IR** 134-135 D 2
Khon ○ **THA** 158-159 E 2
Khondmäl Hills ▲ **IND** 142-143 C 5
Khong Chiam ○ **THA** 158-159 H 3
Khong Khi Sua ○ **THA** 158-159 F 3
Khon Kaen ○ **THA** 158-159 G 2
Khôr Anyär ○ **DJI** 200-201 L 6
Khoräsän = **IR** 134-135 G 1
Khorasgän ○ **IR** 134-135 D 2
Khordha ○ **IND** 142-143 K 5
Khor Fakkan = Haur Fakkān ○ **UAE** 134-135 G 6
Khor Gamdze ○ **VRC** 144-145 M 5
Khorixas ★ **NAM** 216-217 C 10
Khor Khor ○ **IND** 142-143 L 4
Khorlak ○ **NEP** 144-145 P 6
Khossanto ○ **SN** 202-203 E 3
Khost ○ **PK** 134-135 M 3
Khotol Mount ▲ **USA** 20-21 M 4
Khouribga = Khouribga ☆ **MA** 188-189 H 4
Khouribga = **MA** 188-189 H 4
Khourigba ○ **MA** 188-189 H 4
Khowai ○ **IND** 142-143 G 4
Khreum ○ **MYA** 142-143 H 5
Khshwan Mountain ▲ **CDN** 32-33 F 4
Khuang Nai ○ **THA** 158-159 H 3
Khubus ○ **ZA** 220-221 C 4
Khuchinaras ○ **THA** 158-159 H 2
Khudabad ○ **IND** 138-139 D 7
Khudabad ○ **PK** 134-135 M 5
Khudian ○ **PK** 138-139 E 4
Khudzhand = Ḥuǧand ★ **TJ** 136-137 L 4
Khukhan ○ **THA** 158-159 H 3
Khulna ○ **BD** 142-143 F 4
Khums, Al ○ **LAR** 192-193 G 1
Khums, Al ☆ **LAR** (AKM) 192-193 F 1
Khunaniwala ○ **PK** 138-139 E 4
Khunjerab Pass ▲ **PK** 138-139 F 1
Khun Yuam ○ **THA** 142-143 K 6
Khuraburi ○ **THA** 158-159 D 6
Khurai ○ **IND** 138-139 F 7
Khuraiyt ○ **SUD** 200-201 B 6
Khuriga ○ **IND** 138-139 F 5

Kigomasha, Ras ▲ **EAT** 212-213 G 6
Kigosi ~ **EAT** 212-213 C 5
Kigumno ○ **EAK** 212-213 F 4
Kihčik ~ **RUS** 120-121 R 7
Kihei ○ **USA** (HI) 288 J 4
Kihelkonna ○ **EST** 94-95 H 2
Kihnu saar ⊠ **EST** 94-95 J 2
Kiholo ○ **USA** (HI) 288 K 5
Kihurio ○ **EAK** 212-213 G 6
Kii-hantō ⤳ **J** 152-153 G 8
Kii-Nagashima ○ **J** 152-153 G 8
Kii-sanchi ▲ **J** 152-153 F 8
Kii-suidō ≈ 152-153 F 8
Kija ~ **RUS** 114-115 U 7
Kija ~ **RUS** 116-117 E 6
Kija ~ **RUS** 118-119 G 10
Kijaly-Bürta ~ **KA** 124-125 D 4
Kijang ○ **RI** 162-163 F 4
Kijasovo ○ **RUS** 96-97 H 5
Kiji, Île ⊠ **RIM** 196-197 B 5
Kijungu ○ **EAT** 212-213 F 6
Kika ○ **DY** 204-205 E 4
Kikagati ○ **EAU** 212-213 C 4
Kikai-shima ⊠ **J** 152-153 C 10
Kikale ○ **EAT** 212-213 C 5
Kikamba ○ **ZRE** 210-211 L 5
Kikambala ○ **EAK** 212-213 G 5
Kikegtek Island ⊠ **USA** 22-23 O 3
Kikert Lake ○ **CDN** 30-31 N 2
Kikiakrovak River ~ **USA** 20-21 O 2
Kiki Ora ○ **RUS** 88-89 K 4
Kikinda ○ **YU** 100-101 H 2
Kikiongolo ○ **ZRE** 210-211 G 6
Kikkertaruk Island ⊠ **CDN** 36-37 N 4
Kikombo ○ **EAT** 214-215 H 4
Kikonai ○ **J** 152-153 J 4
Kikondja ○ **ZRE** 214-215 D 5
Kikori ○ **PNG** 183 C 4
Kikori River ~ **PNG** 183 B 4
Kikwit ○ **ZRE** 210-211 G 6
Kil ⊕ **S** 86-87 F 7
Kilaguni Lodge ○ **EAK** 212-213 G 5
Kilakkarai ○ **IND** 140-141 H 6
Kilala ○ **EAK** 212-213 F 4
Kilauea ○ **USA** (HI) 288 F 2
Kilauea Crater ▲ **USA** (HI) 288 K 5
Kilauea Lighthouse (Largest Lighthose in the World) ▲ • **USA** (HI) 288 F 2
Kilbeggan = Cill Bheagáin ○ **IRL** 90-91 D 5
Kilbella River ~ **CDN** (BC) 230-231 K 2
Kilbohamn ○ **N** 86-87 F 3
Kilbuck Mountains ▲ **USA** 20-21 K 6
Kilcoy ○ **AUS** 178-179 M 4
Kildala Lake ○ **CDN** (BC) 228-229 J 3
Kildare = Cill Dara ○ **IRL** 90-91 D 5
Kil'din, ostrov ⊠ **RUS** 88-89 M 2
Kildonan ○ **CDN** (BC) 230-231 D 5
Kildonan ○ **ZW** 218-219 F 3
Kildurk ○ **AUS** 172-173 J 4
Kilekale Lake ○ **CDN** 30-31 N 2
Kilembe ○ **ZRE** (BAN) 210-211 G 6
Kilembe ○ **ZRE** (SHA) 214-215 D 4
Kilembi ○ **ZRE** 210-211 L 6
Kileo ○ **ZRE** 210-211 M 5
Kilgana ~ **RUS** 120-121 P 3
Kilganskij massiv ▲ **RUS** 120-121 P 3
Kilgore ○ **USA** (NE) 262-263 F 2
Kilgore ○ **USA** (TX) 264-265 K 6
Kilgoris ○ **EAK** 212-213 E 4
Kili ~ **US** 156-157 F 5
Kilia ○ **PNG** 183 F 5
Kilian, Erg ~ **DZ** 190-191 G 9
Kilibo ○ **DY** 204-205 E 4
Kilifarevo ○ **BG** 102-103 B 6
Kilifas ○ **PNG** 183 A 2
Kilifi ○ **EAK** 212-213 G 5
Kiligwa River ~ **USA** 20-21 L 2
Kilija ○ **UA** 102-103 F 5
Kilikkollür ○ **IND** 140-141 G 5
Kilim ○ **TCH** 206-207 F 3
Kilimanjaro ◻ **EAT** 212-213 F 5
Kilimanjaro ▲ • **EAT** 212-213 F 5
Kilimanjaro Buffalo Lodge ○ **EAK** 212-213 F 5
Kilimanjaro National Park ⊥ •••• **EAT** 212-213 F 5
Kilimatinde ○ **EAT** 212-213 E 6
Kilimbangara ⊠ **SOL** 184 I c 2
Kilindoni ○ **EAT** 214-215 H 4
Kilingi-Nõmme ○ **EST** 94-95 J 2
Kilini, Î-n- ~ **RMM** 196-197 L 5
Kilinochchi ○ **CL** 140-141 H 6
Kilipsärvi ○ **FIN** 88-89 F 2
Kilis ☆ **TR** 128-129 G 4
Kiliuda Bay ≈ 22-23 U 4
Kiljanskij ~ **RUS** 120-121 E 2
Kilju ○ **DVR** 150-151 F 2
Kilkee = Cill Chaoi ○ **IRL** 90-91 C 5
Kilkenny = Cill Chainnigh ☆ • **IRL** 90-91 D 5
Kilkis ○ **GR** 100-101 J 4
Killala Lake ○ **CDN** (ONT) 236-237 B 3
Killaly ○ **CDN** (SAS) 232-233 Q 5
Killam ○ **CDN** (ALB) 232-233 G 4
Killarney ○ **AUS** (NT) 172-173 K 4
Killarney ○ **AUS** (QLD) 178-179 N 2
Killarney ○ **CDN** (MAN) 234-235 D 5
Killarney = Cill Aime ○ **IRL** 90-91 C 6
Killarney Provincial Park ⊥ **CDN** (ONT) 238-239 D 2
Killdeer ○ **CDN** (SAS) 232-233 M 6
Killdeer ○ **USA** (ND) 258-259 E 4
Kill Devil Hills ○ **USA** (NC) 282-283 M 4
Killeen ○ **USA** (TX) 266-267 J 3
Killik River ~ **USA** 20-21 M 2
Killiney Beach ○ **CDN** (BC) 230-231 K 3
Killington Peak ▲ **USA** (VT) 278-279 J 5
Killorglin = Cill Orglan ○ **IRL** 90-91 C 5
Kilmarnock ○ **USA** (VA) 280-281 K 6
Kilmarnock ☆ **RUS** 96-97 G 5
Kil'mez' ○ **RUS** 96-97 H 5
Kilmichael ○ **USA** (MS) 268-269 L 5

Kŏch'ang o ROK 150-151 F 10
Ko Chang ⌒ THA 158-159 E 6
Ko Chang ⌒ THA 158-159 G 4
Ko Chang National Park ⊥ • THA 158-159 G 4
Kochchikade o CL 140-141 H 7
Koch Creek ~ CDN (BC) 230-231 M 4
Kōchi ☆ • J 152-153 E 8
Koch Island ⌒ CDN 24-25 h 6
Koch Peak ▲ USA (MT) 250-251 H 6
Kochtel = Kohtla o EST 94-95 K 2
Kocjubyns'ke o UA 102-103 G 2
Kock o PL 102-103 C 2
Kočki ☆ RUS 124-125 M 1
Kočkoma o RUS 88-89 N 4
Kočkor-Ata o KS 136-137 N 4
Kočkorka o KS 146-147 B 4
Kočubeevskoe o RUS 126-127 D 5
Kočubej o RUS 126-127 G 5
Kočumdek ~ RUS 116-117 F 3
Koda ~ RUS 116-117 J 6
Kodār o IND 140-141 H 2
Kodari o NEP 144-145 E 7
Kodarma o IND 142-143 D 3
Kodiak o USA 22-23 U 4
Kodiak Island ⌒ USA 22-23 U 4
Kodina ~ RUS 88-89 P 5
Kodinār o IND 138-139 C 9
Kodino o RUS 88-89 P 5
Kodiyakkarai o IND 140-141 H 5
Kodjari o BF 202-203 L 4
Kodmo, togga ~ SP 208-209 J 4
Kodok o SUD 206-207 L 4
Kodumuru o IND 140-141 G 3
Kodyma ~ UA 102-103 F 4
Koébonou o CI 202-203 J 5
Koës o NAM 220-221 D 2
Koettlitz Glacier ⊂ ARK 16 F 16
Kofa Game Range ⊥ USA (AZ) 256-257 A 5
Kofa Mountains ▲ USA (AZ) 256-257 A 5
Kofarnihon o TJ 136-137 L 5
Kofelē o ETH 208-209 D 5
Koffiefontein o ZA 220-221 G 4
Kofoed-Hansen Bræ ⊂ GRØ 26-27 o 5
Koforidua ☆ GH 202-203 K 6
Kōfu o J (TOT) 152-153 E 7
Kōfu ☆ J (YMN) 152-153 H 7
Koga o J 152-153 H 6
Kogaluc, Lac ○ CDN 36-37 L 5
Kogaluc, Rivière ~ CDN 36-37 L 5
Kogaluk Bay ≈ 36-37 K 5
Kogaluk River ~ CDN 36-37 S 6
Kogalym o RUS 114-115 N 3
Køge o • DK 86-87 F 9
Køge Bugt ≈ 86-87 F 9
Køge Bugt = Pikiutdleq ≈ 28-29 U 4
Kogel' ~ RUS 114-115 D 3
Kogmanskloof ▲ ZA 220-221 E 6
Kognak River ~ CDN 30-31 U 5
Kogoluktuk River ~ USA 20-21 M 3
Kogon ~ RG 202-203 C 4
Kogrukluk River ~ USA 20-21 L 6
Kogtok River ~ CDN 30-31 V 4
Koğûr o IR 136-137 B 6
Kogyae Strict Nature Reserve ⊥ GH 202-203 K 6
Kohala Mountains ▲ USA (HI) 288 K 4
Kohan o PK 134-135 M 5
Kohāt o • PK 138-139 C 3
Kohāt Pass ▲ PK 138-139 C 3
Kohila o EST 94-95 J 2
Kohil'nik ~ UA 102-103 F 5
Kohima ☆ •• IND 142-143 J 3
Kohinggo = Arundel ⌒ SOL 184 I c 3
Ko Hinh o LAO 156-157 C 6
Koh-i-Patandar ▲ PK 134-135 L 5
Kohler Range ▲ ARK 16 F 25
Kohlu o PK 138-139 B 5
Kohol o RI 166-167 D 3
Kohtla-Järve o •• EST 94-95 K 2
Kohŭng o ROK 150-151 F 10
Kohunlich ∴ • MEX 52-53 K 2
Koiama, Jasiira ⌒ SP 212-213 J 4
Koichab ~ NAM 220-221 C 3
Koichab Pan ○ NAM 220-221 B 3
Koidern o CDN 20-21 U 6
Koidu o WAL 202-203 E 5
Koihoa o IND 140-141 L 5
Koila Kabé ~ SN 202-203 E 3
Koil Island ⌒ PNG 183 C 2
Koilkuntla o IND 140-141 H 3
Koimbani o COM 222-223 C 3
Koimekeah o IND 140-141 L 6
Koin ~ RUS 88-89 V 5
Koindu o WAL 202-203 E 5
Koito o EAK 212-213 G 5
Kojbagar, köli ○ KA 124-125 D 2
Kojda o RUS 88-89 R 3
Kojda ~ RUS 88-89 R 3
Kŏje Do ⌒ ROK 150-151 G 10
Kojgorodok ☆ RUS 96-97 G 3
Kŏjin o ROK 150-151 G 8
Kojmatdag ▲ TM 136-137 D 4
Kojnathun, ozero ○ RUS 112-113 V 4
Kojonup o AUS 176-177 D 6
Kojtoš o US 136-137 K 4
Kojverelan ~ RUS 112-113 R 5
Kojvèrèlanskij krjaž ▲ RUS 112-113 R 5
K'ok'a o ETH 208-209 D 4
K'ok'a Gidib ⊂ ETH 208-209 D 4
K'ok'a Hāyk' ○ ETH 208-209 D 4
Kokand o US 136-137 M 4
Kokanee Glacier Provincial Park ⊥ CDN (BC) 230-231 M 4
Kokani ~ EAK 212-213 G 5
Kökaral o KA 126-127 O 4
Kökaral, tubegi ⌒ KA 126-127 O 4
Kokas o RI 166-167 G 3
Kokatha o AUS 178-179 C 6
Kokča o US 136-137 J 4
Kökcengirsor, köli ○ KA 124-125 G 2
Kokcetau Üstirti ▲ KA 124-125 F 2
Kokenau o RI 166-167 J 4
Kokeragi Point ▲ CDN 30-31 H 3
Kokerboomwoud • NAM 220-221 D 3
Kokerit o GUY 62-63 E 2
Ko Kho Khao ⌒ THA 158-159 E 6
Kokish o CDN (BC) 230-231 C 3
Kok-Jangak o KS 136-137 N 4
Kokkola o FIN 88-89 G 5
Koklapperne ⌒ GRØ 28-29 V 4
Koknese o •• LV 94-95 J 3
Koko o WAN (BEL) 204-205 F 5
Koko o WAN (SOK) 204-205 F 3
Kokoda o PNG 183 D 5
Kokoda Trail • PNG 183 D 5
Kokola o PNG 183 G 2
Kokolik River ~ USA 20-21 K 2
Kokologo o BF 202-203 K 3
Kokomo o USA (IN) 274-275 M 4
Kokonselkä ○ FIN 88-89 H 5
Kokopo o PNG 183 G 3
Kokora, ozero ○ RUS 108-109 d 5
Kokoro ~ RG 202-203 F 3
Kokosa o ETH 208-209 D 5
Kokoso o GH 202-203 K 7
Kokoti Kouamékro o CI 202-203 H 6
Kokoula ~ RG 202-203 D 4
Kokpek o KA 146-147 D 4
Kokpekty o KA 124-125 N 4
Kokrajhar o IND 142-143 G 2
Kokrines Hills ▲ USA 20-21 N 4
Kokruagarok o USA 20-21 O 1
Koksa ~ RUS 124-125 O 3
Koksan o DVR 150-151 F 8
Köksaraj o KA 136-137 L 3
Köksengir, tau ▲ KA (AKT) 126-127 M 5
Köksengir, tau ▲ KA (KZL) 124-125 D 6
Koksoak, Rivière ~ CDN 36-37 P 6
Kokstad o ZA 220-221 J 5
Köksu o KA 136-137 L 4
Köksu ~ KA 124-125 L 6
Koktac, Rivière ~ CDN 36-37 L 5
Koktal o KA 124-125 L 6
Köktas ~ KA 124-125 G 5
Köktöbe, tau ▲ KA 124-125 E 5
Koktokay o VRC 146-147 J 2
Köktyrnak, tubegi ⌒ KA 126-127 O 4
Koku, Tanjung ▲ RI 164-165 G 6
Kokubo o J 152-153 D 9
Kokumbo o CI 202-203 H 6
Kŏkŭm Do ⌒ ROK 150-151 F 10
Ko Kut ⌒ THA 158-159 G 5
Kol o PNG 183 C 3
Kola o CDN (MAN) 234-235 B 5
Kola o RI 166-167 H 4
Kola o RUS 88-89 M 2
Kola, Gorges de ~ • CAM 204-205 K 4
Kola, Pulau ⌒ RI 166-167 H 4
Kolachel o IND 140-141 G 6
Kolāchi ~ PK 134-135 M 5
Kolahun o LB 202-203 E 5
Kolaka o RI 164-165 G 6
Kolan River ~ AUS 178-179 L 3
Ko Lanta ⌒ THA 158-159 E 7
Kola Peninsula = Kol'skij poluostrov ⌒ RUS 88-89 N 2
Kolār o • IND 140-141 H 4
Kolar Gold Fields o IND 140-141 H 4
Kolari o FIN 88-89 G 3
Kolåsen o S 86-87 F 5
Kolasib o IND 142-143 H 3
Kolašin o • YU 100-101 G 3
Kola Town o LB 202-203 G 6
Kolattupuzha o IND 140-141 G 6
Kolāyat o IND 138-139 D 6
Kolbaj, tau ▲ KA 126-127 K 6
Kolbeinsstaðir o IS 86-87 b 2
Kolbio o EAK 212-213 H 4
Kol'covoe, ozero ○ RUS 122-123 Q 4
Kol'čugino ☆ RUS 94-95 Q 3
Kol'čum ~ RUS 114-115 U 5
Kolda ☆ SN 202-203 C 3
Koldaga o TCH 206-207 C 4
Köldenen-Temir ~ KA 126-127 M 3
Kolding o • DK 86-87 D 9
Kole o ZRE (HAU) 210-211 K 2
Kole o ZRE (KOR) 210-211 J 5
Kolebira o IND 142-143 D 4
Kolek"egan ~ RUS 114-115 Q 3
Kolendo o RUS 122-123 K 2
Kolendo, Mount ▲ AUS 180-181 D 2
Kolenovskij, Elan'- o RUS 102-103 M 2
Kolenté ~ RG 202-203 D 4
Kolente ~ RG 202-203 D 5
Koležma o RUS 88-89 N 4
Kolgarin o AUS 176-177 E 6
Kolguev, ostrov ⌒ RUS 88-89 U 2
Kolhāpur o IND (ANP) 140-141 H 2
Kolhāpur o •• IND (MAH) 140-141 F 2
Kolhida ☆ GE 126-127 D 6
Kolhozabad o TJ 136-137 L 6
Koli ▲ FIN 88-89 K 5
Kolia o CI 202-203 G 5
Koliba ~ RG 202-203 D 3
Ko Libong ⌒ THA 158-159 E 7
Koliganek o USA 22-23 S 3
Kolín o •• CZ 92-93 N 3
Kolin o USA (MT) 250-251 K 4
Kolinbiné ~ RMM 202-203 E 2
K'olito o ETH 208-209 D 5
Koljučaja, gora ▲ RUS 112-113 S 3
Koljučin, ostrov ⌒ RUS 112-113 X 3
Koljučinskaja guba ≈ 112-113 X 3
Kolka o •• LV 94-95 H 3
Kolky o UA 102-103 D 2
Kollegal o IND 140-141 G 4
Kolleru Lake ○ IND 140-141 J 2
Kollipara o IND 140-141 J 2
Kollo o RN 204-205 E 2
Kolmackij, porog ~ RUS 88-89 P 3
Kolmakovo o RUS 114-115 P 7
Kolmanskop o NAM 220-221 B 3
Kolmar = Chodzież o • PL 92-93 O 2
Kolmar o • D 92-93 J 3
Kolno o PL 92-93 Q 2
Kolo o EAT 212-213 E 6
Kolo o PL 92-93 P 2
Koloa o USA (HI) 288 F 3
Kolobane o SN 202-203 C 2
Kolobeke o ZRE 210-211 G 4
Kołobrzeg o PL 92-93 N 1
Kolofata o CAM 206-207 B 3
Ko-lok, Sungai o THA 158-159 F 7
Kolokani o RMM 202-203 F 3
Koloko o BF 202-203 H 4
Kolokol, vulkan ▲ RUS 122-123 O 5
Kolokolkova guba ≈ 88-89 W 2
Kolokondé o DY 202-203 L 5
Kolomak o UA 102-103 J 3
Kolomino o RUS 114-115 R 6
Kolomna ☆ •• RUS 94-95 Q 4
Kolomoki Mounds • USA (GA) 284-285 F 5
Kolomonyi o ZRE 210-211 J 6
Kolomyja ☆ UA 102-103 D 3
Kolondieba o RMM 202-203 G 4
Kolondiéba o RMM 202-203 G 4
Kolongotomo o RMM 202-203 H 3
Kolonia ★ FSM 13 G 2
Kolono o RI 164-165 H 6
Kolonodale o RI 164-165 G 4
Kolosovyh, ostrov ⌒ RUS 108-109 W 4
Kolossa ~ RMM 202-203 G 3
Kolotambu = Avu Avu o SOL 184 I e 3
Kolowana-Watobo, Teluk ≈ 164-165 H 6
Kolozero ○ RUS 88-89 M 2
Kolp' ~ RUS 94-95 O 2
Kolpakova ~ RUS 120-121 R 6
Kolpaševo ☆ RUS 114-115 R 5
Kolpino o RUS 94-95 M 2
Kolpny o RUS 94-95 P 5
Kólpos Haniōn ≈ 100-101 J 7
Kólpos Kissámou ≈ 100-101 J 7
Kolpur o PK 134-135 M 4
Kol'skij zaliv ≈ 88-89 M 2
Kolubara ~ YU 100-101 H 2
Kolumadulu Atoll ⌒ MV 140-141 B 6
Koluton ~ KA 124-125 F 3
Kolva ~ RUS 88-89 Y 3
Kolva ~ RUS 108-109 H 8
Kolva ~ RUS 114-115 E 4
Kolvavis ~ RUS 108-109 H 8
Kolvereid o N 86-87 E 4
Kolvica o RUS 88-89 M 3
Kolvickoe, ozero ○ RUS 88-89 M 3
Kolwa o PK 134-135 L 5
Kolwezi o ZRE (SHA) 214-215 C 6
Kolyma ~ RUS 110-111 d 6
Kolyma ~ RUS 110-111 d 7
Kolyma ~ RUS 112-113 H 3
Kolyma ~ RUS 112-113 L 2
Kolyma ~ RUS 120-121 P 2
Kolyma ~ RUS 120-121 M 2
Kolymak ~ RUS 112-113 M 5
Kolymskaja guba ≈ 110-111 d 4
Kolymskaja nizmennost' ○ RUS 110-111 c 5
Kolymskoe o RUS 112-113 K 2
Kolymskoe, vodohranilišče < RUS 120-121 N 3
Kolymskoe nagor'e ▲ RUS 120-121 Q 3
Kolymskoye Nagor'ye = Kolymskoe nagor'e ▲ RUS 120-121 Q 3
Kolyšlej o RUS 96-97 D 7
Kolyvan' ☆ RUS 114-115 R 7
Kol'zat o KA 146-147 E 4
Kom ▲ BG 102-103 C 6
Kom o EAK 212-213 G 3
Kom ~ G 210-211 C 2
Koma o ETH 208-209 C 4
Komagasberge ▲ ZA 220-221 C 4
Komaio o PNG 183 B 4
Komako o PNG 183 C 4
Komanda o ZRE 212-213 B 3
Komandnaja, gora ▲ RUS 122-123 H 3
Komandorskaja kotlovina ⩝ RUS 120-121 V 5
Komandorskaya Basin ⩝ RUS 120-121 V 5
Komandorskie ostrova ⌒ RUS 120-121 W 6
Komarno o CDN (MAN) 234-235 F 4
Komárno o SK 92-93 P 5
Komárom o H 92-93 P 5
Komarovka o RUS 116-117 E 7
Komatipoort o ZA 220-221 K 2
Komatirivier ~ ZA 220-221 K 2
Komatsu o J 152-153 G 6
Komba, Pulau ⌒ RI 166-167 B 5
Kombat o NAM 216-217 D 9
Kombe o ZRE 210-211 K 6
Kombile o WAL 202-203 E 5
Kombissiri o BF 202-203 K 3
Kombo-Itindi o CAM 204-205 H 6
Kombone o CAM 204-205 H 6
Kombongou = Kondio o BF 204-205 E 3
Koméayo o CI 202-203 G 6
Kome Island ⌒ EAT 212-213 D 5
Komenda o GH 202-203 K 7
Komering ~ RI 162-163 F 6
Komfane ~ RI 166-167 H 4
Komga o ZA 220-221 H 6
Komi = Komi, Respublika □ RUS 96-97 G 1
Komin-Yanga o BF 202-203 L 4
Komi-Permyak Autonomous District = Komi-Perm.avt.okrug □ RUS 96-97 H 3
Kommunarsk = Alčevs'k o UA 102-103 L 3
Kommunizma, pik ▲ TJ 136-137 N 5
Komo ~ G 210-211 C 3
Komo o PNG 183 B 4
Komodimini o RMM 202-203 G 3
Komodo o RI 168 D 7
Komodo, Pulau ⌒ RI 168 D 7
Komodo National Park ⊥ ••• RI 168 D 7
Komodou o RG 202-203 F 5
Komono o RCB 210-211 D 5
Komoran, Pulau ⌒ RI 166-167 K 6
Komorane o YU 100-101 H 3
Komoro o J 152-153 H 6
Komosi o ZRE 206-207 D 6
Komotini o GR 100-101 K 4
Kompa o DY 204-205 E 2
Kompiam o PNG 183 B 3
Komponaone, Pulau ⌒ RI 164-165 H 6
Kompot o RI 164-165 J 3
Komrat = Comrat o MD 102-103 F 4
Komsberg ▲ ZA 220-221 E 6
Komsomol o KA (AKT) 126-127 O 2
Komsomol o KA (KST) 124-125 B 3
Komsomolabad o TJ 136-137 M 5
Komsomol cyganaky ≈ 126-127 K 5
Komsomolec, ostrov ⌒ RUS 108-109 Z 1
Komsomol'sk ☆ • RUS 94-95 R 3
Komsomol'sk, Ustjurtdagi o US 136-137 F 2
Komsomol'skij o RUS (CUK) 112-113 R 2
Komsomol'skij o RUS (HMN) 114-115 G 4
Komsomol'skij o RUS (KAR) 88-89 M 4
Komsomol'skij o RUS (KLM)126-127 G 5
Komsomol'skij o RUS (KOM) 108-109 K 8
Komsomol'skij o RUS (MOR) 96-97 D 6
Komsomol'skij zapovednik ⊥ RUS 122-123 G 3
Komsomol'sk-na-Amure ☆ RUS 122-123 G 3
Komsomol'sk na Amure = Komsomol'sk-na-Amure ☆ RUS 122-123 G 3
Komsomol'sk-na-Pečore o RUS 114-115 D 3
Komsomol'skoj Pravdy, ostrova ⌒ RUS 108-109 g 3
Kŏmun Do ⌒ ROK 150-151 F 11
Kon o CAM 204-205 J 6
Kŏn ~ KA 124-125 F 4
Kona o RMM 202-203 J 2
Kona o RN 198-199 D 6
Kona o WAN 204-205 J 4
Kona = Kailua o USA (HI) 288 K 5
Kona Coast ⌒ USA (HI) 288 K 5
Konakovo ☆ RUS 94-95 P 3
Konanmoukro o CI 202-203 H 6
Konar □ AFG 136-137 M 7
Konar, Daryā-ye ~ AFG 138-139 C 2
Konārak o ••• IND 142-143 E 6
Konārak o IR 134-135 J 6
Konar-e Ḫāṣṣ o AFG 138-139 C 2
Konār Tahte o IR 134-135 E 4
Konawa o USA (OK) 264-265 H 4
Konaweha ~ RI 164-165 G 5
Konda o RI 166-167 F 2
Konda ~ RUS 114-115 H 4
Konda ~ RUS 114-115 K 5
Konda ~ RUS 118-119 F 9
Kondagaon o IND 142-143 B 6
Kondakovskaja vozvyšennost' ▲ RUS 110-111 b 4
Kondan, ozero ○ RUS 114-115 K 6
Konde o EAT 212-213 G 6
Kondembaia o WAL 202-203 E 5
Kondinin o AUS 176-177 E 6
Kondinskaja nizmennost' ⌒ RUS 114-115 H 4
Kondinskoe ☆ RUS 114-115 J 5
Kondio = Kombongou o BF 204-205 E 3
Kondoa o EAT 212-213 E 6
Kondoma ~ RUS 124-125 Q 2
Kondopoga ☆ RUS 88-89 N 5
Kondostrov ⌒ RUS 88-89 O 4
Kondratovskaja o RUS 88-89 R 5
Kondromo ~ RUS 116-117 G 4
Kondrovo ☆ RUS 94-95 O 4
Kondue o ZRE 210-211 J 6
Konduga o WAN 204-205 K 3
Konduj-Muhor o RUS 118-119 F 9
Kondyreva ~ RUS 112-113 O 5
Konecbor o RUS 114-115 D 2
Konecbor o RUS (KOM) 88-89 Y 4
Koneng o RI 162-163 B 2
Konėnmyveem ~ RUS 112-113 V 3
Konergino o RUS 112-113 V 4
Köneürgenč ☆ TM 136-137 F 3
Konevaam ~ RUS 112-113 P 2
Konevo o RUS 88-89 P 5
Kong o CAM 204-205 K 6
Kong o • CI 202-203 H 5
Kŏng ~ K 158-159 J 4
Kong, Bandar-e o IR 134-135 F 5
Kongakut River ~ USA 20-21 U 2
Kongasso o CI 202-203 G 6
Kongbeng Caves • RI 164-165 E 3
Kongbo o RCA 206-207 E 6
Kong Christian IX Land ⩝ GRØ 28-29 V 3
Kong Christian X Land ⩝ GRØ 26-27 k 7
Kong Dans Halvø ⌒ GRØ 28-29 U 5
Kongelai o EAK 212-213 E 3
Kong Frederik IX Land ⩝ GRØ 28-29 P 3
Kong Frederik VIII Land ⩝ GRØ 26-27 m 5
Kong Frederik VI Kyst ⩝ GRØ 28-29 T 6
Kong Fu • VRC 154-155 K 4
Konginskij hrebet ▲ RUS 112-113 K 4
Kong Karls Land ⌒ N 84-85 P 3
Kong Leopold og Dronning Astrid land ⩝ ARK 16 F 9
Kongola o NAM 218-219 B 3
Kongolo o ZRE 210-211 L 6
Kongor o LB 202-203 E 6
Kongor o SUD 206-207 K 5
Kong Oscar Fjord ≈ 26-27 n 7
Kongoussi o BF 202-203 K 3
Kongsberg ☆ N 86-87 D 7
Kongsfjorden ≈ 84-85 G 3
Kongsøya ⌒ N 84-85 Q 3
Kongsvinger ☆ • N 86-87 F 6
Kongtongshan • VRC 154-155 E 4
Kongur Shan ▲ VRC 146-147 B 6
Kongwa o EAT 214-215 J 4
Kong Wilhelm Land ⩝ GRØ 26-27 o 6
Koni o ZRE 214-215 D 6
Koni, poluostrov ⌒ RUS 120-121 O 4
Konig, Cape ▲ CDN 24-25 g 6
Königgrätz = Hradec Králové o CZ 92-93 N 3
Konimeh ☆ US 136-137 J 4
Konin ☆ • PL 92-93 P 2
Konin ~ RUS 122-123 G 2
Konina o RMM 202-203 G 3
Konjed Jān o IR 134-135 D 2
Konka ~ UA 102-103 K 4
Könkämäälven ~ S 86-87 K 2
Könkämäeno ~ FIN 88-89 F 2
Konkan ~ IND 138-139 D 9
Konkče, Daryā-ye ~ AFG 136-137 L 6
Konkiep ~ NAM 220-221 C 3
Konko o ZRE 214-215 D 6
Konkoma o ETH 208-209 D 6
Konkouré o RG (KIN) 202-203 D 4
Konkouré ~ RG 202-203 D 4
Kon'kovaja ~ RUS 112-113 K 2
Kon'kovaja, Bol'šaja ~ RUS 112-113 J 2
Konkudera ~ RUS 118-119 F 7
Konkwesso o WAN 204-205 F 3
Konnūr o IND 140-141 F 2
Konobougou o RMM 202-203 G 3
Konogogo o PNG 183 G 2
Konololo o ZRE 210-211 K 3
Konomerume = Donderkamp o SME 62-63 F 3
Konončan ~ RUS 118-119 H 3
Kononda ~ RUS 116-117 M 3
Konongo o GH 202-203 K 6
Konos o PNG 183 F 2
Konoša o RUS 94-95 R 1
Kōnosu o J 152-153 H 6
Konotop o UA 102-103 H 2
Kon Plong o VN 158-159 K 3
Konqi He ~ VRC 146-147 G 5
Konsankoro o RG 202-203 F 5
Konséguéla o RMM 202-203 H 3
Końskie o • PL 92-93 Q 3
Konso o ETH 208-209 C 6
Konstantina, mys ▲ RUS 108-109 N 3
Konstantinopel = İstanbul ☆ ••• TR 128-129 C 2
Konstantinovka ☆ RUS 122-123 B 4
Konstantinovsk o RUS 102-103 M 4
Konstanz o • D 92-93 K 5
Konta o IND 142-143 B 7
Kontagora o WAN 204-205 F 3
Kontagora, River ~ WAN 204-205 F 3
Kontcha o CAM 204-205 K 5
Kontinemo, Área Indígena ⩝ BR 68-69 B 4
Kontiolahti o FIN 88-89 K 5
Kontiomäki o FIN 88-89 K 4
Kontubek o US 136-137 F 2
Kon Tum o VN 158-159 K 3
Konus, gora ▲ RUS (CUK) 112-113 U 3
Konus, gora ▲ RUS (HBR) 120-121 D 5
Konus, ostrov ⌒ RUS 120-121 U 3
Konušin, mys ▲ RUS 88-89 R 3
Konya ☆ •• TR 128-129 E 4
Konza o EAK 212-213 F 4
Konžakovskij Kamen', gora ▲ RUS 114-115 E 5
Konzanso o RMM 202-203 H 4
Konzi ~ ZRE 210-211 F 6
Koobi Fora ∴ • EAK 212-213 F 1
Koocanusa, Lake ○ USA (MT) 250-251 D 3
Koodnanie, Lake ○ AUS 178-179 E 4
Kookooligit Mountains ▲ USA 20-21 E 5
Kookynie o AUS 176-177 F 4
Koolatah o AUS 174-175 G 4
Koolau Range ▲ USA (HI) 288 G 3
Koolen', ozero ○ RUS 112-113 Z 4
Kooline o AUS 172-173 C 7
Koolkootinnie, Lake ○ AUS 178-179 D 4
Koolpinyah o AUS 172-173 K 2
Koolyanobbing o • AUS 176-177 E 5
Koombooloomba o AUS 174-175 H 5
Koonalda Cave • AUS 176-177 K 5
Koondoo o AUS 178-179 H 3
Koongie Park o AUS 172-173 H 5
Koopmansfontein o ZA 220-221 G 4
Koor o RI 166-167 G 2
Koorawatha o AUS 180-181 K 3
Koorda o AUS 176-177 D 5
Koordarrie o AUS 172-173 B 7
Koosharem o USA (UT) 254-255 D 5
Kooskia o USA (ID) 250-251 D 5
Kootenai Indian Reservation ⩝ USA (ID) 250-251 C 3
Kootenai River ~ USA (MT) 250-251 D 3
Kootenay Bay o CDN (BC) 230-231 N 4
Kootenay Indian Reserve ⩝ CDN (BC) 230-231 O 4
Kootenay Lake ○ CDN (BC) 230-231 N 4
Kootenay National Park ⊥ CDN (BC) 230-231 N 2
Kootenay River ~ CDN (BC) 230-231 O 3
Koo Wee Rup o AUS 180-181 H 5
Koozata Lagoon ≈ 20-21 E 5
Kopa o KA 146-147 B 4
Kopa o Z 214-215 F 6
Kopang o RI 168 C 7
Kopanzu o BF 202-203 F 6
Kopaonik ▲ YU 100-101 G 3
Kopargo o DY 202-203 L 5
Kópasker o IS 86-87 e 1
Kopasor, köl ○ KA 126-127 N 4
Kópavogur o IS 86-87 c 2
Ko Payang ⌒ THA 158-159 D 6
Kopbirlik o KA 124-125 K 5
Kopé, Mont ▲ CI 202-203 G 7
Kopejsk o RUS 96-97 M 6
Kopeng o RI 168 D 3
Koper o SLO 100-101 D 2
Kopervik o N 86-87 B 7
Kop'evo o RUS 114-115 U 7
Kop Geçidi ▲ TR 128-129 J 2
Ko Phangan o THA 158-159 E 6
Ko Phangan ⌒ THA 158-159 E 6
Ko Phi ⌒ THA 158-159 E 7
Ko Phra Thong ⌒ MYA 158-159 E 6
Ko Phuket ⌒ •• THA 158-159 E 7
Kopi, Ugol'nye o RUS 112-113 T 4
Kopiago o PNG 183 B 3
Köping ☆ • S 86-87 G 7
Kopingué o CI 202-203 J 5
Koporokendié-Na o RMM 202-203 J 2
Koppa o IND 140-141 F 4
Koppal o IND 140-141 G 3
Koppang ☆ N 86-87 E 6
Kopparberg o S 86-87 G 7
Koppe Dāġ ▲ IR 136-137 E 5
Kopperamanna Bore o AUS 178-179 E 5
Koppi o RUS 122-123 J 4
Koppies o ZA 220-221 H 3
Koppieskraalpan ○ ZA 220-221 E 3
Koprivnica o HR 100-101 F 1
Köprüçay ~ TR 128-129 D 4
Kor, Rūd-e ~ IR 134-135 E 4
Ko Ra ⌒ THA 158-159 E 6
Korab ▲ AL 100-101 H 4
Korabavur pastligi ⩝ US 136-137 E 3
Korača o RUS 102-103 K 2
Ko Racha Noi ⌒ THA 158-159 E 7
Ko Racha Yai ⌒ THA 158-159 E 7
K'orahē o ETH 208-209 G 5
Korakata cuķurligi ⩝ US 136-137 J 4
Korakŭlka ⩝ US 136-137 E 3
Kora National Park ⊥ EAK 212-213 G 4
Korangal o IND 140-141 G 2
Korannaberg ▲ ZA 220-221 F 3
Korān-o-Monğān o AFG 136-137 M 6
Koraon o IND 142-143 C 3
Koraput o IND 142-143 C 6
Korasa o SOL 184 I c 2
Koratagere o IND 140-141 G 4
Ko Rawi ⌒ THA 158-159 E 7
Korbėndja, hrebet ▲ RUS 112-113 K 5
Korbeniči o RUS 94-95 O 1
Korbol o TCH 206-207 C 4
Korbol, Bahr ~ TCH 206-207 C 3
Korbu, Gunung ▲ MAL 162-163 D 2
Korbunčana ~ RUS 116-117 L 3
Korçë ☆ •• AL 100-101 H 4
Korčula o • HR 100-101 F 3
Korčula ⌒ HR 100-101 F 3
Korda o IND 138-139 C 8
Kordestān □ IR 128-129 M 5
Kordié o BF 202-203 J 3
Kord-Kuy o IR 136-137 D 6
Kord Myriem, Hassi < DZ 188-189 K 6
Kordofan = Kurdufān ⩝ SUD 200-201 D 6
Kore o RI 168 D 7
Korea Bay ≈ 150-151 D 8
Korean Folk Village • ROK 150-151 F 9
Koreare o RI 166-167 F 5
Korea Strait ≈ 152-153 C 8
Korec' o UA 102-103 E 2
Korem o ETH 200-201 J 6
Korémairwa o RN 204-205 E 2
Korenevo o RUS 102-103 J 2
Korenovsk o RUS 102-103 L 5
Korepino o RUS 114-115 D 4
Korf o RUS 120-121 V 3
Korfa, zaliv ○ RUS 120-121 V 3
Korgalžyn ☆ KA 124-125 G 3
Korgas o VRC 146-147 E 3
Korgen o N 86-87 F 3
Korgom o RN 198-199 D 6
Korhogo ☆ • CI 202-203 H 5
Koribundu o WAL 202-203 E 6
Korientze o RMM 202-203 J 2
Korim o RI 166-167 J 2
Korinthiakós Kólpos ≈ 100-101 J 5
Kórinthos o GR 100-101 J 6
Korioume o RMM 196-197 J 6
Koripobi o PNG 184 I b 2
Kõris-hegy ▲ • H 92-93 O 5
Korissía o GR 100-101 K 6
Kōriyama o J 152-153 J 6
Korizo, Passe de ▲ TCH 192-193 F 6
Korjaki o RUS 120-121 S 7
Korjakskaja Sopka, vulkan ▲ RUS 120-121 S 7
Korjažma ☆ RUS 88-89 T 6
Korkodon o RUS (MAG) 112-113 H 4
Korkodon ~ RUS 112-113 J 5
Korkodonskij hrebet ▲ RUS 112-113 J 4
Korkut ☆ TR 128-129 J 3
Korkuteli ☆ TR 128-129 D 4
Korla o VRC 146-147 H 5
Korliki o RUS 114-115 R 4
Kormak o CDN (ONT) 236-237 F 5
Kormakitis, Cape ▲ TR 128-129 E 5
Kornake o RN 198-199 C 5
Kornati ⌒ HR 100-101 E 3
Korneevka o KA 124-125 J 3
Kórnik o • PL 92-93 O 2
Koro o CI 202-203 G 5
Koro ⌒ FJI 184 III b 2
Koro o RMM 202-203 J 2
Koroba o PNG 183 B 3
Koroc, Rivière ~ CDN 36-37 R 5
Korodiga o EAT 212-213 F 6
Korodziba o RB 218-219 D 4
Köroğlu Dağları ▲ TR 128-129 D 2
Köroğlu Tepe ▲ TR 128-129 D 2
Korogwe o EAT 212-213 G 6
Korohane o RN 198-199 C 5
Koroit o AUS 180-181 G 5
Korolevu o FJI 184 III a 3
Korom, Bahr ~ TCH 206-207 D 3
Koronadal o RP 160-161 F 9
Korondougou o CI 202-203 G 5
Koronga o RMM 202-203 G 2
Koronga, Mont ▲ RT 202-203 L 5
Koróni o GR 100-101 H 6
Korónia, Límni ○ GR 100-101 J 4
Korontière o DY 202-203 L 4
Koror ★ PAL (CRO) 13 E 2
Körös ~ H 92-93 Q 5
Koro Sea ≈ 184 III b 2
Korosten' o UA 102-103 F 2
Korostyšiv o UA 102-103 F 2
Korotaiha ~ RUS 108-109 K 7
Korotčaevo o RUS 114-115 P 2
Koro Toro o TCH 198-199 J 4
Korovin Island ⌒ USA 22-23 Q 5
Korovin Volcan ▲ USA 22-23 J 6
Korovou o FJI 184 III b 2
Korovou o SOL 184 I b 2
Korpilahti o FIN 88-89 H 5
Korpun o PNG 183 G 3
Korsakow o RUS 122-123 K 5
Korsimoro o BF 202-203 K 3
Korskrogen o S 86-87 G 6
Korsnäs o FIN 88-89 F 5
Korsør o DK 86-87 E 9
Koršunovo o RUS 118-119 E 6
Kortala o SUD 200-201 E 6
Kortkeros o RUS 96-97 G 3
Kortrijk o B 92-93 G 3
Korumburra o • AUS 180-181 H 5
Korup, Park National de ⊥ CAM 204-205 H 6
korvonsaroj Raboti Malik • US 136-137 J 4
Korwai o IND 138-139 G 7
Koryak Autonomous District = Korjakskij avtonomnyj okrug □ RUS 112-113 N 5
Koryťky ~ RUS 108-109 T 8
Kós o •• GR 100-101 L 6
Kós ⌒ GR 100-101 L 6
Kosa o ETH 208-209 C 5
Kosa ☆ RUS 96-97 J 4
kosa Arabats'ka Strilka ⌒ UA 102-103 J 4
kosa Byr'učyj Ostriv ⌒ UA 102-103 J 4
Koš-Agač o RUS 124-125 Q 3
Koš-Agač ☆ RUS (GOR) 124-125 Q 4
Kosaja Gora o • RUS 94-95 P 4
Kosa-Mèèčkyn, ostrov ⌒ RUS 112-113 V 4
Ko Samet National Park • THA 158-159 F 4
Ko Samui ⌒ •• THA 158-159 F 6
Kosbŭlak sor ⩝ KA 126-127 M 5
Kościan o • PL 92-93 O 2
Kościerzyna o • PL 92-93 O 1
Kosciusko o USA (MS) 268-269 L 3
Kosciusko, Mount ▲ AUS 180-181 K 4
Kosciusko Island ⌒ USA 32-33 D 3
Kosciusko National Park ⊥ AUS 180-181 K 4
Kosdäulet, kum ⩝ KA 96-97 F 10
Koš-Dĕbĕ o KS 146-147 B 5
Kose o •• EST 94-95 J 2
Köse ☆ TR 128-129 H 2
Köse Dağları ▲ TR 128-129 G 2
Koses ~ RUS 114-115 R 4
Kosha o SUD 200-201 E 2
Köshetau = Kökšetau ☆ KA 124-125 F 2
Koshi o ZRE 210-211 G 6
Koshikishima-rettō ⌒ J 152-153 C 9
Kosibaai-natuurreservaat ⊥ ZA 220-221 L 3
Kosi Bay ≈ 220-221 L 3
Ko Si Boya ⌒ THA 158-159 E 7
Košice o SK 92-93 Q 4
Košim ~ KA 96-97 G 9
Kosimeer ○ ZA 220-221 L 3
Ko Similan ⌒ THA 158-159 D 6
Kosi Reservoir < NEP 144-145 F 7
Kosistyj o RUS 110-111 G 3
Kosjerić o YU 100-101 G 2
Kos'ju ~ RUS 108-109 H 8
Koskaecodde Lake ○ CDN (NFL) 242-243 N 5
Koškarköl', köli ○ KA 124-125 M 5
Koš-Kohne o AFG 134-135 K 1
Koški ☆ RUS 96-97 G 6
Koskol o KA 124-125 E 4
Koslan o RUS 88-89 U 5
Kosma ~ RUS 88-89 U 4
Kosma ~ RUS 88-89 U 3
Kosminskij Kamen' ▲ RUS 88-89 U 3
Kosminskoe, ozero ○ RUS 88-89 U 3
Košoba o TM 136-137 D 4
Kosong o DVR 150-151 G 8
Kosovo Polje ⌒ YU 100-101 H 3
Kosovska Mitrovica o • YU 100-101 H 3
Kosse o USA (TX) 266-267 L 2
Kosso o CI 202-203 H 7
Kossou, Lac de < CI 202-203 H 6
Kossuth o USA (MS) 268-269 M 2
Kósta o GR 100-101 J 6
Kostanaj ☆ KA 124-125 C 2
Koster o ZA 220-221 H 2
Kostinbrod o BG 102-103 C 6
Kostin Nos, mys ▲ RUS 108-109 E 6
Kostin Šar, proliv ○ RUS 108-109 E 6
Kostomukša o RUS 88-89 L 4
Kostopil' o UA 102-103 E 2
Kostroma o RUS 120-121 U 4
Kostroma ☆ • RUS (KOS) 94-95 R 3
Kostroma ~ RUS 94-95 R 2
Kostrzyn o • PL 92-93 N 2
Kostyantynivka = Južnoukrains'k o UA 102-103 K 3
Kosubosu o WAN 204-205 E 4
Kosubuke o ZRE 210-211 J 6
Ko Surin Nua ⌒ THA 158-159 D 6
Ko Surin Tai ⌒ THA 158-159 D 6
Kos'va ~ RUS 96-97 K 4
Kos'va ~ RUS 114-115 E 5
Kos'va, Bol'šaja ~ RUS 114-115 E 5
Kosvinskij Kamen', gora ▲ RUS 114-115 E 5
Koszalin ☆ • PL 92-93 O 1
Kőszeg o •• H 92-93 O 5
Kota o IND (MAP) 142-143 C 4
Kota o IND (RAJ) 138-139 E 7
Kota, Cascades de la ~ • DY 202-203 L 4
Kotaagung o RI 162-163 F 7
Kotabangun o RI 164-165 E 4
Kotabaru o RI (KSE) 164-165 E 5
Kotabaru o RI (RIA) 162-163 D 5
Kota Belud o MAL 160-161 B 9
Kota Bharu o • MAL 162-163 E 2
Kota Bumi o RI 162-163 F 7
Kot Addu o PK 138-139 C 4
Kotagayah o RI 162-163 F 7
Kotagede o RI 168 D 3
Kota Kinabalu ☆ • MAL 160-161 B 10
Kōtal-e Mollā Yā'qūb ▲ AFG 134-135 M 1
Kota Lenggong o MAL 162-163 D 2
Kotamangalam o IND 140-141 G 5
Kota Marudu o MAL 160-161 B 9
Kotamobagu o RI 164-165 J 3
Kotanopan o RI 162-163 C 4
Ko Tao ⌒ THA 158-159 E 5
Kotapinang o RI 162-163 D 4
Ko Tarutao ⌒ THA 158-159 E 7
Kota Tinggi o • MAL 162-163 E 4
Kotawaringin Teluk ≈ 162-163 J 6
Kotcho Lake ○ CDN 30-31 J 6
Kotcho River ~ CDN 30-31 J 6
Kot Chutta o PK 138-139 C 4
Kot Diji o •• PK 138-139 B 6
Koteľnič o RUS 96-97 F 4
Koteľnikovo o RUS 102-103 N 4
Koteľnyj, ostrov ⌒ RUS 110-111 V 2
Koteľva o UA 102-103 J 2
Kotenko o RUS 110-111 a 4
Kotera ~ RUS 118-119 F 8

348 Kŏch'ang — Kotera

Kotiari ○ SN 202-203 D 3
Kotido ○ EAU 212-213 E 2
Kotira ○ PK 134-135 M 5
Kotjukan ∼ RUS 108-109 f 6
Kotjukan ∼ RUS 110-111 G 4
Kotka ☆ FIN 88-89 J 6
Kot Kapūra ○ IND 138-139 E 4
Kotla Branch ∼ IND 138-139 E 4
Kotlas ☆ RUS 88-89 T 6
Kotlik ○ USA 20-21 J 5
Kot Mūmin ○ PK 138-139 D 3
Koto ○ CAM 204-205 H 6
Kotobi ○ CI 202-203 H 6
Kotongoro II ○ TCH 206-207 D 4
Koton-Karifi ○ WAN 204-205 G 4
Koton-Koro ○ WAN 204-205 F 3
Kotopounga ○ DY 202-203 L 4
Kotor ○ YU 100-101 G 3
Kotor Varoš ○ BIH 100-101 F 2
Kotouba ○ CI 202-203 J 5
Kotoula ○ BF 202-203 G 4
Kotovo ○ RUS 96-97 D 8
Kotovsk ○ RUS 94-95 R 5
Kotovs'k ☆ UA 102-103 F 4
Kotovsk = Hîncești ☆ MD 102-103 F 4
Kot Pūtli ○ IND 138-139 F 6
Kotri ∼ IND 142-143 B 6
Kotri ○ PK 138-139 B 7
Kot Shākir ○ PK 138-139 D 4
Kottagūdem ○ IND 142-143 B 7
Kottakota ○ IND 140-141 H 4
Kottayam ○• IND 140-141 G 6
Kotto ∼ RCA 206-207 F 5
Kottūru ○ IND 140-141 G 3
Kotu ⌒ TON 184 IV a 1
Kotu Group ⌒ TON 184 IV a 1
Kotuj ∼ RUS 108-109 e 6
Kotuj ∼ RUS 108-109 a 7
Kotuj ∼ RUS 116-117 L 2
Kotujkan ∼ RUS 116-117 J 2
Koturdepe ○ TM 136-137 C 5
Kotwa ○ ZW 218-219 G 3
Kotzebue ○ USA 20-21 J 3
Kotzebue Sound ≈ 20-21 J 3
Kouadiokro, Ananda- ○ CI 202-203 H 6
Kouadio-Prikro ○ CI 202-203 H 6
Kouaga ∼ RMM 202-203 E 2
Kouakourou ○ RMM 202-203 H 2
Kouandé ○ DY 202-203 L 4
Kouandikro ○ CI 202-203 H 6
Kouango ○ RCA 206-207 D 6
Kouankan ○ RG 202-203 F 5
Kouassikro ○ CI 202-203 J 6
Kouba Olanga ○ TCH 198-199 J 5
Koubia ○ RG 202-203 E 4
Koubo Abou Azraq ○ TCH 206-207 E 3
Kouchibouguac National Park ⊥ CDN (NB) 240-241 L 4
Koudou, Cascades de ∼• DY 204-205 E 3
Koudougou ☆ BF 202-203 J 3
Kouéré ○ BF 202-203 J 4
Koufey < RN 198-199 F 5
Kouffo ∼ DY 202-203 L 6
Kouga ∼ ZA 220-221 F 6
Kougaberge ▲ ZA 220-221 F 6
Kougnohou ○ RT 202-203 L 6
Kougouleu ○ G 210-211 B 3
Kouibli ○ CI 202-203 G 6
Kouif, El ○ TN 190-191 G 3
Kouilou ▫ RCB 210-211 C 5
Kouilou ∼ RCB 210-211 C 6
Kouka ○ BF 202-203 H 4
Koukdjuak, Great Plain of the ⩦ CDN 28-29 D 3
Koukdjuak River ∼ CDN 28-29 D 3
Kouki ○ RCA 206-207 C 5
Kouklia ○ CY 128-129 E 5
Koukou ○ TCH 206-207 E 3
Koukourou ○ RCA 206-207 E 5
Koukourou ∼ RCA 206-207 E 5
Koukourou-Bamingui, Réserve de faune du ⊥ RCA 206-207 D 5
Koula ○ RMM 202-203 G 3
Koulamoutou ☆ G 210-211 D 4
Koulbo ○ TCH 198-199 K 6
Koulbous ○ SUD 198-199 L 5
Koulé ○ RG 202-203 F 5
Koulé Ekou ▲ DY 204-205 E 4
Koulikoro ○ RMM 202-203 G 3
Koulou ○ RN 204-205 E 2
Koulouguidi ○ RMM 202-203 E 3
Koulountou ∼ SN 202-203 D 3
Koulouoko ∼ BF 202-203 K 3
Koum ○ CAM 206-207 B 4
Kouma ○ RCA 206-207 D 5
Kouma ∼ RCA 206-207 D 6
Koumameyong ○ G 210-211 C 3
Koumantou ○ RMM 202-203 G 4
Koumba ∼ RG 202-203 D 4
Koumbal ○ RCA 206-207 F 4
Koumbala ○ RCA (Bam) 206-207 E 4
Koumbala ∼ RCA 206-207 E 4
Koumbia ○ BF 202-203 J 4
Koumbia ○ RG 202-203 D 4
Koumbi Saleh ∴• RIM 196-197 G 7
Koumbo ○ BF 202-203 K 4
Koumbri ○ BF 202-203 J 3
Koumia ○ RMM 202-203 H 3
Koumogo ○ TCH 206-207 D 4
Koumongou ○ RT 202-203 L 4
Koumongou ∼ RT 202-203 L 4
Koumou ∼ RCA 206-207 F 4
Koumpentoum ○ SN 202-203 C 2
Koumra ○ TCH 206-207 C 4
Kounahiri ○ CI 202-203 H 6
Koundara ○ RG 202-203 D 3
Koundé ○ RCA 206-207 B 5
Koundessong ○ CAM 210-211 D 2
Koundian ○ RMM 202-203 E 3
Koundian ○ RN 202-203 F 4
Koundjourou ○ TCH 198-199 J 6
Koundou ○ RG 202-203 E 5
Koundougou ○ BF 202-203 H 4
Koun-Fao ○ CI 202-203 J 6
Koungheul ○ SN 202-203 C 3
Koungouri ○ TCH 206-207 D 3
Kouniana ○ RMM 202-203 H 3
Kounkané ○ SN 202-203 C 3
Kounradskij ○ KA 124-125 J 5
Kountouata ○ SN 202-203 C 3
Kountze ○ USA (TX) 268-269 F 6
Kouoro ○ RMM 202-203 H 3
Koup ○ ZA 220-221 E 6
Koupé, Mont ▲ CAM 204-205 H 6
Koupéla ○ BF 202-203 K 3
Kouraï ∼ RG 202-203 F 5
Kouraqué ○ RMM 202-203 E 3
Kourémalé ○ RMM 202-203 F 4
Kourgou ○ TCH 206-207 C 3
Kourgui ○ CAM 206-207 B 3
Kouri ○ RMM 202-203 H 3
Kouri Kouri ○ TCH 198-199 H 6
Kourion • CY 128-129 E 5
Kourkéto ○ RMM 202-203 E 2
Kourou ○ F 62-63 H 3
Kourouba ▲ CI 202-203 G 5
Kourouba ○ RMM 202-203 F 3
Koûroudjél ○ RIM 196-197 E 6
Kourougui ∼ BF 202-203 J 3
Kouroukoto ○ RMM 202-203 E 3
Kourouma ○ BF 202-203 H 4
Kourouninnkoto ○ RMM 202-203 F 3
Kouroussa ○ RG 202-203 F 4
Kourtiagou, Réserve de la ⊥ BF 202-203 L 4
Kous ○ NAM 220-221 C 1
Koussa Arma < RN 198-199 F 4
Koussanar ○ SN (SO) 202-203 C 3
Koussanar ∼ SN 202-203 D 2
Koussané ○ RMM 202-203 E 2
Koussane ○ SN 202-203 D 2
Kousseri ○ CAM 198-199 G 6
Koussi, Emi ▲ TCH 198-199 J 3
Koussountou ○ RT 202-203 L 5
Koutaba ○ CAM 204-205 J 6
Koutia Gaïdi ○ SN 202-203 D 2
Koutiala ○ RMM 202-203 H 3
Kouto ○ CI 202-203 G 5
Kouts ○ USA (IN) 274-275 L 3
Kouvola ○ FIN 88-89 J 6
Kouyou ∼ RCB 210-211 F 4
Kova ∼ RUS 116-117 K 6
Kovalam ○• IND 140-141 G 6
Kovalevka ○ KA 124-125 K 2
Kovancılar ☆ TR 128-129 H 3
Kovarzino ○ RUS 94-95 Q 1
Kovdor ○ RUS 88-89 L 3
Kovdozero ○ RUS 88-89 M 3
Kovel' ○ UA 102-103 D 2
Kovenskaja ∼ RUS 114-115 J 4
Kovernino ○ RUS 94-95 S 3
Kovero ○ FIN 88-89 L 5
Kovic, Rivière ∼ CDN 36-37 L 4
Kovik Bay ≈ 36-37 L 4
Kovillur ○ IND 140-141 G 6
Kovilpatti ○ IND 140-141 G 6
Kovin ○ YU 100-101 H 2
Kovkula ○ RUS 88-89 S 5
Kovran ○ RUS 120-121 R 5
Kovriga, gora ▲ RUS 88-89 U 3
Kovrov ☆ RUS 94-95 R 3
Kovūr ○ IND 140-141 H 3
Kovylkino ○ RUS 94-95 S 4
Kowanyama ✕ AUS 174-175 F 4
Kowares ○ NAM 216-217 C 9
Kowloon = Jiulong ○ HK 156-157 J 5
Kowyn's Pass ▲ ZA 220-221 K 2
Koya ○ WAN 198-199 C 6
Koyama ○ RG 202-203 F 6
Koyan, Tanjung ▲ RI 162-163 F 6
Ko Yao Yai ⌒ THA 158-159 E 7
Köyceğiz ☆ TR 128-129 C 4
Koyna Reservoir ○ IND 140-141 E 2
Koyuk ○ USA 20-21 K 4
Koyuk River ∼ USA 20-21 K 4
Koyukuk ○ USA 20-21 M 4
Koyukuk National Wildlife Refuge ⊥ USA 20-21 M 4
Koyukuk River ∼ USA 20-21 M 4
Koyvel'vèergyn ∼ RUS 112-113 V 2
Koza ○ CAM 204-205 K 3
Kožaköl ○ KA 124-125 F 3
Kozan ☆ TR 128-129 F 4
Kozáni ☆• GR 100-101 H 4
Kozel'sk ☆• RUS 94-95 O 4
Koževina, mys ▲ RUS 110-111 Z 2
Koževnikova, buhta ≈ 110-111 G 3
Koževnikovo ○ RUS 114-115 S 6
Kozhikode = Calicut ○• IND 140-141 F 5
Kozienice ○ PL 92-93 Q 3
Kožima ∼ RUS 116-117 G 6
Koźle, Kędzierzyn- ○• PL 92-93 P 3
Kozloduj ○ BG 102-103 C 6
Kozlova ○ RUS 116-117 M 8
Kozlova, mys ▲ RUS 120-121 T 6
Kozlovka ○ RUS 96-97 F 6
Kozluk ☆ TR 128-129 J 3
Koz'modem'jansk ○ RUS 96-97 E 5
Kozok darë ○ US 136-137 F 3
Kožozero ○ RUS 88-89 P 5
Kožuf ▲ MK 100-101 J 4
Kōzu-shima ⌒ J 152-153 H 7
Kožva ○ RUS 88-89 Y 4
Kožva ∼ RUS 88-89 X 4
Kožym ○ RUS 108-109 H 9
Kozyrevsk ○ RUS 120-121 S 5
Kozyrevskij hrebet ▲ RUS 120-121 S 6
Kpako ∼ DY 204-205 E 3
Kpakto ○ GH 202-203 K 5
Kpalbusi ○ GH 202-203 K 5
Kpalimé ○• RT 202-203 L 6
Kpandu ○ GH 202-203 L 6
Kpassa ∼ GH 202-203 L 5
Kpatinga ○ GH 202-203 K 5
Kpedze ○ GH 202-203 L 6
Kpèssi ○ RT 202-203 L 5
Kpèssi, Réserve de ⊥ RT 202-203 L 5
Kpété Béna ○ RT 202-203 L 6
Kpetoe ○ GH 202-203 L 6
Kpimé, Cascade de ∼ RT 202-203 L 6
Kpong ○ GH 202-203 L 6
Kpungan Pass ▲ MYA 142-143 K 2
Kraaifontein ○ ZA 220-221 D 6
Kraairivier ∼ ZA 220-221 H 5
Kraankuil ○ ZA 220-221 G 4
Krabbé ○ RA 78-79 J 4
Krabi ○ THA 158-159 E 6
Krâchéh ○ K 158-159 J 4
Krachi, Kete- ○ GH 202-203 K 6
Kracnooskil's'k vodoschovyšče < UA 102-103 K 3
Kragerø ☆ N 86-87 D 7
Kragujevac ○• YU 100-101 H 2
Krainij ○ RUS 110-111 X 4
Kraj Gorbatka ○ RUS 94-95 R 4
Krajište ▲ YU 100-101 J 3
Krajnij, ostrov ⌒ RUS 120-121 U 3
Krajnovka ○ RUS 126-127 G 6
Kraka hrebet ▲ RUS 96-97 K 7
Kraké ○ DY 204-205 E 5
Kraków ☆••• PL 92-93 P 3
Krakurom ○ GH 202-203 J 6
Krâlanh ○ K 158-159 G 4
Kralendijk ○ NL 60-61 G 1
Kraljevo ○ YU 100-101 H 3
Kramators'k ○ UA 102-103 K 3
Kramatorsk = Kramators'k ○ UA 102-103 K 3
Kramfors ○ S 86-87 H 5
Kranéa ○ GR 100-101 H 5
Kranidi ○ GR 100-101 J 6
Kranj ○ SLO 100-101 E 1
Kransfontein ○ ZA 220-221 J 4
Kranskop ○ ZA 220-221 K 4
Kranuan ○ THA 158-159 G 2
Kranzberg ○ NAM 216-217 C 10
Kraolandia, Área Indígena ✕ BR 68-69 E 6
Krapina ○ HR 100-101 E 1
Krapivinskij ☆ RUS 114-115 T 7
Krapivnaja ○ RUS 120-121 S 6
Krašeninnikova, mys ▲ RUS 120-121 U 4
Krasin, ostrov ⌒ RUS 108-109 a 3
Krasin, zaliv ≈ 112-113 U 1
Krasinka ○ RUS 114-115 U 6
Krasino ○ RUS 108-109 F 6
Kraskino ○ RUS 122-123 D 7
Krāslava ☆•• LV 94-95 K 4
Krasnaja Gorka ☆ RUS 96-97 K 6
Krasnaja Jaruga ○ RUS 102-103 J 2
Krasnaja Poljana ○ RUS 126-127 D 6
Krasnapolle ○ BY 94-95 M 5
Krasneno ○ RUS 112-113 S 4
Krasnij Luč = Krasnyj Luč ○ UA 102-103 L 3
Kraśnik ○ PL 92-93 R 3
Krasni Okny ☆ UA 102-103 F 4
Krasnoarmejsk ☆ KA 124-125 F 2
Krasnoarmejsk ○ RUS (SAR) 96-97 D 8
Krasnoarmejsk ☆ RUS (MOS) 94-95 Q 4
Krasnoarmejsk = Krasnoarmijs'k ○ UA 102-103 K 3
Krasnoarmejskaja ○ RUS 102-103 L 5
Krasnoarmejskij ○ RUS 112-113 Q 2
Krasnoarmejskoe ☆ RUS 96-97 G 7
Krasnoarmijs'k ○ UA 102-103 K 3
Krasnoborsk ○ RUS 88-89 S 6
Krasnodar ☆• RUS 102-103 L 5
Krasnodarskij kraj ▫ RUS 126-127 C 5
Krasnodon ○ UA 102-103 L 3
Krasnoe, ozero ○ RUS 112-113 S 4
Krasnoe Selo ○ RUS 94-95 M 2
Krasnoe Znamja ○ TM 136-137 H 6
Krasnoflotskie, ostrova ⌒ RUS 108-109 c 2
Krasnogorsk ○ RUS 122-123 K 4
Krasnogorskij ○ RUS (CEL) 96-97 M 6
Krasnogorskij ○ RUS (MAR) 96-97 F 5
Krasnogorskoe ☆ RUS 96-97 H 5
Krasnogvardejskij ○ US 136-137 K 5
Krasnoholm ○ RUS 96-97 J 8
Krasnohorivka ○ UA 102-103 K 3
Krasnohrad ○ UA 102-103 J 3
Krasnohvardijs'ke ☆ UA 102-103 J 5
Krasnoj Armii, proliv ≈ 108-109 Z 2
Krasnojarovo ○ RUS 122-123 C 3
Krasnojarsk ☆• RUS 116-117 F 7
Krasnojarskoe, vodohranilišče ○ RUS 116-117 E 8
Krasnokamensk ☆ RUS 118-119 J 10
Krasnokamsk ○ RUS 96-97 J 4
Krasnokutsk ☆ KA 124-125 J 2
Krasnomajskij ○ RUS 94-95 O 3
Krasnoperekops'k ☆• UA 102-103 H 5
Krasnopillja ○ UA 102-103 J 2
Krasnopol'e ○ RUS 122-123 K 4
Krasnoščel'e ○ RUS 88-89 O 3
Krasnosel'kup ○ RUS 114-115 R 2
Krasnoslobodsk ○ RUS (MOR) 94-95 S 4
Krasnoslobodsk ○ RUS (VLG) 96-97 D 9
Krasnotur'insk ○ RUS 114-115 F 5
Krasnoufimsk ☆ RUS 96-97 K 5
Krasnousol'skij ☆ RUS 96-97 K 7
Krasnova, gora ▲ RUS 122-123 K 4
Krasnovišersk ☆ RUS 114-115 D 4
Krasnovodsk = Türkmenbaši ☆ TM 136-137 C 4
Krasnovodskij zaliv ≈ 136-137 C 5
Krasnovodskij zapovednik ⊥ TM 136-137 C 5
Krasnovodskoe plato ▲ TM 136-137 C 4
Krasnoyarsk = Krasnojarsk ☆• RUS 116-117 F 7
Krasnoznamjans'kyj kanal < UA 102-103 H 4
Krasnye Barrikady ○ RUS 96-97 E 10
Krasnyj ○ RUS 102-103 K 5
Krasnyj Aul ○ KA 124-125 M 3
Krasnyj Holm ○ RUS 94-95 P 2
Krasnyj Jar ○ RUS (KMR) 114-115 T 7
Krasnyj Jar ○ RUS (OMS) 114-115 M 7
Krasnyj Jar ○ RUS (VLG) 96-97 D 8
Krasnyj Jar ☆ RUS (AST) 96-97 F 10
Krasnyj Jar ☆ RUS (SAM) 96-97 G 7
Krasnyj Kut ☆ RUS 96-97 E 8
Krasnyj Luč ○ UA 102-103 L 3
Krasnystaw ○ PL 92-93 R 3
Krasnyy Luch = Krasnyj Luč ○ UA 102-103 L 3
Krasuha ○ RUS 94-95 O 2
Kratke Range ▲ PNG 183 C 4
Kratovo ○• MK 100-101 J 3
Krau ○ RI 166-167 L 3
Krebs ○ USA (OK) 264-265 J 4
Krečetovo ○ RUS 94-95 Q 1
Krefeld ○ D 92-93 J 3
Kregbé ○ CI 202-203 J 6
Krekatok Island ⌒ USA 20-21 G 5
Kremenchuk = Kremenčuk ○ UA 102-103 H 3
Kremenčuc'ke vodoschovyšče < UA 102-103 H 3
Kremenčug = Kremenčuk ○ UA 102-103 H 3
Kremenčuk ○ UA 102-103 H 3
Kremenec' ○ UA 102-103 D 2
Kremenec'ki hory • UA 102-103 D 2
Kreminci ○ UA 102-103 D 3
Kreminna ○ UA 102-103 L 3
Kreml' • RUS 96-97 F 10
Kremlin ○ USA (MT) 250-251 J 3
Kremmling ○ USA (CO) 254-255 J 3
Krems an der Donau ○ A 92-93 N 4
Kremsier = Kroměříž ○ CZ 92-93 O 4
Krenicyna, vulkan ▲ RUS 122-123 Q 4
Krenitzin Islands ⌒ USA 22-23 O 6
Kreščenskoe ○ RUS 114-115 Q 7
Kresik Luway • RI 164-165 D 4
Kress ○ USA (TX) 264-265 C 4
Kresta, zaliv ≈ 112-113 V 4
Krestcy ☆ RUS 94-95 N 2
Krest-Hal'džaj ○ RUS 120-121 F 2
Krestjah ○ RUS 118-119 H 4
Krest'janskij ○ US 136-137 L 4
Krestovaja ○ RUS 118-119 F 6
Krestovaja, guba ○ RUS 108-109 F 4
Krestovaja Guba ○ RUS 108-109 F 4
Krestovka ○ RUS 88-89 W 3
Krestovoe ○ RUS 112-113 N 2
Krestovskij, mys ▲ RUS 112-113 L 1
Krestovskij, ostrov ⌒ RUS 112-113 L 1
Krestovyj, pereval ▲ GE 126-127 F 6
Krestovyj, mys ▲ RUS 122-123 S 3
Krestovyj, ostrov ⌒ RUS 110-111 c 4
Kresty ○ RUS 108-109 e 6
Kresty ○ RUS (KIR) 96-97 E 5
Kresty ○ RUS (Mos) 94-95 P 4
Kretinga ○ LT 94-95 G 4
Kreuzburg (Oberschlesien) = Kluczbork ○ PL 92-93 P 3
Kreuznach, Bad ○ D 92-93 J 4
Krėva ○ BY 94-95 K 4
Kriam ○ RI 168 E 3
Kribi ○• CAM 210-211 B 2
Kričal'skaja ∼ RUS 112-113 L 3
Krieger Mountains ▲ CDN 26-27 J 3
Kriel ○ ZA 220-221 J 3
Krigujgun, mys ▲ RUS 112-113 Z 4
Kril'on, mys ▲ RUS 122-123 K 6
Krim-Krim ○ TCH 206-207 B 4
Krishna ∼ IND 140-141 H 2
Krishnagiri ○ IND 140-141 H 4
Krishnarājānagara ○ IND 140-141 G 4
Krishnarajpet ○ IND 140-141 G 4
Kristiansand ☆ N 86-87 C 7
Kristianstad ○ S 86-87 G 8
Kristiansund ☆ N 86-87 C 5
Kristiinankaupunki = Kristinestad ○•• FIN 88-89 F 5
Kristinehamn ☆ S 86-87 G 7
Kristinestad ○•• FIN 88-89 F 5
Kristoffer Bay ≈ 24-25 U 1
Kriti ▫ GR 100-101 K 7
Kriti ⌒ GR 100-101 K 7
Kritiko Pelagos ≈ 100-101 K 6
Kriuša ○ RUS 96-97 F 5
Kriva Palanka ○ MK 100-101 J 3
Krivodol ○ BG 102-103 C 6
Krivoj Rog = Kryvyj Rih ○ UA 102-103 H 4
Krivošeino ☆ RUS 114-115 R 6
Krivyj Rih ○ UA 102-103 H 4
Križevci ○ HR 100-101 F 1
Krjučkovka ○ RUS 96-97 J 8
Krk ⌒ YU 100-101 E 2
Krka ∼ HR 100-101 F 2
Krkonoše ▲ CZ 92-93 N 3
Krkonošský národní park ⊥ CZ 92-93 N 3
Krohnwodoke ○ LB 202-203 G 7
Krokek ○ S 86-87 H 7
Krokodilrivier ∼ ZA 220-221 H 2
Krokom ○ S 86-87 G 5
Krokosua National Park ⊥ GH 202-203 J 6
Krókstjarðarnes ○ IS 86-87 c 2
Krolevec' ○ UA 102-103 H 2
Kroměříž ○ CZ 92-93 O 4
Kronau ○ CDN (SAS) 232-233 O 5
Kronborg Gletscher ⊂ GRØ 28-29 a 2
Krong Kup ○ VN 158-159 K 4
Krŏng Kaôh Kŏng ○ K 158-159 G 5
Krŏng Pa ○ VN 158-159 K 4
Kronkel ∼ RI 166-167 K 5
Kronockaja ∼ RUS 120-121 T 6
Kronockij, mys ▲ RUS 120-121 U 6
Kronockij, zaliv ≈ 120-121 U 6
Kronockij poluostrov ⌣ RUS 120-121 U 6
Kronockij zapovednik ⊥ RUS 120-121 T 6
Kronockoe, ozero ○ RUS 120-121 T 6
Kronprins Christian Land ⩦ GRØ 26-27 q 4
Kronprinsesse Mærtha land ⩦ ARK 16 F 35
Kronprins Olav land ⩦ ARK 16 G 5
Kronshtadt = Kronštadt ○ RUS 94-95 L 2
Kronštadt ○ RUS 94-95 L 2
Kroonstad ○ ZA 220-221 H 3
Kropačevo ○ RUS 96-97 K 6
Kropotkin ○ RUS 102-103 M 5
Krośniewice ○ PL 92-93 P 2
Krosno ☆• PL 92-93 Q 4
Krosno Odrzańskie ○ PL 92-93 N 2
Krotoschin = Krotoszyn ○ PL 92-93 O 3
Krotoszyn ○ PL 92-93 O 3
Krotz Springs ○ USA (LA) 268-269 J 6
Kroya ○ RI 168 C 3
Krško ○ SLO 100-101 E 2
Kručina ∼ RUS 118-119 G 10
Kruet ∼ RI 162-163 B 3
Kruger National Park ⊥•• ZA 218-219 F 6
Krugersdorp ○ ZA 220-221 H 3
Kruglyj, ostrov ⌒ RUS 108-109 V 4
Krui ○ RI 162-163 E 7
Kruidfontein ○ ZA 220-221 E 6
Kruis, Kaap = Cape Cross ▲ NAM 216-217 B 10
Krujë ☆•• AL 100-101 G 4
Krumau = Český Krumlov ○ CZ 92-93 N 4
Krumaye ○ RI 166-167 G 2
Krumë ○•• AL 100-101 H 3
Krumovgrad ○ BG 102-103 D 7
Krung Thep = Bangkok ○ THA 158-159 F 4
Krupanj ○ YU 100-101 G 2
Krusenstern, Cape ▲ USA 20-21 H 3
Kruševac ○• YU 100-101 H 3
Kruševo ○ MK 100-101 H 4
Krušné hory ▲ CZ 92-93 M 3
Krušovene ○ BG 102-103 D 6
Krutec ∼ RUS 96-97 D 7
Krutinka ☆ RUS 114-115 L 7
Krutiška ☆ RUS 124-125 M 2
Krutoberegovo ○ RUS 120-121 U 5
Krutogorova ∼ RUS 120-121 R 6
Krutoj ○ RUS 112-113 N 2
Kruzenšterna, proliv ≈ RUS 122-123 P 4
Kruzof Island ⌒ USA 32-33 B 3
Kryčav ☆ BY 94-95 M 5
Krydor ○ CDN (SAS) 232-233 L 3
Kryktytau hrebet ▲ RUS 96-97 L 7
Krylovo ○ RUS 94-95 G 4
Kryms'ki hory ▲ UA 102-103 H 5
Krynica ○• PL 92-93 Q 4
Kryve Ozero ☆ UA 102-103 G 4
Kryvyj Rih = Krivyj Rih ○ UA 102-103 H 4
'Ksan Indian Village •• CDN 32-33 G 4
Ksar Chellala ○ DZ 190-191 D 3
Ksar El Boukhari ○ DZ 190-191 D 3
Ksar El Hirane ○ DZ 190-191 D 4
Ksar Ghilane ○ TN 190-191 G 4
Ksel, Djebel ▲ DZ 190-191 C 4
Ksenskij ○ RUS 102-103 K 2
Kshwan Mountain ▲ CDN 32-33 F 4
Ksour, Monts des ▲ DZ 190-191 C 4
Ksour Essaf ○ TN 190-191 H 3
Ksour Jelidat ○ TN 190-191 H 4
Kstovo ○ RUS 96-97 D 5
Ktesiphon ∴•• IRQ 128-129 L 6
Kuah ○ MAL 162-163 C 2
Kuala ∼ RI 162-163 C 3
Kuala Baram ○ MAL 162-163 K 2
Kuala Belait ○ BRU 164-165 D 1
Kuala Berang ○ MAL 162-163 E 2
Kuala Dungun ○• MAL 162-163 E 2
Kuala Kangsar ○• MAL 162-163 D 2
Kualakapus ○ RI 164-165 D 5
Kuala Kerau ○ MAL 162-163 E 3
Kualakeriau ○ RI 162-163 K 4
Kuala Krai ○ MAL 162-163 E 2
Kuala Kubu Baharu ○ MAL 162-163 D 3
Kualalangsa ○ RI 162-163 C 2
Kuala Lipis ○• MAL 162-163 E 2
Kuala Lumpur ★•• MAL 162-163 D 3
Kualapembuang ○ RI 162-163 K 6
Kuala Penyu ○ MAL 160-161 A 10
Kuala Pilah ○ MAL 162-163 E 3
Kualapuu ○ USA (HI) 288 H 3
Kuala Selangor ○ MAL 162-163 D 3
Kualasimpang ○ RI 162-163 C 2
Kuala Tahan ○ MAL 162-163 E 2
Kualatanjung ○ RI 162-163 C 3
Kuala Tatau ○ MAL 162-163 K 3
Kuala Terengganu ☆• MAL 162-163 E 2
Kualatungkal ○ RI 162-163 E 5
Kuamut ○ MAL 160-161 B 10
Kuamut ∼ MAL 160-161 B 10
Kuancheng ○ VRC 154-155 L 1
Kuanda ∼ RUS 118-119 H 7
Kuandang ○ RI 164-165 H 3
Kuandian ○ VRC 150-151 E 7
Kuangfu ○ RC 156-157 M 5
Kuantan ☆•• MAL 162-163 E 3
Kuba, zaliv ○ RUS 110-111 O 3
Kuba-Aryta, ostrova ⌒ RUS 110-111 Q 3
Kubalah ∼ RUS 108-109 c 5
Kuban' ∼ RUS 102-103 M 5
Kuban' ∼ RUS 126-127 E 6
Kuban ∼ RUS 126-127 D 5
Kubārā ○ OM 132-133 K 2
Kubari, Mount ▲ PNG 183 C 3
Kubbi ○ SUD 206-207 G 3
Kubbum ○ SUD 206-207 G 3
Kubena ∼ RUS 94-95 R 1
Kubenskoe, ozero ○ RUS 94-95 Q 2
Kuberganja ○ RUS 110-111 Z 6
Kubkain ○ PNG 183 B 3
Kubli ○ WAN 204-205 F 3
Kubli Hill ▲ WAN 204-205 F 3
Kubokawa ○ J 152-153 E 8
Kūbonān ○ IR 134-135 G 3
Kubor Range ▲ PNG 183 C 4
Kubumesaai ○ RI 164-165 D 3
Kubuna ○ PNG 183 D 5
Kubupenelokan ○ RI 168 B 7
Kubutambahan ○ RI 168 B 7
Kūček, Rūd-e Zāb-e ∼ IRQ 128-129 L 4
Kūčesfahān ○ IR 128-129 N 4
Kučevo ○ YU 100-101 H 2
Kuchaiburi ○ IND 142-143 E 4
Kuchi ○ IND 140-141 F 2
Kuching ☆• MAL 162-163 J 4
Kuchino-Erabu-shima ⌒ J 152-153 D 9
Kuchino-shima ⌒ J 152-153 C 10
Kučukskoe, ozero ○ RUS 124-125 L 2
Kučurhan ∼ UA 102-103 F 4
Kuda ○ RI 162-163 K 4
Kuda ∼ RUS 116-117 M 9
Kudāl ○ IND 140-141 E 2
Kudan ○ WAN 204-205 G 3
Kudang ○ WAG 202-203 C 3
Kudani ○ GH 202-203 L 4
Kudat ○ MAL 160-161 B 9
Kudatini ○ IND 140-141 G 3
Kudayn ○ SUD 200-201 E 3
Kudene ○ RI 166-167 K 6
Kūderu ○ IND 140-141 G 3
Kudever' ○ RUS 94-95 L 3
Kudiakof Islands ⌒ USA 22-23 P 5
Kudialčaj ∼ AZ 128-129 N 2
Kudi-Boma ○ ZRE 210-211 D 6
Kudirkos Naumiestis ○•• LT 94-95 H 4
Kudjip ○ PNG 183 C 3
Kudligi ○ IND 140-141 G 3
Kudu ○ WAN 204-205 F 4
Kudu-Kjuël' ○ RUS 118-119 K 6
Kudus ○• RI 168 D 3
Kudymkar ☆ RUS 96-97 J 4
Kueda ☆ RUS 96-97 J 5
Kuedemane ○ RI 162-163 B 2
Kuee ○ USA (HI) 288 K 5
Kuėnga ∼ RUS 118-119 H 9
Kūfa, al- ☆ IRQ 128-129 L 6
Kufrah, Al ▫ LAR 192-193 J 5
Kufstein ○• A 92-93 M 5
Kugaluk River ∼ CDN 20-21 Z 2
Kugaluk River ∼ CDN 24-25 O 6
Kugaly ○ KA 124-125 L 6
Kuganavolok ○ RUS 88-89 O 5
Kugmallit Bay ≈ 20-21 Y 2
Kugong Island ⌒ CDN 36-37 K 6
Kugrua River ∼ USA 20-21 L 1
Kugruk River ∼ USA 20-21 J 4
Kugururok River ∼ USA 20-21 K 2
Kūhak ○ IR (SIS) 134-135 K 5
Kūhak ○ IR (SIS) 134-135 J 3
Kūhdašt ○ IR 134-135 B 2
Kūh-e Baḥūn ▲ IR 134-135 G 5
Kūh-e Binālūd ▲ IR 136-137 F 6
Kūh-e Hūrān ▲ IR 134-135 H 5
Kūh-e Madvār ▲ IR 134-135 F 3
Kūh-e Šāfī ○ AFG 138-139 B 2
Kūh-e Šāh-e Gūlak ▲ IR 128-129 N 5
Kūh-e Šāhū ▲ IR 128-129 M 5
Kūh-e Vāhān ▲ AFG 136-137 N 6
Kūhgīlūye, Būyer Aḥmad-o- ▫ IR 134-135 D 3
Kūhīn ○ IR 128-129 N 4
Kuhmo ○ FIN 88-89 K 4
Kuhmuh ○ RUS 126-127 G 6
Kuhn Ø ⌒ GRØ 26-27 p 6
Kūhpāye ○ IR 134-135 E 2
Kūhpāye, Kūhhā-ye ▲ IR 134-135 G 3
Kuhterin Lug ○ RUS 122-123 C 2
Kuhtuj ∼ RUS 120-121 K 4
Kuhtujskij hrebet ▲ RUS 120-121 K 3
Kui ○ PNG 183 D 4
Kui, Kivori- ○ PNG 183 D 5
Kui Buri ○ THA 158-159 E 4
Kuilsrivier ○ ZA 220-221 D 6
Kuiseb ∼ NAM 220-221 B 1
Kuiseb Canyon ⩦•• NAM 220-221 B 1
Kuito ☆ ANG 216-217 D 6
Kuiu Island ⌒ USA 32-33 C 3
Kuiukta Bay ≈ 22-23 R 4
Kuixingyan • VRC 156-157 L 4
Kuiyang ○ VRC 156-157 D 3
Kuja ∼ RUS 88-89 W 3
Kujama ○ WAN 204-205 G 3
Kujat, Gunung ▲ RI 164-165 E 2
Kujbyšev ☆• RUS 114-115 P 7
Kujbyšev = Bulgar ☆ RUS 96-97 F 6
Kujbyšev = Samara ☆ RUS 96-97 G 7
Kujbyševa, mys ▲ RUS 108-109 Y 1
Kujbyševskij ☆ KA 124-125 E 2
Kujbyševskoe < RUS 96-97 D 5
Kujdusun ○ RUS 120-121 K 2
Kujdusun ∼ RUS 120-121 K 2
Kujgan ○ KA 124-125 J 6
Kujginskij krjaž ▲ RUS 110-111 V 4
Kuji ○ J 152-153 J 4
Kujolri ○ ROK 150-151 G 9
Kujši kumlar •• US 136-137 H 4
Kujtun ☆ RUS 116-117 K 8
Kujūkuri-nada ≈ 152-153 J 7
Kujul ∼ RUS 120-121 V 3
Kujumba ○ RUS 116-117 H 6
Kujū-san ▲ J 152-153 D 8
Kujviveem ∼ RUS 112-113 R 3
Kujwa ○ ROK 150-151 F 11
Kukaklek Lake ○ USA 22-23 T 3
Kukaragi ○ WAN 204-205 G 4
Kukawa ○ WAN 198-199 F 6
Kūkdarjo ∼ US 136-137 G 3
Kuke ○ RB 218-219 B 5
Kukës ☆• AL 100-101 H 3
Kukipi ○ PNG 183 D 5
Kukmor ☆ RUS 96-97 G 5
Kukpowruk River ∼ USA 20-21 J 2
Kukpuk River ∼ USA 20-21 H 2
Kukshi ○ IND 138-139 E 8
Kukuihaele ○ USA (HI) 288 K 4
Kukul'bej, hrebet ▲ RUS 118-119 H 10
Kukuna ○ WAL 202-203 D 5
Kukup ○• MAL 162-163 E 4
Kukur ○ SUD 208-209 A 3
Kukusunda ∼ RUS 110-111 G 5
Kul, Rūd-e ∼ IR 134-135 F 5
Kula ○ BG 102-103 C 6
Kula ☆ TR 128-129 C 3
Kula ○ WAN 204-205 G 6
Kulāchi ○ PK 138-139 C 4
Kulagin ○ KA 96-97 G 9
Kulai ○ MAL 162-163 E 4
Kula Kangri ▲ BHT 142-143 G 1
Kulakovo ○ RUS 116-117 F 6
Kulal, Mount ▲ EAK 212-213 F 2
Kulaly, ostrov ⌒ KA 126-127 H 5
Kula Mawe ○ EAK 212-213 G 3
Kulampanga ○ ZRE 210-211 J 4
Kulandag ▲ TM 136-137 D 4
Kūlandy, aral ⌒ KA 126-127 J 5
Kūlandy, tubegi ⌣ KA 126-127 H 5
Kulankhor ○ VRC 144-145 K 4
Kūlanötpes ∼ KA 124-125 G 4
Kulanutpes ∼ KA 124-125 G 3
Kular ○ RUS 110-111 U 4
Kular, hrebet ▲ RUS 110-111 S 5
Kulasekarapattinam ○ IND 140-141 H 6
Kulassein Island ⌒ RP 160-161 D 9
Kūlatau ○ US 136-137 G 4
Kulawi ○ RI 164-165 F 4
Kulaykili ○ SUD 198-199 L 5
Kulaykili ○ SUD 206-207 G 3
Kul'či ○ RUS 122-123 H 2
Kuldiga ☆•• LV 94-95 G 3
Kul'dino ○ RUS 112-113 H 3
Kul'dur ○ RUS 122-123 D 4
Kule ○ RB 220-221 E 1
Kulebaki ○ RUS 94-95 S 4
Kul'egan ∼ RUS 114-115 N 4
Kulén ○ K 158-159 H 4
Kulenga ∼ RUS 116-117 M 9
Kulgahtah gora ▲ RUS 108-109 X 7
Kulgera ○ AUS 176-177 M 2
Kulgeri ○ IND 140-141 F 3
Kulibi ○ ETH 208-209 E 4
Kulim ○ MAL 162-163 D 2
Kulin ○ AUS 176-177 E 6
Kulina do Médio Juruá, Área Indígena ✕ BR 66-67 B 6
Kuliouou ○ USA (HI) 288 H 3
Kulittalai ○ IND 140-141 H 5
Kuljab ☆ TJ 136-137 L 6
Kuljumbe ∼ RUS 108-109 X 8
Külkuduk ○ US 136-137 H 3
Kulkyne Creek ∼ AUS 178-179 H 6
Kullen ▲ S 86-87 F 8
Kulliparu Conservation Park ⊥ AUS 180-181 C 2
Kullorsuaq ○ GRØ 26-27 W 6
Kulm ○ USA (ND) 258-259 J 5
Kulmaç Dağları ▲ TR 128-129 G 3
Kulmbach ○ D 92-93 L 3
Kulo ○ RI 164-165 K 3
Kuloj ∼ RUS 88-89 R 4
Kulom, Ust'- ○ RUS 96-97 H 3
Kulp ☆ TR 128-129 J 3
Kulpara ○ AUS 180-181 E 3
Kulpawan ∼ GH 202-203 K 4
Kulsary ☆ KA 96-97 J 10
Kulu ○•• IND 138-139 F 4
Kulu ○ RUS (MAG) 120-121 M 3
Kulu ∼ RUS 120-121 L 3
Kulu ☆ TR 128-129 E 3
Kulumadau ○ PNG 183 G 5
Kulunda ☆ RUS 124-125 L 2
Kulundinskaja ravnina ⩦ RUS 124-125 L 3
Kulundinskoe, ozero ○ RUS 124-125 L 2
Kulun-Elbjut ○ RUS 110-111 Y 6
Kulungu ○ ZRE 210-211 F 6
Kulu River ∼ PNG 183 E 3
Kulusuk ○ GRØ 28-29 W 4
Kulusuk Kap Dan ○ GRØ 28-29 W 4
Kulyköl ○ KA 124-125 B 3
Kulyndy Žazygy ⌣ KA 124-125 K 3
Kulynigol ∼ RUS 114-115 R 3
Kulžuktov toglari ▲ US 136-137 H 4
Kum, Kūh-e ▲ IR 134-135 E 3
Kuma ○ RI 164-165 F 4
Kuma ∼ RUS 114-115 J 5
Kuma ∼ RUS 114-115 H 5
Kuma ∼ RUS 126-127 F 5
Kumafa, Pegunungan ▲ RI 166-167 G 3
Kumagaya ○ J 152-153 H 6
Kumahy ∼ RUS 118-119 O 6
Kumai ○ RI 162-163 J 6
Kumait, al- ○ IRQ 128-129 M 6
Kumai Teluk ≈ 162-163 J 6
Kumajri = Gjumri ○ AR 128-129 K 2
Kumak ∼ RUS 96-97 M 8
Kumamba, Kepulauan ⌒ RI 166-167 K 2
Kumamoto ☆• J 152-153 D 8
Kumana ○ CL 140-141 J 7
Kumandan ∼ RI 166-167 G 2
Kumano ○ J 152-153 G 8
Kumano-gawa ∼ J 152-153 F 8
Kumano-nada ≈ 152-153 G 7
Kumanovo ○• MK 100-101 H 3
Kumara ○ NZ 182 C 5
Kumarina Roadhouse ○ AUS 176-177 E 2
Kumarl B Fossicking Area • AUS 176-177 F 6
Kumashi ○ J 152-153 H 3
Kumasi ☆••• GH 202-203 K 6
Kumattur ○ IND 140-141 J 4
Kumayri = Gjumri ○ AR 128-129 K 2
Kumba ○ CAM 204-205 H 6
Kumba ○ ZRE 214-215 C 4
Kumbakonam ○ IND 140-141 H 5
Kumbanikesa ○ SOL 184 I c 2
Kumbarilla ○ AUS 178-179 L 4
Kumbe ○ RI 166-167 L 6
Kumbe ∼ RI 166-167 L 6
Kumbia ○ AUS 178-179 L 4
Kumbla ○ IND 140-141 F 4
Kumbo ○ CAM 204-205 J 5
Kumbwareta ○ PNG 183 C 3
Kum-Dag = Gumdag ○ TM 136-137 D 5
Kūmeğan ○ IR 134-135 C 1
Kumeny ☆ RUS 96-97 F 4
Kumertau ☆ RUS 96-97 J 7
Kume-shima ⌒ J 152-153 B 11
Kūm Gang ∼ ROK 150-151 F 9
Kŭmhwa ○ ROK 150-151 F 8
Kumi ○ EAU 212-213 D 3
Kumi ○ ROK 150-151 G 9
Kumiva Peak ▲ USA (NV) 246-247 F 3
Kumkurgan ○ US 136-137 K 6
Kumla ☆ S 86-87 G 7
Kumlein Fiord ≈ 36-37 S 2
Kumliun, Cape ▲ USA 22-23 S 4
Kumluca ☆ TR 128-129 D 4
Kumo ○ WAN 204-205 J 3
Kumola ∼ KA 124-125 E 5
Kumo-Manyčskij kanal < RUS 126-127 F 5
Kumon Taungdan ▲ MYA 142-143 K 2
Kumroč, hrebet ▲ RUS 120-121 T 6
Kumrovec ○ HR 100-101 E 1
Kumru ☆ TR 128-129 G 2
Kums ○ NAM 220-221 D 4
Kūmsaj ○ KA 126-127 N 3
Kumshe ○ WAN 206-207 B 3
Kŭmsŏng ○ ROK 150-151 F 10
Kumta ○ IND 140-141 F 3
Kumu ∼ RI 162-163 D 4
Kumu ○ ZRE 210-211 K 2
Kumuchuru < RB 218-219 B 6
Kumukahi, Cape ▲ USA (HI) 288 L 5
Kūm Umbū ○• ET 194-195 F 5
Kumusi River ∼ PNG 183 E 5
Kumya ○ DVR 150-151 F 8
Kumžār ○ OM 134-135 G 5
Kuna ○ USA (ID) 252-253 B 3
Kuna Cave ∴• USA (ID) 252-253 B 3

Kotiari — Kuna Cave 349

Lassio ~ **G** 210-211 D 4
Lassul o **PNG** 183 F 3
Last Chance o **USA** (CO) 254-255 M 4
Last Chance Creek ~ **USA** (UT) 254-255 D 6
Last Mountain Lake ⊖ **CDN** (SAS) 232-233 N 4
Lastoursville o **G** 210-211 D 4
Lastovo o **HR** 100-101 F 3
Lastovo ⌒ **HR** 100-101 F 3
Lasu o **PNG** 183 G 3
Las Vegas o **USA** (NM) 256-257 K 3
Las Vegas o·· **USA** (NV) 248-249 J 3
Las Vegas Valley ᴗ **USA** (NV) 248-249 J 3
Latacunga ☆ **EC** 64-65 C 2
Latady Island ⌒ **ARK** 16 F 29
Latah Creek ~ **USA** (WA) 244-245 H 3
Latakia = al-Lāḏiqīya ☆ **SYR** 128-129 F 5
Latakia = Lāḏiqīya, al- ☆ **SYR** 128-129 F 5
Latalata, Pulau ⌒ **RI** 164-165 K 4
Lata Papalang, Bukit ▲ **MAL** 162-163 D 2
Lataro ⌒ **VAN** 184 II a 2
Latas o **RCH** 76-77 C 2
Lätäseno ~ **FIN** 88-89 G 2
Latchford o **CDN** (ONT) 236-237 J 5
Late ⌒ **TON** 184 IV a 1
Lateriquique, Río ~ **PY** 70-71 H 6
Laterriere o **CDN** (QUE) 240-241 D 2
Latham o **AUS** 176-177 D 4
Latham o **USA** (AL) 284-285 C 5
Lathan o **IND** 142-143 J 2
Lathi = Île Sakao ⌒ **VAN** 184 II a 2
Lathom o **CDN** (ALB) 232-233 F 5
Lathu = Île Eléphant ⌒ **VAN** 184 II a 2
Latīfiya, al- o **IRQ** 128-129 L 6
Latik < **RIM** 196-197 G 6
Latimojong Mountains Reserve ⊥ · **RI** 164-165 F 5
Latina ☆ **I** 100-101 D 4
Latinos, Ponta dos ▲ **BR** 74-75 D 9
Lat'juga o **RUS** 88-89 U 4
Latodo o **RI** 168 E 6
Latoma o **RI** 164-165 G 5
Latornell River ~ **CDN** (ALB) 228-229 Q 2
Latorre o **RCH** 76-77 B 5
Latou o **RI** 164-165 G 5
Latouche o **USA** 20-21 R 6
Latouche Island ⌒ **USA** 20-21 R 6
Latouche Treville, Cape ▲ **AUS** 172-173 E 5
Latour o **CDN** (QUE) 240-241 G 2
Látrar o **IS** 86-87 b 1
Latrobe o **AUS** 180-181 J 6
Latrobe o **USA** (PA) 280-281 G 3
Latta o **USA** (SC) 284-285 L 2
Latu o **RI** 166-167 E 3
Latulipe o **CDN** (QUE) 236-237 J 5
Lātūr o **IND** 138-139 F 10
Latura Vati, Tanjung ▲ **RI** 166-167 D 6
Latvia = Latvija ■ **LV** 94-95 J 3
Lau o **PNG** 183 F 3
Lau o **WAN** 204-205 J 4
Lauca, Parque Nacional ⊥ **RCH** 70-71 C 6
Laucala ⌒ **FJI** 184 III c 2
Laudar o **Y** 132-133 D 7
Lauder o **CDN** (MAN) 234-235 C 5
Lauderdale o **USA** (MS) 268-269 M 4
Lauenburg/ Elbe o **D** 92-93 L 2
Lauge Koch Kyst ≐ **GRØ** 26-27 U 5
Laughing Fish Point ▲ **USA** (MI) 270-271 M 4
Laughland Lake ⊖ **CDN** 30-31 X 2
Laughlen, Mount ▲ **AUS** 178-179 C 2
Laughlin o **USA** (NV) 248-249 K 4
Laughlin Peak ▲ **USA** (NM) 256-257 L 2
Lauhkaung o **MYA** 142-143 L 3
Lauiya Nandangarh o **IND** 142-143 D 2
Launceston o **AUS** 180-181 J 6
Launceston o **GB** 90-91 E 6
Launglen o **MYA** 158-159 E 4
Laungmasu o **IND** 142-143 H 4
Launlonbok Islands ⌒ **MYA** 158-159 D 4
Laupahoehoe o **USA** (HI) 288 K 5
Lauqa o **KSA** 130-131 H 3
Laura o **AUS** (QLD) 174-175 H 4
Laura o **AUS** (SA) 180-181 E 2
Laura o **CDN** (SAS) 232-233 L 4
Laura o **USA** (IL) 274-275 J 4
Laura, Kapp ▲ **N** 84-85 P 2
Laurel o **USA** (DE) 280-281 L 5
Laurel o **USA** (FL) 286-287 G 4
Laurel o **USA** (IA) 274-275 F 3
Laurel o **USA** (MD) 280-281 K 4
Laurel o **USA** (MS) 268-269 L 5
Laurel o **USA** (MT) 250-251 L 6
Laurel o **USA** (NE) 262-263 J 2
Laurel o **USA** (VA) 280-281 J 6
Laurel, Cerro ▲ **MEX** 52-53 C 2
Laureles o **ROU** 76-77 K 6
Laureles Grande, Arroyo ~ **ROU** 76-77 J 6
Laurel Hill o **USA** (FL) 286-287 C 1
Laurel River ~ **USA** (KY) 276-277 L 3
Laurel River Lake < **USA** (KY) 276-277 L 3
Laurel Springs o **USA** (NC) 282-283 F 4
Laurelville o **USA** (OH) 280-281 D 4
Laurenceton o **CDN** (NFL) 242-243 N 3
Laurens o **USA** (IA) 274-275 D 2
Laurens o **USA** (SC) 284-285 H 2
Laurentians ≐ **CDN** (QUE) 238-239 H 2
Laurentides o **CDN** (QUE) 238-239 M 3
Laurentides ≐ **CDN** (QUE) 238-239 M 2
Lauri o **MYA** 142-143 J 3
Laurie, Mount ▲ **AUS** 176-177 G 3
Laurie Island ⌒ **ARK** 16 G 32
Laurie Lake ⊖ **CDN** 34-35 E 2
Laurier o **CDN** (MAN) 234-235 D 4
Laurier o **USA** (WA) 244-245 G 2
Laurier, Mont- o **CDN** (QUE) 238-239 K 2
Laurie River o **CDN** 34-35 F 2
Laurinburg o **USA** (NC) 282-283 H 6
Laurium o **USA** (WI) 270-271 K 3
Lauro de Freitas o **BR** 72-73 L 2
Lauro Sodré o **BR** 66-67 F 4
Lausanne ☆ · **CH** 92-93 J 5
Laut, Kampung o **MAL** 162-163 F 4
Laut, Pulau ⌒ **RI** 162-163 H 3
Laut, Pulau ⌒ **RI** 162-163 G 2
Laut, Pulau ⌒ **RI** (KSE) 164-165 E 5
Laut, Selat ≈ 164-165 E 5
Lautaret, Col du ▲ · **F** 90-91 L 9
Lautaro o **RCH** 78-79 C 5
Lautem o **RI** 166-167 D 6
Laut Kecil, Kepulauau ⌒ **RI** 164-165 D 6
Lautoka o **FJI** 184 III a 2
Lauttawar, Danau ⊖ **RI** 162-163 B 2
Lauz, Ǧabal al- ▲ **KSA** 130-131 D 3
Lauzon o **CDN** (QUE) 238-239 O 2
Lava Beds ≐ **USA** (NM) 256-257 J 5
Lava Beds ≐ **USA** (NM) 256-257 H 6
Lava Beds National Monument ∴ **USA** (CA) 246-247 D 2
Lavaca o **USA** (AR) 276-277 A 5
Lavaca, Port o **USA** (TX) 266-267 L 5
Lavaca Bay ≈ **USA** 266-267 L 5
Lavacicle Creek ∴ **USA** (OR) 244-245 E 7
Lava Flow ≐ **USA** (NM) 256-257 H 4
Lava Hot Springs o **USA** (ID) 252-253 F 4
Laval o **CDN** (QUE) 238-239 M 3
Laval ☆ · **F** 90-91 G 7
Lavalle o **RA** 76-77 E 5
La Valle o **USA** (WI) 270-271 H 7
Lāvān, Ǧazīre-ye ⌒ **IR** 134-135 E 5
Lavapié, Punta ▲ **RCH** 78-79 C 4
Lavaur o **F** 90-91 H 10
Lavenham o **CDN** (MAN) 234-235 E 5
La Vérendrye Provincial Réserve ⊥ **CDN** (QUE) 236-237 L 5
Laverlochère o **CDN** (QUE) 236-237 J 5
Laverne o **USA** (OK) 264-265 E 2
Laverton o **AUS** 176-177 G 4
Lavieille, Lake ⊖ **CDN** (ONT) 238-239 G 3
Laviera < **EAT** 212-213 F 6
Lavigne o **CDN** (ONT) 238-239 E 2
Lavik o **N** 86-87 B 6
Lavillette o **CDN** (NB) 240-241 K 3
Lavina o **USA** (MT) 250-251 L 5
Lavon o **USA** (TX) 264-265 H 5
Lavon, Lake ⊖ **USA** (TX) 264-265 H 5
Lavonia o **USA** (GA) 284-285 G 2
Lavoy o **CDN** (ALB) 232-233 G 2
Lavrador, Ribeiro do ~ **BR** 70-71 J 3
Lavras o **BR** 72-73 H 6
Lavrentija o **RUS** 112-113 Z 4
Lavrio o **GR** 100-101 K 6
Lavrova, buhta ⊖ **RUS** 112-113 O 6
Lavrova, proliv ≈ 84-85 f 2
Lavumisa o **SD** 220-221 K 3
Lawang o **RI** 168 E 3
Lawan Gopeng o **MAL** 162-163 D 2
Lawas o **MAL** 164-165 D 1
Lawashi River ~ **CDN** 34-35 P 4
Lawatu o **RI** 164-165 G 5
Lawford Islands ⌒ **CDN** 30-31 N 2
Lawit, Gunung ▲ **RI** 162-163 K 4
Lawksawk o **MYA** 142-143 K 5
Lawn o **USA** (TX) 264-265 E 6
Lawn Bay ≈ 38-39 R 5
Lawn Bay ≈ **CDN** 242-243 N 6
Lawngngaw o **MYA** 142-143 J 2
Lawngtlai o **IND** 142-143 H 4
Lawn Hill o **AUS** 174-175 E 6
Lawnhill o **CDN** (BC) 228-229 C 3
Lawn Hill National Park ⊥ **AUS** 174-175 E 6
Lawowa o **RI** 164-165 H 6
Lawra o **GH** 202-203 J 4
Lawrence o **NZ** 182 B 6
Lawrence o **USA** (KS) 262-263 L 6
Lawrence o **USA** (MA) 278-279 K 6
Lawrence o **USA** (NC) 282-283 K 4
Lawrence o **USA** (NE) 262-263 H 4
Lawrenceburg o **USA** (KY) 276-277 L 2
Lawrenceburg o **USA** (TN) 276-277 H 5
Lawrence Station o **CDN** (NB) 240-241 H 5
Lawrenceville o **USA** (GA) 284-285 G 3
Lawrenceville o **USA** (IL) 274-275 L 6
Lawrenceville o **USA** (VA) 280-281 J 7
Lawrence Wells, Mount ▲ **AUS** 176-177 F 3
Lawtha o **MYA** 142-143 J 4
Lawton o **USA** (ND) 258-259 J 3
Lawton o **USA** (PA) 280-281 K 2
Lawton o **USA** (TX) 264-265 F 4
Lawushi Manda National Park ⊥ **Z** 214-215 F 7
Lay o **BF** 202-203 K 3
Lay o **USA** (CO) 254-255 H 3
Laya o **RG** 202-203 D 5
Laya Dula o **RG** 202-203 E 5
Layang Layang o **MAL** 160-161 A 10
Layar, Tanjung ▲ **RI** 164-165 E 6
Layarat · **MA** 188-189 F 7
Layawng Ga o **MYA** 142-143 K 3
Lay Lake < **USA** (AL) 284-285 D 3
Layo o **PE** 70-71 B 4
Layton o **USA** (FL) 286-287 J 7
Laytonville o **USA** (CA) 246-247 B 4
Lazarev o **RUS** 122-123 J 2
Lazarevac o **YU** 100-101 H 2
Lazarevskoe o **RUS** 126-127 C 6
Lázaro Cárdenas o **MEX** (BCN) 50-51 B 2
Lázaro Cárdenas o **MEX** (MIC) 52-53 C 3
Lazdijai o **LT** 94-95 H 4
Lāze o **IR** 134-135 E 5
Lazio ◻ **I** 100-101 D 3
Lazo o **RUS** 110-111 V 6
Lazo o **RUS** 122-123 E 7
L. Bistrups Bræ ⊂ **GRØ** 26-27 o 5
Lea o **USA** (NM) 256-257 M 6
Léach o **K** 158-159 G 4
Leach Island ⌒ **CDN** (ONT) 236-237 D 5
Leachville o **USA** (AR) 276-277 E 5
Leacross o **CDN** (SAS) 232-233 P 3
Lead o **USA** (SD) 260-261 C 2
Leader o **CDN** (SAS) 232-233 J 5
Lead Hill o **USA** (AR) 276-277 C 4
Leading Tickles o **CDN** (NFL) 242-243 N 3
Leadore o **USA** (ID) 252-253 E 2
Leadpoint o **USA** (WA) 244-245 H 2
Leadville o **USA** (CO) 254-255 J 4
Leaf Bay ≈ 36-37 P 5
Leaf Rapids o **CDN** 34-35 G 2
Leaf River ~ **USA** (MS) 268-269 L 5
League City o **USA** (TX) 268-269 E 7
Leahy o **USA** (WA) 244-245 F 3
Leakesville o **USA** (MS) 268-269 M 5
Leakey o **USA** (TX) 266-267 H 4
Lea Lea o **PNG** 183 D 5
Leamington o **CDN** (ONT) 238-239 C 6
Leamington o **USA** (UT) 254-255 C 4
Leander o **USA** (TX) 266-267 K 3
Leander Point ▲ **AUS** 176-177 C 4
Leandra o **ZA** 220-221 J 3
Leandro o **BR** 68-69 F 5
Leandro N. Alem o **RA** 76-77 K 4
Lea Park o **CDN** (ALB) 232-233 H 2
Learmonth o **AUS** 172-173 B 7
Leary o **USA** (GA) 284-285 F 5
Leasi, Kepulauan ⌒ **RI** 166-167 E 3
Leask o **CDN** (SAS) 232-233 M 2
Leatherwood o **USA** (KY) 276-277 M 3
Leaton State Historic Site, Fort ∴ **USA** (TX) 266-267 C 4
Leavenworth o **USA** (KS) 262-263 M 5
Leavenworth o **USA** (WA) 244-245 E 3
Leavenworth, Fort · **USA** (KS) 262-263 L 5
Leavitt o **CDN** (ALB) 232-233 E 6
Łeba o· **PL** 92-93 O 1
Lebak o **RP** 160-161 F 9
Lebam o **USA** (WA) 244-245 B 4
Lebamba o **G** 210-211 C 5
Leban Condong, Kampung o **MAL** 162-163 E 3
Lébango o **RCB** 210-211 E 3
Lébango ~ **RCB** 210-211 E 3
Lebanon o **USA** (IN) 274-275 M 4
Lebanon o **USA** (KS) 262-263 H 5
Lebanon o **USA** (KY) 276-277 K 3
Lebanon o **USA** (MO) 276-277 C 3
Lebanon o **USA** (NE) 262-263 F 4
Lebanon o **USA** (NH) 278-279 J 5
Lebanon o **USA** (OH) 280-281 B 4
Lebanon o **USA** (OR) 244-245 C 6
Lebanon o **USA** (PA) 280-281 K 3
Lebanon o **USA** (SD) 260-261 G 1
Lebanon o **USA** (TN) 276-277 J 4
Lebanon o **USA** (VA) 280-281 D 7
Lebanon = Lubnān, al- ■ **RL** 128-129 F 5
Lebanon Station o **USA** (FL) 286-287 G 2
Lebap o **TM** 136-137 G 4
Lebbeke o **B** 92-93 H 3
Lebeau o **USA** (LA) 268-269 J 6
Lebec o **USA** (CA) 248-249 F 5
Lebed' ~ **RUS** 124-125 P 2
Lebedjan' o **RUS** 94-95 Q 5
Lebedyn o **UA** 102-103 J 2
Lebel-sur-Quévillon o **CDN** (QUE) 236-237 L 3
Lebida o **ZRE** 210-211 F 5
Lebiolali < **ETH** 208-209 H 5
Lébiri ~ **G** 210-211 D 4
Lebjaž'e ☆ **KA** 124-125 K 3
Lebjaž'e ☆ **RUS** 96-97 F 5
Lebjaž'ja ~ **RUS** 114-115 S 7
Lebo o **USA** (KS) 262-263 L 6
Lebo o **ZRE** 206-207 F 6
Leboma ~ **ZRE** 210-211 F 5
Lébombi ~ **G** 210-211 D 5
Lebombo ▲ **SD** 220-221 K 2
Lebongtandai o **RI** 162-163 D 6
Leboni o **RI** 164-165 G 5
Lebon Régis o **BR** 74-75 E 6
Lębork o· **PL** 92-93 O 1
Lebowa o **ZA** 218-219 E 6
Lebowa (former Homeland, now part of North-Transvaal) ◻ **ZA** 218-219 D 6
Lebowakgomo ☆ **ZA** 220-221 J 2
Lebret o **CDN** (SAS) 232-233 P 5
Lebrija o **E** 98-99 D 6
Lebu o **RCH** 78-79 C 4
Lebuhanbini, Tanjung ▲ **RI** 164-165 F 3
Lecce ☆ · **I** 100-101 G 4
Lecco ☆ **I** 100-101 B 2
Lech ~ **D** 92-93 L 4
Lechang o **VRC** 156-157 H 4
Leche, Laguna de La ⊖ **MEX** 50-51 H 4
Lechiguanas, Islas de las ⌒ **RA** 78-79 K 2
Lechuguilla, Bahía ≈ 50-51 E 5
Lēči o **LV** 94-95 G 3
Le Claire o **USA** (IA) 274-275 H 3
Lecompte o **USA** (LA) 268-269 H 5
Łęczyca o· **PL** 92-93 P 2
Ledang, Gunung ▲ **MAL** (JOH) 162-163 E 3
Ledesma o **E** 98-99 D 4
Ledge o **USA** (MT) 250-251 H 3
Ledge Point o **AUS** 176-177 C 5
Ledjanaja ~ **RUS** 108-109 b 6
Ledjanaja gora ▲ **RUS** 112-113 Q 6
Ledmozero o **RUS** 88-89 M 4
Ledo o **IND** 142-143 J 2
Ledong o **VRC** 156-157 F 7
Ledu o **VRC** 154-155 C 3
Leduc o **CDN** (ALB) 232-233 E 2
Lee o **USA** (NV) 246-247 K 3
Leeburn o **CDN** (ONT) 238-239 B 2
Leech Lake o **USA** (MN) 270-271 D 3
Leech Lake ⊖ **USA** (MN) 270-271 D 3
Leech Lake Indian Reservation X **USA** (MN) 270-271 D 3
Leedale o **CDN** (ALB) 232-233 D 3
Leeds o· **GB** 90-91 G 5
Leeds o **GUY** 62-63 F 2
Leeds o **USA** (AL) 284-285 D 3
Leeds o **USA** (ND) 258-259 H 3
Leeds, Mount ▲ **CDN** 26-27 M 4
Leek o **GB** 90-91 F 5
Leeman o **AUS** 176-177 C 4
Leeman o **USA** (WI) 270-271 K 6
Leer (Ostfriesland) o **D** 92-93 J 2
Leer, Pulau ⌒ **RI** 166-167 H 5
Lees o **USA** (TX) 264-265 C 6
Leesburg o **USA** (FL) 286-287 H 3
Leesburg o **USA** (GA) 284-285 F 5
Leesburg o **USA** (OH) 280-281 C 4
Leesburg o **USA** (VA) 280-281 J 4
Lees Camp o **USA** (OR) 244-245 B 5
Leeston o **NZ** 182 D 5
Leesville o **USA** (LA) 268-269 G 5
Leesville o **USA** (SC) 284-285 J 3
Leesville o **USA** (TX) 266-267 K 4
Leeton o **AUS** 180-181 J 3
Leeudoringstad o **ZA** 220-221 H 3
Leeu-Gamka o **ZA** 220-221 E 6
Leeupoort o **ZA** 220-221 H 2
Leeuwarden ☆ · **NL** 92-93 H 2
Leeuwin, Cape ▲ **AUS** 176-177 C 7
Leeuwin-Naturaliste National Park ⊥ **AUS** 176-177 C 6
Leeuwrivier ~ **ZA** 220-221 F 6
Lee Vining o **USA** (CA) 248-249 E 2
Leeward Islands ⌒ 56 E 2
Leffellier o **CDN** (MAN) 234-235 F 5
Léfini ~ **RCB** 210-211 E 5
Léfini, Réserve de chasse de la ⊥ **RCB** 210-211 E 5
Lefkáda o **GR** 100-101 H 5
Lefkáda ⌒ **GR** 100-101 H 5
Lefkónas o **GR** 100-101 J 4
Lefkosia ★ **CY** 128-129 E 5
Lefo, Mont ▲ **CAM** 204-205 J 6
Lefor o **USA** (ND) 258-259 E 5
Lefors o **USA** (TX) 264-265 D 3
Lefroy, Lake ⊖ **AUS** (WA) 176-177 G 5
Lefroy, Lake ⊖ **AUS** (WA) 176-177 F 5
Legal o **CDN** (ALB) 232-233 E 2
Legape o **RB** 220-221 G 2
Legazpi ☆ **RP** 160-161 E 6
Legend o **CDN** (ALB) 232-233 G 6
Legendre Island ⌒ **AUS** 172-173 C 6
Leggett o **USA** (CA) 246-247 B 4
Leggett o **USA** (TX) 268-269 F 6
Legion Mine o **ZW** 218-219 E 5
Legionnaire, Tunnel du · **MA** 188-189 J 4
Legionowo o **PL** 92-93 Q 2
Legkraal o **ZA** 218-219 E 6
Legnica ☆ · **PL** 92-93 O 3
Legokjawa o **RI** 168 C 3
Le Grand, Mount ▲ **AUS** 176-177 G 6
Leguan Island ⌒ **GUY** 62-63 E 2
Legunditua, Pulau ⌒ **RI** 162-163 F 7
Legune o **AUS** 172-173 J 3
Leh o· **IND** 138-139 F 2
Le Havre o **F** 90-91 H 7
Lehena o **GR** 100-101 H 6
Lehi o **USA** (UT) 254-255 D 3
Lehigh Acres o **USA** (FL) 286-287 H 5
Lehighton o **USA** (PA) 280-281 L 3
Lehman Caves ∴ **USA** (NV) 246-247 L 5
Lehmann o **USA** (TX) 264-265 B 5
Lehr o **USA** (MS) 268-269 K 5
Lehr o **USA** (ND) 258-259 H 5
Lehua Island ⌒ **USA** (HI) 288 E 2
Lehua Landing o **USA** (HI) 288 E 3
Lehututu o **RB** 220-221 E 1
Leiah o **PK** 138-139 C 4
Leibnitz o **A** 92-93 N 5
Leicester o **GB** 90-91 G 5
Leichhardt, Mount ▲ **AUS** 172-173 L 6
Leichhardt Range ▲ **AUS** 174-175 J 7
Leichhardt River ~ **AUS** 174-175 E 5
Leiden o· **NL** 92-93 H 2
Leifs Ø ⌒ **GRØ** 28-29 W 4
Leigh o **USA** (NE) 262-263 J 3
Leigh Creek o **AUS** 178-179 E 6
Leigh Creek South o **AUS** 178-179 E 6
Leighton o **USA** (AL) 284-285 C 2
Leigong Shan ▲ **VRC** 156-157 F 3
Leimebamba o **PE** 64-65 D 5
Leimus o **HN** 52-53 B 4
Leinan o **CDN** (SAS) 232-233 L 5
Leine ~ **D** 92-93 K 2
Leinster o **AUS** 176-177 F 3
Leiper, Kap ▲ **GRØ** 26-27 P 4
Leipzig o **CDN** (SAS) 232-233 K 3
Leipzig o·· **D** 92-93 M 3
Leira ☆ **N** (OPP) 86-87 D 6
Leira ☆ **N** (ROM) 86-87 D 5
Leiria ☆ · **P** 98-99 C 5
Leirvik ☆ **N** 86-87 B 7
Leishan o **VRC** 156-157 F 3
Leisi o **EST** 94-95 H 2
Leisler, Mount ▲ **AUS** 176-177 K 1
Leitchfield o **USA** (KY) 276-277 J 3
Leite, Igarapé do ~ **BR** 66-67 K 5
Leiter o **USA** (WY) 252-253 M 2
Leith o **CDN** (ONT) 238-239 E 4
Leith, Point ▲ **CDN** 30-31 K 3
Leith Harbour o **GB** 78-79 O 7
Leith Peninsula ᴗ **CDN** 30-31 K 3
Leitmeritz = Litoměřice o **CZ** 92-93 N 3
Leitomischl = Litomyšl o **CZ** 92-93 O 4
Leitre o **PNG** 183 A 2
Leiva, Cerro ▲ **CO** 60-61 D 6
Leiyang o **VRC** 156-157 H 3
Leizhou Bandao ᴗ **VRC** 156-157 G 6
Leizhou Wan ≈ 156-157 G 6
Lejac o **CDN** (BC) 228-229 K 2
Lejeune o **CDN** (QUE) 240-241 G 3
Lejeune Marine Corps Base, Camp xx **USA** (NC) 282-283 K 6
Lejone o **LS** 220-221 J 4
Lek ~ **NL** 92-93 H 3
Leka ⌒ **N** 86-87 E 4
Lékana o **RCB** 210-211 E 5
Lekatero o **ZRE** 210-211 J 4
Lekeleka ⌒ **TON** 184 IV a 2
Lékéti ~ **RCB** 210-211 E 5
Lekhcheb o **RIM** 196-197 E 5
Lékila o **G** 210-211 D 4
Lekitobi o **RI** 164-165 J 4
Lekki Lagoon ⊖ **WAN** 204-205 F 5
Leknes o **N** 86-87 F 2
Lekona ~ **RCB** 210-211 E 4
Lékoni o **G** (Hau) 210-211 E 4
Lékoni ~ **G** 210-211 D 4
Lekos ~ **RUS** 114-115 R 3
Lekoumou ◻ **RCB** 210-211 D 5
Leksand o **S** 86-87 G 6
Leksozero ⊖ **RUS** 88-89 L 5
Lekst, Jbel ▲ **MA** 188-189 G 6
Leksula o **RI** 166-167 D 3
Leku o **ETH** 208-209 D 5
Lela o **RI** 166-167 B 6
Lelai, Tanjung ▲ **RI** 164-165 L 3
Lélali ~ **RCB** 210-211 D 5
Leland o **USA** (MS) 268-269 K 3
Lel'čycy o **BY** 94-95 L 6
Lelehudi o **PNG** 183 F 6
Lelepa = Île Leleppa ⌒ **VAN** 184 II b 3
Leleppa, Île = Lelepa ⌒ **VAN** 184 II b 3
Leleque o **RA** 78-79 D 7
Leling o **VRC** 154-155 K 3
Lelingluang o **RI** 166-167 F 5
Lelinta o **RI** 166-167 F 3
Leljuveem ~ **RUS** 112-113 Q 2
Lelogama o **RI** 166-167 B 6
Lélouma o **RG** 202-203 D 4
Lel'vergyrgyn ~ **RUS** 112-113 M 2
Lelydorp ☆ **SME** 62-63 G 3
Lelystad o **NL** 92-93 H 2
Léman, Lac ⊖ **CH** 92-93 J 5
Lemang o **RI** 162-163 E 4
Le Mans o· **F** 90-91 H 8
Lema Shilindi o **ETH** 208-209 F 6
Lematang ~ **RI** 162-163 E 6
Lembar o **RI** 168 C 7
Lembé o **CAM** 204-205 K 6
Lembeh, Pulau ⌒ **RI** 164-165 J 3
Lembeni o **EAT** 212-213 F 5
Lemberg o **CDN** (SAS) 232-233 P 5
Lemberg = L'viv ☆ · **UA** 102-103 D 3
Lembing, Sungai o **MAL** 162-163 E 3
Lembo o **RI** 164-165 H 5
Lemery o **RP** 160-161 D 6
Lemesos o· **CY** 128-129 E 5
Lemfu o **ZRE** 210-211 E 6
Lemhi, Fort ∴ **USA** (ID) 252-253 E 2
Lemhi Pass ▲ **USA** (MT) 250-251 F 7
Lemhi Range ▲ **USA** (ID) 252-253 E 2
Lemhi River ~ **USA** (ID) 250-251 F 6
Lemieux o **CDN** 20-21 Y 7
Lemieux Islands ⌒ **CDN** 36-37 R 2
Lemin o **VRC** 156-157 F 5
Leming o **USA** (TX) 266-267 J 4
Leming o **USA** (TX) 266-267 J 5
Lemitar o **USA** (NM) 256-257 J 4
Lem'ju ~ **RUS** 88-89 X 4
Lem"junskaja vozvyšennost' ▲ **RUS** 88-89 X 4
Lemmenjoen kansallispuisto ⊥ **FIN** 88-89 H 2
Lemmon o **USA** (SD) 260-261 D 1
Lemmon, Mount ▲ **USA** (AZ) 256-257 E 6
Lemoenshoek o **ZA** 220-221 E 6
Lemolemo o **RI** 164-165 L 4
Lemon, Lake ⊖ **USA** (IN) 274-275 M 5
Lemon Creek o **CDN** (BC) 230-231 M 4
Lemon Grove o **USA** 248-249 G 7
le Mont Saint-Michel o··· **F** 90-91 G 7
Lemoore o **USA** (CA) 248-249 E 3
Lemoore Naval Air Station xx **USA** (CA) 248-249 E 3
Lemoyne o **USA** (NE) 262-263 E 3
Lempa, Río ~ **ES** 52-53 K 5
Lempäälä o **FIN** 88-89 G 6
Lempriere o **CDN** (BC) 228-229 P 4
Lemsford o **CDN** (SAS) 232-233 J 5
Lemsid o **MA** 188-189 E 7
Lemtybož o **RUS** 114-115 D 3
Lemu o **WAN** 204-205 G 4
Lemukutan, Pulau ⌒ **RI** 162-163 H 4
Lemva ~ **RUS** 108-109 J 8
Lemvig o **DK** 86-87 D 8
Lemyethna o **MYA** 158-159 C 2
Lena o **CDN** (MAN) 234-235 D 5
Lena ~ **RUS** 10-11 M 2
Lena o **USA** (AR) 276-277 B 6
Lena o **USA** (LA) 268-269 H 5
Lena o **USA** (MS) 268-269 L 4
Lenakel ☆ **VAN** 184 II b 4
Lenangguar o **RI** 168 C 7
Lenapah o **USA** (OK) 264-265 J 2
Lena River Delta = Lena Delta ≈ **RUS** 110-111 P 2
Leñas, Paso de las ▲ **RA** 78-79 D 3
Lençóis o **BR** 72-73 K 2
Lençois, Baía dos ≈ 68-69 F 2
Lençóis Maranhenses, Parque Nacional dos ⊥ **BR** 68-69 G 3
Lençóis Paulista o **BR** 72-73 F 7
Lenda ~ **ZRE** 212-213 B 3
Lendaha ~ **RUS** 116-117 F 6
Lendava o **SLO** 100-101 F 1
Lende o **IR** 134-135 D 3
Lendepas o **NAM** 220-221 D 2
Lendery o **RUS** 88-89 L 5
Lenexa o **USA** (KS) 262-263 M 6
Leney o **CDN** (SAS) 232-233 L 3
Lenge, Bandar-e o· **IR** 134-135 F 5
Lenger ☆ **KA** 136-137 L 3
Lengguru ~ **RI** 166-167 H 3
Lenghu o **VRC** 146-147 L 6
Lenglong Ling ▲ **VRC** 154-155 B 3
Lenglong Ling ▲ **VRC** 154-155 C 3
Lengo o **RCA** 206-207 F 6
Lengoué ~ **RCB** 210-211 E 3
Lengshuijiang o **VRC** 156-157 G 3
Lengshuitan o **VRC** 156-157 G 3
Leng Su Sin o **VN** 156-157 C 5
Lengua de Vaca, Punta ▲ **RCH** 76-77 B 6
Lengulu o **ZRE** 210-211 L 2
Lengwe National Park ⊥ **MW** 218-219 H 3
Lenhovda o **S** 86-87 G 8
Lenin ☆ **TM** 136-137 F 3
Lenina, kanal imeni < **RUS** 126-127 F 6
Lenina, pik ▲ **KS** 136-137 N 5
Lenina, proliv ≈ 108-109 b 3
Leninabad = Hudžand ☆ **TJ** 136-137 L 4
Leninabadskaja oblast' ◻ **TJ** 136-137 K 5
Leninakan = Gjumri o **AR** 128-129 K 2
Lenine o **UA** 102-103 J 5
Leningrad = Sankt-Peterburg ☆··· **RUS** 94-95 M 2
Leningradskaja o **RUS** (KRD) 102-103 L 4
Leningradskaja ~ **RUS** 108-109 d 3
Leningradskij o **RUS** 112-113 U 2
Leningradskij o **TJ** 136-137 M 5
Leningradskij, lednik ⊂ **RUS** 108-109 d 2
Leninogorsk o **KA** 124-125 N 3
Leninogorsk ☆ **RUS** 96-97 H 6
Leninsk o **KA** 126-127 P 5
Leninsk o **RUS** 96-97 D 9
Leninsk o **US** 136-137 N 4
Leninskij o **KA** 124-125 K 2
Leninskij o **TJ** 136-137 L 5
Leninsk-Kuzneckij ☆ **RUS** 114-115 T 7
Leninsk Kuznetskiy = Leninsk-Kuzneckij ☆ **RUS** 114-115 T 7
Leninskoe o **KA** (AKT) 126-127 M 2
Leninskoe ☆ **KA** (KST) 124-125 D 2
Leninskoe o **KS** 136-137 N 4
Leninskoe o **RUS** 96-97 E 4
Lenivaja ~ **RUS** 108-109 X 4
Lenkau o **PNG** 183 D 2
Lenkivci o **UA** 102-103 E 2
Lenkoran' = Lankaran o· **AZ** 128-129 N 3
Lenmalu o **RI** 166-167 F 2
Lennox o **USA** (SD) 260-261 K 3
Lennox, Isla ⌒ **RCH** 80 G 7
Leno-Angarskoe, plato ≐ **RUS** 116-117 L 8
Leno-Angarskoe plato ≐ **RUS** 116-117 L 8
Lenoir o **USA** (NC) 282-283 F 5
Lenoir City o **USA** (TN) 282-283 C 5
Lenora o **USA** (KS) 262-263 G 5
Lenore o **CDN** (MAN) 234-235 C 5
Lenore Lake ~ **CDN** (SAS) 232-233 O 3
Lenox o **USA** (GA) 284-285 G 5
Lenox o **USA** (IA) 274-275 D 4
Lens o **F** 90-91 J 6
Lensk ☆ · **RUS** 118-119 G 5
Lenskie stolby · **RUS** 118-119 N 5
Lenswood o **CDN** (MAN) 234-235 C 2
Lent'evo o **RUS** 94-95 P 2
Lentiira o **FIN** 88-89 K 4
Lentini o **I** 100-101 E 6
Lenwood o **USA** (CA) 248-249 G 5
Lenya o **MYA** 158-159 E 5
Léo o **BF** 202-203 J 4
Leoben o **A** 92-93 N 5
Leofnard o **CDN** (SAS) 232-233 N 3
Léogâne o **RH** 54-55 J 5
Leok o **RI** 164-165 G 3
Leola o **USA** (AR) 276-277 C 6
Leola o **USA** (SD) 260-261 H 1
Leominster o· **GB** 90-91 F 5
Leominster o **USA** (MA) 278-279 K 6
León o· **E** 98-99 E 3
Léon o **F** 90-91 G 10
León o· **MEX** 50-51 J 7
León ☆·· **NIC** 52-53 L 5
Leon o **USA** (IA) 274-275 E 4
Leon o **USA** (OK) 264-265 G 5
León, Cerro ▲ **MEX** 52-53 F 3
León, Cerro ▲ **PY** 70-71 G 7
Leon, De o **USA** (TX) 264-265 F 6
León, Montes de ▲ **E** 98-99 D 3
Leona, La o **YV** 60-61 K 3
Leona, Punta la ▲ **EC** 64-65 B 2
Leonard o **USA** (MN) 270-271 C 3
Leonard o **USA** (ND) 258-259 K 5
Leonard o **USA** (TX) 264-265 H 5
Leonards o **USA** (TX) 264-265 H 5
Leonardtown o **USA** (MD) 280-281 K 5
Leonardville o **NAM** 220-221 D 1
Leonard Wood, Fort xx **USA** (MO) 276-277 C 3
Leona River ~ **USA** (TX) 266-267 H 5
Leoncio Prado o **PE** 64-65 E 3
Leonia o **USA** (ID) 250-251 C 3
Leonidas o **USA** (MI) 272-273 D 5
Leonídio o **GR** 100-101 J 6
Leonidovka ~ **RUS** 122-123 K 4
Leonidovo o **RUS** 122-123 K 4
Leonora o **AUS** 176-177 F 4
Leon River ~ **USA** (TX) 264-265 G 6
Leon River ~ **USA** (TX) 266-267 K 2
Leont'eva, ostrov ⌒ **RUS** 112-113 L 1
León Viejo ∴ · **NIC** 52-53 L 5
Leopold Downs o **AUS** 172-173 G 4
Leopold II, Lac = Lac Mai-Ndombe ⊖ **ZRE** 210-211 G 5
Leopoldina o **BR** 72-73 J 6
Leopold Island ⌒ **CDN** 36-37 S 2
Leopold M'Clintock, Cape ▲ **CDN** 24-25 N 2
Leopoldo de Bulhões o **BR** 72-73 F 4
Leopoldsburg o **B** 92-93 H 3
Léopoldville = Kinshasa ★ · **ZRE** 210-211 E 6
Leoti o **USA** (KS) 262-263 E 6
Léoua o **RCA** 206-207 E 6
Léoura o **BF** 202-203 L 3
Leova ☆ **MD** 102-103 F 4
Leoville o **CDN** (SAS) 232-233 L 2
Leovo = Leova ☆ **MD** 102-103 F 4
Lepanto o **USA** (AR) 276-277 E 5
Lepar, Pulau ⌒ **RI** 162-163 G 6
Lepaterique o **HN** 52-53 L 4
Lepel' ☆ **BY** 94-95 L 4
Lepellé, Rivière ~ **CDN** 36-37 N 4
Lephephe o **RB** 218-219 C 6
Lepine o **CDN** (SAS) 232-233 N 3
Leping o **VRC** 156-157 K 2
Leplja ~ **RUS** 114-115 F 4
Lépoura o **GR** 100-101 K 5
Lepreau o **CDN** (NB) 240-241 J 5
Lepsy o **KA** 124-125 L 5
Lepsy ~ **KA** 124-125 M 6
Leptis Magna = Labdah ∴··· **LAR** 192-193 F 1
Leptokariá o **GR** 100-101 J 4
Leqceïba o **RIM** (BRA) 196-197 C 6
Leqceïba o **RIM** (GOR) 196-197 D 6
Lequena o **RCH** 76-77 C 1
Léraba ~ **CI** 202-203 H 5
Léraba Occidentale ~ **CI** 202-203 H 4
Lérabe o **SN** 196-197 C 6
Lercara Friddi o **I** 100-101 D 6
Lerdo de Tejada o **MEX** 52-53 G 2
Léré o **RMM** 202-203 H 2
Léré o **TCH** 206-207 B 4
Lere o **WAN** (BAU) 204-205 H 4
Lere o **WAN** (KAD) 204-205 H 3
Léré, Lac de ⊖ **TCH** 206-207 B 4
Lérez, Río ~ **E** 98-99 C 3
Lérida = Lleida o·· **E** 98-99 H 4
Lerma o **E** 98-99 F 3
Lerma o **MEX** 52-53 J 2
Lermá, Valle de ≐ **RA** 76-77 E 3
Lerneb o **RMM** 196-197 H 6
Leron Plains o **PNG** 183 D 4
Leros ⌒ **GR** 100-101 L 6
Leross o **CDN** (SAS) 232-233 P 4
Leroy o **CDN** (SAS) 232-233 O 3
Le Roy o **USA** (MN) 270-271 F 7
Lerum ☆ **S** 86-87 F 8
Lerwick o **GB** 90-91 G 1
Ler Zerai < **SUD** 206-207 H 3
Lescoff o **F** 90-91 E 7
Lesdiguières, Lac ⊖ **CDN** 36-37 M 4
Leshan o **VRC** 156-157 C 2
Leshan Dafo · **VRC** 156-157 C 2
Les-Islets-Caribou o **CDN** (QUE) 242-243 A 3
Lesjaskog o **N** 86-87 D 5
Lesjöfors o **S** 86-87 G 7
Leskino o **RUS** 108-109 S 5
Lesko o· **PL** 92-93 R 4
Leskovac o· **YU** 100-101 H 3
Leskovik o· **AL** 100-101 H 4
Leslie o **CDN** (SAS) 232-233 P 4
Leslie o **USA** (AR) 276-277 C 5
Leslie o **USA** (GA) 284-285 F 5
Leslie o **USA** (ID) 252-253 E 3
Leslie o **USA** (MI) 272-273 E 5
Leslie, Kap ▲ **GRØ** 26-27 n 8
Leslieville o **CDN** (ALB) 232-233 D 3
Lesmiegan ~ **RUS** 114-115 G 2
Lesnaja o **RUS** 120-121 T 4
Lesnoj Gorodok o **RUS** 118-119 F 10
Lesnoj Voronež ~ **RUS** 94-95 R 5
Lesogorsk o **RUS** 122-123 K 4
Lesosibirsk o **RUS** 116-117 F 6
Lesotho ■ **LS** 220-221 H 4
Lesozavodsk o **RUS** 122-123 E 6
Lesozavodskij o **RUS** 122-123 M 6
Lesperon o **F** 90-91 G 10
Lessau o **PNG** 183 D 2
Léssé ~ **RCA** 206-207 D 6
Lesser Antilles ≐ 56 B 5
Lesser Hinggan Range = Xiao Hinggan Ling ▲ **VRC** 150-151 F 2
Lesser Slave Lake ⊖ **CDN** 32-33 N 4
Lesser Slave Lake Provincial Park ⊥ **CDN** 32-33 N 4
Lesser Slave River ~ **CDN** 32-33 N 4
Lesser Sunda, Kepulauan ⌒ **RI** 168 C 7
Lesser Sunda Islands = Sunda Kecil, Kepulauan ⌒ **RI** 168 C 6
Lester Prairie o **USA** (MN) 270-271 D 6
Lestijärvi o **FIN** 88-89 H 5
Lestock o **CDN** (SAS) 232-233 O 4
Lesueur, Mount ▲ **AUS** 176-177 C 5
Lesung, Tanjung ▲ **RI** 168 A 3
Lesvos ⌒ **GR** 100-101 L 5
Leszno ☆ · **PL** 92-93 O 3
Letaba o **ZA** 218-219 F 6
Letas, Lac = Tes, Lake ⊖ **VAN** 184 II a 2
Letchworth State Park ⊥ **USA** (NY) 278-279 D 6
Letellier o **CDN** (MAN) 234-235 F 5
Letete o **CDN** (NB) 240-241 J 5
Letfata o **RIM** 196-197 D 6
Lethbridge o **CDN** (NFL) 242-243 P 4
Lethbridge o· **CDN** (ALB) 232-233 F 6
Lethem ☆ **GUY** 62-63 E 4
Leti, Kepulauan ⌒ **RI** 166-167 D 6
Leti, Pulau ⌒ **RI** 166-167 D 6
Letiahau ~ **RB** 218-219 B 5
Leticia o **CO** 66-67 C 5
Leting o **VRC** 154-155 L 2
Letka o **RUS** 96-97 F 4
Letkhokpin o **MYA** 142-143 K 4
Letlhakeng o **RB** 220-221 G 2
Letnica o **BG** 102-103 D 6
Letnij bereg ᴗ **RUS** 88-89 O 4
Letniy Bereg = Letnij bereg ᴗ **RUS** 88-89 O 4
Letnjaja ~ **RUS** 112-113 H 3
Letnjaja Zolotica o **RUS** 88-89 O 4
Letoda o **RI** 166-167 E 6
Letohatchee o **USA** (AL) 284-285 D 4
Letoon ∴··· **TR** 128-129 C 4
Letpadan o **MYA** 158-159 C 2
Letpan o **MYA** 142-143 J 6
Letsitele o **ZA** 218-219 F 6
Letsok-Aw Kyun ⌒ **MYA** 158-159 E 5
Letta o **CAM** 204-205 K 6
Letterkenny o **IRL** 90-91 D 4
Letts o **USA** (IN) 274-275 N 5
Letwurung o **RI** 166-167 E 5
Léuá o **ANG** 216-217 F 5
Leuaniua ⌒ **SOL** 184 I d 1
Leucadia o **USA** (CA) 248-249 G 6
Leupp o **USA** (AZ) 256-257 E 3
Leura o **AUS** 178-179 K 2
Leuser, Gunung ▲ **RI** 162-163 B 3
Leušinskij Tuman, ozero ⊖ **RUS** 114-115 H 5
Leuven o·· **B** 92-93 H 3
Levack o **CDN** (ONT) 238-239 D 2
Levaja Avača ~ **RUS** 120-121 S 7
Levaja Bojarka ~ **RUS** 108-109 b 6
Levaja Bureja ~ **RUS** 122-123 F 3
Levaja Hetta ~ **RUS** 114-115 L 2
Levaja Kamenka ~ **RUS** 110-111 d 6
Levaja Lesnaja ~ **RUS** 120-121 T 4
Levaja Mama ~ **RUS** 118-119 E 7
Levaja Šapina ~ **RUS** 120-121 T 6
Levaja Vetv', kanal < **RUS** 102-103 N 5
Levaja županova ~ **RUS** 120-121 S 6
Levan o **USA** (UT) 254-255 D 4
Levanger o **N** 86-87 E 5
Levante, Riviera di ᴗ **I** 100-101 B 2
Levantine Basin ≃ 128-129 B 6
Levasi o **RUS** 126-127 G 6
Levdiev, ostrov ⌒ **RUS** 108-109 M 7
Level, Isla ⌒ **RCH** 80 C 2

352 Lassio — Level, Isla

Levelland o USA (TX) 264-265 B 5
Leven o GB 90-91 F 3
Leven ~ GB 90-91 F 3
Leven Bank ≃ 222-223 E 4
Leveque, Cape ▲ AUS 172-173 F 4
Lever, Rio ~ BR 68-69 C 7
Leverett Glacier ⌒ ARK 16 E 0
Leverkusen o D 92-93 J 3
Levídi o GR 100-101 J 6
Levin o NZ 182 E 4
Levinópolis o BR 72-73 H 3
Levis o CDN (QUE) 238-239 O 2
Levis, Lac o CDN 30-31 L 4
Levisa Fork ~ USA (KY) 276-277 N 3
Levittown o USA (PA) 280-281 M 3
Levkaditi o GR 100-101 J 5
Levroux o F 90-91 H 8
Levski o BG 102-103 D 6
Levuka o FJI 184 III b 2
Levy Hetagčan ~ RUS 112-113 J 5
Levy Kedon ~ RUS 112-113 K 4
Levy Mamakan ~ RUS 118-119 F 7
Léwa o CAM 204-205 K 5
Lewa o RI 168 D 7
Le Ward o USA (TX) 266-267 L 5
Lewellen o USA (NE) 262-263 D 3
Lewes o USA (DE) 280-281 L 5
Lewes Plateau ≃ CDN 20-21 W 5
Lewin's Cove o CDN (NFL) 242-243 N 5
Lewis o USA (CO) 254-255 G 6
Lewis and Clark Lake o USA (NE) 262-263 G 2
Lewisburg o USA (KY) 276-277 J 4
Lewisburg o USA (OH) 280-281 B 4
Lewisburg o USA (OR) 244-245 B 6
Lewisburg o USA (PA) 280-281 K 3
Lewisburg o USA (TN) 276-277 J 5
Lewisburg o USA (WV) 280-281 F 6
Lewis Creek ~ CDN (SAS) 232-233 N 4
Lewis Hills ▲ CDN (NFL) 242-243 K 4
Lewis Pass ≏ NZ 182 D 5
Lewis Point o CDN 22-23 R 3
Lewisporte o CDN (NFL) 242-243 N 3
Lewis Range ▲ AUS 172-173 J 2
Lewis Range ▲ USA (MT) 250-251 D 3
Lewis River ~ USA (WA) 244-245 C 4
Lewis Smith Lake o USA (AL) 284-285 C 3
Lewiston o USA (ID) 250-251 C 5
Lewiston o USA (ME) 278-279 L 4
Lewiston o USA (MI) 272-273 G 4
Lewiston o USA (MN) 270-271 G 7
Lewiston o USA (UT) 254-255 D 2
Lewistown o USA (IL) 274-275 H 4
Lewistown o USA (MT) 250-251 K 4
Lewistown o USA (PA) 280-281 J 3
Lewisville o USA (AR) 276-277 B 7
Lewisville o USA (TX) 264-265 H 5
Lewisville, Lake o USA (TX) 264-265 H 5
Lewoleba o RI 166-167 B 6
Lewnan o USA 22-23 R 3
Lexa o USA (AR) 276-277 E 6
Lexington o USA (GA) 284-285 G 3
Lexington o USA (KY) 276-277 L 2
Lexington o USA (MI) 272-273 G 4
Lexington o USA (MO) 274-275 D 5
Lexington o USA (MS) 268-269 K 3
Lexington o USA (NC) 282-283 G 5
Lexington o USA (NE) 262-263 G 4
Lexington o USA (OR) 244-245 F 5
Lexington o USA (SC) 284-285 J 2
Lexington o USA (TN) 276-277 G 5
Lexington o USA (TX) 266-267 K 3
Lexington o USA (VA) 280-281 G 6
Lexington Park o USA (MD) 280-281 K 5
Leybourne Islands ⌒ CDN 36-37 R 2
Leyburn o AUS 178-179 L 5
Leye o VRC 156-157 E 4
Leyland o CDN (ALB) 228-229 R 3
Leyson Point o CDN 36-37 J 3
Leyte ⌒ RP 160-161 F 7
Leyte Gulf ≈ RP 160-161 F 7
Lezama o RP 160-161 F 7
Lezhë o ·· AL 100-101 G 4
l-Gadaf, Wādī ~ IRQ 128-129 J 6
l-Gaut, Wādī ~ SYR 194-195 F 5
LG Deux, Réservoir ◁ CDN 38-39 F 2
l'gotny, mys ▲ RUS 120-121 H 5
l'gov o RUS 102-103 J 7
l'govski, Dmitriev o RUS 94-95 O 5
LG Trois, Réservoir de ◁ CDN 38-39 G 2
l-Hail, Wādī ~ SYR 128-129 H 5
Lhari o USA 144-145 J 5
L'Haridon Bight ≈ AUS 176-177 B 3
l-Harit, Wādī ~ ET 194-195 F 5
Lhasa o ·· VRC 144-145 H 6
Lhasa He ~ VRC 144-145 H 6
Lhazê o ·· VRC 144-145 F 6
Lhokseumawe o RI 162-163 B 2
Lhoksukon o RI 162-163 B 1
Lhorong o VRC 144-145 K 5
Lhotse ▲ NEP 144-145 J 5
Lhuntsi o BHT 142-143 G 2
Lhünzê o VRC 144-145 J 6
Li o THA 158-159 E 2
Lia, Tanjung ▲ RI 164-165 H 4
Liambezi, Lake o NAM 218-219 C 3
Liang o RI 164-165 H 4
Liangcheng o VRC (NMZ) 154-155 H 1
Liangdang o VRC (SHA) 154-155 D 5
Lianghe o VRC (SIC) 156-157 F 2
Lianghe o VRC (YUN) 142-143 L 3
Lianghekou o VRC 154-155 D 5
Liangping o VRC 154-155 D 6
Liangpran, Gunung ▲ RI 164-165 D 3
Lianhua o VRC 156-157 H 3
Lianhua Shan ▲ VRC 156-157 J 5
Lianjiang o VRC (FUJ) 156-157 L 4
Lianjiang o VRC (GDG) 156-157 G 6
Lianshan o VRC (GDG) 156-157 H 4

Lianshan o VRC (SIC) 154-155 D 6
Lianshui o VRC 154-155 L 5
Liantang o VRC 156-157 G 4
Lian Xian o VRC 156-157 H 4
Lianyuan o VRC 156-157 G 3
Lianyungang o VRC 154-155 L 4
Lianyungang (Xinpu) o VRC 154-155 L 4
Liaocheng o VRC 154-155 J 3
Liao Dao ⌒ VRC 144-145 M 2
Liaodong Bandao ⌒ VRC 150-151 D 8
Liaodong Wan ≈ VRC 150-151 C 7
Liaodun o VRC 146-147 L 4
Liao He ~ VRC 150-151 D 6
Liaoning □ VRC 150-151 D 7
Liao Shangjingcheng Yizhi ∴· VRC 148-149 O 6
Liaotung, Gulf of = Liaodong Wan ≈ VRC 150-151 C 7
Liaoyang o VRC 150-151 D 7
Liaoyuan o VRC 150-151 E 6
Liaozhong o VRC 150-151 D 7
Liao Zhongjingcheng Yizhi · VRC 148-149 O 7
Liäquatpur o PK 138-139 C 5
Liard Highway II CDN 30-31 H 5
Liard Plateau ▲ CDN 30-31 F 5
Liard River ~ CDN 30-31 G 4
Liat, Pulau ⌒ RI 162-163 G 6
Libano o CO 60-61 D 5
Libano o RA 78-79 J 4
Libanos Gedam, Debre · ETH 208-209 D 4
Libao o VRC 154-155 M 5
Libatemo o RI 164-165 H 5
Libau = Liepaja o LV 94-95 H 4
Libba o WAN 204-205 J 6
Libby o USA (MN) 270-271 E 4
Libby o USA (MT) 250-251 D 3
Libenge o ZRE 210-211 G 2
Liberal o USA (KS) 262-263 F 7
Liberator Lake o USA 20-21 L 2
Liberdade, Rio ~ BR 68-69 B 6
Liberec o ·· CZ 92-93 N 3
Liberia ☆ CR 52-53 B 6
Liberia ■ LB 202-203 C 6
Libertad o RA 76-77 J 6
Libertad o ROU 78-79 L 3
Libertad o YV 60-61 G 3
Libertad, La o ES 52-53 K 5
Libertad, La o HN 52-53 L 4
Libertador General San Martin o RA (JU) 76-77 E 2
Libertador General San Martin o RA (SLU) 78-79 G 2
Liberty o CDN (SAS) 232-233 N 4
Liberty o USA (IN) 274-275 O 5
Liberty o USA (KY) 276-277 L 3
Liberty o USA (ME) 278-279 M 4
Liberty o USA (MS) 268-269 K 4
Liberty o USA (NY) 280-281 M 2
Liberty o USA (SC) 284-285 F 2
Liberty o USA (TN) 276-277 K 4
Liberty o USA (TX) 268-269 F 6
Liberty o USA (UT) 254-255 D 2
Liberty Hill o USA (SC) 284-285 K 2
Liberty Lake o USA (WA) 244-245 H 3
Libertytown o USA (MD) 280-281 J 4
Libjo o RP 160-161 F 7
Libmanan o RP 160-161 E 6
Libode o RZA 220-221 J 5
Liboi o EAK 212-213 H 3
Liboko o ZRE 210-211 H 2
Libono o LS 220-221 H 4
Libourne o F 90-91 G 9
Libradh o ·· AL 100-101 H 4
Libreville ★ o G 210-211 B 2
Librija o CO 60-61 E 4
Libro Point ▲ RP 160-161 C 7
Libuganon ~ RP 160-161 F 9
Libya ■ LAR 192-193 D 4
Libyan Desert = as-Sahrā' al-Lībiyā ± LAR 192-193 K 3
Licancabur, Volcán ▲ RCH 76-77 D 2
Licata o I 100-101 D 6
Lice o TR 128-129 J 3
Licenciado Matienzo o RA 78-79 K 4
Lichang o VRC 154-155 H 6
Licheng o VRC 154-155 H 3
Lichinga o MOC 218-219 H 1
Lichinga, Planalto de ▲ MOC 218-219 H 1
Lichtenburg o RZA 220-221 H 3
Lichteneger, Lac o CDN 38-39 D 2
Licinio de Almeida o BR 72-73 J 3
Liciro o MOC 218-219 J 3
Licking o USA (MO) 276-277 D 3
Licking River ~ USA (KY) 276-277 L 2
Licuare, Rio ~ MOC 218-219 J 2
Licungo, Rio ~ MOC 218-219 J 2
Lida o BY 94-95 J 5
Lidan ~ S 86-87 F 7
Lida Sumtain o USA (NV) 248-249 G 2
Liddon Gulf ≈ 24-25 P 3
Liden o S 86-87 H 5
Lidgerwood o USA (ND) 258-259 K 5
Lidi, Mayo ~ CAM 206-207 A 4
Lidia ~ PE 70-71 B 2
Lidji ~ ZRE 210-211 F 5
Lidjombo o RCA 210-211 F 2
Lidköping o S 86-87 F 7
Lido o RN 204-205 L 2
Lido di Ostia o I 100-101 D 4
Lidskaja ravnina ▲ 94-95 J 5
Lidzbark Warmiński o ·· PL 92-93 Q 1
Liebenthal o CDN (SAS) 232-233 J 5
Liebenthal o USA (KS) 262-263 G 6
Liebig, Mount ▲ AUS 176-177 L 1
Liechtenstein ■ FL 92-93 K 5
Liège o ·· B 92-93 H 3
Lieksa o FIN 88-89 L 5
Liemianzheng o VRC 154-155 H 5
Lienz o A 92-93 M 5
Liepaja o ·· LV 94-95 H 4
Lier = Lier o B 92-93 H 3
Lierre o I 100-101 E 5
Lietnik o USA 20-21 H 2

Lièvre, Rivière du ~ CDN (QUE) 238-239 K 2
Liezen o A 92-93 N 5
Lifamatola, Pulau ⌒ RI 164-165 K 4
Lifford o IRL 90-91 D 4
Lifjell ~ N 86-87 D 7
Lifuka ⌒ TON 184 IV a 1
Lifune ~ ANG 216-217 C 4
Lifupa Lodge o MW 218-219 G 1
Ligao o RP 160-161 E 6
Ligar ~ TCH 206-207 C 4
Lighfoot Lake o USA 176-177 G 4
Light ~ RP 160-161 F 7
Light, Cape ▲ ARK 16 F 30
Lighthouse Beach ⊥ BS 54-55 G 2
Lighthouse Cove o CDN (ONT) 238-239 C 6
Lighthouse Point ▲ USA (FL) 286-287 E 2
Lighthouse Reef ⌒ BH 52-53 L 3
Lightning Creek ~ USA (WY) 252-253 O 3
Lightning Ridge o AUS 178-179 J 5
Lignite o USA (ND) 258-259 E 3
Ligonha, Rio ~ MOC 218-219 H 2
Ligonier o USA (IN) 274-275 N 3
Ligonier o USA (PA) 280-281 G 3
Ligowola o EAT 214-215 J 6
Ligúria ⊙ I 100-101 B 3
Ligurta o USA (AZ) 256-257 A 6
Lihás o GR 100-101 J 5
Lihin, al- o KSA 130-131 F 5
Lihir Group ⌒ PNG 183 G 2
Lihir Island ⌒ PNG 183 G 2
Liholslavľ o RUS 94-95 O 3
Lihou Reefs and Cays ⌒ AUS 174-175 M 5
Lihovskoj o RUS 102-103 M 8
Lihue o · USA (HI) 288 F 3
Lihuel Calel, Parque Nacional ⊥ RA 78-79 G 4
Lihula o EST 94-95 H 2
Liivi Laht ≈ 94-95 H 2
Lijiang o VRC (YUN) 142-143 M 2
Lijiang ·· VRC (GXI) 156-157 G 4
Lik ~ LAO 156-157 C 7
Lik, Pulau ⌒ RI 166-167 K 2
Likala ~ ZRE 210-211 G 3
Likame ~ ZRE 210-211 H 3
Likasi o ZRE 214-215 D 6
Likati o ZRE (Hau) 210-211 J 2
Likati ~ ZRE 210-211 J 2
Likely o CDN (BC) 228-229 N 4
Likely o USA (CA) 246-247 E 2
Likete o ZRE 210-211 J 4
Likisia o RI 166-167 C 6
Likoma Islands ⌒ MW 214-215 H 7
Likoto o ZRE 210-211 K 4
Likouala □ RCB 210-211 F 3
Likouala aux Herbes ~ RCB 210-211 F 3
Likum o PNG 183 D 2
Likuyu o EAT 214-215 J 6
Lilarea o AUS 178-179 H 2
Lilbourn o USA (MO) 276-277 F 4
Liliáni o PK 138-139 D 3
Lilikse o GH 202-203 J 4
Liling o VRC 156-157 H 3
Lilla o PK 138-139 D 3
Lille o F 90-91 J 6
Lille Bælt ≈ DK 86-87 D 9
Lillehammer o N 86-87 E 6
Lille Hellefiskebanke ≈ 28-29 N 4
Lilles, Punta ▲ RCH 78-79 D 2
Lillesand o · N 86-87 D 7
Lillestrøm o N 86-87 E 7
Lillico Point ▲ CDN 36-37 K 6
Lillie o USA (LA) 268-269 H 4
Lillington o USA (NC) 282-283 J 5
Lilliwaup o USA (WA) 244-245 C 3
Lillooet o CDN (BC) 230-231 G 3
Lillooet Lake o CDN (BC) 230-231 F 3
Lillooet Range ▲ CDN (BC) 230-231 G 3
Lillooet River ~ CDN (BC) 230-231 F 3
Lilo o ZRE 210-211 K 4
Lilongwe ★ MW 218-219 H 1
Lilo Viejo o RA 76-77 F 4
Liloy o RP 160-161 E 8
Lily o USA (SD) 260-261 J 1
Lily o USA (WI) 270-271 K 5
Lilydale o AUS 180-181 J 6
Lim o USA (WA) 244-245 G 4
Lim ~ YU 100-101 G 3
Lima o OM 134-135 G 3
Lima ★ ·· PE 64-65 D 8
Lima o PY 76-77 J 2
Lima o USA (MT) 250-251 G 7
Lima o USA (OH) 280-281 B 3
Lima, La o HN 52-53 L 4
Lima, La o RCH 78-79 D 2
Limache o RCH 78-79 D 2
Limal o BOL 70-71 F 5
Liman o RUS 126-127 G 5
Limão, Igarapé do ~ BR 66-67 K 6
Limão do Curuá ~ BR 62-63 J 5
Limapuluh o RI 162-163 C 3
Limar o RI 166-167 G 5
Limari, Rio ~ RCH 78-79 D 2
Limassa o RCA 206-207 F 8
Limasawa Island ⌒ RP 160-161 F 8
Limaú, Rio ~ BR 66-67 G 4
Limay, Río ~ RA 78-79 E 5
Limba Limba ~ EAT 214-215 G 5
Limbang o MAL 164-165 D 1
Limbani o PE 70-71 C 4
Limbaži o LV 94-95 H 3
Limbdi o IND 138-139 C 8
Limbe o MW 218-219 H 2

Limbé o RH 54-55 J 5
Limbé = Victoria o CAM 204-205 H 6
Limbla o AUS 178-179 C 2
Limbo, Pulau ⌒ RI 164-165 J 4
Límboto o RI 164-165 H 3
Limbunan o RP 160-161 E 9
Limbu o RI 164-165 F 5
Limburan o BR 72-73 J 4
Limburg an der Lahn o ·· D 92-93 K 3
Lime ~ USA 244-245 H 6
Lime Acres o ZA 220-221 F 4
Limeira o BR (MIN) 72-73 H 4
Limeira o BR (PAU) 72-73 G 7
Limekiln, Cape ▲ USA 176-177 G 4
Limerick o CDN (NB) 242-243 N 5
Limerick o CDN (SAS) 232-233 M 6
Limerick o USA (ME) 278-279 L 5
Limerick = Luimneach ◉ IRL 90-91 C 5
Limestone o CDN (NB) 242-243 N 5
Limestone o USA (ME) 278-279 O 2
Limestone o USA (MT) 250-251 K 6
Limestone, Lake < USA (TX) 266-267 K 3
Limestone Peak ▲ USA (AZ) 256-257 F 7
Limestone Point ▲ CDN 34-35 G 4
Limestone Rapids ~ CDN 34-35 L 2
Limestone River ~ CDN 34-35 M 2
Limfjorden ≈ 86-87 D 8
Limgytynot ~ RUS 112-113 W 4
Limia, Rio ~ E 98-99 D 3
Limingen o N 86-87 F 4
Liminka o FIN 88-89 J 4
Limmen Bight ≈ 174-175 C 4
Limmen Bight Aboriginal Land X AUS 174-175 C 4
Limmen Bight River ~ AUS 174-175 C 4
Limnos ⌒ GR 100-101 K 5
Limnu ~ RUS 120-121 E 6
Limoeiro o BR 68-69 K 5
Limoeiro do Ajurú o BR 62-63 K 6
Limoeiro do Norte o BR 68-69 J 4
Limoges ★ · F 90-91 H 8
Limon o CO 254-255 M 4
Limonar o C 54-55 H 4
Limousin ⊙ F 90-91 H 9
Limoux o F 90-91 J 10
Limpio o PY 76-77 J 3
Limpopo ~ MOC 218-219 H 5
Limpopo, Rio ~ ZA 218-219 E 6
Limpopo, Rio ~ MOC 220-221 L 2
Limpitýrky ~ RUS 114-115 R 2
Limptēkan ~ RUS 116-117 M 4
Limuru o EAK 212-213 F 4
Lin, Ngọc ▲ VN 158-159 J 3
Linah o KSA 130-131 F 5
Linahamari o RUS 88-89 L 3
Lin'an o VRC 154-155 L 6
Linao Point ▲ RP 160-161 E 9
Linapacan Island ⌒ RP 160-161 C 7
Linapacan Strait ≈ 160-161 C 7
Linares o E 98-99 F 6
Linares o MEX 50-51 K 5
Linares o RCH 78-79 D 3
Linas, Monte ▲ I 100-101 B 5
Lincang o VRC 142-143 M 4
Linchang o VRC 156-157 K 3
Linchuan o VRC 156-157 K 3
Lincoln ☆ NZ 182 D 5
Lincoln o USA (AL) 284-285 D 3
Lincoln o USA (CA) 248-249 E 3
Lincoln o USA (CA) 246-247 D 3
Lincoln o USA (IL) 274-275 J 4
Lincoln o USA (KS) 262-263 G 5
Lincoln o USA (ME) 278-279 N 3
Lincoln o USA (MT) 250-251 G 5
Lincoln o USA (NH) 278-279 L 4
Lincoln o USA (NM) 256-257 K 5
Lincoln o USA (NE) 262-263 K 4
Lincoln Birthplace National Historic Site, Abraham ∴· USA (KY) 276-277 K 3
Lincoln Boyhood National Memorial · USA (IN) 274-275 M 4
Lincoln Caverns ∴ USA (PA) 280-281 H 3
Lincoln City o USA (IN) 274-275 M 4
Lincoln City o USA (OR) 244-245 A 6
Lincoln Highway II USA 180-181 D 2
Lincoln National Park ⊥ AUS 180-181 C 5
Lincoln Sea ≈ 26-27 U 2
Lincoln's New Salem · USA (IL) 274-275 J 3
Lincolnton o USA (GA) 284-285 H 3
Lincolnton o USA (NC) 282-283 F 5
Lind o USA (WA) 244-245 G 4
Linda o USA (CA) 246-247 D 3
Lindadawa o MYA 142-143 J 5
Lindale o USA (TX) 264-265 J 6
Lindau (Bodensee) o ·· D 92-93 K 5
Lindbergh o CDN (ALB) 232-233 H 2
Lindbrook o CDN (ALB) 232-233 F 2
Linde ~ RUS 110-111 M 4
Linde ~ RUS 110-111 M 6
Linde ~ RUS 118-119 M 3
Lindela o MOC 218-219 H 7
Lindeman Group ⌒ AUS 174-175 K 7
Linden o CDN (ALB) 232-233 E 4
Linden o USA (AL) 284-285 C 4
Linden o USA (CA) 246-247 E 3
Linden o USA (NJ) 280-281 M 3
Linden o USA (TN) 276-277 H 5
Linden o USA (TX) 264-265 K 5
Lindenows Fjord ≈ 28-29 T 6
Lindesnes ▲ N 86-87 C 8
Lindhard Ø ⌒ GRØ 26-27 o 5
Lindi o EAT (LIN) 214-215 K 5
Lindi o ZRE 210-211 J 3
Lindian o VRC 150-151 D 4
Lindi Bay ≈ EAT 214-215 K 5
Lindis Pass ≏ NZ 182 B 6
Lindley o ZA 220-221 H 4
Lindleyspoort o ZA 220-221 H 3
Líndos o ·· GR 100-101 M 6

Lindsay o CDN (ONT) 238-239 G 4
Lindsay o USA (CA) 248-249 F 4
Lindsay o USA (MT) 250-251 O 4
Lindsay o USA (OK) 264-265 G 4
Lindsay, Mount ▲ AUS 176-177 K 3
Lindsborg o USA (KS) 262-263 H 6
Lindstrom o USA (MN) 270-271 F 5
Lindström Peninsula ∪ CDN 24-25 e 2
Lindu, Danau o RI 164-165 G 4
Line Islands ⌒ KIB 14-15 N 7
Linejnoe o RUS 96-97 E 10
Linfen o VRC 154-155 G 3
Lingamakki Reservoir ◁ IND 140-141 B 4
Lingayen Gulf ≈ RP 160-161 D 4
Lingbao o VRC 154-155 G 4
Lingbi o VRC 154-155 K 5
Lingbim o CAM 206-207 B 4
Lingen (Ems) o ·· D 92-93 J 2
Lingga o MAL 162-163 J 4
Lingga, Kepulauan ⌒ RI 162-163 F 5
Lingga, Pulau ⌒ RI 162-163 F 5
Lingkeh o RI 164-165 G 5
Lingkobu, Tanjung ▲ RI 164-165 G 5
Lingle o USA (WY) 252-253 O 4
Linglinguiym, buhta ≈ RUS 112-113 R 6
Lingo o USA (NM) 256-257 M 5
Lingomo o ZRE (EQU) 210-211 J 3
Lingomo o ZRE (EQU) 210-211 J 4
Lingqiu o VRC 154-155 J 2
Lingsar o RI 164-165 F 8
Lingshan o VRC 156-157 F 5
Lingshan Dao ⌒ VRC 154-155 M 4
Lingshi o VRC 154-155 G 3
Lingshui o VRC 156-157 G 7
Lingsügür o IND 140-141 C 3
Lingtai o VRC 154-155 D 4
Lingtou o VRC 156-157 F 7
Linguère o SN 202-203 C 2
Lingui o VRC 156-157 G 4
Lingwu o VRC 154-155 E 3
Ling Xian o VRC 156-157 H 3
Lingxiaoyan ·· VRC 156-157 G 5
Lingyuan o VRC 148-149 O 7
Linh, Ngọc ▲ VN 158-159 J 3
Linhai o VRC (HEI) 150-151 J 1
Linhai o VRC (ZHE) 156-157 M 2
Linhares o BR 72-73 K 5
Linhe o VRC 154-155 E 1
Linhenco o ANG 216-217 C 4
Linjiang o VRC 150-151 F 7
Linke Lakes o USA 176-177 G 2
Linkiring o SN 202-203 C 2
Linkou o VRC 150-151 H 5
Linköping o · S 86-87 G 7
Linli o VRC 156-157 G 3
Linlithgow o GB 90-91 F 4
Linn o USA (KS) 262-263 J 5
Linn o USA (MO) 274-275 G 6
Linn o USA (TX) 266-267 J 7
Linn o USA (WV) 280-281 F 4
Linneus o USA (MO) 274-275 E 5
Linping o VRC 156-157 L 5
Linqing o VRC 154-155 J 3
Linqu o VRC 154-155 L 3
Linquan o VRC 154-155 J 5
Lins o BR 72-73 F 7
Linsan o RG 202-203 D 4
Linsell o S 86-87 F 5
Linshu o VRC 154-155 L 4
Linshui o VRC 154-155 E 6
Linstead o JA 54-55 G 5
Linta ~ RM 222-223 D 10
Lintao o VRC 154-155 C 4
Linté o CAM 204-205 J 5
Lintea Tiwolu, Pulau ⌒ RI 164-165 H 6
Linthipe o MW 218-219 H 2
Lintlaw o CDN (SAS) 232-233 P 3
Linton o CDN (QUE) 238-239 S 5
Linton o USA (IN) 274-275 L 6
Linton o USA (ND) 258-259 G 5
Lintong o VRC 154-155 F 4
Linville o USA (NC) 282-283 F 4
Linville Caverns ∴ USA (NC) 282-283 F 5
Linxi o VRC 148-149 O 6
Linxia o VRC 154-155 C 4
Lin Xian o VRC (HEN) 154-155 H 3
Lin Xian o VRC (SHA) 154-155 G 3
Linxiang o VRC 156-157 H 3
Linyanti ~ NAM 218-219 B 4
Linyanti Swamp ~ NAM 218-219 B 4
Linyi o VRC (SHD) 154-155 L 3
Linyi o VRC (SHD) 154-155 K 3
Linz o A 92-93 N 4
Linze o VRC 154-155 B 3
Linzhen o VRC 154-155 F 3
Línzor o RCH 76-77 D 2
Lioana o RP 160-161 E 5
Lioma o MOC 218-219 J 2
Lion, Golfe du ≈ 90-91 J 10
Lion Camp o ZA 218-219 F 1
Lioni, Cachu o CO 60-61 G 5
Lion Park o ZA 220-221 H 2
Lions Den o ZW 218-219 F 3
Lioppa o RI 166-167 C 5
Lios Tuathail = Listowel ◉ IRL 90-91 C 5
Lioua o TCH 198-199 J 6
Liouesso o RCB 210-211 E 3
Lipa o RP 160-161 D 6
Lipale o MOC 218-219 J 2
Lipari o I 100-101 E 5
Lipari, Ísola ⌒ I 100-101 E 5
Lipcani o MD 102-103 E 3
Lipeck o RUS 96-97 F 5
Lipeo, Río ~ RA 76-77 E 2
Liperi o FIN 88-89 L 5
Lipetrén, Sierra ▲ RA 78-79 F 6
Lipin Bor o RUS 94-95 Q 1
Liping o VRC 156-157 F 3

Lipis, Kuala ~ MAL 162-163 E 2
Lipkany = Lipcani o MD 102-103 E 3
Lipki o RUS 94-95 P 5
Lipljan o · YU 100-101 H 3
Lipno o PL 92-93 P 2
Lipno, vodní nádrž ◁ CZ 92-93 N 4
Lipova o RO 102-103 B 4
Lippe ~ D 92-93 K 3
Lippstadt o · D 92-93 K 3
Lipscomb o USA (TX) 264-265 D 2
Lipton o CDN (SAS) 232-233 P 5
Liptougou o BF 202-203 L 3
Liptrap, Cape ▲ AUS 180-181 H 5
Lipu o VRC 156-157 G 4
Liquça = Likisia o RI 166-167 C 6
Lira o EAU 212-213 E 2
Liranga o RCB 210-211 F 4
Lircay o PE 64-65 E 8
Lirung o RI 164-165 J 3
Lisakovsk o KA 124-125 C 2
Lisala o ZRE 210-211 H 2
Lisboa ★ ·· P 98-99 C 5
Lisbon o USA (IL) 274-275 K 3
Lisbon o USA (NY) 278-279 G 5
Lisbon o USA (OH) 280-281 E 3
Lisbon = Lisboa ★ ·· P 98-99 C 5
Lisbon Falls o USA (ME) 278-279 L 4
Lisburn, Cape = Cape Mata'Avea ▲ VAN 184 II a 1
Lisburne, Cape ▲ USA 20-21 G 2
Liscomb o CDN (NS) 240-241 N 5
Liscomb Game Sanction ⊥ CDN (NS) 240-241 N 5
Liscomb Island ⌒ CDN (NS) 240-241 N 5
Liscomb Mills o CDN (NS) 240-241 N 5
Lishan o VRC (SHA) 154-155 G 3
Lishan Z.B. ⊥ · VRC 154-155 G 4
Lishi o VRC (SHA) 154-155 G 3
Lishi o VRC (SHA) 156-157 D 2
Lishu o VRC 150-151 E 6
Lishui o VRC 156-157 L 2
Lisianski Island ⌒ USA 14-15 L 5
Lisičansk = Lysyčans'k o UA 102-103 L 3
Lisica ~ RUS 114-115 O 5
Lisica-Pass ≏ YU 100-101 H 3
Lisieux o · F 90-91 H 7
Lisinskaja buhta ≈ RUS 120-121 W 6
Lisja ~ RUS 112-113 K 3
Lisjanskogo, poluostrov ~ RUS 120-121 M 6
Liski o RUS 102-103 L 2
L'Islet o CDN (QUE) 240-241 E 3
L'Isle-Verte o CDN (QUE) 240-241 F 3
Lismore o AUS (NSW) 178-179 M 5
Lismore o AUS (VIC) 180-181 G 4
Lismore o CDN (NS) 240-241 N 5
Lismore o USA (MN) 270-271 C 7
Lisnaskea o · GB 90-91 D 4
Lisomu, Tanjung ▲ RI 166-167 C 6
Lissadell o AUS 172-173 J 4
Lister o CDN (BC) 230-231 N 4
Lister, Mount ▲ ARK 16 F 17
Lištica = Široki Brijeg o BIH 100-101 F 3
Listowel o CDN (ONT) 238-239 G 5
Listowel = Lios Tuathail ◉ IRL 90-91 C 5
Listvjanka o RUS 116-117 M 10
Lit, al- o KSA 132-133 B 3
Lita o EC 64-65 C 1
Litang o MAL 160-161 C 10
Litang o VRC (GXI) 156-157 F 5
Litang o VRC (SIC) 156-157 B 2
Litáni ~ RL 128-129 F 6
Litanirivier ~ BR 62-63 G 4
Litchfield o CDN (QUE) 246-247 E 3
Litchfield o USA (IL) 274-275 J 6
Litchfield o USA (MN) 270-271 D 5
Litchfield o USA (NE) 262-263 G 3
Litchfield Beach o USA (SC) 284-285 L 3
Litchfield Out Station o AUS 172-173 K 2
Litchfield Park ⊥ AUS 172-173 K 2
Litchfield Park o USA (AZ) 256-257 C 5
Litchville o USA (ND) 258-259 J 5
Lithgow o AUS 180-181 L 2
Lithuania ■ LT 94-95 G 4
Litipára o IND 142-143 G 3
Litke o RUS (ARH) 108-109 F 5
Litke o RUS (HBR) 122-123 J 4
Litke, poluostrov ~ RUS 108-109 J 3
Litke, proliv ≈ 120-121 U 4
Litoměřice o · CZ 92-93 N 3
Litomyšl o CZ 92-93 O 3
Litovko o RUS 122-123 H 5
Littau o USA (WA) 244-245 B 4
Little Abaco Island ⌒ BS 54-55 G 1
Little Abitibi Lake o CDN (ONT) 236-237 H 3
Little Abitibi River ~ CDN (ONT) 236-237 G 2
Little Aden o Y 132-133 D 7
Little America o USA (WY) 252-253 J 4
Little Arkansas River ~ USA (KS) 262-263 H 6
Little Barrier Island ⌒ NZ 182 E 2
Little Bay o CDN (NFL) 242-243 N 3
Little Bay Beach ~ GB 56 D 3
Little Bay de Noc ≈ USA 270-271 L 4
Little Belt Mountains ▲ USA (MT) 250-251 H 4
Little Bitterroot River ~ USA (MT) 250-251 E 4
Little Black River ~ USA 20-21 T 3
Little Blue River ~ USA (KS) 262-263 K 5
Little Blue River ~ USA (NE) 262-263 H 4
Little Bow River ~ CDN (ALB) 232-233 E 5
Little Buffalo River ~ CDN 30-31 N 5
Little Burnt Bay o CDN (NFL) 242-243 N 3
Little Cadotte River ~ CDN 32-33 M 3

Little Cayman ⌒ GB 54-55 E 5
Little Chicago o CDN 30-31 E 2
Little Colorado River ~ USA (AZ) 256-257 F 4
Little Corwallis Island ⌒ CDN 24-25 Y 3
Little Creek o USA (DE) 280-281 L 4
Little Creek Peak ▲ USA (UT) 254-255 D 6
Little Current o CDN (ONT) 238-239 D 3
Little Current River ~ CDN (ONT) 236-237 C 2
Little Current River ~ CDN (ONT) 236-237 B 2
Little Cypress Boyau ~ USA (TX) 264-265 K 6
Little Delta River ~ USA 20-21 R 5
Little Desert ⊥ AUS 180-181 F 4
Little Desert National Park ⊥ AUS 180-181 F 4
Little Diomede Island ⌒ USA 20-21 F 4
Little Exuma Island ⌒ BS 54-55 H 3
Little Falls o USA (MN) 270-271 D 5
Little Falls o USA (NY) 278-279 G 5
Littlefield o USA (AZ) 256-257 B 2
Littlefield o USA (TX) 264-265 B 5
Little Fork o USA (MN) 270-271 E 2
Little Fork River ~ USA (MN) 270-271 E 2
Little Fort o CDN (BC) 230-231 J 2
Little Gold River ~ AUS 172-173 H 4
Little Grand Rapids o CDN (MAN) 234-235 H 2
Little Harbour o BS 54-55 G 2
Little Harbour o CDN (NFL) 242-243 L 3
Little Hocking o USA (OH) 280-281 E 4
Little Humboldt River ~ USA (NV) 246-247 H 2
Little Inagua Island ⌒ BS 54-55 J 4
Little Kanawha River ~ USA (WV) 280-281 E 4
Little Karoo = Klein Karoo ± ZA 220-221 E 6
Little Koniuji Island ⌒ USA 22-23 R 5
Little Lake o USA (CA) 248-249 G 4
Little Lake o USA (MI) 270-271 L 4
Little Lost River ~ USA (ID) 252-253 E 2
Little Lynches River ~ USA (SC) 284-285 L 2
Little Malad River ~ USA (ID) 252-253 F 4
Little Mecatina River ~ CDN 38-39 N 2
Little Miami River ~ USA (OH) 280-281 B 4
Little Missouri River ~ USA (AR) 276-277 B 6
Little Missouri River ~ USA (MT) 250-251 P 6
Little Missouri River ~ USA (ND) 258-259 E 4
Little Moose Island ⌒ CDN (MAN) 234-235 F 3
Little Muddy Creek ~ USA (WY) 252-253 H 5
Little Mud River ~ USA 20-21 O 4
Little Mulberry Creek ~ USA (AL) 284-285 C 4
Little Nemaha River ~ USA (NE) 262-263 L 4
Little Nicobar Island ⌒ IND 140-141 G 8
Little Norway o CDN (CA) 246-247 E 5
Little Osage River ~ USA (MO) 274-275 D 6
Little Pee Dee River ~ USA (SC) 284-285 L 2
Little Pic ~ CDN (ONT) 236-237 B 3
Little Powder River ~ USA (WY) 252-253 N 2
Little Quill Lake o CDN (SAS) 232-233 O 4
Little Ragged Island ⌒ BS 54-55 H 3
Little Rancheria River ~ CDN 20-21 Z 7
Little Rapid Creek ~ CDN 30-31 S 3
Little Red Deer River ~ CDN (ALB) 232-233 D 4
Little Red River ~ USA (AR) 276-277 D 5
Little Ridge o CDN (MAN) 234-235 E 4
Little River o CDN (BC) 230-231 E 4
Little River o USA (AR) 276-277 E 5
Little River ~ USA (GA) 284-285 F 4
Little River ~ USA (GA) 284-285 G 5
Little River ~ USA (LA) 268-269 H 4
Little River ~ USA (NC) 282-283 H 4
Little River ~ USA (NC) 282-283 J 4
Little River ~ USA (OK) 264-265 H 3
Little River ~ USA (TX) 266-267 K 3
Little Rock ☆ USA (AR) 276-277 C 6
Little Rock o USA (WA) 244-245 B 4
Little Ruaha ~ EAT 214-215 H 5
Little Sable Point ▲ USA (MI) 272-273 C 4
Little Sachigo Lake o CDN 34-35 G 4
Little Sahara Recreation Area ⊥ USA (UT) 254-255 C 4
Little Saint Lawrence o CDN (NFL) 242-243 N 5
Little Saint Simons Island ⌒ USA (GA) 284-285 J 3
Little Salkehatchie River ~ USA (SC) 284-285 J 3
Little Salmon Lake o CDN 20-21 X 5
Little Salt Lake o USA (UT) 254-255 C 6
Little Sandy River ~ USA (KY) 276-277 M 2
Little San Salvador Island ⌒ BS 54-55 H 2
Little Sauk o USA (MN) 270-271 D 5
Little Scarcies of Kaba ~ WAL 202-203 D 5
Little Seal River ~ CDN 30-31 W 6
Little Sevier River ~ USA (UT) 254-255 C 6

Little Sioux River ~ USA (IA) 274-275 C 2
Little Sitkin Island ⌒ USA 22-23 F 7
Little Smoky o CDN (ALB) 228-229 R 2
Little Smoky River ~ CDN 32-33 M 4
Little Snake River ~ USA (CO) 254-255 G 3
Little Tallahatchie ~ USA (MS) 268-269 L 2
Little Tallapoosa River ~ USA (AL) 284-285 E 3
Little Tanaga Island ⌒ USA 22-23 H 7
Little Tennessee River ~ USA (NC) 282-283 D 5
Littleton o USA (CO) 254-255 K 4
Littleton o USA (NC) 282-283 K 4
Littleton o USA (NH) 278-279 K 4
Little Traverse Bay ≈ USA 272-273 D 2
Little Valley o USA (CA) 246-247 D 3
Little Valley o USA (NY) 278-279 C 6
Little Wabash River ~ USA (IL) 274-275 K 6
Little White River ~ CDN (ONT) 238-239 B 2
Little Wichita River ~ USA (TX) 264-265 F 5
Little Yellowstone Park ∴ USA (ND) 258-259 K 5
Littoral ◘ CAM 204-205 H 6
Lituhi o EAT 214-215 H 6
Litunde o MOC 218-219 H 1
Litvinova, mys ▲ RUS 108-109 Y 1
Litvinovo o RUS 96-97 F 3
Liu o RI 164-165 G 5
Liuba o VRC 154-155 E 5
Liuchiu Yü ⌒ RC 156-157 M 5
Liucura o RCH 78-79 D 5
Liuhe o VRC 150-151 E 6
Liuheng Dao ⌒ VRC 156-157 N 2
Liujiachang o VRC 154-155 G 6
Liujiang o VRC 156-157 F 4
Liujiaxia Sk. o VRC 154-155 C 4
Liujing o VRC 156-157 G 5
Liukanglu, Pulau ⌒ RI 164-165 G 6
Liuli o EAT 214-215 H 6
Liulin o VRC 154-155 G 3
Liupan Shan ▲ VRC 154-155 D 3
Liupanshan Z.B. ⊥ • VRC 154-155 E 4
Liupanshui o VRC 156-157 D 3
Liúpo o MOC 218-219 K 2
Liushai o VRC 156-157 E 4
Liushipu o VRC 154-155 J 5
Liuwa Plain National Park ⊥ Z 218-219 B 2
Liuxu o VRC 156-157 F 5
Liuyang o VRC 156-157 H 2
Liuzhao Shan ▲ VRC 156-157 D 5
Liuzhi o VRC 156-157 D 3
Liuzhou o • VRC 156-157 F 4
Liuzhuang o VRC 154-155 M 5
Liváli o GR 100-101 K 6
Livadiá o • GR 100-101 J 5
Livani o •• LV 94-95 K 3
Livanovka o KA 124-125 C 2
Livelong o CDN (SAS) 232-233 K 2
Lively o USA (VA) 280-281 K 6
Lively Island ⌒ GB 78-79 L 7
Livengood o USA 20-21 Q 4
Live Oak o USA (CA) 248-249 H 7
Live Oak o USA (FL) 286-287 G 1
Livermore o USA (CA) 248-249 C 2
Livermore o USA (KY) 276-277 H 3
Livermore, Mount ▲ USA (TX) 266-267 C 3
Livermore Falls o USA (ME) 278-279 L 4
Liverpool o AUS 180-181 L 2
Liverpool o CDN (NS) 240-241 L 6
Liverpool o • GB 90-91 F 5
Liverpool, Cape ▲ CDN 24-25 h 4
Liverpool Bay ≈ 20-21 Z 2
Liverpool Range ▲ AUS 178-179 K 6
Liviko Pélagos ≈ 100-101 J 7
Livingston o USA (AL) 284-285 B 4
Livingston o USA (KY) 276-277 L 3
Livingston o USA (LA) 268-269 K 6
Livingston o USA (MT) 250-251 J 6
Livingston o USA (TN) 276-277 K 4
Livingston o USA (TX) 268-269 F 6
Livingston, Lake < USA (TX) 268-269 E 6
Livingstone ☆ Z 218-219 C 3
Livingstone Memorial • Z 214-215 F 7
Livingstonia o • MW 214-215 H 6
Livingston Island ⌒ ARK 16 G 30
Livinstone's Cave • RB 220-221 G 2
Livno o BIH 100-101 F 3
Livny o RUS 94-95 P 5
Livonia o USA (MI) 272-273 F 5
Livorno o I 100-101 C 3
Livradois-Forez, Parc Naturel Régional ⊥ F 90-91 J 9
Livramento do Brumado o BR 72-73 K 2
Liwa o RI 162-163 F 7
Liwā', al- o OM 132-133 K 1
Liwale o EAT 214-215 J 5
Liwonde o MW 218-219 H 2
Liwonde National Park ⊥ MW 218-219 H 2
Li Xian o VRC (GAN) 154-155 D 4
Li Xian o VRC (SIC) 154-155 C 6
Lixin o VRC 154-155 K 5
Lixoúri o GR 100-101 H 5
Lixus ∴ • MA 188-189 H 3
Liyang o VRC 154-155 L 6
Li Yubu o SUD 206-207 H 6
Lizarda o BR 68-69 E 6
Lizard Head Peak ▲ USA (WY) 252-253 J 4
Lizard Island ⌒ AUS 174-175 H 4
Lizard Point ▲ GB 90-91 E 7
Lizard Point Indian Reserve ✕ CDN (MAN) 234-235 C 4
Lizella o USA (GA) 284-285 G 4
Lizotte o CDN (QUE) 240-241 C 2
Lizton o USA (IN) 274-275 M 5
Lizums o LV 94-95 K 3
Ljadova ~ UA 102-103 E 3
Ljady o RUS 94-95 L 2
Ljahovskie ostrova ⌒ RUS 110-111 U 2
Ljaki o AZ 128-129 M 2
Ljamca o RUS 88-89 O 4
Ljamin ~ RUS 114-115 L 4
Ljamin, pervyj ~ RUS 114-115 K 3
Ljamin, vtoroj ~ RUS 114-115 K 3
Ljamskie gory ▲ RUS 108-109 Y 7
Ljangar o TJ 136-137 N 6
Ljangasovo o RUS 96-97 F 4
Ljantorskij o RUS 114-115 M 4
Ljapin ~ RUS 114-115 F 3
Ljapiske ~ RUS 118-119 N 3
Ljig o YU 100-101 H 2
Ljuban' o BY 94-95 L 5
Ljuban' o RUS 94-95 M 2
Ljubanskae vadashovišča < BY 94-95 L 5
Ljubar o UA 102-103 E 3
Ljubercy ☆ RUS 94-95 P 4
Ljubertsy = Ljubercy ☆ RUS 94-95 P 4
Ljubešiv o UA 102-103 D 2
Ljubinskij ☆ RUS 114-115 M 7
Ljubljana ★ SLO 100-101 E 1
Ljubomľ o UA 102-103 D 2
Ljubovija o YU 100-101 G 2
Ljubytino o RUS 94-95 N 2
Ljudinovo o RUS 94-95 O 5
Ljugarn o S 86-87 J 8
Ljukkum ⊥ KA 124-125 K 5
Ljungan ~ S 86-87 H 5
Ljungby ☆ S 86-87 F 8
Ljungdalen o S 86-87 F 5
Ljusdal o S 86-87 H 6
Ljusnan ~ S 86-87 G 6
Ljutoga ~ RUS 122-123 K 5
Lk. Kambera ~ RI 168 E 7
Llaima, Volcán ▲ RCH 78-79 D 5
Llallagua o BOL 70-71 D 6
Llalli o PE 70-71 B 4
Llamara, Salar de o RCH 76-77 C 1
Llançà o E 98-99 J 3
Llancañelo, Laguna y Salina ⊂ RA 78-79 E 3
Llanddovery o GB 90-91 F 6
Llanes o • E 98-99 E 3
Llano o USA (TX) 266-267 J 3
Llano, El o PA 52-53 E 7
Llanobajo o CO 60-61 C 6
Llano Estacado ⌣ USA (TX) 264-265 A 5
Llano Mariato o PA 52-53 D 8
Llano River ~ USA (TX) 266-267 J 3
Llano River, North ~ USA (TX) 266-267 G 3
Llano River, South ~ USA (TX) 266-267 G 3
Llanos, Sierra de los ▲ RA 76-77 D 6
Llanos de Aridane, Los o E 188-189 C 6
Llanquihué o RCH 78-79 C 6
Llanquihué, Lago ⊂ RCH 78-79 C 6
Llao Llao o RA 78-79 D 6
Llaylla o PE 64-65 E 7
Llay-Llay o RCH 78-79 D 2
Lleida o •• E 98-99 H 4
Llera de Canales o MEX 50-51 K 6
Llerena o E 98-99 D 5
Llewellyn Glacier ⊂ CDN 20-21 X 7
Lleyn Peninsula ⌣ GB 90-91 E 5
Llica o BOL 70-71 C 6
Llico o RCH 78-79 C 4
Llíria o E 98-99 G 5
Lliscaya, Cerro ▲ BOL 70-71 C 6
Lloyd o USA (MT) 250-251 K 3
Lloyd Bay ≈ 174-175 G 3
Lloyd Lake ⊂ CDN 32-33 Q 3
Lloydminster o CDN (ALB) 232-233 H 2
Lloyd Rock = The Brothers ⌒ BS 54-55 H 3
Lloyd's Camp o RB 218-219 C 4
Llullaillaco, Volcán ▲ RCH 76-77 C 3
Lluta o PE 70-71 A 5
Lluta, Río ~ RCH 70-71 C 6
l-Miyāh, Wādī ~ SYR 128-129 H 5
l-Murra, al-Buhaira < ET 194-195 F 2
Lo, Île = Loh ⌒ VAN 184 II a 1
Loa o USA (UT) 254-255 D 5
Loa, Caleta ≈ 76-77 B 1
Loa, Río ~ RCH 76-77 C 1
Loandji ~ ANG 216-217 D 4
Loandji ~ ZRE 210-211 G 6
Loange ~ ZRE 210-211 H 6
Loango o ZRE 210-211 D 6
Loanja ~ Z 218-219 C 3
Loano o RI 164-165 G 5
Loary o RP 160-161 F 8
Loban o RUS 88-89 S 4
Lobatse ☆ RB 220-221 G 2
Lobaye ◘ RCA 206-207 C 6
Lobaye ~ RCA 210-211 G 2
Lobaye ~ ZRE 210-211 K 3
Lobé ~ CAM 210-211 C 2
Lobé, Chutes de la = Lobé Falls ~ CAM 210-211 B 2
Lobecks Pass ▲ USA (CA) 248-249 K 5
Lobé Falls = Chutes de la Lobé ~ CAM 210-211 B 2
Lobeke ~ CAM 210-211 F 2
Lobería o RA 78-79 K 5
Łobez o PL 92-93 N 2
Lobi o MW 218-219 H 2
Lobira o SUD 208-209 A 6
Lobito o ANG (BGU) 216-217 B 6
Lobitos o PE 64-65 B 4
Lobo ~ CAM 210-211 D 2
Lobo o RI 166-167 H 3
Loboko o RCB 210-211 F 4
Lobo Lodge o EAT 212-213 E 4
Lobos o RA 78-79 K 3
Lobos, Caño los ⊂ CO 64-65 E 1
Lobos, Cay ⌒ BS 54-55 G 3
Lobos, Cayo ⌒ MEX 52-53 L 2
Lobos, Isla ⌒ MEX 50-51 D 4
Lobos, Islas de ⌒ PE 64-65 B 5
Lobos, Isla ⌒ MEX 50-51 L 7
Lobos, Punta ▲ RA 78-79 J 5
Lobos, Punta ▲ RCH (ATA) 76-77 B 5
Lobos, Punta ▲ RCH (LIB) 78-79 C 3
Lobos, Punta ▲ RCH (TAR) 70-71 B 6
Lobos, Punta ▲ RCH (TAR) 76-77 B 1
Lobos, Río Los ~ MEX 50-51 F 5
Lobos de Afuera, Islas ⌒ PE 64-65 B 5
Lobos de Tierra, Isla ⌒ PE 64-65 B 5
Loboto ▲ RT 202-203 L 6
Lobu o RI 164-165 H 4
Lobuja o RUS 112-113 H 3
Lobutcha Creeks ~ USA (MS) 268-269 L 4
Lobva o RUS 114-115 F 5
Locas de Cahuinari o CO 66-67 B 3
Locate o USA (MT) 250-251 O 5
Loceret o RI 168 D 3
Lochboisdale o GB 90-91 D 3
Loche, La o CDN 32-33 Q 3
Loche, Lac la ⊂ CDN 32-33 Q 3
Loches o • F 90-91 H 8
Loch Fyne ≈ 26-27 p 7
Loch Fyne ≈ 90-91 E 4
Loch Garman = Wexford ☆ IRL 90-91 D 5
Lochgilphead o GB 90-91 E 3
Lochiel o USA (AZ) 256-257 E 7
Lochiel o ZA 220-221 K 3
Lochinvar National Park ⊥ Z 218-219 D 2
Lochinver o GB 90-91 E 2
Loch Linnhe ≈ 90-91 E 3
Loch Lomond ⊂ GB 90-91 E 3
Lochloosa o USA (FL) 286-287 G 2
Lochmaddy o GB 90-91 D 3
Lochnagar ▲ GB 90-91 F 3
Loch Ness ⊂ GB 90-91 E 3
Łochów o PL 92-93 Q 2
Lochsa River ~ USA (ID) 250-251 D 5
Loch Sport o AUS 180-181 J 5
Lock o AUS 180-181 C 2
Lockart o AUS 180-181 H 3
Locke o USA (WA) 244-245 H 2
Lockeport o CDN (NS) 240-241 K 7
Locker Point ▲ CDN 24-25 P 6
Lockesburg o USA (AR) 276-277 A 7
Lockhart o USA (SC) 284-285 J 2
Lockhart o USA (TX) 266-267 K 4
Lockhart, Lake ⊂ AUS 176-177 E 6
Lockhart River ✕ AUS 174-175 G 3
Lockhart River ~ CDN 30-31 P 4
Lockhart River Aboriginal Land ✕ AUS 174-175 G 3
Lock Haven o USA (PA) 280-281 J 2
Lockney o USA (TX) 264-265 C 4
Lockport o CDN (MAN) 234-235 G 4
Lockport o USA (LA) 268-269 K 7
Lockport o USA (NY) 278-279 C 5
Lockwood o USA (CA) 248-249 C 4
Lockwood o USA (MO) 276-277 B 3
Lockwood Hills ▲ USA 20-21 M 3
Lọc Ninh o VN 158-159 J 5
Loco o USA (OK) 264-265 G 4
Loco Hills o USA (NM) 256-257 M 6
Locri o I 100-101 F 5
Locumba, Río ~ PE 70-71 B 5
Locust o USA (IA) 274-275 G 1
Locust o USA (NC) 282-283 G 5
Locust Creek ~ USA (MO) 274-275 E 4
Locust Fork ~ USA (AL) 284-285 D 3
Lod ☆ • IL 130-131 D 2
Loddon River ~ AUS 180-181 G 3
Lodejnoe Pole ☆ RUS 94-95 N 1
Lodève o F 90-91 J 10
Lodge Creek ~ CDN (ALB) 232-233 H 6
Lodge Grass o USA (MT) 250-251 M 6
Lodgepole o CDN (ALB) 232-233 C 2
Lodgepole o USA (NE) 262-263 D 3
Lodgepole o USA (SD) 260-261 D 1
Lodgepole Creek ~ USA (WY) 252-253 O 5
Lodhrān o PK 138-139 C 5
Lodi o • I 100-101 B 2
Lodi o USA (CA) 246-247 D 5
Lodi o USA (OH) 280-281 D 2
Lodi o ZRE 210-211 H 6
Lodié ~ G 210-211 D 3
Løding o N 86-87 G 3
Lødingen o N 86-87 G 2
Lodja o ZRE 210-211 J 5
Lod'ma ~ RUS 88-89 Q 4
Lodmalasin ▲ EAT 212-213 E 5
Lodočnikova, plato ▲ RUS 108-109 e 3
Lodoga o USA (CA) 246-247 C 4
Lodoyo o RI 168 E 4
Lodrani o IND 138-139 C 8
Lodungokwe o EAK 212-213 F 3
Lodwar o EAK 212-213 E 2
Łódź ☆ •• PL 92-93 P 3
Loei o THA 158-159 F 2
Loeka ~ ZRE 210-211 J 2
Loémé ~ RCB 210-211 D 6
Loeng Nok Tha o THA 158-159 H 2
Loeriesfontein o ZA 220-221 D 5
Lofa River ~ LB 202-203 E 6
Lofi o SN 202-203 C 2
Lofoten ⌒ • N 86-87 F 2
Loftahammar o S 86-87 H 8
Lofty Range ▲ AUS 176-177 E 2
Log o RUS 102-103 N 3
Loga o RN 204-205 E 2
Loga o SUD 206-207 K 6
Logan o USA (IA) 274-275 C 3
Logan o USA (KS) 262-263 G 5
Logan o USA (NM) 256-257 M 3
Logan o USA (OH) 280-281 D 4
Logan o USA (UT) 254-255 D 2
Logan o USA (WV) 280-281 D 6
Logan, Mount ▲ •• CDN 20-21 U 6
Logandale o USA (NV) 248-249 K 3
Logan Glacier ⊂ USA 20-21 U 6
Logan Island ⌒ CDN 234-235 P 4
Logan Lake o CDN (BC) 230-231 J 3
Logan Martin Lake < USA (AL) 284-285 D 3
Logan Mountains ▲ CDN 30-31 E 5
Logan Pass ▲ USA (MT) 250-251 F 3
Logan River ~ USA (UT) 254-255 D 2
Logansport o USA (IN) 274-275 M 4
Logansport o USA (LA) 268-269 G 5
Loganton o USA (PA) 280-281 J 2
Loganville o USA (GA) 284-285 G 3
Lōgar ◘ AFG 138-139 B 3
Logas'egan ~ RUS 114-115 J 2
Logaškino o RUS 110-111 d 4
Logata ~ RUS 108-109 c 5
Lögdeälven ~ S 86-87 J 4
Loge ~ ANG 216-217 C 3
Logeloge o EAT 214-215 K 4
Loggieville o CDN (NB) 240-241 K 3
Logobou o BF 202-203 L 4
Logoforok o SUD 212-213 D 2
Logone ~ TCH 206-207 B 3
Logone Birni o CAM 206-207 B 3
Logone Gana o TCH 206-207 B 3
Logone Occidental ◘ TCH 206-207 B 4
Logone Occidental ~ TCH 206-207 B 4
Logone Oriental ◘ TCH 206-207 B 4
Logone Oriental ~ TCH 206-207 C 4
Logozone o DY 204-205 E 5
Logroño o E 98-99 F 3
Løgstør o DK 86-87 D 8
Loh = Île Lo ⌒ VAN 184 II a 1
Lohagara o BD 142-143 F 4
Lohāghāt o IND 144-145 C 6
Lohardaga o IND 142-143 D 4
Lohārghat o IND 142-143 G 3
Lohéac o F 90-91 G 8
Lohiniva o FIN 88-89 H 3
Lohja o FIN 88-89 H 6
Lohjanan o RI 164-165 E 4
Loh Liang o RI 168 D 7
Loi o PNG 183 D 2
Loiborsoit o EAT 212-213 F 5
Loi-kaw ☆ MYA 142-143 K 6
Loile ~ ZRE 210-211 H 4
Loilo ~ ZRE 210-211 J 3
Loimaa o FIN 88-89 G 6
Loima Hills ▲ EAK 212-213 E 2
Loir ~ F 90-91 H 8
Loire ~ F 90-91 H 8
Loiro Poco o BR 66-67 C 2
Lois ~ RI 166-167 C 6
Loiš o US 136-137 K 5
Loi Song ▲ MYA 142-143 K 4
Loita Hills ▲ EAK 212-213 E 4
Loita Plains ⌣ EAK 212-213 E 4
Loja ☆ EC 64-65 C 3
Lojiš ☆ US 136-137 K 5
Lojmola o RUS 88-89 L 6
Lojno o RUS 96-97 H 4
Lokalema o ZRE 210-211 J 3
Lokandu o ZRE 210-211 K 5
Lokan tekojärvi ⊂ FIN 88-89 J 3
Lokata o RI 166-167 F 2
Lokbatan o AZ 128-129 N 2
Lokeli o ZRE 210-211 K 5
Lokichar o EAK 212-213 E 2
Lokichar ~ EAK 212-213 E 2
Lokichogio o EAK 212-213 E 1
Lokila o ZRE 210-211 K 5
Lokitaung o EAK 212-213 E 1
Loknja ☆ RUS 94-95 M 3
Loko o WAN 204-205 G 4
Lokoja o WAN 204-205 G 5
Lokolama o ZRE 210-211 G 5
Lokolia o ZRE 210-211 H 4
Lokolo ~ ZRE 210-211 G 4
Lokomby o RM 222-223 E 9
Lokomo o CAM (Est) 210-211 E 2
Lokomo ~ CAM 210-211 E 2
Lokono o PNG 183 F 2
Lokori o EAK 212-213 F 3
Lokoro ~ ZRE 210-211 H 5
Lokossa ☆ DY 202-203 L 6
Lokot o RUS 94-95 O 5
Lokoti o CAM 206-207 B 5
Lokoundjé ~ CAM 210-211 C 2
Loksiati o SME 62-63 G 3
Loks Land ⌒ CDN 36-37 R 3
Lokutu o ZRE 210-211 J 3
Loky ~ RM 222-223 F 4
Lol o SUD (SR) 206-207 J 5
Lol ~ SUD 206-207 H 4
Lola o ANG 216-217 B 7
Lola o RG 202-203 F 6
Lold o RCH 78-79 D 3
Lole ~ ZRE 210-211 G 5
Lolengi o ZRE 210-211 H 3
Loleta o USA (CA) 246-247 A 3
Lolgorien o EAK 212-213 E 4
Lolland ⌒ DK 86-87 E 9
Lol Lanok < EAT 212-213 F 6
Lolo o USA (MT) 250-251 E 5
Lolobata o RI 164-165 L 3
Lolobau Island ⌒ PNG 183 F 3
Lolobo o CI 202-203 H 6
Loloda Utara, Kepulauan ⌒ RI 164-165 K 2
Lolodorf o CAM 210-211 C 2
Lolo Hot Springs o USA (MT) 250-251 E 5
Lolo Pass ▲ USA (MT) 250-251 E 5
Lolui Island ⌒ EAU 212-213 D 4
Lolvavana ou Patteson, Passage ≈ 184 II b 2
Lolwane o ZA 220-221 F 3
Lolworth o AUS 174-175 H 7
Lolworth Range ▲ AUS 174-175 H 7
Lom o BG 102-103 C 6
Lom ~ CAM 204-205 K 6
Lom ☆ N 86-87 D 6
Loma o ETH 208-209 C 5
Loma o USA (MT) 250-251 J 4
Loma o USA (ND) 258-259 J 3
Loma Alta o USA (TX) 266-267 G 4
Loma Arena o CO 60-61 D 2
Loma Bonita o MEX 52-53 G 2
Loma de Cabrera o DOM 54-55 K 5
Lomako ~ ZRE 210-211 H 3
Lomaloma o FJI 184 III c 2
Lomami o ZRE 210-211 J 4
Lomami ~ ZRE 210-211 K 5
Loma Mountains ▲ WAL 202-203 E 5
Lomas, Las o PE 64-65 B 4
Lomas, Río de ~ PE 64-65 E 9
Loma San Martín ▲ RA 78-79 E 5
Lomas de Arena o USA (TX) 266-267 C 3
Lomas de Vallejos o RA 76-77 J 4
Lomas de Zamora o RA 78-79 K 3
Lomaum o ANG 216-217 C 6
Lomba ~ ANG 216-217 E 7
Lombadina ✕ AUS 172-173 F 4
Lombang o RI 164-165 F 5
Lombarda, Serra ▲ BR 62-63 J 4
Lombardia ◘ I 100-101 B 2
Lombe o ANG 216-217 D 4
Lombe o RI 164-165 H 6
Lomblen (Kawela), Pulau ⌒ RI 166-167 B 6
Lombok o RI (NBA) 168 C 7
Lombok ⌒ RI (NBA) 168 C 7
Lombok, Selat ≈ 168 B 7
Lomé ★ • RT 202-203 L 6
Lomela o ZRE (KOR) 210-211 J 5
Lomela ~ ZRE 210-211 H 4
Lometa o USA (TX) 266-267 J 2
Lomfjorden ≈ 84-85 K 3
Lomié o CAM 210-211 D 2
Loming o SUD 206-207 L 6
Lomitas, Las o RA 76-77 G 3
Lomond o CDN (ALB) 232-233 F 5
Lomonosov Ridge ≃ 16 A 25
Lomovoe o RUS 88-89 Q 4
Lomphăt o K 158-159 J 4
Lompobatang, Gunung ▲ RI 164-165 F 6
Lompoc o USA (CA) 248-249 D 5
Lompopana, Gunung ▲ RI 164-165 F 4
Lompoul o SN 202-203 B 2
Lom Sak o THA 158-159 F 2
Łomża ☆ PL 92-93 R 2
Ló'n ~ VN 158-159 K 4
Lona Bay ≈ 36-37 L 2
Lonambo o EC 64-65 D 2
Lonand o IND 138-139 E 10
Lonāvale o • IND 138-139 D 10
Lončakovo o RUS 122-123 F 5
Loncoche o RCH 78-79 C 5
Loncopangue o RCH 78-79 D 4
Loncopue o RA 78-79 D 5
Londa o IND 140-141 F 3
Londéla-Kayes o RCB 210-211 D 6
Londengo o ANG 216-217 B 6
Londiani o EAK 212-213 E 4
Londolovit o PNG 183 G 2
London o • CDN (ONT) 238-239 D 6
London ★ ••• GB 90-91 G 6
London o USA (KY) 276-277 L 3
London o USA (MN) 270-271 E 7
London o USA (OH) 280-281 C 4
London o USA (TX) 266-267 H 3
Londonderry ☆ • GB 90-91 D 4
Londonderry, Cape ▲ AUS 172-173 H 2
Londonderry, Isla ⌒ RCH 80 E 7
Londrina o BR 72-73 E 7
Lone Butte o CDN (BC) 230-231 H 2
Lonely Mine o ZW 218-219 E 4
Lone Oak o USA (TX) 264-265 J 6
Lone Pine o USA (CA) 248-249 F 3
Lonepine o USA (MT) 250-251 E 4
Lone Pine Indian Reservation ✕ USA (CA) 248-249 F 3
Lone Rock o CDN (SAS) 232-233 J 2
Lone Rock o USA (WI) 274-275 H 1
Lone Star o USA (TX) 264-265 K 6
Lonetree o USA (WY) 252-253 H 5
Long o THA 142-143 L 6
Long o USA (SC) 284-285 M 3
Longa o ANG (CUA) 216-217 E 7
Longa ~ ANG 216-217 C 5
Longa ~ ANG 216-217 E 8
Longa, proliv ≈ 112-113 T 1
Longá, Rio ~ BR 68-69 H 3
Longa-Mavinga, Coutada Pública do ⊥ ANG 216-217 E 8
Long'an o VRC 154-155 L 7
Longana o VAN 184 II a 2
Long Arroyo ~ USA (NM) 256-257 L 5
Longaví, Río ~ RCH 78-79 D 4
Longbao Z.B. ⊥ VRC 144-145 L 4
Long Barn o USA (CA) 246-247 E 5
Long Bay ≈ 48-49 J 3
Long Bay ≈ 54-55 G 6
Long Bay ≈ USA 284-285 M 3
Long Bay Beach ⊥ GB 56 C 2
Long Bay Beach ⊥ • JA 54-55 G 5
Longbeach o CDN (BC) 230-231 M 4
Long Beach o CDN (NFL) 242-243 P 6
Long Beach o USA (CA) 248-249 F 6
Long Beach o USA (NY) 280-281 N 3
Long Beach o USA (SC) 284-285 M 3
Long Beach o USA (WA) 244-245 A 4
Long Beach ⊥ • USA (NJ) 280-281 M 4
Long Beach, Playa de ⊥ • DOM 54-55 K 5
Longboat Key ⌒ USA (FL) 286-287 G 4
Longbow Lake o CDN (ONT) 234-235 J 5
Long Branch o USA (NJ) 280-281 M 3
Long Branch Lake ⊂ USA (MO) 274-275 F 5
Long Canes Creek ~ USA (SC) 284-285 H 2
Long Cay ⌒ BH 52-53 L 3
Long Cay ⌒ BS 54-55 H 3
Longchang o VRC 156-157 D 2
Longchuan o VRC 156-157 J 4
Long Cove o CDN (NFL) 242-243 P 5
Long Creek o CDN (NB) 240-241 J 5
Long Creek o USA (OR) 244-245 F 6
Long Creek ~ USA (NC) 282-283 J 6
Longe ~ ANG 216-217 C 3
Longfengyan • VRC 156-157 K 3
Long Fjord, De ≈ 26-27 d 2
Longford o AUS 180-181 J 6
Longford = An Longfort ☆ IRL 90-91 D 5
Longgang Shan ▲ VRC 150-151 E 6
Longgang Z.B. ⊥ • VRC 156-157 E 5
Longgong • VRC 156-157 D 3
Longgong D. • VRC 156-157 K 2
Long Harbour o CDN (NFL) 242-243 P 5
Longhua o VRC 148-149 N 7
Longhui o VRC 156-157 G 3
Longhushan • VRC 156-157 K 2
Longido o EAT 212-213 F 5
Longikis o RI 164-165 E 4
Longiram o RI 164-165 D 3
Long Island ⌒ AUS 178-179 K 2
Long Island ⌒ BS 54-55 H 3
Long Island ⌒ CDN (NFL) 242-243 N 3
Long Island ⌒ CDN (NFL) 242-243 O 5
Long Island ⌒ CDN (NS) 240-241 J 6
Long Island ⌒ CDN (NWT) 36-37 K 7
Long Island ⌒ PNG 183 D 3
Long Island o USA (KS) 262-263 G 5
Long Island ⌒ USA (NY) 280-281 N 3
Long Island Sound ≈ 36-37 K 7
Long Island Sound ≈ 46-47 M 5
Long Island Sound ≈ USA 280-281 O 2
Longitudinal, Valle ⊥ RCH 78-79 C 4
Longjing o VRC 150-151 G 6
Longkay o RI 164-165 D 3
Long Key ⌒ USA (FL) 286-287 J 7
Longkou o VRC 154-155 M 3
Longlac o CDN (ONT) 236-237 B 3
Long Lake o CDN (ONT) 236-237 B 3
Long Lake o USA (NY) 278-279 G 5
Long Lake o USA (SD) 260-261 G 1
Long Lake o USA (WA) 244-245 H 3
Long Lake ⊂ USA (ND) 258-259 G 5
Long Lake, Indian Reserve ✕ CDN (ONT) 236-237 B 3
Long Lama o MAL 164-165 D 2
Long Lellang o MAL 164-165 D 2
Longlin o VRC 156-157 D 4
Longling o VRC 142-143 L 3
Long Malinau o RI 164-165 E 2
Longmen o VRC 156-157 J 5
Longmen o VRC 156-157 G 6
Longmen Shiku • VRC 154-155 H 4
Longmont o USA (CO) 254-255 K 3
Long Mountains, De ▲ USA 20-21 J 2
Long My o VN 158-159 H 6
Longnan o VRC 156-157 J 4
Longnawan o RI 164-165 D 3
Longo o G 210-211 D 4
Longonjo o ANG 216-217 C 6
Longonot ▲ EAK 212-213 F 4
Longotea o PE 64-65 D 5
Longot"egan ~ RUS 108-109 M 8
Longozabe o RM 222-223 F 7
Long Palai o MAL 164-165 D 2
Long Pine o USA (NE) 262-263 G 2
Long Plain Indian Reserve ✕ CDN (MAN) 234-235 E 5
Long Point o CDN (ONT) 238-239 E 6
Long Point ▲ CDN (MAN) 34-35 G 4
Long Point ▲ CDN (NFL) 242-243 K 4
Long Point ▲ CDN (ONT) 238-239 E 6
Long Point ▲ RP 160-161 C 8
Long Point Bay ⊂ CDN (ONT) 238-239 E 6
Long Prairie o USA (MN) 270-271 D 5
Longquan o VRC 156-157 L 2
Long Range Mountains ▲ CDN (NFL) 242-243 K 5
Longreach o AUS 178-179 H 2
Long Seridan o MAL 164-165 D 1
Longshan o VRC (GDG) 156-157 H 5
Longshan o VRC (HUN) 156-157 F 2
Longsheng o VRC 156-157 F 4
Longshou Shan ▲ VRC 154-155 B 2
Longs Peak ▲ USA (CO) 254-255 K 3
Long Thành o VN 158-159 J 5
Longton o AUS 174-175 H 7
Longue, Pointe ▲ CDN 38-39 E 2
Longueuil o CDN (QUE) 238-239 M 3
Longvale o USA (CA) 246-247 B 4
Long Valley o USA (AZ) 256-257 D 4
Long Valley o USA (SD) 260-261 E 3
Long Valley Junction o USA (UT) 254-255 C 6
Longview o CDN (ALB) 232-233 D 5
Longview o USA (MS) 268-269 M 3
Longview o USA (TX) 264-265 K 6
Longview o USA (WA) 244-245 C 4
Longville o USA (LA) 268-269 G 6
Longwood o USA (FL) 286-287 H 3
Longworth o CDN (BC) 228-229 N 3
Longxi o VRC 154-155 D 4
Long Xian o VRC 154-155 E 4
Long Xuyên ☆ VN 158-159 H 5
Longyan o VRC 156-157 K 4
Longyao o VRC 154-155 J 3
Longyearbyen o N 84-85 J 3
Longyou o VRC 156-157 L 2
Longzhou o VRC 156-157 E 5
Loni Kand o IND 138-139 E 10
Lonkintsy o RM 222-223 F 6
Lonkonia ~ ZRE 210-211 J 5
Lono o USA (AR) 276-277 C 6
Lonoke o USA (AR) 276-277 D 6
Lonquimay o RCH 78-79 D 5
Lonsdale o USA (MN) 270-271 E 6
Lons-le-Saunier o F 90-91 K 8
Lontar o RI 166-167 E 4
Lontar, Pulau ⌒ RI 166-167 E 4
Lontou o RMM 202-203 E 2
Lontra o BR 68-69 C 4
Lontra, Ribeirão ~ BR 72-73 D 6
Lontra, Rio ~ BR 68-69 D 5
Lontué, Río ~ RCH 78-79 D 3
Lonua ~ ZRE 210-211 J 3
Looc o RP (BOH) 160-161 E 8
Looc o RP (ROM) 160-161 D 6
Loogootee o USA (IN) 274-275 M 6
Lookout o USA (CA) 246-247 D 2
Lookout o USA (ME) 278-279 N 4
Lookout, Cape ▲ CDN 34-35 P 3
Lookout, Cape ▲ USA 244-245 B 5
Lookout, Cape ▲ USA (NC) 282-283 L 6
Lookout, Mount ▲ AUS 174-175 H 6
Lookout Mount ▲ USA 20-21 P 3
Lookout Pass ▲ USA (ID) 250-251 D 4
Lookout Point ▲ AUS 174-175 H 4
Lookout Ridge ▲ USA 20-21 L 2
Look Sembuang o MAL 160-161 C 10
Looma o AUS 172-173 G 5
Looma o CDN (ALB) 232-233 E 2
Loomis o CDN (SAS) 232-233 K 6
Loomis o USA (WA) 244-245 F 2
Loongana o AUS 176-177 J 5
Loon Lake o CDN 32-33 Q 4
Loon Lake o USA (WA) 244-245 H 2
Loon Point ▲ CDN 38-39 E 2
Loon River ~ CDN 32-33 N 3
Loop o USA (TX) 264-265 B 6
Loos o CDN (BC) 228-229 O 3
Loosahatchie River ~ USA (TN) 276-277 F 5
Loose Creek o USA (MO) 274-275 G 6
Loost River o USA 20-21 G 4
Lootsberg Pass ▲ ZA 220-221 G 5
Lop o VRC 144-145 C 2
Lopary o RM 222-223 E 9
Lopatina, gora ▲ RUS 122-123 K 3
Lopatino o RUS 96-97 D 7
Lopatka, mys ▲ RUS 122-123 R 3
Lopatka, poluostrov ⌣ RUS 110-111 c 4
Lopburi o THA 158-159 F 3
Lopča ~ RUS 118-119 L 8
Lopeno o USA (TX) 266-267 H 7
Lopevi = Ulveah ⌒ VAN 184 II b 3
Lopez o CO 60-61 C 6
Lopez o RP 160-161 E 6
Lopez, Cap ▲ G 210-211 B 4
López Mateos, Ciudad o MEX 52-53 E 2
Lop Nur ⊂ VRC 146-147 K 5
Lopori ~ ZRE 210-211 H 3
Lopphavet ≈ 86-87 K 1
Lopp Lagoon ≈ 20-21 G 4
Loptjuga ~ RUS 88-89 U 5
Loquilocon o RP 160-161 F 7
Lora, Punta ▲ RCH 78-79 C 3
Lora, Río ~ YV 60-61 E 3
Lora Creek ~ AUS 178-179 C 5
Lorain o USA (OH) 280-281 D 2
Loraine o USA (CA) 248-249 F 4
Loraine o USA (TX) 264-265 D 6
Loralāi o PK 138-139 B 4
Loralāi ~ PK 138-139 B 4
Lorane o USA (OR) 244-245 B 7
Loranstation = Angisoq o GRØ 28-29 S 7
Lordegān o IR 134-135 D 3
Lord Howe Island ⌒ ••• AUS 180-181 N 7
Lord Howe Rise ≃ 13 H 6
Lord Howe Seamounts ≃ 13 H 5
Lord Lindsay River ~ CDN 24-25 Z 5
Lord Loughborough Island ⌒ MYA 158-159 D 5
Lord Mayor Bay ≈ 24-25 a 6
Lordsburg o USA (NM) 256-257 G 6
Lord's Cove o CDN (NFL) 242-243 N 6
Lore o RI 166-167 D 6
Lore Lindu National Park ⊥ • RI 164-165 G 4
Lorella o USA (OR) 244-245 D 8
Loren, Pulau ⌒ RI 168 E 7
Lorena o BR (AMA) 66-67 B 6
Lorena o BR (PAU) 72-73 H 7
Lorena o USA (MS) 268-269 L 4
Lorengau ☆ PNG 183 D 2
Lorentz ~ RI 166-167 K 4
Lorentz Reserve ⊥ • RI 166-167 J 4
Lorenzo o USA (TX) 264-265 C 5
Lōre Rūd ~ AFG 134-135 M 2
Lorestān ◘ IR 134-135 B 2
Loreto o BOL 70-71 E 4
Loreto o BR (MAR) 68-69 F 5
Loreto o BR (MAT) 70-71 H 2
Loreto o CO 66-67 B 4
Loreto o I 100-101 D 3
Loreto o MEX (ZAC) 50-51 J 6
Loreto o • MEX (BCS) 50-51 D 4
Loreto o RP 160-161 F 7
Loreto, Isla ⌒ PE 66-67 B 4
Loretta o USA (WI) 270-271 H 5
Lorette o CDN (MAN) 234-235 G 5
Loretteville o CDN (QUE) 238-239 O 2
Loretto o USA (TN) 276-277 H 5
Lorian Swamp ⊂ EAK 212-213 G 3
Lorica o CO 60-61 D 3
Lorida o USA (FL) 286-287 H 4
Lorient o F 90-91 F 8
Lorillard River ~ CDN 30-31 Y 3
Loring o USA (MT) 250-251 M 3
Loring, Port o CDN (ONT) 238-239 F 3
Lorino o RUS 112-113 Z 4
Loris o USA (SC) 284-285 M 2
Loriscota, Lago ⊂ PE 70-71 B 5
Lorlie o CDN (SAS) 232-233 P 5
Lormes o F 90-91 J 8
Lorn, Firth of ≈ 90-91 E 3
Lorna Downs o AUS 178-179 F 2
Lorne o AUS (QLD) 178-179 J 3
Lorne o AUS (VIC) 180-181 G 5
Lorne o CDN (NS) 240-241 N 5
Lorneville o CDN (NB) 240-241 J 5
Loronyo o SUD 206-207 L 6
Loropéni o BF 202-203 J 4
Loros, Los o RCH 76-77 B 4
Lörrach o D 92-93 J 5
Lorraine o AUS 174-175 E 6
Lorraine ◘ F 90-91 K 7
Lorsch o •• D (HES) 92-93 K 4
Lort, Cabo ▲ RCH 80 C 2
Lorton o USA (NE) 262-263 K 4
Loruk o EAK 212-213 F 3
Lorukumu o EAK 212-213 E 2
Lorzot o TN 190-191 H 5
Los o S 86-87 G 6
Los, Iles de ⌒ RG 202-203 D 5
Losai National Reserve ⊥ EAK 212-213 F 3
Los Angeles o • USA (CA) 248-249 F 5
Los Angeles Aqueduct < USA (CA) 248-249 F 4
Losantville o USA (IN) 274-275 N 4
Losari o RI 168 C 3
Los Cerrillos o USA (NM) 256-257 J 3
Los Coyotes Indian Reservation ✕ USA (CA) 248-249 H 6
Loseya < EAT 212-213 F 6
Los Fresnos o USA (TX) 266-267 K 7
Los Haitises, Parque Nacional ⊥ DOM 54-55 L 5
Losier Canyon ~ USA (TX) 266-267 F 3
Losier Settlement o CDN (NB) 240-241 L 3
Lošinj ⌒ HR 100-101 E 2
Los Mochis o MEX 50-51 E 5
Loso ~ ZRE 210-211 G 4
Losoni o RI 164-165 H 5
Lospalos o RI 166-167 D 6
Los Pinos River ~ USA (NM) 256-257 H 2
Los Reyes Islands ⌒ PNG 183 E 1
Lossiemouth o GB 90-91 F 3
Lossogonoi Plateau ▲ EAT 212-213 F 5
Lost Creek ~ USA (AL) 284-285 C 3
Lost Hills o USA (CA) 248-249 E 4
Lost Maples State Natural Area ⊥ • USA (TX) 266-267 H 4

354 Little Sioux River — Lost Maples State Natural Area

Lost River ○ USA (WV) 280-281 H 4
Lost River Range ▲ USA (ID) 252-253 E 2
Lost Springs ○ USA (WY) 252-253 O 4
Lost Trail Pass ▲ USA (ID) 250-251 F 6
Lostwood ○ USA (ND) 258-259 E 3
Lostwood National Wildlife Refuge ⊥ USA (ND) 258-259 E 3
Losuia ○ PNG 183 F 5
Lot ~ F 90-91 H 9
Lote 15, Cerro ▲ RA 80 E 2
Lotfäbåd ○ IR 136-137 H 6
Lothair ○ USA (MT) 250-251 H 3
Lotikipi Plain ⌣ EAK 212-213 E 1
Loto ○ ZRE (KOR) 210-211 J 5
Loto ○ ZRE 210-211 G 4
Lotoi ~ ZRE 210-211 G 4
Lotsane ~ RB 218-219 D 6
Lott ○ USA (TX) 266-267 K 2
Lotta ~ RUS 88-89 K 2
Lotuke ▲ SUD 208-209 A 6
Lötzen = Giżycko ○ PL 92-93 Q 1
Louangphrabang ▲ LAO 156-157 C 7
Loubetsi ~ RCB 210-211 D 6
Loubomo ○ RCB 210-211 D 6
Loudéac ○ F 90-91 F 7
Loudi ○ VRC 156-157 G 3
Loudima ○ RCB 210-211 D 6
Loudima ~ RCB 210-211 D 6
Loudonville ○ USA (OH) 280-281 D 3
Loudun ○ F 90-91 H 8
Louéssé ○ RCB 210-211 C 5
Louétsi ~ G 210-211 C 5
Louga ○ SN 196-197 B 7
Lougheed Island ○ CDN 24-25 T 2
Loughrea = Baile Locha Riach ○ IRL 90-91 C 5
Lougou ○ DY 204-205 E 3
Louhi ○ RUS 88-89 M 3
Louingui ○ RCB 210-211 E 6
Louisa ○ USA (KY) 276-277 F 7
Louisa Downs ○ AUS 172-173 H 5
Louisbourg ○ CDN (NS) 240-241 P 5
Louisburg ○ USA (KS) 262-263 M 6
Louisburg ○ USA (NC) 282-283 J 4
Louis Creek ○ CDN (BC) 230-231 J 2
Louisdale ○ CDN (NS) 240-241 O 4
Louise ○ USA (TX) 266-267 L 4
Louise, Lake ~ USA 20-21 H 5
Louise Island ○ CDN (BC) 228-229 C 4
Louisiade Archipelago ⌀ PNG 183 G 6
Louisiana ○ USA (MO) 274-275 G 5
Louisiana ▫ USA (LA) 268-269 G 5
Lou Island ○ PNG 183 D 2
Louis Trichardt ○ ZA 218-219 E 6
Louisville ○ CDN (QUE) 238-239 N 2
Louisville ○ USA (CO) 254-255 N 4
Louisville ○ USA (GA) 284-285 H 3
Louisville ○ USA (IL) 274-275 K 6
Louisville ○ USA (KY) 276-277 K 2
Louisville ○ USA (MS) 268-269 L 3
Louisville ○ USA (NE) 262-263 K 4
Louisville Ridge ≃ 14-15 L 10
Louis-XIV, Pointe ○ CDN 36-37 K 7
Loukoléla ○ RCB 210-211 F 4
Loukouo ○ RCB 210-211 D 6
Loukout Mountain ▲ USA (AL) 284-285 E 2
Loulan Gucheng ⋰ VRC 146-147 J 5
Loulé ○ P 98-99 C 6
Loulouni ○ RMM 202-203 H 4
Lou Lou Park ○ USA 254-255 N 5
Loum ○ CAM 204-205 H 6
Loumbi ○ SN 196-197 D 7
Loumbol, Vallée de ~ SN 202-203 H 2
Loumo, Gati- ○ RMM 202-203 H 2
Lournou ○ RCB 210-211 E 6
Loungou ○ RCB 210-211 D 5
Loup, Rivière-du- ○ CDN (QUE) 240-241 F 3
Loup City ○ USA (NE) 262-263 J 4
Loup River ~ USA (NE) 262-263 J 4
Loups Marins, Lacs des ○ CDN 36-37 M 6
Lourdes ○ CDN (NFL) 242-243 K 4
Lourdes ○ F 90-91 G 10
Lourenço ○ BR 62-63 J 4
Lour-Escale ○ SN 202-203 J 4
Lousana ○ CDN (ALB) 232-233 E 3
Lousserie ○ RIM 196-197 E 6
Louta ○ BF 202-203 J 3
Louth ○ AUS 178-179 H 6
Louth ○ GB 90-91 G 5
Louth < RIM 196-197 D 6
Louti, Mayo ~ CAM 204-205 K 3
Loutrå ○ GR 100-101 K 6
Louvain = Leuven ○ · B 92-93 H 3
Louvakou ○ RCB 210-211 D 6
Louvicourt ○ CDN (QUE) 236-237 L 4
Louviers ○ F 90-91 H 7
Louwsburg ○ ZA 220-221 K 3
Lou Yaeger, Lake ○ USA (IL) 274-275 J 5
Lövånger ○ S 86-87 K 4
Lovcova, mys ▲ RUS 122-123 M 6
Love ○ CDN (SAS) 232-233 O 2
Love Beach ~ BS 54-55 G 2
Loveč ☆ BG 102-103 D 6
Lovelady ○ USA (TX) 266-267 E 5
Loveland ○ USA (CO) 254-255 N 4
Loveland Pass ▲ USA (CO) 280-281 B 4
Lovell ○ USA (WY) 252-253 K 2
Lovells ○ USA (MI) 272-273 E 3
Lovelock ○ USA (NV) 246-247 G 3
Lovére ○ I 100-101 K 6
Loverna ○ CDN (SAS) 232-233 J 4
Lovewell Reservoir ~ USA (KS) 262-263 H 5
Lovisa = Loviisa ○ FIN 88-89 L 6
Loving ○ USA (NM) 256-257 L 6
Loving ○ USA (TX) 266-267 F 3
Lovington ○ USA (IL) 274-275 K 5
Lovington ○ USA (NM) 256-257 M 6
Lovisa ○ FIN 88-89 L 6
Lovoi ~ ZRE 214-215 C 5

Lovozero ○ RUS (MUR) 88-89 N 2
Lóvua ○ ANG (LUN) 216-217 F 3
Lóvua ○ ANG (MOX) 214-215 H 3
Lovua ~ ZRE 216-217 H 5
Lovúski, ostrova ~ RUS 122-123 P 4
Low, Cape ▲ CDN 36-37 S 5
Low, Lac ○ CDN 38-39 F 2
Lowakamistik River ~ CDN (ONT) 236-237 J 2
Lowbanks ○ CDN (ONT) 238-239 F 6
Low Bay ≈ 78-79 L 7
Low Cape ▲ USA 22-23 T 4
Lowe Farm ○ CDN (MAN) 234-235 F 5
Lowell ○ USA (IN) 274-275 L 3
Lowell ○ USA (MA) 278-279 K 4
Lowell ○ USA (VT) 278-279 J 4
Lowelli ○ SUD 208-209 A 6
Löwen ~ NAM 220-221 D 3
Lower Arrow Lake ○ CDN (BC) 230-231 L 4
Lower Brule ○ USA (SD) 260-261 G 2
Lower Brule Indian Reservation ⊼ USA (SD) 260-261 G 2
Lower Forster Lake ○ CDN 34-35 D 2
Lower Glenelg National Park ⊥ AUS 180-181 F 5
Lower Gwelo ○ ZW 218-219 E 4
Lower Hutt ○ NZ 182 E 4
Lower Klamath National Wildlife Refuge ⊥ USA (CA) 246-247 D 2
Lower Lake ○ USA (CA) 246-247 C 5
Lower Lake ~ USA (CA) 246-247 C 5
Lower Loteni ○ ZA 220-221 J 4
Lower Lough Erne ~ GB 90-91 D 4
Lower Matecumbe Key ~ USA (FL) 286-287 J 7
Lower Nicola ○ CDN (BC) 230-231 J 3
Lower Otay Reservoir ~ USA (CA) 248-249 H 7
Lower Peach Tree ○ USA (AL) 284-285 C 5
Lower Pensinula ⌣ USA (MI) 272-273 D 3
Lower Post ○ CDN 30-31 N 6
Lower Red Lake ~ USA (MN) 270-271 C 3
Lower Sabie ○ ZA 220-221 K 2
Lower Savage Islands ~ CDN 36-37 O 4
Lower Ship Harbour ○ CDN (NS) 240-241 N 6
Lower Sioux Indian Reservation ⊼ USA (MN) 270-271 D 6
Lower Souris National Wildlife Refuge ⊥ USA (ND) 258-259 G 3
Lower Valley of the Awash ⋯ ETH 208-209 E 3
Lower Zambezi National Park ⊥ Z 218-219 F 2
Lowestoft ○ GB 90-91 H 5
Lowest Point in United States ∴· USA (CA) 248-249 H 3
Łowicz ○ PL 92-93 P 2
Lowman ○ USA (ID) 252-253 C 2
Lowrie Channel ≈ 174-175 J 4
Low Rocky Point ▲ AUS 180-181 H 7
Lowry ○ USA (MN) 270-271 C 5
Lowry Indian Ruins ∴· USA (CO) 254-255 J 6
Lowther Island ~ CDN 24-25 X 3
Lowty, Pico ▲ MEX 50-51 B 4
Lowville ○ USA (NY) 278-279 F 5
Loxahatchee National Wildlife Refuge ⊥ USA (FL) 286-287 J 5
Lò Xo, Đèo ▲ VN 158-159 J 3
Loxton ○ AUS 180-181 F 3
Loxton ○ CDN 220-221 F 5
Loya ~ ZRE 212-213 A 4
Loyada ○ DJI 208-209 F 3
Loyalsock Creek ~ USA (PA) 280-281 K 2
Loyalton ○ USA (CA) 246-247 E 4
Loyangalani ○ EAK 212-213 F 2
Loyauté, Îles ⌀ F 13 H 5
Loyds River ~ CDN (NFL) 242-243 K 4
Loyengo ○ SD 220-221 K 3
Loyoro ○ EAU 212-213 E 2
Loysville ○ USA (PA) 280-281 J 3
Loza ~ RM 222-223 E 5
Lozère, Mont ▲ F 90-91 J 9
Loznica ○ YU 100-101 G 2
Loźnikovo ○ RUS 118-119 H 10
Lozova ○ UA 102-103 K 3
Loz'va ~ RUS 114-115 F 5
L. P. Kochs Fjord ≈ 26-27 c 2
Lua ~ ZRE 210-211 G 4
Luabo ○ MOC 218-219 J 4
Luabo ~ ZRE 210-211 G 5
Luabu ~ ZRE 210-211 G 5
Luacano ○ ANG 216-217 F 4
Luachimo ○ ANG 216-217 F 4
Luachimo ~ ANG 216-217 F 5
Luaco ○ ANG 216-217 F 4
Lua-Dekere ~ ZRE 206-207 D 6
Luadi, Wamba- ○ ZRE 212-213 A 5
Luagungu ○ ZRE 212-213 A 5
Luahula ~ ZRE 212-213 A 4
Luala, Rio ~ MOC 218-219 H 3
Lualaba ~ ZRE 210-211 K 4
Luali ○ ZRE 210-211 C 6
Luama ~ ZRE 212-213 A 6
Luambala, Rio ~ MOC 218-219 H 1
Luampa ○ Z 218-219 D 2
Luampa ~ Z 218-219 D 2
Luampa Kuta ○ Z 218-219 D 2
Lu'an ○ VRC 154-155 K 6
Luana (Luanco) ○ E 98-99 E 3
Luancundo ~ ANG 216-217 D 6
Luanda ▫ ANG 216-217 B 4
Luanda ★· ANG (LDA) 216-217 B 4
Luanda ○ BR (PAR) 72-73 D 7
Luanda ○ BR (PER) 68-69 J 5
Luanda Norte ▫ ANG 216-217 E 4
Luanda Sul ▫ ANG 216-217 D 5

Luando ○ ANG (BIE) 216-217 E 5
Luando, Reserva Natural Integral do ⊥ ANG 216-217 D 5
Luanginga ~ Z 218-219 B 2
Luang Namtha ○ LAO 156-157 B 6
Luang ○ ANG 210-211 D 6
Luangue ○ ANG (LUN) 216-217 F 6
Luangue ~ ANG 216-217 F 6
Luanguinga ~ Z (Lus) 218-219 F 2
Luangwa ~ Z 214-215 F 5
Luangwa ~ Z 214-215 F 5
Luanheca ○ ANG 218-219 B 3
Luanjing ○ VRC 154-155 D 3
Luan He ~ VRC 148-149 N 7
Luannan ○ VRC 154-155 L 2
Luan Xian ○ VRC 154-155 L 2
Luanza ○ ZRE 214-215 E 5
Luapula ~ Z 214-215 E 6
Luapula ~ ZRE 214-215 E 6
Luar, Danau ~ RI 162-163 K 4
Luarca ○ E 98-99 D 3
Luashi ○ ZRE 214-215 B 6
Luashi ~ ZRE 214-215 B 6
Luassingua ~ ANG 216-217 F 6
Luatamba ○ ANG 216-217 F 6
Luatize, Rio ~ MOC 218-219 J 1
Luatize, Rio ~ MOC 218-219 F 2
Luau ○ ANG 214-215 A 5
Lua-Vindu ~ ZRE 210-211 G 2
Luba ○ GQ 210-211 B 6
Lubaantun ∴· BH 52-53 K 3
Lubaczów ○ PL 102-103 C 2
Lubahanbajo ○ RI 168 D 7
Lubalo ○ ANG 216-217 E 4
Lubamba ○ ZRE 214-215 D 6
Lubań ○ PL 92-93 N 3
Lubana eeri ~ LV 94-95 K 3
Lubang ○ RP 160-161 D 4
Lubang Island ~ RP 160-161 D 6
Lubansenshi ~ Z 214-215 E 6
Lubanza ○ ZRE 210-211 H 6
Lubao ○ RP 160-161 D 5
Lubao ~ ZRE 210-211 H 6
Lubartów ○ PL 92-93 R 3
Lubbock ○ USA (TX) 264-265 C 5
Lubbub Creek ~ USA (AL) 284-285 B 3
Lübeck ○··· D 92-93 L 2
Lubefu ○ ZRE (KOR) 210-211 K 6
Lubefu ~ ZRE 210-211 K 6
Lubefu ~ ZRE 210-211 H 6
Lubero ○ ZRE (KIV) 212-213 A 4
Lubero ~ ZRE 212-213 B 4
Lubi ~ ZRE 214-215 B 9
Lubilandji ~ ZRE 214-215 B 4
Lubilanji ~ ZRE 214-215 B 5
Lubile ~ ZRE 214-215 L 5
Lubile ~ ZRE 214-215 D 4
Lubimbi ○ ZW 218-219 D 4
Lubin ○ PL 92-93 O 3
Lubishi ~ ZRE 214-215 C 4
Lublin ☆ PL 92-93 R 3
Lubnán al-Ġarbiya, Ğabal ▲· RL 128-129 F 6
Lubnán aš-Šarqiya, Ğabal ▲· RL 128-129 F 6
Lubny ○ UA 102-103 H 3
Lubok Antu ○ MAL 162-163 J 4
Lubu ○ Z 214-215 F 6
Lubudi ○ ZRE (SHA) 214-215 C 5
Lubudi ~ ZRE 210-211 J 6
Lubudi ~ ZRE 214-215 C 5
Lubue ~ ZRE 210-211 H 5
Lubukalung ~ RI 162-163 D 5
Lubukbargalung ○ RI 162-163 E 6
Lubuklinggau ○ RI 162-163 E 6
Lubukpakan ○ RI 162-163 C 3
Lubuksikaping ○ RI 162-163 D 4
Lubule ~ ZRE 214-215 D 4
Lubumbashi ★· ZRE 214-215 D 6
Lubundji ~ ZRE 214-215 H 6
Lubungu ○ Z 218-219 D 2
Lubushi ~ ZRE 214-215 F 6
Lubutu ○ ZRE 210-211 L 4
Lubutu ~ ZRE 210-211 L 4
Lubwe ○ Z 214-215 E 6
Lucala ○ ANG 216-217 C 4
Lucala ~ ANG 216-217 C 4
Lucan ○ CDN (ONT) 238-239 D 5
Lucanas ○ PE 64-65 E 9
Lucapa ○ ANG 216-217 F 4
Lucas ○ USA (IA) 274-275 E 3
Lucas, Arroyo ~ RA 76-77 H 6
Lucas, Lake ○ AUS 172-173 J 6
Lucca ○ I 100-101 K 5
Lucedale ○ USA (MS) 268-269 M 6
Lučegorsk ○ RUS 122-123 P 5
Lucena ○ RP 160-161 D 6
Lučenec ○ SK 92-93 P 4
Lucera ○ I 100-101 M 4
Lucerna ○ HN 52-53 K 4
Lucerne ○ PE 70-71 C 3
Lucerne ○ USA (CA) 246-247 C 4
Lucerne = Luzern ○ · CH 92-93 K 5
Lucerne Valley ○ USA (CA) 248-249 H 5
Lucero, Lake ○ USA (NM) 256-257 J 6
Luceville ○ CDN (QUE) 240-241 G 2
Lucheng ○ VRC (GXI) 156-157 E 4
Lucheng ○ VRC (SXI) 154-155 J 4
Luchenza ○ MW 218-219 H 3
Luchimva, Rio ~ MOC 218-219 H 2
Lucia ○ USA (CA) 248-249 C 5
Lucia, Lac ○ CDN (QUE) 236-237 K 2
Lucien ○ USA (MS) 268-269 K 5
Lucierivier ~ SME 62-63 F 4
Lucile ○ USA (ID) 250-251 D 7

Lucin ○ USA (UT) 254-255 B 2
Lucindale ○ AUS 180-181 F 4
Lucio V. Mansilla ○ RA 76-77 E 5
Lucipara, Kepulauan ~ RI 166-167 D 4
Lucira ○ ANG 216-217 B 6
Luck ○ USA (WI) 270-271 F 5
Luck = Luc'k ○ UA 102-103 D 2
Luckau ○ D 92-93 M 3
Luckeesarai ○ IND 142-143 E 3
Luckhoff ○ ZA 220-221 G 4
Lucknow ○ CDN (ONT) 238-239 D 5
Lucknow ○ IND 142-143 C 3
Lucky ○ USA (LA) 268-269 H 4
Lucky Bay ≈ AUS 180-181 E 7
Lucky Boy Pass ▲ USA (NV) 246-247 F 5
Lucky Lake ○ CDN (SAS) 232-233 L 5
Lucma ○ PE (CUZ) 64-65 F 8
Lucma ○ PE (LIB) 64-65 C 5
Lucon ○ RP 160-161 D 2
Lúcongpo ○ VRC 154-155 G 6
Lucossa ○ ANG 216-217 G 2
Lucrecia, Cabo ▲ C 54-55 H 4
Lucunde ○ ANG 216-217 C 3
Lucunga ○ ANG 216-217 C 3
Lucunga ~ ANG 216-217 C 3
Lucusse ○ ANG 216-217 F 6
Lucy, Mount ▲ AUS 178-179 B 2
Lucy Creek ○ AUS 178-179 D 3
Lüdåb ○ IR 134-135 D 3
Ludden ○ USA (ND) 258-259 J 5
Lude ○ USA (MN) 270-271 D 2
Lüderitz ★ NAM 220-221 B 3
Lüderitzbaai ≈ 220-221 B 3
Ludhiana ○ IND 138-139 A 4
Ludian ○ VRC 156-157 C 3
Ludimbi ~ ZRE 210-211 K 6
Luding ○ VRC 156-157 C 2
Ludington ○ USA (MI) 272-273 C 4
Ludlow ○ USA (CA) 248-249 H 5
Ludlow ○ USA (SD) 260-261 C 1
Ludlow ○ USA (VT) 278-279 J 5
Ludlow Rieh, Canyon of ∴ USA 24-25 O 2
Ludogorie ⊥ BG 102-103 G 6
Ludowici ○ USA (GA) 284-285 J 5
Ludus ○ RO 102-103 D 4
Ludwigsburg ○ D 92-93 K 4
Ludwigshafen am Rhein ○ D 92-93 J 4
Ludwigslust ○ D 92-93 L 2
Ludza ☆ LV 94-95 K 3
Luebo ○ ZRE 214-215 B 4
Luebo ~ ZRE 210-211 H 6
Lueders ○ USA (TX) 264-265 E 6
Lueki ○ ZRE 210-211 K 5
Lueki ~ ZRE 210-211 K 5
Luele ~ ANG 216-217 F 6
Luena ○ ANG (BAN) 210-211 F 6
Luena ○ ANG (KOR) 210-211 N 6
Luena ○ EAT 214-215 G 4
Luena ~ Z 214-215 D 6
Luena ~ Z 218-219 C 2
Luena ~ Z 218-219 C 2
Luena Flats ~ Z 218-219 C 2
Luengué ○ ANG (CUA) 216-217 E 8
Luengué ~ ANG (CUA) 218-219 C 2
Luengué, Coutada Pública do ⊥ ANG 216-217 E 8
Luenha ~ MOC 218-219 G 3
Lueo ~ ZRE 214-215 B 4
Lueta ~ ZRE 214-215 B 4
Lueta ~ ZRE 214-215 B 4
Lueti ~ ANG 216-217 F 7
Lüeyang ○ VRC 154-155 E 5
Lufeng ○ VRC (GDG) 156-157 J 5
Lufeng ○ VRC (YUN) 156-157 C 4
Lufico ○ ANG 216-217 B 3
Lufije ~ ANG 216-217 D 6
Lufimi ~ ZRE 210-211 G 6
Lufira ~ ZRE 214-215 D 6
Lufira, Lac de retenue de la < ZRE 214-215 D 6
Lufkin ○ USA (TX) 268-269 F 5
Lufu ○ ZRE 210-211 D 6
Lufu ~ ZRE 210-211 L 4
Lufuba ~ Z 214-215 E 6
Lufubu ~ Z 214-215 E 6
Lufuige ~ ANG 214-215 B 7
Lufukwe ~ ZRE 214-215 C 5
Lufupa ~ Z 218-219 C 2
Lufupa ~ Z 218-219 C 2
Lufupa Rest Camp ○ Z 218-219 D 2
Lufwa ~ ZRE 214-215 E 6
Lufwango ~ ZRE 210-211 L 6
Luga ☆ RUS (LNG) 94-95 L 2
Luga ~ RUS 94-95 L 2
Lugait ○ RP 160-161 F 4
Luganga ○ EAT 214-215 H 5
Lugano ○ CH 92-93 K 5
Lugansk = Luhans'k ☆ UA 102-103 L 3
Lugard's Falls ~ EAK 212-213 G 5
Lugazi ○ EAU 212-213 D 3
Luge ○ MOC 218-219 J 1
Lugenda ~ MOC 214-215 J 7
Luggate ○ NZ 182 B 6
Lugo ○ E 98-99 D 3
Lugo ○ I 100-101 C 2
Lugoff ○ USA (SC) 284-285 K 2
Lugogi ~ EAU 212-213 D 3
Lugoj ○ RO 102-103 B 5
Lugovskij ○ RUS 118-119 F 6
Lugu ▲ IND 142-143 H 4
Lugu ○ VRC (SIC) 156-157 C 2
Luguru ○ ZRE 212-213 B 5
Luguruka ○ EAT 214-215 J 5
Lugus Island ~ RP 160-161 D 10
Luhan Shan ▲ VRC 144-145 G 4
Luhans'ke, Stanyčno- ○ UA 102-103 L 3
Luhans'k ○ UA 102-103 L 3

Luhayya, al- ○ Y 132-133 C 6
Luhe ○ VRC (GDG) 156-157 J 5
Luhe ○ VRC (JIA) 154-155 L 5
Luhira ○ EAT 214-215 J 5
Luhit ~ IND 142-143 K 2
Luhoho ~ ZRE 212-213 B 4
Luhombero ○ EAT 214-215 J 5
Luhovicy ☆ RUS 94-95 Q 4
Luhu ○ RI 166-167 D 3
Luhulu ~ ZRE 212-213 B 4
Luhuo ○ VRC 156-157 C 2
Lui ~ ANG 216-217 D 4
Lui ~ Z 218-219 B 3
Luia ~ ANG 216-217 F 3
Luia, Rio ~ MOC 218-219 G 2
Luia, Rio ~ MOC 218-219 G 2
Luiana ○ ANG (CUA) 218-219 B 3
Luiana ~ ANG 218-219 B 3
Luiana, Coutada Pública do ⊥ ANG 216-217 E 8
Luiidži, ostrov ~ RUS 84-85 d 2
Luie ~ ZRE 210-211 H 6
Luik = Liège ☆ · B 92-93 H 3
Luika ~ ZRE 210-211 L 6
Luiko ~ ZRE 212-213 B 6
Luilaka ~ ZRE 210-211 H 5
Luilu ~ ZRE 214-215 B 4
Luimbale ○ ANG 216-217 C 6
Luimneach = Limerick ○ IRL 90-91 C 5
Luinga ○ ANG 216-217 C 4
Luio ~ ANG 216-217 D 6
Luís Correia ○ BR 68-69 H 3
Luís Domingues ○ BR 68-69 F 2
Luishia ○ ZRE 214-215 D 6
Luís L. León, Presa < MEX 50-51 G 3
Luís Tamayo ○ EC 64-65 B 3
Luís Viana ○ BR 68-69 H 6
Luiza ○ ZRE 214-215 B 5
Luiza ~ ZRE 214-215 B 5
Luizavo ~ ANG 216-217 D 6
Luizi ~ ZRE 214-215 D 4
Luján ○ RA 76-77 E 4
Luján ~ RA 76-77 K 3
Luján · RA (BUA) 78-79 K 3
Luján de Cuyo ○ RA 78-79 E 2
Luka ~ ZRE 212-213 B 5
Lukachukai ○ USA (AZ) 256-257 F 2
Lukafu ○ ZRE 214-215 D 6
Lukala ○ ZRE 210-211 D 6
Lukashi ~ ZRE 214-215 C 5
Lukasu ○ ZRE 214-215 C 5
Luke, Mount ▲ AUS 176-177 D 3
Luke Air Force Range ×× USA (CA) 248-249 K 7
Lukedi ~ ZRE 210-211 J 5
Lukenga ○ ZRE 212-213 B 6
Lukenie ~ ZRE 210-211 H 5
Lukeville ○ USA (AZ) 256-257 C 7
Lukimwa ~ EAT 214-215 H 5
Lukojanov ○ RUS 96-97 D 6
Lukolela ○ ZRE (BAN) 210-211 F 4
Lukolela ○ ZRE (KOR) 210-211 K 6
Lukolini ○ EAT 214-215 H 5
Lukonzolwa ○ ZRE 214-215 E 5
Lukos ~ ZW 218-219 D 4
Lukoshi ~ ZRE 214-215 B 6
Lukosi ~ EAT 214-215 J 4
Lukovit ○ BG 102-103 D 6
Lukovnikovo ○ RUS 94-95 O 3
Łuków ○ PL 92-93 R 3
Lukpenenteng ~ RI 164-165 H 4
Luksagu ○ RI 164-165 H 4
Luktah ~ RUS 108-109 Z 5
Lukufo ~ ZRE 214-215 E 6
Lukuga ~ ZRE 212-213 B 6
Lukula ○ ZRE (BAS) 210-211 D 6
Lukula ○ ZRE (SHA) 214-215 D 4
Lukula ~ ZRE 210-211 D 6
Lukula ~ ZRE 210-211 D 6
Lukumbi ~ ZRE 214-215 E 4
Lukumburu ○ EAT 214-215 H 5
Lukunga Swamp ⌣ Z 218-219 D 2
Lukuni ~ ZRE 210-211 H 6
Lukusashi ~ Z 218-219 E 2
Lukushi ~ ZRE 214-215 D 6
Lukusuzi ~ Z 218-219 E 1
Lukusuzi National Park ⊥ Z 214-215 G 7
Lukuswa ~ ZRE 214-215 D 5
Lukuzye ~ Z 218-219 E 1
Lukwasa ○ ZW 218-219 F 1
Lukwila, Gouffre de · ZRE 216-217 D 3
Lula ○ ANG (MS) 268-269 K 2
Lula ~ PE 70-71 D 3
Luleå ○ S 86-87 L 4
Lülebrugaz ○ TR 128-129 B 2
Luliang ○ VRC 156-157 C 4
Lüliang Shan ▲ VRC 154-155 G 3
Lülliáni ○ PK 138-139 E 4
Lulimba ~ ZRE 212-213 B 6
Luling ○ USA (TX) 266-267 K 4
Lulindi ~ ZRE 210-211 L 6
Lulonga ○ ZRE 210-211 G 3
Lulonga ~ ZRE 210-211 G 3
Lulu, Emi ▲ RN 190-191 H 9
Lulung ○ VRC 144-145 D 5
Lulworth, Mount ▲ AUS 176-177 D 3
Luma ~ WAN 204-205 H 4
Luma Cassai ○ ANG 216-217 E 5
Lumajang ○ RI 168 G 4
Lumajangdong Co ○ VRC 144-145 G 5
Lumana ○ ZRE 210-211 K 5
Lumangwe Falls ~ Z 214-215 E 6

Lumata ○ Z 214-215 D 7
Lumba ○ ZRE 206-207 D 6
Lumbala ○ ANG 214-215 B 7
Lumbala N'guimbo ○ ANG 216-217 F 7
Lumbe ~ Z 218-219 B 3
Lumber City ○ USA (GA) 284-285 H 5
Lumbermen's Monument · USA (MI) 272-273 E 3
Lumber River ~ USA (NC) 282-283 H 6
Lumberton ○ CDN (BC) 230-231 M 3
Lumberton ○ USA (MS) 268-269 L 5
Lumberton ○ USA (NC) 282-283 H 6
Lumberton ○ USA (TX) 268-269 F 6
Lumbo ○ MOC 218-219 L 2
Lumbovskij zaliv ≈ 88-89 Q 3
Lumbrera ○ RA 76-77 E 3
Lumby ○ CDN (BC) 230-231 L 3
Lumding ○ IND 142-143 H 3
Lumege ~ ANG 216-217 F 6
Lumeje ○ ANG 216-217 F 6
Lumene ~ ZRE 210-211 H 6
Lumeta ○ ANG 216-217 F 8
Lumholtz National Park ⊥ AUS 174-175 J 5
Lumi ○ PNG 183 B 2
Lumimba ○ Z 214-215 G 7
Luminárias ○ BR 72-73 H 6
Lumoil ○ RI 166-167 E 3
Lumpkin ○ USA (GA) 284-285 F 4
Lumpur ○ RI 162-163 F 6
Lumsden ○ CDN (NFL) 242-243 P 3
Lumsden ○ CDN (SAS) 232-233 O 5
Lumsden ○ NZ 182 B 6
Lumuna ~ ANG 216-217 F 6
Lumut ○ BRU 164-165 D 1
Lumut, Gunung ▲ RI (KTI) 164-165 E 4
Lumut, Gunung ▲ RI (SLT) 164-165 G 4
Lumut, Tanjung ▲ RI 162-163 F 4
Lumwana ○ Z 214-215 D 6
Lun ○ MAU 148-149 G 4
Luna ○ USA (NM) 256-257 G 4
Luna, Laguna de ○ RA 76-77 D 3
Luna, Rio ~ BR 66-67 G 5
Lunahuana ○ PE 64-65 D 8
Lunan Lake ○ CDN 30-31 X 3
Lunan Shilin · VRC 156-157 C 4
Lunar Crater · USA (NV) 246-247 J 5
Lunas, Los ○ USA (NM) 256-257 J 4
Lúnávåda ○ IND 138-139 D 5
Lunca ○ RO 102-103 D 6
Lund ○ CDN (BC) 230-231 J 2
Lund ○ S 86-87 F 9
Lund ○ USA (NV) 246-247 K 4
Lund ○ USA (NV) 246-247 K 5
Lund ○ USA (UT) 254-255 B 6
Lunda, Kasongo- ○ ZRE 216-217 D 3
Lundamilumba ○ EAT (RUK) 214-215 F 4
Lundar ○ CDN (MAN) 234-235 F 4
Lundazi ○ Z 214-215 G 7
Lundazi ~ Z 214-215 G 7
Lundbreck ○ CDN (ALB) 232-233 D 6
Lundu ○ MAL 162-163 H 4
Lundu ~ Z 214-215 G 6
Lüneburg ○·· D 92-93 L 2
Lüneburger Heide ⊥ D 92-93 L 2
Lunenburg ○ CDN (NS) 240-241 M 6
Lunéville ○ · F 90-91 L 7
Lunga ○ MOC 218-219 J 2
Lunga ○ SOL 184 I d 3
Lunga ~ Z 218-219 D 2
Lunga ~ Z 218-219 D 2
Lunga Lunga ○ EAK 212-213 G 6
Lungar Shan ▲ VRC 144-145 D 5
Lunge ○ ANG 216-217 D 6
Lung"egan ~ RUS 114-115 P 4
Lunggar ○ VRC 144-145 D 5
Lungha ~ RUS 118-119 N 4
Lungi ○ WAL 202-203 D 5
Lunglei ○ IND 142-143 H 4
Lungué-Bungo ~ ANG 216-217 F 6
Lunguto ○ RI 164-165 G 3
Lungwebungu ~ Z 218-219 B 1
Luni ~ IND 138-139 D 7
Luninec ○ BY 94-95 K 5
Lunino ○ RUS (NIV) 246-247 G 5
Lunnyj ○ RUS 112-113 H 5
Lunsar ○ WAL 202-203 D 5
Lunsklij, zaliv ≈ RUS 122-123 R 3
Lunyere ~ EAT 214-215 H 5
Lunyuk ○ RI 164-165 F 9
Lunzi ○ Z 214-215 K 6
Luo ○ RI 164-165 G 4
Luo, Rio ~ MOC 218-219 J 3
Luobei ○ VRC 150-151 H 4
Luobuzhuang ○ VRC 146-147 J 6
Luochuan ○ VRC 154-155 F 4
Luodian ○ VRC 156-157 D 4
Luoding ○ VRC 156-157 F 4
Luofushan · VRC 156-157 H 5
Luohe ~ VRC 154-155 H 5
Luojishan ~ VRC 156-157 C 3
Luoning ○ VRC 154-155 G 5
Luoping ○ VRC 156-157 C 4
Luoshan ○ VRC 154-155 J 5
Luoyang ○ VRC 154-155 G 5
Luoyuan ○ VRC 156-157 L 3
Luozi ○ ZRE 210-211 D 6
Lupane ○ ZW 218-219 D 4
Lupar ~ MAL 162-163 J 4
Luperón ○ DOM 54-55 M 4
Lupiliche ○ MOC 214-215 H 6
Lupiro ○ EAT 214-215 J 5

Lupton Channel ≈ 36-37 R 3
Lupuka ○ Z 218-219 B 3
Lupula ○ ANG 216-217 D 7
Luputa ○ ZRE 214-215 B 4
Lupweji ~ ZRE 214-215 E 6
Luqu ○ VRC 154-155 C 4
Luque ○ PY 76-77 J 3
Luquembo ○ ANG 216-217 D 6
Luquillo ○ USA (PR) 286-287 Q 2
Lurahgung ○ RI 168 C 3
Luray ○ USA (KS) 262-263 H 5
Luray ○ USA (VA) 280-281 H 5
Lureco, Rio ~ MOC 218-219 J 1
Lurgan ○ · GB 90-91 D 4
Luribay ○ BOL 70-71 F 5
Lurin, Río ~ PE 64-65 D 8
Lúrio ○ MOC 218-219 L 1
Lúrio ~ MOC 218-219 L 1
Lurton ○ USA (AR) 276-277 B 5
Luruaco ○ CO 60-61 D 2
Lusahunga ○ EAT (KAG) 212-213 C 5
Lusaka ▫ Z 218-219 E 2
Lusaka ★ Z 218-219 E 2
Lusaka ○ ZRE 214-215 C 6
Lusako ○ ZRE 212-213 A 6
Lusamba ○ ZRE 210-211 K 6
Lusambo ○ ZRE 210-211 J 6
Lusancay Islands ⌀ PNG 183 F 5
Lusanga ○ ZRE 210-211 G 6
Lusangi ○ ZRE 212-213 A 6
Luscar ○ CDN (ALB) 228-229 R 3
Luseland ○ CDN (SAS) 232-233 J 3
Lusemfwa ~ Z 218-219 E 1
Lusenga Plain National Park ⊥ Z 214-215 E 6
Lushan ○ VRC (HEN) 154-155 H 5
Lushan ▲ VRC (SHD) 154-155 H 5
Lushan · VRC (JXI) 156-157 J 2
Lushi ○ VRC 154-155 G 5
Lushipuka ~ ZRE 214-215 E 6
Lushoto ○ EAT 212-213 G 6
Lushui ○ VRC (YUN) 142-143 L 3
Lushui ○ VRC (HUB) 156-157 H 2
Lüshun ○ VRC 150-151 G 4
Lusibi ○ Z 218-219 C 3
Lusikisiki ○ ZA 220-221 J 5
Lusinga ○ ZRE 214-215 D 5
Lusitania ○ CO 60-61 D 6
Lusitu ○ EAT 214-215 H 5
Lusk ○ USA (TN) 276-277 K 5
Lusk ○ USA (WY) 252-253 O 4
Lussanhando, Rio ~ MOC 218-219 J 1
Lussenga ○ ANG 216-217 B 3
Lusssso ○ ANG 216-217 C 5
Lustre ○ USA (MT) 250-251 O 3
Lusufu ○ MOC 218-219 L 3
Luswaka ○ Z 214-215 D 6
Lüt, Dašt-e ⊥ IR 134-135 G 2
Lutao ○ RC 156-157 M 5
Lutcher ○ USA (LA) 268-269 K 6
Lutembo ○ ANG 216-217 F 6
Luth ○ SUD 206-207 O 4
Luther Pass ▲ USA (CA) 246-247 F 5
Luthersburg ○ USA (PA) 280-281 H 2
Lutherstadt Wittenberg ○· D 92-93 M 3
Luti ○ SOL 184 I c 2
Luti, River ~ WAN 204-205 K 4
Lutiba ○ USA (TX) 264-265 D 3
Lutilut ○ MYA 158-159 E 4
Lutong ○ MAL 164-165 D 1
Lutope ~ ZW 218-219 E 4
Lutsen ○ USA (MN) 270-271 H 4
Lutshima ○ ZRE 210-211 G 6
Lutshima ~ ZRE 216-217 E 5
Lüttich = Liège ☆ · B 92-93 H 3
Lutuai ○ ANG 216-217 F 6
Lutuhyne ○ UA 102-103 L 3
Lutunguru ○ ZRE 212-213 A 4
Lützow-Holm bukt ≈ 16 G 4
Lutzputs ○ ZA 220-221 E 4
Lutzville ○ ZA 220-221 C 5
Luuq ○ SP 212-213 J 2
Luverne ○ USA (AL) 284-285 D 5
Luverne ○ USA (MN) 270-271 B 7
Luvidjo ~ ZRE 214-215 D 4
Luvilombo ○ ZRE 214-215 D 5
Luvo ○ ANG 216-217 C 2
Luvua ~ ZRE 214-215 E 4
Luvuei ○ ANG 216-217 F 6
Luvunzo ~ ZRE 214-215 C 5
Luwe ~ ZRE 214-215 D 5
Luwegu ~ EAT 214-215 J 5
Luwegu ~ EAT 214-215 H 5
Luwero ○ Z 218-219 F 2
Luwingu ○ Z 214-215 E 6
Luwshi ~ Z 214-215 F 6
Luwowa ~ ZRE 214-215 D 5
Luwuk ○ RI 164-165 H 4
Luwumbu ~ Z 214-215 G 6
Luxapallila Creek ~ USA (AL) 284-285 B 3
Luxembourg ▪ L 92-93 J 4
Luxembourg ★··· L 92-93 J 4
Luxemburg ○ USA (IA) 274-275 G 2
Luxemburg ○ USA (WI) 270-271 L 6
Luxeuil ○ F 90-91 L 8
Luxi ○ VRC (HUN) 156-157 F 2
Luxi ○ VRC (YUN) 142-143 L 3
Luxi ○ VRC (YUN) 156-157 C 4
Luxor = al-Uqsur ○·· ET 194-195 F 5
Luxor = al-Uqsur ·· ET 194-195 F 5
Luxora ○ USA (AR) 276-277 B 5
Luyando ○ PE 64-65 D 6
Luza ☆ RUS 88-89 S 5
Luza ~ RUS 96-97 F 4
Luza ~ RUS 96-97 F 4
Luzern ☆ CH 92-93 K 5
Luzhai ○ VRC 156-157 F 4

Mana ~ RUS 116-117 F 8
Mana o USA (HI) 288 F 2
Manacacias, Río ~ CO 60-61 E 6
Manacapurú o BR 66-67 G 4
Manacapuru, Rio ~ BR 66-67 G 4
Manacas o C 54-55 E 3
Manacor o E 98-99 J 5
Manādir, al- ⊥ UAE 132-133 J 2
Manado ☆ RI 164-165 J 3
Manaffey o USA (PA) 280-281 H 3
Managua ★ NIC 52-53 L 5
Managua, Lago de ⊖ NIC 52-53 L 5
Manāḥa o • Y 132-133 C 6
Manaíra o BR 68-69 J 5
Manajuare o CO 60-61 F 5
Manakana o RM 222-223 E 6
Manakara o RM 222-223 E 9
Manalalondo o RM 222-223 E 7
Manali o • IND 138-139 F 3
Manama o UAE 134-135 G 6
Manama o ZW 218-219 E 5
Manāma, al- ★ • BRN 134-135 D 5
Mānāmadurai o IND 140-141 H 6
Manambaho ~ RM 222-223 D 6
Manambaro o RM 222-223 E 10
Manambolo ~ RM 222-223 D 7
Manambolosy o RM 222-223 F 6
Manambondro o RM 222-223 E 9
Manambovo ~ RM 222-223 D 10
Manamgoora o AUS 174-175 D 5
Manami o RI 166-167 H 3
Manam Island ⌒ PNG 183 C 3
Manamo, Caño ~ YV 60-61 K 3
Manampanihy ~ RM 222-223 E 10
Manampatrana ~ RM 222-223 E 9
Manana, Cachoeira ~ BR 62-63 H 4
Mananantanana ~ RM 222-223 D 8
Mananara ~ RM 222-223 F 6
Mananara Avaratra o RM 222-223 F 6
Manandona o RM 222-223 E 8
Manangatang o AUS 180-181 G 3
Mananjary o RM (FNS) 222-223 F 8
Mananjary ~ RM 222-223 E 8
Manankoro o RMM 202-203 G 4
Manantali, Lac de < RMM 202-203 E 3
Manantenina o RM 222-223 E 10
Mānantoddy o IND 140-141 G 5
Mana Pass ▲ VRC 144-145 B 5
Mana Pools National Park ⊥ ••• ZW 218-219 E 2
Manapouri, Lake ⊖ NZ 182 A 6
Manappārai o IND 140-141 H 5
Manaquiri o BR 66-67 G 4
Manaquiri, Lago ⊖ BR 66-67 G 4
Manari o PNG 183 D 5
Manariã o BR 66-67 D 5
Manas ~ BHT 142-143 G 2
Manas o PE 64-65 D 7
Manas o VRC 146-147 H 3
Manas, gora ▲ KS 136-137 M 3
Manasarowar = Mapam Yumco ⊖ VRC 144-145 C 5
Manas He ~ VRC 146-147 G 3
Manas Hu ⊖ VRC 146-147 H 3
Manaslu ▲ NEP 144-145 E 6
Manassa o USA (CO) 254-255 K 6
Manassas o USA (VA) 280-281 J 5
Manassas National Battlefield Park • USA (VA) 280-281 J 5
Mănăstire Horezu ••• RO 102-103 C 5
Manastir Morača • YU 100-101 G 3
Manastir Ostrog • YU 100-101 G 3
Manas Wildlife Sanctuary ⊥ ••• IND 142-143 G 2
Manatee, Lake < USA (FL) 286-287 G 4
Manatee River ~ USA (FL) 286-287 G 4
Manatí o C 54-55 F 4
Manatí o C 54-55 G 4
Manatí o USA (PR) 286-287 P 2
Manatlán o MEX 52-53 B 2
Manatuto o RI 166-167 C 6
Manau o PNG 183 D 5
Man'aung o MYA 142-143 H 6
Man'aung Kyûn ⌒ MYA 142-143 H 6
Manaure o CO 60-61 E 2
Manaus o BR (MAR) 68-69 E 2
Manaus ☆ BR (AMA) 66-67 G 4
Manavgat ☆ TR 128-129 D 4
Manawoka, Pulau ⌒ RI 166-167 F 4
Mañazo o PE 70-71 B 4
Mānbazār o IND 142-143 E 4
Manbiğ ☆ SYR 128-129 G 4
Manbiri o RMM 202-203 F 3
Mancelona o USA (MI) 272-273 D 3
Mancha, La ⊥ E 98-99 F 5
Manchao, Sierra de ▲ RA 76-77 D 5
Manchar o IND 138-139 D 10
Manche = English Channel ≈ 90-91 F 6
Mancheng Hanmu ∴• VRC 154-155 J 2
Mancherāl o IND 138-139 G 10
Manchester o • GB 90-91 F 5
Manchester o USA (CT) 280-281 O 2
Manchester o USA (GA) 284-285 F 4
Manchester o USA (IA) 274-275 G 2
Manchester o USA (KY) 276-277 M 3
Manchester o USA (NH) 278-279 K 6
Manchester o USA (OH) 280-281 C 5
Manchester o USA (TN) 276-277 J 5
Manchester o USA (VT) 278-279 H 5
Manchester o USA (WI) 270-271 J 7
Manchester Lake ⊖ CDN 30-31 Q 5
Manchhar Lake ⊖ PK 134-135 M 5
Manchioneal o JA 54-55 G 5
Manchok o WAN 204-205 H 4
Manchuria = Dongbei ⊥ VRC 150-151 E 6
Manciano o I 100-101 C 3
Máncora o PE 64-65 B 4
Mancos o USA (CO) 254-255 G 6
Mancos River ~ USA (CO) 254-255 G 6
Mand o PK 134-135 K 5
Mand, Rūd-e ~ IR 134-135 D 4
Manda o EAT (IRI) 214-215 H 6
Manda o EAT (MBE) 214-215 G 4
Manda o ETH 200-201 L 6
Manda o TCH 206-207 D 4
Manda, Parc National de ⊥ TCH 206-207 C 4
Mandabe o RM 222-223 D 8
Mandacaru o BR 68-69 G 3
Mandaguari o BR 72-73 E 7
Mandah = Töhöm o MAU 148-149 J 5
Manda Island ⌒ EAK 212-213 H 5
Mandal ☆ N 86-87 C 7
Mandalay ☆ •• MYA 142-143 K 4
Mandalgov' ☆ MAU 148-149 H 5
Mandali ☆ IRQ 128-129 L 6
Mandal-Ovoo = Šarhulsan o MAU 148-149 G 5
Mandalselva ~ N 86-87 C 7
Mandan o • USA (ND) 258-259 G 5
Mandaon o RP 160-161 E 6
Mandar, Teluk ≈ 164-165 F 5
Mandara Mountains ▲ WAN 204-205 K 3
Mandarin o USA (FL) 286-287 H 1
Mándas o I 100-101 B 5
Mandasor o IND 138-139 E 7
Mandaue o RP 160-161 E 7
Mandélia o TCH 206-207 B 3
Mandera o EAK 212-213 H 2
Manderson o USA (WY) 252-253 L 2
Mandeville o • JA 54-55 G 5
Mandeville o USA (LA) 268-269 K 6
Mandheera o SP 208-209 G 4
Mandi o • IND 138-139 F 4
Mandi, Raudal ~ CO 66-67 B 2
Mandiakui o RMM 202-203 H 3
Mandiana o RG 202-203 F 4
Mandiangin o RI 162-163 C 5
Mandi Bahāuddin o PK 138-139 D 3
Mandi Burewāla o PK 138-139 D 4
Mandié o MOC 218-219 G 3
Mandi Langwé ▲ CAM 204-205 J 6
Mandimba o MOC 218-219 H 2
Mandingues, Monts ▲ RMM 202-203 F 3
Mandioli, Pulau ⌒ RI 164-165 K 4
Mandioré, Lago ⊖ BOL 70-71 J 6
Mandirituba o BR 74-75 F 5
Mandji o G 210-211 C 4
Mandla o IND 142-143 B 4
Mandleshwar o IND 138-139 E 8
Mando o WAN 204-205 G 3
Mandōl o AFG 136-137 M 7
Mandon o RI 166-167 J 2
Mandor o RI 162-163 H 4
Mandora o AUS 172-173 E 5
Mandori o RI 166-167 H 2
Mandoro o ZRE 206-207 J 6
Mandoto o RM 222-223 E 7
Mandoul ~ TCH 206-207 C 4
Mandouri o RT 202-203 L 4
Mandra o PK 138-139 D 3
Mandrare ~ RM 222-223 E 10
Mandrikovo o RUS 112-113 K 3
Mandritsara o RM 222-223 F 5
Mandronarivo o RM 222-223 D 8
Mandrosonoro o RM 222-223 E 8
Mandu o IND 142-143 D 4
Mandul, Pulau ⌒ RI 164-165 E 2
Mandumbua o ANG 216-217 F 7
Mandurah o • AUS 176-177 C 6
Mandúria o I 100-101 F 4
Mandūzai o AFG 138-139 B 3
Māndvi o IND (GUJ) 138-139 D 9
Māndvi o IND (GUJ) 138-139 B 8
Mandya o IND 140-141 G 4
Mané o BF 202-203 K 3
Maneadero o C 54-55 E 3
Maneadero o MEX 50-51 A 2
Mané Kondjo ~ TCH 206-207 D 3
Manengouba, Massif du ▲ CAM 204-205 H 6
Maneromango o EAT 214-215 K 4
Manes o USA (MO) 276-277 C 3
Manevyči o UA 102-103 D 2
Manfalūt o ET 194-195 E 4
Manflas, Río ~ RCH 76-77 C 5
Manfran o RG 202-203 F 5
Manfred Downs o AUS 174-175 F 7
Manfredónia o I 100-101 E 4
Manfredónia, Golfo di ≈ 100-101 F 4
Manga o BF 202-203 K 4
Manga o BR 72-73 J 3
Manga ▲ CAM 204-205 K 5
Manga o PNG 183 G 3
Manga ⊥ RN 198-199 F 6
Mangabeiras, Chapada das ▲ BR 68-69 E 6
Mangada o ZRE 212-213 A 2
Manga Grande o ANG 216-217 B 3
Mangai o PNG 183 F 2
Mangaïzé o RN 202-203 L 2
Mangalia o • RO 102-103 F 6
Mangalmé o TCH 198-199 J 6
Mangalore o AUS 178-179 J 4
Mangalore o • IND 140-141 F 4
Mangalwedha o IND 140-141 F 2
Mangango o Z 218-219 C 2
Māngaon o IND 138-139 D 10
Mangas o USA (NM) 256-257 J 4
Mangatupopo o NZ 182 E 3
Mangawan o IND 142-143 B 3
Mangaweka ▲ NZ 182 F 3
Mangbwalu o ZRE 212-213 C 3
Mangdangshan • VRC 154-155 K 4
Māng Đen, Đèo ▲ VN 158-159 K 3
Mange o PNG 183 D 4
Mange o WAL 202-203 D 5
Mangeni, Hamada ⊥ RN 192-193 E 6
Manggar o RI 162-163 H 6
Manggasi o RI 166-167 J 3
Manggawitu o RI 166-167 G 4
Mangguar, Tanjung ▲ RI 166-167 H 3
Mangham o USA (LA) 268-269 J 4
Mangisor, kōlī ⊖ KA 124-125 F 1
Mangistau, gory ▲ KA 126-127 J 5
Mangit ☆ US 136-137 G 3
Mangkalihat, Tanjung ▲ RI 164-165 F 3
Mangkok, Tanjung ▲ RI 164-165 E 5
Mangkutana o RI 164-165 G 5
Manglares o CO 60-61 C 5
Manglares, Cabo ▲ CO 64-65 C 1
Manglares, Punta ▲ CO 60-61 C 5
Manglares Churute, Reservat E. ⊥ EC 64-65 C 3
Mangla Reservoir < PK 138-139 D 3
Mangnai o VRC 144-145 H 2
Mangnai Zhen o VRC 146-147 K 6
Mangnuc, Lac ⊖ CDN 36-37 L 5
Mango ⌒ TON 184 IV a 2
Mangoaka o RM 222-223 F 4
Mangochi o • MW 218-219 H 2
Mango Creek o BH 52-53 K 3
Mangodara o BF 202-203 H 5
Mangoky ~ RM 222-223 D 9
Mangole, Pulau ⌒ RI 164-165 J 4
Mangole, Selat ≈ 164-165 J 4
Mangom o CAM 204-205 K 5
Mangombe o ZRE 210-211 L 4
Mangonui o NZ 182 D 1
Mangoro ~ RM 222-223 F 7
Mangowra o AUS 174-175 F 5
Māngrol o IND 138-139 C 9
Mangrullo, Cuchilla de ▲ ROU 74-75 D 9
Mangrūl Pīr o IND 138-139 F 9
Mangshan • VRC 154-155 H 4
Mangu o EAK 212-213 F 4
Manguaurcu o EC 64-65 B 4
Mangūchar o PK 134-135 M 4
Mangue o BR 68-69 F 2
Mangueigne o TCH 206-207 E 3
Mangueira, Lagoa ⊖ BR 74-75 D 9
Mangueirinha o BR 74-75 D 5
Manguel Creek o AUS 172-173 F 4
Mangues, Rio dos ~ BR 68-69 D 7
Mangue Seco o BR 68-69 K 7
Mangues Secos, Ponta dos ▲ BR 68-69 G 3
Mangui o VRC 150-151 D 1
Manguito o C 54-55 E 3
Mangum o USA (OK) 264-265 E 4
Mangunça o BR 68-69 F 2
Mangunça, Ilha ⌒ BR 68-69 F 2
Mangungu o ZRE 210-211 F 6
Mangunza o Z 218-219 D 3
Manguohe o VRC 156-157 C 4
Manguredjipa o ZRE 212-213 B 3
Mangut o RUS 118-119 F 11
Mangutiha ~ RUS 114-115 T 3
Mangutiri, Igarapé ~ BR 66-67 D 7
Mang Yang o VN 158-159 K 4
Măng Yang, Đèo ▲ VN 158-159 K 3
Mangyčlak ☆ KA 126-127 J 6
Mangyšlak o KA 126-127 J 6
Mangyšlak, plato ▲ KA 126-127 K 6
Mangyšlakskij zaliv ≈ 126-127 J 5
Mangystau, taulary ▲ KA 126-127 J 5
Manhan = Tögrög o MAU 146-147 L 2
Manhattan o USA (KS) 262-263 K 5
Manhattan o USA (MT) 250-251 H 6
Manhattan o USA (NV) 246-247 H 5
Manhica o MOC 220-221 L 2
Manhuaçu o BR 72-73 J 6
Manhumirim o BR 72-73 K 6
Mani o CO 60-61 E 5
Mani o TCH 198-199 G 6
Mani o WAN 198-199 C 6
Mani o ZRE 214-215 C 4
Mani, Quebrada de ~ RCH 76-77 C 1
Mania ~ RM 222-223 E 8
Maniaçu o BR 72-73 J 2
Maniamba o MOC 214-215 H 7
Mania-Muna o ZRE 214-215 B 5
Manica o MOC 218-219 G 4
Manica ◘ MOC 218-219 G 5
Manicaland ◘ ZW 218-219 F 4
Manicani Island ⌒ RP 160-161 F 7
Manicaragua o C 54-55 F 3
Maniche o RH 54-55 J 5
Manico Point ▲ CDN 36-37 F 3
Manicoré o BR 66-67 G 5
Manicoré, Rio ~ BR 66-67 G 6
Manicorézinho, Rio ~ BR 66-67 G 6
Manicouagan o CDN 38-39 K 3
Manicouagan, Réservoir <••• CDN 38-39 K 3
Manicouagan, Rivière ~ CDN 38-39 K 4
Manicrois, Réservoir < CDN 38-39 K 3
Manifold, Cape ▲ AUS 178-179 L 2
Maniganggo o VRC 144-145 M 5
Manigotagan o CDN (MAN) 234-235 G 3
Maniitsoq o GRØ 28-29 O 4
Maniitsoq = Sukkertoppen o GRØ 28-29 O 4
Manika o ZRE 214-215 C 6
Manila ★ •• RP 160-161 D 5
Manila o USA (AR) 276-277 E 5
Manila o USA (UT) 254-255 F 3
Manila Bay ≈ 160-161 D 5
Manilla o AUS 178-179 L 6
Manily o RUS 112-113 N 5
Manimbaya, Tanjung ▲ RI 164-165 F 4
Maningory ~ RM 222-223 F 6
Maningoza ~ RM 222-223 D 6
Maningrida ⵋ AUS 174-175 C 3
Maninjau o RI 162-163 D 5
Maninjau, Danau ⊖ RI 162-163 D 5
Manipa, Pulau ⌒ RI 166-167 D 3
Manipa, Selat ≈ 166-167 D 3
Manipur ◘ IND 142-143 H 3
Manipur ~ IND 142-143 H 3
Maniqui, Río ~ BOL 70-71 D 4
Manisa ☆ • TR 128-129 B 3
Manisaj ~ KA 126-127 M 4
Manissauá-Miçu, Rio ~ BR 70-71 K 3
Manistee o USA (MI) 272-273 C 3
Manistee River ~ USA (MI) 272-273 D 3
Manistique o USA (MI) 270-271 M 5
Manistique Lake ~ USA (MI) 270-271 N 4
Manistique River ~ USA (MI) 270-271 M 4
Manita pećina •• HR 100-101 E 2
Manito o USA (IL) 274-275 J 4
Manitoba ◘ CDN 34-35 F 3
Manitoba, Lake ⊖ CDN (MAN) 234-235 D 3
Manito Lake ⊖ CDN (SAS) 232-233 J 3
Manitou o CDN (MAN) 234-235 E 5
Manitou o CDN (QUE) 242-243 C 2
Manitou, Lac ⊖ CDN (QUE) 242-243 E 2
Manitou, Rivière ~ CDN (QUE) 242-243 C 2
Manitou Beach o CDN (SAS) 232-233 N 4
Manitou Falls o CDN (ONT) 234-235 K 4
Manitou Island ⌒ USA (MI) 270-271 L 3
Manitou Islands ⌒ USA (MI) 270-271 M 5
Manitou Lake ⊖ CDN (ONT) 238-239 D 3
Manitou Lakes ⊖ CDN (ONT) 234-235 L 5
Manitoulin Island ⌒ CDN (ONT) 238-239 C 3
Manitounuk Sound ≈ 36-37 L 7
Manitou Springs o USA (CO) 254-255 L 5
Manitouwadge o CDN (ONT) 236-237 C 3
Manitowaning o CDN (ONT) 238-239 D 3
Manitowoc o USA (WI) 270-271 L 6
Manitsoq ⌒ GRØ 26-27 X 7
Maniwaki o CDN (QUE) 238-239 K 2
Maniwaki Indian Reservation ⵋ CDN (QUE) 238-239 K 2
Maniwaki Indian Reserve ⵋ CDN (QUE) 238-239 J 2
Maniwori o RI 166-167 H 3
Maniyāchchi o IND 140-141 G 6
Manizales ☆ CO 60-61 D 5
Manja o RM 222-223 D 8
Manjacaze o MOC 220-221 L 2
Manjakandriana o RM 222-223 E 7
Manjakot o PK 138-139 D 2
Manjeri o IND 140-141 G 5
Mānjhand o PK 138-139 B 7
Manjimup o AUS 176-177 D 7
Manjo o CAM 204-205 H 6
Manjou o CAM 204-205 K 6
Manjra ~ IND 138-139 F 10
Mānjra ~ IND 138-139 F 10
Mankanza o ZRE 210-211 G 3
Mankarigu o GH 202-203 K 4
Man Kat o MYA 142-143 L 4
Mankato o USA (KS) 262-263 H 5
Mankato o USA (MN) 270-271 E 6
Mankayane o SD 220-221 K 3
Mankera o PK 138-139 C 4
Mankessim o GH 202-203 K 7
Manki II o CAM 204-205 J 6
Mankim o CAM 204-205 K 6
Mankins o USA (TX) 264-265 F 5
Mankono ☆ CI 202-203 G 5
Mankota o CDN (SAS) 232-233 L 6
Mankpan o GH 202-203 K 5
Mankranso o GH 202-203 K 6
Mankyčlaks, cyganak ≈ 126-127 J 5
Manley Hot Springs o USA 20-21 P 4
Manlius o USA (NY) 278-279 F 6
Manly o USA (IA) 274-275 E 1
Man Na o MYA 142-143 K 4
Manna o RI 162-163 E 7
Mannahill o AUS 180-181 E 2
Manna Hill Gold Field • AUS 180-181 E 2
Mannampitiya o CL 140-141 J 7
Mannar, Gulf of ≈ 140-141 H 6
Mannārgudi o IND 140-141 H 5
Mannar Island ⌒ CL 140-141 H 6
Mannarkkad o IND 140-141 G 5
Manners Creek o AUS 178-179 D 2
Mannheim o • D 92-93 K 4
Manni o VRC 144-145 F 4
Manning o USA (IA) 274-275 C 3
Manning o USA (ND) 258-259 E 4
Manning o USA (SC) 284-285 K 3
Manning, Cape ▲ CDN 24-25 X 3
Manning Park o CDN (BC) 230-231 J 4
Manning Provincial Park ⊥ CDN (BC) 230-231 J 4
Manning Range, Mount ▲ AUS 176-177 E 4
Manning River ~ AUS 178-179 M 6
Manning Strait ≈ 184 I c 2
Mannington o USA (WV) 280-281 F 4
Mann Ranges ▲ AUS 176-177 K 3
Mann River ~ AUS 174-175 C 3
Manns Harbor o USA (NC) 282-283 M 5
Mannville o CDN (ALB) 232-233 G 2
Mano o WAL 202-203 D 5
Manoá Pium, Área Indígena ⵋ BR 62-63 D 4
Mano Junction o WAL 202-203 E 5
Manokwari o RI (IRJ) 166-167 H 2
Manokwari o RI (IRJ) 166-167 H 3
Manolo Fortich o RP 160-161 F 8
Manoma ~ RUS 122-123 G 4
Manombo Atsimo o RM 222-223 C 9
Manometimay o RM 222-223 D 8
Manompana o RM 222-223 F 6
Manonga ~ EAT 212-213 D 5
Manono o ZRE 214-215 D 4
Manonwa o ZRE 210-211 K 6
Manor o CDN (SAS) 232-233 Q 6
Manor o USA (GA) 284-285 H 5
Manor o USA (TX) 266-267 K 3
Mano River o LB 202-203 E 6
Mano River ~ LB 202-203 E 6
Manos, Cueva de las • RA 80 E 3
Manosque o F 90-91 K 10
Manou o RCA 206-207 E 4
Manouane o CDN (QUE) 236-237 O 5
Manouane, Lac ⊖ CDN (QUE) 38-39 J 3
Manouane, Lac ⊖ CDN (QUE) 236-237 O 5
Manouanis, Lac ⊖ CDN 38-39 J 3
Manovo = Tété ~ RCA 206-207 E 4
Manpo o DVR 150-151 F 7
Manresa o E 98-99 H 4
Mānsa o IND 138-139 E 5
Mansa ☆ Z 214-215 E 6
Mansabá o GNB 202-203 C 3
Mansa Konko ☆ • WAG 202-203 C 3
Mansalean o RI 164-165 H 4
Mansavillagra, Arroyo ~ ROU 78-79 M 2
Mānsehra o PK 138-139 D 2
Mansel Island ⌒ CDN 36-37 K 3
Mansfield o AUS 180-181 J 4
Mansfield o GB 90-91 G 5
Mansfield o USA (AR) 276-277 A 5
Mansfield o USA (IN) 274-275 L 5
Mansfield o USA (LA) 268-269 G 4
Mansfield o USA (MA) 278-279 K 6
Mansfield o USA (MO) 276-277 C 3
Mansfield o USA (OH) 280-281 D 3
Mansfield o USA (PA) 280-281 J 2
Mansfield o USA (TX) 264-265 G 6
Mansfield o USA (WA) 244-245 F 3
Mansfield, Mount ▲ USA (VT) 278-279 J 4
Mansfield, Port o USA (TX) 266-267 K 7
Mansha ~ Z 214-215 F 6
Mansi o MYA 142-143 J 3
Mansiari o IND 144-145 C 5
Mansidão o BR 68-69 F 7
Mansijsk, Hanty- ☆ RUS 114-115 K 4
Mansilla o E 98-99 F 3
Mansinam, Pulau ⌒ RI 166-167 H 2
Mansle o F 90-91 H 9
Manso, Rio ~ BR 70-71 K 4
Mansôa o GNB 202-203 C 3
Mansôa, Rio ~ GNB 202-203 C 3
Manso au das Mortes, Rio ~ BR 70-71 K 4
Manson o CDN (MAN) 234-235 B 4
Manson o USA (IA) 274-275 D 2
Manson o USA (WA) 244-245 E 3
Manson Creek o CDN 32-33 H 4
Manso-Nkwanta o GH 202-203 K 6
Mansons Landing o CDN (BC) 230-231 D 3
Mansoura o DZ 190-191 E 2
Mansourah • DZ 188-189 L 3
Mansuar, Pulau ⌒ RI 166-167 F 2
Mansuela o RI 166-167 E 3
Mansuela Reserve ⊥ • RI 166-167 E 3
Mansura o USA (LA) 268-269 H 5
Manṣūra, al- ☆ ET 194-195 E 2
Manṣūriya, al- o Y 132-133 C 6
Mansurlu o TR 128-129 F 4
Manta o DY 202-203 L 4
Manta o EC 64-65 B 2
Manta, Bahía de ≈ 64-65 B 2
Manta, La o CO 60-61 D 3
Mantaba ~ ZRE 210-211 F 5
Mantador o USA (ND) 258-259 L 5
Mantagao Lake ⊖ CDN (MAN) 234-235 F 3
Mantagao River ~ CDN (MAN) 234-235 F 3
Mantalinga o RI 164-165 G 5
Mantalingajan, Mount ▲ RP 160-161 B 8
Mantanzilla, Quebrada ~ RCH 76-77 B 3
Mantario o CDN (SAS) 232-233 J 4
Mantaro, Río ~ PE 64-65 E 8
Manteca o USA (CA) 248-249 C 2
Mantecal o YV (APU) 60-61 G 4
Mantecal o YV (BOL) 60-61 J 4
Manteco, El o YV 60-61 K 4
Mantehage, Pulau ⌒ RI 164-165 J 3
Mantena o BR 72-73 K 5
Mantenga Falls ~ • SD 220-221 K 3
Manteo o USA (NC) 282-283 M 5
Manthani o IND 138-139 G 10
Manti o USA (AL) 284-285 D 5
Manti o USA (UT) 254-255 D 4
Mantiqueira, Serra da ▲ BR 72-73 G 7
Manto o HN 52-53 L 4
Manton o USA (MI) 272-273 D 3
Manton Knob ▲ AUS 176-177 J 3
Mantova o • I 100-101 C 2
Mantralayam o IND 140-141 G 3
Mäntsälä o FIN 88-89 H 6
Mant's Harbour o CDN (NFL) 242-243 P 4
Mantua o C 54-55 C 3
Mantua ~ C 54-55 C 3
Mantuan Downs P.O. o AUS 178-179 J 3
Manturovo o RUS 96-97 D 4
Manú o PE 70-71 B 3
Manu o WAN 198-199 B 6
Manú, Parque Nacional ⊥ ••• PE 70-71 B 2
Manu'a Islands ⌒ USA 184 V c 2
Manubepium o RI 166-167 H 2
Manuel o MEX 50-51 K 6
Manuela, La o RA 78-79 H 4
Manuel Alves, Rio ~ BR 68-69 D 7
Manuel Alves Grande, Rio ~ BR 68-69 E 5
Manuel Alves Pequena, Rio ~ BR 68-69 E 6
Manuel Benavides o MEX 50-51 H 3
Manuel Emídio o BR 68-69 G 5
Manuel Lake ⊖ CDN 30-31 F 2
Manuel Ribas o BR 74-75 E 5
Manuel Rodríguez, Isla ⌒ RCH 80 D 6
Manuel Tames o C 54-55 H 4
Manuel Urbano o BR 66-67 C 7
Manuel Viana o BR 76-77 K 5
Manuel Vitorino o BR 72-73 K 3
Manūğān o IR 134-135 G 5
Manui, Pulau ⌒ RI 164-165 H 5
Manuk ~ RI 168 C 3
Manuk, Pulau ⌒ RI 166-167 F 4
Manukan o RP 160-161 E 8
Manuk Mankax ⌒ RP 160-161 C 10
Manundi, Tanjung ▲ RI 166-167 H 2
Manupampi, Pulau ⌒ RI 166-167 H 2
Manuran, Pulau ⌒ RI 166-167 F 1
Manurimí, Río ~ BOL 70-71 C 2
Manuripe, Río ~ PE 70-71 C 2
Manuripi, Río ~ BOL 70-71 D 2
Manuripi Heath, Natural Reserve ⊥ BOL 70-71 C 2
Manus Island ⌒ PNG 183 D 1
Manvel o USA (ND) 258-259 K 3
Mānvi o IND 140-141 G 2
Manville o USA (WY) 252-253 O 4
Many o USA (LA) 268-269 G 5
Manyame ~ ZW 218-219 F 3
Manyani o EAK 212-213 G 5
Manyara, Lake ⊖ EAT 212-213 E 5
Manyara National Park ⊥ EAT 212-213 E 5
Manyas ☆ TR 128-129 B 2
Manyberries o CDN (ALB) 232-233 H 6
Manyč ~ RUS 102-103 N 5
Manych Depression = Kumo-Manyčskaja vpadina ~ RUS 102-103 M 4
Manyémen o CAM 204-205 H 6
Manyinga o Z 218-219 C 1
Many Island Lake ⊖ CDN (ALB) 232-233 H 5
Manyo o EAT 214-215 F 4
Manyoni o EAT 212-213 E 6
Mānzai o PK 138-139 B 4
Manzai o PK 138-139 C 3
Manzanares o CO 60-61 D 5
Manzanares o • E 98-99 F 5
Manzanillo o C 54-55 G 4
Manzanillo o • MEX 52-53 B 2
Manzanillo, Punta ▲ YV 60-61 G 2
Manzanita o USA (OR) 244-245 B 5
Manzanita Indian Reservation ⵋ USA (CA) 248-249 H 7
Manzano o USA (NM) 256-257 J 4
Manzano, El o RCH 78-79 D 3
Manzengele o ZRE 216-217 D 3
Manzhouli o VRC 148-149 N 3
Manzini o SD 220-221 K 3
Manzurka o RUS 116-117 N 9
Manzurka ~ RUS 116-117 N 9
Mao ☆ • DOM 54-55 K 5
Mao ☆ TCH 198-199 G 5
Maogong o VRC 156-157 F 3
Maojing o VRC 154-155 E 3
Maoke, Pegunungan ▲ RI 166-167 J 4
Maolan Z.B. ⊥ • VRC 156-157 E 4
Mao Ling • VRC 154-155 F 4
Maoming o VRC 156-157 G 6
Maonanzu o VRC 156-157 F 4
Maopora, Pulau ⌒ RI 166-167 D 5
Maospati o RI 168 D 3
Maotou Shan ▲ VRC 142-143 M 3
Mao Xian o VRC 154-155 C 6
Mapaga o RI 164-165 F 4
Mapai o MOC 218-219 G 6
Mapamoiwa o PNG 183 F 5
Mapam Yumco • VRC 144-145 C 5
Mapane o RI 164-165 G 4
Mapangu o ZRE 210-211 H 6
Mapari, Rio ~ BR 66-67 D 4
Mapastepec o MEX 52-53 H 4
Mapat, Pulau ⌒ RI 164-165 E 2
Mapes o CDN (BC) 228-229 L 3
Maphisa o ZW 218-219 E 5
Mapi o RI 166-167 K 5
Mapi ~ RI 166-167 K 5
Mapia, Kepulauan Indonesia ⌒ RI 166-167 H 1
Mapiá, Rio ~ BR 66-67 H 5
Mapichi, Serranía de ▲ YV 60-61 H 5
Mapili o RI 164-165 F 5
Mapinhane o MOC 218-219 H 6
Mapire o YV 60-61 J 4
Mapiri o BOL 70-71 C 4
Mapiri, Rio ~ BOL 70-71 D 4
Mapiri, Rio ~ BOL 70-71 D 2
Mapiripán o CO 60-61 E 6
Maple Bluff o USA (WI) 274-275 J 1
Maple City o USA (MI) 272-273 D 3
Maple Creek o CDN (SAS) 232-233 J 6
Maple Creek ~ CDN (SAS) 232-233 J 5
Maple Ridge o CDN (BC) 230-231 G 4
Maple Ridge o USA (MI) 272-273 F 3
Maplesville o USA (AL) 284-285 D 4
Mapleton o USA (IA) 274-275 C 2
Mapleton o USA (MI) 272-273 D 3
Mapleton o USA (MN) 270-271 E 7
Mapleton o USA (OR) 244-245 B 6
Maple Valley o USA (WA) 244-245 C 3
Mapmakers Seamount ≃ 14-15 J 5
Mapoon ⵋ AUS 174-175 F 3
Mapoon Aboriginal Land ⵋ AUS 174-175 G 2
Mappsville o USA (VA) 280-281 L 6
Maprik o PNG 183 B 2
Mapuca o • IND 140-141 E 3
Mapuera, Rio ~ BR 62-63 E 5
Mapulanguene o MOC 220-221 L 2
Mapunda o ZRE 214-215 C 5
Mapunga o Z 218-219 D 1
Maputi, Pulau ⌒ RI 164-165 F 3
Maputo ◘ MOC 220-221 L 2
Maputo ★ • MOC (MAP) 220-221 L 2
Maputo ~ MOC (MAP) 220-221 L 3
Maputo, Baia do ≈ 220-221 L 3
Maputo, Reserva de Elefantes do ⊥ MOC 220-221 L 3
Maputo, Rio ~ MOC 220-221 L 3
Maputsoe o LS 220-221 H 4
Maqāriyūs, Dair ∴ ET 194-195 E 2
Maqên o VRC 154-155 B 4
Maqên Gangri ▲ VRC 144-145 M 3
Maqrat o Y 132-133 G 6
Maqṭeir ⊥ RIM 196-197 E 4
Maqu o VRC 154-155 B 4
Maquan He (Damqog Zangbo) ~ VRC 144-145 D 5
Maquatua, Rivière ~ CDN 38-39 E 2
Maqueda Channel ≈ 160-161 E 6
Maquela do Zombo o ANG 216-217 C 3
Maqueze o MOC 220-221 L 2
Maquia, Río ~ PE 64-65 E 5
Máquina, La o C 54-55 H 4
Maquinchao o RA 78-79 E 6
Maquinista o BOL 70-71 D 2
Maquinista Levet o RA 78-79 F 2
Maquoketa o USA (IA) 274-275 G 2
Maquoketa River ~ USA (IA) 274-275 G 2
Mar, La ∴ • MEX 52-53 J 3
Mar, Serra do ▲ BR 72-73 H 7
Mar, Serra do ▲ BR 74-75 F 6
Mara ◘ EAT 212-213 E 4
Mara ~ EAT 212-213 E 4
Mara o GUY 62-63 F 2
Mara o ZA 218-219 E 6
Maraã o BR 66-67 E 3
Marabá o BR 68-69 D 4
Marabadiassa o CI 202-203 H 5
Marabahan o RI 164-165 D 5
Marabatua, Pulau ⌒ RI 164-165 D 6
Marabi, al- o KSA 132-133 C 5
Marabitanas o BR 66-67 D 2
Maracá o BR 62-63 J 4
Maracá, Ilha de ⌒ BR 62-63 J 4
Maracaçumé o BR 68-69 F 3
Maracaçumé, Baía do ≈ 68-69 F 2
Maracaçumé, Rio ~ BR 68-69 F 2
Maracaí o BR 72-73 E 7
Maracaibo ☆ YV 60-61 F 2
Maracaibo, Lago de ≈ 60-61 F 2
Maracá-Jipioca, Estação Ecológica ⊥ BR 62-63 J 4
Maracaju o BR 76-77 K 1
Maracaju, Serra de ▲ BR 76-77 K 1
Maracanã o BR 68-69 E 2
Maracanã, Baía de ≈ 68-69 E 2
Maracanã, Rio ~ BR 66-67 H 7
Maracanai, Cachoeira ~ BR 62-63 H 6
Maracanaquará, Planalto ⊥ BR 62-63 H 5
Maracás o BR 72-73 K 2
Maracas Bay Village o TT 60-61 L 2
Maracay ☆ YV 60-61 H 2
Maracoa o CO 60-61 E 6
Maracó Grande, Valle ⌄ RA 78-79 G 4
Maracuni, Río ~ YV 60-61 J 6
Marādah o LAR 192-193 H 3
Maradankadawala o CL 140-141 J 6
Maradi o RN 198-199 C 5
Maradi ☆ RN (MAR) 198-199 C 6
Maradi ◘ RN 198-199 C 6
Maradun o WAN 198-199 C 6
Maraetai o NZ 182 E 2
Marafa o EAK 212-213 G 5
Marag o BR 72-73 L 2
Maragahawewa o CL 140-141 J 6
Marāğe o • IR 128-129 M 4
Maraguay, Punta ▲ YV 60-61 F 2
Marāḥayy o Y 132-133 G 6
Mārahra o IND 138-139 G 6
Marahuaca, Cerro ▲ YV 60-61 J 6
Marais des Cygnes River ~ USA (MO) 274-275 D 6
Marajó, Baía de ≈ 62-63 K 6
Marajó, Ilha de ⌒ BR 62-63 J 6
Marakabei o LS 220-221 J 4
Marakalalo Hills ▲ RB 218-219 D 6
Marakesa o ZRE 210-211 L 3
Maraku o WAN 204-205 H 3
Mara Lake o CDN (BC) 230-231 L 3
Mara Lake ⊖ CDN (BC) 230-231 K 3
Maralal o EAK 212-213 F 3
Maralal National Sanctuary ⊥ EAK 212-213 F 3
Maraldy, kōlī ⊖ KA 124-125 K 2
Marale o HN 52-53 L 4
Maraleda ≈ 80 D 2
Maraleda, Canal ≈ 80 D 2
Marali o RCA 206-207 D 5
Maralinga o AUS 176-177 L 5
Maralinga -Tjarutja Aboriginal Lands ⵋ AUS 176-177 L 4
Maramag o RP 160-161 F 9
Maramasike = Small Malaita ⌒ SOL 184 I e 3
Maramec o USA (OK) 264-265 H 2
Marāmiya, al- o KSA 130-131 E 5
Maramuni o PNG 183 B 3
Maramuni River ~ PNG 183 B 3
Maran o MAL 162-163 E 3
Marān, Kōh-e ▲ PK 134-135 M 4
Marana o USA (AZ) 256-257 D 6
Maranchón, Puerto de ▲ E 98-99 F 4
Marand o • IR 128-129 L 3
Marangu o EAT (KIL) 212-213 F 5
Maranguape o BR 68-69 J 3
Maranhão o BR 66-67 J 4
Maranhão ◘ BR 68-69 E 5
Maranhão, Rio ~ BR 72-73 F 3
Maranhoto o BR 66-67 F 4
Maranoa River ~ AUS 178-179 K 4
Marañón, Río ~ PE 64-65 C 4
Maransabadi, Pulau ⌒ RI 166-167 H 3
Marantale o RI 164-165 G 4
Marantao o RP 160-161 F 9
Maranura o PE 64-65 F 8
Marão o MOC 220-221 M 2
Maraoué ~ CI 202-203 G 6
Maraoué, Parc National de la ⊥ CI 202-203 G 6
Marapa Island ⌒ SOL 184 I e 3
Marapi, Gunung ▲ RI 162-163 D 5
Marapi, Rio ~ BR 62-63 F 5
Marapinim o BR 68-69 F 2
Marapinim, Rio ~ BR 68-69 E 2
Marapiti, Ilha do ⌒ BR 66-67 G 5
Marari, Rio ~ BR 66-67 E 2
Mara River ~ CDN 30-31 P 2
Mara Rosa o BR 72-73 F 2
Mărășești o RO 102-103 E 5
Marāši, al- o Y 132-133 D 5
Marasimsim o MAL 160-161 B 9
Marassu ~ RUS 124-125 Q 2
Marat o US 136-137 J 3
Marat, Ğabal ▲ Y 132-133 G 5
Marata, ford ~ RUS 108-109 c 2
Marateca o P 98-99 C 5
Marathon o AUS 174-175 G 7
Marathon o CDN (ONT) 236-237 B 4
Marathon o USA (FL) 286-287 H 7
Marathon o USA (TX) 266-267 D 3
Maratua, Pulau ⌒ RI 164-165 F 2
Marau o BR 74-75 D 7
Marauiá, Rio ~ BR 66-67 E 2
Marau Island ⌒ SOL 184 I e 4
Maravaam ~ RUS 112-113 U 3
Maravade o IND 140-141 F 2
Maravatío o MEX 52-53 D 2
Marāve Tappe o IR 136-137 D 6
Maravilha o BR 66-67 G 4
Maravilhas o BR 72-73 H 5
Maravilla o BOL 70-71 D 2
Maravillas o MEX 50-51 G 4
Maravillas Creek ~ USA (TX) 266-267 D 4
Marāwah o LAR 192-193 J 1
Marawaka o PNG 183 C 4
Marawi ☆ RP 160-161 F 9
Marawi = Merowe o SUD 200-201 E 3
Marāwi'a, al- o Y 132-133 C 6
Marawiḥ ⌒ UAE 134-135 E 6
Maraxo Patá o BR 62-63 F 5
Marayes o RA 76-77 D 6
Marbella o E 98-99 E 6
Marble o USA (WA) 244-245 H 2
Marble Bar o AUS 172-173 D 6
Marble Canyon o USA (AZ) 256-257 D 2

358 Mana — Marble Canyon

Matak, Pulau ⌒ RI 162-163 G 3
Matakali ○ RI 164-165 F 5
Matakana Island ⌒ NZ 182 F 2
Matakaoa Point ▲ NZ 182 G 2
Matakawau ○ NZ 182 E 2
Matakil, Chutes de ~•• RCA 206-207 E 4
Matala ○ ANG 216-217 C 7
Matala ○ GR 100-101 K 7
Matala ○ IND 140-141 G 2
Matala ○ ZRE 210-211 L 5
Matalaque ○ PE 70-71 B 5
Matale ○ CL 140-141 J 7
Matale ○ ZRE 212-213 B 5
Matam ○ SN 202-203 D 2
Maṭāmah, al- ○ Y 132-133 D 5
Mata Mata ○ ZA 220-221 E 2
Matamatá, Cachoeira ~ BR 66-67 G 6
Matamec ○ CDN (QUE) 242-243 B 2
Matamey ○ RN 198-199 D 6
Matamoros ○ MEX (COA) 50-51 H 5
Matamoros ○ MEX (TAM) 50-51 L 5
Matana ○ BU 212-213 B 5
Matana ○ RI 164-165 G 5
Matana, Danau ○ RI 164-165 G 5
Matanal Point ▲ RP 160-161 E 9
Ma'tan as Sarah ○ LAR 198-199 K 2
Ma'tan Bisciara < LAR 192-193 K 6
Matanda ○ Z 214-215 E 6
Matandu ~ EAT 214-215 K 5
Matane ○ CDN (QUE) 240-241 H 2
Matane, Parc Provincial de ⊥ CDN (QUE) 240-241 H 2
Matanga ○ RI 164-165 H 4
Matanga ○ RM 222-223 E 9
Matankari ○ RN 198-199 B 6
Matantas ○ VAN 184 II a 2
Matanuska River ~ USA 20-21 Q 6
Matanzas ☆ C 54-55 E 3
Matanzas ○ MEX 50-51 J 7
Matanzas ○ YV 60-61 K 3
Matanzilla, Pampa de la ∸ RA 78-79 E 4
Matão ○ BR 72-73 F 6
Mataojo ○ ROU 76-77 J 6
Mataoleo ○ RI 164-165 H 6
Mata Ortiz ○ MEX 50-51 E 2
Matapédia ○ CDN (QUE) 240-241 J 3
Matapédia, Rivière ~ CDN (QUE) 240-241 H 2
Matapi, Cachoeira ~ BR 66-67 F 2
Matapi, Rio ~ BR 62-63 J 5
Mataquito, Río ~ RCH 78-79 C 3
Matara ○ CL 140-141 J 8
Matara ○• ER 200-201 J 5
Matara ○ PE 64-65 C 5
Matará ○ RA 76-77 F 5
Mataraca ○ BR 68-69 L 5
Mataram ☆ RI 168 C 7
Mataranka ○ AUS 174-175 B 4
Mataró ○ E 98-99 J 4
Mataso ⌒ VAN 184 II b 3
Matatiele ○ ZA 220-221 J 5
Matatindoe Point ▲ RP 160-161 E 8
Mataupa ○ PNG 183 F 5
Matauré, Rio ~ BR 66-67 G 5
Matausu ○ RI 164-165 G 6
Matawai ○ NZ 182 F 3
Matawin, Rivière ~ CDN (QUE) 238-239 M 2
Matawin Reservoir ○ CDN (QUE) 238-239 M 2
Matāy ○ ET 194-195 E 3
Matayaya ○ DOM 54-55 K 5
Matechai ○ ANG 216-217 F 5
Matecumbe Key, Lower ⌒ USA (FL) 286-287 J 7
Mategua ○ BOL 70-71 F 3
Matehuala ○ MEX 50-51 J 6
Mateiros ○ BR 68-69 E 7
Matekwe ○ EAT 214-215 K 6
Matela ○ LS 220-221 H 4
Matelot ○ TT 60-61 L 2
Matema ○ EAT 214-215 H 5
Matema ○ MOC 218-219 G 2
Matenge ○ MOC 218-219 G 2
Matera ☆• I 100-101 F 4
Matéri ○ DY 202-203 L 4
Maternillos, Punta ▲ C 54-55 G 4
Mátészalka ○ H 92-93 R 5
Matete ○ ZRE 212-213 A 3
Matetsi ○ ZW 218-219 C 4
Matetsi ~ ZW 218-219 D 4
Mateur ○ TN 190-191 G 2
Matewar ○ RI 166-167 K 2
Mather ○ CDN (MAN) 234-235 D 5
Mätherän ○• IND 138-139 D 10
Matheson ○ CDN (ONT) 236-237 H 4
Matheson Island ○ CDN (MAN) 234-235 G 3
Matheson Point ▲ CDN 24-25 Y 6
Mathews, Lake ○ USA (CA) 248-249 G 6
Mathiassen Brook ~ CDN 36-37 H 2
Mathis ○ USA (TX) 266-267 K 5
Mathiston ○ USA (MS) 268-269 L 3
Mathoura ○ AUS 180-181 H 3
Mathura ○•• IND 138-139 F 6
Mati ~ RUS 120-121 H 4
Matia ~ EAK 212-213 G 4
Matiacoali ○ BF 202-203 L 3
Matiäri ○ PK 138-139 B 7
Matias Cardoso ○ BR 72-73 J 3
Matias Olímpio ○ BR 68-69 G 3
Matías Romero ○ MEX 52-53 G 3
Matibane ○ MOC 218-219 L 2
Maticora, Río ~ YV 60-61 F 2
Matiguás ○ NIC 52-53 B 5
Matilde ○ RA 76-77 G 6
Matilla ○ RCH 70-71 C 7
Matima ○ RB 218-219 C 5
Matina ○ BR 72-73 J 2
Matinenda Lake ○ CDN (ONT) 238-239 C 2
Matinha ○ BR 74-75 F 5
Matiši ○ LV 94-95 J 3
Matjiesfontein ○ ZA 220-221 E 6
Matlahaw Point ▲ CDN (BC) 230-231 C 4
Mātli ○ PK 138-139 B 7
Matlock ○ USA (WA) 244-245 B 3
Matmata ○• TN 190-191 G 4
Matnog ○ RP 160-161 F 6
Mato, El ○ YV 60-61 J 4
Matochkin Shar, Proliv = Matočkin Šar, proliv ≈ RUS 108-109 F 5
Matočkin Šar ○ RUS 108-109 G 5
Matočkin Šar, proliv ≈ RUS 108-109 F 5
Matões ○ BR 68-69 G 4
Matogrossense, Pantanal ~• BR 70-71 J 5
Mato Grosso ◘ BR 70-71 J 3
Mato Grosso, Planalto do ∸ BR 70-71 K 4
Mato Grosso do Sul ◘ BR 70-71 J 6
Mato Guarrojo ○ CO 60-61 F 5
Matola ○ MOC 220-221 L 2
Matondo ○ MOC 218-219 H 3
Matong ○ PNG 183 F 3
Matope ○ MW 218-219 H 2
Matopo ○ ZW 218-219 E 5
Matos, Río ~ BOL 70-71 D 4
Matos Costa ○ BR 74-75 E 6
Matoury ○ F 62-63 H 3
Mato Verde ○ BR 72-73 J 3
Matraca ○ CO 60-61 G 6
Maṭraḥ ○• OM 132-133 L 2
Matras Beach • RI 162-163 G 5
Matroosberg ○ ZA 220-221 D 6
Matru ○ WAL 202-203 D 6
Matrūbah ○ LAR 192-193 K 1
Matsalu Riiklik Looduskaitseala ⊥ EST 94-95 H 2
Matsanga ○ RCB 210-211 D 4
Matsari ○ CAM 204-205 K 6
Matshumbi ○ ZRE 212-213 B 4
Matsiatra ~ RM 222-223 E 8
Matsoandakana ○ RM 222-223 F 5
Matsue ○ J 152-153 E 7
Matsuka ○ G 210-211 B 4
Matsu Liehtao ⌒ RC 156-157 L 3
Matsumae ○ J 152-153 J 4
Matsumoto ○ J 152-153 G 6
Matsu Temple • RC 156-157 M 5
Matsuyama ☆ J 152-153 E 8
Matsuzaka ○ J 152-153 G 7
Mattagami Lake ○ CDN (ONT) 236-237 G 5
Mattagami River ~ CDN (ONT) 236-237 G 3
Mattagami River ~ CDN (ONT) 236-237 F 2
Mattamuskeet Lake ○ USA (NC) 282-283 L 5
Mattaponi River ~ USA (VA) 280-281 J 6
Mattawa ○ CDN (ONT) 238-239 G 2
Mattawa ○ USA (WA) 244-245 F 4
Mattawamkeag ○ USA (ME) 278-279 N 3
Mattawa River Provincial Park ⊥ CDN (ONT) 238-239 F 2
Mattawishkwia River ~ CDN (ONT) 236-237 E 3
Mattawitchewan River ~ CDN (ONT) 236-237 D 3
Matterhorn ▲•• CH 92-93 J 5
Matterhorn ▲ USA (NV) 246-247 K 2
Mattesalja, mys ▲ RUS 108-109 Q 5
Matthews ○ USA (NC) 282-283 G 5
Matthews Ridge ○ GUY 62-63 D 2
Matthew Town ○ BS 54-55 J 4
Mattice ○ CDN (ONT) 236-237 E 3
Mattili ○ IND 142-143 C 6
Mattō ○ J 152-153 G 6
Mattoon ○ USA (IL) 274-275 K 5
Matty Island ⌒ CDN 24-25 Y 6
Matu ○ MAL 162-163 J 3
Matua, ostrov ⌒ RUS 122-123 P 4
Matucana ○ PE 64-65 D 7
Matuda, ozero ○ RUS 108-109 b 5
Matugama ○ CL 140-141 J 7
Matukar ○ PNG 183 C 3
Matuku ⌒ FJI 184 III b 3
Matundu ○ ZRE 206-207 F 6
Matupi, Igarapé ~ BR 66-67 G 6
Ma'tuq ○ SUD 200-201 F 5
Maturín ☆ YV 60-61 K 3
Matusadona National Park ⊥ ZW 218-219 E 3
Matuseviča, fiord ≈ 108-109 b 2
Matveev, ostrov ⌒ RUS 108-109 H 7
Matveevka ○ RUS (ULN) 96-97 F 6
Matveevka ☆ RUS (ORB) 96-97 H 7
Matveev Kurgan ○ RUS 102-103 L 4
Maty-Centre ○ RCB 210-211 E 5
Matykil', ostrov ⌒ RUS 120-121 Q 4
Mau ○ IND (UTP) 142-143 C 3
Mau ○ IND (UTP) 142-143 B 3
Mau, Île = Emao ⌒ VAN 184 II b 3
Mauá ○ BR 72-73 G 7
Maua ○ EAK 212-213 F 3
Maúa ○ MOC 218-219 J 1
Mauba, Wādī ~ Y 132-133 G 5
Mauban ○ RP 160-161 D 5
Maubin ○ MYA 158-159 C 2
Maubisse ○ RI 166-167 C 6
Maud ○ USA (OK) 264-265 H 3
Maud ○ USA (TX) 264-265 K 5
Maude ○ AUS 180-181 H 3
Maué ○ ANG 216-217 E 8
Maués ○ BR 66-67 J 4
Maués, Rio ~ BR 66-67 J 4
Maués-Mirim, Rio ~ BR 66-67 J 4
Maugris < RIM 196-197 C 5
Maui ⌒ USA (HI) 288 J 4
Mauk ○ RI 168 B 3
Maukeli ○ RI 168 E 7
Maulamyaing ○ MYA 158-159 D 2
Maulbronn ○••• D 92-93 K 4
Mauldin ○ USA (SC) 284-285 H 2
Maule, Laguna del ○ RCH 78-79 D 4
Maule, Río ~ RCH 78-79 C 3
Maule o Pehuenche, Paso ▲ RA 78-79 D 4
Maullín ○ RCH 78-79 C 6
Maullín, Bahía ≈ 78-79 C 6
Maumee ○ USA (OH) 280-281 C 2
Maumee River ~ USA (OH) 280-281 B 2
Maumela ○ RI 166-167 C 6
Maumelle, Lake < USA (AR) 276-277 C 6
Maumere ○ RI 166-167 B 6
Maun ☆ RB 218-219 B 4
Mauna Kea ▲ USA (HI) 288 K 5
Maunaloa ○ USA (HI) 288 H 3
Mauna Loa ▲ USA (HI) 288 K 5
Mauneluk River ~ USA 20-21 N 3
Maungmagan Islands ⌒ MYA 158-159 D 3
Maungu ○ EAK 212-213 G 5
Maunoir, Lac ○ CDN 30-31 G 2
Maupertuis, Lac ○ CDN 38-39 J 3
Maupin ○ USA (OR) 244-245 D 5
Mauqaq ○ KSA 130-131 G 4
Maur, Wādī ~ Y 132-133 C 6
Mau Rānipur ○ IND 138-139 G 7
Maure, Col de ▲ F 90-91 L 9
Maurelle Islands Wilderness ⊥ USA 32-33 C 4
Maurepas, Lake ○ USA (LA) 268-269 K 6
Maurepas, Point ▲ CDN (ONT) 236-237 C 5
Mauri, Río ~ PE 70-71 C 5
Maurice, Lac ○ CDN (ONT) 236-237 L 2
Maurice, Lake ○ AUS 176-177 L 4
Maurice Ewing Bank ≃ 6-7 E 14
Mauriceville ○ USA (TX) 268-269 G 6
Mauricio Batista ○ BR 76-77 K 5
Maurine ○ USA (SD) 260-261 D 1
Mauritania = Mawritaniyah ■ RIM 196-197 C 4
Mauritius ■ MS 224 C 7
Maury Channel ≈ 24-25 Y 3
Mausolée • RCA 206-207 D 6
Mauston ○ USA (WI) 270-271 H 7
Mauterndorf ○ A 92-93 M 5
Mauyama ○ WAN 204-205 E 2
Mavaca, Río ~ YV 66-67 E 2
Mävelikara ○ IND 140-141 G 6
Mavengue ○ ANG 216-217 E 8
Mavila ○ PE 70-71 C 2
Mavillette ○ CDN (NS) 240-241 J 6
Mavinga ○ ANG 216-217 F 7
Mavis Reef ⌒ AUS 172-173 F 3
Mavita ○ MOC 218-219 G 4
Mavua ○ Z 218-219 B 2
Mavuè ○ MOC 218-219 G 5
Mavuji ~ EAT 214-215 K 5
Mavunga ~ ANG 216-217 F 6
Mavuradonha ○ ZW 218-219 F 3
Mawa ○ ZRE 210-211 L 2
Mawa-Geti ○ ZRE 210-211 L 2
Mawai ○ MAL 162-163 E 4
Mawanella ○ CL 140-141 J 7
Mawang ○ VRC 156-157 F 2
Mawanga ○ ZRE 216-217 D 3
Mawangdui Hanmu ∴ VRC 156-157 H 2
Mawara Island ⌒ PNG 184 I b 2
Mawasangka ○ RI 164-165 H 6
Māwat ○ IRQ 128-129 L 5
Mawdin ○ MYA 158-159 C 3
Mawefan ○ RI 166-167 H 3
Mawhun ○ MYA 142-143 K 3
Mawlaik ○ MYA 142-143 J 4
Maw Point ▲ USA (NC) 282-283 L 5
Mawson ○ ARK 16 G 7
Max ○ USA (ND) 258-259 F 4
Maxaans ○ SP 208-209 H 6
Maxanguape ○ BR 68-69 L 4
Maxbass ○ USA (ND) 258-259 F 3
Maxcanú ○ MEX 52-53 J 1
Maxeys ○ USA (GA) 284-285 G 3
Maxim ○ CDN (SAS) 232-233 O 6
Maximeville ○ CDN (PEI) 240-241 L 4
Máximo Gómez ○ C 54-55 E 3
Maxixe ○ MOC 218-219 H 6
Maxstone ○ CDN (SAS) 232-233 N 6
Maxville ○ USA (FL) 286-287 G 1
Maxville ○ USA (MT) 250-251 F 5
Maxwell ○ USA (CA) 246-247 C 4
Maxwell ○ USA (NE) 262-263 F 3
Maxwell ○ USA (NM) 256-257 L 2
Maxwell ○ USA (TN) 276-277 J 5
Maxwell Bay ≈ 24-25 b 3
Maxwell Fracture Zone ≃ 6-7 F 4
Maxwelton ○ AUS 174-175 G 7
May ○ PNG 183 A 3
May ○ USA (OK) 264-265 E 2
May ○ USA (TX) 266-267 J 2
May, Kap ▲ GRØ 26-27 Z 2
Maya ○• SUD 200-201 F 6
Maya, La ○ C 54-55 H 4
Maya, Pulau ⌒ RI 162-163 H 5
Mayabandar ○ IND 140-141 L 3
Mayādin, al- ○ SYR 128-129 J 5
Mayaguana Island ⌒ BS 54-55 J 3
Mayaguana Passage ≈ 54-55 J 3
Mayagüez ○ USA (PR) 286-287 O 2
Mayahi ○ RN 198-199 C 6
Mayala ○ ZRE 216-217 D 3
Mayama ○ RCB 210-211 E 5
Mayamaya ○ EAT (DOD) 212-213 E 6
Mayamba ○ ZRE 210-211 F 6
Maya Mountains ▲ BH 52-53 K 3
Mayang ○ VRC 156-157 F 3
Mayanja ~ EAU 212-213 C 3
Mayankwa ○ Z 218-219 B 2
Mayapan ∴• MEX 52-53 K 1
Mayari ○ C 54-55 H 4
Mayarí Arriba ○ C 54-55 H 4
Mayata < RN 198-199 C 5
Maybee ○ USA (MI) 272-273 F 6
Maybell ○ USA (CO) 254-255 G 3
Maybelle River ~ CDN 30-31 O 6
Maych'ew ○ ETH 200-201 J 6
May City ○ USA (IA) 274-275 C 1
May Dara Shet' ~ ETH 208-209 C 3
Maydena ○ AUS 180-181 J 7
Maydh ○ SP (San) 208-209 H 3
Maydh ⌒ SP (San) 208-209 H 3
May Downs ○ AUS 178-179 K 2
Mayel-Samou ~ SN 202-203 D 3
Mayenne ○ F 90-91 G 7
Mayenne ~ F 90-91 G 7
Mayer ○ USA (AZ) 256-257 C 4
Mayerthorpe ○ CDN (ALB) 232-233 C 2
Mayetta ○ USA (KS) 262-263 L 5
Mayfair ○ CDN (SAS) 232-233 L 3
Mayfield ○ CDN (SAS) 232-233 R 6
Mayfield ○ USA (ID) 252-253 C 3
Mayfield ○ USA (KY) 276-277 G 4
Mayfield ○ USA (UT) 254-255 D 4
Mayflower ○ USA (AR) 276-277 C 6
Mayhew Lake ○ USA (MN) 270-271 E 5
Mayhill ○ USA (NM) 256-257 K 6
Mayi, Mbuji- ☆ ZRE 214-215 B 4
May Inlet ≈ 24-25 V 2
May-Jirgui ○ RN 198-199 D 6
Maymont ○ CDN (SAS) 232-233 L 3
Maymūn, Wādī ~ LAR 190-191 H 5
Maymyo ○ MYA 142-143 K 4
Maynard ○ USA (AR) 276-277 E 4
Maynas ∸ PE 64-65 D 3
Mayne River ~ AUS 178-179 F 2
Mayneside ○ AUS 178-179 G 2
Mäyni ○ IND 140-141 F 2
Maynooth ○ CDN (ONT) 238-239 H 3
Maynooth = Maigh Nuad ○ IRL 90-91 D 5
Mayo ○ USA (FL) 286-287 F 1
Mayo, 25 de ○ RA (BUA) 78-79 J 3
Mayo, 25 de ○ RA (MEN) 78-79 E 3
Mayo, 25 de ○ ROU 78-79 L 3
Mayo, Río ~ MEX 50-51 E 4
Mayo, Río ~ PE 64-65 D 5
Mayo, Río ~ RA 80 E 2
Mayo Belwa ○ WAN 204-205 K 4
Mayo Butale ○ WAN 204-205 K 4
Mayo Chehu ○ WAN 204-205 J 4
Mayo Darle ○ CAM 204-205 J 5
Mayo Djoi ○ CAM 206-207 B 4
Mayo Faran ○ WAN 204-205 K 4
Mayo Jarandi ○ WAN 204-205 J 5
Mayo-Kebbi ◘ TCH 206-207 B 3
Mayoko ○ RCB 210-211 D 5
Mayo Lake ○ CDN 20-21 X 5
Mayombé ▲ G 210-211 C 5
Mayo Ndaga ○ WAN 204-205 J 5
Mayon Vulcano ▲ RP 160-161 E 6
Mayo Oulo ○ CAM 204-205 K 4
Mayor Buratovich ○ RA 78-79 H 5
Mayorga ○ RP 160-161 F 7
Mayor Island ⌒ NZ 182 F 2
Mayor Otano ○ PY 76-77 K 4
Mayototo ○ WAL 202-203 E 5
Mayotte ⌒ COM 222-223 D 4
Mayoworth ○ USA (WY) 252-253 M 3
May Pen ○ JA 54-55 G 6
May Point, Cape ▲ USA (DE) 280-281 M 5
Mayqū' ○ KSA 130-131 F 3
Mayraira Point ▲ RP 160-161 D 3
Mayran, Desierto de ∸ MEX 50-51 H 5
May River ~ AUS 172-173 G 4
Maysel ○ USA (WV) 280-281 E 5
Mayson Lake ○ CDN 34-35 C 2
Maysville ○ USA (KY) 276-277 M 2
Maysville ○ USA (MO) 274-275 D 5
Maysville ○ USA (NC) 282-283 K 6
Maysville ○ USA (OK) 264-265 G 4
Maytown ∴ AUS 174-175 H 5
Mayu ≈ 166-167 K 5
Mayu, Pulau ⌒ RI 164-165 K 3
Mayumba ○ G 210-211 C 5
Mayumba ○ ZRE 214-215 E 4
Mayum La ▲ VRC 144-145 D 5
Māyūram ○ IND 140-141 H 5
May Valley ○ USA (CO) 254-255 N 5
Mayville ○ USA (MI) 272-273 F 4
Mayville ○ USA (ND) 258-259 K 4
Mayville ○ USA (NY) 278-279 B 6
Maywood ○ USA (NE) 262-263 F 4
Maza ○ RA 78-79 H 4
Maza ○ WAN 204-205 K 3
Mazabuka ○ Z 218-219 D 2
Mazagão ○ BR 62-63 J 6
Mazagão Velho ○ BR 62-63 J 6
Mazagón ○ E 98-99 D 6
Mazama ○ USA (WA) 244-245 E 2
Mazamari ○ PE 64-65 E 7
Mazamet ○ F 90-91 J 10
Mazan ○ PE 64-65 F 3
Mazandarān ◘ IR 136-137 B 6
Mazar ○ VRC 138-139 F 1
Mazār, Kūh-e ▲ AFG 134-135 L 2
Mazara del Vallo ○ I 100-101 D 6
Mazār-e Adschaeb •• AFG 136-137 K 6
Mazār-e Šarīf ☆ AFG 136-137 K 6
Mazargão ○ BR 70-71 K 4
mazar Karasopy • KA 136-137 K 3
Mazarredo ○ RA 80 G 3
Mazartag ○ VRC 146-147 E 6
Mazar Tag ▲ VRC 146-147 D 6
Mazaruni River ~ GUY 62-63 E 3
Mazarwała ○ VRC 138-139 F 1
Mazatán ○ MEX (CHI) 52-53 H 4
Mazatán ○ MEX (SON) 50-51 D 3
Mazatenango ☆ GCA 52-53 J 4
Mazatlán ○• MEX 50-51 F 6
Mazatzal Peak ▲ USA (AZ) 256-257 D 4
Mazdaǧān, Rūdḫane-ye ~ IR 128-129 N 5
Mažeikiai ☆• LT 94-95 H 3
Mazéla ○ BF 202-203 G 4
Maze Lake ○ CDN 30-31 R 4
Mazenod ○ CDN (SAS) 232-233 M 6
Mazeppa Bay ○ ZA 220-221 J 6
Mazdağı ☆ TR 128-129 J 4
Mazimechopes, Rio ~ MOC 220-221 L 2
Mazinān ○ IR 136-137 E 6
Mazocahui ○ MEX 50-51 D 3
Mazoco ○ MOC 214-215 H 6
Mazo-Cruz ○ PE 70-71 C 5
Mazoe, Rio ~ MOC 218-219 G 3
Mazomeno ○ ZRE 212-213 A 6
Mazomora ○ EAT 214-215 K 4
Mazon ○ USA (IL) 274-275 K 3
Mazong Shan ▲ VRC 148-149 C 7
Mazorca, Isla ⌒ PE 64-65 D 7
Mazoula ○ DZ 190-191 F 6
Mazowe ○ ZW (Mic) 218-219 F 3
Mazowe ~ ZW 218-219 G 3
Mazra'a, al- ○ JOR 130-131 D 2
Mazra'eh Akhund ○ IR 134-135 E 3
Mazrūb ○ SUD 200-201 D 6
Mazsalaca ○•• LV 94-95 J 3
Mazu Miao • VRC 156-157 L 4
Mazunga ○ ZW 218-219 E 5
Mazyr ○ BY 94-95 L 5
Mazzamitla ○ MEX 52-53 C 2
Mba ○ CAM 204-205 J 5
Mbabala ○ Z 218-219 D 3
Mbabane ☆ SD 220-221 K 3
Mbacha ○ WAN 204-205 H 5
Mbadduna ○ SOL 184 I c 3
Mbadi ○ G 210-211 C 5
Mbadjé Akpa ○ RCA 206-207 E 5
Mbaéré ~ RCA 206-207 C 6
Mbagne ○ RIM 196-197 D 6
Mbahiakro ○ CI 202-203 H 6
Mbaiki ☆ RCA 210-211 F 2
Mbakaou ○ CAM 204-205 K 5
Mbakaou, Barrage de < CAM 204-205 K 5
Mbakaou, Lac de < CAM 204-205 K 5
Mbaké ○ SN 202-203 C 2
Mbako ○ RCA 206-207 B 6
Mbala ○• Z 214-215 F 5
Mbalabala ○ ZW 218-219 E 5
Mbalageti ~ EAT 212-213 E 5
Mbalam ○ CAM 210-211 D 2
Mbalambala ○ EAK 212-213 G 4
Mbale ☆• EAU 212-213 E 3
Mbali ~ RCA 206-207 C 6
Mbali-Iboma ○ ZRE 210-211 F 5
Mbalmayo ○ CAM 210-211 C 2
Mbam ~ CAM 204-205 J 6
Mbam, Massif du ▲ CAM 204-205 J 6
Mbama ○ CAM 210-211 D 2
Mbama ○ RCB 210-211 E 4
Mbamba Bay ○ EAT 214-215 H 6
Mbambanakira ○ SOL 184 I d 3
Mbam Minkom ▲ CAM 210-211 C 2
Mbandaka ☆ ZRE 210-211 G 3
Mbandjok ○ CAM 204-205 J 6
Mbandza ○ G 210-211 E 3
Mbandza-Ndounga ○ RCB 210-211 E 6
Mbane ○ SN 196-197 C 6
Mbang ○ CAM 210-211 E 2
Mbanga ○ CAM 204-205 H 6
Mbanga ○ SOL 184 I c 3
Mbangala ~ EAT 214-215 K 6
Mbanika Island ⌒ SOL 184 I d 3
M'banza Congo ☆ ANG 216-217 C 3
Mbanza-Ngungu = Thysville ○ ZRE 210-211 E 6
Mbar ○ SN 202-203 C 2
Mbarang'andu ○ EAT 214-215 J 6
Mbarangandu ~ EAT 214-215 J 6
Mbarara ☆ EAU 212-213 C 4
Mbârek, Hâssei < RIM 196-197 E 6
Mbargué ○ CAM 204-205 K 6
Mbari ~ RCA 206-207 F 6
Mbarizunga Game Reserve ⊥ SUD 206-207 J 6
Mbaswana ○ ZA 220-221 L 3
Mbata ○ RCA 210-211 F 2
Mbati ○ Z 214-215 F 6
Mbava ⌒ SOL 184 I c 2
Mbé ○ CAM 204-205 K 5
Mbé ~ G 210-211 C 3
Mbé ○ RCB 210-211 E 5
Mbeiporo ○ SOL 184 I c 2
Mbéloba ○ RCA 206-207 E 6
Mbemkuru ~ EAT 214-215 K 5
Mbéna ○ RCB 210-211 E 6
Mbengué ○ CI 202-203 H 4
Mbengwi ○ CAM 204-205 J 5
M'Beni ○ COM 222-223 C 3
Mbéré ~ CAM 206-207 B 5
Mberengwa ○ ZW 218-219 E 5
Mbet ○ CAM 204-205 K 6
Mbéti = Alayo ○ RCA 206-207 F 6
Mbéwé ○ CAM 204-205 K 5
Mbeya ◘ EAT 214-215 G 5
Mbeya ☆ EAT (MBE) 214-215 G 5
Mbeya ○ Z 214-215 G 6
Mbi ~ RCA 206-207 C 6
Mbiama ○ WAN 204-205 G 6
Mbié ○ RCB 210-211 E 4
Mbigou ○ G 210-211 C 4
Mbinda ○ RCB 210-211 D 5
Mbinga ○ EAT 214-215 H 6
Mbini ○ GQ 210-211 B 3
Mbita ○ EAK 212-213 E 4
Mbitao ○ CAM 206-207 B 5
Mbitom ○ CAM 204-205 K 6
Mbiyi ○ RCA 206-207 F 5
Mbizi ○ ZW 218-219 F 5
Mbizi Mountains ▲ EAT 214-215 F 4
Mbo ○ RCA 206-207 D 4
Mboké ○ CAM 204-205 K 6
Mboki ○ RCA 206-207 G 6
Mboko ○ ZRE 212-213 B 5
Mbokonimbeti Island = Sandfly Island ⌒ SOL 184 I d 3
Mbokou ~ RCA 206-207 H 6
Mbolo Island ⌒ SOL 184 I d 3
Mbomo ○ G 210-211 E 3
Mbomou ◘ RCA 206-207 F 6
Mbomou ~ RCA 206-207 F 6
Mbon ○ RCB 210-211 E 5
Mbonge ○ CAM 204-205 H 6
Mborokua Island ⌒ SOL 184 I d 3
Mboroma ○ Z 218-219 E 2
Mborong ○ RI 168 E 7
Mboro-sur-Mer ○ SN 202-203 B 2
Mbot ○ CAM 204-205 J 5
Mbouda ○ CAM 204-205 J 6
Mboula ○ CAM 204-205 K 5
Mboula ○ RCA 206-207 C 6
Mbouma ○ CAM 210-211 D 2
Mboune ○ SN 202-203 D 2
Mboungou Badouma ○ G 210-211 D 4
Mbour ○ SN 202-203 B 2
Mbout ○ RIM 196-197 D 6
Mboutou ~ RCA 206-207 G 5
Mbozi ○ EAT 214-215 G 5
Mbozi Meteorit • EAT 214-215 G 5
Mbrès ○• RCA 206-207 D 5
Mbu ~ CAM 204-205 H 6
Mbudi ○ ZRE 210-211 F 6
Mbugwe ○ EAT 212-213 E 5
Mbuji-Mayi ☆ ZRE (KOR) 214-215 B 4
Mbuji-Mayi ~ ZRE 214-215 B 4
Mbuke Islands ⌒ PNG 183 D 2
Mbulu ○ EAT 212-213 E 5
Mbuma ○ SOL 184 I e 3
Mburucuyá ○ RA 76-77 H 5
Mbuyuni ○ EAT (KIL) 212-213 F 6
Mbuyuni ○ EAT (MOR) 214-215 J 4
Mbwamaji ○ EAT 214-215 K 4
Mbwewe ○ EAT 214-215 K 4
McAdam National Park ⊥ PNG 183 D 4
McAdoo ○ USA (TX) 264-265 C 5
McAleese Lake ○ CDN 30-31 U 5
McAlester ○ USA (OK) 264-265 J 4
McAlester Army Ammunition Plant xx USA (OK) 264-265 J 4
McAllen ○ USA (TX) 266-267 J 7
McAllister State Historic Site, Fort • USA (GA) 284-285 J 5
McArthur ○ USA (OH) 280-281 D 4
McArthur Falls ○ CDN (MAN) 234-235 G 4
Mc Arthur River ~ AUS 174-175 D 5
McBee ○ USA (SC) 284-285 K 2
McBeth Fiord ≈ 28-29 F 2
McBeth River ~ CDN 28-29 E 2
McBride ○ CDN (BC) 228-229 O 3
McCall ○ USA (ID) 252-253 B 2
McCall Seamount ≃ 288 J 6
McCallum ○ CDN (NFL) 242-243 M 5
McCamey ○ USA (TX) 266-267 E 2
McCammon ○ USA (ID) 252-253 F 4
McCann Lake ○ CDN 30-31 Q 5
McCarthy ○ USA 20-21 T 6
McCauley Island ⌒ CDN (BC) 228-229 D 3
McCauley Islands ⌒ CDN (BC) 228-229 D 3
McCaulley ○ USA (TX) 264-265 D 6
McCleary ○ USA (WA) 244-245 B 3
McClellan Creek ~ USA (TX) 264-265 D 3
McClellanville ○ USA (SC) 284-285 L 3
Mcclenny ○ USA (FL) 286-287 G 1
McClintock Channel ≈ 24-25 U 4
McClintock Point ▲ CDN 24-25 W 6
McClintock Range ▲ AUS 172-173 H 5
McCloud ○ USA (CA) 246-247 C 2
McCluer Island ⌒ AUS 172-173 L 1
McClure ○ USA (OH) 280-281 C 2
McClure Strait ≈ 24-25 M 3
McClusky ○ USA (ND) 258-259 G 4
McClusky Pass ▲ USA (NV) 246-247 J 4
McColl ○ USA (SC) 284-285 L 2
McComb ○ USA (MS) 268-269 K 5
McConaughy, Lake C.W. ○ USA (NE) 262-263 E 3
McCondy ○ USA (MS) 268-269 M 3
McConkey Hill ▲ AUS 176-177 F 2
McConnells ○ USA (SC) 284-285 J 2
McConnellsburg ○ USA (PA) 280-281 H 4
McConnel Range ▲ CDN 30-31 G 3
McConnel River ~ CDN 30-31 W 5
McConnelsville ○ USA (OH) 280-281 E 4
McCook ○ USA (NE) 262-263 F 4
McCool ○ USA (MS) 268-269 L 3
McCool Junction ○ USA (NE) 262-263 J 4
McCormick ○ USA (SC) 284-285 H 3
McCoy Creek ~ CDN (SAS) 232-233 J 6
McCoy Mountains ▲ USA (CA) 248-249 K 6
McCracken ○ USA (KS) 262-263 G 6
McCreary ○ CDN (MAN) 234-235 D 4
McCredie Springs ○ USA (OR) 244-245 C 7
McCrory ○ USA (AR) 276-277 D 5
McCulloch ○ CDN (BC) 230-231 K 4
McCullough Range ▲ USA (NV) 248-249 J 4
McCusker River ~ CDN 32-33 Q 4
McDavid ○ USA (FL) 286-287 B 1
McDermitt ○ USA (NV) 246-247 H 2
McDonald ○ USA (KS) 262-263 E 5
McDonald Peak ▲ USA (MT) 250-251 F 4
McDonnel, Cape ▲ CDN 30-31 J 2
McDonough ○ USA (GA) 284-285 F 3
Mc Douall Peak ○ AUS 178-179 C 5
McDougal, Lake ○ ZW 218-219 F 6
McDougal Creek ~ CDN 34-35 D 3
McDougall Sound ≈ 24-25 X 3
McDowell ○ USA (AZ) 256-257 D 5
McDowell ○ USA (VA) 280-281 G 5
McDowell Indian Reservation, Fort ⊼ USA (AZ) 256-257 D 5
McDowell River ~ CDN (ONT) 234-235 L 2
Mcensk ○ RUS 94-95 P 5
McEwen ○ USA (TN) 276-277 H 4
McFaddin ○ USA (TX) 266-267 K 5
McFarland ○ USA (CA) 248-249 E 4
McFarlane River ~ CDN 30-31 P 6
McGee ○ CDN (SAS) 232-233 K 4
McGehee ○ USA (AR) 276-277 D 7
McGill ○ USA (NV) 246-247 L 4
McGillivray Bay ≈ 24-25 X 6
McGivney ○ CDN (NB) 240-241 J 4
McGrath ○ USA (AK) 20-21 N 5
McGrath ○ USA (MN) 270-271 E 4
McGregor ○ USA (MN) 270-271 E 4
McGregor ○ USA (ND) 258-259 E 3
McGregor, Lake ○ CDN (ALB) 232-233 F 5
Mc Gregor Range ▲ AUS 178-179 G 4
McGregor River ~ CDN (BC) 228-229 N 2
McGuire, Mount ▲ USA (ID) 250-251 E 6
McHenry River ~ AUS 174-175 G 2
Mcherrah ∸ DZ 188-189 J 7
Mcheta ○ GE 126-127 F 7
Mchinga ○ EAT 214-215 K 5
Mchinji ○ MW 218-219 G 1
M'Chouneche ○ DZ 190-191 F 3
McIlwraith Range ▲ AUS 174-175 G 3
McInnes Lake ○ CDN (ONT) 234-235 K 2
McIntosh ○ USA (SD) 260-261 E 1
McIntosh Lake ○ CDN 34-35 D 3
McIntyre Bay ≈ CDN 228-229 B 2
McIntyre Bay ○ CDN (ONT) 234-235 P 5
McIver's ○ CDN (NFL) 242-243 K 3
McIvor River ~ CDN 30-31 N 6
McKague ○ CDN (SAS) 232-233 P 3
McKay, Mount ▲ AUS 172-173 E 7
McKay Lake ○ CDN (NFL) 38-39 M 2
McKay Lake ○ CDN (ONT) 236-237 B 3
McKay Range ▲ AUS 176-177 F 7
McKeand River ~ CDN 36-37 P 2
McKellar ○ CDN (ONT) 238-239 F 3
McKeller ○ CDN (ONT) 238-239 F 3
McKenna ○ USA (WA) 244-245 C 4
McKenzie ○ USA (AL) 284-285 D 5
McKenzie ○ USA (TN) 276-277 G 4
McKenzie Bridge ○ USA (OR) 244-245 C 6
McKenzie Draw ~ USA (TX) 264-265 B 6
McKenzie River ~ USA (OR) 244-245 C 6
McKinlay ○ AUS 178-179 F 1
McKinlay River ~ AUS 178-179 F 1
McKinley, Mount ▲•• USA 20-21 P 5
McKinney ○ USA (TX) 264-265 H 5
McKinney Mountain ▲ USA (TX) 266-267 D 4
McKinnon ○ USA (WY) 252-253 J 5
McKittrick ○ USA (CA) 248-249 E 4
McLain ○ USA (MS) 268-269 M 5
McLaren Creek ○ AUS 174-175 C 7
Mc Laren Vale ○ AUS 180-181 E 3
McLaughlin ○ USA (SD) 260-261 F 1
McLean ○ CDN (SAS) 232-233 O 5
McLean ○ USA (IL) 274-275 J 4
McLean ○ USA (TX) 264-265 D 3
McLeansboro ○ USA (IL) 274-275 K 6
McLeese Lake ○ CDN (BC) 228-229 M 4
McLeod ○ USA (MT) 250-251 J 6
McLeod ○ USA (ND) 258-259 K 5
McLeod Bay ○ CDN 30-31 O 4
McLeod Lake ○ CDN 32-33 J 4
McLeod River ~ CDN (ALB) 232-233 B 2
McLeod River ~ CDN (ALB) 228-229 R 3
McLeod River ~ CDN (ALB) 232-233 C 2
McLeods Corner ○ USA (MI) 270-271 N 4
McLeod Valley ○ CDN (ALB) 232-233 C 2
McLernon, Lake ○ AUS 172-173 H 5
M'Clintock ○ CDN 34-35 J 2
M'Clintock Inlet ≈ 26-27 M 2
McLoughlin, Mount ▲ USA (OR) 244-245 C 8
McLoughlin Bay ≈ 30-31 U 2
McLure ○ CDN (BC) 230-231 J 2
McMahon ○ CDN (SAS) 232-233 L 5
McManaman Lake ○ CDN 30-31 X 4
McMasterville ○ CDN (QUE) 238-239 M 3
McMillan ○ USA (MI) 270-271 N 4
McMillan, Lake ○ USA (NM) 256-257 L 6
McMinnville ○ USA (OR) 244-245 B 5
McMinnville ○ USA (TN) 276-277 K 5
McMorran ○ CDN (SAS) 232-233 K 4
McMurdo ○ ARK 16 F 17
Mc Murdo Sound ≈ 16 F 17
McMurphy ○ CDN (BC) 230-231 N 2
McMurray ○ USA (WA) 244-245 C 2
McMurtry, Lake ○ USA (OK) 264-265 G 2
McNab Cove ○ CDN (NS) 240-241 P 5
McNary ○ USA (AZ) 256-257 F 4
McNary ○ USA (TX) 266-267 B 2
McNaughton Lake ○ CDN 30-31 U 2
McNeal ○ USA (AZ) 256-257 F 7
McNeill ○ USA (MS) 268-269 L 6
McNeill, Port ○ CDN (BC) 230-231 B 3
McParlon Lake ○ CDN (ONT) 236-237 H 2
McPhee Reservoir < USA (CO) 254-255 G 6
Mc Pherson ▲ AUS 178-179 M 5
McPherson ○ USA (KS) 262-263 J 6
McPhersons Pillar ▲ AUS 176-177 H 2
McQuesten River ~ CDN 20-21 W 5
McRae ○ USA (GA) 284-285 H 4
McRobertson Land ∸ ARK 16 G 7
McTaggart ○ CDN (SAS) 232-233 O 6
McTavish ○ CDN (MAN) 234-235 F 5
McTavish Arm ○ CDN 30-31 K 2
McVicar Arm ○ CDN 30-31 J 3
McVille ○ USA (ND) 258-259 J 4
Mdandu ○ EAT 214-215 H 5
Mdantsane ○ ZA 220-221 H 6
Mdina ○ M 100-101 E 7
M'Doukal ○ DZ 190-191 E 3
M'Drac ○ VN 158-159 K 4
Meacham ○ CDN (SAS) 232-233 N 3
Mead ○ CDN (ONT) 236-237 E 3
Mead ○ USA (NE) 262-263 K 3
Mead, Lake ○ USA (NV) 248-249 K 3
Meade ○ USA (KS) 262-263 F 7
Meade Peak ▲ USA (ID) 252-253 G 4
Meade River ~ USA 20-21 M 2
Meadow ○ USA (TX) 264-265 B 5
Meadow ○ USA (UT) 254-255 C 5
Meadowbank ○ AUS 174-175 H 6
Meadowbank River ~ CDN 30-31 V 3
Meadow Brook Pass ▲ USA (OR) 244-245 G 6
Meadow Creek ○ CDN (BC) 230-231 M 3
Meadow Creek ○ USA (ID) 250-251 C 3
Meadow Lake ○ CDN 32-33 Q 4
Meadow Lake Provincial Park ⊥ CDN 32-33 Q 4
Meadowlands ○ USA (MN) 270-271 F 3
Meadow Portage ○ CDN (MAN) 234-235 D 3
Meadows ○ CDN (MAN) 234-235 F 4
Meadow Valley Range ▲ USA (NV) 248-249 K 2
Meadow Valley Wash ~ USA (NV) 248-249 K 3
Meadville ○ USA (PA) 280-281 F 2
Meaford ○ CDN (ONT) 238-239 E 4

360 **Matak, Pulau — Meaford**

Meakan-dake ▲ J 152-153 L 3
Mealhada o P 98-99 C 4
Méana o RN 202-203 L 2
Meana o TM 136-137 G 6
Meander River o CDN 30-31 L 6
Mearim, Rio ~ BR 68-69 F 4
Meath Park o CDN (SAS) 232-233 N 2
Meaux o F 90-91 J 7
Mebali o RI 164-165 F 5
Mebane o USA (NC) 282-283 H 4
Mebo, Gunung ▲ RI 166-167 G 2
Mebougou o RMM 202-203 G 4
Mebridege ~ ANG 216-217 B 3
Mecanhelas o MOC 218-219 H 2
Mecatan o MEX 50-51 G 7
Mécatina, Cap ▲ CDN (QUE) 242-243 J 2
Mecaya, Río ~ CO 64-65 E 1
Mecca o USA (CA) 248-249 J 6
Mecca = Makka ☆ •• KSA 132-133 A 3
Mecequesse, Rio ~ MOC 218-219 J 2
Mecham, Cape ▲ CDN 24-25 L 3
Mechanicsburg o USA (OH) 280-281 C 3
Mechanicville o USA (NY) 278-279 H 6
Mechàra o ETH 208-209 E 4
Mechelen o • B 92-93 H 3
Méchiméré o TCH 198-199 G 6
Méchins, Les o CDN (QUE) 240-241 J 2
Mechra-Bel-Ksiri o MA 188-189 J 3
Mechra-Benâbbou o MA 188-189 H 4
Mechroha o DZ 190-191 F 2
Mečigmenskij zaliv ≈ 112-113 Y 4
Mecitözü ☆ TR 128-129 F 2
Meckel o USA (KY) 276-277 M 4
Mečkereva ~ RUS 112-113 P 3
Mecklenburger Bucht ≈ D 92-93 L 1
Mecklenburg-Vorpommern ▫ D 92-93 M 2
Meconta o MOC 218-219 K 2
Mecubùri o MOC 218-219 K 2
Mecubùri, Rio ~ MOC 218-219 K 2
Mecúfi o MOC 218-219 L 1
Mecula o MOC 214-215 J 7
Medak o • IND 138-139 G 10
Medan ☆ RI 162-163 C 3
Medan Fair • RI 162-163 C 3
Medang, Pulau ⌒ RI 168 C 7
Medang, Tanjung ▲ RI 162-163 D 3
Medanosa, Punta ▲ RA 80 H 4
Médanos de Coro, Parque Nacional ⊥ YV 60-61 G 2
Medart o USA (FL) 286-287 E 1
Medawachchiya o CL 140-141 J 6
Medd Allah o RMM 202-203 H 2
Médéa ☆ DZ 190-191 D 2
Medeiros o BR 72-73 G 5
Medellín ☆ CO 60-61 D 4
Medelpad ⚍ S 86-87 H 5
Medenine ☆ TN 190-191 H 4
Méderdra o RIM 196-197 C 6
Medford o USA (NJ) 280-281 M 4
Medford o USA (OK) 264-265 G 2
Medford o USA (WI) 270-271 H 5
Medford o • USA (OR) 244-245 C 8
Medgidia o RO 102-103 F 5
Medha o IND 140-141 E 2
Medi o SUD 206-207 K 6
Media Luna o RA 78-79 E 3
Media Luna, Cañada de ~ RA 76-77 F 2
Medianeira o BR 76-77 K 3
Mediapolis o USA (IA) 274-275 G 3
Mediaș o • RO 102-103 D 4
Medical Lake o USA (WA) 244-245 H 3
Medical Springs o USA (OR) 244-245 H 5
Medicine Bow o USA (WY) 252-253 M 5
Medicine Bow Mountains ▲ USA (WY) 252-253 M 5
Medicine Bow Peak ▲ USA (WY) 252-253 M 5
Medicine Creek ~ USA (MO) 274-275 E 5
Medicine Creek ~ USA (NE) 262-263 F 4
Medicine Hat o CDN (ALB) 232-233 H 5
Medicine Lake o USA (MT) 250-251 P 3
Medicine Lake o USA (MT) 250-251 P 3
Medicine Lodge o CDN (ALB) 232-233 B 2
Medicine Lodge o USA (KS) 262-263 H 7
Medicine Lodge River ~ USA (KS) 262-263 G 7
Medicine River ~ CDN (ALB) 232-233 D 3
Medina o BR 72-73 K 4
Medina o CDN (ONT) 238-239 D 5
Medina o USA (ND) 258-259 H 5
Medina o USA (NY) 278-279 C 5
Medina o USA (OH) 280-281 E 2
Medina o USA (TX) 266-267 H 4
Medina = Madina, al- ☆ •• KSA 130-131 F 5
Medina, Río ~ RA 76-77 E 4
Medina Azahara • E 98-99 E 6
Medina del Campo o E 98-99 E 4
Medina de Rioseco o E 98-99 E 4
Médina Gounas o SN 202-203 D 3
Medina Lake o USA (TX) 266-267 J 4
Medina River ~ USA (TX) 266-267 H 4
Medina-Sidonia o E 98-99 E 6
Médina-Yorofoula o SN 202-203 C 3
Médine • TN 190-191 G 3
Medininkai o •• LT 94-95 J 4
Medinipur o IND 142-143 E 4
Medio, Arroyo del ~ RA 78-79 J 2
Medio Creek ~ USA (TX) 266-267 K 5
Mediouna o MA 188-189 H 4
Mediterranean Sea ≈ 8 D 5
Medjebel o DZ 190-191 D 3
Medjerda, Monts de la ▲ DZ 190-191 F 2
Medley o CDN 32-33 P 4
Medley River ~ CDN 32-33 P 4
Mednogorsk o RUS 96-97 K 8
Mednyj, mys ▲ RUS 108-109 a 2
Mednyj, ostrov ⌒ RUS 120-121 W 6
Médoc ⚍ F 90-91 G 9
Mêdog Z.B. ⊥ • VRC 144-145 K 6
Medora o CDN (MAN) 234-235 C 5
Medora o USA (IN) 274-275 M 6
Medora o USA (ND) 258-259 D 5
Medouneu o GQ 210-211 C 3
Medracen, Le • DZ 190-191 F 3
Medrissa o DZ 190-191 C 3
Medstead o CDN (SAS) 232-233 K 2
Medvedica ~ RUS 96-97 D 8
Medvež'e, ozero o RUS 114-115 K 7
Medvež'egorsk ☆ RUS 88-89 N 5
Medvežij, mys ▲ RUS (SAH) 110-111 W 2
Medvežij, mys ▲ RUS (SAH) 110-111 J 2
Medvežij, mys ▲ RUS (SAH) 112-113 M 2
Medvežij, ostrov ⌒ RUS 120-121 G 6
Medvežij, zaliv o RUS 108-109 G 5
Medvež'i ostrova ⌒ RUS 112-113 L 1
Medvež'ja ~ RUS 108-109 e 6
Medvežka o RUS 112-113 M 2
Medyn' o RUS 94-95 O 4
Medynskij Zavorot, mys ▲ RUS 108-109 H 7
Medze o LV 94-95 G 3
Medzilaborce o SK 92-93 Q 4
Mèèčkyn, Kosa-ostrov ⌒ RUS 112-113 V 4
Meekatharra o AUS 176-177 E 3
Meeker o USA (CO) 254-255 H 3
Meek Point ▲ CDN 24-25 J 4
Meeladeen o SP 208-209 J 3
Meeline o AUS 176-177 E 4
Meelpaeg Lake ⊂ CDN (NFL) 242-243 M 4
Meerut o IND 138-139 F 5
Meerzorg o SME 62-63 G 3
Meeteetse o USA (WY) 252-253 K 2
Meeting Creek o CDN (ALB) 232-233 F 3
Mēga o ETH 208-209 D 6
Mega o RI 166-167 F 2
Megalo o ETH 208-209 E 5
Megalópoli o GR 100-101 J 6
Megamo o RI 166-167 F 2
Megantic, Mont ▲ CDN (QUE) 238-239 O 3
Megara o GR 100-101 J 6
Megargel o USA (TX) 264-265 F 5
Megaruma, Rio ~ MOC 218-219 K 1
Megeitia < SUD 200-201 E 5
Megezez ▲ ETH 208-209 D 4
Meghālaya ▫ IND 142-143 G 3
Meghna ~ BD 142-143 G 4
Megion o RUS 114-115 O 4
Mégiscane, Lac ⊂ CDN (QUE) 236-237 N 4
Mégiscane, Rivière ~ CDN (QUE) 236-237 M 4
Megra ~ RUS 88-89 Q 4
Megri o AR 128-129 M 3
Méguet o BF 202-203 K 3
Meguidene ⚍ DZ 190-191 C 6
Mehaiguene, Oued ~ DZ 190-191 D 4
Mehāl Mēda o ETH 208-209 D 3
Mehama o USA (OR) 244-245 C 6
Mehamn o N 86-87 N 1
Mehar o PK 134-135 M 5
Meharry, Mount ▲ AUS 172-173 D 7
Mehdia o DZ 190-191 C 3
Mehe, Küh-e ▲ IR 134-135 H 5
Mehedjibat, Erg ⚍ DZ 190-191 D 8
Mehekar o IND 138-139 F 9
Meherpur o BD 142-143 F 4
Meherrin River ~ USA (VA) 280-281 J 7
Mehmani o IR 134-135 G 5
Mehrābpur o PK 138-139 B 5
Mehrān o IR 134-135 B 2
Mehrān, Rūd-e ~ IR 134-135 E 5
Mehrān, Rūdhāne-ye ~ IR 134-135 F 5
Mehren'ga ~ RUS 88-89 Q 5
Mehrgarh ∴ • PK 134-135 M 4
Mehriz o IR 134-135 F 3
Mehtarlām ☆ • AFG 138-139 C 2
Meia Ponte, Rio ~ BR 72-73 F 5
Meibod o IR 134-135 E 2
Meidāni, Ra's-e ▲ IR 134-135 H 6
Meidānšahr ☆ • AFG 138-139 B 2
Meidougou o CAM 206-207 B 5
Meiganga o CAM 206-207 B 5
Meigs o USA (GA) 284-285 F 5
Meigu o VRC 156-157 C 2
Meihekou o VRC 150-151 E 6
Meiktila o MYA 142-143 J 5
Meili Xue Shan ▲ VRC 144-145 M 6
Meilleur River ~ CDN 30-31 G 5
Meimand o IR 134-135 D 3
Meime o IR 134-135 D 2
Meiningen o • D 92-93 L 3
Meinmagwe o MYA 142-143 H 6
Meio, Ilhéu do ⌒ GNB 202-203 C 4
Meio, Rio da ~ BR 72-73 H 2
Meio, Rio do ~ BR 72-73 K 5
Meio, Rio do ~ BR 68-69 C 4
Meishan o VRC 154-155 C 6
Meißen o • D 92-93 M 3
Meister River ~ CDN 20-21 Z 6
Meitan o VRC 156-157 E 3
Mei Xian o VRC 154-155 E 4
Meizhou o VRC 156-157 K 4
Meizhou Dao ⌒ VRC 156-157 L 4
Mejerda, Oued ~ TN 190-191 G 2
Mejez el Bab o TN 190-191 G 2
Mejia o PE 70-71 B 5
Mejicana, La o RA 76-77 D 5
Mejillones o RCH 76-77 B 2
Mejillones, Quebrada de ~ RCH 76-77 B 2
Mejillones del Sur, Bahía de ≈ 76-77 B 2
Mejnypil'gyno o RUS 112-113 T 5
Mejnypil'gynskij hrebet ▲ RUS 112-113 S 5
Mejo, El o YV 60-61 H 3
Meka o AUS 176-177 D 3
Mékambo o G 210-211 D 3
Mekane Selam o ETH 208-209 D 3
Mékel o CAM 210-211 E 2
Mek'elē ☆ • ETH 200-201 J 6
Mekerrhane, Sebkha ⊂ DZ 190-191 C 7
Mékhé o SN 202-203 B 2
Mekhtar o PK 138-139 B 4
Meki o ETH 208-209 D 4
Mékié ~ CAM 204-205 K 6
Me-kin o MYA 142-143 L 5
Mekinac, Lac ⊂ CDN (QUE) 240-241 C 3
Mekka = Makka ☆ •• KSA 132-133 A 3
Mekmene Ben Amar o DZ 188-189 L 4
Meknassy o TN 190-191 G 3
Meknés = Miknās ☆ MA 188-189 J 4
Meknès = Miknās ☆ MA 188-189 J 4
Meko o WAN 204-205 E 5
Mekomo o CAM 210-211 C 2
Mekong ~ K 158-159 H 4
Mekongga, Pegunungan ▲ RI 164-165 G 5
Mekoryuk o USA 20-21 G 6
Mékrou ~ DY 204-205 E 3
Mel, Ilha do ⌒ BR 74-75 F 5
Melá, Mont ▲ RCA 206-207 F 4
Melado, Río ~ RCH 78-79 D 4
Melak o RI 164-165 D 4
Melaka ▫ MAL 162-163 E 3
Melaka ☆ • MAL 162-163 E 3
Melaka, Selat ≈ 162-163 D 3
Melalih o RI 166-167 F 2
Melanesia ⌒ 13 E 2
Melanesian Basin ≃ 13 G 2
Melanguane o RI 164-165 K 1
Melanieskop ▲ ZA 220-221 J 4
Melati o RI 168 D 3
Melawi ~ RI 162-163 J 4
Melbourne ☆ •• AUS 180-181 H 4
Melbourne o USA (AR) 276-277 D 4
Melbourne o USA (FL) 286-287 J 3
Melbourne o USA (WA) 244-245 B 4
Melbourne Island ⌒ CDN 24-25 T 6
Melchett Lake ⊂ CDN (ONT) 234-235 Q 4
Melchor, Isla ⌒ RCH 80 C 2
Melchor Múzquiz o MEX 50-51 J 4
Meldal ☆ N 86-87 D 5
Meldrum Bay o CDN (ONT) 238-239 B 3
Meldrum Creek o CDN (BC) 228-229 N 4
Meldrum Creek ~ CDN (BC) 228-229 M 4
Mélé o RCA 206-207 E 4
Meleb o CDN (MAN) 234-235 F 4
Mele Bay ≈ 184 II b 3
Meleck o RUS 116-117 E 7
Melehova, proliv ≈ 112-113 L 1
Meleiro o BR 74-75 F 7
Meleiro ⌒ BR 74-75 F 7
Melela, Rio ~ MOC 218-219 J 3
Melenki o RUS 94-95 R 4
Melet Irmağı ~ TR 128-129 G 2
Meleuz ☆ RUS 96-97 J 7
Mélèzes, Rivière aux ~ CDN 36-37 N 6
Melfi o • I 100-101 E 4
Mélfi o TCH 206-207 C 3
Melfort o CDN (NS) 240-241 O 5
Melfort o CDN (SAS) 232-233 O 3
Melgaço o BR 62-63 J 6
Melhus ☆ N 86-87 E 5
Meliandine Lake ⊂ CDN 30-31 X 4
Meliane, Oued ~ TN 190-191 G 2
Melide o E 98-99 C 3
Melides o P 98-99 C 5
Melilla = Melilla o E 98-99 F 7
Melilis, Pulau ⌒ RI 164-165 H 4
Melilla o E 98-99 F 7
Melimoyu, Monte ▲ RCH 78-79 C 7
Melincué o RA 78-79 J 2
Melincué, Laguna ⊂ RA 78-79 J 2
Melinka o RCH 78-79 C 7
Melintang, Danau ⊂ RI 164-165 E 4
Melipeuco o RCH 78-79 D 5
Melipilla o RCH 78-79 D 2
Melita o CDN (MAN) 234-235 C 5
Mélito di Porto Salvo o I 100-101 E 6
Melitopol' o UA 102-103 J 4
Melívia o GR 100-101 J 5
Melk o A 92-93 N 4
Melka Deka o ETH 208-209 F 5
Melka Guba o ETH 208-209 D 6
Melka Kunture • ETH 208-209 D 4
Melka Meri o ETH 208-209 E 6
Melkasa o ETH 208-209 D 4
Melkbosstrand o ZA 220-221 D 6
Melkoe, ozero ⊂ RUS 108-109 X 7
Melkovodnyj, zaliv ⊂ RUS 120-121 U 3
Melkrivier o ZA 220-221 J 2
Mella o C 54-55 H 4
Mellal, Oued ~ MA 188-189 H 4
Mellam o SUD 200-201 B 6
Mellègue, Oued ~ TN 190-191 G 2
Mellemfjord ≈ 28-29 N 2
Mellen o USA (WI) 270-271 H 4
Mellene, Anou < RMM 198-199 B 3
Mellene, Assouf ~ DZ 190-191 C 8
Mellerud ☆ S 86-87 F 7
Mellette o USA (SD) 260-261 H 1
Mellit o SUD 200-201 B 5
Mellizos o RCH 76-77 C 2
Mellizo Sur, Cerro ▲ RCH 80 D 4
Mellon o CDN (BC) 230-231 F 4
Mellouloun, Oued ~ MA 188-189 K 4
Mellwood o USA (AR) 276-277 E 6
Melmoth o ZA 220-221 K 4
Mel'ničnoe o RUS 122-123 F 6
Mel'ničnye, perogi ~ RUS 88-89 O 5
Mělník o CZ 92-93 N 3
Melo o G 210-211 C 2
Melo ☆ ROU 78-79 M 2
Melo, Rio ~ PY 76-77 H 1
Meloco o MOC 218-219 K 1
Melolo o RI 168 E 7
Mélong o CAM 204-205 H 6
Melovoj, mys ▲ KA 126-127 J 6
Melovoj mujisi ▲ KA 126-127 J 6
Melozitna River ~ USA 20-21 N 4
Melrhir, Chott ⊂ DZ 190-191 F 3
Melrose o AUS (WA) 176-177 F 3
Melrose o AUS (SA) 180-181 E 2
Melrose o CDN (NS) 240-241 N 5
Melrose o USA (MN) 270-271 D 5
Melrose o USA (MT) 250-251 F 6
Melrose o USA (NM) 256-257 M 4
Melrose o USA (OR) 244-245 B 7
Melrose o USA (WI) 270-271 H 6
Melstone o USA (MT) 250-251 M 5
Melstrand o USA (MI) 270-271 M 4
Meltaus o FIN 88-89 H 3
Melton o AUS 180-181 H 4
Meluco o MOC 214-215 K 7
Melukua o RI 166-167 E 5
Melume o ZRE 210-211 K 2
Melun ☆ F 90-91 J 7
Melun o MYA 142-143 H 5
Melung Tse Jobo Garu ▲ NEP 144-145 F 6
Melur o IND 140-141 H 5
Melvern Lake ⊂ USA (KS) 262-263 L 6
Melville o CDN (SAS) 232-233 Q 5
Melville o USA (LA) 268-269 J 6
Melville o USA (MT) 250-251 K 5
Melville, Cape ▲ AUS 174-175 H 4
Melville, Cape ▲ RP 160-161 B 9
Melville, Kap ▲ GRØ 26-27 T 5
Melville, Lake ⊂ CDN 38-39 P 2
Melville Bay ≈ 174-175 D 3
Melville Bugt ≈ 26-27 S 6
Melville Hills ▲ CDN 24-25 J 6
Melville Island ⌒ AUS 172-173 K 1
Melville Island ⌒ CDN 24-25 P 3
Melville Land ⚍ GRØ 26-27 k 2
Melville Peninsula ⌣ CDN 24-25 d 6
Melville Sound ≈ 24-25 S 6
Melville Trough ≃ 24-25 Q 3
Melvin River ~ CDN 30-31 L 6
Melvis, La o C 54-55 D 4
Memala o RI 162-163 K 5
Memári o IND 142-143 F 4
Memba o CO 60-61 C 5
Memba o MOC 218-219 L 2
Membalong o RI 162-163 G 6
Membeca, Rio ~ BR 70-71 J 3
Memboro o RI 168 D 7
Membrillo, El o RCH 78-79 D 2
Memel o ZA 220-221 J 3
Memel = Klaipėda ☆ •• LT 94-95 G 4
Memmingen o • D 92-93 L 5
Memo o YV 60-61 H 3
Memori, Tanjung ▲ RI 166-167 H 2
Mempawah o RI 162-163 H 4
Memphis ∴ ••• ET 194-195 E 3
Memphis o USA (MO) 274-275 F 4
Memphis o USA (TX) 264-265 D 4
Memphis o • USA (TN) 276-277 E 5
Memphremagog, Lac ⊂ CDN (QUE) 238-239 N 3
Memramcook o CDN (NB) 240-241 L 4
Ména o RMM 202-203 G 3
Mena o UA 102-103 H 2
Mena o USA (AR) 276-277 A 6
Mena, Wabē ~ ETH 208-209 E 6
Menaa o DZ 190-191 F 3
Menabe ⚍ RM 222-223 D 8
Menahga o USA (MN) 270-271 C 4
Menai ⌒ SY 222-223 E 2
Ménaka o RMM 196-197 M 7
Mènam Kohng (Mekong) ~ LAO 156-157 B 7
Menan o USA (ID) 252-253 G 3
Menanga o RI 164-165 J 4
Menangina o AUS 176-177 F 4
Menarandra ~ RM 222-223 D 10
Menarbu o RI 166-167 H 3
Menard o USA (TX) 266-267 H 3
Menard Fracture Zone ≃ 14-15 R 12
Menaskwagama, Lac ⊂ CDN 38-39 N 3
Menawashei o SUD 200-201 B 6
Menchia o TN 190-191 G 4
Menda ~ RUS 118-119 O 5
Mendale o USA (OH) 280-281 B 2
Mendaña Fracture Zone = Mendana Fracture Zone ≃ 5 B 6
Mendanau, Pulau ⌒ RI 162-163 G 6
Mendawai ~ RI 162-163 K 5
Mendaya o RI 168 D 7
Mende o • F 90-91 J 9
Mendebo ▲ ETH 208-209 D 5
Mendef ~ RUS 116-117 E 7
Mendeleeva, gory ▲ RUS 108-109 J 3
Mendeleevsk ☆ RUS 96-97 H 6
Mendenhall o USA (MS) 268-269 L 5
Mendenhall, Cape ▲ USA 22-23 N 3
Mendenhall Glacier ⊂ USA 32-33 C 2
Mendes o DZ 190-191 C 3
Méndez o EC 64-65 C 3
Méndez o MEX 50-51 K 5
Mendham o CDN (SAS) 232-233 J 5
Mendi o ETH 208-209 B 4
Mendi ☆ PNG 183 B 4
Mendikōl o KA 126-127 O 3
Mendiya-Plage o MA 188-189 H 3
Mendocino o USA (CA) 246-247 B 4
Mendocino, Cape ▲ USA (CA) 246-247 A 3
Mendocino Fracture Zone ≃ 14-15 M 4
Mendocino Pass ▲ USA (CA) 246-247 C 4
Mendol, Pulau ⌒ RI 162-163 E 4
Mendon o USA (IL) 274-275 G 4
Mendon o USA (MO) 274-275 E 5
Mendooran o AUS 178-179 K 6
Mendopolo o SUD 206-207 K 6
Mendota o USA (CA) 248-249 D 3
Mendota o USA (IL) 274-275 J 3
Mendoza o PE 64-65 D 5
Mendoza ▫ RA 78-79 E 3
Mendoza ☆ • RA 78-79 E 2
Mene de Mauroa o YV 60-61 F 2
Menegers Dam o USA (AZ) 256-257 C 7
Mene Grande o YV 60-61 F 3
Menemen ☆ TR 128-129 B 3
Menen o B 92-93 G 3
Menéndez, Lago ⊂ RA 78-79 D 7
Menéndez, Paso de ▲ RCH 78-79 D 7
Menengai Crater • EAK 212-213 F 4
Menesjärvi o FIN 88-89 J 2
Meng ~ CAM 204-205 K 5
Menga o ANG 216-217 C 5
Menga, Puerto de ▲ E 98-99 E 4
Mengam, Mount ▲ PNG 183 C 3
Mengcheng o VRC 154-155 K 5
Menggala o RI 162-163 F 7
Menggari o RI 166-167 H 2
Menghai o VRC 142-143 M 5
Mengkatip o RI 164-165 D 5
Mengkoka, Gunung ▲ RI 164-165 G 5
Mengla o VRC 156-157 B 6
Menglian o VRC 142-143 L 4
Mengong o CAM 210-211 C 2
Mengshan o VRC 156-157 G 4
Ménguémé o CAM 210-211 C 2
Meng Xian o VRC 154-155 H 4
Mengxing o VRC 156-157 B 6
Mengyan o VRC 156-157 F 3
Mengyin o VRC 154-155 K 4
Mengzi o VRC 156-157 C 5
Menidi o GR 100-101 H 5
Menier, Port o CDN (QUE) 242-243 D 3
Menihek Lakes ⊂ CDN 36-37 Q 7
Menindee o AUS 180-181 G 2
Menindee Lake ⊂ AUS 180-181 G 2
Meningie o AUS 180-181 E 3
Mènkèrè ~ RUS 110-111 O 6
Menkerja o RUS 110-111 O 6
Menkjule ~ RUS 120-121 G 2
Menneval o CDN (QUE) 240-241 H 3
Menno o USA (SD) 260-261 J 3
Menoken o USA (ND) 258-259 G 5
Menominee o USA (MI) 270-271 L 5
Menominee Indian Reservation ⅩUSA (WI) 270-271 K 5
Menominee River ~ USA (WI) 270-271 L 5
Menomonee Falls o USA (WI) 274-275 K 1
Menomonie o USA (WI) 270-271 G 6
Menongue ☆ ANG 216-217 D 7
Menorca ⌒ E 98-99 J 4
Men'šikova, mys ▲ RUS 108-109 G 6
Men'šikova, ostrov ⌒ RUS 120-121 H 6
Mentasta Pass ▲ USA 20-21 T 5
Mentawai, Kepulauan ⌒ RI 162-163 C 5
Mentawai Strait = Mentawai, Selat ≈ RI 162-163 C 5
Menteke, kum ⚍ KA 96-97 F 10
Mentmore o USA (NM) 256-257 G 3
Menton o F 90-91 L 10
Mentone o USA (TX) 266-267 D 2
Mentor o USA (OH) 280-281 E 2
Menucos, Bajo de los ⚍ RA 78-79 F 5
Menucos, Los o RA 78-79 E 6
Menukung o RI 162-163 K 5
Menyamya o PNG 183 D 4
Menyapa, Gunung ▲ RI 164-165 E 3
Menyuan o VRC 154-155 B 3
Menza o RUS (CTN) 116-117 O 11
Menza ~ RUS 116-117 O 10
Menzaa ~ RUS 116-117 O 11
Menzel Bourguiba o TN 190-191 G 2
Menzel Chaker o TN 190-191 H 3
Menzelinsk ☆ RUS 96-97 H 6
Menzel Termime o TN 190-191 H 2
Menzie o CDN (MAN) 234-235 C 4
Menzies o AUS 176-177 F 4
Menzies, Mount ▲ ARK 16 F 7
Meoqui o MEX 50-51 G 3
Meota o CDN (SAS) 232-233 K 2
Mepala o ANG 216-217 B 3
Mepica o MOC 218-219 J 2
Mepiskaro, gora ▲ GE 126-127 E 7
Meponda o MOC 218-219 H 1
Mepozo ~ ANG 216-217 B 3
Meppadi o IND 140-141 G 5
Meppel o NL 92-93 J 2
Meppen o D 92-93 J 2
Mepuse, Rio ~ MOC 218-219 H 3
Mequens, Rio ~ BR 70-71 F 3
Mequinenza, Embalse de < E 98-99 H 4
Mequon o USA (WI) 274-275 L 1
Mera o EC 64-65 C 2
Merai o PNG 183 G 3
Merak o RI 168 B 2
Meråker o N 86-87 E 5
Meralaba, Île = Mere Lava ⌒ VAN 184 II b 2
Merama Hill o EAU 212-213 C 4
Meramangye, Lake ⊂ AUS 176-177 M 4
Meramec River ~ USA (MO) 274-275 G 6
Meramec State Park ⊥ USA (MO) 274-275 G 6
Merampi, Pulau ⌒ RI 164-165 K 1
Meran = Merano o I 100-101 C 1
Merangin ~ RI 162-163 D 6
Merano = Meran o I 100-101 C 1
Merapah o AUS 174-175 G 3
Merapi, Gunung ▲ RI 168 D 3
Merasheen Island ⌒ CDN (NFL) 242-243 O 5
Meratswe ~ RB 218-219 C 6
Merauke o RI 166-167 L 6
Merauke ~ RI 166-167 L 6
Mercaderes o CO 60-61 C 7
Mercan Dağları ▲ TR 128-129 H 3
Mercantour, Parc National du ⊥ • F 90-91 L 9
Merced o USA (CA) 248-249 D 2
Mercedario, Cerro ▲ RA 78-79 D 2
Mercedes o RA (BUA) 78-79 K 3
Mercedes o RA (CO) 76-77 H 5
Mercedes o RA (SLU) 78-79 G 2
Mercedes ☆ ROU 78-79 K 2
Mercedes o USA (TX) 266-267 K 7
Mercedes, Ilha das ⌒ BR 70-71 E 2
Mercedes, Las o YV (AMA) 60-61 H 5
Mercedes, Las o YV (GUA) 60-61 H 3
Mercedes, Las o YV (PSA) 60-61 G 3
Merced River ~ USA (CA) 248-249 D 2
Mercer o USA (ND) 258-259 G 4
Mercer o USA (PA) 280-281 F 2
Mercer o USA (TN) 276-277 F 5
Mercer o USA (WI) 270-271 H 4
Mercers Bottom o USA (WV) 280-281 D 5
Merchants Bay ≈ 28-29 J 3
Merčimden ~ RUS 110-111 M 5
Mercoal o CDN (ALB) 228-229 R 3
Mercoya o RMM 202-203 F 3
Mercury o USA (NV) 248-249 J 3
Mercy, Cape ▲ CDN 36-37 S 2
Mercy Bay ≈ 24-25 N 3
Merdani, Hassi < MA 188-189 K 5
Mereb Wenz ~ ETH 200-201 J 5
Merecure o YV 60-61 G 4
Meredith o AUS 180-181 H 4
Meredith o USA (CO) 254-255 J 4
Meredith o USA (NH) 278-279 K 5
Meredith, Cape ▲ GB 78-79 K 7
Meredosia o USA (IL) 274-275 H 5
Meredosia Lake ⊂ USA (IL) 274-275 H 5
Meredoua o DZ 190-191 C 8
Merefa o UA 102-103 K 3
Mereksen o DZ 190-191 G 6
Mere Lava = Île Meralaba ⌒ VAN 184 II b 2
Merenga o RUS 120-121 R 3
Meresichic o MEX 50-51 D 2
Merewa o ETH 208-209 C 5
Merga = Nukhaylah < SUD 200-201 C 3
Mergui o MYA 158-159 E 4
Mergui Archipelago = Myeik Kyûnzu ⌒ MYA 158-159 D 4
Mergui Archipelago = Myeik Kyûnzu ⌒ MYA 158-159 E 4
Merhder Lefâa < MA 188-189 K 4
Meri o CAM 206-207 B 3
Méri o SN 196-197 C 6
Meriç Nehri ~ TR 128-129 B 2
Mérida o • E 98-99 D 5
Mérida ☆ •• MEX 52-53 K 1
Mérida ☆ • YV 60-61 F 3
Mérida, Cordillera de ▲ YV 60-61 F 3
Meriden o USA (CT) 280-281 O 2
Meriden o USA (WY) 252-253 O 5
Meridian o USA (ID) 252-253 B 3
Meridian o USA (MS) 268-269 M 4
Meridian o USA (TX) 266-267 K 2
Meridian Island ⌒ CDN 30-31 K 5
Meridianville o USA (AL) 284-285 D 2
Meridith, Lake ⊂ USA (TX) 264-265 C 3
Meridja o DZ 188-189 K 5
Merig = Île Merigi ⌒ VAN 184 II a 2
Merigi, Île = Merig ⌒ VAN 184 II a 2
Merigur o AUS 180-181 F 3
Méri Harmsuort, mys ▲ RUS 84-85 Y 2
Merikarvia o FIN 88-89 F 6
Merimbula o AUS 180-181 K 4
Merin, Laguna o ROU 74-75 D 9
Meringa o WAN 204-205 K 3
Merino Downs o AUS 178-179 H 2
Merino Jarpa, Isla ⌒ RCH 80 C 3
Merit o MAL 162-163 K 3
Merite Stigbøjlen, Kap ▲ GRØ 26-27 q 4
Merivale o AUS 178-179 K 3
Merkānam o IND 140-141 H 4
Merkel o USA (TX) 264-265 D 6
Merkušina Strelka, poluostrov ⌣ RUS 110-111 Z 3
Merlin o USA (OR) 244-245 B 8
Merluna o AUS 174-175 G 3
Mermaid Reef ⌒ AUS 172-173 D 4
Merna o USA (NE) 262-263 G 3
Merna o USA (WY) 252-253 H 4
Meroe Bank ≃ 182 E 5
Meroe •• SUD 200-201 F 4
Merolia o AUS 176-177 G 4
Meropoh o MAL 162-163 D 2
Meros, Ponta dos ▲ BR 72-73 H 7
Merouana o DZ 190-191 E 3
Merouane, Chott ⊂ DZ 190-191 F 3
Merowe = Marawi o SUD 200-201 E 3
Merredin o AUS 176-177 E 5
Merrick ▲ GB 90-91 E 4
Merrickville o CDN (ONT) 238-239 K 4
Merridale o CDN (MAN) 234-235 B 3
Merrie Range ▲ AUS 176-177 F 2
Merrifield Bay ≈ 36-37 T 7
Merrill o USA (MI) 272-273 E 4
Merrill o USA (MS) 268-269 M 6
Merrill o USA (OR) 244-245 D 8
Merrill o USA (WI) 270-271 J 5
Merrillan o USA (WI) 270-271 H 6
Merrillville o USA (CA) 246-247 E 3
Merrillville o USA (NY) 278-279 H 4
Merrimack River ~ USA (NH) 278-279 K 5
Merriman o USA (NE) 262-263 E 2
Merriman o ZA 220-221 F 5
Merrimerriwa, Mount ▲ AUS 180-181 H 2
Merritt Island ⌒ USA (FL) 286-287 J 3
Merritt o CDN (BC) 230-231 J 3
Merritt Island o USA (FL) 286-287 J 3
Merritt Reservoire ⊂ USA (NE) 262-263 F 2
Merriwa o AUS 180-181 L 2
Mer Rouge o USA (LA) 268-269 J 4
Merry Island ⌒ CDN 36-37 L 7
Merryville o USA (LA) 268-269 G 6
Mersa Fatma o ER 200-201 K 5
Mersa Gulbub o ER 200-201 J 4
Merseburg o • D 92-93 L 3
Mersey ~ GB 90-91 F 5
Mersey River ~ AUS 180-181 J 6
Mersin = İçel o TR 128-129 F 4
Mersing o • MAL 162-163 E 3
Mersrags o LV 94-95 H 3
Merta o IND 138-139 E 6
Merthyr Tydfil o GB 90-91 F 6
Merti o EAK 212-213 G 3
Merting, Kampung o MAL 162-163 E 2
Merti Plateau ▲ EAK 212-213 G 3
Mértola o • P 98-99 D 6
Merton o AUS 180-181 H 4
Mertoutek o DZ 190-191 E 8
Mertule Maryam o ETH 208-209 D 3
Merty Merty o AUS 178-179 F 5
Mertz Glacier ⊂ ARK 16 G 15
Mertzon o USA (TX) 266-267 G 2
Meru o EAK 212-213 G 3
Meru ▲ • EAT 212-213 F 5
Merume Mountains ▲ GUY 62-63 D 3
Meru Mulika Lodge o EAK 212-213 G 3
Meru National Park ⊥ EAK 212-213 G 3
Meruóco o BR 68-69 H 3
Meruíre, Área Indígena Ⅹ BR 72-73 D 3
Merville o CDN (BC) 230-231 D 4
Mervin o CDN (SAS) 232-233 K 2
Merweville o ZA 220-221 E 6
Mëry ☆ BY 94-95 K 4
Meryemana ∴ •• TR 128-129 B 4
Merzifon ☆ TR 128-129 F 2
Mesa o MOC 218-219 K 1
Mesa o RI 164-165 L 3
Mesa o USA (AZ) 256-257 D 5
Mesa o USA (CO) 254-255 G 4
Mesa o USA (ID) 252-253 B 2
Mesa o USA (NM) 256-257 L 5
Mesa o USA (WA) 244-245 G 4
Mesa, Cerro ▲ RA 78-79 E 5
Mesa, La o CO 60-61 D 5
Mesa, La o USA (CA) 248-249 G 7
Mesa, La o USA (NM) 256-257 J 6
Mesa, La o YV 60-61 F 2
Mesabi Range ▲ USA (MN) 270-271 F 3
Mesa de las Tablas o MEX 50-51 J 5
Mesagrós o GR 100-101 J 6
Mesai, Río ~ CO 64-65 F 1
Mešalli o US 136-137 G 4
Mesanak, Pulau ⌒ RI 162-163 F 4
Mesaraba o ZRE 210-211 L 5
Mesa Verde National Park ⊥ ••• USA (CO) 254-255 G 6
Mescalero o USA (NM) 256-257 K 5
Mescalero Apache Indian Reservation Ⅹ USA (NM) 256-257 K 5
Meščerskaja nizmenost' ▲ RUS 94-95 Q 4
Meschetti o SP 212-213 H 3
Meschkakur ▲ MA 188-189 K 4
Mescit Dağları ▲ TR 128-129 J 2
Meseta Baya ▲ RA 78-79 E 5
Meseta de Jaua ▲ YV 60-61 J 5
Meseta de Somuncurá ⚍ RA 78-79 F 6
Meseta el Pedrero ⚍ RA 80 F 3
Mesfinto o ETH 200-201 H 6
Mešginšahr o IR 128-129 M 3
Mesgouez, Lac o CDN 38-39 G 3
Meshik River ~ USA 22-23 R 4
Mesick o USA (MI) 272-273 D 3
Mesilinka River ~ CDN 32-33 H 3
Mesilla o USA (NM) 256-257 J 6
Mesilla, La o GCA 52-53 J 4
Mésima ~ I 100-101 F 5
Mesjagutovo ☆ RUS 96-97 L 6
Mesjid Raya • RI 162-163 C 3
Meškān o IR 136-137 F 6
Meskanaw o CDN (SAS) 232-233 N 3
Meski, Source bleue de • MA 188-189 J 5
Meskiana, Oued ~ DZ 190-191 F 3
Mesklip o ZA 220-221 C 4
Meslo o ETH 208-209 D 5
Mesna ~ RUS 88-89 S 2
Mesndiye o TR 128-129 G 2
Mesogi o CY 128-129 E 5
Mesopotamia ⚍ IRQ 128-129 J 5
Mesopotamia ⚍ RA 76-77 H 6
Mesquakie Indian Settlement Ⅹ USA (IA) 274-275 F 3
Mesquita o BR 72-73 J 5
Mesquite o USA (NV) 248-249 K 3
Mesquite o USA (TX) 264-265 H 6
Messaad o DZ 190-191 D 3
Messalo ~ MOC 214-215 K 7
Messaména o CAM 210-211 D 2
Messaoud, Oued ~ DZ 188-189 L 6
Mess Creek ~ CDN 32-33 E 3
Messeied o MA 188-189 F 6
Messejana o BR 68-69 J 3
Messelesek o RI 164-165 H 4
Messent Conservation Park ⊥ AUS 180-181 E 4
Messier, Canal ≈ 80 C 3
Messina o I 100-101 E 5
Messina o ZA 218-219 F 6
Messina, Stretto di ≈ 100-101 E 5
Messinge, Rio ~ MOC 214-215 H 7
Messiniakos Kólpos ≈ 100-101 J 6
Messojaha ~ RUS 108-109 T 7
Messolóngi o GR 100-101 H 5
Messondo o CAM 210-211 C 2
Messum Crater • NAM 216-217 C 10
Mesters Vig o GRØ 26-27 n 7
Mestia o GE 126-127 E 6
mesto padenija Tungusskogo meteorita • RUS 116-117 L 5
Mesuji ~ RI 162-163 F 7
Mesurado, Cape ▲ LB 202-203 E 6
Meta, Río ~ CO 60-61 E 5
Métabetchouan o CDN (QUE) 240-241 D 2
Metaca o MOC 214-215 J 7
Metagama o CDN (ONT) 236-237 G 5
Meta Incognita Peninsula ⌣ CDN 36-37 O 3
Metairie o USA (LA) 268-269 K 7
Métal, Mont du ▲ DZ 198-199 D 2
Meta Lake ⊂ CDN (ONT) 234-235 Q 4
Metaliferi, Munții ▲ RO 102-103 C 4
Metaline Falls o USA (WA) 244-245 H 2
Metán o RA 76-77 E 3
Metangobalame o MOC 218-219 H 2
Metangula o MOC 214-215 H 7
Metapán o ES 52-53 K 4
Metaponto o • I 100-101 F 4
Metarica o MOC 218-219 J 2
Metchosin o CDN (BC) 230-231 F 5
Metchum ~ CAM 204-205 H 5
Metea o USA (IN) 274-275 M 4
Meteghan o CDN (NS) 240-241 J 6
Metema o ETH 200-201 H 6
Meteóra ••• GR 100-101 H 5
Meteor Crater • USA (AZ) 256-257 D 3
Meteor Creek ~ AUS 178-179 K 3
Meteorit Ø ⌒ GRØ 26-27 S 5
Meteorologist Peninsula ⌣ CDN 24-25 V 1
Metepec o MEX (HGO) 52-53 E 1
Metepec o MEX (PUE) 52-53 E 2
Meteran o PNG 183 F 2
Metet o CAM 210-211 C 2
Metiatoli o PA 52-53 F 7
Methy River ~ CDN 32-33 Q 3
Metil o MOC 218-219 K 3
Metionga Lake ⊂ CDN (ONT) 234-235 N 5
Metiskow o CDN (ALB) 232-233 H 3
Metković o HR 100-101 F 3

Meakan-dake — Metković 361

Metlakatla ○ CDN (BC) 228-229 D 2
Metlakatla ○ USA 32-33 E 4
Metlaoui ○ TN 190-191 G 3
Metlili, Oued ~ DZ 190-191 D 4
Metlili Chaamba ○ DZ 190-191 D 4
Meto, Bayou ~ USA (AR) 276-277 D 6
Metohija ⊥ YU 100-101 H 3
Metoro ○ MOC 218-219 K 1
Metro ○ RI 162-163 F 7
Metropolis ○ USA (IL) 276-277 G 3
Metsera ○ ZRE 210-211 L 5
Métsovo • GR 100-101 H 5
Mettenpherg Creek ~ USA 20-21 O 3
Metter ○ USA (GA) 284-285 H 4
Mettuppālaiyam ○ IND 140-141 G 5
Mettur ○ IND 140-141 G 5
Metu ☆ ETH 208-209 B 4
Metuge ○ MOC 214-215 L 7
Metz ☆• F 90-91 L 7
Metztitlán ○ MEX 52-53 E 1
Meulaboh ○ RI 162-163 B 2
Meureudu ○ RI 162-163 B 2
Meuse ~ B 92-93 H 3
Meuse ~ F 90-91 K 7
Meuse, Côtes de ⊥ F 90-91 K 7
Mēwār ⊥ IND 138-139 D 7
Mexcaltitán ○ MEX 50-51 G 7
Mexia ○ USA (TX) 266-267 L 2
Mexia, Lake < USA (TX) 266-267 L 2
Mexiana, Ilha ⌒ BR 62-63 K 6
Mexicali ☆ MEX 50-51 B 1
Mexican Hat ○ USA (UT) 254-255 F 6
Mexicanos, Laguna Los ○ MEX 50-51 F 3
Mexican Plateau = Altiplanicie Mexicana ▲ MEX 50-51 G 4
Mexican Water ○ USA (AZ) 256-257 F 2
México ▫ MEX 52-53 D 2
Mexico ○ USA (ME) 278-279 L 4
Mexico ○ USA (MO) 274-275 G 5
México, Ciudad de = México ★ ••• MEX 52-53 E 2
México, Golfo de = Gulf of Mexico ≈ 4 E 6
Mexico, Gulf of = México, Golfo de ≈ 4 E 6
Mexico = México ■ MEX 52-53 C 1
Mexico Bay ≈ USA 278-279 E 5
Mexico Beach ○ USA (FL) 286-287 D 2
Mexico City = México, Ciudad de ★ ••• MEX 52-53 E 2
Mexiko ○ USA (NY) 278-279 E 5
Meyāmei ○ IR 136-137 D 6
Meyanodas ○ RI 166-167 F 5
Meydancık ○ TR 128-129 K 2
Meyers Canyon ~ USA (TX) 266-267 E 3
Meyersdale ○ USA (PA) 280-281 G 4
Méyo Centre ○ CAM 210-211 C 2
Meẓada ∴• IL 130-131 D 2
Mezaligon ○ MYA 158-159 C 2
Mezcalapa, Río ~ MEX 52-53 H 3
Mezdra ○ BG 102-103 C 6
Meždurečensk ○ RUS 124-125 Q 2
Meždurečenskij ○ RUS 114-115 H 5
Meždušarskij, ostrov ⌒ RUS 108-109 F 6
Mezen' ○ RUS 88-89 S 4
Mezen' ~ RUS 88-89 T 4
Mézenc, Mont ▲• F 90-91 K 9
Mezenskaja guba ≈ 88-89 R 3
Mezens'kaja Pižma ~ RUS 88-89 U 4
Mézessé ○ CAM 210-211 D 2
Mézessé, Rocher du = Mézessé Rock • CAM 210-211 D 2
Mézessé Rock = Rocher du Mézessé • CAM 210-211 D 2
Mežgornoe, ozero ○ RUS 112-113 W 4
Mézier, Charleville ☆ F 90-91 K 7
Mezón ○ BOL 76-77 E 2
Mežozernyj ○ RUS 96-97 L 6
Mezquita Catedral •• E 98-99 E 6
Mezquital ○ MEX (DGO) 50-51 G 6
Mezquital ○ MEX (TAM) 50-51 L 5
Mezquital, Río ~ MEX 50-51 G 6
Mfou ○ CAM 210-211 C 2
Mfouati ○ RCB 210-211 D 6
Mfum ○ WAN 204-205 H 6
Mgači ○ RUS 122-123 K 3
Mgangerabeli Plains ⊥ EAK 212-213 H 4
Mgbidi ○ WAN 204-205 G 6
Mgende ○ EAT 212-213 C 6
Mgeta ~ EAT 214-215 K 4
Mg.Mu'o'n ○ VN 156-157 C 6
Mgneta, Hassi < MA 188-189 K 4
Mgunga ○ EAT 214-215 J 4
Mhamid ○ MA 188-189 J 6
Mhangura ○ ZW 218-219 F 3
Mhasvād ○ IND 140-141 F 2
Mhlatuze ~ ZA 220-221 K 4
Mi, Enneri ~ TCH 198-199 G 2
Miagao ○ RP 160-161 E 7
Miahuatlán ○ MEX 52-53 F 3
Miahuatlán, Sierra de ▲ MEX 52-53 F 3
Miajadas ○ E 98-99 E 5
Miājlār ○ IND 138-139 C 6
Mial, Oued ~ DZ 190-191 D 6
Miamère ○ RCA 206-207 D 4
Miami ○ USA (AZ) 256-257 E 5
Miami ○ USA (OK) 264-265 K 2
Miami ○ USA (TX) 264-265 D 3
Miami ○• USA (FL) 286-287 J 6
Miami, North ○ USA (FL) 286-287 J 6
Miami Beach ○• USA (FL) 286-287 J 6
Miami Canal < USA (FL) 286-287 J 5
Miami River ~ USA (OH) 280-281 B 4
Miami River ~ USA (OH) 280-281 B 3
Miamo, El ○ YV 62-63 D 2
Miān Channūn ○ PK 138-139 D 4
Miandrivazo ○ RM 222-223 D 7
Miangas, Pulau ⌒ RI 164-165 K 1
Miani ○ PK 138-139 D 3
Miani Hor ≈ 134-135 M 6
Mianmian Shan ▲ VRC 156-157 B 2
Mianmin ○ PNG 183 A 3
Mianning ○ VRC 156-157 C 2
Miānwāli ○ PK 138-139 C 3
Mian Xian ○ VRC 154-155 E 5
Mianyang ○ VRC 154-155 D 6
Mianzhu ○ VRC 154-155 D 6
Miao ~ ZRE 214-215 B 4
Miaodao Qundao ⌒ VRC 150-151 C 8
Miaoergou ○ VRC 146-147 F 3
Miao Li ○ RC 156-157 M 4
Miao Ling ▲ VRC 156-157 E 3
Miaozu ○ VRC 156-157 E 5
Miarinarivo ○ RM 222-223 E 7
Miaru ○ PNG 183 D 5
Miass ☆ RUS (CEL) 96-97 M 6
Miass ~ RUS 96-97 L 6
Miass ~ RUS 114-115 H 7
Miasskoe ☆ RUS 96-97 M 6
Miastko ○ PL 92-93 O 1
Miāti ○ IND 138-139 E 8
Mibalaie ○ ZRE 210-211 H 6
Mibenge ○ Z 214-215 E 6
Mibu Island ⌒ PNG 183 B 5
Mica ○ ZA 220-221 K 2
Mica Creek ○ CDN (BC) 228-229 Q 4
Micaúne ○ MOC 218-219 J 4
Miccosukee, Lake ○ USA (FL) 286-287 F 1
Miccosukee Indian Reservation ⚔ USA (FL) 286-287 J 5
Michael, Lake ○ CDN 36-37 U 7
Michael, Mount ▲ PNG 183 C 4
Michalovce ○ SK 92-93 Q 4
Michel ○ CDN 32-33 Q 3
Michel, Lake ○ CDN (NFL) 242-243 L 2
Michel, Pointe á ▲ CDN (QUE) 240-241 G 2
Michelago ○ AUS 180-181 K 3
Michel Peak ▲ CDN (BC) 228-229 H 3
Michelsen, Cape ▲ CDN 24-25 U 5
Michelson, Mount ▲ USA 20-21 S 2
Miches ○ DOM 54-55 L 5
Michichi ○ CDN (ALB) 232-233 F 4
Michie, Lake ○ USA (NC) 282-283 J 4
Michigamme River ~ USA (MI) 270-271 K 4
Michigan ○ USA (MI) 270-271 M 6
Michigan, Lake ○ USA (MI) 272-273 B 5
Michigan Bar ○ USA (CA) 246-247 D 5
Michigan Center ○ USA (MI) 272-273 E 5
Michigan City ○ USA (IN) 274-275 M 3
Michigan City ○ USA (ND) 258-259 J 3
Michigan Potawatomi Indian Reservation ⚔ USA (MI) 270-271 L 5
Michika ○ RCH 76-77 B 2
Michipicoten Bay ○ CDN (ONT) 236-237 C 5
Michipicoten Island ⌒ CDN (ONT) 236-237 C 5
Michoacan ▫ MEX 52-53 C 2
Michurinsk = Mičurinsk ○ RUS 94-95 R 5
Mico, Río ~ NIC 52-53 B 5
Micronesia ⌒ 14-15 G 6
Microondas ○ MEX 50-51 C 2
Mičurinsk ○ RUS 94-95 R 5
Midal < RN 198-199 B 4
Midale ○ CDN (SAS) 232-233 P 6
Midar ○ MA 188-189 K 3
Midas ○ USA (NV) 246-247 J 2
Midas Şehri ∴• TR 128-129 D 3
Mid-Atlantic Ridge ≃ 6-7 E 5
Midau, Pulau ⌒ RI 162-163 G 3
Mid Baffin ○ CDN 28-29 E 2
Middelburg ☆ NL 92-93 G 3
Middelburg ○ ZA (CAP) 220-221 G 5
Middelburg ○ ZA (TRA) 220-221 J 2
Middelpos ○ ZA 220-221 E 5
Middelveld ⊥ ZA 220-221 G 3
Middelveld ⊥ ZA 220-221 F 4
Middelwit ○ ZA 220-221 H 2
Middendorfa, zaliv ○ RUS 108-109 Y 4
Middle Alkali Lake ○ USA (CA) 246-247 E 2
Middle America Trench ≃ 52-53 F 4
Middle Andaman ⌒ IND 140-141 L 3
Middleboro ○ USA (MA) 278-279 L 7
Middlebro ○ CDN (MAN) 234-235 H 5
Middleburg ○ USA (PA) 280-281 J 3
Middleburgh ○ USA (NY) 278-279 G 6
Middlebury ○ USA (VT) 278-279 H 4
Middlecamp ○ AUS 180-181 F 2
Middle Cay ⌒ JA 54-55 G 6
Middle Channel ~ CDN 20-21 X 2
Middle Creek ~ USA (NC) 282-283 J 5
Middle Fabius River ~ USA (MO) 274-275 F 4
Middle Fiord ≈ 26-27 C 4
Middle Fork ○ USA (IN) 274-275 M 4
Middle Fork ~ USA 20-21 T 4
Middle Fork ~ USA (KY) 276-277 M 3
Middle Fork ~ USA (TN) 276-277 G 4
Middle Fork Chandalar ~ USA 20-21 R 2
Middle Fork John Day River ~ USA (OR) 244-245 F 6
Middle Fork Koyukuk ~ USA 20-21 P 3
Middle Fork Kuskokwim River ~ USA 20-21 N 5
Middle Fork River ~ USA 22-23 Q 3
Middle Fork Salmon River ~ USA (ID) 252-253 C 2
Middle Fork Salt River ~ USA (MO) 274-275 F 5
Middle Gate ○ USA (NV) 246-247 G 4
Middle Ground ≈ 54-55 G 2
Middle Hart River ~ CDN 20-21 W 4
Middle Island ⌒ AUS 176-177 G 7
Middle Lake ○ CDN (SAS) 232-233 N 3
Middle Loup River ~ USA (NE) 262-263 G 3
Middlemount ○ AUS 178-179 K 2
Middle Musquodoboit ○ CDN (NS) 240-241 M 5
Middle Ohio ○ CDN (NS) 240-241 K 7
Middle Park ○ AUS 174-175 G 6
Middle Pease River ~ USA (TX) 264-265 D 4
Middle Rapids ~ CDN 32-33 O 3
Middle Ridge ▲ CDN (NFL) 242-243 N 4
Middle River ~ CDN (BC) 228-229 J 2
Middle River ~ USA (MN) 270-271 B 2
Middle Sackville ○ CDN (NS) 240-241 M 6
Middle Sand Hills ▲ CDN (ALB) 232-233 H 5
Middlesboro ○ USA (KY) 276-277 M 4
Middlesbrough ○ GB 90-91 G 4
Middleton ○ AUS 178-179 F 2
Middleton ○ CDN (NS) 240-241 K 6
Middleton ○ USA (MI) 272-273 E 4
Middleton ○ USA (TN) 276-277 G 5
Middleton ○ USA (WI) 274-275 J 1
Middleton ○ ZA 220-221 G 6
Middleton, Mount ▲ CDN (QUE) 236-237 M 2
Middleton Island ⌒ USA 20-21 R 7
Middletown ○ USA (CA) 246-247 C 5
Middletown ○ USA (CT) 280-281 O 2
Middletown ○ USA (DE) 280-281 L 4
Middletown ○ USA (IA) 274-275 G 4
Middletown ○ USA (NY) 280-281 M 2
Middletown ○ USA (OH) 280-281 C 3
Middletown ○ USA (OH) 280-281 B 4
Middletown ○ USA (PA) 280-281 K 3
Middleville ○ USA (MI) 272-273 D 5
Middleville ○ USA (NY) 278-279 G 5
Middlewood ○ CDN (NS) 240-241 L 6
Midfield ○ USA (TX) 266-267 L 5
Midi, Canal du < F 90-91 J 10
Mid-Indian Basin ≃ 12 F 5
Mid-Indian Ridge ≃ 12 E 5
Midi-Pyrénées ▫ F 90-91 H 10
Midkiff ○ USA (TX) 266-267 F 2
Midland ○ AUS 176-177 C 5
Midland ○ CDN (ONT) 238-239 F 4
Midland ○ USA (CA) 248-249 K 6
Midland ○ USA (MI) 272-273 E 4
Midland ○ USA (SD) 260-261 E 2
Midland ○ USA (TX) 266-267 E 2
Midlander II AUS 178-179 H 2
Midlands ▫ ZW 218-219 E 4
Midlothian ○ USA (TX) 264-265 G 6
Midnab, al- ○ KSA 130-131 J 5
Midongy ⊥ RM 222-223 E 9
Midongy Atsimo ○ RM 222-223 E 9
Midouze ~ F 90-91 G 10
Mid-Pacific-Seamounts ≃ 14-15 H 5
Midpines ○ USA (CA) 248-249 E 2
Midsandur ○ IS 86-87 c 2
Midsayap ○ RP 160-161 F 9
Midsommersø ○ GRØ 26-27 g 2
Midu ○ VRC 142-143 M 3
Midvale Summit ▲ USA (ID) 252-253 B 2
Midville ○ USA (GA) 284-285 H 4
Midway ○ USA (AL) 284-285 E 4
Midway ○ USA (AL) 284-285 C 5
Midway ○ USA (MS) 268-269 K 4
Midway ○ USA (TX) 268-269 E 5
Midway Corner ○ USA (AR) 276-277 E 5
Midway Island ⌒ USA 14-15 L 5
Midway Islands ⌒ USA 20-21 Q 1
Midway Range ▲ CDN (BC) 230-231 L 4
Midway Stores ○ USA (SD) 260-261 J 3
Midway Well ○ USA (CA) 248-249 K 6
Midwest ○ USA (WY) 252-253 M 3
Midwest City ○ USA (OK) 264-265 G 3
Midwestern Highway II AUS 180-181 H 3
Midyat ☆• TR 128-129 J 4
Midyobo ○ GQ 210-211 C 3
Midžor ▲• YU 100-101 J 3
Miechów ○• PL 92-93 Q 3
Międzyrzec Podlaski ○ PL 92-93 R 3
Międzyrzecz ○• PL 92-93 N 2
Mielec ○• PL 92-93 Q 3
Miélékouka ○ RCB 210-211 E 3
Miembwe ○ EAT 214-215 J 5
Mier ○ MEX 50-51 K 4
Miera ○ USA (NM) 256-257 J 4
Miercurea-Ciuc ☆• RO 102-103 D 4
Mieres ○ E 98-99 E 3
Mier y Noriega ○ MEX 50-51 J 6
Mierzeja Wiślana ⌣ PL 92-93 P 1
Mī'ēso ○ ETH 208-209 E 4
Miette Hot Springs ∴• CDN (ALB) 228-229 R 3
Mifflin ○ USA (TN) 276-277 G 5
Migdol ○ ZA 220-221 G 3
Migliónico ○• I 100-101 F 4
Migole ○ EAT 214-215 H 4
Migoli ○ EAT (SIN) 212-213 E 6
Migori ○ EAK 212-213 E 4
Migration Lake ○ CDN 30-31 P 3
Miguasha, Parc Provencial de ⊥ CDN (QUE) 240-241 J 2
Miguel Alemán, Presa < MEX 52-53 F 2
Miguel Alves ○ BR 68-69 G 4
Miguel Auza ○ MEX 50-51 H 5
Miguel Calmon ○ BR 68-69 H 7
Miguel Hidalgo, Presa < MEX 50-51 E 4
Miguel Leão ○ BR 68-69 G 4
Miguelópolis ○ BR 72-73 F 6
Miguel Pereira ○ BR 72-73 J 7
Miguel y Alex Tejada, Meteorite craters: • BOL 70-71 D 6
Migues ○ ROU 78-79 M 3
Mihajlov ☆• RUS 94-95 Q 4
Mihajlovgrad = Monatana ☆ BG 102-103 C 6
Mihajlovka ○ KA 136-137 M 3
Mihajlovka ○ RUS 116-117 M 10
Mihajlovka ○ RUS 122-123 D 7
Mihajlovka ○ RUS (SAH) 120-121 E 3
Mihajlovka ○ RUS (VLG) 102-103 N 2
Mihajlovka, Podyem- ○ RUS 96-97 G 7
Mihajlovo ○ BG 102-103 C 6
Mihajlovsk ○ RUS 96-97 L 5
Mihajlovskij ☆ RUS 124-125 L 3
Mihalıççık ○ TR 128-129 D 3
Mihalkino ○ RUS 112-113 L 2
Mihama ○ J 152-153 G 7
Mihintale ○ CL 140-141 J 6
Mihnevo ○ RUS 94-95 P 4
Miho-wan ≈ 152-153 E 7
Mihrād, al- ⊥ KSA 132-133 H 3
Mihuanoyacu ○ EC 64-65 D 2
Mihumo Chini ○ EAT 214-215 K 5
Mijaki, Kirgiz- ☆ RUS 96-97 J 7
Mijaly ☆ KA 96-97 H 9
Mijek ○ MA 196-197 D 3
Mikado ○ CDN (SAS) 232-233 Q 4
Mikasa ○ J 152-153 J 3
Mikaševičy ○ BY 94-95 K 5
Mikawa-wan ≈ 152-153 G 7
Mikčangda ~ RUS 108-109 Y 7
Mikese ○ EAT 214-215 J 4
Miki ○ ZRE 212-213 B 5
Mikindani ○ EAT 214-215 L 6
Mikkeli ☆ FIN 88-89 J 6
Mikkwa River ~ CDN 32-33 N 3
Miknās ☆ MA 188-189 J 4
Mikojana, zaliv ○ RUS 108-109 e 2
Mikonos ⌒ GR 100-101 K 6
Mikulkin, mys ▲ RUS 88-89 T 3
Mikumi ○ EAT 214-215 J 4
Mikumi Lodge ○ EAT 214-215 J 4
Mikumi National Park ⊥ EAT 214-215 J 4
Mikumi-sanmyaku ▲ J 152-153 H 6
Mikun' ○ RUS 88-89 V 5
Mikuni ○ J 152-153 G 6
Mikwam River ~ CDN (ONT) 236-237 H 3
Mil' ~ RUS 120-121 E 3
Mil', Ust'- ○ RUS 120-121 E 4
Mila ☆ DZ 190-191 F 2
Milaca ○ USA (MN) 270-271 E 5
Milach, In- < RMM 196-197 K 6
Miladummadulu Atoll ⌒ MV 140-141 B 4
Milagres ○ BR (BAH) 72-73 L 2
Milagres ○ BR (CEA) 68-69 J 5
Milagro ○ EC 64-65 C 3
Milagro ○ USA (NM) 256-257 K 4
Milagro, El ○ MEX 50-51 H 3
Milagros ○ RP 160-161 E 6
Milait ⌒ GRØ 28-29 Y 3
Milam ○ USA (TX) 268-269 G 5
Milan ○ USA (GA) 284-285 G 4
Milan ○ USA (IN) 274-275 N 5
Milan ○ USA (KS) 262-263 J 7
Milan ○ USA (MI) 272-273 F 5
Milan ○ USA (MN) 270-271 C 5
Milan ○ USA (MO) 274-275 E 4
Milan ○ USA (NM) 256-257 H 3
Milan ○ USA (TN) 276-277 G 5
Milan = Milano ☆ ••• I 100-101 B 2
Milando ○ ANG 216-217 D 4
Milando, Reserva Especial do ⊥ ANG 216-217 D 4
Milang ○ AUS 180-181 E 3
Milange ○ MOC 218-219 H 3
Milange ○ ZRE 212-213 A 5
Milango ~ RI 164-165 G 3
Milano ☆ ••• I 100-101 B 2
Milano ○ USA (TX) 266-267 L 3
Milanoa ○ RM 222-223 F 4
Milas ☆• TR 128-129 B 4
Milazzo ○ I 100-101 E 5
Milbank ○ USA (SD) 260-261 K 1
Milbanke Sound ≈ 32-33 F 5
Milbanke Sound ≈ CDN 228-229 F 4
Milbridge ○ USA (ME) 278-279 O 4
Milly Milly ○ AUS 176-177 D 3
Milburn ○ USA (NE) 262-263 G 3
Milden ○ CDN (SAS) 232-233 L 4
Mildet ○ MA 188-189 J 4
Mildred ○ CDN (SAS) 232-233 L 2
Mildred ○ USA (MT) 250-251 P 5
Mildura ○ AUS 180-181 G 3
Mildura Gemstone Deposit • AUS 176-177 F 6
Milē ○ ETH 208-209 E 3
Mile ○ VRC 156-157 C 4
Milepa ○ EAT 214-215 F 5
Miles ○ AUS 178-179 L 4
Miles ○ USA (TX) 266-267 G 2
Miles ○ USA (WA) 244-245 G 3
Miles, Cape ▲ CDN 24-25 d 6
Miles City ○ USA (FL) 286-287 H 5
Miles City ○ USA (MT) 250-251 O 5
Milestone ○ CDN (SAS) 232-233 O 6
Milesville ○ USA (SD) 260-261 E 2
Milet ∴• TR 128-129 B 4
Mileura ○ AUS 176-177 D 3
Milē Wenz ~ ETH 208-209 E 3
Milford ○ USA (CA) 246-247 E 3
Milford ○ USA (CT) 280-281 N 2
Milford ○ USA (DE) 280-281 L 5
Milford ○ USA (IA) 274-275 C 1
Milford ○ USA (IL) 274-275 L 4
Milford ○ USA (MA) 278-279 K 6
Milford ○ USA (MI) 272-273 F 5
Milford ○ USA (NE) 262-263 J 4
Milford ○ USA (PA) 280-281 M 2
Milford ○ USA (UT) 254-255 B 5
Milford Lake ○ USA (KS) 262-263 J 5
Milford Sound ≈ 182 A 6
Milford Sound ○ NZ 182 A 6
Milgarra ○ AUS 174-175 F 6
Milgun ○ AUS 176-177 E 2
Mil'guveem ~ RUS 112-113 R 2
Milhara ○ MOC 218-219 K 2
Milhāt ○ IRQ 128-129 K 5
Miliana ○ DZ 190-191 D 2
Milikapiti ⚔ AUS 172-173 K 1
Milim ○ PNG 183 F 3
Milingimbi ⚔ AUS 174-175 C 3
Milijutkêjveem ~ RUS 112-113 W 3
Milkengay Lake ○ AUS 180-181 F 2
Mil'kovo ☆ RUS 120-121 S 6
Milk River ~ 32-33 P 7
Milk River ○ CDN (ALB) 232-233 F 6
Milk River ~ USA (MT) 250-251 J 3
Milk River ~ USA (MT) 250-251 F 3
Milk River Ridge ▲ CDN (ALB) 232-233 F 6
Mill ○ USA (OK) 264-265 H 4
Millaa Millaa ○• AUS 174-175 H 5
Millaroo ○ AUS 174-175 J 7
Millarville ○ CDN (ALB) 232-233 D 5
Millas ○ F 90-91 J 10
Millau ○ F 90-91 J 9
Millboro ○ USA (VA) 280-281 G 5
Millbrook ○ CDN (ONT) 238-239 G 4
Millburne ○ USA (WY) 252-253 H 5
Mill City ○ USA (OR) 244-245 C 6
Milledgeville ○ USA (GA) 284-285 G 3
Milledgeville ○ USA (IL) 274-275 J 3
Mille Lacs, Lac des ○ CDN (ONT) 234-235 N 6
Mille Lacs Lake ○ USA (MN) 270-271 E 4
Millen ○ USA (GA) 284-285 J 4
Millenbeck ○ USA (VA) 280-281 K 6
Miller ○ USA (NE) 262-263 G 4
Miller ○ USA (OK) 264-265 J 4
Miller ○ USA (SD) 260-261 H 2
Miller ○ ZA 220-221 F 6
Miller, Mount ▲ USA 20-21 T 6
Millerdale ○ CDN (SAS) 232-233 K 4
Millerovo ○ RUS 102-103 M 3
Millersburg ○ USA (OH) 280-281 E 3
Millersburg ○ USA (PA) 280-281 K 3
Millers Corners ○ USA (PA) 280-281 H 4
Millers Creek ~ AUS 178-179 C 5
Millers Creek Reservoir < USA (TX) 264-265 E 5
Millersview ○ USA (TX) 266-267 H 2
Millerton ○ BS 54-55 H 3
Millerton ○ CDN (NB) 240-241 K 4
Millerton ○ USA (NY) 280-281 N 2
Millertown ○ CDN (NFL) 242-243 M 4
Millertown Junction ○ CDN (NFL) 242-243 M 3
Millet ○ CDN (ALB) 232-233 E 2
Millett ○ USA (TX) 266-267 H 5
Millevaches, Plateau de ▲ F 90-91 H 9
Millican ○ USA (OR) 244-245 E 7
Millicent ○ AUS 180-181 F 4
Millie ○ AUS 178-179 K 5
Milligan College ○ USA (TN) 282-283 E 4
Milligan Hills ▲ CDN 32-33 K 3
Millington ○ USA (TN) 276-277 F 5
Millinocket ○ USA (ME) 278-279 N 3
Millinocket Lake ○ USA (ME) 278-279 N 3
Mill Iron ○ USA (MT) 250-251 P 6
Mill Island ⌒ ARK 16 G 11
Millmerran ○ AUS 178-179 L 4
Millport ○ USA (AL) 284-285 B 3
Millrose ○ AUS 176-177 F 3
Millry ○ USA (AL) 284-285 B 5
Millsboro ○ USA (DE) 280-281 L 5
Mills Lake ○ CDN 30-31 K 5
Millston ○ USA (WI) 270-271 H 6
Millstream ○ AUS 172-173 C 6
Millstream Chichester National Park ⊥ AUS 172-173 C 6
Milltown ○ CDN (NFL) 242-243 N 5
Milltown ○ USA (IN) 274-275 M 6
Millungera ○ AUS 174-175 F 6
Mill Village ○ CDN (NS) 240-241 L 6
Millville ○ CDN (NB) 240-241 H 4
Millville ○ USA (NJ) 280-281 M 4
Millville ○ USA (PA) 280-281 K 2
Millwood ○ CDN (MAN) 234-235 B 4
Millwood ○ USA (GA) 284-285 H 5
Millwood ○ USA (OH) 280-281 D 3
Millwood ○ USA (WA) 244-245 H 3
Millwood Lake ○ USA (AR) 276-277 A 7
Millyewilpa Lake ○ AUS 178-179 D 4
Milly Milly ○ AUS 176-177 D 3
Milne Bay ≈ 183 F 6
Milne Inlet ≈ 24-25 g 4
Milne Land ⊥ GRØ 26-27 m 8
Milner Lake ○ CDN 38-39 L 2
Milnesand ○ USA (NM) 256-257 M 5
Milnor ○ USA (ND) 258-259 K 5
Milo ○ CDN (ALB) 232-233 F 5
Milo ○ ETH 208-209 F 3
Milo ~ RG 202-203 F 4
Milo ○ USA (ME) 278-279 N 3
Milo ○ USA (OK) 264-265 G 4
Milodon, Cueva del • RCH 80 D 5
Milogradovo ○ RUS 122-123 F 7
Milolii ○ USA (HI) 288 K 5
Milos ⌒ GR 100-101 K 6
Milos ⌒ GR 100-101 K 6
Milot ○ RH 54-55 J 5
Milparinka ○ AUS 178-179 F 5
Milpitas ○ USA (CA) 248-249 C 2
Milpitas Wash ~ USA (CA) 248-249 J 6
Milroy ○ USA (MN) 270-271 C 6
Mil'skaja ravnina ⌣ AZ 128-129 M 3
Milton ○ CDN (NFL) 242-243 P 4
Milton ○ CDN (NS) 240-241 L 6
Milton ○ NZ 182 B 7
Milton ○ USA (DE) 280-281 L 5
Milton ○ USA (FL) 286-287 B 1
Milton ○ USA (IA) 274-275 F 4
Milton ○ USA (ND) 258-259 J 3
Milton ○ USA (OK) 264-265 K 3
Milton ○ USA (PA) 280-281 K 2
Miltona ○ USA (MN) 270-271 C 4
Milton-Freewater ○ USA (OR) 244-245 G 5
Milton Lake ○ CDN 30-31 S 6
Miltonvale ○ USA (KS) 262-263 J 5
Miltou ○ TCH 206-207 C 3
Miluo ○ VRC 156-157 H 2
Milverton ○ CDN (ONT) 238-239 E 5
Milwaukee ○• USA (WI) 274-275 L 1
Milwaukie ○ USA (OR) 244-245 C 5
Mimbelly ○ RCB 210-211 F 2
Mimbres River ~ USA (NM) 256-257 H 6
Mimili (Everard Park) ⚔ AUS 176-177 M 3
Mimiska Lake ○ CDN (ONT) 234-235 P 3
Mi Mi Rocks ▲ AUS 176-177 H 3
Mimizan ○ F 90-91 G 9
Mimongo ○ G 210-211 C 4
Mimouna, Kef ▲ DZ 190-191 D 4
Mimpoutou ○ RCB 210-211 F 2
Mims ○ USA (FL) 286-287 J 3
Mina ~ RI 166-167 C 7
Mina ○ USA (NV) 246-247 G 5
Mina ○ USA (SD) 260-261 H 1
Minā', al- ○ RL 128-129 F 5
Mina, Oued ~ DZ 190-191 C 3
Mina, Salar de la ○ RA 76-77 D 4
Minā' 'Abdallāh ○ KWT 130-131 L 3
Mināb ○• IR 134-135 G 5
Mina Clavero ○ RA 76-77 E 6
Minaçu ○ BR 72-73 F 2
Mina Exploradora ○ RCH 76-77 C 3
Minahasa Semenao djung ~ RI 164-165 G 3
Mina Jebel Ali ○ UAE 134-135 F 6
Minaki ○ CDN (ONT) 234-235 J 5
Mina la Casualidad ○ RA 76-77 C 3
Mina la Juanita ○ RCH 78-79 D 3
Minam ○ USA (OR) 244-245 H 5
Minami-Alps National Park ⊥ J 152-153 H 7
Minami-Daitō ○ J 152-153 D 12
Minamikayabe ○ J 152-153 J 4
Minami-Tane ○ J 152-153 D 9
Minas ○ C 54-55 G 4
Minas ○ RI 162-163 D 4
Minas ☆ ROU 78-79 M 3
Minas, Cerro las ▲ HN 52-53 K 4
Minas, Sierra de las ▲ GCA 52-53 J 4
Minas Basin ≈ 38-39 M 6
Minas Basin ≈ CDN 240-241 L 5
Minas Channel ≈ CDN 240-241 L 5
Minas de Barroterán ○ MEX 50-51 J 4
Minas de Corrales ○ ROU 76-77 K 6
Minas del Oro • CO 60-61 E 4
Minas de Matahambre ○ C 54-55 D 3
Minas do Mimoso ○ BR 68-69 H 7
Minas Gerais ▫ BR 72-73 H 4
Minas Novas ○ BR 72-73 J 4
Minā' Su'ud ○ KWT 130-131 L 3
Minatina Batoche National Historic Park • CDN (SAS) 232-233 M 3
Minatitlán ○ MEX (COL) 52-53 B 2
Minatitlán ○• MEX (VER) 52-53 G 3
Minbu ○ MYA 142-143 J 5
Min Buri ○ THA 158-159 F 4
Minburn ○ CDN (ALB) 232-233 G 2
Minch, The ≈ 90-91 E 3
Minch, The Little ≈ 90-91 D 3
Minchika ○ WAN 204-205 K 3
Minchinābād ○ PK 138-139 D 4
Minchinmávida, Volcán ▲ RCH 78-79 C 7
Minchumina, Lake ○ USA 20-21 O 5
Minco ○ USA (OK) 264-265 G 3
Mindanao ⌒ RP 160-161 G 8
Mindanao Sea ≈ 160-161 E 10
Mindelo ○• CV 202-203 B 5
Minden ○ CDN (ONT) 238-239 G 4
Minden ○• D 92-93 K 2
Minden ○ USA (IA) 274-275 C 3
Minden ○ USA (LA) 268-269 G 4
Minden ○ USA (NE) 262-263 H 4
Minderla ○ RUS 116-117 F 7
Mindif ○• CAM 206-207 B 3
Mindif, Dent de ▲• CAM 206-207 B 3
Mindik ○ PNG 183 D 4
Mindiptana ○ RI 166-167 L 4
Mindjik ○ TCH 206-207 E 3
Mindo ○ EC 64-65 C 2
Mindon ○ MYA 142-143 J 6
Mindona Lake ○ AUS 180-181 G 2
Mindoro ⌒ RP 160-161 D 6
Mindoro Strait ≈ 160-161 D 6
Mindouli ○ RCB 210-211 E 6
Mindourou ○ CAM 210-211 D 2
Minduri ○ BR 72-73 H 6
Mindživan ○ AZ 128-129 M 3
Mine ○ J (NAG) 152-153 C 7
Mine ○ J (YMG) 152-153 D 7
Mine ○ USA (AZ) 256-257 A 5
Mine Centre ○ CDN (ONT) 234-235 L 6
Minehead ○ GB 90-91 F 6
Mineiros ○ BR 72-73 D 4
Mine New Hosco ○ CDN (QUE) 236-237 L 3
Mineola ○ USA (TX) 264-265 J 6
Mineral ○ USA (CA) 246-247 D 3
Mineral, Cerro ▲ RCH 80 E 2
Mineral Hot Springs ○ USA (CO) 254-255 K 5
Mineral'nye Vody ○ RUS 126-127 E 5
Mineral Point ○ USA (WI) 274-275 H 2
Mineral Springs ○ USA (AR) 276-277 B 7
Mineral Wells ○ USA (TX) 264-265 F 6
Miner River ~ CDN 20-21 Z 2
Miners Bird Sanctuary • CDN (ONT) 238-239 C 6
Miners Point ▲ USA 22-23 U 4
Minersville ○ USA (UT) 254-255 C 5
Minerva ○ USA (NY) 278-279 H 5
Minerva ○ USA (OH) 280-281 E 3
Minerva, Presa < C 54-55 F 3
Minette, Bay ○ USA (AL) 284-285 C 6
Minfeng ○ VRC 144-145 D 2
Minford ○ USA (OH) 280-281 D 5
Minga ○ Z 218-219 F 2
Minga ○ ZRE 214-215 D 6
Mingala ○ RCA 206-207 E 6
Mingan ○ CDN (QUE) 242-243 D 2
Mingan, Îles de ⌒ CDN (QUE) 242-243 E 2
Mingan, Rivière ~ CDN (QUE) 242-243 E 2
Minganja ○ ANG 216-217 F 6
Mingao ○ CO 60-61 H 6
Mingary ○ AUS 180-181 F 2
Mingbuloq ○ US 136-137 H 3
Mingbuloq cuкurligi ⊥ US 136-137 H 3
Mingechevir = Mingaçevir ○• AZ 128-129 M 2
Mingechevirskoe vodohranilišče < AZ 128-129 M 2
Mingela ○ AUS 174-175 J 6
Mingenew ○ AUS 176-177 C 4
Minggang ○ VRC 154-155 J 5
Minghoshan = Dunhuang ○• VRC 146-147 M 5
Mingin ○ MYA 142-143 J 4
Ming Ming ○ PNG 183 D 3
Mingo Lake ○ CDN 36-37 N 2
Mingo National Wildlife Refuge ⊥ USA (MO) 276-277 E 3
Mingora ○• PK 138-139 D 2
Mingoyo ○ EAT 214-215 K 6
Ming's Bight ○ CDN (NFL) 242-243 M 3
Mingshui ○ VRC 150-151 E 4
Mingun ○ CAM 204-205 K 6
Mingun ○•• MYA 142-143 J 4
Mingxi ○ MOC 218-219 L 2
Mingxi ○ VRC 156-157 K 3
Minhe Huizu Tuzu Zizhixian ○ VRC 154-155 C 3
Minh Hải ☆ VN 158-159 H 6
Minh Hòa, Hòn ⌒ VN 158-159 H 5
Minhla ○ MYA 142-143 J 6
Minhla ○ MYA 158-159 C 2
Minho, Rio ~ P 98-99 C 4
Minichinas Hills ▲ CDN (SAS) 232-233 M 3
Minicoy Island ⌒ IND 140-141 E 6
Minidoka ○ USA (ID) 252-253 E 4
Minier ○ USA (IL) 274-275 J 4
Minigwal, Lake ~ AUS 176-177 G 4
Minilya Bridge Roadhouse ○ AUS 176-177 B 1
Minilya River ~ AUS 176-177 C 1
Mininian ○ CI 202-203 G 4
Miniota ○ CDN (MAN) 234-235 B 4
Minipi Lake ○ CDN 38-39 O 2
Minisiare, Caño ~ CO 60-61 G 6
Minissa ○ BF 202-203 J 3
Miniss Lake ○ CDN (ONT) 234-235 N 4
Ministro Ramos Mexía ○ RA 78-79 F 6
Minitas, Playa ⊥• DOM 54-55 L 5
Minja ~ RUS 118-119 D 7
Min'jar ○ RUS 96-97 K 6
Min Jiang ~ VRC 154-155 C 5
Min Jiang ~ VRC 156-157 L 3
Min Jiang ~ VRC 156-157 D 2
Minjilang ⚔ AUS 172-173 L 1
Minjip ○ PNG 183 B 3
Minlaton ○ AUS 180-181 D 3
Minle ○ VRC 154-155 B 2
Minna ☆ WAN 204-205 G 4
Minneapolis ○ USA (KS) 262-263 J 5
Minneapolis ○• USA (MN) 270-271 E 6
Minnedosa ○ CDN (MAN) 234-235 D 4
Minneola ○ USA (KS) 262-263 F 7
Minneota ○ USA (MN) 270-271 C 6
Minnesota ○ USA (MN) 270-271 B 4
Minnesota River ~ USA (MN) 270-271 C 6
Minnesott Beach ○ USA (NC) 282-283 L 5
Minnewanka, Lake ○ CDN (ALB) 232-233 C 4
Minnewaukan ○ USA (ND) 258-259 H 3
Minnie Creek ○ AUS 176-177 C 2
Minnies Out Station ○ AUS 174-175 G 5
Minnipa ○ AUS 180-181 C 2
Minnitaki Lake ○ CDN (ONT) 234-235 M 4
Minnkri ○ RMM 196-197 J 6
Miño, Río ~ E 98-99 D 3
Miñoes ○ RA 76-77 H 6
Minong ○ USA (WI) 270-271 G 4
Minonk ○ USA (IL) 274-275 J 4
Minor Hill ○ USA (TN) 276-277 H 5
Minot ○ USA (ND) 258-259 F 3
Minqin ○ VRC 154-155 C 2
Minqing ○ VRC 156-157 L 3
Minquan ○ VRC 154-155 J 4
Min Shan ▲ VRC 154-155 C 5
Minsk ★ BY 94-95 K 5
Mińsk Mazowiecki ○ PL 92-93 Q 2
Minster ○ USA (OH) 280-281 B 3
Minstrel Island ○ CDN (BC) 230-231 C 3
Mintabie ○ AUS 176-177 M 3
Minṭaqat ash Shu'bah ⊥ LAR 192-193 L 2
Minṭaqat Umm Khuwayt ⊥ LAR 192-193 L 2
Mint Hill ○ USA (NC) 282-283 G 5
Mintirib, al- ○ OM 132-133 L 2
Minto ○ CDN (MAN) 234-235 D 5
Minto ○ CDN (NB) 240-241 J 4
Minto ○ CDN (YT) 20-21 W 5
Minto ○ USA (ND) 258-259 K 3
Minto, Lac ○ CDN 36-37 M 6
Minto Inlet ≈ 24-25 N 5
Mintom II ○ CAM 210-211 D 2
Minton ○ CDN (SAS) 232-233 O 6
Mintonas ○ CDN (MAN) 234-235 B 2
Mintonsville ○ USA (NC) 282-283 L 4
Minturn ○ USA (CO) 254-255 J 4
Minūdasht ○ IR 136-137 D 6
Minusinsk ☆ RUS 116-117 E 9
Minvoul ○ G 210-211 D 2
Min Xian ○ VRC 154-155 D 4
Minyā, al- ☆ ET 194-195 E 3
Minzawi, Wādī al- ~ OM 132-133 H 5
Minž gol ~ MAU 148-149 H 3
Mio ○ USA (MI) 272-273 E 3
Miocene ○ CDN (BC) 228-229 N 4
Miosnum, Pulau ⌒ RI 166-167 H 2
Mipia, Lake ○ AUS 178-179 E 3
Miqdādiya, al- ☆ IRQ 128-129 L 6
Miquelon ○ CDN (QUE) 236-237 M 3
Miquelon, Cap ▲ CDN (F) 242-243 M 5
Miquihuana ○ MEX 50-51 K 6
Mira ○ EC 64-65 C 1
Mira ○ P 98-99 C 4
Mira, buhta ≈ 110-111 a 2
Mira, Río ~ EC 64-65 C 1
Mirabel ○ CDN (QUE) 238-239 L 3
Mirabela ○ BR 72-73 H 4
Miracema ○ BR 72-73 J 6
Miracema de Tocantins ○ BR 68-69 D 6
Miracosta ○ PE 64-65 C 5
Mirador ○ BR (AMA) 64-65 F 4
Mirador ○ BR (MAR) 68-69 F 5
Mirador, El ∴• GCA 52-53 K 3
Mirador, Parque Nacional de ⊥ BR 68-69 F 5
Mirador-Dos Lagunas-Río Azul, Parque Nacional ⊥•• GCA 52-53 K 3
Miradouro ○ BR 72-73 J 6
Miraflores ○ BR 66-67 E 4
Miraflores ○ CO (BOY) 60-61 E 5
Miraflores ○ CO (VAU) 66-67 B 2
Mirage Bay ○ CDN 28-29 E 3
Mirāglia, Portella della ▲ I 100-101 E 6
Miragoâne ○ RH 54-55 J 5
Miraj ○ IND 140-141 F 2
Mira Loma ○ USA (CA) 248-249 G 5
Miramar ○ BR 66-67 G 5
Miramar ○ RA 78-79 L 5
Miramichi Bay ≈ 38-39 M 5
Miramichi Bay ≈ CDN 240-241 K 3
Miramichi River ~ CDN (NB) 240-241 J 4
Miram Shāh ○ PK 138-139 C 3
Miran ○ PK 138-139 C 4
Miran ○ VRC 146-147 J 6
Miranda ○ BR (GSU) 70-71 J 7

362 Metlakatla — Miranda

Miranda ○ BR (MAR) 68-69 F 3
Miranda ○ YV 60-61 G 2
Miranda, Lake ○ AUS 176-177 F 3
Miranda, Rio ~ BR 70-71 J 7
Miranda de Ebro ○ E 98-99 F 3
Miranda do Douro ○ P 98-99 D 4
Miranda Downs ○ AUS 174-175 F 5
Mirandela ○ BR 68-69 J 7
Mirandela ○ P 98-99 D 4
Mirandiba ○ BR 68-69 J 6
Mirando City ○ USA (TX) 266-267 H 6
Mirandópolis ○ BR 72-73 E 6
Mirani ○ AUS 178-179 K 1
Miranle da Sura ○ BR 70-71 F 2
Miranorte ○ BR 68-69 D 6
Mirante ○ BR 72-73 K 3
Mirante do Paranapanema ○ BR 72-73 E 7
Mira por vos Cays ⌒ BS 54-55 H 3
Mira por vos Passage ≈ 54-55 H 3
Mirassol ○ BR 72-73 F 6
Mirassol d'Oeste ○ BR 70-71 H 4
Miratu, Área Indígena X BR 66-67 E 4
Miratuba, Lago ○ BR 66-67 H 4
Miravalles ▲ E 98-99 D 3
Miravalles, Volcán ▲ CR 52-53 B 6
Mir Bačče Kūt ○ AFG 138-139 B 2
Mir-Bašir = Terter ○ AZ 128-129 M 2
Mirbāṭ ○ OM 132-133 J 5
Mirebalais ○ RH 54-55 J 5
Mirğāve ○ IR 134-135 J 4
Mirhleft ○ MA 188-189 G 6
Miri ○ MAL 162-163 K 2
Miria ○ RN 198-199 D 6
Miriālgūda ○ IND 140-141 H 2
Miriam Vale ○ AUS 178-179 L 3
Mirim, Lagoa ○ BR 74-75 D 9
Mirim, Lagoa do ○ BR 74-75 F 7
Mirim do Abufari, Paraná ~ BR 66-67 F 5
Mirimire ○ YV 60-61 G 2
Mirina ○ GR 100-101 K 5
Miriñay, Esteros ○ RA 76-77 J 5
Miriñay, Río ~ RA 76-77 J 5
Mirinzal ○ BR 68-69 F 3
Miritiparaná, Río ~ CO 66-67 B 3
Miriye, togga ~ SP 208-209 G 3
Mirjan ○ IND 140-141 F 3
Mirnoe, ozero ○ RUS 114-115 P 6
Mirnyj ○ ARK 16 G 10
Mirnyj ☆• RUS 118-119 F 4
Mirobia ○ RI 166-167 G 3
Mirogi ○ EAK 212-213 E 4
Miroki ○ US 136-137 K 5
Mirond Lake ○ CDN 34-35 E 3
Mirong ○ VRC 156-157 C 5
Mirosławiec ○ PL 92-93 O 2
Mirowāl ○ PK 138-139 E 4
Mirpur Batoro ○ PK 138-139 B 7
Mirpur Khās ○• PK 138-139 B 7
Mirpur Mathelo ○• PK 138-139 B 5
Mirpur Sakro ○ PK 134-135 M 6
Mirra Mitta Bore ○ AUS 178-179 E 4
Mirrngadja Village X AUS 174-175 C 3
Mirror ○ CDN (ALB) 232-233 E 3
Mirror River ~ CDN 32-33 Q 3
Mirrote ○ MOC 218-219 K 1
Mirsale ○ SP 208-209 H 6
Mirtna ○ AUS 178-179 J 1
Mirtóo Pélagos ≈ 100-101 J 6
Miruro ○ MOC 218-219 F 2
Mirwāh ○ PK 138-139 B 7
Mirzā 'Arab, Kūh-e ▲ IR 134-135 J 2
Mirzapur ○ IND 142-143 C 3
Misāha, Bi'r < ET 194-195 C 6
Misaine Bank ≃ 38-39 P 6
Misaki ○ EAT 212-213 E 6
Misaki ○ J (EHI) 152-153 E 8
Misaki ○ J (OSA) 152-153 F 7
Misantla ○ MEX (VER) 52-53 F 2
Misantla ∴• MEX (VER) 52-53 F 2
Misau ○ WAN 204-205 J 3
Misawa ○ J 152-153 J 4
Misaw Lake ○ CDN 30-31 S 6
Miscou Centre ○ CDN (NB) 240-241 L 3
Miscou Island ⌒ CDN (NB) 240-241 L 3
Miscou Point ▲ CDN (NB) 240-241 L 2
Misehkov River ~ CDN (ONT) 234-235 O 3
Misekumaw Lake ○ CDN 30-31 S 6
Misele ○ ZRE 210-211 F 6
Misgund ○ ZA 220-221 F 6
Mishagomish, Lac ○ CDN (QUE) 236-237 M 2
Mishagua, Río ~ PE 64-65 F 7
Mishamo ○ EAT 212-213 C 6
Mishan ○ VRC 150-151 H 5
Mishanattawa River ~ CDN 34-35 N 3
Mishibishu Lake ○ CDN (ONT) 236-237 C 4
Mishicot ○ USA (WI) 270-271 L 6
Mi-shima ⌒ J 152-153 D 7
Misi ○ FIN 88-89 J 3
Misiki ○ PNG 183 B 4
Misión, La ○ MEX 50-51 A 1
Mision de San Fernando ○ MEX 50-51 B 2
Misiones ◘ RA 76-77 K 4
Misiones, Sierra de ▲ RA 76-77 K 4
Miski ○ SUD 200-201 B 5
Miškino ☆ RUS 114-115 G 7
Miškino ☆ RUS (BAS) 96-97 J 6
Miskitos, Cayos ⌒ NIC 52-53 C 4
Miskolc ○ H 92-93 Q 4
Mismār ○ SUD 200-201 G 3
Mismiya, al- ○ SYR 128-129 G 6
Misol-Ha Waterfall ~• MEX 52-53 H 3
Misool, Pulau ⌒ RI 166-167 F 2
Misouminien ○ CI 202-203 J 6
Miṣrāfa, al- ○ Y 132-133 C 6
Misrātah ◘ LAR 192-193 F 1
Misrātah ☆ LAR 192-193 F 1
Misrikh ○ IND 142-143 B 2
Missanabie ○ CDN (ONT) 236-237 D 4
Misseni ○ RMM 202-203 G 4
Missi Falls ~ CDN 34-35 G 2
Missinaibi Lake ○ CDN (ONT) 236-237 E 4
Missinaibi Lake Provincial Park ⊥ CDN (ONT) 236-237 E 4
Missinaibi River ~ CDN (ONT) 236-237 F 2
Missinipe ○ CDN 34-35 D 3
Mission ○ CDN (BC) 230-231 G 4
Mission ○ USA (SD) 260-261 F 3
Mission ○ USA (TX) 266-267 J 7
Mission Beach ○ AUS 174-175 J 5
Missión de San Borja ○ MEX 50-51 C 3
Mission Indian Reservation X USA (CA) 248-249 G 6
Mission Mountains Wilderness Area ⊥ USA (MT) 250-251 F 4
Mission Ridge ○ USA (SD) 260-261 F 2
Mission Valley ○ USA (TX) 266-267 K 5
Mission Viejo ○ USA (CA) 248-249 G 6
Missira ○ SN (SO) 202-203 E 3
Missira ○ SN (SO) 202-203 D 3
Missisagi River ~ CDN (ONT) 238-239 B 2
Missisa Lake ○ CDN 34-35 O 4
Missisicabi, Rivière ~ CDN 38-39 E 3
Missisicabi, Rivière ~ CDN (QUE) 236-237 K 2
Mississagi Provincial Park ⊥ CDN (ONT) 238-239 C 2
Mississagi River Provincial Park ⊥ CDN (ONT) 236-237 F 5
Mississauga ○ CDN (ONT) 238-239 F 5
Mississinewa River ~ USA (IN) 274-275 N 4
Mississippi ◘ USA (MS) 268-269 L 5
Mississippi River ~ USA 4 E 5
Mississippi River Delta ⌣ USA (LA) 268-269 L 7
Mississippi Sound ≈ 48-49 D 4
Mississippi Sound ≈ USA 268-269 L 6
Missoula ○ USA (MT) 250-251 F 5
Missour ○ MA 188-189 K 4
Missouri ◘ USA (MO) 274-275 E 6
Missouri Breaks Wild and Scenic River ⊥ USA (MT) 250-251 K 4
Missouri City ○ USA (TX) 268-269 E 7
Missouri Coteau ⩦ CDN (SAS) 232-233 M 5
Missouri River ~ USA 4 D 4
Missouri Valley ○ USA (IA) 274-275 C 3
Mist ○ USA (OR) 244-245 B 5
Mistake Creek ~ AUS 178-179 G 2
Mistassibi, Rivière ~ CDN (QUE) 236-237 Q 2
Mistassini ○ CDN (QUE) 236-237 P 2
Mistassini ○ CDN (QUE) 240-241 C 2
Mistassini, Lac ○ CDN (QUE) 236-237 P 2
Mistassini, Rivière ~ CDN (QUE) 236-237 Q 3
Mistatim ○ CDN (SAS) 232-233 P 3
Mistawak, Lac ○ CDN (ONT) 236-237 K 3
Mistawak, Rivière ~ CDN (QUE) 236-237 K 3
Mistawasis Indian Reserve X CDN (SAS) 232-233 M 3
Mistelbach an der Zaya ○ A 92-93 O 4
Misterei ○ SUD 198-199 L 6
Misti, Volcán ▲ PE 70-71 B 5
Mistinibi Lake ○ CDN 36-37 R 7
Mistoles, Laguna los ○ RA 76-77 F 6
Mistra ••• GR 100-101 J 6
Mistuskwia River ~ CDN (ONT) 236-237 F 2
Misty Fiords National Monument ⊥• USA 32-33 E 4
Misty Fiords National Monument Wilderness ⊥• USA 32-33 E 4
Misty Lake ○ CDN 30-31 T 6
Misumba ○ ZRE 210-211 H 6
Misumi ○ J 152-153 D 8
Misvær ○ N 86-87 G 3
Mišwara ○ Y 132-133 D 6
Mita, Punta ▲ MEX 52-53 B 1
Mita Hills Dam < Z 218-219 E 2
Mitaho • RM 222-223 C 10
Mita-Mirim ○ BR 66-67 E 3
Mitande ○ MOC 218-219 J 2
Mitare ○ YV 60-61 F 2
Mitau = Jelgava ○•• LV 94-95 H 3
Mitchell ○ AUS 178-179 J 4
Mitchell ○ CDN (ONT) 238-239 D 5
Mitchell ○ USA (GA) 284-285 H 3
Mitchell ○ USA (IN) 274-275 M 6
Mitchell ○ USA (NE) 262-263 C 3
Mitchell ○ USA (OR) 244-245 E 6
Mitchell ○ USA (SD) 260-261 H 3
Mitchell, Mount ▲ USA (NC) 282-283 E 5
Mitchell and Alice Rivers National Park ⊥ AUS 174-175 G 4
Mitchell Highway II AUS 178-179 J 6
Mitchell Lake ○ CDN (BC) 228-229 O 4
Mitchell Lake < USA (AL) 284-285 D 4
Mitchell River ○ AUS 172-173 G 3
Mitchell River ~ AUS 172-173 G 3
Mitchell River ~ AUS 174-175 G 4
Mitchell River National Park ⊥ AUS 180-181 J 4
Mitchell's Bay ○ CDN (ONT) 238-239 C 6
Mitchells Brook ○ CDN (NFL) 242-243 P 5
Mitchelstown = Baile Mhistéala ○ IRL 90-91 C 5
Mitchinamécus, Lac ○ CDN (QUE) 236-237 N 5
Mitchinamecus, Rivière ~ CDN (QUE) 236-237 O 5
Mitémele, Río ~ GQ 210-211 C 3
Mit Ġamr ○ ET 194-195 E 2
Mithankot ○ PK 138-139 C 5
Mitha Tiwāna ○ PK 138-139 D 3
Mithi ○ PK 138-139 B 7
Mithimna ○ GR 100-101 L 5
Miti, Pulau ⌒ RI 164-165 L 3
Mitiamo ○ AUS 180-181 H 4
Mitiaro ⌒ NZ 13 M 4
Mitilíni ☆• GR 100-101 L 5
Mitji ~ SN 202-203 D 3
Mitjušiha, guba ○ RUS 108-109 F 5
Mitla ∴• MEX 52-53 F 3
Mitla, Laguna ≈ 52-53 D 3
Mitlikdavik ○ USA 20-21 K 1
Mito ☆ J 152-153 J 6
Mitoko ○ ZRE 210-211 H 2
Mitole ○ EAT 214-215 K 5
Mitomoni ○ EAT 214-215 H 6
Mitre, Peninsula ⌣ RA 80 H 7
Mitrofania Island ⌒ USA 22-23 R 5
Mitsamiouli ○ COM 222-223 C 3
Mitsinjo ○ RM 222-223 D 5
Mitsio, Nosy ⌒ RM 222-223 F 4
Mits'iwa ○• ER 200-201 J 5
Mits'iwa Channel ≈ 200-201 J 5
Mitsuishi ○ J 152-153 K 3
Mitsushima ○ J 152-153 C 7
Mittagong ○ AUS 180-181 L 3
Mitta Mitta ○ AUS 180-181 J 4
Mittiebah ○ AUS 174-175 D 6
Mittlintown ○ USA (PA) 280-281 J 3
Mitu ☆ CO 66-67 B 2
Mitumba, Monts ▲ ZRE 212-213 B 5
Mitunguu ○ EAK 212-213 F 4
Mitwaba ○ ZRE 214-215 D 5
Mityana ○ EAU 212-213 D 3
Mitzic ○ G 210-211 C 3
Miura-hanto ⌣ J 152-153 H 7
Mius ~ RUS 102-103 L 4
Mivo River ~ PNG 184 I b 2
Mixco ○•• GCA 52-53 J 4
Mixquiahuala ○ MEX 52-53 E 1
Mixteco, Río ~ MEX 52-53 E 2
Mixtlán ○ MEX 52-53 B 1
Miya ○ WAN 204-205 H 3
Miya-gawa ~ J 152-153 G 7
Miyāh, Wādī l- ~ ET 194-195 F 5
Miyake-shima ⌒ J 152-153 H 7
Miyako ○ J 152-153 J 5
Miyakonojō ○ J 152-153 D 9
Miyāndōab ○• IR 128-129 M 4
Miyāne ○• IR 128-129 M 4
Miyanoura-dake ▲ J 152-153 D 9
Miya-shima ⌒•• J 152-153 E 7
Miyazaki ☆ J 152-153 D 9
Miyazu ○ J 152-153 F 7
Miyi ○ VRC 156-157 C 3
Miyoshi ○ J 152-153 E 7
Miyun ○ VRC (BEI) 154-155 K 1
Miyun • VRC (BEI) 154-155 K 1
Mīzāni ○ AFG 134-135 M 2
Mizan Teferi ○ ETH 208-209 B 5
Mizdah ○ LAR 192-193 E 2
Mizen Head ▲ IRL 90-91 C 6
Mizhi ○ VRC 154-155 G 3
Mizil ○ RO 102-103 E 5
Mizo Hills ▲ IND 142-143 H 4
Mizoram ◘ IND 142-143 H 4
Mizpah ○ USA (MT) 250-251 O 5
Mizpah Creek ~ USA (MT) 250-251 O 5
Mizque ○ BOL 70-71 E 5
Mizque, Río ~ BOL 70-71 E 5
Mizur ○ RUS 126-127 F 6
Mizusawa ○ J 152-153 J 5
Mjadzel ☆ BY 94-95 K 4
Mjagostrov ⌒ RUS 88-89 N 4
Mjakit ○ RUS 120-121 P 3
Mjangad = Bajanhošuu ○ MAU 146-147 K 1
Mjanji ○ EAU 212-213 E 3
Mjatis' ~ RUS 110-111 Z 6
Mjölby ☆ S 86-87 G 7
Mjonga ~ EAT (MOR) 214-215 J 4
Mjörn ○ S 86-87 F 8
Mjøsa ○ N 86-87 E 6
Mjurjule ~ RUS 110-111 X 7
Mkambati Nature Reserve ⊥ ZA 220-221 J 5
Mkanga ○ EAT 214-215 H 4
Mkata ○ EAT 212-213 G 6
Mkata ~ EAT 214-215 J 4
Mkoani ○ EAT 212-213 G 6
Mkokotoni ○ EAT 214-215 K 3
Mkomazi Game Reserve ⊥ EAT 212-213 G 6
Mkondoa ~ EAT 214-215 J 4
Mkondowe ○ MW 214-215 H 6
Mkonjowano ○ EAT 214-215 K 6
Mkowe ○ EAK 212-213 H 5
Mkowela ○ EAT 214-215 K 6
Mkujani ○ EAT 212-213 G 6
Mkunumbi ○ EAK 212-213 H 5
Mkuranga ○ EAT 214-215 K 4
Mkushi ○ Z 218-219 E 1
Mkushi ~ Z 218-219 E 2
Mkushi River ○ Z 218-219 E 1
Mkuze ○ ZA (NTL) 220-221 L 3
Mkuze ~ ZA 220-221 K 3
Mkuzi Game Reserve ⊥ ZA 220-221 L 3
Mkwaja ○ EAT 212-213 G 6
Mladá Boleslav ○•• CZ 92-93 N 3
Mladenovac ○• YU 100-101 H 2
Mlala Hills ▲ EAT 214-215 F 4
Mlalo ○ EAT 212-213 G 6
Mlandizi ○ EAT 214-215 K 4
M'lang ○ RP 160-161 F 9
Mława ○ PL 92-93 Q 2
Mlelin ~ RUS 112-113 Q 2
Mlenganapas ▲ ZA 220-221 J 5
Mligasi ~ EAT 212-213 G 6
Mljet ⌒ HR 100-101 F 3
Mmabatho ☆ ZA 220-221 G 2
Mmadinare ○ RB 218-219 D 5
Mmamabula ○ RB 218-219 D 6
Mmashoro ○ RB 218-219 D 5
Mmathethe ○ RB 220-221 G 2
Mmatshumo ○ RB 218-219 C 5
Mnamuk ○ RI 166-167 D 3
Mnanzi ○ EAT 212-213 G 6
Mnarani ∴• EAK 212-213 G 5
Mnjoli Dam < SD 220-221 K 3
Mnogoveršinnyj ○ RUS 122-123 H 2
Mo ~ CAM 204-205 H 6
Mo ~ GH 202-203 L 5
Mô ~ RT 202-203 L 5
Moa ○ C 54-55 H 4
Moa ~ WAL 202-203 E 6
Moa, Pulau ⌒ RI 166-167 E 6
Moa, Rio ~ BR 64-65 F 5
Moab ○ USA (UT) 254-255 F 5
Moabi ○ G 210-211 C 5
Moaco, Rio ~ BR 66-67 C 6
Moai •• RCH 78-79 B 2
Moa Island ⌒ AUS 174-175 G 2
Moala ⌒ FJI 184 III b 3
Mo'allemān ○ IR 136-137 D 7
Mo'allem Kalāyeh ○ IR 136-137 B 6
Moamba ○ MOC 220-221 L 2
Moanda ○ G 210-211 D 4
Moanda ~ ZRE 210-211 G 2
Moapa ○ USA (NV) 248-249 K 3
Moapa River Indian Reservation X USA (NV) 248-249 K 3
Móar Bay ≈ 38-39 E 2
Moatize ○ MOC 218-219 G 3
Moba ○ ZRE 214-215 E 4
Mobara ○ J 152-153 J 7
Mobārak, Kūh ○ IR 134-135 G 6
Mobārake ○ IR 134-135 D 2
Mobaye ☆• RCA 206-207 E 6
Mobayi-Mbongi ○ ZRE 206-207 E 6
Mobdoua < RIM 196-197 G 7
Mobeetie ○ USA (TX) 264-265 D 3
Mobena ○ ZRE 210-211 G 3
Moberly ○ USA (MO) 274-275 F 5
Mobert ○ CDN (ONT) 236-237 C 4
Mobile ○ USA (AZ) 256-257 C 5
Mobile ○• USA (AL) 284-285 B 6
Mobile Bay ⌣ 48-49 D 4
Mobile Bay ≈ USA 284-285 B 6
Mobile River ~ USA (AL) 284-285 B 6
Mobridge ○ USA (SD) 260-261 F 1
Moca ☆ DOM 54-55 K 5
Moca ○ GQ 210-211 B 2
Mocajuba ○ BR 68-69 D 3
Moçambicana ⩦ MOC 218-219 H 5
Moçambique ○ MOC 218-219 L 2
Moçambique, Ilha de ⌒••• MOC 218-219 L 2
Moccasin ○ USA (AZ) 256-257 C 2
Moccasin ○ USA (MT) 250-251 K 4
Mọc Châu ☆ VN 156-157 D 6
Mocha, Isla ⌒ RCH 78-79 C 5
Mochara, Cordillera de ▲ BOL 76-77 E 1
Moche Pyramids • PE 64-65 C 6
Mochirma, Parque Nacionale ⊥ YV 60-61 J 2
Mochis, Los ○ MEX 50-51 E 5
Mọc Hóa ○ VN 158-159 H 5
Mochudi ☆ RB 220-221 H 2
Mochumí ○ PE 64-65 C 5
Mocimboa da Praia ○ MOC 214-215 L 6
Mocimboa do Rovuma ○ MOC 214-215 K 6
Mockonema ○ USA (WA) 244-245 H 4
Mocksville ○ USA (NC) 282-283 G 5
Môco ▲ ANG 216-217 C 6
Mocoa ☆ CO 64-65 D 1
Mocodoene ○ MOC 218-219 H 6
Moções, Rio ~ BR 62-63 K 6
Mocomoco ○ BOL 70-71 C 4
Mocorito ○ MEX 50-51 F 5
Mocotó ○ BR 68-69 E 3
Moctezuma ○ MEX (CHA) 50-51 F 2
Moctezuma ○ MEX (SLP) 50-51 J 6
Moctezuma ○ MEX (SON) 50-51 E 3
Moctezuma, Río ~ MEX 50-51 K 7
Mocuba ○ MOC 218-219 J 3
Mocupe ○ PE 64-65 C 5
Modan ○ RI 166-167 G 3
Modane ○ F 90-91 L 9
Modāsa ○ IND 138-139 D 8
Modderrivier ~ ZA 220-221 G 4
Model ○ USA (CO) 254-255 L 6
Modena ○ I 100-101 C 2
Modena ○ USA (UT) 254-255 B 6
Modesto ○ USA (CA) 248-249 C 2
Modesto Méndez ○ GCA 52-53 K 4
Modjamboli ○ ZRE 210-211 H 2
Modjigo ⩦ RN 198-199 F 4
Modoc Point ○ USA (OR) 244-245 D 8
Modoguhe ○ CI 202-203 G 6
Modot ○ MAU 148-149 J 4
Modriča ○ BIH 100-101 G 2
Moebase ○ MOC 218-219 K 3
Moeilijk, Pulau ⌒ RI 164-165 L 4
Moeko ~ ZRE 210-211 G 2
Moen ○ N 86-87 J 2
Moenkopi ○ USA (AZ) 256-257 D 2
Moenkopi Wash ~ USA (AZ) 256-257 D 2
Moeraki Boulders • NZ 182 C 6
Moerkesung ○ VRC 144-145 E 5
Moero, Lac ○ ZRE 214-215 E 5
Moers ○ D 92-93 J 3
Moe-Yalloum ○ AUS 180-181 J 5
Moffat ○ GB 90-91 F 4
Moffat Creek ~ CDN (BC) 228-229 N 4
Moffat Secton, Mount ⊥ AUS 178-179 J 3
Moffet, Mount ▲ USA 22-23 H 7
Moffet Point ▲ USA 22-23 P 5
Moffit ○ USA (ND) 258-259 G 5
Mofu ○ Z 214-215 F 6
Moga ~ RUS 116-117 O 5
Moga ○ ZRE 210-211 L 4
Mogadishu = Mugdisho ★ SP 212-213 K 2
Mogadouro ○ P 98-99 D 4
Mogalu ○ ZRE 210-211 J 4
Mogami-gawa ~ J 152-153 J 5
Mogangshan • VRC 154-155 L 6
Mogao Ku ••• VRC 146-147 M 5
Mogapinyana ○ RB 218-219 D 6
Mogaung ○ MYA 142-143 K 3
Mogdy ○ RUS (HBR) 122-123 E 3
Mogdy ~ RUS 116-117 M 3
Mogen ○ IR 136-137 D 6
Mogens Heinesens Fjord ≈ 28-29 T 5
Mogi Cruzes ○ BR 72-73 G 7
Mogila ▲ EAK 212-213 E 1
Mogilev = Mahilëv ○• BY 94-95 M 5
Mogilno ○• PL 92-93 O 2
Mogil'nyj Mys ○ RUS 114-115 R 5
Mogi-Mirim ○ BR 72-73 G 7
Mogincual ○ MOC 218-219 L 2
Mogna ○ RA 76-77 C 6
Mogna, Sierra de ▲ RA 76-77 C 6
Mogoča ☆ RUS 118-119 J 9
Mogoi ○ RI 166-167 G 2
Mogojtuj ☆ RUS 118-119 G 10
Mogok ○ MYA 142-143 K 4
Mogollon Mountains ▲ USA (NM) 256-257 G 5
Mogollon Rim ▲ USA (AZ) 256-257 D 4
Mogotes, Punta ▲ RA 78-79 L 5
Mogotoevo, ozero ○ RUS 110-111 b 3
Mogotón, Cerro ▲ NIC 52-53 L 5
Mogou ○ RT 202-203 L 4
Mogroum ○ TCH 206-207 B 3
Mogui Cheng • VRC 146-147 G 2
Mogūye, Bandar-e ○ IR 134-135 F 5
Mogwase ○ ZA 220-221 H 2
Mogzon ○ RUS 118-119 E 10
Mohács ○ H 92-93 P 5
Mohale's Hoek ○ LS 220-221 H 5
Mohall ○ USA (ND) 258-259 F 3
Mohamed 5., Barrage < MA 188-189 K 3
Mohammadābād ○ IR (ESF) 134-135 E 2
Mohammadābād ○ IR (KER) 134-135 G 4
Mohammadābād ○ IR (SIS) 134-135 J 3
Mohammadābād ○ IR (YAZ) 134-135 F 3
Mohammad Āgā ○ AFG 138-139 B 2
Mohammadia ○ DZ 190-191 C 3
Mohammedia ○ MA 188-189 H 4
Mohana ○ IND 142-143 D 6
Mohanganj ○ BD 142-143 G 3
Mohania ○ IND 142-143 C 3
Mohanpur ○ NEP 144-145 F 7
Mohave, Lake ○ USA (NV) 248-249 K 4
Mohawk ○ USA (AZ) 256-257 B 6
Mohawk ○ USA (WI) 270-271 K 3
Mohawk River ~ USA (NY) 278-279 G 6
Mohe ○ VRC 150-151 D 1
Mohej ~ RUS 118-119 E 9
Mohenjo Daro ∴••• PK 138-139 B 6
Mohican, Cape ▲ USA 20-21 G 6
Moho ○ PE 70-71 C 4
Mohol ○ IND 140-141 F 2
Mohon Peak ▲ USA (AZ) 256-257 B 4
Mohoro ○ EAT 214-215 K 5
Mohovaja ~ RUS 108-109 V 6
Mohovaja, gora ▲ RUS 88-89 S 2
Mohrungen = Morąg ○ PL 92-93 P 2
Mohyliv-Podil's'kyj ☆ UA 102-103 E 3
Moiben ○ EAK 212-213 E 3
Moila Point ▲ PNG 184 I b 2
Moili ⌒ COM 222-223 C 4
Moimba ○ ANG 216-217 B 8
Moin ○ CR 52-53 C 7
Moincêr ○ VRC 144-145 C 5
Moinerie, Lac la ○ CDN 36-37 Q 6
Moines, Des ○ USA (NM) 256-257 M 2
Moines River, Des ~ USA (IA) 274-275 D 2
Moira ○ USA (NY) 278-279 G 4
Mo i Rana ○ N 86-87 G 3
Moirang ○ IND 142-143 H 3
Mõisaküla ○ EST 94-95 J 2
Moiseevskaja ○ RUS 94-95 R 1
Moisie ○ CDN (QUE) 242-243 B 2
Moisie, Rivière ~ CDN 38-39 L 3
Moisie, Rivière ~ CDN (QUE) 242-243 B 2
Moison Lake ○ CDN 34-35 H 3
Moissac ○ F 90-91 H 9
Moïssala ○ TCH 206-207 C 4
Moitaco ○ YV 60-61 J 3
Mojáh, El = San Rafael ○ YV 60-61 F 2
Mojave ○ USA (CA) 248-249 F 4
Mojave Desert ⩦ USA (CA) 248-249 G 4
Mojave River ~ USA (CA) 248-249 G 5
Mojero ~ RUS 108-109 f 7
Mojero ~ RUS 116-117 L 2
Mojerokan ~ RUS 116-117 M 2
Mojiang ○ VRC 156-157 B 5
Moji Guaçu, Rio ~ BR 72-73 G 6
Mojiquiçaba ○ BR 72-73 L 4
Mojkovac ○ YU 100-101 G 3
Mojo ○ ETH 208-209 D 4
Mojoagung ○ RI 168 E 3
Mojokerto ○ RI 168 E 3
Mojos, Llanos de ⩦ BOL 70-71 D 4
Mojosari ○ RI 168 E 3
Moju, Rio ~ BR 68-69 D 3
Moju dos Campos ○ BR 66-67 K 4
Moj-Urusta ○ RUS 120-121 N 3
Mojyldy ~ KA 124-125 D 3
Mojynkūm ⩦ KA 124-125 E 5
Mojynty ○ KA 124-125 H 5
Mōka ○ J 152-153 J 6
Mokāma ○ IND 142-143 D 3
Mokambo ○ ZRE 214-215 E 7
Mokau ○ NZ 182 E 3
Mokelumne Aqueduct < USA (CA) 246-247 D 5
Mokelumne Hill ○ USA (CA) 246-247 E 5
Mokgomane ○ RB 220-221 G 2
Mokhotlong ○ LS 220-221 J 4
Mokka = al-Muḫā ○•• Y 132-133 C 7
Mokla ~ RUS 118-119 K 8
Moknine ○ TN 190-191 H 3
Mokoan, Lake ○ AUS 180-181 J 4
Mokobela Pan < RB 218-219 D 5
Mokokchung ○ IND 142-143 J 2
Mokolo ○ CAM 204-205 K 3
Mokolo ~ ZA 220-221 H 2
Mokombe ~ ZRE 210-211 J 4
Mokoreta ○ NZ 182 B 7
Mokoto, Lacs ○ ZRE 212-213 B 4
Mokp'o ○ ROK 150-151 F 10
Mokrous ○ RUS 96-97 E 8
Mokša ~ RUS 94-95 T 5
Mōktama Kwe ≈ 158-159 D 2
Mokwa ○ WAN 204-205 F 4
Mola ~ GH 202-203 K 5
Moladjakit, gora ▲ RUS 116-117 L 3
Molakalmuru ○ IND 140-141 G 3
Molalatau ○ RB 218-219 E 6
Molalē ○ ETH 208-209 D 3
Molalla ○ USA (OR) 244-245 C 5
Molas del Norte, Punta ▲ MEX 52-53 L 1
Molat ⌒ HR 100-101 E 2
Moldary ○ KA 124-125 L 3
Molde ☆ N 86-87 C 5
Moldotau, hrebet ▲ KS 146-147 B 5
Moldova ■ MD 102-103 F 4
Moldova Nouă ○ RO 102-103 B 5
Molegbe ○ ZRE 206-207 E 6
Mole Island ⌒ PNG 183 D 2
Mole Lake Indian Reservation X USA (WI) 270-271 K 5
Mole National Park ⊥ GH 202-203 K 5
Molepolole ☆ RB 220-221 G 2
Moleque, Morro do ▲ BR 74-75 F 7
Mole River ~ AUS 178-179 L 5
Molėtai ○ LT 94-95 J 4
Molfetta ○ I 100-101 F 4
Molibagu ○ RI 164-165 H 3
Molina ○ E 98-99 G 4
Molina ○ RCH 78-79 D 3
Molina de Segura ○ E 98-99 G 5
Moline ○ USA (IL) 274-275 H 3
Moline ○ USA (KS) 262-263 K 7
Moline Mine ∴ AUS 172-173 L 2
Molinggapoto ○ RI 164-165 H 3
Molinillo, Puerto El ▲ E 98-99 F 6
Molino ○ USA (FL) 286-287 B 1
Molinos, Embalse los < RA 76-77 E 6
Molinos, Los ○ USA (CA) 246-247 C 3
Moliro ○ ZRE 214-215 F 5
Molise ◘ I 100-101 E 4
Mol'katy, hrebet ▲ RUS 112-113 J 4
Mollendo ○ PE 70-71 A 5
Mollepata ○ PE 64-65 F 8
Moller, Port ≈ 22-23 Q 5
Mollera, zaliv ○ RUS 108-109 E 5
Mollerusa = Mollerussa ○ E 98-99 H 4
Mollerussa ○ E 98-99 H 4
Molles, Punta ▲ RCH 78-79 D 2
Molo ○ EAK (RIF) 212-213 E 4
Molo ~ EAK 212-213 E 3
Molo ○ MYA 142-143 K 4
Moločna ~ UA 102-103 J 4
Moločnyj lyman ≈ 102-103 J 4
Molocopote ○ BR 62-63 G 5
Molócuè ~ MOC 218-219 J 2
Molócuè, Rio ~ MOC 218-219 J 2
Molodečno = Maladzečna ☆ BY 94-95 K 4
Molodežnaja ○ ARK 16 G 5
Molodežnyj ☆ KA 124-125 H 3
Molodežnyj ○ RUS 120-121 N 2
Molodo ○ RMM 202-203 G 2
Molodo ~ RUS 110-111 N 5
Mologa ~ RUS 94-95 O 2
Molokai ⌒ USA (HI) 288 H 3
Molokai Fracture Zone ≃ 14-15 O 5
Moloma ~ RUS 96-97 E 4
Molona ○ RI 164-165 H 6
Molong ○ AUS 180-181 K 2
Molongda ~ RUS 112-113 L 4
Molongdinskij hrebet ▲ RUS 112-113 L 4
Molopo ~ RB 220-221 E 3
Moloporivier ○ ZA 220-221 G 2
Moloskovicy ○ RUS 94-95 L 2
Moloundou ○ CAM 210-211 E 2
Molsheim ○• F 90-91 L 7
Molt ○ USA (MT) 250-251 L 6
Molteno ○ ZA 220-221 H 5
Moltenopas ▲ ZA 220-221 G 6
Moltke Nunatak ▲ GRØ 26-27 o 4
Moltyrkan ~ RUS 110-111 V 7
Molu, Pulau ⌒ RI 166-167 F 5
Molucca, Laut ≈ 164-165 J 3
Moluccas = Maluku ◘ RI 166-167 D 4
Moluccas = Maluku, Kepulauan ⌒ RI 166-167 J 2
Molucca Sea = Maluku, Laut ≈ RI 164-165 J 4
Molūki ○ AFG 136-137 G 7
Molumbo ○ MOC 218-219 J 2
Molume ○ GH 202-203 J 5
Molus River ○ CDN (NB) 240-241 K 4
Molvo ~ RUS 118-119 H 6
Molwe ○ ZRE 214-215 C 6
Moma ○ MOC 218-219 K 3
Moma ~ RUS 110-111 Y 6
Moma ○ ZRE 214-215 B 4
Moma, Ilha de ⌒ MOC 218-219 K 3
Momaligi ○ WAL 202-203 D 6
Momats ○ RI 166-167 K 4
Mombe ○ Z 218-219 E 2
Mombaca ○ BR 68-69 J 4
Mombasa ○•• EAK 212-213 G 6
Mombasa Marine National Reserve ⊥ EAK 212-213 G 6
Mombenzélé ○ RCB 210-211 F 3
Mombetsu ○ J (HOK) 152-153 K 2
Mombetsu ○ J (HOK) 152-153 K 3
Mombo ○ EAT 212-213 G 6
Mombongo ○ ZRE (HAU) 210-211 J 3
Mombongo ○ ZRE (HAU) 210-211 K 3
Momboyo ~ ZRE 210-211 G 4
Momburn ○ RI 166-167 K 6
Momfafa, Tanjung ▲ RI 166-167 F 2
Mommon, Tanjung ▲ RI 166-167 G 3
Momo ○ RI 164-165 G 4
Momo-Selennjahskaja vpadina ⌣ RUS 110-111 W 5
Momote ○ PNG 183 D 2
Momotombo, Volcán ▲ NIC 52-53 L 5
Mompiche, Ensenada de ≈ 64-65 B 1
Mompog Pass ≈ 160-161 E 6
Mompono ○ ZRE 210-211 H 3
Mompós ○ CO 60-61 D 3
Momskij hrebet ▲ RUS 110-111 Y 6
Momskiy Khrebet = Momskij hrebet ▲ RUS 110-111 Y 6
Møn ⌒ DK 86-87 F 9
Mona ○ USA (UT) 254-255 D 4
Mona, Isla ⌒ USA (PR) 286-287 O 2
Monaco ■ MC 90-91 L 10
Monaco ★• MC 90-91 L 10
Monaco Deep ≃ 6-7 G 5
Monadotua, Pulau ≈ 164-165 J 3
Monadyr ○ KA 124-125 G 4
Monaghan = Muineachán ☆ IRL 90-91 D 4
Monahans ○ USA (TX) 266-267 E 2
Monana ○ G 210-211 D 4
Monango ○ USA (ND) 258-259 J 5
Mona Passage ≈ 56 A 2
Monapo ○ MOC 218-219 L 2
Mona Quimbundo ○ ANG 216-217 E 4
Monarch ○ CDN (ALB) 232-233 E 6
Monarch ○ USA (CO) 254-255 J 5
Monarch ○ USA (MT) 250-251 J 4
Monarch Icefield ⊂ CDN (BC) 228-229 H 4
Monarch Mountain ▲ CDN (BC) 230-231 D 2
Monashee Mountains ▲ CDN (BC) 228-229 P 4
Monashee Provincial Park ⊥ CDN (BC) 230-231 L 3
Monaši ○ UA 102-103 G 4
Monasterace Marina ○ I 100-101 F 5
Monastery ○ CDN (NS) 240-241 O 5
Monastir ☆ TN 190-191 H 3
Monastyrščina ☆ RUS 94-95 M 4
Monatélé ○ CAM 204-205 J 6
Monati, mys ▲ RUS 120-121 W 6
Monboré ○ CAM 206-207 B 4
Moncão ○ BR 68-69 F 3
Mončegorsk ○ RUS 88-89 M 3
Mönchengladbach ○ D 92-93 J 3
Monchy ○ CDN (SAS) 232-233 L 6
Moncks Corner ○ USA (SC) 284-285 K 3
Monclova ○ MEX 50-51 J 4
Monco Bünnyi ○ VRC 144-145 F 5
Moncton ○ CDN (NB) 240-241 L 4
Mondaí ○ BR 74-75 D 6
Mondamin ○ USA (IA) 274-275 B 3
Mondego, Cabo ▲ P 98-99 C 4
Mondego, Rio ~ P 98-99 C 4
Mondjamboli ○ ZRE 210-211 J 2
Mondjuku ○ ZRE 210-211 H 4
Mondo ○ TCH 198-199 G 6
Mondombe ○ ZRE 210-211 J 4
Mondómo ○ CO 60-61 C 6
Mondoñedo ○• E 98-99 D 3
Mondono ○ RI 164-165 H 4
Mondovì ○• I 100-101 A 2
Mondovi ○ USA (WI) 270-271 G 6
Mondragone ○ I 100-101 D 4
Mondrague, Enneri ~ TCH 198-199 H 2
Mondrain Island ⌒ AUS 176-177 G 7
Mondubi, Ponta ▲ BR 74-75 G 5
Monduli ○ EAT 212-213 F 5
Monduran Reservoir < AUS 178-179 L 3
Mondy ○ RUS 116-117 K 10
Moné ~ CAM 204-205 H 6
Moneague ○ JA 54-55 G 5
Monemvassia ○ GR 100-101 J 6
Moneragala ○ CL 140-141 J 7
Moneron, ostrov ⌒ RUS 122-123 J 5
Moneta ○ USA (WY) 252-253 L 3
Monett ○ USA (MO) 276-277 B 4
Monette ○ USA (AR) 276-277 E 5
Money Island = Jinyin Dao ⌒ VRC 158-159 L 2
Monfalcone ○ I 100-101 D 2
Monforte ○ P 98-99 D 5
Monforte (Monforte de Lemos) ○• E 98-99 D 3
Monga ○ ZRE 206-207 F 6
Mongala ~ ZRE 210-211 H 2
Mongalla ○ SUD 206-207 K 6
Mongar ○ BHT 142-143 G 2
Monge ○ EC 64-65 D 3
Mongemputu ○ ZRE 210-211 H 5
Monger, Île ⌒ CDN 38-39 P 3
Mongeri ○ WAL 202-203 E 5
Mongers Lake ○ AUS 176-177 D 4
Monggo ○ RI 166-167 G 2
Monggui ○ RI 166-167 H 2
Möng Hpayak ○ MYA 142-143 L 5
Möng Hsan ○ MYA 142-143 K 5
Möng Hsat ○ MYA 142-143 L 5
Möng Hsu ○ MYA 142-143 L 5
Möng Küng ○ MYA 142-143 K 5
Mongla ○ BD 142-143 F 4
Möng Mit ○ MYA 142-143 K 4
Möng Naí ○ MYA 142-143 K 5
Mongo ☆ TCH 198-199 J 6
Mongočejaha ~ RUS 108-109 S 5
Mongoj ~ RUS 118-119 F 9
Mongol Altajn Nuruu ▲ MAU 146-147 J 1
Mongol Ēls ⩦ MAU 146-147 L 2
Mongolia = Mongol Ard Uls ■ MAU 148-149 E 5
Mongomo ○ GQ 210-211 C 3
Möngönmorit = Bulag ○ MAU 148-149 J 3
Mongonu ○ WAN 198-199 F 6
Mongororo ○ TCH 198-199 L 6
Mongoumba ○ RCA 210-211 G 2
Möng Ping ○ MYA 142-143 L 5
Möng Ton ○ MYA 142-143 L 5
Mongu ☆ Z 218-219 B 2
Mongua ○ ANG 216-217 C 8
Mongubal, Cachoeira do ~ BR 66-67 J 5
Mongubal Grande, Cachoeira ~ BR 66-67 J 5
Monguel ○ RIM 196-197 D 6
Möng Yai ○ MYA 142-143 L 4
Möng Yang ○ MYA 142-143 M 5
Möngyu ○ MYA 142-143 K 4
Mönhbulag ○ MAU 148-149 F 4
Monheagan Island ⌒ USA (ME) 278-279 M 5
Mönhhaan = Bajasgalant ○ MAU 148-149 L 4
Mönh Hajrhan ▲ MAU 146-147 K 2
Moni ○• RI 168 E 7
Monico ○ USA (WI) 270-271 J 5
Monida ○ USA (MT) 250-251 G 7
Monida Pass ▲ USA (ID) 252-253 F 2
Monimpébougou ○ RMM 202-203 H 2
Moni River ~ PNG 183 E 5
Monito, Isla ⌒ USA (PR) 286-287 O 2
Monitor ○ CDN (ALB) 232-233 H 4
Monitor Pass ▲ USA (CA) 246-247 F 5
Monitor Range ▲ USA (NV) 246-247 J 5
Monitos ○ CO 60-61 C 3
Monje ○ RA 78-79 J 2
Monjes, Islas los ⌒ YV 60-61 F 1
Monjolos ○ BR 72-73 H 5
Monkey Bay ○ MW 218-219 H 2
Monkey Mia ○ AUS 176-177 B 2

Miranda — Monkey Mia 363

Moudjéria o **RIM** 196-197 D 6
Moûdros o **GR** 100-101 K 5
Mouenda o **G** 210-211 D 5
Mougalaba, Reserve de la ⊥ **G**
  210-211 C 5
Mougamou o **G** 210-211 D 4
Mouila ✿ **G** 210-211 D 4
Moujia o **RN** 198-199 B 5
Mouka o **RCA** 206-207 E 5
Moukoumbi o **G** 210-211 D 4
Moul < **RN** 198-199 F 5
Moula o **TCH** 206-207 D 4
Moulamein o **AUS** 180-181 H 3
Moulares o **TN** 190-191 G 3
Moulay Bouâzza o **MA** 188-189 H 4
Moulay-Bousselham o **MA** 188-189 H 3
Moulay-Idriss o **MA** 188-189 J 3
Mould Bay o **CDN** 24-25 M 2
Moulêngui Binza o **G** 210-211 C 5
Moulins ✿ **F** 90-91 J 8
Mouli Pouli o **G** 210-211 D 4
Moulmein = Maulamyaing o **MYA**
  158-159 J 4
Moulmein = Maulamyaing o **MYA**
  158-159 J 4
Moulmeingyun o **MYA** 158-159 C 2
Moulouud o **DJI** 208-209 F 3
Moulouya, Oued ~ **MA** 188-189 K 3
Moulton o **USA** (AL) 284-285 C 4
Moulton o **USA** (IA) 274-275 F 4
Moulton o **USA** (TX) 266-267 K 4
Moultrie o **USA** (GA) 284-285 G 5
Moultrie, Lake < **USA** (SC) 284-285 K 3
Moulti Bazar o **BD** 142-143 G 3
Moulvoudoy o **CAM** 206-207 B 3
Mounanko o **CAM** 210-211 B 2
Mound City o **USA** (IL) 276-277 F 3
Mound City o **USA** (KS) 262-263 M 6
Mound City o **USA** (MO) 274-275 C 4
Mound City o **USA** (SD) 260-261 F 1
Mound City Group National Monument ∴
  USA (OH) 280-281 D 4
Moundhill Point ▲ **USA** 22-23 K 6
Moundou ✿ **TCH** 206-207 C 4
Moundridge o **USA** (KS) 262-263 J 6
Mounds o **USA** (IL) 276-277 F 3
Mound State Monument · **USA** (AL)
  284-285 C 4
Moundsville o **USA** (WV) 280-281 F 4
Moundville o **USA** (AL) 284-285 C 3
Moundville o **USA** (AL) 284-285 C 3
Moungoun-dou-sud o **RCB** 210-211 D 5
Moûng Roessei o **K** 158-159 G 4
Mounguel o **CAM** 204-205 K 5
Mount Adams Wilderness ⊥ **USA** (WA)
  244-245 D 4
Mountain o **USA** (WI) 270-271 K 5
Mountainair o **USA** (NM) 256-257 J 4
Mountain Brook o **USA** (AL)
  284-285 C 4
Mountainburg o **USA** (AR) 276-277 A 5
Mountain City o **USA** (NV) 246-247 K 2
Mountain City o **USA** (TN) 282-283 F 4
Mountain Creek ~ **USA** (GA)
  284-285 E 4
Mountain Gate o **USA** (CA) 246-247 C 3
Mountain Grove o **USA** (MO)
  276-277 C 3
Mountain Home o **USA** (AR)
  276-277 C 4
Mountain Home o **USA** (ID) 252-253 C 3
Mountain Home o **USA** (TX)
  266-267 H 3
Mountain Lake o **CDN** 30-31 U 5
Mountain Lake o **USA** (MN)
  270-271 D 7
Mountain Lodge o **EAK** 212-213 F 4
Mountain Park o **CDN** (ALB)
  228-229 R 4
Mountain Pass ⊥ **USA** (CA) 248-249 J 4
Mountain Pine o **USA** (AR) 276-277 B 6
Mountain Point o **USA** 32-33 E 4
Mountain Road o **CDN** (MAN)
  234-235 D 4
Mountainside o **CDN** (MAN)
  234-235 D 4
Mountain Springs o **USA** (NV)
  248-249 J 3
Mountain Valley o **AUS** 174-175 B 4
Mountain View o **CDN** (ALB)
  232-233 E 6
Mountain View o **USA** (AR) 276-277 C 5
Mountain View o **USA** (AZ) 256-257 C 6
Mountain View o **USA** (HI) 288 K 5
Mountain View o **USA** (MO)
  276-277 D 4
Mountain View o **USA** (WV) 280-281 E 6
Mountain View o **USA** (WY) 252-253 H 5
Mountain Village o **USA** 20-21 J 5
Mount Airy o **USA** (MD) 280-281 J 4
Mount Airy o **USA** (NC) 282-283 G 4
Mount Airy o **USA** (VA) 280-281 G 7
Mount Airy Mesa ▲ **USA** (NV)
  246-247 H 4
Mount Allan o **AUS** 172-173 L 7
Mount Alto o **USA** (WV) 280-281 E 5
Mount Amhurst o **AUS** 172-173 K 7
Mount Aspiring National Park ⊥ **NZ**
  182 B 6
Mount Assiniboine Provincial Park ⊥ **CDN**
  (ALB) 232-233 C 4
Mount Augustus o **AUS** 176-177 D 2
Mount Augustus National Park ⊥ **AUS**
  176-177 D 2
Mount Ayliff o **ZA** 220-221 J 5
Mount Barker o **AUS** (SA) 180-181 G 3
Mount Barker o **AUS** (WA) 176-177 D 7
Mount Barnett o **AUS** 172-173 H 4
Mountbatten Indian Reserve ✗ **CDN** (ONT)
  236-237 F 5
Mount Baw Baw o **AUS** 180-181 J 4
Mount Beauty o **AUS** 180-181 J 4
Mount Belview o **USA** (TX) 268-269 F 4
Mount Brockman o **AUS** 172-173 C 7
Mount Buffalo National Park ⊥ **AUS**
  180-181 J 4

Mount Bullion o **USA** (CA) 248-249 D 2
Mount Carleton Provincial Park ⊥ **CDN**
  (NB) 240-241 J 3
Mount Carmel o **USA** (IL) 274-275 L 6
Mount Carmel o **USA** (ND) 258-259 J 2
Mount Carmel Junction o **USA** (UT)
  254-255 C 6
Mount Carrol o **USA** (IL) 274-275 J 2
Mount Celia o **AUS** 176-177 G 4
Mount Charleston o **USA** (NV)
  248-249 J 3
Mount Clemens o **USA** (MI)
  272-273 G 5
Mount Clere o **AUS** 176-177 D 2
Mount Cook o **NZ** 182 C 5
Mount Cook National Park ⊥ ··· **NZ**
  182 C 5
Mount Coolon o **AUS** 178-179 J 1
Mount Croghan o **USA** (SC) 284-285 K 2
Mount Denison o **AUS** 172-173 K 7
Mount Desert Island ⌒ **USA** (ME)
  278-279 N 4
Mount Divide o **AUS** 172-173 E 7
Mount Dora o **USA** (FL) 286-287 H 3
Mount Dora o **USA** (NM) 256-257 N 2
Mount Doreen o **AUS** 172-173 K 7
Mount Douglas o **AUS** 178-179 J 1
Mount Eba o **AUS** 178-179 C 6
Mount Ebenezer o **AUS** 176-177 M 2
Mount Eccles National Park ⊥ **AUS**
  180-181 F 5
Mount Edgar o **AUS** 172-173 E 6
Mount Edziza Provincial Park ⊥ **CDN**
  32-33 E 3
Mount Elizabeth o **AUS** 172-173 H 4
Mount Enterprise o **USA** (TX)
  268-269 F 5
Mount Everest ▲ **NEP** 144-145 F 7
Mount Field National Park ⊥ **AUS**
  180-181 J 7
Mount Fletcher o **ZA** 220-221 J 5
Mount Florance o **AUS** 172-173 C 6
Mount Forest o **CDN** (ONT) 238-239 E 5
Mount Frere o **ZA** 220-221 J 5
Mount Gambier o **AUS** 180-181 F 4
Mount Garnet o **AUS** 174-175 H 5
Mount Gilead o **USA** (NC) 282-283 H 5
Mount Gilead o **USA** (OH) 280-281 D 3
Mount Hagen ✿ ·· **PNG** 183 C 3
Mount Harris Tine Mine Area o **AUS**
  172-173 K 7
Mount Holly o **USA** (NJ) 280-281 M 3
Mount Holly Springs o **USA** (PA)
  280-281 J 3
Mount Hood o **USA** (OR) 244-245 D 5
Mount Hope o **AUS** 180-181 C 3
Mount Horeb o **USA** (WI) 274-275 J 1
Mount House o **AUS** 172-173 G 4
Mount Hutt o **NZ** 182 C 5
Mount Ida o **USA** 176-177 F 4
Mount Ida o **USA** (AR) 276-277 B 6
Mountin Zebra National Park ⊥ **ZA**
  220-221 G 6
Mount Isa o ·· **AUS** 174-175 E 7
Mount Jackson o **AUS** 176-177 E 4
Mount Kaichui ▲ **SOL** 184 I e 3
Mount Kalourat ▲ **SOL** 184 I e 3
Mount Kaputar National Park ⊥ **AUS**
  178-179 L 6
Mount Keith o **AUS** 176-177 F 3
Mount Lakes Wilderness Area ⊥ **USA**
  (OR) 244-245 C 8
Mount Larcom o **AUS** 178-179 L 2
Mount Lofty Range ▲ **AUS** 180-181 E 3
Mount Madden Wheat Bin o **AUS**
  176-177 E 6
Mount Magnet o **AUS** 176-177 D 4
Mount Maitabi ▲ **SOL** 184 I e 2
Mount Mary o **AUS** 180-181 E 3
Mount Meigs o **USA** (AL) 284-285 D 4
Mount Molloy o **AUS** 174-175 H 4
Mount Montgomery o **USA** (NV)
  248-249 F 2
Mount Morgan o · **AUS** 178-179 L 2
Mount Morris o **USA** (MI) 272-273 F 4
Mount Morris o **USA** (WI) 270-271 J 6
Mount Mulgrave o **AUS** 174-175 G 5
Mount Mulligan o **AUS** 174-175 H 5
Mount Narryer o **AUS** 176-177 C 3
Mountnorris Bay ≈ 172-173 L 1
Mount Olive o **USA** (NC) 282-283 J 5
Mount Padbury o **AUS** 176-177 E 2
Mount Paget ▲ **GB** 78-79 O 7
Mount Pearl o **CDN** (NFL) 242-243 Q 5
Mount Perry o **AUS** 178-179 L 3
Mount Pleasant o **USA** (IA) 274-275 G 4
Mount Pleasant o **USA** (MI) 272-273 E 4
Mount Pleasant o **USA** (OH)
  280-281 D 4
Mount Pleasant o **USA** (PA)
  280-281 G 3
Mount Pleasant o **USA** (SC) 284-285 L 4
Mount Pleasant o **USA** (TN)
  276-277 H 5
Mount Pleasant o **USA** (TX) 264-265 K 5
Mount Pleasant o **USA** (UT) 254-255 D 4
Mount Pocono o **USA** (PA) 280-281 L 2
Mount Pulaski o **USA** (IL) 274-275 J 5
Mount Rainier National Park ⊥ **USA** (WA)
  244-245 D 4
Mount Remarkable National Park ⊥ **AUS**
  180-181 D 2
Mount Revelstoke National Park ⊥ **CDN**
  (BC) 230-231 L 2
Mount Richmond National Park ⊥ **AUS**
  180-181 F 5
Mount Robson o **CDN** (BC) 228-229 P 3
Mount Robson Provincial Park ⊥ **CDN**
  (BC) 228-229 Q 4
Mount Rogers National Recreation Area ⊥
  USA (VA) 280-281 F 7
Mount Rupert o **ZA** 220-221 G 4
Mount Rushmore National Memorial ∴
  USA (SD) 260-261 C 3
Mount Sage National Park ⊥ **GB** (VI)
  286-287 P 3
Mount Saint Helens National Volcanic
  Monument ∴ **USA** (WA) 244-245 D 4
Mount -Sandiman o **AUS** 176-177 C 2

Mount Sanford o **AUS** 172-173 K 4
Mount Sasan ▲ **SOL** 184 I d 3
Mount Seymour Provincial Park ⊥ **CDN**
  (BC) 230-231 G 4
Mount Skinner o **AUS** 178-179 L 7
Mount Somers o **NZ** 182 C 5
Mount Spokane State Park ⊥ **USA** (WA)
  244-245 H 3
Mount Sterling o **USA** (IL) 274-275 H 5
Mount Sterling o **USA** (KY) 276-277 M 2
Mount Sterling o **USA** (OH) 280-281 C 4
Mount Sterling o **USA** (WI) 274-275 H 1
Mount Storm Lake o **USA** (WV)
  280-281 G 4
Mount Strzelecki National Park ⊥ **AUS**
  180-181 K 6
Mount Surprise o **AUS** 174-175 H 6
Mount Swan o **AUS** 178-179 C 2
Mount Trumbull o **USA** (AZ)
  256-257 B 2
Mount Union o **USA** (PA) 280-281 J 3
Mount Vernon o **USA** 176-177 E 2
Mount Vernon o **USA** (AL) 284-285 B 5
Mount Vernon o **USA** (GA) 284-285 H 4
Mount Vernon o **USA** (IA) 274-275 G 3
Mount Vernon o **USA** (IL) 274-275 L 7
Mount Vernon o **USA** (IN) 274-275 L 7
Mount Vernon o **USA** (MO) 276-277 B 3
Mount Vernon o **USA** (NY) 244-245 F 6
Mount Vernon o **USA** (OH) 280-281 D 3
Mount Vernon o **USA** (SD) 260-261 H 3
Mount Vernon o **USA** (TX) 264-265 K 5
Mount Vernon o **USA** (WA) 244-245 C 2
Mount Vetters o **AUS** 176-177 F 5
Mount Walker o **AUS** 176-177 E 6
Mount Washington o **USA** (KY)
  276-277 K 2
Mount Wedge o **AUS** (NT) 172-173 L 7
Mount Wedge o **AUS** (SA) 180-181 C 2
Mount William National Park ⊥ **AUS**
  180-181 K 6
Mount Zion o **USA** (IL) 274-275 K 5
Mount Zion o **USA** (MD) 280-281 K 5
Mouping o **VRC** 154-155 M 3
Moura o **BR** 62-63 D 6
Moura o · **P** 98-99 D 5
Moura, Cachoeira ~ **BR** 66-67 H 5
Mourão o **P** 98-99 D 5
Mouray o **TCH** 206-207 E 3
Mourdi, Dépression du ⊥ **TCH**
  198-199 K 3
Mourdiah o **RMM** 202-203 G 2
Mouri Mountains ▲ **WAN** 204-205 J 4
Mourndi o **G** 210-211 C 5
Mouroubra o **AUS** 176-177 D 4
Mouroungoulay o **TCH** 206-207 C 4
Mouscron o **B** 92-93 G 3
Mousgougou o **TCH** 206-207 C 3
Mousôayah o **RG** 202-203 D 5
Moussa, Hassi < **DZ** 190-191 C 4
Moussadey o **RN** 204-205 F 2
Moussafoyo o **TCH** 206-207 D 4
Moussaya o **RG** 202-203 E 4
Moussoro o **TCH** 198-199 H 6
Moustiers-Sainte-Marie o **F** 90-91 L 10
Mouth of the Mekong = Cửa Sông Cửu
  Long ⊥ **VN** 158-159 J 6
Mouth of Wilson o **USA** (VA)
  280-281 F 7
Mouths of the Indus o **PK** 134-135 M 6
Moûtiers o **F** 90-91 L 9
Moutong o **RI** 164-165 G 3
Moutouroua o **CAM** 206-207 B 3
Mouydir, Monts du ▲ **DZ** 190-191 E 8
Mouyonndzi o **RCB** 210-211 D 5
Mouzarak o **TCH** 198-199 G 6
Movila Miresii o **RO** 102-103 E 5
Moville o **USA** (IA) 274-275 E 2
Mowanjum ▲ **AUS** 172-173 F 4
Mowasi o **GUY** 62-63 G 3
Moweaqua o **USA** (IL) 274-275 J 5
Mowewe o **RI** 164-165 G 5
Moxey Town o **BS** 54-55 G 2
Moxico o **ANG** 216-217 E 6
Moxotó, Rio ~ **BR** 68-69 K 6
Moyagee Gemstone Deposit · **AUS**
  176-177 D 3
Moyahua o **MEX** 50-51 H 7
Moyale o **EAK** 212-213 G 2
Moyale o **ETH** 208-209 D 7
Moyamba o **WAL** 202-203 D 6
Moyen Atlas ▲ **MA** 188-189 H 4
Moyen-Chari □ **TCH** 206-207 C 4
Moyeni o **LS** 220-221 H 5
Moyenne Sido o **RCA** 206-207 D 4
Moyie o **CDN** (BC) 230-231 O 4
Moyie River o **CDN** (BC) 230-231 N 4
Moyie Springs o **USA** (ID) 250-251 C 3
Moyne, Lac le o **CDN** 36-37 P 6
Moyo o **RI** 168 C 7
Moyo, Pulau o **RI** 168 C 7
Moyobamba ✿ **PE** 64-65 D 5
Moyock o **USA** (NC) 282-283 L 4
Moyo Pulau Reserve ⊥ **RI** 168 C 7
Moyowosi ~ **EAT** 212-213 C 5
Møysalen ▲ **N** 86-87 G 2
Moyu o **VRC** 144-145 B 4
Mozambique ■ **MOC** 218-219 H 6
Mozambique = Moçambique ■ **MOC**
  218-219 G 6
Mozambique Basin ≃ 6-7 M 6
Mozambique Channel ≈ 222-223 A 7
Mozambique Plateau ≃ 9-9 H 6
Mozambique Plateau = Natal Ridge ≃
  220-221 M 6
Mozdok o **RUS** 126-127 F 6
Mozdûran o **IR** 136-137 G 6
Mozga ✿ **RUS** 96-97 H 3
Mozyr' = Mazyr o **BY** 94-95 L 5
Mpaem o **GH** 202-203 K 6
Mpaka Station o **SD** 220-221 K 3

Mpala o **ZRE** 214-215 E 4
Mpama ~ **RCB** 210-211 E 5
Mpana o **RCB** 210-211 D 5
Mpanda o **EAT** 214-215 F 4
Mpandamatenga o **RB** 218-219 C 4
Mpanga o **EAT** 214-215 F 4
Mpase o **ZRE** 210-211 H 4
Mpataba o **GH** 202-203 J 7
Mpemba o **CAM** 204-205 J 6
Mpepayi o **EAT** (RUV) 214-215 H 5
Mpessoba o **RMM** 202-203 H 3
Mphaki o **LS** 220-221 J 5
Mphoengs o **ZW** 218-219 E 4
Mpiéla o **RMM** 202-203 G 3
Mpigi o **EAU** 212-213 D 3
Mpika o **Z** 214-215 F 6
Mpitimbi o **EAT** (RUV) 214-215 H 5
Mpo o **ZRE** 210-211 G 6
Mpoko ~ **RCA** 206-207 D 6
Mpoko o **ZRE** 210-211 G 6
Mponela o **MW** 218-219 G 1
Mpongwe o **Z** 214-215 E 6
Mporokoso o **Z** 214-215 F 5
Mpoukou o **RCB** 210-211 D 5
Mpoumé, Chute ~ **CAM** 210-211 B 2
Mpouop ~ **CAM** 210-211 D 2
Mpouya o **RCB** 210-211 E 5
Mpraeso o **GH** 202-203 K 6
Mpui o **EAT** 214-215 F 5
Mpulungu o **Z** 214-215 F 5
Mpumalanga o **ZA** 220-221 K 4
Mpume o **ZRE** 210-211 G 6
Mpwapwa o **EAT** 214-215 J 4
Mrakovo o **RUS** 96-97 K 7
Mrara o **DZ** 190-191 G 4
Mrassu ~ **RUS** 124-125 Q 2
Mrčajevci o **YU** 100-101 H 3
Mrezisig < **RMM** 196-197 K 5
M'saken o **TN** 190-191 H 1
Msak Millet ⊥ **LAR** 192-193 D 5
Msandile ~ **Z** 218-219 G 1
Msangasi ~ **EAT** 212-213 G 6
Msanzara ~ **Z** 218-219 F 1
Msata o **EAT** 214-215 J 4
Msembe o **EAT** 214-215 H 4
M'Sila ✿ **DZ** 190-191 E 4
Msima ~ **EAT** 214-215 H 4
Mśinskaja o **RUS** 94-95 L 2
Msoro o **Z** 218-219 F 1
Msta ~ **RUS** 94-95 O 3
Msuna o **ZW** 218-219 D 3
Mszczonów o **PL** 92-93 Q 3
Mtakuja o **EAT** 214-215 F 4
Mtama o **EAT** 214-215 K 6
Mtambo ~ **EAT** 214-215 F 4
Mtandikeni o **EAT** 212-213 G 6
Mtangano Island ⌒ **EAT** 212-213 D 5
Mtarazi Falls ~ **ZW** 218-219 H 3
Mtera Dam < **EAT** 214-215 H 4
Mtina o **EAT** 214-215 J 6
Mtito Andei o **EAK** 212-213 G 4
Mto Wa Mbu o **EAT** 212-213 E 5
Mtubatuba o **ZA** 220-221 K 4
Mtwara ✿ **EAT** 214-215 L 6
Muadiala o **ZRE** 216-217 F 3
Muaguide o **MOC** 214-215 L 7
Mualádzi o **MOC** 218-219 G 2
Muamba o **MOC** 218-219 K 3
Muaná o **BR** 62-63 K 6
Muanda o **ZRE** 216-217 D 6
Muangai o **ANG** 216-217 F 6
Muang Gnômmarat o **LAO** 158-159 H 2
Muang Hiam o **LAO** 156-157 C 6
Muang Hôngsa o **LAO** 156-157 B 7
Muang Houn o **LAO** 156-157 B 6
Muang Huang o **LAO** 156-157 C 6
Muang Khammouan o **LAO** 158-159 J 1
Muang Khôngxédôn o **LAO** 158-159 H 3
Muang Khoua o **LAO** 156-157 C 6
Muang May o **LAO** 158-159 J 3
Muang Namo o **LAO** 156-157 B 6
Muang Nan o **LAO** 156-157 C 6
Muang Ou Thai o **LAO** 156-157 B 5
Muang Pa-Am o **LAO** 156-157 B 7
Muang Pak-Cay o **LAO** 156-157 B 7
Muang Pakbèng o **LAO** 156-157 B 7
Muang Pakxan o **LAO** 156-157 C 7
Muang Phalan o **LAO** 158-159 J 2
Muang Phin o **LAO** 158-159 J 2
Muang Souy o **LAO** 156-157 C 7
Muang Xaignabouri o **LAO** 156-157 B 7
Muang Xay o **LAO** 156-157 B 6
Muang Xépôn o **LAO** 158-159 J 2
Muanza o **MOC** 218-219 H 4
Muanzanza o **ZRE** 216-217 F 3
Muar o · **MAL** 162-163 D 4
Muara o **BRU** 164-165 D 1
Muara o **RI** 162-163 D 6
Muaraaman o **RI** 162-163 D 7
Muaraatap o **RI** 164-165 E 3
Muarabeliti o **RI** 162-163 E 7
Muarabengkal o **RI** 164-165 E 3
Muarabinuangeun o **RI** 168 A 3
Muarabulian o **RI** 162-163 E 6
Muaradua o **RI** 162-163 E 7
Muaraenim o **RI** 162-163 E 6
Muarahalung o **RI** 164-165 E 3
Muarajawa o **RI** 164-165 E 3
Muarakoman o **RI** 164-165 D 4
Muaranayan o **RI** 164-165 D 3
Muararupit o **RI** 162-163 E 6
Muarasimatalu o **RI** 162-163 C 6
Muaratalang o **RI** 162-163 E 6
Muaratebo o **RI** 162-163 E 6
Muaratembesi o **RI** 162-163 E 6
Muarateweh o **RI** 164-165 D 3
Muara Tuang o **MAL** 162-163 J 4
Muarawahau o **RI** 164-165 E 3

Muari, Pulau o **RI** 164-165 K 4
Muâri, Râs ▲ **PK** 134-135 M 6
Muaro Takus Ruins · **RI** 162-163 D 4
Muatua o **MOC** 218-219 K 2
Mubambe o **ZRE** 214-215 F 4
Mubarek o **US** 136-137 L 5
Mubarraz o **KSA** 130-131 L 5
Mubayira o **ZW** 218-219 F 4
Mubende o **EAU** 212-213 C 3
Mubi o **WAN** 204-205 K 3
Mubrani o **RI** 166-167 G 2
Mucaja o **BR** 62-63 D 4
Mucajaí o **BR** 62-63 D 4
Mucajaí, Rio ~ **BR** 62-63 D 4
Mucajaí, Serra ▲ **BR** 60-61 K 6
Mucajaí, Reserva Biológica de ⊥ **BR**
  60-61 K 6
Mucalic, Rivière ~ **CDN** 36-37 Q 5
Mucanha o **MOC** 218-219 F 2
Mucari o **ANG** 216-217 D 4
Muccan o **AUS** 172-173 E 7
Muchalat Inlet ≈ **CDN** 230-231 C 4
Muchea o **AUS** 176-177 C 5
Muchena o **MOC** 218-219 G 2
Muchinga Escarpment ⊥ **Z** 218-219 F 1
Muchinga Mountains ▲ **Z** 214-215 F 7
Muchinka o **Z** 214-215 F 7
Muchuan o **VRC** 156-157 C 4
Muchuchu Ruins ∴ ** ZW** 218-219 F 4
Mucianyu · **VRC** 154-155 K 1
Muckadilla o **AUS** 178-179 K 4
Muckaty o **AUS** 174-175 B 6
Mučnoj, poluostrov ∽ **RUS** 108-109 E 6
Muco, Rio ~ **CO** 60-61 F 5
Mucojo o **MOC** 214-215 L 7
Mucondo o **ANG** 216-217 F 5
Mucope o **ANG** 216-217 C 8
Mucubela o **MOC** 218-219 J 3
Mucucuaú, Rio ~ **BR** 62-63 D 5
Mucujê o **BR** 72-73 K 2
Mucum o **BR** 74-75 E 7
Mucumbura o **MOC** 218-219 F 3
Mucumbura o **ZW** 218-219 F 3
Mucupia o **MOC** 218-219 J 4
Mucur ✿ **TR** 128-129 F 3
Mucúra o **YV** 60-61 F 5
Mucura, Cachoeira da ~ **BR** 68-69 B 5
Mucuri o **BR** 72-73 L 5
Mucurici o **BR** 72-73 K 5
Mucuripe, Ponta de ▲ **BR** 68-69 J 3
Mucuru, Cachoeira ~ **BR** 62-63 H 5
Mucusso o **ANG** 216-217 F 8
Mucusso, Coutada Pública do ⊥ **ANG**
  216-217 F 8
Mucussueje o **ANG** 216-217 F 5
Mûd o **IR** 134-135 H 2
Mudabil, al- o **KSA** 132-133 B 4
Mudairib, al- o **OM** 132-133 L 2
Mudaisis o **OM** 132-133 J 2
Mudâkem, Bi'r < **LAR** 192-193 E 1
Mudanjiang o **VRC** 150-151 G 5
Mudan Jiang ~ **VRC** 150-151 G 5
Mudanya o **TR** 128-129 C 2
Mudarraq o **KSA** 130-131 H 4
Mudawwa o **JOR** 130-131 E 5
Mudây o **OM** 132-133 H 5
Mudbidri o **IND** 140-141 F 4
Mud Butte o **USA** (SD) 260-261 D 2
Muddawa o **KSA** (OK) 264-265 G 4
Muddebihâl o **IND** 140-141 F 3
Muddus nationalpark · **S** 86-87 K 3
Muddy Boggy Creek ~ **USA** (OK)
  264-265 J 4
Muddy Creek ~ **USA** (UT) 254-255 D 5
Muddy Gap o **USA** (WY) 252-253 J 4
Muddy Gap ▲ **USA** (WY) 252-253 L 4
Muddy Pass ▲ **USA** (CO) 254-255 J 3
Mudgal o **IND** 140-141 F 3
Mudgee o · **AUS** 180-181 K 3
Mudgeeraba o · **AUS** 178-179 M 5
Mudhol o **IND** 140-141 F 2
Mudigere o **IND** 140-141 F 4
Mudigubba o **IND** 140-141 G 3
Mudimbi o **ZRE** 216-217 G 3
Mudjatik River ~ **CDN** 34-35 G 2
Mud Island ⌒ **CDN** (NS) 240-241 J 7
Mud Lake o **USA** (ID) 252-253 F 3
Mud Lake < **USA** (KY) 276-277 J 3
Mudug □ **SP** 208-209 J 5
Mudujiaha ~ **RUS** 108-109 S 7
Mudukulattûr o **IND** 140-141 H 6
Muecate o **MOC** 218-219 K 2
Mueda o **MOC** 214-215 K 6
Muelle de los Bueyes o **NIC** 52-53 B 5
Mueller Range ▲ **AUS** 172-173 H 5
Muende o **MOC** 218-219 G 2
Muermos, los o **RCH** 78-79 C 6
Muerte, Meseta de la ~ **RA** 80 D 4
Muerto, Mar ≈ 52-53 G 3
Muerto, Rio ~ **RA** 76-77 F 2
Muertos Trough ≃ 56 A 3
Muezerskij o **RUS** 88-89 M 5
Mufulira o **Z** 214-215 E 7
Mufu Shan ~ **VRC** 156-157 H 2
Mufu Shan ▲ **VRC** 156-157 H 2
Mugâdhar, Dâr o **SUD** 200-201 H 2
Mugâ ▲ **ETH** 208-209 D 4
Mugâira o **KSA** 130-131 F 4
Mugal, Wâdi ~ **SUD** 200-201 G 3
Mugang o **VRC** 156-157 D 4
Mugânia o **EAT** 212-213 D 4
Muganskaja ravnina ⊥ **AZ** 128-129 N 3
Mugâr o **IR** 134-135 H 1
Mugdilsho ~ **SP** 212-213 K 2
Muger o **ETH** 208-209 D 5
Muger Falls ~ **ETH** 208-209 D 4
Muger Wenz ~ **ETH** 208-209 D 4
Muggar Kangri ▲ **VRC** 144-145 F 4
Muggon o **AUS** 176-177 C 3

Mughal Sarai o **IND** 142-143 C 3
Mughsail o **OM** 132-133 H 5
Mûgib, Wâdi l- ~ **JOR** 130-131 D 2
Mugila, Monts ▲ **ZRE** 214-215 E 4
Mugina o **EAT** 212-213 B 6
Muğla ✿ **TR** 128-129 C 4
Mûgodzor, Gora ▲ **KA** 126-127 N 3
Mûhã, al- o **Y** 132-133 C 7
Muhagiriia o **SUD** 206-207 F 3
Muhaiwir o **IRQ** 128-129 J 6
Muhala o **ZRE** 212-213 B 6
Muhammad, Ra's ▲ **ET** 194-195 G 4
Muhammadâbâd o **IND** 142-143 C 2
Muhammadiya o **IRQ** 128-129 K 6
Muhammad Qol o **SUD** 200-201 H 2
Muharraq, al- o **BRN** 130-131 N 5
Muhât o **KSA** 132-133 C 5
Muhazi, Lac o **RWA** 212-213 C 4
Muheit, Wâdi ~ **SUD** 200-201 F 4
Muheza o **EAT** 212-213 G 5
Muhino o **RUS** 118-119 N 9
Mûhldorf am Inn o **D** 92-93 M 4
Muhlig-Hofmann Mountains = Mühlig-
  Hofmann-fjella ▲ **ARK** 16 F 1
Muhlhausen/ Thüringen o · **D** 92-93 L 3
Muhorini o **EAK** 212-213 E 4
Muhor-Konduj o **RUS** 118-119 F 9
Muhoro o **EAK** 116-117 N 10
Muhorsîbir' ~ **RUS** 118-119 F 9
Muhos o **FIN** 88-89 J 4
Muhu saar ⌒ **EST** 94-95 H 2
Muhutwe o **EAT** 212-213 C 4
Muhuwesi ~ **EAT** (RUV) 214-215 J 6
Mui o **ETH** 208-209 B 4
Müi Cà Mau ▲ **VN** 158-159 H 6
Müi Chân Mây ▲ **VN** 158-159 K 2
Müi Diên ▲ **VN** 158-159 K 5
Müi Dôc ▲ **VN** 158-159 J 2
Muidumbe o **MOC** 214-215 L 6
Muié o **ANG** 216-217 F 7
Müi Én ▲ **VN** 158-159 K 4
Müi Gành ▲ **VN** 158-159 K 4
Müi Kê Gà ▲ **VN** 158-159 K 5
Müi Ky Vân ▲ **VN** 158-159 J 5
Müi Lach Quèn ▲ **VN** 156-157 D 7
Müi La Gàn ▲ **VN** 158-159 K 5
Müi Lai ▲ **VN** 158-159 J 2
Müi Nam Trâm ▲ **VN** 158-159 K 3
Müi Nai ▲ **VN** 158-159 H 6
Müi Nay ▲ **VN** 158-159 K 4
Muine o **ANG** 216-217 E 7
Muineachán = Monaghan ✿ **IRL**
  90-91 D 4
Muira, Rio ~ **MOC** 200-201 F 3
Muir Glacier ⊂ **USA** 20-21 W 7
Muiron Islands ⌒ **AUS** 172-173 B 6
Muisma ~ **RUS** 116-117 Z 3
Muisne o **EC** 64-65 B 1
Muite o **MOC** 218-219 K 2
Muitos Capões o **BR** 74-75 E 7
Muiuçu ou Puiuçu, Igarapé ~ **BR**
  66-67 H 6
Muizenberg o **ZA** 220-221 D 7
Muja ~ **RUS** 118-119 F 7
Mujakan ~ **RUS** 118-119 F 7
Mujazzam, Sabkhat o **LAR** 190-191 G 5
Mujeres, Isla ⌒ **MEX** 52-53 L 1
Mujezerskij o **KA** 124-125 H 4
Mujinga ~ **RUS** 118-119 G 6
Mujnak o **US** 136-137 F 3
Mujšin ~ **RUS** 118-119 F 6
Muju o **ROK** 150-151 F 9
Mujunkum ⊥ **KA** 124-125 O 5
Mukah o **MAL** 162-163 K 3
Muka Head ▲ **MAL** 162-163 C 3
Mukala o **ZRE** 210-211 F 6
Mukana o **ZRE** 214-215 D 5
Mukanga o **ZRE** 216-217 F 3
Mukaryjian ~ **RUS** 112-113 Q 5
Mukawo o **PNG** 183 E 5
Mukawa-gawa ~ **J** 152-153 K 3
Mukawwa', Gazirat ⌒ **SUD** 200-201 H 2
Mukdahan o **THA** 158-159 H 2
Mukden = Shenyang o **VRC**
  150-151 D 7
Mukebo o **ZRE** 214-215 E 4
Mukerian o **IND** 138-139 E 3
Muketei River ~ **CDN** (ONT)
  234-235 R 2
Muke T'uri o **ETH** 208-209 D 4
Mukilteo o **USA** (WA) 244-245 C 3
Mukinbudin o **AUS** 176-177 E 5
Mukomuko o **RI** 162-163 D 6
Mukongo o **EAU** 212-213 D 6
Mukry o **TM** 136-137 J 6
Muksu ~ **TJ** 136-137 M 5
Muksuniha ~ **RUS** 108-109 V 6
Muksunuoha-tas, gora ▲ **RUS**
  110-111 X 4
Muktsar o **IND** 138-139 E 4
Mukuku o **Z** 214-215 E 7
Mukulu, Kayembe- o **ZRE** 214-215 D 5
Mukulu, Mutombo- o **ZRE** 214-215 C 4
Mukulushi ~ **ZRE** 214-215 E 6
Mukunsa o **Z** 214-215 F 5
Mukupa Kaoma o **Z** 214-215 F 5
Mukutawa River ~ **CDN** 34-35 H 4
Mûl o **IND** 138-139 G 9
Mula o **E** 98-99 G 5
Mula ~ **PK** 134-135 M 4
Mula, la ▲ **I** 100-101 E 5
Mulalilh, al- o **KSA** 130-131 F 5
Mulaku Atoll ⌒ **MV** 140-141 B 6
Mûlali cukurligi ⊥ **US** 136-137 M 5
Mulam ~ **RUS** 120-121 D 5
Mulamba Gungu, Chute ~ **ZRE**
  214-215 D 5
Mulan o **IND** 138-139 B 8
Mulanay o **RP** 160-161 E 6
Mulanje o **MW** 218-219 H 2
Mulanje Mountains ▲ **MW** 218-219 H 2
Mulanweichang · **VRC** 148-149 N 6
Mulatos o **CO** 60-61 C 3
Mulawa o **PK** 138-139 D 9

Mulbâgal o **IND** 140-141 H 4
Mulberry o **USA** (AR) 276-277 A 5
Mulberry o **USA** (FL) 286-287 H 4
Mulberry o **USA** (AL)
  284-285 C 4
Mulberry Creek ~ **USA** (TX) 264-265 C 4
Mulberry Fork ~ **USA** (AL) 284-285 D 3
Mulberry River ~ **USA** (AR) 276-277 B 5
Mulchatna River ~ **USA** 20-21 N 6
Mulchen o **RCH** 78-79 C 4
Mulchole o **IND** 140-141 G 5
Mulde ~ **D** 92-93 M 3
Muldrow o **USA** (OK) 264-265 K 3
Muleba o **EAT** 212-213 C 4
Mule Creek Junction o **USA** (WY)
  252-253 O 3
Mulegé o · **MEX** 50-51 D 4
Mulembe o **ZRE** 214-215 E 4
Muleshoe o **USA** (TX) 264-265 B 4
Muleta ▲ **ETH** 208-209 E 4
Muleta o **RP** 160-161 F 9
Mulevala o **MOC** 218-219 J 3
Mulga Creek ~ **AUS** 178-179 J 6
Mulgildie o **AUS** 178-179 L 3
Mulgoa ~ **AUS** 20-21 J 3
Mulgul o **AUS** 176-177 E 2
Mulhacén ▲ **E** 98-99 F 6
Mulhouse o · **F** 90-91 L 8
Mulhurst Bay o **CDN** (ALB) 232-233 E 2
Muli ∴ 166-167 K 5 .
Mulia o **RI** 166-167 J 3
Muli Channel ≈ 166-167 K 5
Mulilansolo o **Z** 214-215 G 6
Muling o **VRC** 150-151 H 5
Mulis'ma ~ **RUS** 118-119 O 8
Mûlki o **IND** 140-141 F 4
Mull ⌒ **GB** 90-91 D 3
Mullaittivu o **CL** 140-141 J 6
Mullaley o **AUS** 178-179 K 6
Mullan o **USA** (MT) 250-251 D 4
Mullen o **USA** (NE) 262-263 E 2
Müller, Pegunungan ▲ **RI** 162-163 K 4
Muller Range ▲ **PNG** 183 B 3
Mullet Key ~ **USA** (FL) 286-287 G 4
Mullett Lake < **USA** (MI) 272-273 E 4
Mullewa o **AUS** 176-177 C 4
Mulligan River ~ **AUS** 178-179 E 3
Mullingar o **CDN** (SAS) 232-233 L 2
Mullingar = An Muileann -gCearr o **IRL**
  90-91 D 5
Mullins o **USA** (SC) 284-285 L 2
Mu'muga ~ **RUS** 118-119 O 8
Mulobezi o **Z** 218-219 D 3
Mulonda o **ANG** 216-217 C 7
Mulonga Plain ⊥ **Z** 218-219 B 3
Mulongo o **ZRE** 214-215 D 5
Mulongoie ~ **ZRE** 210-211 L 6
Multai o **IND** 138-139 G 9
Multân o ·· **PK** 138-139 C 4
Mulu o **ETH** 208-209 E 4
Mulu, Gunung ▲ **MAL** 164-165 D 1
Mulungu ~ **ZRE** 214-215 B 5
Mulungushi o **Z** 214-215 E 6
Mulungushi Dam < **Z** 218-219 E 2
Mülûr o **IND** 140-141 H 4
Mulurulu Lake o **AUS** 180-181 G 2
Mulvihill o **CDN** (MAN) 234-235 E 4
Mulym'ja ~ **RUS** 114-115 H 4
Mulyungarie o **AUS** 178-179 F 6
Muma o **ZRE** 210-211 J 2
Mumallah o **SUD** 206-207 G 3
Mumbai = Bombay ✿ **IND** 138-139 D 10
Mumballup o **AUS** 176-177 D 6
Mumbeji o **Z** 218-219 B 1
Mumbleberry o **AUS** 178-179 E 3
Mumbondo o **ANG** 216-217 C 5
Mumbué o **ANG** 216-217 D 6
Mumbwa o **Z** 218-219 D 2
Mume, Swana- o **ZRE** 214-215 D 6
Mumena o **ZRE** 214-215 D 6
Mumeng o **PNG** 183 D 4
Mumias o **EAK** 212-213 E 3
Mumoma o **ZRE** 214-215 B 4
Mumulusan o **RI** 164-165 H 4
Mun o **RI** 166-167 G 4
Muna o **MEX** 52-53 K 1
Muna ~ **RUS** 110-111 R 5
Muna ⌒ **RI** 164-165 G 5
Muna, Dunu- o **RI** 166-167 G 4
Muna, Selat ≈ 164-165 H 5
Münäjšy o **KA** 126-127 K 6
Munakan ~ **RUS** 110-111 M 6
Munarra o **AUS** 176-177 D 4
Munaya ~ **CAM** 204-205 J 5
Muncakabau o **RI** 162-163 D 6
München ✿ **D** 92-93 L 4
Munchique, Parque Nacional ⊥ **CO**
  60-61 C 6
Muncho Lake o **CDN** 30-31 G 6
Muncho Lake Provincial Park ⊥ **CDN**
  30-31 G 6
Muncie o **USA** (IN) 274-275 N 4
Muncoonie Lake West o **AUS**
  178-179 E 3
Munda o **PK** 138-139 C 4
Munda o **SOL** 184 I c 3
Mundabullangana o **AUS** 172-173 D 6
Mundare o **CDN** (ALB) 232-233 F 2
Mundaring o **AUS** 176-177 D 5
Munday o **USA** (TX) 264-265 C 5
Mundemba o **CAM** 204-205 H 6
Mundgod o **IND** 140-141 F 3
Mundico Coelho o **BR** 66-67 J 4
Mundijong o **AUS** 176-177 D 5
Mundiwindi o **AUS** 176-177 E 2
Mundo Novo o **BR** (BAH) 68-69 H 7
Mundo Novo o **BR** (GSU) 76-77 K 2
Mundo Nuevo o **YV** 60-61 J 2
Mundra o **IND** 138-139 B 8
Mundrabilla o **AUS** 176-177 J 5
Mundrabilla Motel o **AUS** 176-177 J 5
Mundubbera o **AUS** 178-179 L 3
Munduoskoe, ozero o **RUS** 108-109 X 8
Mundurucânia, Reserva Florestal ⊥ **BR** (P)
  66-67 J 6
Mundurucânia, Reserva Florestal ⊥ **BR** (P)
  66-67 H 6

Munduručču ~ RUS 118-119 O 5
Mundurucu, Área Indígena ⚔ BR 66-67 J 6
Mündwa o IND 138-139 D 6
Munenga o ANG 216-217 C 5
Munera o E 98-99 F 5
Munford o USA (TN) 276-277 F 5
Munfordville o USA (KY) 276-277 K 3
Mungabroom o AUS 174-175 C 5
Mungallala o AUS 178-179 J 4
Mungallala Creek ~ AUS 178-179 J 5
Mungaoli o IND 138-139 G 7
Mungári o MOC 218-219 G 3
Mungbere o ZRE 212-213 B 2
Munger o IND 142-143 E 3
Mungeranie o AUS 178-179 E 5
Munggurеsak, Tanjung ▲ RI 162-163 H 4
Mungindi o AUS 178-179 K 5
Munglinup o AUS 176-177 F 6
Mungo o ANG (HBO) 216-217 D 5
Mungo o ANG (LUN) 216-217 E 3
Mungo o SME 62-63 G 3
Mungo National Park ⊥ AUS 180-181 G 2
Mungra Badshahpur o IND 142-143 C 3
Munhango o ANG 216-217 E 6
Munhoz o BR 72-73 G 7
Munich = München ☆ D 92-93 L 4
Muniengashi ~ ZRE 218-219 E 1
Muniesa o E 98-99 G 4
Munikan ~ RUS 122-123 F 2
Munim, Rio ~ BR 68-69 G 3
Munimadugu o IND 140-141 G 3
Munising o USA (MI) 270-271 M 4
Muniungu o ZRE 210-211 F 6
Muniz Freire o BR 72-73 K 6
Munkamba ~ RUS 116-117 N 4
Munkumpu o Z 218-219 D 1
Münly, tau ▲ KA 124-125 G 5
Munmarlary o AUS 172-173 L 2
Munn, Cape ▲ CDN 36-37 G 2
Munnat o IND 140-141 G 5
Munnikspoort ▲ ZA 220-221 G 6
Muñoz Gamero, Península ⌣ RCH 80 D 6
Munqaṭi', al- o Y 132-133 D 6
Munro, Mount ▲ AUS 180-181 K 6
Munsan o ROK 150-151 F 9
Munse o RI 164-165 H 6
Munson o CDN (ALB) 232-233 F 4
Munson o USA (FL) 286-287 C 1
Münster o•• D 92-93 J 3
Münster = Müstair o•• CH 92-93 L 5
Munte o RI 164-165 F 3
Munteme o EAU 212-213 C 3
Muntgatsi o EAK 212-213 E 3
Muntilan o RI 168 D 3
Muntok o RI 162-163 F 6
Muntu o EAU 212-213 D 3
Muntu o ZRE 210-211 G 5
Munukata o J 152-153 D 8
Munyamadzi ~ Z 218-219 F 1
Munyaroo Conservation Park ⊥ AUS 180-181 D 2
Munyati ~ ZW 218-219 E 3
Munzur Vadisi Milli Parkı ⊥ TR 128-129 H 3
Muoco o MOC 218-219 J 1
Muodoslompolo o S 86-87 L 3
Muohyang San ▲ DVR 150-151 F 7
Mu'ò'ng Cha o VN 156-157 B 6
Muong Het o LAO 156-157 D 6
Mu'ò'ng Kim o VN 156-157 C 6
Mu'ò'ng Lam o VN 156-157 D 7
Mu'ò'ng Loi o VN 156-157 C 6
Mu'ò'ng Mu'ò'n o VN 156-157 C 6
Mu'ò'ng Pôn o VN 156-157 C 6
Mu'ò'ng Tè ☆ VN 156-157 C 5
Muonio o FIN 88-89 G 3
Muonioälven ~ S 86-87 L 3
Muonionjoki ~ • FIN 88-89 G 3
Muor, Pulau ⌒ RI 164-165 G 3
Muostah, mys ▲ RUS 110-111 R 4
Muostah, ostrov ⌒ RUS 110-111 S 4
Mupa o ANG 216-217 C 8
Mupa ~ MOC 218-219 H 4
Mupa, Parque Nacional da ⊥ ANG 216-217 C 7
Mupamadzi ~ Z 218-219 F 1
Mupele, Chute ~ ZRE 210-211 K 3
Mupfure ~ ZW 218-219 E 3
Muqaddam, Wādī ~ SUD 200-201 E 5
Muqakoori o SP 208-209 H 6
Muqsim, Ğabal ▲ ET 194-195 G 6
Muqšin o OM 132-133 J 4
Muqui o BR 72-73 K 6
Muqui, Rio ~ BR 70-71 F 2
Muqur o AFG 134-135 M 2
Mura o BR 66-67 H 4
Mura ~ RUS 116-117 J 7
Muradiye o TR 128-129 K 3
Muraduagar o IND 138-139 F 5
Murafa ~ UA 102-103 F 3
Murair, Ğazirat ⌒ ET 194-195 G 6
Murakami o J 152-153 H 5
Muralgarra o AUS 176-177 D 4
Murallón, Cerro ▲ RCH 80 D 4
Muramgaon o IND 142-143 B 5
Muramvya o BU 212-213 B 5
Muranga o EAK 212-213 F 4
Murangering o EAK 212-213 E 2
Muraré, Rio ~ BR 62-63 H 5
Muraši o RUS 96-97 F 4
Murat, Château • F 56 E 4
Murat Çayı ~ TR 128-129 K 3
Murat Dağı ▲ TR 128-129 C 3
Murat Nehri ~ TR 128-129 J 3
Muratus, Pegunungan ▲ RI 164-165 D 5
Muravera o I 100-101 B 5
Murbād o IND 138-139 D 10
Murça o P 98-99 D 4
Mürče Ḥūrt o IR 134-135 D 2
Murchinson Range ▲ AUS 174-175 C 7
Murchison o AUS 180-181 H 4
Murchison o NZ 182 D 4
Murchison, Cape ▲ CDN 36-37 R 3
Murchison, Mount ▲ AUS 176-177 D 3
Murchison Falls ~ EAU 212-213 C 2
Murchison Falls National Park ⊥ EAU 212-213 C 2
Murchison Island ⌒ CDN (ONT) 234-235 P 4
Murchison River ~ AUS 176-177 C 3
Murchison River ~ CDN 24-25 a 6
Murchison Settlement Roadhouse o AUS 176-177 C 3
Murchison Sund ≈ 26-27 P 5
Murchisson, Mount ▲ WAN 204-205 H 4
Murcia o E 98-99 G 6
Murcia ◘ E 98-99 G 6
Murder Creek ~ USA (AL) 284-285 D 5
Murdo o USA (SD) 260-261 F 3
Murdochville o CDN (QUE) 240-241 K 2
Murdock o USA (MN) 270-271 C 5
Murdock o USA (NE) 262-263 K 4
Murehwa o ZW 218-219 F 3
Mureji o WAN 204-205 F 4
Murèn, Zun ~ RUS 116-117 L 10
Mureș ~ RO 102-103 D 4
Muret o F 90-91 H 10
Murfreesboro o USA (AR) 276-277 B 6
Murfreesboro o USA (NC) 282-283 K 4
Murfreesboro o USA (TN) 276-277 J 5
Murgab o TJ (GOR) 146-147 B 6
Murgab ~ TJ 136-137 N 5
Murgab o TM 136-137 H 6
Murgab ~ TM 136-137 H 7
Murgaf ~ RUS 112-113 O 4
Murgenella ⚔ AUS 172-173 L 1
Murgenella Wildlife Sanctuary ⊥ AUS 172-173 L 1
Murgha Kibzai o PK 138-139 B 4
Murgho, Hāmūn-i- ⊖ PK 134-135 L 5
Murgon o AUS 178-179 L 4
Murgoo o AUS 176-177 D 3
Murgud o IND 140-141 F 2
Muri o VRC 154-155 B 3
Muriaé o BR 72-73 J 6
Muriaé, Rio ~ BR 72-73 K 6
Murici, Ponta do ▲ BR 68-69 F 3
Muricilândia o BR 68-69 D 5
Muricizal, Rio ~ BR 68-69 D 5
Muridke o PK 138-139 E 4
Muriege o ANG 216-217 F 4
Muriel Lake o CDN 32-33 P 4
Murighiol = Independența o • RO 102-103 F 5
Murillo o CDN (ONT) 234-235 O 6
Murinja o RUS 116-117 N 8
Muritiba o BR 72-73 L 2
Müritz ⊖ D 92-93 M 2
Müritz-National-Park ⊥ D 92-93 M 2
Muriwai o NZ 182 F 3
Murizidié Pass ▲ LAR 192-193 F 6
Murman, zaliv ⊖ RUS 108-109 G 4
Murmanca, buhta ⊖ RUS 108-109 N 3
Murmansk ☆ RUS 88-89 M 2
Murmanskiy Bereg = Murmanskij bereg ⌣ RUS 88-89 M 2
Murmanskoye Rise ≃ 10-11 C 1
Murmaši o RUS 88-89 M 2
Muro Lucano o I 100-101 E 4
Murom ☆ RUS 94-95 S 4
Muroran o J 152-153 J 3
Muros o E 98-99 C 3
Muroto o J 152-153 F 8
Muroto-saki ▲ J 152-153 F 8
Murphy o USA (ID) 252-253 B 3
Murphy o USA (NC) 282-283 C 5
Murphy o USA (OR) 244-245 B 8
Murphy Head ▲ CDN 36-37 S 5
Murphy Hot Springs • USA (ID) 252-253 C 4
Murphysboro o USA (IL) 276-277 F 3
Mürqūm, Kūh-e ▲ IR 134-135 G 2
Murra Murra o AUS 178-179 J 5
Murray o USA (IA) 274-275 E 3
Murray o USA (KY) 276-277 G 4
Murray o USA (UT) 254-255 D 3
Murray, Cape ▲ CDN 24-25 O 2
Murray, Lake o PNG 183 A 4
Murray, Lake < USA (OK) 264-265 G 4
Murray, Lake < USA (SC) 284-285 J 2
Murray Bridge o• AUS 180-181 E 3
Murray Downs o AUS 178-179 C 1
Murray Fracture Zone ≃ 14-15 N 4
Murray Harbour o CDN (NS) 240-241 N 4
Murray Inlet ≈ 24-25 P 3
Murray Islands ⌒ AUS 183 C 5
Murray Maxwell Bay ≈ 24-25 f 5
Murray Range ▲ PNG 183 B 4
Murray River ~ AUS 180-181 E 3
Murray River ~ CDN (BC) 228-229 N 2
Murray River Basin ⩦ AUS 180-181 F 2
Murraysburg o ZA 220-221 F 5
Murray-Sunset National Park ⊥ AUS 180-181 F 3
Murray Town o AUS 180-181 E 2
Murrayville o AUS 180-181 F 3
Murree o PK 138-139 D 3
Murrej, mys ▲ RUS 84-85 b 2
Murri, Rio ~ CO 60-61 C 4
Murroa o MOC 218-219 J 3
Murroe Lake o CDN 30-31 U 6
Murrumbidgee River ~ AUS 180-181 H 3
Murrumburrah o AUS 180-181 K 3
Murrupula o MOC 218-219 K 2
Murrurundi o AUS 178-179 L 6
Murrysville o USA (PA) 280-281 G 3
Murshidābād o• IND 142-143 F 3
Murtajāpur o IND 138-139 F 9
Murtaugh o USA (ID) 252-253 D 4
Murtle Lake ⊖ CDN (BC) 228-229 P 4
Murtle River ~ CDN (BC) 228-229 P 4
Murtoa o AUS 180-181 G 4
Murtovaara o FIN 88-89 K 4
Muru, Rio ~ BR 66-67 B 7
Murua o PNG 183 C 4
Murua Island = Woodlark Island ⌒ PNG 183 G 5
Murual, Lake < USA (TX) 264-265 K 6
Muruchachi o YV 60-61 F 3
Murud o• IND 138-139 D 10
Murud, Gunung ▲ MAL 164-165 D 2
Muruken o PNG 183 C 3
Murun, gora ▲ RUS 118-119 J 6
Murupara o NZ 182 F 3
Muruptumatari ~ RUS 108-109 h 4
Murupu o BR 62-63 D 4
Mururé, Igarapé ~ BR 68-69 C 6
Mururoa Atoll ⌒ F 13 O 5
Murwāra o IND 142-143 B 4
Murwillumbah o AUS 178-179 M 5
Murygino o RUS 96-97 F 4
Mürzzuschlag o A 92-93 N 5
Muş ☆ TR 128-129 J 3
Mūsa, 'Ain • ET 194-195 F 3
Mūsa, Ğabal ▲ ET 194-195 F 3
Mūsā, Ḫōr-e ≈ 134-135 C 3
Mūsā, Wādī o JOR 130-131 D 2
Musa Āli Terara ▲ DJI 200-201 L 6
Musadi o ZRE 210-211 J 5
Mūsā Ḫēl o AFG 138-139 B 3
Musaia o WAL 202-203 E 5
Musaʻid o Q 134-135 D 6
Musaimir o Y 132-133 D 7
Mušairib, Ra's ▲ UAE 134-135 D 6
Mušairifa, al- o SYR 128-129 H 4
Mūsa Khel o PK 138-139 C 3
Mūsa Khel Bāzār o PK 138-139 B 4
Musala ▲ BG 102-103 C 6
Musala, Pulau ⌒ RI 162-163 C 4
Muṣallā, al- o OM 132-133 L 2
Musan o DVR 150-151 G 6
Musandam, Ra's ▲ OM 134-135 G 5
Mūsā Qal'e o AFG 134-135 L 2
Mūsā Qal'e, Rūd-e ~ AFG 134-135 L 2
Musa River ~ PNG 183 E 5
Musashi o J 152-153 D 8
Mušattā, Qaṣr al- ∴• JOR 130-131 E 2
Musawa o WAN 198-199 C 6
Musawwarat, Temples of • SUD 200-201 F 4
Musayyib, al- ☆ IRQ 128-129 L 6
Mušbih, Ğabal ▲ ET 194-195 G 6
Muscat = Masqaṭ ★•• OM 132-133 L 2
Muscatatuck River ~ USA (IN) 274-275 M 6
Muscatine o USA (IA) 274-275 G 3
Muscoda o USA (WI) 274-275 H 1
Muse o USA (OK) 264-265 K 4
Musende o ZRE 210-211 L 6
Musenge o ZRE (KIV) 212-213 B 4
Musenge o ZRE (SHA) 214-215 B 5
Musengezi ~ ZW 218-219 F 3
Museum o• RI 164-165 G 6
Musgrave o AUS 174-175 G 4
Musgrave o CDN (BC) 230-231 F 5
Musgrave, Port ≈ 174-175 F 3
Musgrave Harbour o CDN (NFL) 242-243 P 3
Musgrave Ranges ▲ AUS 176-177 L 3
Mus-Haja, gora ▲ RUS 120-121 J 2
Mushandike Sanctuary ⊥ ZW 218-219 F 5
Mushayfāt o SUD 206-207 K 3
Mushenge o ZRE 210-211 H 6
Mushie o ZRE 210-211 F 5
Mushima o Z 218-219 C 2
Mushipashi o Z 214-215 F 6
Mushota o Z 214-215 E 5
Mushu Island ⌒ PNG 183 B 2
Mūsi ~ IND 140-141 H 2
Musi ~ RI 162-163 F 6
Musidora o CDN (ALB) 232-233 G 2
Musin o WAN 204-205 E 5
Musiri o IND 140-141 H 5
Mūsiyan o IR 134-135 B 2
Muskeg Lake Indian Reservation ⚔ CDN (SAS) 232-233 M 3
Muskego o USA (WI) 274-275 K 2
Muskegon o USA (MI) 272-273 C 4
Muskegon Heights o USA (MI) 272-273 C 4
Muskegon River ~ USA (MI) 272-273 D 4
Muskeg River o CDN (ALB) 228-229 Q 3
Muskeg River ~ CDN 30-31 H 5
Muskingum River ~ USA (OH) 280-281 E 4
Muskira o IND 138-139 G 7
Muskoday Indian Reservation ⚔ CDN (SAS) 232-233 N 2
Muskogee o USA (OK) 264-265 J 3
Muskox Lake ⊖ CDN 30-31 P 3
Muskratdam Lake ⊖ CDN 34-35 L 4
Muskwa o CDN 30-31 H 6
Muskwa River ~ CDN 30-31 H 6
Muskwa River ~ CDN 32-33 N 3
Muslimiya o SYR 128-129 G 4
Muslјumovo ☆ RUS 96-97 H 6
Musoma ☆ EAT 212-213 D 4
Musondweji ~ Z 218-219 C 1
Musongoie o ZRE 214-215 C 5
Mus-Onnjue ~ RUS 118-119 O 7
Musoro o Z 218-219 F 1
Musoshi o ZRE 214-215 D 6
Musquaro, Lac ⊖ CDN (QUE) 242-243 G 2
Musquash o CDN (NB) 240-241 J 5
Musquodoboit Harbour o CDN (NS) 240-241 M 6
Mussel Fork ~ USA (MO) 274-275 F 5
Musselshell o USA (MT) 250-251 L 5
Musselshell River ~ USA (MT) 250-251 L 5
Mussende o ANG 216-217 D 5
Musserra o ANG 216-217 B 3
Mussolo o ANG 216-217 D 4
Mussuma o ANG (MOX) 216-217 F 7
Mussuma ~ ANG 216-217 F 7
Mustāfābād o PK 138-139 D 4
Mustafakemalpaşa ☆ TR 128-129 C 2
Mustahil o ETH 208-209 G 6
Müstair = Münster o•• CH 92-93 L 5
Mustang o NEP 144-145 D 6
Mustang o USA (TX) 264-265 B 6
Mustang Himal ▲ NEP 144-145 D 6
Mustang Island ⌒ USA (TX) 266-267 K 6
Musters, Lago o RA 80 F 2
Mustique Island ⌒ WV 56 E 5
Mustjala o EST 94-95 H 2
Mustvee o EST 94-95 K 2
Musu Dan ▲ DVR 150-151 G 7
Musún, Cerro ▲ NIC 52-53 B 5
Muswellbrook o• AUS 180-181 L 2
Müt o ET 194-195 D 5
Mut ☆ TR 128-129 E 4
Mutá, Ponta do ▲ BR 72-73 L 2
Mutale ~ ZA 218-219 F 6
Mutanda o Z 214-215 D 7
Muṭannā, al ◘ IRQ 130-131 J 2
Mutarara o MOC 218-219 H 3
Mutare ☆• ZW 218-219 G 4
Mutarnee o AUS 174-175 J 6
Muteba, Xá- o ANG 216-217 D 4
Mutenge o Z 218-219 E 1
Mutha o EAK (EAS) 212-213 G 4
Mutha ▲ EAK (EAS) 212-213 G 4
Mutici o BR 68-69 L 6
Mutiene o ZRE 210-211 E 6
Muting o RI 166-167 L 5
Mutinglupa o RP 160-161 D 5
Mutir o EAU 212-213 C 2
Mutis, Gunung ▲ RI 166-167 C 6
Mutki ☆ TR 128-129 J 3
Mutnaja, buhta ⊖ RUS 120-121 S 7
Mutni ~ PK 134-135 M 6
Mutnyj Materik o RUS 88-89 X 4
Mutoko o ZW 218-219 G 3
Mutombo, Bwana- o ZRE 216-217 E 3
Mutombo-Mukulu o ZRE 214-215 C 5
Mutomo o EAK 212-213 G 4
Mutoraj o RUS 116-117 K 5
Mutorashanga o ZW 218-219 F 3
Mutoto o ZRE (KOC) 210-211 J 6
Mutoto o ZRE (SHA) 214-215 E 4
Mutsamudu o• COM 222-223 D 4
Mutshatsha o ZRE 214-215 C 6
Mutsu o J 152-153 J 4
Muttaburra o AUS 178-179 H 2
Mutton Bay o CDN (QUE) 242-243 J 2
Mutüali o MOC 218-219 J 2
Mutukula o EAU 212-213 C 4
Mutum o BR (AMA) 66-67 G 6
Mutum o BR (MIN) 72-73 K 5
Mutum, Cachoeira ~ BR 66-67 J 5
Mutum, Ilha do ⌒ BR 66-67 F 7
Mutum, Rio ~ BR 66-67 C 5
Mutum Biyu o WAN 204-205 J 4
Mutumbo o ANG 216-217 D 6
Mutum Daya o WAN 204-205 J 4
Mutum ou Madeira, Rio ~ BR 70-71 K 5
Mutum Paraná o BR 66-67 E 7
Mutungu-Tari o ZRE 216-217 D 3
Mutuoca, Ilha da ⌒ BR 68-69 F 2
Mutur o CL 140-141 J 6
Mututi, Ilha o BR 62-63 J 6
Mutu-wan ≈ 152-153 J 4
Mutwanga o ZRE 212-213 B 3
Muuriola o FIN 88-89 H 3
Mu Us Shamo ⩦ VRC 154-155 E 2
Muvattupula o IND 140-141 G 6
Muwaih, al- o KSA 130-131 G 6
Muwaiha, Ğabal ▲ UAE 134-135 F 6
Muwailih, al- o KSA 130-131 G 6
Muwassam o KSA 132-133 C 5
Muwo Island ⌒ PNG 183 F 5
Muxima o ANG 216-217 B 4
Muyinga o BU 212-213 C 5
Muy Muy o NIC 52-53 B 5
Muyombe o Z 214-215 G 6
Muyuka o CAM 204-205 H 6
Muyumba o ZRE 214-215 D 4
Muzaffarabad o IND 138-139 D 2
Muzaffargarh o PK 138-139 C 4
Muzaffarnagar o IND 138-139 F 5
Muzaffarpur o IND 142-143 D 2
Muzāhimiya, al- o KSA 130-131 K 5
Muzambinho o BR 72-73 G 6
Muze o MOC 218-219 F 2
Muzej narodnoj architektury i pobutu • UA 102-103 G 2
muzej-usad'ba "Tarhany" • RUS 94-95 S 5
Muzhen o VRC 154-155 K 5
Muži o RUS 114-115 H 2
Mužizi ~ EAU 212-213 C 3
Muzkol, hrebet ▲ TJ 136-137 N 5
Muzo o CO 60-61 D 5
Muzon, Cape ▲ USA 32-33 D 4
Muztag ▲ VRC 144-145 C 2
Muztag ▲ VRC 144-145 F 2
Muztagata ▲ VRC 146-147 B 6
Mvangan o CAM 210-211 C 2
Mveng o CAM 210-211 D 2
Mvengué o CAM 210-211 C 2
Mvera o MW 218-219 H 1
Mvolo o SUD 206-207 J 5
Mvomero o EAT 214-215 J 4
Mvoung ~ G 210-211 D 3
Mvouti o RCB 210-211 D 6
Mvuha o EAT 214-215 J 4
Mvuma o ZW 218-219 F 4
Mvurwi o ZW 218-219 F 3
Mvuvye ~ Z 218-219 F 2
Mwabungu o EAK 212-213 G 6
Mwadi-Kalumbu o ZRE 216-217 E 3
Mwadingusha o ZRE 214-215 D 6
Mwafwe ~ Z 218-219 C 1
Mwaga o EAT 214-215 J 3
Mwala o MW 218-219 H 3
Mwaleshi ~ Z 214-215 F 6
Mwambo o EAT 214-215 L 6
Mwambwa o EAT 214-215 G 6
Mwami o ZW 218-219 E 3
Mwanesi Range ▲ ZW 218-219 F 4
Mwanga o EAT 212-213 F 5
Mwanga o ZRE 212-213 A 4
Mwanga-Ndeke o ZRE 210-211 L 6
Mwangalala o ZRE 214-215 D 6
Mwangia, Pania- o ZRE 214-215 E 4
Mwango o ZRE 214-215 C 4
Mwanibwaghosu o SOL 184 I f 4
Mwanisenga o EAT 212-213 D 6
Mwanza ◘ EAT 212-213 D 5
Mwanza ☆• EAT 212-213 D 5
Mwanza o MW 218-219 H 3
Mwanza o ZRE 214-215 D 4
Mwanza Gulf ⊖ EAT 212-213 D 5
Mwanzangoma ~ ZRE 210-211 J 6
Mwaru ~ EAT 212-213 E 6
Mwatasi o EAT (IRI) 214-215 J 4
Mwatate o EAK 212-213 G 5
Mwatate ~ EAK 212-213 G 5
Mwea National Reserve ⊥ EAK 212-213 F 4
Mweka o ZRE 210-211 H 6
Mwembeshi o Z 218-219 D 2
Mwenda o Z 214-215 E 6
Mwene-Biji o ZRE 214-215 B 5
Mwene-Ditu o ZRE 214-215 B 4
Mwenezi o ZW (Mvi) 218-219 F 5
Mwenezi ~ ZW 218-219 F 5
Mwenga o ZRE 212-213 B 5
Mweru, Lake ⊖ Z 214-215 E 5
Mweru Wantipa, Lake ⊖ Z 214-215 E 5
Mweru Wantipa National Park ⊥ Z 214-215 E 5
Mwilambwe o ZRE 214-215 C 5
Mwimbwi o EAT (RUK) 214-215 F 5
Mwingi o EAK 212-213 G 4
Mwinilunga o Z 214-215 C 6
Mwitika o EAK 212-213 G 4
Mwitikira o EAT (DOD) 214-215 H 4
Mwogo ~ RWA 212-213 B 5
Mwombezhi ~ Z 218-219 C 1
My ~ RUS 122-123 J 2
Mya, Oued ~ DZ 190-191 D 6
Myaing o MYA 142-143 J 5
Myakka City o USA (FL) 286-287 G 4
Myakka Head o USA (FL) 286-287 G 4
Myakka River ~ USA (FL) 286-287 G 4
Myakka River State Park ⊥ USA (FL) 286-287 G 4
Myall Lakes National Park ⊥ AUS 180-181 M 2
Myanaung o MYA 142-143 J 6
Myanmar ■ MYA 142-143 J 5
Mychajlivka o UA 102-103 J 4
Mychla o MYA 142-143 K 6
Mye, Mount ▲ CDN 20-21 Y 5
Myerstown o USA (PA) 280-281 K 3
Myingyan o MYA 142-143 J 5
Myinmoletkat Taung ▲ MYA 158-159 E 4
Myitkyina o MYA 142-143 K 3
Myitnge ~ MYA 142-143 K 5
Myittha o MYA 142-143 K 5
Mykenai •• GR 100-101 J 6
Mykolajiv o UA 102-103 G 4
Mykolajivs'ka cerkva • UA 102-103 C 3
Mykolayiv = Mykolajiv o UA 102-103 G 4
Myky, Área Indígena ⚔ BR 70-71 H 3
Myla o RUS 88-89 V 4
Myla ~ RUS 88-89 V 4
Mylga ~ RUS 120-121 N 2
Mylius Erichsen Land ⩦ GRØ 26-27 m 3
Mylo o USA (ND) 258-259 H 3
Mymensingh o BD 142-143 G 3
Mynämäki o FIN 88-89 F 6
Myndagaj o RUS 120-121 E 3
Mynfontein o ZA 220-221 F 5
Mynsualmas ▲ KA 126-127 L 5
Myohaung o MYA 142-143 H 5
Myoko-san ▲ J 152-153 H 6
Myola o AUS 174-175 F 6
Myola o PNG 183 D 5
Myotha o MYA 142-143 J 5
Myra ∴• TR 128-129 D 4
Myre o N 86-87 G 2
Myrhorod o UA 102-103 H 3
Mýri o IS 86-87 d 2
Myrnam o CDN (ALB) 232-233 G 2
Myronivka ☆ UA 102-103 G 3
Myrtle o CDN (ONT) 238-239 G 4
Myrtle Beach o• USA (SC) 284-285 M 3
Myrtle Creek o USA (OR) 244-245 B 7
Myrtleford o• AUS 180-181 J 4
Myrtle Grove o USA (LA) 268-269 L 7
Myrtle Point o USA (OR) 244-245 A 7
Mysen ☆ N 86-87 E 7
Mys-Kamennyj o RUS 108-109 P 7
Myski o RUS 124-125 P 2
Myškin ☆ RUS 94-95 Q 3
Myškino = Myškin ☆ RUS 94-95 Q 3
Myślenice o• PL 92-93 P 4
My So'n •• VN 158-159 K 3
Mysore o•• IND 140-141 G 4
Mystery Caves ∴ USA (MN) 270-271 F 7
Mys Želanija o RUS 108-109 N 3
Myszyniec o PL 92-93 Q 2
My Tho ☆• VN 158-159 J 5
Mytišči ☆ RUS 94-95 P 4
Mytishchi = Mytišči ☆ RUS 94-95 P 4
Myton o USA (UT) 254-255 E 3
Myvatn • IS 86-87 e 2
Myzeqe ~ AL 100-101 G 4
M'Zab ∴•• DZ 190-191 D 4
M'Zab, Oued ~ DZ 190-191 E 4
Mže ~ CZ 92-93 M 4
Mzenga o EAT 214-215 K 4
Mziha o EAT 212-213 F 6
Mzimba o MW 214-215 G 6
Mzimkulwana Nature Reserve ⊥ ZA 220-221 J 4
Mzuzu ☆ MW 214-215 H 6

N

Naab ~ D 92-93 M 4
Naala o TCH 198-199 G 6
Naalehu o USA (HI) 288 K 5
Na'am o SUD 206-207 J 4
Na'am ~ SUD 206-207 J 4
Na'ama o ET 194-195 G 4
Na'ān, an- o KSA 130-131 K 6
Naantali o• FIN 88-89 G 6
Naas = An Nás ☆ IRL 90-91 D 5
Nababeep o ZA 220-221 C 4
Naban SK ~ VRC 156-157 F 5
Nabar < TCH 198-199 K 3
Nabarlek o AUS 174-175 B 3
Nabas o RP 160-161 E 7
Nabatiya t-Taḥtā ☆ RL 128-129 F 6
Nabavatu o FJI 184 III b 2
Nabawa o AUS 176-177 C 4
Nabawan o MAL 160-161 B 10
Nabberu, Lake ⊖ AUS 176-177 F 2
Nabéré, Réserve Partielle de ⊥ BF 202-203 J 4
Naberera o EAT 212-213 F 6
Naberezhnyye Chelny = Naberežnye Čelny ☆ RUS 96-97 H 6
Naberežnye Čelny ☆ RUS 96-97 H 6
Nabesna River ~ USA 20-21 T 5
Nabeul ☆ TN 190-191 H 2
Nabğa o UAE 134-135 F 6
Nabhāniya, an- o KSA 130-131 H 5
Nabi, Wādī ~ SUD 200-201 F 2
Nabil' ~ RUS 122-123 K 3
Nabilatuk o EAU 212-213 E 2
Nabileque, Pantanal de ⊖ BR 70-71 J 7
Nabileque, Rio ~ BR 70-71 J 7
Nabil'skij, zaliv ⊖ RUS 122-123 K 3
Nabingora o EAU 212-213 C 3
Nabire o RI 166-167 H 3
Nabisar o PK 138-139 B 7
Nabi Šu'aib, Ğabal an- ▲ Y 132-133 C 6
Nabk, an- o KSA 130-131 F 2
Nabljudenij, mys ▲ RUS 120-121 T 3
Naboga o GH 202-203 K 5
Naboomspruit o ZA 220-221 J 2
Nabou o BF 202-203 J 4
Naboulgou o RT 202-203 L 4
Nabouwalu o FJI 184 III b 2
Nabq o ET 194-195 G 3
Nabukjuak Bay ≈ 36-37 L 2
Nābulus = Shekhem ☆ WB 130-131 D 1
Nabuquen, Caño ~ CO 60-61 G 6
Nabusamke o EAU 212-213 D 3
Nabwān o KSA 130-131 G 4
Nacala o MOC 218-219 L 2
Načalovo ☆ RUS 96-97 F 10
Nacaome ☆ HN 52-53 L 5
Nacaroa o MOC 218-219 K 2
Nacebe o BOL 70-71 D 2
Naches o USA (WA) 244-245 E 4
Naches River ~ USA (WA) 244-245 D 4
Nachicapau, Lac ⊖ CDN 36-37 Q 6
Nachingwea o EAT 214-215 K 6
Nāchna o IND 138-139 C 6
Nachtigal, Cap ▲ CAM 210-211 B 2
Nachtigal, Chutes de ~ CAM 204-205 J 6
Nachuge o IND 140-141 L 4
Nachvak Fiord ≈ 36-37 S 5
Načikinskij, mys ▲ RUS 120-121 U 5
Nacimiento Reservoir ⊖ USA (CA) 248-249 D 4
Nacionalni park Brioni ⊥ HR 100-101 D 2
Nacionalni park Kornati ⊥ HR 100-101 E 3
Nacionalni park Kozara ⊥ BIH 100-101 F 2
Nacionalni park Mljet ⊥ HR 100-101 F 3
Nacionalni park Orjen ⊥ YU 100-101 G 3
Nacionalni park Paklenica ⊥• HR 100-101 E 2
Nacionalni park Plitvička Jezera ⊥••• HR 100-101 E 2
Nacional'nyj park "Losinyj ostrov" ⊥ RUS 94-95 P 4
Nackara o AUS 180-181 E 2
Nackawic o CDN (NB) 240-241 H 4
Nacmine o CDN (ALB) 232-233 F 4
Naco o CDN (ALB) 232-233 H 4
Naco ∴• HN 52-53 K 4
Nacogdoches o USA (TX) 268-269 F 5
Nacori Chico o MEX 50-51 E 3
Nacozari de García o MEX 50-51 E 2
Nacula ⌒ FJI 184 III a 2
Ñacuñán o RA 78-79 F 3
Ñacuñán, Reserva Ecológica ⊥ RA 78-79 E 2
Nacyjanal'ny park Belavežskaja pušča ⊥••• BY 94-95 J 5
Nada o USA (TX) 266-267 L 4
Nadawli o GH 202-203 J 4
Nād-e 'Ali o AFG 134-135 L 3
Nāder Šāh Kūt o AFG 138-139 C 2
Nadëžnyj, mys ▲ RUS 110-111 c 2
Nadi o FJI 184 III a 2
Nadi o SUD 200-201 F 3
Nadiād o IND 138-139 D 8
Nadina River o CDN (BC) 228-229 H 3
Nadina River ~ CDN (BC) 228-229 H 3
Nadoba o RT 202-203 L 4
Nadojaha ~ RUS 108-109 N 6
Nador o MA 188-189 K 3
Nadudoturku ozero ⊖ RUS 108-109 U 5
Nadura, Temple of ∴• ET 194-195 E 5
Naduri o FJI 184 III b 2
Nadvirna ☆ UA 102-103 D 3
Nadym o RUS 114-115 N 2
Nadym ~ RUS 114-115 L 3
Nadymskaja Ob' ≈ 108-109 N 8
Nadzab o PNG 183 D 4
Nā'ebābād o AFG 136-137 K 6
Naejangsan National Park ⊥• ROK 150-151 F 10
Næráyfjorden ⩦ N 86-87 C 6
Næstved o• DK 86-87 E 9
Nafada o WAN 204-205 J 3
Nafadj, Baté- o RG 202-203 F 4
Nafadji o SN 202-203 E 3
Nafaq Ahmad Hamdi II ET 194-195 F 2
Nafi o KSA 130-131 H 5
Nafiša o ET 194-195 F 2
Náfpaktos o GR 100-101 H 5
Náfplio o• GR 100-101 J 6
Naft-e Šāh o IR 134-135 A 1
Nafūd ad-Dahi ⩦ KSA 132-133 D 3
Nafūd al-Kubrā, an- ⩦ KSA 130-131 G 3
Nafūd al-'Uraik ⩦ KSA 130-131 H 5
Nafūd as-Sirr ⩦ KSA 130-131 J 5
Nafūsah, Jabal ▲ LAR 192-193 D 2
Nāg o PK 134-135 L 5
Naga o RP (CAS) 160-161 E 6
Naga o RP (CEB) 160-161 E 7
Naǧaf, an- o IRQ 128-129 K 7
Naǧaf, an- ☆ IRQ (NAG) 128-129 L 7
Naǧafābād o IR 134-135 D 2
Nagagami Lake ⊖ CDN (ONT) 236-237 C 3
Nagagami River ~ CDN (ONT) 236-237 D 3
Nagai Island ⌒ USA 22-23 Q 5
Nagai o IND 140-141 F 2
Nāgāland ◘ IND 142-143 J 2
Nag' al-Ma'mariya o ET 194-195 F 5
Nagamangala o IND 140-141 G 4
Nagambie o AUS 180-181 H 4
Nagamisis Provincial Park ⊥ CDN (ONT) 236-237 D 3
Nagam River Mission o PNG 183 B 2
Nagandana o CI 202-203 H 4
Nagano o J 152-153 H 6
Naganuma o J 152-153 J 3
Nagaoka o J 152-153 H 6
Nagaon o IND 142-143 H 2
Nagappattinam o IND 140-141 H 5
Nagara o RMM 202-203 E 2
Nagare Augū ▲ MYA 158-159 C 2
Nagarhole National Park ⊥ IND 140-141 G 4
Nagari o IND 140-141 H 4
Nagarjuna Sāgar ⊖ IND 140-141 H 2
Nagar Karnūl o IND 140-141 H 2
Nagarote o NIC 52-53 L 5
Nagar Pārkar o PK 138-139 C 7
Nagarzê o VRC 144-145 H 6
Nagasaki ☆• J 152-153 C 8
Naga-shima ⌒ J 152-153 D 8
Nāgaur o IND 138-139 D 6
Nagayaman Point ▲ RP 160-161 E 3
Nāgbhir o IND 138-139 G 9
Nagbo o GH 202-203 K 4
Naǧd ⩦ KSA 130-131 G 4
Nage o RI 168 E 7
Nageezi o USA (NM) 256-257 H 2
Nagercoil o IND 140-141 G 6
Nagerīwāla o PK 138-139 C 4
Nag' 'Hammādi o ET 194-195 F 4
Nagichot o SUD 208-209 A 6
Nagina o IND 138-139 G 5
Naglējngynvaam ~ RUS 112-113 O 2
Naglējnyn, gora ▲ RUS 112-113 P 2
Naglējnyn, mys ▲ RUS 112-113 P 2
Nago o J 152-153 B 11
Nāgod o IND 142-143 B 3
Nagor'e o RUS 94-95 Q 3
Nagorno-Karabakh = Dağliq Qarabağ Muxtar Vilayati ◘ AZ 128-129 M 2
Nagornyj o RUS (SAH) 118-119 M 8
Nagornyj ☆ RUS (KOR) 112-113 U 5
Nagorsk ☆ RUS 96-97 G 4
Nagoya ☆• J 152-153 G 7
Nāgpur o IND 138-139 G 9
Nagqu o VRC 144-145 J 5
Nāgrāl o IND 140-141 H 2
Naǧrān ◘ KSA 132-133 D 4
Naǧrān ☆• KSA (NAG) 132-133 D 5
Naǧrān, Wādī ~ Y 132-133 D 5
Nagslaran o RP 160-161 D 5
Nagua ☆ DOM 54-55 L 5
Naguabo o USA (PR) 286-287 Q 2
Nagvaraaluk, Lac ⊖ CDN 36-37 O 4
Nagykanizsa o H 92-93 O 5
Naha o J 152-153 B 11
Na Haeo o THA 158-159 F 2
Nāhan o IND 138-139 F 4
Na Hang ☆ VN 156-157 D 5
Nahang, Rūd-e ~ IR 134-135 K 5
Nahanni Butte o CDN 30-31 H 5
Nahanni National Park ⊥•• CDN 30-31 G 5
Nahara, Orto- o RUS 118-119 G 5
Nahatlatch River ~ CDN (BC) 230-231 G 3
Nahatta ~ RUS 110-111 X 6
Naheleg ⌒ ER 200-201 K 4
Nahīa Lo ☆ VN 156-157 D 6
Nāhid, Bi'r < ET 194-195 D 2
Naḥl, Rūd-e ~ IR 134-135 H 3
Nahlin o CDN 32-33 E 2
Nahlin Plateau ▲ CDN 32-33 D 2
Nahma Junction o USA (MI) 270-271 M 5
Nahmint o CDN (BC) 230-231 E 4
Naho o SOL 184 I e 3
Nahodka o RUS 108-109 R 8
Nahodka o RUS 122-123 E 7
Nahodka, buhta ≈ 108-109 P 8
Nahodka, ostrov ⌒ RUS 112-113 V 1
Nahoi, Cape = Cape Cumberland ▲ VAN 184 II a 2
Nahrin o AFG 136-137 L 6
Nahr Ouessel ~ DZ 190-191 C 3
Nahualate, Río ~ GCA 52-53 J 4
Nahuatzen o MEX 52-53 D 2
Nahuélbuta, Cordillera de ▲ RCH 78-79 C 5
Nahuelbuta, Parque Nacional ⊥ RCH 78-79 C 4
Nahuel Huapi o RA 78-79 D 6
Nahuel Huapi, Lago ⊖ RA 78-79 D 6
Nahuel Huapi, Parque Nacional ⊥ RA 78-79 D 6
Nahuel Mapá o RA 78-79 F 3
Nahum, Hefar ∴• IL 130-131 D 1
Nahunta o USA (GA) 284-285 J 5
Nahuo o VRC 156-157 G 6
Nahwitti o CDN (BC) 230-231 A 3
Nā'ī, an- o KSA 130-131 K 4
Naiams Fort • NAM 220-221 C 3
Naica o MEX 50-51 G 4
Naicam o CDN (SAS) 232-233 O 3
Nā'id Abār o KSA 132-133 C 5
Naidi o FJI 184 III b 2
Nā'if al-'Ağil o IRQ 128-129 L 7
Naihbawi o IND 142-143 H 4
Naij Tal o VRC 144-145 K 3
Naikliu o RI 166-167 B 6
Naikoon Provincial Park ⊥ CDN (BC) 228-229 C 3
Naila o D 92-93 L 3
Nailaga o FJI 184 III a 2
Naiman Qi o VRC 150-151 C 6
Nain o CDN 36-37 T 6
Nāīn o• IR 134-135 E 2
Naini Tāl o• IND 138-139 G 5
Nainpur o IND 142-143 B 4
Naiopue o MOC 218-219 J 2
Nairai ⌒ FJI 184 III b 2
Nairn o GB 90-91 F 3
Nairobi ◘ EAK 212-213 F 4
Nairobi ★ EAK 212-213 F 4
Nairobi National Park ⊥•• EAK 212-213 F 4
Nairoto o MOC 214-215 K 7

366 Munduručču — Nairoto

Naitaba ⌒ FJI 184 III c 2
Naivasha o EAK 212-213 F 4
Naivasha, Lake ⊂⊃ EAK 212-213 F 4
Naiwangaa o EAT 214-215 K 5
Najahan ∼ RUS 112-113 K 5
Najahanskaja guba ≈ RUS 120-121 S 3
Najahanskij hrebet ▲▲ RUS 112-113 K 5
Najasa ∼ C 54-55 G 4
Najba o RUS 110-111 S 4
Najba ∼ RUS 122-123 K 5
Nájera o• E 98-99 F 3
Najibābād o IND 138-139 G 5
Najtingejl, proliv ≈ 84-85 a 2
Najverga ∼ RUS 118-119 G 6
Najzataš, pereval ▲ TJ 136-137 N 6
Nakadōri-shima ⌒ J 152-153 C 8
Na Kae o THA 158-159 H 2
Nakagawa o J 152-153 K 2
Naka-gawa ∼ J 152-153 J 6
Nakamoéka o RCB 210-211 D 6
Nakamura o J 152-153 E 8
Nakanai Mountains ▲▲ PNG 183 F 3
Nakanno o RUS 116-117 O 4
Nakano-shima ⌒ J (KGA) 152-153 C 10
Nakano-shima ⌒ J (SHM) 152-153 E 6
Nakasato o J 152-153 J 4
Naka-Shibetsu o J 152-153 L 3
Nakasongola o EAU 212-213 D 3
Naka-Tane o J 152-153 D 9
Nakatsu o J 152-153 D 8
Nakatsugawa o J 152-153 G 7
Nakchamik Island ⌒ USA 22-23 S 4
Naked Island ⌒ USA 20-21 R 6
Nakel = Nakło nad Notecią o PL 92-93 O 2
Nak'fa o ER 200-201 J 4
Nakhchyvan = Naxçıvan ✩ AZ 128-129 L 3
Nakhichevan = Naxçıvan Muxtar Respublikası □ AZ 128-129 L 3
Nakhon Nayok o THA 158-159 F 3
Nakhon Pathom o THA 158-159 F 4
Nakhonphanon o THA 158-159 H 2
Nakhon Ratchasima o THA 158-159 G 3
Nakhon Sawan o THA 158-159 F 3
Nakhon Si Thammarat o•• THA 158-159 E 6
Nakhon Thai o THA 158-159 F 2
Nakhtarāna o IND 138-139 B 8
Naki-Est o RT 202-203 L 4
Nakina o CDN (ONT) 236-237 B 2
Nakina o USA (NC) 282-283 J 6
Nakitoma o EAU 212-213 D 3
Nakivali, Lake ⊂⊃ EAU 212-213 C 4
Nakkala o CL 140-141 J 7
Naknek o USA 22-23 S 3
Naknek Lake ⊂⊃ USA 22-23 S 3
Nako o BF 202-203 J 4
Nakonde o Z 214-215 G 5
Nakong-Atinia o GH 202-203 K 4
Nakop o NAM 220-221 D 4
Nako-Tombetsu o J 152-153 K 2
Nakpanduri o GH 202-203 K 4
Nakpayili o GH 202-203 L 5
Nakskov o DK 86-87 E 9
Nakson, gora ▲ RUS 116-117 G 3
Naktong Gang ∼ ROK 150-151 G 10
Nakum ∴• GCA 52-53 K 3
Nakuru ✩ EAK 212-213 F 4
Nakuru, Lake ⊂⊃ EAK 212-213 F 4
Nakusp o CDN (BC) 230-231 M 3
Nāl ∼ PK 134-135 L 5
Nalagāmula o IND 140-141 J 4
Nālāgarh o IND 138-139 F 4
Nalajh o MAU 148-149 H 4
Nalatale Ruins ∴• ZW 218-219 E 4
Nālatvād o IND 140-141 G 2
Nalázi o MOC 220-221 L 2
Nalbarra o AUS 176-177 D 4
Nalcayes, Isla ⌒ RCH 80 D 3
Nal'čik ✩ RUS 126-127 E 6
Naldrug o IND 140-141 G 2
Nalgonda o IND 140-141 H 2
Nali o VRC 156-157 F 6
Nalim'e, ozero ⊂⊃ RUS 108-109 V 8
Nalim-Rassoha ∼ RUS 110-111 G 4
Nalimsk o RUS 110-111 d 6
Naliya o IND 138-139 B 8
Näljänkä o FIN 88-89 K 4
Nalkhera o IND 138-139 F 8
Nallıhan ✩ TR 128-129 D 2
Nalong o MYA 142-143 K 3
Nalusuku Pool < Z 218-219 B 3
Nālūt o LAR 190-191 H 5
Nama ∼ NAM 216-217 F 9
Nama o RI 166-167 F 4
Namaa, Tanjung ▲ RI 166-167 E 3
Namaacha o MOC 220-221 L 2
Namacunde o ANG 216-217 C 8
Namacurra o MOC 218-219 J 3
Namadgi National Park ⊥ AUS 180-181 K 3
Namadi, Dag-e ⊂⊃ AFG 134-135 J 2
Namak, Daryā-ye ⊂⊃ IR 134-135 D 1
Namak, Kavir-e ⊂⊃ IR 134-135 G 1
Namak, Küh-e ▲▲ IR 134-135 D 4
Namakan ∼ RUS 108-109 a 6
Namak-e Sirğān, Kavir-e ⊂⊃ IR 134-135 F 4
Namakia o RM 222-223 D 5
Nāmakkal o IND 140-141 H 5
Namaksār ⊂⊃ AFG 134-135 J 3
Namaksar, Kāl-e ⊂⊃ IR 134-135 J 1
Namakwaland ⊥ ZA 220-221 C 4
Namaland ⊥ NAM 220-221 C 3
Namana ∼ RUS 118-119 K 5
Namanga o EAK 212-213 F 5
Namangan o US 136-137 M 4
Namanganskaja oblast' □ US 136-137 M 4
Namanyere o EAT (RUA) 214-215 F 4
Namaö o CDN (ALB) 232-233 E 2
Namapa o MOC 218-219 K 1
Namaponda o MOC 218-219 K 2
Namarrói o MOC 218-219 J 2
Namas o RI 166-167 L 4
Namasagali o EAU 212-213 D 3
Namasale o EAU 212-213 D 3
Namassi o CI 202-203 J 6
Namatanai o PNG 183 G 2
Namatote, Pulau ⌒ RI 166-167 G 3
Namba o ANG 216-217 C 5
Nambazo o MW 218-219 H 2
Nambe Indian Reservation X USA (NM) 256-257 K 3
Namber o RI 166-167 H 2
Nambi o AUS 176-177 F 4
Nambikwara, Área Indígena X BR 70-71 H 3
Nambima, Tanjung ▲ RI 166-167 H 4
Nambolaki, Pulau ⌒ RI 168 E 6
Namboukaha o CI 202-203 H 5
Nambour o AUS 178-179 M 4
Nambuangongo o ANG 216-217 C 4
Nambucca Heads o AUS 178-179 M 6
Nambung National Park ⊥ AUS 176-177 C 5
Namche Bazar o NEP 144-145 F 7
Namchi o IND 142-143 F 2
Nam Chon Reservoir < THA 158-159 E 3
Nam Co ⊂⊃ VRC (XIZ) 144-145 H 5
Nam Co • VRC (XIZ) 144-145 H 5
Namcy ✩• RUS 118-119 O 4
Nam Du, Quần Đảo ⌒ VN 158-159 H 6
Namen = Namur ✩• B 92-93 H 3
Namenalala ⌒ FJI 184 III b 2
Nà Mèo o VN 156-157 D 6
Nametil o MOC 218-219 K 2
Namew Lake ⊂⊃ CDN 34-35 F 3
Namgorab ▲▲ NAM 220-221 C 2
Namhae Do ⌒ ROK 150-151 F 10
Namhan Gang ∼ ROK 150-151 F 9
Nami o MAL 162-163 D 2
Namialo o MOC 218-219 K 2
Namibe □ ANG 216-217 B 7
Namibe ✩• ANG 216-217 B 7
Namibe, Deserto de ⊥ ANG 216-217 A 8
Namibe, Reserva de ⊥ ANG 216-217 B 7
Namibia ■ NAM 216-217 C 10
Namib-Naukluft Park ⊥ NAM 220-221 B 2
Namibwoestyn = Namib Desert ⊥ NAM 216-217 B 9
Namidobe o MOC 218-219 J 3
Namie o J 152-153 J 6
Namies o ZA 220-221 D 4
Namin o IR 128-129 N 3
Namina o MOC 218-219 K 2
Namioka o J 152-153 J 4
Namiquipa o MEX 50-51 F 3
Namiroe, Rio ∼ MOC 218-219 K 2
Namitete o MW 218-219 G 2
Namjagbarwa Feng ▲ VRC 144-145 K 6
Namlan o MYA 142-143 K 4
Namlea o RI 166-167 D 3
Nam Léa, Mount ▲ K 158-159 J 4
Namling o VRC 144-145 G 6
Nam-mawng o MYA 142-143 L 5
Nam Ngum Reservoir ⊂⊃ LAO 156-157 C 7
Namo o RI 164-165 F 4
Namoda, Kaura- o WAN 198-199 C 6
Namoi River ∼ AUS 178-179 K 6
Namon o RT 202-203 L 5
Namor o BR 66-67 F 6
Namorona o RM 222-223 F 8
Nam Ou ∼ LAO 156-157 C 6
Namounou o BF 202-203 L 4
Namous, Oued ∼ DZ 190-191 D 3
Nampa o USA (ID) 252-253 B 3
Nampagan o MYA 142-143 J 3
Nampala o RMM 202-203 H 2
Nam Pat o THA 158-159 F 2
Nampevo o MOC 218-219 J 3
Nampo o DVR 150-151 E 8
Nam Poon o THA 142-143 M 6
Nampuecha o MOC 218-219 L 1
Nampula □ MOC 218-219 K 2
Nampula ✩ MOC (Nam) 218-219 K 2
Namrole o RI 166-167 D 3
Namru o VRC 144-145 C 5
Namsalau = Namysłów o• PL 92-93 O 3
Namsos o N 86-87 E 4
Namsskogan o N 86-87 F 4
Namtabung o RI 166-167 F 6
Namtha o MYA 142-143 J 3
Nam Theun o LAO 158-159 H 2
Nam Tok Chat Trakan National Park ⊥ THA 158-159 F 2
Namtu o MYA 142-143 K 4
Namtumbo o EAT 214-215 J 6
Namu o CDN (BC) 230-231 B 2
Namudi o PNG 183 E 5
Namuiranga o MOC 214-215 L 6
Namukumbo o Z 218-219 D 2
Namuli, Monte ▲ MOC 218-219 J 2
Namuno o MOC 218-219 K 1
Nam Un Reservoir ⊂⊃ THA 158-159 G 2
Namur ✩• B 92-93 H 3
Namur o CDN (QUE) 238-239 L 3
Namur Lake ⊂⊃ CDN 32-33 O 3
Namur Lake Indian Reserve X CDN 32-33 O 3
Namutoni o NAM 216-217 D 9
Namwaan, Pulau ⌒ RI 166-167 F 5
Namwala o Z 218-219 D 2
Namwera o MW 218-219 H 2
Namwŏn o ROK 150-151 F 10
Namy o RUS 110-111 T 5
Namyłdżylah ∼ RUS 118-119 K 5
Namyndykan ∼ RUS 112-113 K 4
Namysłów o• PL 92-93 O 3
Nan o THA 142-143 M 6
Nan, Sa o THA 142-143 M 6
Nana o CAM 206-207 B 5
Nana ∼ RCA 206-207 B 6
Nana Bakassa o RCA (OUH) 206-207 C 5
Nana Bakassa ∼ RCA 206-207 C 5
Nana Barya ∼ TCH 206-207 C 5
Nana Barya, Réserve de la ⊥ RCA 206-207 C 5
Nana Candundo o ANG 214-215 B 6
Nanae o J 152-153 J 4
Nanafalia o USA (AL) 284-285 C 4
Nana-Grébizi □ RCA 206-207 D 5
Nanaimo o CDN (BC) 230-231 F 4
Nanakuli o USA (HI) 288 G 3
Nana-Mambéré □ RCA 206-207 B 6
Nanambinia o AUS 176-177 G 6
Nana Museum of the Arctic • USA 20-21 J 3
Nanango o AUS 178-179 L 4
Nananu-i-ra ⌒ FJI 184 III b 2
Nanao o J 152-153 G 6
Nan'ao Dao ⌒ VRC 156-157 K 5
Nanase o PNG 183 B 4
Nanay, Río ∼ PE 64-65 F 3
Nanbu o VRC 154-155 E 6
Nancay, Arroyo ∼ RA 78-79 K 2
Nance Creek ∼ USA (AL) 284-285 C 2
Nancha o VRC 150-151 G 4
Nanchang ✩• VRC 156-157 J 2
Nancheng o VRC 156-157 K 3
Nanchital o MEX 52-53 G 2
Nanchititla, Parque Natural ⊥ MEX 52-53 D 2
Nanchong o VRC 154-155 E 6
Nanchuan o VRC 156-157 E 2
Nancowry Island ⌒ IND 140-141 L 6
Nancy ✩••• F 90-91 L 7
Nanda Devi ▲••• IND 144-145 C 5
Nandaime o NIC 52-53 L 6
Nandalūr o IND 140-141 H 3
Nandaly o AUS 180-181 G 3
Nandan o VRC 156-157 E 4
Nanded o IND 138-139 F 10
Nandewar Range ▲▲ AUS 178-179 L 6
Nāndghāt o IND 142-143 B 5
Nandi o ZW 218-219 F 5
Nandigāma o IND 140-141 J 2
Nandigram o BD 142-143 F 3
Nandi Hills o• IND 140-141 G 4
Nandikotkūr o IND 140-141 H 3
Nanding Hé ∼ VRC 142-143 L 4
Nandipadu o IND 140-141 H 3
Nandom o GH 202-203 J 4
Nandouta o RT 202-203 L 5
Nandowrie P.O. o AUS 178-179 J 3
Nāndūra o IND 138-139 F 9
Nandurbār o IND 138-139 E 9
Nandyal o IND 140-141 H 3
Nanfeng o VRC 156-157 K 3
Nangade o MOC 214-215 K 6
Nanga Eboko o CAM 204-205 K 6
Nangah Ketungau o RI 162-163 J 4
Nangah Pinoh o RI 162-163 J 5
Nangah Sokan o RI 162-163 J 5
Nangalala X AUS 174-175 C 3
Nanganga o EAT 214-215 K 6
Nanga Parbat ▲ PK 138-139 E 2
Nangarhār □ AFG 138-139 C 2
Nangaroro o RI 168 E 7
Nanga Tamin o MAL 162-163 K 3
Nanga Tayap o RI 162-163 J 5
Nangbéto o RT 202-203 L 6
Nangbéto, Retenue de < RT 202-203 L 6
Nang'egan ∼ RUS 114-115 L 3
Nangin o MYA 158-159 E 5
Nango o J 152-153 D 8
Nangolet o SUD 208-209 A 6
Nangomba o EAT 214-215 K 6
Nangong o VRC 154-155 J 3
Nangqên o VRC 144-145 L 4
Nang Rong o THA 158-159 G 3
Nānguneri o IND 140-141 G 6
Nangunhe Z.B. ⊥• VRC 142-143 L 4
Nangurukuru o EAT 214-215 K 5
Nanguruwe o EAT 214-215 L 6
Nang Xian o VRC 144-145 J 6
Nan Hai ≈ 156-157 J 6
Nanhua o RC 156-157 M 5
Nanhua o VRC 156-157 B 4
Nanhui o VRC 154-155 M 6
Nanika Lake ⊂⊃ CDN (BC) 228-229 G 3
Nanjangud o• IND 140-141 G 4
Nanjian o VRC 142-143 M 3
Nanjiang o VRC 154-155 E 5
Nanjing ✩• VRC 154-155 L 5
Nanjirinji o EAT 214-215 K 5
Nankāna Sāhib o PK 138-139 D 4
Nankang o VRC (GXI) 156-157 F 6
Nankang o VRC (JXI) 156-157 J 4
Nanking = Nanjing ✩• VRC 154-155 L 5
Nankoku o J 152-153 E 8
Nankova o ANG 216-217 E 8
Nankunshan • VRC 156-157 H 5
Nanle o VRC 154-155 J 3
Nanling o VRC 154-155 L 6
Nan Ling ▲▲ VRC 156-157 G 4
Nanlixa o MOC 218-219 J 1
Nannine o AUS 176-177 E 3
Nanning ✩ VRC 156-157 F 5
Nannup o AUS 176-177 C 6
Nano ∼ DY 204-205 E 4
Nanoose Bay o CDN (BC) 230-231 F 4
Nanoro o BF 202-203 J 3
Nanortalik o GRØ 28-29 S 6
Nanortalik Banke ≃ 28-29 R 6
Nanosnyj, ostrov ⌒ RUS 110-111 X 1
Nanpan Jiang ∼ VRC 156-157 D 4
Nanpara o IND 142-143 B 2
Nanpeng Liedao ⌒ VRC 156-157 K 5
Nanping o VRC (FUJ) 156-157 L 3
Nanping o VRC (HUN) 156-157 H 2
Nansebo o ETH 208-209 D 5
Nansei-shotō ⌒ J 152-153 B 11
Nansen, Kap ▲ GRØ (ØGR) 26-27 r 4
Nansen, Kap ▲ GRØ (ØGR) 28-29 a 2
Nansen, Mount ▲ CDN 20-21 W 5
Nansena, ostrov ⌒ RUS 108-109 Z 3
Nansena, ostrov ⌒ RUS (ARH) 84-85 d 2
Nansen Fjord ≈ 28-29 a 2
Nansen Gletscher ⊂ GRØ 26-27 V 6
Nansen Land ⊥ GRØ 26-27 c 2
Nansen Sound ≈ 26-27 E 3
Nanshui SK ∼ VRC 156-157 H 4
Nansio o EAT 212-213 D 5
Nantahala Mountains ▲▲ USA (NC) 282-283 D 5
Nantais, Lac ⊂⊃ CDN 36-37 M 4
Nantamba o PNG 183 F 3
Nantes ✩• F 90-91 G 8
Nanticoke River ∼ USA (MD) 280-281 L 5
Nanton o CDN (ALB) 232-233 E 5
Nanton o GH 202-203 K 5
Nantong o VRC 154-155 M 5
Nantong (Jinsha) o VRC 154-155 M 5
Nantou o RC 156-157 M 5
Nantucket o USA (MA) 278-279 L 7
Nantucket Island ⌒ USA (MA) 278-279 L 7
Nantucket Shoals ≈ 46-47 N 5
Nantucket Sound ≈ USA 278-279 L 7
Nantulo o MOC 214-215 K 7
Nanuku Passage ≈ 184 III c 2
Nanumea ⌒ TUV 13 J 3
Nanuque o BR 72-73 K 4
Nanūr o IR 128-129 M 5
Nanusa, Kepulauan ⌒ RI 164-165 K 1
Nanutarra Roadhouse o AUS 172-173 B 7
Nan Xian o VRC 156-157 H 2
Nanxiao o VRC 156-157 F 5
Nanxijiang • VRC 156-157 M 2
Nanxiong o VRC 156-157 J 4
Nanxu o VRC 156-157 G 4
Nanyamba o EAT 214-215 K 6
Nanyang o VRC 154-155 H 5
Nanyang Hu ∼ VRC 154-155 K 4
Nanyi Hu o VRC 154-155 L 6
Nan-yō o J 152-153 J 5
Nanyuki o EAK 212-213 F 3
Nanzhai o VRC 156-157 F 3
Nanzhang o VRC 154-155 G 6
Nanzhao o VRC 154-155 H 5
Nanzhila o Z (SOU) 218-219 C 3
Nanzhila ∼ Z 218-219 D 3
Nao, Cabo de la ▲ E 98-99 H 5
Naococane, Lac ⊂⊃ CDN 38-39 J 2
Naogaon o BD 142-143 F 3
Não-me-Toque o BR 74-75 D 7
Náoussa o GR 100-101 J 4
Naozhou Dao ⌒ VRC 156-157 G 6
Napa o USA (CA) 246-247 C 5
Napabale Lagoon ⊥•• RI 164-165 H 6
Napacao Point ▲ RP 160-161 F 8
Napadogan o CDN (NB) 240-241 J 4
Napaha o MOC 218-219 K 1
Napaiskak o USA 20-21 K 6
Napaleofú, Arroyo ∼ RA 78-79 K 4
Napanee o CDN (ONT) 238-239 J 4
Napanwainami o RI 166-167 H 3
Napan-yaur o RI 166-167 H 3
Napas o RUS 114-115 R 5
Napassorssuaq Fjord ≈ 28-29 T 6
Napatok Bay ≈ 36-37 S 6
Napavine o USA (WA) 244-245 B 4
Napeitom o EAK 212-213 F 3
Naper o USA (NE) 262-263 G 2
Napido o RI 166-167 H 2
Napier o NZ 182 F 3
Napier o ZA 220-221 D 7
Napier, Mount ▲ AUS 172-173 J 4
Napier Broome Bay ≈ 172-173 H 3
Napier Downs o AUS 172-173 G 4
Napier Mountains ▲▲ ARK 16 G 6
Napier Peninsula ∪ AUS 174-175 C 3
Napier Range ▲▲ AUS 172-173 G 4
Napierville o CDN (QUE) 238-239 M 3
Napinka o CDN (MAN) 234-235 C 5
Naples o USA (FL) 286-287 H 5
Naples o USA (ID) 250-251 C 3
Naples o USA (ME) 278-279 L 5
Naples o USA (SD) 260-261 J 2
Naples o USA (TX) 264-265 K 5
Naples = Nápoli ✩•• I 100-101 E 4
Napo o VRC 156-157 D 5
Napo, Río ∼ EC 64-65 E 2
Napoca, Cluj- ✩• RO 102-103 C 4
Napoleon o USA (IN) 274-275 N 5
Napoleon o USA (ND) 258-259 H 5
Napoleon o USA (OH) 280-281 B 2
Napoleonville o USA (LA) 268-269 J 7
Nápoli ✩•• I 100-101 E 4
Nápoli, Golfo di ≈ 100-101 E 4
Napoopoo o USA (HI) 288 K 5
Nappa Merrie o AUS 178-179 F 4
Napperby o AUS 172-173 L 7
Nappernee o USA (IN) 274-275 M 3
Naqa, Temples of •• SUD 200-201 F 4
Naqada o• ET 194-195 F 5
Naqadeh o• IR 128-129 L 4
Naqb, Ra's an- o JOR 130-131 D 2
Naquen, Serranía de ▲ CO 60-61 G 6
Nār, Umm an- o UAE 134-135 F 6
Nara o AUS 174-175 G 6
Nara ✩•• J 152-153 F 7
Nara o RMM 202-203 G 2
Narač o BY 94-95 K 4
Nāra Canal < PK 138-139 B 7
Naracoorte o AUS 180-181 F 4
Naracoorte Caves Conservation Park ⊥ AUS 180-181 F 4
Naradhan o AUS 180-181 J 2
Naraini o IND 142-143 B 3
Nārāinpur o IND 142-143 B 6
Nārājankher o IND 138-139 F 10
Naramata o CDN (BC) 230-231 K 4
Naran o PK 138-139 D 2
Naran = Hongor o MAU 148-149 L 5
Narandiba o BR 72-73 E 7
Naranjal o EC 64-65 C 3
Naranjas, Punta ▲ PA 52-53 D 8
Naranjito o EC 64-65 C 3
Naranjo ∴• GCA 52-53 K 3
Naranjo o MEX 50-51 E 5
Naranjos o MEX 50-51 K 7
Narao o J 152-153 C 8
Narasannapeta o IND 142-143 D 6
Narasapuram o IND 140-141 J 2
Narasaraopet o IND 140-141 J 2
Narasimharajapura o IND 140-141 F 4
Naratai o RUS 116-117 M 8
Narathiwat ✩ THA 158-159 F 7
Nara Visa o USA (NM) 256-257 M 3
Naravuka o FJI 184 III b 2
Narayangadh o NEP 144-145 E 7
Nārāyangaon o IND 138-139 D 10
Narbonne o F 90-91 J 10
Narcisse o CDN (MAN) 234-235 F 4
Narcondan Island ⌒ IND 158-159 C 4
Narcosli Creek ∼ CDN (BC) 228-229 M 4
Narding River ∼ CDN 24-25 N 6
Naré o RA 76-77 G 6
Narečí, ostrov ⌒ RUS 108-109 O 8
Narega Island ⌒ PNG 183 E 3
Naregal o IND 140-141 F 3
Narembeen o AUS 176-177 E 6
Naréna o RMM 202-203 F 3
Nares Abyssal Plain ≃ 6-7 F 1
Nares Land ⊥ GRØ 26-27 b 2
Nares Stræde ≈ 26-27 O 4
Nares Strait ≈ 26-27 N 4
Narew o PL 92-93 R 2
Narew ∼ PL 92-93 Q 2
Nargund o IND 140-141 F 3
Nāri ∼ PK 134-135 M 4
Nari ∼ PK 134-135 M 4
Narib o NAM 220-221 C 2
Narijn gol ∼ MAU 116-117 F 10
Narijntèèl = Čagaan-Ovoo o MAU 148-149 E 5
Narimanov ✩ RUS 96-97 E 10
Narinda, Helodrano ≈ 222-223 E 5
Narin Nur o VRC 154-155 F 2
Narita o• J 152-153 J 7
Nar'jan-Mar ✩ RUS 88-89 W 3
Narkatiāganj o IND 142-143 D 2
Narmada ∼ IND 138-139 D 9
Narmada ∼ IND 138-139 F 8
Narmajaha ∼ RUS 108-109 L 7
Nārnaul o IND 138-139 F 5
Narndee o AUS 176-177 E 4
Narob ∼ NAM 220-221 C 2
Naroda ∼ RUS 114-115 F 2
Narodnaja, gora ▲ RUS 114-115 F 2
Národní park Šumava ⊥ CZ 92-93 M 4
Naro-Fominsk ✩• RUS 94-95 P 4
Naro Island ⌒ RP 160-161 E 7
Narok o EAK 212-213 E 4
Naro Moru o EAK 212-213 F 4
Narooma o AUS 180-181 L 4
Nārowāl o PK 138-139 E 3
Narrabri o AUS 178-179 K 6
Narracoota o AUS 176-177 E 2
Narragansett Bay ≈ 46-47 N 5
Narragansett Bay ≈ USA 278-279 K 7
Narrandera o AUS 180-181 J 3
Narran Lake ⊂⊃ AUS 178-179 J 5
Narran River ∼ AUS 178-179 J 5
Narraway River ∼ CDN (BC) 228-229 O 2
Narrien Range ▲▲ AUS 178-179 J 2
Narrogin o AUS 176-177 D 6
Narromine o AUS 180-181 K 2
Narrow Cape ▲ USA 22-23 U 4
Narrows o USA (VA) 280-281 F 6
Narrowsburg o USA (NY) 280-281 L 2
Narrows Indian Reserve, The X CDN (MAN) 234-235 E 3
Narryer, Mount ▲ AUS 176-177 D 3
Narsalik o GRØ 28-29 Q 6
Narsampet o IND 140-141 H 2
Narsaq Kujalleg = Frederiksdal o GRØ 28-29 S 6
Narsarsuaq o GRØ 28-29 S 6
Narsimhapur o IND 138-139 G 8
Narsinghgarh o IND 138-139 F 8
Narsipatnam o IND 142-143 C 7
Nart o VRC 148-149 M 6
Narubis o NAM 220-221 D 3
Naru-shima ⌒ J 152-153 C 8
Naruto o J 152-153 F 7
Narva o• EST 94-95 L 2
Narva ∼ RUS 116-117 F 8
Narva laht ≈ 94-95 K 2
Narvik o•• N 86-87 H 2
Narvskoe vodohranilišče < RUS 94-95 L 2
Narwietooma o AUS 176-177 M 1
Nary hrebet ▲▲ RUS 96-97 K 6
Naryilco o AUS 178-179 F 5
Naryn ∼ KA 124-125 J 6
Naryn o KS 146-147 B 5
Naryn ∼ KS 136-137 N 4
Naryn o RUS 116-117 G 10
Naryn ∼ RUS 116-117 G 10
Naryn-Huduk o RUS 126-127 G 5
Narynkol o KA 146-147 E 4
Naryntau, hrebet ▲▲ KS 146-147 C 5
Nasa, Gara ▲ ETH 208-209 B 4
Na'sān, Umm ⌒ BRN 134-135 D 5
Nasanabad o IND 138-139 G 10
Nasarawa o WAN 198-199 B 6
Nasa Test Site xx USA (MS) 268-269 L 6
Năsăud o RO 102-103 D 4
Naschitti o USA (NM) 256-257 G 2
Naselle o USA (WA) 244-245 B 4
Nashan Island ⌒ 160-161 A 7
Nash Harbor o USA 20-21 G 6
Nāshik o IND 138-139 D 10
Nashino, Río ∼ EC 64-65 D 2
Nashū', Wādi an ∼ LAR 192-193 E 4
Nashua o USA (IA) 274-275 F 2
Nashua o USA (MT) 250-251 N 3
Nashua o USA (NH) 278-279 K 6
Nashville o USA (AR) 276-277 B 7
Nashville o USA (GA) 284-285 G 5
Nashville o USA (IL) 274-275 J 6
Nashville o USA (IN) 274-275 M 5
Nashville o USA (KS) 262-263 H 7
Nashville o USA (MI) 272-273 D 5
Nashville o USA (NC) 282-283 K 5
Nashville ✩• USA (TN) 276-277 J 4
Nashville Basin ∪ USA (TN) 276-277 J 4
Nashwaak o CDN (NB) 240-241 J 4
Nashwaak Bridge o CDN (NB) 240-241 J 4
Nashwaak River ∼ CDN (NB) 240-241 J 4
Nashwauk o USA (MN) 270-271 E 3
Nasia o GH 202-203 K 4
Nasia ∼ GH 202-203 K 4
Našice o HR 100-101 G 2
Näsijärvi ⊂⊃ FIN 88-89 G 6
Nasikonis, Tanjung ▲ RI 166-167 B 6
Nāsik Road o IND 138-139 D 10
Nāsipit o RP 160-161 F 8
Nāsir o SUD 208-209 A 4
Nāsir, Buhairat ⊂ ET 194-195 F 6
Nasirābād o IR 136-137 G 7
Nasirābād o PK 134-135 K 5
Nasirābād o PK 138-139 B 5
Nāşirah, Bi'r < LAR 192-193 D 2
Nāşiriya, an- ✩ IRQ 128-129 M 7
Naşiya, Gabal ▲ ET 194-195 F 6
Naskaupi River ∼ CDN 36-37 T 7
Nasmah o LAR 192-193 E 2
Nasolot National Reservoir ⊥ EAK 212-213 E 3
Nasondoye o ZRE 214-215 C 6
Nasorolevu ▲ FJI 184 III b 2
Nāsriganj o IND 142-143 D 3
Naşriyān o IR 134-135 B 2
Nassarawa o WAN 204-205 G 4
Nassau ✩•• BS 54-55 G 2
Nassau, Bahía ≈ 80 G 7
Nassau, Fort • GUY 62-63 F 3
Nassau River ∼ AUS 174-175 F 4
Nassau River ∼ USA (FL) 286-287 H 1
Nassau Sound ≈ USA 286-287 H 1
Nass Basin ⊥ CDN 32-33 F 3
Nasser, Lake = Nāşir, Buhairat ⊂ ET 194-195 F 6
Nassian o CI (BOA) 202-203 J 5
Nassian o CI (FER) 202-203 H 5
Nassoukou o DY 202-203 L 4
Nass River ∼ CDN 32-33 F 4
Nastapoka, Rivière ∼ CDN 36-37 L 6
Nastapoka Islands ⌒ CDN 36-37 L 6
Nastapoka Sound ≈ 36-37 L 6
Nasugbu o RP 160-161 D 5
Nasuraghena o SOL 184 I f 4
Nasva o RUS 94-95 M 3
Nata o•• PA 52-53 D 7
Nata o RB (CEN) 218-219 D 5
Nata ∼ RB 218-219 D 5
Nataboti o RI 166-167 D 3
Natal o BR (TOC) 68-69 D 7
Natal ✩ BR (RNO) 68-69 L 4
Natal o CDN (BC) 230-231 P 4
Natal o RI 162-163 C 4
Natalia o USA (TX) 266-267 J 4
Natalii, buhta ≈ RUS 112-113 R 6
Natalschwelle ≃ 220-221 M 6
Natal Valley ≃ 9 G 9
Natanz o• IR 134-135 D 2
Natar o RI 162-163 F 7
Natara ∼ RUS 110-111 P 5
Nataš, Wādī ∼ ET 194-195 F 5
Natashquan o CDN (QUE) 242-243 G 2
Natashquan, Pointe de ▲ CDN (QUE) 242-243 G 2
Natashquan, Rivière ∼ CDN 38-39 O 3
Natashquan River ∼ CDN 38-39 N 2
Natchamba o RT 202-203 L 5
Natchez o USA (MS) 268-269 J 5
Natchez Trace Parkway • USA (MS) 268-269 K 4
Natchez Trace Parkway • USA (TN) 276-277 H 5
Natchez Trace State Park ⊥ USA (TN) 276-277 G 5
Natchitoches o USA (LA) 268-269 G 5
Nate o IND 140-141 E 2
Natewa Bay ≈ 184 III b 2
Nathahu o MYA 158-159 C 2
Nathalia o AUS 180-181 H 4
Nathan o USA (AR) 276-277 B 6
Nathan River o AUS 174-175 C 4
Na Thawi o THA 158-159 F 7
Nāthdwāra o IND 138-139 D 7
Nathenje o MW 218-219 G 2
Nathia Gali o PK 138-139 D 2
Nathon o THA 158-159 E 6
Nathorst Land ⊥ GRØ 26-27 m 7
Nathorst Land ⊥ N 84-85 J 4
Nathrop o USA (CO) 254-255 J 5
Natiaboani o BF 202-203 L 4
Natingui o BR 74-75 E 5
Nation o USA 20-21 U 4
National Bison Range ⊥ USA (MT) 250-251 E 4
National City o USA (CA) 248-249 G 7
National Parachute Test Range • USA (CA) 248-249 J 7
National Park ⊥ CDN (ONT) 238-239 J 4
National Park o NZ 182 E 3
National Park ⊥ PNG 183 B 4
Nationalpark Bayerischer Wald ⊥ D 92-93 M 4
Nationalpark Berchtesgaden ⊥ D 92-93 M 5
Nationalpark Hochharz ⊥ D 92-93 L 3
Nationalpark i Nørdgrønland og Østgrønland ⊥ GRØ 26-27 e 5
Nationalpark Niedersächsisches Wattenmeer ⊥ D 92-93 J 2
Nationalpark Sächsische Schweiz ⊥ D 92-93 N 3
Nationalpark Schleswig-Holsteinisches Wattenmeer ⊥ D 92-93 K 1
Nationalpark Vorpommersche Boddenlandschaft ⊥ D 92-93 M 1
National Reactor Testing Station xx USA (ID) 252-253 F 3
National Wildlife Refuge ⊥ USA (ID) 252-253 G 3
National Wildlife Refuge ⊥ USA (ID) 252-253 F 3
National Wildlife Refuge ⊥ USA (MN) 270-271 E 5
National Wildlife Refuge ⊥ USA (MN) 270-271 E 4
National Wildlife Refuge ⊥ USA (MT) 250-251 H 4
National Wildlife Refuge ⊥ USA (MT) 250-251 P 3
National Wildlife Refuge ⊥ USA (MT) 250-251 M 3
National Wildlife Refuge ⊥ USA (MT) 250-251 L 5
National Wildlife Refuge ⊥ USA (MT) 250-251 K 5
National Wildlife Refuge ⊥ USA (ND) 258-259 F 4
National Wildlife Refuge ⊥ USA (ND) 258-259 G 5
National Wildlife Refuge ⊥ USA (SD) 260-261 C 2
National Wildlife Refuge ⊥ USA (SD) 260-261 H 1
National Wildlife Refuge ⊥ USA (UT) 254-255 B 4
National Wildlife Refuge ⊥ USA (UT) 254-255 C 2
National Wildlife Refuge ⊥ USA (UT) 254-255 F 3
National Wildlife Refuge ⊥ USA (WI) 270-271 H 6
National Wildlife Refuge ⊥ USA (WY) 252-253 M 4
National Wildlife Refuge and Wilderness Area ⊥ USA (MT) 250-251 H 7
Nation River ∼ CDN 32-33 H 4
Natitingou ✩ DY 202-203 L 4
Natityay, Gabal ▲ ET 194-195 G 6
Native Bay ≈ 36-37 H 3
Native Point ▲ CDN 36-37 H 3
Natividade o BR 68-69 E 7
Natkusiak Peninsula ∪ CDN 24-25 R 4
Natla River ∼ CDN 30-31 E 4
Natmauk o MYA 142-143 J 5
Natong Kuangqu o VRC 156-157 E 2
Nator o BD 142-143 F 3
Natovi o FJI 184 III b 2
Nat River ∼ CDN (ONT) 236-237 F 4
Natron, Lake ⊂⊃ EAT 212-213 F 5
Natron, Trou du • TCH 198-199 H 2
Natrona o USA (WY) 252-253 M 3
Nattam o IND 140-141 H 5
Nattavaara station o S 86-87 K 3
Natukanaoka Pan ⊂⊃ NAM 216-217 C 9
Natuna Besar, Pulau ⌒ RI 162-163 H 2
Natural Arch ∴• USA (KY) 276-277 L 4
Natural Bridge o USA (AL) 284-285 C 2
Natural Bridge ∴• USA (AL) 284-285 C 2
Natural Bridge • USA (FL) 286-287 E 1
Natural Bridges ∴• USA (TN) 276-277 H 5
Natural Bridges National Monument ∴• USA (UT) 254-255 F 6
Natural Bridge State Monument • USA (MT) 250-251 J 6
Natural Dam Salt Lake ⊂⊃ USA (TX) 264-265 C 6
Naturaliste, Cape ▲ AUS (TAS) 180-181 K 6
Naturaliste, Cape ▲ AUS (WA) 176-177 C 6
Naturaliste Plateau ≃ 176-177 B 6
Naturita o USA (CO) 254-255 G 5
Nau o TJ 136-137 L 4
Nauabu o PNG 183 F 6
Nauarai, Bi'r < SUD 200-201 G 2
Nauari o BR 62-63 G 5
Naubise o NEP 144-145 E 7
Nauchas o NAM 220-221 C 1
Naudesberg Pass ▲ ZA 220-221 G 5
Naudesnek ▲ ZA 220-221 J 5
Nauela o MOC 218-219 J 2
Naufal le-Chateau o IR 134-135 D 1
Naufrage o CDN (NS) 240-241 N 4
Naugarh o IND 142-143 C 2
Naujan o RP 160-161 D 6
Naujan Lake ⊂⊃ RP 160-161 D 6
Naukot o PK 138-139 B 7
Naulila o ANG 216-217 C 8
Nauľjaha ∼ RUS 108-109 H 7
Naumatang o RI 166-167 D 5
Naumburg (Saale) o• D 92-93 L 3
Nauna Island ⌒ PNG 183 E 2
Naungmo o MYA 142-143 J 3
Nauru ⌒ NAU 13 H 3
Naushahro Firoz o PK 138-139 B 6
Nausori o FJI 184 III b 3
Nauta o PE 64-65 F 4
Nautanwa o IND 142-143 C 2
Nautilus, Selat ≈ 166-167 G 4
Nautimuk o AUS 180-181 F 4
Nautla o MEX 52-53 F 1
Nautsi o RUS 88-89 K 2
Nauvoo o USA (AL) 284-285 C 3
Nāv o IR 128-129 N 4
Nava o MEX 50-51 J 3
Nava ∼ ZRE 212-213 A 2
Nava de Ricomalillo, La o E 98-99 E 5
Navahrudak ✩ BY 94-95 J 5
Navahrudskae uzvyšša ▲▲ BY 94-95 J 5
Navajo o USA (AZ) 256-257 F 3
Navajo o USA (NM) 256-257 G 3
Navajo C'y o USA (NM) 256-257 H 2
Navajo Indian Reservation X USA (AZ) 256-257 D 2
Navajo Mountain ▲ USA (UT) 254-255 E 6
Navajo National Monument ∴• USA (AZ) 256-257 E 2
Navajo Reservoir < USA (NM) 256-257 H 2
Naval o RP 160-161 F 7
Navalmoral de la Mata o E 98-99 E 5
Navalmorales, Los o E 98-99 E 5
Navan = An Uaimh o IRL 90-91 D 5
Navapara o BD 142-143 F 4
Navapolack ✩•• BY 94-95 L 4
Navapur o IND 138-139 D 9
Navarin, mys ▲ RUS 112-113 U 5
Navarino, Isla ⌒ RCH 80 G 7
Navarino, Pico ▲ RCH 80 G 7
Navarra □ E 98-99 F 3
Navarre o AUS 180-181 G 4
Navarre o CDN (ALB) 232-233 E 3
Navarre o USA (FL) 286-287 C 1
Navarro o RA 78-79 K 3
Navarro o USA (CA) 246-247 B 4
Navarro Mills Lake ⊂⊃ USA (TX) 266-267 L 2
Navas, Las o RP 160-161 F 6
Navašino o RUS 94-95 S 4
Navasota o USA (TX) 266-267 L 3
Navasota River ∼ USA (TX) 266-267 L 3
Navassa Island ⌒ USA 54-55 H 5
Nāve o AFG 134-135 M 2
Navere o RI 166-167 K 3
Navia o E 98-99 D 3
Navidad Bank ≃ 54-55 L 4
Navidad River ∼ USA (TX) 266-267 L 4
Naviraí o BR 76-77 K 2

Naitaba — Naviraí 367

Newport ○ USA (NC) 282-283 L 6
Newport ○ USA (NE) 262-263 G 2
Newport ○ USA (NH) 278-279 J 5
Newport ○ USA (OH) 280-281 B 3
Newport ○ USA (OR) 244-245 A 6
Newport ○ USA (TN) 282-283 D 5
Newport ○ USA (TX) 264-265 F 5
Newport ○ USA (VA) 280-281 F 6
Newport ○ USA (VT) 278-279 J 4
Newport ○ USA (WA) 244-245 H 2
Newport ○• USA (RI) 278-279 K 7
Newport Beach ○ USA (CA) 248-249 G 6
Newport News ○ USA (VA) 280-281 K 7
New Port Richey ○ USA (FL) 286-287 G 3
New Prague ○ USA (MN) 270-271 E 6
New Princeton ○ USA (OR) 244-245 G 7
New Providence ⌒ BS 54-55 G 2
Newquay ○• GB 90-91 E 6
New Raymer ○ USA (CO) 254-255 M 3
New Richland ○ USA (MN) 270-271 E 7
New Richmond ○ CDN (QUE) 240-241 K 2
New Richmond ○ USA (WI) 270-271 F 5
New Ringold ○ USA (OK) 264-265 J 4
New River ∼ GUY 62-63 F 4
New River ∼ USA (AZ) 256-257 C 5
New River ∼ USA (FL) 286-287 E 1
New River ∼ USA (GA) 284-285 G 5
New River ∼ USA (NC) 282-283 F 4
New River ∼ USA (NC) 282-283 K 6
New River ∼ USA (WV) 280-281 F 7
New Roads ○ USA (LA) 268-269 J 6
New Rochelle ○ USA (NY) 280-281 N 3
New Rockford ○ USA (ND) 258-259 H 4
New Ross ○ CDN (NS) 240-241 L 6
New Ross = Ros Mhic Thriúin ○ IRL 90-91 D 5
Newry ○ AUS 172-173 J 4
Newry ○ USA (ME) 278-279 L 4
Newry Island ⌒ AUS 174-175 K 7
New Salem ○ USA (ND) 258-259 F 5
New Schwabenland ∸ ARK 16 F 36
New Sharon ○ USA (IA) 274-275 F 3
New Siberian Islands = Novosibirskie ostrova ⌒ RUS 110-111 Z 3
New Site ○ USA (AL) 284-285 E 3
New Smyrna Beach ○ USA (FL) 286-287 J 2
Newsome ○ USA (TX) 264-265 J 6
New South Wales ◘ AUS 180-181 G 2
New Springs ○ AUS 176-177 F 2
New Stanton ○ USA (PA) 280-281 G 3
Newstead ○ CDN (NFL) 242-243 O 3
New Stuyahok ○ USA 22-23 S 3
New Summerfield ○ USA (TX) 268-269 E 5
Newton ○ USA (GA) 284-285 F 5
Newton ○ USA (IA) 274-275 E 3
Newton ○ USA (IL) 274-275 K 6
Newton ○ USA (KS) 262-263 J 6
Newton ○ USA (MS) 268-269 L 4
Newton ○ USA (NC) 282-283 F 5
Newton ○ USA (NJ) 280-281 M 2
Newton ○ USA (TX) 268-269 G 6
Newton Grove ○ USA (NC) 282-283 J 5
Newton Lake < USA (IL) 274-275 K 6
Newton Mills ○ CDN (NS) 240-241 N 5
Newtontoppen ▲ N 84-85 K 3
Newtown ○ CDN (NFL) 242-243 P 3
New Town ○ USA (ND) 258-259 E 4
Newtownabbey ○ GB 90-91 E 4
Newtown Steward ○ GB 90-91 D 4
New Ulm ○ USA (MN) 270-271 D 6
New Vienna ○ USA (OH) 280-281 C 4
New Waterford ○ CDN (NS) 240-241 P 4
New Waverly ○ USA (TX) 268-269 E 6
New Westminster ○ CDN (BC) 230-231 G 4
New World Island ⌒ CDN (NFL) 242-243 O 3
New York ○• USA (NY) 280-281 N 3
New York ◘ USA (NY) 278-279 E 6
New York Mountains ▲ USA (CA) 248-249 J 4
New York State Thruway II USA (NY) 278-279 F 5
New York State Thruway II USA (NY) 280-281 M 2
New Zealand ■ NZ 182 E 4
New Zealand ⌒ NZ 182 E 4
Nexapa, Río ∼ MEX 52-53 E 2
Nexpa, Río ∼ MEX 52-53 C 2
Neyyāttinkara ○ IND 140-141 G 6
Nezahualcóyotl, Ciudad ○ MEX 52-53 E 2
Nezahualcóyotl, Presa < MEX 52-53 H 3
Neždaninskoe ○ RUS 120-121 H 2
Nežin = Nižyn ○ UA 102-103 G 2
Neznaemyj, zaliv ≈ RUS 108-109 G 5
Neznanovo ○ RUS 94-95 R 4
Nezperce ○ USA (ID) 250-251 C 5
Nez Perce Indian Reservation ⅹ USA (ID) 250-251 C 5
Nez Perce National Historic Park • USA (ID) 250-251 C 5
Nez Perce Pass ▲ USA (ID) 250-251 E 6
Nezpique, Bayou ∼ USA (LA) 268-269 H 6
Nfiss, Oued ∼ MA 188-189 G 5
Ngabang ○ RI 162-163 H 4
Ngabe ○ RCB 210-211 F 5
Ngabordamlu, Tanjung ▲ RI 166-167 H 5
Ngabu ○ MW 218-219 H 3
Ngabwe ○ Z 218-219 D 1
Ngadda, River ∼ WAN 204-205 K 3
Ngadiluwih ○ RI 168 E 3
Ngadza ○ RCA 206-207 E 6
Ngajira ○ EAT 214-215 H 4
Ngala ○ WAN 198-199 G 6
Ngali ○ ZRE 210-211 G 5
Ngalo ○ ZRE 206-207 F 6
Ngalu ○• RI 168 E 8
Ngam ○ CAM 206-207 B 5
Ngam ○ TCH 206-207 C 3
Ngama ○ TCH 206-207 C 3
Ngamakwe ○ ZA 220-221 H 6
Ngambé ○ CAM 204-205 J 6
Ngambé Tikar ○ CAM 204-205 J 6
Ngamdu ○ WAN 204-205 K 3
Ngami, Lake ○ RB 218-219 B 5
Ngamiland ◘ RB 216-217 F 9
Ngamo ○ ZW 218-219 D 4
Ngamring ○ VRC 144-145 F 6
Nganda ○ RCA 206-207 F 6
Nganda ○ SN 202-203 C 3
Ngangala ○ SUD 206-207 K 6
Ngangla Ringco ○ VRC 144-145 D 5
Nganglong Kangri ▲ VRC 144-145 C 4
Nganglong Kangri ▲ VRC 144-145 C 4
Ngangzê Co ○ VRC 144-145 F 5
Nganha, Montagne de ▲ CAM 206-207 B 5
Nganji ○ ZRE 212-213 A 5
Nganjuk ○ RI 168 D 3
Ngantru ○ RI 168 D 3
Nganzi ○ ANG 210-211 D 6
Ngao ○ THA 142-143 L 6
Ngaoui, Mont ▲ CAM 206-207 B 5
Ngaoundal ○ CAM 204-205 K 5
Ngaoundéré ☆ CAM 204-205 K 5
Ngara ○ EAT 212-213 C 5
Ngara ○ MW 214-215 H 6
Ngarama ○ RWA 212-213 C 4
Ngarangou ○ TCH 198-199 G 6
Ngaras ○ RI 162-163 F 7
Ngarimbi ○ EAT 214-215 K 5
Ngarka-Pyrjajaha ∼ RUS 114-115 L 2
Ngarkat Conservation Park ⊥ AUS 180-181 F 3
Ngaso Plain ∸ EAK 212-213 F 2
Ngassao Noum ▲ CAM 206-207 B 4
Ngasumet ○ EAT 212-213 F 6
Ngathainggyaung ○ MYA 158-159 C 2
Ngato ○ CAM 210-211 E 2
Ngawi ○ RI 168 D 3
Ngawihi ○ NZ 182 E 4
Ngayu ∼ ZRE 212-213 B 3
Ngazidja ⌒ COM 222-223 C 3
Ngazun ○ MYA 142-143 J 5
Ngbala ○ RCB 210-211 E 3
Ngerengere ○ EAT 214-215 K 4
Ngezi ∼ ZW 218-219 E 4
Nggatokae ⌒ SOL 184 I d 3
Nggela Pile ⌒ SOL 184 I e 3
Nggela Sule ⌒ SOL 184 I d 3
Nghi Lôc ☆ VN 156-157 D 7
Ngidinga ○ ZRE 210-211 E 6
Ngilikomba ○ SOL 184 I e 3
Ngina ○ ZRE (Ban) 210-211 F 5
Ngina ○ ZRE (HAU) 212-213 A 2
N'Giva ☆ ANG 216-217 C 8
Ngo ○ RCB 210-211 E 5
Ngoa ○ ZRE 212-213 B 2
Ngoassé ○ CAM 210-211 D 2
Ngoc Hiên ○ VN 158-159 H 6
Ngofakiaha ○ RI 164-165 K 3
Ngog Mapubi ○ CAM 210-211 C 2
Ngoila ○ CAM 210-211 E 2
Ngoko ∼ CAM 210-211 E 3
Ngoko ○ RCB 210-211 E 4
Ngoko ∼ RCB 210-211 E 4
Ngoko ○ CAM 210-211 E 2
Ngol Kedju ▲ CAM 204-205 H 5
Ngolo ○ Z 214-215 F 5
Ngolo ○ ZRE 210-211 G 3
Ngolo, Chutes de ∼ RCA 206-207 F 6
Ngolopopo, Tanjung ▲ RI 164-165 L 3
Ngoma ○ NAM 218-219 C 3
Ngoma ○ Z 218-219 C 2
Ngomba ○ EAT 214-215 G 5
Ngomedzap ○ CAM 210-211 C 2
Ngomeni, Ras ▲ EAK 212-213 H 5
Ngomo ○ G 210-211 B 4
Ngom Qu ∼ VRC 144-145 K 4
Ngong ○ CAM 204-205 K 4
Ngong ○ EAK 212-213 F 4
Ngonga ○ CAM 204-205 J 6
Ngoni, Tanjung ▲ RI 166-167 H 5
Ngonye Falls ∼• Z 218-219 B 3
Ngora ○ EAU 212-213 D 3
Ngorengore ○ EAK 212-213 E 4
Ngoring Hu ○ VRC 144-145 L 3
Ngoro ○ CAM 204-205 J 6
Ngorongoro Conservation Area ⊥ EAT (ARV) 212-213 E 5
Ngorongoro Crater ▲••• EAT 212-213 E 5
Ngorongoro Crater Lodge ○ EAT 212-213 E 5
Ngororero ○ RWA 212-213 B 4
Ngoso ○ ZRE 210-211 G 6
Ngoto ○ RCA 206-207 C 6
Ngotwane ∼ RB 220-221 H 2
Ngouanga ∼ RCA 206-207 G 5
Ngoui ○ SN 196-197 D 6
Ngoulemakong ○ CAM 210-211 C 2
Ngoulonkila ○ RCB 210-211 E 5
Ngouma ○ RMM 202-203 J 2
Ngouni ○ G 210-211 D 4
Ngounié ∼ G 210-211 C 4
Ngoura ○ CAM 206-207 B 6
Ngoura ○ TCH 198-199 H 6
Ngouri ○ TCH 198-199 G 6
Ngourti ○ RN 198-199 F 5
Ngoussa ○ DZ 190-191 E 4
Ngoutchèy < TCH 198-199 H 4
Ngoyo ○ RCA 206-207 G 6
Ngoyang ▲ CAM 210-211 C 2
Ngové-Ndogo, Domaine de chasse de ⊥ G 210-211 B 5
Ngoyeboma ○ RCB 210-211 E 3
Ngozi ○ BU 212-213 B 5
Ngudu ○ EAT 212-213 D 5
Nguélémendouka ○ CAM 204-205 K 6
Nguema ○ ZRE 214-215 B 4
Ngui ○ RCA 206-207 F 5
Nguia Bouar ○ RCA 206-207 B 6
Nguigmi ○ RN 198-199 F 5
Nguila ○ CAM 204-205 J 6
Nguini < RN 198-199 D 5
Nguiu ⅹ AUS 172-173 K 1
Ngukurr ⅹ AUS 174-175 C 4
Nguling ○ RI 168 E 3
Nguna ⌒ VAN 184 II b 3
Ngundu ○ ZW 218-219 F 5
Nguni ○ EAK 212-213 G 4
Ngunju, Tanjung ▲ RI 168 E 8
Ngunut ○ RI 168 E 4
Nguroje ○ WAN 204-205 J 5
Ngurore ○ WAN 204-205 K 4
Nguru ○ WAN 198-199 E 6
Nguti ○ CAM 204-205 H 6
Nguyakro ○ CI 202-203 H 6
Nguyên Binh ☆ VN 156-157 D 5
Ngwale ○ EAT 214-215 J 6
Ngwalulu = Maana'oba ⌒ SOL 184 I e 3
Ngwedaung ○ MYA 142-143 K 6
Ngweze ∼ Z 218-219 C 3
Ngwo ○ CAM 204-205 H 5
Ngynesējaha ∼ RUS 108-109 R 6
Nhabe ∼ RB 218-219 B 5
Nhachengue ○ MOC 218-219 H 6
Nhacra ○ GNB 202-203 C 4
Nhamalábue ○ MOC 218-219 H 3
Nhamatanda ○ MOC 218-219 H 4
Nhamunda ○ BR 66-67 J 4
Nhamunda, Rio ∼ BR 62-63 F 6
Nhamundá Mapuera, Área Indígena ⅹ BR 62-63 E 6
Nhandeara ○ BR 72-73 E 6
Nhandu, Rio ∼ BR 66-67 K 7
Nharêa ○ ANG 216-217 D 5
Nha Trang ☆•• VN 158-159 K 4
Nhecolândia ○ BR 70-71 J 6
Nhia ∼ ANG 216-217 C 5
Nhill ○ AUS 180-181 F 4
Nhlangano ○ SD 220-221 K 3
Nho Quan ☆ VN 156-157 D 6
Nhoquim, Igarapé ∼ BR 68-69 C 6
Nhu' Kuân ☆ VN 156-157 D 7
Nhulunbuy (Gove) ○ AUS 174-175 D 3
Niabayo ○ CI 202-203 G 7
Niablé ○ CI 202-203 J 6
Niada ○ RCA 206-207 E 6
Niafounké ○ RMM 202-203 H 2
Niagara ○ USA (ND) 258-259 K 4
Niagara Creek ∼ CDN (BC) 228-229 O 4
Niagara Escarpment ▲ CDN (ONT) 238-239 D 3
Niagara Falls ○ CDN (ONT) 238-239 F 5
Niagara Falls •• CDN (ONT) 238-239 F 5
Niagara Falls ○ USA (NY) 278-279 C 5
Niagara River ∼ 46-47 J 4
Niague ○ CI 202-203 G 7
Niah ○ MAL 162-163 K 3
Niah Caves • MAL 162-163 K 3
Niah National Park ⊥ MAL 162-163 K 3
Niakaramandougou ○ CI 202-203 H 5
Niakhar ○ SN 202-203 B 2
Niaklan ○ LB 202-203 F 7
Nialaha'u Point = Cape Zele'e ▲ SOL 184 I e 3
Niambézaria ○ CI 202-203 H 7
Niamey ◘ RN 204-205 D 1
Niamey ☆• RN (NIA) 204-205 E 2
Niamina ○ RMM 202-203 G 3
Niampak ○ RI 164-165 K 1
Niamtougou ○ RT 202-203 L 5
Niamvoudou ○ CAM 204-205 K 6
Niandakoro ○ RG 202-203 F 4
Niandan ∼ RG 202-203 F 5
Nianfasa ○ CI 202-203 G 5
Nianforando ○ RG 202-203 E 5
Niangandu ○ EAT 214-215 J 4
Niangara ○ ZRE 212-213 A 2
Niangay, Lac ○ RMM 202-203 J 2
Niangoloko ○ BF 202-203 H 4
Niangua River ∼ USA (MO) 276-277 C 3
Niangyuan ○ VRC 156-157 G 4
Nia-Nia ○ ZRE 212-213 A 3
Nianing ○ SN 202-203 B 2
Niantan ∼ RG 202-203 F 4
Niantanina ○ RN 202-203 F 4
Nianyushan SK ∼ VRC 154-155 J 6
Niaoshu Shan ▲ VRC 154-155 D 4
Niapidou ○ CI 202-203 G 7
Niapu ○ ZRE 210-211 L 2
Niaqornaarsuk ○ GRØ 28-29 O 2
Niaqornat ○ GRØ 26-27 Y 8
Niara ○ RG 202-203 E 4
Niari ◘ RCB 210-211 D 5
Niari ∼ RCB 210-211 D 5
Niaro ○ SUD 206-207 K 3
Nias, Pulau ⌒ RI 162-163 B 4
Niassa ◘ MOC 218-219 J 1
Niassa, Lago ○ MOC 214-215 H 7
Niassa, Reserva do ⊥ MOC 214-215 J 7
Niáta ○ GR 100-101 J 6
Niau ⌒ F 13 N 4
Nibinamik Lake ○ CDN (ONT) 234-235 P 2
Nibong, Kampung ○ MAL 162-163 D 2
Nibong Tebal ○ MAL 162-163 D 2
Nica ∼ RUS 114-115 G 6
Nicaragua ○ CDN (QUE) 236-237 P 3
Nicaragua ■ NIC 52-53 A 5
Nicaragua, Lago de ○ NIC 52-53 B 6
Nicasio ○ PE 70-71 B 4
Nicastro ○ I 100-101 F 5
Ničatka, ozero ○ RUS 118-119 H 7
Nicatous Lake ○ USA (ME) 278-279 N 3
Nice ☆• F 90-91 L 10
Niceville ○ USA (FL) 286-287 C 1
Nichicun, Lac ○ CDN 38-39 J 2
Nichinan ○ J 152-153 D 9
Nichlaul ○ IND 142-143 C 2
Nicholas Channel ≈ 54-55 E 3
Nicholasville ○ USA (KY) 276-277 L 3
Nicholl Island ⌒ CDN (NS) 240-241 N 6
Nicholls ○ USA (GA) 284-285 H 5
Nicholls Warm Springs ○ USA (CA) 248-249 K 6
Nicholson ○ AUS 172-173 J 5
Nicholson, Mount ▲ AUS 178-179 K 3
Nicholson Lake ○ CDN (ONT) 236-237 E 5
Nicholson Lake ○ CDN 30-31 S 4
Nicholson Peninsula ∪ CDN 24-25 G 6
Nicholson Range ▲ AUS 176-177 D 3
Nicholson River ∼ AUS 174-175 E 5
Nichols Town ○ BS 54-55 F 2
Nicholsville ○ CDN (NFL) 242-243 L 3
Nicholville ○ USA (NY) 278-279 G 4
Nička ○ TM 136-137 H 6
Nickel Center ○ CDN (ONT) 238-239 E 2
Nickerierivier ∼ SME 62-63 F 3
Nickerson ○ USA (KS) 262-263 H 6
Nickerson ○ USA (MN) 270-271 F 4
Nickol Bay ≈ 172-173 C 6
Nicktown ○ USA (PA) 280-281 H 3
Nicman ○ CDN (QUE) 242-243 B 2
Ničnij Pjandž ○ TJ 136-137 L 6
Nicola ○ CDN (BC) 230-231 J 3
Nicola Mameet Indian Reserve ⅹ CDN (BC) 230-231 J 3
Nicola River ∼ CDN (BC) 230-231 H 3
Nicolás Bruzzone ○ RA 78-79 G 3
Nicolás Levalle ○ RA 78-79 H 5
Nicolet ○ CDN (QUE) 238-239 N 2
Nicolet, Rivière ∼ CDN (QUE) 238-239 N 2
Nicollet ○ USA (MN) 270-271 D 6
Nicondocho, Rio ∼ MOC 218-219 K 1
Nicosia ○ I 100-101 E 6
Nicosia = Lefkosia ☆ CY 128-129 E 5
Nicoya ○ CR 52-53 B 6
Nicoya, Golfo de ≈ 52-53 B 7
Nicoya, Península de ∪ CR 52-53 B 7
Nictau ○ CDN (NB) 240-241 H 3
Nicuadala ○ MOC 218-219 J 3
Nicupa ○ MOC 218-219 K 2
Nida ○•• LT 94-95 G 4
Nida ○ USA (OK) 264-265 H 4
Nidadavole ○ IND 140-141 J 2
Nidelva ∼ N 86-87 D 7
Nidili, ozero ○ RUS 118-119 M 4
Nido, El ○ RP 160-161 C 7
Nidpalli ○ IND 140-141 F 4
Nidri ○ GR 100-101 H 5
Nidym ∼ RUS 116-117 K 4
Nidymkan ∼ RUS 116-117 J 4
Nidzica ○• PL 92-93 Q 2
Niéboré ○ RG 202-203 E 4
Niebüll ○ D 92-93 K 1
Niechorze ○ PL 92-93 N 1
Niedere Tauern ▲ A 92-93 M 5
Niederösterreich ◘ A 92-93 N 4
Niedersachsen ◘ D 92-93 J 2
Niefang ○ GQ 210-211 C 3
Niega ○ BF 202-203 K 3
Niekerkshoop ○ ZA 220-221 F 4
Niellé ○ CI 202-203 H 4
Niellim ○ TCH 206-207 C 4
Niem ○ RCA 206-207 B 5
Niemba ○ ZRE 212-213 B 6
Niemba ∼ ZRE 214-215 E 4
Niemelane < RIM 196-197 E 5
Niemisel ○ S 86-87 L 3
Niéna ○ RMM 202-203 G 4
Nienburg (Weser) ○ D 92-93 K 2
Niénokue, Mont ▲ CI 202-203 G 7
Niéri Ko ∼ SN 202-203 D 3
Nieu Bethesda ○ ZA 220-221 G 5
Nieuw Amsterdam ☆ SME 62-63 G 3
Nieuw Nickerie ☆ SME 62-63 F 3
Nieuwoudtville ○ ZA 220-221 D 5
Nieuwpoort ○ NL 60-61 G 1
Nieva, Río ∼ PE 64-65 D 4
Nieves, Las ○ MEX 50-51 G 4
Niğde ☆• TR 128-129 F 3
Nigei Island ⌒ CDN (BC) 230-231 B 3
Nigel ○ ZA 220-221 J 3
Niger ∼ 9 D 4
Niger ■ RN 198-199 B 4
Niger ◘ WAN 204-205 F 4
Niger Delta ∪ WAN 204-205 F 6
Niger Fan ≃ 9 D 5
Nigeria ■ WAN 204-205 F 4
Night Hawk Lake ○ CDN (ONT) 236-237 H 4
Nightmote ○ USA 20-21 H 6
Nigisaktuvik River ∼ USA 20-21 L 1
Nigu River ∼ USA 20-21 M 2
Niha Settlements • RI 162-163 B 4
Nihing ○ PK 134-135 L 4
Nihing ∼ PK 134-135 K 5
Nihoa ⌒ USA (HI) 288 D 1
Nihonmatsu ○ J 152-153 J 6
Nihuil, El ○ RA 78-79 E 3
Nihuil, Embalse del < RA 78-79 E 3
Nihuil, Salto ∼ RA 78-79 E 3
Niigata ☆ J 152-153 H 6
Niihau ⌒ USA (HI) 288 E 3
Niijima ⌒ J 152-153 H 7
Niimi ○ J 152-153 E 7
Niitsu ○ J 152-153 H 6
Nijadluk Bay ≈ 36-37 R 2
Nijgarh ○ NEP 144-145 E 7
Nijmegen ○• NL 92-93 H 3
Nikeľ ○ RUS 88-89 L 2
Nikiniki ○ RI 166-167 C 6
Nikitinka ○ KA 124-125 N 4
Nikkaluokta ○ S 86-87 J 3
Nikki ○ DY 204-205 E 4
Nikkō ○•• J 152-153 H 6
Nikko National Park ⊥ J 152-153 H 6
Nikoemvon ○ CAM 210-211 C 2
Nikolaev = Mykolajiv ○ UA 102-103 G 4
Nikolaevka ○ KA 124-125 E 1
Nikolaevo ○ RUS 94-95 L 2
Nikolaevsk ○ RUS 96-97 D 8
Nikolaevsk-na-Amure ☆ RUS 122-123 J 2
Nikolaja, mys ▲ RUS 108-109 F 4
Nikolaja, zaliv ○ RUS 122-123 H 2
Nikolka, gora ▲ RUS 120-121 T 6
Nikolo-L'vovskoe ○ RUS 122-123 D 7
Nikoľsk ○ RUS 96-97 D 4
Nikoľsk ○ RUS (PNZ) 96-97 E 7
Nikoľskij = Satpaev ☆ KA 124-125 E 5
Nikoľskoe ○ RUS (AST) 96-97 E 10
Nikoľskoe ○ RUS 96-97 E 9
Nikoľskoe ☆ RUS 120-121 V 6
Nikonga ∼ EAT 212-213 C 5
Nikopol ○ BG 102-103 D 6
Nikopol ○ UA 102-103 J 4
Nikopolis •• GR 100-101 H 5
Nikšahr ○ IR 134-135 J 5
Nikšahr, Rūdhāne-ye ∼ IR 134-135 J 5
Niksar ☆• TR 128-129 G 2
Nikšić ○ YU 100-101 G 3
Nil, an- ∼ ET 194-195 E 3
Nila ○ RI 168 E 7
Nila, Pulau ⌒ RI 166-167 E 5
Nilahué, Estrecho de ∼ RCH 78-79 D 3
Nilakkottai ○ IND 140-141 G 5
Nilan ∼ RUS 122-123 F 3
Niland ○ USA (CA) 248-249 J 6
Nilanga ○ IND 138-139 F 10
Nile ◘ EAU 212-213 C 2
Nile = an-Nil ∼ ET 194-195 E 3
Nile = Nil, an- ∼ SUD 194-195 E 3
Niles ○ USA (MI) 272-273 C 6
Niles ○ USA (OH) 280-281 F 2
Nilgysy ∼ RUS 120-121 L 3
Nilka ○ VRC 146-147 F 4
Nil Kōtal, Kōtal-e ▲ AFG 134-135 M 1
Nilópolis ○ BR 72-73 J 7
Nilsiä ○ FIN 88-89 K 5
Nilt ○ PK 138-139 E 1
Nimach ○ IND 138-139 E 7
Niman ∼ RUS 122-123 E 3
Nimar ∸ IND 138-139 E 9
Nimba, Monts ▲••• RG 202-203 F 6
Nimbāhera ○ IND 138-139 E 7
Nimba Range ∸ LB 202-203 F 6
Nimbin ○ AUS 178-179 M 5
Nimbotong ○ RI 166-167 L 3
Nimburg = Nymburk ○• CZ 92-93 N 3
Nimčan ∼ RUS 112-113 H 3
Nimdè ∼ RUS 116-117 E 3
Nimelen ∼ RUS 122-123 G 2
Nîmes ☆•• F 90-91 K 10
Nimi ∼ RUS 120-121 F 6
Nimingdè ∼ RUS 110-111 Q 6
Nimiuktuk River ∼ USA 20-21 L 2
Nimjat ○ RIM 196-197 C 6
Nim Ka Thāna ○ IND 138-139 E 6
Nim Li Punit ∴• BH 52-53 K 3
Nimmitabel ○ AUS 180-181 K 4
Nimpkish River ∼ CDN (BC) 230-231 C 3
Nimpo Lake ○ CDN (BC) 228-229 J 4
Nimrod ○ USA (MN) 270-271 D 4
Nimrod Lake ○ USA (AR) 276-277 B 6
Nimrōz ◘ AFG 134-135 K 3
Nimrud ∴•• IRQ 128-129 K 4
Nimule ○ SUD 212-213 D 2
Nimule National Park ⊥ SUD 212-213 D 2
Nimún, Punta ▲ MEX 52-53 J 1
Nina ○ NAM 216-217 E 11
Nina, Île = Aniwa Island ⌒ VAN 184 II b 4
Ninā, Wādī ∼ LAR 192-193 F 3
Nina Bang Lake ○ CDN 24-25 g 5
Nina Lake ○ CDN 30-31 X 2
Ninami-Daitō-shima ⌒ J 152-153 D 12
Ninawā ∴•• IRQ 128-129 K 4
Ninawia ◘ IRQ 128-129 J 5
Ninda ○ ANG 216-217 F 7
Nindigully ○ AUS 178-179 K 5
Nine Degree Channel ≈ 140-141 E 6
Nine Mile Falls ○ USA (WA) 244-245 H 3
Ninette ○ CDN (MAN) 234-235 D 5
Ninette ○ NAM 216-217 E 11
Ninetyeast Ridge ≃ 12 G 7
Ninety Mile Beach ∸ AUS 180-181 J 5
Ninety Six ○ USA (SC) 284-285 H 2
Ninety Six National Historic Site ∴• USA (SC) 284-285 H 2
Ninfas, Punta ▲ RA 78-79 G 7
Ninga ○ CDN (MAN) 234-235 D 5
Ningaloo ○ AUS 172-173 A 7
Ning'an ○ VRC 150-151 G 5
Ningan ○ VRC 156-157 C 3
Ningari ○ RMM 202-203 J 2
Ningau Island ⌒ PNG 183 E 3
Ningbo ○• VRC 156-157 M 2
Ningcheng ○ VRC 148-149 O 7
Ningde ○ VRC 156-157 L 3
Ningdu ○ VRC 156-157 J 3
Ningeehak ○ USA 20-21 E 5
Ningera ○ PNG 183 A 2
Ningerum ○ PNG 183 A 3
Ningguo ○ VRC 154-155 L 6
Ninghai ○ VRC 156-157 M 2
Ninghe ○ VRC 154-155 K 2
Ninghua ○ VRC 156-157 K 3
Ningi ○ WAN 204-205 H 3
Ningjin ○ VRC 154-155 K 3
Ningjing Shan ▲ VRC 144-145 L 5
Ningming ○ VRC 156-157 E 5
Ningqiang ○ VRC 154-155 E 5
Ningshan ○ VRC 154-155 F 5
Ningwu ○ VRC 154-155 H 2
Ningxia Huizu Zizhiqu ◘ VRC 154-155 D 3
Ning Xian ○ VRC (GAN) 154-155 E 4
Ning Xian ○ VRC (SXI) 154-155 F 4
Ningxiang ○ VRC 156-157 H 2
Ninh Bình ☆ VN 156-157 D 6
Ninh Hòa ○ VN 158-159 K 4
Ninh So'n ○ VN 158-159 K 5
Ninia ○ RI 166-167 K 4
Ninilchik ○ USA 20-21 P 6
Niniva ⌒ TON 184 IV a 1
Ninive = Ninawā ∴•• IRQ 128-129 K 4
Ninnescah River ∼ USA (KS) 262-263 H 7
Ninnis Glacier ⊂ ARK 16 G 15
Ninocminda ○ GE 126-127 E 7
Ninohe ○ J 152-153 J 4
Nioaque ○ BR 76-77 K 1
Niobrara ○ USA (NE) 262-263 H 2
Niobrara River ∼ USA (NE) 262-263 E 2
Niodior ○ SN 202-203 B 3
Niofouin ○ CI 202-203 G 5
Nioghalvfjerdsfjorden ⊂ GRØ 26-27 o 4
Nioka ○ ZRE (HAU) 212-213 C 2
Nioka ○ ZRE (KOR) 214-215 B 4
Niokolo-Koba ○ SN 202-203 D 3
Niokolo-Koba, Parc National du ⊥•• SN 202-203 D 3
Niono ○ RMM 202-203 H 2
Nionsamoridu ○ RG 202-203 F 5
Niorenge, Rio ∼ MOC 218-219 J 1
Nioro du Rip ○ SN 202-203 C 3
Nioro du Sahel ○ RMM 202-203 F 2
Niort ☆• F 90-91 G 8
Nioût ○ RIM 196-197 G 6
Nipa ○ PNG 183 B 4
Nipáni ○ IND 140-141 F 2
Nipanipa, Tanjung ▲ RI 164-165 H 5
Nipawin ○ CDN (SAS) 232-233 O 2
Nipawin Provincial Park ⊥ CDN 34-35 D 3
Nipe, Bahía de ≈ 54-55 H 4
Nipekamev River ∼ CDN 34-35 D 3
Nipele ∼ NAM 216-217 D 9
Nipgen ○ USA (OH) 280-281 C 4
Niphad ○ IND 138-139 E 9
Nipigon ○ CDN (ONT) 234-235 P 5
Nipigon, Lake ○ CDN (ONT) 234-235 P 5
Nipigon Bay ○ CDN (ONT) 234-235 P 6
Nipigon River ○ CDN (ONT) 234-235 P 5
Nipin River ∼ CDN 32-33 Q 4
Nipiodi ○ MOC 218-219 J 3
Nipishish Lake ○ CDN 36-37 T 7
Nipisi River ∼ CDN 32-33 N 4
Nipissing, Lake ○ CDN (ONT) 238-239 F 2
Nipissing River ∼ CDN (ONT) 238-239 G 3
Nipisso ○ CDN (QUE) 242-243 C 2
Nipisso, Lac ○ CDN (QUE) 242-243 C 2
Nipomo ○ USA (CA) 248-249 D 4
Nippers Harbour ○ CDN (NFL) 242-243 N 3
Nipton ○ USA (CA) 248-249 J 4
Niquelândia ○ BR 72-73 F 3
Nir ○ IR (AZS) 128-129 M 3
Nir ○ IR (YAZ) 134-135 F 3
Nira ○ IND 138-139 E 10
Ñire-Có ○ RA 78-79 E 4
Ñireguao ○ RCH 80 E 2
Nirgua ○ YV 60-61 G 2
Nirmal ○ IND 138-139 G 10
Nirumoar, Pulau ⌒ RI 166-167 K 2
Niš ○ AFG 134-135 L 2
Niš ○•• YU 100-101 H 3
Nisa ○ P 98-99 D 5
Nişāb ○ KSA 130-131 J 3
Nisāb ○ Y 132-133 E 6
Nišan ○ US 136-137 J 5
Niseko Shakotan Otaru-kaigan Quasi National Park ⊥ J 152-153 J 3
Nishi ○ VRC 156-157 G 2
Nishibetsu-gawa ∼ J 152-153 L 3
Nishi-Chugoku-sanchi Quasi National Park ⊥ J 152-153 E 7
Nishi-no-Omote ○ J 152-153 D 9
Nishino-shima ⌒ J 152-153 E 6
Nishi-Okoppe ○ J 152-153 K 2
Nishi-Sonogi-hantō ∪ J 152-153 C 8
Nishi-suidō ≈ 152-153 C 7
Nishnabotna River ∼ USA (IA) 274-275 C 4
Nisi-no-shima ⌒ J 152-153 D 11
Niskibi River ∼ CDN 34-35 M 2
Nisko ○ PL 92-93 R 3
Nisland ○ USA (SD) 260-261 C 2
Nisling River ∼ CDN 20-21 V 5
Nisqually River ∼ USA (WA) 244-245 C 4
Nissan ∼ S 86-87 F 8
Nisséko ○ BF 202-203 J 4
Nisser ○ N 86-87 D 7
Nissiros ⌒ GR 100-101 L 6
Nissum Bredning ≈ 86-87 D 8
Nistru ∼ MD 102-103 F 4
Nistru ∼ MD 102-103 G 4
Niśtūn ○ Y 132-133 H 6
Nisutlin Plateau ▲ CDN 20-21 Z 6
Nisutlin River ∼ CDN 20-21 Y 6
Nita Downs ○ AUS 172-173 E 5
Nitchequon ○ CDN 38-39 J 2
Niterói ○ BR 72-73 J 7
Nith ∼ GB 90-91 F 4
Nitija, gora ▲ RUS 120-121 G 4
Nitinat ○ CDN (BC) 230-231 E 5
Nitinat River ∼ CDN (BC) 230-231 E 5
Niti Pass ▲ VRC 144-145 B 5
Nitmiluk (Katherine Gorge) National Park ⊥•• AUS 172-173 L 3
Nitra ○• SK 92-93 P 4
Nitro ○ USA (WV) 280-281 E 5
Nituj ∼ RUS 122-123 K 4
Niu' Aunofo Point ▲ TON 184 IV a 2
Niuchang ○ VRC 156-157 D 4
Niut, Gunung ▲ RI 162-163 H 4
Niutaca, Corrego ∼ BR 70-71 J 7
Niutoushan ○ VRC 154-155 L 6
Niuwudu, Tanjung ▲ RI 168 E 8
Nivala ○ FIN 88-89 H 5
Niváno ○ PK 134-135 K 5
Nive River ∼ AUS 178-179 J 3
Niverville ○ CDN (MAN) 234-235 F 5
Niviarsiat ▲ GRØ 28-29 T 6
Nivšera ∼ RUS 88-89 W 5
Niwai ○ IND 138-139 E 6
Niwelin Lake ○ CDN 30-31 G 2
Nixon ○ USA (NV) 246-247 F 4
Nixon ○ USA (TX) 266-267 K 4
Niyrakpak Lagoon ≈ 20-21 E 5
Nizāmābād ○ IND 138-139 G 10
Nizām Sāgar ○ IND 138-139 F 10
Nizgan, Rūd-e ∼ AFG 134-135 L 2
Nižnekamsk = Nižnekamsk ☆ RUS 96-97 G 6
Nižnekamskoe Vodohranilishche = Nižnekamskoe vodohr. < RUS 96-97 H 6
Nižnevartovsk = Nižnevartovsk ☆ RUS 114-115 O 4
Nizhniy Novgorod = Nižnij Novgorod ☆•• RUS 94-95 S 3
Nizhniy Tagil = Nižnij Tagil ☆ RUS 96-97 L 5
Nizhnyaya Tunguska = Nižnjaja Tunguska ∼ RUS 116-117 D 3
Nizi ○ ZRE 212-213 C 3
Nizina Sępolska ∪ PL 92-93 Q 1
Nizip ☆ TR 128-129 G 4
Nízke Tatry ▲ SK 92-93 P 4
Nizkij, mys ▲ RUS (CUK) 112-113 U 4
Nizkij, mys ▲ RUS (KOR) 112-113 R 6
Nizkiy Island ⌒ USA 22-23 D 6
Niz'ma ∼ RUS 88-89 T 4
Nižneangarsk ○ RUS 118-119 D 8
Nižnejansk ○ RUS 110-111 V 4
Nižnekamsk ☆ RUS 96-97 G 6
Nižnekamskoe vodohranilišče < RUS 96-97 H 6
Nižnekolymsk ○ RUS 112-113 L 2
Nižnetambovskoe ○ RUS 122-123 H 3
Nižneudinsk ☆ RUS 116-117 J 8
Nižnevartovsk ☆ RUS 114-115 O 4
Nižnie Sergi ☆ RUS 96-97 L 5
Nižnij Bestjah ○ RUS 118-119 O 5
Nižnij Casučej ☆ RUS 118-119 G 10
Nižnij Dvojnik ∼ RUS 88-89 W 4
Nižnij Imbak ∼ RUS 114-115 T 3
Nižnij Ingaš ☆ RUS 116-117 H 7
Nižnij Lomov ○ RUS 94-95 S 5
Nižnij Novgorod ☆•• RUS 94-95 S 3
Nižnij Odes ○ RUS 88-89 X 5
Nižnij Suzun ∼ RUS 124-125 N 1
Nižnij Tagil ☆ RUS 96-97 L 5
Nižnij Viljujkan ∼ RUS 116-117 N 3
Nižnjaja ∼ RUS 108-109 f 5
Nižnjaja Agapa ∼ RUS 108-109 W 6
Nižnjaja Baiha ∼ RUS 114-115 T 2
Nižnjaja Buotankaga ∼ RUS 108-109 W 5
Nižnjaja Cipa ∼ RUS 118-119 F 8
Nižnjaja Čunku ∼ RUS 116-117 H 4
Nižnjaja Kočoma ∼ RUS 116-117 N 4
Nižnjaja Larba ∼ RUS 118-119 L 8
Nižnjaja Peša ○ RUS 88-89 T 3
Nižnjaja Pojma ○ RUS 116-117 H 7
Nižnjaja Suetka ○ RUS 124-125 L 2
Nižnjaja Tajmyra ∼ RUS 108-109 c 4
Nižnjaja Talovaja ∼ RUS 108-109 X 6
Nižnjaja Tavda ☆ RUS 114-115 J 6
Nižnjaja Tunguska ∼ RUS 114-115 U 2
Nižnjaja Tunguska ∼ RUS 116-117 M 4
Nižnjaja Tunguska ∼ RUS 116-117 K 4
Nižnjaja Tunguska ∼ RUS 116-117 N 7
Nižnjaja Tura ○ RUS 96-97 L 4
Nižn Pronge ○ RUS 122-123 J 2
Nižyn ○ UA 102-103 G 2
Nizzana ○ IL 130-131 D 2
Njadajaha ∼ RUS 108-109 T 7
Njagamja, ozero ○ RUS 108-109 X 5
Njagan' ○ RUS 114-115 H 3
Njaiama-Sewafe ○ WAL 202-203 E 5
Njajs ∼ RUS 114-115 F 3
Njakšingda, ozero ○ RUS 116-117 F 2
Njalinskoe ○ RUS 114-115 K 4
Njamakit, gora ▲ RUS 108-109 f 6
Njandoma ○ RUS 88-89 Q 6
Njangus'jaha ∼ RUS 108-109 T 7
Njanneli ∼ RUS 110-111 V 5
Njarövik ○ IS 86-87 b 3
Njarga ∼ RUS 114-115 S 5
Njasviž ☆ BY 94-95 K 5
Njatlongajagun ∼ RUS 114-115 M 3
Njau ○ WAG 202-203 C 3
Njazepetrovsk ☆ RUS 96-97 L 5
Njenje ∼ EAT 214-215 J 5
Njiapanda ○ EAT (MBE) 214-215 G 5
Njinjo ○ EAT 214-215 K 5
Njoko ∼ Z 218-219 C 3
Njombe ○ EAT (IRI) 214-215 H 5
Njombe ∼ EAT 214-215 H 4
Njoro ○ EAK 212-213 E 4
Njuhča ○ RUS (ARH) 88-89 T 5
Njuhča ∼ RUS 88-89 O 5
Njuja ○ RUS (SAH) 118-119 H 5
Njuja ∼ RUS 118-119 G 5
Njuja ∼ RUS 118-119 F 5
Njuja ∼ RUS 118-119 D 5
Njuja ∼ RUS 118-119 E 5
Njuk, ozero ○ RUS 88-89 L 4
Njukčorok ∼ RUS 116-117 L 3
Njukža ∼ RUS 118-119 L 8
Njukža, Ust'- ○ RUS 118-119 K 7
Njun'karakutari ∼ RUS 108-109 f 4
Njun Pelgrimkondre ○ SME 62-63 G 3
Njurba ☆• RUS 118-119 J 4
Njurol'ka ∼ RUS 114-115 O 5
Nkalagu ○ WAN 204-205 G 5
Nkam ∼ CAM 204-205 J 6
Nkamba Lodge ○ Z 214-215 F 5
Nkambe ○ CAM 204-205 J 5
Nkaw ○ ZRE 210-211 G 5
Nkawie ○ GH 202-203 K 6
Nkayi ○ RCB 210-211 D 6
Nkayi ○ ZW 218-219 E 4
Nkeni ∼ RCB 210-211 E 4
Nkhata Bay ○• MW 214-215 H 6
Nkhilé < RIM 196-197 G 6
Nkhotakota ○ MW 214-215 H 7
Nkhotakota Game Reserve ⊥ MW 214-215 G 7
Nkoambang ○ CAM 204-205 K 6
Nkolabona ○ G 210-211 C 3
Nkole ○ Z 214-215 F 6
Nkolmengboua ○ G 210-211 C 2
Nkomfap ○ WAN 204-205 H 5
Nkomi ∼ G 210-211 B 4
Nkomi, Lagune = Fernan Vaz ○ G 210-211 B 4
Nkondwe ○ EAT 212-213 C 6
Nkongjok ○ CAM 204-205 J 6
Nkongsamba ○ CAM 204-205 H 6
Nkon Ngok ○ CAM 204-205 J 6
Nkoranza ○ GH 202-203 K 6
Nkoteng ○ CAM 204-205 K 6
Nkoué ○ RCB 210-211 E 5
Nkourala ○ RMM 202-203 G 4
Nkula Falls ∼ MW 218-219 H 2
Nkulu, Malemba- ○ ZRE 214-215 D 5
Nkundi ○ EAT 214-215 F 4
Nkurenkuru ○ NAM 216-217 E 8
Nkuruman Escarpment ▲ EAK 212-213 F 5
Nkwalini ○ ZA 220-221 K 4
Nkwanta ○ GH (VTA) 202-203 L 5
Nkwanta ○ GH (WTN) 202-203 J 7
Nkwanta, Atasi ○ GH 202-203 K 7
Nkwanta, Manso- ○ GH 202-203 K 6
Nmai Hka ∼ MYA 142-143 L 2
n-Natrūn, Wādī ∼• ET 194-195 E 2
Nnewi ○ WAN 204-205 G 5
No.1, Canal < RA 78-79 L 4
No.2, Canal < RA 78-79 L 4
No.5, Canal < RA 78-79 L 4
No.9, Canal < RA 78-79 L 4
No.11, Canal < RA 78-79 K 4

Newport — No.11, Canal 369

No.12, Canal < RA 78-79 K 4
No.16, Canal < RA 78-79 K 3
Noabanki ○ BD 142-143 F 4
Noakhali ○ BD 142-143 G 4
Noanama ○ CO 60-61 C 5
Noatak ○ USA 20-21 J 3
Noatak National Preserve ⊥ USA 20-21 K 2
Noatak River ~ USA 20-21 M 3
Nobel ○ CDN (ONT) 238-239 E 3
Nobeoka ○ J 152-153 D 8
Nobéré ○ BF 202-203 K 4
Nobleboro ○ USA (NY) 278-279 G 5
Nobleford ○ CDN (ALB) 232-233 E 6
Nobles Nob Mine • AUS 174-175 C 6
Noble's Trail Monument ∴ USA (SD) 260-261 H 2
Noblesville ○ USA (IN) 274-275 M 4
Nobokwe ○ ZA 220-221 H 5
Noboribetsu ○ J 152-153 J 3
Nobres ○ BR 70-71 J 4
Nocina ○ E 98-99 F 3
Nockatunga ○ AUS 178-179 G 4
Nocona ○ USA (TX) 264-265 G 5
Nocuchich ∴• MEX 52-53 K 2
Noda ○ J 152-153 J 4
Nodaway River ~ USA (MO) 274-275 C 4
Noe ○ CI 202-203 J 7
Noefs, Île des ∩ SY 224 C 3
Noel ○ CDN (NS) 240-241 M 5
Noel ○ USA (MO) 276-277 A 4
Noell Lake ⊖ CDN 20-21 Y 2
Noelville ○ CDN (ONT) 238-239 E 2
Noenieput ○ ZA 220-221 E 3
Noépé ○ RT 202-203 L 6
Noetinger ○ RA 78-79 H 2
Nogajskaja step ≐ RUS 126-127 F 5
Nogal ○ USA (NM) 256-257 K 5
Nogales ○ MEX (CHA) 50-51 E 2
Nogales ○ MEX (VER) 52-53 F 2
Nogales ○• MEX (SON) 50-51 D 2
Nogales ○ RCH 78-79 D 2
Nogales ○ USA (AZ) 256-257 E 7
Nogamut ○ USA 20-21 M 6
Nogara ○ ETH 200-201 H 6
Nōgata ○ J 152-153 D 8
Nogent-le-Rotrou ○ F 90-91 H 7
Nogent-sur-Seine ○ F 90-91 J 7
Noginsk ✱• RUS 94-95 Q 4
Nogiri Point ▲ SOL 184 I c 2
Nogliki ✱ RUS 122-123 K 3
Nogoyá ○ RA 78-79 K 2
Nogoyá, Arroyo ~ RA 78-79 K 2
Noguira, Riacho ~ RA 76-77 G 4
Nohar ○ IND 138-139 E 5
Noheji ○ J 152-153 J 4
Nohili Point ▲ USA (HI) 288 F 2
Nohonč, Küh-e ▲ IR 134-135 J 5
Noia ○ E 98-99 C 3
Noice Peninsula ⌣ CDN 24-25 T 1
Noire, Rivière ~ CDN (QUE) 238-239 H 2
Noires, Montagnes ▲▲ RH 54-55 J 5
Noirmoutier, Île de ∩ F 90-91 F 8
Noirmoutier-en-l'Île ○ F 90-91 F 8
Nojabr'sk ○ RUS 114-115 N 3
Nojack ○ CDN (ALB) 232-233 C 2
Nojima-saki ▲ J 152-153 H 7
Nokaneng ○ RB 218-219 B 4
Nokha ○ IND 138-139 D 6
Nokia ○ FIN 88-89 G 6
Nokomis ○ CDN (SAS) 232-233 O 4
Nokomis ○ USA (IL) 274-275 J 5
Nokou ○ TCH 198-199 G 5
Nokoué, Lac ⊖ DY 204-205 E 5
Nokuku ○ VAN 184 II a 2
Nola ○ I 100-101 E 4
Nola ✱• RCA 210-211 F 2
Nolalu ○ CDN (ONT) 234-235 O 6
Nolan ○ USA (TX) 264-265 D 6
Nol'de guba ⊖ RUS 112-113 R 1
Noling ~ RI 164-165 G 5
Nolinsk ✱ RUS 96-97 G 5
Noll ○ ZA 220-221 F 6
Nom ○ VRC 146-147 M 4
Nomad ○ PNG 183 B 4
Nomad River ~ PNG 183 B 4
Noma misaki ▲ J 152-153 D 9
Nomane ○ PNG 183 C 4
Nomansland Point ▲ CDN 34-35 Q 4
Nombre de Dios ○ MEX 50-51 G 6
Nombre de Dios, Cordillera ▲▲ HN 52-53 L 4
Nome ○ USA 20-21 H 4
Nome, Cape ▲ USA 20-21 H 4
Nome-Council-Highway II USA 20-21 H 4
Nome-Taylor-Highway II USA 20-21 H 4
Nomhon ○ VRC 144-145 L 2
Nomtsas ○ NAM 220-221 C 2
Nomuka ∩ TON 184 IV a 2
Nomuka Group ∩ TON 184 IV a 2
Nona, La ○ MEX 50-51 F 6
Nonacho Lake ⊖ CDN 30-31 P 5
Nonagama ○ CL 140-141 J 7
Non Champa ○ THA 158-159 G 2
Nondaltan ○ USA 20-21 N 6
Nondo ○ Z 214-215 F 5
Nong'an ○ VRC 150-151 E 5
Nong Bua ○ THA 158-159 F 3
Nong Bua Daeng ○ THA 158-159 F 2
Nong Bua Khok ○ THA 158-159 F 3
Nong Bua Lamphu ○ THA 158-159 G 2
Nongchang ○ VRC 154-155 F 3
Nong Khae ○ THA 158-159 F 3
Nong Khai ○ THA 158-159 G 2
Nongoma ✱ ZA 220-221 K 3
Nong Phai ○ THA 158-159 F 2
Nong Phok ○ THA 158-159 H 2
Nong Phu ○ THA 158-159 H 3
Nongra Lake ⊖ AUS 172-173 J 5
Nong Rua ○ THA 158-159 G 2
Nongsa ○ RI 162-163 F 4
Nonoava ○ MEX 50-51 F 4
Nonogasta ○ RA 76-77 D 5
Non Thai ○ THA 158-159 G 3
Nooleeye ○ SP 208-209 H 6
Noolyeana Lake ⊖ AUS 178-179 D 4
Noonan ○ USA (ND) 258-259 D 3
Noonday ○ USA (TX) 264-265 J 6
Noondoonia ○ AUS 176-177 G 6
Noonkanbah ○ AUS 172-173 G 5
Noonthorangee Range ▲▲ AUS 178-179 G 6
Noonyereena Hill ▲ AUS 176-177 E 2
Noordoewer ○ NAM 220-221 C 4
Noordzeekanaal < NL 92-93 H 2
Noorvik ○ USA 20-21 K 3
Noosa Heads ○ AUS 178-179 M 4
Nootka ○ CDN (BC) 230-231 C 4
Nootka Island ∩ CDN (BC) 230-231 C 4
Nootka Sound ≈ 32-33 G 7
Nootka Sound ≈ CDN 230-231 C 4
Nopoló ○ MEX 50-51 D 5
Nopoming Provincial Park ⊥ CDN (MAN) 234-235 H 4
Nóqui ○ ANG 216-217 B 2
Nora ○ CDN (SAS) 232-233 P 3
Nora ~ RUS 122-123 D 2
Norah ∩ ER 200-201 K 4
Norala ○ RP 160-161 F 9
Noranside ○ AUS 178-179 E 2
Nora Springs ○ USA (IA) 274-275 F 1
Norassoba ○ RG 202-203 F 4
Norberg ○ N 86-87 D 6
Norberto de la Riesta ○ RA 78-79 K 3
Norcatur ○ USA (KS) 262-263 F 5
Norcross ○ USA (GA) 284-285 F 3
Nord, Île du ∩ SY 224 B 5
Nord = North ◘ CAM 204-205 K 4
Nord, ostrov ∩ RUS 108-109 b 3
Nordaustlandet ∩ N 84-85 L 3
Nordaust-Svalbard naturreservat ⊥ N 84-85 M 3
Nordbruk, ostrov ∩ RUS 84-85 b 3
Nordby ○ DK 86-87 E 9
Nordegg ○ CDN (ALB) 232-233 B 3
Nordegg River ~ CDN (ALB) 232-233 C 3
Norden ○ D 92-93 J 2
Nordenšel'da, arhipelag ∩ RUS 108-109 Z 3
Nordenšel'da, zaliv ⊖ RUS 108-109 G 4
Nordenskiöld Islands ∩ CDN 24-25 W 6
Nordenskiøld Land ≐ N 84-85 J 4
Nordenskiöld River ~ CDN 20-21 W 6
Nordenskiölds Gletscher ⊂ GRØ 28-29 P 2
Nordenskjöld Fjord ≈ 26-27 b 2
Norderney ∩ D 92-93 J 2
Norderstedt ○ D 92-93 K 2
Nordeste ○ ANG 216-217 F 3
Nordfjordeid ✱ N 86-87 B 6
Nordfjorden ≈ 84-85 J 3
Nordfjorden ≈ 86-87 B 6
Nordfold ○ N 86-87 G 3
Nordfriesische Inseln ≐ D 92-93 K 1
Nordgrønland = Avannaarsua ◘ GRØ 26-27 V 4
Nordhausen ○• D 92-93 L 3
Nordhorn ○ D 92-93 J 2
Nordkapp ▲ N 26-27 w 8
Nordkapp ▲ N (SVA) 84-85 L 2
Nordkapp ▲•• N (FIN) 86-87 M 1
Nordkinnhalvøya ⌣ N 86-87 N 1
Nordkvaløy ∩ N 86-87 J 1
Nordli ○ N 86-87 F 4
Nördlingen ○•• D 92-93 L 4
Nordmaling ○ S 86-87 J 5
Nordman ○ USA (ID) 250-251 C 3
Nordostrundingen ▲ GRØ 26-27 t 3
Nord-Ostsee-Kanal < D 92-93 K 1
Nord-Ouest = North-West ◘ CAM 204-205 J 5
Nord-Pas-de-Calais ◘ F 90-91 J 6
Nordreisa ○ N 86-87 K 2
Nordre Isortoq ≈ 28-29 O 3
Nordre Strømfjord ≈ 28-29 O 3
Nordrhein-Westfalen ◘ D 92-93 J 3
Nordvestfjord ≈ 26-27 m 8
Nordvestinskij, aral ∩ KA 96-97 G 10
Nordvest-spitsbergen nasjonalpark ⊥ N 84-85 G 3
Nordvik ○ RUS 110-111 H 3
Nordvik, buhta ≈ 110-111 H 3
Norembega ○ CDN (ONT) 236-237 H 4
Norfolk ○ USA (NE) 262-263 J 2
Norfolk ○ USA (VA) 280-281 K 7
Norfolk, Mount ▲ AUS 180-181 H 6
Norfolk Island ∩ AUS 13 H 5
Norfolk Lake ⊖ USA (AR) 276-277 C 4
Norfolk Ridge ≃ 182 B 1
Norgate ○ CDN (MAN) 234-235 D 4
Nor Harberd ○ AR 128-129 L 2
Norias ○ MEX 50-51 H 5
Norias ○ USA (TX) 266-267 K 7
Noril'ka ~ RUS 108-109 X 7
Noril'sk ○ RUS 108-109 X 7
Noring, Gunung ▲ MAL 162-163 D 2
Noring, Gunung ▲ MAL 162-163 D 2
Norland ○ CDN (ONT) 238-239 G 4
Norlina ○ USA (NC) 282-283 J 4
Normal ○ USA (IL) 274-275 K 4
Norman ○ USA (AR) 276-277 B 6
Norman ○ USA (OK) 264-265 G 3
Norman, Lake < USA (NC) 282-283 G 5
Normanby Island ∩ PNG 183 F 5
Normanby River ~ AUS 174-175 H 4
Normandia ○ BR 62-63 E 4
Normandie ≐ F 90-91 G 7
Normandin ○ CDN (QUE) 240-241 C 2
Normandy ○ USA (TX) 266-267 G 5
Norman Park ○ USA (GA) 284-285 G 5
Norman Range ▲▲ CDN 30-31 F 3
Norman River ~ AUS 174-175 F 6
Norman's Cay ∩ BS 54-55 G 2
Normanton ○ AUS 174-175 F 5
Normantown ○ USA (WV) 280-281 F 5
Normanville ○ AUS 180-181 E 3
Norman Wells ○ CDN 30-31 G 3
Normetal ○ CDN (QUE) 236-237 J 4
Normétal ○ CDN (QUE) 236-237 J 4
Norna, Mount ▲ AUS 174-175 F 7
Norquay ○ CDN (SAS) 232-233 Q 4
Norquinco ○ RA 78-79 D 6
Norråker ○ S 86-87 G 4
Norra Ny ○ S 86-87 F 6
Norra Storfjället ▲ S 86-87 G 4
Norrbotten ≐ S 86-87 K 4
Norris ○ USA (MT) 250-251 H 6
Norris ○ USA (SD) 260-261 E 3
Norris ○ USA (WY) 252-253 H 2
Norris Arm ○ CDN (NFL) 242-243 N 3
Norris Lake ⊖ USA (TN) 282-283 D 4
Norris Point ○ CDN (NFL) 242-243 L 3
Norristown ○ USA (PA) 280-281 L 3
Norrköping ✱• S 86-87 H 7
Norrtälje ○ S 86-87 J 7
Norseman ○ AUS 176-177 F 6
Norsjö ○ S 86-87 J 4
Norsk ○ RUS 122-123 C 2
Norskebanken ≃ 84-85 H 2
Norskehavet ≈ 86-87 E 3
Norske Øer ∩ GRØ 26-27 r 4
Norsup ○ VAN 184 II a 3
Norte, Cabo ▲ EC 64-65 C 10
Norte, Cabo do ▲ BR 62-63 K 5
Norte, Canal do ~ BR 62-63 J 5
Norte, Cayo ∩ MEX 52-53 L 2
Norte, Cerro ▲ RA 80 D 4
Norte, Ponta ▲ CV 202-203 C 5
Norte, Punta ▲ MEX 50-51 E 5
Norte, Serra do ▲▲ BR 70-71 H 2
Norte de Chiapas, Montañe del ▲▲ MEX 52-53 H 3
Norte del Cabo San Antonio, Punta ▲ RA 78-79 L 4
Nortelândia ○ BR 70-71 J 4
North ○ USA (SC) 284-285 J 3
North, Cape ▲ CDN (NS) 240-241 P 3
North = Nord ◘ CAM 204-205 K 4
North Adams ○ USA (MA) 278-279 H 6
North Albany ○ USA (OR) 244-245 B 6
Northam ○ AUS 176-177 D 5
Northam ○ ZA 220-221 H 2
Northampton ○ AUS 176-177 C 4
Northampton ✱ GB 90-91 G 5
Northampton ○ USA (MA) 278-279 J 6
North Andaman ∩ IND 140-141 L 3
North Arm ≈ 24-25 j 5
North Arm ⊖ CDN 30-31 M 4
North Arm ○ GB 78-79 L 7
North Aspy River ~ CDN (NS) 240-241 P 4
North Atlantic Ocean ≈ 6-7 D 6
North Augusta ○ CDN (ONT) 238-239 K 4
North Augusta ○ USA (SC) 284-285 J 3
North Aulatsivik Island ∩ CDN 36-37 S 5
North Australia Basin ≃ 13 C 4
North Balabac Strait ≈ 160-161 B 8
North Baldy ▲ USA (WA) 244-245 H 2
North Banda Basin ≃ 166-167 B 3
North Bannister ○ AUS 176-177 D 6
North Battleford ○ CDN (SAS) 232-233 K 3
North Bay ≈ 36-37 P 3
North Bay ≈ 140-141 L 5
North Bay ○ CDN (ONT) 238-239 F 2
North Bay ○ CDN (NWT) 36-37 O 2
North Bay ○ CDN (ONT) 234-235 P 4
North Belcher Islands ∩ CDN 36-37 K 6
North Belmont ○ USA (NC) 282-283 F 5
North Bend ○ USA (NE) 262-263 K 3
North Bend ○ USA (OR) 244-245 A 7
North Bend ○ USA (WA) 244-245 D 3
North Berwick ○ USA (ME) 278-279 L 5
North Bimini ∩ BS 54-55 F 2
North Bluff ▲ CDN 36-37 O 3
North Bonaparte ○ CDN (BC) 230-231 J 2
North Bonneville ○ USA (WA) 244-245 D 5
North Bosque River ~ USA (TX) 266-267 G 6
North Branch ○ CDN (NFL) 242-243 K 4
North Branch < PK 138-139 D 3
North Branch ○ USA (MN) 270-271 F 5
North Bridge ○ CDN (ONT) 234-235 J 6
North Caicos ∩ GB 54-55 K 4
North Canadian River ~ USA (OK) 264-265 F 3
North Cape ○ CDN (PEI) 240-241 M 3
North Cape ▲ CDN (PEI) 240-241 M 3
North Cape ▲ NZ 182 D 1
North Cape ▲ PNG 183 F 2
North Cape May ○ USA (NJ) 280-281 M 4
North-Cape Province ◘ ZA 220-221 D 4
North Caribou Lake ⊖ CDN (ONT) 234-235 N 2
North Carolina ◘ USA (NC) 282-283 E 5
North Cascades National Park ⊥• USA (WA) 244-245 D 2
North Channel ≈ 90-91 E 4
North Channel ⊖ CDN (ONT) 238-239 B 2
North Charleston ○ USA (SC) 284-285 K 4
North China Plain = Huabei ⌣ VRC 154-155 J 3
North Clymer ○ USA (NY) 278-279 B 6
North Cowden ○ USA (TX) 264-265 B 6
North Cowichan ○ CDN (BC) 230-231 F 5
North Creek ~ AUS 178-179 C 5
North Dakota ◘ USA (ND) 258-259 E 4
North East ◘ RB 218-219 D 6
North East ○ USA (PA) 280-281 G 1
Northeast Cape ▲ USA 20-21 F 5
Northeast Cape Fear River ~ USA (NC) 282-283 K 6
North East Carry ○ USA (ME) 278-279 M 3
Northeast Coast National Scenic Area • RC 156-157 M 4
North Eastern ◘ EAK 212-213 G 3
Northeast Point ▲ BS 54-55 J 3
Northeast Point ▲ BS 54-55 J 4
Northeast Point ▲ BS 54-55 H 2
Northeast Point ▲ CDN (NFL) 38-39 R 2
Northeast Point ▲ CDN (NWT) 24-25 Z 2
Northeast Point ▲ USA 22-23 L 4
Northeast Providence Channel ≈ 54-55 G 2
Northeim ○• D 92-93 K 3
Northern ◘ EAU 212-213 C 2
Northern ◘ MW 214-215 H 6
Northern ◘ Z 214-215 F 6
Northern Arm ○ CDN (NFL) 242-243 N 3
Northern Cay ∩ BH 52-53 L 3
Northern Cheyenne Indian Reservation ✗ USA (MT) 250-251 N 6
Northern Frontier ◘ KSA 130-131 H 3
Northern Indian Lake ⊖ CDN 34-35 H 2
Northern Lau Group ∩ FJI 184 III c 2
Northern Light Lake ⊖ CDN (ONT) 234-235 N 6
Northern Mariana Islands = Mariana Islands ∩ USA 14-15 G 6
Northern Perimeter Highway = Rodovia Perimetral Norte II BR 62-63 F 5
Northern Region ◘ GH 202-203 K 5
Northern Region ◘ SUD 200-201 B 5
Northern Salwati Pulau Reserve ⊥• RI 166-167 F 2
Northern Territory ◘ AUS 174-175 B 6
Northern Yukon National Park ⊥ CDN 20-21 U 2
North Etomi River ~ CDN (MAN) 234-235 G 2
North Fabius River ~ USA (MO) 274-275 F 4
Northfield ○ USA (MN) 270-271 E 6
Northfield ○ USA (TX) 264-265 D 4
North Fiji Basin ≃ 13 J 4
North Fond du Lac ○ USA (WI) 270-271 K 7
North Fork ○ USA (ID) 250-251 F 6
North Fork ○ USA (NV) 246-247 K 2
North Fork ~ USA (ID) 250-251 C 4
North Fork ~ USA (KY) 276-277 M 3
North Fork ~ USA (MO) 274-275 F 4
North Fork ~ USA (MO) 274-275 G 5
North Fork ~ USA (NE) 262-263 K 4
North Fork ~ USA (TN) 276-277 G 4
North Fork ~ USA (TX) 266-267 K 3
North Fork Chandalar ~ USA 20-21 Q 3
North Fork Cimarron River ~ USA (CO) 254-255 N 6
North Fork Clearwater River ~ USA (ID) 250-251 D 5
North Fork Counkee Creek ~ USA (AL) 284-285 E 4
North Fork Holston River ~ USA (VA) 280-281 D 7
North Fork John Day River ~ USA (OR) 244-245 F 5
North Fork Kuskokwim ~ USA 20-21 N 5
North Fork Pavette River ~ USA (ID) 252-253 B 2
North Fork Red River ~ USA (OK) 264-265 E 4
North Fork River ~ USA (WV) 280-281 E 4
North Fork Shenandoah River ~ USA (VA) 280-281 H 5
North Fork Smoky Hill River ~ USA (CO) 254-255 N 4
North Fork Solomon River ~ USA (KS) 262-263 F 5
North French River ~ CDN (ONT) 236-237 G 2
North Frisian Islands = Nordfriesische Inseln ≐ D 92-93 J 1
Northgate ○ CDN (SAS) 232-233 Q 6
Northgate ○ USA (ND) 258-259 E 3
North Head ▲ AUS 176-177 C 5
North Head ○ CDN (NB) 240-241 J 6
North Head ▲ CDN (NFL) 38-39 Q 2
North Head ▲ NZ 182 E 2
North Heart River ~ CDN 32-33 M 3
North Hendon, Cape ▲ CDN 24-25 a 5
North Henik Lake ⊖ CDN 30-31 V 5
Northhome ○ USA (MN) 270-271 D 3
North Horr ○ EAK 212-213 F 2
North Island ∩ AUS (NT) 174-175 D 4
North Island ∩ AUS (WA) 176-177 B 4
North Island ∩ EAK 212-213 F 1
North Island ∩ NZ 182 D 2
North Island ∩ USA (SC) 284-285 L 3
North Jadito Wash ~ USA (AZ) 256-257 E 3
North Judson ○ USA (IN) 274-275 M 3
North Kamloops ○ CDN (BC) 230-231 J 3
North Kitui National Reserve ⊥ EAK 212-213 G 4
North Knife Lake ⊖ CDN 30-31 V 6
North Knife River ~ CDN 30-31 V 6
North Komelik ○ USA (AZ) 256-257 C 6
North Korea = Choson M.I.K. ■ DVR 150-151 G 7
North Lake ○ CDN (NB) 240-241 H 5
North Lakhimpur ○ IND 142-143 J 2
Northland ○ USA (MI) 270-271 L 4
North Land = Severnaja Zemlja ∩ RUS 108-109 c 1
North Las Vegas ○ USA (NV) 248-249 J 3
North Liberty ○ USA (IA) 274-275 G 3
North Limington ○ USA (ME) 278-279 L 5
North Lincoln Land ≐ CDN 24-25 f 2
North Little Rock ○ USA (AR) 276-277 C 6
North Lochaber ○ CDN (NS) 240-241 N 5
North Loup River ~ USA (NE) 262-263 F 2
North Luangwa National Park ⊥ Z 214-215 G 6
North Luconia Shoals ≃ 162-163 K 2
North Lucy ○ USA (NM) 256-257 K 4
North Magnetic Pole = Magnetic Pole Area ARK 24-25 V 3
North Magnetic Pole Area II CDN 24-25 V 3
North Male Atoll ∩ MV 140-141 B 5
North Malosmadulu Atoll ∩ MV 140-141 B 5
North Manchester ○ USA (IN) 274-275 N 3
North Mankato ○ USA (MN) 270-271 D 6
North Milk River ~ CDN (ALB) 232-233 F 6
North Minch ≈ 90-91 E 2
North Moose Lake ⊖ CDN 34-35 F 3
North Muskegon ○ USA (MI) 272-273 C 4
North Myrtle Beach ○ USA (SC) 284-285 M 3
North Nahanni River ~ CDN 30-31 G 4
North Nilandu Atoll ∩ MV 140-141 B 6
North Ossetia = Cægat Irystony Respublikoæ ◘ RUS 126-127 F 6
North Palisade ▲ USA (CA) 248-249 F 2
North Palm Beach ○ USA (FL) 286-287 J 5
North Pangnirtung Fiord ≈ 28-29 H 3
North Pease River ~ USA (TX) 264-265 D 4
North Peninsula ⌣ CDN (ONT) 234-235 P 4
North Peron Island ∩ AUS 172-173 K 2
North Platte ○ USA (NE) 262-263 F 3
North Platte River ~ USA (WY) 252-253 M 4
North Point ▲ USA (MI) 272-273 F 2
North Point ▲ WAN 204-205 F 6
North Pole ≐ 16 A 28
Northport ○ USA (AL) 284-285 C 3
North Port ○ USA (FL) 286-287 G 4
Northport ○ USA (MI) 272-273 D 2
Northport ○ USA (WA) 244-245 H 2
North Portal ○ CDN (SAS) 232-233 Q 6
North Powder ○ USA (OR) 244-245 H 5
North Racoon River ~ USA (IA) 274-275 D 2
North Redstone River ~ CDN 30-31 F 4
North Reef = Bei Jiao ⌒ VRC 158-159 L 2
North Richmond ○ USA (OH) 280-281 F 2
North Rim ○ USA (AZ) 256-257 C 2
North River ○ CDN 30-31 W 6
North River ~ USA (AL) 284-285 C 3
North River ~ USA (MO) 274-275 F 5
North River ~ USA (VA) 280-281 G 6
North Saanich ○ CDN (BC) 230-231 F 5
North Sandwich ○ USA (NH) 278-279 K 5
North Santiam River ~ USA (OR) 244-245 C 6
North Saskatchewan River ~ CDN (ALB) 232-233 F 2
North Scotia Ridge ≃ 6-7 E 14
North Sea ≈ 90-91 D 3
North Seal River ~ CDN 30-31 T 6
North Sentinel Island ∩ IND 140-141 L 4
North Siberian Lowland = Severo-Sibirskaja nizmennost' ⌣ RUS 108-109 W 5
Northside ○ CDN (SAS) 232-233 N 2
North Slope ≐ USA 20-21 K 2
North Solitary Island ∩ AUS 178-179 M 5
North Spicer Island ∩ CDN 24-25 h 6
North Spirit Lake ○ CDN (ONT) 234-235 K 2
North Star ○ AUS 178-179 L 5
North Star ○ CDN (ALB) 32-33 M 3
North Stradbroke Island ∩ AUS 178-179 M 4
North Stratford ○ USA (NH) 278-279 K 4
North Sulphur River ~ USA (TX) 264-265 J 5
North Sydney ○ CDN (NS) 240-241 P 4
North Thames River ~ CDN (ONT) 238-239 D 5
North Thompson River ~ CDN (BC) 228-229 P 4
North Thompson River ~ CDN (BC) 230-231 J 3
North Tonawanda ○ USA (NY) 278-279 C 5
North Truchas Peak ▲ USA (NM) 256-257 K 3
North Tweedsmuir Island ∩ CDN 28-29 C 2
North Twin Island ∩ CDN 34-35 Q 4
North Twin Lake ⊖ CDN (NFL) 242-243 M 3
North Uist ∩ GB 90-91 D 3
Northumberland Isles ∩ AUS 178-179 K 1
Northumberland National Park ⊥ GB 90-91 F 4
Northumberland Ø ∩ GRØ 26-27 O 5
Northumberland Strait ≈ 38-39 M 5
Northumberland Strait ≈ CDN 240-241 L 4
North Umpqua River ~ USA (OR) 244-245 C 7
North Vancouver ○ CDN (BC) 230-231 F 4
North Vernon ○ USA (IN) 274-275 N 6
Northville ○ USA (NY) 278-279 G 5
Northville ○ USA (SD) 260-261 H 1
North Wabasca Lake ⊖ CDN 32-33 O 3
North Washagami Lake ⊖ CDN 34-35 O 3
North Waterford ○ USA (ME) 278-279 L 4
North-West = Nord-Ouest ◘ CAM 204-205 J 5
Northwest Angle Forest Reserve ⊥ CDN (MAN) 234-235 H 5
North West Basin ≐ AUS 176-177 C 2
Northwest Bay ○ CDN (ONT) 234-235 K 6
North West Brooke ○ CDN (NFL) 242-243 P 4
North West Cape ▲ AUS 172-173 B 6
Northwest Cape ▲ USA 20-21 E 5
Northwest Cay ∩ BS 54-55 J 4
North West Coastal Highway II AUS 176-177 C 3
North Western ◘ Z 218-219 C 1
Northwest Feeder ~ CDN 38-39 Q 2
North West Frontier Province ◘ PK 138-139 D 2
Northwest Gander River ~ CDN (NFL) 242-243 N 4
Northwest Highlands ▲▲ GB 90-91 E 3
North West Island ∩ AUS 178-179 L 2
Northwest Pacific Basin ≃ 14-15 G 4
Northwest Point ▲ BS 54-55 J 4
Northwest Providence Channel ≈ 54-55 F 1
North-West Province ◘ ZA 220-221 F 3
North West River ○ CDN 38-39 O 2
North West River ~ CDN (NFL) 242-243 O 4
Northwest Territories ◘ CDN 30-31 D 2
North Wilkesboro ○ USA (NC) 282-283 F 4
North Wind Lake ⊖ CDN (ONT) 234-235 Q 5
Northwood ○ USA (IA) 274-275 E 1
Northwood ○ USA (ND) 258-259 K 4
North Woodstock ○ USA (NH) 278-279 K 4
North York Moors National Park ⊥ GB 90-91 G 4
North Zulch ○ USA (TX) 266-267 L 3
Norton ○ CDN (NB) 240-241 K 5
Norton ○ USA (KS) 262-263 G 5
Norton ○ USA (VA) 280-281 D 7
Norton ○ USA (VT) 278-279 K 4
Norton ○ ZW 218-219 F 3
Norton, Cape ▲ CDN 24-25 Y 6
Norton Bay ≈ 20-21 K 4
Norton Shaw, Cape ▲ CDN 24-25 g 2
Norton Shores ○ USA (MI) 272-273 C 4
Norton Sound ≈ 20-21 H 5
Nortonville ○ USA (KY) 276-277 H 3
Nortonville ○ USA (ND) 258-259 J 5
Norutak Lake ⊖ USA 20-21 N 3
Norwalk ○ USA (CA) 248-249 F 6
Norwalk ○ USA (CT) 280-281 N 2
Norwalk ○ USA (IA) 274-275 E 3
Norwalk ○ USA (OH) 280-281 D 2
Norway ○ USA (KS) 262-263 J 5
Norway ○ USA (MI) 270-271 L 5
Norway = Norge ■ N 86-87 D 7
Norway House ○ CDN 34-35 H 4
Norwegia, Kapp ▲ ARK 16 F 35
Norwegian Basin ≃ 6-7 J 2
Norwegian Bay ≈ 24-25 Z 2
Norwegian Sea ≈ 8 C 1
Norwegian Trench = Norskerenna ≃ N 86-87 B 7
Norwich ○ CDN (ONT) 238-239 E 6
Norwich ○•• GB 90-91 H 5
Norwich ○ USA (CT) 280-281 O 2
Norwich ○ USA (NY) 278-279 F 6
Norwood ○ CDN (ONT) 238-239 H 4
Norwood ○ USA (CO) 254-255 G 5
Norwood ○ USA (LA) 268-269 J 6
Norwood ○ USA (MN) 270-271 E 6
Norwood ○ USA (NC) 282-283 G 5
Nosappu-misaki ▲ J 152-153 L 3
Nosara ○ CR 52-53 B 7
Nose Creek ~ CDN (ALB) 228-229 P 2
Nosehill Creek ~ CDN (ALB) 232-233 B 2
Nose Lake ⊖ CDN 30-31 P 3
Noshiro ○ J 152-153 H 4
Nosive, Farihy ⊖ RM 222-223 F 7
Nosivolo ~ RM 222-223 E 8
Noska ~ RUS 114-115 J 5
Noso ~ RI 166-167 D 3
Nosong, Tanjung ▲ MAL 160-161 A 10
Nosop ~ RB 220-221 E 2
Nosratābād ○• IR 134-135 H 4
Nossa Senhora das Dores ○ BR 68-69 K 7
Nossa Senhora do Livramento ○ BR 70-71 J 4
Nossa Senhora do Socorro ○ BR 68-69 K 7
Nossob ~ NAM 220-221 D 1
Nossob Camp ○ ZA 220-221 E 2
Nossombougou ○ RMM 202-203 G 3
Nosy Varika ○ RM 222-223 F 8
Notakwanon River ~ CDN 36-37 S 7
Notasulga ○ USA (AL) 284-285 E 4
Noteć ~ PL 92-93 N 2
Nothaburi ○ THA 158-159 F 4
Nothern Biak Reserve ⊥• RI 166-167 H 2
Notintsila ○ ZA 220-221 J 5
Nótio Egéo ◘ GR 100-101 L 6
Noto ○ I 100-101 E 6
Notocote ○ MOC 218-219 K 3
Notodden ✱ N 86-87 D 7
Noto-hantō ⌣ J 152-153 G 6
Notora ~ RUS 120-121 F 3
Noto-shima ∩ J 152-153 G 6
Notre-Dame, Monts ▲▲ CDN (QUE) 240-241 D 5
Notre Dame Bay ≈ 38-39 R 4
Notre Dame Bay ≈ CDN 242-243 N 3
Notre-Dame-de-Lorette ○ CDN (QUE) 236-237 Q 3
Notre-Dame-du-Lac ○ CDN (QUE) 240-241 G 3
Notre-Dame-du-Laus ○ CDN (QUE) 238-239 K 2
Notre-Dame-du-Nord ○ CDN (QUE) 236-237 J 5
Notre-Dame-du-Rosaire ○ CDN (QUE) 240-241 D 2
Notre Dame Junction ○ CDN (NFL) 242-243 N 3
Notrees ○ USA (TX) 266-267 E 2
Notsé ○ RT 202-203 L 6
Nott, Mount ▲ AUS 180-181 C 2
Nottawasaga Bay ⊖ CDN (ONT) 238-239 E 4
Nottaway, Rivière ~ CDN 38-39 E 3
Nottaway Rivière ~ CDN (ONT) 236-237 K 1
Nottely Lake < USA (GA) 284-285 F 2
Nottely River ~ USA (GA) 284-285 G 2
Nottingham ○ GB 90-91 G 5
Nottingham Downs ○ AUS 178-179 G 1
Nottingham Island ∩ CDN 36-37 K 3
Nottingham Road ○ ZA 220-221 J 4
Nottoway River ~ USA (VA) 280-281 J 7
Notuken Creek ~ CDN (SAS) 232-233 M 6
Nouâdhibou ✱ RIM 196-197 B 4
Nouâdhibou, Râs ▲ RIM 196-197 B 4
Nouakchott = Nawākshūt ✱• RIM 196-197 C 5
Nouâmghâr ○ RIM 196-197 B 5
Nouazereg < RIM 196-197 D 5
Noubandegān ○ IR 134-135 E 4
Noubarān ○ IR 128-129 N 5
Nouhao ~ BF 202-203 K 4
Nouméa ✱• F 13 H 5
Noumoukiédougou ○ BF 202-203 H 5
Noun ~ CAM 204-205 J 6
Nouna ○ BF 202-203 J 3
Nouna ~ G 210-211 D 3
Noupoort ○ ZA 220-221 G 5
Nourlangie Rock • AUS 172-173 L 2
Noušahr ○• IR 136-137 B 6
Nousūd ○ IR 128-129 M 5
Nouveau-Québec, Cratère du ▲ CDN 36-37 N 4
Nouvelle ○ CDN (QUE) 240-241 J 2
Nouvelle-France, Cap de ▲ CDN 36-37 N 3
Nouvelles Hebrides = Vanuatu ∩ VAN 184 II a 1
Nouzād ○ AFG 134-135 L 2
Nova Alegria ○ BR 72-73 L 4
Nova Aliança ○ BR 72-73 F 6
Nova Almada ○ MOC 218-219 H 4
Nova Almeida ○ BR 72-73 K 6
Nova Alvorada ○ BR 76-77 K 1
Nova Andradina ○ BR 72-73 D 7
Nova Aurora ○ BR 74-75 D 5
Nova Brasilândia ○ BR (MAT) 70-71 K 4
Nova Brasilândia ○ BR (RON) 70-71 F 2
Nova Caipemba ○ ANG 216-217 C 3
Nova Canaã do Norte ○ BR 70-71 K 2
Nova Coimbra ○ MOC 214-215 H 7
Nova Cruz ○ BR 68-69 L 5
Nova Esperança ○ ANG 216-217 C 3
Nova Esperança ○ BR 72-73 D 7
Nova Floresta ○ BR 68-69 J 4
Nova Friburgo ○ BR 72-73 J 7
Nova Gaia ○ ANG 216-217 D 5
Nova Golegã ○ MOC 218-219 G 5
Nova Gradiška ○ HR 100-101 F 2
Nova Granada ○ BR 72-73 F 6
Nova Iguaçu ○ BR 72-73 J 7
Nova Independência ○ BR 72-73 E 6
Nova Itaipe ○ BR 72-73 K 2
Novaja ○ RUS (TMR) 108-109 d 6
Novaja ~ RUS 108-109 e 5
Novaja ~ RUS 110-111 G 2
Novaja Igirma ○ RUS 116-117 L 7
Novaja Inja ○ RUS 120-121 L 4
Novaja Kahovka = Nova Kachovka ○ UA 102-103 H 4
Novaja Ladoga ○ RUS 94-95 N 1
Novaja Ljalja ✱ RUS 114-115 F 5
Novaja Sibir', ostrov ∩ RUS 110-111 a 2
Nova Jorque ○ BR 68-69 F 5
Nova Kachovka ○ UA (HER) 102-103 H 4
Novales, Punta ▲ RA 80 G 2
Nova Lima ○ BR 72-73 J 5
Novalukomi' ○ BY 94-95 L 4
Nova Macajuba ○ BR 68-69 E 2
Nova Mambone ○ MOC 218-219 H 5
Nova Módica ○ BR 72-73 K 5
Nova Nabúri ○ MOC 218-219 K 3
Nova Olímpia ○ BR 72-73 D 7
Nova Olinda ○ BR 66-67 K 4
Nova Olinda, Riachão ~ BR 68-69 G 6
Nova Olinda do Norte ○ BR 66-67 H 4
Nova Prata ○ BR 74-75 E 7
Novara ✱ I 100-101 B 2
Nova Resende ○ BR 72-73 G 6
Nova Roma ○ BR 72-73 G 2
Nova Russas ○ BR 68-69 H 4
Nova Santarém ○ MOC 218-219 H 1
Nova Scotia ◘ CDN (NS) 240-241 K 6
Nova Serrana ○ BR 72-73 H 5
Nova Soure ○ BR 68-69 J 7
Nova Timboteua ○ BR 68-69 E 2
Novato ○ USA (CA) 246-247 C 5
Nova Vandúzi ○ MOC 218-219 G 4
Nova Venécia ○ BR 72-73 K 5
Nova Viçosa ○ BR 72-73 L 4
Nova Vida ○ BR 66-67 C 5
Nova Viseu ○ MOC 214-215 J 7
Nova Vodolaha ○ UA 102-103 J 3
Nova Xavantina ○ BR 72-73 D 3
Novaya Zemlya = Novaja Zemlja ∩ RUS 108-109 E 6
Nova Zagora ○ BG 102-103 E 6
Nova Zembla Island ∩ CDN 26-27 N 7
Nove de Abril, Cachoeira ~ BR 70-71 G 2
Novembro, Cachoeira 15. de ~ BR 70-71 G 3
Nové Zámky ○ SK 92-93 P 5
Novgorod ✱••• RUS 94-95 M 2
Novgorodka ○ RUS 94-95 L 3
Novhorodka ○ UA 102-103 H 3
Novi ○ USA (MI) 272-273 F 5
Novi Iskăr ○ BG 102-103 C 6
Novikbož ○ RUS 88-89 Y 3
Novikovo ○ RUS 122-123 K 5
Novillero ○ MEX 50-51 G 6
Novi Pazar ○ BG 102-103 E 6
Novi Pazar ○ YU 100-101 H 3
Novi Sad ○•• YU 100-101 G 2
Novi Sanžary ○ UA 102-103 J 3
Nóvita ○ CO 60-61 C 5
Novo, Lago ⊖ BR 62-63 J 5
Novo, Rio ~ BR 66-67 J 6
Novo, Rio ~ BR 68-69 B 4
Novo, Rio ~ BR 70-71 E 2
Novo Acordo ○ BR (P) 68-69 B 3
Novo Acordo ○ BR (TOC) 68-69 E 6
Novo Acre ○ BR 72-73 K 2
Novoagansk ○ RUS 114-115 O 4
Novo Airão ○ BR 66-67 G 4
Novoaleksandrovka ○ RUS 116-117 K 8
Novoaleksandrovsk ○ RUS 102-103 M 5
Novoalekseevka = Karagandysay ✱ KA 126-127 L 2
Novoaltajsk ✱ RUS 124-125 N 2
Novoanninskij ○ RUS 102-103 N 2
Novo Areal ○ BR 66-67 E 6
Novo Aripuanã ○ BR 66-67 G 5
Novoazovs'k ○ UA 102-103 L 4

370 No.12, Canal — Novoazovs'k

Novobelokataj ☆ **RUS** 96-97 L 6
Novobogat ○ **KA** 96-97 G 10
Novoburejskij ☆ **RUS** 122-123 C 4
Novočeboksarsk ○ **RUS** 96-97 E 5
Novočerkassk ☆• **RUS** 102-103 M 4
Novočerkasskoe ○ **KA** 124-125 F 3
Novočernorečenskij ○ **RUS** 116-117 E 7
Novocheboksarsk = Novočeboksarsk ○ **RUS** 96-97 E 5
Novocherkassk = Novočerkassk ☆• **RUS** 102-103 M 4
Novo Cruzeiro ○ **BR** 72-73 K 4
Novočuguevka ○ **RUS** 122-123 E 6
Novodvinsk ○ **RUS** 88-89 Q 4
Novoe ○ **RUS** 122-123 E 5
Novoe Čaplino ○ **RUS** 112-113 Y 4
Novoe Mašozero ○ **RUS** 88-89 M 4
Novofedorivka ○ **UA** 102-103 H 4
Novograd-Volynskij = Novohrad-Volyns'kyj ○ **UA** 102-103 E 2
Novo Hamburgo ○ **BR** 74-75 E 7
Novohoperskij ○ **RUS** 102-103 M 2
Novo Horizonte ○ **BR** 72-73 F 6
Novohrad-Volyns'kyj ○ **UA** 102-103 E 2
Novokačalinsk ○ **RUS** 122-123 E 6
Novokašpirskij ○ **RUS** 96-97 F 7
Novokazaly ☆ **KA** 126-127 P 5
Novokievskij Uval ☆ **RUS** 122-123 C 3
Novokubansk ○ **RUS** 102-103 M 5
Novokujbyševsk ○ **RUS** 96-97 F 7
Novokuybyshevsk = Novokujbyševsk ○ **RUS** 96-97 F 7
Novokuzneck ☆ **RUS** 124-125 P 2
Novokuznetsk = Novokuzneck ☆ **RUS** 124-125 P 2
Novolazarevskaja ○ **ARK** 16 F 1
Novo Mesto ○ **SLO** 100-101 E 2
Novomičurinsk ○ **RUS** 94-95 Q 4
Novomihajlovskij ○ **RUS** 126-127 C 5
Novomoskovsk ☆ **RUS** 94-95 Q 4
Novomoskovs'k ○ **UA** 102-103 J 3
Novomoskovsk = Novomoskovs'k ○ **UA** 102-103 J 3
Novo Mundo ○ **BR** 72-73 E 2
Novo Mundo, Igarapé ~ **BR** 70-71 F 2
Novomuraptalovo ○ **RUS** 96-97 J 7
Novonadeždinka ○ **KA** 96-97 J 8
Novonikolaevskij ○ **RUS** 102-103 N 2
Novooleksijivka ○ **UA** 102-103 J 4
Novo Oriente ○ **BR** (CEA) 68-69 H 4
Novo Oriente ○ **BR** (RON) 66-67 F 7
Novoorsk ☆ **RUS** 96-97 L 8
Novo Paraíso ○ **BR** 74-75 D 7
Novo Paraná ○ **BR** 70-71 J 2
Novopavlovsk ○ **RUS** 126-127 E 6
Novo Pensamento ○ **BR** 66-67 F 3
Novopetrovskoe ○ **RUS** 94-95 P 4
Novopokrovka ○ **RUS** 122-123 F 6
Novopokrovskaja ○ **RUS** 102-103 M 5
Novopolock = Navapolack ☆•• **BY** 94-95 L 4
Nôvo Pôrto ○ **BR** 66-67 B 7
Novopskov ○ **UA** 102-103 L 3
Novorossijskoe ○ **KA** 126-127 N 2
Novorybnaja ○ **RUS** 110-111 F 3
Novoržev ☆ **RUS** 94-95 L 3
Novošahtinsk ○ **RUS** 102-103 L 4
Novo São Joaquim ○ **BR** 72-73 D 3
Novosel'e ○ **RUS** 94-95 L 2
Novoselickoe ○ **RUS** 126-127 E 5
Novoselivs'ke ○ **UA** 102-103 H 5
Novoselycja ☆ **UA** 102-103 E 3
Novosemejkino ○ **RUS** 96-97 G 7
Novosergievka ☆ **RUS** 96-97 H 7
Novošešminsk ○ **RUS** 96-97 G 6
Novoshakhtinsk = Novošahtinsk ○ **RUS** 102-103 L 4
Novosibirsk ☆• **RUS** 114-115 R 7
Novosibirskoe vodohranilišče ⊖ **RUS** 124-125 M 1
Novosokol'niki ☆ **RUS** 94-95 M 3
Novotroick ○ **RUS** 96-97 L 8
Novotroickoe ○ **RUS** 122-123 B 3
Novotroickoe ○ **RUS** 122-123 D 4
Novotroitsk = Novotroick ○ **RUS** 96-97 L 8
Novotroji'cke ○ **UA** 102-103 J 4
Novoukrajinka ○ **UA** 102-103 G 3
Novoul'janovsk ○ **RUS** 96-97 F 6
Novouzensk ☆ **RUS** 96-97 F 8
Novovjatsk ○ **RUS** 96-97 F 4
Novovolyns'k ○ **UA** 102-103 D 2
Novovolynsk = Novovolyns'k ○ **UA** 102-103 D 2
Novovoskresenovka ○ **RUS** 118-119 N 9
Novozavidovskij ○ **RUS** 94-95 P 3
Novozemel'skaja vpadina ≃ 108-109 G 6
Novozybkov ○ **BY** 94-95 M 5
Novra ○ **CDN** (MAN) 234-235 B 2
Novska ○ **HR** 100-101 F 2
Nový Bor ○ **CZ** 92-93 N 3
Novye Ljady ○ **RUS** 96-97 K 4
Novye Zjatcy ○ **RUS** 96-97 H 5
Novyj Bor ○ **RUS** 88-89 W 3
Novyj Buh ○ **UA** 102-103 H 4
Nový Jičín ○ **CZ** 92-93 P 4
Novyj Port ○ **RUS** 108-109 P 8
Novyj Tartas ○ **RUS** 114-115 O 7
Novyj Uojan ○ **RUS** 118-119 E 7
Novyj Urengoj ○ **RUS** 114-115 O 1
Novyj Uzen' ○ **KA** 126-127 K 6
Nowashe Lake ⊖ **CDN** 34-35 P 4
Nowa Sól ○ **PL** 92-93 N 3
Nowata ○ **USA** (OK) 264-265 J 2
Nowe ○• **PL** 92-93 P 2
Nowendoc ○ **AUS** 178-179 L 6
Nowgong ○ **IND** 138-139 G 7
Nowitna River ~ **USA** 20-21 N 4
Nowleye Lake ⊖ **CDN** 30-31 T 4
Nowogard ○ **PL** 92-93 N 2
Nowood Creek ~ **USA** (WY) 252-253 L 2
Nowra-Bomaderry ○ **AUS** 180-181 L 3
Nowshehrvirkhan ○ **PK** 138-139 D 4
Nowshera ○ **PK** 138-139 C 3
Nowy Sącz ☆• **PL** 92-93 Q 4
Noxon ○ **USA** (MT) 250-251 D 4
Noxubee National Wildlife Refuge ⊥ **USA** (MS) 268-269 M 3
Noxubee River ~ **USA** (MS) 268-269 M 4
Noya ~ **G** 210-211 B 3
Noyabr'sk = Nojabr'sk ○ **RUS** 114-115 N 3
Noyes Island ∩ **USA** 32-33 D 4
Noyo ○ **USA** (CA) 246-247 B 4
Noyon ○ **F** 90-91 J 7
Nqadubolu ○ **RI** 168 D 7
Nritu Ga ○ **MYA** 142-143 K 2
Nsa ○ **RCB** 210-211 E 5
Nsadzu ○ **Z** 218-219 G 2
Nsakaluba ○ **Z** 214-215 E 6
Nsama ○ **Z** 214-215 E 5
Nsambi ○ **ZRE** 210-211 F 4
Nsanje ○ **MW** 218-219 H 3
Nsawam ○ **GH** 202-203 K 7
Nsawkaw ○ **GH** 202-203 J 6
Nsele ~ **ZRE** 210-211 E 6
Nsem ○ **CAM** 204-205 K 6
Nsiza ○ **ZW** 218-219 E 4
Nsog ○ **GQ** 210-211 C 3
Nsoko ○ **SD** 220-221 K 3
Nsombo ○ **Z** 214-215 E 6
Nsontin ○ **ZRE** 210-211 G 5
Nsukka ○ **WAN** 204-205 G 5
Ntambu ○ **Z** 214-215 C 7
Ntandembele ○ **ZRE** 210-211 F 5
Ntatrat < **RIM** 196-197 C 6
Ntcheu ○ **MW** 218-219 H 2
Ntchisi ○ **MW** 218-219 G 1
Nteko ○ **Z** 214-215 G 5
Ntem ~ **CAM** 210-211 C 2
Ntemwa ○ **Z** 218-219 D 2
Nterguent ○ **RIM** 196-197 D 5
Nthalire ○ **MW** 214-215 G 6
Nthunga ○ **MW** 214-215 H 7
Ntibane ○ **ZA** 220-221 J 5
Ntimaru ○ **EAK** 212-213 E 4
Ntiona ○ **TCH** 198-199 G 5
Ntlenyana, Thabana ▲ **LS** 220-221 J 4
Ntokou ○ **G** 210-211 E 3
Ntomba, Lac ⊖• **ZRE** 210-211 G 4
Ntoum ○ **G** 210-211 B 3
Ntsel, Hassi < **DZ** 190-191 F 7
Ntsou ○ **RCB** 210-211 E 4
Ntui ○ **CAM** 204-205 J 6
Ntungamo ○ **EAU** 212-213 C 4
Ntusi ○ **EAU** 212-213 C 3
Ntwetwe Pan ⊖ **RB** 218-219 C 5
Ntyébougou ○ **RMM** 202-203 G 2
Nu'airiya, an- ○ **KSA** 130-131 L 4
Nuakata Island ∩ **PNG** 183 F 6
Nuaneteze, Rio ~ **MOC** 218-219 F 6
Nuangan ○ **RI** 164-165 J 3
Nuangola ○ **USA** (PA) 280-281 L 2
Nūba, Buḥairat ⊖ **SUD** 200-201 E 2
Nubarašen ○ **AR** 128-129 L 2
Nubeena ○ **AUS** 180-181 J 7
Nubia = Nūba, an- ∸ **SUD** 200-201 D 3
Nubian Desert = Nūba, Ṣaḥrā' an- ∸ **SUD** 200-201 E 2
Nubieber ○ **USA** (CA) 246-247 D 2
Ñuble, Río ~ **RCH** 78-79 C 4
Nuboai ○ **RI** 166-167 J 3
Nučča ~ **RUS** 110-111 W 4
Nucla ○ **USA** (CO) 254-255 G 5
Nucuray, Río ~ **PE** 64-65 D 4
Nudlung Fiord ≈ 28-29 G 2
Nudo Allincapac ▲ **PE** 70-71 B 3
Nudo Aricoma ▲▲ **PE** 70-71 B 4
Nudo Ausangate ▲ **PE** 70-71 B 3
Nudo Chicllaraza ▲ **PE** 64-65 E 8
Nudo de Apolobamba ▲▲ **PE** 70-71 C 4
Nudo de Paramillo ▲ **CO** 60-61 D 4
Nudo de Sunipani ▲ **PE** 70-71 B 4
Nudymi ~ **RUS** 120-121 H 4
Nueces River ~ **USA** (TX) 266-267 H 5
Nueces River, East ~ **USA** (TX) 266-267 G 4
Nueces River, West ~ **USA** (TX) 266-267 G 4
Nueltin Lake ⊖ **CDN** 30-31 U 5
Nuestra Señora del Rosario de Caá Cati ○ **RA** 76-77 J 4
Nueva, Isla ∩ **RCH** 80 G 7
Nueva, La ○ **EC** 64-65 D 1
Nueva Alejandria ○ **PE** 64-65 F 4
Nueva Arcadia ○ **HN** 52-53 K 4
Nueva Ciudad Guerrero ○ **MEX** 50-51 K 4
Nueva Coahuila ○ **MEX** 52-53 J 3
Nueva Constitución ○ **RA** 78-79 F 3
Nueva Era ○ **RP** 160-161 D 4
Nueva Esperanza ○ **RA** (SAE) 76-77 E 4
Nueva Esperanza ○ **RA** (SAE) 76-77 F 4
Nueva Florida ○ **YV** 60-61 G 3
Nueva Galia ○ **RA** 78-79 G 3
Nueva Gerona ☆ **C** 54-55 D 4
Nueva Granada ○ **CO** 60-61 D 3
Nueva Guinea ○ **NIC** 52-53 B 6
Nueva Imperial ○ **RCH** 78-79 C 5
Nueva Italia ○ **PY** 76-77 J 3
Nueva Italia ○ **RA** 76-77 G 5
Nueva Italia de Ruíz ○ **MEX** 52-53 C 2
Nueva Lubecka ○ **RA** 80 E 2
Nueva Ocotepeque ☆ **HN** 52-53 K 4
Nueva Palmira ○ **ROU** 78-79 K 2
Nueva Pompeya ○ **RA** 76-77 G 3
Nueva Rosita ○ **MEX** 50-51 J 4
Nueva San Salvador ☆ **ES** 52-53 K 5
Nuevitas ○ **C** 54-55 G 4
Nuevo, Cayo ∩ **MEX** 52-53 H 1
Nuevo Andoas ○ **PE** 64-65 D 3
Nuevo Campechito ○ **MEX** 52-53 H 2
Nuevo Casas Grandes ○ **MEX** 50-51 F 2
Nuevo Esperanza ○ **PE** 64-65 E 2
Nuevo Laredo ○ **MEX** 50-51 K 4
Nuevo Leon □ **MEX** 50-51 J 4
Nuevo Mundo ○ **CO** 60-61 F 5
Nuevo Mundo, Cerro ▲ **BOL** 76-77 D 1
Nuevo Padilla ○ **MEX** 50-51 K 5
Nuevo Riaño ○ **E** 98-99 E 3
Nuevo Rocafuerte ○ **EC** 64-65 E 2
Nuevo Turino ○ **RA** 76-77 G 6
Nugaal □ **SP** 208-209 H 4
Nugaal, togga ~ **SP** 208-209 J 4
Nuga Nuga, Lake ⊖ **AUS** 178-179 K 3
Nugents Corner ○ **USA** (WA) 244-245 C 2
Nugong, Mount ▲ **AUS** 180-181 J 4
Nugṭat Būlís al Habílíyah ○ **LAR** 192-193 D 1
Nuguaçu ○ **BR** 68-69 H 7
Nuguškoe vodohranilišče < **RUS** 96-97 K 7
Nuḥaib ○ **IRQ** 128-129 K 6
Nuhaida ○ **OM** 132-133 K 2
Nuhaka ○ **NZ** 182 F 3
Núi Lang Bian ▲ **VN** 158-159 K 4
Nuiqsut ○ **USA** 20-21 P 1
Núi Thành ○ **VN** 158-159 K 3
Nuja = Karksi-Nuja ○•• **EST** 94-95 J 2
Nüjang ○ **VRC** 144-145 B 4
Nu Jiang ~ **VRC** 142-143 L 3
Nu Jiang ~ **VRC** 144-145 L 6
Nūkābād ○ **IR** 134-135 J 4
Nuka Bay ≈ 22-23 V 3
Nuka Island ∩ **USA** 22-23 V 3
Nuka River ~ **USA** 20-21 L 2
Nukhaylah < **SUD** 200-201 C 3
Nukiki ○ **SOL** 184 I c 2
Nukko Lake ○ **CDN** (BC) 228-229 L 2
Nukshak, Cape ▲ **USA** 22-23 U 3
Nuku ○ **PNG** 183 B 2
Nuku'alofa ★• **TON** 184 IV a 2
Nukubasaga ∩ **FJI** 184 III c 2
Nuku-Hiva ∩ **F** 13 N 3
Nukuhu ○ **PNG** 183 E 3
Nukulaelae Atoll ∩ **TUV** 13 J 3
Nukus ☆ **US** 136-137 F 3
Nula, El ○ **YV** 60-61 F 4
Nulato ○ **USA** 20-21 L 4
Nulato River ~ **USA** 20-21 L 4
Nuli ○ **ZW** 218-219 F 6
Nullagine ○ **AUS** 172-173 E 6
Nullagine River ~ **AUS** 172-173 E 6
Nulla Nulla ○ **AUS** 174-175 H 6
Nullarbor National Park ⊥ **AUS** 176-177 L 5
Nullarbor Plain ∸ **AUS** 176-177 J 5
Nullarbor Regional Reserve ⊥ **AUS** 176-177 K 5
Nullarbor Roadhouse ○ **AUS** 176-177 L 5
Nuluk River ~ **USA** 20-21 G 4
Num ○ **NEP** 144-145 F 7
Num, Pulau ∩ **RI** 166-167 H 2
Numalla, Lake ⊖ **AUS** 178-179 H 5
Numan ○ **WAN** 204-205 K 4
Nu'mān, Ǧazīrat an- ∩ **KSA** 130-131 D 4
Nū'mān, Ma'arrat an- ○• **SYR** 128-129 G 5
Numancia (Ruinas celtibércas y romanas) ∴• **E** 98-99 F 4
Nu'māniya, an- ☆ **IRQ** 128-129 L 6
Numata ○ **J** (GUM) 152-153 H 6
Numata ○ **J** (HOK) 152-153 J 3
Numatinna ~ **SUD** 206-207 H 5
Numazu ○ **J** 152-153 H 7
Number 24 Well ○ **AUS** 172-173 F 7
Number 35 Well < **AUS** 172-173 G 7
Numbi ○ **ZRE** 212-213 B 4
Numbulwar X **AUS** 174-175 C 4
Numedal ∸ **N** 86-87 D 6
Numfor, Pulau ∩ **RI** 166-167 H 2
Numil Downs ○ **AUS** 174-175 F 6
Numto ○ **RUS** 114-115 L 3
Numto, ozero ⊖ **RUS** 114-115 L 3
Numto, uval ▲▲ **RUS** 114-115 K 3
Numurkah ○ **AUS** 180-181 H 4
Nunalla (abandoned) ○ **CDN** 30-31 W 6
Nunarsuaq ∩ **GRØ** 28-29 U 5
Nunarsuit ∩ **GRØ** 28-29 Q 6
Nunavakanuk Lake ⊖ **USA** 20-21 H 5
Nunavakpak Lake ⊖ **USA** 20-21 J 6
Nunavaugaluk, Lake ⊖ **USA** 22-23 R 3
Nunavik ∪ **GRØ** 26-27 X 8
Nunda ○ **USA** (NY) 278-279 D 6
Nunda ○ **USA** (SD) 260-261 J 2
Nundle ○ **AUS** 178-179 L 6
Nundroo ○ **AUS** 176-177 M 5
Nuneca ○ **USA** (MI) 272-273 C 4
Núñez, Isla ∩ **RCH** 80 D 6
Nungesser Lake ⊖ **CDN** (ONT) 234-235 K 3
Nungo ○ **MOC** 218-219 J 1
Nungwaia ○ **PNG** 183 B 2
Nungwe Bay ○ **EAT** 212-213 D 5
Nunim Lake ⊖ **CDN** 30-31 S 6
Nunivak Island ∩ **USA** 20-21 G 6
Nunjamo ○ **RUS** 112-113 Z 4
Nunjamovaam ~ **RUS** 112-113 X 4
Nunligran ○ **RUS** (CUK) 112-113 T 3
Nunligran ○ **RUS** (CUK) 112-113 X 4
Nunn ○ **USA** (CO) 254-255 L 3
Ñuñoa ○ **PE** 70-71 B 4
Nun River ~ **WAN** 204-205 G 6
Nunukan Timur, Pulau ∩ **RI** 164-165 E 1
Nuora ~ **RUS** 118-119 O 3
Nuoraldžyma ~ **RUS** 118-119 M 4
Nuoro ○ **I** 100-101 B 4
Nuporanga ○ **BR** 72-73 G 6
Nuqay, Jabal ▲▲ **LAR** 192-193 H 6
Nuqruș, Ǧabal ▲ **ET** 194-195 G 5
Nuqūb ○ **Y** 132-133 D 6
Nuqum, Ǧabal ▲ **Y** 132-133 D 6
Nūr ○ **IR** 136-137 B 6
Nūra ○ **KA** (AKT) 126-127 P 3
Nūra ~ **KA** 124-125 J 4
Nūra ~ **KA** 124-125 G 3
Nura ~ **KA** 124-125 H 4
Nūra ~ **KA** 124-125 F 3
Nūra ~ **KA** 124-125 H 4
Nūrābād ○• **IR** (FAR) 134-135 D 3
Nūrābād ○• **IR** (LOR) 134-135 B 1
Nurata ☆ **US** 136-137 J 4
Nurataldy ○ **KA** 124-125 H 4
Nurato tog tizmasi ▲▲ **US** 136-137 J 4
Nur Dağları ▲▲ **TR** 128-129 G 4
Nurei ○ **SUD** 198-199 L 6
Nurek ○ **TJ** 136-137 L 5
Nuremberg = Nürnberg ○ **D** 92-93 L 4
Nūrestān ○• **AFG** 138-139 C 2
Nūr Gāma ○ **PK** 134-135 M 4
Nurhak ☆ **TR** 128-129 G 4
Nurhak Dağı ▲▲ **TR** 128-129 G 3
Nurí ○ **MEX** 50-51 E 3
Nuri •• **SUD** 200-201 E 3
Nuri, Teluk ≈ 162-163 H 5
Nuriootpa ○ **AUS** 180-181 E 3
Nurkaat ○ **RI** 166-167 F 5
Nurlat ☆ **RUS** 96-97 G 6
Nurmes ○ **FIN** 88-89 K 5
Nurmijärvi ○ **FIN** 88-89 K 5
Nürnberg ○ **D** 92-93 L 4
Nurobod ☆ **US** 136-137 K 5
Nurota sovhozi ○ **US** 136-137 K 4
Nūrpur ○ **PK** 138-139 C 4
Nursery ○ **USA** (TX) 266-267 K 5
Nusa Barung, Pulau ∩ **RI** 168 E 4
Nusa Dua ○ **RI** 168 B 7
Nusa Kambangan ∩ **RI** 168 C 3
Nusa Laut, Pulau ∩ **RI** 166-167 E 3
Nusa Tenggara Timur □ **RI** 166-167 B 6
Nusawulan ○ **RI** 166-167 G 4
Nusaybin ☆ **TR** 128-129 J 4
Nusela, Kepulauan ∩ **RI** 166-167 F 2
Nushagak Bay ≈ 22-23 R 3
Nushagak Peninsula ∪ **USA** 22-23 R 3
Nushagak River ~ **USA** 22-23 S 3
Nu Shan ▲▲ **VRC** 142-143 L 2
Nushki ○ **PK** 134-135 L 4
Nutaarmiut ∩ **GRØ** 26-27 X 7
Nutak ○ **CDN** 36-37 T 6
Nutaugè, laguna ≈ 112-113 W 3
Nut Mountain ○ **CDN** (SAS) 232-233 P 3
Nutrias, Las ○ **RA** 78-79 K 5
Nutrioso ○ **USA** (AZ) 256-257 F 5
Nuttal ○ **PK** 138-139 B 5
Nutuvukti Lake ⊖ **USA** 20-21 N 3
Nutwood Downs ○ **AUS** 174-175 C 4
Nuu ○ **EAK** 212-213 G 4
Nuugaatsiaq ○ **GRØ** 26-27 Y 8
Nuuk = Godthåb ☆ **GRØ** 28-29 P 4
Nuuk Kangerluaq ≈ 28-29 P 4
Nuurst ○ **MAU** 148-149 J 4
Nuussuaq Halvø ∪ **GRØ** 28-29 O 1
Nuvuk Point ▲ **CDN** 36-37 R 2
Nuwaibi' al-Muzayyina ○ **ET** 194-195 G 3
Nuwaisib, al- ○ **KWT** 130-131 L 3
Nuwara Eliya ○•• **CL** 140-141 J 7
Nuwefontein ○ **NAM** 220-221 D 3
Nuweh ○ **RI** 166-167 K 5
Nuwekloof ▲ **ZA** 220-221 F 6
Nuwerus ○ **ZA** 220-221 D 5
Nuweveldberge ▲▲ **ZA** 220-221 E 6
Nuy ○ **ZA** 220-221 D 6
Nuyakuk Lake ⊖ **USA** 22-23 R 3
Nuyts Archipelago ∩ **AUS** 176-177 M 6
Nuyts Reefs ∩ **AUS** 176-177 M 6
Nūzvid ○ **IND** 140-141 J 2
Nwa ○ **CAM** 204-205 J 5
Nwanetsi ○ **ZA** 220-221 L 2
N.W. Crocodile Island ∩ **AUS** 174-175 C 2
Nxai Pan ⊖ **RB** 218-219 C 4
Nxai Pan National Park ⊥ **RB** 218-219 C 4
Nya ~ **TCH** 206-207 B 4
Nyabarongo ~ **RWA** 212-213 B 4
Nyabisindu ○ **RWA** 212-213 B 5
Nyadire ~ **ZW** 218-219 G 3
Nyagassola ○ **RG** 202-203 F 3
Nya-Ghezi ○ **ZRE** 212-213 B 5
Nyahanga ○ **EAT** 212-213 D 5
Nyahua ~ **EAT** 212-213 D 6
Nyahururu ○ **EAK** 212-213 F 3
Nyah West ○ **AUS** 180-181 G 3
Nyainqêntanglha Feng ▲ **VRC** 144-145 H 5
Nyainqêntanglha Shan ▲▲ **VRC** 144-145 G 6
Nyainrong ○ **VRC** 144-145 J 4
Nyakahura ○ **EAT** 212-213 C 5
Nyakanazi ○ **EAT** 212-213 C 5
Nyak Co ⊖ **VRC** 144-145 B 4
Nyalā ○ **SUD** 200-201 B 6
Nyalam ○ **VRC** 144-145 F 6
Ny Ålesund ○ **N** 84-85 G 3
Nyali ○ **G** 210-211 C 5
Nyalikungu ○ **EAT** 212-213 D 5
Nyamandhlovu ○ **ZW** 218-219 E 4
Nyamapanda ○ **ZW** 218-219 G 3
Nyamassila ○ **RT** 202-203 L 6
Nyāmati ○ **IND** 140-141 F 3
Nyamirembe ○ **EAT** 212-213 C 5
Nyamlell ○ **SUD** 206-207 H 4
Nyamoko ○ **CAM** 204-205 J 6
Nyamuswa ○ **EAT** (Ma) 212-213 E 4
Nyanding, Khor ~ **SUD** 206-207 L 4
Nyanga ~ **G** 210-211 C 5
Nyanga ○ **RCB** 210-211 C 5
Nyanga ○• **ZW** 218-219 G 4
Nyangamara ○ **EAT** 214-215 K 6
Nyang Qu ○ **VRC** 144-145 G 6
Nyanza □ **EAK** 212-213 E 4
Nyanza-Lac ○ **BU** 212-213 B 6
Nyarling River ~ **CDN** 30-31 M 5
Nyaru ○ **EAK** 212-213 E 3
Nyasa ○ **ZRE** 210-211 L 6
Nyassar ○ **CAM** 206-207 B 5
Nyaungbintho ○ **MYA** 142-143 K 4
Nyaungkhashe ○ **MYA** 158-159 D 2
Nyaunglebin ○ **MYA** 158-159 D 2
Nyaung U ○ **MYA** 142-143 J 5
Nyazura ○ **ZW** 218-219 G 4
Nyazwidzi ~ **ZW** 218-219 F 4
Nybergsund ○ **N** 86-87 F 6
Nybor ○ **RUS** 114-115 D 4
Nyborg ○•• **DK** 86-87 E 9
Nybro ☆ **S** 86-87 G 8
Nyčalah ○ **RUS** 110-111 a 5
Nyda ○ **RUS** 108-109 P 8
Nyda ~ **RUS** 108-109 Q 8
Nyé ~ **G** 210-211 C 2
Nye ○ **USA** (OR) 244-245 G 5
Nyeboe Land ∸ **GRØ** 26-27 W 3
Nyegezi ○ **EAT** (SHI) 212-213 D 5
Nyêmo ○ **VRC** 144-145 G 6
Nyenase ○ **GH** 202-203 K 7
Nyensung ○ **GH** 202-203 K 5
Nyeri ☆ **EAK** 212-213 F 4
Nyeri ▲ **EAU** 212-213 C 2
Ny-Friesland ∪ **N** 84-85 K 3
Nygčekveem ~ **RUS** 112-113 T 5
Nygčigen, mys ▲ **RUS** 112-113 Y 4
Nyibiam ○ **WAN** 204-205 H 4
Nyiel ○ **SUD** 206-207 K 5
Nyika ○ **ZW** 218-219 F 4
Nyikine ○ **SN** 202-203 B 3
Nyima ○ **VRC** 144-145 F 5
Nyimba ○ **Z** 218-219 F 2
Nyiminiama ○ **RMM** 202-203 J 2
Nyingchi ○ **VRC** 144-145 K 6
Nyiragongo ▲ **ZRE** 212-213 B 4
Nyírbátor ○ **H** 92-93 R 5
Nyíregyháza ○ **H** 92-93 Q 5
Nyiri Desert ∸ **EAK** 212-213 F 5
Nyiru Range ▲▲ **EAK** 212-213 F 2
Nyjskij, zaliv ⊖ **RUS** 122-123 K 3
Nykarleby ○ **FIN** 88-89 G 5
Nykia National Park ⊥ **MW** 214-215 G 6
Nykia Plateau ▲▲•• **MW** 214-215 G 6
Nykøbing Falster ○ **DK** 86-87 E 9
Nykøbing Mors ○ **DK** 86-87 D 8
Nyköping ○ **S** 86-87 H 7
Nyland = Uusima ∸ **FIN** 88-89 H 6
Nylrivier ~ **ZA** 220-221 J 2
Nylstroom ○ **ZA** 220-221 J 2
Nymagee ○ **AUS** 180-181 J 2
Nymburk ○• **CZ** 92-93 N 3
Nymphe Bank ≃ 90-91 D 6
Nynäshamn ☆ **S** 86-87 H 7
Nyngan ○ **AUS** 178-179 J 6
Nyoma Rap ○ **IND** 138-139 G 3
Nyong ~ **CAM** 204-205 K 6
Nyons ○ **F** 90-91 K 9
Nyos, Lac ⊖ **CAM** 204-205 J 5
Nyrud ○ **RUS** 88-89 K 2
Nyš ○ **RUS** 122-123 K 3
Nyš ~ **RUS** 122-123 K 3
Nysa ○• **PL** 92-93 O 3
Nysa Kłodzka ~ **PL** 92-93 O 3
Nysa Łużycka ~ **PL** 92-93 N 3
Nyssa ○ **USA** (OR) 244-245 H 7
Nytva ☆ **RUS** 96-97 J 5
Nyudō-saki ▲ **J** 152-153 H 4
Nyumba ya Mungu Reservoir < **EAT** (ARU) 212-213 F 5
Nyunzu ○ **ZRE** 212-213 B 6
Nyvrovo ○ **RUS** 120-121 K 6
Nyžni Sirohozy ○ **UA** 102-103 J 4
Nyžni Torhaji ○ **UA** 102-103 J 4
Nyžn'ohirs'kyj ☆ **UA** 102-103 J 5
Nzako ○ **RCA** 206-207 F 5
Nzako ~ **RCA** 206-207 F 6
Nzambi ○ **RCB** 210-211 C 5
Nzara ○ **SUD** 206-207 J 6
Nzassi ○ **RCB** 210-211 D 6
Nzébéla ○ **RG** 202-203 F 5
Nzega ○ **EAT** 212-213 D 6
Nzérékoré □ **RG** 202-203 F 5
Nzerékoré ☆ **RG** 202-203 F 6
N'Zeto ○ **ANG** 216-217 B 3
Nzi ~ **CI** 202-203 H 6
Nzili, Bahr ~ **RCA** 206-207 F 3
Nzilo, Lac < **ZRE** 214-215 C 6
Nzima ○ **EAT** 212-213 D 5
Nzo ~ **CI** 202-203 G 6
Nzo ○ **RG** 202-203 F 6
N'zo, Réserve de faune du ⊥ **CI** 202-203 G 6
Nzoia ~ **EAK** 212-213 E 3
Nzoro ○ **RCA** 206-207 B 5
Nzoro ~ **ZRE** 212-213 C 2

O

Oā', Wādī al- ~ **KSA** 130-131 F 4
Oahe, Lake ⊖ **USA** (SD) 260-261 F 2
Oahu ∩ **USA** (HI) 288 H 3
Oakbank ○ **AUS** 180-181 F 2
Oak Bay ○ **CDN** (BC) 230-231 F 5
Oak Bluff ○ **CDN** (MAN) 234-235 F 5
Oak Bluffs ○ **USA** (MA) 278-279 L 7
Oakburn ○ **CDN** (MAN) 234-235 C 4
Oak City ○ **USA** (NC) 282-283 K 5
Oak City ○ **USA** (UT) 254-255 C 4
Oak Creek ○ **USA** (CO) 254-255 J 3
Oak Creek ○ **USA** (WI) 274-275 L 2
Oakdale ○ **USA** (CA) 248-249 D 2
Oakdale ○ **USA** (LA) 268-269 H 6
Oakes ○ **USA** (ND) 258-259 J 5
Oakey ○ **AUS** 178-179 L 4
Oakey Creek ~ **AUS** 178-179 L 4
Oak Grove ○ **USA** (LA) 268-269 J 4
Oak Harbor ○ **USA** (OH) 280-281 C 2
Oak Harbor ○ **USA** (WA) 244-245 C 2
Oak Hill ○ **USA** (AL) 284-285 C 5
Oak Hill ○ **USA** (FL) 286-287 J 3
Oak Hill ○ **USA** (OH) 280-281 D 5
Oak Hill ○ **USA** (WV) 280-281 E 6
Oak Hills ○ **AUS** 174-175 H 6
Oakhurst ○ **USA** (CA) 248-249 E 2
Oak Lake ○ **CDN** (MAN) 234-235 C 5
Oak Lake ⊖ **CDN** (MAN) 234-235 C 5
Oakland ○ **CDN** (MAN) 234-235 E 4
Oakland ○ **USA** (CA) 248-249 B 2
Oakland ○ **USA** (IA) 274-275 C 3
Oakland ○ **USA** (IL) 274-275 K 5
Oakland ○ **USA** (MD) 280-281 G 4
Oakland ○ **USA** (MS) 268-269 L 2
Oakland ○ **USA** (NE) 262-263 K 3
Oakland City ○ **USA** (IN) 274-275 L 6
Oakland Park ○ **USA** (FL) 286-287 J 5
Oaklands ○ **AUS** 180-181 J 3
Oak Lawn ○ **USA** (IL) 274-275 L 3
Oak Level ○ **USA** (AL) 284-285 E 3
Oakley ○ **USA** (ID) 252-253 E 4
Oakley ○ **USA** (KS) 262-263 F 5
Oakover River ~ **AUS** 172-173 E 6
Oak Park ○ **USA** (GA) 284-285 H 4
Oak Point ○ **CDN** (MAN) 234-235 F 4
Oak Ridge ○ **USA** (LA) 268-269 J 4
Oakridge ○ **USA** (OR) 244-245 C 7
Oak Ridge ○ **USA** (TN) 282-283 C 4
Oak Ridge ○ **USA** (TX) 268-269 E 6
Oak River ○ **CDN** (MAN) 234-235 C 4
Oakshela ○ **CDN** (SAS) 232-233 Q 5
Oakview ○ **CDN** (MAN) 234-235 E 3
Oak View ○ **USA** (CA) 248-249 E 5
Oakville ○ **CDN** (MAN) 234-235 E 5
Oakville ○ **CDN** (ONT) 238-239 F 5
Oakville ○ **USA** (TX) 266-267 J 5
Oakville ○ **USA** (WA) 244-245 B 4
Oakwood ○ **USA** (IL) 274-275 L 4
Oakwood ○ **USA** (OK) 264-265 F 3
Oakwood ○ **USA** (TN) 276-277 H 4
Oakwood ○ **USA** (TX) 268-269 E 5
Oaky Creek ○ **AUS** 178-179 K 2
Oamaru ○ **NZ** 182 C 6
Oan ○ **RI** 164-165 G 3
Oasis ○ **USA** (CA) 248-249 G 2
Oasis ○ **USA** (NM) 256-257 L 5
Oasis ○ **USA** (NV) 246-247 L 2
Oates Land ∸ **ARK** 16 F 17
Oatlands ○ **AUS** 180-181 J 7
Oatman ○ **USA** (AZ) 256-257 A 3
Oaxaca □ **MEX** 52-53 F 3
Oaxaca de Juárez ☆••• **MEX** 52-53 F 3
Ob' ○ **RUS** 114-115 R 7
Ob' ~ **RUS** 10-11 G 2
Oba ○ **CDN** (ONT) 236-237 D 3
Oba ○ **WAN** 204-205 F 5
Obaa ○ **RI** 166-167 K 5
Obaba ○ **RCB** 210-211 F 4
Obaha ○ **PNG** 183 E 5
Obakamiga Lake ⊖ **CDN** (ONT) 236-237 C 3
Obala ○ **CAM** 204-205 J 6
Obalapuram ○ **IND** 140-141 G 3
Obama ○ **J** 152-153 F 7
Oban ○ **AUS** 178-179 E 1
Oban ○ **CDN** (SAS) 232-233 K 3
Oban ○ **GB** 90-91 E 3
Oban ○ **RCB** 210-211 E 4
Oban ○ **WAN** 204-205 H 6
Obanazawa ○ **J** 152-153 J 5
Oban Hills ▲▲ **WAN** 204-205 H 6
Obanska, Rivière ~ **CDN** (QUE) 236-237 K 2
Obatanga Provincial Park ⊥ **CDN** (ONT) 236-237 C 4
Ōbe ○• **AFG** 134-135 K 1
Obe = Île Aoba ∩ **VAN** 184 II a 2
Obed ○ **CDN** (ALB) 228-229 R 3
Obed River ~ **USA** (TN) 282-283 C 4
Obehie ○ **WAN** 204-205 G 6
Obeiz, hrebet ▲▲ **RUS** 108-109 H 9
Obele ○ **WAN** 204-205 G 5
Obeliai ○ **LT** 94-95 J 4
Obelisco, Monumento el • **YV** 60-61 G 2
Obel-prolaz ▲ **MK** 100-101 J 4
Obera ○• **RA** 76-77 K 4
Oberlin ○ **USA** (KS) 262-263 F 5
Oberlin ○ **USA** (LA) 268-269 H 6
Oberon ○ **AUS** 180-181 K 2
Oberon ○ **CDN** (MAN) 234-235 D 4
Oberösterreich □ **A** 92-93 M 4
Oberpfälzer Wald ∸ **D** 92-93 M 4
Oberstdorf ○• **D** 92-93 L 5
Oberstein, Idar- ○ **D** 92-93 J 4
Obhur ○ **KSA** 132-133 A 3
Obi ○ **WAN** 204-205 H 4
Obi, Pulau ∩ **RI** 164-165 K 4
Obi, Selat ≈ 164-165 K 4
Obiaruku ○ **WAN** 204-205 G 6
Óbidos ○ **BR** 62-63 G 6
Óbidos ○•• **P** 98-99 C 5
Obigarm ○ **TJ** 136-137 L 5
Obihingou ~ **TJ** 136-137 M 5
Obihiro ○ **J** 152-153 K 3
Obilatu, Pulau ∩ **RI** 164-165 K 4
Obilebit, Riacho ~ **PY** 76-77 H 1
Obion ○ **USA** (TN) 276-277 F 4
Obispo Trejo ○ **RA** 76-77 F 6
Obitočna kosa ∪ **UA** 102-103 K 4
Oblačnaja, gora ▲ **RUS** 122-123 F 7
Oblačnyj Golec, gora ▲ **RUS** 120-121 F 5
Oblong ○ **USA** (IL) 274-275 L 6
Obluč'e ○ **RUS** 122-123 D 4
Oblukovina ~ **RUS** 120-121 R 6
Obninsk ○ **RUS** 94-95 P 4
Obo ☆ **RCA** 206-207 H 6
Obo ○ **VRC** 154-155 B 3
Oboa ▲ **EAU** 212-213 E 3
Obock ○ **DJI** 200-201 L 6
Obogu ○ **GH** 202-203 K 6
Obojan ○ **RUS** 102-103 K 2
Obokote ○ **ZRE** 210-211 L 4
Oboli ○ **RCB** 210-211 E 4
Obolo ○ **WAN** 204-205 G 5
Obonga Lake ⊖ **CDN** (ONT) 234-235 O 4
Obout ○ **CAM** 210-211 C 2
Obouya ○ **RCB** 210-211 E 4
Obozerskij ○ **RUS** 88-89 Q 5
Obra ~ **PL** 92-93 N 2
Obregón, Ciudad ○ **MEX** 50-51 E 4
Obrenovac ○ **YU** 100-101 H 2
O'Brien ○ **USA** (OR) 244-245 B 8
O'Brien Creek ~ **USA** (MT) 250-251 J 3
Obrovac ○ **HR** 100-101 E 2
Obručeva, vozvyšennost' ▲▲ **RUS** 120-121 V 7
Obruchev Rise ≃ 14-15 J 2
Obruk Yaylâsı ▲▲ **TR** 128-129 E 3
Obryvistaja, gora ▲ **RUS** 112-113 S 3
Obryvistj, mys ▲ **RUS** 108-109 c 2
Obryvistyj, mys ▲ **RUS** 112-113 M 5
Obščij syrt ▲▲ **RUS** 96-97 F 8
Observatory Hill ▲ **AUS** 176-177 M 4
Observatory Inlet ≈ 32-33 E 4
Obskaja guba ≈ 108-109 P 8
Obskaya Guba = Obskaja guba ≈ **RUS** 108-109 P 8
Obuasi ○ **CI** 202-203 K 6
Obubra ○ **WAN** 204-205 H 5
Obuchiv ○ **UA** 102-103 G 2
Obudu ○ **WAN** 204-205 H 5
Obudu Cattle Ranch ○• **WAN** 204-205 H 5
Obusa ○ **RUS** 116-117 L 9
Obusa ~ **RUS** 116-117 M 9
Obytočna zatoka ≈ 102-103 J 4
Očakiv ○ **UA** 102-103 G 4
Ocala ○ **USA** (FL) 286-287 G 2
Ocalli ○ **PE** 64-65 C 5
Očamčira ○ **GE** 126-127 D 6
Ocampo ○ **MEX** (COA) 50-51 H 4
Ocampo ○ **MEX** (TAM) 50-51 K 6
Ocaña ○ **CO** 60-61 E 3
Ocaña ○ **E** 98-99 F 5
Ocaso ○ **CO** 64-65 F 1
Ocate ○ **USA** (NM) 256-257 K 2
Occidental, Cordillera ▲▲ **RCH** 64-65 C 5
Occidente ○ **CO** 64-65 F 2
Ocean Cape ▲ **USA** 20-21 U 7
Ocean City ○ **USA** (MD) 280-281 L 5
Ocean City ○ **USA** (NJ) 280-281 M 4
Ocean City ○ **USA** (WA) 244-245 A 3
Ocean Falls ○ **CDN** (BC) 228-229 G 4
Ocean Grove-Barwon Heads ○ **AUS** 180-181 H 5
Oceanographer Fracture Zone ≃ 6-7 E 5
Ocean Shores ○ **USA** (WA) 244-245 A 4
Oceanside ○ **USA** (CA) 248-249 G 6
Ocean Springs ○ **USA** (MS) 268-269 M 6
Ocean View ○ **USA** (NJ) 280-281 M 4
Očenyrd, gora ▲ **RUS** 108-109 L 7
Očer ☆ **RUS** 96-97 J 5
Ochiai ○ **J** 152-153 E 7
O'Chiese Indian Reserve X **CDN** (ALB) 232-233 C 3
Ochito ~ **PK** 134-135 M 6
Ochlockonee River ~ **USA** (FL) 286-287 E 1
Ochoa, La ○ **MEX** 50-51 H 5
Ochobo ○ **WAN** 204-205 G 5
Ochopee ○ **USA** (FL) 286-287 H 6
Ocho Rios ○• **JA** 54-55 G 5
Ochre River ○ **CDN** (MAN) 234-235 D 3
Ochtyrka ○ **UA** 102-103 J 2
Ocilla ○ **USA** (GA) 284-285 G 5
Ockelbo ○ **S** 86-87 H 6
Ocmulgee National Monument • **USA** (GA) 284-285 G 4
Ocmulgee River ~ **USA** (GA) 284-285 H 5
Ocmulgee River ~ **USA** (GA) 284-285 G 3
Ocmulgee River ~ **USA** (GA) 284-285 G 4
Ocoa, Bahía de ≈ 54-55 K 5
Ocoa, Sierra de ▲▲ **DOM** 54-55 K 5
Ocoee ○ **USA** (TN) 282-283 C 5
Ocoee, Lake ⊖ **USA** (TN) 282-283 C 5
Ocoña ○ **PE** 70-71 A 5
Ocoña, Río de ~ **PE** 70-71 A 5
Oconee, Lake < **USA** (GA) 284-285 G 3
Oconee River ~ **USA** (GA) 284-285 H 4
Oconee River, North ~ **USA** (GA) 284-285 G 2
Ocongate ○ **PE** 70-71 B 3
O'Connor, Port ○ **USA** (TX) 266-267 L 5
Oconomowoc ○ **USA** (WI) 274-275 K 1
Oconto ○ **USA** (NE) 262-263 G 3
Oconto ○ **USA** (WI) 270-271 L 6
Oconto River ~ **USA** (WI) 270-271 K 6
Ocoruro ○ **PE** 70-71 B 4
Ocós ○ **GCA** 52-53 H 4
Ocosingo ○ **MEX** 52-53 H 3
Ocotal ☆ **NIC** 52-53 L 5
Ocotillo Wells ○ **USA** (CA) 248-249 H 6
Ocotito, El ○ **MEX** 52-53 E 3
Ocotlán ○ **MEX** (JAL) 52-53 C 1
Ocotlán ○• **MEX** (OAX) 52-53 F 3
Ocozocoautla ○ **MEX** 52-53 H 3
Ocracoka Island ∩ **USA** (NC) 282-283 M 5
Ocracoke ○ **USA** (NC) 282-283 M 5
Ocreza, Ribeiro do ~ **P** 98-99 D 5
Ocros ○ **PE** (ANC) 64-65 D 7
Ocros ○ **PE** (AYA) 64-65 F 8
Octavia ○ **USA** (NE) 262-263 J 3
Octotillo ○ **USA** (CA) 248-249 H 7
Octy, Mount ▲ **AUS** 178-179 C 1
Ocú ○• **PA** 52-53 D 8
Ocua ○ **MOC** 218-219 K 1
Očuguj-Botuobuja ~ **RUS** 118-119 G 4
Ocujal ○ **C** 54-55 G 5
Ocumare del Tuy ○ **YV** 60-61 H 2
Ocuri ○ **BOL** 70-71 E 6
Oda ○ **GH** 202-203 K 7
Ódáðahraun ▲▲ **IS** 86-87 e 2
Odaejin ○ **DVR** 150-151 G 7
Odaesan National Park ⊥• **ROK** 150-151 G 9
Odammun ~ **RI** 166-167 K 5
Ōdate ○ **J** 152-153 J 4
Odawara ○ **J** 152-153 H 7
Odde, Oke- ○ **WAN** 204-205 F 4
Odebolt ○ **USA** (IA) 274-275 C 2
Odei River ~ **CDN** 34-35 G 2
Odell ○ **USA** (IN) 274-275 L 4
Odell ○ **USA** (NE) 262-263 K 4
Odell ○ **USA** (TX) 264-265 E 4
Odem ○ **USA** (TX) 266-267 K 6
Odemira ○ **P** 98-99 C 6
Ödemiş ☆ **TR** 128-129 B 3
Odendaalsrus ○ **ZA** 220-221 H 3
Odense ○• **DK** 86-87 E 9
Odenton ○ **USA** (MD) 280-281 K 4
Oder ~ **D** 92-93 N 2
Oderbruch ∸ **D** 92-93 N 2
Odesa ☆•• **UA** 102-103 G 4
Odesa ○ **USA** (NJ) 280-281 L 4
Odessa ○ **CDN** (SAS) 232-233 P 5
Odessa ○ **USA** (MO) 274-275 E 6
Odessa ○ **USA** (TX) 266-267 E 2
Odessa ○ **USA** (WA) 244-245 G 3
Odessa = Odesa ☆•• **UA** (ODS) 102-103 G 4
Odienné ☆• **CI** 202-203 G 5
Odighi ○ **WAN** 204-205 F 5
Odincovo ☆ **RUS** 94-95 P 4
Odiongan ○ **RP** 160-161 D 6
Odjala ○ **G** 210-211 D 4
Odjan, zaliv ⊖ **RUS** 120-121 O 4
Odoev ☆ **RUS** 94-95 P 5
Odomlja ☆ **RUS** 94-95 O 3
Odon ○ **USA** (IN) 274-275 M 6
Ŏdŏngk ○ **K** 158-159 H 5
Odonkawkrom ○ **GH** 202-203 K 6
O'Donnell ○ **USA** (TX) 264-265 C 6
O'Donnell River ~ **AUS** 172-173 H 5
Odorheiu Secuiesc ○ **RO** 102-103 D 4
Odra ~ **PL** 92-93 N 2
Odrus ~ **SUD** 200-201 H 3

Novobelokataj — Odrus **371**

Ongandjera o NAM 216-217 C 8
Ông Cô, Đèo ▲ VN 158-159 K 5
Ongeri o ZRE 210-211 K 6
Ongersrivier ~ ZA 220-221 F 5
Ongi o MAU 148-149 F 5
Ongi gol ~ MAU 148-149 F 4
Ongjin o DVR 150-151 E 9
Ongka o RI 164-165 G 3
Ongkaw o RI 164-165 J 3
Ongkharak o THA 158-159 F 3
Ongniud Qi o VRC 148-149 O 6
Ongoka o ZRE 210-211 L 4
Ongole o IND 140-141 J 3
Ongon o PE 64-65 D 6
Ongon = Havirga o MAU 148-149 L 5
Ongongoro o NAM 216-217 E 10
Ongonyi o RCB 210-211 F 4
Ongoro Gotjari o NAM 216-217 D 11
Onhne o MYA 158-159 D 2
Oni o GE 126-127 E 6
Oni, River ~ WAN 204-205 F 5
Onibe ~ RM 222-223 F 6
Onida o USA (SD) 260-261 F 2
Onide ú Olin, Río ~ RA 80 E 3
Onilahy ~ RM 222-223 G 9
Onin (Fakfak) Peninsula ◡ RI 166-167 F 3
Onioni o PNG 183 E 6
Onion Lake o CDN (SAS) 232-233 J 2
Onitsha ☆ WAN 204-205 G 5
Onive ~ RM 222-223 E 7
Onkamo o FIN 88-89 L 5
Onkivesi o FIN 88-89 J 5
Onnekon ~ RUS 118-119 O 6
Onnës o RUS 120-121 D 3
Onnë-Siligir ~ RUS 110-111 J 6
Ono ⌒ FJI 184 III b 3
Ōno o J 152-153 G 7
Onoko o TCH 206-207 B 3
Onomichi o J 152-153 E 7
Onon ~ RUS 118-119 G 10
Onon gol ~ MAU 148-149 K 3
Onor o RUS 122-123 K 3
Onor ~ RUS 122-123 K 3
Onor, gora ▲ RUS 122-123 K 3
Onot ~ RUS 116-117 K 9
Onoto o YV 60-61 J 3
Onoway o CDN (ALB) 232-233 D 2
Onseepkans o ZA 220-221 D 4
Onslow o AUS 172-173 B 6
Onslow Bay ≈ 48-49 K 2
Onslow Bay ≈ USA 282-283 K 6
Ontake-san ▲ J 152-153 G 7
Ontar o VAN 184 II a 2
Ontaratue River ~ CDN 20-21 Z 3
Ontario ◘ CDN (ONT) 234-235 K 4
Ontario o USA (CA) 248-249 G 5
Ontario o USA (OR) 244-245 H 6
Ontario o USA (WI) 270-271 H 7
Ontario, Lake o 46-47 J 4
Ontario, Lake o 278-279 C 5
Ontario Peninsula ◡ CDN (ONT) 238-239 D 5
Ontmoeting o ZA 220-221 E 3
Ontonagon o USA (MI) 270-271 J 4
Ontonagon River ~ USA (MI) 270-271 J 4
Ontong Java ⌒ SOL 184 I d 1
Ōnuma Quasi National Park ⊥ J 152-153 J 4
Onverwacht ☆ SME 62-63 G 3
Onwul River ~ WAN 204-205 H 5
Onyx o USA (CA) 248-249 F 4
Onyx Cave ∴ USA (AR) 276-277 B 4
Oobagooma o AUS 172-173 G 4
Oodnadatta o AUS 178-179 C 4
Oodnadatta Track II AUS 178-179 C 5
Oodonggo o RI 168 D 7
Oodweyne o SP 208-209 G 4
Ookala o USA (HI) 288 K 4
Ooldea Range ▲ AUS 176-177 L 5
Oolloo o AUS 172-173 K 2
Oologah Lake o USA (OK) 264-265 J 2
Oona River o CDN (BC) 228-229 D 3
Ooratippra o AUS 178-179 D 1
Oorindi o AUS 174-175 F 7
Oos-Londen = East London o• ZA 220-221 H 6
Ooste Lake o CDN (BC) 228-229 H 3
Oostende o• B 92-93 G 3
Oostermoed o ZA 220-221 H 2
Oosterschelde ≈ 92-93 G 3
Ootsa Lake o CDN (BC) 228-229 J 3
Opachuanau Lake o CDN 34-35 G 2
Opaka o BG 102-103 E 6
Opal o CDN (ALB) 232-233 E 2
Opal o USA (WY) 252-253 H 5
Opala ~ RUS 122-123 R 2
Opala o ZRE 210-211 K 4
Opalocka o USA (FL) 286-287 J 6
Opang o RI 164-165 K 4
Opari o SUD 212-213 D 2
Oparino o RUS 96-97 F 4
Opasatika o CDN (ONT) 236-237 F 3
Opasatika Lake o CDN (ONT) 236-237 E 3
Opasatika River ~ CDN (ONT) 236-237 F 2
Opasnyj, mys ▲ RUS (KMC) 120-121 S 7
Opasnyj, mys ▲ RUS (KOR) 120-121 Q 3
Opataca, Lac o CDN (QUE) 236-237 O 2
Opatija o HR 100-101 E 2
Opava o CZ 92-93 O 4
Opawica, Lac o CDN (QUE) 236-237 N 3
Opelika o USA (AL) 284-285 E 4
Opelousas o USA (LA) 268-269 H 6
Opémisca, Lac o CDN (QUE) 236-237 O 3
Opémiska, Mount ▲ CDN (QUE) 236-237 O 3
Open Bay ≈ 183 F 3
Open Bay o PNG 183 F 3
Openshaw o CDN (SAS) 232-233 Q 6
Opeongo Lake o CDN (ONT) 238-239 G 3
Opeta, Lake o EAU 212-213 E 3
Opheim o USA (MT) 250-251 N 3
Ophir o CDN (ONT) 238-239 B 2
Ophir o USA 20-21 M 5
Ophir, Gunung ▲ RI 162-163 C 4
Ophthalmia Range ▲ AUS 172-173 D 7
Opi o WAN 204-205 G 5
Opichén o MEX 52-53 K 1
Opienge o ZRE 212-213 A 3
Opihikao o USA (HI) 288 L 5
Opikeigen Lake o CDN (ONT) 234-235 P 3
Opilija ▲ UA 102-103 D 3
Opinaca, Réservoir < CDN 38-39 F 2
Opinaca, Rivière ~ CDN 38-39 G 2
Opinnagau Lake o CDN 34-35 O 4
Opinnagau River ~ CDN 34-35 P 3
Opiscotéo, Lac o CDN 38-39 K 2
Opiscotiche, Lac o CDN 38-39 L 2
Opišn'a o UA 102-103 J 3
Opitsat o CDN (BC) 230-231 D 4
Opobo o WAN 204-205 G 6
Opočka ☆ RUS 94-95 L 3
Opocopa, Lac o CDN 38-39 L 2
Opoczno o PL 92-93 Q 3
Opole ☆• PL 92-93 O 3
Opopeo o MEX 52-53 D 2
Opornyj o KA 96-97 J 10
Opotiki o NZ 182 F 3
Opp o USA (AL) 284-285 D 5
Oppa-wan ≈ 152-153 J 5
Oppdal ☆ N 86-87 D 5
Opportunity o USA (MT) 250-251 G 5
Opportunity o USA (WA) 244-245 H 3
Opposite Island ⌒ CDN 36-37 H 2
Oppstryn o N 86-87 C 6
Optic Lake o CDN 34-35 F 3
Optima o USA (OK) 264-265 C 2
Optima National Wildlife Refuge ⊥ USA (OK) 264-265 C 2
Optima Reservoir o USA (OK) 264-265 C 2
Opuka ~ RUS 112-113 R 5
Opuka, laguna o RUS 112-113 S 6
Opunake o NZ 182 D 3
Opuntia Lake o CDN (SAS) 232-233 K 4
Opuwo ☆ NAM 216-217 B 9
Oquawka o USA (IL) 274-275 H 4
Oquossoc o USA (ME) 278-279 L 4
Or' ~ KA 126-127 N 3
Or' ~ RUS 96-97 L 8
Or, Cape d' ▲ CDN (NS) 240-241 L 5
Ora o PNG 183 F 3
Ora ~ VAN 184 II a 2
Oraba o EAU 212-213 C 2
Oracle o USA (AZ) 256-257 E 6
Oracle Junction o USA (AZ) 256-257 E 6
Oradea ☆• RO 102-103 B 4
Öræfajökull ▲ IS 86-87 e 2
Orah o WAN 204-205 F 5
Orai o IND 138-139 G 7
Oraibi Wash ~ USA (AZ) 256-257 E 3
Oral ☆ KA 96-97 G 8
Oral ~ KA 96-97 G 9
Ora Loma o USA (CA) 248-249 D 3
Orami o PNG 184 I b 2
Oran = Wahrân ☆•• DZ 188-189 L 3
Oranapai o GUY 62-63 E 2
Orange o AUS 180-181 K 2
Orange o• F 90-91 K 9
Orange o USA (TX) 268-269 G 6
Orange o USA (VA) 280-281 H 5
Orange ~ ZA 220-221 D 4
Orange, Cap ▲ F 62-63 J 3
Orange, Port o USA (FL) 286-287 J 2
Orange Bay ≈ CDN 242-243 M 2
Orangeburg o USA (SC) 284-285 K 3
Orange Cay ⌒ BS 54-55 F 2
Orange Cove o USA (CA) 248-249 E 3
Orangedale o CDN (NS) 240-241 O 5
Orange Fan ≈ 9 E 9
Orange Free State = Oranje-Vrystaat ◘ ZA 220-221 G 4
Orange Grove o USA (TX) 266-267 K 6
Orange Lake o USA (FL) 286-287 G 2
Orange Park o USA (FL) 286-287 H 1
Orangerie Bay ≈ 183 E 6
Orangeville o CDN (ONT) 238-239 E 5
Orangeville o USA (IL) 274-275 J 2
Orangeville o USA (MI) 272-273 D 5
Orange Walk o BH 52-53 K 2
Orangi ~ EAT 212-213 E 5
Orango, Ilha de ⌒ GNB 202-203 B 4
Orangozinho, Ilha de ⌒ GNB 202-203 C 4
Orangutang, mys ▲ RUS 112-113 R 6
Orania o ZA 220-221 G 4
Oranjefontein o ZA 218-219 D 6
Oranjemund o NAM 220-221 C 4
Oranjerivier ~ ZA 220-221 F 4
Oranjestad ☆ ARU 60-61 F 1
Oranjestad ☆•• NA (NA) 56 D 3
Oranjeville o ZA 220-221 J 3
Oranje Vrystaat ◘ ZA 220-221 G 4
Oransbari o RI 166-167 H 2
Oranžeri o RUS 126-127 G 5
Orapa o RB 218-219 C 5
Oras o RP 160-161 F 6
Oratia, Mount ▲ USA 22-23 Q 3
Oratorio o RA 76-77 D 2
Orattanādu o IND 140-141 H 5
Orava o PNG 184 I b 2
Oravita o RO 102-103 B 5
Orb ~ F 90-91 J 10
Orbata, Jebel ▲ TN 190-191 G 3
Orbetello o I 100-101 C 3
Órbigo, Río ~ E 98-99 E 3
Orbost o AUS 180-181 K 4
Orcadas o ARK 16 G 32
Orchard o USA (NE) 262-263 H 2
Orchard City o USA (CO) 254-255 H 5
Orchards o USA (WA) 244-245 C 5
Orchard Valley o USA (WY) 252-253 O 5
Orchardville o USA (IL) 274-275 K 6
Orchila, Isla ⌒ YV 60-61 H 2
Orco ~ I 100-101 A 2
Orcococha, Lago o PE 64-65 E 8
Orcopampa o PE 64-65 F 9
Ord o USA (NE) 262-263 H 3
Ord, Mount ▲ AUS 172-173 G 4
Orda ☆ RUS 96-97 K 5
Orda < TCH 198-199 H 2
Ordale o CDN (SAS) 232-233 M 2
Orderville o USA (UT) 254-255 C 6
Ordes o•• E 98-99 C 3
Ord Mountain ▲ USA (CA) 248-249 H 5
Ordoqui o RA 78-79 J 3
Ordos = Mu Us Shamo ⊥ VRC 154-155 E 2
Ord Regeneration Depot o AUS 172-173 J 4
Ord River ~ AUS 172-173 J 4
Ordu ☆ TR 128-129 G 2
Ordubad o AZ 128-129 M 3
Ordway o USA (CO) 254-255 M 5
Ordynskoe ☆ RUS 124-125 M 1
Ordženikidze ☆ KA 124-125 B 2
Ordžonikidze o UA 102-103 J 4
Ordžonikidzeabad = Kofarnihon o TJ 136-137 L 5
Ore o WAN 204-205 F 5
Örebro ☆• S 86-87 G 7
Ore City o USA (TX) 264-265 K 6
Oredež o RUS 94-95 M 2
Oregon o USA (MO) 274-275 C 5
Oregon o USA (OH) 280-281 C 2
Oregon o USA (WI) 274-275 J 2
Oregon ◘ USA (OR) 244-245 B 7
Oregon Caves National Monument ∴ USA (OR) 244-245 B 8
Oregon City o USA (OR) 244-245 C 5
Oregon Dunes ⊥ USA (OR) 244-245 A 7
Oregon Inlet ≈ USA 282-283 M 5
Orehovo-Zuevo ☆ RUS 94-95 Q 4
Orekhovo-Zuyevo = Orehovo-Zuevo ☆ RUS 94-95 Q 4
Orel o RUS 94-95 P 5
Orel' ~ UA 102-103 J 3
Orel', ozero o RUS 122-123 H 2
Orellana o PE (AMA) 64-65 C 4
Orellana o PE (LOR) 64-65 E 5
Orellana la Vieja o E 98-99 E 5
Orem o USA (UT) 254-255 D 3
Ören o TR 128-129 B 4
Orenburg ☆ RUS 96-97 J 8
Oreng o RI 162-163 B 2
Orense = Ourense o E 98-99 D 3
Orerokpe o WAN 204-205 F 6
Øresund ≈ 86-87 F 9
Oretown o USA (OR) 244-245 B 5
Orewa o NZ 182 E 2
Orford, Port o USA (OR) 244-245 A 8
Organ o USA (NM) 256-257 J 6
Organabo o F 62-63 H 3
Organ Pipe Cactus National Monument ∴ USA (AZ) 256-257 C 6
Orgeev = Orhei ☆ MD 102-103 F 4
Orgūn o AFG 138-139 B 3
Orhaneli ☆ TR 128-129 C 3
Orhangazi o TR 128-129 C 2
Orhei ☆ MD 102-103 F 4
Orhej = Orhei ☆ MD 102-103 F 4
Orhon o MAU 148-149 G 3
Orhon gol ~ MAU 148-149 F 3
Ori ~ RT 202-203 L 5
Orianda, laguna o RUS 112-113 U 5
Orica o HN 52-53 L 4
Orichiv o UA 102-103 J 4
Orick o USA (CA) 246-247 A 2
Orient o USA (SD) 260-261 G 2
Orient o USA (WA) 244-245 G 2
Oriental, Cordillera ▲ DOM 54-55 L 5
Oriental, Cordillera ▲ PE 64-65 D 4
Oriental, Llanura ▲ DOM 54-55 L 5
Orient Bay o CDN (ONT) 234-235 P 5
Oriente o RA 78-79 J 5
Oriente, Cachoeira do ~ BR 66-67 E 7
Orient Point o USA (NY) 280-281 O 2
Orihuela o E 98-99 G 5
Orillia o CDN (ONT) 238-239 F 4
Orin o USA (WY) 252-253 N 4
Orinduik o GUY 62-63 D 3
Orinoca o BOL 70-71 D 6
Orinoco, Delta del ≈ 60-61 L 3
Orinoco, Llanos del ⊥ 60-61 F 5
Orinoco, Río ~ YV 60-61 J 6
Oriomo o PNG 183 B 5
Orion o CDN (ALB) 232-233 H 6
Orion o USA (AL) 284-285 E 5
Orion o USA (AR) 276-277 C 6
Oriska o USA (ND) 258-259 K 5
Orissa ◘ IND 142-143 C 5
Orissaare o EST 94-95 H 2
Oristano o• I 100-101 B 5
Orito o CO 64-65 D 1
Orituco o YV 60-61 H 3
Orituco, Río ~ YV 60-61 H 3
Oritupano, Río ~ YV 60-61 K 3
Orivesi o FIN 88-89 H 6
Oriximiná o BR 62-63 F 6
Orizaba o• MEX 52-53 F 2
Orizaba, Pico de ▲ MEX 52-53 F 2
Orjahovo o BG 102-103 C 6
Orjen ▲ YU 100-101 G 3
Orjus-Miele ~ RUS 118-119 K 7
Orkadiéré o SN 202-203 D 2
Orkanger o N 86-87 D 5
Örkelljunga o S 86-87 F 8
Orkjule, mys ▲ RUS 110-111 S 4
Orkla o N 86-87 D 5
Orkney o CDN (SAS) 232-233 L 6
Orkney o ZA 220-221 H 3
Orkney Islands ⌒ GB 90-91 F 2
Orla o USA (TX) 266-267 D 2
Orlameš o AFG 136-137 K 6
Orland o USA (CA) 246-247 C 4
Orlândia o BR 72-73 G 6
Orlando o• USA (FL) 286-287 H 3
Orleães o BR 74-75 F 7
Orléanais ⌒ F 90-91 H 8
Orléans o F 90-91 H 8
Orleans o USA (IN) 274-275 M 6
Orleans o USA (MA) 278-279 M 7
Orleans o USA (NE) 262-263 G 4
Orleans, Île d' ⌒ CDN (QUE) 240-241 E 4
Orleans Farms o AUS 176-177 G 6
Orle River Game Reserve ⊥ WAN 204-205 G 5
Orlik ☆ RUS 116-117 J 9
Orlinaja gora ▲ RUS 112-113 U 5
Orlinga o RUS 116-117 M 7
Orlinga ~ RUS 116-117 N 8
Orlov Gaj o RUS 96-97 F 8
Orlovka o RUS (NVS) 114-115 O 6
Orlovka ~ RUS 112-113 N 3
Orlovka ~ RUS 112-113 P 4
Orlovka ~ RUS 114-115 T 5
Orlovka ~ RUS 122-123 C 2
Orlovskij o RUS 102-103 N 4
Orlovskij, mys ▲ RUS 88-89 Q 3
Orlovskij hrebet ▲ RUS 112-113 N 3
Orlovskij zaliv ≈ 88-89 Q 3
Orlu o WAN 204-205 G 6
Ormachea, Bosque Petrificado J. • RA 80 F 2
Ormára o PK 134-135 L 6
Ormára, Răs ▲ PK 134-135 L 6
Ormea o• I 100-101 A 2
Ormiston o CDN (SAS) 232-233 N 6
Ormiston Gorge National Park ⊥ AUS 176-177 M 1
Ormoc o RP 160-161 F 7
Ormond Beach o USA (FL) 286-287 H 2
Ormonde Island ⌒ CDN 24-25 e 6
Ormos Almirou ≈ 100-101 K 7
Ormsby o USA (MN) 270-271 D 7
Ormstown o CDN (QUE) 238-239 M 3
Ormtjørn nasjonalpark ⊥ N 86-87 D 6
Orne ~ F 90-91 G 7
Ørnes o N 86-87 F 3
Örnsköldsvik o S 86-87 J 5
Oro, Lac o RMM 196-197 J 6
Oro, Mesa del ▲ USA (NM) 256-257 H 4
Oro, Museo del • CO 60-61 D 5
Oro, Río de ~ RA 76-77 H 4
Oro, Río del ~ MEX 50-51 G 5
Orobayaya o BOL 70-71 F 3
Oro Blanco o USA (AZ) 256-257 D 7
Orocó o BR 68-69 J 6
Orocue o CO 60-61 F 5
Orodara o BF 202-203 H 4
Orodel o• RO 102-103 C 5
Oroek o RUS 110-111 d 7
Orofino o USA (ID) 250-251 C 5
Orog nuur o MAU 148-149 E 5
Orogrande o USA (NM) 256-257 J 6
Orol dengizi = Aral teŋizi ⌒ 126-127 N 5
Orom o EAU 212-213 D 2
Oromocto o CDN (NB) 240-241 J 5
Oromocto Lake o CDN (NB) 240-241 J 5
Oron o RUS 118-119 H 7
Oron o WAN 204-205 H 6
Orondo o USA (WA) 244-245 E 3
Oroners Out Station o AUS 174-175 G 4
Oronga o PNG 183 C 3
Orono o USA (ME) 278-279 N 4
Orono o USA (MN) 270-271 E 6
Oronoquerivier ~ GUY 62-63 F 4
Orope o YV 60-61 E 3
Oropesa o• E 98-99 E 5
Oropesa, Río ~ PE 64-65 F 8
Oroqen Zizhiqi o VRC 150-151 D 2
Oroquieta ☆ RP 160-161 E 8
Orós o BR 68-69 J 5
Orós, Açude < BR 68-69 J 5
Orosei o I 100-101 B 4
Orosháza o H 92-93 Q 5
Orosi o USA (CA) 248-249 E 3
Orosmayo, Río de ~ RA 76-77 D 2
Orotina o CR 52-53 B 7
Orotko, ozero o RUS 110-111 W 4
Orotuk o RUS 120-121 N 2
Orotukan o RUS 120-121 O 2
Orotukan ~ RUS 120-121 O 2
Orovada o USA (NV) 246-247 H 2
Oro Valley o USA (AZ) 256-257 E 6
Oroville o USA (WA) 244-245 F 2
Oroville o• USA (CA) 246-247 D 4
Oroville Reservoir < USA (CA) 246-247 D 4
Oroya, La o PE 64-65 E 7
Orpheus Lake o CDN 30-31 Q 5
Orquídeas, Parque Nacional las ⊥ CO 60-61 C 4
Orr o USA (MN) 270-271 F 2
Orroroo o AUS 180-181 E 2
Orrville o USA (AL) 284-285 C 4
Orša ☆ BY 94-95 M 4
Orsa o S 86-87 G 6
Orsha = Orša ☆ BY 94-95 M 4
Orsk o RUS 96-97 L 8
Ørstavik ☆ N 86-87 C 5
Ortaca ☆ TR 128-129 C 4
Ortaköy o TR 128-129 F 3
Ortasu ~ KA 124-125 J 5
Orte o I 100-101 D 3
Ortega o CO 60-61 D 6
Ortegal, Cabo ▲ E 98-99 D 3
Orteguaza, Río ~ CO 64-65 E 1
Orthez o F 90-91 G 10
Ortho, Río ~ BOL 70-71 D 2
Ortigueira o BR 74-75 E 5
Ortigueira o E 98-99 D 3
Orting o USA (WA) 244-245 C 3
Ortit o GRØ 28-29 V 4
Ortiz o MEX 50-51 D 3
Ort"jagun ~ RUS 114-115 N 4
Ortler = Ortles ▲ I 100-101 C 1
Ortona o I 100-101 E 3
Orto-Nahara o RUS 118-119 G 5
Ortonville o USA (MI) 272-273 F 5
Ortonville o USA (MN) 270-271 B 5
Orto-Surt o RUS 118-119 M 4
Orto-Tokoj o KS 146-147 C 4
Oru o CO 60-61 E 3
Oruhito o NAM 216-217 B 9
Orulgan, hrebet ▲ RUS 110-111 R 5
Orümiye ☆• IR 128-129 L 4
Orümiye, Daryāče-ye o IR 128-129 L 3
Oruro ☆• BOL 70-71 D 5
Orust ⌒ S 86-87 E 7
Orūzgān o AFG (OR) 134-135 M 2
Orūzgān ◘ AFG 134-135 L 2
Orvieto o• I 100-101 D 3
Orville Escarpment ▲ ARK 16 F 30
Orwell o USA (OH) 280-281 F 2
Orzūiye o IR 134-135 G 4
Oržycja ~ UA 102-103 H 3
Orzysz o• PL 92-93 Q 2
Oš ☆ KS 136-137 N 4
Os ☆ N 86-87 E 5
Osa ☆ RUS 116-117 L 9
Osa ☆ RUS (PRM) 96-97 J 5
Oša ~ RUS 114-115 M 6
Osa ~ RUS 116-117 M 9
Osa, Peninsula de ◡ CR 52-53 C 7
Osage o CDN (SAS) 232-233 P 6
Osage o USA (AR) 276-277 B 4
Osage o USA (IA) 274-275 F 1
Osage Beach o USA (MO) 274-275 F 6
Osage City o USA (KS) 262-263 L 6
Osage Fork ~ USA (MO) 276-277 C 3
Osage River ~ USA (MO) 274-275 F 6
Osage River ~ USA (MO) 276-277 A 3
Ōsaka ☆• J 152-153 F 7
Osakarovka o KA 124-125 H 3
Osakarovka = Askarly ☆ KA 124-125 H 3
Ōsaka-wan ≈ 152-153 F 7
Osakis o USA (MN) 270-271 C 5
Osasco o BR 72-73 G 7
Osawatomie o USA (KS) 262-263 M 6
Osborne o CDN (MAN) 234-235 F 5
Osborne o USA (KS) 262-263 H 5
Osburn o USA (ID) 250-251 C 4
Osby o S 86-87 F 8
Osca, Río ~ BOL 70-71 E 5
Oscar o F 62-63 H 4
Oscar II land ⊥ N 84-85 H 3
Oscar Soto Máynes o MEX 50-51 F 3
Osceola o USA (AR) 276-277 F 5
Osceola o USA (IA) 274-275 E 3
Osceola o USA (MO) 274-275 E 6
Osceola o USA (NE) 262-263 J 3
Osceola o USA (SD) 260-261 J 2
Osceola o USA (WI) 270-271 F 5
Oschiri o I 100-101 B 4
Oscoda o USA (MI) 272-273 F 3
Oscura o USA (NM) 256-257 J 5
Oscura, Punta ▲ GQ 210-211 B 2
Oscura Peak ▲ USA (NM) 256-257 J 5
Osetr ~ RUS 94-95 Q 4
Osgood o USA (IN) 274-275 N 5
Osh = Oš ☆ KS 136-137 N 4
Oshakati o NAM 216-217 C 8
Oshamambe o J 152-153 J 3
Oshawa o CDN (ONT) 238-239 G 5
Oshetna River ~ USA 20-21 R 5
Oshika-hanto ◡ J 152-153 J 5
Oshikango o NAM 216-217 C 8
Oshikuku o NAM 216-217 C 8
Ō-shima ⌒ J (TOK) 152-153 H 7
Ō-shima ⌒ J (KGA) 152-153 C 10
Ōshima ⌒ J (TOK) 152-153 H 7
Ō-shima ⌒ J (YMG) 152-153 E 8
Oshima-hantō ◡ J 152-153 J 3
Oshivelo o NAM 216-217 D 9
Oshkosh o USA (NE) 262-263 D 3
Oshkosh o USA (WI) 270-271 K 6
Oshun, River ~ WAN 204-205 F 5
Oshwe o ZRE 210-211 G 5
Osiān o IND 138-139 D 6
Osijek ☆• HR 100-101 G 2
Osilinka River ~ CDN 32-33 H 3
Osinniki ☆ RUS 124-125 P 2
Osinovaja, Bol'šaja ~ RUS 112-113 T 3
Osinovka o RUS 116-117 K 7
Osinovo o RUS 88-89 R 5
Osinovoe Pleso o RUS 114-115 T 7
Osinovskij hrebet ▲ RUS 112-113 S 3
Osinovskij porog •• RUS 114-115 U 4
Oskaloosa o USA (IA) 274-275 F 3
Oskaloosa o USA (KS) 262-263 L 5
Oskarshamn ☆ S 86-87 H 8
Oskélanéo o CDN (QUE) 236-237 N 4
Öskemen o KA 124-125 N 4
Os'kino o RUS 102-103 L 2
Os'kino o RUS 116-117 N 5
Oskoba ~ RUS 116-117 K 6
Os'koto, ozero o RUS 88-89 Y 3
Oskū o IR 128-129 M 4
Osland o CDN (BC) 228-229 D 2
Osler o CDN (SAS) 232-233 M 3
Osljanka, gora ▲ RUS 114-115 E 5
Oslo ☆•• N 86-87 E 7
Oslo o USA (MN) 270-271 A 2
Oslofjorden ≈ 86-87 E 7
Osmānābād o IND 138-139 F 10
Osmancık ☆ TR 128-129 F 2
Osmaneli ☆ TR 128-129 C 2
Osmaniye ☆ TR 128-129 G 4
Osmānnagar o IND 138-139 G 10
Os'mino o RUS 94-95 L 2
Osmo o S 86-87 H 7
Osnabrück o• D 92-93 K 2
Osnaburgh House o CDN (ONT) 234-235 N 3
Ōsnüye o IR 128-129 L 4
Oso o USA (WA) 244-245 D 2
Oso ~ ZRE 212-213 A 4
Oso, El o YV 60-61 J 5
Osogbo o• WAN 204-205 F 5
Osogovski pl. ▲ MK 100-101 J 3
Osório o BR 74-75 E 7
Osório da Fonseca o BR 66-67 H 4
Osorno o E 98-99 E 3
Osorno o RCH 78-79 C 6
Osorno, Volcán ▲ RCH 78-79 C 6
Ososo o WAN 204-205 G 5
Osoyoos o CDN (BC) 230-231 K 4
Osoyoos Indian Reserve X CDN (BC) 230-231 K 4
Osøyra o N 86-87 B 6
Ospasquia Provincial Park ⊥ CDN 34-35 K 4
Ospika River ~ CDN 32-33 H 3
Ospino o YV 60-61 G 3
Osprey o USA (FL) 286-287 G 4
Osprey Reef ⌒ AUS 174-175 J 3
Ossa ▲ P 98-99 D 5
Ossa, Mount ▲ AUS 180-181 J 6
Ossabaw Island ⌒ USA (GA) 284-285 J 5
Ossabaw Sound ≈ USA 284-285 J 5
Ossa de Montiel o E 98-99 F 5
Ossalinskij krjaž ▲ RUS 110-111 c 7
Osse, River ~ WAN 204-205 F 5
Ossélé o RCB 210-211 E 4
Osseo o USA (MN) 270-271 E 5
Osseo o USA (WI) 270-271 G 6
Ossima o PNG 183 A 2
Ossineke o USA (MI) 272-273 F 3
Ossining o USA (NY) 280-281 N 2
Ossokmanuan Lake o CDN 38-39 M 2
Ossora ☆ RUS 120-121 U 4
Ossora, buhta o RUS 120-121 U 4
Ostapazifisches Südpolarbecken ≈ 16 G 27
Ostaškin, kamen' • RUS 114-115 T 7
Ostaškov ☆ RUS 94-95 N 3
Östavall o S 86-87 G 5
Østby o N 86-87 E 5
Oste ~ D 92-93 K 2
Ostenfeld o CDN (MAN) 234-235 G 5
Oster ~ RUS 94-95 N 5
Österbotten = Pohjanmaa ⊥ FIN 88-89 G 5
Österbybruk o S 86-87 H 6
Østerdalen ~ N 86-87 E 6
Östergötland ⊥ S 86-87 G 7
Østerø = Eysturoy ⌒ FR 90-91 D 1
Östersund ☆• S 86-87 G 5
Osterwick o CDN (MAN) 234-235 F 4
Ostfriesische Inseln ⊥ D 92-93 J 2
Østgrønland = Tunu ◘ GRØ 26-27 d 8
Östhammar o S 86-87 J 6
Oštinskij Pogost o RUS 94-95 O 1
Ōštorinān o IR 134-135 C 1
Ostraja, gora ▲ RUS 112-113 P 5
Ostraja, gora ▲ RUS 122-123 E 6
Ostraja, gora ▲ RUS (KOR) 120-121 T 4
Ostrau = Ostrava o CZ 92-93 P 4
Ostrau = Ostrov nad Oslavou o CZ 92-93 N 4
Ostrava o CZ 92-93 P 4
Ostrjak, gora ▲ RUS 112-113 Q 4
Ostróda o• PL 92-93 P 2
Ostrogožsk o RUS 102-103 L 2
Ostrołęka ☆• PL 92-93 Q 2
Ostrov o RO 102-103 E 5
Ostrov ☆ RUS 94-95 L 3
Ostroveršinnyj hrebet ▲ RUS 112-113 N 4
Ostrovnoe o RUS 112-113 N 2
Ostrovnoe o RUS (ORB) 96-97 K 8
Ostrovnoj, mys ▲ RUS 114-115 M 2
Ostrovnoj, zaliv o RUS 120-121 Q 3
Ostrovskoe o RUS 94-95 S 3
ostrov Vozroždenija ⌒ US 136-137 F 2
Ostrowiec Świętokrzyski o PL 92-93 Q 3
Ostrów Mazowiecka o PL 92-93 Q 2
Ostrów Wielkopolski ☆• PL 92-93 O 3
Osttirol ◘ A 92-93 M 5
Ostuni o I 100-101 F 4
Oštorān, Kūh-e ▲ IR 134-135 C 2
Ost Vank • TR 128-129 J 2
O'Sullivan Lake o CDN (ONT) 234-235 Q 4
Ōsumi-hantō ◡ J 152-153 D 9
Ōsumi-kaikyō ≈ 152-153 D 9
Ōsumi-shotō ⌒ J 152-153 D 9
Osuna o E 98-99 E 6
Oswegatchie River ~ USA (NY) 278-279 F 4
Oswego o USA (KS) 262-263 L 7
Oswego o USA (NY) 278-279 E 5
Oswego River ~ USA (NY) 278-279 E 5
Oświęcim o•• PL 92-93 P 3
Ōta o J 152-153 E 7
Otacílio Costa o BR 74-75 E 6
Ōta-gawa ~ J 152-153 E 7
Otago Peninsula ◡•• NZ 182 C 6
Otajkačanskij hrebet ▲ RUS 112-113 J 5
Otaki o NZ 182 E 4
Otakwa o RI 166-167 J 4
Otakwa ~ RI 166-167 J 4
Otaru o J 152-153 J 3
Otasawian River ~ CDN (ONT) 236-237 D 2
Otatal, Cerro ▲ MEX 50-51 D 3
Otavalo o• EC 64-65 C 1
Otavi o NAM 216-217 D 9
Otchinjau o ANG 216-217 B 8
OTC International Satellite Earth Station • AUS 176-177 M 5
O.T.Downs o AUS 174-175 C 5
Otelnuk, Lac o CDN 36-37 P 6
Oterkpolu o GH 202-203 K 6
Otgon Tènger ▲ MAU 148-149 C 4
Otha o IND 138-139 C 9
O'the Cherokees, Lake o USA (OK) 264-265 K 2
Othello o USA (WA) 244-245 F 4
O'the Pines, Lake o USA (TX) 264-265 K 6
Otherside River ~ CDN 30-31 Q 6
Oti ~ GH 202-203 L 5
Oti o RI 164-165 F 4
Oti, Réserve de l' ⊥ RT 202-203 L 4
Otinolândia o BR 72-73 J 3
Otis o USA (NM) 256-257 L 6
Otish, Monts ▲ CDN 38-39 J 2
Otjikondo o NAM 216-217 C 9
Otjikoto Lake • NAM 216-217 D 9
Otjimbingwe o• NAM 216-217 D 11
Otjinene o NAM 216-217 E 10
Otjinhungwa o NAM 216-217 B 8
Otjisemba o NAM 216-217 D 10
Otjitanda o NAM 216-217 B 8
Otjiwarongo ☆ NAM 216-217 D 10
Otjosondjou ~ NAM 216-217 E 10
Otjosondu o NAM 216-217 D 10
Otmök, pereval ▲ KS 136-137 N 3
Otoca o PE 64-65 E 9
Otog Qi o VRC 154-155 E 2
Otog Qian Qi o VRC 154-155 E 2
Otoineppu o J 152-153 K 2
Otola o DY 202-203 L 5
Otorohanga o NZ 182 E 3
Otoskwin River ~ CDN (ONT) 234-235 O 3
Otosquen o CDN (SAS) 232-233 R 2
Ōtoyo o J 152-153 E 8
Otra ~ N 86-87 C 7
Otradnaja o RUS 126-127 D 5
Otradnyj o RUS 96-97 G 7
Ōtranto o I 100-101 G 4
Otranto, Canale d' ≈ 100-101 G 4
Otrožnyj o RUS 112-113 R 4
Otsego o USA (OH) 280-281 E 3
Otsego Lake o USA (NY) 278-279 G 6
Otselic o USA (NY) 278-279 F 6
Ōtsu ☆ J 152-153 F 7
Ōtsuki o J 152-153 H 7
Otta ~ N 86-87 C 5
Ottappidāram o IND 140-141 H 6
Ottawa ★• CDN (ONT) 238-239 K 3
Ottawa o USA (IL) 274-275 K 3
Ottawa o USA (KS) 262-263 L 6
Ottawa o USA (OH) 280-281 B 2
Ottawa Islands ⌒ CDN 36-37 J 5
Ottawa River ~ CDN (ONT) 238-239 F 2
Otte Krupens Fjord ≈ 28-29 U 5
Ottenby o S 86-87 H 8
Otter o CDN (QUE) 242-243 E 3
Otter o USA (MT) 250-251 N 6
Otter, Peaks of ▲ USA (VA) 280-281 G 6
Otterburne o CDN (MAN) 234-235 G 5
Otter Creek o USA (FL) 286-287 G 2
Otter Creek ~ USA (UT) 254-255 D 5
Otter Creek ~ USA (VT) 278-279 H 5
Otter Creek Reserve o USA (UT) 254-255 D 5
Otter Head ▲ CDN (ONT) 236-237 B 4
Otter Island ⌒ CDN (ONT) 236-237 B 4
Otter Island ⌒ USA 22-23 L 4
Otter Lake o CDN (QUE) 238-239 J 3
Otter Lake o USA (MI) 272-273 F 4
Otter Lake o USA (IL) 274-275 J 5
Otterøyane, Von ⌒ N 84-85 M 3
Otter Point ▲ USA 22-23 P 5
Otter Rapids o CDN (ONT) 236-237 G 2
Otter River ~ CDN 34-35 M 4
Otter Rock o USA (OR) 244-245 A 6
Ottertail o USA (MN) 270-271 C 4
Otthon o CDN (SAS) 232-233 Q 4
Otto Fiord ≈ 26-27 F 3
Otto-Sala ~ RUS 110-111 S 7
Ottosdal o ZA 220-221 G 3
Ottoshoop o ZA 220-221 G 2
Ottuk o KS 146-147 C 4
Ottumwa o USA (IA) 274-275 F 3
Otu o CAM 204-205 H 6
Otukamamoan Lake o CDN (ONT) 234-235 L 6
Otukpa o WAN 204-205 G 5
Otumpa o RA 76-77 F 4
Otuquis, Bañados de o BOL 70-71 H 6
Otuquis, Río ~ BOL 70-71 H 6
Oturkpo o WAN 204-205 H 5
Otu Tolu Group ⌒ TON 184 IV a 2
Otuzco o PE 64-65 C 5
Otway o USA (OH) 280-281 C 5
Otway, Cape ▲ AUS 180-181 G 5
Otway, Seno ≈ 80 E 6
Otway National Park ⊥ AUS 180-181 G 5
Otwell o USA (AR) 276-277 E 5
Oua ~ G 210-211 D 3
Ouachita, Lake o USA (AR) 276-277 B 6
Ouachita Mountains ▲ USA (OK) 264-265 J 4
Ouachita River ~ USA (AR) 276-277 C 7
Ouachita River ~ USA (LA) 268-269 J 4
Ouadda o RCA 206-207 F 4
Ouaddaï ◘ TCH 198-199 K 6
Ouâd Nâga o RIM 196-197 C 6
Ouadou ~ RIM 196-197 E 7
Ouagadougou ★ BF 202-203 K 3
Ouagar, I-n- o RN 198-199 C 4
Ouahabou o BF 202-203 J 4
Ouahigouya ☆ BF 202-203 J 3
Ouaka ◘ RCA 206-207 E 6
Ouaka ~ RCA 206-207 E 6
Ouaké o DY 202-203 L 5
Oualâta o RIM 196-197 G 6
Oualâta, Dahr ⊥ RIM 196-197 G 6
Oualia o RMM 202-203 E 3
Oualla ▲ RG 202-203 E 4
Ouallam o RN 204-205 E 1
Ouana ~ G 210-211 D 4
Ouanary o F 62-63 J 3
Ouanazein < TCH 198-199 H 4
Ouanda Djallé o• RCA 206-207 F 4
Ouandago o RCA 206-207 D 5
Ouandja o RCA (Kot) 206-207 F 4
Ouandja ~ RCA 206-207 F 4
Ouandja-Vakaga, Réserve de faune de la ⊥ RCA 206-207 F 4
Ouando o RCA 206-207 G 6
Ouango o RCA 206-207 F 6
Ouangolodougou o CI 202-203 H 5
Ouaninou o• CI 202-203 G 5
Ouara ~ RCA 206-207 G 6
Ouarak o SN 202-203 B 2
Ouareau, Rivière ~ CDN (QUE) 238-239 M 2
Ouargaye o BF 202-203 L 4
Ouargla ☆• DZ 190-191 E 5
Ouaritoufoulout < RMM 196-197 M 6
Ouarkla o CAM 206-207 B 4
Ouarkziz, Jbel ⊥ MA 188-189 F 6
Ouarsenis, Massif de l' ▲ DZ 190-191 C 3
Ouarzazate ☆ MA 188-189 H 5
Ouassa Bamvélé o CAM 204-205 K 6
Ouatagouna o RMM 202-203 L 2
Ouatcha o RN 198-199 D 6
Ouatéré Galafondo o RCA 206-207 D 6
Oubangui ~ RCA 210-211 G 1
Ouchi o VRC 156-157 H 2
Oudâne o• RIM 196-197 E 4
Ouday ~ RIM 196-197 C 4
Oudenaarde o• B 92-93 G 3
Oudjilla o• CAM 206-207 B 3
Oudna • TN 190-191 H 2
Oudtshoorn o ZA 220-221 F 6
Oued el Abiod ~ RIM 196-197 D 6
Oued el Hajar < RMM 196-197 J 5
Oueden Nsa ~ DZ 190-191 D 4
Oued Mimoun ☆ DZ 188-189 L 3
Oued Rhiou o DZ 190-191 C 3
Oued Rhir ⊥ DZ 190-191 F 4
Oued Tlelat o DZ 188-189 L 3
Oued-Zem o MA 188-189 H 4
Oued Zenati o DZ 190-191 F 2
Ouéléssébougou o RMM 202-203 G 4
Ouéllé o CI 202-203 H 6

Ongandjera — Ouéllé 373

Ouémé ~ DY 204-205 E 5
Ouémé = Affon ~ DY 202-203 L 5
Ouenkoro o RMM 202-203 J 4
Ouénou o DY 204-205 E 4
Ouenza o DZ 190-191 G 3
Oué-Oué o DY 204-205 E 4
Ouerrha, Oued ~ MA 188-189 J 3
Ouessa o BF 202-203 J 4
Ouessant ~ F 90-91 E 7
Ouèssè o DY 204-205 E 4
Ouest, Pointe de l' ▲ CDN (QUE) 242-243 D 3
Ouest = West □ CAM 204-205 J 6
Ouezzane o RMA 188-189 J 3
Oufrane o DZ 190-191 C 6
Ougarou o BF 202-203 L 3
Oughterard = Uachtar Ard ~ IRL 90-91 C 5
Ougoué ~ RCB 210-211 D 5
Ouham o RCA 206-207 C 6
Ouham-Pendé □ RCA 206-207 B 5
Ouidah o DY 204-205 E 4
Ouidi o RN 198-199 F 5
Ouinardène o RMM 196-197 K 6
Ouinhi o DY 204-205 E 4
Oujâf ≈ RMM 196-197 D 4
Oujeft o RIM 196-197 D 4
Ou Jiang ~ VRC 156-157 M 2
Ouka ~ RCA 206-207 E 5
Oukaïmeden o MA 188-189 H 5
Oukal o AFG 134-135 J 2
Oukraal o ZA 220-221 D 7
Oukré o RIM 196-197 E 6
Oula, Madina- o RG 202-203 D 5
Oulad Allenda o DZ 190-191 F 4
Ouled Djellal o DZ 190-191 E 3
Ouled Naïl, Monts de ▲ DZ 190-191 D 2
Ouli o CAM 204-205 J 4
Oulmes o MA 188-189 J 4
Oulnina Hill ▲ AUS 180-181 G 2
Oulu ~ FIN 88-89 H 4
Oulu, Bahr ~ RCA 206-207 F 3
Oulujärvi ~ FIN 88-89 H 4
Oulujoki ~ FIN 88-89 H 4
Oum, Bahr ~ TN 190-191 F 4
Oumache o DZ 190-191 E 3
Oumba ~ G 210-211 C 4
Oum-Chalouba o TCH 198-199 K 5
Oumcheggag ~ MA 188-189 J 7
Oum Djerane o DZ 190-191 C 3
Oumé ~ CI 202-203 H 6
Oum el Achar o DZ 188-189 G 6
Oum el Bouaghi ☆ DZ 190-191 F 3
Oum er Rbia, Oued ~ MA 188-189 J 4
Oum-Hadjer o TCH 198-199 J 6
Oumm Debua, Sebkha o MA 188-189 E 7
Oumm ed Droûs Guebli, Sebkhet o RIM 196-197 E 3
Oumm ed Droûs Telli, Sebkhet o RIM 196-197 E 2
Oumm el Khezz o RMM 196-197 E 6
Ounâne, Bir o RMM 196-197 J 4
Ounane, Djebel ▲ DZ 190-191 F 8
Ounara o MA 188-189 G 5
Ounasjoki ~ FIN 88-89 H 3
Ounay, Kôtal-e ▲ AFG 138-139 B 2
Oundou ~ RG 202-203 H 7
Oungre o CDN (SAS) 232-233 P 6
Ounianga Kébir o TCH 198-199 K 3
Ounianga Sérir o TCH 198-199 K 3
Ountivou o RT 202-203 L 6
Ouo o RMM 202-203 J 2
Ouogo o RCA 206-207 C 6
Ouray o USA (CO) 254-255 H 5
Ouray o USA (UT) 254-255 F 3
Ourei ~ RIM 196-197 G 6
Ouré-Kaba o RG 202-203 D 5
Ourém o BR 68-69 E 2
Ourense (Orense) o E 98-99 D 3
Ouret, Oued ~ DZ 190-191 G 8
Ouricana, Serra do ▲ BR 72-73 J 4
Ouricuri o BR 68-69 H 5
Ourikéla o RMM 202-203 H 3
Ourilândia o BR 68-69 C 5
Ourinhos o BR 72-73 F 7
Ourini o TCH 198-199 L 4
Ourique o P 98-99 C 6
Ourlal o DZ 190-191 E 3
Ouro o BR 72-73 F 2
Ouro Amat o SN 202-203 D 2
Ouro Branco o BR 68-69 H 7
Ourofane o RN 198-199 D 5
Ouro Fino o BR 72-73 G 7
Ouro Prêto ~ BR 72-73 J 6
Ouro Preto d'Oeste o BR 70-71 F 2
Ouro Sawabé o RN 202-203 U 3
Ouro Sogui o SN 202-203 D 2
Ourou Rapids ~ WAN 204-205 F 4
Ouro Velho o BR 68-69 K 5
Oursi o BF 202-203 K 2
Oursi, Mare de o BF 202-203 K 2
Ous o RUS 114-115 K 4
Ou-sanmyaku ▲ J 152-153 J 5
Ouse ~ GB 90-91 G 5
Oushutou o VRC 154-155 L 4
Oussouye o SN 202-203 B 3
Oust, Djebel ▲ DZ 188-189 L 4
Outamba-Kilimbi National Park ⊥ WAL 202-203 D 5
Outaouais o CDN (ONT) 238-239 H 2
Outaouais, River ~ CDN (ONT) 238-239 K 3
Outaouais, Rivière des ~ CDN (QUE) 236-237 G 3
Outaouais, Rivière des ~ CDN (QUE) 236-237 G 3
Outaouais, Rivière des ~ CDN (QUE) 238-239 G 3
Outardes, Rivière ~ CDN 38-39 K 3
Outardes, Rivière aux ~ CDN 38-39 K 3

Outardes Quatre, Réservoir < CDN 38-39 K 3
Outat-Oulad-El-Haj o MA 188-189 K 4
Outeid Arkass o RMM 196-197 H 6
Outeniekwaberge ▲ ZA 220-221 E 6
Outer Bill Bailey Bank = Outer Bailey Bank ≈ 90-91 A 1
Outer Hebrides ~ GB 90-91 D 2
Outer Island ~ USA (WI) 270-271 H 3
Outfine o USA (MN) 270-271 E 4
Outing o USA (MN) 270-271 E 4
Outjo o NAM 216-217 D 10
Outlet Bay o CDN 30-31 T 4
Outlook o CDN (SAS) 232-233 L 5
Outlook o USA (MT) 250-251 P 3
Outokumpu o FIN 88-89 K 5
Outoul o DZ 190-191 E 9
Ouzibi ~ G 210-211 C 5
Ouzina o DZ 190-191 E 9
Ouzouda, Cascades d' ~·· MA 188-189 H 4
Ouzzeine, Adrar- ⊥ RMM 196-197 L 5
Ovalau ~ FJI 184 III b 2
Ovalle o RCH 76-77 B 6
Ovamboland ⊥ NAM 216-217 C 9
Ovan o G 210-211 D 3
Ovana, Cerro ▲ YV 60-61 H 5
Ovando o USA (MT) 250-251 F 4
Ovar o P 98-99 C 4
Ovau Island ~ SOL 184 I c 2
Ovcynia, proliv ≈ RUS 108-109 S 5
Ovejas, Cerro de las ▲ RA 78-79 G 2
Ovejería o RA 78-79 F 3
Oveng o CAM 210-211 C 3
Ovens, The .:. CDN (NS) 240-241 L 6
Ovens Natural Park ⊥ CDN (NS) 240-241 L 6
Ovens River ~ AUS 180-181 J 4
Overflowing River ~ CDN 34-35 H 3
Overflowing River ~ CDN (SAS) 232-233 J 2
Overgaard o USA (AZ) 256-257 E 4
Øvergård o N 86-87 J 4
Överkalix o S 86-87 L 3
Overlander Roadhouse o AUS 176-177 C 3
Overland Park o USA (KS) 262-263 M 6
Overton o USA (NV) 248-249 G 6
Overton o USA (TX) 264-265 H 6
Övertorneå o S 86-87 L 3
Øverum o S 86-87 H 8
Ovett o USA (MS) 268-269 L 5
Ovgog ~ RUS 116-117 K 3
Ovid o USA (ID) 252-253 G 4
Ovid o USA (MI) 272-273 E 5
Ovid o USA (NY) 278-279 G 6
Oviedo o DOM 54-55 K 6
Oviedo = Uviéu o ☆ E 98-99 E 3
Ôvögdij ~ MAU 148-149 F 5
Övör-Hangaj □ MAU 148-149 F 5
Ovražnaja, gora ▲ RUS 108-109 j 3
Øvre Anarjokka nasjonalpark ⊥ N 86-87 J 2
Øvre Dividal nasjonalpark ⊥ N 86-87 J 2
Øvre Pasvik Nasjonalpark ⊥ N 86-87 O 2
Øvre Soppero o S 86-87 K 2
Ovruč o UA 102-103 F 2
Ovsjanka o RUS 118-119 N 9
Owaka o NZ 182 B 7
Owalama Range ▲ PNG 183 B 3
Owando o RCB 210-211 E 4
Owa Rafa = Santa Ana Island ~ SOL 184 I f 4
Owase o J 152-153 G 7
Owa Riki = Santa Catalina Island ~ SOL 184 I f 4
Owatonna o USA (MN) 270-271 E 6
Owdoms o USA (SC) 284-285 J 3
Oweenee, Mount ▲ USA 174-175 H 6
Owego o USA (NY) 278-279 F 6
Owen o USA (WI) 270-271 H 6
Owen, Islas ~ RCH 80 C 5
Owen, River ~ WAN 204-205 F 5
Owena o WAN 204-205 G 6
Owen Bay o CDN (BC) 230-231 D 3
Owen Channel ≈ CDN 238-239 D 3
Owen Falls Dam < EAU 212-213 D 3
Owen Fracture Zone ≃ 12 D 4
Owens ~ USA (VA) 280-281 J 5
Owensboro o USA (KY) 276-277 H 3
Owens Lake o USA (CA) 248-249 G 5
Owen Sound o• CDN (ONT) 238-239 E 4
Owen Sound ≈ CDN 238-239 E 4
Owen Springs o AUS 176-177 M 1
Owens River ~ USA (CA) 248-249 F 2
Owen Stanley Range ▲ PNG 183 B 3
Owensville o USA (IN) 274-275 L 6
Owensville o USA (MO) 274-275 G 6
Owenton o USA (KY) 276-277 L 2
Owerri o WAN 204-205 G 6
Owikeno Lake o CDN (BC) 230-231 B 2
Owl Creek ~ USA (WY) 252-253 K 3
Owl Creek Mountains ▲ USA (WY) 252-253 K 3
Owl River o USA 32-33 P 4
Owl River o CDN 34-35 K 2
Owo o WAN 204-205 G 6
Owode o WAN 204-205 E 5
Owosso o USA (MI) 272-273 E 5
Owutu o WAN 204-205 G 6
Owyhee o USA (NV) 246-247 J 2
Owyhee, Lake o USA (OR) 244-245 H 3
Owyhee Ridge ▲ USA (OR) 244-245 H 8
Oxapampa o PE 64-65 E 7
Oxberry o USA (MS) 268-269 K 3
Oxbow o CDN (SAS) 232-233 Q 6
Oxbow o US 220-221 J 4
Oxdrift o CDN (ONT) 234-235 L 5
Oxelösund o S 86-87 H 7
Oxenhope Out Station o AUS 178-179 H 4
Oxford o CDN (NS) 240-241 M 5
Oxford o·· GB 90-91 G 6
Oxford o NZ 182 D 5
Oxford o USA (AL) 284-285 E 4
Oxford o USA (AR) 276-277 D 4
Oxford o USA (IN) 274-275 L 4

Oxford o USA (KS) 262-263 J 7
Oxford o USA (MI) 272-273 F 5
Oxford o USA (MS) 268-269 L 2
Oxford o USA (NC) 282-283 J 4
Oxford o USA (NE) 262-263 G 4
Oxford o USA (OH) 280-281 E 5
Oxford o USA (PA) 280-281 J 5
Oxford House o CDN 34-35 H 3
Oxford House Indian Reserve X CDN 34-35 J 3
Oxford Junction o USA (IA) 274-275 H 3
Oxford Lake o CDN 34-35 H 3
Oxford Peak ▲ USA (ID) 252-253 F 4
Oxley o AUS (NSW) 268-269 M 4
Oxley Highway II AUS 178-179 L 6
Oxnard o USA (CA) 248-249 E 5
Oxville o USA (IL) 274-275 H 5
Oya o MAL 162-163 J 3
Oyabi o RCB 210-211 E 4
Oya-Kannon • J 152-153 H 6
Oyama o CDN (BC) 230-231 K 3
Oyama o J 152-153 H 6
Oyan, River ~ WAN 204-205 D 5
Oyapok ~ F 62-63 H 4
Oyarbide, Cerro ▲ RCH 70-71 B 7
Oyem o G 210-211 C 3
Oyen o CDN (ALB) 232-233 H 4
Øyeren o N 86-87 E 7
Oyé Yeska o TCH 198-199 J 3
Oyo o RCB 210-211 E 4
Oyo o WAN (OYO) 204-205 E 5
Oyo □ WAN 204-205 E 5
Oyou Bezzé Denga o RN 198-199 F 4
Oyoué o G 210-211 C 3
Øyrlandssodden ▲ N 84-85 K 4
Øyslebø o N 86-87 C 7
Oysterville o USA (WA) 244-245 A 4
Özalp o TR 128-129 K 3
Ozamiz o RP 160-161 E 8
Ozark o USA (AL) 284-285 E 5
Ozark o USA (AR) 276-277 B 5
Ozark o USA (MO) 276-277 B 3
Ozark National Scenic Riverways ⊥ USA (MO) 276-277 D 3
Ozark Plateau ▲ USA (MO) 276-277 A 4
Ozarks, Lake of the o USA (MO) 274-275 F 6
Ozark Wonder Cave .:. USA (MO) 276-277 A 4
Ozarów o PL 92-93 Q 3
Özen o KA 126-127 K 6
Ozerki o RUS 96-97 E 5
Ozernaja ~ RUS 108-109 S 6
Ozernaja ~ RUS 120-121 T 5
Ozërnoe o RUS 120-121 M 7
Ozernoj, poluostrov ~ RUS 108-109 U 5
Ozernoj, zaliv ≈ RUS 120-121 U 5
Ozërnyj o RUS 112-113 V 3
Ozerskij o RUS 122-123 R 3
Ozërskoe, Sosnovo o RUS 118-119 E 9
Ozery o RUS 94-95 Q 4
Oždaevo o RUS 122-123 K 5
Ozieri o I 100-101 B 4
Ozimek o PL 92-93 P 3
Özinki o RUS 96-97 F 8
Ozogno ~ RUS 110-111 X 6
Ozogino, ozero o RUS 110-111 a 5
Ozona o USA (TX) 266-267 E 7
Ozondati o NAM 216-217 C 10
Ozone o USA (AR) 276-277 B 5
Ozori o G 210-211 B 4
Ozorków o PL 92-93 P 3
Ozoro o WAN 204-205 G 6
Özu o J 152-153 E 7
Ozuluama o MEX 50-51 L 7
Ozurgeti o GE 126-127 E 7

P

Pa o BF 202-203 J 4
Paakitsup Nunaa ∪ GRØ 28-29 P 2
Paama o VAN 184 II b 3
Paama = Île Pau Uma ~ VAN 184 II b 3
Paamiut = Frederikshåb o GRØ 28-29 Q 5
Pa-an o MYA 158-159 D 2
Paanto o RI 164-165 G 4
Paarl o ZA 220-221 D 6
Pauailo o USA (HI) 288 K 4
Pabal o IND 138-139 E 10
Pabbiring, Kepulauan ~ RI 164-165 F 6
Pabean o RI 164 B 4
Pabedanå o IR 134-135 G 3
Pabellón, El .:. MEX 52-53 J 3
Pabianice o PL 92-93 P 3
Pablo o USA (MT) 250-251 F 4
Pabna o BD 142-143 F 4
Pabradé o LT 94-95 J 4
Pab Range ▲ PK 134-135 M 5
Pacaás Novos, Parque Nacional de ⊥ BR 70-71 F 2
Pacaás Novos, Rio ~ BR 70-71 E 2
Pacaás Novos, Serra dos ▲ BR 70-71 E 2
Pacacocha, Rio ~ BR 64-65 F 4
Pacaembu o BR 72-73 E 6
Pacahuaras, Rio ~ BOL 70-71 D 2
Pacajá, Rio ~ BR 68-69 C 3
Pacajás, Rio ~ BR 68-69 C 3
Pacajus o BR 68-69 J 4
Pacapausa o PE 64-65 E 9
Pacaraima, Sierra ▲ YV 60-61 K 5
Pacaraos o PE 64-65 D 7
Pacasmayo o PE 64-65 C 5
Pacatuba o BR 68-69 J 4
Pacaya-Samiria, Reserva Nacional ⊥ PE 64-65 C 4
Pác Bo o VN 156-157 D 5

Pác Bó o VN 156-157 D 5
Paccha o EC 64-65 C 3
Pacchani o PE 70-71 C 5
Pacet o RI 168 I 3
Pachacámac o EC 64-65 C 3
Pachacámac • PE (LIM) 64-65 D 8
Pachaconas o PE 64-65 F 9
Pachino o RI 164-165 D 5
Pachitea, Rio ~ PE 64-65 E 6
Pacho o CO 60-61 D 5
Pachon, El o RA 78-79 B 6
Pachuca de Soto ☆ MEX 52-53 E 1
Paciá o BR 66-67 E 6
Paciá, Rio ~ BR 66-67 E 6
Paciencia, Llano de la ⊥ RCH 76-77 C 3
Pacific o CDN (BC) 228-229 F 2
Pacific o USA (MO) 274-275 H 6
Pacifica o USA (CA) 248-249 B 2
Pacific Beach o USA (WA) 244-245 A 3
Pacific Grove o USA (CA) 248-249 C 3
Pacific House o USA (CA) 246-247 E 3
Pacific Ocean ≈ 14-15 H 4
Pacific Ranges ▲ CDN (BC) 230-231 D 3
Pacific Rim National Park ⊥ CDN (BC) 230-231 D 5
Pacijan Island ~ RP 160-161 F 7
Paciran o RI 168 E 3
Pacitan o RI 168 D 4
Packington o CDN (QUE) 240-241 G 3
Packsaddle o AUS 178-179 F 6
Packwood o USA (WA) 244-245 C 4
Pác Ma o VN 156-157 C 5
Pacolet o USA (SC) 284-285 J 2
Pacolet River ~ USA (SC) 284-285 J 2
Pacora o PA 52-53 E 7
Pacoval o BR 66-67 K 4
Pacquet o CDN (NFL) 242-243 N 3
Pac Seng o LAO 156-157 C 6
Pacuária da Barra do Longa o ANG 216-217 B 5
Pacuativa o CO 66-67 B 2
Pacucha, Lago o PE 64-65 F 8
Pacul, Rio ~ BR 72-73 H 4
Pacujá o BR 68-69 H 4
Pacuneiro, Rio ~ BR 72-73 D 4
Pacuting, Igarapé ~ BR 66-67 H 7
Padag o RK 134-135 L 4
Padako o CI 202-203 H 7
Padalere o RI 164-165 H 6
Padam o IND 138-139 F 3
Padang o RI 162-163 D 5
Padang, Pulau ~ RI 162-163 E 4
Padang, Selat ≈ 162-163 E 4
Padangan o RI 162-163 H 7
Padangcermin o RI 162-163 F 7
Padangguci o RI 162-163 E 7
Padangpanjang o RI 162-163 D 5
Padang Sidempuan o RI 162-163 C 4
Padang Tikar, Tanjung ▲ RI 162-163 H 5
Padany o RUS 88-89 M 5
Padar, Pulau ~ RI 168 I 7
Padauiri, Rio ~ BR 66-67 E 2
Padawan o CL 140-141 J 6
Padawiya o CL 140-141 J 6
Paddle River ~ CDN 32-33 N 4
Paddock ~ CDN (SAS) 232-233 N 2
Padeabesar, Pulau ~ RI 164-165 H 6
Paden City o USA (WV) 280-281 F 4
Padeniya o CL 140-141 J 6
Paderborn o D 92-93 K 3
Padibe o EAU 212-213 D 2
Padilla o BOL 70-71 E 6
Padillas, Los o USA (NM) 256-257 J 4
Padjelanta nationalpark ⊥ S 86-87 H 3
Padlei (abandoned) o CDN 30-31 V 5
Padloping Island ~ CDN 28-29 J 3
Padma ~ BD 142-143 F 4
Padmanábhapuram o IND 140-141 G 6
Padova ☆ • I 100-101 C 2
Padrauna o IND 142-143 C 2
Padre, Morro do ▲ BR 72-73 G 4
Padre Angel Buodo o RA 78-79 G 4
Padre Bernardo o BR 72-73 F 5
Padre Isla ~ PE 64-65 F 3
Padre Island ~ USA (TX) 266-267 K 6
Padre Island National Seashore ⊥ USA (TX) 266-267 K 6
Padre Paraíso o BR 72-73 J 4
Padriya o NEP 144-145 E 7
Padrón ~ E 98-99 C 3
Padrone, Cape ▲ ZA 220-221 H 6
Paducah o USA (KY) 276-277 G 3
Paducah o USA (TX) 264-265 D 4
Padun o RUS 114-115 J 6
Padun, Vodopad ~ RUS 88-89 O 3
Paduro o PE 64-65 D 7
Paëm o BR 68-69 G 6
Paemleu-Umi ~ USA (HI) 288 K 4
Paeroa o NZ 182 E 2
Paestum ·• I 100-101 E 4
Paete o RP 160-161 D 5
Pafos ~ CY 128-129 E 5
Pafúri o MOC 218-219 F 6
Pafuri ~ ZA 218-219 F 6
Pafuri Gate ~ ZA 218-219 F 6
Pag ~ HR 100-101 E 2
Pagadenbaru o RI 168 I 3
Pagadian o RP 160-161 E 9
Pagai, Kepulauan ~ RI 162-163 C 6
Pagai Selatan, Pulau ~ RI 162-163 C 6
Pagai Utara, Pulau ~ RI 162-163 C 6

Pagalu, Isla de = Annobón ~ GQ 210-211 a 3
Pagan ~ MYA 142-143 J 5
Pagani Bay ≈ 212-213 G 6
Paganzo o RA 76-77 D 6
Pagaralam o RI 162-163 E 7
Pagas Gîrîngaj ~ RI 168 C 7
Pagatan o RI 164-165 G 6
Page o USA (AZ) 256-257 D 3
Page o USA (ND) 258-259 K 4
Page o USA (OK) 264-265 K 4
Pagėgiai o RUS 94-95 G 4
Pageland o USA (SC) 284-285 K 2
Pagergunung o RI 168 C 7
Pagimana o RI 164-165 H 4
Pagmán o AFG 138-139 B 2
Pagoh o MAL 162-163 E 3
Pago Pago o USA 184 V 2
Pagosa Springs o USA (CO) 254-255 H 6
Pagou o BF 202-203 L 3
Pagouda o RT 202-203 L 5
Pagri o VRC 144-145 G 7
Pagu o VRC 156-157 M 2
Paguyaman o RI 164-165 H 4
Paguyaman ~ RI 164-165 H 4
Pagwachuan Lake o CDN (ONT) 236-237 G 4
Pagwachuan River ~ CDN (ONT) 236-237 G 4
Pagwa River o CDN (ONT) 236-237 C 2
Pagwi o PNG 183 B 3
Pahaća ~ RUS 112-113 P 6
Pahači o RUS 112-113 P 6
Pahačinskij hrebet ▲ RUS 112-113 P 6
Pahala o USA (HI) 288 K 5
Pahang □ MAL 162-163 E 3
Pahang ~ MAL 162-163 E 3
Paharpur o BD 142-143 F 3
Pahárpur o PK 138-139 C 3
Pahaska Tepee o USA (WY) 252-253 J 2
Pahiatua o NZ 182 E 4
Pahn Wroal o LB 202-203 F 7
Pahoa o USA (HI) 288 L 5
Pahokee o USA (FL) 286-287 J 5
Pahoturi River ~ PNG 183 B 4
Pah River ~ USA 20-21 N 3
Pahrump o USA (NV) 248-249 J 3
Pahsien Cave • RC 156-157 M 5
Pahu o IND 138-139 E 9
Pahute Peak ▲ USA (NV) 246-247 F 2
Pai o THA 142-143 J 6
Pai, River ~ WAN 204-205 J 4
Paia o USA (HI) 288 J 4
Paicurú, Rio ~ BR 62-63 H 6
Paide o EST 94-95 J 2
Paiela o PNG 183 B 3
Paige o USA (TX) 266-267 K 3
Paiján o PE 64-65 C 5
Päijänne o FIN 88-89 H 6
Paijärvi o FIN 88-89 J 6
Paiko o WAN 204-205 G 4
Pail o PK 138-139 D 3
Paila o USA 50-51 H 5
Paila, Rio ~ BOL 70-71 F 5
Pailillo o K 156-157 H 5
Paillaco o RCH 78-79 C 6
Pailón o BOL 70-71 F 5
Pailou o VRC 148-149 N 7
Paimbu o WAN 204-205 J 4
Paimio o FIN 88-89 G 6
Paim Filho o BR 74-75 E 6
Painan o RI 162-163 D 5
Painan, Teluk ≈ 162-163 D 5
Paine o RCH 78-79 D 4
Paineiras o BR 72-73 H 5
Painel o BR 74-75 F 6
Painesville o USA (OH) 280-281 G 2
Paint Creek ~ USA (OH) 280-281 C 4
Paint Creek Lake < USA (OH) 280-281 C 4
Painted Desert ⊥ USA (AZ) 256-257 D 2
Painted Rock Ranch o USA (CA) 248-249 E 4
Paint Lake o CDN 34-35 G 3
Paint Lake Provincial Park ⊥ CDN 34-35 H 3
Paint Rock o USA (TX) 266-267 H 2
Paint Rock River ~ USA (AL) 284-285 D 2
Paintsville o USA (KY) 276-277 N 3
Paipa o CO 60-61 E 5
Paipote o RCH 76-77 C 6
Paipote, Quebrada ~ RCH 76-77 B 4
Paisano o USA (TX) 266-267 D 7
Paishe o RC 156-157 N 3
Paisley o CDN (ONT) 238-239 D 4
Paisley o GB 90-91 E 4
Paisley o USA (OR) 244-245 E 8
Paita o PE 64-65 B 4
Paita, Bahía de ≈ 64-65 B 4
Paitan, Teluk ≈ 160-161 B 9
Paiton o RI 168 E 3
Pajala o S 86-87 L 3
Pajale o RI 164-165 F 5
Pajapita o GCA 52-53 H 4
Pajaro o CO 60-61 E 2
Pajaros, Islas ~ RCH 76-77 B 6
Pajdugina ~ RUS 114-115 S 5
Pajer, gora ▲ RUS 108-109 L 8
Pajeú, Rio ~ BR 68-69 J 6
Pajona, Cerro ▲ RCH 76-77 C 1
Pajonales, Salar de ~ RCH 76-77 C 3
Pajtug o US 136-137 N 4
Pajule o EAU 212-213 D 2
Pakaá-Nova, Área Indígena X BR 70-71 F 2
Pakabong o PNG 183 B 3
Pakakui o SME 62-63 G 3
Pakapaka o SME 62-63 G 3
Pakaraima Mountains ▲ GUY 62-63 D 3

Pakari o NEP 144-145 F 7
Pakashkan Lake o CDN (ONT) 234-235 N 5
Pak Charang o THA 158-159 G 3
Pakenham o AUS 180-181 H 5
Paket o USA 180-181 H 5
Paki o WAN 204-205 H 3
Pakiangan, Tanjung ▲ RI 168 C 7
Pak Island ~ PNG 183 B 2
Pakistan = Pákistán ■ PK 134-135 K 4
Pakokku o MYA 142-143 J 4
Pakowki Lake o CDN (ALB) 232-233 G 6
Päkpattan o PK 138-139 D 4
Päkpattan Canal < PK 138-139 D 4
Pak Phanang o THA 158-159 F 6
Pakrac o HR 100-101 F 2
Pakri ~ NEP 144-145 D 7
Pakruojis o ~ LT 94-95 H 4
Paksa, mys ▲ RUS 110-111 J 3
Paksa Dinh o CAM 156-157 D 7
Pak To o THA 158-159 E 4
Paktiká □ AFG 138-139 B 3
Paktyä □ AFG 138-139 B 3
Pakuli o RI 164-165 F 5
Pakuliha ~ RUS 114-115 T 2
Pakwach o EAU 212-213 C 2
Pakwash Lake o CDN (ONT) 234-235 K 4
Pakxé o LAO 158-159 H 3
Pal o SN 196-197 B 7
Pala o CDN 206-207 B 7
Pala o USA (CA) 248-249 G 6
Palabaka o RCB 210-211 E 4
Palabora ~ ZA 220-221 J 2
Palabuhanratu o RI 168 B 3
Palabuhanratu, Teluk ≈ 168 B 3
Palace Museum Dalem Loka ★ RI 168 C 7
Palace Wolio, Fort ~· RI 164-165 H 6
Palacios, Gruta del ★ ROU 78-79 L 2
Palacios o BOL (BEN) 70-71 D 3
Palacios o BOL (BEN) 70-71 D 3
Palacios o RA 76-77 G 4
Palácio, Serra do ~ BR 266-267 L 5
Palacios o YV 60-61 H 3
Palacios, Los o C 54-55 D 3
Palacode o IND 140-141 H 4
palac Pereni · UA 102-103 C 3
Palaes o RI 164-165 J 3
Palafox Ruins .:. USA (TX) 266-267 H 6
Palafrugell o E 98-99 J 4
Palagruža ~ HR 100-101 F 3
Palahana o IND 142-143 B 3
Palai, le o F 90-91 F 8
Palaiyam o IND 140-141 H 5
Palala o LB 202-203 F 6
Palala o ZA 220-221 J 2
Palamau National Park ⊥ IND 142-143 D 4
Palame o BR 72-73 M 2
Palamea o RI 164-165 K 4
Palamós o E 98-99 J 4
Palana ☆ RUS 120-121 S 4
Palana ☆ RUS 120-121 T 4
Palanan Bay ≈ 160-161 E 4
Palangán, Küh-e ▲ IR 134-135 J 3
Palangkaraya ☆ RI 162-163 K 6
Palani o IND 140-141 G 5
Palankova o PK 134-135 N 4
Palaoa, Lae o BR 218-219 D 6
Palapye o BW 218-219 D 6
Palasa o RI 164-165 G 3
Palasamudram o IND 140-141 G 4
Palasan Island ~ RP 160-161 E 5
Palasbari o BD 142-143 F 3
Palašt o IR 136-137 B 7
Palatae o RI 164-165 J 4
Palatka ☆ RUS 120-121 O 3
Palatka o USA (FL) 286-287 H 2
Palau ■ PAL (CRO) 13 G 2
Palau o MEX 50-51 J 4
Palauco, Sierra de ▲ RA 78-79 E 3
Palauk o MYA 158-159 E 4
Palavaanskij hrebet ▲ RUS 112-113 T 2
Palaw o MYA 158-159 E 4
Palawan ~ RP 160-161 B 8
Palawan Passage ≈ 160-161 B 8
Palayankottai o IND 140-141 G 6
Palazzo Farnese · I 100-101 D 3
Palazzolo Acréide o I 100-101 E 5
Palca o PE 64-65 E 7
Palca o RCH 70-71 C 6
Palca, Rio de la ~ RA 76-77 C 5
Palcamayo o PE 64-65 E 7
Palcazú, Rio ~ PE 64-65 E 7
Paleiheuwel o ZA 220-221 D 6
Paleleh o RI 164-165 H 3
Paleleh, Pegunungan ▲ RI 164-165 J 3
Palelon o RI 164-165 J 3
Palembang ☆ RI 162-163 F 6
Palena o RCH 78-79 D 7
Palena, Rio ~ RCH 78-79 C 7
Palencia o • E 98-99 E 3
Palencia ★ USA (CA) 248-249 J 6
Palenque o MEX (CHI) 52-53 J 3
Palenque ·• MEX (CHI) 52-53 H 3
Palenque o PA 52-53 E 7
Palenque, Punta ▲ DOM 54-55 K 5
Palenque, Punta ▲ DOM 54-55 K 5
Paleokastritsa o GR 100-101 G 5
Palermo o CO 60-61 D 6
Palermo ☆ • I 100-101 D 5
Palermo o USA (ND) 258-259 E 3
Palermo o USA (ND) 258-259 E 3
Palestina o EC 64-65 C 3
Palestina o RCH 76-77 C 4
Palestina, Cerro ▲ RCH 76-77 C 2
Palestine o USA (AR) 276-277 E 6
Palestine o USA (TX) 268-269 E 5
Palestine, Lake < USA 264-265 J 6
Paletwa o MYA 142-143 H 5
Palevo o RUS 122-123 K 3
Pálghar o IND 138-139 D 10
Palghât o IND 140-141 G 5
Palgrave, Mount ▲ AUS 176-177 C 1
Palha, Rio ~ BR 70-71 G 2
Palhano, Rio ~ BR 68-69 J 4
Palheta o BR 66-67 E 6
Páli o IND 138-139 D 7
Paliaike, Parque Nacional ⊥ RCH 80 F 6
Palian o THA 158-159 F 7
Paliat, Pulau ~ RI 168 E 4
Palimbang o RP 160-161 F 9
Palindi o RI 168 E 8
Palisade o USA (CO) 254-255 G 4
Palisade o USA (NE) 262-263 E 4
Palisades Reservoir < USA (ID) 252-253 G 4
Palit o RI 168 I 7
Pälitäna o ·· IND 138-139 C 9
Palito, El o YV 60-61 G 2
Palito, Raudal o CO 66-67 B 2
Palizada o MEX 52-53 H 2
Paljavaam ~ RUS 112-113 T 2
Palk Bay ≈ 140-141 H 6
Pálkonda o IND 142-143 C 6
Palk Strait ≈ 140-141 H 6
Palkül Co o VRC 144-145 E 6
Palladam o IND 140-141 G 5
Päl Lahara o IND 142-143 D 5
Pallasa, vulkan ▲ RUS 122-123 P 5
Pallasca o PE 64-65 C 6
Pallas-ja Ounastunturin kansallispuisto ⊥ FIN 88-89 H 2
Pallastunturi ▲ ·· FIN 88-89 H 2
Pallegama o CL 140-141 J 7
Pallina, Rio ~ BOL 70-71 D 5
Palling o CDN (BC) 228-229 J 2
Pallisa o EAU 212-213 D 3
Palliser, Cape ▲ NZ 182 E 4
Palliser Bay ≈ NZ 182 E 4
Palliser River ~ CDN (BC) 230-231 O 3
Palma o MOC 214-215 L 6
Palma, La o CO 54-55 D 3
Palma, La o E 188-189 C 6
Palma, La o MEX (NAY) 50-51 G 6
Palma, La o MEX (TAB) 52-53 J 3
Palma, Rio ~ BR 72-73 G 2
Palmácia o BR 68-69 J 4
Palma del Condado, La o E 98-99 D 6
Palma del Rio o E 98-99 D 6
Palma de Mallorca ☆ E 98-99 J 5
Palmales o EC 64-65 B 3
Palmaner o IND 140-141 H 4
Palmar o EC 64-65 B 3
Palmar, El o YV 60-61 J 4
Palmar, Laguna del ~ RA 76-77 G 5
Palmar, Parque Nacional el ⊥ RA 76-77 H 6
Palmar, Represa de < ROU 78-79 L 2
Palmar, Rio ~ YV 60-61 F 3
Palmar, Salto ~ PY 76-77 H 3
Palmar de Cuautla o MEX 50-51 G 6
Palmarejo o YV 60-61 F 2
Palmares o BR (PE) 68-69 L 6
Palmar Grande o RA 76-77 H 4
Palmarin o SN 202-203 B 3
Palmarito o YV 60-61 F 4
Palmar Norte o CR 52-53 E 7
Palmas o BR (PAR) 74-75 D 6
Palmas o BR (TOC) 68-69 D 7
Palmas, Cap ▲ LB 202-203 G 7
Palmas, Barra de ~ SB 52-53 F 1
Palmas, Las ▲ PE 64-65 E 6
Palmas de Gran Canaria, Las ☆ E 188-189 C 6
Palma Sola o RA 76-77 E 2
Palma Soriano o C 54-55 H 4
Pal'mar ~ RUS 112-113 P 5
Palm Bay o USA (FL) 286-287 J 3
Palm Cove o AUS 174-175 H 5
Palmdale o USA (CA) 248-249 F 4
Palmdale o USA (FL) 286-287 H 5
Palm Desert o USA (CA) 248-249 H 6
Palmeira o BR (PAR) 74-75 D 6
Palmeira o CV 202-203 C 5
Palmeira das Missões o BR 74-75 D 6
Palmeira dos Índios o BR 68-69 K 6
Palmeirãndia o BR 68-69 F 3
Palmeirante o BR 68-69 E 5
Palmeiras o BR (BAH) 72-73 J 2
Palmeiras, Rio ~ BR 72-73 E 3
Palmeiras o BR (PIA) 68-69 G 5
Palmeiras, Cachoeira ~ BR 66-67 G 6
Palmeiras, Rio ~ BR 68-69 E 7
Palmeiras, Rio ~ BR 72-73 E 3
Palmeiras do Javari o BR 64-65 F 4
Palmeirinhas, Ponta das ▲ ANG 216-217 B 4
Palmelópolis o BR 72-73 F 2
Palmer o ARK 16 G 30
Palmer o CDN (SAS) 232-233 M 6
Palmer o USA 20-21 O 6
Palmer o USA (TX) 264-265 H 6
Palmer River ~ AUS 176-177 M 2
Palmer River ~ AUS 174-175 G 5
Palmer River ~ USA (MN) 270-271 G 4
Palmerston o CDN (ONT) 238-239 D 4
Palmerston ~ NZ 182 C 6
Palmerston, Cape ▲ AUS 178-179 K 1
Palmerston North o NZ 182 E 4
Palmerston Point ▲ CDN 24-25 X 3
Palmeton o USA (PA) 280-281 J 3
Palmeton P.O. o AUS 174-175 H 4
Palmeta, Riacho ~ RA 76-77 H 4

Pasinler ✩ **TR** 128-129 J 3
Pašino o **RUS** 114-115 R 7
Pasión, Río de la ~ **GCA** 52-53 J 3
Pasir, Tanjung ▲ **MAL** 162-163 J 3
Pasir Panjang o **MAL** 162-163 H 5
Pasir, Tanjung o **RI** 162-163 H 5
Pasirpengarayan o **RI** 162-163 D 4
Pasir Puteh o **MAL** 162-163 E 2
Pasirputih o **RI** 166-167 C 6
Pasitelu, Kepulauan ⌒ **RI** 168 E 6
Påskallavik o **S** 86-87 H 8
Paskenta o **USA** (CA) 246-247 C 4
Pasłęk o **PL** 92-93 P 1
Pasley, Cape ▲ **AUS** 176-177 G 6
Pasley Bay ≈ 24-25 Y 5
Pašman ⌒ **HR** 100-101 E 3
Pasmore River ~ **AUS** 178-179 E 6
Pasni o **PK** 134-135 K 6
Paso o **RI** 166-167 E 3
Paso, El o **USA** (IL) 274-275 J 4
Paso, El o **USA** (TX) 266-267 A 2
Paso de Indios o **RA** 78-79 E 7
Paso de la Laguna o **RA** 76-77 H 6
Paso de las Piedras, Embalse < **RA** 78-79 J 5
Paso de Lesca o **C** 54-55 G 4
Paso del Indio o **80** C 4
Paso de los Algarrobos o **RA** 78-79 F 4
Paso de los Indios o **RA** 78-79 E 7
Paso de los Libres o **RA** 78-79 H 4
Paso de los Toros o **ROU** 78-79 L 2
Paso del Rey o **RA** 78-79 F 2
Paso del Sapo o **RA** 78-79 E 7
Paso del Toro o **MEX** 52-53 F 2
Paso de Ovejas o **MEX** 52-53 F 2
Paso de Patria o **PY** 76-77 H 4
Paso Flores o **RA** 78-79 D 6
Paso Nacional o **MEX** 50-51 H 5
Paso Nuevo o **YV** 60-61 K 3
Paso Real de Macaira o **YV** 60-61 H 3
Paso Real de San Diego o **C** 54-55 D 3
Paso Robles o **USA** (CA) 248-249 D 4
Paso Rodolfo Raballos o **RA** 80 E 3
Paspébiac o **CDN** (QUE) 240-241 K 2
Pasqua o **CDN** (SAS) 232-233 P 3
Pasquatchai River ~ **CDN** 34-35 L 3
Pasquia Hills ▲ **CDN** (SAS) 232-233 P 3
Pasrur o **PK** 138-139 E 3
Passa ⌒ **G** 210-211 E 4
Passa e Fica o **BR** 68-69 L 5
Passagem o **BR** 68-69 L 5
Passagem Franca o **BR** 68-69 G 5
Passage Point ▲ **CDN** 24-25 O 4
Passamaquoddy o **CDN** ≈ 38-39 L 6
Passamaquoddy Bay ≈ **CDN** 240-241 H 5
Passau o **D** 92-93 M 4
Passayten Wilderness Area ⊥ **USA** (WA) 244-245 C 4
Passayten Wilderness Area • **USA** (WA) 244-245 C 4
Pass Christian o **USA** (MS) 268-269 L 6
Passi o **RP** 160-161 E 7
Passi o **SN** 202-203 B 3
Passira o **BR** 68-69 L 5
Pass Island ⌒ **CDN** (NFL) 242-243 M 5
Pass Lake o **CDN** (ONT) 234-235 P 6
Passmore o **CDN** (BC) 230-231 M 4
Passo da Guarda o **BR** 76-77 J 6
Passo Fundo o **BR** 74-75 D 7
Passo Fundo, Represa de < **BR** 74-75 D 6
Passo Real, Represa de < **BR** 74-75 D 7
Passos o **BR** 72-73 G 6
Passu Keah = Panshi Ju ⌒ **VRC** 158-159 L 2
Pastaza, Río ~ **PE** 64-65 D 3
Pasteur o **RA** 78-79 H 3
Pasto o **CO** 64-65 D 1
Pastol Bay ≈ 20-21 J 5
Pastor, El o **MEX** 50-51 G 3
Pastos Bons o **BR** 68-69 F 5
Pastos Chicos, Río o **RA** 76-77 D 2
Pastos Grandes, Sierra de los ▲ **RA** 76-77 D 3
Pastrana o **E** 98-99 F 4
Pastura o **USA** (NM) 256-257 L 4
Pasuruan o **RI** 168 E 5
Pasvalys ✩ **LT** 94-95 J 3
Pasvikelva ~ **N** 86-87 O 2
Pata o **RCA** 206-207 E 4
Pata o **CO** 66-67 B 3
Pata o **SN** 202-203 C 3
Patacamaya o **BOL** 70-71 D 5
Patache, Punta ▲ **RCH** 70-71 B 7
Patadkal o ∴ **IND** 140-141 F 3
Patagonia ⊥ **RA** 80 E 5
Patagonia o **USA** (AZ) 256-257 G 7
Patagónica, Cordillera ▲ **RCH** 80 D 5
Pata Island ⌒ **RP** 160-161 D 10
Pataiya o **IND** 140-141 G 5
Patalasang o **RI** 164-165 F 6
Patambacu ⌒ **ZRE** 210-211 G 5
Patambuco o **PE** 70-71 C 4
Patamuté o **BR** 68-69 J 6
Pātan o **IND** (GUJ) 138-139 D 8
Pātan o **IND** (MAH) 140-141 E 2
Patani o **RI** 164-165 L 3
Patas o **WAN** 204-205 G 4
Patos o **USA** (IA) 274-275 C 2
Patauá, Cachoeira do ~ **BR** 66-67 G 7
Pataula Creek ~ **USA** (GA) 284-285 F 5
Patay Rondos o **PE** 64-65 C 5
Patchepawapoko River ~ **CDN** 34-35 P 4
Patchogue o **USA** (NY) 280-281 N 3
Patea o **NZ** 182 E 3
Pategi o **WAN** 204-205 F 4
Pate Island ⌒ **EAK** 212-213 H 5
Patelilo, Río o **BR** 70-71 J 2
Patensie o **ZA** 220-221 G 6
Paternó o **I** 100-101 E 6
Paternoster o **ZA** 220-221 D 5
Pateros o **USA** (WA) 244-245 F 2
Paterson o **USA** (NJ) 280-281 M 3
Paterson o **ZA** 220-221 G 6
Paterson Inlet ≈ 182 B 7

Paterson Range ▲▲ **AUS** 172-173 F 6
Pathalaia o **IND** (UP) 144-145 E 7
Pathalgaon o **IND** 142-143 J 4
Pathankot o **IND** 138-139 E 3
Pathankot o **NEP** 144-145 E 7
Pathfinder Reservoir < **USA** (WY) 252-253 K 3
Pathin o **THA** 158-159 D 4
Pathlow o **CDN** (SAS) 232-233 O 3
Pāthrud o **IND** 138-139 E 10
Pathum Thani o **THA** 158-159 F 3
Pati o **RI** 168 D 3
Patia o **CO** 60-61 C 6
Patía, Río ~ **CO** 60-61 C 6
Patiala o **IND** 138-139 F 4
Patillas o •• **USA** (PR) 286-287 P 2
Patinti, Selat ≈ 164-165 K 4
Patio Chiquito o **CO** 60-61 F 5
Patiroriolo o **RI** 164-165 G 6
Pativilca o **PE** 64-65 D 7
Pätkai Bum ▲▲ **IND** 142-143 J 2
Patlahara o **NEP** 144-145 E 7
Pátmos ⌒ **GR** 100-101 L 6
Patna o **IND** 142-143 D 3
Patnanungan Island ⌒ **RP** 160-161 E 6
Patnitola o **BD** 142-143 F 3
Patnos o **TR** 128-129 K 3
Pato, Cachoeira do ~ **BR** 62-63 G 6
Pato Branco o **BR** 74-75 D 6
Patoka o **USA** (IL) 274-275 J 4
Patoka Lake < **USA** (IN) 274-275 M 6
Patoka River ~ **USA** (IN) 274-275 L 6
Patomskoe, nagor'e ▲ **RUS** 118-119 F 6
Patonga o **AUS** 172-173 L 2
Patonga o **EAU** 212-213 D 2
Patopsco Reservoir < **USA** (MD) 280-281 K 4
Patos o **BR** (CEA) 68-69 H 3
Patos o **BR** (PA) 68-69 H 3
Patos, Cachoeira dos ~ **BR** 70-71 H 2
Patos, Lagoa dos o **BR** 74-75 E 8
Patos, Río de los ~ **RA** 78-79 E 2
Patos de Minas o **BR** 72-73 G 5
Patos ou São José, Rio dos ~ **BR** 70-71 J 3
Patquia o **RA** 76-77 D 6
Pátra ✩ **GR** 100-101 H 5
Patraikos Kólpos ≈ 100-101 H 5
Patrakeevka o **RUS** 88-89 Q 4
Patreksfjördur ✩ **IS** 86-87 b 2
Patricia o **CDN** (ALB) 232-233 G 5
Patricia o **USA** (TX) 264-265 B 6
Patricios, Los o **CO** 66-67 B 3
Patrick o **USA** (SC) 284-285 L 2
Patrimonio o **BR** 72-73 F 5
Patrocínio o **BR** 72-73 G 5
Pattamada o **IND** 140-141 G 6
Pattani o **THA** 158-159 F 7
Pattaya o •• **THA** 158-159 F 4
Patten River ~ **CDN** (ONT) 236-237 J 3
Patterson o **USA** 172-173 K 4
Patterson o **USA** (CA) 248-249 C 2
Patterson o **USA** (GA) 284-285 H 5
Patterson o **USA** (ID) 252-253 G 3
Patterson o **USA** (LA) 268-269 J 7
Patterson, Mount ▲ **AUS** 176-177 F 2
Patterson, Mount ▲ **CDN** 20-21 X 4
Patterson Pass ▲ **USA** (NV) 246-247 L 5
Patti o **I** 100-101 E 5
Pattison o **USA** (MS) 268-269 K 5
Pattoki o **PK** 138-139 D 4
Pattonsburg o **USA** (MO) 276-277 D 4
Patton o **USA** (MO) 276-277 E 3
Pattullo, Mount ▲ **CDN** 32-33 F 3
Patuakhali o **BD** 142-143 G 4
Patuanak o **CDN** 34-35 G 3
Patuca, Punta ▲ **HN** 54-55 C 7
Patuca, Río ~ **HN** 54-55 C 7
Patuguu o **RI** 168 E 6
Patullo, Mount ▲ **CDN** 36-37 M 3
Patuxent River ~ **USA** (MD) 280-281 K 5
Patuxent River ~ **USA** (MD) 280-281 K 5
Paturau River ~ **NZ** 182 D 4
Pátzcuaro o •• **MEX** 52-53 D 2
Patzímaro o **MEX** 52-53 C 1
Pau ✩ • **F** 90-91 G 10
Pau, Tanjung ▲ **RI** 166-167 B 6
Pau Alto, Río ~ **BR** 72-73 L 4
Paucarbamba o **PE** 64-65 E 8
Paucarcolla o **PE** 70-71 B 4
Paucartambo o **PE** 70-71 B 3
Paucartambo, Río ~ **PE** 64-65 E 7
Pauh o **RI** 162-163 E 6
Pauini o **BR** 66-67 D 6
Pauini, Río ~ **BR** 66-67 F 3
Pauk o **MYA** 142-143 J 5
Paukkung o **MYA** 142-143 J 6
Pauksa Taung ▲ **MYA** 142-143 J 6
Paulaya, Río ~ **HN** 54-55 C 7
Paul B. Johnson State Park ⊥ **USA** (MS) 268-269 L 5
Paul Bunyan & Blue Ox Statue • **USA** (MN) 270-271 D 3
Paulden o **USA** (AZ) 256-257 C 4
Paulding o **USA** (OH) 280-281 B 2
Paulina o **USA** (OR) 244-245 F 6
Paulina Peak ▲ **USA** (OR) 244-245 D 7
Paulinia o **BR** 72-73 G 7
Paulis o **CDN** (NL) 262-263 H 7
Paulista o **BR** 68-69 L 5
Paulistana o **BR** 68-69 J 5
Paulo Afonso o **BR** 68-69 J 6
Paulo Afonso, Parque Nacional ⊥ **BR** 68-69 J 6
Paulo de Faria o **BR** 72-73 F 6
Paulo Ramos o **BR** 68-69 F 4
Paulpietersburg o **ZA** 220-221 K 4
Paul Roux o **ZA** 220-221 H 4
Paul Sauer Dam < **ZA** 220-221 G 6

Paul Spur o **USA** (AZ) 256-257 F 7
Pauls Valley o **USA** (OK) 264-265 G 4
Paungde o **MYA** 158-159 D 2
Paungdawthi o **MYA** 142-143 J 6
Pauni o **IND** 138-139 G 8
Paup o **PNG** 183 B 2
Pauri o **IND** 138-139 F 7
Pausa o **PE** 64-65 E 9
Paute o **EC** 64-65 C 3
Pauto, Río ~ **CO** 60-61 F 5
Pau Uma, Île = Paama ⌒ **VAN** 184 II b 3
Pauwela o **RI** 166-167 L 3
Pauweela o **USA** (HI) 288 J 4
Pāvagada o **IND** 140-141 G 3
Pavant Range ▲▲ **USA** (UT) 254-255 C 5
Pāve o **RI** 128-129 M 5
Pavia o **I** 100-101 C 2
Pavião o **BR** 72-73 K 6
Pavilion o **CDN** (BC) 230-231 H 3
Pavilion o **USA** (NY) 278-279 C 6
Pavilion o **USA** (WY) 252-253 K 3
Pāvilosta o **LV** 94-95 G 3
Pavlikeni o **BG** 102-103 D 6
Pavlodar ✩ **KAZ** 124-125 K 4
Pavlof Bay ≈ 22-23 Q 5
Pavlof Islands ⌒ **USA** 22-23 Q 5
Pavlof Volcano ▲ **USA** 22-23 Q 5
Pavlograd = Pavlohrad o **UA** 102-103 J 3
Pavlogradka ✩ **RUS** 124-125 H 1
Pavlohrad o **UA** 102-103 J 3
Pavlovac o **HR** 100-101 F 2
Pavlovic, Erofej o **RUS** 118-119 L 8
Pavlovka o **RUS** 96-97 J 3
Pavlovo o **RUS** 102-103 M 2
Pavlovsk ✩ **RUS** (LEN) 94-95 M 2
Pavlovsk o **RUS** 102-103 N 4
Pavlovskij Posad ✩ **RUS** 94-95 O 4
Pavlovskoe vodohranilišče < **RUS** 96-97 K 6
Pavlyš o **UA** 102-103 H 3
Pavo o **USA** (GA) 284-285 G 6
Pavon, Arroyo ~ **RA** 78-79 H 2
Pavullo nel Frignano o **I** 100-101 C 2
Pavylon, ozero o **RUS** 110-111 d 5
Pawaia o **PNG** 183 C 4
Pawan ~ **RI** 162-163 J 5
Pawayān o **IND** 144-145 C 6
Pawé ▲ **CAM** 204-205 J 7
Pawhuska o **USA** (OK) 264-265 H 2
Pawleys Island o **USA** (SC) 284-285 L 3
Pawnee o **USA** (OK) 264-265 H 2
Pawnee Bill Museum • **USA** (OK) 264-265 H 2
Pawnee City o **USA** (NE) 262-263 K 4
Pawnee Indian Village ∴ **USA** (KS) 262-263 J 5
Pawnee River ~ **USA** (KS) 262-263 G 6
Pawnee Rock o **USA** (KS) 262-263 H 6
Pawnee Rock State Monument • **USA** (KS) 262-263 H 6
Paw Paw o **USA** (MI) 272-273 M 5
Pawtucket o **USA** (RI) 278-279 K 7
Pawut o **MYA** 158-159 E 4
Paxi ✩ **GR** 100-101 H 5
Paxiúba, Rio ~ **BR** 66-67 G 7
Paxson o **USA** (IL) 274-275 K 4
Paxton o **USA** (NE) 262-263 E 4
Paxville o **USA** (SC) 284-285 K 3
Paya, Parque Nacional La ⊥ **CO** 64-65 E 1
Payahe o **RI** 164-165 K 3
Payakumbuh o **RI** 162-163 D 5
Payang, Gunung ▲ **RI** 164-165 D 3
Payar o **SN** 202-203 C 2
Payas, Cerro ▲ **HN** 54-55 C 7
Payer, Kap ▲ **GRØ** 26-27 b 2
Payer Land ⊥ **GRØ** 26-27 d 2
Payero, Río o **CO** 60-61 F 5
Payette o **USA** (ID) 252-253 B 2
Payette River ~ **USA** (ID) 252-253 B 3
Payne o **USA** (OH) 280-281 B 2
Payne Bay ≈ 36-37 P 4
Paynes Creek o **USA** (CA) 246-247 D 2
Paynes Find o **AUS** 176-177 D 4
Paynesville o **AUS** 180-181 J 4
Paynesville o **USA** (MN) 270-271 D 5
Paynton o **CDN** (SAS) 232-233 K 2
Payogasta o **RA** 76-77 D 3
Payong, Tanjung ▲ **MAL** 162-163 K 3
Paysandú ✩ **ROU** 78-79 J 1
Pays de la Loire □ **F** 90-91 G 8
Payson o **USA** (AZ) 256-257 D 4
Payson o **USA** (UT) 254-255 D 3
Payún, Cerro ▲ **RA** 78-79 E 4
Payyannur o **IND** 140-141 F 4
Paz, Corredera da ~ **BR** 68-69 D 6
Paz, Gruta ∴ **CR** 64-65 D 1
Paz, La o **BOL** 70-71 D 5
Paz, La o **CO** 60-61 E 2
Paz, La o **RA** 52-53 L 4
Paz, La o **MEX** 50-51 E 5
Paz, La o **RA** (COD) 78-79 G 2
Paz, La o **RA** (ERI) 76-77 H 6
Paz, La o **HN** 54-55 B 6
Paz, La o **ROU** 78-79 L 3
Paz, Ribeiro da ~ **BR** 72-73 J 6
Paz, Río de la ~ **BOL** 70-71 D 5
Pazar ✩ **TR** 128-129 J 2
Pazarcik ✩ **TR** 128-129 G 4
Pazardžik ✩ **BG** 102-103 D 6
Paz Centro, La o **NIC** 52-53 L 5
Pazin o **HR** 100-101 D 2
Pazna o **PK** 138-139 B 5
Pazos Kanki o **RA** 78-79 H 3
Pčinja ~ **MK** 100-101 H 4
Pčinja ✩ **BY** 94-95 K 5
Pé de Serra o **BR** 68-69 J 6

Peace River ~ **USA** (FL) 286-287 H 4
Peach Creek ~ **USA** (WV) 280-281 E 6
Peachland o **CDN** (BC) 230-231 K 4
Peach Springs o **USA** (AZ) 256-257 B 3
Peachtree City o **USA** (GA) 284-285 F 3
Peacock Bay ≈ 16 D 26
Peacock Hills ▲ **CDN** 30-31 O 3
Pea Island National Wildlife Refuge ⊥ **USA** (NC) 282-283 N 5
Peak Charles National Park ⊥ **AUS** 176-177 F 6
Peak District National Park ⊥ **GB** 90-91 K 5
Peak Downs Mine • **AUS** 176-179 K 2
Peake o **AUS** 180-181 E 3
Peake Creek ~ **AUS** 178-179 C 5
Peaked Point ▲ **USA** (ME) 66-67 C 7
Peak Hill o **AUS** (NSW) 180-181 K 4
Peak Hill o **AUS** (WA) 176-177 D 3
Peak Mountain ▲ **USA** (CA) 248-249 C 4
Peale, Mount ▲ **USA** (UT) 254-255 F 5
Pearblossom o **USA** (CA) 248-249 G 5
Pearce o **CDN** (ALB) 232-233 G 6
Pearce o **USA** (AZ) 256-257 F 7
Pearce Point ▲ **AUS** 172-173 J 3
Pearcy o **USA** (AR) 268-269 G 4
Peard Bay ≈ 20-21 L 1
Pea Ridge National Military Park • **USA** (AR) 276-277 A 4
Pearisburg o **USA** (VA) 280-281 G 6
Pea River ~ **USA** (AL) 284-285 E 5
Pea River ~ **USA** (AL) 284-285 D 5
Pearland o **USA** (TX) 268-269 E 7
Pearl City o **USA** (HI) 288 H 3
Pearl Harbor ≈ • **USA** 288 G 3
Pearl River ~ **USA** (LA) 268-269 L 6
Pearl River ~ **USA** (MS) 268-269 L 5
Pearsall o **USA** (TX) 266-267 H 5
Pearse Island ⌒ **CDN** 228-229 D 2
Pearson o **USA** (GA) 284-285 H 5
Pearson o **USA** (GA) 284-285 H 5
Pearston o **ZA** 220-221 G 6
Peary Channel ≈ 24-25 U 1
Peary Gletscher C **GRØ** 26-27 U 5
Peary Land ⊥ **GRØ** 26-27 g 2
Pease River ~ **USA** (TX) 264-265 E 4
Peawanuck o **CDN** 34-35 O 4
Peba, Rio ~ **BR** 68-69 D 5
Pebane o **MOC** 218-219 K 3
Pebas o **PE** 66-67 B 4
Pébbel Island ⌒ **GB** 78-79 L 6
Pec ~ **YU** 100-101 H 4
Pečaňka ~ **RUS** 114-115 R 2
Pecangakan o **RI** 168 D 3
Peçanha o **BR** 72-73 J 5
Pecan Island o **USA** (LA) 268-269 H 7
Peças, Ilha das ⌒ **BR** 74-75 F 5
Pecatonica River ~ **USA** (IL) 274-275 J 2
Peçe Sound ≈ 16 D 27
Peene ~ **D** 92-93 M 2
Peeples Valley o **USA** (AZ) 256-257 C 4
Peeramudlayeppa Lake o **AUS** 178-179 D 4
Peera Peera Poolanna Lake o **AUS** 178-179 D 4
Peerless o **CDN** 32-33 Q 4
Peerless o **USA** (MT) 250-251 O 3
Peerless Lake o **CDN** 32-33 N 3
Peers o **CDN** (ALB) 232-233 C 2
Peesane o **CDN** (SAS) 232-233 P 3
Peetz o **USA** (CO) 254-255 M 4
Pegasus Bay ≈ 182 D 5
Pegatan o **RI** 162-163 K 6
Peggys Cove o **CDN** (NS) 240-241 M 6
Peg. Müller ▲ **RI** 162-163 K 5
Pego o **E** 98-99 G 5
Pego o **P** 98-99 C 5
Pegram o **USA** (TN) 276-277 H 4
Pegtymel'skij hrebet ▲ **RUS** 112-113 Z 4
Pegu o **MYA** 158-159 D 2
Peguis Indian Reserve ✕ **CDN** (MAN) 234-235 F 3
Pegunungan, Barisan ▲▲ **RI** 162-163 E 6
Pegyš o **RUS** 88-89 V 3
Péhonko o **DY** 202-203 L 4
Pehuajó o **RA** 78-79 J 3
Pehuén-Co o **RA** 78-79 J 5
Peian Indian Reserve ✕ **CDN** (ALB) 232-233 E 6
Peili o **SUD** 206-207 H 5
Peinata, Cerro ▲ **RA** 80 D 5
Peipsi Järv ~ **EST** 94-95 K 2
Peipus, Lake = Peipsi Järv o **EST** 94-95 K 2
Peixe o **BR** 72-73 F 2
Peixe, Rio do ~ **BR** 74-75 D 6
Peixe, Rio do ~ **BR** 72-73 D 7
Peixe, Rio do ~ **BR** 72-73 G 5
Peixe, Rio do ~ **BR** 72-73 H 3
Peixeboi o **BR** 68-69 E 2
Peixe Couro ou Aquinabo, Rio ~ **BR** 70-71 K 5
Peixes ou de São Francisco, Rio dos ~ **BR** 70-71 J 2
Pei Xian o **VRC** 154-155 K 4
Peixoto, Represa de < **BR** 72-73 G 6
Peixoto de Azevedo o **BR** 70-71 K 2
Peixoto de Azevedo, Rio ~ **BR** 70-71 K 2
Pejantan, Pulau ⌒ **RI** 162-163 G 4
Pekabata o **RI** 164-165 F 6
Pekalongan o **RI** 168 C 4
Pekan o **MAL** 162-163 F 3
Pekanbaru ✩ **RI** 162-163 D 4
Pekin o **USA** (IL) 274-275 J 4
Pekin, Pulau ⌒ **RI** 164-165 E 2
Peking = Beijing ☆ **VRC** 154-155 K 2
Pekinga o **DY** 204-205 J 7
Pekino o **RUS** 94-95 N 5
Peko, Parc National du ⊥ **CI** 202-203 G 6
Peko Mine • **AUS** 174-175 C 6
Pekuřnej, hrebet ▲ **RUS** 112-113 U 5
Pel'ňejnejskoe, ozero o **RUS** 112-113 T 5
Péla o **RG** 202-203 F 6

Pedra Lume o **CV** 202-203 C 5
Pedra Preta o **BR** 70-71 K 5
Pedra Preta, Corredeira da ~ **BR** 68-69 C 5
Pedras, Cachoeira ~ **BR** 68-69 D 7
Pedras Descobertas o **BR** 70-71 J 3
Pedras Grandes o **BR** 74-75 F 7
Pedras Negras • **ANG** 216-217 C 4
Pedras Negras o **BR** 70-71 G 4
Pedras Tinhosas ⌒ **STP** 210-211 b 2
Pelé, Mont ▲ **G** 210-211 C 3
Pélébima o **DY** 202-203 L 5
Pelechuco o **BOL** 70-71 D 4
Peleduj o **RUS** 118-119 F 6
Pelée, Mont ▲ **F** 56 K 4
Pelee, Point ▲ **CDN** 238-239 C 3
Pelee Island ⌒ **CDN** 238-239 C 7
Pelei o **RI** 164-165 H 4
Pelejo o **PE** 64-65 C 5
Pelekech ⊥ **EAK** 212-213 E 2
Pelench o **YV** 60-61 L 3
Peleng, Pulau ⌒ **RI** 164-165 H 4
Peleng, Selat ≈ 164-165 H 4
Pelham o **USA** 174-175 G 6
Pelham o **USA** (AL) 284-285 D 3
Pelhřímov o **CZ** 92-93 N 4
Pelican o **USA** (AK) 32-33 C 6
Pelican, Lac o **CDN** 36-37 N 5
Pelican Lake o **CDN** (MAN) 234-235 C 2
Pelicano, Quebrada del ~ **RCH** 76-77 B 5
Pelican Point (Beach) • **AUS** 176-177 B 4
Pelican Rapids o **CDN** (MAN) 234-235 C 2
Pelican River ~ **CDN** 32-33 O 4
Pelican o **USA** (MN) 270-271 C 3
Pelkan o •• **USA** (MN) 270-271 F 2
Pelikan Narrows o **CDN** 34-35 H 3
Pelikan Rapids o **USA** (MN) 270-271 E 6
Pelileo o **EC** 64-65 C 3
Pelindis, Ponta ▲ **GNB** 202-203 B 4
Pelion o **USA** (SC) 284-285 J 3
Pelkie o **USA** (MI) 270-271 K 4
Pelkosenniemi o **FIN** 88-89 J 3
Pella o **USA** (IA) 274-275 F 3
Pelland o **USA** (MN) 270-271 F 2
Pellatt Lake o **CDN** 30-31 P 3
Pell City o **USA** (AL) 284-285 D 3
Pellegrini o **RA** 78-79 H 4
Pellegrini, Lago o **RA** 78-79 F 5
Pelletier o **CDN** (QUE) 240-241 F 3
Pell Inlet ≈ 24-25 V 3
Pello o **FIN** 88-89 H 3
Pellston o **USA** (MI) 272-273 E 2
Pellworm ⌒ **D** 92-93 K 1
Pelly o **CDN** (SAS) 232-233 R 4
Pelly Bay ≈ 24-25 b 6
Pelly Island ⌒ **CDN** 20-21 X 2
Pelly Lake o **CDN** 30-31 T 3
Pelly Mountains ▲ **CDN** 20-21 Y 6
Pelly Plateau ▲ **CDN** 20-21 W 5
Pelly Point ▲ **CDN** 24-25 W 5
Pelly River ~ **CDN** 20-21 W 5
Pelokang, Pulau ⌒ **RI** 168 D 6
Pelona Mountain ▲ **USA** (NM) 256-257 G 5
Polopónissos ⌒ **GR** 100-101 J 6
Pelopónnisos ⌒ **GR** 100-101 J 6
Peloritani, Monti ▲ **I** 100-101 E 5
Pelotas o **BR** 74-75 E 7
Pelotas, Rio ~ **BR** 74-75 E 7
Pelsart Group ⌒ **AUS** 176-177 B 4
Pelulutegu o **SME** 62-63 G 4
Pelus ⌒ **MAL** 162-163 D 2
Pelusium ∴• **ET** 194-195 F 2
Pelym ⌒ **RUS** 114-115 H 4
Pelymskij Tuman, ozero o **RUS** 114-115 G 4
Pemadumcook Lake o **USA** (ME) 278-279 M 3
Pemalang o **RI** 168 C 4
Pemali, Tanjung ▲ **RI** (SLT) 164-165 H 4
Pemali, Tanjung ▲ **RI** (STG) 164-165 H 4
Pemangil, Pulau ⌒ **MAL** (KED) 162-163 F 3
Pemangkat o **RI** 162-163 H 4
Pemarung, Tanjung ▲ **RI** 164-165 E 4
Pematang Purba o **RI** 162-163 C 4
Pematangsiantar o **RI** 162-163 C 4
Pematangtanabjawa o **RI** 162-163 D 3
Pemba o **MOC** 214-215 L 7
Pemba Z 218-219 D 3
Pemba Channel ≈ 212-213 G 6
Pemba Island ⌒ **EAT** 212-213 G 6
Pembe o **MOC** 218-219 H 6
Pembela o **USA** (WI) 270-271 K 5
Pembina River ~ **CDN** (ALB) 232-233 C 2
Pembina River ~ **CDN** (MAN) 234-235 D 5
Pembine o **USA** (WI) 270-271 K 5
Pembroke o **CDN** (ONT) 238-239 H 3
Pembroke o **GB** 90-91 J 6
Pembroke o **USA** (GA) 284-285 J 4
Pembroke o **USA** (NC) 282-283 H 6
Pembroke, Cape ▲ **CDN** 36-37 J 3
Pembroke Castle • **GB** 90-91 J 6
Pembrokeshire Coast National Park ⊥ **GB** 90-91 H 6
Pemuco o **RCH** 76-77 B 4
Pen o **IND** 138-139 D 10
Peña Blanco o **RCH** 76-77 B 4
Peña del Rosario, Cerro ▲ **MEX** 52-53 E 2

Penafiel o **P** 98-99 C 4
Peñafiel o **E** 98-99 F 4
Peñaflor o **RCH** 78-79 D 2
Peñalara ▲ **E** 98-99 F 3
Penamacor o **P** 98-99 D 4
Penambuan o **RI** 164-165 G 4
Penampang o **MAL** 160-161 B 10
Peña Nevada, Cerro ▲ **MEX** 50-51 K 6

Penang, Pulau ⌒ **MAL** 162-163 D 2
Penanjung Game Park ⊥ **RI** 168 C 3
Penápolis o **BR** 72-73 E 6
Penarak, Kampung o **MAL** 162-163 E 2
Peñaranda de Bracamonte o **E** 98-99 E 4
Peñarroya ▲ **E** 98-99 G 4
Peñarroya-Pueblonuevo o **E** 98-99 E 5
Peñas, Cabo de ▲ **E** 98-99 E 3
Peñas, Golfo de ≈ 80 C 3
Peñas, Las o **RA** 76-77 D 5
Peñas, Sierra de las ▲ **RA** 78-79 G 4
Peñas Blancas o **NIC** 52-53 B 6
Peñasco, Río o **USA** (NM) 256-257 L 6
Peñas Negras o **YV** 60-61 J 4
Pench National Park ⊥ **IND** 138-139 G 8
Penck, Cape ▲ **ARK** 16 G 9
Pendarves o **NZ** 182 C 5
Pendê o **RCA** 206-207 C 5
Pendê ~ **RCA** 206-207 B 5
Pendleton Bay o **CDN** (BC) 228-229 J 2
Pendembu o **WAL** (EAS) 202-203 E 5
Pendembu o **WAL** (NOR) 202-203 D 5
Pendeng o **RI** 162-163 D 3
Pender o **USA** (NE) 262-263 K 2
Pender Bay ≈ 172-173 F 4
Pender Island o **CDN** (BC) 230-231 F 5
Pendjari ~ **DY** 202-203 L 4
Pendjari, Parc National de la ⊥ **DY** 202-203 L 4
Pendjari, Zone Cynégétique de la ⊥ **DY** 202-203 L 4
Pendjua o **ZRE** 210-211 G 4
Pendleton o **USA** (IN) 274-275 N 5
Pendleton o **USA** (OR) 244-245 G 5
Pendopo o **RI** 162-163 E 6
Pend Oreille, Mount ▲ **USA** (ID) 250-251 C 3
Pend Oreille Lake o **USA** (ID) 250-251 C 3
Pend Oreille River ~ **USA** (WA) 244-245 H 2
Pendroy o **USA** (MT) 250-251 G 3
Pendryl o **CDN** (SAS) 232-233 K 5
Pendulium Øer ⌒ **GRØ** 26-27 q 6
Penebangan, Pulau ⌒ **RI** 162-163 H 5
Penebel o **RI** 168 B 7
Peneda ▲ **P** 98-99 C 4
Penedo o **BR** 68-69 K 7
Pene-Katamba o **ZRE** 210-211 K 4
Penela o **P** 98-99 C 4
Pene-Mende o **ZRE** 212-213 B 6
Pénessoulou o **DY** 202-203 L 5
Penet, Tanjung ▲ **RI** 162-163 F 6
Penetanguishene o **CDN** (ONT) 238-239 F 3
Penfro = Pembroke o **GB** 90-91 E 6
Pengalengan o **RI** 168 B 3
Peng'an o **VRC** 154-155 E 6
Penganga ~ **IND** 138-139 G 10
Pengastulan o **RI** 168 B 7
Pengchia Yü ⌒ **RC** 156-157 N 4
Penge o **ZRE** (HAU) 212-213 A 6
Penge o **ZRE** (KOR) 210-211 K 6
Penge, Chute ~ **ZRE** 212-213 H 4
Penghu Islands ⌒ **RC** 156-157 L 5
Pengjie o **VRC** 154-155 M 5
Pengkalan Kubor, Kampung o **MAL** 162-163 E 2
Pengkou o **VRC** 156-157 K 4
Penglai o **VRC** 154-155 M 3
Penglai o **VRC** 156-157 G 7
Penglai Ge • **VRC** 154-155 M 3
Pengshan o **VRC** 154-155 D 6
Pengshui o **VRC** 156-157 F 2
Penguin o **AUS** 180-181 H 6
Penguin Bank ≈ 288 H 4
Penguin Island ⌒ **CDN** (NFL) 242-243 N 5
Penguin Shoal ⌒ **AUS** 172-173 G 2
Pengxi o **VRC** 154-155 D 6
Penhalonga o **ZW** 218-219 G 4
Penhoek Pass ▲ **ZA** 220-221 H 5
Péni o **BF** 202-203 J 4
Peniche o **P** 98-99 C 5
Penida, Nusa ⌒ **RI** 168 B 7
Peninga o **RUS** 88-89 N 4
Pennington o **USA** (AL) 284-285 B 4
Peninsular Development Road ‖ **AUS** 174-175 G 4
Peninsular Lake o **CDN** (ONT) 234-235 P 3
Penitente, Serra do ▲ **BR** 68-69 F 6
Pénjamo o **MEX** 52-53 D 1
Penmarch ✩ **F** 90-91 E 8
Penmarc'h, Pointe de ▲ • **F** 90-91 E 8
Pennādam o **IND** 140-141 H 5
Pennant o **CDN** (SAS) 232-233 K 5
Pennant Point ▲ **CDN** (NS) 240-241 M 6
Penner ~ **IND** 140-141 H 3
Penneshaw o **AUS** 180-181 D 3
Penn Hills o **USA** (PA) 280-281 G 3
Pennines, The ▲▲ **GB** 90-91 K 4
Pennsboro o **USA** (WV) 280-281 F 4
Pennsville o **USA** (NJ) 280-281 L 4
Pennsylvania o **USA** (PA) 280-281 G 2
Pennsylvania TPK ‖ **USA** (PA) 280-281 K 3
Penny o **CDN** (BC) 228-229 N 3
Penny Yan o **USA** (NY) 278-279 D 6
Penny Farms o **USA** (FL) 286-287 H 2
Penny Highlands ▲ **CDN** 28-29 S 3
Penny Ice Cap C **CDN** 28-29 G 3
Pennyroyal Plateau ▲ **USA** (TN) 276-277 J 4
Penny Strait ≈ 24-25 X 2
Peno ✩ **RUS** 94-95 N 3
Penobscot Bay ≈ **USA** 278-279 N 4
Penobscot River ~ **USA** (ME) 278-279 M 3
Penoka o **LB** 202-203 G 7
Penola o **AUS** 180-181 F 4
Peñón Blanco o **MEX** 50-51 H 5
Peñón del Rosario, Cerro ▲ **MEX** 52-53 E 2
Penong o **AUS** 176-177 M 5
Peñón Nevado del Falso Azufre ▲ **RCH** 76-77 C 4
Peñón Nevado del Falso Azufre ▲ **RA** 76-77 C 4

Penonomé o ☆ PA 52-53 D 7
Penot, Mount ▲ VAN 184 II a 3
Penrhyn, Cape ▲ CDN 24-25 f 7
Penrhyn Basin ≃ 13 M 3
Penrith o GB 90-91 F 4
Penrose o CO 254-255 K 5
Pensa o BF 202-203 K 3
Pensacola o USA (FL) 286-287 B 1
Pensacola Bay ≈ 48-49 E 4
Pensacola Bay ≈ USA 286-287 B 1
Pensacola Mountains ▲▲ ARK 16 E 0
Pensamiento, El o BOL 70-71 G 4
Pense o CDN (SAS) 232-233 O 5
Pensepef, mys ▲ CDN 24-25 f 7
Penshurst o AUS 180-181 J 6
Pensilvania o CO 60-61 D 5
Pentáofos o FIN 164-165 J 4
Pentecost o ☆ USA (FL) 286-287 D 1
Pentecost Downs o AUS 172-173 H 4
Pentecostes o BR 68-69 J 3
Pentecost Island = Île Pentecôte ⌐ VAN 184 II b 2
Pentecost Range ▲▲ AUS 172-173 H 3
Pentecost River ~ AUS 172-173 H 3
Pentecôte, Île = Pentecost Island ⌐ VAN 184 II b 2
Penticot, Rivière o CDN (QUE) 242-243 A 3
Pentenga o BF 202-203 J 4
Penticton o CDN (BC) 230-231 K 4
Penticton Indian Reserve 𝕏 CDN (BC) 230-231 K 4
Pentland o AUS 174-175 H 7
Pentland Firth ≈ 90-91 F 2
Pentwater o USA (MI) 272-273 C 4
Penu o RI 164-165 J 4
Penukonda o IND 140-141 G 3
Penwegon o MYA 142-143 K 6
Penwell o USA (TX) 266-267 E 2
Penylan Lake o CDN 30-31 Q 5
Penyu, Kepulauan ⌐ RI 166-167 D 4
Penyu, Teluk ≈ 168 C 3
Penza ☆ RUS 96-97 L 5
Penzance o GB 90-91 E 6
Penzance Lake o CDN 30-31 Q 5
Penze o VRC 154-155 J 2
Penžina ~ RUS 112-113 M 4
Penžinskaja guba ≈ 120-121 T 3
Penžinskij hrebet ▲▲ RUS 120-121 V 3
Peoria o USA (AZ) 256-257 C 5
Peoria o USA (IL) 272-273 D 3
Pep o USA (NM) 256-257 M 5
Pepa o ZRE 214-215 E 4
Pepacton Reservoir o USA (NY) 278-279 G 6
Pepani o ZA 220-221 F 3
Pepeekeo o USA (HI) 288 K 5
Pepita ou Porte Alegre, Rio ~ BR 68-69 B 6
Peque o CDN 30-31 J 6
Pequena, Cachoeira ~ BR 68-69 J 3
Pequeri, Rio ~ BR 70-71 K 5
Pequop Summit ▲ USA (NV) 246-247 L 2
Pequot Lakes o USA (MN) 270-271 D 4
Perabamulih o RI 162-163 F 6
Pérade, La o CDN (QUE) 238-239 N 2
Peraguaizinho, Rio ~ BR 70-71 J 4
Perairyur o IND 140-141 H 5
Perak ⌐ MAL 162-163 D 2
Perak o RI 168 E 3
Perambalur o IND 140-141 H 5
Perämeri ≈ 88-89 G 4
Perapat, Tanjung ▲ MAL 164-165 D 1
Peras-2 ▲ MEX 50-51 G 5
Perbaugan o RI 162-163 C 3
Perbulan o RI 162-163 C 3
Percé o CDN (QUE) 240-241 L 2
Percival o CDN (SAS) 232-233 O 5
Percival Lakes o AUS 172-173 G 6
Percy, Mount ▲ AUS 172-173 G 4
Percy Isles ⌐ AUS 178-179 L 1
Percy Priest Lake, J. o USA (TN) 276-277 J 4
Percy Quin State Park ⊥ USA (MS) 268-269 K 5
Perdekop o ZA 220-221 J 3
Perdida, Rio ~ BR 68-69 H 6
Perdido Bay ≈ USA 286-287 B 1
Perdido River ~ USA (FL) 286-287 B 1
Perdidos, Cachoeira dos ~ BR 70-71 J 4
Perdizes o BR 72-73 G 5
Perdões o BR 72-73 H 6
Perdón, Puerto del ▲ E 98-99 G 3
Perdue o CDN (SAS) 232-233 L 3
Perehins'ke o UA 102-103 D 3
Pereira ☆ CO 60-61 D 5
Pereira, Cachoeira ~ BR 66-67 J 4
Pereira Barreto o BR 72-73 F 6
Pereirinha o BR 66-67 J 7
Perejaslav-Chmel'nyc'kyj o UA 102-103 E 2
Perejastavka o RUS 122-123 F 5
Pereljub ☆ RUS 96-97 L 5
Pereljubovka o KA 126-127 M 3
Peremetnoe ☆ KA 96-97 G 8
Peremul Par ⌐ IND 140-141 B 2
Perené, Río ~ PE 64-65 D 7
Perenjori o AUS 176-177 D 4
Pérerè o DY 204-205 E 4
Pereščepyne o UA 102-103 J 3
Pereslavl'-Zalesskij o ☆ RUS 94-95 Q 3
pereval Kajtezek ▲ TJ 136-137 N 6
Perevolockij o RUS 96-97 J 8
Perevoz o RUS 96-97 J 8
Perevoznaja, guba ≈ RUS 108-109 H 7
Perez o RA 78-79 J 2
Perez o USA (CA) 246-247 D 2
Pergamino o RA 78-79 J 2
Pergamon ∴ TR 128-129 B 3
Perge ∴ TR 128-129 D 4
Pérgola o I 100-101 D 3
Perhentian Besar, Pulau ⌐ MAL (TER) 162-163 E 2

Perho o FIN 88-89 H 5
Perhonjoki ~ FIN 88-89 G 5
Periá, Río ~ BR 68-69 G 3
Peribán de Ramos o MEX 52-53 C 2
Péribonca, Lac o CDN 38-39 J 3
Péribonca, Rivière ~ CDN 38-39 J 3
Péribonka o CDN (QUE) 240-241 C 2
Péribonka o CDN (QUE) 240-241 C 2
Perico o C 54-55 E 3
Perico o USA (TX) 264-265 C 2
Perico Creek ~ USA (TX) 264-265 B 2
Pericos o MEX 50-51 F 5
Peridot o USA (AZ) 256-257 E 5
Périgord o CDN (SAS) 232-233 P 5
Perigoso, Canal o BR 62-63 K 5
Périgueux ☆ F 90-91 H 9
Perijá, Parque Nacional ⊥ YV 60-61 E 3
Perijá, Sierra de ▲▲ YV 60-61 E 3
Peri Lake o AUS 178-179 G 6
Perim = Barim, Gazïrat ⌐ Y 132-133 C 7
Peringat o MAL 162-163 J 2
Periquen o YV 62-63 D 3
Periquito, Cachoeira ~ BR 66-67 K 6
Periquito, Cachoeira ~ BR 66-67 G 6
Pervyj Kurilskij proliv ≈ RUS 122-123 N 6
Peri Suyu ~ TR 128-129 H 3
Peritoro o BR 68-69 F 4
Periyar Lake o IND 140-141 G 6
Perkat, Tanjung ▲ RI 162-163 F 5
Perkins o USA (OK) 264-265 G 3
Perkinstown o USA (WI) 270-271 H 5
Perla, La o USA (TX) 266-267 G 3
Perlas, Archipiélago de las ⌐ PA 52-53 J 7
Perlas, Cayos de ⌐ NIC 52-53 L 5
Perlas, Laguna de ≈ NIC 52-53 L 5
Perlas, Punta de ▲ NIC 52-53 L 5
Perleporten o N 84-85 L 5
Perley o USA (MN) 270-271 B 3
Perley Island ⌐ CDN 36-37 J 5
Perlis ⌐ MAL 162-163 D 2
Perlis, Kuala o MAL 162-163 D 2
Perm' ☆ RUS 96-97 K 4
Perma o DY 202-203 L 4
Perma o USA (MT) 250-251 E 4
Pärmet ▲ AL 100-101 H 4
Permin Land ⌐ GRØ 26-27 Z 3
Pernambuco o BR 68-69 J 6
Pernambuco Abyssal Plain ≃ 6-7 G 8
Pernambut o IND 140-141 H 4
Pernatty Lagoon o AUS 178-179 D 6
Pernhuée, Cordillera de ▲▲ RCH 78-79 D 4
Pernik ☆ BG 102-103 C 6
Pernió o FIN 88-89 G 6
Pernštejn ∙ CZ 92-93 O 4
Perole o CDN 72-73 D 7
Peron North, Cape ▲ AUS 176-177 B 2
Peron Peninsula ⌐ AUS 176-177 B 2
Perote o MEX 52-53 F 2
Perote o USA (AL) 284-285 E 5
Peroto o BOL 70-71 E 4
Perouse Strait, La = Laperuza, proliv ≈ 122-123 J 6
Perow o CDN (BC) 228-229 H 2
Perpignan o ☆ F 90-91 H 10
Perquilauquén, Rio ~ RCH 78-79 D 4
Perrault Falls o CDN (ONT) 234-235 K 4
Perret, Punta ▲ YV 60-61 H 2
Perrin o USA (TX) 264-265 F 5
Perrine o USA (FL) 286-287 J 6
Perrin Vale o AUS 176-177 H 4
Perris o USA (CA) 248-249 G 6
Perrivale o AUS 174-175 G 6
Perro, Laguna del o USA (NM) 256-257 K 4
Perry o CDN (ONT) 236-237 D 5
Perry o USA (FL) 286-287 F 1
Perry o USA (GA) 284-285 G 4
Perry o USA (IA) 274-275 D 2
Perry o USA (MI) 272-273 E 5
Perry o USA (MO) 274-275 G 5
Perry o USA (OK) 264-265 G 2
Perry o USA (TX) 266-267 G 2
Perry o USA 20-21 N 6
Perry Lake o USA (KS) 262-263 L 5
Perry o CDN 30-31 T 2
Perry River ~ CDN (BC) 230-231 L 2
Perryton o USA (TX) 264-265 D 2
Perryville o USA (AK) 22-23 H 5
Perryville o USA (AR) 276-277 C 5
Perryville o USA (MO) 274-275 G 6
Perryville o USA 20-21 N 6
Persalyevo o CDN (ONT) 238-239 G 4
Perse o USA (NH) 278-279 K 6
Persehead o GB 90-91 G 5
Peter Island ⌐ GB (VI) 286-287 R 2
Peter Lake o CDN 30-31 X 4
Peter Lougheed Provincial Park ⊥ CDN (ALB) 232-233 C 5
Petermann Aboriginal Land 𝕏 AUS 176-177 K 2
Petermann Bjerg ▲ GRØ 26-27 I 7
Petermann Fjord ≈ 26-27 U 3
Petermann Gletscher ⊂ GRØ 26-27 U 3
Petermann Ranges ▲▲ AUS 176-177 K 2
Peteroa, Volcán ▲ RA 78-79 D 3
Peter Pond Lake o CDN 32-33 Q 3
Peter Pond Lake Indian Reserve 𝕏 CDN 32-33 Q 4
Peter Richards, Cape ▲ CDN 24-25 M 5
Petersburg o USA (AK) 32-33 X 3
Petersburg o USA (IL) 274-275 J 4
Petersburg o USA (IN) 274-275 L 6
Petersburg o USA (ND) 258-259 K 3
Petersburg o USA (TN) 276-277 J 5
Petersburg o USA (TX) 264-265 D 5
Petersburg o USA (VA) 280-281 J 6
Petersburg o USA (WV) 280-281 H 4
Petersburg Creek-Duncan Salt Chuck Wilderness ⊥ USA 32-33 X 3
Petersburg National Battlefield ∙ USA (VA) 280-281 J 6

Peruhumpenai Mountains Reserve ⊥ · RI 164-165 G 5
Peruibe o BR 74-75 G 5
Peruípe, Rio ~ BR 72-73 L 4
Perumpávúr o IND 140-141 G 6
Perundurai o IND 140-141 G 5
Perung o RI 168 C 7
Perupuk, Tanjung ▲ RI 164-165 F 3
Pervari ☆ TR 128-129 K 4
Perves, Alt de ▲ E 98-99 H 3
Pervomaevka o RUS 116-117 O 9
Pervomaiskyj o UA 102-103 K 3
Pervomajsk ☆ UA (NIK) 102-103 L 3
Pervomajs'k = Pervomajs'k o UA 102-103 L 3
Pervomajs'k o UA 102-103 H 5
Pervomajskij o KA 124-125 N 3
Pervomajskij o RUS 94-95 R 5
Pervomajskij o RUS 118-119 G 10
Pervomajskij o RUS (CEL) 96-97 M 6
Pervomajskij o RUS (ORB) 96-97 G 8
Pervomajskoe o RUS 122-123 K 4
Pervomajskoe o RUS (LEN) 94-95 L 1
Pervomajskoe o RUS 96-97 L 5
Pervyj Mindej o RUS 116-117 L 7
Peša ~ RUS 88-89 T 3
Pésaro o I 100-101 D 3
Pesca, La o MEX 50-51 L 6
Pescadeiros ~ RUS 124-125 O 2
Pescanaja ~ RUS 124-125 O 2
Pesčanaja o RUS 88-89 U 2
Pesčanoe o RUS 88-89 N 5
Pesčanoe ozero o RUS 124-125 L 2
Pesčanokopskoe o RUS 102-103 M 4
Pesčanyj, mys ▲ KA 126-127 J 6
Pesčanyj, mys ▲ RUS 108-109 e 2
Pescara ☆ I 100-101 E 3
Pescara Cassiano o MOC 218-219 H 2
Peščera Kristaličeska ∙ UA 102-103 E 3
Pescovaja, buhta ≈ RUS 112-113 U 1
Peshawar ☆ PK 138-139 C 3
Peshkopi ☆ AL 100-101 H 4
Peshtigo o USA (WI) 270-271 L 5
Peshtigo River ~ USA (WI) 270-271 K 5
Pesjakov, ostrov ⌐ RUS 88-89 Y 2
peski Sëjunasagek ▲ TM 136-137 D 5
Peškovka ▲ KA 126-127 J 6
Pesqueira o BR 68-69 K 6
Pesquería, Rio ~ MEX 50-51 J 4
Peštera o BG 102-103 D 6
Pestovo o RUS 94-95 O 2
Pestravka ☆ RUS 96-97 F 7
Petah Tiqwa ☆ IL 130-131 D 1
Petäjävesi o FIN 88-89 H 5
Petak, Tanjung ▲ RI 164-165 L 3
Petal o USA (MS) 268-269 L 3
Petaling Jaya o MAL 162-163 D 2
Petani, Sungai o MAL 162-163 D 2
Petaquillas o MEX 52-53 E 3
Petatbar o IND 142-143 D 4
Petare o YV 60-61 H 2
Petas, Rio Las ~ BOL 70-71 H 4
Petatlán o MEX 52-53 D 3
Petatuke o Z 218-219 F 2
Petawanga Lake o CDN (ONT) 234-235 P 3
Petcacab o MEX 52-53 K 1
Petchaburi o THA 158-159 E 4
Pété o CAM 206-207 B 3
Pétel, Djoutou- o RG 202-203 D 4
Petén Itzá, Lago o GCA 52-53 K 4
Petenwell Lake o USA (WI) 270-271 J 6
Peterbell o CDN (ONT) 236-237 G 2
Peterborough o AUS (SA) 180-181 E 2
Peterborough o AUS (VIC) 180-181 G 5
Peter Borough o · CDN (ONT) 238-239 G 4
Peterborough o CDN (ONT) 238-239 G 4
Peterborough o USA (NH) 278-279 K 6
Peterhead o GB 90-91 G 5

Peruíbe o RI 162-163 B 2
Peter's Mine o GUY 62-63 E 2
Peterson o CDN (SAS) 232-233 N 3
Peterson o USA (IA) 274-275 C 2
Peterson, ostrov ⌐ RUS 108-109 I 3
Peterstown o USA (WV) 280-281 F 6
Petersville o USA 20-21 P 5
Pethel Peninsula ⌐ CDN 30-31 O 4
Petin o E 98-99 D 3
Petit-Bourg o F 56 E 3
Petit-Cap o CDN (QUE) 242-243 D 3
Petitcodiac o CDN (NB) 240-241 K 5
Petitcodiac River ~ CDN (NB) 240-241 K 5
Petite Bois Island ⌐ USA (MS) 268-269 M 6
Petite Forte o CDN (NFL) 242-243 O 5
Petite Kabylie ▲ DZ 190-191 E 2
Petite-Rivière-de-Île o CDN (NB) 240-241 L 3
Petite Rivière de la Baleine ~ CDN 36-37 L 7
Petite Rivière de Povungnituk ~ CDN 36-37 M 4
Petit Étang o CDN (NS) 240-241 P 4
Petite-Vallée o CDN (QUE) 242-243 C 3
Petit Godve o RH 54-55 J 5
Petit Jardin o CDN (NFL) 242-243 J 4
Petit Jean Mountain ▲ USA (AR) 276-277 C 4
Petit Jean State Park ⊥ USA (AR) 276-277 C 4
Petit Lac des Loups Marins o CDN 36-37 N 6
Petit Lac Manicouagan o CDN 38-39 L 3
Petit Lac Opinaca o CDN 38-39 K 3
Petit Loango, Parc National du ⊥ G 210-211 B 5
Petit Mécatina, Île du ⌐ CDN (QUE) 242-243 J 2
Petit Mécatina, Rivière du ~ CDN 38-39 O 3
Petit Mont Cameroun ▲ CAM 204-205 H 6
Petitot River ~ CDN 30-31 J 6
Petit Point ▲ AUS 176-177 B 2
Petit-Rocher o CDN (NB) 240-241 K 3
Petit-Saguenay o CDN (QUE) 240-241 F 2
Petits-Escoumins o CDN (QUE) 240-241 F 2
Petitsikapau Lake o CDN 36-37 N 4
Petlad o IND 138-139 D 8
Peto o MEX 52-53 K 1
Petoh o MAL 162-163 E 3
Petorca, Rio ~ RCH 78-79 D 2
Petoskey o USA (MI) 272-273 E 2
Petra ∴· JOR 130-131 D 2
Petra, ostrova ⌐ RUS 108-109 k 3
Petra I, ostrov ⌐ ARK 16 G 2
Petra Velikogo, zaliv ≈ 122-123 H 6
Petrel Bank ≃ 22-23 F 6
Petric o BG 102-103 C 7
Petrified Forest o USA (MS) 268-269 K 4
Petrified Forest National Park ∴· USA (AZ) 256-257 F 4
Petrified Wood Park ∴· USA (SD) 260-261 H 1
Petrinja o HR 100-101 F 2
Petrišćevo o RUS 94-95 N 4
Petrivs'ka fortec'a · UA 102-103 K 4
Petro o PK 138-139 C 6
Petrodvorec o RUS 94-95 L 2
Petrograjiyca ☆ RO 102-103 E 4
Petrogani o RO 102-103 C 5
Petrovac o YU 100-101 H 2
Petrovce o RUS 124-125 O 2
Petrovsk o RUS 96-97 D 7
Petrovsk-Zabajkal'skij ☆ RUS 116-117 O 10
Petrov Val o RUS 96-97 D 8
Petrozavodsk ☆ RUS 88-89 N 6
Petrusburg o ZA 220-221 G 4
Petrusdal o NAM 220-221 C 1
Petrus Steyn o ZA 220-221 J 3
Petrusville o ZA 220-221 G 5
Petryav o BY 94-95 L 5
Pettigrew o USA (AR) 276-277 B 5
Pettus o USA (TX) 266-267 H 5
Petty Harbour o CDN (NFL) 242-243 Q 5
Petucalco, Bahía de ≈ 52-53 D 3
Petuhovo ☆ RUS 114-115 O 7
Petuški o RUS (VL) 94-95 Q 3
Peulik, Mount ▲ USA 22-23 H 4
Peumo o RCH 78-79 D 3
Peumo, ozero o RUS 108-109 O 7
Peure ☆ RI 162-163 B 2
Peureula, Tanjung ▲ RI 162-163 B 2

Peureulak o RI 162-163 B 2
Peusangan ~ RI 162-163 B 2
Pevek o RUS 112-113 Q 2
Peyumani, Sierra ▲ YV 60-61 K 5
Peza ~ RUS 88-89 S 4
Pezas o RUS 114-115 T 7
Pézenas o F 90-91 J 10
Pezenka ~ RUS 112-113 M 3
Pežostrov o RUS 88-89 N 4
Pezu o PK 138-139 C 3
Pfarmigan, Cape ▲ CDN 24-25 M 5
Pfarrkirchen o D 92-93 M 4
Pfizner, Mount ▲ AUS 178-179 C 3
Pforzheim o D 92-93 M 4
Phailieng o IND 142-143 H 4
Phalaborwa o ZA 218-219 F 6
Phá Lai o VN 156-157 K 6
Phalodi o IND 138-139 D 6
Phalombe o MW 218-219 H 2
Phältan o IND 140-141 F 2
Phan o THA 142-143 L 6
Phang Khon o THA 158-159 G 2
Phangnga o THA 158-159 E 6
Phanom o THA 158-159 E 6
Phanom Dong Rak ▲▲ THA 158-159 F 4
Phanom Sarakham o THA 158-159 F 4
Phan Rang Tháp Chàm o VN 158-159 K 5
Phan Ri, Vûng ~ VN 158-159 K 5
Phan Thiêt o VN 158-159 K 5
Phantoms Cave = Trou des Fantomes · CAM 210-211 C 2
Pharenda o IND 142-143 C 2
Pharping o NEP 144-145 E 7
Pharr o USA (TX) 266-267 J 7
Phaselis ∴· TR 128-129 D 4
Phatthalung o THA 158-159 F 7
Phayakhapun Phisai o THA 158-159 G 3
Phayao o THA 142-143 L 6
Phayuha Khiri o THA 158-159 F 3
Phedra o SME 62-63 G 3
Phelp River ~ USA 174-175 C 3
Phelps Co o CDN 30-31 S 6
Phelps Lake o USA (NC) 282-283 L 5
Phen o THA 158-159 F 2
Phenix City o USA (AL) 284-285 E 4
Phetchabun o THA 158-159 F 2
Phibun Mangsahan o THA 158-159 H 3
Phichit o THA 158-159 F 2
Phikwe, Selebi- o RB 218-219 E 6
Philadelphia o USA (MS) 268-269 L 4
Philadelphia o · USA (PA) 280-281 L 4
Philae ∴· ET 194-195 F 7
Phil Campbell o USA (AL) 284-285 C 2
Phil Campbell o USA (AL) 284-285 B 2
Philip o USA (SD) 260-261 F 2
Philip Broke, Kap ▲ GRØ 26-27 O 4
Philippeville o B 92-93 H 4
Philippi o USA (WV) 280-281 F 4
Philippi, Lake o AUS 174-175 F 6
Philippi, Monte ▲ RA 80 E 5
Philippine Basin ≃ 14-15 E 6
Philippines = Pilipinas ■ RP 160-161 D 5
Philippines = Pilipinas ⌐ RP 160-161 D 5
Philippine Trench ≃ 160-161 G 6
Philippolis o ZA 220-221 G 5
Philipsburg o USA (MT) 250-251 F 5
Philipsburg o USA (PA) 280-281 H 3
Phillip Island ⌐ AUS 180-181 H 5
Phillips o USA (ME) 278-279 L 4
Phillips o USA (WI) 270-271 H 5
Phillips Arm o CDN (BC) 230-231 D 3
Phillipsburg o USA (KS) 262-263 H 5
Phillipsburg o USA (NJ) 280-281 L 4
Phillips Inlet ≈ 26-27 Q 2
Phillips Mountains ▲▲ ARK 16 F 23
Phillips Point o USA 24-25 P 2
Phillips Range ▲▲ AUS 172-173 G 4
Philo o USA (CA) 246-247 B 4
Philomath o USA (OR) 244-245 B 6
Philpots Island ⌐ CDN 24-25 Q 5
Philpott Lake o USA (VA) 280-281 F 7
Phippen o CDN (SAS) 232-233 K 3
Phippsøya ⌐ N 84-85 M 2
Phitsanulok o THA 158-159 F 2
Phitshane o RB 220-221 G 4
Phnom Penh = Phnum Pénh · K 158-159 H 5
Phnum Pénh ☆ · K 158-159 H 5
Phoenix o USA (AZ) 256-257 C 5
Phoenix ☆ · USA (AZ) 256-257 C 5
Phoenixville o USA (CT) 278-279 J 7
Phoenixville o USA (PA) 280-281 L 3
Phon o THA 158-159 G 3
Phoncharoen o THA 158-159 G 4
Phonda o IND 138-139 E 3
Phongata o IND 138-139 C 5
Phôngsali o LAO 156-157 C 5
Phong Thô o VN 156-157 C 5
Phon Thong o THA 158-159 G 3
Phôn Sa Van o LAO 156-157 C 7
Phoque, Rivière au ~ CDN 36-37 N 7
Phou Khoun o LAO 156-157 C 7
Phrae o THA 142-143 L 6
Phranakhon Si Ayutthaya o ••• THA 158-159 F 3
Phran Kratai o THA 158-159 E 2
Phu Cuong o THA 158-159 J 4
Phú Bài o VN 158-159 J 3
Phú Cát o VN 158-159 K 4
Phu Dén Din ▲ VN 156-157 C 6
Phú Hung o VN 158-159 H 5
Phuket o THA 158-159 E 6
Phukradung o THA 158-159 F 2
Phulabani o IND 138-139 H 4
Phulchari o BD 142-143 F 3

Phuldu o IND 142-143 H 4
Phú Lôc o VN 158-159 J 2
Phú Luong o THA 156-157 D 6
Phumi Ânlóng o K 158-159 G 5
Phumi Bahm o K 158-159 H 4
Phumi Banam o K 158-159 H 5
Phumi Chhlong o K 158-159 H 4
Phumi Chôam Sla o K 158-159 G 4
Phumi Chûb Krau o K 158-159 G 4
Phumi Kâmpóng Trâbêk o K 158-159 H 4
Phumi Khley o K 158-159 G 5
Phumi Krêk o K 158-159 H 4
Phumi Labang Siêk o K 158-159 J 3
Phumi Mlu Prey o K 158-159 H 4
Phumi o Snguôt o K 158-159 H 4
Phumi Pring o K 158-159 H 4
Phumi Sala Vichey o K 158-159 H 4
Phumi Spoe Tbong o K 158-159 H 4
Phumi Sâmraông o K 158-159 G 4
Phumi Taek Sôk o K 158-159 H 4
Phumi Thmâ Pôk o K 158-159 G 4
Phumi Véal Rénh o K 158-159 G 5
Phú My o VN 158-159 K 4
Phú My o VN 158-159 J 5
Phú Nhon o VN 158-159 K 3
Phunpin o THA 158-159 E 6
Phuntsholing o BHT 142-143 F 2
Phu'o'c Long o VN 158-159 H 5
Phu'o'c So'n o VN 158-159 J 3
Phú Quôc, Dào ⌐ VN 158-159 G 5
Phú Qúy o VN 158-159 K 5
Phurkia o IND 138-139 G 4
Phu Sa Phin ▲ VN 156-157 D 6
Phu Tho o VN 156-157 D 6
Phutnaditjhaba o ZA 220-221 J 4
Phutthaisong o THA 158-159 G 3
Phu Yen o THA 158-159 F 2
Plaçabuçu o BR 68-69 K 7
Piaca dos Mineiros o BR 72-73 G 6
Piacenza o I 100-101 C 2
Piamonte o CO 60-61 D 6
Pianag o RP 160-161 D 6
Pianco o BR 68-69 K 5
Piancó, Rio ~ BR 68-69 J 5
Piandang, Tanjung ▲ MAL 162-163 D 2
Piangil o AUS 180-181 G 5
Pianguan o VRC 154-155 G 2
Piankana o ZRE 210-211 E 5
Pianosa, Isola ⌐ I 100-101 C 3
Piapot o CDN (SAS) 232-233 J 5
Piapot Indian Reservation 𝕏 CDN (SAS) 232-233 J 5
Piasecno o PL 92-93 Q 2
Piaski o PL 92-93 R 3
Piatra-Neamţ o · RO 102-103 E 4
Piauí o BR 68-69 G 6
Piauí, Rio ~ BR 68-69 G 6
Piauí, Rio ~ BR 68-69 K 7
Piave ~ I 100-101 D 1
Piaxtla, Punta ▲ MEX 50-51 F 6
Piaxtla, Rio ~ MEX 50-51 F 6
Pibor ~ SUD 208-209 A 5
Pibor Post o SUD 208-209 A 5
Pibrans = Pribram o CZ 92-93 N 4
Pica o YV 60-61 J 3
Pica, La o YV 60-61 H 3
Picacho o USA (AZ) 256-257 D 6
Picacho o USA (NM) 256-257 K 6
Picacho de la Laguna ▲ MEX 50-51 E 6
Picada o BR 70-71 K 5
Picáevo o RUS 94-95 S 5
Picão, Ponta de ▲ BR 70-71 K 5
Pica-Pau, Cachoeira ~ BR 62-63 K 6
Picard o SY 222-223 E 2
Picardie o F 90-91 H 6
Picayune o USA (MS) 268-269 L 6
Picentini, Monti ▲ I 100-101 E 4
Pich o MEX 52-53 J 2
Pichalo, Punta ▲ RCH 70-71 D 6
Pichaman o RCH 78-79 C 3
Pichana, Rio ~ PE 64-65 D 4
Pichanal o RA 76-77 E 2
Picher o USA (OK) 264-265 K 2
Picheugas, Paso ▲ RA 76-77 C 6
Pichilemu o RCH 78-79 C 3
Pichilingue o MEX 50-51 E 5
Pichi Mahuida o RA 78-79 G 4
Pichinche, Volcán ▲ EC 64-65 C 3
Pichilleufu, Cerro ▲ RA 78-79 D 6
Pichis, Río ~ PE 64-65 E 7
Pichor o IND 138-139 F 6
Pichucalco o MEX 52-53 H 3
Pichupichu, Volcán ▲ PE 70-71 B 5
Pic Island ⌐ CDN (ONT) 236-237 B 4
Pickens o USA (MS) 268-269 L 4
Pickens o USA (OK) 264-265 H 4
Pickens o USA (SC) 284-285 H 2
Pickens, Fort · USA (FL) 286-287 B 1
Pickerel Lake o CDN (ONT) 234-235 M 6
Pickerel River ~ CDN (ONT) 238-239 E 3
Pickering o USA (MO) 274-275 D 4
Pickertaramoor 𝕏 AUS 172-173 K 1
Pickford o USA (MI) 272-273 E 2
Pickstown o USA (SD) 260-261 H 3
Pickwick Landing State Park ⊥ USA (TN) 276-277 G 5
Pico ⌐ P 6-7 E 6
Pico, Serra do ▲ BR 72-73 H 4
Pico da Neblina, Parque Nacional do ⊥ BR 66-67 D 2
Pico de Orizaba, Parque Nacional ⊥ MEX 52-53 F 2
Pico de Salamanca o RA 80 G 3
Pico Negro, Cerro ▲ RCH 70-71 C 6
Pico Truncado o RA 80 G 3
Picos o BR 68-69 H 5
Picos, Los o MEX 50-51 H 3

Picota o PE 64-65 D 5
Pic River ~ CDN (ONT) 236-237 B 3
Picton o AUS 180-181 L 3
Picton o CDN (ONT) 238-239 H 4
Picton o NZ 182 E 4
Picton, Isla ⌐ RCH 80 G 7
Pictou o CDN (NS) 240-241 N 5
Pictou Island ⌐ CDN (NS) 240-241 N 5
Pictou Landing o CDN (NS) 240-241 N 5
Picture Butte o CDN (ALB) 232-233 F 6
Pictured Rocks National Lakeshore ⊥ USA (MI) 270-271 M 4
Picturesque Site ∴· RI 166-167 H 2
Picudo, Cerro ▲ RA 80 F 3
Picuí o BR 68-69 K 5
Picunda o RA 78-79 G 4
Picunda, mys ▲ GE 126-127 D 6
Pichín Leufú o RA 78-79 E 5
Picún Leufú, Arroyo ~ RA 78-79 D 5
Picúnleufú, Cerro ▲ RA 78-79 D 5
Picuris Indian Reservation 𝕏 USA (NM) 256-257 K 4
Pidando o DVR 150-151 E 8
Pidarak o PK 134-135 K 6
Pidie, Ujung ▲ RI 162-163 A 2
Pidurutalagala o CL 140-141 J 7
Piebli o CI 202-203 G 5
Piedad de Cavadas, La o MEX 52-53 C 1
Piedade o BR 72-73 G 7
Pié de Palo, Sierra ▲▲ RA 76-77 C 6
Piedmont o USA (AL) 284-285 E 3
Piedmont o USA (MO) 276-277 E 3
Piedmont o USA (SD) 260-261 C 2
Piedmont Lake o USA (OH) 280-281 E 3
Piedmont National Wildlife Refuge ⊥ USA (GA) 284-285 G 3
Piedra, Cerro ▲ RCH 78-79 C 4
Piedrabuena o E 98-99 E 5
Piedra del Águila o RA 78-79 D 6
Piedra de Olla, Cerro ▲ MEX 52-53 F 3
Piedra Echada o RA 78-79 H 5
Piedrahita o E 98-99 E 4
Piedra River ~ USA (CO) 254-255 H 6
Piedras, Las o PE 70-71 C 3
Piedras, Punta ▲ RA 78-79 L 3
Piedras Altas o BR 74-75 D 8
Piedras Blancas o CR 52-53 C 7
Piedras Negras ∴· GCA 52-53 J 3
Piedras Negras o MEX 50-51 J 3
Piedra Sola o ROU 78-79 J 2
Piedras Point o RP 160-161 D 7
Pie Island ⌐ CDN (ONT) 234-235 O 6
Piekenaarskloof ▲ ZA 220-221 D 6
Pieksämäki o FIN 88-89 J 5
Piéla o BF 202-203 K 3
Pielavesi o FIN 88-89 J 5
Pielinen o FIN 88-89 K 5
Pelijekaise nationalpark ⊥ S 86-87 H 3
Pieman River ~ AUS 180-181 H 6
Piemonte o I 100-101 B 2
Pienaarsrivier o ZA 220-221 J 2
Piendamo o CO 60-61 D 6
Pieniężno o PL 92-93 Q 1
Pienza o I 100-101 D 3
Pierce o USA (ID) 250-251 D 5
Pierce o USA (NE) 262-263 J 2
Pierce Inlet, Fort o USA 286-287 J 4
Pierce Lake o CDN 34-35 K 3
Pierceland o CDN 32-33 O 3
Pierceville o USA (KS) 262-263 F 7
Pieres o RA 78-79 K 5
Pierowall o GB 90-91 F 2
Pierre ☆ USA (SD) 260-261 F 2
Pierre Hole o F 62-63 H 4
Pierre Lake o CDN (ONT) 236-237 H 3
Pierrette o F 62-63 H 4
Pierre Verendrye Monument, Fort · USA (SD) 260-261 F 2
Pierreville o CDN (QUE) 238-239 N 2
Pierreville o TT 60-61 L 2
Pierson o CDN (MAN) 234-235 B 5
Pierson o USA (FL) 286-287 H 2
Pierz o USA (MN) 270-271 D 5
Piešťany o SK 92-93 O 4
Pietarsaari = Jakobstad o FIN 88-89 G 5
Pietermaritzburg ☆ ·· ZA 220-221 K 4
Pietersburg o ZA 218-219 E 6
Pietlo o LB 202-203 F 7
Pie Town o USA (NM) 256-257 G 4
Piet Plessis o ZA 220-221 G 3
Piet Retief o ZA 220-221 K 3
Pietroşani o RO 102-103 D 6
Pifo o EC 64-65 C 2
Pigeon Creek ~ USA (AL) 284-285 D 5
Pigeon Forge o USA (NC) 282-283 D 5
Pigeon Hill o CDN (NB) 240-241 L 3
Pigeon Hole o AUS 172-173 K 4
Pigeon Lake o CDN (ALB) 232-233 E 3
Pigeon River ~ CDN (ON) 274-275 N 3
Piggott o USA (AR) 276-277 F 3
Piggs Peak o SD 220-221 K 2
Pigmi o GH 202-203 M 6
Pigué o RA 78-79 H 4
Pigüé, Arroyo ~ RA 78-79 H 4
Pigüm Do ⌐ ROK 150-151 E 10
Pihtipudas o FIN 88-89 H 5
Pihtovyj greben', gora ▲ RUS 114-115 S 7
Pijijiapan o MEX 52-53 H 4
Pikangikum o CDN (ONT) 234-235 K 3
Pikangikum Lake o CDN (ONT) 234-235 J 3
Pikasilla o EST 94-95 K 2
Pikas'vajat ~ RUS 112-113 R 5
Pike Island ⌐ CDN 36-37 M 3
Pike Lake o CDN (SAS) 232-233 M 4
Pikes Peak ▲ USA (CO) 254-255 K 5
Piketberg o ZA 220-221 D 6
Piketon o USA (OH) 280-281 C 4

Pocitos, Salar ⊝ RA 76-77 D 3
Pocoata o BOL 70-71 D 6
Poço de Fora o BR 68-69 J 6
Poçõe o BR 72-73 K 3
Poções o BR 68-69 H 3
Pocomoke City o USA (MD) 280-281 L 5
Pocomoke River ~ USA (MD) 280-281 L 5
Pocomoke Sound ≈ 46-47 K 7
Pocomoke Sound ≈ USA 280-281 L 6
Pocone o BR 70-71 J 5
Poço Redondo o BR 68-69 K 6
Poços de Caldas o BR 72-73 G 6
Poço Verde o BR 68-69 J 7
Pocrane o BR 72-73 K 5
Podbereze o RUS (NVG) 94-95 M 2
Podbereze o RUS (PSK) 94-95 M 3
Podbořany o CZ 92-93 M 3
Podborove o RUS 94-95 L 3
Podčer'e o RUS 114-115 D 3
Podčer'e ~ RUS 114-115 E 3
Poddor'e o RUS 94-95 M 3
Podelga ~ RUS 114-115 R 4
Podena, Kepulauan ∩ RI 166-167 K 3
Podgorenski o RUS 102-103 L 2
Podgorica ★ YU 100-101 G 3
Podgornyj, aral ∩ KA 126-127 J 5
Podile o IND 140-141 H 3
Podil's'ka vysočyna ▲ UA 102-103 D 3
Podkagernaja, buhta ⊂ RUS 120-121 T 3
Podkamennaja ~ RUS 110-111 G 2
Podkamennaja Tunguska ~ RUS 116-117 E 5
Podkamennaya Tunguska = Podkamennaja Tunguska ~ RUS 116-117 E 5
Podkova o BG 102-103 D 7
Podkova, ostrov ∩ RUS 108-109 V 4
Podlomka ~ RUS 88-89 O 5
Podocarpus, Parque Nacional ⊥ EC 64-65 C 4
Podol'sk ★• RUS 94-95 P 4
Podor o SN 196-197 C 6
Podora o RUS 88-89 X 5
Podporože o RUS 94-95 O 1
Podravska Slatina o HR 100-101 F 2
Podupalskij Üstirti ▲ KA 126-127 M 3
Podyem-Mihajlovka o RUS 96-97 G 7
Poe Bank ≃ 158-159 D 6
Poechos, Embalse < PE 64-65 B 4
Poelela, Lagoa ⊝ MOC 218-219 H 7
Poeppel Corner • AUS 178-179 D 3
Pofadder o ZA 220-221 D 4
Pogge II, Chute ~• ZRE 216-217 F 3
Poggibonsi o I 100-101 C 3
Pogibi o RUS 122-123 J 2
Pognoa o BF 202-203 L 4
Pogo o CI 202-203 H 4
Pogoanele o RO 102-103 E 5
Pogorelec o RUS 88-89 S 4
Pogost o RUS 88-89 Q 5
Pogradec ★• AL 100-101 H 4
Pograničnyi o BY 94-95 J 5
Pograničnyj o RUS 122-123 D 6
Pogromni Volcano ▲ USA 22-23 O 5
Poguba, Rio ~ BR 70-71 K 5
Pogynden ~ RUS 112-113 M 2
Pogyndino o RUS 112-113 N 2
Poh o RI 164-165 H 4
Pohang o ROK 150-151 G 9
Pohénégamook o CDN (QUE) 240-241 F 3
Pohiois-li o FIN 88-89 H 4
Pohjanlahti ≈ 86-87 K 5
Pohjanmaa ∴ FIN 88-89 G 5
Pohodsk o RUS 112-113 L 2
Pohvistnevo ★ RUS 96-97 H 7
Poie o ZRE 210-211 J 5
Poi Island ∩ SOL 184 I e 4
Poile, La o CDN (NFL) 242-243 K 5
Poinsett, Lake ⊝ USA (SD) 260-261 J 2
Point, Cap ▲ WL 56 E 4
Point "A" Lake < USA (AL) 284-285 D 5
Point au Fer ∩ USA (LA) 268-269 J 7
Point au Mal o CDN (NFL) 242-243 K 4
Point Baker o USA 32-33 D 3
Point Bickerton o CDN (NS) 240-241 O 5
Pointblank o USA (TX) 268-269 E 6
Point Bridget State Park ⊥ USA 32-33 C 2
Point Dume Beach • USA (CA) 248-249 F 5
Pointe-à-la-Garde o CDN (QUE) 240-241 J 2
Pointe-à-Pitre o F 56 E 3
Pointe-au-Père o CDN (QUE) 240-241 G 2
Pointe-aux-Anglais o CDN (QUE) 242-243 A 3
Pointe-Carleton o CDN (QUE) 242-243 E 3
Pointe des Lataniers o RH 54-55 J 5
Pointe du Bois o CDN (MAN) 234-235 H 4
Pointe-Mistassini o CDN (QUE) 242-243 A 3
Pointe Noire o F 56 E 3
Pointe-Noire ★ RCB 210-211 C 6
Pointe Ouest ▲ RH 54-55 J 4
Pointe Parent o CDN (QUE) 242-243 G 2
Pointe Rivière de l'Artibonite o RH 54-55 J 5
Point Gamble o USA (WA) 244-245 C 3
Point Grondine Indian Reservation ✗ CDN (ONT) 238-239 D 3
Point Harbor o USA (NC) 282-283 M 4
Point Hope o USA 20-21 G 2
Point Judith o USA (RI) 278-279 K 7
Point Lake ⊝ CDN 30-31 N 3
Point Lay o USA 20-21 J 2
Point Leamington o CDN (NFL) 242-243 N 3
Point Lookout o USA (MD) 280-281 K 5
Point Lookout ▲ USA (MD) 280-281 K 5
Point Marion o USA (PA) 280-281 G 4
Point May o CDN (NFL) 242-243 N 6
Point Mc Leay o AUS 180-181 E 3
Point Michaud o CDN (NS) 240-241 P 5
Point of Rocks o USA (MD) 280-281 J 4
Point of Rocks o USA (WY) 252-253 K 5
Point Pedro o CL 140-141 J 6
Point Pelee National Park ⊥ CDN (ONT) 238-239 C 7
Point Pleasant o USA (NJ) 280-281 M 3
Point Pleasant o USA (WV) 280-281 D 5
Point Pleasant State Historic Monument • USA (WV) 280-281 D 5
Point Renfrew o CDN (BC) 230-231 E 5
Point Reyes National Seashore ⊥ USA (CA) 246-247 B 5
Point Salvation Aboriginal Land ✗ AUS 176-177 H 4
Point Samson o AUS 172-173 C 6
Point Stuart ∴ AUS 172-173 K 2
Point Washington o USA (FL) 286-287 C 1
Poisson-Blanc o CDN (QUE) 236-237 P 3
Poissonnier Point ▲ AUS 172-173 D 5
Poitiers ★• F 90-91 H 8
Poitou ⊥ F 90-91 G 8
Poitou-Charentes ◻ F 90-91 G 8
Poivre Atoll ∩ SY 224 C 2
Poix-de-Picardie o F 90-91 H 7
Pojarkovo ★ RUS 122-123 C 4
Pojasovyj kamen' hrebet ▲ RUS 114-115 E 4
Pojezierze Mazurskie ⊥ PL 92-93 P 2
Pojezierze Pomorskie ⊥ PL 92-93 O 2
Pojkovskij o RUS 114-115 L 4
Pojlovajaha ~ RUS 108-109 R 7
Pojlovajaha, Arka- ~ RUS 108-109 Q 8
Pojlu o AZ 128-129 M 2
Pojma ~ RUS 116-117 H 7
Pojmyga ~ RUS 116-117 N 6
Pojo, Río de ~ BOL 70-71 E 5
Pojuca o BR 72-73 L 2
Pojuca, Rio ~ BR 72-73 L 2
Pojuščie peski •• RUS 118-119 D 9
Pokanaevka o RUS 116-117 H 7
Pokaran o IND 138-139 C 6
Pokataroo o AUS 178-179 K 5
Pokemouche o CDN (NB) 240-241 L 3
Pokhara o• NEP 144-145 E 6
Pokigron o SME 62-63 G 3
Po-kil Do ∩ ROK 150-151 F 10
Pokka o FIN 88-89 H 2
Poko o ZRE 210-211 L 2
Pokojnickaja ~ RUS 108-109 U 8
Pokok Sena o MAL 162-163 D 2
Pokoľka ~ RUS 114-115 R 3
Pokrovka o KA 126-127 M 3
Pokrovka o KS 146-147 C 4
Pokrovka o RUS 114-115 O 7
Pokrovsk o RUS (IRK) 116-117 H 8
Pokrovsk ★ RUS (SAH) 118-119 O 5
Pokrovs'ke o UA 102-103 K 4
Pokšen'ga ~ RUS 88-89 R 5
Pokuma o Z 218-219 D 3
Pokur o RUS 114-115 N 4
Pola o RP 160-161 D 6
Pola, La o•• E 98-99 E 3
Polacca o USA (AZ) 256-257 E 3
Polacca Wash ~ USA (AZ) 256-257 E 3
Polače o• HR 100-101 F 3
Polack ★•• BY 94-95 L 4
Pola de Laviana o E 98-99 E 3
Pola de Lena o E 98-99 E 3
Poladpur o IND 140-141 E 2
Polān o IR 134-135 J 6
Polanco o ROU 78-79 M 2
Polanco o RP 160-161 E 8
Poland = Polska ■ PL 92-93 O 3
Polar Bear Provincial Park ⊥ CDN 34-35 N 3
Polaris o USA (MT) 250-251 E 6
Polaris Forland ⊥ GRØ 26-27 U 3
Polar Plateau ▲ ARK 16 E 0
Polatlı o TR 128-129 E 3
Polavaram o IND 142-143 B 7
Polazna o RUS 96-97 K 4
Polcura, Río ~ RCH 78-79 D 4
Pole Abyssal Plain ≃ 16 A 14
Pol-e 'Alam ★ AFG 138-139 B 2
Poleang ~ RI 164-165 G 6
Polebridge o USA (MT) 250-251 E 3
Pol-e Fasā o IR 134-135 E 4
Pol-e Ḥomri o AFG 136-137 L 7
Pol-e Ḥomri, Darryā-ye ~ AFG 136-137 L 7
Pol-e Loušān o IR 128-129 N 4
Pol-e Safid o IR 136-137 C 6
Polessk ★ RUS 94-95 G 4
Polevskoj ★ RUS 96-97 M 5
Polewali o RI 164-165 F 5
Polgahawela o CL 140-141 J 7
Poli o CAM 204-205 K 4
Poli o CY 128-129 E 5
Policastro, Golfo di ≈ 100-101 E 5
Police, Pointe ▲ SY 224 D 2
Policemans Point o AUS 180-181 E 4
Policoro o I 100-101 F 4
Poligiros o GR 100-101 J 4
Polihnitos o GR 100-101 L 5
Polikastro o GR 100-101 J 4
Poliny Osipenko, imeni ★ RUS 122-123 G 2
Polis'ke o UA 102-103 F 2
Politovo o RUS 88-89 U 4
Poliva ~ RUS 116-117 L 6
Polja ~ RUS 94-95 Q 4
Poljakovskij o RUS 118-119 N 9
Poljana o UA 102-103 C 3
Poljarnoe o RUS 110-111 b 4
Poljarnyj o RUS (CUK) 112-113 U 2
Poljarnyj o RUS (MUR) 88-89 M 2
Poljarnyj o RUS (SAH) 110-111 H 6
Poljarnyj hrebet ▲ RUS 120-121 O 2
Poljarnyj Ural ▲ RUS 114-115 E 2
Polk o USA (AL) 284-285 D 4
Polk, Fort ✗✗ USA (LA) 268-269 G 5
Pollāchi o IND 140-141 G 5
Pollença o E 98-99 J 5
Pollilo o RP 160-161 D 5
Pollilo Island ∩ RP 160-161 D 5
Pollilo Islands ∩ RP 160-161 E 5
Pollilo Strait ≈ 160-161 D 5
Pollino, Parco del ⊥ I 100-101 F 5
Pollock o USA (ID) 250-251 C 6
Pollock o USA (LA) 268-269 H 5
Pollock Hills ▲ AUS 172-173 H 7
Pollockville o CDN (ALB) 232-233 G 4
Pol'noj Voronež ~ RUS 94-95 R 5
Polo o USA (IL) 274-275 J 3
Polobaya Grande o PE 70-71 B 5
Polochic, Río ~ GCA 52-53 K 4
Polock = Polack ★•• BY 94-95 L 4
Pologij-Sergeeva, ostrov ∩ RUS 108-109 T 4
Pologoe Zajmišče o RUS 96-97 E 9
Polohy o UA 102-103 K 4
Polom o RUS 96-97 G 4
Polomolok o RP 160-161 F 9
Polonina-Runa hora ▲ UA 102-103 C 3
Polonnaruwa o••• CL 140-141 J 7
Polousnyj krjaž ▲ RUS 110-111 X 5
Polovinnoe, ozero ⊝ RUS 108-109 W 6
Polson o USA (MT) 250-251 E 4
Poltava ★ UA 102-103 J 3
Poltavka ★ RUS 124-125 G 1
Põltsamaa o•• EST 94-95 J 2
Poluj ~ RUS 108-109 M 8
Poluj ~ RUS 114-115 K 2
Polujskaja vozvyšennosť ▲ RUS 114-115 J 2
Polūr o IND 140-141 H 4
Põlva ★ EST 94-95 K 2
Polvadera Peak ▲ USA (NM) 256-257 J 2
Polvār, Rūd-e ~ IR 134-135 E 3
Polvaredas o RA 78-79 K 3
Polvora o PE 64-65 D 5
Polwarth o CDN (SAS) 232-233 M 2
Pölwe = Põlva ★ EST 94-95 K 2
Polyarnyy Ural = Poljarnyj Ural ▲ RUS 114-115 E 2
Polynesia ∩ 14-15 M 7
Polyuc o MEX 52-53 K 2
Poma o ZRE 210-211 K 4
Pomabamba o PE 64-65 D 6
Pomacanchi o PE 70-71 B 3
Pomahuaca o PE 64-65 C 4
Pomarkku o FIN 88-89 F 6
Pomasi, Cerro de ▲ PE 70-71 B 4
Pombal o BR (PA) 68-69 K 5
Pombal o BR (RON) 70-71 F 2
Pombal o P 98-99 C 5
Pombal, Igarapé do ~ BR 68-69 B 5
Pombangi o RI 164-165 G 5
Pombas o BR 66-67 F 3
Pombas, Rio das ~ BR 66-67 G 6
Pombuige ~ ANG 216-217 C 5
Pomene o MOC 218-219 H 6
Pomerene o USA (AZ) 256-257 E 6
Pomeroy o USA (OH) 280-281 D 4
Pomeroy o USA (WA) 244-245 H 4
Pomeroy o ZA 220-221 K 4
Pomfret o ZA 220-221 F 2
Pomio o PNG 183 F 3
Pomme de Terre Lake ⊝ USA (MO) 276-277 B 3
Pomona o RA 78-79 G 5
Pomona o USA (CA) 248-249 G 5
Pomona o USA (KS) 262-263 L 6
Pomona Lake ⊝ USA (KS) 262-263 L 6
Pomorska, Zatoka ≈ 92-93 N 1
Pomorskij proliv ≈ 88-89 U 2
Pomorskoe o RUS 108-109 E 5
Pomos o CY 128-129 E 5
Pompano Beach o USA (FL) 286-287 J 5
Pompei •• I 100-101 E 4
Pompéia o BR 72-73 E 7
Pompeu o BR 72-73 H 5
Pompeys Pillar o USA (MT) 250-251 M 6
Pompeys Pillar • USA (MT) 250-251 M 5
Pom Phra Chunlachomkiao o THA 158-159 F 4
Pompton Lakes o USA (NJ) 280-281 M 3
Pompué, Rio ~ MOC 200-201 F 3
Pomr', zaliv ⊂ RUS 122-123 K 2
Pomut ~ RUS 114-115 K 3
Ponape ∩ FSM 13 G 2
Ponass Lake ⊝ CDN (SAS) 232-233 O 3
Ponazyrevo o RUS 96-97 E 4
Ponca o USA (NE) 262-263 K 2
Ponca City o USA (OK) 264-265 G 2
Ponce o USA (PR) 286-287 P 2
Ponce de Leon o USA (FL) 286-287 D 1
Poncha Springs o USA (CO) 254-255 J 5
Ponchatoula o USA (LA) 268-269 K 6
Poncheville, Lac ⊝ CDN (QUE) 236-237 M 2
Pond o USA (CA) 248-249 E 4
Pond Creek o USA (OK) 264-265 G 2
Pondera Coulee ~ USA (MT) 250-251 H 3
Ponderosa o USA (CA) 248-249 F 3
Pond Fork ~ USA (WV) 280-281 E 6
Pondicherry ◻ IND 140-141 H 5
Pondicherry ★•• IND 140-141 H 5
Pond Inlet ≈ 24-25 h 4
Pond Inlet o CDN 24-25 h 4
Pondosa o USA (CA) 246-247 D 2
Pond River ~ USA (KY) 276-277 H 3
Ponds, Isle of ∩ CDN 38-39 R 2
Ponds Lake, River of ⊝ CDN (NFL) 242-243 L 2
Pondung Lamanggang o RI 162-163 D 6
Poneloya o NIC 52-53 L 5
Ponente, Riviera di ∪ I 100-101 A 3
Ponerečnyj Algan ~ RUS 112-113 R 4
Ponferrada o• E 98-99 D 3
Pônfi ~ MOC 218-219 G 2
Pongai o BR 72-73 F 6
Pongara, Pointe ▲ G 210-211 B 3
Pong Chi o THA 158-159 F 2
Pong Nam Ron o THA 158-159 G 4
Pongo ~ SUD 206-207 H 5
Pongo de Cumbinama ~ PE 64-65 C 4
Pongo de Paquipachango ~ PE 64-65 E 7
Pongola o ZA 220-221 K 3
Pongola ~ ZA 220-221 K 3
Pongolapoortdam < ZA 220-221 L 3
Pongore o ZW 218-219 D 4
Poni ~ BF 202-203 J 4
Ponindilisa, Tanjung ▲ RI 164-165 G 4
Ponio o RT 202-203 L 4
Ponio, Río ~ RCH 76-77 B 6
Ponna o MYA 142-143 J 5
Ponnaiyar ~ IND 140-141 H 4
Ponnāni o IND 140-141 F 5
Ponneri o IND 140-141 J 4
Ponnūru Nidubrolu o IND 140-141 J 2
Ponoj o RUS (MUR) 88-89 Q 3
Ponoj ~ RUS 88-89 N 3
Ponoka o CDN (ALB) 232-233 E 3
Ponomarevka o RUS 114-115 R 6
Ponomarevka ★ RUS (ORB) 96-97 J 7
Ponondougou o CI 202-203 G 5
Ponorogo o RI 168 D 3
Ponrang o RI 164-165 G 5
Ponson Island ∩ RP 160-161 F 7
Ponta o BR 66-67 E 3
Ponta Delgada ∩ P 6-7 E 6
Ponta de Mata o YV 60-61 K 3
Ponta de Pedras o BR 62-63 K 6
Ponta dos Indios o BR 62-63 J 3
Ponta do Sol o CV 202-203 B 5
Ponta do Zumbi o BR 68-69 F 2
Ponta Freitas Morna o ANG 216-217 B 3
Ponta Grande ▲ BR 72-73 L 4
Ponta Grossa o BR 74-75 E 5
Pontal o BR 72-73 F 6
Pontal, Rio do ~ BR 68-69 H 6
Pontalina o BR 72-73 F 4
Pontan River ~ CDN 30-31 L 6
Ponta Porã o BR 76-77 K 2
Pontarlier o• F 90-91 L 8
Pontas de Pedras o BR 68-69 L 5
Pont-Audemer o F 90-91 H 7
Pontchartrain, Lake ⊝ USA (LA) 268-269 K 6
Pontchâteau o F 90-91 F 8
Pont de Suert, el o E 98-99 H 3
Pont du Gard ••• F 90-91 K 10
Ponte Alta, Rio ~ BR 68-69 E 7
Ponte Alta do Tocantins o BR 68-69 E 7
Ponteareas o E 98-99 C 3
Ponte Branca o BR 72-73 D 4
Ponte da Barca o P 98-99 C 4
Ponte de Itabapoana o BR 72-73 K 6
Ponte de Sor o P 98-99 C 5
Ponte Firme o BR 72-73 G 5
Ponteix o CDN (SAS) 232-233 L 6
Ponte Nova o BR 72-73 J 6
Ponte Ribeiro, Lago ⊝ BR 70-71 H 4
Pontes e Lacerda o BR 70-71 H 4
Ponte Serrada o BR 74-75 D 6
Pontevedra o E 98-99 C 3
Pontiac o USA (IL) 274-275 K 4
Pontiac o USA (MI) 272-273 F 5
Pontianak ★ RI 162-163 H 5
Pontian Kecil o MAL 162-163 E 4
Pontic Mountains = Kuzey Anadolu Dağları ▲ TR 10-11 C 4
Pontivy o F 90-91 F 7
Ponto Arari o BR 62-63 J 5
Ponto Busch o BOL 70-71 G 6
Pontoise ★ F 90-91 J 7
Pontokerasia o GR 100-101 J 4
Ponton o CDN 34-35 G 3
Ponton Creek ~ AUS 176-177 G 5
Pontorson o F 90-91 G 7
Pontotoc o USA (MS) 268-269 L 2
Pontotoc o USA (TX) 266-267 J 3
Pontrémoli o• I 100-101 B 2
Pontrillas o CDN (SAS) 232-233 O 2
Pont-Rouge o CDN (QUE) 238-239 O 2
Ponts o E 98-99 H 4
Pontypool o CDN (ONT) 238-239 G 4
Ponuga o PA 52-53 D 8
Pony Express Station ∴ USA (KS) 262-263 K 5
Ponza o I 100-101 D 4
Ponziane, Ísole ∩ I 100-101 D 4
Poochera o AUS 180-181 C 2
Pool ◻ RCB 210-211 E 5
Poole o GB 90-91 G 6
Poole's Monument • AUS 178-179 F 5
Poolesville o USA (MD) 280-281 J 4
Pooley Island ∩ CDN (BC) 228-229 F 4
Pool Malebo ⊝ ZRE 210-211 E 6
Poolowanna Lake ⊝ AUS 178-179 D 4
Pools Cove o CDN (NFL) 242-243 N 5
Poolville o USA (TX) 264-265 G 6
Poonamallee o IND 140-141 J 4
Pooncarie o AUS 180-181 G 2
Pooneryn o CL 140-141 J 6
Poopó o BOL 70-71 D 6
Poopó, Lago de ⊝ BOL 70-71 D 6
Pooppelloe Lake ⊝ AUS 178-179 G 6
Poorman o USA 20-21 N 4
Poor Man Indian Reserve ✗ CDN (SAS) 232-233 O 4
Popa Falls ~• NAM 216-217 F 9
Popayán ★•• CO 60-61 C 6
Popča o RUS 88-89 W 5
Pope o• LV 94-95 G 3
Popenguine o• SN 202-203 B 2
Poperechnoi Island ∩ USA 22-23 Q 5
Poperinge o B 92-93 G 3
Popham Bay ≈ 36-37 R 2
Popham Beach o USA (ME) 278-279 M 5
Popigaj o RUS (TMR) 110-111 H 4
Popigaj ~ RUS 110-111 F 3
Popigaj ~ RUS 110-111 H 4
Popilta Lake ⊝ AUS 180-181 F 2
Poplar o USA (CA) 248-249 E 3
Poplar o USA (MN) 270-271 D 4
Poplar o USA (MT) 250-251 O 3
Poplar o USA (WI) 270-271 G 4
Poplar Bay o CDN (ALB) 232-233 D 2
Poplar Bluff o USA (MO) 276-277 E 4
Poplarfield o CDN (MAN) 234-235 F 4
Poplar Hill o CDN (ONT) 234-235 J 2
Poplar Hill o USA (VA) 280-281 F 6
Poplar Point o CDN (MAN) 234-235 F 4
Poplar Rapids River ~ CDN (ONT) 236-237 G 3
Poplar River ~ CDN 30-31 J 5
Poplar River ~ CDN (MAN) 234-235 G 2
Poplar River ~ CDN (MAN) 234-235 F 2
Poplar River ~ CDN (SAS) 232-233 N 6
Poplarville o USA (MS) 268-269 L 6
Popocatepetl, Volcán ▲•• MEX 52-53 E 2
Popof Island ∩ USA 22-23 Q 5
Popoh o RI 168 D 4
Popokabaka o ZRE 210-211 F 6
Pópoli o I 100-101 D 3
Popomanaseu, Mount = Makarakombu ▲ SOL 184 I e 3
Popondetta ★ PNG 183 E 5
Popovka o RUS (ROS) 102-103 M 3
Popovka ~ RUS 110-111 c 7
Popovka ~ RUS 120-121 P 2
Popovo o BG 102-103 E 6
Popov Porog o RUS 88-89 N 5
Poprad o SK 92-93 Q 4
Poptún o GCA 52-53 K 3
Poquoson o USA (VA) 280-281 K 6
Porāli ~ PK 134-135 M 5
Porangatu o BR 72-73 F 2
Porbandar o• IND 138-139 B 9
Porčaman o AFG 134-135 K 2
Porção, Cachoeira do ~ BR 66-67 B 3
Porcher Island ∩ CDN (BC) 228-229 D 3
Porciúngula o BR 72-73 J 6
Porcos, Riacho dos ~ BR 68-69 J 5
Porcos, Rio dos ~ BR 72-73 H 2
Porcupine o USA 20-21 W 7
Porcupine, Cape ▲ CDN 38-39 Q 2
Porcupine Abyssal Plain ≃ 6-7 H 3
Porcupine Forest Reserve ⊥ CDN (MAN) 234-235 B 2
Porcupine Gorge National Park ⊥ AUS 174-175 H 7
Porcupine Plain o CDN (SAS) 232-233 P 3
Porcupine Plain ⊥ CDN 20-21 V 2
Porcupine Plateau ▲ CDN 20-21 U 3
Porcupine River ~ CDN 30-31 R 6
Porcupine River ~ USA 20-21 U 3
Porcupine State Park ⊥ USA (MI) 270-271 J 4
Pordenone ★• I 100-101 D 2
Pore o CO 60-61 F 5
Porebada o PNG 183 D 5
Porecatu o BR 72-73 E 7
Poreckoe o RUS 96-97 E 6
Porédaka o RG 202-203 D 4
Porekautimbu, Gunung ▲ RI 164-165 G 4
Porga o DY 202-203 L 4
Porgera o PNG 183 B 3
Porhov ★ RUS 94-95 L 3
Pori o FIN 88-89 F 6
Porirua o NZ 182 E 4
Þórisvatn ⊝ IS 86-87 d 2
Porjus o S 86-87 J 3
Pork Peninsula ∪ CDN 30-31 X 4
Porlakshöfn o IS 86-87 c 3
Porlamar o YV 60-61 K 2
Porog o RUS 88-89 P 5
Poro Island ∩ RP 160-161 F 7
Poro Island ∩ SOL 184 I c 2
Poroma o PNG 183 B 4
Poronaj ~ RUS 122-123 K 4
Poronajsk o RUS 122-123 K 4
Porong o RI 168 E 3
Póros o GR 100-101 H 5
Porosozero o RUS 88-89 M 5
Porotos, Punta ▲ RCH 76-77 B 5
Porožsk o RUS 88-89 W 5
Porpoise Bay ≈ 16 G 13
Porquis Junction o CDN (ONT) 236-237 H 4
Porsangen ≈ 86-87 M 1
Porsangerhalvøya ∪ N 86-87 M 1
Porsea o RI 162-163 C 3
Porsgrunn ★ N 86-87 D 7
Þórshöfn o IS 86-87 f 1
Porsild Mountains ▲ CDN 36-37 H 2
Porsuk Çayı ~ TR 128-129 D 3
Port, Le o F 224 B 7
Porta, Rio da ~ BR 68-69 C 5
Porta Ascotan ó del Jardin ▲ BOL 76-77 C 1
Port Adelaide o AUS 180-181 E 3
Portage o CDN (PEI) 240-241 L 4
Portage o USA (AK) 20-21 Q 6
Portage o USA (UT) 254-255 C 2
Portage o USA (WI) 270-271 J 7
Portage Bay ≈ 22-23 T 4
Portage Bay o CDN (MAN) 234-235 E 3
Portage la Prairie o CDN (MAN) 234-235 E 5
Portageville o USA (MO) 276-277 F 4
Portal o USA (ND) 258-259 E 3
Port Alberni o CDN (BC) 230-231 E 4
Port Albion o CDN (BC) 230-231 D 5
Portalegre o•• P 98-99 D 5
Portales o USA (NM) 256-257 M 4
Port Alexander o USA 32-33 C 3
Port Alfred o ZA 220-221 H 6
Port Alice o CDN (BC) 230-231 B 3
Port Allegany o USA (PA) 280-281 H 2
Port Allen o USA (HI) 288 F 3
Port Allen o USA (LA) 268-269 J 6
Port Alma o AUS 178-179 L 2
Port Andrew o USA (WI) 274-275 H 1
Port Antonio o• JA 54-55 G 5
Portão de Baixo, Cachoeira ~ BR 66-67 K 5
Port Arthur o USA (TX) 268-269 G 7
Port Arthur = Lüshun o VRC 150-151 C 8
Port Askaig o GB 90-91 D 4
Port au Choix o CDN (NFL) 242-243 L 2
Port Augusta o• AUS 180-181 D 2
Port au Port Bay ≈ CDN 242-243 K 4
Port au Port Peninsula ∪ CDN (NFL) 242-243 J 4
Port-au-Prince ★• RH 54-55 J 5
Port Austin o USA (MI) 272-273 G 3
Port aux Choix National Historic Park • CDN (NFL) 242-243 L 2
Port Bay, Port au ≈ 38-39 P 4
Port Bell o EAU 212-213 D 3
Port-Bergé = Boriziny o RM 222-223 E 5
Port Blair ★ IND 140-141 L 4
Port Blandfort o CDN (NFL) 242-243 O 4
Port Bolivar o USA (TX) 268-269 F 7
Port Broughton o AUS 180-181 D 2
Port Bruce o CDN (ONT) 238-239 D 6
Port Burwell o CDN (ONT) 238-239 E 6
Port Campbell o AUS 180-181 G 5
Port Campbell National Park ⊥ AUS 180-181 G 5
Port Charlotte o USA (FL) 286-287 G 4
Port Chester o USA (NY) 280-281 N 3
Port Chilkoot o USA 20-21 X 7
Port Clements o CDN (BC) 228-229 B 3
Port Clinton o USA (OH) 280-281 D 2
Port Clyde o USA (ME) 278-279 M 5
Port Coquitlam o CDN (BC) 230-231 G 4
Port-Daniel o CDN (QUE) 240-241 L 2
Port-Daniel, Réserve faunique de ⊥ CDN (QUE) 240-241 L 2
Port-de-Paix ★ RH 54-55 J 5
Port Dickson o• MAL 162-163 D 3
Port Douglas o• AUS 174-175 H 5
Port Dover o CDN (ONT) 238-239 E 6
Port Dufferin o CDN (NS) 240-241 N 6
Porte, La o USA (IN) 274-275 M 3
Porte, La o USA (TX) 268-269 E 7
Port Edward o CDN (BC) 228-229 D 2
Port Edward o ZA 220-221 K 5
Porteira, Cachoeira da ~ BR 66-67 H 7
Porteiras o BR 62-63 F 6
Porteirinha o BR 72-73 J 3
Portél o BR 62-63 J 6
Portel o P 98-99 D 5
Portelândia o BR 72-73 D 4
Port Elgin o CDN (NB) 240-241 L 4
Port Elgin o CDN (ONT) 238-239 D 4
Port Elizabeth o ZA 220-221 G 6
Port Ellen o GB 90-91 D 4
Porteno, Rio ~ RA 76-77 H 3
Porter o CDN (SAS) 232-233 K 3
Porter o USA (WA) 244-245 B 4
Porters Corner o USA (MT) 250-251 F 5
Porterville o USA (CA) 248-249 E 3
Porterville o ZA 220-221 D 6
Port Essington o CDN (BC) 228-229 E 2
Portezuela ▲ BOL 76-77 C 1
Portezuela del Huaytiquina ▲ RCH 76-77 D 2
Portezuela Llullaillaco Norte ▲ RCH 76-77 C 3
Portezuela Pasto Ventura ▲ RA 76-77 D 4
Portezuelo o RCH 78-79 C 4
Portezuelo, El o RA 76-77 E 5
Port Fitzroy o NZ 182 E 2
Port Fourchon o USA (LA) 268-269 K 7
Port Gentil ★ G 210-211 B 4
Port Germein o AUS 180-181 D 2
Port Gibson o USA (MS) 268-269 J 5
Port Grosvenor o ZA 220-221 J 5
Port-Harcourt ★ WAN 204-205 G 6
Port Hardy o CDN (BC) 230-231 B 3
Port Harrison = Inukjuak o CDN 36-37 K 5
Port Hawkesbury o CDN (NS) 240-241 O 5
Port Hedland o AUS 172-173 D 6
Port Heiden o USA 22-23 R 4
Port Henry o USA (NY) 278-279 H 4
Porthill o USA (ID) 250-251 C 3
Port Hillford o CDN (NS) 240-241 O 5
Port Hood o CDN (NS) 240-241 O 4
Port Hope o CDN (ONT) 238-239 G 5
Port Hope o USA (MI) 272-273 G 4
Port Hope Simpson o CDN 38-39 Q 2
Port Howard o GB 78-79 L 6
Port Howe o BS 54-55 H 2
Port Hueneme o USA (CA) 248-249 E 5
Port Huron o USA (MI) 272-273 G 5
Portillo, Paso del ▲ RA 76-77 B 6
Portimão o P 98-99 C 6
Portimo o FIN 88-89 J 3
Portis o USA (KS) 262-263 H 5
Port Isabel o USA (TX) 266-267 K 7
Port Isabel Lighthouse State Historic Site ∴ USA (TX) 266-267 K 7
Port Jackson ≈ 180-181 L 2
Port Jackson o NZ 182 E 2
Port Jefferson o USA (NY) 280-281 N 3
Port Jervis o USA (NY) 280-281 M 2
Port Kenny o AUS 180-181 C 2
Port Kent o USA (NY) 278-279 H 4
Port Láirge = Waterford o• IRL 90-91 D 5
Portland o AUS 180-181 F 5
Portland o USA (IN) 274-275 O 4
Portland o USA (ME) 278-279 L 5
Portland o USA (MI) 272-273 E 5
Portland o USA (OR) 244-245 C 5
Portland o USA (TN) 276-277 J 4
Portland o USA (TX) 266-267 K 6
Portland, Cape ▲ AUS 180-181 J 6
Portland Bay ≈ 180-181 F 5
Portland Bight ≈ 54-55 G 6
Portland Canal ≈ 32-33 E 4
Portland Creek o CDN (NFL) 242-243 L 2
Portland Creek Pond ⊝ CDN (NFL) 242-243 L 2
Portland Inlet ≈ 32-33 E 4
Portland Inlet ≈ CDN 228-229 D 2
Portland Island ∩ NZ 182 F 3
Portland Point ▲ JA 54-55 G 6
Port Langdon ≈ 174-175 D 3
Port Laoise o IRL 90-91 D 5
Port Lincoln o•• AUS 180-181 C 3
Port Lions o USA 22-23 U 4
Portlock Reefs ∩ PNG 183 C 5
Port Loko o WAL 202-203 D 5
Port-Louis o F 56 E 3
Port Louis ★• MS 224 C 7
Port Mac Donnell o AUS 180-181 F 5
Port Macquarie o• AUS 178-179 M 6
Port Maitland o CDN (NS) 240-241 J 7
Port Mansfield o USA (TX) 266-267 K 7
Port Maria o JA 54-55 G 5
Port Mathurin o MS 224 F 6
Port Maurant o GUY 62-63 F 2
Port Mayaca o USA (FL) 286-287 J 5
Port Mc Arthur ≈ 174-175 D 4
Port Mellon o CDN (BC) 230-231 F 4
Port Menier o CDN (QUE) 242-243 D 3
Port Moller o USA 22-23 Q 5
Port Moody o CDN (BC) 230-231 G 4
Portmore o JA 54-55 G 6
Port Moresby ★ PNG 183 D 5
Port Morien o CDN (NS) 240-241 Q 4
Port Neill o AUS 180-181 D 3
Port Nelson o BS 54-55 H 3
Port Nelson (abandoned) o CDN 34-35 K 2
Portneuf, Rivière ~ CDN (QUE) 240-241 F 2
Port Neville o CDN (BC) 230-231 C 3
Portnjagino, ozero ⊝ RUS 110-111 F 2
Port Nolloth o ZA 220-221 C 4
Port Norris o USA (NJ) 280-281 L 4
Port-Nouveau-Québec o CDN 36-37 R 5
Porto o BR 68-69 G 3
Porto o F 98-99 M 3
Porto ★•• P 98-99 C 4
Pôrto Acre o BR 66-67 D 7
Pôrto Alegre o BR 70-71 J 5
Porto Alegre o BR (BAH) 72-73 K 2
Porto Alegre o BR (P) 66-67 J 5
Porto Alegre ★ BR (RSU) 74-75 E 8
Porto-Alegre o STP 210-211 b 2
Porto Alegre do Norte o BR 68-69 C 7
Porto Amazonas o BR 74-75 F 5
Porto Amboim o ANG 216-217 B 5
Porto Antunes o BR 66-67 D 4
Porto Azzurro o I 100-101 C 3
Portobelo o••• PA 52-53 E 7
Porto Belo, Baía de ≈ 74-75 F 6
Porto Belo, Ponta do ▲ BR 74-75 F 6
Porto Bicentenário o BR 70-71 F 2
Porto Braga o BR (AMA) 66-67 E 4
Porto Braga o BR (GSU) 70-71 J 7
Porto Cabello o YV 60-61 G 2
Porto Camargo o BR 72-73 D 7
Porto Cristo o E 98-99 J 5
Porto da Soledade o BR 72-73 G 4
Pôrto de Fora o BR 70-71 K 5
Porto de Pedras o BR 68-69 L 6
Porto do Caititu o BR 68-69 F 4
Porto do Mangue o BR 68-69 K 4
Porto do Moz o BR 62-63 H 6
Porto dos Gaúchos o BR 70-71 J 2
Porto dos Mosteiros o CV 202-203 B 6
Porto Esperanza o RA 76-77 K 4
Porto Esperidião o BR 70-71 H 4
Porto Estrela o BR 70-71 J 4
Porto Euchdes da Cunha o BR 72-73 D 7
Portoferráio o I 100-101 C 3
Porto Ferreira o BR 72-73 G 6
Port of Ness o GB 90-91 D 2
Porto Franco o BR 68-69 E 5
Port of Spain ★ TT 60-61 L 2
Porto Gen. Nac. el Portillo ▲ RA 78-79 E 2
Porto Grande o BR 62-63 J 5
Portogruaro o• I 100-101 D 2
Porto Henrique o MOC 220-221 L 3
Pôrto Jofre o BR 70-71 J 5
Portola o USA (CA) 246-247 E 4
Porto Levante o I 100-101 E 5
Port-Olry o VAN 184 II a 2
Porto Lucena o BR 76-77 K 4
Port Omna = Portumna o IRL 90-91 C 5
Porto Moniz o P 188-189 C 4
Porto Mosquito o CV 202-203 C 6
Pôrto Murtinho o BR 76-77 J 1
Porto Nacional o BR 68-69 D 7
Porto Novo o BR 72-73 J 2
Porto-Novo ★• DY 204-205 E 5
Portonovo o IND 140-141 H 5
Porto Novo, Vila de o CV 202-203 B 5
Porto Quebra o BR 66-67 F 4
Port Orchard o USA (WA) 244-245 C 3
Porto Reis o BR 66-67 E 4
Porto Rico o BR 70-71 D 2
Porto Rolha o BR 70-71 E 2
Porto Santo ∩ P 188-189 C 4
Porto São José o BR 72-73 D 7
Portoscuso o I 100-101 B 5
Porto Seguro o• BR 72-73 L 4
Porto Seguro, Corredeira ~ BR 68-69 B 5
Porto Tolle o I 100-101 D 2
Porto Tórres o I 100-101 B 4
Porto União o BR 74-75 E 6
Pôrto Valter o BR 64-65 F 6
Porto-Vecchio o F 98-99 M 4
Porto Velho ★ BR 66-67 F 7
Portovelo o EC 64-65 C 3
Portoviejo ★ EC 64-65 B 2
Portpatrick o GB 90-91 E 4
Port Perry o CDN (ONT) 238-239 G 4
Port Philip o CDN (NS) 240-241 M 5
Port Pirie o AUS 180-181 D 2
Port Radium o CDN 30-31 L 2
Portree o GB 90-91 D 3
Port Rowan o CDN (ONT) 238-239 E 6
Port Royal o USA (VA) 280-281 J 5
Port Royal National Historic Park • CDN (NS) 240-241 K 6
Port Royal Sound ≈ USA 284-285 K 4
Port Said = Bûr Sa'îd ★ ET 194-195 E 2
Port Saint Joe o USA (FL) 286-287 D 2
Port Saint Johns o ZA 220-221 J 5
Port-Saint-Louis-du-Rhône o F 90-91 K 10
Port Saint Lucie o USA (FL) 286-287 J 4
Portsalon o IRL 90-91 D 4
Port Salut o RH 54-55 J 5
Port Salut, Plage ⊥• RH 54-55 H 5
Port Sanilac o USA (MI) 272-273 G 4
Port Saunders o CDN (NFL) 242-243 L 2
Port Shepstone o ZA 220-221 K 5
Port Simpson o CDN (BC) 228-229 D 2
Portsmouth o GB 90-91 G 6
Portsmouth o USA (IA) 274-275 C 3
Portsmouth o USA (NH) 278-279 L 5
Portsmouth o USA (OH) 280-281 E 5
Portsmouth o USA (VA) 280-281 K 7
Portsmouth o WD 56 E 4
Portsmouth Island ∩ USA (NC) 282-283 L 5
Port Stephens o GB 78-79 K 7

Pocitos, Salar — Port Stephens 379

Puerto Bolivar ○ EC 64-65 C 3
Puerto Boy ○ CO 64-65 E 1
Puerto Boyacá ○ CO 60-61 D 5
Puerto Busch ○ BOL 70-71 J 7
Puerto Cabezas ○ NIC 52-53 C 4
Puerto Caituma ○ GUY 62-63 E 2
Puerto Calvimontes ○ BOL 70-71 E 4
Puerto Canoa ○ BOL 70-71 D 4
Puerto Carabuco ○ BOL 70-71 C 4
Puerto Carare ○ CO 60-61 D 4
Puerto Cardenas ○ PE 64-65 E 2
Puerto Cárdenas ○ RCH 78-79 C 7
Puerto Carreño ☆ CO 60-61 H 4
Puerto Castilla ○ HN 54-55 C 6
Puerto Chacabuco ○ RCH 80 D 2
Puerto Chama ○ YV 60-61 F 3
Puerto Chicama ○ PE 64-65 C 5
Puerto Chicxulub ○ MEX 52-53 K 1
Puerto Cisnes ○ RCH 80 D 2
Puerto Claver ○ CO 60-61 D 4
Puerto Coig ○ RA 80 F 5
Puerto Colombia ○ CO 64-65 E 2
Puerto Colón ○ PY 76-77 J 2
Puerto Constanza ○ RA 78-79 K 2
Puerto Cortés ○ HN 52-53 L 4
Puerto Cumarebo ○ YV 60-61 G 2
Puerto Cunambo ○ PE 64-65 D 3
Puerto de Aseses ○ NIC 52-53 B 6
Puerto de Cayo ○ EC 64-65 B 2
Puerto de la Cruz ○ E 188-189 C 6
Puerto de la Estaca ○ E 188-189 C 7
Puerto de los Angeles, Parque Nacional del ⊥ MEX 50-51 G 6
Puerto del Rosario ○ E 188-189 E 6
Puerto de Luna ○ USA (NM) 256-257 L 4
Puerto de San José ○ GCA 52-53 J 5
Puerto Deseado ○ RA 80 H 3
Puerto Eden ○ RCH 80 C 4
Puerto Ele ○ CO 60-61 F 4
Puerto Escondido ○ MEX (BCS) 50-51 D 5
Puerto Escondido ○• MEX (OAX) 52-53 F 4
Puerto Flores ○ EC 64-65 B 10
Puerto Francisco de Orellana ○ EC 64-65 D 2
Puerto Fuy ○ RCH 78-79 D 5
Puerto Gaitan ○ CO 60-61 E 5
Puerto Galilea ○ PE 64-65 D 3
Puerto Grande ▲ E 98-99 E 5
Puerto Grande ○ EC 64-65 B 3
Puerto Gutierrez ○ CO 60-61 D 5
Puerto Heath ○ BOL 70-71 C 3
Puerto Humbria ○ CO 64-65 D 1
Puerto Inca ○ PE 64-65 E 6
Puerto Ingeniero Ibáñez ○ RCH 80 E 3
Puerto Inirida ☆ CO 60-61 H 6
Puerto Itambey ○ PY 76-77 K 3
Puerto Izozog ○ BOL 70-71 F 6
Puerto Japones ○ BOL 70-71 C 5
Puerto Juárez ○• MEX 52-53 L 1
Puerto La Cruz ○ YV 60-61 J 2
Puerto la Esperanza ○ PY 76-77 J 2
Puerto la Victoria ○ PY 76-77 J 2
Puerto Leguia ○ PE 70-71 B 3
Puerto Leguizamo ○ CO 64-65 E 2
Puerto Leitón ○ BOL 70-71 G 3
Puerto Lempira ☆ HN 54-55 D 7
Puerto Libertad ○ MEX 50-51 C 3
Puerto Libertador ○ CO 60-61 D 4
Puerto Limón ○ CO 64-65 D 1
Puerto Limón ☆•• CR 52-53 C 7
Puertollano ○ E 98-99 E 5
Puerto Llifén ○ RCH 78-79 C 6
Puerto Lobos ○ RA 78-79 G 7
Puerto Lodo ○ CO 60-61 F 1
Puerto Lopez ○ CO 60-61 F 2
Puerto López ○ EC 64-65 B 2
Puerto Lumbreras ○ E 98-99 G 6
Puerto Madero ○ MEX (CHI) 52-53 H 4
Puerto Madero ○ MEX (QR) 52-53 L 2
Puerto Madryn ○ RA 78-79 G 7
Puerto Magdalena ○ MEX 50-51 C 5
Puerto Maldonado ☆ PE 70-71 C 3
Puerto María ○ PY 76-77 J 1
Puerto Masachapa ○ NIC 52-53 L 6
Puerto Montt ☆ RCH 78-79 C 6
Puerto Morazán ○ NIC 52-53 L 5
Puerto Napo ○ EC 64-65 D 2
Puerto Nare ○ CO 60-61 D 4
Puerto Natales ○ RCH 80 D 5
Puerto Navarino ○ RCH 80 F 7
Puerto Ninfas ○ RA 78-79 G 7
Puerto Nuevo ○ CO 60-61 G 5
Puerto Obaldia ○ PA 52-53 F 7
Puerto Octay ○ RCH 78-79 C 6
Puerto Olaya ○ CO 60-61 D 4
Puerto Ospina ○ CO 64-65 E 1
Puerto Padre ○ C 54-55 G 4
Puerto Palomas ○ MEX 52-53 G 3
Puerto Paranay ○ RA 76-77 K 4
Puerto Pardo ○ PE 64-65 D 3
Puerto Patiño ○ BOL 70-71 E 5
Puerto Peñasco ○ MEX 50-51 C 2
Puerto Piedras ○ RCH 78-79 C 7
Puerto Piña ○ PA 52-53 E 8
Puerto Pinasco ○ PY 76-77 J 2
Puerto Pipa ○ PE 66-67 B 4
Puerto Pirámides ○ RA 78-79 G 7
Puerto Pizarro ○ CO (CA) 64-65 F 2
Puerto Pizarro ○ CO (CHO) 60-61 C 5
Puerto Plata ☆• DOM 54-55 K 5
Puerto Porfia ○ CO 60-61 E 5
Puerto Portillo ○ PE 64-65 F 6
Puerto Prado ○ PE 64-65 E 7
Puerto Princesa ☆ RP 160-161 C 8
Puerto Proano ○ EC 64-65 D 3
Puerto Pupuña ○ EC 66-67 B 4
Puerto Puyuguapi ○ RCH 80 D 2
Puerto Quijarro ○ BOL 70-71 J 5
Puerto Quimba ○ PA 52-53 E 7
Puerto Ramírez ○ RCH 78-79 C 7
Puerto Raúl Marín Balmaceda ○ RCH 78-79 C 7
Puerto Rico ○ BOL 70-71 D 2
Puerto Rico ○ PE 64-65 E 7
Puerto Rico □ USA (PR) 286-287 P 2
Puerto Rico ⌒ USA 56 B 2
Puerto Rico Trench ≃ 4 H 6
Puerto Rondon ○ CO 60-61 F 4
Puerto San Antonio ○ RA 78-79 G 6
Puerto San Carlos ○ PE 70-71 B 3
Puerto Sandino ○ NIC 52-53 L 5
Puerto San Julián ○ RA 80 G 4
Puerto San Martin ○ PE 64-65 D 8
Puerto Santa Cruz ○ RA 80 F 5
Puerto Saucedo ○ BOL 70-71 F 3
Puerto Siles ○ BOL 70-71 E 3
Puerto Silvania ○ CO 66-67 B 2
Puerto Suarez ○ BOL 70-71 J 6
Puerto Tacurú Pytá ○ PY 76-77 J 2
Puerto Tamborapa ○ PE 64-65 C 4
Puerto Tejada ○ CO 60-61 C 6
Puerto Tumaco = Sabaloyaco ○ EC 64-65 F 3
Puerto Turumbán ○ GUY 62-63 D 2
Puerto Valencia ○ CO 60-61 G 6
Puerto Vallarta ○• MEX 52-53 B 1
Puerto Varas ○ RCH 78-79 C 6
Puerto Victoria ○ PE 64-65 E 6
Puerto Viejo ○ CR (Car) 52-53 C 7
Puerto Viejo ○ CR (HER) 52-53 B 6
Puerto Villamil ○ EC 64-65 B 10
Puerto Visser ○ RA 80 G 2
Puerto Weber ○ RCH 80 D 5
Puerto Williams ○ RCH 80 G 7
Puerto Yahape ○ RA 76-77 J 4
Puerto Yungay ○ RCH 80 D 3
Puesto Avanzado ○ PE 64-65 D 3
Puesto Esperanza ○ PY 76-77 H 2
Pueyrredón, Lago ⊖ RA 80 E 3
Pugačev ☆ RUS 96-97 F 7
Pugačevo ○ RUS 122-123 K 4
Pugašev muzej uji • KA 96-97 G 8
Puge ○ VRC 156-157 C 3
Puger ○ RI 168 E 4
Puget Sound ≈ 40-41 C 2
Puget Sound ≈ USA 244-245 C 3
Pugima ○ RI 166-167 K 4
Puglia □ I 100-101 E 4
Pugwash ○ CDN (NS) 240-241 M 5
Puhal-e Ḩamir, Kūh-e ▲ IR 134-135 F 5
Puhos ○ FIN 88-89 K 5
Puiatoq ≈ 28-29 T 6
Puig ○ SUD 206-207 J 4
Puig Major ▲ E 98-99 J 5
Puinahua, Canal de < PE 64-65 E 4
Puir ○ RUS 122-123 J 2
Puissortoq Gletscher ⊂ GRØ 28-29 T 5
Pujehun ○ WAL 202-203 E 6
Pujiang ○ VRC (SIC) 154-155 C 6
Pujiang ○ VRC (ZHE) 156-157 L 2
Pujonryong Sanmaek ▲ DVR 150-151 F 7
Pukaki, Lake ⊖ NZ 182 C 5
Pukalani ○ USA (HI) 288 J 4
Puk'ansan National Park ⊥• DVR 150-151 F 9
Pukaskwa National Park ⊥• CDN (ONT) 236-237 B 4
Pukatawagan ○ CDN 34-35 F 3
Pukchong ○ DVR 150-151 G 7
Pukë ☆• AL 100-101 G 3
Pukekohe ○ NZ 182 E 2
Pukota ○ Z 218-219 E 1
Pukšen'ga ~ RUS 88-89 Q 5
Puksubaek San ▲ DVR 150-151 F 7
Pukuanratu ○ RI 162-163 F 7
Pukuatu, Tanjung ▲ RI 166-167 B 7
Pula ○ HR 100-101 D 2
Pula ○ I 100-101 B 5
Pula, Goi- ○ ZRE 214-215 D 4
Pulai ○ RI 164-165 F 3
Pulaksama ○ RI 162-163 B 3
Pulanduta Point ▲ RP 160-161 E 7
Pulangi ~ RP 160-161 F 9
Pulangpisau ○ RI 164-165 D 5
Pular, Cerro ▲ RCH 76-77 C 3
Pularumpi X AUS 172-173 K 1
Pulasi, Pulau ⌒ RI 168 E 6
Pulaski ○ USA (NY) 278-279 E 5
Pulaski ○ USA (TN) 276-277 H 5
Pulaski ○ USA (VA) 280-281 F 6
Pulaski National Monument, Fort • USA (GA) 284-285 K 4
Pulau ○ RI (BEN) 162-163 D 6
Pulau ~ RI 166-167 K 4
Pulau Banding ○ MAL 162-163 D 2
Pulauberingin ○ RI 162-163 E 7
Pulau Penang □ MAL 162-163 D 2
Pulausekopong, Tanjung ▲ RI 162-163 F 7
Pulau Tiga Park ⊥ MAL 160-161 A 10
Pulau Tioman ⌒•• MAL 162-163 F 3
Puławy ○• PL 92-93 Q 3
Puleowine ○ SME 62-63 G 4
Pulguk Sa • ROK 150-151 G 10
Pulicat ○ IND 140-141 J 4
Pulicat Lake ⊖ IND 140-141 J 4
Pulie River ~ PNG 183 E 3
Pulingom ○ IND 140-141 F 4
Pulisan, Tanjung ▲ RI 164-165 J 3
Pulivendla ○ IND 140-141 H 3
Puliyangudi ○ IND 140-141 G 6
Pulkkila ○ FIN 88-89 H 4
Pullman ○ USA (WA) 244-245 H 4
Pullo ○ PE 64-65 F 9
Pulmoddai ○ CL 140-141 J 6
Pulo Buda ⌒ MYA 158-159 E 5
Pulog, Mount ▲ RP 160-161 D 4
Pulozero ○ RUS 88-89 M 2
Pulpit Harbor ○ USA (ME) 278-279 N 4
Pulp River ○ CDN (MAN) 234-235 C 3
Pulpul ○ PNG 183 F 3
Pułtusk ○• PL 92-93 Q 2
Pulu ○ VRC 144-145 C 2
Pülümür ☆ TR 128-129 H 3
Pulupanda ○ RI 164-165 H 5
Puluqui, Isla ⌒ RCH 78-79 C 6
Pulwama ○ IND 138-139 E 3
Puma ○ EAT 212-213 E 6
Puma Yumco ⊖ VRC 144-145 H 6
Pumpville ○ USA (TX) 266-267 F 4
Puna ○ EC 64-65 C 3
Puna, Isla ⌒ EC 64-65 B 3
Punakaiki ○ NZ 182 C 5
Punakha ○ BHT 142-143 F 2
Punalūr ○ IND 140-141 G 6
Punang ○ MAL 164-165 D 1
Punarupka ○ PNG 183 F 3
Punāsa ○ IND 138-139 F 8
Punata ○ BOL 70-71 E 5
Puncak Jaya ▲ RI 166-167 J 4
Puncak Mandala ▲ RI 166-167 L 4
Puncak Trikora ▲ RI 166-167 K 4
Puncak Yamin ▲ RI 166-167 K 4
Punch ○ IND 138-139 E 3
Punchaw ○ CDN (BC) 228-229 L 3
Punda Hamlets ○ PNG 183 A 2
Punda Maria ○ ZA 218-219 F 6
Pundanhar ○ MOC 214-215 L 6
Pune ○• IND 138-139 D 10
Punei, Tanjung ▲ RI 162-163 F 6
Pungai, Kampung ○ MAL 162-163 F 4
Pungali ~ RUS 112-113 H 4
Pungalina ○ AUS 174-175 D 5
Punganuru ○ IND 140-141 H 4
Punggaluku ○ RI 164-165 H 6
Pungo Andongo ○ ANG 216-217 C 4
Púngoe ~ MOC 218-219 G 4
Púngoè, Rio ~ MOC 218-219 G 4
Pungo National Wildlife Refuge ⊥ USA (NC) 282-283 L 5
Pungo River ~ USA (NC) 282-283 L 5
Pungwe Falls ~• ZW 218-219 G 4
Punia ○ ZRE 210-211 L 4
Punilla, La ○ RCH 78-79 D 4
Punilla, Sierra de la ▲ RA 76-77 C 5
Puning ○ VRC 156-157 K 5
Punja ○ RUS 116-117 J 6
Punjab □ IND 138-139 E 4
Punjab □ PK 138-139 C 4
Punkaharju ○ FIN 88-89 K 6
Punkalaidun ○ FIN 88-89 G 6
Punkasalmi = Punkaharju ○ FIN 88-89 K 6
Punkin Center ○ USA (CO) 254-255 M 5
Puno ☆• PE 70-71 B 4
Punos ○ PE 64-65 D 6
Punrun, Lago ⊖ PE 64-65 D 7
Punta, La ○ RA 76-77 E 5
Punta Alegre ○ C 54-55 F 3
Punta Allen ○ MEX 52-53 L 2
Punta Alta ○ RA 78-79 H 5
Punta Arenas ☆ RCH 80 E 6
Punta Arenas, Caleta ≈ 76-77 B 1
Punta Cana ○ DOM 54-55 L 5
Punta Cardón ○ YV 60-61 F 2
Punta Chame ○ PA 52-53 E 7
Punta Corral ○ RA 76-77 F 5
Punta de Balosto ○ RA 76-77 D 4
Punta de Bombon ○ PE 70-71 B 5
Punta de Díaz ○ RCH 76-77 B 5
Punta del Agua ○ RA 78-79 E 3
Punta del Este ○ C 54-55 D 4
Punta Delgada ○ RCH 80 F 6
Punta Delgado ○ RA 78-79 H 7
Punta de los Llanos ○ RA 76-77 D 6
Punta del Viento ○ RCH 76-77 B 5
Punta Eugenia ○ MEX 50-51 B 4
Punta Gorda ○ BH 52-53 K 3
Punta Gorda ○ USA (FL) 286-287 G 5
Punta Gorda, Playa ≐• DOM 54-55 L 5
Punta Mala ▲ PA 52-53 D 8
Punta Negra, Salar ⊖ RCH 76-77 C 3
Punta Norte ○ RA 78-79 H 7
Punta Nueva ○ YV 60-61 K 4
Punta Piaroa ○ YV 60-61 J 6
Puntarenas ☆• CR 52-53 B 7
Puntawolana, Lake ⊖ AUS 178-179 E 5
Punto Alegre ○ BR 62-63 J 6
Punto Catatumbo ○ YV 60-61 E 3
Punto da Barca ○ BR 62-63 K 6
Punto Fijo ○ YV 60-61 F 2
Punto M.O.P. ○ YV 60-61 K 6
Punxsutawney ○ USA (PA) 280-281 H 3
Puolanka ○ FIN 88-89 J 4
Puponga ○ NZ 182 D 4
Pupri ○ IND 142-143 D 2
Pupuan ○ RI 168 B 7
Pupunhas, Ilha ⌒ BR 66-67 F 6
Pupū Pu'e National Parc ⊥ WS 184 V b 1
Pupyr, mys ▲ RUS 112-113 M 5
Puqi ○ VRC 156-157 H 2
Puquina ○ PE 70-71 B 5
Puquio ○ PE 64-65 E 9
Pur ~ RUS 108-109 S 8
Pur ~ RUS 114-115 O 2
Pura ~ RUS 108-109 X 6
Pura, Cachoeira da ~ BR 66-67 H 6
Puracé, Parque Nacional ⊥ CO 60-61 C 6
Puracé, Volcán ▲ CO 60-61 C 6
Purándiro ○ MEX 52-53 D 1
Purangarh ○ IND 140-141 E 2
Puranpur ○ IND 144-145 C 6
Puraquê Ponta ○ BR 66-67 C 2
Purari River ~ PNG 183 C 4
Purbalingga ○ RI 168 C 3
Purcell ○ USA (OK) 264-265 G 3
Purcell Mountains ▲ CDN (BC) 230-231 M 2
Purcell Wilderness Conservancy ⊥• CDN (BC) 230-231 N 3
Purchase Bay ≈ 24-25 N 3
Purchena ○ E 98-99 F 6
Purdum ○ USA (NE) 262-263 F 2
Purdy Islands ⌒ PNG 183 D 2
Pure, Río ~ EC 66-67 C 4
Pureba Conservation Reserve ⊥ AUS 180-181 C 2
Pureh ○ RUS 94-95 S 3
Purepero ○ MEX 52-53 C 2
Puretê ou Purata, Rio ~ BR 66-67 C 4
Purgatoire River ~ USA (CO) 254-255 M 6
Purgatorio ○ YV 62-63 D 2
Puri ○ ANG 216-217 C 3
Puri ○•• IND 142-143 D 6
Puricaure ○ YV 60-61 F 2
Purificacion ○ CO 60-61 D 6
Purificación ○ MEX 52-53 B 2
Purificacion, Río ~ MEX 52-53 B 2
Puring ○ RI 168 C 3
Purinskoe vtoroe, ozero ⊖ RUS 108-109 X 6
Purisima, La ○ MEX 50-51 C 4
Purma ○ EC 64-65 F 3
Purmamarca ○ RA 76-77 E 2
Pūrna ○ IND (MAH) 138-139 F 10
Pūrna ~ IND 138-139 F 9
Pūrna ~ IND 138-139 E 9
Purnač ~ RUS 88-89 P 3
Pūrnia ○ IND 142-143 E 3
Purnong ○ AUS 180-181 E 3
Purpe ○ RUS 114-115 O 2
Purpe ~ RUS 114-115 N 2
Purple Springs ○ CDN (ALB) 232-233 G 6
Purranque ○ RCH 78-79 C 6
Purros ○ NAM 216-217 B 9
Puruarán ○ MEX 52-53 D 2
Puruí, Rio ~ BR 66-67 C 3
Purukcahu ○ RI 164-165 D 4
Puruliya ○ IND 142-143 E 4
Purureche ○ YV 60-61 F 2
Purus, Rio ~ BR 66-67 E 5
Purutu Island ⌒ PNG 183 B 5
Purvachal ≐ IND 142-143 H 4
Pūrvāchal ≐ IND 142-143 H 4
Purvis ○ USA (MS) 268-269 L 5
Purwakarta ○ RI 168 B 3
Purwo, Tanjung ▲ RI 168 B 7
Purwodadi ○ RI 168 D 3
Purwodari ○ RI 168 D 3
Purwokerto ○ RI 168 C 3
Purworejo ○ RI 168 D 3
Puryong ○ DVR 150-151 G 6
Purzell Mount ▲ USA 20-21 M 3
Pusa ○ MAL 162-163 J 4
Pusad ○ IND 138-139 F 10
Pusan ○ ROK 150-151 G 10
Pusat Gajo, Pegunungan ▲ RI 162-163 B 2
Pusegaon ○ IND 140-141 F 2
Pusesāvli ○ IND 140-141 F 2
Pushkar ○ IND 138-139 E 6
Pusisama ○ SOL 184 I c 2
Puškarëva, ostrov ⌒ RUS 112-113 L 1
Puškin ○•• RUS 94-95 M 2
Puškino ○ RUS 96-97 E 8
Puškino = Biljasuvar ○ AZ 128-129 N 3
Puskwaskau River ~ CDN 32-33 M 4
Pušlahta ○ RUS 88-89 O 4
Pušma ☆ RUS 114-115 G 6
Pušnoj ○ RUS 88-89 N 4
Pusok Sa • ROK 150-151 G 9
Püspökladány ○ H 92-93 Q 5
Pustaja ~ RUS 120-121 U 3
Pusticamicca, Lac ⊖ CDN (QUE) 236-237 M 3
Pustoška ☆ RUS 94-95 L 3
Pustunich ○ MEX (CAM) 52-53 J 2
Pustunich ∴• MEX (CAM) 52-53 J 2
Pusuga ○ GH 202-203 K 5
Putahow Lake ⊖ CDN 30-31 T 6
Putahow River ~ CDN 30-31 T 5
Putai ○ RC 156-157 M 5
Putao ○ MYA 142-143 K 2
Puteran, Pulau ⌒ RI 168 B 6
Puthein (Bassein) ○ MYA 158-159 C 2
Puthukkudiyiruppu ○ CL 140-141 J 6
Putia ○ RI 166-167 D 3
Putian ○ VRC 156-157 L 4
Putina ○ PE 70-71 C 4
Putina, Río ~ PE 70-71 C 4
Putineiu ○ RO 102-103 D 6
Puting, Tanjung ▲ RI 162-163 J 6
Putnam ○ USA (CT) 278-279 K 7
Putnam ○ USA (OK) 264-265 F 3
Putnam ○ USA (TX) 264-265 E 6
Putončany ○ RUS 116-117 F 3
Putorana, plato ▲ RUS 108-109 Z 7
Putoranskij zapovednik ⊥ RUS 108-109 a 7
Putre ○ RCH 70-71 C 6
Putsonderwater ○ ZA 220-221 E 4
Puttalam ○ CL 140-141 H 6
Puttalam Lagoon ≈ 140-141 H 6
Puttgarden ○ D 92-93 L 1
Puttur ○ IND (ANP) 140-141 H 4
Puttur ○ IND (KAR) 140-141 F 4
Putty ○ AUS 180-181 L 2
Putumayo, Río ~ PE 66-67 B 4
Putuoshan • VRC 154-155 N 6
Putus, Tanjung ▲ RI 162-163 H 5
Putyvl' ○ UA 102-103 H 2
Puuanahulu ○ USA (HI) 288 K 5
Puuhonua o Honaunau National Historical Park ⊥• USA (HI) 288 K 5
Puukohola Heiau National Historical Park ⊥• USA (HI) 288 K 5
Puula ⊖ FIN 88-89 J 6
Puumala ○ FIN 88-89 K 6
Puu Ulaula ▲ USA (HI) 288 J 4
Puuwai ○ USA (HI) 288 E 3
Pu Xian ○ VRC 154-155 G 3
Puxico ○ USA (MO) 276-277 E 4
Puyallup ○ USA (WA) 244-245 C 3
Puyang ○ VRC 154-155 J 4
Puyca ○ PE 64-65 F 9
Puyehue, Lago ⊖ RCH 78-79 C 6
Puyehue, Parque Nacional ⊥ RCH 78-79 C 6
Puyehue, Volcán ▲ RCH 78-79 C 6
Puy-en-Velay, le ☆•• F 90-91 J 9
Puymorens, Col de ▲ F 90-91 H 10
Puyo ☆ EC 64-65 D 2
Puyuguapi, Canal ≈ 80 D 2
Pūzak, Hāmūn-e ⊖ AFG 134-135 J 3
Puzino ○ RUS 122-123 D 5
Pwalugu ○ GH 202-203 K 4
Pwani □ EAT 214-215 K 4
Pweto ○ ZRE 214-215 E 5
Pwllheli ○ GB 90-91 E 5
PWV = Pretoria Witwatersrand Vereeniging □ ZA 220-221 H 2
Pyachnung ○ MYA 142-143 H 5
Pyanangazu ○ MYA 142-143 K 5
Pyawbwe ○ MYA 142-143 K 5
Pyechin ○ MYA 142-143 H 6
Pye Islands ⌒ USA 20-21 V 3
Pyhäjärvi ○ FIN 88-89 H 5
Pyhäjoki ○ FIN 88-89 H 4
Pyhäjoki ~ FIN 88-89 H 4
Pyhäntä ○ FIN 88-89 J 4
Pyhäselkä ⊖ FIN 88-89 K 5
Pyhätunturi ▲ FIN 88-89 J 3
Pyingaing ○ MYA 142-143 J 4
Pyinmana ○ MYA 142-143 K 6
Pyjakojajaha ~ RUS 108-109 N 6
Pylema ○ RUS 88-89 S 4
Pylginskij hrebet ▲ RUS 112-113 O 7
Pylgovajam ~ RUS 112-113 O 6
Pymatuning Reservoir ⊖ USA (PA) 280-281 F 2
Pymatuning State Park ⊥ USA (PA) 280-281 F 2
Pyngan ○ US 136-137 M 4
Pyonggang ○ DVR 150-151 F 8
Pyongsan ○ DVR 150-151 F 8
Pyongsong ○ DVR 150-151 E 8
P'yŏngt'aek ○ ROK 150-151 F 9
Pyongyang ★ DVR 150-151 E 8
Pyote ○ USA (TX) 266-267 D 2
Pyramid ○ RI 166-167 K 3
Pyramiden ○ N 84-85 K 3
Pyramid Hill ○ AUS 180-181 H 4
Pyramid Lake ⊖ AUS 176-177 F 6
Pyramid Lake ⊖ USA (NV) 246-247 F 3
Pyramid Lake Indian Reservation X USA (NV) 246-247 F 3
Pyramids Mountains ▲ USA (NM) 256-257 G 6
Pyrénées, Parc National des ⊥• F 90-91 G 10
Pyrenees = Pyrénées ▲ F 90-91 G 10
Pyre Peak ▲ USA 22-23 K 6
Pyrjatyn ○ UA 102-103 H 2
Pyrkanaj ▲ RUS 112-113 N 2
Pyrzyce ○• PL 92-93 N 2
Pyščyg ○ RUS 96-97 D 4
Pyšma ~ RUS 96-97 M 5
Pyšma ~ RUS 114-115 J 6
Pyssa ~ RUS 88-89 U 4
Pytalovo = Abrene ☆ RUS 94-95 K 3
Pythonga, Lac ⊖ CDN (QUE) 238-239 J 2
Pyt'-Jah = Pjat'-Jah ○ RUS 114-115 M 4
Pyttegga ▲ N 86-87 C 5
Pyu ○ MYA 142-143 K 6
Pyuthan ○ NEP 144-145 D 6
Pyžina ~ RUS 114-115 R 5

Q

Qa'āmiyāt, al- ≐ KSA 132-133 E 5
Qaanaaq = Thule ☆ GRØ 26-27 Q 5
Qaarsut ○ GRØ 28-29 O 1
Qab ○ VRC 154-155 E 2
Qabane ○ LS 220-221 J 4
Qabr Hūd ○ Y 132-133 F 5
Qacha's Nek ○ LS 220-221 J 5
Qadam ○ SUD 200-201 D 6
Qadamgāh ○ IR 136-137 F 6
Qaḍarif, al- ○ SUD 200-201 G 5
Qādes ○ AFG 134-135 K 1
Qadir Purrān ○ PK 138-139 C 4
Qādisiya, al- □ IRQ 128-129 L 7
Qādisiya, al- ∴• IRQ 128-129 K 5
Qafa ○ OM 132-133 H 5
Qaffāy, al- ⌒ UAE 134-135 D 6
Qagan Nur ○ VRC (NMZ) 154-155 F 2
Qagan Nur ⊖ VRC (JIL) 150-151 E 5
Qagan Nur ⊖ VRC (NMZ) 148-149 M 6
Qagcaka ○ VRC 144-145 C 4
Qagdlumiut ○ GRØ 28-29 S 6
Qahar Youyi Houqi ○ VRC 148-149 L 7
Qahar Youyi Zhongqi ○ VRC 148-149 L 7
Qahāvand ○ IR 134-135 C 1
Qahb, Ğabal al- ▲ KSA 130-131 J 5
Qāhira, al- ★••• ET 194-195 E 2
Qahmah, al- ○ KSA 132-133 B 4
Qā'id, Abū al- ○ KSA 132-133 C 5
Qaidam He ~ VRC 144-145 L 2
Qaidam Pendi ≐ VRC 146-147 L 6
Qāimšahr ○ IR 136-137 C 6
Qaiṣār ○ AFG 136-137 J 7
Qaiwain, Umm al- ○ UAE 134-135 F 6
Qā'iya, al- ○ KSA 130-131 H 5
Qala'an-Nahl ○ SUD 200-201 G 6
Qalamat Nadqān ○ KSA 132-133 G 2
Qalana ○ Y 132-133 G 6
Qalansiya ○ Y 132-133 H 7
Qalāt ○ AFG 134-135 M 2
Qalat al-Hafirah • KSA 130-131 F 5
Qal'at al-Ḥiṣn •• SYR 128-129 G 5
Qal'at al-Mu'azzam ○ KSA 130-131 E 4
Qal'at ar-Rabaḍ ∴• JOR 130-131 D 1
Qalat az Zubaidiyah • KSA 130-131 F 5
Qal'at Ğābir • SYR 128-129 H 5
Qal'at Ḥamidī ○ IRQ 128-129 L 6
Qal'at Ṣalāḥaddīn ∴•• SYR 128-129 G 5
Qal'at Ṣāliḥ ☆ IRQ 128-129 M 7
Qal'at Sam'ān •• SYR 128-129 G 4
Qal'at Sukkar ☆ IRQ 128-129 M 7
Qal'a-ye Nau ☆ AFG 136-137 H 7
Qal'e Dīze ☆ IRQ 128-129 L 4
Qal'e Ra'isi ○ IR 134-135 D 3
Qal'e-ye Kāh ○ AFG 134-135 J 2
Qal'e-ye Mīr Dāvūd ○ AFG 134-135 K 1
Qal'e-ye Panğe ○ AFG 136-137 N 6
Qalhāt ○ OM 132-133 L 2
Qalība, al- ○ KSA 130-131 E 3
Qalluviartuuq, Lac ⊖ CDN 36-37 M 5
Qaltī al-Adusa < SUD 200-201 C 4
Qaltī al-Khudairā < SUD 200-201 C 4
Qaltī Immaseri < SUD 200-201 B 5
Qalyūb ○ ET 194-195 E 2
Qambar ○ PK 134-135 M 5
Qamdo ○ VRC 144-145 L 5
Qamea ⌒ FJI 184 III c 2
Qamīnis ○•• LAR 192-193 J 2
Qāmišlī, al- ☆ SYR 128-129 J 4
Qamṣar ○ IR 134-135 D 2
Qanā ○ KSA 130-131 G 4
Qandahār □ AFG 134-135 L 3
Qandahār ☆•• AFG 134-135 L 3
Qandala ○ SP 208-209 J 3
Qaqortoq = Julianehab ○ GRØ 28-29 R 6
Qāra ○ ET 192-193 L 3
Qāra ○ KSA 130-131 G 3
Qarā', Ğabal al- ▲ OM 132-133 H 5
Qara Āġaǧ, Rūdḫāne-ye ~ IR 134-135 E 4
Qarabāġ ○ AFG (ĠA) 138-139 B 3
Qarabāġ ○ AFG (HE) 134-135 J 1
Qarabāġ ○ AFG (KB) 138-139 B 2
Qara Čāy ~ IR 128-129 N 5
Qara Dāġ ▲ IR 128-129 M 3
Qara Dāġ ▲ IRQ 128-129 L 5
Qara Ertis ~ KA 124-125 O 5
Qaraghandy = Ķaraġandy ☆ KA 124-125 H 4
Qaraghandy = Ķaraghandy ○ KA 124-125 H 4
Qarah Dāġ ▲ IRQ 128-129 K 4
Qarajaqs Isfjord ≈ 28-29 P 1
Qaramqol ○ AFG 136-137 J 6
Qarānqū, Rūd-e ~ IR 128-129 M 4
Qara Qash ~ IND 138-139 G 2
Qara Sū ~ IR 134-135 B 1
Qar'āt ad Dibah, Bi'r < LAR 190-191 G 6
Qardho ○ SP 208-209 J 4
Qardliit Ikerat ≈ 28-29 V 4
Qare Āġāǧ ○ IR 128-129 M 4
Qare Sū ~ IR 136-137 E 6
Qare Żiyā'od-Dīn ○ IR 128-129 L 3
Qarhan ○ VRC 144-145 K 2
Qārloq ○ IR 136-137 E 6
Qarqāī ○ AFG 138-139 C 2
Qarqan He ~ VRC 146-147 H 6
Qarqaraut, Wādī ~ Y 132-133 G 6
Qārūn, Birkat ⊖ ET 194-195 E 3
Qaryah ash Sharqīyah, Al ○ LAR 192-193 E 2
Qaryās, Bi'r < LAR 192-193 G 3
Qaryat Abū Nujaym ○ LAR 192-193 F 2
Qaryat Abū Qurays ○ LAR 192-193 F 2
Qaryatain, al- ○ SYR 128-129 G 5
Qaryat al Fā'idiyah ○ LAR 192-193 J 1
Qaryat al-'Ulyā ○ KSA 130-131 K 4
Qaryat az Zuwaytīnah ○ LAR 192-193 J 2
Qaryat Shumaykh ○ LAR 192-193 E 2
Qarzah, Wādī ~ LAR 192-193 E 2
Qaṣab, Wādī l- ~ IRQ 128-129 K 5
Qaṣabe ▲ IR 128-129 M 3
Qasī bu Hadi ○ LAR 192-193 G 2
Qasigianguit = Christianshåb ○ GRØ 28-29 P 2
Qasir, Sabhat al- ⊖ SYR 128-129 J 5-
Qaṣr, Umm ○ IRQ 130-131 K 2
Qaṣr al-Farāfira ○ ET 194-195 C 4
Qaṣr al-Ḥair • SYR 128-129 H 5
Qaṣr al-Ḥair al-Ġarbī ∴• SYR 128-129 G 5
Qasr al-Harāna ∴• JOR 130-131 E 2
Qasr al Jady ○ LAR 192-193 L 2
Qasr al Kharrūbah ○ LAR 192-193 J 1
Qaṣr al-Mušattā ∴• JOR 130-131 E 2
Qaşr al Qarn ○ LAR 192-193 L 2
Qaṣr 'Amīq ○ IRQ 128-129 J 6
Qaṣr ash Shaqqah ○ LAR 192-193 L 2
Qaṣr aṭ-Ṭūbā ∴• JOR 130-131 E 2
Qaṣr-e Qand ○ IR 134-135 J 5
Qasr-e Šīrīn ○• IR 134-135 A 1
Qasr Ibn Rashid Palace • KSA 130-131 G 4
Qaṣrīk ○ IR 128-129 L 3
Qaṣr Khulayf ○ LAR 192-193 E 4
Qaṣr Larocu ○ LAR 192-193 E 4
Qaṣr Šaqra ∴• IRQ 130-131 K 2
Qassiarsuk ○ GRØ 28-29 S 6
Qassim, al- □ KSA 130-131 H 5
Qa'taba ○ Y 132-133 D 7
Qaṭanā ○ SYR 128-129 G 6
Qatar = Qaṭar ■ Q 134-135 D 6
Qaṭīf, al- ○ KSA 134-135 D 5
Qatliš ○ IR 136-137 E 6
Qaṭn, al- ○ KSA 130-131 K 6
Qaṭn, al- ○ Y 132-133 F 6
Qaṭrāna, al- ○ JOR 130-131 E 2
Qaṭrānī, Ğabal ▲ ET 194-195 E 3
Qaṭrūye ○ IR 134-135 F 4
Qaṭṭār, Ğabal ▲ ET 194-195 F 4
Qattara Depression ≐ ET 194-195 C 3
Qattara Depression = Qattāra, Munhafad al ≐ ET 194-195 C 3
Qawām al-Ḥamza ○ IRQ 128-129 L 7
Qawz Ragab ○ SUD 200-201 G 4
Qāyen ○• IR 134-135 H 2
Qaysan ○ SUD 208-209 B 3
Qayyāra ○ IRQ 128-129 K 5
Qazvīn ○• IR 128-129 N 4
Qeersorfik = Ikamiut ○ GRØ 28-29 P 2
Qelelevu ⌒ FJI 184 III c 2
Qeqertaq ○ GRØ (VGR) 28-29 P 1
Qeqertaq ⌒ GRØ (VGR) 26-27 X 8
Qeqertarssuaq ⌒ GRØ (VGR) 26-27 X 7
Qeqertarssuaq ⌒ GRØ (VGR) 26-27 Y 8
Qeqertarsuaq = Godhavn ○ GRØ 28-29 O 2
Qeqertarsuatsiaat = Fiskenæsset ○ GRØ 28-29 P 5
Qeqertat ○ GRØ 26-27 R 5
Qerri ○ SUD 200-201 F 4
Qešm ○• IR 134-135 G 5
Qešm, Ğazīre-ye ⌒ IR 134-135 G 5
Qezaltepeque ○ ES 52-53 K 5
Qezel ○ AFG 134-135 M 1
Qezel Ūzan, Rūd-e ~ IR 128-129 M 4
Qezel Ūzan Qoli, Čam-e ~ IR 128-129 M 5
Qian'an ○ VRC 150-151 E 5
Qianarteq ⌒ GRØ 28-29 W 4
Qiandaohu • VRC 156-157 L 2
Qianfoshan • VRC 154-155 K 3
Qianfo Yan • VRC 154-155 D 5
Qianheshangyuan ○ VRC 154-155 F 3
Qianjiang ○ VRC (HUB) 154-155 H 6
Qianjiang ○ VRC (SIC) 156-157 F 2
Qianjin ○ VRC 150-151 J 4
Qian Ling ∴• VRC 154-155 F 4
Qianshan ○ VRC (ANH) 154-155 K 6
Qianshan ○ VRC (GDG) 156-157 G 6
Qian Shan ▲ VRC 150-151 D 7
Qianshan • VRC (LIA) 150-151 D 7
Qianwei ○ VRC 156-157 C 2
Qianxi ○ VRC 156-157 E 3
Qian Xian ○ VRC 154-155 F 4
Qianyang ○ VRC (HUN) 156-157 G 3
Qianyang ○ VRC (SXI) 154-155 E 4
Qiaochuan ○ VRC 154-155 E 3
Qiaojdang ○ VRC 156-157 E 5
Qiaojia ○ VRC 156-157 C 3
Qiaojian ○ VRC 156-157 E 5
Qiaowan ○ VRC 148-149 C 7
Qiaozhen ○ VRC 154-155 F 3
Qichoi ○ VRC 156-157 F 6
Qichun ○ VRC 154-155 J 6
Qidong ○ VRC 154-155 M 6
Qidugou ○ VRC 144-145 K 3
Qiemo ○ VRC 146-147 G 6
Qifṭ ○ ET 194-195 F 5
Qijiang ○ VRC 156-157 E 2
Qijiaojing ○ VRC 146-147 K 4
Qila Didār Singh ○ PK 138-139 E 3
Qila Lādgasht ○ PK 134-135 K 5
Qilaotu Shan ▲ VRC 148-149 O 6
Qila Saifullāh ○ PK 138-139 B 4
Qilian ○ VRC 154-155 B 2
Qilian Shan ▲ VRC 146-147 N 6
Qilian Shan ▲ VRC 146-147 O 6
Qilwa ○ KSA 132-133 B 4
Qimen ○ VRC 156-157 K 2
Qinā ☆ ET 194-195 F 4
Qinā, Wādī ~ ET 194-195 F 4
Qin'an ○ VRC 154-155 D 4
Qin Binmayong ∴••• VRC 154-155 F 4
Qing'an ○ VRC 150-151 F 4
Qingchengshan • VRC 154-155 C 6
Qingdao ☆ VRC 154-155 M 3
Qing Donling • VRC 154-155 K 1
Qinggang ○ VRC 150-151 F 4
Qinghai □ VRC 144-145 J 4
Qinghai Hu ⊖ VRC 144-145 M 2
Qinghai Nanshan ▲ VRC 144-145 M 2
Qinghe ○ VRC (HEB) 154-155 J 3
Qinghe ○ VRC (XUZ) 146-147 K 2
Qingjian ○ VRC 154-155 G 3
Qing Jiang ~ VRC 154-155 G 6
Qingkou ○ VRC 156-157 E 3
Qinglan • VRC 156-157 G 7
Qinglong ○ VRC 154-155 L 1
Qinglong D. • VRC 156-157 F 3
Qingping ○ VRC 156-157 F 6
Qingpu ○ VRC 154-155 M 6
Qingshan ○ VRC 154-155 J 6
Qingshizoi ○ VRC 154-155 B 3
Qingshui ○ VRC 154-155 A 2
Qingshuihe ○ VRC (NMZ) 154-155 G 2
Qingshuihe ○ VRC (QIN) 144-145 L 4
Qingshui He ~ VRC 154-155 E 3
Qingtang ○ VRC 156-157 H 4
Qingtian ○ VRC 156-157 M 2
Qingtongxia ○ VRC 154-155 E 2
Qing Xiling • VRC 154-155 J 2
Qingxu ○ VRC 154-155 H 3
Qingyang ○ VRC (ANH) 154-155 K 6
Qingyang ○ VRC (GAN) 154-155 E 3
Qingyuan ○ VRC (GDG) 156-157 H 5
Qingyuan ○ VRC (LIA) 150-151 E 6
Qingyuanshan • VRC 156-157 J 3
Qingyun Huaxuechang • VRC 150-151 G 5
Qingzhang Gaoyuan ≐ VRC 144-145 D 4
Qingzhen ○ VRC 156-157 E 3
Qingzhou ○ VRC 154-155 L 3
Qinhuangdao ○ VRC 154-155 L 2
Qin Ling ▲ VRC 154-155 E 5
Qintang ○ VRC 156-157 F 5
Qinwanglao Shan ▲ VRC 156-157 E 4
Qin Xian ○ VRC 154-155 H 3
Qinyang ○ VRC 154-155 H 4
Qinzhou ○ VRC 156-157 F 6
Qinzhou Wan ≈ 156-157 F 6
Qionghai ○ VRC 156-157 G 7
Qionglai ○ VRC 154-155 C 6
Qionglai Shan ▲ VRC 154-155 C 6
Qiongzhong ○ VRC 156-157 F 7
Qiongzhou Haixia ≈ 156-157 F 6
Qiqian ○ VRC 150-151 C 1
Qiqihar ○ VRC 150-151 D 4
Qiqushan Damiao • VRC 154-155 D 6
Qīr ○ IR 134-135 E 4
Qira ○ VRC 144-145 C 2
Qisba, Ra's ▲ KSA 130-131 D 3
Qisha ○ VRC 156-157 F 6
Qishu ○ VRC 154-155 F 6
Qišla, al- ○ IRQ 130-131 L 3
Qišn ○ Y 132-133 G 6
Qitai ○ VRC 146-147 J 4
Qitaihe ○ VRC 150-151 H 5
Qitbīt, Wādī ~ OM 132-133 J 4
Qitian Ling ▲ VRC 156-157 H 4
Qiubei ○ VRC 156-157 D 4
Qiujin ○ VRC 156-157 J 2
Qixia ○ VRC 154-155 M 3
Qiyang ○ VRC 156-157 G 3
Qiyuanshan • VRC 156-157 L 2
Qizhou Liedao ⌒ VRC 156-157 G 7
Qogir Feng = K2 ▲ VRC 138-139 F 2
Qoğūr ○ IR 128-129 M 4
Qohrūd, Kūhhā-ye ▲ IR 134-135 D 1
Qoltag ▲ VRC 146-147 J 4
Qom ○•• IR 134-135 D 1
Qom, Rūd-e ~ IR 134-135 D 1
Qomolangma Feng = Mount Everest ▲ VRC 144-145 F 7
Qomše ○• IR 134-135 D 2
Qonggyai ○ VRC 144-145 H 6
Qongkol ○ VRC 146-147 H 5
Qooriga Neegro ≈ 208-209 J 5
Qorqī ○ IR 136-137 F 6
Qôrsungnitsoq ⌒ GRØ 28-29 P 2
Qorve ○ IR (HAM) 128-129 N 5
Qorve ○ IR (KOR) 128-129 M 5
Qoryooley ○ SP 212-213 K 3
Qostanay = Ķostanaj ☆ KA 124-125 C 2
Qoṭābād ○ IR 134-135 E 4
Qoṭūr ○ IR 128-129 L 3
Qoṭūr Čāy ~ IR 128-129 L 3
QÞuáng Ngãi ○•• VN 158-159 K 3
Quabbin Reservoir ⊖ USA (MA) 278-279 J 6
Quadeville ○ CDN (ONT) 238-239 H 3
Quadra Island ⌒ CDN (BC) 230-231 D 3
Quadros, Lagoa dos ⊖ BR 74-75 E 7
Quaidabad ○ PK 138-139 C 3

Puerto Bolivar — Quaidabad 381

Quail o USA (TX) 264-265 D 4
Quairading o AUS 176-177 D 6
Quakertown o USA (PA) 280-281 L 3
Qualicum Beach o CDN (BC) 230-231 E 4
Quallene o DZ 190-191 C 8
Quambone o AUS 178-179 J 6
Quamby o AUS 174-175 F 7
Quanah o USA (TX) 264-265 E 4
Quần Dao Nam Du ⌒ VN 158-159 H 6
Quảng Tri ☆ VN 158-159 J 2
Quan Hóa o VN 156-157 D 6
Quantico Marine Corps xx USA (VA) 280-281 J 5
Quanzerbé o RN 202-203 L 2
Quanzhou o VRC (GXI) 156-157 G 4
Quanzhou o• VRC (FUJ) 156-157 L 4
Quapaw o USA (OK) 264-265 K 2
Qu'Appelle o CDN (SAS) 232-233 P 5
Qu'Appelle River ~ CDN (SAS) 232-233 N 5
Quaqtaq o CDN 36-37 P 4
Quaraí o BR 76-77 J 6
Quarkoye o BF 202-203 J 3
Quarryville o USA (PA) 280-281 K 4
Quartier Militaire o MS 224 C 7
Quartu Sant'Elena o I 100-101 B 5
Quartzite Lake o CDN 30-31 W 4
Quartzite Mountain ▲ USA (NV) 248-249 H 2
Quartz Lake o CDN (NWT) 24-25 f 5
Quartz Lake o CDN (ONT) 34-35 O 5
Quartz Mountain o USA (OR) 244-245 E 8
Quartz Mountain State Park ⊥ • USA (OK) 264-265 E 4
Quartzsite o USA (AZ) 256-257 A 5
Quathiaski Cove o CDN (BC) 230-231 D 3
Quatipuru, Ponta de ▲ BR 68-69 E 2
Quatorze de Abril, Cachoeira ~ BR 62-63 G 5
Quatorze de Abril, Rio ~ BR 70-71 G 2
Quatre Cantons, Lac de = Vierwaldstättersee o CH 92-93 K 5
Quatsino Sound ≈ 32-33 F 6
Quatsino Sound ≈ CDN 230-231 A 3
Quay o USA (NM) 256-257 M 4
Qubayyat, al- o RL 128-129 G 5
Qūčān o• IR 136-137 F 6
Qudaiḥ o KSA 134-135 D 5
Qué ~ ANG 216-217 C 7
Queanbeyan, Canberra- o AUS 180-181 K 3
Québec ⊓ CDN 38-39 F 3
Québec ☆ ••• CDN (QUE) 238-239 O 2
Quebo o GNB 202-203 C 4
Quebra-Anzol, Rio ~ BR 72-73 G 5
Quebracho o ROU 76-77 J 6
Quebrada Arriba o YV 60-61 F 2
Quebrada de los Cuervos • ROU 78-79 M 2
Quebrada Honda o CR 52-53 B 6
Quedas o MOC 218-219 G 4
Quedas do Iguaçu o BR 74-75 D 5
Quedas do Lúrio ~• MOC 218-219 L 1
Quedlinburg o• D 92-93 L 3
Queen, De o USA (AR) 276-277 A 6
Queen Alexandra Range ▲ ARK 16 E 0
Queen Bess, Mount ▲ CDN (BC) 230-231 E 2
Queen Charlotte Bay ≈ 78-79 K 6
Queen Charlotte City o CDN (BC) 228-229 B 3
Queen Charlotte Islands ⌒ CDN (BC) 228-229 A 3
Queen Charlotte Islands ⌒ CDN (BC) 228-229 C 4
Queen Charlotte Islands Museum • CDN (BC) 228-229 C 3
Queen Charlotte Mountains ▲ CDN (BC) 228-229 B 4
Queen Charlotte Sound ≈ 32-33 F 6
Queen Charlotte Sound ≈ CDN 228-229 D 5
Queen Charlotte Strait ≈ 32-33 G 6
Queen Charlotte Strait ≈ CDN 230-231 B 2
Queen City o USA (MO) 274-275 F 4
Queen Elizabeth Islands ⌒ CDN 16 B 30
Queen Elizabeth National Park ⊥ EAU 212-213 B 4
Queen Lake, De ~ USA (AR) 276-277 A 6
Queen Mary Land ⊥ ARK 16 G 10
Queen Maud Gulf ≈ 24-25 U 6
Queens Bay o CDN (BC) 230-231 N 4
Queens Cape ▲ CDN 36-37 R 2
Queens Channel ≈ 24-25 X 2
Queenscliff o AUS 180-181 H 5
Queensferry o• GB 90-91 F 4
Queensland ⊓ AUS 174-175 E 6
Queenslander II AUS 174-175 K 7
Queensland Plateau ≃ 174-175 K 5
Queensport o CDN (NS) 240-241 O 5
Queens Sound ≈ 32-33 F 6
Queens Sound ≈ CDN 230-231 A 2
Queenstown o AUS 180-181 H 7
Queenstown o CDN (ALB) 232-233 F 5
Queenstown o•• NZ 182 B 6
Queenstown o ZA 220-221 H 5
Queen Victoria Rock ▲ AUS 176-177 F 5
Que'ergou o VRC 146-147 H 4
Queets o USA (WA) 244-245 A 3
Queguay Grande, Río ~ ROU 78-79 L 2
Quehue o PE 70-71 B 4
Quehué o RA 78-79 G 4
Quehué, Valle de ⌣ RA 78-79 G 4
Queidār o IR 128-129 N 4
Queilén o RCH 78-79 C 7
Queimadas o BR (BAH) 68-69 J 7
Queimadas o BR (PA) 68-69 L 5
Queirós o BR 72-73 E 6
Queiros, Cape ▲ VAN 184 II a 2
Quela o ANG 216-217 D 4
Quélé o CI 202-203 G 4
Quelele o ANG 216-217 E 4
Quelimane ☆ MOC 218-219 J 3
Quellón o RCH 78-79 C 7
Quellouno o PE 64-65 F 8
Quelo o ANG 216-217 B 3
Queluz o BR 72-73 H 7
Quemado o USA (NM) 256-257 G 4
Quemado o USA (TX) 266-267 G 5
Quemado, Cerro ▲ CO 60-61 D 2
Quemado de Güines o C 54-55 E 3
Quemados, Punta de ▲ C 54-55 H 4
Quembo ~ ANG 216-217 E 7
Quemchi o RCH 78-79 C 7
Quemu Quemu o RA 78-79 H 4
Quenco, Cerro ▲ BOL 76-77 E 1
Queñoal, Río ~ BOL 76-77 D 2
Quénomisca, Lac o CDN (ONT) 236-237 M 2
Quepe, Río ~ RCH 78-79 C 5
Quê Phong ☆ VN 156-157 D 7
Quepos o CR 52-53 B 7
Quepos, Punta ▲ CR 52-53 B 7
Quequén o RA 78-79 K 5
Quequén Grande, Río ~ RA 78-79 K 5
Quequén Salado, Río ~ RA 78-79 J 5
Querari o CO 66-67 C 2
Querari, Río ~ CO 66-67 B 2
Querco o PE 64-65 E 8
Querência do Norte o BR 72-73 D 7
Querendaro o MEX 52-53 D 2
Querétaro ⊓ MEX 52-53 D 1
Querétaro ☆ •• MEX (QRO) 52-53 D 1
Quero o EC 64-65 C 2
Querobamba o PE 64-65 F 8
Querocotillo o PE 64-65 C 5
Quesnel o CDN (BC) 228-229 M 4
Quesnel Lake o CDN (BC) 228-229 N 4
Quesnel River ~ CDN (BC) 228-229 M 4
Quesso ☆ RCB (San) 210-211 F 3
Questa o USA (NM) 256-257 K 2
Questro, El o AUS 172-173 H 4
Quetico o CDN (ONT) 234-235 N 6
Quetico Lake o CDN (ONT) 234-235 M 6
Quetico Provincial Park ⊥ CDN (ONT) 234-235 M 6
Quetico Provincial Park ⊥ USA (MN) 270-271 G 2
Quetta ☆ • PK 134-135 M 3
Queue de Turtue, Bayou ~ USA (LA) 268-269 H 6
Queulat, Parque Nacional ⊥ RCH 80 D 2
Queve ~ ANG 216-217 C 5
Quevedo o EC 64-65 C 2
Quevedo, Río ~ EC 64-65 C 2
Quévillon, Lac o CDN (QUE) 236-237 M 3
Quezaltenango ☆ • GCA 52-53 J 4
Quezon o RP 160-161 C 8
Quezon City o RP 160-161 D 5
Qufu o• VRC 154-155 K 4
Quiabaya o BOL 70-71 C 4
Quiaca, La o RA 76-77 E 2
Quiahniztlan • MEX 52-53 F 2
Quiba o ZA 220-221 H 5
Quibala o ANG (CZS) 216-217 C 5
Quibala o ANG (ZAI) 216-217 B 3
Quibaxe o ANG 216-217 C 4
Quibdó ☆ CO 60-61 C 5
Quibell o CDN (ONT) 234-235 K 5
Quiberon o F 90-91 F 8
Quibor o YV 60-61 G 3
Quicabo o ANG 216-217 B 4
Quicacha o PE 64-65 F 9
Quicama, Parque Nacional do ⊥ ANG 216-217 B 4
Quichaura, Cerro ▲ RA 78-79 D 7
Quicksand o USA (KY) 276-277 M 3
Quiculungo o ANG 216-217 C 4
Quidico o RCH 78-79 C 5
Quidong o VRC 156-157 H 3
Quiet Lake o CDN 20-21 Y 6
Quijadas, Sierra las ▲ RA 78-79 F 2
Quijingue o BR 68-69 J 7
Quijotoa o USA (AZ) 256-257 C 6
Quijoux, Col ▲ RCA 206-207 F 4
Quila o MEX 50-51 F 5
Quilán, Cabo ▲ RCH 78-79 B 7
Quilandi o IND 140-141 F 5
Quilca o PE (ARE) 70-71 A 5
Quilca o PE (LIM) 64-65 D 7
Quilcene o USA (WA) 244-245 C 3
Quilchena o CDN (BC) 230-231 J 3
Quilempa o ANG 216-217 B 7
Quilenda o ANG 216-217 C 5
Quilengues o ANG 216-217 C 7
Quillabamba o PE 64-65 F 8
Quillacollo o BOL 70-71 D 5
Quillagua o RCH 76-77 C 1
Quillan o F 90-91 J 10
Quillayute Indian Reservation ⚔ USA (WA) 244-245 A 3
Quillen, Río ~ RCH 78-79 C 5
Quill Lake o CDN (SAS) 232-233 O 3
Quill Lakes o CDN (SAS) 232-233 O 4
Quilmes o RA 78-79 K 3
Quilombo dos Dembos o ANG 216-217 C 4
Quilon o• IND 140-141 G 6
Quilpie o AUS 178-179 H 4
Quilpué o RCH 78-79 D 2
Quilua o MOC 218-219 K 3
Quilu Hu ~ VRC 156-157 C 4
Quimal, Llano del ⊥ RCH 76-77 C 2
Quimantag ▲ VRC 144-145 H 2
Quimbala o ANG 216-217 C 2
Quimbaya o CO 60-61 D 5
Quimbele o ANG 216-217 D 3
Quimet o CDN (ONT) 234-235 P 6
Quimili o RA 76-77 F 4
Quimome, Río ~ BOL 70-71 G 6
Quimper ☆ • F 90-91 E 8
Quinabucasan Point ▲ RP 160-161 E 5
Quinapondan o RP 160-161 F 7
Quinault o USA (WA) 244-245 B 3
Quinault Indian Reservation ⚔ USA (WA) 244-245 A 3
Quinault River ~ USA (WA) 244-245 B 3
Quince Mil o PE 70-71 B 3
Quinchao, Isla ⌒ RCH 78-79 C 7
Quinché, Raudal ~ CO 66-67 B 3
Quincy o USA (FL) 286-287 E 1
Quincy o USA (IL) 274-275 G 5
Quincy o USA (MA) 278-279 L 6
Quincy o USA (WA) 244-245 F 3
Quincy, De o USA (LA) 268-269 G 6
Quincy Hills ▲ USA (IL) 274-275 G 5
Quines o RA 78-79 G 2
Quinga o MOC 218-219 L 2
Quingenge o ANG 216-217 C 6
Quinhagak o USA 22-23 Q 3
Quinhámel o GNB 202-203 C 4
Quiniluban Group ⌒ RP 160-161 D 7
Quinjalca o PE 64-65 D 5
Quinkan Nature Reserve ⊥ AUS 174-175 H 4
Quinlan o USA (TX) 264-265 H 6
Quinn River ~ USA (NV) 246-247 G 2
Quinns Rocks o AUS 176-177 C 5
Quinota o PE 64-65 F 9
Quintana de la Serena o E 98-99 E 5
Quintana Roo ⊓ MEX 52-53 K 2
Quintana Roo, Parque Nacional de ⊥ MEX 52-53 L 1
Quinter o USA (KS) 262-263 F 5
Quintero o RCH 78-79 D 2
Quintero, Bahía ≈ 78-79 D 2
Quintín Banderas o C 54-55 E 3
Quinto, Río ~ RA 78-79 G 2
Quinton o CDN (SAS) 232-233 O 4
Quinton o USA (OK) 264-265 J 3
Quinzala o ANG 216-217 C 3
Quinzau o ANG 216-217 B 3
Quionga o MOC 214-215 L 6
Quiongua o ANG 216-217 C 4
Quiotepec o MEX 52-53 F 3
Quipapa o BR 68-69 K 6
Quipeio o ANG 216-217 C 6
Quipungo o ANG 216-217 C 7
Quirigua ∴ ••• GCA 52-53 K 4
Quirihue o RCH 78-79 C 4
Quirima o ANG 216-217 E 5
Quirindi o AUS 178-179 L 6
Quiriñeo, Cerro ▲ RCH 78-79 D 3
Quirinópolis o BR 72-73 E 5
Quiriquire o YV 60-61 K 3
Quiroga o BOL 70-71 E 6
Quiroga o MEX 52-53 D 2
Quiroga o RA 78-79 J 3
Quiroga, Punta ▲ RA 78-79 G 7
Quiros o YV 60-61 F 2
Quirpon o CDN (NFL) 242-243 N 1
Quiruvilca o PE 64-65 C 5
Quisquiro, Salar de o RCH 76-77 D 2
Quissanga o MOC 214-215 L 7
Quissico o MOC 220-221 M 2
Quitandinha o BR 74-75 F 5
Quitapa o ANG 216-217 E 5
Quitaque o USA (TX) 264-265 C 4
Quiterajo o MOC 214-215 L 6
Quitéria, Rio ~ BR 72-73 E 5
Quiteve o ANG 216-217 C 8
Quitexe o ANG 216-217 C 3
Quitilipi o RA 76-77 G 4
Quitman o USA (AR) 276-277 C 5
Quitman o USA (GA) 284-285 G 6
Quitman o USA (LA) 268-269 H 4
Quitman o USA (MS) 268-269 M 4
Quitman o USA (TX) 264-265 J 6
Quitman Ruins, Fort • USA (TX) 266-267 B 2
Quito ☆ ••• EC 64-65 C 2
Quivira National Wildlife Refuge ⊥ USA (KS) 262-263 H 6
Quivolgo o RCH 78-79 C 3
Quixadá o BR 68-69 J 4
Quixadá o BR 66-67 D 7
Quixada o BR 68-69 J 4
Quixaxe o MOC 218-219 L 2
Quixeramobim o BR 68-69 J 4
Quizenga o ANG 216-217 C 4
Qujiang o VRC 156-157 H 4
Qujing o VRC 156-157 C 4
Qulaita, Umm o Y 132-133 E 7
Qulin o USA (MO) 276-277 E 4
Qumar He ~ VRC 144-145 J 3
Qumar Heyan o VRC 144-145 J 3
Qumarlêb o VRC 144-145 K 3
Qummāh, Ğazīrat ⌒ KSA 132-133 B 5
Qunaiṭira, al- ☆ SYR 128-129 F 6
Qunfuḏa, al- o KSA 132-133 B 4
Quobba o AUS 176-177 B 2
Quobba, Point ▲ AUS 176-177 B 2
Quoich River ~ CDN 30-31 W 2
Quoin, Du o USA (IL) 274-275 J 6
Quoin Head ▲ AUS 176-177 B 2
Quoin Island ⌒ AUS 172-173 J 3
Quoy, Pulau ⌒ RI 166-167 F 1
Qurayd o SUD 206-207 K 3
Qurayyāt o• OM 132-133 L 2
Qurayyāt, al- ⌒ KSA 130-131 E 3
Qurayyāt, al- ☆ • KSA 130-131 E 2
Qurdūd o SUD 206-207 J 3
Qureida o SUD 206-207 G 3
Qurna, al- ☆ IRQ 128-129 M 7
Qurnat as-Saudā' ▲ RL 128-129 G 5
Qurrāṣah o SUD 200-201 F 5
Qūs o ET 194-195 F 5
Quṣaiba o IRQ 128-129 J 5
Quṣair, al- o IRQ 130-131 J 2
Quṣair, al- ☆ SYR 128-129 G 5
Quṣair 'Amra ∴ ••• JOR 130-131 E 2
Quṣay'ir o Y 132-133 G 6
Qusum o VRC 144-145 J 6
Quṭaifa, al- ☆ SYR 128-129 G 6
Qutau ▲ KA 124-125 K 4
Qutdligssat o GRØ 28-29 O 1
Qutdlikorssuit ⌒ GRØ 26-27 W 7
Quthing = Moyeni o LS 220-221 H 5
Qutsigsormiut ⌒ GRØ 28-29 U 5
Quṭū', Ğazīrat ⌒ KSA 132-133 B 4
Quṭūf o UAE 132-133 H 2
Quwair, al- o IRQ 128-129 K 4
Quwāra, al- o KSA 130-131 H 4
Quwu Shan ▲ VRC 154-155 D 3
Qu Xian o VRC 154-155 E 6
Qūxū o VRC 144-145 H 6
Quyāğū o IRQ 128-129 L 5
Quyang o VRC 154-155 J 2
Quyanghai SK ~ VRC 156-157 H 3
Quyen o AUS 180-181 G 3
Quynh Lu'u o VN 156-157 D 7
Quy Nho'n ☆ • VN 158-159 K 4
Qūz, al- o KSA 132-133 B 4
Qūz, al- o Y 132-133 G 6
Quza, al- o Y 132-133 F 6
Quzhou o VRC 156-157 L 2
Qwa Qwa (former homeland) now part of Oranje Vrystaat ⊓ ZA 220-221 J 4
Qyzylorda = Kyzylorda ☆ KA 124-125 D 6

R

Raab ~ A 92-93 N 5
Raadol'naja ~ RUS 122-123 D 6
Raahe o FIN 88-89 H 4
Raanes Peninsula ⌒ CDN 26-27 G 4
Raanujärvi o FIN 88-89 H 3
Raas, Pulau ⌒ RI 168 B 6
Raattama o FIN 88-89 H 2
Rab o• HR 100-101 E 2
Rab ⊥•• HR 100-101 E 2
Raba o• RI 168 D 7
Rabaable o SP 208-209 J 4
Rabad, Qal'at ar- ∴• JOR 130-131 D 1
Rabah o WAN 198-199 B 6
Rabak o SUD 200-201 F 6
Rabal o RI 166-167 H 5
Rabang o VRC 144-145 C 4
Rabaraba o PNG 183 E 5
Rabārika o IND 138-139 C 9
Rabat o M 100-101 E 7
Rabat = Ar-Ribāṭ ☆•• MA 188-189 K 4
Rabat = Victoria o M 100-101 E 6
Rabaul ☆• PNG 183 G 3
Rabba o WAN 204-205 F 4
Rabbād, ar- ⊥ UAE 132-133 J 2
Rabbit Ears Pass ▲ USA (CO) 254-255 J 3
Rabbit Flat Store o AUS 172-173 K 6
Rabbit Lake o CDN (SAS) 232-233 L 2
Rabbit River ~ CDN 30-31 F 6
Rabbitskin River ~ CDN 30-31 J 5
Raber o USA (MI) 270-271 O 4
Rabi ⌒ FJI 184 III c 2
Rabi'a o IRQ 128-129 K 4
Rabia o RI 166-167 F 2
Rabida, Isla ⌒ EC 64-65 B 10
Rābiġ o KSA 130-131 F 6
Rabka o PL 92-93 P 4
Rabkavi Banhatti o IND 140-141 F 2
Rabočeostrovsk o RUS 88-89 N 4
Rabo da Onça o BR 66-67 E 3
Rābor o IR 134-135 G 4
Raboti Malik, korvonsaroj • US 136-137 J 5
Rabt Sbayta ⊥ MA 196-197 C 3
Rabun Bald ▲ USA (GA) 284-285 G 2
Rabwah o PK 138-139 D 4
Rabyanah o LAR 192-193 K 5
Raccoon Cay ⌒ BS 54-55 H 3
Raccoon Creek ~ USA (OH) 280-281 D 5
Raccoon Creek State Park ⊥ USA (PA) 280-281 F 3
Raceland o USA (LA) 268-269 K 7
Race Pond o USA (GA) 284-285 H 6
Rachal o USA (TX) 266-267 J 7
Rachel o USA (NV) 248-249 J 2
Rạch Giá ☆• VN 158-159 H 5
Rachid o RIM 196-197 E 5
Rachiv ☆ UA 102-103 D 3
Racibórz o PL 92-93 P 3
Racine o USA (OH) 280-281 E 5
Racine o USA (WI) 274-275 L 2
Racing River ~ CDN 30-31 G 6
Rackham o CDN (MAN) 234-235 C 4
Rackla Range ▲ CDN 20-21 X 4
Radā' o Y 132-133 D 6
Radama, Nosy ⌒ RM 222-223 E 4
Rădăuţi o RO 102-103 D 4
Radcliff o USA (KY) 276-277 K 3
Radde o RUS 122-123 D 4
Radechiv o UA 102-103 D 2
Radford o USA (AL) 284-285 C 4
Radford o USA (VA) 280-281 F 6
Radford Lake o CDN 30-31 R 4
Radford River ~ CDN 30-31 R 4
Rādhan o PK 134-135 M 5
Rādhānagari o• IND 140-141 E 2
Rādhanpur o IND 138-139 C 8
Radial'naja, gora ▲ RUS 112-113 Q 3
Radimlja • BIH 100-101 F 3
Radio Australia • AUS 172-173 K 2
Radio Australia Station • AUS 176-177 B 2
Radio Telescope • AUS 180-181 K 2
Radioville o USA (IN) 274-275 M 3
Radisson o CDN (QUE) 38-39 F 2
Radisson o CDN (SAS) 232-233 L 3
Radisson, Pointe ▲ CDN 36-37 N 3
Radium Hot Springs o CDN (BC) 230-231 O 3
Radium Springs o USA (NM) 256-257 J 6
Rādkān o IR 136-137 F 6
Radom ☆ PL 92-93 Q 3
Radom o SUD 206-207 G 4
Radomsko o PL 92-93 P 3
Radoviš o MK 100-101 J 4
Radstadt o• A 92-93 M 5
Radužnyj o RUS 114-115 O 3
Radviliškis ☆•• LT 94-95 H 4
Radville o CDN (SAS) 232-233 O 6
Radwan o KSA 130-131 G 6
Radzyń Podlaski o PL 92-93 R 3
Rae o CDN 30-31 L 4
Rāe Bareli o IND 142-143 B 2
Raeford o USA (NC) 282-283 H 6
Rae Isthmus ⌣ CDN 24-25 c 7
Rae Lake o CDN 30-31 L 3
Rae River ~ CDN 24-25 M 6
Raeside, Lake o AUS 176-177 F 4
Raes Junction o NZ 182 B 6
Rae Strait ≈ 24-25 Y 6
Raetihi o NZ 182 E 3
Raevskij ☆ RUS 96-97 J 6
Rafaela o RA 76-77 G 6
Rafael Freyre o C 54-55 G 4
Rafah o AUT 130-131 C 2
Rafaï o RCA 206-207 F 6
Raffingora o ZW 218-219 F 3
Raffin-Kada o WAN 204-205 H 5
Rafhā' o KSA 130-131 H 3
Rafin-Čabas o WAN 204-205 H 4
Rāfit, Ğabal ▲ SUD 200-201 F 2
Rafsai o MA 188-189 J 3
Raft River ~ CDN (BC) 230-231 K 2
Raft River ~ USA (ID) 252-253 E 4
Raft River Mountains ▲ USA (UT) 254-255 B 2
Raga o SUD 206-207 G 4
Raga ~ SUD 206-207 G 4
Ragaing Yōma ▲ MYA 142-143 J 6
Ragama o CL 140-141 H 7
Ragang, Mount ▲ RP 160-161 F 9
Ragay Gulf ≈ 160-161 E 6
Ragged Island ⌒ CDN 36-37 U 7
Ragged Island ⌒ USA (ME) 278-279 N 5
Ragged Island Range ⌒ BS 54-55 H 3
Raghwan o KSA 132-133 A 3
Raglan o NZ 182 E 2
Ragland o USA (NM) 256-257 M 4
Ragley o USA (LA) 268-269 G 6
Rago o USA (KS) 262-263 H 7
Rago nasjonalpark ⊥ N 86-87 G 3
Ragozina, mys ▲ RUS 108-109 N 5
Ragueneau o CDN 38-39 K 4
Ragusa o I 100-101 E 6
Raha o RI 164-165 H 6
Rahad ~ ETH 200-201 H 6
Rahad al-Bardī o SUD 206-207 F 3
Rahama o WAN 204-205 H 3
Rāhatgarh o IND 138-139 G 8
Rahhāliya, ar- o IRQ 128-129 K 6
Rahib < SUD 200-201 C 4
Rāhida, ar- o Y 132-133 D 7
Rahim ki Bāzār o PK 138-139 B 7
Rahimyār Khān o PK 138-139 C 5
Rahmanovka o RUS 96-97 F 8
Rahmanovskie Kljuci o KA 124-125 P 4
Rahmat, Ra's ▲ ER 200-201 L 6
Rahmet o KA 124-125 D 4
Rahole National Reserve ⊥ EAK 212-213 G 3
Råholt o N 86-87 E 6
Rahouia o DZ 190-191 C 3
Rahué o RA 78-79 D 5
Rahue, Río ~ RCH 78-79 C 6
Raiatéa ⌒ F 13 M 4
Rāichūr o• IND 140-141 G 2
Raida o Y 132-133 D 6
Raidāk ~ IND 142-143 F 2
Raiford o USA (FL) 286-287 G 1
Raiganj o IND 142-143 F 3
Raigarh o IND 142-143 C 5
Raijua, Pulau ⌒ RI 168 E 8
Raikal o IND 138-139 G 10
Railroad Pass ▲ USA (NV) 246-247 H 4
Railroad Valley ⌣ USA (NV) 246-247 K 5
Raima, Wādi ~ Y 132-133 C 6
Rain, ar- o KSA 130-131 J 6
Rainbow o USA 20-21 Q 6
Rainbow o USA (OR) 244-245 C 6
Rainbow Beach o AUS 178-179 M 3
Rainbow Bridge National Monument ∴ USA (UT) 254-255 E 6
Rainbow City o USA (AL) 284-285 D 3
Rainbow Falls ~• USA (HI) 288 K 5
Rainbow Lake o CDN 30-31 K 6
Rainier o CDN (ALB) 232-233 F 5
Rainier o USA (OR) 244-245 C 4
Rainier, Mount ▲ USA (WA) 244-245 D 4
Rainpura o IND 140-141 G 3
Rainsville o USA (AL) 284-285 E 2
Rainy Lake o CDN (ONT) 234-235 K 6
Rainy River o CDN (ONT) 234-235 J 6
Rainy River ~ USA (MN) 270-271 E 2
Raipur o IND (MAP) 142-143 B 3
Raipur o IND (MAP) 142-143 B 5
Raisūt o OM 132-133 J 5
Raith o CDN (ONT) 234-235 O 6
Rai Valley o NZ 182 D 4
Rāiwind o PK 138-139 E 4
Raja, Pulau ⌒ RI 168 E 3
Raja Ampat, Kepulauan ⌒ RI 166-167 E 2
Rajada o BR 68-69 H 6
Rajagangapur o IND 142-143 D 4
Rājahmundry o IND 142-143 B 7
Rājākhera o IND 138-139 G 6
Rajampet o IND 140-141 H 3
Rajang o MAL (SAR) 162-163 J 3
Rajang ~ MAL 162-163 K 3
Rājanpur o PK 138-139 C 5
Rājāpalaiyam o IND 140-141 G 6
Rājāpur o IND 140-141 E 2
Rajasthan ⊓ IND 138-139 C 6
Rajčihinsk o RUS 122-123 C 4
Rajga ~ RUS 114-115 S 5
Rājgarh o IND (MAP) 138-139 F 8
Rājgarh o IND (RAJ) 138-139 F 6
Rājgarh o IND (RAJ) 138-139 E 5
Rajgarhat o NEP 144-145 F 7
Rajin o DVR 150-151 H 6
Rajkoke, ostrov ⌒ RUS 122-123 P 4
Rājkot o IND 138-139 C 8
Rājmahāl o IND 142-143 E 3
Rājmahal Hills ▲ IND 142-143 E 3
Rāj-Nāndgaon o IND 142-143 B 5
Rajnera, ostrov ⌒ RUS 84-85 f 2
Rājpiīpla o IND 138-139 D 9
Raj Samund o IND 138-139 D 7
Rajshahi ☆• BD 142-143 F 3
Raka o VRC 144-145 E 6
Rakan, Ra's ▲ Q 134-135 D 5
Rakata, Pulau ⌒ RI 168 A 3
Rakaye o BF 202-203 K 4
Raka Zangpo ~ VRC 144-145 F 6
Rakhni o PK 138-139 B 4
Rakhni ~ PK 138-139 B 5
Rakhshān ~ PK 134-135 K 5
Rakiraki o FJI 184 III b 2
Rakit, Pulau ⌒ RI 168 C 3
Rakitnoe o RUS 122-123 F 6
Rakom o THA 158-159 G 4
Rakonitz = Rakovník o CZ 92-93 M 3
Rakops o RB 218-219 C 5
Rakovník o CZ 92-93 M 3
Rakovskaja o RUS 88-89 Q 5
Rakušečnyj, mys ▲ KA 126-127 J 6
Rakvere ☆•• EST 94-95 K 2
Rakwa o RI 166-167 H 3
Ralco o RCH 78-79 D 4
Rālegaon o IND 138-139 G 9
Raleigh o CDN (NFL) 242-243 N 1
Raleigh o USA (MS) 268-269 L 4
Raleigh ☆ USA (NC) 282-283 J 5
Raleigh Bay ≈ 48-49 K 2
Raleigh Bay ≈ USA 282-283 L 6
Raleigh National Historic Site, Fort • USA (NC) 282-283 M 5
Raleighvallen ~ SME 62-63 F 3
Raleighvallen Voltzberg, National Reservaat ⊥ SME 62-63 F 3
Raley o CDN (ALB) 232-233 E 6
Ralls o USA (TX) 264-265 C 5
Ralph o CDN (SAS) 232-233 P 6
Ralston o USA (NE) 262-263 K 3
Ralston o USA (WA) 244-245 G 4
Ralston o USA (WY) 252-253 K 2
Rama o CDN (SAS) 232-233 P 4
Rama o NIC 52-53 B 5
Rāmabhadrapuram o IND 142-143 C 6
Rama Caída o RA 78-79 E 3
Rāmachandraparam o IND 140-141 K 2
Ramad, Hassi < DZ 190-191 F 6
Ramada, La o RA 76-77 E 4
Ramadas, Las o RCH 76-77 B 6
Ramādī, ar- ☆ IRQ 128-129 K 6
Ramadillas o RCH 76-77 C 1
Ramagiri o IND 140-141 G 3
Ramah o USA (NM) 256-257 G 3
Ramah Navajo Indian Reservation ⚔ USA (NM) 256-257 G 4
Rāmak o AFG 138-139 B 3
Ramalho, Serra do ▲ BR 72-73 H 2
Rāmallāh ☆ WB 130-131 D 2
Ramallo o RA 78-79 J 2
Rāmanāthapuram o IND 140-141 H 6
Rāman Mandi o IND 138-139 E 5
Rāmānuj Ganj o IND 142-143 C 4
Ramardori o RI 166-167 H 2
Ramas, Las = Salitre o EC 64-65 C 2
Rāmasamudram o IND 140-141 G 5
Ramatlabama o ZA 220-221 G 2
Ramayampet o IND 138-139 G 10
Rāmāyapatnam o IND 140-141 J 3
Rambipuji o RI 168 E 4
Rambouillet o F 90-91 H 7
Rambrè o MYA 142-143 H 6
Rambrè ⌒ MYA 142-143 H 6
Rambutyo Island ⌒ PNG 183 D 2
Ramea o CDN (NFL) 242-243 L 5
Ramea Island ⌒ CDN (NFL) 242-243 L 5
Rameau o CDN (QUE) 240-241 L 2
Ramechhap o NEP 144-145 F 7
Rame Head ▲ AUS 180-181 K 4
Ramena o RM 222-223 F 4
Rameški ☆ RUS 94-95 P 3
Rāmeswaram o•• IND 140-141 H 6
Ramey o USA (MN) 270-271 E 5
Ramezān Kalak o IR 134-135 J 5
Rāmganga ~ IND 138-139 G 6
Rāmganj Mandi o IND 138-139 E 7
Ramgarh o BD 142-143 G 4
Rāmgarh o IND 138-139 C 6
Rāmgarh o IND (BIH) 142-143 D 4
Rāmgarh o IND (MAP) 142-143 C 4
Rāmgarh Tāl o IND 142-143 C 2
Rāmhormoz o IR 134-135 C 3
Ramhurst o USA (GA) 284-285 F 2
Ramingining ⚔ AUS 174-175 C 3
Ramis Shet' ~ ETH 208-209 E 4
Ramkan o• IR 134-135 G 5
Ramkhamhaeng National Park ⊥ THA 158-159 E 2
Raml o IRQ 128-129 K 5
Ramla ☆ IL 130-131 D 2
Ramlat al-Ġāfa ⊥ OM 132-133 J 3
Ramlat al-Wahiba ⊥ OM 132-133 L 2
Ramlat as-Sab'atain ⊥ Y 132-133 D 6
Ramlat Rabyanah ⊥ LAR 192-193 J 5
Ramlat Zallāf ⊥ LAR 192-193 E 4
Ramlu ▲ ER 200-201 K 6
Rāmnagar o IND 142-143 B 2
Rāmnagar o IND 138-139 G 5
Rāmnagar o IND 138-139 E 3
Rāmnagor o IND 142-143 B 3
Ramo o ETH 208-209 E 5
Ramon o USA (NM) 256-257 L 4
Ramon, Mitzpé o IL 130-131 D 2
Ramona o USA (CA) 248-249 H 6
Ramonal ∴• MEX 52-53 K 2
Ramones, Los o MEX 50-51 K 5
Ramon Grande, Laguna o PE 64-65 B 4
Ramore o CDN (ONT) 236-237 H 4
Ramos o BR 62-63 H 6
Ramos, Cachoeira ~ BR 70-71 G 2
Ramos, Río de ~ MEX 50-51 G 5
Ramos Arizpe o MEX 50-51 J 5
Ramos Island ⌒ RP 160-161 B 8
Ramos Otero o RA 78-79 K 4
Ramotswa o RB 220-221 G 2
Rampa o ANG 216-217 C 4
Rampart o USA 20-21 P 4
Ramparts River ~ CDN 30-31 D 3
Rāmpur o IND (GUJ) 138-139 D 8
Rāmpur o IND (HIP) 138-139 F 4
Rāmpur o IND (MAP) 142-143 B 4
Rāmpur o IND (ORI) 142-143 D 5
Rāmpur o IND (UTP) 138-139 G 5
Rāmpura o IND 138-139 E 7
Rampur Hāt o IND 142-143 E 3
Ramree = Rambrè o MYA 142-143 H 6
Ramree Island = Rambrè ⌒ MYA 142-143 H 6
Ram River ~ CDN 30-31 H 5
Ram River ~ CDN (ALB) 232-233 C 3
Rams o UAE 134-135 F 6
Rāmsar o• IR 136-137 B 6
Ramsay, Mount ▲ AUS 172-173 H 5
Ramsay Lake o CDN (ONT) 236-237 F 5
Rāmše o IR 134-135 E 3
Ramsele o S 86-87 H 5
Ramseur o USA (NC) 282-283 H 5
Ramsey o CDN (ONT) 236-237 F 5
Ramsey o USA (IL) 274-275 J 5
Ramsey o USA (NC) 282-283 F 5
Ramsgate o• GB 90-91 H 6
Ramsgate o ZA 220-221 K 5
Ramsing o IND 142-143 J 1
Rāmšir o IR 134-135 C 3
Ramsjö o S 86-87 G 5
Ramta, ar ☆ JOR 130-131 E 1
Rāmtek o IND 138-139 G 9
Ramu o BD 142-143 H 5
Ramu o EAK 212-213 H 2
Ramu o NEP 144-145 C 6
Ramu National Park ⊥ PNG 183 C 3
Ramundberget o S 86-87 F 5
Ramu River ~ PNG 183 C 3
Ramusio, Lac o CDN 36-37 S 7
Ramvik o S 86-87 H 5
Ramygala o•• LT 94-95 J 4
Ran o WAN 198-199 G 6
Rana, Danau o RI 166-167 D 3
Rana, La o C 54-55 F 3
Rānahu o PK 138-139 B 7
Ranai o RI 162-163 H 3
Ranakah, Gunung ▲ RI 168 E 7
Rana Pratap Sāgar o IND 138-139 E 7
Ranarmoye ~ RI 166-167 F 5
Ranau o MAL 160-161 B 10
Ranau, Danau o RI 162-163 E 7
Ranbausawa, Tanjung ▲ RI 166-167 J 3
Ranburne o USA (AL) 284-285 E 3
Rancagua ☆ RCH 78-79 D 3
Rancahué, Cerro ▲ RA 78-79 D 5
Rancharia o BR 72-73 E 7
Rancheria, Río ~ CO 60-61 E 2
Rancheria River ~ CDN 30-31 E 5
Ranchester o USA (WY) 252-253 L 2
Ranchi o•• IND 142-143 D 4
Rānchi o•• IND 142-143 D 4
Rānchi Plateau ▲ IND 142-143 D 4
Rancho California o USA (CA) 248-249 G 6
Rancho Cordova o USA (CA) 246-247 D 5
Rancho Queimado o BR 74-75 F 6
Ranchos o RA 78-79 K 3
Rancho Velho o BR 74-75 E 8
Rancho Viejo o MEX 52-53 E 3
Ranchuelo o C 54-55 E 3
Ranco, Lago o RCH 78-79 C 6
Rand o USA (CO) 254-255 J 3
Randa o DJI 208-209 F 3
Randado o USA (TX) 266-267 J 6
Randale ~ DJI 200-201 L 6
Randall Dam, Fort • USA (SD) 260-261 H 3
Randangan-Panua Reserves ⊥• RI 164-165 G 3
Randazzo o I 100-101 E 6
Randberge ▲ ZA 220-221 K 3
Randeggi o WAN 204-205 G 3
Randers o DK 86-87 E 8
Randfontein o ZA 220-221 H 3
Randijaure o S 86-87 J 3
Randle o USA (WA) 244-245 D 4
Randlett o USA (OK) 264-265 F 4
Randolph o USA (KS) 262-263 K 5
Randolph o USA (NE) 262-263 J 2
Randolph o USA (TN) 276-277 F 5
Randolph o USA (UT) 254-255 D 2
Randolph o USA (VT) 278-279 J 5
Random Island ⌒ CDN (NFL) 242-243 P 4
Randowaya o RI 166-167 J 2
Randsburg o USA (CA) 248-249 G 4
Randsfjorden o N 86-87 E 6
Randudongkal o RI 168 C 3
Råneälven ~ S 86-87 K 3
Ranemsletta o N 86-87 E 4
Ranérou o SN 202-203 D 2
Ranfurly o CDN (ALB) 232-233 G 2
Rangaranga o RI 164-165 H 4
Rangasa, Tanjung ▲ RI 164-165 F 5
Range o USA (AL) 284-285 C 5
Rangeley o USA (ME) 278-279 L 4
Rangely o USA (CO) 254-255 G 3
Ranger o CDN (SAS) 232-233 L 2
Ranger o USA (TX) 264-265 F 6
Ranger Brook ~ CDN 36-37 G 3
Rangers Valley o AUS 178-179 H 2
Ranger Uranium Mine • AUS 172-173 L 2
Ranges Valley o AUS 178-179 F 1
Rangia o IND 142-143 G 2
Rangiora o NZ 182 D 5
Rangkasbitung o RI 168 B 3
Rangkul' o TJ 146-147 B 6
Rangnim o DVR 150-151 F 7
Rangnim Sanmaek ▲ DVR 150-151 F 7
Rangoon = Yangon ☆ MYA 158-159 D 2
Rangoon = Yangon ☆•• MYA 158-159 D 2
Rangpo o IND 142-143 F 2
Rangpur o BD 142-143 F 3
Rangpur Canal < PK 138-139 C 4
Rangsang, Pulau ⌒ RI 162-163 E 4
Ranguana Cay ⌒ BH 52-53 K 3
Ranhal o PK 138-139 C 5
Rānibennur o IND 140-141 F 3
Raniganj o IND 142-143 E 4
Rāniganj o IND 142-143 E 2
Rānikhet o• IND 138-139 G 5
Ranikot ∴• PK 138-139 B 7
Rānipettai o IND 140-141 H 4
Rānipur o PK 138-139 B 6
Rāniya ☆ IRQ 128-129 L 4
Ranken Store o AUS 174-175 D 6
Rankin o USA (IL) 274-275 L 4
Rankin o USA (OK) 264-265 E 3
Rankin o USA (TX) 266-267 F 2
Rankin Inlet ≈ 30-31 X 4
Rankin Inlet o CDN 30-31 X 4
Rankin's Pass ▲ ZA 220-221 H 2
Rankins Springs o AUS 180-181 J 2
Rankoshi o J 152-153 J 3
Rannee o RUS 96-97 H 8
Rannes o AUS 178-179 L 3
Rann of Kachchh ⊥ IND 138-139 B 7

382 Quail — Rann of Kachchh

Reyes Creek ▲ USA (CA) 248-249 E 5
Reyes Salgado, Los ○ MEX 52-53 C 2
Reyhanlı ☆ TR 128-129 G 4
Reykjanes Ridge ≃ 6-7 F 3
Reykjanestá ▲ IS 86-87 b 3
Reykjavík ○ CDN (MAN) 234-235 E 3
Reykjavík ★ • IS 86-87 c 2
Reynaud ○ CDN (SAS) 232-233 N 3
Reynolds ○ USA (GA) 284-285 F 4
Reynolds ○ USA (ID) 252-253 B 3
Reynolds ○ USA (IN) 274-275 L 4
Reynolds ○ USA (ND) 258-259 K 4
Reynoldsburg ○ USA (OH) 280-281 D 4
Reynolds Range ▲ AUS 172-173 L 7
Reynosa ○ MEX 50-51 K 4
Reyy ○ • IR 136-137 B 7
Rež ☆ RUS 96-97 M 5
Reza, gora ▲ TM 136-137 F 6
Rēzekne ☆ •• LV 94-95 K 3
Rezina ☆ MD 102-103 F 4
Rēznas ezers ○ • LV 94-95 K 3
Rezovo ○ BG 102-103 E 6
Režvān Šahr ○ IR 128-129 N 4
Rhame ○ USA (ND) 258-259 D 5
Rharb ⊥ MA 188-189 H 3
Rharous ‹ RMM 196-197 L 5
Rhea ○ USA (OK) 264-265 E 3
Rhein ○ CDN (SAS) 232-233 Q 4
Rhein ~ D 92-93 J 3
Rheine ○ D 92-93 J 2
Rheinfall ~ •• CH 92-93 K 5
Rheinland-Pfalz □ D 92-93 J 3
Rheinwaldhorn ▲ CH 92-93 K 5
Rhemilès ‹ DZ 188-189 J 6
Rhems ○ USA (SC) 284-285 L 3
Rheris, Oued ~ MA 188-189 J 5
Rhine ○ USA (GA) 284-285 G 5
Rhine = Rhein ~ D 92-93 K 4
Rhinelander ○ USA (WI) 270-271 J 5
Rhino Camp ○ EAU 212-213 C 2
Rhiou, Oued ~ DZ 190-191 C 3
Rhir, Cap ▲ MA 188-189 G 5
Rhode Island □ USA (RI) 278-279 K 7
Rhode Island ⌒ USA (RI) 278-279 K 7
Rhodes Inyangani National Park ⊥ ZW 218-219 G 4
Rhodes Matopos National Park ⊥ ZW 218-219 E 5
Rhododendron ○ USA (OR) 244-245 D 5
Rhodope Mountains = Rodopi ▲ BG 102-103 C 7
Rhome ○ USA (TX) 264-265 G 5
Rhön ▲ D 92-93 K 3
Rhondda ○ GB 90-91 F 6
Rhône ~ CH 92-93 J 5
Rhône ~ F 90-91 K 10
Rhône-Alpes □ F 90-91 K 9
Rhoraffa, Bir ‹ DZ 190-191 G 5
Rhoufi ○ DZ 190-191 F 3
Rhourd El Baguel ○ DZ 190-191 F 5
Rhum ⌒ GB 90-91 D 3
Rhumel, Oued ~ DZ 190-191 F 2
Rhyolite Ghost Town ∴ • USA (NV) 248-249 H 3
Riaba ○ GQ 210-211 B 2
Ria Celestún Parque Natural ⊥ MEX 52-53 J 1
Riachão ○ BR 68-69 E 5
Riachão, Rio ~ BR 68-69 G 5
Riachão das Neves ○ BR 68-69 F 7
Riachão do Banabuiú ○ BR 68-69 J 4
Riachão do Jacuípe ○ BR 68-69 J 7
Riacho de Santana ○ BR 72-73 J 2
Riacho do Sal ○ BR 68-69 J 6
Riacho dos Machados ○ BR 72-73 J 3
Riachos, Isla de los ⌒ RA 78-79 H 6
Riacho Seco ○ BR 68-69 J 6
Riákia ○ GR 100-101 J 4
Riamkanan, Danau ○ RI 164-165 D 5
Rianápolis ○ BR 72-73 F 3
Riangnom ○ SUD 206-207 K 4
Riaño, Embalse de ‹ E 98-99 E 3
Riau □ RI 162-163 D 5
Riau, Kepulauan ⌒ RI 162-163 F 4
Ribadavia ○ • E 98-99 C 3
Ribadeo ○ E 98-99 D 3
Ribadesella ○ E 98-99 E 3
Ribah ○ WAN 204-205 F 3
Riban'i Manamby ▲ RM 222-223 D 9
Ribariće ○ YU 100-101 H 3
Ribas do Rio Pardo ○ BR 72-73 D 6
Ribāṭ, ar- ○ IRQ 128-129 J 5
Ribatejo ⊥ P 98-99 C 5
Ribāṭ Qila ○ PK 134-135 J 4
Ribáuè ○ MOC 218-219 K 2
Ribe ○ •• DK 86-87 D 9
Ribeira Brava, Vila de ○ CV 202-203 B 5
Ribeira de Cruz ○ CV 202-203 B 5
Ribeira do Pombal ○ BR 68-69 J 7
Ribeira do Pombal, Rio ~ BR 68-69 J 7
Ribeirão ○ BR 68-69 L 6
Ribeirão, Área Indígena ⚔ BR 70-71 E 2
Ribeirão, Rio ~ BR 70-71 E 2
Ribeirão das Neves ○ BR 72-73 H 5
Ribeirão do Pinhal ○ BR 72-73 E 7
Ribeirão Preto ○ BR 72-73 G 6
Ribeiro Gonçalves ○ BR 68-69 F 5
Ribera ○ I 100-101 D 6
Ribera ○ USA (NM) 256-257 K 3
Ribérac ○ F 90-91 H 9
Riberalta ○ BOL 70-71 D 2
Ribniţa ☆ MD 102-103 F 4
Ribnitz-Damgarten ○ D 92-93 M 1
Ribo Escale ○ SN 202-203 C 2
Ribstone ○ CDN (ALB) 232-233 H 3
Ribstone Creek ~ CDN (ALB) 232-233 G 3
Rica, Cañada ~ RA 76-77 F 2
Ricardo ○ USA (TX) 266-267 K 6
Ricardo Flores Magón ○ MEX 50-51 F 3
Ricaute ○ CO 60-61 D 6
Rice ○ USA (CA) 248-249 K 5
Rice ○ USA (TX) 264-265 H 6
Rice ○ USA (WA) 244-245 G 2
Riceboro ○ USA (GA) 284-285 J 5
Rice Hill ○ USA (OR) 244-245 B 7
Rice Historic Site, Fort • USA (ND) 258-259 G 5
Rice Lake ○ CDN (ONT) 238-239 G 4
Rice Lake ○ USA (WI) 270-271 G 5
Rice Terraces •• RP 160-161 D 4
Riceton ○ CDN (SAS) 232-233 O 5
Riceville ○ USA (PA) 280-281 G 2
Rich ○ MA 188-189 J 4
Richan ○ CDN (ONT) 234-235 L 5
Richão do Dantas ○ BR 68-69 K 7
Richão dos Paulos ○ BR 68-69 F 6
Richard Collinson Inlet ≈ 24-25 P 4
Richardsbaai = Richards Bay ○ ZA 220-221 L 4
Richards Bay = Richardsbaai ○ ZA 220-221 L 4
Richards Island ⌒ CDN 20-21 Y 2
Richardson ○ USA (OR) 244-245 B 7
Richardson ○ USA (TX) 264-265 H 6
Richardson, Cape ▲ CDN 24-25 d 6
Richardson Bay ≈ 30-31 M 2
Richardson Island ⌒ CDN 30-31 L 3
Richardson Islands ⌒ CDN 24-25 R 6
Richardson Lake ○ CDN 30-31 O 6
Richardson Mountains ▲ CDN 20-21 W 2
Richardson Point ▲ AUS 180-181 H 6
Richardson River ~ CDN 30-31 L 2
Richardson River ~ CDN 32-33 P 3
Richards Trench ≃ 76-77 B 4
Richard Toll ○ SN 196-197 C 6
Richardton ○ USA (ND) 258-259 E 5
Richburg ○ USA (SC) 284-285 J 2
Riche, Cape ▲ AUS 176-177 E 7
Richelieu, Rivière ~ CDN (QUE) 238-239 M 3
Richer ○ CDN (MAN) 234-235 G 5
Richey ○ USA (MT) 250-251 O 4
Richfield ○ USA (ID) 252-253 D 3
Richfield ○ USA (KS) 262-263 E 7
Richfield ○ USA (NC) 282-283 G 5
Richfield ○ USA (UT) 254-255 C 5
Richfield Springs ○ USA (NY) 278-279 G 6
Richford ○ USA (NY) 278-279 E 6
Richford ○ USA (VT) 278-279 J 4
Richgrove ○ USA (CA) 248-249 E 4
Rich Hill ○ USA (MO) 274-275 D 6
Richibucto ○ CDN (NB) 240-241 L 4
Richibucto 15 Indian Reserve ⚔ • CDN (NB) 240-241 L 4
Richibucto-Village ○ CDN (NB) 240-241 L 4
Richland ○ USA (GA) 284-285 F 4
Richland ○ USA (MO) 276-277 C 3
Richland ○ USA (OR) 244-245 H 6
Richland ○ USA (TX) 266-267 L 2
Richland ○ USA (WA) 244-245 F 4
Richland Balsam ▲ USA (NC) 282-283 E 5
Richland Center ○ USA (WI) 274-275 H 1
Richland Creek ~ USA (TX) 266-267 L 2
Richland Creek Reservoir ○ USA (TX) 264-265 H 6
Richlands ○ USA (VA) 280-281 E 6
Richlands Springs ○ USA (TX) 266-267 J 2
Richmomd ○ USA (MI) 272-273 G 5
Richmond ○ AUS 174-175 G 7
Richmond ○ CDN (BC) 230-231 F 4
Richmond ○ CDN (ONT) 238-239 K 3
Richmond ○ CDN (QUE) 238-239 N 3
Richmond ○ NZ 182 D 4
Richmond ○ USA (CA) 248-249 B 2
Richmond ○ USA (IL) 274-275 K 2
Richmond ○ USA (IN) 274-275 O 5
Richmond ○ USA (KS) 262-263 L 6
Richmond ○ USA (KY) 276-277 L 3
Richmond ○ USA (MO) 274-275 E 5
Richmond ○ USA (OH) 280-281 F 3
Richmond ○ USA (TX) 268-269 E 7
Richmond ☆ USA (VA) 280-281 J 6
Richmond ○ ZA (CAP) 220-221 F 5
Richmond ○ ZA (NTL) 220-221 K 4
Richmond Dale ○ USA (OH) 280-281 D 4
Richmond Hill ○ CDN (ONT) 238-239 F 5
Richmond Hill ○ USA (GA) 284-285 J 5
Richmond Hills ○ AUS 178-179 H 2
Richmond River ~ AUS 178-179 M 5
Richmound ○ CDN (SAS) 232-233 J 5
Rich Mountain ▲ USA (AR) 276-277 A 6
Rich Square ○ USA (NC) 282-283 K 4
Richtersveld National Park ⊥ ZA 220-221 C 4
Richthofen, Mount ▲ AUS 172-173 C 6
Richton ○ USA (MS) 268-269 M 5
Rich Valley ○ CDN (ALB) 232-233 D 2
Richwood ○ USA (WV) 280-281 F 5
Ricinus ○ CDN (ALB) 232-233 D 3
Ricketts, Cape ▲ CDN 24-25 a 3
Rickman ○ USA (TN) 276-277 K 4
Rickwood Caverns • USA (AL) 284-285 D 3
Rico ○ USA (CO) 254-255 G 6
Ricrah ○ PE 64-65 E 7
Ridder, De ○ USA (LA) 268-269 G 6
Riddersprangeт • N 86-87 D 6
Riddle ○ USA (ID) 252-253 B 4
Riddle ○ USA (OR) 244-245 B 8
Rideau Hills ▲ CDN (ONT) 238-239 H 4
Rideau Lake ○ CDN (ONT) 238-239 J 4
Ridge ○ USA (TX) 266-267 L 2
Ridgecrest ○ USA (CA) 248-249 G 4
Ridgedale ○ CDN (SAS) 232-233 O 2
Ridgefield ○ USA (WA) 244-245 C 5
Ridgeland ○ USA (MS) 268-269 K 4
Ridgeland ○ USA (SC) 284-285 K 4
Ridgely ○ USA (TN) 276-277 F 4
Ridge River ~ CDN (ONT) 236-237 D 2
Ridgetown ○ CDN (ONT) 238-239 D 6
Ridgeville ○ CDN (MAN) 234-235 F 5
Ridgeville ○ USA (IN) 274-275 N 4
Ridgeway ○ USA (SC) 284-285 K 2
Ridgewood Summit ▲ USA (CA) 246-247 B 4
Ridgway ○ USA (CO) 254-255 H 5
Ridgway ○ USA (PA) 280-281 H 2
Riding Mountain ▲ CDN (MAN) 234-235 C 4
Riding Mountain National Park ⊥ CDN (MAN) 234-235 C 4
Riding Rock Point ▲ BS 54-55 H 2
Riebeck Bay ≈ 183 E 3
Riebeek Kasteel ○ ZA 220-221 D 6
Riebeek-Oos ○ ZA 220-221 H 6
Riebeekstaad ○ ZA 220-221 H 3
Riecito ○ YV 60-61 G 2
Riecito, Río ~ YV 60-61 G 4
Rieppe ▲ N 86-87 K 2
Riesa ○ D 92-93 M 3
Riesco, Isla ⌒ RCH 80 D 6
Rietavas ○ LT 94-95 G 4
Rietbron ○ ZA 220-221 F 6
Rietfontein ○ NAM 216-217 F 10
Rietfontein ~ NAM 216-217 F 10
Rietfontein ○ ZA 220-221 E 3
Rieti ☆ I 100-101 D 3
Rietrivier ~ ZA 220-221 G 4
Rietse Vloer ○ ZA 220-221 E 5
Rietvlei ○ ZA 220-221 K 4
Rievaulx Abbey •• GB 90-91 G 4
Rifā'i, ar- ☆ IRQ 128-129 M 7
Rifaina ○ BR 72-73 G 6
Riffe Lake ○ USA (WA) 244-245 C 4
Rifle ○ USA (CO) 254-255 H 4
Rifleman Bank ≃ 158-159 L 7
Rift Valley □ EAK 212-213 F 2
Rift Valley ⊥ •• EAK 212-213 F 4
Rift Valley National Park ⊥ ETH 208-209 D 5
Rig, Bandar-e ○ IR 134-135 D 4
Riga, Gulf of = Rīgas Jūras Līcis ≈ LV 94-95 H 3
Rīga = Riga ★ •• LV 94-95 J 3
Riǧā', Umm ○ Y 132-133 D 7
Rigacikun ○ WAN 204-205 G 3
Riǧal Alma' ○ KSA 132-133 C 4
Rīgas Jūras Līcis ≈ 94-95 H 3
Rigaud ○ CDN (QUE) 238-239 L 3
Rigby ○ USA (ID) 252-253 G 3
Riggins ○ USA (ID) 250-251 C 6
Rigolet ○ CDN 36-37 U 7
Rig Rig ○ TCH 198-199 G 5
Rigsdagen, Kap ▲ GRØ 26-27 o 2
Riguldi ○ EST 94-95 H 2
Rihab, ar- ⊥ IRQ 128-129 L 7
Riihimäki ○ FIN 88-89 H 6
Riiser-Larsen halvøy ⊥ ARK 16 G 4
Riisitunturin kansallispuisto ⊥ FIN 88-89 K 3
Riistina ○ FIN 88-89 J 6
Rijau ○ WAN 204-205 F 3
Rijeka ○ HR 100-101 E 2
Rijpfjorden ≈ 84-85 N 2
Rikām Panchū, Gardaneh-ye ▲ IR 134-135 J 5
Rikbaktsa, Área Indígena ⚔ BR 70-71 H 2
Rikorda, mys ▲ RUS 122-123 M 6
Rikorda, proliv ○ RUS 122-123 P 5
Rikuchū-Kaigan National Park ⊥ J 152-153 K 5
Rikumbetsu ○ J 152-153 K 3
Rila ○ • BG 102-103 C 6
Rila ▲ BG 102-103 C 6
Riley ○ USA (KS) 262-263 K 5
Riley ○ USA (OR) 244-245 F 7
Riley, Fort • USA (KS) 262-263 K 5
Rileyville ○ USA (PA) 280-281 L 2
Rillito ○ USA (AZ) 256-257 D 6
Rilski Manastir ••• BG 102-103 C 6
Rima ~ WAN 198-199 B 6
Rima, Wādi ar- ~ KSA 130-131 H 5
Rimac, Río ~ PE 64-65 D 8
Rimbey ○ CDN (ALB) 232-233 D 3
Rime ~ TCH 198-199 J 5
Rimé, Ouadi ~ TCH 198-199 J 6
Rimel ○ USA (WV) 280-281 F 5
Rimini ○ I 100-101 D 2
Rîmnicu Sărat ○ RO 102-103 E 5
Rîmnicu Vîlcea ☆ • RO 102-103 D 5
Rimouski ○ CDN (QUE) 240-241 G 2
Rimouski, Réserve de ⊥ CDN (QUE) 240-241 G 2
Rimrock ○ USA (WA) 244-245 D 4
Rimsko-Korsakovka ○ RUS 96-97 F 8
Rim Village ○ USA (OR) 244-245 C 8
Rinaré ○ BR 68-69 J 4
Rinbung ○ VRC 144-145 G 6
Rinca, Pulau ⌒ RI 168 D 7
Rincão ○ BR 72-73 F 6
Rincón ○ CR 52-53 C 7
Rincón ○ DOM 54-55 K 5
Rincon ○ USA (NM) 256-257 H 6
Rincon ○ • USA (PR) 286-287 O 2
Rincón, Cerro ▲ RA 76-77 D 3
Rincón, Salina del ○ RA 76-77 D 3
Rinconada ○ RA 76-77 D 2
Rinconada ○ USA (NM) 256-257 K 2
Rincón de la Vieja, Parque Nacional ⊥ CR 52-53 B 6
Rincón de la Vieja, Volcán ▲ CR 52-53 B 6
Rincón del Guanal ○ C 54-55 D 4
Rincón de Palometas ○ BOL 70-71 F 5
Rincos de Romos ○ MEX 50-51 H 6
Rincon Valley ○ USA (OR) ...
Rind ~ IND 142-143 B 2
Rindal ☆ N 86-87 D 5
Ringba ○ VRC 154-155 H 6
Ringgi ○ SOL 184 I c 3
Ringgold ○ USA (LA) 268-269 G 4
Ringgold ○ USA (TX) 264-265 G 5
Ringgold Isles ⌒ FJI 184 III c 2
Ringim ○ WAN 198-199 D 6
Ringkøbing ○ DK 86-87 D 8
Ringkøbing Fjord ○ DK 86-87 D 8
Ringling ○ USA (MT) 250-251 J 5
Ringling ○ USA (OK) 264-265 G 4
Ring of Kerry • IRL 90-91 B 6
Ringoma ○ ANG 216-217 D 6
Ringvassøy ⌒ N 86-87 J 2
Ringwood ○ AUS 178-179 C 2
Ringwood ○ USA (OK) 264-265 F 2
Riñihue, Lago ○ RCH 78-79 C 5
Riñinahue ○ RCH 78-79 C 6
Riniquiarí ○ CO 60-61 F 6
Rinjani, Gunung ▲ RI 168 C 7
Rintala ○ RUS 88-89 K 6
Rio ○ GR 100-101 H 5
Río, El ○ DOM 54-55 K 5
Río Abiseo, Parque Nacional ⊥ •• PE 64-65 D 5
Rio Acre, Estação Ecológica ⊥ BR 70-71 B 2
Río Amazonas, Estuário do ~ BR 62-63 K 5
Rio Ariapo ○ BR 66-67 E 2
Río Ariguaisa ○ YV 60-61 E 3
Río Azul ∴ • GCA 52-53 K 3
Riobamba ○ EC 64-65 C 2
Rio Bananal ○ BR 72-73 K 5
Río Bermejo, Valle del ⌣ RA 76-77 C 6
Rio-Biá, Áreas Indígenas ⚔ BR 66-67 D 5
Río Blanco ○ CO 60-61 C 6
Rioblanco ○ CO 60-61 D 6
Rio Blanco ○ USA (CO) 254-255 H 4
Rio Bonito ○ BR (PAR) 74-75 E 5
Rio Bonito ○ BR (RIO) 72-73 J 7
Rio Branco ○ BR (ACR) 64-65 F 6
Rio Branco ○ BR (MAT) 70-71 H 4
Rio Branco ☆ BR (ACR) 66-67 D 7
Río Branco ○ ROU 74-75 D 9
Rio Branco, Área Indígena ⚔ BR 70-71 F 3
Rio Branco, Parque Nacional do ⊥ BR 66-67 F 2
Rio Branco do Sul ○ BR 74-75 F 5
Rio Bravo ○ GCA 52-53 J 4
Río Bravo ○ MEX 50-51 K 5
Río Bravo, Parque Internacional del ⊥ MEX 50-51 H 3
Rio Brilhante ○ BR 76-77 K 1
Río Bueno ○ JA 54-55 G 5
Río Bueno ○ RCH 78-79 C 6
Río Caribe ○ YV 60-61 K 2
Rio Casca ○ BR 72-73 J 6
Río Cauto ○ C 54-55 G 4
Río Ceballos ○ RA 76-77 E 6
Río Chico ○ YV 60-61 J 2
Río Chiquito ○ HN 54-55 C 7
Río Clarillo, Parque Nacional ⊥ RCH 78-79 D 2
Rio Claro ○ BR 72-73 G 7
Rio Claro ○ TT 60-61 L 2
Río Colorado ○ RA 78-79 G 5
Rio Conchas ○ BR (MAT) 70-71 K 3
Rio Conchas ○ BR (MAT) 70-71 K 4
Río Cuarto ○ RA 78-79 G 2
Rio das Pedras ○ MOC 218-219 H 6
Rio de Janeiro □ BR 72-73 J 7
Rio de Janeiro ☆ • BR 72-73 J 7
Rio de Janeiro, Serra do ▲ BR 72-73 H 4
Río de la Plata ≈ 78-79 L 3
Rio Dell ○ USA (CA) 246-247 A 3
Río Deseado, Valle del ⌣ RA 80 F 3
Rio do Pires ○ BR 72-73 J 2
Rio do Prado ○ BR 72-73 K 4
Rio do Sul ○ BR 74-75 F 6
Río Dulce, Parque Nacional ⊥ GCA 52-53 K 4
Río Gallegos ☆ RA 80 F 5
Río Grande ○ BOL 70-71 D 7
Rio Grande ○ BR 74-75 D 9
Río Grande ○ MEX 50-51 H 6
Río Grande ○ RA 80 G 6
Rio Grande ○ USA (NJ) 280-281 M 4
Rio Grande ~ USA (CO) 254-255 J 6
Rio Grande ~ USA (NM) 256-257 J 4
Rio Grande ~ USA (TX) 266-267 G 5
Río Grande, Ciudad de = Río Grande ○ MEX 50-51 H 6
Río Grande, Salar de ○ RA 76-77 C 3
Rio Grande City ○ USA (TX) 266-267 J 7
Rio Grande do Norte □ BR 68-69 K 4
Rio Grande do Sul □ BR 76-77 K 5
Rio Grande Fracture Zone ≃ 6-7 H 11
Rio Grande Plateau ≃ 6-7 G 12
Rio Gregorio, Área Indígena ⚔ BR 66-67 B 7
Rio Guaporé, Área Indígena ⚔ BR 70-71 E 2
Río Guengue ○ RA 80 E 2
Riohacha ☆ CO 60-61 E 2
Río Hato ○ PA 52-53 D 7
Río Hondo ○ GCA 52-53 K 4
Río Hondo, Embalse ‹ RA 76-77 E 4
Río Hondo, Termas de ○ • RA 76-77 E 4
Río Ichilo ○ BOL 70-71 E 5
Rioja ○ PE 64-65 D 5
Rioja, La □ E 98-99 F 3
Rioja, La □ RA 76-77 C 5
Rioja, Llanos de la ⌣ RA 76-77 D 5
Rioja, La ☆ • RA (LAR) 76-77 D 5
Río Lagartos ○ • MEX 52-53 K 1
Río Lagartos, Parque Natural ⊥ MEX 52-53 L 1
Rio Largo ○ BR 68-69 L 6
Riom ○ F 90-91 J 9
Rio Maior ○ P 98-99 C 5
Río Malo ○ RCH 78-79 D 3
Rio Mayo ○ RA 80 E 2
Rio Mequens, Área Indígena ⚔ BR 70-71 G 3
Río Mulatos ○ BOL 70-71 D 6
Riondel ○ CDN (BC) 230-231 N 4
Rio Negrinho ○ BR 74-75 F 6
Rio Negro ○ BR (GSU) 70-71 K 6
Rio Negro ○ BR (GSU) 70-71 J 6
Rio Negro ○ BR (PAR) 74-75 F 6
Rionegro ○ CO 60-61 E 4
Río Negro □ RA 78-79 E 6
Río Negro ○ RCH 78-79 C 6
Rio Negro, Pantanal do ⌣ BR 70-71 J 6
Río Negro, Represa del ‹ ROU 78-79 L 2
Rio Negro, Reserva Florestal do ⊥ BR 66-67 C 2
Rio Negro Ocaiai, Área Indígena ⚔ BR 70-71 E 2
Rioni ~ GE 126-127 E 5
Rio Pardo ○ BR 74-75 D 7
Rio Pardo de Minas ○ BR 72-73 J 3
Río Pilcomayo, Parque Nacional ⊥ RA 76-77 H 3
Río Plátano, Parque Nacional ⊥ •• HN 54-55 C 7
Rio Pomba ○ BR 72-73 J 6
Rio Preto ○ BR 72-73 J 7
Rio Prêto, Serra do ▲ BR 72-73 G 4
Rio Preto da Eva ○ BR 66-67 H 4
Rio Primero ○ RA 76-77 F 6
Río Queguay, Cascadas del ~ ROU 78-79 K 2
Rio Quente • BR 72-73 F 4
Río San Juan ○ DOM 54-55 K 5
Río Seco ○ RA 76-77 E 2
Río Seco ○ YV 60-61 F 2
Río Segundo ○ RA 76-77 F 6
Río Simpsom, Parque Nacional ⊥ RCH 80 D 2
Rio Sono ○ BR 68-69 E 6
Riosucio ○ CO 60-61 D 5
Río Sucio ○ CO 60-61 D 4
Riosucio ○ CO 60-61 C 4
Rio Telha ○ BR 74-75 E 7
Río Tercero, Embalse del ‹ RA 78-79 G 2
Rio Tinto ○ BR 68-69 L 5
Río Tocuyo ○ YV 60-61 G 2
Rio Trombetas, Reserva Biológica do ⊥ BR 62-63 F 6
Riou, Point ▲ USA 20-21 U 7
Rioug ‹ RIM 196-197 E 6
Riou Lake ○ CDN 30-31 Q 6
Rio Verde ○ BR 72-73 E 4
Río Verde ○ MEX 50-51 K 7
Río Verde ○ YV 60-61 H 3
Rio Verde de Mato Grosso ○ BR 70-71 K 6
Rio Verde Grande ~ BR 72-73 J 3
Rio Vermelho ○ BR 72-73 J 5
Río Villegas ○ RA 78-79 D 6
Rio Vista ○ USA (CA) 246-247 D 5
Rio Vista ○ USA (TX) 264-265 G 6
Riozinho ~ BR 66-67 D 6
Riozinho ~ BR 68-69 F 6
Riozinho, Rio ~ BR 66-67 D 4
Riozinho, Rio ~ BR 68-69 B 5
Riozinho do Anfrísio ~ BR 66-67 K 5
Riozinho ou Rio Verde, Rio ~ BR 72-73 E 2
Ripky ○ UA 102-103 G 2
Ripley ○ USA (CA) 248-249 K 6
Ripley ○ USA (KY) 276-277 M 2
Ripley ○ USA (MS) 268-269 M 2
Ripley ○ USA (TN) 276-277 F 5
Ripley ○ USA (WV) 280-281 E 5
Ripoll ○ • E 98-99 J 3
Ripon ○ USA (WI) 270-271 K 7
Ririe ○ USA (ID) 252-253 G 3
Rīšā', Wādī ar- ~ KSA 130-131 H 5
Risālpur ○ PK 138-139 D 2
Risasa ○ ZRE 210-211 K 4
Rishikesh ○ IND 138-139 G 4
Rishiri ○ J 152-153 J 2
Rishirifuji ○ J 152-153 J 2
Rishiri-Rebun National Park ⊥ J 152-153 J 2
Rishiri-suidō ≈ 152-153 J 2
Rishiri-tō ⌒ J 152-153 J 2
Rishon le Ẓiyyon ☆ IL 130-131 D 2
Rising Star ○ USA (TX) 264-265 F 6
Rising Sun ○ USA (IN) 274-275 O 6
Rison ○ USA (AR) 276-277 C 7
Risør ☆ • N 86-87 D 7
Risøyhamn ○ N 86-87 G 2
Rissa ○ N 86-87 E 5
Rissani ○ MA 188-189 J 5
Rištan ○ US 136-137 M 4
Risti ○ EST 94-95 J 2
Ritchie ○ ZA 220-221 G 4
Ritch Island ⌒ CDN 30-31 K 2
Rithi ○ IND 142-143 B 4
Ritiro ○ ANG 216-217 E 8
Rito, El ○ USA (NM) 256-257 J 2
Ritta Island ⌒ USA (FL) 286-287 J 5
Ritter ○ USA (OR) 244-245 F 6
Ritter, Mount ▲ USA (CA) 248-249 E 2
Ritzville ○ USA (WA) 244-245 G 3
Riv ~ UA 102-103 F 3
Rivadavia ○ RA (BUA) 78-79 J 3
Rivadavia ○ RA (MEN) 78-79 E 2
Rivadavia ○ RA (SAJ) 76-77 C 6
Rivadavia ○ RA (SAL) 76-77 F 3
Rivadavia ○ RCH 76-77 B 5
Riva del Garda ○ I 100-101 C 2
Rivalensundet ≈ 84-85 P 3
Rivaš ○ IR 136-137 F 7
Rivas ☆ NIC 52-53 B 6
Rivera ☆ EC 64-65 C 3
Rivera ○ RA 78-79 H 4
Rivera ☆ ROU 76-77 K 6
Riverbank ○ USA (CA) 248-249 D 2
Riverboat Cruise • AUS 180-181 H 4
River Cess ○ LB 202-203 F 7
Rivercourse ○ CDN (ALB) 232-233 H 2
Riverdale ○ USA (CA) 248-249 E 3
Riverdale ○ USA (ND) 258-259 F 4
River Falls ○ USA (WI) 270-271 F 6
Riverhead ○ USA (NY) 280-281 O 3
River Hebert ○ CDN (NS) 240-241 L 5
River Hills ○ CDN (MAN) 234-235 H 4
Riverhurst ○ CDN (SAS) 232-233 M 5
Riverina ⌣ AUS 180-181 H 3
River John ○ CDN (NS) 240-241 M 5
Rivers, Isla ⌒ RCH 80 C 2
River of No Return Wilderness ⊥ USA (ID) 250-251 D 6
River of Ponds ○ CDN (NFL) 242-243 L 2
Rivers ○ CDN (MAN) 234-235 C 4
Rivers □ WAN 204-205 G 6
Rivers, Lake of the ○ CDN (SAS) 232-233 N 6
Riversdal = Riversdale ○ ZA 220-221 E 7
Riversdale ○ BH 52-53 K 3
Riversdale ○ CDN (ONT) 238-239 D 4
Riversdale = Riversdal ○ ZA 220-221 E 7
Riversdale Beach ○ NZ 182 F 4
Riverside ○ AUS 178-179 K 1
Riverside ○ USA (CA) 248-249 G 6
Riverside ○ USA (IA) 274-275 G 3
Riverside ○ USA (ID) 252-253 F 3
Riverside ○ USA (MD) 280-281 J 5
Riverside ○ USA (OR) 244-245 G 7
Riverside ○ USA (TX) 268-269 E 6
Riverside ○ USA (WY) 252-253 M 5
Rivers Inlet ≈ 32-33 G 6
Rivers Inlet ≈ CDN 230-231 B 2
Riversleigh ○ AUS 174-175 E 6
Riverton ○ CDN (MAN) 234-235 G 4
Riverton ○ NZ 182 B 7
Riverton ○ USA (IL) 274-275 J 5
Riverton ○ USA (WY) 252-253 K 3
River Valley ○ CDN (ONT) 238-239 E 2
Riverview ○ CDN (NB) 240-241 L 4
Rivesaltes ○ F 90-91 J 10
Riviera ○ USA (TX) 266-267 K 6
Riviera Beach ○ USA (FL) 286-287 J 5
Riviera Beach ○ USA (TX) 266-267 K 6
Rivière, George ~ CDN 36-37 Q 5
Rivière-à-Pierre ○ CDN (QUE) 238-239 N 2
Rivière-au-Tonnere ○ CDN (QUE) 242-243 D 2
Rivière-aux-Saumons ○ CDN (QUE) 242-243 F 3
Rivière-Bleue ○ CDN (QUE) 240-241 F 3
Rivière-Boisvert ○ CDN (QUE) 236-237 O 3
Rivière-de-la-Chaloupe ○ CDN (QUE) 242-243 F 3
Rivière-Éperlan ○ CDN (QUE) 240-241 F 2
Rivière-Éternité ○ CDN (QUE) 240-241 E 2
Rivière-Pigou ○ CDN (QUE) 242-243 C 2
Rivière Qui Barre ○ CDN (ALB) 232-233 E 2
Rivière Veuve ○ CDN (ONT) 238-239 E 2
Riviersonderend ○ ZA 220-221 D 7
Rivne ○ UA 102-103 E 2
Rivoli ○ I 100-101 A 2
Rivungo ○ ANG 218-219 B 3
Riwat ○ PK 138-139 D 3
Riwoqê ○ VRC 144-145 L 5
Riyāḍ, ar- □ KSA 130-131 J 6
Riyāḍ, ar- ★ •• KSA 130-131 K 5
Riyāḍ al-Ḫabra ○ KSA 130-131 H 4
Riyadh = Riyāḍ, ar- ★ •• KSA 130-131 K 5
Rize ☆ TR 128-129 J 2
Rizhao ○ VRC 154-155 L 4
Rizokarpaso ○ TR 128-129 F 5
Rizzuto, Capo ▲ I 100-101 F 5
Rjabovskij ○ RUS 102-103 M 2
Rjazan' ☆ •• RUS 94-95 Q 4
Rjažsk ☆ • RUS 94-95 R 5
Rjukan ☆ N 86-87 D 7
Rkîz ○ RIM 196-197 C 6
Rkîz, Lac ○ RIM 196-197 C 6
Roadhouse ○ AUS 174-175 B 5
Road River ~ CDN 20-21 X 3
Road Town ☆ •• GB 56 C 2
Road Town ☆ •• GB (VI) 286-287 R 2
Roan Cliffs ▲ USA (UT) 254-255 F 4
Roan Mountain ○ USA (TN) 282-283 E 4
Roanne ○ F 90-91 K 8
Roanoke ○ USA (AL) 284-285 E 3
Roanoke ○ USA (TX) 264-265 G 5
Roanoke ○ USA (VA) 280-281 G 6
Roanoke Island ⌒ USA (NC) 282-283 M 5
Roanoke Rapids ○ USA (NC) 282-283 K 4
Roanoke Rapids Lake ○ USA (NC) 282-283 K 4
Roanoke River ~ USA (NC) 282-283 K 4
Roanoke River ~ USA (VA) 280-281 G 6
Roaring Springs ○ USA (TX) 264-265 D 5
Roaring Springs Ranch ○ USA (OR) 244-245 G 8
Roatán ☆ HN 52-53 L 3
Roatán, Isla de ⌒ HN 52-53 L 3
Robalo, Cachoeira do ~ BR 70-71 K 6
Roban ○ MAL 162-163 J 4
Robanda ○ EAT 212-213 E 5
Robāṭak ○ AFG 136-137 L 6
Robāṭ-e Ǧa'lī ○ AFG 134-135 J 4
Robāṭ-e Ḫān ○ IR 134-135 G 1
Robāṭe Ḫošāb ○ IR 134-135 G 2
Robāṭ-e Ḫošk ○ AFG 134-135 K 2
Robāṭ-e-Mirzā, Kōtal-e ▲ AFG 134-135 K 1
Robāṭ-e Pošt Badām ○ IR 134-135 F 2
Robāṭ-e Sang ○ IR 136-137 F 7
Robāṭ-e Sangī-ye Pāin ○ AFG 134-135 K 1
Robāṭkarīm ○ IR 136-137 B 7
Robb ○ CDN (ALB) 232-233 B 2
Robbeneiland ⌒ ZA 220-221 D 6
Robbies Pass ▲ NAM 216-217 B 9
Robbins ○ USA (NC) 282-283 H 5
Robbins Island ⌒ AUS 180-181 H 6
Robbinsville ○ USA (NC) 282-283 D 5
Robe ○ AUS 180-181 E 4
Robē ○ ETH (Ars) 208-209 D 5
Robē ○ ETH (Bal) 208-209 E 5
Robe, Mount ▲ AUS 178-179 F 6
Robeline ○ USA (LA) 268-269 G 5
Robe River ~ AUS 172-173 B 6
Robersonville ○ USA (NC) 282-283 K 5
Robert, Le ○ F 56 E 4
Roberta ○ USA (GA) 284-285 F 4
Robert Lee ○ USA (TX) 266-267 G 2
Roberts ○ USA (IL) 274-275 K 4
Robert's Arm ○ CDN (NFL) 242-243 N 3
Roberts Creek ○ CDN (BC) 230-231 F 4
Roberts Creek Montain ▲ USA (NV) 246-247 J 4
Robertsdale ○ USA (AL) 284-285 C 6
Robertsganj ○ IND 142-143 C 3
Robertson ○ USA (WY) 252-253 H 5
Robertson ○ ZA 220-221 D 6
Robertson, Kap ▲ GRØ 26-27 O 5
Robertson, Lac ○ CDN (QUE) 242-243 J 2
Robertson, Lake ‹ ZW 218-219 F 3
Robertson Bay ≈ 16 F 18
Robertson Bay ≈ 36-37 K 7
Robertson Fjord ≈ 26-27 P 5
Robertson Range ▲ AUS 172-173 E 7
Robertson River ~ CDN 24-25 e 5
Robertsons Øy ⌒ ARK 16 G 31
Roberts Port ☆ LB 202-203 E 6
Robertville ○ CDN (NB) 240-241 K 3
Roberval ○ CDN (QUE) 240-241 C 2
Robi ○ ETH 208-209 D 4
Robin Falls • AUS 172-173 K 2
Robinhood ○ CDN (SAS) 232-233 J 2
Robins Camp ○ ZW 218-219 C 4
Robinson ○ USA (IL) 274-275 L 5
Robinson ○ USA (ND) 258-259 H 4
Robinson ○ USA (TX) 266-267 K 2
Robinson, Mount ▲ AUS 172-173 D 7
Robinson Island ⌒ ARK 16 G 30
Robinson Pass ▲ ZA 220-221 F 6
Robinson Range ▲ AUS 176-177 E 2
Robinson River ○ AUS 174-175 D 5
Robinson River ~ AUS 174-175 D 5
Robinson River ○ PNG 183 E 6
Robinson Sound ≈ 36-37 R 3
Robinsons River ~ CDN (NFL) 242-243 K 4
Robinson Summit ▲ USA (NV) 246-247 K 4
Robinsonville ○ CDN (NB) 240-241 H 3
Robinvale ○ AUS 180-181 G 3
Robious ○ USA (VA) 280-281 J 6
Robla, La ○ E 98-99 E 3
Roble Alto, Cerro ▲ RCH 78-79 D 2
Robles Junction ○ USA (AZ) 256-257 D 6
Roblin ○ CDN (MAN) 234-235 B 3
Roblin ○ CDN (ONT) 238-239 H 4
Robooksibia ○ RI 166-167 H 2
Rob Roy Island ⌒ SOL 184 I c 2
Robsart ○ CDN (SAS) 232-233 J 6
Robson ○ CDN (BC) 230-231 M 4
Robson, Mount ▲ CDN (BC) 228-229 P 3
Robstown ○ USA (TX) 266-267 K 6
Roby ○ USA (MO) 276-277 C 3
Roby ○ USA (TX) 264-265 D 6
Roca, Cabo da ▲ • P 98-99 C 5
Roca, Península ⌣ RCH 80 D 5
Roça de Bruno ○ BR 68-69 E 2
Roca de la Sierra, La ○ E 98-99 D 5
Rocafuerte ○ EC 64-65 B 2
Rocanville ○ CDN (SAS) 232-233 R 5
Roca Partida, Isla ⌒ MEX 50-51 B 7
Roca Redonda ⌒ EC 64-65 B 9
Rocas, Atol das ⌒ BR 68-69 L 1
Rocas Alijos ⌒ MEX 50-51 B 5
Roça Tapirapé ○ BR 68-69 C 6
Rocha ☆ ROU 78-79 M 3
Rocha, Laguna de ○ ROU 78-79 M 3
Rochebaucourt ○ CDN (QUE) 236-237 L 4
Roche Cabrit ○ F 62-63 H 3
Rochedo ○ BR 70-71 K 6
Rochefort ○ F 90-91 G 9
Rochelle ○ USA (GA) 284-285 G 5
Rochelle ○ USA (IL) 274-275 J 3
Rochelle ○ USA (TX) 266-267 H 2
Rochelle, la ○ CDN (MAN) 234-235 G 5
Rochelle, la ☆ • F 90-91 G 8
Roche River, La ~ CDN 30-31 O 5
Rocher River ○ CDN 30-31 N 5
Roches Point ○ CDN (ONT) 238-239 F 4
Rochester ○ USA (IN) 274-275 M 3
Rochester ○ USA (KY) 276-277 J 3
Rochester ○ USA (MI) 272-273 F 5
Rochester ○ USA (NH) 278-279 L 5
Rochester ○ USA (NY) 278-279 D 5
Rochester ○ USA (TX) 264-265 E 5
Rochester ○ USA (VT) 278-279 J 5
Rochester ○ USA (WA) 244-245 B 4
Rochester ○ • USA (MN) 270-271 F 6
Roche-sur-Yon, la ☆ • F 90-91 G 8
Rochon Sands ○ CDN (ALB) 232-233 F 3
Rock ○ USA (MI) 270-271 L 4
Rock, The ○ AUS 180-181 J 3
Rockall Plateau ≃ 6-7 H 3
Rockall Trough ≃ 6-7 H 3
Rock Bay ○ CDN (BC) 230-231 D 3
Rock Camp ○ USA (WV) 280-281 F 6
Rock Cave ○ USA (WV) 280-281 F 5
Rock Creek ○ CDN (BC) 230-231 K 4
Rock Creek ~ USA (UT) 254-255 E 3
Rockdale ○ USA (TX) 266-267 L 3
Rockefeller National Wildlife Refuge ⊥ USA (LA) 268-269 H 7
Rockefeller Plateau ▲ ARK 16 F 24
Rock Engravings Music Stones • NAM 220-221 C 3
Rock Falls ○ USA (IL) 274-275 J 3
Rockford ○ USA (AL) 284-285 D 4
Rockford ○ USA (IL) 274-275 J 2
Rockford ○ USA (OH) 280-281 B 3
Rockford ○ USA (WA) 244-245 H 3
Rockglen ○ CDN (SAS) 232-233 N 6
Rock Hall ○ USA (MD) 280-281 K 4
Rockhampton ○ AUS 178-179 L 2
Rockhampton Downs ○ AUS 174-175 C 6
Rockhaven ○ CDN (SAS) 232-233 K 3
Rock Hill ○ USA (SC) 284-285 J 2
Rockhouse Island ⌒ CDN 30-31 Y 4
Rockingham ○ USA (NC) 282-283 H 6
Rockingham Bay ≈ 174-175 J 6
Rock Island ○ CDN (QUE) 238-239 N 3
Rock Island ⌒ USA (WI) 270-271 M 5
Rocklake ○ USA (ND) 258-259 H 3
Rock Lake ○ USA (WA) 244-245 H 3
Rockland ○ CDN (ONT) 238-239 K 3
Rockland ○ USA (ID) 252-253 F 4
Rockland ○ USA (ME) 278-279 M 4
Rocklands Reservoir ‹ AUS 180-181 G 4
Rocklea ○ AUS 172-173 C 7
Rockledge ○ USA (FL) 286-287 J 3
Rockmart ○ USA (GA) 284-285 E 2
Rock of Cashel •• IRL 90-91 D 5
Rock Point ○ USA (MD) 280-281 K 5
Rockport ○ USA (IN) 274-275 L 7
Rock Port ○ USA (MO) 274-275 C 4
Rockport ○ USA (TX) 266-267 K 5
Rockport ○ USA (WA) 244-245 D 2
Rock Rapids ○ USA (IA) 274-275 B 1
Rock River ~ CDN 20-21 X 3
Rock River ~ CDN 30-31 F 5
Rock River ○ USA (WY) 252-253 N 5
Rock River ~ USA (IL) 274-275 J 3
Rock River ~ USA (MN) 270-271 B 7

384 Reyes Creek — Rock River

Rock Sound o • BS 54-55 G 2
Rock Springs o USA (AZ) 256-257 C 4
Rock Springs o USA (MT) 250-251 N 5
Rocksprings o USA (TX) 266-267 G 3
Rock Springs o USA (WY) 252-253 J 5
Rockstone o GUY 62-63 E 2
Rockton o AUS 180-181 K 4
Rockville o USA (IN) 274-275 L 5
Rockville o USA (MD) 280-281 J 4
Rockville o USA (NE) 262-263 H 3
Rockville o USA (UT) 254-255 B 6
Rockwall o USA (TX) 264-265 H 6
Rockwell City o USA (IA) 274-275 D 2
Rockwood o USA (ME) 278-279 M 3
Rockwood o USA (TN) 282-283 C 5
Rockwood o USA (TX) 266-267 H 2
Rocky o USA (OK) 264-265 E 3
Rocky Arroyo ∼ USA (NM) 256-257 L 6
Rocky Boy o USA (MT) 250-251 K 3
Rocky Boys Indian Reservation ✕ USA (MT) 250-251 K 3
Rocky Ford o USA (CO) 254-255 M 5
Rocky Fork Lake < USA (OH) 280-281 C 4
Rocky Gap o USA (VA) 280-281 E 6
Rocky Gully o AUS 176-177 D 7
Rocky Harbour o CDN (NFL) 242-243 L 3
Rocky Island Lake ⊖ CDN (ONT) 238-239 C 2
Rocky Lake ⊖ CDN 34-35 F 3
Rocky Mount o USA (NC) 282-283 K 5
Rocky Mount o USA (VA) 280-281 G 6
Rocky Mountain House o CDN (ALB) 232-233 D 3
Rocky Mountain House National Historic Park • CDN (ALB) 232-233 D 3
Rocky Mountain National Park ⊥ USA (CO) 254-255 K 3
Rocky Mountains ▲ 4 B 3
Rocky Mountains Forest Reserve ⊥ CDN (ALB) 232-233 D 6
Rocky Mountains Forest Reserve ⊥ CDN (ALB) 232-233 B 3
Rocky Point o CDN (PEI) 240-241 M 4
Rocky Point ▲ NAM 216-217 B 9
Rockypoint o USA (WY) 252-253 N 2
Rocky Point ▲ USA 20-21 J 4
Rocky Rapids o CDN (ALB) 232-233 D 2
Rocky River ∼ CDN (ALB) 228-229 R 3
Rocky River ∼ USA (NC) 282-283 H 5
Rocky River ∼ USA (NC) 282-283 G 5
Roda, La o E 98-99 F 5
Roda Velha o BR 72-73 H 2
Rōdbār o AFG 134-135 K 3
Rødberg o N 86-87 D 6
Rødbyhavn o DK 86-87 E 9
Roddickton o CDN (NFL) 242-243 M 2
Rodds Bay ≈ 178-179 L 2
Røde Fjord ≈ 26-27 I 8
Rodel o GB 90-91 D 3
Rodelas o BR 68-69 J 6
Rodeo o USA (NM) 256-257 G 7
Rodeo Viejo o PA 52-53 D 7
Roderick Island ⌒ CDN (BC) 228-229 F 4
Rodez ☆ • F 90-91 J 9
Rodgers Bank ≃ 72-73 M 4
Rodi, Tanjung ▲ RI 166-167 B 7
Rodino ☆ RUS 124-125 M 2
Rodnei, Munţii ▲ RO 102-103 D 4
Rodney o USA (MS) 268-269 J 5
Rodney, Cape ▲ NZ 182 E 2
Rodniki o RUS 94-95 R 3
Rodnikovskoe o KA 124-125 H 3
Rododero-Playa, El • CO 60-61 D 2
Ródos ☆ •• GR 100-101 M 6
Ródos ⌒ GR 100-101 M 6
Rodovia Perimetral Norte II BR 62-63 F 5
Rodrigo Arenas Betancourt, Monumento • CO 60-61 E 5
Rodrigues ⌒ MS 12 E 6
Rodrigues ⌒ MS 224 F 6
Rodrigues Ridge ≃ 224 E 6
Rodríguez, Los o MEX 50-51 J 4
Rodžers, buhta ≈ 112-113 V 1
Roe, Lake ⊖ AUS 176-177 G 5
Roebourne o AUS 172-173 C 6
Roebuck Bay ≈ 172-173 F 5
Roebuck Roadhouse o AUS 172-173 F 4
Roedtan o ZA 220-221 J 2
Roe River ∼ AUS 172-173 G 3
Roermond o NL 92-93 J 3
Roeselare o B 92-93 G 3
Roes Welcome Sound ≈ 36-37 F 3
Roff o USA (OK) 264-265 H 4
Rofia o WAN 204-205 F 3
Rogačeva ∼ RUS 108-109 E 6
Rogačevka o RUS 102-103 L 2
Rogačevo o RUS 94-95 P 3
Rogagua, Lago ⊖ BOL 70-71 D 3
Rogaguado o BOL 70-71 E 3
Rogasen = Rogoźno o PL 92-93 O 2
Rogatica o BIH 100-101 G 3
Rogberi o WAL 202-203 D 5
Rogeia Island ⌒ PNG 183 F 6
Rogers o USA (AR) 276-277 A 4
Rogers o USA (ND) 258-259 J 4
Rogers o USA (TX) 266-267 K 3
Rogers, Mount ▲ USA (VA) 280-281 E 7
Rogers City o USA (MI) 272-273 F 2
Rogers Lake ⊖ USA (CA) 248-249 G 5
Rogerson o USA (ID) 252-253 D 4
Rogers Pass ⊖ CDN (BC) 230-231 M 2
Rogers Pass ▲ CDN (BC) 230-231 M 2
Rogers Pass ▲ USA (MT) 250-251 G 4
Rogersville o CDN (NB) 240-241 K 4
Rogersville o USA (AL) 284-285 C 2
Rogersville o USA (TN) 282-283 D 4
Roggeveen Basin ≃ 5 B 8
Roggeveldberge ▲ ZA 220-221 E 5
Rognan o N 86-87 G 3
Rogo o WAN 204-205 G 3
Rogoaguado, Lago ⊖ BOL 70-71 E 3
Rogovaja, Bol'šaja ∼ RUS 108-109 J 8
Rogoźno o PL 92-93 O 2
Rogue River ∼ USA (OR) 244-245 A 8
Rogun o WAN 204-205 F 4
Roha o IND 138-139 D 10
Rohat o IND 138-139 D 7
Rohatyn ☆ UA 102-103 D 3
Rohault, Lac ⊖ CDN (QUE) 236-237 O 3
Rohmojva, gora ▲ RUS 88-89 K 3
Rohri o PK 138-139 B 6
Rohri Canal < PK 138-139 B 6
Rohru o IND 138-139 F 4
Rohtak o IND 138-139 F 5
Rohtak, Rūdḫāne-ye ∼ IR 134-135 K 5
Rohtas Fort • PK 138-139 D 3
Rohuküla o EST 94-95 H 2
Rohwer o USA (AR) 276-277 D 7
Roi Et o THA 158-159 G 2
Roja o •• LV 94-95 H 3
Roja, Punta ▲ RA 80 H 2
Rojas o RA 78-79 J 3
Rojhān o PK 138-139 B 5
Rojo, Cabo ▲ MEX 50-51 L 7
Rojo, Cabo ▲ USA (PR) 286-287 O 3
Rokan o RI 162-163 D 4
Rokan-Kanan ∼ RI 162-163 D 4
Rokan-Kiri ∼ RI 162-163 D 4
Rokeby o AUS 174-175 G 3
Rokeby o CDN (SAS) 232-233 Q 4
Rokeby-Croll Creek National Park ⊥ AUS 174-175 G 3
Rokiškis ☆ •• LT 94-95 J 4
Rokkasho o J 152-153 J 4
Rokom o SUD 206-207 K 6
Rokskij, pereval ▲ RUS 126-127 F 6
Roland o CDN (MAN) 234-235 F 5
Rolândia o BR 72-73 E 7
Røldal o N 86-87 C 7
Roldán o RA 78-79 J 2
Rolette o USA (ND) 258-259 H 3
Rolim de Moura o BR (RON) 70-71 F 3
Rolim de Moura o BR (RON) 70-71 G 2
Roll o USA (AZ) 256-257 B 6
Roll o USA (OK) 264-265 E 3
Rolla ⌒ N 86-87 H 2
Rolla o USA (KS) 262-263 E 7
Rolla o USA (MO) 276-277 D 3
Rolla o USA (ND) 258-259 H 3
Rollapenta o IND 140-141 H 3
Rolleston o AUS 178-179 K 3
Rolleston o NZ 182 D 5
Rollet o CDN (QUE) 236-237 J 5
Rolleville o • BS 54-55 H 3
Rolling Fork o USA (MS) 268-269 K 4
Rolling Fork ∼ USA (KY) 276-277 K 3
Rolling Hills o CDN (ALB) 232-233 G 5
Rolling River Indian Reserve ✕ CDN (MAN) 234-235 D 4
Rollins o USA (MN) 270-271 G 3
Rollins o USA (MT) 250-251 E 4
Rolvsøya ⌒ N 86-87 M 1
Roma o AUS 178-179 K 4
Roma ★ ••• I 100-101 D 4
Roma o LS 220-221 H 4
Roma o S 86-87 J 8
Roma o USA (TX) 266-267 J 7
Roma, Pulau ⌒ RI 166-167 D 5
Romain, Cape ▲ USA (SC) 284-285 L 4
Romaine o CDN (QUE) 242-243 H 2
Romaine, Rivière ∼ CDN 38-39 N 3
Roman o BG 102-103 C 6
Roman o • RO 102-103 E 4
Romana, La ☆ DOM 54-55 L 5
Romanche Fracture Zone ≃ 6-7 G 9
Romancoke o USA (MD) 280-281 K 5
Romanek, Lac ⊖ CDN 36-37 Q 6
Romang, Selat ≈ 166-167 D 5
Romania = România ■ RO 102-103 C 5
Romanina, Bol'šaja ∼ RUS 108-109 c 6
Roman-Koš, hora ▲ UA 102-103 J 5
Romano, Cape ▲ USA (FL) 286-287 H 6
Romano, Cayo ⌒ C 54-55 F 3
Romanovka o RUS 118-119 F 9
Romans-sur-Isère o F 90-91 K 9
Romanzof, Cape ▲ USA 20-21 G 6
Romanzof Mountains ▲ USA 20-21 S 2
Romblon ☆ RP 160-161 E 6
Romblon Island ⌒ RP 160-161 E 6
Romblon Strait ≈ 160-161 E 6
Rome o USA (AL) 284-285 D 5
Rome o USA (GA) 284-285 E 2
Rome o USA (NY) 278-279 F 5
Rome o USA (OH) 280-281 F 2
Rome o USA (OR) 244-245 H 8
Rome o USA (TN) 276-277 J 4
Rome = Roma ★ ••• I 100-101 D 4
Romeo o USA (MI) 272-273 F 5
Romeoville o USA (IL) 274-275 K 3
Romero o USA (TX) 264-265 B 3
Romero, Isla ⌒ RCH 80 C 2
Romer Sø ⊖ GRØ 26-27 q 3
Romita o MEX 52-53 D 1
Rommani o MA 188-189 H 4
Romney o USA (IN) 274-275 M 4
Romney o USA (WV) 280-281 H 4
Romny o RUS 122-123 C 3
Romny o UA 102-103 H 2
Rømø ⌒ DK 86-87 D 9
Romodan o UA 102-103 H 2
Romorantin-Lanthenay o F 90-91 H 8
Rompía o YV 60-61 H 4
Rompin ∼ MAL 162-163 E 3
Romsdalen ∼ N 86-87 C 5
Ronan o USA (MT) 250-251 E 4
Roncador o BR 74-75 D 5
Roncador, Serra do ▲ BR 72-73 E 2
Roncador Reef ⌒ SOL 184 I d 2
Roncesvalles o • E 98-99 G 3
Ronciàre Falls, La ∼ CDN 24-25 L 6
Ronda o E 98-99 E 6
Ronda, Serrania de ▲ E 98-99 E 6
Ronde o DK 86-87 E 8
Ronde, Rivière la ∼ CDN 38-39 L 2
Ronde Island ⌒ WG 56 E 5
Rondon o BR 72-73 D 7
Rondon, Pico ▲ BR 66-67 F 2
Rondon Dopara o BR 68-69 D 4
Rondônia ■ BR 70-71 F 2
Rondonópolis o BR 70-71 K 5
Rond-Point de Gaulle ▲ TCH 198-199 H 3
Rondslottet ▲ N 86-87 D 6
Rondu o IND 138-139 E 2
Rong'an o VRC 156-157 F 4
Rongbuk o VRC 144-145 F 6
Rongchang o VRC 156-157 D 2
Rongcheng o VRC 154-155 N 3
Ronge, La o CDN 34-35 D 3
Ronge, Lac la ⊖ CDN 34-35 D 3
Rongjiang o VRC 156-157 F 4
Rongkong ∼ RI 164-165 G 5
Rong Kwang o THA 142-143 M 6
Rongo o EAK 212-213 E 4
Rongshui o VRC 156-157 F 4
Rõngu o EST 94-95 K 2
Rongxar o VRC 144-145 F 6
Rong Xian o VRC (GXI) 156-157 G 5
Rong Xian o VRC (SIC) 156-157 D 2
Rønne o DK 86-87 G 9
Ronne Bay ≈ 16 F 29
Ronneby ☆ S 86-87 G 8
Rönnöfors o S 86-87 F 5
Ron Phibun o THA 158-159 E 6
Ronsard, Cape ▲ AUS 176-177 B 2
Ronuro, Rio ∼ BR 70-71 K 3
Roodepoort o ZA 220-221 H 3
Roof Butte ▲ USA (AZ) 256-257 F 2
Rooiberge ▲ ZA 220-221 J 4
Rooibokkraal o ZA 220-221 H 2
Rooikloof ▲ ZA 220-221 E 6
Rooikop o NAM 216-217 C 11
Rooikraal o ZA 220-221 J 2
Rooirand ▲ NAM 220-221 C 2
Room, Pulau ⌒ RI 166-167 H 3
Rooney Point ▲ AUS 178-179 M 3
Roopville o USA (GA) 284-285 E 3
Roosendaal o NL 92-93 H 3
Roosevelt o USA (AZ) 256-257 D 5
Roosevelt o USA (OK) 264-265 E 4
Roosevelt o USA (TX) 266-267 G 3
Roosevelt o USA (UT) 254-255 E 3
Roosevelt o USA (WA) 244-245 E 5
Roosevelt, Área Indígena ✕ BR 70-71 G 2
Roosevelt, Mount ▲ CDN 30-31 G 6
Roosevelt, Rio ∼ BR 66-67 G 7
Roosevelt Beach o USA (OR) 244-245 A 6
Roosevelt Campobello International Park ∴ CDN (NB) 240-241 J 6
Roosevelt Fjelde ▲ GRØ 26-27 g 2
Roosevelt Island ⌒ ARK 16 F 21
Roossenekal o ZA 220-221 J 2
Roosville o CDN (BC) 230-231 O 4
Rootok Island ⌒ USA 22-23 O 5
Root River ∼ CDN 30-31 G 4
Root River ∼ USA (MN) 270-271 G 7
Roper Bar o AUS 174-175 C 4
Roper River ∼ AUS 174-175 C 4
Roper Valley o AUS 174-175 C 4
Ropesville o USA (TX) 264-265 B 6
Roquefort o F 90-91 G 9
Roques, Islas los ⌒ YV 60-61 H 2
Roques, Los o YV 60-61 H 2
Roquetas de Mar o E 98-99 F 6
Roraima ■ BR 62-63 D 5
Roraima, Mount ▲ GUY 62-63 D 3
Roraya ∼ RI 164-165 H 6
Rorey Lake ⊖ CDN 30-31 F 2
Rori o RI 166-167 J 2
Rorketon o CDN (MAN) 234-235 D 3
Røros ☆ •• N 86-87 E 5
Rørvik o N 86-87 E 4
Ros' ∼ UA 102-103 G 3
Rosa o CDN (MAN) 234-235 G 5
Rosa, La o YV 60-61 G 3
Rosa, Lake ⊖ BS 54-55 J 4
Rosa, Río Santa ∼ BOL 70-71 D 5
Rosal o BR 72-73 K 6
Rosal' o RUS 94-95 Q 4
Rosal, El o CO 60-61 D 5
Rosal de la Frontera o E 98-99 D 6
Rosalia o USA (WA) 244-245 H 3
Rosalind o CDN (ALB) 232-233 F 3
Rosamond o USA (CA) 248-249 F 5
Rosamoraga o MEX 50-51 G 6
Rosana o BR 72-73 D 7
Rosário o BR 68-69 F 3
Rosario o DOM 54-55 K 5
Rosario o MEX 50-51 E 4
Rosario o PE 70-71 B 4
Rosario o PY 76-77 J 3
Rosario o RA (BUA) 78-79 J 2
Rosario o RA (JU) 76-77 D 2
Rosario o • RA (COD) 78-79 J 2
Rosario o RCH 76-77 B 4
Rosario o RP (BTG) 160-161 D 6
Rosario o RP (LUN) 160-161 D 4
Rosario, Cayo del ⌒ C 54-55 E 4
Rosario, El o MEX (BCN) 50-51 B 2
Rosario, El o MEX (SIN) 50-51 G 6
Rosario, El o YV (BOL) 60-61 J 4
Rosario, El o YV (MON) 60-61 K 3
Rosario, Río ∼ RA 76-77 E 3
Rosario, Río ∼ RA 76-77 D 2
Rosario de la Frontera o • RA 76-77 E 3
Rosario de Lerma o RA 76-77 D 3
Rosario del Ingre o BOL 70-71 F 7
Rosario del Tala o RA 78-79 K 2
Rosário do Catete o BR 68-69 K 7
Rosário do Sul o BR 76-77 K 6
Rosário Oeste o BR 70-71 J 4
Rosarito o MEX (BCN) 50-51 B 3
Rosarito o MEX (BCS) 50-51 D 4
Rosarito o • MEX (BCN) 50-51 A 1
Rosas o CO 60-61 C 6
Rosas, Las o MEX 52-53 H 3
Rosas, Las o RA 78-79 J 2
Rosaspata o PE 70-71 C 4
Rosa Zárate o EC 64-65 C 1
Rosburg o USA (WA) 244-245 B 4
Roscoe o USA (NY) 280-281 M 2
Roscoe o USA (SD) 260-261 G 1
Roscoe o USA (TX) 264-265 D 6
Roscoe River ∼ CDN 24-25 M 6
Roscoff o F 90-91 F 7
Ros Comáin = Roscommon ☆ IRL 90-91 C 5
Roscommon o USA (MI) 272-273 E 3
Roscommon = Ros Comáin ☆ IRL 90-91 C 5
Ros Cré = Roscrea o IRL 90-91 D 5
Roscrea = Ros Cré o IRL 90-91 D 5
Roseau o USA (MN) 270-271 C 2
Roseau ★ WD 56 E 4
Roseau River ∼ USA (MN) 270-271 B 2
Roseau River Wildlife Refuge ⊥ USA (MN) 270-271 B 2
Roseaux o RH 54-55 H 5
Rosebank o CDN (MAN) 234-235 E 5
Rose Belle o MS 224 C 7
Rosebery o AUS 180-181 H 6
Roseblade Lake ⊖ CDN 30-31 V 5
Rose Blanche o CDN (NFL) 242-243 K 5
Roseboro o USA (NC) 282-283 J 6
Rosebud o CDN (ALB) 232-233 F 4
Rose Bud o USA (AR) 276-277 C 5
Rosebud o USA (SD) 260-261 F 3
Rosebud o USA (TX) 266-267 L 2
Rosebud Creek ∼ USA (MT) 250-251 N 6
Rosebud Indian Reservation ✕ USA (SD) 260-261 F 3
Rosebud River ∼ CDN (ALB) 232-233 E 4
Roseburg o USA (OR) 244-245 B 7
Rose City o USA (MI) 272-273 E 3
Rose Creek ∼ CDN (ALB) 232-233 D 3
Rosedale o AUS 178-179 J 2
Rosedale o CDN (ALB) 232-233 F 4
Rosedale o CDN (BC) 230-231 H 4
Rosedale o USA (IN) 274-275 L 5
Rosedale o USA (MS) 268-269 J 3
Rosefield o USA (LA) 268-269 H 5
Roseglen o USA (ND) 258-259 F 4
Rose Harbour o CDN (BC) 228-229 C 4
Rose Hill o MS 224 C 7
Rose Hill o USA (MS) 268-269 L 4
Rose Hill o USA (NC) 282-283 J 6
Rose Island ⌒ BS 54-55 G 2
Roseisle o CDN (MAN) 234-235 F 5
Rose Lake o CDN (BC) 228-229 H 2
Rose Lake o USA (ID) 250-251 C 4
Roseland o USA (LA) 268-269 K 6
Roselle o USA (IL) 274-275 K 3
Rosemount o USA (MN) 270-271 E 6
Rosenberg o USA (TX) 268-269 E 7
Rosenberg = Ružomberok o SK 92-93 P 4
Rosenberg, Sulzbach- o D 92-93 L 4
Rosenburg o CDN (MAN) 234-235 F 3
Rosendal ☆ N 86-87 C 7
Rosendal o ZA 220-221 H 4
Rosenfeld o USA (TX) 266-267 E 3
Rosenheim o D 92-93 M 5
Rosenort o CDN (MAN) 234-235 F 5
Rose Point ▲ CDN (BC) 228-229 C 2
Rose Prairie o CDN 32-33 K 3
Rose River ∼ AUS 174-175 C 3
Roses o USA (PA) 280-281 G 2
Rosetilla o MEX 50-51 G 3
Rosetown o CDN (SAS) 232-233 L 4
Rosetta = Rašīd o • ET 194-195 E 2
Rosette o USA (UT) 254-255 B 2
Rose Valley o CDN (SAS) 232-233 P 3
Rosevear o CDN (ALB) 232-233 B 2
Roseveltpiek ▲ SME 62-63 G 4
Roseville o USA (IL) 274-275 H 4
Roseville Rio o USA (CA) 246-247 D 5
Rosewood o AUS 172-173 J 4
Rosharon o USA (TX) 268-269 E 7
Rosh Pinah o NAM 220-221 C 3
Rosi ∼ IND 138-139 G 5
Rosie Creek o AUS 174-175 C 4
Rosiers, Cap-des- o CDN (QUE) 240-241 L 2
Rosignano Marittima o I 100-101 C 3
Rosignol o GUY 62-63 F 2
Rosillo, Cañada el ∼ RA 76-77 F 2
Roşiori de Vede o RO 102-103 D 5
Rosita, La o CO 60-61 F 5
Rosita, La o NIC 52-53 B 5
Roskilde o •• DK 86-87 F 9
Roslavl' o RUS 94-95 N 5
Roslin o CDN (ONT) 238-239 H 4
Roslyn Lake ⊖ CDN (ONT) 236-237 Q 5
Rosman o USA (NC) 282-283 E 5
Rosmead o ZA 220-221 G 5
Ros Mhic Thriúin = New Ross o IRL 90-91 D 5
Ross, Cape ▲ RP 160-161 C 7
Rossano o I 100-101 F 5
Ross Barnett Reservoir < USA (MS) 268-269 L 4
Ross Bay ≈ 24-25 d 7
Ross Bay Junction o CDN 38-39 L 2
Rosso-Béthio o SN 196-197 B 6
Rossburn o CDN (MAN) 234-235 C 4
Ross City o USA (TX) 264-265 C 6
Rosseau o CDN (ONT) 238-239 F 3
Rosseau, Lake ⊖ CDN (ONT) 238-239 F 3
Rosser o CDN (MAN) 234-235 F 4
Ross Ice Shelf ⊂ ARK 16 E 0
Rossignol, Lac ⊖ CDN 38-39 H 2
Rossignol, Lake ⊖ CDN (NS) 240-241 K 6
Rössing o NAM 216-217 C 11
Ross Inlet ≈ 24-25 c 7
Ross Island ⌒ ARK 16 G 31
Ross Island ⌒ ARK 16 F 17
Ross Island ⌒ CDN 34-35 H 3
Ross Lake ⊖ USA (WA) 244-245 E 2
Rossland o CDN (BC) 230-231 M 4
Rosslare = Ros Láir o IRL 90-91 D 5
Rosso ☆ RIM 196-197 C 6
Rossomaha ∼ RUS 114-115 T 5
Rossošino o RUS 118-119 G 8
Rossouw o ZA 220-221 H 5
Rossport o CDN (ONT) 234-235 Q 6
Ross River o AUS 178-179 C 2
Ross River o CDN (NWT) 20-21 Y 6
Ross River ∼ CDN 20-21 Z 5
Ross Sea ≈ 16 F 19
Rosston o USA (AR) 276-277 B 7
Rosston o USA (OK) 264-265 E 2
Røssvatnet ⊖ N 86-87 F 4
Rossville o AUS 174-175 H 4
Rossville Mission • CDN 34-35 H 4
Rosswood o CDN (BC) 228-229 F 2
Røst o N 86-87 F 3
Rostāq o AFG 136-137 L 6
Rostāq o IR 134-135 E 5
Rosthern o CDN (SAS) 232-233 M 3
Rostock o •• D 92-93 M 1
Rostov ☆ •• RUS 94-95 Q 3
Rostov-na-Donu ☆ RUS 102-103 L 4
Rostraver o USA (PA) 280-281 G 3
Rostrenen o F 90-91 F 7
Roswell o USA (GA) 284-285 F 2
Roswell o USA (NM) 256-257 L 5
Roswell o USA (SD) 260-261 J 2
Rosyth o CDN (ALB) 232-233 G 3
Rotan o USA (TX) 264-265 D 6
Rote = Pulau Roti ⌒ RI 166-167 B 7
Rothenburg ob der Tauber o •• D 92-93 L 4
Rotherham o GB 90-91 G 5
Rothesay o • GB 90-91 E 4
Rothsay o USA (MN) 270-271 B 4
Rothschild o USA (WI) 270-271 J 6
Roti o RI 166-167 B 7
Roti, Pulau ⌒ RI 166-167 B 7
Roti, Selat ≈ 166-167 B 7
Rotifunk o WAL 202-203 D 5
Roto o AUS 180-181 H 2
Rotonda West o USA (FL) 286-287 G 5
Rotondo, Monte ▲ F 98-99 M 3
Rotorua o •• NZ 182 F 3
Rotterdam o • NL 92-93 H 3
Rottnest Island o • AUS (WA) 176-177 C 6
Rottnest Island ⌒ AUS (WA) 176-177 C 6
Rottweil o • D 92-93 K 4
Roualist Bank ≃ 158-159 H 6
Roubaix o F 90-91 J 6
Rouen ☆ • F 90-91 H 7
Rouge, P.K. o RCB 210-211 E 5
Rouge, Rivière ∼ CDN (QUE) 238-239 L 3
Rouge, Rivière ∼ CDN (QUE) 238-239 L 2
Rough River ∼ USA (KY) 276-277 J 3
Rough River Reservoir < USA (KY) 276-277 J 3
Rough Rock o USA (AZ) 256-257 F 2
Rouhia o TN 190-191 G 3
Rouleau o CDN (SAS) 232-233 O 5
Roumsiki o • CAM 204-205 K 3
Roundeyed, Lac ⊖ CDN 38-39 J 2
Roundhead o USA (OH) 280-281 C 3
Round Hill o CDN (ALB) 232-233 F 2
Round Hill o USA (KY) 276-277 J 3
Round House ▲ USA (KS) 262-263 G 6
Round Lake ⊖ CDN (ONT) 238-239 H 3
Round Mountain ▲ AUS 178-179 M 6
Round Mountain o USA (CA) 246-247 D 3
Round Mountain o USA (NV) 246-247 H 5
Round Pond ⊖ CDN (NFL) 242-243 N 4
Round Rock o USA (AZ) 256-257 F 2
Round Rock o USA (TX) 266-267 K 3
Round Spring o USA (MO) 276-277 D 3
Round Spring Cave • USA (MO) 276-277 D 3
Round Top o USA (TX) 266-267 L 3
Roundup o USA (MT) 250-251 L 5
Round Valley Indian Reservation ✕ USA (CA) 246-247 B 4
Rounthwaite o CDN (MAN) 234-235 D 5
Roura o F 62-63 H 3
Rourkela = Raurkela o • IND 142-143 D 4
Rouses Point o USA (NY) 278-279 H 4
Routhierville o CDN (QUE) 240-241 H 2
Rouxdam, P.K. le < ZA 220-221 G 5
Rouxville o ZA 220-221 H 5
Rouyn-Noranda o CDN (QUE) 236-237 J 4
Rovdino o RUS 88-89 R 6
Roven'ky o UA 102-103 L 3
Rover o USA (AR) 276-277 B 6
Rover, Mount ▲ CDN 20-21 U 3
Rovereto o • I 100-101 C 2
Roversi o RA 76-77 G 4
Rovigo ☆ I 100-101 C 2
Rovinari o RO 102-103 C 5
Rovinj o • HR 100-101 D 2
Rovno = Rivne o UA 102-103 E 2
Rovnoe o RUS 96-97 E 8
Rovnyj, mys ▲ RUS 120-121 V 4
Rovnyj, ostrov ⌒ RUS 120-121 U 3
Rovubo ∼ EAT (KAG) 212-213 C 5
Rovuma ∼ MOC 214-215 K 6
Rowala Kot o IND 138-139 D 3
Rowan, Port o CDN (ONT) 238-239 E 6
Rowatt o CDN (SAS) 232-233 O 5
Rowden o USA (TX) 264-265 E 6
Rowdy o USA (KY) 276-277 M 3
Rowena o USA (TX) 266-267 G 2
Rowland o USA (NC) 282-283 H 6
Rowletta o CDN (SAS) 232-233 N 5
Rowley o CDN 24-25 g 6
Rowley Island ⌒ CDN 24-25 h 6
Rowley Lake ⊖ CDN 30-31 R 5
Rowley River ∼ CDN 24-25 j 5
Rowley Shelf ≃ 172-173 C 5
Rowley Shoals ⌒ AUS 172-173 D 4
Roxa, Ilha ⌒ GNB 202-203 C 4
Roxas o RP (ISA) 160-161 D 4
Roxas o RP (MIO) 160-161 D 6
Roxas o RP (PAL) 160-161 C 7
Roxas ☆ RP (CAP) 160-161 E 7
Roxboro o USA (NC) 282-283 J 4
Roxborough Downs o AUS 178-179 E 2
Roxby Downs o AUS 178-179 D 6
Roxie o USA (MS) 268-269 J 5
Roxo, Cap ▲ GNB 202-203 B 3
Roxton o USA (TX) 264-265 J 5
Roxton Falls o CDN (QUE) 238-239 N 3
Roy o USA (MT) 250-251 L 4
Roy o USA (NM) 256-257 L 3
Roy o USA (TX) 264-265 B 4
Roy o USA (UT) 254-255 C 2
Roy, Lac le ⊖ CDN 36-37 M 5
Royal, Mount ▲ CDN (ONT) 234-235 P 5
Royal Center o USA (IN) 274-275 M 4
Royal Charlotte, Bank ≃ 72-73 L 4
Royal Chitawan National Park ⊥ ••• NEP 144-145 E 7
Royal City o USA (WA) 244-245 F 4
Royale, Isle ⌒ USA (MI) 270-271 J 3
Royal Geographical Society Islands ⌒ CDN 24-25 W 6
Royal Gorge • USA (CO) 254-255 K 5
Royal Island ⌒ BS 54-55 G 2
Royal Natal National Park ⊥ ZA 220-221 J 4
Royal National Park ⊥ AUS 180-181 L 3
Royal Palace o • RI 168 D 7
Royal Palm Hammock o USA (FL) 286-287 H 6
Royal Park o CDN (ALB) 232-233 F 2
Royal Society Range ▲ ARK 16 F 16
Royal Soud, Port ≈ 48-49 H 3
Royalties o CDN (ALB) 232-233 D 5
Royalton o USA (MN) 270-271 D 5
Royalton o USA (VT) 278-279 J 5
Royan o • F 90-91 G 9
Roye o F 90-91 J 7
Roy Hill o AUS (WA) 172-173 D 7
Roy Hill ▲ AUS (WA) 172-173 D 7
Røyrvik o N 86-87 F 4
Royston o USA (GA) 284-285 G 2
Rožaje o • YU 100-101 H 3
Różan o PL 92-93 Q 2
Rozdoľne ☆ UA 102-103 H 5
Rozel o USA (KS) 262-263 G 6
Rozet o USA (WY) 252-253 N 2
Rozivka o UA 102-103 K 4
Rožňava o SK 92-93 Q 4
Rozy Ljuksemburga, mys ▲ RUS 108-109 c 1
r-Raṭqa, Wādī ∼ IRQ 128-129 J 6
Rtiščevo o RUS 94-95 S 5
Ruacana o NAM 216-217 C 8
Ruacaná, Quedas do ∼ •• ANG 216-217 C 8
Ruacana Falls ∼ •• NAM 216-217 C 8
Ruaha National Park ⊥ EAT 214-215 H 4
Ruahine Range ▲ NZ 182 F 3
Ru'ais o UAE 134-135 E 6
Ruangwa o EAT 214-215 K 6
Ruapehu, Mount ▲ NZ 182 E 3
Ruapuke Island ⌒ NZ 182 B 7
Ruarwe o MW 214-215 H 6
Ruatahuna o NZ 182 F 3
Ruatoria o NZ 182 G 2
Ruawai o NZ 182 E 2
Rubafu o EAT 212-213 C 4
Rubai'iya, ar- o KSA 130-131 J 4
Rub' al-Ḫālī, ar- ⊥ KSA 132-133 D 4
Rubcovsk o RUS 124-125 M 3
Rubeho Mountains ▲ EAT 214-215 J 4
Rubens, Río ∼ RCH 80 D 6
Ruberong ▲ IND 138-139 F 3
Rubeshibe o J 152-153 K 3
Rubi o ZRE 210-211 K 2
Rubi ∼ ZRE 210-211 K 2
Rubiataba o BR 72-73 F 3
Rubicon River ∼ USA (CA) 246-247 E 5
Rubikon, mys ▲ RUS 112-113 S 6
Rubim o BR 72-73 K 4
Rubinéia o BR 72-73 E 6
Rubio o YV 60-61 E 4
Ruble o USA (IA) 274-275 B 2
Rubondo Island ⌒ EAT 212-213 C 5
Rubondo National Park ⊥ EAT 212-213 C 5
Ruby o USA 20-21 N 4
Ruby o USA (AZ) 256-257 D 7
Ruby Dome ▲ USA (NV) 246-247 K 3
Ruby Lake o CDN (SAS) 232-233 Q 2
Ruby Lake ⊖ USA (NV) 246-247 K 3
Ruby Mountains ▲ USA (NV) 246-247 K 3
Ruby Plains o AUS 172-173 H 5
Ruby Range ▲ CDN 20-21 V 6
Ruby River ∼ USA (MT) 250-251 G 6
Rubys Inn o USA (UT) 254-255 C 6
Rubyvale o AUS 178-179 J 2
Ruby Valley o USA (NV) 246-247 K 3
Rucachoroi, Cerro ▲ RA 78-79 D 5
Rucava o LV 94-95 G 3
Ruch o USA (OR) 244-245 B 8
Ruč'i o RUS 88-89 S 4
Rucio, El o MEX 50-51 H 6
Ruckersville o USA (VA) 280-281 H 5
Rūd o IR 134-135 J 1
Rudal o AUS 180-181 D 2
Rudall River National Park ⊥ AUS 172-173 E 7
Rūdbār o • IR 128-129 N 4
Ruddell o CDN (SAS) 232-233 L 3
Ruddera, buhta ≈ 112-113 W 4
Rūd-e Čalūs ∼ IR 136-137 B 6
Rūd-e Ḥelle ∼ IR 134-135 D 4
Rūdehen o IR 136-137 B 7
Rūd-e Mārūn ∼ IR 134-135 C 3
Rūd-e Šindand ∼ AFG 134-135 K 2
Rudewa o EAT 214-215 H 6
Rūdḫāne-ye 'Aliābād ∼ IR 134-135 J 3
Rūdḫāne-ye Ġarrāhī ∼ IR 134-135 C 3
Rūdḫāne-ye Nekā ∼ IR 136-137 C 6
Rudkøbing o • DK 86-87 E 9
Rudnaja Pristan' o RUS 122-123 G 6
Rudnik ▲ • YU 100-101 H 2
Rudnja ☆ RUS 94-95 M 4
Rudnyj o KA 124-125 C 2
Rudnyy = Rudnyj o KA 124-125 C 2
Rud Ø ⌒ GRØ 28-29 T 5
Rudolf, Lake = Turkana, Lake ⊖ EAK 212-213 F 2
Rudol'fa o RUS 84-85 e 2
Rudol'fa, ostrov ⌒ RUS 84-85 f 2
Rudong o VRC 154-155 M 5
Rūdsar o IR 136-137 B 6
Rudyard o USA (MI) 270-271 O 4
Rudyard o USA (MT) 250-251 J 3
Rue, La o USA (TX) 264-265 K 6
Ruente Nacional o CO 60-61 E 5
Ruenya ∼ ZW 218-219 G 3
Rufā'ah o SUD 200-201 F 5
Ruff Creek o USA (PA) 280-281 F 4
Ruffin o USA (SC) 284-285 K 3
Rufiji ∼ EAT 214-215 J 5
Rufino o BR 62-63 F 6
Rufino o RA 78-79 H 3
Rufisque o SN 202-203 B 2
Rufrufua o RI 166-167 G 3
Rufunsa o Z 218-219 E 2
Rufunsa ∼ Z 218-219 E 2
Rufus o USA (OR) 244-245 E 5
Rufus Lake ⊖ CDN 20-21 Z 2
Rugāji o LV 94-95 K 3
Rugao o VRC 154-155 M 5
Rugby o USA (ND) 258-259 G 3
Rügen ⌒ D 92-93 M 1
Rügenwalde = Darłowo o • PL 92-93 O 1
Rugged Island ⌒ USA 20-21 Q 7
Rugheiwa < SUD 200-201 E 4
Rugufu ∼ EAT 212-213 C 6
Ruḥaimiya, ar- o IRQ 130-131 J 3
Ruhayyah, Ġabal ar- ▲ KSA 130-131 L 4
Ruhengeri o RWA 212-213 B 4
Ruhnu saar ⌒ • EST 94-95 H 3
Ruhudji ∼ EAT 214-215 H 5
Ruhuhu ∼ EAT 214-215 H 6
Rui'an o VRC 156-157 M 3
Rui Barbosa o BR 72-73 K 2
Ruichang o VRC 156-157 J 2
Ruicheng o VRC 154-155 G 4
Ruidosa o USA (TX) 266-267 C 3
Ruidoso o USA (NM) 256-257 K 5
Ruidoso Downs o USA (NM) 256-257 K 5
Ruijin o VRC 156-157 J 4
Ruiki ∼ ZRE 210-211 K 4
Ruili o VRC 142-143 K 3
Ruimte o NAM 220-221 B 1
Ruin Point ▲ CDN 36-37 H 3
Ruins ∴ AUS 176-177 L 5
Ruins of Sambor • K 158-159 H 4
Ruipa o EAT (MOR) 214-215 J 5
Ruiru o EAK 212-213 F 4
Ruisseau-à-Rebours o CDN (QUE) 242-243 C 3
Ruitersbos o ZA 220-221 F 6
Rūjiena o •• LV 94-95 J 3
Ruka o FIN 88-89 K 3
Rukanga o EAK 212-213 G 5
Rukarara ∼ RWA 212-213 B 5
Ruki ∼ ZRE 210-211 G 4
Rukua o RI 164-165 J 6
Rukubji o BHT 142-143 G 2
Rukutama ∼ RUS 122-123 K 4
Rukwa ⊡ EAT 214-215 F 4
Rukwa, Lake ⊖ EAT 214-215 F 4
Rule o USA (TX) 264-265 E 5
Rulenge o EAT 212-213 C 5
Ruleville o USA (MS) 268-269 K 3
Ruma o WAN 198-199 C 6
Ruma o YU 100-101 G 2
Rumāh o KSA 130-131 K 5
Rumahbaru o RI 162-163 B 2
Rumahkai o RI 166-167 E 3
Rumah Kulit o MAL 164-165 D 2
Rumahtinggih o RI 166-167 L 5
Rumaila o IRQ 130-131 K 2
Ruma National Park ⊥ EAK 212-213 E 4
Rumbek o SUD 206-207 J 5
Rumberpon, Pulau ⌒ RI 166-167 H 2
Rumble Beach o CDN (BC) 230-231 B 3
Rum Cay = Mamana Island ⌒ BS 54-55 H 3
Rum Jungle o AUS 172-173 K 2
Rummāna o ET 194-195 F 2
Rumo o BR 68-69 F 2
Rumoi o J 152-153 J 3
Rumonge o BU 212-213 B 5
Rumorosa, La o • MEX 50-51 A 1
Rumphi o MW 214-215 G 6
Rumpi Hills ▲ CAM 204-205 H 6
Rum River ∼ USA (MN) 270-271 E 5
Rumsey o CDN (ALB) 232-233 F 4
Rumuruti o EAK 212-213 F 3
Run, Pulau ⌒ RI 166-167 E 4
Runan o VRC 154-155 J 5
Runaway, Cape ▲ NZ 182 F 2
Runaway Bay o JA 54-55 G 5
Runazi o EAT 212-213 C 5
Runde ∼ ZW 218-219 F 5
Rundeng o RI 162-163 B 3
Rundu ☆ NAM (KV1) 216-217 E 8
Runduma, Pulau ⌒ RI 164-165 J 6
Runge o USA (TX) 266-267 K 5
Rungu o ZRE 212-213 A 2
Rungwa o EAT (RUK) 214-215 F 4
Rungwa o EAT (SIN) 214-215 G 4
Rungwa ∼ EAT 214-215 G 4
Rungwa Game Reserve ⊥ EAT 214-215 G 4
Runmarö ⌒ S 86-87 J 7
Running Springs o USA (CA) 248-249 G 5
Running Water Draw ∼ USA (TX) 264-265 B 4
Runnymede o AUS 174-175 G 7
Runnymede o CDN (SAS) 232-233 R 4
Runton Range ▲ AUS 176-177 G 1
Ruokolahti o FIN 88-89 K 6
Ruoqiang o VRC 146-147 J 6
Ruo Shui ∼ VRC 148-149 D 7
Ruo Shui ∼ VRC 154-155 B 2
Ruovesi o FIN 88-89 H 6
Rupanco, Lago ⊖ RCH 78-79 C 6
Rupanyup o AUS 180-181 G 4
Rupat, Pulau ⌒ RI 162-163 D 4
Rupat, Selat ≈ 162-163 D 4
Rupert o USA (AR) 276-277 C 5
Rupert o USA (ID) 252-253 E 4
Rupert o USA (WV) 280-281 F 6
Rupert, Baie de ⊖ CDN 38-39 E 3
Rupert, Fort o CDN 38-39 E 3
Rupert, Rivière ∼ CDN 38-39 G 3
Rupert, Rivière de ∼ CDN 38-39 E 3
Rupisi o ZW 218-219 G 5
Ruponda o EAT 214-215 K 6
Ruppert Coast ⌒ ARK 16 F 22
Ruqaī', ar- o KSA 130-131 K 4
Ruqayba o SUD 200-201 E 5
Rural Hall o USA (NC) 282-283 G 4
Rurópolis Presidente Médici o BR 66-67 K 5
Rurutu Island ⌒ F 13 M 5
Ruṣāfa, ar- o • SYR 128-129 H 5

Rock Sound — Ruṣāfa, ar- 385

Salmon River ∼ CDN 38-39 Q 3
Salmon River ∼ CDN (BC) 228-229 L 2
Salmon River ∼ CDN (NB) 240-241 K 4
Salmon River ∼ USA 20-21 L 3
Salmon River ∼ USA (ID) 250-251 D 6
Salmon River ∼ USA (ID) 252-253 D 2
Salmon River ∼ USA (NY) 278-279 F 5
Salmon River ∼ USA (NY) 278-279 G 4
Salmon River Mountains ▲ USA (ID) 252-253 B 1
Salmon Valley ○ CDN (BC) 228-229 M 2
Salmo-Priest Wilderness Area ⊥ USA (WA) 244-245 H 2
Salmossi ○ BF 202-203 K 2
Salo ○ FIN 88-89 G 6
Salo ○ RCA 210-211 F 2
Salobra, Ribeiro ∼ BR 70-71 J 7
Salomão, Ilha ⌒ BR 66-67 F 6
Salome ○ USA (AZ) 256-257 B 5
Salonga ∼ ZRE 210-211 H 4
Salonga Nord, Parc National de la ⊥ ··· ZRE 210-211 H 4
Salonga Sud, Parc National de la ⊥ ··· ZRE 210-211 H 4
Salonsa ○ RI 164-165 G 5
Salor, Río ∼ E 98-99 D 5
Salou, Cap de ▲ E 98-99 H 4
Saloum ∼ SN 202-203 C 2
Salpausselkä ⊥ FIN 88-89 H 6
Salsa, Paraná do ∼ BR 66-67 F 5
Salsacate ○ RA 76-77 E 6
Salsberry Pass ▲ USA (CA) 248-249 H 4
Salsipuedes, Canal de ≈ 50-51 C 3
Salsipuedes Grande, Arroyo ∼ ROU 78-79 L 2
Sal'sk ○ RUS 102-103 M 4
Šal'skij ○ RUS 88-89 O 6
Sal'sko-Manyčskaja grjada ▲ RUS 102-103 M 4
Salso ∼ I 100-101 D 6
Salt, as- ☆ JOR 130-131 D 1
Salta ◘ RA 76-77 D 3
Salta ☆ ·· RA (SAL) 76-77 E 3
Saltaim, ozero ○ RUS 114-115 L 6
Salt Basin ○ USA (TX) 266-267 B 2
Salt Cay ⌒ GB 54-55 K 4
Saltcoats ○ CDN (SAS) 232-233 Q 4
Salt Creek ∼ AUS 178-179 F 6
Salt Creek ∼ USA (IL) 274-275 J 4
Salt Creek ∼ USA (NM) 256-257 L 5
Salt Desert = Kavir, Dašt-e ⊥ IR 134-135 E 1
Salt Draw ∼ USA (TX) 266-267 C 2
Salteelva ∼ N 86-87 G 3
Saltery Bay ○ CDN (BC) 230-231 E 4
Saltfjell-Svartisen nasjonalpark ⊥ N 86-87 G 3
Saltfjorden ≈ 86-87 F 3
Salt Flat ○ USA (TX) 266-267 B 2
Salt Fork ∼ USA (KS) 262-263 G 7
Salt Fork Brazos River ∼ USA (TX) 264-265 D 5
Salt Fork Lake ○ USA (OH) 280-281 E 3
Salt Fork Red River ∼ USA (TX) 264-265 D 4
Saltillo ☆ • MEX 50-51 J 5
Saltillo ○ USA (MS) 268-269 M 2
Salt Lake ○ USA (NM) 256-257 M 6
Salt Lake ○ USA (TX) 266-267 C 2
Salt Lake, The ○ AUS 178-179 G 6
Salt Lake City ☆ USA (UT) 254-255 D 3
Salt Lakes ○ AUS 176-177 E 4
Salt March ○ USA (KS) 262-263 H 6
Salto ○ RA 78-79 J 3
Salto ☆ ROU 76-77 J 6
Salto, El ○ MEX (DGO) 50-51 G 6
Salto, El ○ MEX (SLP) 50-51 K 6
Salto, El ○ RCH 78-79 D 3
Salto, El ○ YV 60-61 K 3
Salto, Río ∼ RA 78-79 J 3
Salto da Divisa ○ BR 72-73 L 4
Salto de Cavalo ∼ • ANG 216-217 C 4
Salto de las Rosas ○ RA 78-79 E 3
Salto del Guaíra ☆ PY 76-77 K 3
Salto Grande, Embalse < ROU 76-77 J 6
Salton City ○ USA (CA) 248-249 J 6
Salton Sea ○ USA (CA) 248-249 J 6
Salto Osório, Represa < BR 74-75 D 5
Salto Santiago, Represa de < BR 74-75 D 5
Salt Pan ○ NAM 220-221 D 3
Salt Range ▲ PK 138-139 D 3
Salt River ∼ USA (AZ) 256-257 E 5
Salt River ∼ USA (KY) 276-277 K 3
Salt River ∼ USA (MO) 274-275 G 5
Saltsjöbaden ○ S 86-87 J 7
Salt Spring Island ⌒ CDN (BC) 230-231 F 5
Salt Springs ○ USA (FL) 286-287 H 2
Saltville ○ USA (VA) 280-281 E 7
Saluda ○ USA (SC) 284-285 J 2
Saluda River ∼ USA (SC) 284-285 H 2
Salue Besar, Pulau ⌒ RI 164-165 H 4
Salue Kecil, Pulau ⌒ RI 164-165 H 5
Salue Timpaus, Selat ≈ 164-165 H 4
Salugan ○ RI 164-165 G 3
Salūmbar ○ IND 138-139 E 7
Salus ○ USA (AR) 276-277 B 5
Salut, Îles du ⌒ F 62-63 H 3
Saluta ○ RI 164-165 K 2
Saluzzo ○ I 100-101 A 2
Salvacion ○ RP 160-161 E 7
Salvación, Bahía ≈ 80 C 5
Salvador ☆ ··· BR 72-73 L 2
Salvador ○ CDN (SAS) 232-233 J 3
Salvador, El ■ ES 52-53 K 5
Salvador, Lake ○ USA (LA) 268-269 K 7
Salvador, Passe de ∼ RN 192-193 E 6
Salvador do Sul ○ BR 74-75 E 7
Salvage ○ CDN (NFL) 242-243 P 4
Salvaterra ○ BR 62-63 K 6
Salvaterra ○ E 98-99 C 3
Salvatierra ○ MEX 52-53 D 1
Salvation, Point ▲ AUS 176-177 G 4
Salvator Rosa Section ⊥ AUS 178-179 J 3
Salve Ø ⌒ GRØ 26-27 R 5
Salve River ∼ CDN 30-31 O 6
Salvo ○ USA (NC) 282-283 M 5
Salvus ○ CDN (BC) 228-229 E 2
Salwā, as- ○ KSA 134-135 D 6
Salwā Bahrī ○ ET 194-195 F 5
Salween ∼ MYA 142-143 K 6
Salyan ○ AZ 128-129 N 3
Salyersville ○ USA (KY) 276-277 M 3
Šalyhyne ○ UA 102-103 J 2
Salzberger Bay ≈ 16 F 22
Salzburg ◘ A 92-93 M 5
Salzburg ☆ ·· A 92-93 M 5
Salzgitter ○ D 92-93 L 2
Salzwedel ○ • D 92-93 L 2
Sam ○ G 210-211 C 3
Ša'm, aš ○ UAE 134-135 G 5
Sam, kum ⊥ KA 126-127 L 5
Sama ○ PE 70-71 B 5
Sama, Río ∼ PE 70-71 B 5
Samachique ○ MEX 50-51 F 4
Samachvalavičy ○ BY 94-95 K 5
Samādābād ○ IR 134-135 H 2
Samagaltaj ☆ RUS 116-117 G 10
Samah ∼ MYA 142-143 K 5
Samā'il ○ OM 132-133 L 2
Samaipata • BOL 70-71 F 6
Samak, Tanjung ▲ RI 162-163 F 5
Samakona ○ CI 202-203 G 5
Samakoulou ○ RMM 202-203 F 3
Samal ○ RP 160-161 F 9
Samal, Tanjung ▲ RI 166-167 E 3
Samalá, Río ∼ GCA 52-53 J 4
Samalayuca ○ MEX 50-51 F 2
Samales Group ⌒ RP 160-161 D 9
Samalga Island ⌒ USA 22-23 M 6
Samalga Pass ≈ 22-23 M 6
Samal Island ⌒ RP 160-161 F 9
Sāmalkot ○ IND 142-143 C 7
Samalusi ○ LAR 192-193 J 1
Samālūṭ ○ ET 194-195 E 3
Šamalzāi ○ AFG 134-135 M 3
Samambaia, Rio ∼ BR 72-73 D 7
Šaman, gora • RUS 122-123 H 3
Sam'ān, Qal'at ☆ SYR 128-129 G 4
Samaná ☆ ·· DOM 54-55 L 5
Samaná, Bahía de ≈ 54-55 L 5
Samaná, Cabo ▲ DOM 54-55 L 5
Samaná, Península ∪ DOM 54-55 L 5
Samana Cay ⌒ BS 54-55 J 3
Samana Cays = Atwood Cays ⌒ BS 54-55 J 3
Samanco ○ PE 64-65 C 6
Samandağ ☆ TR 128-129 F 4
Samandré Lake ○ CDN 30-31 M 2
Samanga ○ EAT (KIL) 212-213 F 5
Samanga ○ EAT (LIN) 214-215 K 5
Samangān ○ AFG (SAM) 136-137 L 6
Samangān ◘ AFG 136-137 K 6
Samangan, Rūd-e ∼ AFG 136-137 K 7
Šamaniha ∼ RUS 110-111 d 7
Šamanij kamen' • RUS 116-117 M 8
Šamanka ∼ RUS 120-121 T 4
Samanturai ○ CL 140-141 J 7
Samaqua, Rivière ∼ CDN (QUE) 236-237 Q 3
Samar ⌒ RP 160-161 F 7
Samara ☆ RUS 96-97 G 7
Samara ∼ RUS 96-97 H 7
Samara ∼ UA 102-103 J 3
Samara ∼ UA 102-103 K 3
Samarai ○ PNG 183 F 6
Samarang, Tanjung ▲ MAL 160-161 B 9
Samarga ○ RUS 122-123 H 5
Samarga ∼ RUS 122-123 H 5
Samari ○ PNG 183 B 5
Samariapo ○ YV 60-61 H 5
Samarinda ☆ • RI 164-165 E 4
Samarkand ☆ ·· US 136-137 K 5
Samarkand = Samarkand ☆ ·· US 136-137 K 5
Samarkandskaja oblast' ◘ US 136-137 H 3
Samarqand = Samarkand ☆ ·· US 136-137 K 5
Sāmarrā' ☆ • IRQ 128-129 K 5
Samar Sea ≈ 160-161 F 6
Samarskoe ○ KA 124-125 N 4
Samarskoe vodohranilišče < RUS 96-97 F 7
Samaru ○ WAN 204-205 G 3
Samastipur ○ IND 142-143 D 3
Samate ○ RI 166-167 F 2
Samatiguila ○ • CI 202-203 G 5
Sāmatra ○ IND 138-139 B 8
Samaúma ○ BR 66-67 F 3
Samāwa, as- ☆ IRQ 128-129 L 7
Samba ○ BF 202-203 J 3
Samba ○ IND 138-139 E 3
Samba ○ RCA 206-207 C 6
Samba ∼ RI 162-163 K 5
Samba ○ ZRE (EQU) 210-211 H 3
Samba ○ ZRE (KIV) 210-211 L 6
Samba Caju ○ ANG 216-217 C 4
Sambailo ○ RG 202-203 D 3
Sambalgou ○ BF 202-203 L 3
Sambaliung Pegunungan ▲ RI 164-165 E 3
Sambalpur ○ IND 142-143 C 5
Sambalpur ○ IND 142-143 C 5
Sambao ∼ RM 222-223 D 6
Sambar, Tanjung ▲ RI 162-163 J 6
Sambas ○ RI 162-163 H 4
Sambas ∼ RI 162-163 H 4
Sambau ○ RI 162-163 F 5
Sambava ○ RM 222-223 G 5
Sambazô, Rio ∼ MOC 218-219 H 4
Samberi ○ RI 166-167 H 2
Sambhal ○ IND 138-139 G 5
Sāmbhar Salt Lake ○ IND 138-139 E 6
Sambialgou ○ BF 202-203 L 3
Sambiar ☆ UA 102-103 C 3
Sambirano ∼ RM 222-223 F 4
Sambisumbi ○ SOL 184 I c 2
Sambito, Rio ∼ BR 68-69 H 5
Sambo ○ ANG 216-217 D 6
Sambo ○ RI 164-165 E 4
Samboja ○ RI 164-165 E 4
Samborombón, Bahía ≈ 78-79 L 3
Samborombón, Río ∼ RA 78-79 L 3
Samborondón ○ EC 64-65 C 2
Sambrānī ○ IND 140-141 F 3
Sambriāl ○ PK 138-139 E 3
Sambro ○ CDN (NS) 240-241 M 6
Samburg ○ RUS 108-109 S 8
Samburu ○ EAK 212-213 G 3
Samburu National Reserve ⊥ EAK 212-213 F 3
Sambusu ○ NAM 216-217 E 8
Samch'ŏk ○ ROK 150-151 G 9
Samch'ŏnp'o ○ ROK 150-151 G 10
Samdrup Jonkhar ○ BHT 142-143 G 2
Same ○ EAT 212-213 F 6
Samene, Oued ∼ DZ 190-191 F 7
Sam Ford Fiord ≈ 26-27 P 8
Samfya ○ Z 214-215 E 6
Samha ⌒ Y 132-133 H 7
Samha, al- ○ UAE 134-135 F 6
Šamhor = Šamkir ○ • AZ 128-129 L 2
Sámi ○ GR 100-101 H 5
Sami ○ IND 138-139 C 8
Samia ○ RN 198-199 D 5
Samia, Tanjung ▲ RI 164-165 H 3
Sāmi ji Veri ○ PK 138-139 C 7
Šāmīlī, aš- ○ KSA 130-131 G 4
Samim, Umm as- ⊥ OM 132-133 J 3
Samirā' ○ KSA 130-131 H 4
Samiria, Río ∼ PE 64-65 E 4
Samita ○ KSA 132-133 C 5
Šāmiya, aš- ⊥ IRQ 130-131 K 2
Samjiyon ○ DVR 150-151 G 7
Samka ○ MYA 142-143 K 5
Šamkir = Šamkir ○ • AZ 128-129 L 2
Šammar, Ğabal ▲ KSA 130-131 F 4
Sām Nām ○ VN 156-157 C 6
Samnū ○ LAR 192-193 F 4
Samo ○ CI 202-203 J 7
Samo ○ PNG 183 G 2
Samoa ○ ANG 216-217 F 4
Samoa Basin ≃ 13 L 4
Sāmoa-i-Sisifo ⌒ WS 184 V b 1
Samoded ○ RUS 88-89 Q 5
Samoé ○ RG 202-203 F 6
Samoedskaja Rečka ∼ RUS 108-109 Y 6
Samojlovka ○ RUS 102-103 N 2
Samokov ○ BG 102-103 C 6
Samoleta, ostrov ⌒ RUS 110-111 N 3
Samorogouan ○ BF 202-203 H 4
Sámos ☆ • GR 100-101 L 6
Sámos ⌒ GR 100-101 L 6
Samosir, Pulau ⌒ RI 162-163 C 3
Samothráki ○ GR 100-101 K 4
Samothráki ⌒ GR 100-101 K 4
Samotlor, ozero ○ RUS 114-115 O 4
Sampa ○ GH 202-203 J 6
Sampacho ○ RA 78-79 G 2
Sampadi ○ MAL 162-163 H 4
Sampaga ○ RI 164-165 F 5
Sampaio ○ BR 68-69 E 4
Sampanago, Ruins of • MYA 142-143 K 3
Sampang ○ RI 168 E 3
Sampara ∼ RI 164-165 H 5
Sampelga ○ BF 202-203 L 3
Sampit ○ RI 162-163 K 6
Sampit ∼ RI 162-163 K 6
Sampit Teluk ≈ 162-163 K 6
Sampolawa ○ RI 164-165 H 6
Sampsel ○ USA (MO) 274-275 E 5
Sampun ○ PNG 183 G 3
Sampwe ○ ZRE 214-215 D 5
Sam Rayburn Lake < USA (TX) 268-269 F 5
Samrē ○ ETH 200-201 J 6
Samreboe ○ GH 202-203 J 7
Sams ○ USA (CO) 254-255 H 5
Samsang ○ VRC 144-145 D 5
Samsherpur ○ IND 138-139 D 10
Šamsiya, aš- ○ KSA 130-131 J 4
Samsø ⌒ DK 86-87 E 9
Samson ○ USA (AL) 284-285 D 5
Sām So'n ○ VN 156-157 D 7
Samson Indian Reserve ✕ CDN (ALB) 232-233 E 3
Samsudin Noor • RI 164-165 D 5
Samsun ☆ • TR 128-129 G 2
Samtredia ○ GE 126-127 E 6
Samucumbi ○ ANG 216-217 E 6
Samuel, Represa de < BR 66-67 F 7
Samuels ○ USA (ID) 250-251 C 3
Samuhú ○ RA 76-77 G 4
Samulondo ○ ZRE 214-215 B 5
Samundri ○ PK 138-139 D 4
Samur ∼ AZ 128-129 N 2
Samur-Apšeronskij kanal < AZ 128-129 N 2
Samuro, Raudal ∼ CO 60-61 G 6
Samut Prakan ○ THA 158-159 F 4
Samut Sakhon ○ THA 158-159 F 4
Samut Songkhram ○ THA 158-159 E 4
San ∼ K 158-159 J 3
San ∼ PL 92-93 R 4
San ○ RMM 202-203 H 3
Saña ○ PE 64-65 C 5
Saná ○ Y 132-133 F 5
Şan'ā' ☆ ··· Y 132-133 D 6
Sanā, Wādī ∼ Y 132-133 F 6
Sanaa = Şan'ā' ☆ ··· Y 132-133 D 6
Sanaag ◘ SP 208-209 H 3
Sanaba ○ BF 202-203 J 3
Sanaba ∼ RMM 202-203 F 2
Sanabria ○ CO 60-61 C 6
Sanāfir, Ğazīrat ⌒ KSA 130-131 D 4
Sanaga ∼ CAM 204-205 K 6
San Agusin ○ YV 60-61 H 4
San Agustín, Arroyo ∼ BOL 70-71 D 3
San Agustín de Valle Fértil ○ RA 76-77 D 6
Sanak ○ USA 22-23 P 5
Sanak Island ⌒ USA 22-23 P 5
Sanak Islands ⌒ USA 22-23 P 5
San Alberto ○ CO 60-61 E 4
San Alejandro ○ PE 64-65 E 6
Sanām, as- ⊥ KSA 132-133 G 3
Sanamain, aš- ○ SYR 128-129 G 6
San Ana ○ BR 66-67 C 2
Sanana ○ RI 164-165 J 5
Sanana, Pulau ⌒ RI 164-165 J 5
Sanandağ ☆ • IR 128-129 M 5
Sanando ○ RMM 202-203 G 3
San Andreas ○ USA (CA) 246-247 E 5
San Andrés ○ C 54-55 G 4
San Andres ○ CO 60-61 D 4
San Andres ○ RP 160-161 E 6
San Andrés, Isla de ⌒ CO 52-53 D 5
San Andres, Quebrada de ∼ RCH 76-77 C 4
San Andrés de Giles ○ RA 78-79 K 3
San Andres de Sotavento ○ CO 60-61 D 3
San Andres Mountains ▲ USA (NM) 256-257 J 6
San Andres National Wildlife Refuge • USA (NM) 256-257 J 6
San Andres Point ▲ RP 160-161 D 6
San Andrés y Sauces ○ E 188-189 C 6
San Andros ○ BS 54-55 F 2
Sananduva ○ BR 74-75 E 6
Sanane Besar, Pulau ⌒ RI 168 D 6
Sananferedougou ○ CI 202-203 G 4
San Angelo ○ USA (TX) 266-267 G 2
Sanankoroba ○ RMM 202-203 G 3
San Anselmo ○ USA (CA) 248-249 B 2
San Anton ○ PE 70-71 B 4
San Antônio ○ BH 52-53 K 3
San Antônio ○ BR 62-63 J 5
San Antonio ○ CO 60-61 B 7
San Antonio ○ MEX 50-51 D 6
San Antonio ○ RA 78-79 F 2
San Antonio ○ RCH 78-79 D 2
San Antonio ○ USA (NM) 256-257 J 5
San Antonio ○ • USA (TX) 266-267 J 4
San Antonio ○ YV 60-61 H 6
San Antonio, Cabo ∪ RA 78-79 L 4
San Antonio, Cabo de ▲ C 54-55 C 4
San Antônio, Cachoeira de ○ BR 62-63 H 6
San Antonio, Río ∼ BOL 76-77 D 1
San Antonio, Sierra ▲ MEX 50-51 D 2
San Antonio Bay ≈ 44-45 J 5
San Antonio Bay ≈ 160-161 B 8
San Antonio Bay ≈ USA 266-267 L 5
San Antonio da Tabasca ○ YV 60-61 K 3
San Antonio de Areco ○ RA 78-79 K 3
San Antonio de Esmoraca ○ BOL 76-77 D 1
San Antonio de Esquilache ○ PE 70-71 B 5
San Antonio de Getucha ○ CO 64-65 E 1
San Antonio de Golfo ○ YV 60-61 K 2
San Antonio de los Baños ○ C 54-55 D 3
San Antonio de los Cobres ○ RA 76-77 D 3
San Antonio del Sur ○ C 54-55 H 4
San Antonio de Tamanaco ○ YV 60-61 H 3
San Antonio El Grande ○ MEX 50-51 G 3
San Antonio Huitepec ○ MEX 52-53 F 3
San Antonio Mountain ▲ USA (NM) 256-257 K 6
San Antonio Oeste ○ RA 78-79 G 6
San Antonio River ∼ USA (TX) 266-267 K 5
San Antonio Villalongín ○ MEX 52-53 D 2
San Antonio y Torcuga, Canal < RA 78-79 H 2
San Ardo ○ USA (CA) 248-249 D 3
Sanaroa Island ⌒ PNG 183 F 5
San Augustín ○ CO 60-61 C 6
San Augustín ○ MEX 50-51 B 3
San Augustín ○ RP 160-161 E 6
San Augustín, Parque Arquelógico • CO 60-61 C 7
San Augustine ○ USA (TX) 268-269 F 5
Sanāw ○ Y 132-133 G 5
Sanāwad ○ IND 138-139 F 8
San Bartolo ○ BOL 70-71 D 4
San Bartolo ○ PE 64-65 D 8
San Bartolomé de Tirajana ○ E 188-189 D 7
Sanbei Yangchang ○ VRC 154-155 E 2
San Benedetto del Tronto ○ I 100-101 D 3
San Benedicto, Isla ⌒ MEX 50-51 C 7
San Benito ○ GCA 52-53 K 3
San Benito ○ NIC 52-53 L 5
San Benito ○ USA (TX) 266-267 K 7
San Benito Abad ○ CO 60-61 D 3
San Benito Mountain ▲ USA (CA) 248-249 D 3
San Bernardino ○ USA (CA) 248-249 G 5
San Bernardino Strait ≈ 160-161 F 6
San Bernard National Wildlife Refuge ⊥ USA (TX) 266-267 M 5
San Bernardo ○ RA (BUA) 78-79 J 4
San Bernardo ○ RA (SAF) 76-77 G 5
San Bernardo ○ RCH 78-79 D 2
San Bernardo, Islas de ⌒ CO 60-61 C 3
San Bernardo, Punta ▲ CO 60-61 C 3
San Bernardo del Viento ○ CO 60-61 D 3
San Bernhard River ∼ USA (TX) 268-269 E 7
San Blas ○ MEX (COA) 50-51 J 4
San Blas ○ MEX (SIN) 50-51 E 4
San Blas ○ MEX (NAY) 50-51 G 7
San Blas, Archipiélago de ⌒ ·· PA 52-53 E 7
San Blas, Cape ▲ USA (FL) 286-287 D 2
San Blas, Cordillera de ▲ PA 52-53 E 7
San Borja ○ BOL 70-71 D 4
San Borja, Sierra de ▲ MEX 50-51 C 3
Sanborn ○ USA (MN) 270-271 C 6
Sanbornville ○ USA (NH) 278-279 K 5
San Buenaventura ○ BOL 70-71 D 4
San Buenaventura ○ MEX 50-51 J 4
San Buenaventura, Cordillera de ▲ RA 76-77 C 4
Sanca ○ CDN (BC) 230-231 N 4
Sança ○ MOC 218-219 H 3
San Carlos ○ MEX (BCS) 50-51 C 5
San Carlos ○ MEX (COA) 50-51 J 3
San Carlos ○ MEX (TAM) 50-51 K 5
San Carlos ☆ • NIC 52-53 B 6
San Carlos ○ • PA 52-53 E 7
San Carlos ○ RA (MEN) 78-79 E 2
San Carlos ○ RA (SAE) 76-77 F 5
San Carlos ○ RCH 78-79 D 4
San Carlos ○ ROU 78-79 M 3
San Carlos ○ RP (NED) 160-161 E 7
San Carlos ○ RP (PAN) 160-161 D 5
San Carlos ○ USA (AZ) 256-257 E 5
San Carlos ☆ YV 60-61 G 3
San Carlos, Arroyo ∼ RA 78-79 E 3
San Carlos, Caldera de ▲ GQ 210-211 B 2
San Carlos = Ciudad Quesada ○ CR 52-53 B 6
San Carlos, Punta ▲ MEX 50-51 C 4
San Carlos, Río ∼ CR 52-53 B 6
San Carlos, Río ∼ PY 76-77 H 2
San Carlos Bay ≈ 48-49 G 6
San Carlos Bay ≈ USA 286-287 G 5
San Carlos de Bariloche ○ • RA 78-79 D 6
San Carlos de Bolívar ○ RA 78-79 J 4
San Carlos de Guaroa ○ CO 60-61 E 6
San Carlos del Meta ○ YV 60-61 H 4
San Carlos del Zulia ○ YV 60-61 F 3
San Carlos de Río Negro ○ YV 66-67 D 2
San Carlos Indian Reservation ✕ USA (AZ) 256-257 E 5
San Carlos Lake ○ USA (AZ) 256-257 E 5
San Carlos Yautepec ○ MEX 52-53 F 3
San Cayetano ○ CO 60-61 D 5
San Cayetano ○ RA 78-79 K 5
Sancha ○ VRC (GXI) 156-157 F 4
Sancha ○ VRC (SHA) 154-155 G 2
Sanchakou ○ VRC 146-147 D 6
Sánchez ○ DOM 54-55 L 5
Sánchez, Cerro ▲ RA 80 F 5
Sánchez Magallanes ○ • MEX 52-53 H 2
Sanchi ○ ··· IND 138-139 F 8
Sanchi River ∼ PNG 183 B 2
Sancho, Corrego ∼ BR 68-69 D 6
Sānchor ○ IND 138-139 C 7
San Christóbal, Quebrada ∼ RCH 76-77 C 2
San Cirilo, Cerro ▲ PE 64-65 C 5
San Clara ○ CDN (MAN) 234-235 B 3
San Clemente ○ E 98-99 F 5
San Clemente ○ RCH 78-79 D 3
San Clemente ○ USA (CA) 248-249 G 6
San Clemente del Tuyú ○ RA 78-79 L 4
San Clemente Island ⌒ USA (CA) 248-249 F 7
San Clemente o San Valentín, Cerro ▲ RCH 80 D 3
Sanclerlândia ○ BR 72-73 E 4
Sanco ○ USA (TX) 264-265 D 6
Sancos ○ PE 64-65 F 9
San Cosme y Damián ○ ··· PY 76-77 J 4
San Cristóbal ○ BOL 76-77 D 1
San Cristóbal ○ C 54-55 D 3
San Cristóbal ☆ • DOM 54-55 K 5
San Cristóbal ○ PA 52-53 D 7
San Cristobal ○ RA 76-77 G 6
San Cristóbal ○ RCH 76-77 C 2
San Cristobal ⌒ SOL 184 I e 4
San Cristóbal ☆ YV 60-61 E 3
San Cristóbal, Isla ⌒ EC 64-65 C 10
San Cristóbal, Volcán ▲ NIC 52-53 L 5
San Cristóbal de la Laguna = La Laguna ○ E 188-189 C 6
San Cristóbal de las Casas ○ ·· MEX 52-53 H 3
San Cristobal Trench ≃ 184 I e 4
San Cristobal Wash ∼ USA (AZ) 256-257 B 6
Sancti Spíritu ○ RA 78-79 H 3
Sancti Spíritus ☆ • C 54-55 F 4
Sanctuaire des Addax, Réserve Naturelle Intégrale Dite ⊥ RN 198-199 D 3
Sanctuary ○ CDN (SAS) 232-233 K 5
Sančursk ○ RUS 96-97 E 5
Sancy, Puy de ▲ • F 90-91 J 9
Sand ☆ N 86-87 C 7
Sand ∼ ZA 218-219 E 6
Sandafa al-Far ○ ET 194-195 E 3
Sandakan ○ MAL 160-161 C 10
Sandakan, Teluk ≈ 160-161 B 10
Šāndak Bālā ∼ IR 134-135 H 4
Sandal, ozero ○ RUS 88-89 M 5
Sandama ○ RG 202-203 F 3
Sandando ○ ANG 216-217 F 5
Sandane ☆ N 86-87 C 6
Sandanski ○ BG 102-103 C 7
Sandaré ○ RMM 202-203 E 2
Sand Arroyo River ∼ USA (CO) 254-255 N 6
Sanday ⌒ GB 90-91 F 2
Sandbank Lake ○ CDN 34-35 P 5
Sandberg ○ ZA 220-221 D 6
Sandburg Home National Historic Site, Carl • USA (NC) 282-283 E 5
Sand Creek ∼ USA (CO) 254-255 M 4
Sandefjord ☆ N 86-87 E 7
Sandégué ○ CI 202-203 J 6
Sandema ○ GH 202-203 K 4
Sanderão ○ IND 138-139 D 7
Sanders ○ USA (AZ) 256-257 F 3
Sanderson ○ USA (TX) 266-267 E 3
Sanderson Canyon ∼ USA (TX) 266-267 E 4
Sanderson Lake ○ CDN 30-31 R 5
Sandersville ○ USA (GA) 284-285 H 3
Sandfire Flat Roadhouse ○ AUS 172-173 E 5
Sandfloeggi ▲ N 86-87 C 7
Sandfly Island = Mbokonimbeti Island ⌒ SOL 184 I d 3
Sandford Lake ○ CDN (ONT) 234-235 M 5
Sandhill ○ CDN (ONT) 238-239 F 5
Sandhill ○ USA (MS) 268-269 L 4
Sand Hill ○ USA (MS) 268-269 M 5
Sand Hill River ∼ CDN 38-39 Q 2
Sand Hill River ∼ USA (MN) 270-271 B 3
Sand Hills ▲ USA (NE) 262-263 E 2
Sandhornøy ⌒ N 86-87 G 3
Šandi ○ SUD 200-201 F 4
Sandia ○ PE 70-71 C 4
Sandia Crest ▲ USA (NM) 256-257 J 3
Sandian He ∼ VRC 148-149 M 7
San Diego ○ USA (TX) 266-267 J 6
San Diego ○ • USA (CA) 248-249 G 7
San Diego, Cabo ▲ RA 80 H 7
San Diego de Alcala • USA (CA) 248-249 G 7
San Diego de la Unión ○ MEX 50-51 J 7
Sandies Creek ∼ USA (TX) 266-267 K 4
Sandıklı ☆ TR 128-129 D 3
Sandila ○ IND 142-143 B 2
Sandilands Forest Reserve ⊥ CDN (MAN) 234-235 G 5
Sanding, Pulau ⌒ RI 162-163 D 6
Sanding, Selat ≈ 162-163 D 6
Sandino ○ C 54-55 C 3
San Dionisio del Mar ○ MEX 52-53 G 3
Sand Islands ⌒ USA 20-21 G 5
Sand Lake ○ CDN (ONT) 236-237 D 5
Sand Lake ○ CDN (ONT) 238-239 F 3
Sand Lake ○ CDN (NWT) 30-31 U 3
Sand Lake ○ CDN (ONT) 234-235 J 4
Sandlake ○ USA (OR) 244-245 B 5
Sand Lake ○ USA (OK) 264-265 H 2
Sand Mountains ▲ USA (AL) 284-285 D 2
Sandnes ☆ N 86-87 B 7
Sandnessjøen ○ N 86-87 F 3
Sandoa ○ ZRE 214-215 B 5
Sandomierska, Kotlina ∪ PL 92-93 Q 3
Sandomierz ○ ·· PL 92-93 Q 3
Sandougou ○ CI 202-203 H 6
Sandougou ∼ SN 202-203 C 3
Sandoval ○ USA (IL) 274-275 J 6
Sandover Highway II AUS 178-179 D 1
Sandover River ∼ AUS 178-179 C 1
Sandovo ○ RUS 94-95 P 2
Sandoway ○ MYA 142-143 J 6
Sand Pass ▲ USA (UT) 254-255 B 4
Sand Point ○ CDN (NS) 240-241 O 5
Sand Point ○ USA 22-23 Q 5
Sandpoint ○ USA (ID) 250-251 C 3
Sandrakatsy ○ RM 222-223 F 6
Sandrakota ∼ RM 222-223 F 5
Sandratsino ∼ RM 222-223 F 6
Sandridge ○ CDN (MAN) 234-235 F 4
Šandrin ∼ RUS 110-111 c 4
Sand River ∼ CDN 32-33 P 4
Sandriver ∼ ZA 220-221 H 4
Sandrum ∼ RUS 110-111 d 4
Sandspit ○ CDN (BC) 228-229 C 3
Sand Springs ○ USA (MT) 250-251 M 4
Sand Springs ○ USA (OK) 264-265 H 2
Sandstad ○ N 86-87 D 5
Sandstone ○ AUS 176-177 E 4
Sandstone ○ USA (MN) 270-271 F 4
Sandur ○ IND 140-141 G 3
Sandusky ○ USA (MI) 272-273 G 4
Sandusky ○ USA (OH) 280-281 D 2
Sandusky River ∼ USA (OH) 280-281 C 3
Sandveld Nature Reserve ⊥ ZA 220-221 G 3
Sandvig ○ DK 86-87 G 9
Sandvika ○ S 86-87 F 5
Sandviken ☆ S 86-87 H 6
Sandvisbaai ≈ 220-221 B 1
Sandwich ○ USA (IL) 274-275 K 3
Sandwich, Cape ▲ AUS 174-175 J 6
Sandwich Bay ○ CDN 38-39 Q 2
Sandwich Harbour ○ NAM 220-221 B 1
Sandwip ○ BD 142-143 G 4
Sandwip ⌒ BD 142-143 G 4
Sandwith ○ CDN (SAS) 232-233 K 2
Sandy ○ USA (OR) 244-245 C 5
Sandy ○ USA (UT) 254-255 D 3
Sandy Bar ▲ CDN (MAN) 234-235 F 2
Sandy Bay ○ CDN 34-35 E 3
Sandy Bay Indian Reserve ✕ CDN (MAN) 234-235 E 4
Sandy Beach ○ CDN (ALB) 232-233 D 2
Sandy Bight ≈ 176-177 G 6
Sandy Cape ▲ AUS 178-179 M 3
Sandy Cove ○ CDN (NS) 240-241 J 6
Sandy Creek ∼ AUS 178-179 G 2
Sandy Creek ∼ USA 180-181 H 2
Sandy Creek ∼ USA (NE) 262-263 J 4
Sandy Creek ∼ USA (WY) 252-253 J 4
Sandy Desert ⊥ PK 134-135 K 4
Sandy Harbor Beach ○ USA (NY) 278-279 D 5
Sandy Hills ▲ USA (TX) 264-265 J 6
Sandy Hook ○ USA (KY) 276-277 M 2
Sandy Hook ○ USA (MS) 268-269 L 5
Sandykači ○ TM 136-137 H 6
Sandy Lake ○ CDN (ALB) 32-33 O 4
Sandy Lake ○ CDN (MAN) 234-235 C 4
Sandy Lake ○ CDN (ONT) 34-35 K 4
Sandy Lake ○ CDN (NFL) 242-243 M 3
Sandy Lake ○ CDN (NWT) 20-21 Z 3
Sandy Lake ○ CDN (ONT) 234-235 K 2
Sandy Lake ○ USA (PA) 280-281 F 2
Sandy Lake Indian Reserve ✕ CDN 34-35 K 4
Sandy Point ○ BS 54-55 G 1
Sandy Point ▲ IND 140-141 L 4
Sandy Ridge ○ USA (NC) 282-283 G 4
Sandy River ∼ CDN 36-37 P 7
Sandy River ∼ USA (TN) 276-277 G 4
Sandy Springs ○ USA (OH) 280-281 C 5
San Estanislao ○ CO 60-61 D 2
San Estanislao ○ PY 76-77 J 3
San Esteban ○ HN 54-55 C 7
San Esteban ○ MEX 50-51 C 4
San Estéban, Golfo ≈ 80 C 3
San Esteban, Isla ⌒ MEX 50-51 C 3
San Felipe ○ MEX (GTO) 50-51 J 7
San Felipe ○ MEX (YUC) 52-53 K 1
San Felipe ○ • MEX (BCN) 50-51 B 2
San Felipe ○ RCH 78-79 D 2
San Felipe ☆ YV 60-61 G 2
San Felipe, Bahía ≈ 80 F 6
San Felipe, Castillo de • GCA 52-53 K 4
San Felipe, Cayos de ⌒ C 54-55 D 4
San Felipe, Parque Natural ⊥ MEX 52-53 K 1
San Felipe de Vichayal ○ PE 64-65 B 4
San Felipe Nuevo Mercurio ○ MEX 50-51 H 5
San Felipe Pueblo ○ USA (NM) 256-257 J 3
San Félix ○ YV 60-61 F 2
San Fernando ○ E 98-99 D 6
San Fernando ○ MEX 50-51 K 5
San Fernando ○ RA 76-77 D 4
San Fernando ○ RCH 78-79 D 3
San Fernando ☆ RP (LUN) 160-161 D 4
San Fernando ☆ RP (PAM) 160-161 D 5
San Fernando ○ TT 60-61 L 2
San Fernando ○ USA (CA) 248-249 F 5
San Fernando, Río ∼ BOL 70-71 H 5
San Fernando, Río ∼ MEX 50-51 K 5
San Fernando de Apure ☆ YV 60-61 H 4
San Fernando de Atabapo ○ YV 60-61 H 5
San Fernando del Valle de Catamarca ☆ • RA 76-77 E 5
Sånfjället nationalpark ⊥ S 86-87 F 5
Sanford ○ CDN (MAN) 234-235 F 5
Sanford ○ USA (FL) 286-287 H 3
Sanford ○ USA (ME) 278-279 L 5
Sanford ○ USA (NC) 282-283 H 5
Sanford, Mount ▲ USA 20-21 S 5
Sanford River ∼ AUS 176-177 D 3
San Francisco ○ BOL 70-71 E 5
San Francisco ○ BOL 70-71 E 4
San Francisco ☆ ES 52-53 K 5
San Francisco ○ PE 64-65 F 8
San Francisco ○ RA 76-77 F 6
San Francisco ○ RP 160-161 F 8
San Francisco ○ ·· USA (CA) 248-249 B 2
San Francisco ○ YV 60-61 F 2
San Francisco, Cabo de ▲ EC 64-65 B 1
San Francisco, Igarapé ∼ BR 66-67 C 7
San Francisco, Paso de ▲ RA 76-77 C 4
San Francisco, Río ∼ RA 76-77 C 6
San Francisco, Sierra de ▲ ··· MEX 50-51 C 4
San Francisco Bay ≈ 40-41 C 7
San Francisco Bay ≈ USA 248-249 B 2
San Francisco Creek ∼ USA (TX) 266-267 E 4
San Francisco de Becerra ○ HN 52-53 L 4
San Francisco de Bellocq ○ RA 78-79 J 5
San Francisco de Borja ○ MEX 50-51 F 4
San Francisco de Horizonte ○ MEX 50-51 H 5
San Francisco de Laishi ○ RA 76-77 H 4
San Francisco de la Paz ○ HN 52-53 L 4
San Francisco del Chañar ○ RA 76-77 F 5
San Francisco del Oro ○ MEX 50-51 G 4
San Francisco del Rincón ○ MEX 52-53 D 1
San Francisco de Macoris ☆ DOM 54-55 K 5
San Francisco de Mostazal ○ RCH 78-79 D 2
San Francisco Ixhuatán ○ MEX 52-53 G 3
San Francisco River ∼ USA (AZ) 256-257 F 5
San Francisco River ∼ USA (NM) 256-257 G 5
San Francisco Wash ∼ USA (AZ) 256-257 D 3
San Franciquito ○ MEX 50-51 C 3
Sang ○ GH 202-203 K 5
Sanga ○ ANG 216-217 C 5
Sanga ○ BF 202-203 L 4
Sanga ○ EAU 212-213 C 4
Sanga ○ MOC 214-215 H 7
Sanga ○ • RMM 202-203 J 2
San Gabriel ○ EC 64-65 D 1
San Gabriel da Cachoeira ○ BR 66-67 D 3
San Gabriel Mixtepec ○ MEX 52-53 F 3
San Gabriel Mountains ▲ USA (CA) 248-249 F 5
San Gabriel River ∼ USA (TX) 266-267 K 3
Sangagüey, Volcán ▲ MEX 50-51 G 7
Sanga-Jurjah ∼ RUS 110-111 X 3
Sangala ○ RI 164-165 G 5
San Gallan, Isla ⌒ PE 64-65 D 8
Sangama ○ EAT 214-215 G 5
Sangameshwar ○ IND 140-141 E 2
Sangamner ○ IND 138-139 E 10
Sangamon River ∼ USA (IL) 274-275 J 4
Sangān ○ IR 134-135 J 1
Sanganer ○ IND 138-139 E 6
Sangar ☆ RUS 118-119 N 4
Sangardo ○ RG 202-203 E 5
Sangarh ∼ PK 138-139 C 4
Sangata ○ RI 164-165 E 3
Sangau, Tanjung ▲ RI 162-163 F 5
Sangāv ○ IRQ 128-129 L 5
Sangay, Parque Nacional de ⊥ ··· EC 64-65 C 2
Sangay, Volcan ▲ EC 64-65 C 2
Sangayam ○ RI 164-165 D 5
Sangbast ○ IR 136-137 F 7
Sangbé ○ CAM 204-205 K 5
Sangbor ○ AFG 136-137 H 7
Sang Čarak ○ AFG 136-137 K 7
Sangchris Lake ○ USA (IL) 274-275 J 5
Sange ○ ZRE 214-215 E 4
Sangeang, Pulau ⌒ RI 168 D 7
San Genaro ○ RA 78-79 J 2
Sanger ○ USA (CA) 248-249 E 3
Sanger ○ USA (TX) 264-265 G 5
San Germán ○ • USA (PR) 286-287 O 2
Sanggan He ∼ VRC 154-155 J 1
Sanggau ○ RI 162-163 J 4
Sangha ◘ RCB 210-211 E 3
Sangha ∼ RCB 210-211 F 3
Sangha-Mbaéré ◘ RCA 210-211 E 3
Sanghar ○ PK 138-139 B 6
Sangiang, Pulau ⌒ RI 162-163 F 7
Sangihe, Kepulauan ⌒ RI 164-165 J 2
Sangijn Dalaj ○ MAU 148-149 G 4
Sangijn Dalaj nuur ○ MAU 148-149 D 3
San Gil ○ CO 60-61 E 4
Sangifka ∼ RUS 114-115 Q 4
San Gimignano ○ ··· I 100-101 C 3
Sangin ○ AFG 134-135 L 2
Sangina ∼ RUS 110-111 b 5
Sanginkylä ○ FIN 88-89 J 4
San Giovanni in Fiore ○ I 100-101 F 5

388 Salmon River — San Giovanni in Fiore

Sangir, Kepulauan ⌒ RI 164-165 J 2
Sangir, Pulau ⌒ RI 164-165 J 2
Sangkha Buri ○ THA 158-159 E 3
Sangkulirang ○ RI 164-165 E 3
Sāngla Hill ○ PK 138-139 D 4
Sāngli ○• IND 140-141 F 2
Sanglia Dol (Traditional Village) ○• RI 166-167 F 5
Sangmelima ○• CAM 210-211 D 2
Sango ○ ZW 218-219 F 6
Sangola ○ IND 140-141 F 2
Sangolquí ○ EC 64-65 C 2
Sangonera, Río ~ E 98-99 G 6
Sangoshe ○ RB 218-219 B 4
San Gottardo, Passo del ▲ CH 92-93 K 5
Sangouani ○ CI 202-203 G 5
Sangouiné ○ CI 202-203 G 6
Sangowo ○ RI 164-165 L 2
Sangradouro, Área Indígena ✕ BR 72-73 D 3
Sangraduoro, Rio ~ BR 70-71 J 5
Sangrafa ○ RIM 196-197 D 6
Sangre de Cristo Mountains ▲ USA (CO) 254-255 K 6
San Gregorio ○ MEX 52-53 J 4
San Gregorio ○ PE 64-65 F 6
San Gregorio ○ USA (CA) 248-249 B 2
San Gregorio Carrio ○ ROU 78-79 L 2
Sangre Grande ○ TT 60-61 L 2
Sangrūr ○ IND 138-139 E 4
Sangsang ○ VRC 144-145 F 6
Sangudo ○ CDN (ALB) 232-233 D 2
Sangue, Rio do ~ BR 70-71 H 2
Sanguéya ○ RG 202-203 C 4
Sanguiana ○ RG 202-203 E 4
San Guillermo ○ RP 160-161 D 4
Sangutane, Rio ~ MOC 218-219 G 6
Sangwali ○ NAM 218-219 B 4
Sangzhi ○ VRC 156-157 G 2
Sanhala ○ CI 202-203 G 4
Šanhar ○ RUS 116-117 K 9
San Hilario ○ RA 76-77 H 4
Sâni ○ RIM 196-197 E 6
Sanibel ○ USA (FL) 286-287 G 5
Sanibel Island ⌒ USA (FL) 286-287 G 5
San Ignacio ○ CR 52-53 B 7
San Ignacio ○ MEX (SIN) 50-51 F 6
San Ignacio ○• MEX (BCS) 50-51 C 4
San Ignacio ○ PE 64-65 C 4
San Ignacio ○ PY 76-77 J 4
San Ignacio ○ YV 62-63 D 3
San Ignacio, Isla de ⌒ MEX 50-51 E 5
San Ignacio de Velasco ○ BOL 70-71 G 5
San Ignazio ○ BR 52-53 K 3
San Ildefonso, Cape ▲ RP 160-161 E 4
Sanipas ▲ LS 220-221 J 4
Sanire ○ PE 70-71 B 3
San Isidro ○ NIC 52-53 L 5
San Isidro ○ RA 78-79 K 3
San Isidro ○ USA (TX) 266-267 J 7
San Isidro ○ YV 62-63 D 2
San Isidro de El General ○ CR 52-53 C 7
San Jacinto ○ PE 64-65 B 4
San Jacinto ○ RP 160-161 E 6
San Jacinto, East Fork ~ USA (TX) 268-269 E 6
San Jacinto, Mount ▲ USA (CA) 248-249 H 6
San Jacinto, West Fork ~ USA (TX) 268-269 E 6
San Jaime ○ RA 76-77 H 6
San Janvier ○ E 98-99 G 6
San Javier ○ BOL 70-71 E 4
San Javier ○ MEX 50-51 D 5
San Javier ○ RA (COD) 78-79 G 2
San Javier ○ RA (SAF) 76-77 H 6
San Javier, Río ~ RA 76-77 H 5
San Javier de Loncomilla ○ RCH 78-79 D 3
Sanje ○ EAU 212-213 C 4
San Jeronimo, Isla ⌒ RA 76-77 H 5
Sanjia ○ VRC 156-157 G 5
Sanjiang ○ VRC 156-157 F 4
Sanjiaotang ○ VRC 156-157 M 2
Sanjō ○ J 152-153 H 6
San Joaquim ○ BR 62-63 K 6
San Joaquín ○ MEX 52-53 E 1
San Joaquín ○ RA 78-79 H 3
San Joaquín ○ YV 60-61 H 2
San Joaquin ○ YV 60-61 J 3
San Joaquín, Cerro ▲ EC 64-65 C 10
San Joaquín, Río ~ BOL 70-71 F 3
San Joaquin River ~ USA (CA) 248-249 D 2
San Joaquin Valley ⌣ USA (CA) 248-249 C 2
San Jon ○ USA (NM) 256-257 M 3
San Jorge ○ CO 60-61 G 4
San Jorge ○ RA 76-77 G 6
San Jorge ○ ROU 78-79 M 2
San Jorge, Bahía ≈ 50-51 C 2
San Jorge, Golfo ≈ 80 G 2
San Jorge, Río ~ CO 60-61 D 3
San Jorge Island ⌒ SOL 184 I d 3
San José ○ CO 64-65 D 1
San José ★ CR 52-53 B 7
San José ○ E 98-99 F 6
San José ○ HN 52-53 L 4
San José ○ MEX 50-51 D 4
San José ~ MEX 50-51 E 6
San José ○ PY 76-77 J 3
San José ○ RA (CAT) 76-77 D 4
San José ○ RA (MIS) 76-77 K 4
San Jose ○ RP (MID) 160-161 D 6
San Jose ○ RP (NEC) 160-161 D 5
San Jose ☆ RP (ANT) 160-161 D 7
San Jose ○ USA (CA) 248-249 C 2
San Jose ○ USA (IL) 274-275 J 4
San José ○ YV 60-61 E 2
San José, Golfo ≈ 78-79 G 7
San José, Isla ⌒ MEX 50-51 D 5
San José, Isla ⌒ PA 52-53 E 7
San José, Río ~ RCH 78-79 C 5
San Jose, Rio ~ USA (NM) 256-257 H 4
San José, Volcán ▲ RA 78-79 E 2
San José de Amacuro ○ YV 60-61 L 3
San José de Buja ○ YV 60-61 K 3
San José de Chimbo ○ EC 64-65 C 2
San José de Chiquitos ○••• BOL 70-71 G 5
San José de Dimas ○ MEX 50-51 D 3
San José de Feliciano ○ RA 76-77 H 6
San José de Gracia ○ MEX 50-51 F 4
San José de Guanipa ○ YV 60-61 J 3
San José de Guaribe ○ YV 60-61 J 3
San José de Jáchal ○ RA 76-77 C 6
San José de la Dormida ○ RA 76-77 F 6
San Jose del Alto ○ PE 64-65 C 4
San José de la Mariquina ○ RCH 78-79 C 5
San José de las Lajas ○ C 54-55 D 3
San José del Cabo ○• MEX 50-51 E 6
San José del Guaviare ○ CO 60-61 E 6
San José del Monte ○ RP 160-161 D 5
San José del Morro ○ RA 78-79 G 2
San José del Palmar ○ CO 60-61 C 5
San José del Progreso ○ MEX 52-53 F 3
San José de Maipo ○ RCH 78-79 D 2
San José de Mayo ☆ ROU 78-79 L 3
San José de Ocoa ○ DOM 54-55 K 5
San Jose de Quero ○ PE 64-65 E 8
San José de Raíces ○ MEX 50-51 J 5
San Jose Island ⌒ USA (TX) 266-267 L 6
San José Iturbide ○ MEX 50-51 J 7
San Jose River ~ CDN (BC) 230-231 H 2
Sanju ○ VRC 144-145 B 2
San Juan ○ BOL 70-71 G 6
San Juán ○ BOL 70-71 D 7
San Juan ☆ DOM 54-55 K 5
San Juan ○ PE (ICA) 64-65 E 9
San Juan ○ PE (LOR) 66-67 B 5
San Juan ◘ RA 76-77 C 6
San Juan ☆• RA (SAJ) 76-77 C 6
San Juan ○ RCH 76-77 C 2
San Juan ○ RP 160-161 F 7
San Juan ○ USA (AK) 20-21 Q 6
San Juan ☆••• USA (PR) 286-287 P 2
San Juan, Bahía ≈ 64-65 E 9
San Juan, Cabo ▲ GQ 210-211 B 3
San Juan, Cabo ▲ RA 80 J 7
San Juan, Punta ▲ PE 64-65 E 9
San Juan, Quebrada ~ RCH 76-77 B 5
San Juan, Río ~ BOL 70-71 D 6
San Juan, Río ~ BOL 76-77 E 1
San Juan, Río ~ CO 60-61 C 5
San Juan, Río ~ DOM 54-55 K 5
San Juan, Río ~ MEX 50-51 G 5
San Juan, Río ~ NIC 52-53 B 6
San Juan, Río ~ PY 76-77 H 2
San Juan, Río ~ RA 76-77 C 6
San Juan, Río ~ RA 78-79 F 2
San Juan, Río ~ ROU 78-79 L 3
San Juan, Río ~ YV 60-61 K 2
San Juan Bautista ☆ PY 76-77 J 4
San Juan Bautista ○ RCH 78-79 C 1
San Juan Bautista ○ YV 60-61 K 2
San Juan Capistrano ○ USA (CA) 248-249 G 6
San Juan Chiquihuitlán ○ MEX 52-53 F 3
San Juan de Alacant ○ E 98-99 G 6
San Juan de Alicante = San Juan de Alacant ○ E 98-99 G 5
San Juan de Arama ○ CO 60-61 E 6
San Juan de Colon ○ YV 60-61 E 3
San Juán de Flores ○ HN 52-53 L 4
San Juan de Guadalupe ○ MEX 50-51 H 5
San Juan de la Costa ○ MEX 50-51 D 5
San Juán del Caite ○ HN 52-53 K 4
San Juan del César ○ CO 60-61 E 2
San Juan de Lima, Punta ▲ MEX 52-53 C 2
San Juán de Limay ○ NIC 52-53 L 5
San Juan del Norte, Bahía de ≈ 52-53 C 6
San Juan de los Cayos ○ YV 60-61 G 2
San Juan de los Galdonas ○ YV 60-61 K 2
San Juan de los Lagos ○ MEX 50-51 H 7
San Juan de los Morros ☆ YV 60-61 H 3
San Juan de los Planes ○• MEX 50-51 E 6
San Juan del Río ○ MEX (DGO) 50-51 G 5
San Juan del Río ○ MEX (QRO) 52-53 E 1
San Juán del Sur ○ NIC 52-53 B 6
San Juan de Manpiare ○ YV 60-61 H 5
San Juan de Pastocalle ○ EC 64-65 C 2
San Juan de Sabinas ○ MEX 50-51 J 4
San Juan de Tocoma ○ YV 60-61 K 4
San Juan de Yanac ○ PE 64-65 E 8
San Juan Evangelista ○ MEX 52-53 G 3
San Juan Indian Reservation ✕ USA (NM) 256-257 J 2
San Juan Islands ⌒ USA (WA) 244-245 C 2
San Juanito ○ MEX 50-51 F 4
San Juanito, Isla ⌒ MEX 50-51 F 7
San Juan Ixcaquixtla ○ MEX 52-53 F 2
San Juan Mountains ▲ USA (CO) 254-255 H 6
San Juan National Historic Park ⊥ USA 244-245 B 2
San Juan River ~ USA (CA) 248-249 D 4
San Juan River ~ USA (UT) 254-255 E 6
San Juan Seamount ≃ 248-249 D 6
San Juan y Martínez ○ C 54-55 D 3
San Just, Puerto de ▲ E 98-99 G 4
San Justo ○ RA 76-77 G 6
Sankadiakro ○ CI 202-203 J 6
Sankarani ~ RG 202-203 F 4
Sankarankovil ○ IND 140-141 G 6
Sankari Drug ○ IND 140-141 G 5
Sankha ○ THA 158-159 G 3
Sankosh ○ BHT 142-143 G 2
Sankosh ~ BHT 142-143 F 2
Sankra ○ IND 138-139 G 5
Sankt Gallen ☆••• CH 92-93 K 5
Sankt Gotthardpass = Passo del San Gottardo ▲ CH 92-93 K 5
Sankt Joachimsthal = Jáchymov ○ CZ 92-93 M 3
Sankt Moritz ○• CH 92-93 K 5
Sankt-Peterburg ☆••• RUS 94-95 M 2
Sankt Peter-Ording ○ D 92-93 K 1
Sankt Pölten ☆ A 92-93 N 4
Sankulirang, Teluk ≈ 164-165 F 3
Sankuru ~ ZRE 210-211 J 6
San Leonardo de Yagüe ○ E 98-99 F 4
Sanlifan ○ VRC 154-155 J 6
Şanlı Urfa ☆• TR 128-129 H 4
San Lorenzo ○ BOL 70-71 H 5
San Lorenzo ○ CO 60-61 F 4
San Lorenzo ○ EC (ESM) 64-65 C 1
San Lorenzo ○ EC (MAN) 64-65 B 2
San Lorenzo ○ HN 52-53 L 5
San Lorenzo ○ PE 70-71 C 2
San Lorenzo ○ RA 76-77 H 5
San Lorenzo ○ RP 160-161 E 5
San Lorenzo ○ USA (NM) 256-257 H 6
San Lorenzo ○ USA (PR) 286-287 Q 2
San Lorenzo ○ YV 60-61 E 2
San Lorenzo, Cabo ▲ EC 64-65 B 2
San Lorenzo, Cerro ▲ PE 64-65 C 5
San Lorenzo, Isla ⌒ MEX 50-51 C 3
San Lorenzo, Isla ⌒ PE 64-65 D 8
San Lorenzo, Río ~ MEX 50-51 F 5
San Lorenzo, Río ~ MEX 50-51 K 5
San Lorenzo, Sierra de ▲ E 98-99 F 3
San Louis Pass ≈ USA 268-269 E 7
San Lourdes ○ BOL 70-71 C 2
Sanlúcar de Barrameda ○ E 98-99 D 6
Sanlúcar la Mayor ○ E 98-99 D 6
San Lucas ○ USA (CA) 248-249 C 3
San Lucas, Cabo ▲•• MEX 50-51 E 6
San Luis ○ C 54-55 H 4
San Luis ○ CO 60-61 D 4
San Luis ○ GCA 52-53 K 3
San Luis ○ MEX 50-51 C 1
San Luis ◘ RA 78-79 F 2
San Luis ☆ RA 78-79 F 2
San Luis ○ RCH 76-77 C 4
San Luis ○ ROU 74-75 D 9
San Luis ○ RP 160-161 F 7
San Luis ○ USA (AZ) 256-257 D 6
San Luis ○ USA (CO) 254-255 K 6
San Luis ○ YV 60-61 G 2
San Luis, Lago de ⊖ BOL 70-71 E 3
San Luis, Sierra de ▲ RA 78-79 F 2
San Luis Acatlán ○ MEX 52-53 E 3
San Luis Canal < USA (CA) 248-249 D 3
San Luis Creek ~ USA (CO) 254-255 K 5
San Luis del Cordero ○ MEX 50-51 G 5
San Luis del Palmar ○• RA 76-77 H 4
San Luis de Shuaro ○ PE 64-65 F 7
San Luis Obispo ○ USA (CA) 248-249 D 4
San Luis Potosí ◘ MEX 50-51 H 6
San Luis Potosí ☆•• MEX (SLP) 50-51 J 6
San Luis Reservoir ⊖ USA (CA) 248-249 C 2
San Luis Rey de Francia • USA (CA) 248-249 G 6
San Luis Río Colorado ○• MEX 50-51 B 1
San Luis San Pedro ○ MEX 52-53 D 3
San Luis Valley ⌣ USA (CO) 254-255 K 6
San Luiz de la Paz ○ MEX 50-51 J 7
Sanluri ○ I 100-101 B 5
San Manuel ○ C 54-55 G 4
San Manuel ○ USA (AZ) 256-257 E 6
San Marcial ○ USA (NM) 256-257 J 5
San Marco, Capo ▲ I 100-101 B 5
San Marco, Capo ▲ I 100-101 D 6
San Marcos ○ BR 62-63 K 6
San Marcos ☆ GCA 52-53 J 4
San Marcos ○ MEX 52-53 E 3
San Marcos ○ USA (TX) 266-267 K 4
San Marcos, Isla ⌒ MEX 50-51 C 4
San Marcos, Laguna ≈ 52-53 E 3
San Marcos de Colón ○ HN 52-53 L 5
San Marcos River ~ USA (TX) 266-267 K 4
San Marcus Pass ▲ USA (CA) 248-249 E 5
San Mariano ○ RP 160-161 E 4
San Marino ○ AUS 178-179 C 5
San Marino ■ RSM 100-101 C 3
San Marino ☆• RSM 100-101 D 3
San Martin ○ CO 60-61 E 6
San Martín ⌒ MEX 50-51 A 2
San Martin ○ RA 76-77 E 5
San Martin, Lago ⊖ RA 80 D 4
San Martín, Península ⌒ RCH 80 C 4
San Martín, Río ~ BOL 70-71 F 3
San Martín Chalchicuautla ○ MEX 50-51 K 7
San Martín de los Andes ○ RA 78-79 D 6
San Mateo ○ USA (CA) 248-249 B 2
San Mateo ○ USA (NM) 256-257 H 3
San Mateo ○ YV 60-61 J 3
San Mateo Ixtatán ○ GCA 52-53 J 4
San Mateo Matengo ○ MEX 52-53 E 2
San Mateo Peak ▲ USA (NM) 256-257 H 5
San Matías ○ BOL 70-71 H 5
San Matías, Golfo ≈ 78-79 G 6
Sanmaur ○ CDN (QUE) 236-237 P 5
Sanmen ○ VRC 156-157 M 2
Sanmen Wan ≈ 156-157 M 2
Sanmenxia ○• VRC 154-155 G 4
San Miguel ○ CO 66-67 B 2
San Miguel ○ EC (BOL) 64-65 C 2
San Miguel ○ EC (ESM) 64-65 C 1
San Miguel ☆ ES 52-53 K 5
San Miguel ○ PA (Pan) 52-53 E 7
San Miguel ○ PE 64-65 F 8
San Miguel ○ RA (BUA) 78-79 K 3
San Miguel ○ RA (COR) 76-77 J 4
San Miguel ○ RP 160-161 E 9
San Miguel ○ USA (AZ) 256-257 D 7
San Miguel ○ USA (CA) 248-249 D 4
San Miguel ⌒ USA (CA) 248-249 D 5
San Miguel ○ YV 60-61 J 3
San Miguel, Cerro ▲ BOL 70-71 G 6
San Miguel, Fortaleza • ROU 74-75 D 9
San Miguel, Río ~ BOL 70-71 G 5
San Miguel, Río ~ CO 64-65 D 1
San Miguel, Río ~ MEX 50-51 F 4
San Miguel, Río ~ MEX 50-51 D 3
San Miguel, Sierra ▲ RCH 76-77 C 4
San Miguel, Volcán ▲ ES 52-53 K 5
San Miguel Aloapan ○ MEX 52-53 F 3
San Miguel Bay ≈ 160-161 E 6
San Miguel Creek ~ USA (TX) 266-267 J 5
San Miguel de Allende ○• MEX 52-53 D 1
San Miguel de Baga ○ C 54-55 G 4
San Miguel de Huachi ○ BOL 70-71 D 4
San Miguel del Monte ○ RA 78-79 K 3
San Miguel de Pallaques ○ PE 64-65 C 5
San Miguel de Salcedo ○ EC 64-65 C 2
San Miguel de Tucumán ☆• RA 76-77 E 4
San Miguelito ○ BOL 70-71 C 2
San Miguelito ○ MEX 50-51 E 3
San Miguelito ○ NIC 52-53 B 6
San Miguel River ~ USA (CO) 254-255 G 5
San Miguel Sola de Vega ○ MEX 52-53 F 3
San Miguel Suchixtepec ○ MEX 52-53 F 3
San Miguel Tulancingo ○• MEX 52-53 F 3
Sanming ○ VRC 156-157 K 3
San Narcisco ○ RP 160-161 D 5
Sannaspos ○ ZA 220-221 H 4
San Nicolás ○ BOL 70-71 E 4
San Nicolás ○ MEX 50-51 E 3
San Nicolás, Bahía ≈ 64-65 E 9
San Nicolás de los Arroyos ○ RA 78-79 J 2
San Nicolás de los Garzas ○ MEX 50-51 J 5
San Nicolás de Tolentino ○ E 188-189 D 7
San Nicolas Island ⌒ USA (CA) 248-249 E 6
San Nicolás Tolentino ○ MEX 50-51 J 6
Sannieshof ○ ZA 220-221 G 3
Sannikova ○ RUS 110-111 W 2
Sannikova, proliv ≈ 110-111 W 2
Sanniquellie ☆ LB 202-203 F 6
Sannohe ○ J 152-153 J 4
Sanogasta, Sierra de ▲ RA 76-77 D 5
Sanok ○• PL 92-93 R 4
San Onofre ○ CO 60-61 D 3
Sanosti ○ USA (NM) 256-257 G 2
Sanoyie ○ LB 202-203 F 6
San Pablo ○ BOL 76-77 D 1
San Pablo ○ C 54-55 F 4
San Pablo ○ CO (BOL) 60-61 E 4
San Pablo ○ CO (NAR) 64-65 D 1
San Pablo ○ PE 64-65 C 5
San Pablo ○ RCH 78-79 C 6
San Pablo ○ RP 160-161 D 5
San Pablo ○ YV (ANZ) 60-61 J 3
San Pablo ○ YV (BOL) 60-61 H 4
San Pablo ○ YV (BOL) 60-61 K 4
San Pablo, Punta ▲ MEX 50-51 B 4
San Pablo, Río ~ BOL 70-71 F 4
San Pablo, Río ~ PE 64-65 C 4
San Pablo Balleza ○ MEX 50-51 F 4
San Pablo Bay ≈ 40-41 C 6
San Pablo Bay ≈ USA 246-247 C 5
San Pablo de Balzar, Cordillera de ▲ EC 64-65 B 2
Sanpaka ○ RMM 202-203 F 2
San Pascual ○ RP 160-161 E 6
San Pasqual Indian Reservation ✕ USA (CA) 248-249 H 6
San Pedro ○ BOL 70-71 F 5
San Pedro ~ C 54-55 F 4
San Pédro ○ CI 202-203 G 7
San Pedro ○ CO 60-61 D 4
San Pedro ○ MEX (BCS) 50-51 D 6
San Pedro ○ MEX (CHA) 50-51 G 3
San Pedro ○ MEX (SON) 50-51 D 3
San Pedro ○ MEX (SON) 50-51 C 2
San Pedro ○ PE 70-71 B 2
San Pedro ☆ PY 76-77 J 3
San Pedro ○ RA (BUA) 78-79 K 2
San Pedro ○ RA (JU) 76-77 E 3
San Pedro ○ RA (MIS) 76-77 K 4
San Pedro ○ RA (SAE) 76-77 E 4
San Pedro ○ RCH (ANT) 76-77 C 1
San Pedro ○ RCH (BIO) 78-79 C 4
San Pedro ○ RP 160-161 E 6
San Pedro ○ YV 60-61 K 2
San Pedro, Isla ⌒ RCH 78-79 C 7
San Pedro, Observatorio de • MEX 50-51 B 2
San Pedro, Punta ▲ RCH 76-77 B 3
San Pedro, Río ~ BOL 70-71 E 6
San Pedro, Río ~ BOL 76-77 D 1
San Pedro, Río ~ GCA 52-53 J 3
San Pedro, Río ~ MEX 50-51 F 4
San Pedro, Río ~ MEX 50-51 G 6
San Pedro, Río ~ MEX 52-53 J 3
San Pedro, Río ~ RCH 76-77 C 2
San Pedro, Sierra de ▲ E 98-99 D 5
San Pedro, Volcán ▲ RCH 76-77 C 1
San Pedro Channel ≈ USA 248-249 F 6
San Pedro de Atacama ○• RCH 76-77 C 2
San Pedro de Buena Vista ○ BOL 70-71 E 6
San Pedro de Cachi ○ PE 64-65 E 8
San Pedro de Colalao ○ RA 76-77 E 4
San Pedro de Coris ○ PE 64-65 E 8
San Pedro de Curahuara ○ BOL 70-71 C 5
San Pedro de la Cueva ○ MEX 50-51 E 3
San Pedro de Las Bocas ○ YV 60-61 K 4
San Pedro de las Colonias ○ MEX 50-51 H 5
San Pedro de Lloc ○ PE 64-65 C 5
San Pedro del Norte ○ NIC 52-53 B 5
San Pedro del Paraná ○ PY 76-77 J 4
San Pedro de Macorís ☆ DOM 54-55 L 5
San Pedro de Quemes ○ BOL 70-71 C 7
San Pedro de Urabá ○ CO 60-61 C 3
San Pedro el Alto ○ MEX 52-53 F 3
San Pedro Huamelula ○ MEX 52-53 G 3
San Pedro Lagunillas ○ MEX 50-51 G 7
San Pedro Mártir, Sierra de ▲ MEX 50-51 B 2
San Pedro Nolasco, Isla ⌒ MEX 50-51 D 4
San Pedro Norte ○ RA 76-77 E 6
San Pedro Peak ▲ USA (NM) 256-257 J 2
San Pedro Pochutla ○ MEX 52-53 F 4
San Pedro River ~ USA (AZ) 256-257 E 6
San Pedro Sacatepéquez ○ GCA 52-53 J 4
San Pedro Sula ☆ HN 52-53 K 4
San Pedro Tapanatepec ○ MEX 52-53 G 3
San Pietro, Ísola di ⌒ I 100-101 B 5
Sanpoil River ~ USA (WA) 244-245 G 2
Sanpoku ○ J 152-153 H 5
Sanqingshan • VRC 156-157 L 2
Sanquianga, Parque Nacional ⊥ CO 60-61 B 6
San Quintín ○ MEX 50-51 B 2
San Quintín, Cabo ▲ MEX 50-51 B 2
San Rafael ○ BOL (COC) 70-71 E 5
San Rafael ○ BOL (PAZ) 70-71 C 4
San Rafael ○ BOL (SAC) 70-71 G 5
San Rafael ○ CO 66-67 D 2
San Rafael ○ CR 52-53 B 6
San Rafael ○ MEX (DGO) 50-51 G 5
San Rafael ○ MEX (NL) 50-51 J 5
San Rafael ○ PE 64-65 D 7
San Rafael ○ RA 78-79 E 3
San Rafael, Cabo ▲ DOM 54-55 L 5
San Rafael, Catarate de • EC 64-65 D 2
San Rafael = El Moján ○ YV 60-61 F 2
San Rafael, Glaciar ⊂ RCH 80 D 3
San Rafael, Río ~ BOL 70-71 H 6
San Rafael, Río ~ MEX 50-51 K 6
San Rafael de Curiapo ○ YV 60-61 L 3
San Rafael de Imataca ○ YV 62-63 D 2
San Rafael de Onoto ○ YV 60-61 G 3
San Rafael Knob ▲ USA (UT) 254-255 E 5
San Rafael Mountains ▲ USA (CA) 248-249 D 5
San Rafael River ~ USA (UT) 254-255 E 4
San Ramon ○ BOL 70-71 F 5
San Ramon ○ BOL (BEN) 70-71 E 3
San Ramon ○ BOL (SAC) 70-71 F 4
San Ramón ○ C 54-55 G 4
San Ramón ○ CR 52-53 B 6
San Ramón ○ PE 64-65 D 4
San Ramon ○ PE 64-65 E 7
San Ramón ○ RA 76-77 D 6
San Ramon ○ RCH 76-77 B 6
San Ramon ○ ROU 78-79 M 3
San Ramon ○ RP 160-161 D 9
San Ramón, Río ~ BOL 70-71 G 4
San Ramón de la Nueva Oran ○ RA 76-77 E 2
San Remo ○ I 100-101 A 3
San Roberto ○ MEX 50-51 J 5
San Roque ○ CO 60-61 E 3
San Roque ○ E 98-99 E 6
San Roque ○ MEX 50-51 B 4
San Roque ○ RP 160-161 D 5
San Roque ○ RP 160-161 F 7
San Roque ○ RP (NSA) 160-161 F 6
San Saba ○ USA (TX) 266-267 J 2
San Saba River ~ USA (TX) 266-267 H 3
San Salvador ⌒ BS 54-55 H 2
San Salvador ★• ES 52-53 K 5
San Salvador ○ PE 66-67 B 4
San Salvador ○ RA (CO) 76-77 J 5
San Salvador ○ RA (ERI) 76-77 H 6
San Salvador, Canal de ≈ 64-65 B 10
San Salvador = Guanahani Island ⌒ BS 54-55 H 2
San Salvador, Isla ⌒ EC 64-65 B 10
San Salvador, Río ~ ROU 78-79 L 2
San Salvador de Jujuy ☆ RA 76-77 E 3
San Salvador el Seco ○ MEX 52-53 F 2
Sansanding ○ RMM 202-203 H 3
San Sandrés, Laguna de ⊖ MEX 50-51 L 6
Sansanné-Mango ○ RT 202-203 L 4
Sansārpur ○ IND 144-145 C 6
Sans Bois Creek ~ USA (OK) 264-265 J 3
San Sebastian ○ MEX 52-53 B 1
San Sebastián ○ RA 80 F 6
San Sebastian ○ USA (PR) 286-287 P 2
San Sebastián, Bahía ≈ 80 F 6
San Sebastian de Buenavista ○ CO 60-61 D 3
San Sebastián de la Gomera ○ E 188-189 C 6
San Sebastián de los Reyes ○ E 98-99 F 4
San Sebastião do Uatuma ○ BR 66-67 J 4
Sansepolcro ○ I 100-101 D 3
San Severo ○ I 100-101 E 4
Sansha Wan ≈ 156-157 L 3
Sanshui ○ VRC 156-157 H 5
San Silvestre ○ BOL 70-71 C 2
San Silvestre ○ YV 60-61 F 3
San Simeon ○ USA (CA) 248-249 C 4
San Simon ○ USA (AZ) 256-257 F 6
San Simón, Río ~ BOL 70-71 F 3
San Simon River ~ USA (AZ) 256-257 F 6
Sanso ○ RMM 202-203 G 4
Sans Sault Rapids ~ CDN 30-31 E 3
Sans-Souci ∴• RH 54-55 J 5
Sans Souci ○ USA (MI) 272-273 G 5
Sansui ○ VRC 156-157 F 3
Sansundi ○ RI 166-167 H 2
Sansu-ri ○ DVR 150-151 F 7
Sansynakaç žyrasy ⌒ KA 126-127 O 2
Santa ○ PE 64-65 C 6
Santa ○ USA (ID) 250-251 C 4
Santa, Isla ⌒ PE 64-65 C 6
Santa, Río ~ PE 64-65 D 6
Santa Ana ○ BOL (BEN) 70-71 E 3
Santa Ana ○ BOL (SAC) 70-71 H 6
Santa Ana ○ C 54-55 F 4
Santa Ana ○ CO 60-61 D 3
Santa Ana ○ EC 64-65 B 2
Santa Ana ☆ ES 52-53 K 5
Santa Ana ○ HN 52-53 L 5
Santa Ana ○ MEX (SON) 50-51 D 2
Santa Ana ○ MEX (TAB) 52-53 H 2
Santa Ana ○ PE 64-65 E 9
Santa Ana ○ RA 76-77 K 4
Santa Ana ○ RP 160-161 E 3
Santa Ana ○ USA (CA) 248-249 G 6
Santa Ana ○ YV 60-61 J 3
Santa Ana, Bahía ≈ 50-51 C 4
Santa Ana, Río ~ YV 60-61 E 3
Santa Ana Island ⌒ SOL 184 I f 4
Santa Ana Maya ○ MEX 52-53 D 1
Santa Anna ○ USA (TX) 266-267 H 2
Santa Barbara ○ BR 66-67 D 5
Santa Bárbara ○ BR 72-73 J 5
Santa Barbara ○ CO 60-61 D 5
Santa Bárbara ▲ E 98-99 F 6
Santa Bárbara ☆ HN 52-53 K 4
Santa Bárbara ○ MEX 50-51 G 4
Santa Bárbara ○ RCH 78-79 C 4
Santa Barbara ○• USA (CA) 248-249 E 5
Santa Barbara ○ YV 60-61 F 4
Santa Bárbara ○ YV (AMA) 60-61 H 6
Santa Bárbara ○ YV (ANZ) 60-61 J 3
Santa Bárbara ○ YV (BOL) 60-61 K 4
Santa Bárbara ○ YV (GUA) 60-61 J 3
Santa Bárbara, Parque Nacional ⊥ HN 52-53 K 4
Santa Barbara, Río ~ BOL 70-71 G 5
Santa Bárbara, Serra de ▲ BR 70-71 H 4
Santa Barbara, Sierra de ▲ RA 76-77 E 3
Santa Barbara Channel ≈ 40-41 D 8
Santa Barbara Channel ≈ USA 248-249 D 5
Santa Bárbara do Sul ○ BR 74-75 D 7
Santa Barbara Island ⌒ USA (CA) 248-249 E 6
Santa Brígida ○ BR 68-69 J 6
Santa Casilda ○ MEX 52-53 D 2
Santa Catalina ○ RA 76-77 E 5
Santa Catalina ○ RP 160-161 E 8
Santa Catalina, Arroyo ~ RA 78-79 G 2
Santa Catalina, Gulf of ≈ 40-41 E 9
Santa Catalina, Gulf of ≈ USA 248-249 F 6
Santa Catalina, Isla ⌒ MEX 50-51 D 5
Santa Catalina Island ⌒ USA (CA) 248-249 F 6
Santa Catalina Island = Owa Riki ⌒ SOL 184 I f 4
Santa Catarina ◘ BR 74-75 D 6
Santa Catarina ○ CV 202-203 C 6
Santa Catarina ○ MEX 50-51 J 5
Santa Catarina, Ilha de ⌒ BR 74-75 F 6
Santa Catarina, Río ~ MEX 52-53 E 3
Santa Cecilia ○ BR 74-75 E 6
Santa Clara ○ BR 62-63 J 6
Santa Clara ☆•• C 54-55 F 3
Santa Clara ○ RA 76-77 E 3
Santa Clara ○ USA (UT) 254-255 B 6
Santa Clara ○ YV 60-61 J 3
Santa Clara, Bahía de ≈ 54-55 E 3
Santa Clara, Isla ⌒ RCH 78-79 C 1
Santa Clara, Río ~ MEX 50-51 F 3
Santa Clara, Sierra de ▲ MEX 50-51 C 4
Santa Clara Indian Reservation ✕ USA (NM) 256-257 J 3
Santa Clotilde ○ PE 64-65 F 3
Santa Comba Dão ○ P 98-99 C 4
Santa Cruz ○ BOL 70-71 C 4
Santa Cruz ○ BR (BAH) 68-69 H 6
Santa Cruz ○ BR (GSU) 70-71 J 7
Santa Cruz ○ BR (P) 66-67 J 4
Santa Cruz ○ BR (P) 68-69 B 3
Santa Cruz ○ BR (PAU) 72-73 G 6
Santa Cruz ○ BR (RNO) 68-69 K 5
Santa Cruz ○ BR (RON) 66-67 F 7
Santa Cruz ○ CR 52-53 B 6
Santa Cruz ~ MEX 50-51 E 3
Santa Cruz ○ PE (LIM) 64-65 D 7
Santa Cruz ○ PE (LOR) 64-65 E 4
Santa Cruz ◘ RA 80 E 3
Santa Cruz ○ RCH 78-79 D 3
Santa Cruz ○ RP (DAS) 160-161 F 9
Santa Cruz ○ RP (MAR) 160-161 E 6
Santa Cruz ○ RP (ZAM) 160-161 C 5
Santa Cruz ☆ RP (LAG) 160-161 D 5
Santa Cruz ○ USA (AZ) 256-257 C 7
Santa Cruz ○• USA (CA) 248-249 B 3
Santa-Cruz ○ YV 60-61 G 4
Santa Cruz ○ YV (APU) 60-61 G 4
Santa Cruz ○ YV (BOL) 60-61 K 4
Santa Cruz, Isla ⌒ EC 64-65 B 10
Santa Cruz, Río ~ RA 76-77 E 2
Santa Cruz, Río ~ RA 80 F 5
Santa Cruz Cabrália ○ BR 72-73 L 4
Santa Cruz de Bucaral ○ YV 60-61 G 2
Santa Cruz de Campezo = Santi Kurutze Kanpezu ○ E 98-99 F 3
Santa Cruz de la Palma ○ E 188-189 C 6
Santa Cruz de la Sierra ☆ BOL 70-71 F 5
Santa Cruz del Norte ○ C 54-55 E 3
Santa Cruz del Quiché ☆ GCA 52-53 J 4
Santa Cruz del Sur ○ C 54-55 G 4
Santa Cruz de Mudela ○ E 98-99 F 5
Santa Cruz de Tenerife ☆ E 188-189 C 6
Santa Cruz do Arari ○ BR 62-63 K 6
Santa Cruz do Capibaribe ○ BR 68-69 K 5
Santa Cruz do Sul ○ BR 74-75 D 7
Santa Cruz Island ⌒ USA (CA) 248-249 E 5
Santa Cruz Verapaz ○ GCA 52-53 J 4
Santa de Ayes Laguna Colorada, Parque Nacional ⊥ BOL 76-77 D 2
Santa Doménica Taláo ○ I 100-101 E 5
Santa Elena ○ EC 64-65 B 3
Santa Elena ○ MEX 50-51 H 4
Santa Elena ○ RA 76-77 H 6
Santa Elena ○ YV 60-61 K 3
Santa Elena, Bahía de ≈ 52-53 B 6
Santa Elena, Bahía de ≈ 64-65 B 3
Santa Elena, Cabo ▲ CR 52-53 B 6
Santa Elena, Cerro ▲ RA 80 H 2
Santa Elena, Paso de ▲ RA 78-79 D 3
Santa Elena de Arenales ○ YV 60-61 F 3
Santa Elena de Uairén ○ YV 62-63 D 3
Santa Eleodora ○ RA 78-79 H 3
Santa Eugenia (Ribeira) ○ E 98-99 C 3
Santa Eulalia ○ MEX 50-51 J 3
Santa Eulària del Riu ○ E 98-99 H 5
Santa Fé ○ BR 68-69 J 5
Santa Fé ○ C 54-55 D 3
Santa Fe ○ CO 60-61 F 4
Santa Fé ○ E 98-99 F 6
Santa Fé ○ PA (Dar) 52-53 E 7
Santa Fé ○ PA (Ver) 52-53 D 7
Santa Fé ○ PE 64-65 F 4
Santa Fe ◘ RA 76-77 G 5
Santa Fe ☆• RA (SAF) 76-77 G 6
Santa Fe ○ RP 160-161 D 6
Santa Fe ○ RP 160-161 E 9
Santa Fe ○ USA (TX) 268-269 E 7
Santa Fe ☆• USA (NM) 256-257 K 3
Santa Fe, Isla ⌒ EC 64-65 B 10
Santa Fé de Minas ○ BR 72-73 H 4
Santa Fé do Sul ○ BR 72-73 E 6
Santa Fe River ~ USA (FL) 286-287 G 2
Santa Filomena ○ BR 68-69 F 6
Santa Helena ○ BR (MAR) 68-69 F 3
Santa Helena ○ BR (PAR) 76-77 K 3
Santa Helena ○ CO 60-61 E 6
Santa Helena de Cusima ○ CO 60-61 F 5
Santa Helena de Goiás ○ BR 72-73 E 4
Santai ○ VRC 154-155 D 6
Santa Inês ○ BR (BAH) 72-73 L 2
Santa Inês ○ BR (MAR) 68-69 F 3
Santa Inés ○ YV 60-61 G 2
Santa Ines ○ YV 60-61 J 3
Santa Ines, Bahía ≈ 50-51 D 4
Santa Inés, Isla ⌒ RCH 80 D 6
Santa Isabel ○ MEX 52-53 H 3
Santa Isabel ○ PA 52-53 E 7
Santa Isabel ○ PE 64-65 E 4
Santa Isabel ○ RA 78-79 F 4
Santa Isabel ⌒ SOL 184 I d 2
Santa Isabel ○ USA (PR) 286-287 P 3
Santa Isabel, Cachoeira ~ BR 68-69 D 5
Santa Isabel, Río ~ GCA 52-53 K 4
Santa Isabel do Araguaia ○ BR 68-69 D 5
Santa Isabel d'Oeste ○ BR 74-75 D 5
Santa Isabel do Pará ○ BR 62-63 K 6
Santa Isabel do Preto ○ BR 72-73 H 7
Santa Isabel do Rio Negro ○ BR 66-67 E 3
Santa Júlia ○ BR 66-67 G 6
Santa Lucía ○ C 54-55 D 3
Santa Lucía ○ EC 64-65 C 2
Santa Lucia ○ PE 70-71 B 4
Santa Lucía ○ RA (CO) 76-77 H 5
Santa Lucía ○ RA (SAJ) 76-77 C 6
Santa Lucía ○ ROU 78-79 L 3
Santa Lucía, Río ~ RA 76-77 H 5
Santa Lucía, Río ~ ROU 78-79 L 3
Santa Lucía, Sierra de ▲ MEX 50-51 C 4
Santa Lucia Bank ≃ 248-249 C 5
Santa Lucia Cotzumalguapa ○ GCA 52-53 J 4
Santa Lucia la Reforma ○ GCA 52-53 J 4
Santa Lucia Range ▲ USA (CA) 248-249 C 3
Santa Lugarda, Punta ▲ MEX 50-51 E 4
Santa Luisa ○ RCH 76-77 B 3
Santa Luz ○ BR (BAH) 68-69 J 7
Santa Luz ○ BR (PIA) 68-69 F 6
Santa Luzia ○ BR (BAH) 72-73 L 3
Santa Luzia ○ BR (MAR) 68-69 F 3
Santa Luzia ○ BR (MIN) 72-73 J 5
Santa Luzia ○ BR (PA) 68-69 K 5
Santa Luzia ○ BR (ROR) 62-63 D 5
Santa Luzia, Ilha de ⌒ CV 202-203 B 5
Santa Luzia do Pacuí ○ BR 62-63 J 5
Santa Magdalena ○ RA 78-79 H 3
Santa Margarita, Isla ⌒ MEX 50-51 D 5
Santa Maria ○ ANG 216-217 B 6
Santa Maria ○ BR (AMA) 66-67 H 5
Santa Maria ○ BR (P) 62-63 J 6
Santa Maria ○ BR (RSU) 74-75 D 7
Santa Maria ○ CO 60-61 E 5
Santa Maria ○ CR 52-53 C 7
Santa Maria ○ CV 202-203 C 5
Santa Maria ○ HN 52-53 L 4
Santa Maria ~ PA 52-53 D 7
Santa Maria ○ RA 76-77 F 2
Santa Maria ○ RP 160-161 F 9
Santa Maria ○ USA (CA) 248-249 D 5
Santa María ○ YV 60-61 F 3
Santa María ○ YV (APU) 60-61 H 4
Santa María ○ YV (SUC) 60-61 K 2
Santa Maria, Bahía ≈ 50-51 E 5
Santa María, Boca ≈ 50-51 L 5
Santa Maria, Cabo de ▲ P 98-99 D 6
Santa Maria, Cape ▲ BS 54-55 H 3
Santa Maria, Corredeira ~ BR 66-67 H 6
Santa Maria, Ilha ⌒ EC 64-65 B 10
Santa María, Isla ⌒ RCH 78-79 C 4
Santa María, Laguna de ⊖ MEX 50-51 F 2
Santa Maria, Punta ▲ ROU 78-79 M 3
Santa Maria, Ribeiro ~ BR 68-69 D 5
Santa María, Río ~ BR 76-77 G 3
Santa María, Río ~ MEX 50-51 J 7
Santa María, Río ~ MEX 50-51 F 2
Santa María, Río ~ RA 76-77 E 4
Santa Maria da Vitória ○ BR 72-73 H 2
Santa Maria da Vitória, Mosteiro de •• P 98-99 C 5
Santa Maria de Ipire ○ YV 60-61 J 3
Santa Maria de Itabira ○ BR 72-73 J 5
Santa Maria de Jebitá ○ BR 72-73 K 6
Santa Maria del Camí ○ E 98-99 J 5
Santa María del Oro ○ MEX 50-51 G 5
Santa María de Los Guaicas ○ YV 60-61 J 6
Santa María del Río ○ MEX 50-51 J 7
Santa Maria del Valle ○ PE 64-65 D 6
Santa Maria de Nanay ○ PE 64-65 F 3
Santa Maria de Nieva ○ PE 64-65 D 4
Santa Maria di Léuca, Capo ▲ I 100-101 G 5
Santa Maria do Para ○ BR 68-69 E 2
Santa Maria do Suaçuí ○ BR 72-73 J 5
Santa Maria Ecatepec ○ MEX 52-53 G 3
Santa Maria Eterna ○ BR 72-73 L 3

Sangir, Kepulauan — Santa Maria Eterna 389

Santa Maria Island = Île Gaua ⌒ VAN 184 II a 2
Santa María Zacatepec ○ MEX 52-53 F 3
Santa María Zoquitlán ○ MEX 52-53 F 3
Santa Marta ○ ANG 216-217 B 6
Santa Marta ○ C 54-55 E 3
Santa Marta ✩• CO 60-61 D 2
Santa Marta, Cabo de ▲ BR 74-75 F 7
Santa Monica ○ USA (CA) 248-249 F 5
Santa Monica Mountains National Recreation Area • USA (CA) 248-249 E 5
Santan ○ RI 164-165 E 4
Santan, Tanjung ▲ RI 164-165 E 3
Santana ○ BR (AMA) 66-67 F 3
Santana ○ BR (APA) 62-63 J 6
Santana ○ BR (BAH) 72-73 H 2
Santana ○ BR (P) 68-69 E 3
Santana ○ CO (MET) 60-61 D 6
Santana ○ CO (SAN) 60-61 E 4
Santana ○ P 188-189 C 4
Santana, Área Indígena ✕ BR 70-71 K 4
Santana, Cachoeira ∼ BR 72-73 F 3
Santana, Caverna de • BR 74-75 F 5
Santana, Ilha ⌒ BR 68-69 G 3
Santana, Ribeiro ∼ BR 68-69 C 6
Santana, Rio ∼ BR 68-69 G 6
Santana da Boa Vista ○ BR 74-75 D 8
Santana da Vargem ○ BR 72-73 H 6
Santana de Pirapama ○ BR 72-73 H 5
Santana do Acaraú ○ BR 68-69 H 3
Santana do Araguaia ○ BR 68-69 C 6
Santana do Garambeu ○ BR 72-73 H 6
Santana do Ipanema ○ BR 68-69 K 6
Santana do Itarare ○ BR 72-73 F 7
Santana do Livramento ○ BR 76-77 K 6
Santana do Manhuaçu ○ BR 72-73 K 6
Santana do Matos ○ BR 68-69 K 4
Santander ○• E 98-99 F 3
Santander ○ RP 160-161 E 8
Santander Jiménez ○ MEX 50-51 K 5
Santanilla, Islas = Islas del Cisne ⌒ HN 54-55 D 6
Sant'Antioco ○ I 100-101 B 5
Sant'Antioco, Ísola di ⌒ I 100-101 B 5
Sant Antoni Abat ○ E 98-99 H 5
Santa Olalla del Cala ○ E 98-99 D 6
Santa Paula ○ USA (CA) 248-249 E 5
Santa Pola ○ E 98-99 G 5
Santaquin ○ USA (UT) 254-255 D 4
Santa Quitéria ○ BR 68-69 H 4
Santa Quitéria do Maranhão ○ BR 68-69 G 3
Sant'Arcángelo ○ I 100-101 F 4
Santarém ○ BR 66-67 K 4
Santarém ○• P 98-99 C 5
Santarém, Ponta de ▲ BR 62-63 J 5
Santarém Novo ○ BR 68-69 E 2
Santaren Channel ≈ 54-55 F 2
Santa Rita ∴• BH 52-53 K 2
Santa Rita ○ BR (AMA) 66-67 C 4
Santa Rita ○ BR (PA) 68-69 L 5
Santa Rita ○ CO (CA) 64-65 F 1
Santa Rita ○ CO (VIC) 60-61 G 5
Santa Rita ○ HN 52-53 L 4
Santa Rita ○ MEX 50-51 D 5
Santa Rita ○ PA 52-53 D 7
Santa Rita ○ YV (BOL) 60-61 K 3
Santa Rita ○ YV (GUA) 60-61 H 3
Santa Rita ○ YV (ZUL) 60-61 F 2
Santa Rita, Arroyo ∼ RA 76-77 E 2
Santa Rita, Ilha de ⌒ BR 62-63 F 6
Santa Rita de Caldas ○ BR 72-73 G 7
Santa Rita de Cássia ○ BR 68-69 F 7
Santa Rita do Araguaia ○ BR 72-73 D 4
Santa Rita do Sul ○ BR 74-75 E 8
Santa Rosa ○ BOL (BEN) 70-71 D 4
Santa Rosa ○ BOL (PAN) 70-71 D 2
Santa Rosa ○ BR (CAT) 74-75 F 7
Santa Rosa ○ BR (RON) 70-71 G 3
Santa Rosa ○ BR (ROR) 60-61 K 6
Santa Rosa ○ BR (RSU) 76-77 K 4
Santa Rosa ○ BR (TOC) 68-69 D 7
Santa Rosa ○ CO (CAU) 64-65 D 1
Santa Rosa ○ CO (GU) 60-61 G 6
Santa Rosa ○ CO (VAU) 66-67 B 2
Santa Rosa ○ EC (ELO) 64-65 C 3
Santa Rosa ○ EC (PAS) 64-65 D 3
Santa Rosa ○ MEX (BCS) 50-51 E 6
Santa Rosa ○ MEX (QR) 52-53 K 2
Santa Rosa ○ PE (LOR) 64-65 F 3
Santa Rosa ○ PE (PUN) 70-71 B 4
Santa Rosa ○ RA (CO) 76-77 H 5
Santa Rosa ✩ RA (LAP) 78-79 G 4
Santa Rosa ○ USA (CA) 246-247 C 5
Santa Rosa ○ USA (NM) 256-257 L 4
Santa Rosa ○ YV (ANZ) 60-61 J 3
Santa Rosa ○ YV (APU) 60-61 G 4
Santa Rosa ○ YV (BOL) 60-61 K 4
Santa Rosa, Baja de ≈ 62-63 K 5
Santa Rosa, Cordillera de ▲▲ RA 76-77 C 5
Santa Rosa, Isla ⌒ EC 64-65 C 1
Santa Rosa, Lago ○ BOL 70-71 H 6
Santa Rosa Aboriginal Land ✕ AUS 178-179 C 2
Santa Rosa de Amonadona ○ YV 66-67 D 2
Santa Rosa de Copán ✩ HN 52-53 K 4
Santa Rosa de Cusubamba ○ EC 64-65 C 2
Santa Rosa del Conlara ○ RA 78-79 G 2
Santa Rosa de los Pastos Grandes ○ RA 76-77 D 3
Santa Rosa de Ocopa • PE 64-65 E 7
Santa Rosa de Quijos ○ EC 64-65 D 2
Santa Rosa de Sucumbis ○ EC 64-65 D 1
Santa Rosa de Viterbo ○ BR 72-73 G 6
Santa Rosa dos Dourados ○ BR 72-73 G 5
Santa Rosa Indian Reservation ✕ USA (CA) 248-249 H 6
Santa Rosa Island ⌒ USA (CA) 248-249 D 6
Santa Rosa Island ⌒ USA (FL) 286-287 C 1
Santa Rosa Lake < USA (NM) 256-257 L 3
Santa Rosalía ○• MEX 50-51 C 4
Santa Rosalia ○ YV 60-61 J 4
Santa Rosa Range ▲▲ USA (NV) 246-247 H 2
Santa Rosa Wash ∼ USA (AZ) 256-257 D 6
Šantarskie, ostrova ⌒ RUS 120-121 G 6
Šantarskoe more ≈ 120-121 G 6
Santa Si • VRC 142-143 M 3
Santa Sylvina ○ RA 76-77 G 4
Santa Tecla = Nueva San Salvador ○ ES 52-53 K 5
Santa Teresa ✕ AUS 178-179 C 3
Santa Teresa ○ MEX 50-51 L 5
Santa Teresa ○ RA 78-79 J 2
Santa Teresa ○ YV 60-61 H 2
Santa Teresa, Forteleza • ROU 74-75 D 10
Santa Teresa, Parque Nacional de ⊥ ROU 74-75 D 10
Santa Teresa, Punta ▲ MEX 50-51 D 4
Santa Teresa, Rio ∼ BR 72-73 F 2
Santa Teresa de Goiás ○ BR 72-73 F 2
Santa Teresa di Gallura ○ I 100-101 B 4
Santa Teresinha de Goiás ○ BR 72-73 F 3
Santa Teresita ○ RA 78-79 L 4
Santa Terezinha ○ BR 68-69 C 7
Santa Ursula, Cachoeira ∼ BR 66-67 H 7
Sant' Auta ○ BR 74-75 E 8
Santa Victoria ○ RA 76-77 E 2
Santa Victoria, Río ∼ RA 76-77 E 2
Santa Victoria, Sierra ▲▲ RA 76-77 E 2
Santa Vitória do Palmar ○ BR 74-75 D 9
San-ta-Wani Safari Lodge ○ RB 218-219 B 4
Santa Ynez ○ USA (CA) 248-249 D 5
Santa Ynez Mountains ▲▲ USA (CA) 248-249 D 5
Santa Ysabel ○ USA (CA) 248-249 H 6
Sant Carles de la Ràpita ○ E 98-99 H 4
Sant Celoni ○ E 98-99 J 4
Santchou ○ CAM 204-205 H 6
Santee ○ USA (CA) 248-249 H 7
Santee ○ USA (NE) 262-263 J 2
Santee Indian Reservation ✕ USA (NE) 262-263 J 2
Santee National Wildlife Refuge ⊥ USA (SC) 284-285 K 3
Santee River ∼ USA (SC) 284-285 L 3
Sante Marie Among the Hurons Historic Park • CDN (ONT) 238-239 F 4
San Tempo, Sierra de ▲▲ BOL 76-77 E 2
Sant Feliu de Guíxols ○ E 98-99 J 4
Sant Francesc de Formentera ○ E 98-99 H 5
Santhe ○ MW 218-219 G 1
Santiago ○ BOL 70-71 H 6
Santiago ○ BR 76-77 K 5
Santiago ○ CO 60-61 E 4
Santiago ○ EC 64-65 C 3
Santiago ○ MEX (BCS) 50-51 E 6
Santiago ○ MEX (NL) 50-51 J 5
Santiago ✩ PA 52-53 D 7
Santiago ★•• RCH 78-79 D 2
Santiago ○ RP 160-161 D 4
Santiago, Cabo ▲ RCH 80 C 5
Santiago, Cerro ▲ PA 52-53 D 7
Santiago, Ilha de ⌒ CV 202-203 C 6
Santiago, Punta ▲ GQ 210-211 B 2
Santiago, Rio ∼ PE 64-65 D 3
Santiago, Rio de ∼ MEX 50-51 H 5
Santiago Atitlán ○ GCA 52-53 J 4
Santiago Chazumba ○ MEX 52-53 F 2
Santiago de Cao ○ PE 64-65 C 5
Santiago de Choeorvos ○ PE 64-65 E 8
Santiago de Chuco ○ PE 64-65 C 6
Santiago de Compostela ○••• E 98-99 C 3
Santiago de Cuba ✩•• C 54-55 H 4
Santiago de Cuba, Bahía de ≈ 54-55 G 5
Santiago del Estero □ RA 76-77 E 4
Santiago del Estero ✩ RA (SAE) 76-77 E 4
Santiago de Los Caballeros ○ MEX 50-51 F 5
Santiago de los Cabelloros ✩• DOM 54-55 K 5
Santiago de Machaca ○ BOL 70-71 C 5
Santiago de Pacaguaras ○ BOL 70-71 C 3
Santiago Ixcuintla ○ MEX 50-51 G 7
Santiago Jamiltepec ○ MEX 52-53 F 3
Santiago Maior ○ CV 202-203 C 6
Santiago Maravatío ○ MEX 52-53 D 1
Santiago Mountains ▲▲ USA (TX) 266-267 D 3
Santiago Papasquiaro, Rio ∼ MEX 50-51 G 5
Santiago Peak ▲ USA (TX) 266-267 D 4
Santiago Tamazola ○ MEX 52-53 E 3
Santiago Tuxtla ○• MEX 52-53 G 2
Santiago Yosondúa ○ MEX 52-53 F 3
Santiam Junction ○ USA (OR) 244-245 D 6
Santianna Point ▲ CDN 36-37 G 3
San Tiburcio ○ MEX 50-51 J 5
Santigi ○ RI 164-165 G 3
Santigi, Tanjung ▲ RI (SLT) 164-165 G 3
Santigi, Tanjung ▲ RI (SLT) 164-165 H 4
Santiguila ○ RMM 202-203 G 3
Santipur ○ IND 142-143 B 5
Säntis ▲ CH 92-93 K 5
Santissima Trinità di Saccàrgia • I 100-101 B 4
Sant Joan de Labritja ○ E 98-99 H 5
Sant Jordi, Golf de ≈ 98-99 H 4
Santo ○ USA (TX) 264-265 F 6
Santo/ Malo □ VAN 184 II a 2
Santo Agostinho ○ BR 72-73 K 5
Santo Amaro ○ BR 66-67 B 6
Santo Amore, Ilha de ⌒ BR 72-73 H 7
Santo André ○ ANG 216-217 C 6
Santo André ○ BR (P) 62-63 K 6
Santo André ○ BR (PAU) 72-73 G 7
Santo Ângelo ○• BR 76-77 K 5
Santo Antão, Ilha de ⌒• CV 202-203 B 5
Santo Antonio ○ BR 62-63 F 6
Santo Antonio ○ BR 66-67 G 4
Santo Antônio ○ BR 68-69 L 5
Santo Antônio ○ CV 202-203 C 6
Santo Antonio ○ STP 210-211 b 2
Santo Antônio, Ponta de ▲ BR 68-69 L 5
Santo Antonio, Rio ∼ BR 68-69 D 7
Santo Antônio da Patrulha ○ BR 74-75 E 7
Santo Antonio de Leverger ○ BR 70-71 J 4
Santo Antônio de Lisboa ○ BR 68-69 H 5
Santo Antônio Desejado ○ BR 66-67 D 7
Santo Antônio do Içá ○ BR 66-67 D 4
Santo Antônio do Monte ○ BR 72-73 H 6
Santo Antônio dos Lopes ○ BR 68-69 F 4
Santo Antônio do Sudoeste ○ BR 74-75 D 6
Santo Corazón ○ BOL 70-71 H 5
Santo Domingo ○ C 54-55 E 3
Santo Domingo ○ CO 60-61 D 4
Santo Domingo ★••• DOM 54-55 L 5
Santo Domingo ○ MEX (BCS) 50-51 D 5
Santo Domingo ○ MEX (JAL) 50-51 G 7
Santo Domingo ○ MEX (SLP) 50-51 J 6
Santo Domingo ○ NIC 52-53 B 5
Santo Domingo ○ RA 76-77 F 3
Santo Domingo, Cay ⌒ BS 54-55 H 4
Santo Domingo, Río ∼ MEX 52-53 F 3
Santo Domingo, Río ∼ MEX 52-53 J 3
Santo Domingo, Río ∼ MEX 52-53 H 3
Santo Domingo, Río ∼ YV 60-61 F 3
Santo Domingo de Acobamba ○ PE 64-65 E 7
Santo Domingo de los Colerados ○ EC 64-65 C 2
Santo Domingo Indian Reservation ✕ USA (NM) 256-257 J 3
Santo Domingo Pueblo ○ USA (NM) 256-257 J 3
Santo Domingo Tehuantepec ○• MEX 52-53 G 3
Santo Inácio do Piauí ○ BR 68-69 H 5
San Tomé ○ YV 60-61 J 3
Santoméri ○ GR 100-101 H 6
Santoña ○ E 98-99 F 3
Santonia ○ F 62-63 G 3
Santop ▲ VAN 184 II b 4
Santópolis do Aguapeí ○ BR 72-73 E 6
Santorini = Thíra ⌒•• GR 100-101 K 6
Santos ○ AUS 178-179 F 5
Santos ○ BR 72-73 G 7
Santos, Baía de ≈ 72-73 G 7
Santos, El ○ C 54-55 F 3
Santos, General ✩ RP 160-161 F 9
Santos, Los ○•• PA 52-53 D 8
Santos Dumont ○ BR 72-73 J 6
Santos Lugares ○ RA 76-77 F 4
Santos Mercado ○ BOL 66-67 D 7
Santos Plateau ≃ 6-7 E 11
Santo Tirso ○ P 98-99 C 4
Santo Tomás ○ MEX 50-51 F 3
Santo Tomás ○ MEX 50-51 A 2
Santo Tomás ○ NIC 52-53 B 5
Santo Tomas ○ PE 70-71 A 4
Santo Tomas ○ RP 160-161 F 9
Santo Tomas, Río ∼ PE 64-65 F 9
Santo Tomás, Volcán ▲ GCA 52-53 J 4
Santo Tomé ○ RA (CO) 76-77 J 5
Santo Tomé ○ RA (SAF) 76-77 G 6
Santu Antine, Nuraghe • I 100-101 B 4
Santuaria Nacional de Ampay ⊥ PE 64-65 F 8
Santuario de Flora y Fauna Arauca ⊥ CO 60-61 F 4
Santuario de la Coromoto ○• YV 60-61 G 3
Santuario Nacional Huayllay ⊥ PE 64-65 D 7
Santuario Nacional Pampas del Heath ⊥ BOL 70-71 C 3
Santubong ○ MAL 162-163 J 4
Santu Lussùrgiu ○ I 100-101 B 4
Sanup Plateau ▲▲ USA (AZ) 256-257 B 3
San Vicente ○ BOL 76-77 D 1
San Vicente ✩ ES 52-53 K 5
San Vicente ○ RA 76-77 K 4
San Vicente ○ YV (AMA) 60-61 H 5
San Vicente ○ YV (ANZ) 60-61 J 3
San Vicente ○ YV (SUC) 60-61 K 2
San Vicente, Bahía ≈ 78-79 C 4
San Vicente de Tagua ○ RCH 78-79 D 3
San Vicente Tancuayalab ○ MEX 50-51 K 7
San Víctor ○ GUY 62-63 D 2
San Víctor ○ RA 76-77 H 6
San Vincente de Caguan ○ CO 60-61 D 6
San Vincente de Cañete ○ PE 64-65 D 8
San Vito ○ CR 52-53 C 7
San Vito, Capo ▲ I 100-101 D 5
San Vito, Capo ▲ I 100-101 F 4
San Xavier Indian Reservation ✕ USA (AZ) 256-257 D 6
Sanya ○• VRC 156-157 F 7
Sanya Juu ○ EAT 212-213 F 5
Sanyang ○ VRC 156-157 L 2
Sanyat ad Daffah < LAR 192-193 L 2
Sanyati ○ ZW (Mlw) 218-219 E 3
Sanyati ∼ ZW 218-219 E 3
Sanying ○ VRC 154-155 E 3
San Ysidro ○ USA (NM) 256-257 J 3
Sanyuan ○ VRC 154-155 F 4
Sanza Pombo ○ ANG 216-217 C 3
São Agostinho, Cabo de ▲ BR 68-69 L 6
São Amaro ○• BR 72-73 L 2
São André, Ribeiro ∼ BR 72-73 G 4
São Antônio ○ BR 62-63 D 4
São Antônio ○ BR 66-67 K 6
São Antônio, Cachoeira ∼ BR 66-67 E 7
São Antônio, Rio ∼ BR 72-73 K 2
São Antônio, Rio ∼ BR 72-73 J 5
São Antônio da Abunari ○ BR 62-63 D 6
São Antônio da Platina ○ BR 72-73 E 7
São Antônio das Missões ○ BR 76-77 K 5
São Antônio de Jesus ○ BR 72-73 L 2
São Antônio de Pádua ○ BR 72-73 J 6
São Antônio de Posse ○ BR 72-73 G 7
São Antônio do Amparo ○ BR 72-73 H 6
São Antônio do Jacinto ○ BR 72-73 K 4
São Bartolomeu, Rio ∼ BR 72-73 G 4
São Benedito, Rio ∼ BR 66-67 J 7
São Bento ○ BR (GSU) 70-71 J 6
São Bento ○ BR (MAR) 68-69 F 3
São Bento ○ BR (P) 68-69 E 3
São Bento do Norte ○ BR 68-69 K 4
São Bento do Sul ○ BR 74-75 F 6
São Bento do Una ○ BR 68-69 K 6
São Bernardo ○ BR (MAR) 68-69 G 3
São Bernardo ○ BR (RSU) 76-77 K 5
São Borja ○ BR 76-77 K 5
São Caetano de Odivelas ○ BR 62-63 K 6
São Caitano ○ BR 68-69 K 6
São Canuto ○ BR 76-77 K 5
São Carlos ○ BR (CAT) 74-75 D 6
São Carlos ○ BR (PAU) 72-73 G 7
São Carlos ○ BR (RON) 70-71 E 2
São Cosme ○ BR 62-63 J 6
São Cristóvão ○ ANG 216-217 B 6
São Cristóvão ○• BR 68-69 K 7
São Cruz, Ribeiro de ∼ BR 72-73 G 4
São Desidério ○ BR 72-73 H 2
São Domingos ○ BR 66-67 F 6
São Domingos ○ BR (GOI) 72-73 G 2
São Domingos ∼ BR 70-71 F 3
São Domingos ○ GNB 202-203 B 3
São Domingos, Rio ∼ BR 72-73 G 2
São Domingos, Serra de ▲▲ BR 72-73 G 3
São Domingos da Maranhão ○ BR 68-69 F 4
São Domingos da Prata ○ BR 72-73 J 5
São Domingos do Azeitão ○ BR 68-69 F 5
São Domingos do Capim ○ BR 68-69 E 2
São Efigênia de Minas ○ BR 72-73 J 5
São Estêvão ○ BR 72-73 L 2
São Felício ○ BR 62-63 H 5
São Felix de Balsas ○ BR 68-69 F 5
São Felix do Araguaia ○ BR 68-69 C 7
São Félix do Piauí ○ BR 68-69 G 4
São Felix do Xingu ○ BR 68-69 C 5
São Fidélis ○ BR 72-73 K 6
São Filipe ○ CV 202-203 B 6
São Florêncio, Cachoeira ∼ BR 66-67 H 7
São Francisco ○ BR (GSU) 70-71 J 6
São Francisco ○ BR (MIN) 72-73 H 3
São Francisco ○ BR (P) 68-69 E 3
São Francisco, Cachoeira ∼ BR 66-67 K 5
São Francisco, Ilha de ⌒ BR 74-75 F 6
São Francisco, Rio ∼ BR 66-67 F 7
São Francisco, Rio ∼ BR 68-69 H 6
São Francisco, Rio ∼ BR 72-73 H 3
São Francisco, Serra de ▲▲ BR 74-75 D 5
São Francisco das Chagas ○ BR 62-63 F 6
São Francisco de Assis ○ BR 76-77 K 5
São Francisco de Paula ○ BR 74-75 E 7
São Francisco do Maranhão ○ BR 68-69 G 5
São Francisco do Sul ○ BR 74-75 F 6
São Gabriel ○ BR (CAT) 74-75 F 6
São Gabriel ○ BR (RSU) 76-77 K 6
São Gabriel da Palha ○ BR 72-73 K 5
São Geraldo do Araguaia ○ BR 68-69 D 5
São Gonçalo ○ BR 72-73 J 7
São Gonçalo do Abaeté ○ BR 72-73 H 5
São Gonçalo do Amarante ○ BR 68-69 J 3
São Gonçalo do Para ○ BR 72-73 H 5
São Gonçalo do Rio ○ BR 72-73 J 5
São Gonçalo do Sapucaí ○ BR 72-73 H 6
São Gotardo ○ BR 72-73 G 5
Sao Hill ○ EAT 214-215 H 5
São Inácio ○ BR 72-73 E 7
São Jerônimo ○ BR 74-75 E 7
São Jerônimo, Serra de ▲▲ BR 70-71 K 5
São João ○ BR 66-67 G 5
São João, Ilha de ⌒ BR 68-69 F 2
São João, Ribeiro ∼ BR 72-73 K 4
São João, Rio ∼ BR 72-73 E 2
São João, Serra de ▲▲ BR 74-75 E 5
São João Batista ○ BR 68-69 F 3
São João Batista do Gloria ○ BR 72-73 G 6
São João da Alicança ○ BR 72-73 G 3
São João da Barra ○ BR 72-73 K 6
São João da Barra, Cachoeira ∼ BR 66-67 H 7
São João da Barra, Rio ∼ BR 66-67 H 7
São João da Ponte ○ BR 72-73 H 3
São João da Pracajuba ○ BR 62-63 J 6
São João de Cortes ○ BR 68-69 F 3
São João del Rei ○• BR 72-73 H 6
São João de Meriti ○ BR 72-73 J 7
São João do Araguaia ○ BR 68-69 D 4
São João do Branco, Igarapé ∼ BR 70-71 F 2
São João do Caiuá ○ BR 72-73 D 7
São João do Paraíso ○ BR 72-73 J 3
São João do Paraná ○ BR 66-67 J 7
São João do Piauí ○ BR 68-69 G 6
São João do Sabuji ○ BR 68-69 K 5
São João do Tigre ○ BR 68-69 K 6
São João Evangelista ○ BR 72-73 J 5
São João Nepomuceno ○ BR 72-73 J 6
São Joaquim ○ BR (AMA) 66-67 D 2
São Joaquim ○ BR (CAT) 74-75 F 7
São Joaquim, Parque Nacional de ⊥ BR 74-75 F 7
São Joaquim da Barra ○ BR 72-73 G 6
São Jorge, Ilha ⌒ BR 68-69 F 2
São Jorge do Ivaí ○ BR 72-73 D 7
São José ○ BR (ACR) 66-67 C 7
São José ○ BR (CAT) 74-75 F 6
São José ○ BR (MAR) 68-69 F 3
São José ○ BR (P) 68-69 D 3
São Jóse, Baía ≈ 68-69 G 3
São José, Igarapé ∼ BR 68-69 B 4
São José de Piranhas ○ BR 68-69 J 5
São José de Ribamar ○ BR 68-69 F 3
São José di Mipibu ○ BR 68-69 L 5
São José do Anauá ○ BR 62-63 D 5
São José do Barreiro ○ BR 72-73 H 7
São José do Belmonte ○ BR 68-69 J 5
São José do Caciporé ○ BR 62-63 J 4
São José do Calcado ○ BR 72-73 K 6
São José do Cedro ○ BR 74-75 D 6
São José do Cerrito ○ BR 74-75 E 6
São José do Egito ○ BR 68-69 K 5
São José do Norte ○ BR 74-75 D 9
São José do Peixe ○ BR 68-69 G 5
São José do Prado ○ BR 72-73 L 4
São José do Rio Claro ○ BR 70-71 J 3
São José do Rio Preto ○ BR 72-73 F 6
São José dos Campos ○ BR 72-73 H 7
São José dos Cordeiros ○ BR 68-69 K 5
São José dos Dourados, Rio ∼ BR 72-73 E 6
São José dos Martírios ○ BR 68-69 D 5
São José dos Pinhais ○ BR 74-75 F 5
São José do Xingu ○ BR 68-69 B 7
São Julia do Jurupari ○ BR 62-63 J 5
São Juliana ○ BR 72-73 G 5
Saoleil Ashraf ○ SUD 200-201 G 6
São Lourenço, Pantanal do ∼ BR 70-71 J 5
São Lourenço, Riachão ∼ BR 68-69 G 6
São Lourenço, Rio ∼ BR 70-71 K 5
São Lourenço do Sul ○ BR 74-75 E 8
São Lucas ○ ANG 216-217 D 5
São Lucas, Cachoeira ∼ BR 66-67 H 7
São Luís ○ BR 66-67 G 4
São Luís ○ BR (AMA) 66-67 E 3
São Luís ✩• BR (MAR) 68-69 F 3
São Luís, Cachoeira ∼ BR 66-67 H 7
São Luís, Ilha de ⌒ BR 68-69 F 3
São Luís de Montes Belos ○ BR 72-73 E 4
São Luís do Curu ○ BR 68-69 J 3
São Luís do Paraitinga ○ BR 72-73 H 7
São Luís do Purunã ○ BR 74-75 F 5
São Luís do Quitunde ○ BR 68-69 L 6
São Luís do Tapajós ○ BR 66-67 J 5
São Luís Gonzaga ○ BR 76-77 K 5
São Luís Gonzaga do Maranhão ○ BR 68-69 F 4
São Manuel ○ BR (MAT) 70-71 K 4
São Manuel ○ BR (PAU) 72-73 F 7
São Manuel ou Teles Pires, Rio ∼ BR 70-71 K 2
São Marcos, Área Indígena ✕ BR (MAT) 72-73 D 3
São Marcos, Área Indígena ✕ BR (ROR) 62-63 D 3
São Marcos, Baía de ≈ 68-69 F 3
São Marcos, Rio ∼ BR 72-73 G 4
São Martinho ○ BR 74-75 F 7
São Mateus ○ BR 72-73 L 5
São Mateus, Pico ▲ BR 72-73 K 6
São Mateus do Sul ○ BR 74-75 E 5
São Miguel ○ BR (APA) 62-63 J 5
São Miguel ○ BR (MAT) 72-73 D 2
São Miguel ○ BR (RNO) 68-69 J 5
São Miguel ⌒ P 6-7 E 6
São Miguel, Rio ∼ BR 70-71 F 3
São Miguel, Rio ∼ BR 70-71 J 3
São Miguel Arcanjo ○ BR 72-73 G 7
São Miguel das Missões ○••• BR 76-77 K 5
São Miguel do Araguaia ○ BR 72-73 E 2
São Miguel d'Oeste ○ BR 74-75 D 6
São Miguél do Guama ○ BR 68-69 E 2
São Miguel do Iguaçu ○ BR 76-77 K 3
São Miguel dos Campos ○ BR 68-69 K 6
São Miguel dos Macacos ○ BR 62-63 J 6
São Miguel do Tapuio ○ BR 68-69 H 4
Saona, Isla ⌒ DOM 54-55 L 5
Saône ∼ F 90-91 L 7
São Nicolau ○ ANG 216-217 B 7
São Nicolau ○ BR 76-77 K 5
São Nicolau, Ilha de ⌒ CV 202-203 B 5
São Nicolau, Rio ∼ BR 68-69 H 4
São Onofre, Rio ∼ BR 72-73 J 2
São Paulo ○ BR 72-73 E 6
São Paulo ✩• BR (PAU) 72-73 G 7
São Paulo de Olivença ○ BR 66-67 C 4
São Pedro ○ BR (AMA) 66-67 D 3
São Pedro ○ BR (MIN) 72-73 K 4
São Pedro ○ BR (P) 68-69 C 3
São Pedro ○ BR (PAU) 72-73 G 7
São Pedro ○ BR (RNO) 68-69 L 4
São Pedro ○ CV 202-203 B 5
São Pedro, Ribeiro ∼ BR 72-73 G 4
São Pedro, Rio ∼ BR 70-71 G 2
São Pedro, Rio de ∼ BR 68-69 H 5
São Pedro da Aldeia ○ BR 72-73 J 7
São Pedro da Garça ○ BR 72-73 J 4
São Pedro da Quilemba ○ ANG 216-217 C 4
São Pedro do Butiá ○ BR 76-77 K 5
São Pedro do Icó ○ BR 66-67 C 7
São Pedro do Paraná ○ BR 72-73 D 7
São Pedro do Piauí ○ BR 68-69 G 4
São Pedro dos Crentes ○ BR 68-69 E 5
São Pedro do Sul ○ BR 76-77 K 5
São Raimundo das Mangabeiras ○ BR 68-69 F 5
São Raimundo Nonato ○ BR 68-69 G 6
São Ramão ○ BR 72-73 H 4
São Romão ○ BR 66-67 D 5
São Roque, Cabo de ▲ BR 68-69 L 4
São Roque, Cachoeira ∼ BR 70-71 F 2
São Sebastião ○ BR 72-73 H 7
São Sebastião, Ilha de ⌒ BR 72-73 H 7
São Sebastião, Ponta ▲ MOC 218-219 H 6
São Sebastião da Amoreira ○ BR 72-73 E 7
São Sebastião da Boa Vista ○ BR 62-63 K 6
São Sebastião da Gama ○ BR 72-73 G 6
São Sebastião do Caí ○ BR 74-75 E 7
São Sebastião do Maranhão ○ BR 72-73 J 5
São Sebastião do Paraíso ○ BR 72-73 G 6
São Sebastião do Rio Verde ○ BR 72-73 H 7
São Sebastião dos Poções ○ BR 72-73 H 3
São Sebastião do Tocantins ○ BR 68-69 D 4
São Sepé ○ BR 74-75 D 8
São Simão, Cachoeira ∼ BR 66-67 H 7
São Simão, Ponta ▲ BR 74-75 E 8
São Simão ou Branco, Rio ∼ BR 70-71 F 3
São Teotónio ○ P 98-99 C 6
São Timóteo ○ BR 72-73 J 2
São Tomé ○ BR (APA) 62-63 J 6
São Tomé ○ BR (RIO) 72-73 K 7
São Tomé ★ STP 210-211 b 2
São Tomé ⌒ STP 210-211 b 2
São Tomé, Cabo de ▲ BR 72-73 K 6
São Tomé and Príncipe = São Tomé e Príncipe ■ STP 210-211 B 5
Saoura, Oued ∼ DZ 188-189 L 6
São Valentim ○ BR 74-75 D 6
São Vendelino ○ BR 74-75 E 7
São Vice ○ BR 76-77 K 5
São Vicente ○ BR (ACR) 66-67 B 6
São Vicente ○ BR (GOI) 72-73 G 2
São Vicente ○ BR (GSU) 70-71 J 6
São Vicente ○ BR (MAT) 70-71 K 4
São Vicente ○ BR (P) 62-63 J 6
São Vicente ○ BR (PAU) 72-73 G 7
São Vicente, Cabo de ▲ P 98-99 C 6
São Vicente, Ilha de ⌒ CV 202-203 B 5
São Vicente, Rio ∼ BR 68-69 G 5
São Vicente Ferrer ○ BR 68-69 F 3
Sapang ○ MAL 160-161 C 10
Sapão, Rio ∼ BR 68-69 F 7
Saparua ○ RI 166-167 E 3
Saparua, Pulau ⌒ RI 166-167 E 3
Sapé ○ BR 68-69 L 5
Sape ○ RI 168 D 7
Sape, Selat ≈ 168 D 7
Sapeaçu ○ BR 72-73 L 2
Sapele ○ WAN 204-205 F 6
Sapello ○ USA (NM) 256-257 K 3
Sapelo Island ⌒ USA (GA) 284-285 J 5
Sapelo Sound ≈ USA 284-285 J 5
Sapërnoe ○ RUS 94-95 L 1
Sápes ○ GR 100-101 K 4
Şaphane Dağı ▲ TR 128-129 C 3
Šapina ∼ RUS 120-121 S 6
Sapinero ○ USA (CO) 254-255 H 5
Sapiranga ○ BR 74-75 E 7
Sapiranga do Sul ○ BR 74-75 E 7
Sapi Safari Area ⊥ ZW 218-219 E 2
Šapki ○ RUS 94-95 M 2
Šapkina ∼ RUS 88-89 X 3
Sap Malua ○ THA 158-159 G 3
Sapo, Serrania del ▲▲ PA 52-53 E 8
Sapoba ○ WAN 204-205 F 5
Sapočani ••• YU 100-101 H 3
Sapocoy, Mount ▲ RP 160-161 D 4
Sapodilla Cays ⌒ BH 52-53 K 3
Saponac ○ USA (ME) 278-279 N 3
Saponé ○ BF 202-203 K 3
Sapo Sapo ○ ZRE 210-211 J 6
Saposoa ○ PE 64-65 D 5
Sapouy ○ BF 202-203 K 4
Sappa Creek ∼ USA (KS) 262-263 F 5
Sapphire Mountains ▲▲ USA (MT) 250-251 F 5
Sappho ○ USA (WA) 244-245 A 2
Sapporo ✩• J 152-153 J 3
Sapri ○ I 100-101 E 4
Šapšal'skij hrebet ▲▲ RUS 124-125 Q 3
Sapucaí, Rio ∼ BR 72-73 F 6
Sapucaia ○ BR (AMA) 66-67 J 4
Sapucaia ○ BR (MIN) 72-73 J 6
Sapucaia ○ BR (RIO) 72-73 J 7
Sapudi, Pulau ⌒ RI 168 B 6
Sapuka-Besar, Pulau ⌒ RI 168 D 6
Sapulpa ○ USA (OK) 264-265 H 2
Sapulu ○ RI 168 E 3
Sapulut ○ MAL 160-161 B 10
Saputing Lake ○ CDN 24-25 d 5
Saqadi ○ SUD 200-201 F 6
Sāqain ○ Y 132-133 C 5
Sāqiya ○ IRQ 128-129 K 5
Šaqlāwa ✩ IRQ 128-129 L 4
Saqqaq ○ GRØ 28-29 P 1
Saqqāra ○ ET 194-195 E 3
Saqqara, Pyramids of ∴••• ET 194-195 E 3
Šaqqat al-Ḥarīta ∸ KSA 132-133 D 5
Saqqez ○ IR 128-129 M 4
Şaqr ○ Y 132-133 G 6
Šaqrā' ○ KSA 130-131 J 5
Šaqrā' ○ Y 132-133 D 7
Šaqū ○ IR 134-135 G 5
Ša'r', aš ○ KSA 130-131 J 4
Sara ○ BF 202-203 J 4
Sara ○ RI 166-167 G 3
Sara ○ RP 160-161 E 7
Ša'rā', aš- ○ KSA 132-133 B 3
Sara, Col de ▲ RN 198-199 F 2
Saraar, Bannaanka ∸ SP 208-209 G 4
Sarāb ○ IR 128-129 M 4
Sarāb Dōre ○ IR 134-135 C 2
Saraburi ○ THA 158-159 F 3
Šaraf al-Ba'l ○ KSA 130-131 D 3
Sarafara ∼ SUD 206-207 K 3
Saraf Doungous ○ TCH 198-199 J 6
Saraféré ○ RMM 202-203 J 2
Sarafğegān ○ IR 134-135 D 1
Šarafḥāne ○ IR 128-129 L 3
Šarafiya, aš- ○ KSA 132-133 B 3
Saragosa ○ USA (TX) 266-267 D 2
Saraguro ○ EC 64-65 C 3
Sarah Lake ○ CDN 30-31 L 4
Sarahs ○ TM 136-137 G 6
Sarahsville ○ USA (OH) 280-281 E 4
Sarai ○ RUS 94-95 R 5
Šarā'i', aš- ○ KSA 132-133 A 3
Sarai Gambila ○ PK 138-139 C 3
Saraipali ○ IND 142-143 C 5
Sarajevo ★• BIH 100-101 G 3
Saraj-Ordasy ansambli • KA 136-137 L 3
Sara-Kawa ○ RT 202-203 L 5
Saraktaš ✩ RUS 96-97 K 8
Sarala ○ CI 202-203 G 5
Saraland ○ USA (AL) 284-285 B 6
Saramaccarivier ∼ SME 62-63 G 3
Saramaguacán ∼ C 54-55 G 4
Saran' ○ KA 124-125 H 4
Šaran ✩ RUS 96-97 J 6
Saran, Gunung ▲ RI 162-163 J 5
Saranac Lake ○ USA (NY) 278-279 G 4
Saranac River ∼ USA (NY) 278-279 H 4
Saranda ○ EAT 212-213 E 6
Sarandë ✩•• AL 100-101 H 5
Sarandi ○ BR 74-75 D 6
Sarandi, Arroyo ∼ RA 76-77 H 6
Sarandi del Yí ○ ROU 78-79 M 2
Sarandí de Navarro ○ ROU 78-79 L 2
Sarandi Grande ○ ROU 78-79 L 2
Šaranga ○ RUS 96-97 E 5
Sarangani Bay ≈ 160-161 F 10
Sarangani Island ⌒ RP 160-161 F 10
Saranglayang, Tanjung ▲ RI 162-163 G 6
Sārangpur ○ IND 138-139 F 8
Sarannoe, ozero ○ RUS 120-121 W 6
Saranpauľ ○ RUS 114-115 F 2
Saransk ○ RUS 96-97 D 6
Saranzal ○ BR 68-69 D 4
Šarapov Šar, zaliv ○ RUS 108-109 M 6
Šarapovy koški, ostrova ⌒ RUS 108-109 M 6
Sarapul ✩ RUS 96-97 H 5
Sarapuľskaja vozvyšennosť ▲▲ RUS 96-97 H 5
Šaraqrug ○ SYR 128-129 H 4
Sarār ○ Y 132-133 G 6
Sarare, Área Indígena ✕ BR 70-71 H 4
Sarare, Rio ∼ BR 70-71 H 4
Sarare, Río ∼ YV 60-61 F 4
Sarasota ○ USA (FL) 286-287 G 4
Sarasota Bay ≈ USA 286-287 G 4
Sarata ∼ UA 102-103 F 4
Saratoga ○ USA (AR) 276-277 B 7
Saratoga ○ USA (CA) 248-249 B 2
Saratoga ○ USA (NC) 282-283 K 5
Saratoga ○ USA (WY) 252-253 M 5
Saratoga Hot Springs ∴• USA (WY) 252-253 M 5
Saratoga National Historic Park • USA (NY) 278-279 H 5
Saratoga Springs ○ USA (NY) 278-279 H 5
Saratok ○ MAL 162-163 J 4
Saratov ✩ RUS 96-97 E 8
Saratovskoe vodohranilišče < RUS 96-97 F 7
Saratovskoye Vodokhranilishche = Saratovskoe vodohranil. < RUS 96-97 F 7
Šaraura, aš- ○ KSA 132-133 E 5
Sarāvān ○ IR 134-135 K 5
Saravan ○ LAO 158-159 J 3
Sarawak □ MAL 162-163 J 3
Saray ✩ TR 128-129 B 2
Saraya ○ SN 202-203 E 3
Sarāyān ○ IR 134-135 H 2
Sarayköy ✩ TR 128-129 C 4
Šarbakty ○ KA 124-125 L 3
Sar Bandar ○ IR 134-135 C 3
Sarbāz ○ IR (SIS) 134-135 J 5
Sarbāz ∸ IR 134-135 J 5
Sarbāz, Rūdḫāne-ye ∼ IR 134-135 J 5
Sarbīše ○ IR 134-135 H 2
Šarbītāt ○ OM 132-133 K 5
Šarbītāt, Ra's ▲ OM 132-133 K 5
Sarbulak ○ VRC 146-147 J 2
Sarcee Indian Reservation ✕ CDN (ALB) 232-233 D 5
Sarco ○ RCH 76-77 B 5
Sarcoxie ○ USA (MO) 276-277 A 3
Sarda ∼ NEP 144-145 C 6
Sardarqa ○ RUS 118-119 H 4
Šardara ✩ KA 136-137 L 4
Šardara, kŭm ∸ KA 136-137 K 4
Šardara sukojmasy < KA 136-137 L 4
Sardārshahr ○ IND 138-139 E 5
Sardašt ○ IR (AZG) 128-129 L 4
Sardašt ○ IR (HUZ) 134-135 D 3
Sarde Band < AFG 138-139 B 3
Sardegna □ I 100-101 B 4
Sardegna, Mar di ≃ 98-99 L 4
Sardegna, Punta ⌒ I 100-101 B 4
Sardes ∴•• TR 128-129 C 3
Sardinas ○ EC 64-65 D 2
Sardinata ○ CO 60-61 E 3
Sardinia ○ USA (IN) 274-275 N 5
Sardinia = Sardegna □ I 100-101 B 4
Sardinia = Sardegna ⌒ I 100-101 B 4
Sardis ○ CDN (BC) 230-231 H 4
Sardis ○ USA (GA) 284-285 J 4
Sardis ○ USA (MS) 268-269 L 2
Sardis Lake ○ USA (MS) 268-269 L 2
Sardis Lake ○ USA (OK) 264-265 J 4
Šardonem' ○ RUS 88-89 S 5
Sare, Rumah ○ MAL 164-165 D 1
Sarege, Pulau ⌒ RI 168 D 6
Sar'ein ○• IR 128-129 N 3
Saré Kali ○ RG 202-203 D 4
Sareks nationalpark ⊥ S 86-87 H 3
Saré Ndiaye ○ SN 202-203 C 3
Sar-e Pol ○ AFG 136-137 J 6
Sar-e Pol, Daryā-ye ∼ AFG 136-137 J 6
Sar-e Pol-e Ẕahāb ○• IR 134-135 A 1
Sarepta ○ USA (MS) 268-269 L 2
Saréyamou ○ RMM 196-197 J 6
Sarezckoe, ozero ○ TJ 136-137 N 5
Sarfannguaq ○ GRØ 28-29 O 3
Šarga ○ MAU (GAL) 146-147 M 2
Šarga ○ MAU (HÖG) 148-149 D 3
Šargalant ○ MAU 146-147 K 2
Sargasso Sea ≈ 4 G 5
Sargent ○ USA (NE) 262-263 G 3
Sargent ○ USA (TX) 266-267 M 5
Sargent Icefield ⊂ USA 20-21 Q 6
Sargento, Bahía ≈ 50-51 C 3
Sargento Ayte Victor Sanabria ○ RA 76-77 G 3
Sargents ○ AUS 172-173 K 2
Sargodha ○ PK 138-139 D 3
Sarguľ, ozero ○ RUS 124-125 L 1
Sarh ✩ TCH 206-207 D 4
Sarhād ∸ IR 134-135 J 4
Sarhro, Jbel ▲▲ MA 188-189 H 5
Šarhulsan ○ MAU 148-149 G 5
Sāri ✩• IR 134-135 C 6
Šari ○ KSA 130-131 H 4
Šari, Buhairat < IRQ 128-129 L 5
Saria ⌒ GR 100-101 L 7
Saria ○ IND 138-139 E 3
Sariã, Rio ∼ BR 66-67 E 6

390 Santa Maria Island — Sariã, Rio

Slä ○ MA 188-189 H 3
Slade Point ▲ AUS 174-175 G 2
Slagelse ○ DK 86-87 E 9
Slamet, Gunung ▲ RI 168 C 3
Slancy ✩ RUS 94-95 L 2
Slapout ○ USA (OK) 264-265 D 2
Śląska, Nizina ↘ PL 92-93 N 3
Slate Islands ⌒ CDN (ONT) 236-237 B 4
Slatina ○ RO 102-103 D 5
Slater ○ USA (MO) 274-275 E 4
Slaton ○ USA (TX) 264-265 C 5
Slaughterville ○ USA (OK) 264-265 G 3
Slautnoe ○ RUS 112-113 P 5
Slave Coast ↘ 202-203 L 7
Slave Lake ○ CDN 32-33 N 4
Slave Point ▲ CDN 30-31 M 5
Slave River ~ CDN 30-31 N 5
Slavgorod ✩ RUS 124-125 L 2
Slavharad ○ BY 94-95 M 5
Slavjanka ○ RUS 122-123 G 4
Slavjanka ○ RUS 122-123 D 7
Slavjansk = Slovjans'k ○ UA 102-103 K 3
Slavjansk-na-Kubani ○ RUS 102-103 L 5
Slavkoviči ○ RUS 94-95 L 3
Slavkov u Brna ○ CZ 92-93 O 4
Slavnoe ○ RUS 122-123 N 6
Slavonice ○ CZ 92-93 N 4
Slawi ○ RI 168 C 3
Sławno ○ PL 92-93 O 1
Slayton ○ USA (MN) 270-271 C 7
Sled Lake ○ CDN 34-35 C 3
Sleeman ○ CDN (ONT) 234-235 J 6
Sleeper Islands ⌒ CDN 36-37 U 6
Sleeping Bear Dunes National Lakeshore • USA (MI) 272-273 C 2
Sleeping Giant Provincial Park ⊥ CDN (ONT) 234-235 P 6
Sleepy Eye ○ USA (MN) 270-271 D 6
Sleisbeck Mine ∴ AUS 172-173 L 2
Sletten = Ammassivik ○ GRØ 28-29 S 6
Slidell ○ USA (LA) 268-269 L 6
Slidell ○ USA (TX) 264-265 G 5
Slide Mountain ▲ USA (NY) 280-281 M 4
Slieve League ▲ IRL 90-91 C 4
Sligeach = Sligo ▲ IRL 90-91 C 4
Sligo = Sligeach ○ IRL 90-91 C 4
Slim ○ DZ 190-191 M 4
Slim Creek ○ CDN (BC) 228-229 N 3
Slim River ○ MAL 162-163 D 3
Slipper Island ⌒ NZ 182 E 2
Slite ○ S 86-87 J 8
Sliven ○ BG 102-103 E 6
Sljeme ▲ HR 100-101 E 2
Sljudjanka ○ RUS 116-117 L 10
Šljupočnyj, mys ▲ RUS 112-113 Q 6
Sloan ○ USA (IA) 274-275 B 2
Sloan River ~ CDN 30-31 N 4
S'loboda Bol'šaja Martynovka ○ RUS 102-103 M 4
Slobodskoj ✩ RUS 96-97 G 4
Slobozia ✩ RO 102-103 E 5
Slocan ○ CDN (BC) 230-231 M 4
Slocan Park ○ CDN (BC) 230-231 M 4
Slocan River ~ CDN (BC) 230-231 M 4
Slogen ▲ N 86-87 C 5
Slonim ○ BY 94-95 J 5
Sloping Point ▲ AUS 172-173 C 6
Slovak ○ USA (AR) 276-277 D 6
Slovakia = Slovenská Republika ■ SK 92-93 O 4
Slovenia = Slovenija ■ SLO 100-101 D 2
Slovenské rudohorie ▲ SK 92-93 P 4
Slovjans'k ○ UA 102-103 K 3
Slov'yans'k = Slovjans'k ○ UA 102-103 K 3
Słowiński Park Narodowy ⊥ PL 92-93 O 1
Složnyj, ostrov ⌒ RUS 108-109 X 3
Sluč ○ UA 102-103 E 3
Sluck ○ BY 94-95 K 5
Sludermo = Schluderms ○ I 100-101 C 1
Slunj ○ HR 100-101 E 2
Słupsk ✩ PL 92-93 O 1
Slurry ○ ZA 220-221 G 2
Smackover ○ USA (AR) 276-277 C 7
Småland ↙ S 86-87 F 8
Smålandsstenar ○ S 86-87 F 8
Smaljany ○ BY 94-95 M 4
Smail ○ USA (ID) 252-253 F 2
Small Malaita = Maramasike ⌒ SOL 184 I e 3
Small Point ▲ USA (ME) 278-279 M 5
Smalltree Lake ○ CDN 30-31 R 5
Smallwood Reservoir < CDN 36-37 R 7
Smara ○ MA 188-189 F 7
Smarhon' ○ BY 94-95 L 4
Smart Syndicate Dam < ZA 220-221 F 5
Smeaton ○ CDN (SAS) 232-233 O 2
Smederevo ○ YU 100-101 H 2
Smela = Smila ○ UA 102-103 G 3
Smet, De ○ USA (SD) 260-261 J 2
Smethport ○ USA (PA) 280-281 H 2
Smidovič ○ RUS 108-109 G 4
Smidovič ○ RUS 122-123 E 4
Šmidta, grjada ▲ RUS 110-111 W 1
Šmidta, Mys ○ RUS 112-113 V 2
Šmidta, mys ▲ RUS 110-111 X 2
Šmidta, poluostrov ↘ RUS 120-121 K 6
Smila ○ UA 102-103 G 3
Smiley ○ CDN (SAS) 232-233 J 4
Smiltene ○ LV 94-95 J 3
Smirenski ○ BG 102-103 E 6
Smirneuski ○ BG 102-103 C 6
Smirnyh ○ RUS 122-123 K 4
Smir-Restinga ○ MA 188-189 J 3
Smith ○ CDN 32-33 N 4
Smith, Cape ▲ CDN 36-37 K 4
Smith Arm ○ CDN 30-31 H 2
Smith Bay ≈ 20-21 N 1
Smith Bay ≈ 24-25 g 2
Smith Center ○ USA (KS) 262-263 H 5
Smithdale ○ USA (MS) 268-269 K 5
Smithers ○ CDN (BC) 228-229 G 2
Smithfield ○ USA (NC) 282-283 J 5
Smithfield ○ USA (UT) 254-255 D 2
Smithfield ○ USA (VA) 280-281 K 6
Smith Field ○ USA (WV) 280-281 F 4

Smithfield ○ ZA 220-221 H 5
Smith Inlet ≈ CDN 230-231 B 2
Smith Island ⌒ CDN (NWT) 24-25 f 2
Smith Island ⌒ CDN (NWT) 36-37 K 4
Smith Island ⌒ IND 140-141 L 3
Smithland ○ USA (IA) 274-275 C 2
Smithland ○ USA (TX) 264-265 K 6
Smith Mountain Lake < USA (VA) 280-281 G 6
Smith Peak ▲ USA (ID) 250-251 C 3
Smith Point ▲ USA (TX) 268-269 H 5
Smith Point ○ USA (TX) 268-269 F 7
Smith River ○ USA (CA) 246-247 A 2
Smith River ~ USA 250-251 H 4
Smiths Corner ○ USA (NB) 240-241 K 4
Smiths Falls ○ CDN (ONT) 238-239 J 4
Smiths Ferry ○ USA (ID) 252-253 B 2
Smiths Grove ○ USA (KY) 276-277 J 3
Smithton ○ AUS 180-181 H 6
Smithville ○ CDN (ONT) 238-239 F 5
Smithville ○ USA (GA) 284-285 F 5
Smithville ○ USA (OK) 264-265 K 4
Smithville ○ USA (TN) 276-277 K 4
Smithville ○ USA (TX) 266-267 K 4
Smithville ○ USA (WV) 280-281 E 4
Smithville Reservoir < USA (MO) 274-275 D 5
Smjadovo ○ BG 102-103 H 5
S. M. Jørgensen, Kap ▲ GRØ 28-29 Y 3
Smoke Creek Desert ⟂ USA (NV) 246-247 F 3
Smoke Hole Caverns • USA (WV) 280-281 G 4
Smokey Hill Air National Guard Range • USA (KS) 262-263 J 6
Smoking Tent ○ USA (SAS) 232-233 Q 3
Smoky Bay ○ AUS 176-177 M 6
Smoky Cape ▲ AUS 178-179 M 6
Smoky Falls ○ CDN (ONT) 236-237 E 2
Smoky Falls ~ CDN (ONT) 236-237 F 2
Smoky Hill River ~ USA (CO) 254-255 P 6
Smoky Hill River ~ USA (KS) 262-263 F 6
Smoky Lake ○ CDN 32-33 O 4
Smoky Mountains ▲ USA (ID) 252-253 D 3
Smoky River ~ CDN (ALB) 228-229 P 3
Smøla ⌒ N 86-87 C 5
Smolensk ★ RUS 94-95 N 4
Smolensko-Moskovskaja vozvyšennost' ▲ RUS 94-95 N 4
Smolevici ○ BY 94-95 L 4
Smólikas ▲ GR 100-101 H 4
Smoljan ○ BG 102-103 D 7
Smoljaninovo ○ RUS 122-123 E 7
Smoot ○ USA (WY) 252-253 H 4
Smooth Rock Falls ○ CDN (ONT) 236-237 G 3
Smoothrock Lake ○ CDN (ONT) 234-235 O 4
Smoothstone Lake ○ CDN 34-35 C 3
Smoothstone River ~ CDN 34-35 C 3
Smörfjöll ▲ IS 86-87 f 2
Smuts ○ CDN (SAS) 232-233 M 3
Smyer ○ USA (TX) 264-265 B 5
Smyrna ○ USA (DE) 280-281 L 4
Smyrna ○ USA (GA) 284-285 F 3
Smyrna ○ USA (OH) 280-281 E 3
Smyrna ○ USA (TN) 276-277 J 3
Smyšljaevsk ○ RUS 96-97 G 7
Smyth, Canal ≈ 80 C 5
Snæbai ○ RI 166-167 H 2
Snaefell ▲ GBM 90-91 E 4
Snake and Manjang Caverns • ROK 150-151 F 11
Snake Falls ○ CDN (ONT) 234-235 K 4
Snake Indian River ~ CDN (ALB) 228-229 O 3
Snake Island ⌒ AUS 180-181 J 5
Snake River ~ CDN 20-21 Y 4
Snake River ~ USA (ID) 252-253 B 3
Snake River ~ USA (WA) 244-245 G 4
Snake River Canyon ∴ USA (WA) 244-245 H 4
Snake River Plains ↘ USA (ID) 252-253 F 4
Snape, Pointe ▲ CDN 38-39 E 3
Snape Island ⌒ CDN 36-37 K 7
Snap Point ▲ BS 54-55 G 3
Snare Lake ○ CDN 30-31 M 3
Snare River ~ CDN 30-31 L 4
Snåsa ○ N 86-87 F 4
Snåsvatnet ○ N 86-87 F 4
Snead ○ USA (AL) 284-285 D 2
Sneedville ○ USA (TN) 282-283 D 4
Sneek ○ NL 92-93 H 2
Sneeuberg ▲ ZA 220-221 G 5
Snelling ○ USA (CA) 248-249 D 2
Snellman ○ USA (MN) 270-271 C 3
Snellville ○ USA (GA) 284-285 F 3
Snežka ▲· CZ 92-93 N 3
Snežnaja, gora ▲ RUS 110-111 N 4
Snežnaja, gora ▲ KS 136-137 N 4
Snežnaja gora ▲ RUS 112-113 N 4
Snežnoe ○ RUS 112-113 R 4
Snežnogorsk ○ RUS 108-109 W 7
Snežnogorskij ○ RUS 118-119 N 5
Snežnyj ○ RUS 96-97 E 10
Śnieżka ▲· PL 92-93 N 3
Snihurivka ○ UA 102-103 H 4
Snipe Lake ○ CDN (SAS) 232-233 K 4
Snipe Lake ○ CDN 32-33 M 4
Snøhetta ▲ N 86-87 D 5
Snohomish ○ USA (WA) 244-245 C 2
Snønuten ▲ N 86-87 C 7
Snooks Arm ○ CDN (NFL) 242-243 N 3
Snopa ○ RUS 88-89 T 4
Snoqualmie Pass ⟂ USA 244-245 D 2
Snøta ▲ N 86-87 D 5
Snøtinden ▲ N 86-87 F 3
Snøtoppen ▲ N 84-85 L 2
Snowbank River ~ CDN 24-25 c 7
Snowbird Lake ○ CDN 30-31 S 5

Snowbird Mountains ▲ USA (NC) 282-283 D 5
Snowcrest Mountain ▲ CDN (BC) 230-231 N 4
Snowden ○ CDN (SAS) 232-233 O 2
Snowdon ▲ GB 90-91 D 5
Snowdrift ○ CDN 30-31 O 4
Snowdrift River ~ CDN 30-31 P 4
Snowflake ○ CDN (MAN) 234-235 E 5
Snowflake ○ USA (AZ) 256-257 G 4
Snow Hill ○ USA (MD) 280-281 L 5
Snow Hill ○ USA (NC) 282-283 J 5
Snow Hill Island ⌒ ARK 16 G 31
Snow Lake ○ USA 34-35 F 3
Snow Lake ○ CDN (MAN) 276-277 D 6
Snow Mount ▲ USA (CA) 246-247 C 4
Snowshoe Peak ▲ USA (MT) 250-251 D 7
Snowtown ○ AUS 180-181 L 2
Snowville ○ USA (UT) 254-255 C 2
Snow Water Lake ○ USA (NV) 246-247 L 3
Snowy Mountains ▲ AUS 180-181 K 4
Snowy River ~ AUS 180-181 K 4
Snowy River National Park ⊥ AUS 180-181 K 4
Snug Corner ○ BS 54-55 J 3
Snuöl ○ K 158-159 J 4
Snyde Bay ≈ 36-37 T 6
Snyder ○ USA (AR) 276-277 D 7
Snyder ○ USA (NE) 262-263 K 3
Snyder ○ USA (OK) 264-265 F 4
Soabuwe ○ RI 166-167 E 3
Soacha ○ CO 60-61 E 4
Soalala ○ RM 222-223 D 6
Soamanonga ○ RM 222-223 D 9
Soän ○ PK 138-139 C 3
Soanierana-Ivongo ○ RM 222-223 F 6
Soanindrariny ○ RM 222-223 E 7
Soan River ~ PNG 183 B 3
Soap Lake ○ USA (WA) 244-245 F 3
Soa-Siu ○ RI 164-165 K 3
Soata ○ CO 60-61 E 4
Soavina ○ RM 222-223 F 8
Soavinandriana ○ RM 222-223 E 7
Sob' ○ RUS 108-109 L 8
Sob' ~ RUS 108-109 L 8
Sob ~ UA 102-103 H 3
Soba ○ WAN 204-205 H 3
Sobaecksan National Park ⊥ ROK 150-151 F 9
Sobangourna ○ RMM 202-203 J 2
Sobât ○ SUD 206-207 L 4
Soberbio, El ○ RA 76-77 K 4
Sober Island ⌒ CDN (NS) 240-241 N 6
Sobger ~ RI 166-167 L 3
Sobinka ○ RUS 94-95 R 4
Sobni ○ RUS (MAG) 120-121 O 4
Sobo-Katamuki Quasi National Park ⊥ J 152-153 D 8
Sobolevka, Ust'- ○ RUS 122-123 H 5
Sobolevo ★ RUS 120-121 Q 6
Soboloh ○ RUS 110-111 Y 6
Soboloh-Majan ~ RUS 110-111 P 6
Sobopol ~ RUS 110-111 S 5
Sobor, skala • RUS 122-123 D 3
Sobo-Sise, ostrov ⌒ RUS 110-111 R 3
Sobradinho ○ BR (FED) 72-73 G 3
Sobradinho ○ BR (MAR) 68-69 G 5
Sobradinho ○ BR (RSU) 74-75 D 7
Sobradinho, Represa de < BR 68-69 G 7
Sobrado, Rio ~ BR 72-73 G 2
Sobral ○ BR (ACR) 66-67 B 7
Sobral ○ BR (CEA) 68-69 H 3
Sobtyegan ~ RUS 114-115 J 2
Socavão ○ BR 74-75 F 5
Sochaczew ○ PL 92-93 Q 2
Sochora, Rio ~ BOL 76-77 E 1
Soči ○· RUS 126-127 C 6
Social Circle ○ USA (GA) 284-285 G 3
Society Hill ○ USA (SC) 284-285 L 2
Society Islands = Société, Îles de la ⌒ F 13 M 4
Socompa ○ RA 76-77 C 3
Socorro, Isla ⌒ MEX 50-51 C 7
Socorro ○ BR 72-73 G 7
Socorro ○ CO 60-61 E 4
Socorro ○ USA (NM) 256-257 J 4
Socorro, El ○ CO 60-61 F 4
Socorro, El ○ YV 60-61 H 3
Socorro do Piauí ○ BR 68-69 G 5
Socota ○ RA 76-77 C 3
Socota ○ PE 64-65 C 5
Socotra = Şuquţrā ⌒ Y 132-133 J 7
Sóc Trăng ○ VN 158-159 H 6
Sočur ~ RUS 114-115 U 5
Soda Creek ○ CDN (BC) 228-229 M 4
Soda Lake ○ USA (CA) 248-249 F 3
Soda Lake ○ USA (CA) 248-249 E 4
Sodankylä ○ FIN 88-89 H 3
Soda Springs ○ USA (ID) 252-253 G 4
Soddle Lake ○ CDN 30-31 L 4
Soddy-Daisy ○ USA (TN) 276-277 K 5
Soder, Mount ▲ AUS 176-177 M 1
Sodere ○ ETH 208-209 D 4
Söderfors ○ S 86-87 H 6
Söderhamn ○ S 86-87 H 5
Söderköping ○ S 86-87 H 7
Södertälje ★ S 86-87 H 7
Sidiri ○ SUD 200-201 D 5
Sodium ○ ZA 220-221 F 5
Sodo ○ ETH 208-209 C 5
Södra Vallgrund ○ FIN 88-89 F 5
Soe ○ RI 166-167 C 6
Soekmekaar ○ ZA 218-219 E 6
Soeng Sari ○ THA 158-159 G 3
Soetendalsvlei ~ ZA 220-221 D 7
Sofala ○ MOC (Sof) 218-219 H 5
Sofala ○ MOC 218-219 H 4
Sofara ○ RMM 202-203 H 2
Sofia ~ RM 222-223 E 6
Sofia = Sofija ★· BG 102-103 C 6
Sofija ★★★ BG 102-103 C 6
Sofijsk ○ RUS (HBR) 122-123 F 3
Sofijsk ○ RUS (HBR) 122-123 H 3
Sof Omar caves • ETH 208-209 D 4

Sofporog ○ RUS 88-89 L 4
Şoğa'âbâd ○ IR 134-135 D 2
Sogakofe ○ GH 202-203 L 6
Sogamoso ○ CO 60-61 E 4
Sogamoso, Rio ~ CO 60-61 E 4
Soğanlı Çayı ~ TR 128-129 E 2
Sogda ○ RUS 122-123 E 3
Sogeram River ~ PNG 183 C 3
Sogeri ○ PNG 183 D 5
Søgne ○ N 86-87 C 7
Sognefjorden ≈ 86-87 B 6
Sognesjøen ≈ 86-87 B 6
Sogod ○ RP 160-161 F 7
Sogolle ○ RG 202-203 F 5
Sogolomik ○ PNG 183 A 3
Sogoot ○ MAU 148-149 D 3
Sogoubéni ○ RG 202-203 F 5
Sogra ○ RUS 88-89 T 5
Sõguip'o ○ ROK 150-151 F 11
Söğüt ○ TR 128-129 C 4
Söğütlü Çayı ~ TR 128-129 G 3
Sog Xian ○ VRC 144-145 J 5
Soh ○ IR 136-137 M 5
Sohagi ○ IND 142-143 B 3
Sohei ○ IR 134-135 F 4
Sohela ○ IND 142-143 C 5
Sohonto ○ RUS 108-109 O 7
Sohor, gora ▲ RUS 116-117 M 10
Sohós ○ GR 100-101 J 4
Sohükwen Do ⌒ ROK 150-151 E 10
Soin ○ BF 202-203 J 3
Sointula ○ CDN (BC) 230-231 J 3
Soi Rap, Cu'a ≈ 158-159 J 5
Söja ○ J 152-153 F 7
Sojana ○ RUS 88-89 R 4
Sojat ○ IND 138-139 D 5
Sojda ~ RUS 88-89 O 6
Sojma ~ RUS 88-89 V 3
Sojna ○ RUS 88-89 S 3
Sôjôsôn Man ≈ 150-151 E 9
Sojotoin Point ▲ MAU 148-149 K 4
Sojuznoe ○ KA 126-127 O 2
Sojva ~ RUS 88-89 X 5
Sok ~ RUS 96-97 G 7
Šökaj-Datka mazar • KA 136-137 L 3
Šokal'skogo, mys ▲ RUS 108-109 J 5
Šokal'skogo, proliv ≈ 108-109 d 2
Šokch'o ○ ROK 150-151 G 8
Söke ○ TR 128-129 B 4
Sokele ○ ZRE 214-215 C 5
Sokhumi = Suchumi ★ GE 104 C 5
Soko ○ CI 202-203 J 6
Sokodé ★ RT 202-203 L 5
Sokode Etoe ○ GH 202-203 L 6
Sokol ○ RUS 94-95 R 2
Sokol ○ RUS (MAG) 120-121 O 4
Sokol ○ RUS (SHL) 122-123 K 5
Sokółka ○ PL 92-93 S 2
Sokolo ○ RMM 202-203 G 2
Sokołów Podlaski ○ PL 92-93 R 2
Sokone ○ SN 202-203 B 3
Søkongen ○ GRØ 28-29 a 2
Sokoro, Satama- ○ CI 202-203 H 4
Sokosti ▲ FIN 88-89 K 2
Sokoto □ WAN 204-205 G 2
Sokoto, River ~ WAN 204-205 G 2
Sokoura ○ RMM 202-203 J 3
Sokoura, Satama- ○ CI 202-203 H 4
Šokša ○ RUS 88-89 N 6
Sol ~ IND 138-139 F 4
Sol, Catedral de • CO 60-61 E 5
Sola ○ C 54-55 Q 4
Sola ○ VAN 184 II a 1
Solan ○ IND 138-139 F 4
Solana Beach ○ USA (CA) 248-249 G 7
Solana del Pino ○ E 98-99 D 6
Solander Island ⌒ NZ 182 A 7
Solano ○ YV 66-67 D 2
Solano, Bahia ≈ 80 C 2
Solano, Punta S.F. ▲ CO 60-61 C 4
Solar Observatory • AUS 178-179 K 6
Solarte, Raudal ~ CO 66-67 B 3
Solat, Gunung ▲ RI 164-165 K 3
Solberg ○ S 86-87 H 5
Soldado Monge ○ EC 64-65 D 3
Soldado Pionero, Monumento al • YV 62-63 D 3
Soldatskaja Tašla ○ RUS 96-97 F 7
Soldau = Działdowo ○ PL 92-93 Q 2
Sol de Julio ○ RA 76-77 F 5
Soldier Creek ~ USA (KS) 262-263 L 5
Soldier Point ▲ USA 172-173 K 1
Soldier Summit ⟂ USA (UT) 254-255 D 4
Soldotna ○ USA 20-21 P 6
Soledad ○ CO 60-61 D 2
Soledad ○ USA (CA) 248-249 C 3
Soledad ○ YV 60-61 K 3
Soledad, Isla ⌒ 80 H 7
Soledad, La ○ CO 60-61 F 5
Soledad, La ○ MEX (COA) 50-51 J 4
Soledad, La ○ MEX (DGO) 50-51 G 5
Soledad de Doblado ○ MEX 52-53 F 2
Soledad Díez Gutiérrez ○ MEX 50-51 J 6
Soledade ○ BR (PA) 68-69 K 5
Soledade ○ BR (RSU) 74-75 D 7
Soledade, Cachoeira ~ BR 68-69 B 4
Soledar ○ UA 102-103 L 3
Sølen ▲ N 86-87 E 6
Solenaja ~ RUS 108-109 V 7
Solenoe, ozero ○ RUS 114-115 L 7
Solentiname, Archipiélago de ⌒ NIC 52-53 B 4
Solénýi ~ RUS 96-97 E 10
Solenzo ○ BF 202-203 H 3
Soleure = Solothurn ★ CH 92-93 J 5
Sólgara ~ AFG 136-137 J 5
Solhan ★ TR 128-129 J 3
Solígalič ✩ RUS 94-95 S 2
Soligorsk = Salihorsk ○ BY 94-95 K 5
Solikamsk ✩ RUS 114-115 O 5
Sol-Ileck ✩ RUS 96-97 J 8
Solimões, Rio ~ BR 66-67 F 4

Solingen ○ D 92-93 J 3
Solita ○ CO 64-65 E 1
So'n Đong ★ VN 156-157 E 6
Solitaire ○ NAM 220-221 C 1
Soljanka ~ KA 96-97 P 8
Soljanka ○ RUS 118-119 K 5
Soljanka ○ RUS (SAR) 96-97 G 8
Solleftea ○ S 86-87 H 5
Sóller ○ E 98-99 J 5
Solna ○ BF 202-203 L 3
Solnečnogorsk ✩ RUS 94-95 P 3
Solnečnyj ★ RUS 122-123 G 3
Solo ○ RI 164-165 G 6
Solodniki ○ RUS 96-97 G 9
Solohovskij ○ RUS 102-103 M 3
Šolokša ○ RUS 88-89 L 4
Sololá ★ GCA 52-53 J 4
Sololo ○ EAK 212-213 E 4
Soloma ○ GCA 52-53 J 4
Solomon ○ USA (AZ) 256-257 F 6
Solomon ○ USA (KS) 262-263 J 6
Solomon Islands ■ SOL 184 I b 2
Solomon River ~ USA (KS) 262-263 H 5
Solomons ○ USA (MD) 280-281 K 5
Solomon Sea ≈ 13 G 3
Solon ○ VRC 150-151 C 4
Soloncy ○ RUS (HBR) 122-123 J 2
Soloncy ○ RUS (IRK) 116-117 J 8
Solonešnoe ○ RUS 124-125 O 3
Solongotyn davaa ⟂ MAU 148-149 D 3
Solonópole ○ BR 68-69 J 4
Solon Springs ○ USA (WI) 270-271 Q 4
Solor, Kepulauan ⌒ RI 166-167 B 6
Solor, Pulau ⌒ RI 166-167 B 6
Solothurn ★ CH 92-93 J 5
Solovecke ○ RUS 88-89 N 4
Soloveckie ostrova ⌒ RUS 88-89 N 4
Solov'evsk ○ RUS (AMR) 118-119 M 8
Solov'evsk ○ RUS (CTN) 118-119 G 11
Solsgirth ○ CDN (MAN) 234-235 C 4
Solsona ○ E 98-99 H 4
Solsona ○ RP 160-161 D 2
Soltānābād ○ IR 136-137 F 6
Soltān Bakvā ○ AFG 134-135 K 2
Soltane, Bir < TN 190-191 G 4
Soltānīye • IR 128-129 N 4
Soltau ○ D 92-93 K 2
Soltau, tau ▲ KA 126-127 K 5
Soluntah, ozero ~ RUS 110-111 Y 4
Solusi ○ ZW 218-219 E 5
Solvang ○ USA (CA) 248-249 D 5
Sölvesborg ○ S 86-87 G 8
Solway ○ USA (MN) 270-271 C 3
Solway Firth ≈ GB 90-91 F 4
Solwezi ★ Z 214-215 D 7
Solžavod ○ RUS 116-117 K 5
Söma ○ J 152-153 J 6
Soma ○ TR 128-129 B 3
Soma ○ ZW 218-219 E 4
Somabhula ○ ZW 218-219 E 4
Somadougou ○ RMM 202-203 H 2
Somalia = Soomaaliya ■ SP 212-213 J 2
Somali Basin ≋ 12 D 4
Somalomo ○ CAM 210-211 F 2
Soma Zangpo ~ VRC 144-145 F 5
Sombo ○ ANG 216-217 F 4
Sombo ○ ANG 216-217 F 4
Sombor ○ YU 100-101 G 2
Sombrerete ○ MEX 50-51 H 6
Sombrero ⌒ KAN 56 D 2
Sombrero, El ○ RA 80 F 7
Sombrero, El ○ YV 60-61 H 3
Sombrero Channel ≈ 140-141 L 6
Sombrio, Lagoa ○ BR 74-75 F 7
Som Det ○ THA 158-159 G 2
Somerdale ○ USA (NJ) 280-281 L 4
Somerdale ○ USA (NJ) 280-281 L 4
Somero ○ FIN 88-89 G 6
Somers ○ USA (MT) 250-251 E 7
Somerset ∴ AUS 178-179 J 2
Somerset ○ CDN (MAN) 234-235 E 5
Somerset ○ USA (CA) 248-249 D 2
Somerset ○ USA (CO) 254-255 H 5
Somerset ○ USA (KY) 276-277 L 3
Somerset ○ USA (MI) 272-273 E 5
Somerset ○ USA (PA) 280-281 G 3
Somerset ○ USA (PA) 280-281 L 3
Somerset Aboriginal Land ⚷ AUS 174-175 G 2
Somerset East = Somerset-Oos ○ ZA 220-221 G 6
Somerset Island ⌒ CDN 24-25 Z 4
Somerset-Oos = Somerset-... ○ ZA 220-221 G 6
Somersetwes ○ ZA 220-221 D 7
Somerset ○ USA (OH) 280-281 C 3
Somerville ○ USA (AL) 280-281 M 3
Somerville ○ USA (NJ) 280-281 L 3
Somerville ○ USA (TN) 276-277 E 4
Somerville Lake < USA (TX) 266-267 K 3
Somes Bar ○ USA (CA) 246-247 B 2
Somil ○ ANG 216-217 F 7
Somme ↙ F 90-91 H 4
Sommen ○ S 86-87 G 7
Sommerberry ○ USA (SAS) 232-233 P 5
Sommerton ○ USA (AZ) 256-257 A 6
Sømna ▲ N 86-87 E 4
Somnenija, buhta ≈ RUS 112-113 O 6
Somnija ~ RUS 122-123 J 5
Somokoro ○ CI 202-203 H 4
Somosomo Strait ≈ 184 III b 2
Somoto ★ NIC 52-53 L 5
Sompeta ○ IND 142-143 D 6
Som Poi ○ THA 158-159 G 3
Somra ○ MYA 142-143 J 3
Son ~ IND 142-143 D 3
Sonace ○ GNB 202-203 C 3
Sonaimur ○ BD 142-143 G 4
Sonananga ○ RMM 202-203 G 3
Sonapur ○ IND (ASS) 142-143 J 4
Sonapur ○ IND (ORI) 142-143 C 5
Sonār ~ IND 138-139 G 7
Sonbong ○ DVR 150-151 H 6
Sonchon ○ DVR 150-151 E 8
Soncillo ○ E 98-99 F 3
Sondagsrivier ~ ZA 220-221 G 6
Sønderborg ○ DK 86-87 D 9
Sorab ○ IND 140-141 F 3

Sondershausen ○ D 92-93 L 3
Sondre Isortoq ○ 28-29 O 4
Søndrestrømfjord = Kangerlussuaq ○ GRØ 28-29 P 3
Søndre Upernavik = Upernavik Kujalleq ○ GRØ 26-27 X 7
Sondrio ✩ I 100-101 B 1
Sondu ○ EAK 212-213 E 4
Sonepat ○ IND 138-139 F 5
Song ○ MAL 162-163 K 3
Song ○ WAN 204-205 K 4
Songa ○ ZRE 214-215 C 5
Songawe Lagoon ○ ANG 202-203 L 7
Sông Ba ~ VN 158-159 K 4
Sông Câu ○ VN 156-157 F 8
Sông Cô Chiên ~ VN 158-159 J 5
Sông Cua Dai ~ VN 158-159 K 3
Sông Đồng Nai ~ VN 158-159 J 4
Sông Đa ~ VN 156-157 D 6
Songea ★ EAT 214-215 H 5
Songgato ○ RI 166-167 L 3
Sông Hâu ~ VN 158-159 H 5
Sông Hông ~ VN 156-157 D 5
Songhua Hu < VRC (JIL) 150-151 F 6
Songhua Hu · VRC (JIL) 150-151 F 6
Songhua Jiang ~ VRC 150-151 E 5
Songingo ~ VRC 156-157 C 4
Songir ○ IND 138-139 E 6
Songjiang ○ VRC (JIL) 150-151 G 6
Songjiang ○ VRC (SGH) 154-155 M 6
Sông-Kël, ozero ~ KS 146-147 B 5
Song-Kël, ozero ~ KS 146-147 B 5
Songkhla ★ THA 158-159 G 6
Songkou ○ VRC (FUJ) 156-157 M 4
Song Ling ▲ VRC 154-155 L 1
Sông Lũy ~ VN 158-159 K 5
Songming ○ VRC 156-157 C 4
Sôngnam ○ ROK 150-151 F 9
Songnim ○ DVR 150-151 E 8
Songnisan National Park ⊥ ROK 150-151 F 9
Songo ○ ANG 216-217 C 3
Songo ○ MOC 218-219 G 2
Songololo ○ ZRE 210-211 E 6
Songo Mnara ∴· EAT 214-215 K 5
Songpan ○ VRC 154-155 C 5
Song Phinong ○ THA 158-159 F 3
Songsang ○ IND 142-143 H 3
Songsha ○ VRC 144-145 C 5
Song Shan ▲ VRC 154-155 J 4
Songshang · VRC 154-155 H 4
Sông Tiên ~ VN 158-159 H 5
Songwe ○ EAT 214-215 G 5
Songxian ○ VRC 154-155 H 4
Songyang ○ VRC 156-157 L 2
Songyu Cave • VRC 154-155 G 9
Songzi ○ VRC 154-155 G 6
So'n Hoep ○ VN 158-159 K 5
Sonid Youqi ○ VRC 148-149 L 6
Sonid Zuoqi ○ VRC 148-149 L 6
Soniquera, Cerro ▲ BOL 76-77 D 2
Sonitê, Bishayeh ▲ RUS 108-109 Z 6
Sonjo ○ EAT 212-213 F 5
Sonjol, Gunung ▲ RI 164-165 G 3
Sonkwale Mountains ▲ WAN 204-205 L 5
So'n La ★ VN 156-157 C 6
Son Mbong ○ CDN 210-211 G 2
Sonmiáni Bay ≈ 134-135 M 6
Sonneberg ○ D 92-93 L 3
Sonningdade ○ CDN (SAS) 232-233 L 3
Sono, Rio do ~ BR 68-69 E 6
Sono, Rio do ~ BR 72-73 H 4
Sonoita ○ USA (AZ) 256-257 E 7
Sonoma ○ USA (CA) 246-247 C 5
Sonoma Range ▲ USA (NV) 246-247 H 3
Sonora □ MEX 50-51 B 1
Sonora ○ MEX 50-51 D 3
Sonora ○ USA (CA) 248-249 D 2
Sonora ○ USA (KY) 276-277 J 2
Sonora ○ USA (TX) 264-265 E 7
Sonora, Rio ~ MEX 50-51 D 3
Sonora Aboriginal Land ⚷ CDN (BC) 230-231 D 3
Sonora Junction ○ USA (CA) 246-247 F 5
Sonoran Desert ⟂ USA (AZ) 248-249 K 6
Sonsón ○ CO 60-61 D 4
Sonsonate ★ ES 52-53 K 5
Sonstraal ○ ZA 220-221 F 3
Sonta ○ ZRE 214-215 E 6
So'n Tây, Thị Xã ★ VN 156-157 D 6
Sooke ○ CDN (BC) 230-231 F 5
Sooner Lake < USA (OK) 264-265 G 2
Soos, Tanjung ▲ RI 166-167 E 2
Sooyac ○ SP 212-213 J 3
Sopachuy ○ BOL 70-71 E 6
Sopas, Arroyo ~ ROU 76-77 J 4
Sopau ○ PNG 183 D 2
Sopčapu ○ IND 120-121 Q 5
Sopčoppi ~ USA (FL) 286-287 E 2
Soperton ○ USA (GA) 284-285 H 4
Soperton ○ USA (WI) 270-271 K 5
Sôp Hao ○ LAO 156-157 D 6
Sopi ○ RI 164-165 L 2
Sopi, Tanjung ▲ RI 164-165 L 2
Sopinusa ○ RI 166-167 G 3
Sopo ○ SUD 206-207 H 4
Sopo ~ SUD 206-207 J 4
Sopočnaja ○ RUS 120-121 Q 5
Sopot ○ PL 92-93 O 1
Sop Prap ○ THA 158-159 E 2
Sopron ○ H 92-93 N 5
Sopsoum ○ LAO 156-157 D 6
Soquee River ~ USA (GA) 284-285 G 2
Sôr, Ribeira de ~ P 98-99 D 5
Sora ○ I 100-101 D 4
Sora, Rio do ~ RA 76-77 J 4
Sorab ○ IND 140-141 F 3

Soracaba, Rio ~ BR 72-73 G 7
Sorâh ○ PK 138-139 B 6
Söraksan ▲ ROK 150-151 G 8
Söraksan National Park ⊥ ROK 150-151 G 8
Sora Mboum ○ CAM 206-207 B 5
Sorapa ○ PE 70-71 C 5
Soras, Rio ~ PE 64-65 F 9
Sorata ○ BOL 70-71 C 4
Sörath ○ WAN 138-139 B 6
Sorati-gawa ~ J 152-153 K 3
Sorau ○ WAN 204-205 K 4
Søraust-spitsbergen nat.res ⊥ N 84-85 M 3
Sorbas ○ E 98-99 F 6
Sore ○ F 90-91 G 9
Sorel ○ CDN (QUE) 238-239 M 2
Sorell-Midway Point ○ AUS 180-181 J 7
Sorere ○ EAU 212-213 E 4
Sør-Flatanger ○ N 86-87 E 4
Softa ○ ETH 208-209 D 5
Sorgun ★ TR 128-129 F 3
Sorh, Kôtal-e ▲ AFG 134-135 K 1
Sorh, Kûh-e ▲ IR 134-135 H 3
Sorh, Kûh-e ▲ IR 136-137 G 7
Sorh-ô-Pârsâ ○ AFG 138-139 B 3
Sori ○ DY 204-205 E 3
Soria ✩ E 98-99 F 4
Sorido ○ RI 166-167 J 2
Sorkam ○ RI 162-163 L 3
Sørkapp ▲ N 26-27 v 8
Sørkapp Land ▲ N 84-85 K 4
Sørkappøya ⌒ N 84-85 K 4
Sørli ○ N 86-87 F 4
Sormiento, Canal ≈ 80 C 5
Soro ○ IND 142-143 F 4
Soro = Bahr el Ghazal ~ TCH 198-199 H 5
Sorobango ○ CI 202-203 J 5
Soroca ○ MD 102-103 F 3
Sorocaba ○ BR 72-73 G 7
Soročinsk ✩ RUS 96-97 H 7
Soroki = Soroca ○ MD 102-103 F 3
Sorokino ○ RUS 94-95 L 3
Sorokskaja guba ≈ 88-89 N 4
Sorombéo ○ CAM 206-207 B 4
Sorondideri ○ RI 166-167 H 2
Sorong ○ RI 166-167 F 2
Sororó, Rio ~ BR 68-69 D 4
Soroti ★ EAU 212-213 D 3
Sørøya ▲ N 86-87 L 1
Sørøysundet ≈ N 86-87 L 1
Sorraia, Rio ~ P 98-99 C 5
Sorrento ○ CDN (BC) 230-231 K 3
Sorrento ○ I 100-101 C 4
Sorrento ○ USA (LA) 268-269 K 6
Sorriso ○ BR 70-71 K 3
Sør-Rondane ▲ ARK 16 F 3
Sorsele ○ S 86-87 H 4
Sorsk ○ RUS 116-117 E 8
Sorsogon ○ RP 160-161 F 6
Sørspitsbergen nasjonalpark ⊥ N 84-85 J 4
Sørstraumen ○ N 86-87 K 2
Sort ○ E 98-99 H 3
Šortandy ★ KA 124-125 G 3
Sortavala ○ RUS 88-89 L 6
Sortebræ ⊆ GRØ 28-29 g 2
Sortehest ▲ GRØ 26-27 f 7
Sortija, La ○ RA 78-79 J 7
Sortland ○ N 86-87 G 2
Sorúbií ○ AFG 138-139 B 3
Sørvágen ○ N 86-87 F 3
Sørvágur ○ FR 90-91 D 1
Sorvenok ○ KA 124-125 P 4
Sørvika ○ N 86-87 F 5
Sösan ○ ROK 150-151 F 9
Sösan Haean National Park ⊥ ROK 150-151 F 9
Soscumica, Lac ○ CDN (QUE) 236-237 L 2
Soskie jary ▲ RUS 96-97 G 7
Soseado, El ○ RA 78-79 F 3
Sosnogorsk ○ RUS 88-89 W 5
Sosnove ○ UA 102-103 E 2
Sosnovec, ostrov ⌒ RUS 88-89 Q 3
Sosnovka ○ RUS 110-111 D 8
Sosnovka ○ KA 124-125 L 3
Sosnovka ○ RUS (KIR) 96-97 G 5
Sosnovka ○ RUS (MUR) 88-89 Q 3
Sosnovo-Ozёrskoe ○ RUS 118-119 G 9
Sosnovyj ○ RUS 88-89 M 3
Sosnovyj Bor ○ RUS 114-115 Q 9
Sosnovyj Bor ○ RUS (LEN) 94-95 L 2
Sosnowiec ○ PL 92-93 P 3
Soso Bay ≈ 184 III a 2
Sosogoh ○ MAL 160-161 B 10
Sosok ○ RI 162-163 F 5
Sosso ○ RCA 210-211 E 2
Sosso, Cascades de ~ DY 204-205 E 3
Sossusvlei ~ NAM 220-221 E 2
Šostka ○ UA 102-103 H 2
Sosúa ○ DOM 56-57 L 4
Sos'va ○ RUS (SVR) 114-115 P 5
Sos'va ~ RUS 114-115 Q 5
Sot' ~ RUS 94-95 R 2
Sota ~ DY 204-205 E 3
Sotara, Volcán ▲ CO 60-61 C 6
Sotavento, Ilhas de ~ CV 202-203 B 6
Sotério, Rio ~ BR 70-71 E 2
Sotian ○ RMM 202-203 G 4
Sotik ○ EAK 212-213 E 4
Sotkamo ○ FIN 88-89 K 4
Soto ○ RA 76-77 E 6
Soto, De ○ USA (MO) 274-275 G 1
Soto, Isla ⌒ PE 70-71 C 4
Soto la Marina ○ MEX 50-51 K 6
Sotomayor, Quebrada ~ BOL 76-77 D 1
Sotomayor ○ CO 64-65 D 1
Šotorhūn, Kôtal-e ▲ AFG 134-135 L 1
Sotouboua ○ RT 202-203 L 5
Sotuta ○ MEX 52-53 K 1
Souanké ○ RCB 210-211 E 2
Soubakaniédougou ○ BF 202-203 H 4

Soubakpérou ▲ DY 204-205 E 4
Soubala o RMM 202-203 E 3
Soubané ó RG 202-203 C 4
Soubéira o BF 202-203 K 3
Soubré ☆ CI 202-203 G 7
Soudan o AUS 174-175 D 7
Soudan Bank ≃ 224 C 7
Soudougui o BF 202-203 L 4
Souellaba, Pointe de ▲ CAM 210-211 B 2
Souf ~ DZ 190-191 F 4
Souf, Oued ~ DZ 190-191 D 7
Soufa, Passe de ▲ RIM 196-197 E 7
Soufflets River ~ CDN (NFL) 242-243 M 2
Soufrière o WL 56 E 5
Soufrière, la ▲ F 56 E 3
Sougueur o DZ 190-191 C 3
Souillac o MS 224 C 7
Souk-Ahras o DZ 190-191 F 2
Souk-el-Arab-des-Beni-Hassan o MA 188-189 J 3
Souk-el-Arab-du-Rharb o MA 188-189 H 3
Souk-el-Kella o MA 188-189 J 3
Souk-Jemaâ-des-Oulad-Abbou o MA 188-189 H 4
Soukoukoutane o RN 204-205 E 1
Souk-Tleta-des-Akhasass o MA 188-189 G 5
Sôul ★ ROK 150-151 F 9
Soula, Djebel Adrar ▲ DZ 190-191 G 8
Soulabali o SN 202-203 C 3
Soulis Pond o CDN (NFL) 242-243 O 4
Souma'a Sarà o IR 128-129 N 4
Soummam, Oued ~ DZ 190-191 E 2
Sounders River ~ CDN 36-37 L 2
Sound Hill Cove ≋ 38-39 Q 2
Sounding Creek ~ CDN (ALB) 232-233 H 4
Sounding Lake o CDN (ALB) 232-233 H 4
Sounga o G 210-211 B 5
Soungrougrou ~ SN 202-203 C 3
Source du Nil • RWA 212-213 B 5
Sources, Mont aux ▲ LS 220-221 J 4
Sources Sud du Nil • BU 212-213 B 5
Souris o CDN (MAN) 234-235 C 5
Souris o CDN (PEI) 240-241 N 4
Souris o USA (ND) 258-259 G 3
Souris River ~ CDN (MAN) 234-235 C 5
Souris River ~ CDN (SAS) 232-233 P 6
Souris River ~ USA (ND) 258-259 F 3
Sour Lake o USA (TX) 268-269 F 6
Sourou ~ RMM 202-203 J 3
Souroukaha o CI 202-203 H 5
Sous, Oued ~ MA 188-189 G 5
Sousa o BR 68-69 J 5
Sousel o P 98-99 D 5
Sousse ☆ TN 190-191 H 3
Souterraine, la o F 90-91 H 8
South = Sud o CAM 210-211 C 3
South Africa o ZA 220-221 E 3
South Alligator River ~ AUS 172-173 L 2
Southampton o CDN (NS) 240-241 L 5
Southampton o CDN (ONT) 238-239 D 4
Southampton o • GB 90-91 F 6
Southampton o USA (NY) 280-281 O 3
Southampton, Cape ▲ CDN 36-37 H 3
Southampton Island ⌒ CDN 36-37 G 2
South Andaman ⌒ IND 140-141 L 4
South Andros ⌒ BS 54-55 G 3
South Aulatsivik Island ⌒ CDN 36-37 T 6
South Australia o AUS 178-179 C 4
South Australian Basin ≃ 12 D 6
Southaven o USA (MS) 268-269 G 4
South Baldy ▲ USA (NM) 256-257 H 4
South Banda Basin ≃ RI 166-167 G 3
Southbank o CDN 228-229 J 2
South Baranof Island Wilderness ⊥ USA 32-33 C 3
South Bay ≋ 36-37 H 2
South Bay o CDN (ONT) 234-235 L 3
South Baymouth o CDN (ONT) 238-239 C 3
South Beloit o USA (IL) 274-275 J 2
South Bend o USA (IN) 274-275 M 3
South Bend o USA (OR) 244-245 B 4
South Bend o USA (WA) 244-245 B 4
South Bentinck Arm o CDN (BC) 228-229 H 4
South Bimini ⌒ BS 54-55 F 2
South-Bolton o CDN (QUE) 238-239 N 3
South Boston o USA (VA) 280-281 H 7
South Branch o CDN (NFL) 242-243 J 5
South Branch Potomac River ~ USA (WV) 280-281 H 4
South Brook o CDN (NFL) 242-243 M 3
South Brook o CDN (NFL) 242-243 M 3
South Brookfield o CDN (NS) 240-241 L 6

Southeast Point ▲ BS 54-55 J 3
Southeast Point ▲ BS 54-55 J 3
South End ▲ AUS 172-173 B 6
Southend o CDN 34-35 S 2
Southend-on-Sea o GB 90-91 H 6
Southern o EAU 212-213 C 4
Southern o MW 218-219 H 2
Southern o RB 220-221 F 2
Southern o Z 218-219 C 3
Southern Alps ▲ NZ 182 B 6
Southern Cross o AUS 176-177 E 5
Southern Cross Club o GB 54-55 E 5
Southern Harbour o CDN (NFL) 242-243 P 5
Southern Indian Lake o CDN 34-35 G 2
Southern Kashiji ~ Z 218-219 B 2
Southern Lau Group ⌒ FJI 184 III c 3
Southern Long Cays ⌒ BH 52-53 K 3
Southern Lueti ~ Z 218-219 B 2
Southern National Park ⊥ SUD 206-207 J 7
Southern Pines o USA (NC) 282-283 H 5
Southern Region o SUD 206-207 H 5
Southern Uplands ▲ GB 90-91 E 4
Southern Ute Indian Reservation ☓ USA (CO) 254-255 H 6
Southesk River ~ CDN (ALB) 228-229 R 4
Southesk Tablelands ▲ AUS 172-173 H 6
Southey o CDN (SAS) 232-233 O 5
South Fabius River ~ USA (MO) 274-275 F 4
South Fiji Basin ≃ 13 J 5
South Fork o CDN (SAS) 232-233 K 6
South Fork o USA (CO) 254-255 J 6
South Fork ~ USA (TN) 276-277 G 4
South Fork ~ USA (TN) 276-277 F 5
South Fork ~ USA (VA) 280-281 F 7
South Fork Cumberland River ~ USA (TN) 282-283 C 4
South Fork John Day River ~ USA (OR) 244-245 F 6
South Fork Koyukuk ~ USA 20-21 P 3
South Fork Kuskokwim River ~ USA 20-21 N 5
South Fork Licking River ~ USA (KY) 276-277 L 2
South Fork Owyhee River ~ USA (ID) 252-253 R 4
South Fork Republican River ~ USA (CO) 254-255 N 4
South Fork River ~ USA (WV) 280-281 E 4
South Fork Salmon River ~ USA (ID) 252-253 C 2
South Fork Salt River ~ USA (MO) 274-275 Q 5
South Fork Shenandoah River ~ USA (VA) 280-281 H 5
South Fork Solomon River ~ USA (KS) 262-263 F 5
South Fork Trinity River ~ USA (CA) 246-247 B 3
South Fork White River ~ USA (SD) 260-261 A 3
South Galway o AUS 178-179 G 3
Southgate River ~ CDN (BC) 230-231 K 3
South Grand River ~ USA (MO) 274-275 D 6
South Gut Saint Ann's o CDN (NS) 240-241 P 4
South Harbour o CDN (NS) 240-241 P 4
South Haven o USA (KS) 262-263 J 7
South Haven o USA (MI) 272-273 C 5
South Head o AUS 174-175 G 6
South Heart o CDN (ND) 258-259 F 3
South Heart River ~ CDN 32-33 M 4
South Henik Lake o CDN 30-31 V 5
South Hill o USA (VA) 280-281 H 7
South Horr o EAK 212-213 F 2
South Indian Lake o CDN 34-35 G 2
South Island ⌒ EAK 212-213 F 2
South Island ⌒ NZ 182 B 5
South Junction o CDN (MAN) 234-235 H 5
South Junction o CDN (OR) 244-245 D 6
South Kitui National Reserve ⊥ EAK 212-213 G 4
South Knife River ~ CDN 30-31 V 6
South Korea = Taehan-Min'guk ■ ROK 150-151 G 9
South Lake Tahoe o USA (CA) 246-247 F 5
Southland o USA (TX) 264-265 C 5
South Loup River ~ USA (NE) 262-263 G 3
South Luangwa National Park ⊥ Z 214-215 F 7
South Luconia Shoals ≃ 162-163 K 2
South Lyon o USA (MI) 272-273 F 5
South Magnetic Pole = Magnetic Pole Area II CDN 24-23 T 5
South Male Atoll ⌒ MV 140-141 B 6
South Malosmadulu Atoll ⌒ MV 140-141 B 5
South Milford o CDN (NS) 240-241 K 6
South Milwaukee o USA (WI) 274-275 L 2
South Moose Lake o CDN 34-35 G 4
South Moresby Gwaii Haanas National Reserve ⊥ CDN (BC) 228-229 C 4
South Moresby Gwaii Haanas National Provincial Reserve ⊥ CDN (BC) 228-229 C 4
South Moresby National Park Reserve ⊥ •• CDN (BC) 228-229 C 4
South Mountain o CDN (ONT) 238-239 K 4
South Nahanni ▲ USA (ID) 252-253 B 4
South Nahanni River ~ CDN 30-31 E 4
South Nation River ~ CDN (ONT) 238-239 K 3
South Negril Point ▲ JA 54-55 G 5
South Nilandu Atoll ⌒ MV 140-141 B 6
South Ogden o USA (UT) 254-255 D 2
South Orkneys ⌒ GB 16 G 32

South Ossetia = Jugo-Osetinskaja Avtonomnaja Respublika ○ GE 126-127 F 6
South Pacific Ocean ≈ 14-15 N 11
South Pare Mountains ▲ EAT 212-213 F 6
South Paris o USA (ME) 278-279 L 4
South Pass ▲ USA (CA) 244-245 K 5
South Pass ▲ USA (WY) 252-253 K 4
South Pass City o USA (WY) 252-253 K 4
South Pease River ~ USA (TX) 264-265 D 5
South Pender o CDN (BC) 230-231 N 5
South Peron Island ⌒ AUS 172-173 K 2
South Pittsburg o USA (TN) 276-277 K 5
South Plains o USA (TX) 264-265 C 4
South Platte River ~ USA (CO) 254-255 M 4
South Point ▲ BS 54-55 H 3
South Pole ▲ ARK 16 E 28
South Porcupine o CDN (ONT) 236-237 G 4
Southport o AUS (QLD) 178-179 M 4
Southport o AUS (TAS) 180-181 J 7
Southport o • GB 90-91 F 5
Southport o USA (NC) 282-283 J 7
South Prince of Wales Wilderness ⊥ • USA 32-33 D 4
South Racoon River ~ USA (IA) 274-275 D 2
South Redstone River ~ CDN 30-31 F 4
South River o CDN (ONT) 238-239 F 3
South River ~ CDN (ONT) 238-239 F 3
South River ~ USA (NC) 282-283 J 6
South Rukuru ~ MW 214-215 G 6
South Sandwich Trench ≃ 6-7 G 14
South Saskatchewan River ~ CDN (SAS) 232-233 L 4
South Seal River ~ CDN 34-35 G 2
South Shetlands ⌒ GB 16 G 30
South Shields o GB 90-91 G 4
South Shore o USA (KY) 276-277 N 2
South Shore o USA (SD) 260-261 K 1
Sioux City o USA (NE) 262-263 K 2
South Sioux City o USA (IA) 274-275 B 2
South Slocan o CDN (BC) 230-231 M 4
South Solitary Island ⌒ AUS 178-179 M 6
South Spicer Island ⌒ CDN 24-25 h 6
South Stradbroke Island ⌒ AUS 178-179 M 4
South Sulphur River ~ USA (TX) 264-265 J 5
South Sunday Creek ~ USA (MT) 250-251 N 5
South Tasman Rise ≃ 13 F 7
South Tetagouche o CDN (NB) 240-241 K 3
South Teton Wilderness Area ⊥ USA (WY) 252-253 H 3
South Thompson River ~ CDN (BC) 230-231 K 3
South Tucson o USA (AZ) 256-257 E 6
South Turkana National Reservoir ⊥ EAK 212-213 E 3
South Tweedsmuir Island ⌒ CDN 28-29 C 2
South Twin Island ⌒ CDN 38-39 E 2
South Twin Lake o CDN (NFL) 242-243 N 3
South Uist ⌒ GB 90-91 D 3
South Wabasca Lake o CDN 32-33 O 4
South Wellesley Islands ⌒ AUS 174-175 F 4
South-West = Sud Ouest o CAM 204-205 N 4
South West Cape ▲ AUS 180-181 J 7
Southwest Cape ▲ NZ 182 A 7
South Western Highway II AUS 176-177 C 6
Southwest Gander River ~ CDN (NFL) 242-243 N 4
South West Harbor o USA (ME) 278-279 N 4
Southwest Indian Ridge ≃ 12 B 9
South West Island ⌒ AUS 174-175 N 5
Southwest Miramichi River ~ CDN (NB) 240-241 J 4
Southwest Pacific Basin ≃ 14-15 N 11
Southwest Passage ≈ USA 268-269 H 7
Southwest Point ▲ BS 54-55 H 3
Southwest Point ▲ BS 54-55 G 2
Southwest Point ▲ BS 54-55 J 4
South West Rocks o AUS 178-179 M 6
Southworth o USA (WA) 244-245 C 3
Souto Soares o BR 72-73 K 2
Souvigny o F 90-91 H 8
Sovata o RO 98-99 N 2
Soverato o I 100-101 F 7
Sovereign o CDN (SAS) 232-233 L 4
Sovetabad o US 136-137 N 4
Sovetsk = Nubarašen o AR 128-129 L 2
Sovetsk o RUS (KIR) 96-97 F 5
Sovetsk o RUS (RIF) 94-95 F 3
Sovetskaja o RUS (KRA) 126-127 D 5
Sovetskaja o RUS (STA) 126-127 F 5
Sovetskaja gora ▲ RUS 112-113 V 1
Sovetskij Gavan' o RUS 122-123 R 2
Sovetskij o RUS (MAR) 96-97 F 5
Sovetskoe o RUS 114-115 G 4
Sovetskoe, ozero ~ RUS 108-109 U 8
Sovhoz, Bol'šereckij o RUS 122-123 R 2
Sovpolle o RUS 88-89 S 4
Sowa Pan o RB 218-219 C 5
Soweto o ZA 220-221 H 3
Soy o EAK 212-213 E 3
Sôya-kaikyô ≋ 152-153 K 1
Sôya-misaki ▲ J 152-153 J 2

Soyo o ANG 216-217 B 3
Sož ~ BY 94-95 M 5
Sozak o KA 124-125 F 6
Sozva ~ RUS 88-89 W 3
Spa o • B 92-93 H 3
Spade o USA (TX) 264-265 B 3
Spafar'eva, ostrov ⌒ RUS 120-121 N 4
Spain = España ■ E 98-99 D 4
Spalding o AUS 180-181 E 2
Spalding o CDN (SAS) 232-233 O 3
Spalding o CDN (WI) 270-271 G 5
Spaldings o JA 54-55 G 5
Spanberga, proliv ≋ RUS 122-123 M 7
Spanda, Akra ▲ GR 100-101 J 7
Spangle o USA (WA) 244-245 H 3
Spaniard's Bay o CDN (NFL) 242-243 P 5
Spanish o CDN (ONT) 238-239 D 2
Spanish Fork o USA (UT) 254-255 D 2
Spanish Peak ▲ USA (OR) 244-245 G 6
Spanish Point ▲ AG 56 E 3
Spanish River ~ CDN (ONT) 238-239 D 2
Spanish River Indian Reserve ☓ CDN (ONT) 238-239 C 2
Spanish Town o CDN (VI) 286-287 R 2
Spanish Town o •• JA 54-55 G 6
Spanish Wells o BS 54-55 G 2
Sparbo, Cape ▲ CDN 24-25 e 3
Spárti o GR 100-101 J 6
Sparwood o CDN (BC) 230-231 P 4
Spas-Demensk o RUS 94-95 O 4
Spas-Klepiki ☆ RUS 94-95 P 4
Spasskaja Guba o RUS 88-89 N 3
Spassk-Dal'nij o RUS 122-123 M 6
Spassk-Rjazanskij o RUS 94-95 P 4
Spath Plateau ▲ GRØ 26-27 p 7
Spatsizi Plateau ▲ CDN 32-33 F 3
Spatsizi River ~ CDN 32-33 F 3
Spavinaw Creek ~ USA (OK) 264-265 G 2
Speaks o USA (TX) 266-267 L 4
Spearfish o USA (SD) 260-261 C 2
Spearhole Creek ~ USA 176-177 E 1
Spearman o USA (TX) 264-265 C 2
Special Economic Zone (SEZ) □ VRC 156-157 F 7
Specimen Hill ▲ AUS 178-179 L 3
Speculator o USA (NY) 278-279 G 5
Speed o USA (WV) 280-281 L 5
Speedwell Island ⌒ GB 78-79 L 7
Speers o CDN (SAS) 232-233 L 3
Speery Island ⌒ AZ 202-203 C 8
Speightstown o BDS 56 F 5
Spelle o USA (TX) 266-267 L 4
Spence Bay ≈ 24-25 Z 6
Spence Bay o CDN 24-25 Z 6
Spencer o USA (IA) 274-275 C 1
Spencer o USA (ID) 252-253 F 2
Spencer o USA (IN) 274-275 M 5
Spencer o USA (NE) 262-263 H 2
Spencer o USA (WV) 280-281 E 5
Spencer, Cape ▲ AUS 180-181 J 7
Spencer, Cape ▲ CDN (NB) 240-241 K 5
Spencer, Cape ▲ USA 32-33 B 2
Spencer, Point ▲ USA 20-21 G 4
Spencer Gulf ≋ 180-181 D 3
Spencerville o CDN (ONT) 238-239 K 4
Spencerville o USA (OH) 280-281 B 3
Spences Bridge o CDN (BC) 230-231 K 3
Spéra o AFG 138-139 B 3
Sperling o CDN (MAN) 234-235 F 5
Sperryville o USA (VA) 280-281 H 5
Spessart ▲ D 92-93 K 4
Spetch o CDN (BC) 230-231 G 3
Spey ~ GB 90-91 F 3
Speyer o • D 92-93 K 4
Spezzano Albanese o I 100-101 F 5
Spicewood o USA (TX) 266-267 K 3
Spickard o USA (MO) 274-275 E 4
Spiekeroog o D 92-93 J 2
Spiller Channel ≋ CDN (BC) 228-229 F 4
Spillimacheen o CDN (BC) 230-231 N 3
Špil'-Tarbagannah, gora ▲ RUS 120-121 H 3
Spinazzola o I 100-101 F 4
Spin Böldak o AFG 134-135 M 3
Spin Ğar ▲ AFG 138-139 B 2
Spink o USA (SD) 260-261 K 4
Spirit Falls o USA (WI) 270-271 J 5
Spirit Lake o USA (IA) 274-275 C 1
Spirit Lake o USA (ID) 252-253 L 2
Spiritwood o CDN (SAS) 232-233 L 2
Spiritwood Lake o USA (ND) 258-259 J 4
Spiro o USA (OK) 264-265 K 3
Spišský hrad • SK 92-93 Q 4
Spitak o AR 128-129 L 2
Spit Point ▲ AUS 172-173 D 6
Spitsbergen ⌒ N 84-85 H 3
Spitskopf ▲ N 84-85 H 3
Spittal an der Drau o A 92-93 M 5
Spitzkoppe ▲ NAM 216-217 C 10
Split o •• HR 100-101 F 3
Split, Cape ▲ CDN (NS) 240-241 L 5
Split Island ⌒ CDN 36-37 K 6
Split Lake o CDN (MAN) 34-35 H 2
Split Lake o CDN (MAN) 34-35 J 2
Split Lake Indian Reserve ☓ CDN 34-35 J 2
Split Rock Dam < AUS 178-179 L 6
Spofford o USA (TX) 266-267 G 4
Špogi o LV 94-95 K 3
Spokane o USA (MO) 276-277 B 4

Spokane o • USA (WA) 244-245 H 3
Spokane House • USA (WA) 244-245 H 3
Spokane Indian Reservation ☓ USA (WA) 244-245 H 3
Spokane River ~ USA (WA) 244-245 H 3
Špola o UA 102-103 G 3
Spoleto o • I 100-101 D 3
Spondin o CDN (ALB) 232-233 G 4
Spooner o USA (WI) 270-271 G 5
Spoon River ~ USA (IL) 274-275 H 4
Sporades = Spurádes, Notioi ⌒ GR 100-101 K 6
Sporádes, Vóries ⌒ GR 100-101 J 5
Sporadske, vozero ~ BY 94-95 J 5
Spornoe o RUS 120-121 O 4
Sporyj Navolok, mys ▲ RUS 108-109 N 3
Spotted House o USA (WY) 252-253 N 2
Spotted Island o CDN (NFL) 38-39 R 2
Spotted Range ▲ USA (NV) 248-249 J 3
Sprague o USA (WA) 244-245 H 3
Sprague Island ⌒ CDN (MAN) 234-235 H 5
Sprague River ~ USA (OR) 244-245 D 8
Spray o USA (OR) 244-245 F 6
Spree ~ D 92-93 M 3
Sprenger, Lake ~ USA 176-177 H 2
Sprengisandur ▲ IS 86-87 d 2
Spring Bay ≋ USA 254-255 O 4
Springbok o ZA 220-221 C 4
Springbrook o USA (MN) 270-271 G 5
Spring City o USA (UT) 254-255 N 6
Spring Coulee o CDN (ALB) 232-233 E 6
Spring Creek o AUS 174-175 H 3
Spring Creek ~ USA (TX) 266-267 G 2
Spring Creek ~ USA (TX) 268-269 E 6
Springdale o CDN (NFL) 242-243 M 3
Springdale o USA (AR) 276-277 A 4
Springdale o USA (NM) 256-257 L 2
Springer o USA (NM) 256-257 L 2
Springer o USA (OK) 264-265 G 4
Springer Mountain ▲ USA (GA) 284-285 F 2
Springerville o USA (AZ) 256-257 F 4
Springfield o CDN (MAN) 240-241 K 5
Springfield o USA (CO) 254-255 N 6
Springfield o USA (FL) 286-287 D 1
Springfield o USA (GA) 284-285 J 4
Springfield o USA (IL) 274-275 J 5
Springfield o USA (KY) 276-277 K 3
Springfield o USA (ME) 278-279 N 3
Springfield o USA (MN) 270-271 D 6
Springfield o USA (MO) 276-277 B 3
Springfield o USA (OH) 280-281 C 4
Springfield o USA (OR) 244-245 C 7
Springfield o USA (SD) 260-261 J 4
Springfield o USA (TN) 276-277 J 4
Springfield o USA (VT) 278-279 K 4
Springfield o USA (IL) 274-275 J 5
Springfield Plateau ▲ USA (MO) 276-277 B 3
Springfontein o ZA 220-221 G 5
Spring Garden o GUY 62-63 E 2
Spring Green o USA (WI) 274-275 H 1
Spring Grove o USA (VA) 280-281 K 6
Springhill o CDN (NS) 240-241 L 5
Spring Hill o USA (FL) 286-287 G 4
Spring Hill o USA (KS) 262-263 M 6
Springhill o USA (LA) 268-269 G 4
Springhouse o CDN (BC) 230-231 J 3
Springlake o USA (TX) 264-265 B 4
Spring Lake o USA (NC) 282-283 J 5
Spring Mill State Park • USA (IN) 274-275 M 5
Spring Mountain Ranch State Park ⊥ • USA (NV) 248-249 J 3
Spring Mountains ▲ USA (NV) 248-249 J 3
Springre o AUS 178-179 F 2
Spring River ~ USA (AR) 276-277 D 4
Spring River ~ USA (MO) 276-277 A 3
Springs o ZA 220-221 J 3
Springside o CDN (SAS) 232-233 Q 4
Springs Junction o NZ 182 D 5
Springsure o AUS 178-179 K 3
Springtown o USA (TX) 264-265 G 5
Springvale o AUS 172-173 H 6
Sprinj Vale o AUS 174-175 D 6
Springvale o USA (ME) 278-279 L 5
Springvale Homestead • AUS 172-173 L 3
Spring Valley o CDN (SAS) 232-233 N 6
Spring Valley o USA (CA) 248-249 Q 7
Spring Valley o USA (IL) 274-275 J 3
Spring Valley o USA (MN) 270-271 F 7
Springview o USA (NE) 262-263 G 2
Springville o USA (AL) 284-285 D 3
Springville o USA (CA) 248-249 F 3
Springville o USA (NY) 278-279 D 5
Springville o USA (UT) 254-255 D 3
Springwater o CDN (SAS) 232-233 K 4
Sproat Lake o CDN (BC) 230-231 H 4
Sprouses Corner o USA (VA) 280-281 H 6
Spruce Brook o CDN (NFL) 242-243 K 4
Sprucedale o CDN (ONT) 238-239 F 3
Spruce Grove o CDN (ALB) 232-233 E 3
Spruce Home o CDN (SAS) 232-233 N 2
Spruce Knob ▲ USA (WV) 280-281 G 5
Spruce Knob National Recreation Area ⊥ USA (WV) 280-281 G 5
Spruce Lake o CDN (SAS) 232-233 K 2
Spruce Mountain ▲ USA (NV) 246-247 L 3
Spruce Pine o USA (NC) 282-283 E 5
Spruce River o CDN 30-31 V 6
Spruce Woods Forest Reserve ⊥ CDN (MAN) 234-235 D 5

Spruce Woods Provincial Park ⊥ CDN (MAN) 234-235 D 5
Spur o USA (TX) 264-265 D 5
Spurgeon o USA (IN) 268-269 F 6
Spurn Head ▲ GB 90-91 H 5
Sputinow o CDN (ALB) 232-233 G 3
Squamish o CDN (BC) 230-231 H 4
Squapan Lake o USA (ME) 278-279 N 2
Square Hill ▲ AUS 176-177 H 3
Square Ilands o CDN 38-39 R 2
Square Lake o USA (ME) 278-279 N 1
Squarmish River ~ CDN (BC) 230-231 H 3
Squatec o CDN (QUE) 240-241 G 3
Squaw Creek National Wildlife Refuge ⊥ USA (MO) 274-275 C 4
Squaw House o USA (MN) 270-271 D 3
Squaw River ~ CDN (ONT) 236-237 D 3
Squaw River ~ USA 20-21 K 3
Squillace o USA (WA) 244-245 H 3
Squillace, Golfo di ≋ 100-101 F 6
Squires, Mount ▲ AUS 176-177 G 4
Squirrel River ~ CDN (ONT) 236-237 D 3
Squirrel River ~ USA 20-21 K 3
Sragen o RI 168 D 3
Srbica o YU 100-101 H 3
Srbobran o YU 100-101 G 2
Srebárna, Naroden Park ⊥ ••• BG 102-103 E 5
Sredec o BG 102-103 E 5
Sredinnyj hrebet ▲ RUS 120-121 N 7
Srednebelaja o RUS 122-123 C 3
Srednee Kujto, ozero o RUS 88-89 L 4
Srednekolymsk o RUS 110-111 d 6
Sredneobskaja nizmennost' ▲ RUS 114-115 L 3
Sredne russkaja vozvyšennost' ▲ RUS 94-95 Q 5
Srednij, ostrov ⌒ RUS 108-109 Y 3
Srednij, proliv ≋ 112-113 P 2
Srednij, zaliv ≋ RUS 108-109 M 1
Srednij Ikorec o RUS 102-103 L 3
Srednij Kalar o RUS 118-119 H 6
Srednij Mamakan o RUS 118-119 G 7
Srednij Ural ▲ RUS 114-115 L 5
Srednij Viljujkan ~ RUS 116-117 N 3
Sredni Ural = Srednij Ural ▲ RUS 114-115 L 5
Srednjaja ~ RUS 110-111 K 3
Srednjaja, gora ▲ RUS 108-109 a 4
Srednjaja Kočoma ~ RUS 116-117 N 4
Srednjaja Mokla ~ RUS 118-119 J 4
Srednjaja Olëkma ~ RUS 118-119 K 8
Srednogorie = Pirdop + Zlatica □ BG 102-103 D 6
Šrenk ~ RUS 108-109 Z 4
Srě Noy o K 158-159 H 4
Srě Sbov o K 158-159 J 4
Sretensk o RUS 118-119 H 9
Sribne o UA 102-103 H 2
Sribrodil o BD 142-143 F 3
Sri Dungargarh o IND 138-139 E 5
Srīkākulam o IND 142-143 C 6
Sri Kālahasti o • IND 140-141 H 4
Sri Lanka ■ CL 140-141 J 6
Srinagar ☆ IND 138-139 E 2
Srinakarin National Park ⊥ THA 158-159 F 3
Srinakarin Reservoir < THA 158-159 G 3
Sringeri o IND 140-141 F 4
Srinivāspur o IND 140-141 H 4
Sriperumbudur o IND 140-141 H 4
Srīrāmapura o IND 140-141 G 4
Srirāmpur o IND 138-139 G 10
Srirangam o • IND 140-141 H 5
Srirangapatnam o • IND 140-141 G 4
Srirangarājupuram o IND 140-141 H 3
Srisailam o IND 140-141 H 2
Sri Toi o PK 138-139 B 4
Srivaikuntam o IND 140-141 G 6
Srivardhan o IND 138-139 D 9
Srivilliputtūr o IND 140-141 G 6
Šroda Wielkopolska o PL 92-93 O 2
Srostki o RUS 124-125 O 2
Srungavarapukota o IND 142-143 C 6
ș-Şawāb, Wādī ~ SYR 128-129 J 5
s-Sibū', Wādī ∴• ET 194-195 F 6
Staaten River ~ AUS 174-175 G 5
Staaten River National Park ⊥ AUS 174-175 G 5
Stabburdalen nasjonalpark ⊥ N 86-87 M 1
Stabkirche Urnes ••• N 86-87 C 6
Stackpool o CDN (ONT) 236-237 G 5
Stack Skerry ⌒ GB 90-91 F 2
Stacyville o USA (IA) 274-275 F 1
Stade o D 92-93 K 2
Staduhino o RUS 112-113 O 3
Staffel o USA (AR) 276-277 D 5
Stafford ☆ GB 90-91 F 5
Stafford o USA (KS) 262-263 H 6
Stafford Springs o USA (CT) 280-281 O 2
Stahanov = Kadijivka o UA 102-103 L 3
Staines, Peninsula ⌣ RCH 80 D 5
Staked Plain = Llano Estacado ⌣ USA (TX) 264-265 C 5
Stalingrad = Zarizyn ☆ RUS 94-95 U 5
Stalwart o CDN (SAS) 232-233 N 4
Stamberg, gora ▲ RUS 122-123 K 5
Stamford o AUS 178-179 G 2
Stamford o GB 90-91 G 5
Stamford o USA (CT) 280-281 O 3
Stamford o USA (NY) 278-279 G 6
Stamford o USA (TX) 264-265 E 5
Stamford, Lake < USA (TX) 264-265 E 5
Stamping Ground o USA (KY) 276-277 L 2
Stampriet o NAM 220-221 D 2
Stamps o USA (AR) 276-277 B 7
Stamsund o N 86-87 F 2
Stanberry o USA (MO) 274-275 D 4
Stancionno-Ojašinskij o RUS 114-115 R 7
Standard o CDN (ALB) 232-233 F 4
Standerton o ZA 220-221 J 3
Standing Rock Indian Reservation ☓ USA (SD) 260-261 D 1

Standing Stone State Park ⊥ USA (TN) 276-277 K 4
Standish o USA (MI) 272-273 F 4
Stand Off o CDN (ALB) 232-233 E 6
Stand Rock • USA (WI) 270-271 J 7
Stanfield o USA (AZ) 256-257 D 6
Stanfield o USA (OR) 244-245 F 5
Stanford o USA (KY) 276-277 L 3
Stanford o USA (MT) 250-251 J 4
Stang, Cape ▲ CDN 24-25 U 5
Stanger o ZA 220-221 K 4
Stanhope o AUS 180-181 H 6
Stanhope o CDN (PEI) 240-241 M 4
Stanhope o GB 90-91 F 4
Staniard Creek o BS 54-55 G 2
stanica Bagaevskaja o RUS 102-103 M 4
Staniel Cay Beach ⌣ BS 54-55 G 2
Stanislaus River ~ USA (CA) 246-247 E 5
Stanke Dimitrov = Dupnica o BG 102-103 C 6
Stanley o AUS 180-181 H 6
Stanley o CDN (MAN) 240-241 J 4
Stanley ☆ GB 78-79 M 6
Stanley o USA (ID) 252-253 D 2
Stanley o USA (ND) 258-259 D 3
Stanley o USA (NM) 256-257 K 3
Stanley, Mount ▲ ZRE 212-213 B 3
Stanley, Port o CDN (ONT) 238-239 D 6
Stanley Mission o CDN 34-35 D 3
Stanley Pool o ZRE 210-211 D 5
Stanley Reservoir < IND 140-141 G 5
Stanleyville = Kisangani ☆ ZRE 210-211 K 3
Stanmore o CDN (ALB) 232-233 G 4
Stanmore o ZW 218-219 E 5
Stannard Rock ⌒ USA (MI) 270-271 L 3
Stanovik, hrebet ▲ RUS 118-119 F 11
Stanovoe köli o KA 124-125 F 1
Stanovoe nagor'e ▲ RUS 118-119 E 7
Stanovoj hrebet ▲ RUS 118-119 G 8
Stanovoye Nagor'ye = Stanovoe nagor'e ▲ RUS 118-119 E 7
Stanovoy Khrebet = Stanovoj hrebet ▲ RUS 118-119 L 7
Stansmore Range ▲ AUS 172-173 H 5
Stanthorpe o AUS 178-179 L 5
Stanton o USA (MI) 272-273 P 4
Stanton o USA (ND) 258-259 F 4
Stanton o USA (NE) 262-263 J 3
Stanton o USA (TX) 264-265 C 6
Stanwell o AUS 178-179 L 2
Stanwell Fletcher Lake o CDN 24-25 Y 4
Stanwix National Monument, Fort • USA (NY) 278-279 F 5
Stanwood o USA (MI) 272-273 D 4
Stanyčno-Luhans'ke o UA 102-103 L 3
Stapleford o ZW 218-219 G 4
Staples o CDN (ONT) 238-239 C 6
Staples o USA (MN) 270-271 D 4
Stapleton o USA (NE) 262-263 F 3
Stapylton Bay ≋ 24-25 O 6
Star o CDN 232-233 F 2
Star o USA (MS) 268-269 K 4
Staraja Kulatka o RUS 96-97 E 7
Staraja Majna o RUS 96-97 F 6
Staraja Poltavka o RUS 96-97 F 8
Staraja Russa o RUS 94-95 M 3
Staraja Toropa o RUS 94-95 M 3
Stará L'ubovňa o SK 92-93 Q 4
Staravina o MK 100-101 H 4
Stara Zagora o BG 102-103 D 6
Starboard o CDN (SAS) 232-233 O 3
Star City o CDN (SAS) 232-233 O 3
Star City o USA (AR) 276-277 D 6
Starcke National Park ⊥ AUS 174-175 H 4
Stargard Szczeciński o PL 92-93 N 2
Starica o RUS (AST) 96-97 D 9
Starica o RUS (TVR) 94-95 O 3
Starigrad-Paklenica o HR 100-101 E 2
Stark o USA (KS) 262-263 L 7
Starke o USA (FL) 286-287 G 2
Stark Lake o CDN 30-31 O 4
Starks o USA (LA) 268-269 G 6
Starkville o CDN (SAS) 232-233 O 3
Starkville o USA (MS) 268-269 M 3
Starkweather o USA (ND) 258-259 J 3
Starnberg o D 92-93 L 5
Starnberger See o D 92-93 L 5
Starobaltačevo o RUS 96-97 J 5
Starobeševe o UA 102-103 L 3
Starobíls'k o UA 102-103 L 3
Starokostjantyniv ☆ UA 102-103 E 3
Starominskaja o RUS 102-103 L 4
Staro Orjahovo o BG 102-103 E 6
Staročerbinovskaja o RUS 102-103 L 4
Starosubhangulovo o RUS 96-97 K 7
Starting Point to Baliem Valley •• RI 166-167 K 4
Start Point ▲ GB 90-91 F 6
Start Point to Torajaland ⊥ •• RI 164-165 D 4
Startup o USA (WA) 244-245 D 3
Staryj Oskol o RUS 102-103 K 2
Staryja Darohi o BY 94-95 L 5
State Bridge o USA (CO) 254-255 J 4
State College o USA (PA) 280-281 J 3
State Line o USA (MS) 268-269 M 5
Stateline o USA (NV) 248-249 J 4
Staten Island ⌒ USA (NY) 280-281 M 3
Statenville o USA (GA) 284-285 G 6
Statesboro o USA (GA) 284-285 J 4
Statesville o USA (NC) 282-283 G 5
Statham o USA (GA) 284-285 G 3
Station Nord o GRØ 26-27 r 3
Statue of Liberty ••• USA (NY) 280-281 M 3
Stauffer o CDN (ALB) 232-233 D 4
Stauning Alper ▲ GRØ 26-27 n 7
Staunton o USA (IL) 274-275 J 5
Staunton o USA (VA) 280-281 G 5
Stavanger ☆ N 86-87 B 7

Tabor ○ USA (IA) 274-275 C 4
Tabor ○ USA (SD) 260-261 J 4
Tabor = Tábor ○ CZ 92-93 N 4
Tabora ◘ EAT 212-213 D 6
Tabora ★• EAT (TAB) 212-213 D 6
Tabor City ○ USA (NC) 282-283 J 6
Tabory ★ RUS 114-115 H 5
Tabou ○ BF 202-203 J 4
Tabou ○• CI 202-203 G 7
Tabrinkout < RIM 196-197 C 5
Tabrīz ★•• IR 128-129 M 3
Tábua, Riachão ~ BR 68-69 F 6
Tabuaeran ⌒ KIB 13 L 2
Tabuan, Pulau ⌒ RI 162-163 F 7
Tabubil ○ PNG 183 A 3
Tabudarat ○ RI 164-165 D 5
Tabūk ◘ KSA 130-131 E 4
Tabūk ★ KSA 130-131 E 3
Tabuk ★ RP 160-161 D 4
Tabuleirinho, Cachoeira do ~ BR 62-63 F 6
Tabuleiro ○ BR 76-77 K 6
Tabulga ○ RUS 124-125 K 1
Tabulo ○ RI 164-165 H 3
Tabūr ○ SUD 206-207 F 3
Tabusintac ○ CDN (NB) 240-241 K 3
Tabusintac Indian Reserve ✗ CDN (NB) 240-241 K 3
Tabwemasana ▲ VAN 184 II a 2
Tacabamba ○ PE 64-65 C 5
Tacajó ○ C 54-55 H 4
Tacalaya ○ PE 70-71 B 5
Tacana, Volcán ▲ GCA 52-53 H 4
Tacañitas ○ RA 76-77 F 5
Tacarembó, Río ~ ROU 78-79 M 2
Tacarigua ○ YV 60-61 H 2
Tacarigua, Parque Nacional Laguna de ⊥ YV 60-61 J 2
Tacaratu ○ BR 68-69 J 6
Tacbolubu ○ RP 160-161 B 8
Tachakou ○ VRC 146-147 G 3
Tachdaït, Adrar ▲ RMM 196-197 L 5
Tachee ○ USA (AZ) 256-257 E 2
Tacheng ○ VRC 146-147 F 2
Tachibana-wan ≈ 152-153 D 8
Tachichilte, Isla de ⌒ MEX 50-51 E 5
Tachie ○ CDN (BC) 228-229 K 2
Tachie River ~ CDN (BC) 228-229 K 2
Tachilek ○ MYA 142-143 L 5
Tachiumet < LAR 190-191 H 7
Tacima ○ BR 68-69 L 5
Tacinskij ○ RUS 102-103 M 3
Taciuã, Lago ○ BR 66-67 G 5
Tacloban ★ RP 160-161 F 7
Tacna ★ PE 70-71 B 6
Tacoma ○ USA (WA) 244-245 C 3
Taco Pozo ○ RA 76-77 F 3
Tacora, Volcán ▲ RCH 70-71 C 5
Taco Taco ○ C 54-55 D 3
Tacuane ○ MOC 218-219 J 3
Tacuaras ○ PY 76-77 J 4
Tacuarembó ★ ROU 76-77 K 6
Tacuato ○ YV 60-61 G 2
Tácume • PE 64-65 C 5
Tacunara, Rio ~ BR 68-69 C 7
Tacupare, Cachoeira ~ BR 66-67 K 5
Tacurong ○ RP 160-161 F 9
Tacuru ○ BR 76-77 K 2
Tacutu, Rio ~ BR 62-63 E 4
Tadahadi ○ SOL 184 I e 4
Tadami-gawa ~ J 152-153 H 6
Tadant, Oued ~ DZ 190-191 F 9
Tadao ○ RP 160-161 D 3
Taddert ○ MA 188-189 H 5
Taddert, Tizi-n- ▲ MA 188-189 J 5
Tadebjajaha ○ RUS 108-109 Q 6
Tadek Lake ○ CDN 30-31 F 2
Tadélako < RN 198-199 D 5
Tademaït, Plateau du ▲ DZ 190-191 C 6
Tadenet Lake ○ CDN 24-25 J 6
Tādepallegūdem ○ IND 140-141 J 2
Tadéra, In- < RN 198-199 D 2
Tadio, Lagune ≈ 202-203 H 7
Tadjemout ○ DZ 190-191 D 4
Tadjentourt ▲ DZ 190-191 G 7
Tadjetaret, Oued ~ DZ 190-191 F 9
Tadjmout ○ DZ 190-191 D 8
Tadjoura ○ DJI 208-209 F 3
Tadjoura, Golfe de ≈ 208-209 F 3
Tadjrouna ○ DZ 190-191 D 4
Tadmore ○ CDN (SAS) 232-233 Q 4
Tadmur Palmyra ★•• SYR 128-129 H 5
Tadoba National Park ⊥ IND 138-139 G 9
Tadohae Haesang National Park ⊥• ROK 150-151 F 10
Tadoule Lake ○ CDN 30-31 U 6
Tadoussac ○• CDN (QUE) 240-241 F 2
Tadpatri ○ IND 140-141 H 3
Tadrart, Jabal ▲ DZ 190-191 H 8
Taduna ○ RI 166-167 C 5
Taduno ○ RI 164-165 H 4
Taech'ŏn ○ ROK 150-151 F 9
Taech'ŏngdo ⌒ DVR 150-151 E 9
Taedong Gang ~ DVR 150-151 E 8
Taegu ○ ROK 150-151 G 10
Taehan Haehyŏp ≈ 150-151 F 11
Taehŭksan Do ⌒ ROK 150-151 E 10
Taejŏn ○ ROK 150-151 F 9
Taejŏng ○ ROK 150-151 F 11
Taejŏnpyŏngdo ⌒ ROK 150-151 E 9
T'aepaek ○ ROK 150-151 G 9
Ta'er Si • VRC 154-155 B 3
Taёžnyj ○ RUS 116-117 G 7
Tafalla ○ E 98-99 G 3
Tafarit, Râs ▲ RIM 196-197 B 4
Tafassasset ~ RN 198-199 D 2
Tafassasset, Oued ~ DZ 190-191 G 9
Tafea ◘ VAN 184 II b 4
Tafédek < RN 198-199 C 4
Tafelberg ▲ SME 62-63 F 4
Tafelberg, National Reservaat ⊥ SME 62-63 F 4
Tafermaar ○ RI 166-167 H 5
Tafí del Valle ○• RA 76-77 E 4
Tafila, at- ★ JOR 130-131 D 2
Tafilalt ∴ MA 188-189 J 5
Tafinkar < RMM 196-197 M 7
Tafiré ○ CI 202-203 H 5
Tafraoute ○•• MA 188-189 G 6
Tafreš ○ IR 134-135 D 1
Taft ○ IR 134-135 F 3
Taft ○ USA (CA) 248-249 E 4
Taft ○ USA (TN) 276-277 J 5
Taft ○ USA (TX) 266-267 K 6
Taftān, Kūh-e ▲ IR 134-135 J 4
Tāga ○ WS 184 V a 1
Tagāb ○ AFG 138-139 B 2
Tagab ○ SUD 200-201 E 3
Tagagawik River ~ USA 20-21 L 4
Tagalak Island ⌒ USA 22-23 J 7
Tagânet Keyna < RMM 196-197 J 5
Taganito ○ RP 160-161 F 8
Taganrog ○• RUS 102-103 L 4
Taganrogskij zaliv ≈ 102-103 K 4
Tagant ◘ RIM 196-197 E 5
Tagant ▲ RIM 202-203 B 5
Tagapula Island ⌒ RP 160-161 F 6
Tağarak ○ IR 128-129 N 5
Tagarev, gora ▲ TM 136-137 E 5
Tagari River ~ PNG 183 B 3
Tagaung ○ MYA 142-143 K 4
Tagaytay ○ RP 160-161 D 5
Tagbalé ○ RCA 206-207 E 6
Tagbara ○ RCA 206-207 E 6
Tagbilaran ★ RP 160-161 E 8
Tage, Danau ○ RI 166-167 J 3
Tagelajiabo ○ VRC 144-145 F 4
Taggert ○ USA (IN) 274-275 M 5
Taghit ○ DZ 188-189 K 5
Taghouaji, Massif de ▲ RN 198-199 D 4
Taghum ○ CDN (BC) 230-231 M 4
Tağiābād, Rūdhāne-ye ~ IR 134-135 H 4
Tagish Lake ○ CDN 20-21 X 6
Taglo Point ▲ RP 160-161 E 8
Tagna ~ RUS 116-117 K 9
Tagopah, Tanjung ▲ RI 166-167 G 3
Tagou ○ BF 202-203 L 4
Tagoûrâret < RIM 196-197 G 6
Tagpait ○ RP 160-161 C 8
Tagrina, Oued ~ DZ 198-199 C 2
Tağris ○ IR 136-137 B 7
Taguá ○ BR 68-69 F 7
Tagua, Río ~ CO 60-61 D 6
Taguaruçu, Ribeiro ~ BR 70-71 K 7
Taguas, Río de las ~ RA 76-77 C 5
Taguatinga ○ BR (FED) 72-73 F 3
Taguatinga ○ BR (TOC) 72-73 G 2
Taguay ○ YV 60-61 H 3
Tagum ★ RP 160-161 F 9
Tah, Sebkha ○ MA 188-189 E 7
Tahafo ○ RI 164-165 K 3
Tahalra ∴ DZ 190-191 E 9
Tahalupu ○ RI 166-167 D 3
Tahamiyam ○ SUD 200-201 H 3
Tahan, Gunung ▲ MAL 162-163 E 2
Tahan, Kuala ○ MAL 162-163 E 2
Taḥār ◘ AFG 136-137 L 6
Taharoa ○ NZ 182 E 3
Tahar-Souk ○ MA 188-189 J 3
Tahat ▲ DZ 190-191 E 9
Tahawus ○ USA (NY) 278-279 G 4
Tahe ○ VRC 150-151 E 1
Ṭāheri, Bandar-e ○ IR 134-135 E 5
Tahifet ○ DZ 190-191 F 9
Tahifet, Oued ~ DZ 190-191 F 9
Tahilt ○ MAU 148-149 C 5
Tahiryuak Lake ○ CDN 24-25 Q 5
Tahiti ⌒ F 13 N 4
Tahlāb ~ PK 134-135 K 4
Tahlāb, Dasht-i- ∴ PK 134-135 J 4
Tahoe, Lake ○ USA (CA) 246-247 E 4
Tahoe City ○ USA (CA) 246-247 E 4
Tahoe Lake ○ CDN 24-25 R 5
Tahoka ○ USA (TX) 264-265 C 5
Taholah ○ USA (WA) 244-245 A 3
Tahomi ○ LB 202-203 F 7
Tahoua ◘ RN 198-199 B 5
Tahoua ★ RN (TAH) 198-199 B 5
Tahquamenon Falls State Park ⊥ USA (MI) 270-271 N 4
Tahrami ○ LAR 192-193 F 5
Taḥr-e Ğamšid ○•• IR 134-135 E 4
Tahrou, Oued ~ DZ 190-191 G 8
Tahsis ○ CDN (BC) 230-231 C 4
Taḥṭa ○ ET 194-195 E 4
Tahta ○ RUS 122-123 H 2
Tahta ○ TM 136-137 F 4
Tahta-Bazar ○ TM 136-137 H 7
Tahtakūpir ★ US 136-137 G 3
Tahtakupyr ○ US 136-137 G 3
Tahtali Dağları ▲ TR 128-129 F 3
Tahtamygda ○ RUS 118-119 L 8
Taḥt-e Soleiman, Kūh-e ▲ IR 136-137 B 6
Taht-e Suleimān ○• IR 128-129 M 4
Tahtojama ~ RUS 120-121 Q 3
Tahtojamsk ○ RUS 120-121 Q 3
Tahtsa Lake ○ CDN (BC) 228-229 G 3
Tahuamanu, Río ~ PE 70-71 B 2
Tahulandang ○ RI 164-165 J 2
Tahulandang, Pulau ⌒ RI 164-165 J 2
Tahuna ○ RI 164-165 J 2
Tai ○ CI 202-203 G 7
Taï, Parc National de ⊥•• CI 202-203 G 7
Taiama ○ WAL 202-203 D 5
Tai'an ○ VRC 154-155 K 3
Taibai ○ VRC 154-155 E 4
Taibai Shan ▲ VRC 154-155 E 5
Taibao D. ▲ VRC 154-155 M 3
Taibashan Z.B. ⊥• VRC 154-155 E 5
Taibet ○ DZ 190-191 F 4
Taibique ○ E 188-189 C 7
Taibus Qi ○ VRC 148-149 M 7
Taichung ○ RC 156-157 M 4
Taidalt ○ MA 188-189 G 6
Ṭā'if, aṭ- ○• KSA 132-133 B 3
Taigetos ▲ GR 100-101 J 6
Taigu ○ VRC 154-155 H 3
Taihang Shan ▲ VRC 154-155 H 4
Taihape ○ NZ 182 E 3
Taihe ○ VRC (ANH) 154-155 J 5
Taihe ○ VRC (JXI) 156-157 J 3
Tai Hu ○ VRC (ANH) 154-155 L 6
Taihu ○ VRC (ANH) 154-155 K 6
Tai Hu ○ VRC (JIA) 154-155 M 6
Taihu • VRC (JIA) 154-155 M 6
Taijiang ○ VRC 156-157 F 3
Taikang ○ VRC 154-155 J 4
Taikkyi ○ MYA 158-159 C 2
Tailai ○ VRC 150-151 D 4
Tailako ○ RI 166-167 C 6
Tailem Bend ○ AUS 180-181 E 3
Tailing ○ GUY 62-63 D 2
Taim ○ BR 74-75 D 9
Taimā' ○• KSA 130-131 F 4
Taimana ○ RMM 202-203 G 3
Taimba ○ RUS 116-117 J 5
Taimushan • VRC 156-157 M 3
Tain ○ GB 90-91 E 3
Tainan ○ RC 156-157 M 5
Taínhas ○ BR 74-75 E 7
Taining ○ VRC 156-157 K 3
Taino, Plage ∴• RH 54-55 J 5
Taió ○ BR 74-75 E 6
Taiobeiras ○ BR 72-73 J 3
Taiof Island ⌒ PNG 184 I b 1
Taipei ★•• RC 156-157 M 4
Taiping ○• MAL 162-163 D 2
Taiping ○ VRC (GXI) 156-157 G 5
Taiping ○ VRC (GXI) 156-157 E 5
Taipingchuan ○ VRC 150-151 D 5
Taiping L. ▲ VRC 150-151 C 4
Taipong ○ GUY 62-63 E 3
Täipur ○ IND 142-143 D 3
Ṭair, Ğabal aṭ- ⌒ Y 132-133 B 6
Tairhemt, Tizi-n ▲ MA 188-189 J 4
Taírona, Parque Nacional ⊥•• CO 60-61 D 2
Tais ○ RI 162-163 E 7
Taisha ○ EC 64-65 D 3
Taisha ○• J 152-153 E 7
Taishan ○ VRC (GDG) 156-157 H 5
Taishan ▲••• VRC (SHD) 154-155 K 3
Taishi ○ RC 156-157 M 5
Taishun ○ VRC 156-157 L 3
Taisiya ∴ KSA 130-131 H 3
Taita Hills ▲ EAK 212-213 G 5
Taitaitanopo, Pulau ⌒ RI 162-163 D 6
Taitao, Península de ~ RCH 80 C 3
Taititu ○ BR 66-67 D 5
Taitna Lake ○ CDN 30-31 S 5
Taitung ○ RC 156-157 M 5
Taivalkoski ○ FIN 88-89 K 4
Taiwan ■ RC 156-157 M 5
Taiwan Banks ▲ 156-157 L 5
Taiwan Strait ≈ 156-157 L 5
Tai Xian ○ VRC 154-155 M 5
Taixing ○ VRC 154-155 M 5
Taiyang Dao • VRC 150-151 F 5
Taiyuan ★• VRC 154-155 H 3
Taizhou ○ VRC 154-155 L 5
Taizhou Liedao ⌒ VRC 156-157 M 2
Taizhou Wan ~ VRC 156-157 M 2
Ta'izz ○ Y 132-133 D 7
Tajdon ~ RUS 114-115 T 7
Tajen ○ RC 156-157 M 5
Tajga ○ RUS 114-115 S 6
Tajga ○ RUS (SHL) 122-123 K 4
Tajga ~ RUS 116-117 H 6
Tajgan ○ MAU 148-149 C 4
Tajgonos, mys ▲ RUS 120-121 T 3
Tajgonos, poluostrov ~ RUS 120-121 T 3
Tajicaringa ○ MEX 50-51 G 6
Tajikistan = Tāğikistān ■ TJ 136-137 L 5
Tajima ○ J 152-153 H 6
Tajimi ○ J 152-153 G 7
Tajin, El ∴•• MEX 52-53 F 1
Tajique ○ USA (NM) 256-257 J 4
Tajkanskij, hrebet ▲ RUS 122-123 F 2
Tajlan, köl ○ KA 96-97 G 10
Taj Mahal ••• IND 138-139 G 6
Tajmendra, Bol'šaja ~ RUS 118-119 H 6
Tajmura ~ RUS 116-117 K 4
Tajmylyr ○ RUS 110-111 N 3
Tajmyr, ostrov ⌒ RUS 108-109 a 3
Tajmyr, ozero ○ RUS 108-109 d 4
Tajmyra, mys ▲ RUS 108-109 e 2
Tajmyrskij zaliv ○ RUS 108-109 b 3
Tajnynotskij hrebet ▲ RUS 120-121 T 3
Tajo, Río ~ E 98-99 F 4
Tajšet ★ RUS 116-117 J 8
Tajumulco, Volcán ▲ GCA 52-53 J 4
Tajuña, Río ~ E 98-99 F 4
Tājūrā' ○ LAR 192-193 E 1
Tajura ~ RUS 116-117 N 7
Tak ○ THA 158-159 E 2
Takāb ○ IR 128-129 M 4
Takaba ○ EAK 212-213 H 2
Takachiho ○ J 152-153 D 8
Takahashi ○ J 152-153 E 7
Takahashi-gawa ~ J 152-153 E 7
Takahe, Mount ▲ ARK 16 F 26
Takaka ○ NZ 182 D 4
Takalala ○ RI 164-165 F 6
Takalar ○ RI 164-165 F 6
Takalou ○ TCH 206-207 D 3
Takalous, Oued ~ DZ 190-191 F 9
Takamaka ○ SY 224 D 2
Takamatsu ○ J (EHI) 152-153 E 8
Takamatsu ★• J (KAG) 152-153 F 7
Takan, Gunung ▲ RI 168 C 7
Takanabe ○ J 152-153 D 8
Takanosu ○ J 152-153 J 4
Takaoka ○ J 152-153 G 6
Takapuna ○ NZ 182 E 2
Takara ○ RCA 206-207 E 4
Takara-shima ⌒ J 152-153 C 10
Takasaki ○ J 152-153 H 6
Takatokwane ○ RB 220-221 G 2
Takatsuki ○ J 152-153 F 7
Takatu hrebet ▲ RUS 96-97 K 7
Takaungu ○ EAK 212-213 G 5
Takayama ○ J 152-153 G 6
Takefu ○ J 152-153 G 7
Takengon (Takingeun) ○ RI 162-163 B 2
Takeo ○ J 152-153 C 8
Takeo ○ K 158-159 H 5
Tākestān ○• IR 128-129 N 4
Taketa ○ J 152-153 D 8
Tak Fa ○ THA 158-159 F 3
Takhini River ~ CDN 20-21 W 6
Takhro ○ THA 158-159 G 3
Takht-i-Bahi ∴••• PK 138-139 C 2
Takht-i-Sulaiman ▲ PK 138-139 B 4
Takiéta ○ RN 198-199 D 6
Takikawa ○ J 152-153 J 3
Takinoue ○ J 152-153 K 2
Takis ○ PNG 183 F 3
Takisset, Oued ~ DZ 190-191 H 8
Takiyok, Pointe ▲ CDN 36-37 P 5
Takiyuak Lake ○ CDN 30-31 O 2
Takla Lake ○ CDN 32-33 H 4
Takla Landing ○ CDN 32-33 H 4
Takla Makan Desert = Taklimakan Shamo ∴ VRC 146-147 E 6
Tākli Dhokeshwar ○ IND 138-139 E 10
Taklimakan Shamo ∴ VRC 146-147 E 6
Taknis ○ LAR 192-193 J 1
Takobanda ○ RCA 206-207 E 5
Takoma Park ○ USA (MD) 280-281 K 5
Takoradi ○• GH 202-203 K 7
Takorka ○ RN 198-199 C 6
Takoutala ○ SN 202-203 D 2
Takpamba ○ RT 202-203 L 5
Takpoima ○ LB 202-203 E 6
Takrit ★ IRQ 128-129 K 5
Taksagerbej, grjada ▲ RUS 108-109 a 5
Taksimo ○ RUS 118-119 G 7
Takslesluk Lake ○ USA 20-21 J 6
Takuapa ○ THA 158-159 E 6
Taku Arm ○ CDN 20-21 X 7
Takum ○ WAN 204-205 H 5
Takundi ○ ZRE 210-211 F 6
Taku Plateau ▲ CDN 20-21 Y 7
Taku River ~ CDN 32-33 D 2
Takwa ∴• EAK 212-213 H 5
Tāl ○ IND 138-139 E 8
Tala ○ EAK 212-213 F 4
Tāla ○ IND 142-143 B 4
Tala ○ MEX 52-53 C 1
Tala ○ ROU 78-79 M 3
Tala, Čubuka-gora ▲ RUS 110-111 a 7
Tala, El ○ RA 76-77 E 4
Tala, Río ~ RA 76-77 E 4
Talacasto ○ RA 76-77 C 6
Talacasto, Sierra de ▲ RA 76-77 C 6
Talačyn ★ BY 94-95 L 4
Talagang ○ PK 138-139 D 3
Talagante ○ RCH 78-79 D 2
Talahāt, Ša'ib aṭ- ~ IRQ 128-129 L 7
Talahini ○ CI 202-203 J 5
Talahini-Tomora ○ CI 202-203 J 5
Talaimannar ○ CL 140-141 H 6
Talaivasal ○ IND 140-141 H 5
Talaja ○ RUS 116-117 H 8
Talaja ○ RUS (MAG) 120-121 P 3
Talaja ~ RUS 116-117 H 8
Talakalla ○ IND 140-141 F 3
Talakan ○ RUS (AMR) 122-123 D 3
Talakan ○ RUS (HBR) 122-123 E 4
Talali ○ RUS 122-123 B 3
Talamanca, Cordillera de ▲ CR 52-53 C 7
Talamba ○ PK 138-139 D 4
Talanga ○ HN 52-53 L 4
Talangbetutu ○ RI 162-163 F 6
Talangjauh ○ RI 162-163 F 6
Talangpadung ○ RI 162-163 F 7
Talara ○ PE 64-65 B 4
Talaroo ○ AUS 174-175 G 6
Talas ~ KA 124-125 F 6
Talas ~ KA 124-125 G 6
Talas ★ KS 136-137 N 3
Talas ~ KS 136-137 N 3
Talasea ○ PNG 183 F 3
Talasskij Alatau, hrebet ▲ KA 136-137 M 3
Talata-Ampano ○ RM 222-223 E 8
Talatakoh, Pulau ⌒ RI 164-165 H 4
Talata Mafara ○ WAN 198-199 C 6
Talat at-Timiat ○ KSA 130-131 H 3
Tal' at Damya ∴ MA 188-189 G 7
Talaud, Kepulauan ⌒ RI 164-165 K 1
Talavera, Ilha ⌒ PY 76-77 J 4
Talavera de la Reina ○• E 98-99 E 5
Talawana ○ AUS 172-173 E 7
Talawanta ○ AUS 174-175 F 6
Talawdi ○ SUD 206-207 K 3
Talawe, Mount ▲ PNG 183 E 3
Talawi ○ RI 162-163 D 5
Talbot, Cape ▲ AUS 172-173 H 2
Talbot, Mount ▲ AUS 176-177 J 3
Talbot Glacier ⊂ CDN 24-25 g 2
Talbot Inlet ≈ 24-25 h 2
Talbot Islands ⌒ AUS 183 B 5
Talbot Lake ○ CDN 34-35 G 3
Talbotton ○ USA (GA) 284-285 F 4
Talbragar River ~ AUS 180-181 K 2
Talca ★• RCH 78-79 D 3
Talcahuano ○ RCH 78-79 C 4
Talcan, Isla ⌒ RCH 78-79 C 7
Tālcher ○ IND 142-143 D 5
Talcho ○ RN 204-205 E 1
Talco ○ USA (TX) 264-265 J 5
Tal'daktokon, vozvyšennosť ▲ RUS 116-117 E 2
Taldan ○ RUS 118-119 M 9
Taldom ★ RUS 94-95 P 3
Taldy ~ KA 124-125 J 4
Taldy, Tasty- ★ KA 124-125 E 3
Taldy-Bulak ○ KS 136-137 N 3
Taldyk, pereval ▲ KS 136-137 N 5
Taldykorgan ○ KA 124-125 L 6
Taldyk'organ ○ KA 124-125 L 6
Taldyqorghan = Taldykorgan ★ KA 124-125 L 6
Taleb, Bir < RIM 196-197 F 6
Taleex ○ SP 208-209 J 4
Talegaon ○ IND 138-139 G 9
Tālem ○ IR 128-129 N 4
Talence ○ F 90-91 G 9
Tāleqān ★ AFG 136-137 L 6
Tāleqān Rūd ~ AFG 136-137 L 6
Talequah ○ USA (OK) 264-265 K 3
Tāleš, Kūhhā-ye ▲ IR 128-129 N 4
Taley ○ RCA 206-207 C 5
Talgar ○ KA 146-147 C 4
Talgar, pik ▲ KA 146-147 C 4
Talguharai ○ SUD 200-201 G 3
Talḫāb, Kōtal-e ▲ AFG 134-135 L 1
Talhār ○ PK 138-139 B 7
Taliabu, Pulau ⌒ RI 164-165 J 4
Talibon ○ RP 160-161 F 7
Talibura ○ RI 166-167 B 6
Talica ★ RUS 114-115 G 6
Talicherla ○ IND 140-141 H 3
Talihina ○ USA (OK) 264-265 J 4
Tālikota ○ IND 140-141 G 2
Talimā ○ BR 62-63 G 5
Talimardžan ○ US 136-137 J 5
Talina, Río ~ BOL 76-77 E 1
Taling Chan ○ THA 158-159 F 4
Taliouine ○ MA 188-189 H 5
Taliparamba ○ IND 140-141 F 4
Talipaw ○ RP 160-161 D 10
Talipolo, Tanjung ▲ RI 164-165 F 5
Tali Post ○ SUD 206-207 K 6
Talisay ○ RP 160-161 D 6
Talisayan ○ RP 160-161 F 8
Talisei, Pulau ⌒ RI 164-165 J 3
Taliwang ○ RI 168 C 7
Taljain ~ RUS 112-113 S 4
Tal'jany ○ RUS 116-117 L 9
Talkeetna ○ USA 20-21 P 5
Talkeetna Mountains ▲ USA 20-21 Q 6
Talkeetna River ~ USA 20-21 Q 5
Tall, at- ○ SYR 128-129 G 6
Talladega ○ USA (AL) 284-285 D 3
Talladega Super Speedway • USA (AL) 284-285 D 3
Tall 'Afar ○ IRQ 128-129 K 4
Tallahala Creek ~ USA (MS) 268-269 L 5
Tallahassee ★ USA (FL) 286-287 E 1
Tallahatchie River ~ USA (MS) 268-269 K 3
Tall al-Abyaḍ ★ SYR 128-129 H 4
Tallangatta ○ AUS 180-181 J 4
Tallapoosa ○ USA (GA) 284-285 E 3
Tallapoosa River ~ USA (AL) 284-285 E 3
Tallapoosa River ~ USA (AL) 284-285 D 4
Tallaringa Conservation Park ⊥ AUS 176-177 M 4
Tallassee ○ USA (AL) 284-285 E 4
Tall Birāk ○ SYR 128-129 J 4
Tallering Peak ▲ AUS 176-177 C 4
Talleysville ○ USA (VA) 280-281 J 6
Tall Ğudaida ∴• IRQ 130-131 K 2
Tall Hariri • SYR 128-129 J 5
Tall Huqna ○ IRQ 128-129 K 4
Tallin = Tallinn ★•• EST 94-95 J 2
Tallinn ★•• EST 94-95 J 2
Tallkalā ○ AFG 134-135 K 3
Tall-Kalaḫ ○ SYR 128-129 G 5
Tall Kūšik ○ SYR 128-129 K 4
Tallorutit ⌒ GRØ 28-29 Q 6
Tall Pines ○ CDN (SAS) 232-233 Q 3
Tall Šāgir Bāzār ○• SYR 128-129 J 4
Tall Tamr ○ SYR 128-129 J 4
Tallulah ○ USA (LA) 268-269 J 4
Tall 'Uwainât ○ IRQ 128-129 K 4
Talmage ○ CDN (SAS) 232-233 P 6
Talmage ○ USA (KS) 262-263 J 6
Tal'menka ★ RUS 124-125 N 2
Talmest ○ MA 188-189 G 5
Talnah ○ RUS 108-109 X 7
Taloard ○ IR 134-135 D 3
Taloda ○ IND 138-139 E 9
Taloga ○ USA (OK) 264-265 F 2
Talon ○ RUS 120-121 N 4
Talotajaha ~ RUS 108-109 J 7
Talovaja ○ RUS 102-103 M 2
Talovka ○ RUS 112-113 O 5
Talovka ~ RUS 112-113 N 5
Talovskoe, ozero ○ RUS 120-121 V 3
Talpa ○ USA (TX) 266-267 H 2
Talquin, Lake < USA (FL) 286-287 E 1
Talras < RN 198-199 D 5
Talšand ○ MAU 148-149 C 5
Talsen = Talsi ○•• LV 94-95 H 3
Talsi ○•• LV 94-95 H 3
Talsinnt ○ MA 188-189 K 4
Taltal ○ RCH 76-77 B 3
Taltal, Quebrada de ~ RCH 76-77 B 3
Taltson River ~ CDN 30-31 N 5
Talu ○ RI 162-163 C 4
Taludaa ○ RI 164-165 H 3
Taluk ○ RI 162-163 D 5
Talvār, Rūdḫāne-ye ~ IR 128-129 N 4
Talwood ○ AUS 178-179 K 5
Talyawalka Anabranch ~ AUS 180-181 G 2
Tama ○ RN 198-199 B 5
Tama ○ USA (IA) 274-275 F 3
Tama, Parque Nacional el ⊥ YV 60-61 E 4
Tama Abu, Banjaran ▲ MAL 164-165 D 2
Tamacuari, Pico ▲ BR 66-67 E 2
Ṭamad, aṭ- ○ KSA 130-131 F 5
Tamadan ○ RI 166-167 G 4
Tamafupa < RB 218-219 D 4
Tama-gawa ~ J 152-153 J 5
Tamako ○ RI 164-165 J 2
Tamala = Tolon ○ GH 202-203 K 5
Tamale ★ GH 202-203 K 5
Taman ○ RI 168 C 3
Tamaná, Cerro ▲ CO 60-61 C 5
Tamanaco, Embalse < YV 60-61 J 3
Tamanar ○ MA 188-189 G 5
Tamanco ○ PE 64-65 E 4
Tamandourirt < RMM 196-197 K 5
Tamanduá ○ BR (AMA) 66-67 D 5
Tamanduá ○ BR (MIN) 72-73 J 4
Tamaneke ○ SOL 184 I c 3
Tamango, Parque Nacional ⊥ RCH 80 D 3
Tamanhint ○ LAR 192-193 F 4
Tamani ○ RMM 202-203 G 3
Tamaniquá ○ BR 66-67 F 4
Taman Negra National Park ⊥•• MAL 162-163 E 2
Tamano ○ J 152-153 E 7
Tamanrasset ★•• DZ 190-191 E 9
Tamanrasset, Oued ~ DZ 190-191 D 9
Tamanredjo ○ SME 62-63 G 3
Tamanskij zaliv ≈ 102-103 K 5
Tamaqua ○ USA (PA) 280-281 L 3
Tamaquillo ○ PE 64-65 D 6
Tamar, Alto de ▲ CO 60-61 D 4
Tamarac ○ USA (FL) 286-287 J 5
Tamarack ○ USA (MN) 270-271 E 4
Tamarack Island ⌒ CDN (MAN) 234-235 F 3
Tamarac National Wildlife Refuge ⊥ USA (MN) 270-271 C 3
Tamarana ○ BR 72-73 E 7
Tamarike ○ RI 166-167 L 6
Ṭamarīt ○ OM 132-133 J 5
Tamarou ○ DY 204-205 E 4
Tamaruga, Pampa del ∴ RCH 70-71 C 6
Tamarugal, Pampa del ∴ RCH 76-77 C 1
Tamási ○ H 92-93 P 5
Tamaso ○ SUD 200-201 F 6
Tamassoumit ○ RIM 196-197 D 5
Tamat, Wādī ~ LAR 192-193 G 2
Tamatama ○ YV 60-61 J 6
Tamatave = Toamasina ★ RM 222-223 F 7
Tamaulipas ◘ MEX 50-51 K 6
Tama Wildlife Reserve ⊥ ETH 208-209 C 5
Tamaya, Río ~ PE 64-65 F 6
Tamazula de Gordiano ○ MEX 52-53 C 2
Tamazulapán ○ MEX 52-53 F 3
Tamazunchale ○• MEX 50-51 K 7
Tambach ○ EAK 212-213 E 3
Tambacounda ★ SN 202-203 D 3
Tambakara ○ RMM 202-203 E 2
Tamba Kosi ~ NEP 144-145 F 7
Tambalongang, Pulau ⌒ RI 168 E 6
Tamban ○ RP 160-161 E 6
Tambaqui ○ BR 66-67 F 5
Tambaqui, Cachoeira ~ BOL 66-67 E 7
Tambara ○ MOC 218-219 H 3
Tāmbaram ○ IND 140-141 J 4
Tambarga ○ BF 202-203 L 4
Tambar Springs ○ AUS 178-179 K 6
Tambaur ○ IND 142-143 B 2
Tambawel ○ WAN 198-199 B 6
Tambe ○ ANG 216-217 C 6
També ○ BR 68-69 L 5
Tambea ○ RI 164-165 G 6
Tambea ○• SOL 184 I d 3
Tāmbeibui ○ IND 140-141 L 4
Tambej ○ RUS 108-109 O 6
Tambelan Besar, Pulau ⌒ RI 162-163 G 4
Tambelan Kepulauau ⌒ RI 162-163 G 4
Tambellup ○ AUS 176-177 D 7
Tamberu ○ RI 168 E 3
Tambillo ○ EC 64-65 C 2
Tambillo, Quebrada ~ RCH 76-77 C 1
Tambisan, Pulau ⌒ MAL 160-161 C 10
Tambo ○ AUS 178-179 J 3
Tambo ○ PE 64-65 F 8
Tambo, El ○ CO 60-61 C 6
Tambo, Río ~ PE 64-65 F 7
Tambo, Río ~ PE 70-71 B 5
Tambobamba ○ PE 64-65 F 8
Tambo Colorado • PE 64-65 E 8
Tambo Grande ○ PE 64-65 B 4
Tambohorano ○ RM 222-223 C 6
Tamboli ○ RI 164-165 G 5
Tambopata, Río ~ PE 70-71 C 3
Tambo Ponciano ○ PE 66-67 B 4
Tambo Pucacuro ○ PE 64-65 E 3
Tambor ○ ANG 216-217 B 8
Tambor ○ BR 66-67 F 4
Tambora, Gunung ▲ RI 168 C 7
Tambores ○ ROU 76-77 J 6
Tamboril ○ BR 68-69 H 4
Tamboritha, Mount ▲ AUS 180-181 J 4
Tambo Tambillo ○ BOL 70-71 D 6
Tamboura ○ RCA 206-207 G 6
Tambov ○ RUS 94-95 R 5
Tambovka ○ RUS 122-123 B 3
Tambo Yacu, Río ~ PE 64-65 E 2
Tambrey ∴• AUS 172-173 C 6
Tambu, Teluk ≈ 164-165 F 3
Tambugo ○ RP 160-161 D 4
Tambul ○ PNG 183 B 3
Tambunan ○ MAL 160-161 B 10
Tambura ○ SUD 206-207 H 6
Tambuttegama ○ CL 140-141 J 6
Tamc dabaa ▲ MAU 146-147 L 3
Tāmchakett ○ RIM 196-197 E 6
Tamdibulak ★ US 136-137 J 4
Tam Điệp ★ VN 156-157 D 6
Tamdy ~ KA 124-125 E 4
Tamdytov, toglari ▲ US 136-137 J 4
Tame ○ CO 60-61 F 4
Tâmega, Rio ~ P 98-99 C 4
Tamegroute ○ MA 188-189 J 5
Tamelelt ○ MA 188-189 H 5
Tamelhat ○ DZ 190-191 F 4
Tamenglong ○ IND 142-143 H 3
Tamesi, Río ~ MEX 50-51 K 6
Tamesna ∴ RN 198-199 B 3
Tamewali = Khairpur ○ PK 138-139 D 5
Tamezret ○ TN 190-191 G 4
Tamghas ○ NEP 144-145 D 6
Tamiahua ○ MEX 50-51 L 7
Tamiahua, Laguna de ○ MEX 50-51 L 7
Tamiang ~ RI 162-163 B 2
Tamiang, Ujung ▲ RI 162-163 C 2
Tamica ○ RUS 88-89 P 4
Tami Islands ⌒ PNG 183 D 4
Tamil Nādu ◘ IND 140-141 G 5
Ta'mīn, at- ◘ IRQ 128-129 L 5
Tamir gol ~ MAU 148-149 F 4
Tamitatoala, Rio ~ BR 72-73 D 2
Tāmīya ○ ET 194-195 E 3
Tam Ky ○ VN 158-159 K 3
Tamlelt, Plaine de ∴ MA 188-189 K 4
Tamluk ○ IND 142-143 E 4
Tamma ~ RUS 118-119 O 5
Tammisaari = Ekenäs ○• FIN 88-89 G 7
Tammū, Jabal ▲ LAR 192-193 F 6
Tamnūn ○ Y 132-133 G 6
Tamou ○ RN 204-205 E 2
Tampa ○ ANG (NAM) 216-217 B 7
Tampa ~ ANG 216-217 B 7
Tampa ○ USA (FL) 286-287 G 4
Tampaang, Pulau ⌒ RI 168 C 6
Tampa Bay ≈ 48-49 G 6
Tampa Bay ≈ USA 286-287 G 4
Tampang ○ RI 162-163 E 6
Tampasis ○ MAL 160-161 B 10
Tampéna ○ RN 202-203 L 3
Tampere ○• FIN 88-89 G 6
Tampia Hill ▲ AUS 176-177 E 6
Tampico ○• MEX 50-51 L 6
Tampin ○ MAL 162-163 E 3
Tamp Kōh ○ PK 134-135 J 6
Tampo ○ RI 164-165 H 6
Tampoaga ▲ BF 202-203 L 4
Tampon, Le ○ F 224 B 7
Tamqué, Massif du ▲ RG 202-203 D 3
Tamr, Tall ○ SYR 128-129 J 4
Tamrau, Pegunungan ▲ RI 166-167 G 2
Tamri ○ MA 188-189 G 5
Tamshiyacu ○ PE 64-65 F 3
Tamu ○ MYA 142-143 J 3
Tamūd ○ Y 132-133 F 5
Tamuín ○• MEX 50-51 K 6
Tamur ~ NEP 144-145 F 7
Tamvatvaam ~ RUS 112-113 S 5
Tamworth ○ AUS 178-179 L 6
Tamyš ~ RUS 116-117 H 6
Tana ~ EAK 212-213 G 4
Tana ~ N 86-87 O 1
Tana = Île Tanna ⌒ VAN 184 II b 4
Tana, Lake = T'ana Hayk' ○ ETH 200-201 H 6
Tanabe ○ J 152-153 F 8
Tanaberu ○• RI 164-165 G 6
Tanabi ○ BR 72-73 F 6
Tanabru ○ N 86-87 O 1
Tanaf ○ SN 202-203 C 3
Tanafjorden ≈ 86-87 O 1
Tanaga Island ⌒ USA 22-23 H 7
Tanaga Pass ≈ 22-23 G 7
Tanahbala, Pulau ⌒ RI 162-163 C 5
Tanahgoyang ○ RI 166-167 E 6
Tanahgrogot ○ RI 164-165 E 4
Tanahjampea, Pulau ⌒ RI 168 E 6
Tanahmasa, Pulau ⌒ RI 162-163 C 5
Tanahmerah ○ RI (IRJ) 166-167 G 3
Tanahmerah ○ RI (IRJ) 166-167 L 5
Tanahmerah ○ RI (KTI) 164-165 E 2
Tanahmolala, Pulau ⌒ RI 168 E 6
Tanah Rata ○ MAL 162-163 D 2
Tanahwangko ○ RI 164-165 J 3
Tānai ○ PK 138-139 B 3
Tanakeke ○ RI 164-165 F 6
Tanakeke, Pulau ⌒ RI 164-165 F 6
Tanakpur ○ IND 144-145 C 6
Tanal ○ RMM 202-203 J 2
Tanama ○ BF 202-203 K 3
Tanama ~ RUS 108-109 S 7
Tanamalwila ○ CL 140-141 J 7
Tanami, Mount ▲ AUS 172-173 J 5
Tanami Desert ∴ AUS 172-173 K 5
Tanami Desert Wildlife Sanctuary ⊥ AUS 172-173 K 6
Tanami Mine ∴ AUS 172-173 J 6
Tanami Road II AUS 172-173 J 6
Tân An ★ VN 158-159 J 5
Tanana ○ USA 20-21 O 4
Tanana River ~ USA 20-21 S 4
Tanandava ○ RM 222-223 C 8
Tanani ○ USA 20-21 X 7
Tanantou ○ RG 202-203 F 5
Tana ó Camiña, Quebrada de ~ RCH 70-71 B 6
Tana River Primate National Reserve ⊥ EAK 212-213 H 4
Tanārūt, Wādī ~ LAR 190-191 H 6
Tanatar, ozera ○ RUS 124-125 L 3
Tanba-kochi ▲ J 152-153 F 7
Tanbaoura, Falaise de ▲ RMM 202-203 E 3
Tancheng ○ VRC 154-155 L 4
Tanchon ○ DVR 150-151 G 7
Tanchon Karang ○ MAL 162-163 D 3
Tancitaro, Cerro ▲ MEX 52-53 C 2
Tancitaro, Parque Nacional ⊥ MEX 52-53 C 2
Tancuime ○ MEX 50-51 K 7
Tanda ○ CI 202-203 J 6
Tanda ○• RUS 118-119 P 4
Tanda ~ RUS 120-121 E 2
Tanda, Lac ○ RMM 202-203 H 2
Tandako ○ RG 202-203 C 4
Tandalti ○ SUD 200-201 E 6
Ţăndărei ○ RO 102-103 E 5
Tanderiouel ~ RMM 202-203 K 2
Tandi ○ IND 138-139 F 3
Tandil ○ RA 78-79 K 4
Tandil, Sierra del ▲ RA 78-79 K 4
Tandin ○ MYA 142-143 H 6
Tandjilé ◘ TCH 206-207 C 4
Tandjilé ~ TCH 206-207 B 4
Tandjouaré ○ RT 202-203 L 4
Tāndliānwāla ○ PK 138-139 D 4
Tando Ādam ○ PK 138-139 B 7
Tando Allāhyār ○ PK 138-139 B 7
Tando Bāgo ○ PK 138-139 B 7
Tando Ikram ○ PK 138-139 B 7
Tando Jam ○ PK 138-139 B 7
Tando Muhammad Khān ○ PK 138-139 B 7
Tandou Lake ○ AUS 180-181 G 2
Tandovo, ozero ○ RUS 114-115 O 7
Tando Zinze ○ ANG 210-211 D 6
Tandubatu Island ⌒ RP 160-161 D 10
Tandung ○ RI 164-165 F 5
Tāndūr ○ IND 140-141 G 2
Tanega-shima ⌒ J 152-153 D 9
Taneichi ○ J 152-153 J 4
Tan Emellel ○ DZ 190-191 G 7
Tanemot, Danau ○ RI 166-167 G 2
Tanete ○ RI 164-165 G 6
Taneti, Pulau ⌒ RI 164-165 K 4
Taneytown ○ USA (MD) 280-281 J 4
Tanezrouft ∴ DZ 196-197 K 3
Tanezrouft-Tan-Ahenet ∴ DZ 190-191 C 9
Tanezzruft, Wādī ~ LAR 190-191 H 8
Ṭanf, aṭ- ○ SYR 128-129 H 6
Tanga ◘ EAT 212-213 G 6
Tanga ★ EAT (TAN) 212-213 G 6
Tanga ○ RUS 118-119 E 10
Tanga < TCH 198-199 J 4
Tangadee ○ AUS 176-177 E 2
Tangail ○ BD 142-143 F 3
Tanga Islands ⌒ PNG 183 G 2
Tangale Peak ▲ WAN 204-205 J 4

Tabor — Tangale Peak 399

Tangalle ○ CL 140-141 J 7
Tanganyika, Lac = Lake Tanganyika ⊖ ZRE 214-215 E 3
Tanganyika, Lake = Lac Tanganyika ⊖ BU 214-215 E 3
Tangara ○ BR 68-69 L 5
Tangará da Serra ○ BR 70-71 J 4
Tangarana, Río ~ PE 64-65 E 3
Tangarare ○ SOL 184 I d 3
Tangaye ○ BF 202-203 J 3
Tangent Point ▲ USA 20-21 N 1
Tanger = Tanjah ☆• MA 188-189 J 3
Tangerang ○ RI 168 B 3
Tangermünde ○• D 92-93 L 2
Tanggu ○ VRC 154-155 K 2
Tangguantun ○ VRC 154-155 K 2
Tanggula (Dangla) Shan ▲ VRC 144-145 G 4
Tanggulangin ○ RI 168 E 3
Tanggula Shankou ▲ VRC 144-145 H 4
Tangha ~ RUS 120-121 D 3
Tanghe ○ VRC 154-155 H 5
Tangi ○ PK 138-139 C 2
Tangier ○ CDN (NS) 240-241 N 6
Tangier ○ USA (VA) 280-281 L 6
Tangier = Tanjah ☆• MA 188-189 J 3
Tangier Island ~ USA (VA) 280-281 L 6
Tangier Sound ≈ USA 280-281 L 5
Tangjiahe Z.B. ⊥• VRC 154-155 D 5
Tangkak ○ MAL 162-163 E 3
Tangkoto-Batuangus-Dua Saudara Reserves ⊥• RI 164-165 J 3
Tang La ▲ VRC 144-145 G 7
Tangmai ○ VRC 144-145 K 5
Tangnary ~ RUS 118-119 L 4
Tangorin ○ AUS 178-179 H 1
Tangoutranat = Ti-n-Aguelhaj ○ RMM 196-197 J 6
Tangra Yumco ○ VRC 144-145 F 5
Tangse ○ RI 162-163 A 2
Tangshan ○ VRC 154-155 L 2
Tangu ○ PNG 183 C 3
Tangua ○ CO 64-65 D 1
Tangue River Reservoir < USA (MT) 250-251 N 6
Tanguieta ○ DY 202-203 L 4
Tanguin-Dassouri ○ BF 202-203 K 3
Tangulbei ○ EAK 212-213 F 3
Tangyuan ○ VRC 150-151 G 4
Tân Hiep ○ VN 158-159 H 5
Tánh Linh ○ VN 158-159 J 5
Tanhoj ○ RUS 116-117 M 10
Tanhuijo, Arrecife ⌒ MEX 50-51 L 7
Tani ○ AFG 138-139 B 3
Taniantaweng Shan ▲ VRC 144-145 M 5
Tanichuchí ○ EC 64-65 C 2
Tanimbar, Kepulauan ⌒ RI 166-167 F 6
Taninga ○ MOC 220-221 L 2
Tanintharí ○ MYA 158-159 E 4
Tanintharí ~ MYA 158-159 E 4
Tanipaddi ○ IND 140-141 H 4
Tanis ∴• ET 194-195 E 2
Tanisapata ○ RI 166-167 G 3
Tāniya, Ğabal aṭ- ▲ Y 132-133 E 6
Tanjah ☆• MA 188-189 J 3
Tanjay ○ RP 160-161 E 8
Tan'ju ~ RUS 108-109 L 8
Tanjung ○ RI (JTE) 168 C 3
Tanjung ○ RI (KSE) 164-165 D 5
Tanjung ○ RI (NBA) 168 C 7
Tanjung Api Reserve ⊥• RI 164-165 G 4
Tanjungbalai ○ RI 162-163 C 3
Tanjungbatu ○ RI 164-165 F 2
Tanjungbuaya, Pulau ⌒ RI 164-165 F 3
Tanjungenim ○ RI 162-163 E 6
Tanjungkarang = Bandar Lampung ○ RI 162-163 F 7
Tanjunglolo ○ RI 162-163 D 5
Tanjung Malim ○ MAL 162-163 D 3
Tanjungmangil ○ RI 162-163 F 6
Tanjungmarcang ○ RI 162-163 C 2
Tanjunginiur ○ RI 162-163 F 6
Tanjungpandan ○ RI 162-163 G 6
Tanjung Panjang Reserve ⊥• RI 164-165 G 3
Tanjung Piandang ○ MAL 162-163 D 2
Tanjungpinang ○ RI 162-163 F 4
Tanjungpura ○ RI 162-163 C 3
Tanjungraja ○ RI 162-163 F 6
Tanjungraya ○ RI 162-163 E 7
Tanjungredeb ○ RI 164-165 E 2
Tanjungsaleh, Pulau ⌒ RI 162-163 H 5
Tanjungseloka ○ RI 164-165 E 5
Tanjungselor ○ RI 164-165 E 2
Tanjung Sepat ○ MAL 162-163 D 3
Tanjunguban ○ RI 162-163 F 4
Tanjungwaringin ○ RI 162-163 J 5
Tanjurer ~ RUS 112-113 S 4
Tank ○ PK 138-139 C 3
Tank ○ USA (TX) 266-267 D 3
Tankersley ○ USA (TX) 266-267 G 2
Tankse ○ IND 138-139 G 2
Tankses ~ RUS 114-115 T 4
Tankwa ~ ZA 220-221 D 6
Tankwa-Karoo National Park ⊥ ZA 220-221 D 6
Tân Ky ☆ VN 156-157 D 7
Tanlova ~ RUS 114-115 N 2
Tanlovajaha ~ RUS 108-109 N 8
Tân Minh ○ VN 158-159 J 5
Tanna, Île = Tana ⌒ VAN 184 II b 4
Tannakallu ○ IND 140-141 H 4
Tanner, Mount ▲ CDN (BC) 230-231 L 4
Tanner Bank ≃ 248-249 F 7
Tannin ○ CDN (ONT) 234-235 M 5
Tannum Sands ○ AUS 178-179 L 2
Tannūra, Ra's ○ KSA 134-135 D 5
Tano ~ GH 202-203 J 6
Tano, Tanjung ▲ RI 168 C 7
Tanon Strait ≈ 160-161 E 8
Tanot ○ IND 138-139 C 6
Tanougou ○ DY 202-203 L 4
Tanougou, Cascades de ~• DY 202-203 L 4
Tanout ○ RN 198-199 D 5
Tanouzkka, Sebkhet ⊖ MA 196-197 C 3
Tân Phú ○ VN 158-159 J 5
Tanquary Fiord ≈ 26-27 L 3
Tanque Novo ○ BR 72-73 J 2
Tanque Nuevo ○ MEX 50-51 H 4
Tanque Verde ○ USA (AZ) 256-257 E 6
Tanquinho ○ BR 68-69 J 7
Tansarga ○ BF 202-203 L 4
Tansen ○ NEP 144-145 D 7
Tanshui • RC 156-157 M 4
Tansilla ○ BF 202-203 H 3
Tanşulükh ○ LAR 192-193 J 1
Tanṭā ☆ ET 194-195 E 2
Tantallon ○ CDN (SAS) 232-233 R 5
Tantamayo ○ PE 64-65 D 6
Tan-Tan ☆ MA 188-189 F 6
Tan-Tan-Plage ○ MA 188-189 F 6
Tân Thu'o'ng ○ VN 158-159 J 5
Tan Ti-n-Missaou, Tassili ▲ DZ 196-197 M 4
Tantoyuca ○ MEX 50-51 K 7
Tanūma ○ KSA 132-133 C 4
Tanumbirini ○ AUS 174-175 C 5
Tanumshede ☆ S 86-87 E 7
Tanxi ○ VRC 156-157 F 3
Tanyan ○ MYA 142-143 L 4
Tanzania ■ EAT 214-215 F 3
Tanzilla Plateau ▲ CDN 32-33 E 2
Tanzilla River ~ CDN 32-33 E 2
Taocun ○ VRC 154-155 M 3
Tao He ~ VRC 154-155 C 4
Taohua Dao ⌒ VRC 156-157 N 2
Taohuayuan • VRC 156-157 G 2
Taojiang ○ VRC 156-157 H 2
Taonan ○ VRC 150-151 D 5
Taopa ○ RI 164-165 G 3
Taora ○ SOL 184 I c 2
Taormina ○ I 100-101 E 6
Taos ○••• USA (NM) 256-257 K 2
Taoshan Shouliechang • VRC 150-151 G 4
Taos Indian Reservation ⅄ USA (NM) 256-257 K 2
Taos Pueblo ••• USA (NM) 256-257 K 2
Taouârdeï < RMM 196-197 L 6
Taoudenni ○ RMM 196-197 J 3
Taounate ☆ MA 188-189 J 3
Taourirt ○ MA (Ojd) 188-189 K 3
Taourirt ○ MA (Orz) 188-189 H 5
Taouz ○ MA 188-189 J 5
Taoyuan ○ RC 156-157 M 4
Taoyuan ○ VRC 156-157 G 2
Taoyuan D. • VRC 156-157 K 4
Tapachula ○ MEX 52-53 H 4
Tapah ○ MAL 162-163 D 2
Tapah, Tanjung ▲ RI 162-163 F 6
Tapaiuna, Cachoeira ~ BR 66-67 K 6
Tapaiuna, Ribeiro ~ BR 70-71 J 2
Tapajós, Rio ~ BR 66-67 K 4
Tapajós, Rio ~ BR 66-67 K 5
Tapaktuan ○ RI 162-163 B 3
Tapalpa ○• MEX 52-53 C 2
Tapalqué ○ RA 78-79 J 4
Tapalqué, Arroyo ~ RA 78-79 J 4
Tapan ○ RI 162-163 D 6
Tapanahonirivier ~ SME 62-63 G 4
Tapandulu ○ RI 164-165 F 5
Tapanuli, Teluk ≈ 162-163 C 4
Tapat, Pulau ⌒ RI 164-165 K 4
Tapauá ○ BR 66-67 F 5
Tapauá, Rio ~ BR 66-67 E 5
Tapauá, Rio ~ BR 66-67 D 5
Tapaulama, Tanjung ▲ RI 164-165 H 5
Tapawera ○ NZ 182 D 4
Tapebicuá ○ RA 76-77 J 5
Tapejara ○ BR 74-75 E 7
Tapena ○ BOL 70-71 C 5
Tapenaga, Río ~ RA 76-77 H 4
Tapera ○ BR 66-67 F 3
Tapera, La ○ RCH 80 E 2
Tapera, Rio ~ BR 62-63 D 5
Taperaba ○ BR 62-63 J 5
Taperoá ○ BR 68-69 K 5
Tapes ○ BR 74-75 E 8
Tapes, Ponta de ▲ BR 74-75 E 8
Tapeta ○ LB 202-203 F 6
Taphan Hin ○ THA 158-159 F 2
Tāpi ~ IND 138-139 E 9
Tāpi ~ IND 138-139 F 9
Tapian ○ RI 164-165 E 4
Tapiantana Channel ≈ 160-161 D 9
Tapiantana Group ⌒ RP 160-161 D 9
Tapiche, Río ~ PE 64-65 E 5
Tapini ○ PNG 183 D 5
Tapiocanga, Chapada do ▲ BR 72-73 G 4
Tapira ○ BR 72-73 G 5
Tapiraípe ○ BR 72-73 K 2
Tapirapecó, Sierra ▲ YV 66-67 E 2
Tapirapé Karajá, Área Indígena ⅄ BR 68-69 C 7
Tapiratiba ○ BR 72-73 G 6
Tapiruçu, Cachoeira ~ BR 68-69 E 3
Tapis, Gunung ▲ MAL 162-163 E 2
Tapiú, Cachoeira do ~ BR 62-63 F 6
Tapkaluk Islands ⌒ USA 20-21 M 1
Taplejung ○ NEP 144-145 F 7
Tapoa, La ~ BF (DOS) 204-205 E 2
Tapoa, La ○ BF 202-203 L 3
Tapol ○ TCH 206-207 B 4
Tappahannock ○ USA (VA) 280-281 K 6
Tappalang ○ RI 164-165 F 5
Tappen ○ CDN (BC) 230-231 K 3
Tapsuj ~ RUS 114-115 F 4
Taptugary ○ RUS 118-119 K 9
Tapuaenuku ▲ NZ 182 D 5
Tapul Group ⌒ RP 160-161 D 10
Tapul Island ⌒ RP 160-161 D 10
Tāqa ○ OM 132-133 J 5
Taq-e Bostān ○• IR 128-129 M 4
Taqtaq ○ IRQ 128-129 L 5
Taqtaqāna, aṭ- ○ IRQ 128-129 K 6
Taquara ○ BR 74-75 E 7
Taquari ○ BR 74-75 E 7
Taquari, Pantanal do ⊖ BR 70-71 J 6
Taquari, Rio ~ BR 70-71 J 6
Taquari, Rio ~ BR 72-73 F 7
Taquaritinga ○ BR 72-73 F 6
Taquarituba ○ BR 72-73 F 7
Taques, Los ○ YV 60-61 F 2
Taquili, Isla ⌒ PE 70-71 C 4
Tara ○ AUS 178-179 L 4
Tará ○ BR 68-69 K 6
Tara ☆ RUS (OMS) 114-115 N 6
Tara ~ RUS 114-115 N 6
Tara ~ RUS 114-115 P 6
Tara ~ YU 100-101 G 3
Tara ○ Z 218-219 D 3
Tarā, Ğazirat ⌒ KSA 132-133 B 4
Taraba, River ~ WAN 204-205 J 4
Tarabuco ○ BOL 70-71 E 6
Tarābulus ■ LAR 192-193 E 1
Tarābulus ☆ LAR 192-193 E 1
Tarābulus ○• RL 128-129 F 5
Ṭarābulus ☆• RL 128-129 F 5
Taraca, Golfo de ⊖ BOL 70-71 C 5
Taraco ○ PE 70-71 C 4
Tarād al-Kahf ○ IRQ 128-129 L 7
Taraf, aṭ- ○ KSA 130-131 L 5
Ṭarafiya, aṭ- ○ KSA 130-131 J 4
Tarafo, Ponta ▲ CV 202-203 C 6
Tarag ○ IND 140-141 F 2
Tarāghin ○ LAR 192-193 F 5
Tarahumara, Sierra ▲ MEX 50-51 E 3
Taraira, Río ~ CO 66-67 C 3
Taraire ○ BOL 76-77 F 1
Tarajim ○ WAN 204-205 J 3
Taraka, Mount ▲ PNG 184 I b 2
Tarakan ○ RI 164-165 E 2
Tarakan, Pulau ⌒ RI 164-165 E 2
Tarakbits ○ PNG 183 A 3
Taralga ○ AUS 180-181 K 3
Taramana ○ RI 166-167 C 6
Taranaki Bight, North ≈ 182 E 3
Taranaki Bight, South ≈ 182 E 4
Tarancón ○ E 98-99 F 4
Tarangara ○ TCH 206-207 D 4
Tarangire ~ EAT 212-213 F 6
Tarangire National Park ⊥ EAT 212-213 F 5
Tarangire Safari Camp ○ EAT (ARV) 212-213 F 5
Tarankől, köli ⊖ KA 124-125 F 1
Taranovskij ☆ KA 124-125 C 2
Táranto ☆• I 100-101 F 4
Táranto, Golfo di ≈ 100-101 F 4
Tarapacá ○ CO 66-67 C 4
Tarapacá ○ RCH 70-71 C 6
Tarapoa ○ EC 64-65 D 2
Tarapoto ○ PE 64-65 D 5
Tārāpur ○ IND 138-139 D 10
Taraquá ○ BR 66-67 E 3
Tarara ○ C 54-55 D 3
Tarara ○ PNG 184 I b 2
Tarare ○ F 90-91 K 9
Taras ○ BD 142-143 F 3
Tarasa Dwip Island ⌒ IND 140-141 L 5
Tarascon ○• F 90-91 K 10
Tarasovo ○ RUS 116-117 N 8
Tarasovo ○ RUS (NAO) 88-89 T 3
Tarasovsk ○ RUS 116-117 L 8
Tarat ○ DZ 190-191 G 7
Tarata ○ PE 70-71 B 5
Tarauacá ○ BR 66-67 B 7
Tarauacá, Rio ~ BR 66-67 B 6
Tarawai Island ⌒ PNG 183 B 2
Tarazona ○ E 98-99 G 4
Tarbagataj ○ KA 124-125 M 5
Tarbagataj ☆ RUS 116-117 N 10
Tarbagatay Range = Tarbağataj žotasy ▲ KA 124-125 M 5
Tarbaj ○ EAK 212-213 H 2
Tarbela Reservoir < PK 138-139 D 2
Tarbes ☆ F 90-91 H 10
Tarboro ○ USA (NC) 282-283 K 5
Tarbotvale ○ CDN (NS) 240-241 P 4
Tarcoola ○ AUS 178-179 C 6
Tardie ○ AUS 176-177 D 3
Tardoki-Jani, gora ▲ RUS 122-123 H 4
Tardun ○ AUS 176-177 C 4
Taree ○ AUS 178-179 M 6
Tareja ~ RUS 108-109 Z 4
Taremert-n-Alki, Oued ~ DZ 190-191 E 8
Tarempa, Pulau ⌒ RI 162-163 G 3
Tārendö ○ S 86-87 L 3
Tarfa, Ra's aṭ- ▲ KSA 132-133 C 5
Tarfāwi, Bi'r < IRQ 128-129 K 6
Tarfaya ○ MA 188-189 E 7
Targa < RN 198-199 B 4
Targap ○ KA 146-147 B 4
Targhalāt, Wādi ~ LAR 192-193 F 1
Targhee Pass ▲ USA (ID) 252-253 G 2
Tărgovište ○ BG 102-103 E 6
Targuist ○ MA 188-189 J 3
Tarhaouhaout ∴• DZ 190-191 E 9
Tarhatine, Tizi-n ▲ MA 188-189 H 5
Tarhovo ○ RUS 116-117 E 7
Tarhūnah ■ LAR 192-193 E 1
Tarhūnah ☆• LAR 192-193 E 1
Tari ○ PNG 183 B 3
Tari, Mutungu- ○ ZRE 216-217 D 3
Tariat = Horgo ○ MAU 148-149 D 3
Tarib ○ KSA 132-133 C 4
Tariba ○ YV 60-61 E 4
Taricá ○ PE 64-65 D 6
Tarif ○ UAE 134-135 E 6
Tarifa ○ E 98-99 E 6
Tarija ○ BOL 76-77 E 1
Tarija, Río ~ BOL 76-77 E 1
Tarikere ○ IND 140-141 F 4
Tariku ~ RI 166-167 J 3
Tariku (Rouffaer) ~ RI 166-167 J 3
Tarim ○• Y 132-133 F 5
Tarim Basin = Tarim Pendi ⊥ VRC 146-147 E 6
Tarime ○ EAT 212-213 E 4
Tarim He ~ VRC 146-147 E 5
Tarım Milli Parkı ⊥ TR 128-129 F 3
Tarimoro ○ MEX 52-53 D 1
Tarim Pendi ⊥ VRC 146-147 E 6
Taring ○ RI 162-163 B 3
Taripa ○ RI 164-165 G 4
Tarira ○ BR 66-67 C 2
Tarit, Oued ~ DZ 190-191 D 8
Taritatu ~ RI 166-167 L 3
Taritatu (Idenburg) ~ RI 166-167 K 3
Tarka ~ ZA 220-221 G 6
Tarkastad ○ ZA 220-221 H 6
Tarkio ○ USA (MO) 274-275 C 4
Tarkio ○ USA (MT) 250-251 E 4
Tarkio River ~ USA (IA) 274-275 C 4
Tarko-Sale ☆ RUS 114-115 O 2
Tarkwa ○ GH 202-203 K 7
Tarlac ☆ RP 160-161 D 5
Tarlton Downs ○ AUS 178-179 D 2
Tarma ○ PE 64-65 E 7
Tarmaber Pass ▲ ETH 208-209 D 4
Tarmidā ○ KSA 130-131 J 5
Tarn ~ F 90-91 H 10
Tarn, Gorges du ~•• F 90-91 J 9
Tärnaby ○ S 86-87 G 4
Tarnak Rūd ~ AFG 134-135 M 2
Tarnogskij Gorodok ○ RUS 94-95 S 1
Tarnopol ○ CDN (SAS) 232-233 N 3
Tarnów ☆• PL 92-93 Q 3
Taroa ○ CO 60-61 F 1
Tarobi ○ PNG 183 F 3
Taro Co ⊖ VRC 144-145 E 5
Taroko ○ RC 156-157 M 4
Taroko National Park ⊥• RC 156-157 M 4
Taron ○ PNG 183 G 3
Taronggo ○ RI 164-165 G 4
Taroom ○ AUS 178-179 K 3
Taroudannt ☆• MA 188-189 G 5
Taroum ○ RN 204-205 E 1
Tarpley ○ USA (TX) 266-267 H 4
Tarpon Springs ○ USA (FL) 286-287 G 3
Tarquinia ○ I 100-101 C 3
Tarrafal ○ CV 202-203 B 5
Tarrafal ○ CV 202-203 C 6
Tarrafal ○ CV 202-203 B 5
Tarragona ○ AUS 178-179 H 2
Tarragona ○•• E 98-99 H 4
Tarrajåkkå ~ S 86-87 H 3
Tarraleah ○ AUS 180-181 J 7
Tarrant City ○ USA (AL) 284-285 D 3
Tarras ○ NZ 182 B 6
Tárrega ○ E 98-99 H 4
Tar River ~ USA (NC) 282-283 K 5
Tarso Emissi ▲ TCH 198-199 J 2
Tarsu Musa ▲ TCH 198-199 J 2
Tarsus ☆• TR 128-129 F 4
Tartagal ○ RA 76-77 F 2
Tartagal, Río ~ RA 76-77 F 2
Ṭarṭār, Buhairat aṭ- < IRQ 128-129 K 5
Ṭarṭār, Nahr aṭ- < IRQ 128-129 K 6
Tartaruga ○ BR 72-73 L 2
Tartarugalzinho ○ BR 62-63 J 5
Tartarugas, Cachoeira das ~ BR 68-69 D 4
Tartas ~ RUS 114-115 O 7
Tartrat, Hassi < DZ 188-189 H 7
Tartu ☆•• EST 94-95 K 2
Ṭarṭūs ☆• SYR 128-129 F 5
Tarucani ○ PE 70-71 C 5
Tarucani ○ PE 70-71 B 5
Tarum ~ RI 168 B 3
Taruma ○ BR 70-71 J 6
Tarusa ☆• RUS 94-95 P 4
Tarusan ○ RI 162-163 D 5
Tarūt, Wādi ~ LAR 192-193 E 4
Tarutung ○ RI 162-163 C 3
Tarutyne ☆ UA 102-103 F 4
Tarvagatajn Nuruu ▲ MAU 148-149 D 3
Tarversville ○ USA (GA) 284-285 G 4
Tarves ○ AUS 178-179 H 3
Tarvo, Río ~ BOL 70-71 G 4
Ṭarwāniya ○ UAE 132-133 J 2
Taryng-Ėlge ~ RUS 120-121 E 4
Tarzan ○ USA (TX) 264-265 C 6
Tasabo < WAN 204-205 G 6
Tašāk, Kūh-e ▲ IR 134-135 D 4
Tašanta ○ RUS 124-125 Q 4
Tašauz = Dažhovuz ☆ TM 136-137 F 4
Tašauzskaja oblast' ■ TM 136-137 E 4
Tasböget ☆ KA 124-125 E 6
Taschereau ○ CDN (QUE) 236-237 K 4
Tascosa ○ USA (TX) 264-265 B 3
Tase ○ VRC 144-145 F 6
Tas-Ėekit ~ RUS 110-111 P 4
Taseeva ~ RUS 116-117 G 7
Taseko Lakes ⊖ CDN (BC) 230-231 F 2
Taseko River ~ CDN (BC) 230-231 F 2
Tasermiut ≈ 28-29 S 6
Tasersiaq ≈ 28-29 P 3
Tasersuaq ≈ 28-29 P 3
Taserssuaq ⊖ GRØ (VGR) 28-29 P 4
Taserssuaq ⊖ GRØ (VGR) 28-29 Q 5
Taserssuatsiaq ⊖ GRØ 28-29 P 4
Tasgaon ○ IND 140-141 F 2
Taš Guzar ○ AFG 136-137 K 6
Tashiding ○• IND 142-143 F 2
Tashigang ○ BHT 142-143 G 2
Tashkent = Toškent ☆•• US 136-137 L 4
Tashota ○ CDN (ONT) 234-235 Q 4
Tasiaaluijuaq, Lac ⊖ CDN 36-37 O 5
Tasiat, Lac ⊖ CDN 36-37 M 5
Tasik Bera ⊖ MAL 162-163 E 3
Tasik Chini ⊖ MAL 162-163 E 3
Tasik Kenyir ⊖ MAL 162-163 E 2
Tasikmalaya ○ RI 168 C 3
Tasik Temengur ⊖ MAL 162-163 D 2
Tašina ~ RUS 122-123 D 3
Tašir ○ AR 128-129 L 2
Tasiussaq ⌒ GRØ 26-27 X 7
Tasiussarssuaq ≈ 28-29 P 4
Tas-Jurjah ○ RUS 118-119 F 5
Taskan ○ RUS 120-121 O 2
Taskan ~ RUS 120-121 O 2
Taškent = Toškent ☆•• US 136-137 L 4
Taškentskaja oblast' ■ US 136-137 L 4
Tašķepri ○ TM 136-137 H 7
Taškeprinskoe vodohranilišče < TM 136-137 H 6
Tasker ○ RN 198-199 E 5
Taskesken ○ KA 124-125 M 5
Taşköprü ☆ TR 128-129 E 2
Taskul ○ PNG 183 F 2
Taš-Kumyr ○ KS 136-137 N 4
Tas-Kystabyt, hrebet ▲ RUS 110-111 Y 7
Tašla ☆ RUS 96-97 H 8
Tasman Abyssal Plain ≃ 13 G 6
Tasman Basin ≃ 13 G 7
Tasman Bay ≈ 182 D 4
Tasman Head ▲ AUS 180-181 J 7
Tasman Highway II AUS 180-181 K 6
Tasmania ⌒ AUS 180-181 H 6
Tasman Mountains ▲ NZ 182 D 4
Tasman Peninsula ~•• AUS 180-181 J 7
Tasman Point ▲ AUS 174-175 D 4
Tasman Sea ≈ 13 G 6
Tasmate ○ VAN 184 II a 2
Tășnad ○ RO 102-103 C 4
Taşova ☆ TR 128-129 G 2
Tašqorğān = Hülm ○• AFG 136-137 K 6
Tassara ○ RN 198-199 B 4
Tassa-Takorat < RN 198-199 B 4
Tassedjefit, Erg ⊥ DZ 190-191 D 8
Tasserest < RMM 196-197 M 7
Tassialouc, Lac ⊖ CDN 36-37 N 5
Tassiné ~ DY 204-205 E 3
Tasso Fragoso ○ BR 68-69 F 6
Taštagol ☆ RUS 124-125 P 2
Tastau, gora ▲ KA 124-125 N 5
Tastop ○ KA 136-137 K 3
Tastōp ○ KA 136-137 K 3
Tastuba ○ RUS 96-97 K 6
Taštyp ☆ RUS 124-125 Q 2
Tasty-Taldy ☆ KA 124-125 E 3
Tasu ○ CDN (BC) 228-229 C 4
Tasūğ ○ IR 128-129 L 3
Tāsūki ○• IR 134-135 J 3
Tata ○ H 92-93 P 5
Tata ☆ MA 188-189 H 6
Tatabánya ○ H 92-93 P 5
Tatachikapika River ~ CDN (ONT) 236-237 G 4
Ta Ta Creek ○ CDN (BC) 230-231 O 4
Tata d'Albouri Ndiaye ∴• SN 196-197 C 7
Tataguine ○ SN 202-203 B 2
Tatajachura, Cerro ▲ RCH 70-71 C 6
Tatajuba ○ BR 64-65 F 5
Tatali ○ GH 202-203 L 5
Tatalrose ○ CDN (BC) 228-229 H 3
Tatam ○ RI 164-165 L 3
Tatamagouche ○ CDN (NS) 240-241 M 5
Tata Mailau, Gunung ▲ RI 166-167 C 6
Tatamba ○ SOL 184 I d 3
Tatan ○ KA 124-125 K 4
Tataouine ☆• TN 190-191 H 4
Tatarbunary ○ UA 102-103 F 5
Tatarsk ☆ RUS 114-115 N 7
Tatarskij proliv ≈ 122-123 J 3
Tatarskiy Proliv = Tatarskij proliv ≈ RUS 122-123 J 3
Tatarstan = Respublika Tatarstan ■ RUS 96-97 F 6
Tatau ○ MAL 162-163 K 3
Tatau Island ⌒ PNG 183 F 2
Tatawa ○ RI 166-167 H 3
Tatéma ○ RG 202-203 D 5
Tate River ~ AUS 174-175 G 5
Tateyama ○ J 152-153 H 7
Tate-yama ▲ J 152-153 G 6
Tathlina Lake ⊖ CDN 30-31 L 5
Tathra ○ AUS 180-181 L 4
Tathra National Park ⊥ AUS 176-177 C 4
Tati ~ RB 218-219 D 5
Tātīlt < RIM 196-197 C 5
Tatinnai Lake ⊖ CDN 30-31 V 5
Tatiščevo ○ RUS 96-97 D 8
Tatitlek ○ USA 20-21 R 6
Tat Kha ○ THA 158-159 F 2
Tatkon ○ MYA 142-143 K 5
Tatla Lake ○ CDN (BC) 230-231 E 2
Tatla Lake ⊖ CDN (BC) 230-231 E 2
Tatlanika Creek ~ USA 20-21 Q 4
Tatlatui Provincial Park ⊥ CDN 32-33 G 3
Tatlayoko Lake ○ CDN (BC) 230-231 E 2
Tatlayoko Lake ⊖ CDN (BC) 230-231 E 2
Tatlīt ■ KSA 132-133 C 4
Tatlīt, Wādi ~ KSA 132-133 C 3
Tatlmain Lake ⊖ CDN 20-21 X 5
Tatlow, Mount ▲ CDN (BC) 230-231 F 2
Tatnam, Cape ▲ CDN 34-35 L 2
Tatokou ○ RN 198-199 D 5
Tatra = Tatry ▲ SK 92-93 P 4
Tatry ▲ SK 92-93 P 4
Tatsfield ○ CDN (SAS) 232-233 J 3
Tatshenshini-Alsek Kluane National Park ⊥••• CDN 20-21 U 6
Tatshenshini River ~ CDN 20-21 W 7
Tatta ~ RUS 120-121 E 3
Tattakarai ○ IND 140-141 G 5
Tattannagaripalli ○ IND 140-141 G 4
Tatu, Cachoeira do ~ BR 62-63 H 5
Tatuí ○ BR 72-73 G 7
Tatul, Sierra de ▲ RCH 76-77 B 5
Tatum ○ USA (NM) 256-257 M 5
Tatum ○ USA (TX) 264-265 K 6
Tatumville ○ USA (TN) 276-277 F 4
Tatvan ☆• TR 128-129 K 3
Tau ○ N 86-87 B 7
Ta'u ○ USA 184 V c 2
Tauá ○ BR 68-69 H 4
Tauari ○ BR 68-69 E 2
Taubaté ○ BR 72-73 H 7
Tauberbischofsheim ○• D 92-93 K 4
Tauca ○ PE 64-65 C 6
Taufikia ○ SUD 206-207 K 4
Ta'u Island ⌒ USA 184 V c 2
Tauj ~ RUS 120-121 N 4
Taujskaja guba ≈ 120-121 N 4
Taukum ~ KA 124-125 J 6
Taulihawa ○ NEP 144-145 D 7
Tauliya ○ IRQ 128-129 J 6
Taumarunui ○ NZ 182 E 3
Taumaturgo ○ BR 64-65 F 6
Taum Sauk Mountain ▲ USA (MO) 276-277 E 3
Taunay, Cachoeira ~ BR 70-71 G 2
Taung ○ ZA 220-221 G 3
Taungbon ○ MYA 142-143 J 4
Taungdwingyi ○ MYA 142-143 J 6
Taunggyi ☆ MYA 142-143 K 5
Taungtha ○ MYA 142-143 J 5
Taungthônlôn ▲ MYA 142-143 J 3
Taungup ○ MYA 142-143 J 6
Taunsa ○ PK 138-139 C 4
Taunton ☆ GB 90-91 F 6
Taunton ○ USA (MA) 278-279 K 7
Taupo ○ NZ 182 F 3
Taupo, Lake ⊖ NZ 182 E 3
Tauragė ☆•• LT 94-95 H 4
Tauranga ○ NZ 182 F 2
Taureau, Réservoir ⊖ CDN (QUE) 238-239 M 2
Tauria ○ USA (MO) 276-277 B 4
Tauri River ~ PNG 183 C 4
Tauroa Point ▲ NZ 182 D 1
Taurova ○ RUS 114-115 M 5
Taurus Mountains = Toros Dağları ▲ TR 128-129 D 4
Taus = Domažlice ○ CZ 92-93 M 4
Tau Šalkamür ▲ KA 126-127 P 3
Tauste ○ E 98-99 G 4
Taušyk ○ KA 126-127 J 5
Taušyk ○ KA 126-127 P 2
Tauta ○ PNG 183 C 3
Tavai ○ PY 76-77 K 4
Tavajvaam ~ RUS 112-113 T 4
Tavan Bogd ▲ MAU 146-147 H 1
Tavanei River ~ PNG 183 E 6
Tavani, Mount ▲ VAN 184 II b 3
Tavara ○ SOL 184 I c 3
Tavas ☆ TR 128-129 C 4
Tavda ☆ RUS (SVR) 114-115 H 5
Tavda ~ RUS 114-115 G 5
Tavda ~ RUS 114-115 J 6
Taverner Bay ≈ 28-29 D 3
Tavernier ○ USA (FL) 286-287 J 7
Taveta ○ EAK 212-213 F 5
Taveta ○ EAT 214-215 H 5
Taveuni ⌒ FJI 184 III c 2
Tavira ○• P 98-99 D 6
Tavoliere ~ I 100-101 E 4
Távora, Rio ~ P 98-99 D 4
Tavoy ○ MYA 158-159 E 3
Tavričeskoe ○ RUS 124-125 H 1
Tavşanlı ☆ TR 128-129 C 3
Tavua ○ FJI 184 III a 2
Tavuki ○ FJI 184 III b 3
Tavul Point ▲ PNG 183 G 3
Tavu Na Sici ⌒ FJI 184 III c 3
Tawaeli ○ RI 164-165 F 4
Tawakoni, Lake ⊖ USA (TX) 264-265 H 6
Tawali ○ RI 168 D 7
Tawallah ○ AUS 174-175 C 5
Tawallah Range ▲ AUS 174-175 C 5
Tawang ○• IND 142-143 G 2
Tawa Reservoir < IND 138-139 F 8
Tawargeri ○ IND 140-141 G 3
Tawas City ○ USA (MI) 272-273 F 3
Tawau ○ MAL 160-161 B 10
Tawau Hills Park ⊥ MAL 160-161 B 10
Ṭawīl, aṭ- ⊥ KSA 130-131 F 3
Ṭawīla, aṭ- ○ Y 132-133 C 6
Ṭawīla, Ğazirat ⌒ ET 194-195 F 4
Tawilah ○ SUD 200-201 B 6
Tawitawi Island ⌒ RP 160-161 C 10
Tawlokehn ○ LB 202-203 F 7
Tawma ○ MYA 142-143 K 4
Tawu ○ RC 156-157 M 5
Tāwūq ☆ IRQ 128-129 L 5
Tāwūq Čāy ~ IRQ 128-129 L 5
Tāwurghā' ○ LAR 192-193 F 1
Tāwurghā, Sabkhat ⊖ LAR 192-193 F 1
Taxco ○• MEX 52-53 E 2
Taxco de Alarcon = Taxco ○• MEX 52-53 E 2
Taxi ○ VRC 150-151 F 3
Taxila ○••• PK 138-139 D 3
Taxkorgan ○ VRC 146-147 B 7
Tay ~ GB 90-91 F 3
Tay, Lake ⊖ AUS 176-177 F 6
Tayabamba ○ PE 64-65 D 6
Tayabas Bay ≈ 160-161 D 6
Tayahua ○ MEX 50-51 E 6
Tayan ○ RI 162-163 J 5
Tayandu, Kepulauan ⌒ RI 166-167 F 4
Tayandu, Pulau ⌒ RI 166-167 G 4
Tāyebād ○• IR 134-135 J 1
Tayeeglow ○ SP 208-209 G 6
Tāyin, Wādi ~ OM 132-133 L 2
Taykah ○ LAR 192-193 J 2
Taylor ○ CDN 32-33 K 3
Taylor ○ USA (AK) 20-21 H 4
Taylor ○ USA (AR) 276-277 B 7
Taylor ○ USA (AZ) 256-257 E 4
Taylor ○ USA (NE) 262-263 G 3
Taylor ○ USA (TX) 266-267 K 3
Taylor, Mount ▲ USA (NM) 256-257 H 3
Taylor Canyon ○ USA (NV) 246-247 J 2
Taylor Head ▲ CDN (NS) 240-241 N 6
Taylor Highway II USA 20-21 T 5
Taylor Lake ⊖ CDN 30-31 P 4
Taylor Mountains ▲ USA 20-21 M 6
Taylor Park ○ USA (CO) 254-255 J 5
Taylor River ~ USA (CO) 254-255 J 5
Taylors Falls ○ USA (MN) 270-271 F 5
Taylors Island ○ USA (MD) 280-281 K 5
Taylorsville ○ USA (GA) 284-285 F 2
Taylorsville ○ USA (KY) 276-277 K 2
Taylorsville ○ USA (MS) 268-269 L 5
Taylorsville ○ USA (NC) 282-283 F 5
Taylorsville Lake < USA (KY) 276-277 K 3
Taylorville ○ USA (IL) 274-275 J 5
Taylorville, Lake ⊖ USA (IL) 274-275 J 5
Taymyr, Ozero = Tajmyr, ozero ⊖ RUS 108-109 d 4
Taymyr Autonomous District = Tajmyrskij avtonomnyj okrug ■ RUS 108-109 a 4
Taymyr Peninsula = Tajmyr, poluostrov ~ RUS 108-109 Y 4
Tây Ninh ☆• VN 158-159 J 5
Tayoltita ○ MEX 50-51 G 5
Tayota, Río ~ BOL 70-71 E 4
Tay River ~ CDN 20-21 Y 5
Tây So'n ○ VN 158-159 K 4
Tay Sound ≈ 24-25 g 4
Taytay ○ RP 160-161 C 7
Taytay Bay ≈ 160-161 C 7
Ta Yü ⌒ RC 156-157 L 5
Tayu ○ RI 168 D 3
Tayuling ○ RC 156-157 M 4
Tayyāl, Wādi ~ KSA 130-131 F 3
Tayyāné ○ SYR 128-129 J 5
Tayyibah ○ SUD 200-201 F 5
Taz ~ RUS 108-109 S 8
Taz ~ RUS 114-115 R 2
Taza ☆ MA 188-189 J 3
Tāzah = Taza ☆ MA 188-189 J 3
Tazawa-ko ⊖ J 152-153 J 5
Tazenakht ○ MA 188-189 H 5
Tazerzaït ⊥ RN 198-199 B 3
Tazewell ○ USA (TN) 282-283 D 4
Tazewell ○ USA (VA) 280-281 E 6
Tazgun ○ VRC 146-147 C 6
Taziet, Bi'r < LAR 192-193 E 5
Tazin Lake ⊖ CDN 30-31 P 6
Tazin River ~ CDN 30-31 O 5
Tāzirbū ○ LAR 192-193 J 5
Tazlina Lake ⊖ USA 20-21 R 6
Tazna, Cerro ▲ BOL 70-71 D 7
Tazolé < RN 198-199 D 4
Tazovskaja guba ≈ 108-109 Q 7
Tazovskij ☆ RUS 108-109 S 8
Tazovskij poluostrov ~ RUS 108-109 Q 7
Tazrouk ○ DZ 190-191 F 9
Tazzarine ○ MA 188-189 J 5
Tazzeka, Ibel ▲ MA 188-189 J 3
Tbilisi ☆• GE 126-127 F 7
Tchabal Gangdaba ▲ CAM 204-205 K 5
Tchabal Mbabo ▲ CAM 204-205 K 5
Tchad, Lac ⊖ 198-199 F 6
Tchad, Plaine du ⊥ CAM 206-207 B 3
Tchadaoua ○ RN 198-199 C 6
Tchamba ○ CAM 204-205 K 4
Tchamba ○ RT 202-203 L 5
Tchangsou ○ TCH 206-207 B 4
Tchaourou ○ DY 204-205 E 4
Tchatchou ○ DY 204-205 E 4
Tchentlo Lake ⊖ CDN 32-33 H 4
Tchériba ○ BF 202-203 J 3
Tchetti ○ DY 202-203 L 6
Tchibanga ☆ G 210-211 C 5
Tchibemba ○ ANG 216-217 C 7
Tchie < TCH 198-199 J 4
Tchigai, Plateau du ▲ RN 198-199 G 2
Tchilounga ○ RCB 210-211 C 6
Tchin-Tabaradene ○ RN 198-199 B 5
Tchissakata ○ RCB 210-211 D 6
Tchizalamou ○ RCB 210-211 C 6
Tchollíré ○ CAM 206-207 B 4
Tchula ○ USA (MS) 268-269 K 3
Tczew ○• PL 92-93 P 1
Teá, Rio ~ BR 66-67 E 3
Teacapan ○ MEX 50-51 G 6
Teague ○ USA (TX) 266-267 L 2
Teague, Lake ⊖ AUS 176-177 F 2
Te Anau ○ NZ 182 A 6
Te Anau, Lake ⊖ NZ 182 A 6
Teano Range ▲ AUS 176-177 D 2
Teapa ○ MEX 52-53 H 3
Teapot Dome ⊥ USA (WY) 252-253 M 3
Te Araroa ○ NZ 182 G 2
Te Aroha ○ NZ 182 E 2
Te Awamutu ○ NZ 182 E 3
Teba ○ RI 166-167 J 2
Tebaga, Jebel ▲ TN 190-191 G 4
Tebaram ○ RN 198-199 B 5
Tébe ○ G 210-211 D 4
Tebedu ○ MAL 162-163 J 4
Tebenkopf Bay ≈ 32-33 C 3
Tebenkopf Bay Wilderness ⊥ USA 32-33 C 3
Teben'kova, vulkan ▲ RUS 122-123 M 6
Tebensaj ~ KA 126-127 N 3
Teberda ○ RUS 126-127 D 6
Teberdinskij zapovednik ⊥ RUS 126-127 D 6
Tebesjuak Lake ⊖ CDN 30-31 U 4
Tébessa ☆• DZ 190-191 G 3
Tebez, köl ⊖ KA 126-127 N 3
Tebicuary, Río ~ PY 76-77 J 4
Tebingtinggi ○ RI 162-163 G 2
Tebingtinggi ○ RI 162-163 E 6
Tebingtinggi ○ RI (SUU) 162-163 C 3
Tebo ~ RI 162-163 D 5
Téboura ○ TN 190-191 G 2
Téboursouk ○ TN 190-191 G 2
Tecalitlán ○ MEX 52-53 C 2
Tecamachalco ○ MEX 52-53 F 2
Tecámbaro de Collados ○ MEX 52-53 D 2
Tecate ○• MEX 50-51 A 1
Tecer Dağları ▲ TR 128-129 G 3
Techerène, I-n- < RMM 196-197 K 4
Techia ○ MA 196-197 C 4
Techiman ○ GH 202-203 K 6
Techimpolo ~ ANG 216-217 D 8
Techirimba ○ ANG 216-217 C 5
Techissanha ○ ANG 216-217 D 7
Techongolola ○ ANG 216-217 D 4
Tecka ○ RA 78-79 D 7
Tecka, Rio ~ RA 78-79 D 7
Tecoh ○ MEX 52-53 K 1
Tecojate ○ GCA 52-53 J 5
Tecolote, El ○ MEX 50-51 J 5
Tecoman ○ MEX 52-53 C 2
Tecopa ○ USA (CA) 248-249 H 4
Tecozautla ○ MEX 52-53 E 1
Tecpan de Galeana ○ MEX 52-53 D 3
Tecpatán ○ MEX 52-53 H 3
Tecuala ○ MEX 50-51 G 6
Tecuan, El ○ MEX 52-53 B 1
Tecuci ○ RO 102-103 E 5
Tecumseh ○ CDN (ONT) 238-239 C 6
Tecumseh ○ USA (MI) 272-273 F 6
Tecumseh ○ USA (NE) 262-263 K 4
Tecumseh ○ USA (OK) 264-265 H 3
Ted ○ SP 208-209 F 6
Tedecha Melka ○ ETH 208-209 D 4
Tédéini, I-n- < RN 198-199 D 4
Tedi River ~ PNG 183 A 3
Tedjorar, Adrar ▲ DZ 190-191 E 9
Tedžen ○ TM 136-137 G 6
Tedžen ~ TM 136-137 G 6
Tedžen ~ TM 136-137 G 7
Tedženstroj ○ TM 136-137 G 6
Teebinga Conservation Park ⊥ AUS 180-181 F 3
Teec Nos Pos ○ USA (AZ) 256-257 F 2
Tèèli ☆ RUS 116-117 E 10
Teepee ○ CDN 20-21 X 7
Teepees ○ CDN (ALB) 232-233 E 3
Tees ~ GB 90-91 F 4
Teeswater ○ CDN (ONT) 238-239 D 5
Tefé ○ BR 66-67 E 4
Tefé, Lago ⊖ BR 66-67 E 4
Tefé, Rio ~ BR 66-67 D 5
Tefedest ▲ DZ 190-191 E 8

400 Tangalle — Tefedest

Thomas Hubbard, Cape ▲ **CDN** 26-27 C 3
Thomas Lake, J.B. ⊖ **USA** (TX) 264-265 C 6
Thomas-Müntzer-Stadt Mühlhausen = Mühlhausen o• **D** 92-93 L 3
Thomas Pass ▲ **USA** (UT) 254-255 B 4
Thomas River ~ **AUS** 176-177 D 2
Thomassique o **RH** 54-55 K 5
Thomaston o **USA** (AL) 284-285 C 4
Thomaston o **USA** (GA) 284-285 F 4
Thomaston Corner o **CDN** (NB) 240-241 H 5
Thomasville o **USA** (AL) 284-285 C 5
Thomasville o **USA** (GA) 284-285 G 6
Thomasville o **USA** (NC) 282-283 G 5
Thom Bay o **CDN** 24-25 a 5
Thomonde o **RH** 54-55 K 5
Thompson o **CDN** 34-35 H 3
Thompson o **USA** (ND) 258-259 K 4
Thompson Falls o **USA** (MT) 250-251 D 4
Thompson Island ⌒ **CDN** (ONT) 234-235 O 6
Thompson Pass ▲ **USA** 20-21 S 6
Thompson Peak ▲ **USA** (CA) 246-247 C 2
Thompson River ~ **CDN** (BC) 230-231 H 3
Thompson River ~ **USA** (MO) 274-275 E 4
Thompson River ~ **USA** (MT) 250-251 D 4
Thompson River, North ~ **CDN** (BC) 230-231 K 2
Thompson Sound o **CDN** (BC) 230-231 C 3
Thomsen River ~ **CDN** 24-25 M 4
Thomson o **USA** (GA) 284-285 H 3
Thomson Dam < **AUS** 180-181 J 4
Thomson River ~ **AUS** 178-179 G 3
Thong Pha Phum o **THA** 158-159 E 3
Thongwa o **MYA** 158-159 D 2
Thôn Hai o **VN** 158-159 J 2
Thonon-les-Bains o• **F** 90-91 L 8
Thorburn o **CDN** (NS) 240-241 N 5
Thoreau o **USA** (NM) 256-257 G 3
Thornapple River ~ **USA** (MI) 272-273 D 5
Thornburg o **USA** (IA) 274-275 F 3
Thornbury o **CDN** (ONT) 238-239 E 4
Thorndale o **USA** (TX) 266-267 K 3
Thorndale o **ZA** 218-219 E 6
Thorne o **CDN** (ONT) 238-239 F 2
Thorne o **USA** (NV) 246-247 G 5
Thorne River ~ **CDN** 34-35 L 3
Thornhill o **CDN** (BC) 228-229 F 2
Thorn Hill o **USA** (TN) 282-283 D 4
Thornlea o **CDN** (NFL) 242-243 P 5
Thornloe o **CDN** (ONT) 236-237 J 5
Thornton o **USA** (AR) 276-277 C 7
Thornton o **USA** (IA) 274-275 E 2
Thornton o **USA** (WA) 244-245 H 3
Thorntonia o **AUS** 174-175 E 6
Thorntown o **USA** (IN) 274-275 M 4
Thorp o **USA** (WI) 270-271 H 6
Thorpe Reservoir < **USA** (NC) 282-283 D 5
Thorsby o **CDN** (ALB) 232-233 E 2
Thorshavn = Tórshavn ☆ **FR** 90-91 D 1
Thors Land ∸ **GRØ** 28-29 U 5
Thốt Nốt o **VN** 158-159 H 5
Thou o **BF** 202-203 J 3
Thouars o **F** 90-91 G 8
Thouet ~ **F** 90-91 G 8
Thouin, Cape ▲ **AUS** 172-173 D 6
Thourout = Torhout o **B** 92-93 G 3
Thousand Oaks o **USA** (CA) 248-249 F 5
Thousand Palms o **USA** (CA) 248-249 H 6
Thousand Springs o **USA** (NV) 246-247 L 2
Thrakiko Pelagos ≈ 100-101 K 4
Three Creek o **USA** (ID) 252-253 C 4
Three Creeks o **USA** (AR) 276-277 C 7
Three Forks o **USA** (MT) 250-251 H 6
Three Graces • **AUS** 174-175 C 4
Three Hills o **CDN** (ALB) 232-233 E 4
Threehills Creek ~ **CDN** (ALB) 232-233 E 3
Three Hummock Island ⌒ **AUS** 180-181 H 6
Three Lakes o **USA** (MI) 270-271 K 4
Three Lakes o **USA** (WI) 270-271 J 5
Three Mile Beach ∸ **AUS** 176-177 C 4
Three Mile Rock o **CDN** (NFL) 242-243 L 3
Three Point o **USA** (CA) 248-249 F 5
Three Rivers o **AUS** 176-177 E 2
Three Rivers o **USA** (MI) 272-273 D 6
Three Rivers o **USA** (NM) 256-257 J 5
Three Rivers o **USA** (TX) 266-267 J 5
Three Rocks o **USA** (CA) 248-249 D 3
Three Sisters ▲ **AUS** 178-179 F 3
Three Sisters ▲ **USA** (OR) 244-245 D 6
Three Sisters o **ZA** 220-221 F 5
Three Sisters, The ⌒ **AUS** 174-175 G 2
Three Sisters Islands = Olu Malua ⌒ **SOL** 184 I f 4
Three Springs o **AUS** 176-177 C 4
Three Valley o **CDN** (BC) 230-231 L 3
Three Ways Roadhouse o **AUS** 174-175 C 6
Throat River ~ **CDN** (ONT) 234-235 K 3
Throckmorton o **USA** (TX) 264-265 E 5
Throne o **CDN** (ALB) 232-233 G 3
Throssel, Lake ⊖ **AUS** 176-177 G 3
Throssell Range ▲ **AUS** 172-173 E 6
Thua ~ **EAK** 212-213 G 4
Thuận Châu ☆ **VN** 156-157 C 6
Thubun Lake ⊖ **CDN** 30-31 O 5
Thubun River ~ **CDN** 30-31 O 5
Thuburbo Majus ∴• **TN** 190-191 G 2
Thuchonilini Lake ⊖ **CDN** 30-31 V 5
Thucúc o **VN** 156-157 C 6
Thu Cúc o **VN** 156-157 D 6
Thủ Dầu Một ☆ **VN** 158-159 J 5
Thud Point ▲ **AUS** 174-175 F 3
Thủ Đức o **VN** 158-159 J 5
Thuillier, Mount ▲ **IND** 140-141 L 6
Thul o **PK** 138-139 B 5
Thule = Qaanaaq ☆ **GRØ** 26-27 Q 5
Thuli o **ZW** (Mas) 218-219 E 5
Thuli ~ **ZW** 218-219 E 5
Thuli Safari Area ⊥ **ZW** 218-219 E 5
Thundelarra o **AUS** 176-177 D 4
Thunder Bay o **CDN** (ONT) 234-235 O 6
Thunder Bay ⊖ **CDN** (ONT) 234-235 O 6
Thunder Bay ⊖ **USA** (MI) 272-273 F 3
Thunder Bay ⊖ **USA** (MI) 272-273 F 2
Thunder Bay River ~ **USA** (MI) 272-273 F 2
Thunderbird, Lake < **USA** (OK) 264-265 G 3
Thunderbold o **USA** (GA) 284-285 J 4
Thunder Butte o **USA** (SD) 260-261 E 1
Thunderchild Indian Reservation X **CDN** (SAS) 232-233 K 2
Thunder Creek o **CDN** (SAS) 232-233 M 5
Thunder Hawk o **USA** (SD) 260-261 D 1
Thunder Mount ▲ **USA** 20-21 K 2
Thunder River o **CDN** (BC) 228-229 P 4
Thung Muang o **THA** 142-143 M 6
Thung Salaeng Luang National Park ⊥ **THA** 158-159 F 2
Thung Song o **THA** 158-159 E 6
Thung Wa o **THA** 158-159 E 7
Thung Yai o **THA** 158-159 E 6
Thung Yai Naresuan Wildlife Reserve ⊥••• **THA** 158-159 E 3
Thunkar o **BHT** 142-143 G 2
Thuraiyur o **IND** 140-141 H 5
Thüringen □ **D** 92-93 L 3
Thüringer Wald ▲ **D** 92-93 L 3
Thurles = Durlas o **IRL** 90-91 D 5
Thurlow o **CDN** (BC) 230-231 D 3
Thurmont o **USA** (MD) 280-281 J 4
Thurnwald, Pegunungan ▲ **RI** 166-167 L 4
Thursday Island o•• **AUS** 174-175 G 2
Thurso o **GB** 90-91 F 2
Thurston Island ⌒ **ARK** 16 F 27
Thury, Rivière de ~ **CDN** 36-37 O 5
Thury-Harcourt o **F** 90-91 G 7
Thutade Lake ⊖ **CDN** 32-33 G 3
Thyāvanagi o **IND** 140-141 F 3
Thyborøn o **DK** 86-87 D 8
Thylungra o **AUS** 178-179 G 4
Thymania o **AUS** 178-179 G 2
Thyolo o **MW** 218-219 H 3
Thyou o **BF** 202-203 J 4
Thysville = Mbanza-Ngungu o **ZRE** 210-211 E 6
Tiabaya o **PE** 70-71 B 5
Tiabiga, Mare ⊖• **DY** 202-203 L 4
Tiago o **BR** 62-63 F 6
Tiahualilo de Zaragoza o **MEX** 50-51 H 4
Tiahuanaco • **BOL** 70-71 C 5
Tiahuanacu o **BOL** 70-71 C 5
Tianamé o **RMM** 196-197 L 6
Tianbanjie o **VRC** 156-157 K 2
Tianchang o **VRC** 154-155 L 5
Tianchi • **VRC** 146-147 J 4
Tiandong o **VRC** 156-157 E 5
Tian'e o **VRC** 156-157 E 4
Tiangol Latiéouol ~ **SN** 202-203 C 2
Tiângol Lougguéré ~ **SN** 202-203 C 2
Tianguel-Bory o **RG** 202-203 D 4
Tian Head ▲ **CDN** (BC) 228-229 A 3
Tianjin ☆ **VRC** 154-155 K 2
Tianjin Shi □ **VRC** 154-155 K 2
Tianjun o **VRC** 144-145 M 2
Tiankoura o **BF** 202-203 J 4
Tianlin o **VRC** 156-157 E 4
Tianmen o **VRC** 154-155 H 6
Tianmu Shan ▲ **VRC** 154-155 L 6
Tianmushan • **VRC** 154-155 L 6
Tianmushan Z.B. ⊥• **VRC** 154-155 L 6
Tiansheng o **VRC** 154-155 E 6
Tianshui o **VRC** 154-155 D 4
Tianshuihai o **VRC** 144-145 B 3
Tiantai o **VRC** 156-157 M 2
Tiantaishan • **VRC** 156-157 M 2
Tiantangzhai ▲ **VRC** 154-155 J 6
Tianyahaijao • **VRC** 156-157 F 7
Tianyang o **VRC** 156-157 E 5
Tianzhu o **VRC** (GAN) 154-155 C 3
Tianzhu o **VRC** (GZH) 156-157 F 3
Tianzhushan • **VRC** 154-155 K 6
Tiaraçu o **BR** 76-77 K 6
Tiaret ☆• **DZ** 190-191 C 3
Tías o **E** 188-189 E 6
Tiaski o **SN** 202-203 C 2
Tiassale o **CI** 202-203 H 7
Tibaji o **BR** 74-75 E 5
Tibaji, Rio ~ **BR** 72-73 E 7
Tibana o **CO** 60-61 E 5
Tibati o **CAM** 204-205 K 5
Tibaú o **BR** 68-69 K 4
Tibau, Gunung ▲ **RI** 164-165 D 3
Tibaú do Sul o **BR** 68-69 L 5
Tibba o **PK** 138-139 C 5
Tibboburra o **AUS** 178-179 F 5
Tiberghamine o **DZ** 190-191 C 6
Tibesti ▲ **TCH** 198-199 H 2
Tibesti, Sarir ∸ **LAR** 192-193 G 5
Tibet = Xizang Zizhiqu □ **VRC** 144-145 E 5
Tibi, Pulau ⌒ **RI** 164-165 E 2
Tibiri o **RN** (DOS) 198-199 B 6
Tibiri o **RN** (MAR) 198-199 C 6
Tibirica, Rio ~ **BR** 72-73 E 6
Tibles, Munţii ▲ **RO** 102-103 C 4
Tibni o **SYR** 128-129 H 5
Tibo o **BF** 202-203 J 2
Tibo o **RI** 164-165 F 5
Tibo o **ZRE** 212-213 A 2
Tibung o **RI** 164-165 F 5
Tiburon o•• **RH** 54-55 H 5
Tiburón, Isla ⌒ **MEX** 50-51 C 3
Tica o **MOC** 218-219 H 4
Ticaboo o **USA** (UT) 254-255 E 6
Ticao Island ⌒ **RP** 160-161 E 6
Ticao Pass ≈ 160-161 E 6
Ticatica o **BOL** 70-71 D 7
Tice o **USA** (FL) 286-287 H 5
Tichet < **RMM** 196-197 L 5
Tichît o **RIM** 196-197 F 5
Tichît, Dahr ∸ **RIM** 196-197 F 5
Tichka, Tizi-n- ▲ **MA** 188-189 H 5
Tichkatine, Oued ~ **DZ** 198-199 B 2
T'icho o **ETH** 208-209 D 5
Ticho Brahe, Kap ▲ **GRØ** 28-29 V 4
Tickera o **AUS** 180-181 D 2
Tickfaw River ~ **USA** (LA) 268-269 K 6
Ticonderoga o **USA** (NY) 278-279 H 5
Ticonderoga, Fort • **USA** (NY) 278-279 H 5
Ticsani, Volcán ▲ **PE** 70-71 B 5
Ticul o **MEX** 52-53 K 1
Tidal River o **AUS** 180-181 J 5
Tidangpala o **RI** 164-165 E 2
Tiddim o **MYA** 142-143 H 4
Tiddis ∴• **DZ** 190-191 F 2
Tideridjaouine, Adrar ▲ **DZ** 190-191 C 9
Tiderméné o **RMM** 196-197 M 6
Tidewater o **USA** (LA) 268-269 L 7
Tidewater o **USA** (OR) 244-245 B 6
Tidi Dunes ∸ **RN** 198-199 G 2
Tidikelt, Plaine du ∸ **DZ** 190-191 C 7
Tidirhine, Ibel ▲ **MA** 188-189 J 3
Tidjidit, Erg ∸ **DZ** 190-191 C 9
Tidjikja ☆ **RIM** 196-197 E 5
Tidnish o **CDN** (NS) 240-241 L 5
Tidore, Pulau ⌒•• **RI** 164-165 K 3
Tidore = Soa-Siu o **RI** 164-165 K 3
Tidra, Île ⌒ **RIM** 196-197 B 5
Tidsit, Sebkhet ⊖ **MA** 196-197 C 3
Tiébissou o **CI** 202-203 H 6
Tiéblé o• **BF** 202-203 K 4
Tiéboro o **TCH** 198-199 H 2
Tiefa o **VRC** 150-151 D 6
Tiéfora o **BF** 202-203 H 4
Tiegba o **CI** 202-203 H 7
Tiel o **SN** 202-203 C 2
Tiel, Mayo ~ **CAM** 204-205 K 4
Tieli o **VRC** 150-151 G 4
Tieling o **VRC** 150-151 D 6
Tielong o **VRC** 144-145 B 3
Tielongtan o **VRC** 144-145 B 3
Tielt o **B** 92-93 G 3
Tiéma o **CI** 202-203 G 5
Tiemba ~ **CI** 202-203 G 5
Tiémé o **CI** 202-203 G 5
Tiémélékro o **CI** 202-203 H 6
Tiene o **LB** 202-203 E 6
Tiéningboué o **CI** 202-203 H 5
Tienko o **CI** 202-203 G 4
Tientsin = Tianjin ☆ **VRC** 154-155 K 2
Tiên Yên ☆ **VN** 156-157 E 6
Tiéré o **RMM** 202-203 H 4
Tierfontein o **ZA** 220-221 H 3
Tieri o **AUS** 178-179 K 2
Tierra Amarilla o **USA** (NM) 256-257 J 2
Tierra Blanca o **MEX** 52-53 F 2
Tierra Blanca Creek ~ **USA** (TX) 264-265 B 4
Tierra Colorada o **MEX** 52-53 E 3
Tierra Colorado, Bajo de la ∸ **RA** 78-79 F 7
Tierra del Fuego ⌒ 5 E 10
Tierra del Fuego □ **RA** 80 F 6
Tierra del Fuego, Isla Grande del ⌒ 80 F 6
Tierra del Fuego, Parque Nacional ⊥ **RA** 80 F 7
Tierradentro, Parque Archipiélago • **CO** 60-61 C 6
Tierralta o **CO** 60-61 C 3
Tie Siding o **USA** (WY) 252-253 N 5
Tiétar, Río ~ **E** 98-99 E 5
Tietê o **BR** 72-73 G 7
Tietê, Rio ~ **BR** 72-73 G 7
Tie-Tree Roadhouse o **AUS** 178-179 B 2
Tiev, Shangev- o **WAN** 204-205 H 5
Tieyon o **AUS** 176-177 M 3
Tifernine, Erg ∸ **DZ** 190-191 F 7
Tiffin o **USA** (OH) 280-281 C 2
Tiffin River ~ **USA** (OH) 280-281 B 2
Tiflét o **MA** 188-189 H 4
Tiflis = Tbilisi ★• **GE** 126-127 F 7
Tifore, Pulau ⌒ **RI** 164-165 K 3
Tifrirt < **RIM** 196-197 D 4
Tifton o **USA** (GA) 284-285 G 5
Tifu o **RI** 166-167 D 3
Tiga, Pulau ⌒ **MAL** 160-161 A 10
Tigalda Island ⌒ **USA** 22-23 O 5
Tigapulan, Pegunungan ▲ **RI** 162-163 E 5
Tiga Reservoir < **WAN** 204-205 H 3
Tiga Tarok o **MAL** 160-161 B 9
Tiger o **USA** (WA) 244-245 H 2
Tiger Island ⌒ **GUY** 62-63 E 2
Tighanimines, Gorges de • **DZ** 190-191 F 3
Tighenif o **DZ** 190-191 C 3
Tigi, Danau ⊖ **RI** 166-167 J 4
Tigil' ☆ **RUS** 120-121 S 5
Tigil' ~ **RUS** 120-121 S 5
Tignall o **USA** (GA) 284-285 H 3
Tignère o **CAM** 204-205 K 5
Tigniré < **RIM** 196-197 C 5
Tignish o **CDN** (PEI) 240-241 L 4
Tignuan o **RP** 160-161 D 5
Tigray □ **ETH** 200-201 J 6
Tigre o **RA** 78-79 K 3
Tigre, Arroyo el ~ **RA** 76-77 H 6
Tigre, Cordillera del ▲ **RA** 78-79 E 2
Tigre, El o **CO** 60-61 D 4
Tigre, El ∴• **MEX** 52-53 J 2
Tigre, El o **YV** 60-61 J 3
Tigre, Isla ⌒ **PE** 66-67 B 4
Tigre, Lago del ⊖ **GCA** 52-53 J 3
Tigre, Río ~ **PE** 64-65 E 3
Tigre, Río ~ **YV** 60-61 K 3
Tigre, Sierra del ▲ **RA** 76-77 C 6
Tigre de San Lorenzo, El o **PA** 52-53 D 8
Tigres, Peninsula dos ⌣ **ANG** 216-217 A 8
Tigris ~ 134-135 B 2
Tigris = Diğla ~ **IRQ** 128-129 M 6
Tigrito, El = San José de Guanipa o **YV** 60-61 J 3
Tiguent o **RIM** 196-197 C 6
Tiguézéfene o **RN** 196-197 M 7
Tiguili o **TCH** 206-207 D 3
Tigzerte, Oued ~ **MA** 188-189 G 6
Tigzirt o **DZ** 190-191 E 2
Tihaja ~ **RUS** 120-121 R 5
Tihāma ∸ **Y** 132-133 C 6
Tihāmat aš-Šām ∸ **KSA** 132-133 B 4
Tihodaïne, Erg ∸ **DZ** 190-191 F 8
Tihoreck o **RUS** 102-103 M 5
Tihosuco o **MEX** 52-53 K 1
Tihuatlán o• **MEX** 52-53 F 1
Tihvin ☆ **RUS** 94-95 N 2
Tihvinskaja grjada ▲ **RUS** 94-95 N 2
Tijamuchi, Río ~ **BOL** 70-71 E 4
Tijāra o **IND** 138-139 F 6
Tijeras o **USA** (NM) 256-257 J 3
Tījī o **LAR** 192-193 D 2
Tijo, Tanjung ▲ **RI** 162-163 F 5
Tijoca, Ilha ⌒ **BR** 68-69 E 2
Tijuana o• **MEX** 50-51 A 1
Tijucas o **BR** 74-75 F 6
Tijucas, Ensenada de ≈ 74-75 F 6
Tijucu, Rio ~ **BR** 72-73 F 5
Tika o **CDN** (QUE) 242-243 C 2
Tikal o **GCA** (ELP) 52-53 K 3
Tikal ∴•• **GCA** (ELP) 52-53 K 3
Tikal, Parque Nacional ⊥••• **GCA** 52-53 K 3
Tikamgarh o **IND** 138-139 G 7
Tikanlik o **VRC** 146-147 H 5
Tikaré o **BF** 202-203 K 3
Tikem o **TCH** 206-207 B 4
Tiki Basin ≃ 14-15 P 9
Tikiklut o **USA** 20-21 M 1
Tikkerutuk, Lac ⊖ **CDN** 36-37 L 6
Tiko o **CAM** 204-205 H 6
Tikota o **IND** 140-141 F 2
Tikša o **RUS** 88-89 M 4
Tikšeozero ⊖ **RUS** 88-89 L 3
Tiksi ☆ **RUS** 110-111 R 4
Tiksi, buhta ⊖ **RUS** 110-111 R 4
Tiku o **RI** 162-163 C 5
Tikuna de Feijoal, Área Indígena X **BR** 66-67 C 5
Tikuna São Leopoldo, Área Indígena X **BR** 66-67 C 5
Tiladummati Atoll ⌒ **MV** 140-141 B 4
Tilaiya ⊖ **IND** 142-143 D 3
Tilakvāda o **IND** 138-139 D 9
Tilāl an-Nūba ▲ **SUD** 200-201 E 6
Tilama o **RCH** 78-79 D 2
Tilamuta o **RI** 164-165 H 3
Tilantongo o **MEX** (OAX) 52-53 F 3
Tilantongo ∴• **MEX** (OAX) 52-53 F 3
Tilarán o **CR** 52-53 B 6
Tilburg o **NL** 92-93 H 3
Tilbury o **CDN** (ONT) 238-239 C 6
Tilchuse River ~ **CDN** 30-31 L 2
Tilden o **USA** (NE) 262-263 J 2
Tilden o **USA** (TX) 266-267 J 5
Tilden Lake o **CDN** (ONT) 238-239 F 2
Tilemsen o **MA** 188-189 F 6
Tilemsi, Vallée du ∸ **RMM** 196-197 L 5
Tilford o **USA** (SD) 260-261 C 2
Tilia, Oued ~ **DZ** 190-191 C 7
Tiličiki ☆ **RUS** 112-113 O 6
Tiline o **USA** (KY) 276-277 G 3
Tiljuga ~ **IND** 142-143 E 2
Tillabéri ☆ **RN** 202-203 L 2
Tillamook o **USA** (OR) 244-245 B 5
Tillamook Bay ≈ 40-41 C 3
Tillamook Bay ≈ **USA** 244-245 B 5
Tillanchang Dwip ⌒ **IND** 140-141 L 5
Tillery, Lake < **USA** (NC) 282-283 G 5
Tilley o **CDN** (ALB) 232-233 G 5
Tillman o **USA** (SC) 284-285 J 4
Tillsonburg o **CDN** (ONT) 238-239 E 6
Tilly, Lac ⊖ **CDN** 38-39 G 2
Tilney o **CDN** (SAS) 232-233 N 5
Tiloa o **RN** 204-205 E 1
Tilopozo o **RCH** 76-77 C 2
Tilos ⌒ **GR** 100-101 L 6
Tilpa o **AUS** 178-179 H 6
Tilrempt o **DZ** 190-191 D 4
Tilston o **CDN** (MAN) 234-235 B 5
Tiltil o **RCH** 78-79 D 2
Ţimā o **ET** 194-195 E 4
Timahdite o **MA** 188-189 J 4
Timalchara o **RCH** 70-71 C 6
Timampuu o **RI** 164-165 G 5
Timane, Río ~ **PY** 70-71 G 7
Timanfaya, Parque Nacional de ⊥ **E** 188-189 E 6
Timanskij bereg ⌣ **RUS** 88-89 U 3
Timanskij krjaž ▲ **RUS** 88-89 U 3
Timanskiy Kryazh = Timanskij krjaž ▲ **RUS** 88-89 U 3
Timare o **RI** 166-167 J 4
Timargarha o• **PK** 138-139 C 2
Timaru o **NZ** 182 C 6
Timaševsk o **RUS** 102-103 L 5
Timau o **EAK** 212-213 F 3
Timba o **CO** 60-61 C 6
Timbalier Bay ≈ 44-45 M 5
Timbalier Bay ≈ **USA** 268-269 K 7
Timbalier Island ⌒ **USA** (LA) 268-269 K 7
Timbang, Pulau ⌒ **MAL** 160-161 C 10
Timbaúba o **BR** 68-69 L 5
Timbavati Game Reserve ⊥ **ZA** 220-221 K 2
Timbedgha o **RIM** 196-197 F 6
Timber o **USA** (OR) 244-245 B 5
Timber Creek o **AUS** 172-173 K 3
Timber Creek Lake ⊖ **USA** (KS) 262-263 K 7
Timber Lake o **USA** (SD) 260-261 E 1
Timberlin Lodge Ski Area ⊥ **USA** (OR) 244-245 D 5
Timber Mill o **AUS** 172-173 K 2
Timber Mountain ▲ **USA** (NV) 246-247 K 5
Timberon o **USA** (NM) 256-257 K 6
Timberville o **USA** (VA) 280-281 H 5
Timbiras o **BR** 68-69 G 4
Timbó o **BR** 74-75 F 6
Timbo o **RG** 202-203 E 4
Timboon o **AUS** 180-181 G 5
Timboroa o **EAK** 212-213 E 3
Timbotuba, Ilha do ⌒ **BR** 66-67 D 4
Timboy o **BOL** 76-77 E 1
Timbuktu = Tombouctou o••• **RMM** 196-197 J 6
Timbulun o **RI** 162-163 D 5
Timbuni ~ **RI** 166-167 G 2
Timbunke o **PNG** 183 B 3
Timbun Mata, Pulau ⌒ **MAL** 160-161 C 10
Timeldjame, Oued ~ **DZ** 190-191 D 6
Timelloutine o **DZ** 190-191 G 6
Timétrine, Djebel ▲ **RMM** 196-197 K 5
Timgad o••• **DZ** 190-191 F 3
Timia o **RN** 198-199 D 3
Timiaouine o **RMM** 196-197 L 4
Timika o **RI** 166-167 J 4
Timimoun o• **DZ** 190-191 C 6
Timimoun, Sebkha de ⊖ **DZ** 188-189 L 6
Timirist, Râs ▲ **RIM** 196-197 B 5
Timiş ~ **RO** 102-103 C 5
Timiskaming, Lake= Témiscamingue, Lac ⊖ **CDN** (QUE) 236-237 J 5
Timişoara ☆• **RO** 102-103 B 5
Timissit, Oued ~ **DZ** 190-191 G 6
Timkinskaja ~ **RUS** 112-113 K 2
Timmerkpuk Mountain ▲ **USA** 20-21 J 2
Timmiarmiut o **GRØ** 28-29 U 5
Timmins o **CDN** (ONT) 236-237 G 4
Timmonsville o **USA** (SC) 284-285 L 2
Timms Hill ▲ **USA** (WI) 270-271 H 5
Timna' ∴• **IL** 130-131 D 3
Timoforo ~ **RI** 166-167 G 2
Timok ~ **YU** 100-101 J 2
Timon o **BR** 68-69 G 4
Timonha, Rio ~ **BR** 68-69 H 3
Timonium o **USA** (MD) 280-281 K 4
Timor ⌒ **RI** 166-167 C 6
Timor, Laut ≈ 166-167 D 7
Timor Sea ≈ 172-173 H 2
Timor Trough ≃ 166-167 C 7
Timote o **RA** 78-79 H 3
Timóteo o **BR** 72-73 J 5
Timoudi o **DZ** 188-189 L 6
Timpahute Range ▲ **USA** (NV) 248-249 J 2
Timpanogos Cave National Monument ∴ **USA** (UT) 254-255 D 3
Timpas o **USA** (CO) 254-255 M 6
Timpaus, Pulau ⌒ **RI** 164-165 H 4
Timpson o **USA** (TX) 268-269 F 5
Timpton ~ **RUS** 118-119 N 6
Timra o **S** 86-87 H 5
Tim Raré o **RMM** 196-197 J 6
Tims Ford Lake ⊖ **USA** (TN) 276-277 J 5
Timun o **RI** 162-163 E 4
Timur, Banjaran ▲ **MAL** 162-163 E 2
Timur Digul ~ **RI** 166-167 L 4
Timurni o **IND** 138-139 F 8
Timur Timor □ **RI** 166-167 C 6
Tina ~ **ZA** 220-221 J 5
Tin Abunda, Bi'r < **LAR** 192-193 E 4
Tinaca Point ▲ **RP** 160-161 F 10
Tinaco o **YV** 60-61 G 3
Ti-n-Aguelhaj o **RMM** 196-197 J 6
Tinaja, La o **MEX** 52-53 F 2
Tinaja, Punta ▲ **PE** 70-71 A 5
Ti-n-Akof o **BF** 202-203 K 2
Tin Alkoum < **DZ** 190-191 H 8
Tinambung o **RI** 164-165 F 5
Ti-n-Amzag < **RMM** 196-197 H 6
Tin Amzi, Oued ~ **DZ** 198-199 B 2
Tinangkong o **RI** 164-165 H 4
Tinaroo Falls Reservoir < **AUS** 174-175 H 5
Ti-n-Azabo o **RMM** 196-197 L 6
Ti-n-Bessais < **RIM** 196-197 F 3
Ti-n-Brahim < **RIM** 196-197 C 5
Tindangou o **BF** 202-203 L 4
Tinderry Range ▲ **AUS** 180-181 K 3
Tindila o **RG** 202-203 F 4
Tindivanam o **IND** 140-141 H 4
Tindjassé o **RT** 202-203 L 5
Tindouf ☆• **DZ** 188-189 G 7
Tindouf, Hamada de ∸ **DZ** 188-189 G 7
Tindouf, Sebkha de ⊖ **DZ** 188-189 H 7
Tineba, Pegunungan ▲ **RI** 164-165 G 4
Ti-n-Eguelaï o **RMM** 196-197 J 6
Tineo = Tinéu o **E** 98-99 D 3
Ti-n-Essako o **RMM** 196-197 M 5
Tinfouchy o **DZ** 188-189 J 6
Tin Fouye o **DZ** 190-191 F 6
Tingal ▲ **SUD** 200-201 E 6
Tingambato o **MEX** 52-53 D 2
Tinggi, Pulau ⌒ **MAL** (KED) 162-163 F 3
Tinghert, Hamādat ∸ **LAR** 190-191 F 6
Tinglayan o **RP** 160-161 D 4
Tingmiarmiut ⌒ **GRØ** 28-29 U 5
Tingmiarmiut Fjord ≈ 28-29 T 5
Tingo Maria, Parque Nacional ⊥ **PE** 64-65 D 6
Tingong o **VRC** 156-157 F 4
Tingri o **VRC** 144-145 F 6
Tingsryd ☆ **S** 86-87 G 8
Tingstäde o **S** 86-87 J 8
Tinguá, Parque Nacional de ⊥ **BR** 72-73 J 7
Tingvoll ☆ **N** 86-87 D 5
Tingwon Group ⌒ **PNG** 183 E 2
Tingya o **SUD** 206-207 L 3
Tin Hadjène, Oued ~ **DZ** 190-191 F 8
Tinharé, Ilha de ⌒ **BR** 72-73 L 2
Tinherir o **MA** 188-189 J 5
Tĩnh Gia ☆ **VN** 156-157 D 7
Tini o **SUD** 198-199 L 5
Ti-n-Idnâne < **RMM** 196-197 J 6
Tinigart < **RIM** 196-197 F 5
Tiniroto o **NZ** 182 F 3
Tinis, Wādī ~ **LAR** 192-193 D 5
Tinitan o **RP** 160-161 C 7
Tiniteqilaaq o **GRØ** 28-29 W 4
Tinitonito Bay ≈ 36-37 N 2
Tinjil, Pulau ⌒ **RI** 168 A 3
Tinkisso ~ **RG** 202-203 F 4
Ti-n-Medjouf < **RIM** 196-197 C 5
Tin Merzouga ∸ **DZ** 190-191 H 9
Tin Mountain ▲ **USA** (CA) 248-249 G 3
Tinnie o **USA** (NM) 256-257 K 5
Tinogasta o **RA** 76-77 D 5
Tinombo o **RI** 164-165 G 3
Tinompo o **RI** 164-165 G 5
Tínos o **GR** 100-101 K 6
Tínos ⌒ **GR** 100-101 K 6
Ti-n-Oufart < **RMM** 196-197 K 6
Tinputz o **PNG** 184 I b 1
Tin Rerhoch < **DZ** 198-199 B 2
Tinrhert, Hamada de ∸ **DZ** 190-191 F 6
Tinrhert, Plateau du ▲ **DZ** 190-191 E 7
Tinsman o **USA** (AR) 276-277 C 7
Tin Tadjant ~ **DZ** 196-197 L 4
Tintagel o **CDN** (BC) 228-229 J 2
Tintah o **USA** (MN) 270-271 B 4
Ţinţâne o **RIM** 196-197 E 6
Tin Tarabine < **DZ** 190-191 F 9
Tin Tarabine, Oued ~ **DZ** 190-191 F 9
Ti-n-Tehoun < **RMM** 196-197 J 6
Tintejert, Adrar ▲ **DZ** 190-191 D 8
Tintern Abbey •• **GB** 90-91 F 6
Ti-n-Tijot < **RMM** 196-197 H 6
Tintina o **RA** 76-77 F 4
Tintinara o **AUS** 180-181 F 3
Tintioulen o **RG** 202-203 F 4
Tin Toumma ∸ **RN** 198-199 F 4
Tiny o **CDN** (SAS) 232-233 Q 4
Ti-n-Zaouâtene o **RMM** 196-197 M 5
Tin-Zawatine o **DZ** 196-197 M 5
T'i'o o **ER** 200-201 K 5
Tiobraid Árann = Tipperary o **IRL** 90-91 C 5
Tioga o **USA** (ND) 258-259 E 3
Tioman, Pulau ⌒ **MAL** 162-163 F 3
Tionesta o **USA** (PA) 280-281 G 2
Tionesta Lake ⊖ **USA** (PA) 280-281 G 2
Tioor, Pulau ⌒ **RI** 166-167 F 4
Tiop o **RI** 162-163 D 6
Tioribougou o **RMM** 202-203 G 3
Tioroniaradougou o **CI** 202-203 H 5
Tiou o **BF** 202-203 J 3
Tioughnioga River ~ **USA** (NY) 278-279 E 6
Tiouilît o **RIM** 196-197 B 5
Tiouki o **RMM** 202-203 H 2
Tioussiana o **BF** 202-203 H 4
Tipaza ☆••• **DZ** 190-191 D 2
Tipitapa o• **NIC** 52-53 L 5
Tipitapa, Río ~ **NIC** 52-53 L 5
Tipolo o **RP** 160-161 F 7
Tippecanoe River ~ **USA** (IN) 274-275 M 3
Tipperary o **AUS** 172-173 K 2
Tipperary = Tiobraid Árann o **IRL** 90-91 C 5
Tipton o **USA** (CA) 248-249 E 3
Tipton o **USA** (IA) 274-275 G 3
Tipton o **USA** (IN) 274-275 M 4
Tipton o **USA** (MO) 274-275 F 6
Tipton o **USA** (OK) 264-265 E 4
Tipton, Mount ▲ **USA** (AZ) 256-257 A 3
Tiptonville o **USA** (TN) 276-277 F 4
Tip Top Mountain ▲ **CDN** (ONT) 236-237 B 4
Tiptur o **IND** 140-141 G 4
Tipuani, Río ~ **BOL** 70-71 C 4
Tipuru o **GUY** 62-63 E 3
Tiputini o **EC** 64-65 E 2
Tiquaruçu o **BR** 72-73 L 2
Tiquicheo o **MEX** 52-53 D 2
Tiquié, Rio ~ **BR** 66-67 C 2
Tiquillaca o **PE** 70-71 B 4
Tira, Bol'šaja ~ **RUS** 116-117 M 7
Tiracambu, Serra do ▲ **BR** 68-69 E 4
Tiradentes o **BR** 72-73 H 6
Tirahart, Oued ~ **DZ** 190-191 D 9
Tirān, Ğazīrat ⌒ **KSA** 130-131 D 4
Tirana, La o **RCH** 70-71 C 7
Tiranë ★•• **AL** 100-101 G 4
Tirangole o **SUD** 206-207 L 6
Tiraouene < **RN** 198-199 C 3
T'irarē Shet' ~ **ETH** 200-201 J 6
Tirari Desert ∸ **AUS** 178-179 E 5
Tirasberge ▲ **NAM** 220-221 C 2
Tiraspol ☆ **MD** 102-103 F 4
Tirau o **NZ** 182 E 2
Tirband-e Torkestān, Selsele-ye Kūh-e ▲ **AFG** 136-137 H 7
Tire ☆ **TR** 128-129 B 3
Tire, Kōtal-e ▲ **AFG** 138-139 B 3
Tirebolu o **TR** 128-129 H 2
Tirecatinga, Área Indígena X **BR** 70-71 H 3
Tiree ⌒ **GB** 90-91 D 3
Tirehtjah ~ **RUS** 110-111 a 7
Tirehtjah ~ **RUS** 110-111 P 6
Tirere o **PNG** 183 B 5
Tîrgovişte ☆• **RO** 102-103 D 5
Tîrgu Frumos o **RO** 102-103 E 4
Tirgui < **TCH** 198-199 J 3
Tîrgu Jiu ☆ **RO** 102-103 C 5
Tîrgu Mureş ☆• **RO** 102-103 D 4
Tîrgu Secuiesc o **RO** 102-103 E 4
Tirhatimine < **DZ** 190-191 D 8
Tirhemar, Oued ~ **DZ** 190-191 F 7
Tiri Aguge ~ **TCH** 192-193 H 6
Tiriri o **EAU** 212-213 D 3
Tiririca o **BR** 68-69 G 7
Tiririne, Oued ~ **DZ** 190-191 G 9
Tiriro o **RG** 202-203 F 4
Tiris Zemour □ **RIM** 196-197 E 2
Tîrnăveni o **RO** 102-103 D 4
Tiro o **RG** 202-203 E 5
Tirol □ **A** 92-93 L 5
Tiros o **BR** 72-73 H 5
Tiroungoulou o **RCA** 206-207 F 4
Tirreno, Mar ≈ 100-101 D 5
Tirso ~ **I** 100-101 B 5
Tirso = Lago Omodeo ⊖ **I** 100-101 B 4
Tirthahalli o **IND** 140-141 F 4
Tiruchchendūr o• **IND** 140-141 H 6
Tiruchchirāppalli o• **IND** 140-141 H 5
Tiruchengodu o **IND** 140-141 G 5
Tiruganna o **IND** 140-141 F 4
Tirukkalukkunram o• **IND** 140-141 J 4
Tirukkoyilūr o **IND** 140-141 H 5
Tirumakudal o **IND** 140-141 G 4
Tirumala o• **IND** 140-141 H 4
Tirumangalam o **IND** 140-141 H 6
Tirumullaivāsal o **IND** 140-141 H 5
Tirunelveli o• **IND** 140-141 G 6
Tiruntan o **PE** 64-65 E 5
Tirupati o• **IND** 140-141 H 4
Tirupparangunram • **IND** 140-141 H 6
Tiruppattūr o **IND** 140-141 H 5
Tiruppatūr o **IND** 140-141 H 4
Tirupporur o **IND** 140-141 J 4
Tiruppur o **IND** 140-141 G 5
Tirupuvanam o **IND** 140-141 H 6
Tirutturaippūndi o **IND** 140-141 H 5
Tiruvalaru o **IND** 140-141 H 5
Tiruvalla o **IND** 140-141 G 6
Tiruvannāmalai o• **IND** 140-141 H 4
Tiruvattiyur o **IND** 140-141 J 4
Tiruvūru o **IND** 142-143 B 7
Tirvyjaha ~ **RUS** 108-109 O 6
Ţīs o **IR** 134-135 J 6
Tis ~ **RUS** 116-117 E 6
Tisa ~ **UA** 102-103 C 3
Tisa ~ **YU** 100-101 H 2
Tisaiyanvilai o **IND** 140-141 G 6
Tisdale o **CDN** (SAS) 232-233 O 3
Tisgaon o **IND** 138-139 E 10
Tisgui-Remz o **MA** 188-189 G 6
Tishomingo o **USA** (OK) 264-265 H 4
Tishomingo National Wildlife Refuge ⊥ **USA** (OK) 264-265 H 4
Tišina ~ **RUS** 122-123 D 3
T'is Isat Fwafwatē = Blue Nile Falls ~•• **ETH** 208-209 C 3
Tiska, Pic ▲ **DZ** 190-191 G 9
Tisnaïet, Oued ~ **DZ** 190-191 E 6
Tissa ~ **RUS** 116-117 J 9
Tissamaharama o **CL** 140-141 J 7
Tissān, Hasy < **LAR** 192-193 E 3
Tissemsilt ☆ **DZ** 190-191 C 3
Tista ~ **BD** 142-143 F 2
Tisul' ☆ **RUS** 114-115 U 7
Tisza ~ **H** 92-93 Q 5
Tit o **DZ** (ADR) 190-191 C 7
Tit o **DZ** (TAM) 190-191 E 9
Tit, Suon- o **RUS** 118-119 L 6
Titaluk River ~ **USA** 20-21 N 2
Titao o **BF** 202-203 J 3
Tit-Ary o **RUS** (SAH) 110-111 Q 3
Tit-Ary o **RUS** (SAH) 118-119 N 5
Tite o **GNB** 202-203 C 4
Titicaca, Lago ⊖ **PE** 70-71 C 4
Titicaca, Reserva Nacional ⊥ **PE** 70-71 B 4
Titigading o **RI** 162-163 D 4
Titiwaifuru o **RI** 166-167 K 3
Titiwan, Banjaran ▲ **MAL** 162-163 D 3
Titler o **USA** (OR) 244-245 C 8
Titograd = Podgorica ☆ **YU** 100-101 G 3
Titova Mitrovica = Kosovska Mitrovica o **YU** 100-101 H 3
Titov Drvar o **BIH** 100-101 F 2
Titovo Užice = Užice o **YU** 100-101 H 3
Titov Veles o• **MK** 100-101 H 4
Ti-Tree o **AUS** 178-179 B 2
Titu o **RO** 102-103 D 5
Titule o **ZRE** 210-211 K 2
Titumate o **CO** 60-61 C 3
Titusville o **USA** (FL) 286-287 J 3
Titusville o **USA** (PA) 280-281 G 2
Titwān ☆• **MA** 188-189 J 3
Tiung, Tanjung ▲ **RI** 162-163 G 5
Tiva ~ **EAK** 212-213 G 4
Tivaouane o **SN** 202-203 B 2
Tivoli o **I** 100-101 D 4
Tivoli o **USA** (TX) 266-267 L 5
Tivtejjaha ~ **RUS** 108-109 N 6
Ţiwāl, aţ- o **KSA** 132-133 C 5
Tiwi o **EAK** 212-213 G 6
Tiwori, Teluk ≈ 164-165 G 4
Tiworo, Kepulauan ⌒ **RI** 164-165 H 6
Tiworo, Selat ≈ 164-165 H 6
Tixmul ∴• **MEX** 52-53 K 2
Tixtla de Guerrero o **MEX** 52-53 E 3
Tiya ••• **ETH** 208-209 C 5
Tiyāb o **IR** 134-135 G 5
Tiyo, Pegunungan ▲ **RI** 166-167 H 4
Tizayuca o **MEX** 52-53 E 2
Tizi, Mare de ⊖ **RCA** 206-207 F 3
Tizimín o **MEX** 52-53 K 1
Tizi Ouzou ☆ **DZ** 190-191 E 2
Tiznados, Río ~ **YV** 60-61 H 3
Tiznit ☆ **MA** 188-189 G 6
Tīžtīž o **IR** 128-129 M 5
Tjaneni o **SD** 220-221 K 2
Tjanja o **RUS** 118-119 J 6
Tjanja ~ **RUS** 118-119 K 6
Tjater ~ **RUS** 96-97 J 7
Tjatino o **RUS** 122-123 M 6
Tjatja, vulkan ▲ **RUS** 122-123 M 6
Tjažin ~ **RUS** 114-115 U 6
Tjažinskij ☆ **RUS** 114-115 U 6
Tjeggelvas ⊖ **S** 86-87 H 3
Tjera o **BF** 202-203 H 4
Tjörn ∸ **S** 86-87 E 8
Tjugël'saj o **KS** 146-147 B 5
Tjugjuène ~ **RUS** 118-119 N 4
Tjuhtet ☆ **RUS** 114-115 U 6
Tjukalinsk ☆ **RUS** 114-115 M 7
Tjukjan ~ **RUS** 110-111 L 7
Tjukjan ~ **RUS** 110-111 M 7
Tjukjan ~ **RUS** 118-119 J 4
Tjulender araly ⌒ **KA** 126-127 J 5
Tjulenij, mys ▲ **AZ** 128-129 O 2
Tjul'gan ☆ **RUS** 96-97 K 7
Tjuli o **RUS** 114-115 K 4
Tjumen' ☆ **RUS** 114-115 H 6
Tjung ~ **RUS** 110-111 M 6
Tjung ~ **RUS** 110-111 K 6
Tjung ~ **RUS** 110-111 M 7
Tjung ~ **RUS** 118-119 K 4
Tjungjulju o **RUS** 118-119 P 4
Tjup o **KS** 146-147 D 4
Tjup ~ **KS** 146-147 D 4
Tjuvfjorden ≈ 84-85 M 4
Tkvarčeli o **GE** 126-127 D 6
Tlacoapa o **MEX** 52-53 E 3
Tlacolula o• **MEX** 52-53 F 3
Tlacotalpan o• **MEX** 52-53 G 2
Tlacotepec o **MEX** 52-53 F 2
Tlacuilotepec o **MEX** 52-53 E 1
Tlahuac o **MEX** 52-53 E 2
Tlahuiltepa o **MEX** 52-53 E 1
Tlākshīn, Bi'r < **LAR** 192-193 E 2
Tlalchapa o **MEX** 52-53 D 2
Tlalnepantla o **MEX** 52-53 E 2

402 Thomas Hubbard, Cape — Tlalnepantla

Tlalpan = Tlalnepantla ○ MEX 52-53 E 2
Tlaltenango ○ MEX 50-51 H 7
Tlapacoyan ○ MEX 52-53 F 2
Tlapa del Comonfort ○ MEX 52-53 E 3
Tlapaneco, Río ~ MEX 52-53 E 3
Tlaquepaque ○• MEX 52-53 C 1
Tlaxcala ▫ MEX 52-53 E 2
Tlaxcala ☆• MEX (TLA) 52-53 E 2
Tlaxiaco ○ MEX 52-53 F 3
Tlell ○ CDN (BC) 228-229 C 3
Tlemcen ☆•• DZ 188-189 L 3
Tlemcen, Monts de ▲ DZ 188-189 L 3
Tleta-de-Sidi-Bouguedra ○ MA 188-189 G 4
Tlevak Strait ≈ 32-33 D 4
Tlhakgameng ○ ZA 220-221 G 3
Tljarata ○ RUS 126-127 G 6
Tlokoeng ○ LS 220-221 J 4
Tmassah ○ LAR 192-193 F 4
Tmeïmîchât ○ RIM 196-197 C 4
Tne Haven ○ ZA 220-221 J 6
Tnèkveem ~ RUS 112-113 T 4
To ○ BF 202-203 J 4
Toa Baja ○ USA (PR) 286-287 P 2
Toade, Kepulauan ⌒ RI 164-165 J 2
Toad River ~ CDN 30-31 G 6
Toak ○ VAN 184 II b 3
Toamasina ▫ RM 222-223 F 6
Toamasina ☆ RM (TMA) 222-223 F 7
Toano ○ USA (VA) 280-281 K 6
Toari ○ BR 66-67 D 6
Toaupulai ○ IND 140-141 G 6
Toaya ○ RI 164-165 F 4
Toba ○ CDN (BC) 230-231 E 3
Toba ○ J 152-153 G 7
Toba ○ VRC 144-145 L 5
Toba, Arroyo el ~ RA 76-77 G 5
Toba, Isla ⌒ RA 80 H 2
Tobacco Range ⌒ BH 52-53 K 3
Tobago ⌒ TT 60-61 L 2
Toba Inlet ≈ 32-33 H 6
Toba Inlet ≈ CDN 230-231 E 3
Toba Kākar Range ▲ PK 134-135 M 3
Tobalai, Pulau ⌒ RI 164-165 L 4
Tobalai, Selat ≈ 164-165 L 4
Tobamawu ○ RI 164-165 G 4
Toba River ~ CDN (BC) 230-231 E 3
Tobarra ○ E 98-99 G 5
Toba Tek Singh ○ PK 138-139 D 4
Tobe ○ USA (CO) 254-255 M 6
Tobeatic Game Sanctuary ⊥ CDN (NS) 240-241 K 6
Tobejuba, Isla ⌒ YV 60-61 L 3
Tobelo ○ RI 164-165 K 3
Tobelombang ○ RI 164-165 G 4
Tobermorey ○ AUS 178-179 D 2
Tobermory ○• CDN (ONT) 238-239 D 3
Tobermory ○ GB 90-91 D 3
Tobias Barreto ○ BR 68-69 J 7
Tobin, Kap = Uunarteq ○ GRØ 26-27 p 8
Tobin, Mount ▲ USA (NV) 246-247 H 3
Tobin Lake ○ AUS 172-173 G 6
Tobin Lake ○ CDN (SAS) 232-233 P 2
Tobin Lake ○ CDN (SAS) 232-233 P 2
Tobique 20 Indian Reserve ✗• CDN (NB) 240-241 H 4
Tobique River ~ CDN (NB) 240-241 H 3
Tobishima ⌒ J 152-153 H 5
Toboali ○ RI 162-163 G 6
Tobol ○ KA 124-125 C 2
Tobol ~ RUS 114-115 H 7
Tobol ~ RUS 114-115 J 6
Tobol ~ RUS 124-125 B 3
Toboli ○ RI 164-165 G 4
Tobol'sk ☆• RUS 114-115 K 5
Tobol'skij materik, vozvyšennost' ▲ RUS 114-115 K 5
Tobré ○ DY 204-205 E 3
Tobseda ○ RUS 88-89 W 2
Toby = Morarano ○ RM 222-223 E 8
Tobyčan ~ RUS 110-111 X 7
Tobyš ~ RUS 88-89 V 4
Tobys' ~ RUS 88-89 W 5
Tobyšskaja vozvyšennost' ▲ RUS 88-89 V 3
Toca ○ CO 60-61 E 5
Tocache Nuevo ○ PE 64-65 D 6
Tocaima ○ CO 60-61 D 5
Tocancipa ○ CO 60-61 E 5
Tocantinia ○ BR 68-69 D 6
Tocantinópolis ○ BR 68-69 E 5
Tocantins ▫ BR 68-69 D 7
Tocantins, Rio ~ BR 62-63 K 6
Tocantins, Rio ~ BR 68-69 E 5
Toccoa ○ USA (GA) 284-285 G 2
Toćes ~ RUS 114-115 U 4
Tochatwi Bay ○ CDN 30-31 O 4
Tochcha Lake ○ CDN (BC) 228-229 J 2
Tochi ~ PK 138-139 B 3
Toch'o Do ⌒ ROK 150-151 E 10
Toco ○ ANG 216-217 B 7
Toco ○ RCH 76-77 C 2
Toco ○ TT 60-61 L 2
Tocoa River ~ USA (GA) 284-285 F 2
Toconquis, Cerros de ▲ RA 76-77 D 3
Tocopilla ○ RCH 76-77 B 2
Tocopuri, Cerros de ▲ BOL 76-77 D 2
Tocota ○ RA 76-77 C 6
Tocumwal ○ AUS 180-181 H 3
Tocuyito ○ YV 60-61 G 2
Tocuyo, El ○ YV 60-61 G 3
Tocuyo, Río ~ YV 60-61 G 2
Toda-saki ▲ J 152-153 K 5
Todd River ~ AUS 178-179 C 3
Todeli ○ RI 164-165 J 4
Todenyang ○ EAK 212-213 E 1
Tōdi ▲ CH 92-93 K 5
Todi ○• I 100-101 D 3
Todin ○ BF 202-203 J 3
Todlo ○ RI 166-167 F 2
Todmorden ○ AUS 178-179 C 4
Todos los Santos, Lago ○ RCH 78-79 C 6
Todos os Santos, Baía de ≈ 72-73 L 2
Todos os Santos, Rio ~ BR 72-73 K 4
Todos Santos ○ BOL 70-71 E 5
Todos Santos ○ MEX 50-51 D 6
Todra, Gorges du • MA 188-189 J 5
Todža, ozero = ozero Azas ○ RUS 116-117 H 9
Todžinskaja kotlovina ⚍ RUS 116-117 H 9
Toéguin ○ BF 202-203 K 3
Toekomstig-stuwmeer ○ SME 62-63 F 3
Toéni ○ BF 202-203 J 3
Toéssé ○ BF 202-203 K 4
Toez ○ CO 60-61 C 6
Toffo ○ DY 204-205 E 5
Tofield ○ CDN (ALB) 232-233 F 2
Tofino ○ CDN (BC) 230-231 D 4
Töfsingdalens nationalpark ⊥ S 86-87 F 5
Toga, Île = Toga ⌒ VAN 184 II a 1
Toga = Île Toga ⌒ VAN 184 II a 1
Togafo ○ RI 164-165 K 3
Toganaly ○ AZ 128-129 M 2
Tōgane ○ J 152-153 J 7
Togba < RIM 196-197 E 6
Togdheer ▫ SP 208-209 G 4
Tog Dheer, togga ~ SP 208-209 H 4
Togi ○ J 152-153 G 6
Togiak ○ USA 22-23 Q 3
Togiak Bay ≈ 22-23 Q 3
Togian, Kepulauan ⌒ RI 164-165 G 4
Togian, Pulau ⌒ RI 164-165 G 4
Togme ○ VRC 144-145 H 4
Togni ○ SUD 200-201 G 3
Togo ○ CDN (SAS) 232-233 R 4
Togo ○ PNG 183 B 5
Togo ■ RT 204-205 D 4
Togo ○ USA (MN) 270-271 E 3
Togo, Lac ○ RT 202-203 L 6
Togoba ○ PNG 183 C 3
Togobala ○ CI 202-203 G 5
Togo Hills ▲ GH 202-203 L 6
Togolika ~ RUS 114-115 T 5
Togoromá ○ CO 60-61 C 5
Togou ○ RMM 202-203 H 3
Tōgrög ○ MAU 146-147 L 2
Togtoh ○ VRC 154-155 G 1
Togučin ☆ RUS 114-115 S 7
Togueré-Koumbé ○ RMM 202-203 H 2
Togul ☆ RUS 124-125 P 2
Tog Wajaale ○ SP 208-209 F 4
Togwotee Pass ▲ USA (WY) 252-253 H 3
Togyzak ~ KA 124-125 C 2
Tohāna ○ IND 138-139 E 5
Tohareu, poluostrov ⌒ RUS 122-123 H 2
Tohatchi ○ USA (NM) 256-257 G 3
Tohiatoš ○ US 136-137 F 3
Tohma Çayı ~ TR 128-129 H 3
Tōhoku ○ J 152-153 J 4
Tōhōm ○ MAU 148-149 J 5
Tohomo ~ RUS 116-117 G 5
Tohopekaliga, Lake ○ USA (FL) 286-287 H 3
Tohoun ○ RT 202-203 L 6
Toibalewe ○ IND 140-141 L 4
Toili ○ RI 164-165 H 4
Toineke ○ RI 166-167 C 7
Toison, La ○ RH 54-55 K 5
Toivala ○ FIN 88-89 J 5
Tojo ○ J 152-153 E 7
Tojoku ○ RUS 118-119 K 4
Tojtepa ○ US 136-137 L 4
Tok ~ RUS 96-97 H 7
Tok ~ RUS 118-119 O 8
Toka ○ GUY 62-63 E 4
Tokachi-dake ▲ J 152-153 K 3
Tokachi-gawa ~ J 152-153 K 3
Tokamachi ○ J 152-153 H 6
Tokapalle ○ IND 140-141 H 3
Tōkar ○ SUD 200-201 H 3
Tokara-kaikyō ≈ 152-153 C 9
Tokara-rettō ⌒ J 152-153 C 10
Tokat ☆• TR 128-129 G 2
Tŏkchŏkto ⌒ ROK 150-151 E 9
Tokchon ○ DVR 150-151 F 8
Tok Do ⌒ ROK 150-151 H 9
Tokeland ○ USA (OR) 244-245 A 4
Tokelau Islands ⌒ NZ 13 K 3
Toki ○ TCH 206-207 C 4
Tokio ○ BOL 70-71 C 2
Tokio ○ USA (TX) 264-265 B 5
Tok Junction ○ USA 20-21 T 5
Tokko ○ RUS (SAH) 118-119 K 6
Tokko ~ RUS 118-119 J 6
Tokko ~ RUS 118-119 J 7
Toklat River ~ USA 20-21 P 4
Tokma ○ RUS 116-117 M 6
Tokmak ○ KS 146-147 B 4
Tokmak ○ UA 102-103 J 4
Tokoro ○ J 152-153 L 2
Tokoroa ○ NZ 182 E 3
Tokounou ○ RG 202-203 F 5
Tokrau ~ KA 124-125 J 4
Toksovo ○ RUS 94-95 M 1
Toksum ○ VRC 146-147 J 4
Tokto ○ VRC 146-147 J 4
Toktogul ○ KS 136-137 N 4
Toktogul'skoje vodohranilišče < KS 136-137 N 4
Tokuma ○ RUS 110-111 U 6
Tokunoshima ○ J 152-153 C 11
Tokuno-shima ⌒ J 152-153 C 11
Tokur-Jurjah ~ RUS 112-113 J 4
Tokushima ☆ J 152-153 F 7
Tokuyama ○ J 152-153 D 7
Tokwe ~ ZW 218-219 F 5
Toky, Chute ~ ZRE 212-213 B 3
Tōkyō ☆• J 152-153 H 7
Tōkyō-wan ≈ 152-153 H 7
Tōkyusan National Park ⊥• ROK 150-151 F 10
Tol ○ PNG 183 G 3
Tola, La ○ EC 64-65 C 1
Tolabit ○ RI 164-165 K 3
Tolaga Bay ○ NZ 182 G 3
Tolala ○ RI 164-165 G 5
To' Lan ○ VN 158-159 K 5
Tōlanaro ○• RM 222-223 E 10
Tolapalca, Río ~ BOL 70-71 D 6
Tolar ○ USA (NM) 256-257 M 4
Tolar, Cerro ▲ RCH 76-77 B 1
Tolbazy ☆ RUS 96-97 J 6
Tolbo ○ MAU 146-147 K 1
Tolbo nuur ○ MAU 146-147 J 1
Tolbuhin = Dobrič ○ BG 102-103 E 6
Tolbuzino ○ RUS 118-119 M 9
Toldi ○ GH 202-203 K 5
Tolé ○ PA 52-53 D 7
Tolé ○ RCA 206-207 B 5
Toledo ○ BOL 70-71 D 6
Toledo ○ BR 74-75 D 5
Toledo ○ CDN (ONT) 238-239 K 4
Toledo ○•• E 98-99 E 5
Toledo ○ USA (OH) 280-281 C 2
Toledo ○ USA (OR) 244-245 B 6
Toledo, Montes de ▲ E 98-99 E 5
Toledo Bend Reservoir < USA (TX) 268-269 G 5
Toledo City ○ RP 160-161 E 7
Tolga ○ DZ 190-191 E 3
Tolhuaca, Parque Nacional ⊥ RCH 78-79 D 5
Tolhuin ○ RA 80 G 7
Toli ○ VRC 146-147 F 3
Toliara ▫ RM 222-223 C 9
Toliara ☆ RM (Tla) 222-223 C 9
Tolima A ○ CO 64-65 F 2
Tolimán ○ MEX 52-53 E 1
Tolisain ○ NEP 144-145 C 6
Tolitoli ○ RI 164-165 G 3
Tol'jatti = Stavropol'-na-Volgi ☆ RUS 96-97 F 7
Tol'ka ~ RUS 114-115 Q 3
Tolland ○ CDN (ALB) 232-233 H 2
Tolleson ○ USA (AZ) 256-257 C 5
Tolley ○ USA (ND) 258-259 F 3
Tollhouse ○ USA (CA) 248-249 E 2
Tollja, zaliv ≈ 108-109 d 3
Tolmačovo ○ RUS 94-95 L 2
Tolo ○ ZRE 210-211 G 5
Tolo, Teluk ≈ 164-165 G 5
Tolode ○ LB 202-203 F 6
Tolofu ○ RI 164-165 K 3
Tolokiwa Island ⌒ PNG 183 D 3
Tololalai (Muslim Tombs) ○• RI 168 D 7
Tolon ○• RUS 120-121 E 3
Tolongoina ○ RM 222-223 E 8
Tolono ○ USA (IL) 274-275 K 5
Tolonuu, Pulau ⌒ RI 164-165 L 3
Tolosa ○ E 98-99 F 3
Tolovana River ~ USA 20-21 Q 4
Tolsan Do ⌒ ROK 150-151 F 10
Tolstoi ○ CDN (MAN) 234-235 G 5
Tolstova, mys ▲ RUS 110-111 V 2
Tolstyj, mys ▲ RUS 120-121 W 6
Toltén ○ RCH 78-79 C 5
Toltén, Río ~ RCH 78-79 C 5
Tolu ○ CO 60-61 D 3
Toluca ☆• MEX 52-53 E 2
Toluca de Lerdo = Toluca ☆• MEX 52-53 E 2
Toluk ○ KS 136-137 N 4
Toluviejo ○ CO 60-61 D 3
Tolwe ○ ZA 218-219 E 6
Tol'yatti = Stavropol'-na-Volgi ☆ RUS 96-97 F 7
Tölz, Bad ○ D 92-93 L 5
Tom' ~ RUS 114-115 S 7
Tom' ~ RUS 122-123 D 3
Tom ~ RUS 122-123 D 3
Tom' ~ RUS 124-125 P 1
Tom ○ US 136-137 J 5
Tom ○ USA (OK) 264-265 K 5
Toma ○ BF 202-203 J 3
Toma, La ○ RA 78-79 G 2
Toma, Río la ~ RA 76-77 D 4
Tomah ○ USA (WI) 270-271 H 7
Tomahawk ○ USA (WI) 270-271 J 5
Tomakomai ○ J 152-153 J 3
Tomales Bay ≈ 40-41 C 6
Tomales Bay ≈ USA 246-247 B 5
Tomali ○ RI 164-165 G 4
Tomani ○ MAL 160-161 A 10
Tomanivi ▲ FJI 184 III b 2
Tomar ○ BR 66-67 F 3
Tomar ○•• P 98-99 C 5
Tomara, Talahini- ○ CI 202-203 J 5
Tomari ○ RUS 122-123 K 5
Tomarovka ○ RUS 102-103 K 2
Tomarza ☆ TR 128-129 F 3
Tomas ○ PE 64-65 E 8
Tomás Garrido ○ MEX 52-53 K 2
Tomásia ○ BR 68-69 E 6
Tomaszów Lubelski ○ PL 92-93 R 3
Tomaszów Mazowiecki ○ PL 92-93 P 3
Tomat ○ SUD (Kas) 200-201 G 5
Tomat ○ SUD (NR) 206-207 H 3
Tomatán ○ MEX 50-51 B 3
Tomatlán ○ MEX 52-53 B 2
Tombador, Serra do ▲ BR 70-71 J 2
Tombali, Rio ~ GNB 202-203 C 4
Tomball ○ USA (TX) 268-269 E 6
Tombe ○ ANG 216-217 D 6
Tombe du Camerounais ▲ TCH 198-199 H 3
Tombel ○ CAM 204-205 H 6
Tombetsu, Hama- ○ J 152-153 K 2
Tombetsu, Nakō- ○ J 152-153 K 2
Tombetsu, Shō- ○ J 152-153 K 2
Tombigbee River ~ USA (AL) 284-285 B 4
Tombigbee River ~ USA (AL) 284-285 B 5
Tombigbee River ~ USA (MS) 268-269 M 2
Tombo, Punta ▲•• RA 80 H 2
Tomboco ○ ANG 216-217 B 3
Tombokro ○ CI 202-203 H 6
Tombolo ○ RI 164-165 F 6
Tomboutcou ○••• RMM 196-197 J 6
Tombstone ○ USA (AZ) 256-257 E 7
Tombua ○ ANG 216-217 A 7
Tomé ○ RCH 78-79 C 4
Tome ○ USA (NM) 256-257 J 4
Tomea, Pulau ⌒ RI 164-165 H 6
Tomé-Açu ○ BR 68-69 D 3
Tomelloso ○ E 98-99 F 5
Tomi ~ RCA 206-207 D 6
Tomichi Creek ~ USA (CO) 254-255 J 5
Tomiko ○ CDN (ONT) 238-239 F 2
Tomina, Río ~ BOL 70-71 E 6
Tominé ~ RG 202-203 D 4
Tomingley ○ AUS 180-181 K 2
Tomini ○ RI 164-165 G 3
Tomini, Teluk ≈ 164-165 G 4
Tominián ○ RMM 202-203 H 3
Tomioka ○ J 152-153 H 6
Tomkinson Ranges ▲ AUS 176-177 K 3
Tomma ⌒ N 86-87 F 3
Tommot ○ RUS 118-119 N 6
Tommotskij massiv ▲ RUS 110-111 W 5
Tomo, Río ~ CO 60-61 G 5
Tomochic ○ MEX 50-51 F 3
Tomohon ○ RI 164-165 J 3
Tomori ○ RCA 210-211 E 2
Tomorrit, Mali i ▲ AL 100-101 H 4
Tompira ○ RI 164-165 G 5
Tompi Seleka ○ ZA 220-221 J 2
Tompkins ○ CDN (SAS) 232-233 K 5
Tompkinsville ○ USA (KY) 276-277 K 4
Tompo ○ RI 164-165 G 3
Tompo ○ RUS 120-121 F 2
Tompo ~ RUS 120-121 H 1
Tom Price ○ AUS 172-173 C 7
Tom Price, Mount ▲ AUS 172-173 C 7
Tompuda ~ RUS 118-119 E 8
Tomsk ☆• RUS 114-115 S 6
Toms River ○ USA (NJ) 280-281 M 4
Tom Steed ○ USA (OK) 264-265 E 4
Tomtor ○ RUS (SAH) 110-111 T 6
Tomtor ○ RUS (SAH) 120-121 E 2
Tomu ○ RI 166-167 G 3
Tomur Feng ▲ VRC 146-147 E 4
Tomu River ~ PNG 183 B 4
Tom White, Mount ▲ USA 20-21 T 6
Tonalá ○ MEX (JAL) 52-53 C 1
Tonalá ○• MEX (CHI) 52-53 H 3
Tonami ○ J 152-153 G 6
Tonantins ○ BR 66-67 D 4
Tonasket ○ USA (WA) 244-245 F 2
Tonate ○ F 62-63 H 3
Tonawanda Indian Reservation ✗ USA (NY) 278-279 C 5
Tonb-e Bozorg, Ǧazire-ye ⌒ IR 134-135 F 5
Tonb-e Kuček, Ǧazire-ye ⌒ IR 134-135 F 5
Tonda ○ PNG 183 A 5
Tondano ○ RI 164-165 J 3
Tondano, Danau ○ RI 164-165 J 3
Tonde ○ Z 218-219 E 1
Tønder ○• DK 86-87 D 9
Tondi ○ IND 140-141 H 6
Tondibi ○ RMM 196-197 K 6
Tondidji ○ RMM 202-203 E 3
Tondigamé Goulbi ~ RN 204-205 E 2
Tondi Kiwidi ○ RN 204-205 E 1
Tondon ○ RG 202-203 D 4
Tondong ○ RI 164-165 F 5
Toné ○ BF 202-203 J 4
Tone-gawa ~ J 152-153 H 6
Tonekābon ○ IR 136-137 B 6
Tong ○ SUD 206-207 J 5
Tong ~ SUD 206-207 J 5
Tonga ○ CAM 204-205 J 6
Tonga ○ SUD 206-207 K 4
Tonga ■ TON 184 IV a 1
Tongaat ○ ZA 220-221 K 4
Tongaland ⌒ ZA 220-221 L 3
Tong'an ○ VRC 156-157 L 4
Tonga Ridge ≃ 184 IV a 2
Tongariki ⌒ VAN 184 II b 3
Tongariro National Park ⊥••• NZ 182 E 3
Tongatapu ⌒ TON 184 IV a 2
Tongatapu Group ⌒ TON 184 IV a 2
Tonga Trench ≃ 13 K 4
Tongbai ○ VRC 154-155 H 5
Tongbai Shan ▲ VRC 154-155 H 5
Tongcheng ○ VRC (ANH) 154-155 K 6
Tongcheng ○ VRC (HUB) 156-157 H 2
Tongchon ○ DVR 150-151 F 8
Tongchuan ○ VRC 154-155 F 4
Tongdao ○ VRC 156-157 F 3
Tongde ○ VRC 154-155 B 4
T'ongdo Sa • ROK 150-151 G 10
Tongehatan Point ▲ RP 160-161 D 10
Tongerai, Tanjung ▲ RI 166-167 G 3
Tonggu ○ VRC 156-157 J 2
Tongguan ○ VRC 154-155 G 4
Tongguzbasti ○ VRC 146-147 E 6
Tonggu Zhang ▲ VRC 156-157 K 4
Tonghae ○ ROK 150-151 G 9
Tonghai ○ VRC 156-157 C 4
Tonghaiko ○ VRC 154-155 H 6
Tonghe ○ VRC 150-151 G 5
Tonghua ○ VRC 150-151 E 7
Tong Island ⌒ PNG 183 D 2
Tongjiang ○ VRC (HEI) 150-151 J 4
Tongjiang ○ VRC (SIC) 154-155 E 6
Tongjosŏn Man ≈ 150-151 F 8
Tongko ○ RI 164-165 G 4
Tongkomanino ○ RI 164-165 G 5
Tongku ○ RI 164-165 G 4
Tongliang ○ VRC 156-157 E 2
Tongliao ○ VRC 150-151 D 6
Tongling ○ VRC 154-155 K 6
Tonglu ○ VRC 156-157 L 2
Tongmu ○ VRC 156-157 H 3
Tongnan ○ VRC 154-155 D 6
Tongo ○ RCB 210-211 F 4
Tongoa ⌒ VAN 184 II b 3
Tongobory ○ RM 222-223 D 9
Tongomayél ○ BF 202-203 K 2
Tongren ○ VRC (GZH) 156-157 F 3
Tongren ○ VRC (QIN) 154-155 B 4
Tongsa ○ BHT 142-143 G 2
Tongshan ○ VRC 156-157 J 2
Tongshi ○• VRC 156-157 F 7
Tongtian He ~ VRC 144-145 L 4
Tongue ○• GB 90-91 E 2
Tongue River ~ USA (MT) 250-251 N 6
Tonguo ~ RUS 118-119 K 4
Tonguro, Río ~ BR 72-73 D 2
Tongxiang ○ VRC 154-155 M 6
Tongxin ○ VRC 154-155 D 3
Tongyu ○ VRC (JIL) 150-151 D 5
Tongyu ○ VRC (SHA) 154-155 H 3
Tongzi ○ VRC 156-157 E 2
Tonhil = Zujl ○ MAU 146-147 L 2
Tonichi ○ MEX 50-51 E 3
Tonila ○ MEX 52-53 C 2
Tonimuca, Raudal ~ CO 66-67 B 3
Tonina ○ CO 60-61 H 6
Toniná ∴• MEX 52-53 H 3
Tonk ○ IND 138-139 E 6
Tonka ○ RMM 196-197 J 6
Tonkawa ○ USA (OK) 264-265 G 2
Tonkensval ~ SME 62-63 F 3
Tonki Cape ▲ USA 22-23 V 3
Tonkin ○ CDN (SAS) 232-233 Q 4
Tonkin, Gulf of ≈ 156-157 E 6
Tonkui, Mont ▲ CI 202-203 G 6
Tônlé Sab ○ K 158-159 H 4
Tonnerre ○ F 90-91 J 8
Tōno ○ J 152-153 J 5
Tonoda ~ RUS 118-119 G 6
Tonono ○ RA 76-77 F 2
Tonopah ○ USA (AZ) 256-257 C 5
Tonopah ○ USA (NV) 246-247 H 5
Tonopah Test Range Atomic Energy Commission ✗✗ USA (NV) 248-249 H 2
Tonoro ○ YV 60-61 K 3
Tonosí ○ PA 52-53 D 8
Tonosyō ○ J 152-153 F 7
Tonotha ○ RB 218-219 D 5
Tonquil Island ⌒ RP 160-161 D 10
Ton Sai ○ THA 158-159 F 7
Tønsberg ☆ N 86-87 E 7
Tonsina ○ USA 20-21 S 6
Tonstad ☆ N 86-87 C 7
Tontado, Caleta ≈ 76-77 B 5
Tontal, Sierra del ▲ RA 76-77 C 6
Tontelbos ○ ZA 220-221 E 5
Tonto, Río ~ MEX 52-53 F 2
Tonto Basin ○ USA (AZ) 256-257 D 5
Tonto National Monument • USA (AZ) 256-257 D 5
Tonumea ⌒ TON 184 IV a 2
Tonya ☆ TR 128-129 H 2
Tony Creek ~ CDN (ALB) 228-229 R 2
Tonzona River ~ USA 20-21 O 5
Toobanna ○ AUS 174-175 J 6
Toobli ○ LB 202-203 F 6
Toodyay ○ AUS 176-177 D 5
Tooele ○ USA (UT) 254-255 C 3
To Okena ○ PNG 183 D 4
Toolebuc ○ AUS 178-179 F 2
Toolik River ~ USA 20-21 Q 2
Toolondo ○ AUS 180-181 F 4
Tooloombilla ○ AUS 178-179 K 3
Toompine ○ AUS 178-179 H 4
Toomula ○ AUS 174-175 J 6
Tooncatchyin Creek ~ AUS 178-179 E 5
Toora-Hem ☆ RUS 116-117 H 9
Toormt ○ MAU 116-117 F 10
Toornaarsuk ⌒ GRØ 28-29 Q 6
Toowoomba ○ AUS 178-179 L 4
Top, Ozero = Topozero ○ RUS 88-89 M 4
Topagoruk River ~ USA 20-21 N 1
Topanga ○ USA (CA) 248-249 F 5
Topar ○ KA 124-125 J 6
Topasovėj, ostrov ⌒ RUS 108-109 M 7
Topawa ○ USA (AZ) 256-257 D 7
Topaz ○ USA (CA) 246-247 F 5
Topaz Lake ○ USA (NV) 246-247 F 5
Topeka ☆ USA (KS) 262-263 L 5
Topía ○ MEX 50-51 F 5
Topia ~ RCA 206-207 C 6
Topia, Quebrada ~ MEX 50-51 F 5
Topko, gora ▲ RUS 120-121 G 5
Topley ○ CDN (BC) 228-229 H 2
Topley Landing ○ CDN (BC) 228-229 H 2
Toplita ○• RO 102-103 D 4
Topocalma, Punta ▲ RCH 78-79 C 3
Topock ○ USA (AZ) 256-257 A 4
Top of the World Provincial Park ⊥ CDN (BC) 230-231 O 4
Topografičeskaja, grjada ▲ RUS 108-109 Z 4
Topol ○ RUS 116-117 G 7
Topola ○• YU 100-101 H 2
Topoli ○ ZRE 212-213 A 2
Topolinoe ○ RUS 120-121 F 1
Topolobampo ○ MEX 50-51 E 5
Topolovgrad ○ BG 102-103 E 6
Topolovka ○ RUS 120-121 T 3
Topozero ○ RUS 88-89 M 4
Toppenish ○ USA (WA) 244-245 E 4
Toppi-misaki ▲ J 152-153 J 4
Toprakkale ∴• TR 128-129 G 4
Tops, Mount ▲ AUS 178-179 B 1
Topsfield ○ USA (ME) 278-279 O 3
Top Springs ○ AUS (NT) 172-173 K 4
Top Springs ○ AUS (NT) 174-175 C 5
Topura ○ PNG 183 F 6
Topyrakkala • US 136-137 G 4
Toquerville ○ USA (UT) 254-255 B 6
Tor ○ ETH 208-209 A 5
Toramarkog ○ VRC 144-145 L 4
Torata ○ PE 70-71 B 5
Torbanlea ○ AUS 178-179 M 3
Torbat-e Ǧām ○• IR 136-137 G 7
Torbat-e Heidarīye ○• IR 136-137 F 7
Torbay ○ AUS 176-177 D 7
Torbay ○ CDN (NFL) 242-243 Q 5
Tor Bay ≈ CDN 240-241 O 5
Torbay ○ GB 90-91 F 6
Torboy ○ USA (WA) 244-245 G 2
Torch River ~ CDN (SAS) 232-233 P 2
Tordenskjold, Kap ▲ GRØ 28-29 T 6
Tordesillas ○ E 98-99 E 4
Tōre ○ S 86-87 L 4
Torej, Zun, ozero ○ RUS 118-119 H 10
Torell Land ⚍ N 84-85 K 4
Torellō ○ E 98-99 J 3
Torenur ○ IND 140-141 F 4
Toreo Bugis ○ RI 164-165 H 5
Torǧaj ○ KA (KST) 126-127 P 3
Torǧaj ~ KA 124-125 D 3
Torǧaj ~ KA 126-127 P 3
Torǧaj kolaty ~ KA 126-127 P 3
Torǧaj üstirti ▲ KA 124-125 B 3
Torgau ○• D 92-93 M 3
Torgun ~ RUS 96-97 E 8
Torhout ○ B 92-93 G 3
Tori ○ RMM 202-203 J 3
Toribio ○ CO 60-61 C 6
Tori-Bossito ○ DY 204-205 E 5
Torino ☆• I 100-101 A 2
Torino, Cachoeira do ~ BR 62-63 F 6
Tori-shima ⌒ J 152-153 C 11
Torit ○ SUD 206-207 L 6
Toritama ○ BR 68-69 K 6
Toriu ○ PNG 183 F 3
Toriud ○ IR 136-137 D 7
Torje, Barun, ozero ○ RUS 118-119 G 10
Torkamān ○ IR 128-129 M 4
Torkemān, Bandar-e ○ IR 136-137 D 6
Torlu River ~ PNG 183 F 3
Tormentor, ozero ○ RUS 114-115 P 4
Torment, Point ▲ AUS 172-173 F 4
Tormes, Río ~ E 98-99 E 4
Tormosin ○ RUS 102-103 N 3
Tornado Mountain ▲ CDN (BC) 230-231 P 4
Torneälven ~ S 86-87 L 3
Torneträsk ○• S 86-87 J 2
Torngat Mountains ▲ CDN 36-37 R 5
Tornik ▲ YU 100-101 G 3
Tornio ○ FIN 88-89 H 4
Tornionjoki ~ FIN 88-89 G 3
Tornquist ○ RA 78-79 H 5
Toro ○ E 98-99 E 4
Toro ○ EAU 212-213 C 3
Toro, Cerro del ▲ RA 76-77 C 5
Toro, Isla del ⌒ MEX 50-51 L 7
Toro, Lago del ○ RCH 80 D 5
Toro, Punta ▲ RCH 78-79 D 2
Torobuku ○ RI 164-165 H 6
Torodi ○ RN 202-203 L 3
Toro Doum < TCH 198-199 H 4
Toro Game Reservat ⊥ EAU 212-213 C 3
Torokina ○ PNG 184 I b 2
Toro Kinkéné ○ CI 202-203 H 5
Torokoroba ○ RMM 202-203 G 3
Törökszentmiklós ○ H 92-93 Q 5
Torola, Río ~ ES 52-53 K 5
Torom ○ RUS 120-121 F 6
Torom ~ RUS 120-121 F 6
Toro Negro, Sierra del ▲ RA 76-77 C 5
Toronto ☆• CDN (ONT) 238-239 F 5
Toronto ○ USA (KS) 262-263 L 7
Toronto Lake ○ USA (KS) 262-263 L 7
Toropec ☆ RUS 94-95 M 3
Toroq ○ IR 136-137 F 6
Tororo ○ EAU 212-213 E 3
Torqabe ○ IR 136-137 F 6
Torquato Severo ○ BR 76-77 K 6
Torquay ○ CDN (SAS) 232-233 P 6
Torquinie, Lake ○ AUS 178-179 E 3
Torrabaai ○ NAM 216-217 B 10
Torrance ○ USA (CA) 248-249 F 6
Torrão ○ P 98-99 C 5
Torrealba ○ YV 60-61 J 3
Torre del Greco ○ I 100-101 E 4
Torre de Moncorvo ○ P 98-99 D 4
Torrelaguna ○ E 98-99 F 4
Torrelavega ○ E 98-99 E 3
Torremolinos ○ E 98-99 E 6
Torrens, Cape ▲ CDN 24-25 a 2
Torrens, Lake ○ AUS 178-179 D 6
Torrens Creek ○ AUS 174-175 H 7
Torrens Creek ~ AUS 178-179 H 2
Torrens River ~ CDN (ALB) 228-229 P 2
Torreón ○ MEX 50-51 H 5
Torreon ○ USA (NM) 256-257 H 3
Torre-Pacheco ○ E 98-99 G 6
Torres ○• BR 74-75 F 7
Torres, Îles = Torres Islands ⌒ VAN 184 II a 1
Torres del Paine ○ RCH 80 D 5
Torres del Paine, Parque Nacional ⊥•• RCH 80 D 5
Torres Islands = Îles Torres ⌒ VAN 184 II a 1
Torres Martinez Indian Reservation ✗ USA (CA) 248-249 H 6
Torres Novas ○ P 98-99 C 5
Torres Selat ≈ 183 A 5
Torres Strait ≈ 174-175 F 1
Torres Vedras ○ P 98-99 C 5
Torrevieja ○ E 98-99 G 6
Torrey ○ USA (UT) 254-255 D 5
Torricelli Mountains ▲ PNG 183 B 2
Torrijos ○ E 98-99 E 5
Torrington ○ CDN (ALB) 232-233 E 4
Torrington ○ USA (CT) 280-281 N 2
Torrington ○ USA (WY) 252-253 O 4
Torrock ○ TCH 206-207 B 4
Torrön ○ S 86-87 F 5
Torsås ☆ S 86-87 H 8
Torsby ☆• S 86-87 F 6
Torset, Oued ~ DZ 190-191 G 8
Tórshavn ☆ FR 90-91 D 1
Torsö ⌒ S 86-87 F 7
Torssuqatak ≈ 28-29 P 2
Tortas, Cachoeira das ~ BR 70-71 J 4
Tortel ○ RCH 80 D 3
Tortiya ○• CI 202-203 H 5
Törtköl ○ KA 136-137 L 3
Tortola ⌒ GB 56 C 2
Tortola ⌒ GB (VI) 286-287 R 2
Tórtoles de Esgueva ○ E 98-99 E 4
Tortona ○ I 100-101 B 2
Tortosa ○ E 98-99 H 4
Tortosa, Cabo de ▲ E 98-99 H 4
Tortue, Ile de la ⌒ RH 54-55 J 4
Tortuga, Isla ⌒ MEX 50-51 D 4
Tortuga, Isla La ⌒ YV 60-61 J 2
Tortuguero, Parque Nacional ⊥ CR 52-53 C 6
Tortuguilla ○ C 54-55 H 5
Tortum ☆ TR 128-129 J 2
Torue ○ RI 164-165 G 4
Torul ☆ TR 128-129 H 2
Toruń ☆•• PL 92-93 P 2
Torup ○ S 86-87 F 8
Tõrva ○•• EST 94-95 J 2
Torwood ○ AUS 174-175 G 5
Tory ○ RUS 116-117 L 10
Tory Hill ○ CDN (ONT) 238-239 G 4
Toržkovskaja grjada ▲ RUS 94-95 O 3
Toržok ☆ RUS 94-95 O 3
Torzym ○ PL 92-93 N 2
Tosagua ○ EC 64-65 B 2
Tosari ○ RI 168 E 3
Tosa-shimizu ○ J 152-153 E 8
Tosa-wan ≈ 152-153 E 8
Tosca ○ ZA 220-221 F 2
Toscana ▫ I 100-101 C 3
Toscas, Las ○ RA (BUA) 78-79 J 3
Toscas, Las ○ RA (SAF) 76-77 H 5
Toscas, Las ○ ROU 78-79 M 2
Toshām ○ IND 138-139 E 5
Toshima ⌒ J 152-153 H 7
Toshino-Kumano National Park ⊥ J 152-153 G 7
Tosi ○ SUD 206-207 K 3
Toškent ☆•• US 136-137 L 4
Toškuduk, kumlik ⚍ US 136-137 G 3
Toškŭrgon ○ US 136-137 K 5
Tosno ☆ RUS 94-95 M 2
Tosoncengel ○ MAU 148-149 D 3
Toson Hu ○ VRC 144-145 L 2
Tostado ○ RA 76-77 G 5
Tõstamaa ○ EST 94-95 H 2
Toston ○ USA (MT) 250-251 H 5
Tošviska ○ RUS 88-89 W 3
Tosya ☆ TR 128-129 F 2
Tot ○ EAK 212-213 E 3
Totaranui ○ NZ 182 D 4
Toteng ○ RB 218-219 B 5
Tôtes ○ F 90-91 H 7
Totias ○ SP 212-213 J 2
Tot'ma ○ RUS 94-95 S 2
Totnes ○ CDN (SAS) 232-233 K 4
Totnes Fiord ≈ 28-29 J 3
Totness ☆ SME 62-63 F 3
Toto ○ ANG 216-217 C 3
Toto ○ WAN 204-205 G 4
Totogan Creek ~ CDN (ONT) 234-235 O 2
Totogan Lake ○ CDN (ONT) 234-235 O 2
Totoglag ○ VAN 184 II a 1
Totok ○ RI 164-165 J 3
Totolán ○ MEX 52-53 C 1
Totolapan ○ MEX 52-53 F 3
Totomai, Monts ▲ RN 198-199 G 2
Totonicapán ☆• GCA 52-53 J 4
Totora ○ BOL (COC) 70-71 E 5
Totora ○ BOL (ORU) 70-71 C 5
Totoral ○ RCH 76-77 B 4
Totoral, Quebrada del ~ RCH 76-77 B 5
Totoralejos ○ RA 76-77 E 5
Totoras ○ RA 78-79 J 2
Totota ○ LB 202-203 F 6
Totoya ⌒ FJI 184 III c 3
Totta ~ RUS 120-121 G 5
Tottan Range ▲ ARK 16 F 35
Totten Glacier ⊂ ARK 16 G 12
Tottenham ○ AUS 180-181 J 2
Tottenham ○ CDN (ONT) 238-239 F 4
Tottori ☆ J 152-153 F 7
Totumito ○ YV 60-61 F 4
Totydèottajaha, Bol'šaja ~ RUS 108-109 T 8
Touâjîl ○ RIM 196-197 D 3
Touak Fiord ≈ 36-37 S 2
Touâret < RN 198-199 C 2
Touaris, Djebel ▲ DZ 188-189 K 6
Touat ⚍ DZ 188-189 L 7
Touba ○ CI 202-203 G 5
Touba ○• SN 202-203 C 2
Toubacouta ○ SN 202-203 B 3
Toubéré Bafal ○ SN 202-203 D 2
Toubkal, Ibel ▲ MA 188-189 H 5
Touboro ○ CAM 206-207 B 5
Toubouto, Chutes de ~• RCA 206-207 B 6
Toucha, Djebel ▲ DZ 188-189 L 5
Touchet ○ USA (WA) 244-245 G 4
Toucy ○ F 90-91 J 8
Toueyyirât < RMM 196-197 J 5
Tougan ○ BF 202-203 J 3
Tougé ○ RG 202-203 E 4
Touggourt ○• DZ 190-191 F 4
Tougnifili ○ RG 202-203 C 4
Tougouri ○ BF 202-203 K 3
Tougoutaou < RN 198-199 C 5
Touijinet < RIM 196-197 F 5
Touil, Hâssi < RIM 196-197 H 6
Touila, Bir < TN 190-191 G 4
Toujil ○ RIM 196-197 E 7
Toukoto ○ RMM 202-203 F 3
Toukountouna ○ DY 202-203 L 4
Toul ○ F 90-91 K 7
Touléplou ○ CI 202-203 F 6
Touliu ○ RC 156-157 M 5
Toulnustouc, Rivière ~ CDN 38-39 K 4
Toulon ☆ F 90-91 K 10
Toulon ○ USA (IL) 274-275 J 3
Toulou, Abri des • RCA 206-207 E 4
Touloungа ○ TCH 206-207 D 3
Toulouse ☆•• F 90-91 H 10
Toumbélaga < RN 198-199 C 5
Toumodi ○ CI 202-203 H 6
Toumoundjila ○ RN 202-203 G 2
Tounassine, Hamada ⚍ DZ 188-189 H 6
Tounfafi ○ RN 198-199 B 5
Toungo ○ WAN 204-205 K 4
Toungoo ○ MYA 142-143 K 6
Toungour < TCH 198-199 J 4
Toura ~ BF 202-203 K 3
Toura ○ DY 204-205 E 3
Touragondi ○ AFG 136-137 H 7
Tourassinne < RIM 196-197 E 2
Tourba ○ TCH 198-199 G 6
Tourcoing ○ F 90-91 J 6
Touré Kounda ○ SN 202-203 D 3
Tour Ham ○ AFG 138-139 C 2
Touriñán, Cabo ▲ E 98-99 C 3
Tourine ○ RIM 196-197 E 3
Tournai ○• B 92-93 G 3
Tournavista ○ PE 64-65 E 6
Tourndé, Oued ~ DZ 190-191 H 9
Tourni ○ BF 202-203 H 4
Tournus ○ F 90-91 K 8
Touros ○ BR 68-69 L 4
Tourou ▲ CAM 204-205 K 3
Touroua ○ CAM 204-205 K 4
Tourougoumbé ○ RMM 202-203 F 2
Tourouкoro ○ BF 202-203 H 4
Tours ○ F 90-91 H 8
Tour Village, De ○ USA (MI) 272-273 F 2

Tlalpan — Tour Village, De 403

Touside, Pic ▲ TCH 198-199 H 2
Toussoro, Mont ▲ RCA 206-207 F 4
Toutes Aides o CDN (MAN) 234-235 D 3
Toutoukro o CI 202-203 H 5
Touwsrivier o ZA 220-221 E 6
Touwsrivier ~ ZA 220-221 E 6
Töv ▫ MAU 148-149 G 4
Tovar o YV 60-61 F 3
Tovar Donoso o EC 64-65 C 1
Tovarkovskij o RUS 94-95 Q 5
Tovdalselva ~ N 86-87 D 7
Tovuz o AZ 128-129 L 2
Tow o USA (TX) 266-267 J 3
Towada o J 152-153 J 4
Towada-Hachimantai National Park ⊥ J 152-153 J 4
Towada Hachimantai National Park ⊥ J 152-153 J 5
Towada-ko • J 152-153 J 4
Towakaima o GUY 62-63 D 2
Towanda o USA (KS) 262-263 K 7
Towanda o USA (PA) 280-281 K 2
Towaoc o USA (CO) 254-255 G 6
Towari o RI 164-165 G 6
Towe o LB 202-203 F 6
Tower o USA (MN) 270-271 F 3
Towera o AUS 176-177 C 1
Towerhill Creek ~ AUS 178-179 H 1
Tower Peak ▲ AUS 176-177 G 6
Tower-Roosevelt o USA (WY) 252-253 H 2
Towla o ZW 218-219 E 5
Town Creek o USA (AL) 284-285 C 2
Town Creek ~ USA (AL) 284-285 C 2
Town Creek ~ USA (AL) 284-285 D 2
Town Creek Indian Mound • USA (NC) 282-283 H 5
Towne Pass ▲ USA (CA) 248-249 G 3
Towner o USA (CO) 254-255 N 5
Towner o USA (ND) 258-259 G 3
Townley o USA (AL) 284-285 C 3
Townsend o USA (GA) 284-285 J 5
Townsend o USA (MT) 250-251 H 5
Townsend o USA (WI) 270-271 K 5
Townsend Lake o CDN 30-31 W 4
Townsend Ridges ▲ AUS 176-177 J 3
Townshend o USA (VT) 278-279 J 5
Townshend Island ⌒ AUS 178-179 L 2
Towns River ~ AUS 174-175 C 4
Townsville o• AUS 174-175 J 6
Towson o USA (MD) 280-281 K 4
Towuti, Danau o RI 164-165 G 5
Toxkan He ~ VRC 146-147 D 5
Toyah o USA (TX) 266-267 D 2
Toyah, Lake o USA (TX) 266-267 D 2
Toyah Creek ~ USA (TX) 266-267 D 2
Toyahvale o USA (TX) 266-267 D 3
Tōya-ko o J 152-153 J 3
Toyama ☆ J 152-153 G 6
Toyama-wan ≈ 152-153 G 6
Toyo o J 152-153 F 8
Toyohashi o J 152-153 G 7
Toyokawa o J 152-153 G 7
Toyooka o J 152-153 F 7
Toyota o J 152-153 G 7
Toyotomi o J 152-153 J 2
Tozer, Mount ▲ AUS 174-175 G 3
Tozeur ☆• TN 190-191 G 4
Tozitna River ~ USA 20-21 O 4
Trabária, Bocca ▲ I 100-101 D 3
Trà Bồng o VN 158-159 K 3
Trabzon ☆•• TR 128-129 H 2
Tracadie o CDN (NB) 240-241 L 3
Tracadie o CDN (PEI) 240-241 O 4
Trácino o I 100-101 D 6
Tracy o CDN (NB) 240-241 J 5
Tracy o USA (AZ) 256-257 C 6
Tracy o USA (CA) 248-249 C 2
Tracy o USA (MN) 270-271 C 6
Tracy Arm Fords Terror Wilderness ⊥ • USA 32-33 D 3
Tracy City o USA (TN) 276-277 K 5
Tradewater River ~ USA (KY) 276-277 H 3
Trading River ~ CDN (ONT) 234-235 O 3
Traditional Villages • RI 168 D 7
Tradit. Villages o• RI 168 D 7
Traela, Punta de ▲ RCH 78-79 D 2
Trænstaven ⌒ N 86-87 E 3
Traer o USA (IA) 274-275 F 2
Tragacete o E 98-99 G 4
Traiguén o RCH 78-79 C 5
Traiguen, Isla ⌒ RCH 80 D 2
Trail o CDN (BC) 230-231 M 4
Trail o USA (MN) 270-271 C 3
Trail o USA (OR) 244-245 C 8
Trail City o USA (SD) 260-261 F 1
Traill Ø ⌒ GRØ 26-27 o 7
Traine River ~ AUS 172-173 H 4
Traipu o BR 68-69 K 6
Traíra, Serra do ▲ BR 66-67 C 3
Trairão, Rio ~ BR 68-69 C 5
Trairi o BR 68-69 J 3
Trajgorodskaja ~ RUS 114-115 P 4
Trakai ☆ LT 94-95 J 4
Trakan Phut Phon o THA 158-159 H 3
Trakošćan • HR 100-101 E 1
Trakt o RUS 88-89 V 5
Tralee = Trá Lí ☆ IRL 90-91 C 5
Trá Lí = Tralee ☆ IRL 90-91 C 5
Trallwng = Welshpool o• GB 90-91 F 5
Tramandaí o BR 74-75 E 7
Tramanu ~ RI 166-167 B 6
Trammel Fork ~ USA (KY) 276-277 J 4
Trampa, La o PE 64-65 B 5
Tramping Lake o CDN (SAS) 232-233 K 3
Tramping Lake o CDN (SAS) 232-233 K 3
Trà My o VN 158-159 K 3
Trăn o BG 102-103 C 6
Tranås ☆ S 86-87 G 7
Tranche-sur-Mer, la o F 90-91 G 8
Trang o THA 158-159 E 7
Trangan, Pulau ⌒ RI 166-167 H 5
Tràng Bàng o VN 158-159 J 5
Trangie o AUS 180-181 J 2
Tranomaro o RM 222-223 E 10
Tranoroa o RM 222-223 D 10
Tranqui, Isla ⌒ RCH 78-79 C 7
Tranquille o CDN (BC) 230-231 J 3
Trans Africa Route = Route transafricaine II WAN 204-205 G 5
Trānsāh o IR 128-129 M 4
Trans-Amazon Highway = Transamazônica II BR 66-67 H 6
Transamazônica II BR 66-67 H 6
Trans-Australian-Railway II AUS 176-177 K 5
Trans-Canada-Highway • CDN 230-231 H 3
Transhimalaya = Gangdisê Shan ▲ 144-145 C 5
Transkei (former Homeland, now part of East-Cape) ▫ ZA 220-221 H 5
Transsib II• RUS 118-119 E 10
Transsua o CI 202-203 J 6
Transylvania = Transilvani, Podişul ⌣ RO 102-103 C 4
Transylvanian Alps = Carpaţii Meridionali ▲ RO 100-101 J 2
Tranum o MAL 162-163 D 3
Tranzitnyj o RUS 112-113 V 3
Trà Ôn o VN 158-159 H 6
Trapalco, Cerro ▲ RA 78-79 E 6
Trapalcó, Salinas o RA 78-79 F 5
Trápani o I 100-101 D 5
Traralgon o AUS 180-181 J 5
Traras, Monts des ▲ DZ 188-189 L 3
Trarza ▫ RIM 196-197 C 5
Trârza ⩨ RIM 196-197 C 6
Trasimeno, Lago o I 100-101 D 3
Traskwood o USA (AR) 276-277 C 6
Trás os Montes e Alto Douro ⩨ P 98-99 D 4
Trat o THA 158-159 G 4
Trautenau = Trutnov o CZ 92-93 N 3
Trautfetter ~ RUS 108-109 d 4
Travaillant Lake o CDN 20-21 Z 3
Travelers Rest o USA (SC) 284-285 H 2
Traveler's Rest State Historic Site • USA (GA) 284-285 G 2
Travellers Lake o AUS 180-181 F 2
Travellers Rest • USA (MT) 250-251 E 5
Travemünde o D 92-93 L 2
Travers, Mount ▲ NZ 182 D 5
Traverse, Lake o USA (SD) 260-261 K 1
Traverse City o USA (MI) 272-273 D 3
Traverse Peak ▲ USA 20-21 L 4
Travers Reservoir o CDN (ALB) 232-233 F 5
Travesía del Tunuyán ⩨ RA 78-79 F 2
Travesía Puntana ⩨ RA 78-79 F 3
Travessia de Caju ~ BR 68-69 D 5
Travessia do Jacuzao ~ BR 68-69 D 5
Trà Vinh o VN 158-159 J 6
Travis, Lake < USA (TX) 266-267 K 3
Travka ~ RUS 112-113 P 4
Trawas o RI 162-163 E 6
Trayning o AUS 176-177 D 5
Traynor o CDN (SAS) 232-233 K 3
Trbovlje o SLO 100-101 E 1
Tre ⌒ VN 158-159 K 4
Treasure Beach o JA 54-55 G 6
Treasure Island o USA (FL) 286-287 G 4
Treasury Islands ⌒ SOL 184 I b 2
Třebíč o CZ 92-93 N 4
Trebinje o BIH 100-101 G 3
Trebisacce o I 100-101 F 5
Trebitsch = Třebíč o CZ 92-93 N 4
Treelon o CDN (SAS) 232-233 K 6
Tree River ~ CDN 20-21 Y 3
Tree River ~ CDN 30-31 O 2
Treesbank o CDN (MAN) 234-235 D 5
Trees Point ▲ CDN 26-27 J 3
Trego o USA (MT) 250-251 E 3
Trego o USA (WI) 270-271 G 5
Trehbugornyj, mys ▲ RUS 108-109 P 7
Treherne o CDN (MAN) 234-235 E 5
Treinta y Tres ☆ ROU 78-79 M 2
Trelew o RA 78-79 G 7
Trelleborg o S 86-87 F 9
Tremblant, Mont ▲ CDN (QUE) 238-239 L 2
Trembleur Lake o CDN (BC) 228-229 J 2
Tremen, Volcán ▲ RA 78-79 D 4
Tremiti, Ísole ⌒ I 100-101 E 3
Tremont o USA (PA) 280-281 K 3
Tremonton o USA (UT) 254-255 C 2
Tremp o E 98-99 H 3
Trena o ETH 208-209 E 3
Trenary o USA (MI) 270-271 M 4
Trenche, Rivière o CDN (QUE) 236-237 P 4
Trenčín o SK 92-93 P 4
Trenčín = Trentschin o SK 92-93 P 4
Trenggalek o RI 168 D 4
Trenque Lauquen o RA 78-79 H 3
Trent ~ GB 90-91 F 5
Trent o USA (TX) 264-265 D 6
Trente-et-un Milles, Lac des o CDN (QUE) 238-239 K 2
Trentino -Alto Ádige ▫ I 100-101 C 1
Trento ☆• I 100-101 C 1
Trenton o CDN (ONT) 238-239 H 4
Trenton o USA (FL) 286-287 G 2
Trenton o USA (GA) 284-285 E 2
Trenton o USA (IL) 274-275 J 6
Trenton o USA (MI) 272-273 F 5
Trenton o USA (MO) 274-275 E 4
Trenton o USA (NC) 282-283 K 5
Trenton o USA (NE) 262-263 E 4
Trenton o USA (TN) 276-277 G 5
Trenton ☆ USA (NJ) 280-281 M 3
Trent River ~ CDN (ONT) 238-239 H 4
Trent River ~ USA (NC) 282-283 K 5
Trepassey o CDN (NFL) 242-243 P 6
Trepassey Bay ≈ 38-39 S 5
Trepassey Bay ≈ CDN 242-243 P 6
Trephina Gorge ⊥ AUS 178-179 C 2
Tréport, Le o F 90-91 H 6
Tres Altos, Cerro ▲ RA 78-79 E 2
Tres Arboles o• ROU 78-79 L 2
Tres Arroyos o RA 78-79 J 5
Três Barracas, Cachoeira ~ BR 66-67 G 7
Três Bicos o BR 74-75 E 5
Tres Bocas o RA 78-79 K 2
Três Casas o BR 66-67 F 6
Tres Cerros ▲ RA 78-79 D 7
Três Corações o BR 72-73 H 6
Tres Cruces o BOL 70-71 F 5
Tres Cruces, Arroyo ~ ROU 76-77 J 6
Tres Cruces, Cerro ▲ MEX 52-53 H 4
Tres Cruces, Cerro ▲ RCH 76-77 C 4
Três de Maio o BR 76-77 K 4
Tres Esquinas o CO 64-65 E 1
Três Ilhas, Cachoeira das ~ BR 66-67 J 7
Três Irmãos, Cachoeira dos ~ BR 70-71 H 2
Três Irmãos, Serra dos ▲ BR 66-67 E 7
Tres Isletas o RA 76-77 G 4
Treska ~ MK 100-101 H 4
Três Lagoas o BR 72-73 E 6
Tres Lagos o RA 80 E 4
Tres Mapejos o BOL 70-71 E 2
Três Marias o BR 72-73 H 5
Três Marias, Represa < BR 72-73 H 5
Tres Matas, Las o YV 60-61 J 3
Tres Mojones o RA 76-77 G 4
Tres Montes, Cabo ▲ RCH 80 C 3
Tres Montes, Península ⌣ RCH 80 C 3
Tres Morros o RA 76-77 E 2
Tres Palacios ~ USA (TX) 266-267 L 5
Tres Palmas o CO 60-61 D 3
Três Palmeiras o BR 74-75 D 6
Tres Palos, Laguna o MEX 52-53 E 3
Três Passos o BR 74-75 D 6
Tres Picos, Cerro ▲ RA 78-79 J 5
Tres Piedras o USA (NM) 256-257 K 2
Três Praias o BR 66-67 D 7
Tres Puntas ▲ GCA 52-53 K 4
Tres Puntas, Cabo ▲ RA 80 H 3
Três Ranchos o BR 72-73 G 5
Três Rios o BR 72-73 J 7
Tres Unidos o PE 64-65 E 4
Tres Valles o MEX 52-53 F 2
Três Vendas o BR 76-77 K 6
Tres Virgenes, Volcán de las ▲ MEX 50-51 C 4
Tres Zapotes ∴• MEX 52-53 G 2
Tretes o• RI 168 E 3
Tretij, ostrov ⌒ RUS 120-121 U 3
Tret'jakovo o RUS 124-125 M 3
Treuburg = Olecko o PL 92-93 R 1
Treuenbrietzen o D 92-93 M 2
Treuer Range ▲ AUS 172-173 K 7
Trève, Lac la o CDN (ONT) 236-237 N 3
Trevelín o RA 78-79 D 7
Treviglio o I 100-101 B 2
Treviso o BR 74-75 F 7
Treviso ☆ I 100-101 D 2
Trevlac o USA (IN) 274-275 M 5
Trewdate o CDN (SAS) 232-233 M 5
Triabunna o AUS 180-181 J 7
Triang o MAL 162-163 E 3
Triangle o CDN 32-33 M 4
Triangle o USA (NC) 282-283 F 5
Triangle o ZW 218-219 F 5
Triángulos, Arrecifes ⌒ MEX 52-53 H 1
Trianon o RH 54-55 J 5
Tribugá o CO 60-61 C 5
Tribugá, Golfo de ≈ 60-61 C 5
Tribune o CDN (SAS) 232-233 P 6
Tribune o USA (KS) 262-263 E 6
Tricase o I 100-101 G 5
Trichur o• IND 140-141 G 5
Trici o BR 68-69 H 4
Tri City o USA (KY) 276-277 G 4
Trida o AUS 180-181 H 2
Tridell o USA (UT) 254-255 F 3
Trident o USA (MT) 250-251 H 6
Trident Peak ▲ USA (NV) 246-247 G 2
Trier o••• D 92-93 J 4
Trieste ☆• I 100-101 D 2
Trieste, Golfo di ≈ 100-101 D 2
Trieste, Gulf of = Trieste, Golfo di ≈ I 100-101 D 2
Triglav ▲ SLO 100-101 D 1
Triglavski Narodni Park ⊥ SLO 100-101 D 1
Trigo, El o RA 78-79 K 3
Trigonon o GR 100-101 H 4
Trikala o• GR 100-101 H 5
Trikkandiyur o IND 140-141 F 5
Trikonamadu o CL 140-141 J 6
Trillbar o AUS 176-177 D 2
Trilsbeck Lake o CDN (ONT) 236-237 D 2
Trim = Baile Átha Troim ☆• IRL 90-91 D 5
Trimble o USA (MO) 274-275 D 5
Trincheras, Las o YV 60-61 J 4
Trincomalee o• CL 140-141 J 6
Trindade o BR (GOI) 72-73 F 4
Trindade o BR (PER) 68-69 H 5
Trindade o BR (ROR) 62-63 D 5
Tring o PNG 183 B 2
Trinidad ☆ BOL 70-71 F 4
Trinidad o••• C 54-55 F 4
Trinidad o CO 60-61 F 5
Trinidad o••• PY 76-77 K 4
Trinidad ☆ ROU 78-79 L 2
Trinidad ⌒ TT 60-61 L 2
Trinidad o USA (CA) 246-247 A 2
Trinidad o USA (CO) 254-255 L 6
Trinidad, Golfo ≈ 80 C 4
Trinidad, Isla ⌒ RA 78-79 J 5
Trinidad, Laguna o PY 70-71 G 7
Trinidad and Tobago ▪ TT 60-61 L 2
Trinidad de Arauca, La o YV 60-61 G 4
Trinidade o BR 68-69 D 3
Trinidade, Ilha da ⌒ BR 66-67 H 4
Trinitaria, La o MEX 52-53 H 3
Trinity o CDN (NFL) 242-243 P 4
Trinity o USA (TX) 268-269 E 6
Trinity Bay ≈ 38-39 S 5
Trinity Bay ≈ CDN 242-243 P 5
Trinity Center o USA (CA) 246-247 C 3
Trinity East o CDN (NFL) 242-243 P 4
Trinity Islands ⌒ USA 22-23 T 4
Trinity Range ▲ USA (NV) 246-247 F 4
Trinity River ~ USA (CA) 246-247 B 3
Trinity River ~ USA (TX) 264-265 H 6
Trinity River ~ USA (TX) 266-267 L 2
Trinity River ~ USA (TX) 268-269 F 6
Trinity Site • USA (NM) 256-257 J 5
Trinkat Island ⌒ IND 140-141 L 5
Triolet o MS 224 C 7
Trion o USA (GA) 284-285 E 2
Trios o BR 62-63 G 4
Trípoli o GR 100-101 J 6
Tripoli = Tarābulus o• RL 128-129 F 5
Tripolis = Tarābulus ★ LAR 192-193 E 1
Tripolitania = Tarābulus ⩨ LAR 192-193 D 2
Tripp o USA (SD) 260-261 J 3
Tripton o USA (UT) 254-255 D 5
Tripura ▫ IND 142-143 G 4
Tristan da Cunha Fracture Zone ≃ 6-7 G 12
Tristao, Iles ⌒ RG 202-203 C 4
Triste, Golfo ≈ 60-61 H 2
Triste, Monte ▲ RA 78-79 G 7
Tristeza, Cuchilla de la ▲ RA 78-79 E 3
Trisul ▲ IND 138-139 G 4
Trisuli ~ NEP 144-145 E 7
Trisuli Bazar o NEP 144-145 E 7
Triton, Teluk ≈ 166-167 H 3
Triton Island = Zhongjian Dao ⌒ VRC 158-159 L 3
Triune o USA (TN) 276-277 J 5
Triunfo o BR 74-75 E 7
Triunfo, El o MEX 52-53 J 3
Triunfo, Igarapé ~ BR 68-69 B 5
Triunvirato o RA 78-79 J 3
Trivalea-Moşteni o RO 102-103 D 5
Trivandrum ☆• IND 140-141 G 6
Trnava o SK 92-93 O 4
Trobriand Islands ⌒ PNG 183 F 5
Trocana, Ilha ⌒ BR 66-67 F 5
Trocatá, Área Indígena ✗ BR 68-69 D 3
Trochu o CDN (ALB) 232-233 E 4
Trocoman, Río ~ RA 78-79 D 4
Troebratskij o KA 124-125 E 1
Trofors o N 86-87 F 4
Trogir o•• HR 100-101 F 3
Troick o RUS 116-117 G 7
Troick ☆ RUS (CEL) 96-97 M 6
Troickij o RUS 114-115 G 6
Troicko-Pečorsk ☆ RUS 114-115 D 3
Trois Fourches, Cap des ▲ MA 188-189 K 3
Trois-Îlets, Les o F 56 E 4
Trois-Pistoles o CDN (QUE) 240-241 F 2
Trois Rivières o CDN (QUE) 238-239 N 2
Trois Rivières, des o RCA 206-207 G 5
Trois Rivières, Les ~ RH 54-55 J 5
Trois Sauts o F 62-63 H 4
Trojan o BG 102-103 D 6
Trojes, Las o HN 52-53 B 4
Trojnoj, ostrov ⌒ RUS 108-109 U 4
Trolla < TCH 198-199 G 5
Trollhättan ☆ S 86-87 F 7
Trolltindane ▲•• N 86-87 C 5
Tromai, Baía do ≈ 68-69 F 2
Tromai, Rio ~ BR 68-69 F 2
Trombetas, Rio ~ BR 62-63 F 5
Trom"egan ~ RUS 114-115 M 3
Tromelin, Île ⌒ F 12 D 6
Trompsburg o ZA 220-221 G 5
Tromsø ☆• N 86-87 J 2
Trona o USA (CA) 248-249 G 4
Tronador, Cerro ▲ RCH 78-79 C 6
Troncal, La o EC 64-65 C 3
Troncos, Los o BOL 70-71 F 5
Troncoso o MEX 50-51 H 6
Trondheim ☆•• N 86-87 E 5
Trondheimsfjorden ≈ 86-87 D 5
Troodos ▲ CY 128-129 E 5
Troodos, Kirchen von = Ekklisia ••• CY 128-129 E 5
Tropas, Rio das ~ BR 66-67 J 6
Tropea o I 100-101 E 5
Tropêco Grande, Cachoeira do ~ BR 72-73 F 2
Tropia, Ponta ▲ BR 68-69 H 3
Tropico, El o C 54-55 E 3
Tropic of Cancer 6-7 D 6
Tropic of Cancer Monument • MEX 50-51 E 6
Tropic of Capricorn 6-7 H 11
Tropojë o AL 100-101 H 3
Troppau = Opava o CZ 92-93 O 4
Trosna o RUS 94-95 O 5
Trostjanec' o UA 102-103 J 2
Trotters o USA (ND) 258-259 D 4
Troubador Shoal ≃ 166-167 E 6
Troughton Island ⌒ AUS 172-173 H 2
Trouin o RH 54-55 J 5
Troup o USA (TX) 264-265 J 6
Trousdale o USA (TN) 276-277 K 5
Troutbeck o ZW 218-219 G 4
Trout Creek o CDN (ONT) 238-239 F 3
Trout Creek o USA (MT) 250-251 D 4
Trout Creek ~ USA (AZ) 256-257 B 3
Trout Lake o CDN (BC) 230-231 M 3
Trout Lake o CDN (NWT) 30-31 J 5
Trout Lake o CDN (BC) 230-231 M 3
Trout Lake o CDN (NWT) 30-31 J 5
Trout Lake o CDN (ONT) 234-235 K 3
Trout Lake o USA (MI) 270-271 N 4
Trout Lake o USA (WA) 244-245 D 5
Trout River o CDN (NFL) 242-243 K 3
Trout River ~ CDN 30-31 J 5
Trout River ~ CDN 30-31 G 6
Trout River ~ CDN 32-33 N 3
Troux aux Cerfs • MS 224 C 7
Trovoada, Cachoeira da ~ BR 66-67 K 5
Trowulan o RI 168 E 3
Troy o USA (AL) 284-285 E 5
Troy o USA (ID) 250-251 C 5
Troy o USA (IN) 274-275 M 7
Troy o USA (KS) 262-263 L 5
Troy o USA (MO) 274-275 H 6
Troy o USA (MT) 250-251 D 3
Troy o USA (NC) 282-283 H 5
Troy o USA (NY) 278-279 H 6
Troy o USA (OH) 280-281 B 3
Troy o USA (OR) 244-245 H 5
Troy o USA (PA) 280-281 K 2
Troya, Rio de la ~ RA 76-77 C 5
Troya, Rio la ~ RA 76-77 C 4
Troyes ☆• F 90-91 K 7
Troy Peak ▲ USA (NV) 246-247 K 5
Trpanj o HR 100-101 F 3
Trstenik o YU 100-101 H 3
Truandó, Río ~ CO 60-61 C 4
Truant Island ⌒ AUS 174-175 D 2
Trubčevsk o RUS 94-95 N 5
Truchas o USA (NM) 256-257 K 2
Truckee o USA (CA) 246-247 E 4
Truckee River ~ USA (NV) 246-247 F 4
Truck Island ⌒ FSM 13 G 2
Trucu o BR 68-69 J 5
True, Cape ▲ CDN 36-37 R 3
Truesdale o USA (MO) 274-275 G 6
Trufanova o RUS 88-89 S 4
Truite, Lac-à-la- o CDN (QUE) 236-237 K 5
Trujillo o• E 98-99 E 5
Trujillo ☆ HN 54-55 C 7
Trujillo ☆• PE 64-65 C 6
Trujillo o USA (NM) 256-257 L 3
Trujillo ☆ YV 60-61 F 3
Truman o USA (MN) 270-271 D 7
Trumann o USA (AR) 276-277 E 5
Truman National Historic Site, Harry S. • USA (MO) 274-275 D 5
Trumbull, Mount ▲ USA (AZ) 256-257 B 2
Trumon o RI 162-163 B 3
Trùng Khánh ☆ VN 156-157 E 5
Trung Liên o VN 156-157 C 5
Trừng Lớn, Hòn ⌒ VN 158-159 J 6
Trunkey Creek o AUS 180-181 K 2
Truro o CDN (NS) 240-241 M 5
Truro o USA (IA) 274-275 E 3
Trusan o MAL 164-165 D 1
Truscott o USA (TX) 264-265 E 5
Trus Madi, Gunung ▲ MAL 160-161 B 10
Trutch o CDN 32-33 J 3
Truth or Consequences o USA (NM) 256-257 H 5
Trutnov o CZ 92-93 N 3
Truva (Troja) ∴•• TR 128-129 B 3
Truxno o USA (LA) 268-269 H 4
Truxton o USA (AZ) 256-257 B 3
Tryon o USA (NE) 262-263 F 3
Tryon Island ⌒ AUS 178-179 L 2
Tryphena o NZ 182 E 2
Trzebnica o• PL 92-93 O 3
Trzemeszno o PL 92-93 O 2
Tsacha Lake o CDN (BC) 228-229 K 3
Tsadumu o IND 140-141 H 4
Tsagaan ▲ MAU 148-149 E 2
Tsala Apopka Lake o USA (FL) 286-287 G 3
Tsalwor Lake o CDN 30-31 P 6
Tsama I o RCB 210-211 E 4
Tsamai o WAN 198-199 B 6
Tsandi o NAM 216-217 C 8
Tsangano o MOC 218-219 H 2
Tsanyawa o WAN 198-199 C 6
Tsaramandroso o RM 222-223 E 6
Tsaranonenana o RM 222-223 F 5
Tsaratanana o RM (MJG) 222-223 E 6
Tsaratanana ▲ RM 222-223 F 4
Tsarisberge ▲ NAM 220-221 C 2
Tsarishoogte Pass ▲ NAM 220-221 C 2
Tsau o RB 218-219 B 5
Tsauchab ~ NAM 220-221 B 2
Tsavo o EAK 212-213 G 5
Tsavo ~ EAK 212-213 G 5
Tsavo East National Park ⊥ EAK 212-213 G 5
Tsavo Safari Camp o EAK 212-213 G 5
Tsavo West National Park ⊥ EAK 212-213 F 5
Tsawah o LAR 192-193 E 4
Tsawwassen o CDN (BC) 230-231 F 4
Tsazar o IND 138-139 F 3
Tschida, Lake o USA (ND) 258-259 F 5
Tseikuru o EAK 212-213 G 4
Tselinograd = Akmola o KA 124-125 G 3
Tsembo o RCB 210-211 D 5
Tseminyu o IND 142-143 J 3
Tses o NAM 220-221 D 2
Tsévié o RT 202-203 L 6
Tshabong ☆ RB 220-221 F 3
Tshako o ZRE 214-215 B 5
Tshala o ZRE 214-215 B 5
Tshane o RB 220-221 E 2
Tshela o ZRE 210-211 D 6
Tshenga-Oshwe o ZRE 210-211 J 5
Tshesebe o RB 218-219 D 5
Tshibala o ZRE 216-217 F 3
Tshibamba o ZRE 214-215 B 5
Tshibambula o ZRE 210-211 J 6
Tshibeke o ZRE 212-213 B 5
Tshibuka o ZRE 216-217 F 3
Tshibwika o ZRE 216-217 F 4
Tshidilamolomo o ZA 220-221 G 2
Tshie o ZRE 214-215 B 5
Tshikapa o ZRE 216-217 F 3
Tshikapa ~ ZRE 216-217 F 3
Tshikula o ZRE 216-217 F 3
Tshilenge o ZRE 214-215 B 4
Tshimbalanga o ZRE 214-215 B 5
Tshimboko o ZRE 214-215 C 4
Tshimbulu o ZRE 214-215 B 4
Tshimbungu o ZRE 214-215 B 5
Tshintshanku o ZRE 214-215 B 4
Tshipise o ZA 218-219 F 6
Tshisenda o ZRE 214-215 D 7
Tshisenge o ZRE 216-217 F 3
Tshisonge o ZRE 214-215 B 5
Tshitadi o ZRE 216-217 F 3
Tshitanzu o ZRE 214-215 B 5
Tshkheenickh River ~ CDN (BC) 228-229 E 2
Tshofa o ZRE 210-211 K 6
Tshokwane o ZA 220-221 K 2
Tsholotsho o ZW 218-219 D 4
Tshongwe o ZRE 214-215 C 4
Tshootsha = Kalkfontein o RB 216-217 F 11
Tshopo ~ ZRE 210-211 K 3
Tshuapa ~ ZRE 210-211 H 4
Tshunga, Chutes ~ ZRE 210-211 K 3
Tsiafajavona ▲ RM 222-223 E 7
Tsiaki o RCB 210-211 D 5
Tsianaloka o RM 222-223 D 8
Tsiazompaniry o RM 222-223 E 7
Tsimafana o RM 222-223 D 7
Tsimanampetsotsa, Farihy o RM 222-223 C 10
Tsimazava o RM 222-223 D 8
Tsimlyanskoye Vodokhranilishche = Cimljanskoe vodohranil. < RUS 102-103 N 4
Tsimpsean Indian Reserve ✗ CDN (BC) 228-229 D 2
Tsineng o ZA 220-221 F 3
Tsingtao = Qingdao ☆ VRC 154-155 M 3
Tsingy de Bamaraha Strict Nature Reserve ⊥••• RM 222-223 D 7
Tsiningia o RM 222-223 E 5
Tsinjoarivo o RM 222-223 E 7
Tsinjomitondraka o RM 222-223 E 5
Tsinjomorona ~ RM 222-223 F 5
Tsintsabis o NAM 216-217 D 9
Tsiombe o RM 222-223 D 10
Tsiribihina ~ RM 222-223 D 7
Tsiroanomandidy o RM 222-223 E 7
Tsitondroina o RM 222-223 E 8
Tsitsikamma National Park ⊥ ZA 220-221 G 7
Tsitsutl Peak ▲ CDN (BC) 228-229 J 4
Tsivory o RM 222-223 E 10
Tsoe o RB 218-219 C 5
Tsogstsalu o IND 138-139 G 2
Tsolo o ZA 220-221 J 5
Tsomo o ZA (CAP) 220-221 H 6
Tsomo ~ ZA 220-221 H 5
Tso Morari o IND 138-139 G 3
Tsu ☆ J 152-153 G 7
Tsubata o J 152-153 G 6
Tsuchiura o J 152-153 J 6
Tsugaru Quasi National Park ⊥ J 152-153 J 4
Tsugaru Strait = Tsugaru-kaikyō ≈ J 152-153 J 4
Tsu Lake o CDN 30-31 N 5
Tsuli o RB 218-219 D 4
Tsumbiri o ZRE 210-211 F 5
Tsumeb ☆ NAM 216-217 D 9
Tsumkwe ☆ NAM 216-217 F 9
Tsuruga o J 152-153 G 7
Tsurugi-san ▲ J 152-153 F 8
Tsurui o J 152-153 L 3
Tsuruoka o J 152-153 H 5
Tsushima ⌒ J 152-153 C 7
Tsuyama o J 152-153 E 7
Tswaane o RB (GHA) 216-217 F 11
Tswaane o RB (KWE) 218-219 B 6
Ṭ-Ṭarfa, Wādī ~ ET 194-195 E 3
Ṭ-Ṭarṭar, Wādī ~ IRQ 128-129 K 5
Ṭ-Ṭarṭār, Wādī ~ IRQ 128-129 K 5
Ttati, Laguna o RA 76-77 H 5
Ṭ-Ṭawīl, Wādī ~ IRQ 128-129 J 5
Ṭ-Ṭūbal, Wādī ~ IRQ 128-129 K 6
Tu ~ RUS 118-119 N 9
Tua, Tanjung ▲ RI 162-163 F 7
Tuaim = Tuam o IRL 90-91 C 5
Tual o RI 166-167 G 4
Tuam = Tuaim o IRL 90-91 C 5
Tuambli o CI 202-203 F 6
Tuameseh, Tanjung ▲ RI 166-167 C 6
Tuam Island ⌒ PNG 183 E 3
Tuamotu Archipel ⌒ F 13 N 4
Tuamotu Archipelago = Tuamotu, Îles ⌒ F 13 N 4
Tuần Giáo ☆ VN 156-157 C 6
Tuangku, Pulau ⌒ RI 162-163 B 3
Tuanxi o VRC 156-157 E 3
Tuapse o RUS 126-127 C 5
Tuaran o MAL 160-161 B 9
Tuare o RI 164-165 G 4
Tua River ~ PNG 183 C 4
Tuba ~ RUS 116-117 F 9
Ṭūbā, Qaṣr at- ∴• JOR 130-131 E 2
Tubac o USA (AZ) 256-257 D 7
Tuba City o USA (AZ) 256-257 D 2
Tubaiq, Ğabal at- ▲ KSA 130-131 F 3
Tuban o RI 168 E 3
Tubarão o BR 74-75 F 7
Tubarão Latunde, Área Indígena ✗ BR 70-71 G 3
Ṭūbās o WB 130-131 D 1
Tubau o MAL 162-163 K 3
Tubbataha Reefs ⌒••• RP 160-161 C 8
Tubek Būzačy ~ KA 96-97 G 10
Tubek Būzačy ~ KA 126-127 J 5
Tubek Tub-Karagan ~ KA 126-127 J 5
Tubeya o ZRE 214-215 B 4
Tubğa, Wādī ~ KSA 130-131 F 5
Tubili Point ▲ RP 160-161 D 6
Tübingen o• D 92-93 K 4
Tubisyimita o RI 166-167 G 2
Tubkaragan, mujisi ▲ KA 126-127 J 5
Tubmanburg o LB 202-203 E 6
Tubo, River ~ WAN 204-205 G 3
Tuborg Fondets Land ⩨ GRØ 26-27 o 4
Ṭubruq ▫ LAR 192-193 K 2
Ṭubruq ☆ LAR 192-193 K 1
Tubuai Islands = Australes, Îles ⌒ F 13 M 5
Tuburan o RP 160-161 E 7
Tucacas o YV 60-61 G 2
Tucano o BR 68-69 J 7
Tucapel, Punta ▲ RCH 78-79 C 4
Tucavaca, Río ~ BOL 70-71 H 6
Tucha River ~ CDN 30-31 E 6
Tucheng o VRC 156-157 D 3
Tuchitua o CDN 30-31 E 5
Tuchola o PL 92-93 O 2
Tuchoľka o UA 102-103 C 3
Tuckanarra o AUS 176-177 E 3
Tucker o USA (AR) 276-277 D 6
Tucker o USA (TX) 268-269 E 5
Tucker Bay ≈ 16 F 18
Tuckerman o USA (AR) 276-277 D 5
Tuckerton o USA (NJ) 280-281 M 4
Tuckfield, Mount ▲ AUS 172-173 G 5
Tucson o• USA (AZ) 256-257 E 6
Tucuco, Río ~ YV 60-61 E 3
Tucum, Corredeira do ~ BR 70-71 J 4
Tucumã o BR 66-67 H 6
Tucumán ▫ RA 76-77 E 4
Tucumari Mountain ▲ USA (NM) 256-257 M 3
Tucumcari o USA (NM) 256-257 M 3
Tucuña o CO 66-67 B 2
Tucunare, Raudal ~ CO 66-67 B 2
Tucupido o YV 60-61 J 3
Tucupita ☆ YV 60-61 K 3
Tucuriba o BR 66-67 H 5
Tucuriba, Corredeira ~ BR 66-67 H 5
Tucuruí o BR 68-69 D 3
Tucuruí, Represa de < BR 68-69 D 4
Tucutibapo o CO 66-67 D 2
Tucu-Tucu o RA 80 E 4
Tūdakūl, kūli o US 136-137 J 5
Tudela o• E 98-99 G 3
Tudela o RP 160-161 E 8
Tudu o EST 94-95 K 2
Tudun Wada o WAN 204-205 H 3
Tuekta o RUS 124-125 O 3
Tuena o AUS 180-181 K 3
Tueré, Rio ~ BR 68-69 C 4
Tuetue o RI 164-165 H 6
Tufanbeyli ☆ TR 128-129 G 3
Tuffnell o CDN (SAS) 232-233 P 4
Tufi o PNG 183 E 5
Tug o VRC 154-155 F 2
Tugaloo Lake < USA (GA) 284-285 G 2
Tugaloo River ~ USA (GA) 284-285 G 2
Tugaske o CDN (SAS) 232-233 M 5
Tugela ~ ZA 220-221 K 4
Tugela Ferry o ZA 220-221 K 4
Tug Fork ~ USA (WV) 280-281 E 6
Tug Hill ▲ USA (NY) 278-279 F 5
Tugidak Island ⌒ USA 22-23 T 4
Tugtorqortôq ⌒ GRØ 26-27 W 7
Tugtulik ⌒ GRØ 28-29 O 2
Tugu o GH 202-203 K 5
Tuguegarao ☆ RP 160-161 D 4
Tugulym ☆ RUS 114-115 H 6
Tugur o RUS 122-123 G 2
Tugur ~ RUS 122-123 G 2
Tugurskij poluostrov ⌣ RUS 122-123 G 2
Tugurskij zaliv ≈ 122-123 G 2
Tuguttur ~ RUS 110-111 F 4
Tugyi o MYA 158-159 C 2
Tuhan, Wādī ~ Y 132-133 D 7
Tuhsigat ~ RUS 114-115 O 5
Tui o•• E 98-99 C 3
Tuichi, Río ~ BOL 70-71 C 4
Tuina o RCH 76-77 C 2
Tuineje o E 188-189 D 6
Tuisen o IND 142-143 H 4
Tuitán o MEX 50-51 G 5
Tuiué o BR 66-67 F 5
Tuj ~ RUS 114-115 M 6
Tujau, Tanjung ▲ RI 166-167 D 5
Tujmazy ☆ RUS 96-97 H 6
Tujn gol ~ MAU 148-149 E 5
Tujun ~ RUS 122-123 E 3
Tukalan ~ RUS 108-109 e 7
Tukan ~ RUS 114-115 M 5
Tukangbesi, Kepulauan ⌒ RI 164-165 H 6
Tukarak Island ⌒ CDN 36-37 K 6
Tukayel o ETH 208-209 G 4
Tuki o SOL 184 I c 2
Tukola Tolha o VRC 144-145 K 3
Tukosmera ▲ VAN 184 II b 4
Tūkrah o• LAR 192-193 J 1
Tuktoyaktuk o CDN 20-21 Y 2
Tukulan ~ RUS 120-121 E 2
Tukums ☆• LV 94-95 H 3
Tukuringra, hrebet ▲ RUS 118-119 M 8
Tukuyu o EAT 214-215 G 5
Tula o EAK (COA) 212-213 G 4
Tula ~ EAK 212-213 G 4
Tula o MEX 50-51 K 6
Tula ☆•• RUS 94-95 P 4
Tulā o Y 132-133 C 6
Tulach Mhór = Tullamore o IRL 90-91 D 5
Tula de Allende o• MEX 52-53 E 1
Tuladenggi o RI 164-165 G 3
Tula Hill ▲• WAN 204-205 J 4
Tūlak o• AFG 134-135 K 2
Tulalip Indian Reservation ✗ USA (WA) 244-245 C 2
Tulameen o CDN (BC) 230-231 J 4
Tulameen River ~ CDN (BC) 230-231 J 4
Tulancingo o MEX 52-53 E 1
Tulare o USA (CA) 248-249 E 3
Tulare o USA (SD) 260-261 H 2
Tulare Lake o USA (CA) 248-249 E 4
Tularosa o USA (NM) 256-257 J 5
Tularosa Basin ⌣ USA (NM) 256-257 J 6
Tularosa River ~ USA (NM) 256-257 G 5
Tulate o GCA 52-53 J 4
Tula Yiri o WAN 204-205 J 4
Tulbagh o• ZA 220-221 D 6
Tulcan ☆ EC 64-65 D 1
Tulcea ☆• RO 102-103 F 5
Tul'čyn ☆ UA 102-103 F 3
Tule, El o MEX 50-51 J 3
Tule, Estero del ~ MEX 50-51 F 5
Tuléar = Toliara ☆• RM 222-223 C 9
Tulebaevo o KA 124-125 L 5
Tule Creek ~ USA (TX) 264-265 C 4
Tulehu o RI 166-167 E 3
Tulelake o USA (CA) 246-247 D 2
Tule Lake o USA (CA) 246-247 D 2
Tule Lake National Wildlife Refuge ⊥ USA (CA) 246-247 D 2
Tulema Lake o CDN 30-31 U 4
Tulen' o RUS 116-117 H 7
Tule River Indian Reservation ✗ USA (CA) 248-249 F 3
Tuleta o USA (TX) 266-267 K 5
Tulia o USA (TX) 264-265 C 4
Tuli Block Farms ⩨ RB 218-219 D 6
Tulik Volcano ▲ USA 22-23 M 6
Tulipan o MEX 52-53 J 3
Tuljapur o IND 140-141 G 2
Tullahoma o USA (TN) 276-277 J 5
Tullamore o AUS 180-181 J 2
Tullamore = Tulach Mhór o IRL 90-91 D 5
Tulle ☆• F 90-91 H 9
Tullibigeal o AUS 180-181 J 2

404 Touside, Pic — Tullibigeal

Tullos o USA (LA) 268-269 H 5
Tullulah Falls o USA (GA) 284-285 G 2
Tullus o SUD 206-207 G 3
Tully o AUS 174-175 H 5
Tully Range ▲ AUS 178-179 G 2
Tuloma ~ RUS 88-89 M 2
Tulppio o FIN 88-89 K 3
Tulsa o• USA (OK) 264-265 J 2
Tulsequah o CDN 32-33 D 2
Tulsipur o IND 142-143 C 2
Tulu o PNG 183 D 1
Tulua o CO 60-61 C 5
Tulu Āmara Terara ▲ ETH 208-209 C 4
Tulu Bolo o ETH 208-209 D 4
Tuluca o BR 66-67 C 2
Tuluksak o USA 20-21 K 6
Tūlūl al-Ašaqif ▲ JOR 130-131 E 1
Tulúm o MEX (QR) 52-53 L 1
Tulúm ∴•• MEX (QR) 52-53 L 1
Tulumayo, Río ~ PE 64-65 E 7
Tulume o ZRE 214-215 B 4
Tulun ☆ RUS 116-117 K 8
Tulungagung o RI 168 D 4
Tulungselapan o RI 162-163 F 6
Tulu Welel ▲ ETH 208-209 B 4
Tulvinskaja vozvyšennost' ▲ RUS 96-97 K 5
Tuma o RUS 94-95 R 4
Tuma, Río ~ NIC 52-53 B 5
Ṯūma, Wādī ~ IRQ 128-129 K 6
Tumacacori National Monument • USA (AZ) 256-257 D 7
Tumaco o CO 60-61 B 7
Tumaco, Ensenada de ≈ 60-61 B 7
Tumagabok o RP 160-161 D 6
Tumair o KSA 130-131 J 5
Tuma Island ⌒ PNG 183 F 5
Tumalin o RP 160-161 D 5
Tumalo o USA (OR) 244-245 D 6
Tuman Gang ~ DVR 150-151 G 6
Tumannyj o RUS 88-89 N 2
Tumanšet ~ RUS 116-117 H 8
Tumanskij hrebet ▲ RUS 120-121 Q 3
Tumara ~ RUS 118-119 P 3
Tumat o RUS 110-111 W 4
Tumat, Khor ~ SUD 208-209 B 3
Tumatskaja, protoka Bol'šaja ~ RUS 110-111 Q 3
Tumba ☆ S 86-87 H 7
Tumba o ZRE 210-211 J 5
Tumbanglahung o RI 164-165 D 4
Tumbarumba o AUS 180-181 J 3
Tumbengu ~ ZRE 210-211 J 4
Tumbes ☆ PE 64-65 B 3
Tumbes, Bahía de ≈ 64-65 B 3
Tumbes, Península de ⌣ RCH 78-79 C 4
Tumbes, Punta ▲ RCH 78-79 C 4
Tumbler Ridge o CDN 32-33 K 4
Tumbu o RI 164-165 F 5
Tumbwe o ZRE 214-215 D 6
Tumby Bay o AUS 180-181 D 3
Tumd Youqi o VRC 154-155 G 1
Tumd Zuoqi o VRC 154-155 G 1
Tumen o VRC 150-151 G 6
Tumèncogt = Hanhöhij o MAU 148-149 L 4
Tumen Jiang ~ VRC 150-151 G 6
Tumeremo o YV 62-63 D 2
Tumgaon o IND 142-143 C 5
Tumindao Island ⌒ RP 160-161 C 10
Tumkūr o IND 140-141 G 4
Tumlingtar o NEP 144-145 F 7
Tumnin ~ RUS 122-123 H 4
Tumoiscatio del Ruiz o MEX 52-53 C 2
Tumpang o• RI 168 E 4
Tumpu, Gunung ▲ RI 164-165 H 4
Tumputiga, Gunung ▲ RI 164-165 H 4
Tumrok, hrebet ▲ RUS 120-121 S 6
Tumsar o IND 138-139 G 9
Tumu o GH 202-203 K 4
Tumucumaque, Parque Indígena do ⚔ BR 62-63 G 4
Tumucumaque, Serra do ▲ BR 62-63 G 4
Tumul o RUS 118-119 P 4
Tumupasa o BOL 70-71 D 4
Tumureng o GUY 62-63 D 2
Tumut o AUS 180-181 K 3
Tumwater o USA (WA) 244-245 C 3
Tuna o GH 202-203 J 5
Tu Na, Đèo ▲ VN 158-159 K 4
Tuna Gain o RI 166-167 G 3
Tunago Lake o CDN 30-31 G 2
Tunaida o ET 194-195 D 5
Tunajča, ozero o RUS 122-123 K 5
Tūnali Sālang • AFG 136-137 L 7
Tunapa, Cerro ▲ BOL 70-71 D 6
Tunapuna o TT 60-61 L 2
Tunas, Las ☆ C 54-55 G 4
Tunas, Sierra de las ▲ RA 78-79 J 4
Tunas de Zaza o C 54-55 F 4
Tunas Grandes, Lagunas las o RA 78-79 H 3
Tunaydibah o SUD 200-201 G 6
Tunceli ☆ TR 128-129 H 3
Tunchang o VRC 156-157 G 7
Tuncurry o AUS 180-181 M 2
Tunda, Pulau ⌒ RI 168 B 2
Tundak ~ RUS 118-119 H 8
Tund las Raices • RCH 78-79 D 5
Tundulu o Z 214-215 E 5
Tunduma o EAT 214-215 G 5
Tunduru o EAT 214-215 J 6
Tundyk ~ KA 124-125 K 4
Tundža ~ BG 102-103 E 6
Tunertooq ⌒ GRØ 28-29 P 2
Tunga o WAN 204-205 H 4
Tungabhadra ~ IND 140-141 G 3
Tungabhadra Reservoir o IND 140-141 G 3
Tungaru o SUD 206-207 K 3
Tungawan o RP 160-161 E 9
Tungaztarim o VRC 144-145 D 2
Tungho o RC 156-157 M 5
Tungi o BD 142-143 G 4
Tungir ~ RUS 118-119 K 8
Tungirskij, hrebet ▲ RUS 118-119 J 8
Tungkaranasam o RI 164-165 E 5
Tungku o MAL (SAB) 160-161 C 10
Tungku o MAL (SAR) 162-163 K 3
Tungokočen o RUS 118-119 G 9
Tungor o RUS 122-123 K 2
Tungshih o RC 156-157 M 4
Tungsten o CDN 30-31 E 5
Tungurahua, Volcán ▲ EC 64-65 C 2
Tungurča ~ RUS 118-119 K 7
Tunguru o EAT 212-213 D 5
Tunguskaja vozvyšennost' ▲ RUS 88-89 M 4
Tungusskoe-Centralʹno, plato ⛰ RUS 116-117 K 5
Tunguwatu o RI 166-167 H 4
Tunhèl o MAU 148-149 H 3
Tuni o IND 142-143 C 7
Tunia, La o CO 64-65 F 1
Tunica o USA (MS) 268-269 K 2
Tunis ★••• TN 190-191 H 2
Tunis o USA (TX) 266-267 L 3
Tunis, Golfe de ≈ 190-191 H 2
Tunisia = Tunisiyah ■ TN 190-191 G 4
Tunja ☆ CO 60-61 E 5
Tunkal ~ RI 162-163 E 5
Tunkhannock o USA (PA) 280-281 L 2
Tunku Abdul Rahman National Park ⊥ MAL 160-161 A 9
Tunnel Creek National Park ⊥ AUS 172-173 G 4
Tunnsjøen o N 86-87 F 4
Tunqiu o VRC 156-157 F 4
Tuntum o BR 68-69 F 4
Tuntutuliak o USA 20-21 J 6
Tunu = Østgrønland ◘ GRØ 26-27 d 8
Tunuí, Cachoeira ~ BR 66-67 C 2
Tunulic, Rivière ~ CDN 36-37 Q 5
Tunulliarfik ≈ 28-29 R 6
Tununak o USA 20-21 H 6
Tunungayualok Island ⌒ CDN 36-37 T 6
Tununuk o CDN 20-21 Y 2
Tunuyan o RA 78-79 E 2
Tunuyán, Río ~ RA 78-79 F 2
Tunuyan, Sierra de ▲ RA 78-79 E 2
Tunuyánviejo, Río ~ RA 78-79 F 2
Tuoa Creek ~ PNG 183 C 4
Tuobuja o RUS 118-119 L 4
Tuo Jiang ~ VRC 156-157 D 2
Tuokechikemili o VRC 144-145 E 4
Tuolba ~ RUS 118-119 L 5
Tuolbačan ~ RUS 118-119 L 5
Tuōl Kruōs o K 158-159 G 4
Tuolumne o USA (CA) 248-249 D 2
Tuolumne River ~ USA (CA) 248-249 D 2
Tu'o'ng Du'o'ng ☆ VN 156-157 D 7
Tuora ~ RUS 118-119 M 6
Tuora-Sis, hrebet ▲ RUS 110-111 Q 4
Tuostah ~ RUS 110-111 V 6
Tuotuo He ~ VRC 144-145 H 3
Tuotuo Heyan o VRC 144-145 J 3
Tupã o BR 72-73 E 6
Tupaciguara o BR 72-73 F 5
Tupambaé o ROU 78-79 M 2
Tupana, Rio ~ BR 66-67 G 5
Tupanaci o BR 68-69 J 6
Tupanatinga o BR 68-69 K 6
Tupanciretã o BR 74-75 D 7
Tuparrito, Caño ~ CO 60-61 G 5
Tuparrito, Caño ~ CO 60-61 G 5
Tuparro, Río ~ CO 60-61 G 5
Tupé II o BR 66-67 D 2
Tupelo o USA (AR) 276-277 D 5
Tupelo o USA (MS) 268-269 M 2
Tupelo o USA (OK) 264-265 H 4
Tupelo National Battlefield ∴ USA (MS) 268-269 M 2
Tupik ☆ RUS 118-119 J 8
Tupilco o MEX 52-53 H 2
Tupim, Rio ~ BR 72-73 K 2
Tupinambarana, Ilha ⌒ BR 66-67 J 4
Tupinier, Kap ▲ GRØ 28-29 b 2
Tupiratins o BR 68-69 E 6
Tupitina o MEX 52-53 C 2
Tupiza o BOL 76-77 E 1
Tupiza, Río ~ BOL 76-77 E 1
Tupper o CDN 32-33 K 4
Tupper Lake o USA (NY) 278-279 G 4
Tupran o IND 140-141 H 2
Tupungato o RA 78-79 E 2
Tupungato, Cerro ▲ RA 78-79 E 2
Tupure o YV 60-61 F 2
Tuquan o VRC 150-151 C 5
Tuque, La o CDN (QUE) 240-241 C 3
Tuquerres o CO 64-65 D 1
Tuqu Gang ≈ 156-157 F 7
Ṭūr, aṭ- o Y 132-133 C 6
Tura o IND 142-143 G 3
Tura ~ PA 52-53 F 8
Tura ☆ RUS (EVN) 116-117 K 3
Tura ~ RUS 96-97 L 4
Tura ~ RUS 114-115 H 6
Tura ~ RUS 114-115 J 6
Tura ~ RUS 118-119 F 10
Tura o VRC 144-145 F 2
Turaba o KSA (HAI) 130-131 H 3
Turaba o KSA (MAK) 132-133 B 3
Turagua, Serranía ▲ YV 60-61 J 4
Turaif o KSA 130-131 F 2
Turaif o SYR 128-129 H 5
Turakurgan o US 136-137 M 4
Turama ~ RUS 116-117 H 5
Turama River ~ PNG 183 B 4
Turan ☆ RUS 116-117 F 9
Turangi o NZ 182 E 3
Turan Lowland = Turan persligi ⌣ TM 10-11 F 4
Turan Lowland = Turanskaja nizmennost' ⌣ 136-137 F 5
Tūran ojlety = Turan persligi = Turon Pasttekisligi ⌣ KA 136-137 F 5
Turan persligi = Turon Pasttekisligi = Tūran ojlety ⌣ TM 136-137 F 5
Turāq al-ʿIlab ▲ SYR 128-129 H 6
Turba o EST 94-95 J 2
Turba, at- o Y 132-133 D 7
Turba, at- o Y 132-133 C 7
Turbaco o CO 60-61 D 2
Turbat o PK 134-135 K 6
Turbeville o USA (SC) 284-285 K 3
Turbihal o IND 140-141 G 3
Turbio, El o RA 80 D 5
Turbio, Río ~ RA 80 E 5
Turbio, Río ~ RCH 76-77 C 4
Turbio, Río ~ RCH 76-77 B 5
Turbo o CO 60-61 C 3
Turbón, Raudal el ~ CO 66-67 B 2
Turco o BOL 70-71 C 6
Turco, Río ~ BOL 70-71 C 6
Turda o RO 102-103 C 4
Tūrda ≺ SUD 206-207 J 3
Turee Creek o AUS (WA) 176-177 E 1
Turee Creek ~ AUS 176-177 D 1
Turek o PL 92-93 P 2
Turen o RI 168 E 4
Turgen ~ KA 146-147 C 4
Türgen ▲ MAU 116-117 E 11
Turgeon, Rivière ~ CDN (QUE) 236-237 J 3
Turgut o TR 128-129 D 3
Turgutlu ☆ TR 128-129 B 3
Turhal ☆• TR 128-129 G 2
Türi o EST 94-95 J 2
Turi, Igarapé ~ BR 66-67 D 3
Turia, Río ~ E 98-99 G 4
Turiaçu o BR 68-69 F 2
Turiaçu, Baía de ≈ 68-69 F 2
Turiaçu, Rio ~ BR 68-69 F 3
Turiamo o YV 60-61 H 2
Turiančaj ~ AZ 128-129 M 2
Turiani o EAT 214-215 J 4
Turiba o YV 60-61 H 4
Turin o CDN (ALB) 232-233 F 6
Turin o USA (IA) 274-275 C 2
Turin = Torino ☆• I 100-101 A 2
Turinsk ☆ RUS 114-115 G 5
Turinskaja ravnina ⌣ RUS 114-115 G 6
Turinskaja Sloboda ☆ RUS 114-115 H 6
Tur'ja o RUS 88-89 V 5
Turka o RUS 116-117 O 9
Turka ~ RUS 118-119 E 9
Turka ☆ UA 102-103 C 3
Turkana ⛰ EAK 212-213 E 2
Turkana, Lake o EAK (Eas) 212-213 F 2
Turkestan o KA 136-137 L 3
Turkestanskij hrebet ▲ US 136-137 K 5
Turkestanskij kanal ≺ KA 136-137 L 3
Turkey o USA (TX) 264-265 D 4
Turkey = Türkiye ■ TR 128-129 C 3
Turkey Creek o AUS 172-173 J 4
Turkey Creek o USA (LA) 268-269 H 6
Turkey Creek ~ USA (NE) 262-263 J 4
Turkey Creek ~ USA (OK) 264-265 G 2
Turkey Creek ~ USA (SC) 284-285 J 2
Turkey Flat o USA (AZ) 256-257 F 6
Turkey Mountain ▲ AUS 178-179 L 4
Turkey Point o CDN (ONT) 238-239 E 6
Turkey River ~ USA (IA) 274-275 G 2
Turkistan ☆ KA 136-137 L 3
Türkmen Dağı ▲ TR 128-129 D 3
Turkmenistan = Türkmenistan ■ TM 136-137 D 5
Turkmen-Kala o TM 136-137 H 6
Turkmenskij zaliv ≈ 136-137 C 5
Türkoğlu ☆ TR 128-129 G 4
Turks and Caicos Islands ⌒ GB 54-55 K 3
Turks Islands ⌒ GB 54-55 K 4
Turku = Åbo ☆• FIN 88-89 G 6
Turkwel ~ EAK 212-213 E 2
Turkwel Gorge Reservoir ≺ EAK 212-213 E 3
Turlock o USA (CA) 248-249 D 2
Turmalina o BR 72-73 J 4
Turmantas o LT 94-95 K 4
Turn o USA (NM) 256-257 J 4
Turnagain, Cape ▲ NZ 182 F 4
Turnagain Arm ≈ 20-21 P 6
Turnagain Island ⌒ AUS 174-175 G 1
Turnagain Point ▲ CDN 24-25 R 6
Turnagain River ~ CDN 30-31 E 6
Turneffe Islands ⌒ BH 52-53 L 3
Turner o USA (ME) 278-279 L 4
Turner o USA (MT) 250-251 L 3
Turner o USA (OR) 244-245 C 6
Turner Lake o CDN 32-33 Q 3
Turner Ø ⌒ GRØ 28-29 d 2
Turner River ~ AUS 172-173 D 6
Turners Peninsula ⌣ WAL 202-203 D 6
Turnersville o USA (TX) 266-267 K 2
Turner Turnpike II USA (OK) 264-265 G 3
Turner Valley o CDN (ALB) 232-233 D 5
Turnerville o USA (SD) 260-261 K 2
Turnhout o B 92-93 H 3
Turnpike Creek ~ USA (GA) 284-285 H 5
Turnu Măgurele o RO 102-103 D 6
Turočak ☆ RUS 124-125 P 2
Turon o USA (KS) 262-263 H 7
Turon Pasttekisligi = Turan persligi = Tūran ojlety ⌣ US 136-137 F 5
Turpan o VRC 146-147 J 4
Turpan Pendi ⛰ VRC 146-147 J 4
Turpin o USA (OK) 264-265 D 2
Türpsal = Järve o EST 94-95 K 2
Turra • SUD 200-201 B 6
Turrell o USA (AR) 276-277 E 5
Turrialba o CR 52-53 C 7
Tursāq o IRQ 128-129 L 6
Tursuntskij Tuman, ozero o RUS 114-115 G 4
Tursunzade o TJ 136-137 L 5
Turt o MAU 148-149 E 2
Turt (Hanh) o MAU 148-149 E 2
Turtas ~ RUS 114-115 K 5
Türtkül ☆ US 136-137 G 4
Turtle Creek Reservoir o USA (IN) 274-275 L 5
Turtle Farm • GB 54-55 E 5
Turtleford o CDN (SAS) 232-233 K 2
Turtle Head Island ⌒ AUS 183 B 6
Turtle Islands ⌒ RP 160-161 C 9
Turtle Islands Marine Park ⊥ MAL 160-161 C 9
Turtle Lake o CDN (SAS) 232-233 K 2
Turtle Lake o USA (ND) 258-259 G 4
Turtle Lake o USA (WI) 270-271 F 5
Turtle Mountain ▲ CDN (MAN) 234-235 C 5
Turtle Mountain Indian Reservation ⚔ USA (ND) 258-259 H 3
Turton Lake o CDN 30-31 G 3
Turu ~ RUS 116-117 M 3
Turu, Wangasi- o GH 202-203 K 5
Turu Cay Island ⌒ AUS 183 A 5
Turuchipa, Río ~ BOL 70-71 E 6
Turugart Shankou ▲ VRC 146-147 B 5
Turuhan ~ RUS 108-109 V 8
Turuhan ~ RUS 114-115 T 2
Turuhansk o RUS 114-115 T 2
Turuhanskaja nizmennost' ⌣ RUS 114-115 T 2
Turuktah, mys ▲ RUS 110-111 W 4
Turuna, Rio ~ BR 62-63 F 5
Turuntaevo o RUS (TOM) 114-115 T 6
Turuntaevo ☆ RUS (BUR) 116-117 N 9
Turvânia o BR 72-73 E 4
Turvo, Rio ~ BR 72-73 E 4
Turvo, Rio ~ BR 72-73 F 6
Turvolândia o BR 72-73 H 6
Turwi ~ ZW 218-219 F 5
Tūs o IR 136-137 F 6
Tušama ~ RUS 116-117 K 7
Tuscaloosa o USA (AL) 284-285 C 3
Tuscaloosa, Lake ≺ USA (AL) 284-285 C 3
Tuscánia o• I 100-101 C 3
Tuscarora o USA (NV) 246-247 J 2
Tuscola o USA (IL) 274-275 K 5
Tuscola o USA (TX) 264-265 E 6
Tusculum o USA (TN) 282-283 E 4
Tuscumbia o USA (AL) 284-285 B 2
Tuscumbia o USA (MO) 274-275 F 6
Tusenøyane ⌒ N 84-85 M 4
Tushar Mountains ▲ USA (UT) 254-255 C 5
Tušig=Zèltèr o MAU 148-149 G 2
Tuskegee o• USA (AL) 284-285 E 4
Tuskegee Institute National Historic Site • USA (AL) 284-285 E 4
Tustumena Lake o USA 20-21 P 6
Tutaev ☆•• RUS 94-95 Q 3
Tutak ☆ TR 128-129 K 3
Tuticorin o IND 140-141 H 6
Tutóia o BR 68-69 G 3
Tutoko, Mount ▲ NZ 182 B 6
Tutončana ~ RUS 116-117 F 2
Tutong o BRU 164-165 D 1
Tutrakan o BG 102-103 E 5
Tuttle o USA (ND) 258-259 H 4
Tuttle o USA (OK) 264-265 G 3
Tuttle Creek Lake o USA (KS) 262-263 K 5
Tuttle Town o USA (CA) 246-247 E 5
Tuttosoni, Nuraghe • I 100-101 B 4
Tutuaca o MEX 50-51 F 3
Tutuala o RI 166-167 D 6
Tutuba ⌒ VAN 184 II a 2
Tutuila Island ⌒ USA 184 V b 2
Tutukpene o GH 202-203 L 5
Tutume o RB 218-219 D 5
Tutup, Tanjung ▲ MAL 160-161 C 10
Tutupa o RI 164-165 K 4
Tutura o RUS 116-117 M 8
Tutura ~ RUS 116-117 M 8
Tutwiler o USA (MS) 268-269 K 3
Tuul gol ~ MAU 148-149 G 4
Tuusniemi o FIN 88-89 K 5
Tuva = Tuva, Respublika ◘ RUS 116-117 F 10
Tuvšinširèè = S èrgèlèn o MAU 148-149 K 4
Ṭuwaiq, Ǧabal ▲ KSA 130-131 J 5
Ṭuwaiq, Ǧabal ▲ KSA 132-133 D 3
Tūwal o KSA 130-131 F 6
Tuxcueca o MEX 52-53 C 1
Tuxedni Bay ≈ 20-21 O 6
Tuxford o CDN (SAS) 232-233 N 5
Tuxpan o MEX (NAY) 50-51 G 7
Tuxpan o• MEX (JAL) 52-53 C 2
Tuxpan, Río ~ MEX 52-53 F 1
Tuxpan de Rodríguez Cano o MEX 52-53 F 1
Tuxtla, Sierra de los ▲ MEX 52-53 G 2
Tuxtla Gutiérrez ☆• MEX 52-53 H 3
Tuy, Río ~ YV 60-61 H 2
Tuya River ~ CDN 32-33 E 2
Tuyên Quang ☆ VN 156-157 D 6
Tuy Hòa o VN 158-159 K 4
Tuy Phong o VN 158-159 K 5
Tüyserkān o• IR 134-135 C 1
Tüzdyköl o KA 136-137 M 3
Tuz Gölü o TR 128-129 E 3
Ṭūz Ḫūrmātū ☆ IRQ 128-129 L 5
Tuzigoot National Monument • USA (AZ) 256-257 D 4
Tuzla o• BIH 100-101 G 2
Tuzla Çayı ~ TR 128-129 J 3
Tuzlov ~ RUS 102-103 L 4
Tuzluca ☆ TR 128-129 K 2
Tuzule o ZRE 214-215 B 4
Tværá o FR 90-91 D 1
Tveitsund o N 86-87 D 7
Tver' ☆•• RUS 94-95 P 3
Tverrfjellì ~ N 86-87 D 5
TV Tower • USA (MN) 270-271 A 3
Tweed o CDN (ONT) 238-239 H 4
Tweed ~ GB 90-91 F 4
Tweed Heads o AUS 178-179 M 5
Tweedsmuir Provincial Park ⊥ CDN (BC) 228-229 H 3
Tweefontein o ZA 220-221 D 6
Tweeling o ZA 220-221 J 3
Twee Rivier o NAM 220-221 D 2
Twee Rivieren o ZA 220-221 E 3
Tweespruit o ZA 220-221 H 4
Twelve Apostles, The •• AUS 180-181 G 5
Twentynine Palms o USA (CA) 248-249 H 5
Twentynine Palms Indian Reservation ⚔ USA (CA) 248-249 H 5
Twentynine Palms Marine Corps Base xx USA (CA) 248-249 H 5
Twilight Cove ≈ 176-177 H 6
Twillingate o CDN (NFL) 242-243 O 3
Twin Bridges o USA (MT) 250-251 G 6
Twin Butte o CDN (ALB) 232-233 E 6
Twin Buttes Reservoir ≺ USA (TX) 266-267 G 2
Twin City o CDN (ONT) 234-235 O 6
Twin City o USA (GA) 284-285 H 4
Twin Falls o USA (ID) 252-253 D 4
Twingge o MYA 142-143 K 4
Twingi o Z 214-215 E 6
Twin Mount ▲ USA 20-21 T 4
Twin Mountain o USA (NH) 278-279 K 4
Twin Oaks Reservoir o USA (TX) 266-267 L 2
Twin Peaks o AUS 176-177 C 3
Twin Sisters o USA (TX) 266-267 J 3
Twin Summit ▲ USA (NV) 246-247 J 3
Twin Valley o USA (MN) 270-271 C 3
Twisp o USA (WA) 244-245 E 2
Twitty o USA (TX) 264-265 D 3
Twitya River ~ CDN 30-31 E 4
Twizel o NZ 182 C 6
Two Brothers ⌒ CDN 36-37 J 5
Two Buttes o USA (CO) 254-255 N 6
Two Buttes Creek ~ USA (CO) 254-255 N 6
Two Creeks o CDN (MAN) 234-235 B 4
Two Creeks o USA (WI) 270-271 L 6
Twodot o USA (MT) 250-251 J 5
Twofold Bay ≈ 180-181 K 4
Two Harbors o USA (MN) 270-271 G 3
Two Headed Island ⌒ USA 22-23 U 4
Two Hills o CDN (ALB) 232-233 G 2
Two Inlets o USA (MN) 270-271 C 3
Two Medicine River ~ USA (MT) 250-251 F 3
Twopete Mountain ▲ CDN 20-21 Y 5
Two Rivers o USA (WI) 270-271 L 6
Two Rocks o AUS 176-177 C 5
Twyfelfontein • NAM 216-217 C 10
Tyara, Cayo ⌒ NIC 52-53 C 5
Tybee Island o USA (GA) 284-285 K 4
Tyčany ~ RUS 116-117 H 5
Tychy o PL 92-93 P 3
Tydyotta ~ RUS 114-115 O 2
Tye o CDN (BC) 230-231 N 4
Tyélé o RMM 202-203 G 3
Tygart Lake o USA (WV) 280-281 F 4
Tygart River ~ USA (WV) 280-281 F 4
Tygarts Creek ~ USA (KY) 276-277 M 2
Tygda o RUS 118-119 N 9
Tygda ~ RUS 118-119 N 9
Tyger River ~ USA (SC) 284-285 J 2
Tygh Valley o USA (OR) 244-245 D 5
Tyjebas, cyganak ≈ 126-127 N 4
Tyf ~ RUS 120-121 F 6
Tylawa o PL 92-93 Q 4
Tyler o USA (TX) 264-265 J 6
Tyler o USA (WA) 244-245 H 3
Tyler o USA (WV) 280-281 F 4
Tylertown o USA (MS) 268-269 K 5
Tylgovajam ~ RUS 112-113 O 6
Tylihul ~ UA 102-103 G 4
Tylihul's'kyj lyman ≈ 102-103 G 4
Tylnoj ~ RUS 112-113 M 5
Tym ~ RUS 114-115 T 4
Tym ~ RUS 114-115 Q 5
Tym' ~ RUS 122-123 K 3
Tym, Ust'- o RUS 114-115 Q 5
Tymerokan ~ RUS 116-117 F 2
Tymlat ☆ RUS 120-121 U 4
Tymna ~ RUS 118-119 O 8
Tymna, laguna ≈ 112-113 U 4
Tymovskoe ☆ RUS 122-123 K 3
Tympyčan, Ùèl' ~ RUS 118-119 E 5
Tympylykan ~ RUS 118-119 L 3
Tymtej ~ RUS 120-121 L 2
Tynda ☆ RUS 118-119 M 8
Tynda ~ RUS 118-119 N 9
Tyndall o CDN (MAN) 234-235 G 4
Tyndall o USA (SD) 260-261 J 4
Tyndall Air Force Base xx USA (FL) 286-287 D 1
Tyndik ~ KA 124-125 K 3
Tyndrum o GB 90-91 E 3
Tyne ~ GB 90-91 G 4
Tynep ~ RUS 114-115 U 3
Tyner o USA (KY) 276-277 M 3
Tyne Valley o CDN (PEI) 240-241 M 4
Tynset ☆ N 86-87 E 5
Typical Torajan Villages ⚔•• RI 164-165 F 5
Typtygir, kòli o KA 124-125 D 2
Tyr ∴•• RL 128-129 F 6
Tyrifjorden o N 86-87 E 6
Tyrkan ~ RUS 120-121 E 5
Tyrma o RUS (HBR) 122-123 E 3
Tyrma ~ RUS 122-123 D 3
Tyrma ~ RUS 122-123 E 4
Tyrnyauz o RUS 126-127 E 6
Tyro o USA (AR) 276-277 D 7
Tyrone o USA (GA) 284-285 H 3
Tyrone o USA (NM) 256-257 G 6
Tyrone o USA (OK) 264-265 C 2
Tyrone o USA (PA) 280-281 H 3
Tyrrell, Lake o AUS 180-181 G 3
Tyrrell Lake o CDN 30-31 R 4
Tyrrhenian Basin ≃ 100-101 C 5
Tyrrhenian Sea ≈ 100-101 C 5
Tyrs Bjerge ▲ GRØ 28-29 U 5
Tyrtova, ostrov ⌒ RUS 108-109 b 3
Tyry ~ RUS 120-121 K 2
Tyškanbaj o KA 126-127 P 2
Tysnesøy ~ N 86-87 B 6
Tytyf, ozero o RUS 112-113 P 3
Tyumen' = Tjumen' ☆ RUS 114-115 H 6
Tzaneen o ZA 218-219 F 6
Tzinteel o MEX 52-53 H 3
Tziscao o MEX 52-53 J 3
Tzonconejo, Río ~ MEX 52-53 J 3
Tzucacab o MEX 52-53 K 1

U

Uaçá, Área Indígena ⚔ BR 62-63 J 4
Uacaca, Cachoeira ~ CO 66-67 C 2
Uachtar Ard = Oughterard o IRL 90-91 C 5
Uaco Cungo o ANG 216-217 C 5
Uacuru, Cachoeira ~ BR 70-71 G 2
Ua'ili, Wādī al- ~ KSA 130-131 F 2
Uala, zaliv o RUS 120-121 V 3
Uamba o ANG 216-217 D 3
Uanda o AUS 178-179 H 1
Uanga ~ RUS 122-123 K 2
Uangando ~ ANG 216-217 D 8
Uape o MOC 218-219 K 3
Uapuí, Cachoeira ~ BR 66-67 C 2
Uarges ▲ EAK 212-213 F 3
Uar Igarore ≺ SP 212-213 J 3
Uarini o BR 66-67 F 4
Uarini, Rio ~ BR 66-67 D 5
Uaroo o AUS 172-173 B 7
Uati-Paraná, Área Indígena ⚔ BR 66-67 D 4
Uatuma, Rio ~ BR 66-67 H 4
Uauá o BR 68-69 J 6
Uauaretê o BR 66-67 C 2
Uaupés, Rio ~ BR 66-67 D 2
Uaus, Ra's ▲ OM 132-133 J 5
Uavala ~ ANG 216-217 D 8
Uaxactún ∴• GCA 52-53 K 3
Uaza ▲ ETH 200-201 J 6
Ub o YU 100-101 H 2
Ubá o BR 72-73 J 6
Uba ~ KA 124-125 N 3
Uba o WAN 204-205 K 3
Übagan ~ KA 124-125 D 2
Ubaí o BR 72-73 H 4
Ubai o PNG 183 F 3
'Ubaid ≺ SUD 200-201 B 6
Ubaila o IRQ 128-129 J 6
'Ubaila, al- o KSA 132-133 G 2
Ubaitaba o BR 72-73 L 3
Ubajay o RA 76-77 H 6
Ubaldino Taques o BR 74-75 E 6
Ubangi ~ ZRE 210-211 F 3
Ubangui ~ ZRE 206-207 D 6
Ubaporanga o BR 72-73 J 5
Ubar ∴• OM 132-133 H 4
Ubarc' ~ BY 94-95 K 6
Ubatã o BR 72-73 L 3
Ubate o CO 60-61 E 5
Ubatuba o BR 72-73 H 7
Ubauro o PK 138-139 B 5
'Ubayyid, Wādī l- ~ IRQ 128-129 J 7
Ube o J 152-153 D 8
Úbeda o E 98-99 F 5
Ubehebe Crater • USA (CA) 248-249 G 3
Ubekendt Ejland ⌒ GRØ 26-27 Y 8
Uberaba o BR 72-73 G 5
Uberaba, Lago o BR 70-71 J 5
Uberaba, Rio ~ BR 72-73 F 5
Uberlândia o BR (MIN) 72-73 F 5
Uberlândia o BR (ROR) 62-63 E 5
Ubia, Gunung (Gunung Leonard Darwin) ▲ RI 166-167 J 4
Ubiaja o WAN 204-205 G 5
Ubina o BOL 70-71 D 7
Ubinskoe o RUS 114-115 P 7
Ubinskoe, ozero o RUS 114-115 P 7
Ubirajara o BR 72-73 F 7
Ubirr o AUS 172-173 L 2
Ubit ≺ WAN 204-205 H 6
Ubojnaja ~ RUS 108-109 U 5
Ubol Rat Reservoir o THA 158-159 G 2
Ubombo ▲ ZA 220-221 L 3
Ubon Ratchathani o THA 158-159 H 3
Ubovka o RUS 122-123 F 6
Ubundu o ZRE 210-211 K 4
Uč-Adži o TM 136-137 H 5
Učaly ☆ RUS 96-97 L 6
Učami ~ RUS 116-117 F 4
Ucapinima o CO 66-67 C 2
Ucaral o KA 124-125 M 5
Ucayali, Río ~ PE 64-65 F 4
Učdepe o TM 136-137 H 6
Uch o•• PK 138-139 C 5
Ucharonidge o AUS 174-175 C 5
Uchee Creek ~ USA (AL) 284-285 E 4
Uchiura-wan ≈ 152-153 J 3
Uchiza o PE 64-65 D 6
Učkeken o RUS 126-127 E 6
Učkuduk ☆ US 136-137 H 3
Učkurgan o US 136-137 N 4
Ucluelet o CDN (BC) 230-231 D 5
Učničihija ~ RUS 112-113 P 5
Ucross o USA (WY) 252-253 M 2
Učsaj o US 136-137 F 3
Učtagankum ⛰ TM 136-137 E 4
Úcua o ANG 216-217 C 4
Učur ~ RUS 120-121 F 6
Uda ~ RUS 116-117 O 10
Uda ~ RUS 116-117 J 8
Uda ~ RUS 118-119 E 9
Uda ~ RUS 120-121 D 6
Udačnyj o RUS 110-111 J 6
Udagamandalam o IND 140-141 G 5
Udaipur o IND 142-143 E 5
'Udaib, al- o KSA 130-131 E 4
'Udaiba, 'Uqlat al- o KSA 130-131 K 3
'Udaid, al- o UAE 134-135 D 6
Udaipur o IND (RAJ) 138-139 D 7
Udaipur o IND (TRI) 142-143 G 4
Udaiyarpalaiyam o IND 140-141 H 5
Udaquiola o RA 78-79 K 4
Udayagiri o IND 140-141 H 3
Udbina o HR 100-101 E 2
Uddeholm o• S 86-87 F 6
Uddevalla ☆ S 86-87 E 7
Uddjaure o S 86-87 H 4
Udè, Ulan ☆• RUS 116-117 N 10
Udegi o WAN 204-205 G 4
Udgir o IND 138-139 F 10
Udhampur o IND 138-139 E 3
Udi o WAN 204-205 G 5
Údine ☆• I 100-101 D 1
Udinsk o RUS 122-123 H 2
Udintsev Fracture Zone ≃ 14-15 N 13
Udispattu o CL 140-141 J 7
Udja ~ RUS 110-111 L 4
Udmurtia = Udmurtskaja Respublika ◘ RUS 96-97 H 5
Udobnaja o RUS 126-127 D 5
Udobnaja, buhta o RUS 108-109 b 2
Udokan, hrebet ▲ RUS 118-119 J 7
Udon Thani o THA 158-159 G 2
Udova ~ RUS 120-121 R 6
Udpūdi o IND 140-141 F 2
Udskaja guba o RUS 120-121 F 6
Udskoe o RUS 120-121 F 6
Udubaddawa o CL 140-141 H 7
Udumalaippettai o IND 140-141 G 5
Udupi o IND 140-141 F 4
Udu Point ▲ FJI 184 III c 2
Udy ~ RUS 102-103 K 2
Udyhyn ~ RUS 120-121 D 6
Udyl', ozero o RUS 122-123 H 2
Udzhar = Ucar o AZ 128-129 M 2
Uebonti o RI 164-165 G 4
Ueca ▲ ETH 208-209 C 4
Ueda o J 152-153 H 6
Uedinenija, ostrov ⌒ RUS 108-109 U 3
Uekuli o RI 164-165 G 4
Uèle ~ RUS 110-111 K 3
Uele ~ ZRE 210-211 J 2
Uèlen o• RUS 112-113 a 3
Uelgi, ozero o RUS 96-97 M 6
Uèl'-Siktjah ~ RUS 110-111 P 5
Uèl'-Tympyčan ~ RUS 118-119 E 5
Uelzen o D 92-93 L 2
Uembje, Lagoa o MOC 220-221 L 2
Ueno o J 152-153 G 7
Uere ~ ZRE 206-207 H 6
Ueré, Rio ~ BR 66-67 D 5
Ufa ☆ RUS (BAS) 96-97 J 6
Ufa ~ RUS 96-97 K 5
Ufeyn o SP 208-209 J 3
Ufimskoe plato ▲ RUS 96-97 K 6
Uftjuga ~ RUS 88-89 T 6
Ugab ~ NAM 216-217 D 9
Ugahan o RUS 118-119 G 6
Ugak Island ⌒ USA 22-23 U 4
Ugāle o LV 94-95 H 3
Ugalla o EAT 212-213 C 6
Ugalla ~ EAT 212-213 C 6
Ugalla River Game Reserve ⊥ EAT (TAB) 212-213 C 6
Ugamak Island ⌒ USA 22-23 O 5
Uganda ■ EAU 212-213 C 2
Uganik Island ⌒ USA 22-23 U 4
Ugarit ∴•• SYR 128-129 F 5
Ugashik Bay ≈ 22-23 R 4
Ugashik Lake o USA 22-23 S 4
Ugatkyn ~ RUS 112-113 Q 3
Ugba o WAN 204-205 H 5
Ugbala o WAN 204-205 G 6
Ugbenu o WAN 204-205 F 5
Ugep o WAN 204-205 H 6
Ughelli o WAN 204-205 F 6
Ugie o ZA 220-221 J 5
Ugjokfok Bay ≈ 36-37 T 7
Ugjut o KS 146-147 B 5
Uglegorsk o RUS 122-123 K 4
Ugleural'skij o RUS 96-97 K 4
Uglič ☆•• RUS 94-95 Q 3
Uglovoe o RUS 122-123 C 3
Uglovoe, ozero o RUS 108-109 Z 1
Ugo o WAN 204-205 G 5
Ugojan o RUS 118-119 M 6
Ugol'naja ~ RUS 108-109 c 4
Ugol'naja, buhta o RUS 112-113 U 5
Ugol'noe o RUS 110-111 b 7
Ugol'nye Kopi o RUS 112-113 T 4
Ugol'nyj o RUS 118-119 M 7
Ugol'nyj, mys ▲ RUS 120-121 U 3
Ugra o RUS 94-95 O 4
Ugssugtussoq ≈ 28-29 V 4
Uḫaiḍir ∴• IRQ 128-129 K 6
Uhen o WAN 204-205 F 5
Uherské Hradiště o CZ 92-93 O 4
Uhi o WAN 204-205 G 5
Uhiere o WAN 204-205 F 5
Úhlava ~ CZ 92-93 M 4
Uhlenhorst o NAM 220-221 C 1
Uhma ~ RUS 88-89 W 5
Uholovo ☆ RUS 94-95 R 5
Uhrichsville o USA (OH) 280-281 E 3
Uhta o RUS (KOM) 88-89 W 5
Uhta ~ RUS 88-89 W 5
Uhuru Peak ▲ EAT 212-213 F 5
Uib o NAM 216-217 D 9
Uíge ◘ ANG 216-217 C 3
Uíge ☆ ANG (UIG) 216-217 C 3
Uiha ⌒ TON 184 IV a 1
Ŭijŏngbu o ROK 150-151 F 9
Uiju o DVR 150-151 E 7
Uinskoe ☆ RUS 96-97 K 5
Uintah and Ouray Indian Reservation ⚔ USA (UT) 254-255 E 3
Uinta Mountains ▲ USA (UT) 254-255 E 3
Uinta River ~ USA (UT) 254-255 E 3
Uiraponru o BR 70-71 H 4
Uiraúna o BR 68-69 J 5
Uis Myn o NAM 216-217 C 10
Ŭisŏng o ROK 150-151 G 9
Uitenhage o ZA 220-221 G 6
Uivak, Cape ▲ CDN 36-37 S 5
Uivaq ⌒ GRØ 28-29 U 5
Uizèn o MAU 148-149 H 5
Uj ~ RUS 96-97 L 6
Uj ~ RUS 114-115 K 6
Uj ~ RUS 114-115 G 7
Ujali o WAN 204-205 G 5
Ujaly o KA (KZL) 126-127 O 5
Ujaly o KA (MNG) 126-127 L 5
Ujaly o TJ 136-137 L 5
Ujan ~ RUS 120-121 E 5
Ujana ~ RUS 120-121 F 2
Ujandina ~ RUS 110-111 Z 5
Ujar ☆ RUS 116-117 G 8
Ujdah ☆ MA 188-189 L 3
Ujelang ⌒ MAI 13 H 2
Uji o J 152-153 F 7
Uji-guntō ⌒ J 152-153 C 9
Ujiji o• EAT 212-213 B 6
Ujil ~ KA 96-97 H 9
Ujil ~ KA 126-127 L 3
Ujir, Pulau ⌒ RI 166-167 H 4
Ujjain o IND 138-139 E 8
Ujmen' ~ RUS 124-125 P 3
Ujohbilang o RI 164-165 D 3
Ujskoe o RUS 96-97 M 6
Ujuk o KA 136-137 M 3
Ujuk ~ RUS 116-117 F 10
Ujukskij, hrebet ▲ RUS 116-117 F 10
Ujungbatu o RI 162-163 D 4

Tullos — Ujungbatu 405

Venézia ☆••• I 100-101 D 2
Venézia, Golfo di ≈ 100-101 D 2
Venezuela ■ YV 60-61 F 3
Venezuela, Golfo de ≈ 60-61 F 2
Venezuela Basin ≃ 5 E 3
Vengurla o IND 140-141 E 3
Veniaminof Volcano ▲ USA 22-23 R 4
Venice o USA (FL) 286-287 G 4
Venice o USA (LA) 268-269 L 7
Venice, Gulf of = Venézia, Golfo di ≈ I 100-101 D 2
Venice = Venézia ☆••• I 100-101 D 2
Venjan o S 86-87 F 6
Venkatagiri o IND 140-141 H 4
Venlo o NL 92-93 J 3
Venray o NL 92-93 H 3
Venta o LT 94-95 H 3
Venta, La o MEX (TAB) 52-53 G 2
Venta, La ∴• MEX (TAB) 52-53 G 2
Venta de Baños o E 98-99 E 4
Ventana o USA (AZ) 256-257 C 6
Ventana, La o MEX 50-51 J 6
Ventanas o EC 64-65 C 2
Ventanas, Las o YV 60-61 H 4
Ventania o BR 74-75 E 5
Ventas con Peña Aguilera, Las o E 98-99 E 5
Ventersburg o ZA 220-221 H 4
Ventersdorp o ZA 220-221 H 3
Venterstad o ZA 220-221 G 5
Ventisquero, Cerro ▲ RA 78-79 D 6
Ventosa, La o MEX 52-53 G 3
Ventoux, Mont ▲ F 90-91 K 9
Ventspils ☆•• LV 94-95 G 3
Ventuari, Río ~ YV 60-61 H 5
Ventura o• USA (CA) 248-249 E 5
Venujeuo o RUS 108-109 O 6
Venus o USA (FL) 286-287 H 4
Venus o USA (NE) 262-263 H 2
Venustiano Carranza o MEX 52-53 H 3
Venustiano Carranza, Presa o MEX 50-51 J 4
Venustiono Carranza o MEX 52-53 C 2
Veppur o IND 140-141 H 5
Ver, Horej- o RUS 88-89 Y 3
Vera o BR 70-71 K 3
Vera o CDN (SAS) 232-233 J 3
Vera o RA 76-77 G 5
Vera o USA (TX) 264-265 E 5
Vera, Bahía ≈ 80 H 2
Vera, Cape ▲ CDN 24-25 b 2
Vera, Laguna o PY 76-77 J 4
Veracruz o MEX (BCN) 50-51 B 1
Veracruz o• MEX 52-53 F 2
Veracruz ▫ MEX 52-53 E 1
Verada da Redenção ~ BR 68-69 G 7
Verada do Buriti ~ BR 68-69 G 7
Verada Tábua ou Rio Salitre ~ BR 68-69 H 7
Verado de Côcos ~ BR 72-73 H 2
Veranópolis o BR 74-75 E 7
Vere Meso = Île Moso ⌒ VAN 184 II b 3
Veraval o IND 138-139 C 9
Verbano = Lago Maggiore o I 100-101 B 2
Verbena o USA (AL) 284-285 D 4
Verbljud, gora ▲ RUS 108-109 f 3
Verbrande Berg • NAM 216-217 C 10
Verchères o CDN (QUE) 238-239 M 3
Verchivceve o UA 102-103 J 3
Verchnie Jarnki o RUS 112-113 L 2
Verchnjadzvimsk ☆ BY 94-95 K 4
Verchn'odniprovs'k o UA 102-103 J 3
Verdalsøra o N 86-87 E 5
Verde, Arroyo ~ RA 78-79 G 6
Verde, Bahía ≈ 78-79 H 5
Verde, Cay ⌒ BS 54-55 H 3
Verde, Laguna o RA 78-79 E 7
Verde, Península ⌣ RA 78-79 H 5
Verde, Punta ▲ EC 64-65 C 1
Verde, Rio ~ BR 70-71 K 3
Verde, Rio ~ BR 72-73 D 6
Verde, Rio ~ BR 72-73 E 5
Verde, Rio ~ BR 72-73 G 4
Verde, Río ~ MEX 50-51 K 7
Verde, Río ~ MEX 52-53 C 1
Verde, Río ~ MEX 52-53 F 3
Verde, Río ~ PY 70-71 J 6
Verde, Río ~ PY 76-77 H 2
Verde Hot Springs o USA (AZ) 256-257 D 4
Verde Island ⌒ RP 160-161 D 6
Verde Island Passage ≈ 160-161 D 6
Verde River ~ USA (AZ) 256-257 D 4
Verdigre o USA (NE) 262-263 H 2
Verdigris Lake o CDN (ALB) 232-233 F 6
Verdigris River ~ USA (KS) 262-263 L 7
Verdigris River ~ USA (OK) 264-265 J 2
Verdinho, Rio ~ BR 72-73 E 4
Verdon ~ F 90-91 L 10
Verdon-sur-Mer, le o F 90-91 G 9
Verdun o• F 90-91 K 7
Verdun o ROU 78-79 M 2
Verdun, Pampa ⊥ RA 80 E 3
Vereda Pimenteira ~ BR 68-69 G 6
Vereeniging o ZA 220-221 H 3
Veregin o CDN (SAS) 232-233 Q 4
Verena o ZA 220-221 J 2
Vereščagino o RUS 114-115 T 2
Vereščagino ☆ RUS (PRM) 96-97 J 4
Verestovo, ozero o RUS 94-95 P 3
Vergara o ROU 74-75 D 9
Vergareña, La o YV 60-61 K 4
Vergas o USA (MN) 270-271 C 4
Vergel, El o MEX 50-51 F 4
Vergeleë o ZA 220-221 G 2
Vergement o AUS 178-179 G 2
Vergennes o USA (VT) 278-279 H 4
Vergi o EST 94-95 K 2
Vergne, La o USA (TN) 276-277 J 4
Verhalen o USA (TX) 266-267 D 2
Verhnee Ondomozero o RUS 88-89 P 3
Verhneimbatsk o RUS 114-115 U 3
Verhnejarkeevo ☆ RUS 96-97 J 6
Verhnekamskaja vozvyšennost' ▲ RUS 96-97 H 4
Verhnekarahbahskij kanal < AZ 128-129 M 2
Verhnekarelina o RUS 116-117 N 7
Verhnekolymskoe, nagor'e ▲ RUS 120-121 M 2
Verhnespasskoe o RUS 96-97 D 4
Verhne tazovskaja vozvyšennost' ▲ RUS 114-115 Q 3
Verhnetazovskij, zapovednik ⊥ RUS 114-115 R 3
Verhnetulomskii o RUS 88-89 L 2
Verhnetulomskoe Vodohranilišče < RUS 88-89 L 2
Verhneural'sk ☆ RUS 96-97 L 7
Verhneural'skoe vodohranilišče < RUS 96-97 L 7
Verhnevažskaja vozvyšennost' ▲ RUS 94-95 R 1
Verhneviljujsk ☆ RUS 118-119 K 4
Verhnevym'skaja grada ▲ RUS 88-89 V 4
Verhnezejsk o RUS 118-119 O 8
Verhnezejskaja ravnina ⌣ RUS 118-119 N 8
Verhnie Kigi ☆ RUS 96-97 L 6
Verhnie Tatyšly ☆ RUS 96-97 J 5
Verhnie Usugli ☆ RUS 118-119 G 9
Verhnij Balygyčan o RUS 112-113 H 5
Verhnij Baskunčak o RUS 96-97 E 9
Verhnij Enisej ~ RUS 116-117 F 10
Verhnij Kužebar o RUS 116-117 F 9
Verhnij Mel'gin ~ RUS 122-123 D 3
Verhnij Paren' o RUS 112-113 M 5
Verhnij Suzun ~ RUS 124-125 N 2
Verhnij Toguzak ~ RUS 124-125 B 2
Verhnij Turukan ~ RUS 116-117 L 3
Verhnij Ufalej o RUS 96-97 M 5
Verhnij Uslon ☆ RUS 96-97 F 6
Verhnjaja Agapa ~ RUS 108-109 W 6
Verhnjaja Amga o RUS 118-119 N 6
Verhnjaja Angara ~ RUS 118-119 E 7
Verhnjaja Baiha ~ RUS 114-115 S 2
Verhnjaja Čunku ~ RUS 116-117 J 4
Verhnjaja Kočoma ~ RUS 116-117 N 5
Verhnjaja Kuènga o RUS 118-119 H 9
Verhnjaja Larba ~ RUS 118-119 L 8
Verhnjaja Mokla ~ RUS 118-119 J 8
Verhnjaja Pyšma ☆ RUS 96-97 M 5
Verhnjaja Salda ☆ RUS 96-97 M 4
Verhnjaja Sarčiha ~ RUS 114-115 U 3
Verhnjaja Tajmyra ~ RUS 108-109 a 4
Verhnjaja Tomba ~ RUS 116-117 N 2
Verhnjaja Viljujka ~ RUS 116-117 M 2
Verhnjaja Zolotica o RUS 88-89 Q 4
Verhojansk o RUS 110-111 T 6
Verhojanskij hrebet ▲ RUS 110-111 Q 5
Verhotupova, ostrov ⌒ RUS 120-121 V 4
Verhotur'e ☆ RUS 96-97 M 4
Véria o• GR 100-101 J 4
Verín o E 98-99 D 4
Verkhoyanskiy Khrebet = Verhojanskij hrebet ▲ RUS 110-111 Q 5
Verkola o RUS 88-89 S 5
Verkykerskop o ZA 220-221 J 3
Verlegenhuken ▲ N 84-85 K 2
Vermasse o RI 166-167 D 6
Vermelha, Serra ▲ BR 68-69 F 6
Vermelha, Serra ▲ BR 72-73 E 7
Vermelho, Rio ~ BR 68-69 E 6
Vermelho, Rio ~ BR 68-69 D 5
Vermelho, Rio ~ BR 68-69 C 5
Vermelho, Rio ~ BR 68-69 J 7
Vermelho, Rio ~ BR 72-73 E 3
Vermilion o CDN (ALB) 232-233 H 2
Vermilion o USA (OH) 280-281 D 2
Vermilion, Lake o USA (IL) 274-275 L 4
Vermilion Bay ≈ 44-45 L 5
Vermilion Bay o CDN (ONT) 234-235 K 5
Vermilion Bay ≈ USA 268-269 H 7
Vermilion Hills ▲ CDN (SAS) 232-233 M 5
Vermilion Lake o CDN (ONT) 234-235 L 4
Vermilion Lake o USA (MN) 270-271 F 3
Vermilion River ~ CDN (ALB) 232-233 G 2
Vermilion River ~ USA (LA) 268-269 H 7
Vermillion o USA (SD) 260-261 K 4
Vermillion River ~ CDN (ONT) 238-239 C 2
Vermillion River ~ USA (IL) 274-275 J 3
Vermillion River ~ USA (SD) 260-261 J 3
Vermillon, Rivière ~ CDN (QUE) 236-237 P 5
Vermont o USA (IL) 274-275 H 4
Vermont ▫ USA (VT) 278-279 J 5
Vernal o USA (UT) 254-255 F 3
Vernalis o USA (CA) 248-249 C 2
Verner o CDN (ONT) 238-239 E 2
Verneuil-sur-Avre o F 90-91 H 7
Verneuk Pan o ZA 220-221 E 4
Vernia, La o USA (TX) 266-267 J 4
Vernoe o RUS 122-123 C 3
Vernon o CDN (BC) 230-231 K 3
Vernon o F 90-91 H 7
Vernon o USA (AL) 284-285 B 3
Vernon o USA (AZ) 256-257 F 4
Vernon o USA (CT) 280-281 O 2
Vernon o USA (FL) 286-287 D 1
Vernon o USA (IN) 274-275 N 6
Vernon o USA (LA) 268-269 H 4
Vernon o USA (OH) 280-281 F 2
Vernon o USA (TX) 264-265 E 4
Vernon o USA (UT) 254-255 C 3
Vernon, Lake < USA (LA) 268-269 G 5
Vernon Bridge o CDN (PEI) 240-241 N 4
Vernon Center o USA (MN) 270-271 D 7
Vernon Creek ~ USA (IN) 274-275 N 5
Vernon Hill o USA (VA) 280-281 G 7
Vernonia o USA (OR) 244-245 B 5
Vernon Islands ⌒ AUS 172-173 K 2
Vero Beach o USA (FL) 286-287 J 4
Verona o CDN (ONT) 238-239 J 4
Verona ☆•• I 100-101 C 2
Verona o USA (ND) 258-259 J 5
Verónica o RA 78-79 L 3
Veron Range ▲ PNG 183 G 3
Verret, Lake o USA (LA) 268-269 J 7
Versailles ☆••• F 90-91 J 7
Versailles o USA (IN) 274-275 N 5
Versailles o USA (KY) 276-277 L 2
Versailles o USA (MO) 274-275 F 6
Versailles o USA (OH) 280-281 B 3
Versalles o CO 60-61 C 5
Veršina-Tuojdah, gora ▲ RUS 110-111 W 7
Veršino-Darasunskij o RUS 118-119 G 9
Veršiny, Čelno- ☆ RUS 96-97 G 6
Versteende Woud • NAM 216-217 C 10
Vert, Cap ▲ SN 202-203 B 2
Verte, Rivière ~ CDN (QUE) 240-241 G 3
Vertentes o BR 68-69 L 5
Vertientes o C 54-55 F 4
Vertijievka o UA 102-103 G 2
Vert Island ⌒ CDN (ONT) 234-235 P 6
Vértiz o RA 78-79 H 3
Verulam o ZA 220-221 K 4
Verviers o B 92-93 H 3
Verwoert Tunnels II ZA 218-219 E 6
Verwood o CDN (SAS) 232-233 N 6
Vesali, Ruins of • MYA 142-143 H 5
Ves'egonsk o RUS 94-95 P 2
Vesele o UA 102-103 J 4
Veselovskoe o RUS 124-125 L 1
Veselovskoe vodohranilišče < RUS 102-103 M 4
Vesennij o RUS 112-113 N 3
Vešenskaja o RUS 102-103 M 3
Vesljana o RUS 88-89 V 5
Vesljana ~ RUS 88-89 V 5
Vesoul ☆ F 90-91 L 8
Vestaburg o USA (MI) 272-273 E 4
Vestbygd o N 86-87 C 7
Vesterålen ⌒ N 86-87 G 2
Vesterø Havn o DK 86-87 E 8
Vestfjorden ≈ 86-87 G 3
Vestfonna ⊂ N 84-85 L 3
Vestgrønland = Kitaa ▫ GRØ 26-27 b 5
Vestmannaeyjar o IS (RAN) 86-87 c 3
Vestmannaeyjar ⌒ IS (RAN) 86-87 c 3
Vestnik, buhta o RUS 122-123 R 3
Vestvågøy ⌒ N 86-87 F 2
Vesúvio ▲ I 100-101 E 4
Veszprém o H 92-93 O 5
Veta, La o USA (CO) 254-255 K 6
Vetal o USA (SD) 260-261 E 3
Vetauua ⌒ FJI 184 III c 1
Veteran o CDN (ALB) 232-233 G 4
Vetlanda ☆• S 86-87 G 8
Vetluga o RUS (GOR) 96-97 D 5
Vetluga ~ RUS 96-97 E 4
Vetlužskij o RUS 96-97 D 5
Vetovo o BG 102-103 E 6
Vetrenyj pojas, krjaž ▲ RUS 88-89 N 5
Vetrivier ~ ZA 220-221 H 4
Vetryna o BY 94-95 L 4
Vetvejskij hrebet ▲ RUS 120-121 V 3
Vevay o USA (IN) 274-275 N 6
Vévi o GR 100-101 H 4
Veyo o USA (UT) 254-255 B 6
Vezdehodnaja ~ RUS 108-109 j 4
Vézelay o•• F 90-91 J 8
Vežen ▲ BG 102-103 D 6
Vézère ~ F 90-91 H 9
V. Gradište o YU 100-101 H 2
Vi o S 86-87 H 5
Viacha o BOL 70-71 C 5
Viahtu o RUS 122-123 K 3
Viahtu ~ RUS 122-123 J 3
Viai Island ⌒ PNG 183 C 2
Vialadougou o CI 202-203 G 5
Viale o RA 76-77 H 6
Viamão o BR 74-75 E 8
Vian o USA (OK) 264-265 K 3
Viana o ANG 216-217 B 4
Viana o BR (ESP) 72-73 K 6
Viana o BR (MAR) 68-69 F 3
Viana o BR (P) 62-63 J 6
Viana do Castelo o• P 98-99 C 4
Viangchan ★ LAO 158-159 G 2
Viangphoukha o LAO 156-157 B 6
Vianópolis o BR 72-73 F 4
Viar, Río ~ E 98-99 E 6
Viaréggio o I 100-101 C 3
Via River ~ PNG 183 E 3
Vibank o CDN (SAS) 232-233 P 5
Vibora, La o MEX 50-51 H 4
Viboras o USA (TX) 266-267 J 7
Víboras, Las o RA 76-77 E 3
Viborg o DK 86-87 D 8
Vic o E 98-99 J 4
Vicebck o BY 94-95 M 4
Vic-en-Bigorre o F 90-91 H 10
Vicência o BR 68-69 L 5
Vicente Franco o BR 68-69 E 3
Vicente Guerrero o MEX 52-53 L 1
Vicente Guerrero o MEX (DGO) 50-51 H 6
Vicente Guerrero o MEX (TLA) 52-53 E 2
Vicente Noble o DOM 54-55 K 5
Vicenza ☆• I 100-101 C 2
Viceroy o CDN (SAS) 232-233 N 6
Vicertópolis o BR 72-73 E 6
Vichada, Río ~ CO 60-61 G 5
Vichadero o ROU 76-77 K 6
Vichy o F 90-91 J 8
Vichy o USA (MO) 274-275 G 6
Vici o USA (OK) 264-265 E 2
Vicksburg o USA (AZ) 256-257 B 5
Vicksburg o USA (MS) 268-269 K 4
Vicksburg National Military Park • USA (MS) 268-269 K 4
Viçosa o BR (ALA) 68-69 K 6
Viçosa o BR (MIN) 72-73 J 6
Viçosa do Ceará o BR 68-69 H 3
Victor o CDN (SAS) 232-233 L 2
Victor o USA (CO) 254-255 K 5
Victor o USA (ID) 252-253 G 3
Victor o USA (MT) 250-251 E 5
Victor o USA (NY) 278-279 D 6
Victor o USA (SD) 260-261 K 1
Victor, Lac o CDN (QUE) 242-243 G 2
Victor, Mount ▲ AUS 180-181 E 2
Victor Emanuel Range ▲ PNG 183 A 3
Victor Harbor o AUS 180-181 E 3
Victoria ▫ AUS 180-181 H 4
Victoria o BOL 70-71 D 2
Victoria o CDN (NFL) 242-243 P 5
Victoria ☆• CDN (BC) 230-231 F 5
Victoria o CO 60-61 D 5
Victoria ☆•• HK 156-157 J 5
Victoria o M 100-101 E 6
Victoria o RA 78-79 J 2
Victoria o RCH 78-79 C 5
Victoria o SME 62-63 G 3
Victoria ★• SY 224 D 2
Victoria o USA (KS) 262-263 G 6
Victoria o USA (MS) 268-269 L 2
Victoria o USA (TX) 266-267 K 5
Victoria o USA (VA) 280-281 H 7
Victoria, Isla ⌒ RCH 80 C 2
Victoria, La o YV (APU) 60-61 F 4
Victoria, La o YV (ARA) 60-61 H 2
Victoria, Lake o AUS 180-181 F 3
Victoria, Lake o EAT 212-213 D 4
Victoria, Monte ▲ RCH 80 E 6
Victoria, Mount ▲ MYA 142-143 H 5
Victoria, Mount ▲ PNG 183 D 5
Victoria, Sierra de la ▲ RA 76-77 K 3
Victoria and Albert Mountains ▲ CDN 26-27 L 4
Victoria Beach o CDN (MAN) 234-235 G 4
Victoria Beach o CDN (NS) 240-241 K 6
Victoria Bridge o CDN (NS) 240-241 P 5
Victoria de Durango = Durango ☆• MEX 50-51 G 5
Victoria Falls ~••• Z 218-219 C 3
Victoria Falls National Park ⊥ ZW 218-219 C 3
Victoria Fjord ≈ 26-27 a 2
Victoria Head ▲ CDN 26-27 N 4
Victoria Highway II AUS 172-173 J 3
Victoria Hill o BS 54-55 H 2
Victoria Island ⌒ CDN 24-25 O 5
Victoria Island ⌒ CDN (ONT) 234-235 O 6
Victoria Lake o CDN (NFL) 242-243 L 4
Victoria Land ⊥ ARK 16 F 16
Victoria Nile ~ EAU 212-213 C 2
Victoria Peak ▲ BH 52-53 K 3
Victoria Peak ▲ CDN (BC) 230-231 C 3
Victoria Peak ▲ USA (TX) 266-267 C 2
Victoria River ~ AUS (NT) 172-173 K 3
Victoria River ~ AUS 172-173 J 3
Victoria River ~ CDN (NFL) 242-243 M 4
Victoria River Downs o AUS 172-173 K 4
Victorias o RP 160-161 E 7
Victoria Strait ≈ 24-25 V 6
Victoria Vale o AUS 174-175 G 6
Victoriaville o CDN (QUE) 238-239 O 2
Victoria West o ZA 220-221 F 5
Victorica o RA 78-79 G 4
Victorino o C 54-55 G 4
Victor Rosales o MEX 50-51 H 6
Victorville o USA (CA) 248-249 G 5
Victory, Mount ▲ PNG 183 E 5
Vičuga ☆ RUS 94-95 R 3
Vicuña o RCH (COQ) 76-77 B 6
Vicuña o RCH (MAC) 80 F 7
Vicuña Mackenna o RA 78-79 G 2
Vicus • PE 64-65 B 4
Vida o USA (MT) 250-251 O 4
Vida o USA (OR) 244-245 C 6
Vidal o PE 64-65 F 3
Vidal o USA (CA) 248-249 K 5
Vidalia o USA (GA) 284-285 H 4
Vidalia o USA (LA) 268-269 J 5
Vidamlja o BY 94-95 H 5
Vidapanakallu o IND 140-141 G 3
Vidauri o USA (TX) 266-267 K 5
Videira o BR 74-75 E 6
Vidhareidhi = Viðareiði o FR 90-91 D 1
Vidim o RUS 116-117 L 7
Vidin o BG 102-103 C 6
Vidisha o IND 138-139 F 8
Vidor o USA (TX) 268-269 G 6
Vidora o CDN (SAS) 232-233 J 6
Vidzy o BY 94-95 K 4
Viedgesville o ZA 220-221 J 5
Viedma ☆ RA 78-79 H 6
Viedma, Lago o RA 80 D 4
Vieira Grande, Canal do ~ BR 62-63 J 6
Vieja, Punta la ▲ RCH 78-79 C 3
Vieja, Sierra ▲ USA (TX) 266-267 C 3
Viejitas, Caño las ~ CO 60-61 F 6
Viejo, El o NIC 52-53 L 5
Viejo, Mission o USA (CA) 248-249 G 6
Viejo, Río ~ RA 76-77 F 5
Vielha e Mijaran o E 98-99 H 3
Viella-Mitg Arán = Vielha e Mijaran o E 98-99 H 3
Vienna o USA (GA) 284-285 G 4
Vienna o USA (IL) 276-277 G 3
Vienna o USA (MD) 280-281 L 5
Vienna o USA (MO) 274-275 G 6
Vienna o USA (VA) 280-281 J 5
Vienna o USA (WV) 280-281 E 4
Vienna = Wien ★•• A 92-93 O 4
Vienne o F 90-91 K 9
Vienne ~ F 90-91 H 8
Vientiane = Viangchan ★ LAO 158-159 G 2
Viento, Cordillera del ▲ RA 78-79 D 4
Viento, Puerto del ▲ E 98-99 E 6
Vientos, Los o RCH 76-77 C 3
Vientos, Paso de los ≈ 54-55 H 5
Vieques, Isla de ⌒ USA (PR) 286-287 Q 2
Vieques Passage ≈ USA 286-287 Q 2
Vieremä o FIN 88-89 J 5
Vierwaldstätter See o CH 92-93 K 5
Vierzon o F 90-91 J 8
Viesca o MEX 50-51 H 5
Viesite o LV 94-95 J 3
Vieste o I 100-101 F 4
Vietas o S 86-87 J 3
Vietnam = Việt Nam ■ VN 158-159 K 2
Việt Tri ☆ VN 156-157 D 6
Viêt Vinh ☆ VN 156-157 D 5
Vieux-Comptoir, Lac du o CDN 38-39 F 2
Vieux-Comptoir, Rivière du ~ CDN 38-39 E 2
Vieux Fort o WL 56 E 5
View o USA (TX) 264-265 E 6
Vieytes o RA 78-79 L 3
Vigan ☆ RP 160-161 D 4
Vigan, le o F 90-91 J 10
Vigia o BR 62-63 K 6
Vigía, El o YV 60-61 F 3
Vigia Chico o MEX 52-53 L 2
Vigía de Curvaradó o CO 60-61 C 4
Vigía del Fuerte o CO 60-61 C 4
Vigil o USA (CO) 254-255 L 6
Vigo o E 98-99 C 3
Vihanti o FIN 88-89 H 4
Vihari o PK 138-139 D 4
Vihorevka o RUS 116-117 K 7
Vihren ▲ BG 102-103 C 7
Vihti o FIN 88-89 H 6
Viisanmäki o FIN 88-89 J 5
Viitasaari o FIN 88-89 H 5
Viitna o•• EST 94-95 K 2
Vijayadurg o IND 140-141 E 2
Vijayanagar o IND 138-139 D 8
Vijayāpati o IND 140-141 G 6
Vijayapura o IND 140-141 G 4
Vijayapuri o IND 140-141 H 2
Vijayawada o• IND 140-141 J 2
Vik ☆ IS 86-87 d 3
Vik o N 86-87 C 6
Vikajärvi o FIN 88-89 J 3
Vikārābād o IND 140-141 G 2
Vikeke o RI 166-167 D 6
Vikenara Point ▲ SOL 184 I d 3
Vikersund ☆ N 86-87 D 7
Viking o CDN (ALB) 232-233 G 2
Vikna ⌒ N 86-87 E 4
Viksøyri ☆ N 86-87 C 6
Viktoria = Labuan o MAL 160-161 A 10
Viktorija, ostrov ⌒ RUS 84-85 U 2
Vikulova, mys ▲ RUS 108-109 H 4
Vila Aurora o BR 68-69 E 3
Vila Bela da Santíssima Trinidade o BR 70-71 H 4
Vila Coutinho o MOC 218-219 H 2
Vila de Ribeira Brava o CV 202-203 B 5
Vila de Sal-Rei o CV 202-203 C 5
Vila de Sena o MOC 218-219 H 3
Vila do Maio o CV 202-203 C 6
Vila dos Remédios o BR 68-69 L 1
Vila Flor o ANG 216-217 C 6
Vilafranca del Penedès o E 98-99 H 4
Vila Franca de Xira o P 98-99 C 5
Vilagarcía de Arousa o• E 98-99 C 3
Vila Gomes da Costa o MOC 220-221 L 2
Vilaine ~ F 90-91 G 8
Vila Ipixuna o BR 68-69 E 3
Vilakalaka o VAN 184 II a 2
Vila Maria Pia o CV 202-203 B 5
Vila Martins o BR 66-67 C 6
Vila Meriti o BR 66-67 H 5
Vilanandro, Tanjona ▲ RM 222-223 D 6
Vila Nazaré o BR 66-67 E 4
Vilanculos o MOC 218-219 H 5
Viljäni o•• LV 94-95 K 3
Vila Nova o ANG 216-217 D 6
Vila Nova o BR (PAR) 74-75 D 5
Vila Nova o BR (RSU) 74-75 D 8
Vila Nova da Fronteira o MOC 218-219 H 3
Vila Nova de Foz Côa o P 98-99 D 4
Vila Nova do Seles o ANG 216-217 C 5
Vilanova i la Geltrú o E 98-99 H 4
Vila Nova Laranjeiras o BR 74-75 D 5
Vila Nova Sintra o CV 202-203 B 6
Vila Porto Franco o BR 66-67 H 6
Vila-real o E 98-99 G 5
Vila Real o P 98-99 D 4
Vila Real de Santo António o P 98-99 D 6
Vilar Formoso o P 98-99 D 4
Vila Rica o BR 68-69 C 6
Vilarinho do Monte o BR 62-63 H 6
Vilas, Los o RCH 76-77 B 6
Vila Sagrado Coração de Jesus o BR 66-67 H 5
Vila Tambaquí o BR 66-67 E 4
Vila Tepequem o BR 62-63 D 4
Vila Velha o BR 62-63 J 4
Vila Velha o BR 72-73 K 6
Vila Velha de Ródão o P 98-99 D 5
Vilavila o PE 70-71 B 4
Vilca o PE 64-65 E 8
Vilcabamba o EC 64-65 C 4
Vilcabamba • PE 64-65 F 8
Vilcabamba, Cordillera ▲ PE 64-65 F 8
Vilcanota, Cordillera de ▲ PE 70-71 B 3
Vilcas Huaman o PE 64-65 F 8
Vilčeka, Zemlja ⌒ RUS 84-85 f 2
Vilches o E 98-99 F 5
Vilcún o RCH 78-79 C 5
Vilcún, Río ~ RCH 78-79 C 5
Vilejka ☆ BY 94-95 K 4
Vilelas o RA 76-77 F 4
Vilhelmina o• S 86-87 H 4
Vilhena o BR 70-71 G 3
Viliga ~ RUS 120-121 R 3
Viliginskij, mys ▲ RUS 120-121 R 3
Viljandi ☆•• EST 94-95 J 2
Viljoenskroon o ZA 220-221 H 3
Viljučinskaja buhta o RUS 120-121 S 7
Viljuj ~ RUS 116-117 M 3
Viljuj ~ RUS 118-119 D 3
Viljuj ~ RUS 118-119 G 4
Viljučan ~ RUS 118-119 G 4
Viljujsk ☆• RUS 118-119 K 4
Viljujskoe vodohranilišče o RUS 118-119 E 4
Vil'kickogo, ostrov ⌒ RUS 108-109 Q 5
Vil'kickogo, proliv ≈ 108-109 d 3
Vilkija o LT 94-95 H 4
Vil'kitskogo, Proliv = Vil'kickogo, proliv ≈ RUS 108-109 d 3
Villa Abecia o BOL 70-71 E 7
Villa Ahumada o MEX 50-51 F 2
Villa Alcaraz o RA 76-77 H 6
Villa Alemana o RCH 78-79 D 2
Villa Ana o RA 76-77 H 5
Villa Angela o RA 76-77 G 4
Villa Atuel o RA 78-79 F 3
Villa Azueta o MEX 52-53 G 2
Villaba o RP 160-161 F 7
Villa Berthet o RA 76-77 G 4
Villablino o E 98-99 D 3
Villa Brana o RA 76-77 F 4
Villa Bruzual o YV 60-61 G 3
Villacañas o E 98-99 F 5
Villa Cañas o RA 78-79 J 3
Villa Candelaria o RA 76-77 F 5
Villa Carlos Paz o RA 76-77 E 6
Villacarrillo o E 98-99 F 5
Villach o A 92-93 M 5
Villa Constitución o RA 78-79 J 2
Villa Corona o MEX 52-53 C 1
Villa Coronado o MEX 50-51 G 4
Villa de Cazones o MEX 52-53 F 1
Villa de Cos o MEX 50-51 H 6
Villa de Cura o YV 60-61 H 2
Villa de García o MEX 50-51 J 5
Villa de Leiva o•• CO 60-61 E 5
Villa del Rosario o RA 76-77 F 6
Villa del Rosario o YV 60-61 E 2
Villa de Orestes o MEX 50-51 G 4
Villa de Reyes o MEX 50-51 J 7
Villa de Sari o MEX 50-51 D 3
Villadiego o E 98-99 E 3
Villa Dolores o RA 76-77 E 6
Villa Figueroa o RA 76-77 F 4
Villa Flores o MEX 52-53 H 3
Villafranca del Bierzo o E 98-99 D 3
Village Cove o CDN (NFL) 242-243 O 3
Village Creek ~ USA (TX) 268-269 F 6
Villa General Belgrano o RA 76-77 E 6
Villa General Güemes o RA 76-77 H 3
Villa General Roca o RA 78-79 F 2
Villa General San Martín o RA 76-77 C 6
Village of Yesteryear • USA (MN) 270-271 E 7
Villa Gesell o RA 78-79 L 4
Villa Gobernador Gálvez o RA 78-79 J 2
Villagran o MEX 50-51 K 5
Villaguay o RA 76-77 H 6
Villaguay Grande, Arroyo ~ RA 76-77 H 6
Villa Hermosa o MEX 52-53 C 1
Villahermosa o MEX (CAM) 52-53 K 3
Villahermosa ☆• MEX (TAB) 52-53 H 3
Villa Hidalgo o MEX (DGO) 50-51 G 4
Villa Hidalgo o MEX (JAL) 50-51 H 7
Villa Hidalgo o MEX (SON) 50-51 E 2
Villa Huidobra o RA 78-79 G 3
Villa Insurgentes o MEX 50-51 D 5
Villa Joyosa o E 98-99 G 5
Villa Juárez o MEX 50-51 J 6
Villa Larca o RA 78-79 G 2
Villalba o E 98-99 D 3
Villalbín o PY 76-77 H 4
Villaldama o MEX 50-51 J 4
Villa Lola o YV 60-61 K 4
Villalonga o RA 78-79 H 5
Villalpando o E 98-99 E 4
Villa Mainero o MEX 50-51 K 5
Villa María o RA 78-79 H 2
Villa Martin o BOL 70-71 D 7
Villamartín o E 98-99 E 6
Villa Mascardi o RA 78-79 D 6
Villa Mazán o RA 76-77 D 5
Villa Media Agua o RA 76-77 C 6
Villa Mercedes o RA 76-77 E 4
Villa Mills o CR 52-53 C 7
Villamontes o BOL 76-77 F 1
Villanow o USA (GA) 284-285 E 2
Villanueva o CO 60-61 E 2
Villanueva o MEX 50-51 H 6
Villa Nueva o RA 76-77 C 6
Villanueva o USA (NM) 256-257 K 3
Villanueva de Córdoba o E 98-99 E 5
Villanueva de los Castillejos o E 98-99 D 6
Villanueva de los Infantes o E 98-99 F 5
Villanueva y Geltrú = Vilanova i la Geltrú o E 98-99 H 4
Villa Ocampo o MEX 50-51 G 4
Villa Ocampo o RA 76-77 H 5
Villa O'Higgins o RCH 80 D 4
Villa Ojo de Agua o RA 76-77 F 5
Villa Oliva o PY (CEN) 76-77 J 3
Villa Oliva o PY (NEE) 76-77 J 4
Villa Ortega o RCH 80 E 2
Villapinzon o CO 60-61 E 5
Villarcayo o E 98-99 F 3
Villard o RH 54-55 J 5
Villardecierivos o E 98-99 D 4
Villa Reducción o RA 78-79 H 2
Villa Regina o RA 78-79 F 5
Villa Rica o USA (GA) 284-285 F 3
Villarpando o DOM 54-55 K 5
Villarreal de los Infantes = Vila-real o E 98-99 G 5
Villarrica ☆ PY 76-77 J 3
Villarrica o RCH 78-79 C 5
Villarrica, Lago o RCH 78-79 C 5
Villarrica, Parque Nacional ⊥ RCH 78-79 C 5
Villarrica, Volcán ▲ RCH 78-79 D 5
Villarrobledo o E 98-99 F 5
Villa Salvadorita o NIC 52-53 L 5
Villa San Martín o RA 76-77 E 5
Villa Santa Rita de Catuna o RA 76-77 D 6
Villasimius o I 100-101 B 5
Villa Talavera o BOL 70-71 E 6
Villa Toquepala o PE 70-71 B 5
Villatoya o E 98-99 G 5
Villa Tunari o BOL 70-71 E 5
Villa Unión o MEX 50-51 J 3
Villa Unión o MEX (DGO) 50-51 G 6
Villa Unión o MEX (SIN) 50-51 F 6
Villa Unión o RA 76-77 C 5
Villa Valeria o RA 78-79 G 3
Villa Vásquez o DOM 54-55 K 5
Villavicencio ☆ CO 60-61 E 5
Villaviciosa o• E 98-99 E 3
Villazon o RA 76-77 E 2
Villebon, Lac o CDN (QUE) 236-237 L 5
Ville de Lameque o CDN (NB) 240-241 L 3
Villefranche-de-Rouergue o F 90-91 J 9
Villefranche-sur-Saône o F 90-91 K 9
Villeguera, La o YV 60-61 H 4
Ville-Marie o CDN (QUE) 236-237 J 5
Villemontel o CDN (QUE) 236-237 K 4
Villena o E 98-99 G 5
Villeneuve o CDN (ALB) 232-233 E 2
Villeneuve-sur-Lot o F 90-91 H 9
Ville Platte o USA (LA) 268-269 H 6
Villeroy o CDN (QUE) 238-239 O 2
Villeurbanne o F 90-91 K 9
Villicún, Sierra de ▲ RA 76-77 C 6
Villiers o ZA 220-221 J 3
Villisca o USA (IA) 274-275 D 4
Vilnes o N 86-87 B 6
Vilnius ★•• LT 94-95 J 4
Vil'njans'k o UA 102-103 J 4
Vil'nohirs'k o UA 102-103 J 3
Vilonia o USA (AR) 276-277 C 5
Vils ~ D 92-93 L 4
Vil'šany o UA 102-103 J 2
Vilyuyskoye Vodokhranilishche = Viljujskoe vodohranilišče < RUS 118-119 E 4
Vimieiro o P 98-99 D 5
Vimioso o P 98-99 D 4
Vimmerby ☆• S 86-87 G 8
Vina ~ CAM 204-205 K 5
Vina o USA (AL) 284-285 B 2
Vina, Chute de la ~• CAM 204-205 K 5
Viña, La o RA (CAT) 76-77 E 5
Viña, La o RA (SAL) 76-77 E 3
Viña del Mar o RCH 78-79 D 2
Vinalhaven o USA (ME) 278-279 N 4
Vinalhaven Island ⌒ USA (ME) 278-279 N 4
Vinanivao o RM 222-223 G 5
Vinaròs o E 98-99 H 4
Vinători o RO 102-103 C 5
Vincelotte, Lac o CDN 36-37 N 7
Vincennes o USA (IN) 274-275 L 6
Vincennes Bay ≈ 16 G 11
Vincent o USA (AL) 284-285 D 3
Vincent o USA (TX) 264-265 C 6
Vinces o EC 64-65 C 2
Vinchina o RA 76-77 C 5
Vinchina, Río ~ RA 76-77 C 5
Vindelälven ~ S 86-87 J 4
Vindeln o S 86-87 J 4
Vindhya Range ▲ IND 138-139 E 8
Vinegar Hill ▲ USA (OR) 244-245 G 6
Vine Grove o USA (KY) 276-277 K 3
Vineland o USA (CO) 254-255 L 5
Vineland o USA (NJ) 280-281 L 4
Viner Nejstadt, ostrov ⌒ RUS 84-85 f 2
Vingåker ☆ S 86-87 G 7
Vingerklip • NAM 216-217 C 10
Vinh ☆ VN 156-157 D 7
Vinhais o P 98-99 D 4
Vinh Bắc Bộ ≈ 156-157 E 6
Vinh Cam Ranh ≈ 158-159 K 5
Vinh Cây Du'o'ng ≈ 158-159 H 5
Vinh Diên Châu ≈ 156-157 D 7
Vinhedo o BR 72-73 G 7
Vĩnh Hy o VN 158-159 K 5
Vĩnh Kim o VN 158-159 K 3
Vĩnh Lọc ☆ VN 156-157 D 6
Vĩnh Long o VN 158-159 H 5
Vinh Pham Thiêy ≈ 158-159 K 5
Vĩnh Yên ☆ VN 156-157 D 6
Vinita o USA (OK) 264-265 J 2
Vinju Mare o RO 102-103 C 5
Vinkovci o HR 100-101 G 2
Vinnica = Vinnycja ☆ UA 102-103 F 3
Vinnycja ☆ UA 102-103 F 3
Vinnytsya = Vinnycja ☆ UA 102-103 F 3
Vinson o USA (OK) 264-265 E 4
Vinson, Mount ▲ ARK 16 F 28
Vinstra ☆ N 86-87 D 6
Vinsulla o CDN (BC) 230-231 J 3
Vinter Øer ⌒ GRØ 26-27 W 6
Vinton o USA (IA) 274-275 F 2
Vinton o USA (LA) 268-269 G 6
Vinton o USA (OH) 280-281 D 5
Vinukonda o IND 140-141 H 2
Vinza o RCB 210-211 E 5
Vinzili o RUS 114-115 H 6
Viola o USA (IL) 274-275 H 3
Viola o USA (KS) 262-263 J 7
Viola o USA (WI) 274-275 H 1
Violaineville o G 210-211 C 3
Violeta, La o RA 78-79 J 2
Vioolsdrif o ZA 220-221 C 4
Viphya Mountains ▲ MW 214-215 G 7
Vipos, Río ~ RA 76-77 E 4
Vir o TJ 136-137 M 6
Virac ☆ RP 160-161 F 6
Viração, Cachoeira da ~ BR 62-63 G 6
Virac Point ▲ RP 160-161 F 6
Viradouro o BR 72-73 F 6
Vira-e-Volta, Cachoeira ~ BR 68-69 C 3
Viraganur o IND 140-141 H 5
Virago Sound ≈ CDN 228-229 B 2
Viramgām o IND 138-139 D 8
Viranşehir ☆ TR 128-129 H 4
Virapalle o IND 140-141 H 3
Virār o IND 138-139 D 10
Virarājendrapet o IND 140-141 F 4
Virāwah o PK 138-139 C 7
Virden o CDN (MAN) 234-235 C 5
Virden o USA (IL) 274-275 J 5
Virden o USA (NM) 256-257 G 6
Virei o ANG 216-217 B 7
Virgem da Lapa o BR 72-73 J 4
Virgen, La o NIC 52-53 B 6
Virgen de las Lajas, Santuario • CO 64-65 D 1
Virgen del Carmen, Canal < RA 76-77 F 3
Virgilina o USA (VA) 280-281 H 7
Virgin Gorda ⌒ GB 56 C 2
Virgin Gorda ⌒ GB (VI) 286-287 R 2
Virginia o AUS 180-181 E 3
Virginia o USA (IL) 274-275 H 5
Virginia o USA (MN) 270-271 F 3
Virginia ▫ USA (VA) 280-281 G 6
Virginia o ZA 220-221 H 4
Virginia Beach o USA (VA) 280-281 L 7
Virginia City o USA (MT) 250-251 H 6
Virginia City o USA (NV) 246-247 F 4
Virginia Dale o USA (CO) 254-255 K 3
Virginia Falls ~ CDN 30-31 F 5
Virginiatown o CDN (ONT) 236-237 J 4
Virgin Islands ⌒ GB (VI) 286-287 R 2
Virgin Islands (United Kingdom) ▫ GB (VI) 286-287 R 2

408 Venézia — Virgin Islands

Virgin Islands (United States) □ **USA** (VI) 286-287 R 2
Virgin Islands National Park ⊥ **USA** (VI) 286-287 R 2
Virgin Mountains ▲ **USA** (NV) 248-249 K 3
Virgin Passage ≈ 56 C 2
Virgin Passage ≈ **USA** 286-287 Q 2
Virgin River ~ **USA** (NV) 248-249 K 3
Virgolândia o **BR** 72-73 J 5
Virihaure o **S** 86-87 H 3
Virojoki = Virolahti o **FIN** 88-89 J 6
Virolahti o **FIN** 88-89 J 6
Viroqua o **USA** (WI) 274-275 H 1
Virovitica o **HR** 100-101 F 2
Virrat o **FIN** 88-89 G 5
Virtsu o **EST** 94-95 H 2
Viru o **PE** 64-65 C 6
Virudó o **CO** 60-61 C 5
Virudunagar o **IND** 140-141 G 6
Virunga, Parc National des ⊥ ··· **ZRE** 212-213 B 4
Vis o **HR** 100-101 F 3
Vis ⌒ **HR** 100-101 F 3
Vis ~ **NAM** 220-221 C 2
Visaginas ☆ **LT** 94-95 K 4
Visalia o **USA** (CA) 248-249 E 3
Visayan Sea ≈ 160-161 E 7
Visayas ⌒ **RP** 160-161 E 7
Visby ☆ ·· **S** 86-87 J 8
Viscount o **CDN** (SAS) 232-233 N 4
Viscount Melville Sound ≈ 24-25 P 3
Višegrad o · **BIH** 100-101 G 3
Višera ~ **RUS** 88-89 V 5
Višera ~ **RUS** 114-115 D 4
Viseu ☆ · **P** 98-99 D 4
Vishākhapatnam o ·· **IND** 142-143 C 7
Visicsa, Río ~ **BOL** 70-71 D 6
Visim ~ **RUS** 114-115 F 3
Visimskij zapovednik ⊥ **RUS** 96-97 L 5
Visita o **BR** 66-67 H 6
Visite, La o **RH** 54-55 J 5
Višneva o **BY** 94-95 K 4
Višnevka ☆ **KA** 124-125 H 3
Visočica ▲ **HR** 100-101 E 2
Visoko o **BIH** 100-101 G 3
Visrivier o **ZA** (CAP) 220-221 G 5
Visrivier ~ **ZA** 220-221 E 5
Visrivierafgronde Park ⊥ **NAM** 220-221 D 3
Visriviercanyon ·· **NAM** 220-221 C 3
Visrivier Canyon Park, Ai-Ais and ⊥ **NAM** 220-221 C 3
Vista o **CDN** (MAN) 234-235 C 4
Vista o **USA** (CA) 248-249 G 6
Vista Alegre o **ANG** 216-217 C 4
Vista Alegre o **BR** (AMA) 66-67 E 3
Vista Alegre o **BR** (AMA) 66-67 C 6
Vista River ~ **CDN** 24-25 c 4
Visuvisu Point ▲ **SOL** 184 I c 2
Visviri o **RCH** 70-71 C 5
Vit ~ **BG** 102-103 D 6
Vita o **CDN** (MAN) 234-235 G 5
Vita o **IND** 140-141 F 2
Vitberget ▲ **S** 86-87 L 3
Vitebsk = Vicebck o **BY** 94-95 M 4
Viterbo ☆ · **I** 100-101 D 3
Vitgenštejna, mys ▲ **RUS** 112-113 R 6
Vithalapur o **IND** 138-139 D 8
Vị Thanh o **VN** 158-159 H 6
Vitiaz Strait ≈ 183 D 3
Vitigudino o **E** 98-99 D 4
Viti Levu ⌒ **FJI** 184 III a 2
Vitim o **RUS** (SAH) 118-119 F 6
Vitim ~ **RUS** 118-119 F 6
Vitimkan ~ **RUS** 118-119 E 8
Vitimskij o **RUS** 118-119 F 6
Vitimskij zapovednik ⊥ **RUS** 118-119 H 7
Vitimskoe ploskogor'e ∸ **RUS** 118-119 F 9
Vitimskoye Ploskogor'ye = Vitimskoe ploskogor'e ∸ **RUS** 118-119 F 9
Vitiones, Lago de los o **BOL** 70-71 H 6
Vitolište o **MK** 100-101 H 4
Vitóna o **BR** 76-77 K 5
Vitor o **PE** 70-71 B 5
Vitoria o **BR** 68-69 B 3
Vitória ☆ **BR** 72-73 K 6
Vitória da Conquista o **BR** 72-73 K 3
Vitória de Santo Antão o **BR** 68-69 L 6
Vitória do Mearim o **BR** 68-69 F 3
Vitoria-Gasteiz o · **E** 98-99 F 3
Vitória Seamount ≃ 72-73 M 6
Vitorino o **BR** 74-75 D 6
Vitorino Freire o **BR** 68-69 F 4
Vitoša, Naroden Park ⊥ **BG** 102-103 C 6
Vitré o **F** 90-91 G 7
Vitry-le-François o **F** 90-91 K 7
Vitshumbi o · **ZRE** 212-213 B 4
Vitsyebsk = Vicebck o **BY** 94-95 M 4
Vittangi o **S** 86-87 K 3
Vittel o · **F** 90-91 K 7
Vittichi, Río ~ **BOL** 70-71 E 7
Vittória o **I** 100-101 E 6
Vittorio Vèneto o **I** 100-101 D 1
Vityaz Depth ≃ 122-123 O 6
Viuda, Isla La ⌒ **PE** 64-65 C 6
Viuda, La o **YV** 60-61 K 3
Viudas de Oriente o **MEX** 50-51 H 6
Vivario o **F** 98-99 M 3
Viveiro o **E** 98-99 D 3
Vivero, El o **YV** 60-61 H 4
Vivi ~ **RUS** 116-117 H 4
Vivi ~ **RUS** 116-117 G 2
Vivi, ozero o **RUS** 116-117 G 2
Vivian o **CDN** (MAN) 234-235 G 5
Vivian o **USA** (LA) 268-269 G 4
Vivian o **USA** (SD) 260-261 F 3
Vivo o **ZA** 218-219 E 6
Vivonne Bay ≈ 180-181 D 4
Vivoratá, Arroyo ~ **RA** 78-79 L 4
Vivorillo, Cayos ⌒ **HN** 54-55 D 7
Viwa ⌒ **FJI** 184 III a 2
Vižas ~ **RUS** 88-89 S 3
Vizcachas, Meseta de las ∸ **RCH** 80 D 5
Vizcachillas, Cerro ▲ **BOL** 76-77 D 2
Vizcaíno, Desierto de ∸ **MEX** 50-51 C 4
Vizcaino, Peninsula de ⌣ **MEX** 50-51 B 4
Vizcaíno, Reserva de la Biósfera El ⊥ ··· **MEX** 50-51 B 4
Vizcaya, Golfo de ≈ 90-91 G 10
Vizcaya, Golfo de ≈ 98-99 G 3
Vize, ostrov ⌒ **RUS** 84-85 p 3
Vizeu o **BR** 68-69 E 2
Vizianagaram o **IND** 142-143 C 6
Vizien, Rivière ~ **CDN** 36-37 N 5
Vizille o **F** 90-91 K 9
Vizinga o **RUS** 96-97 G 3
Vizzini o **I** 100-101 E 6
Vjalozero o **RUS** 88-89 N 3
Vjartsilja o **RUS** 88-89 L 5
Vjatka ~ **RUS** 96-97 H 4
Vjatskie Poljany ☆ **RUS** 96-97 G 5
Vjazemskij o **RUS** 122-123 F 5
Vjaz'ma ☆ **RUS** 94-95 O 4
Vjazniki o **RUS** 94-95 S 3
Vjosës, Lumi i ~ **AL** 100-101 G 4
Vlaanderen □ **B** 92-93 H 3
Vladičin Han o **YU** 100-101 J 3
Vladikavkaz ☆ **RUS** 126-127 F 6
Vladimir ☆ ··· **RUS** 94-95 R 3
Vladimirovka o **KA** 124-125 F 2
Vladimirovka o **RUS** 122-123 K 3
Vladimirovo o **RUS** 122-123 K 4
Vladivostok o **RUS** 122-123 D 7
Vlaşca, Drăgăneşti- o **RO** 102-103 D 5
Vlasenica o **BIH** 100-101 G 2
Vlas'evo o **RUS** 122-123 J 2
Vlasovo o **RUS** 110-111 U 4
V. Lelija ▲ **BIH** 100-101 G 3
Vlieland ⌒ **NL** 92-93 H 2
Vliets o **USA** (KS) 262-263 K 5
Vlissingen o **NL** 92-93 G 3
Vlkolínec o ··· **SK** 92-93 P 4
Vlorë ☆ ·· **AL** 100-101 G 4
Vltava ~ **CZ** 92-93 N 4
Vnutrennjaja guba o **RUS** 120-121 T 3
Vobkent o **US** 136-137 J 4
Voč' ~ **RUS** 96-97 J 3
Voca o **USA** (TX) 266-267 H 2
Vodla ~ **RUS** 88-89 O 6
Vodlozero, ozero o **RUS** 88-89 O 5
Vodnyj o **RUS** 88-89 W 5
Vodopadnyj, mys ▲ **RUS** 120-121 U 3
Vogan o **RT** 202-203 L 6
Vogar o **CDN** (MAN) 234-235 E 4
Vogelkop = Doberai Peninsula ⌣ **RI** 166-167 F 2
Vogulka ~ **RUS** 114-115 G 3
Vogul'skij Kamen', gora ▲ **RUS** 114-115 E 4
Vogvazdino o **RUS** 88-89 V 5
Vohémar = Iharana o **RM** 222-223 G 4
Vohilava o **RM** 222-223 F 8
Vohilengo o **RM** 222-223 F 6
Vohimena o **RM** 222-223 F 6
Vohimena ▲ **RM** 222-223 E 10
Vohimena, Tanjona ▲ **RM** 222-223 D 10
Vohipeno o **RM** 222-223 E 9
Vohitra ~ **RM** 222-223 F 7
Vohitraivo o **RM** 222-223 F 6
Võhma o **EST** 94-95 H 2
Võhma o ·· **EST** 94-95 J 2
Vohma o **RUS** 96-97 E 4
Voi o **EAK** 212-213 G 5
Voi ~ **EAK** 212-213 G 5
Voi o **VN** 156-157 E 7
Voinjama ☆ **LB** 202-203 F 5
Voiron o **F** 90-91 K 9
Voisey Bay ≈ 36-37 T 6
Voja, Ust'- o **RUS** 114-115 D 2
Voja, Ust'- o **RUS** (KOM) 88-89 Y 4
Vojampolka o **RUS** 120-121 S 4
Vojampolka (Matëraja) ~ **RUS** 120-121 S 4
Vojampolka (Žilovaja) ~ **RUS** 120-121 S 4
Vojejkov šelfovyi lednik ⌒ **ARK** 16 G 13
Vojkarsyn'inskij massiv ▲ **RUS** 114-115 F 2
Vojkor ~ **RUS** 114-115 G 2
Vojnica o **RUS** 88-89 L 4
Vojvareto, ozero o **RUS** 108-109 P 7
Vojvož o **RUS** 88-89 X 5
Vokeo Island ⌒ **PNG** 183 C 2
Vokre, Hosséré ▲ **CAM** 204-205 K 4
Vol' ~ **RUS** 88-89 W 5
Volborg o **USA** (MT) 250-251 O 6
Volcán o **PA** 52-53 C 7
Volcán o **RA** 76-77 E 2
Volcán, El o **RCH** 78-79 D 2
Volcán Barú, Parque Nacionale ⊥ ·· **PA** 52-53 C 7
Volcán de Colima, Parque Nacional ⊥ **MEX** 52-53 C 2
Volčanka ~ **RUS** 108-109 Z 6
Volcano o **USA** (HI) 288 K 5
Volcans, Parc National des ⊥ **ZRE** 212-213 B 4
Volčansk o **RUS** 114-115 F 5
Volcán Tupungato, Parque Provincial ⊥ **RA** 78-79 E 2
Volčiha ☆ **RUS** 124-125 M 3
Volda ☆ **N** 86-87 C 5
Vol'dino o **RUS** 88-89 X 5
Volens o **USA** (VA) 280-281 G 7
Volga ~ **RUS** 94-95 N 3
Volga ~ **RUS** 96-97 E 8
Volga ~ **RUS** 96-97 E 10
Volga ~ **RUS** 96-97 F 10
Volga ~ **RUS** 126-127 G 5
Volga-Baltic Waterway = Volgo-Baltijskij kanal < **RUS** 94-95 P 1
Volgo-Baltijskij kanal < **RUS** 94-95 P 1
Volgodonsk o **RUS** 102-103 N 4
Volgo-Donskoi kanal < **RUS** 102-103 N 3
Volgograd = Zarizyn ☆ · **RUS** 96-97 D 9
Volgogradskoe vodohranilišče < **RUS** (SAR) 96-97 E 8
Volgogradskoe vodohranilišče < **RUS** (VLG) 96-97 D 9
Volgogradskoye Vodokhranilishche = Volgogradskoe vodohranil. < **RUS** 96-97 D 9
Volhov o **RUS** (LEN) 94-95 N 2
Volhov ~ **RUS** 94-95 N 2
Volímes o **GR** 100-101 H 6
Volksrust o **ZA** 220-221 J 3
Volna, gora ▲ **RUS** 112-113 H 5
Volnovacha o **UA** 102-103 K 4
Voločanka o **RUS** 108-109 a 6
Voločys'k ☆ **UA** 102-103 E 3
Volodarsk ☆ **KA** 124-125 F 2
Volodarsk o **RUS** 94-95 S 3
Volodarskij ☆ **RUS** 96-97 F 10
Volodino o **RUS** 114-115 S 6
Volodymyr-Volyns'kyj o **UA** 102-103 D 2
Vologda ☆ · **RUS** 94-95 Q 2
Volokolamsk o · **RUS** 94-95 O 3
Volokonovka o **RUS** 102-103 K 2
Volokovaja o **RUS** 88-89 U 3
Volokvynejtkon, gora ▲ **RUS** 112-113 R 5
Volop o **ZA** 220-221 F 4
Vólos o · **GR** 100-101 J 5
Volosovo ☆ **RUS** 94-95 L 2
Volot o **RUS** 94-95 M 3
Volquart Boon Kyst ∸ **GRØ** 26-27 o 8
Volšepahk, gora ▲ **RUS** 88-89 M 2
Vol'sk ☆ **RUS** 96-97 E 7
Volstruisleegte o **ZA** 220-221 F 6
Volta ~ **GH** 202-203 L 7
Volta Blanche ~ **BF** 202-203 K 3
Voltaire, Cape ▲ **AUS** 172-173 G 3
Volta Lake < **GH** 202-203 K 5
Volta Noire ~ **BF** 202-203 J 4
Volta Redonda o **BR** 72-73 H 7
Volta Region □ **GH** 202-203 L 5
Volta Rouge ~ **BF** 202-203 K 4
Volterra o **I** 100-101 C 3
Volturino, Monte ▲ **I** 100-101 E 4
Volturno ~ **I** 100-101 E 4
Voltzberg ▲ **SME** 62-63 F 3
Volubilis ∴ ·· **MA** 188-189 J 3
Vólvi, Limni o **GR** 100-101 J 4
Volyns'ka vysočyna ▲ **UA** 102-103 D 2
Volyns'kyj, Novohrad- o **UA** 102-103 E 2
Volyns'kyj, Volodymyr- o **UA** 102-103 D 2
Volzhskiy = Volžskij o **RUS** 96-97 D 9
Volžsk o **RUS** 96-97 F 6
Volžskij o **RUS** 96-97 D 9
Volžsko-Kamskij zapovednik ⊥ **RUS** 96-97 F 6
Vom o **WAN** 204-205 H 4
Vonavona = Parara ⌒ **SOL** 184 I c 3
Vonda o **CDN** (SAS) 232-233 M 3
Vondanka o **RUS** 96-97 E 4
Vondrove o **RM** 222-223 D 8
Vondrozo o **RM** 222-223 E 9
Von Frank Mountain ▲ **USA** 20-21 N 5
Vónitsa o **GR** 100-101 H 5
Von Lindequist Gate < **NAM** 216-217 D 9
Von Ormy o **USA** (TX) 266-267 J 4
Vontimitta o **IND** 140-141 H 3
Voon, Tarso ▲ **TCH** 198-199 H 2
Voortrekker fort · **ZA** 220-221 K 2
Vopnafjarðurgrunn ≃ 86-87 g 1
Vopnafjörður ≈ 86-87 f 2
Vopnafjörður o **IS** 86-87 f 2
Voranava ☆ **BY** 94-95 J 4
Voranga ~ **RUS** 118-119 L 3
Vorarlberg □ **A** 92-93 K 5
Vordingborg o · **DK** 86-87 E 9
Vóreio Egéo □ **GR** 100-101 K 5
Vorenža o **RUS** 88-89 N 5
Vorgašor o **RUS** 108-109 K 8
Vóries Sporádes ⌣ **GR** 100-101 J 5
Vøringfossen ·· **N** 86-87 C 6
Vöring Plateau ≃ 6-7 K 2
Vor'ja ~ **RUS** 114-115 G 3
Vorkuta ☆ **RUS** 108-109 K 8
Vorkuta ~ **RUS** 108-109 K 8
Vorma ~ **N** 86-87 E 6
Vormamay o **AFG** 138-139 B 3
Vormsi saar ⌒ **EST** 94-95 H 2
Vorob'evo o **RUS** 114-115 O 6
Vorogovka ~ **RUS** 116-117 E 5
Vorona ~ **RUS** 94-95 S 5
Vorona ~ **RUS** 102-103 N 2
Voroncovka o **RUS** 118-119 F 6
Voroncovo o **RUS** 108-109 U 6
Voroneț o ··· **RO** 102-103 D 4
Voronež o **RUS** 102-103 L 2
Voronež ~ **RUS** 94-95 Q 5
Voronezh = Voronež o **RUS** 102-103 L 2
Voronina, ostrov ⌒ **RUS** 108-109 a 2
Voron'ja ~ **RUS** 88-89 N 2
Voronov, mys ▲ **RUS** 88-89 R 3
Vorošilovgrad = Luhans'k ☆ **UA** 102-103 L 3
Vorotan ~ **AR** 128-129 L 3
Vorotynec o **RUS** 96-97 D 5
Vorožba o **UA** 102-103 J 2
Vorskla ~ **RUS** 102-103 J 2
Vorsma o **RUS** 94-95 S 4
Vorstershoop o **ZA** 220-221 F 2
Võrtsjärv järv o **EST** 94-95 K 2
Võru ☆ ·· **EST** 94-95 K 3
Vosburg o **ZA** 220-221 F 5
Vose o **TJ** 136-137 L 6
Vosges ▲ **F** 90-91 K 8
Voskopojë o · **AL** 100-101 H 4
Voskresenovka o **RUS** 122-123 C 3
Voskresensk ☆ · **RUS** 94-95 Q 4
Voskresenskoe o **RUS** 94-95 P 3
Voskresenskogo, buhta o **RUS** 108-109 X 4
Voss o **USA** (TX) 266-267 H 2
Vossavangen o · **N** 86-87 C 6
Vostočnaja, kosa ⌒ **RUS** 108-109 R 5
Vostočnaja Handyga ~ **RUS** 120-121 G 2
Vostočnoe Munozero o **RUS** 88-89 N 3
Vostočno-Sahalinskie gory ▲ **RUS** 122-123 K 3
Vostočnyj, proliv ≈ 110-111 H 2
Vostočnyj o **RUS** (CUK) 112-113 W 3
Vostočnyj o **RUS** (SHL) 122-123 K 4
Vostočnyj hrebet ▲ **RUS** 120-121 S 7
Vostočnyj Kamennyj, ostrov ⌒ **RUS** 108-109 U 4
Vostočnyj Sinij, hrebet ▲ **RUS** 122-123 E 7
Vostočnyj Tannu-Ola, hrebet ▲ **RUS** 116-117 F 10
Vostok o **ARK** 16 F 11
Vostok o **RUS** 122-123 F 5
Votaw o **USA** (TX) 268-269 F 6
Votkinsk ☆ **RUS** 96-97 J 5
Votkinskoe vodohranilišče < **RUS** 96-97 J 5
Votkinskoye Vodohranilishche = Votkinskoe vodohranilišče < **RUS** 96-97 J 5
Vot Tande ⌒ **VAN** 184 II a 1
Votuporanga o **BR** 72-73 F 6
Vouga o **ANG** 216-217 D 6
Vouga, Rio ~ **P** 98-99 C 4
Vouka o **RCB** 210-211 D 5
Vouliagméni o **GR** 100-101 J 6
Vouzela o **P** 98-99 C 4
Vovča ~ **UA** 102-103 J 3
Vovča ~ **UA** 102-103 K 3
Vovčans'k o **UA** 102-103 K 2
Vovodo ~ **RCA** 206-207 G 5
Voxna o **S** 86-87 G 6
Voyageurs National Park ⊥ **USA** (MN) 270-271 F 2
Vože, ozero o **RUS** 94-95 Q 1
Vožega o **RUS** 94-95 R 1
Vožgora o **RUS** 88-89 U 4
Voznesens'k o **UA** 102-103 G 4
Voznesenskoe o **RUS** 94-95 S 4
Vozroždenie o **RUS** 96-97 F 7
Vozroždenije otasi ⌒ **US** 136-137 F 2
Vozvraščenija, gora ▲ **RUS** 122-123 K 4
vpadina Assake-Audan ⌣ **US** 136-137 E 3
Vraca o **BG** 102-103 C 6
Vrangelja, mys ▲ **RUS** 120-121 H 6
Vrangelja, ostrov ⌒ **RUS** 112-113 U 1
Vranica ▲ **BIH** 100-101 F 2
Vrăška čuka, Prohod ▲ **BG** 102-103 C 6
Vrbas ~ **BIH** 100-101 F 2
Vrede o **ZA** 220-221 J 3
Vredefort o **ZA** 220-221 H 3
Vredenburg o **ZA** 220-221 C 6
Vredendal o **ZA** 220-221 D 5
Vredeshoop o **NAM** 220-221 D 3
Vreed-en-Hoop o **GUY** 62-63 E 2
Vreede Stein o **GUY** 62-63 E 2
Vriddhāchalam o **IND** 140-141 H 5
Vrigstad o **S** 86-87 G 8
Vríssa o **GR** 100-101 L 5
Vroolijk, Pulau ⌒ **RI** 164-165 L 4
Vršac o · **YU** 100-101 H 2
Vryburg o **ZA** 220-221 G 3
Vryheid o **ZA** 220-221 K 3
Vsesvjats'kyj kostel · **UA** 102-103 C 3
Vsevidof, Mount ▲ **USA** 22-23 M 6
Vsevidof Island ⌒ **USA** 22-23 M 6
Vsevoložsk ☆ **RUS** 94-95 M 1
Vstrečnyj o **RUS** 112-113 N 3
Vtoroj Kuril'skij proliv o **RUS** 122-123 R 3
Vuadil' o **US** 136-137 M 4
Vube o **ZRE** 212-213 A 2
Vui-Uata Nova Itália, Área Indígena X **BR** 66-67 C 4
Vuka ~ **HR** 100-101 G 2
Vukovar o · **HR** 100-101 G 2
Vuktyl ☆ **RUS** 114-115 D 3
Vulavu o **SOL** 184 I d 3
Vulcan o **CDN** (ALB) 232-233 E 5
Vulcano, Ísola ⌒ **I** 100-101 E 5
Vulcan Shoal ⌒ **AUS** 172-173 G 2
Vulkannyj hrebet ▲ **RUS** 112-113 N 3
Vulsinio = Lago di Bolsena o **I** 100-101 C 3
Vúlture, Monte ▲ **I** 100-101 E 4
Vulture Mine o **USA** (AZ) 256-257 C 5
Vul'vyveem ~ **RUS** 112-113 T 3
Vumba Gardens ⊥ **ZW** 218-219 G 4
Vumba Mountains ▲ **ZW** 218-219 G 4
Vũng Hôn Khói ≈ 158-159 K 4
Vũng Lâng Mai ≈ 158-159 K 4
Vũng Tàu ☆ · **VN** 158-159 J 5
Vunisea o **FJI** 184 III b 3
Vuokatti o **FIN** 88-89 K 4
Vuolijoki o **FIN** 88-89 J 4
Vuollerim o **S** 86-87 K 3
Vuolvojaure o **S** 86-87 J 3
Vuotso o **FIN** 88-89 J 2
Vuranggo o **SOL** 184 I c 2
Vurnary o **RUS** 96-97 E 6
Vuxikou o **VRC** 154-155 L 6
Vwaza Game Reserve ⊥ **MW** 214-215 G 6
Vya o **USA** (NV) 246-247 F 2
Vyaparla o **IND** 140-141 H 2
Vybor o **RUS** 94-95 L 3
Vyborg ☆ · **RUS** 94-95 L 1
Vyčegda ~ **RUS** 88-89 W 6
Vydrino o **RUS** 116-117 M 10
Vydropužsk o **RUS** 94-95 O 3
Vyezžij Log o **RUS** 116-117 F 8
Vygoniči o **RUS** 94-95 O 5
Vygozero o **RUS** 88-89 N 5
Vyhanaščanskoe, vozero o **BY** 94-95 J 5
Vyhodnoj, mys ▲ **RUS** 108-109 G 5
Vyja ~ **RUS** 88-89 S 5
Vyksa ☆ **RUS** 94-95 S 4
Vylkove o **UA** 102-103 F 5
Vym' ~ **RUS** 88-89 V 4
Vym' ~ **RUS** 88-89 V 5
Vyngajaha ~ **RUS** 114-115 O 2
Vyngapurovskij o **RUS** 114-115 O 3
Vyra o **RUS** 94-95 L 2
Vys', gora ▲ **RUS** 112-113 H 5
Vyšhorod o **UA** 102-103 G 2
Vyšnij Voloček ☆ **RUS** 94-95 O 3
Vysokae o **BY** 94-95 H 5
Vysokaja, gora ▲ **RUS** 122-123 N 6
Vysokaja Gora ☆ **RUS** 96-97 F 6
Vysokaja gora ▲ **RUS** 120-121 V 4
Vysokaja Parma vozvyšennost' ▲ **RUS** 114-115 E 4
Vysokij, mys ▲ **RUS** (KOR) 112-113 R 6
Vysokij, mys ▲ **RUS** (SAH) 110-111 a 2
Vysokogornyj o **RUS** 122-123 H 3
Vytegra ☆ · **RUS** 88-89 O 6
Vyvenka o **RUS** (KOR) 120-121 V 3
Vyvenka ~ **RUS** 112-113 P 6
Vyvenka ~ **RUS** 120-121 V 3

W

Wa o **CI** 202-203 F 6
Wa ☆ · **GH** 202-203 J 4
Waaheen, togga ~ **SP** 208-209 G 3
Waajid o **SP** 212-213 J 2
Waal ~ **NL** 92-93 H 3
Waangyi-Garawa Aboriginal Land X **AUS** 174-175 D 6
Waar, Pulau ⌒ **RI** 166-167 H 3
Waara o **RI** 164-165 H 6
Waarlangier, Tanjung ▲ **RI** 166-167 G 5
Waat o **SUD** 206-207 L 4
Wababimiga Lake o **CDN** (ONT) 236-237 B 2
Wabag ☆ · **PNG** 183 B 3
Wabakimi Lake o **CDN** (ONT) 234-235 O 4
Wabakimi Provincial Park ⊥ **CDN** (ONT) 234-235 O 4
Wabamun o **CDN** (ALB) 232-233 D 2
Wabamun Lake o **CDN** (ALB) 232-233 D 2
Wabana o **CDN** (NFL) 242-243 Q 5
Wabasca Indian Reserve X **CDN** 32-33 O 4
Wabasca River ~ **CDN** 32-33 N 3
Wabash o **USA** (IN) 274-275 N 4
Wabasha o **USA** (MN) 270-271 F 6
Wabash River ~ **USA** (IL) 274-275 L 5
Wabash River ~ **USA** (IL) 274-275 L 6
Wabash River ~ **USA** (IN) 274-275 N 4
Wabash River ~ **USA** (IN) 274-275 L 4
Wabassi River ~ **CDN** (ONT) 234-235 R 3
Wabbaseka o **USA** (AR) 276-277 D 6
Wabbwood o **CDN** (ONT) 238-239 D 2
Wabē Shebelē Wenz ~ **ETH** 208-209 E 5
Wabigoon Lake o **CDN** (ONT) 234-235 L 5
Wabimeig Lake o **CDN** 34-35 O 5
Wabinosh Lake o **CDN** (ONT) 234-235 O 4
Wabo o **PNG** 183 C 4
Wabowden o **CDN** 34-35 G 3
Wabron o **CDN** (BC) 230-231 K 2
Wabuda o **PNG** 183 B 5
Wabuda Island ⌒ **PNG** 183 B 5
Wabuk Point ▲ **CDN** 34-35 O 3
Waburton Bay o **CDN** 30-31 N 4
Wabuska o **USA** (NV) 246-247 F 4
Waccamaw, Lake o **USA** (NC) 282-283 J 6
Waccasassa Bay ≈ 48-49 G 5
Waccasassa Bay ≈ **USA** 286-287 G 2
Waccassa River ~ **USA** (FL) 286-287 G 2
Wachapreague o **USA** (VA) 280-281 L 6
Wach'īlē o **ETH** 208-209 D 6
Waci o **RI** 164-165 L 3
Waco o **CDN** 38-39 M 3
Waco o **USA** (TN) 276-277 H 5
Waco o **USA** (TX) 266-267 K 2
Waco, Lake o **USA** (TX) 266-267 K 2
Waconda Lake o **USA** (KS) 262-263 H 5
Waconia o **USA** (MN) 270-271 E 6
Wacuach, Lac o **CDN** 36-37 Q 7
Wad o **PK** 134-135 M 5
Wada'ah o **SUD** 200-201 B 6
Wadalai o **PNG** 183 F 5
Wadamago o **SP** 208-209 H 4
Wad an-Nail o **SUD** 200-201 G 6
Wadau o **PNG** 183 D 3
Wadayama o **J** 152-153 F 7
Wad Bandah o **SUD** 200-201 C 6
Wad Ban Naqa o **SUD** 200-201 F 4
Wadbilliga National Park ⊥ **AUS** 180-181 K 4
Waddān o · **LAR** 192-193 G 3
Waddān, Jabal ▲ **LAR** 192-193 G 3
Waddell Bay ≈ 36-37 Q 3
Waddenzee ≈ 92-93 H 2
Waddikee o **AUS** 180-181 D 2
Waddington, Mount ▲ **CDN** 230-231 D 2
Waddy Point ▲ **AUS** 178-179 M 3
Wade o **USA** (MS) 268-269 M 6
Wade Lake o **CDN** 36-37 R 7
Wadena o **CDN** (SAS) 232-233 P 4
Wadena o **USA** (MN) 270-271 C 4
Wadesboro o **USA** (NC) 282-283 G 6
Wadeye o **AUS** 172-173 J 3
Wad Ḥāmid o **SUD** 200-201 F 4
Wadham Islands ⌒ **CDN** (NFL) 242-243 P 3
Wad Hassib o **SUD** 206-207 H 3
Wadhope o **CDN** (MAN) 234-235 H 4
Wadi o **IND** 140-141 G 2
Wādī Ğimal, Ğazīrat ⌒ **ET** 194-195 G 5
Wādī Ḥalfā o **SUD** 200-201 E 2
Wādī Seidna o **SUD** 200-201 F 5
Wadley o **USA** (AL) 284-285 E 3
Wadley o **USA** (GA) 284-285 H 4
Wād Madanī ☆ **SUD** 200-201 F 5
Wad Nafarein o **SUD** 200-201 F 6
Wadomari o **J** 152-153 C 11
Wad Rāwah o **SUD** 200-201 F 5
Wadsworth o **USA** (NV) 246-247 F 4
Wadsworth o **USA** (TX) 266-267 M 5
Waeldern o **USA** (TX) 266-267 K 4
Waenhuiskrans o **ZA** 220-221 E 7
Waeplau o **RI** 166-167 D 3
Waeputih o **RI** 166-167 D 3
Waerana o **RI** 168 E 7
Wafangdian o **VRC** 150-151 C 8
Wafra, al- o **KWT** 130-131 K 3
Wagait Aboriginal Land X **AUS** 172-173 K 2
Wagan o **PNG** 183 D 4
Waga River ~ **PNG** 183 B 4
Wagau o **PNG** 183 D 4
Wagdari o **IND** 140-141 G 2
Wagener o **USA** (SC) 284-285 J 3
Wageningen o **SME** 62-63 F 3
Wager, Isla ⌒ **RCH** 80 C 3
Wager Bay ≈ 30-31 Z 3
Wageseri o **RI** 166-167 K 2
Wagga Wagga o **AUS** 180-181 J 3
Wağh, al- o **KSA** 130-131 E 4
Waghai o **IND** 138-139 D 9
Waghete o **RI** 166-167 J 4
Wağid, Ğabal al- ▲ **KSA** 132-133 D 4
Wagin o **AUS** 176-177 D 6
Waglisla o **CDN** (BC) 228-229 F 4
Wagner o **BR** 72-73 K 2
Wagner o **USA** (SD) 260-261 H 3
Wagny = Ouana ~ **G** 210-211 D 4
Wagoner o **USA** (OK) 264-265 J 3
Wagon Mound o **USA** (NM) 256-257 L 2
Wagontire o **USA** (OR) 244-245 F 7
Wagram o **USA** (NC) 282-283 H 6
Wągrowiec o · **PL** 92-93 O 2
Wagwalcook o **CDN** (NS) 240-241 P 4
Waha o **RI** 164-165 H 6
Waha o **USA** (ID) 250-251 C 5
Wahabu o **GH** 202-203 J 4
Wahai o **RI** 166-167 E 3
Wahala o **RT** 202-203 L 6
Wah Cantonment o **PK** 138-139 D 3
Wahi o **PK** 134-135 M 6
Wahiawa o **USA** (HI) 288 G 3
Wahlbergøya ⌒ **N** 84-85 L 3
Wahlebone Cape ▲ **USA** 22-23 N 6
Wahlenbergfjorden ≈ 84-85 L 3
Wahoo o **USA** (NE) 262-263 K 3
Wahpeton o **USA** (ND) 258-259 L 5
Wahrān ☆ **DZ** 188-189 L 3
Wahroonga o **AUS** 176-177 C 2
Wai o **IND** 140-141 E 2
Waiakoa o **USA** (HI) 288 J 4
Waialua o **USA** (HI) 288 J 3
Waialua o **USA** (HI) 288 G 3
Waian o **RC** 156-157 L 5
Waianae o **USA** (HI) 288 G 3
Waiãpi, Área Indígena X **BR** 62-63 H 5
Waiau o **NZ** 182 D 5
Waibula o **PNG** 183 F 5
Waidhān o **IND** 142-143 C 3
Waidhofen an der Thaya o **A** 92-93 N 4
Waidu o **WAL** 202-203 E 5
Waigen Lakes o **AUS** 176-177 K 3
Waigeo, Pulau ⌒ **RI** 166-167 F 2
Waihau Bay o **NZ** 182 F 2
Waihi o **NZ** 182 E 2
Waiji, Pulau ⌒ **RI** 166-167 F 2
Waikabubak o · **RI** 168 D 7
Waikaia o **NZ** 182 B 6
Waikaremoana o **NZ** 182 F 3
Waikawa o **NZ** 182 B 7
Waikelo o **RI** 168 D 7
Waikerie o **AUS** 180-181 E 3
Waikii o **USA** (HI) 288 K 5
Waikiki Beach < · **USA** (HI) 288 H 3
Wailapa o **VAN** 184 II a 2
Wailea o **USA** (HI) 288 J 4
Wailebe o **RI** 166-167 B 6
Wailua o **USA** (HI) 288 F 2
Wailua Falls ~ · **USA** (HI) 288 J 4
Wailuku o · **USA** (HI) 288 J 4
Waimanalo Beach o **USA** (HI) 288 H 3
Waimanguar o **RI** 168 D 7
Waimate o **NZ** 182 C 6
Waimea o **USA** (HI) 288 G 3
Waimea Canyon ⌣ · **USA** (HI) 288 F 2
Waimenda o **RI** 164-165 G 5
Waimiri Atroari, Área Indígena X **BR** 62-63 D 6
Wainganga ~ **IND** 138-139 G 9
Waingapu o **RI** 168 E 7
Waini River ~ **GUY** 62-63 E 1
Wainwright o **CDN** (ALB) 232-233 H 3
Wainwright o **USA** 20-21 L 1
Waiouru o **NZ** 182 E 3
Waipa o **RI** 166-167 J 3
Waipah o **USA** (HI) 288 G 3
Waipara o **NZ** 182 D 5
Waipawa o **NZ** 182 F 3
Waipio o **USA** (HI) 288 K 4
Waipoua Kauri Forest · **NZ** 182 D 1
Waipukang o **RI** 166-167 B 6
Waipukurau o **NZ** 182 F 4
Wair o **RI** 166-167 G 4
Waira o **PNG** (GUL) 183 B 4
Waira o **PNG** (GUL) 183 C 4
Wairaha ~ **SOL** 184 I e 3
Wairoa o **NZ** 182 F 3
Wairunu o **RI** 166-167 B 6
Waisa o **PNG** 183 C 4
Waitakaruru o **NZ** 182 E 2
Waitaki o **NZ** 182 C 6
Waitaki River ~ **NZ** 182 C 6
Waitangi o ·· **NZ** 182 E 1
Waitara o **NZ** 182 E 3
Waitati o **NZ** 182 C 6
Waite o **USA** (ME) 278-279 O 3
Waitomo Caves · **NZ** 182 E 3
Waitsburg o **USA** (WA) 244-245 G 4
Waitville o **CDN** (SAS) 232-233 N 3
Waiuku o **NZ** 182 E 2
Waiwa o **PNG** 183 E 5
Waiwai o **GUY** 62-63 E 5
Waiwerang o **RI** 166-167 B 6
Waje o **WAN** 204-205 G 4
Wajima o **J** 152-153 G 6
Wajir o **EAK** 212-213 H 3
Waka o **ETH** 208-209 C 5
Waka o **RI** 168 E 7
Waka o **USA** (TX) 264-265 D 2
Waka o **ZRE** (EQU) 210-211 H 3
Waka o **ZRE** (EQU) 210-211 H 4
Waka, Tanjung ▲ **RI** 166-167 D 3
Wakaf Tapai o **MAL** 162-163 E 2
Wakami Lake Provincial Park ⊥ **CDN** (ONT) 236-237 F 5
Wakamoek o **RI** 166-167 F 2
Wakarusa River ~ **USA** (KS) 262-263 L 6
Wakasa-wan ≈ 152-153 F 7
Wakasawan Quasi National Park ⊥ **J** 152-153 F 7
Wakatin o **RI** 166-167 D 3
Wakatipu, Lake o **NZ** 182 B 6
Wakaw o **CDN** (SAS) 232-233 N 3
Wakay o **SME** 62-63 F 3
Wakaya ⌒ **FJI** 184 III b 2
Wakayama ☆ **J** 152-153 F 7
Wakde, Pulau ⌒ **RI** 166-167 K 2
Wakeeny o **USA** (KS) 262-263 G 5
Wakefield o **CDN** (QUE) 238-239 K 3
Wakefield o **NZ** 182 D 4
Wakefield o **USA** (MI) 270-271 J 4
Wakefield o **USA** (NE) 262-263 K 2
Wakefield o **USA** (RI) 278-279 K 7
Wakefield o **USA** (VA) 280-281 K 7
Wakefield River ~ **AUS** 180-181 E 3
Wake Forest o **USA** (NC) 282-283 J 5
Wakeham, Rivière ~ **CDN** 36-37 N 4
Wakeman River ~ **CDN** (BC) 230-231 C 2
Wakingku o **RI** 164-165 H 6
Wakinosawa o **J** 152-153 J 4
Wakkanai o **J** 152-153 J 2
Wakkerstrom o **ZA** 220-221 K 3
Waklarok o **USA** 20-21 H 5
Wako o **PNG** 183 E 4
Wakomata Lake o **CDN** (ONT) 238-239 B 2
Wakonassin River ~ **CDN** (ONT) 238-239 C 2
Wakonda o **USA** (SD) 260-261 J 3
Wakoo o **AUS** 180-181 H 3
Wakool River ~ **AUS** 180-181 G 3
Wakopa o **CDN** (MAN) 234-235 D 5
Wakulla Springs · **USA** (FL) 286-287 E 1
Wakunai o **PNG** 184 I b 1
Wakusimi River ~ **CDN** (ONT) 236-237 F 4
Wakwayokwastic River ~ **CDN** (ONT) 236-237 H 3
Wala ~ **EAT** 212-213 D 6
Walachia ∸ **RO** 102-103 D 6
Wālājāpet o **IND** 140-141 H 4
Walakpa o **USA** 20-21 M 1
Walambele o **GH** 202-203 K 4
Wálamo, El o **MEX** 50-51 F 6
Walanae ~ **RI** 164-165 G 6
Wal Athiang o **SUD** 206-207 J 5
Wałbrzych ☆ · **PL** 92-93 O 3
Walbundrie o **AUS** 180-181 J 3
Walcha o **AUS** 178-179 L 6
Walckenaer, Teluk ≈ 166-167 K 3
Walcott o **CDN** (BC) 228-229 H 2
Walcott o **USA** (WY) 252-253 M 5
Walcott Inlet ≈ 172-173 G 4
Wałcz o · **PL** 92-93 O 2
Waldburg o **AUS** 176-177 D 2
Waldburg Range ▲ **AUS** 176-177 D 2
Waldeck o **CDN** (SAS) 232-233 L 5
Walden o **CDN** (ONT) 238-239 D 2
Walden o **USA** (CO) 254-255 J 3
Walden o **USA** (NY) 280-281 M 2
Waldenburg o **USA** (AR) 276-277 E 5
Walden Ridge ▲ **USA** (TN) 276-277 K 5
Waldersee o **CDN** (MAN) 234-235 D 4
Waldheim o **CDN** (SAS) 232-233 M 3
Waldo o **USA** (AR) 276-277 B 7
Waldo o **USA** (FL) 286-287 G 2
Waldo o **USA** (OH) 280-281 C 3
Waldorf o **USA** (MD) 280-281 K 5
Waldport o **USA** (OR) 244-245 A 6
Waldron o **CDN** (SAS) 232-233 Q 5
Waldron o **USA** (AR) 276-277 A 6
Walea, Selat ≈ 164-165 H 4
Waleabahi, Pulau ⌒ **RI** 164-165 H 4
Waleakodi, Pulau ⌒ **RI** 164-165 H 4
Waleri o **RI** 168 D 3
Wales □ **GB** 90-91 E 5
Wales o **USA** 20-21 F 4
Wales o **USA** (UT) 254-255 D 4
Wales Island ⌒ **CDN** 24-25 c 6
Wales Island ⌒ **CDN** (BC) 228-229 D 2
Walewale o **GH** 202-203 K 4
Walfe, Chute ~ **ZRE** 210-211 J 6
Walgett o **AUS** 178-179 K 6
Walgra o **AUS** 178-179 E 1
Walgreen Coast ⌣ **ARK** 16 F 26
Walhalla o **USA** (MI) 272-273 C 4
Walhalla o **USA** (ND) 258-259 K 3
Walhalla o **USA** (SC) 284-285 G 2
Walhalla Historic Site ∴ **USA** (ND) 258-259 K 3
Walikale o **ZRE** 212-213 B 4
Walir, Pulau ⌒ **RI** 166-167 G 4
Walis Island ⌒ **PNG** 183 B 2
Walk = Valga ☆ ·· **EST** 94-95 K 3
Walker o **USA** (IA) 274-275 G 2
Walker o **USA** (MI) 272-273 D 4
Walker o **USA** (MN) 270-271 D 3
Walker o **USA** (SD) 260-261 E 1
Walker, Mount ▲ **CDN** 24-25 Z 4
Walker Baldwin Range ▲ **CDN** 24-25 S 3
Walker Bay ≈ 24-25 N 5
Walker Bay ≈ 220-221 D 7
Walker Creek ~ **AUS** 176-177 M 2
Walker Lake o **CDN** (MAN) 34-35 H 3
Walker Lake o **CDN** (NWT) 30-31 Y 2
Walker Lake o **USA** (AK) 20-21 N 3
Walker Lake o **USA** (NV) 246-247 G 5
Walker Mountains ▲ **ARK** 16 F 26
Walker Pass ▲ **USA** (CA) 248-249 F 4
Walker River ~ **AUS** 174-175 C 3
Walker River ~ **USA** (NV) 246-247 F 5
Walker River Indian Reservation X **USA** (NV) 246-247 G 4
Walkerston o **AUS** 178-179 K 1
Walkerton o **CDN** (ONT) 238-239 D 4
Walkerton o **USA** (IN) 274-275 M 3
Walkerville o **AUS** 180-181 H 5
Walkerville o **USA** (MI) 272-273 C 4
Wall o **USA** (SD) 260-261 D 2
Wall o **USA** (TX) 266-267 G 2
Wall, Mount ▲ **AUS** 172-173 C 7
Wallabi Group ⌒ **AUS** 176-177 B 4
Wallace o **CDN** (NS) 240-241 M 5
Wallace o **USA** (ID) 250-251 D 4
Wallace o **USA** (NC) 282-283 K 6
Wallace o **USA** (NE) 262-263 E 4
Wallaceburg o **CDN** (ONT) 238-239 C 6
Wallace River o **CDN** 30-31 W 5
Wallachisch Meseritsch = Valašské Meziříčí o **CZ** 92-93 O 4
Wallal Downs o **AUS** 172-173 E 5
Wallambin, L. o **AUS** 176-177 D 5
Wallam Creek ~ **AUS** 178-179 J 5
Wallareenya o **AUS** 172-173 D 6
Wallaroo o **AUS** 180-181 D 2

Virgin Islands — Wallaroo 409

Walla Walla o USA (WA) 244-245 G 4
Wallekraal o ZA 220-221 C 5
Wallenpaupack, Lake ⊂ USA (PA) 280-281 L 2
Wallhallow o AUS 174-175 C 5
Wallingford o USA (VT) 278-279 J 5
Wallis o USA (TX) 266-267 L 4
Walliser Alpen ▲ CH 92-93 J 5
Wallis Lake ⊂ AUS 180-181 M 2
Wallkill River ∼ USA (NY) 280-281 M 2
Walløe, Kap ▲ GRØ 28-29 T 6
Wallonie ◘ B 92-93 H 3
Wallowa o USA (OR) 244-245 H 5
Wallowa Mountains ▲ USA (OR) 244-245 H 5
Walls of China, The • AUS 180-181 G 2
Wallula o USA (WA) 244-245 G 4
Wallumbilla o AUS 178-179 K 4
Walmanpa-Warlpiri Aboriginal Land ✕ AUS 172-173 K 5
Walnut o USA (CA) 248-249 B 2
Walnut o USA (IL) 274-275 J 3
Walnut o USA (MS) 268-269 M 2
Walnut Canyon National Monument ∴ USA (AZ) 256-257 D 3
Walnut Cove o USA (NC) 282-283 G 4
Walnut Creek o USA (AZ) 256-257 C 4
Walnut Creek ∼ USA (KS) 262-263 G 6
Walnut Grove o USA (MN) 270-271 C 6
Walnut Grove o USA (MO) 276-277 B 3
Walnut Grove o USA (TN) 276-277 G 5
Walnut Hill o USA (AL) 284-285 E 4
Walnut Ridge o USA (AR) 276-277 E 4
Walnut River ∼ USA (KS) 262-263 J 7
Walparous o CDN (ALB) 232-233 D 4
Walpeup o AUS 180-181 G 3
Walpole o AUS 176-177 D 7
Walpole o CDN (SAS) 232-233 R 6
Walpole Island Indian Reserve ✕ CDN (ONT) 238-239 C 6
Walrus Island ⌒ USA 22-23 Q 4
Walrus Islands ⌒ USA 22-23 Q 3
Walrus Islands State Game Sanctuary ⊥ USA 22-23 Q 3
Walsall o GB 90-91 G 5
Walsenburg o USA (CO) 254-255 L 6
Walsh o CDN (ALB) 232-233 H 6
Walsh o USA (CO) 254-255 N 6
Walsh River ∼ AUS 174-175 H 5
Walsingham, Cape ▲ CDN 28-29 K 3
Walsrode o D 92-93 K 2
Walterboro o USA (SC) 284-285 K 4
Walterhill o USA (TN) 276-277 J 5
Walter James Range ▲ AUS 176-177 K 2
Walters o USA (OK) 264-265 F 4
Waltershausen Gletscher ⊂ GRØ 26-27 n 6
Walthall o USA (MS) 268-269 L 3
Waltham Station o CDN (QUE) 238-239 J 3
Walthill o USA (NE) 262-263 K 2
Waltman o USA (WY) 252-253 L 3
Walton o CDN (NS) 240-241 L 5
Walton o USA (IN) 274-275 M 4
Walton o USA (KY) 276-277 L 2
Walton o USA (NY) 278-279 F 6
Walton, Mount ▲ AUS 176-177 F 5
Walue o RI 164-165 H 6
Walungu o ZRE 212-213 B 5
Walvisbaai ≈ 220-221 B 1
Walvisbaai = Walvis Bay ✩• NAM 220-221 B 1
Walvis Bay ✩• NAM 220-221 B 1
Walvis Ridge ≃ 6-7 K 11
Walworth o USA (WI) 274-275 K 2
Wamal o RI 166-167 K 6
Wamala, Lake ⊂ EAU 212-213 C 3
Wamanfo o GH 202-203 J 6
Wamar, Pulau ⌒ RI 166-167 H 4
Wamaza o ZRE 210-211 L 6
Wamba o EAK 212-213 F 3
Wamba ⩦ WAN 204-205 H 4
Wamba o ZRE 212-213 B 2
Wamba ∼ ZRE 216-217 D 3
Wamba-Luadi o ZRE 216-217 D 3
Wamba Mountains ▲ WAN 204-205 J 5
Wamdé Tabal ▲ BF 202-203 K 2
Wamego o USA (KS) 262-263 K 5
Wamena o RI 166-167 K 4
Wamera Island ⌒ PNG 183 F 5
Wami ∼ EAT 214-215 K 4
Wamis o LAR 192-193 E 2
Wamoi Falls ∼ PNG 183 B 4
Wamonket, Tanjung ▲ RI 166-167 F 2
Wampembe o EAT 214-215 F 4
Wamsutter o USA (WY) 252-253 L 5
Wamtakin, Mount ▲ PNG 183 A 3
Wāna o PK 138-139 B 3
Wanaaring o AUS 178-179 H 5
Wanaka o NZ 182 B 6
Wanaka, Lake ⊂ NZ 182 B 6
Wanapitae Lake ⊂ CDN (ONT) 238-239 E 2
Wanapitei o CDN (ONT) 238-239 E 2
Wanapitei River ∼ CDN (ONT) 236-237 G 5
Wanapitei River ∼ CDN (ONT) 238-239 E 2
Wanasabari o RI 164-165 H 6
Wanau o RI 166-167 G 2
Wanblee o USA (SD) 260-261 E 3
Wanbu o VRC 156-157 J 2
Wanci o RI 164-165 H 6
Wandagee o AUS 176-177 C 1
Wandai (Homeyo) o RI 166-167 J 3
Wandamen, Teluk ≈ 166-167 H 3
Wandamen Peninsula ⌒ RI 166-167 H 3
Wanda Shan ▲ VRC 150-151 H 5
Wandel, Kap ▲ GRØ 28-29 X 3
Wandering River ∼ CDN 32-33 O 4
Wanderlândia o BR 68-69 E 5
Wanding o VRC 142-143 L 3
Wando o PNG 183 A 5
Wando o ROK 150-151 F 10
Wandoan o AUS 178-179 K 4
Wandokai o PNG 183 D 4
Wanesabe o RI 168 C 7
Waneta o CDN (BC) 230-231 M 4
Wanfotang Shiku • VRC 150-151 C 7
Wang o PNG 183 G 2
Wanga o ZRE 212-213 B 2
Wanga Mountains ▲ WAN 204-205 J 5
Wanganui o NZ 182 E 3
Wanganui River ∼ NZ 182 E 3
Wangaratta o AUS 180-181 J 4
Wangary o AUS 180-181 C 3
Wangasi-Turu o GH 202-203 K 5
Wangcang o VRC 154-155 E 5
Wangcheng o VRC 156-157 H 2
Wangdi Phodrang o BHT 142-143 F 2
Wangerooge ⌒ D 92-93 J 2
Wanggamet, Gunung ▲ RI 168 E 8
Wanggao o VRC 156-157 G 4
Wanggar o RI 166-167 H 3
Wanggar ∼ RI 166-167 H 3
Wangi o AUS 172-173 K 2
Wāngi o IND 138-139 E 10
Wangianna o AUS 178-179 D 5
Wangiwangi, Pulau ⌒ RI 164-165 H 6
Wangjiang o VRC 154-155 K 6
Wangjie o VRC 156-157 B 5
Wangkí, Río = Coco o Segovia ∼ HN 52-53 B 4
Wangmo o VRC 156-157 E 4
Wang Nam Yen o THA 158-159 G 4
Wangon o RI 168 C 3
Wangpan Yang ≈ 154-155 M 6
Wang Sam Mo o THA 158-159 G 2
Wang Saphung o THA 158-159 F 2
Wang Thong o THA 158-159 F 2
Wang Wiset o THA 158-159 E 7
Wangziguan o VRC 154-155 D 5
Wanham o CDN 32-33 L 4
Wan Hsa-la o MYA 142-143 L 5
Wanhuayan • VRC 156-157 H 4
Wani o IND 138-139 G 9
Wanie-Rukula o ZRE 210-211 K 3
Wanigela o PNG 183 E 5
Wānkāner o IND 138-139 C 8
Wanless o CDN 34-35 F 3
Wanleweeyn o SP 212-213 K 2
Wan Long o MYA 142-143 L 4
Wanlong o VRC 154-155 E 6
Wanna o AUS 176-177 D 1
Wanna Lakes ⊂ AUS 176-177 K 4
Wannarra o AUS 176-177 D 4
Wannaska o USA (MN) 270-271 C 2
Wannian o VRC 156-157 K 2
Wannian Temple o VRC 156-157 C 2
Wannianxue ▲ VRC 154-155 C 6
Wanning o VRC 156-157 G 7
Wannon River ∼ AUS 180-181 F 4
Wannoo o AUS 176-177 C 3
Wanparti o IND 140-141 H 2
Wan Pong o MYA 142-143 L 5
Wanqing o VRC 150-151 G 6
Wanshan Qundao ⌒ VRC 156-157 J 6
Wansra o RI 166-167 H 2
Wantang o VRC 156-157 C 5
Wantoat o PNG 183 D 4
Wan Xian o VRC 154-155 F 6
Wanyuan o VRC 154-155 F 5
Wanzai o VRC 156-157 J 2
Waogena o RI 164-165 H 6
Wapah o CDN (MAN) 234-235 E 3
Wapakoneta o USA (OH) 280-281 B 3
Wapanucka o USA (OK) 264-265 H 4
Wapaseese River ∼ CDN 34-35 L 3
Wapato o USA (WA) 244-245 E 4
Wapawekka Hills ▲ CDN 34-35 D 3
Wapawekka Lake ⊂ CDN 34-35 D 3
Wapella o CDN (SAS) 232-233 R 5
Wapello o USA (IA) 274-275 G 3
Wapenamanda o PNG 183 B 3
Wapet Camp o AUS 172-173 B 6
Wāpi o IND 138-139 D 9
Wapikopa Lake ⊂ CDN (ONT) 234-235 P 2
Wapi Pathum o THA 158-159 G 3
Wapiti o CDN (ALB) 228-229 P 2
Wapiti o USA (WY) 252-253 J 2
Wapoga ∼ RI 166-167 J 3
Wapomaru o RI 164-165 H 6
Wapotih o RI 166-167 D 3
Wappapello o USA (MO) 276-277 E 4
Wappapello, Lake ⊂ USA (MO) 276-277 E 4
Waprak o RI 166-167 H 3
Wapsipinicon River ∼ USA (IA) 274-275 G 2
Wapta Icefield ⊂ CDN (ALB) 232-233 B 4
Wapuli o GH 202-203 L 5
Wapumba Island ⌒ PNG 183 B 5
Waputik Icefield ⊂ CDN (ALB) 232-233 B 4
Wara o WAN 204-205 F 3
Waradi ‹ EAK 212-213 H 3
Warakaraket, Pulau ⌒ RI 166-167 F 3
Warakurna ✕ AUS 176-177 K 2
Warambif o PNG 183 G 3
Warandab o ETH 208-209 G 5
Waranga Basin ‹ AUS 180-181 H 4
Warangal o• IND 138-139 G 10
Wararisbari, Tanjung ▲ RI 166-167 J 2
Waratah o AUS 180-181 H 6
Wara Wara Mountains. ▲ WAL 202-203 E 5
Warbreccan o AUS 178-179 G 3
Warburg o CDN (ALB) 232-233 D 2
Warburton o AUS (VIC) 180-181 H 4
Warburton ✕ AUS (WA) 176-177 J 3
Warburton o ZA 220-221 K 3
Warburton Creek ∼ AUS 178-179 E 4
Warburton Range ▲ AUS 176-177 J 3
Warburton Range Aboriginal Land ✕ AUS 176-177 J 2
Ward o NZ 182 E 4
Warda o USA (TX) 266-267 L 3
Wardak ◘ AFG 138-139 B 2
Wardang Island ⌒ AUS 180-181 D 3
Ward Cove o USA 32-33 E 4
Wardé o RMM 202-203 G 2
Warden o USA (WA) 244-245 F 4
Warden o ZA 220-221 J 3
Wardha o IND (MAH) 138-139 G 9
Wardha ∼ IND 138-139 G 9
Wardha ∼ IND 138-139 G 10
War Dhugulle ‹ SP 212-213 K 2
Ward Hunt, Cape ▲ PNG 183 E 5
Ward Hunt Island ⌒ CDN 26-27 N 2
Ward Hunt Strait ≈ 183 F 5
Ward Inlet ≈ 36-37 Q 3
Wardlaw, Kap ▲ GRØ 26-27 p 8
Wardlow o CDN (ALB) 232-233 G 5
Wardner o CDN (BC) 230-231 O 4
Wardo o RI 166-167 H 2
Ware o CDN 32-33 H 3
Wareham o USA (MA) 278-279 L 7
Waren o RI 166-167 J 3
Waren ∼ RI 166-167 J 3
Waren (Müritz) o• D 92-93 M 2
Warenda o AUS 178-179 F 2
Wares Crossroads o USA (VA) 280-281 J 5
Warfallah, Ra's ▲ LAR 192-193 F 3
War Galoh o SP 208-209 H 5
Wariai, Tanjung ▲ RI 166-167 F 2
Warialda o AUS 178-179 L 5
Waria River ∼ PNG 183 D 4
Wāri Godri o IND 138-139 E 10
Wari Island ⌒ PNG 183 F 6
Warilau o RI 166-167 H 4
Warilau, Pulau ⌒ RI 166-167 H 4
Warin Chamrap o THA 158-159 H 3
Waring Mountains ▲ USA 20-21 K 3
Wario River ∼ PNG 183 B 3
Wāris Aliganj o IND 142-143 D 3
Warkopi o RI 166-167 H 2
Warkworth o NZ 182 E 2
Warman o CDN (SAS) 232-233 M 3
Warmandi o RI 166-167 G 2
Warmbad o NAM 220-221 D 4
Warmbad o ZA 220-221 J 2
Warm Baths = Warmbad o ZA 220-221 J 2
Warm Creek Ranch o USA (NV) 246-247 K 3
Warming Land ⩦ GRØ 26-27 Y 3
Warminster o USA (PA) 280-281 L 3
Warm Springs o USA (NV) 246-247 J 5
Warm Springs o USA (OR) 244-245 D 6
Warm Springs o USA (VA) 280-281 G 5
Warm Springs Indian Reservation ✕ USA (OR) 244-245 D 6
Warnemünde o D 92-93 M 1
Warner o CDN (ALB) 232-233 F 6
Warner o USA (OK) 264-265 J 3
Warner o USA (SD) 260-261 H 1
Warner Pass ▲ USA (OR) 244-245 E 8
Warner Range ▲ USA (CA) 246-247 E 2
Warner Robins o USA (GA) 284-285 G 4
Warner Springs o USA (CA) 248-249 H 6
Warnes o RA 78-79 J 3
Warning, Mount ▲ AUS 178-179 M 5
Warnock o USA (KY) 276-277 N 2
Warnow ∼ D 92-93 L 2
Waromge, Teluk ≈ 166-167 F 2
Warooka o AUS 180-181 D 3
Waroona o AUS 176-177 C 6
Waropen, Teluk ≈ 166-167 J 2
Waropko o RI 166-167 L 4
Warora o IND 138-139 G 9
Warra o AUS 178-179 L 4
Warrabri ✕ AUS 178-179 C 1
Warracknabeal o AUS 180-181 G 4
Warragul o AUS 180-181 H 5
Warrakalanna, Lake ⊂ AUS 178-179 E 5
Warrakunta Point ▲ AUS 174-175 C 4
Warralakin o AUS 176-177 E 5
Warral Island ⌒ AUS 183 B 6
Warrandirinna, Lake ⊂ AUS 178-179 D 4
Warrawagine o AUS 172-173 E 6
Warrego Highway II AUS 178-179 J 4
Warrego Mine • AUS 174-175 B 6
Warrego Range ▲ AUS 178-179 H 3
Warrego River ∼ AUS 178-179 H 4
Warren o AUS 178-179 J 6
Warren o CDN (MAN) 234-235 F 4
Warren o USA (AR) 276-277 C 7
Warren o USA (AZ) 256-257 F 7
Warren o USA (ID) 250-251 D 6
Warren o USA (IL) 274-275 H 2
Warren o USA (IN) 274-275 N 4
Warren o USA (MI) 272-273 F 5
Warren o USA (MN) 270-271 B 2
Warren o USA (MT) 250-251 L 6
Warren o USA (NH) 278-279 K 5
Warren o USA (OH) 280-281 F 2
Warren o USA (PA) 280-281 G 2
Warren o USA (TX) 268-269 F 6
Warrendale o USA (PA) 280-281 F 3
Warrender, Port o AUS 172-173 G 3
Warren Point ▲ CDN 20-21 Y 2
Warrensburg o USA (MO) 274-275 E 6
Warrensburg o USA (NY) 278-279 H 5
Warrens Landing o CDN 34-35 H 4
Warrenton o USA (GA) 284-285 H 3
Warrenton o USA (OR) 244-245 B 4
Warrenton o USA (VA) 280-281 J 5
Warrenton o ZA 220-221 G 4
Warren Vale o AUS 174-175 F 6
Warri o WAN 204-205 F 6
Warriedar o AUS 176-177 D 4
Warriedar Hill ▲ AUS 176-177 D 4
Warriner Creek ∼ AUS 178-179 D 5
Warrington o USA (FL) 286-287 B 1
Warrington Bay ≈ 24-25 N 3
Warrior o USA (AL) 284-285 D 3
Warrior Creek ∼ USA (GA) 284-285 G 5
Warrior Reefs ⌒ AUS 174-175 G 2
Warri River ∼ WAN 204-205 F 6
Warri Warri Creek ∼ AUS 178-179 F 5
Warrnambool o AUS 180-181 G 5
Warroad o USA (MN) 270-271 C 2
Warrumbungle National Park ⊥ AUS 178-179 K 6
Warrumbungle Range ▲ AUS 178-179 K 6
Warruwi ✕ AUS 174-175 B 2
Warsa o RI 166-167 H 2
Warsaw o USA (IN) 274-275 N 3
Warsaw o USA (KY) 276-277 L 2
Warsaw o USA (MO) 274-275 E 6
Warsaw o USA (NC) 282-283 J 6
Warsaw o USA (NY) 278-279 C 6
Warsaw = Warszawa ★••• PL 92-93 Q 2
Warshi o IND 138-139 F 10
Warshiikh o SP 212-213 K 2
Warszawa ★••• PL 92-93 Q 2
Warta ∼ PL 92-93 O 2
Wartburg o USA (TN) 282-283 C 4
Wartime o CDN (SAS) 232-233 K 4
Warton, Monte ▲ RCH 80 D 6
Waru o RI (JTI) 168 E 3
Waru o RI (KTI) 164-165 E 4
Waru o RI (MAL) 166-167 F 3
Warud o IND 138-139 G 9
Waruta ∼ RI 166-167 L 3
Warwick o AUS 178-179 L 5
Warwick o CDN (ALB) 232-233 F 2
Warwick ✩• GB 90-91 G 5
Warwick o USA (GA) 284-285 G 5
Warwick o USA (ND) 258-259 J 4
Warwick o USA (NY) 280-281 M 2
Warwick o USA (OK) 264-265 H 3
Warwick Channel ≈ 174-175 D 4
Warwick Downs O.S. o AUS 178-179 E 1
Waryori ∼ RI 166-167 G 2
Warzazāt = Ouarzazate ✩ MA 188-189 H 5
Wasa o CDN (BC) 230-231 O 4
Wasaga Beach o CDN (ONT) 238-239 E 4
Wasagaming o CDN (MAN) 234-235 D 4
Wasagu o WAN 204-205 F 3
Wasai o RI 166-167 F 2
Wasalangka o RI 164-165 H 6
Wasatch Plateau ▲ USA (UT) 254-255 D 4
Wasatch Range ▲ USA (ID) 252-253 G 4
Wasatch Range ▲ USA (UT) 254-255 D 4
Wasco o USA (CA) 248-249 E 4
Wasco o USA (OR) 244-245 E 5
Wase o WAN 204-205 H 4
Wase, River ∼ WAN 204-205 H 4
Waseca o CDN (SAS) 232-233 J 2
Waseca o USA (MN) 270-271 E 6
Wasel o CDN (ALB) 232-233 F 2
Washackie Wilderness Area ⊥ USA (WY) 252-253 J 3
Washago o CDN (ONT) 238-239 F 4
Washakie Needles ▲ USA (WY) 252-253 J 3
Washāp o PK 134-135 K 5
Washburn o USA (ME) 278-279 N 2
Washburn o USA (ND) 258-259 G 4
Washburn o USA (TX) 264-265 C 3
Washburn o USA (WI) 270-271 H 4
Washburne Lake ⊂ CDN 24-25 S 5
Washi Lake ⊂ CDN (ONT) 234-235 Q 3
Wāshim o IND 138-139 F 9
Washington o USA (AR) 276-277 B 7
Washington o USA (GA) 284-285 H 3
Washington o USA (IA) 274-275 G 3
Washington o USA (IL) 274-275 J 4
Washington o USA (IN) 274-275 L 6
Washington o USA (KS) 262-263 J 5
Washington o USA (MO) 274-275 G 6
Washington o USA (MS) 268-269 J 5
Washington o USA (NC) 282-283 K 5
Washington o USA (NE) 262-263 K 3
Washington o USA (NJ) 280-281 M 3
Washington o USA (OH) 280-281 C 4
Washington o USA (PA) 280-281 F 3
Washington o USA (UT) 254-255 B 6
Washington o USA (WI) 270-271 M 5
Washington ◘ USA (WA) 244-245 B 4
Washington ★• USA (DC) 280-281 J 5
Washington, Mount ▲ USA (NH) 278-279 K 4
Washington/ Slagbaai, National Reservaat ⊥ NL 60-61 G 1
Washington Birthplace National Monument, George • USA (VA) 280-281 K 5
Washington Island ⌒ USA (WI) 270-271 M 5
Washington Land ⩦ GRØ 26-27 R 3
Washington National Monument, Booker T. • USA (VA) 280-281 G 6
Washington Pass ▲ USA (WA) 244-245 E 2
Washita o USA (AR) 276-277 B 6
Washita, Fort ∴ USA (OK) 264-265 H 4
Washita River ∼ USA (OK) 264-265 G 4
Washita River ∼ USA (TX) 264-265 D 3
Washougal o USA (WA) 244-245 C 5
Washow Bay ⊂ CDN (MAN) 234-235 G 3
Washowng ✩ MYA 142-143 K 3
Washpool National Park ⊥ AUS 178-179 M 5
Washtucna o USA (WA) 244-245 G 4
Wāshūk o PK 134-135 L 5
Wasian o RI 166-167 G 2
Wasile o RI 164-165 K 3
Wasilla o USA 20-21 Q 6
Wasimi o WAN 204-205 E 4
Wasini Island ⌒ EAK 212-213 G 6
Wasini Marine National Park ⊥ EAK 212-213 G 6
Wāsiqa, al- o KSA 132-133 B 4
Wasir, Pulau ⌒ RI 166-167 H 4
Wāsiṭ ◘ IRQ 128-129 L 6
Wāsiṭ ∴• IRQ 128-129 M 6
Wāsiṭa, al- o KSA 130-131 F 6
Waskaganish = Fort Rupert o CDN 38-39 E 3
Waskahigan River ∼ CDN (ALB) 228-229 R 2
Waskaiowaka Lake ⊂ CDN 34-35 H 2
Waskesiu Lake o CDN (SAS) 232-233 M 2
Waskesiu Lake ⊂ CDN (SAS) 232-233 M 2
Waskom o USA (TX) 264-265 K 6
Wasletan o RI 166-167 F 5
Wasola o USA (MO) 276-277 C 4
Waspam o NIC 52-53 B 4
Waspuk, Río ∼ NIC 52-53 B 4
Wassadou o SN 202-203 C 3
Wassamu o J 152-153 K 2
Wassaw Island ⌒ USA (GA) 284-285 K 5
Wassaw Sound ≈ USA 284-285 K 5
Wasserburg am Inn o D 92-93 M 4
Wassou o RG 202-203 D 4
Wasta o USA (SD) 260-261 D 2
Wasu o PNG 183 D 3
Wasua o PNG 183 B 5
Wasum o PNG 183 E 4
Waswanipi o CDN (ONT) 236-237 M 3
Waswanipi, Lac ⊂ CDN (QUE) 236-237 M 3
Waswanipi, Rivière ∼ CDN (QUE) 236-237 M 3
Waswanipi Indian Réserve ✕ CDN (QUE) 236-237 M 3
Wata o RI 164-165 G 5
Waṭā, al- ⩦ OM 132-133 K 3
Watalgan o AUS 178-179 M 3
Watam o PNG 183 C 2
Watam o RI 164-165 L 3
Watambayoli o RI 164-165 G 4
Watampone o RI 164-165 G 6
Watamu Marine National Park ⊥ EAK 212-213 G 5
Watansoppeng o RI 164-165 F 6
Watar o IND 140-141 E 2
Watarais o PNG 183 D 4
Watarrka National Park ⊥•• AUS 176-177 L 2
Wataugа Lake ⊂ USA (TN) 282-283 F 4
Watawa o RI 166-167 D 3
Watee o SOL 184 I f 4
Waterberge ▲ ZA 220-221 H 2
Waterberg Plateau Park ⊥ NAM 216-217 D 10
Waterbury o USA (CT) 280-281 N 2
Waterbury o USA (VT) 278-279 J 4
Waterbury Lake ⊂ CDN 30-31 R 6
Water Cay ⌒ BS 54-55 H 3
Water Cay ⌒ GB 54-55 J 4
Wateree Lake ‹ USA (SC) 284-285 K 2
Wateree River ∼ USA (SC) 284-285 K 2
Waterford o AUS 178-179 E 2
Waterford o ZA 220-221 G 6
Waterford = Port Láirge ✩• IRL 90-91 D 5
Waterfound River ∼ CDN 30-31 R 6
Watergap o USA (KY) 276-277 N 3
Waterhen o CDN (MAN) 234-235 D 3
Waterhen Indian Reserve ✕ CDN (MAN) 234-235 D 3
Waterhen Lake ⊂ CDN (MAN) 234-235 D 2
Waterhen Lake ⊂ CDN (SAS) 32-33 Q 4
Waterhen River ∼ CDN 32-33 Q 4
Waterhouse River ∼ AUS 174-175 B 4
Waterloo o AUS 172-173 J 4
Waterloo o B 92-93 H 3
Waterloo o CDN (ONT) 238-239 E 5
Waterloo o CDN (QUE) 238-239 N 3
Waterloo o USA (AL) 284-285 B 2
Waterloo o USA (IA) 274-275 F 2
Waterloo o USA (IL) 274-275 H 6
Waterloo o USA (NY) 278-279 E 6
Waterloo o WAL 202-203 D 5
Waterman o USA (OR) 244-245 G 5
Waterpoort o ZA 218-219 E 6
Waterproof o USA (LA) 268-269 J 5
Waters o USA (MI) 272-273 E 3
Watersmeet o USA (MI) 270-271 J 4
Waterton Glacier International Peace Park ⊥ USA (MT) 250-251 E 3
Waterton Lakes National Park ⊥ CDN (ALB) 232-233 D 6
Waterton Park o CDN (ALB) 232-233 E 6
Waterton River ∼ CDN (ALB) 232-233 E 6
Watertown o USA (MN) 270-271 E 6
Watertown o USA (NY) 278-279 F 5
Watertown o USA (SD) 260-261 J 2
Watertown o USA (TN) 276-277 J 4
Watertown o USA (WI) 274-275 K 1
Waterval-Boven o• ZA 220-221 K 2
Water Valley o CDN (ALB) 232-233 D 4
Water Valley o USA (MS) 268-269 L 2
Water Valley o USA (TX) 266-267 G 2
Waterville o CDN (QUE) 238-239 O 3
Waterville o USA (KS) 262-263 K 5
Waterville o USA (ME) 278-279 M 4
Waterville o USA (MN) 270-271 E 6
Waterville o USA (WA) 244-245 E 3
Waterville = An Coireán o IRL 90-91 B 6
Watervliet o USA (MI) 272-273 C 5
Watford o CDN (ONT) 238-239 D 6
Watford o GB 90-91 G 6
Watford City o USA (ND) 258-259 D 4
Wathaman Lake ⊂ CDN 34-35 D 2
Watheroo o AUS 176-177 D 5
Watheroo National Park ⊥ AUS 176-177 C 5
Watino o CDN 32-33 M 4
Watkin Bjerge ▲ GRØ 28-29 a 2
Watkins Glen o USA (NY) 278-279 E 6
Watkinsville o USA (GA) 284-285 G 3
Watkins Woolen Mill State Historic Site • USA (MO) 274-275 D 5
Watmuri o RI 166-167 F 5
Watnil o RI 166-167 G 4
Watoa Island ⌒ PNG 183 F 5
Watom Island ⌒ PNG 183 G 3
Watonga o USA (OK) 264-265 F 3
Watpi o PNG 183 G 3
Watri o RMM 202-203 F 2
Watrous o CDN (SAS) 232-233 N 4
Watrous o USA (NM) 256-257 L 3
Watrupun o RI 166-167 E 5
Watsa o ZRE 212-213 B 2
Watseka o USA (IL) 274-275 L 4
Watsi o ZRE 210-211 H 4
Watsikengo o ZRE 210-211 H 4
Watson o AUS 176-177 L 5
Watson o CDN (SAS) 232-233 O 3
Watson o USA (AR) 276-277 D 7
Watson Lake o CDN 30-31 E 5
Watson River ∼ AUS 174-175 F 3
Watsonville o USA (CA) 248-249 C 3
Watt, Mount ▲ CDN (BC) 228-229 O 4
Watta, Hiré- o CI 202-203 H 6
Wattegama o CL 140-141 J 7
Watterson Lake ⊂ CDN 30-31 U 5
Watt Hills ▲ AUS 176-177 F 5
Wattiwarriganna Creek ∼ AUS 178-179 C 5
Watts Bar Lake ⊂ USA (TN) 282-283 C 5
Wattsview o CDN (MAN) 234-235 B 4
Wattsville o USA (VA) 280-281 L 6
Watubela, Kepulauan ⌒ RI 166-167 F 4
Watukebo, Tanjung ▲ RI 168 G 4
Watumanuk, Tanjung ▲ RI 168 E 7
Watumohai, Gunung ▲ RI 164-165 H 6
Watunea o RI 164-165 H 6
Watupati, Tanjung ▲ RI 166-167 E 6
Watutau o RI 164-165 G 4
Wau o PNG 183 D 4
Wau o RI 166-167 G 2
Wau o SUD 206-207 H 5
Wāu ∼ SUD 206-207 H 5
Waubaushene o CDN (ONT) 238-239 F 4
Waubay o USA (SD) 260-261 J 1
Waubra o AUS 180-181 G 4
Wauchope o AUS (NSW) 178-179 M 6
Wauchope o AUS (NT) 174-175 C 7
Wauchope o CDN (SAS) 232-233 R 6
Wauconda o USA (WA) 244-245 G 2
Waukaringa o AUS 180-181 E 2
Waukarlycarly, Lake ⊂ AUS 172-173 E 6
Waukegan o USA (IL) 274-275 L 2
Waukena o USA (CA) 248-249 E 3
Waukesha o USA (WI) 274-275 K 1
Waukon o USA (IA) 274-275 G 1
Wauneta o USA (NE) 262-263 E 4
Waupaca o USA (WI) 270-271 J 6
Waupun o USA (WI) 270-271 K 7
Waurika o USA (OK) 264-265 G 4
Waurika Lake ⊂ USA (OK) 264-265 F 4
Wausau o USA (WI) 270-271 J 6
Wausaukee o USA (WI) 270-271 L 5
Wautoma o USA (WI) 270-271 J 6
Wauwatosa o USA (WI) 274-275 K 1
Wave Hill o AUS 172-173 K 4
Waverley o CDN (NS) 240-241 M 6
Waverley Game Sanctuary ⊥ CDN (NS) 240-241 M 6
Waverly o USA (GA) 284-285 J 5
Waverly o USA (IA) 274-275 F 2
Waverly o USA (IL) 274-275 J 5
Waverly o USA (MO) 274-275 E 5
Waverly o USA (NE) 262-263 K 4
Waverly o USA (NY) 278-279 E 6
Waverly o USA (OH) 280-281 D 4
Waverly o USA (TN) 276-277 H 4
Waverly o USA (VA) 280-281 J 6
Waverly Hall o USA (GA) 284-285 F 4
Wave Rock •• AUS 176-177 E 6
Wawa o CDN (ONT) 236-237 D 5
Wawa o WAN 204-205 F 4
Wawa, Río = Río Huahua ∼ NIC 52-53 B 4
Wawagosic, Rivière ∼ CDN (QUE) 236-237 K 3
Wawalalindu o RI 164-165 H 5
Wāw al Kabir o LAR 192-193 G 5
Wawan o RP 160-161 D 6
Wawanesa o CDN (MAN) 234-235 D 5
Wawawai o USA (WA) 244-245 H 4
Wawiwa Island ⌒ PNG 183 F 5
Wawo o RI 164-165 G 5
Wawoi River ∼ PNG 183 B 4
Wawolandawe o RI 164-165 H 5
Waworada o RI 168 D 7
Waworada, Teluk ≈ 168 D 7
Wawota o CDN (SAS) 232-233 Q 6
Wawotobi o RI 164-165 H 5
Wawousu o RI 164-165 H 6
Waxahachie o USA (TX) 264-265 H 6
Waxxari o VRC 146-147 H 6
Way, Lake ⊂ AUS 176-177 F 3
Waya ⌒ FJI 184 III a 2
Wayabula o RI 164-165 L 2
Wayag, Pulau ⌒ RI 166-167 F 1
Wayamli o RI 164-165 L 3
Wayamli, Tanjung ▲ RI 164-165 L 3
Wayaua o RI 164-165 K 4
Waycross o USA (GA) 284-285 H 5
Wayerton o CDN (NB) 240-241 K 3
Waygay o RI (MAL) 164-165 J 4
Waygay o RI (MAL) 164-165 J 5
Wayhaya o RI 166-167 J 4
Waykadai o RI 164-165 J 4
Waykilo o RI 164-165 J 4
Wayland o USA (KY) 276-277 N 3
Wayland o USA (MI) 272-273 D 5
Wayland o USA (NY) 278-279 D 6
Wayne o CDN (ALB) 232-233 F 4
Wayne o USA (AL) 284-285 C 4
Wayne o USA (MI) 272-273 F 5
Wayne o USA (NE) 262-263 J 2
Wayne o USA (WV) 280-281 D 5
Wayne City o USA (IL) 274-275 K 6
Waynesboro o USA (GA) 284-285 H 3
Waynesboro o USA (MS) 268-269 M 5
Waynesboro o USA (PA) 280-281 J 4
Waynesboro o USA (TN) 276-277 H 5
Waynesboro o USA (VA) 280-281 H 5
Waynesburg o USA (KY) 276-277 L 3
Waynesburg o USA (PA) 280-281 F 4
Waynesville o USA (GA) 284-285 J 5
Waynesville o USA (MO) 276-277 C 3
Waynesville o USA (NC) 282-283 E 5
Waynoka o USA (OK) 264-265 F 2
Wayongon o MYA 142-143 J 3
Wayside o USA (NE) 262-263 C 2
Wayside o USA (VA) 280-281 J 6
Waza o CAM 206-207 B 3
Waza, Parc National de ⊥ CAM 206-207 B 3
Wāzaḥwa = Vāzahā o AFG 138-139 B 3
Wazān = Ouezzane o MA 188-189 J 3
Wāzin o LAR 190-191 H 5
Wazirābād o PK 138-139 E 3
W du Niger, Parc National du ⊥ BF 204-205 E 2
We o CAM 204-205 J 5
Weagamow Lake o CDN (ONT) 234-235 M 2
Weagamow Lake ⊂ CDN (ONT) 234-235 M 2
Weald o CDN (ALB) 232-233 B 2
Weam o PNG 183 A 5
Weasua o LB 202-203 E 6
Weatherall Bay ≈ 24-25 S 2
Weatherford o USA (OK) 264-265 F 3
Weatherford o USA (TX) 264-265 G 6
Weaton o USA (MD) 280-281 J 4
Weaver o USA (MN) 270-271 G 6
Weaver Lake ⊂ CDN (MAN) 234-235 G 2
Weaverville o USA (CA) 246-247 C 3
Weaverville o USA (NC) 282-283 E 5
Webb o CDN (SAS) 232-233 K 5
Webb o USA (TX) 266-267 H 6
Webb, Mount ▲ AUS 172-173 J 7
Webb City o USA (MO) 276-277 A 3
Webbers Falls Lake ‹ USA (OK) 264-265 J 3
Webb Gemstone Deposit • AUS 176-177 E 3
Webbville o USA (KY) 276-277 N 2
Webequie o CDN (ONT) 234-235 Q 2
Weber o NZ 182 F 4
Weber o USA (AR) 276-277 D 6
Webster o USA (MA) 278-279 K 6
Webster o USA (ND) 258-259 J 3
Webster o USA (NY) 278-279 D 5
Webster o USA (SD) 260-261 J 1
Webster City o USA (IA) 274-275 E 2
Webster Reservoir ⊂ USA (KS) 262-263 G 5
Webster Springs o USA (WV) 280-281 F 5
Webuye o EAK 212-213 E 3
Wech'echa ▲ ETH 208-209 D 4
Weches o USA (TX) 268-269 E 5
Wecho Lake ⊂ CDN 30-31 N 4
Wecho River ∼ CDN 30-31 M 4
Weda o RI 164-165 K 3
Weda, Teluk ≈ 164-165 L 3
Wedangkau o RI 166-167 F 5
Weddell Island ⌒ GB 78-79 K 6
Weddell Sea ≈ ARK 16 F 32
Wedderburn o AUS 180-181 G 4
Weddin Mountain National Park ⊥ AUS 180-181 K 2
Wedel Jarlsberg Land ⩦ N 84-85 J 4
Wedgefield o USA (SC) 284-285 K 3
Wedge Island ⌒ AUS 176-177 C 5
Wedge Mountain ▲ CDN (BC) 230-231 G 3
Wedge Point o CDN (NS) 240-241 K 7
Wednesday Island ⌒ AUS 183 B 6
Wedowee o USA (AL) 284-285 E 3
Weduar o RI 166-167 G 4
Weduar, Tanjung ▲ RI 166-167 G 4
Wedweil o SUD 206-207 H 4
Weebubbie Caves ⊥ AUS 176-177 K 5
Weed o USA (CA) 246-247 C 2
Weed o USA (NM) 256-257 K 6
Weed Patch Hill ▲ USA (IN) 274-275 M 5
Weedville o USA (PA) 280-281 H 2
Weeim, Pulau ⌒ RI 166-167 F 2
Weekes o CDN (SAS) 232-233 Q 3
Weeki Wachee Spring • USA (FL) 286-287 G 3
Weeks o USA (LA) 268-269 J 7
Weelarrana o AUS 176-177 F 1
Weelhamby Lake ⊂ AUS 176-177 D 4
Weemarie, Lake ⊂ AUS 178-179 E 3
Weenen o ZA 220-221 K 4
Weeping Water o USA (NE) 262-263 K 4
Weesatche o USA (TX) 266-267 K 5
Weethalle o AUS 180-181 J 2
Wee Waa o AUS 178-179 K 6
Wegdraai o ZA 220-221 E 4
Wegener-Inlandeis ⊂ ARK 16 F 36
Węgorzewo o• PL 92-93 Q 1
Weh, Pulau ⌒ RI 162-163 A 2
Wehni o ETH 200-201 H 6
Weichang o VRC 148-149 N 7
Weiden in der Oberpfalz o D 92-93 M 4
Weidman o USA (MI) 272-273 E 4
Weifang o VRC 154-155 L 3
Weihai o VRC 154-155 N 3
Wei He ∼ VRC 154-155 E 4
Wei He ∼ VRC 154-155 J 4
Weihui o VRC 154-155 J 4
Weila o GH 202-203 K 5
Weilmoringle o AUS 178-179 J 5
Weimar o•• D 92-93 L 3
Weimar o USA (TX) 266-267 L 4
Wein, Bur ▲ EAK 212-213 H 2
Weinan o VRC 154-155 F 4
Weiner o USA (AR) 276-277 E 5
Weinert o USA (TX) 264-265 E 5
Weining o VRC 156-157 D 3
Weipa o AUS 174-175 F 3
Weipa South ✕ AUS 174-175 F 3
Weirdale o CDN (SAS) 232-233 N 2
Weir River ∼ AUS 178-179 K 5
Weir River o CDN (MAN) 34-35 J 2
Weir River ∼ CDN 34-35 K 2
Weirton o USA (OH) 280-281 F 3
Weiser o USA (ID) 252-253 B 2
Weiser River ∼ USA (ID) 252-253 B 2
Weishan o VRC 154-155 K 4
Weishan Hu ∼ VRC 154-155 K 4
Weishi o VRC 154-155 J 4
Weiss o USA (LA) 268-269 K 6
Weiss Lake ‹ USA (AL) 284-285 E 2
Weitchpec o USA (CA) 246-247 B 2
Weitou o VRC 156-157 L 4
Weixi o VRC 142-143 L 2
Wei Xian o VRC 154-155 J 3
Weixin o VRC 156-157 D 3
Weiya o VRC 146-147 M 5
Weiyuan o VRC (GAN) 154-155 D 4
Weiyuan o VRC (SIC) 156-157 D 2
Weizhou Dao ⌒ VRC 156-157 F 6
Wekakura Point ▲ NZ 182 D 4
Weko o ZRE 210-211 K 3
Wekusko o CDN 34-35 G 3
Wekusko Lake ⊂ CDN 34-35 G 3
Welab o RI 166-167 K 6
Welanpela o CL 140-141 J 7

410 Walla Walla — Welanpela

Contributors/Credits

MACMILLAN
A Simon & Schuster Macmillan Company
1633 Broadway, New York, NY 10019

Copyright © 1996 RV Reise- und
Verkehrsverlag Munich · Stuttgart,
Germany, updated 1998
Maps copyright © 1996 Geo Data,
Werder/H., Germany, updated 1998

First United States edition 1996

All rights reserved. No part of this book
may be reproduced or transmitted in any
form or by any means electronic or me-
chanical, including photocopying, record-
ing, or by any information storage and
retrieval system now or hereafter invented, without permission in writing of the
Publisher.

MACMILLAN is a registered trademark of
Macmillan, Inc.

Library of Congress Cataloging-in-
Publication Data
The Macmillan world atlas.
    p.   cm.
  Includes index.
  ISBN 0-02-862244-8
  1. Atlases.   I. Macmillan Publishers.
G1021.M2382   1995 ‹G&M›
912–dc20   95–34908   CIP   MAP

Cartography

Editors-in-Chief/Project Directors
Dieter Meinhardt, Heinz-Jürgen Newe,
Eberhard Schäfer, Stuttgart

Editorial Staff
Hannelore Anders, Werder/H.
Marianne Bartsch, Leipzig
Ralf van den Berg, Stuttgart
Francesco Bover, Barcelona
Markus Burkhardt, Leipzig
Vaclav Cerny, Stuttgart
Klaus Dorenburg, Leipzig
Werner Drapak, Stuttgart
Heinz Eckert, Leipzig
Gisela Gaebler, Leipzig
Karin Gehrmann, Werder/H.
Kai Gründler, Leipzig
Angela Jaehne, Werder/H.
Eva-Maria Jahnke, Leipzig
Erika Klimpel, Leipzig
Karl-Heinz Klimpel, Leipzig
Renate Krahl, Werder/H.
Beate Laus, Werder/H.
Uwe Lipfert, Leipzig
Christoph Lutze, Stuttgart
Winfried Maigler, Stuttgart
Frank Meitzen, Leipzig
Hans-Jochen Poetzsch, Leipzig
Folker Rhaesen, Leipzig
Klaus Schaefer, Werder/H.
Helmut Schaub, Stuttgart
Irmgard Sigg, Stuttgart
Rüdiger Werr, Stuttgart
Gabriele Wiemann, Werder/H.
Erwin Woska, Werder/H.

Cartography Relief Artists
Kai Gründler, Leizpig
Eberhard von Harsdorf, Siegsdorf
Prof. Dr. Christian Herrmann, Karlsruhe
Bruno Witzky, Stuttgart

Computer Cartographers
Directors: Michael Menzel,
Wolfgang Severin, Stuttgart,
Andreas Westermann, Berlin

Vitor Vicente Antunes, Berlin
Antoinette Beckert, Berlin

Kerstin Budig, Berlin
Heike Czeglars, Leipzig
Martin Eisenmann, Stuttgart
Friedrich Enßle, Berlin
Joachim Eppler, Stuttgart
Ramona Fabian, Leipzig
Natascha Fischer, Stuttgart
Gerhard Geller, Stuttgart
Margot Graf, Leipzig
Jana Grundke, Leipzig
Beate Jankowski, Stuttgart
Kristine Keppler, Stuttgart
Gudrun Kolditz, Leipzig
Doris Kordisch, Leipzig
Ute Krasselt, Leipzig
Hannelore Kühsel, Leipzig
Hanno Lehning, Berlin
Helga Mickel, Leipzig
Karin Oelzner, Leipzig
Jörg Wagner, Stuttgart
Ulrich Zeiler, Leipzig
Kathrin Zimmer, Leipzig

Technology
Director: Bernd Hlawatsch, Stuttgart
Elke Bellstedt, Stuttgart
Joachim Drück, Stuttgart
Erika Rieger, Stuttgart
Olaf Untermann, Stuttgart
Walter Zimmermann, Stuttgart

Typesetting
Directors: Gabriele Stuke, Jörg Wulfes,
Stuttgart
Frank Barchet, Stuttgart
Thomas Ellinger, Stuttgart
Karin Krüger, Leipzig
Elfriede Salomo, Leipzig
Hannelore Scherer, Leipzig
Mario Spalj, Stuttgart
Judith Winter, Tübingen

Final Checking
Director: Hartmut Voit, Stuttgart
Bernd Hilberer, Stuttgart

Independent Contributors and Consultants

Institut für Angewandte Geodäsie,
Frankfurt/M.
UNESCO, World Heritage Center, Paris,
Vesna Vujicic
Moscow Aerogeodetic Enterprise,
Moscow,
  Dr. Alexander Borodko
Academia Sinica, Nanking,
  Prof. Zhang Longsheng
  Mrs. Liu Xiaomei
Kartografie Praha A.S., Prague,
  Jiří Kucera
Cartographia Ltd, Sofia,
  Ivan Petrov
Maplan Warszawa, Warsaw,
  H. Michal Siwicki
Prof. Dr. Christian Herrmann,
  Karlsruhe
Prof. Dr. Wilfried Fiedler, Munich
Prof. Dr. Heinrich Lamping,
  Frankfurt/M.
Kartographisches Büro Messer,
  Pfungstadt
Internationales Landkartenhaus,
  Stuttgart
Birgit Kapper-Wichtler, Buhlenberg
Beate Siewert-Mayer, Tübingen
Dr. Martin Coy, Tübingen
Dr. Wolfgang Frank, Remshalden
Martin Friedrich, Tübingen
Henryk Gorski, Warsaw
Jörg Haas, Rottenburg
Ernst-Dieter Zeidler, Potsdam
Peter Krause, Regensburg
Studio für Landkartentechnik,
  Norderstedt

Jochen Layer, Fellbach
Angelika Palczynski, Heidelberg
Susanne Priemer, Esslingen
Maryland Cartographics, Columbia MD
European Map Graphics,
  Finchampstead (Berkshire)
GeoSystems, Lancaster PA
Timothy J. Carter, Comfort TX

Text and Photo Division

Editor-in-Chief/Project Director
Carlo Lauer, Prisma Verlag GmbH,
Munich

Publisher
Natalie Chapman, Macmillan USA,
New York

Editor
Armin Sinnwell, Prisma Verlag GmbH,
Munich

Assistant Editors
Raphaela Moczynski, Prisma Verlag
GmbH, Munich
Jennifer Webb, Macmillan USA,
New York

Production Editor
Maria Massey, Macmillan USA,
New York

Photo Editor
Sabine Geese, Prisma Verlag GmbH,
Munich

Texts
Dr. Ambros Brucker, Gräfelfing
Dr. Christoph Schneider, Düsseldorf

Translation
GAIA Text, Munich

Illustrations
Satellite Imagery
GEOSPACE-Beckel Satellitenbilddaten,
Bad Ischl, Salzburg
© Satellite images:
  GEOSPACE/EURIMAGE/EOSAT
© Original data: EOSAT 1994

Photographers
Abbreviations: AKG – Archiv für Kunst
und Geschichte; B&U – B&U International Picture Service; IFA – IFA-Bilder-
team; TG – Transglobe Agency; TIB –
The Image Bank; TSW – Tony Stone
Worldwide

Photo credits
I NASA; 1 (center left/cl) AKG; 1 (top to
bottom) Hans Wolf/TIB, David W.
Hamilton/TIB, Ben Simmons/TG, TIB,
Albrecht G. Schaefer, Luis Castaneda/
TIB), Rauh/PhotoPress, B&U, Magnus
Reitz/TIB, Eric Meola/TIB; 17 (cl) AKG,
17 (left column: top to bottom) Zefa,
J. Gnass/Zefa, Norbert Rosing/Silvestris,
Hansgeorg Arndt/Silvestris, W. Allgö-
wer/IFA, Norbert Rosing/Silvestris, TSW,
Derek Trask/TG, 17 (right column: top
to bottom) Scholz/Bavaria, Hunter/IFA,
Kokta/IFA, Fuhrmann/PhotoPress, Do-
novan Reese/TSW, Glen Allison/TSW,
A. Schein/Zefa, John J. Wood/Photo-
Press, Cosmo Condina/TSW, Chris
Haigh/ TSW, Rob Boudreau/TSW; 57
(cl) AKG, 57 (top to bottom) Koene/
TG, Diaf/IFA, Michael Scott/TSW, Mar-
tin Wendler/Silvestris, R. McLeod/TG,
TIB, L. Veiga/TIB, Giuliano Colliva/TIB,
A.N.T./Silvestris, R. McLeod/TG, A.N.T./
Silvestris; 81 (cl) AKG, 81 (top to bot-
tom) Damm/Zefa, Magnus Rietz/TIB,

Jürgens Ost+Europa Photo, UPA/IFA,
Jeff Hunter/TIB, Wolfgang Korall/Silve-
stris, Konrad Wothe/Silvestris, Everts/
IFA, A. Gallant/TIB, Backhaus/Zefa, Jür-
gens Ost+ Europa Photo; 105 (cl) AKG,
105 (left column: top to bottom) Jür-
gens Ost+Europa Photo, Jürgens Ost+
Europa Photo, Hubert Manfred/Bava-
ria, Aberham/IFA, Ben Simmons/TG,
Jürgens Ost+Europa Photo, A. Filatow/
APN/Nowosti, Hubert Manfred/Bava-
ria, Gerd Ludwig/Visum, 105 (center
column: top to bottom) Jürgens Ost+
Europa Photo, M. Theis/TG, Richard
Elliott/TSW, Ben Edwards/TSW, Rolf
Richardson/TG, Everts/IFA, David
Sutherland/TSW, Hoa-Qui/Silvestris,
Roland Birke/Agentur Hilleke, Alex
Stewart/TIB, Andreas Gruschke/Agen-
tur Hilleke, 105 (right column: top to
bottom) B&U, Terry Madison/TIB, K.
Stration/TG, Romilly Lockyer/TIB, IFA,
Glen Hillson/TSW, Paul Chesley/TSW,
Chris Haigh/TSW, Nigel Dickinson/
TSW, Bail/IFA, Paul Chesley/TSW; 169
(cl) Interfoto, 169 (top to bottom)
Clemens Emmler, Gottschalk/IFA, Voll-
mer/IFA, Albrecht G. Schaefer, Albrecht
G. Schaefer, Siebig/IFA, P. Arnold/IFA,
BCI/IFA; 185 (cl) AKG, 185 (left co-
lumn: top to bottom) Kiepke/Photo-
Press, Werner Gartung, Diaf/IFA, Erika
Graddock/Silvestris, Hoa-Qui/Silvestris,
Werner Gartung, Werner Gartung,
Obremski/TIB, 185 (right column: top
to bottom) Diaf/IFA, Aberham/IFA,
Fiedler/IFA, Sally Mayman/TSW,
Herbert Schaible/TIB, Nicholas
Parfitt/TSW, Stefan Meyers/Silvestrsi,
Chris Harvey/TSW, Aberham/IFA, Kon-
rad Wothe/Silvestris, Hoa-Qui/Silve-
stris; 225 (cl) AKG, 225 (left column:
top to bottom) M. Braunger/Agentur
Hilleke, Wunsch/IFA, Hunter/IFA, Hans
Schmied/Silvestris, Georg French/Bava-
ria, Diaf/IFA, Glück/IFA, Hunter/IFA,
Krämer/IFA, 225 (center column: top
to bottom) The Telegraph/Bavaria, M.
Braunger/Agentur Hilleke, Nowitz/IFA,
Sunwind/Bavaria, Nägele/IFA, Krämer/
IFA, Picture Finders/Bavaria, Picture
Finders/Bavaria, David Ball/Bavaria,
Comnet/IFA, M. Braunger/Agentur
Hilleke, 225 (right column: top to
bottom) Osborne/IFA, PhotoPress, M.
Braunger/Agentur Hilleke, Picture
Finders/Bavaria, Helga Lade, Bavaria,
BCI/IFA, M. Braunger/Agentur Hilleke,
P. Graf/IFA, Oertel/IFA, FPG/Bavaria.

Cover Design
Iris Jeromnimon, Macmillan USA,
New York

Production
Design, Layout
Pro Design, Munich
Typographischer Betrieb Walter Biering
& Hans Numberger, Munich

Reproduction
Worldscan, Munich

Repro Director
Wolfgang Mudrak, Munich

Manufacture
Bernhard Mörk, Stuttgart

General Manufacture
Graficas Estella, Estella, Spain

Printed in Spain
10 9 8 7 6 5 4 3